The Garland Encyclopedia of World Music
Volume 3

The United States and Canada

THE GARLAND ENCYCLOPEDIA OF WORLD MUSIC

Volume 1
AFRICA
edited by Ruth M. Stone

Volume 2
**SOUTH AMERICA, MEXICO,
CENTRAL AMERICA, AND THE CARIBBEAN**
edited by Dale A. Olsen and Daniel E. Sheehy

Volume 3
THE UNITED STATES AND CANADA
edited by Ellen Koskoff

Volume 4
SOUTHEAST ASIA
edited by Terry E. Miller and Sean Williams

Volume 5
SOUTH ASIA: THE INDIAN SUBCONTINENT
edited by Alison Arnold

Volume 6
THE MIDDLE EAST
edited by Virginia Danielson, Scott Marcus, and Dwight Reynolds

Volume 7
EAST ASIA: CHINA, JAPAN, AND KOREA
edited by Robert C. Provine, Yosihiko Tokumaru, and J. Lawrence Witzleben

Volume 8
EUROPE
edited by Timothy Rice, James Porter, and Christopher Goertzen

Volume 9
AUSTRALIA AND THE PACIFIC ISLANDS
edited by Adrienne L. Kaeppler and J. Wainwright Love

Volume 10
THE WORLD'S MUSIC: GENERAL PERSPECTIVES AND REFERENCE TOOLS

Advisory Editors
Bruno Nettl and Ruth M. Stone

Founding Editors
James Porter and Timothy Rice

The Garland Encyclopedia of World Music
Volume 3

The United States and Canada

Ellen Koskoff
Editor

GARLAND PUBLISHING, INC.
A member of the Taylor and Francis Group
New York and London
2001

The initial planning of *The Garland Encyclopedia of World Music* was assisted by a grant from the National Endowment for the Humanities.

Library of Congress Cataloging-in-Publication Data

The Garland encyclopedia of world music / [advisory editors, Bruno Nettl and Ruth M. Stone; founding editors, James Porter and Timothy Rice].
    p. cm.
    Includes bibliographical references, discographies, and indexes.
    Contents: v. 3. The United States and Canada / Ellen Koskoff, editor
    ISBN 0-8240-6040-7 (alk. paper)
    1. Music—Encyclopedias.   2. Folk music—Encyclopedias.   3. Popular music—Encyclopedias.
  I. Nettl, Bruno, 1930–   II. Stone, Ruth M.   III. Porter, James, 1937–   IV. Rice, Timothy, 1945–
  ML100.G16   2001
  780'.9—dc21

97-9671
CIP
MN

For Garland Publishing:

Vice President: Linda Hollick
Publishing Director: Sylvia K. Miller
Project Editor: Laura Kathleen Smid
Assistant Editor: Gillian Rodger
Director of Production: Laura-Ann Robb
Copyeditor: JoEllen Ausanka
Indexer: Marilyn Bliss
Music Typesetter: Hyunjung Choi
Text Typesetter: Stratford Publishing Services
Cartographer: Mapping Specialists Limited, Madison, Wisconsin
Cover Designer: Lawrence Wolfson Design, New York

Cover Illustration: Jazz street musician in San Francisco. © Bill Bachmann

The section "The Impact of Race on American Musical Scholarship" in "Race, Ethnicity, and Nationhood" was adapted from "Introduction: Music and Race, Their Past, Their Presence" in *Music and the Radical Imagination,* eds. Ronald Radano and Philip V. Bohlman (University of Chicago Press, 2000).

"Indian and Pakistani Music" by Alison Arnold originally appeared as "North America" in volume 5 of *The Garland Encyclopedia of World Music (South Asia: The Indian Subcontinent).*

The section "Jazz 1914–1939" in "Four Views of Music in Canada" was adapted from the book *Such Melodious Racket: The Lost History of Jazz in Canada 1914–1949,* by Mark Miller (The Mercury Press, Toronto, 1997).

"Cantonese Music in Vancouver" was adapted from the article "Cantonese Music Societies of Vancouver: A Social and Historical Survey," by Alan Thrasher and Huang Jinpei, *Canadian Folk Music Journal* 21(1993): 31–39.

Printed on acid-free, 250-year-life paper
Manufactured in the United States of America

Contents

Part 3
Musical Cultures and Regions   363

Audio Examples

The following examples are included on the accompanying audio compact disc packaged with this volume. Track numbers are also indicated on the pages listed below for easy reference to text discussions. Complete notes on each example may be found on pages 1310–1312.

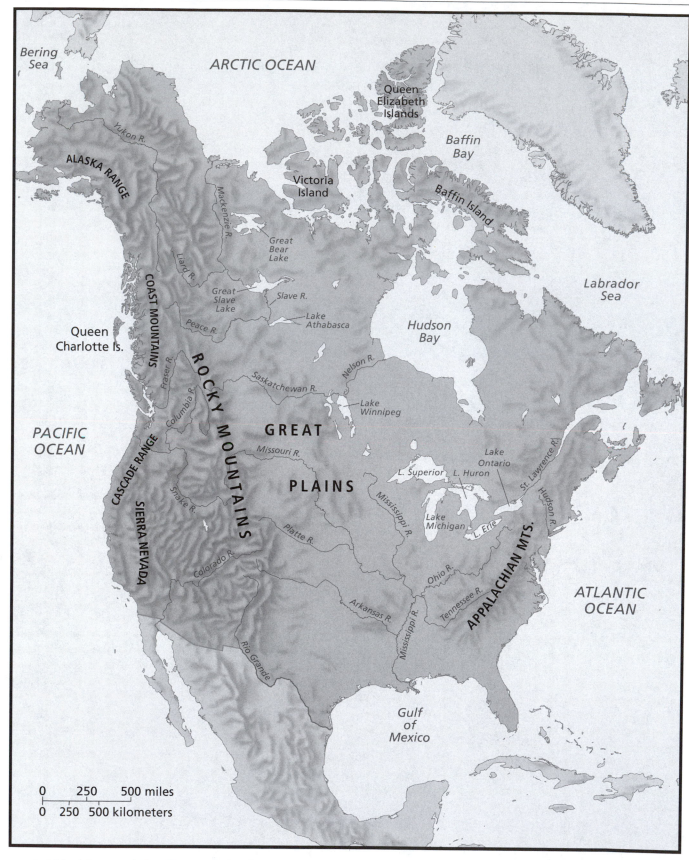

ARCTIC OCEAN

Bering
Sea

Queen
Elizabeth
Islands

*Baffin
Bay*

ALASKA RANGE

Victoria
Island

Yukon R.

Mackenzie R.

Great
Bear
Lake

Baffin Island

*Labrador
Sea*

Liard R.

COAST MOUNTAINS

Great
Slave
Lake

Slave R.

Peace R.

Lake
Athabasca

*Hudson
Bay*

Queen
Charlotte Is.

Fraser R.

R O C K Y   M O U N T A I N S

Saskatchewan R.

Nelson R.

*PACIFIC
OCEAN*

Columbia R.

Lake
Winnipeg

CASCADE RANGE

Missouri R.

GREAT

Lake
Ontario

St. Lawrence R.

Snake R.

L. Superior

L. Huron

SIERRA NEVADA

PLAINS

Lake
Michigan

Hudson R.

Platte R.

Mississippi R.

L. Erie

APPALACHIAN MTS.

Colorado R.

Ohio R.

*ATLANTIC
OCEAN*

Arkansas R.

Tennessee R.

Mississippi R.

Rio Grande

Gulf
of
Mexico

0	250	500 miles
0	250	500 kilometers

MAP 1   United States and Canada topographical

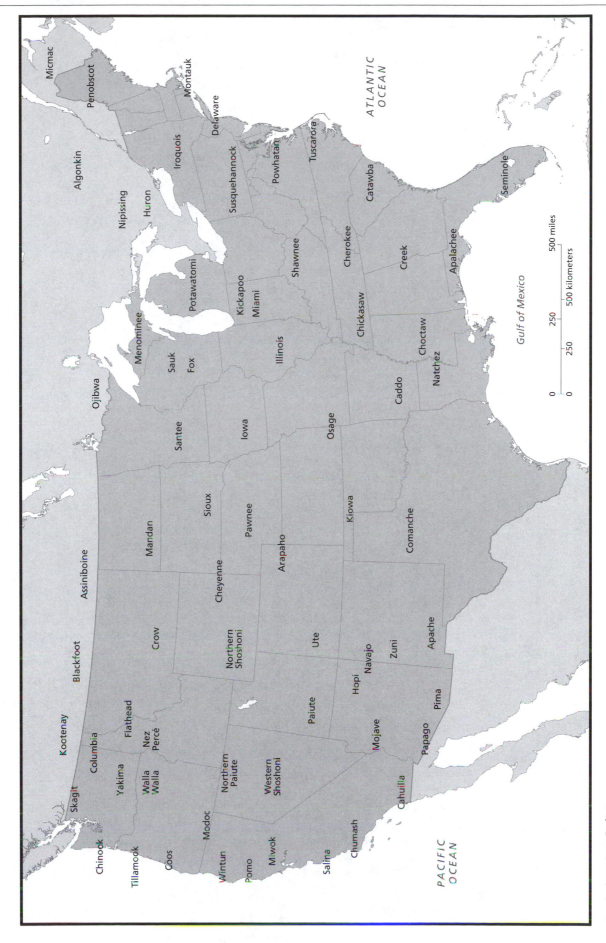

MAP 2   American Indians

MAP 3 First Nations

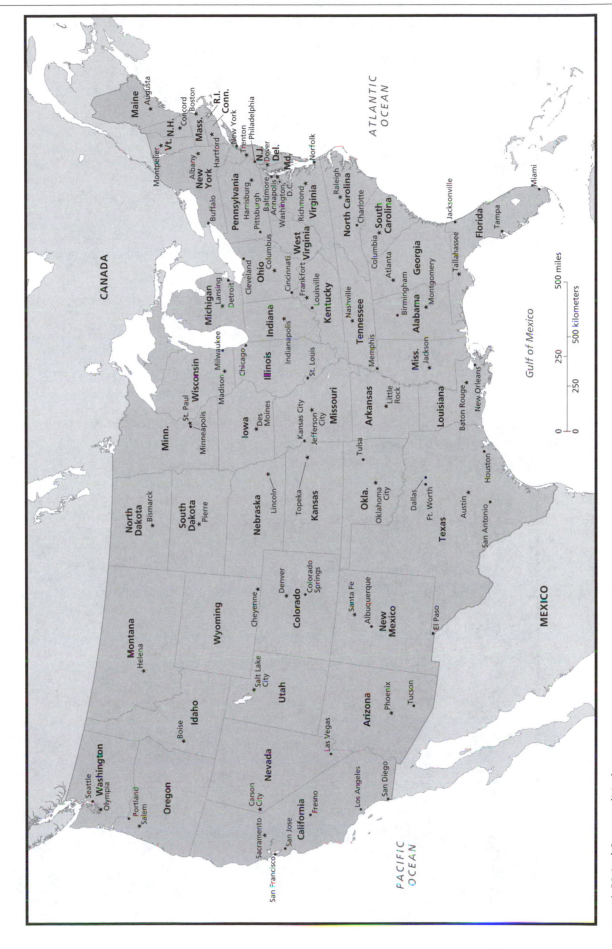

MAP 4 United States, political

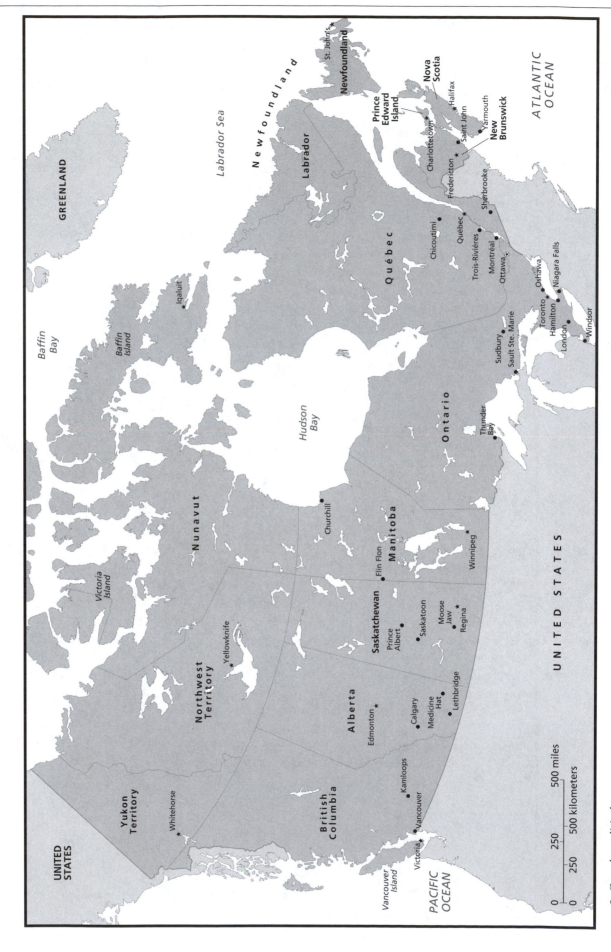

MAP 5 Canada, political

About *The Garland Encyclopedia of World Music*

Scholars have created many kinds of encyclopedias devoted to preserving and transmitting knowledge about the world. The study of music has itself been the subject of numerous encyclopedias in many languages. Yet until now the term *music encyclopedia* has been synonymous with surveys of the history, theory, and performance practice of European-based traditions.

In July 1988, the editors of *The Garland Encyclopedia of World Music* gathered for a meeting to determine the nature and scope of a massive new undertaking. For this, the first encyclopedia devoted to the music of all the world's peoples, the editors decided against the traditional alphabetic approach to compartmentalizing knowledge from A to Z. Instead, they chose a geographic approach, with each volume devoted to a single region and coverage assigned to the world's experts on specific music cultures.

For several decades, ethnomusicologists (following the practice of previous generations of comparative musicologists) have been documenting the music of the world through fieldwork, recording, and analysis. Now, for the first time, they have created an encyclopedia that summarizes in one place the major findings that have resulted from the explosion in such documentation since the 1960s. The volumes in the series comprise contributions from all those specialists who have from the start defined the field of ethnomusicology: anthropologists, linguists, dance ethnologists, cultural historians, and performers. This multidisciplinary approach continues to enrich the field, and future generations of students and scholars will find *The Garland Encyclopedia of World Music* to be an invaluable resource that contributes to knowledge in all its varieties.

Each volume has a similar design and organization: three large sections that cover the major topics of a region from broad general issues to specific music practices. Each section consists of articles written by leading researchers, and extensive glossaries and indexes give the reader easy access to terms, names, and places of interest.

Part 1: an introduction to the region, its culture, and its music as well as a survey of previous music scholarship and research

Part 2: major issues and processes that link the musics of the region

Part 3: detailed accounts of individual music cultures

The editors of each volume have determined how this three-part structure is to be constructed and applied depending on the nature of their regions of interest. The concepts covered in Part 2 will therefore differ from volume to volume; likewise, the articles in Part 3 might be about the music of nations, ethnic groups, islands, or subregions. The picture of music presented in each volume is thus comprehensive yet remains focused on critical ideas and issues.

Complementing the texts of the encyclopedia's articles are numerous illustrations: photographs, drawings, maps, charts, song texts, and musical examples. At the end of each volume is a useful set of study and research tools, including a glossary of terms, lists of audio and visual resources, and an extensive bibliography. An audio compact disc will be found inside the back cover of each volume, with sound examples that are linked (with a ⊙ in the margin) to discussions in the text.

The Garland Encyclopedia of World Music represents the work of hundreds of specialists guided by a team of distinguished editors. With a sense of pride, Garland Publishing offers this new series to readers everywhere.

Preface

This volume on the music of the United States and Canada is the first ever to present a unified historical and contemporary picture of musical life in these two countries. Based on years of historical research and ethnographic fieldwork, the volume presents a rich variety of social and musical traditions, from hip-hop to the Celtic revival in Cape Breton, from Subarctic Inuit drumming to indie pop in Champaign-Urbana, from rock and roll to concert life in nineteenth-century Boston. Over 125 authors from fields such as ethnomusicology, historical musicology, folklore, and popular music studies have combined their talent and expertise here to create an inclusive portrait of musical life in the United States and Canada, where music is seen as not only as sound-structure—a materialization of shared ideas and values—but also as a basic human social behavior of equal importance and meaning to all.

Many fine histories and contemporary accounts of music in the United States and Canada exist today, perhaps more than for any other world area except Europe, but this volume, like the others in *The Garland Encyclopedia of World Music,* is different in many ways. Rather than organizing the material chronologically—as in most standard histories, which favor urban-based, classical musical traditions—or alphabetically—as in most standard encyclopedias, which do not organize material within an overall narrative structure—this volume, like the others in the series, focuses on a variety of organizational principles, using specific social and cultural contexts, issues of musical identity, and geography to frame its musical stories. This, we feel, creates more realistic pictures of musical life in these two countries, ones that come closer to the interactive nature of musical cultures and the variety of ways music is actually experienced by people living in a pluralistic society. Thus, one of the goals for this volume is not only to provide the most current research on the music of these two countries, as well as a wealth of resources for future study, but also to provide a variety of organizational schemes by which readers can develop their own paths through the vast maze of musics and musical experiences these two countries hold.

Obviously not every music that has ever existed or exists today in the United States and Canada is discussed here. That would certainly have taken far more space than one volume and the result would not have been any more complete upon its publication than the present volume, as new musics are continuously being created and old ones given new meanings. As certain decisions had to be made concerning content, we decided to favor musics that are not normally discussed in standard histories, and to put less weight on (but not exclude) certain classical and popular genres on which many fine books and other resources already exist.

Some editorial issues were decided early in the process of organizing the ten-volume *Garland Encyclopedia of World Music* series. Perhaps the most significant for our volume was the decision to focus on the United States and Canada as a cultural and musical unit (rather than on North America, a more common, modern-day political designation) and to place the varied traditions of Mexico and the Caribbean in volume two, which is devoted to the musics of South and Central America. However, no presentation of music, especially in the United States, would be complete without a discussion of these musics and the important roles they have played in the development of popular and classical genres in the United States. So, although Mexico and the Caribbean are not treated here as separate regions, the influence of their music and musical practices is reflected in many discussions found throughout the volume.

Other decisions focused on differences in organizational style, perspective, and language found in English, French, and Spanish discourses on music. While the official language of the United States is English, a large percentage of the population speaks Spanish as well, and in Canada, both English and French are official languages. Thus, certain inconsistencies in spelling, bibliographic style, and perspective that would normally be standardized in an encyclopedia or dictionary began to appear early in the editing process. Since we wanted the articles in this volume to reflect, not to gloss over or "correct," historical, ethnic, and language differences, we allowed for certain differences, especially in perspective and bibliographic style.

Two additional editorial decisions deserve mention here. First, the decision was made to remove the hyphen often used to designate certain ethnic communities, such as in the terms "African-American" or "Chinese-Canadian." This is a tricky issue, not without political implications. As all people now living in the United States and Canada (including American Indians/First Nations peoples) either emigrated or were forcibly brought here from somewhere else, we felt the dual-citizenship nature of the hyphenated term was not necessary or appropriate. Further, as the hyphen is used most often to label distinct "ethnic" groups, as opposed to "mainstream" western and northern European groups, it brings up the question of what is and what is not considered "ethnic" and "ethnic music." It is our view that if the common meaning of "ethnic" is what is characteristic of a particular group of people, then we are all "ethnics" of some sort or another and all of our musics can be considered "ethnic musics."

Finally, people living in the United States and Canada (as well as in Mexico and Central and South America) are all citizens of the Americas and are, technically, all Americans. However, as there is no one word to describe people living in the United States, most people, even Canadians, refer to the United States of America simply as "America" and those living there as "Americans." We have attempted to keep the use of the word *America* (when referring only to the United States) to a minimum here, but occasionally it has slipped in when it just seemed simplest to use it.

HOW THIS VOLUME IS ORGANIZED

Like the others in *The Garland Encyclopedia of World Music* series, this volume is organized into three large sections. Part 1 presents an overview of the musical history and historiography of these two countries, seen as one cultural unit.

Music in social and cultural contexts

Part 2, "Music in Social and Cultural Contexts," was written collaboratively by U.S and Canadian writers and presents first a variety of articles exploring issues—such as musical identity, including class, race, ethnicity and nationhood, gender and religion—that cross cultural and political boundaries. A section on music in "Diverse Environments" deals with the importance of place—not only geographic, but also cultural "place"—discussing, among other things, music for the stage, the concert hall, film, and dance, and music in business and technology. "Processes and Institutions" examines some of the institutions that affect music and music making in the United States and Canada, such as music schools and other teaching and learning contexts, as well as the role of government and politics in music making. Part 2 concludes with a section, "Border Crossings and Fusions," that examines the social and musical processes of acculturation and synthesis whereby different musics are borrowed, adapted, exchanged, interwoven, or merged into one another.

Snapshots

In part 2, and throughout the rest of volume, musical genres as well as small "ethno-graphic moments" are introduced in the form of "Snapshots." This is somewhat of a departure from the other volumes in *The Garland Encyclopedia of World Music* series and reflects a growing understanding that music, like all aspects of human behavior, is located within specific, often highly dynamic contexts. Musical Snapshots, like photographic snapshots, represent only tiny, specific moments, but each moment has a history leading up to it and a future life after it passes, and can be seen, understood, and interpreted quite differently depending on the perspectives of the person framing the shot and the viewer.

We have included a large number of Snapshot genres here, some of which may not seem to be logically connected to each other as in a standard history or textbook, but rather, may be connected to the basic ideas found in the more general articles that precede them. In other words, specific Snapshots were placed within or after certain articles because they provided especially good examples of concepts introduced in those articles, but many of the Snapshots could have been placed elsewhere to illustrate other ideas as well. We hope the somewhat arbitrary placement of the Snapshots will encourage the reader to engage in a more interactive way with the material. Again, we wanted this volume to present not only facts about certain musics but also to suggest that music has multiple, often simultaneous meanings.

Musical cultures and regions

Part 3, the largest section of the book, examines the musical cultures of American Indian/First Nations peoples, the United States, and Canada in three separate sections. The American Indian/First Nations section discusses the first inhabitants of this area and how different kinds of contemporary music, as well as traditional ceremony and ritual, infuse daily life among these peoples as they continue to adapt to rapid social and economic changes. It is organized geographically and tribally, without respect to the political boundaries of the United States and Canada.

The section on music in the United States begins with an overview of musical traditions in this country, presenting materials historically and chronologically accord-ing to different national, religious, and racial groups, as in the sections that follow, using the metaphor of different musical "streams" to organize the information. This is followed by an examination of the musics of the various groups of people who have come to the United States and the role each has played in the development of music there. African American, Hispanic American, European American, and Asian Ameri-can musics and musicians are discussed more fully in each of these sections.

We recognize that one of the problems of organizing musical information in the United States according to the origin of its inhabitants, especially given the country's history of racism, is that it tends to mark race, "ethnicity," and sometimes class as the most essential features of identity. While these are certainly important aspects of indi-vidual and group identity (if freely chosen and not imposed from the outside), they are not always the only important or relevant ones. Furthermore, as more and more people from different parts of the world—many with mixed heritages in their native lands—emigrate to the United States, meet, interact, marry, and have children of many com-bined racial and ethnic backgrounds, who is to decide which race, ethnicity, or class is significant? And who is to decide which music is influenced by which of these factors? Ultimately the answers must be negotiated between the music-makers, the pieces of music, and those who experience the music—all of whom may communicate or assign different meanings, associations, and values to the music and musical experience. Thus, as the realities of social and musical identity are far more subtle than these gross categories suggest, the reader is cautioned to use them as starting, not ending, points.

The final section on the music of Canada is organized according to the regions of Canada itself, moving east to west across this vast country. As in the section on music in the United States, this one begins with a large overview of music in Canada, arranged geographically in anticipation of the smaller sections to follow. The music of each region is organized similarly, with an overview presented first, followed by discussion of the musics of the various groups who have formed sizeable communities in these regions. The differences in organizational style between the three large sections devoted to music of the American Indians/First Nations, the United States, and Canada reflect major differences in these nations' images of themselves as social and musical entities—differences that will become more apparent as the reader uses this volume.

Research tools

Throughout the volume various research tools are available to readers, beginning with a table of contents showing the major articles as well as the Snapshots embedded within and between them. Each article (including Snapshots) begins with an outline of the important headings within the article, so users can immediately see what discussions will follow. Most articles contain illustrations in the form of photographs, musical examples (written in Western notation), and charts. Large maps can be found in the front matter that show the numerous American Indian/First Nations communities discussed within, as well as the political division of the United States and Canada into states, provinces, and territories. Each article concludes with a bibliography listing relevant books, articles, recordings, films, videos, and occasionally websites. Cross-references in brackets such as "[see POPULAR MUSIC FOR THE PARLOR AND STAGE]" provide links to other articles in the volume.

Glossary and index

Because this encyclopedia is organized thematically and not alphabetically, musical genres, instruments, and theoretic concepts, along with many other terms, are listed and defined with page references in the glossary. Musicians' names, titles of pieces, and names of social groups and organizations are found with page references in the index. These tools, like the cross-references within the articles, can be used not only to identify certain people and define concepts, but also to link many articles together.

Compact disc

A compact disc found on the inside back cover provides listening examples for many of the articles contained within the volume. Some of these have been taken from the authors' own field tapes; some come from commercial recordings; and some have been graciously donated by the Smithsonian Institution's Folkways Collection. We have tried to provide a varied sampling of musics found in the United States and Canada, while also recognizing that, with a rising interest in "folk" and "world musics," many fine recordings of traditional and newly composed and arranged musics exist and are easily available today.

ACKNOWLEDGMENTS

No project of this size could possibly be completed without the work and support of many people and institutions. First, my heartfelt thanks and gratitude go to the authors whose work is represented here and to their teachers, collaborators, and informants who provided the strength and substance of this work; their combined expertise and their commitment to and respect for the world's musics are what give this volume its vitality, authenticity, and integrity. I am also especially grateful for the authors' patience and willingness to work under sometimes stressful deadlines. I also wish to acknowledge the fine work of my three predecessors, Jeff Todd Titon, Deane L. Root, and Doris J. Dyen, who at various earlier times were the editors of this volume; I am grateful for their vision and for their initial work in organizing and shepherding the volume along its sometimes rocky path.

Thanks also to the many people at Garland/Routledge, especially Leo Balk, the original founding father of this project, who, over twelve years ago, first envisioned *The Garland Encyclopedia of World Music*, and who lovingly watched over it for many years; and Richard Wallis, who helped enormously, not only with organizational and editorial advice, but also with continuing warm friendship and a steady stream of Internet jokes. I am also grateful to Soo Mee Kwon and Gillian Rodger of Garland who provided needed encouragement and advice, and always kept me moving, laughing, and eating chocolate. Others at Garland/Routledge who have joined this project later in its journey to publication—Richard Carlin, music editor, and Laura Smid, project editor, also deserve warm thanks, especially Laura for her attention to nitty-gritty details that I may have missed. I am also grateful to Stratford Publishing, the company that handled the production of this volume, especially to Judith Ashkenaz and Linda DeMasi, who were able to take my infinite scraps of paper, pictures, musical examples, and other bits of this puzzle and assemble them into a beautiful and lively form.

I sincerely thank my team of volume advisors—Beverley Diamond, Charlotte Frisbie, Judy McCulloh, Lester Monts, and Robert Walser—who helped with the organization and recruitment of authors, as well as with later readings of articles; and Beverley Diamond, Victoria Levine, Portia Maultsby, Dan Sheehy, Steve Loza, and Terry Miller, who acted as subeditors for each of the major sections and who read and re-read articles, making invaluable comments and suggestions.

I am also especially grateful to my ethnomusicology colleagues who often gave me support in the form of a good listening ear or a shoulder to lean on. Other *Garland Encyclopedia of World Music* volume editors, Terry Miller, Alison Arnold, Ruth Stone, and Virginia Danielson, were always available to me and often provided needed encouragement to keep moving when the stacks of articles seemed too high; Beverley Diamond, in her role as a volume adviser, subeditor, author, and donator of pictures, always acted as friend, colleague, and supporter as well. I would also like to acknowledge Terry Miller and T. Temple Tuttle (who, sadly, died during the completion of this volume) for their wonderful pictures; and Tony Seeger, D. Atesh Sonneborn, and the Smithsonian Institution for the use of many recorded examples.

Closer to home were those people who worked with (or tolerated) me on a daily, ongoing basis, and to these I owe a tremendous debt of gratitude, mainly for not losing their patience or their commitment to seeing this volume completed. Sara W. Nicholson and Heidi Owen, both musicology graduate students at the Eastman School of Music, were invaluable as assistants and always a pleasure to work with. Thanks also to the Eastman School for its support in many ways. Finally, my gratitude and love go to my husband, Robert Morris, and my son, David Morris, for their constant encouragement and support, even when it meant that Mom was unavailable to watch the latest *Roseanne* re-run or to make dinner, and whose echoes of "Go work on Garland!" still linger in my ears.

—ELLEN KOSKOFF

Editorial Advisers

Volume Advisers

Beverley Diamond
York University, North York, Ontario

Charlotte J. Frisbie
Southern Illinois University of Edwardsville

Judy McCulloh
University of Illinois Press

Lester Monts
University of Michigan–Ann Arbor

Robert Walser
University of California at Los Angeles

Consulting Editors

Beverley Diamond
York University, North York, Ontario

Victoria Lindsay Levine
Colorado College, Colorado Springs

Steven Loza
University of California at Los Angeles

Portia K. Maultsby
Indiana University–Bloomington
    With contributions by Mellonee V. Burnim,
    Indiana University–Bloomington

Terry E. Miller
Kent State University, Kent, Ohio

Daniel Sheehy
National Endowment for the Arts, Washington, D.C.

Contributing Authors

Alison Arnold
Cary, North Carolina, U.S.A.

Susan M. Asai
Northeastern University
Boston, Massachusetts, U.S.A.

Gage Averill
New York University
New York, New York, U.S.A.

Nicole Beaudry
University of Québec at Montréal
Montréal, Québec, Canada

Barbara Benary
Gamelan Son of Lion
New York, New York, U.S.A.

Wesley Berg
University of Alberta
Edmonton, Alberta, Canada

Barry Bergey
Folk Arts Program National Endowment
   for the Arts
Washington, D.C., U.S.A.

Jody Berland
York University
North York, Ontario, Canada

Stephen Blum
City University of New York
New York, New York, U.S.A.

Jane Bowers
University of Wisconsin at Milwaukee
Milwaukee, Wisconsin, U.S.A.

Rob Bowman
York University
North York, Ontario, Canada

Mellonee V. Burnim
Indiana University
Bloomington, Indiana, U.S.A.

Patricia Shehan Campbell
University of Washington
Seattle, Washington, U.S.A.

Raoul F. Camus
City University of New York
New York, New York, U.S.A.

Amy Catlin
University of California at Los Angeles
Los Angeles, California, U.S.A.

Brian Cherwick
University of Alberta
Edmonton, Alberta, Canada

Dale Cockrell
Vanderbilt University
Nashville, Tennessee, U.S.A.

Frank J. Cipolla
State University of New York
Buffalo, New York, U.S.A.

Judith R. Cohen
York University
North York, Ontario, Canada

Susan C. Cook
University of Wisconsin
Madison, Wisconsin, U.S.A.

Steven Cornelius
Bowling Green State University
Bowling Green, Ohio, U.S.A.

James R. Cowdery
City University of New York
New York, New York, U. S. A.

Michael Daley
York University
North York, Ontario, Canada

Beverley Diamond
York University
North York, Ontario, Canada

Jody Diamond
American Gamelan Institute,
    Dartmouth College
Lebanon, New Hampshire, U.S.A.

Jacqueline Cogdell DjeDje
University of California at Los Angeles
Los Angeles, California, U.S.A.

Jon Dueck
University of Alberta
Edmonton, Alberta, Canada

Kate Dunlay
DunGreen Music
Halifax, Nova Scotia, Canada

Robin Elliott
University College Dublin
Dublin, Ireland

Dena J. Epstein
University of Chicago, Emerita
Chicago, Illinois, U.S.A.

David Evans
University of Memphis
Memphis, Tennessee, U.S.A.

Susan Fast
McMaster University
Hamilton, Ontario, Canada

Kai Fikentscher
City University of New York
New York, New York, U.S.A.

Robert Fink
University of California, Los Angeles
Los Angeles, California, U.S.A.

Charlotte J. Frisbie
Southern Illinois University at
    Edwardsville
Edwardsville, Illinois, U.S.A.

Annemarie Gallaugher
York University
North York, Ontario, Canada

Reebee Garofalo
University of Massachusetts Boston
Boston, Massachusetts, U.S.A.

Christopher Goertzen
Earlham College
Richmond, Indiana, U.S.A.

Erik D. Gooding
Indiana University
Bloomington, Indiana, U.S.A.

Linda J. Goodman
Museum of New Mexico
Santa Fe, New Mexico, U.S.A.

Judith A. Gray
Library of Congress
Washington, D.C., U.S.A.

Pauline Greenhill
University of Winnipeg
Winnipeg, Manitoba, Canada

Ain Haas
Indiana University-Perdue University
    Indianapolis
Indianapolis, Indiana, U.S.A.

J. Richard Haefer
Arizona State University
Tempe, Arizona, U.S.A.

Rob Haskins
Eastman School of Music
University of Rochester
Rochester, New York, U.S.A.

Dorothea Hast
Southern Connecticut State University
New Haven, Connecticut, U.S.A.

Charlotte Heth
Smithsonian Institution
Washington, D.C., U.S.A.

Fred Ho
Brooklyn, New York, U.S.A.

Okon Hwang
Eastern Connecticut State University
Willimantic, Connecticut, U.S.A.

Huang Jinpei
University of British Columbia
Vancouver, British Columbia, Canada

Anahid Kassabian
Fordham University
Bronx, New York, U.S.A.

Joann W. Kealiinohomoku
Northern Arizona University
Flagstaff, Arizona, U.S.A.

William Kearns
University of Colorado
Boulder, Colorado, U.S.A.

Richard Keeling
Oakland, California, U.S.A.

Elaine Keillor
Carleton University
Ottawa, Ontario, Canada

Susan Key
Stanford University
Palo Alto, California, U.S.A.

James Kimball
State University of New York
Geneseo, New York, U.S.A.

James R. Kippen
University of Toronto
Toronto, Ontario, Canada

Rita Klinger
Cleveland State University
Cleveland, Ohio, U.S.A.

Ellen Koskoff
Eastman School of Music
University of Rochester
Rochester, New York, U.S.A.

Carolyn H. Krasnow
Los Angeles, California, U.S.A.

Holly Kruse
La Salle University
Philadelphia, Pennsylvania, U. S. A

Anne Lederman
Toronto, Ontario, Canada

Marie-Thérèse Lefebvre
University of Montréal
Montréal, Québec, Canada

James K. Leger
New Mexico Highlands University
Las Vegas, New Mexico, U.S.A.

Victoria Lindsay Levine
Colorado College
Colorado Springs, Colorado, U.S.A.

Mark Levy
University of Oregon
Eugene, Oregon, U.S.A.

Tamara E. Livingston
University of Illinois
Champaign-Urbana, Illinois, U. S. A.

Steven Loza
University of California at Los Angeles
Los Angeles, California, U.S.A.

Peter Manuel
City University of New York
New York, New York, U.S.A.

Irene Markoff
York University
North York, Ontario, Canada

Claire Martin
School of Oriental and African Studies
London, England

Portia K. Maultsby
Indiana University
Bloomington, Indiana, U.S.A.

Andra McCartney
Concordia University
Montréal, Québec, Canada

Anne Dhu McLucas
University of Oregon
Eugene, Oregon, U.S.A.

Edward Meadows
San Diego State University
San Diego, California, U.S.A.

F. Mark Mealing
Community College, Emeritus
Kaslo, British Columbia, Canada

Rebecca S. Miller
Wesleyan University
Middletown, Connecticut, U.S.A.

Mark Miller
Toronto, Ontario, Canada

Terry E. Miller
Kent State University
Kent, Ohio, U.S.A.

Ingrid Monson
Washington University
St. Louis, Missouri, U.S.A.

Val Morrison
University Québec
Montréal, Québec, Canada

Peter Narváez
Memorial University of Newfoundland
St. John's, Newfoundland, Canada

Sara Nicholson
Eastman School of Music
University of Rochester
Rochester, New York, U.S.A.

Phong T. Nguyễn
Cleveland Heights, Ohio, U.S.A.

Dawn M. Norfleet
New York, New York, U. S. A.

Karen Pegley
York University
North York, Ontario, Canada

Ron Pen
University of Kentucky
Lexington, Kentucky, U.S.A.

Jennifer C. Post
Middlebury College
Middlebury, Vermont, U.S.A.

Katherine K. Preston
The College of William and Mary
Williamsburg, Virginia, U.S.A.

Regula Burckhardt Qureshi
University of Alberta
Edmonton, Alberta, Canada

Ronald Radano
University of Wisconsin
Madison, Wisconsin, U.S.A.

Carl Rahkonen
Indiana University of Pennsylvania
Indiana, Pennsylvania, U.S.A.

Anne K. Rasmussen
College of William and Mary
Williamsburg, Virginia, U.S.A.

Adelaida Reyes
Jersey City State College
Jersey City, New Jersey, U.S.A.

José R. Reyna
California State University at Bakersfield
Bakersfield, California, U.S.A.

Thomas L. Riis
University of Colorado
Boulder, Colorado, U.S.A.

Brenda M. Romero
University of Colorado
Boulder, Colorado, U.S.A.

Neil V. Rosenberg
Memorial University of Newfoundland
St. John's, Newfoundland, Canada

Jennifer Rycenga
San Jose State University
San Jose, California, U.S.A.

Sam-Ang Sam
Reston, Virginia, U.S.A.

David Sanjek
Broadcast Music Incorporated
New York, New York, U.S.A.

George Dimitri Sawa
Toronto, Ontario, Canada

Denise A. Seachrist
Kent State University
Kent, Ohio, U.S.A.

Anthony Seeger
University of California at Los Angeles
Los Angeles, California, U.S.A.

Daniel Sheehy
National Endowment for the Arts
Washington, D.C., U.S.A.

John Shepherd
Carleton University
Ottawa, Ontario, Canada

Zoe C. Sherinian
Franklin and Marshall College
Lancaster, Pennsylvania, U.S.A.

Mark Slobin
Wesleyan University
Middletown, Connecticut, U.S.A.

Gordon E. Smith
Queen's University
Kingston, Ontario, Canada

D. Atesh Sonneborn
Smithsonian Institution
Washington, D.C., U.S.A.

Norman Stanfield
University of British Columbia
Vancouver, British Columbia, Canada

Amy Ku'uleialoha Stillman
University of Michigan
Ann Arbor, Michigan, U.S.A.

Will Straw
McGill University
Montréal, Québec, Canada

Janet L. Sturman
University of Arizona
Tuscon, Arizona, U.S.A.

Paul Théberge
University of Western Ontario
London, Ontario, Canada

Alan R. Thrasher
University of British Columbia
Vancouver, British Columbia, Canada

Judith Tick
Northeastern University
Boston, Massachusetts, U.S.A.

Ricardo D. Trimillos
University of Hawai'i
Honolulu, Hawai'i, U.S.A.

Nancy F. Vogan
Mount Allison University
Sackville, New Brunswick, Canada

Jeremy Wallach
University of Pennsylvania
Philadelphia, Pennsylvania, U.S.A.

Mary Jane Warner
York University
North York, Ontario, Canada

Robert Witmer
York University
North York, Ontario, Canada

Charles K. Wolfe
Middle Tennessee State University
Murfreesboro, Tennessee, U.S.A.

Josephine R. B. Wright
The College of Wooster
Wooster, Ohio, U.S.A.

Su Zheng
Wesleyan University
Middletown, Connecticut, U.S.A.

Andrew M. Zinck
University of Prince Edward Island
Charlottetown, Prince Edward Island,
Canada

Part 1
The United States and Canada as a Musical Area

The United States and Canada are home to people and communities from virtually every nation in the world. The sheer variety and liveliness of the social and musical traditions in these two countries reflect over twelve thousand years of history and interaction that continue to help define them as musical cultures in today's world. From centuries-old practices, such as performing mimetic dances at harvest time, to newer ones, such as the marketing of popular music; from the political performances of nineteenth-century minstrel shows to those of the great concert halls of New York, Toronto, or Los Angeles; music making in the United States and Canada has always been and continues to be a mixture of traditional and modern practices creatively blended to adapt and adjust to changing social conditions and musical meanings. This volume is a testament to the creativity and perseverance of individuals and communities who have kept alive the cherished traditions of the past while creating new possibilities for a musical future.

Latin-flavored street music in New York City. Photo by Terry Miller, 1981.

Musical Profile of the
United States and Canada
Ellen Koskoff

The Land and Its People Today
The United States and Canada as a Unified Musical Culture
Differences in Musical Cultures

Together, Canada—the modern world's second largest country in area—and the United States—the fourth largest—cover over 7,384,000 square miles of land, approximately 90 percent of the continent of North America. From its highest points, Mt. McKinley in Alaska and Mt. Logan in the Yukon, to its lowest, in Death Valley, California, this enormous land area (roughly 13 percent of the Earth's total) encompasses deserts, imposing mountain ranges, polar ice caps, lush woodlands, rain forests, rich prairies, six time zones, and more than 310,000,000 people of varying ethnicities, languages, and histories (Crystal 1999).

Unity in diversity is a common phrase often used today to describe the people and social contexts of the United States and Canada. It is an apt one, for although these two close neighbors share much in the way of geography, institutions, language, and music and therefore can be seen as a cultural and political unit, the people who live in these countries are also highly diverse in the expression of their own social and musical identities, as nations and as nations within nations. Home to people of virtually all of the world's social, ethnic, religious, and language groups, the United States and Canada have embedded within their history, government, and national consciousness the twin ideals of democracy and equal human rights; although not always realized, these ideals have motivated much political, social, and musical activity within their borders.

Any discussion of music in the United States and Canada must take into account the various contexts of its creation, performance, and meanings. What part do specific geographical, historical, and cultural contexts play in music making among highly diverse social and cultural groups? How are various group and individual identities realized or marked through music and its performance? How do people and their musics interact, merge, or separate from one another to form distinct entities? This essay attempts to answer some of these questions by examining the musical cultures of the United States and Canada through various wide-angle lenses or windows, the first framing a picture of a shared musical culture in which similar patterns of social structure and musical identity are discussed, the second framing another picture, of distinct musical cultures in which the focus is on issues of difference. Finally issues of social and musical interaction are addressed, in which the resulting pictures are far more fluid, amorphous, and blurred and in which identities are contested, negotiated, and continually in flux.

Such frames are for the most part artificial constructions designed to highlight or privilege certain features of musical culture over others; life lived by real people "on the ground," so to speak, is often far more complex, interactive, and unpredictable. These large frames of discussion, then, are to be taken more as guideposts than as true pictures, pointing the way to musical and social streams that have had and continue to have implications for the people and musics of the United States and Canada. The reader is urged to look more closely at specific articles and especially at the ethnographic Snapshots found throughout this volume.

THE LAND AND ITS PEOPLE TODAY

Together the United States and Canada extend east to west from the Atlantic Ocean to the Pacific and north to south from the northern polar cap to the Rio Grande River, which forms the natural boundary between the United States and Mexico. Northeast Canada is separated from Greenland in the east by Baffin Bay; in the northwest, the Beaufort Sea flows into the Arctic Ocean. The southeast United States is framed by the Gulf of Mexico; the southwestern portion by the Pacific Ocean. Alaska, off the northwestern coast of Canada and separated from the easternmost tip of Russia by the Bering Strait, shares far more in terms of topography, climate, and natural resources with northwestern Canada than with the contiguous United States, while Hawai'i, forming one of the many island chains in the South Pacific, shares much with the culture of Polynesia.

Both the east coast plain, framed on the west by the Appalachian Mountains, and the Canadian Shield dominate the eastern portion of the United States and Canada, while the great prairies and plains dominate the central portion of both countries. The mammoth mountain chains—the Eastern and Western Cordilleras (stretching parallel to the Pacific Ocean from Cape Horn at the tip of South America to the Aleutians in Alaska), which encompass the Sierra Nevada, Rocky, and Cascade Mountains in the United States and the Cordillera Chain (including the Rocky, Cassian, and Mackenzie Mountains) in Canada—provide a natural north–south barrier giving way to the lowlands and deserts of the west and southwest coasts of the United States.

Major inland waterways include in the east the St. Lawrence River (Canada) and the Hudson, Delaware, and Potomac Rivers (United States), which flow east into the Atlantic; the dominating central river system, including the Red, Mississippi, and Missouri Rivers, which flow into the Gulf of Mexico; the western Mackenzie (Canada), which flows into the Beaufort Sea; and the Columbia and Colorado Rivers (United States), which flow into the Pacific. The Great Lakes, which share their borders with both Canada and the United States, as well as the Hudson's Bay of Canada, also provide tremendous natural resources today as they did for these countries' earliest inhabitants, as well as dominating the inland waterways system of trade and early land ownership.

Geographical barriers, such as the imposing mountain chains shared by the United States and Canada and the often harsh climate at both temperature extremes, in earlier times often made interaction between social groups difficult; thus musical and other forms of expressive cultural exchanges were fairly limited until the nineteenth century, although American Indian/First Nations groups before that time had developed extensive trade networks among themselves and with the first European traders and settlers.

Political and social organization

Today the United States and Canada are divided politically into the fifty states of the United States and into the ten provinces and three territories of Canada, the third territory, Nunavut, having been established on 1 April 1999. In addition, the United States also has a number of other formal dependencies, such as Puerto Rico, the Virgin

The United States and Canada share a similar political, social, and musical history and yet have also maintained their own distinct identities and expressive modalities, especially in the present day.

Islands, and Samoa, which will only be briefly mentioned in this volume. [See THE GARLAND ENCYCLOPEDIA OF WORLD MUSIC, VOL. 2, SOUTH AMERICA, MEXICO, CENTRAL AMERICA, AND THE CARIBBEAN, AND VOL. 9, AUSTRALIA AND THE PACIFIC ISLANDS, for fuller discussion of these people and their musics.] Canada is considered an independent nation within the British Commonwealth, while the United States is a federal republic, both related forms of democracy in which local and national leaders are elected by the citizenry or appointed by elected officials.

The population of these two countries reflects both their political and social history and current demographic patterns of immigration and settlement. The following information is based on recent census data for the United States (1997) and for Canada (1996), and although the major statistics are presented here, they do not do justice to the variety of subgroups, languages, and ethnicities embedded within these categories [for more specific data please refer to OVERVIEW OF MUSIC IN THE UNITED STATES, p. 519; OVERVIEW OF MUSIC IN CANADA, p. 1066; and other sectional articles].

The first inhabitants—American Indians, Eskimo, and Aleut in the United States, and First Nations, Inuit, and Métis in Canada—are today a small minority of the total population (approximately 5 percent) spread somewhat unevenly throughout the two countries. The majority of American Indian/First Nations peoples today live in the southwest, northeast, and plains areas of the United States and in Ontario, the Plains Provinces, and British Columbia of Canada, with the newest territory, Nunavut, containing a substantial majority of Inuit. Many American Indian/First Nations peoples continue to live today in rural areas or on reservations, often in very depressed economic conditions (especially in the United States, which had a harsher policy than Canada's toward their welfare), while others, especially in the twentieth century, have migrated to large urban areas to find work.

By far the largest population of both countries (about 75 percent of the total) derives from Europe, predominantly Britain and France (about 70 percent of the European total). Obviously many aspects of our federal and local governments, social and political institutions, religions, official languages (English in the United States; English and French in Canada), economies, and musical institutions and values derive from these nations. Sizable populations of Germans, Italians, Ukrainians, Dutch, Scandinavians, Hungarians, and Greeks also live within the United States and Canada, predominantly in urban areas, although Ukrainians and Scandinavians especially played a large part in the westward expansion and rural settlement of these countries in the eighteenth and nineteenth centuries.

The remaining 20 percent of the population is divided among the growing African American/Canadian population (about 10 percent of the total) originally transported from West Africa during both countries' periods of slavery; people of Hispanic origin (Mexican, Caribbean, Central and South American)—the largest growing minority population, representing about 8 percent of the total; and Asian communities (Chinese, Filipino, Japanese, Indian, Korean, Vietnamese, Lao) and Pacific Islanders (predominantly Hawaiians and Tongans), about 2 percent of the total. Again, these statistics are somewhat misleading, especially in Canada, where about 90 percent of the population lives on about 12 percent of the land. In the province of Québec, for example, the population is about 90 percent of French origin, whereas in Newfoundland it is approximately 90 percent of British origin.

About 75 percent of the population of the United States and about 85 percent of the Canadian population live within large urban areas, such as New York, Chicago, and Los Angeles, Toronto, Montréal, and Vancouver, with most of the Canadian population concentrated along the southern border with the United States. The overwhelming majority of the population of both countries is Christian (about 80 percent), with Protestants comprising about 53 percent in the United States and Catholics comprising the largest group (49 percent) in Canada. Sizable Jewish and Muslim populations as well as a growing number of Buddhists, Sikhs, and Hindus have also emigrated to these countries, especially during the twentieth century.

The United States and Canada share a similar political, social, and musical history and yet have also maintained their own distinct identities and expressive modalities, especially in the present day. Other articles in this volume present historical and ethnographic portraits of music and music making in the United States and Canada as separate nations. In the U.S. section, the concentration is on that country's various ethnicities and their development of musical traditions; the Canadian section concentrates on the regional development of musical and social communities [see OVERVIEW OF MUSIC IN THE UNITED STATES, p. 519; OVERVIEW OF MUSIC IN CANADA, p. 1066; other, more specific articles]. This difference in organizational style and content is one of the many you will encounter here, and it reflects less a difference in the actual facts concerning the development of musical cultures in these two countries than a difference in the styles of social and musical scholarship that have developed separately and of concepts of history, music, and nationality that are embedded within Canadian and U.S. notions of themselves as music makers. The following sections of this article will attempt to synthesize those two approaches by taking an overall chronological view of the combined social and musical histories of the two countries and showing, first, various similar trends and, second, major distinctions between the two.

THE UNITED STATES AND CANADA AS A UNIFIED MUSICAL CULTURE

The earliest inhabitants

The original inhabitants of the United States and Canada were the ancestors of the American Indian/First Nations peoples believed to have emigrated here from what is now the westernmost portion of Russia through the Bering Strait in two great waves (c. 18,000 B.C.E. and 12,000 B.C.E.). Centuries before the Europeans arrived, American Indian/First Nations peoples had developed extensive cultures based on hunting, fishing, and small-scale farming that were sustained by a traditional life infused with music and ritual activity.

Specific contexts for musical performance included ceremonies surrounding the yearly cycles of spring/summer and fall/winter activities, including hunting songs (often revealed in dreams) and planting (often including mimetic dancing) and harvesting (thanksgiving) songs and dances, as well as shamanistic practices, including individual and community healing ceremonies. Among the Plains Indians, song practices associated with medicine bundles and with war dances were also common. In the Northwest, among the Haida, Salish, and Athapaskan, potlatches (large feasts characterized by gift giving to all participants) were frequently held, as well as ceremonies accompanying totem pole carving and installation. Some music, such as gambling, game, and love songs, addressed daily social and communal life, while other kinds of music commemorated historical or mythical events. Social dance songs, such as the women's shuffle dances of the Iroquois Confederacy in the northeast United States and southeast Canada, were also performed.

The social structure of most American Indian/First Nations communities traditionally was divided along gender and age lines, with men and women having clearly delineated and equally valued tasks and responsibilities to the group throughout their adult lives. Puberty, marriage, and death rituals were common practices ensuring safe and orderly passage into, through, and beyond life. Puberty rituals, perhaps the most extensive of the life-cycle rituals, often involved separating the young men and women from the community for a period of time, during which the elders would teach them the history and mythology of their group as well as its secret songs and ceremonies.

Many American Indian/First Nations peoples, such as the Inuit/Eskimo living in harsh northern climates, remained fairly isolated and scattered from one another, while others, such as the Plains Indians in the central United States and Canada or the Woodlands Indians in the East, developed by the fifteenth and sixteenth century C.E. large and powerful hunting and trading networks made up of many independent communities tied together through elaborate exchange economies. The intertribal meeting, later to develop into the powwow, became an important context for the exchange not only of food and gossip but also of songs and dances.

Although traditional American Indian/First Nations song and dance was quite varied in terms of its performance contexts and meanings, musically it shared certain basic features: most of the music was vocal, monophonic (one line) or heterophonic (one line performed in different simultaneous variations), with frequent use of vocables (syllables that are phonetically related but have no referential meaning in the local language) (figure 1). No separate instrumental traditions existed, although instruments such as the drum and rattle were frequently used to accompany song. The drum, especially, had deep power and significance for early communities and became in later times a source of much contention between aboriginal peoples and Christian colonists and other settlers, who regularly banned its use.

FIGURE I   Today it is quite common for members of contemporary American Indian groups to visit local schools to teach children something of Indian music and ceremonies. Here, Golden Eagle, from Cleveland, Ohio, is working with elementary school students, who studied with him during a week-long residency preparing meals and performing American Indian rituals. Photo by T. Temple Tuttle, n.d.

From colonies to nations: 1600–1800

Although there is some evidence for early Norse contact in Newfoundland c. 990 C.E., the first permanent European settlements were made by the Spanish in 1565 in modern-day St. Augustine, Florida; the French at Port Royal in Nova Scotia in 1605; and the British in Jamestown, now in Virginia, in 1607. The early visitors were mainly traders sent by various governments and business interests in Europe in hopes of establishing ties with the Indians, who would help them in the lucrative fur trade. By the early seventeenth century, American Indian/First Nations peoples in the East had a fully established economy based on fishing and hunting and had developed skills that proved essential to European survival. With the traders came also notions of private ownership and a money-based economy. Missionaries from Spain and France arrived soon after, bringing with them a radically different spiritual worldview based on the hierarchic principles of Christianity and on early modern European notions of class.

Along with the early traders and clerics came their music, their musical instruments, and their ideas of what music was and was not. By the mid-eighteenth century English and French ballads and other popular secular musics of the day were commonplace, as were British regimental bands, fife and drum field or marching bands, and string orchestras playing the latest minuets and gavottes from Europe to entertain the landed gentry in the southern U.S. colonies, Newfoundland, New France (present-day Québec, claimed in 1607 for the French crown by Samuel de Champlain [1567–1635]), and Acadia (present-day Nova Scotia).

Various forms of hymns, psalmody, and Christian liturgical music had also become commonplace within European communities in the East, promoted in the United States by the singing schools that sprang up, especially in New England, and in Canada by the British Anglican and the French Roman Catholic churches, which controlled land ownership and much of the cultural life of New France. Gradually, as European-derived communities began to grow and social and musical institutions began to develop, new or newly adapted music, composed and performed within the Canadian and U.S. contexts, also began to appear in the form of French *voyageur* ballads, Anglo American ballads, theatrical music, and hymns composed and taught by singing masters and clerics.

Interactions between Europeans and American Indian/First Nations peoples were frequent especially in Canada, where the children of aboriginals and Europeans (especially the French) known as Métis began to develop their own separate language and expressive culture. In the United States, as more and more land was taken by European settlements, Indian lands began to shrink, and communities that had once roamed freely were forced to develop new forms of economy and social interaction based on European models. Furthermore, disturbed by the powerful drumming of many Indian groups with whom they had contact, Europeans began to ban its use in Indian ceremonies, describing it as sinful and primitive [see SOURCES, SCHOLARSHIP, AND HISTORIOGRAPHY, p. 21].

Many revitalizing movements, such as that of the Iroquoian Handsome Lake, who established the Longhouse religion in 1799, attempted to help Indian communities face the swift social, religious, and political changes (not to mention diseases such as tuberculosis and smallpox) brought by the Europeans, and much Indian music developed at the time addresses the destruction of their traditional way of life. Some musical interaction took place, such as the development of the *katachina* ceremony (Indian/Spanish) and the Métis fiddling tradition (Indian/French/Celtic). However, such interaction was limited for many reasons, not the least of which was that European concepts of music, especially secular forms such as ballads, dances, or marching band music, and of notation whereby music was written down were initially unknown to the Indians, who viewed what they did as prayer, ritual, or ceremony—in other words, as religious and social, as well as "sounded," behavior.

In constant fear of uprisings, slave owners frequently banned, as they had with aboriginals, the use of drums and certain dances.

Slavery was introduced into the United States in 1619 and in Canada in 1689; by 1800 over a million blacks, of mainly West African and Caribbean descent, were living within these two countries (about 95 percent of them in the United States). The majority of slaves in Canada were not imported directly from West Africa, however, but were brought in as property with the Loyalists (those who remained loyal to the British crown following the American Revolution in 1776), who emigrated from the United States in great numbers in the late eighteenth century. Slavery as an institution was far less entrenched in Canada than in the United States and was abolished somewhat earlier there, first in Nova Scotia in 1787 and in Upper Canada (present-day Ontario) in 1793. It would take another seventy years and the Civil War (1861–1865) for the United States to abolish slavery as a legal institution, and during that time thousands of runaway slaves passed through the Underground Railroad, a system of interconnected hiding places that took them north via the Great Lakes from the United States into Canada, through cities such as Detroit, Buffalo, and Rochester. Frequently African American songs such as "Follow the Drinking Gourd" (the Big Dipper, shaped like a ladle) were used as musical/linguistic codes to give directions to runaways.

The slaves imported from the coastal areas of West Africa and the Caribbean often brought with them small, portable musical instruments such as drums and gourd rattles as well as a vast and rich tradition of song, dance, ritual, and ceremony (figure 2). Because the slaves were frequently separated from their families, first in Africa and then again in North America, much of the integrity and cohesiveness of their many musical cultures was lost. Furthermore, in constant fear of uprisings, slave owners frequently banned, as they had with aboriginals, the use of drums and certain dances (regarded by

FIGURE 2   Members of St. John's Spiritual Baptist Church in the Flatbush neighborhood of Brooklyn, New York, sing a hymn from the Church of England's *Hymns Ancient and Modern.* The Spiritual Baptist faith probably originated in St. Vincent Island in the east Caribbean, then flourished in Trinidad, but through immigrants it also thrives in New York City and Toronto. Photo by Terry Miller, 1989.

the European gentry as indecent). Slave culture, especially in the United States, thus developed its own unique "American" musical tradition based on calls, cries, and other forms of vocal musics that enabled slaves to communicate their feelings as well as vital bits of information through their performance [see TWO VIEWS OF MUSIC, RACE, AND ETHNICITY, p. 76].

In the eighteenth century, as a result of various treaties negotiated in Europe between the British and French following the Peace of Utrecht in 1713 and the French and Indian War (known in Europe as part of the Seven Years War, 1756–1763), the French lost control of most of their formerly claimed territory in Canada, ceding it to Britain. Many French living in what was then Acadia (present-day Nova Scotia) were forcibly removed to the Louisiana Territory, a French-controlled portion of the southeastern United States, where they interacted with Africans and Indians primarily from the Caribbean, creating a new and vital Cajun culture with its own language dialects and musical traditions.

By the end of the sixteenth century Spanish clerics had established a thriving mission culture predominantly in the upper Rio Grande Valley in New Mexico, bringing with them, either directly from Spain or via Mexico, Spanish sacred music in the form of the *alabado* 'religious ballads related to Catholic plainchant' and religious theatrical forms such as Christmas and Easter plays. They also frequently imported musical instruments from Europe, including organs, which were installed within their newly built churches (Kingman 1998:53). Secular music also traveled from Mexico and through Spanish-held territories in what is now the southwestern United States. As mestizo culture (a blending of Spanish, West African, and American Indian cultures) developed, new forms such as the *corrido* 'ballad' and later *conjunto* 'ensemble music' became popular along the Rio Grande and throughout the southwestern United States. European, predominantly German and Czech, immigration to Mexico also introduced various popular dances such as the polka and the quintessential polka band instrument, the button accordion, which became a mainstay of various later-developed Mexican ensembles.

Westward expansion: 1800–1900

By the beginning of the nineteenth century, the new United States of America and the two Canadas were established. (Upper Canada, present-day Ontario, and Lower Canada, present-day Québec, were united in 1840 and merged with other Atlantic provinces into the Dominion of Canada in 1867.) Boundaries between these two nations were firmly drawn by 1850 and their capitals settled in Washington, District of Columbia (1800), and Ottawa, Province of Ontario (1867).

The nineteenth century is marked in both countries by westward expansion to the Pacific Ocean; by the immigration of many European groups, as well as Chinese and Japanese; by the building of the transcontinental railways; by the gold rushes of the 1850s in the United States and in the Yukon in the 1890s; by various policies, especially those of the U.S. government, surrounding the taking of Indian land, forcible Indian migration, and war; and by discriminatory practices aimed at both American Indian/First Nations peoples and African Americans. Both countries expanded their land holdings through purchases with European and Mexican powers and through such business enterprises as the Hudson's Bay Company, which sold the land now known as the Province of Manitoba and the Northwest Territories to the newly formed Dominion of Canada in 1869.

By 1850 the United States had acquired most of its southeastern territory from France through the Louisiana Purchase (1803), Florida from Spain (1819), and much of the Southwest (Texas, California, Arizona, Nevada, New Mexico, Utah, parts of Colorado, Oklahoma, and Wyoming) from Mexico through the treaty of Guadalupe Hidalgo signed at the end of the Mexican–American War in 1848. The last large chunks of land to be added to the United States were Alaska, sold by Russia in 1867, and Hawai'i, previously an independent republic and annexed in 1898, although both would not become states until the middle of the twentieth century (Chiswick 1992: 41–42; 429–430).

Sizable communities of Germans, Scandinavians, Italians, Ukrainians, and, in the mid- to late nineteenth century, Greeks, Hungarians, and Southern and Eastern Europeans, among others, emigrated to the United States and Canada during this time, capitalizing on both countries' offers of inexpensive farm land and land grants in the great prairie states and provinces. With these communities came their music, including sacred Moravian hymns, Lutheran chorales, and Orthodox Russian, Greek, and other Eastern Orthodox practices. German and Scandinavian communities, especially, modeled their musical activities after those they had enjoyed in Europe, and soon various orchestras, town bands, choral societies, "liederkranz" 'singing circles', and Ukrainian *bandura* 'long-necked chordophone' orchestras were established. Italians, too, brought their own European musical culture to the New World in the form of opera and popular and folk music traditions. And the Irish, emigrating to escape the potato famine and difficult economic conditions in their homeland, brought their rich folk song, fiddling, and Celtic dance traditions, settling primarily in the growing eastern cities.

As the major cities in the East and Midwest—New York, Philadelphia, Chicago, Toronto, and Montréal—began to grow, large communities developed that could sustain middle- and upper-middle-class European-derived musical institutions such as concert halls, opera houses, theaters, and schools modeled after their European counterparts. Classical concert music began to flourish, at first based on European models but later taking on its own "American" character, based in part on the adoption and adaptation of various indigenous and newly arrived folk traditions.

In the rural U.S. South other rich traditions slowly emerged: (1) the African American spiritual and black gospel hymn, originally part of worship service but later adapted for concert use by choirs such as the Wiregrass Sacred Harp Singers (figure 3); (2) white gospel hymns, originally evolved from the shape-note tradition and the nineteenth-century camp meeting and produced by the hundreds by composers such as Dwight Moody (1837–1899), Ira Sankey (1840–1908), and Fanny Jane Crosby (1820–1915), among others; (3) early blues, based on African American musical and linguistic forms such as field cries and hollers; and (4) country ("hillbilly") music, originally evolved from the Scottish and English ballad tradition that flourished there.

With the division of music into essentially urban and rural contexts, a regional–class hierarchy began to develop in the United States and Canada that had both an east–west and north–south split. Furthermore, the social–critical rhetoric of the time, found in newspapers, music journals, and other publications, revealed a European bias that still exists in some quarters today. Music and musical activities in the larger East Coast cities and continuing close ties with British and other European composers and teaching methods (especially in Canada), for example, began to be constructed as more "refined," and "sophisticated" (much like contemporary European urban concert music), whereas the predominantly rural southern (in the United States) and western areas of both countries began to be seen as "rustic," "coarse," and, in the case of fiddle music, "the devil's work" (much like European peasant music of the nostalgic past). These class distinctions would become more complex and embedded within notions of separate American and Canadian musics developed in the twentieth century.

Westward expansion in the United States and Canada, of course, resulted in the shrinking of American Indian/First Nations lands and the continued destruction, especially in the United States, of the Indian way of life. In the 1880s frequent wars broke

FIGURE 3   Henry Japeth Jackson of Ozark, Alabama's, Wiregrass Sacred Harp Singers explains the four-shape note system (fasola) at a workshop during Kent State University's annual folk festival. Photo by Terry Miller, 1989.

FIGURE 4   Two Métis women sitting in a Canadian prairie field. The woman on the left is holding a small scraper; the one on the right, a button accordion. Photo by Carl Kalbfleish, courtesy Saskatchewan Archive Board (#R-A 14, 337).

out between the United States cavalry and members of the Sioux nation, for example. As in the East among the Iroquois a century earlier, Plains Indians developed new and creative ceremonies and rituals to counteract the destruction of their material and spiritual lives. Perhaps the best known was the short-lived Ghost Dance religion that emerged in the 1880s, immediately traveling northward into Canada, which espoused revivalist beliefs in the coming of a new world free of white men, without sickness or hunger, and marked by the return of the buffalo. Misinterpreted as war dances, Ghost Dance ceremonies were banned and interactions between the army and the Sioux grew worse, culminating in the devastating massacre at Wounded Knee in 1890 [see MUSICAL INTERACTIONS, p. 480].

First Nations peoples in Canada, although also facing discriminatory practices, were treated with somewhat more dignity than were their U.S. counterparts. For example, they were not forcibly removed and transported westward, as were many American Indians, such as the Seminole in the southern United States in the mid-nineteenth century, but rather emigrated on their own to find work and better living conditions. And the Métis, who wished to separate themselves from both the French community in Québec and the Prairies Indian communities, declared their own nationhood under the leadership of Louis Riel (1844–1885) in the Red River Valley of Saskatchewan, where they were ultimately defeated in the late 1880s. Certain musical fusions, such as the adoption and adaptation of the European-derived brass band tradition by the Northwest Coast Indians, mark this period as one of continuous social and musical interaction (figure 4).

In the mid- to late nineteenth century, two events—the completion of the transcontinental railroad and the gold rushes (spawning their own repertoire of ballads) in both countries—established new patterns of immigration and social and musical exchange. Chinese and Japanese workers were brought to both the United States and Canada in the 1850s to work as miners and later to help complete the railway. With them they brought Asian religious beliefs and practices as well as their own classical, theatrical, dance, and folk music traditions. The Cantonese, for example, established a large community in Vancouver, British Columbia, that quickly supported a number of Chinese opera and theater associations [see CANTONESE MUSIC IN VANCOUVER, p. 1260]. Never a majority in western Canada, the British worked with other Europeans primarily as farmers, performing agrarian-associated musical repertoires such as ballads, seasonal song cycles, and ceremonial music for weddings and Christian services.

Changing patterns in the twentieth century

As most of the articles in this volume discuss contemporary music and musical practices and their immediate histories in the twentieth century, this section will simply present some of the major political, social, and musical trends of this time. The reader is encouraged to read more about these trends in specific articles listed in the Table of Contents, p. v.

Perhaps the major factors affecting the growth (and, occasionally, the demise) of musical traditions in the United States and Canada during the twentieth century were: (1) the development of mass media and related technologies and the resulting commodification of folk, popular, and religious musics; (2) new patterns of immigration resulting in the influx of large groups of people, predominantly from Southern Europe, Asia, and the Caribbean, especially between 1880 and 1920, which brought about new governmental policies concerning immigration, the status of citizens, and the construction of "ethnicity" and "multiculturalism" through revivals and other forms of cultural display; (3) the development of an American/Canadian-defined classical music tradition; and (4) the rapid growth of institutions that supported the collection, study, and teaching of U.S./Canadian-born musics.

By the mid-twentieth century one could experience music from all over the world through recordings and even witness its performance in own's living room through the medium of television.

Certainly the invention of the radio in the late nineteenth century and the rise of recording and broadcasting technology in the late nineteenth and early twentieth century, along with the completion of the transcontinental railroads and highways, made it easier for people and their musics to travel and to interact over greater and greater geographic, linguistic, and social distances. Now it was not necessary to make music yourself or even to travel to the local concert hall, church, powwow, or fiddling festival to hear musical performances. By the mid-twentieth century one could experience music from all over the world through recordings and even witness its performance in one's living room through the medium of television.

Perhaps one of the most profound social and musical changes that occurred when this new technology was introduced was that for the first time in human history, musical sound itself (not just its abstraction in the form of notation) could be captured and materialized. This made it far easier for people to conceptualize music as a "thing" rather than as human social and interactive behavior, for people to "own" music, and, ultimately, for music and its performance to become a commodity within the rapidly changing capitalist economies of the modern world. Of course, this technology also made new sounds possible and far more available to many more people and thus became a source of new creative techniques for composers, performers, and other musicians. At the beginning of the twenty-first century it is possible, through electronic media such as CDs, audio- and videocassettes, computers, and other digital formats, for anyone (with the economic means to do so) to listen to, download, even edit any recorded music from any part of the world.

A major wave of immigration at the end of the nineteenth century through World War I (c. 1880–1918) also changed the face of the United States and Canada. Although smaller communities had emigrated from the seventeenth century onwards, large groups of Ashkenazic Jews from Eastern Europe and Russia; Chinese, primarily from Canton; Doukhobors, a religious group from Russia, under the leadership of Peter Veregin; and Muslim Arabs from the Middle East began arriving in large numbers at that time, settling primarily in large urban areas such as New York, Chicago, Edmonton, and Vancouver or, as in the case of the Doukhobors, in the farming communities of British Columbia. With them they brought not only their folk and dance traditions but also liturgical, theatrical, and classical musics. Many Jews, for example, who had been cantors or instrumental musicians in Eastern Europe, joined newly established symphony orchestras. Others, such as Irving Berlin (1888–1989) and Al Jolson (1886–1950), quickly found their way to Tin Pan Alley (the colloquial name given to the New York City district where popular songs were written and sold), to the burgeoning film industry in Los Angeles, or to the vaudeville stage. Still others, such as the Brooklyn-born Richard Tucker (1914–1975), became famous opera stars.

The first half of the twentieth century also saw the development of African American styles, such as gospel music (through the efforts of Thomas A. Dorsey [1899–1993] and others); the blues of Muddy Waters (1918–1953), Bessie Smith (1894–1937), and countless others; the ragtime of Scott Joplin (1868–1917); and early jazz forms performed and recorded by King Oliver (1885–1938) and Jelly Roll Morton (1885–1941) developed in large urban areas such as New Orleans, Chicago, Kansas City, and Montréal. And, of course, in the white rural South, the popularity of "hillbilly," "cowboy," or country music, made popular by the recordings of Jimmy Rodgers (1897–1933) and the prodigious Carter Family, among many others, would spread through radio programs such as *Grand Ole Opry* and ultimately merge with the blues in midcentury to form early rock and roll.

Hispanic music, too, began to emerge as a growing force, especially in the southern ballad tradition (*corrido*) and in popular dance music as more and more people from Mexico and the Caribbean entered the United States and Canada and began to establish communities. Dances such as the *habanera, son,* rumba, mambo and cha-cha-chá from Cuba, Puerto Rico, Haiti, and other Caribbean islands, performed in venues such as the Palladium Ballroom in New York City by bandleaders Xavier Cugat (1900–1990) and Tito Puente (1925–2000), among others, became wildly popular in the 1940s and 1950s, especially in large urban areas such as New York, Los Angeles, and Toronto.

The new wave of immigration, as well as newfound economic and social mobility for African Americans and African Canadians, however, soon ushered in a wave of conservatism where laws such as the Chinese Restriction Act in Canada (1923–1947), the quota system in the United States (1921–1965), and the "separate but equal" doctrine (established in 1896 to keep public facilities such as schools, restaurants, and so on segregated by race; overthrown in 1954) in the United States, restricted the immigration and mobility of certain groups, most notably Chinese, Japanese, Jews, and African Americans, and discriminatory practices against these and other groups were common. By midcentury, however, American Indian/First Nations peoples had become citizens through the 1942 Citizens Act in the United States and the Canadian Citizenship Act of 1947.

One of the outcomes of a new ethnic and political consciousness in the United States and Canada at midcentury was the renewal of interest in roots and in old-time, Old World, or traditional musics. This interest crystallized in the 1950s and 1960s in the form of revivals, festivals, and other forms of cultural display where members of different groups could perform old musics in new settings for new audiences (figure 5) and where largely white, young, middle-class audiences could come together to participate in group musical experiences, such as hootenannies and sing-ins, where various

FIGURE 5 A typical Appalachian string band, consisting of (*left to right*) banjo, two guitars, fiddle, mandolin, and guitar, performing at the National Folk Festival near Cleveland, Ohio. Photo by Terry Miller, 1984.

governmental policies such as school segregation, the Vietnam War, or the authority of their parents could be protested. Folk singers such as Pete Seeger, Joan Baez, and the Kingston Trio in the United States and Gordon Lightfoot, Joni Mitchell, and Buffy Sainte-Marie in Canada became not only national singing stars, but also national heros to a younger generation of idealistic "flower children." Canada was especially committed to the ideals of ethnic diversity, forming the Royal Commission on Bilingualism and Biculturalism in 1963 and gradually developing support for multiculturalism, as entrenched in the Multicultural Act of 1988.

Classical music traditions in the United States and Canada during the twentieth century also developed in similar but slowly diverging ways. One pattern that both countries shared, however, was a growing interest in separating culturally from Europe and in forming authentic American and Canadian forms and institutions. As early as the mid-nineteenth century, certain "nativist" composers such as George Frederick Bristow (1825–1898) and Louis Moreau Gottschalk (1829–1869) in the United States and, in Canada, Calixa Lavallée (1842–1891), the composer of the present Canadian national anthem, "O Canada," and Alexis Constant (1858–1918), among others, were beginning to speak of the need to establish independent musical identities, separate not only from Europe but also from each other (Kingman 1998:289–296; McGee 1985:74–81).

By the early twentieth century, U.S. composers such as Edward MacDowell (1860–1908), Henry F. Gilbert (1868–1928), and Arthur Farwell (1872–1952) were consciously incorporating American Indian and African American songs into their classical compositions, one example being Gilbert's symphonic poem, *Dance in Place Congo* (1906–1908), based on African American tunes performed by southern blacks during the Reconstruction period following the Civil War. Perhaps the best known U.S. composers in the 1920s and beyond whose works are most clearly defined as American are Charles Ives (1874–1954), Virgil Thomson (1896–1989), and Aaron Copland (1900–1990), whose works painted musical pictures of an idealized America in midcentury. Examples are Ives's *Three Places in New England* (1904–1914) and the *Concord Sonata* (1911–1915), Thomson's music to accompany the film *The Plow That Broke the Plains* (1936) and Copland's ballets *Appalachian Spring* (1944) and *Billy the Kid* (1938). Truly revolutionary musics, notations, and technologies were to come later, generally between 1950 and 1970, in the new, electronic musics of John Cage (1912–1992), Milton Babbitt (b. 1916), Elliott Carter (b. 1908), and Morton Subotnick (b. 1933) [see ELECTRONIC CONCERT MUSIC, p. 252].

Although similar efforts were being made to assert a national aesthetic in Canada, Canadian composers were more likely to study in England or France as part of their training and to compose pieces based on preestablished European models. One such composer, Claude Champagne (1891–1965), studied in Paris but attempted to infuse his work with a Canadian consciousness, especially in works such as *Suite Canadienne* and *Images du Canada français,* in which he tried to depict musically the French Canadian countryside. In addition to his prolific composing, R. Murray Schafer (b. 1933), perhaps Canada's best-known composer in the mid- to late twentieth century, established in the late 1960s the World Soundscape Project at Simon Fraser University (McGee 1985:91–97, 136–137).

Finally, as educational institutions began to develop and grow within the two countries, so too did an interest in music scholarship, the collection and study of the musics not only of the great European masters through their own notations but also of the many groups of people who had migrated to the United States and Canada, through ethnographic fieldwork based primarily on the oral/aural tradition. Collectors such as Sir Francis James Child and Cecil Sharp (British American ballads and folk materials), Frances Densmore (American Indian materials), Alan and John Lomax (early blues, ballads, and much else) in the United States and Roy MacKenzie, Kenneth

Peacock, Helen Creighton, and Edith Fowke (English ballad tradition, mainly in the Atlantic provinces), among others, in Canada, contributed greatly to our understanding of music as human social behavior as well as beautifully organized sound.

Some lingering (and unifying) effects of European social and musical hegemony

Despite the rich and ever-increasing variety of social, cultural, and religious groups that have always been a part of the cultural portrait of the United States and Canada, European (primarily British) language, political, social, and economic structures have largely prevailed into the twenty-first century. With them have also come European-derived discourses surrounding the dissemination and production of music in the New World.

For example, the primary scholarly divisions and canonization of music into classical, folk, and popular musics that dominated the formal teaching of music in the twentieth century in major institutions such as the University of Toronto and McGill University in Canada and the Juilliard School and the Peabody and New England Conservatories of Music, as well as major university music schools such as those of Michigan, Illinois, Indiana, California, and Rochester (Eastman School of Music), continue to define music as a largely European-derived, class-based phenomenon. However, as Timothy Rice has pointed out in his introduction to *The Garland Encyclopedia of Music,* vol. 8, *Europe,* these artificial divisions were largely invented as a European nationalist strategy in the nineteenth century to distinguish among the cultivated, literate, and monied elite (classical), the agrarian-based rural peasant class (folk), and the urban working middle class (popular) (2000:2). Such distinctions, still perpetuated today in U.S. and Canadian educational institutions as well as in the display bins of the large book and recording retailers, tend to further perpetuate other class-based distinctions such as literacy, education, and economic standing—clearly privileging musical notation over the oral/aural tradition, "formal" music learning over "informal," and the material aspects of music making, such as the use of (ever more complicated and expensive) musical instruments, over the solo voice. European notions of music—and even the word *music* itself—however, initially had little to do with American Indian/First Nations or early immigrant ideas of sound as ritually and spiritually rooted in social and ceremonial life, or as efficacious in bringing about a successful hunt, the growth of crops, or a healthy baby. As various social, political, and musical institutions were gradually put into place and have largely persisted into the twenty-first century, the inheritance from Europe is still strongly felt in the New World (especially in Canada), while at the same time it is frequently contested.

DIFFERENCES IN MUSICAL CULTURES

So far, this essay has concentrated on the shared social, political, and musical histories of the United States and Canada. But there is also much that separates these two countries into distinct musical cultures. Discussed here are some of these issues, such as the construction of separate, nationally based social and musical identities in each country; the relationships that the United States and Canada have maintained with Europe as well as with each other; the role of government in the development of different musical institutions and policies; and a new way to conceptualize music and social identity within the context of two pluralistic nations.

Separate national and musical identities

Various metaphors—"rainbow," "salad bowl," "mosaic"—have frequently been used in the rhetoric of social critics and others to describe the ethnic, racial, and social diversity of the United States and Canada. Among them, perhaps the term *melting pot,* taken from Israel Zangwill's (1864–1926) play about the Jewish immigrant experience, "The Melting Pot" (1914), is the most enduring (at least in the United States), if not the

Perhaps the major polarizations that have been used variously to construct a positive (or negative) picture of the unity of the United States and Canada, as well as its diversity, have been the black/white (United States) and French/English (Canada) dichotomies, which have infused especially the written musical histories of both countries.

most accurately descriptive of actual life and social interaction. The history of these two countries is, rather, marked as in many modern nation-states by the ebb and flow of nationalism—constructed predominantly during war or difficult economic times, when individual or group identities are minimized and discriminatory practices are more in evidence—and pride in diversity, seen most often during periods of relative economic ease, when specific social identities are valorized, often commodified, and an interest in civil rights becomes more prominent.

The United States and Canada have had different political and social histories, creating musical stories that reflect these differences. Perhaps the most obvious difference between the two countries is their geography: the contiguous United States shares a long southern border with Mexico, and immigration from this country, as well as from the countries of Spain (through Mexico), Central America, and the Caribbean, has been constant over many centuries. Spanish, Mexican, and other Latin musics have made enormous contributions to the musics of the United States for many years, first through the long-established missions in the South and West, later through various border traditions such as the *corrido* and *conjunto,* and most recently through popular dances, songs, and styles, such as *salsa,* and various musical elements, such as rhythmic complexity, that have been adopted by rock and jazz musicians (figure 6).

On the opposite end of the continent, the northern coast of Canada faces the Arctic Ocean and the polar ice cap, and rugged, often hostile living conditions there have made settlement difficult even in the present day. A growing popular music industry in the Yukon has distinguished northern Canada, but Hispanic music, so much a part of

FIGURE 6   Latin-flavored street music in New York City. Photo by Terry Miller, 1981.

the U.S. musical landscape, was, until the late twentieth century, found less in Canada, with one major exception: Caribana, held in Toronto every summer and billed as one of the world's largest Afro-Caribbean festivals.

Another geographic consideration that has affected the development of distinct U.S. and Canadian musical personalities has been polarization of the coasts, mentioned earlier. In the United States, although an east–west distinction is present, especially in more recent times, the division between north and south is primary, having been solidified through centuries of difference in settlement patterns, economic institutions, and issues surrounding slavery. But in Canada the primary split has always been east–west, with the major cities of Toronto and Montréal being settled and "gentrified" long before the "rustic" western cities of Edmonton and Vancouver. These distinctions have been most apparent in the development of various musical styles and institutions, such as performance halls and schools.

In constructing many national identities over the centuries, both the United States and Canada have frequently concentrated on, negotiated, or polarized different ethnic/ racial groups—especially in relation to the overarching hegemony of primarily western and northern European "mainstream" culture. In certain contexts such as music festivals and contests, this polarization served positively to highlight distinctive features of specific groups that distinguish them within the mosaic or rainbow of North American culture as a whole. More frequently, however, such discriminations have served a negative purpose, resulting in the restriction and subjugation of certain groups, most notably American Indian/First Nations peoples and African Americans. These ethnic tensions have had a major impact on the growth and development of musical styles and genres within these two countries, as many articles in this volume attest.

Perhaps the major polarizations that have been used variously to construct a positive (or negative) picture of the unity of the United States and Canada, as well as its diversity, have been the black/white (United States) and French/English (Canada) dichotomies, which have infused especially the written musical histories of both countries [see SOURCES, SCHOLARSHIP, and HISTORIOGRAPHY, p. 21]. In the United States, the black/white racial divide has historically created artificial but divisive barriers to musical interaction and to the recognition especially of African American and Hispanic contributions to a complete musical portrait. The lasting effects of slavery in the form of discriminatory practices, such as those preventing black performers from playing in certain contexts, are still, albeit perhaps more subtly, affecting the ways in which black and white performers are received and accepted today, although late-twentieth-century forms such as rock and rap have catapulted many black performers to international stardom.

In Canada, where slavery never became the settled institution it was in the United States, the French/English polarity has historically taken precedence. The original European settlers in Canada were the French, and its first name, New France, reflected this influence until the mid-eighteenth century, when New France gave way to the British-controlled Two Canadas. The legacy of French control has been felt to the present day in Canada in the recognition of French as an official language, in the growing separatist movements in Québec and elsewhere, in musical traditions, an example being *chansonnier*, that flourish in Canada but not in the United States, and in the growth of a separate culture, that of the Métis (descendants of Indians and French).

One final feature of U.S. and Canadian identity that will be discussed here is their respective relationship to Europe. Although Canada, especially in more recent times, has begun to assert its own musical "Canadian-ness," it still maintains strong ties to Europe, especially to Britain and France, whereas composers and other musicians in the United States have made a more conscious turn away from Europe, attempting to construct a uniquely "American" (that is, U.S.) musical identity.

The relationship of the United States and Canada to each other

A discussion of the music of the United States and Canada would not be complete without acknowledging the unequal power relations between the two countries in terms of musical production and dissemination [see OVERVIEW OF MUSIC IN CANADA, p. 1066]. Although larger than the United States in terms of land mass, Canada has about one-tenth the population, and new towns are still growing rapidly, especially in the West. Canadians frequently joke that their country has no separate identity and that it is, in reality, the fifty-first state, while people living in the United States often refer either pejoratively or nostalgically to Canada as "our partner to the North," an ill-defined place where life is rugged, untamed, and still "pure," but often constructed as weaker and undervalued.

Although all communities that have lived in these two countries, no matter what their origins, have always participated in musical and social activities of various kinds, until the twentieth century and the growth of electronic technology, neither country was considered (at least by the standards of European classical music) to be especially musically sophisticated. In the eighteenth and nineteenth centuries, for example, musical performances, such as those of the "Swedish Nightingale," Jenny Lind (1820–1887), and others were frequently imported from Europe for the edification of American audiences, and ensembles and theatrical troupes from the United States sometimes toured Canada. With the advent of radio, television, film, and computer technology, however, the United States has become a world leader in music composition and production, especially within popular music, and genres such as rock, rap, jazz, and country and western music, which were born and developed within unique social and musical contexts of the United States, and have become the world's most popular musics. In addition, the North American Free Trade Agreement (NAFTA) enacted with Canada in 1989 (and with Mexico in 1994) has caused some concern in Canada that the United States will simply drain all of its natural, economic, and musical resources, leaving it unable to compete in today's world.

The Canadian government has taken certain measures in response to these developments to ensure the performance of Canadian music, especially on the radio. From its earliest days, the Canadian Broadcasting Corporation (CBC) was one of the largest patrons of Canadian orchestral and band music, broadcasting this music weekly across the country. When many radio stations in Canada began adopting the popular music formats of the United States in the 1970s and 1980s, the Canadian government enacted the Cancon regulations, requiring FM stations to play a certain percentage of Canadian music each day. In addition, both English- and French-run music publishing businesses have taken protective measures to ensure the dissemination of Canadian music [see FOUR VIEWS OF MUSIC IN CANADA, p. 1101].

Musical and social interactions

Another way of understanding how music and social identity work together in Canada and the United States is to see all forms of identity, even nationalistic ones, as constantly in flux and continuously negotiated in the context of everyday and ritual life. For example, although we may conceptualize Canada and the United States as two separate and distinct political entities (separated by a thick border on the map), ethnic, social, religious, and other kinds of groups freely cross such borders, creating different kinds of cultural boundaries that are far more fluid, permeable, and changeable. Music can be seen as a marker of certain aspects of one's identity at any given moment and is often used by individuals or groups to help define themselves in relation to others and as a means for others to define them as well. A German American brass band marching down the street during Oktoberfest, for example, may be an important way of demonstrating a German community's pride in its ethnicity, but each individual member of this community may be many other things besides a German American (such as a

Lutheran, a woman, a white person, and so on). Similarly, many teenagers in the United States and Canada enjoy contemporary popular music, and one's whole identity as a "punk" or "nerd" can rest on the strength of what band one listens to, but years later, those same teenagers may look back on those musical and identity choices as childish or silly.

In his work with different musical communities, Mark Slobin (1993), among others, has suggested that we begin to rethink our notions of musical and social identity as fixed and simplistic, instead seeing them as constructed over a lifetime, based on the interaction and relative importance of several factors, including one's ethnicity, nationality, religion, gender, affinity groups, and many others, elements that carry different weight or meaning at specific times (see also Koskoff 1980) (figures 7 and 8). And because we are all social and musical beings who interact with others, there is always the potential for identities and musics to intermingle and cross borders, creating new groups, new musics, and new interactions. Thus as we move into the twenty-first century we should not be surprised to see new musical and social forms develop, such as Northwest Indian brass bands, French Indian blues, Celtic revivalists who are Jewish (and *klezmer* clarinetists who are not), African American classical composers, and

FIGURES 7 and 8   Young Cambodian girls and boys sing and dance at the National Heritage Festival, Washington, D.C., 1980. Social identities such as gender and age are frequently performed through music and dance. The girls in figure 7, for example, use specific movements and gestures that define them as young (probably unmarried), graceful, and refined women, while the boys in figure 8 perform using the single-headed *skor chhaiyaim* drums and masks, denoting their status within Cambodian culture as young and powerful men. Photo by Terry E. Miller.

female percussionists, as well as unlikely musical combinations, such as Ukrainian country, American Indian gospel, or Christian rock, because these combinations are natural within the rich and complex contexts of social and musical plurality that define the United States and Canada today.

REFERENCES

Alba, Richard D. 1990. *Ethnic Identity: The Transformation of White America.* New Haven, Conn.: Yale University Press.

Allen, James Paul. 1988. *We the People: An Atlas of America's Ethnic Diversity.* New York: Macmillan.

Auerbach, Susan. 1994. *Encyclopedia of Multiculturalism.* New York: Marshall Cavendish.

Breton, Raymond. 1980. *Cultural Boundaries and the Cohesion of Canada.* Montréal: Institute for Research on Public Policy.

Chase, Gilbert. 1987. *America's Music: From the Pilgrims to the Present.* Urbana: University of Illinois Press.

Chiswick, Barry R., ed. 1992. *Immigration, Language and Ethnicity: Canada and the United States.* Washington, D.C.: AEI Press.

Crawford, Richard. 1993. *The American Musical Landscape.* Berkeley: University of California Press.

Crystal, David. 1999. *The Cambridge Factfinder.* 3rd ed. Cambridge: Cambridge University Press.

Denisoff, R. Serge. 1983. *Sing a Song of Social Significance.* 2nd ed. Bowling Green, Ohio: Bowling Green State University Press.

Diamond, Beverley and Robert Witmer, eds. 1994. *Canadian Music: Issues of Hegemony and Identity.* Toronto: Canadian Scholars' Press, Inc.

Driedger, Leo, ed. 1978. *The Canadian Ethnic Mosaic.* Canadian Ethnic Studies Association Series 6. Toronto: McClelland and Stewart, Ltd.

———. 1999. *Immigrant Canada: Demographic, Economic, and Social Challenges.* Toronto: University of Toronto Press.

Hamm, Charles. 1983. *Music in the New World.* New York: Norton.

Hitchcock, H. Wiley. 1988. *Music in the United States: A Historical Introduction.* 3rd ed. Englewood Cliffs, N.J.: Prentice-Hall.

Kallmann, Helmut. 1960. *A History of Music in Canada, 1534–1914.* Toronto: University of Toronto Press.

Kallmann, Helmut, Gilles Potvin, and Kenneth Winters, eds. 1992. *Encyclopedia of Music in Canada.* 2nd edition. Toronto: University of Toronto Press.

Katkin, Wendy F., Ned Landsman, and Andrea Tyree, eds. 1998. *Beyond Pluralism: The Conception of Groups and Group Identities in America.* Urbana: University of Illinois Press.

Kingman, Daniel. 1998. *American Music: A Panorama.* New York: Schirmer Books.

Koskoff, Ellen. 1980. *The Musical Self.* Pittsburgh: University of Pittsburgh, External Studies Program.

Lipset, Seymour Martin. 1990. *Continental Divide: The Values and Institutions of the United States and Canada.* New York: Routledge.

Lornell, Kip, and Anne K. Rasmussen, eds. 1997. *Musics of Multicultural America: A Study of Twelve Musical Communities.* New York: Schirmer Books.

Magocsi, Paul, ed. 1988. *Encyclopedia of Canada's Peoples.* Toronto: University of Toronto Press.

McGee, Timothy J. 1985. *The Music of Canada.* New York: Norton.

McGee, Timothy J., ed. 1995. *Taking a Stand., Essays in Honour of John Beckwith.* Toronto: University of Toronto Press.

Rice, Timothy, Christopher Goertzen, and James Porter, eds. 2000. *The Garland Encyclopedia of World Music.* Vol. 8, *Europe.* New York: Garland Publishers.

Schafer, R. Murray. 1984. *R. Murray Schafer on Canadian Music.* Bancroft, Ont.: Arcana Editions.

Slobin, Mark. 1993. *Sub-Cultural Sounds: Micromusics of the West.* Hanover, N.H.: University Press of New England.

Sonneck, Oscar George Theodore. 1983. *Oscar Sonneck and American Music.* Urbana: University of Illinois Press.

Tawa, Nicholas E. 1982. *A Sound of Strangers: Musical Culture, Acculturation, and the Post–Civil War Ethnic American.* Metuchen, N.J.: Scarecrow Press.

———. 1987. *Art Music in the American Society: The Condition of Art Music in the Late Twentieth Century.* Metuchen, N.J.: Scarecrow Press.

———. 1990. *The Way to Tin Pan Alley: American Popular Song.* New York: Schirmer Books.

Thernstrom, Stephan, et al., eds. 1980. *Harvard Encyclopedia of American Ethnic Groups.* Cambridge: Belknap Press of Harvard University Press.

Sources, Scholarship, and Historiography
Stephen Blum

Attitudes toward Music and History
Sacred Histories
The Politics of Musical Identities (Nineteenth and Twentieth Centuries)

Musical knowledge is everywhere one of the necessities of communal life, in large part because musicians, dancers, and ceremonial specialists can articulate and explore attitudes toward older and newer ways of living together. The musical practices of most North American communities have combined idioms, styles, and genres introduced at various times, and performances are often charged with references to social and cultural history.

ATTITUDES TOWARD MUSIC AND HISTORY

Representations of history are as diverse as are the modes of musical communication in North America. The diverse populations of the United States and Canada have developed various ways of defining and interpreting relationships between the past and the present. Some of these attitudes toward history rely heavily on musical communication. To a significant extent, communities have identified themselves through their musical practices and through avoidance of certain practices; each community has acceded to some pressures for change while resisting others.

Identities

Historical consciousness is fundamental to the experiences of conquered peoples, settlers, colonists, slaves, immigrants, and their descendants, not least because no group can avoid contact with others. Writings on music and its history are linked in various ways to performances that are spoken, sung, or danced rather than written and that are staged, recorded, broadcast, or filmed rather than printed. The following discussion is concerned mainly with published writings, casting occasional glances toward other media of communication.

Cultural interaction

From the sixteenth century to the present, all genres of writing in North America have been profoundly affected by perceptions of changing relationships among descendants of the European colonists, descendants of the Native Americans they killed or displaced, and descendants of the African slaves they imported. The implications of this point for the writing of music history were first addressed in the 1940s and 1950s by the musicologist Charles Seeger (1886–1979). Seeger emphasized the continuous reciprocal influence between oral and written transmission in music as well as in other cultural practices (1945). As chief of the music division of the Pan American Union from 1941 to 1953, he advocated the comparative study of "acculturation," or culture contact, throughout the Americas.

Seeger (1957, 1961) attempted an impartial view of the types of contact between rural and urban populations and between the dominant population of European ancestry and the minorities of African and Amerindian ancestry. He was particularly concerned with the "effective hegemony of neo-European traditions" and with the restrictions placed on musicality in the "predominantly verbal universe" of North America (Seeger 1940:322, 1957:281). Through making their own music, people discover "what is common (or strange) between them" (Seeger 1939:148–149) in ways that may transcend the limitations of verbal communication and of consuming the music made by others. Seeger's formulations of these points may now appear somewhat naive when we consider the continuous interplay among producers and consumers and the numerous respects in which language both constitutes and inhibits the practices of musicians and listeners alike. (Whether or not musical communication can be as sharply separated from verbal communication as Seeger believed is very much open to question.)

Nonetheless, studies of North American music history strongly support Seeger's thesis that in subordinating the American Indian and African populations to the European, language has been a far more powerful tool of symbolic violence, compared with music. As dominated groups have tried to reaffirm their identity and solidarity through musical performance, members of the dominant groups have sought to neutralize these efforts both by misrepresenting the musical practices of their "inferiors" and by denying the human significance of music altogether.

At present it is difficult to imagine a "neutral viewpoint from which to examine in equal perspective the unusually concentrated and continuous acculturation between oral and written traditions in the Americas" (Seeger 1945:341). If "neutrality" is unattainable, at least we can acknowledge frankly the different vantage points from which North Americans attempt to understand music and history.

Who is musical?

As European concepts of music were adapted to North American conditions, ambivalent attitudes toward the value of music were projected onto images of American Indians and African Americans: musicality was often taken as a symptom of racial inferiority. The concerns of the European colonists and their descendants also resulted in deep-seated and enduring anxieties that North American civilization might not provide an appropriate environment for musical art and science. Thomas Jefferson, for example, glanced with envy toward Italy, where "music is cultivated by every class of men," and in a letter of 8 June 1778 to Giovanni Fabbroni he complained that his "passion for music" could not be fulfilled in a country where music remained "in a state of deplorable barbarism" (Jefferson 1984:761). His widely read *Notes on the State of Virginia* (1787) presented an influential view of the alleged "inferiority" of blacks, despite their evident musical "gifts." Arguing that "in music they are more generally gifted than the whites with accurate ears for tune and time," Jefferson added that blacks were "capable of imagining" short pieces of music but might not be "equal to the composition of a more extensive run of melody, or of complicated harmony." It was consistent with Jefferson's notions of the mental inferiority of blacks to acknowledge their musical inclinations while finding that "their existence appears to participate more of sensation than reflection" (1984 [1787]:265–226).

The questions "Who is musical?" and "Can music flourish here?" are inextricably linked to the question "How will peoples of different origin live together on this continent?" Many of the stories told by music historians have served as mechanisms of exclusion and segregation: some ways of writing history and criticism allow one to write so as not to know what one is missing. At its infrequent best, musical scholarship has helped North Americans to hear one another, often in circumstances that did not encourage close listening.

SACRED HISTORIES

New France

Conversion of the heathen

The French interests in expansion of the fur trade and conversion of the heathen required close attention to the customs and cultures of North American Indians. In compiling information on the musical life of indigenous peoples, the Recollet and Jesuit missionaries looked for signs of innate musicality that might facilitate the work of Christianizing and "civilizing" the Indians. They found many such signs, and the seventeenth-century *Jesuit Relations* are replete with stories of "little savages [who] have learned to sing beautiful hymns in their own language" (Thwaites 1896–1901, 57:61, 63). Jesuit accounts of indigenous ceremonies generally described the singing as "very disagreeable" or "sombre and unpleasant" (Thwaites 1896–1901, 5:27, 6:183), but there is evidence that some missionaries may have drawn on indigenous tunes and rhythms as they translated hymns and spiritual songs into native languages (Bailey 1937:156).

It was a modest step toward acknowledging the common humanity of the colonizer and the native and their mutual involvement in the North American history to come when the French missionaries and travelers recognized that American Indians, like "most of the nations of the earth," sing "for recreation and for devotion" (Bailey 1937:156). In Virginia as well, European observers of Indians noted that "their divotion is most in songes" (Stevenson 1973b:401). In the eyes of the Jesuit Father François Nau, the fact that all prayers of the Indians of Caughnawaga "were done in singing" was a sign of the mental inferiority of savages: "[S]ong is necessary to our savages, who are not generally capable of a sustained application of intelligence" (in Amtmann 1976:234).

The strongest affirmation of the Indians' capacity to advance from natural music to musical art and science was voiced by Father Francesco Bressani:

> I do not doubt that they are capable of the sciences, they have a harmonious and excellent ear for music, but theirs is different and somehow more martial than ours. It is not taught as an art, but the most proficient esteem it as one of the gifts of nature. (Kennedy 1950:139)

Father Lalemant declared his confidence in the ability of at least some Indians to equal the standard of performance in France itself: "[T]he nuns of France do not sing more agreeably than some savage women here" (Thwaites 1896–1901, 60:145).

Natural virtue

Beliefs in the natural virtue of Indians were expressed by French observers who praised them not only for their aptitude in learning Christian hymns but also for avoiding "immodesty" in their dances (Lescarbot 1609) and for rejecting the profane songs of Europeans (Sagard-Théodat 1636). In their histories of North America, both Lescarbot and Sagard-Théodat sought to edify their European readers with images of uncorrupted and noble savages. Such images were reproduced in a substantial body of French literature, extending from the *Jesuit Relations* and other seventeenth-century histories to philosophical and literary works of the eighteenth and early nineteenth centuries.

Regular singing, in whatever form, left no room for individuals to produce idiosyncratic renditions of familiar melodies, since several of these at once were thought to result in "an horrid Medly of confused and disorderly Noises."

French interest in the natural man of the North American wilderness also involved efforts to notate Indian melodies, resulting in the publication of no fewer than fourteen tunes during the seventeenth and eighteenth centuries (Stevenson 1973a). In contrast, the earliest surviving notations of North American Indian melodies by English and Spanish travelers and administrators date from the late eighteenth and early nineteenth centuries, respectively (Stevenson 1973a:8–13; 1973b:408).

New England

Union and distance

Of the many criteria by which genres of music are differentiated, perhaps the most important for North Americans is the difference between musical actions that unite performers with others and those that create or maintain distance between groups or individuals. Each musical genre is characterized by a specific configuration of attitudes, enhancing integration on some levels and favoring segregation on others. For the Puritans who established colonies in New England, the aim of singing spiritual songs was to "feel our selves come into an Holy *Symphony* with the Saints who had their *Hearts burning* within them, when they *sang* these things unto the Lord," in the words of the theologian Cotton Mather (1721:13).

The Puritans understood their Great Migration to New England as "a heavenly translation from corrupt to more pure churches" and as "the establishment of the Holy Commonwealth . . . preparatory to the great event" (Allin and Shepard 1648:8; Bercovitch 1978:38). They lived in anticipation of a "brighter day wherein East & West shall sing the song of the Lamb" (Bercovitch 1978:75; Shepard 1648:30). The fund of topics, images, and rhetorical devices accumulated in writings and speeches on "New England's Errand into the Wilderness" (Danforth 1671) remained influential in much American literature and oratory of the eighteenth, nineteenth, and twentieth centuries, including the literature on music. For example, the style and spirit of the Puritan jeremiads, in which clerics excoriated New Englanders for manifold failures in carrying out their mission, is readily apparent in the writings of the composer Charles Ives (1874–1954).

Perfecting the Holy Commonwealth

The need to perfect the Holy Commonwealth had both short- and long-term implications for American attitudes toward music and history. The Covenant of Grace by which God had established the conditions of salvation required individuals to ask themselves whether or not they had been received into the covenant; those who gave convincing testimony of their conversion were henceforth numbered among the "visible saints." Constant anxiety over "declension" and "degeneration" was expressed in assessments of every field of activity, including psalmody. Spokesmen for the cultural consensus could not accept "any Loose, Defective, Irregular way, that this, or that People, have Accustomed themselves unto" (Chauncey 1728). Writing was essential to the transmission of cultural knowledge in "small things," such as psalmody, as well as in more important matters. The commonwealth must not depend upon "the uncertain and doubtful Conveyance of *Oral Tradition*" (Symmes 1720:8).

There was no reason why the New Jerusalem constructed in New England could not equal the sacred music of the Temple, as described in the Old Testament (especially I Chronicles 15:16–22, II Chronicles 5:12–13, and the Psalms). According to the Reverend Thomas Walter (1696–1725), this music had used the three voices, bass, medius, and treble (Walter 1721); according to the composer William Billings (1746–1800), it was "more than probable" that Guido of Arezzo, establishing the modern tonal system, had "by some means or other availed himself of King David's Scale" (Billings 1794:xiii).

Among the long-term consequences of the effort to build a model Christian society were the continuing inclination of many Americans to think of themselves as actors on a world stage; a tendency to interpret the lives of individuals according to various conceptions of the nation's mission; and an abiding interest in music designed for people of average capacities—the "people's song," as it was called by the composer and publisher George F. Root (1825–1895). These consequences are no less apparent in American histories of secular music than in the histories of salvation.

The continuous attempts to define a mainstream American culture have inevitably produced many images of errant or deviant behavior, some of them closely linked to conceptions of musicality. The controversy of 1636–1638 over the so-called Antinomian heresy is an exemplary instance of conflict between proponents of social and religious order and an individual, Anne Hutchinson, who claimed to have experienced direct revelations and promptings from the Holy Ghost. The ecstasy that Mrs. Hutchinson attributed to an experience of communion with the Holy Ghost was found by her accusers and judges to have been a delusion inspired by the devil. Although no musical issues were explicitly raised in this controversy, the history of American music is marked by continual tension and conflict between defenders of order and partisans of ecstasy (Hamm 1976).

Regular singing

A powerful rationale for the cultivation of an orderly, well-regulated music was constructed in the 1720s by advocates of regular singing. The sermons and pamphlets generated by the effort to subdue "the confused Noise of a Wilderness" (Mather 1721:23) through regular singing have been interpreted by later music historians as cardinal documents of North American musical thought. The values and arguments of the reform movement were endorsed without qualification by historians of the nineteenth and early twentieth centuries (including Hood 1846; Howard 1931; Ritter 1883; Thayer 1846–1847). By the mid-twentieth century, music historians had begun to consider both sides in the controversy, rereading the diatribes against "the usual way of singing" in order to understand the values of its countless followers (Britton 1950; Chase 1987[1955]:22–40; Hamm 1983:31–41).

In urban areas regular singing entailed learning to read music from notation, so that all worshipers could sing one standard version of a psalm or hymn tune, note by note, in perfect unison. In rural New England, however, a similarly regular manner of performance had to be achieved without the use of notation. Worshipers were urged to learn the standard tunes by ear and to match their voices as closely as possible as they moved from one note to the next (Osterhout 1986). Regular singing, in whatever form, left no room for individuals to produce idiosyncratic renditions of familiar melodies, since several of these at once were thought to result in "an horrid Medly of confused and disorderly Noises" (Walter 1721:2).

Regular singing required some degree of contact with music theory: the theoretical introductions of many tunebooks summarized "the laws of time and tune" and "the rules of composition" while explaining how to read notation and how to sing properly. Largely adapted from British publications, notably William Tans'ur's *New Musical Grammar* (1746), these works were the first North American attempts to publish compendia of musical knowledge.

Histories in performance

Legitimate knowledge

Knowledge is stored in order to be used in performances and other actions. People often find it necessary to defend the legitimacy of their knowledge from real or imagined challengers. During a winter ceremonial held in 1895 by three Kwakiutl tribes at Fort Rupert, British Columbia, Canada, a member of one tribe addressed the others as follows:

> I am going to tell you the story of this Cannibal dancer, which will show you that we, Koskimo . . . do not steal winter dances from you, Kwa'g•ul, nor from other tribes. All the winter dances were given to us by the Maker of Man in the beginning of the world. (Boas 1966:214)

Kwakiutl shamans were sometimes called upon not only to demonstrate their power to effect cures but to tell how they had acquired their arts—so that others might judge which of their powers were real and which were fraudulent.

Interpretation

In many situations, performers and other actors must learn how to interpret writings if they wish to be regarded as fully knowledgeable. Different types of control limit the range of acceptable interpretations. For example, sequences of songs performed by priests of the Ojibwa Grand Medicine Society (*mitewiwin*) contained information pertaining to Ojibwa migrations and to the origins of the *mite* rituals. In some performance contexts, priests would describe the meanings and purposes of songs before performing them (Vennum 1978:756). This was particularly necessary as initiates were examined on their knowledge before being promoted to one of the higher degrees in the society. The priests' capacities to remember sequences of songs and their meanings were enhanced by the use of pictographs inscribed on birch bark scrolls.

Writers may shape their narratives by adapting the format of a public ceremony. When the anthropologist Paul Radin offered to pay him for writing an autobiography in the Winnebago syllabary, Sam Blowsnake (b. 1875) drew upon his experience of public confession in the peyote cult as he described his life before and after conversion to the cult:

> I claimed that I had been blessed by spirits. . . . I was, of course, not telling the truth, for I had never felt the stirring of anything of that kind within me; . . . I would say that I was blessed by a Grizzly-Bear spirit, that it had blessed me with the power of being uncontrollable; that I had been taught certain songs and these I would sing at the top of my voice. (Radin 1963 [1920]:27–28, 53, 55)

Many of the major documents of North American music history, like Blowsnake's autobiography, result from the actions of writers who were obliged to reinterpret the meanings of familiar genres of performance. Frederick Douglass (1817–1895) explained why he "did not, when a slave, understand the deep meaning of those rude and apparently incoherent songs," the African American spirituals: "I was myself within the circle; so that I neither saw nor heard as those without might see and hear." As a writer, he could inform his readers that "every tone was a testimony against slavery, and a prayer to God for deliverance from chains" (1845:37). African American religious and musical practices, which had long invoked the sacred history of the children of Israel and their redemption from slavery, became politicized as the meanings of the practices were spelled out in writing.

THE POLITICS OF MUSICAL IDENTITIES (NINETEENTH AND TWENTIETH CENTURIES)

Progress

In assessing their own musicality and that of American Indians and African Americans, European Americans emphasized capacities for growth and improvement. Narratives of musical progress and backwardness, printed in numerous periodicals and books, were linked to narratives of progress in religion, commerce, level of education, or all of these at once.

Musical publics

The several musical publics of the United States in the early nineteenth century were classified by Thomas Hastings (1784–1872), a composer and compiler of sacred music, as "an uncultivated, a laborious, a military, a refined, and a fashionable class of community." Hastings believed that all five classes "may readily unite in their fondness for rhythm, . . . and they may all, under certain circumstances, be delighted with simplicity in melody or harmony." He was also certain that "the arts are necessarily progressive" (1822:152, 131).

Publication of biographies and anecdotes about noteworthy musicians, native and foreign, was one way in which the refined and fashionable classes could keep abreast of progress. The first U.S. periodical entirely devoted to writing about music was *The Euterpeiad* (Boston, 1820–1823), edited by John Rowe Parker with the aim of "carefully compiling and collating—A Brief History of Music from the earliest Ages—Cherish a classical taste—Watch the progress of the Art—Excite the emulation of genius," and so on. Much of the biographical material from *The Euterpeiad* was reprinted in Parker's *A Musical Biography: or Sketches of the Lives and Writings of Eminent Musical Characters* (1824)—the first in a series of such books, followed by William Smith Porter's *The Musical Cyclopedia* (1834), John Weeks Moore's *Complete Encyclopaedia of Music* (1852, with an *Appendix* in 1875) and a three-volume *Cyclopedia of Music and Musicians* (1888–1890) by John Denison Champlin Jr. and William Foster Apthorp. In all of these works, musical biography was a central concern.

Modern musical science

Such compilations of musical knowledge in written form were heavily dependent on publications obtained from Europe. In preparing his *Musical Cyclopedia,* Porter used the large library accumulated by Lowell Mason (1792–1872), the most powerful voice of musical reform in nineteenth-century North America. Mason believed that "modern musical science," most fully revealed in the works of Handel and Beethoven, provided a solid foundation for congregational song, the "plain and simple" style that his colleague Hastings termed "a most delicate medium between vulgarity on the one hand, and undue refinement on the other" (Hastings and Warriner 1836:iii). In 1839 Mason published three articles on the history of music in the United States, emphasizing the failings of sacred music in New England prior to his reforms.

Aiming at the "improvement and universal diffusion" of music (Mason 1853:iv), Mason and his numerous associates created a network of institutions through which thousands of North Americans received instruction in "the laws of time and tune." When music education was introduced in the public schools of Boston in the late 1830s, Mason's colleagues hailed the initiation of "a great revolution in the musical character of the American people" (Eliot 1841:320). Half a century later, in the first attempt at a history of "popular and the higher musical education" in the United States, Mason was portrayed as the "founder of national music" and the leading figure in "a complete revolution in the character and objects of all musical activity in America" (Mathews 1889:35). In these statements, *revolution* is synonymous with thoroughgoing *reform,* based on public education.

Gagnon extended the theory of "ancient tonality" to folk song when, in 1865, he published a collection of one hundred *Chansons populaires du Canada* without accompaniment.

Controversies

An opposing view of "the general cultivation of taste" (Thayer 1852:170) questioned the possibility of bridging the gap between the practice of "common choirs" and the proper performance of musical masterpieces. Alexander Wheelock Thayer (1817–1897) and other contributors to *Dwight's Journal of Music* (Boston, 1852–1881) argued that popular participation in church music served at best to create audiences who might learn to appreciate the "classics" of German instrumental music, "the established models of form and method in the art of composition" (*Dwight's Journal of Music* 1(13 [1852]:100). Thayer's great contribution to musical scholarship was his biography of Beethoven (1866–1879), rather than his early studies of the history of psalmody in New England (1846–1847). He can be regarded as the first North American scholar to undertake studies of music history based on criticism of primary sources.

American discussions of progress referred to aims that were not easily reconciled: the development of musical art and science, "the improvement and universal diffusion of music" in the United States through the creation of appropriate institutions, and the cultivation of taste according to the "highest" standards. The efforts of musical societies to "improve" or "raise" the level of musical taste were one of the main topics treated in the histories and surveys of musical life that North Americans began to publish toward the end of the nineteenth century (for examples, Harrison 1898 and 1908; Mathews 1889; Ritter 1883; Smith 1881–1882; Torrington 1898). The first histories of North American musical societies to be published dealt with the Handel and Haydn Society of Boston (Perkins and Dwight 1883) and the Société Musicale Sainte-Cécile of Québec City (1881).

North American writings on the subject of musical progress also include explanations and justifications of resistance to progress. In Québec, organists could not agree on whether to use modern harmonic progressions, with leading tones, in accompanying plainchant. According to the French theorists Fétis, d'Ortigue, and Niedermeyer, such harmonies were both symptoms and causes of "subjectivity" and "restlessness," and they were foreign to the "objective" spirit of Catholicism. A debate conducted in the newspaper *Le Courrier du Canada* in 1860 centered on this theory as presented by Pierre-Minier Lagacé (1830–1884) in *Les chants d'église . . . harmonisés pour l'orgue suivant les principes de la tonalité gregorienne* (1860). Lagacé's main opponent was Antoine Dessane (1826–1873), a brilliant student at the Paris Conservatoire before he left France in 1849 to become organist at the Basilica of Notre-Dame in Québec City; his most eloquent defender was Ernest Gagnon (1834–1915), organist at the Église St-Jean-Baptiste and a former pupil of Dessane's. Gagnon extended the theory of "ancient tonality" to folk song when, in 1865, he published a collection of one hundred *Chansons populaires du Canada* without accompaniment. The Québécois, he argued, had upheld the faith of their ancestors by resisting the temptation to adjust their traditional melodies to "modern tonality." Many subsequent writers on folk song, in English as well as in French, concerned themselves with its alleged relationships to plainchant and the church modes.

"Genuine folksong"

Late-nineteenth-century studies of English-language folk song were concerned mainly with ballads, thought to have been created at a much earlier stage of social evolution. Francis James Child (1825–1896) published a corpus of 305 *English and Scottish Popular Ballads* (1882–1898). He treated his texts as survivals from a time "anterior to the appearance of the poetry of art," dismissing the "vulgar ballads of our day" as "products of a low kind of *art*" (Wilgus 1959:7–9). Some of Child's successors became interested in what people were actually singing, and their activities as collectors gradually undermined the notion that "genuine folksong" was almost extinct.

In each decade from the 1860s on, some North American publications have been aimed at preserving music that was considered "genuine" while other publications have celebrated "progress." The white abolitionists who compiled *Slave Songs of the United States* believed that "these relics of a state of society which has passed away should be preserved while it is still possible" (Allen, Ware, and Garrison 1867:iii).

"Music of the most classical order"

Whereas the authors of *Slave Songs of the United States* were deeply impressed by the "creative power" of the "half-barbarous people" who lived on the Port Royal Islands, James Monroe Trotter (1842–1892) sought to inform his readers that "notwithstanding their lack of scientific knowledge of music, colored men, as instrumentalists, have long furnished most of the best music that has been produced in nearly all the Southern states." In his *Music and Some Highly Musical People* (1878), which outlines the careers of well over forty African American musicians and touring groups, Trotter wished to demonstrate that African Americans had successfully created and performed "music of the most classical order" (1878:326–327, 111). The publication of collective biographies of musicians, initiated by John Rowe Parker, came to include African American musicians by the efforts of an African American writer.

Projects

Institutions and collaborations

In the late nineteenth and early twentieth centuries, North Americans began to undertake more ambitious programs of musical research, some of which depended on the support of newly established museums, libraries, government bureaus, and professional associations (figure 1). New types of collaboration among scholars with different backgrounds and skills produced work of lasting value.

The Peabody Museum of American Archaeology and Ethnology and the Bureau of American Ethnology published several monographs by Alice Fletcher (1838–1923) and her collaborator Francis La Flesche (1857–1932), the son of an Omaha Indian mother and a father of mixed French and Ponca parentage. Fletcher's "Five Indian Ceremonies" (1884) includes, along with notations of music, description of ceremonial actions and detailed notes on how the author acquired her information. La Flesche's suggestion that Fletcher write down melodies he sang for her led to "A Study of Omaha Indian Music" (1893), the product of ten years' work, in which John Comfort Fillmore (1843–1898) also participated. In "The Omaha Tribe" (1970[1911]), Fletcher and La Flesche tried "to make so far as possible the Omaha his own interpreter" by emphasizing Omaha beliefs and values (1970[1911]:30)—for which they were criticized by anthropologists advocating a more scientific approach.

Several other monographs published by the Bureau of American Ethnology and by the U.S. National Museum included notation of music and song texts. With musical assistance from Fletcher and, after her death, from Helen H. Roberts (1888–1985), La Flesche produced four large volumes, *The Osage Tribe* (1921–1930), describing multiple versions of ceremonies as they were understood and practiced by members of

FIGURE I   Important Resources for the Study of Music in the United States and Canada

Establishment of Organizations Involved in the Support of Musical Scholarship, Including Archives and Publication Projects (Selective List)

1842	Museum Branch, Geological Survey of Canada (renamed National Museum of Canada in 1927; renamed Canadian Museum of Civilization in 1987)	
1866	Peabody Museum of American Archaeology and Ethnology, Harvard University	
1876	Music Teachers National Association	
1879	Bureau of Ethnology, Smithsonian Institution (later Bureau of American Ethnology)	
1888	American Folklore Society	
1896	Music Department (later Division), Library of Congress	
1902	American Anthropological Association	
1903	Society of the Southwest, Los Angeles	
1907	Music Supervisors National Conference (later Music Educators National Conference)	
1907	Internationale Musik-Gesellschaft, United States Section (disbanded 1916)	
1910	Division of Anthropology, Museum Branch, Geological Survey of Canada (1957, Folklore Section created)	
1919	Society for the Publication of American Music (disbanded 1969)	
1928	Archive of American Folk-Song, Library of Congress (now part of Archives of Folk Culture, American Folklife Center)	
1931	Music Library Association	
1931	New York Musicological Society (disbanded 1934)	
1933	American Society for Comparative Musicology (disbanded 1937)	
1934	American Musicological Society	
1936	Archives of Folk and Primitive Music, Columbia University (transferred to Indiana University as Archives of Traditional Music, 1948)	

1938	Society for the Preservation and Encouragement of Barber Shop Quartet Singing	
1942	Les Amis de la Bonne Chanson (an outgrowth of the 1937 Congrès de la langue française)	
1944	Archives de Folklore, Laval University, Québec	
1944	Canadian Music Council	
1945	Institute of Renaissance and Baroque Music (renamed American Institute of Musicology, 1946)	
1955	Society for Ethnomusicology	
1956	Canadian Folk Music Society / Société canadienne de musique folklorique (renamed Société canadienne pour les traditions musicales, 1988; Canadian Society for Musical Traditions, 1989)	
1957	Canada Council	
1957	College Music Society	
1959	Canadian Music Educators Association	
1959	Canadian Music Centre, Toronto (Montréal office, 1973)	
1960	Society for Asian Music, New York	
1964	Country Music Foundation, Nashville, Tenn.	
1964	John Edwards Memorial Foundation, UCLA (collection acquired by University of North Carolina, Chapel Hill, 1983; now part of Southern Folklife Collection)	
1965	Canadian Association of University Schools of Music (renamed Canadian University Music Society, 1981)	
1965	National Endowment for the Humanities	
1966	American Society of University Composers	
1966	Ethnology Division and Folklore Division (created from Anthropology Division), National Museum of Canada (renamed	

	Canadian Centre for Folk Culture Studies, 1970, and Canadian Ethnology Service, 1974)
1968	American Music Research Center, Dominican College, San Rafael, Calif. (moved to University of Colorado, Boulder, 1988)
1970	Music Division, National Library of Canada
1971	American Musical Instrument Society
1972	Center for Southern Folklore, Memphis
1973	Canadian Music Research Council
1973	Center for Acadian and Creole Folklore, University of Southwestern Louisiana
1974	American Society for Jewish Music
1974	Centre for American Music, Keele University, England
1975	The Sonneck Society (renamed The Sonneck Society for American Music, 1992, renamed The Society for American Music, 1999)
1977	Social Sciences and Humanities Research Council of Canada
1978	Institute for Research in Black American Music, Fisk University, Nashville, Tenn.
1978	Society for Music Theory
1980	Association pour l'avancement de la recherche en musique du Québec
1981	International Association for the Study of Popular Music (branches in Canada and United States)
1982	Canadian Musical Heritage Society, Ottawa
1983	Center for Black Music Research, Columbia College, Chicago
1984	Institute for Canadian Music, University of Toronto

different clans. Large collections of texts in the Kwakiutl language, also including some notation of music, were published by the anthropologist Franz Boas (1858–1942), assisted by George Hunt (of mixed Tlingit-Scots parentage but raised among the Kwakiutl and taught by Boas to write in Kwakiutl). It was Hunt who wrote down the Kwakiutl text quoted earlier. With respect to contemporary history, James Mooney's study of "The Ghost Dance Religion and the Sioux Outbreak of 1890" (1896) contained a small anthology of recent songs in several American languages.

Recordings

No less valuable than the publication of ethnographic texts were the wax cylinder recordings made by North American scholars beginning in the 1890s; many of these were deposited in such institutions as the American Museum of Natural History (New York), the Southwest Museum (Los Angeles), and the National Museum of Canada (Ottawa). As head of the anthropology department at the last named institution, Marius Barbeau (1883–1969) collected music of Canadian Indians, then turned increasingly to French-Canadian folklore and recorded thousands of songs, many of which he transcribed and published. On a much smaller scale, Charles F. Lummis (1859–1928) recorded American Indian music and Hispanic American folklore in the Southwest (for transcriptions of twenty of his recordings see Lummis and Farwell 1929 [1923]). Hundreds of Indian songs were recorded and transcribed by Frances Densmore (1867–1957), who was assisted by native speakers in transcribing and translating the song texts (see, for example, Densmore 1918).

The first scholars to record substantial numbers of Anglo-American folk songs were Robert W. Gordon (1888–1961), founder of the Archive of American Folk-Song at the Library of Congress, and John A. Lomax (1867–1948), his successor as director of the archive. Gordon was particularly interested in evidence of musical interaction between African Americans and European Americans (see Gordon 1938). Lomax and his son Alan were extraordinarily successful in recording African American music in several southern states, with emphasis on work songs, early blues, and other genres they considered "authentic" (for examples of their notations see Lomax and Lomax 1934).

Professionalism

The creation and development of large collections of research materials made it possible for scholars to criticize false conceptions of North American cultural history with arguments supported by evidence. Yet the extent to which scholars could make their voices heard in public life was quite another matter. The institutions of professionalized scholarship established separate domains for ethnography, folklore, and music. A considerable number of scholars felt that their interests were discouraged or excluded by the policies and practices of the institutions and professional associations in all three domains. The professional networks remained under the control of men, and women were often treated unfairly.

Oscar Sonneck (1873–1928), who served as chief of the Music Division of the Library of Congress from 1902 to 1917, did as much as anyone to shape the directions of musicology in the United States. He developed the library's holdings to support research on the history of European music and research on "music in America," seeing the former as prerequisite to the latter. Sonneck recognized the bibliographic weakness of the existing histories of U.S. music (Elson 1904; Farwell and Darby 1915; Hubbard 1910; Mathews 1889; Ritter 1883), which he termed "compilations" rather than "works of research in the stricter sense" (Sonneck 1921 [1916]:324). His own writings on such topics as early opera and early concert life in the United States were the first to be based on critical assessment of the sources.

A musician's 'stock-in-trade' is knowledge, the product of study and practice, which he is able to sell according to its extent and quality.

Sonneck was convinced that "the cultivation of art is practically a city-bred function of the human mind" and that both African American music and "the Indian's musical system" were "ethnomusically too different from our inherited European system" to permit meaningful interchange in musical life and musical scholarship (Sonneck 1916 [1913]:135, 140–141). By means of these exclusions, based on "race," he was able to maintain that "music as a commodity, music as a factor of esthetic culture, music as a power for spiritual uplift, and music as a nuisance, is substantially the same here as abroad" (Sonneck 1916 [1913]:139).

Sonneck's vision of "a methodologically correct and abundant literature of city and state musical histories" (Sonneck 1916 [1913]:132) was not to be realized quickly. As late as 1965, Joseph Kerman proposed "A Profile for American Musicology," which found nothing worth studying in nineteenth-century American music or in Indian and African American music apart from jazz. In the first half of the twentieth century, the small number of North Americans who mastered European techniques of musical scholarship confined their research to European music, with very few exceptions. Works that fully satisfied Sonneck's criteria for "research in the stricter sense" began to appear regularly in the 1960s, among them Helmut Kallmann's *A History of Music in Canada 1534–1914* (1960), Hans Nathan's *Dan Emmett and the Rise of Early Negro Minstrelsy* (1962), Irving Lowens's *Music and Musicians in Early America* (1964), Ralph Daniel's *The Anthem in New England before 1800* (1966), Robert Stevenson's *Protestant Church Music in America* (1966), and Richard Crawford's *Andrew Law, American Psalmodist* (1968). By 1975, when the Sonneck Society was formed, many North American scholars were engaged in research projects that did not conform to Kerman's myopic "Profile." It was also in the 1960s and 1970s that academic institutions in the United States began, very slowly, to dismantle the terrible legacy of racism.

The primary sources for musical research may be understood as notations of music and other written documents (following Sonneck); sound and video recordings (following Seeger 1940); or all of these in various combinations, as in Charles Hamm's *Music in the New World* (1983), the first history of U.S. music based in large part on the author's experience with primary sources.

Resources and interpretations

The history of primary sources includes their creation, identification and collection, storage and classification, reproduction, and interpretation. H. Wiley Hitchcock suggests that "no culture before ours has had such a fantastic variety of means for *creating*, not just preserving, the raw materials from which history is written" (1968:11). North Americans have also created several types of venues in which histories are interpreted: concert series, revues, traveling shows, folk festivals, ethnic fairs, intertribal powwows, birthday tributes to famous musicians, museums, exhibitions, and halls of fame, among others.

Autobiographies

Some of the most important primary sources are musicians' autobiographies, of which an enormous number have been published in the United States (and a relatively small number in Canada). The autobiographies are particularly valuable in spelling out musicians' perceptions of the public spaces in which they worked. The cornetist Herbert L. Clarke (1865–1945), who worked extensively in both Canada and the United States, described musical knowledge as the indispensable "capital" one needs in a free market where "all have an equal chance to rise to success, provided they have the initial talent, and work properly and conscientiously": "A musician's 'stock-in-trade' is knowledge, the product of study and practice, which he is able to sell according to its extent and quality" (Clarke 1934:73, 60). The autobiography of the African American musician Perry Bradford (1893–1970) paints a very different picture:

> I guess it's about time I get my "nickle's worth" of credit for the part I played as one of the pioneers that started our girls and boys, in the hectic twenties, swinging, playing and recording the "Blues 'N Rhythms." . . . I get so hot and bothered and I feel lower down than a doodle-bug every time I hear some smart promoters who own those over-commercialized musicians—body and soul—with "Life to Grave" contracts—shouting that their chattel-slaves created all this down-home music. (Bradford 1965:13, 29)

Bradford's complaint shows how much is at stake for musicians who watch music history in the making and try, as he did, "to trick the trickster" (1965:90).

Interviews

Even more numerous than published autobiographies are interviews and oral histories. Major collections of interviews with jazz musicians are housed in the William Ransom Hogan Jazz Archive at Tulane University and in the Institute of Jazz Studies at Rutgers University, Newark, New Jersey. The American Music Oral History project at Yale University contains extensive interviews with associates of several important musicians (among them Ives, Hindemith, Ellington, and Copland). Such collections allow historians to compare styles of writing with styles of speaking.

Stage performances

Through writings, interviews, and public performances, many North American musicians have tried to correct what they perceived as misrepresentations of music history. The first Carnegie Hall "Concert of Negro Music," presented in 1912 by James Reese Europe (1881–1919), was described in the *New York Age* as "the first organized attempt . . . to show to the public of New York what the Negro race has done and can do in music" ("Black Music Concerts . . ." 1978:74). One African American writer insisted that this program would show that "classical music is not the only kind that requires preparation and intelligent interpretation" ("Black Music Concerts . . ." 1978:75).

A considerable number of the scholars who set out to document and notate various kinds of music in the first half of the twentieth century also found it desirable or even necessary to sponsor stage performances. In 1919, eight years after his first expedition to record French-Canadian folklore, Barbeau, with his collaborator Édouard-Zotique Massicotte (1867–1947), initiated a series, *Soirées du bon vieux temps,* at the Bibliothèque St.-Sulpice in Montréal. A similar series, the enormously successful *Veillées du bon vieux temps,* was produced at the Monument National in Montréal from 1921 to 1941 and became an important forum for artists who drew upon the folklore of Québec in innovative ways. Madame Bolduc (1894–1941), one of the supreme reinterpreters of Québécois traditions, began to compose songs after her first public appearances as a singer in the *Veillées* (1927).

FIGURE 2   Katherine Dunham, c. 1950.
© Bettmann/CORBIS.

FIGURE 3   Dizzy Gillespie.

In the early 1930s Zora Neale Hurston (1891–1960) was more interested in mounting stage presentations of African American folklore than in publishing the material she had collected in Florida, but her patron, Mrs. Rufus Osgood Mason, insisted on publication in book form. Hurston's revue or "concert," *The Great Day*, was presented in New York (1932) and in revised form with different titles at Rollins College in Florida (1933) and in Chicago (1934) before her book, *Mules and Men*, appeared in 1935. Her aim in these concerts was "to show what beauty and appeal there was in genuine Negro material, as against the Broadway concept, and it went over" (Hurston 1995 [1935]:194, 208).

The complementarity of stage performances and publications in the historiography of North American music is also well illustrated by the work of several anthropologists, dancers, and instrumentalists in the 1940s. With the publications of Melville Herskovits (1895–1963) and his student Richard Waterman (1914–1971), the dances of Katherine Dunham (b. 1912, figure 2) and Pearl Primus (1919–1994), and the music of Dizzy Gillespie (1917–1992, figure 3) and Chano Pozo (1915–1948), many (though certainly not all) North Americans began to understand the breadth and depth of the African musical heritage of both Americas, North and South. For many decades, writers and lecturers in the United States had debated the question of whether black Americans had or had not retained any cultural or "racial" memories of Africa, without recognizing the need for comparative study of histories and cultures of African populations in many parts of the New World. Herskovits, Dunham, and Gillespie were not the first North Americans to acquire firsthand experience of Afro-Caribbean religions, dance, and music, but their work established a solid basis for further exploration of African practices and their transformations in the Americas (see Dunham 1983 [1947]; Gillespie 1979:233, 317–325, 289–291, 483–485; Herskovits 1966 [1945]).

Access

Most North Americans now have some degree of access to resources that can be used in interpreting our history and music history. Our needs as interpreters are sufficiently diverse that our only realistic course of action is to agree to disagree, in the hope that we may arrive at a better understanding of our differences. Resources can be widely distributed—as commercial recordings, videotapes, facsimiles of notated music, and so on. Criticism of poor interpretations can be articulated in publications and performances. The rather considerable costs of musical scholarship are justified each time that one person produces a good interpretation.

REFERENCES

Allen, William Francis, Charles Pickard Ware, and Lucy McKim Garrison. 1867. *Slave Songs of the United States*. New York: A. Simpson.

Allin, John, and Thomas Shepard. 1648. *A Defense of the Answer*. London: pr. by R. Cotes for Andrew Crooke. New ed. as Shepard, *A Treatise of Liturgies*. London: pr. by E. Cotes for Andrew Crooke, 1653.

Amtmann, Willy. 1976. *La Musique au Québec 1600–1875*. Montréal: Les Éditions de l'Homme.

Austin, William W. 1975. *"Susanna," "Jeanie," and "The Old Folks at Home": The Songs of Stephen C. Foster from His Time to Ours*. New York: Macmillan.

Bailey, Alfred G. 1937. *The Conflict of European and Eastern Algonkian Cultures 1504–1700*. Saint John: New Brunswick Museum.

Beckwith, John, and Frederick A. Hall, eds. 1988. *Musical Canada: Words and Music Honouring*

Helmut Kallmann. Toronto: University of Toronto Press.

Bercovitch, Sacvan. 1978. *The American Jeremiad*. Madison: University of Wisconsin Press.

Billings, William. 1794. *The Continental Harmony*. Boston: Isaiah Thomas and Ebenezer T. Andrews.

"Black Music Concerts in Carnegie Hall, 1912–1915." 1978. *The Black Perspective in Music* 6:71–88.

Boas, Franz. 1966. *Kwakiutl Ethnography*, ed. Helen Codere. Chicago: University of Chicago Press.

Bradford, Perry. 1965. *Born with the Blues*. New York: Oak Publications.

Britton, Allen P. 1950. "Theoretical Introductions in American Tune-Books to 1800." Ph.D. dissertation, University of Michigan.

Carpenter, Carole Henderson. 1979. *Many Voices: A Study of Folklore Activities in Canada and Their*

Role in Canadian Culture. Ottawa: National Museums of Canada.

Champlin, John Denison Jr., and William Foster Apthorp. 1888–1890. *Cyclopedia of Music and Musicians.* 3 vols. New York: C. Scribner's Sons.

Chase, Gilbert. 1987[1955]. *America's Music, from the Pilgrims to the Present.* 3rd ed., rev. Urbana: University of Illinois Press.

Chauncey, Nathaniel. 1728. *Regular Singing Defended and Proved to Be the Only True Way of Singing the Songs of the Lord.* New London, Conn.: T. Green.

Child, Francis James. 1882–1898. *The English and Scottish Popular Ballads.* Boston: Houghton, Mifflin.

Clarke, Herbert L. 1934. *How I Became a Cornetist: The Autobiography of a Cornet-playing Pilgrim's Progress.* St. Louis, Mo.: J. L. Huber.

Crawford, Richard. 1968. *Andrew Law, American Psalmodist.* Evanston, Ill.: Northwestern University Press.

———. 1993. *The American Musical Landscape.* Berkeley: University of California Press.

Danforth, Samuel. 1671. *A Brief Recognition of New-Englands Errand into the Wilderness.* Cambridge, Mass.: S. G. and M. J.

Daniel, Ralph. 1966. *The Anthem in New England before 1800.* Evanston, Ill.: Northwestern University Press.

Densmore, Frances. 1918. *Teton Sioux Music and Culture.* Washington, D.C.: U.S. Government Printing Office. Bureau of American Ethnology, Bulletin 61. Reprint, Lincoln: University of Nebraska Press, 1992.

Douglass, Frederick. 1845. *Narrative of the Life of Frederick Douglass, an American Slave.* Cambridge, Mass.: Harvard University Press, 1960.

Dunham, Katherine. 1983[1947]. *Dances of Haiti.* Los Angeles: Center for Afro-American Studies, UCLA.

Dwight, John Sullivan, ed. 1852–1881. *Dwight's Journal of Music.* Boston: Houghton, Osgood.

Eliot, Samuel Atkins. 1841. "Music in America." *North American* 52:320–338.

Elson, Louis Charles. 1904. *The History of American Music.* New York: Macmillan.

Epstein, Dena J. 1977. *Sinful Tunes and Spirituals: Black Folk Music to the Civil War.* Urbana: University of Illinois Press.

Farwell, Arthur, and W. Dermot Darby. 1915. *Music in America.* The Art of Music, vol. 4. New York: The National Society of Music.

Fletcher, Alice C. 1884. "Five Indian Ceremonies." *16th Annual Report of the Peabody Museum* 3:260–333.

———. 1893. "A Study of Omaha Indian Music." *Archaeological and Ethnological Papers of the Peabody Museum* 1:237-287.

Fletcher, Alice C., and Francis La Flesche. 1970 [1911]. "The Omaha Tribe." In *27th Annual Report of the U.S. Bureau of American Ethnology to*

the Secretary of the Smithsonian Institution, *1905–06,* 19–672. Reprint, New York: Johnson Reprint.

Gagnon, Ernest. 1865. *Chansons populaires du Canada.* Québec: Bureau du "Foyer canadien."

Gillespie, Dizzy, with Al Fraser. 1979. *To Be, or Not . . . to Bop: Memoirs.* New York: Doubleday.

Gordon, Robert W. 1938. *Folk-songs of America.* New York: National Service Bureau.

Hamm, Charles. 1976. "The Ecstatic and the Didactic: A Pattern in American Music." In *Current Thought in Musicology,* ed. John W. Grubbs, 14–62. Austin: University of Texas Press.

———. 1983. *Music in the New World.* New York: Norton.

[Harrison, Susie Frances]. 1898. "Historical Sketch of Music in Canada." In *Canada: An Encyclopedia of the Country,* ed. John C. Hopkins, vol. 4, 389–394. Toronto: Linscott.

———. 1908. "Canada." In *History of Foreign Music,* ed. W. L. Hubbard, 229–241. Vol. 3 of *The American History and Encyclopedia of Music.* New York: Irving Squire.

Hastings, Thomas. 1822. *A Dissertation on Musical Taste.* Albany, N.Y.: Websters and Skinners. Reprint, New York: Da Capo Press, 1974.

Hastings, Thomas, and Solomon Warriner. 1836. *Musica Sacra, or Utica and Springfield Collections United.* 10th ed. Utica, N.Y.: William Williams.

Herskovits, Melville J. 1966[1945]. "Problem, Method and Theory in Afroamerican Studies." Reprinted in Herskovits, *The New World Negro: Selected Papers in Afroamerican Studies,* 49–61. Bloomington: Indiana University Press.

Historique de la Société musicale Sainte-Cécile de Québec. 1881. Québec: Société musicale Sainte-Cécile.

Hitchcock, H. Wiley. 1968. "A Monumenta Americana?" *Music Library Association Notes* 25:5–11.

Hood, George. 1846. *History of Music in New England; with Biographical Sketches of Reformers and Psalmists.* Boston: Wilkins, Carter.

Howard, John Tasker. 1931. *Our American Music: Three Hundred Years of It.* New York: Crowell. Rev. eds., 1939, 1946, 1965.

Hubbard, W. L., ed. 1910. *History of American Music.* Vol. 8 of *The American History and Encyclopedia of Music.* New York: Irving Squire.

Hurston, Zora Neale. 1995[1935]. *Mules and Men.* New ed. in Zora Neale Hurston, *Folklore, Memoirs, and Other Writings,* ed. Cheryl A. Wall, 1–267. New York: The Library of America.

Jefferson, Thomas. 1984 [1787]. *Notes on the State of Virginia.* New ed. in Thomas Jefferson, *Writings,* ed. Merrill D. Peterson. New York: The Library of America.

Kallmann, Helmut. 1960. *A History of Music in Canada 1534–1914.* Toronto: University of Toronto Press.

Kennedy, John H. 1950. *Jesuit and Savage in New France.* New Haven, Conn.: Yale University Press.

Kerman, Joseph. 1965. "A Profile for American Musicology." *Journal of the American Musicological Society* 18:61–69.

La Flesche, Francis. 1921–1930. *The Osage Tribe.* Bureau of American Ethnology, Annual Reports 36, 39, 43, 45. Washington, D.C.: U.S. Government Printing Office.

Lagacé, Pierre-Minier. 1860. *Les chants d'église en usage dans le province ecclésiastique de Québec, harmonisés pour l'orgue suivant les principes de la tonalité grégorienne.* Paris: H. Bossange et fils.

Lescarbot, Marc. 1609. *Histoire de la Nouvelle France.* Paris: Jean Milon.

Levine, Lawrence W. 1977. *Black Culture and Black Consciousness: Afro-American Folk Thought from Slavery to Freedom.* New York: Oxford University Press.

———. 1988. *Highbrow/Lowbrow: The Emergence of Cultural Hierarchy in America.* Cambridge, Mass.: Harvard University Press.

Lomax, John A., and Alan Lomax. 1934. *American Ballads and Folk Songs.* New York: Macmillan.

Lowens, Irving. 1964. *Music and Musicians in Early America.* New York: Norton.

Lummis, Charles F., and Arthur Farwell. 1929 [1923]. *Spanish Songs of Old California.* New York: G. Schirmer.

Mason, Lowell. 1839. "Historical Sketches of Sacred and Church Music, from the Earliest Times to the Present." *The Boston Musical Gazette* 1:51, 57, 65–66, 83, 97–98, 105, 113, 122, 130, 139.

———1853. *Musical Letters from Abroad.* Boston: Oliver Ditson.

Mather, Cotton. 1721. *The Accomplished Singer.* Boston: B. Green.

Mathews, W. S. B. 1889. *A Hundred Years of Music in America.* Chicago: G. L. Howe.

Mooney, James. 1896. "The Ghost Dance Religion and the Sioux Outbreak of 1890." *14th Annual Report of the Bureau of American Ethnology.* Washington, D.C.: U.S. Government Printing Office.

Moore, John Weeks. 1852. *Complete Encyclopaedia of Music.* Boston: Oliver Ditson.

———. 1875. *Appendix to Encyclopaedia of Music.* Boston: Oliver Diston.

Nathan, Hans. 1962. *Dan Emmett and the Rise of Early Negro Minstrelsy.* Norman: University of Oklahoma Press.

Osterhout, Paul R. 1986. "Note Reading and Regular Singing in Eighteenth-Century New England." *American Music* 4:125–144.

Parker, John Rowe. 1824. *A Musical Biography: or Sketches of the Lives and Writings of Eminent Musical Characters.* Boston: Stone & Forell.

———, ed.1820–1823. *The Euterpeiad: or, Musical Intelligencer, Devoted to the Diffusion of Musical Information and Belles Lettres.*

Perkins, C. C., and J. S. Dwight. 1883. *History of the Handel and Haydn Society of Boston, Massachusetts.* Vol. 1. Boston: A Mudge.

Porter, William Smith. 1834. *The Musical Cyclopedia: The Principles of Music Considered as a Science and an Art.* Boston: James Loring.

Radin, Paul. 1963 [1920]. *The Autobiography of a Winnebago Indian.* Reprint, New York: Dover.

Ritter, Frédéric Louis. 1883. *Music in America.* New York: Scribner's.

Sagard-Théodat, Gabriel. 1636. *Histoire du Canada et voyages que les frères mineurs Recollects y ont faicts pour la conversion des infideles.* Paris: C. Sonnius.

Seeger, Charles. 1939. "Grass Roots for American Composers." *Modern Music* 16:143–149.

———. 1940. "Folk Music as a Source of Social History." In *The Cultural Approach to History,* ed. Carolyn F. Ware, 316–323. New York: Columbia University Press.

———. 1945. "Music in the Americas: Oral and Written Traditions in the Americas." *Bulletin of the Pan American Union* 79:290–293, 341–344.

———. 1957. "Music and Class Structure in the United States." *American Quarterly* 9:281–294.

———. 1961. "The Cultivation of Various European Traditions in the Americas." *International Musicological Society Report of the Eighth Congress, New York, 1961,* 1:364–375.

Shepard, Thomas. 1648. *The Clear Sun-shine of the Gospel.* London: by R. Cotes.

Smith, Gustave. 1881–1882. "Du mouvement musical en Canada." *L'Album musical* (Montréal). 12 installments.

Sonneck, O. G. 1916 [1913]. *A Survey of Music in America.* Reprinted in O. G. Sonneck, *Suum Cuique: Essays on Music,* 121–124. New York: G. Schirmer.

———. 1921 [1916]. "The History of Music in America: A Few Suggestions." Reprinted in O. G. Sonneck, *Miscellaneous Studies in the History of Music,* 324–344. New York: Macmillan.

Stevenson, Robert. 1966. *Protestant Church Music in America.* New York: Norton.

———. 1970. *Philosophies of American Music History.* Washington, D.C.: Library of Congress.

———. 1973a. "Written Sources for Indian Music until 1882." *Ethnomusicology* 17:1–40.

———. 1973b. "English Sources for Indian Music until 1882." *Ethnomusicology* 17:399–442.

———. 1977–1978. "American Musical Scholarship: Parker to Thayer." *19th-Century Music* 1:191–210.

Stuckey, Sterling. 1987. *Slave Culture: Nationalist Theory and the Foundations of Black America.* New York: Oxford University Press.

Symmes, Thomas. 1720. *The Reasonableness of Regular Singing.* Boston: B. Green.

Tan'sur, William. 1746. *A New Musical Grammar: or, the Harmonical Spectator.* London: Jacob Robinson.

Thayer, A. W. 1846–1847. [Series of short notices on New England psalmody]. *The World of Music* 4:14–15, 18–19, 22, 26–27, 30–31, 34–35, 38–39, 42–43, 58, 62.

———. 1852. "A Letter from A.W.T. on Oratorio Practice, American Voices, &c." *Dwight's Journal of Music* 1(22):170.

———. 1866–1879. *Ludwig van Beethovens Leben*, ed. H. Deiters, 3 vols. Berlin: F. Schneider. English version, *The Life of Ludwig Van Beethoven*, ed. and rev. H. Deiters and H. Riemann, with additions by H. E. Krehbiel, 3 vols. New York: The Beethoven Association.

Thwaites, Reuben Gold, ed. 1896–1901. *The Jesuit Relations and Allied Documents: Travels and Explorations of the Jesuit Missionaries in New France, 1610–1791.* 73 vols. Cleveland, Ohio: Burrows.

Torrington, F. H. 1898. "Musical Progress in Canada." In *Canada: An Encyclopedia of the Country,* ed. John C. Hopkins, vol. 4, 383–386. Toronto: Linscott.

Trotter, James Monroe. 1878. *Music and Some Highly Musical People.* Boston: Lee and Shepard.

Vennum, Thomas Jr. 1978. "Ojibwa Origin-Migration Songs of the *mitewiwin.*" *Journal of American Folklore* 91:753–791.

Walter, Thomas. 1721. *The Grounds and Rules of Musick Explained.* Boston: J. Franklin for Samuel Garrish.

———. 1722. *The Sweet Psalmist of Israel.* Boston: J. Franklin for S. Gerrish.

Wilgus, D. K. 1959. *Anglo-American Folksong Scholarship since 1898.* New Brunswick, N.J.: Rutgers University Press.

Part 2
Music in Social and Cultural Contexts

The musics of the United States and Canada express the beliefs and values of a wide variety of individuals and communities. To understand the totality of music in these countries today we must look beyond the music itself to a broader picture of the contexts in which this music is made and understood. The contexts discussed here focus on social, cultural, and historical identities and the roles they play in music making; on the many environments in which music takes place; on social processes such as music learning; on institutions that affect who makes music and for what purpose; and on various forms of interaction by which people and their musics cross social and cultural boundaries. Treating the United States and Canada as a unified cultural area, most of the articles presented in this section were written by scholars and musicians from those countries. Specific musical genres and ethnographic scenes are presented between articles in the form of "Snapshots," which are meant to provide good examples of concepts discussed in the articles rather than to define these concepts.

Male dancing at powow, Grand Portage, Minnesota. © Richard Hamilton Smith/ CORBIS.

Section 1
Issues of Identity

Certain issues of individual and group identity have had historical significance in, and continue to affect, the musical lives of those living in the United States and Canada. Although there is considerable mobility within and among identities, with some more freely chosen than others, all affect music and music making. One's socioeconomic class, for instance, might influence whether or not one takes private music lessons as a child; one's race, ethnicity, or gender might direct one toward or away from certain musical instruments, genres, or learning opportunities; and one's religion might be a major factor in the kinds of music one experiences as a child. Categories of identity are both self- and other-defined, as are musical paths and choices, but they need not totally govern one's musical life. Thus, the categories of identity presented here are not to be taken as fixed or immutable, but rather as suggestions of the varied factors that often affect music and music making within these two countries.

Members of the Douglas Middle School Mariachi Band, Douglas, Arizona. © Jan Butchofsky-Houser/CORBIS.

Class

Anne Dhu McLucas
Jon Dueck
Regula Burckhardt Qureshi

Music and Class in the United States—Anne Dhu McLucas
Music and Class in Canada—Jon Dueck, Regula Burckhardt Qureshi

It has become a basic tenet of ethnomusicology that "any particular kind of music can only be understood in terms of the criteria of the group or society which makes and appreciates that music" (Shepherd et al. 1977:1). If this is so, then it follows that the socioeconomic group to which an individual belongs—his or her "class"—must be a strong determinant (though certainly not the only one) in decoding the meaning of a particular kind of music created or enjoyed by that person. In surveying the wide variety of genres and styles of music in North America, it is clear that social class has a great deal to do not only with the creation of music but also with its consumption, its meaning within society, and its modes of study. Music serves as a potent symbol that carries a generally agreed on meaning for the members of a particular group, even though that meaning may not be clearly articulated by any one member of the group. The meaning is carried in both the actual sound of the music and in the social networks that are necessary to sustain its performance.

MUSIC AND CLASS IN THE UNITED STATES

Charles Hamm (1991) divides music of the United States through World War I into "classical, industrial, and invisible music," with "classical," or "art," music serving largely the needs of the elite classes (upper and upper-middle socioeconomic groups) and "industrial," or, as some would term it, popular or commercial, music serving the large mass of middle-class and working-class groups. The term *invisible music* is what Hamm uses to cover the nineteenth-century musical traditions of American Indians, slaves, and certain other ethnic groups whose music communicated within their own groups without reaching the outside world; hence its "invisibility" (295–305). Charles Seeger (1957) makes similar distinctions among folk, fine art, and popular musics and also underlines the special tensions caused by the presence of classes in a country with an equalitarian view of itself and the contradictions this has brought to the musical expressions of culture.

More recently Mark Slobin (1993) has written convincingly about how larger structures may cut across all of these divisions, describing a "superculture" that refers to the mainstream musics of nation-states; the micromusics of families, neighborhoods, associations, and other voluntary and involuntary groups that form "subcultures"; and, finally, those forces that cross the boundaries of both of the former categories, most particularly the industrial and the diasporic "intercultures." Social class plays a role in all of these, but it is important to see our current situation as one that is part of "a planet in flux, with a population that is creating 'imagined worlds' based both on hard reality and on fantasy . . . ," in which "no one parameter is paramount—not populations, money, ideology, media, or technology—and each factor is only partly dependent on the other" (Slobin 1993:15).

How class influences musical transmission: Oral tradition

However characterized, these broad groupings of music have relevance to social class in terms of how they communicate their meanings and how they are transmitted. For example, in preliterate and pretechnological societies, musical communication takes place in face-to-face situations and exists without notation or reproduction. Musical utterances therefore cannot be isolated and examined at leisure, a fact that affects not only how they are heard but also how they are created and what values they carry with them. Music comes "packaged" with the person who transmits it; therefore its meaning is always socially determined and socially relevant. Music must be remembered in order to be transmitted; thus, fixed thematic formulas become important. And music often carries the value of traditionalism, as "what is non-traditional—cast in recognized themes and formulas—is dangerous because it is slippery and unmanageable" (Ong 1969:640–641).

In the United States today, there are very few, if any, preliterate musical cultures extant and beyond the reach of the technologies that have changed the way music is transmitted and remembered, but their histories remain, and some of their music has been collected. These oral traditions remain as a pool of memory from which other musics draw, whether it be the British American and Irish American traditional vocal and instrumental tunes that form the backbone of country music and bluegrass or the individual Native American oral traditions that are now amalgamated into an ongoing and very active powwow culture, in which the older traditions are augmented with cassette and compact disc performances traded among various Indian nations. Particularly important is the ever-renewing resource of oral musical traditions of black Americans, originally brought over as slaves, a particular and artificially created lower class.

The United States in an industrial age: A mostly middle-class culture

The beginning of the industrial age in Europe coincided with and probably helped cause profound changes in how music was composed and received. In contrast to the face-to-face interactions of oral tradition, the advent of the middle class brought the commercial exchange of music for money, and the clients for it multiplied from the single patron of feudal times to a concert audience, simultaneously creating a wider gulf between the musician and the audience, with whom the musician no longer had a personal relationship. Music "became an element in a new code of power, that of the solvent consumer, the bourgeoisie. It became an element of social status" (Attali 1985:49–50).

At the height of this development, with public concerts and music publishing becoming primary modes of musical dissemination, the United States was born. The religious separatists who helped colonize this new country did not participate in the developing European bourgeois concert culture. Rather, they maintained various religious and secular communal musical traditions, many of them oral. Not surprisingly, tensions between their democratic, communally based version of music and the newer, consumer-culture version were built into the fabric of this new nation, and continue to surface in many ways.

In addition, the first layers of immigration to the new country were largely from Britain, where the attitude toward music on the part of the upper class was also ambivalent (Leppert 1988:13–16). Alongside a small, quasi-aristocratic "gentry" of old political and moneyed influence, the new country divided into a socioeconomic elite—the wealthier merchants, lawyers, and professionals—a middle class that was economically upwardly mobile, and the "mechanics," or laborers. For example, in Boston the two latter classes mixed freely in the cultural arena until the nineteenth century, when "members of the middle class began to distance themselves from both the working class and the upper class" (Broyles 1992:92).

The cross-cutting influence of democracy

The cross-currents thus created in the new country included religious versus commercial and secular attitudes toward music, pro-American attitudes versus art music seen as a foreign influence; music as a money-making arena versus music seen as elevating and above commercialism. Perhaps most important, and a recurring theme in American music, were (and are) the special problems that the exercise of democratic ideals bring to an art form transplanted from an aristocratic Europe. What music is accessible to the populace? How do citizens become educated to "higher" aesthetic experiences? What is the appropriate music for a democracy? Composers, educators, music businessmen, and occasionally even politicians have grappled with these questions. Even the history of patronage by the elite classes has recently been characterized as having a "democratizing spirit" (Locke 1993).

The cross-cutting influence of commercialism

Just as pervasive an influence as democracy is that of commercialism, which became a factor in American music making as early as the mid-eighteenth century with the advent of the singing schools, in which equal parts of idealism, aesthetic concern, and entrepreneurial spirit motivated the peripatetic singing masters. Often of the working class, the singing masters, such as the Boston tanner William Billings or the farmer, liquor merchant, and horse breeder Justin Morgan, nonetheless taught the children of both middle and upper classes (Bandel 1981; Crawford 1993).

Early on, the democratic ideal of educating the masses to appreciate art music was intertwined with commercialism as it became apparent to publishing companies and instrument manufacturers that the educational market would be a lucrative one. This alliance, formed in the early nineteenth century, perhaps earliest in Boston, under the guidance of composer and educator Lowell Mason, is still with us today, especially in the music industry's various interactions with public schools. A new level of commercialism that uses the notion of class to target particular audiences is that of geodemographics and lifestyle analysis in which the profile of each subgroup is ascertained and radio or television advertising uses music to reach that subgroup, a trend explored in more detail later. At the other end of the spectrum, contemporary art music, which since the early nineteenth century has been developing an ideology of individuality, has narrowed its audience to an elite few and must therefore survive on charitable donations by powerful institutions or individuals (Brackett 1993).

The capacity of consumer culture to absorb the music of other classes

The pervasiveness of the commercial side of our society touches music of virtually every class. For example, the songs of the rural working class, created in oral traditions, have been appropriated to make money for those who "discovered" them, and classical music is used for the marketing of almost anything to almost anyone [see MARKETING CLASSICAL MUSIC, p. 268]. The most distant-seeming kinds of music are now consumed, sampled, and reused for new purposes. Put colorfully about one form of music, "we are witnessing the mulching or composting of classical music, and its reintegration into a musical life as a kind of commercial health food product. Classical music 'links' appear everywhere, in film and TV scores, in commercials, in rock (especially heavy metal rock), where the romantic rhetoric enters from the horror film, on Broadway, and in everybody's orchestrations" (Sahl 1986:527). In a less alarmist mode, Slobin describes the same phenomenon as one of freedom of choice: "Omnivorous consumers, we take in any musical nourishment" (Slobin 1993:17).

Differences between passive consumption and active creation

Consumption of music as a product is only part of the overall picture. Music is also being created, and although the percentage of active creators of music compared to passive consumers is quite low—Charles Seeger estimated less than 1 percent (Seeger 1957), the class associations of the creators range from the working-class and middle-class "garage-rock" bands to the highly educated classical composers of the conservatory, with increasing links between the two groups as rock composers become interested in further training and sometimes turn toward universities.

During hard economic times, music has provided a viable alternative to factory jobs or manual labor. Benny Goodman and many other Depression-era swing musicians escaped the grinding labor experienced by their parents and siblings by cultivating their musical talents, often turning professional at early ages (Bindas 1992). The WPA Federal Music Project, as well as the short-lived attempts of the New York composers of the 1930s such as Aaron Copland, Marc Blitzstein, Elie Siegmeister, and others to organize themselves around social causes in the Young Composer's Group and the Composer's Collective, provided outlets, if not much remuneration, for art music composers (Bindas 1995; Oja 1988).

Does the urge to create music fall along class lines? That we have music created by all classes would seem to speak against the idea that one class has dominance in the area of creation. The type, quantity, and commercial viability of music of different classes may vary considerably, but the urge to create exists everywhere.

Historiography of the field

Scholarly interest in social class as it affects music is largely a phenomenon of the twentieth century, and it occurred later for music than for the other arts. This is not to say that there are not many observations concerning class from earlier periods; the issue of how social class intersects with music has been of interest to observers for centuries. In our own country we can find evidence in the diaries of people such as the music-loving seventeenth-century Massachusetts judge Samuel Sewall (Lambert 1985) and the nineteenth-century George Templeton Strong, the opinionated and verbose diarist, critic, and member of New York City's elite social register (Lawrence, 1995 [1988]), as well as in newspapers, journals, histories, and biographies. The more recent scholarly interest in such material has a European backdrop, with the works of Theodor Adorno, Walter Wiora, Walter Salmen, Ivan Supicic, and Jacques Attali focusing largely on art music traditions, sometimes contrasted with popular music, and Simon Frith, Christopher Small, Phillip D. Tagg, and others writing about popular musics from a more Marxist perspective. The serious and comprehensive study of American music must inevitably deal with social class, and certain topics have brought it to the forefront: opera and concert music (Ahlquist 1997; Broyles 1992; Preston 1993); minstrel shows (Cockrell 1997; Lott 1993; Saxton 1975); work songs and songs about work (Cohen 1981; Green 1972, 1991, 1993; Korson 1927; Lomax and Lomax 1947); the development of country music (Conrad 1988; DiMaggio 1972; Malone 1985); and folk music and the folk music revival (Cohen 1991; Denisoff 1971; Rosenberg 1993; Seeger 1957).

Straightforward sociological studies of music have also provided some data (Adorno 1973, 1988; Schuessler 1980; Supičić 1987), and more recently the study of format radio, television, and geodemographics and its applications to music have brought the issue of class into the marketing of music (Barnes 1988; Rodman 1997; White 1997). Each of these topics will be explored briefly here.

As the Astor Place Theater had been built exclusively by the upper class to house its favorite Italian opera, with many discouragements offered to the middle- and lower-class general public, the resentment that boiled over into the streets and that eventually caused the demise of the Astor Place Company was in hindsight hardly a surprise.

Some intersections of music and class

Music of the elite: Opera and concert music

Class consciousness in nineteenth-century music was most clearly displayed in the newly opened urban opera houses and concert halls. Eighteenth-century opera in the colonies and the new nation was originally in the tradition of British ballad opera, itself a genre embodying a middle- and lower-class satire of aristocratic conventions. As in Britain, the American public for this sort of opera ranged from working class to elite, and as the genre developed into English-language comic opera, the plots and the music continued to provide something for each layer of society (Ahlquist 1997:9). In addition, these works were often played as "afterpieces" to the popular plays of the day, which were likewise attended by many levels of society (Levine 1988). In the nineteenth century, as touring stars from Europe and later whole operatic troupes began to come to the United States, the repertoire changed to continuously sung opera; by the 1830s it was often sung in a foreign language (Preston 1993:4–5).

Reception varied between cities and more rural areas: audiences in small communities, such as the small southern and western towns and the mining camps, were surprisingly heterogeneous in class makeup and were open to the wide variety of entertainment that made its way to the western outposts of the developing country. City audiences tended to be more stratified, with the positioning of the classes literally on display in the various tiers of theaters, or largely segregated by class, as people congregated in different theaters to witness, variously, Italian or English opera, minstrel shows, melodrama, and so on.

The most infamous of the incidents arising from the class differentiations and the tensions arising from them was the Astor Place Riot of May 1849, "an altercation ostensibly prompted by a feud between the British actor William Charles Macready and the American actor Edwin Forrest, but in reality a class conflict: the rich versus the poor, the aristocracy versus American democrats" (Preston 1993:141). As the Astor Place Theater had been built exclusively by the upper class to house its favorite Italian opera, with many discouragements offered to the middle- and lower-class general public (such as uncomfortable seating with bad sight lines to the stage), the resentment that boiled over into the streets and that eventually caused the demise of the Astor Place Company was in hindsight hardly a surprise. By the late nineteenth century, according to Deane Root, New York theaters were situated along class and ethnic lines in three general zones according to the ethnic composition and income level of their neighborhood and the programs they characteristically offered (Root 1981:174–175).

Music of the nineteenth-century working class: Minstrel shows

At the other end of the social and entertainment spectrum of the mid-nineteenth century, although sometimes sharing the same stages as opera, were the minstrel shows. As Alexander Saxton puts it most succinctly, "Minstrel shows expressed class identification and hostility" (1975:4). Growing out of strong working-class roots in rural cele-

FIGURE I   Poster advertising Baird's Mammoth Minstrels, c. 1880. The four dancing figures parody polite dancing styles with grotesquely and overly large physical movements. Illustration © Bettmann/CORBIS.

brations and urban rowdiness, and a long British American tradition of white men blackening their faces for both theatrical and folk presentations (Cockrell 1997), the blackface minstrel show appeared in more or less crystallized form in the 1840s, performed and composed mainly by white men of urban origin. It thrived through the 1870s, when it was absorbed into vaudeville and other forms, but in both the United States and Britain as late as the 1980s it put forth late-blooming offshoots designed to satirize class divisions: "The original foursome of undifferentiated musicians expanded into a line in which customary position corresponded roughly to class identification. The end men, who always played tambourine and bones, were lower class . . . the middleman, or interlocutor, served as a bogus mouthpiece for the high culture" (Saxton 1975:9–11) (figure 1).

Work songs and songs about work

After the music of some of the theatrical entertainments of the nineteenth century, such as minstrel shows, which were clearly geared to the urban working class, the clearest example of music made by and for the working class is the labor songs, which have comprised a large and variegated strand of our national heritage from the beginning. Classification of these songs is fluid; cross-cutting the occupation of the singer-composer are issues of whether the song is descriptive or accompanies work, whether it has entered an oral tradition or is the expression of a single moment in time, and whether it is descriptive or political (or sometimes both). Archie Green defines many such distinctions, in particular distinguishing between an industrial song and one merely describing the life of a worker by contrasting two of the best known ballads dealing with West Virginians. "John Henry" is characterized as a true industrial ballad, while "John Hardy" is a lyrical ballad that happens to deal with a coal miner (Green 1972:9). Green also discusses other hierarchies of the laboring folk, listing peasant, worker, miner, unionist, radical, and communist, but goes on to say that "such scholastic hair-splitting breaks down when the life histories of particular miner organizers are pursued" (Green 1972:18). His account of the life of Aunt Molly Jackson, miner's wife, midwife-nurse, singer-songwriter, and at times communist labor organizer, illustrates this statement. But he holds to the essential folklike nature of the laborers' societies, writing, "Miners,

FIGURE 2   Bill Monroe (1911–1996), the "Father of Bluegrass," found commercial success in the 1940s and 1950s with music drawn from his folk roots. He was inducted into the Country Music Hall of Fame in 1970. Photo © Bettmann/ CORBIS.

neither tribal nor rural, are sufficiently linked by the centripetal nature of their work to behave, in part, as the peasantry does" (Green 1972:23).

Country music

The popular genre of country music intersects the world of work songs. The major themes of country music are work, freedom, and alienation, appearing in approximately one-sixth of all Top 20 selections (Dimaggio 1972). Country music is itself a commercial offshoot of the traditional song and instrumental music of the South, formerly carried on in an oral tradition. Consequently, from the start country music was an eclectic mix, which included ancient British ballads, Americanized versions of these, sacred songs, minstrel tunes, rudimentary blues, and songs of many sorts absorbed from the commercial popular music industry over the years (figure 2). Over the century it has grown from a homegrown and heartfelt music, expressing working-class identity, into a commercial music, produced by others to appeal to a working-class identity, whether or not its listeners are actually working class (Peterson 1992:37, 59). The symbolic meaning of country music as the declared favorite music of New England–educated, upper-class President George Bush, as making him more "of the people," is unmistakable (Malone 1990).

Folk music and the folk revival

The "invisible musics," which have persisted for centuries in pockets of oral tradition all over the United States, have surfaced into the visible, commercial market at various times in the history of this country. In doing so, they have often crossed class lines in interesting and complex ways. The minstrel shows, for example, had their roots at least in part in oral tradition, although probably less of the southern blacks they pretended to portray than of the British-Irish-American men performing in them. The middle-class white composers and performers of minstrelsy (until after the Civil War, when blacks also formed minstrel troupes) used music derived from that of the rural working class to entertain audiences of the urban working class.

In the early history of the recording industry, the market for "race" and "hillbilly" records (commercial designations for music aimed largely at rural black and white working-class audiences) used performers from those classes. But the profits from the recordings went almost solely to the middle-class producers who hired the traditional performers. In the case of hillbilly music, some performers went on to develop country music and became the later well-paid stars. Later on, in the 1950s, the "smoother" and usually white performers often covered the songs of earlier black and white performers. This practice went on quite visibly in rock and roll, where performers like Elvis Presley and the Beatles became wealthy, as well as in the folk revival, where the Kingston Trio, Pete Seeger, and others sang songs collected from traditional performers for radio, recordings, and college performances. Although the intent of record producers of the folk revival was perhaps not as crassly commercial as that of rock and roll's producers, the shift in values and class lines was probably even sharper. Rock and roll was a translation of a largely black working-class music into an urban white working-class music, which later spread to the youth of every class. The folk revival took the music of rural whites and blacks and purveyed it directly to the elite, college-educated youth (Cantwell 1993:40–43).

For example, in tracing the career of folk revival singer Pete Seeger from his early days of idealism with his radical singing collective, The Almanac Singers, to his later commercial popularity, Robert Lumer writes: "Ironically, the folk music alternative to commercial mass music could only be popularized by making it a commercial music, ultimately changing its nature" (1991:53). Seeger himself was a Harvard dropout, son of the well-known composer-musicologist, Charles Seeger—hardly a man of the working class or "peasantry" (figure 3). Nor were the many college students who followed

FIGURE 3   Pete Seeger, playing his banjo, appeared at the HUAC hearing on 18 August 1955. Seeger's early idealism had brought him to the attention of this committee. Photo © Bettmann/ CORBIS.

Seeger, the Kingston Trio, Joan Baez, Judy Collins, and others into the folk revival. "Why American college students should want to express the ideas and emotions of the downtrodden and the heartbroken, of garage mechanics and millworkers and miners and backwoods farmers, is in itself an interesting question. But there is certainly good reason for students today to find the world brutal and threatening, and one suspects that when they sing about the burdens and sorrows of the Negro, for example, they are singing out of their own state of mind as well" (Montgomery 1960:118). For at least some of these students, the folk revival meant a complete change in lifestyle and the adoption of some of the values that were seen to go with folk culture: less reliance on money and its accumulation; more concern with community; pursuit of participatory, not vicarious, recreation; and political goals that resisted centralization of power while taking into account global and ecological concerns.

Format radio, television, and geodemographics

The "subcultures" of which Slobin writes are in clear evidence on North American radio stations. Since the 1950s, when the Top 40 radio format was devised to help radio recover its market after television had taken over center stage, differential programming has become more and more refined in order to target advertising to particular audiences. Recorded music now provides well over 50 percent of all radio air time (the percentage is even higher for FM radio), according to Jody Berland (1990:180), and musical profiles have been constructed on the researched tastes of targeted audiences. These tastes are also in part a result of formatting, so the process is a circular one: target audiences are identified and their musical tastes researched, and these tastes are reinforced by development of a playlist of records that will appeal to the target audience. Although the demographics of each format are not explicitly class based, many of the parameters relate to class, as in a profile of New Age (abbreviated as NAC—"New Age Contemporary") stations in which they are characterized as playing "Beautiful Music for Yuppies: 25–54, usually upper middle class" (Barnes: 1988:35).

Television, although not so closely formatted by channel, nonetheless uses the whole spectrum of musical styles that target particular audiences, especially in the construction of commercials designed to sell products. For example, a recent study of two commercials contrasts the music used to sell a Chevrolet truck (Bob Seger's "Like a Rock") to a presumably working-class audience—men with hard hats are depicted in the commercial—while the newly composed music for an Infiniti sedan with an expensive wood-paneled interior uses the "classical" connotations of tonal chamber music featuring woodwinds, along with the visual images of an elegant country house with cobblestone driveway, to sell to an upper-class audience and those aspiring to it (Rodman 1997).

Such marketing depends on the presence of "taste cultures" reflecting the long-term consumption patterns of those who share certain demographic variables, such as race, social class, region, and gender. However, there is evidence that social mobility and the availability of inexpensive music through electronic technology is causing instead the formation of "culture classes," or groupings of individuals who share similar consumption patterns regardless of social class (Lewis 1975). Country music, mentioned earlier, is an example of a music that is enjoyed by groups far removed from the classes for and by which this music was originally developed.

Geodemographic and lifestyle data are relatively new and sophisticated marketing tools that depend on socioeconomic class—accessed either by locality or by taste culture, among other characteristics—and are used to target customers (Sleight 1997). In these fields, musical tastes are both a sign of the lifestyle as well as a communication tool to use in capturing a particular customer. This marketing strategy is perhaps the ultimate extreme of the cross influences noted earlier—commercialism and democracy. While class was always a factor in the choices people have made concerning the music

Although concepts of class hegemony and identity (in the Marxist or Weberian sense) are central to present-day ethnomusicological study and well developed in the discipline of sociology in Canada, they have yet to be fully explored by scholars of Canadian music.

they make or listen to, at the beginning of the twenty-first century it has become a tool wielded at times to manipulate consumers into making certain choices. The consumer is presumably always "free" to choose among a wide variety of musics, in a way that was probably not possible in earlier societies; however, the influences on that consumer are also more pervasive and persuasive—and certainly more researched—than in any previous time.

The importance of an individual's socioeconomic class in determining musical taste, creativity, and consumption is probably less now than it was earlier in the century, but it continues to be a factor, if at times an unseen one, even in current cultural decisions. Paying attention to the history of its development in America, as well as looking for its traces in contemporary culture, can illuminate sides of musical choices that might otherwise go unnoticed.

—ANNE DHU McLUCAS

MUSIC AND CLASS IN CANADA

Class, or, more specifically, class hierarchy, denotes unequal group identities derived from differential access to wealth and power. While stopping short of directly addressing class per se, Beverley Diamond and Robert Witmer (1994:1) suggest that ideas of hegemony and identity may be "well worn" in most of the humanities and social sciences, but they are "less familiar" to the student of Canadian music. Although concepts of class hegemony and identity (in the Marxist or Weberian sense) are central to present-day ethnomusicological study and well developed in the discipline of sociology in Canada, they have yet to be fully explored by scholars of Canadian music.

Origins of a capitalist class structure in Canada

Sociologist Joanne Naiman writes that "Canada . . . came late to the Industrial Revolution" (Naiman 1997:85). Unlike the United States, which, with Britain, experienced rapid capitalist development in the late eighteenth century, Canada, as first a French and then a British colony, remained more or less a resource-based colonial economy until the late nineteenth century, providing fish, furs, and timber to the colonial powers. Because of this, a manufacturing base was slow to develop, and Canada's society prior to the late nineteenth century was largely rural and agrarian. This is true for both English Canada and what is now Québec, which retained a French seigneurial system of property rights even after the ascension of the British as a colonial power in 1763. Thus while an inequitable racial class structure developed early between the European colonizers and the Native peoples of Canada, modern capitalist class structure developed later in Canada than it did in the United States.

A capitalist boom in Canada did occur in the late nineteenth century when workers and capital arrived from Britain, Continental Europe, and the United States. The majority of the production took place within the primary sector involving the processing of resources such as lumber into paper. In addition, capital poured into the development of the railroad, an essential transportation infrastructure linking the resources of Western Canada to the Eastern centers of trade and commerce, Toronto and Montréal. Capitalist class structure in Canada developed as its rural resource-based economies became linked to production, trade, and commerce.

Canadian class structure(s)

Today the Canadian economy includes all sectors of a modern capitalist economy, but it retains a strong emphasis on resource and primary sector economies. As with the United States, a rapid expansion of the middle class occurred after World War II, and the middle and working classes have been increasingly marginalized since the mid-1970s. Anton Allahar and James Côté estimate that presently 1.1 percent of the Canadian population is upper class (or the owning class), 26.5 percent is middle class (including the professional sector), 63.7 percent is working class, and 8.7 percent is lower class (that is, poor or unemployed) (Allahar and Côté 1998:35).

According to John Porter's seminal study (1969), what is notable about Canadian class structure is a relatively coherent economic and political elite whose members are of predominantly British and also French Canadian descent and are located in metropolitan Ontario and Québec. Professional and working classes are more socially mobile as well as ethnically diverse, with continuing immigration reinforcing bonds of ethnicity over class. On the other hand, racist antagonism contributes to lower-class immobility. Clearly, Canadian class structure has been strongly marked by the hegemonic control as well as by the racial, regional, linguistic, and cultural tensions that characterized the development of capitalism in Canada.

The most central racial tension in Canada has been between persons of European descent and aboriginal persons. Joanne Naiman notes that the poorest part of the Canadian population includes a disproportionate amount of aboriginal persons (1997:214). Canada's history of marginalizing its indigenous population has left a legacy of structural and cultural inequity that is proving difficult to overcome—particularly for aboriginal urban dwellers.

The regional tensions that characterize Canadian history, that is, the tensions between the less advantaged periphery and the economic core of central Canada, with its urban centers of Toronto and Montréal, continue to the present. The resource-based economies of the Canadian West and the Maritimes struggle for a more central place in the Canadian political economy, but power (and, indeed, population) continues to be concentrated in central Canada.

The most central regional tension in Canada is linguistic: the tension between French Canada, especially Québec, and Canada's English-speaking majority. Christian Dufour's important work *Le défi québécois* (1990) traces the history of Québec's relationship with English Canada. Québec was doubly colonized: it remained a resource base for English Canada, which exported those resources not to the French colonial power but to Britain. The middle class developed later in Québec than it did in English Canada, after the end of the seigneurial system of property rights; however, with its development a large nationalist movement, favoring secession from Canada, flowered in Québec. Québec's economic marginality (excepting of course Montréal) and secessionist nationalism continue to the present day.

Finally, cultural inequalities persist in Canada despite its official multicultural policies. Sociologist M. Reza Nakhaie notes that there is a wide range of scholarly debate about the hierarchy of ethnic groups in Canada: while most scholars recognize that certain ethnic groups are marginalized by Canadian society in that they are pressured to be assimilated into its linguistic and cultural mainstream, they differ in their analyses of the possibility of resistance by these groups (Nakhaie 1999:233–234). That ethnic and aboriginal groups in Canada do pursue strategies of resistance, however, is noteworthy and renders visible the tension between the cultural mainstream of Canada and Canada's

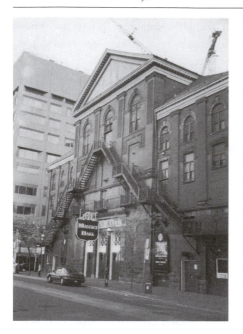

FIGURE 4   Massey Music Hall, Toronto. This hall, which was given to the city by the Massey family, opened in 1894. At that time Toronto had no concert halls suitable to host classical music performance. Massey Hall became the premier classical concert hall for this city. Photo by Gillian Rodger, 2000.

cultural periphery. Thus while class stratification is a reality in Canada, it is most often discussed in terms of its racial, regional, linguistic, and cultural ramifications.

Canadian music and class structures

Marked by colonial rule until independence in 1867, Canada's political elites established musical institutions that remain to this day rooted in Central Canada and are strongly marked by English as well as French elite culture (figure 4). Thus Canadian music generally means concert music by Canadian composers, while the Canadian Broadcasting Corporation's FM network airs and patronizes Western art music performance almost exclusively. Canadian folk music, on the other hand, has received institutional patronage as the musical heritage of the two founding nations. Both English and French Canadian folk songs have also served to voice rural and working-class concerns as well as to gloss "Old Country" nostalgia. More recently, singer-songwriters across the country have begun to use folk as well as popular music idioms to shape an individually based Canadian musical identity that fits comfortably within consumer capitalism, bypassing tensions between groups.

The dialogue surrounding aboriginal identity in music is highlighted in the story of Micmac fiddler Lee Cremo told by Gordon Smith (1994). Cremo, a Cape Breton Islander, learned to fiddle from his father and became enormously successful as a performer both in Canada and abroad. Nonaboriginal persons viewed Cremo as one of the best Maritime fiddlers, playing Cape Breton–style (Scottish origin) fiddle. On the other hand, Micmac interviewees saw Cremo as representing a syncretic blend of Cape Breton musical style and traditional Micmac performance styles and values. For the Micmac, then, Cremo was exemplary of a successful way to assert Micmac identity while participating in Canadian (Maritime) society.

Music can also express the regional tensions of Canada: John Lehr (1994) addresses the process whereby country music has become a symbol of the Canadian West (versus the East, that is, metropolitan central Canada). Lehr suggests that while in the U.S. context country music is identified with the rural South, in Canada the regional conflict runs East–West, and Canadian country songwriters employ place names of both the United States and the Canadian West to valorize the "West of North America" as a general region. For example, the Canadian country lyrics of Ian Tyson assert a new geography of Canada, with the West an exemplar of what is free and good—the agricultural and the natural—while the great urban spaces of the East (central Canada) are positioned as a sort of Babylon in contrast.

Linguistic identity remains a continuing site of contest in relation to Canadian political hegemony. Christian Dufour discusses the role of radio in marking Québec as both francophone and distinct from Canada as nation. Dufour suggests that France as a nation (not Canada) has become a cultural marker of national identity for Québec; Canada is marked as a place where a distinct history and culture is seen as both lost and exploited (Dufour 1990:92). On the other hand, the Canadian Broadcasting Corporation (CBC), which controls national radio and television, can index both a creation of "Canadian" space and a simultaneous suppression of regional, racial, and cultural differences. Jody Berland (1998) describes CBC Radio's singular programming across Canada as defining, in the case of the variety-oriented CBC Radio 2, a "'public' space" on the airwaves, regardless of place within Canada, and on the other hand a "blandly homogenous" musical world in the case of the classical music–oriented CBC Radio 1. This national radio presence and Dufour's French-language radio exist in tension with each other, particularly in Québec.

Doreen Klassen's discussion (1989) of the Plautdeutscha Owend, a Low German–language musical celebration of the southern Manitoba Mennonites, reveals the complexity of music as involved in discourses of ethnicity in Canada. The Mennonites of southern Manitoba by and large arrived from Ukraine, retaining their language, Low

German, or Plautdeutsch [see MUSIC OF CHRISTIAN MINORITIES, p. 1237]. Over time they began to assimilate to the anglophone mainstream of Canadian culture. However, in the late 1960s, Mennonites began to celebrate their linguistic tradition through evenings of songs and drama in Low German, called Plautdeutscha Owend. While one might view this musical tradition as a site of resistance against assimilation, Klassen notes that the Canadian government began pursuing an official policy of multiculturalism at this time, thus encouraging events such as the Plautdeutscha Owend. This policy of multiculturalism on the one hand recognized the diversity of culture in Canada and on the other was intended to relativize the cultural struggles of Québec. Thus, the Plautdeutscha Owend can be read as a complex phenomenon representing both a site of resistance and a function of Canadian hegemony.

A different instance of the musical struggle for ethnic recognition may be found among South Asian Canadians, who see their classical music as equivalent to and enriching the elite domain of Canadian music. Indian music thus becomes a powerful tool for breaking ethnic boundaries to join a Canadian cultural elite. At the same time, Indian music is cultivated internally as a powerful index of South Asian heritage, regardless of class (Qureshi 1972). Significant here is the assertion of agency indexed by a music that is not only "ethnic" but non-Western as well.

The picture of Canadian music and class that arises from these writings on Canadian music does not align simply with materialist notions of class; rather, it reflects the complex and multifaceted experience of class in Canada as embodied in popular and scholarly discourse. The tensions surrounding the origins of a capitalist class structure in Canada are central to these discourses: each binary (aboriginal–nonaboriginal, Québec–English Canada, and so on) keys into a basic social experience of have versus have-not.

—JON DUECK, REGULA BURCKHARDT QURESHI

REFERENCES

Adorno, Theodor. 1973 [1948]. *Philosophy of Modern Music.* Trans. Anne G. Mitchell and Wesley V. Blomster. New York: Seabury Press.

———. 1988. *Introduction to the Sociology of Music.* Trans. E. B. Ashton. New York: Continuum.

Ahlquist, Karen. 1997. *Democracy at the Opera: Music, Theater, and Culture in New York City, 1815–60.* Chicago: University of Illinois Press.

Allahar, Anton L., and James E. Côté. 1998. *Richer and Poorer: The Structure of Inequality in Canada.* Toronto: James Lorimer and Company.

Attali, Jacques. 1985. *Noise: The Political Economy of Music.* Minneapolis: University of Minnesota Press.

Bandel, Betty. 1981. *Sing the Lord's Song in a Strange Land: The Life of Justin Morgan.* Rutherford, N.J.: Fairleigh Dickinson University Press.

Barnes, Ken. 1988. "Top 40 Radio: A Fragment of the Imagination." In *Facing the Music,* ed. Simon Frith, 8–50. New York: Pantheon Books.

Berland, Jody. 1990. "Radio Space and Industrial Time: Music Formats, Local Narratives and Technological Mediation." *Popular Music* 9(2):179–192.

———. 1998. "Locating Listening: Technological Space, Popular Music, and Canadian Mediations." In *The Place of Music,* ed. Andrew Leyshon, David Matless, and George Revill, 129–150. New York: The Guilford Press

Bindas, Kenneth J. 1992. "Race, Class, and Ethnicity among Swing Musicians." In *America's Musical Pulse: Popular Music in Twentieth-Century Society,* ed. Kenneth J. Bindas, 73–82. Westport, Conn.: Praeger.

———. 1995. *All of This Music Belongs to the Nation: The WPA's Federal Music Project and American Society.* Knoxville: University of Tennessee Press.

Brackett, David. 1993. "Economics and Aesthetics in Contemporary Art Music." *Stanford Humanities Review* 3(2):49–59.

Broyles, Michael. 1992. *"Music of the Highest Class": Elitism and Populism in Antebellum Boston.* New Haven, Conn.: Yale University Press.

Cantwell, Robert. 1993. "When We Were Good: Class and Culture in the Folk Revival." In *Transforming Tradition,* ed. Neil V. Rosenburg, 35–60. Urbana: University of Illinois Press.

Cockrell, Dale. 1997. *Demons of Disorder: Early Blackface Minstrels and Their World.* Cambridge: Cambridge University Press.

Cohen, Norm. 1981. *Long Steel Rail: The Railroad in American Folksong.* Urbana: University of Illinois Press.

———. 1991. Notes to "Folk Song America: A 20th Century Revival." Notes for *Smithsonian Collection of Recordings* R 046/P6 21489. Compact disc.

Conrad, Charles. 1988. "Work Songs, Hegemony, and Illusions of Self." *Critical Studies in Mass Communication* 5(3):179–201.

Crawford, Richard. 1990. "'Ancient Music' and the Europeanizing of American Psalmody, 1800–1810." In *A Celebration of American Music: Words and Music in Honor of H. Wiley Hitchcock,* ed. Richard Crawford, R. Allen Lott, and Carol J. Oja, 225–255. Ann Arbor: University of Michigan Press.

———. 1993. *The American Musical Landscape.* Berkeley: University of California Press.

Denisoff, R. Serge. 1971. *Great Day Coming: Folk Music and the American Left.* Chicago: University of Illinois Press.

Diamond, Beverley, and Robert Witmer, eds. 1994. *Canadian Music: Issues of Hegemony and Identity.* Toronto: Canadian Scholars' Press.

DiMaggio, Paul. 1972. "Country Music: Ballad of the Silent Majority." In *The Sounds of Social Change,* ed. R. Denisoff and R. Peterson, 31–56. Chicago: Rand McNally.

———. 1982. "Cultural Entrepreneurship in Nineteenth-Century Boston: The Creation of an Organizational Base for High Culture in America." In *Rethinking Popular Culture: Contemporary Perspectives in Cultural Studies,* ed. Chandra Mukerji and Michael Schudson. Berkeley: University of California Press.

Dufour, Christian. 1990. *Le défi québécois /A Canadian Challenge.* Lantzville, B.C. and Halifax: Oolichan Books and L'Institut de recherches politiques.

Forcese, Dennis. 1997 [1975]. *The Canadian Class Structure.* 4th ed. Toronto: McGraw-Hill Ryerson.

Frith, Simon. 1978. *The Sociology of Rock.* London: Constable.

Green, Archie. 1972. *Only a Miner: Studies in Recorded Coal-Mining Songs.* Urbana: University of Illinois Press.

———. 1991. "Labor Song: An Ambiguous Legacy." *Journal of Folklore Research* 28(2–3): 93–102.

———. 1993. *Songs about Work: Essays in Occupational Culture for Richard A. Reuss.* Bloomington: Folklore Institute, Indiana University.

Hamm, Charles. 1991. "The USA: Classical, Industrial and Invisible Music." In *The Late Romantic Era: From the Mid-Nineteenth Century to World War I,* ed. Jim Samson, 295– 326. Englewood Cliffs, N.J.: Prentice-Hall.

Klassen, Doreen. 1989. *Singing Mennonite: Low German Songs among the Mennonites.* Winnipeg: University of Manitoba Press.

Korson, George. 1927. *Songs and Ballads of the Anthracite Miner.* New York: F. H. Hitchcock.

———. 1964. *Minstrels of the Mine Patch: Songs and Stories of the Anthracite Industry.* Hatboro, Pa: Folkore Associates.

Lambert, Barbara, ed. 1985. *Music in Colonial Massachusetts, 1630–1820.* 2 vols. Boston: The Colonial Society of Massachusetts.

Lawrence, Vera Brodsky. 1995 [1988]. *Strong on Music: The New York Music Scene in the Days of George Templeton Strong, 1836–1878.* 2 vols. Chicago: Chicago University Press.

Lehr, John. 1994. "As Canadian as Possible . . . under the Circumstances: Regional Myths, Images of Place and National Identity in Canadian Country Music." In *Canadian Music: Issues of Hegemony and Identity,* ed., Beverley Diamond and Robert Witmer, 269–282. Toronto: Canadian Scholars' Press.

Leppert, Richard. 1988. *Music and Image: Domesticity, Ideology and Socio-Cultural Formation in Eighteenth-Century England.* Cambridge: Cambridge University Press.

Levine, Lawrence. 1988. *Highbrow/Lowbrow: The Emergence of Cultural Hierarchy in America.* Cambridge: Harvard University Press.

Lewis, George H. 1975. "Cultural Socialization and the Development of Taste Cultures and Culture Classes in American Popular Music: Existing Evidence and Proposed Research Directions." *Popular Music and Society* 4(4): 226–241.

Locke, Ralph P. 1993. "Music Lovers, Patrons, and the 'Sacralization' of Culture in America." *Nineteenth Century Music* 17(2):149–173.

Lomax, John, and Alan Lomax. 1947. *Folk Song USA.* New York: Duell, Sloan and Pearce.

Lott, Eric. 1993. *Love and Theft: Blackface Minstrelsy and the American Working Class.* New York: Oxford University Press.

Lumer, Robert. 1991. "Peter Seeger and the Attempt to Revive the Folk Music Process." *Popular Music and Society* 15(1):45–58.

McConachie, Bruce A. 1988. "New York Operagoing, 1825–50: Creating an Elite Social Ritual," *American Music* 6(2):181–192.

Malone, Bill C. 1985. *Country Music, U.S.A.* Austin: University of Texas Press.

———. 1990. "Classic Country Music." Notes to *Classic Country Music: A Smithsonian Collection.*

Montgomery, Susan. 1960. "The Folk Furor." *Mademoiselle* December, 98–99, 118.

Naiman, Joanne. 1997. *How Societies Work: Class, Power and Change in a Canadian Context.* Concord, Ont.: Irwin Publishing.

Nakhaie, M. Reza. 1999. *Debates on Social Inequality: Class, Gender and Ethnicity in Canada.* Toronto: Harcourt Brace.

Oja, Carol. 1988. "Composer with a Conscience: Elie Siegmeister in Profile." *American Music* 16(2):158–180.

Ong, Walter. 1969. "World as View and World as Event." *American Anthropologist* 71:634–647.

Peterson, Richard A. 1992. "Class Unconsciousness in Country Music." In *You Wrote My Life: Lyrical Themes in Country Music,* ed. Melton A. McLaurin and Richard A. Peterson, 35–62. Philadelphia: Gordon and Breach.

Porter, John. 1969. *The Vertical Mosaic: An Analysis of Social Class and Power in Canada.* Toronto: University of Toronto Press.

Preston, Katherine. 1993. *Opera on the Road: Traveling Opera Troupes in the United States, 1825–60.* Urbana: University of Illinois Press.

Qureshi, Regula Burckhardt. 1972. "Ethnomusicological Research among Canadian Communities of Arab and East Indian Origin." *Ethnomusicology* 16(3):381–396.

Rodman, Ronald. 1997. "And Now an Ideology from Our Sponsor: Musical Style and Semiosis in American Television Commercials." *College Music Symposium* 37:21–48.

Root, Deane L. 1981. *American Popular Stage Music: 1860–1880.* Ann Arbor, Mich.: UMI Research Press.

Rosenberg, Neil V., ed. 1993. *Transforming Tradition: Folk Music Revivals Examined.* Chicago: University of Illinois Press.

Russell, Philip A. 1997. "Musical Tastes and Society." In *The Social Psychology of Music,* ed. David J. Hargreaves and Adrian C. North, 141–158. Oxford: Oxford University Press.

Sahl, Michael. 1986. "Thoughts on the State of Classical Music in the United States." *Musical Quarterly* 72(4):523–527.

Salmen, Walter, ed. 1983 [1971]. *The Social Status of the Professional Musician from the Middle Ages to the Nineteenth Century.* Trans. Herbert Kaufman and Barbara Reisner. New York: Pendragon Press.

Saxton, Alexander. 1975. "Blackface Minstrelsy and Jacksonian Ideology." *American Quarterly* 29:3–28.

Schuessler, Karl F. 1980. *Musical Taste and Socioeconomic Background,* New York: Arno Press.

Seeger, Charles. 1957. "Music and Class Structure in the United States." *American Quarterly* 9(3):281–294.

Shepherd, John, Phil Virden, Graham Vulliamy, and Trevor Wishart, eds. 1977. *Whose Music? A Sociology of Musical Languages.* New Brunswick, N.J.: Transaction Books.

Sleight, Peter. 1997. *Targeting Customers: How to Use Geodemographic and Lifestyle Data in Your Business,* 2nd ed. Henley-on-Thames, Eng.: NTC Publications.

Slobin, Mark. 1993. *Subcultural Sounds: Micromusics of the West.* Hanover, N.H.: Wesleyan University Press.

Small, Christopher. 1996. *Music, Society, Education.* Hanover, N.H.: University Press of New England.

Smith, Gordon E. 1994. "Lee Cremo: Narratives about a Micmac Fiddler." In *Canadian Music: Issues of Hegemony and Identity,* ed. Beverley Diamond and Robert Witmer, 541–556. Toronto: Canadian Scholars' Press.

Supičić, Ivan. 1987. *Music in Society: A Guide to the Sociology of Music (Elementi sociologije muzike).* Stuyvesant, N.Y.: Pendragon Press.

Tagg, Phillip D. 1979. "Kojak: 50 Seconds of Television Music: Toward the Analysis of Affect in Popular Music." Ph.D. dissertation, University of Goteborg.

Walser, Robert. 1993. *Running with the Devil: Power, Gender, and Madness in Heavy Metal Music.* Hanover, N.H.: University Press of New England.

White, John. 1997. "Radio Formats and the Transformation of Musical Style: Codes and Cultural Values in the Remaking of Tunes." *College Music Symposium* 37:1–12.

Wiora, Walter. 1994. "Der Musikalische Ausdruck von Ständen und Klassen in eigenen Stilen." *International Review of the Aesthetics and Sociology of Music* 25(1–2):93–113.

Snapshot:
Two Views of Music and Class
Tamara E. Livingston
Katherine K. Preston

Revivals—Tamara E. Livingston
Scene: 25 April 1857, New York City—Katherine K. Preston

Issues of group and social identity, such as class, are always intertwined with music making, as illustrated in the following two examples. Although quite different in their subject matter, historical context, and treatment of class issues, both relate specific musical practices to the American middle classes of the nineteenth and twentieth centuries, highlighting the range of musical choices available during these times.

REVIVALS

Social movements calling themselves music revivals are a prominent feature of the twentieth-century musical landscape. Music revivals have occurred in the United States, Canada, Germany, England, Brazil, India, Russia, Scotland, and elsewhere. Their focus is as wide-ranging as their geographical spread; they span from the revival of a single instrument—the harpsichord, the Northumbrian small-pipe, the lute—to the re-creation of entire popular, indigenous, or art music traditions—traditional jazz, American folk song, early music.

Music revivals are defined as social movements that strive to restore musical systems that have disappeared (or are believed to be disappearing) for the benefit of contemporary society. What distinguishes music revivals from musical fads or trends is the overt political and cultural agenda expressed by revivalists themselves. Through the re-creation of a past music system, defined by Neil Rosenberg as "contextual aggregates of shared repertoire, instrumentation, and performance-style generally perceived as being historically and culturally bounded by such factors as class, ethnicity, race, religions, commerce, and art" (1993:177), revivalists position themselves in opposition to the contemporary cultural mainstream, align themselves with a particular historical lineage, and offer a cultural alternative in which legitimacy is grounded in claims of authenticity and historical fidelity.

Music revivals are middle-class phenomena that play an important role in the formulation and maintenance of identity for subgroups of disaffected individuals. Thus revivalist ideologies tend to be constructed on certain modes of thinking and structured experiences that are shared by the middle class. These include the division of culture into modern and traditional; the emphasis on cultural products instead of processes; the objectification, commodification, and rationalization of various aspects of life; and the imagined community of the nation, among others (Turino 1996), all of which play an important role, to a lesser or greater extent, in music revivalism.

Revivalist ideology and discourse

The most important tenet of revivalist ideology is the historical continuity and authenticity of the revivalist practice. In the case of indigenous music revivals, the term *folk music* is often employed to refer to music with a long history outside consumer culture that contains the essence or seeds of a national cultural expression. In other types of revivals, authenticity is based on written source interpretation or on the re-creation of certain recorded performances. In revivalist discourse, historical continuity is often used to imply authenticity and vice versa, and both in turn are used to imply positive social value. Exactly how these concepts are mapped onto the repertoire, instrumentation, playing style, and interpretation of revivalist music will vary, but what is notable is that these values and distinctions are made, debated, and defended.

The educational aspect of revivals is another characteristic trait; once the aesthetic code referencing historical continuity and authenticity has been determined and reified through performance, recordings, and written and spoken discourse, it must be passed on to novice revivalists in order to ensure the correct maintenance of the tradition. Core revivalists also engage in efforts to educate the general public, in the hope of gaining new converts as well as to foster a widespread appreciation of their music. Lecture-demonstrations, public television appearances, and recordings with informative liner notes are examples of revivalist pedagogical venues.

Core revivalists

Music revivals are almost always initiated by a group of individuals who feel a strong affinity for and commitment to the musical tradition. Almost invariably they are scholars and collectors, and many are amateur musicians as well. Using their connections with institutions, the recording industry, radio, and television, they frequently act the role of cultural producer in promoting the revival.

Core revivalists are responsible for formulating the tradition's repertoire, stylistic features, and history. In the process an aesthetic code is constructed on what is believed to be a stylistic common denominator derived from individual performances and/or written and oral sources. This is transformed into the essence of the style that is then used to judge revivalist performances. Although aspects of this transformation may be historically verifiable, what core revivalists really do is create a new ethos, musical style, and aesthetic code strongly influenced by their revivalist ideology and personal preferences.

Cultural politics are inherent in music revivals regardless of the type of music being revived or the intentions of those involved. Because revivalists select, appropriate, and codify certain aspects of culture, they construct an aesthetic code in the process. Rosenberg notes that some scholars view revivalists in a negative way as "cultural intervenors," whereas others see revivals as a manifestation of social consensus (1993: pp. 19–20). The political ramifications of revivals become even more complex with the involvement of state institutions, the recording and entertainment industry, and academic institutions.

Revivalist community

Revival followers are more than just fans; they are members of an imagined community held together by common beliefs and activities arising from their shared middle-class position. These include dissatisfaction with the status quo, devotion to a musical system as a cultural alternative, and participation in revivalist activities. Peter Narváez notes that many revivalists experience a similar series of emotional and aesthetic states in the course of their involvement: participants initially experience a state of ecstatic revelation on discovering the revived music; this is followed by the desire to seek out more of the same experience from recordings, books, and so on and the reification of the experience by attending performance events. In some cases this leads to the eventual accommodation of new aesthetic codes based on the old, traditional codes, but no longer restricted by concerns for authenticity (1993).

The revivalist community is reinforced through participation in activities such as organizational meetings, informal gatherings, concerts, festivals, and competitions. It is at these events that revivalists meet each other face-to-face to share repertoire and playing techniques, to discuss the strengths and weaknesses of artists within the tradition, to actively learn and experience the revivalist ethos and aesthetic code at work, and to socialize among other insiders. These events are fundamental to a revival's success, for they supplement what can be learned from recordings and books with lived experiences and direct human contact.

As the community grows it tends to diversify, and factions may arise that challenge dominant revivalist assumptions. The ebb and flow nature of revivalist experience is mirrored by the processual aspect of revivals themselves; more often than not revivals go through a cycle of boom and bust before they break down completely.

Revivalist industries

An industry consisting of nonprofit and/or commercial enterprises catering to the revivalist market, including concert promotions, sales of recordings, newsletters, pedagogical publications, instruments, and supplies, may develop to serve the new revivalist market. Not only does the industry serve to perpetuate revivalist doctrine and practices, but it acts as a valuable adjunct to organizations for the formation and maintenance of a tight-knit community based on shared consumption patterns. The commodification of revivalist traditions begins well before an industry emerges, however, starting with the initial objectification of the musical practice by transforming it into a thing that can be restored, and it is furthered each time the practice is distilled into words and printed music, fixed in time and space by sound recordings and videotapes, and offered for public consumption on stage, radio, or television. Public success and longevity of musical revivals depends in part on the strength and vitality of such industries, although problems can arise when revivalist concerns for authenticity compete with industry demands for marketability.

The balalaika orchestra revival in the United States

A brief overview of the balalaika orchestra revival in the United States serves to illustrate some of the most prominent features of music revivals. The transformation of the balalaika, a triangular, three-stringed Russian folk instrument, into a concert instrument began with its discovery by nobleman Vassily Andreyev in the 1880s (Belevich 1988). Intrigued by its sound, Andreyev engaged a luthier to build a balalaika suitable for concert performances. In a short time Andreyev had mastered the instrument and was giving concerts that dazzled elite Russian society. Inspired by his success as a balalaika soloist, he decided to create an orchestra consisting of balalaikas and *domras* 'round-bodied Russian folk instrument played with a pick' of various sizes. Andreyev and his balalaika ensemble were so well received at home that they began to tour abroad, appearing in concert halls in Paris, London, and Berlin. In 1910 and again in 1911 Andreyev's group gave concerts in the United States. Balalaika orchestras formed by Russian and East European emigrés and supported by the Russian Orthodox Church soon arose in St. Louis (1910), Chicago (1911), New York (1912), Philadelphia (1920), and Detroit (1926). These groups strove to pass on the teachings of Andreyev to their peers and children, thereby celebrating their Russian heritage.

By the early 1960s, the political climate was beginning to change, and younger generations of Russian Americans became interested in reviving the balalaika orchestra from the early twentieth century.

In Russia the October Revolution (1917) brought about radical political changes; among these was the use of the balalaika orchestra as a means of furthering socialist ideology. Professional balalaika orchestras modeled after Andreyev's group were developed and supported by the Soviet state. Although these groups were presented by the Soviets as representative of regional folk music, they were composed of highly trained professionals who strove for a technical virtuosity and precision that rivaled Western art music. Nevertheless, these groups were and continue to be looked upon as role models for balalaika groups in the United States and elsewhere.

The burst of activity stimulated by Andreyev's visits to the United States came to an end with World War II, and the ensuing McCarthy era forced many groups to restrict their activities. During this time Russian instruments were difficult to find, and anything having to do with Russian culture was viewed with suspicion. By the early 1960s, however, the political climate was beginning to change, and younger generations of Russian Americans became interested in reviving the balalaika orchestra from the early twentieth century. The appearance of long-playing recordings of orchestras helped to stimulate interest. Old instruments were dug out of attics, and veterans from the old orchestras, including Sergei Larionoff, Luke Bakoota, and Mark Selivan, were sought out to guide their efforts and interests.

The revival began with the foundation of the Balalaika and Domra Society of New York in 1961, founded by veteran performers Mark Selivan, Jack Raymond, and Alexander Kuchma. These revivalists were not interested in reviving Russian folk music as it existed in peasant villages. Instead their aim was to revive the balalaika orchestra as it was conceived of by its founder, Vassily Andreyev. Thus only three-stringed instruments of the *balalaika* and *domra* family tuned in Andreyev concert tuning (in fourths) were to be used. Other standards, for example, playing the prima or standard-size balalaika with the fingertip instead of a plectrum, were also passed down by the Society.

By the late 1970s a number of different babalaika orchestras and performers were operating throughout the United States. It was felt that the creation of a national organization would bring these disparate groups together and serve as a clearinghouse for importing Russian instruments, books, and music, so the Balalaika and Domra Association of America was created in 1978 by musicians Lynn Carpenter, Charley Rappaport, and Steve Wolownik. The group produces a regular newsletter and sponsors annual conventions. Most years, instrumentalists from Russia and/or East Europe are invited to act as teachers and performers, thus allowing novices to learn from accomplished performers of the tradition. The conventions are an important aspect of maintaining the revivalist community, which has grown from a small group of Russian emigrés and their descendants to include both Slavs and non-Slavs alike (figure 1).

Musical revivals are both a middle-class product of and a reaction against modernity. The appearance of a great number of revivals across the globe is a generalized response within the middle sectors of a society to specific local and historical crises. The fluidity and dialectical nature of revivals, however, make each one a unique phenomenon in time and space, appropriate for that culture at that point in history. Music

FIGURE 1   "Rodina" Balalaika and Domra Convention, University of Illinois, Urbana, 1993. Photo by Bibs Ekkel.

revivals, then, provide fertile ground for the study of music as a site for social action and political contention in times of social stress and for the study of the articulation of class identity through musical performance.

—TAMARA E. LIVINGSTON

SCENE: 25 APRIL 1857, NEW YORK CITY

Urban Americans who lived during the middle of the nineteenth century had available to them a surprisingly varied and sophisticated range of concert and musical theatrical opportunities. To a scholar, one of the most arresting characteristics of this concert life is how fairly oblivious it was to the clear-cut social and class identities we associate today with "popular" or "art" musics. This blurring of modern categories of class-based preferences for specific styles of music is illustrated here by a snapshot description from an imaginary case study. Although the account here is fictitious, most of the scheduled performances and venues mentioned are not. Furthermore, the account was inspired by the entertainment activities of a young Philadelphia bookkeeper, N. Beekley, who recorded in his 1849 diary the concert and theatrical performances he attended on a regular basis.

In the early evening hours of a New York City Saturday in late April 1857, a pair of young men are discovered strolling south, down Broadway, in the vicinity of Union Square. The day is pleasant for late April—sunny and warm. The street is jammed with cabs, buggies, delivery wagons driven by swearing hostlers, even a lone barouche with a driver in livery, all of them jockeying for position in the thoroughfare and inching forward as a space becomes available. The sidewalks are not nearly so crowded, but there are shoppers laden with packages, Irish servant girls with baskets of purchases from the market, hucksters, children playing tag from the stoops of the houses lining the street, and others—like Paul Steepleson and his friend Martin Wallack—just out for a late-afternoon constitutional. The two men are in their early twenties; they both work for an accounting firm as bookkeepers; neither is married; each lives in a boardinghouse nearby. They are trying to decide what to do for the evening's entertainment, which, they have decided, should be either theatrical or musical in nature.

The two briefly join a small crowd gathered around an organ-grinder playing an entertaining version of "Listen to the Mocking Bird," the popular Septimus Winner

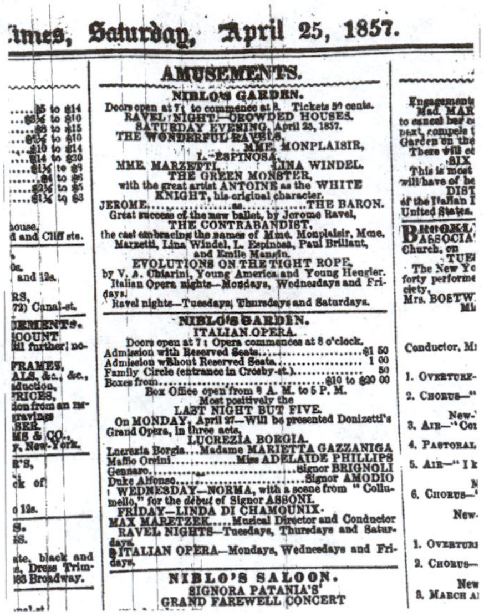

FIGURE 2 The Amusements Column, *New York Times,* Saturday 25 April 1857, showing the operatic offerings available to New Yorkers at Niblo's Garden during the coming week.

song that everyone has been whistling for nearly two years. At the end of the tune the stooped and heavily bearded man—he is one of dozens of organ-grinders occupying the street corners of Manhattan, most of them recent German or Italian immigrants—bends down to collect coins that passersby have tossed onto the pavement at his feet. He wipes the sweat from his glistening forehead with a large, extremely tattered handkerchief, then, lest he lose his listeners, quickly resumes his miniconcert by launching into "The Brindisi" from *La Traviata.* Steepleson and Wallack listen for another several moments, then Paul digs into his pocket and retrieves a coin for the musician. He nudges his companion (who had been studying the "Amusements" section of the *New York Times*), and they resume their perambulations (figure 2).

"Did you manage to see Anna de la Grange as Violetta last December?" Martin asks his companion. "She sang with Maurice Strakosch's company at the Academy. I went with Miss Hampstead, and it was worth every penny."

"No," Paul responds. "I tried to get tickets but the one night I was free the Academy was sold out. But I heard Marietta Gazzaniga with Max Maretzek's company at Niblo's Gardens just last week and enjoyed it a lot." He takes the newspaper from his friend and scans the columns. "Here, let me look at that a moment—what's on at the Academy tonight? Nothing . . . nothing. . . . Oh, here. The Philharmonic Society. It's their last concert of the season. Theodore Eisfeld is conducting. It doesn't say what they're going to play, but Maria Brainerd and Henry Timm are the guests. Doors open at 6:30." He pulls out his watch. "We have time, and the Academy's just ahead—what do you think?"

"What are the other options?" Martin takes the paper back and inspects the column. "I went to their last concert and it was mobbed—even in the Academy! But I was seated next to two rowdies who were fairly rude and noisy. Let's keep looking." The two continue walking, dodging passersby.

"Hmmm. Mrs. Jameson is doing a concert—violin, French horn, piano, bass—no, that's next Wednesday. Never mind. Hey!" He looks up and grins mischievously at his companion. "We can always go down to Mlle. Caroline Vezien's Dancing Academy on Howard Street. There'll be some music there! It says here, 'Grand Ball on Wednesday and Saturday Evenings—'"

Paul—who suffers from the social misfortune of being a clumsy dancer—grimaces and snatches the newspaper from his friend. The two are standing in the middle of the sidewalk, and the stream of pedestrians, only slightly abated, ebbs and flows around them.

"Oh, look here," Paul points to an advertisement. "The Ravel Family is at Niblo's Gardens tonight. You know, they're those French pantomimists or acrobats or whatever you call them. Have you ever seen them? I think I'd rather do that than the Philharmonic Society, and tickets are the same price, fifty cents."

"Let's walk on down to Niblo's and see what the placards look like," Martin responds. "I've seen them, but it's been a long while."

The two continue strolling south on Broadway. The sidewalks are beginning to clear out as late afternoon becomes early evening and the crush of humanity disappears into side streets, homes, and shops. They pause at Astor Place, in the shadow of the ill-fated and now-defunct Opera House, to allow a short funeral procession to pass. At the front is a small brass band of about twelve instrumentalists wearing musicians' uniforms and playing cornets and various sizes of saxhorns. They march slowly and rather raggedly, but their playing is dignified and suitable—they are playing a slow dirge, and the clip-clop of horses' hooves provides a rhythmic counterpoint. Behind the musicians is the crepe-draped undertaker's hearse, drawn by two black horses, and behind the hearse are four or five buggies with their windows shuttered. Most of the passersby, like Steepleson and Wallack, stand quietly and respectfully as the procession passes en route to the cemetery.

A few moments later the two young men pause at the corner of Bond and Broadway to look at the playbills posted in front of Burton's New Theater.

"I didn't know Louisa Pyne was back in town," Paul comments. "Look, they're doing *Fra Diavolo* tonight. I heard the Pyne and Harrison company last year—they did *Bohemian Girl*—and they were pretty good. The staging and scenery aren't as spectacular as with Maretzek's or Strakosch's companies, but I like the English opera, and Pyne and Harrison do a good job with *Fra Diavolo*. Besides, Miss Pyne is a delightful soprano."

"Yes, this is definitely a possibility," Martin responds. He checks the sign, and tickets are still available. As the curtain time is a good hour away, however, they still have time to stroll. "Let's think about this but go on down to Niblo's and look at the playbills, all right?"

The two young men saunter down the street. The nature of their fellow pedestrians has changed. Gone are the workers heading homeward. The scampering children and produce-laden servants have all but disappeared into the row houses on Broadway and up and down the cross streets, as it is time for the evening meal. They have been replaced by individuals more like Wallack and Steepleson—young men and women heading out for their evening's entertainment or older couples out for a stroll, enjoying the balmy spring weekend evening.

Paul suddenly stops and points across the street, which is still crowded with conveyances. "There's what I feel like doing tonight," he exclaims, pointing to Buckley's Serenaders' New Hall at 585 Broadway. "It looks like The Serenaders are doing an Old Folks' Concert and 'Essence of Old Virginny' tonight. They're the best blackface minstrels I've ever seen!"

Martin, catching his friend's enthusiasm, folds the newspaper. "I saw them do *Bone Squash Diavolo* last month–you know, that's a burlesque of *Fra Diavolo*. The Serenaders had all the characters and all the songs down pat. They even had a playbill that burlesqued the names of the Pyne and Harrison singers! I've never seen this show, and I feel like a good laugh."

The two dash across the street, dodging the almost stationary vehicles clogging the artery, and buy tickets for the blackface minstrel show. Paul tosses the *Times* into a rubbish basket, and the two friends disappear into the theater.

—Katherine K. Preston

REFERENCES

Allen, Matthew Harp. 1997. "Rewriting the Script for South Indian Dance." *The Drama Review* 41(3):155.

Anderson, Benedict. 1983. *Imagined Communities.* London: Verso.

Beekley, N. 1849. "Diary." Manuscripts Collection. American Antiquarian Society. Worcester, MA.

Belevich, Alexander. 1988. "History of the Balalaika." *Balalaika and Domra Association of America Newsletter* 11(1):8, 11.

Bohlman, Philip V. 1988. *The Study of Folk Music in the Modern World.* Bloomington: Indiana University Press.

Boyes, Georgina. 1993. *The Imagined Village: Culture, Ideology and the English Folk Revival.* Manchester, Eng.: Manchester University Press.

Feintuch, Burt. 1993. "Musical Revival as Musical Transformation." In *Transforming Tradition: Folk Music Revivals Examined,* ed. Neil V. Rosenberg. Urbana: University of Illinois Press.

Frigyesi, Judit. 1996. "The Aesthetic of the Hungarian Revival Movement." In *Retuning Culture: Musical Changes in Central and Eastern Europe,* ed. Mark Slobin, 54–75. Durham, N.C.: Duke University Press.

Goertzen, Chris. 1997. *Fiddling for Norway: Revival and Identity.* Chicago: University of Chicago Press.

Groom, Bob. 1971. *The Blues Revival.* London: November Books Ltd.

Haskell, Harry. 1988. *The Early Music Revival: A History.* London: Thames and Hudson.

Hazen, Margaret and Robert. 1987. *The Music Men. An Illustrated History of Brass Bands in America, 1800–1920.* Washington, D.C.: Smithsonian Institution Press.

Hobsbawm, Eric. 1983. "Introduction: Inventing Traditions." In *The Invention of Tradition,* ed. Eric Hobsbawm and Terence Ranger, 1–14. Cambridge: Cambridge University Press.

Ireland, Joseph. *Records of the New York Stage from 1750 to 1860.* 1968 [1866–1867]. New York: Burt Franklin.

Katz, Ruth. 1970. "Mannerism and Cultural Change: An Ethnomusicological Example." *Current Anthropology* 11(4–5):465–475.

Keil, Charles. 1985. "People's Music Comparatively: Style and Stereotype, Class and Hegemony." *Dialectical Anthropology* 10:119–130.

Kenyon, Nicholas. 1988. *Authenticity and Early Music: A Symposium.* Oxford: Oxford University Press.

Kivy, Peter. 1995. *Authenticities: Philosophical Reflections on Music Performance.* Ithaca, N.Y.: Cornell University Press.

Le Huray, Peter. 1990. *Authenticity in Performance: Eighteenth-Century Case Studies.* Cambridge: Cambridge University Press.

Leppard, Raymond. 1988. *Authenticity in Music.* Portland, Ore.: Amadeus Press.

Levin, Theodore. 1996. "Dmitri Pokrovsky and the Russian Folk Music Revival Movement." In *Retuning Culture: Musical Changes in Central and Eastern Europe,* ed. Mark Slobin, 14–36. Durham, N.C.: Duke University Press.

Linton, Ralph. 1943. "Nativistic Movements." *American Anthropologist* 45:230–240.

MacKinnon, Niall. 1994. *The British Folk Scene: Musical Performance and Social Identity.* Buckingham: Open University Press.

Mattfeld, Julius. 1952. *Variety Musical Cavalcade, 1620–1950. A Chronology of Vocal and Instrumental Music Popular in the United States.* New York: Prentice-Hall.

McKay, Ian. 1994. *The Quest of the Folk: Antimodernism and Cultural Selection in Twentieth-Century Nova Scotia.* Montréal: McGill-Queen's University Press.

Monro, Ailie. 1984. *The Folk Music Revival in Scotland.* London: Kahn and Averill.

Morrison, Craig. 1996. *Go Cat Go!: Rockabilly and Its Makers.* Urbana: University of Illinois Press.

Narváez, Peter. 1993. "Living Blues Journal: The Paradoxical Aesthetics of the Blues Revival." In *Transforming Tradition: Folk Music Revivals Examined,* ed. Neil V. Rosenberg, 241–257. Urbana: University of Illinois Press.

Narváez, Peter, and Martin Laba, eds. 1986. *Media Sense: The Folklore–Popular Culture Continuum.* Bowling Green, Ohio: Bowling Green State University Popular Press.

New York Times. 1857. 25 April.

Niles, Christina. 1978. "The Revival of the Latvian *Kokle* in America." *Selected Reports in Ethnomusicology* 3(1):211–239.

Odell, George C. D. 1931. *Annals of the New York Stage.* Vol. 6. New York: Columbia University Press.

Peña, Manuel. 1985. "From Ranchero to Jaiton: Ethnicity and Class in Texas-Mexican Music." *Ethnomusicology* 29(1):29–55.

Preston, Katherine. 1993. *Opera on the Road: Traveling Opera Troupes in the United States, 1825–1860.* Urbana: University of Illinois Press.

Romero, Raul R. 1994. "Black Music and Identity in Peru: Reconstruction and Revival of Afro-Peruvian Musical Traditions." In *Music and Black Ethnicity: The Caribbean and South America,* ed. Gerard H. Béhague, 307–330. Miami: University of Miami North-South Center.

Rosenberg, Neil V. 1993. *Transforming Tradition: Folk Music Revivals Examined.* Urbana: University of Illinois Press.

Shanet, Howard. 1975. *Philharmonic: A History of New York's Orchestra.* New York: Doubleday.

Slobin, Mark. 1983. "Rethinking 'Revival' of American Ethnic Music," *New York Folklore* 9:37–44.

———. 1984. "The Neo-Klezmer Movement and Euro-American Musical Revivalism." *Journal of American Folklore* 97:98–104.

Smith, Anthony D. 1981. *The Ethnic Revival.* Cambridge: Cambridge University Press.

Taruskin, Richard, Daniel Leech-Wilkinson, Nicholas Temperley, and Robert Winter. 1984. "The Limits of Authenticity: A Discussion." *Early Music* 12(1):1–25.

Turino, Thomas. 1991. "The History of a Peruvian Panpipe Style and the Politics of Interpretation." In *Ethnomusicology and Modern Music History,* ed. Stephen Blum, Philip V. Bohlman, and Daniel M. Neuman, 121–138. Urbana: University of Illinois Press.

———. 1994a. "Nationalism and the Folklorization of Music in Peru." Unpublished paper. University of Illinois.

———. 1994b. "Zimbabwean Guitar Music and Musical Nationalism, 1955–1980." Unpublished paper. University of Illinois.

———. 1996. "Nationalism and the Spread of Cosmopolitanism in Zimbabwean Music." Unpublished paper. University of Illinois.

Turner, Frederick. 1994. *Remembering Song: Encounters with the New Orleans Jazz Tradition.* New York: Da Capo.

Wallace, Anthony F. C. 1956. "Revitalization Movements." *American Anthropologist* 58:264–281.

Whisnant, David. 1983. *All That Is Native and Fine: The Politics of Culture in an American Region.* Chapel Hill: University of North Carolina Press.

Race, Ethnicity, and Nationhood

Ronald Radano (United States)
Michael Daley (Canada)

Music's Racial Precursors in the United States: African "Noise"
The Emergence of the Concept of "Negro Music"
Spirituals and the Rise of Modern "Black Music"
The Impact of Race on American Musical Scholarship
Music, Race, Ethnicity, and Nationhood in Canada

Notions of difference, constructed in racial, ethnic, or national discourses, historically developed quite differently in the United States and Canada, so too did the histories of music scholarship concerning these markers. This article highlights the ways in which the two countries have conceptualized and constructed difference and how different musics have come to take on different meanings within these contexts.

MUSIC'S RACIAL PRECURSORS IN THE UNITED STATES: AFRICAN "NOISE"

Among the many social determinations of musical meaning in the United States, none has proven more powerful and enduring than that of race. At the onset of the new millennium, music's racial aspect carries forward the burden of its long memory, charting the extent of black and white relations. The relationship of race to music is so fundamental to the American experience that it identifies a crucial linkage or even an archetype. What we may call the racio-musical dynamic not only informs modern notions of color and difference; it can be traced to the very seat of their formation over two hundred years ago.

As an ideology, the concept of race would seem inextricably related to all musical categories and artists, from folk to classical, from Madonna to Aaron Copland. Typically, however, the extent of racial influence is downplayed in favor of more "colorless" distinctions of personality and style. Indeed, most Americans, and particularly those of the white majority, fail to recognize race's impact on music, except when it intervenes directly in representation and judgment. The appeal of Paul Whiteman in the 1920s and the public fascination with rap artists such as Vanilla Ice stand as exceptions to a rule of musical racelessness, which defers discussions of difference to the realm of African American artistry. Accordingly, the innovations of rap, jazz, gospel, and blues are not only representative American forms but color-coded ones, subsumed under the broad category of "black music" [see AFRICAN AMERICAN MUSICS: OVERVIEW, p. 572].

The designation of African American music as quintessentially racial emerged out of the trajectories of colonial relations taking shape in the early modern era. While already a concept existing in Europe before the Renaissance, *race* acquired its specific, modern meaning by the seventeenth century, replacing the vague category of *nation* that had previously distinguished people of color from Europeans and European Americans (Hudson 1996). Africans in particular were singled out as the weakest of humanity's links, to the point at which the black phenotype became widely acknowledged as a signifier of intellectual and moral inferiority. By the late eighteenth century, the social weaknesses of blacks were deemed irreversible and endemic to the "species," an assumption that helped to justify the practice of slavery (Davis 1999[1975]; Wood 1997).

The appearance of a racially determined "Negro music," in its turn, took shape within this setting as it simultaneously proposed a critical challenge to a facile racialist orthodoxy. While providing sonic evidence of the difference between black and white, Negro music also complicated race-based distinctions because of its formation within the common ground of American cultural expression. As will be seen, the power of black music can be understood historically as something that emerged as much from this inherently unstable racial economy as it did from qualities typically attributed to the music itself. The magnitude of its power eventually carried into other realms, suffusing American social and intellectual perspectives (including those of musical scholarship) with a discernible racial cast.

In her seminal studies of African American music, Dena Epstein first observed the remarkable gaps in information common to virtually all documentary evidence from the colonial era (Epstein 1963, 1973, 1977). Despite a scrupulous, painstaking review of a multitude of historical sources, she could only account for a handful of references to African-based performance appearing in North American texts on music. This prompted her to turn to the somewhat more abundant documentation from Jamaica and Barbados in order to shape a narrative of early New World black music. As important as Epstein's research proved, however, its emphasis on Caribbean sources masked the significance of such a startling documentary blankness. The silence characterizing the early history of African American music spoke volumes about the musical and racial attitudes among white literate classes, whose opinions played a profound role in the casting of the foundational relationship of race and music.

Music as a conscious, rational ordering of sound presupposes human articulation and intervention. Notwithstanding the most radical vanguard proposals, music without humanity cannot logically exist. It is useful to bear this logic in mind when observing musical representations of Africans and African Americans from eighteenth-century colonial North America. Aside from the occasional mention, black music would seem to have been virtually absent even among the sizable African populations of Virginia and South Carolina. Although New World Africans surely possessed their own concepts for understanding the sounds they made, these concepts were rarely recognized by southern planters, northern visitors, or European travelers. Within the circumstances of the dominant white public sphere, African American music had literally yet to come into being. It remained invisible and unheard, having been precluded from the possibility of existence by Euro-Western assumptions of African intellectual inferiority. As mere earthly utterance, slave expression was little more than a sounding practice, a determinedly unmusical form relegated to a place well beneath the high plain of civilization.

The occasional references, nonetheless, provide insight into the European comprehension of African performances and, in turn, into how this understanding helped to determine racio-musical categories. Musical practices, when acknowledged, were typically framed within a discourse that characterized the array of discrete performance practices as so many versions of "noise." These fragmentary references to singing, instrumental playing, preaching, and bodily movement appeared as passing asides, such as the comment in a letter by Lady Oglethorpe from 1736 that referred to the "dismal and incessant blare" of an African slave playing a conch horn (Head 1893). In the texts of Anglican evangelists, however, the discussions—still nearly always fleeting—sometimes showed greater sensitivity to slave musical potential, in part because the ministers had witnessed singing practices as part of the humanizing activity of religious conversion. James Meacham stands out for his vivid description of a nocturnal performance, in which he relies on the age-old trope of the "natural musician": "I awakened in raptures of Heaven by the sweet Echo of Singing . . . among the dear Black people (who my Soul loves). I scarcely ever heard anything to equal it upon the earth" (Historical Papers 1912:88). More commonly, however, even clergymen, when they chose to speak, dismissed these natural inclinations as merely expressions of excess. "Commonly," John Leland observed in 1790, "[blacks] are more noisy in time of preaching than the whites and are more subject to bodily exercise, and if they meet with an encouragement in these things, they grow extravagant" (Raboteau 1978:61).

References to African American music in European travelogues

These shadow texts of New World performance are more or less consistent with those appearing in the travelogues of European explorers and missionaries who visited Africa and the Caribbean in the seventeenth and eighteenth centuries. In the travel accounts, African-sounding practices were commonly portrayed as a cacophony that reflected native fetishism: "Their musical instruments are various, and very numerous; but all of them yield a horrid and barbarous shocking sound; the chief of them are the mentioned horns . . . which by blowing they produce a sort of extravagant noise" (Bosman 1705:394). Occasionally the comments seemed more generous. African accounts, in fact, suggest a greater propensity on the part of the European travelers to acknowledge a black musicality while also implying—in ways anticipating romantic notions of "barbarism" (Berlin 1999:85)—that the fruits of this musical labor bore no resemblance to civilized expression. In his official account of a court performance at the residence of the Emperor of Fez and Morocco, the British royal servant John Windhus juxtaposed images of music and the natural landscape to imply an organic relation. "The governor had his music with him. . . . [One performer] beat time to their music, by striking the palm of his hands together, very loud and well. This part of the country abounds with fine oranges, lemons, citrons, olives, grapes, figs, melons, pomegranates, and apricots" (Windhus 1725:448). If the practice of black sounding had achieved Euro-Western recognition as "music," it had done so as one of the many forms of marginally human production existing in an ambiguous conceptual space. Moroccan court music was not music as such but a peculiarly coherent sensation existing between civilized utterance and the ambient manifestations of nature.

A general skepticism about Negro musicality, then, pervaded modern Euro-Western thought into the eighteenth century. By the latter part of the century this skepticism, as it was represented in the African travelogues, had grown particularly strident in ways consistent with the rigid determinations of black inferiority emerging in European philosophical opinion (Horsman 1981; Pratt 1992; Pieterse 1992). The virtual absence of musical references in the North American literature leaves open to speculation the likelihood of a parallel shift among white colonists. Given what we know about the existing representations, however, it is perhaps reasonable to assume that American white attitudes about Negro musical proficiency followed a similar course of development. Indeed, the opinions probably grew even harsher, for American whites were motivated not only by European intellectual abstractions but also by the social and economic realities of slavery, which by mid-century had created—by virtue of the middle passage and natural birth—a conspicuous population of displaced Africans and African Americans. As monied whites recognized the economic advantages of slavery, the rate of slave importations increased. With slavery in place, whites were socially and economically motivated to justify its continuation, arguing that the moral and intellectual "weaknesses" of blacks were not only common, but irreversible. Modern ideologies of race and the practice of chattel slavery worked hand in hand, one reinforcing the other: if African slaves were inferior they could be enslaved; the enslavement of Africans was proof of their inferiority (Davis 1999 [1973]; Jordan 1968). As living

The departure from call and response and the new emphasis on harmony, together with the broadscale institutional efforts to remove blacks from white congregations, worked to craft a racio-musical defense against the encroaching "noise" of blackness.

commodities positioned below the category of human, their musical capacities were, at best, difficult to discern. As a consequence, they went largely unrecorded.

The irrefutable evidence of black humanity also continually challenged the certainty of white supremacy. As blacks and whites lived together, labored together, and engaged in various forms of worship and play, they grew to share common forms and expressions that contradicted the assumption of racially based difference. These commonalities were revealed in multiple musical ways. Even the occasional reports toward the end of the eighteenth century provide a sense of the developing musical cross play that had accompanied the formation of discernibly American cultural expression. In Virginia, slaves performed Anglo-based fiddling tunes for white dances (sometimes called "Congos") [see ENGLISH AND SCOTTISH MUSIC, p. 831] and engaged with whites in corn-shucking rituals that reflected processes of cultural exchange in both directions. Farther south and to the north, blacks played in marches and parades, drumming alongside white soldiers and civilians, while black and white singers increasingly joined together in Christian worship (Abrahams 1992; Camus 1980; Southern 1997). These musical articulations were as widely challenged as they were applauded and appeared alongside the literal voicings of black protestation against slavery that coursed through New England after the Revolution (Litwack 1961). By the end of the eighteenth century, a black sounding presence had already grown familiar enough—at least in the broadest, comparative terms—to contradict the easy dismissals of African American music as noise. Ironically, however, with each step toward musical familiarity, black sounding seemed to Europeans and European Americans farther from their own musical conventions. If acculturation would eventually position black sounding securely within the European category of "music," it would also determine that music out of the bounds of reasonable, cultivated expression. The threat of an encroaching racial sameness inspired the naming of black performance as the epitome of racial difference.

THE EMERGENCE OF THE CONCEPT OF "NEGRO MUSIC"

By the 1830s, reports of "Negro music" had become conspicuous, marking its transformation from a prior noise. These commentaries appeared in a variety of public and private sources that brought to wide attention a new awareness of a formally coherent African American performance. As public acknowledgments of musical form, the depictions were significant, reflecting the changing attitudes of northerners who increasingly recognized the humanity and reasonableness of African Americans. Despite this shift, the texts perpetuated the image of black sound as a form of excess, figured differently according to the political positions of observers. Typically, these portraits took two forms. The first reflected the antislavery sentiments of the abolitionist movement, which represented black song in its slave narratives and newspapers as the tragic expression of a noble people caught in struggle (Douglass 1845). The second depicted black music as a debased kind of primitive glee, staged in performance by white men in blackface. While tracing dramatically different social figures, the representations shared in their caricatures a reliance on stereotypes of authenticity and folk nature. If slave song was the consummate expression of sorrow, voicing the most profound form of human emotion, so was it a perverse form of musical play that revealed the natural frivolity and animal-like senselessness of blacks. That northern white working-class performers were principally responsible for the latter invention suggests an effort on their part to celebrate blackness in order to distance it (and an emerging African American working class) from their own racial status. As both David Roediger and Eric Lott have suggested, blackface performance played a key formative role in the evolution of whiteness as a racial category (Lott 1993; Roediger 1991).

The documentation of Negro music in the 1830s, then, announced a new northern public construction of black difference that had emerged as a consequence of interracial familiarity and sameness. Yet as much as this new conception emerged from the circumstances of northern public culture, it was also informed by prior racial encounters in western and southern rural areas during the rise of the camp meetings. These events, which appeared rather suddenly around 1800, spread from Kentucky across much of the United States, providing a sacred forum for musical engagement (Hatch 1989). Appealing to the poorest and most desperate sectors of the population, the meetings brought together literally thousands of worshipers who gathered for a period of several days. Initially the camp meetings were strenuously abolitionist in nature, routinely welcoming free blacks and even slaves into the open-air congregations. If after the events blacks and whites went their separate ways, they carried with them singing practices constituted within an interracial environment, subsequently documented in the overwhelmingly common parallels of "black" and "white" songs in Christian tunebooks (Epstein 1983; Jackson 1943). Indeed, Anglo and black singing practices appeared to be related, particularly among the lowest classes, who introduced African, Scottish, and Irish styles into the mix of "spiritual song."

With the emergence of a recognizable Negro music in the 1830s, however, singing masters began working assiduously to stress performance practices that appeared to favor white significations. The departure from call and response and the new emphasis on harmony, together with the broadscale institutional efforts to remove blacks from white congregations (commencing already by the 1810s), worked to craft a raciomusical defense against the encroaching "noise" of blackness. While slave and free singing had most likely already reflected recognizable distinctions based on the peculiar concentrations of African and European musical peoples, a new ideological separation heightened these distinctions and, most likely, prompted the invention of new ones out of the existing intercultural matrix. And although the evidence remains ambiguous, it appears that to some extent at least, white musical practices emerged in both the North and the South as a consequence of prior sharing (Hamm 1983; Steel 1988).

This conscious effort on the part of whites to distinguish themselves musically from blacks took place at some distance from the local circumstances of slaves. To be sure, slaves had developed their own performance practices from the various combinations of African approaches and hybrids that had become by the early nineteenth century (if not before) patently "African American." Significantly, however, the emergence of slave musical distinctiveness also took shape with respect to the same codes of difference that had developed out of the larger framework of black and white relations. Evidence suggests that slaves too had recognized difference and had worked from it in crafting a sound world distinctively their own. Given the contentious nature of the master/slave relation, it is likely that slave musical practices developed along similarly contested lines. Constructed within a racially relational circumstance, slaves' difference resisted as it expressed European presence. As slaves advanced vocal practices, devised distinctive, recognizably African-derived performance modes such as patting and shouting, and engaged in instrumental music making on banjo and fiddle, they continually shaped these approaches within the contexts of intercultural familiarity. It would not be too much to say, then, that black difference emerges dialectically—particularly in the circumstances of the camp meetings and the relatively interracial Virginia plantations—casting an "authentic" slave sound from a prior, "inauthentic" European–African sharing.

The interracial character of antebellum slave expression, in turn, had a subversive effect on the integrity of supremacist racial categories. The music of slaves, which had become deeply loved and admired by whites across the South, seemed almost to define the sonic environment as a whole. Reports from the time repeatedly refer to black song as a veritable natural force that welled up from waterways and wafted over fields and villages: "[T]he music [of the slaves]," a planter wrote, "made the hills and dells of Virginia vocal with its merry notes" (Smith 1852). So popular had slave songs become that whites would frequently pay (with liquor, coins, or other means) for the pleasure of hearing them, contributing to an economy whereby the master's possession (the slave) produced within itself a salable commodity for personal profit (Criswell 1973 [1852]; Gilmore 1862). The selling of black performative difference became deeply situated within the relations of whites and blacks, exacerbating its manufacture to challenge the extent of white generosity. (Those who did not pay could be subject to critique in performance. See, for example, Jacobs 1971 [1861]). In this way, black difference took shape within and against the norms of white expectation. It was a recognizable music for purchase that white southerners could not wholly access without undermining the integrity of whiteness as such. Built on the negation of a distressing racial noise, black music emerges as something fulfilling a public sense of familiarity while simultaneously challenging racial stability. As a result, it would repeatedly complicate notions of race as it helped to define them.

SPIRITUALS AND THE RISE OF MODERN "BLACK MUSIC"

By the 1860s, the twin social forces of blackface minstrelsy and southern slave song had converged in public performances and representations, overwhelming northern audiences during and after the Civil War. Rendered publicly as *spirituals* (a term probably developing interracially from the former "spiritual song"), these songs would be celebrated as the wondrous achievements of a possessed people, representing a kind of miracle of sound. First described by northern visitors to the sea islands around 1860, the songs would grow in popularity, soon to be documented in the form of published lyrics and notations that circulated among northern and southern people. By the 1870s the songs were being sung professionally by blacks themselves, most notably by the Fisk University Jubilee Singers, whose famous tours of the United States and Europe made black music a common symbol of pleasure and leisure in western societies (figure 1).

Significantly, these renderings of black music were not actual slave songs but rather second-level representations of the already inauthentic expressions that had evolved interculturally within the particular locales of southern plantations. Refigured in notation and performed according to practices introduced by northern white teachers, the spirituals of the Fisk singers and other singing groups identified yet another level of racially based cultural interplay that spoke to a legacy of interracial involvement. Nonetheless, these hybrids would carry meaning across black and white cultures, informing practices as they were repeatedly recast within the particular circumstances of communities across the nation. Later specifications, notably the rhythmic qualities *hot, rag, jazz,* and *swing,* contributed additional levels of meaning to the musical formation of racial difference (Gilroy 1993; Radano 1996, 2000).

By the turn of the twentieth century, black music had come to define, perhaps more than any other cultural expression, the difference between black and white, even as its actual history betrayed repetitions of cross-racial influence. It was this sound that DuBois named black people's gift to America, a form whose paradoxical racial markers revealed the true source of its affective power (DuBois 1992 [1903]). Indeed, the emo-

FIGURE 1   The Jubilee Singers of Fisk University, c. 1875. © Hulton-Deutsch Collection/ CORBIS.

JUBILEE SINGERS

MAGGIE PORTER.   E. W. WATKINS.   H. D. ALEXANDER.   F. J. LOUDIN.   THOMAS RUTLING.

JENNIE JACKSON.   MABEL LEWIS.   ELLA SHEPPARD.   MAGGIE CARNES.   AMERICA W. ROBINSON.

tional potency of black music derived not from some mythic concentration of racial essence but from its instability as a racial marker. It offered to African Americans a sense of "blackness" accessed ironically through the interracial American whole, as it provided for European Americans the imagination of a national completion that depended on the concept of race being beyond whiteness as such (figure 2).

THE IMPACT OF RACE ON AMERICAN MUSICAL SCHOLARSHIP

The development of American musicological research is commonly portrayed as an extension and elaboration of German scholarly practices of *Musikwissenschaft,* which emerged in the late nineteenth century (Krader 1980). Within the scheme proposed by Guido Adler (1885), interpretation proceeds as a scientific quest for music's natural law, in which stylistic change follows the model of organicism (Allen 1939; Kerman 1985). Ethnomusicological practice develops in its turn from a related comparative orientation (*vergleichende Musikwissenschaft* 'comparative musicology'), which Adler classifies as part of the analytical development of systematic musicology. The histories of the discipline that appear after World War II commonly build on this perspective, concentrating on the evolution of methodological procedure set apart from the vagaries of social and ideological change. The intellectual history of music scholarship follows the formula of positivism, consistent with internalist studies of style that have occupied the disciplines for decades. Acknowledging the impact of black music within the very texture of American musical experience, however, suggests a different kind of history, one less concerned with European legacies than with the ideologies that construct "Europe" and "European music" as supraracial categories. The section that follows proposes an alternative history, a view of American musical scholastics rewritten as if race were to define its very center.

American musicology emerged during the early twentieth century alongside the institutions of high culture that defined the United States's artistic coming of age (DiMaggio 1982). As patrician classes forged institutions to propagate an elite sense of

FIGURE 2   W. E. B. DuBois (1868–1963), professor, civil rights activist, and writer. One of his best known works is *The Souls of Black Folk* (1903). © CORBIS.

Whereas music historians resisted the power of racial ideas in describing musical experience, ethnographers embraced it, above all, to exalt difference.

refinement, so did colleges and universities introduce a pedagogy that reinforced the liberal ideology of the Enlightenment through the appreciation of cultivated arts. From the beginning the directive was to edify and to educate, to build on nineteenth-century affirmations of taste in response to the aesthetically and morally deficient popular arts overtaking public culture at the time (Crawford 1983). Founding patrons focused specifically on securing a canon comprising the major works of the European common practice era, together with genres of choral music and musical composition that reinforced a common aesthetic judgment. As expressions of culture, these repertoires seemed to rise above matters of ideology and race. They did so, however, by limiting representation to European masterworks, to those emblems of civilization that grew up within the frames of whiteness. As black music defined something beyond the realm of civilized expression, it was cordoned off within the bounds of race during a Jim Crow era.

The contradictions inherent in the racial construction of music in the United States had profound repercussions on the emerging disciplines of musicology. Notwithstanding the work of Oscar Sonneck, together with nationalist (yet exclusively white-centered) writers on folk and band musics, historical musicology remained most obviously committed to the study of European and European American art-musical achievements. This orientation no doubt developed from multiple incentives, social, experiential, geographic, and otherwise. The discipline's commitment to art, to "music itself," expressed above all a progressive desire to move beyond the racial stereotypes contaminating public consciousness, to transcend the regressive impulses of the United States's own colonizing, imperial past. In doing so, however, musicology did not solve these issues but merely deferred them. Possessing the option to focus beyond race, white scholars could claim an enlightened racelessness that betrayed race and class privilege and, in certain circumstances—particularly when the conversation turned to nationalist musical practices—a clear desire to maintain a Euro-centered aesthetic preserve (Elson 1900; Sonneck 1983 [1927]). It is precisely the tenacity with which historical musicology has claimed the European and European American traditions as its principal purpose that reveals the enduring force of race in our musical understanding.

Ethnomusicology's historical narrative similarly shares a genealogical relation with a nineteenth-century racial music. Yet whereas music historians resisted the power of racial ideas in describing musical experience, ethnographers embraced it, above all, to exalt difference. The first musical ethnographers openly acknowledged music's difference along racial lines: in the depictions of ballads collected by Francis James Child and his Harvard colleagues, in the forms of blackness that preoccupied William Francis Allen (1867) and other students of slave song, in the "imperialist nostalgia" that characterized the multitude of essays on the music of Native Americans appearing directly after their massacre (Rosaldo 1989). In these pursuits, ethnographers sought to locate the "missing link" of authenticity that had defined since Rousseau both the completion and the unraveling of civilization. Yet whereas for Rousseau such contradictions developed within a sturdier sense of European superiority (that paradoxically sought to challenge aristocratic confidence), for American ethnographers they revealed the inconsistencies of racial logic in a divided nation. The desire for and contempt of racial Others pervaded the ethnographic accounts that rapidly proliferated after the Civil War, leading a well-known observer of Native American music to strategically dismiss in one of the final paragraphs of her monograph the artistic value of "primitive song" (Densmore 1909). As discourses, these ideas circulated widely across the culture. Indeed, such contradictions even showed up in the work of W. E. B. DuBois, that inimitable advocate of African American culture, who cast disparaging comments about the "brothers and sisters" responsible for a music "the greatest this side the seas" (DuBois 1992 [1903]; see also West 1989). The unrelenting power and appeal of "race music" would increasingly complicate the emergence of scholarly ethnographic practice, as the exaltation of science intersected with racial fantasies established the nation's common sense.

Race music

These trajectories of popular race music were perhaps more important in the making of modern musical ethnography than any other single influence. Their appeal established the frames of reference in which modern narratives of difference would be written, refashioned according to nineteenth-century racialist assumptions to express the musical imaginations of early modernism. Accordingly, the distinctions one makes among scholarship, journalism, and entertainment grow complicated, given the extent to which all these rhetorics betray racial sensibilities consistent with early modernism (Torgovnick 1990). In Dorothy Scarborough's *On the Trail of Negro Folk-Songs* (1925), for example, one encounters the voice of blackface, just as it bears resemblances to the authenticity that informs the primitivist rhetoric of Harlem Renaissance writers. The 1932 cartoon image of Betty Boop traipsing across the African jungle (in fear of the "spook" facial image of a disembodied Louis Armstrong) carries forth significations of exoticism and danger that define the black image in anti-Negro social criticism and even in the fieldwork depictions of the WPA and Library of Congress (Carby 1998; Gabbard 1996:205). These racialisms, moreover, informed even the most scientific observations. In his early exercise in mechanical transcription (phonophotography), for example, Milton Metfessel chose as his laboratory specimen the "Negro voice," dissecting the physicality of African American sonic renderings (Metfessel 1928). This is not to conflate the many dimensions of musical representation, whose purpose, quality, and achievement varied widely. It is rather to identify the network of discourses in which the conversation about race music was taking place. As well, it seems not too much to say that racial difference consumed talk about music, a fact that carries profound significance when one observes the growth of academic studies in ethnomusicology.

It is against this social background that the modern discipline of ethnomusicology emerged. At once it embodied these racial notions as it worked purposely to establish a higher ground of representation. Recognizing the racialisms that so preoccupied scholars in the 1920s and 1930s, those of the post–World War II era sought to remove racial matters from the academic discourse. Unlike Europeanists, however, who merely displaced racial music, scholars of world music were forced to face it directly while searching strategically for better analytical models. For this they turned to the discipline of cultural anthropology and particularly to the perspective of "cultural relativism" established in the work of Franz Boas, which offered a way of disrupting the aesthetic hierarchy that had preoccupied Europeanist studies. In its stead they proposed a kind of cultural egalitarianism that relegated aestheticist concerns—beyond the intracultural explorations of David MacAllester, Alan Merriam, and others—to mere judgments of taste. Stressing above all the objective claims of science, ethnomusicology provided for music studies the outline of a new Enlightenment Project, consistent with the calls for the "end of ideology" that would emerge in the late 1950s and 1960s (Bell 1960). That these calls, however laudable, also revealed a new kind of imperialism consistent with

U. S. world dominance rarely entered into the reflections of the discipline's mission (for noteworthy exceptions, see Agawu 1992; Gourlay 1982; Keil 1982). Absent too was the discussion of race, which seemed to evaporate from the scholarly discourse in the attempt to reach a higher intellectual order.

An influential yet curiously underrecognized text in this "unspoken history" was Melville Herskovits's monumental *Myth of the Negro Past* (1941), which outlined a culture-based way of expressing essentialist positions once framed in racial terms. His dual emphases on culture over race and on the processes of transmission enabling diasporic continuities helped scholars to maintain arguments about musical essence without succumbing to the problematic views of biological determinism. Although Herskovits himself devoted only marginal attention to musical matters, his students, notably Alan Merriam and Richard Waterman, were instrumental in transposing this interpretive apparatus to the emerging ethnomusicological discipline. In the work of both Merriam and Waterman one observes a commanding devotion to scientific objectivity as a way of transcending racial pitfalls together with versions of the modern racial-musical intertext. Waterman's theories of "hot rhythm" owe an unmistakable legacy to the racializing of music, just as his musical applications of the anthropological theory of syncretism, in which African American music was observed as a melding of European and African similarities, may be read as a metaphor of the integrationist debates consuming mid-century American liberal thought (Waterman 1948, 1952). Merriam's vigorous demands for scientific practice similarly revealed progressive political sentiments. Yet in the end they could not obscure the extent to which he succumbed to the primitive myth of African ferocity—such as when he proposed Henry Stanley's narrative of "Bandussuma at Usiri" as an unparalleled depiction "of the emotional impact of African rhythm" (Merriam 1959)—any more than the achievements of Alan Lomax can deny the "pornotropic" rhetoric of his early studies of folk song style (Lomax 1959; McClintock 1995).

Black music's invention within the American cultural landscape emerged as a consequence of the nation's racial boundaries. Its exclusivity and power derive from contradictions inherent in a racial ideology that defines black music as something at once Other and constituted within the social Same. Accordingly, musical qualities of difference that took shape in a circumstance of intercultural familiarity supplied the paradoxical symbols of racial particularism and nationalism: black music could simultaneously define slavery and represent the sonic embodiment of America. By the twentieth century, the rising presence of black music had a profound impact on the public understanding of race and music, to the point of influencing the evolution of scholarly engagement. The language of the musicologies, together with the experience of music overall, would continually operate in constant contact with this fundamental racial dynamic.

—Ronald Radano

MUSIC, RACE, ETHNICITY, AND NATIONHOOD IN CANADA

It is something of a cliché to compare Canada's "cultural mosaic" to the United States's "melting pot." The analogy is not entirely accurate, but, like most stereotypes, it has a grain of truth. Both the United States and Canada are composed of a large number of ethnic, racial, cultural, and linguistic groups that sometimes overlap quite freely. But this is a purely descriptive account and is probably true of most of the world's nations at present. The dialectic between African American and European American cultures that has dominated discourses about the music of the United States has no obvious counterpart in Canada. Unlike the way in which the United States is viewed as being bifurcated along black/white racial and cultural lines, Canada is seen as a conglomeration of several "nations" that are constituted along ethnic, racial, and linguistic lines. As Beverley Diamond has pointed out, these lines are fragile in both theory and practice, and music plays an important role in "the maintenance of this fragile solidarity" (Diamond 1994:5).

The fragmented character of Canadian musical culture is somewhat abetted by the government's official policy on multiculturalism, which was introduced in 1971. As described by Augie Fleras and Jean Leonard Elliot, within a multicultural society "[r]acial or ethnic minorities are entitled to recognition of their culture as well as to attainment of equality at political, social, and economic levels. Ethnocultural differences are thought of as an integral part of Canadian life and promoted through active government intervention" (Fleras and Elliot 1992a:54). In some ways this is an institutionalization of the "mosaic" trope, although in actual practice there is considerable intolerance and pressure from some quarters for identifiable minorities to assimilate. Neil Bissoondath argues that multicultural policy has come to take on a "cult" quality, in that public challenges to its orthodoxy are strictly proscribed and usually dismissed as racism. Bissoondath argues that multicultural policy esteems exotic Otherness over Canadian identity and thus impairs community-building across the usual borders (1994). Thus Canada is replete each year with heritage festivals, which often present developmentally frozen, stereotyped versions of ethnic musical traditions. Canadian musical culture is characterized by a montage of large and small ethnic enclaves. There exists relatively little syncretism among groups, other than the sometime mixing of any of the heritage musics with the hegemonic English–Canadian popular music for the purposes of commercial crossover. This may be an overly pessimistic view, as the tourist culture of heritage festivals sometimes obscures actual acculturative forces in action. More obviously syncretic musics are beginning to appear among the youth cultures of second-generation immigrant populations, for example, Bhangra, which is a synthesis of hip-hop and Punjabi traditional music (Warwick 1996).

The First Nations of Canada, a group that is estimated to number up to one and one-half million in this country, with fifty-three different languages, covers a wide range of musical genres that divide along linguistic, regional, age, and class lines. Nonetheless, the "Indian" is a stereotype in the Canadian music industry. Otherwise disparate artists such as Susan Aglukark, Buffy Sainte-Marie (figure 3), and Kashtin are often conflated under an essentialized, exoticized rubric for marketing purposes. As a rule, the First Nations artists that have received widespread acclaim have borrowed heavily from mainstream styles. An example is Kashtin, a group from the remote Maliotenan reserve (800 kilometers north of Montréal), whose lyrics were invariably written in the Innu language. Some Native musicians have embraced popular styles that are strongly identified with African Americans, including Chicago blues and rap [see Musical Interactions, p. 480]. These styles are then adapted to accommodate lyrics addressing Native concerns and issues.

The black population of Canada is not insignificant, estimated at 573,860 by the mid-1990s. The largest concentration is in Toronto and may in fact be much higher due to heavy immigration from the Caribbean in the last twenty years [see African Canadian Music, pp. 1132, 1169, 1211]. Several black communities, many of them refuges for slaves who escaped via the Underground Railroad, were prominent in the nineteenth century in parts of Ontario and Nova Scotia, although these communities scattered to urban areas over time. There were also several black communities on the prairies in the years prior to the Civil War. Important enclaves of black music include Montréal, where significant numbers of black slaves were employed as domestic servants as early as 1783. The Montréal Black Community Youth Choir (1974–1981) was succeeded by the successful Montréal Jubilation Gospel Choir. Black performers played to racially mixed audiences in Montréal from the 1920s, and African Canadians have continued to play a significant role in the Montréal jazz scene. In Toronto, a vital hip-hop scene developed in the 1990s. Several Torontonian rappers, for example, Dream Warriors and UBAD, highlight a Caribbean identity in their lyrics and visual images.

FIGURE 3   Canadian singer Buffy Sainte-Marie. Photo courtesy the BMI Archives.

If one were to insist on naming a Canadian dichotomy analogous to the United States's black/white divide, the French/English one would probably do. In popular discourse, language is sometimes conflated with race; for example, Beverley Diamond, in interviews with French Saskatchewaners, heard stories of people being told to "speak white" when they dared use the French language (Diamond, 1999). Canada's two official languages instantiate an enduring difference. Canada's popular musical artists are divided primarily along lines of sung language; vocalists who sing in French rarely gain exposure in mainstream media outlets until they cross over linguistically. (There are exceptions to this, including the female pop singer Mitsou.) One of the few Canadian figures to gain true national popularity was Don Messer, who, as an instrumental performer, could be embraced by both Francophones and Anglophones. Linguistic identity could be effaced for the moment (Rosenberg 1990:238). The Canadian popular music industry has in recent years depended on two music video cable channels, the English-language MuchMusic and the French-language Musique Plus (both channels are owned and operated by the same media conglomerate, ChumCity) [see MUCHMUSIC AND MUSIQUEPLUS, p. 250]. The musical repertoires featured on each channel are nearly mutually exclusive, and the difference is wholly constituted in the sung languages of the artists.

Music is sometimes used to aid in the constitution of nationhood in Canada, especially in localized contexts. In the early 1990s, Cape Breton fiddle music gained national popularity and became a metonymic representation of the Maritime provinces and, for some, Canada in general [see CELTIC REVIVAL IN CAPE BRETON, p. 1127]. Through a strategy that is part ideological work and part savvy marketing, Cape Breton fiddling has become for many the epitome of the Canadian sound. As Neil Rosenberg points out, "region has become ethnicity" in the case of the Maritimes (1990: 238). This powerful melding of identities has allowed East Coast traditional music to resonate as perhaps the most plausible example of Canadian music. Furthermore, fiddle music has been cross-pollinated with pop and rock elements to create a palatable commercial blend, a strategy reminiscent of 1980s world beat productions.

—MICHAEL DALEY

REFERENCES

Abrahams, Roger D. 1992. *Singing the Master: The Emergence of African American Culture in the Plantation South.* New York: Pantheon.

Adler, Guido. 1885. "Umfang, Methode und Ziel der Musikwissenschaft." *Vierteljahrsschrift für Musikwissenschaft* 1:5–20.

Agawu, Kofi. 1992. "Representing African Music." *Critical Inquiry* 18(2):246–266.

Allen, Warren Dwight. 1939. *Philosophies of Music History.* New York: American Book Company.

Allen, William Francis, Lucy McKim Garrison, and Charles Pickard Ware, eds. 1867. *Slave Songs of the United States.* New York: A. Simpson and Co.

Bell, Daniel. 1960. *The End of Ideology: On the Exhaustion of Political Ideas in the Fifties.* Glencoe, IL: Free Press.

Berlin, Isaiah. 1999. *The Roots of Romanticism.* Ed. Henry Hardy. Princeton, N.J.: Princeton University Press.

Bissoondath, Neil. 1994. *Selling Illusions: The Cult of Multiculturalism in Canada.* Toronto: Penguin Books.

Bosman, William. 1705. "Chief Factor for the Dutch at the Castle of St. George D' Elmina," English Translation from the Dutch. In *A General Collection . . . ,* ed. John Pinkerton, 16:394. London: Longman, Hunt, Rees, and Orme.

Camus, Raoul François. 1980. "Military Music of Colonial Boston." In *Music in Colonial Massachusetts, 1630–1820,* vol 1: *Music in Public Places,* 75–103. Boston: The Colonial Society of Massachusetts and the University Press of Virginia.

Carby, Hazel. 1998. *Race Men.* Cambridge: Harvard University Press.

Crawford, Richard. 1983. "Musical Learning in Nineteenth-Century America." *American Music* 1(1):1–11.

Criswell, Robert. 1973 [1852]. *"Uncle Tom's Cabin" Contrasted with Buckingham Hall, the Planter's Home; Or, A Fair View of Both Sides of the Slavery Question.* New York: AMS Press.

Davis, David Brion. 1999 [1975]. *The Problem of Slavery in the Age of Revolution, 1770–1823.* New York: Oxford University Press.

Densmore, Frances. 1909. "Scale Formation in Primitive Music." *American Anthropologist* 11(1):1–12.

Diamond, Beverley. 1994. "Issues of Hegemony and Identity in Canadian Music." In *Canadian Music: Issues of Hegemony and Identity,* ed. Beverley Diamond and Bob Witmer, 1–22. Toronto: Canadian Scholars' Press.

———. 1999. Personal communication, 6 December.

Diamond, Beverley, and Bob Witmer, eds. 1994. *Canadian Music: Issues of Hegemony and Identity.* Toronto: Canadian Scholars' Press.

DiMaggio, Paul. 1982. "Cultural Entrepreneurship in Nineteenth-Century Boston: The Creation of an Organizational Base for High Culture in America." *Media, Culture, and Society* 4(January):33–50, 303–322.

Douglass, Frederick. 1845. *The Narrative of the Life of Frederick Douglass, an American Slave, Written by Himself.* Boston: The Anti-Slavery Office.

DuBois, W. E. B. 1992 [1903]. *The Souls of Black Folk.* Ed. Henry Louis Gates Jr. New York: Bantam.

Elson, Louis Charles. 1900. *The National Music of America and Its Sources.* Boston: L. C. Page.

Epstein, Dena. 1963. "Slave Music in the United States before 1860: A Survey of Sources, pts. I–II." *Notes of the Music Library Association* 20(Spring):195–212; (Summer):377–390.

———. 1973. "African Music in British and French America." *Musical Quarterly* 59(January):61–91.

———. 1977. *Sinful Tunes and Spirituals: Black Folk Music to the Civil War.* Urbana: University of Illinois Press.

———. 1983. "A White Origin for the Black Spiritual? An Invalid Theory and How It Grew." *American Music* 1(2):53–59.

Fleras, Augie, and Jean Leonard Elliot. 1992a. *Multiculturalism in Canada: The Challenge of Diversity.* Scarborough, Ont.: Nelson Canada.

———. 1992b. *The "Nations Within": Aboriginal-State Relations in Canada, the United States, and New Zealand.* Toronto: Oxford University Press.

Gabbard, Krin. 1996. *Jammin' at the Margins: Jazz and the American Cinema.* Chicago: University of Chicago Press.

Gilmore, James Robert. 1862. *Among the Pines; Or, South in Secession-Time.* 6th ed. New York: J. R. Gilmore.

Gilroy, Paul. 1993. *The Black Atlantic: Modernity and Double Consciousness.* Cambridge: Harvard University Press.

Gourlay, Kenneth A. 1982. "Towards a Humanizing Ethnomusicology." *Ethnomusicology* 26(3):411–420.

Hamm, Charles. 1983. *Music in the New World.* New York: Norton.

Hatch, Nathan O. 1989. *The Democratization of American Christianity.* New Haven, Conn.: Yale University Press.

Head, Franklin H. 1893. "The Legends of Jekyl Island." *New England Magazine,* n.s., 8(May):393–399.

Herskovits, Melville. 1941. *The Myth of the Negro Past.* New York: Harper and Brothers.

Historical Papers. 1912. Series IX. Trinity College Historical Society and the North Carolina Conference Historical Society.

Horsman, Reginald. 1981. *Race and Manifest Destiny: The Origins of American Racial Anglo-Saxonism.* Cambridge: Harvard University Press.

Hudson, Nicholas. 1996. "From 'Nation' to 'Race': The Origin of Racial Classification in Eighteenth-Century Thought." *Eighteenth-Century Studies* 29(3):247–264.

Jackson, George Pullen. 1943. *White and Negro Spirituals.* Locust Valley N.Y.: J. J. Augustin.

Jacobs, Harriet Brent. 1971 [1861]. *Incidents in the Life of a Slave Girl. Written by Herself.* Ed.

Lydia Maria Child. New York: Harcourt Brace Jovanovich.

Jordan, Winthrop D. 1968. *White over Black: American Attitudes toward the Negro, 1550–1812.* Chapel Hill: University of North Carolina Press.

Keil, Charles. 1982. "Applied Ethnomusicology and a Rebirth of Music from the Spirit of Tragedy." *Ethnomusicology* 26(3):407–411.

Kerman, Joseph. 1985. *Contemplating Music: Challenges to Musicology.* Cambridge: Harvard University Press.

Krader, Barbara. 1980. "Ethnomusicology." In *The New Grove Dictionary of Music and Musicians,* ed. Stanley Sadie. London: Macmillan.

Litwack, Leon F. 1961. *North of Slavery: The Negro in the Free States, 1790–1860.* Chicago: University of Chicago Press.

Lomax, Alan. 1959. "Folk Song Style." *American Anthropologist* 61:927–954.

Lott, Eric. 1993. *Love and Theft: Blackface Minstrelsy and the American Working Class.* New York: Oxford University Press.

McClintock, Anne. 1995. *Imperial Leather: Race, Gender, and Sexuality in the Colonial Context.* New York: Routledge.

Merriam, Alan P. 1959. "African Music." In *Continuity and Change in African Cultures,* ed. William R. Bascom and Melville J. Herskovits, 49–86. Chicago: University of Chicago Press.

Metfessel, Milton F. 1928. *Phonophotography in Folk Music: American Negro Songs in New Notation.* Chapel Hill: University of North Carolina Press.

Pieterse, Jan Nederveen. 1992. *Black on White: Images of Africa and Blacks in Western Popular Culture.* New Haven, Conn.: Yale University Press.

Pinkerton, John, ed. 1808–1814. *A General Collection of the Best and Most Interesting Voyages and Travels in All Parts of the World: Many of Which Are Now First Translated into English: Digested on a New Plan.* London: Longman, Hurst, Rees, and Orme.

Pratt, Mary Louise. 1992. *Imperial Eyes: Travel Writing and Transculturation.* New York: Routledge.

Raboteau, Albert J. 1978. *Slave Religion: The "Invisible Institution" in the Antebellum South.* New York: Oxford University Press.

Radano, Ronald. 1996. "Denoting Difference: The Writing of the Slave Spirituals." *Critical Inquiry* 22(Spring):506–544.

———. 2000. "Hot Fantasies: American Modernism and the Idea of Black Rhythm." In *Music and the Racial Imagination,* ed. Ronald Radano and Philip V. Bohlman, 459–480. Chicago Studies in Ethnomusicology. Chicago: University of Chicago Press.

Roediger, David R. 1991. *The Wages of Whiteness: Race and the Making of the American Working Class.* New York: Verso.

Rosaldo, Renato. 1989. "Imperialist Nostalgia." *Representations* 26(Spring):107–122.

Rosenberg, Neil V. 1990. "Whose Music Is Canadian Country Music? A Precis." In *CanMus Documents 5: Ethnomusicology in Canada,* ed. Bob Witmer and Beverley Diamond, 236–238. Toronto: Institute for Canadian Studies.

Scarborough, Dorothy. 1925. *On the Trail of Negro Folk-Songs.* Cambridge: Harvard University Press.

Smith, William L. 1852. *Life at the South; Or, "Uncle Tom's Cabin" as It Is. Being Narratives, Scenes, and Incidents in the Real "Life of the Lowly."* Buffalo, N.Y.: George H. Derby and Company.

Sonneck, Oscar. 1983 [1927]. "An American School of Composition: Do We Want and Need It?" In *Oscar Sonneck and American Music,* ed. William Lichtenwanger, 158–166. Urbana: University of Illinois Press.

Southern, Eileen. 1997. *The Music of Black Americans: A History.* 3rd ed. New York: Norton.

Steel, David Warren. 1988. "Lazarus Jones and *The Southern Minstrel* (1849)." *American Music* 6(2):123–157.

Torgovnick, Marianna. 1990. *Gone Primitive: Savage Intellects, Modern Lives.* Chicago: University of Chicago Press.

Warwick, Jacqueline. 1996. "'Can Anyone Dance to This Music?': Bhangra and South Asian Youth in Toronto." Master's thesis, York University.

Waterman, Richard. 1948. "'Hot' Rhythm in Negro Music." *Journal of the American Musicological Society* 1(1):24–37.

———. 1952. "African Influence in the Music of the Americas." In *Acculturation in the Americas,* ed. Sol Tax, 207–218. Chicago: University of Chicago Press.

West, Cornel. 1989. *The American Evasion of Philosophy: A Genealogy of Pragmatism.* Madison: University of Wisconsin Press.

Windhus, John. 1725. "A Journey to Mequinez, The Residence of the Present Emperor of Fez and Morocco." In *A General Collection . . . ,* ed. John Pinkerton, 15;448. London: Longman, Hurst, Rees, and Orme.

Wood, Betty. 1997. *The Origins of American Slavery: Freedom and Bondage in the English Colonies.* New York: Hill and Wang.

Snapshot:
Two Views of Music, Race, Ethnicity, and Nationhood

Charles K. Wolfe
Jacqueline Cogdell DjeDje

Country and Western—Charles K. Wolfe
African American Cries, Calls, and Hollers—Jacqueline Cogdell DjeDje

Most music in the world is associated with a specific geographical place or with a specific group of people. Indeed, music—its creation and performance—is often so embedded within these contexts that it is difficult, if not impossible, to separate them. Here are two kinds of music, each linked to a different historical, social, and ethnic context, that have developed in the United States within the past two centuries.

COUNTRY AND WESTERN

Country music is a vernacular form of American popular music that traditionally has been associated with the Southeast and with the rural Midwest. It is generally characterized by an emotive and highly ornamented singing style, an instrumental accompaniment that relies heavily on small ensembles of stringed instruments, and a repertoire that has been derived from and influenced by older folk balladry and nineteenth-century popular song. Although the actual term *Country Music* did not gain widespread acceptance until the 1940s, the music itself emerged as a commercial art form in the years from 1922 to 1927. The music's involvement with the mass media—especially radio and phonograph records—has always been heavy, and many feel that this involvement is one of the essential distinctive features of the genre. The first center for the music was Atlanta, Georgia, but in later years locations like Chicago; Los Angeles; Cincinnati; Charlotte, North Carolina; and, finally, Nashville served as hubs. At various times, starting in the 1940s, country music impinged significantly on mainstream popular music, but it routinely became self-conscious about its own identity and retrenched to reaffirm its traditional roots. The music has been generally conservative in a number of ways—politically, musically, socially, philosophically, and even technically. It has frequently served in many ways as the rear guard in the parade of American music.

The roots of country music

The roots of country music singing are found in the oral tradition of balladry that accompanied Scottish and Irish immigrants into the Southeast in the nineteenth century [see ENGLISH AND SCOTTISH MUSIC, p. 831; IRISH MUSIC, p. 842]. In this tra-

FIGURE I   The father of bluegrass music and "old-time" country legend Bill Monroe (1911–1996). Photo courtesy Charles K. Wolfe.

dition, the old songs of love and death were performed unaccompanied, often in a freemeter style, using so-called gapped scales, and often sung at full volume and at the very top of the singer's range. This "high lonesome sound" became an element of later country singing that gave it a soulful, strident quality that one heard in major singers like Hank Williams, Roy Acuff, Bill Monroe (figure 1), and Dolly Parton. Most of these modern singers experienced at least some firsthand contact with older, precommercial ballad singing. Another key stylistic element is what older singers called "snaking the melody," in which an individual word or syllable may be stretched over a number of notes, as is heard in recordings by the Texas singer Lefty Frizzell and the California singer Merle Haggard. Country vocal ornamentation includes the use of scoops and slurs; the use of "feathering" at the ends of lines (a short glissando up to a glottal stop); the deliberate dropping of a beat or measure between lines; the use of falsetto, either as a high keening or as some sort of yodel; and an emphasis on nasality and head tones. Notions of vocal harmony were derived from southern gospel music singing schools and song books, although often sung a full octave above the printed sources. At various points in country music's development, major singers broke with this older style and eschewed newer, smoother styles that were derived from mainstream pop singers like Bing Crosby; such smooth singers included Red Foley (in the 1940s), Jim Reeves (in the 1950s), and Eddy Arnold (1950s–1960s).

The instruments of country music

The three main instruments associated with country music are the fiddle, the banjo, and the guitar. The fiddle was a staple in the Scots-Irish culture, and Americans were staging fiddling contests as early as the 1760s. Light and easily portable, the fiddle soon found its way into the rural Southeast, along with a battery of tunes carried across the water. Thus "Miss McLeod's Reel" became "Did You Ever Did See a Devil, Uncle Joe," and dozens of new songs emerged as fiddlers plied their solitary wares at country dances, barnwarmings, county fairs, auctions, and political rallies. A variety of unorthodox tunings emerged, such as what many called "cross tuning" (A-E-A-E) to get a harmonic drone effect. By the turn of the twentieth century, the fiddle had become the anchor for string bands and was being used less and less as a solo instrument.

For years it has been accepted that the banjo was an African instrument first brought to this country by slaves; we now know that its roots reach far into the culture of subSaharan Africa, with some references to a banjolike instrument dating as far back as thirteenth century Mali. Through its use in minstrel shows in the 1840s, the banjo made its way into Anglo-American musical circles and into the hands of rural southerners. Here it also was subjected to unorthodox, unEuropean tuning systems (especially complicated by the addition of a fifth drone string in the 1840s) and to a rich variety of tonal textures brought about by homemade skin heads and handcarved fingerboards. Although the instrument was a favorite of many pioneer performers, such as Tennessee's Uncle Dave Macon, the banjo fell out of favor in the 1940s as the music became smoother, only to reemerge in the 1950s as the centerpiece of a new subgenre, bluegrass, at the hands of innovator Earl Scruggs [see BLUEGRASS, p. 158].

The central icon for country music, however, was the third and most recent addition to this trio of instruments: the guitar. The guitar had been a part of the American musical landscape for most of the nineteenth century, but with its gut strings and soft sound, it was looked upon as a refined parlor instrument, suitable for young ladies to strum on. Then, around the turn of the twentieth century, two things happened to change this. Guitar makers began using steel strings on their instruments and reinforcing the neck and tailpiece to accommodate the greater stress. These strings, often played with flat or finger picks, gave the guitar much more volume and brightness and allowed it to take its place in the string bands of the day. The second important change occurred when the giant mail order firms of Sears, Roebuck and Montgomery Ward began selling inexpensive guitars by mail. Unlike other folk instruments such as the banjo or dulcimer, the guitar was not easy for amateurs to make, and the cheap Sears Silvertones and Supertones went all over the South. As musicians became more proficient, they aspired to a better guitar, the best being the flat-topped Martin (originated in Pennsylvania before the Civil War) or the arch-top Gibson (dating from the 1890s); these two models are still considered the standards for country music today. By the 1920s, the guitar had made its way into rural southern string bands; many veteran country performers can even remember the first time they saw the guitar and how it changed the nature of both singing and instrumental music.

Major figures

The 1920s–1940s

The commercialization of what would become country music began in 1922 and 1923, with the first recordings by Texas fiddler Eck Robertson ("Sallie Gooden," Victor 1922) and Georgian Fiddlin' John Carson ("The Little Old Log Cabin in the Lane," OKeh 1923). With these releases, the big commercial record companies from the Northeast realized that there was an untapped market among southern audiences for this kind of "hill country" or "old time" music, and they wasted no time in sending talent scouts into the area to set up temporary studios. One such studio, set up by A & R man Ralph Peer in Bristol, Tennessee, struck paydirt almost immediately. It yielded a singing trio from nearby Maces Spring, Virginia, named the Carter Family, who had a knack for taking old mountain songs, putting harmony to them, and arranging them for guitar and autoharp accompaniment (figure 2). Their recordings of songs like "Bury Me under the Weeping Willow Tree" (Victor 1928) and "Wildwood Flower" (Victor 1929) became standards. The Carter singing style and harmony is still heard today, as is the "thumbstroke" guitar style perfected by Maybelle Carter. A day after the Carters were discovered, Jimmie Rodgers, a young singer from Mississippi, appeared before Peer. Rodgers offered a unique singing style heavily influenced by blues and cowboy songs; the Rodgers forte was a pliant, expressive voice and an ability to break into falsetto phrasing on refrains—a technique that became forever associated with his career song "Blue Yodel" (or "Blue Yodel No. 1," Victor 1928). These two acts dominated early country music; they sold more records than any other act and had more influence. Although Rodgers died prematurely in 1933, the Carters continued to work on records and radio until their breakup in 1943. Other important first-generation performers included the banjoist and songster Uncle Dave Macon, the singer Charlie Poole, the Georgia string band the Skillet Lickers, and the ballad singer Bradley Kincaid.

During country music's second decade, the 1930s, performers quickly found they could use income from radio shows and personal appearances to become fulltime professionals. This led to a dramatic increase in technical proficiency as well as an increase in original songs and styles. Innovations during this time, in fact, often led to new subgenres within the music. One was the soft, plaintive close-harmony duet singing exemplified by groups such as the Blue Sky Boys (Bill and Earl Bolick) and the Delmore Brothers (Alton and Rabon). Best-selling records from this style included sentimental pieces like "I'm Just Here to Get My Baby Out of Jail" and "What Would You Give in Exchange for Your Soul?" When Texas yodeler Gene Autry left his spot on WLS Chicago radio to go to Hollywood to try his hand at films, he started another subgenre built on the image of the singing cowboy. Soon hundreds of singers, including many in the Southeast, were adapting a cowboy image and repertoire. The third major innovation, western swing, also came from the Southwest. Popularized, though not invented, by Texasborn Bob Wills, the music merged old-time fiddle breakdowns, blues, and *norteño* music with the uptempo swing style of bands such as Benny Goodman's and

FIGURE 2   The Carter Sisters, Helen and June, and Mother Maybelle Carter, c. 1960s. Photo courtesy Charles K. Wolfe.

Jimmie Lunceford's [see TEJANO MUSIC, p. 770]. During World War II, Wills transplanted his music to California, where it flourished and led to an entire musical scene in the southern part of the state.

By the 1940s, radio had become even more important, and powerful shows like WSM Nashville's *Grand Ole Opry,* WLS Chicago's *National Barn Dance,* and WWVA's *Wheeling Jamboree* were attracting national attention for the music. During and after the war, the Armed Forces Radio Network recorded a number of country programs and sent them around the world to various GI outposts, further spreading the music to audiences that had never heard it. For a time, because it was full of smooth-singing Bing Crosby imitators, country seemed about to lose its identity, but this was rejuvenated by two rough-hewn but powerful singing stylists, Texan Ernest Tubb and Alabaman Hank Williams. Turning their back on the idealized imagery of the movie cowboy as well as the sentimental songs about death and children, these singers addressed the problems of the modern-day working class: drinking, divorce, lost love, and money. Tubb's "Walking the Floor over You" (Decca 1941) and Williams's "Lovesick Blues" (MGM 1949) became emblematic of the new style and defined a direction that still continues today. Other stylists of note during the late 1940s and early 1950s included Roy Acuff, Lefty Frizzell (figure 3), Red Foley, and Faron Young. Women, who had been generally discouraged from professional country by public opinion, had found an early role model in singing cowgirl Patsy Montana, who had a huge hit in 1936 with "I Want to Be a Cowboy's Sweetheart" (ARC). In 1952, women found an even stronger model in Tennessean Kitty Wells, whose "It Wasn't God Who Made Honkytonk Angels" (Decca) showed that a song from a women's point of view could become a best-seller [see GENDER AND SEXUALITY, p. 87].

By now new instruments were helping define what was being called "Country and Western Music." The electric amplified guitar was featured on many of Ernest Tubb's recordings in the 1940s, as well as in many western swing bands; it soon became the lead instrument in the country band. In the 1920s numerous musicians had also adapted the acoustic Hawaiian guitar to country music, eventually resulting in the manufacture in the 1930s of the dobro, or resonator guitar, that was also played with a metal slide. Emerging in the 1940s was a solid-body amplified steel guitar called a "lap

FIGURE 3   Singer and guitarist Lefty Frizzell, who was noted for his distinctive vocal style, c. 1950s. Photo courtesy Charles K. Wolfe.

By the 1990s dynamic performers like Shania Twain were openly exploiting a provocative sexual image in the new video medium and were outselling almost all of their male counterparts.

steel," and in the late 1940s many players began to experiment with a "pedal steel," a flat steel guitar on a stand attached to a series of rods and pedals that allowed the performer to alter the string pitches and modulate chords. The pedal steel soon became country's most distinctive instrument: no other popular music genre utilized it. Early pioneers with the instrument included West Coast studio musician Speedy West, Nashville session man Bud Isaacs, and Grand Ole Opry performer Buddy Emmons. Webb Pierce's hit recording of "Slowly" (Decca 1954), featuring Isaac's work, inspired hundreds of guitarists around the country and helped make the pedal steel the central icon it is today.

The 1950s–1970s

By the early 1950s Nashville had emerged as the geographical center for country music. One reason for this was that WSM's radio show *Grand Ole Opry* had emerged after the war as the nation's most popular country radio show, and many leading performers had moved to Nashville to be near it. The city was also becoming a center for country music publishing, with the formation of the first nationally successful firm, Acuff-Rose, in 1942. In addition to publishing the works of Hank Williams, Roy Acuff, Charles and Ira Louvin, the Everly Brothers, Don Gibson, and Roy Orbison, the company aggressively marketed its wares to pop music producers. Nashville could also boast a cadre of superior studio engineers, and by 1946 two of them had set up the first permanent studio in town. This led major record companies to come to town to record and to open branch offices in the 1950s.

All of this eventually evolved into a phenomenon called "the Nashville studio system," which nurtured a new generation of specialized musicians who did little but play in recording studios. Producers like Chet Atkins and Owen Bradley, both musicians themselves, set up an assembly-line type of system in which performers would come into a studio without a band and would be given a studio band of crack technicians for backing on the record. (Among the best of these background musicians were guitarists Grady Martin and Harold Bradley, fiddler Tommy Jackson, and steel player Jerry Byrd.) While the music was clean and competent, the system left little room for innovation, and by the 1960s it was being blamed for a blandness that was infecting the music. Newer generations of session musicians have remedied that to some extent, and the session system was still in place in the 1990s.

Country's predictable musical settings of the 1950s were especially vulnerable to the rise of rock and roll. As youth stars like Elvis Presley and Carl Perkins began to add a drum kit to their stage shows and added a heavy beat to the loud electric guitars, country bookings plummeted. Although Presley, from Memphis, began his career touring with country package shows, the new teenaged record-buying fans had little interest in the established Opry stars. Some country stars, such as Marty Robbins, tried to accommodate the new sound by exploring the hybrid genre called "rockabilly," a country sound with a strong beat. It did help weather the storm, and by the 1960s a new generation of singers and songwriters was arriving in Nashville to rejuvenate the

FIGURE 4   Born in 1933 in Central Texas, Willie Nelson became synonymous with Country and Western music. A songwriter, performer and poet, Nelson expresses in his music both the dark and light sides of life. © Philip Gould/CORBIS.

music. These included Willie Nelson (figure 4), Waylon Jennings, Patsy Cline, Don Gibson, Tom T. Hall, Kris Kristofferson, Harlan Howard, and George Jones. Writers like Hall, Howard, and Kristofferson were especially adept at turning away from the commonplace clichés of country lyrics and experimenting with new song forms and subject matter. Kentuckian Loretta Lynn, a protégée of Cline's, gave women fans a new voice in the country repertoire with songs like "One's on the Way" (Decca 1971). From the Bakersfield area in California came two of the most popular singer-songwriters of the 1960–1980 era, Buck Owens and Merle Haggard. It was Haggard's songs like "Working Man Blues" and "Okie from Muskogee" that helped restore a social sensibility in the music.

The 1980s to the present

In 1980, with the release of the film *Urban Cowboy,* country music found itself threatening once again to "go pop." New artists like Mickey Gilley and Johnny Lee, as well as light rock acts like the Eagles and Linda Ronstadt, soon married the dance hall beat to new, hip lyrics like Lee's "Lookin' for Love in All the Wrong Places" (Full Moon 1980). During this time a number of veteran rock musicians from the sixties and seventies moved to Nashville and made their presence felt in the studios. But by the mid-1980s a countertrend emerged in the person of North Carolinian Randy Travis, who refurbished the themes and styles of Hank Williams and Lefty Frizzell. The so-called new traditionalism also won new respect for established performers like George Jones and Tammy Wynette and helped pave the way for a new generation of singers like Alan Jackson and George Strait.

Women, who had been a crucial part of the music since the Carter Family, came totally into their own in the mid-1980s. Suddenly the bestselling *Billboard* charts were full of new hits by K.T. Oslin, Reba McEntire, Tanya Tucker, Emmylou Harris, Dolly Parton, and The Judds, among others. By the 1990s dynamic performers such as Shania Twain were openly exploiting a provocative sexual image in the new video medium and were outselling almost all of their male counterparts.

In the 1990s, the various independent record and publishing companies that defined Nashville and country music were being purchased by larger corporations, and much of the artistic control over the music was passing out of Nashville, or into the hands of executives who cared little for music at all. The spectacular success of Oklahoman Garth Brooks in the late nineties showed that aggressive corporate marketing could increase profit margins far beyond any Nashville expectations. Within a span of seventy years, country had expanded far beyond a niche music for a specific audience to a nationwide phenomenon and a major international commercial success. Although still largely centered in Nashville, the music by the year 2000 could boast of fans, media outlets, and concert venues all over the country.

—CHARLES K. WOLFE

AFRICAN AMERICAN CRIES, CALLS, AND HOLLERS

African American cries, calls, and hollers are topics often excluded from the examination of black folk music. Until recently most scholars have devoted attention to the study of religious forms, blues, and jazz. As a result there are gaps in our knowledge and understanding of black folk music culture, and some secular forms have not been preserved. This is unfortunate, because secular songs, particularly those created during the seventeenth and eighteenth centuries, told of the slaves' loves, work, and floggings and expressed the slaves' moods and the reality of their oppression. They sang of the proud defiance of the runaway, the courage of the black rebels, the stupidity of the patrolers,

TRACK
1

the heartlessness of the slave traders, and the kindness and cruelty of masters (Blassingame 1979 [1972]:115).

In early years one of the major reasons for the lack of documentation was that most song collecting took place on plantations where slaves, having been converted to Christianity, came to regard dancing as sinful and no longer indulged in it. There were collectors who realized that they might be neglecting an important repertoire in failing to record nonreligious music, but apparently they were in the minority. The fact that texts of dance songs tended to be nonsensical may have also discouraged some investigators (Southern 1997:170–171).

Work songs in African American culture

Before the 1800s, descriptions of music to accompany work were found only sparingly in the writings of travelers, slave traders, and slave owners. A few investigators after the Civil War began to realize the importance of work songs and other types of black secular music, but little effort was made to document this music systematically. For example, in the 1867 publication of *Slave Songs of the United States,* John McKim states:

> We must look among their nonreligious songs for the purest specimens of negro minstrelsy. . . . Some of the best *pure negro* songs I have ever heard were those that used to be sung by the black stevedores, or perhaps the crews themselves, of the West India vessels, loading and unloading at the wharves in Philadelphia and Baltimore. I have stood for more than an hour, often, listening to them, as they hoisted and lowered the hogsheads and boxes of their cargoes; one man taking the burden of the song (and the slack of the rope) and the others striking in with the chorus. They would sing in this way more than a dozen different songs in an hour . . . generally rather innocent and proper in their language, and strangely attractive in their music; and with a volume of voice that reached a square or two away. (Allen 1983:153)

The meaning and significance of work songs depended upon context. The work experience represented a secondary environment and was far less important in determining the slaves' personality than was the social organization of their primary environment, the slave quarters (Blassingame 1979 [1972]:105–106). However, knowing about the music performed and created during work is essential, because through work songs enslaved blacks expressed their deep-seated feelings about their conditions, attitudes towards whites, longings, and interpersonal relationships with loved ones and family members.

In most instances, slaves were required to perform music while working, for slave owners realized the impact that music making had on the work experience. For example, many masters encouraged slaves to sing as they went about their work, believing that they were more productive when they sang (Bailey 1992:41). "When at work I have no objection to their whistling or singing some lively time, but no drawling tunes are allowed in the field, for their motions are almost certain to keep time with the music" (Epstein 1977:162). An article from 1895 states:

> The singing of the slaves at work was regarded by their masters as almost indispensable to the quick and proper performance of the labor, and the leaders of the singings were often excused from work so that they might the better attend to their part of the business. Wharf laborers were selected and retained largely because of their ability as singers, a good singer being regarded as worth more on the wharves then a laborer who merely did his work and kept still about it. . . . In canning establishments in Baltimore, the leading singers are actually paid more by their employers, showing that their leading has a distinct money value from the capitalist's point of view. ("Negro Folk Songs" 1976 [1895]:150–151)

Most writers concur that the singing of songs assisted the physical labor and helped arouse and keep up the energy of work. In such situations, it did not matter if the songs were religious or secular. In communal group labor, songs provided a rhythm to coordinate physical activity involved in work (figure 5). Singing thus relieved the tedium and made the time pass more quickly. Even when the work was performed by one individual and a group was not involved, songs provided "psychic benefits that were no less important then the physical stabilization they afforded" (Levine 1977:212). Eileen Southern explains that the lone worker performed a different type of song. Because the worker had no need to coordinate work movements with others, songs tended to take on the nature of a deeply personal utterance. Tempo, text, melody—all these things reflected the person's mood of the moment. If the worker was happy, fingers flew and the work song cheered all who might be listening; if the worker was melancholy, the same song might be sung so mournfully as to slow up the activity and to depress all within hearing (1997:161).

FIGURE 5   Song is used to provide rhythm and coordinate work in groups. This is evident in this photo of "Lightning" and a group of men working at Darrington State Prison Farm, Sandy Point, Texas, April 1934. Photo from the Collection of the Library of Congress.

Research on the cry, call, and holler

There are few pre–Civil War sources that include references to the cry, call, holler, or whoop, even though some investigators believe this music evolved during slavery (Ramsey 1960). Dena Epstein believes that "perhaps the people who heard them then did not know how to describe them, or possibly they did not consider them worth mentioning" (1977:182). However, Glenn Hinson suggests that field hollers "developed primarily after the Civil War, when black farmers were able to work alone on land they owned or sharecropped rather than in the work crews of the plantations" (1978:1).

One of the first descriptions of the call is found in writings of Frederick Law Olmstead, a journalist/landscape architect who traveled in the South between 1853 and 1854:

> At midnight I was awakened by loud laughter, and, looking out, saw that the loading gang of negroes had made a fire and were enjoying a right merry repast. Suddenly, one raised such a sound as I never heard before, a long, loud, musical shout, rising, and falling, and breaking into falsetto, his voice ringing through the woods in the clear, frosty night air, like a bugle call. As he finished, the melody was caught up by another, and then, another, and then by several in chorus. (1976 [1856]:140–141)

In other early sources, descriptions refer to the sounds that slaves made while working in the fields on plantations and farms or made by those who worked with animals (Southern and Wright 1990). It is noteworthy that in most of the early literature, the terminology for cry, call, holler, or whoop was used interchangeably; writers did not associate a specific term with a distinct context, function, or performance style. One of the reasons is that blacks in different geographical locations referred to the music by different names. According to Harold Courlander cries and calls of the open spaces were called corn field hollers, cotton field hollers, or just hollers (1963:82). In Alabama, the term *whooping* was used, whereas people in other regions referred to these musical sounds as "loud mouthing." While all the terms are still used, contemporary scholars have attempted to make distinctions between them. Whereas the street cry is an urban form usually sung to call attention to goods or services for sale (Epstein 1977:181; James 1973:6), the field holler is associated with slavery and/or rural farm life (Courlander 1963). David Evans (1978) explains that field hollers were very loosely structured unaccompanied songs sung by farm workers and other manual laborers. They often contained falsetto singing, moaning, humming, or whistling. Some had no words at all, while others might repeat a single verse over and over. Some had more developed texts. They dealt with working conditions, stubborn mules, the hot sun, and, inevitably, with the singer's woman.

Dance cry—the oldest and most vital of all cries—
performed when a person naturally gives out a
statement of joy while dancing.

Several descriptions have been written about the use of the cry, call, and holler in the post-Emancipation era and the early twentieth century. Eugene D. Genovese's interpretation regarding the significance of the holler is noteworthy. Like others, he believes that this form of music spread during and after Reconstruction, when work patterns fragmented. Hollers provided a counterpart to plantation work songs but ranged beyond a direct concern with labor to a concern with the most personal expressions of life's travail. As such, they created a piercing history of the impact of hardship and sorrow on solitary black men. They represented a burning negative statement of the blacks' desire for community in labor as well as in life generally. As positive expressions they provided a form for a highly individualistic self-expression among a people whose very collectivity desperately required methods of individual self-assertion in order to combat the debilitating thrust of slavery's paternalistic aggression (1974:324). Thomas V. Talley, a professor at Fisk University who was involved in some sociological investigations near Tuskegee, Alabama, during the early 1900s, gives an account of calls that he heard:

> In the afternoon, when the Negro laborers were going home from the fields and occasionally during the day, these laborers on one plantation would utter loud musical "calls" and these "calls" would be answered by musical responses from the laborers on other plantations. These calls and responses had no peculiar significance. They were only for whatever pleasure these Negroes found. . . . Dr. William H. Sheppard, many years a missionary in Congo, Africa, upon inquiry, tells me that similar calls and responses obtain there, though not so musical. He also tells me that the calls have a meaning there. There are calls and responses for those lost in the forest, for fire, for the approach of enemies, etc. These Alabama Negro calls, however, had no meaning, and yet the calls and responses so fitted into each other as to make a little complete tune. (1922:277–278)

Later in the account Talley, using musical transcriptions, describes the stylistic differences between calls in Alabama and Tennessee (1922:279–283).

The Classification of Cries, Calls, and Hollers
The research of Willis Laurence James (1970, 1973) and Harold Courlander (1963) is important, for these scholars are among the few who have attempted to classify the cry and call systematically. In "The Romance of the Negro Folk Cry in America" (1973), James uses cry as a catchall term to describe musical statements and sounds that have different functions in various contexts:

1. call—the most common: the sound produced by a man who gives orders to a group of men at work; a musical statement which asks something for or from someone else, or pronounces judgement;
2. street cry—the most significant, familiar, and self-respecting of all cries: a musical statement used to sell an item or product; can be regarded as a species of the work song;

3. religious cry—a subtle, musical use of the voice by a preacher in presenting a sermon;

4. field cry (corn field whoop)—a brief statement frequently heard in silent, open country; signifies a loneliness of spirit due to isolation of the worker, or serves as a signal to someone nearby, or merely as a bit of self-indulgence;

5. night cry—musical statement that gives a feeling of relaxation and self expression; may be performed at night while traveling at night as a personal serenade or as a signal in the dark;

6. dance cry—the oldest and most vital of all cries—performed when a person naturally gives out a statement of joy while dancing;

7. water cry, performed by workers who have served as boatmen, roustabouts, longshoremen, rafthaulers, and fishermen. (430–444)

In *Afro-American Music* (1970), James uses performance style as a basis for categorizing various types of cries—plain cry, florid cry, coloratura cry, and wordless cry—inferring that each can be used in other types of musical forms (also see discussion in Cureau 1980:19–20). Courlander (1963) bases his discussion on information obtained from performers in Alabama. Whereas the call is used to communicate messages of all kinds—to bring people in from the fields, to summon them to work, to attract the attention of a girl in the distance, to signal hunting dogs, or simply to make one's presence known—the cry is simply a form of self-expression, a vocalization of some emotion. It does not have to have a theme or fit into any kind of musical or formal structure. It is short and free and consists of a single music statement or a series of statements that reflect any number of moods—homesickness, loneliness, lovesickness, contentment, exuberance. A man working under the hot sun might give voice to such a cry on impulse, directing it to the world, or to the fields around him, or perhaps to himself. It might be filled with exuberance or melancholy. It might consist of a long "hoh-hoo," stretched out and embellished with intricate ornamentation of a kind virtually impossible to notate; or it might be a phrase like "I'm hot and hungry," or simply "pickin' cotton, yohhoo." Hinson states that hollers in North Carolina were short shouted songs embellished with falsetto phrasing and interrupted by yodel-like cries. As in the group work songs, hollers drew upon the body of traditional lyrics or were improvised by a singer while working. Some hollers had no words but were just complex combinations of sounds expressing one's state of mind or communicating a particular message to others (1978:1).

Although the cry, call, and holler are rarely performed as separate and distinct music types in modern culture, the performance style is still very much a part of the African American musical tradition, found, for example in the recordings of songs by Alan Lomax (1956). Not only are elements found in various religious forms as well, Evans (1978) believes that field hollers also contributed the basic vocal material to the early blues.

—JACQUELINE COGDELL DJEDJE

REFERENCES

Allen, William Francis. 1983 [1867]. "General Characteristics of Slave Music." In *Readings in Black American Music,* 2nd ed., ed. Eileen Southern, 149–174. New York: Norton.

Bailey, Ben E. 1992. "Music in Slave Era Mississippi." *The Journal of Mississippi History* 54(1):29–58.

Barrow, David C. 1882. "A Georgia Corn-Shucking." *The Century Magazine* 24(n.s.2):873–878.

Blassingame, John W. 1979 [1972]. *The Slave Community: Plantation Life in the Antebellum South.* Rev. and enl. ed. New York: Oxford University Press.

Botkin, Benjamin Albert. 1959 [1942]. Notes to *Negro Work Songs and Calls.* Library of Congress, Division of Music, Recording Laboratory AAFS L8. LP disk.

Browne, Ray B. 1954. "Some Notes on the Southern Holler." *Journal of American Folklore* (67):73–77.

Bufwack, Mary A., and Robert K. Oermann. 1993. *Finding Her Voice: The Saga of Women in Country Music.* New York: Crown.

Courlander, Harold. 1956. *Negro Folk Music of Alabama.* Folkways Records FE 4417.

————. 1963. *Negro Folk Music U.S.A.* New York: Columbia University Press.

Cureau, Rebecca. 1980. "Black Folklore, Musicology and Willis Laurence James." *Negro History Bulletin* 43(1):16–20.

Epstein, Dena J. 1977. *Sinful Tunes and Spirituals: Black Folk Music to the Civil War.* Urbana: University of Illinois Press.

Evans, David. 1978. Notes to *Let's Get Loose: Folk and Popular Blues Styles from the Beginnings to the Early 1940s.* New World Records NW 290. LP disk.

Genovese, Eugene D. 1974 [1972]. *Roll, Jordan, Roll: The World Slaves Made.* New York: Pantheon Books.

Hinson, Glenn. 1978. Notes to *Eight-Hand Sets and Holy Steps: Traditional Black Music of North Carolina.* North Carolina Department of Cultural Resources Crossroad C-101. Cassette.

Horstman, Dorothy. 1975. *Sing Your Heart Out, Country Boy.* Rev. ed. Nashville: Country Music Foundation Press.

James, Willis Laurence. 1970. *Afro-American Music: A Demonstration Recording by Dr. Willis James.* ASCH Records AA702. LP disk.

———. 1973 [1955]. "The Romance of the Negro Folk Cry in America." In *Mother Wit from the Laughing Barrel,* ed. Alan Dundes, 430–444. Englewood Cliffs, N.J.: Prentice-Hall.

Kingsbury, Paul, ed. 1996. *The Country Reader.* Nashville: Vanderbilt University Press and Country Music Foundation Press.

———. 1998. *The Encyclopedia of Country Music.* New York: Oxford University Press.

Levine, Lawrence W. 1977. *Black Culture and Black Consciousness: Afro-American Folk Thought from Slavery to Freedom.* New York: Oxford University Press.

Lomax, Alan. 1956 [1942]. *Afro-American Spirituals, Work Songs and Ballads,* record notes. Library of Congress, Division of Music, Recording Laboratory AAFS L3. LP disk.

Lornell, Christopher "Kip" 1978. *Non-Blues Secular Black Music,* record notes. BRI Records BRI 001. LP disk.

Malone, Bill C. 1985. *Country Music U.S.A.* Rev ed. Austin: University of Texas Press.

McCallum, Brenda. 1988. "Songs of Work and Songs of Worship: Sanctifying Black Unionism in the Southern City of Steel." *New York Folklore* 14(12):9–33.

"Negro Folk Songs." 1976 [1895]. *The Black Perspective in Music* 4(2):145–151.

Olmstead, Frederick Law. 1976 [1856]. "Negro Jodling: The Carolina Yell." *The Black Perspective in Music* 4(2):140–141.

Peabody, Charles. 1976 [1903]. "Notes on Negro Music." *The Black Perspective in Music* 4(2): 133–137.

Peterson, Richard, 1997. *Creating Country Music: Fabricating Authenticity.* Chicago: University of Chicago Press.

Porterfield, Nolan. 1979. *Jimmie Rodgers: The Life and Times of America's Blue Yodeller.* Urbana: University of Illinois Press.

Ramsey, Frederic. 1960. Notes to *Been Here and Gone.* Folkways Records FA 2659. LP disk.

Southern, Eileen. 1997 [1983, 1971]. *The Music of Black Americans: A History.* 3rd ed. New York: Norton.

Southern, Eileen, and Josephine Wright, comps. 1990. *African American Traditions in Song, Sermon, Tale, and Dance, 1600s–1920: An Annotated Bibliography of Literature, Collections, and Artworks.* Westport, Conn.: Greenwood Press.

Talley, Thomas V. 1922. *Negro Folk Rhymes: Wise and Otherwise.* New York: Macmillan Co.

Townsend, Charles, 1976. *San Antonio Rose: The Life and Times of Bob Wills.* Urbana: University of Illinois Press.

Whitburn, Joel, 1994. *Top Country Singles, 1944–93.* Menominee Falls, Wisc.: Record Research.

Wolfe, Charles K. 1976. *Tennessee Strings: The Story of Country Music in Tennessee.* Knoxville: The University of Tennessee Press.

———. 1989. "Thomas Talley's Negro Folk Rhymes." *Tennessee Folklore Society Bulletin* 53(3):104–111.

———. 1999. *A Good Natured Riot: The Birth of the Grand Ole Opry.* Nashville: Vanderbilt University Press and the Country Music Hall of Fame.

Gender and Sexuality

Susan C. Cook (United States)
Andra McCartney (Canada)

Gender as a Defining Category of Difference
Gender Ideologies in the Nineteenth and Early Twentieth Centuries
Research into Music and Gender
Music and Gender within Specific Contexts

Gender as an analytic category and interpretive focus has become increasingly central to music research of all kinds. The concept of gender is generally understood to describe the means or systems by which cultures and social groups create, display, transmit, and enforce biological sexual difference; that is, gender theory describes how a culture makes sense of what it means to be male and female. Given the almost universal practice of patriarchy, which gives some men power over all women and many other men, gender roles typically enact and thereby perpetuate unequal power relations. Thus behaviors and other social practices described as masculine are not only different from those identified as feminine but typically carry more cultural prestige and power.

GENDER AS A DEFINING CATEGORY OF DIFFERENCE

In North America, the ideologies of masculinity frequently incorporate a fear of the feminine, because femininity, like the female sex, is less socially valued and valuable. Such gender imbalance further shapes other cultural relationships, especially assumptions about social power and worth. The influential Cartesian mind/body duality accords greater significance and importance to the rational mind—typically understood as "masculine"—over the irrational and "feminized" body. Similarly, notions of the "civilized" and civilization have been masculinized, and male "primitives," including most men of color, have been placed in subordinate or feminized positions regardless of their biological sex (Torgovnick 1997). As well, given the considerable political and cultural power the United States has in comparison to Canada, Canadian scholars of either sex may thus find themselves in feminized positions vis-à-vis their U.S. colleagues. On the other hand, recent research on Canadian concert music (McCartney 1999) indicates the development of images of rugged northernness by Canadian composers that construct Canadian music as particularly masculine in relation to the music of a feminized United States.

Gender roles, while often portrayed as dichotomies or opposites, are highly mutable and frequently contradictory, changing over time and place and in response to social realities of all kinds. Although gender roles may be understood as normative and self-evident by their cultural practitioners, the explication and interpretation of the gendering process requires great care and contextualization to understand how power relationships function and change on a day-to-day basis and over time. For example, men and women may share roles and attributes and regularly or occasionally take part in certain behaviors or activities typically assigned to the other sex. However, some gender transgressions may be more permissible than others, depending on other sociopolitical realities. Acknowledging and exploring gender dynamics allows scholars to see behaviors and activities—music making among them—as socially and culturally shaped and shaping rather than biologically determined and essential.

The academic field of women's studies, which grew out of the political activism of second-wave feminism in the 1970s, is largely responsible for the scholarly attention paid to gender and its various processes. Many early women's studies scholars came from the social sciences (sociology, anthropology, and psychology), literary studies, or history, and their work, in its interdisciplinary nature, frequently drew upon the new critical and theoretical perspectives of poststructuralism, post-Freudian psychoanalytical thought, and other postcolonial and postmodern theoretical perspectives.

While much early feminist scholarship, in its desire to both identify and remedy patriarchal practices, was often involved in pointed sociopolitical critiques, feminist thought itself faced challenges about its own exclusionary, even at times simplistic, practices. Working-class women, women of color, and lesbians demonstrated how gender rarely, if ever, functions as an isolated cultural construction. Rather, as a dynamic process, gender intersects with other cultural constructions such as race, ethnicity, class, sexuality, ability, and country of origin (Collins 1990; Driedger 1991; Higginbotham 1992; Hull, Scott, and Smith 1982; O'Brien 1989; Rich 1983; Terborg-Penn and Harley 1978). These categories of difference act upon each other to create a complex web of interrelationships of power and prestige. Thus, for example, race shapes the practice of gender in that women of white European descent, while inferior to their male counterparts, have many more claims to power than African American or First Nation women. And "whiteness" no less than "blackness" is a socially constituted category whose meaning has changed over time (Hill 1997).

Such a nuanced understanding of gender has been particularly important for research focusing on North America, with its history of unequal power relations among indigenous peoples and European colonials (Valaskakis 1993), the U.S. experience of slavery and institutionalized racism, and the dominance of the United States as a political power. Current gender theory challenges scholars to acknowledge and account for their own biases and how their experience of the normative practices of their own cultures, especially the culture of academe, can blind them to the many unequal workings of power from which they might benefit (Christensen 1997; Embree 1994; Harris 1991).

The recognition of the intersection of gender with other cultural constructions in the formation of identity has also influenced forms of representation in feminist writings. Québecois feminist writers began to integrate French psychoanalytic theory and semiotics into an aesthetic of writing the body (Gagnon 1989). Experiences of complex, raced, gendered, and classed identities inform innovative theoretical approaches in the cross-genre writing of contemporary feminist authors in Canada (Williamson 1993).

Although early gender research focused almost entirely on how women came to understand and act out their feminine roles, men have gender, too; beliefs about male behavior, manliness, and masculinity were and are constructed and normalized over time and are frequently racially charged. White masculinity thus exists in tension not only with notions of femininity and homophobic fears of effeminacy but also with black masculinity (Bederman 1995; Carby 1998; Harper 1996). Explorations of the gendering of men are increasing, often through the growing presence of men's studies, but women still carry the burden of gender, so work that makes gender central to its interpretive analysis remains overwhelmingly focused on women or female subjectivity.

Gay and lesbian scholarship, which emerged in the 1980s, and "queer theory" of the 1990s problematized gender further by foregrounding sexuality as another kind of difference and critiquing presumptions of "compulsory heterosexuality" while raising issues about the social meanings of the erotic, pleasure, and desire (Lorde 1984; Rich 1983; Sedgwick 1985, 1990). This research starts from the premise expressed by Foucault (1978) and others that sexuality, which has normatively been understood as heterosexuality, is culturally defined, and its practices have changed over time and place and complicate the workings of other categories of difference. While some scholars such as Butler (1990) question whether biological sex difference exists or is itself another cultural construction, other scholars have explored how the presumptions of heterosexuality as the "normal," and thus only, mode of sexual desire influence cultural behaviors and practices by both heterosexuals and individuals who define themselves as outside the domain and privileges of heterosexuality.

Music education researchers, especially in Canada, have also begun to analyze how gender affects the formation of musicians. These studies include the role of informal cultural contexts such as the children's playground in the development and maintenance of children's songs (Caputo 1990) and institutional contexts, such as the mentoring relationship as it affects the formation of contemporary composers and performers (Lamb 1999).

GENDER IDEOLOGIES IN THE NINETEENTH AND EARLY TWENTIETH CENTURIES

Although musical practices themselves reinforce sociocultural hierarchies of power, music making in the United States and Canada has historically been a feminized activity. Due largely to the constructions of nineteenth-century gender ideologies, in which middle- and upper-class men and women were understood as acting in separate and unequal arenas (often described as public and private spheres), certain kinds of music making and music appreciation came to be understood as activities appropriate to middle- and upper-class femininity as "feminine accomplishments." Training in female seminaries, colleges, and even within public coeducational universities identified music—typically singing or playing the piano within the home and teaching amateurs—as women's work, not unlike embroidery, quilting, or the later academic discipline of home economics. Furthermore, growing out of nineteenth-century European American notions of music's transcendent power, certain kinds of music became associated with moral uplift, which similarly was a white woman's purview, given her position as the guardian of domesticity and goodness within the middle- and upper-class home.

Men, especially in countries like Canada and the United States, which were still being actively colonized or settled, required practical training in business and agriculture; the arts and other recreational pursuits were luxuries thus left to women with class privilege who had the resources of leisure time and money. This separation of men's business and women's arts may have been more extreme in recently settled areas such as the American West and Canada and less obvious in established urban centers. For instance, in Canada prior to 1920 women's participation in major orchestras was significant, whereas many U.S. orchestras of the same period barred female participation (Keillor 1995). After 1920, women began to be barred from Canadian orchestras as well. Yet men still maintained a great deal of power within this feminized space, because gender ideology permitted them to make musical activities their public careers, something not readily possible for women. Thus men remained the most privileged performers and teachers, especially in academe.

Particular musical activities, such as the powerful roles of conductor or composer of large-scale symphonic and operatic repertoires, remained largely off-limits to women of all classes as well as to nonwhite or working-class men. Women who challenged these practices and sought public careers as performers or composers often did

"Acting like a man" rendered a female musician open
to criticism regarding her femininity and sexuality;
those who persisted in masculine careers often found
themselves judged abnormal.

FIGURE 1   American composer Amy Beach
(1867–1944) was an active composer and performer in the United States and Europe in the
early twentieth century. Photo from the collection at the Library of Congress.

so at great personal cost. "Acting like a man" rendered a female musician open to criticism regarding her femininity and sexuality; those who persisted in masculine careers
often found themselves judged abnormal.

With the growing power of the nineteenth-century suffrage movement in the
United States and Canada, antiwomen attitudes in general became more prevalent
and fears about the feminization of culture more acute (Douglas 1988). Similarly,
the turn of the twentieth century witnessed the earliest scholarly discussions of homosexuality and homosexuals, or "gender inverts" as Richard Kraft-Ebbing called them.
This gave rise to homophobic and misogynistic beliefs that attempted to counter fears
of music making as a female, and thus effeminizing, activity (Brett et al. 1994; Parsons
Smith 1994).

The granting of suffrage in the United States in 1920 and in Canada between 1916
and 1940 (as suffrage was granted separately at the federal and provincial levels), along
with other political and educational reforms, helped bring about real changes in many
women's lives. Although white middle- and upper-class women were frequently the
greatest beneficiaries of these changes, as the twentieth century progressed, women
gained greater—if rarely full—parity with men in many public and professional arenas
of music. Women composers of modern concert music, for example, were no longer a
rarity, and a number, including Violet Archer and Barbara Pentland in Canada and Amy
Beach (figure 1) and Miriam Gideon in the United States, attained recognition.

RESEARCH INTO MUSIC AND GENDER

As was true of scholarship in virtually all disciplines of the humanities and arts before
the advent of women's studies, music research took as a presumptive point of departure
male behavior, typically the public activities of male performers and composers. The
very real contributions and activities of women, which often took place within the
home or in the context of amateur music making, remained invisible, inaudible, and
thus inferior by scholarly standards. Although early research, especially in folklore and
ethnomusicology, identified complementary or separate musical activities among men
and women, it rarely explored these differences further or identified how musical
power and prestige were negotiated or how musical practices themselves reproduced or
reinforced how men and women understood their social-sexual roles.

The recognition of gender as a force in culture and thus in musical life emerged as
disciplines responded to the political influences of the 1970s women's movement, the
subsequent creation of the academic discipline of women's studies, and other challenges to traditional paradigms of thought. Although music scholarship, especially in
music history and music theory, lagged behind other areas of the arts and humanities
in incorporating feminist theories, today there is a growing body of research that identifies gender as a perspective that cannot be ignored if music scholarship makes any
claim at being substantive, complete, and reflecting the multiple realities of human
lives and cultures.

Such research starts from the assumption that both music activities and behaviors are shaped by gender practices and that these musical practices themselves further shape cultural beliefs. What men and women *do* in music matters; it influences how they understand themselves—and are understood by others—as gendered subjects. In tandem with other categories of difference, gender ideologies have helped dictate who has had access to music's cultural power through training and use of specific instruments, what repertoires have been created and valued, how listeners participate in or consume musics, and how musical activities or individual performers have been financially sustained and supported. Furthermore, feminist scholars also recognize that musical scholarship and its methodologies have been marked by gendered notions of power and privilege. Topics or activities deemed especially worthy of scholarly study have typically been those areas of music making understood as either most powerful and important, thus "masculine," or most inaccessible to female participation or participation by "feminized" individuals whether male or female.

As a corrective to the scholarly inattention to women's culture and women's music making, some gender and feminist work within historical musicology and ethnomusicology provides a compensatory approach that centers on women as the musical subjects, typically as performers or composers within the already privileged concert repertoires or in geographical areas or genres already explored by ethnomusicologists. This approach continues as female participation grows within music professions (Block 1992; Bowers and Tick 1986; Groh 1991; Herndon and Ziegler 1990; Keeling 1989; Kennedy and Polansky 1996; Koskoff 1989; Neuls-Bates 1996; Pendle 1997). Along these same lines, recording companies early on began to feature or single out the work of women composers, publishing companies devoted themselves to finding lost and out-of-print work, and contemporary women composers, performers, and scholars in the United States and Canada organized professional societies such as American Women Composers, the Association of Canadian Women Composers/L'association des femmes compositeurs Canadiennes, and, later, the International Alliance for Women in Music to promote their work and focus attention on female creativity (Boone 1984; Hall 1984). Scholarly conferences began to provide important public forums for a wide range of research and performance (Boroff 1987; Cash 1991; Drakich et al. 1995). Compensatory histories have also emerged in feminist studies of jazz, popular, and folk music (Kivi 1992; Sawa 1991; Smith and Alstrup 1995). In addition, journalistic literature of female popular, jazz, and classical musicians has also increased (Diamond 2000).

Other groundbreaking work (Clément 1988; Cook and Tsou 1994; Koskoff 1989; McClary 1991; Pegley 1998; Solie 1993b) began to challenge the norms of musical scholarship further by identifying new kinds of female music making or demonstrating how musical genres and specific instrumental and texted works can encode and transmit misogynistic and patriarchal ideologies through musical means. Much of this work drew on contemporaneous literary theory and critical historical methodologies that posit multiple readings or interpretations of any given work or focus on discourse strategies that examine the shaping power of language and texted materials—informal and formal, written and spoken—that further invest works and activities with social meaning.

While ethnomusicology's recognition of music practices as reflecting social beliefs and structures influenced musicological scholarship, feminist ethnomusicologists turned to new anthropological perspectives that emphasized the multiplicity of social practices and the need for self-reflexive scholarly positions that allow the voices of cultural informants to emerge more clearly in dialogue with the researcher, and they generally challenged preconceptions about ethnography and fieldwork (Abu-Lughod 1990; Barz and Cooley 1997). This dialogic research explores various forms of positioning, such as researchers approaching each other as informants to explore their gender and sexuality in relation to musical performances (Pegley and Caputo 1994) or scholars exploring their own gender and sexual formation in relation to music making (Lamb 1997).

Recent ethnographic work in Canada has taken gender as well as other forms of identity into account in the research process. The comparison of several oral histories, for example, can allow a researcher to compare clearly articulated gender issues discussed by some informants with those that are enacted (but not articulated) by others (Diamond 2000). Some recent biographical work on women musicians interprets the oral histories of several informants simultaneously, defined according to a similar identity as Canadian musicians (Kivi 1992), Québécois composers (Lefebvre 1991), or Canadian electroacoustic composers (McCartney 1995). This strategy allows the researcher to discuss similar experiences and to create a heightened sense of community through dialogue among the informants, while also noting aspects of experience that are not shared. Informants are sometimes included in the writing and editorial process, allowing them more control over how their voices are heard (Diamond 2000).

Feminist ethnomusicology reexamined methodological tenets such as the structuralist binary of public and private, sought to redefine the place or scholarly role of the ethnomusicologist, and called for a great attention to gender throughout the field of ethnomusicology (Jones 1991; Koskoff 1993; Monson 1997; Post 1994; Robertson 1993). Scholars have also drawn attention to the important early research carried out by female scholars such as Frances Densmore, Alice Fletcher, and Natalie Curtis, work that was often undervalued at the time because the women did not (and could not) possess the necessary anthropological or musical professional credentials (Myers 1992; Rahkonen 1998).

Recent writing in ethnomusicology has also focused on the ethnographic position of researchers and the challenges of writing about gender in cross-cultural contexts (Diamond 2000). Ethnomusicological projects also give researchers the opportunity to study how traditional forms survive and change in new contexts as ethnic groups migrate into different North American communities. In these studies, gender can be analyzed in terms of how it intersects with the traditions of the country of origin and the expectations of the new culture (Cohen 1987, 1989).

In addition, explorations into listening as an activity with its own history and cultural context suggests that the relationships between musical works and their listeners or consumers, while complicated and highly individual, are also gendered. The action of listening may provide a crucial place for individuals to construct a sense of self that can both reproduce or contest dominant beliefs about gender and sexuality (Horowitz 1994; Hubbs 1996; Rabinowitz 1993). As literary scholars have theorized about "resisting readers" who actively read against a narrative and its claims of truth, so too listeners may choose strategies that allow them to redefine or resist the masculinist or heterosexist presumptions of certain performers or specific musical practices and activities to fit their own self-definitions (Coates 1997; Douglas 1995; Ehrenreich et al. 1992; Fetterley 1978; Ortega 1998; Rycenga 1997). Listeners repeatedly find ways to use particular kinds of music for their own ends, as in the phenomenon of Riot Grrls, young women who redefine the aggressive masculinist discourse strategies of punk rock music to empower their own actions (Cateforis and Humphreys 1997; Wald 1998) (figure 2). Other consumers have created separatist genres such as women's music, whose often explicitly lesbian identity not only influences musical structures and texts but also determines how this kind of popular music is marketed and under what conditions it might be heard (Lont 1992; Post 1995; Tilchen 1984).

FIGURE 2   Based in Olympia, Washington, the band Sleater-Kinney exemplifies the spirit of the riot-grrrl movement. Their songs often question traditional notions of success and express both anger and emotional vulnerability. Photo by John Clark, courtesy the BMI Archives.

MUSIC AND GENDER WITHIN SPECIFIC CONTEXTS

The following discussion is intended to be suggestive of the range of work, much of it interdisciplinary, that explicitly addresses the dynamic role of gender within the many musical practices found in North America.

Concert music

Some of the earliest works that made women's music making a central focus were biographical studies of women composers and performers of European American concert music (Ammer 1980; Eastman and McGee 1983; Proctor 1980; Tick 1983). In Canada, a notable work honoring composer Violet Archer (Qureshi et al. 1995) attends to issues of voice, authority, and representation, grounded in the experiences of Archer's former students and colleagues, many of whom have contributed to the volume. Further research recovered the lives and activities of African American women in the United States, exploring how they negotiated the cultural constructions of femininity as well as race within the privileged concert repertoires (Brown 1993; Green 1983; Handy 1992; McGinty 1992; Wright 1992). Four notable biographical studies are those of U.S. composers Ruth Crawford (Tick 1997), Amy Beach (Block 1998), and Pauline Oliveros (Mockus 1999), and early feminist musicologist Sophie Drinker (Solie 1993a). All four studies provide complicated explications of gender, sexuality, racial ideologies, class privilege, and national identity as central to specific musical practices, the writing of music history, and the musical lives of their subjects. The careers and writings of male composers of "classical" music have also provided a means for exploring various relationships between masculinity and musicality and musical style (Parsons Smith 1994; Spizizen 1993; Tick 1993).

Not unlike feminist scholars who challenged the systems of cultural prestige by celebrating quilt making, romance novels, and other aspects of "woman's culture" that had been ignored, music scholars began to examine and reinterpret undervalued repertoires of European American music, such as so-called parlor or salon music and magazine music, and venues, such as settlement houses, where women exercised a great deal of power or where women acted as primary consumers (Feldman 1990; Green 1998; Key 1995; Koza 1991; Lang 1998; Miller 1994; Tyler 1992). Similarly, the neglected area of patronage has received attention, acknowledging the crucial roles women played in the creation and maintenance of music life as patrons or through music clubs, such as the Women's Musical Club of Toronto, begun in 1898 (Elliott 1997; Locke and Barr 1997), the Winnipeg club, inaugurated in 1894, or the Hamilton club, the oldest in Canada, begun in 1889 [see The Toronto Women's Musical Club, p. 1207]. Often women's musical clubs in Canada are the oldest surviving musical organizations in their communities, providing scholarships to young musicians and hosting concerts in which Canadian and women performers are prominent. While acknowledging women's continued inferior political status and how their patronage often sustained musical repertoires that were closed to female creators, this research sheds light on underexplored institutional structures and helps refine and redefine issues of female agency and power, as well as demonstrating how inextricably linked gender systems are with the systems of race and class.

Apart from the examinations of women's lives and activities, other studies have explored how aspects of music life and culture have been talked and written about in ways that show the gendering of music within larger social frameworks and practices. Such critical interpretations of these discourse strategies include how modern music maintained its masculinity in the face of feminized culture, how technology has become a masculine domain that has influenced the consumption of hi-fi stereos in the 1950s as well as the current accessibility of electronic and computer music composition, and how the academic field of music study perpetuates exclusive if not misogynistic practices (Detels 1994; Keightley 1996; McCartney 1994a, 1994b; Theberge 1997; "Toward a Feminist Music Theory" 1994) [See Technology and Media, p. 235].

TRACK 2

Native American/First Nation musics

Ethnomusicologists interested in exploring the gender-music dynamic have turned to the many differentiated musical practices of Native Americans and First Nation

Rock music's emphasis on electric guitar and drums—both instruments still largely viewed as inappropriate for girls to learn—continues to mark it as a music men make and women listen to.

peoples. Many of these practices are sex-segregated, although often understood within the culture as complementary rather than separatist (Cavanagh 1989). Women may have control over specific ritual or life-cycle celebrations in which they exercise enormous power while still being forbidden from other music-making activities such as ceremonial drum circles played at pan-Indian powwows. Following a path not unlike that of compensatory scholarship found elsewhere, ethnomusicologists have often explored the activities of individual women (Giglio 1994; Little Coyote and Giglio 1997; Vander 1988) as well as specifically female-identified practices such as puberty rituals (Keeling 1989; Shapiro and Talamantez 1986). Other scholars have attempted to document how women's musical roles have changed over time, acknowledging that musical practices and gender are both systems in flux, changing in response to social and political realities. In some cases, scholars identify how women have adopted formerly male-identified roles, such as drumming, and how the clear differentiation of musical behaviors along sex lines has blurred or eroded as the activities of men and women have changed (Gonzalez 1998; Hatton 1986; Vander 1988).

Popular musics

The postmodern critic Andreas Huyssen (1986) has suggested that in the West mass culture—or practices and activities associated with popular taste—presents another feminized cultural space. Popular culture, by definition, does not partake of the timelessness associated with "high art," itself a historically constructed category, but rather embodies novelty, changeability, faddishness, and malleability, all attributes often associated with women and contributing to their lesser cultural value (Levine 1988). This perspective can be borne out in music studies in which popular musics have only recently received the kind of scholarly attention presumed for so-called classical or concert repertoires. For the purpose of this study, the term *popular music* is used in the most inclusive way possible to encompass a wide variety of traditions and repertoires that have been judged outside the normative limits of concert and classical Western music, for example, Anglo-American balladry, sheet music and popular song, blues, jazz, rock and roll, country, klezmer, and so on.

Several women such as La Bolduc in Québec earlier in this century and, more recently, Rita MacNeil from Canada's Maritimes have become prominent public figures through their participation in the area of folk-derived songwriting. Compensatory histories of female folk musicians situate their work within a genre that has often been defined in terms of traditionally male occupations such as lumbering and fishing. Studies using extensive interviews and unpublished materials have rediscovered the lives and work of such musicians as Katherine Gallagher (Tye 1995) and La Rena Clark (Rahn and Fowke 1994). The association of folk music with political consciousness, from seventeenth-century broadsides to contemporary women-identified music, makes this genre a potent location for the recognition and elaboration of gender issues. From 1961, with the start of the Mariposa festival, a web of independent folk festivals has grown in Canada to support this music.

FIGURE 3   The Amazon chorus was an innovation of mid-nineteenth-century popular theater that provided the largely male audience with a mass display of the female form. This image, which was printed in the *National Police Gazette* on 15 November 1884, had the following caption: "Walking into their Affections: How a manager at Tombstone, Arizona, utilized his pretty waiter girls as Marching Amazons."

Popular musics, in order to be indeed popular and populist, have often relied on amateur music making, industrialization, and changing mass media, such as the growth of the sheet music industry, mass production of the parlor piano in the last decades of the nineteenth century, and the emergence of recorded sound technology in the early twentieth century. The domestic venues of popular music often encouraged female participation, and thus women found opportunities as creators of popular song or even as public performers within popular entertainments such as vaudeville. Women still participated in clearly gendered and frequently sexualized ways visible in the kinds of repertoire chosen, how they learned repertoire, and the kinds of roles they might play on stage (Antelyes 1994; Cook 1994; Rodger 1998) (figure 3). However, while adhering to gender norms, situations could arise that demonstrate the malleability of gender and suggest how women may adapt or redefine notions of masculinity and femininity in their participation. For example, in a family without sons, a firstborn daughter might join her father as a singer, or during times of war, when male musicians were drafted, female instrumentalists might find greater—and unusual—opportunities for public performance (Tucker 1996, 1997, 1998).

Female instrumentalists often faced the same kinds of prohibitions that faced women in so-called high art repertoires (MacLeod 1993). Singing and playing the piano remained the most appropriate ways for women to take part in popular musics, and singers, male or female, were frequently not accorded the same prestige as instrumentalists were. Women who played the saxophone, drums, upright bass, or other "masculine" instruments faced almost insurmountable difficulties in pursuing professional careers except within the context of all-women ensembles (Kivi 1992). Rock music's emphasis on electric guitar and drums—both instruments still largely viewed as inappropriate for girls to learn—continues to mark it as a music men make and women listen to (McSwain 1995; Waksman 1999.) Even women singers who pursue the masculinized vocal genres of rap, heavy metal, or punk encounter opposition coming from their attempts to cross gendered musical lines (Berry 1994; Cateforis and Humphreys 1997). An increasing reliance on MIDI technology in popular music also raises questions of gender in contemporary technology-based musical education (Pegley 1995), in which MIDI technology is often perceived as a masculine domain. Regardless of its challenges and limitations, popular music, in its many varieties and musical possibilities, remains particularly attractive and accessible to women.

Writing on popular musics—both informal and formal—while understandably embodying a compensatory history approach initially (Cooper 1996; Dahl 1984; Douglas 1995; Gaar 1992; McDonnell and Powers 1995; O'Brien 1996; O'Dair 1997),

FIGURE 4   Queen Latifah, a prominent and highly successful rap artist since the early 1990s, has advocated equality and unity within the black community through her music. Photo by Randee St. Nicholas, courtesy the BMI Archives.

continues to reflect a separate-yet-not-equal practice as visible in special "women-only" issues of *Rolling Stone* or other journals and magazines devoted to specific kinds of popular musics. Although such publications acknowledge a female presence, the kind of separate treatment popular female performers receive marks them as not central or crucial to the continuation of the genre as a whole (Aparicio 1998; Peraino 1998). If they can be relegated to one issue of a magazine a year or to a sole chapter in a book, they do not need to be integrated into an entire study, and thus the gender issues that the presence of women raise remain marginalized, as do the contested meanings and multiple behaviors of masculinity.

The popular traditions of blues, gospel, and rhythm and blues (and later hip-hop and rap) provided women, most often African American, with continued career opportunities, although ones still marked by race and gender. Some of the earliest popular recording stars in the United States were black women blues singers whose success and performative power called into question their repertoires, which might seem to perpetuate images of women as passive victims (Carby 1990 [1986]; Harrison 1988) [see BLUES, p. 637; HIP-HOP AND RAP, p. 692]. Similarly, women as gospel performers, although often prohibited from preaching in the pulpit, might find their music making a place of power from which to reconstruct gender behaviors (Carby 1991; Kirk-Duggan 1997). Rap is frequently depicted in the mainstream popular press as an undifferentiated kind of music almost exclusively voicing black male aggression and misogynist violence, but female rap artists have constantly presented alternative models of black femininity (figure 4). While relying on rap's musical and textural modes, these female creators subvert beliefs about femininity and musicianship, masculinity and racial difference and call into question simplistic and reductive approaches to rap as a musical category (Berry 1994; Gaunt 1995, 1997; Keyes 1993; Rose 1994).

Jazz has attained significant scholarly and cultural prestige, and compensatory histories (Dahl 1984; Gourse 1996) have argued for the important contributions of women performers, arrangers, and composers. More recently, scholars have begun to explore jazz's complicated racial meanings and roles in the changing ideologies of black manhood and white masculinity as well as addressing the complicated issues facing black women, whose public presence has often been controversial (Carby 1998; Cook 1992; Davis 1998; Four the Moment 1989; Monson 1995; Peretti 1992).

Rock music, loosely defined, has been an especially powerful kind of popular music in this century, one that allows for many explorations regarding the connections between music and identity. While women have played enormously important roles as performers and consumers of rock-based musics, as with most other traditions, rock remains a male-dominated field as well as an industry that is still largely controlled by white Americans. Likewise, within the emerging field of popular music study, scholars have overwhelmingly focused on rock-based genres to the exclusion of other genres and popular musics existing before 1960. Some of the earliest scholarship on rock music came from sociologists who recognized the importance of this new kind of popular music in the courtship activities of adolescents (Horton 1956–1957). More recently, scholars have examined the ways in which rock music helps individuals construct and identify themselves as sexualized and gendered beings (Frith 1996; Pegley and Caputo 1994; Shepherd 1991; Wald 1998; Walser 1993) (figure 5). Several recent scholarly collections have specifically brought gender to the forefront by examining connoisseurship, consumption, and the musical sounds themselves (Swiss et al. 1998; Whiteley 1997).

The creation of MTV in the United States (1981) and MuchMusic in Canada (1984) and the growing importance of music videos have provided other means to examine and critique the gendered meanings and strategies of rock and other kinds of popular music [see MUCHMUSIC AND MUSIQUEPLUS, p. 250]. Although many music

FIGURE 5   Poison (L-R: Bret Michaels, singer; Bobby Dall, bass; Rikki Rockett, drums; C. C. Deville, guitar), who reunited for a reunion tour in 1999, typified the glam side of the heavy metal scene in the late 1980s and 1990s. Photo courtesy the BMI Archives.

videos have been widely criticized for their highly eroticized images of women and depictions of misogynist violence, this new media can provide women performers such as Cyndi Lauper, Queen Latifah, and Annie Lennox with the means to present, challenge, and subvert ideologies about public performance, musical power, and femininity (Berry 1994; Lewis 1990; Roberts 1996; Sawchuk 1989). Analysis of music television stations such as MTV and MuchMusic reveals how programming decisions in these institutions both reflect and maintain gendered and raced categories within each country (Pegley 1999).

Country music has provided a way for male and female performers, typically white, to challenge class presumptions. Although widely popular with listening audiences, country music remains a marginalized genre, a music often satirized for its lack of class status and its connection with the undervalued and "backward" South. Indeed, country music's initial self-definition in the 1940s as "country and western" was a means to legitimate its lower-class roots through connections with the then-popular western cowboy hero, whose positive image of masculinity replaced that of the uneducated southern hillbilly (figure 6). Recent scholarship demonstrates how country music provides another means to explore the multiple intersections of gender, class, and race. Women both as consumers and as popular performers continue to rework and negotiate the multiple oppressions of their lives, often creating powerful subversive strategies in the face of the contradictions of gender, class, and regional ethnicity (Bufwack and Oermann 1993; Lang 1998; Wilson 1998).

FIGURE 6   Clint Black, one of the most successful country and western singers of the 1990s, in a pose that invokes a rugged, clean-cut masculinity and country roots. Photo by Jim McGuire, courtesy the BMI Archives.

Ethnic-identified musics

The North American continent, once believed to be predominantly English-speaking, Anglo-identified, and Christian, is now understood to be multicultural, and, especially in its large urban areas such as Toronto and New York City, it displays a marked variety of ethnic practices that further reveal a range of behaviors and responses to assimilation and retention. Ethnic musics have received growing scholarly attention and recognition for the ways in which they construct ethnic identities among recently emigrated peoples to Canada and the United States as well as in the descendants of immigrants wishing to reclaim an ethnic heritage. Many of these musics reflect the process of crossover, which suggests the fuzzy, ambiguous borders of both ethnic categories and musical genres themselves (Anzaldúa 1987; Brackett 1994; Liera-Schwichtenberg 1998).

FIGURE 7   Cuban born singer Celia Cruz is often referred to as the queen of salsa. She began her performing career in the United States with Tito Puente's band and was awarded a National Medal of the Arts in 1994 for her services to music. Photo courtesy the BMI Archives.

Once again gender acts as part of the overall shaping process, often in tension with beliefs about change and the need to be faithful to past traditions.

The musics of Latin America (itself an ambiguous category that subsumes many different ethnic and national practices) have been influential in North American musical and theatrical traditions although often in ways that reinscribe gendered and racial stereotypes about "macho" masculinity and sexually available femininity (Sandoval-Sanchez 1999). Among Puerto Rican communities, the music of salsa reflects through its continual transformation the complex constructions of national and ethnic identity. As Aparicio (1998) cogently demonstrates, it is a rich musical practice that presents contradictions and tensions between traditional patriarchal beliefs and practices and the presence and popularity of female performers such as Celia Cruz, who reconstruct salsa as a space for women to negotiate femininity and masculinity (figure 7). *Conjunto,* a music associated with the Mexican American, or Tejano, communities in Texas, similarly has become a musical space for testing patriarchal practices and ethnic identity, as seen in the popularity of the Tejana singer Selena (Liera-Schwichtenberg 1998; Valdez and Halley 1996) [see TEJANO MUSICA, p. 770].

In Asian American communities, which reflect a wide variety of national and regional practices, karaoke is often central to celebrations of ethnic identity. The popularity and specific practices of karaoke reflect gender beliefs regarding the public sphere, access to technology, and maintenance of a heterosexual social order (Lum 1996; Wong 1994).

A variety of Jewish musical practices reflects the growing diversity within conservative and reformed traditions and separatist orthodox groups such as Hasidim. The growing presence of women in positions of power as rabbis and cantors in Reformed Judaism has called into question traditional beliefs about the suspect power of the female voice (Koskoff 1993, 1995; Slobin 1989). The resurgence of klezmer, a music associated with East European Jewish wedding practices and performed in North America in the early decades of this century, has provoked discussions about the presence of female musicians in what traditionally was a male-only tradition as well as about the construction of Jewish masculinity and heterosexuality (Baade 1998) [see JEWISH MUSIC, p. 933].

Dance

While central to much popular music and frequently part of many Native American and First Nation rituals, dance, as an embodied activity with its own movement language and possibility for metaphorical meaning, remains underexplored. This lack of scholarly attention reflects another legacy of the Cartesian mind/body hierarchy, as dance so clearly resides in the feminized body (Cook 1999). As scholars rightly suggest, however, dance practices and the discourses surrounding them have been crucial to understanding racial ideologies and the exoticized "Other" in North America (Cook 1998; Desmond 1997; Frith 1996). As has been suggested regarding the activity of listeners and fans, dance often provides an important site for negotiating and subverting the social constructions of race, gender, and sexuality (Gaunt 1998; McRobbie 1984; Ventura 1985) [see DANCE, p. 206].

The recognition of gender as a socially shaping force that is itself shaped by historical, political, and social contexts effectively challenges all modes of research. While gender analysis cannot be claimed to be part of all current musical scholarship, a growing number of scholars recognizes that gender marks the activities they explore in some way, and whether they choose to make it central to their analysis or not, it remains an acknowledged force with which to be reckoned. Scholars who ignore gender completely can be held accountable for presenting skewed and distorted analyses of musical activities and for being blind to the workings of power within musical systems. As scholars continue to refine and rework theoretical understandings of how femininities and masculinities are constructed and reconstructed, performed and acted upon in different times and places, they underscore music's centrality to that shaping process. Music and music making emerge as central to the way individuals understand themselves as social beings in relationship to others.

REFERENCES

Abu-Lughod, Leila. 1990. "Can There Be a Feminist Ethnography?" *Women and Performance* 5(1): 7–27.

Ammer, Christine. 1980. *Unsung: A History of Women in American Music.* Westport, Conn.: Greenwood Press.

Antelyes, Peter. 1994. "Red Hot Mamas: Bessie Smith, Sophie Tucker and the Ethnic Maternal Voice in American Popular Song." In *Embodied Voices: Representing Female Vocality in Western Culture,* ed. Leslie C. Dunn and Nancy A. Jones, 212–229. New York: Cambridge University Press.

Anzaldúa, Gloria. 1987. *Borderlands/La Frontera: The New Mestiza.* San Francisco: Spinsters/Aunt Lute.

Aparicio, Frances R. 1998. *Listening to Salsa: Gender, Latin Popular Music, and Puerto Rican Cultures.* Middletown, Conn.: Wesleyan University Press.

Baade, Christina L. 1998. "Jewzak and Heavy Shtetl: Creating Identity and Asserting Authenticity in the Neo-Klezmer Movement." *Monatshefte* 90(2):208–219.

Barz, Gregory F., and Timothy J. Cooley, eds. 1997. *Shadows in the Field: New Perspectives for Fieldwork in Ethnomusicology.* New York: Oxford University Press.

Bederman, Gail. 1995. *Manliness and Civilization: A Cultural History of Gender and Race in the United States, 1880–1917.* Chicago: University of Chicago Press.

Berry, Venise. 1994. "Feminine or Masculine: The Conflicting Nature of Female Images in Rap Music." In *Cecilia Reclaimed,* ed. Susan C. Cook and Judy S. Tsou, 183–201. Urbana: University of Illinois Press.

Block, Adrienne Fried. 1992. "Two Virtuoso Performers in Boston: Jenny Lind and Camilla Urso." In *New Perspectives on Music,* ed. Josephine Wright, 355–372. Warren, Mich.: Harmonie Park Press.

———. 1998. *Amy Beach, Passionate Victorian.* New York: Oxford University Press.

Boone, Clara Lyle. 1984. "Women's Composers' Upbeat: Arsis Press." In *The Musical Woman 1,* ed. Judith Lang Zaimont, 98–104. Westport, Conn.: Greenwood Press.

Boroff, Edith. 1987. "Spreading the Good News: Conferences on Women in Music." In *The Musical Woman 2,* ed. Judith Lang Zaimont, 335–346. Westport, Conn.: Greenwood Press.

Bowers, Jane, and Judith Tick, eds. 1986. *Women Making Music: The Western Art Tradition, 1150–1950.* Urbana: University of Illinois Press.

Brackett, David. 1992. "James Brown's 'Superbad' and the Double-Voiced Utterance." *Popular Music* 11(3):309–324.

———. 1994. "The Politics and Practice of 'Crossover' in American Popular Music, 1963–1965." *Musical Quarterly* 78(4):774–797.

Brett, Philip, Elizabeth Wood, and Gary C. Thomas, eds. 1994. *Queering the Pitch: The New Gay and Lesbian Musicology.* New York: Routledge.

Brown, Rae Linda. 1993. "The Woman's Symphony Orchestra of Chicago and Florence B. Price's Piano Concerto in One Movement." *American Music* 11(2):185–205.

Bufwack, Mary A., and Robert K. Oermann. 1993. *Finding Her Voice: The Saga of Women in Country Music.* New York: Crown.

Butler, Judith. 1990. *Gender Trouble.* New York: Routledge.

Caputo, Virginia. 1990. "Canadian English-Language Children's Songs in Toronto Schools." *Canadian Folk Music Journal* 18:4–12.

Carby, Hazel. 1990 [1986]. "It Jus Be's Dat Way Sometimes: The Sexual Politics of Women's Blues." In *Unequal Sisters: A Multicultural Reader in U.S. Women's History,* ed. Ellen Carol DuBois and Vicki L. Ruiz, 238–249. New York: Routledge.

———.1991. "In Body and Spirit: Representing Black Women Musicians." *Black Music Research Journal* 11(2):177–192.

———. 1998. *Race Men.* Cambridge: Harvard University Press.

Cash, Alice H. 1991. "Conference Report: Feminist Theory and Music: Toward a Common Language." *Journal of Musicology* 9(4):521–532.

Cateforis, Theo, and Elena Humphreys. 1997. "Constructing Communities and Identities: Riot Grrl New York City." In *Musics of Multicultural America,* ed. Kip Lornell and Anne K. Rasmussen, 317–342. New York: Prentice Hall.

Cavanagh, Beverley (Diamond). 1989. "Writing about Music and Gender in the Sub-Arctic Algonquian Area." In *Women in North American Music: Six Essays,* ed. Richard Keeling, 55–66. Special Series, no. 6. Bloomington, Ind.: The Society for Ethnomusicology.

Christensen, Kimberly. 1997. "'With Whom Do You Believe Your Lot Is Cast?' White Feminists and Racism." *Signs* 22(3):617–648.

Clément, Catherine. 1988. *Opera, or the Undoing of Women.* Trans. Betsy Wong. Minneapolis: University of Minnesota Press.

Coates, Norma. 1997. "(R)evolution Now?: Rock and the Political Potential of Gender." In *Sexing the Groove,* ed. Sheila Whiteley, 50–64. New York: Routledge.

Cohen, Judith R. 1987. "'Ya salio de la mar': Judeo-Spanish Wedding Songs among Moroccan Jews in Canada." In *Women and Music in Cross-Cultural Perspective,* ed. Ellen Koskoff, 55–68. Westport, Conn.: Greenwood Press.

———. 1989. "Judeo-Spanish Songs in the Sephardic Communities of Montréal and Toronto." Ph.D. dissertation, University of Montréal.

Collins, Patricia Hill. 1990. *Black Feminist Thought.* New York: Routledge.

Cook, Susan C. 1992. "Listening to Billie Holiday: Intersections of Race and Gender." *Sonneck Society Bulletin* 18(3):94–97.

———. 1994. "'Cursed Was She': Gender and Power in American Balladry." In *Cecilia Reclaimed: Feminist Perspectives on Gender and Music,* ed. Susan C. Cook and Judy S. Tsou, 202–224. Urbana: University of Illinois Press.

———. 1998. "Passionless Dancing and the Passionate Reform: Respectability, Modernism, and the Social Dancing of Irene and Vernon Castle." In *The Passion of Music and Dance: Body, Gender, Sexuality,* ed. William Washabaugh, 133–150. Oxford, England: Berg Press.

———. 1999. "Watching Our Step: Embodying Research, Telling Stories." In *Audible Traces: Gender, Identity, and Music,* ed. Lydia Hamessley and Elaine Barkin, 177–212. Zurich: Carciofoli Press.

Cook, Susan C., and Judy S. Tsou, eds. 1994. *Cecilia Reclaimed: Feminist Perspectives on Gender and Music.* Urbana: University of Illinois Press.

Cooper, Sarah, ed. 1996. *Girls, Girls, Girls: Essays on Women and Music.* New York: New York University Press.

Dahl, Linda. 1984. *Stormy Weather: The Music and Lives of a Century of Jazzwomen.* New York: Pantheon.

Davis, Angela Y. 1998. *Blues Legacies and Black Feminism: Gertrude "Ma" Rainey, Bessie Smith, and Billie Holiday.* New York: Pantheon.

Davitt, Pat. 1993. "Songs for Ourselves, Revisited: A Dialogue between Maggie Benston and the Rest of the Euphoniously Feminist and Non-Performing Quintet." *Canadian Woman Studies* 13(2):21–24.

Desmond, Jane C. 1997. "Embodying Difference: Issues in Dance and Cultural Studies." In *Everynight Life: Culture and Dance in Latino America,* ed. Celeste Frasier Delgado and José Esteban

Muñoz, 33–64. Durham, N.C.: Duke University Press.

Detels, Claire. 1994. "Autonomist/Formalist Aesthetics, Music Theory, and the Feminist Paradigm of Soft Boundaries." *The Journal of Aesthetics and Arts Criticism* 52(1):113–126.

Diamond, Beverley. 2000. "The Interpretation of Gender Issues in Musical Life Stories of Prince Edward Islanders." In *Gender and Music: Negotiating Shifting Worlds,* ed. Beverley Diamond, 99–139. Urbana: University of Illinois Press.

Diamond, Beverley, and Robert Witmer, eds. 1994. *Canadian Music: Issues of Hegemony and Identity.* Toronto: Canadian Scholars' Press.

Douglas, Ann. 1988. *The Femininization of American Culture.* New York: Anchor Press.

Douglas, Susan J. 1995. *Where the Girls Are: Growing Up Female with the Mass Media.* New York: Times Books.

Drakich, Janice, Edward Kovarik, and Ramona Lumpkin. 1995. *With a Song in Her Heart: A Celebration of Canadian Women Composers.* Windsor, Ont.: University of Windsor Humanities Research Group.

Driedger, Diane. 1991. "Women with Disabilities: Naming Oppression." *Resources for Feminist Research* 20(1–2):5–9.

Eastman, Sheila Jane, and Timothy J. McGee. 1983. *Barbara Pentland.* Toronto: University of Toronto Press.

Ehrenreich, Barbara, Elizabeth Hess, and Gloria Jacobs. 1992. "Beatlemania: Girls Just Want to Have Fun." In *The Adoring Audience: Fan Culture and Popular Media,* ed. Lisa A. Lewis, 84–106. New York: Routledge.

Elliott, Robin. 1997. *Counterpoint to a City: The First One Hundred Years of the Women's Musical Club of Toronto.* Toronto: ECW Press.

Embree, Sonja. 1994. "Mommy Dearest: Women's Studies and the Search for Identity." In *Who Is This We? Absence of Community,* ed. Eleanor Godway and Geraldine Finn, 83–100. Montréal: Black Rose.

Feldman, Ann E. 1990. "Being Heard: Women Composers and Patrons at the 1893 World's Columbian Exposition." *Notes* 47(1):7–20.

Fetterley, Judith. 1978. *The Resisting Reader: A Feminist Approach to American Fiction.* Bloomington: Indiana University Press.

Foucault, Michel. 1978. *The History of Sexuality,* vol. 1, *An Introduction.* Trans. Robert Hurley. New York: Random House.

Four the Moment. "Four the Moment." In *Feminism: From Pressure to Politics,* ed. Angela Miles and Geraldine Finn, 345–352. Montréal: Black Rose, 1989.

Fowke, Edith, and Jay Rahn. 1994. *A Family Heritage: The Story and Songs of LaRena Clark.* Calgary: University of Calgary Press.

Frith, Simon. 1996. *Performing Rites: On the Value of Popular Music.* Cambridge: Harvard University Press.

Gaar, Gillian G. 1992. *She's a Rebel: The History of Women in Rock & Roll.* Seattle: Seal Press.

Gagnon, Madeleine. 1989. "My Body in Writing." In *Feminism: From Pressure to Politics,* ed. Angela Miles and Geraldine Finn, 375–388. Montréal: Black Rose.

Gaunt, Kyra. 1995. "African-American Women between Hopscotch and Hip-hop: 'Must Be the Music (That's Turnin' Me On).'" In *Feminism, Multiculturalism and the Media: Global Diversities,* ed. Angharad Valdivia, 277–308. Thousand Oaks, Calif.: Sage Publications.

———. 1997. "Translating Double-Dutch to Hip-hop: The Musical Vernacular of Black Girls' Play." In *Language, Rhythm and Sound: Black Popular Cultures into the Twenty-First Century,* ed. Joseph K. Adjaye and Adrianne R. Andrews, 146–163. Pittsburgh: University of Pittsburgh Press.

———. 1998. "Dancin' in the Street to a Black Girl's Beat: Music, Gender, and the 'Ins and Outs' of Double-Dutch." In *Generations of Youth: Youth Cultures and History in Twentieth-Century America,* ed. Joe Austin and Mike Williard, 272–292. New York: New York University Press.

Giglio, Virginia. 1994. *Southern Cheyenne Women's Songs.* Norman: University of Oklahoma Press.

Gonzalez, Anita. 1998. "Powwow Dancing and Native Rap: American Indian Dance Patronage and the Politics of Spirituality." *Proceedings Society of Dance History Scholars,* 227–233. Riverside, Calif.: Society of Dance History Scholars.

Gourse, Leslie. 1996. *Madame Jazz: Contemporary Women Instrumentalists.* New York: Oxford University Press.

Green, Mildred Denby. 1983. *Black Women Composers: A Genesis.* Boston: Twayne.

Green, Shannon. 1998. "'Art for Life's Sake': Music Schools and Activities in U.S. Social Settlement Houses, 1892–1942." Ph.D. dissertation, University of Wisconsin–Madison.

Groh, Jan Bell. 1991. *Evening the Score: Women in Music and the Legacy of Frédérique Petrides.* Fayetteville: University of Arkansas.

Hall, Marnie. 1984. "Chronicling Women Composers on Disc." In *The Musical Woman 1,* ed. Judith Lang Zaimont, 83–97. Westport, Conn.: Greenwood Press.

Handy, D. Antoinette. 1981. *Black Women in American Bands and Orchestras.* Metuchen, N.J.: Scarecrow.

———. 1992. "Black Women and American Orchestras: An Update." In *New Perspectives on Music,* ed. Josephine Wright, 451–462. Warren, Mich.: Harmonie Park Press.

Harper, Phillip Brian. 1996. *Are We Not Men?: Masculine Anxiety and the Problem of African-American Identity.* New York: Oxford University Press.

Harris, Debbie Wise. 1991. "Colonizing Mohawk Women: Representation of Women in the Mainstream Media." *Resources for Feminist Research* 20(1–2):15–20.

Harrison, Daphne Duval. 1988. *Black Pearls: Blues Queens of the 1920's.* New Brunswick, N.J.: Rutgers University Press.

Hatton, Orin T. 1986. "In the Tradition: Grass Dance Musical Style and Female Pow-wow Singers." *Ethnomusicology* 30(2):197–222.

Herndon, Marcia, and Susanne Ziegler, eds. 1990. *Music, Gender, and Culture.* Wilhelmshaven, Germany: F. Noetzel.

Higginbotham, Evelyn Brooks. 1992. "African-American Women's History and the Metalanguage of Race." *Signs* 17(2):251–274.

Hill, Mike, ed. 1997. *Whiteness: A Critical Reader.* New York: New York University Press.

Horowitz, Joseph. 1994. "Finding a 'Real Self': American Women and the Wagner Cult of the Late Nineteenth Century." *Musical Quarterly* 78(2):189–205.

Horton, Donald. 1956–1957. "The Dialogue of Courtship in Popular Songs." *American Journal of Sociology* 62(6):569–578.

Hubbs, Nadine. 1996. "Music of the 'Fourth Gender': Morrissey and the Sexual Politics of Melodic Contour." *Genders* 23:266–296.

Hull, Gloria T., Patricia Bell Scott, and Barbara Smith, eds. 1982. *All the Women Are White, and All the Blacks Are Men, but Some of Us Are Brave: Black Women's Studies.* Old Westbury, N.Y.: Feminist Press.

Huyssen, Andreas. 1986. "Mass Culture as Woman: Modernism's Other." In *Studies in Entertainment,* ed. Tania Modleski, 188–207. Bloomington: Indiana University Press.

Jones, Jafran. 1991. "Women in Non-Western Music." In *Women and Music: A History,* ed. Karin Pendle, 314–330. Bloomington: Indiana University Press.

Keeling, Richard, ed. 1989. *Women in North American Indian Music: Six Essays.* Special Series, no. 6. Bloomington, Ind.: The Society for Ethnomusicology.

Keightley, Keir. 1996. "'Turn It Down!' She Shrieked: Gender, Domestic Space, and High Fidelity, 1948–59." *Popular Music* 15(2):149–178.

Keillor, Elaine. 1995. "Are We Really 'Minorish?" *With a Song in Her Heart: A Celebration of Canadian Women Composers,* ed. Janice Drakich, Edward Kovarik, and Ramona Lumpkin, 61–66. Windsor: University of Windsor.

Kennedy, John, and Larry Polansky. 1996. "'Total Eclipse': The Music of Johanna Magdalena Beyer, An Introduction and Preliminary Annotated Checklist." *Musical Quarterly* 80(4):719–778.

Key, Susan. 1995. "Sound and Sentimentality: Nostalgia in the Songs of Stephen Foster." *American Music* 13(2):145–166.

Keyes, Cheryl L. 1993. "We're More Than a Novelty, Boys: Strategies of Female Rappers in the Rap Music Tradition." In *Feminist Messages: Coding in Women's Folk Culture,* ed. Joan N. Radner, 203–220. Urbana: University of Illinois Press.

Kirk-Duggan, Cheryl A. 1997. *Exorcizing Evil: A Womanist Perspective on the Spirituals.* Maryknoll, N.Y.: Orbis Books.

Kivi, K. Linda. 1992. *Canadian Women Making Music.* Toronto: Green Dragon Press.

Koskoff, Ellen. 1993. "Miriam Sings Her Song: The Self and the Other in Anthropological Discourse." In *Musicology and Difference,* ed. Ruth A. Solie, 149–163. Berkeley: University of California Press.

———. 1995. "The Language of the Heart: Men, Women, and Music in Lubavitcher Life." In *New World Hasidism: Ethnographic Studies of Hasidic Jews in America,* ed. Jane S. Belcove-Shalin, 87–106. Albany: State University of New York Press.

———, ed. 1989. *Women and Music in Cross-Cultural Perspective.* Urbana: University of Illinois Press.

Koza, Julia Eklund. 1991. "Music and the Feminine Sphere: Images of Women as Musicians in Godey's Lady's Book, 1830–1877." *Musical Quarterly* 75(2):103–129.

Kydd, Roseanne. "Jean Coulthard: Revised View." *Soundnotes* (Spring/Summer):14–24.

Lamb, Roberta. 1997. "Music Trouble: Desire, Discourse, Education." *Canadian University Music Review* 18(1): 84–98.

———. 1999. "'I Never Really Thought about It': Master/apprentice as Pedagogy in Music." In *Equity and How to Get It: Rescuing Graduate Studies,* ed. Kay Armatage, 213–238. Toronto: Thanna Publications.

Lang, Amy Schrager. 1998. "Jim Crow and the Pale Maiden: Gender, Color, and Class in Stephen Foster's 'Hard Times.'" In *Reading Country Music,* ed. Cecelia Tichi, 378–388. Durham, N.C.: Duke University Press.

Lefebvre, Marie-Thérèse. 1991. *La création musicale des femmes au Québec.* Montréal: Editions du remue-menage, 1991.

Levine, Lawrence W. 1988. *Highbrow/Lowbrow: The Emergence of Cultural Hierarchy in America.* Cambridge: Harvard University Press.

Lewis, Lisa A. 1990. *Gender Politics and MTV.* Philadelphia: Temple University Press.

Liera-Schwichtenberg, Ramona. 1998. "Crossing Over: Selena's Tejano Music and the Discourse of Borderlands." In *Mapping the Beat,* ed. Thomas Swiss, John Sloop, and Andrew Herman, 205–218. Malden, Mass.: Blackwell Publishers.

Little Coyote, Bertha, and Virginia Giglio. 1997. *Leaving Everything Behind: The Songs and Memories of a Cheyenne Woman.* Norman: University of Oklahoma Press.

Locke, Ralph, and Cyrilla Barr, eds. 1997. *Cultivating Music in America: Women Patrons and Activists since 1860.* Berkeley: University of California Press.

Lont, Cynthia M. 1992. "Women's Music: No Longer a Small Private Party." In *Rockin' the Boat: Mass Music and Mass Movements,* ed. Reebee Garofalo, 241–253. Boston: South End.

Lorde, Audre. 1984. "Uses of the Erotic: The Erotic as Power." In *Sister Outsider: Essays and Speeches,* 53–55. Freedom, Calif.: Crossing Press.

Lum, Casey Man Kong. 1996. *Search of a Voice: Karaoke and the Construction of Identity in Chinese America.* Mahwah, N.J.: Lawrence Erlbaum Associates.

MacLeod, Beth Abelson. 1993. "Whence Comes the Lady Tympanist: Gender and Instrumental Musicians in America, 1853–1990." *Journal of Social History* 27(2):291–308.

McCartney, Andra. 1994a. "Inventing Metaphors and Metaphors for Invention: Women Composers' Voices in the Discourse of Electroacoustic Music." In *Canadian Music: Issues of Hegemony and Identity,* ed. Beverley Diamond and Robert Witmer, 491–502. Toronto: Canadian Scholars' Press.

———. 1994b. "Creating Worlds for My Music to Exist: How Women Composers of Electroacoustic Music Make Place for Their Voices." Master's thesis, York University Graduate Program in Music.

———. 1995. "Inventing Images: Constructing and Contesting Gender in Thinking about Electroacoustic Music." *Leonardo Music Journal* 5:57–66.

———. 1999. "Sounding Places: Situated Conversations through the Soundscape Compositions of Hildegard Westerkamp." Ph.D. dissertation, York University Graduate Program in Music.

McClary, Susan. 1991. *Feminine Endings: Music, Gender, Sexuality.* Minneapolis: University of Minnesota Press.

McDonnell, Evelyn, and Ann Powers. 1995. *Rock She Wrote.* New York: Delta.

McGinty, Doris Evans. 1992. "Black Women in the Music of Washington, D.C., 1900–20." In *New Perspectives on Music,* ed. Josephine Wright, 409–450. Warren, Mich.: Harmonie Park Press.

McRobbie, Angela. 1984. "Dance and Social Fantasy." In *Gender and Generation,* ed. Angela McRobbie and Mica Nava, 130–161. London: Macmillan.

McSwain, Rebecca. 1995. "The Power of the Electric Guitar." *Popular Music and Society* 19(Winter):21–40.

Miller, Bonny H. 1994. "Ladies' Companion, Ladies' Canon? Women Composers in American Magazines from Godey's to the Ladies Home Journal." In *Cecilia Reclaimed,* ed. Susan C. Cook and Judy S. Tsou, 156–182. Urbana: University of Illinois.

Mockus, Martha. 1999. "Sounding Out: Lesbian Feminism and the Music of Pauline Oliveros." Ph.D. dissertation, University of Minnesota.

Monson, Ingrid. 1995. "The Problem with White Hipness: Race, Gender, and Cultural Conceptions in Jazz Historical Discourse." *Journal of the American Musicological Society* 48(3):396–422.

———. 1997. "Music and Anthropology of Gender and Cultural Identity." *Women and Music* 1:24–32.

Myers, Helen, ed. 1992. *Ethnomusicology: An Introduction.* New York: Norton.

Neuls-Bates, Carol. 1996 [1982]. *Women in Music: An Anthology of Source Readings from the Middle Ages to the Present.* 2nd ed. Boston: Northeastern University Press.

O'Brien, Lucy. 1996. *She Bop: The Definitive History of Women in Rock, Pop and Soul.* New York: Penguin.

O'Brien, Mary. 1989. "Feminist Praxis." In *Feminism: From Pressure to Politics,* ed. Angela Miles and Geraldine Finn, 327–344. Montréal: Black Rose.

O'Dair, Barbara, ed. 1997. *Trouble Girls: The Rolling Stone Book of Women in Rock.* New York: Random House.

Ortega, Teresa. 1998. "'My Name Is Sue! How Do You Do?': Johnny Cash as Lesbian Icon." In *Reading Country Music,* ed. Cecelia Tichi, 222–233. Durham, N.C.: Duke University Press.

Parsons Smith, Catherine. 1994. "A Distinguishing Virility: Feminism and Modernism in American Art." In *Cecilia Reclaimed: Feminist Perspectives on Women and Music,* ed. Susan C. Cook and Judy S. Tsou, 90–106. Urbana: University of Illinois Press.

Pegley, Karen. 1995. "'Places, Everyone': Gender and the Non-Neutrality of Music Technology." *The Recorder* 37(2):55–59.

———. 1998. "Femme Fatale and Lesbian Representation in Alban Berg's Lulu." In *Encrypted Messages in Alban Berg's Music,* ed. Siglind Bruhn, 249–277. New York: Garland Press.

———. 1999. "An Analysis of the Construction of Gendered, Racial, and National Identities on MTV (U.S.) and MuchMusic (Canada)." Ph.D. dissertation, York University Graduate Program in Music.

Pegley, Karen, and Virginia Caputo. 1994. "Growing up Female(s): Retrospective Thoughts on Musical Preferences and Meanings." In *Queering the Pitch: The New Gay and Lesbian Musicology,* ed. Philip Brett, Elizabeth Wood, and Gary C. Thomas, 297–313. New York: Routledge.

Pendle, Karin, ed. 1997. "American Women Composers." *Contemporary Music Review* 16(1/2).

Peraino, Judith. 1998. "PJ Harvey's 'Man-Size Sextet' and the Inaccessible, Inescapable Gender." *Women and Music* 2:47–63.

Peretti, Burton W. 1992. *The Creation of Jazz: Music, Race, and Culture in Urban America.* Urbana: University of Illinois Press.

Post, Jennifer C. 1994. "Erasing the Boundaries between Public and Private in Women's Performance Traditions." In *Cecilia Reclaimed,* ed. Susan C. Cook and Judy S. Tsou, 35–51. Urbana: University of Illinois Press.

Post, Laura. 1995. "Cris Williamson, Tret Fure: Women's Music and the Folk Mainstream." *Sing Out!* 40(2):40–49.

Proctor, George A. 1980. *Canadian Music of the Twentieth Century.* Toronto: University of Toronto Press.

Qureshi, Regula, et al., ed. 1995. *Voices of Women: Essays in Honour of Violet Archer. Canadian University Music Review* 16(1).

Rabinowitz, Peter J. 1993. "'With Our Own Dominant Passions': Gottschalk, Gender, and the Power of Listening." *Nineteenth-Century Music* 16(3):242–252.

Rahkonen, Carl. 1998. "Special Bibliography: Natalie Curtis (1875–1921)." *Ethnomusicology* 42(3):511–522.

Rich, Adrienne. 1983. "Compulsory Heterosexuality and Lesbian Existence." In *The Signs Reader: Women, Gender, and Scholarship,* ed. Elizabeth Abel and Emily K. Abel, 139–168. Chicago: University of Chicago Press.

Roberts, Robin. 1996. *Ladies First: Women in Music Videos.* Jackson: University of Mississippi Press.

Robertson, Carol E. 1993. "The Ethnomusicologist as Midwife." In *Musicology and Difference: Gender and Sexuality in Music Scholarship,* ed. Ruth A. Solie, 107–124. Berkeley: University of California Press.

Rodger, Gillian. 1998. "Male Impersonation on the North American Variety and Vaudeville Stage." Ph.D. dissertation, University of Pittsburgh.

Rose, Tricia. 1994. *Black Noise: Rap Music and Black Culture in Contemporary America.* Hanover, N.H.: University Press of New England.

Rycenga, Jennifer. 1997. "Sisterhood: A Loving Lesbian Ear Listens to Progressive Heterosexual Women's Rock Music." In *Keeping Score: Music, Disciplinarity, Culture,* ed. David Schwarz, Anahid Kassabian, and Lawrence Siegel, 203–228. Charlottesville: University Press of Virginia.

Sabourin, Carmen. 1995. "Vers une approche critique de la théorie schenkérienne." *Canadian University Music Review* 15(1):1–43.

———. 1997. "La critique féministe étasunienne en musique: Pertinence en milieu francophone Québecois." *Canadian University Music Review* 18(1):99–118.

Sandoval-Sanchez, Alberto. 1999. *José, Can You See? Latinos On and Off Broadway.* Madison: University of Wisconsin Press.

Sawa, Suzanne Myers. 1991. "The Story of Dahlia Obadia: Moroccos, Israel, Canada." *Canadian Folk Music Journal* 19:32–39.

Sawchuk, Kimberly Anne. 1989. "Towards a Feminist Analysis of 'Women in Rock Music: Patti Smith's "Gloria." ' " *Atlantis* 14(2):44–54.

Schwartz, Ellen. 1988. *Born a Woman.* Winlaw, B.C.: Polestar.

Sedgwick, Eve Kosofsky. 1985. *Between Men: English Literature and Male Homosocial Desire.* New York: Columbia University Press.

———. 1990. *Epistemology of the Closet.* Berkeley: University of California Press.

Shapiro, Anne Dhu, and Inés Talamantez. 1986. "The Mescalero Girls' Puberty Ceremony." *Yearbook of the International Council for Traditional Music* 18:77–90.

Shepherd, John. 1991. *Music as Social Text.* Cambridge: Polity Press.

Slobin, Mark. 1989. *Chosen Voices: The Story of the American Cantorate.* Urbana: University of Illinois Press.

Smith, Gordon E., and Kevin Alstrup. 1995. "Words and Music by Rita Joe: Dialogic Ethnomusicology." *Canadian Folk Music Journal* 23:35–53.

Solie, Ruth A. 1993a. "Women's History and Music History: The Feminist Historiography of Sophie Drinker." *Journal of Women's History* 5(2):8–31.

———, ed. 1993b. *Musicology and Difference: Gender and Sexuality in Music Scholarship.* Berkeley: University of California Press.

Spizizen, Louise. 1993. "Johana and Roy Harris: Marrying a *Real* Composer." *Musical Quarterly* 77(4):579–606.

Swiss, Thomas, John Sloop, and Andrew Herman, eds. 1998. *Mapping the Beat: Popular Music and Contemporary Theory.* Malden, Mass.: Blackwell Publishers.

Terborg-Penn, Rosalyn, and Sharon Harley, eds. 1978. *The Afro-American Woman: Struggles and Images.* Port Washington, N.Y.: Kennikat Press.

Theberge, Paul. 1997. *Any Sound You Can Imagine: Making Music/Consuming Technology.* Hanover, N.H.: University Press of New England.

Tick, Judith. 1983. *American Women Composers before 1870.* Rochester, N.Y.: University of Rochester.

———. 1993. "Charles Ives and Gender Ideology." In *Musicology and Difference: Gender and Sexuality in Music Scholarship.* ed. Ruth A. Solie, 83–106. Berkeley: University of California Press.

———. 1997. *Ruth Crawford: A Composer's Search for American Music.* New York: Oxford University Press.

Tilchen, Maida. 1984. "Lesbians and Women's Music." In *Women Identified Women,* ed. Trudy Darty and Sandee Potter, 287–303. Palo Alto, Calif.: Mayfield Publishing Company.

Torgovnick, Marianna. 1997. *Primitive Passions: Men, Women, and the Quest for Ecstasy.* Chicago: University of Chicago Press.

"Toward a Feminist Music Theory." 1994. *Perspectives of New Music* 32(1):6–88.

Truax, Barry. 1996. "Sounds and Sources in Powers of Two: Towards a Contemporary Myth." *Organised Sound* 1(1):13–21.

Tucker, Sherrie. 1996. "'And, Fellas, They're American Girls!' On the Road with the Sharon Rogers All-Girl Band." *Frontiers* 16(2/3):128–160.

———. 1997. "Telling Performances: Jazz History Remembered and Remade by the Women in the Band." *Women and Music* 1:12–23.

———. 1998. "Female Big Bands, Male Mass Audiences: Gendered Performances in a Theater of War." *Women and Music* 2:64–89.

Tye, Diane. 1995. "Katherine Gallagher and the World of Women's Folksong." *Atlantis* 20(1):101–111.

Tyler, Linda L. 1992. "Poetry and Commerce Hand in Hand: Music in American Department Stores, 1880–1930." *Journal of the American Musicological Society* 45(1):75–120.

Valaskakis, Gail Guthrie. 1993. "Postcards of My Past: The Indian as Artifact." In *Relocating Cultural Studies: Developments in Theory and Research,* ed. Valda Blundell, John Shepherd, and Ian Taylor, 155–170. London: Routledge.

Valdez, Avelardo, and Jeffrey A. Halley. 1996. "Gender in the Culture of Mexican American Conjunto Music." *Gender and Society* 10(2):148–167.

Vander, Judith. 1988. *Songprints: The Musical Experience of Five Shoshone Women.* Urbana: University of Illinois Press.

Ventura, Michael. 1985. "White Boys Dancing." In *Shadow Dancing in the USA,* 42–51. Los Angeles: J. P. Tarchor.

Waksman, Steve. 1999. *Instruments of Desire: The Electric Guitar and the Shaping of Musical Experience.* Cambridge: Harvard University Press.

Wald, Gayle. 1998. "Just a Girl? Rock Music, Feminism, and the Cultural Construction of Female Youth." *Signs* 23(3):585–610.

Walser, Robert. 1993. *Running with the Devil: Power, Gender, and Madness in Heavy Metal Music.* Middletown, Conn.: Wesleyan University Press.

Weller, Nik. 1993. "Alternative Music." *Canadian Woman Studies* 14(1):36–37.

Whiteley, Sheila, ed. 1997. *Sexing the Groove: Popular Music and Gender.* New York: Routledge.

Williamson, Janice. 1993. *Sounding Differences: Conversations with Seventeen Canadian Writers.* Toronto: University of Toronto Press.

Wilson, Pamela. 1998. "Mountains of Contradictions: Gender, Class, and Region in the Star Image of Dolly Parton." In *Reading Country Music,* ed. Cecelia Tichi, 98–120. Durham, N.C.: Duke University Press.

Wong, Deborah. 1994. "I Want the Microphone: Mass Mediation and Agency in Asian-American Popular Music," *TDR* 38(3):152–167.

Wright, Josephine. 1992. "Black Women in Classical Music in Boston during the Late Nineteenth Century: Profiles of Leadership." In *New Perspectives on Music,* ed. Josephine Wright, 373–408. Warren, Mich.: Harmonie Park Press.

Snapshot:
Gendering Music
Jane Bowers
Zoe C. Sherinian
Susan Fast

Mama Yancey and the Blues—Jane Bowers
K.D.Llang and Gender Performance—Zoe C. Sherinian
Heavy Metal and the Construction of Masculinity: Led Zeppelin—Susan Fast

Only within the past twenty years or so has gender been used as a category of analysis to contextualize music within broader social and cultural processes. The three "case studies" presented here show some of the current paradigms that researchers are using today to position both women and men into specific music making contexts.

MAMA YANCEY AND THE BLUES

When the blues, originally a folk music, emerged from its underground status in the 1890s and continued to evolve in the early twentieth century, it was associated mainly with male singers and instrumentalists [see BLUES, p. 637]. Undoubtedly this had to do with blues performance contexts—streets, riverboats, railroad stations, pool halls, bars, brothels, house parties, dances, and jailhouses. But women frequently sang the blues for themselves, and two female singers were reported among the earliest singers of the blues in traveling shows—Ophelia ("Black Alfalfa") Simpson, who composed a blues in 1898 while in jail for killing her husband and later performed it in Dr. Parker's Medicine Show, and Gertrude "Ma" Rainey, a professional entertainer, who added blues singing to her stage act in 1902. Rainey later went on to become one of the most famous of all popular blues singers and a prolific recording artist.

Women and the blues

The blues increased in popularity during World War I, and in 1920 black female vocalists began to record blues songs commercially. When these singers, who specialized in vaudeville blues, appeared in public, they were often billed as "queens" of the blues and dressed and acted the part. Perhaps the greatest of them all was Bessie Smith. But women singers did not dominate the market for long. Soon record companies began going south for material, and by 1926 the majority of the new singers being recorded were men who sang in a less citified, more traditional style. Moreover, women were scarce in the rural blues cultures that had developed in the Mississippi Delta, East Texas, and the Piedmont. William Barlow (1989) suggests three main reasons for this paucity: their heavy workloads as both mothers of large families and workers in the cotton fields, the physical danger and stigma of a woman traveling alone, and the double

In "Make Me a Pallet on the Floor," in which she drew upon an old, sometimes highly pornographic song from the South Central region, her theme seems to have been not only sex but also a request for tenderness and friendship and perhaps help as well under adverse circumstances.

standard that branded female blues artists as "fallen women" while it touted male artists as "free men." Nancy Levine (1993) points out that women also often played a supportive or subsidiary role with male blues musicians with whom they were associated. Religion was another significant obstacle to women's involvement in the blues, as blues were often considered to be "the devil's music."

Recently Peter Aschoff (1995) has pointed to a further impediment for female blues singers: because the social role of the "bluesman" is quite gender specific, women can never occupy the role of bluesman without gender ambiguity. Aschoff proposes that the tough legendary women who were able to handle the life of a bluesman—Memphis Minnie, Lucille Bogan, and Louise Johnson—were made by life into bluesmen even if they weren't born to it. Unlike vaudeville blues singers, "real blues women" lived the same life as the men, and they gained much of their social authority and sexual power from their ambiguous occupation of male social role and position.

Blues texts focus first and foremost on the relationship between the sexes, and they grant women the opportunity to sing more freely of their sexual interests and appetites than do most other forms of American vocal music. Daphne Duval Harrison notes that women's blues of the 1920s employed the bragging, signifying language of males to boast of fine physical attributes and high-powered sexual ability. It was not just the lyrics but also women's "throaty growls, coy expressions, and sensuous movements" (1988:109) that did the trick. Hazel Carby (1990) also views these blues as both articulating a cultural and political struggle directed against the objectification of female sexuality and trying to reclaim women's bodies as the sexual and sensuous objects of women's song. Ann duCille, on the other hand, has called into question "the utopian trend in contemporary cultural criticism that readily reads resistance in such privileged, so-called authentically black discourses as the classic blues of the 1920s" (1993:67) and suggests that probably few black women "lived the kind of sexually liberated lives or held the kind of freewheeling values refracted in the blues" (72). Angela Davis (1998) has yet a different take on the sexual language of the blues, arguing that the affirmations of sexual autonomy and open expressions of female sexual desire announced in women's blues songs gave historical voice to the possibilities of equality not articulated elsewhere. She further contends (Davis 1990) that while the blues incorporated a new consciousness about private love relationships, in many ways the interpersonal relationships sung about in the blues functioned as metaphors for the freedom black people sought from the brutal realities encountered in postslavery America.

More generally, Sandra Lieb (1981) points out that women's vaudeville blues describe a considerably narrower range of human experience than do men's folk blues, whether because women's activities were actually more physically and geographically limited than men's or because the public and record companies demanded from female singers more songs about love than about other subjects. Lieb also observes that women's blues ignore many major events in women's lives: birth and motherhood, childhood and children, adolescence, family relations, old age (except for an occasional mocking reference), and formal religion or church affairs.

Mama Yancey

One blues singer whom we might look at in greater detail is Estelle "Mama" Yancey (1896–1986), a traditional musician primarily active in Chicago. Although she belonged to the same generation as such vaudeville blues singers as Bessie Smith, her musical development was totally unlike theirs. Rather than singing in vaudeville or tent shows, theaters, or cabarets, she performed informally at gatherings in her own home with her husband, Jimmy Yancey (1900–1951)—a noted blues and boogie-woogie pianist—as well as at a limited circle of house parties in Chicago's South Side black ghetto. During certain periods of her life, she also participated in limited club and concert dates, especially during her husband's final years and again after 1977, when pianist Erwin Helfer brought her back out of "retirement" to sing primarily at clubs and local festivals. Her recording career was limited to seven sessions, two with Jimmy Yancey (1943, 1951) and the remaining ones with Don Ewell (1952), Little Brother Montgomery (1961), Art Hodes (1965), Erwin Helfer (1982–1983), and Axel Zwingenberger (1982–1983).

Mama Yancey was hardly a professional singer. She rarely sought out singing engagements on her own, and her life was primarily filled with homemaking, friends, family, and occasional work outside the home as a domestic or Democratic party precinct captain for her ward. She had no training in singing; she just picked it up hearing other people do the blues and other kinds of music. Indeed, a theme that runs through a number of interviews with Yancey is the role that her father, and later her husband, played in inhibiting her music making. She told Barbara Dane that although she and Jimmy would sing and play together "constantly" at home, he would not let her get out and sing for anybody else until they recorded for the Session label in 1943 (Dane 1964). She also alleged that her husband told her to throw her guitar in the garbage can; he didn't want her to do anything musical except sing for him.

Preferring to sing and record a handful of songs again and again, Mama Yancey had a central repertoire of only about seven songs, although she recorded some twenty-four altogether and improvised others in public and private performances. Most of her repertory consisted of the blues, but she occasionally sang and recorded nonblues songs. Apart from one of her great favorites, "Make Me a Pallet on the Floor," each time she sang a particular song she reconstructed it, drawing on one or more core stanzas that she reconstituted and rearranged at the time of performance, often combining them with other new or preexistent stanzas as well.

Most of her songs were loosely based on older songs passed down through the oral tradition or disseminated widely through recordings. But Mama Yancey never copied any other singer's version of a song, only borrowed certain lines and stanzas, which she put together in her own unique way. Her songs, typically enough, deal mainly with love relationships, as, for example, her "How Long Blues," in which she elaborates on her mistreatment by her man. The theme of being mistreated is one of the central themes of blues songs generally, and a number of ideas in the song are conventional, yet she creates a striking persona of a strong, upright woman who is able to "stand more trouble than any gal my size" and who is trying hard to teach her lover right from wrong.

In "Make Me a Pallet on the Floor," in which she drew upon an old, sometimes highly pornographic song from the South Central region, her theme seems to have been not only sex but also a request for tenderness and friendship and perhaps help as well under adverse circumstances. In "Four O'Clock Blues," related in part to other singers' versions of "Death Letter Blues," she illustrates a deep grieving process and teaches a lesson in how to deal with the final loss of a loved one. When faced with the departure of her lover in "Santa Fe Blues," she tries to catch up with him instead of abandoning herself to sorrow. In the comic song "Monkey Woman [or "Monkey Man] Blues," she scolds another woman for telling her man everything and advises her to "just let him know you're the boss, baby, and he'll come under too." She brags in "Weekly Blues" about having a different man for every day of the week and tells other women to follow her example. Of course, the character she created in her songs—the woman who had every right to be her own woman, the autonomous person who knuckled under to no one—was the expression of an ideal, but it is clear that it was closely related to her own life, personality, and values. Because Mama Yancey did not cultivate the role of entertainer or have to maintain a large repertoire for professional reasons, the handful of songs she chose to sing over and over was very close to her as an individual and as a woman.

In terms of her self-presentation as a singer, dressing elegantly and being theatrical were never important to Mama Yancey. Furthermore, she deplored the commercialization of the blues and the idea that younger singers were singing songs they did not really feel just to entertain a crowd or to make a hit. In 1964 she told Barbara Dane, "You don't sing blues from just your mind, to go out there and clown for a whole lot of people. Blues is what . . . comes from your heart" (Dane 1964). Thus she was very much concerned with feeling in singing, and her style at its best was intense, moving, and powerful. She also made effective use of scoops, slides, and sobs; rhythmic complexity; and a variety of vocal timbres ranging from lyrical singing through speech-song [see AFRICAN AMERICAN CRIES, CALLS AND HOLLERS, p. 81].

Mama Yancey's blues themes and messages were deeply grounded in her experience of being a woman. In addition, she frequently made statements about how singing on the stage was no life for a married woman, which seem to have reflected a specifically female perspective. Another aspect of her musical activity related to gender was the fact that she specialized in singing, which was typical for women blues musicians of her age group, rather than in both singing and playing.

In her late years, Mama Yancey was blind and so crippled by arthritis that she had to be carried onto the stage (figure 1). Yet she continued to sing with vitality, power, and humor. When Harriet Choice reviewed Mama Yancey's Chicago Jazz Festival appearance in 1979, she reported that the singer received a spontaneous standing ovation, "not because of endurance, but because Mama Yancey still knows how to tell a story, to sing the blues" (1979:6).

—JANE BOWERS

FIGURE 1   Estelle "Mama" Yancey, flanked by Erwin Helfer and S. P. Leary, after a 1978 performance. Photo by Dale Shigley. Copyright 1985 by Dale Shigley; reproduced courtesy Scott Shigley.

FIGURE 2   k. d. lang challenges mainstream America's definitions of "female" with her powerfully butch performance style, 1990s. Photo courtesy the BMI Archives.

K. D. LANG AND GENDER PERFORMANCE

On 24 February 1993 at the Grammy Awards, five women were nominated for Best Female Pop Vocalist—a category that might be considered to represent the definitive voice of mainstream popular femininity in America. When the announcer, Patti LaBelle, opened the envelope, she set the tone for the crowning of the new pop vocal queen by declaring, "Ooh, I'm scared of you!" and then sang the first line of k. d. lang's song "Constant Craving." lang, dressed in a black sea captain–style tux, kissed her mother, who was sitting next to her, and strode toward the stage. What was LaBelle afraid of? Was it k. d. lang's vocal abilities, her richly androgynous or butch (a type of lesbian gender or public style) persona? Or was it her performance art package of ironic social commentary that incited fear in the hearts of some and lust in the bodies of many?

Although lang had received a Grammy for Best Female Country Vocalist in 1990, the 1993 Grammy Awards program may have been the first time many mainstream American viewers had seen her on television, although Canadians have known of this local Alberta country gal since the mid-1980s. Did this tux-clad, richly androgynous person fit the image of the voice of mainstream femininity that America expected (figure 2)?

In a pre-Grammy interview with talk show hosts Regis Philbin and Kathie Lee Gifford, lang commented on the surprise fact that she had been nominated for four Grammys, including Song of the Year and Album of the Year. She said, "Maybe next year they will nominate me for Best Male Vocalist." Was she joking, or was she serious about her voice being considered in the male gender category? Or did she dislike the gendering of her voice at all?

Is lang female, or does her lesbian sexual preference and her particularly butch style put her in another gender category? Is her voice in a gender category of its own? And if so, how does her voice, her music, and its performance create this category? To appreciate fully the k. d. lang phenomenon, its history, and the role of her commanding voice we must examine how she dresses her voice in a context of what she calls "cross-pollinized" performance art (Lemon 1992:38).

When she had the most to lose or gain, Kathy played it conservatively feminine.

Harvest of Seven Years: Cropped and Chronicled (1991) is a one-hour package covering seven years of television and video production that brings k. d. out in a multiplicity of performance situations. Her cross-pollinized style repertoire includes rock-a-billy surfer, punk, honky-tonk, yodeling, polka, torch song, and 1940s jazz. She uses vocal and performance invocations of Elvis, Hank Williams, Hank Snow, Patsy Kline, and the crooners, and she presents herself in multiple costume codes, including that of an androgynous cowpoke, a 1950s homemaker, a lonesome cowboy in a nudie suit, a 1940s crooner in a zoot suit, and a soft butch lesbian kicking back at home in a tee shirt, jeans, and Doc Martens.

k. d. lang performs for and to both the mainstream music industry and a lesbian subculture. She uses her voice and body to negotiate a more fluid definition of the category of female vocalist—one in which subjectivity is simultaneously outspokenly female, multiply gendered, and lesbian. She plays with country music's strict gender coding of vocal range and texture. Her ironic gender play and vocal drag simultaneously invoke and subvert male vocal styles and performance gestures. Her lyrics and videography contain codes from her lesbian subculture that allow her to be herself by enacting a butch subjectivity that communicates with her lesbian culture while playing with, but still surviving in, the mainstream.

In this interpretation of k. d. lang's music the category of woman is theorized as socially constructed in sex/gender ideology systems reified by or produced by her music. Three points are important here. First, Western heterosexual ideology equating sexuality with gender is imposed on bodies and voices (Butler 1990, 1991; De Lauretis 1991). Gays, lesbians, and others who reject this heterosexual system are able to construct different and even multiple gender identities that lie outside this economy. However, members of this queer subculture may still be in dialogue with the superculture. Second, male impersonation by a woman can invoke yet subvert masculine subjectivity and the naturalized gender dichotomy, thus determining the totality of gender construction and challenging the power regimes of mainstream music culture that keep women in their place. Third, k. d. lang uses her biologically female voice to construct a subcultural gender. Here is an alternative female voice whose vociferousness refuses to remain closeted. Its use produces lesbian agency through ambivalent and multiple gender performance.

It is the naturalization of voice in American popular music culture that most often defines one's musical gender and performance style identity. The assertions that one can sound black or gay, or that men sing bass and women sing soprano, are reflections of the culturally constructed gendering of human vocal chords. The human voice is a biological instrument that actually has a much larger range potential than is taught or exhibited in popular music. k. d. lang references these vocal gender norms, parodies them, transverses them, and ultimately undermines them in her music.

lang's typical vocal range, which I refer to here as low alto, extends from E below middle C to the F above, although there are instances when it extends as low as C below middle C (almost as low as the average tenor). Thus, lang's use of a low female vocal range in country and pop music styles, where the norm is for women to sing much higher, marks her vocal gender as ambiguous and even threatening. When she accompanies this low alto with imitations of male vocal personas and male drag as well as a variety of seductive timbres, she challenges the hegemonic female gender ideology and regime of compulsive heterosexuality ascribed to the category Best Female Vocalist.

Early years

k. d. lang's first period of success, during which she appeared on country music television shows and independent videos with a punk-a-billy band, showed examples of her early play with gender constructions. Kathy Lang's first media break was an appearance in 1984 on a local Edmonton country star search show called *Sun Country.* In this performance, included on the video autobiography *Harvest of Seven Years,* she is dressed in a relatively conservative, feminine outfit (black dress, white cowgirl boots, and makeup). She delivered relatively little physical gender play or unfeminine stage behavior. In other words, she looked like a girl. However, the power of her talented low-alto voice and the active subjectivity in her lyrics broke through her feminine facade to make her sexuality suspect. This video clip, which stands in stark contrast to her later subversive play, shows the way she negotiated her gender performance within the music industry. When she had the most to lose or gain, Kathy played it conservatively feminine.

That same year, "k. d." lang (note that the initials do not indicate the singer's gender) made two independent videos with a rock-a-billy punk band. The satirical lyrics and stage behavior in these performances take a full feminist turn. The song "Polly Ann" satirizes the 1950s white-bread consumer homemaker while simultaneously commenting on the use of women's bodies and feminine gender to sell products. The title doubles as the name for a brand of white bread and for the "soft and fresh" female who is sexually desired by this polyester-clad homemaker, who looks like a man in female drag. lang expresses this homoerotic behavior visually while singing the line, "I don't want breadsticks, I don't want buns. But if it's Polly Ann, I'll save all the crumbs." Her satire is produced vocally through a two-octave jump from her usual low-alto range to piercing operatic soprano wails. In the chorus of the video, her all-male backup singers pretend to be surfers, singing Beach Boy–style falsetto lines while she sprays them with the phallic water hose she has appropriated. At the end of the song, she exposes the housewife as a drag persona by taking off her wig, but the viewer is doubly shocked because what we thought to be a female singer looks like a man with a butch haircut or a mean, threatening punker in cat glasses.

The sexual desire lang shows in her songs is not necessarily directed toward a man. Indeed, she told *The Advocate,* "I'm certainly not singing about the Marlboro man when I'm up there" (Lemon 1992:38). She likes to make it clear that she writes love songs that can be applied to any relationship (with God or one's mother, for example), facilitating this through the use of "I" or "you" instead of "he" or "she." This ambiguity permits the listener to question the direction of her sexual or passionate gestures. In a hierarchic sex/gender power system, ambiguous identity performance creates difference or play, leaving room for alternative interpretations by those who want to see it. When asked why she thought country music had not embraced her, she replied, "Because they did not want someone who looked like me, who thought like me, who spoke out like me" (Lemon 1992:38). Thus, k. d. lang's persona works very much as a masquerade within the mainstream music industry. The irony of the masquerade is its lack of fit, "so that we see the face behind the mask, the mask does not quite fit, and the masquerade is never quite successful; or rather, it is successful as a masquerade not an embodiment" (De Lauretis 1991:244).

In her video performance of the song "Pay Dirt," lang references the voices, honky-tonk style, performance gestures, clothes, and personas of Hank Snow and Elvis

Presley. Her low-alto range nicely matches the high lonesome tenor aesthetic of these singers. However, through writing her own ironic lyrics and singing them in her alto timbre she appropriates these male personas and voices as her own. Her voice really sounds like Elvis's, yet the vocal timbre and physical cues reveal the woman under the country nudie suit—although not the typical country female singer. Thus an alternative subjectivity is produced through this ambivalence and irony.

"Pay Dirt," from a country music television performance filmed in 1986, is an example of the prowork song genre often seen in country music. It is a commentary on materialistic people who want something for nothing, people who would rather pray or gamble than work for a living and who only want a relationship with someone with money. This money or "wad of dough" is half of the construction of the desire, "half the price of a tease and a flirt." In the verses of this song, lang uses a country twang vocal style, and in the chorus she clearly imitates Elvis, including his lip curl, vibrating falsetto leaps, and body twists. Her outfit, an off-green nudie suit she claims to have found in Hank Snow's garbage, is out of date enough to be humorous as country drag. She even accessorizes it with a scarf tie, typical black hat, and fake sideburns.

This performance challenges our conception of lang's sexual identity as heterosexual feminine female. Instead she becomes a deviant feminist challenging the malecentric control of subjectivity within the country music industry by claiming the voice and persona of famous sexual male figures. She becomes a gender cyborg, showing homage to these personas through the musical and gestural performance of their identifying codes while simultaneously being irreverently blasphemous to the phallocentric heterosexual regime by appropriating these voices as her own, stepping out of the assigned feminine gender role of her voice and behavior, yet all the while insisting that she is female.

This alternative subjectivity is also a code of lesbian identity, a way of surviving and communicating one's sexual preference as different and outside of the heterosexual regime. Looking and acting "butch" is not an imitation of male heterosexuality within lesbian subculture but a deconstruction through inversion of the hegemony that requires female bodies to be heterosexually feminine, to be objectified, inactive, controlled, and the negated mirror of male subjectivity. As lang said in *The Advocate*:

> I am completely a woman. My body is completely a woman's body. I think the male thing is just a way of surviving—outside. Inside I'm completely a woman. The stage gives you the emancipation to do things. Because you know there has always been cross-dressing on stage—always since theater began. And it's the place to do it. It's about art transcending sex. But still retaining sexual elements. (Lemon 1992:42)

Shadowland

k. d. lang's sexual construction of lesbian desire and subjectivity become more focused in her Shadowland period of the late 1980s. She moved away from the honky-tonk and rock-a-billy style toward blues/pop torch songs, losing much of the twang but allowing greater passion to be expressed in her vocal technique.

"Pullin Back the Reins" is a love song that personifies a soft butch style. "Soft butch" is a lesbian category of multiple gender in which a biological female embodies masculine codes of strength yet can simultaneously direct feminine qualities, particularly seduction, toward another woman. Through her gestures, expression of feelings, and dress, lang claims mainstream masculine gender codes of strength and control. Yet through her vocal range, the intensity of vocal emotion, and her description of her relationship in the song's lyrics she softens this masculinity, visually and aurally creating a sensitive lesbian masculinity. Those privy to queer subcultural codes read that lang is a *lesbian* woman through her butch style, the direction of her passion toward a feminine beloved, and the ambiguity created through mixing gender codes.

There are several codes in *Harvest of Seven Years* that announce her soft butch subjectivity. lang sports a typical late-1980s lesbian buzz hair cut. Her handsome tailored suit hides her breasts and waist, while the camera does little to objectify "feminine" parts of her body. The visual focus is on her hands, shoulders, and face, which all show her strength. Yet the soft light filter and soft curtains of the stage, in the same rust color as her suit, feminize this masculine look. lang evokes the icon of the cowboy through her appropriation of John Wayne's powerful masculine hand gesture. Yet her hands also evoke the feminine when she touches her face—replicating the wind as a metaphor for her lover's kiss. Furthermore, she uses her hands to create feminine passion as she sings, "All that we had ran away with a will of its own." Finally, her eyes also reinforce these multiple gender codes. She looks directly into the camera when making the John Wayne gesture—creating male subjectivity—then swoons with her eyes at the thought of her lover's "wild and free" soul.

The lyrics demonstrate her attempt to maintain control while her feelings gallop wildly. The use of the coded horse-riding metaphor is sexually suggestive, evoking images of women reaching orgasm while horseback riding. The lyrics speak of sharing power and finding a balance between waiting and trust, a cherished ideal in lesbian relationships. Her voice covers a mid-alto range, female yet not particularly feminine by pop or country standards. Finally, she plays air guitar during the guitar solo, a gesture usually the privilege of male rock musicians. Thus, k.d. lang visually and aurally mixes mainstream gender codes in this performance. Through intentional ambiguity and gender fusion, lang claims a space in which she creates her lesbian butch subjectivity.

—ZOE C. SHERINIAN

HEAVY METAL AND THE CONSTRUCTION OF MASCULINITY: LED ZEPPELIN

FIGURE 3   Led's Zeppelin's Robert Plant, 1990s. Photo by Ross Halfin, courtesy the BMI Archives.

The group Led Zeppelin (1968–1980) is often cited as the progenitor of heavy metal or hard rock, genres of music that have been dominated by male performers. The prevalent view of gender construction in this music has focused attention on the ways in which both visual images and musical sounds reinforce stereotypical notions of masculinity. As Simon Frith and Angela McRobbie characterized it in their influential 1978 article "Rock and Sexuality," these performers and their music can be "aggressive, dominating, and boastful, and they constantly seek to remind the audience of their prowess, their control" (1990:372). Frith and McRobbie, and many others since, have indeed referred to this kind of music as "cock rock" because of its celebration of machismo and masculine sexuality. Many metal performers, Led Zeppelin's Robert Plant (figure 3) among them, choose to bare their chests in performance and to wear tight pants that emphasize their genitals, thereby flaunting their biologically male physical attributes by putting these on display for their audiences. Typical gestures made in performance, such as taking a wide-legged firm stance or picking up the microphone stand and walking around with it, have been interpreted as demonstrations of male strength and power.

Hard rock as masculine

The guitar player—or better, the guitar "hero"—is central to hard rock and metal and has also been linked with the notion of masculine power and control. Typically, the guitarist is a virtuoso player, whose mastery of the instrument can also be interpreted as signifying dominance and control over it. The electric guitar has also often been thought of as a metaphor for the phallus because of its shape and the position in which it is often held (slung around the hips) and because the way in which it is played suggests masturbation. The sound of much of the music—very loud and rhythmically insistent—has also often been associated with masculine sexuality, the loudness suggesting, again,

Rivalry gave way to Plant's urging Page on during a guitar solo, responding to his musical gestures with moans and sighs, imploring Page to "push, push," suggesting that he stretch himself further in terms of musical direction.

domination and power; the rhythmic insistence, male thrusting during intercourse. Metal singers display power through the use of high, strained registers and plenty of distortion, the latter of which especially can be viewed, as Robert Walser has expressed it, as "a signal of extreme power and intense expression by overflowing its channels and materializing the exceptional effort that produces it" (1993:42).

These powerful images of masculinity, as well as the relationships among band members, especially between singer and guitarist, acted out in performance have been described as opportunities for male bonding not only among band members but, as Deena Weinstein (1991) has pointed out, among band members and the males in their audiences. The enactments of power and control have been thought to be especially compelling for young men and further, to young *white* men (almost all metal performers are white as well), less so for women [see TWO VIEWS OF MUSIC, RACE, ETHNICITY, AND NATIONHOOD, p. 76; BLUES, p. 637]. Lyrically, the songs often celebrate male sexuality (in a tradition largely taken over from the blues), create escapist fantasy narratives, or explore spiritual life through a mixture of Christian, Eastern, ancient, and other religious themes and symbols.

These generalizations certainly hold to some degree, but the arguments need to be much more subtly made, taking into account the differences that inhere among groups and individual performers and, certainly, taking greater stock of how and why the audience consumes the music and images. Here I will take up three issues with respect to Led Zeppelin's constructions of gender to begin to problematize issues around masculinity in this music: the sound of the music, the visual imagery, and the reception of the band by fans.

Led Zeppelin and "cock rock"

One of the quintessential "cock rock" songs is surely Led Zeppelin's "Whole Lotta Love," the lyric of which (mostly taken from bluesman Willie Dixon's song "You Need Love") is about sexual gratification. It is not so much the lyric that has attracted attention, however, as it is Plant's performance, which, with its generally intense expression, moans, and screams, can be read as an enactment of sex, complete with orgasm. Because Plant is biologically male, and because there are references in the lyrics to his maleness and his partner's femaleness, this song is generally viewed as a boastful, arrogant display of machismo. The riff, one of guitarist Jimmy Page's most famous ones, seems to reinforce the idea that this song is being sung from a masculine perspective, each beat of the measure articulated by a stroke on the guitar, the regularity and speed of these gestures suggesting, perhaps, male thrusting during intercourse, as well as the approach of sexual climax.

But this is quite a superficial reading. First, the nearly hysterical emotional landscape suggested by Plant's singing has traditionally been associated with women, not men; although this is an essentialist idea, it is nonetheless the way in which hysterical behavior has traditionally been coded—it is not a behavior associated with men who are "in control." Second, there are several points, not simply one, throughout the song at which Plant would seem to reach climax, and this idea of multiple climaxes also suggests a feminine identity for Plant in the song. The insistent riff subsides twice during the song as well, making way for an experimental section of electronic music in the first instance and a guitar solo in the second. These moments have been interpreted by Steve Waksman as interruptions of the phallic insistence of the riff, the electronic section, in fact, as a "crisis in the representation of phallic potency" (1996). I would argue (perhaps because I am a woman) that these moments are less a crisis than they are an enrichment of the sexual experience being enacted. The electronic section introduces washes of sound to which Plant responds, suggesting that these sounds may represent a partner for him; with the guitar solo, a completely new voice is introduced into the narrative, a third party, so to speak, who moves the song in yet another direction.

Another consideration of gender construction in "Whole Lotta Love" is that in some cases—perhaps many—the song is not understood in isolation but within the context of other Led Zeppelin songs, and while the band is known for producing some of the heaviest rock music ever, their recorded output also includes a considerable number of acoustically based songs or songs in which acoustic and electric elements are blended. In other words, while the group was interested in creating an identity that included macho posturing, this identity is not monolithic and is not understood, at least by avid fans, in isolation. The acoustically based love song "Tangerine," for example, suggests intimacy and vulnerability in its musical as well as lyrical narrative. In this song, Page begins to play the introduction and then stops, suggesting that he has made a mistake, which he allows to remain on the final recording. He then counts himself in and begins again, allowing the listener to be a party to his error, to make himself vulnerable to his audience. He does play a solo on the electric guitar in "Tangerine," but it is a fleeting sign of power and confidence. The solo is too short—it climaxes too soon, reaching a fevered high point without sufficient development—and the acoustic chorus of the song, which has been delayed by the guitar solo, quickly reappears. Page's usual ability to create a transcendent guitar solo within a piece, which, as Robert Walser (1993) points out, is an essential element of the style and an essential factor in the construction of the powerful masculine guitar hero, has been curtailed here, demonstrating frustrated desire, perhaps also impotence, and in any case fallibility, imperfection, and vulnerability.

Equally problematic are the visual images in this band. Although Page, for example, certainly enacts elements of the typical macho "cock rocker" figure (he is Simon Frith's prime example of the style), his appearance often contradicts this image. Page's machismo poses are always uneasily negotiated through his slender, lanky frame, the delicacy of his features, the way in which he so often bends his body inward in collapse as he plays, signifying the "frailty" that journalistic writers have commented on—especially in early days, but even today to some extent—and the childlike qualities of his face. Quite aside from the sometimes frilly or glittery clothes that he wore, or his curling-ironed long hair, his body, face, and elfin gestures (*Melody Maker* journalist Chris Welch once called them "feline") have an androgynous quality that is difficult to ignore.

The relationship between Page and Plant on stage is certainly partly about male comaraderie and competition. The two would often engage in a kind of sparring during which Page would play a musical gesture on his guitar that Plant was then expected to imitate. The gestures would become increasingly higher, often driving Plant past the uppermost reaches of his vocal range, and eventually forcing him to concede failure to Page. Sometimes, however, this kind of rivalry gave way to Plant's urging Page on during a guitar solo, responding to his musical gestures with moans and sighs, imploring Page to "push, push," suggesting that he stretch himself further in terms of musical direction. These exchanges have interesting possibilities in terms of gender construction, for they cast Plant in the role of feminine other to Page's masculine guitar hero: Plant begs Page for more, for him to push harder, and responds to Page's musical gestures as if they were a lover's caresses.

Much has been said about how the majority of the audience for heavy metal is male and how the music and images reproduce hegemonic constructions of white suburban male identity. This is certainly true to an extent, but the culture of heavy metal cannot be so unproblematically interpreted in terms of gender. As Robert Walser reports (1993), by the late 1980s, nearly half of the audience for heavy metal was female. In the ethnographic study of Led Zeppelin fans that I conducted for the book *Led Zeppelin, Rock Culture, and Subjectivity* (Fast 2001), a third of the people who responded were women, all of whom were avid fans. Many of these women find the music and images erotic, and many appropriate the demonstrations of "masculine" power for themselves, finding the images and music empowering, not frightening (as Frith and McRobbie [1990] suggested they were to women). Walser (1993) also reports that there is significant interest in heavy metal by gay men, who view some metal videos as erotic fantasies. Sue Wise (1990) has argued that popular music performers may, through their music, also serve the function of platonic friend. According to Wise, Elvis Presley was always there for her, even when she was lonely or feeling depressed. In my experience, this has been true as well for both men and women consuming Led Zeppelin's music. Fans may relate to the music and images as sources of strength and to those who made the music as sharing similar values, trials and tribulations.

Some imagery and lyrics in metal are decidedly misogynistic, and the arguments I make here are not intended to excuse or justify those that are. Rather, I would call for a closer examination of images and music, a differentiation among various performers in terms of their constructions of gender, and interviews with those who consume the music and images in order to understand what and how they relate to the genre.

—SUSAN FAST

REFERENCES

Aschoff, Peter. 1995. Unpublished manuscript, including sections entitled "'Bluesman' as a Gender Specific Social Role," "Gender and Sex in the Blues," and "The Bluesman as a Mythic and Social Figure."

Barlow, William. 1989. *"Looking Up at Down": The Emergence of Blues Culture.* Philadelphia: Temple University Press.

Blackman, Inge and Kathryn Perry. 1990. "Skirting the Issue: Lesbian Fashion for the 1990s." *Feminist Review* 34(Spring): 67–78.

Butler, Judith. 1990. *Gender Trouble.* New York: Routledge.

———. 1991. "Imitation and Gender Insubordination." In *Inside/Out,* ed. Diana Fuss, 13–31. New York: Routledge.

Carby, Hazel. 1990 [1986]. "It Jus Be's Dat Way Sometime: The Sexual Politics of Women's Blues." In *Unequal Sisters: A Multicultural Reader in U.S. Women's History,* ed. Ellen Carol DuBois and Vicki L. Ruiz, 238–249. New York: Routledge.

Case, Sue-Ellen. 1988. "Towards a Butch-Femme Aesthetic." In *Making Spectacle: Feminist Essays on Contemporary Women's Theatre,* ed. Lynda Hart, 282–299. Ann Arbor: University of Michigan Press.

Choice, Harriet. 1979. "Carter's Alto, Arrangements Give Fest Memorable Moments." *Chicago Tribune,* 31 August, sec. 6, 6.

Cunningham, Patricia. 1991. *Dress and Popular Culture.* Bowling Green, Ohio: Bowling Green State University Press.

Dane, Barbara (with Pete Welding). 1964. Interview of Estelle "Mama" Yancey. Chicago, 23 September. Barbara Dane Collection, Archive of Folk Culture, Library of Congress, tape A–24.

Davis, Angela. 1990. "Black Women and Music: A Historical Legacy of Struggle." In *Wild Women in the Whirlwind: Afra-American Culture and the Contemporary Literary Renaissance,* 3–21. New Brunswick: Rutgers University Press.

———. 1998. *Blues Legacies and Black Feminism: Gertrude "Ma" Rainey, Bessie Smith, and Billie Holiday.* New York: Pantheon Books.

Davis, Stephen. 1985. *The Led Zeppelin Saga: Hammer of the Gods.* New York: Ballantine.

De Lauretis, Teresa. 1991. "Queer Theory: Lesbian and Gay Sexualities: An Introduction." *Differences* 3(2):iii–xviii.

Devor, Holly. 1989. *Gender Blending: Confronting the Limits of Duality.* Bloomington: Indiana University Press.

duCille, Ann. 1993. "Blues Notes on Black Sexuality: Sex and the Texts of the Twenties and Thirties." In *The Coupling Convention: Sex, Text, and Tradition in Black Women's Fiction,* 66–85. New York: Oxford University Press.

Ehrenreich, Barbara, Elizabeth Hess, and Gloria Jacobs. 1986. *Re-making Love: The Feminization of Sex.* New York: Doubleday.

Faderman, Lillian. 1991. *Odd Girls and Twilight Lovers.* New York: Penguin.

Fast, Susan. 2001. *Led Zeppelin, Rock Culture and Subjectivity.* New York: Oxford University Press.

———. 1999. "Rethinking Issues of Gender and Sexuality in Led Zeppelin: A Woman's View of Pleasure and Power in Hard Rock," *American Music* 17(3):245–299.

Foucault, Michel. 1978. *The History of Sexuality.* New York: Penguin.

Frith, Simon, and Angela McRobbie. 1990. "Rock and Sexuality." In *On Record: Rock, Pop and the Written Word,* ed. Simon Frith and Andrew Goodwin, 277–292. New York: Routledge.

Fuss, Diana. 1991. *Inside/Out: Lesbian Theories, Gay Theories.* New York: Routledge.

Halberstam, Judith. 1998. *Female Masculinity.* Durham, N.C.: Duke University Press.

Haraway, Donna. 1990. "A Manifesto for Cyborgs: Science, Technology, and Socialist Feminism in the 1980's." In *Feminism/Postmodernism,* ed. Linda Nicholson, 190–233. New York: Routledge.

Harrison, Daphne Duval. 1988. *Black Pearls: Blues Queens of the 1920s.* New Brunswick, N.J.: Rutgers University Press.

Irigaray, Luce. 1985. *This Sex Which Is Not One.* Ithaca, N.Y.: Cornell University Press.

lang, k. d. 1991. *Harvest of Seven Years (Cropped and Chronicled).* Warner Reprise Video, WB38234.

Lemon, Brendon. 1992. "k.d. lang: Virgin Territory." *The Advocate,* (605):34–46.

Levine, Nancy J. 1993. "'She Plays Blues Like a Man': Gender Bending the Country Blueswomen." *Blues Revue Quarterly* 7:34–38.

Lieb, Sandra R. 1981. *Mother of the Blues: A Study of Ma Rainey.* Amherst: University of Massachusetts Press.

Loulan, JoAnn. 1990. *The Lesbian Erotic Dance: Butch, Femme, Androgyny, and Other Rhythms.* San Francisco: Spinster Book Company.

Malone, Bill, and Judith McCulloh. 1975. *Stars of Country Music.* Urbana: University of Illinois Press.

Nash, Alanna. 1988. *Behind Closed Doors: Talking with the Legends of Country Music.* New York: Knopf.

Reynolds, Simon, and Joy Press. 1995. *The Sex Revolts: Gender, Rebellion and Rock 'n' Roll.* Cambridge: Harvard University Press.

Riley, Denise. 1988. *"Am I That Name?" Feminism and the Category of "Women" in History.* Minneapolis: University of Minnesota Press.

Robertson, Carol. 1987. "Power and Gender in the Musical Experiences of Women." In *Women and Music in Cross-Cultural Perspective,* ed. Ellen Koskoff, 225–245. Urbana: University of Illinois Press.

Scott, Joan. 1989. "Gender: A Useful Category of Historical Analysis." In *Coming to Terms: Feminism, Theory, Politics,* ed. Elizabeth Weed, 225–245. New York: Routledge.

Shepherd, John. 1991. "Music and Male Hegemony." In *Music as Social Text,* 152–173. Cambridge, England: Polity Press.

Stein, Arlene. 1992. "All Dressed Up, But No Place to Go? Style Wars and the New Lesbianism." In *The Persistent Desire: A Butch-Femme Reader,* ed. Joan Nestle, 431–439. Boston: Alyson Publications.

Straw, Will. 1993. "Characterizing Rock Music Culture: the Case of Heavy Metal." In *The Cultural Studies Reader,* ed. Simon During, 368–381. New York: Routledge.

Waksman, Steve. 1996. "Every Inch of My Love: Led Zeppelin and the Problem of Cock Rock." *Journal of Popular Music Studies* 8:5–25.

Walser, Robert. 1993. *Running with the Devil: Power Gender and Madness in Heavy Metal Music.* Hanover, N.H.: University Press of New England.

Weinstein, Deena. 1991. *Heavy Metal: A Cultural Sociology.* New York: Lexington Books.

Welch, Chris. 1977. "Zeppelin over America," *Melody Maker* (25 June) :30.

Whiteley, Sheila, ed. 1997. *Sexing the Groove: Popular Music and Gender.* New York: Routledge.

Wise, Sue. 1990. "Sexing Elvis." In *On Record: Rock, Pop and the Written Word,* ed. Simon Frith and Andrew Goodwin, 390–398. London: Routledge.

Religion
Terry E. Miller

Few religions anywhere, especially in the United States, lack some kind of musical expression, as long as we understand music to include all performance that has musical qualities, including chant and other forms of heightened speech, unaccompanied song, instrumental music by itself or as vocal accompaniment, and mediated music. Although this may seem self-evident, to many Americans music means instrumental music. We accept the logic of the Primitive Baptist elder from North Carolina who commented, "We don't have any music in our church. All we do is sing," while continuing to give music its broadest meaning.

It is safe to say that the United States is as diverse in religions as any nation on earth. As a nation composed primarily of people who left other places, Americans brought ideas of individual expression and freedom of religion on a scale hitherto unknown. *The Encyclopedia of American Religions* (Melton 1989) includes entries for at least 1,186 separately named religious bodies in twenty-four categories. The vast majority of adherents likely belong to a much smaller number, for in this list the Roman Catholic Church counts as one along with the Absolute Predestinarian Primitive Baptist Church and the Universal Church of Psychic Science. Melton's list also includes non-European and/or non-Christian faiths present in the United States, including Judaism, Baha'i, Satanism, Rosicrucianism, theosophical societies, Buddhism (figure 1), Hinduism, Islam, and Shinto. Accounting for music in all these faiths would be an impossibility. Thus, we will emphasize Christianity, arguably the religion of the vast majority of worshipers in the United States, while taking into account the many adherents of non-Christian religions as well [see OVERVIEW OF MUSIC IN THE UNITED STATES, p. 519].

References to these religious bodies easily create a terminological minefield. Shall each be called a religion, a church, a denomination, a sect, or a cult? We will use *religion* here to denote a major category of faith, such as Christian, Buddhist, or Jewish; *denomination* or *church* to denote a named organized religious body, such as Baptist, Russian Orthodox, or Spiritualist; and *sect* to refer to subdenominations or breakaway groups, such as Primitive Baptist or Lutheran (Missouri Synod). The term *cult,* sometimes used to describe groups that demonstrate an unusual devotion to and admiration of a particular leader, will be avoided. Faiths described as cults often carry a negative image among mainstream Christians, and people who feel they have found the one

true faith, even if known only to a single inspired leader who dictates all of the group's beliefs and practices, usually resent being called members of a cult. The term *faith* will be used here to denote religions generally.

It is impossible to make any general statements about music and religion in the United States. The question of music has not even been raised in much of the existing literature on American religious practices. American ethnomusicology has not generally focused on religious practices, but folklore studies, which do, rarely say much about music. It is safe to say that the study of religious musical expression remains one of the least tapped but richest veins of American life. Because of the context—worship and personal expression—such research is especially difficult both for investigators, who are often nonbelievers, and for practitioners who, as believers, expect visitors to show more than a detached, scientific interest. Titon (1985) has explored three aspects of this relationship, calling them "role," "stance," and "identity." For purposes of research it has been necessary to consider religions as human expressions, subject to all the variety, biases, and weaknesses typical of humans.

Finally, there is the question of whether to call these practices American religions or religions in America. The difference turns on the question of whether a given faith was brought without change to the United States or underwent change as a result of being there. We view the latter as falling on the "American religion" end of the continuum and the former on the "religion in America" end. It follows that a study of music in American religions would be of greater interest here, because of the potential uniqueness of religious development in this country, than would be a study of religions in America, as the latter might include unchanged musical expressions from Europe, Asia, Africa, Latin America, the Caribbean, and Oceania.

MUSIC AND RELIGIOUS IDENTITY

Each faith is best defined by a combination of beliefs (or doctrine) and practices. Beliefs include both articulated (spoken or written) and unarticulated thoughts about the nature of the spiritual world and the individual adherent's place in that order. Practices include most of the human activities and patterns of ritual that express and realize these beliefs. Isolating practices and beliefs from each other, however, is problematic, for they become so intertwined that both have equal weight in defining a given faith.

Both white and black churches perform types of gospel music, but despite their having common roots, these have become completely differentiated.

Particular practices may become the hallmarks of a faith, the special characteristics that differentiate it from all others. Although these differences may at times seem trivial to outsiders, they can be absolutely fundamental to practitioners. These may include behaviors such as using wine, grape juice, or water for communion; using a common cup or individual glasses; singing with or without accompaniment; using only the King James Bible or allowing other translations; and encouraging or discouraging manifestations of the spirit during services.

Music is a primary identifier in a surprising number of religions. One basic question in many faiths, for example, is whether or not to allow instrumental accompaniment. Should accompaniment be restricted to the piano or organ, or can one include the violin (traditionally the "devil's fiddle"), brass instruments, and drums? In many nineteenth-century American churches the violin was forbidden, but the violoncello, called "the Lord's fiddle," was acceptable. The Old Regular Baptists from eastern Kentucky consider the unique sound of their high-tessitura lined hymns to be part of their sect's identity, and changing this practice would detract from, if not destroy, that identity. Russian Orthodox services sound distinct from Bulgarian Orthodox services because of musical style. Liturgical churches, usually derived from historical European denominations, often avoid evangelical and especially gospel hymns because these hymns are believed to detract from the churches' sophisticated and reserved identities. And a surprising number of sects, such as the Church of God and Saints of Christ and the Old Order Amish, maintain musical traditions not found in any other group.

AUSTERITY AND SENSUALITY: JEAN CALVIN'S SHADOW OVER AMERICAN RELIGION

The United States at the beginning of the twenty-first century is a vibrant, multiethnic, multicultural society, but there is also much discussion of and tension over issues of morality, especially the cultural politics advocated by the religious right. Simplified, these attitudes appeal to old-fashioned morals, obedience to a Christian God, family values, abstinence, self-sufficiency, and all other habits that, in the words of their practitioners, "made this country great." The Founding Fathers were primarily of English extraction. Many who followed were Scottish and German. The majority were Protestants who believed in religious individuality. Protestantism itself was and continues to be a continuum extending from those who broke with the Roman Catholic Church but only modified its worship patterns (for example, Lutherans, Episcopalians) and those who departed as far as possible from Roman Catholic worship. The latter followed reformers of various stripes, some more radical than others. Jean (or John) Calvin (1509–1564), a French churchman who spent several years of exile in Switzerland because of his anti-Rome views, espoused what became the mainstream views of the resulting Reformed churches, both on the Continent (German, Dutch, French [Huguenots]) and in the British Isles.

Calvin and his followers objected to most worship practices that were deemed sensual (the "bells and smells" of Roman Catholicism), as well as vestments, stained glass, the crucifix, and other traits of liturgical religion. Planted by John Knox in Scotland's rocky soil, Calvin's ideas grew quickly. In England they brought years of tension and civil war between Roman Catholics or Anglicans and "puritans" (Calvinists). For many Americans whose forefathers were avid followers of Calvinism, these austere attitudes remain embedded in their psyches and continue to be expressed in American politics, emerging most clearly in such controversies as that over the National Endowment for the Arts. Cultural conservatism in the United States is a retention of Calvinism, but Calvinism is also reflected in American attitudes toward alcohol, sex, and most other "sins of the flesh."

Musically, Calvin allowed only the singing of versified psalms. Although Calvin's followers used instrumental accompaniment in Switzerland, English and Scottish Calvinists preferred the unaccompanied singing of simple melodies. Certain of their performance practices, such as lining out the psalms (called "precenting" among the Scots), have survived in the United States among certain white Appalachian sects as well as among most black Baptists, although the psalms have been largely replaced by hymns. A great many musical controversies throughout America's history have reflected a continuing tension between Calvinistic preferences for austerity and tradition as opposed to rich liturgical and secularized modern practices.

DICHOTOMIES: A SURVEY OF POSSIBILITIES FOR THE STUDY OF RELIGION AND MUSIC

In approaching any given faith, one can ask a number of questions about a particular group's values and uses of music. Following are nine such questions, posed here as dichotomies—two opposing positions, each pair representing the ends of a continuum. Each set of dichotomies reflects a basic defining issue of primary importance to social, cultural, and religious identity in North America.

Mainstream and folk religions

Mainstream denominations tend to be highly centralized and standardized and are found over a broad geographical area. Most are of foreign origin; they are sometimes described as "historical churches." Typical examples include the Roman Catholic Church, the Orthodox traditions, and the main bodies of the Lutheran, Methodist, Presbyterian, Episcopal, and other such denominations. Folk churches, perhaps better described as sects, tend to be small in scale, restricted in geography, and idiosyncratic in practice, if not in belief. A great many faiths fall somewhere between these two, with characteristics of both. For many reasons, the music found at the folk end of this scale tends to be of greater interest to researchers than that at the mainstream end. However, although North America is rich in folk-type churches, where musical expression is greatly varied and sometimes archaic, many are local and cannot be researched easily.

Urban and rural contexts

The urban–rural dichotomy—perhaps more useful in the past than in the present as a result of demographic changes especially since World War II—nevertheless retains some relevance, especially in terms of music. Urban churches, especially the larger mainstream congregations, are more likely to have instruments, in particular large pipe organ installations, and choirs. In the nineteenth century, it was also common in urban churches to accompany singing with a violoncello, and the old European Baroque custom of thorough bass accompaniment persisted in such churches until the late nineteenth century (Dana 1875). Although rural folk churches have become part of the urban environment because of migrations, rural churches are unlikely to have more than a piano, pump organ (in the past), or electronic organ. Archaic performance practices such as lining out, singing from shape-note notation, and chanted sermons are more likely found in isolated rural areas than in towns or cities. The term *rural* can denote both churches located in vast agricultural areas such as Illinois, where mainstream historical churches dominated (some speaking German until the early twentieth century) and those in isolated areas, such as Appalachia, where independent local sects predominate.

Black and white socioreligious groups

Although the United States is ostensibly an integrated society, it tends to remain segregated in terms of religious association. Few churches, none of them mainstream, would exclude members of any race or ethnicity, but in practice, churches are either white, predominantly white, or black. Black denominations—primarily Baptist and Methodist—formed out of historically white denominations after the Civil War, and by the end of the nineteenth century newly founded sects proliferated. Black and white styles of worship tend to remain distinctive, especially in terms of performance practices and repertoire. For example, both white and black churches perform types of gospel music, but despite their having common roots, these have become completely differentiated. In present-day America, however, many traits hitherto considered black have been absorbed by white society, and one can now encounter white and mixed choirs singing and behaving like black choirs.

Class and ethnicity as factors in religious practice

Although one might hope that religious doctrines would overcome class differences, people still prefer to associate with others of similar class and lifestyle. Churches are, after all, aspects of human organization and tend to reflect the ethnic, economic, and political orientations of the secular world. Whether fair or not, many people associate particular denominations with particular classes because these stereotypes are, or have been, more or less true. Ethnic-based denominations or congregations, even when associated with otherwise broad-based mainstream groups, tend to retain traits from the homeland. Consequently, one encounters a Korean Presbyterian church, a Hungarian Jewish temple, an English Lutheran church, a Polish Catholic church, or an African American Islamic mosque. Many of these faiths worship with distinctive musical traditions. In terms of class, few churches are clearly based on a single economic category, but members of the working and professional classes do tend to gravitate toward separate congregations of like membership, and this factor often determines the style of worship as well. Whether right or wrong, people sometimes refer to "country club" or "silk-stocking" churches, or to emotional congregations as "holy rollers."

Emotion and evangelicalism in religious practice

The degree of emotional expression during worship may say nothing of individual sincerity but often says a great deal about culture and tradition, as such behaviors are learned within one's own socioreligious context. Most denominations and sects follow typical patterns of behavior that usually correlate with socioeconomic status, ethnic background, and sometimes geographical origin. At the restrained end of the scale one finds many of the historical denominations, especially those originating in the British Isles and northern Europe. For the most part, orthodox Christian faiths, Judaism, and especially the Asian-derived religions are also restrained. At the emotional end are those faiths that are described as "pentecostal" or, in the case of black churches, "sanctified." Here one encounters the "gifts of the spirit," including glossolalia (speaking in tongues) and being "slain in the spirit." Emotional expression is typically found wherever evangelism is strong, and music has long been an important tool for encouraging conversion. At the extreme end of the scale one encounters music that brings the worshiper to a state of ecstasy or even trance through repetition and extreme volume combined with emotional words encouraging surrender to the Lord. Although both are Baptist, a member of a Missionary Baptist church is much more likely to exhibit emotional behavior than a Primitive Baptist, as the former sect is evangelical and the latter sect is predestinarian, eliminating any appeal to conversion. Similar to this scale is one that considers impersonal aloofness at one end and a personal relationship with God at the other. Such aloofness may derive from a more philosophical, intellectual, or abstract approach to religion, whereas the personal view is well expressed in the gospel hymn "What a Friend We Have in Jesus."

Liturgy and spontaneity in religious practice

Liturgical worship follows a fixed pattern of events. The archetypal liturgy is the Roman Catholic and Orthodox Mass, a symbolic reenactment of Christ's Last Supper. Most historical denominations resulting from the Reformation, including the Lutheran and Episcopal churches, retain liturgies that in some respect follow, or at least echo, the Mass format. Although liturgy is part of Methodist and Presbyterian tradition, little remains in practice. Any church celebrating communion, however, in retaining this basic rite is practicing some form of liturgy.

Virtually all liturgies require music. In the most elaborate rituals there is a great variety of music, from congregational hymns and responses to chants sung by the priest and choir. In less elaborate rituals only fragments of the Mass remain, such as a Kyrie response, a foreshortened Gloria, and a spoken Creed. At the other end of the scale are patterns that, though fixed, are not liturgical in any historical sense, as well as worship patterns that strive for spontaneity. Much of this seeming spontaneity, however, derives from long-standing and more or less fixed patterns of behavior. There is also a strong tradition of conscious antiliturgicalism that sometimes manifested itself in declarations against "romanism" and "popishness." William Walker's *Southern Harmony* [1854] included the song "The Romish Lady," whose first stanza begins "There was a Romish lady brought up in popery, Her mother always taught her the priest she must obey." Books such as Justin D. Fulton's *Rome in America* (Boston 1872) and Isaac Kelso's *Danger in the Dark: A Tale of Intrigue and Priestcraft* (Cincinnati 1855) spread a virulent suspicion of both Roman Catholicism and practices associated with it.

Primitive (antimodern) and modern ideologies

The term *primitive,* far from being pejorative, is usually interpreted by practitioners as meaning "in the manner of the first-century Christians" and is worn as a badge of honor by a number of American sects espousing this idea, especially the Primitive Baptists (also called "Hardshell Baptists" because of their alleged refusal to consider alternative—that is, "modern"—ideas). Strict primitives admit no practice unless explicitly endorsed by precept or example in the Bible's New Testament. Only four rites are allowed: baptism, foot washing, communion, and marriage. At the primitive end of the scale one is likely to find unaccompanied singing; archaic practices such as lined hymnody and chanted preaching; and a rejection of such modern practices as Sunday School, missionary activity, or the use of printed bulletins. Typically, these sects are male dominated, following Paul's comments in his epistles on the place of women. Perhaps the most primitive people in the United States are the Old Order Amish, who shun musical instruments, gasoline-powered vehicles, electricity, and modern dress. At the modern end of the scale are churches that exist in the modern world both socially and technologically, using modern media according to their means. Some churches, such as those of Roman Catholicism, have willingly dispensed with the use of Latin and Gregorian chant in favor of the vernacular and newly composed tunes, sometimes accompanied by guitars. The extreme end includes churches where so-called political correctness has been institutionalized, especially through the degendering of standard prayers (for example, in the Lord's Prayer, changing "Our Father" to "Our Father/ Mother") and hymns (for example, adding "Faith of Our Mothers" to "Faith of Our Fathers"). The terms *conservative* and *liberal* might appear to be synonymous with *primitive* and *modern,* but the former terms more likely connote attitudes toward doctrine,

The organist accompanies congregational hymn singing, responses, choir anthems, and solos and may improvise "walking music" during brief gaps in the service or provide a quiet musical atmosphere during communion.

lifestyle, and politics than to musical practices. Modern churches may allow somewhat exceptional practices such as dance, drama, mediated music, and the performance of long, concerted works such as cantatas, oratorios, and masses by classical composers.

Music as performance and as self-expression

At the performance end of the scale, people perform musical compositions created, in most cases, by others; at the self-expression end people use some aspect of a composition—perhaps the melody—as the departure point for their own emotional expression through the medium of often improvised music. The concepts are fundamentally different, for a performer is self-consciously aware of being a medium for someone else's thoughts and can contribute only minimally to the performance. Concerned about performance issues, musicians may experience anxiety, regrets about wrong notes, uncertainty about reception, and a desire to behave appropriately in terms of dress, gesture, and overall demeanor. In some traditions, especially those of Asia, performers must chant the sacred texts with exactitude. At the opposite end of this continuum, musical expression is confident, without concerns for right or wrong notes or for obeying the wishes of the original composer; the performer uses the music merely as a medium for conveying sincerity of feeling and concern for the souls of others. In a broadly generalized sense, this is a fundamental difference between white and black worship in the United States.

Otherworldly and worldly contexts for religious practice

The atmosphere for worship is created by both physical and conceptual elements. Religions and denominations that strive for otherworldliness favor buildings that remove the worshiper from the ordinary world through sheer size, and through the use of stained glass windows, statuary, murals, icons, elaborate altars, officiants dressed in sacred vestments, flickering candles, and the smell of incense. The most sensuous buildings are those of the various Orthodox traditions and Roman Catholicism, although Episcopal cathedrals strive for this as well. Musical expression, too, tends to be ethereal, especially through the use of otherworldly heightened speech, whether the drone and melody of Greek Orthodox chant or the monophonic Gregorian chant of Roman Catholic churches of the recent past. These denominations, when they can, prefer to re-create the architecture and decoration of buildings from their geographical origins, giving the United States many styles prefixed with "neo" (for example, neobaroque, with the churches' vaulted ceilings painted to look like heaven itself). At the worldly end of the scale are church buildings called meeting houses, built as simply as possible, lacking stained glass, adornments, and even basic Christian symbols other than perhaps a cross and a print of Warner Sallman's *Head of Christ*. Most often associated with austere, Calvinistic sects such as the Old Regular Baptists, such buildings may double as dining halls or meeting rooms. No attempt is made to isolate the worshiper from the secular, which is easily seen through the clear windows. Officiants wear the same styles of clothing as those worn by worshipers, including slacks and open-collared shirt or skirt and blouse. Singing tends to be unelaborated, often unaccompanied. Otherworldliness is conceptual; a baptized member is no longer "living in the world," and preaching may take the elder into an altered state, even a trance, during which the Lord speaks through him. Worldliness and unworldliness coexist in different ways at each end of this spectrum.

MUSIC OF A MAINSTREAM DENOMINATION: THE EPISCOPAL CHURCH

The music of the Episcopal Church can be plotted on the foregoing nine continua to represent a more or less typical model of mainstream music. Every denomination is unique in some respects (the differences seem greatest to those closest to the church in question), but, for example, any skilled church musician (organist–choir director) will be able to function in virtually any mainstream church, even if called for emergency duty. The music of the Episcopal Church is consistent throughout the United States because it is a highly centralized body with its own hymnal and other publications.

Episcopal churches offer the possibility of many kinds of services depending on the day and time, but two predominate—Morning Prayer and Holy Communion. All liturgical texts are found in the *Book of Common Prayer* supplemented by a denominational hymnal. Three entities provide virtually all music: the congregation (with choir and organ), the choir (with or without a soloist and organ), and the organist (occasionally with a solo instrument such as violin, oboe, or trumpet). Larger parishes, however, might have multiple choirs and perhaps a bell choir as well. The duties of playing the organ and directing the choir may be separate or combined. The organist provides continuity through the playing of compositions, both historical (for example, Bach) and contemporary (such as Healy Willan), that mark important points in the service (prelude and postlude, marking the beginning and ending) or accompany a specific function (for example, the collection of offerings). The organist also accompanies congregational hymn singing, responses, choir anthems, and solos, and may improvise "walking music" during brief gaps in the service or provide a quiet musical atmosphere during communion. The congregation is invited to sing hymns and liturgical responses, whereas the choir leads all congregational singing, sings certain liturgical responses alone, and sings at least one anthem, either alone or during the offering. In some parishes the priest may chant the beginnings of certain texts that are elsewhere spoken. Services typically last an hour. The musical traditions of the Episcopal Church are heavily English in both hymnody and choral literature, but the church embraces all kinds of classical music, its hymnal has become more and more eclectic (now including a greater portion of American folk hymns as well as some gospel hymns), and organists may play whatever they please, both sacred and classical-secular.

Episcopal churches are primarily urban- and town-centered. Congregations are predominantly white, but there are also black parishes. Although the church has a reputation for being an institution associated with the upper class, in the United States membership is broad-based and includes many working-class people. Emotion is generally restrained, behavior seems to be dignified, and the service is among the most liturgical, providing a somewhat otherworldly atmosphere. Episcopalians take pride in their traditions, but they are not antimodern; and although their emotions may be as deeply felt as those of other Christians, they tend not to exhibit them, especially through music, which is considered as performance more than as individual expression.

MUSIC OF A NONMAINSTREAM WHITE SECT:
THE OLD REGULAR BAPTISTS OF JESUS CHRIST

The Old Regular Baptists of Jesus Christ evolved out of the Great Awakening (1739–1742), being a compromise between the predestinarian Regular Baptists and the newly awakened evangelical New Lights on the frontiers of early-nineteenth-century North Carolina and Kentucky. Originally confined to several eastern Kentucky counties, where they remain strong, many Old Regular Baptists moved north after World War II, seeking employment in Indiana, Ohio, and Michigan. They also founded churches in these states, where they maintain their patterns virtually without change. Although they are not predestinarian like their distant cousins, the Primitive Baptists, the Old Regulars are also nonevangelical, understanding that each individual has a chance to accept conversion when God offers it. One's name is placed in the Lamb's Book of Life (containing the names of the elect, according to the Book of Revelation) upon baptism by immersion, performed throughout the year outdoors, preferably in moving water (that is, in a stream rather than a pond).

The Old Regulars typify the American folk church in that they are a little-known rural sect whose ministers (called elders) require no training, whose buildings (called meeting houses) are extremely plain, and whose singing and preaching reflect archaic practices. Virtually all members are hard-working country people, many of them coal miners; most of those who have postsecondary education are teachers. Most Old Regular congregations are white, but there are a few black congregations as well whose practices differ little from those of their white brethren. Emotional expression is confined to a few fixed behaviors: women, who otherwise must keep silent (except in singing), may shout (a cathartic release of tension expressed as shouting, crying, and waving the arms); men preach spontaneously. Being Baptists, they do not manifest the gifts of the spirit. Each church meets one weekend a month, on both Sunday morning and the Saturday before. Although their services follow a fixed order—thirty minutes of songs, opening sermon, song, prayer, one to three sermons, song (for altar call and offering), and announcements—they are not liturgical (figure 2). Both sermons and prayers are spontaneous, with sermons typically delivered in a heightened speech that resembles an auctioneer's chant. Besides the rites of passage found in baptism and marriage, their major annual service is foot washing and communion, reserved for members. Services typically last three or more hours, especially for communion or baptism. Old Regular Baptists are antimodern; they wish to be primitive, that is, to preserve practices associated with the early, first-century church. Although their buildings are ordinary and worldly, baptism transfers Old Regulars from the world into a suspended state of waiting for the Lord. Overall, the Old Regulars live a fairly severe form of Calvinism, shunning pleasure of every kind but without expressing an overt doctrine of holiness.

FIGURE 2   Two elders of the Old Regular Baptist Church of Jesus Christ, originally from eastern Kentucky, baptize a new member by immersion outdoors near Medina, Ohio. Photo by Terry E. Miller, 1980.

Old Regular Baptist singing preserves both the lining out of hymns and hetero-phonic performance of monophonic tunes, practices that were much debated in New England during the early eighteenth century. Lining out originated in England, where it was recommended in the *Directory for Publick Worship,* a Calvinist-Presbyterian document, in 1645. Although Calvinism allowed only the singing of psalms, the Baptists embraced hymns during the eighteenth and nineteenth centuries; the Old Regular Baptist song repertoire now includes both historical hymn texts as well as newly written ballads, many by members. Without announcement, any male member may begin singing, after which the others, as they recognize the song, join in. Only the leader uses a hymnal (a book with only the words), while the others pick up the words from the prompting of the line. The timbre is nasal and the tessitura high.

MUSIC OF A MAINSTREAM BLACK DENOMINATION: MISSIONARY BAPTISTS

The first independent African American denominations to form after the Civil War were the Baptists and Methodists, but by the end of the nineteenth century many new denominations and sects appeared, the majority being sanctified (pentecostal) [see RELIGIOUS MUSIC, p. 624]. The Baptists have remained the most visible and main-stream black denomination, however, and membership spans virtually the entire range of social strata. Although there are many Baptist sects, the Missionary Baptists predominate. Many older members of northern churches migrated from the South, from both rural and urban areas, but in the North virtually all churches are urban. Services follow a fixed but nonliturgical order that varies from church to church, the sermon and altar call being perhaps the most important segments. Emotional outbursts are most likely to take place during climaxes in the choral and solo gospel numbers, and many churches have nurses on duty to assist members who "get happy"—that is, engage in shouting, crying, and holy dancing—or in some cases faint. Their rituals are relatively short and plain, including marriage, baptism by immersion in a tank behind the pulpit, and communion (sometimes with foot washing). Throughout the year the congregation observes numerous memorials and anniversaries, the pastor's being the most important. Many Sunday afternoons and evenings are spent visiting other Baptist churches or hosting visits.

Music plays a major role in black Baptist services, and most music is performed by the choirs, soloists, ministers, and musicians. The congregation does little more than sing one or two hymns. Medium to large churches may have five or more choirs, including a sanctuary (mixed) choir, male chorus, female chorus, young people's choir, high school choir, and youth choir. In addition there is an organist, a pianist, and nowadays usually a drum set player, electric guitarist, and more. Other than the organist's or director's charts, little musical notation is used; virtually all music is taught by rote to the choirs by directors who may have heard the composition on a recording and arranged it for their particular forces (figure 3).

Many Baptist churches preserve virtually the entire range of black sacred music. Lay leaders may open the service with spirituals sung the old way, lined hymns (called "Dr. Watts," "long meter," or "raising an old hymn"), and chanted prayers. The choirs offer a full range of gospel styles, from early James Cleveland to the latest Andrae Crouch, and new works by local musicians. The service begins with a grand procession of the main choir dressed in colorful robes bearing a symbol of the church's name. Congregational hymns, mostly of the gospel type but enlivened by improvised accompaniments, are sung slowly, with little vocal improvisation. Depending on the social status of the church, emotions range from restrained to "hot," the wealthiest churches being the most restrained and most similar to white churches.

Preaching has musical qualities, too. Most ministers begin preaching on a particular biblical text, constantly reiterating a central theme. Indeed, the black preacher is perhaps the most skilled and effective orator in American society today, something

Singer-composers usually receive songs in part or whole from a "song angel" and then teach them to the choir, which is capable of instant harmonization using complex chromatic harmonies and semi-independence of parts, especially the bass.

FIGURE 3   The adult choir of the Ocala, Florida, Covenant Missionary Baptist Church rehearses for the Sunday service. Photo by Terry E. Miller, 1987.

familiar to any American who has heard speeches by black politicians, be they ministers or not. As the sermon progresses, it takes on a more rhythmic delivery, which gradually focuses on a reciting pitch. As it becomes more melodic, one senses a shift from the text to a more generalized flow of thoughts. At an appropriate point, often signaled by the minister to the organist, the musicians take their places and begin accompanying the sermon with exclamatory chords and short harmonic passages. After reaching one or more climaxes, during which he may loosen his tie and shift to an off-the-pulpit microphone, the minister cools down quickly, moving to the altar call and prayer requests. After two to three hours, the service is over.

MUSIC OF A UNIQUE DENOMINATION: THE CHURCH OF GOD AND SAINTS OF CHRIST

Founded in Oklahoma in 1896 by former slave William Saunders Crowdy, the Church of God and Saints of Christ (hereafter CGSC) is unique in the United States not only for its beliefs, practices, and costumes but also for a self-sufficient musical tradition without equal that constitutes more than half of any service. Prophet Crowdy's visions formed the basis for most beliefs and practices, although he also brought much Masonic ritual and paraphernalia into the church. Though Christian, the CGSC is Old Testament–oriented, with members calling their churches tabernacles, worshiping on the Sabbath (Saturday), and having a rabbi as one of the church officials. The church's complex hierarchy includes several bishops (one of them the Chief Executive Officer), deacons, elders, a board of presbytery, and officials unique to the CGSC, such as Grandfather Abraham, Grandmother Sarah, and the National Exhorter. The CGSC

FIGURE 5   A group of singers offers a special song at the annual Passover of the Church of God and Saints of Christ. Photo by Terry E. Miller, 1999.

has tabernacles in twenty-seven American cities, but most are small and remain obscure. A succession dispute occurred at the death of the Prophet in 1908, and many of Crowdy's descendants formed a second division called by the same name for many years. Now under the control of Rabbi Levi S. Plummer, this larger branch gradually adopted Judaism during the 1950s and 1960s and eventually changed its name to Temple Beth-El, with headquarters in Belleville, Virginia. Both branches have additional tabernacles in Jamaica, Canada (comprising Jamaicans), South Africa, Zimbabwe, and the United Kingdom.

The majority of members usually sing in the a cappella choir, whose singing is joined by most officiants and even by members of the congregation, which has no singing otherwise. Led by a chorister, the choir opens the service and sings throughout, especially during the testimony period, which can last more than an hour (figure 5). Climaxing the service before the sermon is the choir's grand march, consisting of intricate formations and patterns that lead to the rear of the tabernacle, where female members put on crowns before marching to the front, genuflecting to the officiants, and resuming their seats. Singing may account for up to two-thirds of the three- to four-hour service. There is a hierarchy of music officials, including Chorister, District Chorister, Chief Chorister, Superintendent of Singers, and Minister of Music.

The CGSC repertoire is primarily songs of their own composition, although nothing more than the words is ever written down. Singer-composers usually receive songs in part or whole from a "song angel" and then teach them to the choir, which is capable of instant harmonization using complex chromatic harmonies and semi-independence of parts, especially the bass. Some songs are quite long and elaborate, even in multiple sections; others are shorter and sometimes strophic. After the adults have marched, the children are invited to march and sing as well. Because they lead their own songs, there is a tendency for them to choose more contemporary songs, known from the media but sung in CGSC style. No one knows how many songs exist, as old ones are forgotten and new ones learned continuously. Songs become known throughout the church because most members spend eight days together each year for their annual Passover, which begins on April 13 with the eating of the Paschal Lamb and continues with two long services daily. On Singer's Day each choir sings its newest songs, now preserved and learned through the use of tape recorders.

MUSIC AND AMERICAN RELIGIONS

The musics practiced in the endless variety of religions of the United States embrace historical styles as well as express migration patterns from Europe, Africa, Central and South America, and Asia. Music serves many roles, from an edifying cultural experience to a way of expressing one's profoundest feelings about the nature of life, salvation, and the afterlife. The field is so rich because most churchgoers recognize the necessity of making their own music, in contrast to the general population, which more often experiences music through the media. Although the mainstream denominations offer few surprises for researchers, as one moves to the "folk" end of the spectrum, the limitless musical inventiveness of American worshipers becomes apparent.

REFERENCES

Crawford, Richard, ed. 1984. *The Core Repertory of Early American Psalmody.* Recent Researches in American Music, vols. 11 and 12. Madison, Wisc.: A-R Editions.

Dana, William H. 1875. *Dana's Practical Thorough Base (The Art of Playing Church Music).* Warren, Ohio: Dana's Musical Institute.

Epstein, Dena J. 1981. *Sinful Tunes and Spirituals: Black Folk Music to the Civil War.* Urbana: University of Illinois Press.

Eskew, Harry, David W. Music, and Paul A. Richardson. 1994. *Singing Baptists: Studies in Baptist Hymnody in America.* Nashville, Tenn.: Church Street Press.

Fulton, Justin D. 1872. *Rome in America.* Boston: Howard Gannett.

Gould, Nathaniel D. 1972 [1853]. *Church Music in America, Comprising Its History and Its Peculiarities of Different Periods with Cursory Remarks. . . .* New York: AMS Press.

Heilbut, Tony. 1971. *The Gospel Sound: Good News and Bad Times.* New York: Simon and Schuster.

Hood, George. 1970 [1846]. *A History of Music in New England: With Biographical Sketches of Reformers and Psalmists.* New York: Johnson Reprint Corp.

Hurston, Zora Neale. 1983. *The Sanctified Church.* Berkeley, Calif.: Turtle Island.

Jackson, George Pullen. 1965 [1933]. *White Spirituals in the Southern Uplands.* New York: Dover.

Kelso, Isaac. 1855. *Danger in the Dark: A Tale of Intrigue and Priestcraft.* 31st ed. Cincinnati: Queen City Publishing House.

Lovell, John Jr. 1972. *Black Song: The Forge and the Flame.* New York: Macmillan.

Melton, J. Gordon. 1989. *The Encyclopedia of American Religions.* 3rd ed. Detroit: Gale Research.

Montell, William Lynwood. 1991. *Singing the Glory Down: Amateur Gospel Music in South Central Kentucky, 1900–1990.* Lexington: University Press of Kentucky.

Patterson, Beverly Bush. 1995. *The Sound of the Dove: Singing in Appalachian Primitive Baptist Churches.* Urbana: University of Illinois Press.

Ricks, George Robinson. 1977. *Some Aspects of the Religious Music of the United States Negro.* New York: Arno Press.

Titon, Jeff Todd. 1985. "Stance, Role, and Identity in Fieldwork among Folk Baptists and Pentecostals." *American Music* 3(1):16–24.

Walker, William. 1966 [1854]. *The Southern Harmony, and Musical Companion.* Rev. ed. Los Angeles: Pro Musicamericana.

Snapshot:
Three Views of Music and Religion
Jennifer Rycenga
Denise A. Seachrist
Elaine Keillor

The Influence of Asian Religious Ideas on American Music—Jennifer Rycenga
The Shakers—Denise A. Seachrist
Sharon: "Make a Joyful Noise"—Elaine Keillor

Religious practices of all sorts have flourished in the United States and Canada. Some religions and their musics, originally brought here from other parts of the world, have remained relatively unchanged, while others have developed in new and distinctive ways. The three views of music and religion presented in this Snapshot, while not a comprehensive survey of the hundreds of musico-religious groups in the United States and Canada, do serve to illustrate the tremendous variety and creativity of religious and musical practice here, both historically and in contemporary times.

THE INFLUENCE OF ASIAN RELIGIOUS IDEAS ON AMERICAN MUSIC

Asian religious ideas pervade twentieth-century American music even more than Asian musical influences do. This surprising cross-cultural narrative weaves together strands of orientalism, war, imperialism, commerce, counterculture, and immigration.

The religious traditions of Asia discussed herein—Hinduism, Buddhism, and Taoism—have reached North America in three principal ways. Countercultural contact came first, enabled by translations of major Asian religious texts. Second, increased contact between Asian nations and the United States and Canada occurred via cultural and intellectual exchanges as well as through commerce and war, starting from the mid-nineteenth century. While such contact fueled orientalism around Asian religions, ongoing human contact exposed these ideas to Americans outside of intellectual or aesthetic coteries (soldiers, businesspeople, jazz musicians). Third, Asian religions have become established, institutionally and culturally, through immigration to North America. The most recent immigrants, particularly from Tibet, have had the widest musical impact.

But why have religious concepts had musical influence? The perceived body/mind dualism of Western traditions is offset by the concrete religious practices, such as meditation and yoga, encouraged in Asian religions. Immanent Asian cosmologies that locate the sacred in matter as well as spirit encourage different philosophic approaches to time, sound, and form.

Countercultural movements

Countercultural movements go against the grain of the dominant culture. In religious terms, in North America after European conquest, this has meant rejection of Christianity (and, to a lesser extent, Judaism). Buddhism and Hinduism serve as perfect foils for this impulse, presenting highly literate traditions with cosmological presuppositions radically different from those of monotheism. Ideas like karma, *samsara* 'reincarnation', *moksa* 'enlightenment', and nirvana derive from the concept that ignorance of our true situation is what blocks spiritual progress—not sin or human guilt.

Awareness of Asian religious ideas among American intellectuals dates from the early nineteenth century. Ralph Waldo Emerson read Hindu texts in translation; his poem "Brahma" is a gloss on the *Bhagavad Gita*. The Transcendentalist journal *The Dial* published the first partial translation of the Buddhist *Lotus Sutra* in 1844. The World's Parliament of Religions, held in Chicago in 1893, brought leading practitioners of Asian religions to the United States, most notably Swami Vivekananda from the Hindu Ramakrishna Mission (Vedanta Society) and Zen master Shaku Soen from Japan. It was Shaku's disciple D. T. Suzuki (1870–1966) whose two extended stays in the United States made an impact on American music. Paul Carus (1852–1919), the American publisher of Open Court Books, worked with Suzuki in the early years of the century; he later set Buddhist hymns to Western music (Verhoeven 1998:207–208).

The epochal breakthrough for countercultural Buddhism and American music came with John Cage's (1912–1992) attendance at Suzuki's Columbia lectures of the early 1950s. Like those of other luminaries who attended, including Gary Snyder, Allen Ginsburg, Erich Fromm, Karen Horney, and Philip Kapleau, Cage's impressions reflected the Beat Zen phenomenon. However, while Beat Zen often devolved into sheer eclecticism, Cage's musical thought was entirely transformed by this encounter.

Cage's interest in Asian religions began in the 1940s, when he had a student, Gita Sarabhai, who conveyed that in her Indian tradition "the purpose of music is to sober and quiet the mind, thus making it susceptible to divine influences" (Revill 1992:90). Cage read the aesthetic writings of Ananda Coomaraswamy (1877–1947), particularly on the theory of *rasa* (the Indian aesthetics of representing emotional states), and the sayings of Ramakrishna; these Hindu influences were applied in Cage's *The Seasons*.

Imbibing D. T. Suzuki's brand of Zen Buddhism yielded an austere removal of expression and personality from music. Letting sounds exist for themselves, apart from human intentions, was something Cage learned directly from Suzuki's lecture style, as reported in a famous anecdote: "Suzuki never spoke loudly. When the weather was good, the windows were open, and the airplanes leaving La Guardia flew directly overhead from time to time, drowning out whatever he had to say. He never repeated what had been said during the passage of the airplane" (Revill 1992:109).

Zen offered Cage the means for excising personality: discipline. Drawing on the Taoist I Ching, Cage developed "a means as strict as sitting cross-legged, namely the use of chance operations" to generate sound. This resulted in the role of the composer shifting "from that of making choices to that of asking questions" (Fields 1986:196).

Cage's transformation culminated with the famous *4'33"*, a composition in which a pianist approaches the piano but plays nothing for the designated length. The piece consists of the ambient sounds in the concert hall and the questions in the minds of the listeners. The seeming arbitrariness of the length and form of the piece reflects Suzuki's understanding of Zen practice, in which "'[b]eing religious' is at once a critical enterprise and a willingness to be transformed by these 'contrivances,'" such as meditation, study, and *koans* (paralexical puzzles meant to thwart rational consciousness) (Dornish 1986:2).

The removal of ego was central for Cage. He had long sought to erase the distinction between music and noise, resenting composers' imposition of their agendas upon the givenness of sound. He reinterpreted the definition given by Gita Sarabhai, understanding divine influences as "all the things that happen in creation. There's nothing that isn't" (Revill 1992:90). This fulfills what Suzuki had predicted/described of the Zen artist: "When the mind, now abiding in its isness—which, to use Zen verbalism, is not isness—and thus free from intellectual complexities and moralistic attachments of every description, surveys the world of the senses in all its multiplicities, it discovers in it all sorts of values hitherto hidden from sight. Here opens to the artist a world full of wonders and miracles" (Suzuki 1959:17).

Pauline Oliveros, in her "Sonic Meditations," explores similar concerns, explicitly in sonic relationships between sentient beings: "she developed a theory of sonic awareness in which the goals of music are ritual, ceremony, healing, and humanism; beauty, rather than the goal, is a by-product" (Edwards with Lassetter 1991:229). Likewise, jazz saxophonist Steve Lacy absorbed countercultural conceptions of Taoism, which resulted in his allowing his reed to indicate which notes were playable on any given night and which also accounted for the always unfinished nature of his first composition, "The Way" (figure 1). Philip Glass credits John Cage's book *Silence* (1961) with introducing him to Buddhist concepts, even though he was already practicing yoga in the early 1960s. Glass specifically says that Asian religions have not influenced the sound of his music. Rather, they have aided his "development of compassion and equanimity and mindfulness" and enabled him to perceive his music as a form of spiritual practice (Tweed and Prothero 1999:347).

FIGURE I   Score of "The Way," by Steve Lacy.

Coltrane reflected on this in his choice of instrumentation, explaining his need for two bass players: "I want more of the sense of the expansion of time. I want the time to be more plastic."

Increased contact: John Coltrane and the dissemination of Asian thought in jazz

Because jazz musicians often found greater respect outside of the United States, international jazz tours became a jazz institution from the 1920s onward. After World War II, these tours increasingly included Asian countries, particularly Japan. World War II and the Korean and Vietnam Wars also created increased contact between working-class soldiers and Asian thought; one enduring result of this is the proliferation of martial arts in North America.

The musical and spiritual journey of John Coltrane can be viewed from the perspective of Asian influences. In 1957, his life and career endangered by excessive drug use, Coltrane went "cold turkey" and claimed to have experienced "a spiritual awakening" (Berendt 1975:107). By 1958 he was practicing yoga, eating health food, and reading Eastern philosophy. His explorations were public knowledge by 1962, when he said: "I believe in all religions" (Berendt 1975:107). At this point, Coltrane's interests included Asian musics, particularly the improvisatory traditions of India (Collier 1978: 485; Porter 1983:127–128). Coltrane came to know Ravi Shankar, even naming his son Ravi (Priestley 1987:52).

This combination of Asian religious ideas with modal improvisation can be heard in all of Coltrane's music of the 1960s, but it is most explicit on the album *Om*. The composition evokes world music by using mbiras 'African thumb pianos', gongs, and low-voiced chanting, while remaining essentially an avant-garde jazz improvisation. But the focus of the piece is on a specifically Hindu idea—the idea of Om, in Coltrane's words, "the first vibration—that sound, that spirit which set everything else into being. It is The Word from which all men and everything else comes, including all possible sounds that men can make vocally. It is the first syllable, the primal word, the word of Power" (Hentoff 1968). This description is saturated with Hindu philosophy concerning the mantric syllable, which is echoed in the Upanishadic verses that open the composition and invoke Vedic ritual. The recited words, preceded and followed by an intensely chanted Om, convey the ritual intent of the piece: the search for universals in sound (Rivelli and Levin 1979 [1970]:123).

This search for the universal raises the larger cultural context of *Om*'s 1965 recording. In the midst of 1960s radical activism, from the civil rights movement to the anti–Vietnam War activities, this album merited special criticism from Amiri Baraka for being apolitical music, "ultra-metaphysical where you get a lot of 'Om-m-m-m-m' in it" (Priestley 1987:56). The album cover displays "The Omulet," an amulet of flower power and religious eclecticism (figure 2). This search for a universal religious meaning in music pulls away from both the narrative specificities of Christian mythology and the history of Black struggles in the United States. Likewise, the different perspective on time that Asian religious traditions offered was less linear in its direction. Coltrane reflected on this in his choice of instrumentation, explaining his need for two bass players: "I want more of the sense of the expansion of time. I want the time to be more plastic" (Hentoff 1968). The connection to meditative practices, including yoga,

FIGURE 2   Album cover of John Coltrane's *Om*.

which employ a nonteleological sense of time, is evident here. The combination of discipline and freedom needed in improvisational musics, and the articulation of that dynamic in Indian thought, was attractive to many jazz musicians, especially those who, for ideological reasons, were looking outside of European traditions (Blancq 1983:81).

Like John Cage, Coltrane attempted to substitute the perceived universalism of sound in Asian traditions for the finitude of musical ego. Cecil Taylor noted that with Trane "it was a matter of music, it was never a matter of personality. Music was all he was concerned with" (Priestley 1987:36). What this meant concretely, though, was the precedence of sound over music; in the words of Alice Coltrane, "[h]e always felt that sound was the first manifestation in creation before music" (Cole 1993:173). These are Asian-influenced insights that again bear comparison to Cage's.

Coltrane's influence put jazz musicians in the vanguard of introducing Asian thought into popular music. Sonny Rollins reexamined his music and spirituality in the light of Coltrane's impact and spent time studying Zen in Japan and living in an ashram in India. Alice Coltrane continued her husband's legacy, literally connecting to Asian spirituality when she "made a pilgrimage to India and studied Hinduism and Buddhism; she took a Hindu name, and she believes that John Coltrane—had he lived longer—would also have gone this way" (Berendt 1975:115). Coltrane's influence percolated into rock music as well, preceding even the Beatles' embrace of Transcendental Meditation: Roger McGuinn of the Byrds credits a tape of Coltrane's "India and Africa" with inspiring the psychedelic opening of "Eight Miles High" (Thomas 1975:198–199).

Immigration: Tibetan Buddhism and the complexity of esoteric religion

The invasion and occupation of Tibet by China in the 1950s created a diaspora of Tibetan Buddhist (Vajrayana) practitioners to India, the United States, Canada, and Europe. In North America in particular, Tibetan teachers have established teaching institutes that combine transmittal of Vajrayana Buddhism with the political cause of Tibetan freedom. The establishment of the Naropa Institute by Chögyan Trungpa in Boulder, Colorado, in 1974 was a signal event in this still-developing movement; John Cage was on the faculty in its first year (Prebish 1999:148).

The influence of Tibetan Buddhism on American music has come through musicians who have embraced the political cause of Tibet's restoration. The Free Tibet Concert, held in Golden Gate Park in San Francisco in 1996 and featuring The Smashing Pumpkins and Rage Against the Machine, is one high-profile example of this. Another prominent instance is found in the Beastie Boys' rap setting of "Bodhisattva Vow." Ensemble member Adam Youch credits a brief meeting with the Dalai Lama as the inspiration for this composition and for Youch's own conversion to Buddhism (Tweed and Prothero 1999:349).

The homology in thought between a technically esoteric religion—one requiring initiation, precise symbolic meanings, and intensive, graded study—and the styles of rap and alternative rock emerges in relation to temporality and texture: time is intensive rather than extensive, and the textures themselves are dense and multilayered, whether one is discussing a mandala or a rap mix [see HIP-HOP AND RAP, p. 692].

There is an extensive embrace of the mystique of Tibet within popular culture. This orientalization of Tibet, maintained for centuries, fits an agenda of spiritualization in the New Age, what Lopez calls the "Shangri-la Syndrome" (1998). Tibetan immigration, Vajrayana study centers, and interest in the Tibetan political cause have all dovetailed with the growth of New Age music [see NEW AGE, p. 345]. This has also encouraged crossover ventures, as in the 1993 Lollapalooza festival, when the "Namgyal monks of Tibet performed purification rituals and sacred dances" to inaugurate each day's festivities (Tweed and Prothero 1999:349).

—JENNIFER RYCENGA

THE SHAKERS

The daughter of a poor blacksmith, Ann Lees (b. Manchester, England, 29 February 1736; d. Watervliet, New York, 8 September 1784) was an illiterate cotton factory worker who in 1758 converted to the Shaking Quakers, a radical offshoot of the English Quakers that had adopted the French Camisards' ritual practices of shaking, shouting, dancing, whirling, and singing in tongues when the spirit came upon them. In 1770, during a period of religious persecution by the English authorities, Lees was imprisoned for participation in noisy worship services. In the course of her incarceration, she experienced a series of revelations and visions that convinced her that she was the female embodiment of God's dual personality and, therefore, the second Incarnation of Christ. This reembodiment in the female was essential to her religious views, which required a restoration of all things to harmony and balance. Lees and her followers believed Christ to be the actual Spirit of God, who had chosen to live as a man the first time but must appear as a woman the second time.

A subsequent revelation in 1774 inspired Lees to persuade her husband, brother, and six other followers to emigrate with her to America to establish a church in the New World. In 1776, this small group of believers settled in the woods at Niskayuna, New York (now Watervliet, near Albany), where within five years their religious community was enlarged by converts from nearby settlements and spread throughout New England. During the community's zenith in the 1840s, records indicate approximately six thousand members, residing in twenty Shaker villages from Maine to Indiana and Kentucky, enrolled in the church. Thus the Shakers were by far the most successful of all the nineteenth-century American communal societies.

Religious beliefs

The Shakers were one of the many religious groups classified as communitarian. They hoped to achieve the perfect society by selfless adherence to strict principles of social-spiritual unanimity, and many were adamantly convinced that a new era of history was emerging. Because they believed in the end of a current phase of historical time and the beginning of a new age of perfection that would last an entire millennium, the Shakers have come to be known as a millenarian group.

Officially known as the United Society of Believers in Christ's Second Appearing, the Shakers organized their lives around work and prayer. Brotherly love and communal labor were encouraged, with men and women treated as equals, but because there was no sexual mating, the sect depended on new recruits for its survival. Lee (her name was shortened after she settled in America), known to her followers as Mother Ann, believed that sexual lust impeded Christ's work and insisted that only through celibacy could men and women further his kingdom on Earth. Her unhappy marriage to Abraham Stanley, a blacksmith, in 1762 probably contributed to her affirmation that sexual intercourse was the root of all evil. Stanley and Lee had four children, all of whom died in infancy.

Although often persecuted for pacifism or for bizarre beliefs falsely attributed to them, the Shakers won admiration for their model farms and orderly, prosperous communities. Dedicated to productive labor as well as to a life of perfection, Shaker communities flourished economically, and the simple beauty, functionalism, and craftsmanship of their meetinghouses, barns, furniture, and artifacts have had a significant influence on American design and culture. Their industry and ingenuity produced numerous (usually unpatented) inventions, including the screw propeller, a turbine waterwheel, a threshing machine, the circular saw, and the common clothespin, to name just these few. Noted for their fair dealing in exchanges with outsiders, the Shakers were the first to package and market seeds and were once the largest producers of medicinal herbs in the United States.

Musical style

Accounts of early Shaker ritual report of dancing and singing with unrestrained gestures and embellished vocal displays. From the beginning, dancing in the presence of the Holy Spirit was an essential element of Shaker worship. Citing nineteen scripture passages instructing one to dance for the Lord, the Shakers reasoned that they should praise the Lord with their entire bodies, and because they thought one could not improve on God's most perfect instrument, the human voice, Shaker music was always performed a cappella and in unison. It was not until the 1870s that the Shakers began to purchase organs and pianos, to study song books of other denominations, and to compose hymns with four-part harmony.

The Shakers left a legacy of over ten thousand religious songs and dance tunes, preserved in almost eight hundred manuscripts and a few printed tunebooks, the two most notable being Isaac N. Youngs's *A Short Abridgment of the Rules of Music* (1846 [1843]) and Russel Haskell's *A Musical Expositor* (1847), both of which detailed Shaker music theory, notation, and tunes. Shaker songs had only one stanza of text, while their hymns had two or more stanzas. The first Shaker songs were wordless tunes that were hummed, and they remained wordless until the period of the Great Awakening.

Emphasizing "gifts" or spiritual revelation, many Shakers dictated their hymns and dance tunes to scribes who later arranged the melodies into manuscript hymnals. Besides texts in English, there is a proliferation of lyrics consisting of nonsense syllables or vocables and words imitative of American Indian and African American dialects, which broadly suggests that Shaker scribes made the first transcriptions of these musics. As illustrated by "Simple Gifts," composed by Elder Joseph Brackett in 1848 at the Shaker community in Alfred, Maine (the tune used by Aaron Copland for the variations near the end of his collaboration with famed choreographer Martha Graham in the ballet *Appalachian Spring*), Shaker music combined pentatonic melodies with rhythms imposed by the textual prosody.

Elder Richard McNemar, known as the "Father of Shaker Music," composed more hymns and anthems than any other Shaker. The musical notation in the Shaker manuscripts is of several types: shape-note notation, conventional "round-note" notation, and letter notation (identified by Patterson 1979), to which were joined conventional rhythmic values. Four types of letter notation have been identified: capital, small, linear, and cursive.

The decline of the Shakers

In 1780 Mother Ann was imprisoned for treason because of her pacifist doctrines and her refusal to sign an oath of allegiance. She was soon released, however, and in 1781–1783 toured New England. According to witnesses, she performed a number of miracles during her trips, including healing the sick by the laying on of hands. Following Mother Ann's death in 1784, the society was in decline and forced to advertise for members, emphasizing physical comfort as well as spiritual values. The Shaker church came under the leadership of Elder Joseph Meacham and Eldress Lucy Wright, who together worked out the communal pattern that was to be the distinctive Shaker social organization.

As America industrialized and the country expanded west following the Civil War, Shaker communities gradually declined. By 1905 there were only one thousand members, and by the third quarter of the twentieth century they were all but extinct. Presently, the sect claims seven members, all living the celibate lifestyle and following the religious doctrine of the Shaker church in the sole surviving Shaker community, located in Sabbathday Lake, Maine.

—DENISE A. SEACHRIST

SHARON: "MAKE A JOYFUL NOISE"

In spite of the frontier conditions in Ontario until 1850, the vision of just one person could result in a plethora of musical activity. Such a person was David Willson (1788–1866), born in New York state of Irish Presbyterian immigrants. In 1801 he settled north of present-day Toronto. Initially worshiping with the Quakers, Willson frequently closed his sermon by singing a stanza rather than intoning as was the custom with Quaker elders. By 1812, when Quakers were being fined or imprisoned for not taking part in the war, a group met in Willson's own home. In Willson's view the British Crown that persecuted them was the uncaring biblical Pharaoh, and Hope (renamed Sharon in 1841) was to be the new Jerusalem, from which they would reunite the Christian and Jewish faiths in a peaceable kingdom.

In 1817 Willson was attempting to incorporate congregational singing within his sect's meetings for worship. He based the religious authority to use music on the many references to singing and instruments in the Old Testament. Because music must be a spontaneous expression of the Inner Light, before 1845 a hymn was never repeated. Willson wrote new words, thus creating thousands of hymns, sung to a fixed set of melodies for each service in a "lining-out" procedure, in which a leader sings a line and the congregation repeats it.

Willson and his wife formed a choir within the girls' school they established, and by 1819 this small choir of "virgins" performed at the beginning and end of each service. The group, now known as the Children of Peace, commissioned a barrel organ from Richard Coates (1778–1886), a painter and bandmaster originally from England. In 1819 the Children of Peace completed their first meetinghouse (later known as the Music Hall), a perfectly square building that had a platform at its center on which the barrel organ was placed with musicians seated around it. Coates organized a ten-to-thirteen-piece band in 1820 that accompanied the choir.

FIGURE 3   1848 Coates organ, Sharon Temple. Photo by author, 1999.

Of the seven organs known to have been built by Coates in Canada, three were for the Children of Peace. The first barrel organ consisted of 133 pipes and four stops covering a compass of thirty-seven notes. A single individual would play the instrument by pumping the bellows with his left foot to force air into the appropriate pipes while turning the crank with his left hand to revolve the barrel. The barrel was equipped with pins and bridges fixed to open certain pipes, thus making the required pitches. At the same time the right hand could operate the stops. For the organ's installation Coates pinned two barrels of ten tunes each, all European in origin except for "China." When a tune did not fill one complete revolution of the barrel, Coates chose to fill this gap with his own composed interlude. In 1848 Coates completed a keyboard organ of tracker action, a forty-nine-note manual, and four ranks of 188 wooden pipes for the second meetinghouse (figure 3).

The Children of Peace built the three-tiered, symmetrical, "wedding-cake-like" Temple (1825–1831) that was used for fifteen special services annually (figure 4). Members were called to the Temple by the sound of a trumpet. They gathered at the meetinghouse and formed a procession led by the band and choir. The band entered first by the Temple's east door and climbed "Jacob's Ladder" to the musicians' gallery on the second floor. As the congregation entered and divided, men on one side, women on the other, the musicians played and the choir assembled around the central ark, which held the open Bible, singing one of David Willson's "Songs for the Altar." Music is referred to as "manna from heaven" in Willson's writings, and it is likely that beginning in the 1820s the choir and band were performing the seventeen anthems among other complex works found in the Coates manuscripts for the Feasts of the Passover, the First Fruits, and the Illumination.

FIGURE 4   Sharon Temple. Photo by author, 1999.

FIGURE 5   The doctrine of equality displayed on the property at the Sharon Temple. At lower left is a picture of the first meetinghouse, later known as Music Hall. Photo by author, 1999.

Because of the sect's belief in equality for all, resulting in a complete rejection of a class system as had been established by the British, and the establishment of Willson's friendships with reformers such as William Lyon Mackenzie, the band and choir performed for numerous secular occasions and particularly political rallies throughout the region (figure 5). Through the 1820s and into the early 1830s the band consisted of string and wind instruments. Becoming a woodwind, brass, and percussion ensemble, the band in 1844 requested money to buy new instruments in order to further improve the performance standard on sacred and secular occasions. Membership in the band fluctuated over the years. It began as solely made up of men but later included some women players. The band also urged the sect to adopt a style of congregational unison singing. From 1846 to 1848 Daniel Cory, a music teacher from Boston, gave the sect members systematic training in singing.

Functioning as a marching band or an instrumental ensemble, the band could play alone, accompany the choir, or be accompanied by choir and organ. Extant descriptions of performances at Sharon indicate that (1) three- or four-part mixed choir, unaccompanied or doubled by organ or instruments, (2) three- or four-part choir, women only or men only, (3) a unison of men's or women's voices with organ or instruments supplying harmony, or (4) solo voice with instrumental accompaniment were commonly heard at Sharon.

More manuscripts and published music books used in this community exist than for any other location in nineteenth-century Ontario. *Ira Doan's Book, Hester Hannah's Book,* and *The Keyboard Book* include selections from English ballad opera and comic opera, oratorio numbers, British military band music, dances, and marches, solo songs, duets, glees, and folk tunes. Not only known for their sacred music performances, the Sharon community was in the mid-nineteenth century the place to hear the most current music—its bandleader would go to Boston annually and note down the newest repertoire by ear. In 1860 the sect purchased silver instruments in Boston for $1,500, and the band became known as the Sharon Silver Band. Some newspaper reports refer to it as the oldest and best civilian band in Canada. The band continued to give concerts throughout the region into the 1870s but gradually, with changing political and economic conditions, the foundation of the sect's beliefs dissipated. By 1889 the Children of Peace ceased to exist. Its legacy for compromise, peacekeeping, and for "making a joyous noise" can be found in Canadian identity today.

—ELAINE KEILLOR

REFERENCES

Andrews, Edward Deming. 1962 [1940]. *The Gift to Be Simple: Songs, Dances and Rituals of the American Shakers.* New York: Dover Publications.

———. 1963 [1953]. *The People Called Shakers.* New York: Dover Publications.

Berendt, Joachim. 1975. *The Jazz Book: From New Orleans to Rock and Free Jazz.* Trans. Dan Morgenstern and Helmut and Barbara Bredigkeit. Westport, Conn.: Lawrence Hill and Co.

Blancq, Charles. 1983. *Sonny Rollins: The Journey of a Jazzman.* Boston: Twayne Publishers.

Cage, John. 1961. *Silence: Lectures and Writings.* Middletown, Conn.: Wesleyan University Press.

Cole, Bill. 1993 [1976]. *John Coltrane.* New York: Da Capo.

Collier, James Lincoln. 1978. *The Making of Jazz: A Comprehensive History.* Boston: Houghton Mifflin.

Coltrane, John. 1968. *Om.* Impulse A-9140. LP disk.

Cook, Harold E. 1973. *Shaker Music: A Manifestation of American Folk Culture.* Lewisburg, Pa.: Bucknell University Press.

Desroche, Henri. 1971. *The American Shakers.* Amherst: University of Massachusetts Press.

Dornish, Margaret H. 1986. "Wisdom and Means: D. T. Suzuki's Theology of Culture." Unpublished paper, delivered to the Pacific Coast Theological Society. Berkeley, California. February.

Edwards, J. Michelle, with Leslie Lassetter. 1991. "North America since 1920." In *Women and Music: A History,* ed. Karin Pendle, 211–257. Bloomington: Indiana University Press.

Ellwood, Robert S. Jr. 1979. *Alternative Altars: Unconventional and Eastern Spirituality in America.* Chicago: University of Chicago Press.

———. 1987. "Buddhism in the West." In *Encyclopedia of Religion.* ed. Mircea Eliade, 2:436–439. New York: Macmillan Reference.

Evans, Frederick W. 1974 [1875]. *Shaker Music.* New York: AMS Press.

Fields, Rick. 1986. *How the Swans Came to the Lake: A Narrative History of Buddhism in America.* Rev. ed. Boston: Shambala.

Fiofore, Tam. 1971. "Re-entry: The New Orbit of Sonny Rollins." *Downbeat* 38(17):14–15, 39(14 October).

Hall, Roger L. 1992. *Love Is Little.* Rochester, N.Y.: Sampler Records. 9222. Compact disc.

Haskell, Russel. 1847. *A Musical Expositor.* New York: G. W. Wood.

Hentoff, Nat. 1968. Liner notes for John Coltrane, *Om.* Impulse A-9140. LP disk.

Kansas City Chorale. 1998. *Alleluia.* Charlottesville, Va.: Nimbus. NI 5568. Compact disc.

Lacy, Steve. 1987. *Prospectus.* Newton Center, Mass.: Margun Music.

Lopez, Donald S. Jr. 1998. *Prisoners of Shangri-La: Tibetan Buddhism and the West.* Chicago: University of Chicago Press.

McCabe, Daniel. 1997. *An American Idyll.* Buffalo, N.Y.: Fleur de Son Classics. FDS 57924. Compact disc.

Mertens, Wim. 1983. *American Minimal Music: La Monte Young, Terry Riley, Steve Reich, Philip Glass.* Trans. J. Hautekiet. New York: Alexander Broude.

Needleman, Jacob. 1970. *The New Religions.* Garden City, N.Y.: Doubleday.

Oliveros, Pauline. 1984. *Software for People.* Baltimore, Md.: Smith Publications.

Patterson, Daniel W. 1979. *The Shaker Spiritual.* Princeton, N.J.: Princeton University Press.

Porter, Lewis. 1983. *John Coltrane's Music of 1960 through 1967: Jazz Improvisation as Composition.* Ph.D. dissertation, Brandeis University.

Prebish, Charles S. 1979. *American Buddhism.* North Scituate, Mass.: Duxbury Press.

———. 1999. *Luminous Passage: The Practice and Study of Buddhism in America.* Berkeley: University of California Press.

Priestley, Brian. 1987. *John Coltrane.* Jazz Masters Series. London: Apollo Press.

Revill, David. 1992. *The Roaring Silence: John Cage: A Life.* New York: Arcade Publishing.

Richmond, Mary L. 1977. *Shaker Literature: A Bibliography.* Hanover, N.H.: University Press of New England.

Rivelli, Pauline, and Robert Levin, eds. 1979 [1970]. *Giants of Black Music* (originally published as *The Black Giants*). New York: Da Capo.

Roszak, Theodore. 1969. *The Making of a Counter Culture: Reflections on the Technocratic Society and Its Youthful Opposition.* Garden City, N.Y.: Doubleday Anchor.

Rudhyar, Dane. 1961 [1933]. "Oriental Influence in American Music." In *American Composers on American Music: A Symposium,* ed. Henry Cowell, 184–185. New York: Frederick Ungar Publishing Co.

Schau, Barbara Ann. 1985. "Sharon's Musical Past." *The York Pioneer* 80:17–31.

Schrauwers, Albert. 1993. *Awaiting the Millennium: The Children of Peace and the Village of Hope 1812–1889.* Toronto: University of Toronto Press.

Stein, Stephen J. 1992. *The Shaker Experience in America.* New Haven, Conn.: Yale University Press.

Suzuki, D. T. 1959. *Zen and Japanese Culture.* Bollingen Series. New York: Pantheon.

Thomas, J. C. 1975. *Chasin' the Trane: The Music and Mystique of John Coltrane.* Garden City, N.Y.: Doubleday.

Tweed, Thomas A. 1992. *The American Encounter with Buddhism, 1844–1912: Victorian Culture and the Limits of Dissent.* Bloomington: Indiana University Press.

Tweed, Thomas A., and Stephen Prothero, eds. 1999. *Asian Religions in America: A Documentary History.* New York: Oxford University Press.

Verhoeven, Martin. 1998. "Americanizing the Buddha: Paul Carus and the Transformation of Asian Thought." In *The Faces of Buddhism in America,* ed. Charles S. Prebish and Kenneth K. Tanaka, 207–227. Berkeley: University of California Press.

Yellin, Victor Fell. 1980. "Shakers, American." In *The New Grove Dictionary of Music and Musicians,* ed. Stanley Sadie. London: Macmillan.

Yellin, Victor Fell, and H. Wiley Hitchcock. 1986. "Shaker Music." In *The New Grove Dictionary of American Music,* ed. H. Wiley Hitchcock and Stanley Sadie. London: Macmillan.

Youngs, Isaac N. 1846 [1843]. *A Short Abridgement of the Rules of Music.* New Lebanon, N.Y.: Shaker Society.

Section 2
Diverse Environments

Historically, in the United States and Canada, the specific ecological, historical, and geographic space someone inhabited—be it rural farm community, great urban center, arctic fishing village, or swampy woodland—often determined the kinds of music that person experienced. Today, with almost everyone in these countries owning radios, televisions, and a multitude of electronic recording and listening devices, most of the world's musics are available for all to experience. But before the advent of such technology, people and musics were far less mobile, and those living in communities outside large urban centers often had to travel great distances to interact musically with their neighbors or to see traveling opera troupes and other popular and concert music performances. In this section, we discuss the role of geographical place and how it has helped shape and define certain musical traditions in the United States and Canada. In addition, we also examine "place" more symbolically, as meaning a specific but not necessarily geographic historical or contemporary context such as a concert or dance hall, a vaudeville stage, or the music industry.

Old-time fiddler and fiddle maker Cliff Hardesty at the Hale Farm Harvest Festival north of Akron, Ohio. Photo by Terry E. Miller, 1985.

Place
Gordon E. Smith

Historical Paradigms
Further Sources and Historical Performance Contexts
Rural and Urban Music: Models in Traditional Franco-Canadian Song Collecting
Rural and Urban Music: Models in Anglo-American Traditional Song Collecting
Recent Paradigms
Current Paradigms: Identity and Place

The terms *rural, suburban,* and *urban* are interpreted in varied, sometimes overlapping ways with respect to music. Historical and ideological processes have driven the discourse on musical contexts in North America, shaping definitions, attitudes, and ethnographic paradigms. In the past, ideas of authenticity and originality have dominated approaches toward North American music and helped to establish what have become well-entrenched assumptions, often viewed as dualities. One of the most widely known of these considers rural as old, pure, and untainted (oral tradition) versus urban as modern, developed, and therefore tainted within an ethnographic context (written tradition). In recent years (from about the 1960s), such dichotomies have been modified by unavoidable yet creative processes of cultural and technological change. Contextual boundaries of region, class, gender, and ethnicity are increasingly determining the ways different musics are viewed and, indeed, are created and performed. In addition, a sense of place, and individual experience, have modified older paradigms based on evolutionary patterns of musical style, class, and national difference. In both historical and more current frameworks, music is viewed as a significant symbol of identity. Borrowing ideas and techniques from other disciplines (anthropology, linguistics, gender studies, critical theory), ethnomusicologists increasingly view the importance of studying context as a means of understanding the diverse processes that determine the creation and production of music in the contemporary world. In this respect, implicit notions in the labels *rural, suburban,* and *urban* are often blurred and diverse when considered in current perspectives.

This article first traces the kinds of music and music making associated with these categories from the colonial period in Canada and the United States through the 1950s with a view to highlighting major ideological trends as well as relevant literature. Then the discussion moves to developments in the continental context over the last forty years. Throughout, reference is made to specific musical contexts that demonstrate some of the emergent parameters of music in such diverse cultural contexts.

HISTORICAL PARADIGMS

During the colonial period (seventeenth to nineteenth centuries) musical life in the United States and Canada showed similarities and differences, which derived from historical, geographic, and demographic factors. Although Canada was visited by newcomers first in the fifteenth and sixteenth centuries (the Vikings, John Cabot, Jacques Cartier, Samuel de Champlain), European immigration patterns to North America in the eighteenth and nineteenth centuries greatly favored the United States, partly because of obvious geographic and climatic advantages. This continuous migration coincided with the ongoing Industrial Revolution and its subsequent social and political upheaval. In comparison with the United States, which assumed independence from Britain in 1776, Canada did not become a Dominion (four politically connected provinces; nine by 1905) until 1867 and did not actually assume its current configuration of ten provinces (plus two territories) until 1949, when Newfoundland voted narrowly to join the Canadian confederation. Colonial ties with Britain were not broken officially until 1982. A major cultural and linguistic difference between Canada and the United States is that constitutionally Canada consists of English- and French-speaking peoples as well as First Nations peoples; the United States can be viewed historically in terms of geographical divisions, northern and southern, with a strong and culturally influential presence of African American and Native peoples. Through the colonization period of the eighteenth and nineteenth centuries, the creation and production of music in both countries assumed social and cultural significance deriving variously from hierarchical configurations based on political, economic, social, and gender considerations.

In historical terms, folk/traditional music was associated with rural contexts, while concert/art music was associated with urban contexts. Another duality—professional and amateur music performance—also can be considered, with the former usually associated with urban contexts and the latter often centered in smaller regional communities. At times, especially in the nineteenth century, the two categories overlapped, reflecting changing societal patterns.

A useful strategy here is to consider ways in which commentators and scholars have viewed music (art, traditional, popular) in their writings, thereby delineating frameworks for musical contexts. In historiographic terms, music history in both the United States and Canada shares one common theme [see SOURCES, SCHOLARSHIP, HISTORIOGRAPHY, p. 21]. In various ways, most, if not all, American and Canadian writers adopt a colonialist perspective: Europe is viewed as the starting point, and the story is told in evolutionary terms centered on the Western art music canon. As Americanist Richard Crawford observes, "[N]o fact about the writing of American music history is more characteristic than the looming presence of Europe. Scholars of music are trained and acculturated to think of European music history as their norm. Whether as provider, exploiter, or authority figure, whether in the foreground or background, Europe is the powerful 'other'" (Crawford 1993:6). Canadian musicologist Helmut Kallmann's oft-cited "harvest" metaphor, which refers to music in Canada in the colonial period as a process of "planting of seeds rather than the harvesting of fruits," and his defining themes of transplantation, assimilation, and the search for identity in Canadian music represent more than a coincidental parallel (Kallmann 1987 [1960]:3, 5).

Two comparable studies that critique the historiographic situation from a current perspective and, in different ways, discuss terminology and boundaries around diverse musics are Crawford (United States) (1993) and Beverley Diamond (Canada) (1994). Noting H. Wiley Hitchcock's widely borrowed distinction between "cultivated" and "vernacular" traditions, for example, Crawford builds his critique of U. S. music historiography (using four texts: Gilbert Chase [1987 (1955)], Wilfrid Mellers [1964], H. Wiley Hitchcock [1988 (1969)], and Charles Hamm [1983]) around a typology of two "polar opposites": cosmopolitan and provincial. While the former refers to the "inevitable European hegemony," the latter is characterized by a more experimental attitude based on "finding value chiefly from divergence from European practices" (Crawford 1993:7). Through a process of examining different narrative levels (for example, intent, proportion, organization, metaphor) in three well-known texts on Canadian music (Helmut Kallmann [1987 (1960)], Clifford Ford [1982], and Timothy McGee [1985]), Diamond raises a number of pertinent questions regarding historiographic issues and boundaries in Canadian musical scholarship, such as regional versus urban representation, or, as she puts it, "who gets advantaged, legitimized, disadvantaged or ignored" in these narratives (Diamond 1994:165). In Diamond's comparison among the three Canadian texts and the American texts by Hamm and Daniel Kingman (1989 [1979]), she observes that aside from some obvious differences (for example, absence, ahistoricization, and separation of native music cultures within the overall story), there are more marked differences. For example, there is much more attention paid to popular, "vernacular," traditions in the U.S. texts and less emphasis on urban centers and regional communities in the United States; conversely, more attention is paid to the pre–eighteenth century period in the Canadian texts (Diamond 1994:164). Such comparisons demonstrate the historically entrenched notions of the rural/urban divide as well as a reluctance on the part of many to recognize the musical experience of those outside of the mainstream: immigrant groups, ethnic minorities, aboriginal peoples, and women. Issues surrounding cultural hierarchical patterns in the United States are also discussed in Levine (1988).

FURTHER SOURCES AND HISTORICAL PERFORMANCE CONTEXTS

Along with these texts, the reader should consult the bourgeoning literature on North American music that demonstrates these and other historiographic issues as well as different and similar approaches toward rural, suburban, and urban music. In various ways, these texts emphasize historical narrative frameworks as well as more specific topics, such as musical "streams," time periods, and local, regional, and comparative perspectives (U.S. texts: Chase 1987 [1955]; McCue 1977; Mellers 1964; Rockwell 1983; Canadian texts: Beckwith and Hall 1988; McGee 1995; Proctor 1980). The volumes of essays by the pioneer musicologist and librarian Oscar Sonneck (1873–1928) (Lichtenwanger 1983), and musicologist Charles Seeger (1886–1979) (Seeger 1977) contain articulate views on different U.S. musical contexts. Similarly, for the Canadian setting, the collected essays of conductor, composer, teacher, and administrator Ernest MacMillan (1893–1973) present a particular picture (that is, an art music, urban perspective from the mid-twentieth-century period) of the Canadian musical scene (Morey 1997), and the essays by composer, teacher, and administrator John Beckwith (b. 1927) represent a lifetime of activity devoted to promoting the creation and performance of Canadian music (CanMus, to use Beckwith's term) (Beckwith 1997). Beckwith is of special importance because of his knowledge of the North American musical scene, and he has written on comparative aspects of American and Canadian music, notably hymn-singing traditions. This research has helped to dislodge some of the notions about "what is good or *real* music?," as well as demonstrating the potential for considering diverse contextual boundaries.

An effective paradigm with which to examine diverse musical contexts in the colonial North American period is that of performance. Although most writers describe performance contexts from the hegemonic perspective of European superiority, the variety of kinds of performance demonstrates defined and overlapping boundaries between rural, suburban, and urban. In the nineteenth century in both countries, local musical organizations increasingly appeared; for example, most "musical societies," as they were known in Canada, were choral, as it took less time to perfect a level of expertise as a vocalist than as an instrumentalist. Performances of large-scale vocal compositions (oratorios, operas, and so on) often used the resources of instrumentalists from other centers.

An illustration is provided by one of Canada's most well known musicians, Calixa Lavallée (1842–1891), performer, composer, and administrator, who spent more than a dozen years touring and working in the United States. In 1879, to commemorate the arrival of the new governor-general to Canada, Lavallée composed a cantata and assembled more than three hundred musicians for the performance in Québec City; the performers consisted of choristers and band members from the area, plus instrumentalists from other Canadian and American cities. The conclusion of the piece was a simultaneous contrapuntal rendition of "God Save the Queen," "Vive la Canadienne," and "Comin' Thro' the Rye." Kallmann writes that this caused a "sensation" and that "the combination of these songs symbolized the friendship between the French and British elements of Canada" (1987 [1960]:137). Of course this combination of songs (including "Comin' Thro' the Rye") also symbolized the friendship and cooperation between the Canada and United States.

Moreover, this event represents the different, often typically combined, layers of nineteenth-century urban musical performance: solo and ensemble singing, band and orchestral traditions, popular, patriotic, and traditional music, amateur and professional music making, and local and other (outside) resources. Music may be considered a significant symbol in such colonial contexts, a socially rooted phenomenon that provided continuity and a sense of identity. Later, in the twentieth century, competitive music festivals, community concerts, and performing groups provided significant social and cultural contexts for music making in both urban settings and, especially, smaller communities, fostered ties between regions, and helped to create pride in local music making efforts.

RURAL AND URBAN MUSIC: MODELS IN TRADITIONAL FRANCO-CANADIAN SONG COLLECTING

The divide between rural and urban music was a theme in Ernest Gagnon's *Chansons populaires du Canada,* a seminal collection of one hundred French/French-Canadian songs, published first in 1865, with a second edition in 1880 and many reprintings through to the 1950s. Gagnon's collection was recognized in both his native Québec and France by leaders of the folk song movement for its inclusion of music as well as texts (unusual for the nineteenth century, with its pervasive emphasis on text collecting), as well as for his fieldwork descriptions, scrupulous attention to detail in the transcriptions, concordances with French sources, and musical analysis (Smith 1990). In addition to separating rural and urban repertoires with a view toward establishing the "authentic" product and developing hypotheses on issues of origin, thereby anticipating later ideas in folk song scholarship, Gagnon was also forward looking in his awareness of different purposes and levels of detail in transcription as well as in his distinction between rhythmic types. Notwithstanding Gagnon's idealized and typically romantic view of the folk, within the North American context in the 1860s the Gagnon collection is an unusual example of folk song scholarship, which was tied to the emerging nationalist context in Québec as well as to French models in France. Significantly, Gagnon and his contemporaries associated folk music with the rural countryside and concert music with the urban setting.

Gagnon's conception of the *le peuple* 'the people'—the word *folk* is never used— was in some respects similar to that of his successors' conception of the folk in both Franco and Anglo traditions. A level of ethnographic authority—borrowing James Clifford's (1988) term—frames the distance Gagnon leaves between himself and the people the song collection is about. The dualism of "us" and "them"—needless to say a persistent issue in ethnomusicology—is evident first in Gagnon's privileged background, which included a multifaceted formal education in music, literature, and history. As part of a small intelligentsia in Québec City, Gagnon idealized the *chanson populaire* 'popular song' as a living artifact of a chosen (uneducated) people. Gagnon's comment in the preface to his collection about the notated parts of the *Chansons populaires* not

Herder and the Grimms conceived of folk music as a group-created expression of the soul of the people and, by extension, the nation.

being his work, but the work of that "elusive composer known as the people" is qualified by "people not educated in music." Gagnon's notion of the people was part of a literary and historical movement characterized by a historical and patriotic orientation and a deeply Roman Catholic spirit. His notion of the people—especially their moral superiority—was also a romantic one, inspired by nineteenth-century French writers on music such as François-Joseph Fétis and other contemporaries.

Gagnon's eminent successor, Marius Barbeau (1883–1969) shared Gagnon's educated background and status within political and academic spheres. Barbeau expanded significantly upon Gagnon's documentation ideas, incorporating into his (Barbeau's) research not just Franco-Canadian folk song but also First Nations music and traditions. Barbeau's efforts to popularize songs, and also to demonstrate their artistic merit and potential for new musical compositions, are well known. His *Soirées du bon Vieux Temps,* organized with Édouard-Zotique Massicotte and devoted to the performance of songs, tales, and dances, began in Montréal in 1919 at the Bibliothèque Saint-Sulpice (renamed the Bibliothèque nationale du Québec), and the *Veillées du Bon Vieux Temps,* which took place between 1919 and 1941 at the Monument national in Montréal, are examples. The more than a dozen Canadian Pacific Railway folk and handicraft festivals held across Canada (except in Atlantic Canada), which Barbeau organized with the Canadian Public Radio publicist John Murray Gibbon, resulted in live performances by traditional musicians and compositions and arrangements of a variety of traditional music by composers (at the two festivals held in Québec City in 1927 and 1928). Historically, these festivals are regarded as an important early effort to break down barriers between art and traditional music and societal and ethnic groups, to demonstrate the Canadian mosaic of cultures that Gibbon espoused, and to promote tourism in and around the railway's luxury hotels.

In 1928 in Asheville, North Carolina, the lawyer Bascom Lamar Lunsford, a well-known performer, lecturer, and collector, organized a folk song and dance festival that became an annual event drawing people from near and far, marking the beginning of the important folk festival movement in the United States (Rosenberg 1993:6). As cultural producers, Barbeau (National Museum, Ottawa), Robert W. Gordon (Archive of American Folk Song, Library of Congress), and John and Alan Lomax (U.S. Library of Congress), among others, were determined and prolific collectors, classifiers, and popularizers of folk traditions, whose multiple efforts bore fruit in the period following World War II with the expansion of public archives, university folklore programs, and general public interest in traditional lifeways. An important corollary here, as Rosenberg observes, is that "[f]ascination with folk music is a pervasive legacy in North American culture," and the transplantation of folk tunes, songs, and dances from the rural plantation to the urban stage actually occurred in the United States as early as the 1830s, resulting in blackface minstrelsy—"an early folk song revival"—[see RACE, ETHNICITY, AND NATIONHOOD, p. 63; POPULAR MUSIC OF THE PARLOR AND STAGE, p. 179], and, later, in the blues and other popular music forms (Rosenberg 1993:4–5).

RURAL AND URBAN MUSIC: MODELS IN ANGLO-AMERICAN
TRADITIONAL SONG COLLECTING

In the nineteenth-century United States, folk song collectors and scholars followed the romantic ideology of separating rural and urban music and established influential theories of folk song origin. As in Britain, ballad (folk song) study in the United States and in Canada (from the 1920s) was carried out first by literary scholars—later called folklorists—who conceived the ballad texts as relics of an antiquated past. The highly influential work of the Harvard English professor Francis James Child (1825–1896), his student George Lyman Kittredge (1860–1941), and their followers was rooted in the seminal ideals regarding the folk of the pioneer German collectors Jacob (1785–1863) and Wilhelm (1786–1859) Grimm and Johann Gottfried Herder (1744–1803). Herder and the Grimms conceived of folk music as a group-created expression of the soul of the people and, by extension, the nation: "From Herder and the Grimms, the Folk bore witness, in the eloquent simplicity of their lives, to that anonymous warmth of their common culture, to the *Gemeinschaft*—that ideal type of society bound together by tradition, custom, and faith, and permanently rooted over generations in small uncommercialized communities" (McKay 1994:12). Following from this lead, scholars such as Child and Kittredge promoted the idea of communal creation by which the folk created collectively. Opposition to this view was voiced strongly by both British and American scholars, such as Andrew Lang (1895) and Louise Pound (1921), who argued convincingly that folk songs were not communally composed but were the creation of individual composers. These opposing positions were reconciled in the work of the American folklorist Phillips Barry (1880–1937), who developed the widely held theory of communal recreation, which advocated individual composition reflecting the spirit of a community, and subsequent variation through processes of oral tradition (Myers 1993:36–37). Throughout the nineteenth century, attitudes toward the folk were rooted in a rural stance that was shaped by a distance between the collector/scholar and the folk. The site of the folk was rural and pastoral, whereas that of the collector was urban and modern—distancing that was noted earlier within the Québec context.

The pastoral view of the folk dominated the influential work of U.S. and Canadian collectors well into the twentieth century, at least until the 1960s. In varying guises, collectors conceived of their informants in idealized, folkloric ways. Commenting from a more current perspective, Philip Bohlman has observed "a conservative undertow" in much of this folk song scholarship and at the basis of this conservatism four corresponding ideological stances: collection, classification, revival, and canonization (Bohlman 1988:xix).

One sees in the work of many collectors a frontier between themselves and their roles as collectors and preservers, and their consultants. The folk are presented as the bearers of stories and songs characterized by oral transmission, traditionalism, and anonymity. At the same time, there was the belief on the part of the collectors that this lore did not truly belong to the folk and that it could be saved only if it was transferred to other hands and other, more modern (that is, urban) means of cultural transmission and preservation. In the minds of many collectors, the folk were a disappearing breed living on the edges of civilization; they had to be searched out and persuaded to part with what they knew.

Intrinsic to this cult-of-the-folk thinking is the idea of the prolific informant—an individual who knows or remembers in some cases hundreds of songs. Philéas Bédard (Barbeau), Angelo Dornan and Ben Henneberry (Creighton), LaRena Clark (Fowke), Huddie Ledbetter ("Leadbelly") (John Lomax), and Joe Scott and Larry Gorman (Edward Ives) were treasured facilitators of some of the most prodigious work of their respective collectors. In retrospect, one wonders if the *discovery* of these individuals was

FIGURE I   Helen Creighton and Norman
McGrath, Victoria Beach 1947. Courtesy of Public Archives of Nova Scotia, Album 14.155.

FIGURE I   Helen Creighton and Norman McGrath, Victoria Beach 1947. Courtesy of Public Archives of Nova Scotia, Album 14.155.

as important as the documentation of their respective repertoires. Without doubt, the idea of the prolific informant was related to the preservationist belief that such individuals were a dying breed.

An illustration is found in the work of one of the most prodigious Canadian collectors, Helen Creighton (1899–1989) (figure 1). One scholar has identified the theme of paternalism in some of Creighton's work, as well as that her apparent obliviousness to certain historical, social, cultural, and racial facts stemmed from her class perspective as a whole (Creighton came from an educated, privileged, and urban background). She believed that there were havens of unspoiled folk in Nova Scotia but that they were fast disappearing. "The time is pressing, because life is changing and the radio is introducing new music into homes which only knew the old," Creighton wrote to a likeminded Barbeau in 1947. "If we wish to retain our treasures, we must do so at once, or the opportunity will be gone." Regarding her search for ballads in southwestern Nova Scotia, Creighton continued by reporting that there were "pitifully few songs" (meaning, of course, what she called "traditional songs"): "Between the old people having passed away, and the radio bringing a new form of entertainment, there is nothing left to get. . . . Occasionally a singer would be found who can sing a verse or two of a ballad, but a real old timer who can sing from dawn to dark and never repeat could not be found" (McKay 1994:105).

Indeed, Barbeau and the French folklore school in Québec, as well as many U.S. collectors, shared Creighton's belief in the pressing necessity to conduct tireless fieldwork before "it was too late." Typically, Barbeau also distinguished between the authentic folk product and that which had been tainted by popular "modern" urban music. In the preface to his 1946 collection *Alouette* he wrote that his efforts to "popularize" the "chanson populaire" had been exploited by people for commercial purposes and cites the *La Bonne Chanson* series as an example of a popular "modern" repertoire mistakenly taken by people to represent the folk song tradition. Like many of their generation, Barbeau and Creighton drew a line between newly composed popular song and the rich and old tradition of folk song.

RECENT PARADIGMS

Creighton's concern about the effects of the radio resulting in "new music" and "a new form of entertainment" signified a genuine fear of change. The perception of change brought on by modernism and urbanism, coupled with its resultant industrial and technological development, was that it would decay and disintegrate the ideological sense of innocence that characterized collectors' invented cult of the folk. Within the context of scholarly research prior to the 1950s, when ethnomusicology emerged as a recognized field of study, attention was focused on the rural. A crucial shift in approach was away from the idea of comparing musical systems in the world toward gaining an understanding of the diverse contexts that create music, as well as the emergent processes of musical change. In the past fifty years, the study of traditional music in its once bounded rural context has broadened to include the urban setting. In various ways, ethnomusicologists have adapted anthropological concepts in their work, notably ideas surrounding the interaction of different musics—such as traditional, ethnic, Western—represented in, for example, syncretism, or the blending of similar (compatible) cultural traits to create new, mixed forms. Modernization, westernization, and urbanization are further concepts that have been identified to help explain change processes in music (Nettl 1978, 1985)

Urban ethnomusicology in the United States focused first on the movement of African American music from the rural South to the urban North. Charles Keil's *Urban Blues* (1966) is considered a landmark publication in this domain. Other examples include A. Reyes Schramm's *The Role of Music in the Interaction of Black Americans and Hispanos in New York City's East Harlem* (1975) and, for a more general overview reflecting the increasing diversity of approaches, S. Erdely's "Ethnic Music in America" (1979). Similarly, Canadian ethnomusicology, including urban ethnomusicology and research into the music of ethnic groups, is surveyed thoroughly with complete bibliographic listings in Diamond and Robbins (1992). Of particular interest with respect to the rural, suburban, and urban matrix is the folk festival movement in both the United States and Canada, which, in many fundamental respects, signified the changing social and political climate from the late 1950s [see REVIVALS, p. 55]. No longer intended as vehicles to simply educate and valorize folk traditions, folk festivals increasingly became large public forums for musical performance and political statement (for example, Newport, Rhode Island, in the United States; Mariposa, Ontario, in Canada).

The folk revival phenomenon was closely connected to and mirrored the changing political, cultural, and social landscape in the 1960s. Indeed, the terms *revival* and *revitalization* have become part of the vocabulary of ethnomusicologists working with ethnic musics in urban settings and with music culture in First Nations communities, to cite two pervasive contexts [see MUSICAL INTERACTIONS, p. 480]. As Alan Jabbour observes, these phenomena were not new cultural developments, and included other important musical movements such as bluegrass, rhythm and blues, the polka movement, the Indian powwow movement, rock and roll, and other forms and genres of popular music, as well as folk song (1993:xii).

CURRENT PARADIGMS: IDENTITY AND PLACE

The mixing of musical genres has become widespread in many diverse contexts in North America. This reality is part of postmodern circumstances that presume that no single social code, aesthetic perspective, or musical system is preeminent. In this setting the rural, suburban, and urban matrix of earlier contexts is disrupted and blurred; musical creativity is plural, hetereogeneous, and, more than ever, socially rooted. Interdisciplinarity is increasingly a major formative part of ethnomusicology. Ideas and developments in gender studies, critical theory, and cultural studies, among other areas, have influenced shifting directions and the confluence of ethnographic boundaries in

Cremo is an engaging performer who loves to play varied music in any context—from a large public concert to his own kitchen—and his music is built on his own identity as a creative artist and that of the people he proudly represents.

fieldwork and ethnomusicological texts. In diverse contexts music is regarded increasingly as a means of bounding identity and place. In the large body of literature on related topics, for example, see Witmer (1990) and Diamond and Witmer (1994) for the Canadian context and beyond and Koskoff (1989), Titon (1988), and Barz and Cooley (1997) for the U.S. context and beyond.

The conflation of boundaries and cultural interaction between ethnic groups is illustrated in the music culture of many North American communities, including cities and parts of cities as well as smaller regional communities. A case in point is the Mi'kmaq reserve of Eskasoni, Cape Breton Island, Nova Scotia, in Canada, the largest Native reserve in Atlantic Canada, with a population of approximately three thousand [see ATLANTIC CANADA: OVERVIEW, p. 1114]. Eskasoni is considered "rural," in that it is somewhat isolated, located on the shores of the Bras d'Or Lakes some twenty-five miles from Sydney, the nearest urban center. As in many Native communities in North America, music making in Eskasoni serves as a means of reaffirming Mi'kmaq tradition and asserting native identity. Music making is diverse and is typically connected to a social, religious, or political context, such as a powwow, dance, house party, church service, or the installation of a new chief. Typical are syncretic levels of styles and individual and group distinctiveness. For example, fiddler Lee Cremo's playing is a mixture of Scottish (Cape Breton), French Canadian, and Native influences. From an outside perspective, Lee Cremo is viewed as a talented borrower of non-Mi'kmaq musical practices; from the inside perspective he personifies a blending of cultural traditions, which has come to be seen as a positive value among the Mi'kmaq.

There is a striking level of difference in these interpretations (Smith 1994:541–556). The disparate narratives concerning an individual such as Lee Cremo reveal the ongoing cognitive dissonance between Natives and non-Natives. It is also significant that Lee is seen by some as the embodiment of the struggle for contested identities in the Maritime provinces of Canada. In this context, Lee's "Nativeness" is not simply an aspect of Mi'kmaq identity but is representative of the struggles for identity and cultural survival by other Maritime minority groups such as Gaelic-speaking people, African Canadians, and Acadians. Cremo is an engaging performer who loves to play varied music in any context—from a large public concert to his own kitchen—and his music is built on his own identity as a creative artist and that of the people he proudly represents.

As a point of regional comparison, if one looks beyond the Eskasoni community to the rich, pervasive musical activity on the rest of Cape Breton Island, some of the same themes are found, particularly among current performers. Well-known examples— locally, nationally, and internationally—are the Barra MacNeils and the Rankins family groups, and fiddlers Natalie MacMaster and Ashley MacIsaac [see THE CELTIC REVIVAL IN CAPE BRETON, p. 1127]. In diverse and creative ways, the musical production of such performers demonstrates combinations of Celtic tradition and popular musics, as well as a powerful sense of place and personal interpretation. In this mix, individual, local, rural, suburban, urban, and other parameters are deliberately and typically blurred. For example, one of Natalie MacMaster's recent CDs is titled *No Boundaries*.

Contextual factors are more than ever cultural determinants in diverse musical environments. Technological forces (with their urban focus), demographic patterns (rural to urban migration and the abundance of immigrant communities in urban settings), and the emergence of strong regional musical voices are formative influences on musical production today. However, in addition to and concomitant with these emergent influences, music continues to be used by musicians as social actors in specific situations to erect boundaries, to maintain distinctions between us and them, and to confirm a sense of place. Indeed, questions of identity and authenticity are still present, if now in ever more complex cultural and ethnic configurations. As Anya Royce observes, the power of ethnic identity "is perceived and interpreted differently by individuals and groups, whether they are users of ethnicity, observers of ethnicity, or analysts of ethnicity" (1982:1).

REFERENCES

Allen, Ray, and Lois Wilcken, eds. 1998. *Island Sounds in the Global City: Caribbean Popular Music and Identity in New York*. New York: Brooklyn College and New York Folklore Society and the Institute for Studies in American Music.

Barbeau, Marius. 1946. *Alouette*. Montréal: Thériens.

Barz, Gregory F., and Timothy J. Cooley, eds. 1997. *Shadows in the Field: New Perspectives for Fieldwork in Ethnomusicology*. New York: Oxford University Press.

Beckwith, John. 1997. *Music Papers: Articles and Talks by a Canadian Composer 1961–1994*. Ottawa: Golden Dog Press.

Beckwith, John, and Frederick A. Hall. 1988. *Musical Canada: Words and Music Honouring Helmut Kallmann*. Toronto: University of Toronto Press.

Bohlman, Philip V. 1988. *The Study of Folk Music in the Modern World*. Bloomington: Indiana University Press.

Chase, Gilbert. 1987 [1955]. *America's Music: From the Pilgrims to the Present*. New York: McGraw-Hill.

Child, Francis James. 1883–1898. *The English and Scottish Popular Ballads*.

Clifford, James. 1988. *The Predicament of Culture: Twentieth-Century Ethnography, Literature, and Art*. Cambridge: Harvard University Press.

Crawford, Richard. 1993. *The American Musical Landscape*. Berkeley: University of California Press.

Diamond, Beverley. 1994. "Narratives in Canadian Music History." In *Canadian Music: Issues of Hegemony and Identity*, ed. Beverley Diamond and Robert Witmer, 139–171. Toronto: Canadian Scholars' Press.

Diamond, Beverley, and James Robbins. 1992. "Ethnomusicology." In *Encyclopedia of Music in Canada*, ed. Helmut Kallmann et al., 422–431. Toronto: University of Toronto.

Diamond, Beverley, and Robert Witmer, eds. 1994. *Canadian Music: Issues of Hegemony and Identity*. Toronto: Canadian Scholars' Press.

Erdely, S. 1979. "Ethnic Music in the United States: an Overview." *Yearbook of the International Folk Music Council* 9:114–137.

Fétis, François-Joseph. "Résumé philosophique de la musique." In *Biographie Universelle des Musiciens*. Brussels: Leroux.

Ford, Clifford. 1982. *Canada's Music: An Historical Survey*. Toronto: GLC Publishers.

Gagnon, Ernest. 1935 [1865, 1880]. *Chansons populaires du Canada*. Montréal: Beauchemin.

Hamm, Charles. 1983. *Music in the New World*. New York: Norton.

Hitchcock, Wiley. 1988 [1969]. *Music in the United States: A Historical Introduction*. Englewood Cliffs, N.J.: Prentice-Hall.

Jabbour, Alan. 1993. "Foreword." In *Transforming Tradition: Folk Music Revivals Examined*, ed. Neil Rosenberg. Urbana: University of Illinois Press.

Kallmann, Helmut. 1987 [1960]. *A History of Music in Canada 1534–1914*. Toronto: University of Toronto Press.

Keil, Charles. 1966. *Urban Blues*. Chicago: University of Chicago Press.

Kingman, Daniel. 1989 [1979]. *American Music: A Panorama*. New York: Schirmer.

Koskoff, Ellen, ed. 1989. *Women and Music in Cross-Cultural Perspective*. Urbana: University of Illinois Press.

Lang, Andrew. 1895. *Border Ballads*. London: Lawrence and Bullen.

Levine, Lawrence. 1988. *Highbrow/Lowbrow: The Emergence of Cultural Hierarchy in America*. Cambridge: Harvard University Press.

Lichtenwanger, William, ed. 1983. *Oscar Sonneck and American Music*. Urbana: University of Illinois Press.

McCue, George, ed. 1977. *Music in American Society 1776–1976: From Puritan Hymn to Synthesizer*. New Brunswick, N.J.: Transaction Books.

McGee, Timothy J. 1985. *The Music of Canada*. New York: Norton.

———, ed. 1995. *Taking a Stand: Essays in Honour of John Beckwith*. Toronto: University of Toronto Press.

McKay, Ian. 1994. *The Quest of the Folk: Antimodernism and Cultural Selection in Twentieth-Century Nova Scotia*. Montréal: McGill-Queen's Press.

Mellers, Wilfrid. 1964. *Music in a New Found Land: Themes and Developments in the History of American Music*. London: Barrie and Rockcliffe.

Mishler, Craig. 1993. *The Crooked Stovepipe: Athapaskan Fiddle Music and Square Dancing in Northeast Alaska and Northwest Canada*. Urbana: University of Illinois Press.

Morey, Carl, ed. 1997. *MacMillan on Music: Essays on Music by Sir Ernest MacMillan*. Toronto: Dundern Press.

Myers, Helen. 1993. "British-Americans." In *Ethnomusicology: Historical and Regional Studies*, ed. Helen Myers, 36–45. New York: Norton.

Nettl, Bruno. 1985. *The Western Impact on World Music: Change, Adaptation, and Survival*. New York: Schirmer.

———. 1992. "Ethical Concerns and New Directions: Recent Directions in Ethnomusicology." In *Ethnomusicology: An Introduction*, ed. Helen Myers, 375–399. New York: Norton.

———, ed. 1978. *Eight Urban Musical Cultures: Tradition and Change*. Urbana: University of Illinois Press.

Paredes, Américo, and Ellen Stekert, eds. 1971. *The Urban Experience and Folk Tradition*. American Folklore Society Bibliographical and Special Series 22. Austin: University of Texas Press.

Pound, Louise. (1921). *Poetic Origins of the Ballad*. New York: Macmillan.

Proctor, George. 1980. *Canadian Music of the Twentieth Century*. Toronto: University of Toronto Press.

Rockwell, John. 1983. *All American Music*. New York: Knopf.

Rosenberg, Neil, ed. 1993. *Transforming Tradition: Folk Music Revivals Examined*. Urbana: University of Illinois Press.

Royce, Anya Peterson. 1982. *Ethnic Identity: Strategies of Diversity.* Bloomington: Indiana University Press.

Schramm, A. Reyes. 1975. "The Role of Music in the Interaction of Black Americans and Hispanos in New York City's East Harlem." Ph.D. dissertation, Columbia University.

Seeger, Charles. 1977. *Studies in Musicology 1935–1975.* Berkeley: University of California Press.

Smith, Gordon E. 1990. "Fieldwork and Ernest Gagnon's *Chansons populaires du Canada.*" In *Ethnomusicology in Canada: Proceedings of the First Conference on Ethnomusicology in Canada,* ed. Robert Witmer, 300–306. Toronto: Institute for Canadian Music.

———. 1994. "Lee Cremo: Narratives about a Micmac Fiddler." In *Canadian Music: Issues of Hegemony and Identity,* ed. Beverley Diamond and Robert Witmer, 541–556. Toronto: Canadian Scholars' Press.

Titon, Jeff Todd. 1988. *Powerhouse for God: Speech, Chant, and Song in an Appalachian Baptist Church.* Austin: University of Texas Press.

Witmer, Robert, ed. 1990. *Ethnomusicology in Canada: Proceedings of the First Conference on Ethnomusicology in Canada.* Toronto: Institute for Canadian Music.

Snapshot:
How Music and Place Intertwine
Jennifer C. Post
Neil V. Rosenberg
Holly Kruse

New England Ballads—Jennifer C. Post
Bluegrass—Neil V. Rosenberg
Indie Pop in Champaign-Urbana, Illinois—Holly Kruse

Often a specific geographical area, such as a farmstead, village, or small town, becomes the locus for a specific kind of musical culture. Such is the case in the following three examples, taken from the rural American landscape, one from northern New England, one from the rural South, and the last from the Midwest. These musics, with roots primarily in British culture, developed and grew quite differently in the United States and have come even to this day to be associated with their own unique geography.

NEW ENGLAND BALLADS

Northern New England is a unique cultural region in the United States. Because of the area's physical geography, settlement patterns, and relative isolation from urban centers before the middle of the twentieth century, its musical traditions exhibit a particularly close connection between musical performance and economic and social practices.

Early northern New England residents were primarily Irish, English, and Scottish settlers who arrived from Europe and southern New England beginning in the eighteenth century [see ENGLISH AND SCOTTISH MUSIC, p. 831; IRISH MUSIC, p. 842]. In the nineteenth and twentieth centuries the European American population grew with the arrival of settlers from Canada and Europe who joined the growing rural and urban work forces, yet the region has remained strongly Anglo-American. The primary livelihood for many was farming, although later, as commercial enterprises arrived, some residents moved out of the rural sphere to work in mills, lumberyards, and other industries.

The geographical landscape that northern New England settlers adopted and adapted to was a many-layered one. The spatial organization of individuals and families that settled in the rural sphere was closely tied to its physical and cultural geography. When families settled on hillsides and in villages they joined neighborhoods that were dependent on one another for support. Social obligation became a critical factor in their everyday lives, and the resulting reciprocity turned into a pattern of farm mutuality that played a major role in family and community survival.

Active musical traditions accompanied work and play, provided entertainment, reinforced social roles, and contributed to the establishment and maintenance of a cultural identity. British Isles and North American ballads and lyric songs, popular songs and tunes, hymns and dance pieces dominated the diverse repertoires of the residents and were performed at events that took place regularly in families, neighborhoods, and occupational groups. Shared musical ideas in the family or household and among neighbors and other members of the community enriched each tradition. These practices continued until the mid-1940s, when major cultural, social and economic changes finally moved the traditions away from localized practices and into the mainstream.

Community singing

Families and neighbors gathered to sing not only for entertainment but also in conjunction with work they shared. The same groups that met to sing and dance regularly provided help for one another during times of need. Thus sharing songs helped bond families and communities. When residents assembled to share ballads, popular songs, and hymns the occasion was sometimes referred to as a sing, social, or party. In northern New Hampshire an eighty-eight-year-old man remembers gatherings when neighbors and friends sang together.

> A lot of people used to come when they had them parties. The way they used to handle them parties, lots of times . . . they'd ask people to sing. Someone that they knew that really could. And that was quite a lot of entertainment. And once in a while they'd spring a song the rest hadn't heard, then oh boy! That was wonderful. It was probably a song they learnt when they were younger, before they knew them. (Covill 1988)

Some families sang in the evening during parlor or kitchen gatherings. Repertoires were broad and included traditional ballads and popular songs. Two sisters in central Vermont remember their father's songs:

> Sometimes, when we had company, and sometimes when we was all alone he used to sit there and sing those songs. And he taught us the Woodmen's Song there [figure 1], and that's how we learned our ABC's. In the dining room [we] had a big table, of course, for a big family. And we used to sit around that and sing. And then sometimes we'd go in what they called the parlor—the livin' room. And my brother and my sister'd play the organ and we'd sing. (Vaara and Leonard 1989)

FIGURE 1 "Woodmen's Song" (Woodsman's Alphabet).

1. A is the axe that you very well know
   And B is the boys that can use them also
   C is the chopping that soon will begin
   And D is the danger we always stand in.

CHORUS
Oh merry my boys, oh merry are we
No mortal on earth are as happy as we
Hi derry, ho derry, hi derry down
When the shantymen's well and there's nothing goes wrong.

2. E is the echo that rings through the woods
   And F is the foreman the boss of the gang
   G is the grindstone so swiftly will smooth
   And H is the handle so slippery and smooth.

CHORUS

3. I is the iron we mark our spruce with
   J is the joefle the boy of the ring
   K is the keen edge our axes will keep
   And L is the lice that keeps you from sleep.

CHORUS

4. M is the moss we stuff our camps with
   N is the needle we sew our pants with
   O is the owl that hoots out at night
   And P is the pine that we always fall right.

CHORUS

5. Q is the quarrel we do not allow
   R is the river we draw our logs through
   S is the sled so stout and so strong
   And T is the team that we draw them along.

CHORUS

6. U is the use we put our teams to
   V is the valley we build our roads through
   W's the woods that we leave in the spring
   And now you have heard all I'm going for to sing.

CHORUS

(Ed Dragon, Ripton, Vermont, 8–9-38)

In addition to singing, residents also recited songs and poems referred to as recitations or speaking pieces. Ballads or narrative songs such as "Brave Wolfe," "Young Charlotte," and "Barbara Allen" were especially popular, because they told stories about events and emotions that residents could easily relate to.

Songs, either spoken or sung, were transmitted both orally and in print, in song books, song sheets, manuscript books, and scrapbooks. A New Hampshire woman discussed a scrapbook of newsprint songs and poems she compiled in the 1920s to preserve her family's songs.

> I clipped them out of a paper that was sent out, I think it was a weekly paper. And every week there'd be one page of old songs and pieces. My mother couldn't sing— she spoke pieces. And a lot of the entertainment back then was: people would get together in the evening, there might be two or three that would speak pieces, then some of 'em would sing. They'd entertain each other. That was the entertainment. (Haynes 1987)

Communal singing also took place when friends met informally to share work or at gatherings when neighbors socialized at the end of a long work week. These gatherings were gender-specific at some times, although at others they were made up of young couples; frequently they were broad intergenerational events [see GENDER AND SEXUALITY, p. 87]. We find references in diaries and oral histories to bees for quilting, apple paring, hops picking, and corn husking, as well as to shared labor for haying and barn raising. Typically, a social time with food, dancing, and singing followed an intense period of labor, especially communal labor. In addition to dance tunes, songs, including game songs, were popular among children and adults at these socials.

Singing at work

Songs frequently accompanied women's and men's daily work, especially on the farm. Singing played an important part in daily life, especially to provide relaxation while working and to ease work loads. In fact, singing as an adjunct to work is referred to more often than is any other type of song performance by women. Many women sang to their children, and to themselves, while they worked. The songs distracted them from the pressures of work and kept the children occupied while finishing their household chores. One central Vermont resident remembers her mother's singing in the early years of the twentieth century:

> When my mother was mopping, Marion and I had to sit on the woodbox and she would be singing. Of course we would be bored! We would say: "Oh mother, sing 'Cabbage and Meat'" [figure 2], or "sing about the fish. . . ." She also sang at the sink while doing dishes. She sang the songs that she heard her father sing. (Pierce 1984)

FIGURE 2   "Cabbage and Meat" (The Half Hitch).

1. A noble lord in Plymouth did dwell
   He had a fine daughter, a beautiful gal
   A young man of fortune, and riches supplied
   He courted this fair maid to make her his bride
   To make her his bride
   He courted this fair maid—to make her his bride.

2. He courted her long and he gained her love
   At length this fair maiden intend him to prove
   From the time that she owned him, she fairly denied
   She told him right off, she'd not be his bride
   She'd not be his bride
   She told him right off, she'd not be his bride.

3. Then he said, "Straight home I will steer,"
   And many an oath under her he did swear
   He swore he would wed the first woman he see
   If she was as mean as a beggar could be.
   As a beggar could be
   If she was as mean as a beggar could be.

4. She ordered her servants this man to delay
   Her rings and her jewels she soon laid away
   She dressed herself in the worst rags she could find
   She looked like the devil before and behind
   Before and behind
   She looked like the devil before and behind.

5. She clapped her hands on the chimney back
   She crocked her face all over so black
   Then down the road she flew like a witch
   With her petticoats heisted upon the half hitch
   Upon the half hitch
   With her petticoats heisted upon the half hitch.

6. Soon this young man come riding along
   She stumbled before him she scarcely could stand
   With her old shoes on her feet all tread off askew
   He soon overtook her and said, "Who be you?"
   And said, "Who be you?"
   He soon overtook her and said, "Who be you?"
   (*spoken*) "I'm a woman, I s'pose."

7. This answer grieved him much to the heart
   He wished from his very life he might part
   Then he wished that he had been buried
   And then he did ask her and if she was married
   And if she was married
   And then he did ask her and if she was married
   (*spoken*) "No, I ain't."

8. This answer suited him much like the rest
   It lay very heavy and hard on his breast
   He found by his oath he must make her his bride
   And then he did ask her behind him to ride
   Behind him to ride
   And then he did ask her behind him to ride
   (*spoken*) "Your horse'll throw me, I know he will."

9. "O no, O no, my horse he will not."
   So on behind him a-straddle she got
   His heart it did fail him. He dare not go home
   For his parents would say, "I'm surely undone.
   I'm surely undone."
   For his parents would say, "I'm surely undone."

10. So to a neighbor with whom he was great
    The truth of the story he dared to relate
    He said, "Here with my neighbor you may tarry
    And in a few days, with you I will marry
    With you I will marry
    And in a few days, with you I will marry"
    (*spoken*) "You won't, I know you won't."

11. He vowed that he would and straight home he did go
    He acquainted his father and mother also
    Of what had befallen him, how he had sworn
    His parents said to him, "For that don't you mourn.
    For that don't you mourn."
    His parents said to him, "For that don't you mourn."

12. "Don't break your vows but bring home your girl
    We'll fix her up, and she'll do very well."
    The day was appointed, they invited the guests
    And then they intended the bride for to dress
    The bride for to dress
    And then they intended the bride for to dress
    (*spoken*) "Be married in my old clothes, I s'pose."

13. Married they were and sat down to eat
    With her hands she clawed out the cabbage and meat
    The pudding it burned her fingers so bad
    She licked 'em, she wiped 'em along on her rags
    Along on her rags
    She licked 'em, she wiped 'em along on her rags.

14. Hotter than ever, she at it again
    Soon they did laugh 'til their sides were in pain
    Soon they did say, "My jewel, my bride
    Come sit yourself down by your true lover's side
    By your true lover's side
    Come sit yourself down by your true lover's side."
    (*spoken*) "Sit in the corner, I s'pose, where I used to."

15. Some were glad and very much pleased
    Others were sorry and very much grieved
    They asked them to bed the truth to decide
    And then they invited both bridegroom and bride
    Both bridegroom and bride
    And then they invited both bridegroom and bride
    (*spoken*) "Give me a light and I'll go alone."
    They gave her a light, what could she want more
    And showed her the way up to the chamber door
    (*spoken*) "Husband, when you hear my old shoe go
        'klonk' then you may come."

16. Up in the chamber she went klonking about
    His parents said to him, "What you think she's about?"
    "O mother, O mother, say not one word
    Not one bit of comfort to me this world can afford.
    This world can afford.
    Not one bit of comfort to me this world can afford."

17. At length they heard her old shoe go klonk
    They gave him a light and bade him go along
    "I choose to go in the dark," he said
    "For I very well know the way to my bed.
    The way to my bed.
    For I very well know the way to my bed."

18. He jumped into bed, his back to his bride
    She rolled and she tumbled from side unto side
    She rolled and she tumbled, the bed it did squeak
    He said unto her, "Why can't you lie still?
    Why can't you lie still?"
    And he said unto her, "Why can't you lie still?"
    (*spoken*) "I want a light to unpin my clothes."

19. He ordered a light her clothes to unpin
    Behold she was dressed in the finest of things
    When he turned over her face to behold
    It was fairer to him than silver or gold
    Than silver or gold
    It was fairer to him than silver or gold.

20. Up they got and a frolic they had
    Many a heart it was merry and glad
    They looked like two flowers just springing from
        bloom
    With many fair lasses who wished them much joy.
    Who wished them much joy.
    With many fair lasses who wished them much joy.

(Pierce 1984)

Children also heard singing while working outside the home. The repertoire and singing style inside the house was different from that employed in the outbuildings of a farm. A man from northern New Hampshire who lived with his grandparents when he was young learned sentimental ballads and hymns from his grandmother. From his grandfather, a blacksmith, he heard primarily British ballads and songs.

Northern New England farming families often sent men to spend winters in the woods to cut timber in preparation for the spring log drives. In the lumber camps, men frequently assembled on Saturday evenings after a long week of work, to entertain one another with dancing, fiddling, storytelling, recitations, and songs. Anglo-American songs popular in the camps included lumbering ballads with tragic themes such as "The Jam on Gerry's Rock" (figure 3) or "Peter Amberley," humorous songs, and satirical pieces about local people and events, as well as more sentimental songs. The musical environment in some of the camps was competitive. Men challenged one another to perform and encouraged some to create new songs. Ballads about tragedies reminded the singers and their audiences about the constant dangers of working in the woods.

FIGURE 3   Jack Monroe ("The Jam on Gerry's Rock").

1. Concerning a young shanty boy,
   With courage bold and brave.
   'Twas at the jam on Gary's Rock,
   He met his watery grave.

2. It was on Sunday morning,
   As you will plainly hear.
   Our logs they piled up mountains high,
   We could not keep them clear.

3. The foreman says "Turn out brave boys,
   With hearts devote from fear
   We'll break the jam on Gary's Rock
   And for Ingleston's we will steer."

4. Some of them were willing,
   Whilst others they were not,
   To work on jams on Sunday,
   They did not think they'd ought.

5. But six of our Canadian boys
   Soon volunteered to go
   To break the jam on Gary's Rock
   With our foreman Jack Monroe.

6. They had not rolled off many logs
   When they heard his clear voice say,
   "I'd have you boys be on your guard,
   For the jam will soon give way."

7. Those words were scarcely spoken
   When the jam did break and go,
   And it carried off those six brave youths,
   And the foreman Jack Monroe.

8. Some of the mangled bodies,
   Afloating down did go,
   While crushed and bleeding near the bank
   Lie that of young Monroe.

9. They took him from his watery grave,
   Brushed back his raven hair.
   There was one fair maid among them,
   Whose sad cries roamed the air.

10. There was one fair maid among them,
    A girl from Saginaw town,
    Whose moans and sighs rose to the skies,
    For her loved one who'd gone down.

11. Fair Clara was a noble girl,
    A riverman's true friend.
    Who with her widowed mother,
    Lived at the river's bend.

12. The foreman of her own true love,
    Her wages to her did pay
    And the shantyboys to her made up
    A generous purse next day.

13. But Clara did not long survive,
    Her heart broke with her grief.
    And scarcely three months after,
    Death came to her relief.

14. And when the time had passed and gone
    And she was called to go,
    Her last request was granted,
    To be laid by Jack Monroe.

(Elmer George, N. Montpelier, Vermont, 11-16-44)

For many rural residents, active social singing has been replaced by listening. Those once active in community singing report that they are involved in a more passive tradition today.

Despite the close relationship between singing and work, the use of songs to regulate work was found in limited spheres in northern New England. On the Maine coast sailors sang shanties to coordinate specific work activities on the ships, especially hoisting sails and anchors. While shanties had a critical function in the work on sailing vessels, they were also popular among lumbermen in the camps (some of whom worked winters in the woods and summers on the sea), where they were sung purely for entertainment.

Changes in the twentieth century

Today northern New England families and neighbors seldom socialize with songs in homes and community spaces, although social dancing continues to be popular in many rural and urban communities. The lifestyle changes that began to affect most Americans in the early years of the twentieth century have decreased opportunities for sharing in families and neighborhoods. On the farms, widespread mechanization has altered rural social practices that have in turn affected family and community repertoires and overall performance practice.

For many rural residents, active social singing has been replaced by listening. Those once active in community singing report that they are involved in a more passive tradition today. Gradually they have become listeners—of the radio and audio recordings—and viewers—of television and videos—rather than active participants in musical events as performers. This behavior is reflected in repertoires and performance practices throughout the region.

Songs and their social function have also been altered by professional singers and the commercialization encouraged by the song industry. Singers in northern New England now regularly interact with musicians from other regions and countries. This naturally contributes to the development of new songs and styles. At public events where "the old songs" are occasionally presented, older singers are viewed as remnants of the past; younger singers offer new and revised songs that less often repeat and re-create images of the past, than comment on the present. Rather than representing broad sentiments and issues targeting an intergenerational community, they speak to a single generation, or social group, of listeners. The environment has changed and so have the songs that northern New England communities support.

—Jennifer C. Post

BLUEGRASS

The American musical form known as bluegrass takes its name from the band of Grand Ole Opry star Bill Monroe (1911–1996), the Blue Grass Boys (figure 4). Kentucky native Monroe began developing this music in 1939 when he formed his band. By the late 1940s other musicians who had worked with him, seen his performances, and heard his broadcasts and recordings were copying instrumentation, performance

FIGURE 4   Bill Monroe (center) and his Blue Grass Boys (Kenny Baker, Vic Jordan, Roland White, James Monroe) at Chautauqua Park, Franklin, Ohio, 8 September 1969. Photo by Carl Fleischhauer.

styles, repertoire, and other details of his and his band's special country music sound [see COUNTRY AND WESTERN, p. 76].

TRACK 4

In addition to Monroe, who continued to perform with his Blue Grass Boys until six months before his death at age 84 in September 1996, other significant performers are Lester Flatt and Earl Scruggs (together from 1948 to 1969), Don Reno and Red Smiley (1952–1964), the Stanley Brothers (1947–1966), Ralph Stanley (since 1967), Jim and Jesse McReynolds (since 1947), the Osborne Brothers (since 1953), Jimmy Martin (since 1956), the Country Gentlemen (since 1957), Del McCoury (since 1968), the Seldom Scene (since 1971), Doyle Lawson and Quicksilver (since 1979), Hot Rize (1978–1990), the Nashville Bluegrass Band (since 1984), and Alison Krauss and Union Station (since 1984).

Review of previous scholarship

The word *bluegrass* was first used to describe this music in print in 1956. The first serious descriptive writing about it was done by folk music enthusiasts (Rinzler 1957; Lass 1958; Seeger 1959), who stressed its divergence from mainstream commercial country music and its close ties to Appalachian folk music. The first scholarly work was that of L. Mayne Smith, whose 1964 thesis under the supervision of Alan P. Merriam led to an introductory article in the *Journal of American Folklore* (Smith 1965). Since then, folklorists have contributed the lion's share of the scholarship on this music, a form invariably performed by bands rather than individual musicians. Significant dissertations focusing on primary instruments have been written about the banjo (Adler 1980); mandolin (Hambly 1977, a study that covers other aspects of that instrument); and fiddle (Spielman 1975, like Hambly, a survey that covers a larger body of music but includes bluegrass).

The growth of interest in the music following the festival movement that began in the late 1960s led to several popular works, the best of which was by Bob Artis (1975) [see REVIVALS, p. 55]. In the mid-1980s two book-length studies explored the meaning of bluegrass as cultural artifact and symbol (Cantwell 1984) and analyzed its history (Rosenberg 1985). Meanwhile, other studies have examined facets such as diffusion (Adler 1974; Hale 1983; Hambly 1980) and the cultural milieu of the bluegrass festival, including jam sessions (Adler 1985; Kisliuk 1988) and foodways (Adler 1988). Although an in-depth ethnomusicological analysis of the musical dimensions of this complex style and its offshoots is lacking, considerable transcription and analysis has been done for the pragmatic purpose of teaching, as reflected in such works as Trischka and Wernick (1988).

Insider conceptions of music

Bluegrass is thought by those who participate in it to have a definite history reaching back no further than the 1940s, when Bill Monroe formulated the style and introduced the key repertoire. Monroe was working within what is now called country music (then "hillbilly"), and bluegrass followers still think of the music as a special kind of country music. It is, however, also thought to represent or incorporate various other forms related to bluegrass as roots, influences, or elements. These forms include fiddle music, "old-time music," folk music, blues, jazz, and so forth. It is therefore typical of many contemporary forms in that it is perceived to be in its origins a populist blend of folk, popular, and elite musics. It is unique in situating this blend in the rural culture of the southern Appalachian mountains, a region of the United States that includes portions of West Virginia, eastern Kentucky and Tennessee, northern Georgia and Alabama, and western South Carolina, North Carolina, and Virginia. Although this region historically has been the site of the most bluegrass activity, it is important to know that many influential bluegrass musicians, including western Kentuckian Monroe, are from other parts of the rural upland South.

Those who participate in bluegrass also believe it has other cultural associations, specifically with the white working-class rural population of the upland South in the United States. Again, a symbolic level of representation is perceived to lie behind this cultural association: namely, the cultural roots of these people, mainly in the British Isles but also with other European and African American connections [see EUROPEAN AMERICAN MUSICS: OVERVIEW, p. 820; AFRICAN AMERICAN MUSICS: OVERVIEW, p. 572].

Bluegrass is thought to have typical performance contexts that can be divided into three general categories. The first is the formal concert in which a proscenium device exists—at least a microphone connected to a sound amplification (PA) system and usually including a stage. Here the musicians present themselves standing side by side in a line facing the audience. In this context musicians generally follow set arrangements for each piece performed, although some improvisation may occur. The second is the informal music session in which musicians stand in a circle and play for one another. Here arrangements may be negotiated during performance rather than set beforehand. The third context is more specialized—the recording session or radio broadcast with no audience, which combines aspects of the first two contexts: formal-context arrangements and informal-context proxemics. Some specialized contexts, such as church services, onstage jams at festivals, and so on, may call for modification of these performance expectations.

Audiences for the formal concert vary according to the nature of the event. At shows and festivals listeners sit in chairs facing and listening to the musicians; in bars (clubs) patrons at tables drink, talk, listen, and occasionally dance to the music; at square dances (which are not nearly as common an event for bluegrass bands as are shows, festivals, and club dates) most of the audience dances. Audiences for informal music sessions stand around outside of the circle, listening and sometimes commenting or making requests.

A high proportion of those who regularly follow bluegrass music are themselves musicians. In this sense, bluegrass is a "musician's music": concert audiences often contain a high number of musicians, and the informal sessions are considered an essential aspect of the spirit of the music. Those who have studied these events report varying amounts of competition shaped by rules often described in the music's popular literature as "jam session etiquette."

This is a music in which both vocal and instrumental skills are required. Bluegrass is performed by singers who use stringed instruments—guitar, banjo, mandolin, fiddle, string bass, Dobro steel guitar—both to carry along the music and to accompany singing. Audience members, whether they are musicians or not, expect certain standards of musical competence in both realms. A competent performance must therefore not merely present a musical text that is acceptable, but must also demonstrate both individual virtuosity and the ability of all band members to work closely to produce a coordinated and integrated sound.

Aesthetics and affect, or the power to move

Bluegrass is, then, an ensemble music in which there is a constant shifting of focus—from one individual to another and between individuals and groups. Largely unspoken musical rules about acceptable rhythm and melody/harmony ensure that the boundaries between individual expression and group cohesion are mutually understood, allowing members of a band to mesh in a collective expression that allows for individual presentation.

Each musical piece is structured to enable instrumentalists to perform roles that vary between their support of the other musicians/vocalists in the ensemble and the display of their own personal skills. Musicians try not to get in each other's way or upstage one another, by adhering to accepted modes of performance—"rhythm," "backup," "filling," "lead"—all of which will be discussed later.

The vocal dimension of the music, which is embedded in its instrumental presentation—that is, the instruments are generally heard before, after, and surrounding the singing—displays a similar range of opportunity. Solo vocalists are free to ornament the melody and in various other ways to assert personality through style. Duets, a combination of "lead" (melody) and "tenor" (a harmony part sung above the melody), allow for less of this, but there is still room for a considerable amount of freedom in structuring the harmony part so that the polyphonic dimensions of bluegrass duets can be as important as the harmonic ones. Trios and quartets, on the other hand, require a considerable degree of coordination and are carefully worked out so as to ensure that each individual (lead, tenor, baritone, and bass) is always singing a different note from those of the others.

The way in which bluegrass bands actually work out the details of this interaction varies considerably. Some aspects, like the subordination of instruments to vocal solos, are so basic to the music that they are not discussed except in terms of evaluation of the skill of the instrumentalist to do what is expected in that context. Others, like the decision about which instrument will solo at what place in the song, must be worked out before or, in a jam session, negotiated by eye contact and a sense of hierarchy in the group. Although musicians are expected to know how to sing certain harmony parts, a new song may present problems in structuring a trio or quartet that will require rehearsal to arrive at an acceptable arrangement.

In all of these processes the band structure may range from one in which a recognized leader makes decisions about who does what to an egalitarian situation in which all band members participate in the process. Frequently band names tell about how this works: in Bill Monroe and the Blue Grass Boys (five to seven members), the decisions were made by Bill Monroe, while in Spectrum (four members) consensus ruled (Lightfoot 1983). In jam session contexts decisions like these are negotiated in an ad hoc situation in which it is not unusual to find a hierarchy emerging, based on skill, knowledge, experience, and assertiveness.

History of bluegrass

Bluegrass began as a radio and record music, in the band of a musician who was an innovative commercial musician associated with the most popular hillbilly radio jamboree of the years between 1940 and 1960. It did not spring from a specific locale; it was viewed by its creator and his audiences as a modern statement in country music of the values associated with old-time music of the rural upland South. This music included instrumental tunes associated with dances and frolics, religious songs associated

At the same time, bluegrass was becoming increasingly marginal in the world of country music. Bluegrass was considered hopelessly out of date, embarrassingly down home, and a commercial liability because it appealed only to older rural people.

with Protestant fundamentalism, traditional ballads and lyrics, favorite popular songs from the past, and newly composed songs often modeled on these older ones—all dealing in various ways with events and emotions, affairs of the heart, nostalgia for the old rural home, and the stress of modern urban life. This repertoire was set to a music form that developed from earlier traditional string band music but was more tightly integrated, faster, and demanded greater musical skills. It was presented in concerts, shows that mixed various elements of repertoire in formulaic ways to focus on the featured musicians as performers and to present certain topics—here the fiddle tune, there the bandleader's latest record, next the comedy routine, then the religious songs, and so on—in a certain format.

The 1940s

The earliest followers of this music were working-class men and women from the rural upland South. Many were recent migrants from farms or villages to urban centers where the men found factory jobs. For these people it was an exciting new music based on familiar patterns associated with home, the past, the country, the old church, or the family. Its novel aspects—the heightened musical skills and the greater performance integration it demanded—paralleled their experiences in the modern urban world, where assembly lines and crowded streets demanded that individuality be curbed and regulated in the name of progress. For them it was a music that simultaneously clung to the past and embraced the present.

In the late 1940s younger musicians from this group began to form bands that closely copied Bill Monroe's music, and by the mid-1950s they were calling their music bluegrass. They made records, toured in the South, Southwest, Midwest, and border states along the Mason-Dixon line, performed in daily shows on small radio and television stations in the South, and played at working-class hillbilly bars in the migrant centers of Cincinnati, Detroit, Columbus, Pittsburgh, Baltimore, and Washington, D.C. In all of these settings bluegrass was still presented and experienced mainly as a regional type of country music.

The 1950s and early 1960s

In the mid-1950s the music was discovered by followers of folk music from the revival movement that eventually grew into a commercial boom following the popularity of groups like the Kingston Trio in the late 1950s. This new audience was generally young, urban, and middle class, mainly from outside the South. Bluegrass first appealed to them because it included the five-string banjo, popularized by revival leader Pete Seeger as a folk instrument [see TECHNOLOGY AND MEDIA, p. 235]. Also appealing were aspects of the repertoire that they identified as traditional. Bluegrass bands began to appear at folk festivals and folk music clubs in New York, Los Angeles, and Boston. By the early 1960s musicians from this new audience were forming bands, and a few of the outstanding ones were working in established southern bands.

At the same time, bluegrass was becoming increasingly marginal in the world of country music. The advent of rock and roll in the mid-1950s presented a commercial threat to country music marked by declining record sales and a drop in radio exposure [see ROCK, p. 347]. Establishing a trade association, the Country Music Association (CMA), the industry sought to protect and regain old markets and to penetrate mainstream urban popular music markets. In this context bluegrass was considered hopelessly out of date, embarrassingly down home, and a commercial liability because it appealed only to older rural people.

The mid-1960s through the 1980s

In 1965 the first bluegrass festival was held. It marked the beginning of a major shift in the social focus of bluegrass. At the festival the best known of bluegrass bands performed in three days of concerts much like those they had been presenting since the late 1940s. They also spoke informally about their skills from the stage in workshops—performance events borrowed from folk festivals. Instrument and band contests were held. Many who attended camped on the festival grounds, and informal jam sessions were carried on around the clock. On the final day of the festival a gospel concert was held in the morning, and in the afternoon Bill Monroe was honored as "the father of bluegrass" in an event that saw many of the musicians who had apprenticed with him come onstage to re-create various versions of the Blue Grass Boys in order to perform their recorded repertoire—a kind of staged jam session. The audience was a mixture of ages, classes, and regions, which belied the CMA perception that had marginalized the music.

In the next decade the festival movement (by the early 1970s there were more than five hundred per year, held mainly in the South and Midwest but also as far afield as Canada, Japan, and Europe) was the center of an emerging bluegrass community with its own infrastructure. In addition to the presentation of annual weekend festivals, regional clubs were formed, monthly magazines were published, weekly radio shows initiated, instrument companies founded, and instructional methods published. By 1984 when the International Bluegrass Music Association, a trade association, was established, the music itself had become a historical phenomenon, and the venues in which it was performed were the focus of community. Its early roots in the rural upland South were not forgotten but were increasingly seen in symbolic terms. Meanwhile performances continued to be evaluated in terms of developed standards for the music, with stress on "lonesome" vocals and "driving" instrumentals.

Bluegrass as a musical system

Bluegrass is a musical system that integrates two subsystems, one involving solo and group vocal roles and the other, musical instrument band roles. The characteristic musical forms in bluegrass are two-part strophic pieces that, like gospel song and much popular music, tend to be two to four minutes in length and to repeat the strophe five to ten times. A typical song begins with an instrumental introduction, usually half the strophe. The complete strophe, performed vocally, follows, typically with the first half (verse) performed by a soloist and the second (chorus) by additional vocalists who join the soloist, singing harmony parts. An instrumental break of a half strophe follows, and the pattern repeats for two or three more strophes. Generally each instrumental section features a different instrument. Instrumental pieces follow a similar pattern in which the various instruments take turns performing two-part strophic tunes.

Within this framework, in which four to six musicians sing and play instruments, there is typically a central focus, the lead instrument or vocal. When the lead singer is at the center, the instruments provide support on two levels: rhythm, consisting of single notes or chords played on the major beats; and backup, consisting of ornamental textures, antiphonal riffs, and harmonic countermelodies, all conceived of as supporting or decorating the vocalist's melody. Additional vocalists who join the lead singer play supporting roles, singing harmonic parts above and below the melody. Considerable value is placed on the careful orchestration of such parts, to the extent that "good" duets, trios, and quartets are often experienced by seasoned enthusiastic listeners as polyphonic textures. When instruments are central, their role resembles that of the vocalist; there is the expectation that they are playing a melody to which the other instrumental parts are subordinate. As with vocals, various kinds of backup reflect this hierarchy.

Bluegrass genres

Broadly speaking, bluegrass is divided into three genres: secular songs, sacred songs, and instrumentals. Each of these is subdivided in various ways according to structure of its music. For example, secular songs can be characterized in terms of the vocal parts used (duet, trio) or tempo (waltz, slow, medium, fast); sacred songs can be "bass lead" or a cappella, have lyric content, or feature instruments or voices.

Vocal styles

Bluegrass voice production is shaped by the emphasis imparted to the music by Bill Monroe's practice of singing at the top of his range, often described as the "high, lonesome sound." Vocal textures are generally clear, with a tendency toward the use of head tones, and the most emulated singers have been those whose range is toward the high end. Stylistic influences have, however, varied over the years, with influence from mainstream American popular vocalists being reflected at every point. Thus early bluegrass lead singers like Clyde Moody and Jim Eanes reflected smooth "crooner" influences, while later singers have followed trends in mainstream country music, rock, and other forms. In general, though, the details of earlier southern folk styles can be seen in recurrent details of vocal style, such as the breaking of final notes upward and melismatic ornamentation. In vocal harmonizing emphasis is placed upon blend and coordination, with the subordination of personal style to the concept of a tight duet, trio, or quartet, as discussed earlier.

Instruments

Bluegrass instruments include the guitar, fiddle, mandolin, five-string banjo, bass, and Dobro steel guitar. Strong emphasis is placed on the use of acoustic (nonelectrified) instruments. With a few significant exceptions the only electrified instrument heard in bluegrass has been the electric bass. Generally one of each instrument is used in a bluegrass band, although two fiddles (playing in harmony) are occasionally used, as are two guitars (one playing rhythm, the other lead). Banjos and mandolins are rarely doubled for lead harmony, and then usually only on recordings or at jam sessions.

Bluegrass musicians seek instruments that have a broad dynamic range and can be played at great volume so as to "cut" (be heard) through the sounds of the other instruments or crowd noise. Certain makes and styles of instruments are preferred—in particular the Martin D (Dreadnought) series guitars, Gibson Mastertone banjos of the type produced in the 1930s, and Gibson F5 Master Model mandolins, developed in the 1920s by acoustical engineer Lloyd Loar. Considerable attention is paid to instruments as icons within the music: old "original" guitars, banjos, and mandolins fetch high prices and serve as models for modern re-creations, both manufactured and handmade. Fiddles and basses are chosen more on the basis of personal preference.

Instrumental styles

Today bluegrass instrumentals are generally kept in standard tuning, with the fiddle tuned to G–D–A–E, the guitar to E–A–D–G–B–E, and so on. Some combination of the I–IV–V chords is most common, with the passing use of the II–V and the relative minor. Echoing the consciously held association with older forms of mountain folk music is the use of the VII chord, often in a I–VII–V or I–IV–VII sequence. The circle of fifths progression is also found. Seventh chords are used in a passing way; augmented chords, suspensions, and other chordal techniques are used infrequently.

A few instrumental showpieces may involve special tunings of the most common lead instruments: the banjo, fiddle, or mandolin. In the early years the influential bands tuned a half step (one fret) above standard pitch. Various reasons were advanced for this practice: it was easier to keep the instruments in tune, it gave a brighter sound, it brought the instruments closer to the keys used for high pitched vocals, and it discouraged other musicians from butting into backstage practice and jam sessions.

Bluegrass instruments are played in styles that depend more or less on open (that is, unfretted) strings that are allowed to ring (are not damped). The major exception to this rule occurs with the fiddle and, in a more general way, when musicians are playing rhythm on lead instruments, at which time damped chords are used to provide percussive rhythm on the offbeat. Although high value is placed on the ability to play in any key, the preferred keys are G, A, B, C, D, and E major. The major keys of F and B-flat are also used, but less commonly. Banjos and guitars use capos frequently, playing in the various keys using two or three standard sets of chord formations associated with several major keys, the most common being G.

The banjo

The instrument with a style most closely identified uniquely with bluegrass is the banjo. This instrument, with its four main strings tuned to produce a G-major chord and its short drone fifth string tuned to the tonic, is played in a style introduced by North Carolinian Earl Scruggs, who developed it from traditional styles in his home. The steel strings of the banjo are plucked by the thumb, index, and middle fingers— hence the style is described as "three-finger picking." Picks (plastic for the thumb, metal for the other two fingers) are worn, which produce a bright, pinging sound, particularly when they are used to pick close to the bridge for lead work. Scruggs's style produces a series of eighth-note arpeggios, formulaic harmonic phrases in which the melody is embedded. These formulae are shaped by right hand "rolls"—sequences limited by the rule that any single digit never strikes the same string twice in a row, so that all rolls involve alternating finger-string patterns. The combination of right-hand rolls with left-hand fingerings results in "licks," or melodic phrases. Later developments in bluegrass banjo have been characterized by growing complexities in both hands, with a tendency to move toward arpeggios perceived as melodic or chromatic rather than harmonic. Some of these have been shaped by the desire to closely emulate fiddle melodies.

The guitar

Early bluegrass guitar players followed country music practice of their time in using thumb and index finger picks on the right hand to play rhythm, but this is now rare, and most bluegrass guitarists use a plectrum (flat pick). Rhythm is played using chords that combine fretted and unfretted strings, all of which are allowed to ring. Generally all six strings are played with strokes that emphasize the major pulses or have a responsorial relationship to the vocal or instrumental lead being accompanied, but runs, successive single-note phrases played on the lower strings, are a staple of the style. These are heard most often as transitions between chords and at the midpoints and ends of strophes. Lead guitar breaks are like solos on other bluegrass instruments, grounded in the melody and tending to move toward a statement based on chord structures.

With the advent of multiple speed turntables in the mid-1950s, banjo pickers sometimes played along with records at half speed to learn rolls and licks.

The mandolin

The mandolin, which has eight strings in double courses tuned like those of a violin, is fretted and played with a plectrum. A number of techniques are used by mandolinists playing lead, from tremolo on one to three strings (used on slower pieces) to single-note melodic techniques, including fiddle tunes, statements grounded in blues phrasing, and arpeggios across three strings in the style of the bluegrass banjo, a style invented by Jesse McReynolds and called "cross-picking." Rhythm on the mandolin consists of three- or four-note chords in which all strings are fretted and quickly damped after they are struck, producing a percussive effect. These "chop chords" are usually played on the offbeat.

The fiddle and bass

A variety of styles are used by bluegrass fiddlers depending upon the musical context. Unlike the old-time traditional fiddling from which techniques for this instrument developed, bluegrass fiddling ranges from pop-influenced use of long sweeping phrases to jazz-tinged shuffle rhythms involving rocked bows and double or triple stops, to melodic, harmonic, and chromatic single-note arpeggios. Bluegrass fiddlers are also expected to play outside of first position and do so most effectively in double stops on the upper reaches of the fingerboard. Bluegrass fiddle solos often place such available techniques in contrast. One might open with a flurry of single-note phrases, then shift to a shuffle, and close with a series of long held chords. Backup techniques include bouncing the portion of the bow closest to the nut (frog) on the strings close to the bridge to achieve a percussive sound on the offbeat.

The bass player generally provides notes central to the harmonic structure of the piece, roots and fifths, playing on the downbeats. More adventurous style leaders have extended the technique to provide a "walking" bass, where all the major beats are used and harmonic elaboration is heard.

The Dobro guitar

The Dobro is a mechanically amplified guitar invented in the 1920s in which the bridge is suspended on a metallic device incorporating one or more spun aluminum cones underneath a metal plate. It is used as a Hawaiian-style guitar, tuned to an open chord, with the strings raised high off the fretboard, and stopped not with frets but with a steel bar slid along the strings [see POLYNESIAN MUSIC, p. 1047]. This early "steel guitar" (steel referring to the bar held in the left hand; on the right hand are picks like those worn by the banjoist) was integrated into bluegrass during the middle 1950s by Buck "Uncle Josh" Graves in the Flatt and Scruggs band; Graves's style was like typical country steel on slower pieces but used Scruggs's right-hand banjo techniques on uptempo ones.

Music education and transmission

In the first decade and a half of its existence bluegrass skills were mastered by a relatively small number of people, essentially concentrated in a handful of bands. During this period most people first heard the music over the radio in live broadcasts or saw the same groups who were broadcasting at various concert venues. Phonograph recordings, either broadcast or purchased and played at home, constituted the other major source for hearing the music during its formative years.

Individuals wishing to learn the music (in the early years, generally boys and young men) learned through a variety of informal means. Recorded performances served as models for text, tune, and key. With the advent of multiple speed turntables in the mid-1950s, banjo pickers sometimes played along with records at half speed to learn rolls and licks. Souvenir autograph-picture-song books sold by bands at personal appearances provided texts as well as photographic clues to standards of dress, orientation around the microphone, and preferred instruments. Close observation of performers in concert venues was another learning tactic, and beginners would ask musicians to show them instrumental techniques when they spoke to them at autograph sessions after performances. In general, more conscious effort went into learning instrumental techniques than into singing.

Once individuals mastered an instrument to the extent that they could play in a band situation, they then became apprentices to the older musicians in the band and would be taught in a pragmatic piecemeal way what they needed to know to help the band, particularly arrangements and repertoire, by more experienced musicians in rehearsals or warm-ups and during travel to performance venues. There is little evidence of formal lessons during the early years of bluegrass.

As the music diffused geographically and socially from its southern working-class origins during the late 1950s and early 1960s, larger numbers of people became proficient in its skills. As the music became more widely known, informal performance at jam sessions and parties grew in importance as another context available for learning by observation and participation. In the mid-1960s books that taught banjo through the use of tablature ("tabs") and musical scores began appearing. The festival movement that began in 1965 created an even larger market for formal instruction; private lessons and lessons through music stores became common. Early festivals had workshops in which well-known musicians demonstrated their skills. Opportunities for informal performance as a learning device were also expanded by the festivals, where campers could learn from one another. The markets created by festival-goers who wished to learn or improve their skills led to an explosion of published teaching material for instrumentalists, including books (often with sound sheets or other ancillary recordings), cassettes (with ancillary tablature), and monthly magazines with tablature for all the instruments at various levels of skill. Eventually such publications became available for vocal style and part singing. By the end of the 1980s videocassettes had been added to the range of available teaching materials. Today a range of informal and formal ways exist by which the music is learned and transmitted. Recent formal techniques have not so much supplanted the older informal techniques as added to them. In addition several academic institutions include courses on bluegrass musical techniques and business skills in their curricula.

Music and creativity

Although early scholarship placed considerable emphasis on the traditional aspects of the bluegrass repertoire, the commercial milieu in which the music emerged and continues to exist has always created demand for the composition of new songs and tunes. Bill Monroe's leadership in this aspect of the music was particularly marked. A number of his compositions, such as "Uncle Pen" and "Blue Moon of Kentucky," have become standards, and the fact that he based many of his love songs on personal experience has served as an example for other bluegrass songwriters. Instrumental pieces may be programmatic in various ways, suggesting dance ("Blue Grass Stomp"), recalling region ("Cheyenne"), mimicking technology ("Train 45"), and so forth.

Creativity may also be expressed in arrangements of repertoire received from tradition. Flatt and Scruggs devised a showy arrangement for the well-known old frolic tune "Cripple Creek," which has been emulated on record by many bands. In general, arrangement techniques include decisions about the structuring and situating of vocal harmonies, the nature and sequence of instrumental breaks, choices of tempo and key, and beginnings and endings. Solos become trios, waltzes are re-created as up-tempo 4/4 pieces, instrumental breaks are performed in harmony or split among several instruments, and so on. Creativity is also expected in the form of improvisation, particularly in instrumental breaks, which are perceived as opportunities for self-expression, and, in a more general way, during jam sessions.

In evaluating a competent performance in concert, as much attention is paid to the proper balance between voices, between instruments, and between the two as is paid to how well the performers' musical material is realized. Thus the details of sound system technology and use, ability to properly use microphones, instrument quality with respect to tone and volume, and other factors that affect balance are central in execution. In informal performances, more attention is paid to exhibitions of individual skill, and much emphasis is placed upon the etiquette of jam sessions. Here the focus is on the way in which individual musicians negotiate breaks according to "turns" based on a balance of interaction with attention to relative competence. In these settings arrangements are negotiated.

Music and identity

Bluegrass music in its earliest years was the focus for regional and class identity, an extension of the vernacular music of the rural upland South. The strong religious component reflected another identity, with close ties to class and region; the instrumental music served the dual purpose of allowing for the expression of individual identity and symbolizing the dance and frolic music identified with rural community life. The texts of the songs are pretty evenly divided between those that deal with events and feelings that are the result of having to leave one's home (family, community, region) and those which focus on the dynamics of interpersonal relations between men and women (courtship, love, romance, marriage, and separation).

As bluegrass diverged from mainstream country music in the late 1950s, it acquired an additional identity for some followers of being a form of country music that had preserved old values and not sold out to the pop music industry. In a similar way it attracted the attention of folk music followers in part because it used no electric instruments, which were, to the urban and middle-class folk enthusiasts, symbolic of the alienation of modern life. It was also attractive because those aspects that its audience recognized in it tied it to a region and class they perceived as distinctly different and "folk." After the mid-1960s festival movement bluegrass music itself became a community with both business and social dimensions that constituted a new aspect of identity subsuming those that had gone before.

—NEIL V. ROSENBERG

INDIE POP IN CHAMPAIGN-URBANA, ILLINOIS

Champaign-Urbana, Illinois, is home to a large state university and has been an active site of independent (or "indie") pop and rock music production for well over a decade. Champaign is a fairly typical college town, but unlike Athens, Georgia, or Austin, Texas, Champaign-Urbana has not occupied a central position in the history of music making practices and/or styles outside the mainstream music industry. Despite this, Champaign-Urbana has spawned many indie pop/rock bands that have been regionally popular and even nationally known, including, in the 1980s, the Elvis Brothers, Turning Curious, the Farmboys, Weird Summer, and Combo Audio. By the early 1990s Champaign was home to several alternative acts that had signed major label deals—such as Poster Children, Adam Schmitt, and Titanic Love Affair—and to small independent labels like Parasol and 12 Inch Records.

Key players in Champaign-Urbana indie pop

Indie labels

The Parasol label is part of the growth in independent labels in the United States that began in the 1980s and that has been accompanied by an increase in the number of bands recording their music (as opposed to simply performing it live). Many of these bands record for very small labels that are unable to pay them (or solo artists) advances before recording; however, larger indies like Touch and Go and Frontier are able to fund the production of records and videos. Very few indie pop or rock bands in communities like Champaign-Urbana record for large indies, however; many more release records for micro-indies like Parasol.

Parasol exists at the intersection of two distinct vectors: (1) the emergence of the seven-inch single as an important marketing tool in indie music, especially, indie pop, and (2) the history of indie music production in Champaign-Urbana. The rise of the underground seven-inch market seems to have coincided with the mainstream industry's determination that the vinyl phonograph record was no longer a profitable, and therefore viable, format. Independent labels, and especially smaller indies, were reluctant to abandon the cheap vinyl format for CDs, as many did not have the available capital to invest in CD production, and most indies did not want to be relegated to the production and distribution of cassette tapes. Undoubtedly, part of vinyl's appeal to independent companies selling alternative rock and pop is that the major labels' effort to make the format obsolete in effect makes whatever appears on vinyl, especially in the seven-inch format, seem to be in opposition to the mainstream. Furthermore, the format caters to a rather select audience: those who still own, or are willing to purchase, turntable technology.

Throughout the 1980s, a number of indie pop and rock bands appeared in Champaign-Urbana, and several released albums, singles, and/or tapes on such local labels as Office, Trashcan, and Popsicle. The existence of small local labels and the availability of cheap recording equipment enabled bands to make recordings available locally without relying on signing major label or major indie deals. According to Trashcan's founder, its entire purpose was "to break the local scene" (Springer 1989:8)

Indeed, a 1989 local newspaper article declared that "Champaign-Urbana is on the verge of becoming a trendsetting music scene with national influence" (Springer 1989:8). Although this optimistic prediction has yet to come to pass, several local artists have major label or major indie deals, including Poster Children, who released records on indies Frontier, Twin Tone, and Sub Pop and who now record for Sire; Hum, currently signed to RCA, but who have released records on independent labels like Dedicated, 12 Inch Records, and Mud (a Parasol affiliated label); and until recently, former Champaign musicians Ric Menck and Paul Chastain, whose band Velvet Crush recorded for Warner Brothers in the United States and Creation in Britain.

The sense that Champaign-Urbana is a regional scene of some national significance is undoubtedly important to the visibility of labels like Parasol, yet Parasol has not had as much success selling records in Champaign-Urbana as it has through mail order. For instance, singles by Champaign music scene veteran Nick Rudd have not sold well in Champaign: his first single on Parasol sold eighty copies in England and

Music scene participants are for the most part aware of some version of local music history and place themselves within that tradition, whether it is in Champaign's indie pop scene, San Francisco's punk scene, or Seattle's grunge scene.

one at Record Swap, the store at which he works. Although those in the greater indie pop subculture see Parasol as important in getting local music to the public, Geoff Merritt argues that despite a roster laden with local talent, he's not doing them much good in the local area. He recalls a time in the early eighties when there was more of a sense of community in the Champaign scene:

> It used to be a single came out in this town and everybody bought it. *Stabs in the Dark* [a 1982 compilation album of Champaign indie pop and rock bands] came out and everybody bought it whether they liked the stuff or not, because it was local. . . . I guess there's something wrong with putting out 45s because a lot of people don't even own turntables anymore, but even so, people should buy this stuff. (Merritt 1991)

Thus it was at the moment in the 1990s that the Champaign scene was most in the national spotlight that one of its key participants saw the scene as least cohesive.

Radio

One virtual nonparticipant in the local indie pop/rock scene historically has been the University of Illinois's student-run radio station, WPGU. From its establishment in 1967 until relatively recently, WPGU was an album rock station, and this made the station a site of contention. Indeed, a local musician remarked in the early 1990s, "I'm always so blown away when I go to another town and I hear their college radio station, because PGU is—I hate to get on anyone's case—but they're really awful" (Schmitt 1992). In the early 1990s, WPGU switched to a "top of the alternative charts" format.

However, most music scene participants saw this shift to another commercial format as not particularly adventurous, and thus for most Champaign-Urbana listeners who wish to hear nonformatted alternative music radio shows, the only option is the community radio station, WEFT. As a community radio station, WEFT's overall philosophy is to provide the community with programming that is not otherwise available, and in Champaign-Urbana, this includes independent pop and rock. Within its programming mix, alternative rock and pop occupy about 20 percent of WEFT's slots. WEFT also devotes slots to a number of other types of music and programming that are not otherwise available in the area, including alternative news and information, world music, bluegrass, folk, and jazz. For listeners looking for nonmajor label alternative rock/pop on the radio in Champaign-Urbana, WEFT can be a rather frustrating source of material. As a local musician notes, WEFT is "so sporadic, it's hard to know when you turn it on what you're going to be hearing."

Venues

Live performance venues have also been a source of frustration for musicians and other music scene participants. By the early 1990s there were two clubs in Champaign that booked indie acts, Mabel's and the Blind Pig, but most local indie musicians complain that Mabel's, the larger of the two venues and the one that is located near campus, is essentially closed to them. This was not always true: during much of the 1980s Mabel's was the primary performing venue for local alternative acts. However, in recent years the club has booked more mainstream local acts, prompting Geoff Merritt of Parasol Records to state that "Mabel's doesn't book bands like ours for various reasons" (Merritt 1991). However, a local musician adds that with the opening in 1990 of the Blind Pig, a club located away from campus, "it's been both easier and better for bands to find a place to play." Still, The Blind Pig is often criticized for its small size, heat, and location, and the limited number of venues means Champaign-Urbana musicians often find their home base one of the harder markets to enter (Schmitt 1992).

The importance of local identity

Indie music, more than most forms of pop and rock music in the United States, has been identified by locality (Athens, Seattle, Austin, Minneapolis, Champaign, Olympia, and so on), by both participants and those outside particular scenes; therefore, the way in which indie music is understood in relation to notions of local identity merits examination. Localities are constituted by geographical boundaries, by networks of social relationships, and by a sense of local history.

Placing one's participation within this context is a way of asserting the importance of one's position in local music history. For instance, a particular Champaign musician constructs his involvement in local music as "pioneering" by articulating his band's relationship in time and space to other bands and local scenes. He claims, "I think we were one of the first completely original local alternative college bands, after the Vertebrats—there was probably no one before them. We were sort of paralleling what the Replacements were doing in Minneapolis without even knowing or hearing of them" (Gerard 1991). By locating his band on a level of importance similar to that of a seminal local band and a nationally prominent band, the musician identifies his band as one of local and possibly even national importance, at least within the confines of his narrative.

Indeed, music scene participants are for the most part aware of some version of local music history and place themselves within that tradition, whether it is in Champaign's indie pop scene, San Francisco's punk scene, or Seattle's grunge scene. Participants are part of social formations in which existing musical practices and traditions impact emerging music.

Yet identification of a "Champaign scene" in the 1990s came at a time when participants were being connected in some way with entities that were both defined by and transcended locality, for example, Parasol and the other, "local" indie pop seven-inch labels like Slumberland, or Poster Children and other, harder rocking indie bands like Minneapolis's Soul Asylum. On a more tangible level, a Champaign indie musician explains the role played by touring in making interlocal connectons: "People come to me asking about certain people in certain towns. Tonight I'm going to go see Die Kreuzen, who we always used to stay with every time we played Milwaukee. If they were in town, they expected to stay with us. We're part of a group where you see someone every six months or every three months" (Gerard 1991).

Interlocal networks such as these, because they bring institutions and people in disparate local scenes together in broader systems of cultural production and dissemination, underscore the degree to which economic structures of college music are interrelated in numerous ways with social practices.

Indie music's local scenes and socioeconomic structures can, in the end, be seen as overlapping networks, in which musical knowledge, genre, geography, and position in the independent music business locate subjects within one or more networks. Shared musical knowledge and practices are important in the formation and maintenance of interlocal social and economic networks and thus make it impossible to ever understand a formation like the Champaign-Urbana music scene in isolation.

—HOLLY KRUSE

REFERENCES

Adler, Tom. 1974. "The Concept of Nidality and Its Potential Application to Folklore." In *Conceptual Problems in Contemporary Folklore Study,* ed. Gerald Cashion, 1–5. Bloomington, Ind.: Folklore Forum.

———. 1980. "The Acquisition of Traditional Competence: Folk-Musical and Folk-Cultural Learning Among Bluegrass Banjo Players." Ph.D. dissertation, Indiana University.

———. 1985. "Dueling Banjos: Overt and Covert Competition in Amateur Bluegrass Performance." *John Edwards Memorial Foundation Quarterly* 19:9–16.

———. 1988. "Bluegrass Music and Meal-Fried Potatoes: Food, Festival, Community." In *"We Gather Together": Food and Festival in American Life,* ed. Theodore C. Humphrey and Lin T. Humphrey, 195–204. Ann Arbor, Mich.: UMI Research Press.

Artis, Bob. 1975. *Bluegrass.* New York: Hawthorne.

Bourdieu, Pierre. 1993. *The Field of Cultural Production,* ed. Randal Johnson. New York: Columbia University Press.

Cantwell, Bob. 1984. *Bluegrass Breakdown.* Urbana: University of Illinois Press.

Child, Francis James. 1882–1898. *The English and Scottish Popular Ballads.* Boston: Houghton, Mifflin.

Cohen, Sara. 1991. *Rock Culture in Liverpool: Popular Music in the Making.* Oxford: Oxford University Press.

———. 1993. "Ethnography and Popular Music Studies." *Popular Music* 12(2):123–138.

Colcord, Joanna C. 1938. *Songs of American Sailormen.* New York: Norton.

Covill, Clyde. 1988. Personal interview, September.

Finnegan, Ruth. 1989. *The Hidden Musicians: Music-Making in an English Town.* Cambridge: Cambridge University Press.

Flatt, Lester, and Earl Scruggs. 1991. *Flatt & Scruggs, 1948–1959.* Notes by Neil V. Rosenberg. Bear Family BCD 15472. Compact disc.

Gerard, Don. 1991. Personal interview, 19 December.

Hale, Tony. 1983. "A Comparison of Bluegrass Music Diffusion in the United States and New Zealand." Master's thesis, Memphis State University.

Hambly, Scott. 1977. "Mandolins in the United States: An Industrial and Sociological History

since 1880." Ph.D. dissertation, University of Pennsylvania.

———. 1980. "San Francisco Bay Area Bluegrass and Bluegrass Musicians: A Study in Regional Characteristics." *JEMF Quarterly* 16:110–120.

Haynes, Ardes. 1987. Personal interview, June.

Hills and Home: Thirty Years of Bluegrass. 1976. Compiled, edited, and with notes by Neil V. Rosenberg. New World Records NW 225. LP disk.

Hot Rize. 1990. *Take It Home.* Sugar Hill SH-CD-3784. Compact disc.

Ives, Edward. 1978. *Joe Scott: The Woodsman Songmaker.* Urbana: University of Illinois Press.

Kisliuk, Michelle. 1988. "'A Special Kind of Courtesy': Action at a Bluegrass Festival Jam Session." *The Drama Review* 32:141–155.

Krauss, Alison. 1990. *I've Got That Old Feeling.* Rounder CD 0275. Compact disc.

Kruse, Holly. 1993. "Subcultural Identity in Alternative Music Culture." *Popular Music* 12(1):33–41.

Lass, Roger. 1958. "Bluegrass." *Caravan* 12:20–23.

Laws, George Malcolm. 1950. *Native American Balladry: A Descriptive Study and a Bibliographical Syllabus.* Philadelphia: American Folklore Society.

———. 1957. *American Balladry from British Broadsides: A Guide for Students and Collectors of Traditional Song.* Philadelphia: American Folklore Society.

Lawson, Doyle, and Quicksilver. 1990 [1979]. *Rock My Soul.* Sugar Hill SH-CD-3717. Compact disc.

Lightfoot, William E. 1983. "Playing Outside: Spectrum." *Appalachian Journal* 10:194–198.

Martin, Jimmy. 1990. *You Don't Know My Mind: 1956–1966.* Notes by Neil V. Rosenberg. Rounder CD SS 21. Compact disc.

Merritt, Geoff. 1991. Personal interview, 19 December.

Monroe, Bill. 1989. *Blue Grass 1950–1958.* Notes by Neil V. Rosenberg and Charles K. Wolfe. Bear Family BCD 15423. Compact disc.

———. *The Original Blue Grass Band.* 1978 [1946–1947]. Notes by Neil V. Rosenberg. Rounder SS 06. LP disk.

Mountain Music Bluegrass Style. 1991 [1959]. Recorded, edited, and with notes by Mike Seeger. Smithsonian/Folkways CD SF 40038. Compact disc.

Negus, Keith. 1992. *Producing Pop: Culture and Conflict in the Popular Music Industry.* London: Edward Arnold.

The Osborne Brothers. 1991 [1986]. *Once More Vols. 1 and 2.* Notes by Sonny Osborne. Sugar Hill SH-CD 2203. Compact disc.

Pickering, Michael. 1982. *Village Song and Culture: A Study Based on the Blunt Collection of Song from Adderbury, North Oxfordshire.* London: Croom Helm.

Pierce, Marjorie. 1984. Personal interview, October.

Redhead, Steve. 1990. *The End-of-the-Century Party: Youth and Pop Towards 2000.* Manchester, Eng.: Manchester University Press.

Rinzler, Ralph. 1957. Notes to *American Banjo Scruggs Style.* Folkways FA 2314. LP disk.

Rosenberg, Neil V. 1985. *Bluegrass: A History.* Urbana: University of Illinois Press.

Schmitt, Adam. 1992. Personal interview, 17 June.

Seeger, Mike. 1959. Notes to *Mountain Music Bluegrass Style.* Folkways FA 2318. LP disk.

The Seldom Scene. 1990 [1973]. *Act 3.* Rebel CD 1528. Compact disc.

Shank, Barry. 1994. *Dissonant Identities: The Rock 'n' Roll Scene in Austin, Texas.* Hanover. N.H.: Wesleyan University Press.

Smith, L. Mayne. 1965. "An Introduction to Bluegrass." *Journal of American Folklore* 78:245–256.

Spielman, Earl V. 1975. "Traditional North American Fiddling: A Methodology for the Historical and Comparative Analytical Style Study of Instrumental Music Traditions." Ph.D. dissertation, University of Wisconsin.

Springer, P. Gregory. 1989. "Back to the Garage." *Champaign-Urbana News-Gazette,* 17(February):8–9, Weekend Section.

The Stanley Brothers. 1990 [c. 1964]. *Long Journey Home.* Notes by Bill Vernon. Rebel CD 1110. Compact disc.

Straw, Will. 1991. "Systems of Articulation, Logics of Change: Communities and Scenes in Popular Music." *Cultural Studies* 5(3):368–388.

Trischka, Tony, and Pete Wernick. 1988. *Masters of the 5-String Banjo.* New York: Oak Publications.

Vaara, Elizabeth, and Lula Leonard. 1989. Personal interview, June.

Orchestral and Chamber Music in the Twentieth Century
Rob Haskins

Concert Music from 1900 to 1945
Destructions and Rebirths: 1945 to 2000

One way to examine the importance of place in the development of a music culture is to examine the social and cultural institutions constructed to present and transmit specific kinds of music. The concert hall, long associated in Europe and the United States with the Western classical tradition, still reigns as the most important venue for symphonic and chamber music performed today. But through the twentieth century and into the twenty-first, new possibilities for public performance have begun to emerge.

Like the music of any other culture, twentieth-century American chamber and symphonic music was conceived, written, and performed in response to specific cultural institutions. Although these institutions have both changed and intersected each other numerous times, each has particular kinds of venues and practices that can be identified, and these, in turn, have had some impact on the types of music that have been heard (or not heard) there. Space limitations do not permit a comprehensive account of every composer and style that our country has witnessed during this century, but I hope that the following sketch will give an indication of the ways in which some important composers have created the most exciting work possible as they worked within the many practices and ideologies that resided within various streams of twentieth-century American instrumental music.

CONCERT MUSIC FROM 1900 TO 1945

At the turn of the twentieth century, such typical musical institutions as orchestras, chamber groups, and opera companies all reflected a primary commitment to the Western European concert music tradition [see OVERVIEW OF MUSIC IN THE UNITED STATES p. 519; CONCERT MUSIC AT THE END OF THE NINETEENTH CENTURY, p. 554]. The few American composers who held academic posts—for example, John Knowles Paine (1839–1906) and Horatio Parker (1863–1919), who taught at Harvard and Yale respectively—had themselves studied in Europe and were meticulous but thoroughly conservative craftsmen. Younger Americans who wanted to devote themselves to composition studied with them or with similar pedagogues. Many also studied in Europe, either in Germany with such composers as Engelbert Humperdinck (1854–1921) and Joseph Rheinberger (1839–1901) or in France with Vincent d'Indy (1851–1931). Some younger composers took this solid training as a base from which they could absorb more current European concerns. Charles Tomlinson Griffes (1884–1920), for instance, was influenced by impressionism and knew some music by both Schoenberg and Stravinsky; the Boston Symphony premiered his tone poem *The Pleasure Dome of Kubla Khan* (1919) in the last year of his short and financially troubled life.

Other young American composers from the period, however, responded to their conservative training by a more thoroughgoing rejection of it. In the symphonic and chamber music of Charles Ives (1874–1954), nearly all of which was completed by 1921, we find such modernistic traits as polyrhythm, extreme dissonance, and an attitude toward earlier music that ranged from simple quotation to allusion (with or without subtle transformation)—all this despite the fact that Ives was practically unaware of European contemporary music. Ives's appropriation of other musics within his own remains a powerful evocation of America's heterogeneous culture. Carl Ruggles (1876–1971) developed for himself a painstaking and completely intuitive method of composing; of a small handful of works he allowed to be released (he destroyed any pieces he felt to be unsatisfactory), his orchestral *Sun-Treader* (1926–1931) is his best known work. Nevertheless, it is important to remember that neither composer had much impact until the 1930s or even later, because the then-existing musical institutions were unable and probably unwilling to perform such works. Ives made his living selling insurance; Ruggles struggled with various odd jobs and the support of patrons until he found a more lucrative career as a painter.

Developing an American identity

In the 1920s and 1930s composers attempted to establish an American identity through ever more diverse stylistic choices; more important, support from institutions both old and new gave their work increased visibility. George Gershwin (1898–1937) was essentially self-taught as a composer and began his successful career writing popular songs and a string of hit Broadway musicals. His *Rhapsody in Blue* (1924) was probably the most successful work in the movement to bring jazz into the concert hall, but, ironically, it is better known today through lush arrangements for full symphony orchestra that have necessarily smoothed out the vernacular idiosyncrasies of its original performance style. Henry Cowell (1897–1965), born in California, was one of the so-called ultramodernists; he was already writing piano music that exploited tone clusters (played with the fist or forearm) when he came under the enlightened tutelage of Charles Seeger (1886–1979). In 1917–1918, during his time with Seeger, Cowell wrote an important compositional and theoretical primer, *New Musical Resources* (1996 [1930]). Cowell's concert tours to Europe and Russia inspired him to help American composers organize performances and publications of their music; this he did through the quarterly *New Music* (1927–1957) and through his leadership, from 1929 to 1933, of the Pan American Association of Composers (1928–1934) founded by Edgard Varèse (1883–1965). Finally, a large number of composers who had trained under the great French pedagogue Nadia Boulanger (1887–1979) worked to establish a more populist, but distinctly symphonic, American idiom. Of a number of symphonies produced by these composers, perhaps the best known is the Third Symphony (1938) by Roy Harris (1898–1979). In this work, a number of traits appear that mark an American symphonic sound later taken up by many composers of the period: massive but spacious textures; a new emphasis on vital, syncopated rhythms (sometimes referring to popular music traditions); and a rich harmonic palette based on compounds of simple major and minor chords in different keys and inversions (for example, an A-major triad in root position above a C-major triad in second inversion). This great flowering of the American symphony found favor in concert halls across the country, and such organizations as the Koussevitzky Music Foundation (est. 1942) helped support the production of such works through its commissioning program.

DESTRUCTIONS AND REBIRTHS: 1945 TO 2000

Another important site of activity for symphonic and chamber music was in the universities and conservatories, whose music departments were coming of age just after World War II. The Jewish exodus brought many composers, scholars, and their families to this country. Among composers, Paul Hindemith (1895–1963), whose wife was Jewish, was at Yale, and Arnold Schoenberg (1874–1951) was at the University of Southern California and the University of California at Los Angeles. More than a few composers from Nadia Boulanger's tutelage, including Harris and Walter Piston (1894–1976), found a haven in academia as well. But another powerful group of composers, especially Milton Babbitt (b. 1916), who taught both at Princeton and Juilliard, came to even greater prominence in the 1950s and 1960s. Through his activities as theorist, composer, and pedagogue, Babbitt explored the limits of the twelve-tone system and indeed extended those limits in fascinating and exciting directions. The extreme complexity and precision that his music required led him to turn away, for a time, from large orchestral pieces—the disastrous Cleveland Symphony Orchestra performance of his *Relata I* (1965) is the most famous example of the problems musicians faced in playing his music—to electronic music and also to smaller chamber ensembles (especially string quartet). Such complex music challenged some musicians, who created their own ensembles (many of which were affiliated with colleges or universities) to tackle their difficulties and to commission new works. Among these groups, the best known are the Contemporary Chamber Ensemble, the Da Capo Chamber Players, the Juilliard String Quartet, the Fine Arts Quartet, and the American Composers Orchestra.

John Cage and his influence

The growing prominence of John Cage (1912–1992) (figure 1) in the 1960s had a profound impact on certain sectors of music making within the university system and on a new generation of younger, "independent" composers as well. Cage himself held no extensive academic appointment, although he did teach occasional classes at the New School for Social Research between 1956 and 1960; he also held fellowships at Wesleyan University (1960–1961, 1970–1971), the University of Illinois (1967–1969), and other institutions. Many of Cage's works were eagerly performed in universities and colleges.

Cage's long personal and professional partnership with the choreographer Merce Cunningham (b. 1919) led him and others naturally toward theater; one can, for instance, see the influence of such rarefied music-theater pieces especially in the chamber music with voice of George Crumb (b. 1929), another university composer who for many years taught at the University of Pennsylvania. Cage's continuing support from New York artists frequently led to performances of his music that were often outside traditional venues for concert music. Indeed, like Babbitt, he had unsatisfactory and even unhappy experiences with symphony orchestras earlier in his career, as in the New York Philharmonic's miserable performances of *Atlas Eclipticalis* (1961). In the final years of his life, however, Cage fulfilled many commissions with over forty instrumental works collectively known as the Number Pieces; these works—one example is *Fourteen* (1990), a work for bowed piano and thirteen instruments—represent his final thoughts on chamber and orchestral composition.

Around the same time, a rich experimental tradition on the West Coast resulted in some unusual chamber music that explored simple collections of pitches at great length. The *Trio for Strings* (1958) by La Monte Young (b. 1935) was an extremely early work, one that began the musical style known as Minimalism; a work that achieved even greater fame was a chamber work for variable ensemble, *In C* (1964) by Terry Riley (b. 1935). By this time, Young had already moved to New York, where in 1961 he and Richard Maxfield (1927–1969) produced a famous series of concerts in

FIGURE 1   John Cage with his cat Losa, New York, September 1991. Photo by Rene Block, courtesy John Cage Trust.

Glass's ensemble with its relatively stable instrumentation of electric keyboards, winds, and soprano voice, became the prototype of a new kind of amplified chamber music.

the downtown New York loft of Cage's friend Yoko Ono (b. 1933). These concerts are said to have begun the so-called Downtown tradition, a large and fairly loose-knit community of composers and performers whose work did not fit in academic settings or in the traditional venues for concert music.

Minimalism

Certainly many of these composers followed in the tradition of Cage and his students at the New School for Social Research (for example, the conceptual performance art of the Fluxus group, some of whom had been in Cage's composition class). Of all the various styles of music that emerged from the Downtown tradition, however, the most conspicuous was that by the younger minimalist composers. The most prominent of these were Steve Reich (b. 1936), who had participated in the *In C* premiere, and Philip Glass (b. 1937). New York's art community had strong ties with both men. After Reich and Glass established their own ensembles to play their own music, many of their early performances were in artists' lofts or galleries (for instance, a notable pair of concerts at the Whitney Museum's *Anti Illusion* exhibit in 1969). Glass's ensemble in particular, with its relatively stable instrumentation of electric keyboards, winds, and soprano voice, became the prototype of a new kind of amplified chamber music.

Around the same time, several composers with strong academic backgrounds and pedigrees turned away from their earlier, more complex music and begun exploring new possibilities for tonality. George Rochberg's (b. 1918) "Concord" String Quartets (Nos. 4–5, 1977–1979) juxtapose tonal and atonal styles within a movement. Some, like String Quartet No. 5, are almost entirely tonal. The trend hit younger composers as well, as in the famous series of pieces based on Lewis Carroll's *Alice's Adventures in Wonderland,* written between 1969 and 1986 by David Del Tredici (b. 1937). After some resistance, the "Neoromantic" movement gained considerably more visibility, most obviously in the series of New York Philharmonic concerts produced by Jacob Druckman (1928–1996) during the 1982–1983 season; these concerts were advertised with the description "Since 1968: A New Romanticism?"

Composer-performers

In the late 1980s and 1990s there has been further splintering, though the essential character of all these musical environments has changed very little. Orchestra concerts remain largely devoted to the music of the past, with only occasional offerings from living American composers. The preoccupation with a "new tonality" has felt a sharp counteraction from younger composers, and many other older ones have reached out to a wider harmonic palette as well. For example, the luminescent, sophisticated neo-romantic-cum-minimalist style of John Adams (b. 1947), as seen in such works as *Harmonium* (1980), has given way to a more dissonant and rhythmically complex idiom in such works as his Violin Concerto (1993). And of course some elder statesmen have continued to produce works in their chosen idiom: Babbitt, for instance,

FIGURE 2   The Bang on a Can All-Stars, a collective of composers and performers, c. 1990s. Photo by Peter Sterling. Reproduced with permission.

FIGURE 2   The Bang on a Can All-Stars, a collective of composers and performers, c. 1990s. Photo by Peter Sterling. Reproduced with permission.

steadily produces new works, sometimes for larger forces; one of the most recent is his Second Piano Concerto (1999).

The vanguard of minimalists has also moved in ever divergent paths. After a few orchestral commissions, including the brilliant *Variations for Winds, Strings and Keyboards* (1979), Reich turned away from the symphonic repertoire and now concentrates almost entirely on medium-sized chamber ensembles (both his own and others in America and Europe) that usually include amplification. Glass's amazing ensemble of amplified winds, keyboards, and voice continues to tour regularly, but he also seems to be turning increasingly to such conventional instrumental genres as string quartet and symphonies (five of both). His newer music, of which Symphony No. 2 (1992) is perhaps the most impressive recent example, combines the melodic, harmonic, and rhythmic hallmarks of his work in a more comprehensive, symphonic-style discourse than he has attempted before.

The model of the composer-performer popularized by Reich and Glass continues to hold sway with younger composers. Many of these individuals continue to play out the wide variety of options for composers in America. Some, who no longer feel that they need be bound to any particular style or ideology, eagerly embrace a wide variety of styles and manner in their work. This group, which Kyle Gann has dubbed Totalists (1997), includes such composers as Michael Gordon (b. 1956), whose string orchestra, electronics, and video "opera" *Weather* (1997) shows a typical range of utterance and traceable influences. These individuals have more often than not formed their own collectives to produce concerts largely devoted to their own work. Most famous, perhaps, is the Bang on a Can All-Stars, a group under the artistic leadership of Gordon, David Lang (b. 1957), and Julia Wolfe (b. 1958) (figure 2). In the face of ever more dire predictions for symphony orchestras in the twenty-first century, the growing number of such ensembles suggests that their influence may become even more pervasive in the foreseeable future.

REFERENCES

Babbitt, Milton. 1970. "On *Relata I.*" *Perspectives of New Music* 9(1):1–22.

———. 1987. *Words about Music.* Ed. Stephen Dembski and Joseph N. Straus. Madison: University of Wisconsin Press.

Cowell, Henry. 1996 [1930]. *New Musical Resources.* New York and Cambridge: Cambridge University Press.

Duckworth, William. 1995. *Talking Music. Conversations with John Cage, Philip Glass, Laurie Anderson, and Five Generations of American Experimental Composers.* New York: Schirmer Books.

Gagne, Cole, and Tracy Caras. 1982. *Soundpieces: Interviews with American Composers.* Metuchen, N.J.: Scarecrow Press.

Gann, Kyle. 1997. *American Music in the Twentieth Century.* New York: Schirmer Books.

Glass, Philip. 1987. *Music by Philip Glass.* New York: Harper and Row.

Hitchcock, H. Wiley, and Kyle Gann. 2000. *Music in the United States: A Historical Introduction.* 4th ed. Englewood Cliffs, N.J.: Prentice-Hall.

Howard, John Tasker. 1941. *Our Contemporary Composers: American Music in the Twentieth Century.* New York: Thomas Y. Crowell.

Kostelanetz, Richard, ed. 1990 [1970]. *John Cage: An Anthology.* New York: Da Capo.

Morgan, Robert P. 1992. *Twentieth-Century Music.* New York: Norton.

Noss, Luther. 1989. *Paul Hindemith in the United States.* Urbana: University of Illinois Press.

Nyman, Michael. 1999 [1974]. *Experimental Music: Cage and Beyond.* 2nd ed. New York: Schirmer Books.

Potter, Keith. 2000. *Four Musical Minimalists: La Monte Young, Terry Riley, Steve Reich, Philip Glass.* New York and Cambridge: Cambridge University Press.

Pritchett, James. 1993. *The Music of John Cage.* New York and Cambridge: Cambridge University Press.

Reich, Steve. 1974. *Writings about Music.* Halifax: Press of Nova Scotia College of Art and Design.

Rochberg, George. 1984. *The Aesthetics of Survival: A Composer's View of Twentieth-Century Music.* Ann Arbor: University of Michigan Press.

Schiff, David. 1997. *George Gershwin: Rhapsody in Blue.* New York and Cambridge: Cambridge University Press.

Schwarz, K. Robert. 1996. *Minimalists.* London: Phaidon.

Slonimsky, Nicolas. 1997. *Baker's Biographical Dictionary of Twentieth-Century Classical Musicians.* Ed. Laura Kuhn. New York: Schirmer Books.

Stehman, Dan. 1984. *Roy Harris: An American Musical Pioneer.* Boston: Twayne Publishers.

Strickland, Edward. 1991. *American Composers: Dialogues on Contemporary Music.* Bloomington: Indiana University Press.

Tawa, Nicholas. 1995. *American Composers and Their Public: A Critical Look.* Metuchen, N.J.: Scarecrow.

Thomson, Virgil. 1971. *American Music since 1910.* New York: Holt, Rinehart and Winston.

Tischler, Barbara L. 1986. *An American Music: The Search for an American Musical Identity.* New York: Oxford University Press.

Watkins, Glenn. 1988. *Soundings: Music in the Twentieth Century.* New York: Schirmer Books.

Popular Music of the Parlor and Stage

Dale Cockrell (United States)
Andrew M. Zinck (Canada)

Little is known about non-Native secular music in seventeenth-century America. Music for pleasure was surely a part of many lives. Still it seems clear that nothing like popular music, as it is understood today, existed. Conditions for its growth were first met in the eighteenth century, with the development of a vibrant middle-class culture with the requisite leisure time, disposable income, widespread literacy, and urbanization. Further, as nearly all of the American middle class was white, this new music assumed a white audience and was reflective of Anglo-Saxon social, political, and aesthetic values.

The relationship between the stage, with its professional performers, and the parlor, with its dedicated amateurs, has been a particularly dynamic part of popular music's history. The broadest outline finds popular music of the eighteenth century conceived for the stage, with profit accruing to the performers and producers from ticket sales, and, conversely, that of the twentieth century intended for consumption in the home, to the monetary benefit of the producers. The nineteenth century cultivated an important role for both venues and both forms of production. Music for the parlor, a more private form of amateur expression, needed a highly developed system of dissemination, and it matured later, when a sophisticated industry for its production, marketing, and distribution first came about.

THE EIGHTEENTH CENTURY: EUROPEAN HERITAGE

Musical theater was not a term the eighteenth century would have recognized, as a small orchestra and singers were expected to be part of all theatrical occasions. Instrumental music, purposely unobtrusive, was background to plays and other dramatic presentations. Songs with greater intrinsic interest to audiences were more in the foreground and were often interpolated into plays or featured between plays or acts of plays, yet they too remained relatively minor aspects of the evening's entertainment. In such incidental ways was music heard at the first North American theater, an unimposing structure built in 1716 in Williamsburg, Virginia.

Ballad opera

Only with ballad operas, produced first in the New World Theatre in Charleston, South Carolina, in 1735, did music appear in North American theater. Ballad opera was a form of comic opera, developed in England in the 1720s, that derided high opera by using simple, direct, spoken dialogue and by incorporating short, singable songs in the vernacular, usually set to well-known folk tunes. *The Beggar's Opera, The Virgin Unmasked, The Devil to Pay, The Honest Yorkshireman,* and *The Mock Doctor* were some of the most performed ballad operas of the period. In almost all of these, and the dozens of others heard in the United States, common lower- or middle-class characters prevailed at the expense of those of the upper classes. The settings were usually urban and the plots direct and comprehensible (as opposed to those of Italian operas), often enlivened by touches of humor or satire. Americans themselves wrote and produced several ballad operas in the last third of the century. *The Disappointment, or The Force of Credulity* by Andrew Barton was the first written by a resident of this country. Four days before its opening in Philadelphia in 1767 it was canceled as "it contains personal Reflections, [and] is unfit for the stage," according to the *Pennsylvania Gazette* (22 April 1767). The plot, based on life, satirized several local leaders who undoubtedly had a hand in seeing that the opera never opened. There were eighteen songs, and, typical for the genre, they ranged in musical complexity from a quasi-art song by English composer Thomas Arne to traditional folk ballads to the folk tune "Yankee Doodle." None of these songs maintained the original or traditional texts, but rather substituted plot-specific lyrics. This technique, already centuries old, served the eighteenth century well, and many songs of the period were topical and original in text but set to familiar and proven tunes, including most of the popular "broadside ballads." In its directness, its intention to please, and its willingness to identify with its audience by opposing the values, affectations, and modes of expression associated with the upper classes, the ballad opera established important precedents for the development of popular music. In the music's reliance upon a commonly known body of tunes in the oral tradition, popular music's roots in folk culture is manifest.

Songs for the middle class

Popular songs of a less common, more genteel nature were heard at pleasure gardens in the larger cities, in subscription concerts, and, eventually, in the homes of solidly prosperous middle-class Americans. They were more technically sophisticated than those heard in ballad operas and appealed to the small group of musically literate. These songs proved important for laying the foundation of the business aspect of popular music, for they were disseminated widely in sheet music form. Networks of professional composers and arrangers, publishers, and music dealers were developed to produce this sort of music. Research has identified the most popular of these songs. One such list (Hamm 1979:479) names the ten most liked songs: "The Galley Slave" (William Reeve), "Lullaby" (Stephen Storace), "Henry's Cottage Maid" (Ignaz Pleyel), "Life Let Us Cherish" (Hans Georg Nägeli), "Since Then I'm Doom'd" (anonymous), "The Little Sailor Boy" (Benjamin Carr), "Within a Mile of Edinburgh" (James Hook), "Lucy, or Selim's Complaint" (James Hook), "The Silver Moon" (James Hook), and "I Have a Silent Sorrow Here" (Alexander Reinagle).

Observations made about these representative songs apply generally to the hundreds of similar ones that filled the bins of music publishers in New York, Boston, Philadelphia, and Charleston. One notes, for example, that only two of them were written by musicians living in America (Carr and Reinagle), and eight were imported. Not surprisingly, this is music firmly rooted in English and European styles of the time. Usually these mostly strophic songs have texts that range from a nostalgic regard for a lost, romanticized past, to pastoral perfection, to an appeal to the fullness of life—all ideals shared by the middle class. They do not have preexistent melodies set to substitute texts; all were freshly composed. Typically, the melody is fresh and charming, conjunct in its voice leading, of about an octave in range, with a predictable contour that moves from low to high and ends where it began. Phrase structure is such that the first part of a melody demands completion of a second part. There is a great deal of melodic repetition, with phrases often forming an ABAB pattern or something similar. Harmonies are rooted firmly in the functional system of tonality and are limited generally to the tonic, dominant, and subdominant. Almost all are in major keys. Rhythms and meters are not adventuresome, but tend to be lively. Each song takes two to four minutes to perform, generally needing only a singer and an accompanist at the keyboard, likely a piano. The songs are similar to European art music of the period but simpler in style. In fact, Mozart, Haydn, and Beethoven all wrote and arranged songs that were intended to appeal to broad audiences, that entertained rather than challenged, and that brought them ready remuneration from publishers wanting such songs to turn a handy profit. Not only does this list of stylistic characteristics give definition to a particular group of songs from the end of the eighteenth century, it serves well for popular song into the next century.

THE NINETEENTH CENTURY: THE DEVELOPMENT OF A NORTH AMERICAN POPULAR MUSIC

Popular musics of many kinds became much more important to Americans in the nineteenth century, so that by century's end no one, of whatever social class, economic standing, ethnic, religious, or racial group, was untouched. Audiences flooded to theaters, concert halls, grand halls, opera houses, saloons, wherever music was to be heard performed by accomplished musicians. At the same time, American homes rang out with the sound of the latest hit tune. Arguably, musical literacy reached a peak unmatched since, supported in large part by a highly developed popular music industry structure.

Early century

Opera

The American middle class early in the nineteenth century patronized musical theater modeled after that in England, with music composed by Englishmen and imported or by immigrants from England. These were generally comic operas in English, the ballad opera form having lost favor. Texts tended to reflect the pastoral aesthetic of the pleasure gardens; the music was more complex than that heard in ballad opera and was written by a single composer. Americans took to the English and Italian *bel canto* 'beautiful singing' opera as well, in part as a result of the efforts of Lorenzo Da Ponte (1749–1838), librettist for Mozart's operas *Don Giovanni* and *The Marriage of Figaro* among others, who emigrated to the United States in 1805. Da Ponte aided in the great success enjoyed by the Manuel García troupe of opera singers in 1825, a pivotal moment in the history of opera in the United States. Most important for our purposes, the melodic, harmonic and rhythmic style of this music worked its way directly into the popular musical idiom. In addition, many of the arias were translated, or received completely new texts, and in these versions they became popular songs.

The influence of the style was pervasive throughout Europe and America. Composers in England were affected, principally Michael William Balfe (1808–1870) and William Vincent Wallace (1812–1865), who produced important operas including, respectively, *The Bohemian Girl* (1843) and *Maritana* (1845), both of which incorporated Italian opera idioms. These works were imported to the United States and received with great acclaim. From them came arias that attained high popularity, perhaps most significantly "I Dreamt That I Dwelt in Marble Halls" from *The Bohemian Girl*. Songs like these featured Italianate melodies, vocal pyrotechnics, and arpeggiated accompaniment, but in forms simpler than found in Italian operas and more accessible to the amateur.

Many respectable Americans had long been suspicious of the theater, and Russell countered this by advertising the educational benefits of "An Evening with Henry Russell." He might discourse through song on issues ranging from social reform to marriage.

Musical theater

There appears already to have been a distinction in the early nineteenth century between opera and musical theater. The latter was more the domain of the lower middle and working classes, and it was less specific to large American cities. Theater music tended to be more comic and varied than opera and was clearly descended from ballad operas of the eighteenth century. It also spoke more directly to the needs, wishes, hopes and anxieties of its audience. Three theatrical genres were particularly important for the history of early-nineteenth-century popular music: the melodrama, the circus, and minstrelsy. Melodrama was the most popular type of theater of the day, with its energetic plot turning around heroism, exaggerated dramatic effects, sentimentality, and, especially, villainy. Songs and incidental music were interpolated and, although certainly of secondary importance, rode to popularity with the fortunes of the play. Music was associated with the circus from at least the 1780s, and proscenium stages regularly complemented the circus ring by the 1790s. Bands, orchestras, ballet troupes, singers, and actors were accepted parts of the circus retinue. Small stage pieces, usually of skit length, featured songs and incidental music.

The most far-reaching aspect of circus theater was the development of a genre featuring white men in blackface makeup who ostensibly dressed, sang, and danced like African Americans and called themselves minstrels. The first of these to establish a wide reputation was George Washington Dixon (1801–1861). His performances of "Coal Black Rose," "Long Tailed Blue," and, especially, "Zip Coon" captivated audiences and contributed to significant publication of these songs. The last two songs in their texts helped define the stage persona of the "darkie dandy." "Zip Coon" (the tune to which is today better known as "Turkey in the Straw") employed a mild form of syncopation and was thus an early acknowledgment of the musical influence of African Americans. Thomas Dartmouth Rice (1808–1860), who first "jumped Jim Crow'" in 1830, was even more popular than Dixon. His signature song was the first American song to become a hit in Europe. Textually, it established the comic southern slave persona on the popular stage [see RACE, ETHNICITY, AND NATIONHOOD, p. 63].

Parlor music

Parlor music of mass appeal can almost be said to begin with the publication by Thomas Moore (1779–1852) of the *Irish Melodies* in 1808. Issued in seven volumes, these were poems of a highly sentimental, often nationalistic, altogether "romantic" and bittersweet nature that were set by accomplished musicians of the day to folk tunes, generally Irish in origin. Songs such as "Believe Me If All Those Endearing Young Charms," "The Last Rose of Summer," and "The Harp That Once Thro Tara's Halls" spoke of nostalgia for a place, time, and loved ones left behind, a subject sure to appeal to emigrant North Americans. With these songs, parlor music came to much wider social and economic circles than before.

John Hill Hewitt (1801–1890) was the first American to compose parlor songs and market them successfully. Reared in a family of professional musicians and publishers, he was early prepared for a life in the music business. His songs were based on the English pleasure garden style, with texts of a simple, narrative type. "The Minstrel's Return'd from the War" (1825) was Hewitt's first successful song. It was direct and to the point, easy enough for modest talents. Stylistically it is of a type that characterizes parlor music for much of the rest of the century. In it an eight-measure introduction for the keyboard establishes key, meter, and mood; the primary melody is heard in the verse, sung by a vocalist, in a form that is gracefully conjunct with a climactic high point toward the end; phrases are of regular length and complement each other; harmonies are limited to the tonic, subdominant, and dominant. The text to "The Minstrel's Return'd" was an important part of its appeal. The verses tell of a musician-soldier who must once again put down the guitar and take up the sword; home, family, and the nation are the institutions duty calls him to protect. The song was realistic and directed to the experiences of its audience. Beyond the success of this and others of his songs, Hewitt's importance lay in his understanding of the business of popular music and in his considerable technical and imaginative skills. He was versed in many styles of music and synthesized them convincingly. Hewitt was one of the first songwriters to perceive that mainstream cultural values were tending away from primary support for the communal social unit toward centralizing the importance of the family. His music expressed this understanding, particularly in the development of songs "for the heart and hearth," which later would be called parlor songs.

Midcentury

This most dynamic period in the history of American popular music is characterized by a symbiotic relationship between the stage and the parlor. Songs were produced for initial performance in theaters, then were bought as sheet music for consumption at home.

The concert

The most important new development was that of the popular concert. No longer were songs for public presentation introduced as part of a play or show; rather, they came to stand on their own. Most important to the initial development of this idea in the United States was the cosmopolitan Henry Russell (1812–1900). Born of Jewish parents in provincial England, he trained and performed in London and Italy. Around 1835, he immigrated to Canada and from there moved to Rochester, New York. He developed the concept of the performer-songwriter who traveled widely giving frequent concerts for ordinary people. Many respectable Americans had long been suspicious of the theater, and Russell countered this by advertising the educational benefits of "An Evening with Henry Russell." He might discourse through song on issues ranging from social reform to marriage. Nearly all of his songs were also highly entertaining, often because of their melodramatic qualities. Throughout, middle-class social values would be endorsed, such as respect for family, God, and motherhood and nostalgic regard for the past.

Stylistically his music was shaped by the influence of Italian opera and a strong sense of drama. Many of Russell's most important songs, such as "The Maniac" (1840), were long, grand, and sweeping, like opera, with ample opportunity for histrionics. These served well for Russell the performer, for he was obviously a charismatic stage presence. Shortly after the applause died and the receipts were counted, he would board the technological wonder of the age, the railroad, travel to the next town, and repeat his success. By such seeding of his music, Henry Russell changed the landscape of popular music in the United States.

The Rainer Family of singers from the European Tyrol came to the United States in 1839, and with them arrived the ingredients for establishing the next wave of public popular music performance. Their music was based on the four-part glee; texts were religious or uplifting; their stage personae were without affectation and thoroughly respectable. Altogether they and their music celebrated the developing cornerstone of North American society—the family. In emulation, hundreds of "singing families" were heard throughout the land over the next three decades, each hoping to reap the same bonanza enjoyed by the Rainers.

The most successful of these groups by far was the Hutchinson Family Singers. By 1843, this quartet had become likely the best known and most influential musicians in the United States, as hundreds of thousands heard them in the 1840s, the decade of the group's greatest success. The Hutchinsons even managed to take American music abroad, with a highly successful year-long tour of England, Ireland, and Scotland.

Russell's influence on the Hutchinsons was to be even more important than that of the Rainers. They sang many of his songs, adopted many of his touring techniques, and attempted to educate and persuade their audiences in a manner similar to that of Russell. More than Russell, though, they made the issues of social reform central to their message. Through their music they advocated temperance, communal living, women's rights, dress reform, food reform, medical reform, universal suffrage, and, most explosively, the abolition of slavery. The Hutchinsons were part of a world in transition, from an epoch when religion explained and provided meaning to the modern era with its regard for science. They sang about their confusing, complicated, fluid times and established popular music's essential mission: to articulate the common thoughts of the day.

Songs sung early by the Hutchinsons in their career were glees and ballads by Russell. Soon, though, they began to sing their own compositions, which characteristically featured new words to old music. Among these were "The Old Granite State," the strongly abolitionist "Get Off the Track" (somewhat ironically set to the minstrel show song "Old Dan Tucker"), "King Alcohol," and "Axes to Grind." Their songs were relatively simple in melody, rhythm, harmony, and form; accompaniments were easy enough for someone of moderate skills. Their performances of popular songs set new standards. Not unusual in the effusive praise that followed the Hutchinsons was that of the reporter who wrote: "The multitude who heard them will bear me witness, that they transcended the very province of mere music" (*Herald of Freedom,* 14 June 1844). The quartet sound they achieved featured a close, "sweet" blend; attention was paid to "natural" singing; the intonation was perfect; the words were projected forcefully and were cleanly articulated; accompaniment was provided by the singers themselves on stringed instruments (violins, a cello, sometimes a guitar); the stage manner was easy and unaffected. A typical audience found values they revered reinforced in song, especially those about directness and simplicity of behavior, centralizing the family. Beyond that was regard for what it was to be an American. A typical program would find all songs written by Americans, espousing American values, hopes, and ideals. The catalogue of their unique contributions to American popular music—simplicity and naturalness of approach, sweet blended sound, clear enunciation, expression of a wide range of pertinent social values, aggressive advertising of their product—still applied to popular music in the mid-twentieth century.

Blackface minstrelsy

In 1843, the year of the Hutchinsons' ascendancy, four blackface minstrels in New York City, who modeled themselves after characters like those portrayed by Dixon and Rice, banded together to present the first complete minstrel show, establishing thereby the most popular form of musical theater in the nineteenth century. They called themselves the Virginia Minstrels (although none was from Virginia). The instruments they played—fiddle, banjo, bones, and tambourine—established the core ensemble for the minstrel show. Very soon after their first appearance together in early 1843, competing troupes formed, with names like Christy Minstrels (figure 1), Ethiopian Serenaders,

FIGURE I   Handbill for a performance by the Original Christy Minstrels, 14 May 1855. Photo courtesy the Foster Hall Collection, Center for American Music, University of Pittsburgh Library System.

Buckley's New Orleans Serenaders, Kentucky Minstrels, and White's Minstrels. By century's end, hundreds, perhaps thousands, of such troupes had been established and scattered throughout the English-speaking world.

The structure of the minstrel show was obviously influenced by the singing families. Four to six performers, each of whom combined singing, playing, and dramatic talents, joined together to present a full evening of entertainment, with various soloistic and ensemble, vocal and instrumental, musical and theatrical combinations possible. Explicitly about American concerns, the show was implicitly filled with social commentary. One issue, of course, was American racism and slavery. Presumably the songs, stump speeches, humor, and images reflected the views held by many in the audience: that the black man was ludicrous, stupid, tasteless, ugly, sexually adventurous, a dancer of wild abandon, and a great lover of music, all racial stereotypes that lived on into the twentieth century. Significantly, another message was that the black was in almost all ways beneath the white and, also fundamentally, a southern problem. Another issue, less obvious, was class. White working-class rituals in Europe and America had long used blackface to grant the player a moment outside of normal status and position, an opportunity often seized to criticize those who oppressed and contained the underclasses. In its early years, minstrelsy seems to have sometimes functioned in a somewhat like manner.

The early minstrel show followed the form of the blackface minstrel skits of the 1830s: a part depicting the ludicrous urban dandy (the "Zip Coon" paradigm) was followed by a section treating the ridiculous southern slave (as in "Jim Crow"). The music itself was little changed from that of the solo minstrels. Many of the tunes were from the Anglo-American fiddle tune dance tradition, and few showed any influence of true African American music, with its layered and syncopated rhythms. Subject matter expanded only in that more songs about women were sung, an especially popular example being "Miss Lucy Long" by minstrel Billy Whitlock, which, like many early minstrel songs, was not a narrative but consisted of isolated and unrelated vignettes revolving around the central character.

Only in the 1850s did the structure of the minstrel show change significantly. At that time a third section, called the "olio," was added in the middle. This part of the evening presented skits, gags, jokes, and songs, all in blackface; frequently middle-class virtues and institutions were made the butts of the jokes. The first section evolved toward a variety show of sorts, often delivered without the adornment of blackface makeup. The songs sung in this section were much more genteel than heard heretofore in the minstrel show, often had nothing whatsoever to do with the black man, were sometimes sung without dialect, and represented the best effort of the mid-nineteenth-century stage to co-opt the parlor. It was so successful that a wide range of music came to be considered appropriate for the minstrel shows. Technically the structure of the minstrel show (and its complement, the singing family concert) reinforced the development of the chorus section of the typical midcentury song. When the ensemble joined together at the refrain, often in sweet harmony supporting the song's most compelling melody, it was almost inevitable that this would be the song's most important musical moment and give it its definition. The last section of the show continued to ridicule the southern slave, but it was expanded, produced more cohesively, and concluded rousingly with the "walkaround" song, a grand finale of which the best known today is Dan Emmett's "Dixie" (1859).

In its theatrical effect, the minstrel was leagues beyond the singing families. For decades nothing on the American stage could match the showstopping mix of makeup and costumes, lively repartee (typically between the "endmen"—Mr. Bones and Mr. Tambo—set up by the master-of-ceremonies, or the "interlocutor"), the malaprop-filled stump speeches, humorous impersonations (often of women), skits, dances, and songs. The show was a swirl of sound and image, bathos and pathos, weird and wonderful,

The period of Foster's greatest songs, the 1850s, coincides with one of the most highly wrought and fateful decades in American history. Foster's songs reflect the building political storm and stake out a strong position on the slavery issue.

FIGURE 2   Stephen Collins Foster (1826–1864). Photo courtesy the Foster Hall Collection, Center for American Music, University of Pittsburgh Library System.

otherworldly and very much in touch with the most sensitive social and political nerves in the mid-century United States.

The main characteristic of the minstrel show in its early years was that of a poignant but showy novelty, much as the circus from which it sprang. It presented stereotypes, treated in less-than-human ways. Historically new popular theatrical genres fail if they do not eventually confront the essentially human qualities of their subjects, which is to say, their audience; novelty wears thin. The minstrel show might have been a brilliant, brassy, loud, noisy flash but for the music of Stephen Collins Foster (1826–1864), whose timely genius added a completely new dimension to it (figure 2).

Stephen Foster

A native of Pittsburgh, Foster grew up drawn to music and the theater. Even in his teens he performed as a minstrel and composed songs characteristic of the time for that stage, of which "Oh! Susanna" (published in 1847) is the most famous. Textually, like "Miss Lucy Long," it is nonnarrative, and vignettelike. Musically derived from the Anglo-American fiddle tune repertoire, the song adds an additional measure of rhythmic excitement and places greater emphasis on the refrain. The songs he wrote up to about 1850 (which include the well-known "Gwine to Run All Night [Camptown Races]") gained for Foster such fame that he was able to quit a bookkeeping job and become America's first full-time popular songwriter, a venture at which he was quite successful.

The period of Foster's greatest songs, the 1850s, coincides with one of the most highly wrought and fateful decades in American history. Foster's songs reflect the building political storm and stake out a strong position on the slavery issue. A brief summary of some of the most important and representative songs will make the point and demonstrate the progression in Foster's expression from that of the conventional minstrel show to one of radical progressivism.

"Oh! Lemuel" (1850) is representative of the day's conventions. The caricature it draws is of dark skins, huge lips, big feet, laziness, and predispositions toward dance and music. The music is catchy, with simple harmonies; the rhythms are danceable and mildly syncopated. In its day a novelty song that inaccurately depicted southern slave life, it painted images that northern audiences wanted drawn.

Another song, "Old Folks at Home" (1851), quickly became Foster's most popular and remains today perhaps his best-known. Like "Oh! Lemuel," it features exaggerated dialect and represents carefree plantation slave life. Unlike earlier minstrel songs, though, this one tells a story of a person with feelings something like those felt by the audience: someone is longing for bygone days, a dear mother, and a cozy home. The subject, a slave, has become one with whom the audience can empathize to some extent and with whom the values of home and family are shared. Humanity links the slave and the person being moved by the song. Music reinforces the alliance. Although it is still simple and, typically for Foster, everything serves its purpose with great economy, it is more highly polished than earlier songs and manages to exude a sentimental

FIGURE 3   The cover of the sheet music for "Jeanie with the Light Brown Hair," a nostalgic song composed by Stephen Foster in 1856. Photo courtesy the Foster Hall Collection, Center for American Music, University of Pittsburgh Library System.

melancholy. In many ways "Old Folks" is stylistically similar to the day's parlor songs, which were about white, middle-class sentiments, concerns, and values.

The next year brought "Massa's in de Cold Ground" (1852) from Foster's pen. To some degree the song did not challenge important stereotypes: the demeaning dialect is still there, the plantation image holds, slaves continue to be helpless and childlike, music remains their palliative, "Ole Massa" is kindly and good. Contrary to the old model, though, this song is a deeply felt expression of affection for a deceased parent figure. The use of a nostalgic, sentimental idiom heretofore associated with white working- and middle-class popular music draws a compelling analogy between the feelings of those in the audience and the real humans that happen to be enslaved.

"My Old Kentucky Home, Good Night" (1853) confirms the radical shift Foster was working out in his minstrel show songs. First, with this song he abandoned forever the use of dialect; the black man sings using the white man's language. The first verse of the song paints a family picture of happy times on the placid, peaceful southern plantation. Verses two and three, though, tell of the wrenching experience of leaving family, friends, and home, for, most tragically, this man has been sold downriver, where a slave's life of backbreaking work and death await him. Certain aspects of "My Old Kentucky Home" are common to the time—romantic love, nostalgia, death, tragedy—but they had largely applied to parlor songs before this time. The usage of such devices in the context of a song about slavery was unusual. Although Foster's music does not step outside the period's conventions, except perhaps for the finely developed chorus, it is so well formed that it convinces utterly of the song's sincerity. Text and music work together to compel the audience to confront the horror of slavery. Given the enormous popularity of this and later minstrel show songs by Foster in the same vein, the blatant message undoubtedly affected working-class minstrel show audiences that would soon be called on to shed their blood to bring about the end of slavery in the United States.

Foster wrote songs other than those for the minstrel show. Many of these were "Irish songs," after the type established by Thomas Moore. "Sweetly She Sleeps, My Alice Fair," "Comrades, Fill No Glass for Me," "Gentle Annie," and "Jeanie with the Light Brown Hair" (figure 3) are examples. Texts were elegiac, morose, nostalgic, nearly always bittersweet. The melodies were frequently pentatonic, like those in the *Irish Melodies.* Other Foster songs were influenced by Italian opera styles. "Wilt Thou Be Gone, Love?," which is a setting of the balcony scene from *Romeo and Juliet,* is stylistically much like a *scena* from an Italian opera of the period; "Beautiful Dreamer" is aria-like. The old-fashioned pleasure garden style is also represented in Foster's canon. "What Must a Fairy's Dream Be?," "Stay, Summer Breath," and "Once I Loved Thee" are capable of categorization almost by title alone; the music is in a major key, diatonic, controlled, with square-cut rhythms, again like most pleasure garden songs.

TRACK 5

Stephen Foster's importance for popular music is hard to overestimate. He was among the first to realize that the parlor was gaining ascendancy over the stage as the primary venue for popular music. Even his most theatrical music, the minstrel show songs, were capable of successful performance in the home. He seemed to know instinctively that popular songs had to be synthesized from musical and textual elements already understood and treasured by the audience, that a popular song was a kind of democratic imperative that had to come from the people instead of being dictated to them. And over all is an indefinable, deft touch for melody that is of the order of genius. Likely his music is still today, world over, the best known and most loved of any ever composed.

Songs of the Civil War

The Civil War (1861–1865) is the pivotal event in the history of the United States. It divided and destroyed, dramatized and traumatized. Important national attitudes and institutions forged in that crucible of fire still guide Americans today. Given that singing was important to the nation in a way unimaginable now, it is not surprising that popular song chronicled and reflected the dimensions of the conflict. Significantly, the scale of the war transcended the ability of the theater to represent it, and the music of the Civil War was not fashioned for it. However, the American hearth had become an important enough symbol for social and cultural values that it was big enough to absorb some of the emotions unleashed in the four years of battle. It was, of course, the family back home that needed to comprehend and express the emotions generated by the battlefield, from victory to defeat, glory to death, horror to comic relief. Accordingly the songs of the Civil War were largely parlor songs.

Three important categories of Civil War songs are discernible: those of patriotic nature, those of soldiering life, and those manifestly dealing with home life. Two of the best known songs to come out of the war fall into the first category: "The Battle Hymn of the Republic" (1862) and "Dixie" (1859, but popularized during the war), the former an almost missionary anthem for the North, the latter a celebration of the South. Both of these songs had powerful, rousing choruses, indicative of the direction being taken by popular music. Only two other patriotic songs approached these in popularity: George F. Root's "The Battle Cry of Freedom" (1863), which was apparently sung by some northern troops as they went into battle, and southerner Harry Macarthy's "The Bonnie Blue Flag" (1861).

Songs about soldiering life were more generally published in the North—reasonable, when one considers that many southerners knew firsthand what was involved. Some of these were lighthearted, often about food. Others were deadly serious and served to help those at home bridge the emotional and physical gap between the safety of home and the dangers faced by husbands, sons, and brothers in the field. Root's "Tramp! Tramp! Tramp! (The Prisoner's Hope)" (1864) was about being a prisoner of war, and pointed out that prisoners too served the cause, in this case, the northern cause (figure 4). Its message hit home, and the song sold one hundred thousand copies within six months. Walter Kittredge's "Tenting on the Old Camp Ground" (1864), composed at the war's midpoint, confesses that war was not only glory: suffering, pain, misery, and death were also constant companions. Other highly popular songs also confronted the ultimate reality of soldiering. Given the higher ratio of casualties to population, perhaps it is not surprising that two of the most powerful songs were written by southerners. John Hill Hewitt's "All Quiet along the Potomac Tonight" (1864) is about a lone picket, afraid, far from home, who dies from a lucky enemy shot in the still of the night, undeserving of his fate. The soldier is ignored even in death, for the newspaper reports: "Not an officer lost! Only one of the men / Moaning out all alone the death rattle, / All quiet along the Potomac tonight!"

Will S. Hays (1837–1907), a Kentuckian who wrote both verse and music, was typical of southern songwriters during the period in that his music was heavily flavored by Italian and Irish styles. His "The Drummer Boy of Shiloh" (1862) communicates effectively the innocence and righteousness of the little drummer boy against his cruel, unjust death. The song contains practically a lexicon of mid-century, middle-class values: religion, home, family, and veneration for parents. Other songs addressed romantic love. One especially powerful example was Henry Tucker's "Weeping, Sad and Lonely, or When This Cruel War Is Over" (1862). Here the loved one at home is anxious about the fate of her soldier; soldiers, too, sang this song and thus affirmed their belief in the steadfastness of those back home. Important songs about the women in the dreams of soldiers were "Lorena" (1857) and "Aura Lea" (1861). Millions of men in the fields longing for and singing about idealized American womanhood confirmed the genre and placed it at the center of popular music for many decades to come. And finally, a great song of hope and yearning: "When Johnny Comes Marching Home"

FIGURE 4   The Civil War song "Tramp! Tramp! Tramp!," composed by George F. Root in 1864, expressed the view of a northern prisoner of war. Photo courtesy the Foster Hall Collection, Center for American Music, University of Pittsburgh Library System.

(1863) by Patrick S. Gilmore, a song devoid of artifice, lending genuineness and dignity to the verse, the pentatonic melody a throwback to a perceived simpler and happier time. The chorus, which begins with an exuberant "Hurrah, Hurrah," is an opportunity for all to express joy in rebuilt community.

Before the Civil War the South had been at or near the center of American musical life. The first theaters and opera houses in the United States were built there, and the first operas and ballad operas were heard there. The southern states of Virginia and Maryland were the only states that did not ban theater during the Revolutionary War; pleasure gardens thrived, as did a music-publishing industry. John Hill Hewitt was the first important composer of American popular song. The war destroyed all this, and the South played almost no part in the history of popular music again until the mid-twentieth century.

Canadian popular music in the nineteenth century

Canada came under the sway of the culture of the American Northeast even earlier than did the American South. The country enjoyed a vital theatrical life in the eighteenth century, but it was mostly imported from Great Britain or from the United States. In the realm of light opera, Joseph Quesnel (1746–1809) stands out as Canada's first composer for the genre. *Colas et Colinette,* which Quesnel described as a "comedy in prose intermixed with ariettes," was composed in 1789 and produced the following year in Montréal. The fourteen musical numbers closely follow the model of music heard in many French operas of the day, revealing the composer's familiarity with contemporary musical developments overseas. Unfortunately Quesnel was a rarity; only a small number of composers and playwrights managed to arrange performances of their works in Canada. Most successful Canadian operetta composers of the nineteenth and early twentieth century were actually expatriates living in the United States, such as Calixa Lavallée (1842–1891), Geoffrey O'Hara (1882–1966), and Clarence Lucas (1866–1947). Oscar Telgmann (c. 1855–1946) was a notable exception; after the premiere of his "military opera" *Leo, the Royal Cadet* (1889), the work received over 150 performances in Canada over a period of forty years, setting a record for a Canadian theatrical work that was not surpassed until the late twentieth century. Not only composers but also important Canadian-born musicians of the period, such as Eva Tanguay (1879–1947) (figure 5) and May Irwin (1862–1938), also emigrated to the United States to establish their careers. By 1865, the die had been cast; popular music and its business in North America, for the rest of the century and beyond, was to reflect the culture and image of the great urban American centers.

Late century

The decade and a half after the American Civil War witnessed the maturity of popular music. Songs were composed, published, bought, and sung in vast numbers; by one estimate, 250,000 different song titles and editions were available for purchase in 1870. The songs themselves were highly stylized. Nearly all began with a keyboard introduction that introduced the primary melody; typically there were two to four narrative verses that would be sung solo, each of sixteen measures divided into four phrases in the pattern AABC, ABAC, AABA, or ABCB; the song climaxed with a four-part chorus and concluded with a short keyboard postlude.

Parlor music

The majority of songs were written for consumption in the home. Not surprisingly, they reinforced values held by the owners of middle-class parlors. A master of the genre was Henry Clay Work (1832–1884). He first made his mark composing songs relating to the war; his "Kingdom Coming" (1862) and "Marching through Georgia" (1865)

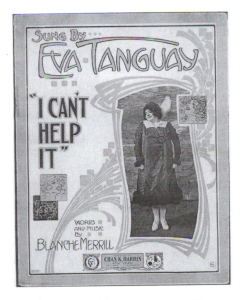

FIGURE 5   The Canadian performer Eva Tanguay (1879–1947) became notorious as a risqué and daring performer on America's vaudeville and burlesque stages. Tanguay is shown here on the cover of sheet music for one of her songs, "I Can't Help It," published in 1910. Sheet music from the collection of Gillian Rodger.

By century's end, millions of amateur pianists, generally women, were playing a range of piano music in the same physical environment as the parlor song and conceiving of it as popular music for the piano.

were both extremely popular. Although he produced many of his best songs in the war period, his muse returned in 1875 to inspire "Grandfather's Clock," perhaps the most popular song of the decade, one claimed to have sold 800,000 copies. Musically it fits exactly the prototype outlined in the previous paragraph. The narrative is of a man's life and the clock that accompanies him throughout. It affirmed social values such as family, home, religion, and more abstract notions like the work ethic and materialism. Other popular parlor songs filled comfortable and familiar niches. Thomas P. Westendorf's "I'll Take You Home Again, Kathleen" (1876) is nostalgic, a wistful memory of home and young love. "Sweet Genevieve" (1869) by Henry Tucker, to a text by George Cooper, is a sentimental ballad about a past love; H. P. Danks's "Silver Threads among the Gold" (1873) treats mature romantic love. Alice Hawthorne, the pseudonym for Septimus Winner, succeeded with a quasi-sacred duet, "Whispering Hope" (1868).

Americans learned about these and the day's many other popular songs in ways both old and familiar and new and different. It was often still the case that songs were first heard in the minstrel show or on the vaudeville stage, then bought for the parlor. But as Americans learned more and more how to make music by paying for lessons with private teachers and less and less in public singing schools, music teachers became the conduit for dissemination.

The piano was the supreme parlor instrument of the last part of the century and publishers nearly always assumed a piano would be accompanying their songs [see THE PIANO AND WOMEN OF ACCOMPLISHMENT, p. 561]. But an important body of popular music for piano alone arose during the century. Early in the century, pieces for orchestra had been available in simple keyboard arrangements. Music by composers such as Haydn, Clementi, and Beethoven was published in such manner. Waltzes were also popular. In all cases, amateur keyboardists of modest skills could perform and enjoy these works. By midcentury, other popular dance forms were finding favor on music stands, polkas, mazurkas, and schottisches among them. Variations on popular songs and programmatic pieces were also popular. Depending on the skill of the pianist, a complicated piece that today might be called "classical," such as a Polonaise by Chopin, might have been played in the nineteenth century alongside "Variations on 'Old Folks at Home.'" By century's end, millions of amateur pianists, generally women, were playing a range of piano music in the same physical environment as the parlor song and conceiving of it as popular music for the piano.

Stylistically, popular music of the 1880s differed little from that of the decade before, either in text or in music. One historian wrote that the years of this decade "represent the bridge from an exciting past to a still more exciting future . . . [and] might be counted largely as measures of rest" (Spaeth 1948:212). Important developments were at the business end of the industry. Before, popular songs were sold by music dealers and publishers who tried to cover the gamut of music in the United States [see THE MUSIC INDUSTRY, p. 256]. A single publisher might issue piano sonatas, string quartets, fiddle music, operettas, banjo instructors, popular songs, and so on. The publishing firms of Thomas B. Harms (established in 1881) and M. Witmark and Sons (1885) came into business with the intention to publish only popular music, and other like-minded publishers soon followed. With their focus concentrated, production, management, advertising, marketing, and dissemination skills were honed much beyond those of old-style publishers. By decade's end the mechanism for manufacturing popular music on a large scale was in place.

The history of the parlor song in the last decade of the century is dominated by the creative work of two men: Paul Dresser (1857–1906) and Charles K. Harris (1867–1930). Dresser's best known songs were mainly sentimental ballads of the type popular around the time of the Civil War. "On the Banks of the Wabash" (1899) and "My Gal Sal" (1905) could have been written by Stephen Foster but for the more complex harmonies and greater musical attention to the chorus. Other songs by Dresser, though, such as "Just Tell Them That You Saw Me" (1895) and "She Went to the City" (1904), dealt with the problems brought about by urbanism. Charles K. Harris's "After the Ball" (1892) first received wide attention when it was interpolated into an important musical play in 1892. The song is one of innumerable waltz-songs of the period, with a maudlin, highly sentimental narrative in multiple verses. Primary musical interest is located in the chorus, today perhaps the only part of the song still known. It was claimed that five million copies were sold, making it perhaps the most popular song of the time. Other Harris songs, such as "Just behind the Times" (1896) and "Hello Central, Give Me Heaven" (1901), were less successful but still sold perhaps a million copies each, pointing to the growing size of the industry. Harris may have been an even better businessman than songwriter. He was one of the first to publish and distribute his own songs and even served as the model for the covers of many. His musical and business skills combined to make of him one of the wealthiest and most influential of those in the business at the turn of the twentieth century.

Theater music

Two important types of theater music dominated the last third of the century, with the minstrel show in its golden maturity and musical comedy in its infancy.

Minstrelsy

The minstrel show moved toward a much larger troupe of performers and, concomitantly, a greater variety of entertainment. Twenty or even thirty blackface entertainers came to make up some gigantic minstrel lines. Although women impersonators were important from the early years of the genre and continued to be so, the production now accepted women blackface performers, expanding the range of entertainment possibilities.

Before and during the Civil War, the issue of slavery was central to the minstrel show, sometimes explicitly, more often implicitly. With emancipation, white consciences were cleansed, and slavery moved to the political back burner. In fact, the plight of the black man was perhaps even more desperate, for slavery had provided at least day-to-day support. The minstrel show dealt with large-scale human tragedy and Jim Crow legislation by reflecting nostalgically on the days of slavery.

Two songwriters for the minstrel show stand out during the period, and both wrote songs of this type. Will S. Hays's highly popular "The Little Old Cabin in the Lane" (1871) is a good example: A sample of lines includes:

> Dar was a happy time to me, 'twas many years ago,
> When de darkies used to gather round de door,
> When dey used to dance an' sing at night, I played de ole banjo,
> But alas, I cannot play it any more.

Bostonian C. A. White set these verses in his "The Old Home Ain't What It Used to Be" (1874):

> Oh, the old home ain't what it used to be,
> The banjo and fiddle has gone,
> And no more you hear the darkies singing,
> Among the sugar cane and corn.
> Now the old man would rather lived and died,
> In the home where his children were born,
> But when freedom came to the colored man,
> He left the cotton field and corn.
> No, the old home ain't what it used to be,
> The change makes me sad and forlorn,
> For no more we hear the darkies singing,
> Among the sugar cane and corn.

Both of these verses could have been composed before 1850, so strong was the regression, as if Stephen Foster had never composed his great songs. To further compound this astonishing development, White's song was made famous by the Georgia Minstrels, the first important minstrel troupe made up of black men.

The admission of blacks to the minstrel show was one of the most important developments of the period. For the first time, the black man had a central place on the American stage, and many took advantage of it. The most important black songwriter for the minstrel stage was James Bland (1854–1911), and he provided the genre with some of the biggest hits of the period. His songs did not challenge the show's prevailing social message. "Carry Me Back to Old Virginny" (1878), for example, includes the lines:

> Massa and missis have long gone before me,
> Soon we will meet on that bright and golden shore,
> There we'll be happy and free from all sorrow,
> There's where we'll meet and we'll never part no more.

On the surface it is surprising that a dignified African American like Bland would so willingly distort the truth of his race's past, almost to belittle it. In fact there was general dissatisfaction by blacks in the American theater with the demeaning stage roles assigned them. By way of explanation, black historian and musician James Weldon Johnson wrote that "[t]he general spirit of the race was one of hopelessness or acquiescence. The only way to survival seemed along the road of sheer opportunism and of conformity to the triumphant materialism of the age" (Johnson 1930:127). The nineteenth-century audience dictated terms to the stage, and it mattered little if the voice behind the blackface belonged to a white man or a black man.

An important new branch of the musical theater was born out of the minstrel show. In 1865 the doors first opened to Tony Pastor's Opera House, and with this the age of vaudeville began. Like the minstrel show, it consisted of a range of entertainments, yet the point of reference was not racism but ethnicity and urbanism. In 1871 Ned Harrigan, from the Irish neighborhoods of New York City and formerly a blackface minstrel, collaborated with Tony Hart to develop this new genre further. Their "Mulligan Guard" skits lampooned nearly all the groups making up urban America and, in turn, urban working-class audiences. The songs, usually by David Braham, were out of a typical mold but emphasized the chorus and added a dash of brassy energy, suitable for a public, staged form of music. Harrigan, Hart, and Braham recognized that the American landscape was by then as much urban as rural. Their shows and songs were among the first to reflect this new truth.

Musical comedy

The birth of what came to be called the musical comedy occurred from a synthesis of existent theatrical elements. Of crucial importance is *The Black Crook* (1866). This five-hour extravaganza combined a plot based loosely on *Faust* with melodrama, dance, music, extraordinary special effects, and mild eroticism. This "most Resplendent, Grand and Costly Production ever presented on this continent" (*New York Times,* 12 September 1866) dazzled far beyond any previous theatrical conception. Other shows of the sort followed, most successfully, *Evangeline* (1874) and *Adonis* (1884). These three, and dozens of others like them, established a high tone by often borrowing from the idioms of art music and setting them to "serious" literature. The operettas of Offenbach (1819–1880) and of Gilbert (1836–1911) and Sullivan (1842–1900) in the 1870s and 1880s issued along the same line and appealed to the same audience. With notable exceptions, few of the songs from these works achieved wide popularity. This line of composition, realized perhaps best in John Philip Sousa's *El Capitan* (1895) and Gustave Kerker's *The Belle of New York* (1897), continued through the end of the nineteenth century and flourished at the beginning of the twentieth century in works by Johann Strauss (*Die Fledermaus,* 1874), Franz Lehár (*Die lustige Witwe,* 1906), Rudolf Friml (*Rose-Marie,* 1924), and Sigmund Romberg (*The Student Prince,* 1924). Victor Herbert (1859–1924) is especially important in this development; his more than forty operettas included the popular *Babes in Toyland* (1903), *Mlle. Modiste* (1905), *The Red Mill* (1906), *Naughty Marietta* (1910), and *Sweethearts* (1913). Although Herbert's songs are more technically demanding than many popular songs of the time, with more adventuresome harmonies and wider vocal ranges, many of them achieved considerable popularity, especially "Kiss Me Again" from *Mlle. Modiste.*

Another musical line from *The Black Crook* led toward more accessible, and popular, musical theater. From operetta this theater learned of serious concern for plot and musical consistency; from vaudeville and the minstrel show came a dynamic energy and concern for the audience's wishes. The revolution was not won overnight, of course, and the fledgling musical comedy form of the 1890s and the 1900s exhibited traits that only more or less adhere to a latter-day definition of the genre. Common throughout, though, is a special place for the music and a belief that the music alone could lead to successful musical theater. An early example is the historic *A Trip to China-town* (1890). Although the plot was contrived, the music was beguiling, and a record was established of 657 performances. Songs by Percy Gaunt and other songwriters carried the show.

The most important name on the musical stage during this time, and one of the most important for any time, was that of George M. Cohan (1878–1942). His *Little Johnny Jones* (1904) is a watershed. It borrowed heavily from vaudeville but was called "a musical play"; rooted deeply in audience-held values, its intention was to please. Cohan's music was utterly infectious, in part because it was among the first to exploit the new syncopated rhythms of ragtime. Although simple in construction (nearly always introduction-verse-chorus-verse-chorus) and relatively limited in its scope, his songs worked perfectly on the stage. "Yankee Doodle Boy" and "Give My Regards to Broadway" (both from *Little Johnny Jones*) are examples of his anthemlike marches; the title song to *Forty-Five Minutes from Broadway* (1906) is one of Cohan's waltz-songs; "Mary's a Grand Old Name" from the same show is an example of his sentimental ballads. Cohan's musicals were optimistic in an age of such, wrapped in kindly American virtues and unabashedly chauvinistic about the city, especially New York. If he did not invent the musical comedy, and by some accounts he did, George M. Cohan certainly

By early in the century, important publishers of popular sheet music had located around each other, in offices and buildings strung along West 28th Street in New York City. Anecdotal evidence has it that the incessant clanging of cheap pianos lent the area its name—Tin Pan Alley—and by extension named an era and a style in popular music.

bears primary responsibility for developing it and for associating it with New York's famous street, Broadway.

The 1890s also saw the synthesis of elements that led to the development of black musical comedy. Like so much theater of the nineteenth century, its germinal source was the minstrel show. In fact, the first important black production, *The Octoroon* (1895), was only slightly more cohesive in plot than a typical minstrel show. Will Marion Cook's (1869–1944) *Clorindy, or The Origin of the Cakewalk* (1898) and Bob Cole's (1863–1911) *A Trip to Coontown* (1898), the first musical written, directed, and performed by African American artists, were loosely joined, vaudeville-like productions. One notices from the titles that the subject matter, again like that of the minstrel shows, was ersatz African American culture. The music was more varied than that found in white musical theater, primarily because black musicals expanded the range to include the new syncopated songs of the time. The early twentieth century saw more breakthroughs, especially with *In Dahomey* (1903) by the comic duo George Walker and Bert Williams, the first all-black show to play at a major Broadway theater. *Shuffle Along* (1921), a major Broadway success by composer Eubie Blake (1883–1983) and lyricist Noble Sissle (1889–1975), capped the early history of the genre with a work of top-quality music and a plot that dealt implicitly with the role of the African American in American culture.

THE TWENTIETH CENTURY: TIN PAN ALLEY AND THE DEVELOPMENT OF THE MUSICAL IN THE UNITED STATES

The history of stage and parlor music in the twentieth century is much cleaner and more succinct than that of the nineteenth century. The lines of development are fewer and simpler, and extensive research has identified the most important developments. As was the case through much of the nineteenth century, Canada largely followed the lead of the United States.

Tin Pan Alley

Perhaps the single most significant factor in the history of twentieth-century popular music was the consolidation of its commercial aspects. By early in the century, important publishers of popular sheet music had located around each other, in offices and buildings strung along West 28th Street in New York City. Anecdotal evidence has it that the incessant clanging of cheap pianos lent the area its name—Tin Pan Alley—and by extension named an era and a style in popular music.

Centralization of the business led to standardization of the medium. Structurally, there was an introduction for the piano, usually of eight measures, which introduced primary melodic material; a verse of perhaps sixteen measures of undistinguished melodic content, whose primary function was to establish the song's dramatic situation; and a lyrical section of thirty-two measures broken up into four eight-bar phrases in the symbolic order of AABA (more rarely, ABAB, AABC, or ABCA), which contained the most interesting music. This last section, called the chorus, became so much the heart of the song that by the 1930s songwriters often omitted the verse altogether, and its length actually lent the genre its name ("thirty-two-bar form"). Melodies typically spanned slightly more than an octave, were conjunct, and were contoured gracefully from low to high back to low. Harmonies were relatively simple, with few excursions outside the tonic-subdominant-dominant relationship, and were triadic, diatonic, tonal, and generally in major. Modulations, if they occurred at all, were limited to the B section of the chorus (called the "release"). Metrically, duple meters heavily dominated the choruses. Rhythmically, songs often featured mild syncopation. Lyrically, the expression "moon-June-spoon songs" joined three of the most important themes, all having to do with romantic love, far and away the primary concern.

Music published by Tin Pan Alley in the first third of the century generally followed traditional paths of distribution into the American home through the local music store. A consumer might go there on his or her own to try out the newest songs before purchasing or might have been encouraged to do so by another amateur or a music teacher. Songs received a real boost if they were integrated into successful musical comedies or into revues, which were responsible for introducing an inordinate number of hits to American audiences. Similar to vaudeville in many ways, revues appealed to a more elite audience and usually featured a central theme, often satirical, but were not unified by plot. Songs, dances, and chorus lines of beautiful young women were featured, especially in famous productions of the Follies by Florenz Ziegfeld Jr. The revue was especially popular and important in Canada, and some of the most important Canadian musicians served their apprenticeships there. From the perspective of Tin Pan Alley, though, revues and musical comedies were merely marketing outlets that might lead to enhanced sales of sheet music, the industry's bread and butter (figure 6).

The impact of new technologies

Important technological developments played a large part in finally destabilizing the traditionally symbiotic relationship between stage and parlor music. One of these was the phonograph, which with its limit of about four minutes per disk filled the needs of popular song nicely. By as early as the 1910s, North Americans were spending millions on gramophone disks, purchasing songs for home consumption that, for the first time, did not require performance skills. In 1929 in the United States alone, $120 million were spent on phonograph recordings, most for songs that had never been heard by the consumer on stage nor were sung in the home from sheet music. Recordings tended to feature the performer as much as, or more than, the song, and those by John McCormack or Caruso (early) or, later, Bing Crosby or Frank Sinatra were especially treasured. (The passive audience relationship to the genre was to have profound implications by mid-century.) Still, although technology altered the actual object sold, it affected the manner of writing successful songs hardly at all.

Commercial radio first began in North America in 1920 and in the long run may have changed popular music more profoundly than did the phonograph. The vehicle was, for one thing, a perfect advertising medium for popular songs. If a publisher could manage to place a new song in a prime-time broadcast, it would be heard free in millions of homes. If liked by the audience, the next day would find manifold orders placed for the music. This one-shot phenomenon encouraged conservatism on the industry, to stick with that which worked at the time. A by-product of radio changed significantly the performance styles associated with popular music. The mechanical recording horn had long served the phonograph industry but could not meet the demands of radio for electronic transmission. The electric microphone was developed, applied to the recording process, and allowed "crooners" such as Fred Astaire, Crosby, and Sinatra to quickly gain ascendancy over the earlier, more operatic recording stars.

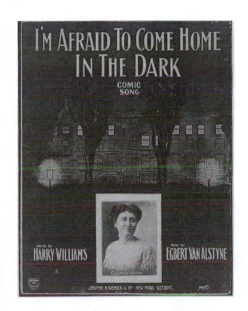

FIGURE 6   One marketing tactic of music publishers was to feature the images of famous performers on the cover of sheet music. "I'm Afraid to Come Home in the Dark," published in 1907, appeared with pictures of at least three different actresses in the inset. This cover features the vaudeville performer Clarice Vance; different versions of the same music depict the musical comedy stars May Vokes and Della Fox. Sheet music from the collection of Gillian Rodger.

Developers of the "talkies" (movies with sound) suspected from the first that popular music would be important to the genre: Al Jolson's famous first words in *The Jazz Singer* (1927)—"You ain't heard nothing yet!"—were followed immediately by his rendering of "My Mammy." Within two years motion pictures were being made that were essentially Broadway musicals for celluloid. A successful movie with a successful song generated tremendous profits, first from ticket receipts, then from sheet music sales. Again, the tendency was toward "safe" songs from "safe" songwriters, generally recruited from Tin Pan Alley to serve Hollywood.

The songwriters

Altogether, the period from 1910 to 1955 was considered a golden era for the popular song. Legions of songwriters and lyricists were in New York City, under contract to the publishing firms with nothing more or less to do than turn out new songs, at which they succeeded with some of the most finely crafted songs of any period in Western music history. Any representative list will inevitably omit many fine musicians. But surely among the most important were the legends Irving Berlin, Jerome Kern, George Gershwin, Cole Porter, Richard Rodgers, Harry Warren, Harold Arlen, Vincent Youmans, and Hoagy Carmichael.

Of this group, Berlin (1888–1990) must surely have composed the greatest number of enduring songs. To mention only a few: "Alexander's Ragtime Band," "Oh How I Hate to Get Up in the Morning," "Always," "Shaking the Blues Away," "Blue Skies," "A Pretty Girl Is Like a Melody," "Puttin' on the Ritz," "Let's Have Another Cup of Coffee," "How Deep Is the Ocean," "Easter Parade," "Heat Wave," "Cheek to Cheek," "God Bless America," "White Christmas," and "There's No Business Like Show Business." Like many successful popular songwriters of his generation, he was an immigrant; his nearly classical melodies and harmonies manifest the strong influence of European music.

Jerome Kern (1885–1945) is one of the few to be mentioned in the same breath with Berlin. His music was more meticulously fashioned, with more adventuresome harmonies than Berlin's. "Smoke Gets in Your Eyes," for example, approaches the harmonic complexity of an art song by a classical music composer like Maurice Ravel. Kern mainly composed songs that fit into larger frameworks (such as musical comedies, operettas, and movies). More than any other songwriter of Tin Pan Alley, he is responsible for bridging the gap between the high style of operetta and the high-energy, accessible musical comedy style of George M. Cohan. His concern for the close integration of plot, song lyrics, and music set the standard for subsequent musical theater. *Show Boat* (1927) in particular was a watershed, a musical that left earlier, more loosely constructed musicals far behind. The libretto, with the treatment of racial issues primary, was explosive for its time and later.

George Gershwin (1898–1937) was a more flexible composer than most. He wrote important popular songs, but also *Rhapsody in Blue, An American in Paris,* preludes for the piano, and the opera *Porgy and Bess,* all of which enjoyed success as art music. Much more than most Tin Pan Alley songwriters, Gershwin was concerned with the "Fascinatin' Rhythm" of jazz. His music is typically heavily syncopated, with a bluesy feel about it. His harmonies are also more complex than most popular song composers, even those of Kern, and often include ninth and eleventh chords, much like those then being heard in jazz. Modulations occur frequently in his songs. Although the conventional thirty-two-bar song form remained intact, in nearly all other ways Gershwin was poised at the end of his tragically short life to further fuse the qualities of popular and art music.

Cole Porter (1891–1964) was an exception to many rules governing Tin Pan Alley. Born in Indiana to wealth and a non–Eastern European heritage, he received his musical training in the finest American and European schools. Because he was less dependent on the need for his music's commercial success, his songs are idiosyncratic and iconoclastic. Musically, there is a suave refinement that follows from Porter's training in art music. But it is the texts, written by Porter himself, that give his songs their originality. He treated controversial, noncommercial subjects like alcohol and drug addiction, prostitution, and sexual indulgence, but also endorsed elegance, sophistication, and urbanity. That his songs achieved popularity spoke for a time that wished to avoid the harsh realities of a world in severe economic depression, one sandwiched between the unspeakable horrors of two world wars.

The songs of Richard Rodgers (1902–1979) generally came to attention because of their inclusion in his extraordinarily successful string of Broadway musicals, *Oklahoma!* (1943), *Carousel* (1945), *South Pacific* (1949), *The King and I* (1951), and *The Sound of Music* (1959) primary among them. His music is always graceful and tastefully done, if predictably out of the Tin Pan Alley mold. His lyricists, of whom Lorenz Hart and Oscar Hammerstein II were among the best in the business, provided him with material suitable for his genius. Theatrical context governed Rodgers's muse—*Oklahoma!* approaches a kind of vernacular opera in its structural integrity—and the songs have been judged and appreciated accordingly. As the theatrical situations changed so did Rodgers's songs; he could and did write waltz-songs, jazzy songs, sentimental love songs, and novelty songs if the occasion demanded.

The achievements of these and other giants of Tin Pan Alley set a remarkable standard of professional craftsmanship. From what had been something much like a cottage industry in the nineteenth century, songwriting, in their capable hands, became a profession and a business. But the more songwriting became a business, the more it seemed to lose touch with those who supported it. The strength of the business's structure, especially in its advertising, marketing, and distribution, managed to sustain and nurture it for many years. However, there is some truth to the charge leveled at Tin Pan Alley that its songs were escapist and aimed at white upper- and middle-class urbanites, with no sense of the dramatic social, political, and economic events swirling through the society during a most tumultuous half century. The 1940s exposed the first fault lines, when some songs with a country music flavor came into brief favor. The 1950s found the business quaking, especially with the advent of rock and roll. Music based in the experience of the majority who lived outside New York City, that spoke of real lives, hopes, joys, sorrows, and anxieties, proved devastating competition for music that was associated with the tastes and values of a well-heeled, urbane minority.

Tin Pan Alley's legacy

With the death of Tin Pan Alley came the demise of parlor music. The new music of the 1950s was consumed by buying a recording or listening to a radio broadcast; it was almost never played and sung at the piano. Private musical experience became something quite different from what it had been before, characterized by the much more passive action of turning on a piece of electronic equipment.

American musical theater, though, has remained something of a force in the culture, although it no longer has the vitality it exhibited in the 1920s and 1930s. The musical comedy line that extended through Richard Rodgers continued, for example, in the work of composers like Stephen Sondheim (b. 1930). His musicals, such as *Company* (1970), *A Little Night Music* (1973), *Sweeney Todd* (1979), and *Sunday in the Park with George* (1984), obviously perpetuate the tradition, although certain others of his works challenge the conventional dramaturgy of the musical comedy. His only song to achieve widespread popularity outside the theater is "Send in the Clowns," which is a general commentary on the current contribution of musical comedies to popular musical culture.

Another strain of musical theater has better accommodated new musical and cultural values. Arguably this began with *West Side Story* (1957), music by Leonard

The Broadway model, while attractive to those seeking a large audience, often proved to be frustrating for many involved in the musical theater scene in Canada.

Bernstein (1918–1990) to Sondheim's lyrics. A modern-day retelling of the Romeo and Juliet myth set in a Puerto Rican neighborhood of New York City, the book (by Arthur Laurents) is not about middle- or upper-class life, and the music is vibrant with new and exciting rhythms. The 1960s saw the trend continue, especially with *Hair* (1967) by the Canadian Galt MacDermot (b. 1929), a rock- and soul-laced celebration of hippiedom. Andrew Lloyd Webber's (b. 1948) *Jesus Christ Superstar* (1971) is of this same line, as are his *Cats* (1982) and *Phantom of the Opera* (1988), two of the most important musicals of the 1980s (figure 7).

CANADIAN POPULAR MUSIC FOR THE THEATER IN THE TWENTIETH CENTURY

Unlike the history of musical theater in the United States, whose roots extend back to a rich indigenous tradition of vaudeville and minstrel shows through the nineteenth century, the Canadian reality is quite different. In the nineteenth century Canadian musical and theatrical production was strongly influenced by American activities through tours and imported shows. An indigenous form of musical theater did not really begin to thrive in Canada until the twentieth century, and, although an American cultural influence was inevitable, a distinctive type of musical theater developed in part as a creative response to this American presence.

Although the minstrel phenomenon in Canada was limited to occasional tours by American performers and a few celebrated Canadian stars, the concept of a humorous musical show with skits created the basis for what became the twentieth century's most successful form of indigenous musical theater in Canada: the musical revue. The combination of songs, dances, and comedic skits proved to be a popular format for many successful satires that focused on timely Canadian topics while frequently and deliberately shunning the polish and flash associated with the popular American shows.

One of the first successful revues involved an all-male soldier group called the Dumbells, formed in 1917. After a protracted engagement on the front lines in Europe during World War I, the Dumbells continued to perform as a civilian ensemble, touring extensively in Canada before becoming the first all-Canadian show to play on Broadway in 1921. Attempts to revive the Dumbell tradition during World War II resulted in shows organized by the various branches of the armed forces, such as *The Army Show* and *Meet the Navy*. The entertaining performances of the Dumbells and their spin-offs served to popularize the revue format in Canada.

The musical revue found fertile ground in major urban centers, where informal club shows prospered. In Montréal, *Fridolinons!*, by Gratiens Gélinas (1909–1999), combined satirical skits with musical material derived primarily from traditional French Canadian sources. It enjoyed a lengthy run—from 1938 to 1946. This show strongly influenced Mavor Moore's (b. 1919) Toronto-based *Spring Thaw* (1948–1972), which is today considered to be one of the most significant developments in the history of modern Canadian musical theater. *Spring Thaw*'s greatest legacy has perhaps been the long list of Canadian musical and stage performers who thereby received valuable performance opportunities and experience and who, in many cases, formed the

FIGURE 7   The Pantages Theatre, Yonge Street, Toronto. This theater, built in the early twentieth century, was the premier vaudeville house for Toronto and part of the Keith Vaudeville Circuit. Renovated in the late 1980s, the theater was home to the Toronto production of *Phantom of the Opera*. Photo by Gillian Rodger, 2000.

backbone of later musical theater in Canada. The success of *Spring Thaw* inspired many imitators. The best known of these was the celebrated spoof *My Fur Lady,* produced at McGill University in 1957 and using a loose plot as a framework for poking fun at Canadian political issues. Many of the songs in this revue were composed by Galt MacDermot, who later wrote the music for the U.S. countercultural musical *Hair* and several other musicals.

An indigenous Canadian revue tradition continued into the 1970s, although productions were scaled down considerably in order to accommodate performances in the intimate cabaret theaters that were becoming popular. As these cabaret spaces gradually closed down in the 1980s, the revue was superseded in popularity by the integrated musical. Despite this, however, the musical revue has continued to play an important role in the Canadian musical theater scene.

The birth of the modern Canadian musical is generally identified with Mavor Moore, whose efforts to create an indigenous musical theater began in 1955 with his celebrated tribute to the Canadian humorist Stephen Leacock, entitled *Sunshine Town.* After his successful 1956 follow-up, *The Optimist* (an adaptation of *Candide*), Moore planned to create a series of original Canadian musicals. Although this did not actually materialize, he demonstrated that it was possible to create a specifically Canadian brand of musical theater.

In 1964 Moore established the Charlottetown Festival in Prince Edward Island as a showcase for Canadian theater, and under Alan Lund (Moore's eventual successor as director) the festival became a focal point for the development of indigenous musicals. In 1965 the festival commissioned Norman Campbell and Don Harron to expand their 1956 television musical special, *Anne of Green Gables,* into a full-length musical for the stage. Mavor Moore and Elaine Campbell supplied additional lyrics for the new production. Based on Lucy Maud Montgomery's popular novel, *Anne of Green Gables* quickly became the mainstay of the Charlottetown Festival. Now heralded as a family classic, the show has been produced each summer at the festival since its debut, making it the most popular production in the history of Canadian musical theater.

A number of other worthy productions born at the Charlottetown Festival have not found the success of *Anne of Green Gables. Johnny Belinda* (1968), Moore's collaboration with John Fenwick (b. 1932), ranks as the second most popular Charlottetown show after *Anne,* but it has been performed only sporadically since its 1968 debut. Cliff Jones's *Kronborg: 1582,* a rock musical based on *Hamlet,* enjoyed success at the Festival and on tour in 1974 and 1975, but it was soon transformed into an expensive spectacle that met with disaster when it premiered on Broadway as *Rockabye Hamlet* (1976). The Broadway model, while attractive to those seeking a large audience, often proved to be frustrating for many involved in the musical theater scene in Canada.

The 1970s witnessed a period of experiments that actively moved away from the Broadway model. George Ryga's classic play *The Ecstasy of Rita Joe* (1967) was transformed into a musical through the addition of a folk-oriented score by Ann Mortifee (b. 1947). Ken Mitchell's (b. 1940) 1975 "country opera" *Cruel Tears,* with music by Henry and the Dumptrucks, rewrote *Othello* as a prairie trucker's story set to bluegrass and country music. The most notable show to appear in the 1970s was John Gray's (b. 1946) *Billy Bishop Goes to War* (1978), a musical account of Canada's most famous flying ace in World War I. Written for just one singer-actor who must play eighteen different roles, and accompanied only by a pianist on the stage, *Billy Bishop* blended elements of intimate comedic revues with those of traditional musicals to forge a new type of Canadian musical theater. The show enjoyed a four-year run with national and international tours, eventually spawning over 150 amateur and commercial productions throughout the United States. John Gray has continued to create his unique brand of musical theater and has since become the best-known contemporary Canadian composer in the field.

FIGURE 8   The Royal Alexandra Theatre, King Street West, Canada's oldest continuously operating theater, has been home to a number of large-scale musical productions, including *Jane Eyre, Les Miserables,* and *Rent.*

In 1985, an all-Canadian production of Andrew Lloyd Webber's *Cats* in Toronto marked a turning point for Canadian musical theater. The success of the production demonstrated for the first time the long-term viability of commercial musical theater in Canada. A number of large-scale musicals followed *Cats,* creating a burgeoning musical theater community in Toronto (figure 8), and, despite the fact that most of the shows were essentially "franchise musicals" (attempts to recreate faithfully the original New York or London productions), the proliferation of large-budget mega-musicals spawned a new movement to create original Canadian musicals of a similar scale, including *Napoleon* (1994), with music by Timothy Williams and lyrics by Andrew Sabiston; Vincent de Tourdonnet's musical tale about Joan of Arc, entitled *Jeanne* (1995); *Jane Eyre* (1996), a collaboration of composer Paul Gordon and John Caird, drawing inspiration from Charlotte Brontë's 1847 gothic romance; and *Ragtime* (1998), with a score by Stephen Flaherty and lyrics by Lynn Ahrens. Although each of these musicals received mixed reviews, together they signaled that indigenous commercial musical theater had finally gained a foothold in Canada. With the successful appearance of *Ragtime* on Broadway (which resulted in four Tony awards for the show in 1998), it was clear that Canadian musical theatre was also finding a new audience in the United States.

THE INFLUENCE OF THE MOVIES

More than Broadway, the movie house has become the venue for new, widely popular musical theater. The extraordinary success of *Saturday Night Fever* in 1977 generated a string of high-energy, dance-filled films. Among the most important are *Hair* (1979, originally a Broadway musical), *Fame* (1980), *Flashdance* (1983), and *Dirty Dancing* (1987). Many films of the period from the mid-1960s situate music near the plot's center, where it usually symbolizes a set of social values subscribed to by the day's youth.

Nearly all of these movies were musically derivative, in that they simply affirmed prevailing musical directions. The typical contemporary film musical is not much closer to the forefront of the day's developments in popular music than was the Tin Pan Alley–derived musical comedy. The centers of North American popular music production are no longer to be found on 28th Street, on Broadway, or in Hollywood, all of which controlled musical taste through their representation of culture. Production, instead, has become more localized and more responsive to local values and traditions. In this way, at least, the state of contemporary popular music resembles more its distant, and much less its recent, past.

REFERENCES

After the Ball: A Treasury of Turn-of-the-Century Popular Songs. Elektra-Nonesuch 79148-2. Compact disc.

American Dreamer: Songs of Stephen Foster. 1992. Angel CDC 07777–54621-28. Compact disc.

American Popular Song: Six Decades of Songwriters and Singers. 1984. Smithsonian R031 P7 17983. Compact disc.

Austin, William W. 1987. *"Susanna," "Jeanie," and "The Old Folks at Home": The Songs of Stephen C. Foster from His Time to Ours.* 2nd ed. Urbana: University of Illinois Press.

Burrows, Malcolm. 1989. "Marketing the Megahits." *Canadian Theatre Review* 61:5–12.

Campbell, Norman. 1984. *Anne of Green Gables.* Ready Records LR045. Compact disc.

Cockrell, Dale. 1989. *Excelsior: Journals of the Hutchinson Family Singers, 1842–1846.* Sociology of Music Series 5. Stuyvesant, N.Y.: Pendragon Press.

————. 1997. *Demons of Disorder: Early Blackface Minstrels and Their World.* American Theatre and Drama Series 3. Cambridge: Cambridge University Press.

Cooper, Dorith R., ed. 1991. *Opera and Operetta Excerpts I.* The Canadian Musical Heritage, vol. 10. Ottawa: Canadian Musical Heritage Society.

Crawford, Richard, ed. 1977. *The Civil War Songbook: Complete Original Sheet Music for 37 Songs.* New York: Dover.

An Evening with Henry Russell. 1977. Nonesuch H71338. LP disk.

Ewen, David. 1962. *Popular American Composers, from Revolutionary Times to the Present.* New York: H. W. Wilson, Co.

————. 1977. *All the Years of American Popular Music.* Englewood Cliffs, N.J.: Prentice-Hall.

Fiske, Roger. 1973. *English Theater Music in the Eighteenth Century.* London: Oxford University Press.

Ford, Clifford. 1982. *Canada's Music: An Historical Survey.* Agincourt, Ont.: GLC Publishers.

Glass, Paul, ed., and Louis C. Singer, arr. 1975. *Singing Soldiers: A History of the Civil War in Song.* New York: Da Capo.

Gray, John. *Billy Bishop Goes to War.* 1979. Tapestry Records GD7372. LP disk.

The Great American Composers: Cole Porter. 1989. CBS C21/2 7926. Compact disc.

The Great American Composers: George and Ira Gershwin. 1989. CBS C21/2 7925. Compact disc.

The Great American Composers: Irving Berlin. 1989. CBS C21/2 7929. Compact disc.

The Great American Composers: Jerome Kern. 1990. CBS C21/2 7973. Compact disc.

The Great American Composers: Rodgers and Hart. 1990. CBS C21/2 7971. Compact disc.

Greenberg, Joel. 1996. "Montréal/Toronto . . . But Our Own?" *Canadian Theatre Review* 86:49–51.

Hamm, Charles. 1979. *Yesterdays: Popular Song in America.* New York: Norton.

Hitchcock, H. Wiley, and Stanley Sadie, eds. 1986. *The New Grove Dictionary of American Music.* London: Macmillan.

Harwell, Richard B. 1950. *Confederate Music.* Chapel Hill: University of North Carolina Press.

Jackson, Richard. 1976. *Popular Songs of Nineteenth-Century America.* New York: Dover.

Johnson, James Weldon. 1930. *Black Manhattan.* New York: Knopf.

Johnston, Denis. 1992. "Knowing What They Want: Musical Theatre in Vancouver." *Canadian Theatre Review* 72:11–15.

Kallmann, Helmut, Gilles Potvin, and Kenneth Winters, eds. 1992. *Encyclopedia of Music in Canada.* 2nd ed. Toronto: Toronto University Press.

Levine, Lawrence W. 1988. *Highbrow/Lowbrow: The Emergence of Cultural Hierarchy in America.* Cambridge: Harvard University Press.

Loesser, Arthur. 1954. *Men, Women, and Pianos: A Social History.* New York: Simon and Schuster.

Loney, Glenn, ed. 1984. *Musical Theater in America: Papers and Proceedings of the Conference on the Musical Theater in America.* Contributions in Drama and Theater Studies 8. Westport, Conn.: Greenwood Press.

Lott, Eric. 1993. *Love and Theft: Blackface Minstrelsy and the American Working Class.* New York: Oxford University Press.

Manning-Albert, Jacqui. 1996. "What More Could You Ask For? A Conversation on Musical Theatre in Canada." *Canadian Theatre Review* 72:4–10.

McGee, Timothy J. 1985. *The Music of Canada.* New York: Norton.

Marks, Edward B. 1934. *They All Sang: From Tony Pastor to Rudy Vallee.* New York: Viking Press.

Mates, Julian. 1985. *America's Musical Stage: Two Hundred Years of Musical Theater.* Contributions in Drama and Theater Studies, 18. Westport, Conn.: Greenwood Press.

Moore's Irish Melodies. 1984. Nonesuch 79059. LP disk.

Nathan, Hans. 1962. *Dan Emmett and the Rise of Early Negro Minstrelsy.* Norman: University of Oklahoma Press.

Paskman, Daily, and Sigmund Spaeth. 1928. *"Gentlemen, Be Seated!": A Parade of the Old-Time Minstrels.* New York: Doubleday, Doran and Co.

Popular Music in Jacksonian America. 1982. Musical Heritage Society MHS 834561. LP disk.

Porter, Susan L. 1991. *With an Air Debonair: Musical Theater in America, 1785–1815.* Washington, D.C.: Smithsonian Institution Press.

Preston, Katherine K. 1993. *Opera on the Road: Traveling Opera Companies in the United States, 1825–60.* Urbana: University of Illinois Press.

Riis, Thomas L. 1989. *Just before Jazz: Black Musical Theater in New York, 1890–1915.* Washington, D.C.: Smithsonian Institution Press.

Root, Deane L. 1981. *American Popular Stage Music 1860–1880.* Studies in Musicology 44. Ann Arbor, Mich.: UMI Research Press.

Sacks, Howard L., and Judith R. Sacks. 1993. *Way Up North in Dixie: A Black Family's Claim to the Confederate Anthem.* Washington, D.C.: Smithsonian Institution Press.

Sadie, Stanley, ed. 1980. *The New Grove Dictionary of Music and Musicians.* London: Macmillan.

Saunders, Steven, and Deane L. Root, eds. 1990. *The Music of Stephen C. Foster.* Washington, D.C.: Smithsonian Institution Press.

Sanjek, Russell. 1988. *American Popular Music and Its Business: The First Four Hundred Years.* New York: Oxford University Press.

Scott, Derek. 1989. *The Singing Bourgeois: Songs of the Victorian Drawing Room and Parlour.* Milton Keynes, Eng.: Open University Press.

The Smithsonian Collection of American Musical Theater: Shows, Songs, and Stars. 1989. Smithsonian RD 036 A4 20483. Compact disc.

Songs by Henry Clay Work. 1975. Nonesuch H71317. LP disk.

Songs of the Civil War. 1991. New World Records 202. Compact disc.

Spaeth, Sigmund. 1948. *A History of Popular Music in America.* New York: Random House.

Stuart, Ross. 1977. "Song in a Minor Key: Canada's Musical Theater." *Canadian Theater Review* 15:50–75.

Swain, Joseph P. 1990. *The Broadway Musical: A Critical and Musical Survey.* New York: Oxford University Press.

Tawa, Nicholas E. 1980. *Sweet Songs for Gentle Americans: The Parlor Song in America, 1790–1860.* Bowling Green, Ohio: Bowling Green University Popular Press.

————. 1982. *A Sound of Strangers: Musical Culture, Acculturation, and the Post-Civil War Ethnic American.* Metuchen, N.J.: Scarecrow.

————. 1984. *A Music for the Millions: Antebellum Democratic Attitudes and the Birth of American Popular Music.* New York: Pendragon.

Toll, Robert. 1974. *Blacking Up: The Minstrel Show in Nineteenth-Century America.* New York: Oxford University Press.

Vaudeville: Songs of the Great Ladies of the Musical Stage. 1976. Nonesuch H71330. LP disk.

Virga, Patricia H. 1982. *The American Opera to 1790.* Studies in Musicology 61. Ann Arbor, Mich.: UMI Research Press.

Wilder, Alec. 1972. *American Popular Song: The Great Innovators, 1900–1950.* New York: Oxford University Press.

Woll, Allen. 1989. *Black Musical Theater: From Coontown to Dreamgirls.* Baton Rouge: Louisiana State University Press.

Yerbury, Grace D. 1971. *Song in America, from Early Times to about 1850.* Metuchen, N.J.: Scarecrow Press.

Film
Anahid Kassabian

Silent Films
Early Sound Movies (to 1950)
1950s and 1960s
1970s to the Present

Music in film serves a variety of purposes. The overall style or musical vocabulary of the score may serve a number of functions. It may provide geographic or temporal information or express emotional value. In a particular scene, the music may be produced by someone within the scene (source music) or by an outside force (dramatic scoring). It may represent one of the characters in the scene or comment on something happening or that has not yet happened. The music, along with the rest of the soundtrack, produces a sense of space by the way it is mixed. It may be a theme from within the film or a quotation from other music. It may begin and end obviously (an unusual strategy), or slowly fade in and out, or hide under other sounds (a technique known as "sneaking"). In these and many other ways, film music provides clues to the listener as to why it is there and what it is doing.

Before describing the history of music in U.S. feature films, several important exceptions are worth noting. First, and perhaps least obviously, musicals are generally bracketed from the history of film music, as are cartoons. Both animation and musicals are organized by different relationships between image and sound and between narrative and music. One mark of these differences is in production practices: in both cases, visuals are cut to music, rather than the music being composed and edited to the already edited image track. Also not foregrounded in this brief history are documentary scores and music for avant-garde and experimental films or industrial and educational videos. Wonderful new scholarship is beginning to appear in each of these areas, but it remains to be seen whether or not they should be connected to more mainstream feature film musical practices.

SILENT FILMS

Films have always—or almost always—had music. Silent film theaters had orchestras (of varying sizes) or organists or pianists. Books of music like Erno Rapee's *Encyclopedia of Music for Pictures* (1978) were published to provide ideas for music appropriate to a scene and were catalogued by mood or event (for example, "sad," "chase," "horses," and so on). Many films were sent out with lists of musical selections, called cue sheets, already made for them. On one line of the cue sheet would be the name of the scene, the name of the tune, and a duration; on the second would be a few measures of the melody of the song. These cue sheets depended on good organists or pianists and were probably not followed in any precise way. Some films had scores written specifically for them (for example, *The Birth of a Nation,* 1915, music by D. W. Griffith and Joseph Carl Brail), in some cases by known composers.

EARLY SOUND MOVIES (TO 1950)

Explanations for the presence of music in silent films vary: some say it was an inheritance from theater, others that it covered projector noise, and still others that it made the two-dimensional image appear three-dimensional and thus less "ghostly." Whatever the early reasons, music became a part of sound films as well. At first sound films were given musical tracks the way silent films were, from preexisting popular or nineteenth-century Western art ("classical") music. In the 1930s this practice became less and less common, in favor of original scores composed for the particular film. While some filmmakers and composers were exploring possible image-music relations, most films used music simply as reinforcement.

During this period Hollywood studios started hiring composers trained in European art music to write scores for films. Among the most well known of these composers are Erich Wolfgang Korngold (*The Adventures of Robin Hood,* 1938), Max Steiner (*King Kong,* 1933), Miklos Rozsa (*Spellbound,* 1945), and Dmitri Tiomkin (*High Noon,* 1952), all European immigrants. The major U.S.-born composers of this group were Alfred Newman (*Blood and Sand,* 1941) and Victor Young (*For Whom the Bell Tolls,* 1943). These composers began to develop a vocabulary for mainstream British and American film music, a vocabulary based predominantly on German late-romantic practices. It was designed to meet the demands of studios and directors to support, as unobtrusively as possible, the rest of the film.

By the 1940s the vocabulary and practices were solidly established. The most important Hollywood composer of this period was Bernard Herrmann (*Citizen Kane,* 1941), who refined the practices of the thirties through more careful, more limited, and more unusual instrumentations. Hollywood set the standards of cinematography, editing, sound, and music that in the United States marginalized other models as "art films" and would continue to do so for many years to come.

1950s AND 1960s

Breaks with the symphonic, European art-music style first began in the 1950s. Although jazz of various kinds had always been a part of filmmaking through musicals and animation, it was the exception in scoring throughout the thirties and forties. In the fifties, however, Alex North (*A Streetcar Named Desire,* 1951), Leonard Rosenman (*Rebel without a Cause,* 1955), and Elmer Bernstein (*The Man with the Golden Arm,* 1955) all wrote jazz-influenced scores, making room for more use of contemporary sounds within the parameters of the Hollywood tradition. Jazz began to take hold in Hollywood not as it was heard elsewhere, but as new features for the symphonic score. One advantage jazz had was its smaller, less expensive orchestration; another was the increasing numbers of American composers who, influenced by jazz harmonies and rhythms, were scoring films. Foremost among these was Henry Mancini (*The Pink Panther,* 1964), who is generally considered to have paved the way for a new generation of film composers.

The experiments and expansion of the fifties continued in the sixties, adding some new possibilities and consolidating others. In the United States, Quincy Jones (*In the Heat of the Night,* 1967) and Lalo Schifrin (*Cool Hand Luke,* 1967) took advantage of the acceptance of new musical vocabularies. John Barry (*Dr. No,* 1962) added some rock and some medieval styles to the scoring repertoire. Maurice Jarre (*Is Paris Burning?,* 1968) used the most traditional romantic vocabulary to build epic scores for epic films. Ennio Morricone (*The Battle of Algiers,* 1966) commanded a dizzying array of styles and a sense of humor and irony in his work on spaghetti Westerns, mysteries, dramas, farces, and so on. His score for *A Fistful of Dollars* (1964), like his score for *The Good, the Bad, and the Ugly* (1967), helped define the sound of Clint Eastwood's early career.

1970s TO THE PRESENT

The consolidation of the sixties continued throughout the seventies, with one major innovation. John Williams (*Star Wars,* 1977, figure 1), Bill Conti (*Rocky,* 1976), and Jerry Goldsmith (*Planet of the Apes,* 1968) revitalized the symphonic score, using existing practices and vocabularies to create scores, like Williams's one for *Jaws* (1975), that were highly memorable. This return to romanticism has defined the sound of several genres for two decades, and Williams and Goldsmith are still among its most important practitioners. In general, though, the seventies did not bring much new musical material to the film soundtrack.

In the eighties, however, several major new trends came into film scoring. The first was the use of obviously synthesized sounds, such as those used in Vangelis's Academy Award–winning score for *Chariots of Fire* (1981), with its very un-Hollywood sound. Similarly, Tangerine Dream's soundtracks for the films *Risky Business* (1983), Firestarter (1984), and *Red Heat* (1988) and Giorgio Moroder's contributions to, for example, *Flashdance* (1983), *Metropolis* (1984), and *Top Gun* (1986) brought these new, synthesized sounds into Hollywood's repertoire. The second new development, related to the first, was the use of avant-garde musicians, not only for the music of avant-garde films (such as Philip Glass's score for *Koyaanisqatsi,* 1983), but also for more mainstream films such as Jonathan Demme's *Something Wild* (1986), which had music by David Byrne, Laurie Anderson, and John Cale, or Bertolucci's *The Last Emperor* (1987), whose Academy Award–winning score was written by Ryuichi Sakamoto, David Byrne, and Cong Su. A third new trend, again related to the others, was the solid establishment of the rock score, with original music written in rock musical vocabularies for films such as *Against All Odds* (1984) and *Stakeout* (1987), many showing the direct influence of Jan Hammer's groundbreaking musical direction for the TV series *Miami Vice* (1984–1989).

One final point to be made about 1980s film scoring takes us directly back to the very beginnings of film. Since the advent of sound on film, there have been some few Hollywood films, like *American Graffiti* (1973) whose scores are built almost entirely on preexisting popular songs. In the 1980s, however, this kind of compiled soundtrack became a very significant trend, as Kathryn Kalinak describes in her book on music and the classical Hollywood film:

> Since many composers of pop scores were already established in the record industry, scores such as those for *The Graduate* (1967), *Butch Cassidy and the Sundance Kid* (1969), and *Goodbye Columbus* (1969) were also easily marketed as records, and frequently outgrossed the films they were composed for. In the seventies producers capitalized on the pop score's ability to create an audience for a film and began the practice of premarketing a film's songs. (Kalinak 1992:186)

A trend, beginning perhaps with *The Big Chill* (1983), illustrates one very important source for a film's music: a group of songs that preexist the movie, often by decades. These songs are taken from one or more genres that evoke a certain period (doo-wop, acid rock), an identity (alternative, disco, rhythm and blues), a geography (country, rap), and more. Currently this method of scoring films so totally dominates our sense of soundtracks that almost every film ends with popular song credits and a soundtrack album is released for every film.

FIGURE I   Composer-conductor John Williams, 1980. © Bettmann/CORBIS.

REFERENCES

Brown, Royal S. 1994. *Overtones and Undertones: Reading Film Music.* Berkeley: University of California Press.

Eisler, Hanns, and Theodor Adorno. 1947. *Composing for the Films.* New York: Oxford University Press.

Flinn, Caryl. 1992. *Strains of Utopia: Gender, Nostalgia, and Hollywood Film Music.* Princeton, N.J.: Princeton University Press.

Gorbman, Claudia. 1987. *Unheard Melodies: Narrative Film Music.* Bloomington: Indiana University Press.

Kalinak, Kathryn. 1992. *Settling the Score: Music and the Classical Hollywood Film.* Madison: University of Wisconsin Press.

Kassabian, Anahid. 2000. *Hearing Film: Tracking Identifications in Contemporary Hollywood Film Music.* New York: Routledge.

Marks, Martin. 1997. *Music and the Silent Film: Contexts and Case Studies, 1895–1924.* New York: Oxford University Press.

Rapee, Erno. 1978 [1970]. *Encyclopedia of Music for Pictures.* New York: Ayer Co.

Smith, Jeff. 1998. *The Sounds of Commerce: Marketing Popular Film Music.* New York: Columbia University Press.

Dance
Joann W. Kealiinohomoku
Mary Jane Warner

Music and Dance in the United States
Music and Dance in Canada

MUSIC AND DANCE IN THE UNITED STATES

Dance in the United States exists in more forms than is immediately apparent. In addition to the highly visible dance seen on television and in performance, traditional dances are performed in ethnic enclaves, recreational dancing takes place in many social situations, dance classes are held to promote health and well-being, and dance is often part of religious ritual.

The Scope of Dance

Dance and music are performatory, and their relationship is synergistic. Both are produced by the human body engaged in extraordinary transformative behaviors that express and influence affective culture.

Music and dance are major hallmarks of humanity. Music occurs when humans produce organized and symbolically affective sounds that are perceived aurally by audiences. Dance occurs when humans produce organized and symbolically affective bodily movements that are perceived visually by audiences. However, music and dance are interdependent. Practitioners of music and dance share certain commonalities. Musicians perform selected rhythmic bodily movements. As well, dancers employ all aspects of musicality, although sound is not considered a definitive feature of dance.

In fact, dance events incorporate acoustic elements as accompanying sounds. Distinctions blur when the performer is both dancer and musician. Self-accompanying dancers may use their bodies as sound-producing instruments for singing or for body percussion such as hand clapping. They may carry or wear sound-producing items such as rattles or shoes with taps. Musicians who dance are showcased on television channels such as MTV and VH1, where musicians rhythmically gesticulate and move. It is thus difficult to say whether an artist like Michael Jackson is a singer who dances or a dancer who sings.

The diversity and vitality of dance in the United States is suggested by three categories of participation by dancers—vocation, pastime, and heteronomy—and three categories of participation by those who watch dance—for pleasure, to reaffirm social identity, and for professional reasons.

FIGURE I   Ballet dancer and a dancer from Chaksam-pa, the Tibetan Dance and Opera Company compare movement techniques with one another during Tibet Week in Flagstaff, Arizona. Photo by John Running, 1995.

Why dance?

Dancing as vocation

Dancing is a profession that develops from inspiration, talent, training, or inheritance. In order to distinguish between those for whom dancing is a vocation and those for whom it is not, in this article the former will be capitalized, identified as Dancers rather than as dancers. Most Dancers consider themselves to be artists, and whenever possible their dance art is also their occupation. In order for a person to be a Dancer within his or her own culture, that culture must traditionally recognize that role. For example, Native American cultures do not recognize the role of Dancer. American Indians who have become Dancers have done so outside of their cultures. Maria Tallchief (Osage) and Jock Soto (Navajo/Puerto Rican) are famous classical ballet Dancers who happen to be Indians, but they are not Indian Dancers.

Vocational Dancers are performers, choreographers, teachers, or dedicated students. Venues for Dancers are studios, concert halls, theaters, exhibition arenas, and electronic media. Vocational dance genres include classical ballet, contemporary concert dance, show dance, jazz, and tap. Besides those genres, the United States is enriched by multicultural dance art genres such as hula (Hawaiian), flamenco (Spanish Gypsy), *kathakali* (North Indian), and *butoh* (contemporary Japanese).

There are a number of traditional Dance companies for which Dance is an art, such as Chaksam-pa, The Tibetan Dance and Opera Company (figure 1), and The Royal Cambodian Dancers. Other dance companies, such as the Ballet Folklorico (representing regions of Mexico) and the American Indian Dance Theater, have theatricalized their traditional dances.

Some celebrated dancers

Isadora Duncan (1878–1927) revolutionized concert dance when she turned to the ancient Greeks and naturalism for inspiration while deliberately ignoring ballet and show dancing. She is considered to be the progenitor of modern dance in North America. Bill (Bojangles) Robinson (1878–1949), the most famous tap dancer of his day, performed in several movies, including three with child star Shirley Temple. In 1946, to recognize his sixty-year contribution to show business, New York City's mayor, William O'Dwyer, proclaimed "Bill Robinson Day." Contemporary Canadian ice dancer Kurt Browning trained as a hockey player, became a champion figure skater, and then studied classical ballet. Today he adapts several dance genres for his ice dancing choreography and performances. Nalani Kanaka'ole and Pualani Kanaka'ole Kanahele, both *kumu hula* 'hula master teachers', continue the family legacy of hula inherited from their late mother, Edith Kanaka'ole. Their *halau hula* 'hula guild', Halau 'O Kekuhi, has toured widely and has been featured on PBS television programs. In 1993 the sisters were named National Heritage Fellows by the National Endowment for the Arts.

Challenges for Dancers

Vocational dancing is a high-risk occupation. Training to be a Dancer takes several years and total dedication, but the number of years a person can expect to perform are few. As with other athletic activities, debilitating injuries are occupational hazards. The demands on concert Dancers are formidable. Dancers take extreme measures to achieve the perfect body. Many Dancers, especially young women, suffer from eating disorders—anorexia and bulimia—when they strive to become thin enough to satisfy their own and their teachers' aesthetic demands. Ballet Dancers have been known to have their feet surgically standardized for *pointe* work—dancing on the tips of the toes supported by blocked slippers ("toe shoes").

Training to be a Dancer takes several years and total dedication, but the number of years a person can expect to perform are few.

Dancers spend long hours auditioning for even the most inconsequential positions in the chorus. Show business provides employment for thousands of Dancers, but because shows have limited runs and employment with a dance company is usually seasonal, many Dancers are all too familiar with unemployment checks. Dancers also have special expenses. For example, they must take daily classes (figure 2), and because their bodies are their instruments, their clothing is important—they need special rehearsal clothing and shoes. Often custom made, shoes are a major expense, needing frequent replacement, sometimes after a single concert.

In order to support themselves and their careers, most Dancers need supplemental employment (such as waiting on tables in restaurants, which damages feet and exhausts bodies already overextended by hours of daily classes and rehearsals). Except for a very few stars, most Dancers have little financial security, unless they perform in ongoing commercial ventures such as Las Vegas shows or in a few large ballet companies in major cities.

With no established system of patronage to support them, independent Dancers and their companies piece together support from grants, teaching, and ticket sales to limited audiences during limited seasons. Those with their own companies struggle for funds to mount shows and pay other Dancers to be in their concerts. The U.S. government sets aside funds for the arts, and every state has an arts council that helps underwrite worthy dance projects, but government funding is still woefully inadequate.

To build successful careers, some Dancers avoid the dance capitals of the United States and Canada. Seattle, Washington, for example, is currently attracting numerous Dancers, and regional dance companies such as those in Boulder, Colorado, and Atlanta, Georgia, have become more and more important. The faculties of several fine

FIGURE 2   Ballet dancer stretching at the barre, an essential exercise. Photo by John Running, 1987.

university dance programs choose to work within academic environments that encourage their efforts to develop dancers and present their works. Many Dancers live where their spouses work. In order to continue to dance, they teach or join other Dancers in the community to work out and present occasional community performances.

Who are the vocational Dancers?

Many more women than men become, or train to become, Dancers. Families discourage their sons from careers with uncertain financial futures. In addition, mainstream North America stigmatizes classical ballet and contemporary concert dance as unmanly, although some dance genres, such as tap dancing and ethnic dances such as flamenco and *kathakali,* do not carry the same stigma.

Dancers come from all ethnic backgrounds, although minorities in the larger society are also minorities in the professional dance world. The majority of professional Dancers come from middle-income families who can afford dance lessons for their children. This contrasts with the nineteenth and early twentieth centuries, when most professional Dancers were from theatrical families that were considered to be low class.

Pastime

For some individuals, dancing is an avidly pursued hobby. They invest significant time and money in taking lessons, attending workshops, practicing, and buying costumes, tapes, and CDs. The hobby of dancing has many forms.

Hula

Hula, performed by serious avocational dancers over the past three decades, is an interpretive revival of embodied Hawaiian expressive culture, a result of a "Hawaiian Renaissance." Hula is culturally Hawaiian, but being of Hawaiian ancestry is not a prerequisite to participating in a modern *halau,* and many Asian Americans and European Americans adopt Hawaiianness as their ethnicity of choice. *Halau* members today are usually in their teens or twenties.

As a performance form hula exemplifies the synergy of texts, music, and dance. The dance accompanies and illustrates the sung or chanted texts. What appears to be hip swinging is actually stepping from side to side with flexed knees while the upper torso is upright and still. Hula gestures and apparel extend the dancers' silhouettes horizontally rather than vertically, and the thin body of the classical ballet dancer is not admired in hula dancers. Hula people dance barefooted unless performing in a particular style from the nineteenth century. In today's hula environment, women and men, slender and heavyset, participate in perhaps equal numbers [see POLYNESIAN MUSIC, p. 1047].

Folk dancing

The topic of folk dancing is controversial among scholars because it is challenging to define, beginning with the question Who are the folk? Nevertheless, in its commonly understood description it is a popular pastime in the United States. Folk dancers perform mainly European dances for recreational reasons with no concern for the dancers' original contexts and purposes. The dances have been codified in set routines and established guidelines so that dancers from anywhere in the United States can immediately dance with one another. They are formally referred to by folk dance hobbyists as International Folk Dances, although groups sometimes specialize in a particular style, such as British, Scandinavian, or Balkan dances [see EUROPEAN AMERICAN MUSICS, p. 819].

Women's costumes typically include full skirts with "peasant" blouses; men wear casual slacks and shirts. The characteristics of European folk dancing include upright, still torsos and heads; hand and arm gestures limited to set positions on hips, above the shoulders, or in contact with other dancers; and emphasis on complicated floor patterns (figures) for couples or groups. Folk dancing is team dancing par excellence that requires a large performance space such as a gym or community hall.

Every weekend folk dance enthusiasts from all over the United States flock to classes and workshops. The majority of folk dancers are middle-income, young to middle-aged European American men and women. Folk dancers only incidentally have the same heritage as the cultures represented by the dances they perform.

Ethnic dancing

In the last few decades avocational dancers have become attracted to the dances, even the specific dance genres, of cultural "others," most of which are not part of International Folk Dance repertoires. For example, adapted West African–style dancing and culture are the passion of many Americans, and most teachers of West African–style dancing welcome students from every ethnic background. Many European Americans find that the dynamic rhythms and total bodily involvement introduced from West Africa are more fun and challenging than those of dances from their own backgrounds.

Belly dancing, adapted from women's dances of the Middle East, has become fashionable among many women of all ages. Enthusiasts diligently practice this format of dance that demands coordinated muscle isolations, and they learn to play the *zils* 'finger cymbals' (figure 3). An absorbing task is preparing individualized costumes, for which they select diaphanous fabrics as well as sound-producing paraphernalia such as girdles, bracelets, and anklets hung with jingles.

Summer is the main time for intensive workshops for avocational dancers. Groups of International Folk Dancers travel to many parts of the world to observe and learn new dances. Ethnic dancers attend workshops such as Bulgarian dance camps in Massachusetts and California, a dance camp in New Mexico designed for complete immersion in Central Asian dance and culture, and a workshop/conference in New York City on *capoeira*, an African Brazilian martial arts dance.

Ballroom dancing

Avocational ballroom dancers have annual local, regional, and national competitions. The annual national competitions, aired on television, include finalists from both the United States and Canada. Competitors must perform several dances, including waltz, foxtrot, swing, and several Latin forms such as tango and rumba. Performance stan-

FIGURE 3   A belly dancer in traditional costume, including finger cymbals (*zils*). Adapted from women's dances of the Middle East, belly dancing has an enthusiastic following among women of all ages. Photo by John Running, 1977.

dards are strict, and competitors are graded according to their success in achieving the standards. According to Juliet Prowse, former Hollywood film dancer and television host for the national competitions, women competitors spend thousands of dollars on dance gowns that they wear only once. The majority of competitive ballroom dancers are young to middle-aged European Americans in the middle-income range. There are countless ballroom studios all over North America.

Competitive powwow dancing

Successful Indian powwow dance competitors follow the powwow circuit throughout North America and finance their trips with prize monies from winning dance competitions. They love the exhilaration of dancing and reuniting with friends all over the United States. Plains Indian dance–style powwow dances are further divided into Southern Plains and Northern Plains styles, and various genres are judged separately, such as Fancy and Grass dances for men, and Shawl and Jingle dances for women [see PLAINS, p. 440].

Recreation

Recreational dancing is for pleasure, refreshment, diversion, excitement, and, incidentally for exercise.

Children and youths

Organized play dances for children, such as "Ring-Around-a-Rosy," are tried and true, and children of all ages and ethnic groups seem to dance spontaneously whenever they hear music. African American children, for example, often have circle dances in which each child takes a turn to do his or her best moves. Youngsters dance tricky jumping rope patterns, self-accompanied by chanted rhymes.

Youths are empowered by social dancing because it channels energy, crystallizes a generational image, enables contact with people of like interests, and can even express rebellion. Contemporary social dancing for youths usually happens at ad hoc gatherings. The hallmark for performance is improvisational dancing using known dance styles that are determined by, and take their names from, current music genres.

Dance moves vary from jumping up and down, smooth free-flowing motions, and movements that depend on muscle isolation. Fads differ from city to city, but generally they include dances and music made popular through the media, especially television channels MTV and VH1. A famous television show, aired daily since the 1950s, is the *American Bandstand,* hosted by Dick Clark, where mostly European American teenagers perform current popular dances. Don Cornelius's *Soul Train,* also aired weekly since 1978, is the African American counterpart of *American Bandstand.*

High school students from all racial and economic backgrounds dance whenever and wherever they can—during lunch hours, after school, and especially on the weekends, with street dancing, club dancing, and house dancing. With dances such as rap and hip-hop, it is not essential to dance in couples; young people often "dance alone together."

Personal contacts are made by some teenagers and young adults in an astounding way. In slam dancing dancers, and even band members, forcefully bang into one another, sometimes throwing themselves from the bandstand or stage face down into the crowd, with faith that people in the audience will catch them before they crash to the floor. Some clubs set aside a special space, called the mosh pit, for this activity. Slam dancing came to America from England in the late 1970s, where it was an outgrowth of punk dancing.

Many young adults from all walks of life choose social dancing for their preferred recreational activity (figure 4). In nightclubs, dance halls, coffeehouses, and homes

In slam dancing dancers, and even band members, forcefully bang into one another, sometimes throwing themselves from the bandstand or stage face down into the crowd, with faith that people in the audience will catch them before they crash to the floor.

FIGURE 4   Disco dancers Marne Lucas and Steve Hunt show their form in a dance hall in Portland, Oregon. Photo by Dawn Kish, 1997.

they dance varieties of jazz dance, rock, and funk. Latino dances such as *tejano* and salsa are favorites in many places. Reggae is popular, and because of its spiritual messages it seems to inspire free dancing. *Ska,* another popular dance, is a fusion of Jamaican reggae with other music styles and dance movements influenced by skank, jive, and bop.

New dance styles frequently begin in New York or Los Angeles, where both regular clubs and avant-garde dance venues can be found in abandoned warehouses and other industrial buildings. Perhaps the most important characteristic of popular dancing in the United States is that it is dynamic, with new moves, themes, elements of risk, and expressions of rebellion.

Adults and families

Swing

Dancing can also be nostalgic. Although the roots of swing are in the African American jazz of the 1920s, and the genre had peaked in popularity by World War II, swing has been rediscovered with astounding vitality. Performed exuberantly in clubs, it is also the rage for ballroom dance classes. People of all backgrounds and ages try to emulate the masters such as Frankie Manning, now in his eighties, who still teaches and dances in Harlem. As part of the current nostalgia craze, Manning has been interviewed several times for media events, where he recalls how he first discovered swing dancing and later invented the movements that came to be called aerials. There are dozens of varieties of swing, ranging from Arthur Murray shag to West Coast swing. The Internet yields a huge amount of information about swing.

Country

All over North America, young to middle-aged, mostly European American couples enjoy country dancing. Beginners can learn the basics at bars where the cover charge includes free dance lessons. Country dance fans can dance at home and in the bars along with the hundreds of nonprofessionals who flock to perform on *Club Dance* and *Prime Time Country,* live television shows broadcast from Nashville, Tennessee [see COUNTRY AND WESTERN, p. 73].

In contrast to many social dances mentioned above, country dances are gender dependent (figure 5). Couples embrace while the man steers the woman backward as they circle counterclockwise around the room. Sometimes dancers regroup into double rows for line dancing. Country dance steps include the schottische, polka, a touch of rock, and hand clapping for accents. The form is clearly from the British Isles but has been adapted as an American idiom [see CONTRA DANCE, p. 230].

By seasoning the moves with rhythmic bouncing, a fairly uniform way of dressing, a folksy mood, and hosts who speak with a Country and Western twang (a cross between hillbilly and Texas drawl), this dance form is called an American original. The preferred attire includes cowboy boots, blue jeans, sometimes very short skirts for women, western shirts, and cowboy hats for men.

FIGURE 5   In gender-dependent country dancing
and ballroom dancing, shown here, dancing
couples embrace. Photo by John Running, 1992.

Regional variations

In reservation Border Towns, towns near Indian reservations that are visited frequently by Indians for shopping and recreation, Indians in cowboy clothes and huge silver belt buckles love Country-and-Western dancing. In central and southern Arizona, Tohono O'odham (formerly called Papago) Indians dance the popular *waila*. The word *waila* is derived from the Spanish word *baile,* meaning "dance." This version of Country-and-Western dance and music is said to have come across the Mexican border in the mid-nineteenth century, when popular Mexican music was influenced by the polka imported by German settlers from the Rio Grande Valley in Texas.

Other kinds of social dances include polka parties in Milwaukee, salsa parties on the East Coast, "flat foot" dancing in Appalachia, contredanses by the Métis near the Canadian border, and open circle dancing at Balkan and Greek restaurants throughout North America [see MÉTIS, p. 404]. The Inuit of Canada and Alaska dance jigs and reels introduced by whalers, as well as more ancient Drum Dancing, and Freeze Dancing (similar to the game of statues) [see ARCTIC CANADA AND ALASKA, p. 374; SUB-ARCTIC CANADA, p. 383].

Many families enjoy weekly social events. Country and Western, salsa, and *waila* are often enjoyed as family activities. Square dancing is also popular. Contra dance clubs are increasing in numbers. In the southeastern United States, Cajun families have weekly socials with music and dance adapted from Nova Scotia Acadian traditions. At Jewish gatherings, Israeli dancing is hugely popular. On the East and West Coasts of the United States, organized groups have "Umbrella Dances," when mostly European Americans of all ages meet for several hours of free, improvisational dancing to recorded music of every genre.

Exclusive recreational dancing

After an intense day of ceremonial dancing, Taos Pueblo Indians, who are uniquely influenced by neighboring Plains Indians, retreat to the Blue Mountains. There they relax and have fun while singing and dancing 49ers throughout the night. Recreational pan-tribal, often humorous, songs and dances said to have originated with the Kiowa after they watched travelers going to California during the gold rush of 1849, 49ers are performed after a powwow or other serious event. (For various accounts of 49ers, see Feder 1964.)

Self-expression

Although it can be argued that all dancing is expressive, the character of self-expression is shaped by one's cultural body language.

American Indian attitudes toward individualistic dancing

Indian tribes differ in their attitudes toward self-expressive dances. They are unheard of among the Pueblo Indians, who always seek conformity and anonymity. Masks, headdresses, makeup, and hairpieces conceal the identity of Pueblo dancers. In contrast, Plains dancing is individualistic. This is consonant with the Plains Indian tradition whereby a youth's vision quest bestowed a personal song and dance, and dance outfits were designed as private metaphors.

It is logical that modern pantribal powwow dancing, also individualistic, is modeled after Plains dancing. Powwow dancers develop individualistic dance features of signature moves and clothing. They make elaborate outfits with a great investment of time and money. Some Pueblo Indians participate in pan-Indian powwows, but when they do, they emulate Plains style and not Pueblo style. This allows Pueblo Indians to dance expressively while protecting Pueblo values.

West African dance influence

Individualistic movements characterize much West African dancing. Not surprisingly, derivatives of West African dance, such as jazz dancing, also include improvisational movements. Indeed, most popular dances in North America have been influenced by West African dance styles and are very individualistic.

Interpretive dance

After Isadora Duncan danced barefoot and uncorseted, interpretive dancing became an ongoing popular vehicle for self-expression, especially among European American women. Some take dance classes not to become great dancers but to gain skills in expressing themselves freely with their bodies. Quite in contrast is the structured interpretive dance hobby of practicing to dance in a group at amateur programs. The tap dance groups of Dancin' Grannies, for example, are springing up all over North America. These are autonomous groups of vigorous older women who learn to tap dance in carefully rehearsed routines, dressed in snazzy outfits, wearing tap shoes, and often carrying hats and canes. They perform at municipal functions where they and their audiences delight one another.

Heteronomy

Heteronomous dances are designed for some reason other than dancing and are subject to external controls and restrictions. Heteronomous (applied) dances are used for human engineering, therapy, human relations, problem solving, community solidarity, and for religious and political reasons.

Mind/body well-being through dance

Dancing engenders a feeling of well-being, control, enhanced awareness, and inspiration. Some Asian dancing, for example, includes danced Zen meditations and danced martial art forms such as tai kwon do and t'ai chi ch'uan. Increasingly there is also interest in dance as a healing art.

Aerobic dance

Aerobic dance is calisthenics performed to music. Its specific agenda is weight control and physical fitness. The copyrighted form requires aerobic dance leaders to be certified, but the name has become generic for any dance with a similar agenda. Aerobic dance has become a popular pastime, with national competitions for individuals and groups. Men as well as women, especially young adults, primarily European Americans, from all economic backgrounds, participate in aerobic dancing. Members of the work force dance during lunch breaks or after work. Individuals can dance at home accompanied by televised aerobic dance programs. Aerobic dancers wear exercise clothing and characteristically keep bottles of drinking water close at hand.

Dance therapy

Dance therapy treats emotional and physical problems. Dance therapy was extemporized until the mid-1960s, when it became an acknowledged field. Today dance therapists must be formally trained and certified. Dance as therapy is also used by psychologists and clinicians to resolve interpersonal dilemmas and for personal development through individual and group dance experiences. Senior citizens are encouraged to dance for social engagement and physical fitness.

Prevention of societal dysfunction

Youths involved in creative dance can prevent or resolve social problems. For example, a former Los Angeles gang member testifies that his life was turned around when he discovered the power of creative dance. He now teaches dance to youths at risk, in the public schools and in his own studio. He recently established a performance company with many of those youths.

Community solidarity

Dancers perform at critical times during school athletic events to encourage the athletes, stimulate fans' enthusiasm, and give spirit to the entire school community. The dancers are usually pompon girls, cheerleaders, and drill teams, who are selected through fierce competition. Once chosen, they attend training camps during the summers. During the school year they rehearse several hours a week. The dancers must maintain good grades or be dismissed from the team. They are rewarded by learning teamwork, discipline, and self-respect. Dancing can also be used to meet more general goals. For example, charity balls are held as annual fundraisers for community institutions such as hospitals or to raise money for special projects such as support for a political candidate.

Dance as ritual work

Among the Hopi Indians of northern Arizona, dance events are often ritual work. Without dance, Hopis say, the world would come to an end. Dances are aesthetically pleasing so that everyone will think happy thoughts and thus contribute to the energy needed for good results. Religious ideas become visible when they are danced. Dancing styles match the preferred mode of spiritual expression. Hopi dancers fast and deprive themselves of sleep before dancing, and their dancing is sober, carefully planned, and meticulously executed. In contrast, at those Christian churches that focus on personally receiving the Holy Spirit, such as the Holiness churches, some dancing members experience dissociation, incited by the driving music and the call-and-response speech and song by the minister and congregation. A person overtaken by the Spirit may become catatonic or dance to a frenzy before collapsing on the floor while others in the congregation gather around, perhaps to prevent others from stepping on him or her or to cover a woman to maintain her modesty. Upon recovering from such a cathartic experience, the person often claims to feel refreshed and will continue to participate in the service with dancelike movements [see RELIGION, p. 116].

Identity maintenance

Another form of heteronomy is the use of dances as identity markers and to establish cultural boundaries. The modern Native American powwow is an example. The participants in intertribal powwows celebrate their Indianness. They also signal mes-

Hopi dancers fast and deprive themselves of sleep before dancing, and their dancing is sober, carefully planned, and meticulously executed.

sages of solidarity and pride to mainstream North American society. In the 1950s and 1960s non-Indian hobbyists participated in powwows, but contemporary pan-Indian powwows are exclusive. Non-Indians are invited to join in only during the occasional Friendship dances.

Dance clubs throughout North America—Polish, Mexican, Irish, and others—remind young people of their cultural heritage and help them embody it. For over fifty years the annual Holiday Folk Festival has celebrated the multiplicity of cultures in Milwaukee, Wisconsin. Dancers proudly display their dance cultures and enjoy the admiration of the audiences. Dancing can also be a signature for specific events. Examples are the first dance by the bride and groom at a wedding reception, the fifteenth birthday party of a Mexican American woman, and the presidential Inaugural Ball.

Cultural continuity

Dancers are embodied culture carriers, and dance cultures achieve continuity through their maintenance or adaptation. Following are two examples of how dance helps to maintain cultural continuity.

Hopi Indians

The Hopi of northern Arizona live in their traditional homeland and have never incorporated Christianity into their belief system. Hopi people schedule their lives according to an established ritual calendar, with ceremonies that last several days in a *kiva,* the semi-subterranean ceremonial chamber associated with Pueblo Indian communities in the Southwest. Ritual dances performed in the plazas, and usually open to the public, are really the concluding segments of *kiva* ceremonies. For ten months each year, ceremonial dances are performed by members of ritual societies that belong to matrilineal clans. But in August and January there are optional pleasure dances of the butterfly and buffalo genres, at which unmarried girls invite their favorite paternal nephews to be their partners.

This recognition of paternal relatives strengthens family ties. Dance events reaffirm Hopi history, worldview, values, and dedication to the Hopi way. Hopis are obliged to sponsor four dances during their lifetime and should participate in at least four other dance events sponsored by someone else.

Immigrants to North America

Except for indigenous populations, the United States is an immigrant society. Normally assimilated into mainstream culture, immigrants to this country often retrieve their cultural heritage on festive occasions through displays of food, clothing, dance, and music.

There is a patchwork of ethnic neighborhoods in many cities such as residential New York City that sponsor traditional celebrations, often religious or commemorative, in which dance is a featured activity. To welcome the New Year in Chinatowns throughout the United States, for example, acrobatic teams dance under a huge cloth dragon to chase away evil and bring in good luck. Every August, Japanese and Okinawan Americans perform a dance to commemorate their ancestors, just as their ancestors danced every August in Japan. The Bon Odori, as the ceremonial dance event is called, is usually performed in the courtyard of a Buddhist temple. The dancers circle in single file around a platform where musicians accompany them with folk songs. Basque communities in California and Nevada have a festival network to celebrate their common heritage. They visit first one community, then another, each regularly hosting a festival of dance and music on an assigned saint's day.

Adaptive strategies

Syncretism

Other groups keep their cultures alive by adapting introduced elements. Although living on their traditional lands, Pueblo Indian tribes in New Mexico incorporated aspects of colonial Spanish culture. They profess both their ancestral religious beliefs and Roman Catholicism; both are reflected in their dance events. Pueblo Indians of New Mexico perform appropriate dances according to their proper seasons: animal dances are performed in winter and corn dances in summer (figure 6), but now their

FIGURE 6   Pueblo Indian corn dancers at San Ildefonso Pueblo, New Mexico. Photo by John Running, 1985.

performances are scheduled on saints' days. Likewise, the Yaqui Indians of southern Arizona still have a traditional deer dancer and three or four *pascolas,* the traditional sacred clowns who dance with the deer dancer and who serve in the official capacity as the hosts of a Yaqui fiesta, but now they are allied with the Yaqui Catholic Church sodalities as they perform their annual syncretistic Passion of Christ.

Borrowing

Unlike concert musicians who usually re-create works from an established repertoire, contemporary modern dancers make their own pieces, and they are always searching for new materials to incorporate into their choreography. Other cultures have been a mother lode for new choreographic ideas. Although contemporary modern dance and classical ballet choreographers disdain borrowing material from other choreographers in the same discipline, until recently non-Western materials were considered to be in the public domain. For example, Michael Smuin choreographed a version of Kabuki for the San Francisco Ballet, which was performed on pointe.

Dancers from throughout the world visit the United States. Many of them stay to teach and perform, and when they return home they leave images of their styles and movement vocabulary. Choreographers today worry about charges of cultural trespass. But, as with the surge for World Music, there is a developing World Dance, a fusion by usually mutual consent.

Reactionary

In the 1940s, twenty years before the "Black Is Beautiful" movement, some young African American men founded fraternities to affirm pride and solidarity. They perfected a form of step dancing performed with strongly accented spoken cadences and percussive foot work in heavy shoes. A modern version of this dancing, executed by the men of the Gamma chapter of the Omega Psi Phi fraternity, can be seen in the video series *Dancing.* Modeled after this form, young people of all races have step dancing groups under the auspices of the Baha'i faith who tour from city to city, performing and carrying messages of brotherhood.

Bhangra, a Bengali farmers' dance, was revitalized in England by the sons of Punjabi immigrant families. Not farmers themselves, the sons sought a way to celebrate their parents' legacy, and to redress discrimination against East Indians. The exciting *bhangra* brought enthusiasm and new pride to the Punjabi community in England. It is now becoming popular in Canada and is also recorded in the television series *Dancing.*

Canadian Ukrainian communities were concerned lest their culture be lost because their young people were attracted to Canadian popular culture. Festivals and competitive dancing were strategic solutions. The Ukrainian community of Vegreville, Alberta, Canada, holds an annual summer festival. It features dance competitions, both traditional and choreographed, for children and young adults, for soloists, couples and groups, for males and females separately and together. Dance practices are held all year, and all year the dancers embody their cultural heritage. The festival also empowers the Ukrainian community economically and by establishing cultural boundaries [see UKRAINIAN MUSIC, p. 1241].

In Hawai'i, after years of performing hula to satisfy tourists, young Islanders demanded to learn the old traditions before the elders, repositories of cultural knowledge, had passed away. The Hawaiian Renaissance that began at the end of the 1950s was flourishing by the mid-1960s. The results of this renaissance still resonate. As in the Ukrainian communities, Hawaiian leaders developed competitions that aroused excitement for the real hula, and the revived Hawaiian culture began to play a major role in the lives of young people. The most famous annual competitive event is the Merry Monarch Festival, first held in 1963. It commemorates the last Hawaiian king,

Kalākaua, (reigned 1874–1891), who resurrected the hula from the underground, where it had hidden for years from disapproving outside forces.

Because the original rationale and context for the hula are long gone, the competitive festival is a modern strategy of revival and survival. It engenders the enthusiasm of a football game for the crowds that cheer wildly for their favorite *halau*. All of Hawai'i is caught up in the Renaissance, and anyone who is willing to undergo the rigorous hula training may participate regardless of ancestry. Whereas the American Indian and the Ukrainian dances are participant exclusive, Hawaiian dances are participant inclusive.

Political

By opening the Hawaiian Renaissance to everyone regardless of ancestry, a critical mass of people in Hawai'i ensures Hawaiian cultural viability. The hula festival sends a powerful message to administrators and politicians, who must support the Renaissance or lose credibility. Hawaiian studies flourish in the schools. Hundreds of dedicated dancers belong to *halaus*. *Kumu hula* are engrossed in uncovering old chants and dances as well as composing new chants and choreographing them. The Hawaiian Renaissance, embodied in the hula, is omnipresent in Hawai'i. Newly empowered Hawaiians demand correction of past inequities, and with the support of their non-Hawaiian neighbors, many are working toward reestablishing Hawaiian sovereignty.

Tibetans and the Royal Cambodian Dancers fled their nations because of social catastrophes. In 1959 the Dalai Lama and many followers, fleeing the Chinese Communist takeover in Tibet, escaped to India, where they were granted asylum. The first institution His Holiness established in exile was the Tibetan Institute for the Performing Arts (TIPA) on the principle that Tibetan culture would not thrive if the arts were lost. TIPA graduates use their artistry to educate the outside world about Tibetan culture and the plight of Tibet. Some of the most gifted graduates moved to San Francisco, where in 1989 they founded Chaksam-pa, The Tibetan Dance and Opera Company. Its very presence calls attention to Tibet. It has toured North America three times and performs for the Dalai Lama when he visits the Americas.

The Cambodian Court Dancers in the United States are the few who escaped from the mass assassination of their company by the Pol Pot regime. The survivors keep their dance traditions alive by performing in North America. Both the Tibetan Dancers and the Cambodian Dancers perform to influence public opinion and Western governmental policies.

Why watch dance?

For pleasure

Loyal aficionados, attending dance concerts whenever possible, are aesthetically nourished by the experience. At the same time, vocational Dancers depend upon the give-and-take from informed and appreciative audiences. Some people identify empathetically with dancing. Observers become kinesthetically involved, and this heady experience transforms audiences vicariously. This phenomenon is especially effective for religious and culturally potent dances. Millions of people attend show dance performances, such as musical theater, Las Vegas extravaganzas, and New York City's Radio City Music Hall's Rockettes. Millions more watch dance on television programs, especially on the MTV and VH1 networks, or have seen the PBS series *Dance in America,* which has aired more than seventy programs since 1976.

To reaffirm social identity

Audiences experience dances to reaffirm their shared cultural heritage, an example being Mexican Americans who attend *Cinco de Mayo* celebrations (figure 7).

When there is dancing in public places such as Washington Square in New York City or on the streets of San Francisco, people are irresistibly drawn to watch it.

FIGURE 7   Mexican Americans celebrating *Cinco de Mayo* in Flagstaff, Arizona. Photo by John Running, 1992.

Dance schools present annual student recitals, and across North America loyal families and neighbors come to show support for the performers. Whole communities attend Native American dance events even though but a small percentage may be dancing. Congregations attend religious services, such as Santería services in New York City, to reaffirm their values even though but a few members are moved to dance [see AFRO-CUBAN MUSIC, p. 783].

When there is dancing in public places such as Washington Square in New York City or on the streets of San Francisco, people are irresistibly drawn to watch it. These nondancing participants become an instant community that responds appropriately by nodding their heads, tapping their feet, and applauding.

For professional reasons

Critics, photographers, talent scouts, medical specialists, and researchers watch dancing for professional reasons. Critics center their attention on concert dancing. In the past few years critics have reframed their attitudes and skills to be able to critique dances from non-Western cultures. They keep on the cutting edge of their profession through the Dance Critics Association.

Dancing is a favorite subject for photographers, and some establish their reputations as dance specialists. Dance medicine, body work, and physical therapy for dancers are important emerging fields. Dance ethnologists and other researchers observe dancers and dance events in the field for empirical studies and to gather data.

The state of dance today

The robust health of dance in the United States is revealed by the successful strategies that create, research, transmit, and preserve dance: classes and workshops, public performances, festivals, competitions, political events, public and private funding, social pressure, cultural demands, revivals, syncretism and other adaptations, organizations, publications, preservation, and scholarly studies.

The dance mosaic of North America has become evident and its many parts acknowledged and honored in the twentieth to the twenty-first century. Respected dancers and treasured dances are seen as part of the North American heritage. New methods have been developed to honor, research, and preserve dance materials. Libraries, museums, and archives dedicated to dance are being expanded or newly established. The Pew Foundation is pouring millions of dollars into grants distributed by the Washington, D.C.–based NIPAD (National Initiative to Preserve American Dance) for large dance organizations to catalog, document, and preserve historical dance data.

Dance has also become a subject for serious historical, technical, pedagogical, and anthropological scholarship. CORD (Congress on Research in Dance), founded in 1967, is an international organization that encourages research in all aspects of dance and has been instrumental in building a body of literature on dance scholarship. Professional conferences are held annually by CORD as well as by the American Dance Guild, Dance Educators of America, Dance/USA, Dance Critics Association, and the Society for Dance History Scholars.

The Dance Collection of the New York Public Library for the Performing Arts, founded in 1944, is the largest and most comprehensive archive in the world devoted to the documentation of dance. It chronicles dance in all its manifestations—ballet, modern, social, folk, and ethnic. Its 30,600 reference books account for only 3 percent of its holdings. It has thousands of films, video- and audiotapes, and an amazing collection of iconography, as well as over one million manuscript items. In addition, the collection staff does its own filming and recording and has produced hundreds of hours of oral history interviews.

Rudolf von Laban (1879–1958) developed a system of movement notation that made it possible to record dance scores as music notation records music scores. Called Labanotation in North America and Kinetography Laban in Europe, it is taught at the Dance Notation Bureau in New York City, where Labanotators prepare for certification by the bureau. Another aspect of Laban's work, called Effort/Shape, was developed by Irmgard Bartenieff, who founded the Laban Institute of Movement Studies in the United States, where a graduate becomes a CMA (Certified Movement Analyst). Effort/Shape was the method of analysis used for the Alan Lomax project "Choreometrics" (1974).

The anthropology of dance is now an established field of study. On the forefront are scholars Gertrude Prokosch Kurath, Adrienne L. Kaeppler, Joann W. Kealiino-homoku, Anya Peterson Royce, Jill Sweet, Judith Lynne Hanna, and Drid Williams. Indiana University has a major graduate program in the anthropology of dance.

For dancers there are numerous workshops, summer programs, and competitions in classical ballet, modern dance, tap, and jazz. The American Dance Festival convenes several weeks every summer in Durham, North Carolina. The University of the Dance, founded by Ted Shawn, also meets for several weeks every summer at Jacob's Pillow, Massachusetts.

Cultural diversity may be a rallying cry, but multicultural approaches to dance are mixed. On the one hand, there is enthusiasm for alternative dance forms. During the summer of 1996 publicly advertised workshops focused on at least twenty-five ethnic dance cultures, such as Estonian, Greek, Uzbeki, Philippine, Dutch, Irish, Soweto street dance, and Morris. In 1996, forty groups were selected from the 150 that auditioned to participate in the eighteenth season of the San Francisco Ethnic Dance Festival for dancers and dances that culturally represent the San Francisco area. Amazingly, three thousand people came to watch the auditions. Many times that number attended the performances.

On the other hand, few university dance departments include curricula that reach beyond standard Western concert dance genres. In the hundreds of degree programs in the United States, only a handful offer classes in non-Western dance disciplines, and they are limited primarily to Spanish flamenco, West African, and Caribbean dancing. Notable exceptions of culturally eclectic university dance programs are found at Florida International University, the University of California at Los Angeles, the University of Hawai'i, and Wesleyan University in Connecticut.

Dance is increasingly enmeshed with high technology, and many dance-related sites are on the World Wide Web. For the 1996 Olympics in Atlanta, technologists and engineers collaborated with choreographer David Parsons on his work "Timepiece," which included virtual dancers performing with real dancers.

Despite increasing dance activity and interest, the value of dance continues to be underestimated by politicians, educators, and the general North American public. The United States National Endowment for the Arts is constantly threatened with extinction because many politicians insist the performing arts should not be supported by public tax monies. In recent years several university dance programs have been reduced or even eliminated. Dance is seldom included in public schools, except sometimes as part of physical education. Dance in public education is considered to be frivolous. The shining exception is North Carolina, a state that successfully mandates dance in its public school curricula—a model for other states and regions.

The challenge in the twenty-first century is for every citizen of North America to understand that dance is wedded to music and that life would be intolerable without it. Dance is essential to human life, worthy of support, valuable in school curricula, important for research, and part of the measure of a culture's identity.

—JOANN W. KEALIINOHOMOKU

MUSIC AND DANCE IN CANADA

Canadians are engaged in dance as observers, as participants in recreational settings, and as professional dancers, teachers, choreographers, therapists, and administrators of dance organizations. Because the country is home to people from many cultures, the range of dance forms is unusually rich.

Native peoples

The traditions of the earliest inhabitants—Indians and Inuit—were threatened by Western civilization, but in the last three decades of the twentieth century native culture received increased support. There are numerous tribes across Canada, each with its own songs and dances. For example, the Northwest Pacific Coast Indians interweave songs and dances with a floating movement quality. Animal masks are often worn, and dancers usually repeat dances four times or execute them making four circles. Athapaskans in the northern areas of western Canada perform "happy" dance songs, with both men and women wearing beaded caribou skin tunics, feathered headdresses, and beaded dance mittens. They sway their bodies side to side while in a circle formation. The Plains Indians in western Canada celebrate the annual Sun Dance gathered around a tall pole symbolizing the joining of heaven and earth. Songs and dances continue for hours with breaks for social dancing. Powwows are also popular. Dancers wearing elaborate costumes travel on the powwow circuit to compete for prizes and socialize during the summer. The Eastern Woodlands Indians, in the area from the Great Lakes to the Atlantic, celebrate each season with ceremonies that include about forty dance suites. These events are followed by social dancing [see MUSICS OF THE AMERICAN INDIAN/FIRST NATIONS IN THE UNITED STATES AND CANADA, p. 365].

Québécois tradition

Evidence exists of French settlers dancing at a masque performed at Port Royal in 1606. The French brought a strong dance tradition with them that often featured the square or longways formation. Step dancing or gigue also remains popular, with emphasis on complex, rhythmical footwork. The dance tradition is passed down, usually from father to child. Historically, Québécois families danced regularly in their homes, but the impact of television precipitated a decline in this practice. To counteract this trend, revival workshops are sponsored by the Fédération des loisiers-danse du Québec.

English community

The square dance remains the most popular dance performed by Anglophones. Scottish and Irish descendants maintain their dance traditions by enrolling their children in Irish or Scottish dance lessons. Competitions are held regularly, with dancers competing both nationally and internationally. Many Scottish adults enjoy country dancing through classes and social balls, especially in Ontario and the Maritimes. More recently, step dancing has grown in popularity, with regularly held competitions. Although old-timers tend to maintain the traditional style, younger participants now use taps to amplify the sound. Newfoundlanders perform step dances with intricate footwork close to the ground. Square, longways, and pantomimic dance games are also done by groups of dancers.

Later immigrants

Canada encourages immigrants to retain their heritage through an official policy of multiculturalism. Most large cities, especially Montréal, Toronto, and Vancouver, attract a culturally diverse population. During the last hundred years, there have been several waves of immigration since Confederation (1867), including northern Europeans in the late nineteenth century, southern Europeans after World War II, and immigrants from Third World countries after 1960. Many immigrants enrolled their Canadian-born children in ethnic dance classes in order to maintain cultural links. Toronto is one of the most ethnically diverse cities in the world, with immigrants representing more than 150 countries.

Since the Centennial and Expo 67, cultural traditions, and especially dancing, have been maintained across Canada. Many ethnic communities offer dance instruction; older children and young adults often participate in performance ensembles. Ukrainian and Hungarian groups in several cities have ensembles that tour extensively.

Toronto's Caribana was initiated in 1967 in order to celebrate the city's black community [see CARIBANA, p. 1207] and has grown into the largest Caribbean festival in North America, with a parade featuring music, dancing, and spectacular costumes. Over time, Caribana spawned similar festivals, such as Ottawa's Fête-Caribe and Montréal's Carifiesta, and in 1969 Leon and Zena Kossar established the Toronto Caravan, a nine-day event in which various communities share their culture. Displays, food, and performances by costumed dancers are traditionally followed by audience members participating in a simple dance. Similar events are now held in other cities.

Performers of non-Western dance

Across Canada, there are dancers highly trained in non-Western forms who work almost exclusively as dancers and teachers. There is a strong presence of East Indian dancers in Toronto, Vancouver, Ottawa, and Montréal. Some, such as Menaka Thakkar (figure 8) and Lata Pada in Toronto and Jai Govinda and Roger Sinha in Vancouver, offer extensive training and give regular performances.

FIGURE 8　Menaka Thakkar, Canada's most famous classical East Indian dancer, performing in the *Bharata Natyam* style.

Initially, funding was available only to mainstream ballet and modern dance companies, but since the early 1980s arts organizations have become more inclusive.

FIGURE 9   William Lau portraying a female in a Peking Opera production in Toronto.

There are also Chinese dance groups in Toronto and Vancouver (figure 9). Some teach only Chinese folk dancing, but others offer training that incorporates classical ballet. The Xing Dance Theatre in Toronto and Vancouver's Lorita Leung Dancers perform regularly. Korean and Filipino dance groups have also been established, primarily in Toronto.

Both African and Afro-Caribbean dance groups have emerged that offer training and provide a performance outlet through an attached company. Several groups, such as COBA (Collective of Black Artists), focus on West African dance (figure 10). Toronto's Ballet Creole and Canboulay Dance Theatre combine Caribbean forms with ballet and modern dance, and across Canada there are also Spanish and Middle Eastern dance companies, both of which are especially popular with women of all ages.

Most dance groups are not restricted to people from the sponsoring ethnic group, but attract a mix of interested dancers. There is a strong trend toward the fusion of dance styles. Vancouver's Kokoro blends Japanese *butoh* and modern; Toronto's Aminurta Kang fuses Mongolian and modern; and Montréal's Zelma Badu combines Ghanaian and modern dance. Several dancers from different cultures have worked together to create new dance works that blend the characteristics of each dance form.

Western theatrical forms

Major government and corporate funding still goes to the three largest dance companies—the National Ballet of Canada, Les Grands Ballets Canadiens, and the Royal Winnipeg Ballet—and to the more established modern dance groups—Toronto Dance Theatre, Dancemakers, and Le Groupe de la Place Royale. Most dancers supplement

FIGURE 10   Dancer from COBA (Collective of Black Artists) performing a West African dance. Photo by Joan Border, c. 1997.

their income with unemployment insurance. There is a burgeoning community of independent dance artists. Toronto's annual FFIDA (Fringe Festival of Independent Dance Artists) attracts dancers both locally and internationally. Other dancers are employed in musicals, summer theater, commercial shows, and videos. Some work in movement therapies such as Pilates or Alexander technique.

Social dance

Ballroom dancing is practiced across Canada, with many schools offering instruction and entering couples in local and national competitions. In the western provinces, Country and Western, square, and line dancing are popular, especially with seniors. There are many folk dance groups, often connected with universities, which teach international (mostly European) folk dancing in regular classes and workshops. Latin American dance has become increasingly popular with the recent influx of immigrants from Central and South America (figure 11). Rap and hip-hop are enjoyed by school-aged youngsters. Aerobics classes are offered by many recreational centers.

Dance in education

Ballet, jazz, tap, and modern dance are taught in local studios, and students often take graded examinations through organizations such as the Royal Academy of Dancing. Highly talented students audition annually to attend professional schools, such as the National Ballet School or L'École supérieure de danse.

In the 1990s dance was introduced into the public school system in several provinces. Because education is a provincial, not a federal, responsibility, the curricula are different across Canada but usually focus on creative work in the early grades and on the principles of modern dance in the senior grades. Most school boards require that the multicultural makeup of the school be acknowledged by the introduction of dances from diverse cultures.

At the postsecondary level, dance degree programs are offered at several universities, including Simon Fraser University, York University, and the Université du Québec à Montréal. Most provide a strong liberal arts background coupled with intensive dance training in modern dance and ballet.

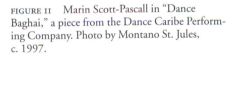

FIGURE 11   Marin Scott-Pascall in "Dance Baghai," a piece from the Dance Caribe Performing Company. Photo by Montano St. Jules, c. 1997.

Government support

Grants are available at the federal, provincial, and local levels for dance companies and artists. Funding began in 1957 with the founding of the Canada Council, and provincial and local arts councils emerged soon after. Grants are awarded by arm's-length committees composed of members of the arts community. Initially, funding was available only to mainstream ballet and modern dance companies, but since the early 1980s arts organizations have become more inclusive. New policies recognize the prominence of classical and fusion forms in addition to ballet and modern, but despite the increased number of eligible dance artists, funding has decreased dramatically, with various governments needing to rely increasingly on corporate sponsorship.

Dance resources

Most provinces officially sponsor organizations such as Dance Ontario, Dance Saskatchewan, and the Vancouver Dance Centre that disseminate information to the broad dance community and serve as dance advocates. Numerous websites have emerged, covering everything from theatrical dance companies to Country and Western and line dancing. The Dancer Transition Resource Centre provides advice and grants for professional dancers making the change to a new career. Dance Collection Danse, in Toronto, serves as an archive for Canadian theatrical dance materials and regularly publishes books on Canadian dance. Major dance collections are housed at York University, the Metropolitan Toronto Reference Library, the University of Waterloo, and the Vancouver Public Library.

—Mary Jane Warner

REFERENCES

Amin. Vols. 1–2. San Antonio, Texas: International Folk Culture Center.

Arabesque: A Magazine of International Dance. Vols. 1–22. New York: Arabesque.

Attitudes and Arabesques. Vols. 1–20. Menlo Park, Calif.: Getz Dance Library.

Casey, Betty. 1985. *Dance Across Texas.* Austin: University of Texas Press.

Cohen, Selma Jeanne, ed. 1998. *International Encyclopedia of Dance.* New York: Oxford University Press.

Collier, Cliff, and Pierre Guilmette. 1982. *Dance Resources in Canadian Libraries.* Ottawa: National Library of Canada.

Cornell, Katherine. 1999. "Dance Defined: An Examination of Canadian Cultural Policy on Multicultural Dance." In *Continents in Movement: Proceedings of the International Conference of The Meeting of Cultures in Dance History,* 45–50. Oieras, Portugal, 1998.

Dance Magazine. Vols. 1–74. Oakland, Calif.: Dance Magazine.

Dance Research Journal. Vols. 1–31. Brockport, N.Y.: CORD (Congress on Research in Dance).

Dance/USA Journal: For Professionals in Dance. Vols. 1–18. Washington, D.C.

Davis, Mary B., ed. 1994. *Native America in the Twentieth Century: An Encyclopedia.* New York: Garland.

DCA News. New York: Dance Critics Association.

Feder, Norman. 1964. "Origins of the Oklahoma Forty-Nine Dance." *Ethnomusicology* 8(3):290–294.

Kealiinohomoku, Joann W. 1972. "Folk Dance." In *Folklore and Folklife,* ed. Richard M. Dorson, 381–404. Chicago: University of Chicago Press.

———. 1976. "Theory and Methods for an Anthropological Study of Dance." Ph.D. dissertation, Indiana University.

———. 1978. "Hopi Social Dance Events and How They Function." *Discover,* 27–38. Santa Fe, N.M.: School of American Research.

———. 1998. "Folk Dance." In *Academic American Encyclopedia,* vol. 8, 199–201. Danbury, Conn.: Grolier.

Kurath, Gertrude. 1968. *Dance and Song Rituals of Six Nations Reserve.* Bulletin No. 220. Ottawa: National Museum.

Lau, William. 1991. "Chinese Dance Experience in Canadian Society: An Investigation of Four Chinese Dance Groups in Toronto." Master's thesis, York University.

Lomax, Alan. 1974. *Dance and Human History.* Berkeley: University of California Extension for Media and Independent Learning. Videocassette.

Lutz, Maija M. 1978. "The Effects of Acculturation on Eskimo Music of Cumberland Peninsula." Mercury Series, Canadian Ethnology Service Paper No. 41. Ottawa: National Museum of Man.

———. 1982. "Musical Traditions of the Labrador Coast Inuit." Mercury Series, Canadian Ethnology Service Paper No. 79. Ottawa: National Museum of Man.

Macpherson, Susan, ed. 2000. *Encyclopedia of Theatre Dance in Canada.* Toronto: Dance Collection/Danse Press.

Naimpally, Anuradha. 1988. "The Teaching of Bharata Natyam in Canada: Modifications within the Canadian Context." Master's thesis, York University.

Odom, Selma, and Mary Jane Warner, eds. 1994, 1997. *Canadian Dance Studies,* vols. 1 and 2. Toronto: York University, Graduate Programme in Dance.

Quigley, Colin. 1985. *Close to the Floor: Folk Dance in Newfoundland.* St. John's: Memorial University of Newfoundland.

Van Zile, Judy. 1982. *The Japanese Bon Dance in Hawaii.* Kailua, Hawai'i: Press Pacifica.

Viltis: A Magazine of Folklore and Folk Dance. Vols. 1–57. Milwaukee: International Institute of Wisconsin.

Voyer, Simonne. 1986. *La Danse traditionnelle dans l'est du Canada: Quadrilles et cotillons.* Québec: Les Presses de l'Université Laval.

Warner, Mary Jane. 1998. "Canada: Dance Education." In *International Encyclopedia of Dance,* ed. Selma Jeanne Cohen, 2:46–48. New York: Oxford University Press.

Wyman, Max. 1989. *Dance Canada: An Illustrated History.* Vancouver: Douglas and McIntyre.

Snapshot:
Two Popular Dance Forms
Carolyn H. Krasnow
Dorothea Hast

Disco—Carolyn H. Krasnow
Contra Dance—Dorothea Hast

Although almost any dance form could be used to illustrate the importance of movement and music in the creation and maintenance of social, gender, political, and/or ethnic identity in North America, two forms—disco and contra dance—are especially useful. Both imported from Western Europe, each with its own distinct historical and social context, disco and contra dance gained acceptance and developed along their own paths in North America. Disco, a form of dance first developed in France following World War II, became wildly popular in the United States in the 1970s and 1980s and led to the development of other popular urban dance forms. Contra dance—imported from England—developed initially in the rural communities of eighteenth- and nineteenth-century America and continues today in both rural and revivalist urban settings as a social dance of immense popularity.

DISCO

The term *disco* is a shortened form of discothèque, a French word meaning "record library," and refers generally to dance clubs that play recorded music rather than using live bands. The first venues to call themselves discothèques developed in France during the German occupation of World War II, when jazz was banned and underground clubs that wanted to continue playing it were forced to rely on contraband albums rather than live acts. Discothèques flourished in many cities after the war, playing dance music and popularizing steps like the Twist and the Peppermint Twist (named after The Peppermint Lounge, a New York disco). The mass popularity of discothèques declined in the mid-1960s as developments in rock began to move toward a more improvisational style that favored undemonstrative, individualistic dancing over the flamboyant displays typical of discos and that lent itself more to concert venues than to record mixes. Dance music and dance halls regained mass popularity in the mid-1970s, sparking a dance craze that would last through the decade. It is this period that has come to be most associated with the discothèque and whose music and dance are referred to simply as disco.

The revival of dance hall culture after its decline in the 1960s began as a localized, virtually underground scene in neighborhood clubs and parties in East Coast cities, particularly New York. Most clubs were located in areas where the dominant rock of

"Death to disco" slogans began appearing on tee shirts and elsewhere, radio stations featured antidisco call-in shows and promoted disco-free weekends, and some deejays began smashing disco records on the air.

the pop charts had less of a grip, particularly in African American and Caribbean communities where rhythm and blues, funk, salsa, and other dance musics continued to flourish. Discos also took hold in the emerging gay communities in New York's Greenwich Village and Fire Island. Underground gay clubs had been around for some time and had tended to rely on recorded music, as it was often difficult to find live bands to play at these clubs, but it was not until the post-Stonewall era (after 1969) that the clubs made their impact felt beyond their immediate communities. The emerging disco scene became a site where groups on the margins of the mainstream culture (which was reflected in rock) constituted alternative communities.

Rhythm and blues disco

The music circulating at these clubs in the early 1970s came primarily from independent rhythm and blues labels, although deejays tended to use a wide variety of musics on the dance floor, ranging from hard rock to African pop. Companies such as Philadelphia International produced dance music based in rhythm and blues and funk but with an increased emphasis on layers of tightly arranged strings, horns, and backing vocals. It was an urbane sound—smooth but also pulsing and edgy—whose combinations of strong dance riffs with rich timbres and arrangements worked well on huge dance-floor sound systems. Songs in this vein, by groups such as the O'Jays and Harold Melvin and the Bluenotes, found consistent success on the rhythm and blues charts and, increasingly, on the pop charts as well, paving the way for the emergence and success of new dance-oriented labels such as T.K. Records in Miami. By the middle of the decade, hits from these producers and the surprise chart success of seemingly obscure club hits such as Manu Dibango's "Soul Makossa" gave dance music significant momentum; the huge success of Van McCoy's "The Hustle" in 1975—both the song and the dance that went with it—turned disco into a national trend.

Eurodisco

Clubs spread across the country and, until the end of the 1970s, remained one of the most popular forms of entertainment. The music, too, continued to expand and increase its success on the charts. Rhythm and blues disco was joined by Eurodisco, a style from the continent that relied largely on synthesized instrumentation and effects. Lacking the footing in the rhythm and blues idioms that carried American disco, Eurodisco sounded more purely electronic, often more futuristic. Some tunes were long, thematic works that were closer to film scores. But it shared with its American counterpart the favored disco beat and tempo (mostly in the range of 110 to 140 beats per minute), which worked well for dancers and for deejays trying to keep transitions smooth. It also demonstrated a similar regard for meticulous, intricate production and the resulting rich layers of sound. Donna Summer, an American recording artist in Germany with Giorgio Moroder, was Eurodisco's most prominent star. Most of the other big stars in the United States (Gloria Gaynor, Chic, Sister Sledge, and others) were of the r and b school [see R&B AND SOUL, p. 667; FUNK, p. 680].

The disco ethos

Rhythm and blues disco and Eurodisco shared with the many other idiosyncratic disco hits an ability to rekindle interest in dance halls and dancing. Rock had put great emphasis on its stars, but because disco circulated almost entirely through records, stars were less dominant; instead, the focus was on the dancers themselves and on the social milieu of the club. In this way discos recalled earlier times, when dance clubs, from the smallest neighborhood gathering places to the most elite nightclubs, were focal points of entertainment. Discos revived the popularity of showy choreography for couples and groups (line dances) as well as elaborate freestyle solo and couple dancing that made the dancers the stars. This tendency was highlighted by the film *Saturday Night Fever* in 1977. Steps like the Hustle and the Bus Stop harkened back to earlier dance crazes like the Lindy Hop and the Jitterbug, reviving a long tradition of popular dance culture (including a renewed interest in dance schools and contests) that had largely disappeared during the height of sixties rock. Some dances, like the Tango Hustle and the Swing, were simply updated versions of the older Tango and Lindy Hop.

This is not to say that disco functioned as a nostalgia movement, however. Although aspects of the dancing and milieu resembled those of earlier eras, almost everything else about disco club culture indicated a heightened attention to contemporary mores and styles. Following the legacy of the sixties in overturning old taboos, disco publicly celebrated the sexual revolution, welcoming it as a vital expression of modern social experience. This ethos manifested itself in some of the explicit moves common on dance floors (as the dance called the Bump suggests) and in the liberal dress code, which in many places allowed for hitherto unimaginable displays of undress. It was also evident in the casual acceptance at many discos of open homosexuality, which was still taboo in most other contexts, and in its implicit sanctioning of public sexual activity at the clubs. The sensual culture of disco constituted a brave-new-world aesthetic, one that embraced, and happily exaggerated, the look of modern life.

Disco culture

This ultramodern sensibility was further evident in other aspects of disco style. While some dances were reminiscent of earlier modes, with flowing skirts and high heels recalling the elegant ballroom dancing of earlier eras, others were meant to evoke a science fiction world of robots, an image often enhanced sartorially by futuristic compositions of metallic fabrics and glittering body paint. Club decor, too, often strove for this effect. In New York City, Xenon featured a spaceship that would descend over the crowd, while Studio 54 decorated its postindustrial-looking space with hundreds of pulsing lights and manufactured fog. Xenon and Studio 54 were particularly lavish clubs, but their basic sensibility was common throughout the scene: flashing lights, strobes, and other visual effects as well as engulfing sound systems dominated these venues, while the music filling the spaces was itself replete with the newest advances in sound engineering. Deejaying also demonstrated a preoccupation with new technologies, as deejays pioneered new mixing techniques using multiple turntables and speed controls to produce a seamless transition between songs. The constant stream of sound, without any jarring changes in tempo or even a missed beat, was an important musical innovation in dance-hall culture, and the deejays who maneuvered sound and lights effectively were themselves treated as disco stars.

Rock fans, including critics and deejays, were hostile toward disco from the start; as the disco phenomenon grew toward the end of the 1970s, so did the antagonism. "Death to disco" slogans began appearing on tee shirts and elsewhere, radio stations featured antidisco call-in shows and promoted disco-free weekends, and some deejays began smashing disco records on the air. In 1979 one deejay in Chicago outdid all others by sponsoring a disco demolition rally at Comiskey Park, at which disco records were collected and demolished by explosives on the field. Rock fans justified their violent opposition in aesthetic terms—that good music was being driven from the radio by technology-laden dance music—and celebrated the death of disco at the end of the decade. From another perspective, the war on disco was one in which music coming from the margins was viewed as an invading force that threatened the dominance of European American rock: in the name of freeing the airwaves, rock fans, most of them European Americans, gleefully destroyed records made predominantly by African American artists.

The disco legacy

Disco did lose its huge national following after 1979, but critics who celebrated its death underestimated the lasting impact of its innovations. The mixing techniques pioneered by deejays at clubs and dance parties served as the foundation of the virtuosic turntable art of rap deejays that redefined musicianship starting in 1979. And disco style—production values, mixing techniques, club milieu—would survive and constitute the essence of house and techno, which have dominated club scenes since the 1980s and, like rap, reenvisioned music and dance culture.

—Carolyn H. Krasnow

CONTRA DANCE

Contemporary contra dances may be described as progressive figure dances involving two or more couples who dance together in two lines called a set. Each dance consists of several basic figures combined from a stock vocabulary. Dancers move symmetrically through choreographed floor tracks set to tunes each thirty-two measures in length—one time through the music equals one time through the entire dance sequence. The dance and music will typically repeat over and over again in performance, depending on the number of couples in a set. Dancers use a kind of lilting walking step through most of the figures.

Couples are either active, progressing down the set as a pair during each time through the dance, or inactive and progressing up the set. A traditional core unit in the set is the group of four, composed of an active couple and their neighbors, an inactive couple. For each time through the dance, each couple has a new set of neighbors. Dancers interact with their partners for such figures as "balance and swing," with their neighbors during figures such as "star right" or "circle right," and with the entire set during figures such as "forward and back in long lines." It is this combination of dancing with a partner, dancing with many neighbors, and working as a team during the course of each dance that makes contra dancing a unique form of American participatory dance and one that promotes a high degree of interpersonal interaction and community spirit (figure 1).

Contra dance music

The current contra dance music repertoire is a blend of dance-tune traditions. Many tunes are of Irish, Scottish, English, French Canadian, Cape Breton, and American origin, and some date back to eighteenth-century sources. Tunes such as "Hull's Victory," "Chorus Jig," and "Flowers of Edinburgh" became New England standards (now referred to as "old chestnuts") by the end of the nineteenth century and are still associated with contra dances of the same name (figure 2). Most tunes that enter the repertoire now are not associated with specific dances and retain associations with their ethnic origins. Newly composed tunes also make up a significant portion of the repertoire.

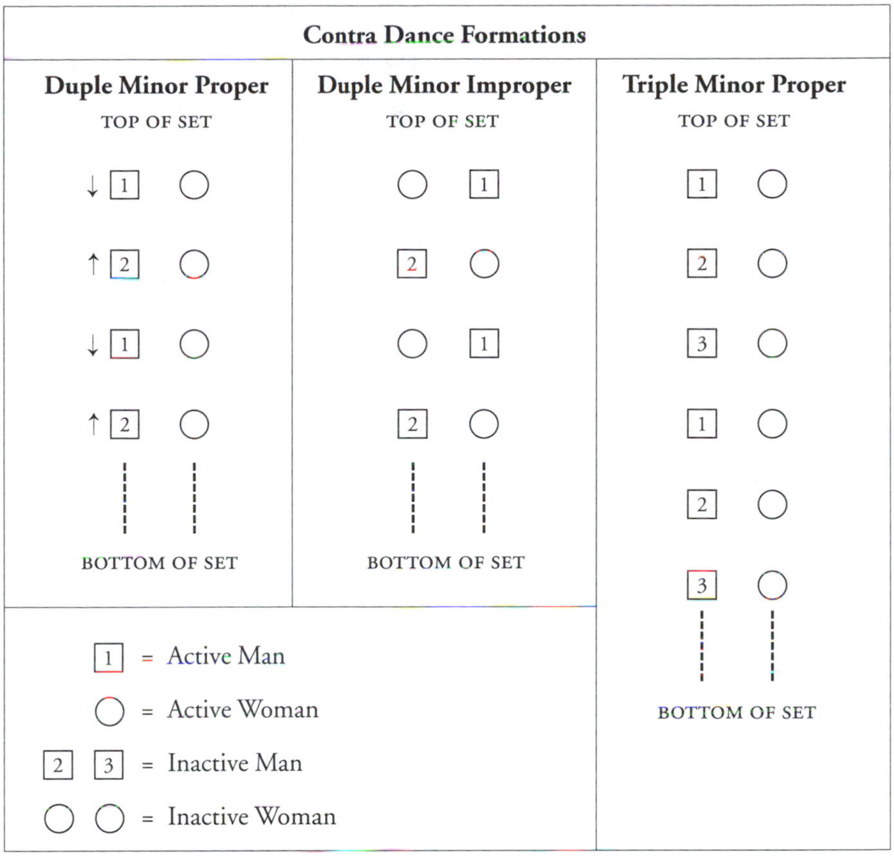

FIGURE 1   To form a traditional contra dance set, the dancers stand in two lines extending from the caller and band to the opposite end of the room. In one kind of set (duple proper), men are on one side and women on the other. In a duple improper set, men and women vary in each line.

Contra Dance Formations

Duple Minor Proper	**Duple Minor Improper**	**Triple Minor Proper**
TOP OF SET	TOP OF SET	TOP OF SET

1 = Active Man
○ = Active Woman
2 3 = Inactive Man
○ ○ = Inactive Woman

Lady of the Lake	
A1	First couple cross over, balance and swing the one below (16).
A2	First couple balance and swing in the middle (16).
B1	First couple down center and back. (16)
B2	Cast off; all right and left through (16).

FIGURE 2   Notation for one of the old chestnuts in the New England contra dance repertoire. Note the regularity of the phrasing. Figures conform to one strain of the music (8 bars or 16 steps). The inactives do not move until B2.

Regardless of nationality, contemporary contra dance tunes usually adhere to the widely shared parameters of the Anglo-Irish-American fiddle tune structure. Most fiddle tunes have two parts, an A section and a B section, each eight measures long. These sections are repeated in performance to create a form that is thirty-two measures long (AABB)—the average length of a contra. The tune types most commonly played are reels (in 4/4), hornpipes (in 4/4), jigs (in 6/8), and marches (in 2/4). In contemporary performance practice, tunes are for the most part interchangeable—any tune that adheres to this basic structure can potentially be used for any dance. Although bands or callers may try to match tunes with dances, citing mood, emotion, flow, smoothness, or bounce as important concerns, individual tunes do not often become associated with a particular dance and are usually changed for the next performance. Bands often string together tunes to form medleys during the course of one contra in order to add melodic variety, both for the players and for the dancers.

The contra dance event

As a social participatory dance form, contra dance performance involves a caller, musicians, and dancers. Dances take place on a regular basis at specified venues, including churches, town halls, and grange halls. All of these locations have wooden floors, which are important for the dancers, and all have live music. The bands usually consist of at least three players, with fiddle and piano as core instruments. Other instruments may include flute, concertina, accordion, mandolin, tin whistle, clarinet, guitar, and bass. Contra dance events are open to the public at a nominal cost, and anyone can join in without attending a class. Many dancers travel considerable distances to attend dances that are organized by local callers, bands, or committees. They may be held on a weekly, biweekly, or monthly basis, and each has its regulars as a well as a varying percentage of casual participants and newcomers.

Contra dance, as an accessible, ensemble-oriented, participatory dance and music form, provided a link between an old New England tradition, popular mediated folk music, and counterculture values.

Contra dance history in New England

Contra dances are part of a larger genre of figure dances called country dances—a generic term for group, mixed-sex dances in line, square, and round formation. Originating in England before the sixteenth century, these dances became the most popular urban social dance genre in the eighteenth century. Exported to America as well as throughout Europe, country dances played an important role in the expressive culture of the colonists. By the mid-eighteenth century, the terms "country dance," "progressive longways formation," and "longways for as many as will" became synonymous as the circle and square formations dropped out of fashion. By the 1780s, Americans began to call these dances *contras,* although both *country* and *contra* were used interchangeably throughout the nineteenth century.

John Griffiths, an itinerant dancing master in New England, was the first to publish collections of country dances in America in the 1780s. His 1788 publication, *A Collection of the Newest and Most Fashionable Country Dances and Cotillions,* contained twenty-nine contras. Unlike most of the earlier English collections, Griffith's anthology contained instructions for dances without accompanying musical notation or indications of how the music matched the dance.

By the mid-nineteenth century, new dances such as the waltz, polka, and quadrille became enormously popular in both urban and rural settings in the United States. The quadrille, a country dance in square formation, was exported from France to England around 1815 and soon after to America, where it quickly became a favorite dance form. Quadrille bands were employed to accompany the dances, and a large body of music repertoire was published in parts for the typical quadrille band of first violin, second violin, clarinet, two cornets, bass, flute, viola, cello, trombone, and piano, as well as for smaller ensembles.

Folk histories record that contras were gradually displaced by the introduction of the quadrille and the new couple dances. Extant mid- to late-nineteenth-century dance manuals seem to substantiate this theory. Although contras were increasingly equated with quadrilles (as country dances) in order to differentiate them from the popular round or couple dances, many of the quadrille call-books that were published at this time made little or no reference to contras. Contra dance tunes that appeared in printed anthologies such as Elias Howe's *Musicians Omnibus* (c. 1861–1882) were a small and fairly static core of repertoire. Howe, a prolific Boston music publisher, as well as other publishers of the day, recycled the same repertoire of tunes linked to dances (often with dance directions printed directly underneath the score) over and over again. Many of these, however, were popular fiddle tunes in their own right, including "The Flowers of Edinburgh," "Fisher's Hornpipe," and "Money Musk."

Although sources suggest that contras were out of favor in urban areas during this period, the fact that they continued to appear in print suggests that they were still performed in northeastern cities, at least for home entertainment. It is also likely that they were performed in certain regions and contexts more than others. Dances that were held in rural New England kitchens (called "kitchen junkets") might have included more contras than dance events sponsored by a club, society, church, fraternal organization, or business in New York City. Because the dancers of the mid- to late-nineteenth century apparently liked a mix of dance formations and rhythms, ranging from the large group dances to waltzes, polkas, and schottisches, it appears that even in urban areas one or two contras would often be thrown in to round out an evening's program.

Twentieth-century revivals

By the end of the nineteenth century, quadrilles and contras were both considered old-fashioned participatory dance forms. In the mid-1920s, however, Henry Ford helped to initiate what he called a "square dance revival," which brought squares and some contras, as well as old-time fiddling and fiddle contests, into the U.S. mainstream as a highly mediated reaction against contemporary music and dance genres such as jazz, tango, and the Charleston. By using the contemporary media of his day, including recordings, radio, newspapers, and books, Ford launched a reactionary campaign, but one that brought square dancing and square dance music into homes, schools, town halls, and automobile showrooms across the country.

Mid- to late twentieth century

Although interest in square dance peaked by the late 1920s, a new generation of enthusiasts emerged during the early 1940s. By the mid-1940s, square dancing had become popular at both urban and rural public dance events throughout the country and was included in the physical education curriculum in many public schools. As square dancing became more popular, the square dance club became an organizational model around which a small commercial industry thrived. Contra dances played little part in the square dance movement, although some callers continued to use them. Ralph Page, a square dance caller from Keene, New Hampshire, was an important proponent of contras and taught them all over the United States, Europe, and Japan. He was probably the first touring caller to specialize in New England material, and he always included contras at his dance events. As caller, composer, and choreographer, his influence on the next generation of callers was considerable.

By the 1960s, the "longways for as many as will" contra formation emerged again as a genre in its own right, but this time as part of an oppositional youth subculture. Dudley Laufman, a dance caller and musician from Boston, adopted southern New Hampshire as his new home, where he was one of a few key individuals at the center of this resurgence of contra dance. He acted as a catalyst for creating what is now a nationwide grassroots network of dancers, callers, and musicians. It was at this time that dance events began to be called contra dances, in order to differentiate them from the more mainstream square dances. Although the name of the event changed, dances other than contras were usually danced, including traditional squares, circle mixers, and couple dances such as waltzes, polkas, and *hambos* (a Swedish couple dance).

Participants were primarily white urbanites of college age, many of whom had similar social values stemming from opposition to the Vietnam War and a belief in living an alternative, communal, and rural lifestyle. Contra dance, as an accessible, ensemble-oriented, participatory dance and music form, provided a link between an old New England tradition, popular mediated folk music, and counterculture values. Mobility was a key element in the transmission of the genre, as participants were travelers and transitory college students. Therefore, although the revitalization of contra dance took place in New England, people were contra dancing and playing contra dance music in many cities and college towns throughout the United States by the mid-1970s.

The contra dance community today

At the beginning of the twenty-first century, the activity continues to grow nationally and to attract new participants, but it has lost its oppositional status as part of a youth culture. Many of the dancers, musicians, and callers are in their thirties and forties, although people of all ages attend dances. The tradition itself has been transformed over time by the inclusion of thousands of new dances and tunes and by changes in performance style. It is hard to locate contra dancers as a group, except as a collection of individuals brought together by their love of dancing. In many ways, the contra dance community is formed on the dance floor and maintained through the regular repetition of dancing and music making at specific dance events. On a larger scale it can be viewed as part of a noncorporate national movement or network in which participants know of one another through dance calendars, travel, recordings, touring callers and bands, dance camps, newsletters, and the Internet but are not bound together by any national organization. Contra dance is also a genre of participatory dance placed under the umbrella of all that is folk dance, a relationship often reinforced and celebrated at numerous traditional music and dance festivals where contra dance is featured along with social dances and traditional music from around the world.

—Dorothea Hast

REFERENCES

Bealle, John. 1989. "American Folklore Revival: A Study of an Old-Time Music and Dance Community." Ph.D. dissertation, Indiana University.

George, Nelson. 1989. "Crossover: The Death of Rhythm and Blues (1975–1979)." In *The Death of Rhythm & Blues,* ed. 129–143. New York: E. P. Dutton.

Goldman, Albert. 1978. *Disco.* New York: Hawthorn.

Griffiths, John. 1788. *A Collection of the Newest and Most Fashionable Country Dances and Cotillions, The Greater Part by Mr. John Griffiths, Dancing Master, in Providence.* Providence, R.I.

Hast, Dorothea. 1993. "Performance, Transformation, and Community: Contra Dance in New England." *Dance Research Journal* 25(1):21–32.

———. 1994. "Music, Dance, and Community: Contra Dance in New England." Ph.D. dissertation, Wesleyan University.

Hendrickson, Charles Cyril. 1989. *Early American Dance and Music: John Griffiths, Dancing Master, 29 Country Dances.* Sandy Hook, Conn.: The Hendrickson Group.

Hillgrove, Thomas. 1864. *A Complete Practical Guide to the Art of Dancing.* New York: Dick and Fitzgerald.

Holden, Stephen. 1979. "The Evolution of a Dance Craze." *Rolling Stone* 289:29–30.

Howe, Elias. 1858. *Howes Complete Ball-Room Hand Book.* Boston: Brown, Taggard, and Chase.

———. c. 1861. *Musicians Omnibus.* Boston: Elias Howe.

Jennings, Larry. 1983. *Zesty Contras.* Cambridge, Mass.: New England Folk Festival Association.

Keller, Kate Van Winkle. 1989. *Early American Dance and Music: John Griffiths, Eighteenth-Century Itinerant Dancing Master.* Sandy Hook, Conn.: The Hendrickson Group.

Keller, Kate Van Winkle, and Ralph Sweet. 1975. *A Choice Selection of American Country Dances of the Revolutionary Era 1775–1795.* New York: Country Song and Dance Society.

Krasnow, Carolyn. 1993. "Fear and Loathing in the Seventies: Race, Sexuality, and Disco." *Stanford Humanities Review* 3(2):37–45.

Melanson, Jim, et al. 1975. "The Disco Phenomenon Goes On and On." *Billboard* 87:D-2–38.

Mooney, Hugh. 1980. "Disco: A Music for the 1980s?" *Popular Music and Society* 7(2):84–94.

Parkes, Tony. 1992. *Contra Dance Calling.* Bedford, Mass.: Hands Four Books.

Shannon, Doug. 1982. *Off the Record: The Disco Concept.* Cleveland: Pacesetter.

Shaw, Arnold. 1986. "The Disco Craze." In *Black Popular Music in America,* ed. 249–256. New York: Schirmer.

Smucker, Tom. 1980. "Disco." In *The Rolling Stone Illustrated History of Rock and Roll,* ed. Jim Miller, 425–434. New York: Random House/Rolling Stone Press.

Tolman, Beth, and Ralph Page. 1976. *The Country Dance Book.* Brattleboro, Vt.: The Stephen Greene Press.

Villari, Jack, and Kathleen Sims Villari. 1978. *Disco Dance Steps.* Secaucus, N.J.: Chartwell.

Technology and Media

Anthony Seeger
Paul Théberge

A Model of Music Performance—Anthony Seeger
Conceptualization of a Music Performance—Anthony Seeger
Music, Technology, and Media in the United States—Anthony Seeger
Music, Technology, and Media in Canada—Paul Théberge

The sounds of music cannot be separated from the technology involved in their conception, performance, transmission, and audience reception because the technology is an integral part of the sounds themselves. By technology I mean a manner of accomplishing a task, especially using technical processes, methods or knowledge.

With the exception of the unamplified human voice, unaccompanied or accompanied by naturally occurring objects such as stones or sticks used as musical instruments, some technology is involved in the production of all music. The use of new technological processes has increased tremendously during the past few hundred years, partly as a result of the evolution of many kinds of music into commodities that are marketed and through which money or other rewards are obtained not only by the musicians but also by others involved in music's creation, performance, and dissemination. Yet even in areas where musical performances confer prestige rather than income, technological innovations have in many cases transformed the sounds themselves. Virtually every aspect of the music of North America has been affected by technological changes during the past five hundred years.

Composers and performers can produce a variety of sounds, limited largely by their cultural traditions, their ideas, and the technology they are using. Yet, composers and performers carry out only two of the many roles that may be involved in a musical performance. Consider the number of people required to present a symphony orchestra or a touring popular music band today. They include publicists, printers, ushers, stagehands, security personnel, concession workers, and sound engineers, to name just a few. Although musicians and composers often take advantage of new technical possibilities, many other figures are involved in the process of technological development—from technology-introducing outsiders to systematic inventors, craftspeople, patent officers, government agencies, lawyers, manufacturers, marketers, stores, and salespeople. Sometimes a technology has appeared and lingered, waiting for some other development to spark its widespread use. Entire industries have sprung up, profited, withered, gone bankrupt, or been transformed by changing uses of technology in musical composition, transmission, performance, and reception.

A MODEL OF MUSIC PERFORMANCE

To simplify matters for this discussion, consider a simple model of musical performance. Following writings by Alan Merriam (1964) and others, any musical performance includes a process of conceptualization, a performance location, a performance by musicians that creates a flow of sound waves, a carrier that moves those waves from the performers to the audience, the audience itself, and the evaluation of the performance by the audience, the musicians, the conceptualizers, and other interested parties. Each of these elements may have several distinct parts, and they interact with each other (figure 1).

CONCEPTUALIZATION	PERFORMANCE	PERFORMANCE	SOUND CARRIER	AUDIENCE	EVALUATION
composition & planning the performance	space: location of performers & audiences	musicians create sounds or voice &/or instruments	air, amplifier, audio/video recording	group/indiv. & cultural background	by all participants

FIGURE I   Elements of a musical performance.

Here is an example of a simple performance: a parent wants to put a baby to sleep and plans to sing a lullaby; he or she either makes up a lullaby or recalls an existing one (conceptualization). The performance space is the child's bedroom with low light and relative silence; the musical instrument producing the stream of sound waves is the parent's unaccompanied voice; the voice is carried directly through the air, without the mediation of any equipment; the audience is a solitary child. If the child reacts by falling asleep (an evaluation of the event of a sort), the parent will consider the performance to have been a success and probably try the same thing again. If, however, the parent sings the same song to the child on a noisy street corner (different performance space), the child may not fall asleep. The parent might then try changing the performance space (to the bedroom), or he or she might sing a different song (different conceptualization and different stream of sound waves), use a prerecorded lullaby, or stop trying to put the child to sleep.

The lullaby example illustrates that a change in any one of the elements of a musical performance event may stimulate or require changes in the others. Thus, preparing a composition for a large performance space without amplification might encourage a composer to increase the number of instruments on each part. Or the composer's desire for more instruments on each part might inspire the construction of larger performance spaces—even if only temporary tents. The availability of amplifiers and large speakers, on the other hand, might enable the use of fewer musicians and softer instruments. If the audience is an individual at home and the signal carrier is a radio broadcast or an audio recording, then the conceptualization of the performance might change and the production and carrier of the sound would differ greatly from that of a live concert. A change in the sonic capabilities of musical instruments (sound producers) may stimulate composers to new genres and composition techniques, which might themselves result in new types of performance events. In every case, the evaluation of the audience—broadly defined to include the composer, the performers, the listeners, the producers, the financiers, and all the other figures involved in the performance and dissemination of music—plays an important role in whether that type of performance will be repeated. If all parties dislike it, the performance is not likely to be repeated; if one aspect is criticized it might be changed; if the carrying medium is criticized it might be improved.

Certainly, many of the most obvious technological transformations of music developed as a result of the introduction of new (or transformed) musical instruments and the invention of sound recording and playback. Yet some changes in musical performances are offshoots of wider-reaching social and technological transformations that have occurred in North America—and throughout the world—during the past five hundred years. Changing settlement patterns and improved transportation in both rural and urban areas facilitated audience attendance and musicians' travel. An emerging social class with leisure time and a high evaluation of music created new markets for musical instruments, music boxes, and music playback machines. Audience expectations of comfort (padded seats and air conditioning, to name only two) have altered the acoustics of many performance spaces at the same time as the study of acoustics itself has modified the design of spaces in which music is performed. Sound recording, invented in 1877, radio transmissions beginning in the 1920s, "talking" (or "singing") movies in the 1930s, and television since the 1950s have all been parts of a dramatic technological and aesthetic transformation of musical performance from a face-to-face encounter with the performer to an experience in which a "medium" is inserted between the performance event and the hearing of it—a medium that enables more distant listening and also imposes certain constraints on the musicians.

The same technological developments that influenced musical performance have also stimulated the growth of many music-related institutions, including media libraries and archives (unthinkable without sound recording), Musicology and Ethnomusicology departments and their associated electronic analysis and composition laboratories, university specializations in music technology and field recording techniques, professional societies with regular meetings in far-flung parts of the country or the world, and multi-volume encyclopedias of music.

—ANTHONY SEEGER

CONCEPTUALIZATION OF A MUSIC PERFORMANCE

The kinds of conceptualization required for a musical performance vary from culture to culture and from event to event within any given culture. The planning of a musical performance, whether a new composition or an ancient ritual repeated without changes, usually includes an evaluation of the technology for the performance itself (the acoustics of the space, the characteristics of the instruments to be used), the medium to be used for transmission, and the interests and preferences of the audience. Although composition technology has altered dramatically in the past half-century, most of the changes affecting conceptualization have appeared in other aspects of the performance event, described next.

Performance space

Performance spaces have changed dramatically during the past five hundred years. In general they have become larger, as have the audiences for musical performances. It may be argued that the appearance of a large middle class that considered musical performances to be prestigious and desirable created the demand for larger venues. The emerging need to pay performers more money has stimulated the use of larger performance venues and audio recordings, often altering the sounds themselves. Earlier performance spaces continue to be used, however. Unamplified places of religious worship and the kitchen and porch are still places where music is performed and appreciated. While some earlier locations continue to be popular, many new locations have been added since the colonial period, including music halls, sports stadiums, radio, television, and the Internet. The architectural design of performance spaces is complex, and poor acoustics today are often compensated for by sound reinforcement using loudspeakers. Instruments abandoned because they were not loud enough for large performance spaces have returned since the use of amplification.

While the significance of performance spaces continues today (for example, certain music is usually sung in a church; other music is never sung in a church), transmission

Musical performance is defined here as the actual production of the sounds themselves by musicians or machines.

media and amplified sounds have altered some of the spatial requirements for musical performances. The acoustics of space can even be replicated electronically. Although neither the performers nor the audience ever appeared in a cathedral, the sounds may seem to have been produced there and give the listener the illusion of being there with the performers.

Musical performance

Musical performance is defined here as the actual production of the sounds themselves by musicians or machines. Musical instruments, the playing techniques appropriate to human bodies using specific physical artifacts, and vocal styles are important features of musical performance. Important technological innovations here include the modification and invention of new musical instruments, the reinforcement of a sound by adding more instruments of a given kind, and the encouragement of new musical styles by electric amplification.

—ANTHONY SEEGER

MUSIC, TECHNOLOGY, AND MEDIA IN THE UNITED STATES

In the precolonial period, prior to 1492, North American Indians employed a variety of technologies in the manufacture of musical instruments. The acoustic knowledge and skill used to produce even an apparently simple rattle, flute, or drum should not be underestimated, even though the production may require few implements and no machines. Many decisions made in the manufacture of a traditional instrument are based on past experience and experimentation. Technology need not be complex to have a profound influence on musical sounds.

The simplest form of technological change occurs when a community borrows a new technology from another community. Innovations were certainly passed from one American Indian group to another—one might adopt the musical instruments or singing style of another, modifying them to its own preferences. The process of inter-tribal musical exchange continues into the beginning of the twenty-first century with the widespread adaptation of the Plains Indian drum manufacture and singing style at intertribal powwows—facilitated by books, recordings, and videotapes.

During the first three hundred years after 1492, most parts of North America were colonies of European powers. Their colonial status affected both their technology and musical styles. Colonialism is partly characterized by the dominant relationship between the colonial power and its subject colonies in which the colonies provide raw materials to the mother country and purchase finished products from it. Most colonies were prohibited by law from a number of manufacturing activities. Their economic dependency was often paralleled by a cultural dependency. The musical dependency of North America on Europe (especially England, France, and Spain) continued even after the United States became independent in the eighteenth century. Until the mid-nineteenth century most of the musical genres and performance styles of the wealthy were imported from, or directly imitative of, the mother countries. The less wealthy rural dwellers often passed their traditions within the community, made their own instruments out of materials at hand, and transmitted their music without music publishers or imported instruments. Enslaved Africans and American Indians often continued to practice earlier musical traditions on a reduced scale in the framework of large and terrible changes in their lives and in the face of religious and secular influences from European settlers. Because of regional isolation, personal preference, and artistic innovation, the musical instruments of rural North America varied widely from place to place and instrument maker to instrument maker.

Instruments

Some European immigrants to North America brought with them skills with which they set up industries in the United States. For example, makers of keyboard instruments came as early as the late 1700s, but they did not begin to transform the existing European technology until the 1830s. The establishment of the United States as a nation, with copyright and patents stipulated in its constitution, was an important factor in the independent development of musical technology within that country.

The piano

With the nineteenth century came the industrialization and standardization of many musical instruments and the replacement of certain ensembles by new ones. The history of the piano is especially significant because of the large numbers manufactured and sold, the stimulus piano sales gave to the sheet music publishing industry, and the role the piano has long played in music education. Encouraged to innovate by the system of patents and the possibility of profits, nineteenth-century U.S. innovations in piano technology (the development of the one-piece metal frame being probably the most important) transformed the industry from one based in England and France to one based in the United States, just as much of manufacture of keyboards (acoustic and electronic) in the late twentieth century would move the center of production to Asia. The piano was capable of playing many genres, from European classical music to locally popular barroom dance music, and it was found in many middle-class homes as well as in churches, brothels, bars, and other venues in which musical performance was a significant feature (but not necessarily the entire focus) of the events taking place therein. The automatic, or player, piano, which played the encoded contents (long rolls of perforated paper or cardboard), was one of the earliest and most accurate sound recording devices developed in the nineteenth century, and the digital keyboard is a central part of contemporary popular music. The development of the piano has acoustic, technical, and social components, all of which influence the use of the instrument today.

The banjo

The banjo also underwent major transformations in the late nineteenth and early twentieth centuries (the number of patents for banjos peaked in the 1920s). Unlike the piano, whose manufacturers emigrated from Europe, the original banjo makers and players were the descendants of enslaved Africans. Partly in response to the use of the banjo in larger halls and in ensembles, the instrument was transformed from a homemade, fretless, gut-stringed instrument with a skin stretched over a variety of types of resonators to an industrially produced, fretted, metal-stringed, resonator-equipped instrument capable of a louder and more "accurate" sound when playing with bands in large concert halls. Playing techniques, the ethnic identity of many of the performers, and attitudes about the banjo itself also changed with the technological modernization of the instrument—a process probably common to the transformation of many musical instruments.

New instruments

Technological developments not only transformed existing instruments like the piano and the banjo, they enabled the manufacture and use of entirely new instruments. Many musical instruments were invented and patented in the nineteenth century, some of them in Europe and some in the United States and Canada. One of these was the accordion (patented in 1829, Vienna), whose loud volume and ability to play chords resulted in its widespread adoption for dance bands. In some places the accordion replaced earlier dance music ensembles, just as the brass band replaced the fife and drum at public events and spectacles during the same century. The autoharp, a chorded zither, was patented in the United States in 1882 and was selling nearly three thousand units a week in the 1890s. The autoharp practically disappeared in the early twentieth century but became popular again during the folk music revival partly because of the influence of 1930s recordings of the Carter family and those they inspired—an example of how an influential musician or group can spark the popularization of an instrument.

In some cases instruments developed from musicians' specific wishes. The sousaphone, a type of tuba, was manufactured for John Philip Sousa in the 1890s. Pete Seeger's use of a three-fret extension on his five-string banjo led to manufacture of extra-long-necked banjos, including Vega's Pete Seeger Model in the 1960s. In other cases musicians simply had instruments specially made for them—some preferring extra-wide necks, others preferring the use of certain woods. Some instruments were invented to the extent that their very name is a trademark. The Dobro guitar was originally developed by John Dopyera and his brothers in 1926 (the name combines their name and relationship) in response to a demand for a louder guitar. This instrument, although supplanted in the 1940s by the electric guitar, continued to be used in country music and other genres.

As was the case with the Dobro guitar, part of the evolution of musical instrument manufacture was devoted to producing louder instruments (or those with brighter timbres) that could be played in larger performance spaces. The evolution of performance venues and the development of instrument technology to a certain extent paralleled one another until the invention of electronic sound amplification using microphones, amplifiers, and loudspeakers made it possible to use quieter instruments and vocal styles and still be heard in a large hall. The invention of loudspeaker systems itself also launched a new wave of instrument invention and manufacture that would take advantage of the new possibilities.

Electronic and synthesized instruments

Electric amplifiers and loudspeakers, which improved rapidly after World War II, developed along with new instruments. Important among these were the electric guitar and the electric keyboard. The electric guitar was more than an amplified guitar; its design permitted a number of performance styles that were not previously possible. In addition to the amplification of the strings themselves, the electronic signals produced by the instrument could be modified in a number of ways that added to its flexibility. The electronic keyboard is also capable of many sounds impossible to produce on the instrument from which it evolved.

The digitalization of sound waves sparked another wave of instrument invention that transformed the conceptualization, performance, and analysis of music. The MIDI synthesizer permitted musicians to compose on the keyboard with virtually unlimited sonic capabilities, play back their compositions, and even print certain kinds of scores. Digitalization has modified the conceptualization of both composers and producers, the production of the sounds, some of the performance spaces, and some of the media through which music can be transferred—increasingly over telephone lines on the Internet. It has also led to lawsuits (particularly in the area of digital quotation or sampling in some genres) and to the redefinition of intellectual property in music and other domains.

Throughout the entire spectrum of musical activities, the second half of the twentieth century was the occasion of constant technological innovation in musical instruments and consequent change in performance. Some instruments have changed little, although they are often amplified in performance, like the jaw harp, whose quiet overtones could scarcely be heard a foot away until the microphone could amplify them. In other cases the instruments themselves are new, and the use of signal modification or previously recorded sounds that are played along with the live performance have at times blurred the line between performance and the playback of a recording. There is no indication that this evolution will slow down in the near future—although at times musicians revert to acoustic instruments in order to take advantage of the potentials of the earlier instruments.

Sound carriers and dissemination

Dissemination in this sense means simply how the sounds get from the performers to the audience(s). It is easy to contrast the transmission of a musical piece by oral/aural face-to-face transmission with the impersonality and wide scope of the Internet, but transmission needs to be considered as a continuum in which many of its forms may be used at the same time by different members of a community. Technology may add new dimensions and possibilities, but older forms often continue, albeit at a reduced rate: children still teach their playmates clapping rhythms in school yards, even as they learn other music from books prepared by music publishers and taught in school music classes, or from audio recordings, radio, television, and the Internet. Innovations do not necessarily replace earlier traditions; they are used to create new ones.

The technology for dissemination includes transmission directly through the air to the audience, without any intermediaries and without amplification; the use of published scores to enable distant performers to play the music for new audiences; the use of microphones and amplifiers for sound reinforcement; and the development of various kinds of recording devices (audio, film, and video) that typically involve producers and whose development is influenced the idiosyncrasies of each medium.

Music publishing

If the dissemination of music through the air may be considered the most traditional form of music transmission, music publishing is probably the second oldest. The publication and sale of song books, hymnbooks, and scores in North America dates back to the eighteenth century. During the nineteenth century and into the early twentieth century, sheet music and song books were the most important media for disseminating popular and religious songs as well as other forms of music. Such publications were abundant and provide an important source for the study of American music before the advent of the recording industry. Songs from the musical theater, vaudeville songs, and a large variety of genres were published and disseminated with piano transcriptions. Some music publishers sent groups of musicians on tour to promote their copyrighted books—anticipating by decades the practice of popular music groups going on tour to promote their record companies' recordings. The growth of music publishing paralleled the growth of music education in North America. Here a dissemination technology awaited an educational movement. Some form of music education—especially vocal training and piano lessons—came to be considered part of general education, and particularly appropriate for women.

Music publishing was more than a means for disseminating music. It was also a big business—a mass medium. Some of Stephen Foster's songs sold over one hundred thousand copies each in the 1850s. Music publishers became a powerful force in the entertainment industry of the late nineteenth and early twentieth centuries, and their

The early years of the recording industry were complicated by lawsuits over patent infringements and the simultaneous presence in the market of competing technologies.

influence can be seen in the copyright law of 1909, which protected composers and print music publishers but did not include a provision for performers and audio recording. During the twentieth century the sales of audio recordings gradually exceeded the sales of sheet music, and music publishers increasingly became the administrators of intellectual property rather than actual disseminators of published music.

Sound recording

The most significant technological development in North American music was certainly the invention of the audio recorder, with its subsequent evolution through a number of different technologies to the compact disc and Internet. The history of the development of recorded sound, from its initial invention toward the end of the nineteenth century to its ubiquitous presence at the start of the twenty-first century, is an important area for ethnomusicological and historical research on the impact of technology on music specifically and on culture in general.

To summarize a complex history, in 1877 Thomas Edison created a recording device consisting of a rotating tinfoil cylinder into which he sang "Mary Had a Little Lamb"; he then played it back. Edison considered his invention of principal interest to businesses—for dictating letters, for recording important events (such as deathbed statements), and for entertainment. He did not, at the outset, consider prerecorded music to be a particularly important use of the machine. Other inventors, however, quickly saw the potential of prerecorded entertainment. Interestingly, the companies that specialized in music publishing and the production of song books did not expand into recorded sound. Later many of them would be bought by recording companies, which also controlled massive amounts of intellectual property.

The early years of the recording industry were complicated by lawsuits over patent infringements and the simultaneous presence in the market of competing technologies—somewhat similar to the early years of home video in the twentieth century with the competing technologies of Beta and VHS technology, and to the early years of the computer industry in which a number of incompatible operating systems were available simultaneously.

Early audio recordings were not all of music. Popular subjects included vaudeville recitations, speeches, humor, and other nonmusical items. As a disk might cost as much as a worker's weekly wage, early recordings were often used in slot machines. The first musical star with a "big hit" was Enrico Caruso (1873–1921), whose recordings were the first to sell over a million copies in the twentieth century. It was to be followed by many more.

The far-reaching influence of recorded sound

The recording industry developed steadily with the help of a number of technological innovations, including electric (rather than direct) recording, the standardized 78-rpm disk, the 45-rpm single, the 33⅓-rpm long-playing record, the audiocassette, and the compact disc. By the 1950s the impact of recorded sound on all aspects of music—musicians, composers, performers, performance spaces, and audiences—was tremendous. Some analysts have argued that recordings enabled people to hear musical sounds in entirely new ways and created entirely new attitudes toward performances of all kinds.

The invention of recording technology certainly stimulated the comparative study of music and the development of ethnomusicology. Most musicology, to the extent that it existed, was based on the study of written documents. Only with the invention of the cylinder recorder was it possible to reliably fix and then study sounds that had no scores. Only when sound was a transcribable onto physical objects could it become part of museum collections and the subject of reanalysis and dissemination. Jesse Walter Fewkes is generally credited with some of the first ethnographic field recordings—of Passamoquoddy Indian songs and narratives performed by Noel Josephs and Peter Selmore, recorded in Calais, Maine, in March 1890. Many cylinder recordings were made at the 1896 Chicago World's Fair, including some of the earliest of a number of non-Western musicians who attended the fair. In 1899 the first audio archive was founded in Vienna, to be followed by audio archives in Berlin and, later, in the United States and Canada.

The new recording technology not only created new possibilities, it imposed certain limitations. Early cylinder and disk recorders had a great impact on performers and their musical performances. Both the cylinder and Emile Berliner's disks shared a common feature—they had limited fidelity and could only play three to five minutes of music at a time. Musicians therefore had to distill their performances into that limited period. Thus dance tunes that might have been played for fifteen minutes and long ballads that might have gone on for more than ten minutes were reduced to about three minutes. Until the development of the long-playing (LP) record, the medium served popular music better than longer classical pieces. A number of other performance traits can be traced to the early history of recording technology.

The widespread adoption of recorded sound had a profound influence on the lives of performers. At the same time as they opened new opportunities for some musicians, recordings certainly had a negative effect on others. Many performers began to make their living as studio musicians, while others were put out of work by the replacement of live performers with jukeboxes and other playback devices.

Recorded sound had a huge impact on audiences as well as on musicians and the academic study of music. North Americans soon became accustomed to listening to music from a machine, far from the performers. Performances became "mediated" in the sense that there was an intermediate stage between their production and the audience's hearing them, and also objectified and subject to repeated listening, collection, sale, archiving, rediscovery, and reissues. The music of the mid- to late-twentieth century was repeatedly influenced by recordings; later recordings were often strongly influenced by earlier ones—as in the case of the folk music revival and rock and roll. A generation of English rock musicians may never have seen live blues performers when they started their careers, but they certainly had listened to them.

Radio, "talking pictures," and television

The invention of wireless transmission was transformed into full-blown commercial radio broadcasting in the 1920s, with the some of the earliest stations established in that year. Like early recordings, early radio programming was quite varied, but it quickly focused more and more on music. Radio stations presented a variety of musical forms, and as early as 1922 country or "hillbilly" music was featured on a number of stations. Nashville's WSM's *Barn Dance* began in 1925 and later achieved international renown as the *Grand Ole Opry.* Because the programming was free, many people first heard traditions they came to enjoy and even to perform on radio broadcasts. By the late 1930s, the majority of radio programming consisted of popular and "light" music.

The trio of radio, audio recordings, and music publishing soon became closely linked, as music publishers, record companies, and artists realized the promotional value of radio play. What people heard on the radio they often wanted to buy for their home listening. The different parts of the entertainment industry did not agree, however, on the distribution of radio income to artists and music publishers. The history of radio reveals repeated conflicts between the networks and the music publishers. In the United States, regulation by the Federal Communications Commission (FCC) has also played an important role in shaping music through a number of its rulings on programming.

Radio had some unintended influences on vocal performance style, for example, the development of "crooning." Radio engineers found it easier to amplify a soft voice than to modify a loud one, and so a combination of microphone technology and radio practice strongly influenced the growth of the soft-voiced crooning style by vocalists from the 1920s on. Musicians learned to exploit the possibilities of evolving microphone, radio, and loudspeaker technology as the century wore on, but they may have been encouraged to do so by technicians and the limitations of their equipment.

In addition to inventing the cylinder recorder, Thomas Edison developed a machine that combined sound and moving visual images at the end of the nineteenth century. But it was not until the 1930s that cinema films with sound tracks became commonplace. Film music soon became an important part of the production, both as background sound and as part of the feature itself. Film sound tracks, issued on recordings and for a while also in the form of sheet music, were very popular from the beginning and continued to be so throughout the century.

Although invented in the 1920s, television only became a mass medium in the 1950s, a time of tremendous expansion of television into homes and its appropriation of the lion's share of the audience during the evening hours. Although music never became the central focus of television as it had been for radio, some influential shows introduced new artists (Elvis Presley, the Beatles, and others) to large audiences. Cable television—whose signals are distributed by cable rather than transmitted through the air—and home satellite dish reception were other technological breakthroughs that permitted programmers and viewers access to a larger number of channels. This opened the door for more varied programming and for the real emergence of television as a music medium. The use of television as an independent musical medium—one in which the visual aspects of the performance have a compositional and interpretative significance of their own—began with MTV (Music Television), distributed by cable television, and spread to other cable channels. MTV went far beyond the televised performances that typified earlier televised music events and began to present elaborate visual dramas that depicted the content or the mood of the song rather than just the images of the performing musicians. Like other innovations before it, MTV inspired some performers and producers and influenced some audiences to imagine music in a new way, and video became a staple of the popular music industry.

Cable television was initially viewed as an opportunity to add greater diversity in television programming. Yet with radio, films, television, and cable channels, a close alliance among music publishers, record companies, artists, composers, and the new media grew into a unified whole with the consolidation of the entertainment industry into massive multimedia corporations such as Sony, Time-Warner, and BMG in the 1990s.

Computers and music

In the 1980s the use of home computers became widespread. At first the technical limitations of computers prevented most of them from being very useful for the production or dissemination of music. By the 1990s, however, various computer formats had emerged that suggested some larger long-term changes in the way musical sounds are produced, assembled, and distributed. One of the innovations was the MIDI interface, which primarily influenced the conceptualization and performance of music. Another was the CD-ROM (Compact Disc Read-Only Memory, available in various formats), which enabled programmers to present music, text, photographs, and moving images on a single computer disc. The emergence of the World Wide Web (WWW) on the Internet enabled computer users to access sound, photographs, and moving images, to download them, and to manipulate them in a variety of ways. Distributing sounds through the Internet is considerably faster than mailing a compact disc to a store to sell to a consumer, and every indication is that the dissemination of music will be once again transformed by a technological innovation. Yet all of these have posed new problems for the existing music industry, which continues to be transformed by technology.

Audiences

An audience, those people who hear and evaluate performances, including producers, performers, reviewers, financiers and the general public, is an essential part of musical performances. North American audiences have been exposed to more and more music as the evolving media appear in more and more domains of their lives—in workplaces, automobiles, stores, elevators, and (through the portable cassette and compact disc player) in almost any other location or activity. Transformed into consumers by purveyors of commercial music, North Americans of all ages have been profoundly affected by the technological changes within musical performance and have to some extent directed those changes by their acceptance or rejection of the performances. Audiences are more complex than the theories that reduce them to consumers, or status-and-power hungry manipulators, or mindless automatons. Musical preferences often vary by social class, ethnic group, age, and gender. Yet many North Americans are conversant with several different musical styles and are at once performers (of a small repertoire), teachers (of favorite genres), and consumers (of a much larger repertoire) who are deeply attached to and moved by certain kinds of music.

The audience technology that most influenced the recording industry in the late twentieth century were the audio and video recorder. The ability of consumers to make copies of performances for their own use—called piracy by the industry—may have had a profound effect on the number and price of commercial recordings sold.

In the market system that dominates contemporary musical performance, when an audience abandons a musical style it is relegated to sound archives and libraries. There it becomes the object of research and a resource for future musical revitalization.

From the first manufacture of instruments to the use of computers for the production and dissemination of musical sound and images, technology has been an intimate part of musical conceptualization, performance, and evaluation. Because of this, technology employed in musical performances must be considered as carefully as the structures of the sounds themselves in order to understand what music is today, how it became what it is, and where it might be taken in the future.

—Anthony Seeger

MUSIC, TECHNOLOGY, AND MEDIA IN CANADA

Although the population of Canada is relatively small, it possesses nevertheless one of the highest rates of per capita consumption of recorded music in the world. Thus much like other affluent and industrialized societies, Canadians' love of music is intimately tied to a fascination with and a dependency on contemporary media and technology. And although the origins of much of this technology lie, for the most part, outside its borders, Canadians have made a number of significant contributions to the development of music, media, and technology during the past century.

Certainly the conditions in which Canada experienced its early history—with its combination of an immense geographical territory, harsh climate, and a relatively

Test broadcasts were conducted on a semiregular basis at station XWA in Montréal as early as 1919, establishing it as the first regularly operating broadcast facility in the world (according to most accounts); however, fears developed quickly during the 1920s concerning the perceived domination of Canadian airwaves by U.S. broadcasters.

sparse and largely rural population—were not conducive to the development of a strong musical culture or a solid industrial economy. It was not until the end of the nineteenth century that musical instrument manufacturing (especially piano and organ manufacture) reached significant proportions, and by 1901 Canadian exports of musical instruments (based largely on the export of reed organs) surpassed imports for the first time (Kallmann 1960). The publishing of periodicals devoted to music (an important medium of support to both musical culture and the instrument trades) was also a precarious industry, with many titles having publishing runs of only a few years because of the relatively small size of the urban population and an inadequate advertising base. By the final decade of the twentieth century, however, some eighty-five firms were engaged in the manufacture of music related products. These firms and their operations varied considerably, ranging from Québec luthier Paul Champagne, whose hand-crafted guitars are known throughout North America despite the fact that he manages to produce only about fourteen instruments a year, to Sabian Ltd. of New Brunswick, reputed to be the second leading cymbal manufacturer in the world, producing some two hundred thousand instruments annually, including a series of hand-hammered bronze instruments (Allen 1990). The instrument trades and the consumer market also matured to the point at which a number of specialized music periodicals were able to amass adequate resources and a secure, albeit relatively small, readership.

Innovations in instrument technology

The significance of instrument technologies within musical culture, however, cannot be limited to a simple assessment of the relative health of the instrument manufacturing and periodical publishing sectors; innovations in instrument design can have far-reaching influence on our concepts of what music is and can be and on the character of musical composition, performance, and reception. During the 1950s and 1960s, for example, inventor Hugh LeCaine, an engineer at the National Research Council of Canada, produced a series of unique and innovative electronic instruments for the fledgling experimental music studios located at the University of Toronto and at McGill University in Montréal. Composers from all parts of North America came to the studios to explore the possibilities offered by his unique instrument designs. Although none of his instruments was ever successfully brought to the marketplace, his influence on a generation of composers during this critical early period of experimentation with electronic means of production was considerable (Young 1989).

Even with instruments produced by commercial enterprises, the functional source of technical innovations can be unpredictable and may be found in virtually any sector of musical culture, reversing, in some cases, the conventional relationship between manufacturers and consumers of technology. While engaged in a variety of musical projects during the 1970s, including film, record and jingle production, Vancouver musician Ralph Dyck designed a makeshift digital device that enabled him to control the output of his synthesizers and synchronize them to a multitrack tape recorder. His design was taken up and further developed by the Roland Corporation of Japan and eventually marketed 1977 as the MC-8, one of the first polyphonic digital sequencers introduced into the commercial marketplace (Vail 1990).

Public and private media

As important as musical instrument technologies are for the practice of music, certainly no technical innovation of the past one hundred years has had as far-reaching an impact as the invention of sound recording and the subsequent development of the recording and broadcast industries. The beginnings of a domestic sound recording industry were established in Canada in 1899 when Emile Berliner set up his gramophone operations in Montréal (the Columbia Phonograph Company followed suit in Toronto in 1904); prior to this time, all phonographs and gramophones had been imported into Canada from the United States. Berliner decided to begin manufacturing gramophone machines and records in Canada for two reasons: first, to establish a base from which to protect his patents, many of which were being contested in the United States, and, second, to exploit the francophone market in Québec. Shortly after the turn of the century, Berliner began producing records for the French Canadian market, first from imported masters and later from domestically produced recordings of French Canadian artists as well (Moogk 1975). Thus the character of the Canadian record industry was established, from the outset, as essentially a branch plant operation with links to larger, international concerns—a character that continues to influence its development to the present day.

A similar pattern of development appeared to take root with the advent of radio broadcasting but resulted in a very different outcome [see Four Views of Music in Canada, p. 1101]. Test broadcasts were conducted on a semiregular basis at station XWA in Montréal as early as 1919, establishing it as the first regularly operating broadcast facility in the world (according to most accounts); however, fears developed quickly during the 1920s concerning the perceived domination of Canadian airwaves by U.S. broadcasters. Indeed, by the end of the decade the largest Canadian stations were affiliated with the U.S. networks. The report of a royal commission in 1929 led to the Broadcasting Act of 1932 that established, in principal, the public ownership of the airwaves and the creation of the Canadian Radio Broadcasting Commission (CRBC) for their management. In practice, what eventually developed, however, was a mixed system consisting of a publicly owned national broadcaster—the Canadian Broadcasting Corporation (CBC) was created as the result of a second broadcasting act in 1936—and a set of privately owned local and regional broadcasters. By 1958 both public and private sectors were regarded as equal and allowed to develop parallel national networks. The establishment of this mixed system formed the basis of the unique character of Canadian broadcasting. While the content of privately owned broadcasting closely resembled that found on the U.S. commercial networks, the CBC busied itself with the creation of cultural and educational programming and developed a large technical infrastructure by linking local, regional, and national facilities, including services devoted to both English- and French-speaking populations as well as a northern service addressing the needs of the aboriginal peoples (the latter eventually attaining its own independent facilities as well).

Despite the legislated public ownership of the airwaves, however, Canadian musicians and independent record companies complained that Canadian music was still not effectively reaching Canadian listeners. In 1971, the fortunes of the Canadian record industry and radio broadcasters were essentially linked when the Canadian Radio and Television Commission (CRTC) instituted a set of Canadian content regulations ensuring that a minimum percentage of broadcast time would be devoted to Canadian music. The success of the content regulations was hotly debated both within and outside Canada and was followed in the mid-1980s by government programs that directly subsidized the production of Canadian records and music videos.

What is important about these various attempts to legislate the character of broadcasting structure and content in Canada is the degree to which they bear testimony to the complex interplay between music, media, and technology, on the one hand, and Canadian social, political and economic realities, on the other. Ironically, while much of the impetus behind the regulation of the broadcast sector has stemmed from a nationalist cultural agenda that sought to protect Canada from a perceived threat from outside its borders (Dorland 1996), Canadian media have in recent decades had considerable success in penetrating the cultural space of other countries: for example, MuchMusic, a Canadian music video alternative to the U.S.-based MTV, provides music programming to cable services around the world; it has also successfully marketed its broadcast format and established joint ventures in Argentina (MuchaMusica), the United States (MuchMusic USA), and Finland (Jyrki) [see Two Forms of Electronic Music, p. 250].

The innovations of Glenn Gould

In addition to their impact on Canadian politics and economy (but certainly not separate from them), sound recording and broadcasting have also had a profound influence on the character of musical performance and reception. Perhaps nowhere in the world of music has this influence been so acutely felt and so eloquently expressed as in the career of the renowned Canadian pianist and broadcaster Glenn Gould (1932–1982) (figure 2). Gould, more than most musical performers before or after him, realized the potential of electronic technologies to radically transform the music making process. In 1964 he abandoned the concert hall, arguing that it had become an anachronism, and devoted his career to exploring the possibilities offered by the media of sound recording, radio, and television broadcasting. Although he was regarded by many as a mere eccentric, Gould's ideas were grounded in a thorough reevaluation of his artistic practice, including the use of tape editing not only to enhance the technical perfection of his recorded performances but also as an integral part of his interpretive process; experimentation with microphone placement to increase the clarity and intimacy of his recordings; and an exploration of the spatial aspects of sound reproduction. Furthermore, Gould argued that sound recording could play an important part in breaking down the specialized roles of composer, performer, and audience and that it

FIGURE 2   Glenn Gould animatedly playing the piano. © Bettmann/CORBIS.

fostered a more active form of listener involvement in music making (Gould 1966). Moving beyond the boundaries of conventional music, he also produced a series of innovative radio documentaries for the CBC. Based on musical or, in cases such as *The Idea of North,* distinctly Canadian themes, Gould explored the musical potential embodied in the spoken word and applied principles of musical form to the documentary genre.

Gould's ideas and creative practice highlight the fact that technologies are never truly "finished" at the design or manufacturing stage; rather, they only realize their full potential when they are put to innovative and creative uses (Théberge 1997). In popular music, the recording studio is itself a kind of metatechnology, consisting of a variety of specialized devices for the recording and manipulation of sound, a precisely engineered configuration of acoustic spaces, and a flexible, though highly coordinated, system of labor. A number of Canadians, such as David Foster (working primarily in Los Angeles) and Daniel Lanois (who has worked in studios throughout the world), have earned reputations for their ability to combine the roles of musician, arranger, producer, and/or sound engineer and have placed their unique stamp on the recorded sound of numerous international artists with whom they have worked.

During the past century, changes in musical instrument technology, publishing, sound recording, radio, and music television have exerted powerful influences on musical cultures throughout the world. The responses to these forces, however, have not been uniform, and in Canada, especially, the character of its unique political, socioeconomic, cultural, and artistic heritage has been as important a factor in determining its responses as the attributes of the technologies themselves.

—Paul Théberge

REFERENCES

Allen, Richard. 1990. "Made in Canada: The Markets, the Manufacturers, the Merchandise." *Canadian Music Trades* 12(1):22–38.

Attali, Jacques. 1979. *Noise.* Manchester, Eng.: Manchester University Press.

Benson, Barbara Elna. 1945. *Music and Sound Systems in Industry.* New York: McGraw-Hill.

Chanan, Michael. 1994. *Musica Pratica: The Social Practice of Western Music from Gregorian Chant to Postmodernism.* London: Verso.

———. 1995. *Repeated Takes: A Short History of Recording and Its Effects on Music.* London: Verso.

Clark, Kenneth S. 1929. *Music in Industry.* New York: National Bureau for the Advancement of Music.

Crawford, Richard. 1993. *The American Musical Landscape.* Berkeley: University of California Press.

Dorland, Michael. 1996. *The Cultural Industries in Canada: Problems, Policies and Prospects.* Toronto: James Lorimer and Co.

Eisenberg, Evan. 1987. *The Recording Angel: Music, Records and Culture from Aristotle to Zappa.* New York: McGraw-Hill.

Fewkes, Jesse Walter. 1890. *Contributions to Passamaquoddy Folk-Lore.* Boston: n.p.

Frith, Simon. 1987. "The Industrialization of Popular Music." In *Popular Music and Communication,* ed. James Lull, 53–78. Newbury Park, Calif.: Sage.

———, ed. 1993. *Music and Copyright.* Edinburgh: Edinburgh University Press.

Gould, Glenn. 1966. "The Prospects of Recording." *High Fidelity* 16:46–63.

Hoover, Cynthia Adams. 1969. *Harpsichords and Clavichords.* Washington, D.C.: Smithsonian Institution Press.

Kallmann, Helmut. 1960. *A History of Music in Canada 1534–1914.* Toronto: University of Toronto Press.

Kallmann, Helmut, Gilles Potvin, and Kenneth Winters, eds. 1992. *Encyclopedia of Music in Canada.* 2nd ed. Toronto: University of Toronto Press.

Liang, David. 1991. "A Voice without a Face: Popular Music and the Phonograph in the 1890s." *Popular Music* 10(1):1–10.

Linn, Karen. 1991. *That Half-Barbaric Twang: The Banjo in American Popular Culture.* Urbana: University of Illinois Press.

Malm, Krister, and Roger Wallace. 1992. *Media Policy and Music Activity.* London: Routledge.

Marco, Guy A., ed. 1993. *Encyclopedia of Recorded Sound in the United States.* New York: Garland.

Merriam, Alan. 1964. *The Anthropology of Music.* Chicago: Northwestern University Press.

Millard, André. 1995. *America on Record: A History of Recorded Sound.* Cambridge: Cambridge University Press.

Moogk, Edward B. 1975. *Roll Back the Years: A History of Canadian Recorded Sound and Its Legacy, Genesis to 1930.* Ottawa: National Library of Canada.

Read, Oliver, and Walter L. Welch. 1959. *From Tinfoil to Stereo: Evolution of the Phonograph.* Indianapolis: Howard W. Sams and Co.

Théberge, Paul. 1997. *Any Sound You Can Imagine: Making Music/Consuming Technology.* Hanover, N.H.: University Press of New England.

Vail, Mark. 1990. "Vintage Synths: The Roland MC-8 Micro Composer." *Keyboard* 16(10):116–117.

Young, Gayle. 1989. *The Sackbut Blues: Hugh Le Caine, Pioneer in Electronic Music.* Ottawa: National Museum of Science and Technology.

Snapshot:
Two Forms of Electronic Music
Karen Pegley
Rob Haskins

MuchMusic and MusiquePlus—Karen Pegley
Electronic Concert Music—Rob Haskins

Certainly nothing has affected the composition, performance, production, and dissemination of music in the twentieth century more than electronic technology. Part of our everyday lives, electronic media such as radio, television, synthesizers, and computers have forever changed the ways we make and receive music. Here are two examples showing the profound effects of electronics on two very different musics.

MUCHMUSIC AND MUSIQUEPLUS

MuchMusic, the first of a series of Canadian specialty stations dedicated to airing music videos and music-related programming, was licensed by the Canadian Radio-Television and Telecommunications Commission (CRTC) to CHUM Ltd. in 1984. The decision to license CHUM over its competitors was influenced by the highly successful music video programming on Citytv, a CHUM-owned, Toronto-based station (LaPointe1984). Once licensed, MuchMusic, with media mogul Moses Znaimer as president and executive producer and John Martin as director of music programming, began airing from the Citytv Building in Toronto as a pay-tv station, becoming part of the basic cable service later in 1989 (Miller 1992).

MuchMusic was heralded as "Canadian MTV" before it even went on the air (LaPointe 1984); given MTV's significant cultural presence internationally, this comparison perhaps was unavoidable. Indeed, MuchMusic, like MTV, has emphasized the Top 40 playlist in its programming. Other, more subtle programming differences, however, now distinguish it from its American counterpart, including a larger proportion of multicultural content (on programs like *ClipTrip*), more attention to regional musical practices (*MuchEast* and *MuchWest*), and a wider playlist with more historical depth and breadth (Pegley 1999).

Governmental regulations also have contributed to MuchMusic's distinctive programming: to obtain its license, the station agreed to devote a portion of its air time to "Canadian content," a set of criteria defined by the CRTC, whereby two "audio components" must be Canadian based (the music or lyrics were written by a Canadian, the artist is Canadian, and/or the performance/production take place in Canada) and at least one "video component" is Canadian (the director, production company, or production facilities). The proportion of Canadian content videos aired was negotiated at 10 percent for MuchMusic's first year, increasing gradually to 30 percent. Although this posed a challenge initially, meeting this quota has become considerably easier since Canadian artists such as Bryan Adams, Celine Dion, Shania Twain, and others now enjoy both domestic and international success (in part due to MuchMusic's initiatives). Today the station exceeds the minimum quota, frequently featuring new little-known Canadian bands vis-à-vis individual videos (*Indie Spotlight*) and within thematic programs (*The New Music*).

Some of MuchMusic's other distinguishing features are directly traceable to the Citytv environment. Self-described as "the world's first television facility without studios," indoor and outdoor locations surrounding the Citytv Building frequently are transformed into temporary filming sets, breaking down traditional barriers separating front and back regions. Audience members are encouraged to gather in and around the primary ground-level set, allowing MuchMusic to create a sense of connectedness between audience members, VJs, and visiting performers. MuchMusic tapes live while street-front cameras reveal day or nighttime; this creates a time-inflected environment that contributes to the station's heightened spacial and temporal specificities (figure 1).

The French-language specialty service MusiquePlus was launched in 1986 with Znaimer once again executive producer and Pierre Marchand as director of programming. When this Montréal-based station began airing, the total repertoire of French-language videos totaled only twenty-six; accordingly, MusiquePlus had to import much of its programming from English-based MuchMusic. By 1994, through a series of initiatives, the number of French-language videos was well over six hundred (Chiasson 1994); today MusiquePlus airs at least 35 percent French-language videos (including those from outside Québec), making the station distinct from both MuchMusic and MTV. MusiquePlus's style also differs from that of the older stations because of its unique target audience: a result of Québec's low birth rate (the province is consistently below the Canadian national average), the twelve-to-seventeen-year-old teen population of Québec comprises only 9.6 percent of the overall population. As a result, 71 percent of MusiquePlus viewers are between eighteen and forty-nine, with a substantial 36 percent over the age of thirty-five. In fact, the average viewer in 1992 was twenty-eight years old, four years older than the average employee (McElgunn 1992; Chiasson 1994).

FIGURE 1 Alanis Morissette performing on MuchMusic. Photo by Barry Roden. Photo courtesy MuchMusic.

In *Cartridge Music* (1960), the performers insert small objects into phonograph cartridges; they then strike or rub the objects, and the amplified sounds that those actions produce constitute the piece.

A significant contributor to the proliferation of Canadian (and particularly French Canadian) videos is VideoFACT (Foundation to Assist Canadian Talent), established in 1984 by Znaimer and Bernie Finkelstein to provide financial assistance to Canadian artists for creating videos. Applicants must meet the Canadian content regulations; if successful, they can receive up to 50 percent of the production costs of their videos to a maximum of $15,000. Since its inception, VideoFACT has awarded more than $12.6 million to aid the production of over one thousand four hundred videos, assisting the early careers of performers like k.d. lang, Celine Dion, Sarah McLachlan, and Loreena McKennitt, among others [see GENDERING MUSIC, p. 103]. Today VideoFACT is sponsored by MuchMusic and MusiquePlus as well as MuchMoreMusic, the latest specialty service targeting the twenty-five-plus market. As part of MuchMoreMusic's 1998 licensing agreement, the station also outlined its commitment to further support Canadian artists by creating PromoFACT, a program within VideoFACT to assist in the development of electronic press kits and web sites.

Throughout the 1990s, the CHUM/Citytv network has extended beyond its domestic borders, establishing stations in Argentina (MuchaMusica 1992), the United States (MuchUSA 1994), and Mexico (MuchMusic 1995). *Jyrki,* a highly-successful ninety-minute after-school programming using the Citytv/MuchMusic format, was introduced in Helsinki, Finland, shortly thereafter. Given its international successes and rapid growth, the claim that Citytv/MuchMusic is an important "alternative [Canadian] export for the next millennium" (Smallbridge 1996) may, within the realm of Canadian cultural industries, prove accurate.

—KAREN PEGLEY

ELECTRONIC CONCERT MUSIC

To American composers trained in the literature and traditions of concert music, electronic music was an exciting new terrain with unimagined possibilities. Indeed, experimental composers such as John Cage (1912–1992) believed that electronic technology would not only inspire a new music unique to its possibilities but would also make a permanent impact on composition for conventional acoustic instruments (Cage 1961:7–12). But the medium proved even more flexible in its appeal to the American entertainment industry (especially film, television, and popular music). In turn, these media have had some measure of influence on both the composition and performance of American concert music, thus revealing a fascinating blurring of cultural boundaries. This article briefly touches on some (though certainly not all) of the major figures within American concert music that involves electronic technology and suggests some of the influences that have made their presence felt from outside the realms of that tradition.

The earliest American activity with electronic music began with composition that involved the tape recorder, following the French techniques of *musique concrète* in which composers used natural sounds that they altered and/or superimposed with the device. At first there was no institutional support for such work, and composers shared resources, often with individuals in the commercial sector. Hundreds of prerecorded sounds in Cage's *Williams Mix* (1952), for example, came from the library in the studio of Louis (1920–1989) and Bebe (b. 1927) Barron. (The Barrons are best known for the soundtrack they produced for the 1956 science fiction film *Forbidden Planet*.) Around the same time, Vladimir Ussachevsky (1911–1990) began his famous experiments with tape music composition. Unlike Cage, whose *Williams Mix* is a dense collage of sound assembled entirely by chance-determined splices, Ussachevsky favored a combination of traditional and nontraditional sounds. Pieces like his *Sonic Contours* (1952) include elaborate piano textures built up with tape delay as well as the rerecorded sounds of a piano and human speech at different speeds; nevertheless, the overall shape and character of the work is quite conventional.

In part, Ussachevsky's academic affiliation with Columbia University helped him and his colleague Otto Luening (1900–1996) to gain increased visibility for the new electronic music. Certainly it found a secure base of support in the university setting; the Columbia–Princeton Electronic Music Center, which Ussachevsky and Luening helped to establish in the early 1950s, became a model for many other American universities and music conservatories. One of the Columbia–Princeton Center's major pieces of equipment was a large device originally developed at the RCA laboratories in Princeton for the purpose of reproducing traditional instrumental sounds for popular music. This device, which became known as the RCA Synthesizer, was eventually acquired for Columbia–Princeton and used in the electronic music of Luening, Ussachevsky, and, quite importantly, Milton Babbitt (b. 1916). It was Babbitt who, in his desires to extend the principles of twelve-tone composition into the domains of timbre, duration, and volume, found in the RCA Synthesizer the ideal medium for realizing his stimulating ideas (Babbitt 1962, 1964). His completed works for synthesizer were always on tape in their final form; they ranged from compositions for synthesizer alone (*Composition for Synthesizer*, 1961) to later works that combined a live performer with tape (*Reflections*, for piano and tape, 1975).

Babbitt, of course, was an important music scholar as well as a composer; in his electronic music he attempted to make a profound break with conventional musical patterns in the spirit of humanistic research that the university environment fostered (Babbitt 1996 [1958]). And although both his works and his attitudes have been much criticized (the latter generally distorted), he has always hoped that listeners will attempt to find meaningful pathways of understanding through his music; for the electronic works, most of which are not completely notated, that process is difficult, though it has begun (Morris 1997).

Other composers in the 1960s of even more radical bent found in electronic technology a surprising variety of possibilities for live performance. On the West Coast, Pauline Oliveros (b. 1932) helped codirect the San Francisco Tape Music Center, a locus for many experimental projects. She and Richard Maxfield (1927–1969) pioneered techniques of live performance with electronics; one example, Oliveros's *I of IV* (1966), uses tape delay and mixer feedback systems. In the Midwest, the interdisciplinary ONCE group (based in Ann Arbor, Michigan, although not officially affiliated with the university there) involved architects, dancers, theater performers, and filmmakers, as well as such composers as Robert Ashley (b. 1930) and Roger Reynolds (b. 1934). Ashley's *Wolfman* (1964), a shocking piece that uses extreme amplification and feedback to change both live speaking and tape, is a notorious example of his theatrical work. Cage's own forays into live electronics covered a typical range of possibilities that mirrored the frenzied pluralism of the 1960s. In *Cartridge Music* (1960), the performers insert small objects into phonograph cartridges; they then strike or rub the objects, and the amplified sounds that those actions produce constitute the piece. Many of the works in the

Variations series (1958–1967) similarly involve amplification, sometimes of everyday actions. In a more elegant use of technology, the piece *Reunion* (1968) involves a chessboard rigged with photoresistors; moves in an actual chess game (between Cage and Marcel Duchamp at the premiere) trigger live electronic music composed by David Tudor (1926–1996), Gordon Mumma (b. 1935), David Behrman (b. 1937), and Lowell Cross (b. 1938). Cross (1999) documents the technology and performances of the work.

Throughout the 1960s, designers labored to produce commercial music synthesizers for use in professional and academic studio settings; one of the best known was Robert Moog (b. 1934). In 1968, Moog's name became a household word with the release of the Columbia record *Switched-On Bach,* and a great number of people became powerfully aware of the musical potentials of Moog's synthesizer. This album, a collection of imaginative Bach transcriptions conceived and performed by Wendy Carlos (b. 1939), brought to the fore fascinating issues of electronic "orchestration." Carlos, herself a student of Ussachevsky's, explored a combination of imaginative programming and recording techniques in subsequent albums, especially *The Well-Tempered Synthesizer* (1969). The variety of sound combinations and textures that she achieved through all these techniques served her well in her own music; her important work *Timesteps* (1971) demonstrated how the electronic medium could serve a composer who wanted to explore electronic sounds within the context of a more accessible concert music.

As the technology continued to develop, designers made synthesizers ever more portable in an attempt to interest popular musicians in them. And while many certainly took advantage of the new synthesizers, some younger concert music composers took on the technology for their own performances. The most famous examples from the 1970s are the minimalists Philip Glass (b. 1937) and David Borden (b. 1938). Glass used Farfisa organs in the early years of his own Philip Glass Ensemble, a group of amplified keyboards and winds with voice. Later, after the composer-performer Michael Riesman (b. 1943) joined the ensemble, a variety of new synthesizers came on board as well, all programmed and maintained by Riesman. Borden's Mother Mallard Portable Masterpiece Co. was the first all-Moog ensemble; it still includes a MiniMoog in its instrumentarium. The repetitive rhythms and modal textures of such works as Glass's *Music in Twelve Parts* (1971–1974) and Borden's *The Continuing Story of Counterpoint* (1976–1987) have much in common with the art rock of the period. Indeed, as minimalism became more pervasive in the late 1970s and 1980s the style could be found frequently in contemporary rock music; its spirit stills finds a home in the dance music known generally (and somewhat imprecisely) as Electronica [see ROCK, p. 347]. John Adams (b. 1947) has used the synthesizer in almost every one of his major orchestral works and operas; the synthesizer part in his *Chamber Symphony* (1994) is just as important as the parts for the remaining members of the ensemble.

An important chapter in the history of American electronic music concerns work done with mainframe and microcomputers. Max Mathews (b. 1926) pioneered techniques using computers to generate sound in the late 1950s during his work at Bell Laboratories. Lejaren Hiller (1924–1994) used mainframe computers both to construct algorithms (which would made compositional decisions) and to make sound. Charles Dodge (b. 1942) and Paul Lansky (b. 1944) have done extensive work with the creation of user-friendly software for computer sound synthesis, and some of their important work has involved the synthesis of human speech. Lansky's *Six Fantasies on a Poem by Thomas Campion* (1978–1979) is one of the most important such works. Another composer, Tod Machover (b. 1953), has developed "hyperinstruments"— conventional musical instruments equipped with sensors that send musical signals to computers for additional processing and even real-time elaboration. His *Begin Again Again . . .* (1993) was written for the cellist Yo Yo Ma (b. 1955). Hiller, Dodge, Lansky, and Machover all held or hold university appointments, but similar computer-based technology has also been championed by composers who prefer to work outside the academy. Of these, the best known and most promising is Scott Johnson (b. 1952); Johnson's "Soliloquy" from *How It Happens* (1991) combines the recorded voice of the left-wing journalist I. F. Stone (1907–1989) with string quartet. Johnson bases the rhythms and pitch material of the music on Stone's voice (which he sometimes repeats or otherwise modifies) in subtle and extremely moving ways.

Electronic and computer technology is increasingly pervasive in the United States. It has allowed people from a wide variety of cultural backgrounds to make their own music; and it will continue to allow the production of musics both avant-garde and conventional, but always with sounds largely unimagined and otherwise unavailable.

—ROB HASKINS

REFERENCES

Babbitt, Milton. 1962. "Twelve-Tone Rhythmic Structure and the Electronic Medium." *Perspectives of New Music* 1(1):49–79.

———. 1964. "An Introduction to the RCA Synthesizer." *Journal of Music Theory* 8(2):251–265.

———. 1996 [1958]. "The Composer as Specialist [originally, Who Cares if You Listen?]." In *Classic Essays on Twentieth-Century Music: A Continuing Symposium*, ed. Richard Kostelanetz et al., 161–167. New York: Schirmer Books.

Cage, John. 1961. *Silence: Lectures and Writings.* Middletown, Conn.: Wesleyan University Press.

Carlos, Wendy. 1999 (1974). *Switched-on boxed set.* Minneapolis, Minn.: East Side Digital. Compact disk.

Chadabe, Joel. 1997. *Electric Sound: The Past and Promise of Electronic Music.* Englewood Cliffs, N.J.: Prentice Hall.

Chiasson, Gail. 1994. "MusiquePlus Gets Its Break." *Marketing,* 16 May:18.

Cross, Lowell. 1999. "Reunion: John Cage, Marcel Duchamp, Electronic Music and Chess." *Leonardo Music Journal* 9:35–42.

DeLio, Thomas. 1984. *Circumscribing the Open Universe.* Lanham, Md.: University Press of America.

Dunn, David. 1996. "A History of Electronic Music Pioneers." In *Classic Essays on Twentieth-Century Music: A Continuing Symposium*, ed. Richard Kostelanetz et al., 87–123. New York: Schirmer Books.

Gagne, Cole, and Tracy Caras. 1982. *Soundpieces: Interviews with American Composers.* Metuchen, N.J.: Scarecrow Press.

James, Richard. 1987. "ONCE: Microcosm of the 1960s Musical and Multimedia Avant-Garde." *American Music* 5:359–390.

LaPointe, Kirk. 1984. "CHUM to Offer Canadian 'MTV.'" *Billboard,* April 14:3, 61.

Manning, Peter. 1993. *Electronic and Computer Music.* Oxford: Clarendon Press.

McElgunn, Jim. 1992. "Musique Plus Is Selling to Its Own Beat." *Marketing,* 8 June:24.

Miller, Mark. 1992. "MuchMusic." In *Encyclopedia of Music in Canada,* 2nd ed., ed. Helmut Kallman et al., 895. Toronto: University of Toronto Press.

Morris, Robert. 1997. "Milton Babbitt's Electronic Music: The Medium and the Message." *Perspectives of New Music* 35(2):85–99.

Ondishko, Denise Michelle. 1990. "Six Fantasies on a Poem by Thomas Campion: Synthesis and Evolution of Paul Lansky's Music Compositions." Ph.D. dissertation, University of Rochester, Eastman School of Music.

Pegley, Karen. 1999. "An Analysis of the Construction of National, Racial and Gendered Identities on MuchMusic (Canada) and MTV (US)." Ph.D. dissertation, York University.

Perry, Jeffrey. 1996. "The Inner Voices of Simple Things: A Conversation with Paul Lansky." *Perspectives of New Music* 34(2):40–60.

Slonimsky, Nicolas. 1997. *Baker's Biographical Dictionary of Twentieth-Century Classical Musicians.* Ed. Laura Kuhn. New York: Schirmer Books.

Smallbridge, Justin. 1996. "Think Global, Act Loco." *Canadian Business,* June:43–56.

The Music Industry
David Sanjek (United States)
Will Straw (Canada)

Any discussion of the music industry must involve an examination of music's creators, producers, and consumers, or, those who write, sell, and listen to music. The relationship among these three constituencies has never has been equal in the sense of who profits from the merchandising of the music itself or who controls how that music is created or marketed. For the most part, those who sell music have occupied the principal position of power, although the ways in which they have wielded that power or reaped its rewards have differed over time. The examination of two factors, law and technology, is crucial to an analysis of the music industry [see THE MUSIC INDUSTRY, p. 705].

COPYRIGHT LAW

The protection of intellectual property as prescribed by U.S. copyright statutes has metamorphosed over the years and is at the present time in the process of revision. Recent legislation has extended the number of years a piece of music receives protection before it enters the public domain. The Sonny Bono Copyright Extension Act, passed in 1998, extends the term of copyright by twenty years. In Canada, the most recent copyright act granted protection for a period of fifty years following the death of the author. The language contained in the copyright statutes codifies not only how a writer is to be protected from the misuse of his or her works but also, in a more implicit manner, what the law considers to be musical. The tenets of American copyright law reinforce certain Western European cultural standards, key among them the emphasis upon melody and harmony as the principal if not sole determinants of musical form. Any composition that is rooted instead in rhythm or texture, a definition that encompasses much work by non–Western European writers and performers, is not denied protection but remains less easily assimilated.

Furthermore, the original U.S. copyright act, which became law in 1790, reinforces the language contained in the Constitution defining intellectual property as a relationship between users and creators in order to establish what has been called the "promotion of learning" policy. The Constitutional provision respecting copyright reads, "The Congress shall have Power . . . To promote the Progress of Science and useful Arts, by securing for limited Times to Authors and Inventors the exclusive Right to their respective Writings and Discoveries" (U.S. Constitution, Article I, Section 8). To this day, copyright specialists and legislators continue to debate who should retain the most attention and thereby secure the greatest rights: the public, which benefits from the promotion of knowledge, or the individuals, who stand to profit from the making and merchandising of that knowledge. At the same time, it should be added that those who stand to profit from "Writings and Discoveries" need not be the person or persons who brought them into being, the holder of an individual copyright (musical or otherwise) often having played no part in the creation of the work.

Changes in the copyright statutes have also reflected the ongoing evolution of technology. The law, however, consistently lags behind the introduction of each novel technology by at least some fifteen years, argues legal scholar Paul Goldstein (1994). Every time a new means of creating or disseminating music is developed, marketed, and accepted by the American public, the law must be revised to ensure that the creators and marketers of music receive proper compensation for its use. Careful study of history shows that profits have always been made far sooner by the manufacturers of communications technologies than by the creators whose work the technology features. It was not until 1831 that the U.S. copyright law even mentioned music as a form of culture that required systematic protection. During the more than 120 years since the Law of Queen Anne first recognized the rights of protection of authors, any number of profit-making communications technologies have made their appearance. It might seem at times that the producers of recording and playback equipment conceive of music simply as a means of selling their products. Despite the fact that music might seem to them a secondary consideration, the statutes have always placed primary emphasis upon creators and enforced their control of the material those technologies permit to exist.

EARLY NINETEENTH CENTURY

During the first half of the nineteenth century the principal player in the music industry was the publisher. Sheet music was the customary means by which popular music was sold and its writers compensated. Much of the material was engraved rather than set with movable type. The engraving process permitted elegant cover illustrations as well as allowing notation to be easily corrected. Copyright law did not require publishers to pay royalties for any non–American printed materials, a fact that abetted American businessmen in their presumption that work by their own countrymen was aesthetically inferior to that of Europeans and certainly more expensive to produce. Consequently, only one-tenth of the music printed in the United States in the first quarter of the nineteenth century was by native Americans. This stigma remained for quite some time, for as the twentieth century began, 70 percent of all piano rolls and recordings were by foreign composers.

The terms under which American composers sold their works were onerous. Most music was purchased outright by the publisher, and only the most successful writers were permitted any royalties. Even Stephen Foster was awarded just 10 percent of the retail price of all music sold after production costs were recouped [see POPULAR MUSIC OF THE PARLOR AND STAGE, p. 179]. Unequal as these terms appear, they exceeded the customary five or ten dollars at best, and a meal or a bottle of alcohol at worst, for which many, if not most, writers exchanged their wares. The stranglehold publishers exerted upon the industry intensified in 1855 when the Board of Music Trade of the United States was established by the twenty-five leading publishing houses. Begun as a means of regulating the price of copyright-free foreign music, the association soon constituted a monopoly by fixing prices, eradicating any independent operations, and, in effect, creating the canon of American composition without effective competition or legislative oversight.

Sentimental parlor ballads and quartet-songs found favor within the bourgeois domestic sphere, while the "cheap" music associated with the rambunctious environment of the concert saloon and dance hall frequented by the working classes carved out a separate universe.

Studies of Canadian music publishing in the nineteenth century note that large numbers of Canadian composers published their sheet music in the United States, rather than in their home country, in order to be protected in the much larger market to the south. After passage of the Berne Copyright Convention of 1886, British publishers were no longer required to publish sheet music in Canada in order to compete with imported, illegal American reprints. They focused their attention on the U.S. market, establishing branches there and producing sheet music for sale in both the United States and Canada.

Early-nineteenth-century consumers

The principal customers for sheet music during the first half of the nineteenth century were music teachers, who accounted for half the sales. They purchased material through mail order at a 50 percent discount and then in turn marketed it at a profit to their students. Following the Civil War, those students, many of them now members of the nation's burgeoning middle class, assembled private collections of sheet music for home performance. Their choice of material reflected the developing schism between social classes. As Lawrence Levine (1988) and others have argued, the cultural repertoire, as well as public spaces shared by diverse elements of the American public, began to fragment along the lines of class, ethnic origin, and race once the hierarchy between "high" and "low" culture took hold [see CLASS, p. 42; RACE, ETHNICITY, AND NATIONHOOD, p. 63]. Sentimental parlor ballads and quartet-songs found favor within the bourgeois domestic sphere, while the "cheap" music associated with the rambunctious environment of the concert saloon and dance hall frequented by the working classes carved out a separate universe.

Marketing

Publishers appealed to these divergent audiences with equally diverse marketing strategies. Middle- and upper-class consumers were enticed by the leading mainstream publishers with material that lyrically mirrored their ideological presuppositions as well as by elaborate cover designs that ratified their sentimental vision of the "good life." Those upstart firms that competed with members of the Board of Music Trade began to apply to the merchandising of music that appealed to a mainstream audience the same mass marketing techniques that governed the sale of domestic goods. Salesmen discovered the value of constant repetition, a process that came to be known as "song plugging," and proceeded to drill their wares into the public consciousness. This was done in music stores or on the stage through financial arrangements with well-known stars. Such techniques would prove particularly useful when the intellectual property statutes were amended in 1891 by the establishment of reciprocal international copyright. No longer could one publish foreign music free of charge, although the major firms possessed the fiscal resources to refine their appeals to the domestic, middle-class public that played and sang together in the parlor.

LATE NINETEENTH CENTURY

As the twentieth century arrived, the music industry had become a major business. Sheet music sold for from twenty-five to sixty cents a copy, and the wholesale value of its domestic sales tripled from 1890 to 1909, rising from $1.7 million to $5.5 million. Newly formed aggressive firms, such as those owned by the Witmark brothers and Edward B. Marks, led the way and took advantage of changes in the way music was consumed. Technological aids to the appreciation of music began to take over, for no longer was domestic performance by amateurs or public performance by professionals the principal means by which music was consumed or merchandised. The player had been replaced by the listener. Technology made it possible to enjoy music without human agency. Innovations such as the phonograph and the piano roll offered novel means of hearing as well as marketing music. For some, this process augmented the breadth of the musical audience, introducing them to material they could neither perform themselves nor hear in person. For others, it irreparably severed the appreciation of music from instrumental competency and reified music as a consumable commodity by individuals in isolation, thereby eradicating the communal solidarity that public performance among the immediate circle of family and friends had once encouraged.

The player piano

The process of musical reification was abetted by the Aeolian Company's launching of the player piano, the Pianola, in 1902. Their public relations campaign, however, was stymied by a legal point: neither the courts nor the Congress was able to determine whether the mechanical reproduction of music was an infringement of the copyright laws. Aeolian chose to ignore these complications and amassed a catalogue of more than eight thousand compositions to which it added three thousand more annually. It further circumvented the established statutes by cementing unpublicized agreements with a number of firms. These companies signed a thirty-five-year agreement under which Aeolian could claim exclusive rights to their catalogues, with a stipulation that a royalty of 10 percent would be paid if the issue of infringement were resolved in court in the copyright owners' favor.

Aeolian's actions clearly bordered on monopolistic practices, a claim urged upon the courts by competing piano roll manufacturers and others in the recording industry. Roused to action, the government enacted a compulsory licensing provision as part of the Copyright Act of 1909. For the first time in the country's history, the price for the use of a piece of private property was codified by federal law. To that end, a royalty of two cents for each piano roll, phonograph record, or cylinder manufactured had to be paid to the copyright holder. Furthermore, no single company or individual could stake exclusive claim to a piece of music. Once permission was granted for the mechanical reproduction of a work, it was to be offered for the same price to anyone who wished to use it. Ironically, Aeolian in the end gained more from the claims against it than it lost: from then on the company was required to pay two cents rather than the ten cents it set out to convey to copyright owners.

At the same time, the company's questionable business practices led to the establishment of the right of composers to be compensated for the mechanical reproduction of their work. This right applied equally to the phonograph, and the public appetite for recordings fed not only the pockets of newly established record companies but also those of the writers of materials these companies released. Society had entered the age of multimedia and with it the proliferation of the means of profiting from the creation, recording, and mass marketing of music. A provision of the Copyright Act of 1909 also initiated a "public right" in the guarantee of the exclusive right "to perform the copyrighted work publicly for profit if it be a musical composition and for the purpose of public performance for profit." By virtue of this passage, writers and publishers stood to be compensated for the use of their music in any public forum. However, it would

FIGURE 1   Cover to the sheet music *Nobody Lied* (*When They Said That I Cried Over You*) as sung by Karyl Norman (George Paduzzi), a flamboyant female impersonator who billed himself as "The Creole Fashionplate." The cover clearly links this piece to Norman's repertoire and also gives him credit as lyricist. Photo courtesy Gillian Rodger.

be a few years before they capitalized upon this privilege and established standardized means of compensation.

Tin Pan Alley

Although both the pianola and phonograph upped the ante of potential revenues to creators and marketers, live performance remained the principal domain for the exploitation of music. Publishers developed sophisticated means of getting their material before the eager public that filled vaudeville theaters and other venues of public amusement. Those Manhattan-based publishing companies that collectively came to be known as Tin Pan Alley made use of popular entertainers who performed their material in return for above- or under-the-table compensation, a practice that came to be known as pay for play or Payola. Pictures of performers were displayed on the covers of sheet music, or firms would offer them the exclusive right to perform a particular composition in their acts. On other occasions, a performer would receive credit and compensation as one of a song's writers even if he or she had no formal musical skills whatsoever (figure 1). Bandleaders and instrumentalists were plied with free sheet music or offered elaborate folders that ostentatiously featured a publisher's name. Professional marketers, known in the industry as song pluggers, hawked their clients' wares (sometimes written by the pluggers themselves) through a variety of means that included public performance in music stores or planting individuals in theaters who "requested" predetermined material by popular performers.

Even the new technology of motion pictures was employed for promotional ends. Illustrated reproductions of song lyrics, known as stereopticon slides, were offered to theater owners free of charge during the first decade of the century. This led to the advent of the public "sing-along," and publishers frequently commissioned songs written exclusively for this format. Whatever the means of merchandising, music was becoming a more and more profitable commercial commodity, a fact underscored by the rising costs of promotion. By the middle of the 1890s, it cost as much as $1300 to launch a single song. Fewer than half of those individual compositions made back their investment, and only one out of every two hundred songs secured a profit.

American Society of Composers, Authors and Publishers (ASCAP)

Despite the fact that the 1909 revision of the Copyright Act instituted payment for public performance, few composers or publishers took advantage of that fact for no codified system was in place to assure reimbursement. In 1913, six writers and publishers, including the preeminent theatrical composer of the day, Victor Herbert, banded together to rectify the matter and founded the American Society of Composers, Authors and Publishers (ASCAP). Convinced that no single individual or corporate entity could monitor all potential performances of its intellectual property, the membership pooled its interests and, by combining its individual catalogues into an inclusive body of compositions, proposed to require any users of that music to take out a license for the entire repertoire. The result was, in effect, a private organization for the enforcement of a public law and the principle of performing rights.

In order to guarantee ASCAP's legal standing the membership sued several establishments that it felt used music without appropriate compensation. The first case, *Church v. Hilliard* (1914), took on the hotel industry on behalf of a nonmember publisher, the John Church Company (Ryan 1985:19–20). The case alleged that the performance of John Philip Sousa's "From Maine to Oregon" in the dining room of New York City's Hotel Vanderbilt constituted a for-profit occasion even if no special admission charge was required to hear the composition. The hotel countered that music was no more than a portion of the establishment's general environment. The courts ruled in favor of the John Church Company that Sousa's piece would not have been performed were the Vanderbilt management unconvinced that the music would draw customers. To reinforce this claim and circumvent a local court's overturning of *Church v. Hilliard,* ASCAP, in the person of Victor Herbert, sued Shanley's Cabaret of New York City, where it was alleged his composition "Sweethearts" was sung on more than one occasion to dinner guests. While a lower court ruled in Shanley's favor, the case was officially decided for Herbert and the other defendants by the Supreme Court on the basis of the dramatic-work licensing provision of the copyright law.

In 1917, the U.S. Supreme Court justices declared that the public performance of music contributed to the ability of an establishment to make profits even if no special admission was charged for that music. ASCAP now possessed a legal precedent, and the performance license became a boon to writers and publishers. At the same time, ASCAP's membership was a select, and far from representative, sample of the nation's writers of music. Being admitted required a publisher to have been in business for no less than a year, and a writer had to have had no fewer than five of his works "regularly published," an obscure attribution meaning that it had been released by an ASCAP member. Applicants were then required to solicit the sponsorship of two members of the ASCAP board before they finally received the approval of the membership committee. Needless to say, this series of obstacles restricted the organization to a body of like-minded individuals. As a result, ASCAP possessed a virtual lock on all compensation for public performances of music. This led, as shall be seen, to recurring battles with other portions of the entertainment industry.

EARLY TWENTIETH CENTURY

Records

The adoption by the public of novel communications technologies, the sound recording and radio in particular, multiplied not only the means by which writers and publishers of music could be compensated but also the kinds of entities that were required to take out performance licenses. The year 1920 saw the demise of sheet music's hegemony as the preeminent means by which the public purchased music. A 50 percent increase in production costs followed a printers' strike and concurrent paper shortage that led in turn to the abandonment by a number of chain stores of their sheet music departments. Phonograph records had became the medium of choice. Writers and publishers thereafter flocked to record company offices with material in hand. The success of George Stoddard's "Mary" in 1913 indicated how lucrative the record trade could be. Rejected by every New York City–based publisher, Stoddard took his song to RCA Victor Records and earned $15,000 in mechanical royalties—a predetermined figure for each record sold—when the disk sold 300,000 copies in only three months. Stoddard's success illustrated to many other songwriters the need to avoid the middleman and open their own publishing firms. Irving Berlin, for example, had earned almost $160,000 annually during the period of World War I, but once he took his interests in his own hands and touted his material to the record industry, his profits grew exponentially. The Berlin composition "Say It with Music" sold 375,000 printed copies in a seventy-five-week period but more than one million records and 100,000 piano rolls, the profits from which flowed back to Berlin's pockets.

Radio

Radio was introduced as a widely available commercial medium in 1920 and took the public by storm. What was at first an amateur medium became a national addiction. In 1922, the number of active stations jumped from twenty-eight in January to 570 in December. Eager for material to put on the air, station managers sought the assistance

BMI turned to many of those individuals and forms of composition that ASCAP had not seen fit to admit into their ranks. As a result, the writers and publishers of many indigenous genres—blues, jazz, country, bluegrass, and, later, rock and roll, to name a few—were able to profit as never before from the public use of their work.

of the music industry in finding musicians and material for them to play. Although the radio was for the public essentially an opportunity to hear "free music," ASCAP saw to it that the broadcasters paid an appropriate rate for use of its repertoire. Radio executives in turn argued that the performance of music over the air was tantamount to free advertising and that their contribution to the popularity of a growing body of indigenous composition and performance ought to absolve them of any undue expenses. Eager not to upset a tenuous relationship and to preserve radio as a lucrative promotional tool, ASCAP initially collected from broadcasters in 1925 only $58,478.05—under 10 percent of the medium's total income that year. However, as the public acceptance of radio grew and profits rose, so too did license fees paid to ASCAP; in 1929, they accounted for nearly 35 percent of total income: $619,398.94 out of $1,777,288.08. Broadcast executives found these figures less and less acceptable, but it would be a decade before they obtained an alternative source of licensed music.

Movies

Motion pictures have routinely featured music, even during the silent period, although the scores for some time amounted to little more than cobbled-together fragments of well-known concert music warhorses [see FILM, p. 202]. Accompanists drew upon thumb indexes of themes, most notably Erno Rapée's *Motion Picture Moods for Pianists and Organists* (1924), to heighten the emotions of silent features. Songs specifically written to tie in with motion pictures date back as early as 1918, when Charles N. Daniels penned the popular "Mickey (Pretty Mickey)" for the Mabel Normand vehicle of the same name. However, such material failed more often than it succeeded, and it was not until the multimillion-copy sales of Rapee's song "Charmaine," used as the theme song of the 1926 feature *What Price Glory?*, that music publishers began more systematically to exploit the motion picture. The following year Rapee once again succeeded with "Diane," the theme for *Seventh Heaven*. The release of Warner Brothers's Al Jolson vehicle, *The Jazz Singer*, marked the advent of the sound film. With the ascendance of talking pictures and the increased use of interpolated music, ASCAP quickly moved to establish a rate structure for the use of that music. Just as quickly, the film companies, rather than be beholden to East Coast publishers for materials to use in the "All Talking All Singing All Dancing" movies the public desired, began to purchase firms with remarkable speed. Warners, for example, picked up M. Witmark and Sons and the Dreyfus music interests. Despite the fact that just a few years later the Depression would erode the attraction of musical features and cause studios to curtail their Tin Pan Alley interests, the acquisition of a variety of media by a single corporate entity paved the way for the institutional "synergy" that pervades the mass entertainment industry at the turn of the twenty-first century.

FIGURE 2   Ralph Peer (1892–1960). Famous record producer, A and R man, and publisher. Peer supervised the primal commercial recordings of blues (Mamie Smith's "Crazy Blues," 1920) and country music (Fiddlin' John Carson's "Little Old Log Cabin," 1923). In 1928, he founded the Southern Music Company in conjunction with Victor Records and took sole ownership in 1932. Photo courtesy BMI Archives.

Formation of Broadcast Music Inc. (BMI)

ASCAP's desire to maximize the profitability of all communications media led it routinely to raise its rates, particularly in the broadcasting field. Radio station owners complained that in the absence of an alternative licensing organization, they were forced to comply with exorbitant fees or risk not being able to broadcast any music whatsoever. Furthermore, live music accounted for a good deal of what went out over the airwaves and a healthy percentage of the annual performance record tabulated by ASCAP. As sheet music sales fell and record royalties fluctuated, radio licensing fees comprised the lion's share of ASCAP's annual income. At first payments called for 2 percent of a station's revenue from the sales of advertising time, but this rose to 5 percent in 1936 as part of a contract that would expire four years later. In dollar figures, ASCAP licensing payments between 1931 and 1939 rose from $960,000 to $4.3 million, a jump of 448 percent (Sanjek and Sanjek 1996:176). The National Association of Broadcasters was founded in 1923 as an intermediary between ASCAP and the radio industry. Its president, Neville Miller, feared that licensing fees might double under a new agreement and proposed the formation of an alternative performance licensing agency. To that end, some six hundred broadcasting organizations pledged sums equal to 50 percent of their 1937 ASCAP payments to provide capital and operating funds for the establishment of Broadcast Music Inc. (BMI). In order to develop a catalog of music, BMI turned to many of those individuals and forms of composition that ASCAP had not seen fit to admit into their ranks. As a result, the writers and publishers of many indigenous genres—blues, jazz, country, bluegrass, and, later, rock and roll, to name a few—were able to profit as never before from the public use of their work. At the same time, the landscape of commercial American music became more diversified and reflected, as it had not before, the divergent traditions of our national culture (figure 2).

MID-TWENTIETH CENTURY

During the 1940s the domination of the music industry by a handful of publishers and recording companies diminished for a number of reasons. Key among them were the effects of the strike called by James Petrillo, president of the American Federation of Musicians, in 1942. Alarmed by the erosion of his members' earnings by the replacement of live performance on radio with the phenomenon of "disk jockeys," who played recorded (or "canned," as it was called pejoratively) music, Petrillo followed through on his threat to pull all union members out of recording studios unless the major labels renegotiated their union contract. The labels balked, and the strike lasted until 1944. During that time, World War II preoccupied the American public and brought an influx of rural residents to metropolitan centers to work at factories dedicated to the war effort. The opportunity of obtaining some of these people's newfound disposable income attracted entrepreneurs eager to enter the record business. They proceeded to cement agreements with the musicians' union and thereafter supply the public with music that took their minds off the conflict overseas. During this period and the immediate postwar economic boom, any number of small companies sprang up (for example, Aladdin, Chess, Duke-Peacock, and King) and established the commercial viability of forms of performance the major record labels had ignored or inefficiently marketed: blues, rhythm and blues, and country music principal among them. Innovative technologies—including the reel-to-reel tape recorder, magnetic tape, and the newly developed playback configurations, the 33-⅓-rpm LP and the 45-rpm single—aided these entrepreneurs. Furthermore, at war's end the growth of the economy, the retreat of urban dwellers to the suburbs, and the proliferation of that new generational entity, the teenager, offered a plethora of opportunities for the music industry to exploit a cash-ready and music-eager population (figure 3).

FIGURE 3   Ahmet Ertegun (1924–). Cofounder in 1947 of the Atlantic Records label and a senior statesman in the music industry. Ertegun, along with his partners Jerry Wexler and his brother Nesuhi, released some of the most successful records in popular history, including R&B classics by Ray Charles, Ruth Brown, and Aretha Franklin, and rock landmarks by the Rolling Stones, Cream, and Led Zeppelin. Photo courtesy BMI Archives.

POST–WORLD WAR II

The music industry has undergone many changes since the end of World War II. Three of the most crucial are the absorption of independent record labels by multinational media conglomerates; the introduction of sophisticated technologies that render pre-existing formats obsolete; and the synergistic interfusion of diverse media by Fortune 500 corporations to maximize the means by which music, and other forms of entertainment, are sold. In effect, what was once an enterprise dominated by a large number of avaricious but culturally savvy entrepreneurs has succumbed to the kind of gigantism that rules the global economy unabated by either the desires of the consumer or the political will of government bodies.

The small-scale operations that began to come into being during the AFM strike and proliferated thereafter have succumbed one after the other to the superior capabilities and substantial profit margins of the major record labels. At the present time, five companies (Sony Music Group, Universal Music Group, Warner Music Group, BMG, and EMI) account for virtually 80 percent of global record sales. They therefore dictate what the public will be able to hear. For the major companies, the currently operating independent companies serve two principal ends: to act as systems for career development (known in the industry as "farm teams") whereby new artists develop audiences and illustrate their potential marketability, or to fulfill the needs the majors consider fiscally insupportable, by uncovering a niche for those forms of music or individual artists that will never command the interest of the majority of the record-buying public. While it is inarguable that more music can be purchased at the present time than ever before, the question remains whether the bottom-line mentality of multinational conglomerates, for which music is but one of many products, will ever be able to serve the needs of progressive or experimental musicians, let alone the purveyors of those indigenous forms of expression, such as blues, jazz, gospel, and bluegrass to name a few, that they consider to be outmoded or inaccessible.

NEW TECHNOLOGIES

The proliferation of formats upon which music can be recorded as well as played back has affected the industry since its beginning. Whether the public wishes it or not, technologies routinely replace one another, the promise of improved acoustics overriding, for many consumers, the expense of trading in what they are led to believe is outmoded equipment. At the same time, the manufacturers of musical technology often seem to treat music itself in an indifferent manner. More often than not, it is acoustic imperatives, not aesthetic requirements, that routinely have led to the development and marketing of many if not most technological breakthroughs. The introduction of the 33-⅓-rpm LP record in 1948 and the 45-rpm single in 1950 encouraged what the industry (not the consumer) called the "battle of the speeds." The survival of these two formats and the decimation of the 78-rpm disk were, one imagines, less a result of consumer preferences than of the $5 million advertising budget that RCA Victor spent on the 45-rpm disk. Similarly, the recent hegemony of the compact disc over the LP disk and the promotion of digital technology as the industry standard for acoustic reproduction force one to ask whether the determination of what qualifies as superior sound technology arises from a musical or a mercenary analysis.

It must be added that the technological innovations of the past half-century have redefined the nature of the writer and performer as well as that of the compositional process itself. The reel-to-reel recorder and magnetic tape it employed (invented by German scientists during World War II) allowed the studio to become the place not merely where music was reproduced but also where it could in the fullest sense be created. The ability to edit one performance with another, to correct flaws, and to employ the many effects permitted by multitrack technology liberated musicians from the need simply to re-create live performances before a microphone. Instead, they could treat a studio session as but one piece in a complex process, in which prerecorded material is synthesized into a final product, much as the many takes of a scene in a motion picture are assembled by a film editor into a seamless whole. This further augmented the role and responsibilities of the engineer, as well as that of the producer, or A and R (artists and repertoire) man, as the person in charge of the recording session was known for many years, so that they were virtually coequal with the writer and the performer. More recently, the use of the computer, specifically the digital sampler, has permitted the practice of programming and composing to become virtually synonymous. The fact that one can transform any sound into digital code and then enter it into a composition unleashes a wealth of possibilities for how sound can be employed as well as what music itself might be.

THE CANADIAN MUSIC INDUSTRY IN THE TWENTIETH CENTURY

The first commercial recordings pressed in Canada were issued in 1900 by the E. Berliner Company of Montréal. In the beginning, as throughout its history, the Canadian recording industry has been dominated by foreign-owned companies. The absence of a strong national film industry throughout the twentieth century and the fragmentary, undeveloped character of radio in Canada (until the beginnings of public broadcasting in the 1930s) deprived Canada of the most important channels through which musical careers could be launched. Nevertheless, the existence of significant tariffs on imported recordings has led multinational firms to open branch plants within Canada, pressing records for the Canadian market rather than simply importing them from the United States or elsewhere. Although these subsidiaries (such as Columbia or, later, Capitol Records) have principally been engaged in pressing versions of American or U.K. repertoire for the Canadian market, they have also provided the pressing and distribution facilities through which smaller, Canadian-owned firms have found a way to produce and disseminate national repertoire.

Until the 1970s, English Canadian performers seeking commercial success within the music industries typically moved to the United States. Notable examples of such performers include Guy Lombardo, Percy Faith, country singers Wilf Carter and Hank Snow, and post–World War II vocal groups such as the Diamonds or the Crew Cuts. French Canadian performers were more likely to remain within Canada, finding local success in the folk or *chansonnier* styles popular within Québec and in other parts of the country with French-speaking populations. The fragility of the Canadian recording industry may be traced in part to Canada's small population (roughly one-tenth that of the United States) and to Canada's proximity to the United States (whose cultural industries have typically dominated Canada).

During the 1960s, performers and cultural critics frustrated by the lack of opportunity for English Canadian musical performers began exerting pressure on the federal government to devise means to protect and support a national recording industry. One result of this was the introduction in the early 1970s of so-called "Canadian Content" quotas, which required that radio broadcasters include a designated percentage of Canadian music within their playlists. In 2000, this quota, for private broadcasters of popular music, was 35 percent. (For broadcasters of classical music or jazz, these quotas are lower.) Also in the early 1970s multinational record companies operating within Canada developed coast-to-coast distribution systems (so-called "branch distribution") that mirrored those set up by the same companies in the United States during this period. Having organized national distribution, multinational firms such as Warner began entering into agreements with Canadian-owned firms to distribute their recordings across the country.

Both these events contributed to a significant boost in the health of the Canadian recording industry. Increased access to radio playlists helped to boost sales for Canadian artists such as the rock groups April Wine or Harmonium. A two-tiered industry

In the 1990s, several performers of Canadian origin, including Celine Dion, Shania Twain, Bryan Adams, and Alanis Morrissette, became among the most successful popular music stars in the world. Nevertheless, the effect of their success on a national industry is difficult to discern.

structure, in which multinational firms affiliated with domestic companies for whom they provided distribution, allowed small, locally based companies to concentrate on artist-and-repertoire activities. Attic, Aquarius, True North, and Stony Plain are among the important Canadian-owned record companies that have flourished since the early 1970s as a result of these developments.

In the 1980s, the federal government offered further support to a Canadian recording industry through the establishment of the Sound Recording Development Program, which disburses approximately five million dollars annually to support the production, promotion, and distribution of musical recordings.

Also in the 1980s, the introduction of MuchMusic and MusiquePlus, national music video channels, served as a further stimulus to the production and sales of Canadian music [see MUCHMUSIC AND MUSIQUEPLUS, p. 250]. In the 1990s, several performers of Canadian origin, including Celine Dion, Shania Twain, Bryan Adams, and Alanis Morissette, became among the most successful popular music stars in the world. Nevertheless, the effect of their success on a national industry is difficult to discern. All these performers are signed to the U.S. branches of major recording companies rather than to their Canadian subsidiaries, so that their record sales do not benefit the Canadian industry in any direct sense.

Although Canada's large size has long made the distribution of musical recordings in English-Canada a difficult and expensive undertaking, the market for French-language recordings is more easily served by small, independent firms that operate within the boundaries of Québec. The fate of a Canadian recording industry will be determined in large measure by the effect of trade initiatives (such as the North American Free Trade Agreement), which have eliminated all tariffs on the importation of sound recordings into Canada. Over time this may result in the emergence of north-south distribution patterns, which bring recordings into Canada from pressing plants in the United States and eliminate the need for Canadian subsidiaries of multinational firms. It should be noted that the largest music company in the world, Universal Music, is owned by the Canadian-based Seagram company. Nevertheless, Universal's corporate headquarters are located outside Canada, in the United States.

Finally, for all the innovations available to the writer or performer, the power in the music industry remains in the hands of the businessmen for whom they work. Such has always been the case for creative individuals, but what stands out at the present time is not only the degree to which power remains in the hands of a limited number of corporations (the five recording enterprises previously enumerated) but also the fact that conglomerates, for whom music (or any other form of entertainment) is not their principal source of income, have acquired businesses affiliated to the mass media as but one of the enterprises they control. One is led to wonder if the corporate gigantism that seems to rule the public arena will reduce music to little more than an asset among many other assets, no more or less important than soap flakes, automobiles, or military weapons. The activities of the music-loving entrepreneur would appear to be long gone or at least in short supply. "Synergy" remains the buzzword of the hour. The drive on the part of many businesses is to participate as carriers and program creators on the "information highway," which is believed to be the principal means by which we will in the future receive virtually all our information and entertainment. Whether such communications technology will be a benefit or a detriment to the creation and appreciation of music remains to be seen.

REFERENCES

Breen, Marcus. 1995. "The End of the World as We Know It: Popular Music's Cultural Mobility." *Cultural Studies* 9(3):486–504.

Burnett, Robert. 1996. *The Global Jukebox.* London: Routledge.

Dannen, Frederic. 1990. *Record Men: Power Brokers and Fast Money inside the Music Business.* New York: Times Books.

Eliot, Marc. 1989. *Rockonomics: The Money behind the Music.* New York: Franklin Watts.

Frith, Simon. 1981. *Sound Effects: Youth, Leisure and the Politics of Rock and Roll.* New York: Pantheon.

Garofalo, Reebee, and Steve Chapple. 1977. *Rock & Roll Is Here to Pay: The History and Politics of the Music Industry.* Chicago: Nelson Hall.

Goldstein, Paul. 1994. *Copyright's Highway: From Gutenberg to the Celestial Jukebox.* New York: Hill and Wang.

Kraft, James P. 1996. *Stage to Studio: Musicians and the Sound Revolution, 1890–1950.* Baltimore: Johns Hopkins University Press.

Levine, Lawrence. 1988. *Highbrow/Lowbrow: The Emergence of Cultural Hierarchy in America.* Cambridge: Harvard University Press.

Negus, Keith. 1992. *Producing Pop: Culture and Conflict in the Pop Music Industry.* London: Edward Arnold.

O'Neill, Patrick B. 1993. "The Impact of Copyright Legislation upon the Publication of Sheet Music in Canada, Prior to 1924." *Journal of Canadian Studies* 28(3):105–122.

Rapée, Erno. 1924. *Motion Picture Moods for Pianists and Organists: A Rapid-reference Collection of Selected Pieces, Adapted to Fifty-two Moods and Situations.* New York: G. Schirmer.

———. 1978 [1970]. *Encyclopedia of Music for Pictures.* New York: Ayer Co.

Ryan, John. 1985. *The Production of Culture in the Music Music Industry: The ASCAP–BMI Controversy.* Lanham, Md.: University Press of America.

Sanjek, David. 1997. "Popular Music and the Synergy of Corporate Culture." In *Mapping the Beat: Popular Music and Contemporary Theory,* ed. Thomas Swiss, John Sloop, and Andrew Herman, 171–186. London: Blackwell.

Sanjek, David, and Russell Sanjek. 1996. *Pennies from Heaven: The American Popular Music Business in the Twentieth Century.* New York: DaCapo Press.

Straw, Will. 1996. "Sound Recording." In *The Cultural Industries in Canada,* ed. Michael Dorland, 95–117. Toronto: James Lorimer and Company

Snapshot:
Marketing Classical Music
Robert Fink

The Mass Marketing of Music
Borders Books and Music, Rochester, New York

Let's go shopping. Most North American devotees of classical music would deny that the packaged goods on display in the classical section of a record store represent the essence of art music. But "art for art's sake" means little in an HMV (His Master's Voice) megastore, where the values and structures of meaning associated with the historic canon of Western classical music confront directly the power of late capitalist mass marketing.

THE MASS MARKETING OF MUSIC

Most scholars of consumer culture agree that the distinctive features of a mass market—mass production, national distribution of standardized products, the creation of distinctive corporate logos, media advertising—first came together in late-nineteenth-century America (Strasser 1989). Nationally advertised brands either displaced locally distributed staples (Uneeda Biscuit, Ivory Soap) or created huge new markets for previously exclusive luxury items (Eastman Kodak, Ford). Music, in its live performance both a locally produced staple and an elite luxury, had to undergo a fundamental transformation to be mass marketed: the invention of sound recording provided the impetus for music's national distribution and branding (see TECHNOLOGY AND MEDIA, p. 235). One of the most recognizable brand logos in the early mass-market days was RCA's mascot "Nipper," the dog transfixed by His Master's Voice as it emerged from the gramophone's horn (figure 1).

But 78-rpm disks had technical limitations: three minutes per side meant that an opera recording, spread over fifteen disks that could cost a month's salary, was still a luxury item. These bulky "albums" were marketed on a small scale to consumers already socialized into the appreciation of locally produced art music in performance.

Mass marketing and distribution of classical music had to wait until after World War II, when the economies of scale made possible by magnetic tape recording and the long-playing record led to the first true mass consumption of art music. In the fifty years since the introduction of the LP in 1948, national retail chains and the huge multinational media conglomerates that supply them have thoroughly transformed the way Western society consumes and values classical music. We have moved from a system of

FIGURE 1 "Nipper" listening to His Master's Voice, RCA logo. © Bettmann/CORBIS.

social relations, controlled by networks of patronage, personal instruction, and group interaction, to a system of objects, controlled by advertising, mass marketing, and individual consumption (Attali 1985; Baudrillard 1996 [1968], 1970). At the record store, in the neatly stacked rows of brightly packaged shiny discs, we confront the system of (classical music) objects in all its disorienting complexity. Sometimes this system of objects passively reinterprets traditional art music ideology for the commodity age, but just as often it dramatically disrupts many of classical music's most cherished beliefs.

In the mass market system of (consumer) objects commodities are not simply useful things; thanks to brand advertising, they signify, and in consuming them we consume meaning as well as value. The function of marketing and advertising is not just to sell goods but to construct their meaning, to imbue commodities with signifying power (see Jhally 1987; Lears 1994; Twitchell 1996). Consumption as "invidious display" (Veblen 1899) is an old idea, with many obvious applications to the history of Western classical music (Levine 1988; Weber 1975). On the other hand, the prospect that the cultural meaning of music in an industrialized mass society could be constituted primarily through consuming musical works in (mass-marketed) commodity form—buying and listening to recordings—has caused intense anxiety (Adorno 1991).

Classical musicians only become aware of marketing per se negatively, when the meanings it constructs as it attempts to sell performers or recordings fail to harmonize with previous ideologies of art music (Horowitz 1987; Lebrecht 1997). But from an ethnographic perspective the interference between classical music as idealized in cultural tradition and as materialized in a system of mass-marketed commodities provides crucial data. A preliminary ethnography of the classical section of Borders Books and Music in Rochester, New York, taken on the afternoon of 14 October 1997, documents a real, if low-key, conflict between the remnants of classical music's performance culture and what we might call CD culture.

BORDERS BOOKS AND MUSIC, ROCHESTER, NEW YORK

Actually, in its large-scale structure the system of musical objects constructed by Borders and its suppliers reinforces some key aspects of classical music traditions. Like almost any store that expects significant traffic in classical music recordings, Borders rigidly segregates classical music from all other types of music. At the largest record stores, the classical section is often acoustically sealed off from the rest of the store and decorated more conservatively, with a simulacrum of more luxury. This retail strategy translates the claims for aesthetic autonomy made on behalf of Western art music into material terms, even inflecting them with the same slight tinge of class consciousness. (The separate space of classical music is also the locus of an ersatz gentility.) One might note that this separate section only exists because a select few stores devote a wildly disproportionate amount of floor space to classical music; its very appearance is limited to a network of boutiques where consumers can indulge the fiction that their extremely exotic taste is still at the center of the world's musics.

As you enter the large rectangle of the record department, the classical music section is on your left. (Studies show that consumers overwhelmingly turn to the right as they enter a new space; as in the world at large, no one wanders into classical music by mistake.) Classical music extends halfway up the left-hand wall and halfway along the far wall; it is bisected by racks of videotapes in the far left corner. Along that back wall it abuts the jazz section, sensibly enough; jazz is the "black classical music" and is rapidly approaching classical music's canonicity, aestheticism, and cultural marginalization. But the rest of the classical section is bordered by a riot of exotic and flagrantly "nonclassical" musics: soundtracks, yes, but also reggae and world music, rap, electronica, ska, funk, and soul.

This strange border zone becomes clear only after you have traversed the entire store, which reproduces the generic landscape inside the mind of a typical upper-middle-class consumer quite precisely. Along the right (dominant) wall is pop-rock, by far the largest section, arranged alphabetically by artist. Facing off uneasily against the rock colossus along the left wall is classical, also arranged alphabetically. Between are "borderline" exotic and dance musics—African, Latin, Asian—that occupy the same marginal place in the system of musical objects as in the Western musical imagination.

The bulk of classical recordings is organized by composer; here the system of objects reinforces the traditional Western emphasis on individual creativity and "genius" quite handily. (The overwhelming recorded preponderance of a few "great" composers goes without saying.) This materialized canon of the great composers is physically segregated from mongrel classical recordings categorized in other ways. Past the video racks are budget recordings, operas (by title, not by composer), recordings of famous and historical performers, collections by instrument type and by chronological period, and, farthest from Bach and Beethoven, "greatest hits" albums and collections organized on extramusical themes.

But only half of these thematic collections are in the bins; the rest are prominently displayed in special fixtures. If the bins largely reinforce traditional classical music values, these display racks are where those values take a beating. Of the several kinds of marketing displays visible at Borders on this afternoon, two show "CD culture," the new system of musical objects, under construction most clearly.

Towering garishly over the understated wooden bins is a large rotating metal stand. Its twelve-by-four-inch slots are filled with identically styled CDs, whose intentionally crude bright yellow and red covers grab the eye. Each CD bears a cartoon figure holding up a poster/blackboard, on which is chalked *Beethoven* [Bach, Brahms, Romantic Music, Puccini] *for Dummies*. The *Classical Music for Dummies* (Pogue and Speck, 1997) series is a collaboration between EMI Records and IDG Books, which first used the *X for Dummies* rubric to sell instructional computer books, and it recasts classical music's vaunted cultural autonomy in a new, unflattering light. "Classics for the Rest of Us!" the covers announce, echoing a famous slogan coined for the Apple Macintosh; classical music is still an autonomous realm, but the prospective consumer is now located firmly outside its suddenly rather exotic and geeky precincts. Here classical music has become Other.

Classical Music for Dummies turns the notion of "high" art upside down. Art music is difficult, not like great art or literature, but difficult like badly written computer manuals, and these CDs, which include some rudimentary educational software, provide a "Fun and Easy Way" to master it. Nobody buys *Windows 95 for Dummies* because he or she actually feels stupid; we are responding to the promise that the stripped-down knowledge it contains is purely instrumental (in other words, I don't really care about this, just tell me what I need to get the job done). The idea that connoisseurship of art music could be reduced to such pure instrumentality ("Get to Know the Real Rimsky-Korsakov and Have the Ultimate Listening Experience") erases music for music's sake from the system of objects. Within the system, all music, like all computer equipment, is functional.

However ironic its outsider attitude toward art music's aesthetic of disinterested intellectuality, *Classical Music for Dummies* does at least leave the canon in place: almost every title is devoted to the work of one famous composer. But scan the classical section's most prominent display case, devoted to new major label releases, and an even more disorienting picture emerges. This is the first rack you see as you enter the section, and in October 1997 it was completely under the control of Polygram's Deutsche Grammophon subsidiary, providing a particularly clear picture of one conglomerate's view of the system of musical objects. The canon is in ruins: of the thirty-five slots, only seven used a composer's name to attract the eye, and most of those were reissues.

Most trumpeted a celebrity performer, usually a singer or violinist, with the music a distinctly secondary consideration. (Fully six slots went to a single Pavarotti collection; three to Cecilia Bartoli; two to Bryn Terfel; eight other slots were selling either a voice or a violin.) Media tie-ins abounded: a new recording of Vivaldi's *Four Seasons* was linked to the Weather Channel, while another release echoed late-night TV infomercials by offering *The Only Opera CD You'll Ever Need* ("hundreds of excerpts on one incredible CD!").

And thus the new system of (musical) objects displaces the old system of social relations. Should we mourn? In one sense, "Western classical music" does reveal itself as another fragile indigenous musical culture, as vulnerable as any to the destructive encroachment of technology and capital. But I would argue that the system of musical objects is ultimately liberating. If we move out of the embattled classical section and browse among those other musics, we can find a new anticanon of serious music, a new set of sociomusical relations mediated quite happily by technology and commodity exchange, and a hardy growth of that perennial, art. CD culture is alive and well.

Even the ethnomusicologist can see him- or herself reflected in the system's transforming mirror. On Borders's classical best-seller list that week was a compilation disc called *Tune Your Brain* (1997), a collection of classical music sorted by mood and designed to accompany a self-help book of the same title. The cover blurb: "Ethnomusicologist Elizabeth Miles shows how you can use music as a mood-enhancement tool—finding just the right sounds to help you handle anxiety, enhance your creativity, boost your IQ, control pain, get motivated, have better sex, and more." We have met the Other—and they are us.

REFERENCES

Adorno, Theodore. 1991 [1944]. "The Culture Industry: Enlightenment as Mass Deception." In *Dialectic of Enlightenment,* ed. Theodore Adorno and Max Horkheimer. New York: Continuum.

Attali, Jacques. 1985. *Noise: The Political Economy of Music.* Trans. Brian Massumi. Minneapolis: University of Minnesota Press.

Bach for Dummies. 1996. EMI 7243 5 66270 0 0. Compact disc.

Baudrillard, Jean. 1970. *La société de la consommation.* Paris: Gallimard.

———. 1996 [1968]. *The System of Objects.* Trans. James Benedict. London: Verso.

Beethoven for Dummies. EMI 7243 5 66264 0 9. Compact disc.

Brahms for Dummies. 1996. EMI 7243 5 66272 0 8. Compact disc.

Fox, Stephen. 1984. *The Mirror Makers: A History of American Advertising.* New York: Morrow.

Horowitz, Joseph. 1987. *Understanding Toscanini.* New York: Knopf.

Jhally, Sut. 1987. *The Codes of Advertising.* New York: St. Martin's Press.

Lears, Jackson. 1994. *Fables of Abundance.* New York: Basic Books.

Lebrecht, Norman. 1997. *Who Killed Classical Music? Maestros, Managers, and Corporate Politics.* Secaucus, N.J.: Birch Lane Press.

Levine, Lawrence. 1988. *Highbrow/Lowbrow: The Emergence of Cultural Hierarchy in America.* Cambridge: Harvard University Press.

McLuhan, Marshall. 1964. *Understanding Media: The Extensions of Man.* New York: McGraw-Hill.

Miles, Elizabeth. 1997. *Tune Your Brain: Using Music to Manage Your Mind, Body, and Mood.* New York: Berkley Books.

Pogue, David, and Scott Speck. 1997. *Classical Music for Dummies.* Foster City, Calif.: IDG Books.

Puccini for Dummies. 1997. EMI 7243 5 66404 0 5. Compact disc.

Romantic Music for Dummies. 1997. EMI 7243 5 66561 0 9. Compact disc.

Strasser, Susan 1989. *Satisfaction Guaranteed: The Making of the American Mass Market.* New York: Pantheon.

Tune Your Brain: Music to Manage Your Mind, Body, and Mood. 1997. Focus/Deutsche Grammophon 289 457 853–2. Compact disc.

Twitchell, James. 1996. *AdcultUSA: The Triumph of Advertising in American Culture.* New York: Columbia University Press.

Veblen, Thorstein. 1899. *The Theory of the Leisure Class.* New York: Macmillan.

Weber, William. 1975. *Music and the Middle Class: The Social Structure of Concert Life in London, Paris and Vienna.* London: Croom Helm Press.

Section 3
Processes and Institutions

The learning and teaching of music has taken many forms within the United States and Canada, from the singing schools of Lowell Mason to the shape note traditions of the rural south, from the European-inherited schools of classical music to the American traveling singing master, from the notated score of the diva's studio to the oral/aural tradition of the back porch. Part of this history is bound up with the development of various school music education programs in both countries and their role in socializing children to be musical "Americans" or "Canadians." Government, too, has played its part in the encouragement and regulation of musical practices in these two countries. Governmental agencies such as the National Endowments for the Arts and Humanities in the United States and the Canadian Radio-Television and Telecommunications Commission (CRTC) have been crucial to the development of various musical cultures within their borders.

Grandfather teaching banjo to grandson, Issaquah, Washington. © Walter Hodges/ CORBIS.

Learning
Patricia Shehan Campbell
Rita Klinger

Historical Perspectives
Practices in Elementary Schools
Practices in Secondary Schools
In the Community
In the Lives of Children
Research Trends

Learning is the acquisition and short- or long-term retention of knowledge, skills, and values. Musical learning is the amassing of knowledge about music: its repertoire, performance techniques, and meanings. It broadly encompasses formal and informal contexts, within social institutions such as schools and churches as well as beyond them—in communities and families and among friends. There are numerous conceptions of musical learning, with various words employed to describe how people come to know music: schooling, education (instruction and pedagogy), training, socialization, and enculturation. Of these, education in music or through music (or music education) usually refers to the teaching of music in elementary and secondary schools and to collegiate programs that prepare teachers for the profession. It may be paired with schooling to indicate musical activities and sequential instruction in the teacher-directed groups of state-operated schools, where the continued survival of a group's heritage and its cultural identity are assured through the curriculum of bands, choirs, orchestras, and "general music" classes. Education in music typically concerns the learning of music as performance as well as for its historical and theoretical aspects; this type of learning occurs in formal settings that include conservatories and university schools and departments of music. Training involves the conscious efforts of teachers and students in the transmission and acquisition of knowledge through experiences relegated to some but not all members of a culture; professional teachers and parents often provide musical training to children in their developmental years. Music is also learned through the less formal process of socialization, whereby a group or institution inculcates its beliefs and values in its membership to ensure that its members continue to act in approved ways and hold particular shared beliefs. Socialization is a broader enterprise than schooling or training, extending from music in schools and lessons to the manner in which young people pick up knowledge from personal insight through participation in the activities of a group and thus adopt a set of ideas or skills as well as a way of life. An even broader view of musical learning is enculturation, the totality of life—customs, values, occupations, and recreations—that is known through the experience and context of a sociocultural group. A particular repertoire and the characteristic features of music are known by virtue of growing up and living within a cultural (or subcultural) group.

HISTORICAL PERSPECTIVES

The history of music education in North America has been shaped by social circumstances beginning with the interaction between church and community. In Canada, the participation of Roman Catholic clerics in the organization of choirs and training of its choristers began in Québec ("New France") in 1626. Singing and piano lessons were offered by religious orders in their convents in the mid-eighteenth century, while Protestant-backed music schools for private instrumental learning spread rapidly following the founding of the first musical school in Montréal in 1789. The first instances of music education in the United States were linked to worship activities within the Protestant church and the perceived need of its leaders to train singers in notational literacy for the purpose of congregational psalm singing. With the establishment of singing schools in the eighteenth century, homes, barns, and schoolhouses became the earliest venues of nightly music reading sessions taught by traveling singing school masters that included William Billings and Francis Hopkinson. In urban areas such as Boston, Philadelphia, and Savannah, singing schools developed into singing societies by the late 1700s.

Music in the school curriculum

Private academies in the United States offered children instruction on violin, cello, piano, and other orchestral instruments, but public school music was first offered in Boston in the late 1830s. Extramusical claims in three categories—moral, intellectual and physical—were raised to justify the place of music in the curriculum. Through the efforts of bank clerk and singing teacher Lowell Mason, who espoused the principles of "sound before symbol" and experiential learning advocated by Swiss educational reformer Johann Heinrich Pestalozzi (1746–1827), vocal music education was admitted into the curriculum of not only Boston but also Buffalo, Pittsburgh, Louisville, Cincinnati, Chicago, Washington, D.C., Cleveland, San Francisco, and St. Louis. By the early 1850s Mason had established widespread standards for public school music through his many travels to eastern and midwestern cities to discuss and demonstrate his pedagogical method. The development of "music conventions" at this time for the discussion and demonstration of music in schools soon led to Mason's establishment of a prototype for longer terms of training teachers in music and its pedagogy.

In a similar manner, Egerton Ryerson, the first superintendent of education in western Canada, was impressed by the educational processes of Pestalozzi and also of Jean Jacques Rousseau. He perceived vocal music as a vehicle for promoting middle-class values, and he recognized the potential of music to foster loyalty and patriotism in Canadian life. Rather than designate specialist music teachers, however, Ryerson supported the training of regular classroom teachers in the Hullah system of singing. Canada's first official school curriculum guide was published in 1870. Music was prescribed for all grades, singing was a recommended activity for morning opening exercises, and the tonic sol-fa method (for French-Canadians, solfège) was included to enable children to read music. The music course for primary and intermediate students at the end of the nineteenth century recommended simple airs, rounds, and songs in two parts to be taught in four weekly lessons. Beyond the schools, Canadians could avail themselves of music instruction through choral societies and church choirs as well as activity in instrumental music such as regimental bands.

Throughout the nineteenth century, efforts to establish music as a curricular subject in North America was contained mostly to vocal music in elementary schools. Although music instruction could be found in girls' schools, ladies' colleges, and select seminaries, it was rarely found in boys' private schools or in grammar schools geared toward the provision of traditional academic studies. Occasional mention is given to a school operetta or festival, but such events are more anomalies than an indication of a

FIGURE I   Fasola nota-
tion, from Patricia Shehan
Campbell's *Lessons from
the World*, 66.

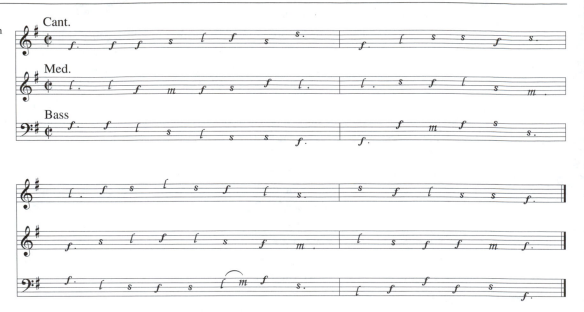

pattern of activity. In Canada even more so than in the United States, music was
crowded out of the picture by academic subjects that enjoyed higher political priority.

When the American educator Luther Whiting Mason had succeeded in establishing music in the primary schools of Cincinnati, he then went on to develop both primary and secondary school music in the Boston schools in the 1860s. His graded
music series, The National Music Course (1870), was a set of four books and a chart
for the teaching of musical notation, one of which was widely adapted. During the 1880s
and 1890s, teachers and textbook publishers (such as Silver Burdett, the American
Book Company, and Ginn) presented their views on the use of shape-note, tonic sol-fa,
and the fixed *do* methods of instruction and on whether to emphasize singing for its
own sake over the goals of notational literacy (figure 1). Vocal music began to be well
established in elementary school classrooms through the dispersion of textbooks and
the establishment of teacher training institutes sponsored by the textbook companies.

A critical mass of supervisors and teachers of music was developing, so that American music educators had developed a music section within the National Education
Association by the 1890s. In 1910, the Music Supervisors National Conference was
formed to promote music in the public schools, and annual meetings and quarterly
issues of the *Music Supervisors Bulletin* were distributed to the membership. The organization was renamed the Music Educators National Conference (MENC) in 1934,
and the monthly periodical became the *Music Educators Journal*. Canadians created
short-lived music sections within the Dominion Educational Association and the
National Council of Education but by the 1920s were participating in the American
conferences. The Canadian Federation of Music Teacher Associations was established
in 1935; its concerns ranged from the licensing of private music teachers to the facilita-
tion of uniform standards of examinations. In 1959, the Canadian Music Educators'
Association was organized to support the interests of public school music teachers.

The rise and development of music programs

The rise of choirs in secondary schools was achieved as a direct outgrowth of vocal
music instruction in elementary schools but was also due to the presence of singing in
the community through churches and professional and amateur singing societies. By
the end of the nineteenth century, four-part choral singing was a common curricular
choice in American high schools. Courses in listening, instrumental performing, music
history, and theory began to appear in isolated places. The invention of the player

piano and the phonograph brought a new emphasis to the high school curriculum through music appreciation courses. Frances E. Clark was engaged by the Victor Gramophone Company in 1911 to design instructional materials that were linked to their recordings, and a new pedagogical movement for all ages and learning stages, led by the state-of-the-art technology, was born [see THE MUSIC INDUSTRY, p. 256]. In the 1920s and 1930s regular radio broadcasts of concerts with commentary by conductor Walter Damrosch introduced millions of schoolchildren to symphonic masterworks; soon in Canada Roy Fenwick's *Musical Homework* program was showcasing performances of school ensembles.

Instrumental music instruction in the United States was offered mostly as a private enterprise through most of the nineteenth century, and strings were far more popular than winds. The band music of Patrick Gilmore's community peace jubilees in the post–Civil War era influenced John Philip Sousa, Frederick Innes, and others of the school band movement of the early twentieth century. Instrumental music activity, particularly through orchestras, became prominent in schools before World War I. With the discharge of enthusiastic bandsmen from the military at the end of the war, there was a rapid growth in school bands and in the study of wind and percussion music. The beginning of a national school band competition in 1923 brought considerable attention and interest, so that in less than two decades, the number of participating schools had soared from a mere handful (concentrated mostly in the Midwest) to 24,000 bands spread across the United States. Will Earhart, who in 1898 established a high school orchestra in Richmond, Indiana, set the standard for other orchestras to follow. Joseph Maddy persuaded industrialist George Eastman to give ten thousand dollars worth of instruments to Rochester, New York, thereby developing another model of a school orchestra program. By the early 1930s, a school's musical reputation began to be judged largely by the quality of its instrumental performance programs.

Beginning with the development of school choirs as extracurricular activities, Canadian high schools began to develop music as part of the curriculum between the wars. Instruction on musical instruments from the late nineteenth through the early twentieth century was achieved largely through private means, or in churches or community centers. The establishment in 1902 of local music examinations, based upon the practices of the Associated Board of the Royal Schools of Music in London, ensured that students of piano, organ, violin, and cello were following a detailed syllabus that led to the development of high standards of musical performance. Following World War II, music curricular offerings began to appear in rural areas, and massed singing events with choirs of a thousand children led to further recognition of music as a viable subject for inclusion within the curriculum. In Canada's secondary schools, first vocal music and later instrumental teaching predominated through the early to the mid-twentieth century, and finally a more equitable balance between the two offerings was attained by the 1960s.

Training of music supervisors

Unlike high school principals, music supervisors at the turn of the twentieth century were usually without normal school training. Many supervisors were self-taught and had not graduated from high school, were given minimal training by publisher-sponsored summer schools, or, by World War I, were trained musicians but without professional training in music education. The first normal school for the preparation of music teachers was established in Potsdam, New York, by Julia Ettie Crane in 1884, but it was not until the 1920s that a four-year degree program in music education was developed at Oberlin Conservatory in Ohio. In Canada, universities began to train specialist teachers of music in the 1940s. By the middle of the century, licensed (or certificated) music teachers were able to graduate with bachelor's degrees in music or

Federal policies and funds that had been designed to strengthen and nurture national development in the arts through school and community programs in the 1950s and 1960s weakened and in some cases were abandoned by the 1970s and 1980s.

music education. Practices varied, in that some states and provinces integrated licensing requirements within the bachelor's degree program, while others required a fifth year beyond the bachelor's degree or even a master's degree. In an era of increasing specialization, many states and provinces that began with an all-encompassing "music K–12" certificate turned toward separate vocal/choral, instrumental, or general music areas at either the elementary or secondary level by the end of the century.

A wave of music aptitude (talent) and achievement assessment, brought on by the broader educational movement in comprehensive intelligence testing, swept the United States in the opening decades of the century. Carl Seashore's *Measures of Musical Talent,* first proposed in 1912, was published in 1919 and was principally intended to measure musical sensitivity to small gradients of difference in pitch and rhythm as a means of guiding parents and teachers in their choices of musical involvement for children and youth. This atomistic assessment of aptitude was controversial, and other tests, including those by Jacob Kwalwasser and Peter Dykema, Raleigh Drake, E. Thayer Gaston, and Edwin E. Gordon, attempted a broader review of musical sensitivity. Standardized achievement tests by Kwalwasser and Ruch and Knuth in the 1930s and Gordon and Colwell in the mid-1960s were designed to measure musical accomplishments, including the recognition of symbols and the aural ability to detect errors, but they have had limited use.

The writings and teachings of Rousseau, Pestalozzi, and later John Dewey continued to influence music education practices in the twentieth century as newer music-specific philosophies emerged. Utilitarian views on music justified the inclusion of music in formal educational settings, as it was seen as a tool to strengthen other areas of the curriculum. In the 1930s Dewey's "art as experience" sought to turn the ordinary passive exposure to art into an active, enriching, educational encounter and paved the way for the Susanne Langer–inspired "Music as Aesthetic Education" movement in which the intrinsic qualities of music ultimately enrich the quality of life for students beyond the formal educational experience.

Music programs in the second half of the twentieth century

The second half of the twentieth century was a roller-coaster ride of growth, stability, and, since the late 1970s, decrease of support for music in schools in the United States and Canada. Federal policies and funds that had been designed to strengthen and nurture national development in the arts through school and community programs in the 1950s and 1960s weakened and in some cases were abandoned by the 1970s and 1980s. A movement to support distinctive Canadian cultural and artistic traditions and forms was in evidence in midcentury but suffered cutbacks within two decades. Large performing ensembles, particularly wind bands, flourished in high schools, while orchestras decreased in size and number (this despite the growth of Suzuki-styled training of young string players in community settings outside the schools). As musical styles changed, so did curricular offerings. Jazz was introduced to schools in the 1950s and within the next two decades was a viable alternative for secondary students to the more traditional ensembles. Courses in "youth music" and "rock music" also began to flourish as a nonperformance option for secondary school students.

In the United States, the introduction of the Carl Orff and Zoltán Kodály pedagogies in the 1960s soon brought about a fusion of the two perspectives in many elementary classrooms, with children singing folk songs via the tonic sol-fa method, performing folk dances, creating instrumental and movement pieces, and playing recorders, xylophones, and other percussion instruments. Until the 1960s, the most common activity in music in Canadian schools was singing from song collections such as *High Road of Song* and *La Bonne Chanson,* but when Canadians embraced the Kodály method and its rigorous development of vocal and literacy skills, music instruction was revitalized in key cities like Calgary, Toronto, and Vancouver. The Orff-Schulwerk method has received somewhat less attention by Canadians than by Americans, but its emphasis on improvisation has nonetheless been felt in most elementary music classrooms.

Computer technology is evident throughout North America in the establishment of keyboard labs for developing aural and notational literacy skills and for their use in facilitating composition activity and recording projects by students. The promotion of creativity in the classroom has been more theory than practice in American classrooms, but in Canada the development of "sound pieces" and the use of traditional music have been particularly prominent in the last three decades. Composer R. Murray Schafer has created an approach to the development of musical sensitivity involving exercises for keen listening and the creative exploration of sound leading to composition. His books and widespread demonstrations have addressed means for musical expression for the young and musically naive.

Since the early 1980s, both policy statements and curricular practices have been directed toward the inclusion of music from many diverse populations of North America. In the United States, African and African American traditions have been strongly integrated into choirs and music classes for children, and drumming ensembles in middle and high schools are on the rise. Native American and, to a lesser extent, Latin American and Asian musical cultures are also featured in the materials published since 1990. In Canada, music from the "First Peoples" (Native Canadians), as well as from French and Celtic cultures, is increasingly performed. Eastern European and Middle Eastern communities in Toronto have been the source and impetus of the greater presence of these musical traditions in the schools, while in Vancouver the considerable Chinese population has inspired the inclusion of *luogu* 'percussion' ensembles, songs, and folk dances of China into classes of music for children.

PRACTICES IN ELEMENTARY SCHOOLS

Formal music instruction in the elementary schools (elementary schools in North America generally include kindergarten through fifth or sixth grade, or ages five through twelve) is typically offered in the form of thirty- to forty-five-minute general music lessons. When music specialist teachers are employed, students may receive instruction from once to three times a week; some schools have optional choirs for children in fourth through sixth grades. Many schools also offer instruction in Western orchestral or wind band instruments, with the opportunity to perform in ensembles beginning in fourth or fifth grade.

The purpose of general music in the elementary school is to introduce children to a wide variety of music through songs, dances, movement, dramatic play, and the use of classroom instruments. Singing, which occupies much of the general music lesson, is often viewed by music teachers as the primary means by which to educate young students about the formal elements of music and musical structures. Song repertoire ranges from patriotic, seasonal, and holiday songs to international, popular, and art songs. Students often accompany their singing with an assortment of small pitched and unpitched percussion instruments such as rhythm sticks, claves, hand drums, wood blocks, triangles, maracas, and xylophones (figure 2).

Elementary school music teachers provide numerous services to the school community. Most elementary schools stage several assembly programs during the year for parents and the community, often centering on seasonal or curricular themes. All-school sings, prevalent during the 1950s and 1960s, are once again gaining popularity. The elementary school music teacher also supports the general curriculum by providing musical materials and information for the integration of music that reinforces the social studies, math, science, and language arts areas of the curriculum. In Canada as well as in an increasing number of U. S. schools (particularly in urban areas), the responsibility for teaching music may rest fully in the hands of classroom teachers who are likely to use music as entertainment, as an ambiance for other classroom activities, or as a means of setting the scene for a particular season or special event (figure 3).

Teachers of elementary school music commonly continue and extend their education by seeking certification in one of several pedagogical trends that have grown in popularity since their introduction in North America during the 1960s. Formal training in the pedagogical practices associated with Orff-Schulwerk, Kodály, Suzuki, Dalcroze, and Gordon is available at various sites in the United States and Canada. Teachers can pursue multilevel certificates endorsed by national associations or even master's degrees in these pedagogical approaches. Comprehensive Musicianship is another curricular approach which, while having no certification process, was widely espoused by teachers in the 1960s and is still practiced.

Each of the influential pedagogical methods offers strategies, materials, and experiences for motivating young students to actively sing, listen, create, perform, and move to music. Although similar in many ways (all are to some extent rooted in the belief that music is experiential), each approach emphasizes different facets of music making. Emile Jaques-Dalcroze (1865–1950), Swiss musician and professor of solfège at the Geneva Conservatory of Music, believed in the use of the whole body to express rhythm and sound. Through movement, fixed-*do* solfège, and improvisation one emerged with individual, expressive musicianship. Those following a Dalcroze-based approach advocate experiencing music first through an auditory stimulus, then responding physically and mentally, and finally expressing the response through movement. Zoltán Kodály (1883–1967), Hungarian composer and professor of composition, theory, and solfège at the Liszt Academy in Budapest, believed in the importance

FIGURE 2   Children on rhythmic percussion instruments. B. F. Day Elementary School, Seattle, Washington. Photo by Jerry Gay, 1993.

FIGURE 3   Children associating sounds of pitches with notation. B. F. Day Elementary School, Seattle, Washington. Photo by Jerry Gay, 1993.

of musical literacy. According to Kodály, a musician should strive to read music in the same way as one might read a book. Through singing folk songs of the musical mother tongue and the use of relative solfège and rhythm mnemonics, one could extract the essential musical ideas leading toward understanding and skill in Western art music. Teachers in a Kodály-inspired curriculum advocate the long-term, unconscious preparation of selected musical skills, followed by the presentation of newly acquired musical skills in an additive spiral over time. Carl Orff (1895–1983), known primarily as a composer, founded the approach known as Orff-Schulwerk, an experiential method rooted in rhythm and improvisation. Fundamental to the method is the notion that feeling precedes understanding. Music is taught through speech, movement, and childhood songs that are usually accompanied by layered ostinati patterns on small percussion and pitched instruments such as xylophones and metallophones, often referred to as "Orff Instrumentarium." The Orff process for teaching includes guided experiences in exploration, imitation, and improvisation. Edwin Gordon (1927–), American music researcher and educator, created a music learning sequence of instruction based on his Music Learning Theory. This instruction includes strategies and materials for developing rhythmic and melodic "audiation," the term Gordon coined to represent inner hearing, or internally thinking music with understanding. Rhythmic and tonal patterns are introduced sequentially with the aid of mnemonics as children sing, move, and create music. Shinichi Suzuki (1898–1998), Japanese violinist, educator and philosopher, developed the system known as Talent Education, or the Mother-Tongue Method, for nurturing innate musical abilities. Originally developed for violin instruction, the system now includes materials and methods for teaching cello, piano, and flute. Central to the pedagogy is an early start, parental involvement, and the delay of the music reading process until basic instrumental readiness has been established. Comprehensive Musicianship, a literature-based approach to teaching music by integrating and relating all musical components, grew out of the Young Composers Project (1959) and the Contemporary Music Project (1963), both funded by the Ford Foundation. With a focus on relating various areas of musical study, students learn about common structural elements in music and experience music as listeners, composers, and performers.

PRACTICES IN SECONDARY SCHOOLS

Music in the secondary schools of the United States and Canada may be either an elective or a mandated course, depending on the educational guidelines set by the state or provincial board. It is common for regional policies to require the study of music for students in middle or junior high school (ages twelve to fourteen), while in high school musical study is one among several elective courses in the arts and humanities. In the United States, student participation in music electives in high schools ranges from 5 to 15 percent, depending on the nature of the electives, the competitive electives in other arts subjects, and other factors relative to the socioeconomic status and cultural values of families and communities to which students belong. In Canada, it is an accepted fact that instrumental music instruction is more likely to occur beyond or in addition to the public school curriculum—in community, Saturday, weekend or night schools—while choral music activities are evident in schools as well as in churches and other community-wide organizations. Other course offerings in music are available under the categories "general," "appreciation," or "advanced placement" (AP), although the greatest emphasis is on group instruction within performing ensembles rather than private applied lessons or nonperformance classes; nine out of ten music enrollments in U. S. high schools are in performing organizations.

Performing ensembles are well suited to adolescent needs for recognition, self- and social identity, and active and participatory learning. Concert bands and marching bands are popular electives in U. S. schools. Marching bands are as regional as they are

Enrollments have multiplied for nontraditional ensembles such as Trinidadian steel drum and African drumming ensembles, guitar and keyboard classes, and courses in composition, songwriting, and musical theater.

seasonal: in the autumn, there are few midwestern and southern high school football teams without a large and spirited band to cheer them on and play the halftime entertainment, while high schools on both coasts are apt to have smaller "pep bands" that are extracurricular clubs rather than curricular classes. The corps style of marching is increasingly popular, in which a large percussion section perfects a set piece for all performances to be played in military style to the choreographed dancing of flag twirlers and drum majors. Enrollment in concert, symphonic, or wind bands may often overlap with membership in marching bands, and in many schools there is an automatic transfer of membership from one to the other in late November. Repertoires of wind, symphonic, and concert bands consist of serious musical forms composed expressly for these ensembles (largely by American composers) and occasional transcriptions of classical art music pieces, while marching bands are as likely to play "Louie, Louie" and medleys of currently popular songs and show tunes as they are to give yet another rendition of the school's alma mater (figure 4).

Orchestras that in the opening decades of the twentieth century attracted the attention of the finest young musicians in the schools began shrinking in size as wind ensembles grew in popularity. Enrollments have multiplied for nontraditional ensembles such as Trinidadian steel drum and African drumming ensembles, guitar and keyboard classes, and courses in composition, songwriting, and musical theater. Middle schools and junior high schools provide short-term courses on a variety of musical subjects, and this exposure leads students to commit to longer periods of selected high school study.

Jazz ensembles attract students who play in other instrumental ensembles or who "graduate" after several years from one of the larger ensembles to an interest in jazz-

FIGURE 4   High school students play in a regional jazz festival.

FIGURE 5 Vocal jazz performers.

style improvisation. Most high school curricula feature swing-style big bands, or stage bands, and some offer small combos and classes in jazz improvisation. Because jazz is still perceived by some educators as marginal to the mainstream concert band tradition, the ensemble rehearsals are often scheduled before or at the end of the school day. Despite this, many high school musicians commit themselves to jazz for the personally expressive avenue it allows them, a sense of building individual identity within a collective venture.

Secondary students frequently select from various choral opportunities, including mixed a cappella and accompanied choirs for beginners and more advanced singers, same gender choirs, and smaller ensembles such as madrigal, vocal jazz, and swing or show choirs (figure 5). In some regions of North America such as the upper Midwest, choral ensembles are strong because of the participation by adults in church and community choirs (and thus parental support of the high school programs that feed these choirs). At the same time, choral programs in urban schools with many African American students may have small enrollments due to the nature of students' involvement in the gospel choirs of their churches. Concerts are the prime motivators for ensemble classes, with December and spring programs as rather lavish indicators of what students have learned.

IN THE COMMUNITY

Since the first settlements in the colonies, in New England, New France, and New Spain, there has been spontaneous and untutored music making by people in song, dance, and instrumental playing. Churches first and then schools provided young people with access to musical knowledge and skills, but musical learning was widespread in other contexts as well. A spectrum of formal to informal contexts for learning music still exists, from other established institutions that engage in the education and training of musicians to the casual or even coincidental learning of music that occurs even when it is not particularly intended. At the formal end of the spectrum, instrumental lessons, choir activities, musicianship and "exploratory music" classes are available to students of all ages in nearly every community, while informally, music is made by garage bands and in home-styled jam sessions and is further available to listeners through recordings and the media of radio, television, and videotapes [see TECHNOLOGY AND MEDIA, p. 235].

Private music instruction is widespread. In storefront studios, community centers, and homes of musicians (or the homes of students to which the teachers travel), students of all ages are taught technique and repertoire for piano, keyboard, guitar, drums, saxophone, voice, and a host of band, orchestral, and even ethnic instruments (for example, West African percussion). Weekly and monthly fee contracts are set by individual teachers, periodic recitals are arranged in local churches, and students are expected to learn weekly exercises, practice pieces, and recital repertoire. A typical thirty-minute lesson engages the student in performance of the week's assigned work, and teachers may perform with the student, issue verbal comments while the student performs, or demonstrate passages or whole pieces themselves. A private teacher of piano may run in her home studio thirty to forty lessons per week, in which an adult clientele will comprise her daytime schedule while the after-school and Saturday morning time will be filled by children and adolescents at the beginning and intermediate levels of instruction. Music stores may hire performers or salespeople who can also teach and who do so in separate rooms or even sound-attenuated booths. The rental of instruments with an option to buy can be a successful means of bringing the student into contact with technique, repertoire, and eventually the ownership of an instrument.

Select children's choirs have flourished in the United States and Canada over the past several decades. These tuition-based organizations usually include several levels of groups that children have the opportunity to qualify for and pass through. Children at age six or seven are eligible to audition for training choirs and, through subsequent auditions, move on to intermediate and advanced performing and touring choirs. With community-based boards of directors and financial support from tuition as well as public and private sources, children's choirs from Toronto to San Francisco have gained public attention through concerts and professionally produced CDs. Choral series from music publishers such as Boosey and Hawkes and Oxford abound under the names of distinguished children's choral directors.

Children are often enculturated into the music of their varied communities—enclaves of ethnicities, races, classes, and social groups. These communities embrace their music, giving much effort to the creation, maintenance, and transfer of individual and group identity through the music they make. For Mexican American children, important styles like mariachi (in California and the Southwest) and *conjunto* (in Texas) may engage them as dancers or even performers. Children in midwestern communities of Poles, Germans, Czechs, and Bohemians flock with their parents to weddings and old-world "national day" celebrations that feature polka bands. A recent mushrooming of interest by Irish Americans in their Celtic roots has drawn many children to group step dance lessons. Countless numbers of African American children participate in the religious music of children's gospel choirs and congregational singing.

In the early 1980s a keen interest developed in the provision of music instruction for young children. Spurred by a growing number of parents who were interested in the holistic education of their infants, toddlers, and preschoolers, and furthered by the lore of the "Mozart effect," in which it is believed that musical training will enhance intellectual development, a wave of national and local community organizations was established to coordinate exploratory musical experiences for children from the earliest age. Kindermusik is best known among them for its certified training of teachers who run classes in song, instrumental play, and movement for young children and their parents in their homes, church social halls, and community centers. Audio- and video-taped instruction, as well as televised series such as *Barney and Friends, Mr. Rogers' Neighborhood, Sesame Street,* and *Teletubbies,* has been influential in exposing children to musical styles and activities.

Adolescent involvement in music may turn toward the organization of rock bands. These bands usually begin in basements or garages, where friends and classmates gather on weekends and evenings to listen to and imitate the songs of their favorite performers on guitars, small keyboards, and often makeshift drum sets. Concentrated, analytical listening and repeated trials to "play the song like the recording" give structure to the rehearsals. For each new song that is targeted for learning, a musical leader functions as "expert," principal "on-site transmitter," and model, leading the group through its acquisition of the various melodic, rhythmic, and harmonic components of a song. Often these bands stay private, but occasionally some attain their goals of playing dances at schools, shopping malls, and teen clubs.

IN THE LIVES OF CHILDREN

In the corners of their rooms, yards, schools, and throughout their play (and often work) with friends, classmates, neighbors, and family members, there is a steady current of children's own music that underlies their activity. Music is on the minds of children and in their voices and bodies. As they converse, walk or run, eat, play games, manipulate toys, or ride bikes, they sing, chant, and move in rhythmic ways. Children engage in making music because it is their intention to do so, and they also make music even when they are unaware that it *is* music. They use music for its many functions, and many will explain in considerable detail what music is important to them, and why.

Children begin their musical involvement in the nuclear culture of their family, with lullabies sung by parents and grandparents and songs that are sung for waking, dressing, and eating. Siblings add to the repertoire, as do child care workers, and their playful song texts extend to family and friends, animals, the weather, and transportation. Children's musical knowledge spreads from this primary source in ever-widening circles, and soon they are singing the songs of characters on television programs and videotapes and songs they have learned from their playmates. By school age, children enter into the realm of singing games, clapping chants, and regular and purposeful rhythms. They jump rope, toss balls, and even count out team members through songs and chants, preserving songs that have lived for many generations within these games and rituals as well as occasionally contributing new material.

Parents, teachers, and professional songwriters often establish that songs suited for children should be simple in rhythm, sparse in pitch information, and quaint in their texts. Yet songs that children invent, refashion, or learn from other children and then preserve intact may often consist of greater musical complexities and diverse texts. Their musical grammar arises without, and often prior to, formal instruction. "Ring around the Rosy," "Bluebird," "Little Sally Walker," and "A-Tisket A-Tasket" are classic singing games that have been played for many generations, while "My Mama Told Me," "My Sailor," and "Apple on a Stick" are long-standing interactive chants in which children stand in pairs or occasionally in circles and lines, clapping, patting, stamping, snapping fingers, and moving their bodies in complex patterns that complement the chant or song.

Children's spontaneous songs are typically open-ended, with beginnings and endings unpredictably developing from and returning to their playful interaction with toys and other children. Some are intermediary forms, performances that sit between speaking and singing. Open musical forms may use a single rhythmic or melodic phrase repeatedly, often with one phrase joined to or launching another phrase. Often children's musical expressions are a blend of bits of songs and rhythms they have known but that are refashioned into new arrangements that match the children's own musical knowledge, skills, and inclinations.

Children learn songs, games, rhymes, and lullabies not only from teachers but also from parents, grandparents, siblings, and friends. Children teach each other music on the playground, in the school bus, at scout meetings, or in their backyards. The teaching and learning process is informal, holistic, and typically quite successful. Children's

Among music educators the thrust of research has been to seek answers to questions that arise in the instructional process, such that research is derived from, and further informs, teaching and learning practices.

musical genres such as jump-rope and ball-bouncing chants, rhymes, hand-clapping and street games, and sporting event cheers have been passed down through generations of children and continue to flourish anywhere that children congregate informally.

RESEARCH TRENDS

The study of music and learning has attracted music educators on faculties in tertiary institutions and students in graduate music education programs to issues of teaching method and sequence, teacher behaviors, and student reactions and outcomes. Research by psychologists, sociologists, anthropologists, and folklorists, as well as music theorists and ethnomusicologists, has raised large issues of music perception and cognition and music as a transmissional and enculturative process. Among music educators the thrust of research has been to seek answers to questions that arise in the instructional process. The founding of the *Journal of Research in Music Education* in 1953, within the Music Educators National Conference (MENC), was testimony to the growing interest by teachers in finding solutions to their practical problems and in contributing to theories of music education. Early articles were often historical in nature or descriptive of particular school programs and their challenges, but by 1970 the majority of articles were experimental or consisted of surveys and correlations. Special research groups were formed by the MENC in 1978, calling themselves by their interest areas: Affective, Creativity, Early Childhood, Gender Studies, General, History, Instructional Strategies, Learning and Development, Measurement and Evaluation, Perception, Philosophy, and Social Sciences.

In addition to the biennial conferences that feature sessions and the popular, research poster exhibit area, there have been since the late 1970s numerous research symposia and other gatherings. The Ann Arbor Symposium was spread over three meetings in 1978, 1979, and 1981 and explored the relationship between music education and behavioral psychology through interactions among specialists in both fields. The 1984 Wesleyan Symposium attempted to achieve understandings among music educators, anthropologists, and ethnomusicologists on music, its role in culture, and its means of transmission. In the last part of the twentieth century, researchers gathered to examine research method (behavioral and qualitative in particular) and pressing issues (multiculturalism and technology) or to pay tribute to outstanding educators and educational researchers (Charles Leonard, Carl E. Seashore).

Research by music educators has encompassed many issues. The *Handbook of Research on Music Teaching and Learning* (Colwell 1992) delivers a review of research in fifty-four chapters, ranging from philosophical foundations to comparative music education, including disparate articles on auditory-visual perception and musical behavior, technology, keyboard music, and students with disabilities. A recent anthology of research in music education (Price 1998) presents notable research over four decades in the following categories: philosophical conceptualizations; historical conceptualizations; children's perception, discrimination, and performance abilities; performance and adult discrimination; teacher behavior and student response; observing and evaluating music teaching; responses to music; reinforcement and music; special populations in music; multicultural issues and music. Research by music educators has often been behavioral in approach, in which a large selection of studies has examined preference behaviors and the step-by-step process by which a performance skill is shaped. Recent efforts to understand the nature of music learning and instruction are moving beyond music and education to the discovery of what insights the disciplines of psychology, sociology, and anthropology can offer the field.

REFERENCES

Campbell, Patricia Shehan. 1991. *Lessons from the World: A Cross-Cultural Guide to Music Teaching and Learning.* New York: Schirmer Books.

Carder, Polly, ed. 1990. *The Eclectic Curriculum in American Music Education.* Rev. 2nd ed. Reston, Va.: Music Educators National Conference.

Choksy, Lois, Robert Abramson, David Woods, and Avon Gillespie. 1986. *Teaching Music in the Twentieth Century.* Englewood Cliffs, N.J.: Prentice-Hall.

Colwell, Richard. 1992. *Handbook of Research on Music Teaching and Learning.* New York: Schirmer Books.

Dann, Hollis Ellsworth, et al., comp. [1943–1944]. *The High Road of Song.* Toronto: W. J. Gage & Co.

Green, J. Paul, and Nancy F. Vogan. 1991. *Music Education in Canada: A Historical Account.* Toronto: University of Toronto Press.

La Bonne Chanson: A Program of French Songs. [1978]. Cambridge CRS 2775.

Mark, Michael L. 1996. *Contemporary Music Education.* New York: Schirmer Books.

Mark, Michael L., and Charles L. Gary. 1992. *A History of American Music Education.* New York: Schirmer Books.

Price, Harry F. 1998. *Music Education Research: An Anthology from the Journal of Research in Music Education.* Reston, Va.: Music Educators National Conference.

Government and Politics
Barry Bergey

Regulation of the Arts
Conservation of the Arts
Presentation of the Arts
Public Policy in the 1990s

The impact of public policy on music cannot easily be untangled from a general consideration of the historical relationship between government and the arts. In the United States and Canada the engine of public policy has several times jumped the track on the journey toward the establishment of a coherent cultural agenda. Alexis de Tocqueville noted that citizens in a democracy are not indifferent to the arts, but "they cultivate them after their own fashion and bring to the task their own peculiar qualifications and deficiencies" (1945[1835]:2:41). The peculiar nature of democratic systems seems indeed to have contributed to an equally peculiar combination of policies and programs meant to address the arts in both Canada and the United States.

Not until after World War II was there a serious attempt on the part of either government to create a federal arts council. The Canadian Arts Council was formed in 1957, and the National Endowment for the Arts in the United States was not created until 1965. Both agencies were decentralized systems of public support for the arts, roughly modeled on the British Arts Council (established in 1945). Their function was not to create or enact a public arts policy, such as a ministry of culture might, but to fund artistic organizations and artistic activity at arm's length through an independent, peer-panel system. The level of support for the arts councils from each government remains minuscule: around one-twentieth of one percent of the federal budget in Canada and less than one-hundredth of one percent of the budget in the United States.

Although public policy on the arts has been notable more for its absence than its presence, other governmental instruments—including cultural preservation projects, work relief endeavors, foreign policy and exchange programs, governmental arts centers, and national artistic ensembles—have affected artists. Indirect aspects of policy, such as regulations in the form of tax laws, postal rates, and copyright legislation, also apply. Although the public support of music reflects no single coherent cultural strategy, a historical survey reveals three areas of governmental involvement: regulation, conservation, and presentation.

REGULATION OF THE ARTS

Governmental involvement with the arts in Canada and the United States took its earliest form as legislation establishing the right of private ownership of artistic products and ideas.

Copyright

In both countries, copyright provides for the protection of intellectual or creative property, extending to fifty years beyond the life of the creator. In the case of music, it addresses the right to copy, print, sell, arrange, record, or publicly perform a work. Infringement of copyright can be penalized by injunction, exacting financial remuneration for the copyright owner, fines, and in some cases imprisonment. Copyright serves political and social systems based on individual ownership and an artistic marketplace but does not sufficiently address the concept of collective ownership (Seeger 1992). International copyright builds on the Berne Copyright Union, an agreement reached at the Berne Convention in 1886 and revised frequently in subsequent years. The Universal Copyright Convention (UNESCO Convention), concluded at Geneva in 1952 and later revised, provides the basis for international copyright agreements.

In December 1996 representatives of 160 countries met in Geneva and reached agreement on treaties affecting copyright issues. Under the auspices of the World Intellectual Property Organization of the United Nations, these treaties would protect owners from computer-generated copies of musical recordings from the Internet. It is still necessary for these treaties to be ratified by legislative bodies of the various countries.

In Canada

Canadian copyright laws draw on British statutes enacted as early as 1709. In 1832 the provincial Statutes of Lower Canada established copyright protection for writers and composers, and in 1841 the statute was extended to Upper Canada. The registration of a Canadian publication through deposit in the Office of the Registrar and the Legislative Library (Ottawa) was introduced in 1859. At that time only seven musical publications, all hymnbooks, had copyrights. The first sheet music registered was Martin Lazare's "Canadian National Air" (1859), and Maria Stisted's "The Rose of Ontario Waltz" (1868) was the first musical item in the numerical register of copyrights (Kallmann et al. 1992:233). In 1921 Canadian copyright law was extended to protect the mechanical reproduction of musical works. The National Library of Canada in Ottawa and the Bibliothèque national du Québec in Montréal have become the repositories of copyrighted works.

In the United States

In the United States copyright was established by the Constitution (framed in 1787, effective 4 March 1789): Article One, Section Eight granted Congress the legislative power to "promote the Progress of Science and useful Arts, by securing for limited Times to Authors and Inventors the exclusive Right to their respective Writings and Discoveries." By 1790 Congress had legislated the details of the copyright process, including applications, registrations, deposits, renewals, and enforcement (Anderson 1989). The first musical work registered for copyright was Andrew Adgate's *Rudiments of Music,* entered 18 November 1790 and extant as only a title page. Benjamin Carr's *Ellen Arise: A Ballad* and *The Little Sailor Boy: A Ballad* (1798) were the first complete deposits. A significant change in the law occurred in 1831 after Noah Webster, author of spelling books and a renowned dictionary, successfully argued to bring U.S. law into conformity with European statutes. For the first time, musical compositions were covered by copyright; until then, music was registered only in book form.

Responsibility for copyright shifted among several offices, but an 1870 statute mandated the Library of Congress as the sole repository for copyright materials, and all previously accumulated registrations and deposits were transferred there. Deposited materials were increasingly utilized as part of the library's general collection. In 1972 a revision of the copyright law expanded coverage to include recorded materials. As a result, the library's Recorded Sound Division, set up in 1939 to cover commercial materials and recordings generated by the Works Progress Administration (WPA), grew exponentially. By 1996, approximately two million recordings had gone on deposit in the Motion Picture, Broadcasting, and Recorded Sound Division.

In cultural warfare

While copyright is a way for governments to legislate individual artists' rights, nations also have used regulation to protect cultural integrity: "The arts lie at the heart of the cultural sovereignty battle. The spirit of a nation is expressed through the creative act, and the arts, by definition, are the focus of that activity" (*Funding of the Arts in Canada* . . . 1986:26). In an effort to defend Canadian music from incursions by U.S. culture through the airwaves, the Canadian Radio-Television and Telecommunications Commission enacted in the 1970s a law requiring that 30 percent of all music played on AM radio during prime time be Canadian; on the FM band the regulations varied, requiring 30 percent Canadian content for classical music and 70 percent for popular music. On the other hand, only 13.8 percent of the recordings purchased in record stores in Canada are by Canadian artists. As defined by the Broadcasting Act of 1991, music is Canadian if two of four requirements are Canadian: music, artist, performance, or lyrics (*Canada's Culture* . . . 1995: 32). Ownership of radio and television broadcasting companies by foreigners is also regulated in Canada.

The 1989 United States–Canada Trade Agreement, also known as the Free Trade Agreement, spurred a debate on issues involving cultural products. Canadians fought for the exclusion of cultural industries from trade liberalization: "When Americans discussed trade in culture, they usually talked in terms of culture as a commodity, whereas Canadians (and Europeans) generally speak in terms of heritage, national identity, and social well-being" (Kestin 1992:164). For the most part, the cultural sector in Canada was protected from trade deregulation. In 1994 a trade war was nearly precipitated when there was a move by the Canadian Radio-Television Telecommunications Commission to ban Country Music Television, a Nashville-owned country music cable station, from Canada in favor of the Canadian-owned Country Network.

Another near border skirmish between the United States and Canada brings to light an additional type of regulation, immigration policy, that can affect musicians and other performing artists. The U.S. Congress passed the Immigration Act of 1990, scheduled to take effect, after a period of public comment, in October 1991. This law made it considerably more difficult for artists and entertainers to enter the United States by limiting the number of visas available, tightening eligibility, and complicating application procedures. After much protest from U.S. arts presenters and other governments, Canada in particular, legislation was passed easing the protectionist restrictions.

Other aspects of governmental provenance also affect the arts. Most crucial in the United States is the allowance of federal tax deductions and local property tax exemptions. Further benefits are extended to arts organizations through tax and postal regulations. Special postal rates offered to nonprofit organizations indirectly support artistic institutions and their programs, and tax regulations exempt nonprofit organizations from local property taxes and allow individual deductions for contributions to nonprofit arts organizations. Tax-related support of cultural institutions in the United States has been estimated to amount to more than three times the direct cash support (Schuster 1985:44).

CONSERVATION OF THE ARTS

Copyright laws in both Canada and the United States in effect created the first significant repositories of musical materials in those countries. However, technologies new in the nineteenth century, combined with a growing interest in the study of culture, led to an era of documentation of musical performance, often supported by governments in the name of preserving the cultural patrimony.

American Indian/First Nations music

Anthropologists and folklorists in the 1890s were beginning to explore the importance of music in human culture. The invention of the cylinder phonograph and its commercial availability in 1889 opened up the possibility of documenting and reproducing musical performances for the purpose of study and entertainment [see TECHNOLOGY AND MEDIA, p. 235]. Anthropologist Jesse Walter Fewkes, field-testing a recording device on a visit to the Passamaquoddy Indians of Maine in March 1890, made the first recording of Native American music. His interest was in documentation "as a means of preserving the songs and tales of races which are fast becoming extinct" (Fewkes 1890:257) [see MUSIC OF THE AMERICAN INDIANS/FIRST NATIONS IN THE UNITED STATES AND CANADA, p. 365].

In Canada

In 1841 Queen Victoria granted money for the creation of the Geological and Natural History Survey of Canada (based in Montréal), and by the 1890s James A. Teit, a survey-team member who had worked with Franz Boas, had recorded songs among tribes in British Columbia. An anthropology division within the museum branch of the survey was created in 1910, and Edward Sapir, a German-born and U.S.-educated social anthropologist and linguist, was appointed its head. In 1911 the museum was moved to the Victoria Museum in Ottawa. In 1927 the museum adopted a new name, National Museum of Canada, later changed to National Museum of Man and in 1987 to Canadian Museum of Civilization.

The first work of musical interest done for the new division was W. H. Mechling's transcription of Malecite and Micmac songs in New Brunswick in 1911. The same year, Sapir hired Marius Barbeau as staff ethnologist. For the next forty years, Barbeau was the central figure in the collection of Canadian traditional music. He and his colleagues recorded approximately three thousand songs on wax cylinders among thirty-one Indian tribes of the Northwest Coast, Eastern Woodlands, and Plains.

In the United States

In the United States the earliest governmental documentation of American Indians also came about as an offshoot of geological and geographic surveys. The Bureau of Ethnology, later named Bureau of American Ethnology, was established in 1879 under the purview of the Smithsonian Institution. Major John Wesley Powell, a Civil War veteran and head of the bureau, encouraged the documentation of Native American culture in all of its aspects. Influenced by the prevailing evolutionist belief that Indian culture was gradually being assimilated and would inevitably be lost, early ethnologists with the bureau conceived of their mission as providing a window on humankind's "primitive" past and a record of a disappearing present. They sought "the completion of a systematic and well-rounded record of the tribes for historic and scientific purposes before their aboriginal characteristics and culture are too greatly modified or are completely lost" (*Annual Report . . .* 1908:29).

The staff of the bureau was small, and much work was done by unsalaried consultants, many of whom were self-educated. Alice Cunningham Fletcher, a pioneer student of Indian music, studied a variety of tribes of the Great Plains, collaborating with Francis La Flesche, son of an Omaha chief.

Frances Densmore, inspired by Fletcher, became the most prolific documenter of Native American music of the early twentieth century. Between 1907 and 1941, from thirty-seven cultures, she recorded nearly two thousand cylinders of music, and she wrote nearly a dozen monographs and numerous articles on Indian music. Reared in Red Wing, Minnesota, and trained as a classical pianist, she believed that the music she collected could become a basis for new American compositions. Her work, most of it

In the United States, the accumulation of musical items at the Library of Congress as a result of the copyright law necessitated the accommodation of physical and bureaucratic structures for musical materials, including the establishment of a separate music section in 1897.

under the auspices of the Bureau of American Ethnology, resulted in significant publications on Chippewa and Teton Sioux music.

Non-Native music

In both Canada and the United States, documentation of musics other than those considered aboriginal was somewhat slower to materialize.

In Canada

Between 1915 and 1930 Marius Barbeau and his associates in French Canada recorded over 6,700 folk songs. Carmen Roy, who in 1966 became director of the National Museum's folklore division, continued research into French-Canadian folklore and music, documenting over 2,500 folk songs by the late 1960s.

Work recording the Anglo-Saxon music of Canada came much later, as Helen Creighton began documenting music of the Maritimes for the museum in 1947. However, before that, between 1928 and 1942, she financed her own field trips to collect music in Nova Scotia. In 1943–1944 and 1948, the U.S. Library of Congress provided her with recording equipment. In 1961 her *Maritime Folk Songs,* containing 170 songs, was published, and in 1964 the museum published her *Gaelic Songs in Nova Scotia.* In 1965 the museum published the three volumes of *Songs of the Newfoundland Outports* containing over four hundred songs collected by Kenneth Peacock over a ten-year period.

In the 1950s and 1960s there was a geographic and cultural broadening of documentary activities through the National Museum of Canada. In 1957 a Folklore Section was created within the Anthropology Division. Kenneth Peacock began surveying smaller ethnic communities in central and western Canada, and in 1966 the museum published *Twenty Ethnic Songs from Western Canada,* containing songs he had collected in Doukhobor, Mennonite, German, Hungarian, Ukrainian, and Czech communities. Also, the museum and the Canada Council cosponsored research by Robert B. Klymasz into the Ukrainian communities of the prairie region of Canada, beginning in 1963. The federal government's multicultural policy announced in 1971 further encouraged expansion of the museum's mandate to document ethnic music.

In 1970 the Folklore Division was renamed the Canadian Center for Folk Culture Studies. The Ethnology Service by 1980 included seven thousand tapes and wax cylinders of music, while the Center for Folk Culture Studies had some two hundred collections of folk songs and instrumental music on more than three thousand wax cylinders and five thousand tapes. From time to time, Canadian governmental institutions have also supported documentation of traditional music: in 1941 the National Film Board engaged Laura Boulton to make a trip across Canada recording ethnic communities, including Eskimo and Indian.

Lamenting the work left to be done in Canada, Kenneth Peacock (1969:88–89) wrote:

> Only a small proportion of our traditional folk music has been made available to the academic community, the creative musician, and the public at large. . . . Up to

the present, folk-music research in Canada has largely been carried on by a few dedicated individuals working in comparative isolation. Few institutions of higher learning offer courses where students may learn the techniques of collecting, documenting, archiving, transcribing, analyzing, and publishing folk-music materials. There is no institute of ethnomusicology. The miracle of it all is that we have done as well as we have in preserving and disseminating our traditional folk music.

In the United States

In the United States, the accumulation of musical items at the Library of Congress as a result of the copyright law necessitated the accommodation of physical and bureaucratic structures for musical materials, including the establishment of a separate music section in 1897. No less important in the library's early history was the vision of such leaders as Herbert Putnam, librarian of Congress from 1899 to 1930, and Oscar Sonneck, hired to be the chief of the Music Division in 1902. Sonneck initiated a program of acquisition, classification, cataloging, and research. His visionary interests, including his attempt, in his words, "to catch the music of the future," allowed him to lay the foundation for an American field of musicology and to leave behind at the Library of Congress in 1917 one of the largest and most diverse music libraries in the world (Anderson 1989:130).

For documenting American musical traditions in the 1920s, the Library of Congress turned to a more fieldwork-based approach. Carl Engel, who succeeded Sonneck, continued Sonneck's expansionist policies and reported to the librarian in 1928 that there was a pressing need for a great centralized collection of American folk songs. This interest in indigenous music was spurred by the presence of collections of folk material in prestigious European institutions and the trend among composers to draw on folk music to create a distinctly national music.

The Archive of American Folk-Song was established in 1928. Robert Winslow Gordon, a scholar of folklore, a folk song collector, and a freelance writer, was named director (Bartis 1982). Gordon, writing to Engel in 1927 before his appointment, said in a prescient comment about his plans to document folk culture: "I'll bet a cookie that a hundred years from now the backers of such a national project would be better remembered by this nation than the man who offered $10,000 or $15,000 or $25,000 for a new stunt aeroplane flight" (Kodish 1986:156). During his tenure he collected music in a number of states, he continually experimented with new technological advances in recording equipment, and he investigated copyright claims for such popular songs as "The Wreck of Old 97" and "Oh! Susanna" However, his individualistic personality, lack of attention to administrative details, and penchant for esoteric research put him at odds with the library administration. In 1932, the Great Depression and a scarcity of available funds from the private sector provided the administrators with an opportunity to quietly let him go.

In 1931 the distinguished folk song collector John A. Lomax had contacted the Library of Congress to inquire about borrowing recording equipment to record African American work songs in Texas prisons. Lomax had made some of the earliest English-language American cylinder recordings of music when recording cowboy songs between 1906 and 1910 for his publication *Cowboy Songs and Other Frontier Ballads* (1910). He asserted: "The book had one distinction which no one recognized at the time. It was the first collection of native American folk songs ever printed along with the music of the songs. This music had been taken down in field recordings, and such music as there existed on the cylinders then transcribed through the use of earphones" (1947:77).

John Lomax and his son, Alan, went out on the road. From the Archive of Folk-Song in 1933 they received a shipment of equipment, first to record on cylinders and then on disks. The Lomaxes collected material for the archive and for *American Ballads and Folk Songs* (1934) through a publishing contract with Macmillan, funding from the American Council of Learned Societies, and later a grant from the Carnegie Corporation of New York.

In 1934, upon Engel's insistence, John Lomax accepted the position of Honorary Curator of the Archive of American Folk-Song for a salary of $1.00 per month. The father and son continued to collect, including on trips to Texas, Louisiana, and other southern states. The era of the Lomax family's association with the archive marked the period of the most intense fieldwork and documentation of American musical traditions in the history of the United States.

In fiscal year 1938 the U.S. Congress made the Archive of American Folk-Song part of the central library budget for the first time. Alan Lomax was the first archive employee paid by congressional funds, with the title assistant-in-charge, while his father remained honorary consultant and curator. The Lomaxes brought to the library a new vision that combined intensive field documentation and public outreach based on their work. Performing artists were brought to the library to record, a radio series done jointly with the Columbia Broadcasting System was initiated, and a series of published recordings based on fieldwork was started.

A field trip in 1941–1942 by Alan Lomax to Mississippi to document music and narrative marked the last major field documentation by archive staff for more than a decade. With the war, most activity was curtailed. Alan Lomax resigned in 1942, but he continued to work on radio projects for the Office of War Information and the U.S. military.

By 1936 several Depression-era federal relief projects had begun feeding into the archive. Harold Spivacke, Chief of the Music Division of the Library of Congress, was a member of the national committee of the WPA Music Program. Musical documentation recorded by a few state music projects and materials from the Resettlement Administration were transferred to the Archive of American Folk-Song. In particular, a collecting expedition in the South by Herbert Halpert of the WPA Federal Theater Project in 1939 was funded through a joint committee on folk arts, chaired by Benjamin A. Botkin of the Federal Writers' Project. With the assistance of the WPA and Charles Seeger, *Check-List of Recorded Songs in the English Language in the Library of Congress Archive of American Folk Song to July, 1940* was researched and published in 1942.

The Recording Laboratory, created at the Library of Congress in 1940 to accommodate the archive's recording and duplicating ventures, plus commercial recordings, radio recordings, electrical transcriptions, and WPA-generated recordings, began to play a more active role in musical programs at the library, including the release of a series of albums, *Folk Music of the United States*. In succeeding years there was a decline of staff fieldwork, but there was an increase in acquisitions through duplication, gifts, purchases, and transfers from other federal agencies. The recording series and documentation-equipment loan program continue.

In 1976 the American Folklife Preservation Act established the American Folklife Center at the Library of Congress with a mandate to preserve and present American folklife. This legislation provided the first official definition of folklife: "The traditional expressive culture shared within the various groups in the United States: familial, ethnic, occupational, religious, regional" (Loomis 1983:26). The Archive of American Folk-Song, renamed Archive of Folk Culture in 1981, became part of the American Folklife Center, which initiated several broad-based fieldwork projects, most of them documenting music as one facet of the project.

The Federal Cylinder Project, initiated by the center in 1979, was intended to preserve and disseminate earlier ethnographic recordings, many of them made under the auspices of the Bureau of Ethnology. Tribal groups have benefited from the repatriation of rare and in some cases forgotten musical repertoires inscribed on wax. The Archive of Folk Culture has holdings that include 53,000 sound recordings, 1,250,000 manuscripts, 220,000 photographs, 450 moving image materials, and 26,000 printed items (Jabbour 1996b).

The Music Division of the Library of Congress, having actively solicited composers' manuscripts, maintains an extensive collection of European and American works. Special private trust funds, the first of their kind in the federal government, have allowed the library to purchase important work, acquire five Stradivarius instruments, maintain resident chamber ensembles (such as the Juilliard Quartet), sponsor ongoing musical programs, and commission new works (including Aaron Copland's *Appalachian Spring*). The Music Division contains over eight million items, with strong collections of chamber music, opera, popular music, and American musical theater.

PRESENTATION OF THE ARTS

Direct federal support of artists and artistic presentations in any significant way is a development of the late twentieth century. As early as 1778 Thomas Jefferson, the fiddling president, lamented that "the bounds of an American fortune will not admit the indulgence of a domestic band of musicians, yet I have thought that a passion for music might be reconciled with that economy which we are obliged to observe" (1992 [1778]:363).

In both the United States and Canada the first governmental support of musicians actually occurred through the subsidy of military bands. The U.S. Marine Band, organized in 1798 and conducted by John Philip Sousa from 1880 to 1892, predated by two years the government's move to the District of Columbia. Supporters of the National Endowment for the Arts frequently point out that the budget to support military bands in the United States is double the entire budget of the National Endowment for the Arts.

In Canada

The Canadian government began to investigate government support of the arts after World War II. The Massey Commission recommended the creation of an arts council based on the British Council, created by Royal Charter in 1945. Critic Northrop Frye hailed the Massey Commission Report of 1951 as "a landmark in the history of Canadian culture, not merely because it recommended a Canada Council, but because it signified the end of cultural laissez-faire and assumed that the country itself had a responsibility for fostering its own culture" (*The Canada Council 33rd Annual Report* . . . 1990:6).

The Canada Council, created by an act of Parliament in 1957, was designed to give support to professional artists and arts organizations using the peer-review process. In 1998–1999 the council distributed $112 million (Canadian), nearly three dollars per citizen, to arts programs and organizations. Historically, between 17 and 19 percent of the allocation has supported music and opera. Almost two-thirds of that amount goes to nine orchestras and eight opera companies for operating support, and most of the rest goes to orchestras and opera companies for project grants. There is little evidence that the council supports to any measurable degree the music of ethnic or folk cultures. In 1990 its Opera and Music Section held a meeting involving musicians who practice non-European music to develop a program that would accommodate music from all cultures. In March 1995 the Canada Council published its strategic plan, *The Canada Council: A Design for the Future,* setting its priorities as maintaining grant budgets and supporting creation, production, distribution and dissemination of Canadian artists and works of art.

The Canada Council represents only 4.6 percent of the governmental expenditure for arts and culture. Two-thirds of the government's allocation to culture goes to the Canadian Broadcasting Corporation, amounting to nearly $765 million (Canadian)

Canadian observers note that there seems to be a growing tension between the urban centers and the rural provinces in both cultural and political policy.

annually. The Royal Commission on Radio Broadcasting (Aird Commission) recommended a state-owned radio system, expressing concern about the penetration of U.S. broadcasting into Canada and the perceived chaos in U.S. radio because of the lack of regulation. Prime Minister R. B. Bennett said: "This country must be assured of complete Canadian control of broadcasting from Canadian sources, free from foreign interference or influence. Without such control radio broadcasting can never become a great agency for communication of matters of national thought and ideals, and without such control it can never be the agency by which national consciousness may be fostered and sustained and national unity still further strengthened" (Meisel and Van Loon 1987:284).

The CBC provides both AM and FM radio service and television service in French and English, the official languages of Canada. The CBC saw its greatest growth after World War II. It has sponsored competitions for young composers and talent festivals. For regular live broadcasts, it has sponsored a variety of musical ensembles, including the CBC Opera Company, the CBC Québec Chamber Orchestra, the CBC Symphony Orchestra (Toronto), the CBC Vancouver Chamber Orchestra, and the CBC Winnipeg Orchestra. The CBC has historically been the country's principal employer of musicians who play "serious music."

In the area of recording, the CBC International Service, founded in 1945 to provide Canadian composers and musicians record distribution abroad through the RCI label, had a catalogue of over five hundred recordings by 1980. The CBC-SM (Serious Music) label, begun in 1966, was initiated to produce phonograph records by Canadian performers. When discontinued (in 1980), it had a catalogue of 350 disks featuring recordings largely by Canadian orchestras. The CBC-LM (Light Music) label, with a catalogue of 450 recordings by 1980, featured Canadian jazz and popular music.

The year 1995 marked the beginning of a three-year period of reductions targeted to shrink the CBC budget by a third over three years. In response, the Corporation has initiated a process of downsizing and is looking to advertising and other sources of funding to make up the difference.

The National Arts Centre, completed in 1969, was a centennial arts project of the Canadian government. Located in Ottawa, it is the home of the National Arts Centre Orchestra. It presents musical series that include classical, baroque, and pop music. Cutbacks in governmental funding in the 1980s led to the curtailment of some programs and the suspension of the Centre's annual productions of operas.

In 1993 the Department of Canadian Heritage was given the responsibility of overseeing the issues and implementation of cultural policy. The Minister of Canadian Heritage serves as the link between various cultural agencies and Parliament. In Canada, with an arm's-length system of support, the municipal arts councils and provincial arts councils collectively spend more on culture than the federal government. Canadian observers note that there seems to be a growing tension between the urban centers and the rural provinces in both cultural and political policy: "In all probability the public perception of elitism will be that the fault lies in the length of the arm, rather than in the persistence of the values of dominant groups to the exclusion of most of the other groups in Canadian society" (Cohnstaedt 1992:179).

In the United States

Direct federal support of the arts advanced like the mythical slow train through Arkansas—riders on the train were said to comment that the train would have to speed up to stop. George Washington remarked that "the arts and sciences are essential to the prosperity of the state and to the ornament and happiness of human life," and Senator Jacob Javits, during hearings in 1965, the year of the creation of the National Endowment for the Arts, noted: "Federal concern with the arts goes back a very long way— way back to George Washington's time. We have not done too much about it" (Mankin 1976:62). The birth of an arts-funding agency within the U.S. government culminated a long period of gestation marked by debate about the government's proper role with regard to the arts.

The New Deal emergency relief programs yielded the U.S. government's first serious forays into support for artists and the presentation of artistic programs. The Civil Works Administration, created 9 November 1933, provided money for work relief, and in some states amateur orchestras, bands, and chamber ensembles were formed to give free concerts in libraries, museums, hospitals, and schools. On 6 May 1935 the Works Progress Administration (WPA) was created, and in August the Federal Arts Projects were initiated. Several issues emerged, including whether the artists employed should be professional or amateur and whether admission should be charged for programs: "The difficulty was that as time went on and the rival claims of professional versus amateur art defined themselves, the approval of the cognoscenti became more compelling than the applause of the commoner" (McDonald 1969:186).

Directed by Nikolai Sokoloff, a Russian immigrant and former conductor of the Cleveland Symphony, the Federal Music Project had five goals: providing employment assistance for musicians, establishing high standards through classification of these musicians, stimulating community interest, creating an intelligent musical public, and demonstrating to the public the constructive work being done by the federal government in the face of the depression (Bindas 1995:1). When the Federal Music Project was created, there were eleven recognized symphony orchestras in the United States, but by 1938 there were thirty-four orchestras employing 2,533 musicians. Other presentational projects included funding for operas, composers' contests, a composers' forum, music-teacher training, and the radio broadcasting of music.

Controversy within Congress concerning the Federal Theater Program and political and administrative wrangling led to the dismantling of the federal arts programs in 1939 and the gradual transfer of responsibility to the states. The federal cultural program ceased to exist for all practical purposes, except in support of the war effort. Virgil Thomson commented that the Federal Music Project was primarily responsible for establishing the credibility of symphonic music in America. The performance of American works by orchestras more than doubled from 1939 to 1943, and compositions by Thomson, Aaron Copland, Roy Harris, Elie Siegmeister and William Schuman can be directly linked to FMP activities (Bindas 1995:109).

The next concerted governmental involvement with the arts came during the cold war and involved international cultural exchange. As early as 1936 the U.S. government had initiated a cultural program to counteract Germany's cultural offensive in Latin America. After 1941 this Division of Cultural Relations was absorbed into the Office of War Information.

In the 1950s attention was drawn to the supposition that the United States was losing the cultural war to the Soviet Union with its active program of sending athletes, scientists, writers, and performing artists abroad. In response, the United States Information Agency (USIA) was created in 1953 to coordinate educational, cultural, and information activities overseas and to arrange musical tours of artists in the fields of classical, jazz, and folk music. The Voice of America was developed to tell America's story via the radio waves. Critics of the USIA have pointed out that its position has never been secure; it has appeared independent at times, and at other periods it has looked like an arm of the State Department. Of the administrative confusion, former USIA Director George Allen is said to have commented that "only the U.S. government could invent a system under which one agency sends the fiddler abroad and another the fiddle" (Mulcahy 1982:292). Operating under the name Arts America and with a limited annual budget, static at approximately $1.3 million for more than two decades, the USIA continued to sponsor approximately fifteen tours of American musical artists a year until 1996, when it was disbanded as a result of budget cuts, with some of its functions transferred to the State Department.

The idea of an independent domestic arts agency within the U.S. government surfaced in the 1950s. Jacob Javits pointed out in 1954 that the United States was almost unique in the world in that its government gave no financial support to public arts. As late as 1953 Helen Thompson, executive secretary of the American Symphony Orchestra League (ASOL), testified to a House subcommittee that 91 percent of the ASOL members opposed federal subsidies for fear of governmental control (Larson 1983:82).

On the election of John F. Kennedy as president, the climate for governmental support of the arts seemed to improve, beginning with the invitation of 155 leading figures of the arts and sciences to the inauguration. In August 1961, Arthur Goldberg, secretary of labor, helped settle the strike of musicians at the Metropolitan Opera. Some would say his intervention was the first sign of an official governmental policy on the arts.

In 1961 a House committee began to investigate the economic plight of performing artists in the United States. The same year, Kennedy asked August Heckscher to join the White House staff as a special consultant on the arts. Heckscher's 1963 report, *The Arts and the National Government,* supported a governmental arts program. Already there were thirteen arts councils, at least in embryonic stages, at the state level.

The National Endowments for the Arts and Humanities

On 29 September 1965 the National Foundation for the Arts and Humanities bill was signed by President Lyndon Johnson, bringing into existence the National Endowments for the Arts and Humanities. The National Endowment for the Arts (NEA) budget of 1966 was approximately $2.5 million. The same year, the Ford Foundation, a private eleemosynary trust, announced it would disburse $85 million for symphony orchestras alone. The NEA was set up to allocate money by artistic discipline in the form of matching grants to nonprofit organizations and individuals using a peer-panel system of review. The budget of the National Endowment for the Arts during the tenure of its second chairman, Nancy Hanks (1969–1977), increased tenfold. From 1980 until 1996, the NEA budget varied between $150 and $174 million.

By directly subsidizing artists and artistic activity, the NEA provides but one tier of a multilayered system of public support, which includes regional, state, and local agencies. When all forms of direct public subsidy on the state and local levels are combined, per capita subvention represents approximately three dollars per person in the United States (Schuster 1985:45). In 1986 the aggregate appropriations of state arts councils exceeded for the first time the disbursements of the NEA.

The earliest state arts councils predated the NEA, many of which were originally formed to support urban-based symphonies and museums. With this longer history of public funding for musical organizations, and benefitting from a well-institutionalized field, music projects and institutions have historically received a respectable percentage of the NEA budgeting pie. In fiscal year 2000, musical institutions and projects were granted nearly 23 percent of the grant monies in the competitive categories of NEA funding. This represents grants in three agency disciplines: Music, 16.8 percent; Opera, 4 percent; and Musical Theater, 2 percent. Of the grants under the Music discipline, which includes jazz but not folk or traditional music, roughly 62 percent supported projects of symphony orchestras, 12 percent funded jazz projects, 11 percent went to chamber ensembles, and 4.2 percent underwrote activities of choral groups. The remaining funds supported a variety of projects, including 3.4 percent to contemporary/new music activities, 4.3 percent to support the work of composers or solo artists, 2.5 percent to underwrite activities of music schools, and .7 percent to culturally specific or world music programs. One indicator of the impact of federal funding on musical institutions is revealed in statistics concerning the growth of the field: between 1965 and 1990, the number of orchestras in the United States grew from 110 to 230, the number of opera companies grew from 27 to 120, and the number of musical theaters grew from twenty-two to fifty-six (*Arts in America* . . . 1990:38). These figures include only orchestras with budgets over $280,000.

In 1974 the NEA Music Program created a subcategory, Jazz/Folk/Ethnic Music; in 1976 Jazz and Folk Music were separated into separate categories. In 1974 Alan Jabbour was appointed to the staff of Special Projects, the NEA research and development program, as a specialist in folk arts and Bess Lomax Hawes succeeded him in 1977, when he became director of the American Folklife Center at the Library of Congress. In 1978 the Folk Arts Program was established as a separate, multidisciplinary endowment program to support music, crafts, dance, and verbal arts. During Hawes's tenure, the budget of the program grew to nearly $4 million, roughly 2 percent of the NEA budget.

Although allocated a small budget, the Folk Arts Program under Hawes, daughter of John A. Lomax, dispensed a powerful and far-reaching philosophy of cultural equity, which combined elements of conservation and presentation. Hawes has said, "The folk arts need what the fine arts need: chances to be heard and seen, a reasonable financial return for effort, a knowledgeable and informed audience, an opportunity to reach children and young people, tough aesthetic criticism, respectful attention to matters of documentation and history" (1985) A policy of funding was developed to support the traditional and folk arts of small cultural communities. In addition to supporting festivals, workshops, tours, and documentation of traditional artists, the Folk Arts Program developed the National Heritage Fellowships to honor master traditional artists and initiated artistic apprenticeships to aid in the perpetuation and refinement of endangered artistic skills.

In the United States, unlike Canada, nationally subsidized radio plays a minor role in the support of music. The federally appropriated budget for the Corporation for Public Broadcasting, a conduit for federal funds to nonprofit radio and television stations, was $340 million for 2001. While National Public Radio (NPR) has increased its listenership, the emphasis in programming has been on news and public affairs. The new and expanded audience for public radio stations seems to exhibit a greater eclecticism when it comes to musical taste, and individual stations exercise great independence in their core programming. Listeners—once patrons of Western classical music—no longer accord this music a privileged position; instead, they seek varied programming, including folk, jazz, rock, world, country, bluegrass, and new age styles (Peterson 1990). In an address to NPR's annual conference in 1989, Peter Pennekamp, former vice president of NPR's Cultural and Program Services, stated: "Our cultural assumptions that listeners want to just hear popular and classical music from a European viewpoint don't work anymore" (Ouelette 1989:32).

The Smithsonian Institution

Although George Washington had in his farewell address (1796) recommended the establishment of a national institution of learning, it was not until the 1830s that federal

Some writers opposed the writing, recording, mechanical reproduction, and copyrighting of music as the ultimate agents of commodification and reification of culture, while lawmakers attempted to broaden copyright protection to include new technologies such as the Internet.

plans for such an entity took shape. With a bequest of £104,960 (worth $508,318.46) from James Smithson, the Smithsonian Institution was founded in 1846. It was the original home of the Bureau of American Ethnology. Technically a public–private hybrid, it receives about 85 percent of its funding from the government.

In 1967 James Morris, director of the Museum Service, became the director of a newly formed section, the Division of the Performing Arts. Soon S. Dillon Ripley, secretary of the Smithsonian, championed a folk festival on the Mall. Ralph Rinzler, member of the board of directors of the Newport Folk Festival, was hired by the Performing Arts Division to direct the first Festival of American Folklife, and under his leadership the annual festival expanded the purview of its presentations of folklife to include music, dance, craft, oral traditions, and foodways. The 1976 Festival of American Folklife, celebrating the country's bicentennial, was a landmark exposition featuring traditional artists representing every region of the United States and the work of artists from thirty-eight countries as well.

In 1977 a separate Office of Folklife Programs was established at the Smithsonian. This office, later renamed the Center for Folklife Programs and Cultural Studies, has conducted field research and documentation, published books and audiovisual materials, and established an internal archive. In 1987 the Smithsonian acquired the Folkways Records catalogue and archive of Moses Asch, including more than two thousand recordings of traditional musicians and speech. The new Smithsonian Folkways continues to release new recordings, some in conjunction with festival programs, focusing largely on traditional folk music.

The Smithsonian's Division of Performing Arts, continuing independently, developed programs in jazz, chamber music, country music, American musical theater, and African American culture. In addition to conferences and resident ensembles of jazz and chamber music, this division released significant series of historic recordings. In 1983 it was disbanded, but aspects of its program continue under the auspices of the National Museum of American History and the Resident Associates Program, the privately funded community education wing of the Smithsonian. Also, the Division of Musical Instruments, located within the National Museum of American History, has one of the largest collections of musical instruments in the world.

Other federal agencies

The year 1971 saw the development of two federally subsidized performing arts facilities. During the summer, the U.S. Department of the Interior opened Wolf Trap Farm Park near Washington, D.C., the first such park under the supervision of the National Park Service. In September, the John F. Kennedy Center for the Performing Arts opened on the banks of the Potomac; it contains an opera house, a concert hall, a theater, and a cinema and is the home of the National Symphony Orchestra.

The direct programmatic subsidy of music in both the United States and Canada must be viewed in the context of support for the arts in general. It is difficult to measure the impact of this support: in the United States public monies represent less than

10 percent of the income of orchestras, while their counterparts in Canada receive 35 percent of their income from that source. As the relative real value of the dollars granted declines, the leveraging effect of federal dollars and the symbolic value of governmental recognition of an arts institution's quality have become more and more the prevailing arguments for the continuation of direct governmental support.

PUBLIC POLICY IN THE 1990s

The 1990s ushered in a period of reexamination and debate with regard to public policy and the arts. Court cases involving recorded samples and control of previously recorded material called into question the concept of individual ownership and copyright. Issues regarding individual ownership of musical content or style and the appropriation of musical traditions of other cultures by pop musicians were debated (Seeger 1992). Some writers opposed the writing, recording, mechanical reproduction, and copyrighting of music as the ultimate agents of commodification and reification of culture (Keil 1994:228–229), while lawmakers attempted to broaden copyright protection to include new technologies such as the Internet. Recent amendments to the Canadian Copyright Act provide neighboring rights, extending copyright protection in the sound recording industry from authors and producers to include performers. Canada has also introduced a private copying levy on blank audio recording media to compensate Canadian composers/authors, music publishers, performers, and producers.

Legislators in the United States and Canada challenged the assumption that taxpayers should support the arts, however parsimoniously. With a new political dynamic in the U.S. Congress, the 1996 budget for the NEA was reduced by 40 percent to $99 million (thirty-eight cents per citizen), and the staff was reduced by almost half. Individual granting programs such as Music were discontinued and funding was instituted under general categories such as Heritage and Preservation, Education and Access, Creation and Presentation, and Planning and Stabilization. All individual fellowships were eliminated with the exception of Literature Fellowships and honorific awards such as National Heritage and Jazz Masters Fellowships. In 1997, the U.S. House of Representatives voted to defund the National Endowment for the Arts, a decision that was reversed by the Senate, however, through fiscal year 2000, the NEA budget remained flat.

While the debate about public funding of the arts appears to be ongoing in the United States, primarily fueled by issues related to religion, sexual content, and morality, in Canada cuts in funding for the arts have been more modest and seem more directly a consequence of general governmental fiscal retrenchment. In 1995 a 9 percent cut in the Canada Council budget was announced to take effect over a three-year period, with a 50 percent reduction in administrative costs. In 1999 the Standing Committee on Canadian Heritage of the House of Commons issued a report called *A Sense of Place—A Sense of Being: The Evolving Role of the Federal Government in Support of Culture in Canada*. This report identifies a distinctive Canadian model of cultural affirmation that "focuses on the development of a healthy cultural marketplace, freedom of choice for consumers and the principle of access to Canadian cultural materials (*A Sense of Place* 1999:7). Examining six key elements—creation, training, distribution, preservation, and consumption—the report reaffirms the role of governmental support for artistic activitiy in a geographically dispersed and culturally diverse country.

Just as issues related to nationalistic self-identity and sovereignty provided some of the impetus for the creation of Canadian and U.S. policies on the arts, political realignments called into question the desirability of using culture as a diplomatic tool. The dismantling of the Arts America Program of the United States Information Agency in 1996 virtually ended any serious government sponsorship of musical groups or arts programs abroad. Canada has continued vigorously to use culture as a tool of diplomacy. The Department of Foreign Affairs released a white paper proclaiming that the projection of Canadian culture and values is one of its three pillars of foreign policy, along with security and prosperity ("Two-edged Sword . . ." 1997: 7). Foreign Affairs devotes $6.3 million (Canadian) to export culture. A recent report of the Cultural Industries Sectoral Advisory Group on International Trade to the Department of Foreign Affairs and International Trade entitled *Canadian Culture in a Global World* (1999) positions arts and culture as a central issue in Canadian economic and cultural identity and diversity.

In both Canada and the United States there is a renewed interest in issues related to the role of arts in education. In 1992 the Canada Council and the Social Sciences and Humanities Research Council initiated a study to lead to a plan to enhance arts literacy through education [see LEARNING, p. 274]. The Goals 2000: Educate America Act did not include the arts as a core subject when standards were originally conceived in 1989. The move toward establishing educational standards and testing for them is still vigorously debated, but the Music Educators' National Conference has been very active in developing and striving to implement standards in music. Music is now one of four arts disciplines described in *National Standards for Arts Education: What Every Young American Should Know* (1994).

The once clear line between the "fine arts" and the "popular arts" has also become less and less discernable. Increased mobility and worldwide systems of communication brought citizens into contact with a variety of aesthetic traditions. Richard Peterson (1990) argues that a "new aesthetic" will develop in music, combining elements of jazz, rock, folk, and traditional classical music into one style, which will challenge the classical Western art-music aesthetic. However, Alan Lomax has appealed for preservation of the variety of musical aesthetics deeply rooted in distinct cultural traditions and warns against cultural "gray-out" reflected in the "oppressive dullness and psychic distress of those areas where centralized music industries exploiting the star system and controlling the communications system, put the local musician out of work and silence folksong, tribal ritual, local popular festivities and regional culture" (1977:126).

Herbert Gans, reconsidering his dichotomy of popular culture and high culture, points out that high culture is becoming less influential because of "the declining credibility of its claim that its cultural standards are universal" (1992:99; see also Levine 1988), and Charles Keil and Steven Feld write of the "obsolescence of high culture" and the quaint residues that we know as written music (Keil and Feld 1994:21).

Surveys (Peterson et al. 1996; Zill and Robinson 1994; Miller 1996) of public participation in the arts reveal a growing eclecticism in the tastes of the music listening public and a graying demographic for both the consumers of and contributors to the arts and, in particular, classical music. There seems to be a growing appreciation that in the field of music there are many "taste cultures" (Gans 1992).

Recent studies have pointed to the need for funders and policymakers to broaden and deepen connections with artists and their public (Larson 1997; Peterson et al. 1996; *The Arts and the Public Purpose* . . . 1997). As parties to the general discussion about public policy and the arts, the diverse and far-reaching worlds of music echo an evolving mix of voices of governmental agencies, artists, arts organizations, aesthetic communities and audiences. Governmental agencies that lay the tracks for the engine of public policy may need to traverse new and uncharted terrain to serve the artistic vitality and cultural variety of their citizenry.

REFERENCES

Anderson, Gillian B. 1989. "Putting the Experience of the World at the Nation's Command: Music at the Library of Congress, 1800–1917." *Journal of the American Musicological Society* 42:108–148.

Annual Report of the Board of Regents of the Smithsonian Institution for the Year Ending 30 June 1907. 1908. Washington, D.C.: Government Printing Office.

The Arts and the Public Purpose. 1997. New York: The American Assembly.

Arts in America 1990: The Bridge between Creativity and Community. 1990. Washington, D.C.: National Endowment for the Arts.

Bartis, Peter. 1982. "A History of the Archive of Folk Song at the Library of Congress: The First Fifty Years." Ph.D. dissertation, University of Pennsylvania.

Bindas, Kenneth J. 1995. *All of This Music Belongs to the Nation: The WPA's Federal Music Project and American Society, 1935–1939.* Knoxville: University of Tennessee Press.

The Canada Council: A Design For the Future. 1995. Ottawa: Canada Council.

The Canada Council 33rd Annual Report, 1989–1990. 1990. Ottawa: Canada Council.

Canada's Culture, Heritage and Identity: A Statistical Perspective. 1995. Ottawa: Ministry of Industry.

Canadian Culture in a Global World. 1999. Ottawa: Department of Foreign Affairs and International Trade.

Check-List of Recorded Songs in the English Language in the Archive of American Folk Song to July, 1940. 1942. Washington, D.C.: Library of Congress.

Cohnstaedt, Joy. 1992. "Shoulder to Fingertip: Arm's Length and Points between in Canadian Cultural Policy." In *Culture and Democracy: Social and Ethical Issues in Public Support for the Arts and Humanities,* ed. Andrew Buchwalter, 169–180. Boulder, Colo.: Westview Press.

Creighton, Helen. 1961. *Maritime Folk Songs.* Toronto: The Ryerson Press.

Creighton, Helen, and Calum MacLeod. 1964. *Gaelic Songs in Nova Scotia.* Ottawa: National Museum of Canada.

Fewkes, Jesse Walter. 1890. "A Contribution to Passamaquoddy Folklore." *Journal of American Folklore* 3:257–280.

Funding of the Arts in Canada to the Year 2000. 1986. Ottawa: Government of Canada.

Gans, Herbert. 1992. "American Popular Culture and High Culture in a Changing Class Structure." In *Public Policy and the Aesthetic Interest: Critical Essays on Defining Cultural and Educational Relations,* ed. Ralph A. Smith and Ronald Berman, 91–104. Urbana: University of Illinois Press.

Hawes, Bess Lomax. 1985. "Remarks delivered before an international cultural forum in Budapest, Hungary, October." Unpublished manuscript.

Jabbour, Alan. 1996a. "The American Folklife Center: A Twenty-Year Retrospective." *Folklife Center News* 18(1, 2):3–19.

———. 1996b. "The American Folklife Center: A Twenty-Year Retrospective (Part 2)." *Folklife Center News* 18(3, 4):3–23.

Jefferson, Thomas. 1992 [1778]. *The Life and Selected Writings of Thomas Jefferson.* Ed. Adrienne Koch and William Peden. New York: Modern Library.

Kallmann, Helmut, Gilles Potvin, and Kenneth Winters, eds. 1992. *Encyclopedia of Music in Canada.* 2nd ed. Toronto: University of Toronto Press.

Keil, Charles. 1994. "On Civilization, Cultural Studies, and Copyright." In *Music Grooves,* ed. Charles Keil and Steven Feld, 227–231. Chicago: University of Chicago Press.

Keil, Charles, and Steven Feld, eds. 1994. *Music Grooves.* Chicago: University of Chicago Press.

Kestin, Myles. 1992. "The Canada–U.S. Free Trade Agreement: Provisions Directly and Indirectly Affecting Trade in Cultural Product." In *Cultural Economics,* ed. Ruth Towse and Abdul Khakee, 163–171. Berlin: Springer-Verlag.

Kodish, Debora. 1986. *Good Friends and Bad Enemies: Robert Winslow Gordon and the Study of American Folksong.* Urbana: University of Illinois Press.

Larson, Gary O. 1983. *The Reluctant Patron: The United States Government and the Arts, 1943–1965.* Philadelphia: University of Pennsylvania Press.

———. [1997]. *American Canvas: An Arts Legacy for Our Communities.* Washington, D.C.: National Endowment for the Arts.

Levine, Lawrence W. 1988. *Highbrow/Lowbrow.* Cambridge: Harvard University Press.

Lomax, Alan. 1977. "An Appeal for Cultural Equity." *Journal of Communications* 27:125–138.

Lomax, John. 1910. *Cowboy Songs and Other Frontier Ballads.* New York: Sturgis and Walton.

———. 1947. *Adventures of a Ballad Hunter.* New York: Macmillan.

Lomax, John, and Alan Lomax. 1934. *American Ballads and Folk Songs.* New York: Macmillan.

Loomis, Ormond, ed. 1983. *Cultural Conservation: The Preservation of Cultural Heritage in the United States.* Washington, D.C.: Library of Congress.

Mankin, Lawrence David. 1976. "The National Government and the Arts: From the Great Depression to 1973." Ph.D. dissertation, University of Illinois.

Margolis, Michael, ed. 1994. *Free Expression, Public Support, and Censorship: Examining Government's Role in the Arts in Canada and the United States.* Lanham, Md.: University Press of America.

McDonald, William F. 1969. *Federal Relief Administration and the Arts: The Origins and Administrative History of the Arts Projects of the Works Progress Administration.* Columbus: Ohio State University Press.

Meisel, John, and Jean Van Loon. 1987. "Cultivating the Bushgarden: Cultural Policy in Canada." In *The Patron State: Government and the Arts in Europe, North America and Japan,* ed. Milton C. Cummings Jr. and Richard S. Katz, 226–310. New York: Oxford University Press.

Miller, Judith. 1996. "Aging Audiences Point to a Grim Arts Future." *New York Times,* 12 February, A1, C12.

Mulcahy, Kevin V. 1982. "Cultural Diplomacy: Foreign Policy and the Exchange Programs." In *Public Policy and the Arts,* ed. Kevin V. Mulcahy

and C. Richard Swaim, 269–301. Boulder, Colo.: Westview Press.

National Standards for Arts Education: What Every Young American Should Know and Be Able to Do in the Arts. 1994. Reston, Va.: Music Educators National Conference.

Ouelette, Dan. 1989. "National Public Radio." *Pulse!* October, 32–36.

Peacock, Kenneth. 1965. *Songs of the Newfoundland Outports.* 3 vols. Ottawa: National Museum of Canada.

———. 1966. *Twenty Ethnic Songs from Western Canada.* Ottawa: National Museum of Canada.

———. 1969. "Folk and Aboriginal Music." In *Aspects of Music in Canada,* ed. Arnold Walter, 62–89. Toronto: University of Toronto Press.

Peterson, Elizabeth. 1996. *The Changing Faces of Tradition: A Report on the Folk and Traditional Arts in the United States.* Washington, D.C.: National Endowment for the Arts.

Peterson, Richard A. 1990. "Audience and Industry Origins of the Crisis in Classical Music Programming: Toward World Music." In *The Future of the Arts: Public Policy and Arts Research,* ed. David Pankratz and Valerie B. Morris, 210–213. New York: Praeger.

Peterson, Richard A., Darren E. Sherkat, Judith Huggins Balfe, and Rolf Meyerson. 1996. *Age and Arts Participation with a Focus on the Baby Boom Cohort.* National Endowment for the Arts Research Division Report 34. Santa Ana, Calif.: Seven Locks Press.

Porterfield, Nolan. 1996. *Last Cavalier: The Life and Times of John A. Lomax, 1867–1948.* Urbana: University of Illinois Press.

Schneider, Howard. 1997. "Canada's Culture War Questioned." *The Washington Post,* 15 February, A29.

Schuster, J. Mark Davidson. 1985. *Supporting the Arts: An International Comparative Study.* Washington, D.C.: National Endowment for the Arts.

Seeger, Anthony. 1992. "Ethnomusicology and Music Law." *Ethnomusicology* 36(2):345–359.

A Sense of Place—A Sense of Being: The Evolving Role of the Federal Government in Support of Culture in Canada. 1999. 9th Report, Standing Committee on Canadian Heritage. Ottawa: House of Commons.

Tocqueville, Alexis de. 1945 [1835]. *Democracy in America.* Trans. Francis Bowen. 2 vols. New York: Vintage Books.

"Two-edged sword of arts funding." 1997. *The (Montréal) Gazette,* 17 March, 7.

U. S. Senate. 1963. *The Arts and the National Government.* 88th Cong., 1st sess.S. Doc. 28.

Zill, Nicholas, and John Robinson. 1994. "Name that Tune." *American Demographics* 16:22–27.

Snapshot:
Four Views of Music, Government, and Politics

Steven Cornelius
Charlotte J. Frisbie
John Shepherd

Campaign Music in the United States—Steven Cornelius
A Navajo Medicine Bundle Is Repatriated—Charlotte J. Frisbie
Government, Politics, and Popular Music in Canada—John Shepherd
Protest Music of the 1960s—Steven Cornelius

Music, government, and politics are frequently intertwined in interesting ways, as these four views show. For example, sometimes music is used to further a political party or cause; sometimes music and its composition and production are regulated by governmental controls; and, occasionally, a government's legal system can provide a context for the negotiation of musical rights and privileges.

CAMPAIGN MUSIC IN THE UNITED STATES

There had never been a parade quite like this one. Revolutionary War vintage artillery headed the gathering. Following behind was the carriage of Daniel Webster, some one thousand banners, eight log cabin floats (one with a working chimney, another that had traveled—delegates inside—from Pennsylvania), an assortment of marching bands, plenty of hard cider, and other sundry paraphernalia. In all, as many as twenty-five thousand people may have marched through the Baltimore streets on that 4 May 1840 morning.

Such was the scene that met the ratification of William Henry Harrison and John Tyler as the Whig nominees in that year's presidential race. "Tippecanoe and Tyler too" was the rallying cry. Raucous throughout the route, the multitudes reached fever pitch when passing Music Hall, singing, "And with them we'll beat little Van, Van, Van / Van is a used up man." Inside, some 248 Democrats were drearily engaged in the business of renominating their own candidate, President Martin Van Buren. American politics would never be the same.

Beginning with the Harrison campaign, music became an important ingredient in the tapestry that made up the American political landscape. While literature created images that posters, banners, and buttons projected, songs—led by glee clubs or distributed in pamphlet form—were used to arouse popular enthusiasm. No one at the time would have argued that the music—most of which venerated the party's candidate, some which vituperated the opposition—held much in the way of artistic merit. Aesthetic quality, however, hardly mattered. Campaign songs were utilitarian. Simple in construction, the texts were sometimes witty. More likely, however, they consisted of strings of banal, yet vivid, clichés.

The songs tended to share a number of features. Typically, they were constructed in pastiche fashion with words attached to well-known preexisting melodies. During the mid-1800s, for example, innumerable campaign texts were set to "Yankee Doodle," "Old Dan Tucker," and other popular tunes. When new melodies were composed, the simple tunes were easy to both sing and remember. For those willing to take chances and able to work within a short time frame, there was money to be made writing campaign songs. The music had to be published and sold quickly, for as the election grew near, value would decrease, effectively reaching zero after the election.

Notwithstanding their short-term appeal, campaign songs remained an important segment of the music publishing business from Harrison's 1840 campaign until after World War II. Amateurs and professionals—including Stephen Foster, Paul Dresser, Gus Edwards, and Irving Berlin—made contributions. Interestingly, most songs were written for profit by individuals with no particular political allegiance [see POPULAR MUSIC OF THE PARLOR AND STAGE, p. 179].

Early history

Emerging as the uncontested leader in a young nation in which party politics did not yet exist, George Washington was the subject of more than a handful of song texts. None of them, however, could accurately be called campaign songs. Perhaps credit for the first campaign song should go to Robert Treat Paine Jr., who, in support of Federalist John Adams, set verses to the melody "To Anacreon in Heaven" (the tune later used for "The Star Spangled Banner") and titled his 1798 song "Adams and Liberty."

> Ye sons of Columbia who bravely have fought,
> For those rights which unstained from your sires have descended,
> May you long taste the blessings your valor has bought.
> And your sons reap the soil which your father defended. (Silber 1971:23)

For the elections that followed—the campaigns of Madison, Monroe, Adams, Jackson, and Van Buren—songs were penned, but music played little part in the election process.

Harrison to Lincoln: a twenty-year snapshot

The role of music changed dramatically during the Harrison race. The Whigs created around Harrison, known as "General Mum" for his unwillingness to articulate his stand on issues, a campaign of propaganda, paraphernalia, and theater in which, for the first time, hundreds of thousands of Americans took active part in the election process. It was a "campaign of songs" in which, as Philip Hone remarked, Harrison became the first man ever "sung into the Presidency" (Tuckerman 1889:177).

The song texts manufactured for Harrison something he could hardly have created with his own politics: the image of a steadfast common man's hero. Harrison's reputation was founded on his role as commanding officer in the 1811 battle at Tippecanoe Creek, Indiana, where his seasoned forces defeated the outnumbered warriors led by Tecumseh. Building on that exploit—as well as a timely satirical editorial in the *Baltimore Republican* newspaper (Gunderson 1977 [1957]:74) that suggested the ex-general might best serve his country if he were put up with "a barrel of hard cider" to "sit the remainder of his days in his log cabin"—this well-born Ohioan slipped a few rungs down the social ladder and was transformed into a common man's hero. Supporting the facade, *The Log Cabin Songbook*—put together by publisher Horace Greeley and available at eight dollars per hundred—was distributed through campaign headquarters. At seventy-two pages, the book included fifty-five songs and illustrations (Gunderson 1977 [1957]:124; Miles 1990:xxvii). It was immaterial that Harrison's image had little to do with reality. The slogan "Tippecanoe and Tyler too" soon rang throughout the land as astute Whig song makers polished the mythology. The words to

"Should Brave Old Soldiers Be Forgot?," sung to the tune of "Auld Lang Syne," are
typical:

> No ruffled shirt, no silken hose,
> No airs does TIP display;
> But like the "pith of worth" he goes
> In homespun "hoddin-grey."
> Upon his board there ne'er appeared
> The costly "sparkling wine,"
> But plain "hard cider" such as cheered
> In days of old lang syne. (Silber 1971:34–35)

Not all Whig campaign songs focused on Harrison. Van Buren had—unlike his opponent—a clear national record upon which to be judged. As president he had endured
the 1837 financial panic, an Indian war in Florida, and criticism for his reluctance
to annex Texas. The lampoon "Van Buren," while addressing no particulars, allowed
political foes to cast an image of the man that seemed as iniquitous as Harrison's
glossed image was steadfast.

> Who never did a noble deed:
> Who of the people took no heed?
> Who is the worst of tyrant's breed?
> Van Buren! (*Sing Along with Millard Fillmore:* album notes)

Although music may have marched Harrison into the presidency, reliance on image
quickly got the best of him. He was in office just one month before perishing from
pneumonia, an illness contracted shortly after he refused to wear a hat and coat to his
cold and rainy inauguration.

Upon ascending to the presidency, Harrison's vice president, the independent-
thinking John Tyler, soon lost party support. That left the door open for Henry Clay.
Clay, who had lost the 1840 nomination to Harrison, rallied supporters to build an
internecine campaign for the 1844 Whig nomination. Curiously, he built upon Harrison's enduring popularity. "Tippecanoe—but not Tyler too!" was the refurbished slogan. Harrison's songs were readapted as well. "Tip and Ty" was refashioned with the
lyrics "Do you know a traitor viler, viler, viler / Than Tyler."

"Tip and Ty" and over 180 other songs were available in *The Clay Minstrel; or,
National Songster* (Littell 1884). The first edition, which comprised some 388 pages,
came prefixed with a "sketch of the life, public services, and character of Henry Clay."

Daniel Decatur Emmett's 1843 "Old Dan Tucker" and other songs of blackface
minstrels were frequently adapted for campaign use. Only occasionally, however, did
the minstrel literary style appear in presidential campaign songs, as in "Clare de
Kitchen" from *The Clay Minstrel:*

> O hush! who come yonder!—oh! dem's de Whig boys,
> Dey bringin' Massa Clay—by golly what a noise;
> Dis nigger better *colonize*—but hark, what dey say,
> "You must *all* clare de kitchen for Massa Henry Clay!" (Littell 1844:126–127)

Clay was eventually opposed by the Democrat James K. Polk, an expansionist from
Tennessee who ultimately won the presidency by taking a firm stand in supporting the
annexation of Texas and (with the slogan "Fifty-four Forty or Fight") demanding all of
the Oregon territory for the United States. Adding songs to slogans, the Democrats

came up with new sets of words to the tunes for "Yankee Doodle" and "Old Dan Tucker." To the former they sang:

> Come raise the banner, raise it high,
> Ye Democrats so handy;
> Let songs of triumph rend the sky
> For "Yankee Doodle Dandy."
>
> Clear the track boys, how they run,
> The Whigs we're just surprisin',
> Soon we'll send to "Kingdom come"
> H. Clay and Frelinghuysen! (Brand 1960:5)

In reworking Emmett's song, the Democrats took the unusual step of including a political stand:

> A Psalm we don't object to sing,
> But Uncle Sam is now the thing,
> He cries, "For Polk and Dallas go,"
> And save Texas from Mexico. (Silber 1971:51)

Meanwhile, a third party, the antislavery Liberty Party, sang of social iniquities. *The Liberty Minstrel* contained such songs as "The Fugitive Slave to the Christian," "Negro Boy Sold for a Watch," and "Slave Girl Mourning Her Father."

The 1848 election pitted Whig Zachary Taylor against Lewis Cass. Once again, as in 1844, both candidates were profoundly centrist with, one might argue, little to distinguish them but songs. As they had with Harrison, Whigs built on Taylor's (Mexican American) war exploits while fashioning down-home appeal. Sung to the melody of "Yankee Doodle," the song "Rough and Ready" from the 1846 *Rough and Ready Songster* is an example.

> His foes may slander as they can,
> And bluster at his manners,
> Who cares a fig? He's just the man
> To lead the Yankee banners. (Silber 1971:55)

In the 1852 election, the last in which the crumbling Whig party would nominate a candidate, the primary issues were slavery and preservation of the Union. Election songs generally avoided the issue of slavery altogether, and focused instead on the military records of Whig Winfield Scott and Democrat Franklin Pierce. By 1856 there was no turning back on the slave question, and songs of the newly formed Republican party—initially a sectional group primarily made up of disgruntled northern Whigs, Democrats, and "free soilers" (antislavery activists who represented the interests of the homesteaders)—echoed that developing reality. Sung for Republican candidate John Charles Frémont to the tune of "Old Dan Tucker," the song "March to Freedom" hailed:

> The millions heard the thrilling cry,
> It warmed the blood, it fired the eye:
> "Free Speech, free pen, free soil want we—
> And FREMONT to lead to victory!"
> Out of the way, Old Buchanan!
> For we have out an honest man on!

Like celestial novas, third parties have been dramatic, passionate, and generally short-lived, yet have contributed much to the campaign songbook.

Out of the way, each wriggling doughface,
Freedom's car will knock you no place. (Silber 1971:70)

While a Republican victory would almost certainly have resulted in the quick dissolution of the Union, ultimately the moderate Pennsylvania Democrat James Buchanan could do little better. Buchanan sought to hold a slippery middle ground by affirming his personal aversion to slavery while simultaneously supporting laws that upheld the southern states' right to hold slaves. Some Democrat campaign songs, however, demonstrated little of Buchanan's moderation:

Free speech, free niggers, and Frémont
Now seems to be the go
But these crazy Nigger-Worshippers,
The Union would destroy. (Silber 1971:72)

During this and the next two elections, minstrel and ballad writer Stephen Foster contributed songs first for Buchanan and later—although the published words were probably updated after Foster's death—for George B. McClellan, the dismissed Commander of the Army of the Potomac, who ran against Lincoln in 1864. Along with Foster, another important campaign song writer was John W. Hutchinson of the well-known midcentury family singing troupe. Besides compiling *Hutchinson's Republican Songster, for the Campaign of 1860,* the Hutchinson family proved to be strong advocates of both abolition and women's suffrage.

Later-nineteenth-century campaigns

Post–Civil War songwriting generally continued in the same vein; style continued to be more important than substance, and songs focused on topical issues of the day. In 1872 the breakaway Liberal Republican Party nominated publisher Horace Greeley to lead the campaign against the corruption-ridden Grant administration. Although Greeley had never held political office, throughout the 1850s he had used his position as founder and editor of the *New York Tribune* to speak out against slavery. Unfortunately for his 1872 campaign, Greeley had also opposed Lincoln's 1864 reelection and later supported the bail fund for Confederate president Jefferson Davis. These facts gave the Republicans more than ample musical fodder, as in "Hurrah! Hurrah for Grant and Wilson" from the *National Republican Grant and Wilson Campaign Song Book* (tune: "John Brown's Body"/"Glory, Hallelujah"):

We'll hang the "Lib'ral" Greeley on a sour apple tree,
Because he bailed Jeff Davis and he set the traitor free;
He never can be president, as you can plainly see,
As we go marching on. (Silber 1971:108)

Despite the Republican smear campaign, Greeley managed to pull in over 40 percent of the popular vote. He died before the electoral college met. Not surprisingly, songs referencing "Old Tippecanoe" were revived for the campaign of 1888 when Republican Civil War veteran Benjamin Harrison, grandson of William Henry Harrison, ran against, and narrowly defeated, incumbent Grover Cleveland.

TRACK 6

Minority parties

Like celestial novas, third parties have been dramatic, passionate, and generally short-lived, yet have contributed much to the campaign songbook.

The Greenback Party

"The National Greenback Rally," taken from the *Greenback Labor Songster* of 1878 and sung to the tune "America" ("God Save the King"), is typical of hard-hitting "nothing to lose, everything to gain" minority party politics:

> The workingmen have brains,
> They are not bound with chains
> to party hacks.
> After next voting day,
> When the sons of toil have sway,
> They'll wipe the frauds away
> With more Greenbacks. (Lawrence 1878:46)

The Prohibition Party

Although founded in 1869—and still active in rural areas today—it was not until the elections of 1888 and 1892 that the mostly evangelical Protestant–based Prohibition Party had much effect in national elections. Although they never won at the national level, their political message was heard; in 1919 the Eighteenth Amendment to the Constitution began the Prohibition era, and political purpose and song were woven together. Published in 1878, *The National Temperance Songster* opens with the following preface:

> The wonderful progress which the cause of Temperance is now making in this country and the great interest taken in it by thousands of our people, seem to demand a collection of Bright and Thrilling Original Temperance Songs, issued in cheap form, and in their character acceptable to the masses who love to *sing* their enthusiasm into practical effect, for the saving of the tempted and the encouragement of all co-workers in a Good Cause. (Moffitt 1878)

Inside, one finds thirty-one songs. All are set to popular melodies of the time. "Our Land Redeemed," set to the melody of "America," is typical:

> My country! broad and fine,
> Cursed by both beer and wine,
> Of thee I sing;
> Land where my fathers died,
> Land which King George defied
> And slavery set aside,
> Thy deeds shall ring. (Moffitt 1878:15)

The Socialist Party

Replacing the fragmented Socialist Labor Party in 1901, the Socialist Party under the leadership of Eugene Debs had limited impact through 1920. Debs ran for president five times between 1900 and 1920 and managed to garner 6 percent of the vote in 1912.

Your work, my work,
All of us working to bring the day
When the wage slaves shall be free men,
And the children shall joyfully play. (Kerr 1901)

The Progressive Party

The dashing Theodore Roosevelt inspired more than a few songs when running as a Republican in 1904. The song most associated with that shoe-in campaign was the 1896 minstrel march "(There'll be) A Hot Time in the Old Town (Tonight)." In 1912, after a four-year hiatus, Roosevelt returned to politics but was stunned by not receiving the Republican nomination over incumbent William Howard Taft. Preconvention songs had focused on Roosevelt's dynamic qualities. During his presidential campaign with the newly formed Progressive (or Bull Moose) Party it was "Onward Christian Soldiers" and "The Battle Hymn of the Republic" that were most emblematic.

Although Truman would hold off Dewey and retain the presidency in 1948, songs from Woody Guthrie and appearances by Pete Seeger for Progressive candidate Henry Wallace inspired Alan Lomax to dub this "the first singing campaign since Lincoln's" (Klein 1980:347). Perhaps it was, but Wallace received just one million votes.

Women's suffrage

Although not a political party per se, and generally fought at the state rather than national level, mention must also be made of the women's suffrage movement. The movement gathered force alongside the antislavery movement in the decades preceding the Civil War and inspired considerable singing until national victory was achieved in 1920 with the passing of the Nineteenth Amendment.

Political campaign songs in the second half of the twentieth century

While the twentieth century saw inspirational outbursts of song from third parties and an occasional memorable tune produced for major party candidates, as an institution the campaign song has been in steady decline since World War I. Throughout the 1950s Tin Pan Alley writers continued to turn out songs, but the glee clubs and bands that were central to earlier campaign rallies had disappeared.

In 1932 the Democratic Party rallied behind Franklin Delano Roosevelt, who brought his New Deal politics and a sense of hope to a Depression-weary populace. The tune most associated with the campaign was the 1929 "Happy Days Are Here Again." Although the song has been associated with the Democratic Party ever since, it is rarely heard outside the context of the national convention and plays no role in the business of winning elections.

Since then, a few songs have managed to become popular. Irving Berlin wrote the song "They Like Ike" for his 1950 musical *Call Me Madam.* Sung by three "congressmen" and with Eisenhower himself in the opening-night Broadway audience, the song was an instant success. With the title changed to "I Like Ike" it became a rallying point in the 1952 Eisenhower campaign. Eight years later, it was refurbished film music—the 1959 song "High Hopes" from *Hole in the Head*—that animated the Kennedy campaign, while Nixon's Republicans sang "Here Comes Nixon" to the 1853 tune "Good Night, Ladies."

Since the emergence of television in the 1950s, the focus on staged media events has generally relegated campaign songs to the background. That development has meant the demise of many of the more material aspects of political culture found in earlier campaigns. We still encounter political paraphernalia—elephants and donkeys, silly hats, posters, and buttons—within the context of conventions in the United States, but almost nothing remains of the song-singing, banner-waving, participatory styles that typified campaign rallies of earlier generations.

In recent years, Ronald Reagan used his relationship with the Beach Boys to political advantage, and Bill Clinton capitalized on his ability to play the saxophone. Yet in those and similar cases, music has been only peripheral, a prop used to enhance or solidify image. As for songs that focus on political figures, while they continue to exist, most—such as the satirical adaptations of popular songs devised by pianist-comedian Mark Russell, or the political comedy troupe Capital Steps—are lampoons.

—STEVEN CORNELIUS

A NAVAJO MEDICINE BUNDLE IS REPATRIATED

The Native American Graves Protection and Repatriation Act (NAGPRA) was enacted in 1990 to achieve two objectives: to protect Native American human remains, funerary objects, sacred objects, and objects of cultural patrimony presently on federal or tribal lands; and to repatriate Native American human remains, associated funerary objects, sacred objects, and objects of cultural patrimony currently held or controlled by federal agencies and museums. The law and subsequent regulations provide methods for identifying objects, determining rights of descendants, and retrieving and repatriating that property to Native Americans. As such, it can be viewed as human rights legislation.

This discussion focuses on a 1996 court case in New Mexico concerned with testing the legal protection afforded by NAGPRA to "objects of cultural patrimony" or items having ongoing historical, cultural, or traditional importance central to the Native groups covered by the law. These cultural items are of such importance that they may *not* be alienated, appropriated, or conveyed by any individual group member. The test case, *Richard N. Corrow v. United States of America,* in which I served as a non-Navajo "expert witness" because of my research on Navajo medicine bundles (Frisbie 1987, 1993), was the first jury trial in the nation under the criminal provisions of NAGPRA. The combined efforts of the FBI, National Park Service, U.S. Fish and Wildlife Service, and the Bureau of Indian Affairs resulted in the arrest of Richard Nelson Corrow, age fifty-four, for trafficking in protected cultural items and for possessing bird feathers protected by the Migratory Bird Treaty Act. Because the case involved a dealer in Native American religious items and a Santa Fe gallery, and because the Antique Tribal Art Dealers Association filed an *amicus curiae* 'friend of the court' brief in support of Corrow's appeal, various aspects of it were reported in Ron McCoy's Legal Briefs column of *American Indian Art Magazine* (Summer 1998:25, 29), *The Indian Trader* (October 1996:8), and the *A.T.A.D.A.* (Antique Tribal Art Dealers Association) *Newsletter* (July 1996:4–8), as well as in the *Navajo Times* (3 October 1996: 1–2, 5; 10 October 1996:5), various regional newspapers, and *Common Ground* (Summer 1996:9).

Briefly, the particulars were as follows. Ray Winnie, a well-known Navajo ceremonial practitioner (medicine man, chanter, or *hataali*), who lived in Lukachukai, Arizona, died in 1991 without making provisions for the transmission/disposition of the *jish* 'medicine bundle' he used when performing the Nightway (one of the major nine-night sacred ceremonials during which masked deities, the *Yé'ii*[s] 'Supernatural Beings, Giants' or *Yeibichei* 'God Impersonators,' may appear (see Faris 1990). *Jish* are considered to be sacred and alive by Navajos. As comparable to "living gods," they require appropriate care at all times, whether in use in ritual settings or in storage. While a number of options exist among Navajos for the acquisition, transmission, and disposition of *jish*, it is understood that medicine bundles should not be sold to non-Navajos involved in making a profit by buying and selling "esoteric art" in the international marketplace. Instead, the sacred, living medicine bundles belong in the hands of qualified Navajos who live within the boundaries of the four sacred mountains.

After Corrow arrived in Santa Fe with two suitcases and one cardboard box on 9 December 1994, he was apprehended and charged with trafficking in Native American cultural items and selling protected bird feathers from the golden eagle, great horned owl, and buteoine hawk.

Corrow, owner of Artifacts Display Stands in Scottsdale, Arizona, and a buyer/seller of Navajo religious items, traveled to Lukachukai, Arizona, after Winnie's death and visited his eighty-one-year-old widow, Fannie, in her hogan in the presence of her granddaughter and other family members. After several visits, Fannie showed Corrow some of her husband's ceremonial equipment, among which was the Nightway *jish,* which included twenty-two ceremonial masks. Corrow then said he wanted to buy the *jish* and some other items in order to give them to a younger Navajo man in Utah, who was learning the Nightway. After negotiation, in August 1993 Corrow paid $10,000 to Fannie Winnie for the Nightway *jish,* five headdresses, and other items.

In November 1994 the owners of East-West Trading Company in Santa Fe, Bo Icelar and Jimmy Luman, contacted Corrow, saying they had a wealthy Chicago surgeon interested in buying a set of Nightway masks. The alleged buyer was James Tanner, an undercover agent for the National Park Service who was helping in the federal investigation of questionable activities at the East-West gallery. Photographs of Corrow's recent purchase revealed eagle and owl feathers on several of the ceremonial items. Agent Tanner agreed to pay $70,000 for the Nightway *jish,* with $50,000 to go to Corrow and the remainder to the store's coowners. After Corrow arrived in Santa Fe with two suitcases and one cardboard box on 9 December 1994, he was apprehended and charged with trafficking in Native American cultural items and selling protected bird feathers from the golden eagle, great horned owl, and buteoine hawk. The store's owners were also apprehended for making an illegal sale involving feathers of protected birds.

The trial, finally scheduled for April 1996 in Albuquerque's U.S. District Court of New Mexico, began with pretrial hearings on 11, 15, and 19 April; the jury trial followed from 22 through 25 April. Testimony focused on the cultural patrimony status of the Nightway *jish* and other aspects of Navajo religion and traditional law, especially the diversity of Navajo options for transmission and disposition of medicine bundles. Paula Burnett, assistant U.S. attorney, led the prosecution, and Alonzo J. Padilla, the defense; Judge James A. Parker presided. Among the government witnesses, in addition to federal agents involved in investigative aspects of the case, were Alfred Yazzie, a well-respected Nightway chanter who also works for the Navajo Nation Historic Preservation Office; Harry Walters, Navajo anthropologist and director of the Ned Hatathli Cultural Center Museum at Diné College; and myself. The defense called Fannie Winnie and some members of her family, as well as two singers, Jackson Gillis and Billy Yellow, from Monument Valley, and a younger Navajo, Harrison Begay, said to be learning the Nightway. The jury found Corrow guilty of trafficking in objects of cultural patrimony and of possessing (but not selling) protected feathers. At his hearing on 2 July, in accordance with penalties facing first-time NAGPRA offenders, he was sentenced to two concurrent five-year probatory terms and one hundred hours of community service to benefit the Navajo Nation.

On 26 September 1996 the Nightway medicine bundle was repatriated, first through a transfer ceremony in the U.S. District Attorney's Office in Albuquerque, attended by Albert Hale, then president of the Navajo Nation, Alfred Yazzie, other Historic Preservation Office personnel U.S. Attorney John Kelly; and invited guests. Corrow was denied entrance, as his intention of appealing his conviction was already known. After the transfer, the medicine bundle traveled back to Blue Canyon, Arizona, where it went through an all-night cleansing and welcoming home ceremony on 26–27 September before being returned to Wilbert Williams of Deer Springs, the maternal grandson of the chanter who had first acquired the bundle. Finally, after needed repairs, the *jish* was put back into use during a nine-night Nightway ceremonial in Blue Gap, 4–11 October. Those of us who had assisted the government in prosecuting its case against Corrow participated, by invitation, in this ceremony, the final phase of repatriating this particular medicine bundle.

On 21 October, Corrow appealed his conviction to the U.S. Court of Appeals, Tenth Circuit, Denver; his appeal was accompanied by the brief from the Antique Tribal Art Dealers Association. The Denver Court upheld the District Court's decisions (Case No. 96-2185, published 11 July 1997). On 31 December 1997, Corrow filed another appeal, this time with the U.S. Supreme Court. On 23 February 1998, that court, without comment, denied his request, thus finally bringing this case to an end.

—CHARLOTTE J. FRISBIE

GOVERNMENT, POLITICS, AND POPULAR MUSIC IN CANADA

Canada was established as an independent country in 1867 through the British North America Act. The history and development of music and culture in Canada has been distinct from that of the United States in three respects. First, the country from the earliest times has in practice, if not through government policy, maintained its English and French bilingual and bicultural character. Bilingualism and biculturalism since the time of the Trudeau government in the late 1960s have been official policies of succeeding federal governments and from time to time of a number of provincial and municipal governments where it has been felt that demographic patterns warrant it. Such has been the strength of the presence of the French language and French culture in the Province of Québec that, since the 1970s, the issue of independent status as a country for Québec has been a recurring trope of national politics.

Second, because the formation of Canada involved relations with Britain and France that were less confrontational than those between the United States and Britain when the new nation was formed, there have been stronger ties in Canada to European heritages. While Canadian music and culture evidence much of the populism that has characterized U.S. music and culture, they evidence also more prominent traces of the legacy of European high culture. Finally, it is arguable that Canada has maintained a different kind of relationship to immigrant cultures than has the United States. In contrast to the U.S. "melting pot," Canada's increasingly diverse ethnic character has been marked by a greater degree of cultural and linguistic autonomy for ethnic groups. Multiculturalism has been a federal government policy since the late 1960s.

A final important element in understanding the relations of government and politics to music in Canada is Canada's situation as geographically the second largest country in the world, with a relatively small population (approximately 30,000,000 in 2000) spread from the Atlantic to the Pacific, and concentrated close to what has been characterized as the longest friendly border in the world. During the second half of the twentieth century, Canada was the United States's biggest trading partner. The character of this proximity to the country that during the course of the twentieth century became the most powerful in the world has demonstrably affected government policy with regard to music and culture in Canada.

Government, politics, and popular music

A major concern that has driven a good part of federal government policy toward culture and the media since World War II has been that Canadian culture would not be able to maintain its distinctiveness and would, instead, be absorbed as part of the increasing spread of U.S. popular culture around the world. Canada has felt especially vulnerable in this respect, because the vast majority of its population is concentrated near the Canada–U.S. border, within easy reach of U.S. radio and television broadcasts. As Robert Wright observes, "Direct government involvement in the so-called cultural industries—a reasoned and consistent effort to protect Canada from absorption into the mass culture of the United States—became the policy of federal governments beginning in the mid-1950s" (1987:27).

The scene for state intervention in the realm of popular music was set in the late 1960s, when, as part of the national fervor surrounding centennial celebrations, the perception grew that a distinctively Canadian (and distinctly "un-American") form of popular music was being developed by singer-songwriters such as Gordon Lightfoot, Anne Murray, Neil Young, Joni Mitchell, and Bruce Cockburn. Although, as Wright points out, "It was the natural affinity of Canadians for the American folk tradition and their uniquely ambivalent perception of American society, not anti-Americanism, that accounted for their remarkable ascendance as heroes of the Sixties generation" (1987:39), the perception in Canada was that the music of these singer-songwriters spoke of a peaceable, rural, and tranquil nation, to be contrasted with the nation to the south, regarded as urban and as being characterized by civil unrest and violence. This alignment of music with nationalist aspirations was repeated a decade later in Québec, when Gilles Vigneault and his music became intimately associated with the 1980 referendum on independence. Vigneault was disillusioned when the referendum failed, and he largely withdrew from public and musical life.

CanCon regulations

On the national front, it was only after the departure from Canada of artists such as Guy Lombardo, Percy Faith, the Diamonds, and, most notably, Paul Anka, that the federal government enacted legislation to actively promote Canadian popular music. While federal government support for Canada's cultural industries can be traced back to the mid-1950s, support for music was slow. As late as 1970, *Rolling Stone* magazine observed that Canada "was notorious for virtual non-support of its own talent" in popular music (Rodriguez 1970). In January 1970 the Canadian Radio-television and Telecommunication Commission (CRTC: the federal regulatory body for Canadian broadcasting and telecommunications) ruled that 30 percent of music radio programming must be Canadian. In order to count as Canadian under these Canadian content (CanCon) rules, music had to fulfill two of four criteria: the music had to be composed by a Canadian, the lyrics had to be written by a Canadian, the music had to be performed by a Canadian, or the music had to be recorded in Canada (Shuker 1994:63).

These regulations were of mixed effectiveness, and not universally welcomed. First, there was a feeling on the part of some already established Canadian performers such as Gordon Lightfoot that future success by Canadians would be attributed to government "meddling" rather than to talent. In 1971 Lightfoot observed: "Well, the CRTC did absolutely nothing for me, I didn't want it, I didn't need it . . . and I don't like it. They can ruin you, man. Canadian content is fine if you're not doing well" (Wright 1987:30). Second, many radio stations got around the regulation by playing their Canadian quota at off-peak hours, such as the early morning. Third, although in the long term the CanCon rules can be argued to have had a beneficial effect on the growing prominence of Canadian performers during the second half of the twentieth century by encouraging a greater need for recordings of Canadian performers, the effects on the Canadian recording industry have been questionable. As Jody Berland observed in 1988: "The eight largest record companies in Canada are foreign-owned; eighty-nine percent of the revenues from the Canadian domestic market goes to multinationals. Their interest in Canadian music is restricted to those recordings which are marketed across the continent" (1988:349).

Finally, the CanCon rules can be argued to have had little effect on the development of any distinctively Canadian forms of popular music. The argument is that policies such as these have helped Canadians become successful in a transnational marketplace performing music essentially indistinguishable from other transnational music, rather than fostering music internationally recognizable as "Canadian." In addition, anomalies arise in terms of what can and cannot be counted as Canadian. For example, in 1991 a Bryan Adams international hit could not be counted as Canadian, because it only fulfilled one of the CanCon criteria. As a result, Adams was ineligible for a Juno, the Canadian equivalent of the U.S. Grammy. The public controversy that followed led to a change in the regulations.

The Sound Recording Development Program

Essentially the same kinds of criticism have been made of the Sound Recording Development Program (SRDP), established in 1986 (Laroche 1988). The program's purpose was to stimulate the production of Canadian content recordings and the development of the Canadian industry infrastructure. Yet, as Berland notes, the preference for supporting those recordings that can be marketed continentally "also shapes current government programs for subsidizing domestic recording" (1988:349). Concerns about the effectiveness of the CanCon rules and the SRDP led, in the mid-1990s, to the establishment of a federal Task Force on the Future of the Canadian Music Industry. However, in some sectors, the CanCon rules were clearly having an effect. Linda Daniel (1999), for example, reports that in the 1990s, many country music radio stations applying to the CRTC for licenses were undertaking to play more than the required Canadian quota, which by this time was 35 percent, in order to maximize their chances of submitting successful applications. In the context of this increase, it should also be noted that in 1988, the CRTC required an increase from 30 to 50 percent for all popular music programming on the CBC's (Canadian Broadcasting Corporation's) radio network, it being the country's government-funded public broadcasting institution. Parallel developments also occurred in the case of French-language popular music. On 1 July 1990, the CRTC ruled that French-language radio stations had to meet the requirement that 65 percent of the vocal music they played be in French (Grenier 1993:119).

Although a continuing subject for discussion, it seems likely that the background for the rise to prominence of a number of Canadian artists during the late twentieth century (for example, Céline Dion, Alanis Morissette, Sarah McLachlan, and Shania Twain) was set in part by federal government policies with respect to radio and the music industries in general. Such policies have served also to foster music of a more regional and local character.

—JOHN SHEPHERD

PROTEST MUSIC OF THE 1960S

Dominated early on by the civil rights movement and later the Vietnam War, the 1960s marked a time in which vigorously opposed constituencies endeavored to stamp their moral and political visions onto the national soul. During this time, protest music, one of many vehicles used to advance, reflect, and comment upon the decade's frictions, gained a brief and unprecedented importance.

Considering young people's obvious stake in the war's progression, one might have expected a large amount of protest music to come out of mainstream rock and roll. But, in fact, relatively little did.

FIGURE I   Joan Baez walking arm in arm with Martin Luther King Jr. in Granada, Mississippi, 1966. Courtesy Bob Fitch.

The folk song revival movement

As the 1960s began, probably the strongest activist voice in American music was folk singer Pete Seeger (b. 1919). In the 1940s Seeger had performed with the Almanac Singers and later the Weavers. In the early 1950s, a time when his "If I Had a Hammer" was considered subversive, Seeger's left-wing politics got him blacklisted by much of the entertainment industry. Ultimately, however, Seeger's determination to continue performing, combined with a dogged adherence to principle, provided an essential catalyst for the folk song revival movement in which a new generation of singers—nourished by the politics of Seeger and Woody Guthrie, the blues of Leadbelly and Robert Johnson, and the expressions of solidarity found within black spirituals—forged their styles in the coffeehouses and bars of New York City's Greenwich Village.

At the forefront was Joan Baez (b. 1941), who became involved in the civil rights movement in 1961 and in 1963 led an estimated 350,000 people in a performance of "We Shall Overcome" at the Washington, D.C., rally where Martin Luther King Jr. gave his "I have a dream" speech. Equally active in the movement against the Vietnam War, Baez was performing in Hanoi during the height of the 1972 American Christmas bombing campaign. As a composer she contributed the melancholy "Saigon Bride" (figure 1).

Although determined not to be typecast by politics or musical style, the enigmatic Bob Dylan (b. 1941) nevertheless contributed a number of important songs to both the civil rights and antiwar movements. These include "Blowin' in the Wind," "The Times They Are A-Changin'," "Oxford Town," "Masters of War," "A Hard Rain's A-Gonna Fall," and the Woody Guthrie–modeled "Talking World War III Blues." Dylan's songs, covered by the trio of Peter, Paul, and Mary, were firmly in the folk idiom; covers by the Byrds and other pop groups soon followed.

The military experience of 1960 draftee Tom Paxton inspired a number of songs, including, "The Willing Conscript" (in which a still-innocent GI politely asks his drill sergeant for clearer directions in how to kill), "Talking Vietnam Pot Luck Blues," and later the mordant "Lyndon Johnson Told the Nation." Phil Ochs (1940–1976) contributed music to both the civil rights and antiwar movements with "Ballad of Medgar Evers," "Talking Cuban Missile Crisis," "Talking Vietnam," and his widely popular "The Draft Dodger Rag."

"Eve of Destruction" and beyond

Early on, politics went virtually unnoticed in the rebellious but unfocused world of rock and roll [see ROCK, p. 347]. Then in 1965, and following President Lyndon B. Johnson's year-long escalation of troop deployment, the gravelly-voiced Barry McGuire released "Eve of Destruction," a wide-ranging folk song–like anthem that discussed social injustice from Selma, Alabama, to Vietnam. Hugely popular despite being barred from airplay on ABC affiliate radio stations, "Eve of Destruction" went on to reach the number one spot in the *Billboard* pop charts.

While McGuire's song brought the pop music audience one of its first truly political songs, in 1965 a majority of Americans still supported their government's involvement in Vietnam. Not surprisingly, "Eve of Destruction" quickly inspired a counterreaction when The Spokesmen released the anticommunist pro–Vietnam War "Dawn of Correction." In fact, promilitary country songs had been on the upswing all year. In Nashville, songwriter Tom T. Hall's "Hello Viet Nam" was such a strong seller that he quickly wrote three more in a similar vein.

A number of country songs sent threats to those who refused to support military policy. Kris Kristofferson's "Viet Nam Blues" features the simmering rage of a soldier on orders to Vietnam who happens to stumble into a Washington, D.C., antiwar protest. "Wish You Were Here, Buddy," sung by 1950s pop crooner Pat Boone, closes with the following narrative: "And when the whole damn mess is through / I'll put away my rifle and my uniform / And I'll come lookin' for you."

The most disciplined and, commercially, the most successful of the promilitary songs was Staff Sergeant Barry Sadler's 1966 "Ballad of the Green Berets." The single sold two million copies in five weeks. Yet despite the assurances of Sadler, military morale was slumping. By the mid-1960s acts of civil disobedience in both the United States and Vietnam signaled the beginning of the GI antiwar movement.

Parody songs became common. Sadler's melody was reset a number of times, one example being Grace Mora Newman's "Fort Hood Three," which honors soldiers who in 1966 refused orders to board a plane bound for Vietnam. Says one of Newman's verses, "Side by side we walk as men. / Brothers one until the end. / Black and white we think alike. / We will save but not take lives."

Other parodies, such as Tuli Kupferberg's "National Interest March," portrayed a world gone mad. Set to the tune of "Battle Hymn of the Republic," the chorus maniacally chants: "Gory, gory, give 'em napalm, / Gory, gory, drop the A-bomb, / Gory, gory make it H-bomb, / Cause it's in the national interest."

As the decade progressed, an increasing number of off-base "GI coffeehouses" were established. There GIs could find antiwar literature and music whose sale had been banned in the base PX. A live music circuit developed around the coffeehouses where musicians (such as Barbara Dane, who in 1971 recorded a live album titled *FTA!: Songs of the GI Resistance*), sang about the Vietnam War, civil rights, and other social issues.

Perhaps the most memorable antiwar song of the decade was Berkeley-based Country Joe and the Fish's 1965 "I-Feel-Like-I'm-Fixin'-to-Die-Rag." The song's combination of jug band style and cheerfully apocalyptic lyrics—"And it's 1–2-3, What're we fightin' for / Don't ask me, I don't give a damn / Next stop is Vietnam / And it's 5–6-7, open up the pearly gates / There ain't no time to wonder why / (Whoopee!) We're all gonna die"—seemed to sum up the decade's insanity. Lacking the Fish's wry humor, but along the same lines, was The Fugs' machine gun sound effect–enhanced 1966 release "Kill for Peace." Advised those lyrics: "If you don't like a people or the way that they talk, / If you don't like their manners or the way that they walk, / Kill, kill, kill for peace."

On the folk rock side, Donovan (1965) and others would go on to record Buffy Sainte-Marie's "Universal Soldier," while Simon and Garfunkel released three trenchant antiwar songs on their 1966 album *Parsley, Sage, Rosemary and Thyme,* including, "Scarborough Fair/Canticle" and "7 O'Clock News/Silent Night." Arlo Guthrie took a gentle swipe at the era's convoluted morals in his autobiographical folk song/monologue "Alice's Restaurant" (1967). The following year Pete Seeger won a battle with the CBS censors and caught national attention with the performance of his biting "Waist Deep in the Big Muddy" on the nationally televised *Smothers Brothers Comedy Hour.*

Considering young people's obvious stake in the war's progression, one might have expected a large amount of protest music to come out of mainstream rock and roll.

But, in fact, relatively little did. There were songs of generalized discontent, like The Rolling Stones' "(I Can't Get No) Satisfaction" (1965), but the most incisive material, such as The Doors' "The End" (1967), came from the fringe or, as in the case of Jimi Hendrix's soaring Woodstock performance of "The Star Spangled Banner" (1969), from a moment of singular inspiration.

In general, pop music tended to be reactive rather than proactive. Following the 1968 Tet Offensive, as Americans turned increasingly against the war, the music industry increased its antiwar output. Some songs, like John Lennon's pacifist "Give Peace a Chance" (1969), called for renewal. The message in others, such as the call for revolution in Jefferson Airplane's 1969 "Volunteers," however, was taken seriously by virtually no one. Additional releases included Eric Burdon and the Animals' "Sky Pilot" (1968), The Doors' "Unknown Soldier" (1968), and Steppenwolf's "Draft Resister" (1969).

A curious spin within the generally right-wing country music sound occurred in 1969 when The Flying Burrito Brothers released their antidraft tune "My Uncle." That same year, and perhaps in response to the threats posted in earlier songs like "Wish You Were Here, Buddy," the Byrds released "Drug Store Truck Drivin' Man," in which the song's Ku Klux Klan–affiliated protagonist is advised to get out of town while he still can.

The end of the era

As the 1970s opened, the war pounded on in Vietnam and so did the protest movement at home. Peace talks, in progress since 1968, made slow headway, and despite the fact that troop counts were reduced from a 1969 high of 540,000 to 160,000 by the end of 1971, the war's breadth and death count continued to grow. Antiwar songs continued to be produced as well, but most, like "Ohio," Crosby, Stills, Nash, and Young's popular response to the 4 May 1970 National Guard shooting of four students at Kent State University, seemed inspired as much by market potential as political conviction.

Ultimately, almost every major section of the pop music business offered up some sort of anti–Vietnam War anthem. But as these songs now expressed the sentiments of the nation's majority, there was little actual protest associated with them. Perhaps they are best described as pop songs with a topical message. For example, at Motown The Temptations released "Ball of Confusion" (1970) and Edwin Starr recorded "War" (1970). The following year reggae star Jimmy Cliff recorded "Viet Nam," while in Los Angeles the Beach Boys, hardly an ensemble at the political forefront, produced "Student Demonstration Time."

—Steven Cornelius

REFERENCES

Brand, Oscar. 1960. *Election Songs of the United States*. New York: Folkways Records. FH5280. LP disk.

Berland, Jody. 1988. "Locating Listening: Technological Space, Popular Music, Canadian Mediations." *Cultural Studies* 2(3):343–358.

Clark, George W. 1845. *The Liberty Minstrel*. Boston: Leavitt and Alden.

Dane, Barbara. 1971. *FTA!: Songs of the GI Resistance Sung by Barbara Dane with GI's*. Brooklyn, N.Y.: Paredon Records. P1003. LP disk.

Dane, Barbara, and Irwin Silber. 1969. *The Vietnam Songbook*. New York: The Guardian.

Daniel, Linda J. 1999. "Singing Out! Canadian Women in Country Music." D.Ed dissertation,

Ontario Institute for the Study of Education, University of Toronto.

Dunaway, David King. 1981. *How Can I Keep From Singing: Pete Seeger*. New York: McGraw Hill Book Company.

Ewen, David, ed. 1966. *American Popular Songs from the Revolutinary War to the Present*. New York: Random House.

Faris, James C. 1990. *The Nightway: A History and a History of Documentation of a Navajo Ceremonial*. Albuquerque: University of New Mexico Press.

Fischer, Roger A. 1988. *Tippecanoe and Trinkets Too: The Material Culture of American Presidential Campaigns 1828–1984*. Urbana: University of Illinois Press.

Frisbie, Charlotte J. 1987. *Navajo Medicine Bundles or Jish: Acquisition, Transmission, and Disposition in the Past and Present*. Albuquerque: University of New Mexico Press.

———. 1993. "NAGPRA and the Repatriation of Jish." In *Papers from the Third, Fourth, and Sixth Navajo Studies Conferences*, ed. June-el Piper, 119–128. Window Rock, Ariz.: Navajo Nation Historic Preservation Department.

Greeley, Horace. 1872. *The Autobiography of Horace Greeley; or Recollections of a Busy Life*. New York: E. B. Treat.

Grenier, Line. 1993. "Policing French-Language Music on Canadian Radio: The Twilight of the Popular Record Era?" In *Rock and Popular Music: Politics, Policies, Institutions*, ed. Tony Bennett,

Simon Frith, Lawrence Grossberg, John Shepherd, and Graeme Turner, 119–141. London: Routledge.

Gunderson, Robert Gray. 1977 [1957]. *The Log-Cabin Campaign.* Westport, Conn.: Greenwood Press.

Hampton, Wayne. 1986. *Guerrilla Minstrels.* Knoxville: University of Tennessee Press.

Hutchinson, John W. 1860. *Hutchinson's Republican Songster, for the Campaign of 1860.* New York: O. Hutchinson.

Kerr, Charles H. 1901. *Socialist Songs with Music.* Chicago: Charles H. Kerr and Company.

Klein, Joe. 1980. *Woody Guthrie: A Life.* New York: Knopf.

Laroche, Karyna. 1988. "The Sound Development Recording Program: Making Music to Maintain Hegemony." Master's thesis, School of Canadian Studies, Carleton University.

Lawrence, Benjamin M. 1878. *The National Greenback Labor Songster.* New York: D. M. Bennett.

Littell, John S. 1844. *The Clay Minstrel; or, National Songster, to Which Is Prefixed a Sketch of the Life, Public Services, and Character of Henry Clay.* New York: Greeley and M'Elrath.

Lund, Jens. 1975. "Socio-Political Aspects of Right-Wing Music." Master's thesis, Bowling Green State University.

Miles, William. 1990. *Songs, Odes, Glees and Ballads: A Bibliography of American Presidential Campaign Songsters.* Music Reference Collection 27. New York: Greenwood Press.

Moffitt, W. O. 1878. *The National Temperance Songster.* Debuque, Iowa: Gay and Schermerhorn.

Robbins, Mary Susannah, ed. 1999. *Against the Vietnam War: Writings by Activists.* Syracuse, N.Y.: Syracuse University Press.

Rodriguez, Juan. March 19, 1970. "Jesse Winchester's Trip to Canda," *Rolling Stone.*

Sanjek, Russell. 1988. *American Popular Music and Its Business: The First Four Hundred Years. Volume II: From 1790 to 1909.* New York: Oxford University Press.

Shuker, Roy. 1994. *Understanding Popular Music.* London: Routledge.

Silber, Irwin. 1971. *Songs America Voted By.* Harrisburg, Pa.: Stackpole Books.

Simon, Paul and Art Garfunkel. 1966. *Parsley, Sage, Rosemary, and Thyme.* Columbia CL2563. LP disk.

Sing along with Millard Fillmore: The Life Album of Presidential Campaign Songs. Columbia Mono-CL 2260. LP disk.

Tuckerman, Bayard, ed. 1889. *The Diary of Philip Hone,* 1828–1851, vol. 2. New York: Dodd, Mead and Company.

Wright, Robert A. 1987. "'Dream, Comfort, Memory, Despair': Canadian Popular Musicians and the Dilemma of Nationalism, 1968–1972." *Journal of Canadian Studies* 22(4):27–43.

Section 4
Border Crossings and Fusions

Living within the context of a highly diverse, pluralistic society in which a variety of social and musical interactions are always possible has enabled people in the United States and Canada to develop musical cultures that are, at times, identified by strong cultural boundaries, and at other times, highly integrative products of creative social and musical mergers. Many of the genres of music we experience today, such as country and western, rock, and certain concert musics, are the result of musical and social mixtures that created new forms and meanings for music, as well as for other expressions of social and cultural identity. This section discusses the processes of musical acculturation and synthesis (the borrowing, adaptation and/or merging of different musical elements) as they have occurred in various contexts within the United States and Canada as disparate peoples have moved and settled close to each other and have shared their lives and musics.

Fusions and bordercrossings of all kinds occur naturally between and among musical cultures. Here, Ken Zuckerman, a classically-trained western musician plays the sarod, a North Indian solo instrument. Zuckerman, who has studied under Ali Akbar Khan for twenty-five years and is recognized worldwide as a master of the sarod, is the Director of the Ali Akbar School in Basel, Switzerland. Photo courtesy of Heiner Grieder, 1997.

Blurring the Boundaries
of Social and Musical Identities
James R. Cowdery
Anne Lederman

Border Crossings—James R. Cowdery
Border Crossings: Some Random Notes from Canada—Anne Lederman

BORDER CROSSINGS

The folk festival presenter on the phone was telling our band something we had heard before. Yes, we played Irish traditional music, which she was interested in presenting. Yes, we had studied the music thoroughly, and we could play it in an authentic manner. Yes, we had built up a good-sized local audience, so people would come to hear us. But we weren't Irish. We didn't even act like Irish musicians, who (according to her) projected a proper reverence for their traditional music and culture. We conducted ourselves on stage like the middle-class American college students we were, speaking and behaving in ways that were grounded in our own culture and experiences. The name of our group, How To Change a Flat Tire, evoked the culture that produced The Velvet Underground and The Mothers of Invention, not the one that produced The Chieftains and The Boys of the Lough. Finally, despite our ability to play our instruments in a recognizable (if rather generalized) Irish style, we insisted on experimenting with complex group arrangements that she considered unsuitable for the simple, pure folk music of our mentors. We were appropriating a music that was not rightly ours and treating it, she felt, with disrespect. Our music smelled of privileged Americans plundering and debasing the fragile heritage of a culture of poor farmers and laborers. Of course we disagreed, and we tried to explain ourselves: we felt that we were Americans playing Irish music in a way that made cultural sense to us and to our American audience. (The festival presenter must have felt some of the ambiguity of the situation herself, because she ended up hiring us for her folk festival—and changing her mind the next day.)

Anthony Barrand, who was born and raised in England and moved to the United States as a young man, provides another point of view, involving the traditional English outdoor seasonal rituals known as morris dancing. When his group of American morris dancers performs in the United States, with their repertoire of tunes and dances from England and new ones derived from traditional models, he resolutely tells curious onlookers that what they are watching is American dancing. Although the original style, tunes, and dances came from England, their offering is an American event, not an English one; to characterize it otherwise would be to suggest that the activity was independent of the context of its performance.

In their own ways, both of these examples involve the idea that affect and meaning are not simply artifacts of their original cultural contexts: they also are processes that are inextricably intertwined with the time, place, and community in which they currently occur [see DIVERSE ENVIRONMENTS, p. 141]. Indeed, the very concept of original culture is a problematic one. In the mid- twentieth century, some ethnomusicologists who had revisited sites of earlier fieldwork to find once-meaningful practices discarded in favor of mass-mediated popular culture propounded a gloomy prophecy of cultural gray-out: the beautiful old traditional genres and styles were being abandoned for drab modern ones, and eventually the world's wonderful diversity would disappear, replaced by one big, gray cultural monolith (Lomax 1968:4). But this theory misses two important points: eventually, some people will not remain satisfied with insipid cultural forms (witness, for example, the rise of punk, rap, and other defiant musics out of the bland, safe commercialism of disco in the 1980s); and any perception of an original, static culture is a mirage—throughout human history people have created, explored, and developed music in ways that respond to the vital nature of all cultures.

Musical practices have evolved in relation to cultural dynamics in North America in various ways, often involving the generation of new musical genres, repertoires, and styles. While examples may not always represent a literal crossing of political or geographical borders, they share a movement away from some prior physical and/or psychological location of musical practices and meanings toward a new meeting place mapped by new cultural developments and demands. And in comparing physical borders to conceptual ones, we must remember that although both may become war zones, conceptual space always has room for a new region, delineated with a new border.

These metaphoric crossings may be seen in two general categories, characterized by congenial horticultural metaphors: transplanting and hybridizing. If a tree is transplanted from one ecosystem to a new one, it may or may not be able to thrive at all; if it does, it may have to adapt in one or more ways to its new climate. Such transplantings can be done formally, as in the conscious introduction of a plant from a different habitat, or they may occur informally, as in the accidental stowaway seeds that brought certain nonindigenous wildflowers to North America from Europe. Hybridizing involves mergers of species—usually intentional—that create new and genetically viable ones. Such hybridizing may take place in the mind of one person, such as a classical or jazz composer who is influenced by elements of other musics, or it may be the result of cross-cultural contacts, such as the myriad African American genres that arose from the interaction of African rhythmic and formal practices with the European harmonic system. And as we have already seen, issues of appropriation and power may come into play in both hybridizing and transplanting. What does it mean to use someone else's music? Are various musics just collections of sounds, like colors on a painter's palette, to be combined at the whim of the artist? Different people will answer such questions in different ways.

Transplanting

Formal procedures

Barrand was not the first person to institute morris dancing in North America. When the English musician and folklorist Cecil Sharp visited the United States in the mid-1910s to teach and collect folk songs, he enlisted May Gadd, a young Englishwoman, to help to establish the Country Dance and Song Society of America as a branch of the English Country Dance Society. Gadd presided over the teaching of morris and country dancing in the northeast United States for almost fifty years through various venues, notably at Pinewoods Camp near Plymouth, Massachusetts. In the late 1960s the Pinewoods Morris Men took their dancing to the streets of Cambridge (Massachusetts), bringing their music and dancing to the public in a replication of morris events in England. Numerous American morris groups descended from Gadd's teaching have followed, including Barrand's Marlboro Morris Men in Vermont, touring for local street performances in the spring just as the morris groups in England have done for several generations. Since the mid-1970s some of these American groups—like the Marlboro Men—have started to develop new dances and tunes as well, ensuring a thriving creative pulse (Barrand 1991).

This, therefore, was a kind of transplanting that involved a certain amount of formal, institutional support. A host institution was found or founded, teachers were hired, and people who wanted to participate gravitated to the established centers, perhaps later establishing their own centers elsewhere. This relative formality mirrors the comparatively formal nature of morris events, in which a set number of dancers and a solo musician perform carefully rehearsed musical and choreographic compositions that involve little or no latitude for spontaneous embellishment (excluding the improvisatory role of the Fool). The creation of new tunes and dances—a practice that is still somewhat controversial among more conservative practitioners—takes place within this established framework. Similarly, Scottish highland bagpipe regiments have been organized throughout the United States and Canada, each with a specific name and leader, performing set repertoires of tunes played in unison and precisely executed marching formations, with much difference of opinion concerning the desirability of composing and playing new tunes. More broadly, ethnomusicology programs such as those at Wesleyan University in Connecticut or the University of California in Los Angeles have established performing groups in African, Asian, and other world musics, hiring master musicians from abroad as teachers. These activities have sometimes spawned new local groups as well, such as the Boston Village Gamelan in Massachusetts, which performs traditional Central Javanese gamelan music, and Gamelan Son of Lion in New York City, which performs new compositions by American and other composers.

Informal processes

The Irish tradition adapted by How To Change a Flat Tire had been transplanted to North America in a less formal way. Immigrants from Ireland who played the music brought their songs and instruments along when they could, sometimes as their most prized possessions from home. When Francis O'Neill arrived in Chicago in the late nineteenth century, he found a thriving community of players of the music, and as he rose to the rank of superintendent of police (the equivalent of today's chief of police), he made every possible effort to nurture and expand this community. (During his tenure as superintendent, it was much rumored in Ireland that a good man who was a skilled player of traditional music and was able to emigrate would have little trouble landing a job on the Chicago police force.) And New York City became the home of virtually whole transplanted musical communities from Ireland in what was later called a golden age of Irish music in New York in the first three decades of the twentieth century (Miller 1996).

While the transplanting of Irish traditional music was sometimes nurtured by institutions such as the New York Gaelic League or the Chicago police force, it was not at all dependent on them. To extend the horticultural metaphor, it was more like the spreading of wildflowers than the cultivation of gardens. Again, the informality of the process reflects the informality of a typical Irish music session, in which any number of musicians—playing any suitable instruments with varying degrees of proficiency—can participate freely, spontaneously embellishing the melodies in accordance with each one's own individual skill and temperament. The same structural informality can be found in the music making of certain other transplanted cultural groups in North America—Caribbean and South American, for example—echoing the relative informality of the musical transplantation process itself. Of course, these are not sharp generic distinctions: one may encounter informal sessions among Scottish highland pipers and morris dancers, and one can find structured, formal presentations of Irish, Caribbean, and South American musics. But the relationships between the usual methods of transplantation and the usual structures of musical events are notable.

Whatever the degree of formality involved, immigrants brought their music to North America, and it thrived there as long as it continued to be valued, sometimes going through periods of decline and renewal. Africans who were sold as slaves brought their music too, but their captivity proved as harsh to their music as it was to their bodies and souls, so adaptation was the only key to survival. Concerns over the sanctioning of pagan rituals and the possibility that drums could be used to send incendiary signals, along with the tried-and-true practice of subjugating people by obliterating their cultural heritage, led North American slaveholders to forbid drumming among their slaves and to ban cultural events that replicated African ones. Only in a few isolated pockets—for example, in and around New Orleans—could true transplantations of African music actually thrive.

Hybridizing

Cross-cultural contacts

As suggested earlier, African and musical elements, forms, and practices could sometimes survive through adaptation. Ecstatic singing and dancing—even trance and spirit possession—might be sanctioned if they were framed in Christian worship. Some slaves mastered European instruments and genres for the entertainment of their captors, incorporating various African musical practices for their own recreation. Many slave owners came to believe that such religious and recreational usages contributed significantly to their slaves' contentment, lessening the possibility of rebellion. Field hollers and other kinds of work songs founded on African models seemed to spark more spirited labor among the slaves, invigorating workers and increasing output, so these genres were allowed to develop and thrive. LeRoi Jones (Amiri Baraka) has noted that only first-generation slaves were African; their children were American (Jones 1963). Similarly, second-generation slave music in North America was seldom purely African: it was African American, a hybrid. Today the story of African American music is one of the richest accounts of hybridization in recorded history, involving the development of blues, jazz, and the foundations of virtually all contemporary popular music.

Musical hybridization has often been the result of close contact between ethnic groups—perhaps literally involving intermarriage, or sometimes just due to proximity in residence and work. The minglings of Scottish and French communities produced distinctive musical styles and repertoires in Nova Scotia and Québec, just as interactions among Scottish, Irish, and English immigrants generated new songs, tunes, and techniques in Appalachia and New England. *Tejano* music arose along the U.S. border with Mexico, reflecting the cultural mixing and social tensions of the region. The music that became known as jazz, with its particular mixtures of African American performing styles and European instruments and harmonic practices, largely developed in the Creole community of New Orleans, where blacks and whites fraternized more freely than they could in most other parts of the world. Sometimes such interethnic developments have involved a commingling of older and newer forms: contemporary klezmer music, for example, arose out of contacts in the United States between jazz players and immigrant European Jewish traditional musicians, just as salsa evolved among jazz musicians and immigrants from Cuba and other Caribbean and South American countries.

Here the picture starts to get more complex, as we start to perceive hybrids mixing with hybrids. We can see, for example, Appalachian music leaving the high mountains in the early twentieth century as hillbilly music (also known as old time or, in a more recent development, as bluegrass) and joining forces with early rhythm and blues to

Musical hybridization bespeaks the formulation of a contemporary identity rooted in older values and practices, in a sense saying: we are thriving in the modern world, while our heritage continues to nurture and inspire us

become country and western, with mid-century jazz to become western swing, or with rock and roll to become rockabilly music. We can see the music of transplanted French Canadians combining with the local African American traditions in Louisiana to become Cajun music and further recombining with rhythm and blues to become zydeco. First Nation cultures are also a part of this picture: witness the development of Native American fiddle traditions in Canada and the many mixtures by Native American musicians of genres and elements of their older traditions with country, rock, jazz, folk, and new age musical styles. Such developments articulate historically situated redefinitions of identity in response to changing social situations. Specific individual examples are notable too: the Irish-American rock band Black 47 has been known to mix traditional Irish fiddle tunes with rapping over hip-hop beats. In all of these cases, musical hybridization bespeaks the formulation of a contemporary identity rooted in older values and practices, in a sense saying: we are thriving in the modern world, while our heritage continues to nurture and inspire us.

Constructed musical identities

Heritage, however, cannot always be so clearly defined. Many North Americans grow up without any particular feeling of belonging to a specific ethnic group, and some who do eventually find that the range of expression provided by their ethnic background is not sufficient for their needs. Such people may be satisfied by the mass-mediated music that is easily available to them, or they might construct a different sense of belonging, founded more on choice than on family history or mainstream allegiance. They might gravitate toward what Mark Slobin has called affinity groups: communities bound together not by ethnicity but by attraction to particular cultural practices, such as music (1993). And affinity groups can generate their own musical hybrids. Young white musicians who were more attracted to African American genres than to European-based popular musics contributed significantly to the development of rock and roll. Most of the participants in the folk revival of the 1950s did not grow up with Appalachian or other traditional musics. They discovered these musics as young adults, were attracted to them, and developed their own musical styles, drawing on what they imbibed from them. Sometimes such affinity-driven musicians go deeper into the cultures that produced their adopted music—studying or apprenticing with Appalachian or African American musicians, for example—and they may reach high levels of technical and expressive proficiency.

From the idea of affinity we can branch into more complex kinds of musical borrowings. The Canadian singer and songwriter Loreena McKennitt uses instruments from a number of cultures—the harp, whistle, bodhrán 'drum', and uilleann pipes of Ireland; the electric guitar, bass, keyboards, and drums of rock music; string and percussion instruments from India, and so on—to construct a kind of imaginary ethnicity that mixes images of the world of the ancient Celts with a contemporary identity. Her strong commercial success indicates that a large number of people feel a powerful affinity with this kind of ideally constructed culture. Groups like The Chicago Art Ensemble combine the instruments and techniques of jazz with African instruments and experimental improvisational forms to evoke a broadly based cultural identity, rooted equally in African, African American, and contemporary experimental musics. A number of jazz groups include instruments (and sometimes players) from Africa, the Caribbean, or South America, suggesting a kind of black identity that spans geographic boundaries. The Ottawa-based multiethnic group Seventh Fire presents socially conscious songs that mix Native and Latin American sounds with elements of reggae and punk, envisioning a kind of pan-subcultural identity. Some composers of contemporary folk, popular, and new age music take this kind of generalized identity even further, combining instruments and techniques from every corner of the earth as an articulation of a pan-human identity: the harmonious juxtaposition of sounds from different cultures becomes a metaphor for peaceful coexistence in a utopian global village.

Composers

Constructed identity takes on another dimension when we consider the border crossings of North American classical composers. (I use the word *classical* more to indicate the usual venues for performances of this music than to tag all of these composers with one label; there is little consensus among them regarding identifications like classical, art, serious, concert, and so on.) Wishing to develop a specifically American compositional voice, mid-twentieth-century composers like Aaron Copland and Roy Harris sometimes borrowed American folk tunes for their compositions (Copland's use of the Shaker song "Simple Gifts" in his 1944 ballet *Appalachian Spring* is a prominent example), but more often they brought abstractions of what they perceived as folk elements into their music, inspired by what Béla Bartók and other European composers had done with abstracted elements of their own countries' folk traditions. Like these Europeans, they wanted to forge a uniquely American sound that was identifiably rooted in European classical traditions—a generalized national identity within a larger, established genre.

Other composers have a less nationalistic agenda but are attracted to the fresh palette of sounds offered by instruments, forms, and techniques from other cultures. Such composers may gravitate toward the kind of institutional ethnomusicology programs described above, where they can find such instruments and people who can play them. Lou Harrison, for example, was so inspired by his studies of Indonesian gamelan music that he founded his own American gamelan group and composed a sizable repertoire of new music for it, often with parts for European instruments and voices as well. Harrison doesn't imagine that he is articulating a Javanese American identity; rather, he envisions something akin to the kind of harmonious blendings sought by the contemporary folk, popular, and new age composers mentioned here, but with a classical sensibility. There is a certain tradition for imagining a pan-human identity in European classical music already: some of its past practitioners maintained that it was a universal music that transcended time and place (Nettl 1983:36–38). European classical music has a long history of adopting and adapting instruments from other cultures already—string instruments from Arabic countries, percussion instruments from Turkey, and so on—so composers like Harrison often see their work as a natural development rather than as a clever curiosity.

While composers like Aaron Copland and Roy Harris expanded the range of Western classical music to include a distinctive American voice by incorporating elements of American traditional musics, composers like Harrison and his teacher, Henry Cowell, took a less regional stance, making room for influences from any and every part of the world. Rooted in Western classical music, they worked to broaden its scope from within. Other composers have come from different cultural roots, establishing antihegemonic subcultural voices that contest the supremacy of European classical traditions while still making some use of their affective powers. Jazz composers like

Ornette Coleman have created works that develop an authentically African American sound within Western classical music. The rock guitarist and composer Frank Zappa combined forces with classical musicians for a number of his projects, even collaborating with the celebrated conductor and composer Pierre Boulez. Working in the opposite direction, some heavy metal guitarists have assiduously studied classical music theory and compositions—particularly the works of Baroque composers like Vivaldi and Bach—to broaden their scope for composing and improvising. Nor is classical music the only genre to inspire such cross-pollinations: Fred Wei-han Ho, for example, brings his jazz background to the forging of a contemporary Asian American musical voice, sometimes combining Chinese and jazz instruments and styles to produce compositions and performances that can be heard as an enrichment of both musics' expressive capabilities and as a challenging—even subversive—articulation of subcultural identity.

Issues

All men are brothers?

As these last examples suggest, the musical discourse of identity can involve more than just the establishment and maintenance of a real or idealized ethnicity. Identity also includes conceptions of the individual or group in relation to larger aspects of society.

In the wake of World War II, the United States saw a considerable resurgence of parochialism—xenophobia, bigotry, and class resentment—underscored by the anticommunist fervor of the House Un-American Activities Committee (HUAC). In 1948 Pete Seeger, Lee Hays, Fred Hellerman, and Ronnie Gilbert—four musicians who deplored such conservative developments—began singing together informally. They soon became The Weavers (taking their name from a German play about a rebellion among weavers in medieval England), and by 1950 The Weavers had become a successful performing group, playing acoustic guitar and banjo and singing songs from various parts of the United States as well as from other countries: songs of many lands (figure 1). Their first hit record, "Goodnight Irene," presented a song by the African American musician Huddie Ledbetter (publicly known as Leadbelly). Subsequent successes included "Wimoweh," a song that the South African composer Solomon Linda had based on a traditional Zulu chant; "Tzena Tzena," an adaptation of a Yiddish folk song; the Appalachian "On Top of Old Smoky"; and "The Hammer Song" ("If I Had a Hammer"), composed by Hays and Seeger. The overall message was eminently antiparochial: all men are brothers, and music is a particularly potent and attractive vehicle for the unification and empowerment of the world's oppressed peoples (Cantwell 1996).

But why should these comfortably middle-class young white Americans appoint themselves the spokespeople for the earth's oppressed? They had acquired record deals and concert and television engagements, they were pleasant and safe-looking, and their performances projected a feeling of good clean fun, not angry defiance. Certainly they believed that their relatively privileged position in society enabled them—even compelled them—to use their prominence to champion the voiceless masses, and in a dismal episode in American popular music history, they were hounded out of the music business by HUAC in 1953. But despite their best intentions and subsequent persecution, in retrospect one might ask whether the result of the Weavers's efforts was real social redress or just the commercial commodification of other peoples' songs, involving the inevitable dilution of meaning caused by replacing the cultural context in which the songs arose with a sanitized, mass-mediated one. When considerations of political, social, and economic power enter the picture, musical border crossings can take on a new dimension.

FIGURE I   The Weavers, c. 1951 (*left to right:* Pete Seeger, Lee Hays, Ronnie Gilbert, Fred Hellerman). Photo courtesy Harold Leventhal Management.

The case raises more questions than it answers. Pete Seeger went on to become a significant figure in the civil rights and antiwar movements of the 1960s and continues to address social issues in song well into old age. He scrupulously honored his sources—for example, tracking down Solomon Linda's widow to ensure that she shared in the proceeds from "Wimoweh"—and he often donated his own profits to activist social organizations. Does it matter that his father was a distinguished musicologist instead of a coal miner? Or when John Hammond Jr. expertly performs the music of Robert Johnson and Blind Willie McTell, does it matter that his father was a prosperous entrepreneur instead of a sharecropper? Besides, how many other musicians, white or black, are currently espousing the rural blues repertoires and styles of the 1930s?

Appropriation and power

Consider the white rhythm and blues musicians in the 1950s who recorded cover versions of songs by black musicians, reaping financial rewards from the racist radio and television stations who wouldn't present African American artists but were happy to turn a profit from their songs. Until comparatively recently, the American mass media consistently have tried to put a white face on any successful black music. Benny Goodman was dubbed the king of swing, Elvis Presley the king of rock and roll (the term

African American musicians have long played the musics of neighboring white communities—barn dances, polkas, popular songs, and so on—as well as their own community's music, but that was because they needed to do so in order to eke out a living as musicians.

rock and roll was itself a kind of white subterfuge for supplanting the racially loaded term rhythm and blues). But whatever the motives of music business operatives, these artists were all drawn to their professions through a sincere love of the music. Why shouldn't they follow their affinity and garner financial rewards if they could? Can we define absolutely the point beyond which affinity becomes appropriation?

The issue of power is salient. African American musicians have long played the musics of neighboring white communities—barn dances, polkas, popular songs, and so on—as well as their own community's music, but that was because they needed to do so in order to eke out a living as musicians. The recordings that survive from the blues boom of the 1920s and 1930s give a one-sided picture of these artist's repertoires, as the recording companies wanted to record only their blues songs to satisfy the current market trend. Listening to Alan Lomax's recordings of Sid Hemphill's group in Mississippi in 1942, it is hard to believe that the personnel was the same from one song to the next, so complete was their ability to render local white music as well as their own African American traditions. These musicians appear to have had a real affinity with all of the music they played, but one cannot ignore the fact that they needed to be able to satisfy a broad range of clientele in order to survive as musicians. By contrast, white musicians have usually performed African American music out of choice rather than necessity. As some of these musicians have pointed out, their participation does not deplete a resource: they are not taking music away from anyone—indeed, they may help to increase audiences for the music they espouse, leading listeners back to their sources.

Again, if there is an issue here it is one of social and economic power, which may be related to race or, more broadly, to the social stratification of people and genres. Consider, for example, the popular crossover recordings that are much promoted by the classical music industry, in which classical musicians perform nonclassical musics. When the celebrated violinist Itzhak Perlman chose to perform klezmer music in the 1990s, he was soon guaranteed a major recording contract, a substantial promotional budget, and an hour-long special program on Public Television (which has been aired several times, becoming something of a crossover staple). But when the banjo player Bill Crofut (a former student of Pete Seeger's) wanted to make recordings of classical music on folk instruments, he had to pay all the production costs out of his own pocket and spend two years trying to interest record companies in publishing and distributing the recordings. The relative merits of the Crofut and Perlman projects are not the point here: the issue is who had access to the power structures and rewards of the lucrative crossover media—the classical musician playing folk music or the folk musician playing classical music—and why. One could argue that Perlman had proven that his name could sell a large number of recordings, while Crofut had not, but one could also argue that Perlman had long enjoyed the backing of the classical music establishment and therefore had had much more opportunity to develop and demonstrate his commercial potential.

For the future

Here are some questions we might ask: Does a person's pursuit of a musical affinity have the result—intended or not—of usurping a more authoritative musician's share in the marketplace? Does it change the original meaning of the music in ways that neutralize potentially controversial expressions and reduce the impact of vital cultural symbols? What kinds of power structures are involved, and how do they interact? Some ethnomusicologists maintain that scholars must be wary of imposing their own moral judgments on musical practices; others insist that it is their duty to recognize and censure inequities wherever they find them. Certainly, it is important for those involved in the study of musical border crossings to contemplate questions such as those raised above, and it is just as important to refrain from oversimplifying our perceptions of situations in order to answer them.

—JAMES R. COWDERY

BORDER CROSSINGS: SOME RANDOM NOTES FROM CANADA

What happens when musical cultures collide? Or sit down to tea, chat over the fence or end up on the same dance floor in a small community? Or when one listens at the window of another, not daring to go inside? In North American contexts these sorts of things have been going on for a very long time—between First Nations themselves, between First Nation and European, European and African, European and European, Canadian and U.S. cultures, and, eventually, virtually all of the older cultures in the world with North American cultures. What happens seems to depend largely on the concentration of the cultures involved, the common ground they have, and what they represent to each other in terms of symbolic power and desirability.

James Cowdery talks of transplantation and hybridization, but those processes essentially preserve the genetic structures of the originals, even if two or more are grafted together. This does not account for the great crucible of human creativity that takes elements from various places, catalyzes and transforms them, and synthesizes entirely new expressions that are far greater than the sum of their parts. It is far more than a genetic transplanting or grafting that happens; it is elemental transformation.

Certainly, cultures are brought here, but they quickly follow their own path. Where concentrations are high enough and people isolated enough, the New World paths remained relatively monocultural for a time, as in Cape Breton and Québec. These New World cultures developed with little or no contact with the Old for some time, only to reestablish connections in the twentieth century through mass media. This allowed them to preserve certain elements lost in the Old World, although it is hard to compare musical styles when one has disappeared. But even these relatively isolated musics have changed under the influence of other musics. And, of course, songs reflect New World experiences. Cultural affinity with "the old country" often leads to new cross-pollination when contact is reestablished—a revival of the hurdy-gurdy and a new interest in Breton music in Québec, for example. But both New and Old World practices are strong in their own identity at this point.

Let's look at a much more recent case in point—African music arriving in the past twenty years to Canadian urban centers. Versions of rural outdoor festivals are transplanted to banquet halls. Chiefdoms are chosen, honorary, and symbolic, not inherited. Events that took days in the old country happen in one night here, inevitably Saturday because of the North American work week. Libations are still poured on the floor, but someone has to get a mop. Relatively young, inexperienced musicians become the "master drummers," and a Canadian African music is born.

Contrast this with the earlier experience of African music in the United States. Then, the concentration was not high enough of any one culture, so that Africans in the United States were dealing with each other's radically different traditions as well as with European music, and in a culturally repressive, soul-numbing situation. Much more was lost under these conditions. But nobody takes up a new musical style because he or she is forced to. On some level, African slaves must actually have liked at least some of the European music they heard (and probably enjoyed making fun of the rest) just as, eventually, European North Americans liked what they heard in the blues bars. In Canada, a similar repression of Native traditions was tried in many areas, and where people were moved and ended up with others of radically different cultures, it generally worked. But this was their home territory and there were comparatively more of them, so Native people often found ways to preserve the older traditions, secretly if necessary. Where concentrations of people are high, cultures develop, although never quite the way they did in another place. When they are not, experience has shown that much is lost.

But what happens when a whole palette of sound, developed under one cultural world view, is perceived by people whose understanding of the world is very different? Perhaps they do not even perceive certain aspects that are too far outside their own experience. Where there is common ground, information can be taken in. What is not liked is ignored. But what is not understood is possibly not even perceived. I believe this process is as active today in the world as it was when Native fiddlers adopted something approximating the European modal system and the steady rhythms of the fiddling, but not the phrasing or the forms, which were, in all likelihood, too far outside their cultural understanding. How many North Americans today fail to understand spiritual and philosophical aspects of other musics, for example, and go merely for the sounds of the instruments? After all, most music in North America is no longer performed for spiritual reasons, and perhaps we are perceptually handicapped from seeing those sorts of things.

Where there is enough common ground, a musician from one tradition can copy the traditions of another, eventually, perhaps, consciously experimenting with putting them together, as has happened with klezmer and jazz musicians. In fact, if the lessons of North America have taught us anything, it is that there is enough common ground between virtually any two given cultures for synthesis to be possible on some level, if the desire is there. It is the details that get interesting, and, for want of a better word, the politics.

Not all cultures that are exposed to each other do come together. In the eighteenth century Europeans found Native music, for the most part, savage and unpleasant, which is pretty much what they thought of the people themselves. But today, learning Native music is often seen as a desirable thing, symbolizing values such as respect for the land and spiritual harmony. From the other side, Native people often parodied the staid concert traditions of Europe but could relate to aspects of their social and dance musics. So although some combinations don't take, Canadians have been adopting traditions outside their own for a very long time, from the Scottish fiddle/dance practices taken up by Native, French, and Métis, to the Irish and mixed French/English songs in the camps, taken up by men of many backgrounds, to British murder ballads sung by the descendants of slaves in Nova Scotia, down to modern revivals and adoptions of just about anything.

And what of today, when so many peoples the world over are abandoning their traditional musical expressions in favor of North American popular ones? Perhaps North American music is a symbol of other aspects of North American culture that they want. Ironically, this is happening as many North Americans are busy pursuing the same process in reverse, involving themselves in older musical cultures around the world. Perhaps they are starved for depth and for music whose purpose is something other than commercial. So, on the one hand, we have those who would abandon their traditions for North American popularity, not realizing it is their traditions that are most likely to make them popular here, and, on the other, those who are hoping immigrants will teach them the "old ways." Here in Canada, as these various worldviews experience each other right now, some interesting new chapters on cultural exchange are being written.

—ANNE LEDERMAN

REFERENCES

Barrand, Anthony G. 1991. *Six Fools and a Dancer: The Timeless Way of the Morris.* Plainfield, Vt.: Northern Harmony.

Cantwell, Robert. 1996. *When We Were Good: The Folk Revival.* Cambridge: Harvard University Press.

Jones, LeRoi (Amiri Baraka). 1963. *Blues People.* New York: Morrow Quill.

Lomax, Alan. 1968. *Folk Song Style and Culture.* Washington, D.C.: American Association for the Advancement of Science.

Miller, Rebecca. 1996. "Irish Traditional and Popular Music in New York City: Identity and Social Change, 1930–1975." In *The New York Irish,* ed. Ronald H. Bayor and Timothy J. Meagher, 481–507. Baltimore: Johns Hopkins University Press.

Nettl, Bruno. 1983. *The Study of Ethnomusicology: Twenty-nine Issues and Concepts.* Urbana: University of Illinois Press.

Slobin, Mark. 1993. *Subcultural Sounds: Micro-musics of the West.* Hanover, N.H.: Wesleyan University Press.

Snapshot: Five Fusions

Fred Ho
Jeremy Wallach
Beverley Diamond
Ron Pen
Rob Bowman and Sara Nicholson

New and Experimental Genres—Fred Ho
World Beat—Jeremy Wallach
Intercultural Traditions on the Canadian Prairies—Beverley Diamond
New Age—Ron Pen
Rock—Rob Bowman and Sara Nicholson

Musical interactions are a natural process of social and cultural exchange. People living side by side hear and experiment with each other's musics in the same ways as with language, art, and all other forms of expressive culture. In the United States and Canada, where the diversity of social and cultural groups is extraordinarily rich and at a time when new technologies are making it increasingly possible to manipulate sound, opportunities for musical borrowings, border crossings, fusions, and other forms of musical interaction abound. As the views presented here show, however, the borrowing and adaption of others' musics carries with it ethical and often legal problems that need to be examined carefully and resolved.

NEW AND EXPERIMENTAL GENRES

Since the middle of the twentieth century, the human community has become, as Marshall McLuhan phrased, a global village. Cartographers have mapped every corner of the earth; technology—expanding at a phenomenal rate, through mass communication and mass transportation—has shortened distances to literally the push of a button, making physical travel possible within hours; achievements in the field of aerospace have made it possible to photograph the planet from space; international political, economic, legal and cultural bodies have emerged; and every facet of human existence has become increasingly interconnected and interdependent in a global, planetary context.

The second half of the twentieth century also marked two major shifts in geopolitical power. Former Western European colonial powers lost significantly to the rising economic and military dominance of the United States as a superpower. As part of the decline of European colonialism, former European colonies in Africa, Asia, Central and South America, and the Pacific Islands gained independence and emerged as significant forces in international affairs. These developments had impact on the American musical processes and practices during the latter half of the twentieth century.

Since the 1950s, various forms of experimentation have occurred among existing musical styles, genres, and idioms. For example, crossovers between European-derived concert or classical music (that is, music requiring formal training, usually in academic institutions or conservatories, primarily notated, and performed in concert venues) and African American traditions such as jazz, and between one or the other of these musical traditions and world or "ethnic" musics, have become increasingly common. Despite what artists and others may claim, however, musical and cultural borrowings and mixings cannot be divorced from the sociopolitical power relations existing between cultural and social groups, and hence are not value-neutral. The debate surrounding what constitutes respectful borrowing/mixing/blending and what constitutes "rip-off" (or cultural imperialism) is at its core an issue less about artistic motives and integrity and much more about oppressor–oppressed relations mirrored in the economic and political struggle between various cultural groups.

Experimentation in classical music from 1950 to the present

During the 1950s, composers and performers of American concert music and jazz, such as Gunther Schuller, the Modern Jazz Quartet, Gerry Mulligan, Gil Evans, Stan Kenton, and others, experimented with jazz using ensembles that fused classical and jazz styles. The movement they brought into existence, "Third Stream," was for the most part an effort by jazz composers and players to adopt some of the conventions of the more acceptable classical music—such as its heavy reliance upon notation (and minimizing of improvisation) and its formal presentation in concert halls with performers wearing tuxedos, performing in a "cool" style devoid of "hot" guttural blues-based playing. The music of composers Claude Debussy and Samuel Barber also influenced the style of Third Stream Jazz.

Other composers and performers sought to revitalize and transform canonized classical music in U.S. society. John Cage, deemed an iconoclast, led the way. In the 1950s, Cage studied Zen Buddhism and used the principles of the Chinese *I Ching* 'Book of Changes' in developing a compositional and performance approach based upon indeterminacy or chance. As international travel and contact with other cultures introduced world music into American society, particularly in higher education institutions, more and more white American composers and musicians began to explore non-Western musical approaches, instrumentation and principles. These included Steve Reich, who in the 1970s studied and incorporated Indonesian gamelan music, Ghanaian drumming, and Hebrew cantillation into his music developing a popular and influential minimalist/systems/process/repetitive trend, and Lou Harrison, whose interest and study in Asian/Pacific musics was incorporated in his highly composed works that call for Asian traditional instruments in combination with Western ones. Other composers, based on the West Coast with its proximity and access to the Pacific Rim, who have experimented in combining Eastern and Western idioms include Terry Riley and Colin McPhee. The influence of Eastern music, particularly in the area of invariable temperament and fractional or microtonal pitch, is evident in the work of Harry Partch, who creates his own instruments to supersede diatonicism.

While the generation of American classically trained composers and performers of the 1950s and 1960s was to look to world music for inspiration in experimenting with concert music, the trend since the 1970s has been to incorporate American popular idioms (which are primarily African American forms). This has been the procedure of a younger generation of classically trained composers, including Meredith Monk, Philip Glass, Robert Telson, and Laurie Anderson. The success of such groups as the Kronos Quartet—a classical string quartet spiced up with punk haircuts and high-fashion designer clothing instead of the staid tuxedo—performing an eclectic repertoire of commissioned work and covers of Jimi Hendrix and Thelonious Monk, has shown the alliance between classical and popular music to be a fruitful one.

The "Third World" revolution as inspiration

The 1950s and 1960s was a period of rising African independence and national liberation movements. On 6 March 1957, in winning its independence from British colonial rule, Ghana became the first independent sub-Saharan African nation-state. The movement's leader and first president was Kwame Nkrumah, who espoused pan-Africanism, the unity of peoples of African descent both on the mother continent and throughout the diaspora. In the United States, African American jazz artists were inspired by the vision of pan-Africanism and began to explore musical collaborations with African musicians. Collaborations included those of pianist-composer Randy Weston with North African Moroccan musicians, saxophonist Johnny Griffen with an oud master musician in a late-1950s recording, and John Coltrane with Nigerian drummer Olatunji, among others. Drummer Max Roach traveled to Ghana to study traditional West African drumming. The jazz avant-garde of the 1960s was in part looking to world music sources in its search for the new and in its hope to liberate pitch and meter from western European conventions.

In American rock and popular music, as part of the 1960s countercultural and antiestablishment thrust, world music—especially from the "Third World"—was embraced and explored. Beatles member George Harrison collaborated with Indian sitarist Ravi Shankar, which subsequently helped to popularize South Asian music in the United States; the late Brian Jones, a member of the Rolling Stones, collaborated and recorded with Jajouka musicians from the Atlas Mountains of Morocco during the late 1960s; and years later, saxophonist-composer Ornette Coleman and the New York City contemporary klezmer group The Klezmatics would also concertize with the musicians from Jajouka.

Multicultural hybrid forms

Emerging in the early 1960s in New York City's Latino (primarily Puerto Rican) community was a new form of dance music, salsa, that blended earlier popular Cuban dance forms with jazz and rock. This uniquely North American urban music, while a song-based form, developed increasingly complex horn arrangements and virtuosic solo artistry as it drew from jazz influences. By the 1970s, salsa was undergoing a profound renaissance, paralleling the social, political, and cultural upsurge for liberation and equality among Latinos in the United States and throughout the Caribbean and Central and South America. Composer/bandleader/performers such as Eddie Palmieri and the late Bobby Paunetto were among the leading innovators. Palmieri recorded entire album-length extended suites. Along with the blues, salsa has become an indigenous American musical form with international popularity and influence.

In the mid-1970s, primarily in the San Francisco Bay Area, Asian/Pacific American musicians and composers—many from an avant-garde jazz orientation—were experimenting with traditional and folk musics from their ancestral Pacific Rim cultures. A loose community of Asian American jazz musicians, including Bay Area residents Russel Baba, Paul Yamazaki, and Jeanne Aiko Mercer, would become pioneers in combining traditional Japanese instrumentation and idioms with improvisational free jazz. By the mid-1980s, a number of Asian/Pacific American musicians scattered across the United States, including baritone saxophonist-composer Fred Ho of New York City, bassist Mark Izu, pianist Jon Jang, *koto* player Miya Masaoka of the Bay Area, pianist Glenn Horiuchi of Southern California, *taiko* drummer Kenny Endo of Hawai'i, and others, would experiment in developing an Asian American sound that wedded African American traditions with Asian/Pacific concepts. A more commercial pop fusion of Japanese and American rock/soul styles was spearheaded by the predominantly Japanese American band Hiroshima of Los Angeles.

During his time as a student in Wesleyan University's world music and jazz studies programs, Iranian American tenor saxophonist Hafez Modirzadeh innovated a major new theoretical and performance approach to musical fusions—what he terms "chromodal discourse." Modirzadeh has developed a way of playing the tenor saxophone using Persian temperament via a system of alternative fingerings and has applied it to jazz improvisation, including improvisations based on vertically based chord changes as, for example, in John Coltrane's "Giant Steps." Chromodal discourse is a cross-cultural theoretical and practical application and may possibly be the first significant new theoretical development in American jazz within the past two decades.

Similarly, Royal Hartigan, a drum set player and another former longtime Wesleyan University student, added a highly developed adaptation of West African (Ghanaian) and other world and ethnic rhythms to the Western trap drum set. The multiple rhythms and meters of various world music rhythmic forms are fluently incorporated into his playing of the drum set. His book, *West African Rhythms for the Drum Set* (1995) presents a detailed exposition of cross-cultural performance and a breakthrough method that shows a new way of playing the drum set by incorporating traditional Ghanaian rhythmic forms.

Creolization and resistance

As rap and hip-hop have emerged from their underground New York City/South Bronx–based origins to become a major U.S. pop cultural influence, cross-cultural fusions with ethnic/world music sources have been part of the multicultural mix. American youth-based music making has fused with South Asian (*bhangra*), Native American (through such groups as W.O.R—WithOut Reservation), and Caribbean idioms. The Caribbean has a particular fecundity for cultural mixing given its colonial/plantation sociohistorical development, including forms such as Jamaican ska, reggae, calypso, Dominican merengue, Puerto Rican bomba/plena, Cuban mambo, and so on. In a similar sociocultural development, Hawaii has also generated hybrid musical-cultural forms, from the Japanese American *hole hole bushi* 'immigrant women plantation workers songs' to today's popular/commercial style, Jawaiian (from the words *Jah*, representing the influence of Rastafarian reggae and the mellifluous Hawaiian *hula ku'i*). Earlier in the twentieth century, Hawaiian guitar virtuoso Sol Hoopi pioneered a hula blues styles, and Hawaiian twelve-string slack key guitar has introduced an interesting and unique regional, multicultural American modal and tuning system.

—FRED HO

WORLD BEAT

World beat refers to a hybrid musical form that combines European American popular music with selected elements from Latin American, African, Asian, Caribbean, Australian, European, and/or North American vernacular musics. The term is often contrasted with "world music," a label that describes non-Western folk and traditional art musics marketed to Western audiences—musics that lack obvious Western pop influences.

Musical characteristics

World beat recordings usually contain musical features typical of world popular musics: chordal polyphony, danceable rhythm, verse-chorus pop song structure, electronic and electrified instruments, and Western equal-temperament tuning. In addition, the "beat" that forms an underlying rhythmic framework for the exotic timbres of world beat's stylistic fusions is often an African American–derived backbeat, similar to that used in rock music.

Common world music ingredients in the world beat musical mixture include Indian classical instruments, Afro-Brazilian percussion, the Australian aboriginal *didgeridu*,

The phrase *world music* was coined in 1987 at a meeting of British music business figures as a way to promote musics of non-Western peoples as popular music genres in their own right, instead of as mere curiosities stuck in the back corners of record stores.

Indonesian gamelan music, Andalusian flamenco guitars, and Eastern European folk melodies; by far the most frequent sources of inspiration for world beat artists today are sub-Saharan African drumming traditions and Celtic folk music. Popular mass-mediated genres that have crossed over into the world beat market include Algerian *rai,* Congolese *soukous,* South African *mbaqanga* and *iscathamiya,* South Asian *qawwali,* Ghanaian *highlife,* Nigerian *juju,* Jamaican *reggae,* and Trinidadian *soca.*

Creating a market for world beat

Although the sounds of world beat come from all over the globe, as a marketing category it is primarily a British import. The phrase *world music* was coined in 1987 at a meeting of British music business figures as a way to promote musics of non-Western peoples as popular music genres in their own right, instead of as mere curiosities stuck in the back corners of record stores (Spencer 1992). Many music retailers agreed to use the category, and the formerly impoverished section in the back devoted to "international" music was expanded and diversified. In the 1980s, because of the popularity of albums by Paul Simon, David Byrne, Peter Gabriel, and others, many commentators predicted that world beat, recognized as the most accessible variety of world music, would become a major popular music genre in North America, rivaling rock itself. This claim, which arose during one of the periodic "crises" in the commercial and artistic viability of mainstream rock music, was overly optimistic (or perhaps premature). At the close of the 1990s, world music/world beat remains a marginal but stable genre in the North American music market, akin to jazz and folk (that is, less than 3 percent of total annual sales). In fact, many record store chains still use the antiquated "international" label to classify their world beat recordings, although these sections are certainly larger and more diverse than ever before. *Billboard* magazine introduced its world music album chart in 1990, and the first Best World Music Album Grammy was awarded a year later (to Grateful Dead percussionist Mickey Hart's *Planet Drum* album).

World beat aficionados often possess a highly sophisticated knowledge of their favorite genres, and their expertise is often beyond that of professional ethnomusicologists. The most comprehensive reference work for this type of music, *World Music: The Rough Guide* (Broughton et al. 1994), contains thirteen lengthy chapters covering exhaustively all the major musical regions of the world. Not surprisingly, the continent of Africa is covered in five different chapters, whereas East and Southeast Asia are combined in a single chapter entitled "The Far East." Nevertheless, the guide does cover the careers of such Asian musical megastars as Rhoma Irama, Lata Mangeshkar, and Oum Kalthoum, who are hugely popular in their own countries but are virtually unknown to European American audiences.

Graceland and its critics

The greatest boost to world beat's commercial visibility was a 1986 album by the popular American singer-songwriter Paul Simon, whose *Graceland* almost singlehandedly carved out a space for African musicians in the European American mainstream. The album's phenomenal success inspired countless other musicians. The album is indeed a masterpiece, an effective combination of quirky songwriting and striking musical eclecticism. The Zulu a capella group Ladysmith Black Mambazo is the best known of Simon's *Graceland* collaborators, but the album also contains contributions from (among others) Senegalese pop star Youssou N'Dour, Nigerian pedal steel guitarist Demola Adepoju, the Boyoyo Boys (a mbaqanga group from Soweto), Angeleno roots-rock band Los Lobos, and a zydeco group, Good Rockin' Dopsie and the Twisters. According to the album's liner notes, Simon chose to work with the latter two North American groups because their accordion-and-saxophone-driven compositions reminded him of the music of South Africa.

Graceland remains a highly controversial work. Indeed, a veritable cottage industry has grown up around debating the ethics, politics, and aesthetics of this seminal album. Portions of the album were recorded in South Africa (at Ovation Studios in Johannesburg) in direct violation of the United Nations–sponsored cultural boycott of South Africa. Critics have also voiced concerns about ownership; the songs on the album are copyrighted by Paul Simon alone. Without proper writing credits, the other musicians who contributed to *Graceland* cannot collect royalties.

Despite the problematic conditions of its production, even *Graceland*'s detractors admit that the songs on the record are musically compelling. Nonetheless, while Paul Simon's album provides an attractive blueprint for subsequent world beat collaborations, the difficult ethical issues regarding artistic control, ownership, and global politics raised by *Graceland* continue to haunt such endeavors.

Collaborations

Ethical considerations aside, the most artistically successful world beat recordings capitalize on musical affinities between different styles. Ry Cooder, the American slide guitarist, has won two world music Grammy awards for his collaborations with V. M. Bhatt, an Indian musician who plays Hindustani classical music on a modified Western guitar, and Ali Farka Toure, a Malian *griot* and *kora* virtuoso. Cooder has also displayed his uncanny ability to blend stylistically with different musics and musicians on albums recorded with Okinawan folksinger Shoukichi Kina and Hawaiian guitarist Gabby Pahinui. Mickey Hart's Planet Drum project features a number of very accomplished percussionists from different world traditions, including the Hindustani *tabla* virtuoso Zakir Hussein. Like many American world beat musicians, Hart is also an active producer of world music recordings, and he has used his fame as percussionist for the Grateful Dead to promote both his world music and world beat projects.

A dramatic example of cross-cultural musical fusion can be found on Kongar-ol Ondar's album *Back Tuva Future* (1999). The title indexes a typical preoccupation with juxtaposing "ancient" and "modern" musical styles found among North American world beat fans and promoters. Ondar, a Tuvan throat singer who is so popular in his home region that he has been compared to Elvis, has produced an extraordinary recording with his American collaborators that combines Tuvan folk melodies and throat-singing techniques with slickly produced rap, funk, country, and even Native American chanting. The album features contributions from American country and western music star Willie Nelson, and, more strangely, some posthumous percussion and vocal recordings by the renowned American physicist Richard Feynman are also added to the mix. The resulting rustic hybrid was dubbed "country and eastern" by one concert promoter.

While world beat collaborations between American and non-Western musicians can raise difficult ethical questions, more controversial still is the related practice of technologically plundering the sounds and grooves of world music to be reused in new compositions.

Technological appropriations

New sonic possibilities

The orientation of U.S. and Canadian music producers toward the cultivation of original and exotic sounds, a quest frequently aided by digital audio technologies (Théberge 1997), has led to the increasing incorporation of the sounds of the *didgeridu,* sitar, gamelan, North Indian *tabla* drums, the Japanese *shakuhachi,* and other "ethnic" instruments into American pop, rock, rap, and jazz recordings (not to mention the soundtracks to countless television commercials and movies).

Vocal samples of Bulgarian choirs, Tibetan monks, and Tuvan throat singers are also mixed into new compositions. The highly distinctive sounds of African Pygmy chants have been sampled by artists including Herbie Hancock and Madonna (who actually sampled the Hancock track). Steven Feld, one of world beat's most outspoken critics, claims that such appropriation is yet another form of colonial exploitation, in which the music of non-Western primitives become "raw material" for further processing and refinement in the metropole by bourgeois artists (1996). Feld's objection is powerful, but the appropriative practices enabled by new musical technologies will no doubt continue to make the "exotic" sounds of world music ever more ubiquitous in the North American music scene.

Producing world beat

Recording a world beat album "involves more than adding rock instruments to traditional music, or superimposing different musical styles; it is also a question of imposing sophisticated sound ideals and recording techniques typical for rock music" (Van Peer 1999:383). While world music purists continue to stress the authenticity of unadulterated field recordings, state-of-the-art multitrack recording studios define the sound of world beat. Most major releases are the product of hundreds of hours of overdubbing, editing, and mixing. In many cases traditional instruments are recorded with various electronic effects, such as chorus and reverberation, that alter the instrumental timbre. Sometimes the sounds of these instruments are sampled and approximated on an electronic keyboard.

Studio technologies have begun to erode the distinction between world music and world beat. With the more recent technical advances in portable recording, particularly the invention of digital audio tape, coupled with the now common practice of re-recording and remixing field recordings in a multitrack recording studio prior to their commercial release, the line between sophisticated studio productions and "raw" aural documentation has blurred. Feld (1994a) has argued that record companies intentionally try to collapse the distinction between world beat and world music, part of a strategy to lend the aura of authenticity to the former and pop trendiness to the latter. If this is indeed the case, their attempt has been remarkably successful.

The impact of world beat on American music

Beginning in the late 1980s, world beat became a significant influence on popular music as a whole. Tracy Chapman's debut album (1988), one of the best rock albums of that decade, features an electric *sitar* and Afro-Latin percussion performed by Paulinho Da Costa. More recently, the soundtrack to the film *Dead Man Walking* (1995) includes two stunning collaborations between Pearl Jam frontman Eddie Vedder and the late *qawwali* master Nusrat Fateh Ali Khan. But does the true impact of world beat extend beyond these instances of crossover?

Music for the next millennium?

It is difficult to predict the commercial and artistic future of world music/world beat in North America. Many commentators predict that an overall increase in global awareness will characterize North America in the twenty-first century, and they see world music as part of that emerging consciousness. In truth the appearance of world music/world beat is typical of the period of post-1960s genre fragmentation in the North American popular music market, which gathered speed in the 1980s and 1990s. This same period saw the invention of numerous new genres of varying degrees of commercial viability, including rap, techno, New Age, dance hall, "smooth jazz" and house music.

In the United States, of course, ignorance of even basic world geography is widespread, and any step toward greater understanding of other countries would certainly be welcome. However, many academic critics of world beat point out the lack of explicit political commentary in the music of the most popular artists. (Again, Paul Simon's solipsistic, "Me Decade" lyrics on *Graceland,* which made no mention of apartheid, were a cause of some concern to critics.) Cultural critic Timothy Taylor derides world music as "music for grown-ups, music as wallpaper, music that does not, on its reasonably attractive and accessible surface, raise sticky problems about misogyny, racism, colonialism, what have you" (1997:6). It is certainly possible to relate the popularity of world beat among middle-aged middle-class baby boomers to their embrace of New Age, adult acoustic, alternative, and even country music as more pleasant choices than discordant 1980s and 1990s youth musics like metal, rap, and hard-core. Certainly neocolonialism, poverty, exploitation, human rights violations, and other assorted miseries of the contemporary globalized world do not figure prominently in the music of Youssou N'Dour or the Gipsy Kings. But it is also true that world beat is often linked to progressive causes, especially environmental conservation and protecting the rights of indigenous people.

In fact, world beat may ultimately owe its existence to the so-called charity-rock phenomenon, which raised awareness about international human rights issues, famine in Ethiopia, and South African apartheid in the 1980s, and also had the effect of exposing Western pop stars to the popular musics of other countries, particularly sub-Saharan Africa (Garofalo 1997:387–389). Among these artists was Paul Simon, who participated in the USA for Africa project.

Another important, if unintended, consequence of world beat's popularity is the discipline of ethnomusicology's increased visibility and importance in American universities. Throughout the 1990s, introduction to world music classes were among the most popular offerings in college music departments, guaranteeing the usefulness of ethnomusicologists in an era of academic downsizing. Although many ethnomusicologists continue to denounce world beat, it is clear that this genre has contributed to the relevance of their research in the eyes of the general public and widened that research's potential audience.

World beat in historical perspective

The historical development of twentieth-century American popular music has been characterized by the emergence of new hybrid genres that combine diverse nonelite vernacular styles with elements from commercial pop. Often these new styles are introduced to the mainstream public via musical popularizers who present a watered-down, familiarized version, which then leaves consumers hungry for the "real thing." These cycles of appropriation, commercialization, and the pursuit of authenticity have played a central role in the historical development of ragtime, jazz, swing, blues, country, rock, and rap music. Despite the exotic origins of much world beat music, the aesthetic and political debates that surround it appear to be the result of similar cultural dynamics. It is therefore not surprising that debates about authenticity and "selling out" that characterize rock music discourse have now been carried over to discussions of world beat artists.

The attraction of novel timbres and musical techniques, a cosmopolitan but unchallenging sense of global citizenship, and fantasies of community and premodern

The label "fusion" suggests one type of interaction, but the topic cannot be addressed adequately without reference to other types of interaction, such as compartmentalization, parody, and others—that is, to border making as well as border crossing

wholeness all undoubtably play a role in world music/world beat's (modest) commercial success in Canada and the United States, as does a genuine interest in the creative musical endeavors of other peoples. There can be no doubt, however, that the production, marketing, and promotion of these musics are part of a recurring process of musical popularization that has long been a feature of the North American musical landscape.

Finally, the possibility exists that world beat will become a genuine grassroots music among young people in North America. The increasing number of non-Western performing ensembles on North American college campuses (usually Javanese or Balinese gamelan, West African drumming groups, or Arab music ensembles) have exposed America's youth to non-Western sounds, playing techniques, and repertoires and may encourage some world beat consumers to become producers of new, unforeseen musical hybrids.

—JEREMY WALLACH

INTERCULTURAL TRADITIONS ON THE CANADIAN PRAIRIES

Musical fusion is a phrase that occurs most often in discussions of recent cross-cultural musical alliances. Sometimes these discussions allude to the enormous late-twentieth-century demographic shifts that have resulted in unprecedented diversity in contemporary North American societies. Sometimes they relate to the urgent postcolonial issues of appropriation and intellectual property rights. It is, however, instructive to look at the topic with regard to earlier historical periods. As the multicultural nature of North American society has existed since the sixteenth century and was certainly recognized as distinctive by the late nineteenth century, musical interaction is a rich and varied subject of inquiry in this context. In addition, the label "fusion" suggests one type of interaction, but the topic cannot be addressed adequately without reference to other types of interaction, such as compartmentalization, parody, and others—that is, to border making as well as border crossing. This article examines several instances of musical interaction on the Canadian prairies since the 1920s. It considers genres and performance contexts that facilitated social interaction whether or not the music itself embodied diverse stylistic references, types of cross-cultural commentary including parodies of cultural stereotypes, and various stylistic juxtapositions and/or syntheses.

The prairies are an appropriate region for this exploration, as in both the United States and Canada, the encouragement of large-scale immigration from Northern, Eastern, and Western Europe in particular in the late nineteenth century resulted in a society that effectively had no majority and no mainstream. The cultural diversity in architecture, religion, and foodways is already represented as emblematic of the prairies in writings of the 1920s such as Victoria Hayward's *Romantic Canada* in which she observes "a mosaic of vast dimensions and great breadth, essayed of the Prairie"

(1922:187). The policy of block settlement, whereby all homesteaders of, for instance, Swedish or Icelandic descent located in the same area, worked against cultural interaction. Furthermore, the important objective of language maintenance was, for many, another reason for discouraging interaction. Despite these factors, however, musical exchange and collaboration did occur, unevenly and in many forms.

Genres and performance events that facilitated social interaction

Classical music performance or folk performance in classically influenced arrangements at concert venues attracted individuals from different ethnocultural backgrounds. Hence, the *Encyclopedia of Music in Canada* might report that in Winnipeg, oratorio soloists were "drawn from the Anglo-Saxon, French, Mennonite, and Ukrainian communities" (Kallmann et al. 1992). But this multiethnic involvement did not necessarily encourage musical fusion. Many choirs were established between the first and second world wars, for instance, precisely to preserve repertoire in the language of their homeland. Male voices were especially popular, and separate Icelandic, Norwegian, Swedish, Polish, and Jewish choirs flourished in Winnipeg during this period. Increasingly in the post–World War II period, however, the audiences for culturally specific performance became more diverse. Hence, the Saskatoon-based Yevshan Ukrainian Orchestra (est. 1974) defines a mandate to perform Ukrainian Canadian works but enjoys the patronage of a broader social spectrum. Similarly, large-scale music and dance shows became popular in Western Canada, performed by ensembles such as Edmonton's Dnipro Ensemble (choirs, orchestra, and dancers) or Winnipeg's Hoosli Ukrainian Folk Ensemble.

Potentially more conducive to social interaction were festivals. A series of events that were extraordinarily forward looking for their time were the folk song and handicraft festivals of the 1920s organized by John Murray Gibbon to celebrate the newly built hotels affiliated with the Canadian Pacific Railway (CPR). Organizers including folklorist Marius Barbeau and composer Ernest Macmillan insisted on celebrating cultural diversity by inviting regional representatives of different musical and craft practices and by setting folk music for classical ensembles. The majority of these festivals took place either in Québec City or on the prairies. The Winnipeg Festival of 1927, significantly labeled the "New Canadian Folk Song and Handicraft Festival," featured performers and craftsmen of "European Continental extraction" from nineteen different nations, a much more diverse representation than found in previous festivals. The Regina festival in 1928 featured thirty different ethnic groups (figure 1).

Musical fusion was not the objective of the CPR Festival organizers (although the appropriation of folk music by composers such as Macmillan was fusion of a sort), but the juxtaposition of many different musical traditions was a model that would continue to effect a degree of social interaction. It is not surprising, then, that a 1949 anniversary concert in Winnipeg, organized by local Ukrainians, boasted of its inclusion of Estonian, Hungarian, Latvian, Lithuanian, Polish, Ukrainian, and Yugoslav Canadians. Similarly, the spirit of cultural diversity was reinforced in multilingual radio programs such as those hosted by the Edmonton-based Czech musician Gaby Haas in the 1950s. By the 1980s, the culturally diverse Winnipeg Folk Festival (est. 1974) had become the largest event of its kind in North America (Kallmann, et al. 1992:1415).

More recently, musical juxtaposition sometimes serves to crosscut ethnic solidarities. Hence, for example, francophone artists in Western Canada have produced two CDs (entitled RADO for Regroupement des Artistes Del 'Ouest Canadien) featuring musicians of widely varying cultural backgrounds, including Acadians, Québécois, and West Africans. Linguistic solidarity, in this case, facilitates ethnocultural border crossing.

FIGURE I   Unidentified banjo and mandolin players in Saskatchewan where, in the post–World War II years, Filipinos constituted one of the eight largest cultural groups. Photo courtesy the Saskatchewan Archives Board.

Cross-cultural musical commentary, borrowing, and fusion

It is clear that the relationships among different ethnocultural communities varied enormously. As Robert Klymasz has observed, part of the variation relates to a rural–urban distinction; he characterized the former as "tight ethnic enclaves" (1972:373), the latter as having more dispersed populations. Additionally, one generation's friendships might not be maintained by the next generation. The custom of parodying different ethnicities also became entrenched in some musical practices. Even today, for instance, the French pop band Les Zed, whose members include individuals of French, Ukrainian, and English descent, includes a parody of a German polka and the fiddle ensemble. Cleaver's World performs various regional and ethnic styles, one of which uses the parallel thirds of Ukrainian *bandura* ensemble arrangements. Two (among many) early instances of rather consistent musical interaction are in the areas of Métis song and fiddle repertoires and Ukrainian country music.

Métis fusions

A distinctive aspect of the Canadian constitution, vis-à-vis the United States, is the recognition of the Métis—people of mixed First Nations and other (usually European) descent—as an aboriginal people alongside the First Nations and Inuit [see MÉTIS, p. 404]. Although it is essential to recognize that Métis reside in all parts of Canada and in adjacent areas of the United States such as Turtle Mountain, North Dakota, the largest and oldest group comprises those people who descend from marriages of Cree or Ojibwe and French settlers in the mid-nineteenth-century Red River settlement near Winnipeg. Their language is Michif, characterized by a combination of Cree verbs and French nouns. Hence, cultural fusion is fundamental to their very definition as a people.

Métis musical practices include songs as well as instrumental musics that are generally fiddle based. Songs may be linguistically adapted from French chanson (see, for example, the text "Il y avait une belle fille" performed by the well-known Manitoban Métis singer Joe Venne alongside "standard" French [Kallmann, et al. 1992:851] as well as tune adaptations studied by folklorist Donald Deschenes [1993]). In many cases, the texts move from French to Michif, or English. Others songs are original compositions, some of which articulate aspects of Métis experience. The martyred Louis Riel composed a number of these, including "La Métisse," in which he foresees a proud destiny for his people.

Perhaps more distinctive are the dance musics of the Métis. Both set dances and step dances or clogging, the latter with a distinctive sideways step, are widely practiced, and fiddle music continues to be the accompaniment of choice. Unique choreographies have been developed by Métis dancers. Stories abound about the Métis love of dancing (as collected by ethnomusicologist Lynn Whidden in Grand Rapides, Alberta, for instance), particularly when popular tunes such as the "Red River Jig" (an adaptation of a tune that is widely known in Québec as "La Grande Gigue Simple," often performed in duple meter in Métis contexts) is played. Among the best known prairie Métis recording artists are Andy DeJarlis and Lawrence Houle. Distinctive elements of Métis fiddle style include asymmetrical phrases, which ethnomusicologist Anne Lederman (1991) relates to rhythmic patterns in the Cree or Ojibwe languages, and percussion instruments such as rattles.

Ukrainian fusions

After over a century of residence in Canada, it is not surprising that Ukrainian musicians have also created various fusions between the musics they hold in their memories or hear on contemporary Ukrainian recordings and diverse North American popular music styles they encounter. Ukrainian fiddlers have maintained a culturally specific repertoire (the older genres of which include *kozatchok, kolomyka,* and *holub*) as well as distinctive styles of ornamentation. String bands often include the *tsymbaly*, the hammered dulcimer of the Ukraine.

The genre that has had scholarly attention, however, is Ukrainian country music. In the early 1970s, folklorist Klymasz (1972) studied 514 items from forty-two recordings by such artists as Mickey and Bunny [Sklepowich], Mae Chwaluk, Peter Hnatiuk, and the Semcuk sisters. He observed the extensive use of macaronic texts (in English and Ukrainian), the incorporation of *tsymbaly* in many recordings, and the canonization of a small subset of the most popular songs. He noted that English songs selected for adaptation often had features that were compatible with common patterns in Ukrainian folk song, such as the use of ten-syllable lines with a mid-line break.

Other fusions

The topic of musical fusion is generally addressed in Canada as in the United States with reference to musical practices that embody cultural diversity. In this framework, Native American blues or hip-hop artists such as Murray Porter, Jani Lauzon, or TKO, collaborations between pop bands and symphony orchestras (for example, Spirit of the West and the Vancouver Symphony), Asian classical and jazz (for example, the work of Toronto *er hu* player George Gao), the folk rock of Ashley McIsaac, the eclectic styles of music performed in the course of R. Murray Schafer's "Wolf Project," or the host of world music bands active in every major urban center might be the sorts of subjects that would normally be explored in this article. Instead, this discussion has looked back historically to a region of the country where musical interaction occurred as a result of the diverse immigration patterns that led to its settlement. This approach raises relevant questions about the way we frame issues of musical fusion particularly by emphasizing the inherent tension between bounded community and crossover, as well as the variety of strategies employed in the representation of cultural interaction.

—BEVERLEY DIAMOND

NEW AGE

New Age music, a twentieth-century instrumental popular style, may be defined by its spiritual purpose rather than by its salient musical characteristics. As Suzanne Doucet, founder of the International New Age Music Network, has noted, "New Age music distinguishes itself not by style, performance, technique, or personality, but by its nature, which is contemplative rather than entertaining" (Doucet 1988:9). Thus, New Age music may be considered a normative style based on an aesthetic that emphasizes the contemplative function of music as a medium for physical and emotional healing.

New Age music is also a popular form of entertainment. It is an important marketing category that is distinguished by its mass media support and transmission system. New Age sound embraces a diverse range of contemporary influences, such as eclectic world music influences, static harmonies, avoidance of a direct beat, electronic-influenced timbres, use of nature-derived sounds, consonant harmonies, layering of musical events, and a spontaneous and improvised approach.

The two different aspects of New Age—the spiritual and the commercial—have made it difficult to assign it a single identity based exclusively on either purpose or musical considerations. New Age musicians themselves seem incapable of constructing a single definition that will embrace the multiplicity of musical styles. The genre seems to celebrate individual vision and personal expression. Chip Davis, founder of American Gramophone Records, called it "uncategorizable instrumental music" (Heckman 1987:N-3). Windham Hill record label co-founder Anne Robinson termed it "new acoustic impressionistic music" (Walsh 1986:82). Eddie Jobson characterized the style as "a soundtrack for the movie of the mind" (Doerschuk 1988:38), while composer

New Age musical style became dependent on commercial distribution, yet its image and sound were, and still are, particularly antithetical to mass media.

Lucia Hwong suggests it is "music that springs from a world culture" (Walsh 1986:82). Suzanne Doucet has provided perhaps the best and most comprehensive and frequently cited definition of this genre:

> New Age music is instrumental. . . . Instrumental music bypasses the intellectual center, going directly to the right half of the brain, which is more intuitive and imaginative than the left half. It has something in common with jazz, in that both styles are improvisational. But jazz is not designed to relax; instead it builds up tension towards a climax. New Age music is the opposite. It relaxes and heals. You can expand your consciousness by listening. (Doerschuk 1988:39)

New Age music 1965–1990

Although the use of the term *New Age* in reference to music was not used self-consciously until 1976, the underlying philosophies and concept of a New Age movement were generated in the mid-1960s in association with the idealism generated by the dawning of the Age of Aquarius. One of the pioneers of the style, Steve Halpern, a psychologist and composer, conceived of this music as an "anti-frantic alternative, which unlike other musics . . . has no driving beat or compelling harmonic or melodic progression" (Richardson 1986:60). In 1965 Halpern initiated studies to examine the healing effects of music. This provided the impetus for his therapeutic recordings that were distributed through alternative markets such as book and health food stores.

Other musicians who were influenced by this aesthetic began to develop the musical aspects of the style. Tony Scott's *Music for Zen Meditation* (1983 [1964]) is generally considered the first commercial New Age recording. In combining the world music influence of Japanese instruments and performers (*koto* and *shakuhachi*) with a focus on contemplative improvisations, graced by titles such as "Is All Not One?" and "Satori," Scott's recording provided a template for subsequent releases.

Concurrently, a support network of independent record labels evolved to produce and distribute the burgeoning style. Anne Robinson and Will Ackerman founded Windham Hill Records in 1976 and released their first recording, *In Search of the Turtle's Navel* that year. By 1983 Windham Hill pianist George Winston became the first New Age star with his recordings *Autumn, December,* and *Winter into Spring,* and the label became practically synonymous with New Age style.

New Age music also reached a growing segment of the public through expanded radio exposure. Stephen Hill's *Music from the Hearts of Space,* the first weekly radio program devoted entirely to New Age music, was carried on 245 public radio stations by 1988. In February 1987 KMET in Los Angeles, which changed its call letters to KTWV ("The Wave"), became the first completely New Age commercial radio station. Subsequently other stations integrated New Age recordings into various light jazz and easy listening formats.

By 1986 the commercial success of New Age music insured its absorption within the music industry. Accordingly, the first National Academy of Recording Arts Award

(Grammy) in the New Age category was presented in 1987, and on 29 October 1988 *Billboard* issued its first New Age music chart. Certainly New Age music was now acknowledged as a vital music market, but, according to Suzanne Doucet, the music had by this time become "subject to the disease it was trying to heal" (Doucet 1988:9). As was the case with other popular musical styles, there existed an uneasy dissonance between the medium and the message. New Age musical style became dependent on commercial distribution, yet its image and sound were, and still are, particularly antithetical to mass media.

New Age music today

Today the term *New Age* incorporates a welter of musical categories that are only loosely connected to the original manifestations of the style. Categories such as meditative/trance, space, acoustic, cross-cultural, vocal, jazz-fusion, healing/stress release, crossover classical, progressive/electronic, and popular/commercial present the many facets of the New Age, from the pure acoustic piano of George Winston to the lush synthesizer of Yanni, from the crossover pop of Mannheim Steamroller to the experimental ambient sound of Brian Eno.

—RON PEN

ROCK

The history of rock music can be seen as a confluence of intersecting streams of musical styles and social interactions. Clearly divided into an early "rock and roll" period, heavily influenced by rhythm and blues, and later into a plethora of "rock" styles influenced by new technology and media, rock is the quintessential music of youth.

Rock and Roll

The term *rock and roll* historically has had three different but related meanings. First, it has commonly functioned, much like the word *jazz,* as an umbrella term that designates a range of postwar musical styles that have evolved over time in a weblike fashion from a number of late 1940s styles of rhythm and blues, pop, and country music. In the case of rock and roll, the overriding unifying factor has been the primary target audience for the music—white youth. In this sense rock and roll is often used interchangeably with the short form rock and is often, although not always, understood in opposition to pop music, rock being considered by critics and fans alike as in one way or another more "authentic" than pop. Rock and roll and rock have also been routinely associated with youth disaffection, and, at various moments in time, each has served as the focal point for what can be termed moral panics within the hegemonic culture. Various definitions/usages of the term in this first sense subsume under the term *rock and roll* genres of rhythm and blues that have garnered a substantial white audience, such as black rock and roll, doo-wop, girl group, soul, funk, and rap alongside styles produced and consumed nearly exclusively by whites, such as grunge, progressive rock, folk rock, punk, and heavy metal.

Second, rock and roll has commonly been used to designate a range of popular music styles that flourished from the late 1940s through the mid-1960s. By 1966 and 1967 new styles began to emerge that were different enough from the roots of rock and roll to be designated under the short form rock. The latter was assumed at the time to denote more "serious" music that involved higher levels of musicianship (for example, the work of Cream, Jimi Hendrix, and the Mothers of Invention), borrowed various features from Western classical and world musics (such as the Beatles's work on *Revolver* and *Sgt. Pepper's Lonely Hearts Club Band* as well as the first two Velvet Underground albums), used much more complex formal structures and production techniques (for example, the Doors's "The End," the Beatles's "Tomorrow Never Knows," the Beach Boys's "Good Vibrations"), addressed deeper and/or wider ranging issues with more poetically informed lyrics (for example, the work of Bob Dylan, the Band, and the Doors), and ceased to function only or, in the case of some groups, primarily as dance music and instead was designed for serious listening and contemplation. Part of the change to rock was a concomitant shift in designation of the musicians involved with these styles; once referred to as entertainers, they were now considered to be artists. The latter term was tied up with a range of values derived from nineteenth-century conventions and included the notion that the artist was somehow special and thereby removed from everyday norms and constraints, and that the rock musician as artist was obliged to develop or progress in his art with each subsequent release. All of these changes took place within the context of the development of FM radio, the full-length 33-⅓-rpm LP disk's becoming more important than the 45-rpm single, the publication of the first serious North American magazines dedicated to discussing these musics (*Crawdaddy* and *Rolling Stone*), and the publication of the first books on the subject (*Rock and Other Four Letter Words* (1968) by J. Marks and *The World of Rock* (1968) by John Gabree). The primary audience for both rock and roll and rock under these definitions was again white youth.

Finally, rock and roll has at times been used in a more strictly musicological sense to designate a particular style of dance-oriented, high-energy, loud, up-tempo, blues-based music that is predicated on a groove in which bass drum and bass guitar (upright bass in the earliest recordings and live performances) accent beats one and three, a back beat (on beats two and four) is played on the snare (often in tandem with another instrument such as rhythm guitar or piano), and a ride pattern consisting of straight eighth notes is played on the ride cymbal or closed hi-hat. One of the primary distinguishing features of this style is the use of rhythm guitar and/or piano to play an added sixth chordal pattern in straight eighth notes (root and fifth on the onbeats; root and sixth on the offbeats—derived from boogie-woogie piano playing) to accompany a vocal line that is also primarily sung in eighths. The typical performing force for rock and roll in this sense consists of electric lead guitar, electric rhythm guitar, bass and drums, and, at times, piano. In the 1950s a tenor saxophone was used by virtually all black as well as some white rock and roll musicians as the primary lead instrument. Both the electric guitar and saxophone were often played in ways that distorted their tone, adding to the primal energy of the music and its primary appeal to youth. Prior to the advent of punk in the mid-1970s, rock and roll lyrics (as opposed to those of rock) were exclusively youth focused, largely concerned with idealized, often sexualized boy-girl relationships (usually from the point of view of the male protagonist), rock and roll, cars, and no school.

The original recordings designated by this use of the term in this third sense were by Little Richard, Chuck Berry, Elvis Presley, and Jerry Lee Lewis. In the early and mid-1960s, British Invasion groups such as the Beatles, the Dave Clark Five, and the Rolling Stones, as well as American groups such as the Beach Boys, often played in this style (all four groups routinely recording cover versions of Chuck Berry tunes on their earliest albums). In the late 1960s Creedence Clearwater Revival and the Rolling Stones were the primary exponents of this style (although most groups of the time, including those as disparate as the Grateful Dead, the Byrds, the Velvet Underground, and Led Zeppelin, would play the occasional song in this style). Punk groups in the mid- and late 1970s such as the Sex Pistols and the Ramones and later groups such as the Georgia Satellites in the mid-1980s and the Black Crowes in the 1990s all continued playing music that clearly fit into the style of 1950s rock and roll as originally articulated by Chuck Berry.

In all three usages of the term, rock and roll, in contrast to the earlier Tin Pan Alley tradition of white popular music, prioritizes the performer over the composer, the recording over the song [see POPULAR MUSIC OF THE PARLOR AND STAGE, p. 179]. As such, rock and roll has been, for the most part, the product of an oral-based culture that has repeatedly found itself in tension with capitalistic business practices governed by the notions of authorship and ownership. The result has been ongoing inequities in which individuals are privileged for the purposes of both remuneration and historical recognition as the composers of music which, in essence, was created through group effort. Further serving to demarcate rock and roll from earlier forms of white popular music in North America is the fact that much of the music subsumed under all three definitions conveys a heightened sense of immediate and overt emotional engagement. Finally, in all three usages of the term it is understood that rock and roll originated initially in the United States and over time spread throughout North America, into the United Kingdom and the rest of Europe, and eventually to the Middle East, South America, South Asia, and, in the case of soul, funk and rap, into Sub-Saharan Africa. Given limited space, this article will discuss rock and roll as articulated in the second definition, limiting the discussion to the advent and development of the music from the late 1940s through the late 1950s.

Early references to rock and roll

The two words *rock* and *roll* can be found separately in several examples of African American music recorded in the 1920s, in all cases referring to partying in the broadest sense and more particularly serving as a euphemism for sex, as in, "We're going to rock and roll all night" [see R & B AND SOUL, p. 667]. By the 1930s the terms could be found coupled, as in rock and roll, referring to raucous dance music with a big beat. References in African American records to rock and roll increased exponentially in the 1940s, referring in a variety of senses to partying, rocking music, and/or sex.

The term was first used to refer to styles of postwar music in the early 1950s by disc jockey Alan Freed, who called his radio show on Cleveland station WJW the *Moondog Rock 'n' Roll Party*. When Freed debuted his show in the fall of 1951, he was one of the first white disc jockeys to play black rhythm and blues for the consumption of a largely white audience. In a segregated society such a phenomenon necessitated a new term. Freed said as much himself when he told Theodore Irwin in an interview that appeared in *Pageant* in 1957 that he decided to use rock and roll as a euphemism for rhythm and blues in an attempt to disassociate the music from any and all racial stigma "in order to cultivate a wider audience." The bottom line was that when African Americans consumed this music it was called rhythm and blues; when European Americans consumed the same music, it was called rock and roll. *Rock and roll,* then, was initially a sociologically conceived term to designate the consumption of a particular music by a different demographic defined by race.

Black appeal radio

Although there had always been a small group of whites who had avidly consumed various forms of black recorded music, the phenomenon grew to the point of having economic impact with the advent in 1947 and 1948 of what historian Bill Barlow (1999) has referred to as black appeal radio stations. Prior to the late 1940s the FCC had restricted the number of radio stations in each market to between three and five [see THE MUSIC INDUSTRY, p. 256]. The major networks (NBC, CBS, and Mutual) accounted for the majority of these licenses and, not surprisingly, lobbied successfully for many years to maintain these restrictions. The overwhelming majority of programming broadcast by these stations was produced by and targeted toward European Americans. The situation changed in 1947 when the networks began focusing their energies and money on the new medium of television, ceased pressuring the FCC to restrict radio licenses, and sold many of their affiliated stations at bargain basement prices to local entrepreneurs.

It is not a coincidence that Elvis Presley moved to Memphis as a thirteen-year-old in the same year that WDIA began targeting its programming to the black populace in the mid-South.

Advertisers also quickly moved to television, and, consequently, between 1948 and 1952 radio income derived from advertising revenue dropped by 38 percent. Paradoxically, while radio income was plummeting, the FCC was relaxing its restrictions on licenses. By 1952 the number of radio stations in most markets had doubled, the proportion of those being network affiliates dropping from a high of 97 percent in 1947 to a low of 30 percent in 1955.

The new owners of these radio stations were faced with a double bind: there were now twice the number of stations competing for advertising revenue that had shrunk across the board by nearly 40 percent. Consequently, most independent radio stations could not afford to produce what up to that point had been standard radio fare—drama and comedy programs—nor could they afford to pay musicians for live radio broadcasts. To lower their overhead, the majority of stations were forced to spend most of their broadcast day paying what later became known as disc jockeys to spin records. To open up new advertising streams, a number of stations, often in desperation, began tailoring their programming to the needs and interests of a previously neglected demographic, African Americans. The result was black appeal stations, the most famous being WDIA in Memphis and WLAC in Nashville. In 1949 there were four such stations. By 1954 there were two hundred, that number doubling to four hundred by 1956.

Black appeal stations played a mixture of jump blues, club blues, bar band blues, honking tenor sax instrumentals, vocal group records, boogie piano records, and gospel. While to varying degrees it is possible to segregate society, making it difficult for whites to actively consume black musical culture in a performance context, it is impossible to segregate airwaves. Once stations such as WDIA began programming black music from dawn to dusk, any white teenager who chose to could spin his or her radio dial and consume an unending diet of all forms of rhythm and blues. It is not a coincidence that Elvis Presley moved to Memphis as a thirteen-year-old in the same year that WDIA began targeting its programming to the black populace in the mid-South. Presley was among the first generation of white teenagers whose soundscape could consist of a steady diet of rhythm and blues alongside country and Tin Pan Alley pop fare.

In the late 1940s relatively few whites listened to such stations or attempted to purchase records they heard on black appeal stations. Slowly but steadily these numbers grew so that by 1951 enough white teenagers were wanting to purchase the black rhythm and blues recordings they heard on black appeal stations that retail stores in white neighborhoods began to take notice and consequently started to stock a small number of black recordings issued by independent labels such as Specialty, Modern, Aladdin, Chess, Atlantic, Peacock, and Imperial. Retailers who primarily served a black clientele began to notice an increasing number of white teenagers frequenting their stores as well. One such retailer was Leo Mintz, who owned Record Rendezvous in Cleveland. Fascinated by this development, Mintz suggested to his friend, classical disc jockey Alan Freed, that potentially there was substantial money to be made programming black rhythm and blues to white youth. Thus was born Freed's *Moondog Rock 'n' Roll Party.*

Early rock and roll

Various commentators over the years have argued over what should be considered the first rock and roll record. Sun Records owner Sam Phillips and rock historian Robert Palmer have both argued for "Rocket 88," released on Chess in 1951 by Jackie Brenston and his Delta Cats. Others have suggested "It's Too Soon to Know" by the Orioles, first issued in 1948 by the tiny independent It's A Natural and subsequently picked up by Jubilee Records, while still others have referenced "Cry" by Johnny Ray, released by Columbia in 1951. Such arguments, of course, are fruitless. It is simply not possible to establish what was the first rock and roll record, as criteria will vary widely depending upon who is making the selection. It is interesting, though, to look at the reasons why "Rocket 88," "It's Too Soon to Know," or "Cry" might be considered as early prototypical examples of this music.

The Orioles are widely acknowledged to be the first rhythm and blues (as distinct from jazz and/or pop) vocal group. "It's Too Soon to Know" was their first charting single, reaching No. 1 on *Billboard's* Race Juke Box chart, No. 2 on *Billboard's* Race Sales chart, and, more important for this discussion, No. 13 on *Billboard's* pop chart (the race charts were designed to measure black consumption, while the pop charts were designed to measure airplay on white-oriented radio stations as well as sales to white consumers). As such, the Orioles were the first black artists recording in a new style to garner substantial airplay on white radio stations and to sell significant numbers of records to white consumers.

"Rocket 88" was also a No. 1 hit on the race charts, which in 1949 were renamed the Rhythm and Blues charts, but did not register on the pop charts. Theoretically, the record was not consumed by a large number of European Americans. "Rocket 88," though, was perhaps the first record to prominently feature distorted electric guitar. This, combined with a lyric that consisted of a series of automotive/sexual metaphors, a for-the-time frantic tempo, and an extended tenor sax solo involving overblowing, distortion, and cracked notes, makes the song, from a musicological point of view, an early recording containing many of the seminal features of rock and roll.

Finally, "Cry" was the first nationally successful record by a white singer to display a level of emotional outpouring that was completely foreign to the Tin Pan Alley aesthetic that had dominated white pop music in North America throughout the twentieth century. Significantly, it reached No. 1 on the Rhythm and Blues Juke Box and Sales charts as well as on the pop charts.

Taken together, these three recordings articulate a number of the central tropes embodied in the earliest uses of the term rock and roll: the consumption on a large scale of black popular culture by white youth; music that is youth oriented in terms of the use of distortion, fast tempos, and lyrical concerns; and the production of music by white artists that, to one degree or another, manifests a substantial debt to black music especially in terms of the articulation of overt emotional catharsis.

Rock and roll hits the charts

The first black records to begin to show up with regularity on the pop charts, thereby demonstrating substantial white consumption, were by black vocal groups (the Ravens in 1947, the Deep River Boys and the Orioles in 1948, Billy Ward and the Dominoes in 1951). In 1952 and 1953 New Orleans rhythm and blues star Fats Domino had two minor pop hits. New York–based singer Ruth Brown and vocal groups the Four Tunes and the Orioles also charted pop in 1953, but it was not until 1954 that a sizable number of black artists achieved hits on the pop charts, including the Crows ("Gee"), the Drifters ("Honey Love"), Hank Ballard and the Midnighters ("Work with Me Annie"), and the Chords ("Sh-Boom"). It is significant that Fats Domino was the only solo black male artist associated with rock and roll to achieve crossover success prior to 1955. Black vocal groups and female vocalists were less sexually threatening to white males and thereby more easily garnered white radio play and proved easier on both pragmatic and psychological levels for white youth to consume.

Covers

With the advent of black artists on independent labels beginning to penetrate the pop charts, the major labels (Columbia, RCA, Decca, Capitol, Mercury, and MGM), which had previously controlled the pop market, began to routinely "cover" with white artists any black recording that exhibited signs of crossing over. The most famous example of this was the Crew Cuts's cover on Mercury of the Chords's "Sh-Boom," originally issued on the Atlantic subsidiary Cat Records in the summer of 1954. The Chords released "Sh-Boom" on 19 June 1954. Two weeks later, on 3 July, their record entered the rhythm and blues charts, immediately charting pop as well. That same week Mercury rushed the Crew Cuts into the studio to cover the song. On 10 July the cover version entered the pop charts. Eventually the Chords reached the No. 2 spot on the rhythm and blues charts while peaking at No. 5 on the pop charts. The Crew Cuts's version vaulted to the No. 1 spot on the pop charts, where it stayed for nine weeks, making their record far and away the best-selling disc of the year.

For the next few years, the covering of black rhythm and blues records originally released on independent labels, by white artists on major labels (and, in the case of Pat Boone and the Fontane Sisters, who both recorded for Dot Records, on independent labels) proliferated. Prominent examples include Georgia Gibbs's cover on Mercury of LaVern Baker's "Tweedly Dee," originally released on Atlantic, the McGuire Sisters' cover on Coral (a subsidiary of Decca) of the Moonglows' "Sincerely," originally released by Chess, and Pat Boone's multiple covers on Dot of Little Richard and Fats Domino recordings originally issued on Specialty and Imperial. In 1954 alone nine of the Top Ten rhythm and blues songs of the year were covered by white pop artists (the lone exception being blues guitarist Guitar Slim's "The Things That I Used to Do," released on Specialty). Many rhythm and blues stars were bitter about this practice, as the cover versions clearly took potential sales and royalties away from the originators of the music.

It is important to note, though, that in the prerock world of pop cover versions were a routine part of the business, so much so that between 1946 and 1950, 70 percent of the records that entered the Pop Top Ten appeared in more than one version. It is also worth noting that at the same time major labels were covering rhythm and blues/rock and roll records originally released on independent labels, they were also covering the odd country tune that showed signs of potential pop success. Finally, it was not uncommon for black rhythm and blues artists recording for independent labels to cover white pop tunes originally issued on major labels. (Ironically, the Chords' "Sh-Boom" was originally intended as the B side of their cover of white pop singer Patti Page's "Cross over the Bridge.") The cover syndrome, then, was not necessarily based on racism, as is often asserted. Instead, it was a standard practice within the business to garner and control market share practiced by both major and independent labels with white and black artists. In the early and mid-1950s, though, the specific nature of the practice developed both racial implications and ramifications. By 1956 the cover syndrome abated, as the black originals began routinely to outsell the white covers, and the major labels had begun to sign the first young white rock and roll artists such as Elvis Presley (RCA), Gene Vincent (Capitol), and Johnny Burnette and the Rock 'n' Roll Trio (Decca) in their attempt to meet the demand of white youth for this new style of music.

In the 1950s rock and roll substantially changed the political economy of the record industry. Between 1954 and 1959 gross sales in the industry grew from $213 million a year to $603 million. At the same time, independent labels with new, often black artists began to acquire a significant share of the pie, resulting in the Top Four firm concentration ratio for Top Ten pop hits dropping from 74 percent to 34 percent. The most telling fact, however, was that independent labels issued 69 percent of all rock and roll hits that charted pop between 1955 and 1959, representing 30 percent of all hits on the pop charts.

The year 1955 clearly marked the watershed as black rock and rollers Little Richard, Chuck Berry and Bo Diddley all enjoyed their first hits (for Specialty and Chess), Fats Domino enjoyed his first Top Ten pop hit (after twelve Top Ten rhythm and blues hits between 1950 and early 1955, all released on Imperial), and white rock artist Bill Haley and the Comets reached the No. 1 spot for eight weeks straight with the rerelease of "(We're Gonna) Rock around the Clock," which was also featured in the film Blackboard Jungle. By March 1956 Elvis Presley would begin to chart nationally. Equally telling is the fact that in 1954 major labels released forty-two of the fifty top-selling singles, while in 1955 that number had dropped to seventeen of the fifty top-selling singles as the pop charts became inundated with rock and roll records released on independent labels.

Early white rock and roll artists

It is not surprising that the first examples of music made by white artists that was called rock and roll combined elements of country and pop music with rhythm and blues. Elvis Presley's first five releases on Sun Records in 1954 and 1955 all combined one rhythm and blues song with one country song. In all cases Presley modified the songs, adding substantial rhythm and blues elements to his recordings of country material and, similarly, adding country and pop elements to his versions of rhythm and blues songs. Subsequent white rock and roll artists including Billy Lee Riley, Carl Perkins, and Buddy Holly all stated that it was hearing Presley's unique fusion of rhythm and blues, country and pop that made them realize that they could combine the black music they had been hearing for several years on black appeal stations with the country and occasional pop material they had begun to play as professional musicians. This new style was called rockabilly, the name itself being a hybrid of the terms for black rock and roll and white hillbilly music.

Presley was not the only artist experimenting with the cross-pollination of black and white styles. Many aspects of Chuck Berry's multistring guitar style can be traced to country guitarists such as Chet Atkins, while his predilection for text-heavy extended linear narratives also resonates with long-standing country practices. It is instructive in this regard to note that Berry's first single and first hit, "Maybelline," was a rewrite of a public domain country fiddle tune known as "Ida Red." By the mid-1950s Tin Pan Alley songwriters clearly recognized that rock and roll was a combination of the two main tributaries of vernacular white and black musics. Max Freedman, the author of a number of Tin Pan Alley chestnuts including "Sioux City Sue," took the melody from Hank Williams's 1949 country hit "Move It On Over," added a riff section based on rhythm and blues star Jimmy Liggins's recording "Shuffleshuck," and wrote lyrics about rocking for what was seen by many as the clarion call of the era, "(We're Gonna) Rock around the Clock."

Early reactions to rock and roll

From the broadcasts of black appeal radio stations in the late 1940s to Alan Freed's first rock and roll dance concerts in Cleveland in the early 1950s to the large-scale package tours of the mid- and late 1950s, rock and roll presented the United States with a music that was being consumed by both black and white youth and, beginning in the mid-1950s, that was being produced by black and white artists. In essence, rock and roll represented the first public phenomenon since the Great Awakening at the beginning of the nineteenth century that was integrated on this scale. As such, it threatened

Much of the anti–rock and roll sentiment was fueled by Asa Carter, the head of the North Alabama Citizens' Council (NACC) and a member of the Ku Klux Klan.

the segregated status quo that was at the time the norm throughout the country, albeit more overtly in the South.

Although it seems that no one was disturbed enough to comment in 1951 when Billy Ward and the Dominoes entered the pop charts with "Sixty Minute Man," a song that, although humorous, sonically portrays ejaculation, by the mid-1950s church groups, local governments, police authorities, and white citizens' councils began actively to denounce rock and roll, connecting it in an unholy alliance to race, sex, and delinquency. Three significant developments provided the context for the anti–rock and roll sentiment of the mid-1950s: (1) the civil rights struggle, manifest in the 1954 *Brown vs. Board of Education* judgment, the May 1955 admonishment of the Supreme Court to move with "all deliberate speed" toward integrating public education, and the beginning of the Montgomery bus boycott in December 1955, all of which threatened substantial change to the American system of apartheid; (2) black rhythm and blues recordings began regularly to outsell white covers, meaning the black presence on the pop charts became much more significant; and (3) Elvis Presley's sexualized movements on stage, broadcast to one and all on national television, suggested what could happen if white youth immersed themselves in African American musical culture.

Rock and roll was quickly connected by those who opposed it to issues of morality including juvenile delinquency and premarital sex, racial miscegenation, anti-Christian practice, and communism. Much of the anti–rock and roll sentiment was fueled by Asa Carter, the head of the North Alabama Citizens' Council (NACC) and a member of the Ku Klux Klan. In April 1956 members of the statewide coordinating Alabama Citizens' Council assaulted Nat King Cole on stage in Birmingham when Cole sang a duet with white pop singer June Christy. The NACC's magazine, *The Southerner*, subsequently published pictures of Cole and June Christy with inflammatory captions such as "Cole and Your Daughter" and "Cole and His White Women." *The Southerner* also accused the NAACP of deliberately trying to corrupt white teenagers with rock and roll. .

The widespread press coverage that followed the attack on Cole provided Carter and his group with a national stage. In *Newsweek* Carter was quoted as saying that "[rock and roll] is the basic heavy beat of Negroes. It appeals to the very base of man, brings out the animalism and vulgarity (*Newsweek,* 23 April 1956, 32). In *The Southerner,* Carter wrote [it will erode the] entire moral structure of man, Christianity, of spirituality in Holy marriage . . . all the white man has built through his devotion to God" (*The Southerner,* March 1956, 6).

In May 1956 Carter's group carried placards outside the Birmingham Municipal Auditorium protesting a whites-only concert performed by an interracial group of artists including Bill Haley and the Comets, Bo Diddley, and LaVern Baker. Their signs proclaimed, "Jungle Music promotes integration," "bebop promotes communism," "Jungle Music aids delinquency," and "Churches must speak out against these anti-Christ forces" (*Birmingham News,* 21 May 1956, 1/6, 30). Carter subsequently wrote to the mayor of Birmingham protesting the use of the Municipal Auditorium "for indecent and vulgar performances by Africans before our white children." By December 1956 the Municipal Auditorium was instructed not to book any type of event with an interracial cast of performers.

Fueled by the publicity accorded Carter, anti–rock and roll sentiment spread throughout the South and eventually the rest of the country. In the summer of 1956 Louisiana passed a law that prohibited interracial dancing, social functions, and entertainment. In July the San Antonio Parks Department banned rock and roll from jukeboxes at the city's swimming pools. Throughout the rest of the summer and into the fall numerous city councils across the country simply banned rock and roll performances. Aiding and abetting such egregious attempts at censorship were racist statements made by the Very Reverend John Carroll in Boston ("Rock and roll inflames and excites youth like jungle tom-toms" (*Variety*, 23 April 1956, 32) and Hartford psychiatrist Dr. Francis J. Braceland, who called rock and roll a "tribalistic and cannibalistic" style of music, a "communicable disease" (*New York Times*, 28 March 1956, 33). Even President Eisenhower saw fit to state publicly that "[rock and roll] represents some kind of change in our standards. What has happened to our concepts of beauty, decency and morality?"

Although their politics were clearly spurious, the anti–rock and roll forces were in a sense quite right. Rock and roll in the 1950s did promise to transform American society. Many of the white teens who consumed this new exciting music made by black artists and found themselves dancing at public concerts, oftentimes alongside black kids, began to question the racist status quo that governed America. A number of those white teenagers would grow up, go to college, and participate actively in the civil rights movement of the early 1960s. Rock and roll, in effect, resocialized a number of white youth and played a part in the long struggle to end the system of American apartheid.

The early splintering of rock and roll

By the early 1960s, the major labels, aided by the tightening of radio playlists due to the payola scandal and the rise of the Top 40 format, regained control of the pop market and began to promote and distribute a safer, softer, more pop-oriented version of the music, now performed by white teen idols such as Paul Anka, Ricky Nelson, and Johnny Burnette. A small number of American artists and producers, including Phil Spector, Link Wray, and the Beach Boys, pioneered new variants of rock and roll music in this period, but it would not be until the British Invasion in 1964, led by the Beatles, the Dave Clark Five, the Rolling Stones, and others, that rock and roll would return full force for a couple of years before mutating into various new styles subsumed under the term *rock*.

Rock itself would mutate in a myriad number of directions over the next three-and-a-half decades, at various points incorporating influences from folk, jazz, renaissance, baroque, classical, romantic, avant-garde, "new music," blues, *norteno, tejano,* Celtic, reggae, Native, and various so-called world musics. While rock would continue to be primarily produced and consumed by white youth, the age range of the audience would expand upward as the original fans of the music in the 1950s and 1960s grew older. This expanded demographic produced a number of tensions as rock became heavily stratified in the late 1970s, many newer styles such as punk, new wave, various forms of heavy metal, grunge, rap, and dance musics being actively positioned in opposition to the music of the late 1960s and early 1970s, the latter now renamed "classic rock."

The myriad styles of dance music that came to prominence in the 1980s and 1990s, including various forms of techno, house, garage, drum and bass, and jungle, in particular, were proclaimed by many as signaling the "death of rock," the mythology of rock no longer serving to demonstrably unify white youth on a mass scale. Finally, as the demographic that embraced rock in the 1960s and 1970s began to experience material success, earlier styles that had originally been considered oppositional began to be incorporated into advertising for such hegemonic consumer items as cars, banking services, and clothes, further undermining the power and meaning that rock and roll once enjoyed.

—ROB BOWMAN

Rock since the 1970s

Although popular music is by definition a commercial art form, rock artists through the latter half of the twentieth and into the twenty-first century have consistently rebelled against the establishment of which they are a part. The consciously constructed image of the rock artist as the outsider, a marginalized member of society, resonated with a large audience and challenged the comfortable image and music of more mainstream groups, specifically rock's more commercially acceptable counterpart, Top 40. In the last three decades of the twentieth century, the gulf between rock and Top 40 widened further as the rock genre fragmented into myriad subgenres. No longer attracting the homogenous audience of the 1950s, rock music of the late 1960s and beyond captivated a similarly fragmented and expanding audience of teens and baby boomers. As these audiences grew, so too did record sales, topping one billion dollars for the first time in 1967 and quadrupling over the next decade. Often the gulf between rock and Top 40 was exploited by artists who maintained the attitude and appearance of outsiders while achieving great success on the pop charts; this tendency can be traced throughout this period, from Led Zeppelin to Guns n' Roses.

Early fusions

Led Zeppelin, an outgrowth of the 1960s group The Yardbirds, released two albums in the late 1960s, although it achieved its pinnacle of popularity during the 1970s. Heavily blues influenced, Led Zeppelin routinely performed medleys of songs by Elvis Presley and Robert Johnson in concert. Zeppelin's recordings are an amalgamation of this prominent blues influence, fantasy-based lyrics, and a loud, distorted sound similar to hard rock forerunner Cream. Zeppelin's music strongly contrasted the softer sound of 1970s pop that appealed to a more conservative audience. Although Zeppelin achieved great musical success, the band's on and off stage behavior, along with Jimmy Page's preoccupation with the occult figure Aleister Crowley, lent the band a mysterious and dangerous image. Contemporaries including Bad Company (the first band signed to Led Zeppelin's label Swan Song) and Aerosmith offered a more commercially acceptable Zeppelin-influenced music that also remained popular during the 1970s.

Groups including Yes, Pink Floyd, King Crimson, Genesis, and Emerson Lake and Palmer (ELP) began to incorporate increasingly sophisticated formal, harmonic, and rhythmic structures into their music, referred to as progressive rock ("prog rock"), art rock, or classical rock, in the late 1960s and into the 1970s. Influenced by the technical virtuosity of Eric Clapton and Jimi Hendrix, the complexity of classical music, and the experimental nature of later Beatles recordings, many of these groups appealed to a particular subculture comprising young musicians themselves, searching for more intricate and contemplative music. Such groups maintained this small but consistent fan base through the 1980s and 1990s. Meanwhile, bands such as Blood, Sweat, and Tears, The Mahavishnu Orchestra, Weather Report, and Return to Forever were influenced by Miles Davis's recordings of the late 1960s and combined jazz-based elements with the aforementioned musical complexity to create the art-rock subgenre of jazz rock or jazz-rock fusion.

As Led Zeppelin's popularity rose and progressive rock found its niche audience, fellow Englishman Ozzy Osbourne joined another blues-based rock group, Earth, later known as Black Sabbath. The band's eponymous debut album in 1970, followed by *Paranoid* (1970), codified the heavy metal sound. The blues influence played a subtler role in Black Sabbath's music, which Osbourne and band mates imbued with slower tempos, darker lyrics filled with references to the occult, and an ominous stage presence. Often cited as the seminal heavy metal band, Black Sabbath inspired—at least in part—the heavy metal music popular throughout the 1980s.

"Glam" and punk rock

Between 1970 and 1975, Lou Reed (former Velvet Underground singer), David Bowie, The New York Dolls, and others created a music that departed from the hard rock of Led Zeppelin and Black Sabbath and foreshadowed the punk rock movement soon to follow. Variously termed glamour ("glam") rock, glimmer rock, or glitter rock, the music of Bowie and his contemporaries shared much of punk rock's minimalistic sound but contained relatively more harmonic variety, a polished musical production, and a manicured stage dress. Androgyny was integral to the stage personae of these performers, achieved by their donning women's clothing along with heavily applied makeup [see GENDER AND SEXUALITY, p. 87].

The Sex Pistols, the Clash, the Damned and other British groups spearheaded the punk rock movement of the late 1970s, which was—as were all previous rock movements—decidedly antiestablishment. In contrast to previous movements, punk rockers rebelled not just against society's mores but also against current trends in both pop and rock music as well as the seemingly monolithic recording industry. Punk groups dispensed with guitar solos and any other displays of technical prowess in favor of a simple chordal texture and standard 4/4 drum beats—both reminiscent of 1950s rock and roll—played at breakneck tempos. The use of fast tempos and heavy distortion, coupled with politically charged lyrics that the singer more often screamed than sang, created a stark contrast to the polished, heavily produced sound of disco as well as to the sounds of progressive and mainstream rock. Joe Strummer of the Clash characterized this style: "[I]magine in your mind an ELP [Emerson, Lake, and Palmer] number, then imagine punk rock like a blow torch sweeping across it. That to me is what punk rock did" (Szatmary 1996:238).

American punk rock groups, including The Ramones, Iggy Pop, and, later, the Dead Kennedys, were also forming at this time. The shunning of such groups by radio station executives on both sides of the Atlantic only reinforced their authenticity and cult status. Although the Ramones borrowed some of their sound from the New York Dolls, they and other punk rockers rebelled against the glitzy, polished appearance of glimmer rock. In contrast, performers displayed ripped clothing, dyed hair, and safety pins as jewelry, mimicking in appearance the "do-it-yourself" punk sound.

The intentionally extreme dress and notorious behavior of punk rock groups, particularly The Sex Pistols, rendered them virtually unmarketable. Thus, some groups lessened their rebellious look and sound to create a cleaner, more marketable music dubbed New Wave. Groups including Blondie and the Go Go's began their careers in the New York City punk scene but then reworked their sounds and later achieved great commercial success. Similarly, bands like the Police and Generation X (with Billy Idol) attempted to create a style that offered a compromise between punk and pop. Many punk rock groups viewed New Wave and hybrid styles as sanitized versions of punk, manufactured by artists who had "sold out." The notoriety of early punk bands spawned punk chic, a mode of dress adopted by Top 40 artists as well as the general public. The ripped clothes and spiked hair that were once shocking were now commonplace and mass-marketable—punk had lost its edge. Although punk rock groups seemingly vanished, numerous bands remained active in the underground scene through the 1980s and resurfaced in the early 1990s.

Heavy (and other) metal groups

The heavy metal genre of the 1980s synthesized the sound of predecessors Black Sabbath, Deep Purple, and Led Zeppelin with the look of 1970s glamour rock. Glam rockers including Mötley Crüe, Poison, and Cinderella paradoxically combined Bowie's

The product of Generation X malaise, grunge lyrics reflect a sense of disillusionment and uselessness.

androgynous look with overtly sexual lyrics that, along with the band's cover art and videos, consistently objectified women. Female artists constructed a curious subgenre of this trend, exemplified by Vixen and Lita Ford, who adopted the musical style, stage persona, and lyrical sexual aggressiveness of 1980s heavy metal. Other heavy metal and hard rock bands of the 1980s recaptured the guitar virtuosity of the late 1960s and early 1970s dormant during the punk rock craze. Metallica, Anthrax, and Judas Priest played speed metal, or thrash, identified by the use of fast tempos and rapid double bass drum attacks. Death metal bands including Slayer, Death, and Obituary combined speed metal and satanic, often violent lyrics sung with vocal distortion. The negative reaction to misogynist themes in heavy metal prompted Tipper Gore to found the Parents' Music Resource Center (PMRC) in 1985, an organization that targeted this music she termed "porn rock" (Gore 1987).

In the last years of the 1980s, and briefly into the 1990s, Guns n' Roses commanded the radio and marketplace. Selling over fifteen million copies, the band's debut album, *Appetite for Destruction* (1987), was the second-biggest-selling debut album in rock history. With a guitar-based sound, Axl Rose's unique vocal delivery, and the band's intriguing stage presence, Guns n' Roses managed to make a subcultural phenomenon mainstream. The band, however, quickly unraveled after the somewhat disappointing release of its fifth album, *The Spaghetti Incident* (1993).

Grunge

The rapid decline of audience interest in heavy metal has been attributed to the burgeoning Seattle grunge scene of the early 1990s. Led by Nirvana and other bands signed to the independent label Sub Pop, grunge musicians combined a gritty punk rock sound with less politically charged lyrics and other pop elements. With Nirvana's release of its major label debut album *Nevermind* (1991), punk found a mass audience. Similar to the punk movement of the late 1970s, grunge eschewed the visual excesses of 1980s rock and spawned its own mode of dress, including flannel shirts, often worn over long underwear, paired with tattered jeans and combat boots. The product of Generation X malaise, grunge lyrics reflect a sense of disillusionment and uselessness.

Like 1970s punk and 1980s heavy metal music, grunge, too, splintered into a variety of subgenres. The year 1991 saw the emergence of a group of female rock artists collectively known as Riot Grrrls who explored issues of feminine sexuality and celebrated anger through their music. These latter-day punks, led by Bikini Kill, Hole, and Babes in Toyland, adopted punk and grunge elements and co-opted previously derogatory terms targeted at women to further empower themselves and their music. In the mid-1990s, bands including Greenday and the Offspring created a new punk-pop hybrid with faster tempos, more melodic lines, and a less downtrodden sentiment. Seattle groups including Soundgarden, Pearl Jam, and Alice in Chains injected Nirvana's formula with decidedly heavy metal riffs.

Rap-influenced rock

Rap music, popular since the late 1970s, heavily influenced a group of hard-rock bands, now referred to as rap rock groups, beginning with the Red Hot Chili Peppers [see HIP-HOP AND RAP, p. 692]. In the mid- to late 1990s, however, bands including Korn, Limp Bizkit, and the Kottonmouth Kings added a heavy metal element to rap rock and have garnered recent success. These bands not only frequently employ rap lyrics but also incorporate samples into the fiber of their music.

The consistent, weblike proliferation of rock subgenres as well as the lack of historical perspective renders a linear, evolutionary history of rock music of the past three decades both impossible and undesirable. A certain theme or trope can, however, be traced through the years—something one could call the "paradox of rock": the tendency of rock artists to achieve popularity by consciously and aggressively resisting popularizing mechanisms. The disjunction between pop and rock continues to evolve as rock fractures into more and more subgenres. Furthermore, aided by different recording media technology and new innovations in the transmission of rock—specifically Napster and other Internet organizations—the future of rock is unclear. Although rock as a musical genre is no longer the monolith it was in its early years, the profusion of artists and music assures its longevity.

—SARA NICHOLSON

REFERENCES

Barlow, William. 1999. *Voice Over: The Making of Black Radio.* Philadelphia: Temple University Press.

Berry, Chuck. 1987. *Chuck Berry: The Autobiography.* New York: Harmony Books.

Birosek, Patti Jean. 1989. *The New Age Music Guide.* New York: Collier Books.

Brackett, David. 1995. *Interpreting Popular Music.* Cambridge: Cambridge University Press.

Broughton, Simon, et al., eds. 1994. *World Music: The Rough Guide.* London: Rough Guides.

Broven, John. 1978. *Rhythm & Blues in New Orleans.* Gretna, La.: Pelican Publishing.

Brown, Charles T. 1983. *The Rock and Roll Story: From the Sounds of Rebellion to an American Art Form.* Englewood Cliffs, N.J.: Prentice-Hall.

Buzzell, John ed. 1986. "Mister 'Rock 'n' Roll' Alan Freed." *Los Angeles: National Rock 'n' Roll Archives,* 18.

Chapman, Tracy. 1988. *Tracy Chapman.* Elektra.

Charlton, Katherine. 1994. *Rock Music Styles: A History.* Boston: McGraw-Hill.

Christgau, Robert. 1998. *Grown Up All Wrong: 75 Great Rock and Pop Artists from Vaudeville to Techno.* Cambridge: Harvard University Press.

Covach, John, and Graeme M. Boone, eds. 1997. *Understanding Rock: Essays in Musical Analysis.* New York: Oxford University Press.

Davis, Stephen. 1985. *Hammer of the Gods: The Led Zeppelin Saga.* New York: Ballantine Books.

Day, Richard. 1998. "Identity, Diversity and the Mosaic Metaphor: The National Jewel as the Canadian Thing." *Topia. Canadian Journal of Cultural Studies* 2:42–66.

De Curtis, Anthony, ed. 1992. *Present Tense: Rock & Roll and Culture.* Durham, N.C.: Duke University Press.

Deschenes, Donald. 1993. "Les Chansons de Joe Venne, Métis." *Canadian Folk Music Journal* 21:3–11.

Dickerson, James. 1996. *Goin' Back to Memphis: A Century of Blues, Rock and Roll, and Glorious Soul.* New York: Schirmer Books.

Doerschuk, Bob. 1988. "New Age Hits Middle Age: Confronting the Betrayal of Noble Ideals." *Keyboard,* October, 36–40.

Dorough, Prince. 1992. *Popular-Music Culture in America.* New York: Ardsley House.

Doucet, Suzanne. 1988. "Success Has Diluted New Age Music." *Rolling Stone,* 18 June, 9.

Eremo, Judie, ed. 1989. *New Age Musicians.* Milwaukee, Wisc.: Hal Leonard Publishing Corporation.

Escott, Colin, and Martin Hawkins. 1991. *Good Rockin' Tonight: Sun Records and the Birth of Rock 'n' Roll.* New York: St. Martin's Press.

Feld, Steven. 1994a. "From Schizophonia to Schismogenesis: Notes on the Discourses of World Music and World Beat." In *Music Grooves: Essays and Dialogues,* ed. Charles Keil and Steven Feld, 257–289. Chicago: University of Chicago Press.

———. 1994b. "Notes on 'World Beat.'" In *Music Grooves: Essays and Dialogues,* ed. Charles Keil and Steven Feld, 238–246. Chicago: University of Chicago Press.

———. 1996. "Pygmy POP: A Genealogy of Schizophonic Mimesis." *Yearbook for Traditional Music* 28:1–35.

Friedlander, Paul. 1996. *Rock and Roll: A Social History.* Boulder, Colo.: Westview Press.

Frith, Simon. 1996. *Performing Rites: On the Value of Popular Music.* Cambridge: Harvard University Press.

Frith, Simon, and Andrew Goodwin, eds. 1990. *On Record: Rock, Pop, and the Written Word.* New York: Pantheon.

Gabree, John. 1968. *The World of Rock.* Greenwich, Conn.: Fawcett Publications.

Garofalo, Reebee. 1997. *Rockin' Out: Popular Music in the U.S.A.* Boston: Allyn and Bacon.

Gart, Galen, ed. 1986. *First Pressings: The History of Rhythm and Blues.* Vol. 1–8 (1948–1958). Milford, N.H.: Big Nickel Publications.

Gibbon, Roy W. 1980. "'La Grande Gigue Simple' and 'The Red River Jig.'" *Canadian Folk Music Journal* 8:40–48.

Gillett, Charlie. 1970. *The Sound of The City: The Rise of Rock and Roll.* London: Souvenir Press.

Gore, Tipper. 1987. *Raising PG Kids in an X-Rated Society.* Nashville: Abingdon Press.

Groia, Philip. 1983. *They All Sang on the Corner: A Second Look at New York City's Rhythm and Blues Vocal Groups.* West Hempstead, N.Y.: Phillie Dee Enterprises.

Guralnick, Peter. 1994. *Last Train to Memphis: The Rise of Elvis Presley.* New York: Little, Brown.

Hannusch, Jeff. 1985. *I Hear You Knockin': The Sound of New Orleans Rhythm and Blues.* Ville Platte, La.: Swallow Books.

Hartigan, Royal. 1995. *West African Rhythms for the Drum Set.* Miami, Fla.: Warner Bros. Publications.

Hayward, Victoria. 1922. *Romantic Canada.* Toronto: The Macmillan Company of Canada.

Heckman, Don. 1987. "New Age Talent: Vital Voices from the Melting Pot." *Billboard,* October, N-3, N-5.

Hill, Trent. 1992. "The Enemy Within: Censorship in Rock Music in the 1950s." In *Present Tense: Rock & Roll and Culture,* ed. Anthony DeCurtis. Durham, N.C.: Duke University Press.

Jackson, John. 1991. *Big Beat Heat: Alan Freed and the Early Years of Rock & Roll.* New York: Schirmer Books.

Kallmann, H., et al., eds. 1992. *Encyclopedia of Canadian Music.* 2nd ed. Toronto: University of Toronto Press.

Klymasz, Robert. 1972. "'Sounds You Never Heard Before': Ukrainian Country Music in Western Canada." *Ethnomusicology* 16(3):381–396.

Kocandrle, Mirek. 1988. *The History of Rock and Roll: A Selective Discography.* Boston: G. K. Hall and Co.

Laing, Dave. 1985. *One Chord Wonders: Power and Meaning in Punk Rock.* Philadelphia: Open University Press.

Lederman, Anne. 1991. "Old Indian and Métis Fiddling in Manitoba: Origins, Structure, and Questions of Syncretism." *Canadian Folk Music Journal* 18:40–60.

Leighton, David. 1982. *Artists, Builders and Dreamers: 50 Years at the Banff School.* Toronto: McClellen and Stewart.

Lysloff, René T.A. 1997. "Mozart in Mirrorshades: Ethnomusicology, Technology, and the Politics of Representation." *Ethnomusicology* 41(2):206–19.

Marcus, Greil. 1975. *Mystery Train: Images of America in Rock 'n' Roll Music.* New York: E. P. Dutton.

Marks, J. 1968. *Rock and Other Four Letter Words.* New York: Bantam Books.

Mayer, Margaret M. 1994. *The American Dream: American Popular Music.* Bethesda, Md.: Front Desk Publishing.

Meintjes, Louise. 1990. "Paul Simon's *Graceland,* South Africa, and the Mediation of Musical Meaning." *Ethnomusicology* 34(1):37–73.

Middleton, Richard. 1990. *Studying Popular Music.* Milton Keynes, Eng.: Open University Press.

Ondar, Kongar-ol. 1999. *Back Tuva Future.* Warner Bros. 9 47131–2. Compact disc.

Pavlow, Big Al. 1983. *The R & B Book: A Disc-History of Rhythm and Blues.* Providence, R.I.: Music House Publishing.

Peterson, Richard A., and David G. Berger. 1975. "Cycles in Symbol Production and the Case of Popular Music." *American Sociological Review* 40.

Pruter, Robert. 1996. *Doowop: The Chicago Scene.* Urbana: University of Illinois Press.

Regroupement des Artistes Del Ouest Canadien. (1994). *RADO '95.* CBC Radio, L'Association des artistes de la Saskatchewan. Galas compact disc Gala9501.

Richardson, Derk. 1986. "The Sounds of Sominex." *Mother Jones,* November, 60.

Sakolsky, Ron, and Fred Ho.1995. *Sounding Off: Music as Subversion/Resistance/Revolution.* New York: Autonomedia.

Sanjek, Russell, and David Sanjek. 1991. *American Popular Music Business in the 20th Century.* New York: Oxford University Press.

Scaruffi, Piero. 1996. *Enciclopedia della Musica New Age, Elettronica, Ambientale, Pan-Etnica.* Padua, Italy: Arcana Ed.

Scott, Tony. 1983 [1964]. *Music for Zen Meditation.* Verve 817–209-2.

Simon, Paul. 1986. *Graceland.* Warner Bros. 9 26098–2. Compact disc.

Spencer, Peter. 1992. *World Beat: A Listener's Guide to Contemporary World Music on CD.* Pennington, N.J.: A Capella Books.

Sweeney, Philip. 1992. *The Virgin Directory of World Music.* New York: Henry Holt.

Szatmary, David P. 1996. *A Time to Rock: A Social History of Rock-and-Roll.* New York: Schirmer Books.

Taylor, Timothy D. 1997. *Global Pop: World Music, World Markets.* New York: Routledge.

Théberge, Paul. 1997. *Any Sound You Can Imagine: Making Music/Consuming Technology.* Hanover, N.H.: University Press of New England.

Tosches, Nick. 1984. *Unsung Heroes of Rock 'n' Roll.* New York: Charles Scribner's Sons.

Van Peer, René. 1999. "Taking the World for a Spin in Europe: An Insider's Look at the World Music Recording Business." *Ethnomusicology* 43(2):374–384.

Walser, Robert. 1993. *Running with the Devil: Power, Gender, and Madness in Heavy Metal Music.* Hanover, N.H.: Wesleyan University Press.

Walsh, Michael. 1986. "New Age Comes of Age." *Time,* 1 September, 82–83.

Ward, Brian. 1998. *Just My Soul Responding: Rhythm and Blues, Black Consciousness and Race Relations.* Berkeley: University of California Press.

Ward, Ed, Geoffrey Stokes, and Ken Tucker. 1986. *Rock of Ages: The Rolling Stone History of Rock & Roll.* New York: Rolling Stone Press.

Whidden, Lynn. 1992. "Métis." In *Encyclopedia of Canadian Music,* 2nd ed., ed. H. Kallmann et al. Toronto: University of Toronto Press

Whitburn, Joel. 1986. *Pop Memories 1890–1954: The History of American Popular Music.* Menomonee Falls, Wisc.: Record Research.

———. 1991. *Top Pop Singles: 1955–1990.* Menomonee Falls, Wisc.: Record Research.

———. 1996. *Top R&B Singles: 1942–1995.* Menomonee Falls, Wisc.: Record Research.

White, Charles. 1984. *The Life and Times of Little Richard: The Quasar of Rock.* New York: Harmony Books.

White, George R. 1995. *Bo Diddley: Living Legend.* Surrey, Eng.: Castle Communications.

Whitely, Sheila. 1992. *The Space between Notes: Rock and the Counter-Culture.* New York: Routledge.

Winston, George. (1980). *Autumn.* Windham Hill.

———. (1982). *December.* Windham Hill.

———. (1982). *Winter into Spring.* Windham Hill.

Part 3
Musical Cultures and Regions

Here we examine the distinctive musical cultures of the modern-day countries we know as Canada and the United States and the American Indian/First Nations peoples who reside within these geographic borders. The earliest inhabitants of North America, who arrived over fifteen thousand years ago, have successfully retained elements of their traditional social and ritual lives within new contexts, as well as creatively developing new musical forms that situate them within contemporary times. Groups from Africa, Europe, South and Central America, and Asia have arrived more recently (since the late sixteenth century), also bringing with them their own musics, musical instruments, and concepts of music, and have adjusted in varying ways to changing environments and social conditions. Each tradition has contributed much to the contemporary musical landscape within the United States and Canada as people have continued to negotiate issues of social and musical plurality.

A zydeco musician plays the frottoir, a percussion instrument modeled after a washboard, at Richard's, a club in Lawtell, Louisiana. © Philip Gould/CORBIS.

Section 1
Music of the American Indians/ First Nations in the United States and Canada

American Indians/First Nations peoples comprise a variety of social, linguistic, and musical groups, from the Choctaw living in the great swamp lands of the southeastern United States to the Inuit of the newest north Canadian territory, Nunavut; from the powerful six-nation Iroquois confederacy located in western New York and southern Ontario to the scattered villages of the Eskimo (as the Inuit are called in the United States) of Alaska. First Nations peoples in Canada also include the Métis, of Indian and predominantly French heritage, who form a separate social group with their own language as well as their own cultural and musical identity. Despite a wide variety of languages, physical environments, and musical cultures, however, most American Indians and First Nations peoples share a common history of European interaction and of rapid social and economic change brought about by European immigration and expansion. Various revivals of traditional musics, such as accompanied the Longhouse tradition in the early nineteenth century, and the development of much music and ritual over the past one hundred years, such as that associated with the Ghost Dance religion and the Native American Church, address these concerns, while contemporary musical forms such as rock and country and western music have also attracted Native musicians.

A Choctaw woman dances for tourists, Phoenix, Arizona. © Buddy Mays/CORBIS.

Overview
Charlotte Heth

History of Research
Musical Characteristics
Song Texts
Musical Origins and Sources
Social and Gender Considerations
Learning and Tradition in Native American Music

The first Americans (the American Indians, or Native Americans, or First Peoples) have for centuries valued music as integral to their lives. Creation narratives, migration stories, magic formulas, and ancient ceremonial practices tell of music. Archaeologists have found Indian musical instruments and pictographs of singing and dancing from as early as 600 C.E. and from areas as far apart as the mounds of the Southeast and the cliff dwellings of the Southwest. Although styles differ within tribal groups and among individuals, the variety of the music is infinite, due largely to its constant recreation and improvisation.

The migration of Native peoples over time has encouraged musical interaction and exchange. Historically, North America was a great and open hunting and fishing ground for many native peoples. They came together for subsistence and farming activities, marriage, religious, ceremonial, or trading purposes, often ignoring national and state boundaries and formal tribal borders created largely after white occupation. In the nineteenth century, the U.S. and Canadian governments forced Indian peoples to leave their ancestral homelands, later establishing reservations and allotments. In the twentieth century, Indian people began leaving their reservations, migrating in the 1930s to work on commercial farms and later in the 1940s to work in industries and to join the armed forces. Starting in the 1950s, government agents urged many Indians to relocate and moved them, for job training, from all parts of the United States to big cities in the West and Midwest. One way they made their lives happier in the cities was to form powwow clubs and social dance clubs with other urban Indians, often from different tribes. By the turn of the twentieth century, Indians had begun to travel back and forth between cities and their homelands for family and ceremonial events specific to their own tribal groups.

Sacred narratives, legends, music, and dance enable today's Native American people to carry on those ceremonies and traditions critical to Indian life. Originating from the Creator, other deities, guardian spirits, and animal spirits, or from respected human storytellers and composers, their ceremonies are simultaneously ancient and modern. They rely on memory and reenactment, not written words, thus transcending generations and cultural boundaries. Even traditional apparel and dance regalia tell stories about the makers, wearers, and symbols important to the nation, tribe, village, clan, family, or individual. We find in studying these spoken histories, song texts and sacred narratives—often called myths, creation stories or Indian literature—that they are much more than extraordinary tales. These oral histories concern the land and the spirits of the land, the important animals and plants, the history of the people, and their religious and moral beliefs. The worldview embodied in the stories when taken together tells us how various Indian peoples look at their lives in relation to the rest of the world. These philosophies frequently control how the people represent themselves through music and dance. This overview provides general background information on issues and concepts in American Indian music. A brief history of research on Native music is followed by a survey of musical characteristics, song texts, musical origins and sources, social and gender considerations, and learning and tradition in American Indian music. The subsequent articles on specific culture areas and topics in Native North American music provide more detailed information on what is introduced here.

HISTORY OF RESEARCH

To our knowledge, although Native peoples have always valued music highly, its significance was largely overlooked by most early writers—the travelers, missionaries, and soldiers who thought it quaint, comical, savage, or hard on the ears. After these very early accounts we proceed to the era of the curiosity seekers. Throughout much of the nineteenth century, authors transcribed Indian songs from memory and published them in various reports and journals in Europe and the United States. In the last two decades of the nineteenth century and in the early twentieth century, musicologists and scientists began collecting and analyzing Indian music. These early collectors provided the academic world with theories on "primitive" music and also gave the world's composers new melodic and rhythmic material for works based on Indian themes [see RACE, ETHNICITY, AND NATIONHOOD, p. 63]. Some of the composers who later used Indian music as the basis for composition were Victor Herbert (1859–1924), Frederick Burton (1861–1909), Edward MacDowell (1861–1908), Arthur Farwell (1872–1952), Henry F. Gilbert (1868–1928), Thurlow Lieurance (1878–1963), Charles Wakefield Cadman (1881–1946), Charles Tomlinson Griffes (1880–1920), Mario Castelnuovo-Tedesco (1895–1968), and Elliott Carter (1908–).

After 1900, comparative musicologists such as Natalie Curtis (1875–1921), Helen Roberts (1888–?), George Herzog (1901–1983), and Frances Densmore (1867–1957) started systematically collecting and analyzing Indian music of many tribes and nations. The most prolific of these authors was Densmore, who from 1903 until 1959 published more than 120 books, monographs, and articles on American Indian music. Since the 1950s, ethnomusicologists who focused their research on Native American music have included David McAllester, Gertrude Kurath, Ida Halpern, Alan Merriam, Bruno Nettl, Donald Roberts, James Howard, William Powers, and many others, including several contributors to this volume. Yet the importance of American Indian music is found not in its impact on modern scholarship and composition, but in the traditions and values it expresses to and for Indian people.

MUSICAL CHARACTERISTICS

In Indian music, the voice is the most important instrument. Vocal music includes solo pieces, responsorial songs in which the leader and chorus take turns, unison chorus songs, and multipart songs, some with rattle and/or drum accompaniment. Although most singers use a drum to set the beat and cue the dancers, rattles and sometimes whistles are also common. The singers perform for the most part in their native languages, but many songs include vocables (nontranslatable syllables, such as *he, ya, ho, we,* and so on) that are used to carry the melody.

Usually the songs begin with a soft, slow, stately drum beat and get louder and faster throughout the song. Hard and soft drum beats, accented patterns, rattle and drum tremolos, and shouts enliven the performance. These often signal important words, repeats, and changes of movement or direction for the singers and dancers. Many of these musical characteristics—the words, the number of repetitions, the instruments, and the way the singers work together—come from a particular world-view and depend largely on the dance or ceremony being performed.

SONG TEXTS

Many of the most ancient and unchanging songs are not intended to be sung in public or translated for the uninitiated. Indian people reserve these songs for ceremonial occasions, which are often sacred and secret. They usually do not allow them to be recorded or made available for study. In contrast to these songs, ritual speeches performed at public ceremonial events often sound musical because they employ rhythm and melody not found in everyday language. These are not usually secret, because any speaker of that particular Indian language can understand them. Often the speakers refer to the event that is happening and explain its significance. For example, during his ritual speech preceding a Stomp Dance, a Cherokee speaker might discuss singing, dancing, being happy, and shaking turtle shell rattles all night.

Often historical and current events take their place in songs. Probably the best known Navajo song is "Shi' naasha'," composed in 1868 to mark the Navajos' release from four years of internment at Fort Sumner, New Mexico (1864–1868). The text expresses the people's joy in returning to their homeland. Unlike many other Navajo songs, almost every syllable in the text is translatable. The words of the first verse may be freely translated as:

> I am walking, alive
> Where I am is beautiful
> I am still walking (lonely, sad, or nostalgic).

In "Shi' naasha'," vocables are used only to indicate the beginning and ending phrase of each section; the same vocable phrase, *"he ya he ne ya,"* also marks the end of the song.

Many tribes and nations have composed flag songs or national anthems in their own languages and styles. These are performed at the beginning of a powwow or other traditional event. The songs are treated seriously: all of the people stand, the men remove their hats, and no dancing occurs. The free translation of the Sioux "Flag Song" (in Lakota) is:

> The flag of the United States will fly forever;
> Under it the people will grow and prosper;
> Therefore have I (fought for my country).

Its form is typical of Plains songs, and the vocables occur in the same way they do in the Rabbit Dance, discussed below.

The subjects of songs tend to reinforce important aspects of culture. The first of nine San Juan Pueblo Butterfly Dances, a ladies' choice partner dance performed in the spring, speaks of how the corn is growing, starting from the sprout, and describes the green leaves, the red flower, and finally the white ear. It gives thanks to Mother Earth, who produced that ear. The first section of the song is the *wasa* or 'entrance,' sung entirely in vocables. The second section, the dance proper, not only contains vocables but also includes Tewa words about growing corn.

The placement of words in songs can occur in a number of ways: whole texts, words sprinkled throughout, alternating phrases or verses with vocables, and words performed in improvisatory fashion. A Northern Plains Rabbit Dance with English words employs a typical placement for texts in Plains powwow songs:

A vocables (leader)
A vocables (chorus echoes leaders)
B vocables (all)
C text (all):

Hey Sweetheart, I always think of you
I wonder if you are alone tonight hai yai
I wonder if you are thinking of me
Hai yai we ya hai ya.

D vocables (all)

The entire song is then repeated, beginning with the second A section.

In the Cherokee Stomp Dance, the call–response style allows the leader some freedom to improvise. After each song in the cycle is established with vocables, the leader moves temporarily into a higher register and can improvise if he likes. He can add Cherokee words, the chorus can harmonize briefly, the melody can be altered, and the dancers can clap hands and add special hand and arm motions as they face the fire. The leader does not have to add words; he can sing the entire song with vocables if he so desires. The songs in the cycle are separated by shouts that are also part of the music. One Cherokee song with words speaks of the Stomp Dance, the particular song being used and its ancient origin, the tobacco, and the group assembled at the Stomp Ground. Another talks about the song itself, how it starts quickly, and how beautiful it is.

A few singers have incorporated American popular tunes and words into social dance songs, such as "Jambalaya" and "Sugar in the Morning" for the Navajo, "Dixie" for the Hopi, and "Amazing Grace" (in a Buffalo Dance song) for Jemez Pueblo.

MUSICAL ORIGINS AND SOURCES

The origins of Native American music are many and varied. Some are described as coming from creation stories, individual inspiration, dreams, visions, personal or group experiences, purposeful composition, collaborative efforts, reworking time-tested models, buying, selling, inheriting, or misappropriating. Indian composers and singers cite many examples of music being taught or given by supernatural means. For example, Changing Woman, a central character from Navajo mythology, is the architect for the creation of the world and sings the world into being. The Navajo songs performed by the Singer (a ceremonial leader) can reunite or restore the order of the universe and appease the forces of evil. The Lakota people trace the Pipe Ceremony and Buffalo Calf Pipe Song to White Buffalo Woman, who taught the ceremony to the people, then departed, later being transformed into a white buffalo. The warriors who founded the Lakota Fox Society followed the sound of singing to an old fox who taught them the first songs and rules for their men's association. On the Plains, songs were often described not as taught but as given to humans by guardian spirits such as the fox. These songs were theoretically learned in one sitting.

Some Indian people still fast and seek visions that may include songs taught by animal or other guardian spirits. Furthermore, songs can be inspired by the sounds of nature—rivers, winds, or animals. Winnebago singers consider the drum as a source of songs and also recognize that songs come from or exist in the air. Singers often talk of catching songs. In addition, songs are given, sold, or exchanged with other people for many reasons, such as when ceremonial activities and objects are transferred, when people are initiated into societies, when power is transferred, or in recognition of honor and friendship.

Native American composers use varying techniques to express their artistry. Some cultures encourage creativity, while others require exact duplication of music from year

Pueblo songs are said to possess the power to lure needed game animals to the hunters who provide food, and they also have the power to regulate the agricultural cycle.

to year. Most tribal groups express an active need for new compositions, while also maintaining as many of the ancient songs as possible. Improvisatory techniques, particularly in call–response songs, are a type of composition. The numbers of verses and repetitions the singers can use are often based on sacred numbers. When an old song or ceremony is revived, it is often renewed or updated in some fashion.

In some communities, musicians do not compose new pieces because of the revered origin of the age-old songs. The Cherokee provide an example: a Cherokee origin story concerns a monster known as Stonecoat. This cannibal monster introduced death to the Cherokee by eating the livers of unsuspecting villagers. To weaken him, the medicine men positioned seven menstruating women in his path (seven is a Cherokee sacred number). As he passed each woman in succession, he became weaker and finally was captured and burned. While he was burning in the fire, Stonecoat sang all the songs that the Cherokee will ever need for dances, magic, and curing and instructed the people as to the songs' uses. Because of this supernatural origin for music, the Cherokee usually do not compose songs, preferring to express their creativity through improvisation. The forms of music found in the Stomp Dance and various animal and agricultural songs, particularly the responsorial songs, allow for several types of improvisation in words, melodies, and lengths.

Among Pueblo singers, being able to compose new songs is often as important as being able to remember old ones, so that composing can be summed up in four words: interest, tune, words, and memory, all adding up to talent. In singing both the new and older songs, the Pueblo men strive for perfect unison and faithful reproduction of songs from performance to performance. Pueblo songs are said to possess the power to lure needed game animals to the hunters who provide food, and they also have the power to regulate the agricultural cycle.

SOCIAL AND GENDER CONSIDERATIONS

In Native American musical settings, an audience is rarely defined. Most tribal members participate in dances and ceremonies, and visitors are often asked to join in. The audience reaction and interaction can therefore be determined by the extent to which the people gathered together endorse the musicians through active participation. They may join the singing and dancing or add shouts, ululations (high-pitched, wordless, rhythmic cries), and whistles to show approval, or may show disapproval by boycotting or other negative actions.

In many reservation or rural settings where tribal members live near each other, all or most of the community members are expected to participate in music and dance events, such as powwows, ceremonies, social dances, fiddle festivals, and hymn singings. Plains women often show approval by singing *lulus* or 'ululations' for honor or encouragement. The lead dancer at a powwow will sometimes blow a whistle, praising the singers and calling for a repetition. If a Cherokee man does not lead the Stomp Dance well, or if he is of poor character, the women will not dance behind him with their leg rattles, and he has to leave the circle. By contrast, a young singer just learning to lead brings out all of the people to dance with him and support his efforts.

Women can participate as singers, dancers, and instrumentalists in many events, but in others they must observe custom and not partake [see GENDER AND SEXUALITY, p. 87]. Dances and songs for women only are few in number. In the Northeast and Southeast, there are a few ceremonial and social dances for women. In these, one or a few men provide the music, or, more recently, a women's singing group is featured. Ordinarily the women may sing softly while they dance, accompanying themselves with rattles worn on their legs. In California and the Great Basin, there are hand game songs for women by themselves. And in California and the Northwest Coast, there are many medicine songs, love songs, and other influential songs that are exclusively for women.

Dozens of ceremonies, songs, and dances throughout North America cannot be performed without women. Although the Southeastern women provide accompaniment by shaking their leg rattles for various animal, friendship, and closing dances, they have regular singing roles in the Horse and Ball Game dances. The Ojibway women's dances in Wisconsin include a section in which the men drop out and the women sing alone, highlighting the words of the song. The Iroquois social dances also require the participation of women, particularly as dancers. Women's dances are the most popular type of song in singing contests, with all-female ensembles participating in recent times.

Both men and women of the Kashia Pomo of California sang the musical repertoire for curing, dancing, and other ceremonial activities. Both played the double whistles, and all accompanied themselves with clapping sticks. Further north in California, the Brush Dance of the Yurok, Karok, and Hupa focuses the group's energy on a sick child and the medicine woman sitting near the fire in the center of the dancing pit. The woman sings to cure the child, while male and female Brush Dancers sing and dance. The only rhythmic accompaniment is provided by the girls, whose shells and beads sewn onto their dresses and dance aprons clink in time to the music. Either men or women can sing "Light," or secular, Brush Dance songs, while a male chorus accompanies the soloist, but only men can sing the "Heavy," or spiritual songs.

The Sun Dance of the Great Plains and Great Basin requires the presence and participation of women in various roles. Sioux women pledgers dance, carry the pipes to the sacred circle, and make sacrificial offerings. They also sing behind the drummers during the social dances, as do the Arapaho and Shoshone women. Until the 1980s, Shoshone women still remembered and sang Ghost Dance songs, although the ritual was discontinued in the 1930s.

In the Southwest, with its rich musical variety, women have many roles to play. The Navajo and Apache girls' puberty ceremonies are centered on women and their activities. In these ceremonies, women sing, dance, and interpret ritual singing. The Pueblo women are accustomed to choosing their male dancing partners for many dances and often participate equally in the Basket, Corn, Harvest, Comanche, Butterfly, Dog, and Buffalo Dances. They even serve as instrumentalists by playing a notched-stick rasp in the Basket Dance. The sticks that are components of the rasp itself have gender designations as male and female. The Cloud Dance at San Juan Pueblo features four pairs of women who dance as Corn Maidens, representing four colors of corn. They dance in front of the male chorus, at times entering and leaving the men's ranks.

Ordinarily, both men and women can sing lullabies. Love songs, magic songs, and curing songs often have both male and female versions. Mescalero Apache women even compose love songs. In the Bird Songs of the Southern California Indians, both men and women sing and dance in unison, playing rattles. And one cannot imagine a powwow without the participation of women as dancers and backup singers.

Music and dance can serve as metaphors for life ways. In music, as in life, women serve as leaders, equals, or supporters; they perform alone, together, with men, or subordinate to men; they make instruments, compose music, and retain, transmit, and revive songs and cultures; they serve as evaluators and critics of music, of dance, and of both male and female performers; they can be the focal points or sponsors of ceremonial and musical events; they can cure or be cured, and they can pledge themselves in music and dance to live in this world and struggle for the good of all.

LEARNING AND TRADITION IN NATIVE AMERICAN MUSIC

Native American music, outside of movies and popular contemporary recordings, is little known to the general public in North America because traditional Indian musical events are rarely advertised. Often the organizers charge low admission prices, or the events are free of charge. The composers usually create their music without reading notation or using finely tuned instruments, outside of purely instrumental pieces or those based on Western models, such as some hymns and fiddle tunes. Famous only locally or in "Indian Country," the best singers customarily do not take lessons in American Indian music but instead learn by participating in performances [see LEARNING, p. 274]. They or their families and friends make their own instruments and special clothing and earn very little money, if any, practicing their arts.

These people and their communities organize and participate in festivals, social dances, games, special ceremonies, family and clan events, hymn singings, powwows, and medicine rites. Some Indian people live on reservations or in small towns or villages, but others live in major cities. They use the word *traditional* to cover various activities and practices. Often being traditional means adhering to the oldest norms: languages, religions, artistic forms, everyday customs, and individual behavior. More recently, the word refers to modern practices based on those norms. In other instances it may refer to a time period before technological advances. It may even indicate categories of dance, music, and dress that are derived from ancient, established practices.

Songs are integral to the Indian peoples who created them and still use them. Music pervades Indian life, starting with creation stories and ending with death and memorial songs. American Indian music is important not only because it influences modern American society, but also because it emphasizes the traditions and values of Indian people. This oral tradition has survived solely because the music and dance were too important to be allowed to die.

REFERENCES

Curtis, Natalie. 1905. *Songs of Ancient America: Three Pueblo Indian Corn-Grinding Songs from Laguna, New Mexico.* New York: Schirmer.

———. 1907. *The Indians' Book: An Offering by the American Indians of Indian Lore, Musical and Narrative, to Form a Record of the Songs and Legends of their Race.* New York: Harper.

———. 1920a. *Dawn Song.* Based on a Cheyenne Indian song for male chorus, tenor solo, and flute or oboe obbligato. New York: Schirmer.

———. 1920b. *Victory Song.* Pawnee Indian. New York: Schirmer.

Densmore, Frances. 1910–1913. *Chippewa Music.* 2 vols. Bureau of American Ethnology Bulletin 45, 53. Washington, D.C.: Smithsonian Institution.

———. 1918. *Teton Sioux Music.* Washington, D.C.: Smithsonian Institution.

———. 1921. *Indian Action Songs.* Boston: C. C. Birchard.

———. 1922. *Northern Ute Music.* Bureau of American Ethnology Bulletin 75. Washington, D.C.: Smithsonian Institution.

———. 1923. *Mandan and Hidatsa Music.* Bureau of American Ethnology Bulletin 80. Washington, D.C.: Smithsonian Institution.

———. 1926. *The American Indians and Their Music.* New York: The Woman's Press.

———. 1929. *Chippewa Customs.* Bureau of American Ethnology Bulletin 86. Washington, D.C.: Smithsonian Institution.

———. 1929. *Papago Music.* Bureau of American Ethnology Bulletin 90. Washington, D.C.: Smithsonian Institution.

———. 1932. *Menominee Music.* Bureau of American Ethnology Bulletin 102. Washington, D.C.: Smithsonian Institution.

———. 1936. *Cheyenne and Arapaho Music.* Southwest Museum Papers, no. 10. Los Angeles: Southwest Museum.

———. 1939. *Nootka and Quileute Music.* Bureau of American Ethnology Bulletin 124. Washington, D.C.: Smithsonian Institution.

———. 1942. "The Study of Indian Music." From the Annual Report of the Smithsonian Institution for 1941. Publication 3671. Washington, D.C.: U.S. Government Printing Office.

———. 1953. "The Use of Music in the Treatment of the Sick by American Indians." From the Annual Report of the Smithsonian Institution for 1952. Publication 4128. Washington, D.C.: U.S. Government Printing Office.

———. 1957. *Music of Acoma, Isleta, Cochiti, and Zuñi Pueblos.* Bureau of American Ethnology Bulletin 165. Washington, D.C.: Smithsonian Institution.

———. 1972 [1943]. *Choctaw Music.* New York: Da Capo.

Halpern, Ida. 1967. *Indian Music of the Pacific Northwest Coast.* Collected and recorded by Ida Halpern. Folkways Records FE 4523. LP disk.

———. 1974. *Nootka Indian Music of the Pacific Northwest Coast.* Collected, recorded, and annotated by Ida Halpern. Folkways Records FE 4524. LP disk.

———. 1981. *Kwakiutl: Indian Music of the Pacific Northwest.* Collected, recorded, and annotated by Ida Halpern. Folkways Records. LP disk.

———. 1986. *Haida Indian Music of the Pacific Northwest.* Recorded and annotated by Ida Halpern. Folkways Records. LP disk.

Herzog, George. 1936. *Research in Primitive and Folk Music in the United States: A Survey.* Washington, D.C.: American Council of Learned Societies.

———. 1937. "A Comparison of Pueblo and Pima Musical Styles." Ph.D. dissertation, Columbia University.

Howard, James Henri. 1968. *The Southeastern Ceremonial Complex and Its Interpretation.* Columbia: Missouri Archaeological Society.

———. 1981. *Shawnee!: The Ceremonialism of a Native Indian Tribe and Its Cultural Background.* Athens: Ohio University Press.

———. 1984. *The Canadian Sioux.* Lincoln: University of Nebraska Press.

Howard, James Henri, and Victoria Lindsay Levine. 1990. *Choctaw Music and Dance.* Foreword by Bruno Nettl. Norman: University of Oklahoma Press.

Kurath, Gertrude Prokosch. 1966. *Michigan Indian Festivals.* Ann Arbor, Mich.: Ann Arbor Publishers.

———. 1968. *Dance and Song Rituals of Six Nations Reserve, Ontario.* Bulletin of the National Museum of Canada, no. 220; Folklore series, no. 4. Ottawa: Queen's Printer.

———. 1977. *Iroquois Music and Dance: Ceremonial Arts of Two Seneca Longhouses.* St. Clair Shores, Mich.: Scholarly Press.

———. 1981. *Tutelo Rituals on Six Nations Reserve, Ontario.* Ann Arbor, Mich.: Society for Ethnomusicology.

McAllester, David P. 1964. *Peyote music.* New York: Johnson Reprint Corporation.

———. 1973. *Enemy Way Music: A Study of Social and Esthetic Values as Seen in Navaho Music.* Milwood, N.Y.: Kraus Reprint Co.

———. 1980. *Hogans: Navajo Houses and House Songs,* translated and arranged by David P. McAllester. Middletown, Conn.: Wesleyan University Press.

Merriam, Alan P. 1967. *Ethnomusicology of the Flathead Indians.* Chicago: Aldine.

Nettl, Bruno. 1954. *North American Indian Musical Styles.* Memoirs of the American Folklore Society, vol. 45. Philadelphia: American Folklore Society.

———. 1979. *An Historical Album of Blackfoot Indian Music.* New York: Folkways Records.

———. 1989. *Blackfoot Musical Thought: Comparative Perspectives.* Kent, Ohio: Kent State University Press.

Powers, William K. 1977. *Oglala Religion.* Lincoln: University of Nebraska Press.

———. 1982. *Yuwipi, Vision and Experience in Oglala.* Lincoln: University of Nebraska Press.

———. 1987. *Beyond the Vision: Essays on American Indian.* The Civilization of the American Indian Series, vol. 184. Norman: University of Oklahoma Press.

———. 1990a. *War Dance: Plains Indian Musical Performance.* Tucson: University of Arizona Press.

———. 1990b. *Voices from the Spirit World: Lakota Ghost Dance Songs.* Kendall Park, N.J.: Lakota Books.

———. 1998. *Lakota Cosmos: Religion and the Reinvention of Culture.* Kendall Park, N.J.: Lakota Books.

Roberts, Helen H. 1933. *Form in Primitive Music: An Analytical and Comparative Study of the Melodic Form of Some Ancient Southern California Indian Songs.* American Library of Musicology. New York: Norton.

———. 1936. *Musical Areas in Aboriginal North America.* Publications in Anthropology 12. New Haven, Conn.: Yale University Press.

Roberts, Helen H., and Morris Swadesh. 1955. *Songs of the Nootka Indians of Western Vancouver Island.* Philadelphia: American Philosophical Society.

Arctic Canada and Alaska
Nicole Beaudry

Culture of the Arctic
Musical Performance
Singing, Drumming, and Dancing in the Arctic
Musical Styles
Historical Transformations of Music and Culture
Scholarship

The Arctic encompasses an immense area ranging from the Atlantic to the Pacific Oceans across the highest portion of the North American continent. This vast area features a variety of ecosystems and landscapes and hosts several different cultural and linguistic groups. Two large and distinct musical cultures will be discussed in this article: those of the Western Arctic and those of the Central and Eastern Arctic.

CULTURE OF THE ARCTIC

Arctic peoples belong to the Eskimo-Aleut linguistic family, which is divided into three principal linguistic groups: the Aleut, Yupik, and Inupiat speakers. The Aleut speakers, who occupy islands extending into the Pacific in southern Alaska, are divided into eastern and western branches. The Yupik inhabit Bering Sea coastal areas and inland regions along the Kuskokwim and Yukon rivers and deltas. Yupik divides into two main dialects, Siberian and Central. The Inupiat are by far the largest group, ranging from northern Alaska to northeastern Canada and Greenland. In Canada, Inupiat people refer to themselves as Inuit. Thus, one must distinguish among the Mackenzie Delta Inuit, the Copper, Netsilik, Iglulik, and Caribou Inuit, the south Baffinland Inuit, and the Inuit of Québec and Labrador Coast. In theory, all Inupiat groups share the same language, but important dialectical and cultural differences exist.

Relationship to other culture areas

Typical of the Arctic populations is their relative isolation from non-Eskimoan cultures. However, North American Arctic populations share a circumpolar continuum with Siberian and Greenland Inuit. The Arctic's southern margin is characterized by a no-man's land, the Barrens, used sporadically by Arctic peoples on hunting and fishing expeditions. In the past, Inuit and Indian bands met in this neutral zone, often at war with one another but also proceeding to exchanges of goods during more peaceful episodes.

Subsistence patterns and other aspects of precontact society

Arctic populations were traditionally nomadic, mostly traveling along game animal migration routes. For food, clothing, and habitation materials, they relied mostly on

FIGURE I   Inuit women creating a soft voice-modulated sound by vibrating a seagull quill (*suluk*) gently between their teeth. Photo by Nicole Beaudry, Inukjuaq, Arctic Québec (Canada) 1978.

sea mammals (whale, walrus, seal) and large land mammals (caribou, bear), supplementing these with waterfowl (duck, geese), ptarmigan, hare, and clear- and saltwater fish. The recent emphasis on fox and wolf trapping is due to the development of a European-based fur-trading economy.

Although driftwood was a relatively reliable source of wood, the absence of trees led to the development of the ice-dome house (igloo), which was made of snow and ice—material readily available most of the year. In winter, Western Arctic peoples also used a hide-covered semisubterranean dwelling.

MUSICAL PERFORMANCE

Music making in the Arctic primarily involves the voice and the drum. Many song types are exclusively vocal, while the use of one or several drums is mostly restricted to large gathering celebrations. Even if songs have been composed expressly for the drum dance, they can be sung on intimate occasions without drumming and dancing, especially if they recount anecdotes concerning the singer's life or if they express personal feelings and emotions. However, the drum is never played by itself, only to accompany singing or dancing.

Drums and other sound producers

With very few exceptions, the only drum construction principle prevailing in the Arctic areas involves stretching an animal skin over a relatively thin round wood frame. A handle is attached to the frame with lacing and a tongue-and-groove adjustment. However, there are important regional structural differences in performance practices between those of the Western and the Eastern and Central Arctic. A drummer is free to decorate with painted motifs on rims or handles, for his own pleasure or to symbolize the special relationship with his familiars. Only in the Western Arctic do we find another type of drum, the box drum, used in the specific context of the wolf dance.

Buzzers, bull-roarers, and whistles also existed in all Arctic regions but did not feature prominently as music makers. Long ago in the Eastern Arctic, the metal Jew's harp appeared, probably obtained from European fishermen and whalers. No doubt it became popular because it produced a better sound than did the goose-feather quill (figure 1). The creation of a crude box fiddle was probably also inspired by encounters with sailor crews, who always had a fiddler along in their expeditions (figure 2).

FIGURE 2   Inuit woman making a modern violin sound like the old Inuit three-string box violin (*tautik*). She slides her bow across the three open strings alternately (notice the absence of a fourth string), thus creating rhythmic patterns rather than melodic ones. Photo by Nicole Beaudry, Ivujivik, Arctic Québec (Canada), 1978.

SINGING, DRUMMING, AND DANCING IN THE ARCTIC

The term *personal songs* (in Central and Eastern Arctic, *pisirk*) designates songs that express a person's emotions and feelings or recount favorite anecdotes. These are composed either singly or for drum dances. There are also songs to address the spirits, asking for their protection against dangers, illness, or evil. An individual's own magic songs and formulas were used to influence climatic events, such as bad weather or extremely high winds. Shamans get in touch with spirit helpers through their songs, and sometimes their drums, and can thus effect cures or foretell events. Such songs are also part of the Western Arctic drum dance repertoire.

A great number of Inuit games require songs in order to be played properly, including juggling, hide-and-seek, rhymes, riddles, string games, and laughter-seeking games. Also, quite a few games use sounds as the game element, requiring vocal abilities from a player even though these sounds do not qualify as songs. The best known of these games is the Eastern Arctic *katajjaq,* in which two women standing very close to one another, face to face, repeatedly utter some predetermined sound patterns—words, animal cries, or melodic fragments. Their voices, alternating among a variety of vocal qualities—respiration patterns, registers, shape of mouth, voicedness, and voicelessness—follow each other as in Western *contrapuntal* imitation. Because of the rapid breathing, the game requires endurance and quick reflexes on the part of the players, and often the game becomes competitive. Most of the time, however, laughter and fun take precedence over winning or losing. *Katajjaq*-type sounds are also used in a similar game found predominantly in the Central Arctic (but not in the Western Arctic) in which words are part of a series (with narrative intent or not) rather than repeated (figure 3).

Few songs are exclusively reserved for children. However, one children's song (*aqausiq*), typical of the Central and Eastern Arctic, symbolizes the special connection between a child and one or several close-kin adults. Thus, a young child may own several such songs and cherish them throughout his or her life. These songs use diminutive forms of the child's name or words pertaining to realities that warrant close attention. Finally, the widespread tradition of storytelling—myth, legends, or personal anecdotes—also occasionally features songs. Dialogues between human or animal characters, the imitation of animal cries, or the expression of special feelings and forebodings are often expressed in song.

Drum dancing in the Western Arctic

Drum dancing in the Western Arctic is an essential ingredient of annual rituals. Even informal drum dances are often held at the end of festivals or interspersed with more formal events. Many festivals are held in order to please the spirits of animals slain in the past year and to make sure they are satisfied with the hunters who have killed them. Such deference to animal spirits ensures that the species will allow more killing, therefore promising the group's survival for another year. The Bladder Feast among the Yupik and, among the Inupiat, the Whale Feast were the most elaborate and significant.

Another important feast complex concerns the relationship between the living and the souls of deceased relatives. A funeral ritual and a memorial ritual performed several years later are essential to this relationship. These festivals nearly always involve guests from other villages to whom gifts are offered. Potlatching, or gift giving, is elaborately ritualized, as are costuming, the wearing of masks, and feasting. Subjects of songs and their related mimetic dances pertain to the relationship among hosts, guests, and the deceased person (or group of persons) honored by the event.

A group of drummers—as many as are available—sits or stands in a semicircle facing the audience. They sing the songs composed and rehearsed especially for the occasion or chosen from an older repertoire. The dancers, both men and woman, stand in front of them, forming a circle or a double semicircle facing the audience. They do not

FIGURE 3   Eight-year old Inuit girl learning to play *katajjaq* with an older woman. Photo by Nicole Beaudry, Ivujivik, Arctic Québec (Canada), 1978.

sing. In general, the dancers stand in one spot, bouncing lightly, up and down by flexing their knees in time with the drumbeats, with only the arms and upper body performing the expressive movements. Men and women perform identical motions, but men tend to move more vigorously than women. In some men-only dances, for example, they leap and move around more freely but still in synchrony with the drumbeats. Dances and festivals are held in one of the large men's houses (*kasigi*) belonging to the family group hosting the event. Of course, dancing also occurs, especially in summer, when small bands of performers simply want to enjoy themselves (figure 4).

Central and Eastern Arctic drum dance

In the Central and Eastern Arctic drum-dancing tradition a single drum dancer performs, surrounded by close relatives who sing the songs he composed. This usually takes place inside a large snow-house, the *qaggi,* erected especially for the communal feasts, games, and dances that take place when the small nomadic bands gather in one location for a long period of time. The drum dancer performs until he runs out of songs or until he tires playing the heavy drum. He then is replaced by another, then another, and so forth. Thus, being a good drum dancer entails composing interesting songs but also demonstrating strength and endurance. Dance motions, mainly performed with the upper body, are relatively free and adjusted to the swaying of the drum that moves so that its rim meets the stick on one side, then on the opposite side. The drum dancer moves around inside the circle formed by the audience. He dances to songs telling personal stories, freely expressing the emotions engendered in him with body movements and with improvised cries and yells.

A partnership system also exists in this region, usually two men (song cousins) who dance and sing humorously to and about each other. Each man's songs expose the other's idiosyncrasies publicly, making everyone laugh good-naturedly. However, such song competitions might take on a grim meaning when a serious conflict arises between two people or two families. This must be resolved publicly, in a drum dance duel. Songs of ridicule are then carefully prepared, and the singer/dancer who elicits the most laughter from the audience wins his case. In extreme cases, such as murder or theft, the loser might find himself in a life-threatening position if he is forbidden to participate in food-and-work sharing networks essential for survival in the Arctic. The drum dance thus functions in community life at many different levels: as entertainment, as an expression of personal emotions, as an amusing competition, or as a severe form of social sanction.

MUSICAL STYLES

When discussing the Arctic singer's voice qualities, one must distinguish between private and public performances. With the exception of the unusual Eastern Arctic vocal games, context rather than genre determines the vocal style. The soft, gentle voice used in private settings is sometimes transformed for character illustration in a story. However, in the public performances of drum dance, the singers must use a loud, resonant voice to compete with the booming drums. In the Western Arctic, loudness sometimes entails nasality. In the Eastern Arctic, the single drum dancer punctuates the song's words and movements with cries of indeterminate length and pitch, emphasizing his feelings about his song.

The singing is monophonic, with unison or octave doublings when men and women sing together. In several communities of the West Coast of Hudson's Bay (Eastern Arctic), singers sometimes double melodies at the interval of the fifth or fourth. Some scholars believed this to be a rare example of Arctic polyphony, but it is probably best to speak of an expanded form of unison, in which a woman's voice, higher than a man's, sings in perfect parallelism.

The best known of these games is the Eastern Arctic *katajjaq,* in which two women standing very close to one another, face to face, repeatedly utter some predetermined sound patterns—words, animal cries, or melodic fragments.

FIGURE 4   Yupik youngsters—boys kneeling, girls standing—dancing at a gift-giving drum dance given in honor of their coming of age. Notice the handheld dance fans typical of this area. Photo by Nicole Beaudry, Alakanuk, Alaska, 1981.

Song texts

Different genres require different song text styles, of which there are many regional variants. In general, text treatment is syllabic, with the occasional lengthening of a vowel on one or two pitches or on a long sustained tone, softly articulated with glottal pulsations. In many areas, consonants are somewhat softened, especially at the beginnings and ends of songs, thus making some words indistinct. Most of the time, meanings are conveyed through textual symbolism, imagery, and indirect references, using only a few meaningful words at a time. Words are interspersed with vocables, the most typical throughout the Arctic being some variant of the syllables "ai-ya-ya" or "ai-ya-yanga." At times these vocables serve to emphasize feelings or to fill in incomplete thoughts; in addition, they frequently begin and end phrases. They are used so consistently throughout the Arctic that songs typically called *pisirk* (the meaning of which varies from region to region) are often simply called "ai-ya-ya."

Song structures and characteristics

With the exception of a number of through-composed game songs, most Arctic song structures are strophic; that is, one or several melodic phrases are repeated with some melodic variation while the text is modified. Phrase length is determined by the number of words that need to be said, and sections made of one or several phrases are set off by lengthened notes on a single vowel.

The number of pitches and their range varies widely according to genre and area. In general, most songs use six different pitches. Magical songs and story songs use fewer pitches, small ranges, and frequent monotone repetitions, whereas game songs and drum-dance songs use the most pitches and wider ranges, sometimes as much as a tenth or a twelfth. Songs are characterized by numerous textual repetitions, sometimes featuring short two- or three-note melodic-rhythmic motifs (for example, Eastern Arctic game songs, magical songs, *aqausiq*) or four- or five-note melodic motifs whose rhythms derive from the nature of the text (for example, Alaska drum-dance songs). In general, there is no metric regularity because rhythm is determined by word length and accentuation and thus retains a recitative-like style. In the case of drum dances the drums beat a regular pulse of even-spaced single or double beats (the first being slightly shorter than the second). The pulse itself is not differentiated by accents. Interestingly, the natural melodic pulses often do not correspond to the regular drum pulse, with which the movements of the dancers are synchronized. Thus, an Eastern Arctic drum dancer who sings his own songs marks one pulse with his body and his drum and another with his voice. In the Western Arctic, the even-spaced beats are sometimes grouped by leaving one pulse unbeaten at regular intervals. Sometimes these pulse groups are danced to without song (as in the Yupik drum dances) and constitute refrain-type material between song strophes.

HISTORICAL TRANSFORMATIONS OF MUSIC AND CULTURE

Arctic regions were the last of the North American continent to be invaded by non-indigenous people, such as Europeans. Their many subareas sustained the invasion at different times and to different degrees. To generalize, it is convenient to distinguish three stages during which ceremonial and musical traditions were altered and new ones adopted.

Exploration

In the Eastern Arctic, one can trace early Viking explorations from the tenth century; however, we know little of the contacts the newcomers were able to establish with the natives. European exploration in search of a passage to the Orient or for new commercially profitable territories continued sporadically until the early twentieth century. Explorers remained mostly in coastal areas, not yet intending to settle on the North American continent. In the sixteenth, seventeenth, and eighteenth centuries, whalers from Europe's west coast came frequently to the Labrador coast, briefly traveled inland up the Saint Lawrence River, or followed the Arctic coast as far as the Mackenzie Delta in search of whales and of places to transform whale blubber into oil. Western Arctic regions attracted Europeans and Russians from the seventeenth century on.

All of these early visitors made contact with the natives, exchanging food and warm clothing for firearms, tools and utensils, or trinkets. Natives were invited aboard their boats and into their camps, where they witnessed merry singing and fiddling sessions. Some believe these occasions inspired the resourceful Inuit to make their own fiddle, which resulted in a crude imitation of the European violin, made from an irregularly shaped rectangular wooden box on which two or three strings were stretched. A short bow made from a willow branch strung with caribou sinew was used on the open strings, and today's rare recordings mostly feature rhythmic patterns rather than melodic ones. The enduring taste for fiddling and square dancing [see Contra Dance, p. 230] most probably originated from these first encounters and experiences.

European settlement

From the early seventeenth century in the East, the eighteenth century in Alaska, and the early nineteenth century in the interior Northwest, explorations were intensified, especially inland, as Russia, England, and France wanted to consolidate what they considered to be their possessions in the new territories for the purpose of establishing a fur trade economy [see Subarctic Canada, p. 383]. Mining prospectors, trappers, museum collectors, teachers, and missionaries followed explorers, intent on realizing profit or on educating these "poor people." Together, they influenced the northern native lifestyle and traditions, altering them in many important ways. For example, the transformation of the native sustenance economy into a market economy resulted in a new focus on trading posts and the goods available there—new foods, tools, utensils, firearms, and alcohol. Unwilling to relinquish their age-old nomadic lifestyle, the natives were nevertheless forced to adapt to a new yearly traveling cycle. Missionaries, both Roman Catholic and Protestant, did their best to Christianize the natives, condemning native religious ideologies and practices while attempting to educate them in European terms. They also introduced special days (such as Christmas and Easter) into the annual feast cycle. Children spent many months in residential schools, away from their families and normal environment, forced into learning a new language and new customs and sometimes forgetting the old ones.

Permanent settlements

In the mid-twentieth century, most settlements around trading posts officially became villages or communities and school became compulsory, thus transforming nomadic lives into sedentary ones. Family patterns and relationships were modified as women stayed in the settlements with the children who attended school while men went out hunting for limited periods of time. The communities steadily became organized, thus removing the people further and further away from their former lifestyles. The traditional context is still alive in many older people's memories, especially those who have lived the old way of life, but youngsters who have never lived "in the bush" or "out on the land" now focus on a wider world context and have become their own agents of transformation.

Briefly stated then, the move toward permanent settlements, Christianization, and technological transformation are three important factors in the evolution of Arctic native cultural and musical traditions and values. Christian hymn-singing at church or at home, fiddle tunes, also played on accordion, and square dancing all developed in different areas according to the origins of the settlers in the area. Moravian missionaries in Labrador, for example, taught four-part singing and fanfare instruments to the extent that these are now considered true "Eskimo" music, whereas Russian Orthodox harmonies were integrated into Yupik hymn-singing. Hymns and folk songs were translated into each group's language and are now considered to be part of their respective musical traditions. In the Western Arctic, the numerous traditional ceremonies merged into one or two annual festivals. Everywhere in the North, a new calendar of festivities has more or less substituted for the traditional cycles. For example, Christmas and New Year, determined by the Christian calendar, were readily adopted because of their relationship to winter solstice ritual activities. They became times for gift giving, drum dancing, and many communal activities. Other celebrations, such as the Fourth of July in the United States and Dominion Day in Canada, have been made official by each country's authorities.

Changing tastes and contexts

As communities were created, general stores carried more and more items from the south, among which records, cassettes, and now CDs are chosen by the store owners who have helped to fashion native musical tastes. Thus, country music has become one of the most popular styles, closely followed by folk styles and pop and rock styles [see MUSICAL INTERACTIONS, p. 480; COUNTRY AND WESTERN, p. 76; POPULAR MUSIC OF THE PARLOR AND STAGE, p. 179; ROCK, p. 347]. Now northern people travel extensively and bring back musical flavors from elsewhere on the continent and around the world. European American musical instruments such as guitars (acoustic or electric), electric pianos, and drums sets were, and continue to be, readily adopted, along with impressive amplifying and recording paraphernalia. Across the Arctic, local radio and television stations have been important for the promotion of native music and events, at times producing records and videotapes available to the public.

Since the late 1960s, rock groups have sprung up in most communities, and several singers have become popular with their very personal songs telling of their land, their ancestors, and also their difficulties in adapting to these new contexts. One major transformation concerns the traditional approach to musical occasions. In their traditional settings, northern people focused on communal traditions, of which musical expression was a part. Nowadays, aside from the large annual festivals, a musical performance focuses on an individual singer or on a small group of performers. Thus, a musical elite is now defined by its productivity and its popularity in the Arctic.

SCHOLARSHIP

Written sources focusing on Arctic musical traditions date from the beginning of the intensive exploration and settlement of this region (fifteenth century) and extend across the continent. Ships came to the northern coastal areas from several European countries, sending people to investigate the new land's resources, to evaluate its economic potential, and to inventory the fauna, flora, and sometimes the human residents. Thus, early scholarship came to rely on explorers' and ship captains' diaries and on the writings of early observers. Missionaries' journals and registers, as well as fur-trading companies' accounts, also enable us to reconstruct the history of specific areas and traditions.

Important ethnological investigation was carried out throughout the North from the late nineteenth century on, often including lengthy descriptions of feasts and ceremonies as well as observations of the more private magical rituals and shamanic practices. In the Western Arctic, W. Dall (1870), Frank A. Golder (1907), Edward W. Nelson (1983 [1899]), John Murdoch (1892) and L. Zagoskin (Michael 1967), among others, provide invaluable information about the pre-twentieth-century era. Among the wealth of ethnological investigations conducted up to and around the mid-twentieth century, the work of Margaret Lantis (1947), W. Oswalt (1963, 1972), Robert F. Spencer (1959) and J. Van Stone (1964, 1967) are particularly useful. For the Central and Eastern Arctic, the work of Franz Boas (1888) in the late nineteenth century, as well as the exploratory expeditions of Knud Rasmussen in the Canadian Arctic in the early 1920s, provide a solid basis for any study of the Arctic. These last resulted in a series of publications on the Netsilik (1931), the Iglulik (with T. Mathiassen, 1929), the Caribou (1930), and (with K. Birket-Smith) the Copper Eskimos (1932). Later ethnographers such as David Damas and John Honigmann, among others, provide the essential backdrop to musical events.

Ethnomusicological research in the Arctic has blossomed since the mid-twentieth century. Before that, research had been scattered and sporadic. In Alaska, the numerous publications of Thomas F. Johnston (1975, 1976a, 1976b) in several regions of Alaska attest to the tirelessness of this field-worker. Lorraine D. Koranda (1964, 1972, 1980) and M. Stryker (1966) have both published extensive recordings. Koranda's publications also make a valuable contribution to the study of Inupiat and Yupik music. Diamond Jenness's report on the 1913–1918 Canadian Arctic expedition (1922) included a volume on the songs of the Copper Eskimos (written with Helen Roberts). A small number of early-twentieth-century recordings made by Comer, Jenness, Leden and those of Laura Boulton (Caribou and Alaska, 1954) in the mid-twentieth century, encouraged subsequent research on regional and historical differences. Since then, numerous recordings, published and unpublished, bear witness to the recognition of the importance of Inuit music making by ethnographers and ethnomusicologists alike. Issues such as culture change, acculturation, expression through text, song, game, and dance have been given careful consideration in the works of Nicole Beaudry (1978, 1984, 1986), Beverley Cavanagh (1982), Patricia Dewar (1990), Maija Lutz (1978), Jean-Jacques Nattiez and his research team (1980, 1988, 1989, 1993), Ramon Pelinski et al. (1979), and Paula Thistle (1992). Today, research is very effectively carried out by, or in collaboration with, native cultural centers and researchers.

REFERENCES

Beaudry, Nicole. 1978. "Le katajjaq: Un jeu inuit traditionnel." Études/Inuit/Studies 2(1):35–53.

———. 1984. Inuit Traditional Songs and Games. Canadian Broadcasting Corporation, Northern Québec Service. SQN 108. LP disk.

———. 1986. "La danse à tambour des Esquimaux yupik du sud-ouest de l'Alaska: performance et contexte." Ph.D. dissertation, Université de Montréal.

Beaudry, Nicole, Claude-Yves Charron and Denise Harvey. 1976. Inuit Games and Songs. Auvidis D8032 (LP), Unesco Collection. AD 090.

Béclart d'Harcourt, Marguerite. 1928. "Le Système pentaphone dans les chants des Copper Eskimos." Proceedings of the 22nd Session of the International Congress of Americanists 2:15–23.

Birket-Smith, Kaj. 1929. "The Caribou Eskimo: Material and Social Life." Report of the Fifth Thule Expedition (1921–1924, vol. 5, parts 1 and 2). Copenhagen: Gyldendalske Boghandel.

Boas, Franz. 1888. The Central Eskimo. Sixth Annual Report of the Bureau of American Ethnology. Washington: Smithsonian Institution.

Boulton, Laura. 1954. The Eskimos of Hudson Bay and Alaska. Folkways Records FE 4444. LP disk.

Bours, Etienne. 1991. *Musiques des peuples de l'Arctique: analyse discographique.* Belgique: Médiathèque de la communauté Française de Belgique.

Cavanagh, Beverley. 1982. *Music of the Netsilik Eskimo: A Study of Stability and Change.* 2 vols. Mercury Series 82. Ottawa: National Museum of Man. Record included. LP disk.

Dall, William H. 1870. *Alaska and Its Resources.* Boston: Lee and Shepard. Reprint, New York: Amo Press, 1970.

Dewar, Patricia. 1990. "A Historical and Interpretive Study of Inuit Drum-Dance in the Canadian Central Arctic: The Meaning Expressed in Dance, Culture and Performance." Ph.D. dissertation, University of Alberta.

Estreicher, Zygmunt. 1948a. "La musique des Esquimaux-Caribous." *Bulletin de La Société châteloise de géographie* 5(1):1–54.

———. 1948b. "La polyphonie chez les Esquimaux." *Journal de la Société des Américanistes de Paris* 37:259–268.

Fienup-Riordan, Ann. 1983. *The Nelson Island Eskimo: Social Structure and Ritual Distribution.* Anchorage: Alaska Pacific University Press.

Fulcomer, Ann. 1898. "An Eskimo 'Kashim'." *American Anthropologist* 11:55–58.

Golder, Frank A. 1907. "Songs and Stories of the Aleuts with Transcriptions from Veniaminov." *Journal of American Folklore* 20:132–142.

Hawkes, Ernest W. 1913. *The Inviting-In Feast of the Alaskan Eskimo.* Anthropological Series 3, Memoir 45. Ottawa: Canadian Geological Survey.

———. 1914. *The Dance Festivals of the Alaskan Eskimos.* University of Pennsylvania Anthropological Publications 6(2):1–41.

Honigmann, John J. 1962. *Social Networks in Great Whah River: Notes on an Eskimo, Montagnais-Naskapi and Euro-Canadian Community.* Anthropological Series No. 54. Ottawa: National Museum of Canada Bulletin.

Jenness, Diamond, with Helen Roberts. 1922. "The Life of the Copper Eskimos." In *Report of the Canadian Arctic Expedition, 1913–1918,* vol.12, part A. Ottawa: F. A. Acland.

Johnston, Thomas F. 1975. "Eskimo Music of the Northern Interior Alaska." *Polar Notes* 14:54–57.

———. 1976a. *Eskimo Music, a Comparative Circumpolar Study.* Mercury Series 32. Ottawa: National Museum of Man.

———. 1976b. "The Eskimo Songs of Northwestern Alaska." *Arctic* 29(1):7–19.

Koranda, Lorraine. 1964. "Some Traditional Songs of the Alaskan Eskimos." *Alaska University Anthropological Papers* 12:17–32.

———. 1972. *Alaskan Eskimo Songs and Stories.* Seattle: University of Washington Press.

———. 1980. "Music of the Alaskan Eskimos." In *Musics of Many Cultures,* ed. Elizabeth May, 332–362. Berkeley: University of California Press.

Lantis, Margaret. 1947. *Alaskan Eskimo Ceremonialism.* Monograph 11. Seattle: American Ethnological Society.

Le Mouël, J. F., and M. Le Mouël. n.d. *Music of the Inuit. The Copper Eskimo Tradition.* Unesco Collection, Musical Atlas. EMI-Odon 64-2402781. LP disk.

Lutz, Maija. 1978. *The Effects of Acculturation on Eskimo Music of Cumberland Sound Peninsula.* Mercury Series 41. Ottawa: National Museum of Man. Record included.

———. 1982. *Musical Traditions of the Labrador Coast Inuit.* Mercury Series 79. Ottawa: National Museum of Man.

Michael, Henry, N. 1967. *Lieutenant Zagoskin's Travels in Russian America, 1842–1844.* Arctic Institute of North America, Anthropology of the North, Translations from Russian Sources 7. Toronto: University of Toronto Press.

Morrow, Phyllis. 1984. "It Is Time for Drumming: A Summary of Recent Research on Yupik Ceremonialism." *Études/Inuit/Studies* 2:113–139.

Murdoch, John. 1892. *The Ethnological Results of the Point Barrow Expedition.* Report of the Bureau of American Ethnology 11. Washington, D.C.: Smithsonian Institution.

Nattiez, Jean-Jacques. 1980. "Le disque de musique amérindienne: introduction à l'écoute des disques de musique inuit." *Recherches amérindiennes au Québec* 10(2):110–122.

———. 1988. "La danse à tambour chez les Inuit igloolik (Nord de la Terre de Baffin)." *Recherches amérindiennes au Québec* 18(4):37–48.

———. 1989. *Jeux vocaux des Inuit (Inuit du Caribou, Netsilik et Igloolik).* Ocora. CD HM83.

———. 1993. *Inuit Iglulik.* Museum Collection Berlin CD 19. Compact disc.

Nelson, Edward W. 1983 [1899]. *The Eskimo about Bering Strait.* Report of the American Bureau of Ethnology 18, part 1. Washington, D.C.: Smithsonian Institution Press.

Oswalt, W. 1963. *Napaskiak, an Alaskan Eskimo Community.* Tucson: Univ. of Arizona Press.

———. 1972. "The Eskimos of Western Alaska." In *Alaskan Native Material Culture,* ed. W. Oswalt. Fairbanks University of Alaska Museum: 73–95.

Pelinski, Ramon, et al. 1979. *Inuit Songs from Eskimo Point.* Mercury Series 60. Ottawa: National Museum of Man. Record included. LP disk.

Rasmussen, Knud. 1930. "The Intellectual Culture of the Caribou Eskimos." In *Report of the Fifth Thule Expedition, 1921–1924,* vol. 7, part 2. Copenhagen: Gyldendalske Boghandel.

———. 1931. "The Netsilik Eskimos: Social Life and Spiritual Culture." In *Report of the Fifth Thule Expedition, 1921–1924,* vol. 8. Copenhagen: Gyldendalske Boghandel.

Rasmussen, Knud, and T. Mathiassen. 1929. "The Intellectual Culture of the Iglulik Eskimos." In *Report of the Fifth Thule Expedition, 1921–1924,* vol. 7, part 1. Copenhagen: Gyldendalske Boghandel.

Rasmussen, Knud, and K. Birket-Smith. 1932. "The Copper Eskimos." *In Report of the Fifth Thule Expedition, 1921–1924,* vol. 9, part 2. Copenhagen: Gyldendalske Boghandel.

Ray, Dorothy Jean. 1975. *Eskimo Masks, Art and Ceremony.* Vancouver: J. J. Douglas Ltd.

Roberts, Helen, and Diamond Jenness. 1925. "Songs of the Copper Eskimos." In *Report of the Canadian Arctic Expedition, 1913–1918,* vol. 14. Ottawa: F. A. Ackland.

Ross, W. Gillies. 1984. "The Earliest Sound Recordings among the North American Inuit." *Arctic* 37(3):291–292.

Spencer, Robert F. 1959. *The North Alaskan Eskimo, a Study on Ecology and Society.* Bureau of American Ethnology Bulletin 171. Washington, D.C.: Smithsonian Institution.

Sryker, Miriam. 1966. *Eskimo Songs from Alaska.* Record FE 4069 and booklet. New York: Folkways.

Sturtevant, William C., and David Damas, eds. 1984. *Handbook of North American Indians,* vol. 5: *Arctic.* Washington, D.C.: Smithsonian Institution.

Suluk, Donald. 1983. "Some Thoughts on Traditional Inuit Music." *Inuktitut* 54:24–30.

Suluk, Donald, and Alice Suluk. n.d. *Inuit Songs and Dances.* Canadian Broadcasting Corporation, Northern Québec Services. Cassette.

Thistle, Paula. 1992. "Drum Dance Songs of the Iglulik Inuit and the Northern Baffin Island Area." Ph.D. dissertation, Université de Montréal.

Van Stone, James. 1964. "Some Aspects of Religious Change among Native Inhabitants of West Alaska of the Northwest Territories." *Arctic Anthropology* 2(2):21–24.

———. 1967. *Eskimos of the Nushagak River, an Ethnographic History.* Seattle: University of Washington Press.

Victor-Howe, Anne-Marie. 1994. "Songs and Dances of the St. Lawrence Island Eskimos." *Études/Inuit/Studies* 18(1–2):173–182.

Subarctic Canada
Nicole Beaudry

Like the Arctic, Subarctic regions range across the North American continent, except for some portions of the Pacific coastal areas occupied by the Northwest Coast populations. The most widely accepted boundary between the Arctic and the Subarctic is the "tree line," a more or less well-defined line weaving north and south of the Arctic Circle indicating the zone where tree growth becomes significant. As one moves south from the sparsely forested zone featuring mostly black spruce, tree growth increases to include other conifers, birch, poplar, and willow. Thus, Subarctic populations inhabit a large forested territory south of and contiguous to the Arctic [see ARCTIC CANADA AND ALASKA, p, 374].

CULTURE OF THE SUBARCTIC

Subarctic regions host two major linguistic families, the North Athapaskan and the Algonquian, each of which is subdivided into numerous tribal entities speaking mutually unintelligible languages and identified by distinctive cultural traits. Although there is a remarkable diversity of ecocultural classifications possible, the musical traditions discussed here will relate solely to these two large linguistic families.

The Subarctic Athapaskan population is historically linked with Athapaskans in the southwestern United States. However, for thousands of years their paths have diverged, and North and South Athapaskans have developed separately. The North Athapaskan family features an east-west split generally marked by the Rocky Mountains and the Mackenzie River, which also includes a mountainous plateau area called the Cordillera. The recent political boundary between Canada and the United States further enhances the separation between Alaskan natives and those who inhabit Canada's Yukon and Northwest Territories, northern British Columbia, and Alberta. Tribal groups are too numerous to list (Sturtevant and Helm 1981).

The northern branch of the Algonquian family is dispersed across vast territories west of Hudson's Bay and east of James Bay into the provinces of Ontario, Québec, and Labrador. The northernmost areas are inhabited by the Cree and Montagnais or Innu peoples (including the Naskapi), as well as the Attikamek, Algonquin, and Northern Ojibwa just north of the Saint Lawrence Valley.

Relationship to other culture areas

The Barrens, a treeless no-man's land used sporadically by Arctic populations, serves the Subarctic peoples more consistently as they follow the migrating caribou herds. Many Native as well as non-Native stories document the existence of conflicts between Inuit and Indians in this zone. Northwest Athapaskans have also entertained relationships with non-Athapaskan groups west of the Rockies. Thus, several common traits are shared among certain gift-giving ceremonies (potlatch feasts) of the Northwest Coast tribes, the Northwestern Athapaskans (both Alaskan and Canadian), and the Southwestern Arctic Yupik, whereas the ceremonial traditions east of the Rockies differ considerably. The Northeastern Athapaskans have sustained contacts, both hostile and friendly, mainly with (Algonquian) Cree and with Northern Plains groups [see PLAINS, p. 440].

In the southeastern section of the Subarctic, Algonquian groups are contiguous with other members of the Algonquian family (southern branch) who are not considered Subarctic peoples. Rather, they are usually included with the tribes that live in the Eastern Woodlands, Great Lakes, or Plains regions.

Subsistence patterns and other aspects of precontact society

Subarctic peoples were traditionally nomadic, although their travels were only marginally determined by the migrating caribou herds. Instead, small hunting bands traveled within relatively well-defined territories, fishing and hunting along the numerous lakes and rivers. The size of groups varied according to each tribe's yearly cycle, and their rituals alternated between individual or intimate small group rituals and celebrations by large gatherings during feasts and ceremonies.

Although only the northernmost Subarctic inhabitants relied on caribou for food, clothing, and lodging, all the Subarctic populations had access to the same animals: moose, bear, beaver, muskrat, and many other small mammals, as well as an abundance of waterfowl and fish species. The recent shift from hunting animals for subsistence to hunting them for their fur emphasizes the development of a European-based fur-trading economy.

MUSICAL PERFORMANCE

As in the Arctic, music making relies mostly on the voice and the drum. However, drumming practice is more pervasive within Subarctic regions.

Drums and other sound producers

The principle of the single-membrane frame drum is common to all Subarctic tribes, although size, inscribed designs, decorations, and performance practice vary according to region (figure 1). For example, Algonquian frame drums can have two membranes tied to either side of the same frame. Smaller in size than most of the Arctic frame drums, Subarctic drums also differ by their lack of a handle. The player holds the cross-lacing knotted at the back (figure 2) with one hand and with the other beats the drum with a thin stick. The somewhat larger and heavier Innu (Algonquian) drum is often suspended from one of the lodge's frame poles during a performance.

Another feature of Subarctic drums is the nearly constant presence of snare strings. Athapaskan drums use from one to three (rarely four) snare strings across the top of the drum. Sometimes a snare string is also placed on the drum's underside. Moreover, on most Algonquian drums and on some Athapaskan drums (although rarely), a number of small bird bones or porcupine quills are attached to the snares, which increases the buzzing sound produced when the drum is beaten. Painted designs on the skins, decoration of the frame, or the addition of colored ribbons are left to the taste and private symbolism of drummers who own their drums. Drums belonging to the community remain anonymous.

FIGURE I   Drawing illustrating Arctic and Subarctic drumming performance techniques. Illustration by François Girard. *Top left:* In the Western Arctic Inupiat groups of drummers, usually seated, hit their drums from below, either the rim with the stick, or the center of the membrane in order to produce different timbres and volumes. They are singing for dancers in front of them. *Top right:* In the Western Arctic Yupik groups of drummers, usually seated, hit their drums from above, always in the center of the membrane. They are singing for the dancers in front of them. *Center:* In the Central and Eastern Arctic, the single Inuit drummer rotates his (usually) large drum so that his sticks alternately hits one, then the other underside rim. He dances as he is drumming to a song sung by a group of singers seated around him. *Bottom left:* The Subarctic Athapaskan groups of drummers, usually standing, use their handheld drums while singing for the dancers. They hit the middle of the membrane with a small stick, setting off the buzzing snare strings strung across the top. *Bottom right:* A single Subarctic Algonquian drummer, usually seated, uses his drum in private song communication with his spirits. His drum hangs from the structure of the tent; it is immobilized with one hand while the other, holding a stick, hits the middle of the membrane on the top side. The buzzing of the snare string(s) is enhanced by attaching small bones or porcupine quills. More rarely, drumming with the same technique is used for group celebrations.

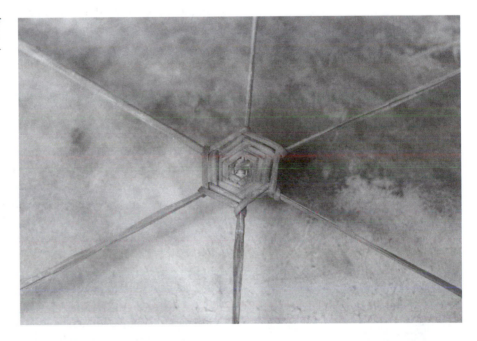

FIGURE 2   Detail of knotted lacing at the back of an Athapaskan frame drum made in 1988. Photo by Nicole Beaudry, Fort Franklin, Northwest Territories (Canada), 1989.

Painted designs on the skins, decoration of the frame, or the addition of colored ribbons are left to the taste and private symbolism of drummers who own their drums.

Rattles as well as buzzers, bull-roarers, whistles, and sticks were also traditionally used throughout the Subarctic, but information remains scanty regarding their probable former use in ceremonial contexts. For some time now, they have functioned mostly as children's toys. Some of these noisemakers may have once served as substitutes for the drum (for example, the two sticks used in the West Athapaskan Feast for the Dead). These were used for ritual reasons or when no drum was available.

SONGS AND SINGING IN THE SUBARCTIC

In the Subarctic the expression *personal songs* refers to songs expressing strong feelings of joy, sadness, wistfulness, or longing. In English, these songs have been glossed as love songs, happy songs, mourning songs, and pleasure songs. Among the Athapaskans, only a listener who knows the singer well truly understands his song, because the actual texts hardly ever refer directly to feelings. It is the singer who chooses whether or not to explain the meaning of the song after singing it.

Dream-songs

Dream-songs (for example, guardian-spirit songs, animal songs, hunting songs) emanate from dreams or visions that occur at any time during a person's adult life. They come from one's guardian-spirit(s) who can be called upon in times of need such as famine, illness, bad weather, or when one has lost his way. These very private songs cannot be made public or used without sufficient reason lest they lose their potency. In theory, Athapaskans do not usually sound the drum with these songs, but several cases of private drumming have been reported. Northern Algonquian dream-songs are mainly related to hunting. Once a hunter acquires one or several songs, he then uses them to envision the animals (mostly moose or caribou) he wishes to kill. The hunter sings with his drum close to his face. The buzzing sound (caused by snare strings and attachments) creates the proper conversational atmosphere required by the relationship with the singer's guardian-spirit. Thus, the drum constitutes a powerful tool, essential to hunting preparations, to be handled cautiously and respectfully. Texts of such songs are in general indecipherable to outside listeners.

Northern Algonquian dream-songs are also used in other divinatory contexts, such as the shaking tent (or conjuring tent) ceremony, during which one or several men known for their ability to see beyond the ordinary world enter a small tent and use their songs to call the spirits, who signal their presence and power by producing weird noises and by shaking and rocking the tent, sometimes throwing it to the ground.

Lullabies, storytelling, and gaming songs

Most Subarctic tribes also sing or hum to their babies. These lullabies, or crooning songs, are often simple formulas passed on through generations of mothers, who also improvise new songs and soothing sounds as the need arises. Storytelling is also very important, either for recounting imaginary or real-life events and anecdotes or for recounting myths. All kinds of stories include songs or specific intonations. The Atha-

FIGURE 3   Athapaskan men singing their team song at the beginning of the gambling game (*udzi*). They are mockingly imitating the gestures of the other team's captain who is trying to guess which of each man's hands hides a token. No one has yet been eliminated and the drums remain silent. Photo by Nicole Beaudry, Fort Norman, Northwest Territories (Canada), 1989.

paskans, for example, favor the many humorous anecdotes of the trickster cycle, in which Raven often sings and talks loudly or makes awful noises. Story characters may sing of sadness or fear or tell of unexpectedly hearing a mysterious voice singing in a tree or near a river. Story songs are usually short and consist mostly of one or two repeated words and vocables.

The Northern Algonquian have no games that require songs. This is notably different from the Arctic context, where so many games feature songs or require vocal ability. Nearly all Northern Athapaskans play a unique guessing-gambling game that includes singing and drumming. Eastern Athapaskans start their game of *udzi* by having two teams challenge each other with songs. Much laughter and teasing goes on during this preparatory phase (figure 3). Later, while guessing is taking place, eliminated guessed-out players stand behind the remaining members of their team and begin to drum loudly while vocalizing an indefinite vocable on one or two tones. Loud and intense drumming is meant to support teammates and perhaps to distract opponents (figure 4).

FIGURE 4   Athapaskan men playing the game *udzi*. One team's captain indicates his guesses with gestures while the other team's men still hide their tokens in their closed fists. Behind them, loud drumming and vocalizing by those who have just been "guessed-out" enhances the atmosphere of excitement and intense concentration. Photo by Nicole Beaudry, Fort Norman, Northwest Territories (Canada), 1989.

DRUM DANCING

There are numerous forms and occasions for drum dancing throughout the Subarctic. Some are linked exclusively with geographic areas, such as the Western Athapaskan potlatch, the Eastern Athapaskan drum dance and tea dance, and the Northeastern Algonquian feast dance.

The Western Athapaskan potlatch ceremony

West Athapaskan communities hold potlatch-type ceremonies akin to Northwest Coast potlatching. Feasting and gift giving, as well as costuming, singing, and drum dancing, are the principal activities at these ceremonies. Several reasons justify hosting a potlatch, such as marking a child's first game killing, to celebrate someone's return to health, or in atonement for a bad action. In the most important ceremony, the living honor and complete their obligations toward a deceased relative. Variously referred to as the Feast for the Dead, the Stick Dance, or *Hi'o,* depending on group or region, this ceremony lasts several days, during which several forms of music-making occur.

Despite numerous regional variations, certain basic principles of potlatch ceremonies can be stated. The Interior Alaska tribes, for example, open festivities with a potlatch song (or lucky song) without dance or drum. They then sing sorry songs, mourning songs especially composed for the deceased person being honored. For several hours, women relatives of the deceased form a half circle and move sunwise (clockwise), using small side steps while slowly swinging their arms in an arc in front of them. This dance might be accompanied by sticks rhythmically clapped together. The slow tempo and the brief sung sentences repeated in a near-sobbing voice resemble the wailing heard at funerals.

Once the mourning is over, guests are fed and offered gifts (clothing and various goods) that are sometimes danced around before being handed over. After the meal more energetic dances in a variety of styles are accompanied by one or several drums. The dances might enact certain gestures of characters or animals mentioned in the song text or stylize the meaning of the song. All those present may join in the multilayered circle in which men generally dance closer to the center. Everyone sings, but dancing in two opposing lines is rare. This might be a remnant from a very old, and not well documented, tradition of war dancing, or it might imitate Scottish immigrants' dances. In the Stick Dance, a pole that was brought in at the beginning of festivities is taken out after several days, danced around the village, and finally broken and thrown into the river.

The Eastern Athapaskan drum dance and tea dance

The Eastern Athapaskans have a tradition of dancing in a sunwise circle to the even-pulsed rhythm of several drums. Drum beats are single or double. Drum-dance songs come from prophets, people who have been visited in dreams or visions by celestial beings who gave them messages and songs to be transmitted to their communities. Drum-dance songs are of two kinds: prayer songs, with drumming but no dancing, and the dance songs proper, in which everyone might join the circle at any time. Drum dances are held for a number of reasons, such as weddings, funerals, chief investitures, and the arrival of special guests.

Also typical of the Eastern Athapaskan groups is the tea dance, a sunwise circle dance in which the beat is marked not by drums but by the feet of the dancers stomping hard on the ground. The dancers move slowly around the circle, standing sideways and facing the center. Early tea dances were held in the open, at times of large group gatherings, especially in spring when the group reassembled for the caribou hunt. The relatively recent custom of tea drinking while feasting may explain the English designation. Songs for the tea dance are utterly different from drum-dance songs. Frequently they are composed on the spur of the moment as a form of teasing between people who have not seen each other for a long time.

Northern Algonquian feast dance

Northern Algonquian drumming is mainly related to hunting preparations and divination. However, in the nomadic past, after a successful hunt or during the summer when small bands congregated near the coast, feasts (*makushan*) were held to celebrate weddings, successful hunts, or other happy occasions. At the end of such feasts, one man would start singing and drumming, and soon others would start dancing, moving forward in a sunwise circle with a small shuffling step. The first singer eventually would be replaced by another.

VOCAL QUALITY OF SUBARCTIC SINGING

Subarctic vocal quality is somewhat determined by performance context. Private, intimate circumstances call for a soft, gentle voice. However, the Athapaskan drum dance and gambling games require that the men sing in a loud, nasal, and tense voice. As songs often begin in the singers' upper range, the men must revert to a near-falsetto voice, thus switching back and forth between near-falsetto and near-normal voices. Singing is monophonic and in unison, with some octave doubling differentiating men's and women's voices. The long sustained tones of phrase endings are characterized by strong glottal pulsations, which in their extreme form (such as in the mourning potlatch songs of the West Athapaskans) resemble sobbing.

MUSICAL STYLES

Song texts and structures

Although only a handful of Subarctic song texts are available, some generalizations arise from field-workers' reports. Most Athapaskan song texts are strophic, containing one word or, more rarely, two or three words. To understand the meaning of a song, a listener must be familiar with the particular context of the singer. Words are treated syllabically, and musical phrases begin and end with vocables, most frequently *heye, heya, hinna,* and so on, or a combination of these. Vocables often merge with word endings, thus lengthening the word in a manner that sometimes makes it difficult to understand.

Northern Algonquian hunting songs use brief phrases repeated several times rather than isolated words. Words are not meant to be understood. Rather, they are part of the intimate act of addressing the singer's spiritual helper. Thus, they are pronounced with minimal consonant sounds, and the singer's voice is projected inward, somewhat buried beneath the sound of the drum and its buzzing snares. Text treatment appears to be mostly syllabic (one note to a syllable), but it is difficult to distinguish whether or not melisma-like syllables (many notes to one syllable) result from the vocalization of consonants. Spoken words often interrupt the melodic flow, providing explanations about the meaning of the song without revealing individual song words.

Most Athapaskan songs are strophic: although words may change, melodies tend to be repeated quite strictly, with adjustments to rhythm and accent when a word change results in the addition of a number of syllables. A true refrain, separate from the strophe, is rare, but because strophe endings are uniform (numerous repetitions of vocables on a focus tone), phrase endings can be considered as refrain-type sections. The concept of strophic is further highlighted in Northern Algonquian songs, in which short phrases containing several words, rarely vocables, are repeated over and over with near exactness.

Tonal organization

Eastern Athapaskan songs present a variety of tonal organizations. For instance, personal feeling songs feature the most variable melodic contour and much disjunct motion; drum-dance songs follow a general pattern of an upward leap (a fifth, sixth, or

As songs often begin in the singers' upper range, the men must revert to a near-falsetto voice, thus switching back and forth between near-falsetto and near-normal voices. Singing is monophonic and in unison, with some octave doubling differentiating men's and women's voices.

octave) and a gradual descent to a starting tone, outlining a triad. Tea dance songs and *udzi* game songs have a more restricted range, usually within a fourth or a fifth, and play with the two notes outlining a third. Stories featuring private animal spirit songs tend to be sung in a rapid monotone or in two-tone word repetitions. Recent recordings allow us to hear firm pitches, although a certain amount of ornamentation is frequent. However, it is difficult to assess whether this is a truly ancient manner of singing or whether in this region westernized music education has fostered such a singing style.

In contrast, the Northern Algonquian singing style features much more fluidity from one tone to another. Slurring and sliding are frequent, as well as attacks that accentuate the strong beat note. Northern Algonquian songs use a much smaller range than Athapaskan songs, most often falling within a third or a fourth. Melodic patterns are repeated, but numerous tonal and microtonal variations are possible. Word length determines rhythmic groupings, but the blurring of consonants may also blur the exact articulation of the notes.

HISTORICAL TRANSFORMATIONS

Exploration, European settlement, and permanent settlements

Most of what has been said about the Arctic regions concerning the Europeans' development of land-based ownership to increase their power and to further their economies is also true of the Subarctic regions. Thus, exploration and, later, settlement, brought a contingent of travelers, adventurers, missionaries, and merchants who were an important factor in change, affecting the yearly cycle of traveling and the gathering patterns of these traditionally nomadic people, who increasingly gravitated around the trading post and mission and the material and spiritual wares these centers offered. The process of creating permanent settlements was more or less completed by the end of the 1950s, when schools in the villages allowed children to remain in their own villages instead of going far away to residential schools. Family disruptions were caused in part by demands on hunters to travel away from the settlements for trapping while the rest of the family remained in the community, tied to a school calendar unrelated to native lifestyles and seasonal needs.

In the Eastern Subarctic, systematic exploration started around the end of the fifteenth century, from the coastal areas along the Atlantic or on the north shore of the Gulf of Saint Lawrence, very slowly reaching inland. Early on, Jesuit missionaries and others traveled to remote areas north of the Saint Lawrence River and along the coast of the Labrador Peninsula to live with and Christianize Indian bands. They were well established and influential throughout the seventeenth, eighteenth, and nineteenth centuries. However, the Northern Algonquian peoples were most affected by the missionaries (then mostly Anglican) from the mid-nineteenth century on (figure 5).

Athapaskan peoples west of the Rockies had been able to obtain trade goods through exchange with the neighboring West Coast peoples before being the subject of explorations. East of the Rockies, the Mackenzie River became the main north–south

travel route of voyagers and merchants from the eighteenth century. In all Athapaskan regions, inland exploration did not intensify much before the middle of the nineteenth century. Newcomers then included mining prospectors and gold miners, nonnative trappers, and collectors for museums. Roman Catholic (Oblate) and Church of England missionaries and eventually those from other Protestant denominations competed in the race to conquer "lost" souls. As in the Arctic, people adopted several new festive periods in the year such as Christmas, New Year, and Easter, July first (in Canada) and fourth (in Alaska), and, for East Athapaskans, a Treaty Day that became the occasion for a large intertribal annual summer gathering.

Changing tastes and contexts

Some studies show how missionaries have relied heavily on the teaching of hymns to attract native peoples to their religion by systematically translating the words into native languages. Thus, Christian hymn-singing became a part of native life and remains important until today.

Among the Athapaskans, the appearance of prophets around the end of the nineteenth century shows that some of the missionaries' teachings were integrated into native cultures, creating a religious synthesis of traditional native beliefs and Christian ideologies. These dreamers or visionaries became influential through their own teachings by encouraging people (especially Eastern Athapaskans) to dance to songs sent from "Heaven," accompanied by drums.

Voyagers and trading post agents left their legacy in the form of French and Scottish fiddling (or accordion-playing) and square-dancing traditions. In most Subarctic groups, these seem to coexist happily with native forms of music making, whereas some groups, such as the Athapaskan Gwich'in, have totally replaced drum dancing with square dancing and have set aside, if not forgotten, most of their original musical traditions.

As in the Arctic, country music, folk styles, blues, and rock music are influenced by availability in the stores, through the media, and through people's love of travel and exchange. Modern instruments and sound paraphernalia are available to youngsters, many of whom belong to bands that perform locally but also attend many types of festivals and gatherings. Singers' words focus mainly on their love of the land or express personal feelings, including difficulties associated with the definition of their modern identity.

SCHOLARSHIP

Early written sources focusing on musical traditions in the Subarctic regions are few. Some of the explorers who came mostly to investigate land resources and potential were curious enough about the inhabitants to record what they saw, but not much was written about music. Traders' and missionaries' journals also contain information, although in the case of the latter, one must at times deduce the meanings behind their indignant commentaries. Genuine interest for musical traditions developed at such a late date that, until this present article, no clear delimitation of a musical area was ever made.

In the East, the Jesuit Relations (1611–1672) constitute an invaluable document, and some passages of the diaries of Jacques Cartier, Champlain, and others describe natives encountered on the north shore of the Gulf of Saint Lawrence. From the end of the nineteenth century to the mid-twentieth century, early ethnographers such as John M. Cooper (1944), Regina Flannery (1936), and I. Hallowell (1926, 1942), Frank G. Speck (1977 [1935]), Lucien Turner (1894), among others addressed the otherwise little known matters of religion, magic, and recreation. These issues were more carefully researched by later scholars such as Richard Preston (1975), R. Savard (1971), Adrian Tanner (1979), and Sylvie Vincent (1982). True ethnomusicology never thrived in this area, although important research was accomplished by Beverley Diamond among the Innu (1994) and Lynn Whidden (1985, 1986) among the Cree.

For the Athapaskans, Alexander Mackenzie, Samuel Hearne, and John Franklin in the late eighteenth and early nineteenth centuries provide invaluable insights on native customs. Except for the writings of Émile Petitot, O.M.I. (1876), a late-nineteenth-century missionary, linguist, and ethnographer, interesting observations and ethnological studies only began in the early twentieth century, although until the 1970s they remained widely scattered and limited in scope. Some of the first recordings on wax cylinder of a variety of songs were collected in 1914 in the Subarctic by Alden Mason (1946), who lived among the Slavey in the 1910s. Since World War II an explosion of ethnological research has provided essential source material for ethnmusicological studies, especially about religious practices, social and political organization, and kinship systems. Important authors include M. Asch (Slavey, 1988), J.-G. Goulet (South Slavey, 1981, 1998), Marie-Françoise Guédon (1974), June Helm (Dogrib, 1981) and Robert McKennan (Upper Tanana, 1959), Cornelius Osgood (North Slavey, 1932; Kutchin, 1936; Tanaina, 1937; Ingalik, 1958; Han, 1971), Robin Ridington (Beaver, 1971), R. Slobodin (Kutchin, 1975), and David Merrill Smith (Chippewyan, 1973). Ethnomusicological studies began to appear from the end of the 1970s, first with the doctoral work of Michael Asch and with the numerous publications by Thomas Johnston (Koyukon and other West Athapaskans, 1978 and n.d.). More recently, the work of Nicole Beaudry (North Slavey, 1992), Elaine Keillor (Dogrib, 1985), and Craig Mischler (Kutchin, 1974), continues to unfold.

REFERENCES

Asch, Michael. 1988. *Kinship and the Drum Dance in a Northern Community*. Edmonton: The Boreal Institute for Northern Studies.

Beaudry, Nicole. 1992. "The Language of Dreams: Songs of the Dene Indians (Canada)." *The World of Music* 34(2):72–90.

Caroll, Ginger. 1972. "Stick Dance." *Alaska Journal* 2(2):28–33.

Cavanagh, B. 1985. "Les mythes et la musique naskapis." *Recherches amérindiennes au Québec* 15(4):5–18.

Clark, Annette McFadyen. 1970. "Koyukon Athapaskan Ceremonialism." *Western Canadian Journal of Anthropology* 2(1):80–88.

Cooper, John M. 1944. "The Shaking Tent Rite among Plains and Forest Algonquians." *Primitive Man* 17(3–4):60–84.

Cronk, Sam M., et al. 1988. "Celebration: Native Events in Eastern Canada." *Folklife Annual* 1987: 70–85.

Diamond Cavanagh, Beverley. 1989. "Music and Gender in the Sub-Arctic Algonkian Area." In

Women in North American Indian Music: Six Essays, ed. Richard Keeling, 55–66. SEM Special Series, No. 6. Bloomington, Ind.: Society for Ethnomusicology.

Diamond, Beverley, et al. 1994. *Visions of Sound: Musical Instruments of First Nations Communities in Northeast America.* Chicago: University of Chicago Press.

Flannery, Regina. 1936. "Some Aspects of James Bay Recreative Culture." *Primitive Man* 9(4):49–56.

Goulet, Jean-Guy. 1981. "Religious Dualism among Athapaskan Catholics." *Revue canadienne d'anthropologie* 3(1):1–18.

———. 1998. *Ways of Knowing—Experience, Knowledge and Power Among the Dene Tha.* Vancouver: University of British Columbia Press.

Guédon, Marie-Françoise. 1974. *People of Tetlin, Why Are You Singing?* Mercury Series 9. Ottawa: National Museum of Man.

Hallowell, Irving A. 1926. "Bear Ceremonialism in the Northern Hemisphere." *American Anthropologist* 28:1–175.

———. 1942. *The Role of Conjuring in Saulteaux Society.* Philadelphia: Publication of the Philadelphia Anthropological Society 2 (Reprinted in 1971).

Helm, June, ed. 1981. "Subarctic." In *Handbook of North American Indians,* vol. 6. Washington, D.C.: Smithsonian Institution.

Honigmann, John J. 1954. *The Kaska Indians: An Ethnographic Reconstruction.* Publications in *Anthropology* 51. New Haven, Conn.: Yale University.

Jenness, Diamond. 1935. *The Ojibwa Indians of Parry Sound, Their Social and Religious Life.* Bulletin 78. Ottawa: Department of Mines, National Museum of Canada.

———. 1943. *The Carrier Indians of the Bulkley River: Their Social and Religious Life.* Bureau of Ethnology Paper 25, Bulletin 133. Washington, D.C.: Smithsonian Institution.

———. 1943. *The Sekani Indians of British Columbia.* Bulletin 84, Anthropological Series 20. Ottawa: Department of Mines and Resources.

Jetté, Jules. 1911. "On the Superstitions of the Ten'a Indians." *Anthropos* 6:95–108, 241–259, 602–723.

Johnston, Thomas F., et al. 1978. *Koyukan Athapaskan Dance Songs.* Anchorage, Alaska: National Bilingual Materials Development Center.

———. n.d. *The Social Role of Alaskan Potlatch Dancing.* Fairbanks: University of Alaska.

Jones, Owen R. Jr. 1972. *Music of the Algonkians: Woodland Indians (Cree, Montagnais, Naskapi).* Folkways FE 4253. LP disk.

Keillor, Elaine. 1985. "Les tambours des Athapascans du nord." *Recherches amérindiennes au Québec* 15(4):43–52.

Kroul, Mary V. 1974. "Definitional Domains of the Koyukon Athapaskan Potlatch." *Arctic Anthropology* 11 (supplement): 39–47.

Laplante, Louise, and José Mailhot. 1972. "Essai d'analyse d'un chant montagnais." *Recherches amérindiennes au Québec* 2(2):2–19.

Loyens, William J. 1964. "The Koyukon Feast for the Dead." *Arctic Anthropology* 2(2):133–148.

———. 1965. *The Chandalar Kutchin.* Technical Paper 17. Montréal: Arctic Institute of North America.

Mason, Alden F. 1946. *Notes on the Indians of the Great Slave Lake Area.* Publications in Anthropology 34. New Haven, Conn.: Yale University.

McKennan, Robert A. 1959. *The Upper Tanana Indians.* Publications in Anthropology 55. New Haven, Conn.: Yale University.

Mishler, Craig. 1974. *Music of the Alaskan Kutchin Indians.* Folkways FE 4070. LP disk.

———. 1981. "Gwich'in Athapaskan Music and Dance: An Ethnography and Ethnohistory." Ph.D. dissertation, University of Texas.

———. 1993. *The Crooked Stovepipe: Athapaskan Fiddle Music and Square Dancing in Northeast Alaska and Northwest Canada.* Urbana: University of Illinois Press.

Moore, Pat, and Angela Wheelock, eds. 1990. *Wolverine Myths and Visions: Dene Traditions from Northern Alberta.* Edmonton: University of Alberta Press.

Osgood, Cornelius. 1932. *The Ethnography of the Great Bear Lake Indians.* Bulletin 70. Ottawa: National Museum of Canada.

———. 1936. *Contributions to the Ethnography of the Kutchin.* Publications in Anthropology 14. New Haven, Conn.: Yale University.

———. 1937. *The Ethnography of the Tanaina.* Publications in Anthropology 16. New Haven, Conn.: Yale University.

———. 1958. *Ingalik Social Culture.* Publications in Anthropology 53. New Haven, Conn.: Yale University.

———. 1971. *The Han Indians: A Compilation of Ethnographic and Historical Data on the Alaska-Yukon Boundary Area.* Publications in Anthropology 74. New Haven, Conn.: Yale University.

Petitot, Émile, O.M.I. 1876. *Monographie des Dènè-Dindjié.* Paris: Leroux.

Preston, Richard. 1975. *Cree Narrative: Expressing the Personal Meaning of Events.* Mercury Series 30. Ottawa: National Museum of Canada.

Ridington, Robin. 1971. "Beaver Dreaming and Singing." In *Pilot Not Commander: Essays in Memory of Diamond Jenness,* ed. P. Lotz and J. Lotz, 115–128. Ottawa: Anthropologica.

———. 1978. *Swan People: A Study of the Dunne-Za Prophet Dance.* Mercury Series 38. Ottawa: National Museum of Man.

Savard, Rémi. 1971. *Carcajon et le sens du monde: récits montagnais-naskapis.* Montréal. Bibliothéque Nationale du Québec.

Savoie, Donat, ed. 1970. "The Loucheux Indians." In *The Amerindians of the Canadian Northwest in the Nineteenth Century, as seen by Émile Petitot,* vol 2. Northern Science Research Project MDRP 10. Ottawa: Department of Indian and Northern Affairs.

Slobodin, Richard, ed. 1975. *Proceedings of the Northern Athapaskan Conference, 1971.* Mercury Series No. 27. Ottawa: National Museum of Man.

Smith, David Merrill. 1973. *Inkonze: Magico-Religious Beliefs of Contact Traditional Chippewyan Trading at Fort Resolution, Northwest Territories, Canada.* Mercury Series 6. Ottawa: National Museum of Man.

Speck, Frank G. 1977 [1935]. *Naskapi: The Savage Hunters of the Labrador Peninsula.* Norman: University of Oklahoma Press.

Sturtevant, William C., and June Helm, eds. 1981. *Handbook of North American Indians,* Vol. 6: *Subarctic.* Washington, D.C.: Smithsonian Institution.

Tanner, Adrian. 1979. *Bringing Home Animals: Religious Ideology and Mode of Production of the Mistassini Cree Hunters.* Institute of Social and Economic Research, Social and Economic Studies 23. Memorial University of Newfoundland.

Turner, Lucien. 1894. "Ethnology of the Ungava District, Hudson Bay Territory." In *Eleventh Annual Report of the Bureau of American Ethnology for the Years 1889–1890,* vol. 5, 159–350. Washington, D.C.: Smithsonian Institution.

Vincent, Sylvie, ed. 1982. *Puamuna-Montagnais Hunting Songs.* Canadian Broadcasting Corporation, Northern Québec Service SQN 100. LP disk.

Whidden, Lynn. 1985. "Les hymnes, une anomalie parmi les chants traditionnels des Cris du nord." *Recherches amérindiennes au Québec* 15(4):29–36.

———. 1986. "An Ethnomusicological Study of the Traditional Songs of the Chisasibi Cree." Ph.D. dissertation, Université de Montréal.

Northwest Coast
Linda J. Goodman

Along or near the rugged coastline from Yakutat Bay in southeastern Alaska to the Northern California coast of North America live numerous fishing, hunting, and sea-faring tribes. Several of the better known groups include the Tlingit, Haida, Tsimshian, Bella Bella (who now call themselves Heiltsuk), Bella Coola (now known as Nuxalk), Kwakiutl (who now call themselves Kwá-kwa-kya-wakw), Nootka (now known as Núu-chá-nulth or Westcoast), Makah, Coast Salish, Quileute, Quinault, Chinook, Tillamook, and Yurok. Cool mists and abundant rainfall allow the growth of dense vegetation throughout this temperate rain forest region. Traditionally the native peoples harvested a wide variety of fauna and flora from both land and sea for food as well as for the creation of utilitarian and ornamental objects such as masks, drums, rattles, clothing, houses, canoes, and totem poles. Women preserved and stored large quantities of surplus fish and other food, thus allowing time for development of a complex social and political organization as well as a rich musical and ceremonial life.

Northwest Coast social structure, hierarchically organized, included chiefs and their royal families, commoners, and slaves. A combination of heredity and wealth determined one's place in the system. Each lineage or extended family had its own chief, a wealthy and powerful man who owned many rights and privileges, including specific land areas, fishing grounds, shellfish and berry tracts, hereditary art motifs, family names, and also songs, dances, costumes, masks, and ceremonies.

SONG OWNERSHIP

The predominant concept governing Northwest Coast music was, and still is, song ownership. Songs are considered privately owned pieces of personal property, and strict, but unwritten rules regulate their use, precise ownership, inheritance, procedures for learning, and proper methods for buying, selling, giving away, or loaning them to chiefs or other upper-class Indian persons. In the past, chiefs owned the most important songs (those that emphasized their power, wealth, and status); commoners (collaterally related to a chief) owned less important songs, and slaves (prisoners of war and their children born in captivity) in most cases were not allowed to own songs.

CONTEXTS FOR MUSICAL PERFORMANCE

Although music functioned in a variety of ways among the Northwest Coast tribes, first, and perhaps most important, it supported and reinforced the sociopolitical organization. Certain songs maintained and perpetuated the system of chiefs, separated different classes of people (chiefs from non-chiefs), and united families related to a chief (those who performed for him and otherwise received recognition by being related to him).

The potlatch ceremony

Traditionally hosted by a chief, this ceremony reinforced his position while celebrating significant family occasions: a new birth, a girl's puberty, a wedding, a death, or the formal transfer of rights and privileges to the chief's heir, usually his oldest son or his sister's oldest son. Specially invited guests witnessed these events and the associated musical performances, then were paid in gifts and money to remember and to teach their children.

Other ceremonies and major musical occasions

Briefly summarized, various secret rituals and initiation ceremonies used personally owned songs in the teaching of youngsters and in the public performances that followed. Life-cycle ceremonies (for birth, puberty, marriage, and death) included small private rites followed by a large public feast and/or potlatch hosted by a chief. Curing songs and special rattles were used by both male and female Indian doctors in healing individual patients. Guardian spirit songs, sought by most men and some women, brought special power and assisted the owner throughout life. War songs, sung by individuals and by groups both before and after battles, were used first to strengthen resolve and later to celebrate victories. Whaling, practiced primarily by the Nootkans, Makahs, Quileutes, and Quinaults, involved many secret rituals as well as songs, first to ensure a successful hunt, then to tow the giant treasure safely back to land. Several types of entertainment songs were performed for a variety of occasions or activities: breaks between serious parts of major ceremonies; bone gambling games; small, friendly gatherings; drinking; and courtship. Also included in this group were lullabies and songs sung as integral parts of lengthy stories told primarily to children.

MAJOR HISTORICAL CHANGES

Over the years, as Northwest Coast Indian cultures have been significantly affected by the outside world, many songs and some ceremonies have disappeared; others have survived although in modified form. Major ceremonies were outlawed by the United States and Canadian governments in the 1880s. Gradually many songs were forgotten before the laws were repealed in the 1930s in the United States and in 1951 in Canada. During the same period, the hierarchical system of chiefs, commoners, and slaves disappeared. Thus today chiefly lines of descent are no longer always clear, nor are the lines of inheritance. A few tribes manage to maintain their hereditary chiefs; others, however, have no chiefs, and in general, the corpus of songs belonging to the chiefs has shrunk. Frequently, the result is feuding among the descendants of the old chiefs over song ownership rights and thus legitimate performance claims. Song ownership remains a guiding concept, but its realization has become far more complex.

Changes in many other areas of musical life are quite apparent as well. Most of the older forms of life-cycle ceremonies have vanished and been replaced by potlatch ceremonies, often hosted by any family that claims a relationship to a former chief and thus the ownership of his songs. Curing ceremonies along with most of their music have largely disappeared, as have war and whaling songs. The same is generally true for personal power ceremonies and songs, except among the Coast Salish tribes, where spirit dancing has gained strength in recent years and new songs continue to be created. Shaker Indian religious services, begun in the 1880s, continue to combine elements of native and Christian beliefs and use special songs for healing as well as other purposes. Throughout most of this region, secret rituals, ceremonies, and much of the accompanying music disappeared long ago; however, a few of these songs have survived and are now performed at potlatches, especially among the Makah and Nootkans. A variety of other important musical and ceremonial occasions, such as the Kwakiutl Winter Ceremony, have also survived in modified form.

THREE CONTEMPORARY NORTHWEST COAST MUSICAL GENRES

The following three ceremonies and their music continue to reinforce cultural values for tribes, villages, and families, while providing a renewed sense of strength and purpose for individuals.

Coast Salish spirit dancing (winter dancing)

The acquisition of a personal guardian spirit and its powerful accompanying song(s) has been and continues to be the most important element in the religious life of many Coast Salish peoples living in western British Columbia and western Washington State. Because each of these tribes has its own special ways in which individuals acquire spirit power and display it at these ceremonies, only a few general characteristics can be related here.

The ceremony

Usually a young man or woman acquires a guardian spirit either through a spontaneous vision experience or else by being "captured" in the proper ritual manner. Over several days, this person's individual spirit song and dance, first received during the vision, is "brought out," practiced, and perfected. Its first public performance occurs when the novice is initiated at a spirit dancing ceremony. Because the spirit helper of each experienced dancer re-enters its owner's body every winter and makes him or her "sick," a spirit dancing ceremony must be held in order to soothe the spirit, seek its goodwill for continued help, and then remove it so it will not harm its owner.

In the smokehouse, a large, rectangular wooden structure where the ceremony is held, the spirit dancers at a Coast Salish Winter Dance begin by "warming up"—each dancer performs for a short time in front of his or her own seat, accompanied by a few drummers and singers, thus ensuring the proper mood. A number of dancers doing this simultaneously create cacophonous sound.

When the warming up is completed, the "work" of the evening begins—a modified form of potlatch that includes performances of inherited songs and masked dances. The host(s) and/or hostess(es) either give or receive special honors—usually revered ancestral names—that audience members witness and are paid to remember. Finally, many hours later, the spirit dancing begins, first with new initiates, who are called "babies," then with regular dancers who were initiated in previous years. One after the other, each dancer performs alone in a prearranged sequential order. New dancers wear face paint, a costume, special hat, and deer-hoof rattles on knees and ankles, and each carries a wooden staff. Each initiate gasps, shouts, and moans while acquiring the spirit power and starting his or her own song. The song is continued by a group of drummers, usually male, who also sing as they follow the dancer around the floor. Occasionally a female relative may lead the song of a particular dancer. Only women who are close relatives of the dancer are allowed to join the group of drummers on the floor and accompany the dancer around the smokehouse. Those in the audience who know the song sing and drum from their seats, thus creating a powerful musical sound that emanates from all sides of the room. At the appropriate time, the dancer, imbued with spirit power, begins to dance in a counterclockwise circuit, moving between the central fires and the people sitting on platforms along the walls.

As the dancer performs, a spouse or close relative gives money to ten or twelve spectators who are thus selected to help the dancer regain his or her place without falling. It is a bad sign if the dancer stumbles or falls while dancing or being seated. Therefore, these individuals position themselves on either side of the dancer's place and help lower him or her into it when the dancing is completed. Once the dancer is seated, the cries and moans gradually diminish as the guardian spirit leaves his or her body. For many hours this sequence of events continues, with one dancer following another, until all have completed their performances. When the entire ceremony is finished, the participants feel cleansed, renewed, and strengthened.

The music: Coast Salish spirit dancing songs

Personal spirit dancing songs are usually begun by the owner, who is soon joined by the drummers (usually male) and knowledgeable audience members of both sexes, all of whom could be said to create a loosely structured chorus. Other musical characteristics include cries, moans, and sighs indicative of a trance state; vocal ornaments such as pulsations, turns, trills, and slides or slurs on final notes; a considerable amount of two- to five-part singing (which Jamie Cunningham terms "singing in parallel harmony" [1995]); and instrumental accompaniment provided by handheld frame drums, beating sticks, hand clapping, and deer-hoof rattles. A drum tremolo is usually heard during the chantlike beginning of a song, followed in later sections by loud, steady drum beats at a moderate or fast tempo. The tempo normally changes several times over the course of the song. Each song is divided into several sections with a definite pause between them.

Recently created songs consist entirely of vocables, while many older songs include one or several short lines of meaningful Salish text surrounded by vocables. A succinct translation of one old song states, "He walks as a human being, but he is not one" (Roberts and Haeberlin 1918:503).

Makah potlatch

The ceremony

Even though it has been modified over the years, the potlatch ceremony, as performed by members of the Makah tribe (the southernmost branch of the Nootkans), continues to thrive. Held most often for life-cycle celebrations, as previously described, the potlatch is the only remaining traditional ceremony performed by descendants of the old Makah chiefly families. Now called a "party" or "potlatch party" and involving much planning and practice, this ceremony is held to honor an important person, to display family-owned privileges such as songs, dances, masks, and costumes, and sometimes to transfer songs and other hereditary rights in the appropriate manner.

The ceremony includes the performance of several family-owned dinner songs that precede the serving of a lavish feast in the village community hall. Afterward the actual potlatch begins as the speaker announces the purpose of the gathering and introduces the visiting tribes and special guests. In a prearranged order, members of each visiting tribe sing and dance a pair of their family-owned potlatch songs, then give away gifts and money as payment for witnessing the performance of these treasured privileges. This portion of the potlatch often lasts many hours, with one family after another singing, dancing, and giving away. Members of the Makah tribe are the last to perform and give away.

Near the end of the party, the host family takes its turn. Members often perform many more than two of their family-owned songs, then give away vast quantities of gifts and money, a gesture important for maintaining their prestige in the community. At this time, the host may give a song to a relative or other deserving person, and the audience is paid for witnessing this transfer. Often the potlatch ends (some eight to

They place themselves in a large, open U-shaped formation, then dance in place, rotating 180 degrees, arms moving in a graceful pattern from right to left to right.

FIGURE 1   Singing and drumming, Helma Swan leads other family members in a Swan family song performed in honor of Oliver Ward Jr. at his Memorial Potlatch, Neah Bay, Washington, 10 October 1998. Photo by Linda J. Goodman.

sixteen hours after it began) with the singing of several social songs by the performers and audience.

Songs performed at contemporary Makah (and Nootkan) potlatches include mainly family-owned Wolf, Grizzly Bear, Thunderbird, Eagle, and Hámatsa dances (cannibal dances received from the Kwakiutl tribe through marriage). Family members may sing their own songs or else ask the Makah chorus (comprised of both men and women) to provide the music (figure 1). The choruses of several other Nootkan tribes are composed entirely of male singers, and occasionally, the Makah follow this older pattern as well.

Gendered dance roles

Male and female dance roles are quite different. Normally each dance includes one or two lead male dancers dressed in appropriate costumes and masks. From an initial crouching position, they rise at the appropriate place in the song and begin to dance in a counterclockwise circuit around the room. Frequently the dancers imitate the movements of the animal or creature they are impersonating, and they always end their dance at the point where it began (figure 2). Women perform as "background" or "backup" dancers, providing support for the men. They place themselves in a large, open U-shaped formation, then dance in place, rotating 180 degrees, arms moving in a graceful pattern from right to left to right. If no men in the family are available to perform as lead dancers, women are sometimes now allowed to do so, or nonfamily males are publicly paid to dance for the family.

FIGURE 2 Makah Wolf Dance performed at Oliver Ward Jr. Memorial Potlatch, Neah Bay, Washington, October 10, 1998. The central characters, two masked Wolf Dancers, crouch in the center of the dance floor, ready to rise and leap back into motion when they hear the proper drum beat. They are surrounded by women dancers who wear black dance shawls and provide "background" or "backup." The audience, lining the walls of the community hall, watches intently. Photo by Linda J. Goodman.

The music: Makah family-owned potlatch songs

Often a song leader will start each family-owned dance song, which is then continued by a chorus using handheld frame drums and singing mostly in a low to medium range. Vocal ornaments, especially turns, grace notes, and final descending slurs, are common, as are long extended opening and/or closing notes. Most melodies begin with a rising pattern followed by an undulating and/or descending shape. Song structure often consists of several sections that are repeated a variable number of times. Strong, steady drumbeats, played at a moderate tempo, may change once or several times at specific places in a song. Short syncopated sections are common. Voices and drums are synchronized in some songs, not in others.

Song texts consist largely of vocables; however, some songs have one or several short lines of lexical text that remind performers and audience of the underlying story that many of them learned as children, for example, "I am dancing in the air and dancing round and round" (Densmore 1939:101). New songs are seldom composed for these ceremonies.

Kwakiutl winter ceremony

The ceremony

Also known as the Cedar Bark Dance because this material plays a significant part in many of the dances and proceedings, the Winter Ceremony, or *Tséyka,* continues to maintain its important position in marriages and in memorial observances among the Southern Kwakiutl of British Columbia. Formerly of great religious significance, this ceremony, which over time has been reduced in length and complexity, is now performed primarily to enhance the rank of the host family, to validate its hereditary privileges (including numerous names, songs, dances, masks, and crests), and to initiate its young in a variety of dance traditions that must be renewed from generation to generation. The art, music, and drama of the event, also important considerations, are carefully planned and rehearsed ahead of time.

Formerly continuing for several weeks or more, the contemporary Winter Ceremony lasts only one to two days and is held in a village community hall or reconstructed big house. The proceedings open with a mourning ceremony that includes special songs and other related activities, all of which end before dark. This is followed by the display of important family privileges in the course of the initiation of young people (mostly males, but some females as well) into various dance traditions. Underlying themes, based on ancient myths, involve the initiate's encounter and kidnapping by a particular spirit that takes him or her away for a period of time while bestowing supernatural powers. Then, during the Winter Ceremony the novice returns, the spirit is exorcized, and the initiate is calmed or tamed. The novice inherits the right to his or her particular dance performance from an ancestor who went through this same experience in the past.

The Hámatsa

The primary character in this dance drama, the *Hámatsa* or Cannibal Man, is traditionally the son of a chief. According to the myth, the novice, first carried off by the Cannibal Spirit, returns in a wild state and desires to eat human corpses. The Kwakiutl masterfully create sensational stage effects to simulate such cannibal activities and a host of other equally amazing dramatic effects during the course of the Winter Ceremony. The *Hámatsa* first dances in his wild state, wearing a costume of hemlock branches and squatting low on the floor. At his next appearance he dances in an upright position while wearing red cedar bark—indicative of his taming (figure 3). At the sound of certain words in the song, however, he becomes wild once again, his dance attendants are unable to hold him, and he escapes from the house.

Then, one after the other, the *Hámatsa*'s three giant bird associates, wearing magnificent masks and costumes, move onto the floor and perform slow, stately dances (figure 4). When they depart, the *Hámatsa* returns, calm, for his final tame dance, performed in an upright position while wearing red cedar bark. Lastly, his female attendant leads the women in a dance symbolizing his successful taming.

Other dances

Many other dances are also a part of the Winter Ceremony. They too are based on old myths and include specific activities and songs. When no face mask is involved, the owner usually performs his or her own dance. If a mask is worn, however, the owner often hires someone else to wear it and dance for him or her (Holm 1995). Dances consist of one or more counterclockwise circuits of the big house, with the dancer pivoting whenever each end of the house is reached. Each character has special songs and a specific cry, behaves and dances in a recognizable manner, but usually does not sing while dancing.

At the end of the Winter Ceremony, performers remove their cedar bark head rings, and the assembled group sings one final song, stating that calmness has returned. A potlatch finalizes the preceding events; usually no further singing and dancing occur, just the giving away of money and gifts to the witnesses. Afterwards, the entire group sings a "Happy Song," concluding the entire ceremony.

The music: Kwakiutl Winter Ceremony songs

A song leader, aside from beginning and leading most songs, usually calls out the words of each verse before it is sung by the chorus. Sitting at the back of the hall, the chorus consists of a number of male singers who perform with a rather loose, open vocal sound in a low to medium register while beating out the rhythm with wooden batons on a raised wooden plank (a plank drum) in front of them. Formerly a wooden box drum and now a manufactured bass drum or one or more single-headed hand drums supplement the plank drum. Vocal ornaments include quavers, pulsations, turns, slides, and descending slurs on final notes. Melodic lines often undulate and/or descend. Voices and drums sometimes are, but often are not, synchronized for many of the Winter Ceremony songs. Syncopation is common. Rhythmic patterns are often complex, sometimes remaining constant, at other times changing during the course of a song. Many songs begin with a fast tremolo on the plank drum, which then moves into a steady rhythmic pattern.

FIGURE 3   Kwakiutl *Hámatsa* dancer Joe Seaweed, wearing a red cedar bark headband, arm bands, and neck rings, raises his left arm in a typical *Hámatsa* motion as he dances upright during a Winter Ceremony held at Ft. Rupert, British Columbia, in 1963. His attendant, James Wallas, wearing a button blanket and a cedar bark neck ring and holding a traditional round rattle, stands beside him. The giant image of a raven, a crest belonging to the host family, appears on the canvas curtain behind the performers. Photo by Bill Holm.

FIGURE 4   A Giant Long-Beaked Bird *(Hohokw)* Dance performed as part of the *Hámatsa* during a Kwakiutl Winter Ceremony held at Alert Bay, British Columbia in 1976. The beak of this wild supernatural creature was used, it is said, "to crack the skulls of men and eat their brains." Red cedar bark fringe partially hides the dancer's body as he adeptly maneuvers the five- to six-foot-long beak while his attendant watches closely. Photo by Bill Holm.

Winter Ceremony songs often include both vocables and meaningful words. Specific calls or vocal sounds are associated with certain characters. For example, the *Hámatsa* shouts "Haap! Haap!" and the words "Ham, Hamai" always appear in *Hámatsa* songs. These are references to the Kwakiutl word *hamáp* 'to eat'. Many *Hámatsa* song texts describe carrying corpses, chewing and eating various body parts, and swallowing men whole and alive. In the past, new songs were often created for those who received *Hámatsa* or other dance privileges. Today, few new songs are composed; most young dancers perform to the songs of their predecessors. When new songs are made, the words (as in days past) often refer to former mistakes or incidents embarrassing to the dancer, while seeming to speak only of certain ceremonial activities. One has to know specific details of these events in order to catch the subtle secondary message of the song.

SUMMARY OF NORTHWEST COAST MUSICAL CHARACTERISTICS

1. Voice quality is, in general, fairly open and relaxed. Songs are normally sung in a low to middle register with numerous vocal ornaments, especially vocal pulsations and descending slurs at ends of phrases. Perhaps more common in the past than in the present, small rises in pitch often occur at the beginnings of phrases or repetitions of sections of songs.

2. Song texts are of two basic types: those that consist entirely of vocables, and those that are a combination of meaningful words and vocables. Settings are usually syllabic or neumatic (a few pitches are used for each texted syllable).

3. Musical texture is primarily monophonic: songs are usually begun by a solo song leader and then continued by a chorus, all of whom sing the same melodic line. Although not as frequently as in the past, two- to five-part parallel harmonies still may be heard in some songs, especially among the Coast Salish.

4. Musical form does not fall into any easily definable pattern. Many songs are strophic; others are not. Most songs are divided into sections that repeat once or several times. Short motifs or phrases often provide the underlying structure of a song and can be varied and repeated numerous times.

5. Melodic range varies from a second to a tenth; however, ranges of a third to an octave are most common.

6. Melodic lines are generally undulating or descending in contour. Ends of phrases often descend and/or flatten on one pitch that is either extended or repeated numerous times.

7. Scales generally vary from three to seven tones, with four-, five-, and six-tone scales perhaps being most common. Scales that include quarter tones are present but do not predominate.

8. Duple and triple meters are most common, but compound meters can also be heard. Groups of two and three beats may be used alternately within a song or may be played and sung simultaneously creating cross-rhythms. Syncopations occur moderately often. It is proper for voices and drums to be synchronized for some songs but out of synchronization for others.

9. Musical instruments commonly used today include handheld frame drums, long plank drums, carved wooden rattles, deer-hoof rattles, and carved wooden whistles in a variety of sizes and shapes.

10. Long, extended vowel sounds, heard at beginnings or endings of many songs, often are representative of supernatural beings. Other extramusical sounds and cries have a similar connection, as does the use of drum tremolo and the blowing of whistles.

Two different types of vocal composition can be heard, the first being a recitative or chant type that centers on one pitch, includes many meaningful words, and is

Melodic lines are generally undulating or descending in contour. Ends of phrases often descend and/or flatten on one pitch that is either extended or repeated numerous times.

accompanied by drum or rattle tremolo only. The second type may be described as a song with a rising and falling melody line, either a mixture of vocables and words or just vocables alone, and one or several distinctive drum beat patterns.

REFERENCES

Altman, George J. 1947. "Guardian Spirit Dances of the Salish." *Masterkey* 21(4):155–160.

Amoss, Pamela. 1978. *Coast Salish Spirit Dancing.* Seattle: University of Washington Press.

———. 1995. Personal communication.

Barbeau, Marius. 1951. "Tsimshian Songs." In *The Tsimshian: Their Arts and Music,* ed. Marian Smith, 95–280. New York: American Ethnological Society Publications, 18.

Barnett, Homer G. 1938. "The Coast Salish of Canada." *American Anthropologist,* n.s. 40(1): 118–141.

Boas, Franz. 1888. "On Certain Songs and Dances of the Kwakiutl." *Journal of American Folklore* 1(1):49–64.

———. 1890. "The Nootka." *British Association for the Advancement of Science Annual Meeting,* Report 60:582–604, 668–679.

———. 1897. "The Social Organization and the Secret Societies of the Kwakiutl Indians." *Report of the U.S. National Museum for 1895.* Washington, D.C., 311–738.

———. 1966. *Kwakiutl Ethnography.* Ed. Helen Codere. Chicago: University of Chicago Press.

Boley, Ray. 1975. *Stick Game Songs by Joe Washington (Lummi).* Canyon Records 6124. LP disk.

Codere, Helen. 1950. *Fighting with Property.* Monograph 18. Seattle: American Ethnological Society.

Cole, Douglas, and Ira Chaikin. 1990. *An Iron Hand upon the People: The Law against the Potlatch on the Northwest Coast.* Seattle: University of Washington Press.

Colson, Elizabeth. 1953. *The Makah Indians.* Minneapolis: University of Minnesota Press.

Cunningham, Jamie. 1995. Personal communication.

Cunningham, Jamie, and Pamela Amoss. 1999. "Song Traditions of the Indian Shaker Church." In *Spirit of the First People: Native American Music Traditions of Washington State,* ed. Willie Smyth and Esmé Ryan, 117–133. Seattle: University of Washington Press.

Curtis, Edward S. 1913. "Salishan Tribes of the Coast." In *The North American Indian,* vol. 9, ed. Frederick W. Hodge, 3–227. Norwood, Mass.: Plimpton Press.

———. 1915. "The Kwakiutl." In *The North American Indian,* vol. 10, ed. Frederick W. Hodge, 3–366. Norwood, Mass.: Plimpton Press.

———. 1916. "The Nootka." In *The North American Indian,* vol. 11, ed. Frederick W. Hodge, 3–113. Norwood, Mass.: Plimpton Press.

de Laguna, Frederica. 1972. *Under Mount Saint Elias: The History and Culture of the Yakutat Tlingit.* Washington, D.C.: Smithsonian Institution Press.

Densmore, Frances. 1939. *Nootka and Quileute Music.* Bureau of American Ethnology Bulletin 124. Washington, D.C.: Smithsonian Institution.

———. 1943. *Music of the Indians of British Columbia.* Bureau of American Ethnology Bulletin 136. Washington, D.C.: Smithsonian Institution.

———. 1952. *Songs of the Nootka and Quileute.* Library of Congress AAFS L32. LP disk.

Drucker, Philip. 1940. "Kwakiutl Dancing Societies." *Anthropological Records* 2(6):201–230. Berkeley: University of California Press.

———. 1951. *The Northern and Central Nootkan Tribes.* Bureau of American Ethnology Bulletin 144. Washington, D.C.: Smithsonian Institution.

———. 1963. *Indians of the Northwest Coast.* Garden City, N.Y.: The Natural History Press.

———. 1965. *Cultures of the North Pacific Coast.* San Francisco: Chandler Publishing Company.

Drucker, Philip, and Robert F. Heizer. 1967. *To Make My Name Good: A Reexamination of the Southern Kwakiutl Potlatch.* Berkeley: University of California Press.

Eells, Myron. 1985. *The Indians of Puget Sound: The Notebooks of Myron Eells.* Ed. George P. Castile. Seattle: University of Washington Press.

Enrico, John, and Wendy Bross Stuart. 1996. *Northern Haida Songs.* Lincoln: University of Nebraska Press.

Ernst, Alice. 1952. *The Wolf Ritual of the Northwest Coast.* Eugene: University of Oregon Press.

Ford, Clellan S. 1941. *Smoke from Their Fires: The Life of a Kwakiutl Chief.* New Haven, Conn.: Yale University Press.

Frachtenberg, Leo J. 1921. "The Ceremonial Societies of the Quileute Indians." *American Anthropologist,* n.s., 23:320–352.

Garfield, Viola, Paul S. Wingert, and Marius Barbeau. 1951. *The Tsimshian: Their Arts and Music.* American Ethnological Society Publication 18. New York: J. J. Augustin.

George, Graham. 1962. "Songs of the Salish Indians of British Columbia." *International Folk Music Journal* 14:22–29.

Goodman, Linda J. 1977. *Music and Dance in Northwest Coast Indian Life.* Occasional Papers, vol. III, Music and Dance Series no. 3. Tsaile, Ariz.: Navajo Community College Press.

———. 1978. "This Is My Song: The Role of Song as Symbol in Makah Life." Ph.D. dissertation, Washington State University.

———. 1986. "Nootka." In *The New Grove Dictionary of American Music,* ed. H. Wylie Hitchcock and Stanley Sadie, 3:380–382. London: Macmillan.

———. 1991. "Traditional Music in Makah Life." In *A Time of Gathering: Native Heritage in Washington State,* ed. Robin K. Wright, 223–233. Seattle: University of Washington Press.

———. 1992. "Aspects of Spiritual and Political Power in Chiefs' Songs of the Makah Indians." *The World of Music* 34(2):23–42.

———. n.d. *Singing the Songs of My Ancestors: The Makah Life and Music of Helma Swan.* Norman: University of Oklahoma Press, in press.

Goodman, Linda J., and Helma Swan. 1999. "Makah Music: Preserving the Traditions." In *Spirit of the First People: Native American Music Traditions of Washington State,* ed. Willie Smyth and Esmé Ryan, 81–105. Seattle: University of Washington Press.

Haeberlin, Herman, and Erna Gunther. 1930. *The Indians of Puget Sound.* Seattle: University of Washington Press.

Halpern, Ida. 1967. *Indian Music of the Pacific Northwest.* Ethnic Folkways Record Library FE 4523. LP disk.

———. 1968. "Music of the B.C. Northwest Coast Indians." In *Centennial Workshop on Ethnomusicology,* 23–42. Vancouver: University of British Columbia.

———. 1974. *Nootka Indian Music of the Pacific Northwest Coast.* Ethnic Folkways Record Library FE 4524. LP disk.

———. n.d. *Kwakiutl, Indian Music of the Pacific Northwest.* Ethnic Folkways Record Library FE 4122. LP disk.

Herzog, George. 1949. "Salish Music." In *Indians of the Urban Northwest,* ed. Marian W. Smith, 93–109. New York: Columbia University Press.

Holm, Bill. 1977. "Traditional and Contemporary Kwakiutl Winter Dance." *Arctic Anthropology* 14(1):5–24.

———. 1978. Unpublished class notes for a course entitled "Dance and Drama of the Northwest Coast Indians," University of Washington, Seattle.

———. 1983. *Smokey-Top: The Art and Times of Willy Seaweed.* Thomas Burke Memorial Washington State Museum, Monograph 3. Seattle: University of Washington Press.

———. 1990. "Kwakiutl: Winter Ceremonies." In *Handbook of North American Indians,* vol. 7, *Northwest Coast,* ed. William C. Sturtevant and Wayne Suttles, 378–386. Washington, D.C.: Smithsonian Institution.

———. 1995. Personal communication.

Jenness, Diamond. 1955. *The Faith of a Coast Salish Indian.* Anthropology in British Columbia, Memoir no. 3. Victoria: British Columbia Provincial Museum.

Jilek, Wolfgang. 1974. *Salish Indian Mental Health and Culture Change: Psychohygienic and Therapeutic Aspects of the Guardian Spirit Ceremonial.* Toronto: Holt, Rinehart and Winston.

———. 1982. *Indian Healing: Shamanic Ceremonialism in the Pacific Northwest Today.* Surrey, B.C.: Hancock House.

Johnston, Thomas F. 1975. "A Historical Perspective on Tlingit Music." *The Indian Historian* 8(1):3–8.

———. 1986–88. "Tlingit Dance, Music and Society." *Acta Ethnographica Academiae Scientiarm Hungaricae* 34:283–324.

Kew, Michael. 1970. "Coast Salish Ceremonial Life: Status and Identity in a Modern Village." Ph.D. dissertation, University of Washington.

Kolstee, Anton F. 1977. "Bella Coola Indian Music: A Study of the Interaction Between Northwest Coast Indian Musical Structures and Their Functional Context." Master's thesis, University of British Columbia.

McIlwraith, Thomas F. 1948. *The Bella Coola Indians,* 2 vols. Toronto: University of Toronto Press.

Mohling, Virginia Gill. 1957. "Twana Spirit Power Songs." Master's thesis, University of Washington.

Mulder, Jean. 1994. "Structural Organization in Coast Tsimshian Music." *Ethnomusicology* 38(1):81–125.

Murdock, George P. 1936. "Rank and Potlatch among the Haida." *Anthropology* 13. New Haven, Conn.: Yale University Publications.

Myers, Helen. 1986. "Salish." In *The New Grove Dictionary of American Music,* ed. H. Wylie Hitchcock and Stanley Sadie, 122–124. London: Macmillan.

Nettl, Bruno. 1954. *North American Indian Musical Styles.* American Folklore Society Memoir 45. Philadelphia: American Folklore Society.

Peck, Elizabeth. 1973. "Songs of the Bogachiel: An Examination of the Music Owned by a Prestigious Quileute Family." Master's thesis, Washington State University.

Rhodes, Willard. 1950. *Northwest (Puget Sound).* Library of Congress AFS L34. LP disk.

Roberts, Helen H., and Herman K. Haeberlin. 1918. "Some Songs of the Puget Sound Salish." *Journal of American Folklore* 31(122):496–520.

Roberts, Helen H., and Morris Swadesh. 1955. "Songs of the Nootka Indians of Western Vancouver Island." *Transactions of the American Philosophical Society,* n.s., 45(3):199–327.

Rohner, Ronald P., and Evelyn C. Rohner. 1970. *The Kwakiutl Indians of British Columbia.* New York: Holt, Rinehart, and Winston.

Sapir, Edward. 1911. "Some Aspects of Nootka Language and Culture." *American Anthropologist,* n.s., 13:15–28.

———. 1913. "A Girl's Puberty Ceremony among the Nootka." *Transactions of the Royal Society of Canada,* 3rd ser., 7(2):67–80.

Sapir, Edward, and Morris Swadesh. 1939. *Nootka Texts: Tales and Ethnological Narratives.* Special Publication of the Linguistic Society of America. Philadelphia: University of Pennsylvania. Reprinted: AMS Press, New York, 1978.

———. 1955. "Native Accounts of Nootka Ethnography." *International Journal of American Linguistics* 21(4, part 2):1–457. Reprinted: New York: AMS Press, 1978.

Smyth, Willie, and Esmé Ryan, eds. 1999. *Spirit of the First People: Native American Music Traditions of Washington State.* Seattle: University of Washington Press.

Spradley, James P. 1969. *Guests Never Leave Hungry: The Autobiography of James Sewid, a Kwakiutl Indian.* New Haven: Yale University Press.

Sproat, Gilbert. 1868. *Scenes and Studies of Savage Life.* London: Smith, Edler, and Company.

Stuart, Wendy. 1972. *Gambling Music of the Coast Salish Indians.* Mercury Series 3. Ottawa: National Museum of Man, Ethnology Division.

Suttles, Wayne. 1987. "Spirit Dancing and the Persistence of Native Culture among the Coast Salish." In *Coast Salish Essays,* 199–208. Seattle: University of Washington Press.

Swan, James G. 1870. *The Indians of Cape Flattery.* Smithsonian Contributions to Knowledge, vol. 16, article 8. Smithsonian Institution Publication 220. Washington, D.C.: Smithsonian Institution.

Swanton, John R. 1912. *Haida Songs.* Publications of the American Ethnological Society 3:1–63.

Williams, Vivian. 1962. "Analysis of Skagit Music." Master's thesis, University of Washington.

Métis
Anne Lederman

Métis peoples, in the simplest terms, are those of mixed French and Native ancestry. However, defining Métis identity and culture is far from simple. The word came into common use in the 1800s on the Canadian prairies for the children of French traders and Native women, largely Cree and Ojibwa. These intermarriages spawned a syncretic culture, including distinctive languages called *Mitchif* (or *Métchif*) as well as clothing, food, and music. But Métis peoples live in every province and territory of Canada and many of the northern states, roughly following the old east–west fur trade routes with some expansion northward and southward. It is therefore difficult to draw clear dividing lines between Métis, French and aboriginal peoples, and aspects of Métis musical traditions extend into Native, Inuit, and French communities.

Since 1982, Métis peoples have been officially recognized as one of three aboriginal peoples in Canada, the others being Inuit and First Nations. This allows them to apply for card-carrying status as members of the Métis Nation, based on the two principles of self-identification and community acceptance. However, various historical factors have complicated such identification. These include old laws that allowed only non-Native peoples to own land or hold certain kinds of jobs, so that many denied their Native ancestry. Alternatively, some denied their non-Native ancestry in order to qualify for the rights granted Native peoples. Many people still do not know, or have only recently discovered, that they in fact have a mixed heritage, because it was in their parents', grandparents' or great-grandparents' best interest to deny it. One branch of Mitchif, Mitchif-Cree, has recently been acknowledged officially as a distinct language, but other versions are still considered dialects of French, Cree, or Ojibwe, making Métis identification more problematic. Also, because of the historical situation, many Métis peoples today speak only English, French, or Native languages. Interestingly, the idea that Métis identity could be based on culture, rather than bloodlines, is gaining currency. This means that it is through music and other cultural expressions passed down in one's family that people may most easily come to a recognition of their Métis heritage (Chrétien 1996). This makes the study and understanding of Métis traditions increasingly important.

Métis culture is perhaps best thought of as a complex of traditions with regional and even family variations. "Métis musical traditions are actually expressed along a continuum, with Native and white elements at either end" (Chrétien 1996:56). Given the many different aboriginal cultures involved over such a wide territory, it is surprising that recent studies reveal as much common ground as they do. What these studies show is a distinctive fiddle and dance tradition that combines elements of Scottish, French-Canadian, American, and Native cultures and which shares some common elements from Acadia to Alaska. There is also a legacy of songs in Mitchif and French.

FIDDLING AND DANCING

Fiddling was so central to Métis culture and so identified with it at one time that Turtle Mountain players say, "There's no Metchif without no fiddle. The dancin' and the fiddle and the Metchif, they're all the same" (Leary 1992:27). "The Sioux would say . . . when he played one of these [a fiddle], they knew he was a Metchif" (Leary 1992:22). Largely a male practice until recently, the fiddle tradition involves a style of playing and a certain core repertoire that can be directly traced to the fur trade in early Canada. This article will examine what is known about this syncretic style throughout its range, even as it occurs among peoples who do not identify themselves as Métis but as French or Saulteaux, Chippewa, Cree, Athapaskan, or other aboriginal cultures.

Our knowledge of early Métis music comes from diaries, letters, and writings of non-Métis writers and from twentieth-century collections of oral traditions still active in these communities. By all accounts, fiddling for dancing became the mainstay of fur trade culture in the nineteenth century. It was adopted by French, Native, Métis, and Scots alike and in many areas replaced older Native musical traditions, especially as laws were passed banning Native religious practices in the late 1800s. There are only two in-depth studies of the Métis/Native style of fiddling: that of Anne Lederman in Saulteaux communities of western Manitoba (1986) and that of Craig Mishler in Gwich'in communities in Alaska and the Yukon (1993). These are augmented by anecdotal evidence from many other areas, especially Saskatchewan and the Turtle Mountain region of North Dakota, which has cultural and family ties with Manitoba. Evidence from Ontario suggests that many of the features of the older style are still active in Cree communities in the north, but that more southern Métis communities are influenced by Ottawa Valley French and Irish practice. However, there are still large gaps in our current knowledge.

CULTURAL INFLUENCES

The most noticeably distinctive feature of the older northwest Métis fiddle repertoire is its highly asymmetric phrasing, a feature of much traditional Native song. This means that rather than the common two-section, four-phrase, thirty-two-bar form of Scottish tradition, forms vary widely from tune to tune, with no standard phrase length, number of phrases, or repeat patterns. In Manitoba, for example, it is not uncommon for a tune to have phrases that vary in length between three and nine beats that may or may not repeat, with phrases of five beats being especially common. The degree of irregularity in forms varies from place to place, but current evidence would suggest it is highest in communities where aboriginal languages are spoken.

TRACK 8

Older fiddling exhibits other features of old Native song as well, such as introductory and tag phrases, overlapping phrases, embellished cadences, and descending melodic contours. In this sense, it is not unlike the Mitchif language, which, in one version, is described as having a largely French vocabulary and an Algonkian/Ojibwe/Cree grammatical structure (Bakker 1992). Similarly, the fiddle tradition can be thought of as having a largely Scottish and French vocabulary and a Native structure. All of these structural features can be seen by comparing a Scottish version of a well-known tune with one of its Métis versions (figure 1).

Native influence is also evident in attitudes surrounding fiddling. For example, there is often a sense of personal ownership of particular versions of tunes. "If someone heard you playing his tunes, he'd walk up to you and say, 'Hey, you play your own

FIGURE 1A "Haste to the Wedding," from *1001 Fiddle Tunes,* a 1940s reprint of *Ryan's Mammoth Collection,* originally published c. 1880, United States.

FIGURE 1B "The Wedding Tune," as played by Willie Mousseau, Ebb and Flow Manitoba, c. 1984. Transcription by Anne Lederman, field collection.

tunes'" (Lederman 1987a). Some do not feel the tunes should be recorded, and there are stories of tapes having been fatefully erased after a player dies, sometimes in rather mysterious ways. In Turtle Mountain, older players sometimes put rattlesnake rattles or other natural objects inside their fiddles, while in Alaska they are known to decorate them with such Native symbols as feathers, ribbons, or beadwork. In Ontario, Chiga Groulx speaks of the fiddle as having a soul, of the wood as being alive, a belief echoed on the prairies (Chrétien 1996:140).

ASPECTS OF STYLE

Clogging patterns involving both feet to accompany fiddling are common in Métis, Native and French-Canadian areas. This is a feature unique to North American fiddling and seems to have developed in fur-trade culture. Whether it was of French-Canadian or Native origin, we will probably never know. However, there are some interesting differences between Québécois and Métis/Native practice. Figure 2 shows the rhythms most commonly found in Métis/Native areas.

In Québec, players do not generally clog in 6/8 rhythm, and although some use the 2/4 rhythm given here, Québécois players also frequently fill in the pattern (figure 3). Some Québec players have a pattern for waltzes as well, while most Métis waltzes are played to a steady foot on every beat.

FIGURE 2   Clogging patterns in 2/4 and 6/8 from Ebb and Flow Manitoba. *R* denotes the right foot, *L* the left foot, although some patterns are reversed.

FIGURE 3   A standard Québécois clogging pattern for a reel.

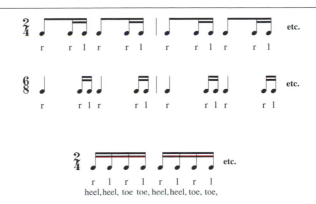

Altered tunings are used in both Manitoba, Turtle Mountain, and Alaska/Yukon, most commonly A–D–A–E (from lowest to highest) and A–E–A–E. These are common in older Scottish tradition, as well as in Québec and U.S. styles. A–E–A–C♯ and a "drop D" tuning—D–D–A–D—also occur in Manitoba, possibly from American influence. Also in Manitoba, tunes in A–E–A–C♯ and A–E–A–E are sometimes called "devil tunes," and there are reports that older players were afraid to play them for fear the devil would appear. In Alaska/Yukon, this type of story seems to be confined to one particular tune (Mishler 1993:56).

Bowing in the older style uses short, generally separate strokes mixed with two-note slurs, similar to French-Canadian bowing. However, there seems to be a generally stronger off-beat accent than in Québec, especially in 6/8 tunes, resulting in two-note chords on accented notes. Some players practice what they call "double-stringing," that is, playing extra open strings along with the melody. According to reports this was much more popular in the past in all areas than it is now.

As in other North American fiddle traditions, older players tend to vary the tunes every time they play them, whereas younger players often have only one version of a tune. In Métis practice, these variations can involve changes of phrasing and structure as well as notes. Cadences, especially, frequently change length as players choose to emphasize these key notes by repeating and embellishing them.

The fiddle was generally unaccompanied until guitars came into use in the mid-twentieth century. Sometimes a second fiddle was used, doubling the melody, playing in octaves, or playing drones or chords. In Turtle Mountain, one two-note chord is sometimes played on every beat throughout the tune with an "off-the-string" bow (lifted after each stroke). This is called "bucking" or "le boss" and was also used to teach. "One would beat out the time on the strings like the drum while the other one played. That's how the young ones learned" (Leary 1992:24).

REPERTOIRE

Written descriptions of social events at fur trade posts on Hudson's Bay and in the settlement of Red River (later Winnipeg) from the early 1800s report a repertoire of Scottish strathspeys, jigs, and reels, played by "Indian" fiddlers "to the vigorous accompaniment of the foot. We have known men to carry an extra pair of moccasins, so that when one pair was worn out on the rough floor they might not be at a loss" (Macbeth 1971:54). Although strathspeys have largely disappeared, jigs, marches, and reels of Scottish derivation often referred to simply as "quadrilles" or "old Scotch reels," were still a mainstay of older players' repertoires in Manitoba in the 1980s. More than three hundred have been recorded from one player alone, Grandy Fagnan of Camperville, Manitoba. The Scottish forebears of some of these tunes are obvious, as in the "Haste to the Wedding" example (figure 1), and it is possible that further comparison with older Orkney, Shetland, and Scottish repertoire would reveal sources of many others.

The dance is a test of endurance and skill and even in community settings has always been somewhat competitive, both in the number and complexity of steps.

However, this pursuit is complicated by two factors: first, the tunes have been greatly altered in Métis tradition, often making comparison with older tunes difficult; and second, the older repertoire is reported to have almost completely disappeared in the Orkneys. In any case, although such explorations may be a matter of historical curiosity, they tell us little about Métis culture.

In all areas, older tunes are named for their dances—"Red River Jig," "Duck Dance," "Rabbit Dance," "Reel of Four," "Reel of Eight," "Hook Dance" (also called "Brandy" or "Drops of Brandy"), "La Double Gigue" ("Double Jig" in Alaska/Yukon), and "Handkerchief Dance" (or "Scarf Dance"), all of which are well known on both the prairies and in Yukon/Alaska. These appear to be directly related to older dances from the Orkney and Shetland Islands. Each dance seems to have one particular tune associated with it in any given area in North America, but not always the same one in every place. Although a few of the tunes are well known ("Macdonald's Reel" for a "Reel of Eight," "Fisher's Hornpipe" for "La Double Gigue"), others have proved more elusive.

There are obvious Québécois connections in both tunes and dances, further revealed by the use of the term *jig* in English for simple rather than compound meter, corresponding to the French use of the word *gigue* for simple time step-dance tunes. Thus, "La gigue de la rivière rouge" (in Québec, "La grande gigue simple") translates into "Red River Jig" and "La double gigue" into "Double Jig," with both being in simple duple time (although irregular), not in 6/8. It is possible that much of this older Scottish-derived repertoire came northwest from Québec. Some tunes, such as "Le brandy/Drops of Brandy" and "La grand gigue simple/Red River Jig," are regular in form in Québec and asymmetric in Métis culture, whereas others, such as "La double gigue," are irregular in both areas.

On the prairies other one-tune couple dances such as the "Seven-Step," "The Butterfly," and "The Waltz Quadrille" have been adopted that do not seem to be known in Yukon/Alaska. In both areas, though, there is a whole range of dances from more recent Canadian and American sources that can be done to any number of tunes, including three-part quadrille sets of first change, second change, and breakdown, polkas, waltzes, schottisches, fox-trots, one-steps, and two-steps. Common on the prairies but seemingly unknown in Yukon/Alaska is the "sideways polka" that usually kicks off a dance as a warm-up and acts as filler between dances. Couples do a basic polka step in side-by-side formation, all facing the same direction, in a big circle around the floor, while the fiddler plays any number of tunes of his choosing. It would seem that the Red River Jig serves this "filler" function in Yukon/Alaska, whereas on the prairies, the Red River Jig was generally saved for one special time of night, usually just before midnight and the supper break.

Players have learned other names for older tunes as they hear them from others or see them on recordings. "'Early on, I never did hear them call a name on a tune. . . . 'Whiskey Before Breakfast' . . . that was a 'Reel of Eight.' The first time I heard a name for that was Andy de Jarlis'" (Leary 1992:24). Many common Anglo-North American tunes are known by name, such as "Devil's Dream," "Soldier's Joy," "Flowers of Edinburgh," "Girl I Left Behind Me," "Turkey in the Straw," "Arkansas Traveler," and others. These tunes generally exhibit less irregularity in phrasing, suggesting they came into the repertoire more recently. In parts of northern Ontario, "Sainte Anne's Reel" is thought of as particularly Métis.

Tunes adopted from Ukrainian, Swedish, Icelandic, and English settlers all entered the prairie repertoire from the late 1800s on. In the twentieth century, more tunes came into the repertoire from radio and recordings. Especially popular on the prairies are tunes from Andy de Jarlis, a French Métis fiddler from Woodridge, Manitoba, who recorded thirty-three records of traditional and original tunes, many of the former in somewhat "straightened" versions. It is not uncommon to hear older players say that Andy changed the older tunes.

STEP DANCING AND THE RED RIVER JIG

West of Ontario, the Red River Jig (figure 4) is considered a cornerstone of traditional Métis culture. While still played in James Bay and northern Ontario, however, it is not common in more southerly Ontario Métis communities. The term *Red River Jig* has become generic for both step dancing in general, also called simply "jigging," and the tune now almost universally played for it. Interestingly, there are reports in Manitoba of another "Red River Jig" tune having been used in the past (Lederman 1987a), a tune known to some Acadian fiddlers. Also, as with other tunes, it seems to have been a point of pride to have one's own version of "Red River Jig" at one time, but the one recorded by Andy de Jarlis in the 1950s is most commonly heard today.

There are many regional variations in exactly how and when the Red River Jig is done, such as whether or not an individual, a couple, or several of either take to the floor simultaneously, the preferred posture, and whether the dance is done at a specific time (Prairies) or whenever the dancers wish it (Yukon/Alaska), but some features are common throughout. A two-part tune, the dance involves a basic time step on the high part and a number of individual steps on the low part that vary from person to person. The dance is a test of endurance and skill and even in community settings has always been somewhat competitive, both in the number and complexity of steps. Some dancers proudly attest to knowing thirty or more individual steps. In some areas a very straight posture with little movement besides that of the feet is prized (Winnipeg and Yukon/Alaska), while in others, the body is bent over almost double to the floor (witnessed by the author in The Pas, Manitoba).

The Red River Jig is done by both men and women, and although many attest that their style and steps were different in the past, the women's footwork involving smaller steps and less athletic movements, this seems to be less true today. While it is still a mainstay at social dances, it has also been done in formal competitions since at least the 1930s in Manitoba. In competition, men and women, boys and girls usually compete separately and do only three fancy steps each on which they are judged. At some contests, they preserve the circling movements common to community dances, while at others, such as that held at Le Festival de Voyageur every winter in St. Boniface, Manitoba, a small square is marked on the floor within which the dancer must stay.

In most Métis communities, jigging is done throughout all group dances as well. Usually dancers do the basic time step of the Red River Jig, adapted to 6/8 when necessary, although in some northern areas 6/8 is hardly ever played. However, some dancers will go into other fancy steps, especially during parts of the dances where they are not active. On the prairies, this practice of jigging constantly through all group dances is considered a way of distinguishing Métis communities from non-Métis ones.

Many Métis fiddlers have recorded over the years, although, ironically, the older style has reappeared recently. Andy de Jarlis was probably the first prairie Métis player to record, followed by Reg Bouvette and Marcel Meilleur, Emile Spence, Mel Bedard,

FIGURE 4   "Red River Jig," as played by Lawrence "Teddy Boy" Houle, 1985. Transcription by Anne Lederman, field collection.

Eugene Laderoute, Cliff Maytwayashing, Lawrence "Teddy Boy" Houle, John Arcand, Calvin Volrath and others. Sunshine Records of Winnipeg released many recordings of Native and Métis players from the 1960s on, but very little of this repertoire is in the older style. More recently in Ontario, Sinclair Cheechoo and James Cheechoo of Moose Factory have recorded older repertoire, and Bill Stevens in the Yukon has two independent releases. Anthology collections that document at least some aspects of older style are also available (Lederman 1987a, b; Mishler 1974, 1984). Michael Loukinen's film *Medicine Fiddle* (1992) is an excellent introduction to the subject.

SONGS

Many French songs dating back several centuries are part of Métis song repertoire, again often carried west with voyagers and frequently adapted locally. In addition, many songs were composed on the prairies specifically about Métis experience, especially during the nineteenth century, when political consciousness of the Métis as a distinct people was strong. Some of these songs were written down at the time by their authors or others, and many have survived for generations in oral tradition to be written down by collectors in the twentieth century. However, as Mitchif was often not considered a real language and/or was not always understood by transcribers, many of these songs have been rendered in standard French, not in their probable Mitchif origins. As a testament to the difficulties around the Mitchif language, one well-known song, "La lettre de sang" (sometimes called the "Louis Riel Song," although probably not composed by him) has been transcribed by three different collectors from the same singer, two from the same original recording, all resulting in fairly different versions of the words (Thomas 1993:12–18). Sometimes collectors acknowledge they have changed the words, either because they could not understand the original or decided they did not make sense (Cass-Beggs 1967:11).

Louis Riel did write songs, several of which survive, but the best-known song-writer of the last century is Pierre Falcon, known as "The Bard of the Prairies" or "Pierre the Rhymester," as he is represented in a literary work of the day (Laut 1900). His repertoire spans a fifty-year period from about 1816 to 1869. He wrote many songs describing important political events, such as his most famous one, "La Bataille des Sept Chênes" (The Battle of Seven Oaks) commemorating the 1816 altercation between *bois brulées* (literally, "burnt wood," another name for the Métis) and the newly arrived Selkirk settlers. The song became even more popular later in the century as a rallying cry during the two Riel Rebellions. Falcon's songs were generally set to older French melodies (MacLeod 1959) and were frequently "chanson a répondre" in style.

Henri Létourneau, curator of La Musée de Saint Boniface, gathered a large collection of songs from both Métis and French singers from the 1950s on, but these have not been published. Available song collections of all or partially Métis material include Cass-Beggs (1967), Ferland (1979), MacLeod (1959), and a recent collection by Lynn Whiddon for school use that has some songs in Mitchif (1993).

Contemporary Métis songwriters such as Laura Vinson, Shingoose, Edgar Desjarlais, Winston Wuttunee, and Don Freed have continued to write about Métis social and political experience, mostly in English. Also, mainstream country music has became extremely popular throughout Métis communities, and, in some areas, bluegrass is also popular [see COUNTRY AND WESTERN, p. 76; BLUEGRASS, p. 158]. More recently, young people are forming blues and rock bands [see BLUES, p. 637; ROCK, p. 347]. Current dances in prairie Métis communities are often a combination of country songs on drums, electric bass and guitars mixed with old Métis fiddle dances.

REFERENCES

Bakker, Peter. 1992. *"A Language of our Own": The Genesis of Michif, The Mixed Cree-French Language of the Canadian Métis.* Amsterdam: University of Amsterdam.

Bouvette, Reg. n.d. *Red River Jig.* Sunshine Records SSB 402. LP disk and cassette.

Cass-Beggs, Barbara. 1967. *Seven Métis Songs.* Don Mills: BMI Canada.

Cheechoo, James. 1998. *Shay Chee Man.* Kwishkegun Productions JCCS 01. Compact disc and cassette.

Chrétien, Annette. 1996. "'Mattawa, Where the Waters Meet': The Question of Identity in Métis Culture." Master's thesis, University of Ottawa.

DeJarlis, Andy. n.d. *Back Again.* Sunshine Records SSB 434. Cassette.

Duchênes, Donald. n.d. "Les chansons de Joe Venne, Métis." *Canadian Folk Music Journal* 21:3–11.

Ferland, Marcien. 1979. *Chansons à répondre du Manitoba.* Ottawa: Les Éditions du Blé.

Freed, Don, and Prince Albert students. 1996. *Singing About the Métis.* Bush League Records BL8. Cassette.

Gibbons, Roy. 1980a. "'La Grande Gigue Simple' and the 'Red River Jig': A Comparative Study of Two Regional Styles of a Traditional Fiddle Tune." *Canadian Folk Music Journal* 8:40–48.

———. 1980b. "Ethnomusicology of the Métis in Alberta and Saskatchewan: A Distinct Cultural Display of Anglo-Celtic, French and Native Elements." Audiotape, Video Collection, and Field Report. Canadian Centre for Folk Culture Studies, National Museum of Civilization.

Heth, Charlotte, producer. *Wood That Sings: Indian Fiddle Music of the Americas.* Smithsonian Folkways SF 40472.

Houle, Lawrence. 1986. *Lawrence "Teddy Boy" Houle.* Sunshine Records SSBCT 442. LP disk and cassette.

Institute of Alaska Native Arts. 1987. *Interior Tunes: Athapaskan Old-Time Music.* Fairbanks: Institute of Alaska Native Arts.

Laut, Agnes. 1900. *Lords of the North.* Toronto: Ryerson Press.

Leary, James, editor. 1992. "Medicine Fiddle: A Humanities Discussion Guide." Booklet to accompany film, *Medicine Fiddle.* Marquette, Mich.: Northern Michigan University.

Lederman, Anne. 1984. "Fiddling in Western Manitoba." Audiotape Collection and Field Report. Canadian Centre for Folk Culture Studies, Canadian Museum of Civilization.

———. 1986. "Old Native and Métis Fiddling in Two Manitoba Communities: Camperville and Ebb and Flow." Master's thesis, York University.

———. 1987a. *Old Native and Métis Fiddling in Manitoba,* vols. I and II. Falcon Productions FP 187, FP 287. Compact discs.

———. 1987b. "Instrumental Music: The Three Sisters." In *Canadian Folk Music Bulletin* 21(2):17–22.

———. 1988. "Old Indian and Métis Fiddling in Manitoba: Origins, Structure and the Question of Syncretism." *The Canadian Journal of Native Studies* 8 (2):205–230. First published in *Canadian Folk Music Journal* 19:40–60.

———. 1989. "Dancing in Western Manitoba." Videotape Collection and Field Report. Canadian Centre for Folk Culture Studies, Canadian Museum of Civilization.

———. 1990. "The Drops of Brandy: Several Versions of a Métis Fiddle Tune." *Canadian Folk Music Bulletin* 24(1):3–11.

Loukinen, Michael. 1992. *Medicine Fiddle.* Marquette, Mich.: Up North Films.

Macbeth, R. G. 1971. *The Selkirk Settlers in Real Life.* Toronto: William Briggs.

MacLeod, Margaret Arnett. 1959. *Songs of Old Manitoba.* Toronto: The Ryerson Press.

Meilleur, Marcel. *Hooked on Fiddle.* Sunshine Records SSB 433.

Mishler, Craig. 1974. *Music of the Alaskan Kutchin Indians.* Folkways FE 4070. LP disk.

———. 1984. *Turtle Mountain Music.* Folkways FES 4140. Compact disc.

———. 1993. *The Crooked Stovepipe.* Urbana: University of Illinois Press.

———. 1999. "Athabascan Fiddlers and Dancers." *Fiddler Magazine* 6(2):4–8.

Peterson, Jacquelin, and J. Brown, eds. 1987. *The New Peoples: Being and Becoming Métis in North America.* Winnipeg: University of Manitoba Press.

Stevens, Bill. 1995. *Alaska Gwich'in Fiddler.* N.p.

Thomas, Philip J. 1993. "The 'Louis Riel Song': A Perspective." *Canadian Folk Music Journal* 21:12–18.

Whiddon, Lynn. 1989. "SMEA Prairie Music Project 1988–89." *Canadian Folk Music Bulletin* 23(3):7–9.

———. 1990. "A Note on Métis Music: Songs From the SMEA Project." *Canadian Folk Music Bulletin* 24(1):12–24.

———. 1992. "Métis." In *Encyclopedia of Music in Canada,* 2nd ed., ed. Helmut Kallman, Gilles Potvin, and Kenneth Winters, 851–852. Toronto: University of Toronto Press.

———. 1993. *Métis Songs: Visiting was the Métis Way.* New York: Gabriel Dumont Institute.

California
Richard Keeling

Northwestern California
Northeastern California
North-Central California
San Joaquin Valley and Adjacent Foothills of the Sierra Nevadas
Southern California

Before contact with Europeans, California was extremely rich in natural resources such as acorn-bearing oak trees, salmon, deer, elk, and smaller game animals. It was one of the most densely populated and culturally variegated areas in all of North America: at least sixty-four mutually unintelligible languages were spoken, representing twenty-one language families, and the indigenous cultures of various subregions within the state were strikingly diverse. Indians of California were also among the last in North America to have their lives greatly altered by contact with whites. Native civilizations of the central coast and Southern California were severely devastated by the Spanish Catholic missionization that took place between 1769 and 1832, but those of the northern counties and Sierra Nevada regions were relatively untouched by outsiders before the Gold Rush of 1850. Despite the genocide that followed, there are many areas in which traditional songs and dances are still being performed. The ethnographic situation is so complex that one needs to provide separate accounts for five distinct subareas of traditional music.

NORTHWESTERN CALIFORNIA

A unique and relatively self-contained civilization developed among Indians of the region encompassing modern Humboldt, Del Norte, and Siskiyou counties. This civilization centered on the Yurok, Karok, and Hupa tribes but was also shared to a lesser extent by neighboring groups such as the Wiyot, Tolowa, Chilula, and Whilkut. In some respects these cultures can be viewed as belonging to the Northwest Coast culture area—for example, they share ideas about the importance of wealth and status in native society or the performance of a First Salmon Ceremony—but their rituals and music are distinctively Californian and without close parallels elsewhere.

Important contexts for performance

Two of the most important ceremonies are the White Deerskin Dance and the Jump Dance. Comparable to New Year celebrations, they are also deeply religious in character, as their purpose is to renew the world and purify it from the polluting influence of human beings. The music for these ceremonies is slow to moderate in tempo, and the singers (always men) often seem to have a "sobbing" quality in their voices, as if they were crying. These dances are still being performed regularly, but because they are considered too sacred for public demonstrations, the music can only be heard by those who attend the actual ceremonies or obtain recordings from archives.

By contrast, songs of the Brush Dance are often sung in public. This is also a religious ceremony, traditionally held to cure a sick child, but even though it is a sacred event it is also an occasion for having fun. There are "heavy songs" and "light songs" heard during the Brush Dance, but even the more religious heavy songs have a strongly rhythmic feeling that derives from the contrast between a repeated bass pattern (sung by the group) and the syncopated solo part that is sung by the lead singer.

The basic texture can be heard in the recorded example, although it should be noted that there are only two "helpers" on this recording, while many more would be heard in an actual Brush Dance. The soloist starts alone, and after a few phrases the others begin their ostinato. This is done softly at first, but the ensemble becomes increasingly louder and more markedly rhythmic until it reaches a peak of volume and intensity toward the end, when the lead singer terminates the song rather abruptly with a closing flourish or shout. The solo part of this Brush Dance heavy song (first rendition) is transcribed in figure 1. As indicated, the melodic form can be conceived as

FIGURE I   Brush Dance heavy song sung by Ewing Davis (Hupa) and recorded by Frank Quinn in 1956. Transcription by Richard Keeling (1992).

This is done softly at first, but the ensemble becomes increasingly louder and more markedly rhythmic until it reaches a peak of volume and intensity toward the end, when the lead singer terminates the song rather abruptly with a closing flourish or shout.

consisting of three main parts (ABB[1]), the last including some extended improvisation as the song reaches a peak of emotion. All of these songs are relatively short in duration, generally about one minute, and each is sung three times with considerable variation in an actual dance. This type of counterpoint is very rare in Native American music, but some form of it occurs in nearly all types of group singing from this area.

The most prominent contexts for contemporary public singing are the White Deerskin Dance, Jump Dance, Brush Dance, and gambling songs. Other ceremonies that have greatly declined but still occur occasionally are the War Dance, Kick Dance (a curing ritual for female shamans), and Flower Dance (a puberty ceremony for girls).

Musical style

Each of these contexts has its own musical style—most readily identified by a distinctive bass pattern—but it is also possible to identify general characteristics that hold for nearly all styles of group singing from this area. The basic traits are as follows:

1. The solo part often has a sobbing quality, and there is much tension, pulsation, nasality, and sliding.
2. The song texts most often consist of vocables rather than words, and the setting is melismatic (many pitches sung to one syllable).
3. The musical texture features a solo part and some type of bass part sung by the group.
4. The melodic form is typically strophic or through-composed, and songs usually include a contrasting phrase or groups of phrases sung at a higher pitch level than the opening melodic phrases.
5. The melodic range is extremely wide, usually an octave or more and often as wide as a twelfth.
6. The melodic contour is typically descending.
7. Scales are most often five tones.
8. Simple meters (simple or compound duple [2/4 or 6/8]) are the general rule, although dropped or added beats are frequent, and there is a tendency toward syncopation; irregular (changing) meters or complex (additive) meters are rare.
9. The solo part may include some of the bass part's melodic motives, especially at the end of phrases, and there is a general tendency for the solo part to begin in a high register, then descend gradually so as to merge with the bass part at the end of phrases.

In precontact times, shamanism (performed by female "Indian doctors") and use of medicine songs for magical purposes was highly developed among the groups of this area. More than one thousand sound recordings have been collected from this area in the years since 1900. These are mainly available at the Phoebe Hearst Museum (University of California, Berkeley) and at the American Folklife Center (Library of Congress, Washington, D.C.).

NORTHEASTERN CALIFORNIA

Songs and dances of the Modoc, Achumawi, Atsugewi, Yana, and other tribes of Modoc and Lassen counties are much less well known. In precontact times, the ceremonial life of this region seems to have been less developed than elsewhere in California, and the main contexts for public singing were a girl's puberty ceremony and gambling games. Nearly all historical recordings that have been collected in this area fit the profile of animal songs as described above. Recently this has become a sort of international zone, musically speaking. One can hear pan-Indian singing at an annual powwow in Susanville, while on other occasions such as the Maidu Bear Dance one hears hand-game (gambling) songs performed by Indians from various tribes of California and Nevada as well as other vocal music in the North-Central style discussed below [see MUSICAL INTERACTIONS, p. 480; GREAT BASIN, p. 420].

NORTH-CENTRAL CALIFORNIA

This large musical style area stretches from Mendocino and Sonoma counties in the west, across the Sacramento Valley and eastward into the adjacent northern Sierra Nevada range. Major tribal groups include the Pomo, Yuki, Nomlaki, Patwin, Maidu, Konkow, Nisenan, and Miwok.

Contexts for music performance

Music and ceremonial life throughout this region were very complex in precontact times, when a number of different cultures and religious systems existed. During the past 150 years there have been major transformations in music and spiritual life, mainly through the influence of the Ghost Dance during the 1870s and the subsequent emergence of what has been called the Dreamer religion or Bole-Maru cult. Still, it is clearly best to think of this as a unified musical area in the context of a general survey.

In ancient times many of these tribes shared a ceremonial complex that has been called the Kuksu religion. In a sense these rituals were similar to those of the (Northwestern) World Renewal ceremonies, as they were intended to renew and preserve the natural world, but dance rituals of the Kuksu religion also featured impersonations of supernatural beings. These dances were held in large, semisubterranean ceremonial houses or roundhouses. Today, these are sometimes known as Bighead dances, because of a costume the main dancer wears, but in fact the Bighead is only one of several deities and animals that were imitated in earlier times. In most areas the spirit impersonations were connected with initiation rites into men's secret societies. Boys would be taken into the roundhouses by their adult male sponsors and then subjected to formalized ordeals, such as being frightened or shot at with false arrows. The younger members were allowed to dance as smaller deities such as Duck, Goose, Coyote, or Deer. Later, as they became older and more knowledgeable, they would perhaps be permitted to impersonate more important deities such as the Cloud, the Woman, the Bighead, or the Grizzly Bear.

Musical style

Throughout this area the various tribes also perform secular dances such as the Shakehead Dance or the Pomo Ball Dance, and these illustrate the basic style of group singing in the region. This music resembles the Northwestern style in that it is contrapuntal, but the nature of the counterpoint is very different. In North-Central California, the solo part is augmented by another basically rhythmic part known as "the rock." This accompaniment is sung by one person, and the singing itself is called "holding rock." In addition to the soloist and the rock there is the rhythmic beating of clapsticks (played by the singers) and often the sound of whistles blown by dancers, so that the whole musical texture is fairly complex. The basic characteristics of the style can be summarized as follows:

1. The vocal delivery is tense and forceful, but there is less nasality, pulsation, glottalization, and glissando than in Northwestern singing.
2. The song texts usually consist of vocables rather than words, and the setting of the text is syllabic (one pitch for one word).
3. The musical texture includes a solo vocal part, a vocal accompaniment (the rock) sung by an individual, and rhythmic support by instruments such as the clapstick and single-pitched whistles.
4. The typical melodic form consists of one or two phrases repeated with variation, but there is often a contrasting section sung at a higher pitch level. Native singers call this contrasting section "the turn," and it corresponds in type to what George Herzog (1928:193) and Bruno Nettl (1954:18–19) have called "the rise."
5. The melodic range is moderate, usually between a fifth and an octave.
6. The contour is typically level or undulating.
7. Three-, four-, and five-tone scales are the most typical, and half steps or minor second intervals are common.
8. Simple meters such as 2/4 and 3/4 and complex meters—especially an 8/8 measure comprising 3+3+2—are about equally represented.
9. The rhythmic complexity of the singing is connected to a sophisticated formalization of dance, as there are several different step patterns associated with particular types of vocal rhythm.

Generally speaking, published sources on native culture and ritual life in this region are fairly numerous and of good quality, while studies of the music itself are less satisfactory for one reason or another. Many historical recordings from this area may be found at the Phoebe Hearst Museum of Anthropology, the Archives of Traditional Music (Indiana University), and the American Folklife Center.

SAN JOAQUIN VALLEY AND ADJACENT FOOTHILLS OF THE SIERRA NEVADAS

Music and culture among the various Yokuts tribes of this area differ sharply from those of the North-Central area. Although instruments such as the clapstick and cocoon rattle are known in both regions, the Yokuts' musical style has greater affinity with that of their easterly neighbors the Monache (Western Mono) and other tribes of the Great Basin area [see GREAT BASIN, p. 420]. There are also certain cultural connections to Southern California, as mourning rituals and initiation ceremonies involving the drinking of crushed datura roots (jimson weed or *toloache*) were widespread throughout both the San Joaquin Valley and among Southern California tribes in aboriginal times.

Through drinking various narcotic substances, young adults in this area expected to have visions or hallucinations in which they formed relations with a guardian spirit. The connection with a spirit helper was often symbolized by a song, and titles such as "Eagle Song," "Coyote Song," "Owl Song," and "Beaver Song" generally derive from relationships of this sort. Hand-game songs and mourning songs are also very prominent in the Yokuts' repertoires.

Musical style

In this singing the vocal delivery is much softer and more relaxed than in the Northwestern and North-Central styles discussed previously, and rather than employing some form of counterpoint the Yokuts ensemble style has a unison texture: that is, when there are two or more singers they sing the same melody together. Most important, there is a distinctive type of melodic form or structure that is very common in recordings from this area. In many of the songs, each phrase of the music is sung twice, so that many of the songs have an AABB structure. This type of paired patterning is common in songs of the Ghost Dance, but the historical basis of this correspondence is not well understood [see MUSICAL INTERACTIONS, p. 480].

Precontact rituals as described above are no longer performed, but singers who demonstrate traditional music (especially hand-game songs) can still be found. Yokuts culture and religion are described in some detail in the literature. Recordings are available at the Hearst Museum of Anthropology and at the American Folklife Center.

SOUTHERN CALIFORNIA

The entire area south of the Tehachapi mountain range can be viewed as a fairly unified region, including tribal groups such as the Luiseño, Serrano, Cahuilla, Diegueño (or Ipai and Tipai), and Mohave. This is another international zone in which Californian musical traditions have a strong relationship with those of other native peoples to the east. From a comparative perspective, the most striking element in the public singing of this region is the presence of songs that are sung in groups or series. These song-cycles are mythological: that is, each song depicts a particular image or event, and, strung together in a series, these songs reveal a history of events that took place shortly after the world was created. In earlier times there were more than a hundred songs in some of the cycles, so that singing an entire cycle took some time. Many different cycles were known. These can be considered a form of literature as much as music, and similar traditions of epic poetry are found among other Indian peoples of the greater Southwest culture area, for example, the Havasupai and Walapai of Arizona and the Yaquis of Arizona and northwestern Mexico.

Contexts for musical performance

In earlier times, these songs were recited as part of a very complex ceremonial life. There were two main categories of ceremonies: (1) various rituals to initiate adolescents of either sex as they approached adulthood and (2) other types of ceremonies to mourn the passing of tribal members. Today, much of the early ceremonial life has been lost, and many of the song-cycles have been forgotten. However, the cycle known as Bird Songs is still being performed in a style that Indians believe has been handed down continuously since the era described in the mythic texts themselves. The words derive from an ancient language that is no longer spoken or understood by modern singers, and the music itself varies in style from stately, chantlike introductory songs to highly syncopated melodies with catchy rhythms.

Musical style

The general profile for public singing in the Southern California region can be given as follows:

1. The vocal delivery is fairly soft and relaxed, but the most comfortable range of the singing is lower than that of the San Joaquin Valley (Yokuts) tribes. The total melodic range is moderate (usually from a fifth to an octave).
2. The songs have words in an archaic language no longer understood by modern singers, and the setting of the text is syllabic.
3. All singers perform the same melody in unison, with regular rhythmic accompaniment by seed-rattles.
4. The melodic form is best classified as complex litany; that is, the songs consist of one or two phrases repeated over and over but typically include a contrasting section sung at higher pitch level (the rise).
5. The contour is typically level or undulating.
6. Scales are usually six or occasionally five tones.

While certain types of polyphony have been noted among tribes of the Northwest Coast, true rhythmic counterpoint is much more prevalent in California than in other regions of North America.

7. Complex and irregular meters are very common.
8. The songs are strung together into lengthy cycles or series.

There are some excellent sources on earlier music and culture of this area. These include Herzog (1928), Kroeber (1976 [1925]), Roberts (1933), and Waterman (1910). Historical recordings can be found at the Hearst Museum of Anthropology and the American Folklife Center.

From this survey we can see that it is not easy to generalize about California Indian music, but it does seem possible to note certain traits that distinguish it from other areas of Native American music. The presence of vocal counterpoint as a basic element in public singing is one of the most distinctive characteristics. While certain types of polyphony have been noted among tribes of the Northwest Coast, true rhythmic counterpoint is much more prevalent in California than in other regions of North America. Contrapuntal styles have been described here among the Northwestern and North-Central California nations, but other types of counterpoint are also evident in historical sources and archival recordings of music pertaining to certain earlier rituals of Southern California groups.

Another unique feature pertains to musical form or structure. The formal device of including repeated or new melodic material sung at a higher pitch level than the opening phrases of a song (the rise) was first identified as a basic feature of Mohave and Diegueño Indian singing by Herzog (1928:193). Years later, Nettl (1954:18–19) argued that the rise was widespread in California and highly distinctive of the region as a whole. Nettl's study was based on limited evidence, but it seems clear now that various forms of the rise are indeed present throughout much of California, even in musical styles and performance contexts that are otherwise quite diverse. This musical structure is much less common in the adjacent culture areas or elsewhere in North America.

Finally, it should be noted that California Indian peoples have been fairly resistant to external or modernizing influences relating to music and ceremonial activities. The Ghost Dance had an impact here, but neither the Ghost Dance nor the Native American Church were embraced in California as they were, for example, in the adjacent Great Basin area. Pan-Indian powwows have recently become popular in urban areas, especially among Indian people from other states. But Native Californians on rural reservations have generally tended to place much importance on maintaining their own tribal music and dance traditions above all others.

REFERENCES

Angulo, Jaime de, and Marguerite Béclard d'Harcourt. 1931. "La Musique des Indiens de la Californie du Nord." *Journal de la Société des Americanistes de Paris* 23(1):189–228.

Barrett, Samuel A. 1963. *The Hupa Jump Dance at Hupa, 1962.* Kroeber Anthropological Society Papers, vol. 28. Berkeley: University of California, 73–85.

Cummins, Marjorie. 1979. *The Tachi Yokuts Indians of the San Joaquin Valley: Their Lives, Songs, and Stories.* Fresno, Calif.: Pioneer Publishing.

Densmore, Frances. 1958. *Music of the Maidu Indians of California.* Los Angeles: Southwest Museum.

Gifford, Edward. 1955. *Central Miwok Ceremonies.* University of California Anthropological Records, vol. 14, no. 4. Berkeley, 261–318.

Goldschmidt, Walter, and Harold Driver. 1940. *The Hupa White Deerskin Dance.* University of California Publications in American Archeology and Ethnology, vol. 35. Berkeley, 103–142.

Hall, Jody C., and Bruno Nettl. 1955. "Musical Style of the Modoc." *Southwestern Journal of Anthropology* 11:58–66.

Halpern, Abraham M. 1988. *Southeastern Pomo Ceremonials: The Kuksu Cult and Its Successors.* University of California Anthropological Records, vol. 29. Berkeley.

Hatch, James. 1958. *Tachi Yokuts Music.* Kroeber Anthropological Society Papers, vol. 19. Berkeley: University of California, 47–66.

Herzog, George. 1928. "The Yuman Musical Style." *Journal of American Folklore* 41(160):183–231.

Keeling, Richard H. 1992. *Cry for Luck: Sacred Song and Speech among the Yurok, Hupa, and Karok Indians of Northwestern California.* Berkeley: University of California Press.

Kroeber, Alfred L. 1976 [1925]. *Handbook of the Indians of California.* Bureau of American Ethnology Bulletin 78. New York: Dover Publications.

Kroeber, Alfred L., and Edward W. Gifford. 1949. *World Renewal: A Cult System of Native Northwest California.* University of California Anthropological Records, vol. 21, no. 1. Berkeley, 1–210.

Meighan, Clement, and Francis Riddell. 1972. *The Maru Cult of the Pomo Indians.* Southwest Museum Papers, no. 23. Los Angeles: Southwest Museum.

Merriam, Alan P., and Robert F. G. Spier. 1958. *Chukchansi Yokuts Songs.* Proceedings of the 33rd International Congress of Americanists, San José,

Costa Rica. San José: Impreso por la Editorial Lehmann.

Nettl, Bruno. 1954. *North American Indian Musical Styles.* Philadelphia: American Folklore Society.

———. 1965. "The Songs of Ishi: Musical Style of the Yahi Indians." *Musical Quarterly* 51(3): 460–477.

Roberts, Helen H. 1933. *Form in Primitive Music: An Analytical and Comparative Study of the Melodic Form of Some Ancient Southern Californian Indian Songs.* New York: Norton.

Wallace, William J. 1978. "Music and Musical Instruments." In *Handbook of North American Indians,* vol. 8: *California,* ed. William C. Sturtevant and Robert F. Heiser, 642–648. Washington, D.C.: Smithsonian Institution.

Waterman, Thomas T. 1910. *The Religious Practices of the Diegueno Indians.* University of California Publications in American Archeology and Ethnology, vol. 8, no. 6. Berkeley, 271–358.

Great Basin
Brenda M. Romero

The Great Basin Indians inhabited an area that now includes much of Utah and Nevada and parts of Colorado, Wyoming, Idaho, Oregon, and California, as well as the northern fringes of Arizona and New Mexico. The Basin—a sink area, also referred to as a desert plateau—includes the mountainous areas of the Humboldt Range of Nevada, the Wasatch Range of Utah, and the Rocky Mountains of Colorado, as well as other uplands, all of which provide essential forests and winter snows to the region. The mountains also block rainfall, however, creating a very arid and harsh environment in most of the region. Over the ten thousand years that Native peoples have lived here they have experienced the gradual drying of an area originally covered with bodies of water, including the Great Salt Lake of Utah, which is much smaller than it once was.

HISTORY AND CULTURE

Agricultural communities of the Fremont culture had disappeared by the fourteenth century. Survival has depended on fishing and hunting, primarily for small game and other edible creatures, and on seasonal foraging migrations from mountain ridges to lowland marshes in search of food, water, firewood, and material with which to make baskets and other utensils. Before contact with Europeans people often dispersed into small groups, especially family units or bands of families, convening with each other and with neighboring Indian groups for extended periods in places where food was abundant. This included communal antelope, rabbit, or grasshopper drives (Waldman 1985:36). The most important Basin crop was the piñon nut, and elaborate rituals accompanied the initiation of its early autumn harvest, including celebratory social Round Dances. The harvest itself lasted for weeks. The Shoshone considered the chokecherry a sacred food, and its harvest was also an occasion of elaborate rituals.

The peoples occupying the Basin today are primarily Numic speakers (of the northern branch of the Uto-Aztecan language family), whose ancestors arrived in this area from the South about 1000 C.E. They include the Paiutes, Shoshones, Bannocks, Utes (Weeminuche or Weenuche), and Kawaiisu. The Washo, who live in the area bordering California and Nevada, speak a Hokan language in common with the Pomo and various other, primarily northern California, groups. Distinct regional identities are applied to the Northern Paiutes, the Owens Valley Paiutes, and the Southern Paiutes, who are linguistically closer to the Utes and the Kawaiisu than to the other

Paiute groups. The Shoshones divide into Western, Eastern, and Northern groups, the latter traditionally associated with a Paiute group called Bannocks.

The introduction of the horse further delineated regional tribal differences. Wherever the land was favorable for sustaining horses, as for the Northern and Eastern Shoshones and the Utes, traditional lifeways were supplemented by buffalo hunting. These groups also adopted buffalo skin clothing and tipis and began to need and use chiefs to coordinate the buffalo hunt and to deal with enemies encountered on the plains, which included the Nez Perces and the Flathead from the Columbia Plateau, the region north of the Great Basin. The Arapaho were hostile, as were the Hidatsas, who became formidable after obtaining firearms from whites in the 1700s. The horse further gave some Basin tribes unfair advantage over others, and some took Indian captives to sell as slaves to the Spanish.

THE GHOST DANCE

Beliefs in ghosts and a fear of the dead have always been common among American Indians, and in the Basin many believed that ghosts wanted to abduct the living and take them to the other world [see MUSICAL INTERACTIONS, p. 480]. It is somewhat surprising, therefore, that the Ghost Dance gained as much momentum as it did, and many attribute this to the influence of Christian beliefs about heaven.

The Ghost Dance phenomenon was preceded by Eastern native revivalist movements dating as far back as the 1760s. The Ghost Dance itself is believed to have been dreamed a century later by a Walker Lake–Walker River Northern Paiute prophet named Wodziwob. Another Paiute, named Ta'vibo, from the Walker Lake, Nevada, area, spread the teachings that included returning to the old ways of life and the resurrection of the dead. Around 1886 Ta'vibo's son Wovoka (Jack Wilson), a Northern Paiute medicine man, fused the teachings (already influenced by the Mormon missionaries of Utah) with Christian ideas he had acquired when he worked for a Presbyterian family named Wilson. Wovoka articulated a messianic promise that the Ghost Dance would restore life to what it had been or better than it had been before the advent of the whites; the buffalo would return and whites would disappear.

The movement quickly spread among up to thirty-five nations, encompassing over sixty thousand Indians at a time when white settlers armed with guns had reduced the Indian population to fewer than three hundred thousand by the end of the nineteenth century. (At the time of the conquest, the Indian population in North America was at least two and one-half million—the conservative government estimate; recent systematic scholarly estimates average around fifteen million.) The Ghost Dance was forbidden following the massacre of more than two hundred Lakotas at Wounded Knee in 1890, but Great Basin groups continued to sing Ghost Dance songs in association with a ritual for good health. Among the Wind River Shoshones, Judith Vander (1997) documented that Naraya songs rooted in Ghost Dance beliefs continued to be sung by some women for their own and others' physical well-being until the early 1980s, although most Shoshones had abandoned the beliefs and repertoire by 1940.

Music of the Ghost Dance

George Herzog noted a strong Great Basin influence in Ghost Dance songs, reflected in the paired phrasing that is the main stylistic identifier of this region (1935:413–415). This is a simple repetition of both the melody and text of each of the two or three phrases that make up the song, for example:

> E'yehe'! they are new—
> E'yehe'! they are new—
> The bed coverings,
> The bed coverings. (Mooney 1973 [1896]:963)

Wovoka articulated a messianic promise that the Ghost Dance would restore life to what it had been or better than it had been before the advent of the whites; the buffalo would return and whites would disappear.

Songs were received in the trance state induced by the Ghost Dance, in which hundreds of participants formed concentric circles, stepping to the left and dragging the right foot, while the songs and dance got faster and faster. The stamping and dragging created a fine dust two or three inches high on the ground, and every so often someone would scoop some in his hands and toss it high into the air (perhaps recalling the biblical phrase "dust to dust"). The song above was received by a woman who, in her trance, was taken to a large camp where all the tipis, beds, and interior furniture were made of new buffalo skins.

Traditional ideas about ghosts held that they took human and other forms, including that of a whirlwind. In the following song the spiraling movement of the whirlwind becomes Father, who wears crow feathers, re-creating the spirit through which the dancers are to be borne upward to the new spirit world.

> Our father, the whirlwind,
> Our father, the whirlwind,
> Now wears the headdress of crow feathers,
> Now wears the headdress of crow feathers. (Mooney 1973 [1896]:970)

CONTEXTS FOR MUSICAL PERFORMANCE

For the Great Basin groups, as for all American Indian nations, music is integral to ceremony. Among the ceremonies that traditionally marked the ritual cycle were the previously mentioned harvest festivals, birthing and naming ceremonies, puberty ceremonies, mourning ceremonies, dances related to war, the Bear Dance among the Utes, and the Sun Dance among the Utes and Shoshones. Today the prominent public ceremonies remain the Sun Dance and the Bear Dance. The Sun Dance in this area has never included the sacrificial practices of the Plains groups' Sun Dances, although it is accompanied by fasting and dancing in the direct sun. The songs honor the essential life-sustaining sun. In times past, the rhythm was provided by stamping a buckskin-covered willow bough with deer hooves tied on top.

The Bear Dance

Disillusionment following the Ghost Dance brought changes in some ceremonies. The Bear Dance became focused on gaining good health, rather than on propitiating bears, making Ute hunters successful, and making men and women successful in their sex lives. The Bear Dance participants now began to fast for four days prior to the ceremony, often collapsing (as dancers had collapsed into a trance during the Ghost Dance), to be revived by shamans with musical rasps. All of the Ute groups adopted the Bear Dance, as did the Southern Paiutes and the Walapai, Havasupai, and Mohave peoples of the Southwest culture area (Jorgensen 1986:663).

The actual ceremony seems to have been maintained with little change for hundreds of years. A description of the Bear Dance was published in the May 1996 *Weenuche Smoke Signals,* the local newspaper of the Mountain Utes in Towaoc, Colorado, in preparation for the ceremony that is held there for four days over the Memo-

FIGURE 1   Poster advertising the 107th Annual
Beardance, Towaoc, Colorado, 30 May–3 June,
1996.

rial Day weekend (figure 1). The article reinforces beliefs that Utes and the Bear People
are related because they live on the mountain together, that the Bear Dance is a healing
ceremonial, and that the music makes the people feel good. A celebration of spring and
a new beginning for the Indian people, the Bear Dance is danced in a specially constructed arbor, with an opening to the east and the singers positioned on the west side.
The dance is ladies' choice, but they cannot dance with their close male relatives. To
dance with one's husband implies jealousy and bad luck. A "catman" with a long stick
is in charge of keeping the dancers in order; he uses the stick to "cut" the line, when
couples start dancing back and forth together. If a dancer falls, a circle is drawn around
the couple and they must sit there until a prayer is done for them. The dance goes on
from late morning until midnight or later. The final song of the Bear Dance is a contest
to see who will outlast the other, the dancers or the singers. In the past, a feast followed
the Bear Dance; today's feast takes place at noon on a chosen day, and as many as five
or more cows are butchered to feed the entire village and the many visitors. The food is
blessed by a Bear Dance "chief."

Music of the Bear Dance

Paul Rudy, a composer who analyzed a series of Bear Dance songs spanning a sixty-year
period from 1914 to 1974, confirms a strong continuity of song style over time (1993),
and this is corroborated by Thomas Vennum Jr. (1986:694). Rudy's transcription of a
Ute Bear Dance song, sung by Henry Williams and recorded by Willard Rhodes sometime between 1936 and 1951 (Rhodes 1984), begins with a brief repeated eighth-note
introduction that was played by rubbing a stick or metal rod over a notched stick,
a rasp the Utes call *morache*, that is traditionally held over a basket used as a resonator.
I have observed recent performances beginning with a tremolo introduction, during
which time the catman makes sure the lines are ordered and everyone is ready. The
eighth-note pattern usually begins at the end of the introduction and functions as a signal to the dancers that the dance is about to begin. The eighth notes continue in subsequent verses, with a strong emphasis on the first eighth note's coinciding with the
accented downstroke of the stick or metal rod on the rasp, in contrast to the unaccented upstroke.

Rudy's analyses (1993) indicate that the songs consistently start high and descend
to the end of the phrase, in some cases beginning the second phrase a fourth or fifth
below the initial tone. Although there may be symmetry in the use of paired phrasing,
the second phrase may be extended with a pulsation on the tonic, a feature also found

at the end of the verse. The pulsation often includes rhythmic gestures. The length of the extension varies, but at the ends of verses it is often four long notes punctuated by a break in the middle. Rudy describes the extension as a strong identifier of Bear Dance songs over time. The paired phrase structure in Bear Dance songs is not necessarily simple repetition, but may use contrastive technique. The number of times that verses are repeated also varies, and songs are often started by a leader and answered by the group after the first phrase.

Figure 2 is a transcription of the first two verses of a Bear Dance song recorded and released commercially in 1974 by the Southern Ute Singers from Ignacio, Colorado. Subsequent verses, not seen in this transcription, are repeated exactly. Some Bear Dance texts referring to bears and deceased ancestors are still considered sacred by elders, although most songs are more socially oriented. As in the past, Bear Dance texts may carry images from the past year, including amusing gossip and commentaries on male/female relationships and notable events, but a somewhat standard repertoire appears to be emerging. Many contemporary Bear Dance songs rely heavily on vocables, with the use of *ya* or *heya* at the ends of verses and sometimes individual phrases.

The Bear Dance ceremonial today

Today the Bear Dance is the center focus of a complex of ongoing activities, including competitive men's and women's softball tournaments for cash prizes up to $750 for first place; Bear Dance hand game competitions for cash prizes up to $4,000 plus jackets for the first-place team; and a Bear Dance powwow with a $500 contest special on Saturday night. The Bear Dance goes on continuously in the large circular Bear Dance arbor described above, beginning daily around 11:00 A.M. Following the Bear Dance

FIGURE 2   Bear Dance Song No. 6, as performed by the Southern Ute Singers and recorded in 1974 (Canyon Records). Transcription by Paul Rudy.

each evening, many gather to share 49ers, humorous social songs with English lyrics, until late into the night.

The Native American Church

Another Great Basin response to the disillusionment following the Ghost Dance was the more private pan-Indian ceremony of the Native American Church ("The Tipi Way"), in which prayers are offered to Jesus, God, and Mary in addition to Peyote. The hallucinogenic cactus is considered a sacred medicine and a medium for communication with spiritual wisdom. The peyote cult arrived in the Great Basin around the turn of the twentieth century, but became the dominant religion only on the Ute Mountain Reservation. Although the ceremony is basically the same everywhere, some variations occur due to the differences in traditional belief systems among the various Basin groups (Stewart 1986:673).

Studies conducted in recent times confirm the cactus's active antibiotic properties, and today the Shoshones refer to members of the peyote religion as Medicine Eaters. Peter Furst, the noted scholar of the peyote religion among the Huichol people of Mexico (1987), confirms that song and ritual are essential to a positive healing experience in peyote ceremonies. Although the ceremony is basically the same, the songs may derive from various sources in any given location. Vennum (1986:696) documented that the Ute Mountain repertoire consisted primarily of Mescalero Apache songs. Opening and closing songs are fixed, as is a song for the midnight break. Additionally, individuals contribute songs from their own repertoires.

Other holistic private curing ceremonies use prayer, herbal medicines, and songs specifically identified with the herbs used. As in the peyote rituals, songs help the patient to receive the emotional, physical, and intellectual properties of the plant that will bring about a rebalancing with nature and therefore a cure (Knight 1977). The common sweat lodge ceremony also follows a ritual format and usually incorporates drum-accompanied singing. Among the more secular musical events are the contemporary powwow and ancient Indian gambling stick or bone games, still intensely popular wherever groups gather. The Utes have incorporated the traditional stick or bone games, accompanied by singing, into some of their casinos.

MUSICAL INSTRUMENTS OF THE GREAT BASIN

The Great Basin is generally considered to have been limited in its use of musical instruments, although this may have been an outside observation of the result of culture disruption [see MUSICAL INSTRUMENTS, p. 472]. Among the sound-producing instruments, the Utes distinguished between some whose sounds were important in ceremony and those used to make music. The bull-roarer was used to make the wind blow and clear away clouds. The Great Basin is unique in the use of the hunting bow as a musical instrument by plucking or bowing the string. Hoof rattles were tied to the two ends of a stick or were sewn on dresses to accompany dances. Whistles were made of bones or elderberry bush, and flutes of elderberry wood were used by men to court women. Drums were made by stretching rawhide over willow hoops and tying underneath; they were beaten with a mallet. Today the rasp is made of ax handles and is played with a metal rod. Many men, and sometimes women, sing Bear Dance songs and play their *moraches* simultaneously, using a large (ten-foot) rectangular box covered with a sheet of corrugated tin as a resonator. It is common to amplify the voices.

SINGING STYLE

Monophonic or unison singing is the rule in the Basin area. The two Ghost Dance song texts above demonstrate the use of vocables as well as word phrasing. A combination of both is also common in the Great Basin. Vocables may connote the animal

Songs are gifts of Peyote [the Great Spirit] and should be taken for what they are, rather than being talked about and analyzed.

nations in some instances; other times they might preserve words from ancient languages, or they may simply represent an ingenious use of sound for rhythmic or other musical effects. The use of vocables may be based on pan-Indian ideas of the sacredness of sound itself, and they greatly facilitate singing with people who do not speak the same language. Thus, vocables reflect the free borrowing or trading of songs among Native peoples. Words in general are used in a highly connotative fashion, and song interpretation is difficult except for culture members or for those with a clear understanding of both the particular language and fashion. The Paiutes and Utes also related stories through songs, often using an improvisatory, syllabic style (a single syllable set to a single tone).

Bear Dance songs also make frequent use of syncopation, belying the general belief that there is little rhythmic variety in Basin songs. Vennum (1986:696) points out that religious movements such as the Ghost Dance and the Native American Church exposed Basin peoples to new and different repertoires and styles. Cross-tribal influences have continued to be more and more important as pan-Indian contexts have increased and developed through mutual performance venues such as the powwow. Vennum (1986:682) arrives at three possible musical areas within the Basin region: Northeastern, Western, and Southwestern, as marked by bordering cultural influences, instrument distribution, genres, and styles.

Generally speaking, then, Basin song styles incorporate an open sound with an avoidance of high pitches except for specific purposes. The use of song as prayer has limited the range that songs encompass, which in some types spans only a fourth. Frances Densmore's systematic analyses of 110 Ute songs (1922:34) from the early part of the twentieth century indicate that the majority fell within a range of six to twelve notes. Interestingly, Sun and Bear Dance songs typically did not use seven tones, while healing songs were very likely to use seven tones, implying that the genres were differentiated melodically.

Rudy's transcriptions (1993) indicate that over time some Bear Dance songs consistently start high and descend to the end of a phrase, typically spanning an octave or an octave and a fourth. The loudness of the singing depends on the context. For example, singing Bear Dance songs requires the singers to sing as loudly as they can in order to balance the loud "growl" of the multiple rasping *morache*s. For this reason, singing for the Bear Dance is a test of the singer's stamina. When present, dynamics, as well as other musical parameters, are most often in the service of emotional expression. Alan P. Merriam noted the following values for Washo Peyote songs that can be shown to apply to sacred singing among American Indians in general (d'Azevedo 1972:7):

1. The most important thing about a song is that it is like a prayer. It has a unity and power of its own that cannot be "broke [sic] into parts."
2. Songs are gifts of Peyote [the Great Spirit] and should be taken for what they are, rather than being talked about and analyzed.

3. Singing a song at the wrong time, or talking about it, may spoil it so that it loses its power.

4. Certain songs are to be admired for their intricacy, and the singer who can learn them is also admired.

5. There is a certain length of time a song should be sung to feel right; it has to build up a certain amount of emotion and concentration in the singer and the listener.

REFERENCES

d'Azevedo, Warren L. 1972. *Washo-Peyote Songs: Songs of the American Indian Native Church-Peyotist.* Twelve-page reprint of a 1957 study by Alan P. Merriam and Warren L. d'Azevedo. Ethnic Folkways Library Album No. FE 4384. LP disk.

Densmore, Frances. 1922. *Northern Ute Music.* Bureau of American Ethnology Bulletin 75. Washington, D.C.: Smithsonian Institution.

Furst, Peter. 1987. Personal communication.

Herzog, George. 1935. "Plains Ghost Dance and Great Basin Music." *American Anthropologist* 38(3):403–419.

Hultkranz, Åke. 1986. "Mythology and Religious Concepts." In *Handbook of North American Indians.* Vol. 11: *Great Basin,* ed. William C. Sturtevant, and Warren L. d'Azevedo, 630–640. Washington, D.C.: Smithsonian Institution.

Jorgensen, Joseph G. 1986. "Ghost Dance, Bear Dance, and Sun Dance." In *Handbook of North American Indians.* Vol. 11, *Great Basin,* ed. William C. Sturtevant and Warren L. d'Azevedo, 338–367. Washington, D.C.: Smithsonian Institute.

Knight, Terry. 1977. Public lecture on "Ute Mountain Elder." *The Use of Herbs in Ute Society.* Boulder: Henderson Museum, University of Colorado.

Laubin, Reginald, and Gladys Laubin. 1977. *Indian Dances of North America: Their Importance to Indian Life.* Norman: University of Oklahoma Press.

Lowie, Robert. 1915. *Dances and Societies of the Plains Shoshone.* Anthropological Papers of the American Museum of Natural History, vol. 11, no. 1, 803–835.

———. 1919. *The Sun Dance of the Shoshone, Ute, and Hidatsa.* Anthropological Papers of the American Museum of Natural History, vol. 16, no. 5, 387–431.

Mooney, James. 1973 [1896]. *The Ghost Dance Religion and Wounded Knee.* Reprint of the Fourteenth Annual Report (Part 2) of the Bureau of Ethnology to the Smithsonian Institution, 1892–93; *The Ghost-Dance Religion and the Sioux Outbreak of 1890.* Mineola, N.Y.: Dover Publications.

Rhodes, Willard, ed. 1984. *Music of the American Indian, Great Basin: Paiute, Washo, Ute, Bannock, Shoshone.* Library of Congress Archive of Folk Culture, Recording Laboratory AFS L38. Cassette.

Romero, Brenda M. 1988. "Two Native American Trance Contexts." Paper delivered at the Southern California Chapter of the Society of Ethnomusicology Annual Meeting, University of California, San Diego. 6 March 1988.

Rudy, Paul. 1993. "Ute Bear Dance Songs." Unpublished paper for doctoral seminar in American Indian Music, University of Colorado, Boulder.

Sapir, Edward. 1910. "Song Recitative in Paiute Mythology." *Journal of American Folklore* 23: 455–472.

Shimkin, Demitri B. 1953. *The Wind River Shoshone Sun Dance.* Bureau of American Ethnology Bulletin 151. Washington, D.C.: Smithsonian Institution, 399–491.

Stewart, Omer C. 1986. "The Peyote Religion." In *Handbook of North American Indians.* Vol. 11: *Great Basin,* ed. William C. Sturtevant and Warren L. d'Azevedo, 673–681. Washington, D.C.: Smithsonian Institute.

Southern Ute Singers. 1974. Canyon Records CR-6113-C.

Vander, Judith. 1986. *Ghost Dance Song and Religion of a Wind Shoshone Woman.* University of California at Los Angeles, Program in Ethnomusicology.

———. 1996. *Songprints: The Musical Experience of Five Shoshone Women.* Urbana: University of Illinois Press.

———. 1997. *Shoshone Ghost Dance Religion: Poetry Songs and Great Basin Context.* Urbana: University of Illinois Press.

Vennum, Thomas Jr. 1986. "Music." In *Handbook of North American Indians.* Vol. 11: *Great Basin,* ed. William C. Sturtevant and Warren L. d'Azevedo, 682–704. Washington, D.C.: Smithsonian Institution.

Waldman, Carl. 1985. *Atlas of the North American Indian.* Maps and illustrations by Molly Braun. New York: Facts on File.

Weenuche Smoke Signals. 1996. 2 May.

Woodhead, Henry, ed. 1995. *The American Indians: Indians of the Western Range.* Alexandria, Va.: Time-Life Books.

Southwest

J. Richard Haefer

The Pueblos
The Athabascans
The Yumans, Pais, and Paiutes
The O'odham
The Yaquis

The Southwest is one of the most complex areas of Native American cultures in the United States, comprising eight major Indian languages and dozens of different cultures. Geographically the area includes the modern states of Arizona and New Mexico, with the tribal lands of several cultures overlapping the bordering states of California, Utah, Colorado, and Texas as well as the Mexican state of Sonora. The more inclusive Greater Southwest, however, includes additional cultures living in Southern California, Nevada, Colorado, Texas, and Northern Mexico [see CALIFORNIA, p. 412; TEJANA MUSICA, p. 770]. A dated though interesting presentation of information about the region may be found in Bertha P. Dutton's *Indians of the American Southwest* (1975), while Charlotte J. Frisbie (1977) has compiled an excellent bibliographic survey of studies written between 1880 and the late 1970s, and Greg Gombert (1994) presents the most complete discographic data for North American Indian music as a whole. Selected ritual drama issues pertinent to Southwest cultures are found in Frisbie (1989 [1980]).

Cultures living in this area today may be grouped as Pueblo, Athabascan, Yuman, Pai, O'odham, and Yaquis. The pueblos include the Tiwa-speaking villages of Taos, Picurís, Sandía, and Isleta; the Tewa-speaking San Juan, Santa Clara, San Ildefonso, Pojoaque, Nambé, and Tesuque (as well as Tewas living in the village of Hano in Hopi country); the Tanoan village of Jémez; the Keresan speakers of Acoma, Laguna, Zia, Santa Ana, San Felipe, Santo Domingo, and Cochiti; and the two distinct languages of the Zuni (the Westernmost pueblo of New Mexico) and the Hopi of Northern Arizona. Two additional pueblos were founded by Indians who fled with the Spaniards following the Pueblo revolt of 1690 and settled near present-day Las Cruces, New Mexico, and El Paso, Texas. The two major Athabascan cultures are the Navajo (Diné) and Apache (including several major subdivisions). Among the Yumans are the *ranchería* 'those who live on small ranches rather than in villages' peoples known as Mohave, Cocopah, Quechan, and Maricopa, with the Pai including the Hualapai and Havasupai, while the O'odham include the Tohono O'odham (formerly known as the Papago) and the Pima (locally referred to as the Akimel O'odham). The most recent immigrants to the Southwest are the Yaqui, who speak the Cahitan language.

The climate of the Southwest varies from low, sandy desert to mountain peaks well above the tree line in height. Most of the Southwestern cultures adapted to a single environment, although some like the Tohono O'odham moved between the summer desert fields and the winter mountain homes, while the Apache were more nomadic. Summer rainfalls provided moisture for basic crops such as corn and beans even in the desert, while roots, nuts, and fruit could be harvested at the higher elevations. Wildlife was abundant throughout the region, especially rabbits and deer in the foothills. The pueblo peoples lived in multi-storied "cities" made of rock and adobe, while the desert peoples lived in single rooms of waddle and dab construction; the more nomadic Athabascans used both temporary and more permanent structures.

Precontact cultures include the Eastern and Western Anasazi of the four corners area, the Mogollon of east-central Arizona and west-central New Mexico, the Hohokam of central Arizona, the Hakataya from central Arizona to southwestern California, and the O'otam of southern Arizona and northwestern Mexico. Trade routes abounded throughout the area not only linking Mexico to the south with the northern and central United States but also providing valuable items from the ocean (salt, shells) for domestic and ceremonial use in the Southwest. Although no one knows for sure why these peoples abandoned their village and *rancheria* sites, those who came after them often continued to ply the same trade routes, providing interaction between the historic cultures now living in the area.

THE PUEBLOS

The people of the pueblos (from the Spanish for *town*) had established permanent villages by early in the second millennium C.E., many located along the Rio Grande as it flows through central New Mexico and others placed on top of protective mesas to the west. Having obtained domestic crops such as corn from their neighbors to the south, the pueblo peoples were and still are farmers, with a ceremonial calendar derived from an agrarian cycle.

Comprising more than twenty villages speaking six major languages, culturally the pueblo peoples are very similar. Pueblo music and dance may be generalized as the most complex and varied in the United States. Pueblo songs tend to be complex and lengthy, lasting several minutes. Scales may be pentatonic, hexatonic, or heptatonic, while rhythms consist of numerous lengths and may include duple and triple metric alternation. Melodic contours may be in descending terraced style, while phrasing tends to be long and intense. Song forms may be either through-composed or of the incomplete repetition type. Singing style often uses a low pitch and a deep growling sound, heightened by masks sometimes worn by the performers.

The songs of the Hopi and Zuni to the west tend to be more complex than those of the eastern pueblos. Songs are often composed communally by groups of men in the *kivas* 'meeting rooms for sacred societies, usually underground in each village'. The most thorough presentation of Tewa music and dance, including native terminology and concepts concerning song, is found in Gertrude P. Kurath with Antonio Garcia (1970). The most prominent sound instruments include the gourd container rattle, hoof and bell suspension rattles, the log drum played by a solitary person, and rasps of various shapes and sizes. Instruments are associated with specific song genres or ceremonies and often have symbolic connotations in addition to their use as sound instruments.

Social dances such as round dances and two-steps are found at nearly every pueblo. Others, such as the Butterfly Dance, are performed only at specific pueblos such as Hopi and San Juan, while some may be considered social at one culture and ceremonial at another. Often pueblos exchange dances between villages, so one might find a Zuni dance being performed at a Hopi village, sometimes seriously, other times in jest or even derisively. Other dances have been borrowed from contact with neighboring cultures to the east and north such as the arrow, hoop and eagle dances, and the "comanche" dance.

However, most songs and dances are an inseparable part of the ceremonial life of the pueblos. Some ceremonial dances may relate to the agrarian or hunting rites, and others to more recent borrowings from the Spanish Catholics. The names of the following dances/ceremonies, for example describe the agrarian connection: green and blue corn dances, harvest, cloud, basket, rainbow dances; deer, antelope, buffalo, turtle, mountain sheep dances; and the *matachin.* Parts or even all of the ceremonies may be secret and performed within the *kivas,* where only members of a society are privileged to attend, while other aspects of the ceremony include dancing in the open streets and squares of the pueblos, where the public, including non-puebloans, may attend. Dancers are often masked and perform as supernatural beings generically known as *kachinas* or *katsinas* (over 250 known entities including such modern ones as Mickey Mouse), which are also represented in carved wooden figurines used to instruct the children in the pueblo worldview (see Ortiz 1969). In modern times specific dances are also associated with Catholic saints' days, especially those related to the patron of the village.

Several ceremonials stand out as unique among the pueblos. In the Rio Grande pueblos public performances of corn dances are the culmination of multiday purification rites held in the *kivas* by various societies. Corn is the most sacred plant among the pueblos, having been a staple of pueblo society since it was introduced from Mexico well before the coming of the Spaniards. Corn dances recount the planting, germination, growth (with its need for life-sustaining rain), maturation, and harvesting of the plant and are, therefore, summer dances. Animal dances are usually line dances, with the performers dressed in costumes symbolic of the animals and using motions that pantomime those of the animals. Ceremonies usually begin in the *kivas* and move to the public streets or plazas. The dancers are accompanied by a single male drummer and a chorus of male singers. Jill D. Sweet (1985) presents an excellent description of Rio Grande pueblo dances. The *matachin* dance is an example of an acculturated ceremony mixing traditional line dancing and music with European instruments (violin and guitar) and elements of contra dancing.

In Hopi land the *kachina* cycle begins with the earliest major ceremonial (*powamú*) in February. It is nine days in length and is often referred to as the bean dance, although there are many aspects, including the initiating of young men and curing. Closely connected is the *pálulukoñ,* or horned water-serpent dance. Various *kachina* dances continue throughout the spring until the performance of *niman* in July that brings the *kachina* cycle to a close. Perhaps the best known dance of the Hopi is the snake dance, celebrated by the snake and antelope societies in August, and presented in alternating years with the flute dance. The men and boys collect snakes from the surrounding desert and bring them to the *kiva* over a four-day period. For the public dance concluding the ceremony the members of the two societies line up opposite one another in the plaza. A wooden plank drum covers the *sípapu* or symbolic entrance to the underworld around which society members dance, holding the snakes in their hands and mouths while other members sing the requisite songs. At the end of the ceremony the snakes are covered with corn meal and then released to take the prayers of the Hopi to the four corners of the world and to the underworld.

Among the Zuni the *shalako* (celebrated in late November or early December) is the most spectacular of the ceremonies that outsiders are able to view. It is a combination of fertility dance and house-blessing ceremony danced by masked impersonators as a reenactment of the creation and migration of the Zuni people from their sacred lake village to the "middle place." The ceremony is controlled by the leaders (*cacique*) of the six *kivas* (one for each cardinal direction plus the zenith and nadir), each of whom provides a group of masked *katsina* dancers. This ritual closes the Zuni ceremonial year (Gonzales 1968).

Pueblo ceremonials often include the use of sacred clowns, sometimes called *koshari,* who function as custodians of the masks and organizers of the dance preparations, and also serve to keep the spectators in line during the public portions of events. Nearly all pueblo dances include the use of masks, either of *kachinas* or animals (Brown 1962), and elaborate costumes. Each item of apparel is significant, from body paint to the tiniest shell or gourd decoration. Feather and cotton tufts are symbolic of clouds and sky, gourd rattles imitate the sound of rain, and women's headdresses or *tablitas* are carved or decorated with sun, moon, and other objects of nature. The colors are also chosen with specific meaning: turquoise signifies the sky, yellow is for corn pollen, red is for life, and so forth.

THE ATHABASCANS

The Athabascans of the Southwest, the Navajo and Apache, migrated into their present-day locations at least by the beginning of the sixteenth century, and probably earlier, moving down the eastern slopes of the Rockies and eventually west to the four corners area and central and southern Arizona and New Mexico. As nomadic hunters and gatherers, the Athabascans lived in small groups or bands with emphasis more on the individual than the group, although clan relations were and are still of importance for tracing one's ancestors and establishing reciprocal relationships and responsibilities.

The Apache

The Apache maintained mobility far longer than the Navajo, spreading as far east as present-day Kansas and Oklahoma—where they are known as the Kiowa-Apache—and as far South as northern Mexico, finally settling into the following areas in the mid- to late nineteenth century: the Jicarilla Apache in northwestern New Mexico, the Mescalero Apache in southern New Mexico, the Chiricahua in southeastern Arizona, and the Western Apache (including the White Mountain, Cibeque, San Carlos, and Northern and Southern Tonto) in central and eastern Arizona. The name *Apache* is probably derived from the Zuni term for enemy (*ápachu*), as the settled Indians of the area referred to these intruders.

The extended family or band—based on a matrilineal system—constituted the political and economic unit of Apache life. Clan groupings extended beyond bands and strongly affected ceremonial and secular aspects of life. Cousins referred to one another as brother or sister, and intermarriage was forbidden. Today larger village groups abound, but clan relationships are still important. Most present-day reservation lands contain ample natural resources for lumbering, ranching, and entertainment (both summer and winter sports and gaming), providing both tribal and individual incomes.

Apache musical style is characterized by the alternating of melodic choruses with recitative-like verses that often invoke the thirty-two deities of the people. Vocal tension and nasality are present, with some use of falsetto singing in the choruses and a release of tension and a more guttural sound in the verses. Choruses tend to use consonant–vowel clusters, while the verses are texted. The choruses have a distinctive triadic sound, with much use of an interval approximating a third. Rhythmically, Apache songs usually use two note values, one being one-half length of the other. Songs are performed by groups of individuals (often four in number), with the water drum (a small pot with buckskin head) as a sound instrument. Dancers frequently wear or carry bells as part of their costume.

Apache ceremonial activities tend to focus on the individual, with curing often the intent of the activities that include singing, the use of yellow powder (corn pollen), dancing, and additional actions. Deities include the Mountain Gods or *gan* (often portrayed by masked young male dancers, especially in public portions of ceremonies), White Shell Woman, Bear and Snake gods, and Monster Slayer.

At night the *gan,* painted and attired in their headdresses, appear and dance around the bonfire, another indication of the strong spiritual nature of the rite.

The Navajo

In contrast to the continuous mobility of the Apache, the Navajo chose to become more settled after reaching the Four Corners area (where Colorado, New Mexico, Arizona, and Utah all touch), cultivating fields and later raising sheep. It is believed that the Navajo maintained more of a positive relationship with their pueblo neighbors than did the Apache. The land base of the Navajo is extensive, with the present-day reservation being the largest in the country. Several smaller areas in the vicinity, including Ramah, Alamo or Puertocito, Cañoncito, and the checkerboard area in northwestern New Mexico, are also home to numerous Navajo families.

Navajo tend to live in family groupings or small communities. The clan structure is still of utmost importance for ceremonials and lifeways. The herding of sheep and goats is still a significant way of life especially for more conservative families, while many earn their living through the cash economy of arts and crafts (especially the prized Navajo rugs and silverwork), industry, and commerce, while revenues from natural resources (timber, uranium, coal, and so on) provide supplemental income and finance tribal affairs.

There are two basic Navajo musical styles: the high piercing falsetto of the *yei* songs and the lower less tense style of most other songs. Generally there is a light nasality with few, if any, pulsations. The range may vary from medium to large (especially in the *yei* songs), and, as in Apache song, the interval of a third is frequently found. Rhythmic values are similar (often just a long and a short of half value). Songs are nearly always sung only by men.

TRACK 10

Song in Navajo culture is most frequently used to restore and maintain the harmony of the people with nature and as such focuses on the individual. The estrangement of man from his environment (known as "sickness") calls for a number of different ceremonials, consisting of miniature dramas (often connected with parts of the creation myth) in which the sick person, his family, and the ceremonial practitioner and his singers all participate. The use of sand painting and the singing of chants are a part of each ceremony of which some 500 paintings and more than fifty ceremonials have been identified. Typically a sing or "way" lasts for several days and nights, during which time evil and danger are banished and, through invocation and prayer, harmony is reestablished with the Navajo deities (Frisbie and McAllester 1978). The gourd rattle and the pottery water drum are the most common instruments used with the songs.

Numerous ceremonies called ways are performed by the Navajo, with Enemyway, Nightway, and Blessingway the most common; others include Windway, Red Antway, and Mountainway (Wyman 1962, 1965, 1970, 1975). Nightway and Blessingway include private and public aspects and numerous songs or chants. Blessingway is performed to invoke good within the people, and although it is the shortest and simplest way, it is also considered by many to be the most sacred. Parts of Blessingway may be included within other ways. In the Nightway (a nine-day complex of ceremonials) personifications of the male and female deities known as the *yei* sing striking falsetto songs, each begun with the cry of the *yei.* A clown, providing levity by imitating the *yei* and generally acting like a buffoon, accompanies the dancers. In the public portion of the Enemyway the social dance songs, often collectively called "squaw dance songs," (though the term is considered unacceptable today) include Circle Dance, Sway, and Skip Dance songs. These songs, more melodic than other genres, generally use only consonant–vowel clusters rather than texts.

Since the middle of the twentieth century, the Peyote cult has made substantial inroads in Navajo culture, more so than in other Southwestern cultures. Most likely adopted from the Utes or from the Southern Plains, the Navajo have added elements of traditional Navajo ceremonialism to the typical Peyote pan-Indian and Christian environment. Today the Peyote cult is officially known as the Native American Church, with legal status including the possession of and use of the peyote button.

Several nontraditional music styles are performed by Navajos and Apache today. The Sun Downers are just one of several Navajo country and western bands, and rock groups like Xit are also popular today. Mormon songs are performed by some Navajos and several Apache gospel groups are well-known [see MUSICAL INTERACTIONS, p. 480].

The girl's puberty ceremony

Both the Apache and Navajo perform a similar ceremony for the coming of age of female members of the culture. Called *kinaldá* by the Navajo (Frisbie 1993 [1967]) and *nai'es* by the Apache, this ceremony is perhaps the most important ceremony for the Apache. (Extensive descriptions of the Apache ceremony are presented in Basso [1966] and Farrar [1989 (1980)], while Frisbie documents a very similar observance for their Navajo cousins.) Originally held at the time of first menses, the rite, among the Apache, is now often held simultaneously with other public events such as a Fourth of July or Labor Day celebration, including a rodeo, queen contest, tribal and public dancing, carnival, and so on. The girl entering womanhood symbolically becomes White Painted Woman and thereby becomes a model for all the women of the culture and possessor of great powers during the ritual. In private parts of the ceremony she is instructed in the history and mythology of the culture by the shaman leader, while in public appearances she demonstrates the stamina necessary for a strong healthy life by dancing and running. At night the *gan* 'personification of Apache deities', painted and attired in their headdresses, appear and dance around the bonfire, another indication of the strong spiritual nature of the rite. Following the ceremony the girl is considered sacred and powerful until cleansed and is often approached with requests to perform cures or other blessings.

THE YUMANS, PAIS, AND PAIUTES

Along the Colorado River from northern Arizona to the Mexican border live the Paiute, Pai, and Yuman peoples. Late 1940s relocation practices brought several Hopi, Navajo, and Havasupai families to this area, and today they live interspersed with the local peoples. The most prominent are the Yumans: the Mohave, Quechan, Cocopah and Maricopa. Surrounded by low mountains, the Yumans live in the valley along the lower Colorado River, a flowing oasis in the Arizona desert. Modern dams, canals, and irrigation have led to some farming, and more recent wage-based economy, especially involving recreational activities along the river, has led to a localized village lifestyle different from the more traditional *ranchería* settlement. Traditionally the Yumans were of a rather fierce war-like nature and defensive of their lands. Early in the nineteenth century the Maricopa, due to disagreements with the other Yuman tribes, moved up the Gila River, where they eventually settled with the Pimas in central Arizona, with Piman ceremonial activities largely replacing their Yuman traditions in the twentieth century.

The Yumans speak a language of the Hokan–Siouan family. They are sparse in number, ranging from a few hundred Cocopah to a few thousand Mohave, and many of the traditional lifeways are no longer practiced, although a recent resurgence of cultural interest has led to language studies and a revival of songs and ceremonies. Traditional ceremonies included funeral ceremonies, with the cremation of the dead accompanied by singing and dancing; singing associated with war, hunting, agriculture, and myths; and dancing, incorporating both circular and line dancing. Dreaming, an important means of communication with one's ancestors and with other beings, was an inspiration for song and ceremony as well as an influence on important tribal decisions. Today these ceremonies are mostly extinct, and the major song genre remaining is that of the bird dance.

Songs use a type of song-language-variant of spoken Yuman, and most people are unable to interpret their meaning. Texts are usually organized into song cycles or series often describing a journey, with geographical details from the Yuman land base. Both words and melodies are normally learned through dreams. Song cycles also outline the temporal events of an evening of storytelling, with specific songs for the early evening and others for late night.

A unique feature of the melody of Yuman songs is the "rise," a section of the piece sung usually a fourth or fifth higher. A typical formal structure might be: a a' a a' b b' a a' a^5 a' b b' a a' a^5 a', although as many as four different melodic phrases may be found in a song. Rhythmically, Yuman songs are somewhat complex, often employing a triplet figure together with two or three different note values. It is hypothesized that the text line strongly influences both the rhythmic and formal aspects of a song.

Musical instruments employed by the Yumans include the basket drum and the gourd rattle, while a cane flute was used in the past. A common household basket of woven yucca fibers (approximately fourteen inches in diameter by four inches deep) is inverted and either placed on the ground or held against the chest by one hand. The basket is struck either with a single willow stick or a bundle of arrow weed sticks (eight to twelve sticks approximately two feet long). When struck with the latter the sound is enhanced by the sound of the sticks striking each other as well as the basket. One to three baskets are struck by one to four singers depending upon the number of dancers. The gourd rattles are usually globular in shape, with pottery rattle elements (though today buckshot is often used) and handles made from ironwood. They may be painted a solid color or in a geometric pattern. Smaller rattles with a brighter sound are usually used for the bird dance songs today. In the past deer hoof suspension rattles were used with the cremation songs, and cocoon rattles, similar to those of the Yaqui, were used for deer dance songs. The flutes, made of two lengths of a local river cane, were of the internal duct type, with a cloth or leather block at the middle node and three or four finger holes in the lower portion of the tube. Little is known about the use of this instrument.

The Havasupai and the Hualapai live along the upper Colorado River. They are also speakers of the Yuman language, and their names mean "of the blue-green water" and "pine tree folk." The Havasupai live at the bottom of Cataract Canyon near the western end of the Grand Canyon. Although they are traditionally hunters, gatherers, and farmers, the main Havasupai economic activity today is the tourist industry. Little is known about their ceremonial life and use of song, although many aspects are similar to those of their Yuman relatives, such as the use of funeral songs and circle and line dances. In the past, a ceremony using masked dancers was performed possibly as a harvest or rain dance. The Hualapai live on the plateau above and to the west of the Supais centering on the village of Peach Springs. Their economic and ceremonial life parallels that of the Supai, with perhaps more emphasis on the position of the shaman and use of songs for curing.

The Yavapai (from the Yuman for "People of the Sun") live on the plateaus of central Arizona. Traditionally hunters and gatherers, they were seminomadic, moving with the food supplies and living in small bands or family groups. Eventually they were relocated to the San Carlos Reservation and are sometimes still given the misnomer "Mohave Apache," though there has been much intermarriage between the two groups. Today most live in Fort McDowell, Camp Verde, Prescott, or Payson.

The Paiutes are often associated with the Yuman people because of their geographical proximity, although as members of the Uto-Aztecan language family, they speak a Numic tongue of the Shoshoni. The Kaibab Paiutes live in North Arizona and the Shivwits in Southwestern Utah. Today they are one of the smallest Indian groups, with just a few hundred people. Little is known about their ceremonial life, although circular social dancing was common and songs were used to accompany the playing of hand games. The music style is similar to that of the Northern Paiutes. The Chemehuevi, Southern Paiutes who established themselves along the lower Colorado River, are often confused with the Yumans and since the 1970s have lived with them. Most of their Pai customs have been replaced by Yuman practices.

THE O'ODHAM

The O'odham or Piman-speaking peoples of the Uto-Aztecan family include the Akimel O'odham, or Pimas, and the Tohono O'odham, once known as the Papago. The former, literally the "River People," are so named because they lived along the Salt and Gila rivers in Central Arizona, while the latter are the "Desert People," living in the Sonoran desert of Southern Arizona and Northwestern Sonora, Mexico. The River People lived in stable villages, using an elaborate canal system to water their fields, while the Desert People moved between the winter villages in the foothills—with constant water sources—and their related summer villages on the desert floor, where they diverted run-off water from the summer rains to grow corn, beans, and squash. Both peoples also hunted and gathered. Today they live primarily in a wage-based economy with incomes from federal or tribal government, farming, ranching, mining, gaming, or—for the Pimas—from commercial or industrial labor.

Because of their location along the major waterways of Arizona, the Pimas came under stronger outside influences earlier than their neighbors to the South. They were also subjected to Protestant missionization that stifled traditional practices, so that by the early twentieth century only individual curing rites performed in secrecy and a few social dances were still held. Since the 1970s a concerted effort to regain tribal traditions has led to a revival of many Piman social dances such as the basket dance and, more recently, the Girl's Puberty ceremony. The Desert People, however, were missionized by the Catholics, who permitted most "Indian" activities to continue, thereby preserving a continuous music tradition to the present.

The O'odham singing style may be characterized as rather soft, with a low degree of tension and medium to high nasality. Melodies tend to be descending in shape, although the range of each phrase is limited. Songs normally have from three to five phrases, often of unequal length. The form is a modified incomplete repetition set in repeating pairs, for example, aabcd aabcd abcd abcd. Generally (and following O'odham theory) songs are repeated in multiples of four (Haefer 1981). Songs are also grouped in sets or cycles (also in multiples of four), with each cycle organized into subgroups based on a performance circuit of "sundown" songs, "middle of the night" songs, and "sun raising" songs.

Songs are learned through dreams, which provide a contact for the O'odham with the world of animals and various natural phenomena to which were given all songs by the "Creator Being" at the beginning of time. The "giving" of the songs to O'odham establishes a special relationship between giver and receiver. An inherent naming principal for songs is based on the twofold principle of song giver and action or song use, for example, *ban wusota ñe'i*, 'coyote [giver] blowing [use] song' or *ban keihina ñe'i* 'coyote [giver] kick step [action] song'. Songs are always texted (without consonant–vowel clusters), and the subject of the text may be about the donor or another aspect of O'odham life, often portraying a journey.

Musical instruments are called *ñeicuda* 'song makers' by the O'odham, as they are an integral part of the song. Most often used today are gourd rattles and the basket

The most important communal ritual still practiced today is the *gohimeli* ceremony of the Tohono. Held in late July or early August after the arrival of the summer rains, this four-night ceremony includes the fermentation of saguaro cactus wine, singing, and dancing, and concludes with ritual speaking and excessive drinking of the new wine.

drum, similar to that of the Yuman described above. The basket may be either rubbed or struck, and, like the shaking of the rattle, the motion is changed to signal the "turning" of the song (the change from full to incomplete repetition and back). The rasping stick is often used with curing songs and previously existed in two types. Specific instruments are used for certain types of songs.

Although traditionally many different ceremonies were performed by the O'odham, such as the *wi:gita* or harvest ceremony, today only four are normally encountered: the *keihina, celkona,* curing (*ḍuajida* and *wusota*), and *gohimeli.* The *keihina* is the traditional round or social dance, a circular movement with males and females interlocked at the elbows. Since the middle of the twentieth century this dance has largely been supplanted by the modern *waila,* or chicken scratch. The *celkona* was a traditional inter-village ritual enacted between Tohono and Akimal for the sharing of food, dance, and socialization (Haefer 1977) that was revived in the 1960s as a modern expression of O'odham culture. Cures are usually private ceremonies involving only the sick person and a few members of the immediate family together with the doctor and singers. The process is twofold, comprising the diagnosis, using *ḍuajida* songs, and the actual cure or blowing with *wusota* songs. The purpose of the cure is to establish an ongoing relationship between the sick person and the offended being or element that is causing the sickness (Bahr and Haefer 1974). Therefore, a person is not "healed" in the Western sense; rather, a harmonious relationship between sick person and causer of the illness is established, lasting for the life of the person.

The most important communal ritual still practiced today is the *gohimeli* ceremony of the Tohono. Held in late July or early August after the arrival of the summer rains, this four-night ceremony includes the fermentation of saguaro cactus wine, singing, and dancing, and concludes with ritual speaking and excessive drinking of the new wine until—through regurgitation—one symbolically cleanses one's self and renews the relationship between man and his world.

The *waila* (named from the Spanish *baile,* and called "chicken scratch" by the Anglos) is an acculturated music and dance genre that began in the middle of the nineteenth century (Haefer 1977). Today modern electric instruments (guitar, bass, and even sometimes a synthesizer) together with the saxophone, accordion, and trap set substitute for the acoustic instruments of the previous century. The music is borrowed from the *norteño* tradition of Sonora, Mexico (which in turn had borrowed the early tunes from European settlers in the southwest United States and northern Mexico), and include polkas, schottisches, two-steps, and *cumbias.* Probably the most interesting aspect of *waila* is the way in which it was adapted to O'odham ways as a replacement for the traditional *keihina.* Although in Mexico much of the music may have texts, in the United States *waila* is strictly an instrumental genre. Today one is likely to find a celebration such as a house blessing, anniversary, or birthday beginning with a Catholic Mass, followed by a feast, perhaps entertainment dancing by Yaqui *matachin,* and a short *keihina,* and concluding with an all night *waila.*

THE YAQUIS

The Cahitan-speaking Yaqui Indians originally lived in Northwestern Mexico with seven traditional villages along the mouth of the Río Yaqui. From their first contact with the Spanish in the middle of the sixteenth century, they strongly resisted the takeover of their land, which led to nearly continuous warfare. In the late nineteenth century, many Yaqui were captured and relocated as far south as the Yucatan and even to the Philippine Islands, where today an isolated community still resides. At this same time, many Yaqui fled to the United States, settling near Tucson (Pascua and Barrio Libre), Marana, Eloy, Guadalupe, and Scottsdale, Arizona (Spicer 1970). In the 1970s formal recognition was given to the Pascua Tribe of Arizona and the village of New Pascua was established on government land to the north of the O'odham San Xavier Reservation.

Economic life for the Yaqui in Arizona has nearly always been dependent upon a wage-based standard, with the men working in the cotton fields or at other ranch or trade occupations. Though their languages are significantly different, a loose relationship has existed between the Yaqui and the O'odham at least since the middle of the nineteenth century, with the O'odham apparently "borrowing" the *pascola* dance (masked dancers often referred to as old men of the fiesta, dancing to harp and violin music) and possibly some of the music and instrumentation for the *waila* from the Yaqui, though the latter do not play *waila*.

Painter (1986) presents the most extensive discussion of Arizona Yaqui lifeways. She divides the ceremonial organization of the Yaqui into five groups:

1. the Church Group (including the *maestros* 'masters or leaders' and *cantoras* 'female singers', who lead Catholic prayers and the singing of *alabanzas* and *alabados* 'Praise songs', and the *santos* 'saints' or Holy Figures)
2. the *matachinis* (dancers of the *matachina*)
3. the *Kohtumbre Ya'ura* (the *caballeros* 'horse men's society' and the *fariseos* 'pharisees')
4. the native dancers (the deer and *pascola*)
5. the military society

The *matachinis* orchestrate the ceremonial cycle from Easter to Ash Wednesday, while the *Kohtumbre Ya'ura* organize activities during the Lenten season, although their activities overlap these divisions. Ceremonial activities today are based closely on the Catholic Liturgical Year, with Lent, Holy Week, and the Feast of the Holy Cross being most important and other activities such as mourning celebrations, birthdays or anniversaries having a strong Catholic influence.

Yaqui music consists of two parallel traditions: traditional songs and instrumentation and the pseudo-European music of the *pascola* and the *matachin,* both influenced by Catholicism. Deer songs are sung to the accompaniment of a half-gourd drum and two rasps. The drum and the gourd resonators of the rasps are inverted in pans of water, which helps to amplify the sound. The songs are texted (Evers and Molina 1987) and sung in a rather guttural style, with simple rhythms and melodies encompassing a moderate range. The texts speak of the worldview of the Yaqui, stressing the flora and fauna of the area and the relation of man to *sialig* 'the flower world.' This metaphor has been adapted from the Catholic symbolism that depicts the blood of Jesus falling on the cross and being transformed into beautiful flowers, and from the traditional Yaqui belief of that other world known as the flower world.

The *pascolas* and *matachin* dance to the music of violin, harp, and guitar. Although the instruments are European, the melodies are native in origin and feature several short phrases repeated, varied, and alternated throughout the length of the piece. Ceremonies are organized on a nighttime cycle, with the tuning of the instruments changing as the cycle progresses and with specific songs assigned to various parts of the night. Near the midpoint of the night the harpist will play alone for a brief time, showing his versatility at playing both melody and harmonic accompaniment (using the tonic, dominant, and subdominant chords that are applied to the traditional violin melodies). *Pascola* also dance to the *tampaleo,* an internal duct, two-holed flute played with the left hand, while a fourteen-inch double-sided drum is beaten with the right hand.

Pascolas and deer dancers will perform at separate times, alternating with one another, and at times together during the night. At one point in the ceremony the *pascola* (dancing in groups of three) will imitate the stalking of the deer by coyotes, eventually capturing the deer dancer. The *pascolas* wear belts with seven hawks bells (representing the seven traditional villages) around their waists and long strings of cocoon rattles (*teneboim*) wrapped around their legs from the ankles to the knees. They also use a hand held systrum jingle rattle, carried on entrance and exit and placed in the belt in the center of the back during most of the dance. The carved wooden masks they wear are symbols of either animals or humans. Their movements are basically intricate foot motions in elaborate rhythms. The deer dancer, wearing the head of a deer on his head, carries two gourd rattles in his hands and mimics the movements of the deer in his dance. Often at the same time as the men are dancing *pascola* and deer, the women in a nearby ramada will be reciting prayers in Yaqui, Latin, and/or Spanish, a sign of the mixture of traditional and Catholic rituals.

The *matachin* dance, accompanied by violin and guitar, is a complicated line dance of the contra-dance type with distinct European origins [see CONTRA DANCE, p. 230]. The dancers are all male although one young boy will wear a white dress, symbolizing *malinchi* (the first Indian convert). The dance at one time was thought to represent the conquest by the Christians of the Aztecs (originally the Moors in the Spanish version), although today that belief is not held by the Yaqui. Each dancer wears a decorative crown and carries a gourd rattle and a symbolic staff. All take a yearly vow to the Blessed Virgin Mary. For the Yaqui the dance is religious and performed for a blessing, and although they may be "hired" by the O'odham to perform either privately or publicly, their personal religious vow is maintained. And although the *matachin* dance is found throughout the Southwest, the elements of humor and fighting found in the Pueblo versions are not present for the Yaqui.

The most important and most documented ceremony of the Yaqui is often referred to as the Easter Ceremony, although it takes place throughout the Lenten season. While public portions are held in the plaza in front of the Yaqui chapel (located beside the Church of the Roman Rite), additional ceremonies are practiced by the vowed members and their families in their homes and headquarters. Public portions include the recitation of prayers and singing of songs by the Church Group in the chapel, with dancing in the plaza by the *fariseos,* their subgroup the *chapayekas,* and the *caballeros.* All are under vows to Jesus. Painter (1986:184–240) presents the most recent detailed synopsis of this ceremony. Although the Yaqui, as other Southwest Native peoples, allow visits by all to the public portions of their ceremonies, they do not allow cameras, recorders, or even notebooks.

The diversity of music in the Southwest is exemplified by the presence within this two-state region of many different music style areas (as defined by Nettl 1954), including Great Basin, Athabascan, Pueblo, California-Yuman, and the subclass of Piman, as well as elements of Plains style and the contemporary Peyote and powwow genres. Combined with the many popular nontraditional musics, the Southwest continues to be one of the most interesting Native music domains in North America.

REFERENCES

Bahr, Donald M., and Richard J. Haefer. 1974. *Piman Shamanism and Staying Sickness (Ka:cim Mumkidag).* Tucson: University of Arizona Press.

Bahr, Donald M., et al. 1978. "Song in Piman Curing." *Ethnomusicology* 22(1):89–122.

Bahti, Tom. 1964. *An Introduction to Southwestern Indian Arts and Crafts.* Flagstaff, Ariz.: KC Publications.

————. 1970. *Southwestern Indian Ceremonials.* Flagstaff, Ariz.: KC Publications.

Basso, Keith H. 1966. "Gift of Changing Woman." Bureau of American Ethnology Bulletin 196, 76. Washington, D.C.: Smithsonian Institution.

Brown, Donald N. 1962. *Masks, Mantas, and Moccasins: Dance Costumes of the Pueblo Indians.* Colorado Springs: Taylor Museum.

Dutton, Bertha P. 1975. *Indians of the American Southwest.* Englewood Cliffs, N.J.: Prentice-Hall.

Evers, Larry, and Felipe S. Molina, eds. 1987. *Yaqui Deer Songs, Maso Bwikam.* Tucson: University of Arizona Press.

Farrar, Clair R. 1989 [1980]. "Singing for Life: The Mescalero Apache Girls' Puberty Ceremony." In *Southwest Indian Ritual Drama,* ed. Charlotte J. Frisbie. Prospect Heights, Ill.: Waveland Press.

Frisbie, Charlotte J. 1977. *Music and Dance Research of Southwestern United States Indians: Past Trends, Present Activities and Suggestions for Future Research.* Detroit Studies in Music Bibliography 36. Detroit: Information Coordinators.

————. 1993 [1967]. *Kinaaldá. A Study of the Navajo Girls' Puberty Ceremony.* Middletown, Conn.: Wesleyan University Press.

————, ed. 1989 [1980]. *Southwest Indian Ritual Drama.* Prospect Heights, Ill.: Waveland Press, Inc.

————, and David P. McAllester. 1978. *Navajo Blessingway Singer: The Autobiography of Frank Mitchell, 1881–1967.* Tucson: University of Arizona Press.

Gombert, Greg. 1994. *A Guide to Native American Music Recordings.* Fort Collins, Colo.: Multi Cultural Publishing.

Gonzales, Clara. 1968. *The Shalakos are Coming.* Santa Fe: Museum of New Mexico Press.

Haefer, J. Richard. 1977. *Papago Music and Dance.* Tsalie, Ariz.: Navajo Community College Press.

————. 1981. *Musical Thought in Papago Culture.* Ann Arbor, Mich.: University Microfilms.

————. 1986. "Chicken Scratch [*Waila*]." In *The New Grove Dictionary of American Music,* ed. H. Wiley Hitchcock and Stanley Sadie, 1:425–26. London: Macmillan.

————. 1989 [1980]. "O'odham Celkona: The Papago Skipping Dance." In *Southwest Indian Ritual Drama,* ed. Charlotte J. Frisbie. Prospect Heights, Ill.: Waveland Press.

Hinton, Leanne. 1984. *Havasupai Songs: A Linguistic Perspective.* Tubingen, Germany: Gunter Narr Verlag.

Kurath, Gertrude P. with Antonio Garcia. 1970. *Music and Dance of the Tewa Pueblos.* Museum of New Mexico Records 8. Santa Fe: Museum of New Mexico Press.

McAllister, David P. 1954. *Enemyway Music: Papers of the Peabody Museum of American Archaeology and Ethnology,* Harvard University, vol. 41, no. 3.

————. 1961. *Indian Music in the Southwest.* Colorado Springs: Taylor Museum.

Nettl, Bruno. 1954. *North American Indian Musical Styles.* Memoirs of the American Folklore Society 45. Philadelphia: American Folklore Society.

Ortiz, Alfonso. 1969. *The Tewa World.* Chicago: University of Chicago Press.

————, ed. 1979. *Southwest.* Vol. 9, *Handbook of North American Indians,* ed. William Sturtevant. Washington, D.C.: Smithsonian Institution.

————, ed. 1983. *Southwest.* Vol. 10. *Handbook of North American Indians,* ed. William Sturtevant. Washington, D.C.: Smithsonian Institution.

Painter, Muriel Thayer. 1986. *With Good Heart: Yaqui Beliefs and Ceremonies in Pascua Village.* Tucson: University of Arizona Press.

Rodriguez, Sylvia. 1996. *The Matchines Dance: Ritual Symbolism and Interethnic Relations in the Upper Rio Grande Valley.* Albuquerque: University of New Mexico Press.

Russell, Frank. 1975. *The Pima Indians.* New ed. With introduction, citation sources, and bibliography by Bernard Fontana. Tucson: University of Arizona Press.

Spicer, Edward H. 1970. *Cycles of Conquest.* Tucson: University of Arizona Press.

Spier, Leslie. 1928. "Havasupai Ethnography." *Anthropological Papers of the American Museum of Natural History* 29(3).

Sweet, Jill D. 1985. *Dances of the Tewa Pueblo Indians.* Santa Fe: School of American Research.

Underhill, Ruth Murray. 1973 [1938]. *Singing for Power: The Song Magic of the Papago Indians of Southern Arizona.* New York: Ballantine Books.

Wyman, Leland Clifton. 1962. *The Windways of the Navajo.* Colorado Springs: Taylor Museum.

————. 1965. *The Red Antway of the Navajo.* Navajo Religion Series 5. Santa Fe: Museum of Navajo Ceremonial Art.

————. 1970. *Blessingway.* Tucson: University of Arizona Press.

————. 1975. *The Mountainway of the Navajo.* Tucson: University of Arizona Press.

Plains
Erik D. Gooding

Geographically, the Plains region of North America extends southward from Alberta, Saskatchewan, and Manitoba to Texas. The western boundary follows the Rocky Mountains, while the eastern boundary loosely follows the Mississippi River Valley. Within this vast expanse are two distinguishable environmental subregions, the Prairies and the High Plains. Tribal groups within the boundaries of the Prairie-Plains regions interacted with groups in neighboring culture areas, thus creating few distinct cultural boundaries.

The Prairie subregion, located in the eastern half of the Plains region, was historically home to semisedentary horticulturalist tribes: the Pawnee, Arikara, Mandan, Hidatsa, Omaha, Ponca, Iowa, Otoe, Missouri, Kansa, Osage, Quapaw, Wichita and Kitsai. This area was characterized by tall grasses and more moisture in the form of humidity and rainfall than its western neighbor, the High Plains, received. The peoples of the Prairies relied on a diverse economic base of horticulture and hunting. The High Plains subregion was historically home to the Plains Indians, the nomadic buffalo hunters, including the Sioux, Assiniboine, Stoney, Blackfoot, Sarcee, Plains Cree, Plains Ojibwa, Gros Ventre, Arapaho, Crow, Kiowa, Kiowa-Apache, Lipan Apache, Comanche, Cheyenne, and Tonkawa. This area received less rainfall and moisture than did the Prairie region and was characterized by a variety of short grasses. Linguistically, the entire Plains region was diverse, including members of six language families: Siouan, Caddoan, Algonquian, Athapascan, Uto-Aztecan, and Kiowa-Tanoan, plus one language isolate, Tonkawa.

EARLY HISTORY AND CULTURE

The history of Plains Indians and their music from first contact with Europeans to the present can be characterized as one of cultural florescence, followed by cultural destruction, then by cultural regeneration. The historical picture of the people of the Plains region began to be documented with the arrival on the Plains of Spanish, French, English, and, later, American explorers, travelers, traders, missionaries, and military. During the early years of contact the classic attributes of Plains Indian cultures were forming and flourishing: large communal buffalo hunts, the horse culture, intertribal raiding and warfare, men's societies, and tribal ceremonies. Variation exists among Plains cultures, such as the differences between nomadic hunting groups and sedentary horticultural-based groups, but many aspects of Plains life and music are common throughout the whole area. Plains music, which is primarily vocal, is integral to Plains cultures. Singing, either by individuals or in groups, encompasses all aspects of life.

The importance of song to early Plains life

In the Plains region, singing accompanied all aspects of life, especially political life. Important rituals, known variously as the calumet or adoption ceremony, for example, were used to establish peace between groups. Governing organizations of Plains peoples also employed song as a medium of expression and communication.

Music also played a key role in Plains religions, both formally and informally. The dialogue between higher powers and individuals is expressed through song in many important Plains religious ceremonies, such as the Sun Dance, bundle ceremonies, and the vision quest. Organizations and societies with religious functions, either for shamanism or curing, relied heavily on musical performance.

Many of the economic aspects of Plains life were also accompanied by music. Song was the medium used by many in asking for assistance in hunting, either in the communal buffalo hunts or individual occurrences, and was an integral part of the process of reaching trade agreements between groups through rituals, frequently being used as an object of trade.

Singing by women and men was also important to the social life of the Plains peoples. From lullabies to memorial songs at funeral rites, the life cycle was accentuated by song. Courting was assisted by the use of flutes, one of the few musical instruments used by Plains Indians. Various organizations, such as those women's societies based on the production of beadwork or quill work, used singing as an entertainment activity. Many children's games were accompanied by songs, and singing was a popular activity by itself. Dancing was also a key social activity and was always accompanied by a variety of song forms.

Men's warrior societies, one of the classic attributes of Plains cultures, relied on song for several purposes. Songs were used to document the successes of intertribal warfare as well as to recount individual exploits, known as coups. Many of these societies accompanied their social dances with songs particular to their groups, using song as a vehicle of group identity.

Early contact with Europeans in the United States

During the early years of contact with Europeans, Plains peoples had limited interaction with the outsiders. Explorers traveled through the Plains, often with native guides, but the first forms of close interactions were with traders and missionaries beginning in the 1600s. Europeans brought their own musical traditions with them, which in turn were introduced to their native hosts. These early contacts with outsiders brought more than trade goods and divine guidance in the form of Christianity to the Plains; they also brought disease and epidemics. In the 1700s and the 1800s, numerous epidemics of cholera and smallpox swept through the Plains peoples, ravaging their populations. The horse was also introduced into the Plains during the early years of contact, and by the early 1800s the use of the horse had spread throughout Plains groups. With the addition of the horse and European trade goods, Plains cultures flourished and thrived during these early years of contact.

The nineteenth century

At the beginning of the nineteenth century, a new foreign presence came onto the Plains—the Americans. With the Louisiana Purchase in 1803 and the expedition of Lewis and Clark beginning in the following year, this time of cultural florescence and the independent ways of life of Plains Indians was beginning to end. In the early years

From lullabies to memorial songs at funeral rites, the life cycle was accentuated by song. Courting was assisted by the use of flutes, one of the few musical instruments used by Plains Indians.

of the nineteenth century the United States government initiated a policy toward Plains Indians intended to destroy their traditional cultures and force them to assimilate into the dominant American society, and measures were enacted in the mid-1800s in order to break down their economic, religious, political, and social systems. The first of these measures was a series of treaties that began to define and reduce the Indian land base. By the middle of the nineteenth century, the migration of settlers from the eastern United States had escalated. This expansion onto the Plains led to increased interaction, which was often hostile. From the 1850s to the 1880s numerous military encounters occurred throughout the Plains, including the Minnesota Sioux War, the Sand Creek Massacre, the Battle of the Little Big Horn, and the Wounded Knee Massacre.

In the 1850s and 1860s a series of treaties to establish early reservation boundaries was signed on the Plains. With the separation of Plains Indians into reservations located on the Northern and Southern Plains, two separate music and dance traditions, although based on common heritages, began to emerge. In 1870, under Grant's Peace Policy, these reservations were placed under the control of various Christian denominations. Reservation life took its toll on the cultures of Plains Indians. The prereservation economic system based on the hunting of buffalo was entirely eliminated when buffalo herds were destroyed in the 1870s.

FIGURE 1   Indian drummers from the Cass Lake Reservation beating the drum during the 4th of July Indian celebration commemorating the signing of a peace treaty between the Chippewa and Sioux, 1938. Photo courtesy the Minnesota Historical Society.

Traditional religions also came under attack. In 1880 the Sun Dance was banned, and in the period between 1881 and 1885 the Office of Indian Affairs outlawed a wide variety of Indian customs. Church mission schools were established as well, and Indian children were removed from their homes and from traditional cultures. In addition, the basic social systems of Plains Indians came under attack in the reservation setting. Traditional social activities were discouraged or banned, and social systems based on band and family structures were eroded by the establishment of the reservation communities and the distribution of land among families as formalized by the General Allotment (Dawes) Act of 1887.

The confinement of Indian peoples to reservations on the Plains and the cessation of intertribal warfare led to a decline of the warrior ethos, and warrior societies, which were key aspects of Indian culture, were divested of their power. Prestige and honor, concepts often associated with the ability to become a leader or to marry, were typically earned through warfare and raiding. With these avenues eliminated, young men were left with uncertain futures, driving some to suicide.

New religious movements and their associated musical styles entered the Plains region in response to the breakdown of traditional cultures. These included the Ghost Dance religion and Peyote religion, both of which are discussed further in this volume [see MUSICAL INTERACTIONS, p. 480].

The early twentieth century

America's involvement in World War I provided a new outlet for the warrior traditions of Plains Indians. Many young men joined the armed forces, and with their participation came a brief revival of warrior musical traditions. During the war, older dance forms previously banned were allowed to be performed on many reservations, often in order to raise funds for the war effort. The victorious soldiers returned to large-scale homecoming celebrations, reminiscent of the victory celebrations of the prereservation intertribal warfare days.

In the 1920s various Indian rights societies were organized in the United States in opposition to federal Indian policy. Their criticisms of government policies were echoed in the Meriam Report of 1928, commissioned by the Bureau of Indian Affairs. Further reform in Indian policy began when John Collier, a leader in the Indian rights movement, was appointed commissioner of Indian affairs in 1933. In 1934 Collier introduced the Indian Reorganization Act (IRA), which, in contrast to previous assimilationist policies of the federal government, gave legal sanction to tribal holdings, encouraged the formation of tribal governments, granted religious freedom, and promoted the survival of arts, crafts, and other native traditions (figure 1). In 1936 the Oklahoma Indian Welfare Act was passed, a measure similar to the IRA for Indians in Oklahoma.

Mid-twentieth century to the present

With this change in policy, rituals and traditional customs that had been driven out of public forums returned. Tragically, many rituals and customs were lost with the passing of a whole generation of elders during the early 1900s. These elders, who were born before the establishment of reservations, were unable or unwilling to pass on much of their traditional knowledge, including that of music and dance, because of government policies and restrictions. However, many music and dance forms developed in modified versions at this time, and many new forms were created as well. Social dances became an important locus for many Indian communities, providing forums for expression and creativity.

Indian involvement in World War II renewed interest in early warrior society music and dance forms from prereservation days and from World War I. Following World War II, U.S. Indian policy returned to the assimilation of American Indians into the general population as well as the termination of government support for certain groups. The relocation program provided assistance for reservation Indians to migrate to large urban centers, including Denver, Los Angeles, Minneapolis, and Chicago. With this relocation of Indians came a migration of music and dance forms from reservations to urban centers, where traditions from numerous tribes were able to blend and merge. As music and dance forms spread across the Plains, new media were found for performance. Several radio programs emerged in the 1950s and 1960s, such as the *Indians for Indians Hour* and *Moccasin Time,* that introduced music forms to large Indian and non-Indian audiences.

In the 1950s numerous revivals of secular and religious music and dance forms occurred. On the Northern Plains the Sun Dance was revived among several groups, while on the Southern Plains men's societies were revived among the Kiowa, Comanche, and Ponca. Other forms that were suppressed at the turn of the century also returned to prominence in the 1950s and 1960s among both Northern and Southern Plains groups.

In the 1960s and 1970s, in conjunction with the Vietnam War, the activism of the general U.S. population was mirrored in its Indian population. Concerns with civil rights were reflected in conferences and the creation of numerous organizations in the United States. This activism and sense of freedom influenced certain music and dance forms, including the acceptance and the increased role and participation of women in traditionally male events.

In the 1970s and 1980s the U.S. government passed several policies favorable to American Indians, including the American Indian Religious Freedom Act in 1978, the Indian Civil Rights Act in 1986, and the Indian Gaming Regulatory Act in 1988. In the 1980s and 1990s, the U.S. government began to reestablish trust relationships with groups that had been terminated by earlier policy. Today, Plains peoples are experiencing a new cultural florescence, one in which music plays a highly visible and important role.

PLAINS MUSIC

Research and scholarship

The study of Plains music can be said to have begun when European and American explorers, missionaries, and military moved onto the Great Plains. Writings from the seventeenth and eighteenth centuries documenting these early encounters provide limited glimpses into the musical worlds of the native people. Little is known of the musical traditions on the Plains before the mid- to late nineteenth century, when the academic study of native North American music began, assisted by the invention of sound-recording technology.

Early academic research in the 1880s and 1890s by Theodore Baker (1882), James Owen Dorsey n.d., Alice C. Fletcher (1893), Walter McClintock (1968), and James Mooney (1973 [1896]), among others, was sponsored by a variety of institutions including the Smithsonian Institution's Bureau of American Ethnology. From their work, and from the academic influence of Franz Boas and his students at Columbia University, the study of Native American music became an established part of the emerging academic disciplines of anthropology, folklore, and ethnomusicology.

In the early 1900s, numerous studies of Plains music were undertaken, including Frances Densmore's work with the Teton and Sioux (1918), Mandan and Hidatsa (1923), Pawnee (1929), and Cheyenne and Arapaho (1936). Other works of this time, such as Natalie Curtis's *The Indians Book* (1907), surveyed the music of American Indians and included sections on the Plains. In addition to studies that were primarily devoted to American Indian and Plains music, many ethnographic works of the early twentieth century contained descriptions and discussions of Plains music embedded within their larger presentations.

Throughout the twentieth century, Plains cultures have been the object of numerous studies. Bruno Nettl's work with the Arapaho (1954) and Blackfoot (1989), for example, has figured prominently not only in Plains studies but in ethnomusicology at large. In recent years, dissertations and theses in anthropology, ethnomusicology, and folklore have been undertaken with a variety of Plains groups, including the Crow, Gros Ventre, Northern Arapaho, Kiowa, Blackfeet, and Southern Cheyenne.

MUSICAL STYLES

From these works that build upon the knowledge gained by our predecessors, we can begin to speak of the characteristics of the Plains musical style.

Vocal music

The basic traits of Plains vocal music can be described as follows: the vocal quality is marked by tenseness, with pulsations on longer tones. Vocal quality is also influenced by the sound system of each language, such as the presence of nasal vowels. Glissandos are present at the ends of phrases and of the songs themselves. Musical texture varies between solo and group singing. Plains songs are typically monophonic, with women's parts approximately an octave above the men's. There are rare instances of polyphonic singing in certain peyote songs. The musical form of Plains song is AABCBC, and songs typically begin with an introductory line or phrase sung solo that is repeated (sometimes interrupted) by another solo singer or by the group. This is known as the "second." From the second, the song moves into the main body or chorus, divided into two verses. In solo singing, the introductory line is followed by the main body of the song.

Song texts consist of both words and vocables, either separate or in combination. Vocables, or nonlexical syllables, are formed from the sound system of the specific language of the singer and are primarily vowel sounds in combination with initial consonants. The melodic range is typically greater than an octave. The melodic contour is terraced and descending, with each phrase beginning lower than the start of the previous phrase. There is a predominance of five- and four-tone scales, with the average range being a tenth. Major seconds and minor thirds are the most common melodic intervals. Finally, most Plains singing has a rhythmic accompaniment, provided primarily by a drum but also by various types of rattles and bells that are worn or shaken by the dancers. Drum rhythm varies depending on the type of song or dance and ranges from an unaccented beat to an accented 1-2 beat to a steady tremolo.

Instrumental music

Several types of musical instruments exist on the Plains [see MUSICAL INSTRUMENTS, p. 472]. Membranophones, such as hand drums or small drums, are used typically to accompany solo singing, and larger wooden drums or commercially manufactured bass drums with either commercially made drum heads or with hide drum heads are used to accompany group singing. Other forms of drums, such as stretched rawhides, are used as well. Several aerophones (flutes and whistles) are also common to the Plains. Traditionally, flutes were end blown and were made of certain types of wood, with varying numbers of finger holes. These were used in courting. Whistles were used in conjunction with dancing, either blown in the Sun Dance or blown over drums to encourage the singers (figure 2). Rattles, which are idiophones, were also used in religious rituals, as well as secular dances.

FIGURE 2   A traditional dancer blows his whistle over the Badlands Singers Drum at the 1994 Milk River Days Powwow, Ft. Belknap, Montana. Photo by Erik D. Gooding.

SOCIETY, MUSIC, AND DANCE: YESTERDAY AND TODAY

Various societies such as men's warrior societies, women's societies, and religious and social societies have been significant outlets for Plains music and dance. Many of these

The powwow is a complex of features that centers on various music and dance forms that have persisted in a historical continuum from the mid-1800s to the present through a certain flexibility and adaptability that met the ever-changing needs of its participants.

exist today in some form. A number have persisted in their original form to the present, while others have been modified through time. Still others were eliminated in the past by government policies and were revived in the twentieth century. Like other contemporary Plains Indians music and dance forms, they are thriving.

The Plains powwow

One of the most visible music and dance forms of today, which has its origins in the traditional men's societies, is the powwow. The powwow is a complex of features that centers on various music and dance forms that have persisted in a historical continuum from the mid-1800s to the present through a certain flexibility and adaptability that met the ever-changing needs of its participants. Originating on the Central Plains among the Ponca, Omaha, Pawnee, and Sioux, from the fusion of various societal forms (Omaha, Iruska, Inlonshka, and Hethuska), the powwow complex adapted to the social, political, economic and religious changes that accompanied the breakdown of traditional Plains cultures. In response to these pressures, the powwow developed into a more strictly social form allowing for prestige to be earned through dancing and singing abilities, lessening the importance of warrior society elements. The powwow adapted again as the United States and its Indian citizens entered the world wars, bringing back to the forefront the elements emphasizing honor. Since 1950 the powwow complex has retained elements from each of its functions: honoring, entertainment, economic and social prestige, and the expression of identity. As the complex spread throughout the Plains in the mid-1800s, each tribe contributed to it or made some part of it uniquely its own. Today powwows still express this original tribalism through individual dance outfits, language, singing, and traditions. The flexibility of the powwow allows it to be interpreted on individual, tribal, or regional levels and to remain culturally relevant as an outlet for expression of specific tribal and generalized Indian identity [see MUSICAL INTERACTIONS, p. 480].

There is a variety of powwow forms today, but the most distinctive difference is between those of the Northern and Southern Plains. With the relocation of tribal groups either to Indian Territory (present-day Oklahoma) or to reservations on the Northern Plains, two early forms of the powwow began to develop independently. Intertribal exchange within these geographical regions in the late 1880s and early 1900s led to many tribal variations on the same form. In the mid-1900s, a variety of factors, including relocation policies and improved transportation, led to increased exchange and mutual borrowing between the two geographic regions.

Although many elements are common to both Northern and Southern powwows, each has developed from the influences of the tribal groups within its region. The structure of a song is basically the same in the two regions, although the pitch range of the songs differs. Music of the Northern Plains is sung at a higher pitch than that of the Southern Plains. Dance styles have been exchanged between regions, but each region has its particular version. The movement of the dancers around the arena varies according to the tribal traditions and is either clockwise or counterclockwise.

Context and structure of the powwow

Within these two geographic regions, the powwow has a basic common form regardless of its general purpose and location. Powwows can be held for recreation, competition, and honoring, and on a family, community, tribal, or regional level. They may be held in outdoor arbors that are either temporary or permanent, in specially built structures, in gymnasiums, or in large modern arenas. Powwows may be one-day events, occurring only in the evening, or they may be multiday events, sometimes beginning on a Thursday and ending late on Sunday night or even early Monday morning. The following is a typical program of a powwow, listing the dances and their musical accompaniment.

Grand Entry/Parade

This dance leads off most powwows and serves as a way of bringing the dancers into the dance arena. The dancers enter dancing in a predetermined order, beginning with flag bearers and followed by head dancers, royalty, male dancers, women dancers, and, finally, children.

Flag Song

This song functions similarly to the national anthem at sporting events and usually employs native language texts. It is generally followed by an invocation of some kind. These songs are also sung at sporting events and special occasions, such as high school graduations.

Veterans'/victory songs

These can be sung following the invocation or at any other time during a dance session, especially at the end of a dance as a way to conclude. These songs tell of the actions of Native American soldiers and their involvement in various conflicts.

Round Dance

Based on a basic side step, this form of social dancing appears in a variety of forms throughout the Plains. Each dance has a different connection to a particular society or origin, and the songs are derived from these sources as well.

FIGURE 3   Larry Yazzie, champion Mesquakie Fancy Dancer. Photo by Erik D. Gooding.

Intertribal Dance

The most common dances at powwows are these simple dances in which all can participate. They follow the basic toe-heel dance step and are dispersed between other dances, typically in groupings, throughout dance sessions.

Two-Step/Rabbit Dance

These are male-female partner dances in which the dancers glide along while maintaining some form of contact with each other, typically by holding hands or interlocking their arms. These dances are ladies' choice. Songs that accompany the dances are typically love songs and are among certain groups the few texts that are sung from a female perspective.

Contest dances

These are contests that are specific to each dance style. Men's dance styles include Straight, Traditional, Grass, and Fancy (figure 3), while women's dance styles include Traditional, Fancy Shawl, and Jingle. These styles vary between tribal groups and between regions. Each style has specific songs for contest dancing. Typically, each style will have two different contest dances, the first known as a straight song, and the second, a trick song. Trick songs are specific to each dance style and have elements that

FIGURE 4   Dakota Hotain Singers performing an
honor song at the 1995 Sioux Valley Powwow,
Sioux Valley, Manitoba. Photo by Erik D.
Gooding.

require the dancer to perform certain trick movements or to have mastered the ability
to follow unexpected starts and stops in the songs. Trick songs can also be sung as exhibition dances or specials.

Exhibition/specials

These include a variety of older society-based dances that have been secularized and
that are now used for contests and exhibitions, such as the sneak-up, crow hop, snake
and buffalo dances, and slide songs. Each retains certain attributes of the music of these
earlier forms. In some areas, switch dancing has become a recent exhibition fad, in
which a male dancer will dance in the style of a female and vice versa. This occurs
in varying degrees, from the simple to the complex, when the dancer actually dresses in
the appropriate clothing for the dance.

Honor songs

These songs and their accompanying dances are used within the powwow as a mechanism for honoring individuals, such as head dancers, committee members, and graduates, as well as the deceased (figure 4).

Other contemporary music and dance forms

Other contemporary music and dance forms are also based on earlier societal forms.
Gourd dancing (figure 5) is practiced by numerous tribes, primarily in Oklahoma,
where its strongest adherents are the Kiowa and Comanche. The basic structure is
common to all and allows for the overlay of specific tribal attributes, thus enabling the
Gourd Dance, like the powwow, to become a vehicle for tribal identity. The dance is
named for the characteristic rattle, made from gourds in earlier times, which was held
in the hand and shaken in time with the drum. The basic dance is the characteristic
bobbing up and down in place in a circle around a large drum and singers, who set up
in the middle of the dance arena. This movement is followed by the basic toe-heel step,
when at certain times the dancers advance toward the center. There are variations, such
as in the organization of the dancers on the dance floor in either a circular formation or
a line. Songs are sung in groupings, called sets. Each session has a certain number of
sets that build in intensity, climaxing at the end of the dance.

The Southern Plains is also home to several other societies that are based on earlier
forms. The Tonkonga, or Black Legs Society, of the Kiowa is an example of a revived

military society that plays an important role in Kiowa life and is thriving today. It was revived in 1958 by younger veterans led by Gus Palmer Sr., and the older veterans taught the society's songs, dances, and traditions that are performed biannually today. In addition to their ceremonies, the Black Legs provide various services to the Kiowa people throughout the year, such as acting as color guards and assisting in mourning rituals.

The Osage, Ponca, and Comanche, who all reside in Oklahoma, also practice variations of the men's formal War Dance. Performed either tribally or by districts, these dances follow the strict rules of early-twentieth-century warrior society dances that are organized for societies whose members performed specific duties during their dances, such as the whip men, who today encourage dancers to dance and fulfill the role of modern-day arena directors. The dancers wear the Southern Plains straight dance outfits, with specific tribal attributes, and they dance to songs that often speak of the exploits and honors earned by their ancestors in battle.

Plains guessing games

Throughout the Plains, a common recreational activity, based on the hiding of an object while another guesses its location (for example, which hand it is in), is played by two or more people divided into teams. Known variously as the hand game or moccasin game, this guessing game is accompanied by singing. Songs are sung while one group is hiding and then again when the other group is attempting to guess. Typically, the participants are the singers, and the song texts reflect the action of the game. For example, when a team is attempting to guess, a process accomplished through an elaborate system of hand signals, the team that has hidden the object will sing songs that taunt the other team and attempt to distract it from guessing. The rules of these games vary from group to group, but most have a system of counting with sticks to determine the winner (figure 6). In the late 1800s and early 1900s, hand games were used as divination tools to predict the future. Among the Pawnee, the hand game was associated with the Ghost Dance movement.

RECORDING SOURCES

Major collections of Plains music can be found at the Library of Congress in Washington, D.C., and at the Archives of Traditional Music at Indiana University. Numerous commercial recording companies carry Plains recordings. The major companies include Canyon Records, Sound of America Records, Indian House, Sweetgrass Records, Sunshine Records, and Indian Records. Commercial releases are currently being produced in compact disc and audiocassette formats, either as studio or live recordings. Singing groups today may have numerous recordings available, sometimes as many as ten or more.

FIGURE 6   The hand game set used at the opening of Ft. Belknap Community College. Photo by Erik D. Gooding. 1994.

REFERENCES

Baker, Theodore. 1882. *Über die Musik der Nordamerikanischen Wilden*. Leipzig, Germany: Breitkopf und Härtel.

Black Bear, Ben Sr., and R. D. Theisz. 1976. *Songs and Dances of the Lakota*. Rosebud, S. Dak.: Sinte Gleska College.

Callahan, Alice A. 1990. *The Osage Ceremonial Dance I'n-Lon-Schka*. Norman: University of Oklahoma Press.

Curtis, Natalie. 1907. *The Indians Book*. New York: Harper & Brothers.

Densmore, Frances. 1918. *Teton Sioux Music*. Bureau of American Ethnology Bulletin 61. Washington, D.C.: Smithsonian Institution.

———. 1923. *Mandan and Hidatsa Music*. Bureau of American Ethnology Bulletin 93. Washington, D.C.: Smithsonian Institution.

———. 1929. *Pawnee Music*. Bureau of American Ethnology Bulletin 80. Washington, D.C.: Smithsonian Institution.

———. 1936. *Cheyenne and Arapaho Music*. Los Angeles: Southwest Museum.

Dorsey, James Owen. (n.d.) *Osage Traditions*. Washington, D.C.: Government Printing Office.

Fletcher, Alice C. 1893. *A Study of Omaha Indian Music*. Archaeological and Ethnological Papers of the Peabody Museum, vol. 1, no. 5. Cambridge: Harvard University Press.

Giglio, Virginia. 1994. *Southern Cheyenne Women's Songs*. Norman: University of Oklahoma Press.

Gooding, Erik D. 1998. "Songs of the People: Plains Indian Commercial Recordings, 1968–1996." *Notes* 55:37–67.

Hatton, Orin T. 1974. "Performance Practices of Northern Plains Pow-wow Singing Groups." In *Yearbook of Inter-American Musical Research*, vol. 10, 123–37.

———. 1986. "In the Tradition: Grass Dance Musical Style and Female Pow-wow Singers." *Ethnomusicology* 30:197–222.

———. 1990. Power and Performance in Gros Ventre War Expedition Songs. Canadian Ethnology Service Mercury Series Paper 114. Canadian Museum of Civilization.

Howard, James H. 1976. "The Plains Gourd Dance as a Revitalization Movement." *American Ethnologist* 3:243–258.

Huenemann, Lynn F. 1992. "Northern Plains Dance." In *Native American Dance: Ceremonies and Social Traditions,* ed. Charlotte Heth, 125–147. Washington, D.C.: Smithsonian Institution.

Kavanagh, Thomas W. 1992. "Southern Plains Dance: Tradition and Dynamism." In *Native American Dance: Ceremonies and Social Traditions,* ed. Charlotte Heth, 105–123. Washington, D.C.: Smithsonian Institution.

Lassiter, Luke E. *The Power of Kiowa Song: A Collaborative Ethnography*. Tucson: University of Arizona Press.

McClintock, Walter. 1968. *The Old North Trail; Or, Life, Legends and Religion of the Blackfeet Indians*. Lincoln: University of Nebraska Press.

Meadows, William C., and Gus Palmer Sr. 1992. "Tonkonga: The Kiowa Black Legs Military Society." In *Native American Dance: Ceremonies and Social Traditions,* ed. Charlotte Heth, 116–117. Washington, D.C.: Smithsonian Institution.

Mooney, James. 1973 [1896]. *The Ghost-Dance Religion and Wounded Knee*. Reprint of the Fourteenth Annual Report (Part 2) of the Bureau of Ethnology to the Smithsonian Institution, 1892–93: *The Ghost-Dance Religion and the Sioux Outbreak of 1890*. Mineola, N.Y.: Dover Press.

Nettl, Bruno. 1954. *North American Musical Styles*. Philadelphia: American Folklore Society.

———. 1989. *Blackfoot Musical Thought*. Kent, Ohio: Kent State University Press.

Powers, William K. 1968. "Contemporary Oglala Music and Dance: Pan-Indianism Versus Pan-Tetonism." *Ethnomusicology* 12:352–371.

———. 1990. *War Dance: Plains Indians Musical Performance*. Tucson: University of Arizona Press.

Great Lakes

Brenda M. Romero

The largest and most influential group of the Great Lakes area, the Anishinaabeg (sing., Anishinaabe), or First People, are Algonquian-speaking peoples. They are said to have been guided to this region in ancient times by prophecies that warned of their annihilation if they did not leave the area around the Gulf of St. Lawrence and foretold that food would grow on the water in the new homeland (Woodhead 1994:22). Wild rice has always been the staple of the "three fires" who live around the Great Lakes: the Ojibwe (pronounced Ojibway; also known as Chippewa), who live around Lake Superior (Minnesota and northern Wisconsin); the Potawatomi, who live on the eastern shores of Lake Michigan (with communities in central Wisconsin, Kansas, and Oklahoma); and the Ottawa (Odawa in Canada), who live on Manitoulin Island (between Lake Huron and Georgian Bay) and on the northern tip of the peninsula between Lake Michigan and Lake Huron.

HISTORY AND SOCIAL ORGANIZATION

During the ancient migration, mostly by canoe, the Potawatomi safeguarded the sacred fire used to light all fires along the epic trip. The Ottawa took on the job of trading, and the Ojibwe became the protectors of the spiritual beliefs. During the migration the Anishinaabeg were given signs, the last of which appeared at what is today Madeleine Island, a sacred site that became a center of spiritual activity. The migration, which took many generations, was preserved on birch bark scrolls in the form of epic songs of the *Midéwiwin,* loosely translated as 'things done to the sound of the drum,' or Grand Medicine Society, which emerged among the Ojibwe and subsequently spread throughout the general area as the Medicine Lodge Society.

Algonquian-speakers in the Great Lakes area are often grouped with the more easterly Woodland Indians. The Anishinaabeg, together with the Menominee (today in Wisconsin), the Kickapoo (many displaced to Mexico), the Sac-Fox (today in Kansas, Iowa, and Oklahoma), the Miami and the Illinois (today in Illinois), are known as the Central Algonquians (in addition to the Eastern Algonquian, Subarctic Algonquian [Eastern Canada], and the Iroquoian-speakers). Other groups from this area include the Siouan-speaking Winnebago (today in Nebraska and Wisconsin) and the Iroquoian-speaking Huron. Affiliations are not necessarily indications of cultural homogeneity, as many differences exist within groups as a result of regional, historical, social, economic, and cultural variation. The Ojibwe are themselves divided into four different groups (Northern, Southeastern, Southwestern, and Plains), and it is only since 1975 that these groups have reclaimed Anishinaabeg as their original name. As is true of most North American Indians, the most isolated groups have retained more of their ancient customs and beliefs.

A patrilineal clan system operates among most of the Great Lakes groups, and except for the Anishinaabeg, they divide into moieties based on either clan or birth order, depending on the group. Children join the father's clan, which has its own spiritual guardian (*manitou*) associated with a totem animal, and exogamy, marriage outside the clan, has always been the rule. Particular clans provided leadership in former times (Crane and Loon clans among the Ojibwe; Thunderbird among the Winnebago) (Woodhead 1994:93–95). Wartime leadership was different from peacetime leadership. Tattoos were used for decoration and body paint preserved personal totems and other ritual or decorative signs (Densmore 1979:37–38; Woodhead 1994:42).

The French arrived in the early 1600s and with them the fur trade, which had a devastating impact on various aspects of Native culture over time. Of crucial significance, the fur trade marked a departure from traditional value systems that held to killing animals almost entirely for subsistence and always with appropriate prayers, songs, and ceremonies that thanked the animals for sacrificing themselves so that humans might live (Wapp 2000). The fur trade also exacerbated old hostilities and sparked new ones between the lakes groups (allied with the French) and the Eastern Iroquois (allied with the British) until the mid-seventeenth century and with their former allies, the Dakotas, in the eighteenth century. Many Indians learned to speak French in addition to their native languages, and the high rate of French and Native intermarriage eventually produced a large population of mixed-blood *métis,* who eventually played a large role in the fur trade.

Many Lakes Indians fought against encroachment by British settlers in the eighteenth century but allied with the British against the colonists (referred to as "Big Knives") after the American Revolution. War, a generous alcohol trade, and various European diseases, to which the Indians had no immunity, greatly undermined the strength of the lakes groups, and many were killed or removed from the region. Some whites offered bounties for Indian scalps until the late nineteenth century. The Anishinaabeg managed to hold on to some of their lands, as did a small group of Winnebagos. Today the Ojibwe comprise the largest lakes population, at around two hundred thousand. Close ties continue between some lakes groups and their Canadian counterparts.

LIFEWAYS

Agriculture, large game hunting, wild rice production, and fishing formed distinct subsistence patterns in the Great Lakes area. Emphasis was placed on harvesting the resources most easily preserved in large quantities for winter and in times of scarcity (Tanner 1987:21–22). Corn, beans, and squash were cultivated as staples by 1000 C.E., and potatoes were cultivated after European contact. Fishing, often from birch bark canoes, went on all year, and a wide variety of ancient fishing and preserving techniques are still used today. People also still harvest and preserve wild rice and berries in the fall. In former times the Anishinaabeg and other groups prepared in September to move in small bands to winter camps in the forest to hunt deer, bear, and moose. The portable wigwam, a pole-and-bent-sapling frame covered with sheets of birch bark and cattail matting in a characteristic dome shape, was easily erected over frames left in place the year before.

Winter was also the time for telling sacred tales, which were often accompanied by a drum. In March and April the people moved to the sugarbush, or maple grounds, where they remained until the sap stopped flowing and sturgeon fishing began.

Reunited into a community after months of living in isolated winter quarters, the people celebrated the most important intertribal Maple Sugar Festival as an occasion for giving thanks. Medicine and social dances, adoptions and councils took place at this time. In general, group seasonal food gathering provided opportunities to visit with other families not seen for months, and much gambling, singing, and dancing to the drum took place after a hard day's work. Thanksgiving feasts dedicated to the sun and to the spirit of the particular plant took place as each crop was ready, and in November they offered thanks to the spirits of the game animals that would sustain them during the winter. Smoking the sacred pipe preceded ritual songs such as the following:

> Spring Thanksgiving
> We have endured the ordeal of winter
> the hunger, the winds, the pain of sickness,
> and lived on.
> We grieve for those Grandparents, Parents,
> Children, and Lovers who have gone.
> Once again we shall see the snows melt
> taste the flowing sap, touch the budding seeds.
> smell the whitening flowers, know the renewal of life (Johnston 1990:144).

Wild rice (actually a cereal grass) is considered a sacred food, and elaborate rules governed its harvest and use in former times. It was tended in family plots but was not cultivated until the twentieth century, although there remains a fear that its *manitou* 'spirit' will be lost through cultivation (Woodhead 1994:173). First Fruits or Game ceremonies accompanied the first preparation of each seasonal food, and special ceremonies and songs still accompany first harvests today.

European contact brought many changes that can be only briefly alluded to here. It had always been important to decorate garments to please the personal guardian spirits, and women of the Great Lakes area practiced quillwork, moose-hair embroidery, and the weaving of stringy bark into sashes and bags. Around 1750 most groups of this region began to integrate wool, glass beads, and the art of silk appliqué, or ribbonwork, mostly in floral designs. Although the art of silk appliqué has largely died out, the floral designs are still copied in beadwork by Native Americans across the United States today, and ribbons have become an integral part of shirts worn by Native men as formal attire.

The lakes groups lost most of the 25,000 square miles of reservations that had been assigned to them since the early nineteenth century, mostly through government intervention. After the decline of the fur trade in the late nineteenth century and the timber trade in the early twentieth century, a great deal of relocation took place to the urban centers of Chicago, Detroit, and Minneapolis, among others. Today treaty rights to traditional hunting, fishing, and harvesting grounds off the reservation allow for some of the traditional lifeways to continue. Wild rice is big business that nonetheless offers opportunities for participation in the customs and rituals that still surround it. Gaming casinos have provided an enormous boost to Native economies, allowing for the construction of colleges, schools, housing, and community centers through which the old traditions are revitalized. Michigan Indian Day, on 4 September every year, is one of several important regional celebrations that lend impetus to the process of revitalization.

In 1963 the Great Lakes Intertribal Council (GLITC) began as a community action agency of the Federal Office for Economic Opportunity. The consortium includes federally recognized Indian tribes in Wisconsin and Upper Michigan, who assist each other in a delivery system of services and programs that helps them assume

The production of musical sound implies a spiritual responsibility that has never been taken lightly.

greater responsibility for their own communities. Tribal chairs or their representatives comprise the GLITC board of directors, who represent the Bad River, Lac Courte Oreilles, Lac du Flambeau, and Red Cliff bands of Lake Superior Chippewa, the Sokaogon (Mole Lake) and St. Croix Chippewa, the Forest County Potawatomi, the Oneida and Ho Chunk Nations, the Stockbridge-Munsee and Menominee peoples of Wisconsin, and the Lac Vieux Desert people of Michigan. The central office is located in Lac du Flambeau, Wisconsin. Important issues and decisions are discussed in an intertribal forum, "but by long-standing custom, public comment and policy implementation is reserved to the member tribes through their elected representatives" (http://www.glitc.org/glitc.htm).

BELIEF SYSTEMS

For the Anishinaabeg, the world was created by *Gitche Manitou,* the Master of Life (or Great Spirit), from whom all good things come. Groups around the Great Lakes traditionally believe in a host of *manitou* (also *manido,* plural *manidog*) spirits that inhabit everything, the most important of which are the sun, the moon, thunder, lightning, the four winds, and the thunderbird (eagle) *manitous.* Shamans are important for their roles in communicating with *manitous,* as well as for their understanding of the healing powers of herbs and plants. These practitioners also exert a great deal of healing psychological influence through the words of songs when they administer their medicines. The spirit of evil is personified in a mythical cannibalistic giant that represents excess and encourages moderation. A third important mythical figure is *Winebojo,* both trickster and bringer of good things, who taught the people about the wild rice, corn, tobacco, and medicinal plants.

The Medicine Lodge represents the oldest religion of this area, although it is in decline (Wapp 2000) and "mostly defunct" (Vennum 1989:16). Engraved pictographs on birch bark scrolls served as memory aids during the long and complicated Medicine Dance (*Midéwiwin,* or *Midé,* among the Ojibwe) rituals, accompanied by a water drum and rattles (Vennum 1978). Where practiced, participation in the *Midé* requires payment and the renunciation of alcohol, as well as study of the secret knowledge. Women participate fully in the *Midé,* singing its ritual songs in a low, tenor range characteristic of sacred *Midé* singing in general (Vennum 1989:17).

When President Ulysses S. Grant put missionary boards in charge of reservations, the process of evangelizing the lakes groups to Christianity began (although few ever completely abandoned their Native beliefs). Soon after, in 1877, the lakes peoples received the Drum Dance from the Dakota. The beliefs that accompanied the dance indicated that Turkey Tailfeather Woman had escaped the cavalry and hidden in a lake for four days (the details vary in different versions). During that time she received instructions in the construction of a big drum and its ceremonial use, which would unite native peoples. This created the sacred Drum Religion and gave the people hope at the lowest point in their history. According to Thomas Vennum Jr. (1982:45), the big drum used in today's intertribal powwow is the direct descendant of the early drum ceremony disseminated in the Drum (Dream) Dance. The Drum Religion continues today, and the songs of the sacred Drum Dance are believed to be those given to Turkey Tailfeather Woman herself (Vennum 1982:92). In Wisconsin in 1910, Frances Densmore documented the ritual of exchange when the Lac du Flambeau Chippewa presented the Drum Dance to the Menominee. Although both the Chippewa and the Menominee danced to their own songs before and after the ceremony, the songs at important points of the Drum Dance itself were in Dakota (Sioux) (Densmore 1913:144).

Not all of the region's groups adhered to the Drum Religion, many turning to Christianity and smaller numbers to the Native American Church (peyotism) during the twentieth century. Nonetheless, Dakota music has had a strong influence on traditional music of the lakes area, leading Vennum (1997:24) to consider it the eastern-most part of a northern plains culture area. Although there are differences in the music of this region's groups, the following discussion centers almost exclusively on the Ojibwe, whose music culture represents a prototype for the area.

THE ROLES OF TRADITIONAL MUSIC AND INSTRUMENTS

As with other American Indian groups, Native music in the Great Lakes region is traditionally religious in nature and important to ceremonies, games, social songs, courtship, storytelling, and healing. The production of musical sound implies a spiritual responsibility that has never been taken lightly.

Songs

Songs have always been particularly important in expressing respect and devotion for the personal and other *manitou* spirits, and many derive from dreams. Sacred hunting songs, for example, were meant to invoke the help of the hunted animal's *manitou,* and each species had a song. These songs appear to have declined in recent years.

Because dreams are considered the source of knowledge and wisdom, the vision quest was formerly a part of the initiation of all male children at puberty (and continues in traditional families today). Sacred songs received in dreams or in vision quests have been passed down from generation to generation, although today they may be heard in various contexts, including moccasin gambling games. Songs used in courtship (including flute songs) and wartime taunts are not considered sacred. Songs and ceremonies could be bought and were often learned from neighboring Native groups, as noted above for the Drum Dance. Individuals have always learned songs from other groups whenever possible, and the origin and location of songs is well known. Individuals do not traditionally own songs.

Musical instruments

The lakes groups use various types of rattles and drums, and flute music was formerly used in courtship or to surreptitiously warn the village of an impending attack from a rival group. A contemporary Ojibwe flute player, "Grandpa" Hollis Littlecreek, applies traditional ideas about healing through music to his flute playing. He criticizes Western flute playing as being too fast and maintains that the held notes are all important to the soothing and healing quality of Indian flute playing (Littlecreek 1997). Musical instruments include sacred and secular ones. The most important instrument is the drum, of which Densmore identified four types with varying degrees of loudness. She also mentioned an early Ojibwe war drum that preceded the use of the large drum introduced by the Dakotas (Densmore 1913:145).

The *Midéwiwin* uses the sacred water drum, customarily averaging about sixteen inches tall and ten inches in diameter, with hole and plug for filling and emptying with water, and played with a curved stick that represents the head and eye of the loon (Densmore 1979:96). The War Dance, moccasin games, and curing songs use a round

FIGURE I   Young woman in jingle dress.

wooden frame drum, about eighteen inches in diameter and two and one-half inches wide, although the size may vary. Small frame drums played in moccasin games often use cords, held in place with short sticks against the drumhead, as snares. The Drum Dance uses a large two-headed drum, similar in appearance to the European bass drum (which is also used). It is important to paint the drum in a prescribed manner for sacred observances. Traditionally, big drums are not allowed to touch the ground, and it is still common to see them supported by ornamented and feathered stakes facing the four directions. The long mallets resemble cattails with long stems. The cattail shape makes an excellent mallet for the large drum, and it is hard not to see it also as an association with the watery location of Turkey Tailfeather Woman's vision.

Rattles, mostly used in *Midéwiwin* meetings, were traditionally made by attaching a stick handle to animal horns, hide (moose scrotum), wood, or birch bark containers filled with corn kernels, pebbles, buckshot, or small bones. Some whistles were used as signaling instruments, and these might be placed in a war bundle and made to sound, as if it were the residing *manitou*. Some of the rattle's sacredness is imparted to the jingle dance dress that originated among the Ojibwe and is seen in the modern pow-wow (figure 1). One of the stories associated with the dance holds that the daughter of a powerful spiritual leader fell deathly ill. He received a visionary dream in which he was instructed to make a dress, on which he was to attach many jingles fashioned of the tin lids of snuffboxes, for his daughter to dance in. He did as instructed, and she recovered from her illness. The jingle dress makes a soft rattling sound as the wearer moves and dances. Today the jingles are not taken from the snuffboxes themselves but from large tin sheets on which the snuff lids are perforated in small circles. A good jingle maker can "turn" five hundred flat tin circles into jingles in one day.

RESEARCH ON THE MUSIC OF THE GREAT LAKES GROUPS

Based on extensive documentation, Densmore (1913:2) concluded that the Ojibwe preferred melody and musical sound over words and language, except in love songs and some of the *Midé* songs. Word accents could change or vocables could be added in order to fit the melody. The voice nonetheless seemed independent from the drumbeat, which was placed slightly before or after the voice, as is still the style here and in many other North American Indian song traditions. Vennum (1997:2) cites language loss as the reason for an increasing number of songs using only vocables by the late twentieth century. Except for flute melodies, which alternated with sung texts, all instruments accompanied singing.

Turn-of-the-century recordings of the Ojibwe outnumber those of any other Native group (Vennum 1980:44). The first recordings of Ojibwe music were made in 1869 by Alice Fletcher in Washington, D.C., when a delegation from Leech Lake was there protesting treaty violations of timber rights (Vennum 1997:4). Soon after, Frederick Burton collected 180 songs and published the transcriptions. The largest collection of Ojibwe songs, comprising over five hundred wax cylinder recordings, was collected by Densmore, and much of what is known about the songs comes from her early work (1913). Densmore also collected 140 Menominee songs of this area (Densmore 1932). Albert B. Reagan collected many songs in the Nett Lake area in this early period, and overall Ojibwe recordings are well represented geographically. Rituals of the *Midéwiwin* were documented by Walter J. Hoffman after living for three years at the White Earth Reservation in Minnesota (1885–1886), but he did not transcribe many of the songs, dismissing them as unworthy of his attention (Vennum 1980:47).

Densmore (1913) classified the songs as social or for the *Midéwiwin*. Among the social songs she listed dream songs, personal in nature and from supernatural sources; war songs, of which there were dream songs of individual warriors, war charms and medicine songs, war expedition songs, and war success songs; love songs; moccasin game songs; a Begging Dance acquired from the Sioux; songs connected with gifts; Pipe Dance songs; songs for children; and Woman's Dance songs, also acquired from the matrilineal Sioux. Among the songs of the *Midé* Densmore listed ceremonial songs, initiation songs, ceremonial songs for a dying chief, songs to ensure success, songs for curing, songs for medicines, and love-charm songs.

Gertrude Prokosch Kurath's analyses of Great Lakes traditional vocalization revealed pulsation on sustained notes, glides, grade notes, and a neutral third, or "blue note." With much insight, she noted that transcription could only "conform to Indian concept . . . by omitting key and time signatures, by lightening metrical divisions, [and] by indicating blue notes with plus or minus signs" (Kurath 1956:12). The older songs use three, four, or five tones that progress downward and end on the main tone and would typically be performed four times. Six-tone, diatonic, and modal scales are usually a Western influence (Kurath 1956:13). Since Kurath's research, however, many changes have occurred.

Vennum has done the most work on Ojibwe song since Densmore, collecting songs among the southwestern bands in the same areas where Densmore did her research and re-transcribing her wax cylinder recordings for greater accuracy. He states (1980:44) that some genres were and still are exceptional and must be studied separately. My own research suggests that this is partly because so much musical "borrowing" or "receiving" from other groups has taken place (a phenomenon commonly seen throughout North America) that musical form may be or may once have been specific to an accommodated genre. Kurath (1956:13) notes the ways that recurrent Great Lakes song forms intermixed with the forms of neighboring groups, creating distinct regional types. European tendencies were associated with the east and the St. Lawrence River, and Native tendencies with the Southwest. Vennum (1997) also attests to the disappearance of many of the sacred genres that Densmore recorded and provides excellent examples of nonsacred, contemporary moccasin game, story, dream, and love songs, along with highly mainstream urban styles.

GREAT LAKES MUSICAL CULTURE TODAY

Although solo prayer singing might be prominent in difficult times (winter in particular), group singing was and still is very important in traditional Anishinaabe cultures, especially at summer gatherings. Group singing accompanied group work in the past as it does today. Songs and stories accompanied the various phases of ricing, but the older songs have been lost. Group songs accompanying the hulling of wild rice after parching were forgotten after the 1930s, when mechanization took over that stage of the processing (Vennum 1989:14–15). Although Ojibwe women in the past enjoyed nearly the same musical roles as men, today the powwow is the only context in which women have begun to reclaim those roles, albeit with difficulty.

Spoken native language tends to correlate negatively with adaptation to mainstream culture, but language is reinforced when the economy is strong. Today familiar mainstream Christian hymns and Christmas carols are sung in Ojibwe by singer-fiddler Lawrence "Teddy Boy" Houle and others. The Ojibwe rock singer Keith Secola uses the native language sparingly but includes traditional Indian melodies reinterpreted in a rock idiom. The melody he uses in "Indian Cars" (Vennum 1997), for instance, is remarkably similar to a rabbit song sung in a much slower and quieter style by contemporary Oneida singer Joanne Shenandoah (1995).

Three contexts continue to provide ample opportunity for the sharing and development of traditional music ceremonials: the modern powwow and ricings (both of which have also become symbols of Indian identity), and wakes. The late twentieth century saw the revival of moccasin gambling games accompanied by singing, even though words are now commonly replaced by vocables (Vennum 1997).

Song types that still exist among the lakes groups that are not discussed here are unaccompanied love songs, songs for children, peyote songs, and Christian hymns with native texts [see MUSICAL INTERACTIONS, p. 480]. The last, similar to Christmas carols, usually retain the original European American melodies with texts translated into native languages. Finally, Native peoples have not neglected the instrumental folk traditions of mainstream culture, and the fiddle music of surrounding areas has become a part of the musical cultures of the Ojibwe and the Plains Chippewa (Métis). In this case, the pieces are played much as they are played among mainstream fiddlers.

Contemporary Ojibwe song form reflects Dakota influence and defines the Ojibwe powwow style. It contains three unique features: a double introduction; a main melody composed of phrases related to the introduction, ending with a cadential formula; and the restatement of the main melody, without the introductory phrases. Religious songs end here, while secular songs end with a coda, which is the incomplete repetition of the main melody. Drum patterns signal the end. The number of times the coda is performed depends on the context of the performance (Vennum 1980). The transcription below represents a version of this form (figure 2).

There are many ways in which traditional songs can find a place in contemporary life. The "Ojibwe Air Force Song," from the Lac Court Oreilles Reservation in Wisconsin, came in a dream to an Ojibwe man whose son was in the Air Force during World War II. Typical of old Ojibwe protective songs that anticipated a safe return from battle, this prayerful Ojibwe powwow song refers to a modern situation that soldiers can relate to: "While I am flying around in the sky, I know that I will come to land safely upon the earth" (*Honor the Earth Powwow* 1991). The melodic material encompasses one octave plus a perfect fifth and descends in the typical Plains powwow style. Kathy Kucsan, while a graduate student at the University of Colorado, Boulder, transcribed the song in 1993. She suggested that the descent of the melodic line might symbolize the safe descent. I conclude this article with her transcription of this contemporary Ojibwe powwow song (Kucsan 1993):

FIGURE 2   "Ojibwe Air Force Song," transcription by Kathy Kucsan, 1993.

REFERENCES

Densmore, Frances. 1913. *Chippewa Music*. Vol. 2. Bureau of American Ethnology Bulletin 53. Washington, D.C.: Smithsonian Institution.

———. 1932. *Menominee Music*. Bureau of American Ethnology Bulletin 102. Washington, D.C.: Smithsonian Institution.

———. 1979. *Chippewa Customs*. Minneapolis, Minn: Minnesota Historical Society Press.

Healing Songs of the American Indians. 1965. Notes by Charles Hofmann. Ethnic Folkways Library FE 4251. LP disk.

Hickerson, Harold. 1988. *The Chippewa and Their Neighbors: A Study in Ethnohistory*. Prospect Heights, Ill.: Waveland Press.

Hoffman, Walter J. 1885–1886. *The Midéwiwin or "Grand Medicine Society" of the Ojibwe*. Bureau of American Ethnology Annual Report 7:143–300.

Hofmann, Charles. 1965. "Frances Densmore and the Music of the American Indians." Liner notes for *Healing Songs of the American Indians*. Ethnic Folkways Library FE 4251. LP disk.

Honor the Earth Powwow: Songs of the Great Lakes Indians. 1991. Thomas Vennum Jr., notes; Mickey Hart, Jens McVoy, and Thomas Vennum Jr., research and recording. Rykodisc RACS 0199.

Johnston, Basil. 1976. *Ojibway Heritage*. Lincoln: University of Nebraska Press.

———. 1990. *Ojibway Ceremonies*. Lincoln: University of Nebraska Press.

Kucsan, Kathy. 1993. "Ojibwa Musical Culture." Unpublished paper. Boulder: University of Colorado.

Kurath, Gertrude Prokosch. 1956. "Voices of the Waterways." Liner notes for *Songs and Dances of the Great Lakes Indians*. Monograph Series of the Ethnic Folkways Library. Smithsonian-Folkways Recordings P 1003. LP disk.

———. 1966. *Michigan Indian Festivals*. Ann Arbor, Mich.: Ann Arbor Publishers.

Littlecreek, Hollis. 1997. Personal communication.

Ojibway Music from Minnesota. 1997. Notes by Thomas Vennum Jr. Minnesota Historical Society. Compact disc.

Paredes, J. A., ed. 1980. *Anishinaabe: Six Studies of Modern Chippewa*. Tallahassee: University Presses of Florida.

Parthun, Paul. 1976. "Ojibwe Music in Minnesota." Ph.D. dissertation, University of Minnesota.

Plains Chippewa/Métis Music from Turtle Mountain: Drums, Fiddles, Chansons and Rock and Roll. 1992. Smithsonian/Folkways SF 40411. Compact disc.

Ritzenthaler, Robert E., and Pat Ritzenthaler. 1970. *The Woodland Indians of the Western Great Lakes*. New York: Natural History Press.

Shenandoah, Joanne, with Peter Kater. 1995. *Lifeblood*. Silver Wave Records SC 809. Compact disc.

Songs of the Chippewa, Volume I: Game and Social Dance Songs. 1977. Recording and liner notes by Paul Parthun. Smithsonian-Folkways FE 4392.

Songs and Dances of the Great Lakes Indians. 1956. Recording and liner notes by Gertrude Prokosch Kurath. Monograph Series of the Ethnic Folkways Library. Smithsonian-Folkways Recordings P 1003. LP disk.

Tanner, Helen Hornbeck, ed. 1987. *Atlas of Great Lakes Indian History*. Norman: University of Oklahoma Press.

Vennum, Thomas Jr. 1978. "Ojibwe Origin-Migration Songs of the *Mitewiwin*." *Journal of American Folklore* 91:753–791.

———. 1980. "A History of Ojibwe Song Form." *Selected Reports in Ethnomusicology* 3(2):43–75.

———. 1982. *The Ojibwe Dance Drum: Its History and Construction*. Smithsonian Folklife Studies, No. 2. Washington, D.C.: Smithsonian Institution Press.

———. 1989. "The Changing Role of Women in Ojibwe Music History." In *Women in North American Indian Music*, ed. Richard Keeling, 13–21. Ann Arbor, Mich.: Society for Ethnomusicology.

———. 1997. Booklet notes to *Ojibway Music from Minnesota*. Minnesota Historical Society. Compact disc.

Wapp, Ed. 2000. Personal communication.

Woodhead, Henry, ed. 1994. *The American Indians: People of the Lakes*. Alexandria, Va.: Time-Life Books.

Wood That Sings: Indian Fiddle Music of the Americas. 1997. Smithsonian Folkways SF CD 40472. Compact disc.

Websites:

www.nativeculture.com

www.glitc.org/glitc.htm

Northeast
Victoria Lindsay Levine

The Northeast Indians inhabited what is now New England, the mid-Atlantic states, the tidewater zones of Virginia and North Carolina, and Canadian territory from the lower Great Lakes to Nova Scotia. The region contains two major geographical divisions: the coastal zone and the Saint Lawrence lowlands. The coastal zone includes the eastern seaboard from Nova Scotia to North Carolina; much of this area is separated from the interior by the Appalachian Mountains. The Saint Lawrence lowlands include southern Ontario, northern New York, and the Saint Lawrence and Susquehanna River valleys.

EARLY HISTORY AND CULTURE

At the time of contact with Europeans, the Northeast was thickly forested with coniferous and deciduous trees, providing a rich variety of nuts, berries, and other wild fruits and vegetables as well as abundant fish and game. The climate of the region alternates between cold winters with deep snow, and hot summers; the peoples who lived in the northernmost reaches of the area employed winter survival techniques similar to those used in the Subarctic region [see SUBARCTIC CANADA p. 383].

Northeast Indians are culturally related to Southeastern tribes as well as to the Algonkian-speaking peoples of the western Great Lakes and Prairie regions. The dominant language families of the Northeast are Iroquoian and Algonkian. The Iroquoian languages include Seneca, Cayuga, Onondaga, Mohawk, Oneida, and Tuscarora. The Algonkian languages include Micmac, Maliseet, Passamaquoddy, Eastern and Western Abenaki (including Penobscot), and Delaware (Lenape). The coastal Algonkian languages spoken in southern New England, Virginia, and the Carolinas, such as Massachusett, Narragansett, Powhatan, Nanticoke, and many others, have been extinct for more than a century.

Northeast Indians are descended from Woodland traditions, which developed in the eastern United States after 400 C.E. Woodland peoples grew maize, squash, beans, and other crops in addition to hunting, fishing, and gathering wild foods. Woodland settlements were semisedentary, and villages were moved periodically as the soil in an area became depleted. Warfare and raiding were intense during this period; many Woodland communities were protected by palisades. At the time of contact with Europeans in the fifteenth and sixteenth centuries, most Northeast Indians lived in relatively

The traditional music of some other eastern Algonkians, such as the Micmac, Penobscot, and Delaware, became moribund during the twentieth century but is currently being revitalized.

small, autonomous villages; alliances with neighboring communities were fluid and temporary. The modern tribes grew out of these informal alliances that became more permanent as a result of contact.

The League of the Iroquois

By the early seventeenth century, five of the Iroquoian tribes—the Mohawk, Oneida, Onondaga, Cayuga, and Seneca—had established a confederacy known as the Five Nations or the League of the Iroquois. Other Iroquoian groups in the region were eventually dispersed by or incorporated into the Five Nations. Some southern Siouan and Iroquoian speakers such as the Tutelo and Tuscarora began migrating to the north in the seventeenth century to escape the colonists. Around 1722 the Tuscarora were adopted by the League of the Iroquois, which became known thereafter as the Six Nations. The Tutelo were among the dislocated peoples who subsequently found homes among the Six Nations. After the Revolutionary War, some members of the League remained in their homelands, while others resettled in Ontario, depending upon which side they had taken in the war. The Six Nations Reserve was established near Brantford, Ontario, in 1847; it remains the largest Iroquois reservation in North America.

Algonkian-speaking peoples

The Algonkian-speaking peoples of the Northeast generally did not fare as well as the Iroquoians. Several coastal Algonkian cultures were completely destroyed during the seventeenth century by disease epidemics and warfare with the colonists; the survivors from some of these communities were absorbed by the Delaware. The Delaware lived in several independent but related bands in the Delaware River valley during the early seventeenth century; their history involves a complex series of migrations, along with repeated divisions and consolidations. Ultimately some Delaware people were absorbed by the Iroquois and others moved to Wisconsin, but most were eventually settled in Oklahoma. The Algonkian-speakers in New England and the Maritime Provinces, including the Micmac, Maliseet, Penobscot, and Passamaquoddy, have endured many changes but continue to live within their homelands. These groups were part of a political and ceremonial alliance known as the Wabanaki Confederacy, which was active from the mid-eighteenth century through the late nineteenth century.

CONTEXTS FOR MUSICAL PERFORMANCE

Because the southern-coastal Algonkians suffered the most complete cultural destruction after contact, very little is known about their indigenous music. The traditional music of some other eastern Algonkians, such as the Micmac, Penobscot, and Delaware, became moribund during the twentieth century but is currently being revitalized. Iroquoian peoples continue to perform native music in a variety of contexts, including the seasonal thanksgiving ceremonies of the Handsome Lake or Longhouse religion, the curing rituals of medicine societies such as the False Face and Husk Face

Societies, and the Feast of the Dead. In addition, Northeast Indians now participate in a variety of pan-Indian and syncretic musical styles, Christian hymns and gospel music, and European American classical, folk, and popular music [see MUSICAL INTERACTIONS, p. 480].

MUSICAL STYLES

Songs

Northeast Indians use a moderately relaxed and open vocal quality in traditional songs, emphasizing the middle or lower range. Vocal pulsations articulate phrase endings in some Northeast styles; aspirated attacks and releases, as well as vocal glides, are common. Northeast Indian song texts consist of vocables with some lines of lexical text; the texts are often humorous in social dance songs. Many Northeast Indian songs feature antiphony; the leader sings a short melodic phrase and is answered by the dancers in unblended unison, with the women doubling the men at the octave in some tribes. Some dance songs are performed as solos or duets by one or two head singers.

Diverse strophic, sectional, and iterative forms are used in Northeast Indian music. Songs in strophic form may have an introduction performed as a solo by the head singer; sectional songs sometimes use a phrase design that may be diagrammed as AABAB or AABABA. Many different scale types exist in the Northeast, although there is a predilection for five-tone scales. Most Northeast Indian songs employ melodic contours that descend or undulate with a descending inflection; these songs generally have an ambitus of an octave or more, although certain genres have a small scale and narrow range. Most dance songs have relatively simple, symmetrical rhythmic structures, although songs with small scales tend to be more complex rhythmically.

Instruments

A variety of musical instruments are indigenous to the Northeast, including many kinds of container rattles [see MUSICAL INSTRUMENTS, p. 472]. Iroquoian peoples use different rattles to accompany different genres of dance music; cow horn rattles accompany Social Dance songs, while rattles made of bark, gourds, or turtle shells are used in ceremonial music. Other idiophones used in the Northeast include striking sticks (Tutelo), rasps (Seneca), pounding sticks (Seneca), plank drums (Maliseet), and deerhide drums (Delaware). Small water drums are used throughout the Northeast; some double-headed hand drums are indigenous to the region, as is a kind of snare drum used in Penobscot shamanism. Drums are played with wooden drumsticks throughout this region. Other instruments indigenous to the Northeast include flageolets and flutes, which are played as solo instruments.

TWO IMPORTANT GENRES

Iroquois Social Dance songs and Delaware Big House songs are two of the most important genres of Northeast Indian music.

Iroquois Social Dance songs

The Iroquois perform Social Dances during ceremonies associated with the Longhouse religion, which was founded by the Seneca prophet Handsome Lake in 1799. Longhouse ceremonies are communal expressions of thanksgiving and renewal; they are held inside a rectangular council house with a stove or fireplace at each end and two rows of benches along each wall. As it is important to maintain a good feeling throughout a Longhouse ceremony, Social Dances are performed during and after more intense, sacred rituals, to entertain and provide an element of humor. Iroquois Social Dances are similar to the Social Dances of other eastern tribes; they are performed in single-file lines or by couples and move counterclockwise around the Longhouse. The

Social Dance repertoire contains about nineteen different dances, including the Standing Quiver Dance, Women's Dance, animal dances, and dances obtained from other eastern tribes, such as the Alligator Dance (received from the Seminole) or the Delaware Skin Dance.

An evening of Iroquois social dancing usually opens with the Standing Quiver Dance, which has also been known as the Warrior's Dance, Trotting Dance, Old Man's Cane Dance, or Stomp Dance. A large number of discrete songs exists in this genre, all of which are identified by the generic title of Standing Quiver Dance. These songs are very short and fast and are performed as a set in rapid succession; the leader sings short phrases and is answered by the male dancers in unblended unison. This genre showcases the song leader's unique vocal style and quality as well as his knowledge of the repertoire. Unlike other Iroquois Social Dance songs that employ strophic and sectional forms, Standing Quiver Dance songs feature an iterative form. Melodic contours in these songs are level or undulate with a descending inflection. These songs tend to have narrow ranges, and scales with three, four, or five pitches predominate. Standing Quiver Dance songs are usually in duple meter and feature simple rhythmic patterns, compared to the rhythms in other Iroquois musical genres. The song texts are primarily vocables, but sometimes humorous words are added, and new texts are composed regularly. Standing Quiver Dance songs are performed without instrumental accompaniment. In form, style, and function, they resemble the Stomp Dances performed by many Eastern Woodland peoples.

Delaware Big House songs

The Delaware experienced dramatic culture change during the seventeenth and eighteenth centuries. By the early nineteenth century, their most important religious ritual was the Big House ceremony that developed from an annual harvest observance combined with the performance of songs received in vision quests. The Big House ceremony was held in the spring at planting time and again in the fall after the corn harvest. The entire event lasted six, eight, or twelve nights and included many subrituals, each accompanied by its own musical genre. The ceremony took place inside a rectangular log cabin called a Big House; the structure had no windows and was sited east to west, with a door and a fire at each end. The sponsor of the event held a turtle shell rattle while reciting a stylized narrative of his vision experience; then he danced counterclockwise around the Big House, singing the song he had received in the vision. Those who wished to do so could dance single file behind the sponsor; the women danced in a separate line. After the sponsor had completed his performance, he passed the rattle to another participant, who presented his vision narrative and song. The ceremony ended when the rattle had been passed once around the entire circle of participants.

The Delaware vision experience was highly personal, and therefore each Delaware vision song is stylistically idiosyncratic. Big House songs use a great variety of scales, ranging from three to seven tones. The lengths of melodic phrases can vary within a song, and meter changes frequently in some songs. Several kinds of melodic contours are used, including broadly undulating lines, melodies that begin high and gradually descend, and melodies that begin low but leap upward. The visionary was assisted in his performance by two head singers, who sang the vision songs while playing a deerhide drum. Actually an idiophone, this instrument was made from a dried deerhide, which was folded into an oblong packet framed by four wooden slats and bound together with deerhide thongs. The drum was played by striking the slats with narrow wooden paddles. The last Big House ceremony took place in 1924, although vision songs remained in the musical repertoire of some Oklahoma Delawares until the 1980s.

SCHOLARSHIP

The historical sources on Northeast Indian musical cultures are some of the richest available for native North America. French missionaries and explorers of the seventeenth and eighteenth centuries described the music, dance, and ceremonialism of the Huron and other Iroquoian-speaking peoples. Ethnographic work in the region began in the mid-nineteenth century with Lewis Henry Morgan (1962 [1851]), and scholarly interest in Northeast Indian musics began a few decades later with John Reade (1887), Alexander Cringan (1900), Ernest Gagnon (1907), and most importantly, Marius Barbeau (1915). From the 1930s through the 1960s, significant contributions to the ethnomusicology of the Northeast were made by William Fenton (1936, 1940), Gertrude Kurath (1964, 1968), and Frank Speck (1949; Speck and Herzog, 1942). Elizabeth Tooker has published a valuable study of the Iroquois Midwinter Ceremony (1970), while Robert Adams (1991 [1977]) studied Delaware music and dance. Several ethnomusicologists have undertaken research on diverse aspects of Northeast Indian music since 1980, including Beverley Diamond, M. Sam Cronk, Franziska von Rosen (1994), and Ron LaFrance (1992). Archival recordings of Northeast Indian music are preserved by the Library of Congress Federal Cylinder Program and the Archives of Traditional Music at Indiana University.

REFERENCES

Adams, Robert H. 1991 [1977]. *Songs of Our Grandfathers: Music of the Unami Delaware Indians.* Dewey, Okla.: Touching Leaves Indian Crafts.

Barbeau, C. Marius. 1915. *Huron and Wyandot Mythology.* Canadian Department of Mines, Geological Survey Memoirs 80, Anthropological Series no. 11.

Cringan, Alexander. 1900. *Pagan Dance Songs of the Iroquois.* Ontario Education Department: Archaeological Report for 1899, 168–189.

Diamond, Beverley, M. Sam Cronk, and Franziska von Rosen. 1994. *Visions of Sound: Musical Instruments of First Nations Communities in Northeastern America.* Chicago: University of Chicago Press.

Fenton, William N. 1936. "An Outline of Seneca Ceremonies at Coldspring Longhouse." In *Publications in Anthropology* 9. New Haven, Conn.: Yale University.

———. 1940. *Masked Medicine Societies of the Iroquois.* Annual Report of the Smithsonian Institution for 1940. Washington, D.C.: Government Printing Office, 397–429.

———. 1942. *Songs from the Iroquois Longhouse.* Library of Congress AFS L6. LP disk.

———. 1948. *Seneca Songs from Coldspring Longhouse.* Library of Congress AFS L17. LP disk.

———. 1978. *Iroquois Social Dance Songs.* 3 vols. Iroqrafts, Ont.: Ohsweken.

Gagnon, Ernest. 1907. "Les Sauvages de l'Amérique et l'art musical." In *Proceedings of the International Congress of Americanists* (1906), 179–189. Québec: International Congress of Americanists.

Kurath, Gertrude Prokosch. 1964. *Iroquois Music and Dance: Ceremonial Arts of Two Seneca Longhouses.* Bureau of American Ethnology Bulletin 187. Washington, D.C.: Smithsonian Institution.

———. 1968. *Dance and Song Rituals of Six Nations Reserve, Ontario.* National Museum of Canada Bulletin 220.

LaFrance, Ron. 1992. "Inside the Longhouse: Dances of the Haudenosaunee." In *Native American Dance: Ceremonies and Social Traditions,* ed. Charlotte Heth, 19–32. Washington, D.C.: Smithsonian Institution.

Morgan, Lewis Henry. 1962 [1851]. *League of the Ho-dé-no-sau-nee or Iroquois.* Secaucus, N.J.: Citadel Press.

Reade, John. 1887. "Some Wabanaki Songs." *Transactions of the Royal Society of Canada* 5(2):1–8.

Rhodes, Willard. n.d. *Delaware, Cherokee, Choctaw, Creek.* Library of Congress AFS L37. LP disk.

Riemer, Mary Frances. 1980. *Seneca Social Dance Music.* Smithsonian Folkways Recordings FE 4072. Compact disc.

Speck, Frank Gouldsmith. 1949. *Midwinter Rites of the Cayuga Longhouse.* Philadelphia: University of Pennsylvania Press.

Speck, Frank G., and George Herzog. 1942. *The Tutelo Adoption Ceremony: Reclothing the Living in the Name of the Dead.* Harrisburg: Pennsylvania Historical Commission.

Tooker, Elizabeth. 1970. *The Iroquois Ceremony of Midwinter.* Syracuse, N.Y.: Syracuse University Press.

Trigger, Bruce G., ed. 1978. *Northeast.* Vol. 15, *Handbook of North American Indians.* Washington, D.C.: Smithsonian Institution Press.

Southeast
Victoria Lindsay Levine

Early History and Culture
Contexts for Music Performance
Musical Styles
Two Important Genres
Scholarship

Southeastern Indians originally inhabited the present states of North Carolina, South Carolina, Georgia, Florida, Tennessee, Alabama, Mississippi, Louisiana, and those parts of Illinois, Kentucky, Missouri, and Arkansas that border the Mississippi River. The climate throughout this region is mild, although snow falls at the higher elevations and the southernmost reaches are nearly tropical. The region contains three distinct natural environments: the coastal plain, the southern Piedmont, and the southern part of the Appalachian Mountains. The coastal plain covers roughly three-fourths of the region. With its meandering rivers, marshes, and cypress stands, it was rich in wild vegetables and fruits as well as game animals, birds, fish, and shellfish at the time of contact with Europeans. Between the coastal plain and the Appalachian highlands is the Piedmont, a plateau about one hundred fifty miles wide. The Piedmont, like the southern Appalachians, was densely forested with deciduous and evergreen trees; it was inhabited by large herds of deer as well as many other game animals and birds.

EARLY HISTORY AND CULTURE

Southeast Indians have cultural ties to tribes from the Northeast and the eastern Plains and may have had contact with peoples from the interior of Mexico in the distant past [see NORTHEAST, p. 461; PLAINS, p. 440]. The dominant language family of the area is Muskhogean, which includes the languages of the Choctaw, Chickasaw, Muskogee (Creek), Seminole, Alibamu (Alabama), Coushatta (Koasati), Mikasuki, Hitchiti, and other tribes. Related to the Muskhogean family are the languages spoken by the Natchez and Tunica. Other Southeast language families include Iroquoian (Cherokee), Siouan (Ofo, Biloxi, Catawba, and others), Yuchi, and Caddo. In addition, some Southeast Indians spoke the Mobilian trade language, a lingua franca used for intertribal communication.

Most Southern Indians are descended from the Mississippian peoples who flourished throughout the Southeast after about 800 C.E. The Mississippians grew maize, squash, beans, and other crops, but also hunted, fished, and gathered wild foods. The Mississippians lived in semisedentary towns with stratified social organizations. They built large earthen temple mounds with flattened tops that were used for ceremonial purposes as well as for the homes of religious leaders. Mississippians were in the process of social reorganization at the time of contact with Europeans in the sixteenth century. Although it is difficult to trace the precise origins of the modern Southern tribes, many evidently formed during the early contact period. In some instances, larger, more intact societies assimilated smaller groups with which they had alliances. In other cases, small, previously separate groups banded together in informal confederacies.

After the Revolutionary War, the U.S. government initiated an aggressive campaign to assimilate the Southern Indians; government agents and missionaries urged them to learn English and to adopt European American customs. Beginning in the 1830s, the government moved most Southern Indians to the Indian Territory. The Indians refer to this episode as the Trail of Tears because of the tragic losses they suffered. In the 1890s, the United States terminated tribal governments in the Indian Territory, which became the state of Oklahoma in 1907. Most Southern tribes now have two divisions. The eastern division includes descendants of those who avoided removal from their homelands in the nineteenth century, and the much larger western division includes descendants of those who underwent removal.

CONTEXTS FOR MUSIC PERFORMANCE

Centuries of intense pressure to assimilate, and the complete destruction of many smaller tribes, have taken a heavy toll on native music of the Southeast. However, many Southeast Indians continue to perform indigenous music in a variety of contexts, including private medicine rituals, sacred festivals such as the Green Corn ceremony, and folkloric or educational exhibitions. Since the 1970s, some Southeast groups, such as the Choctaw and Chickasaw, have revitalized moribund music and dance traditions. Many Southeast Indians now participate in powwow music, Plains Indian flute music, Christian hymn-singing with Indian language texts, gospel music, and European American classical, folk, and popular music, in addition to indigenous music.

MUSICAL STYLES

In traditional vocal repertoires, Southeast Indians generally employ a moderately relaxed and open vocal style. Exceptions include the Caddo, whose vocal quality is tense and nasal. In addition, some genres, such as Stomp Dance songs, feature a variety of extended vocal techniques that include yodeling, rapid vibrato, and heavily aspirated attacks and releases.

Songs

Southeast Indian song texts consist primarily of vocables, although some lines of lexical text may appear in dance songs as well as in medicine songs. Most Southeast dance songs employ antiphony; the leader sings a call, and the dancers respond in unblended unison, the women doubling the men at the octave in some songs. Some dance songs are performed as solos by the leader, and a few are performed by the dancers in unblended unison. Medicine songs are sung as solos in a barely audible voice, in order to protect the religious content of this genre.

Songs from the Southeast region feature tremendous variety in form and design, including diverse sectional and strophic forms with intricate, often asymmetrical phrase patterns. Some songs begin with an unmetered solo introduction. Frequent metric changes within songs, complex rhythmic relationships between music and choreography, syncopation, and *sforzandi* characterize Southeast Indian approaches to rhythm. Although a variety of scale types are used, there is a predilection for anhemitonic scales with four, five, or six pitches. The melodic contours of most Southeast Indian dance songs feature an overall descent or undulation with a descending inflection; these melodies usually have an ambitus of an octave or more. Medicine songs and certain ritual songs, by contrast, employ a predominantly level contour with a narrow range, a scale of three or fewer pitches, and iterative form.

The first song features dense, energetic antiphonal exchanges between the leader and male dancers; the melodic contour is predominantly level, the tempo is fast, and the chorus echoes the leader's call. At a specific point in the first song, the dancing starts, to the accompaniment of the shell-shakers.

Instruments

Many Southeast dance songs are performed without instrumental accompaniment, although some dances feature a drum, a pair of striking sticks, or a rattle. Southeast drums, which are always played with a drumstick, include water drums, cylinder drums, and double-headed hand drums; in this region, drums are more often used in medicine rituals than in communal dances. Southeast rattles are of the container type, including gourd, turtle shell, and coconut shell hand rattles. Leg rattles, made of clusters of turtle shells or evaporated milk cans, accompany Stomp Dances; they are worn on each leg by women dancers, called shell-shakers, who skillfully control their movements to produce a vigorous rhythm during specific parts of the song. Other instruments from the Southeast include cane flutes or whistles, played solo in medicine rituals, and sleigh bells that are worn as part of a dancer's outfit.

TWO IMPORTANT GENRES

Two of the most important genres of Southeast Indian music are Creek Stomp Dance songs and Choctaw Social Dance songs.

Creek Stomp Dance songs

Creek Stomp Dance songs are performed during the Green Corn ceremony or Busk, an abbreviation of the Creek word *boskita*. The Green Corn ceremony originated during the Mississippian era and was widespread throughout the Southeast at the time of contact with Europeans. It is an annual festival of world renewal, held in the summer when the new corn crop is ripe. The ceremony takes place at a square ground, a sacred outdoor area defined by brush arbors on four sides. The ceremony lasts from two to four days and involves many components, including purification rites, feasts, orations, prayers, and daytime dances, such as the Ribbon Dance and the Feather Dance, each of which has its own symbolism, meaning, and religious function. Stomp Dances are one of several distinct genres performed at night during the Green Corn ceremony, and the entire night dance event is often referred to as a Stomp Dance. Stomp Dances are sometimes performed as interludes between the daytime dances and are frequently done on other occasions during the year. The men of the community take turns leading Stomp Dance sets; each set includes several short songs performed in nearly continuous succession.

Creek Stomp Dance songs are among the most dramatic in Native North America. Each set is introduced with a brief, stylized recitation by the leader, to which the male dancers respond with shouts. The introduction develops seamlessly into the first song of the set, sung while the dance line is forming, as the participants walk counterclockwise around the circle. The first song features dense, energetic antiphonal exchanges between the leader and male dancers; the melodic contour is predominantly level, the tempo is fast, and the chorus echoes the leader's call. At a specific point in the first song, the dancing starts, to the accompaniment of the shell-shakers. The end of the song is articulated by a formulaic call of indefinite pitch, answered by a shout from the dancers, and the shell-shakers pause momentarily.

The second song begins almost immediately and differs from the first in that the leader gradually begins to improvise longer calls with wider ranges, more varied melodic contours, and more complex rhythms; the dancers respond in unison with one fixed phrase throughout the song. The set continues in this manner, with a short break between each song and a progressive broadening and lengthening of musical components in each successive song. By the last song in the set, the leader's calls are relatively long and intricate, exploiting his full vocal range and expressive capabilities, while the dancers may elaborate their response with three-part harmony. The cumulative musical effect evokes the image of sound spiraling outward from the center in concentric circles.

Choctaw Social Dance songs

Choctaw Social Dance songs are now performed in diverse secular contexts such as folkloric demonstrations and educational programs, but the genre originated with the Ballgame ceremonial cycle. The Ballgame existed in some form throughout the Eastern Woodlands and Great Lakes regions and was the forerunner of lacrosse. Yet the Ballgame was more than a sport; for the Choctaw, it was a complex sacred festival that integrated healing and communal ritual to effect world renewal. Four discrete musical genres were associated with the Choctaw Ballgame: healer's music, personal songs performed by the ball players, music for the communal Ballplay Dance performed prior to the game, and music for the communal dances performed throughout the night after the game. The communal night dances have been reinterpreted and recontextualized as Social Dance or Stomp Dance music. This is an exceptionally rich repertoire, including at least fourteen different choreographies and over ninety songs, most of which permit improvisation by the song leader. The dances move counterclockwise in a circle and include line dances as well as couples dances.

Choctaw Social Dance songs feature a variety of forms and designs, depending upon the type of dance they accompany. In addition to iterative and sectional forms, several Choctaw dance songs employ a kind of strophic form that is widespread throughout the East. Songs in strophic form usually have a slow introduction that is sometimes unmetered and may be performed as a solo by the song leader. The introduction is followed by a strophe that is faster in tempo and is repeated as often as necessary for the dancers to complete one full circuit around the dance ground. Each song in strophic form has a unique internal design that can involve frequent changes in texture, tempo, or melodic style; in some songs, musical changes signal a change in the choreography (figures 1 and 2).

FIGURE 1   Choctaw Drunk Dance song, performed by Adam Sampson. Transcription by Victoria Lindsay Levine, 1990.

FIGURE 2   Choctaw Drunk Dance. Photo by
James Howard, 1977.

SCHOLARSHIP

The ethnomusicological literature on the Southeast is surprisingly slim, given the size
and significance of the region. Accounts written by explorers and missionaries in the
seventeenth, eighteenth, and nineteenth centuries contain some information on native
Southeast music, but these reports are of poor quality compared to the historical materials available for other regions. In the early twentieth century, pioneer ethnographers
such as James Mooney (1890, 1891), David Bushnell (1909), and Frank Speck (1909,
1911) wrote about the music of the Cherokee, Choctaw, Yuchi, and Creek peoples,
providing song transcriptions in each case. Frances Densmore (1937, 1943a, 1943b,
1958) began ethnomusicological research in the Southeast during the 1930s; her
recordings and reports on music of the Choctaw, Seminole, Chitimacha, and Alibamu
are invaluable today. Scholarly interest in the music of this region increased in the late
1960s, particularly among Native American ethnomusicologists such as Marcia Herndon (1971, 1980) and Charlotte Heth (1975, 1979) (Cherokee), David Draper (1980)
(Choctaw), and Edwin Schupman Jr. (1984) (Creek). Aspects of Choctaw musical
culture have been studied by James Howard (1990) and by Victoria Lindsay Levine
(1993, 1997a, 1997b), who has also researched the music of Louisiana Indians.
Archival recordings of Southeast American Indian music are available through the
Library of Congress Federal Cylinder Project and the Archives of Traditional Music at
Indiana University.

REFERENCES

Anon. 1971, 1974. *American Indian Music of the
Mississippi Choctaws, vols. 1–2.* United Sound
Recorders USR 3519, USR 7133. LP disk.

Anon. 1976. *Songs of the Caddo.* Canyon Records
C 6146. LP disk.

Anon. 1970. *Songs of the Muskogee Creek, pts. 1-2.*
Indian House IH 3001, IH 3002. LP disk.

Anon. 1978. *Stomp Dance, vols. 1–2.* Indian House
IH 3003, IH 3004. LP disk.

Bushnell, David I. 1909. *The Choctaws of Bayou
Lacomb, St. Tammany Parish, Louisiana.* Bureau of
American Ethnology Bulletin no. 48. Washington,
D.C.: Smithsonian Institution.

Densmore, Frances. 1937. "The Alabama Indians
and Their Music." In *Straight Texas,* ed. J. Frank
Dobie, 270–293. Publications of the Texas Folklore Society.

———. 1943a. *A Search for Songs Among the
Chitimacha Indians of Louisiana.* Bureau of Ameri-
can Ethnology Bulletin No. 133. Washington,
D.C.: Government Printing Office.

———. 1943b. *Choctaw Music.* Bureau of American Ethnology Bulletin No. 136. Washington,
D.C.: Smithsonian Institution.

————.1958. *Seminole Music.* Bureau of American Ethnology Bulletin No. 141. Washington, D.C.: Smithsonian Institution.

————. 1972. *Songs of the Seminole Indians of Florida.* Ethnic Folkways FE 4383. LP disk.

Draper, David. 1980. "Occasions for the Performance of Native Choctaw Music." *Selected Reports in Ethnomusicology* 3(2):147–173.

————. 1983. "Breath in Music: Concept and Practice among the Choctaw Indians." *Selected Reports in Ethnomusicology* 4:285–300.

Herndon, Marcia. 1971. "The Cherokee Ballgame Cycle: An Ethnomusicologist's View." *Ethnomusicology* 15:339–352.

————. 1980. "Fox, Owl, and Raven." *Selected Reports in Ethnomusicology* 3(2):175–192.

Heth, Charlotte Wilson. 1975. "The Stomp Dance of the Oklahoma Cherokee: A Study of Contemporary Practice with Special Reference to the Illinois District Council Ground." Unpublished Ph.D. dissertation, University of California at Los Angeles.

————. 1976. *Songs of Earth, Water, Fire, and Sky: Music of the American Indians.* New World Records NW 246. LP disk.

————. 1979. "Stylistic Similarities in Cherokee and Iroquois Music." *Journal of Cherokee Studies* 4(3):128–162.

Howard, James H., and Victoria Lindsay Levine. 1990. *Choctaw Music and Dance.* Norman: University of Oklahoma Press.

Hudson, Charles. 1976. *The Southeastern Indians.* Knoxville: University of Tennessee Press.

Levine, Victoria Lindsay. 1991. "Arzelie Langley and a Lost Pantribal Tradition." In *Ethnomusicology and Modern Music History,* ed. Stephen Blum, Philip Bohlman, and Daniel Neuman, 190–206. Urbana: University of Illinois Press.

————. 1993. "Musical Revitalization among the Choctaw." *American Music* 11(4):391–411.

————. 1997a. "Music, Myth, and Medicine in the Choctaw Indian Ballgame." In *Enchanting Powers: Music in the World's Religions,* ed. Lawrence Sullivan, 189–218. Cambridge: Harvard University Center for the Study of World Religions.

————. 1997b. "Text and Context in Choctaw Social Dance Songs." *Florida Anthropologist* 50(4):183–187.

Mooney, James. 1890. "The Cherokee Ball Play." *American Anthropologist* (old series) 3(2):105–132.

————. 1891. *Sacred Formulas of the Cherokees.* Bureau of American Ethnology Annual Report (1885–1886) 7:301–409. Washington, D.C.: U. S. Government Printing Office.

Ned, Buster. 1976–1977. *Choctaw-Chickasaw Dance Songs,* vols. 1–2. Mannsville, Okla.: Choctaw-Chickasaw Heritage Committee. LP disk.

Rhodes, Willard. n.d. *Delaware, Cherokee, Choctaw, Creek.* Library of Congress AFS L37. LP.

Schupman, Edwin, Jr. 1984. "Current Musical Practices of the Creek Indians as Examined Through the Green Corn Ceremonies of the Tulsa Cedar River and Fish Pond Stomp Grounds." Unpublished master's thesis, Miami University of Oxford, Ohio.

Speck, Frank Gouldsmith. 1909. *Ethnology of the Yuchi Indians.* University of Pennsylvania. The University Museum Anthropological Publications 1(1):1–154.

————. 1911. *Ceremonial Songs of the Creek and Yuchi Indians.* University of Pennsylvania. The University Museum Anthropological Publications 50(2):157–245.

Speck, Frank G., and Leonard Broom. 1983. *Cherokee Dance and Drama,* 2nd ed. Norman: University of Oklahoma Press.

Music Instruments
J. Richard Haefer

Two Music Instrument Classification Systems
Instrument Types

The term *music instruments* is a misnomer for North American Indian cultures, as Indian languages do not possess the lexeme *music* within their native vocabularies. Although there may be some justification for using the designator *sound instruments,* such a class would also include other objects not related to music. Therefore we must look to the cultures themselves to see the terms or designators used by Indian peoples to refer to those items called music instruments in Western culture. Although no North American Indian culture has a word for music, nearly every culture has a term for song and a term referring to objects we call music instruments. Two examples will suffice, one from the Seneca of the Northeast and the other from the Tohono O'odham of the Southwest.

TWO MUSIC INSTRUMENT CLASSIFICATION SYSTEMS

In an article describing the music of the Coldspring Longhouse, Harold C. Conklin and William C. Sturtevant (1953) describe a taxonomic system developed from Senecan cultural concepts and discuss what the Seneca call *yotēnotáhkhwaśhoȯ* 'singing tools.' This term is used by the Seneca because sound instruments like the great turtle shell rattle and the water drum are said to be "those things used for propping up the songs," that is, they are tools that help make the song. In other words, one cannot have song without the use of singing tools or what we might call music instruments.

A similar concept is found in the southwestern United States among the Tohono O'odham. Formerly referred to in the literature as the Papago, Tohono O'odham literally means *desert people.* Within this culture music instruments are called *ñe'icuda* 'song makers' (Haefer 1982). This is distinct from *ñe'ikuḍ* 'song things,' an invalid lexeme to the O'odham. The gourd rattle, basket drum, and scraping sticks of the O'odham are items necessary to make or produce *ñe'i* 'song' in their culture. Without these instruments song could not exist, and furthermore, when one learns or dreams (*cu:kud*) a song he also learns what *ñe'icuda* to use, how to use it, and when and where to sing the song.

One might wonder why an invalid lexeme, *ñe'ikuḍ,* was introduced above. In O'odham some music instruments are referred to as *piastakuḍ.* The root *piasta* is borrowed from the Spanish lexeme *fiesta;* the suffix *–kuḍ* in the Piman language refers to a 'thing of' something—in this case a thing of a fiesta. Instruments such as the saxophone, guitar, bass, and drum set—used to perform *waila* 'chicken scratch' music, are literally "things of the fiesta," not *ñe'icuḍa* 'song makers.' They could not be song makers, as the music played at these dances is not *ñe'i* or O'odham song but rather polkas, schottisches, and two-steps borrowed from nineteenth-century Mexico. And although the O'odham "own" *waila,* it is not considered to be of the same class as their own music (Haefer 1982, n.d.). Hence among the O'odham we find two very different categories of music instruments: song makers and fiesta things.

The basic O'odham concepts stated above may be expanded to present a more complete taxonomy of sound instruments in O'odham culture. O'odham instruments may be grouped according to origin: O'odham origin or non-O'odham origin. The four types of song makers are obviously of O'odham origin, but so are the cane flute and the bullroarer. The latter is also of the type "thing of" as it is but one of many items that were used in the *wi:gita* 'harvest celebration.' As such it does not make songs but is integral to the successful completion of the ceremony. The cane flute is said "to be sung into" rather than "played."

Of non-O'odham origin are those music instruments, many of European origin, introduced during the nineteenth century from Mexican and Yaqui musicians. Descriptive names have been given to the taxonomic classes (plucked, blown, bowed, pulled, and so on), while some specific instruments have European derived names (*wi:olin* for violin or *a:pa* from the Spanish for harp (*arpa*), and others use O'odham terms (*ge'e tambio* for big drum). The Yaqui cocoon rattle and *coyole* belt rattle are also considered of the class *piastakuḍ.*

INSTRUMENT TYPES

Several methods for the scientific classification of music instruments have been devised over the years. Probably the most significant for comparing sound instruments cross culturally is that of von Hornbostel and Sachs (1961 [1914]). They based their classification on the method of producing sound in each instrument type: idiophone—in which the body of the instrument vibrates; membranophone—a vibrating skin; aerophone—a vibrating column of air; and chordophone—a vibrating string. Although this approach is easy for cross-cultural understanding and will be adopted to describe North American Indian instruments below, it is also important to remember the significance of the individual cultural conceptions of music instruments presented above.

Few studies of North American Indian individual sound instruments have been written (Driver 1953 on the rasp is one example), but brief preliminary information about instrument distribution patterns may be found in Brown (1967), and Haefer (1975), Roberts (1936), and prehistoric studies include those by Brown (1967, 1971) and Driver (1953). A major study of the sound instruments of one culture area (the Northeast) is that by Diamond et al. (1994). Most additional information concerning music instruments consists of brief mentions within larger ethnographic studies.

Idiophones

Idiophones are those instruments that produce sound by vibrations of the surface area of the instrument themselves, such as rattles and clappers. This class is by far the largest group of instruments in both prehistoric and historic times for North American Indians and is best discussed by looking at various subgroups.

Body movements

The most readily accessible idiophone is the human body, although few reports of body movements as an intentional producer of music sound exist for North America. In the Northwest Coast and Northern California areas hand clapping is used to accompany song. Body movements, especially those of dancers, may produce sound indirectly by the movement of clothing that may have jingles or bells attached. The stamping of feet might also be considered a part of the body sound continuum, especially in the South.

The three most predominant idiophones in North America are the notched sticks and the suspension and container rattles.

Notched stick rasps

Found predominantly in the Great Basin and the Southwest, the rasp is also scattered through the lower Mississippi Valley, the Plains, and the Northeast. The rasp consists usually of a length of wood or bone with a series of notches or teeth cut along one side. This is then scraped by another stick or often by a scapular bone to produce a grating sound. Resonators are made from inverted baskets, half gourds, or even a hole in the ground covered by metal or hide. In some areas (especially the Pueblos) the rasp is highly decorated and carried in the hands of dancers, therefore used without resonators. In the southern Mississippi area an alligator skin may be used as a rasp, and inverted baskets are rubbed as rasps in Arizona.

Rattles

Suspension or jingle rattles

Suspension rattles are made by suspending objects from a stick or other device so that when shaken the objects strike one another and produce sound. Although found throughout the United States, the most dense concentration of suspension rattles is in the area from the Mexican border north along the west side of the Rockies and into Canada. The elements suspended from the stick include animal hooves (predominantly deer or mountain sheep) and claws (especially bear), tin jingles, bones, or bird beaks, with hooves being the most widespread. These rattle elements may be suspended from a stick, a cord, or a ring, or tied to the body of a dancer or to clothing. A correlation between this instrument and its use with a girl's puberty ceremonies is discussed by Driver and Reisenburg (1950). Suspension rattles may also be found hanging from the ceiling or from poles within a ceremonial structure, and small groups of suspension objects may be attached to other instruments such as drums and whistles.

Container rattles

By far the most widespread and varied sound instrument in North American Indian cultures is the container rattle—found everywhere except in the Arctic. The major variant of container rattles is the material from which the container itself is made. Traditionally made from materials available in the local environment, at the beginning of the twenty-first century many materials are now widely distributed and sold from culture to culture.

Container rattles are made from gourds in the South (particularly the Southwest), from cow and buffalo hide (including the scrotum) on the Plains, wood in the Northwest, bark in the Northeast and the Great Lakes area, and turtle shells (box turtles in the South and terrapins in the Northeast). Other local and less frequently used variants include coconuts (Southeast), basketry (Northwest Coast and Southwest), copper (Northwest Coast), cocoon shells (Southwest and California), bark (Great Lakes), small animal skulls (Northeast and Great Lakes), and pottery (Pueblos).

Beaters

Two sticks may be struck together to produce a rhythmic accompaniment in the Southeast and on the Plateau—as part of the hand game—and larger logs or poles may also be beaten on the Plateau. Wooden boxes or simple wood planks are beaten on the Northwest Coast. Planks may be placed over a hole to increase the resonance of the instrument; when played by stepping on them, they are often erroneously called "foot drums." Hollowed logs or half logs are also found in the Northwest. In the Northeast, plains, and the Pueblos a beater may be made by rolling a dried deer or sheep skin into a bundle and striking it with sticks.

Other sound instruments may alternately be played as beaters, such as the bark and turtle rattles of the Northeast that may be struck against a wooden bench instead of shaken to produce sound. The Yuman, Piman, and Navajo peoples use an inverted basket, striking it with a single stick or with bundles of sticks that also simultaneously strike each other, while the Yaqui place an inverted half gourd in a pail of water and strike it. Many of these items are referred to as drums or drums without skins. A specialized type of beater, the clapper, consists of split sticks (often hollowed out) that are clapped together. These are found along the Pacific Coast from Southern California to Alaska.

Bells and stones

Both pottery and metal (usually copper) bells are found throughout the Southwest and up the Mississippi valley. They may be either of the clapper or internal pebble type. Along the Rio Grande, peoples often suspended rectangular stones of about twelve inches in length. These were struck with another stone to produce specific tones.

Other idiophones

Prehistoric findings of idiophones include rasps made of deer bones, the horns of mountain sheep, the scapula bone of antelope, and the ribs of elk, as well as those made of wood. Although found throughout the United States, these instruments were located predominantly in the Plains and Southwest and date from c. 500 C.E. to the time of contact with Europeans. Percussion stones from about the fourteenth century were found only in the Pueblo area along the Rio Grande, while copper bells (and clay bells made in imitation of the copper ones) date from about 1000 C.E. and were distributed along the trade routes from Mexico through the Mississippi Valley region. Prehistoric shaken idiophones include strung rattles of deer hooves, rabbit bones, pieces of wood, and even Conus shells (small conical seashells) traded from Mexico. Few prehistoric container rattles have been found; the materials used include gourds, box turtle shells, and few examples of hide and clay.

Recent innovations in the production of idiophones include the specialization and use of gourds of different sizes and shapes (for example, the small gourd of the Peyote cult), and the introduction of new containers (for example, the use of tin salt or pepper shakers for the container rattles of the Gourd Dance). Various materials are used today as substitutes for traditional containers, such as evaporated milk tins for gourds (Southwest), sometimes covered with quill work in imitation of hide rattles on the Plains. When tied in clusters, milk tins substitute for the traditional box turtle rattles of the Southeast.

Membranophones

Drums using a stretched skin are found in several different variations based on the number of skin heads, the shape and size (and in turn the number of people playing them), and whether or not they contain water. A few examples of simple skin drums consisting of a loose skin tied to four stakes (or even held by people) and struck with a beater by a single person are found in the central area west of the Rockies and on the Northern Plains.

Frame drum

The most prevalent North American Indian drum is the frame drum with either a single or a double head—often erroneously called a "hand drum" or "tambourine" drum. It is found throughout the entire continent except in lower California and parts of Arizona. Typically the drum is made from a circular frame, traditionally a bent stave

Examples of modern plastic polyvinylchloride (PVC) pipe used to make the frame of water drums are found among the Iroquois. The Apache sometimes use part of a truck inner tube to cover their water drums. During the middle of the twentieth century some groups substituted marching band bass drums turned on their side for use at powwows.

of wood, although the "cheese box" became a popular substitute in the late nineteenth century. When the frame is covered with a single head, the skin is usually knotted together in the back to form a grip for the hand. Double-headed frame drums have a handle of hide thongs attached to the top of the instrument. Local variants would include the Eskimo *someak,* which is single headed with a short handle of wood, ivory or bone on the lower side of the instrument. The diameter of frame drums varies from four inches to more than thirty inches, although the typical size on the Northern Plains is about fifteen inches. The depth of the frame varies from the small one-inch Eskimo frame to one of three or four inches. The frame drum is normally held in one hand and struck with a beater held in the other hand.

The log drum

The so-called log drum consists of an instrument with one or two hide heads (usually the latter) that may vary in diameter and height depending on the region. The instrument is so named because traditionally it was made by hollowing out a log, although similar instruments were made by using barrel staves following contact with Europeans. In the Southwest the drum is usually rather small in diameter (about twelve to fourteen inches) but fairly tall (twenty-four to thirty-six inches) and is normally played by a single person.

On the Plains and in the Great Lakes and Northeast the log drum is usually of a larger diameter than height and is played by more than one person. Although traditionally made from a large log, the use of barrel staves is more prominent today and is sometimes even considered "traditional" as those by the Ojibwa drum maker Mr. William Benishi Baker (Vennum 1982). This is the style of instrument that has become associated with the contemporary powwow and is often referred to as a powwow drum. Among the Pueblos both shapes and sizes of log drum are found, and the choice of instrument varies with the use or ceremonial activity.

Double-sided drums

Square- or rectangular-shaped double-sided drums are found in northern California and consist of a hide stretched over both sides of a rectangular wooden frame usually about four inches deep. In the Plains area small circular rattle drums are made by bending a sapling into a circle of about six to eight inches diameter and covering it with hide on both sides after inserting rattle elements. The internal elements strike the membrane when shaken, and sometimes these instruments are also used as a beater for a larger drum.

Water drums

Water drums vary from the oldest, traditional style consisting of a pottery vessel used by the Navajo to the modern ones made from cooking pots. The Navajo instrument consists of an elongated pottery vessel covered by a buckskin tied around the lip of the pot. In the Great Lakes region and the Northeast wooden containers are partially filled with water and covered by a skin head held on by an outer ring. The Ojibwa and

Menominee use a hollowed-out log about fifteen inches tall, while the members of the Iroquois Confederation use small containers (about four to five inches tall) made from staves, probably devised from nail kegs brought from Europe. The Apache make their water drum from a cooking pot with the handle removed. A more specialized water drum is that associated with the Peyote religion (the Native American Church) and made from a heavy metal cooking pot. The head is laced on in a star pattern as prescribed by the norms of the religion.

Water drums often have materials placed inside of them based on the ceremonial significance or the use of the instruments. These materials include ashes, corn or corn pollen, tobacco, and other similar materials and are usually placed within the instrument in a ritual fashion. The drum sticks used with water drums are usually not padded and often are shaped in an inverted "L" or a small circular hoop. The Navajo water drum is usually struck with a stick made from bundles of arrowweed wrapped with yucca.

Other membranophones

No membranophones from prehistoric times have been found in the present, though it must be conceded that instruments similar to those used today would not have survived over long periods of exposure to the elements. Not many items have been used as substitutes for membranophones. Early in this century the Pima Indians used an inverted cardboard box as a "drum," although this is technically an idiophone and not a membranophone. Examples of modern plastic polyvinylchloride (PVC) pipe used to make the frame of water drums are found among the Iroquois. The Apache sometimes use part of a truck inner tube to cover their water drums. During the middle of the twentieth century some groups substituted marching band bass drums turned on their side for use at powwows. However, others strongly resisted the use of such non-Indian drums, even refusing to participate in a powwow when a band drum was present. This practice began to fade by the 1990s.

Aerophones

Instruments that use a column of vibrating air to produce sound include flutes, whistles, reed instruments, trumpets, and the bullroarer.

Flutes

The most widespread aerophone is the flute, although different characteristics, such as the number of sound holes and the type of material used, vary across the continent. The Indian flute is of the internal duct type with a hollowed interior tube containing a block, usually of the same material as the tube, that diverts the air stream to an exterior cap that directs the air across a lip, causing the air column to split and vibrate, producing the actual sound. Flute stops (finger holes) vary from one to nine depending on the culture (for example, three for the O'odham, four for the Yuman, more among peoples in the Northern Plains). Flutes are made from cedar (Sioux and Northern Plains) and various other woods (like box elder), cane (O'odham, Yuman), bark (Northeast and Northwest), pottery (Rio Grande area), and even bone. Globular wooden flutes are found in the Northwest. Nearly all North American Indian flutes are end blown, but side-blown instruments are reported for the Plateau, and the nose flute was apparently used in the Great Basin in the distant past.

Whistles

Whistles are most commonly made from bone, usually the leg bone of an eagle on the Plains, although cane and wooden whistles are found in California and the Northwest Coast. The interior deflector of whistles is normally a piece of pitch or resin, and the lower end of the instrument may also be plugged with similar material. Bone whistles are commonly decorated with either direct painting or etching, or covered with quill or bead work (on the Plains). In the Northern Plains the distal end of wooden whistles is usually splayed and often carved as a bird head, while on the Northwest Coast globular whistles may look like a human head. More unusual are individual tubes connected in panpipe style. In California, pairs of bones or pieces of cane are found as panpipes, and Densmore (1923) reports groups of quill tubes used among the Mandan.

Reeds

Reed instruments are unique to the Northwest Coast area, found less frequently in the Arctic, Subarctic, and Northern Great Basin areas. Reeds of either the ribbon type (of grass or other fiber) or the beating reed type (made of thin wood or metal strips) are placed inside the hollow chamber of the instrument. The size of the instruments vary from one and one-half inches to over eighteen inches in length. Most have only one reed chamber, although some Northwest Coast instruments have as many as five. With the exception of bird and animal calls, reed instruments are seldom encountered today. A similar instrument was used by the Hopi and made by placing a piece of reed between two stones, similar to the Zuni reed instrument called *bitsitsi*.

Other aerophones

Horns (often referred to erroneously as trumpets) made from shells, wood, or bark are found scattered from Southern Florida through the Southwest, in the Northwest Coast area and the Subarctic. Nearly always used for signaling, they were not considered as song instruments in the United States.

The bullroarer, another nonsong sound instrument, is used by many cultures in the Western United States. Consisting of one or occasionally two flat pieces of wood attached to a long cord, the bullroarer is swung over the head. A sound like rushing wind is produced when the wood begins to spin on its axis, creating a column of moving air. The purpose of this instrument varies from child's toy to ceremonial object; some are said to represent symbolically the sound of wind, thunder, and rain, or "spirit voices." Whirling disks on cords are also sound producers, although used only as toys.

Modern substitutes for aerophones consist mainly in the use of readily available, easy to work materials, for example, PVC or copper pipe for flutes. Occasionally manufactured whistles or animal calls are also used. Within the past hundred years metal gas pipes or gun barrels were at times fashioned into flutes, but such materials are hard to work with. In most cultures the use of aerophones has nearly vanished, though the Plains flute, or so-called love flute, has seen a resurgence in recent years.

Archaeological finds include examples of bullroarers (of shell and wood) as well as bone and wooden flutes and whistles, and large conch shell trumpets in the Southwest (especially along the Mexican trade routes in the United States). Among the Hopewellian cultures were found bone whistles and panpipes of bone and copper.

Chordophones

Few chordophones are found in indigenous North America. The music bow, a single string stretched across a bent wood stick (originating from the hunting bow), was probably a pre-Columbian instrument. It was struck with a small stick or arrow, and the mouth of the performer was used as a resonator. The music bow was found only in a narrow band from the Southern Plains of Texas through the Great Basin, Plateau, and into southern Canada and also along the Mississippi River valley. Presumably used only as a self-delectitive (for self entertainment) sound producer, the instrument has fallen out of use.

The Apache "fiddle" is a variation of the music bow with European influences. The Apache make this instrument from a stalk of the yucca plant which is split in half and hollowed out except for the two ends. The two halves are bound together and sealed with pitch and cords. The outer surface of the yucca is often decorated with red or yellow paints in geometrical and anthropomorphic designs. The instrument may have one or two strings (the former most common) that are permanently fastened to one end of the body, while the opposite end is attached to a peg, which is used to tighten the tension of the string, thereby tuning the instrument. The fiddle is played with a bow (usually with a high arch similar to early European bows) and held against the upper chest. A true melody instrument, the Apache fiddle with a soft, raspy sound is also a self-delectitive instrument.

In the Northwest and the Arctic instruments have been found that resemble early contact European string instruments, especially some Russian folk instruments. In both the northern and southern extremes of the continent, European violins, guitars, and harps have been adapted to Indian ways and used to accompany dance, with the melodies being of Indian origin and the harmonies of European origin. No archaeological finds of string instruments have been reported.

The instrumentarium of the Indians of North America has always been large and varied. While some instruments, notably aerophones, have ceased to be used (the Plains flute being an exception), other instruments of non-Indian origins have been borrowed by many Indian cultures. This borrowing might be better termed adapting, as illustrated in the O'odham use of instruments in the *waila*. North American Indian music cultures remain vital, ever-changing cultural phenomena and, consequently, their instrumentarium also remains dynamic and vigorous.

REFERENCES

Brown, Donald N. 1967. "Distribution of Sound Instruments in Prehistoric Southwestern United States." *Ethnomusicology* 11(1):71–90.

———. 1971. "Ethnomusicology and the Prehistoric Southwest." *Ethnomusicology* 15(3): 361–378.

Conklin, Harold C., and William C. Sturtevant. 1953. "Seneca Indian Singing Tools at Coldspring Longhouse." *Proceedings of the American Philosophical Society* 97:262–290.

Densmore, Frances. 1923. *Mandan and Hidatsa Music.* Bureau of American Ethnology Bulletin 80. Washington, D.C.: Smithsonian Institution.

Diamond, Beverley, M. Sam Cronk, and Franziska von Rosen. 1994. *Visions of Sound: Musical Instruments of First Nations Communities in Northeastern America.* Chicago Studies in Ethnomusicology. Chicago: University of Chicago Press.

Driver, Harold E. 1953. "The Spatial and Temporal Distribution of the Musical Rasp in the New World." *Anthropos* 48:578–592.

Driver, Harold E., and S. H. Reisenburg. 1950. *Hoof Rattles and Girls' Puberty Rites in North and South America,* Indiana University Publications in Anthropology and Linguistics, Memoir IV.

Haefer, J. Richard. 1975. "North American Indian Musical Instruments: Some Organological Distribution Problems." *Journal of the American Musical Instrument Society* 1:56–85.

———. 1982. "Musical Thought in Papago Culture." Ph.D. dissertation, University of Illinois.

———. n.d. *Making the Song: North American Indian Sound Instruments.* In press.

Roberts, Helen.1936. *Musical Areas in Aboriginal North America.* Publications in Anthropology 12. New Haven, Conn.: Yale University.

Vennum, Thomas Jr. 1982. *The Ojibwe Dance Drum: Its History and Construction.* Smithsonian Folklife Studies, 2. Washington, D.C.: Smithsonian Institution.

von Hornbostel, Eric, and Curt Sachs. 1961 [1914]. "Systematik der Musikinstrumente. Ein Versuch." *Zeitschrift für Ethnologie,* Jahrg. Translated by Anthony Baines and Klaus P. Wachsman as "Classification of Musical Instruments," *Galpin Society Journal* 14:3–29.

Musical Interactions
Victoria Lindsay Levine
Judith A. Gray

The Powwow
Christian Hymnody
Music and Nativism
Peyote Music
Indian Shaker Church
Contemporary Musics

Social and musical interaction occurs between and among all people living within a common geographical area. Before contact with Europeans, American Indian/First Nations peoples interacted for centuries with each other; following the arrival of the French, Spanish, and English, among others, interactions between Indian and non-Indian peoples often took place within the context of Christian missionization. More recently, Indian/First Nations groups have joined to create new contexts for the performance of Indian identity. The six musical cultures presented in this article show a variety of adaptive strategies used by American Indian/First Nations peoples to both renegotiate and maintain traditional beliefs within new social and musical environments.

THE POWWOW

Pan-Indianism, pantribalism, and intertribalism are terms used to describe a Native American strategy for effecting musical and cultural change. This strategy involves the adoption by one community of a musical repertoire indigenous to another, in a process that facilitates the renegotiation of ethnic boundaries and perpetuates native concepts, beliefs, values, and aesthetic expression in new social or geographical environments. Many Native Americans choose to participate in one or more pantribal musics; at the same time, they may maintain their indigenous music in separate contexts. There are several examples of pantribalism in the history of Native American music, including the repertoires associated with the Ghost Dance and the Native American Church. Currently, the most popular and widespread pantribal music belongs to the powwow.

The powwow is a multifaceted, multivalent intertribal celebration with historical roots in the rituals of nineteenth-century men's organizations among the Plains Indians, including the Inloshka, Hethuska, and Iruska Societies of the Kansa, Omaha, Ponca, and Pawnee tribes. The ceremonies performed by these organizations celebrated acts of heroism carried out by experienced warriors and included music, dance, and feasting. These ceremonies spread throughout the Plains during the second half of the nineteenth century and developed into the Grass Dance, Omaha Dance, or Crow Dance. In the late nineteenth century, some tribes performed the Grass Dance in conjunction with the Ghost Dance or Sun Dance; other tribes blended it with the Drum or Dream Dance ceremony.

By the early twentieth century, the Grass Dance had combined components of several ceremonies with newly created elements, and the style of the music and dance, as well as associated concepts and practices, had begun to diverge between the Northern and Southern Plains tribes. At the same time, European Americans were using the term powwow to refer to Indian council meetings or other assemblies; the word powwow derives from *pauau*, an Algonkian name for curing rituals. Native Americans gradually adopted this word to describe the music and dance event that had grown out of the Grass Dance, and by the 1950s the word powwow was widely used.

Contexts for the powwow

The federal government initiated the Indian relocation program in 1949, offering incentives to Indians who moved from reservations to urban areas. This move brought together people of widely separated tribes and stimulated the development of the powwow. The involvement of non-Indian hobbyists, particularly during the 1960s, and the Indian Awareness movement of the 1970s further contributed to the growth and spread of powwows. Today they occur virtually every weekend throughout Indian country, on reservations as well as in urban centers. The participants are men, women, and children of all ages, from tribes all over North America and from diverse educational and socioeconomic backgrounds. A dynamic, dramatic, and innovative expressive form, the powwow has become a mainstay of Indian life and culture and is a powerful manifestation of Indian identity.

Powwow organization and structure differ somewhat from place to place, according to local concepts and traditions. Ideally, powwows are held outdoors, but during the winter months, school gymnasiums, community centers, or indoor sports arenas offer comfortable alternatives. Longer powwows held outdoors during the summer months usually involve encampments and provide an opportunity for joyous family reunions and homecomings. Powwows vary in length from one evening to a week, depending on the season and location of the event. Powwows may be sponsored by families, tribes, civic organizations, or student associations, and they are held for various reasons, from fund-raising for charitable causes to honoring a family member. Scholars have often characterized the powwow as a secular event, but this is contradicted by its origin in religious ceremonialism, by certain ritual practices (such as the treatment of fallen feathers), and by the spirituality many participants express.

There are two main types of powwow, called Northern Plains and Southern Plains, which differ from one another in details of content and style.

Northern Plains powwows

Northern Plains powwows begin with a Grand Entry, or parade entrance of the participants into the dance circle. The parade is led by an honor guard, composed of local American Indian veterans, who carry the American flag into the dance ground. The Grand Entry is accompanied by a special parade song; spectators stand during the Grand Entry to honor the dancers. After the posting of the colors, a Flag Song is performed, as dancers and spectators stand. Many tribes have their own Flag Song that honors the American flag with an Indian-language text set in Plains musical style. Next, an invocation is offered in an Indian language as well as in English, reflecting either Native American or Christian religious beliefs. A member of the organizing committee welcomes the participants and introduces the principals, which include the Host Drum, Head Man Dancer, Head Lady Dancer, Arena Director, and Announcer. At large powwows there may be additional principals, such as a Head Boy Dancer, Head Girl Dancer, and Princess (who represent the sponsors of the event). After these preliminaries, the main program begins.

Scholars have often characterized the powwow as a secular event, but this is contradicted by its origin in religious ceremonialism, by certain ritual practices (such as the treatment of fallen feathers), and by the spirituality many participants express.

The War Dance

The powwow focuses on the intertribal War Dance, also known as Grass Dance, Omaha Dance, Wolf Dance, or Intertribal Dance. In the War Dance, many dancers perform simultaneously, each with his or her own spontaneous choreography. Although each dancer wears a unique outfit and uses individualized dance steps, seven main styles are recognized: Men's Straight, Men's Traditional, Men's Grass Dance, Men's Fancy Dance, Women's Traditional, Women's Jingle Dress, and Women's Fancy Shawl. The Men's Traditional dance style emphasizes a flat toe-heel step, with sharp head and upper-body movements simulating an alert tracker, while the Fancy Dance style features vigorous high steps, intricate footwork, and rapid spins that frequently change direction. The Men's Grass Dance is marked by fluid whole body movements, accented by precise footwork and head movements. Women's Traditional dancers perform graceful, stately movements, flexing their knees in place or dancing in barely perceptible toe-heel steps around the arena. Women's Jingle Dress employs two styles of footwork; during a straight song they use the toe-heel step, while during the slide song they perform a modified side-step, keeping upper body movements to a minimum. Women's Fancy Shawl steps are athletic and dynamic, with intricate footwork and frequent spins, paralleling the Men's Fancy Dance styles.

The Men's Traditional outfit includes a fringed dance apron, a feather bustle worn at the waist, and either a roach headdress (made of porcupine hair standing upright on the dancer's head, with one or two upright feathers) or a headdress made of animal skin. The Men's Grass Dance outfit is brilliantly colored and consists of a heavily fringed cape, pants and apron, and a roach headdress; Grass Dancers do not wear feather bustles. The Men's Fancy Dance outfit includes the dance apron and two large, vivid feather bustles, worn at the waist and shoulders, with two smaller bustles on the upper arms, as well as a roach headdress. The Straight Dance outfit consists of either a dark tradecloth suit (leggings, apron, and vest) or buckskin leggings with tradecloth accessories. Besides these fundamental components, the outfit is marked by a dragger, trailing from the back of the dancer's neck to the floor, made of either otter hide or metal conchos. The outfit is completed with a roach headdress. The Women's Traditional outfit includes a full-length fringed buckskin or tradecloth dress covered with elaborate beadwork, cowrie shells, elk teeth, or dentalium shells. Women's Jingle Dress dancers wear knee-length brightly colored dresses with tin-cone shaped jingles sewn on in rows. The Women's Fancy Shawl outfit includes a knee-length cloth dress, a beaded or sequined cape, and a fringed shawl decorated with ribbon appliqué. Both men and women dancers wear beaded moccasins, jewelry, and other accessories; most carry hand-crafted paraphernalia having symbolic significance. Dancers who belong to tribes from outside the Plains area often incorporate features of their tribal dress into their powwow attire. Powwow outfits, which are in themselves works of art, take months or years to assemble and include items made by the dancer as well as gifts received from family and friends.

Intertribal Dances are interspersed with other dances, including the Sneak-up Dance, which pantomimes warriors sneaking up on and fighting with an enemy, social dances (Round Dance, Rabbit Dance, Crow Hop, Two-Step, or Owl Dance), and exhibition dances, performed by one or two dancers at a time, such as the Hoop Dance. When members of a tribe from outside the Plains culture area are present, they may perform dances from their indigenous repertoire as exhibition numbers. At certain points during the event, Honor Songs and Giveaways or Specials take place. Honor Songs are performed in memory of one or more relatives, or to honor a specific person or family present at the event; those being honored dance around the arena, accompanied by family and friends. Giveaways involve the distribution of gifts and express appreciation for an individual, family, or group. After the program has proceeded in this manner for some time, contest dances may be held, in which dancers classified by age, sex, and style of outfit compete for prizes. The program concludes around midnight.

Southern Plains powwows

Southern Plains powwows differ from the Northern format in that additional activities precede the War Dance program; the colors are posted, and a Flag Song is performed, followed by two or more hours of Gourd Dances, a genre that developed during the 1940s on the basis of rituals associated with warrior societies. The outfit worn for Gourd Dances includes a ribbon shirt with everyday slacks and shoes, or fatigues with combat boots, with a red and blue broadcloth shoulder blanket and a red or blue fringed sash tied around the waist. Gourd dancers wear military ribbons, pins, or beaded rosettes on their shoulder blankets. In his right hand, each Gourd dancer carries a rattle made from an aluminum salt shaker, which he uses to accompany the songs. The songs are performed in sets that increase progressively in intensity. At first the dancers stand in a circle, flexing their knees in time to the song; as the set continues, they take small toe-heel steps toward the middle of the circle, culminating in a brief display of vigorous footwork. Gourd Dances began as a male genre, but women now also participate. After a dinner break the Grand Entry takes place, and the program follows a plan similar to that of the Northern Plains powwow, although the categories of dress, musical style, and dance names are somewhat different. After the conclusion of the powwow program, the dancers change into street clothes and then may perform Forty-Nine Dances (a social dance genre) until dawn.

Musical characteristics

The music featured at powwows derives from Plains Indian styles; new War Dance songs are composed regularly, and the repertoire changes continually [see PLAINS, p. 440]. The fundamental powwow musical ensemble is called a drum group, or simply a drum, and includes three to six or more singers. They use a nasal, extremely tense vocal style with heavy pulsations on sustained tones and slides at phrase endings. Powwow singers must have clear, loud voices, in order to be heard above the drum and the dancers. Most War Dance songs start high and cover an octave or more in range; Northern singers often use falsetto at the "push-up," or beginning, of the song, while Southern singers generally use a lower average range. Song texts consist primarily of fixed vocable patterns, but some lines of lexical text may be inserted, particularly in Flag and Honor songs. Occasionally songs with English-language texts are performed, primarily at urban powwows and in social dance songs. The drum was initially a male ensemble, but many women now sing with drum groups and compose War Dance songs.

The scales in powwow songs tend to use four or five pitches. Melodies usually start high and descend by steps, a contour scholars call terraced descent. Standard War

Dance songs employ a strophic (incomplete repetition) form. The strophe begins with a push-up or lead, a brief introduction performed by the song leader and then repeated or seconded, with some variations, by the other singers. The second half of the strophe, or chorus, contains two or more phrases, sung heterophonically; the chorus is then repeated. The strophe may be diagrammed as AA'BCBC; the phrase endings of the lead, second, and subsequent phrases are articulated by certain melodic and rhythmic patterns. One strophe is repeated several times, and at the end of the song, the final two phrases of the chorus are reiterated as a coda or tail. Variations on this basic form are found in Crow Hop and some other contest songs.

The musical instrument most characteristic of the powwow is the large bass drum; the drum group sits in a circle around the drum, and each singer plays it with a padded stick [see MUSICAL INSTRUMENTS, p. 472]. The drumbeat slightly precedes the melodic beat, a rhythmic complexity that the singers maintain throughout a song (drum groups from outside the Plains culture area do not always adhere to this practice). In War Dance songs, the drum supports the underlying pulse of the song in steady duple beats. Occasionally the drummers perform a series of honor beats or heart beats, in which the first beat of a duple pair is heavily accented. Other powwow instruments include an eagle bone or metal whistle, carried by some male dancers, and bells worn on dancers' outfits.

Scholarship

The first scholars to research pantribalism and powwows were James Howard (1955) and Gertrude Kurath (1957), who became interested in intertribal events during the 1950s. During the 1960s, Bruno Nettl began writing about powwows in the course of his broader research on Blackfoot musical culture, while William Powers began his lifelong study of Lakota music and dance (1990). Powwow scholarship emerged as a central topic in research on American Indian music during the 1980s with the work of Thomas Vennum Jr., Robert Witmer, Orin T. Hatton (1986), and many others. Archival recordings of powwow music are available from the Library of Congress; numerous commercial recordings are available from Canyon Records, Indian House, and other sources.

—VICTORIA LINDSAY LEVINE

CHRISTIAN HYMNODY

The presence of Christian hymnody within Native American communities is a reminder of the history of contact between indigenous groups and European American culture. Whether it was originally imposed from without or absorbed through conversion, example, and personal relationships, Christianity was foreign to the Western Hemisphere; correspondingly, students of Indian traditions have tended to look upon Christian elements as evidence of acculturation. But this, like all generalizations, conceals complex interrelationships.

The musical consequences of the initial missionizing reflect at least two different approaches to the process. French Jesuits in the St. Lawrence River Valley, for example, often lived in Indian communities, learned the language, and wrote prayers and hymns in that language, typically using European tunes but incorporating textual references to indigenous names, familiar objects, and so on. One example is the song identified as the "first North American Christmas carol" and known in English as "Twas in the Moon of Wintertime." Written in the Huron language in 1642 by Père Jean de Brébeuf, the song used a sixteenth-century French folk melody called "Une Jeune Pucelle." In this sung version of the Christmas story, the shepherds of Israel became hunters, the baby's swaddling clothes were furs, and so on. Priests such as Father Brébeuf thus attempted to meet their parishioners part way, not relying solely on the Latin mass. They did, however, choose European tunes, not surprising given the fact that their reports to their superiors, compiled in the *Jesuit Relations,* contain less-than-complimentary comments about native song styles, which the Jesuits apparently neither understood nor enjoyed.

At the other side of the continent, much of the missionizing was undertaken by Spanish priests (primarily Franciscans after Jesuits were ejected from the New World in 1767). In many places they built missions around which native people were expected to settle. (Groups that are now reclaiming their indigenous names have long been known principally by the name of these mission communities, such as "Juaneño band of Mission Indians," Gabrielinos, or Luiseños.) Although prayers were simplified and doctrines explained in ways that could facilitate conversions, the music of the Catholic Church does not appear to have been particularly modified. Native people in mission settings, like other non-Latin-speaking people up into the twentieth century, learned the music of the Church without necessarily understanding the texts.

There were, of course, many intermediate forms of contact, each with musical implications. In some cases, Christianity was simply a precarious overlay on the native culture. But over the course of five centuries, the European-introduced religion has become more intertwined in the daily lives of some Indian people (sometimes, but not always, to the exclusion of traditional ways). In a public television program aired in 1994, for example, the governor of one of the southwestern pueblos, noting that pueblo people had initially pretended to convert in order to survive, went on to ask, "At some point, did we forget we were pretending?"

Documentation efforts, beginning with Theodore Baker's 1880 dissertation and the cylinder recordings made between 1890 and the early 1940s by people such as Jesse Walter Fewkes, Alice Cunningham Fletcher, and Frances Densmore, have focused primarily on indigenous traditions, sometimes deliberately excluding genres seen as "mixed." Densmore, for example, sought out the oldest singers in a community, the people most likely to know the older ceremonial songs. When confronted with the "strange mixture of Roman Catholicism, paganism, and individual originality" in Yaqui villages, she found the music "pleasing in style, somewhat plaintive, and [resembling] that heard at the 'Mexican dances' in other parts of southern Arizona" (Densmore 1932:154). Transcribing two examples of such "modern songs" accompanied by guitar, she noted that the rest were so similar "that the songs here presented were considered sufficient." Yet the Yaqui themselves asserted that the music accompanied by guitar, violin, harp, or other stringed instruments was also Yaqui and that "Mexican songs are different" (Densmore 1932:23).

Anthropologists such as Edward Spicer later documented the cultural complexity and creative expressivity that are apparent in the Yaqui Easter celebration: each Holy Saturday, when Pascola dancers (accompanied by drum and flute) and the Deer Dancer (accompanied by gourd rattles, rasp, and a half-gourd drum floating in a container of water) use real and metaphorical flowers as "weapons" of divine grace in a struggle with the Soldiers of Rome and the Judases who kill Jesus and try to overthrow the church, the core Christian narrative is caught up in the values and even the geography of the Yaqui world. The flowers and the references in Deer songs to the "flower-covered holy heaven" (Evers and Molina 1987:56) are associated not only with the Virgin Mary but also with the innocence of children and with the *huya aniya* 'forest world', the "region of untamed things into which [human] influence does not extend" (Evers and Molina 1987:64).

There are, then, in Indian communities, many varieties of Christian-derived music as well as Christian-influenced musical traditions that no longer are attached very directly with Christian worship. Some music practices, such as the use of prepared hymnals, originated outside native communities but were and are intended for use by Christian Indian people, even those in remote areas. The resulting mingling of traditions is apparent, for example, in *The Utkiaguik Inupiat Hymn Book,* printed in Mexico

When confronted with the "strange mixture of Roman Catholicism, paganism, and individual originality" in Yaqui villages, she found the music "pleasing in style, somewhat plaintive, and [resembling] that heard at the 'Mexican dances' in other parts of southern Arizona."

in 1959, a compilation of non-Indian religious songs translated into an indigenous language. The hymnal, edited by the Reverend William Wartes, missionary to the north Arctic slope from 1951 to 1958, consists of English-titled, Inupiat-texted songs such as "In the Sweet Bye and Bye," "Rock of Ages," "O Little Town of Bethlehem," "Is My Name Written There," and "The Old Rugged Cross." Credit for the translations of the songs into Inupiat is given to two early missionaries as well as to several other people, including the Reverend Roy Ahmaogak, an ordained native minister. The one original Eskimo hymn in the compilation also has an English name: "Oh How Joyful." Hymnals of this kind provide only the texts; the melodies would have been learned orally. In one case, the hymn is identified solely by the name of its melody and poetic meter ("Miriam 7,8,6"). Hymnals such as this reflect the tastes and Christian musical traditions of the compilers (whether non-Indians or members of the specific tribal community). We can expect that the song choices made at a Lutheran mission would be different from those available in a Catholic or Baptist setting.

There are many recordings of Christian music traditions distributed commercially that serve primarily native audiences (the Canyon/Drumbeat Records releases, for example, by the Chinle [Navajo] Galileans, Johnny Curtis [Apache Gospel singer], the Gospel Light Singers, and the South Family Gospel Singers). Other recordings, such as the home-produced cassettes by the Cherokee Indian Choir under the direction of J. B. Dreadfulwater, are sold principally by the performers themselves at events, in a manner comparable to the selling of the drum recordings that are often available at powwows. Other recordings seem to be aimed as much at a non-Indian audience as to people of the community. Among these are documentary recordings such as the two-volume series *Music of the Orthodox Church in Alaska*. Produced with support from the National Endowments of the Arts and Humanities, these cassettes are filled with hymns and liturgies in English, Aleut, Tlingit, and Slavonic. Also on the cassettes are recordings of the church bells of Sitka and of a parish in the Pribilofs, sounds that would carry the most meaning for people who have attended those particular churches. Finally, there are the purely archival documentation projects such as the one of hymns by the Ole Smoke Seneca Singers at the Native American Bible Church (Basom, New York) recorded on the Tonawanda reservation in New York in 1974, now in the Archive of Folk Culture at the Library of Congress.

To round out the picture, we should also note that some Christian elements appear in non-Christian contexts. Among these are peyote religion songs, described below, that incorporate references to Jesus.

MUSIC AND NATIVISM

Musical style is influenced by song genre. Songs adopted from other traditions—and serving as a template for new compositions—in many cases retain stylistic features not otherwise found in songs of communities in which they are subsequently used. Such is the case, for example, with Ghost Dance and peyote songs.

Ghost Dance songs

The Ghost Dance was a revivalist religion, the first manifestation of which came around 1870 with the preachings of Wodziwob, a Northern Paiute prophet, at traditional gatherings when people customarily had Round Dances [see PLAINS, p. 440; CALIFORNIA, p. 412]. The interest in Wodziwob's ideas spread to many tribes in California but disappeared rather quickly among the Paiute themselves. The more well-known religion began with the visions that came to another Paiute man, Wovoka, around 1887. He subsequently prophesied the reunion of all Indian people, living and dead, in a regenerated world, free to live without sickness or death according to traditional ways; white people would disappear, the buffalo would return. Emissaries going from tribe to tribe spread the word to many Great Basin as well as Plains communities, together with the songs and decorated shirts that went along with the dance rituals. The Plains Ghost Dance observances, misunderstood by non-Indians as war dances, led to the tragedy of Wounded Knee in 1890 where Sioux ghost dancers were killed by U.S. soldiers.

The Ghost Dance songs found on recordings or transcribed in the 1896 Ghost Dance monograph by James Mooney (1973 [1896]) all have the paired phrase structure and limited range characteristic of songs from the Great Basin. Most songs are short and, unlike many Indian song genres, fully texted rather than based on vocables. They are usually sung unaccompanied.

Probably the earliest ethnographic recordings of Ghost Dance songs were those made on 18 March 1895 by Alice Fletcher, who recorded "New Religion" songs sung by Left Hand and Row of Lodges, two Southern Arapaho men who were visiting Washington, D.C., as members of a Cheyenne and Arapaho delegation. Ghost Dance songs were also the first commercially listed recordings of Indian music, although probably *not* as performed by native singers. Arapaho, Kiowa, Comanche, and Caddo Ghost Dance songs (together with Kiowa peyote songs and a Paiute gambling song) appeared in the catalog of Emile Berliner's National Gramophone Company around 1896 together with information that the songs had been recorded in Washington, D.C., on 11 July 1894. The songs are identified by their numbers in the Mooney monograph, and it appears that the singer may have been James Mooney himself or his brother Charles.

Although no longer sung within the a ritual context, Ghost Dance songs remain in the memory of some singers. See particularly the accounts of the Great Basin Ghost Dance [Naraya] songs known by Emily Hill and Dorothy Tappay, two Wind River Shoshone women who worked with ethnomusicologist Judith Vander (1997).

PEYOTE MUSIC

The peyote religion, centered on the eating of hallucinogenic peyote cactus "buttons," was introduced from Mexico to the southern plains around the 1880s and spread from there in all directions. It was formally incorporated in Oklahoma in 1918 as the Native American Church [see PLAINS, p. 440]. A syncretic religion, peyotism draws on a combination of native beliefs and practices with some added Christian symbolism. Songs are a major and distinguishing portion of the ritual.

The night-long ceremony that takes place in a special tipi includes groups of four songs by every person present (or by their designated representative), each song repeated four times. Four special songs are sung by the ceremony leader at designated times during the night: the Opening Song, Night Water Song, Morning Sunrise Song, and Closing Song. Peyote songs are sung by individuals who accompany themselves by shaking a gourd rattle decorated with characteristic peyote motifs and colors; the person to the right of the singer also accompanies the songs with a rapid, even drumbeat on a small water drum made from an iron pot. (During intervals between the songs in a set, the drummer may press a thumb into the moistened head of the drum, thus tightening it and making the drum pitch rise.)

Peyote song texts consist primarily of vocables, with a characteristic ending formula: "he ne ne yo way." Like Ghost Dance songs, peyote songs typically have paired phrases. In many communities, this repertoire exists completely separately from songs of very different styles that are more traditional for that group.

INDIAN SHAKER CHURCH

In 1882, John Slocum, a Squaxin man from the Puget Sound area, was believed to have died. But he miraculously revived and proclaimed a revelation from God promising salvation and powerful medicine to Indian people who would give up drinking, gambling, smoking, and the use of native shamans. A year later, Slocum again fell ill. His wife, Mary, while praying over him, started to shake violently. Many believed that Slocum was once again restored due to her trembling. Followers who listened to his message subsequently experienced the same shaking, hence the name of the religion based on Slocum's teachings.

The Shaker Church (not to be confused with the Shaker religion of the East Coast [see THE SHAKERS, p. 134]) has features drawn from indigenous guardian spirit beliefs as well as from Christian practices that missionaries had introduced, and in fact some people participate in rituals belonging both to the "Indian Way" and to the Shaker religion or other branches of Christianity. Shakers believe in God, in his son, Jesus, and in the Spirit and repeat the sign of the cross three times before and after each prayer. They have Sunday services as well as meetings to cure sickness, to convert, and to hear testimonials resulting from members' direct revelations. There are Shaker churches affiliated with several organizations not only in the Puget Sound area but also in eastern Washington, Oregon, British Columbia, and California. Although the number of members has never been very high, the Shaker Church is much respected for its good influence.

At services, the whole congregation sings hymns accompanied by a steady accompaniment of hand bells while marching in place or processing counterclockwise three times around the church. The songs, although reminiscent of evangelical Protestant hymns, have a distinctive style and are received by individuals in dreams. (The song's recipient must be present when the song is sung.) Shaker hymns characteristically have a heartfelt, expressive quality in their performance, a large tonal range, relatively equal upward and downward intervals, and little syncopation; the tempo typically increases as the song continues. The vocable *hai* is used quite consistently in the texts. Willard Rhodes, whose Puget Sound collections contain twenty-nine Shaker hymns, found a few examples of heterophony in them (n.d., 1954).

CONTEMPORARY MUSICS

New circumstances, new occasions, and new technologies come to people in all cultures. Such changes over time frequently find expression in music. Similar to its definition in Western classical music circles, however, the term *contemporary music* does not include all varieties of newly created American Indian music. It does *not* simply mean "newly composed music"; instead, "contemporary" is usually applied to nontraditional genres, to musical categories not exclusively linked to Indian culture—folk music, rock and roll, country and western, New Age, and reggae, for example. Such music is produced by everything from full orchestra to accordions, saxophones to electronic keyboards.

The involvement of Indian musicians in these kinds of music is evident in the fact that one-third of the pages in *A Guide to Native American Music Recordings,* compiled and edited by Greg Gombert (1994), are devoted to what he calls "Crossover Music Styles"—adult acoustic alternative, blues, chicken scratch, children's, classical, comedy, country, country and western, educational, folk (and fiddle), gospel, jazz, Native American flute, New Age, rap, reggae (and ska), rock (alternative and standard), rockabilly (and rhythm and blues), and world beat. And many of the recordings that have won Juno [the Canadian equivalent of a Grammy] or Indie [Association for Independent Music] awards in the "Aboriginal" or "Native American" categories are in crossover genres—Jerry Alfred's "Etsi Shon" and Joanne Shenandoah's "Matriarch," for example. Recordings are submitted to the sponsoring association by record labels and voted on by members of the associations or by category specialists, few of whom are probably of native background.

Questions about definitions and boundaries come up periodically concerning art, literature, and music created by Native American people: if the painting or sculpture doesn't somehow "look" Indian, is it Indian art, or is it better described as art created by a Native American artist? If a book or poem does not address Indian concerns or incorporate images drawn from specifically tribal community life, is it a Native American work, or should it simply be labeled as a work created by an Indian writer? Is a given composition "Indian music," particularly if it makes no use of or allusions to traits typically associated with Indian songs, such as vocables, drums, rattles, and so on? Is the definition dependent on musical content or on the ethnicity of its creators and performers, or on some combination of traits?

Possible answers to such questions become still more complex when we look at audiences and marketing. Some of the contemporary genres are directed principally to non-Indian audiences. New Age recordings, for example, are often flute-based "reveries" with titles that suggest dreaming or visions, ceremonies, spiritual journeys, and the like. Every element from cover art to album title to information about the artists may be shaped with an eye toward an audience (and potential market) among those who reach out for connections with the natural world and who perceive non-European-American people as having privileged contacts with that world. Given that there are many New Age recordings by non-Indian musicians, the question remains whether those recordings by native composers and performers are best classified as "Indian music" or as New Age music by Indian people. At this point in time, there may be as many different answers as there are composers and performers of the genre. But the category under which a potential customer finds a recording has real economic consequences for the musicians.

Other crossover genres, while utilizing nonindigenous instruments and repertoire, for example, still speak primarily to an Indian audience [see FIVE FUSIONS, p. 334]. Among them are songs using all the musical devices of mainstream rock and roll but filled with in-group references that affirm what is particularly "Indian." A classic case is the 1960s–70s political rock of the group called XIT: "Nothing could be finer than a 49'er" on the album *Relocation* uses the mainstream genre to praise a specifically Indian social dance type. The text includes references to a classic Forty-Nine Dance song about a "one-eyed Ford." The rock song fades out at the end, until the listener can hear a drum group actually performing that Forty-Nine Dance song. The success of the song depends on the audience's familiarity with both repertoires. A parallel situation occurs with the comedy "Indian Chipmunks" recordings; the humor lies in the juxtaposition of popular culture references, tunes, and texts ("Peter Cottontail," here entitled the "Yuk-a-day Rabbit Dance") with Indian musical devices such as vocables and in-group allusions to powwow behavior, for example. Those who are amused solely by the use of the high-pitched voice of Alvin Ahoy-Boy and his cohorts miss much of the humor.

Still other crossover genres are firmly linked with native communities. One of the most popular is *waila* (a word derived from *baile*, the Spanish word for social dance) music of the Tohono O'odham people of Arizona [see SOUTHWEST, p. 428]. *Waila* (sometimes identified as "chicken scratch") bands are descended from fiddle ensembles that existed early in the twentieth century; current instrumentation includes accordions, saxophones, trumpets, drum sets, and electric basses. The repertoire consists of genres reflecting German and Hispanic influences: polkas, *chotis* (schottisches), two-steps, *cumbias*. Some pieces are taken from popular culture (such as arrangements of "Ghost Riders in the Sky"). But there is no question that *waila* is distinctively Tohono O'odham music. Recent *waila* festivals as well as workshops for O'odham youth in the Tucson area emphasize cultural continuity and O'odham identity.

—JUDITH A. GRAY

REFERENCES

Amoss, Pamela. 1978. *Coast Salish Spirit Dancing: The Survival of an Ancestral Religion.* Seattle: University of Washington Press.

———. 1990. "The Indian Shaker Church." In *Handbook of North American Indians.* Vol. 7: *Northwest Coast,* ed. Wayne Suttles, ed. 633–639. Washington, D.C.: Smithsonian Institution Press.

Arapaho Music and Spoken Word Collection. The Alice Cunningham Fletcher Collection. Archive of Folk Culture, Library of Congress AFS 20308 and 20324.

Baker, Theodor. 1882. *Über die Musik der nordamerikanischen Wilden.* Leipzig: Breitkopf and Härtel. Reprinted with English translation by Ann Buckley as: Baker, Theodore. 1976. *On the Music of the North American Indians.* Source Materials and Studies in Ethnomusicology IX. Buren, The Netherlands: Frits Knuf.

Boley, Raymond. 1976. *Gourd Dance Songs of the Kiowa.* Canyon Records C-6148.

Densmore, Frances. 1932. *Yuman Music.* Bureau of American Ethnology Bulletin No. 110. Washington, D.C.: Smithsonian Institution.

Evers, Larry, and Felipe S. Molina. 1987. *Yaqui Deer Songs: Maso Bwikan: a Native American Poetry.* Tucson: Sun Tracks, University of Arizona Press.

Gombert, Greg. 1994. *A Guide to Native American Music Recordings.* Fort Collins, Colo: Multi Cultural Publishing.

Hatton, Orin T. 1986. "In the Tradition: Grass Dance Musical Style and Female Pow-wow Singers." *Ethnomusicology* 30(2):197–222.

Howard, James H. 1955. "The Pan-Indian Culture of Oklahoma." *Scientific Monthly* 18(5):215–220.

———. 1983. "Pan-Indianism in Native American Music and Dance." *Ethnomusicology* 27(1):71–82.

Huenemann, Lynn F. 1992. "Northern Plains Dance." In *Native American Dance: Ceremonies and Social Traditions,* ed. Charlotte Heth, 125–147. Washington, D.C.: Smithsonian Institution Press.

Indian Chipmunks, vol. 2–. 1983. Indian Sounds IS 3031. Cassette.

Isaacs, Tony. 1969. *Kiowa 49: War Expedition Songs.* Indian House IH 2505.

Kavanagh, Thomas W. 1992. "Southern Plains Dance: Tradition and Dynamics." In *Native American Dance: Ceremonies and Social Traditions,* ed. Charlotte Heth, 105–123. Washington, D.C.: Smithsonian Institution Press.

Kurath, Gertrude Prokosch. 1957. "Pan-Indianism in Great Lakes Tribal Festivals." *Journal of American Folklore* 70(2):179–182.

Mooney, James. 1973 [1896]. *The Ghost-Dance Religion and Wounded Knee.* Reprint of the Fourteenth Annual Report (Part 2) of the Bureau of Ethnology to the Smithsonian Institution, 1892–93: *The Ghost-Dance Religion and the Sioux Outbreak of 1890.*

Music of the Orthodox Church in Alaska. 1981. Vol. 1—Tlingit Orthodox Liturgical Music. Vol. 2—Aleut Orthodox Liturgical Music. Anchorage, Alaska: St. Innocent Orthodox Church. 2 cassettes.

Powers, William K. 1990. *War Dance: Plains Indian Musical Performance.* Tucson: University of Arizona Press.

Relocation. Originally Canyon Records C-7121, released in 1977. Since 1990, available on compact disc and cassette as S.O.A.R. 131 [Sound of America Record].

Rhodes, Willard. n.d. *Indian Songs of Today.* Library of Congress AFS L36.

———. 1954. *Music of the American Indian from the Archive of Folk Culture: Northwest (Puget Sound).* Library of Congress AFS L34. Accompanying booklet revised in 1984.

Roberts, Chris. 1992. *Pow-wow Country.* Helena, Mont.: American and World Geographic Publishing.

Vander, Judith. 1997. *Shoshone Ghost Dance Religion: Poetry Songs and Great Basin Context.* Urbana: University of Illinois Press.

Vennum, Thomas Jr. 1973. *Chippewa Grass Dance Songs: The Kingbird Singers of Ponemah, Minnesota.* Canyon Records C-6106.

———. 1982. *The Ojibway Dance Drum: Its History and Construction.* Smithsonian Folklife Studies 2. Washington, D.C.: Smithsonian Institution Press.

Wartes, William, ed. 1959. *The Utkiaguik Inupiat Hymn Book.* Printed in Mexico.

American Indian Musical Repatriation

Charlotte J. Frisbie

No encyclopedic volume dealing with musical cultures of American Indians at the beginning of the twenty-first century would be complete without consideration of at least one of the many federal laws recently passed to expand earlier adjudicated American Indian rights of self-determination and sovereignty (1975) and religious freedom (1978, with amendments in 1993 and 1994). Although not clear from its title, the 1990 Native American Graves Protection and Repatriation Act (NAGPRA) has implications for individuals, groups, and institutions interested in American Indian music makers and their diverse musics, musical knowledge, and cultures.

BACKGROUND

Repatriation is a multifaceted global phenomenon, one that intersects with complex, ever-changing issues of concern to those involved in museums, archives (audio/visual/other), art/antiquities/exotica collecting and marketing, ethics, international/national/state/American Indian law (especially contested ideas about copyright, ownership, and property—be it individual, group, cultural, or intellectual), and the rights of indigenous peoples as well as all other humans in today's complex nation states.

Our world today

Our postmodern, fragmented, global society is characterized by disappearing biological and cultural diversity; rampant ecological exploitation; rapid technological developments; consumerism; neocolonialism; Eurocentric hegemony; appropriation; misrepresentation; commodification; contested and reinvented identities, traditions, and histories; authentic reproductions; shifting/disappearing borders; military strife; overpopulation; biopiracy; inequities in power and politics; and numerous other issues. Thus the literature surrounding NAGPRA is diverse, and understandings of the law must be derived from delving into many disciplines and resources, such as archaeology; physical anthropology; art; museum; and legal journals; auction house (and on-line) catalogs; conference volumes; state, federal, and international documents; and discussions and publications of the United Nations and its various subcommittees and commissions (Messenger 1989; "Intellectual Property Rights" 1991; Posey and Dutfield 1996; Nason 1997).

Native Americans live in the global world and thus experience all of these larger issues as well as the repercussions of legal and attitudinal shifts in the United States during the twentieth century. Among the latter are enforced relocation; federal mismanagement of trust funds and reservation resources; poverty; continuing ethnic and racial stereotyping, misrepresentation, and misinterpretation; prejudice, misunderstanding, and degradation; poisoned lands; unending challenges to land, resource, and religious freedom rights; defamation and loss of sacred lands; and appropriation and exploitation of cultural practices and beliefs (including music) by New Agers, "would-be Indians," plastic Indians, and white shamans from without, and plastic shamans or fake/instant medicine people from within (see, for examples, Browner 1995; Kealiinohomoku 1986; Rose 1984, 1992; Welch 1997, as well as tribal newspapers, *Indian Country Today*, and journals such as *Native Americas, Native Peoples, American Indian Quarterly, American Indian Culture and Research Journal, Akwe:kon Journal* and *Cultural Survival Quarterly*).

But despite pouring energies, resources, and personnel into the problems represented by the Black Hills, Big Mountain, Chief Illiniwek, Mount Graham, and all the rest, today's tribes and nations are increasingly exercising their sovereign rights and continuing the decolonization process by re-appropriating their own voices, reaffirming their heritages, and celebrating their cultural traditions. As the publications previously cited, along with Roberts (1994) and others demonstrate, through many developments, such as cultural preservation/heritage programs; tribally owned and operated, community-based, living museums (for example, the National Museum of the American Indian [NMAI] in Washington, D.C.), archives, and/or cultural centers; active participation in broadcasting, film, theater, and other arts; websites; colleges; historic preservation offices; and research approval boards), American Indians are actively reclaiming their cultural histories and cultural patrimony, restoring and retaining their languages, recovering and reinstating traditional practices, laws, and knowledge, and taking control of presenting, representing, and interpreting themselves and their identities, cultures, histories, and traditions for national and international audiences. Many of these revitalization projects have roots in the 1970s and continue to expand through incorporation into the schools, tribal fairs and festivals, and beyond.

History of repatriation

Repatriation as a global phenomenon has its roots in the 1960s, when many nations achieved independence from colonialism and began to rediscover and reclaim their ethnic heritages, histories, roots, and traditional practices. Questions about ownership, collection, and marketing began to rock the art collecting and museum worlds. The 1969 European Archaeological Convention and the 1970 UNESCO Convention on Preventing Illicit Imports and Exports in the United States provided an impetus for many changes in the 1970s. Museums and professional organizations undertook revisions in acquisition, exhibition, deaccessioning policies, and ethical codes. The Smithsonian Institution began its Native American archival research internship (1973) and museum training (1976) programs, and the Native American Rights Fund (NARF) emerged (1970) and started assisting groups, some of which were already using other legal aid groups, the FBI, publicity, travels, negotiation, and confrontation to locate and repatriate ceremonial materials lost through theft, illicit sales, and other means of appropriation. A number of states also passed laws controlling archaeological excavations and their results, and some museums began of their own accord to return ceremonial materials in their collections, be these masks, musical instruments, medicine bundles, or recordings of religious songs and dances. Discussion of the political, social, economic, and intellectual climate in these times and Navajo, Pueblo, Iroquois, and Blackfoot examples can be found in Frisbie (1987:337–348); Merrill, Ladd, and Ferguson (1993) consider the lengthy process involved in repatriating Zuni War Gods.

THE LAW

The Native American Graves Protection and Repatriation Act, Public Law 101-601, of 16 November 1990, makes it possible for federally recognized tribes, Alaskan native villages and corporations, and native Hawaiians to reclaim ancestral human remains and funerary objects excavated from federal/tribal lands and housed in institutions receiving federal funds. It further provides for the recovery of sacred objects and objects of cultural patrimony (those having ongoing historical, traditional, or cultural importance central to the group or culture itself) that left home in earlier times. Various sections defined relevant terms and established deadlines for the mandated collection summaries, inventories, and notifications required from agencies and institutions, as well as the procedures for requesting and negotiating repatriation. Section four established fines and imprisonment for illegal trafficking in Native American human remains and cultural items, some of which are also covered by the 1979 Archaeological Resources Protection Act (ARPA).

While repatriations stemming from all three areas covered by NAGPRA—human remains, grave goods, and cultural patrimony—are ongoing today, human remains have had the most media coverage, especially since the discovery of Kennewick Man in July 1996 and the ensuing conflicting interpretations, claims, and current attempts to amend NAGPRA in favor of scientific research. The magnitude of the human remains problem, foreshadowed by Anna Lee Walters's 1988 novel, *Ghost Singer,* continues. For example, the University of Nebraska is now negotiating the return of 1,702 remains, and the Smithsonian's National Museum of Natural History will repatriate over 15,000 individuals and more than a million artifacts in the future, in addition to the four thousand remains returned since 1991, and the highly publicized 7 May 1999 repatriation of Ishi's brain (Foster 1999; Marks 1999). Additionally, Kennewick, Spirit Cave, and other finds contributing evidence of early diversity have recently led to serious challenges of archaeological explanations of the peopling of the New World (Begley and Murr 1999; Brace and Nelson 1999; Johansen 1999:36–47).

For those interested in American Indian musics, Section C of NAGPRA, which addresses cultural patrimony, is the most relevant. Cultural patrimony includes cultural knowledge and "artifacts" used in practicing this knowledge, thus covering ceremonial knowledge and its associated tangible equipment—masks, ritual poles, sacred textiles, medicine bundles, musical instruments, and other items.

AMERICAN INDIAN REACTIONS TO NAGPRA

A glance at the numerous sources that document repatriation claims, intentions to repatriate, and completed returns suggests that all tribes and nations are interested in the return of everything covered under NAGPRA. However, this is not the case. While the calls for repatriation from museums, audio/visual/other archives, and elsewhere are, in general, increasing, reactions are diverse. Today's world is very different from that traversed by Edith Fewkes, Frances Densmore, and Helen Roberts, and other early collectors dedicated to salvage ethnography. Ethical concerns and sensibilities have changed, along with recording technology. While cultural preservation and renewal programs have widespread support, attitudes about sharing knowledge are diverse and in many places more restrictive, with unresolved debates over access to knowledge by some insiders as well as outsiders. And some Indian communities are now closed to outside researchers.

Perhaps the rule of thumb is that there are no comprehensive procedures that can be followed for repatriation. Many tribes and nations have cultural resource management or traditional cultural properties offices, advisory committees (staffed with ceremonialists, elders, and traditionalists, as well as archivists, curators, and educators), procedures for reviewing NAGPRA inventories, and policies on repatriation. But groups have different attitudes about what should and should not come home, and, if

For those choosing to have their cultural materials returned, bringing the past back provides proof of the endurance, integrity, persistence, vitality, and survival of values, worldviews, songs, dances, and other cultural practices.

so, when, where, and how it should be handled, what should then be done with it, by whom, and for what purposes. Not all are interested in receiving ancestral remains or mortuary goods, or materials surrounded by unknown circumstances of appropriation and use/abuse, or unclear collection and preservation histories (Donovan 1999; Lee 1992). Additionally, there are other potential problems of contested claims, questionable credentials, internal factionalism, and the like. As all involved in repatriation know, each situation is unique and must be handled individually, with serious consideration of ethical, contextual, historical, political, economic, and legal perspectives before consultations start. Sensitivity is necessary throughout the complex, lengthy negotiation process.

Today many cultural patrimony claims have already been successfully completed and others are in final negotiation. Some examples include the sacred pole returned to the Omaha, wampum belts to Six Nations Iroquois Confederacy Grand River, musical instruments to Seneca Nations, and a Dogrib Lodge returned to the Northwest Territories in 1997 by the University of Iowa. More recently, a Wounded Knee Ghost Dance shirt, obtained in 1891, was repatriated to Lakota Sioux (via the Cultural Heritage Center Museum in Pierre, South Dakota) from the Kelvingrove Museum, Glasgow, Scotland, in July 1999, after fourteen years of effort by descendants of Wounded Knee ("Ghost Dance Shirt Returned" 1999). Those interested in tracking intended and completed repatriations can turn to numerous sources, including: *The Federal Register,* the Legal Briefs column in *American Indian Art, Common Ground: Archaeology and Ethnography in the Public Interest* (National Park Service quarterly with columns on NAGPRA news), *Cultural Resource Management,* numerous websites for NAGPRA (including the data base for contact people, grant applications, updates), *Anthropology Today, Cultural Survival Quarterly, American Indian Culture and Research Journal,* tribal newspapers, *Indian Country Today, NARF Legal Review* and other reports, *Phonographic Bulletin* (Journal of International Association of Sound Archives), *American Indian Law Review, Association for Indian Affairs, Inc., Native American Report,* and *Arizona State Law Journal* as well as other state and university law journals, especially from 1992 on.

The benefits of NAGPRA are verbalized in a variety of ways by American Indians. Even those who have opted not to claim ancestral remains praise the new climate of open dialogue in which Indians, as culture bearers, are being asked to advise museums and archives on policies concerning access, use, exhibit, preservation, and appropriate treatment of culturally specific and sensitive collections. New collaborative partnerships are being forged, new projects envisioned, new ideas exchanged among Indians and between Indians and outsiders. Meanwhile, new museums and cultural centers continue to be developed or opened by tribes and nations. One example is the Mashantucket Pequot Museum in southeastern Connecticut, opened on 11 August 1998 and now called the largest native built and operated museum in North America. Nationally, on 2 February 1999, NMAI's Cultural Resources Center was officially blessed.

For those choosing to have their cultural materials returned, bringing the past back provides proof of the endurance, integrity, persistence, vitality, and survival of values, worldviews, songs, dances, and other cultural practices. Repatriated materials reaffirm continuity and have helped stimulate both short- and long-term cultural retention, renewal, and reaffirmation programs, archival and oral history projects, transmission of cultural knowledge to the younger generation, and the like. Understanding and celebrating the past can revitalize the present, while shaping and injecting hope into the future. Interested individuals can reclaim older practices, re-create community and tribal identities, and even augment understandings of the histories of songs, dances, festivals, and other cultural practices by verifying their antiquity. But of utmost importance is understanding that the roles given to repatriated materials by American Indians is for them as sovereign nations to decide, not outsiders.

REPATRIATION OF AMERICAN INDIAN MUSICS BY INSTITUTIONS

To review the repatriation efforts of those interested in American Indian musics, music makers, and musical knowledge in cultural contexts, attention needs to be given to both institutional repatriation programs and individual efforts supportive of the spirit of NAGPRA.

The Federal Cylinder Project

Two of the three institutional projects mentioned here occurred or were started before NAGPRA was passed in 1990. The first, the Federal Cylinder Project (FCP) is, to date, the largest repatriation project undertaken by any world archive. The FCP was the brainchild of the American Folklife Center (AFC) at the Library of Congress, in conjunction with the Smithsonian Institution, the Bureau of Indian Affairs, and other federal agencies. The AFC was established through the 1976 American Folklife Preservation Act, Public Law 94-201, and the Archive of American Folk-Song, established in 1928, became part of it, with a name change in 1978.

Begun in 1979, the FCP set out to "preserve, document, catalog, and disseminate information contained in . . . early field recordings" (done by the Bureau of American Ethnology [BAE] employees, Helen Heffron Roberts, and others) (Gray 1991:32). Other public and private institutions and various federal agencies contributed their holdings, which resulted in a collection of over ten thousand cylinders spanning the years 1890 to 1942. Of these, 7,500–8,000 were of Native American music and spoken word.

In 1985, after completing much of the copying onto preservation tape, identifying and cataloging contents, and after a dry-run trip to the Omaha of Macy, Nebraska, in 1983 (Lee 1992), the FCP, with support from the Ford Foundation, entered its dissemination phase, or the time when the resulting tapes were made available to their communities of origin. First, the FCP sponsored a meeting with representatives from American Indian communities to discuss strategies and potential problems. Then, the contacts began. Where there was interest in having copies of archived materials returned, communities were in charge of the setting up and the details of the repatriation event. The FCP staff returned materials along with catalogs and supplementary information on resources. If asked, they also spent time consulting about establishing or expanding existing cultural programs, sources of funding, and so on. They were not in the business of telling American Indians what to do or how to use the repatriated materials. Rather, they helped with duplicating the cylinders, cataloging, and disseminating, and then departed.

Over time, numerous individuals were involved in the FCP including Tom Vennum, Maria LaVigna, Ron Walcott, Erika Brady, Dorothy Sara Lee, Judith Gray, and Ed Schupman. To date, some of the Indian communities in Florida, North Carolina, Oklahoma, Montana, Washington, Wisconsin, Minnesota, Idaho, Iowa, Nebraska,

Arizona, New Mexico, Arkansas, Mississippi, Maine, and British Columbia have chosen to have copies of their archived materials returned. Over one hundred communities have been visited or contacted through the FCP since 1979. This does not count the hundreds of individual American Indians who annually continue to search for cultural heritage materials at the Library of Congress, which houses the country's largest collection of early recordings of Native American music.

Between 1984 and 1990 five of the eight catalogs planned for the FCP were published (American Folklife Center 1984a, 1984b, 1985, 1988, 1990). Cataloging is still in process on the remaining three (Plains, Pueblo, and Navajo, Southwest II and III) (Gray 1999a). As Judith Gray, who sees herself as the "last remnant" of the FCP, notes, "Work still remains to be done, not only with the cylinders but with the other collections. . . . Dissemination now [also] takes other forms as more and more cultural preservation folks come to D.C.; there's much more information and intentionality out there now, and some of the early FCP strategies wouldn't make much sense any more" (Gray 1999b).

Further information on the FCP can be found in numerous issues of the *Folklife Center News*. Various staff members have also published comments about the process, hopes and dreams, challenges, and diverse experiences associated with the FCP, in addition to their editorial work on the catalogs.

The Lowie Museum of Anthropology

The second institutional project involved the duplication and repatriation of musical, linguistic, and other materials housed at the Lowie Museum of Anthropology (now the Phoebe Apperson Hearst Museum) to their communities of origin in California. By the early 1980s this institution's collection included more than five thousand songs and spoken narratives. Richard Keeling (1984a, 1984b, 1988), an active participant in the repatriation project, has documented its details.

Wesleyan University World Music Archives

The third institutional repatriation occurred in 1992–1993 when David P. McAllester, in a response to some Navajo requests and visits, spearheaded the repatriation of copies of four collections of Navajo ceremonial recordings in the Wesleyan University World Music Archives to two different places on the reservation. The Ned A. Hatathli Cultural Center/Museum at Navajo Community College (now Diné College), Tsaile, Arizona received one of the collections, and three individuals involved in a newly formed Institute of Cultural Integrity, the others. (The latter has since collapsed from lack of political and financial support.) A participant, Robert Lancefield (1993, 1998), has described this repatriation. Elsewhere, McAllester (1984) has considered a myriad of ethical issues connected with the preservation and still unresolved (in 1999) disposition of a film he made of the Blessingway ceremony in 1957.

ROLES FOR INDIVIDUALS IN THE REPATRIATION OF AMERICAN INDIAN MUSICS

Besides the duplication and return of audio materials from these sources and more informal programs at other archives, other repatriation activities by students of American Indian musics that have helped or could facilitate American Indian programs of cultural renewal and preservation need consideration. Many roles are available to those interested in championing the repatriation of musical knowledge, its performances, and associated equipment, if and when assistance is requested by American Indians. Most of these are of the cultural broker, mediator, or support staff variety, as the goal is to empower indigenous efforts at achieving their own programs of cultural preservation, renewal, and sometimes participation in larger world music scenes and markets.

In addition to leaving copies of research results with those who contribute the information, if those with whom one works agree, one should also leave or later deposit copies of research results with tribal museums, cultural centers, archives, colleges, or other appropriate sites. Now it is not uncommon for such deposits to be among the conditions agreed to when securing research permits from tribal research boards. Given diverse cultural protocols and different ideas about intellectual property and access thereto, one needs to understand many issues in this area. One should also donate copies of works generated later from such information, be these in print, compact disc or audio cassette, videocassette, CD-Rom, or other formats. One should also be prepared to replace (often at personal expense) such deposits with individuals or institutions over time, should they be lost, stolen, or otherwise destroyed.

The very fact of documenting/recording events can help future cultural preservation efforts if the results are safeguarded as well as disseminated to individuals and/or communities of origin. Future generations may be able to reconstruct songs, dances, ceremonies, or other practices not passed on through oral tradition for any number of reasons with appropriate access to documentation. Here, for examples, one can turn to almost any of the publications by individuals interested in American Indian musics (see all of the entries on music in the Smithsonian Institution volumes of the *Handbook of North American Indians,* as well as the publications of scholars and collectors).

Another kind of work that facilitates repatriation is that which helps make museums and archives more accessible. Here, histories of collections (Brady 1985; Gray 1990) and guides and catalogs to collections of interest to American Indians (Korson and Hickerson [1969] for the Willard Rhodes collection at AFS; Lee [1979] and Seeger and Spear [1987] for the Archives of Traditional Music, Indiana University; Keeling [1991] for the Lowie Museum; and the FCP catalogs) are noteworthy. In addition to preparing such documents, one can assist Native peoples in their searches for cultural materials by providing information about collections, locations, policies, and contact people, existing catalogs, funding, and other resources, such as Dyal (1985), and sometimes even facilitating visits to museums and archives. If one is a donor of collections, working to facilitate contemporary people's access to their own heritage is also important. See, for example, Johansen (1998) for problems experienced by Joanne Shenandoah when wanting access to and copies of Fenton's collection of Oneida materials, despite the 1942 and 1946 American Folklore Society albums based on Fenton's work for the Library of Congress; Browner (1995:190–194) discusses other problems involving Fenton's activities. Of equal use are annotated bibliographies and discographies; for one example, see Keeling (1997).

Given the diverse issues with which repatriation intersects, one should work to educate professional and public audiences about the changing global complexities of copyright laws, intellectual property rights, and the implications these have for ethics of collecting, roles of museums and archives, professional methodologies, committees on and codes of ethics, and so on. For example, see Ethical Codes of various professional organizations or Ethical Dilemma Columns in *Anthropology Newsletter.* In the spirit of applied/action ethnomusicology or Public Sector Ethnomusicology ("Music and the Public Interest" 1992), there is still much to be done, some of which is already under way.

Where outside scholars are still welcome, one should, on request, get involved in collaborative efforts with indigenous peoples interested in recording/preserving/documenting their musical cultures. For a few examples of successful collaborations, see Diamond, Cronk, and von Rosen (1994), Frisbie and Tso (1993), Howard and Levine (1990), Keeling (1993), Lang and Risling (1997), Vander (1986, 1988, 1997), and Vennum (1982), as well as the ongoing collaborative efforts of Levine, Jackson, and Yuchi ceremonial leaders on Yuchi Oklahoma Indian social dance music (Jackson 1999).

Another version of this involvement is to assist with both the production of cassettes and CDs (and accompanying liner notes) of archived cultural heritage and the dissemination of the results to cultures of origin. Such work may take years and may involve further field research (given the mysteries of the documentation left with some

One should also work to empower and legitimize indigenous music makers, improve their legal protections and compensations, and enhance the marketing of their commercial endeavors, if they are so interested.

collections) and helping with final selections. It may also involve combining the results of one's own work with that of others. Three of many examples include the collaborative FCP/Omaha of Macy LP/cassette album, *Omaha Indian Music,* based on the Alice Fletcher and Frances La Flesche collection and presented to the community in 1985; *Navajo Songs* recorded by Laura Boulton in 1933 and 1940 (1992); and Thomas Vennum Jr.'s efforts on *Honor the Earth Powwow: Songs of the Great Lakes Indians,* 1991.

One should also work to empower and legitimize indigenous music makers, improve their legal protections and compensations, and enhance the marketing of their commercial endeavors, if they are so interested. This entails involvement in global issues, be these music equity, human rights, or the politics of amplification, appropriation, and commercialization as these apply to music makers. Examples include Steven Feld's continuing commitments to Rain Forest realities, and the Endangered Music Project Series started in 1993—coproduced by Alan Jabbour for the American Folklife Center and Mickey Hart of Rykodisc and 360° Productions—where treasures taken from threatened cultural traditions and housed at the American Folklife Center are being remastered and made accessible to international audiences while also being repatriated, to musicians and communities of origin.

In her study of the appropriation of Native North American music, Browner (1995:202–205) illustrates some other possibilities. One example is provided by the collaboration between Navajo/Ute Native American flute artist R. Carlos Nakai and non-Native Arizona composer James DeMars that has led to a number of works, including the 1991 flute-orchestral concerto "Spirit Horses" and the 1993 three-movement "Two World Symphony," both recorded on Canyon Records. Another example is the 1995 Milwaukee Ballet Company's production of *Dream Dances.* Conceived by the Potawatomi Nation and underwritten by their Milwaukee Bingo Casino, *Dream Dances* was based on this Nation's successful reclamation of its songs from the 1979 work *Potawatomi Legends* by non-Native Wisconsin-born composer Otto Luening. This three-way collaboration involved an Indian Nation, an Ojibwe artistic director and choreographer of the Milwaukee Ballet, Dane LaFontsee, and a non-Native composer supportive of repatriating the songs he had learned in his youth from tribal members and later used in creating *Potawatomi Legends.*

Another kind of direct contribution that can be made to the owners of musical knowledge and practices is to use one's training and skills, upon request, to assist in legal battles, whether focused on sacred landscapes, aboriginal land claims and rights, repatriation of ceremonial paraphernalia, or comparable problems. While there may be no direct parallels in archived collections of American Indian music to the song maps Roseman (1998) discusses for the Malaysian Rain Forest, or the songs now politically important in land claims of Australian aboriginal groups (Ellis 1992; Koch 1985, 1989, 1997; Tatar 1985; Wild 1992), or the potentials of collections in Papua New Guinea (Niles 1992), the political implications of archived sounds in today's world should not be overlooked.

Individual legal assistance may also be possible. For example, on the basis of my work with Navajo medicine bundles or *jish* (Frisbie 1987, 1993), I now help, in and out of the courtroom, with investigative and prosecution efforts aimed at returning *jish* to the Navajo Nation. Other Navajo medicine bundle repatriations continue. For example, in September 1999, after thirteen years of effort, federal investigators arrested John Patrick Williams, who had stolen a *jish* in 1986, and were able to retrieve and repatriate the medicine bundle after tracing its journey through three art galleries and one private collector (Shebala 1999a, 1999b). Aspects of this case were presented on ABC's *Nightline,* 28 September 1999.

In addition to doing action anthropology/ethnomusicology by applying one's knowledge in ways that facilitate the return of contested cultural patrimony, those interested in American Indian musics and music makers can help educate the public about NAGPRA in the print/sound/video materials we produce for classroom use. To do so effectively, of course, requires staying current with American Indian legal and political issues, the work of NARF on behalf of tribes and nations, and further developments in the complex issues that intersect with NAGPRA and its implementation.

There are also many new possibilities as various tribes and nations repatriate and rebury human remains and bring other things home through NAGPRA. Already new uses are being made of older ceremonial practices, and new procedures are emerging. Music is also involved in preparing for legal battles over defamed sacred sites, celebrating or grieving the outcomes, and commemorating tribal anniversaries, returns of historical treaties (even if these are copies that come by loan), and so on. As always, at least some of the musics of American Indians continue to document and express reactions to current experiences on and off the reservation in local, national, and international worlds. Future generations will incorporate these expressions into their understandings of their pasts, if current generations choose to document them.

At present, roles for outsiders interested in American Indian musics, musical knowledge, and music makers vary with tribes and nations and range from nonexistent, through tenuous and volatile, to firmly established collaborative efforts. A commitment to staying current on relevant developments and a firm respect for American Indian sovereignty and self-determination can help outsiders look forward to the challenges of the twenty-first century.

REFERENCES

American Folklife Center. 1984–1990. *The Federal Cylinder Project: A Guide to Field Cylinder Collections in Federal Agencies.* Washington, D.C.: American Folklife Center, Library of Congress.

———. 1984a. "Introduction and Inventory," ed. Erika Brady, Maria LaVigna, Dorothy Sara Lee, and Thomas Vennum. Vol. 1, *The Federal Cylinder Project.*

———. 1984b. "Early Anthologies," ed. Dorothy Sara Lee. Vol. 8, *The Federal Cylinder Project.*

———. 1985. "Northeastern Indian Catalog," ed. Judith A. Gray; "Southeastern Indian Catalog," ed. Dorothy Sara Lee. Vol. 2, *The Federal Cylinder Project.*

———. 1988. "Great Basin/Plateau Indian Catalog," "Northwest Coast/Arctic Indian Catalog," ed. Judith A. Gray. Vol. 3, *The Federal Cylinder Project.*

———. 1990. "California Indian Catalog"; "Middle and South American Indian Catalog"; "Southwestern Indian Catalog-I (non-Pueblo and non-Navajo)," ed. Judith A. Gray and Edwin J. Schupman Jr. Vol. 5, *The Federal Cylinder Project.*

Arizona State Law Journal. 1992. Vol. 24(1).

Begley, Sharon, and Andrew Murr. 1999. "The First Americans." *Newsweek,* 26 April, 50–57.

Boulton, Laura. 1992 [1933, 1940/1992]. *Navajo Songs.* Notes by Charlotte J. Frisbie and David P. McAllester. Smithsonian Folkways CD SF 40403. Compact disc.

Brace, C. Loring, and A. Russell Nelson. 1999. "The Peopling of the Americas: Anglo Stereotypes and Native American Realities." *General Anthropology* 5(2):1, 2–9.

Brady, Erika. 1985. "Bringing the Voices Home: The Omaha Pow-wow Revisited." *Folklife Center News* 8(4):7–10.

———. 1988. "The Bureau of American Ethnology, Folklore, Fieldwork, and the Federal Government in the Late Nineteenth and Early Twentieth Centuries." In *The Conservation of Culture: Folklorists and the Public Sector,* ed. Burt Feintuch, 35–45. Lexington: University Press of Kentucky.

———. 1999. *A Spiral Way: How the Phonograph Changed Ethnography.* Jackson: University Press of Mississippi.

Brown, Michael. 1998. "Can Culture Be Copyrighted?" *Current Anthropology* 39(2):193–222.

Browner, Tara Colleen. 1995. "Transposing Cultures: The Appropriation of Native North American Musics, 1890–1990." Ph.D. dissertation, University of Michigan.

Bruner, Edward. 1994. "Abraham Lincoln as Authentic Reproduction: A Critique of Postmodernism." *American Anthropologist* 96(2):397–415.

Diamond, Beverley, M. Sam Cronk, and Franziska von Rosen. 1994. *Musical Instruments of First Nations Communities in Northeastern America.* Chicago: University of Chicago Press.

Donovan, Bill. 1999. "Nation Being Selective in What Is Returned Home." *Navajo Times,* 1 April, A–1, 2.

Dyal, Susan. 1985. *Preserving Traditional Arts: A Toolkit for Native American Communities.* Los Angeles: University of California American Indian Studies Center.

Ellis, Catherine. 1992. "Living Preservation: Problems of Cultural Exchange with Central Australian Traditional Performers." In *Music and Dance of Aboriginal Australia and the South Pacific: The Effects of Documentation on the Living Tradition,* ed. Alice M. Moyle, 155–170. Sydney: University of Sydney.

Farnell, Brenda. 1998. "Retire the Chief." *Anthropology Newsletter* 39(4):1, 4.

Foster, George M. 1999. "Responsibility for Ishi." *Anthropology News* 40(7):5–6.

Frisbie, Charlotte J. 1987. *Navajo Medicine Bundles, or Jish: Acquisition, Transmission, and Disposition in the Past and Present.* Albuquerque: University of New Mexico Press.

———. 1993. "NAGPRA and the Repatriation of Jish." In *Papers from the Third, Fourth, and Sixth Navajo Studies Conferences,* ed. June-el Piper, 119–128. Window Rock, Ariz: Navajo Nation Historic Preservation Department.

Frisbie, Charlotte J., and Eddie Tso. 1993. "The Navajo Ceremonial Practitioners Registry." *Journal of the Southwest* 35 (1):53–92.

Gable, Eric, and Richard Handler. 1996. "After Authenticity at an American Heritage Site." *American Anthropologist* 98(3):569–578.

"Ghost Dance Shirt Returned." 1999. *Navajo Times,* 5 August, A:7, 9.

Gray, Judith A. 1989. "Early Ethnographic Recordings in Today's Indian Communities: Federal Agencies and the Federal Cylinder Project." In *Songs of Indian Territory: Native American Music Traditions of Oklahoma,* ed. Willie Smyth, 49–55. Oklahoma City: Center of the American Indian.

———. 1990. "Documenting Native America with Sound Recordings: The First Hundred Years of Federal Involvement." *Folklife Center News* 12(1):4–7.

———. 1991. "The Songs Come Home: The Federal Cylinder Project." *CRM (Cultural Resource Management)* 14(5):32–35.

———. 1997. "Returning Music to the Makers: The Library of Congress, American Indians, and the Federal Cylinder Project." *Cultural Survival Quarterly* 20(4):42–44.

———. 1999a. Personal communication, 21 July.

———. 1999b. Personal communication, 7 September.

Greenfield, Jeanette. 1989. *The Return of Cultural Treasures.* Cambridge: Cambridge University Press.

Howard, James H., and Victoria Lindsay Levine. 1990. *Choctaw Music and Dance.* Norman: University of Oklahoma Press.

Howarth, Rea, and Marguerite Carroll. 1998. "Cultural Treasures for Sale." *American Indian Report: Indian Country's News Magazine* 14(6):14–17.

"Intellectual Property Rights: The Politics of Ownership." 1991. *Cultural Survival Quarterly* 15(1).

Jackson, Jason Baird. 1999. "Indians and Scholars Join Forces to Document the Dance Music of Oklahoma's Yuchi Tribe." *Folklife Center News* 21(2):3–6.

Johansen, Bruce E. 1998. "Fenton: Scholar and Polemicist." *Native Americas* 15(4):60–63.

———. 1999. "Great White Hope? Kennewick Man, the Facts, the Fantasies, and the Stakes." *Native Americas* 16(1):36–47.

Kealiinohomoku, Joann W. 1986. "The Would-Be Indian." In *Explorations in Ethnomusicology: Essays in Honor of David P. McAllester,* ed. Charlotte J. Frisbie, 111–126. Detroit Monographs in Musicology 9. Detroit: Information Coordinators.

Keeling, Richard. 1984a. "The Archive as Disseminator of Culture: Returning California Indian Music to Its Sources." *Phonographic Bulletin* 38:44–54.

———. 1984b. "Tribal Music and Cultural Revival." In *Sharing a Heritage: American Indian Arts.* Contemporary American Indian Issues Series 5:165–173. Los Angeles: University of California American Indian Studies Center.

———. 1988. "Returning California Indian Music to Its Source." Unpublished paper.

———. 1991. *A Guide to Early Field Recordings (1900–1949) at the Lowie Museum of Anthropology* [now Phoebe Apperson Hearst Museum of Anthropology]. Berkeley: University of California Press.

———. 1993. *Cry for Luck: Sacred Song and Speech among the Yurok, Hupa, and Karok Indians of Northwestern California.* Berkeley: University of California Press.

———. 1997. *North American Indian Music: A Guide to Published Sources and Selected Recordings (1535–1995).* Garland Library of Music Ethnology 5. New York: Garland Publishing Company.

Killion, Thomas, William Sturtevant, Dennis Stanford, and David Hurt. 1999. "The Facts About Ishi's Brain." *Anthropology News* 40(6):9.

Koch, Grace. 1985. "Who Are the Guardians? Problems in Retrieval at an Ethnographic Sound Archive." *Phonographic Bulletin* 43:17–23.

———. 1989. "The Music Tape Archive of the AIAS Library." *Australian Aboriginal Studies* 1:50–53.

———. 1997. "Songs, Land Rights, and Archives in Australia." *Cultural Survival Quarterly* 20(4):38–41.

Korson, Rae, and Joseph C. Hickerson. 1969. "The Willard Rhodes Collection of American Indian Music in the Archive of Folk Song." *Ethnomusicology* 13(2):296–304.

Lancefield, Robert C. 1993. *On the Repatriation of Recorded Sound from Ethnomusicological Archives: A Survey of Some of the Issues Pertaining to People's Access to Documentation of Their Musical Heritage.* Master's thesis, Wesleyan University.

———. 1998. "Musical Traces, Retraceable Paths: The Repatriation of Recorded Sound." *Journal of Folklore Research* 35(1):47–68.

Lang, Julian, and Lyn Risling. 1997. "Singing the Songs Back to Life: A California Romance of Cultural Recovery." *Native Americas* 14(1):50–55.

Lee, Dorothy Sara. 1979. *Native North American Music and Oral Data: A Catalogue of Sound Recordings 1893–1976 (at the Archives of Traditional Music, Indiana University).* Bloomington: Indiana University Press.

———. 1992. "Historic Recordings and Contemporary Native American Culture: Returning Materials to Native American Communities." In *Music and Dance of Aboriginal Australia and the South Pacific: The Effects of Documentation on the Living Tradition,* ed. Alice M. Moyle, 24–39. Sydney: University of Sydney.

Marks, Jonathan. 1999. "They Saved Ishi's Brain!" *Anthropology Newsletter* 40(4):22.

McAllester, David P. 1984. "A Problem in Ethics." In *Problems and Solutions: Occasional Papers in Musicology Presented to Alice M. Moyle,* ed. Jamie C. Kassler and Jill Stubington, 279–289. Sydney: Hale and Iremonger.

McCoy, Ron. 1998. "Legal Briefs: NAGPRA Case Before U.S. Supreme Court." *American Indian Art* 23(3):25, 29.

Merrill, William L., Edmund J. Ladd, and T. J. Ferguson. 1993. "The Return of the Ahayu:da: Lessons for Repatriation from Zuni Pueblo and the Smithsonian Institution." *Current Anthropology* 34(5):523–567.

Messenger, Phyllis Mauch, ed. 1989. *The Ethics of Collecting Cultural Property: Whose Culture? Whose Property?* Albuquerque: University of New Mexico Press.

Montejo, Victor D. 1999. "Becoming Maya? Appropriation of the White Shaman." *Native Americas* 16(1):58–61.

"Music and the Public Interest." 1992. *Ethnomusicology* 36(3).

Nason, James D. 1997. "Native American Intellectual Property Rights: Issues in the Control of Esoteric Knowledge." In *Borrowed Power: Essays on Cultural Appropriation,* ed. Bruce Ziff and Pratima V. Rao, 237–254. New Brunswick, N.J.: Rutgers University Press.

Niles, Don. 1992. "Collection, Preservation, and Dissemination: The Institute of Papua New Guinea Studies as the Center for the Study of All Papua New Guinea Music." In *Music and Dance of Aboriginal Australia and the South Pacific: The Effects of Documentation on the Living Tradition,* ed. Alice M. Moyle, 59–78. Sydney: University of Sydney.

Omaha Indian Music. n.d. American Folklife Center L71.

Posey, Darrell A., and Graham Dutfield. 1996. *Beyond Intellectual Property Rights: Toward Traditional Resource Rights for Indigenous Peoples and Local Communities.* Canada: International Development Research Center.

Ridington, Robin. 1993. "A Sacred Object as Text: Reclaiming the Sacred Pole of the Omaha." *American Indian Quarterly* 17:83–99.

Ridington, Robin, and Dennis Hastings. 1997. *Blessing for a Long Time: The Sacred Pole of the Omaha Tribe.* Lincoln: University of Nebraska Press.

Roberts, Carla. 1994. "Object, Subject, and Practitioner: Native Americans and Cultural Institutions. Native American Expressive Culture." *Akwe:kon Journal* 11(3–4):22–29.

Rockafellar, Nancy, and Orin Starn. 1999. "Ishi's Brain." *Current Anthropology* 40(4):413–415.

Rose, Jerome C., Thomas J. Green, and Victoria D. Green. 1996. "NAGPRA Is Forever: Osteology and the Repatriation of Skeletons." *Annual Review of Anthropology* 25:81–104.

Rose, Wendy. 1984. "Just What's All This Fuss About Whiteshamanism Anyway?" In *Coyote Was Here: Essays on Contemporary Native American Literary and Political Mobilization,* ed. Bo Scholer, 13–25.

———. 1992. "The Great Pretenders: Further Reflections on Whiteshamanism." In *The State of Native America: Genocide, Colonization, and Resistance,* ed. M. Annette Jaimes, 403–421. Boston: South End Press.

Roseman, Marina. 1998. "Singers of the Landscape: Song, History, and Property Rights in the Malaysian Rain Forest." *American Anthropologist* 100(1):106–121.

Schuldenrein, Joseph. 1999. "Charting a Middle Ground in the NAGPRA Controversy: Secularism in Context." *SAA Bulletin* 17(4):22–23, 33.

Schupman, Edwin J. Jr. 1988. "Northern Cheyennes Preserve Tribal Culture." *Folklife Center News* 10(2):10–13.

Seeger, Anthony. 1986. "Role of Sound Archives in Ethnomusicology Today." *Ethnomusicology* 30(2):261–276.

———. 1991a. "After the Alligator Swallows Your Microphone: The Future(?) of Field Recordings." In *Essays in Honor of Frank J. Gillis,* ed. Nancy Cassell McEntire, et al., 37–49. Discourse in Ethnomusicology 3. Bloomington, Ind.: Ethnomusicology Publications Group.

———. 1991b. "Singing Other People's Songs." *Cultural Survival Quarterly* 15(3):36–39.

———. 1992. "Ethnomusicology and Music Law." *Ethnomusicology* 36(3):345–359.

———. 1996. "Ethnomusicologists, Archives, Professional Organizations, and the Shifting Ethics of Intellectual Property." *Yearbook of Traditional Music* 28:87–105.

———. 1997. "Introduction," as guest ed., to "Traditional Music in Community Life: Aspects of Performance, Recordings, and Preservation." *Cultural Survival Quarterly* 20(4):20–22.

———. 1999. "Happy Birthday, ATM: Ethnographic Futures of the Archives of the 21st Century." RESOUND (A Quarterly of the Archives of Traditional Music, Indiana University): 1–3.

Seeger, Anthony, and Louise S. Spear, eds. 1987. *Early Field Recordings: A Catalogue of the Cylinder Collections at the Indiana University Archives of Traditional Music.* Bloomington: Indiana University Press.

Shebala, Marley. 1999a. "Elders Attend Homecoming of the Holy Ones." *Navajo Times,* 23 September, A:1, 2.

———. 1999b. "Sacred Artifacts Took Long Road Home." *Navajo Times,* 23 September, A:1, 2.

Slobin, Mark. 1992. "Ethical Issues." In *Ethnomusicology: An Introduction,* ed. Helen Myers, 329–336. Norton/Grove Handbooks in Music. New York: Norton.

Tatar, Elizabeth. 1985. "Returning to the Source: A Review of the Dissemination Program at the Audio-Recording Collections, Bernice Pauahi Bishop Museum." *Phonographic Bulletin* 41:41–46.

Turner, Terence, and Carole Nagengast, guest eds. 1997. "Universal Human Rights vs. Cultural Relativity." Special issue of *Journal of Anthropological Research* 53(3).

Vander, Judith. 1986. *Ghost Dance Songs and Religion of a Wind River Shoshone Woman.* Urbana: University of Illinois Press.

———. 1988. *Songprints: The Musical Experience of Five Shoshone Women.* Urbana: University of Illinois Press.

———. 1997. *Shoshone Ghost Dance Religion: Poetry Songs and Great Basin Context.* Urbana: University of Illinois Press.

Vennum, Thomas Jr. 1982. *The Ojibwa Dance Drum: Its History and Construction.* Smithsonian Folklife Studies 2. Washington, D.C.: Smithsonian Institution Press.

———. 1991. *Honor the Earth Powwow: Songs of the Great Lakes Indians.* 360° Productions/ Rykodisc RACS 0199. Compact disc.

Walcott, Ronald. 1982. "The Federal Cylinder Project." *Phonographic Bulletin* 33:13–22.

Walters, Anna Lee. 1988. *Ghost Singer.* Flagstaff, Ariz.: Northland Publishing Company.

Welch, John R. 1997. "White Eyes' Lies and the Battle for Dzil/Nchaa Si'an (Mount Graham)." *American Indian Quarterly* 21(1):75–109.

Wild, Stephen. 1992. "Issues in the Collection, Preservation and Dissemination of Traditional Music: The Case of Aboriginal Australia." In *Music and Dance of Aboriginal Australia and the South Pacific: The Effects of Documentation on the Living Tradition,* ed. Alice M. Moyle, 7–22. Sydney: University of Sydney.

Section 2
The United States

Here we discuss the four major groups of "recent" arrivals to the United States: African Americans, Hispanic Americans, European Americans, and Asian Americans, examining the history of their immigration (or in the case of African Americans their forcible removal from African communities and placement in the United States), the growth of communities, and the contribution of various musics, musicians, instruments, and musical ideas to the total mosaic of American musical culture. We begin this section with an article addressing issues of identity and interaction that are specific to the United States, followed by a general overview of U.S. musical history and four views of music in the United States that hint at the variety of music making here, both historically and in contemporary times. Organized roughly in the order of their arrival here, discussions of these four groups reveal, among other things, a variety of settlement patterns and the establishment of different social and musical institutions, as well as different forms of musical transmission and religious expression.

Yankee Doodle 1776, lithograph based on a painting by A. M. Willard. © CORBIS.

Identity, Diversity, and Interaction
Adelaida Reyes

Identity: The Concept and Its Evolution
Music and Identity: A Historical Perspective

Who are we? This question arises from a profound human need for identity that comes to being when consciousness of difference begins. In the United States, the question draws added significance from the country's history as a nation-state. Though born out of a successful rebellion against the British and ultimately taking a different form of government, the United States adopted the basic features, particularly the civic, from the English model. One did not have to be born American; one could *become* an American through citizenship: "To be or to become an American, a person did not have to be of any particular national, linguistic, religious or ethnic background. All he [*sic*] had to do was commit himself to the political ideology centered on the abstract ideals of liberty, equality and republicanism" (Gleason 1980:32). More than a decade later, Liah Greenfeld reasserted the principle: "In contrast to the European nations, where the primacy of the nation over the individual imposed general uniformity, the unchallenged primacy of the individual [in the United States] allowed—even guaranteed—plurality of tastes, views, attachments, aspirations and self-definitions, within the national framework. Pluralism was built into the system" (1992:482). Diversity, therefore, was not an unintended consequence of migrations from Europe, Asia, and Africa, nor merely an accident of history, but part of the ideological foundation of the new nation-state. It was an intrinsic part of American self-definition.

Diversity is thus embedded in the country's soundscape. If, for example, one drives cross-country with the radio on, one can hear pan-Indian music, Greek bouzouki music, polkas, klezmer, sitar and *tabla* ensembles, Cantonese opera, salsa, merengue, country and western, jazz, blues, rap music, Ghanaian drumming, Buddhist chant, Jewish cantorial singing, music for belly dancing, folk songs from different parts of the world, the sounds of the Metropolitan Opera, a catalog of so-called world musics following one another as one radio station moves out of range and is replaced by another on the airwaves and as one segment of America's listening public is replaced by another. Musical life gives abundant evidence of a population within which is represented every country in the modern world—evidence that supports the United States' claim to be a country of immigrants and the contention that the immigrant is the archetypal American (Gleason 1980). No wonder, then, that throughout the United States, the question Who are we? resounds because the constituent populations change as do the replies, depending on the intellectual climate, the temper of the times, and the tools that become available to those who ask and those who respond.

IDENTITY: THE CONCEPT AND ITS EVOLUTION

The term *identity* comes from the Latin *idem* 'same' and has been part of English usage since at least the fourteenth century. Mathematics, logic, and psychology have continued to use the term, with its original emphasis on sameness or equivalence. In the nineteenth century, as the social sciences took on studies of identity in general and national identity in particular, sameness in the sense of general uniformity prevailed as well. The European nation-state expected the boundaries of *Kulturnation* 'the national culture' and *Staatsnation* 'the state's legal and political system' to coincide (Meinecke 1908); the nation's and the citizens' identity were to grow out of what they had in common—their shared language, values, norms, and traditions.

The primacy of national identity and its association with cultural identity grew out of a long chain of events. The collapse of feudalism, the rise of secularization and urbanization, and the demise of the Austro-Hungarian and Ottoman empires, with their echoes of the Holy Roman Empire, its fluid borders, inclusivity, multinationality, and multilinguality, set the stage for the emergence of the European nation-state— exclusive, homogeneous, and territorially bounded—and made national identity "the principal surviving factor in an individual's sense of identity" (Pfaff 1993:44). The relationship of nationalism to ethnicity, two factors that together form the principal wellsprings of identity, is reflected in their etymology: ethnicity (from the Greek *etnikos*) came to English via the Latin *nasci, natio* 'something born.'

The nature of identity

Identity can be examined in terms of its basic components.

Human agency

Identity requires a minimal pair—a self and an other (whether an individual or a group)—because identity is not only a statement of who a group *is* and what it identifies itself *as,* it is also a statement that expresses *to* someone an identification *with* and difference *from* an other on some grounds.

A medium

Identity is conveyed through something perceivable: an object, an act, a music, an art, a language, a banner that serves as label, insignia, diacritic, or emblem. These tag a human group and, in the literal sense of identity as sameness or oneness, they in turn assume the identity of the group. Those who pledge allegiance to the American flag proclaim their American identity. The piece of cloth with stars and stripes imprinted on it is rarely described as such; it is identified as an *American* flag.

Some objects or forms of behavior mark identity more readily than others. Language, for example, is highly indicative because it penetrates all areas of daily life and because it has referential meanings. Music, less pervasive in daily life than language, more flexible and manipulable as a vehicle of or instrument for meaning, is more ambiguous as a marker. It therefore requires more deliberate action from human agents, more interventions—from history, from language, from convention—to fulfill its assigned function. Thus, the effectiveness of national anthems to symbolize national identity, for example, is enhanced by their texts, usually patriotic in nature. The French identity of tunes that have been used for decades in Louisiana is reinforced by historical evidence of French origins. And convention has cemented the association of certain songs with certain affiliations—"Happy Days Are Here Again" with the Democratic political party, for example.

The tango is frequently identified as Vietnamese by Vietnamese at their New Year's Day celebrations in the United States; it is identified as Latin American in most other American contexts.

The components and their use

Identity presupposes human action motivated by perceptions of likeness or difference that must be communicated to others through perceivable means. Thus, the power of a jingle or a musical phrase to identify a product, a radio station, or a television program is not inherent; it is bestowed by convention. Identity always implicates the means by which it is communicated, the people who use them, and the circumstances of their use.

In actual usage, the components of identity vary in emphasis, form, and function. The choice of markers may be arbitrary or based on iconic or onomatopoetic relations; their customary meanings may undergo radical alteration even when the forms do not, and the perceptions of self and other may change. Identity, therefore, as recent scholarship has demonstrated, is responsive to changes in context, is socially negotiated, and is reinventable.

Variability in emphasis

Sometimes the focus is on markers. The singing of a national anthem and the raising of a flag at the Olympic Games, for example, signal the national identity of a victorious athlete or team. Sometimes the emphasis is on ascription, on who people say they are or on what identity they impute to the things they create. The significance now given to ascription is partly an acknowledgment of the multiple identities that contemporary life imposes and requires. Depending on context, for example, immigrants may insist on their American-ness, or they may insist on their dual identity as hyphenated Americans. The tango is frequently identified as Vietnamese by Vietnamese at their New Year's Day celebrations in the United States; it is identified as Latin American in most other American contexts.

The current emphasis on ascription is also a corrective to earlier practices in which outsiders to a group unilaterally imputed—or denied—identity. "Negro," for example, was a label imposed on African Americans by colonialists without the consent of those they were labeling. It ascribed to "Negroes" an identity based on race while denying them an identity as American citizens.

Often the emphasis is on the grounds for differentiation (figure 1). In the first decades of the nineteenth century, for example, religion emerged as such a ground when an influx of Irish Roman Catholics disturbed the complacency of the mostly English Protestant resident population. Acts of violence such as the burning of Catholic churches underscored the stigmatization of Catholicism. Slavery, which began to take root in America in the earliest days of colonialism, became a dramatic and, to a large extent, defining issue in American political and social life before the Civil War. It also became a basis for identification with—or differentiation from—its supporters, a development that found expression in a large body of songs exemplified by *Slave Songs of the United States,* published in 1867 by the abolitionists William Francis Allen, Charles Pickard Ware, and Lucy McKim Garrison. The deepening focus on gender as basis for claiming an identity and the use of music for that purpose are reflected in the burgeoning literature on the subject—for example, Jane Bowers and Judith Tick (1986), Marcia J. Citron (1993), Richard Keeling (1989), and Ellen Koskoff (1987).

FIGURE I Events in American history that coincide with shifts in emphasis on components of identity—from an emphasis on difference (from) to an emphasis on sameness (as) or identification (with).

Period (approximate)	Events tending to emphasize differentiation from	Events tending to emphasize likeness (identification as)
1776–1814		Nation building; creates a unitary identity based on ideology.
1815–1860	Sectional tensions arising from large influx of Irish Catholic immigrants lead to religion-based differentiation.	
1861–1879		Participation of immigrants in support of the Union during the Civil War reduces suspicion of the foreign-born. Subsequent need for labor in the industrializing nation supports tolerance.
1880–1929	Rising animosities based on nationality and race are manifested in the Chinese Exclusion Act (1882) and National Origins Act (1924). The melting pot concept that supported Americanization as Anglo-Saxonization becomes popular.	
1930s–1940s		Depression forces the nation to focus on bread-and-butter issues. The need to win in World War II reinforces the need for unity, and victory feeds national pride.
1950s–1980s	The reemergence of animosities based on race and national origin is manifested in civil rights and Black Power movements. The influx of non-Caucasian immigrants and refugees made possible by the reform of immigration laws, the undermining of confidence due to the Vietnam War, and Watergate add impetus to differentiation.	

Variability in form and function

Changes in form and/or function of one or more of the components reflect the dynamic nature of identity. "We Shall Overcome," a song widely recognized as a symbol of the civil rights movement and the Black Power movement, was originally a Christian church hymn. In 1972, in New York City's East Harlem, its function was broadened to become a rallying cry, sung weekly at processions organized to mobilize the community in its fight against drugs. Subordinating their differences in ethnic identity to their shared identity as members of the East Harlem community, African Americans and Latinos who organized and attended the rallies sang the strophes of "We Shall Overcome" alternately in English and in Spanish to signal their unity and dedication to a common cause. In each of these cases, the same song, with some modification, was used by different groups for different though related purposes in different contexts. Similarly, the West Indian carnival in New York, with its elaborate costumes, steel drum bands, and dances that hark back to the Caribbean homeland, is recognized by both the West Indian and non–West Indian communities as distinctively West Indian in form despite some fundamental changes in function. Once a pre-Lenten event, the carnival is now both a proud symbol of West Indian identity and part of West Indians' celebration of Labor Day, an American national holiday.

Identity recapitulated

Identity is a concept that changes in the way it is manifested, studied, and interpreted. It implies diversity—at the very least, a self and an other. It implies interaction—at the very least, a self acknowledging and being acknowledged by an other. It implies an object or behavior, something perceivable, through which the message of identity may be conveyed and understood. And it implies conventions and dynamic processes that habitually engage these components with each other on the basis of perceived likeness and difference.

MUSIC AND IDENTITY: A HISTORICAL PERSPECTIVE

From a contemporary ethnomusicological point of view, the study of music as a dimension of identity delineation or construction requires an account of music as both an object or act that marks the identity of something else *and* an object or act that itself has been assigned or partakes of an identity. Until the first half of the twentieth century, musical scholarship concentrated on the study of existing forms rather than on the processes and circumstances of identity construction.

Late-nineteenth- and early-twentieth-century scholarship

From the European or Eurocentric point of view, American music hardly existed in the late nineteenth and early twentieth centuries. F. L. Ritter, in the first comprehensive history of American music, *Music in America* (1883), noted "the utter absence of national people's poetry and music in America" (quoted in Chase 1987 [1955]:xvi). As late as 1931, John Tasker Howard devoted one of eighteen chapters of *Our American Music* to "folk music." The chapter also dealt with Native American music and composers who used American folk materials. All levels of academic and political discourse were permeated by the concepts of national identity and of Darwinian evolution that played prominent roles in European intellectual life during the nineteenth century.

Despite the historically grounded differences between the European and the American nation-states, those concepts dominated studies of culture and identity in the United States. Their penetration into studies of musical culture came in no small measure from their compatibility with ethnomusicology's early choice of subject matter: so-called simple, self-contained, homogeneous societies with a degree of stability that made them seem static and with a degree of insularity that made them seem free— or capable of being seen as free—from external influences. Identity could therefore be taken as immanent, internally generated, unitary, and shaped independently of forces from outside the society or the group. From this point of view, a cultural label used to identify a society or group is equally and automatically applicable to its music.

Early studies

In the United States, these practices and intellectual predilections were taken to be particularly sustainable in studies of Native Americans. Unlike the plantation settings where African slaves had lived in close proximity to their Anglo-European masters, the reservations were believed to have allowed the Native Americans to live in relative isolation and to maintain many of their traditional ways. Thus there was a substantial body of work on Native American cultures, all of it by outsiders. Identity, assumed to be a property inherent to the music makers and users, was not an issue in studies of music. Scholars concentrated on description (using Western European frames of reference and terminology), transcription (in Western notation), and collection (in manuscript form or on wax cylinders). Most of the references to music were part of the ethnographic literature.

Early work on Native American music was exemplified by Theodore Baker's on Seneca songs (1882) and the output of Frances Densmore who from the time she began her work with Native American music in 1895 until fifty years later devoted her efforts to collecting and documenting Native American musics. The majority of her studies were published by the Bureau of American Ethnology under the auspices of which she did the bulk of her research.

These early studies responded to a general interest in the exotic and to an interest in the location of so-called primitive and less civilized peoples within an evolutionary framework. The underlying question was What features identified them as such in the rank order of cultures worldwide? Subsequently, the emphasis on describing, collecting, and documenting that continued well into the twentieth century became a response to the perception that these cultures were threatened by extinction. In this respect, scholarly focus shifted from the evolutionary ranking of cultures in general to the study of specific ways of life in specific locations. Identity was an assumption, not an object of investigation.

Musical identity and cultural relativism

In the last quarter of the nineteenth century, work began that was to change significantly the way culture and musical identity would come to be regarded. Spearheading the activities was the anthropologist Franz Boas, who undertook an intensive pioneering field-based investigation into the culture of the Eskimo, the Kwakiutl, the Salish, and other groups in British Columbia. His approach was holistic, based on the premise that a full account of a culture cannot exclude its music, art, language, and other forms of expressive culture, as these reflect a people's mental processes. One of the greatest contributions that came out of the Kwakiutl studies in particular (most comprehensively presented in *Kwakiutl Ethnography,* published posthumously in 1966) was what eventually came to be known as cultural relativism, a view that emphasized the uniqueness and incommensurability of cultures. It had an especially strong impact on cultural identity because it loosened the then tight grip of the evolutionary point of view. Freed from the constraints of ranking, cultures could be investigated in their own terms, and, with the help of intensive fieldwork, their special character or their identity could be made manifest through culture traits: those elements and patterns that distinguish one culture from another and make it unique. Music, established as a cultural product, was thus recontextualized, its universe broadened from that of sheer sound to that of social act. As object of investigation, it became not just an autonomous structure with its own internal logic but an entity dependent upon culture for its meaning and function.

It would be some time before the full impact of this insight would be felt in studies of music and identity, but a new framework had clearly been put in place. The work of Alice Cunningham Fletcher (1884) and her collaborators, John Comfort Fillmore and Francis La Flesche, on the Omaha (1893) and of Jesse Walter Fewkes on the Passamaquoddy (1890) and the Zuni (1891) bear the marks of Boas's influence in their concern for fieldwork and for describing the music in context. But it was Boas's student George Herzog, trained in both musicology and anthropology, who most clearly illustrated the use of musical traits, the analog of culture traits, in identifying a music and, subsequently, a musical style. In his study of the Ghost Dance songs (1935), he charted and tabulated the features of his musical corpus, using and adapting terms borrowed from Western European art music (scales, melodic range, phrase, finals) to arrive at what was distinctive in this musical repertoire.

In time, Herzog realized that traits, singly or in sets, could not be confined within the boundaries of a culture group. His investigation of the distribution of traits across cultural boundaries, represented by "The Yuman Musical Style" (1928), laid the groundwork for what in the middle of the twentieth century was to become known as the musical area, the typological equivalent of anthropology's culture area.

Music, established as a cultural product, was thus recontextualized, its universe broadened from that of sheer sound to that of social act.

The persistence of old paradigms

Boas's innovations and insights, however, did not replace earlier assumptions about culture and identity; they complemented, competed with, or paralleled other ways of thinking. Studies of music as acoustic phenomenon continued to predominate, as did the assumption that the identity of the music derived a priori from the identity—presumed to be monolithic—of its national or tribal culture of origin. What needed to be discovered, therefore, were the historical evidence of provenance to establish lineage, correspondences between past and present forms that authenticated and corroborated the assumption of identity, and features intrinsic to the music that made it unique. These methodological imperatives help explain the importance given to studying "the folk" as repositories of national identity and the preference for villages or relatively insular settings as fieldwork sites.

Until the first half of the twentieth century, musical scholarship in the United States dealt with the country's diversity in terms of three major groups: the Anglo-American, the Native American, and the African American. Collecting music mainly for purposes of documentation and cataloging followed along these lines. Studies of Anglo-American music focused on ballads and folk songs, the British provenance of which gave their materials the kind of legitimacy and authenticity that were important considerations at the time. D. K. Wilgus's *Anglo-American Folksong Scholarship since 1898* (1959) exemplifies these efforts. In 1910, John Lomax began collecting cowboy songs (then considered American folk songs), and in the mid-1930s he expanded his activities to collect African American songs with the help of his son, Alan. Native American groups and their music continued to be studied as isolates; music continued to be treated either as ethnographic fact or as object of musicological analysis, but seldom if ever both.

The music of African Americans posed difficult problems. In a climate in which identity was still thought of in terms of oneness with the forms of a traditional homeland and with authenticated descent from a specific cultural lineage, ascription of African American identity was contingent on extricating the African from the American. But this was rendered extremely difficult if not impossible by the interpenetration of the musics brought about by the historical and political contexts within which Anglo- and African Americans had interacted since the days of slavery, as well as by the character of their contact, first in plantation settings and subsequently in densely populated urban areas. In the beginning, evidence of African origin depended on those who had had direct experience with Africa and who identified the music on the basis of what they associated with West African traits. But with the emergence of such forms as minstrel songs, spirituals, ragtime, gospel, blues, and jazz, problems of identity increased in complexity. Nonetheless, the collection of music called Afro-American or Negro folk song proceeded apace even as isolated efforts such as that by Henry Edward Krehbiel (1913) called for a more "scientific" investigation.

Others outside of the three major groups were treated marginally in the formulation of a national identity. Restrictive immigration policies, the ideal of assimilation, and the melting pot metaphor continued to hold sway. To a very large extent, the first half of the twentieth century was an extension of the last decade of the nineteenth.

World War II and its aftermath

For a brief period during World War II, there arose in the United States a conscious effort to represent national identity as monolithic rather than as a composite with culturally distinct parts. In the international arena in which the war had thrust the country, the United States was to be recognized not through its internal diversity but through contrast with the non-American others. To this end, the U.S. government encouraged studies of the "American character." In one such effort, *And Keep Your Powder Dry: An Anthropologist Looks at Americans* (1942), Margaret Mead took the cultural relativism of her mentor, Franz Boas, and combined it with ideas from Sigmund Freud's studies of personality. Similarly, Gilbert Chase's *America's Music,* first published in 1955, sought a holistic treatment of its subject matter. The book was conceived at about the time when the author, working at the Library of Congress in Washington, D.C., came under the influence of Charles Seeger, who was working on America's folk music with his wife, Ruth, and the Lomaxes (John and Alan). Chase's characterization of American music was also a reaction to Oscar Sonneck's observation that Americans writing about music do so not as Americans but as Europeans looking for continuities with Europe. Chase argued that American music was unique and demanded to be studied as such.

Irving Sablosky embarked on a similar course when he sought to discover what was "peculiarly American about the music composed and performed in the United States." The volume *American Music* (1969), part of a series on American civilization edited by Daniel Boorstin, was the result.

Attempts to formulate a generalized national identity and its musical counterpart in the United States, however, were short-lived. The culture contacts hastened and intensified by World War II helped raise serious questions about the limits of cultural relativism. With the war won, the country's attention was drawn once again to differences within. It would take time for these developments to have an impact on musical scholarship, which continued to rely heavily on oneness or continuity with culture of origin as a necessary condition for the legitimation of identity. But it was no longer possible to ignore the inevitability of variation on traditional forms.

Postwar perspectives on the study of music and identity

Anglo-American studies, dominated by studies of ballads that had been defined largely in terms of their historic British provenance, sought new insights by looking not only for the earliest versions that were presumed most likely the closest to the original but for variants that had evolved in the North American environment. The towering work on this subject was Bertrand H. Bronson's *The Traditional Tunes of the Child Ballads with Their Texts, According to the Extant Records of Great Britain and America* (1959–1972). Charles Seeger, in his highly detailed study of the ballad "Barbara Allen" (1966), discussed identity in the context of a tune family according to which a tune's identity is established through its relation to a "skeleton"—a reconstruction of the tune's essential features arrived at through an analysis of all possible variants. This was a contribution both to the "classificatory and naming" function of identity and identification and to the "very concrete sensory phenomenon" that serves the purpose of recognition.

Native American studies benefited from the growing implementation of the concept of music in cultural context. David McAllester's *Enemy Way Music* (1954), Alan Merriam's *Ethnomusicology of the Flathead Indians* (1967), and, a few decades later, Marcia Herndon's work on the Cherokee Ballgame cycle (1971), Bruno Nettl's *Blackfoot Indian Musical Thought* (1989), and Judith Vander's *Songprints* (1988) exemplified this trend. The musical area concept, adapted from anthropology's culture area, offered new grounds for identifying music that transcended tribal, cultural, and geopolitical boundaries. Given incipient form by George Herzog and explored by Helen Heffron Roberts in *Musical Areas in Aboriginal North America* (1970 [1936]), the concept was treated more fully in Bruno Nettl's *North American Indian Musical Styles* (1954) and its revised version (1969).

It was in the realm of African American music that issues of identity raised the most provocative questions. Melville Herskovits (*The Myth of the Negro Past,* 1958 [1941]) and, subsequently, his former student Richard Waterman (1967), concerned themselves with Africanisms or musical survivals as markers of Africanness in African American music. But their studies departed from the framework of cultural relativism by taking change as a basic premise and by looking for identity markers after, in the course of, despite, or as a consequence of interaction with other cultural groups.

Toward the fourth quarter of the twentieth century, the pendulum of American musical identity studies finally began to swing away from both its European orientation and the view of identity as primordial. The exclusivity imposed by the model of the European nation-state and manifested in such legislation as the Exclusion Act of 1882, which restricted the entry of Asians to the United States, and the Immigration Act of 1924, which imposed quotas based on national origins and showed its exclusionary bias by favoring those "more readily assimilable" (U.S. Senate 1950:455), was reversed by the immigration reform legislation of 1964 and 1965. This development let loose the forces of ethnic consciousness that had been rising since the second quarter of the twentieth century, when a large number of African Americans migrated from the South to the urban North. The return of African Americans who had served during World War II helped consolidate African American political power, giving impetus to the civil rights movement and the Black Power movement of the 1960s. Latino migration, which had begun with a trickle at the beginning of the twentieth century, swelled significantly, impelled by political and economic conditions in Latin America and the Caribbean. The success of the Black Power movement encouraged Native Americans and Latinos to follow suit, giving rise to the pan-Indian and pan-Latino movements. Intra- and intergroup differences notwithstanding, the movements demonstrated the negotiability of ethnic boundaries on all fronts: in the arts, in music, in politics, and in social relations.

World War II had brought unprecedented numbers of Americans in the military service face to face with cultural diversity abroad. A few years after the war, that range of diversity arrived in the United States in the form of new immigrants and refugees. If the cumulative effects of these events had not sufficed, the fragmenting effects of the Vietnam War on American society compelled the country to look beyond assimilation for a social dynamic that would lend cohesion to its diversity.

As globalization, transnationalism, and the movement of people, goods, and ideas gained momentum, replicating worldwide features of diversity that had long been quintessentially American, the paradigm shift took hold. What Ulf Hannerz had called "the replication of uniformity," so dependent on virtually indelible, fixed forms, gave way to the variability and negotiability that are presupposed by "the organization of difference" (Barth 1969; Hannerz 1990). Identity could no longer be thought of as static, unitary, or immutable; it had become multiplex, emergent, and dynamic, contingent not only on the changing needs of the identifying subject but on the Other from which the subject seeks to be distinguished. As Fredrik Barth had argued decades earlier, common culture was the consequence of, not a precondition to, ethnic group organization (1969:11). The growing confidence in the emergent nature of American musical identity was given voice by Richard Crawford in the foreword to the third edition of Chase's *America's Music:*

[T]he essence of American musical life . . . lay not only in those branches that emulated Old World models but also in the complexity and disorderedness of the whole—in short, in the *discontinuities* of the New World's musical life with the Old. It is precisely in the author's perception of America's *difference* from Europe that the viewpoint of *America's Music* is rooted. (1987 [1955]; emphasis in the original)

This was one of the most forceful signals that in musical scholarship, too, the replication of uniformity had begun to give way to the organization of diversity.

Vestiges of identity as "the 'same' [*idem*] that varies," as Chambers (1994:118) described it, remain in such works as Keyes (1996) and Walser (1995), which trace elements of rap music to African roots. But a trend toward examining the "doubleness" inherent in genres from jazz to salsa to *pizmon*—doubleness in terms of having a dual cultural identity—which does no violence to and in fact enhances musical structural integration, has clearly emerged in works such as that of Ingrid Monson (1996) on jazz and jazz musicians and Kay Kaufman Shelemay (1999) on Syrian American Jews.

Pluralism: beyond ideology

The tension between the *unum* and the *pluribus* in the American motto *"E pluribus unum"* has always been a fundamental dialectic in American life. On the level of ideology pluralism reigned, but its realization has always been problematic. Changing metaphors have reflected the difficulties. The homogenizing melting pot that celebrates oneness induced by assimilation has given way to the mosaic, the salad bowl, and the rainbow. The diversity that these recent metaphors celebrate finds expression everywhere: in ethnic festivals, in performances of music and dance, and in other types of cultural expression that are public manifestations of ethnic pride (figure 2). Government entities such as the National Endowment for the Arts in the United States encourage the conservation, growth, and practice of musical traditions from all of the nation's constituent cultural groups. Government recognition of outstanding musicians from these groups is exemplified by the National Heritage Awards, which gives each of them the stamp of American identity. The creative energy that the embrace of diversity has released has legitimized and encouraged such hybrid forms as *salsoul*, Korean rap, and Latin jazz.

The continuing influx of new immigrants and the constantly changing social milieu continually call for new ways of reconciling aspirations toward oneness and the strong desire on the part of immigrant groups to perpetuate their cultural identity (figure 3). The parvenu–pariah dichotomy, for example, used by Hannah Arendt in her exploration of German Jewish identity, has been applied to behavior of all kinds,

FIGURE 2   A Tet (Vietnamese New Year) celebration in Chinatown, New York City. On the left is that quintessential symbol of American identity, the Statue of Liberty, with the flag of precommunist Vietnam streaming from it. Just to the right of it is the American flag. The proceedings are being stage-lit and the sounds mixed and regulated with the technology seen in the foreground. Photo by Adelaida Reyes, January 1990.

The homogenizing melting pot that celebrates one-ness induced by assimilation has given way to the mosaic, the salad bowl, and the rainbow. The diversity that these recent metaphors celebrate finds expression everywhere: in ethnic festivals, in performances of music and dance, and in other types of cultural expression that are public manifestations of ethnic pride.

FIGURE 3   The Saigon City Mall in Houston, Texas, with the skyscrapers of downtown Houston in the background. Two of the street signs are in English (Milam and Drew) and two are in Vietnamese. Photo courtesy Kay K. Shelemay. June 1999.

artistic and otherwise. The parvenu is said to court the acceptance of the larger society by sacrificing distinctiveness; the pariah insists on that distinctiveness at the cost of remaining an outsider (Rothstein 1999:9). Music performers from African American rappers to Latin American global pop stars to American opera singers who record popular songs walk the tightrope between their dual identities, at times leaning more heavily on one side than on the other, at other times creating coherence out of their dichotomous identities.

American tunes such as "I'm a Yankee Doodle Dandy," "Take Me Out to the Ballgame," and "Ol' Man River" are sometimes used in the Jewish ritual of Simhat Torah—a practice met with consternation by some and delight by other members of the community—as a reflection of the struggle to integrate the historical Jewish identity with the contemporary American one (Summit 1993). Cajuns who wish to signal their difference from non-Cajun Americans sing songs in Cajun French even when the language is no longer spoken or even comprehended, whereas for those whose preferred identification is with the larger American society, the choice of repertoire is country music in English (Emoff 1998).

Disciplinary repercussions

By the 1970s, the ineradicability of cultural diversity in complex societies and its significance in identity construction had become canonical in virtually all of the social sciences. In the musical world, the reality of multiple ascribed identities has become manifest in the many different musical repertoires that have become part not only of daily life but also of academic offerings. Competence in more than one musical language became increasingly common. Klezmer musicians one day may be jazz performers or symphony orchestra members the next.

These developments slowly began to be reflected in ethnomusicological fieldwork, data gathering, and method as a whole. By the last quarter of the twentieth century, the near-exclusiveness of fieldwork in relatively insular locations where orderliness was equated with homogeneity gave way to fieldwork in urban areas where diversity is at the core of social and musical life and where heterogeneity is functional and systemic.

The linked issues of (im)migration, diversity, and musical identity have given additional impetus to the integration of the musical and the ethnographic in ethnomusicological explanation. The admissibility of hybridity as a valid subject for investigation and the negotiability of cultural boundaries have subverted the need to keep groups conceptually insulated from each other. The positive value now assigned to diversity and the reality of America's growing cultural heterogeneity have made obsolescent the compartmentalization of American musical identity into Anglo-American, African American, and Native American.

The old pattern of immigration, which involved leaving a homeland for good or for long periods of time before contact could be reestablished, has been replaced by a pattern of frequent contacts made possible by modern transportation and communication facilities. The result is a further multiplication of identities, with the option of reinforcing whichever promise to be socially effective. The resettlement process has thus become more complex and a sense of belonging more elusive, making it necessary continually to "redefine what it means to be [or to become] American" (Sontag and Dugger 1998:28).

Problems are being reformulated. The notions of home, of culture of origin, of place—in contradistinction to space as sites of identity construction—are repeatedly calling for reinterpretation. Ironically, however, these notions, so central to ethnomusicological research, were not subjected to the scrutiny they deserved until two factors, one helped along by the other, made their impact felt: the rise of ethnic consciousness in the 1960s and the legitimation in the early 1970s of doing fieldwork in one's "own backyard."

Ethnicity

Like *identity,* the term *ethnicity* seems to have been resuscitated. Glazer and Moynihan (1975) report that it did not appear in the *Oxford English Dictionary* until its 1972 *Supplement* recorded usage of the term for the first time by David Riesman in 1953. At about the same time in the 1950s, identity was (re)discovered or reconceptualized by Erik H. Erikson, who argued that identity and identity crisis were born of immigration and Americanization (Gleason 1980). It is in a modern sense, therefore, that Gleason claims ethnicity to be "a dimension of American identity" and Thernstrom (1980) contends that it is "a central theme—perhaps the central theme—of American history." In 1993, Moynihan declared the nation "the highest form of ethnic group denoting a subjective state of mind . . . but also, almost always, an objective claim to forms of territorial autonomy" (1993:4–5).

The foundation of what came to be known as new ethnicity was laid by Fredrik Barth in the introduction to *Ethnic Groups and Boundaries: The Social Organization of Difference* (1969). He argued that ethnic identity is not a matter of cultural form or of the personnel who constitute ethnic group membership. Like other types of identity, ethnic identity calls for cultural markers to signal membership, but such markers are not where ethnicity resides. Rather, identity is defined by the boundary created as a consequence of groups' differentiating themselves from one another on grounds that group members claim are cultural. This allows ethnic identity to persist despite changes in the cultural forms used as markers or changes in the individuals who constitute the ethnic group membership; herein lies ethnicity's particular applicability to the rapidly changing, largely immigrant population of the United States and the dynamics of group interaction. The combination of emotional ties engendered by invoking cultural validation and their instrumental (in the sociological sense of functional or utilitarian) efficacy holds together ethnic group members and makes ethnicity a powerful cohesive as well as potentially explosive force.

Implications for ethnomusicological field work

These changes in theoretical framework were inevitably felt on the level of fieldwork. Ethnic identity now required study not only of the forms and the people to whom identity was being ascribed but also of those who were presumed to be the Others. Markers did not have to be primordial or authenticated by historical evidence; their status as cultural could be imputed. Identity construction required at least two groups who could not be isolated from each other by predetermined boundaries; it was their interaction based on their perception of difference from each other that created the boundaries that define identity. All these called for drastic departures from practices that ethnomusicologists had held dear: fieldwork in simple, insular societies with predetermined boundaries; the marginal or nonexistent Other; the uncompromising authenticity of what can be considered cultural forms. But they also freed ethnomusicologists to do fieldwork in their own backyards, there finally to study identity in the context of American cultural diversity.

Ethnicity and ethnomusicology

Until the 1970s, the label *ethnic* was applied to the musical analog of the U.S. Census Bureau's definition of immigrants as "the foreign-born or their children." Whether those musics were being practiced in their native environments in the context of their own cultures and were being heard in the United States only through sound recordings or special concert performances, or whether they were being practiced in the United States as part of the American mosaic did not matter. Recordings of the music of Pygmies from the Ituri forest were as likely as the New York Puerto Rican *bombas* and *plenas* to be called ethnic music. And although by this time ethnomusicologists had begun to work in urban areas, the prevalent approach simulated what Barth had called isolationist—treating groups as though they were self-contained.

In the late 1970s, efforts were made to incorporate social science insights on ethnicity into ethnomusicological thinking (see, for example, Reyes Schramm 1979), but the use of the term *ethnic music* continued to suffer from confusion. Often it was taken to be interchangeable with *folk music*. As late as 1989, John Blacking saw the need to challenge "the myth of 'ethnic music'," seeing the label as an "obnoxious and derogatory term" for something that is presumed to be the product of some "folk collective" (Blacking 1989). But the intensification of work in urban areas with their inevitably heterogeneous populations made the interaction between cultural groups increasingly difficult to ignore; indeed, sociology and anthropology had established such diversity as a defining attribute of urban areas. Musical data that corroborated this finding began to accumulate, but the methodological imperatives suggested by the data found their way more readily into ethnomusicological work outside North America.

Early efforts in the United States were understandably tentative. Joseph Blum's article on salsa (1978) argued that this Latin popular "ethnic" genre (he used the quotation marks around the term) was a proper subject for ethnomusicological investigation. Two volumes of *Selected Reports in Ethnomusicology*, the first on European immigrant groups (Porter 1978) and the second on Asian musics in the United States (Jairazbhoy and de Vale 1985), though not dealing with these groups methodologically as ethnic groups, indicated the status of ethnic music studies until the 1980s. Data gathered by Linda Fujie from a Japanese Buddhist group in New York, as well as data from New York City's East Harlem, were interpreted in terms of ethnicity in Reyes

Schramm (1979). Recent works that exemplify the growing interest in the music of ethnic groups and issues of identity are Manuel Peña's *The Texas-Mexican Conjunto* (1985), Jane Sugarman's study of the Prespa Albanians (1989) in the United States and Canada, and Paula Savaglio's article on Polish Americans in Detroit (1996). Mark Slobin's "small musics living in big systems" (1993) and the ways in which such musics get designated as "ours" or "theirs" carry echoes or fingerprints of ethnic identification. Almost imperceptibly, the term *ethnic music* in ethnomusicological studies of groups in the United States entered the arena of studies of identity. Ethnic music came to be understood as the music of groups that distinguish themselves from others within a larger society through the use of markers perceived to be cultural.

The contemporary situation

To illustrate ethnomusicology's relative neglect of identity as object of study, Barbara Krader in 1987 noted that the term *identity* did not appear in the text or index of Alan Merriam's *Anthropology of Music* (1964) or Bruno Nettl's *Study of Ethnomusicology: Twenty-nine Issues and Concepts* (1983). The reverse is now true: identity as something ascribed to music and/or as something that music serves to ascribe to something or someone else is fast becoming ubiquitous. Patterns and trends are not yet clearly discernible, but perhaps indicative of where scholarship on American identity might be headed are two recent articles. One, by Thomas Turino (1999), elevates identity to a higher level of abstraction and focuses on the nature of identity construction itself, using Charles Sanders Peirce's theory of signs to explore the semiotic character of both identity formation and music. The other, by the critic Michael Kimmelman (1999), addresses the problem of American identity specifically; although he is writing on art in general, his assessments apply to music as well:

> Throughout our history, the notion has prevailed that there could be a distinctly American art, as if a particular form or style might encapsulate the nation's identity. Assimilation was an underlying assumption. . . . But . . . we're so diverse culturally: the goal of a synthetic American art remains illusory because the idea of an American identity is, in the end, an illusion. . . . Diversity is a prevailing theme in American art at this moment.

The pendulum appears to have swung all the way to the other side. American national identity has broken loose from the expectations raised by the European model of the nation-state, sameness or homogeneity has made way for diversity, and pluralism has become a defining feature of the American musical scene. Whether the idea of an American identity in the arts is indeed an illusion is now open to fresh debate.

REFERENCES

Allen, William Francis, Charles Pickard Ware, and Lucy McKim Garrison. 1951 [1867]. *Slave Songs of the United States.* New York: Peter Smith.

Baker, Theodore. 1882. *Über die Musik der nord-amerikanischen Wilden.* Leipzig: Breitkopf u. Härtel.

Barth, Fredrik. 1969. Introduction to *Ethnic Groups and Boundaries: The Social Organization of Difference,* ed. Fredrik Barth, 9–38. Boston: Little, Brown.

Blacking, John. 1989. "Challenging the Myth of 'Ethnic' Music: First Performances of a New Song in an African Oral Tradition, 1961." *Yearbook for Traditional Music* 21:17–24.

Blum, Joséph. 1978. "Problems of Salsa Research." *Ethnomusicology* 12(1): 137–149.

Boas, Franz. 1966. *Kwakiutl Ethnography,* ed. Helen Codere. Chicago: University of Chicago Press.

Boorstin, Daniel. 1958–1974. *The Americans.* 3 vols.: *The Colonial Experience* (New York: Random House, 1958); *The National Experience* (New York: Random House, 1973); *The Democratic Experience* (New York: Vintage Books, 1974).

Bowers, Jane, and Judith Tick, eds. 1986. *Women Making Music: The Western Art Tradition, 1150–1950.* Urbana: University of Illinois Press.

Bronson, B. H. 1959–1972. *The Traditional Tunes of the Child Ballads with Their Texts, According to the Extant Records of Great Britain and America.* Princeton, N.J.: Princeton University Press.

Chambers, Iain. 1994. *Migrancy, Culture, Identity.* London and New York: Routledge.

Chase, Gilbert. 1987 [1955]. *America's Music: From the Pilgrims to the Present.* 3rd ed. Urbana: University of Illinois Press.

Citron, Marcia J. 1993. *Gender and the Musical Canon.* Cambridge and New York: Cambridge University Press.

Eaklor, Vicki L. 1988. *American Antislavery Songs: A Collection and Analysis.* New York and Westport, Conn.: Greenwood Press.

Emoff, Ron. 1998. "A Cajun Poetics of Loss and Longing." *Ethnomusicology* 42(2):283–301.

Erikson, Erik H. 1950. "Reflections on the American Identity." In *Childhood and Society,* 237–283. New York: Norton.

Fewkes, J. Walter. 1890. "A Contribution to Passamaquoddy Folk-lore. *Journal of American Folklore* 1:257–280.

———. 1891. "A Few Summer Ceremonials at Zuni Pueblo." *Journal of American Ethnology and Archaeology* 1:1–91.

Fletcher, Alice C. 1884. "The Wawan or Pipe Dance of the Omahas." *Annual Report,* 308–333. Cambridge, Mass.: Peabody Museum of American Archaeology and Ethnology, Harvard University.

Fletcher, Alice C., Francis La Flesche, and John C. Fillmore. 1893. *A Study of Omaha Indian Music.* Peabody Museum Archaeological and Ethnological Papers, vol. 1, no. 5. Cambridge, Mass.: Peabody Museum of American Archaeology and Ethnology, Harvard University.

Glazer, Nathan, and Daniel P. Moynihan, eds. 1975. *Ethnicity: Theory and Experience.* Cambridge, Mass.: Harvard University Press.

Gleason, Philip. 1980. "American Identity and Americanization." In *Harvard Encyclopedia for American Ethnic Groups,* ed. Stephan Thernstrom, Ann Orlov, and Oscar Handlin, 31–58. Cambridge, Mass.: Harvard University Press.

Greenfeld, Liah. 1992. *Nationalism: Five Roads to Modernity.* Cambridge, Mass.: Harvard University Press.

Hannerz, Ulf. 1990. "Cosmopolitans and Locals in World Culture." In *Global Culture, Nationalism, Globalization and Modernity,* ed. Mike Featherstone. London: Sage.

Herndon, Marcia. 1971. "The Cherokee Ballgame Cycle: An Ethnomusicologist's View." *Ethnomusicology* 15(3):339–352.

Herskovits, Melville J. 1958 [1941]. *The Myth of the Negro Past.* Boston: Beacon Press.

Herzog, George. 1928. "The Yuman Musical Style." *Journal of American Folklore* 41(160): 182–231.

———. 1935. "Plains Ghost Dance and Great Basin Music." *American Anthropologist* 37:403–419.

Howard, John Tasker. 1931. *Our American Music.* New York: Thomas Y. Crowell.

Jairazbhoy, Nazir, and Sue Carole de Vale, eds. 1985. *Asian Music in North America.* Vol. 6 of *Selected Reports in Ethnomusicology.* Los Angeles: University of California Press.

Keeling, Richard, ed. 1989. *Women in North American Music: Six Essays.* Bloomington: Indiana University Press.

Keyes, Cheryl L. 1996. "At the Crossroads: Rap Music and Its African Nexus." *Ethnomusicology* 40(2):223–248.

Kimmelman, Michael. 1999. "A Century of Art: Just How American Was It?" *The New York Times,* 18 April, 37.

Koskoff, Ellen, ed. 1987. *Women and Music in Cross-Cultural Perspective.* Westport, Conn.: Greenwood Press.

Krader, Barbara. 1987. "Slavic Folk Music: Forms of Singing and Self-Identity." *Ethnomusicology* 31(1):9–17.

Krehbiel, Henry Edward. 1913. *Afro-American Folksongs: A Study in Racial and National Music.* New York: Schirmer.

Lomax, John. 1922. *Cowboy Songs and Other Frontier Ballads.* New York: Macmillan.

McAllester, David P. 1954. *Enemy Way Music.* Cambridge, Mass.: Peabody Museum of American Archaeology and Ethnology, Harvard University.

Mead, Margaret. 1942. *And Keep Your Powder Dry: An Anthropologist Looks at America.* New York: William Morrow.

Meinecke, Friedrich. 1908. *Cosmopolitanism and the National State.* Trans. Robert B. Kimber. Princeton, N.J.: Princeton University Press.

Merriam, Alan P. 1964. *The Anthropology of Music.* Evanston, Ill.: Northwestern University Press.

———. 1967. *Ethnomusicology of the Flathead Indians.* Chicago: Aldine Press.

Monson, Ingrid. 1996. *Saying Something: Jazz Improvisation and Interaction.* Chicago: University of Chicago Press.

Moynihan, Daniel Patrick. 1993. *Pandaemonium: Ethnicity in International Politics.* New York: Oxford University Press.

Myers, Helen, ed. 1993. *Ethnomusicology: Historical and Regional Studies.* The Norton/Grove Handbooks in Music. New York: W. W. Norton.

Nettl, Bruno. 1954. *North American Indian Musical Styles.* Philadelphia: American Folklore Society.

———. 1969. "Musical Areas Reconsidered: A Critique of North American Indian Research." In *Essays in Musicology in Honor of Dragan Plamenac on his 70th Birthday,* ed. Gustav Reese and Robert Snow, 181. Pittsburgh: Pittsburgh University Press.

———. 1983. *The Study of Ethnomusicology. Twenty-nine Issues and Concepts.* Urbana: University of Illinois Press.

———. 1989. *Blackfoot Indian Musical Thought: Comparative Perspectives.* Kent, Ohio: Kent State University Press.

Peña, Manuel. 1985. *The Texas-Mexican Conjunto: History of a Working-Class Music.* Austin: University of Texas Press.

Pfaff, William. 1993. *The Wrath of Nations: Civilization and the Furies of Nationalism.* New York: Simon and Schuster.

Porter, James, ed. 1978. *Selected Reports in Ethnomusicology* 3(1). Los Angeles: University of California Press.

Reyes, Adelaida. 1999. *Songs of the Caged, Songs of the Free: Music and the Vietnamese Refugee Experience.* Philadelphia: Temple University Press.

Reyes Schramm, Adelaida. 1979. "'Ethnic Music,' the Urban Area, and Ethnomusicology." *Sociologus* 29(1):1–21.

Ritter, Frederic Louis. 1883. *Music in America.* New York: Charles Scribner & Sons.

Roberts, Helen Heffron. 1970 [1936]. *Musical Areas in Aboriginal North America.* Yale University Publications in Anthropology, no. 12. New Haven, Conn.: Yale University Press.

Rothstein, Edward. 1999. "Faced with 'Parvenu' or 'Pariah,' Ellison Settled on 'Artist.'" *The New York Times,* 15 May, B9.

Sablosky, Irving L. 1969. *American Music.* Chicago: University of Chicago Press.

Savaglio, Paula. 1996. "Polka Bands and Choral Groups: The Musical Self-Representation of Polish-Americans in Detroit." *Ethnomusicology* 40(1):35–47.

Seeger, Charles. 1966. "Versions and Variants of 'Barbara Allen.'" *Selected Reports in Ethnomusicology* 1(1)120–167. Los Angeles: University of California Press.

Shelemay, Kay Kaufman. 1999. *Let Jasmine Rain Down: Song and Remembrance Among Syrian Jews.* Chicago: University of Chicago Press.

Slobin, Mark. 1993. *Subcultural Sounds: Micromusics of the West.* Hanover & London: Wesleyan University Press.

Sontag, Deborah, and Celia W. Dugger. 1998. "The New Immigrant Tide: A Shuttle Between Worlds." *The New York Times,* 19 July, 1, 28.

Stokes, Martin, ed. 1994. *Ethnicity, Identity and Music: The Musical Construction of Place.* Oxford and Providence, R.I.: Berg.

Sugarman, Jane C. 1989. "The Nightingale and the Partridge: Singing and Gender among Prespa Albanians." *Ethnomusicology* 33(2):191–215.

Summit, Jeffrey A. 1993. "'I'm a Yankee Doodle Dandy'?: Identity and Melody at an American *Simhat Torah* Celebration." *Ethnomusicology* 37(1):41–62.

Thernstrom, Stephan. 1980. Introduction to *Harvard Encyclopedia of American Ethnic Groups,* ed. Stephan Thernstrom, Ann Orlov, and Oscar Handlin, v–x. Cambridge, Mass.: Harvard University Press.

———. 1982. Foreword to *Concepts of Ethnicity,* ed. William Petersen, Michael Novak, and Philip Gleason, v–vi. Cambridge, Mass.: The Belknap Press of Harvard University Press.

Turino, Thomas. 1999. "Signs of Imagination, Identity, and Experience: A Peircian Semiotic Theory of Music." *Ethnomusicology* 43(2):221–255.

U.S. Senate. 1950. Committee on the Judiciary. *The Immigration Systems of the United States.*

Vander, Judith. 1988. *Songprints: The Musical Experience of Five Shoshone Women.* Urbana and Chicago: University of Illinois Press.

Walser, Robert. 1995. "Rhythm, Rhyme and Rhetoric in the Music of Public Enemy." *Ethnomusicology* 39(2):193–217.

Waterman, Richard A. 1967 [1952]. "African Influence on the Music of the Americas." In *Acculturation in the Americas, Proceedings and Selected papers of the XXIXth International Congress of Americanists,* ed. S. Tax, 207–218. Chicago: University of Illinois Press.

Wilcken, Lois E. 1991. "Music Folklore among Haitians in New York: Staged Representations and the Negotiation of Identity." Ph.D. dissertation, Columbia University.

Wilgus, D. K. 1959. *Anglo-American Folksong Scholarship since 1898.* New Brunswick, N.J.: Rutgers University Press.

Zheng, Su de San. 1993. "Immigrant Music and Transnational Discourse: Chinese American Music Culture in New York City." Ph.D. dissertation, Wesleyan University.

Overview of Music in the United States
William Kearns

Ethnic Music
Religious Music
Concert Music
Theater Music
Popular Music
The Future

On looking at the breadth of the United States, although we are first impressed by its heterogeneity, at the same time we search for a core that gives us an identity as a nation. We view our music in much the same way—marveling at its many ethnicities, noting its various uses, exclaiming at its numerous types, and often wondering what makes them "American." This essay divides the various and diverse forms of American music into five large, overlapping categories: ethnic music, religious music, concert or art music, theater music, and popular music, each having its own history, aesthetics, and social context for its uses.

ETHNIC MUSIC

Most Americans are proud of having a distinct, other-than-American ancestry that blends easily with a basic political and cultural allegiance to the United States. This section deals with those ethnic musics that have had a major influence upon our entire culture [see IDENTITY, DIVERSITY, AND INTERACTION, p. 504].

Anglo and Irish American

Although colonial America was divided among several European powers, the first major immigrations were from the British Isles. They extended from the seventeenth-century Atlantic coast settlements until the large Irish influx during the mid-nineteenth century. Our major religious movements and much of our musical theater, popular, and folk music have been in tandem with those of Great Britain [see ENGLISH AND SCOTTISH MUSIC, p. 831; IRISH MUSIC, p. 842].

Anglo-American folk song

The work of Harvard professor James Francis Child (1825–1896) during the late nineteenth century in classifying over three hundred of the oldest English and Scottish popular ballads ("Barbara Allen," "Lady Isabelle and the Elf Knight," and "The Farmer's Curst Wife" are among the more popular) and the discovery somewhat later by English folk song specialist Cecil Sharp of a rich lode of these songs in the Appalachian mountain region gave the United States an important Anglo identity at the turn of the twentieth century.

FIGURE I   *Singing Cowboy,* Thomas Eakins (1844–1916), courtesy Metropolitan Museum of Art.

The Anglo-American folk tradition has made important contributions to several of our musical streams. Many of our cowboy songs are new texts set to older Anglo-American tunes. (For example, "Streets of Laredo," or "Dying Cowboy," is a parody of an eighteenth-century British song, "The Unfortunate Rake.") The folk music of other occupational groups—sailors, lumberjacks, railroaders, miners, and oil riggers—also draws heavily on Anglo sources (figure 1).

During the folk song revival of the 1950s–1960s, Bob Dylan, Joan Baez, and groups such as the Kingston Trio gave the Anglo-American repertoire a national prominence as popular music and created new songs within the musical style and subject matter. Earlier, in the 1930s and 1940s, Woody Guthrie, the Weavers, and others had influenced protest movements with this same repertoire.

Country music

Rural popular music in its various phases—hillbilly, country, and Nashville—has drawn upon the Anglo-American tradition both substantively and spiritually [see COUNTRY AND WESTERN, p. 76]. Country music is the largest popular-music genre with a persistent Anglo identification. It was born as hillbilly music in the 1920s in the same rural southern Appalachia that Cecil Sharp had mined for folk songs a few years earlier. Hillbilly, or country, music resulted from the collusion of this isolated culture with commercial recording and radio companies. At first it was considered a regional music, but commercialization and social change made it national by the 1930s. Hillbilly music soon had its stars: the Carter Family and, later, Roy Acuff and Chet Atkins representing the core Appalachian tradition; Jimmie Rodgers infusing it with blues and yodeling; Bob Wills expanding it into western and blending it with jazz; and Gene Autry and Roy Rogers providing its strong and pervasive link with cowboy movie culture.

Country music has continued to have its converts throughout the nation. The realism of many songs (dealing with broken relationships, alcohol, self-pity) and nostalgia for a rural Arcadia has an appeal to a working class with minimal formal education but a strong desire to assert feelings distinctive to their lives. Many country music fans share a political, social, and spiritual conservatism.

Country music has its own corporate structure and its own capital, Nashville, Tennessee. The name of its entertainment mecca, Grand Ole Opry, is a satirical expression tossed at elite society. Although the music itself has been buffeted by the forces of jazz, the blues, rock, and schmaltz, it manages to keep an identity reminding one of the twang of guitars, the agility of fiddles, and the nasality and hard consonant sounds of the rural voice. It also has had its own search for roots, an important one being bluegrass music. Among its pantheon of stars since World War II, those who seem most deeply imbued with its idealistic core have been Hank Williams, Patsy Cline, Bill Monroe, Merle Haggard, Willie Nelson, Waylon Jennings, Johnny Cash, Emmylou Harris, and Dwight Yoakam. It shows every indication of persisting as an important popular music.

Irish music

A major impact on our nineteenth-century popular song came from Thomas Moore's *Irish Melodies* (1808–1834), first published in England. The sentimentality and tunefulness of two of the most popular songs from that series, "The Harp That Once Thro' Tara's Halls" and "The Last Rose of Summer," is evident in the work of our major song composers such as Stephen Foster. The Irish song continued to claim its share of the mass culture, popular song market throughout the late nineteenth and early twentieth centuries, for such songs as "My Wild Irish Rose" (1899) were learned by ear and sung by many Americans, regardless of their ethnic identity.

Patriotic and popular song

The United States and the British Isles share a large body of patriotic and popular song. The tune source for our national anthem is "To Anacreon in Heaven" (1775), composed for an English gentlemen's convivial society. In the original lyrics the Greek poet Anacreon instructs the society's members to "entwine the myrtle of Venus with Bacchus's vine." Just how and why the melody composed for these words became a favorite for patriotic parodies in the United States during the Federalist era remains a mystery. Eighty-five are recorded between 1790 and 1818, among which is Francis Scott Key's "Star Spangled Banner" in 1814 (Marrocco & Gleason 1964:280). The text and tune have remained coupled as our national anthem to this day, informally before 1933 and officially thereafter by congressional action [see FOUR VIEW OF MUSIC, GOVERNMENT, AND POLITICS, p. 304]. Its numerous performances are a mirror of our changing tastes, from the lifting, waltzlike renditions of our nineteenth-century dance orchestras and brass bands to soulful embellishments by popular-music performers in today's climate of diversity.

Others of our national songs are wedded to England. The tune for "My Country 'Tis of Thee" is also the British "God Save the King (Queen)"; "Yankee Doodle," sung by British troops during the American Revolution to deride their ill-trained, hayseed adversaries, crossed the lines and became a rallying song for the Continentals. Other national songs not directly linked to England but in the Anglo tradition are Katherine Lee Bates's poem "America, the Beautiful" (1895), which by 1910 had found its permanent tune in Samuel Augustus Ward's "Materna" (1882), from the white gospel tradition; and Julia Ward Howe's "Battle Hymn of the Republic" (1862), which was set to the tune of the rather disreputable "John Brown's Body" (1861), whose previous incarnation had been a Methodist camp-meeting song, "Say Brothers, Will You Meet Us" (1858).

Hispanic American music

Early religious music

Catholic priests were an important part of the Spanish incursions into Florida, New Mexico, and California during the sixteenth through the eighteenth centuries. They not only served colonists but also proselytized Native Americans. The latter were particularly susceptible to music, and the missions echoed with both traditional and newly composed service music [see SOUTH AMERICAN, CENTRAL AMERICAN, MEXICAN, AND CARIBBEAN MUSICS, p. 717].

Influence of Latin rhythms on American music

Language has been a factor in keeping Hispanic song out of the mainstream; however, Latin dance rhythms have been an integral part of our classical and popular music from the nineteenth century forward.

New Orleans–born Louis Moreau Gottschalk (1829–1869) was one of our earliest classical composers to draw on Hispanic music. Drawing on memories of his youth and keeping his ear close to the ground during his various travels, he used such rhythms as the habeñera and tango as well as Caribbean folk song in his piano music. Many other American composers who followed, from Henry Gilbert (1868–1928; *Dance in the Place Congo*, 1906) to Aaron Copland (1900–1990; *Danzon cubano*, 1944) have drawn on Latin and the hybrid Afro-Caribbean musical cultures for at least a part of their compositional activity.

In popular music, Latin rhythms have maintained a nearly continuous presence in the face of predominant European and black influences from the late nineteenth century to today. The tango can be found in ragtime and early jazz. During the 1930s, the rumba was popularized by Latin bandleader Xavier Cugat, and by the 1940s Cuban

The salsa, from Cuba, has pushed beyond ephemeral status to typify contemporary Latin American dance music.

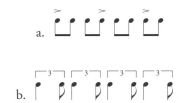

FIGURE 2   Popular American rhythms: *a*, duple-based Latin rhythm; *b*, African American swing beat.

percussion (conga) had infiltrated the leading big bands such as those of Dizzy Gillespie and Stan Kenton. The incisive, duple-based Latin rhythm, with its syncopated accents, offers a strong contrast to the rounded swing beat of African American derivation (figure 2).

The Latin music craze continued into the post–World War II years, with many dance fads such as the mambo and the cha-cha of the 1950s, the samba and bossa nova of the 1960s, reggae of the 1970s, salsa of the 1980s, and the macarena of the 1990s. Many of these are Caribbean in origin. Among them, the salsa, from Cuba, has pushed beyond ephemeral status to typify contemporary Latin American dance music. A dense, polyrhythmic texture undergirds short, ostinato melodies performed by small groups of brass, woodwinds, or voices.

Mexican American or conjunto music

Just as food from the northern provinces of Mexico became a part of American cuisine throughout the United States during the 1980s and 1990s, so music from the *norteño* Mexican folk tradition has become increasingly popular [see Tejano Musica, p. 770]. The Texas-Mexican border has been a dynamic musical area breeding *conjunto* music. The instrumentation consists of button accordion, twelve-string bass guitar, double bass, and drums. The preferred song is the *polca,* a vocal form of the polka, with its fast tempo and melody harmonized in thirds or sixths.

Popular Mexican American dance music includes the polka, schottische, waltz, mazurka, *redowa,* and cotillion, usually performed by fiddle and guitar. These titles reveal the assimilative power of much Mexican American music.

An important ballad, or storytelling, form is the *corrido.* Examples are "Homenaje a John F. Kennedy" by José Morante and "Gregorio Cortez," a ballad about an early-twentieth-century Chicano folk hero whose life and violent death symbolize the tensions along the Texas-Mexican border (Spottswood 1978: 963, 1268).

Present-day Latin popular music

The changing face of America in the early twenty-first century undoubtedly will be more inclusive of not only Latin dance music but also Latin song. Immigration projections for the United States during the next generation show the largest increase will be among the Spanish-speaking groups. The older areas of Hispanic settlement—the Southwest, Florida, New York, and Chicago—will move toward bilingualism, and some of this explosive growth will be felt in other parts of the country as well. Already increasing national interest in Hispanic popular song is evident in the sensation created by Ricky Martin and the late Latina singer Selena. Younger Hispanic Americans are interested in a melding of their own heritage with that of mainstream American popular music. For example, the singer El Vez is second-generation Mexican American and an impersonator of Elvis Presley; Marc Anthony and India, singers of a new salsa that has generous portions of rhythm and blues as well as hip-hop, have brisk record sales and can be heard over Spanish radio stations in the New York area. Similarly, *Rock en*

Español, 'Spanish rock,' can be in numerous rock styles but always with an evident Latin beat.

African American music

Second only to the Anglo tradition, African American music has asserted an enormous influence on nearly every aspect of United States' musical culture [see AFRICAN AMERICAN MUSICS, p. 571]. It is omnipresent in urban popular music, and many of its stylistic characteristics—glissandos, blue notes, incantatory melodies, improvisatory patterns—can be found even in today's Anglo-derived country music. Hispanic-Caribbean music is also heavily saturated with African characteristics, an expected outcome of the heterogeneous culture of that region [see LATIN CARIBBEAN MUSIC, p. 790]. Our classical music, to the extent that it has defined itself through ethnic characteristics, has drawn heavily on both African American repertory and style.

Unlike the European or Asian immigrant groups, who have brought much of their culture with them, blacks were forcibly separated from their African heritage. Although some African elements survived, blacks built an essentially new African American culture strongly marked by their subordinate social condition as slaves. Their speech became a dialect of the prevailing English tongue; their religion, a distinctive form of Protestantism; their clothes, food, and social interaction evolved from their unique cultural circumstances. Among the great musical forms that have arisen from African American culture are the spiritual and the blues.

The spiritual

The spiritual, or religious folk song coalesced before the Civil War from musical fragments and singing practices of the slaves and the religion they learned from their masters. Christianity was one of the few privileges granted to slaves, and the homilies and lessons of the Bible, often interpreted through white hymnodists such as Isaac Watts, became the nucleus from which blacks built their own musical idiom. Snatches of scripture and religious poetry were remade into vernacular phrases that were frequently subject to repetition, alternation of leader with choral response, elaboration, and improvisation [see FOLK TRADITIONS, p. 592; RELIGIOUS MUSIC, p. 624].

At the close of the slavery period, three whites who had firsthand experience with antebellum black culture published a remarkable anthology that remains one of our basic repositories of the early spiritual (Allen et al. 1951 [1867]). Some are sung yet today: "Roll, Jordan, Roll" (figure 3), "Old Ship of Zion," "Lay This Body Down," and "Michael, Row the Boat Ashore." The compilers commented in the preface on many

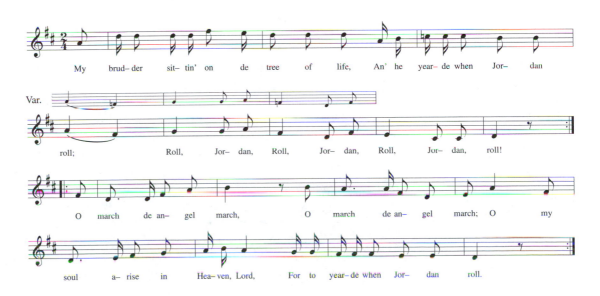

FIGURE 3   Spiritual, "Roll, Jordan, Roll," from *Slave Songs of the United States,* 1867.

FIGURE 4 The Fisk (University) Jubilee Singers popularized the concert spiritual throughout the United States and Europe. From *The American History and Encyclopedia of Music.* W. L. Hubbard, ed., 1910.

FIGURE 4 The Fisk (University) Jubilee Singers popularized the concert spiritual throughout the United States and Europe. From *The American History and Encyclopedia of Music.* W. L. Hubbard, ed., 1910.

aspects of performance that they had observed and that we have come to associate with black performance generally:

> The lead singer starts the words of each verse, often improvising, and the others . . . strike the refrain, or even join the solo . . . and seem to follow their own whims . . . so as to produce the effect of a marvelous complication and variety. (1951:2–3)

Because of the printing of spirituals and the education of blacks following the Civil War at colleges such as Fisk University of Nashville and Hampton Institute in Virginia, the improvisatory features of the folk spirituals disappeared. Nevertheless, the tunes, harmonies, rhythms, and texts were sufficiently vivid to attract worldwide attention when presented by groups such as the Fisk Jubilee Singers in the late nineteenth century (figure 4), and distinguished black recitalists of the early twentieth century—including Roland Hayes, Paul Robeson, and Marian Anderson—transformed the spiritual into an art song. By this time, however, the black community had turned to gospel music as a more vital religious expression.

The blues

Few musical genres born in the United States have been so influential as the blues [see BLUES, p. 637]. Both their melancholy nature and cathartic effect give the blues a central position in twentieth-century popular music. The structure of the blues is remarkable both in its simplicity—the most common pattern is a three-line stanza, AAB rhyme scheme, set to a twelve-bar, three-phase harmonic progression: I, IV–I, V^7–I— and in its seemingly endless capacity for variation.

The blues emerged a distinctive folk type around the turn of the twentieth century along with black ballads (for example, "John Hardy" and "John Henry") and gospel music. It soon evolved into both rural and urban types. Performers of the former type are the itinerant bluesmen "Blind Lemon" Jefferson of Texas and Robert Johnson and Charley Patton of Mississippi. The singer and his guitar seem to be a single voice of despair, with the instrument echoing the vocal inflections in the time-honored leader-response manner.

Urban blues achieved national popularity during the 1920s through the work of three celebrated female singers—Mamie Smith, Gertrude "Ma" Rainey, and the best known, Bessie Smith. Black theater and race recordings were principal means of dissemination. Shortly before World War I, W. C. Handy introduced the blues into popular music with the "St. Louis Blues" and "Memphis Blues" and earned the title "King of the Blues." Jazz bands of the 1920s frequently performed lively pieces using the twelve-bar blues form. Thereafter nearly every type of popular music has devoted part of its repertoire to the blues in form and spirit.

American Indian music

The earliest of the groups inhabiting the United States is the American Indian. Many Americans have attended powwows, often organized by a pan-Indian or intertribal association, and witnessed or possibly participated in ceremonial dancing and singing, along with sampling native food and purchasing crafts. Some have visited a reservation, such as a New Mexican pueblo, and observed the corn or turtle dances or the *katichina* ceremony (the latter based on the interaction of Spanish and Pueblo cultures over the past four hundred years). Nearly everyone is aware of Native American musical motives, or caricatures of them, that pervade mass culture: the chant resembling a Plains Indian war cry sung by sports fans, or the soundtracks for the popular "cowboy and indian" movies of the mid-twentieth century [see MUSIC OF THE AMERICAN INDIAN/FIRST NATIONS IN THE UNITED STATES AND CANADA, p. 365].

Predominantly white America has had an ambivalent attitude toward Native Americans (figure 5). It has venerated the American Indian as a "noble savage," unaffected by a despoiling civilization. For example, American literature is studded with laudatory images, such as the Delaware Mohican Ungas in James Fenimore Cooper's *The Last of the Mohicans* (1826) or the immersion of white army officer John Dunbar in Comanche culture from Michael Blake's *Dances with Wolves* (1988). A more frequent image of Native Americans has been that of cruel warriors who vigorously resisted the European colonization of the New World.

But the New World was a very old one to the various Indian populations at the time of the first European settlements. They had come to the Americas many thousands of centuries before Europeans. Those Indians that remained in North America were scattered among diversified geographic areas. This vast expanse was so sparsely settled that the total Indian population at the time of early European colonization was about that of a mid-sized metropolitan area such as Denver or Kansas City: from one million to two million people. The numerous tribes that lived in what is now the United States had highly varying social structures, from the nomadic hunting and gathering groups of the Great Plains to the settled, agricultural villages of the East and the western deserts. What they all shared, however, was a preindustrial cultural homogeneity regarding beliefs, legends, rituals, and music.

FIGURE 5   *The Indian Bear Dance.* Many Americans learned about Native American culture by means of Currier and Ives lithography such as this.

The singer and his guitar seem to be a single voice of despair, with the instrument echoing the vocal inflections in the time-honored leader-response manner.

Features of American Indian music

Native American music is largely vocal and monophonic. Songs often follow a descending, scalar contour with rhythmic pulsations on the longer notes. Vocables are interspersed with meaningful text. Drums and rattles usually supply an underlying beat. A piece can often be lengthy, consisting of several songs or phrases, often modified on repetition. A leader may start a song or motive, and the group joins in, sometimes splintering the monophonic texture into heterophony. Extended pieces are sometimes punctuated by falsetto cries or even casual conversation. Some songs take on the shape of verse-refrain or leader-response, but they rarely use harmony or counterpoint.

American Indian ceremonies

Indian ceremonies feature dance as well as song. Since Native American religions are naturalistic, nearly all activity falls under their purview: the changing seasons; beseeching the gods for successful hunting, bountiful crops, or good health; warding off evil spirits; and giving thanks for blessings already bestowed. The topics of songs include the many activities of daily life: games, love, nature, animals, legends, and significant historical events. Modern-day Navajos, for example, sing of "Old Glory Raising on Iwo Jima," and the Sioux, a "Memorial Song," commemorating the Korean War (*Authentic Music of the American Indian* c. 1970 record 1, side 2, #s 7 and 8).

These generalizations about Native American music can only offer an expectation for the novice listener, who would on further exploration be confounded by its very diversity. A good place to begin is the recording *Songs of Earth, Water, Fire, and Sky* (Heth 1976), which includes many different types of songs from nine tribes whose origins encompass the entire United States. Over a century of ethnological work has deepened our respect for Indian culture. Values such as living in harmony with nature, conservation, cooperation, respect for tradition, and reverence for the universe are characteristics of Indian culture that other American ethnic groups have come to admire.

Asian American music

Asian Americans are a rapidly growing ethnic group in the United States. Countries such as Korea, Vietnam, China, and India have more than doubled the size of their respective groups here since 1980. East Asia and the surrounding area has the largest population and cultural diversity of any continent. It consists of the Far East (China, Korea, Japan, the Philippines), Southeast Asia (Vietnam, Laos, Cambodia, Indonesia), South Asia (the Indian subcontinent), and Oceania (Micronesia, Melanesia, Polynesia, the Malay archipelago). The music we hear from these regions, performed by touring professionals and immigrants, ranges from highly cultivated art and traditional genres to folk and popular forms, the latter often a hybrid of Western and Asian styles [see ASIAN AMERICAN MUSICS, p. 947].

Chinese and Japanese immigration

The earliest Asian immigrants, from south China, came to California to work in the gold fields and on major construction projects and to open small businesses. Entertainers soon followed, and Cantonese opera troupes regularly visited San Francisco and other cities during the late nineteenth century. After restrictions were made on Chinese immigration during the 1880s, Japanese immigrants fulfilled the unending demand for labor and established a sizable ethnic group of their own in the United States. A second immigration from China, this time from the north, followed the 1940s civil war there. The Chinese American cultural base was enlarged to include Peking opera as well as various kinds of instrumental and choral music. Chinese and Japanese communities can be found in all major United States metropolitan areas.

Bicultural musical activity

Asian American cultures have held on to many of their traditional instruments and genres but have also adapted them to American forms such as jazz. Fusion Japanese American groups draw on the sonorities of such traditional instruments as the *koto* 'zither', *shamisen* 'lute', *shakuhachi* 'end-blown flute', and the very popular *taiko* 'drum.' The American public has become aware of Japanese music and dance through such events as the traditional O-Bon Festivals held in Buddhist temples, the Nisei (second-generation) Week Festival of Los Angeles, and various cherry blossom festivals held in major cities.

Asian Americans sometimes bring with them a Western music that had been transplanted to their homelands earlier in the nineteenth century. The Philippine and Indonesian cultures were heavily influenced during their colonial periods under Western governments. Missionaries taught Western hymn tunes in Korea, China, and Japan during the late nineteenth century. Some Japanese students today sing Stephen Foster's songs in Japanese, a legacy, perhaps, of the work of American educator Luther Whiting Mason, who set up a program for training Japanese music teachers in Western music during the 1880s.

Hawai'i: a cross section of musical cultures

The Hawaiian archipelago is our foremost multicultural state [see POLYNESIAN MUSIC, p. 1047]. The oldest cultural layer is from Polynesia and includes the hula, dances that integrate religious and historical texts, and the *mele hula,* dance-chants accompanied by drums, rattles, bamboo pipes, and shell trumpets. Following the arrival of Captain Cook in 1778, Hawai'i became open to immigration from modern Polynesia, Asia, Europe, and America. Each culture has left its deposit: Protestant hymns, European opera and oratorio, the part songs of German singing societies, and Japanese court music. Even the ukulele is descended from the Atlantic Portuguese colony of Madeira. The native Hawaiian court established its own European-styled military band in the nineteenth century. After Hawai'i became a U.S. territory in 1900 and a state in 1959, its musical institutions and schools were increasingly Americanized; nevertheless, much remains to remind us of Hawai'i's history and many cultures: hula chant underlaid with Western harmonic progressions and accompanied by steel guitar and ukulele is a syncretization of old and new, East and West.

European American music

French music

Although France struggled valiantly during the mid-eighteenth century to control the Great Lakes as well as the Mississippi and Ohio River valleys, its ethnic enclaves today are restricted largely to the Northeast, bordering the Canadian province of Québec, and to the Cajun culture in southwest Louisiana [see FRENCH MUSIC, p. 854]. The

Northeast celebrates the culture of Old France and relives the experiences of the voyageurs in such songs as "Alouette," in other songs from bawdy to spiritual, in dances such as the quadrille, and in fiddle music.

Cajun culture, however, has captured the interest of present-day America at large. These descendants of French Acadians have clung to a dialect of French while evolving a distinctively southern rural way of life. Many restaurants throughout the United States feature Cajun food, and Cajun music has made its niche in popular music. The older style such as the *fais dodo* 'country dance,' akin to hillbilly music, exists alongside zydeco, which is a blending of black styles with the traditional.

German-speaking and Scandinavian American music

German-speaking Moravians were among the numerous groups who came to the New World with the intention of maintaining autonomous religious communities [see CENTRAL EASTERN EUROPEAN MUSIC/EASTERN EUROPEAN MUSIC, p. 908; SCANDINAVIAN AND BALTIC MUSIC, p. 866]. Settling principally in Pennsylvania and North Carolina during the eighteenth century, they created or brought with them religious and chamber music on a par with the classical music of Europe. Today's Moravians continue to have a rich musical tradition. The Amish and Mennonite religious sects chose to maintain a more rigid cultural isolation. Resisting technological evolution and changing fashions, they also preserve even today much of their earlier singing traditions.

Nineteenth-century immigration from the various German-speaking parts of Europe profoundly affected United States musical culture. Both in the East and in the Midwest—Milwaukee, Cincinnati, St. Louis, Louisville, and many smaller communities—orchestras, bands, and choral societies blossomed. The *Liederkranz,* 'singing group,' was at first intended to preserve Germanic culture; however, many evolved to become major community organizations inclusive of other ethnic backgrounds. For example, the annual *Saengerfest* in the Cincinnati-Louisville region, organized in 1849, became the Cincinnati May Festival by 1873 and continues to be a musical event for the entire community today.

The Lutheran church and its rich musical tradition is common to both German and Scandinavian immigrants. Although less numerous than immigrants from Germany, Scandinavian Americans have made a distinctive contribution to multiethnic America. Settling primarily in the upper Midwest in the mid-nineteenth century, they preserved much of their own culture from church music to folk ballads. The popular Paul Bunyan lumberjack stories suggest a Scandinavian American adapted to the national tall-tale folk tradition. Like German ethnic groups, the Scandinavians have a robust choral tradition.

Italian music

Italian Americans are a sizable minority in the United States, numbering over fourteen million through the fourth generation [see ITALIAN MUSIC, p. 860]. Many came from the poorer central and southern areas of Italy and have maintained a strong, conservative folk tradition here. Drawing on the rich musical heritage of their homeland, Italian Americans and nationals who have spent an appreciable part of their lives in the United States have played a prominent role in American music, both classical and popular. Arturo Toscanini is foremost among several Italian conductors who have led American orchestras, and Italian singers from Enrico Caruso to Luciano Pavarotti have been prominent in American opera houses. Singers such as Frank Sinatra, Perry Como, Dean Martin, Tony Bennett, and Vic Damone have turned their lyrical heritage into a popular bel canto of immense appeal.

Balkan and Eastern European music

Influence of the church

As with immigrant groups from other parts of Europe, the church has played a major role in preserving the ethnic identities of the various cultures from the Balkans and Eastern Europe: the Roman Catholic church for Polish, Czech, and Hungarian immigrants and the various national Orthodox churches for Russian and Balkan immigrants [see SOUTHEASTERN EUROPEAN (BALKAN) MUSIC, p. 919]. The choral music of the Russian Orthodox Church, the product of an ancient liturgy as well as of Russia's major composers, has reached out beyond its ethnic enclave to have a national appeal as a form of classical music.

The relation of the Greek Orthodox Church to the various Greek American communities throughout the United States is an illustration of how the church not only bonds the ethnic community but clarifies its relation to culture at large. Many activities are under the aegis of the church—baptisms, weddings, picnics, and festivals—and feature ethnic dancing and music. Some churches offer instruction in the Greek language and culture to the descendants of immigrants, thus attempting to keep the ethnic heritage alive. Saints' days are often commemorated as "name days" in the homes of those bearing a particular saint's name, and the singing of Greek folk songs, particularly among first-generation Greek Americans, is a popular activity. Societies closely related to the church, such as the Order of AHEPA (American Hellenic Educational Progressive Association), sponsor community as well as regional and national events. Churches in urban areas hold festivals often lasting for several days, inviting the community at large to learn about the Orthodox religion and to share in the food, dance, and music of Greek culture. Greek Americans are a fairly sizable ethnic group; however, the structure of their activities described above is typical of the numerous other ethnic groups from Eastern Europe and the Balkans.

Dance music

East European and Balkan dances have a popular appeal reaching far beyond their respective ethnic groups. Polish dance music such as the *varsovienne,* the mazurka, and particularly the polka (of Bohemian origin) have captured the popular imagination since the nineteenth century. The polka craze extended well into the twentieth century. That its identity is now panethnic is evident in that one of the most popular polka bandleaders of the post–World War II period, Frankie Yankovich, is of Slovenian descent, and the universally popular song "The Beer Barrel Polka" underwent a metamorphosis during the 1930s from Czech to German and English.

Balkan dances, especially Greek, have had a special appeal in this country. Most are line dances with simple gliding steps. They afford opportunity for social mixing. The additive rhythms of many Greek song-dances—7/8 (3+2+2 or 2+2+3) or 8/8 (4+2+2 or 3+3+2)—give them a distinctive, graceful quality. These line dances are a decided contrast to those of the Anglo-American tradition such as the Virginia reel.

Instruments

The instruments native to Eastern Europe and the Balkans have a fascination for most Americans. Russian balalaika ensembles have attracted audiences beyond the ethnic community. The Croatian-Serbian *tambura* has been popularized by the Popovich Brothers' Yugoslavian Tamburitza Orchestra, founded in 1925. The Greek *bouzouki,* the balalaika, the *tambura*—all make distinctive ethnic statements; however, the accordion, of Viennese origin, is the panethnic instrument common to many of the ensembles of Central and Eastern Europe, and in the polka bands it becomes the principal one. Other pan-European instruments popular in these bands are the violin, clarinet, and drums. Modern ethnic bands often feature electronic keyboards capable of a variety of sounds.

The Greek *bouzouki,* the balalaika, the *tambura*—
all make distinctive ethnic statements; however,
the accordion, of Viennese origin, is the panethnic
instrument common to many of the ensembles of
Central and Eastern Europe, and in the polka bands
it becomes the principal one.

Hungarian American music

Like German Americans, Hungarian Americans emphasize singing societies and have
made important contributions to American classical music. The association of Hungarian folk music with "Gypsy" music, however, has achieved mass appeal in the form
of popular songs, usually with a free rhythm, sustained notes, and a form with alternating slow and quick sections (*verbunkos* style). Victor Herbert's "Romany Life," subtitled "Song à la *Czardas*" (1898), has these features.

Jewish American music

The vast majority of American Jews have immigrated since the mid-nineteenth century
from Central and Eastern Europe [see JEWISH MUSIC, p. 933]. Yiddish is the spoken
language common to these various groups, along with the various Hebrew liturgies of
the Jewish religion. Although the cantorial music of the Orthodox liturgy has maintained close identity to European practice, its richness of melody and sophisticated
production have been cited as spilling over into the popular songs of Jewish composers
such as George Gershwin, Richard Rodgers, and Jerome Kern. The classical virtuosity
of cantorial singing is evident in the fact that both Jan Peerce and Richard Tucker
moved easily from liturgical singing to opera.

Jewish folk and popular music is as varied as the many regions from which the
immigrants have come. The minor mode and augmented second intervals, characteristic of much Eastern Europe, Balkan, and Middle Eastern music, have become easily
identifiable to the general public. The popular *klezmer* bands have further strengthened the association of Jewish music with those regions. At its peak during the early
twentieth century, Yiddish song constituted the largest body of non-English popular
music published in the United States; however, few of these songs became generally
known outside of the Jewish community.

Islamic American music

Recent immigration from West and Central Asia, the Indian subcontinent, and Africa,
as well as the conversion of some African Americans to the Muslim faith, has resulted
in the establishment of a significant and growing Islamic community in the United
States [see MIDDLE EASTERN MUSIC, p. 1028]. Islamic chanting of the Koran and the
call to prayer are traditional musical features practiced in worship; however, one may
expect the emergence of an Islamic American syncretic style if the experience of other
ethnic groups in America holds true in this case.

RELIGIOUS MUSIC

Religious music in its various forms is an important part of our musical culture. Oratorios, cantatas, and instrumental music, particularly music for organ, play an important
role in our classical concert tradition. Psalm and hymn singing on religious and social
occasions and in music education was a major activity until well into the nineteenth

century. Our folk music is heavily invested with religious ideas, and many secular folk tunes have been joined with sacred texts in our hymnody. Both white and black gospel as well as contemporary Christian music are major segments of urban popular music. Much country music reflects Christian fundamentalist values, and piety similarly has been an important topic in popular song. Here we will trace the main currents of religious music throughout our history [see RELIGION, p. 116].

New England psalmody in the seventeenth and eighteenth centuries

Early religious practice

The religious migrations to the New World during the seventeenth century were numerous and varied: Spanish to the Southwest, French Huguenots to Florida, German-speaking Protestants and Quakers to Pennsylvania, Catholics to Maryland, Dutch Protestants to New York, and Moravians to North Carolina and Pennsylvania. The most extensive was English to New England.

The music of the English Puritans and its development, called psalmody, not only thrived in New England during the seventeenth and eighteenth centuries but also fathered both the sophisticated hymnody of urban areas and the folk hymnody of the rural South and West during the nineteenth century. Excepting a few hymns and psalms, such as the "Old Hundredth" (Psalm 100), now used as the doxology ("Praise God from Whom All Blessings Flow") in the Protestant service, this early great wave of psalmody is now spent.

In its heyday, however, psalmody dominated New England life much as popular music does in the United States today. The singing of the Psalms of David in unison was a principal activity in the seventeenth-century Puritan service, and performing them at home, sometimes in parts, was a popular secular activity. By the eighteenth century, the term had come to embrace not only musical settings of the psalms but also the hymns, anthems, and fuguing tunes that were the repertoire for church as well as for instructional and recreational use.

The singing schools and their composers

During the eighteenth century, singing schools, usually of a few months' duration, were held to combat musical illiteracy and to master the increasingly varied and difficult repertoire. Singing schools created the better trained singers who would eventually be organized during the nineteenth century into choirs. Singing schools also mark the beginning of class instruction in music that was to become an essential part of public school curricula in the nineteenth century.

The teachers of the singing schools were also our first school of native-born American composers. They traveled among different communities, offering classes and teaching youngsters to sing "by note" rather than "by rote" from newly published tune books containing their own and others' compositions. William Billings (1746–1800) is the best known and most prolific among them. His patriotic hymn "Chester" is among our cherished pieces from the Revolutionary War (figure 6).

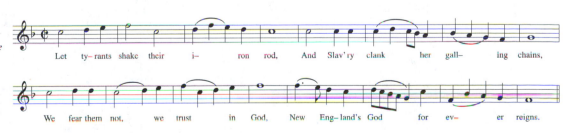

FIGURE 6 The tenor (melody) for "Chester," by William Billings, from *The Singing Master's Assistant,* Boston, 1778.

Let ty—rants shake their i— ron rod, And Slav'ry clank her gall— ing chains,

We fear them not, we trust in God, New Eng—land's God for ev— er reigns.

Church music in the nineteenth century

Urban hymnody

The first of the two religious music traditions spawned by New England psalmody can aptly be called urban hymnody, for it flourished in the established churches of our cities and larger communities. Its practitioners considered earlier psalmody uncouth and rewrote some of the older tunes they deemed worthy of preservation in the new European "scientific" manner, as is evident in Thomas Hastings's reworking of Lewis Edson's fuguing tune "Lenox" (Stevenson 1966:67).

"Scientific" music's leading practitioner, Lowell Mason (figure 7), sought to bring Europe and America together by setting hymn texts to melodies (usually unidentified) of masters such as Mozart and harmonizing them in the European classical manner. These arrangers were also composers, for original pieces such as Mason's "My Faith Looks Up to Thee" ("Olivet") and Hastings's "Rock of Ages" ("Toplady") (figure 8), can still be heard in our older, established churches.

Mason's zeal for improving both the quality and instruction of music makes him an important musical figure in a century dominated by the ideal of self-improvement in all walks of life. He inaugurated public school music instruction in the United States by offering classes in the Boston schools beginning in 1841. He traveled extensively, teaching teachers how to teach and choir directors how to improve their choirs. The sale of his school music tutors and church hymnals raised musical literacy generally and, incidentally, made him a wealthy man.

Mason's and Hastings's work led to a flowering of church music in the nineteenth century. Literary giants such as John Greenleaf Whittier, James Russell Lowell, and Henry Wadsworth Longfellow wrote hymns of high quality, and American composers wrote anthems, oratorios, and hymn tunes in a cosmopolitan style comparable to that of their European counterparts. An important part of the U.S. classical music tradition in the late nineteenth century can be found in the larger religious music forms.

Rural hymnody

The second offshoot of New England psalmody can be called rural or frontier hymnody, which was practiced in the rural Midwest and South. It was a far more obedient offspring than was urban hymnody, preserving intact the "primitive" older anthems, hymns, and fuguing tunes. Composers of this shape-note hymnody (so-called because of the differently shaped note heads used to facilitate reading) also added many folk hymns and spirituals to the original New England repertoire. The writing of the new tunesmiths was sometimes even more rugged and individualistic than that of the

FIGURE 7   Nineteenth-century composer, arranger, and educator Lowell Mason. From *The American History and Encyclopedia of Music*, W. L. Hubbard, ed.

FIGURE 8   Thomas Hastings's "Rock of Ages" (1831), as found in *The New Laudes Domini*, 1892.

FIGURE 9 "Amazing Grace," as found in William Walker's, *Southern Harmony,* 1854 ed.

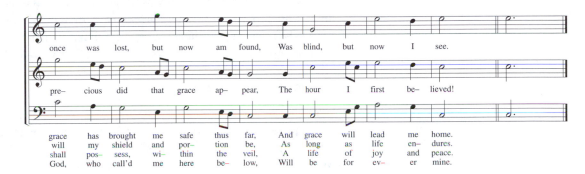

earlier New Englanders. A case in point is the coupling of a text, John Newton's "Amazing Grace" (1789), with the setting of the folk tune "New Britain," in the 1858 edition of William Walker's *Southern Harmony* (figure 9).

Rural hymnody atrophied as the United States became increasingly industrialized following the Civil War. Nevertheless, pockets of continuous use remain in parts of the South and Southwest, largely because of the dedication of rural singing societies, which often restrict their singing to just one particular tune book. *The Sacred Harp* (1844) has been by far the most popular. This tune book was used at singing conventions in Georgia and Texas before World War II, and since the folk music revival of the 1960s, Sacred Harp societies have appeared in nearly every state of the union.

White gospel music

Much religious vigor in the United States today comes from the Pentecostal churches, both white and black, which emphasize the intensely personal, emotional experience characteristic of revival meetings. The United States has had several periods of fervent revivalism over a period of the past three centuries. All but the last period produced a significant body of music and a particular musical style that later became absorbed, at least in part, by the established, denominational churches.

The First Great Awakening, occurring in the early eighteenth century, was led by George Whitefield, who encouraged the singing of hymns by Isaac Watts and, later, the Wesleys. More emotional and literary hymns gradually replaced the older, stern psalms, and the more sanguine quality of verse supported the musical flowering of the New England school.

The Second Great Awakening at the turn of the nineteenth century was even more radical. In the large camp meetings, many held in frontier regions of the country such as Kentucky, the revival song as we know it, consisting of short, repetitive refrains and call-and-response techniques, emerged as an important type of religious music. By midcentury, a simple, personal hymn writing permeated other areas of church music, particularly Sunday school songs, such as William Bradbury's "Jesus Loves Me" (1862), and sentimental devotional hymns, such as poet Fanny Crosby's "Blessed Assurance" (1873).

A third intensive revival period began with the collaboration of the charismatic preacher Dwight Moody and his song leader, Ira A. Sankey, in the 1870s, and was followed by the preaching of Billy Sunday and his musical counterpart, Homer Rodeheaver, after the turn of the twentieth century. Sankey and another composer, P. L. Bliss, virtually coined the word *gospel* for the newer, lighter religious verses and their catchy musical settings. A rich store of music comes from this period, such as Joseph Brackett's "Simple Gifts" (1848), which is frequently heard in its art music setting by Aaron Copland. So successful was this body of music that a fourth and most recent revival period, headed by Billy Graham following World War II, has continued to rely on it.

During the twentieth century, white gospel music has came to take its place as an important popular music independent of revival movements or denominational hymnody. Through publishing houses, recordings, and radio, it has maintained a continuous impact on the public, particularly in the South and Midwest.

Contemporary church music

The classical tradition

Much present-day music in the long-established denominational churches has drawn upon the large historical reservoir of the Western art music tradition, and new works are often commissioned, largely from classical-music composers. Thus, the goal of the nineteenth century to elevate church music to that of the classical tradition appears to have been reached.

The communal music of these churches has no one distinctive style as did the music of the nineteenth century. Rather, the vast hymn literature has become increasingly eclectic and ecumenical, not only maintaining its own direct line from Lowell Mason but also drawing on the popular gospel tradition on the one hand and multicultural or ethnic sources on the other.

The popular tradition

During the late twentieth century, two new phenomena of urban church activity emerged: television ministries and nondenominational pastoral churches. Both handle massive numbers of people, use business marketing techniques, and rely on emotional appeal similar to that of the Pentecostal movements. Their music is drawn from the more egalitarian gospel tradition or contemporary popular music. The pastoral churches frequently employ rock bands or gospel choirs and sing hymns of simple, repetitive melodic construction. They are the fastest growing congregations among the vast majority of American Protestants (Trueheart 1996).

Black gospel music

The religious music showing the most vitality today is black gospel. Emerging as a genre at the end of the nineteenth century, its antecedents are found in the flourishing white gospel tradition on the one hand and the venerable black spiritual tradition on the other. Unlike the concert spiritual, which by the twentieth century had left its black folk roots and was becoming part of an international art music tradition, black gospel remained firmly rooted in popular music.

Throughout the early twentieth century, black gospel music flourished in both the Pentecostal and the older denominations. The leading pioneers were Charles Albert Tinley (1851–1933) and Thomas A. Dorsey (1899–1993). Special gospel choirs grew up alongside more traditional ones as gospel music increasingly became a more integral part of black church services.

The gospel performance style is highly emotive and in many ways draws on early black folk traditions, such as the ring shout, antiphonal singing, shuffling from foot to foot, hand clapping, and solo interpolations. The phrase structure of many songs lends itself to extensive repetition and the building of a fervency or spiritual catharsis. In this respect, gospel music is much like its secular counterpart, soul music. Extremely high soprano singing and driving, hard-edged choral delivery characterize much ecstatic gospel singing, although the medium is varied enough to include a smoother, less urgent vocal style and complex enough to accommodate the sophisticated harmonies and elaborate improvisation of jazz. Various instruments are used to support choral and solo singing, including percussion, banjo, and, more recently, guitar, piano, electronic organ, and various wind instruments.

Black gospel music has extended far beyond the church service. By the 1920s numerous singers were making recordings, and in the 1930s Dorsey founded the first publishing house dedicated to gospel music. Sister Rosetta Tharpe pushed gospel singing into the wider sphere of popular music with her recording "Rock Me" (1938). She was followed by gospel queen Mahalia Jackson (1911–1972), who drew on both the traditional black Baptist and the secular blues heritages to gain a popularity extending far beyond the black community. Male quartets, among which the Golden Gate is best known, have been a mainstay in the gospel concert tradition since nearly the beginning of the century. The importance of black gospel music is demonstrated in numerous festivals held throughout the country and the increasing number of colleges in which gospel choirs have become a part of their musical programs.

Black gospel music demonstrates a remarkable fusion of religious and popular styles. Many popular black singers, among them Aretha Franklin, Ray Charles, Della Reese, and Dionne Warwick, have gospel music roots. Hardly a major event transpires today, from a presidential inauguration to a nationally celebrated athletic event, that does not feature a gospel choir or gospel-rooted singer, black or white.

CONCERT MUSIC

Although other kinds of music are sometimes presented in concert, the primary venue for classical music is a setting for an audience [see FOUR VIEWS OF MUSIC IN THE UNITED STATES, p. 554] whose principal activity is to listen. In the concert hall, we are expected to give performers our undivided attention, and for this effort we anticipate receiving both pleasure and enlightenment. First we will look at various kinds of concert activity; then we will examine the concept of "classical" music in the United States as it evolved from the eighteenth through the twentieth centuries.

Choral music

Choral societies

Choral music as a concert activity had its beginning with the Stoughton (Massachusetts) Musical Society in 1786, which remains active today. Other early extant groups include the Handel and Haydn Society of Boston, founded in 1815, and the New York [City] Oratorio Society, organized by Leopold Damrosch in 1873. Many choral organizations sponsor festivals. Among the best known are the Bethlehem Bach, the Cincinnati May, and the Worcester, Massachusetts, Festivals. Also, many universities have organized choral unions, large "town-gown" ensembles for the purpose of performing major choral works.

During the nineteenth century, choral societies, in both England and the United States, were an important feature of concert life. Although choral festivals no longer have a central position in concert life, major choral works, both traditional and modern, continue to be performed, usually in conjunction with community or university orchestras.

Twentieth-century professional and collegiate groups

A few fully professional choral groups existed at various times in the twentieth century, among them well-known African American ensembles—the Eva Jessye Choir and the

Hall Johnson Choir. Fred Waring's Pennsylvanians, consisting of both choral and instrumental groups, spanned much of the century and was undoubtedly the most popular and influential force for lighter choral music throughout that time. Groups organized by Roger Wagner, Gregg Smith, and especially Robert Shaw set the standard for the performance of more extended and serious choral compositions.

The twentieth century also witnessed a strong blossoming of concert choral music in colleges and universities throughout the country. Much emphasis has been placed on a cappella singing. Both professional and collegiate choruses today draw on the rich repertoire of Western music tradition as well as contemporary works.

Band music

Nineteenth-century bands

The town band was a major means for introducing the "classics" to America's broad hinterland during the nineteenth century [see BANDS, p. 563]. Overtures, potpourris of opera arias, and arrangements of famous classical pieces can be found on programs of numerous town bands, along with marches, dances, and arrangements of popular songs. During the earlier and mid-nineteenth century, amateur brass bands existed in nearly every town. A noted band historian has estimated that some three thousand ensembles, including sixty thousand performers, existed in the decade before the Civil War (Camus 1986).

Following the Civil War, Patrick Gilmore toured the country with one of the early professional symphonic groups, the Twenty-second Regimental Band of New York. Such bands were larger than brass bands and consisted of woodwinds, brass, and percussion. John Philip Sousa, after directing the U.S. Marine Band for more than a decade, organized a civilian band of his own in 1892 and soon after brought the professional symphonic band movement to the peak of its popularity.

Twentieth-century and contemporary bands

During the early twentieth century, Sousa's was the leading of several professional bands that toured internationally and maintained summer residencies in leading amusement parks. Programs continued to be inclusive of both classical and popular traditions, consisting of orchestral transcriptions, opera excerpts, medleys, suites, marches, popular songs, and, above all, solos featuring the phenomenal virtuosity of musicians such as cornetists Herbert L. Clarke and Frank Simon, trombonist Arthur Pryor, violinist Maud Powell, and leading singers of the day.

The professional and service bands became models for the band movement in secondary schools and colleges. After the professional and municipal bands waned during the mid-twentieth century, the band movement was taken over by the schools and continues to flourish today at a high artistic level in many universities.

Some schools have also developed wind ensembles, following the lead of Frederick Fennell at the University of Rochester's (New York) Eastman School of Music in 1952. Wind ensembles have created an alternative sound to that of the massive symphonic band by having single performers on a part. Their repertoire consists largely of works commissioned from leading composers.

Orchestra music

Early orchestras

Eighteenth- and early nineteenth-century orchestras existed in major cities such as New York, Philadelphia, Baltimore, Boston, and Charleston. They were little more than chamber groups, their activities centering on the theater, with an occasional concert. The New York Philharmonic Society was permanently established in 1842, and other existing major orchestras followed closer to the turn of the twentieth century:

FIGURE 10   Theodore Thomas, German American conductor of the Chicago Symphony Orchestra, 1891–1905. From *The American History and Encyclopedia of Music*, W. L. Hubbard, ed., 1910.

Boston, 1881; Chicago, 1891; Cincinnati and Pittsburgh, 1895; Philadelphia, 1900; Minneapolis (now Minnesota), 1903; San Francisco, 1911; Baltimore, 1914; Cleveland, 1918; and Los Angeles, 1919. All of these fully professional ensembles were preceded by various amateur and semiprofessional groups.

The major stimulus to the orchestra movement in the United States during the nineteenth century came from German immigration. The Germania Musical Society, consisting of twenty-five musicians, toured America between 1848 and 1854 and created a demand for German classical and early romantic music. Theodore Thomas (1835–1905) (figure 10), who came to the United States as a teenager, was to become the most important conductor in nineteenth-century America. At first he toured from coast to coast with his own orchestra, consisting mostly of German immigrants. He then became the central figure in many musical events in Chicago and Cincinnati, as well as New York. He capped his career by organizing in 1891 the Chicago Symphony Orchestra which he conducted until his death.

Orchestras Today

In the twentieth century, the symphony orchestra has become the nexus of classical-music concert activity. Orchestras have been criticized for placing emphasis on earlier masterpieces rather than contemporary music. Orchestral programming varies widely, however, and, as all-purpose musical organizations, most ensembles try to provide for a variety of community needs—the edification of classical music, the entertainment of pops concerts, and the education of youth. Hardly a schoolchild throughout the United States lacks the opportunity both to see and hear an orchestra at various times in his or her school program. Thus, today's orchestras appear to fulfill the multifarious role of the nineteenth-century bands.

The virtuoso tradition

Nineteenth-century European virtuosos crisscrossed the country, strengthening the growing appetite for classical music. Soprano Jenny Lind, the "Swedish Nightingale," is foremost and best remembered. After establishing a successful European operatic career during the 1840s, Lind accepted P. T. Barnum's invitation to tour America in 1850, where she remained for two and a half years. Nearly equaling Lind in celebrity status was Norwegian violinist Ole Bull, who made frequent tours of the United States from the 1840s until his death in 1880.

Louis Moreau Gottschalk (figure 11) was the only American-born musician to achieve fame as a touring virtuoso comparable to Lind and Bull. He found it necessary to establish his reputation in Europe before returning to the United States for his first round of tours (1853–1856) and later for a three-year period during the Civil War. He also toured the Caribbean islands and South America.

Virtuosos continued to be an important feature of concert life in the twentieth century. Prokofiev, Rachmaninov, and Bartók were three leading composers who supported themselves, in part, by performing their own music here. African Americans such as tenor Roland Hayes and contralto Marian Anderson established their reputations on the concert stage rather than in opera houses. Amelita Galli-Curci, Enrico Caruso, John McCormack, Rosa Ponselle, Risë Stevens, Lawrence Tibbett, Jerome Hines, Jessye Norman—the list goes on and on—have been or are well-known opera singers who have also attracted large concert audiences throughout the country.

Chamber music

During the nineteenth century, chamber music found a venue on the concert stage. The Music Performance Trust Fund of Philadelphia and the Mendelssohn Quintette Club of Boston are two among various community organizations that sponsored chamber music concerts before the Civil War. The late nineteenth and early twentieth

FIGURE 11   Louis Moreau Gottschalk. From *Notes of a Pianist*, 1881.

Nineteenth-century European virtuosos crisscrossed the country, strengthening the growing appetite for classical music.

centuries saw the flourishing of the Kneisel and the Flonzaly string quartets; thereafter, many such groups toured the country—among them the Budapest, Hungarian, Pro Arte, Juilliard, Cleveland, and Emerson quartets—and several affiliated themselves with conservatories and universities.

The American composer during the nineteenth century

European art music overwhelmed the United States during the nineteenth century, just as it continues to be virtually synonymous with classical music today. Although acquiring compositional skill was a first priority for our early composers, some drew on the American environment for inspiration. Early Federalist immigrant composers, such as Alexander Reinagle and Benjamin Carr, incorporated patriotic airs into a few of their compositions; a generation later, A. P. Heinrich used tunes such as "Yankee Doodle" as well as programmatic effects describing the scenic beauty of the New World in his *Dawning of Music in Kentucky.* Gottschalk drew heavily on the vernacular music touching his life, from the folk songs of his New Orleans youth to the patriotic and minstrel music popular during his touring days.

At midcentury Philadelphia's William Henry Fry and New York's George Bristow were composing symphonies, operas, and chamber music. They were demanding more recognition for the American composer but were preoccupied with matching the European ideal of excellence rather than creating a distinctively American sound. The same can be said for a group of late-nineteenth-century composers from New England— John Knowles Paine, Arthur Foote, George Chadwick, Horatio Parker, Amy Beach, and Charles Martin Loeffler—who clearly match all but the very major European composers in quantity and quality. They were preparing the way for the Great American Composer, about whom critic John Van Cleve wrote: "There must be indeed much good writing before a genius of the first order can find a mellow leaf-loam deep enough for the ramifying amplitude of his mighty thoughts" ("Americanism in Music" 1899:96).

The search for an American music

Toward the end of the nineteenth century, younger European composers were drawing on the folk music of their respective countries as an antidote to the Germanic style then dominating classical music. Among them was Antonín Dvořák, who had come to America in 1892 to become the director of the National Conservatory of Music in New York. His counsel on what sort of music Americans should be writing was eagerly sought by many, and he provided both compositions and words. His most famous "demonstration" piece was the *Symphony from the New World,* premiered by the New York Philharmonic in December 1893. At the same time he urged American composers to draw on their own folk sources, particularly black and Indian, as he had apparently done in his American compositions.

The appeal of using folk music of the so-called lower classes as a source for a national art can be traced to the late-eighteenth-century German philosopher Johann

Gottfried von Herder, who asserted that any vital belles lettres had to stem from the base, vernacular language of the folk. Certainly Herder's idea fit well with American egalitarian ideals, and Dvořák's influence broadened the course of future American classical music to include indigenous as well as sophisticated features.

Classical music in the early twentieth century

The Indianist composers

A younger generation of composers hastened to Dvořák's call and, for a brief time, the so-called Indianist composers flourished. Among the better known are Arthur Farwell and Charles Wakefield Cadman. Cadman made an intense study of American Indian music, visited the Omaha and Winnebago reservations, and gave lecture-recitals with a Native American singer, Princess Tsianina Redfeather. His "Land of the Sky-blue Water," from a set of *Indian Songs,* op. 45 (1909), crossed over into popular music and became a best-seller. In addition to writing music on Indian themes, Farwell organized the Wa-Wan Press (1901–1912), which became the principal voice of composers using indigenous music.

African American influence on classical music

African American music, rather than Indian, became a more fertile and enduring source of inspiration for classical music. Spiritual melodies played their part, but jazz became the primary vernacular source after World War I. George Gershwin used "blue" notes and syncopation in such popular works as *Rhapsody in Blue, An American in Paris,* and the Piano Concerto in F. His opera, *Porgy and Bess,* drew deeply on many other features of black folk music.

Composers more wholly committed to classical music than Gershwin, such as Aaron Copland (Piano Concerto, 1926), were also drawing on the jazz idiom. Rhythm appears to be an obvious feature. Syncopation, from folk through jazz and into concert music, was seen as an important device in fulfilling Herder's concept of an artistic link between low and high cultures, thus producing a genuinely American music.

The Anglo folk influence

Copland, Virgil Thomson, and Roy Harris are among the best known composers who explored yet other ways to Americanize concert music around World War II. They broadened the base of ethnic influence on classical music by including actual hymn tunes, folk songs, and nursery tunes, as well as their harmonies, from the European, principally Anglo, repertoire. Copland's use of sparse, widely spaced, and pandiatonic chords, along with bright orchestral colors, has come to suggest somehow the vastness and openness of our plains and mountains. That this pastoral image is quite different from our preoccupation with industry and technology makes it no less important, for it preserves in art the nostalgia for a rural heritage that has nearly vanished. The "American Wave" style has continued to be popular in concert and film music (Hitchcock 1988:218).

The great American composer?

At the beginning of the twentieth century stands our most enigmatic composer, Charles Ives. Ives embraced the nostalgia of his nineteenth-century upbringing in both its vernacular and classical aspects. At the same time he turned to experimental ideas that continue to occupy us even today. Virtually unknown while he was composing during the first two decades of the twentieth century, he has since become the inspiration for successive generations of composers. The bits of Americana that emerge as collages in his music, the contrasting sound planes, the extreme range of his textures from harsh dissonances to soothing consonances, the contrasting of polyrhythmic complexities with simple vernacular rhythms, the occasional rhapsodic and atonal passages merging into the most satisfying formal and tonal procedures—these have all set the eclectic stage for the composers of today.

Classical music at mid-twentieth century

Serial music

During the last half of the twentieth century, classical music split into a number of types; however, these tended to stem from either the internationalist-progressive or the nationalist-vernacular traditions hewed during the late nineteenth and early twentieth centuries. During the 1920s, when Gershwin was following the nationalist road of fusing jazz with classical forms, other composers were pursuing a different course that led them far beyond the prevailing concepts of tonality, melody, harmony, and form. The sound structures of immigrant composer Edgard Varèse and the noise making of West Coast composer Henry Cowell, however iconoclastic their ideas appeared to be at first, are now seen as having been solidly rooted in the progressivist desire to evolve new sounds and ways of manipulating music, just as the Europeans were doing.

The serialists were also a part of the internationalist way of thinking. Austrian composer Arnold Schoenberg saw his own evolution from late-romantic music through atonality to serialism as an inevitable progression in the Grand Western Tradition. Serialism is a technique of composing based on a logical organization of tones rather than adherence to key feeling and traditional melodic-harmonic principles. A refugee in the United States during the World War II period, Schoenberg reached out to a generation of American composers from the 1940s through the 1960s, many of whom also wrote serial music. The resulting musical textures were startling to most classical music lovers, who felt abandoned by the rapid evolution music was undergoing. Leading post–World War II composers Roger Sessions and Elliott Carter, although not strictly serialists, wrote compositions with melodic-harmonic textures akin to serialism. Another, Milton Babbitt, became a part of the internationalist group that embraced total serialism, the expansion of mathematical techniques to rhythm and tone color (Schoenberg's practice was restricted to melody and harmony).

Electronic music

At the same time Babbitt also became a leading proponent of electronic music, which has resulted in astonishing innovations in melody, harmony, rhythm, form, and particularly tone color. Whether in its *musique concrète* form (tape manipulation of natural sounds) or as a music produced synthetically, electronic music offered the composer a means of making music unfettered by the limitations of the human performer or traditional instruments. But electronic composition has not become a major classical music style. Ironically, electronic techniques are more prevalent in today's popular and commercial music. Thus, electronic music appears to be finding its place as a tool in many types of music, but it is a master in none.

Chance music

Yet another part of the internationalist tradition is the most radical of all, that exemplified in the music of John Cage. Rather than drawing on the European tradition as his aesthetic base, Cage combined the fascination of sound per se with philosophical and procedural ideas from the East [see ORCHESTRAL AND CHAMBER MUSIC IN THE TWENTIETH CENTURY, p. 173]. The result is a music that emphasizes process over product, unrelated sounds over tonal hierarchy, sound mass over linear pitches, and, above all, chance over control.

The middle of the road

Certainly the majority of twentieth-century American composers can be classed as neither radical innovators nor vernacularists. Some followed a more conservative cast, using ideas, textures, and forms closer to the ones of the past. Others used some avant-garde and vernacular effects, but rarely to the extent of alienating the listening public. Composers such as Howard Hanson, Peter Mennin, William Schuman, Samuel Barber, Ned Rorem, Leonard Bernstein, and Morton Gould appeared to place emphasis on traditional craft and its gradual evolution.

Classical music in the late twentieth century

Minimalism

First minimalism during the 1970s and then the new romanticism of the 1980s blunted the leading edge that the avant-garde styles—serialism, electronic music, and chance—had enjoyed in the years following World War II. By concentrating on one or a few musical elements (for La Monte Young, harmony and temperament; for Steve Reich, rhythm) and by methodically adding to or subtracting from melodic-rhythmic cells in a very controlled manner, the minimalists offer a listening experience entirely different from that of serialism. Instead of frequent changes of numerous musical components, minimalism is the slow evolution of one or a few. The serialist's risk of bewildering the public is replaced by the minimalist's danger of boring it. Minimalism has its radical aspect, but its reductionist goals have frequently resulted in simpler, more consonant, harmonies and readily discernible melodic patterns. Thus minimalism had a broader appeal than most novel movements have had. Philip Glass used minimalist musical techniques in operatic, film, and popular music. John Adams has combined the repetitive, propulsive, slowly evolving rhythms of minimalism with more traditional lyrical melody in such works as *Harmonium* (1980) and *Harmonielehre* (1985).

From new romanticism to extended eclecticism

The new romantic movement began with a number of composers whose purpose was to recapture the communicative power that music of the nineteenth century had held for its audiences and still has for today's listeners. It has now evolved into many different approaches. Although the name suggests a regression—and melody, harmony, counterpoint, and rhythmic continuity often follow more traditional approaches—the music nevertheless sounds fresh. Sometimes it deals very directly with neohistoricism by means of nostalgia, embracing large portions of tunes, styles, and literary sources from the past, such as David Del Tredici's *Alice* orchestral pieces (1968–1985), which use Lewis Carroll's famous stories as inspiration, or William Bolcom's Symphony No. 3 (1979), which juxtaposes pointillistic writing with the lushness of past popular music. Some composers wrestle with traditional compositional procedures, such as are found in John Harbison's cantata *The Flight into Egypt* (1987), subtitled "A Sacred Ricercar," in which imitative points gradually draw together and spread out again. Orchestral virtuosity can be found in Joan Tower's *Silver Ladders* (1986) featuring extended solos for clarinet, oboe, marimba, and trumpet, as well as in Ellen Taaffe Zwilich's "Cello" Symphony (No. 2, 1985), which features the entire cello section.

Composers are also increasingly embracing the music of non-Western cultures, and nowhere has the search for inspiration been more apparent than in the Pacific rim. One of the most dedicated is Lou Harrison (b. 1917), who has directed a company producing Chinese music and has used many Asian instruments in his works. He has both constructed and written for gamelan (Indonesian orchestra). Chinese-American composer Chou Wen-chung (b. 1923) has made an impressive fusion of Chinese and Western idioms in his compositions.

Our growing awareness of the past and our increasing knowledge of many cultures have ushered in what might be called a time of extended eclecticism. Today's composers are shaping these historical and multicultural resources according to their individual creative inclinations.

Even frontier towns of the nineteenth century had their "opera houses," just as nearly every city today has some form of musical theater.

THEATER MUSIC

Even frontier towns of the nineteenth century had their "opera houses," just as nearly every city today has some form of musical theater. Local companies rent space in available halls; dinner theaters are found in numerous communities; many schools and colleges mount one or more productions of musicals or opera a year; and thousands regularly flock to New York City, the center for theater music, to see the latest shows. Thus, music theater is nearly as pervasive at the community and national level as is instrumental music. Here we will observe the evolution of musical theater from its eighteenth-century forms through its many divergencies during the nineteenth and twentieth centuries [see POPULAR MUSIC OF THE PARLOR AND STAGE, p. 179].

Music-theater forms in the eighteenth and nineteenth centuries

Ballad, comic, and other opera types

Our early music theater was quite similar to today's musical in that dialogue alternated with music: folk or popular tunes set to new lyrics for ballad operas, and freshly composed arias and ensembles for the more musically and dramatically complex comic operas. Beginning with *The Beggar's Opera* (London 1728) by poet John Gay, with music chosen and arranged by J. C. Pepusch, the form became enormously popular in both England and the United States throughout the eighteenth and early nineteenth centuries. A few are of American origin (*Tammany,* 1794, music by James Hewitt). Over nine hundred different ballad and comic operas were performed in the United States during their heyday, 1785–1815 (Porter 1991).

British-derived ballad and comic operas were gradually replaced in the early nineteenth century by more elitist operatic forms on the one hand and by the vernacular musical theater on the other. Italian opera, particularly Rossini's *La Cenerentola,* became very popular in its English, and considerably altered version, *Cinderella,* during the 1830s and 1840s (Graziano 1994). Operas in their original languages were also heard—French in New Orleans, Italian and later German in New York. In the latter city, various foreign and native companies supplied elite opera culminating in the establishment of the Metropolitan Opera in 1883.

Blackface minstrelsy

Vernacular music theater captured the interest of egalitarian America, and by far the most popular musico-dramatic form for the entire century was blackface minstrelsy, or "Ethiopian Opera." Because it drew primarily on lower class, particularly black, culture for its material, minstrelsy was viewed with alarm by white America's upper classes. Their musical spokesman, critic John Sullivan Dwight, inadvertently acknowledged the popularity of minstrel songs by describing their effect as a "breaking out . . . like a morbid irritation of the skin" (*Dwight's Journal of Music* 1853:54). During the antebellum period, the ragtag figure (Jim Crow) and the swell (Zip Coon) were the principal black caricatures through which the social conventions of the day could be ridiculed (figure 12).

FIGURE 12   Black minstrel types: Jim Crow (left) and Zip Coon (right), c. 1840s.

What sort of music fit the raucous skits of minstrelsy? The banjo, tambourine, fiddle, and bones (clappers) were the instruments of choice. Most lyrics called for fast tempos, diverse, frequently syncopated rhythms, and melodies of flat contour and short duration. Acrobatic dancing was featured along with these patter songs. "Old Dan Tucker" (figure 13) is a typical minstrel song that is still used today for country square dancing.

Minstrel songs and dances sprang from the depth of the Anglo folk tradition. Their dressing, syncopation, and dialect were an imitation of the black folk tradition. A few pieces, such as Dan Emmett's "Dixie" and Stephen Foster's "Oh! Susanna" and "Old Folks at Home," have transcended both the period and the genre.

Following the Civil War minstrel troupes became much larger and their acts more varied. Blacks themselves donned burnt cork and became professional minstrels. Black performer James Bland wrote "Carry Me Back to Ole Virginny" and "In the Evening by the Moonlight," which have an eloquence far removed from minstrelsy's bumptious beginnings. The focus remained, however, on entertainment through ethnic stereotype. A dignified white interlocutor engaged a motley group of endmen in blackface, and backing them at times were a sizable chorus and orchestra.

FIGURE 13   "Old Dan Tucker," from *Minstrel Songs Old and New,* Boston, 1882.

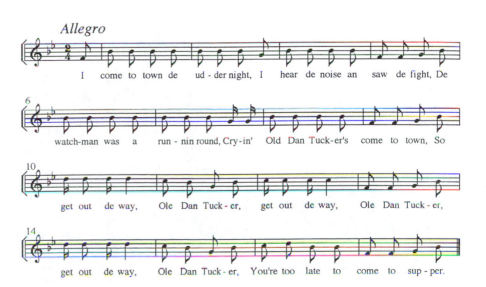

Minstrelsy reached its zenith in the late nineteenth century, but remnants lingered on in twentieth-century vaudeville. Two popular entertainers, Al Jolson and Eddie Cantor, used blackface and sang songs that were the offspring of minstrelsy ("Mammy," "Dinah," "Alabamy Bound"). At the local and regional levels, thousands of lodges, clubs, schools, and other social organizations pooled their talents and presented amateur minstrel shows; however, World War II brought an end to tolerance for blackface minstrelsy.

Antecedents to the contemporary musical

Today's musical has many forerunners. Its basic structure, the alternation of dialogue with music veering toward the popular, reveals its distant ancestry in the eighteenth-century ballad/comic opera. More immediate progenitors are the multifarious theatrical activities from the 1860s on, such as the extravaganza, pantomime, burlesque, operetta, and farce-comedy. The last two are very important predecessors, and operetta continued to compete successfully with the musical during the early twentieth century.

Operetta

Operetta differs from opera by using not only more popular music but also spoken dialogue. The American variety is closely tied to its European counterparts, the operettas of the English team of W. S. Gilbert and Arthur Sullivan and those of French composer Jacques Offenbach. American composers who sampled the genre are Reginald De Koven (*Robin Hood,* 1891), John Philip Sousa (*El Capitan,* 1896), and Victor Herbert (*The Fortune Teller,* 1898; *Mlle. Modiste,* 1905; *Naughty Marietta,* 1910). All three composers' works had immediate popularity, and Herbert's continued to have appeal well into the twentieth century, when the operettas of Rudolph Friml (*Rose-Marie,* 1924; *The Vagabond King,* 1925) and Sigmund Romberg (*The Student Prince,* 1924; *The Desert Song,* 1926) held the New York stage. Hollywood was to expand the popularity of the operetta enormously. Jeanette MacDonald and Nelson Eddy became America's sweethearts in filmed versions of Herbert's *Naughty Marietta* (1935) and *Sweethearts* (1938), Friml's *Rose-Marie* (1936), and Romberg's *New Moon* (1940).

From farce-comedies to "book" musicals

The second forerunner of today's musical sprang from the variety shows of the late nineteenth century. The farce-comedy was a dramatic form that was to feed into the vernacular side of the twentieth-century musical. These 1870s dramatic skits, such as *The Mulligan Guards' Ball* by Edward Harrigan and Tony Hart, with songs by English immigrant composer David Braham, drew on the daily life of the New York Irish for their stories.

By the 1890s, productions were beginning to assume a full-blown form like today's musicals. Among the first is *A Trip to Chinatown* (1891), a "book" musical or a full evening's production held together by a single story. Its plot, humorous happenings of urbanites, is flexible enough to allow continuing changes in both text and music. Among its two best-known interpolations are "The Bowery," by the show's principal composer, Percy Gaunt, and Charles K. Harris's "After the Ball."

Humor, flexibility in the use of plot and music, stories about ordinary people, and popular songs that transcend their theatrical connection—these are leading characteristics of the early-twentieth-century musical comedy. Other defining characteristics came from the musicals of George M. Cohan (*Little Johnny Jones,* 1904; *George Washington, Jr.,* 1906), whose unapologetic patriotism and catchy syncopated tunes ("Give My Regards to Broadway," 1904) were not only long-lived but also gave the genre a closer alliance with nationalism and cutting-edge vernacular styles.

The twentieth-century musical

By the early twentieth century, musical theater was firmly established in three areas: the musical revue, the operetta, and the musical comedy. Only the musical comedy was to continue to evolve, absorbing new dramatic directions and increasing in musical depth until the term *comedy* became an insufficient description. An important key to the musical's success continued to be its close alliance with the popular or hit song. The leading songwriters for the musicals at midcentury are identical with those for popular music itself: Jerome Kern (musicals leading to *Show Boat,* 1927); Irving Berlin (revues *Ziegfeld Follies,* 1927; *Music Box Revues,* 1921–1924; *This Is the Army,* 1942; and musicals *Annie Get Your Gun,* 1946; *Call Me Madam,* 1950); George Gershwin (*George White's Scandals,* musical satires *Strike Up the Band,* 1930, and *Of Thee I Sing,* 1931; the musical *Girl Crazy,* 1932; and the folk opera *Porgy and Bess,* 1935); Cole Porter (various 1930s musicals; *Kiss Me, Kate,* 1948; *Can-Can,* 1953); Richard Rodgers (numerous musicals spanning the 1930s–1950s, the most successful being *Oklahoma!,* 1943; *South Pacific,* 1948; *The King and I,* 1951); Frank Loesser (*Guys and Dolls,* 1950; *The Most Happy Fella,* 1956); and Frederick Loewe (*Brigadoon,* 1947; *My Fair Lady,* 1956; *Camelot,* 1960). These shows were all very popular in their time. Many became movie musicals, and some continue to be revived on Broadway, in national tours, and in regional theater. They have become the standards, enduring monuments of a period sometimes referred to as the Golden Age of the American musical.

In addition to the popular songwriters of the mid-twentieth century, classically trained composers wrote successful musicals. Kurt Weill (*Lady in the Dark,* 1940) and Leonard Bernstein (*West Side Story,* 1957) contributed significantly to raising the level of musical complexity in the American musical, which now displayed such features as more continuous music, varied song forms, ensemble segments, major dance and pantomime sequences, impressionist harmony, and contrapuntal devices.

The direction of musical theater in the late twentieth century was fragmented. Stephen Sondheim (*A Little Night Music,* 1973; *Pacific Overtures,* 1976; *Sweeney Todd,* 1979; *Sunday in the Park with George,* 1984; *Into the Woods,* 1987) has been mentioned frequently as the one composer who continued to follow the direction of the previous Golden Age musicals toward increasing dramatic depth and musical sophistication. In doing so, however, he largely abandoned the musical's historic link with popular song and its large middle-class audience. English composer Andrew Lloyd Webber's musicals (*Jesus Christ Superstar,* 1971; *Evita,* 1978; *Phantom of the Opera,* 1987) combined spectacle with memorable tunes and have secured the allegiance from the middle class that Rodgers and Hammerstein and Lerner and Loewe commanded at midcentury. In 1997, Lloyd Webber's *Cats* (1982) surpassed Hamlisch and Kleban's *A Chorus Line* (1975) as the longest-running musical on Broadway.

The musicals of the mid-1990s revealed both the heterogeneity and the resilience of the musical as our favorite form of theater. *Rent* (1996), which is still on Broadway at the turn of the twenty-first century, parodies the opera *La Bohème* and updates for the younger rock generation the enduring theme of Bohemian life and love; *Bring in 'da Noise/Bring in 'da Funk* (1996) was one in a long line of musicals celebrating blackness and athletic dancing.

American opera

Only occasionally have American composers been successful in grand opera; rather, most have developed other musico-dramatic structures. Such composers include Virgil Thomson, who in *Four Saints in Three Acts* (1934) and *Mother of Us All* (1947), both with lyrics by Gertrude Stein, developed distinctively American speech rhythms in his music; Marc Blitzstein, whose plays in music *The Cradle Will Rock* (1937) and *Regina* (1949), the latter after Lillian Hellman's *The Little Foxes,* used vernacular musical types such as the

An increase in the number of independent film makers and the demise of studio composers and orchestras are important factors undergirding the musical heterogeneity we can expect from today's films.

popular song and the blues; and Douglas Moore, who evoked American history with *The Devil and Daniel Webster* (1939) and *The Ballad of Baby Doe* (1958). Most of these works have been performed with some frequency throughout the country as have others by Carlisle Floyd (*Susanna,* 1954), Aaron Copland (*The Tender Land,* 1954), Robert Ward (*The Crucible,* 1961), and Italian-born Gian Carlo Menotti (*The Medium* and *The Telephone,* 1946; *The Consul,* 1950; *Amahl and the Night Visitors,* 1951).

Music and film

The most far reaching and influential performing-art form is film, which touches the lives of nearly everyone [see FILM, p. 202]. Just as recordings and radio have vastly increased music's availability, so the movies and television have made dramatic entertainment widespread. Although music appears infrequently in stage drama, it has become a nearly constant companion to film. Only occasionally noticed, movie music is nevertheless meant to perform the important function of sustaining and enhancing the feeling appropriate to the action on the screen.

Silent films

The so-called silent films of the early twentieth century were far from quiet, for a pianist, a small ensemble, or even a major orchestra in the large urban movie palaces was ever present. The pastiche tradition, so prevalent in earlier dramatic forms, is evident here: preexisting music of different composers was often chosen to fit the dramatic contingencies of the film. "Cue sheets" for individual films were sometimes issued, and catalogs of dramatic situations and emotions were developed, with recommended pieces listed under each category. Publishers issued special arrangements of classical and light-classical music as well as freshly composed musical segments to fit particular moods. In all, the public was exposed to a wide variety of music.

Sound films

Following the introduction of the sound track, theater orchestras were replaced by Hollywood studio orchestras, and, beginning in the 1930s, single composers increasingly wrote original music for individual films. Their principal concern was fitting appropriate music to the dramatic situation, not demonstrating their individuality; nevertheless, the major composers of midcentury—Dimitri Tiomkin, Franz Waxman, Miklos Rozsa, Max Steiner, Alfred Newman, and Bernard Herrmann—did manage to achieve a semblance of individual style and some recognition. Most wrote in a neo-romantic, symphonic idiom easily absorbed by the moviegoing public. Other styles occasionally appear, for popular music—Dixieland, jazz, swing, rock—has been used for appropriate dramatic material. Science fiction, psychological, and suspense dramas have afforded opportunity for dissonant, atonal, and electronic musical underscoring. An increase in the number of independent filmmakers and the demise of studio composers and orchestras are important factors undergirding the musical heterogeneity we can expect from today's films.

POPULAR MUSIC

Throughout this essay we have dealt with aspects of popular music that were pertinent to ethnic, religious, concert, and theater musics. Here we will examine popular music's remaining aspects—the major historical styles preceding the twentieth century and two major contemporary forms—jazz and rock.

The diversity of popular music is apparent when one walks into a music store and is confronted by various classifications posted on signs over the CD bins. The Grammy Awards, presented yearly by the National Academy of Recording Arts and Sciences, also afford some idea of the spectrum of genres: rock, rhythm and blues, country, soul, gospel, pop, new age, jazz, jazz fusion, Latin pop, tropical Latin, Mexican American, traditional blues, traditional folk, polka, reggae, and various types of rap. Some categories are inclusive of others, and many reveal their ethnic derivation. Although any one of us might show an interest in only a few, we do recognize *all* as popular music.

Such variety fosters the common perception that popular music today no longer has the core that it had in the past, that it has split into many fragments revealing our cultural dichotomies: young/old, rich/poor, white/black, Latin/North American, ethnic/mainstream. Actually, popular music has always been diverse, but one or a few styles have tended to dominate and influence the others, just as rock shapes nearly all of the popular music of our present culture. As we wend our way through these many types and styles, we must keep in mind that the touchstone of all popular music is the song (and sometimes the dance): readily comprehensible, performable without special musical training, and loved by large numbers of people.

Popular song in the eighteenth and nineteenth centuries

During the Federal period at the end of the eighteenth century, popular songs were published that ran the gamut from folk and national songs to airs from the current Anglo-American theater and concert part-songs. They reveal the United States in its infancy as an agrarian, seafaring nation, still closely tied to the mother country but fiercely proud of its independence.

The nineteenth century witnessed the change of popular song from music for different social groups to mass-produced and mass-distributed sheet music more or less the same for all audiences. Nevertheless, a diversity of song topics was maintained. In addition to love songs, songs were written about politics, wars, social issues, occupations, inventions, sports, tragedies, comic situations, geographical locations, and travels, among other topics. The thoughts of the people and their reactions to sometimes bewildering change are found in the large number of songs celebrating an earlier, seemingly simpler, time. Indeed, nostalgia in various forms—for family, the home place, various artifacts, childhood friends, or a sweetheart—is an important category of nineteenth-century popular music.

Undoubtedly the best known popular song composer of the nineteenth century is Stephen Foster (1826–1864) (figure 14). He wrote hit songs in the important genres of his day—the minstrel song ("Oh! Susanna"), the plantation song ("Old Folks at Home"), and the genteel love song ("Jeanie with the Light Brown Hair"). A dozen or so of his songs remained popular well into the twentieth century.

Popular music at the turn of the twentieth century

Ragtime

Ragtime attained some respectability as a middle-class popular music during the first two decades of the twentieth century. Its roots were disparate—folk and popular song and dance—with the primary focus on syncopation. This vital form of rhythmic displacement (figure 15), with the many accents falling between regular beats, had

FIGURE 14   Stephen Foster, from *The American History and Encyclopedia of Music,* W. L. Hubbard, ed., 1910.

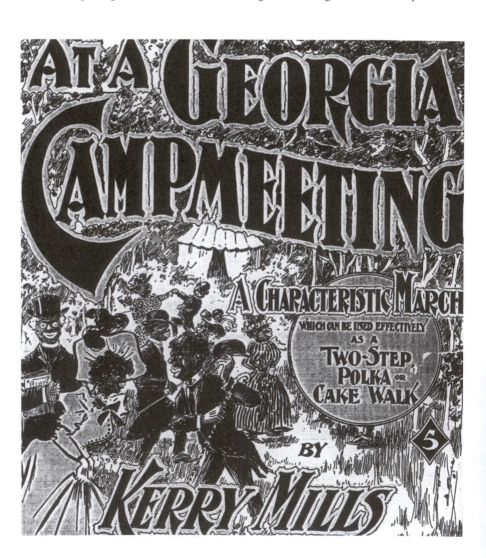

FIGURE 15   Ragtime rhythmic displacement.

heretofore been confined largely to minstrelsy but had spilled over into popular music of the 1890s and 1900s, principally as "coon" songs that satirized blacks. Kerry Mills's "At a Georgia Camp Meeting" is an example (figure 16).

Ragtime became even more popular as purely instrumental piano music, and Scott Joplin, among its many practitioner-composers, has become ragtime's foremost historical figure. His "Maple Leaf Rag" is an American classic (figure 17). Its sectional form, with one repeated strain following another, parallels that of the quickstep march, such as Sousa's "Stars and Stripes Forever."

The Tin Pan Alley song

The term *Tin Pan Alley* originally signified a specific locale in New York City that was the headquarters for many popular song publishers. It has also come to mean a type of early-twentieth-century song suitable for mass distribution. Its consumers consisted of the traditional, agrarian middle class, a rapidly expanding urban working class, and the newly arrived immigrant populations. The song topics are as heterogeneous as the interests of these varied groups, but the music and lyrics are formulaic. The composers and librettists sought to grab or hook the listener with simple, highly repetitive melodies and harmonies and with rigidly metered, heavily rhymed lyrics, replete with assonances ("June," "moon," "spoon") and consonances ("fuzzy-wuzzy," "tick-tock"). The song was meant to strike listeners as something recognizable but with a novel melodic or poetic twist. Although creativity was reduced sometimes to a single catchy effect, a surprising number of memorable songs have emerged from the Gay Nineties

FIGURE 16   Cover for "At a Georgia Campmeeting," 1902.

FIGURE 17   "Maple Leaf Rag," by Scott Joplin, 1899.

and the following decade (Charles K. Harris's "After the Ball"; Harry Dacre's "Bicycle Built for Two"; Joseph E. Howard and Ida Emerson's "Hello! My Baby"; Paul Dresser's "On the Banks of the Wabash"; Charles B. Lawlor and James W. Blake's "The Sidewalks of New York"; Albert von Tilzer's "Take Me Out to the Ball Game"; Frank L. Stanton and Ethelbert Nevin's "Mighty Lak' a Rose").

The twentieth century: from jazz to rock

The jazz-age popular song (1920–1955)

The formulaic song continued to be the basis of songwriting during the jazz age; however, in the hands of composers such as George Gershwin, Harold Arlen, Hoagy Carmichael, Cole Porter, Jerome Kern, and, of course, Irving Berlin, popular song achieved what many consider to be its Golden Age [see JAZZ, p. 650]. The emotional emphasis is found in the chorus or refrain, with the extended verse or storytelling sections of the older 1890s songs such as "After the Ball" reduced to a forgettable introduction. Many aficionados of jazz-age popular songs such as "Blue Skies" (Berlin, 1927), "Star Dust" (Carmichael, 1929), "Embraceable You" (Gershwin, 1930), "Easy to Love" (Porter, 1936), "That Old Black Magic" (Arlen, 1943), and "Long Ago and Far Away" (Kern, 1944) can sing entire choruses from memory but often don't recognize their corresponding verse sections. In the jazz-age song, melody and harmony became more integral and the latter more complex, with seventh and ninth chords, more unusual chord progressions, chromaticism, and unexpected key changes. These textural features, along with the sumptuous arrangements of the big bands and studio

In the jazz-age song, melody and harmony became more integral and the latter more complex, with seventh and ninth chords, more unusual chord progressions, chromaticism, and unexpected key changes.

orchestras, made the jazz-age song appear more sophisticated than those of earlier periods. Indeed, without leaving its vernacular roots completely, the popular song approached the art song during the jazz age.

1920s jazz

Emerging from turn-of-the-century genres such as ragtime, blues, and popular song, jazz acquired a distinctive identity by the 1920s, with minor variant localizations found in New Orleans, Chicago, Kansas City, and New York. Some of early jazz's most endearing characters—Bix Beiderbecke, Louis Armstrong, Jelly Roll Morton, Sidney Bechet—caught the country's, indeed the world's, attention. A typical performing group ranged from six to ten players, and the repertoire consisted of popular songs and blues structures often played at a "hot" or rapid tempo. Improvisation became an important feature of jazz performance at this time, and the improvisatory section for soloist or dueling soloists was adapted by other types of popular music, including later jazz, country music, and rock. The jazz of the 1920s lives on today as Dixieland music.

The swing era and beyond

Jazz reached the peak of its influence as a popular genre during the 1930s–1940s in the form of swing, as performed by the big bands (fifteen to twenty pieces) of Benny Goodman, Duke Ellington, Glenn Miller, and Harry James or their chamber-music counterparts, combos. The big band era will always be identified with World War II, and many of that generation consider it to be the peak of the jazz movement. Big bands were capable of demonstrating exciting rhythmic precision in fast pieces and luxuriant harmony on slower ballads.

During the 1940s–1950s, swing evolved into bebop and its counterpart, cool jazz, followed by the progressive jazz of the 1950s and 1960s and several other types thereafter. Emphasis on improvisation and harmonic-rhythmic sophistication are features of these later phases of jazz, which moved to the periphery if not out of popular music altogether.

The transition to rock

The first rock music coalesced during the 1950s out of two different ethnic types: white country music and black rhythm and blues. Elvis Presley has become the legendary figure effecting this merger into a radically different style, rock and roll, which was to replace jazz as the major popular music form. Rock and roll soon turned into rock during the 1960s, the era of the Beach Boys, the Doors, the Rolling Stones, and, above all, the Beatles. This period is often considered the high point of rock, just as swing was a similar apex for the jazz era. The last thirty years of the century witnessed fewer changes in rock, although numerous subgenres and fusions of various styles occurred [see ROCK, p. 347].

The sociopolitical concomitants of the rock era—post–World War II prosperity and a vague dissatisfaction with materialistic complacency, the increasing empowerment of young people, the relaxing of moral constraints, the tensions created by a prolonged cold war, racial divisions, the assassinations of Martin Luther King Jr. and John and Robert Kennedy, and the unpopular Vietnam War—created a general disillusionment with all forms of authority: parental, generational, and governmental. Popular music, always a mirror of social attitudes and issues, was to reflect this tension in the 1969 Woodstock Festival, a coming together of major rock celebrities and legions of young people on rain-soaked farm pastures in the lower Catskills of New York. The folk protest movement (led by Bob Dylan and Joan Baez), as well as Woodstock and a few festivals in its wake, at the peak of rock's confrontational period. Although certain groups continued to assault societal norms, rock, for the most part, settled into a less adversarial role as undergirding most of the world's popular music.

A comparison of jazz with rock

Rock is different from jazz in many ways. The rock sound is electronically produced or amplified; jazz is acoustic—that is, the sound of the instruments and the voice is not changed by amplification. The rock ensemble consists basically of guitars, keyboards, and percussion; the jazz ensemble, of winds (choirs of brasses and saxophones for big bands), piano, guitar, string bass, and percussion. The steady quadruple beat of 1920s jazz, with its more sophisticated treatment in 1930s–1940s swing, was replaced by the strong backbeat of rock (figure 18). The rock singing style marks a complete break with the classical music singing tradition. The smooth crooning of jazz vocalists such as Frank Sinatra still retained a vestige of the bel canto tradition; whereas the raspy, strident quality of rock singers such as Bruce Springsteen is evidence of popular music's complete emancipation from a classical vocal production.

Jazz and rock performers are quite different in both demeanor and dress. The understatement of most jazz performers contrasts vividly with frequently extravagant rock gesticulations. During jazz's heyday, its performers dressed in conventional or business clothing associated with the professional classes. Rock performers often appear in various states of striking or working-class costuming, suggesting an indifference to, even arrogance toward, mainstream society.

The principal means of dissemination for both rock and jazz is the recording; however, their live performance venues are different. Even in the heyday of swing, jazz thought of itself as a service to dancing, hence the common appellation *dance band*. The 1920s jazz bands appeared in speakeasies or clubs, and the big bands of the 1930s and 1940s frequently performed in large dance pavilions throughout the country. Concerts were a less frequent activity, although personalities such as the singer Judy Garland could command large, appreciative audiences.

Rock, like jazz, is performed in clubs and bars, but during the 1960s rock frequently became heard as concert music in large halls and, by the 1970s, even in stadiums. The music was bolstered by huge amplification and spectacular lighting, and the massive crowds became enthusiastic participants in these "happenings."

The rock-age song

The rock-age song largely abandoned the evolution of the popular song toward harmonic sophistication. Simpler, often modal, harmonies prevail. The archlike contours of many jazz-age melodies gave way to short, repetitive phrases, with "doo-wop" ensembles backing or echoing the principal singer.

The rock song is frequently written by its own or other performers rather than by the specialist composers characteristic of the jazz age. It is increasingly created for musicals, revues, or movies, but it usually is heard as a vehicle for the performer in concert, on audio recordings, or on MTV. Characteristically it has no elaborate introduction, and it usually ends by fading away on a repeated riff. The song appears to be simply *there*, to be tuned in and out at the listener's will. Its lyrics are more graphic than those

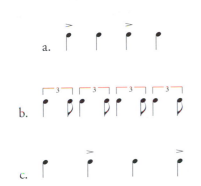

FIGURE 18   Three popular beats that emerged in the twentieth century: *a,* duple jazz beat; *b,* swing beat; *c,* rock backbeat.

of the jazz song and are frequently criticized for their vulgarity. Nevertheless, perennial popular-song themes such as love in its many manifestations, from despair to exultation, are a major part of the rock repertoire.

Rock's significant songs have played a major role in defining our society and have often mediated among many diverse groups, sometimes spanning more than one generation. The Beatles's "Yesterday"; Chuck Berry's "Maybelline"; James Brown's "Say It Loud, I'm Black and I'm Proud"; the Byrds' "Mister Tambourine Man"; Johnny Cash's "Folsom Prison Blues"; Fats Domino's "Blueberry Hill"; Bob Dylan's "Blowin' in the Wind"; Aretha Franklin's "Respect"; Marvin Gaye's "What's Going On?"; the Jefferson Airplane's "White Rabbit"; Led Zeppelin's "Stairway to Heaven"; Elvis Presley's "Heartbreak Hotel"; the Rolling Stones' "I Can't Get No Satisfaction"; Simon and Garfunkel's "Bridge Over Troubled Water"; Bruce Springsteen's "Born in the U.S.A."; U2's "Sunday, Bloody Sunday"; Van Halen's "Running with the Devil"; and Muddy Waters's "Hoochie Coochie Man"—these titles, together with the many different styles represented by their performers, suggest the immense diversity of popular music with rock as its core over the past half-century.

From rock to rap

During the past two decades, a genre of rock known as rap or hip-hop has emerged with strength and commanding recognition as a major style on its own [see HIP-HOP AND RAP, p. 692]. Much of rap is defiant, stemming from black youths' confronting a society that seems indifferent to, or inept at, solving the enormous social problems of urban minorities. Gangsta rap ("Cop Killer," performed by Ice T) has been the genre's most outspoken form, yet rap is also an entertainment form that reaches beyond race and gender. It has had its white (Beastie Boys) as well as female (Blondie) performers, and music meant primarily for dancing or humor. "Dissing" (insulting) and boasting ("Sucker MCs," performed by Run-D.M.C.) are also features of rap.

Like many other forms of popular music, rap's purely musical components—the rhythm of vernacular poetry recited over a repetitive, timbral-rhythmic background—have given it a popularity that overpowers its confrontational aspect. Radio stations playing only rap music can be found in many communities, and hip-hoppers turn their automobiles into powerful cruising sound systems.

Rap's immediate ancestry can be traced to disco music and its emphasis on mechanical reproduction. In its infancy, the disc jockey, or deejay, was composer-performer. By rerecording the repetitive instrumental breaks or fragments of other rock recordings, by "scratching" (spinning a record back and forth against the needle), and, later, by using drum machines and synthesizing new sound, the deejay created a music based entirely on modern technology.

The technique of rapping over this prerecorded sound material is a most radical change for popular song. If rap were to proliferate as rock has done for the past fifty years, electronics and speech-rhythm would replace song as the principal vehicle for popular music. As rap merges with other popular music forms, however, melody of a type that most people can remember, and even perform, will probably prevail.

THE FUTURE

In the twenty-first century, many of the defining national characteristics framing our music will endure: our individualism, egalitarianism, belief in pragmatism, and idealism about ourselves as a people on whom so much good fortune has been bestowed. Our economic and political activity has become increasingly world centered, and our music will undoubtedly reflect that tendency as well.

At the beginning of the twentieth century, we considered our society to be a melting pot for many cultures. We now liken the efflorescences of these cultures to a salad bowl, mosaic, or rainbow, where both integration and individualization are continuously at work. Composer Normand Lockwood, whose life spanned nearly the entire century, has compared the process to "a melding hand of cards, and maybe we're still shuffling them" (Lockwood 1996). Undoubtedly we will continue to have many defining moments in American music, and they will be ever changing.

REFERENCES

Allen, William Francis, Charles Pickard Ware, and Lucy McKim Garrison, comp. 1951 [1867]. *Slave Songs of the United States.* New York: Peter Smith.

"Americanism in Music." 1899. *The American Monthly Review of Reviews.* January.

Authentic Music of the American Indian. c. 1970. Everest Records 3450/3. (Record 1, side 2, #s 7 and 8).

Bordman, Gerald. 1986. *American Musical Theatre: A Chronicle.* New York: Oxford University Press.

Béhague, Gerard. 1979. *Music in Latin America: An Introduction.* Englewood Cliffs, N.J.: Prentice-Hall.

Bronson, Bertrand H. 1976. *The Singing Tradition of Child's Popular Ballads.* Abridgment of *The Traditional Tunes of the Child Ballads.* 4 vols., 1959–1972. Princeton, N.J.: Princeton University Press.

Burton, Bryan. 1993. *Moving within the Circle: Contemporary Native American Music and Dance.* Danbury, Conn.: World Music Press.

Camus, Raoul. 1986. "Bands." In *The New Grove Dictionary of American Music,* ed. H. Wiley Hitchcock and Stanley Sadie, 1:130. London and New York: Macmillan.

Chase, Gilbert. 1987. *America's Music: From the Pilgrims to the Present.* 3rd ed. Urbana: University of Illinois Press.

Crawford, Richard. 1993. *The American Musical Landscape.* Berkeley: University of California Press.

Dwight's Journal of Music. 1853. 19 November.

Graziano, John, ed. 1994. "Italian Opera in English: 'Cinderella' (1831)." In *Nineteenth-Century American Musical Theater,* ed. Deane L. Root, 3: New York: Garland.

Hamm, Charles. 1979. *Yesterdays: Popular Song in America.* New York: Norton.

Heth, Charlotte, ed. 1976. *New World Records.* Vol. 1. New York, N246. LP disk

Hitchcock, H. Wiley. 1988. *Music in the United States.* 3rd ed. Englewood Cliffs, N.J.: Prentice Hall.

Hubbard, W. L., ed. 1910. *The American History and Encyclopedia of Music.* Irving Squire.

Kingman, Daniel. 1998. *American Music: A Panorama.* Concise 3rd ed. New York: Schirmer Books.

Lockwood, Normand. 1996. Letter to author, 29 June.

Lomax, Alan. 1975. *The Folk Songs of North America.* New York: Doubleday/Dolphin.

Manuel, Peter L. 1988. *Popular Musics of the Non-Western World: An Introductory Survey.* New York: Oxford University Press.

Marrocco, W. Thomas, and Harold Gleason. 1964. *Music in America.* New York: Norton.

Oliver, Paul. 1998. *The Story of the Blues.* New Ed. Boston: Northeastern University Press.

Peña, Manuel H. 1985. *The Texas-Mexican Conjunto: History of a Working Class Music.* Austin: University of Texas Press.

Porter, Susan L. 1991. *With an Air Debonair: Musical Theater in America, 1785–1815.* Appendix A, 425–500. Washington, D.C.: Smithsonian Institution Press.

Slobin, Mark. 1982. *Tenement Songs: The Popular Music of the Jewish Immigrants.* Urbana: University of Illinois Press.

Southern, Eileen. 1997. *The Music of Black Americans: A History.* 3rd ed. New York: Norton.

Spottswood, Richard K., ed. 1976. *Folk Music in America.* Library of Congress, Music Division. LP disk.

Stevenson, Robert. 1966. *Protestant Church Music in America.* New York: Norton.

Stuessy, Joe. 1990. *Rock and Roll: Its History and Stylistic Development.* Englewood Cliffs, N.J.: Prentice-Hall.

Tawa, Nicholas. 1982. *A Sound of Strangers: Musical Culture, Acculturation, and the Post–Civil War Ethnic American.* Metuchen, N.J.: Scarecrow Press.

Trueheart, Charles. 1996. "Welcome to the Next Church." *The Atlantic Monthly,* August, 37–58.

Ward, Ed, Geoffrey Stokes, and Ken Tucker. 1986. *Rock of Ages: The Rolling Stone History of Rock and Roll.* New York: Rolling Stone Press/Summit Books.

Snapshot: Four Views of Music in the United States
Katherine K. Preston
Susan Key
Judith Tick
Frank J. Cipolla and Raoul F. Camus

Concert Music at the End of the Nineteenth Century—*Katherine K. Preston*
Ethnic Radio—*Susan Key*
The Piano and Women of Accomplishment—*Judith Tick*
Bands—*Frank J. Cipolla, Raoul F. Camus*

Following are four different views of music in American life, some taken from the nineteenth and early twentieth centuries, others from our own time. These four are not meant to represent the totality of musical activity in the United States but are presented here because each portrays a unique snapshot of musical life within a particular historical or social context that helps define us as a country. Readers are encouraged to consult cross-referenced articles within this one for further information about many related musical activities.

CONCERT MUSIC AT THE END OF THE NINETEENTH CENTURY

The term *concert music* is a useful phrase in the context of late-twentieth-century musical life, for we all know what a concert is: an activity that focuses on the live performance of music. The liveness of the performance is an important distinction, for live performances today (most of which are concerts) have a special status distinct from the much more ubiquitous recordings or broadcast music that fill our lives (and that often function as background sound). Also implied by the term *concert* is the fact that music is the principal raison d'être for the event: at all classical-music concerts—and even at most modern pop and rock concerts—music is not background noise or ancillary to whatever else is happening, it is the main attraction. Further embedded in a twentieth-century concept of concert life and concert music are class signifiers associated with different categories or styles of music. The distinctions (stereotypical as they might be) that are applied to different kinds of music, whether broad ("art" or "classical" music as opposed to "popular" or "vernacular" music) or specific (different types of music, such as rap, classical, jazz, punk, heavy metal, classic rock, folk, or opera, all of which appeal to very different sorts of people), are part of our knowledge of those types of music. Everyone knows, whether subconsciously or overtly, that a concert by the Juilliard String Quartet and one by Puff Daddy exist in different musical universes between which there is often very little communication or overlapping audiences and repertoires.

The phrase *concert music,* however, even though it is commonly used in reference to musical activity of the nineteenth century, is much less suitable in this context, primarily because the term's connotations are specific to conditions inherent to the twentieth century. A discussion of nineteenth-century concert activity in the United States, therefore, must highlight some of these basic differences.

How does concert music today differ from that of the late nineteenth century? It differs significantly, and in complicated ways, for the twentieth-century attitudes toward music that we take for granted were in the process of evolution a hundred years ago. The first difference should be obvious: music in the nineteenth century was performed live, by either professional or amateur musicians (rare was the middle-class family that did not include a member who was at least modestly proficient on an instrument). Consequently, the special category that concerts enjoy today as live performances did not exist in the nineteenth century, for concerts then, in fact, were only a minute percentage of the possible live performances available to Americans. Second, the idea of music as an entity that can stand alone (as opposed to music as something essentially utilitarian) gained wide acceptance in the European cultural sphere (including the United States) over the course of the nineteenth century. This should not suggest that there was little musical activity in the United States during the eighteenth or early nineteenth centuries, but rather that concert activity per se was but a small (albeit growing) portion of a musical culture that was rich and diverse. Finally, it is crucial to realize that the clear-cut distinctions between musical styles and the class and status signifiers that we associate with different types of music in the late twentieth century were in the process of formation but were far from fully defined in the late nineteenth century. During this period there emerged the basic idea that different types of music and different repertoires could be crafted to appeal to specific and distinct subgroups of the population. This led, of course, to the concept of niche marketing, which became an accepted part of musical life in the twentieth century [see CLASS, p. 42; MARKETING CLASSICAL MUSIC, p. 268].

Musical activity in the United States, 1850–1900

For a majority of nineteenth-century Americans, music was primarily utilitarian in function. It was sometimes serious (church music), sometimes frivolous (ditties), sometimes background sound (much theater music). Occasionally it was essential to the featured activity (dance music), but more commonly it was not. Music was ubiquitous, arguably almost as ubiquitous to nineteenth-century Americans as it is to their twentieth- and twenty-first-century descendants. Dancing, for example, was the most popular and widespread form of social activity, and this obviously required the services of musicians—whether a pair of fiddlers for a rural barn dance in western New York, a string and wind band hired for a town ball in Raleigh, North Carolina, or sisters playing four-hands arrangements on the parlor piano for a family party in Philadelphia [see DANCE, p. 206]. Urban Americans, furthermore, attended the theater regularly, and every theater had some semblance of an orchestra: music accompanied almost all theatrical productions, whether dramatic fare by Shakespeare or Sheridan, blackface minstrelsy, opera (Italian, French, or English), pantomime, dance, variety show, or melodrama [see POPULAR MUSIC OF THE PARLOR AND STAGE, p. 179]. Nineteenth-century Americans also regularly hired journeymen musicians to perform music for special events such as dinners, weddings, parades, commencements, boat parties, bicycle races, picnics, and funerals. Americans of all backgrounds heard and performed music in their churches [see RELIGION, p. 116]. They sang work songs to ease manual labor and lullabies to put babies to sleep; they also entertained themselves with at-home performances of instrumental and vocal music with a frequency difficult to imagine today. These were all venues for the performance of music that was utilitarian, entertaining, and ubiquitous in nineteenth-century American life.

Concerts in large cities

Concerts, in the twentieth-century sense of the term, functioned as one small component of this wealth of musical activity. They were varied in nature. There were performances by local musicians and by visiting virtuosos, by amateur groups as well as by professional performers. They were also wonderfully varied in repertoire: generally a concert at midcentury would feature a marvelous mixture of performers (singers and various combinations of instrumentalists) performing an incongruous (by twentieth-century standards) hodgepodge of compositions. They were also broad based in terms of audience. The clear-cut stratification of audiences along lines of class, education, and even ethnicity that is so much a part of modern concert-going was not yet a major factor at midcentury: many different peoples attended many different kinds of concerts; furthermore, there was a great deal of shared repertoire among concerts given by different kinds of performers.

Large cities in the United States generally had a richer and more diverse concert life than did small towns and villages, but the denizens of both enjoyed concert performances by some of the best professional touring musicians—instrumentalists, ensembles, and singers—that Europe had to offer. Pianists, singers, and ensembles began touring the United States, Canada, and Mexico during the late 1830s and the 1840s; by the middle of the century tours by pianists (Sigismund Thalberg, Hans von Bülow, Leopold de Meyer, Alfred Jaëll), violinists (Camilla Urso, Ole Bull, Henri Vieuxtemps), singers (Henriette Sontag, Jenny Lind, Adelina Patti, Christine Nilsson, and dozens of others), and ensembles (the Germania Orchestra and the Saxonia Band) were rather commonplace. European artists, who regularly mounted tours of Europe and even Asia, had expanded into North America because it was a wonderful and lucrative new market: many of these performers stuffed their pockets with American dollars before heading back to London, Milan, or Paris. Such itinerant virtuoso performers appeared regularly in North American urban areas, but they also filled in the gaps between cities on their itineraries with one- or two-night stands in smaller towns and villages en route. After the mid-1860s the stream of European performers was augmented by Americans—pianist Louis Moreau Gottschalk, bands headed by Patrick Sarsfield Gilmore and John Philip Sousa, and Theodore Thomas's Orchestra, to name but a few, who also performed concerts widely in American cities, towns, and villages.

Local, amateur concerts

In addition to concerts by the itinerant professionals, there were also occasional concerts offered by local amateur music makers, usually as a social outlet, sometimes as a benefit performance to raise funds for charity. Amateur choral societies and clubs could be found in cities, villages, and towns all over the United States at midcentury: an amateur choral tradition transplanted from the United Kingdom flourished in the United States during the nineteenth century, and the influx of German immigrants, especially after the late 1840s, resulted in the formation of hundreds of *Saengerbund, Musikvereinen*, and Arion Musical Societies [see CENTRAL EUROPEAN MUSIC, p. 884; EASTERN EUROPEAN MUSIC, p. 908]. Amateur brass bands also could be found all over the United States during the nineteenth century. Americans in small towns and large cities joined these choral and instrumental groups for social interchange and musical enjoyment; other Americans attended their concerts to see and hear friends and family members performing. It is worth noting, however, that the numerous local professional musicians who lived and worked in most American towns and cities rarely mounted concerts (except for the occasional benefit performance); they were much too busy performing the ubiquitous utilitarian music (for dances, the theater, parades, and the like) that made up a majority of Americans' musical landscape. This bolsters the contention that concerts, per se, made up but a small percentage of Americans' musical experiences at midcentury.

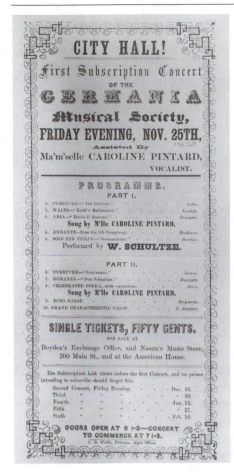

FIGURE I A typical eighteenth-century concert program from an 1853 performance at City Hall, Worcester, Massachusetts, by the Germania Orchestra, a European ensemble that toured the United States at midcentury with the expressed intention of introducing Americans to a "higher class" of music. The ensemble, however, mixed the repertoire, including various operatic selections, a movement from Beethoven's Fifth Symphony, and several dances—a waltz, a polka, and two galops. Illustration courtesy Graphic Arts Collection of the American Antiquarian Society, Worcester, Massachusetts.

Traveling concerts

The vast majority of concerts during the second half of the century were designed to attract as broad a segment of the (primarily middle-class) population as possible. When opera singers were not touring the country with a company, they formed concert troupes—several singers, perhaps a violinist and a pianist—and took their show on the road, performing a mixture of foreign-language arias, English translations of operatic "gems," traditional Scotch or Irish ballads, and instrumental works. Pianists and violinists played their own showy, virtuosic compositions, adaptations from the operatic stage, and sets of variations on familiar popular tunes. Local brass bands—when performing in a band shell in a town center, on the lawn of a resort, or during an interlude in an athletic event—played a similar repertoire, arranged for brass instruments. Even ensembles such as the Germania Orchestra, which toured the United States with the overt intention of introducing to Americans the "better" sort of European repertoire, offered varied programs to attract a wide range of auditors (figure 1).

Many Americans attended concerts because of the celebrity of the featured performer: the frenzied public reception of the Swedish soprano Jenny Lind on her American tour (1850–1852) was far from unique. Midcentury audiences generally wished to be entertained, diverted, and bedazzled; this desire persisted among much of the population for the remainder of the century. Since the repertoire of concerts was so broad (and so shared by different types of performers), a concert by an itinerant singer generally would attract audiences of the same social and economic makeup as that given by a virtuoso pianist or violinist, or even by an ensemble (a singing family like the Hutchinsons, for example) or an individual performing what we today would consider primarily popular music. And the audiences of local amateur choral societies, although perhaps attracted to the concert for personal reasons, were not unlike other concert audiences in terms of social or economic makeup or a desire to be entertained.

Changes in the status of concert musics

There were, of course, exceptions to this rather idealized picture of American concertgoing homogeneity. Even in the first half of the century there were proselytizers for the elevation of music from the status of entertainment and diversion, individuals who believed that Americans should follow the example of those Europeans who were beginning to consider music an art rather than a utilitarian activity. As the century wore on, and as the new Romantic-period attitudes toward the function of music became more widespread in Europe, those Americans of like mind grew in number and influence and began to effect a change in American concertgoing. The agents for this change were editors of music periodicals and, especially, the founders and directors of the professional ensembles that began to proliferate in the larger American cities after midcentury. Many of these ensembles were founded and nurtured by German immigrant musicians who overtly promoted "serious" or "weighty" music to the American public, encouraged the adoption of a new attitude toward a particular repertoire of music (that known today as classical), and marketed this style of music to a special segment of the population. The kind of concertgoing associated with performances by these ensembles required of audience members a completely different attitude: music no longer as entertainment but rather as a serious art that demanded study and close attention. Many of the directors of amateur choral societies (especially after midcentury) similarly set out to convert both their ensemble members and their (relatively) captive audiences to this very different Romantic-period notion about the function of music. As a result, during the second half of the nineteenth century there was a concomitant growth in this particular segment of the American concertgoing public. There was also increasing reception throughout American society of the idea that some music was so different from the rest that it should be regarded as art and that this music should be heard only in the contexts of special

Urban popular music soon forged with the new
medium a mutually beneficial alliance that
endures to this day.

concerts (which, of course, did not include any examples of the lower, "baser" entertainment forms of music) and by audiences comprised of special people (those educated sufficiently to understand and appreciate the repertoire).

By the end of the nineteenth century, concertgoing was clearly acquiring many of the characteristics we associate with classical concert life in the twentieth century: the identification of certain audiences with particular repertoires, the ranking of different styles of music (some "better" than others), and the disappearance of shared repertoires. Some concerts represented music for edification and as such had acquired the cachet of the legitimate and the significant, as opposed to the utilitarian, which had became, in the eyes of some, inferior and second rate. By century's end concerts still represented only a small proportion of Americans' live-music experiences. In other important ways, however, this aspect of musical life had changed significantly from what concertgoing meant to mid-nineteenth century Americans.

—KATHERINE K. PRESTON

ETHNIC RADIO

The impact of radio broadcasting on musical life in the United States can hardly be overestimated. At one end of the artistic spectrum, both traditional European masterworks and avant-garde compositions reached audiences of unprecedented proportions. At the other, hillbilly and other rural genres found new commercial outlets. Urban popular music soon forged with the new medium a mutually beneficial alliance that endures to this day. The early years of broadcasting also saw the growth of new institutional mechanisms for musical creation, consumption, and dissemination. Most powerful were the three networks, beginning with NBC in 1926, whose enormous resources and national reach created a new type of musical occasion.

Like any technology that reconfigures methods of musical dissemination, radio inevitably produced as a corollary a broader and deeper cultural reconfiguration of the relationship of music to class, gender, and race. During its first two decades, the new medium challenged class boundaries of fine-art music, replaced the female-dominated parlor with the male-dominated broadcasting studio, altered the music making habits of Americans across the economic spectrum, and allowed ethnic communities to both reach out across geographic and cultural boundaries and admit outside influences into their most intimate domestic spaces.

After World War II, radio's role in American life maintained its importance but changed crucial aspects of its broadcasting practices. The evolution from the largely haphazard broadcasting patterns of radio's early years to the narrowly formatted structure of post–World War II radio had particularly significant implications for America's ethnically diverse musical landscape. Following is a short historical sketch of the early relationship between radio and music, its change after World War II, and the subsequent impact on two ethnic musical styles in the United States.

Historical background

Radio's early stage as a technological curiosity gave way in 1922 to commercial viability, and by the time the stock market crashed in 1929 the "wireless" was a fixture in nearly 40 percent of American homes [see TECHNOLOGY AND MEDIA, p. 235]. National networks (NBC in 1926, CBS in 1927, Mutual in 1934) extended broadcasting's geographic reach and made possible more ambitious programs. In addition, a string of nonprofit stations affiliated with universities provided educational programs. Although radio gave Americans the latest sports, news, and drama, its backbone, as measured by programming hours and contemporary commentary, was music.

Radio's approach to music programming in the United States was greatly affected by its institutional configuration. The Federal Radio Commission (FRC), founded in 1927 and replaced in 1934 by the Federal Communications Commission (FCC), exerted pressure on broadcasters to balance pleasing the public with programming in the public interest. Networks responded with "sustaining," or noncommercial, programs designed to convince legislators that no extensive regulation was necessary. Although sustaining programs generally reflected the networks' more highbrow efforts, a significant number of commercial programs were also aimed at the general population, such as the symphonic broadcasts sponsored by General Motors and Firestone [see CLASS, p. 42].

Reflecting these various pressures, music programming in the early days of commercial radio consisted of an eclectic mix of classical, salon, jazz, sacred, and popular music performed live. In its earliest years, amateur performers could be heard even in large cities, but by the Depression, networks and large stations employed professional musicians. All three networks had music departments, their own in-house orchestras, composers, and arrangers; as a result, musicians played the entire spectrum of music, from symphony concerts to background music for radio drama. Often disparate styles were included within the same program, designed with "something for everyone" in the family audience.

By the late 1930s, it was clear that radio's dual imperatives—to serve the public interest and to earn maximum profits—were incompatible. New audience measurement techniques helped networks and their advertisers understand the conflict, and gradually network executives stressed profit over more abstract cultural good by tailoring their programs to the largest possible audience. This strategy diminished the demand for fine-art music and correspondingly increased the demand for popular music. The beginning of World War II accelerated the decline of cultural broadcasting by highlighting radio's role as a disseminator of news and by blunting possible attention from the FCC. The war years saw a quick end to sustaining programs.

A number of factors led to the narrow formats introduced in the post–World War II period and still characteristic of radio programming today. The advent of commercial television pressured radio broadcasters to define a new niche for their industry. With radio no longer the center of family entertainment, broadcasters had to develop a new mode of use. The invention of the transistor allowed the size of radio sets to shrink and thus encouraged a more individual, personal relationship with radio. Simultaneously, broadcasters changed the dominant format from live to recorded music. The development of Top 40 formats promoted repetition of a few hits at the expense of variety.

Two important styles on radio

White rural music

From the earliest days of radio's popularity, local rural white music could be heard on southern stations beginning with WSB in Atlanta, Georgia, in 1922. WBAP, initiated in Fort Worth, Texas, in January 1923, played programs of square dance music to overwhelming response, encouraging numerous imitators. Best known, of course, is WSM in Nashville, Tennessee, whose *WSM Barn Dance* was inaugurated in 1925 and renamed *Grand Ole Opry* in 1927. WSM expanded to a high-powered station in 1932 and could be heard all over the South; *Grand Ole Opry* became a national program in 1939. As far north as Chicago, WLS featured *National Barn Dance,* which went national in 1933. Even during the Depression, when the recording industry suffered, radio persisted as a major outlet for white rural music.

Economic and technological factors encouraged the growth of rural white style on radio. Conflicts with ASCAP (American Society of Composers, Authors, and Publishers) over royalties for broadcast music surfaced early in the decade and peaked during 1940–1941, when broadcasters refused to use any ASCAP material and formed their own competitor, Broadcast Music International (BMI). As ASCAP had a stranglehold on the established Tin Pan Alley composers, BMI became an outlet for less established, rural and black styles [see POPULAR MUSIC OF THE PARLOR AND STAGE, p. 179; THE MUSIC INDUSTRY, p. 256]. After World War II, the invention of electromagnetic tape made recording less cumbersome and expensive, thus encouraging independents outside the New York City establishment.

By the post–World War II era, the music now called country was poised to become a major commercial force along with a revitalized recording industry, as live performances gave way to the disc jockey format [see COUNTRY AND WESTERN, p. 76]. By 1949 over six hundred radio stations featured live country performers, not just in the South but in all regions; California represented an especially rich source of country music on radio; and KXLA in Pasadena may well have been the first all-country radio station.

Country music stations moved toward the Top 40 format of rock stations, thus at once homogenizing their repertoires and broadcasting to a greater audience. Even *Grand Ole Opry* evolved from a local, idiosyncratic show to one featuring stars and ambitious advertising. Hank Williams joined the show in 1949; he, along with crooners and honky-tonk singers, defined the style for coast-to-coast audiences. By the end of the 1950s, the success of country music inevitably sparked countertendencies: the absorbing of influences from other styles and a simultaneous attempt to revive the earlier, purer style.

Race music

African American music also reflected the enormous impact of radio. Coincidental to the development of the medium was the migration of African Americans from the South to northern cities in the post–World War II era. Radio assumed a dual role as both a connection to the faraway community and a symbol of its dislocation. Black music provided a separate marketing challenge for the music industry, which responded by attempting to create a niche market. Although recordings were easier to target selectively, radio broadcasting of African American music quickly found outlets. Radio was crucial to the spread of swing; it also introduced thousands of Americans to gospel music in the 1930s and 1940s, including broadcasts of church services. *Billboard* has produced, since the late 1940s, charts of black music on radio.

Like its hillbilly counterpart, race music was poised to become a major commercial force in the 1950s. And as it had done for hillbilly music, the establishment of BMI and the invention of electromagnetic tape stimulated the growth of race music. The power of radio to cross ethnic boundaries was demonstrated during this period. The radio broadcasting of black music allowed white fans to become familiar with rhythm and blues, as both black and white disk jockeys broadcast in the 1950s to a teenage audience restless with pop standards. Soul stations in the 1960s took over the position of catering to mostly black audiences [see R & B AND SOUL, p. 667].

The development of black radio differed from that of white radio because of its economic structure. Black radio stations had a different economic relationship to their communities: the owners were nearly always white, while the musicians and disk jockeys were black. They depended on advertising revenue from white businesses and thus were constrained in an important way. Even so, black radio made contributions to the political dynamic of the postwar period. In the 1950s and 1960s, for example, civil rights speeches may have been more explicit, but musical styles also carried an implicit political meaning. By functioning as the voices of their communities, broadcasters played an important role in the civil rights movement.

Both white and black music on radio thus demonstrate the paradoxical effect of this medium: at once breaking the boundaries of communities and creating new ones. That radio broadcasts of hitherto isolated styles had far-reaching musical consequences is undeniable. The development of rock and roll, which drew from both rural white and black musical sources, revolutionized the musical industry [see ROCK, p. 347]. Given the reaction to rock and the way it functioned to simulate the youth community, it could be argued that the technology of radio had even more far-reaching consequences on the cultural life of the United States.

—SUSAN KEY

THE PIANO AND WOMEN OF ACCOMPLISHMENT

The single most important instrument in American musical history—the piano—stands in complex and fascinating relationship to the class of people who have been its predominant constituency—women. As a commodity, the piano has its own material history, replete with stunning statistics that document its growth in consumer popularity: from 1829 when one out of every 4800 Americans bought a piano, to 1910, when the figures rose to one out of 252 and 350,000 pianos were produced in one year. The power of such an expanding market made the great American piano manufacturing firms like Chickering and Steinway the nineteenth-century equivalent of Chrysler and General Motors in the twentieth.

If the American automobile has been gendered male from the beginning of its history, then the American piano has been gendered female. It is hardly a coincidence that this growth in the piano industry coincided with an equally extraordinary rise in the numbers of women employed as musicians and music teachers during roughly the same period. Between 1870 and 1910—decades when the number of people employed in the profession of music and music teaching increased about nine times over—the percentage of women employed in the profession almost doubled, growing from 36 percent in 1870 to 66 percent in 1910 [see LEARNING, p. 274]. The stage was now set for a quintessential American experience:

> On my sixth birthday my mother did two things. She took me out on the front porch with great mystery, brought out her sewing basket, and gave me my first lesson in darning socks. Later she took my hand to head me down the street to another surprise. This she did [in] a sort of mixture of solemnity and triumph, for it represented something she had wanted and been deprived of all during her childhood. She took me to my first piano lesson. (Ruth Crawford Seeger in Tick 1997:4)

FIGURE 2   Ruth Crawford Seeger, composer, piano teacher, folk music educator, and advocate, c. 1927. She left her own conservative training behind in her work as a teacher, integrating improvisation and folk music into the studies of her many piano students in the Washington, D.C., area. Photo courtesy Fernand de Gueldre.

We turn this memory of Ruth Crawford Seeger (figure 2), now acknowledged as a pioneering composer of early American modernism, into a ritual of cultural history: of being introduced to music education by "taking piano" from a lady in the neighborhood, who owned one of the few grand pianos in town and who ran marathon recitals on hot Sunday afternoons in June.

The late-nineteenth-, early-twentieth-century model of a grand piano with the logo "Our Pet" emblazoned in the name-space above the keyboard recently discovered in an antique store in New England portrays a different point in the gendered musical life cycle: a fashionable young mother plays the piano for her dancing daughter.

Because such ordinary experiences ground the musical life of a society, historians explore the assumptions and values that underlie them. An earlier generation of historians produced social history, such as Arthur Loesser's still valuable *Men, Women, and Pianos* (1954); newer academic criticism based on cultural studies borrows critical tools from semiotics, iconography, and feminist theory. A case in point is Richard Leppert's reading of the sign *piano* as "a floating signifier, a semantic pendulum that swung in extreme arc between social stability and social change, to be understood against the increasingly complex and contradictory social position in the nineteenth century of both art music itself and its female and male practitioners" (1993:153). Leppert's observations could easily be applied to nineteenth-century American society as well as to Victorian England. Cynthia Hoover has written that "the piano has played an important role in American life since the late eighteenth century, when learning the instrument was considered a genteel occupation for young ladies" (1986:559). The late-nineteenth-, early-twentieth-century model of a grand piano with the logo "Our Pet" emblazoned in the name-space above the keyboard recently discovered in an antique store in New England portrays a different point in the gendered musical life cycle: a fashionable young mother plays the piano for her dancing daughter.

Primary sources for both social history and cultural criticism enrich our understanding of the piano as social signifier. To iconographic evidence (paintings, photographs, advertisements) that supply the sight as well the sound of music, and its embodied practice, we also add eighteenth- and nineteenth-century etiquette books, treatises on women's education, and curricular materials from female academies or seminaries, as private schools were then called. In the nineteenth and twentieth centuries, such sources expand to mass market magazines such as *Miss Godey's Lady's Book* or *Etude Magazine*. We need only cite a few examples to convey the immediacy such sources bring to our understanding of music as social expression. An advertisement in an eighteenth-century newspaper for a "Miss Ball . . . newly arrived from London," offering lessons in "singing, playing on the spinet, dancing, and all sorts of needle-work" (Tick 1986:13), reminds us of the link between decorative craft (now so highly prized) and decorative music (still so typically scorned). Recollections of James Huneker, a prominent music critic in the early 1900s, turn the tradition of music as a feminine accomplishment into the American counterpart of Chinese foot-binding in order to herald the new relationship between gender and the piano as a sign of modernity:

> Passed away is the girl who played the piano in the stiff Victorian drawing rooms of our mothers. . . . The piano girl was forced to practice at the keyboard, even if without talent. Every girl played the piano, not to play was a stigma of poverty. The new girl is too busy to play the piano unless she has the gift; then she plays with consuming earnestness. We listen to her, for we know that this is an age of specialization, an age when woman is coming into her own . . . so our poets no longer make sonnets to our Ladies of Ivories, nor are budding girls chained to the piano." (1904:285)

It does not take a feminist to perceive the extent to which such cultural practice both enabled and constrained women. For every man (such as the composer Charles Ives or the educator Walter Damrosch) who decried the feminization of American music, there was a professionally aspiring female musician battling the ghost of our "Lady of Ivory." The legacy of achievement of American women pianists, piano composers, and piano educators stands in relief against this background, their history still being documented and integrated into our understanding of the American musical past.

—JUDITH TICK

BANDS

The American band, represented across the land by countless bandstands ornamenting village greens, has long been a sprightly part of life in American towns and cities. Band musicians, smartly uniformed, have accompanied soldiers as they went off to war and welcomed them on their return home. They have led funeral processions and enlivened parades on the Fourth of July and on other national holidays. In the concert hall and on the sports field, in front of a local factory or on the steps of the nation's Capitol, the band has filled our ears with music and our eyes with colorful pageantry, serving throughout American history as a focal point for entertainment and an integral part of our sociocultural development. No civic holiday, ceremony, memorial, or festive occasion, then and now, would be considered complete without a band to provide inspiring and entertaining music.

European heritage

European musical customs and traditions arrived with the colonists, with the snare drum filling an important and necessary function in colonial life: it set the cadence for marching men and beat out warnings, signals, and orders for both military and civil events. A fife or bagpipe was often added for melodic interest in sounding the camp duty calls that regulated military life. Each company had its field musicians, usually soldiers with some musical training who were taught the necessary calls and marches by drum and fife majors.

Early in the eighteenth century another European tradition, the hautboys, provided a bright note in several American cities. In contrast to field musicians, these bandsmen were professionals hired by military officers to provide music for ceremonies, concerts, social occasions, and entertainment. The hautboys usually included three oboes and a bass oboe or bassoon, with drums. When, by the middle of the eighteenth century, two French horns were added to provide a contrasting timbre, the ensemble became known as the *Harmoniemusik* 'band of music'. Clarinets were introduced shortly after the horns, and trumpets were sometimes used for flourishes or signals. An ideal *Harmoniemusik* was composed of paired oboes, clarinets, bassoons, and horns, without drums.

British regimental bands gave concerts in New York, Boston, and Philadelphia before the Revolutionary War, and Americans soon followed with bands of their own. During the Revolution, the Third and Fourth Regiments of Continental Artillery formed bands that served throughout the eight-year war. Both regimental bands achieved reputations that surpassed those of all other musical groups then in existence and established a musical standard that succeeding bands strove to attain.

By the end of the eighteenth century, an interest in Turkish instruments—bass drum, cymbals, triangle, and tambourine—spread across Western Europe and subsequently across the Atlantic, thus adding to the band's resources. Further instrumental developments in the Federal period included the use of the piccolo, serpent, bass horn, bass clarinet, and trombone. Woodwind instruments became more complex with the addition of new keys. Although the distinction between band and field music was retained, combinations of the two became frequent, and the snare drum, once a field instrument exclusively, became an integral part of both.

Nineteenth century

The development of the keyed-bugle in the early part of the nineteenth century helped shape the future composition of American bands. This new instrument became known on this side of the Atlantic through the virtuoso playing of Richard Willis at West Point and Edward (Ned) Kendall in Boston. Another virtuoso performer was Francis Johnson, an African American composer who was also the leader of the Washington Guards Band of Philadelphia, which he organized after the War of 1812.

The popularity of the keyed-bugle and the adaptation of the key principle to larger brass instruments (ophicleides and bass horns) led to the formation of all-brass bands. The Boston Brass Band, founded in 1835 under the leadership of Ned Kendall, is often credited with being the first, and it was soon followed by the Dodworth Band of New York and the American Band of Providence, Rhode Island. The keyed-bugle presented by members of the American Band to their leader, Joseph Greene, now in the collection of the Rhode Island Historical Society, is one of the finest surviving examples of these instruments.

The 1840s saw further changes as valved, over-the-shoulder brass instruments were developed. These instruments projected the sound to the rear, a marked advantage for units marching behind the band. Simultaneously, in Paris, Adolphe Sax developed the saxhorn family of valved brass instruments noted for good intonation and uniform mellow tone. The cornet, already an established band instrument in Europe, was also exported to this country.

One of the finest bands of the antebellum period was New York's Dodworth Band. The best known "star" of the Dodworth Band was the nineteenth-century conductor Theodore Thomas. Other Dodworth musicians included cornet soloist Alessandro Liberati and baritone horn soloists Carlo Cappa and David L. Downing, each of whom later became famous as the leader of his own band.

Thomas Dodworth Sr. and his eldest son, Allen, began playing in New York City bands shortly after their arrival from England in the mid-1820s. By the mid-1830s they developed a band under their own name that eventually included the four Dodworth sons (Allen, Harvey, Charles, and Thomas Jr.). Each of the Dodworths was proficient on more than one instrument, and all were prolific composers. The family had a virtual monopoly on society band activity, writing, publishing, and selling music, teaching popular dance steps (Allen ran a highly successful ballroom dance studio), and playing for fashionable balls, society parties, and civic celebrations, They were also influential in establishing the New York Philharmonic Orchestra Society in 1842. Four family members were in the orchestra, and, in addition, Allen Dodworth was elected the society's first treasurer.

The golden age

The golden period of the American brass band was the 1850s, during which time instruments became more fully developed and amateur and professional organizations flourished. Although the emphasis on brass brought forth new bands and new band compositions, woodwinds never went out of favor. European bandmasters, especially those from Italy (the most notable being Francis Scala, leader of the U.S. Marine Band), who settled in this country favored reed instruments over brass. Consequently, brass band music of the 1850s often included extra parts for woodwind instruments.

During the Civil War, a great many new bands came into being. Documentation of these organizations is often sketchy, but through regimental histories and diaries

much can be learned about the music that marked this war-ravaged era. Clad in elaborate dress uniforms, exotic Zouave costumes, or in the standard blue or gray, bandsmen were present at the major battles, cheering and bolstering spirits with music, or providing additional service on occasion as aides in military hospitals (figure 3).

Of the collections of music that survive from this period, the band books of the Third New Hampshire Regiment Band, the Twenty-sixth North Carolina Band, and the Twenty-fifth Massachusetts Volunteer Infantry Band are especially noteworthy. They contain an abundance of music composed or arranged by leading bandmasters, with Claudio Grafulla, bandmaster of the Seventh Regiment Band of New York, being the most prominent. Other famous Civil War bandmasters were Gustavus Ingalls, Thomas Coates, and George Ives (father of composer Charles Ives). Without question, however, the greatest bandmaster to emerge from this era was Patrick S. Gilmore (1829–1892).

Patrick S. Gilmore

Gilmore was born in Ireland but emigrated to the United States in 1849. He settled in Boston, where he began his career in the early 1850s as a member of Ordway's Aeolian Vocalists, a minstrel group he helped form and in which he played the tambourine and, on occasion, a cornet solo. He subsequently held several bandmaster posts in the Boston area, and in 1859, his reputation firmly established, he organized Gilmore's Band, a new band for which he assumed all financial and business responsibilities.

With the coming of the Civil War, Gilmore and his band enlisted to serve with the Twenty-fourth Massachusetts Infantry Regiment; later he helped organize many bands as part of the Massachusetts Civil War effort. In 1864, Gilmore accompanied two of these bands to New Orleans, and while there he organized the music for the inauguration of Michael Hahn as governor of Louisiana, utilizing hundreds of bandsmen, a chorus of six thousand, a battery of cannons, and the simultaneous ringing of all the church bells of the city. Those forces were on an even grander scale for the two gigantic festivals he later presented in Boston, the National Peace Jubilee in 1869 and the World Peace Jubilee in 1871, which brought him both national and international attention and fame. In 1873 Gilmore accepted an invitation to provide the music for the Twenty-second Regiment of New York and organized a new band that he developed into the premiere professional ensemble in the United States. During the late 1870s and throughout the 1880s, the Gilmore Band performed at Manhattan Beach each summer, toured extensively in the spring and fall, and presented a concert series each winter in New York.

John Philip Sousa

In 1891, John Philip Sousa (1854–1932), then leader of the U.S. Marine Band, made a short tour with that organization under the auspices of David Blakely, Patrick Gilmore's former business manager. The following year, Blakely convinced Sousa to resign from the service to form a professional civilian band. Sousa's ability as a dynamic

Except for armed forces bands, most professional and recreational musical organizations have disappeared, leaving colleges and universities as the inheritors of the great American band tradition.

FIGURE 4   "The President's Own" U.S. Marine Band, John Philip Sousa, director (on podium), 1891. Photo courtesy of the U.S. Marine Band, Washington, D.C.

leader and composer were the chief reasons for his meteoric rise, and under Blakely's management Sousa began to reap the financial rewards of his music. The Sousa Band toured extensively throughout the United States, with four tours of Europe and a world tour (figure 4).

During World War I he organized a very large band for the U.S. Navy and then resumed his concert schedule with his own organization after the war. No bandmaster, before or since, achieved such international popularity or was as honored with as many trophies, medals, and honorary degrees.

The twentieth century

At the turn of the century, increases in population and the development of rail transportation contributed to the popularity of all kinds of traveling bands. Several all-female bands came into vogue, the most notable being Helen May Butler and Her Ladies Brass Band (figure 5), which traveled extensively (especially in the Midwest), performing in concert halls and at state fairs; the Ladies Ideal Band from Mauston, Wisconsin; and the Keota, Iowa, Ladies Band.

The main force of early-twentieth-century bands, however, belongs to individuals such as David Reeves, Alessandro Liberati, Giuseppe Creatore, Bohumir Kryl, Jean Missud, Frederick Innes, and, later, Arthur Pryor, Patrick Conway, and Edwin Franko Goldman. These men led professional bands of the first order, and their popularity continued through the opening quarter of the twentieth century. Increasing competi-

FIGURE 5 Helen May Butler and Her Ladies Brass Band, 1910. Smithsonian Institution.

tion from radio and phonograph records eventually led to a decline in the demand for live performances by these great bands and bandmasters but also brought into prominence some excellent industrial bands, which, through their radio broadcasts, provided entertaining programs and helped to promote their sponsor's product.

 Except for armed forces bands, most professional and recreational musical organizations have disappeared, leaving colleges and universities as the inheritors of the great American band tradition. The University of Illinois Concert Band under Albert Austin Harding, followed by the University of Michigan Symphonic Band under William D. Revelli and the Eastman Wind Ensemble (figure 6) developed by Frederick Fennell in 1952, set standards of excellence surpassing those of many professional orchestras.

FIGURE 6 The Eastman Wind Ensemble, Donald Hunsberger, music director, February 1998, in preparation for the 1998 concert tour of Japan sponsored by the Sony Corporation. Photo by John Widman.

Circus bands

Circus bands also hold a unique position in the historical development of bands in America. Elaborate circus parades, with highly decorative bandwagons in the lead, evolved in the 1850s. The circus band was unique, too, in the kinds of music it performed and in the tempo and style of its presentation. From his first post at the Ringling-Barnum Band in 1919 to his retirement fifty years later, Merle Evans was the best known circus bandleader, famous for playing the cornet with one hand and leading the band with the other. In the midst of the excitement, noise, and fun of the circus, the responsibilities of the circus bandleader are often overlooked. Split-second timing in setting the tempo for performance is essential, but in case of accident or emergency, a disaster march is played, a piece recognized on the lot as a warning and a call for help if things go wrong—fire being the greatest fear. Today, the heyday of the Big Top has passed and with it the parading, sound, and ballyhoo of the circus band and bandwagon.

Funeral bands

Another tradition that has come to an end is the minstrel band, whose popularity for a time paralleled that of circus musicians. One special kind of band that has managed to survive in diminished numbers is the New Orleans Brass Funeral Band. In the Reconstruction period following the Civil War, many benevolent social clubs arose. Burial processions for deceased members were important events for these groups. The band traditionally played a solemn, slow march to the cemetery and something lively and cheerful on its return, which often included an early kind of jazz improvisation on a theme. King Oliver, Bunk Johnson, Kid Ory, and Louis Armstrong are a few of the musicians who got their start in these street bands. Ragtime was another form of popular music that found its way into the band's repertoire [see RELIGIOUS MUSIC, p. 624; BLUES, p. 637].

Professional and amateur music making, sophisticated programs in concert halls and outdoor entertainments are what constitute the Great American Band. It has been developing for more than two hundred years, and its continued growth proves that the tradition is alive and will hopefully flourish for generations to come.

—FRANK J. CIPOLLA AND RAOUL F. CAMUS

REFERENCES

Adler, Tom. 1974. "The Concept of Nidality and Its Potential Application to Folklore." In *Conceptual Problems in Contemporary Folklore Study,* ed. Gerald Cashion, 1–5. Bloomington, Ind.: Folklore Forum.

Band Music Guide. 1989. 9th ed. Northfield, Ill.: The Instrumentalist Company.

Barlow, William. 1998. *Voice Over: The Making of Black Radio.* Philadelphia: Temple University Press.

Bierley, Paul. 1984. *The Works of John Philip Sousa.* Columbus, Ohio: Integrity Press.

———. 1986. *John Philip Sousa, American Phenomenon.* Rev. ed. Columbus, Ohio: Integrity Press.

Bly, Leon J. 1977. "The March in American Society." Ph.D. dissertation, University of Miami.

Bridges, Glenn D. 1965. *Pioneers in Brass.* Detroit: Sherwood Publications.

Broyles, Michael. 1992. *"Music of the Highest Class": Elitism and Populism in Antebellum Boston.* New Haven, Conn.: Yale University Press.

———. 1999. "Art Music from 1860 to 1920." In *The Cambridge History of American Music,* ed. David Nicholls, 214–254. Cambridge: Cambridge University Press.

Bryant, Carolyn. 1975. *And the Band Played On, 1776–1976.* Washington, D.C.: Smithsonian Institution Press.

Bufkin, William A. 1973. "Union Bands of the Civil War (1826–65): Instrumentation and Score Analysis." Ph.D. dissertation, Louisiana State University.

Camus, Raoul F. 1986a. "Bands." In *The New Grove Dictionary of American Music,* ed. H. Wiley Hitchcock and Stanley Sadie, 1:127–137. London: Macmillan.

———. 1986b. "Military Music." In *The New Grove Dictionary of American Music,* ed. H. Wiley Hitchcock and Stanley Sadie, 3:228–230. London: Macmillan.

———. 1989. "Early American Wind and Ceremonial Music 1636–1836." *The National Tune Index,* phase 2. New York: University Music Editions.

———. 1992. *American Wind and Percussion Music.* Three Centuries of American Music, Vol. 12. Boston: G. K. Hall.

———. 1993 [1976]. *Military Music of the American Revolution.* Westerville, Ohio: Integrity Press.

Carpenter, Kenneth W. 1970. "A History of the United States Marine Band." Ph.D. dissertation, University of Iowa.

Cipolla, Frank J. 1978. "Annotated Guide for the Study and Performance of Nineteenth Century Band Music in the United States." *Journal of Band Research* 14(1): 22–40.

———. 1979–1980. "A Bibliography of Dissertations Relative to the Study of Bands and Band Music." *Journal of Band Research* 15(1):1–31; 16(1):29–36.

Cipolla, Frank, J., and Donald Hunsberger, eds. 1994. *The Wind Ensemble and Its Repertoire.* Rochester, N.Y.: University of Rochester Press.

Clappé, Arthur A. 1911. *The Wind-Band and Its Instruments.* New York: Henry Holt.

Cone, John Frederick. 1983. *First Rival of the Metropolitan Opera*. New York: Columbia University Press.

Crawford Seeger, Ruth. 1997. "Unpublished autobiographical sketch." In *Ruth Crawford Seeger: A Composer's Search for American Music,* by Judith Tick. New York: Oxford University Press.

Dana, William H. 1878. *J. W. Pepper's Practical Guide and Study to the Secret of Arranging Band Music or, the Amateur's Guide*. Philadelphia: J. W. Pepper.

Dodworth, Allen. 1853. *Dodworth's Brass Band School*. New York: H. B. Dodworth. Reprint, St. Paul, Minn.: Paul Mayberry, [n.d.].

Eliason, Robert E. 1972. *Keyed Bugles in the United States*. Washington, D.C.: Smithsonian Institution Press.

Fennell, Frederick. 1954. *Time and the Winds*. Kenosha, Wis.: G. Leblanc Company.

Fong-Torres, Ben. 1998. *The Hits Just Keep on Coming: The History of Top 40 Radio*. San Francisco: Miller Freeman Books.

Foster, William P. 1955. "Band Pageantry." Ed.D. dissertation, Columbia University.

Garofalo, Robert, and Mark Elrod. 1985. *A Pictorial History of Civil War Era Musical Instruments and Military Bands*. Charleston, W.Va.: Pictorial Histories, 1985.

Goldman, Richard Franko. 1946. *The Concert Band*. New York: Rinehart.

———. 1974 [1961]. *The Wind Band*. Westport, Conn.: Greenwood Press, 1974.

Hall, Harry H. 1980 [1963]. *A Johnny Reb Band from Salem*. New York: Da Capo.

Haugen, Einar, and Camilla Cai. 1993. *Ole Bull: Norway's Romantic Musician and Cosmopolitan Patriot*. Madison: University of Wisconsin Press.

Haynie, Jerry T. 1971. "The Changing Role of the Band in American Colleges and Universities (1900–1968)." Ph.D. dissertation, Peabody College.

Hazen, Margaret Hindle, and Robert M. Hazen. 1987. *The Music Men. An Illustrated History of Brass Bands in America, 1800–1920*. Washington, D.C.: Smithsonian Institution Press.

Heintzelman, Thomas D. 1988. "Adult Concert Band Participation in the United States." D.M.E. dissertation, Indiana University.

Hines, Michele. 1997. *Radio Voices: American Broadcasting, 1922–1952*. Minneapolis: University of Minnesota Press.

Hoover, Cynthia Adams. 1986. "Piano(forte)." In *The New Grove Dictionary of American Music,* ed. H. Wiley Hitchcock and Stanley Sadie, 3: 559–562. London: Macmillan.

Hot Rize. *Take It Home*. 1990. Sugar Hill SH-CD-3784. Compact disc.

Huneker, James. 1904. *Overtones*. New York: Charles Scribner's Sons.

Hunt, Charles B. 1949. "The American Wind Band, Its Function as a Medium in Contemporary Music." Ph.D. dissertation, University of California, Los Angeles.

Johnson, H. Earle. 1953. "The Germania Musical Society." *The Musical Quarterly* 39(1): 75–93.

Krauss, Alison. *I've Got That Old Feeling*. 1990. Rounder CD 0275. Compact disc.

Kreitner, Kenneth. 1990. *Discoursing Sweet Music: Brass Bands and Community Life in Turn-of-the-Century Pennsylvania*. Urbana: University of Illinois Press.

Lawson, Doyle, and Quicksilver. *Rock My Soul*. 1990 [1979]. Sugar Hill SH-CD-3717. Compact disc.

Leppert, Richard. 1993. *The Sight of Sound: Music, Representation, and the History of the Body*. Berkeley: University of California Press.

Lightfoot, William E. "Playing Outside: Spectrum." *Appalachian Journal* 10:194–198.

Loesser, Arthur. 1954. *Men, Women, and Pianos: A Social History*. New York: Simon and Schuster.

Lord, Francis Alfred, and Arthur Wise. 1979 [1966]. *Bands and Drummer Boys of the Civil War*. New York: Da Capo.

Lott, R. Allen. 1986. "The American Concert Tours of Leopold de Meyer, Henri Hertz, and Sigismond Thalberg." Ph.D. dissertation, City University of New York.

Manfredo, Joseph. 1995. *Influences on the Development of the Instrumentation of the American Collegiate Wind Band and Attempts for Standardization of the Instrumentation from 1905–1941*. Alta Musica, vol. 17. Tutzing, Germany: Hans Schneider.

Martin, George Whitney. 1983. *The Damrosch Dynasty: America's First Family of Music*. Boston: Houghton Mifflin.

Martin, Peter John. 1983. "A Status Study of Community Bands in the United States." Ph.D. dissertation, Northwestern University.

Mates, Julian. 1985. *American's Musical Stage: Two Hundred Years of Musical Theater*. Westport, Conn.: Greenwood Press.

McCarrell, Lamar Keith. 1971. "A Historical Review of the College Band Movement from 1875 to 1969." Ph.D. dissertation, Florida State University.

Milburn, David Allen. 1982. "The Development of the Wind Ensemble in the United States (1952–1982)." D.M.A. dissertation, Catholic University of America.

Newsom, Jon. 1979. "The American Brass Band Movement." *The Quarterly Journal of the Library of Congress* 36:115–139.

Olson, Kenneth E. 1981. *Music and Musket: Bands and Bandsmen of the American Civil War*. Westport, Conn.: Greenwood Press.

Osborne Brothers. *Once More*. 1991 [1986]. Notes by Sonny Osborne. Sugar Hill SH-CD 2203. Compact disc.

Patton, G. F. 1875. *A Practical Guide to the Arrangement of Band Music*. Leipzig, Germany: John F. Stratton.

Preston, Katherine K. 1992. *Music for Hire: A Study of Professional Musicians in Washington (1877–1900)*. Stuyvesant, N.Y.: Pendragon Press.

———. 1993. *Opera on the Road: Traveling Opera Troupes in the United States, 1825–1860*. Urbana: University of Illinois Press.

———. 1999. "Art Music from 1800 to 1860." In *The Cambridge History of American Music,* ed. David Nicholls, 186–213. Cambridge: Cambridge University Press.

Railsback, Thomas C., and John P. Langellier. 1987. *The Drums Would Roll: A Pictorial History of U.S. Army Bands on the American Frontier, 1866–1900*. Poole, England: Arms and Armour Press.

Rehrig, William H. 1991. *The Heritage Encyclopedia of Band Music: Composers and Their Music*. Ed. Paul Bierley. 2 vols. Westerville, Ohio: Integrity Press.

Rinzler, Ralph. 1957. Notes to *American Banjo Scruggs Style*. Folkways FA 2314. LP disks.

Rocco, Emma S. 1990. *Italian Wind Bands: A Surviving Tradition in the Milltowns of Lawrence and Beaver Counties of Pennsylvania*. New York: Garland.

Schabas, Ezra. 1989. *Theodore Thomas: America's Conductor and Builder of Orchestras, 1835–1905*. Urbana: University of Illinois Press.

Schafer, William J., with Richard B. Allen. 1977. *Brass Bands and New Orleans Jazz*. Baton Rouge: Louisiana State University Press.

Schwartz, Harry Wayne. 1975 [1957]. *Bands of America*. New York: Da Capo Press.

Seldom Scene. *Act 3*. 1990 [1973]. Rebel CD 1528. Compact disc.

Shanet, Howard. 1975. *Philharmonic. A History of New York's Orchestra*. New York: Doubleday.

Smith, Norman E. 1986. *March Music Notes*. Lake Charles, La.: Program Note Press.

Starr, S. Frederick. 1995. *Bamboula! The Life and Times of Louis Moreau Gottschalk*. New York: Oxford University Press.

Tick, Judith. 1986. "Passed Away Is the 'Piano Girl': Changes in American Musical Life, 1970–1900." In *Women Making Music,* ed. Jane Bowers and Judith Tick. Urbana: University of Illinois Press.

———. 1997. *Ruth Crawford Seeger: A Composer's Search for American Music*. New York: Oxford University Press.

Ward, Brian. 1998. *Just My Soul Responding: Rhythm and Blues, Black Consciousness, and Race Relations*. Berkeley: University of California Press.

White, William C. 1944. *A History of Military Music in America*. New York: Exposition Press.

Whitwell, David. 1985. *A Concise History of the Wind Band*. Northridge, Calif.: Winds.

Wright, Al G., and Stanley Newcomb. 1970. *Bands of the World*. Evanston, Ill.: The Instrumentalist Co.

Zander, Marjorie Thomas. 1962. "The Brass Band Funeral and Related Negro Burial Customs." Master's thesis, University of North Carolina, Chapel Hill.

Section 2a
African American Musics

The first African Americans were forcibly taken from their home communities, mainly in West Africa, and brought in the early seventeenth century to what would become the United States. Slaves in the cotton- and tobacco-based economy of the rural South were frequently separated from families and supporting communities once they arrived, and after slavery ended in 1865 they continued to be subjected to harsh and demeaning discriminatory practices. Much of the early music history of African Americans reflects these social and economic conditions, as well as the importance of the church in reestablishing strong communities and providing various contexts for musical performance. Early forms, such as field cries and hollers, early blues, and other folk traditions, as well as spirituals and early musical theater, grew from a synthesis of predominantly West African and Western European musics and developed over time into musical forms and styles that today permeate all of American music. Musics such as jazz, blues, early rock and roll, soul, and rap, among many others, would not exist today without the creative contributions of African American musicians, entrepreneurs, and recording companies. In addition to these and many other forms, African Americans have also made important contributions to American theater and to classical music traditions as performers, composers, and patrons.

Two gospel singers, Atlanta, Georgia.
© Bob Krist/CORBIS.

Overview
Portia K. Maultsby
Mellonee V. Burnim
with contributions from Susan Oehler

Antebellum Perspectives
The Post–Civil War Era
A Cultural Renaissance in Harlem and Jim Crow in the South
Civil Rights, Black Power, and the Black Arts Movement
Advancing to the Twenty-First Century

Beginning with descriptions of African music making during the seventeenth century recorded by casual observers, the study of African-derived musics in the United States has evolved into a dynamic area of scholarly investigation. The proliferation of methods from various disciplines of scholarly engagement has changed and enriched this field of study over the past centuries. Many students of African American music, for example, employed the tools of Western-derived musical analysis, which emphasized the study of music as sound, focusing on elements of structure and technique. Historical musicologists approached their study largely through the exploration of primary documents such as newspapers, manuscripts, organizational records, personal letters, and diaries, which they combined with secondary sources and musical analysis to produce descriptive and analytical narratives on this tradition. In contrast, scholars from such fields as anthropology, ethnomusicology, sociology, cultural studies, and history, to name only a few, employed models that acknowledged the importance of culture and the social milieu in determining the character of musical traditions. In ethnographic-centered studies, such scholars collected field research data as a method for establishing music making as a process grounded in culture-specific meaning. Still another approach to the study of African American music combined components from anthropological and musicological models, employing a qualitative framework to interpret quantitative data. In the last decade of the twentieth century, many scholars expanded these models to include methodological and analytical approaches from various other disciplines.

As the breadth and depth of scholarship in African American music evolved, so did the foci of study and their underlying assumptions. While issues of race, culture, and class were recurrent themes in narratives on African American music, such diverse topics as origins, representation, identity, aesthetics, commodification, and appropriation, as well as gender, diasporic connections, and the politics of music, became standard to scholarly inquiry in the late twentieth century. Yet both the character or tone of writing on African American music and the content have been defined largely by the prevailing American sociocultural milieux.

Similarly, the overall scope of scholarship in African American music became more inclusive, with virtually every dimension considered worthy of study. The hierarchy of musical values that ranked African American music as inherently inferior to musics of European descent was, in large part, dismantled. As new genres of black music emerged, an accompanying domain of scholarly inquiry soon followed, although some genres received attention more readily than others. As the movement of African Americans within the larger American society became less circumscribed, as the impact of the presence of African Americans was more strongly felt in the United States, and as African American voices assumed greater acceptance and prominence in articulating their own perspectives in writings, the spectrum of scholarship on African American music consequently broadened.

ANTEBELLUM PERSPECTIVES

Music making by people of African descent became a subject of interest beginning with descriptions of the Middle Passage, where music making during the process of "dancing the slaves," the method employed to exercise slave cargo, documented the transfer of African instruments and musical practices to the New World (Epstein 1977:8–17). By the third decade of the seventeenth century, accounts of New World music making by African slaves as observed by slaveholders, travelers, and missionaries began to surface. Such sources as diaries, journals, reports, and memoirs provided firsthand documentation of the activities of blacks, noting the importance of dance in African music making and the use of antiphony as a recurrent musical structure, as well as the ubiquitous circle that served as a contextual frame to organize those present at the event. Almost uniformly, early European observers commented on the profound distinction they identified between their own musical values and those of the slave populace. Equating slave practices with "uncivilized" African rituals, Europeans most typically interpreted the music making of blacks with such pejorative terms as "barbaric," "wild," and "nonsensical." Other important sources documenting musical activity among slaves were advertisements for runaway slaves that identified their musical skills.

Even though perspectives presented in many of these early works unveiled Eurocentric cultural bias, they nonetheless are invaluable primary documents for studies on African American music. Authors Dena Epstein (1977), Eileen Southern (1983b [1971]), Southern and Josephene Wright (1990), and Bruce Jackson (1967) offer a representative sampling of works that either compiled or assessed these early writings.

THE POST–CIVIL WAR ERA

The major debate on African American music, which expanded over a century, centered on its origin and authenticity. Until the onset of the Civil War in 1861, the distinct repertoire and musical traditions of African Americans were hardly known outside the South. The exposure of northern whites to African Americans came in 1843 through the introduction of minstrelsy, a form of entertainment consisting of novelty acts, dialogue, and musical presentations in which whites blackened their faces in caricature of African Americans. Despite the promotion of these productions as authentic, minstrel audiences had virtually no firsthand knowledge of the music of slaves that could allow them to judge the accuracy of their evolving representation. Knowledge of authentic African American music as performed by African Americans themselves became more widespread with the 1866 formation and subsequent national and international tours of the Fisk Jubilee Singers. The success of the Fisk effort prompted the establishment of similar ensembles at other newly formed institutions of higher learning dedicated to the education and training of former slaves. Public interest in this distinct repertoire led to the proliferation of printed collections of Negro spirituals.

The early twentieth century

Between 1910 and 1929, more than one hundred collections of Negro spirituals appeared, approximately four times the number published between 1890 and 1909

Without ever having heard performances of either African or African American music firsthand, Wallaschek advanced an analysis of Negro spirituals that labeled them as "very much overrated," explaining that "as a rule they are mere imitations of European compositions which the negroes have picked up and served again with slight variations."

(Lovell 1972:19, 95). Prefacing this early-twentieth-century publication flurry was *Slave Songs of the United States* (1867), the first collection of Negro spirituals ever to be published. Its compilers, William Allen, Charles Ware, and Lucy McKim Garrison, were all graduates of Harvard University, drawn to the Georgia Sea Islands in response to the abolitionist call for assistance to instruct the newly emancipated slave population. The three were not folklorists, anthropologists, or musicologists, and their training in music represented that of the "dedicated amateur" at best. Their personal fascination with the music and collective desire to make these songs known to the general public prompted their compilation of 136 songs, most of which were Negro spirituals (Epstein 1977:321–326).

Slave Songs of the United States stands out in the establishment of scholarship in African American music for several reasons. First, the preface detailed the content and character of music sung in the second half of the nineteenth century by the people known as the Gullah, considered to be the group of African Americans who exhibited the greatest range of African retentions in the United States. Second, the collectors expressed their inability to transcribe live performances of melodies as sung by blacks, acknowledging the overall complexity of the repertoire, which posed great challenges in accurately representing the musical nuances in conventional Western notation. (Allen, Ware, and Garrison 1965 [1867]:10). The fundamental problem of "how to notate with conventional symbols a music that did not conform to conventional rules" (Epstein 1977:328) was shared by Lucy McKim Garrison, the most musically literate of the group. She lamented:

> It is difficult to express the entire character of these negro [*sic*] ballads by mere musical notes and signs. The odd turns made in the throat, and the curious rhythmic effect produced by single voices chiming in at different irregular intervals, seem almost as impossible to place on the score as the singing of birds or the tones of an Aeolian Harp. (Allen, Ware, and Garrison 1965 [1867]:10)

Third, *Slave Songs* documented the widespread interest in the music of African Americans especially among northern whites, as well as the general acknowledgment of African American music as a form of expressive behavior *distinct* from that of whites. The collection includes contributors, mainly northern whites, who submitted music, text, or both of songs they had first heard during the Civil War (Epstein 1977:325).

Public reaction to the publication of *Slave Songs* was mixed. As Dena Epstein noted, most music journals ignored it; others labeled the collection as "curious," and its content as "wild," "irregular," "pathetic," and "strange." The 1868 review in Lippincott Magazine declared that "it was hardly worth while to try to perpetuate this trash, vulgarity and profanity by putting it in print." Although a second edition was reissued in 1871, the collection later sank into oblivion (Epstein 1977:339–340).

However, the response to *Slave Songs* in the abolitionist publication *National Anti-Slavery Standard* is instructive in understanding the ensuing direction of scholarship in

African American music. Referring to the contents as both "remarkable and valuable alike to observer and historical student," the author advanced the argument that the repertoire, not merely the performance style, of African Americans represented an *original* contribution to both the character and content of the American musical landscape (Epstein 1977:338). Reviewing her own publication in *The Nation* in 1867, editor Lucy McKim Garrison and her husband, Wendell, reinforced this view of the originality of the collection's content:

> We utter no new truth when we affirm that whatever of nationality there is in the music of America she owes to her dusky children. . . . The negroes in their turn imitate the whites, but they show their peculiar musical genius as much in their imitations as in their compositions. A "white tune," so to speak, adopted and sung by them "in their own way" becomes a different thing. The words may be simply mangled, but the music is changed under an inspiration; it becomes a vital force. Hence the difficulty of accrediting authorship; to say how much is pure African, how much Methodist or Baptist camp-meeting. Where did the camp-meeting songs come from? Why might they not as likely emanate from black as from white worshippers? (Epstein 1977:337)

As more collections of Negro spirituals emerged following the successful national and international tours of performing ensembles such as the Fisk Jubilee Singers and their imitators at Hampton Institute in Virginia—who pioneered the performance of the Negro spiritual as "art song"—views of the authenticity of African American spirituals proliferated. Upon hearing the Jubilee Singers during their first 1871 tour, for example, Dr. Cuyler, pastor of the Lafayette Avenue Presbyterian Church of Brooklyn, showered the group with praise for the "magnetism" of their music, which "moved and melted" a "cultivated Brooklyn assemblage" in a way he had never before seen (Marsh 1971 [1876]:32). This and similar descriptions further documented the unique character of the performance—one that differed from that of European American "cultivated" whites.

Beginnings of the origins controversy

In his book *Primitive Music* (1970 [1893]) the Viennese philosopher Richard Wallaschek was the first to challenge claims to the originality of the Negro spiritual. Without ever having heard performances of either African or African American music firsthand, Wallaschek advanced an analysis of Negro spirituals that labeled them as "very much overrated," explaining that "as a rule they are mere imitations of European compositions which the negroes have picked up and served again with slight variations" (60). Wallaschek's thesis, based on his review of transcriptions from the 1867 collection *Slave Songs,* sparked what is now frequently referred to in African American music historiography as the origins controversy—the effort to ascribe either African or European origins to the Negro spiritual. This debate continued well into the last quarter of the twentieth century and attracted both black and white researchers from various disciplines, whose scholarly impartiality was often questionable.

Primary proponents of the European origins were three southern American professors—Newman Ivy White (1965 [1928]), Guy B. Johnson (1930), and George Pullen Jackson (1933, 1975 [1943]). Their fields of expertise were English, sociology, and German respectively and they taught at Duke, Vanderbilt, and the University of North Carolina. These writers advanced an argument that in large part supported Wallaschek's; their methods, however, differed. Whereas music was not a part of White's analysis, Jackson compared both texts and tunes of fasola song books, which reputedly represented the song traditions practiced by whites during the camp meetings of the Second Great Awakening. Similarly, Johnson analyzed melodic and rhythmic patterns as well as pitch intervals, using camp meeting song books as his point of departure. Jackson's comparison of 892 black tunes with 555 white tunes yields what he defines as 116 "genetic relationships." Despite this huge disparity, he concluded that the hymnody of whites provided the foundation for Negro spirituals, even though the songs underwent radical transformation in the transfer from one culture to another.

Arguments posed by writers who supported the thesis of the originality of Negro spirituals were often equally tenuous. Henry Krehbiel, for example, argued in his work *Afro-American Folksongs* (1962 [1914]) that whites did not have the type of culture needed to create Negro spirituals. In 1925, black writers James Weldon Johnson and J. Rosamond Johnson in their collection *American Negro Spirituals* advanced a charge of prejudice toward those who challenged the African-based origin of the spiritual and at the same time contended that the character of the Negro spiritual resulted in part from "native musical instinct and talent" (1989 [1925]:14, 17).

This scholarly debate, initiated in the nineteenth century, attracted attention well into the latter half of the twentieth century. A 1963 essay in *Ethnomusicology* by Richard Waterman (figure 1) entitled "On Flogging a Dead Horse: Lessons Learned from the Africanisms Controversy," outlined some of the main issues in the debate. First, Waterman noted that before the 1930s African music was *not* a part of the analytical equation. He cited as illustrative examples Wallaschek's view that African music bore no relationship to black music in the United States and ethnomusicologist Erich von Hornbostel's assertion that African and European music were too different to blend (Waterman 1963:84). Any efforts to determine or deny a distinctive, African-based character in Negro spirituals was at best speculative, without the consideration of musical values that had been retained in the cultural memory of the slave populous.

Waterman also pointed to the relative merit of writers in the origins debate. In some instances, scholars based their arguments on texts exclusively. In those treatises that considered music, analyses were often based on transcriptions that were no more accurate than those represented in the 1867 *Slave Songs* volume. In both cases, authors reduced the most distinctive feature of the music sung by blacks—the dynamic character of the actual performance—to a mere skeletal representation on the Western musical score. Because they ignored the improvisatory style and aesthetic principles associated with African American musical performance, the conclusions they drew from these minimalist musical sketches were inherently flawed.

As the origins debate continued into the 1940s, anthropologists and folklorists expanded the analytical frame to include ethnography. The writings of such scholars as anthropologists Melville Herskovits (1958 [1942]) (figure 2) and Richard Waterman (1943, 1967 [1952]) and folklorist Alan Lomax (1978 [1968]) reflected a wholesale shift from the trend of using a priori assumptions to interpret African American music, electing instead to generate answers based on evidence that surfaced in the ethnographic data. With data collected during extensive fieldwork in Africa and the diaspora, the debate advanced to a new level of more concrete comparison of African American music in contrast not only to European American practice but to African traditions as well.

During the 1960s, the origins debate finally achieved closure with the acknowledgment of syncretism that forged the unique character of spirituals as a genre grounded in African-derived musical values yet shaped into its distinctiveness as a direct result of the North American sociocultural experience. In addition to Waterman (1963), William Wescott (1977), William Tallmadge (1981), Dena Epstein (1983), and John Garst (1986), among others, provided contemporary critiques of the origins controversy.

FIGURE 1   Richard Waterman, c. 1970. Photo courtesy Christopher A. Waterman.

FIGURE 2   Melville J. Herskovits, 1950s. Photo courtesy Photographs and Prints Division, Schomburg Center for Research in Black Culture, The New York Public Library; Astor, Lenox and Tilden Foundations.

A CULTURAL RENAISSANCE IN HARLEM AND JIM CROW IN THE SOUTH

Beginning in the 1920s, new voices surfaced in the narratives on African American music. Black intellectuals and musicians joined white critics and scholars in assessing the flourishing musical activity among African Americans, which changed the sound-scape of the American mainstream and simultaneously contributed to new musical expressions across the Atlantic.

In distinguishing between "high" and "low," "art" and "popular" forms of expression based on a hierarchy of musical values, race and class became major themes in the literature published on Negro spirituals, blues, and jazz between the 1920s and 1950s. Beginning with highly successful musical productions on Broadway in the 1920s, the genres of blues and jazz moved beyond the borders of the African American community through recordings and radio. The Negro spiritual was transformed from choral to solo arrangement and performed on the concert stage by both blacks and whites. During this period, Hall Johnson and Eva Jessye formed the first black professional choruses.

The Harlem Renaissance

The 1920s also ushered in a literary and artistic movement among African Americans labeled the Harlem Renaissance—an era of intense flowering and celebration of African American culture in the city of New York. Leaders of the Harlem Renaissance included a group of intellectuals, among them poet Langston Hughes and philosopher Alain Locke, who committed themselves to advancing the status of African American literary and expressive forms by transforming vernacular traditions into what were perceived as "higher" art forms. Participants in the Harlem Renaissance argued for African American self-acceptance, embracing both faults and shortcomings (Locke 1992 [1925]:11). At the same time, a more subliminal yet widely accepted point of view existed, one that minimized or ignored any characteristics of African American culture that might be considered less than desirable (DuBois 1995 [1926]).

This ideological schism translated in at least two ways into scholarship on African American music produced during the Harlem Renaissance. First, discussions of African American music continued to focus on the Negro spiritual to the virtual exclusion of the emerging vernacular forms of blues and jazz. Second, though the spiritual received much scholarly attention, it was typically discussed through an assimilationist filter—viewed as a rich, though undeveloped, musical resource waiting to be tapped and raised to higher musical plane (Locke 1992 [1925]:200).

Composer Harry T. Burleigh (1866–1949) (figure 3), the first to arrange the Negro spiritual for solo voice, spoke of his chagrin and disappointment when audiences reacted with laughter to his incorporation of "folksongs" into his concerts. Black critics at Washington and Boston newspapers questioned his choice of repertoire as well as his judgment for having made the selection. Black performers, composers, and scholars, from Burleigh to Locke to DuBois, consistently promoted a desire to reconfigure or "elevate" the spiritual by placing it within a European compositional frame. Upon transformation, the music was considered to be more accessible and more readily appreciated by nonblack audiences (Johnson and Johnson 1989 [1925, 1926]:48).

Contrary to this assimilationist perspective, such writers as folklorist and novelist Zora Neale Hurston and poet Langston Hughes did not consider the works of composers and arrangers based on Negro spirituals as representative of this tradition. Hurston contended that such works by Harry T. Burleigh, J. Rosamond Johnson (1873–1954) (figure 4), Nathaniel Dett (1882–1943) (figure 5), John Work (1901–1967), and Hall Johnson (1888–1970), among others, were "all good work and beautiful, but not the spirituals" (Hurston 1976 [1935]:344). She and Hughes argued unapologetically for the proliferation of the Negro spiritual and all vernacular forms of African American expression in their original form, without modification.

FIGURE 3   Harry Burleigh, 1916. Photo courtesy Photographs and Prints Division, Schomburg Center for Research in Black Culture, The New York Public Library; Astor, Lenox and Tilden Foundations.

FIGURE 4   J. Rosamond Johnson, c. 1930. Photo courtesy Photographs and Prints Division, Schomburg Center for Research in Black Culture, The New York Public Library; Astor, Lenox and Tilden Foundations.

Citing polarized views of the Negro spirituals,
Hughes argues: "[M]any an upper-class Negro
church, even now, would not dream of employing
a spiritual in its services. The drab melodies in
white folks' hymnbooks are much to be preferred.
'We want to worship the Lord correctly and quietly.'"

FIGURE 5   Nathaniel Dett, 1920s. Photo
courtesy Photographs and Prints Division,
Schomburg Center for Research in Black
Culture, The New York Public Library; Astor,
Lenox and Tilden Foundations.

This view expanded the dissenting Harlem Renaissance voice to include the variable of class, highlighting the tension that existed among the African American populace about what constituted desirable self-defining qualities. In his 1926 publication "The Negro Artist and the Racial Mountain," Hughes strongly castigated those African Americans who adopted and celebrated facets of European American culture while simultaneously denigrating or ignoring the indigenous musics and traditions created by African Americans in this country. Citing polarized views of the Negro spirituals, Hughes argues: "[M]any an upper-class Negro church, even now, would not dream of employing a spiritual in its services. The drab melodies in white folks' hymnbooks are much to be preferred. 'We want to worship the Lord correctly and quietly. We don't believe in "shouting." Let's be dull like the Nordics,' they say in effect" (1976 [1926]:307). Hughes's treatise explored the realm of aesthetic value among African Americans, stridently labeling members of the educated black elite as devoid of pride in what he referred to as "racial culture."

As black intellectuals of the Harlem Renaissance movement grappled with issues of race and class to redefine the character and significance of African American music in the broader American culture, they restricted their discussion largely to the Negro spiritual. Meanwhile, African American artists made inroads to greater commercial opportunities and direct presence in popular American music. By 1920 James Reese Europe's Clef Club Symphony Orchestra had performed "syncopated" compositions many times at Carnegie Hall. The Original Dixieland Jazz Band, a white group from New Orleans, in 1920 had recorded the first commercial release of jazz at a time when white-owned recording companies aimed products only at the tastes of white consumers. Like Burleigh's spirituals, arrangements of blues by black vaudeville bandleaders W. C. Handy and Perry Bradford strongly appealed to markets of black consumers, first as sheet music and later as recordings known as "race records" (Handy 1991 [1941]; Bradford 1965; Barlow 1989).

Under Prohibition, blues and jazz performers interacted in urban clubs extensively, emphasizing the conversant nature of the two distinct genres (Barlow 1989: 292–294). Recordings featuring black vaudeville blues performer-songwriters like Bessie Smith and others, backed by jazz instrumentalists, caught the attention of white critics and hipsters, who often saw the urban strains of blues and jazz, if not all of black music, as one impervious style. For example, a white reviewer of Mamie Smith wrote for the *Dallas Journal* in 1921:

> [Smith's] "Hounds" give more spontaneous . . . harmony in a minute than the average so-called "jazz" orchestra could give during an entire year of effort. But this is only natural, as, since time immemorial, Negroes have been masters of folk melodies and ragtime tunes, and modern jazz is nothing more than ragtime with a little moonshine jazz. ("Mamie Smith Co." 1921:6)

Music critics also viewed rural blues styles, commercially available on race records, as a more primitive predecessor or folk root of jazz.

Collecting and recording

Collectors and scholars of folk song led the academic study and documentary recording of blues and other African American vernacular music for the first half of the twentieth century. Although research on spirituals was far more prevalent, predominantly southern white folklorists published descriptions and some analyses of blues in the 1910s and 1920s that echoed the stereotypical or superficial assessments of spirituals and black life (Lomax 1917; Odum 1911; White 1965 [1928]). Lyrics often provided the basis for folkloristic analysis of blues as an oral tradition. Secondarily treated (if at all), musical aspects of blues typically were evaluated through standards of Western European art music, which belied the importance of the performance aesthetic. Of prevailing concern beginning in the mid-1920s was the authenticity of blues and the contact of performers with commercially produced recordings, as addressed by Dorothy Scarborough (1963 [1925]) among others.

Most folklorists, who expected vernacular music to be the natural expression of an unsophisticated ethnic community (Bauman 1993:xiii–xiv; Roberts 1993), focused on blues in rural contexts as a representative of a mass black voice, even as African American migrants increasingly created an urban presence after each world war. The evaluative views of jazz critics during the 1930s and 1940s, which presented blues as a subsidiary, shifted the focus from folk versus popular blues to rural versus urban, employing the hierarchical classifications of "preclassic" or "country blues," "classic," and "postclassic" styles (Blesh 1946; Jones 1946).

Although ethnocentric interpretations dominated blues literature in the era of racial segregation, black intellectuals introduced a different perspective to this field of study. In the 1930s, folklorist Zora Neale Hurston and poet Sterling Brown wrote brief narratives that presented blues as a black vernacular art in its own right—one performed in social settings to vivify and comment on the experiences of black laborers or workers (Brown 1958 [1930]; Hurston 1978 [1935]). Similarly, although rarely before the 1960s, a few researchers interpreted the blues and its meaning through the accounts of African Americans who lived the blues experience (Oster 1969; Work 1940).

Blues scholar David Evans (1982:95–96) has noted that between the 1930s and 1940s, folklorists focused on making and archiving field recordings of blues songs to a greater degree than publishing analytical studies about them. The recordings made by researchers John Lomax (figure 6) and his son Alan (figure 7) in the 1930s and early 1940s are significant contributions in this area of research. As part of a larger recording project to document folk music as an art of common Americans for the Archive of Folk Song at the Library of Congress, the field recordings of the blues featured performers Huddie "Leadbelly" Ledbetter, Jelly Roll Morton, Big Bill Broonzy, and Vera Hall, among others (Lomax 1993:xii).

African American academics participated as paid field researchers, assisting the Lomaxes to elicit information from a southern black populace cautious about revealing social criticism to whites. Alan Lomax's 1993 memoir indicated that he sought a dual goal through collaborations in field research with Boasian-trained folklorist Zora Neale Hurston in 1935 and later projects with sociologist Charles Johnson and composer John Wesley Work III. In addition to countering his racial position as a white southerner, Alan Lomax also reasoned that in working on a project with the Archive of Folk Song, "black lettered intellectuals might overcome their prejudices against the oral traditions of the rural and unlettered blacks" (Lomax 1993:xii). Work's chapter on blues in *American Negro Songs and Spirituals* (1940) suggested that his views were compatible with Alan Lomax's, because Work used field research and musicological methods oriented to African American aesthetic values in his analysis of blues.

Field recordings provided researchers with information to sketch a fuller portrait of the settings and aims of African American musical performance in the era of legalized segregation. Some blues sound documents, for example, unveiled lyric themes that

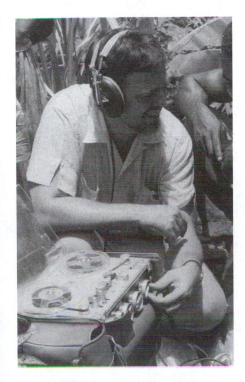

FIGURE 6   John Lomax, 1940s. Courtesy the Alan Lomax Archives.

FIGURE 7   Alan Lomax, Dominica 1962. Courtesy the Alan Lomax Archives.

directly criticized white oppression—songs that white-owned commercial companies would not have recorded or released (Gellert 1936, 1939, 1966).

The scholarship on blues revealed the same theoretical and ideological bias that prevailed in studies on ragtime and jazz. Although different in approach and perspective, the two major studies of ragtime, by Rudi Blesh and Harriet Janis (1971 [1966]) and Edward Berlin (1980), established ragtime as a precursor of what later became known as jazz and as both oral and written composition. The assessment of both forms in literature follows a similar trajectory. Focusing on the "racial" character of African American music, the first accounts of ragtime and jazz were basically reviews of recordings and performances or commentaries by music critics and performing musicians on both sides of the Atlantic. Published in American and European newspapers and in popular and jazz magazines, these narratives were shaped by the prevailing sociocultural milieux in America and the musical values of writers trained or with backgrounds in European classical traditions, which relegated ragtime and jazz to an inferior status. When ragtime and jazz were described as "peculiar," "primitive," and "discordant" by critics, black musicians challenged this stereotypical characterization, offering their cultural interpretation of the sound aesthetic. In "A Negro Explains Jazz" (1919), bandleader and composer James Reese Europe described the technique used to produce "peculiar" sounds, maintaining that they were expressions natural to black musicians: "With the brass instruments we put in mutes and made [*sic*] a whirling motion with the tongue, at the same time blowing full pressure. With wind instruments we pinch the mouthpiece and blow hard. This produces the peculiar sound which you all know" (Europe 1999 [1919]:13).

Despite such defenses, members of the black middle class joined their white counterparts in criticizing jazz and its black performers. Dave Peyton, for example, who wrote for the widely circulated African American newspaper *Chicago Defender*, heralded the anticipated demise of jazz, commenting in 1928: "Things are fast changing in the music game. Jazz is on the wane, and the better class of music is coming back into favor with the critical public" (Peyton 1999 [1928]:59). As a trained classical pianist, Peyton frequently compared jazz musicians to those performing in symphony orchestras and evaluated the artistic merit of jazz employing the standards applied to European classical traditions. Writings on jazz gradually expanded into book-length historical narratives (Osgood 1926). Preserving the basic content, tone, and perspective of writings published during the first two decades of the twentieth century, the authors examined a number of issues introduced earlier in more detail, including the concept of "hot jazz" (Panassié 1970 [1936]); jazz's bicultural heritage (Sargeant 1975 [1938]); comparative studies on hot jazz and swing (Panassié 1960 [1942]); and jazz as classical music (Hodeir 1979 [1956]). Other narratives were biographical in orientation (Armstrong 1993 [1936]); many of them focused on the human conditions of musicians—personal tragedies and self-destructive behaviors—as well as ethnically prescribed notions (Ramsey and Smith 1939). The research model drew from commercial recordings, published reviews, and anecdotes, which produced a narrow interpretation of the tradition. Moreover, and with few exceptions, American critics limited their reviews of jazz bands to those musicians who performed in and broadcast from white venues. As noted by music critic John Hammond (1977), the black performers identified by African Americans as major jazz figures were omitted from or treated as footnotes in many early accounts of the genre.

In the 1940s jazz criticism acquired a different tone when a younger generation of African American musicians introduced a new aesthetic to the tradition in the creation of bebop. Most critics responded negatively to the radical changes in musical language that distinguished bebop from earlier jazz styles. "The birth of this style," according to Scott DeVeaux, "coincided with the revival of New Orleans jazz, prompting a frequently acrimonious, occasionally hysterical war of words that did much to polarize the jazz community into opposing sides: the progressives and the 'moldy figs'" (1991:538). Music critics, record reviewers, and musicians either defended or berated bebop's originality, evaluating its merit using the musical values associated with New Orleans jazz and swing (Gendron 1995). Regardless of the position taken, their arguments reinforced the Eurocentric biases that prevailed in the writings of earlier decades (Blesh 1946; Hodeir 1979 [1956]; Stearns 1956; Ulanov 1952; Williams 1981 [1959]).

CIVIL RIGHTS, BLACK POWER, AND THE BLACK ARTS MOVEMENT

The advent of the civil rights movement in the 1950s and its national explosion in the 1960s and 1970s led to the introduction of African American studies into the academy. The student-generated push for a more inclusive curriculum—one that embraced the study of black life and culture in its totality, rural and urban—led to the formulation of new theoretical models of analysis. During this period, a generation of scholars emerged who directed their energies toward bringing a broader and more objective interpretation to the study of African American history and culture. Unlike much of the earlier scholarship, research in this era emphasized the perspectives and activities of African Americans themselves. The existence of a profound and pervasive African American voice in defining the nuances of African American music and culture reshaped and redefined the character, content, and quality of scholarship in African American music. In 1971 musicologist Eileen Southern (figure 8) published a groundbreaking, comprehensive historical narrative, *The Music of Black Americans: A History* (1983a [1971]), which traced the development of African American music from its African origins through the emergence of twentieth-century forms. Southern's treatise modeled, in part, two earlier historical studies on African American music published by blacks during the late nineteenth century and the first half of the twentieth. The first, *Music and Some Highly Musical People* (1881 [1878]), by James Monroe Trotter, focused exclusively on the achievements of African Americans in the Western art music tradition. The other, Maud Cuney-Hare's *Negro Musicians and Their Music* (1974 [1936]), built on Trotter's work but notably expanded the discussion to "explore the whole sweep of black musical activity, from its folk to art traditions, and to trace its development from the African roots to the present (that is, the 1930s)" (Southern 1983a [1971]: 452). A historical approach to the study of blacks in the classical music tradition remained prevalent. Two periodicals, *The Black Perspective in Music* (1973–1991), edited by Eileen Southern, and *The Black Music Research Journal* (1980–present) edited by Samuel A. Floyd Jr. (figure 9), are key resources advancing emergent scholarship in this area.

FIGURE 8   Eileen Southern, early 1980s. Photo courtesy Eileen Southern.

FIGURE 9   Samuel A. Floyd Jr. (*left*) and scholar J. H. Kwabena Nketia (*right*) 16 April 1997. Photo by Bob Kusel. Courtesy Center for Black Music Research, Columbia College, Chicago.

Scholars adopted and studied blues as a metaphor for a dynamic portrait of black struggles against racism in varied social-historical contexts.

Blues scholarship

While the historical musicologists continued chronicling the history of African American music and the achievements of African American musicians, black studies scholars began challenging earlier approaches to cultural analysis that misinterpreted African American music as a social-historical mirror of a monolithic and pathological black experience. Beginning with LeRoi Jones's (now Amiri Baraka) articulation in *Blues People: Negro Music in White America* (1963), scholars studied blues as a metaphor for a dynamic portrait of black struggles against racism in varied social-historical contexts. Literary specialists Larry Neal (1987 [1972]) and Albert Murray (1976) reconfigured blues and its meanings by emphasizing the importance of understanding blues in relation to both African Americans' interactions in performance and the experiences of black people in America. Others further developed aspects of these themes to reinterpret blues in the dynamic black cultural perspective, as in works by musicologist Daphne Duval Harrison (1988), communications scholar William Barlow (1989), literary theorist Houston A. Baker (1984), theologian James H. Cone (1972), feminist scholars Hazel Carby (1986) and Angela Y. Davis (1998), interdisciplinary scholar-performer Julio Finn (1992 [1986]), and others.

Another body of scholarship focused on the recording history of individual blues performers and their approaches to musical performance. The primarily British and white American researchers were involved in the blues revival, an outgrowth of the urban folk revival movement that embraced rural blues as pure folk music (Cohen 1995; Jackson 1993). Led by authors Samuel Charters (1959) and Paul Oliver (1963 [1960]), they portrayed the blues as a static tradition most ably represented in commercial recordings of the 1920s to 1940s. The recordings served as artifacts for literary and psychosocial readings of blues lyrics used to paint a monolithic portrait of black life. Revivalists interpreted contemporary blues through filters of both their romantic notions of rural southern black life and their expectations that "modern" (urban) lifestyles produced degenerate folk music. Within this context, revivalists imposed aesthetic standards and assigned meanings to blues with the aim of preserving an "authentic" blues tradition.

The research activities of these blues aficionados, record collectors, journalists, and academics expanded over time, as did the methodology used to investigate various issues. Moving beyond overarching studies of the origin, form, and meaning of blues, some writers catalogued blues recordings or performers (Dixon and Godrich 1963; Harris 1993 [1979]). The interview, modeled after folkloristic field recordings, became a primary mode of seeking connections between the art and lives of blues performers (Charters 1975; Howling Wolf 1970; Oliver 1965). Others examined regional musical styles through historical or ethnographic studies of performers (Evans 1971, 1982; Rowe 1981 [1975]; Titon 1994 [1977]). Despite the gradual inclusion of performers' views, the prolific revivalist publications as a whole represented a "reprinting," according to blues guitarist Buddy Guy (1970), or romantic construction, of black cultural life that has maintained many stereotypes (Titon 1993).

The retrospective gaze of revivalist blues publications often overshadowed investigations of blues performances favored by black blues audiences of the time. Charles Keil noted in *Urban Blues,* a pioneering examination of the most popular artists among 1960s black blues markets: "[Stylistic] changes from folk to urban blues have taken place. With the emergence and maturation of B. B. King, Jr. Parker, and Bobby Bland we have the models for nearly all contemporary blues forms" (1966:68). Keil's *Urban Blues* and, to a more limited extent, William Ferris Jr.'s *Blues from the Delta* (1970) applied ethnographic research methods to analyze blues performances as cultural processes in black social settings, a technique also rare in the often literary or historical approach of most black studies scholars.

Ethnographic approaches permitted definitions of blues centered on the broader perspectives of African Americans who participated in blues performances, whether in urban, rural, or commercial settings. Prominent blues performers such as Willie Dixon (with Snowden 1989) and David "Honeyboy" Edwards (1997) collaborated with writers to produce life stories that similarly provided a fuller and less sensationalized portrait of their contributions as musicians in their own voice. Revivalist constructions and widely ranging research methods continue, however, and analyses of blues music and its performers must be read critically (O'Neil 1993:375–376).

Jazz scholarship

Similar to material published on the blues, the literature on jazz published during the 1950s and 1960s reflected a general trend of two perspectives, one common to blacks and one common to whites. The activism associated with the Civil Rights and Black Power movements influenced a range of responses to the ideology of an integrated society, one that heightened the awareness of a racial identity among African Americans. As jazz became completely entrenched in every aspect of American life and proclaimed as *American* music, and as new styles emerged from musical innovation, the tradition acquired new identities and associations. These and other changes generated tension and debate among members of the jazz community—musicians and critics alike—in which the issues of race, class, generation, and identity became central themes. The major point of contention was how to define jazz and from whose perspective.

By the 1950s, for example, bebop had become identified with a younger generation of black musicians. At the same time, a commodified swing style and a classical-oriented small group and symphonic style became associated with white musicians who appealed to white middle-class audiences. While most critics, along with the older generation of black jazz musicians, relegated bebop to the margins of jazz by ignoring or debasing it, they expressed ambivalence about the commodified white swing bands that featured pop singers. Yet "faced with a bebop movement dominated by African American musicians," according to Bernard Gendron, the virtually all-white jazz journals seemed always to be in search of a "great white hope" (Elworth 1995:69). Steven Elworth noted that, in an effort to reinvent jazz for the white middle class, the influential jazz critic Martin Williams and composer-musician Gunther Schuller promoted an intellectual approach to jazz—a concept that recast jazz in the mold of European classical tradition as exemplified in cool and Third Stream jazz. While ignoring bebop and its derivative hard bop style, jazz critics heralded these new styles as markers of a new era in jazz. Moreover, their writings, based primarily on recordings and a musicological analysis of transcribed recordings, reduced jazz to an intellectual discourse. Countering this form of appropriation and reclaiming jazz as black cultural expression, African American musicians drew elements from black vernacular and popular forms to highlight a black racial identity (Elworth 1995; Leonard 1962).

Supporting this effort and providing a uniquely black perspective on contemporary jazz styles were literary critics affiliated with the 1960s black arts movement. African

American writers such as A. B. Spellman (1970 [1966]), LeRoi Jones (Amiri Baraka) (1967), and Larry Neal (1987 [1972]) believed that a valid criticism of jazz could evolve only from an understanding of the underlying philosophies and local cultural references that produced it. Interpreting the creation and meaning of performance of jazz within a black sociopolitical and cultural context, they vigorously defended the artistic merit of bebop, hard bop, and free jazz (the last style emerged in the 1960s) (Thomas 1995). This approach influenced the writings of budding young scholars such as Frank Kofsky (1970), whose works complemented the autobiographies and related narratives that proliferated over the following two decades (Ellington 1976 [1973]; Gillespie and Fraser 1979; Taylor 1993 [1977]).

Popular music scholarship

The recurring themes of race, identity, and appropriation in jazz scholarship were also prevalent in writing on black popular music. Despite the profound influence of contemporary black popular forms on mainstream American popular forms, this area of study rested on the margins of academic scholarship until the 1960s and was treated, if at all, as a footnote in most narratives on rock and rock and roll. While most academics ignored the tradition, questioning the artistic merit of a music produced and mass marketed as a commodity, journalists deemphasized its significance, promoting instead the derivative and adaptive forms of black music popularized by white artists. Bringing attention to this issue, Arnold Shaw, in the introduction to his book *Honkers and Shouters: The Golden Years of Rhythm and Blues* (1978), wrote: "The fact is that in its beginnings rock 'n' roll was derivative rhythm and blues. . . . Yet the relation of R&B to the past and its contribution to the future have been slighted, and until now there has been no comprehensive history of its rise and development" (xv).

Although limited in numbers, the first lengthy studies on black popular music were descriptive treatments of performers, hit recordings, regional styles, and record labels (Broven 1978 [1974]; Gillett 1974; Larkin 1970; Shaw 1970, 1978). Black journalist Phyl Garland in *The Sound of Soul* (1969), however, introduced a radically different approach that established the significance of context in interpreting popular musical genres. To determine what she called ethnic forces that helped shape the character of soul music, Garland traced the emergence of earlier black musical traditions, relating them to historical events and black cultural practices. Moreover, she examined soul music as an appropriated commodity, examining the practices of the music industry that prevented blacks from becoming the "Kings" and "Queens" of their own music.

This landmark study provided the model for a more substantive and culture-specific treatment of black popular music adopted by scholars such as Michael Haralambos in his ethnographic study *Right On: From Blues to Soul in Black America* (1975). Other noteworthy works, although descriptive rather than analytical in treatment, are historical narratives (Gillett 1983 [1970]; Hoare 1975) and historical profiles of specific musical styles or traditions. Subsequent studies drew primarily from empirical research and interviews with musicians (Guralnick 1986; Hirshey 1984). With the publication of *The Death of Rhythm and Blues* in 1988 by music critic Nelson George, issues of race, class, and culture came to the foreground and were interwoven with concepts of identity, authenticity, and the politics of the music industry. These themes became central to studies published in the 1990s.

Gospel music scholarship

Similar to the initial exclusion of black popular music from scholarly study, the first lengthy narrative written on African American gospel music, a genre that began to emerge in its most salient and enduring form during the 1930s, did not appear until 1960. "Some Aspects of the Religious Music of the United States Negro: An Ethnomusicological Study with Special Emphasis on the Gospel Tradition," a dissertation written by George Robinson Ricks through the department of anthropology at Northwestern University, "combines extensive field research in black churches in the North and South, interviews of performers, publishers and composers of gospel music and statistical analysis of intervals, tempo, melody and mode to show the relationship between styles of black religious music and the cultural background of exponents of the tradition" (Burnim 1980:18–19).

For the next twenty years, Ricks's dissertation was the most thorough, comprehensive, and insightful study of gospel music available. A very limited number of extended works on gospel music appeared over the next two decades, written primarily by music producers and journalists (Heilbut 1971) and ministers and civil rights activists (Walker 1979). The approach and content of such works were typically plagued by inappropriate, inadequate, or nonexistent research designs or by unsupported conjecture. As a form of music that distinguished the worship of all major African American denominations, Baptist, Methodist, and Pentecostal, gospel music was largely ignored in academic realms until scholar-performer Pearl Williams-Jones (1975, 1977) produced two pioneering works on the performance aesthetic of Pentecostal churches.

The decade of the 1980s ushered in a climate of increased scholarly attention to the gospel music genre. As the music received increasing media coverage on radio and television and in film, an accompanying body of scholarship has evolved. Topics of study have broadened from the rather perfunctory descriptive writing characteristic of the formative years to include ethnographic studies of culturally defined aesthetic values among choirs and quartets (Burnim 1980; Jackson 1988), historical treatments of pioneering gospel composers (Harris 1992; Reagon 1992), regional studies (Allen 1991; Lornell 1988; DjeDje 1998), musical analyses (Boyer 1985, 1992a–e), gospel publishing (Boyer 1992b), gospel announcers (Pollard 2000a), gospel piano styles (Kalil 1993), gospel musicals (Pollard 2000b), and the influence of gospel on popular music (Maultsby 1992).

As a relatively new domain of scholarly inquiry, the study of gospel music is no longer an ignored topic. Although the quality of the existing gospel music literature is uneven, there are pockets of excellence that invite new directives. Theoretical perspectives of scholars in gospel music have advanced from the initial preoccupation of defining gospel in opposition to Western European music, distinguishing gospel from the Negro spiritual, or producing trait lists believed to define meaning. Gospel music research has clearly benefited from the lessons learned in the study of earlier forms of African American music. From the beginning, the voices of gospel music tradition bearers have been an integral part of the analytical equation, contributing in significant ways to the growing body of knowledge in this area.

The Africanisms debate revisited

The spirit of the 1960s also generated a resurgence of interest in the Africanisms debate. The seminal work of historians John Blassingame (1979 [1972]), Lawrence Levine (1977), and Sterling Stuckey (1987) advanced the study of the African musical continuum among African Americans in the United States by placing music in a holistic cultural frame that embraced dance, art, language, drama, and religion. These more integrated approaches viewed culture as a dynamic process of continuity and change, one that permitted the conceptual transfer of musical values, ideals, and behaviors through such mechanisms as syncretism and reinterpretation. The work of scholars J. H. Kwabena Nketia (1973, 1981) (figure 9), Olly Wilson (1974, 1981, 1992) (figure 10), Portia Maultsby (1990), Ernest Brown (1990), and Gerhard Kubik (1999) are prime examples that reflect this conceptual approach to the study of links between the musics of Africans and African Americans in the United States.

FIGURE 10   Olly Wilson, c. 1990. Photo courtesy Olly Wilson.

Although hip-hop was described as "noise" by its detractors, Tricia Rose contended that "[r]ap's black sonic forces are very much an outgrowth of black cultural traditions, the post-industrial transformation of urban life, and the contemporary technological terrain."

ADVANCING TO THE TWENTY-FIRST CENTURY

Scholarly studies on African American music exploded in the 1990s, largely as a result of the cross-cultural and transnational popularity of hip-hop music and culture. The exposure of hip-hop culture through Hollywood films, MTV (Music Television) and BET (Black Entertainment Television), mainstream advertising, and popular culture magazines generated a curiosity about the harsh realities of inner city life and a corresponding set of cultural values and social norms that differed from those of mainstream society. As the tradition became entrenched in the mainstream, so did stereotypical and controversial representations of urban black life. The criticism and controversy that surrounded hip-hop and its commercial exploitation attracted the attention of scholars from an array of disciplines.

Building on the writings of journalists Nelson George, Greg Tate, Harry Allen, James Bernard, John Leland, James Spady, Havelock Nelson, Alan Light, and S. H. Ferenado Jr., among others, scholars sought to explain the phenomenology of this culture and its cross-cultural appeal. Employing research methods and analytical models from the fields of sociology, literary theory, cultural studies, and history, their works framed hip-hop music as a product of inner city black communities plagued by decades of institutional racism, social inequalities, political maneuvering, and governmental neglect, and as a unique form of vernacular expression (Baker 1993; Dyson 1991, 1993:3–22; Perkins, 1996; Potter 1995; Shusterman 1991). Inspired by the feminist writings of such authors as bell hooks (1988, 1990, 1992), issues of gender became central to scholarly inquiry on hip-hop, especially the representation of women, feminist perspectives, and the role of women as songwriters, producers, and executives in establishing new musical directions (Berry 1994a; Forman 1994; Keyes 1993; Niesel 1997; Roberts 1991; Rose 1994).

They and other writers examined technological aspects and aesthetic principles that intertwine to produce hip-hop's distinctive sound (Allen 1988; Bartlett 1994; Dimitriadis 1996; Rose 1994:62–96; Salaam 1995). Although hip-hop was described as "noise" by its detractors, Rose contended: "Rap's black sonic forces are very much an outgrowth of black cultural traditions, the post-industrial transformation of urban life, and the contemporary technological terrain" (1994:63). In an analysis of hip-hop using musicological and ethnomusicological methods, Robert Walser (1995) and Cheryl Keyes (1996) linked the sound, structure, and technique to cultural traditions of Africa and the diaspora. Music theorists also used a similar approach to analyze the performance aesthetic of soul music (Brackett 1992) and to investigate the relationship between music sound and identity in both national and transnational contexts (Krims 2000).

Increases in the national and transnational consumption of black popular music inspired new investigations on the racial politics of the music industry and the economic impact of crosscultural marketing by Chapple and Garofalo in *Rock 'n' Roll Is Here to Pay* (1977). A decade later, other writers from various disciplines continued this area of investigation (Brackett 1994; Early 1995; Garofalo 1990; George 1988). The worldwide explosion of hip-hop generated many different representations of the genre.

Employing a range of interdisciplinary approaches, scholars examined both local and global conditions that encouraged the production of hip-hop and the construction of related yet imagined identities in non-American contexts (Mitchell 1995; Elflein 1998; Krims 2000; Mitchell n.d.).

The theoretical perspectives of cultural studies scholars Stuart Hall (Hall and du Gay, 1996; Morley and Chen 1996) and Paul Gilroy (1993a, 1993b) inspired a new field of research on the reciprocal influence of black American music on Africa and its diasporic cultures in which issues of identity, ethnicity, and representation became the focus (Erlmann 1999; Hamm 1988; Lipsitz 1994; Kalumbu 1999; Williams 1995).

The 1990s also witnessed new approaches in scholarly studies on jazz. The works of Burton Peretti (1992), William Kenney (1993), and David Stowe (1994), for example, framed culture as significant in shaping and defining various styles of jazz. Applying ethnographic research, Paul Berliner (1994) and Ingrid Monson (1996) examined musical processes as a manifestation of black cultural values and social behavior. Their use of empirical data and musicological analysis filtered through the interpretation of performing musicians distinguished these two works from other studies on Jazz.

The development of interdisciplinary approaches to studies on jazz, blues, and popular styles motivated the use of music as a research tool in other disciplines. Historian Brian Ward, for example, examined "the relationship between black protest and consciousness, race relations, and Rhythm and Blues music [rhythm and blues, soul, and funk]" (1998:4). Similarly, historian Craig Werner (1999) drew from a range of black popular styles to expose the multiple and heterophonic voices of black people as a way to generate dialogues about race relations since World War II. Such applications generated new voices in the interpretation of historical events and social conditions that affected life in America during the second half of the twentieth century.

Over a period of four centuries, the study of African American music advanced from the early descriptive accounts of musical performance by casual observers, the Eurocentric analyses of structure and technique, and subjective interpretations of meaning and significance to a more holistic understanding of music making as a set of black cultural practices associated with specific historical, sociocultural, and political contexts. Approaches to the study of this tradition also changed from nonexistent methodologies to the use of a single research and analytical model and then to the combination of multiple approaches from various disciplinary areas. Although the literature on African American music is uneven in quality, it presents varying interpretations, including those of African Americans, whose views were excluded from the musical canon before the 1970s and 1980s. The last decade of the twentieth century witnessed new trends in black music production as the tradition became appropriated and reinvented in global contexts. Such developments generated new research initiatives that will further broaden the study of African American music and culture in the twenty-first century.

REFERENCES

Allen, Ernest Jr. 1996. "Making the Strong Survive: The Contours and Contradictions of Message Rap." In *Droppin' Science: Critical Essays on Rap Music and Hip-Hop Culture*, ed. William Eric Perkins, 158–191. Philadelphia: Temple University Press.

Allen, Harry. 1988. "Hip-Hop Hi-Tech: A Sampler of Men, Music, and Machines." *The Village Voice*, Consumer Electronics Special 1(1):9–11.

Allen, Ray. 1991. *Singing in the Spirit: African American Sacred Quartets in New York City.* Philadelphia: University of Pennsylvania Press.

Allen, William Francis, Charles Ware, and Lucy McKim Garrison, eds. 1965 [1867]. *Slave Songs of the United States.* New York: Oak Publications.

Armstrong, Louis. 1993 [1936]. *Swing That Music.* New York: Da Capo.

Baker, Houston A. 1984. *Blues, Ideology, and Afro-American Literature: A Vernacular Theory.* Chicago: University of Chicago Press.

———. 1993. *Black Studies, Rap, and the Academy.* Chicago: University of Chicago Press.

Barlow, William. 1989. *"Looking Up at Down": The Emergence of Blues Culture.* Philadelphia: Temple University Press.

Bartlett, Andrew. 1994. "Airshafts, Loudspeakers, and the Hip Hop Sample: Contexts and African American Musical Aesthetics." *African American Review* 28(4): 639–652.

Bastin, Bruce. 1995 [1986]. *Red River Blues.* Urbana: University of Illinois Press.

Bauman, Richard, ed. 1993. "Introduction." In *Folklore and Culture on the Texas-Mexican Border* [Essays by Américo Parades], ix–xxiii. Austin:

Center for Mexican American Studies, University of Texas.

Berendt, Joachim-Ernst. 1975. *The Jazz Book: From New Orleans to Rock and Free Jazz.* Trans. Dan Morgenstern and Helmut and Barbara Bredigkeit. New York: Lawrence Hill.

Berlin, Edward A. 1980. *Ragtime: A Musical and Cultural History.* Berkeley: University of California Press.

Berliner, Paul F. 1994. *Thinking in Jazz: The Infinite Art of Improvisation.* Chicago: University of Chicago Press.

Berry, Venise T. 1994a. "Feminine or Masculine: The Conflicting Nature of Female Images in Rap Music." In *Cecilia Reclaimed. Feminist Perspectives on Gender Music,* ed. Susan Cook, 163–201. Urbana: University of Illinois Press.

———. 1994b. "Redeeming the Rap Music Experience." In *Adolescents and Their Music: If It's Too Loud, You're Too Old,* ed. Jonathon S. Epstein, 165–187. New York: Garland Publishing.

Blassingame, John W. 1979 [1972]. *The Slave Community: Plantation Life in the Antebellum South.* New York: Oxford University Press.

Blesh, Rudi. 1946. *Shining Trumpets. A History of Jazz.* New York: Knopf.

Blesh, Rudi, and Harriet Janis. 1971 [1966]. *They All Played Ragtime.* 4th ed. New York: Oak Publications.

Blues Unlimited. London: BU Publications.

Bowman, Rob. 1997. *Soulsville U.S.A.: The Story of Stax Records.* New York: Schirmer Books.

Boyer, Horace. 1985. "A Comparative Analysis of Traditional and Contemporary Gospel Music." In *More Than Dancing,* ed. Irene V. Jackson, 127–145. Westport, Conn.: Greenwood Press.

———. 1992a. "Charles Albert Tindley: Progenitor of African American Gospel Music." In *We'll Understand It Better By and By,* ed. Bernice Johnson Reagon, 53–78. Washington, D.C.: Smithsonian Institution Press.

———. 1992b. "Kenneth Morris: Composer and Dean of Black Gospel Music Publishers." In *We'll Understand It Better By and By,* ed. Bernice Johnson Reagon, 309–327. Washington, D.C.: Smithsonian Institution Press.

———. 1992c. "Lucie E. Campbell: Composer for the National Baptist Convention." In *We'll Understand It Better By and By,* ed. Bernice Johnson Reagon, 81–108. Washington, D.C.: Smithsonian Institution Press.

———. 1992d. "Roberta Martin: Innovator of Modern Gospel Music." In *We'll Understand It Better By and By,* ed. Bernice Johnson Reagon, 275–286. Washington, D.C.: Smithsonian Institution Press.

———. 1992e. "Take My Hand, Precious Lord, Lead Me On." In *We'll Understand It Better By and By,* ed. Bernice Johnson Reagon, 141–163. Washington, D.C.: Smithsonian Institution Press.

———. 1992f. "William Herbert Brewster: The Eloquent Poet." In *We'll Understand It Better By*

and By, ed. Bernice Johnson Reagon, 211–231. Washington, D.C.: Smithsonian Institution Press.

Brackett, David. 1992. "James Brown's 'Superbad' and the Double-Voiced Utterance." *Popular Music* 11(3):309–323.

———. 1994. "The Politics and Practice of 'Cross-Over' in American Popular Music, 1963–1965." *Musical Quarterly* 78(4):774–779.

Bradford, Perry. 1965. *Born with the Blues: Perry Bradford's Own Story.* New York: Oak Publications.

Broven, John. 1978 [1974]. *Rhythm and Blues in New Orleans.* Gretna, La.: Pelican Publishing.

Brown, Ernest. 1990. "Something from Nothing and More from Something." *Selected Reports in Ethnomusicology* 8:275–291.

Brown, Sterling. 1958 [1930]. "The Blues as Folk Poetry." In *The Book of Negro Folklore,* ed. Langston Hughes and Arna Bontemps, 371–397. New York: Dodd, Mead.

Burnim, Mellonee. 1980. "The Black Gospel Music Tradition: Symbol of Ethnicity." Ph.D. dissertation, Indiana University.

———. 1985. "The Black Gospel Tradition: A Complex of Ideology, Aesthetic, and Behavior." In *More Than Dancing,* ed. Irene V. Jackson, 147–167. Westport, Conn.: Greenwood Press.

Carby, Hazel. 1986. "'It Jus' Be's Dat Way Sometime': The Sexual Politics of Women's Blues." *Radical America* 20(4):9–24.

Cashmore, Ellis. 1997. *The Black Culture Industry.* New York: Routledge.

Chapple, Steve, and Reebee Garofalo. 1977. *Rock 'n' Roll Is Here to Pay: The History of Politics in the Music Industry.* Chicago: Nelson-Hall.

Charters, Samuel B. 1959. *The Country Blues.* New York: Rinehart.

———. 1967. *The Bluesmen: The Story and the Music of the Men Who Made the Blues.* New York: Oak Publications.

———. 1975. *The Legacy of the Blues: A Glimpse into the Art and the Lives of Twelve Great Bluesmen: An Informal Study.* London: Calder and Boyars.

Charters, Samuel B., and Leonard Kunstadt. 1962. *Jazz: A History of the New York Scene.* Garden City, N.Y.: Doubleday.

Cohen, Ronald D., ed. 1995. *"Wasn't That a Time!": Firsthand Accounts of the Folk Music Revival.* Metuchen, N.J.: The Scarecrow Press.

Collins, Patricia H. 1990. *Black Feminist Thought: Knowledge, Consciousness, and the Politics of Empowerment.* Boston: Unwin Hyman.

Cone, James H. 1972. *The Spirituals and the Blues: An Interpretation.* New York: Seabury Press.

Cuney-Hare, Maud. 1974 [1936]. *Negro Musicians and Their Music.* New York: Da Capo.

Davis, Angela Y. 1998. *Blues Legacies and Black Feminism: Gertrude "Ma" Rainey, Bessie Smith, and Billie Holiday.* New York: Pantheon.

DeVeaux, Scott. 1991. "Constructing the Jazz Tradition: Jazz Historiography." *Black American Literature Forum* 25(3):525–560.

Dimitriadis, Greg. 1996. "Hip Hop: From Live Performance to Mediated Narrative." *Popular Music* 15(2):179–194.

Dixon, Robert M. W., and John Godrich. 1963. *Blues and Gospel Records (1902–1942).* Middlesex, Eng.: Storyville.

Dixon, Wheeler Winston. 1989. "Urban Black American Music in the Late 1980s: The 'Word' as Cultural Signifier." *The Midwest Quarterly* 30(2):229–241.

Dixon, Willie, with Don Snowden. 1989. *I Am the Blues: The Willie Dixon Story.* New York: Da Capo.

DjeDje, Jacqueline Cogdell. 1998. "The California Black Gospel Music Tradition: A Confluence of Musical Styles and Cultures." In *California Soul: Music of African Americans in the West,* ed. Jacqueline Cogdell DjeDje and Eddie Meadows, 124–175. Berkeley: University of California Press.

DuBois, W. E. B. 1995 [1926]. "Criteria of Negro Art." In *A Reader: DuBois,* ed. David Levering Lewis, 509–515. New York: Da Capo.

Dyson, Michael E. 1991. "Performance, Protest, and Prophecy in the Culture of Hip-Hop." In *The Emergence of Black and the Emergency of Rap,* special issue of *Black Sacred Music* 5(1):13–24.

———. 1993. *Reflecting Black African American Cultural Criticism.* Minneapolis: University of Minnesota Press.

———. 1996. *Between God and Gangsta Rap: Bearing Witness to Black Culture.* New York: Oxford University Press.

Early, Gerald Lyn. 1995. *One Nation under a Groove: Motown and American Culture.* Hopewell, N.J.: Ecco Press.

Edwards, David "Honeyboy." 1997. *The World Don't Owe Me Nothing: The Life and Times of Delta Bluesman "Honeyboy" Edwards.* Chicago: Chicago Review Press.

Elflein, Dietmar. 1998. "From Krauts with Attitudes to Turks with Attitudes: Some Aspects of Hip-Hop History in Germany." *Popular Music* 17(3):255–264.

Ellington, Duke. 1976 [1973]. *Music Is My Mistress.* New York: Da Capo.

Ellison, Mary. 1989. "The Blues in American Poetry." In *Extensions of the Blues,* 107–70. New York: Riverrun Press.

Elworth, Steven B. 1995. "Jazz in Crisis, 1948–1958: Ideology and Representation." In *Jazz among the Discourses,* ed. Krin Gabbard, 57–75. Durham, N.C.: Duke University Press.

Epstein, Dena J. 1977. *Sinful Tunes and Spirituals: Black Folk Music to the Civil War.* Urbana: University of Illinois Press.

———. 1983. "A White Origin for the Black Spiritual? An Invalid Theory and How It Grew." *American Music* 1(2):53–59.

Erlmann, Veit. 1999. *Music, Modernity and the Global Imagination: South Africa and the West.* New York: Oxford University Press.

Eure, Joseph D., and James G. Spady, eds. 1991. *Nation Conscious Rap.* New York: PC International Press.

Europe, James Reese. 1999 [1919]. "A Negro Explains 'Jazz.'" In *Keeping Time: Readings in Jazz History,* ed. Robert Walser, 12–14. New York: Oxford University Press.

Evans, David. 1971. *Tommy Johnson.* London: Studio Vista.

———. 1982. *Big Road Blues: Tradition and Creativity in the Folk Blues.* Berkeley: University of California Press.

Fernando, S. H. Jr. 1994. *The New Beats: Exploring the Music, Culture and Attitudes of Hip-Hop.* New York: Anchor Books/Doubleday.

Ferris, William Jr. 1970. *Blues from the Delta.* London: Studio Vista.

Finn, Julio. 1992 [1986]. *The Bluesman: The Musical Heritage of Black Men and Women in the Americas.* New York: Interlink Books.

Forman, Murray. 1994. "'Movin' Closer to an Independent Funk': Black Feminist Theory, Standpoint, and Women in Rap." *Women's Studies* 23(l):35–55.

Gabbard, Krin, ed. 1995. *Jazz among the Discourses.* Durham, N.C.: Duke University Press.

Garland, Phyl. 1969. *The Sound of Soul.* Chicago: H. Regnery.

Garofalo, Reebee. 1990. "Crossing Over: 1939–1989." In *Split Image: African Americans in the Mass Media,* ed. Jannette L. Dates and William Barlow, 57–121. Washington, D.C.: Howard University Press.

Garon, Paul. 2000. *White Blues.* Available at http://www.bluesworld.com/whiteblues.html.

Garst, John F. 1986. "Mutual Reinforcement and the Origins of Spirituals." *American Music* 4(4):390–424.

Gellert, Lawrence. 1936. *Negro Songs of Protest.* New York: Carl Fischer.

———, coll. 1939. *Me and My Captain.* New York: Hours Press.

———. 1966. Interview by Richard Reuss. In *Lawrence Gellert Interviews.* Indiana University Archives of Traditional Music 84-302-F, ATL 9178.

Gendron, Bernard. 1995. "'Moldy Figgs' and Modernists: Jazz at War (1942–1946)." In *Jazz among the Discourses,* ed. Krin Gabbard, 31–56. Durham, N.C.: Duke University Press.

George, Nelson. 1988. *The Death of Rhythm & Blues.* New York: Pantheon.

———. 1998. *Hip-Hop America.* New York: Viking.

Gillespie, Dizzy, and Al Fraser. 1979. *To Be or Not to Bop: Memoirs.* New York: Doubleday.

Gillett, Charlie. 1974. *Making Tracks: Atlantic Records and the Growth of a Multi-Billion Dollar Industry.* New York: Dutton.

———. 1983 [1970]. *The Sound of the City.* New York: Outerbridge and Dienstfrey.

Gilroy, Paul. 1993a. *The Black Atlantic: Modernity and Double Consciousness.* Cambridge: Harvard University Press.

———. 1993b. *Small Acts: Thoughts on the Politics of Black Cultures.* New York: Serpent's Tail.

Guillory, Monique, and Richard C. Green. 1998. *Soul: Black Power, Politics, and Pleasure.* New York: New York University Press.

Guralnick, Peter. 1986. *Sweet Soul Music: Rhythm and Blues and the Southern Dream of Freedom.* New York: Harper and Row.

Guy, Buddy. 1970. "Living Blues Interview: Buddy Guy." *Living Blues* 1:3–9.

Hall, Stuart, and Paul du Gay, eds. 1996. *Questions of Cultural Identity.* Thousand Oaks, Calif.: Sage.

Hamm, Charles. 1988. *Afro-American Music, South Africa, and Apartheid.* ISAM Monograph 28. Brooklyn, N.Y.: Institute for Studies in American Music.

Hammond, John. 1977. *On Record: An Autobiography.* New York: Ridge Press.

Handy, William C. 1991 [1941]. *Father of the Blues: An Autobiography.* Ed. Arna Bontemps. New York: Da Capo.

Hannusch, Jeff. 1985. *I Hear You Knockin': The Sound of New Orleans Rhythm & Blues.* Ville Platte, La.: Swallow Publications.

Haralambos, Michael. 1975. *Right on: From Blues to Soul in Black America.* New York: Drake Publishers.

Harris, Michael W. 1992. *The Rise of Gospel Blues: The Music of Thomas Andrew Dorsey in the Urban Church.* New York: Oxford University Press.

Harris, Sheldon. 1993 [1979]. *Blues Who's Who: A Biographical Dictionary of Blues Singers.* New York: Da Capo.

Harrison, Daphne Duval. 1988. *Black Pearls: Blues Queens of the 1920s.* New Brunswick, N.J.: Rutgers University Press.

Heilbut, Anthony. 1971. *The Gospel Sound: Good News and Bad Times.* New York: Simon and Schuster.

Hentoff, Nat. 1961. *The Jazz Life.* New York: Dial Press.

Herskovits, Melville. 1958 [1942]. *The Myth of the Negro Past.* Boston: Beacon Press.

Hickerson, Joe. 1995. "Overviews." In *"Wasn't That a Time!": Firsthand Accounts of the Folk Music Revival,* ed. Ronald D. Cohen, 13–23. Metuchen, N.J.: The Scarecrow Press.

Hirshey, Gerri. 1984. *Nowhere to Run: The Story of Soul Music.* New York: Times Books.

Hoare, Ian, ed. 1975. *The Soul Book.* London: E. Methuen.

Hodeir, André. 1979 [1956]. *Jazz: Its Evolution and Essence.* Trans. David Noakes. New York: Grove Press.

hooks, bell. 1988. *Talking Back: Thinking Feminist, Thinking Black.* Toronto: Between the Lines.

———. 1990. *Yearning: Race, Gender and Cultural Politics.* Boston: South End Press.

———. 1992. *Black Looks: Race and Representation.* Boston: South End Press.

Hornbostel, Erich Von. 1926. "American Negro Songs." *The International Review of Missions* 15(60): 748–753.

Howling Wolf. 1970. "Interview." *Living Blues* 1(1):13–17.

Hughes, Langston. 1976 [1926]. "The Negro Artist and the Racial Mountain." In *Voices from the Harlem Renaissance,* ed. Nathan Huggins, 305–307. New York: Oxford University Press.

Hurston, Zora Neale. 1976 [1935]. "Spirituals and Neo-Spirituals." In *Voices from the Harlem Renaissance,* ed. Nathan Huggins, 344–347. New York: Oxford University Press.

———. 1978 [1935]. "Card Game." In *Mules and Men,* 152–159. Bloomington: Indiana University Press.

Jackson, Bruce. 1993. "The Folksong Revival." In *Transforming Tradition: Folk Music Revivals Examined,* ed. Neil V. Rosenberg, 73–83. Urbana: University of Illinois Press.

———, ed. 1967. *The Negro and His Folklore in Nineteenth-Century Periodicals.* Austin: The University of Texas Press.

Jackson, George P. 1933. *White Spirituals in the Southern Uplands.* Chapel Hill: University of North Carolina Press.

———. 1975 [1943]. *White and Negro Spirituals: Their Life-Span and Kinship.* New York: Da Capo.

Jackson, Joyce. 1988. "The Performing Black Sacred Quartet: An Expression of Cultural Values and Aesthetics." Ph.D. dissertation, Indiana University.

Joe, Radcliffe A. 1980. *This Business of Disco.* New York: Billboard Books.

Johnson, Guy B. 1930. *Folk Culture on St. Helena Island, South Carolina.* Chapel Hill: University of North Carolina Press.

Johnson, James W., and J. Rosamond Johnson. 1989 [1925, 1926]. *American Negro Spirituals, I and II.* New York: Da Capo.

Jones, LeRoi [Amiri Baraka]. 1963. *Blues People: Negro Music in White America.* New York: Morrow.

———. 1967. *Black Music.* New York: Morrow.

Jones, Max. 1946. "On Blues." In *The PL Yearbook of Jazz 1946,* ed. Albert McCarthy, 72–107. London: Editions Poetry.

Kalil, Timothy M. 1993. "The Role of the Great Migration of African Americans to Chicago in the Development of Traditional Black Gospel Piano by Thomas A. Dorsey circa 1930." Ph.D. dissertation, Indiana University.

Kalumbu, Isaac. 1999. "The Process of Creation and Production of Popular Music in Zimbabwe." Ph.D. dissertation, Indiana University.

Keil, Charles. 1966. *Urban Blues.* Chicago: The University of Chicago Press.

Living Blues: A Journal of the Black American Blues Tradition. Jackson: Center for the Study of Southern Culture, University of Mississippi.

Kelley, Robin D. G. 1994. *Race Rebels: Culture, Politics, and the Black Working Class.* New York: The Free Press.

———. 1997. *Yo' Mama's DisFUNKtional!: Fighting the Culture Wars in Urban America.* Boston: Beacon Press.

Kenney, William H. 1993. *Chicago Jazz: A Cultural History 1904–1930.* New York: Oxford University Press.

Keyes, Cheryl. 1993. "We're More Than a Novelty, Boys: Strategies of Female Rappers in the Rap Music Tradition." In *Feminist Messages: Coding in Women's Folk Culture,* ed. J. N. Radner, 203–220. Urbana: University of Illinois Press.

———. 1996. "At the Crossroads: Rap Music and Its African Nexus." *Ethnomusicology* 40(2):223–247.

Kofsky, Frank. 1970. *Black Nationalism and the Revolution in Music.* New York: Pathfinder Press.

Krehbiel, Henry. 1962 [1914]. *Afro-American Folk Songs.* New York: Frederick Ungar.

Krims, Adam. 2000. *Rap Music and the Poetics of Identity.* Cambridge: Cambridge University Press.

Kubik, Gerhard. 1999. *Africa and the Blues.* Jackson: University of Mississippi Press.

Larkin, Rochelle. 1970. *Soul Music.* New York: Lancer Books.

Laubenstein, Paul Fritz. 1930. "Race Values in Aframerican Music." *Musical Quarterly* 16(3): 378–403.

Leonard, Neil. 1962. *Jazz and the White Americans: The Acceptance of a New Art Form.* Chicago: The University of Chicago Press.

Levine, Lawrence W. 1977. *Black Culture and Black Consciousness.* New York: Oxford University Press.

Lipsitz, George. 1994. *Dangerous Crossroads: Popular Music, Postmodernism and the Poetics of Place.* London: Verso.

Locke, Alain. 1969 [1936]. *The Negro and His Music.* New York: Arno Press.

———, ed. 1992 [1925]. *The New Negro: Voices of the Harlem Renaissance.* New York: Atheneum.

Lomax, Alan. 1978 [1968]. *Folk Song Style and Culture.* New Brunswick, N.J.: Transaction Books.

———. 1993. *Land Where the Blues Began.* New York: Pantheon.

Lomax, Alan, and John Avery Lomax. 1936. *Negro Folk Songs as Sung by Leadbelly.* New York: Macmillan.

Lomax, John. 1917. "Self-Pity in Negro Folk-Songs." *The Nation* 105:141–145.

Lornell, Kip. 1988. *Happy in the Service of the Lord: Afro-American Gospel Quartets in Memphis.* Urbana: University of Illinois Press.

Lovell, John. 1972. *Black Song: The Forge and the Flame.* New York: Macmillan.

Luane, Clarence. 1993. "Rap, Race and Politics." *Race & Class* 35(l):41–56.

"Mamie Smith Co." 1921. *Chicago Defender,* Movie and Stage Department, 2 April, 6.

Marsh, J. B. T. 1971 [1876]. *The Story of the Jubilee Singers: With Their Songs.* New York: AMS Press.

Maultsby, Portia K. 1990. "Africanisms in African American Music." In *Africanisms in American Culture,* ed. Joseph Holloway, 185–210. Bloomington: Indiana University Press.

———. 1992. "The Impact of Gospel Music on the Secular Music Industry." In *We'll Understand It Better By and By,* ed. Bernice Johnson Reagon, 19–33. Washington, D.C.: Smithsonian Institution Press.

Mitchell, Tony. 1995. "Questions of Style: Notes on Italian Hip Hop." *Popular Music* 14(3):333–348.

———, ed. n.d. *Global Noise: Rap and Hip Hop outside the U.S.A.* Hanover, N.H.: Wesleyan University Press. Forthcoming.

Monson, Ingrid. 1996. *Saying Something: Jazz Improvisation and Interaction.* Chicago: University of Chicago Press.

Morley, David, and Kuan-Hsing Chen, eds. 1996. *Stuart Hall. Critical Dialogues in Cultural Studies.* New York: Routledge.

Murray, Albert. 1976. *Stomping the Blues.* New York: McGraw-Hill.

Neal, Larry. 1987 [1972]. "The Ethos of the Blues." In *Visions of a Liberated Future: Black Arts Movement Writings,* ed. Michael Schwartz, 107–117. New York: Thunder's Mouth.

Neal, Mark Anthony. 1999. *What the Music Said: Black Popular Music and Black Popular Culture.* New York: Routledge.

Niesel, Jeff. 1997. "Hip-Hop Matters: Rewriting the Sexual Politics of Rap Music." In *Third Wave Agenda: Being Feminist, Doing Feminism,* ed. Leslie Haywood and J. Drake, 239–254. Minneapolis: University of Minnesota Press.

Nketia, J. H. Kwabena. 1973. "The Study of African and Afro-American Music." *The Black Perspective in Music* 1(1):7–15.

———. 1977. "African Roots of Music in the Americas: An African View." In *Report of the 12th Congress,* ed. Daniel Heartz and Bonnie C. Wade, 82–88. Berkeley: American Musicological Society.

Odum, Howard. 1911. "Folk-Song and Folk-Poetry as Found in the Secular Songs of the Southern Negroes." *Journal of American Folklore* 24:255–294, 351–396.

Oliver, Paul. 1963 [1960]. *The Meaning of the Blues.* New York: Collier Books.

———. 1965. *Conversation with the Blues.* New York: Horizon Press.

———. 1969. *The Story of the Blues.* Philadelphia: Chilton.

O'Neil, Jim. 1993. "I Once Was Lost, But Now I'm Found: The Blues Revival of the 1960s." In *Nothing but the Blues: The Music and the Musicians,* ed. Lawrence Cohn, 347–387. New York: Abbeville.

Osgood, Henry O. 1926. *So This Is Jazz.* Boston: Little, Brown.

Oster, Harry. 1969. *Living Country Blues.* Detroit: Folklore Associates.

Panassié, Hugues. 1960 [1942]. *The Real Jazz.* Rev. ed. New York: Barnes.

———. 1970 [1936]. *Hot Jazz: The Guide to Swing Music.* Westport, Conn.: Negro Universities Press.

Pankake, John. 1995. "Transcript of Conference Presentation for Section on 'Folk Magazine.'" In *"Wasn't That a time!: Firsthand Accounts of the Folk Music Revival,* ed. Ronald D. Cohen, 105–114. Metuchen, N.J.: The Scarecrow Press.

Pearson, Barry Lee. 1990. *Virginia Piedmont Blues: The Lives and Art of Two Virginia Bluesmen.* Philadelphia: University of Pennsylvania Press.

Peretti, Burton W. 1992. *The Creation of Jazz: Music, Race and Culture in Urban America.* Urbana: University of Illinois Press.

Perkins, William Eric, ed. 1996. *Droppin' Science: Critical Essays on Rap Music and Hip Hop Culture.* Philadelphia: Temple University Press.

Peyton, Dave. 1999 [1928]. "A Black Journalist Criticizes Jazz." In *Keeping Time: Readings in Jazz History,* ed. Robert Walser, 57–59. New York: Oxford University Press.

Pollard, Deborah Smith. 2000a. "Gospel Announcers (Disc Jockeys): What They Do and Why It Matters." *Arkansas Review: A Journal of Delta Studies* 31(2):87–101.

———. 2000b. "The Phenomenon Known as the Gospel Musical Stage Play." *The CEA Critic* 62(3):1–17.

———. n.d. "Edna Tatum: A Gospel Announcer and Narrator in Performance." *Womanist Research* 3(2). Forthcoming.

Potter, Russell A. 1995. *Spectacular Vernaculars: Hip-Hop and the Politics of Postmodernism.* Albany: State University of New York Press.

Pruter, Robert. 1991. *Chicago Soul.* Urbana: University of Illinois Press.

———. 1996. *Doowop: The Chicago Scene.* Urbana: University of Illinois Press.

Quinn, Michael. 1996. "'Never Shoulda Been Let Out the Penitentiary': Gangsta Rap and the Struggle over Racial Identity." *Cultural Critique* 34(3):65–89.

Ramsey, Frederic Jr., and Charles Edward Smith, eds. 1939. *Jazzmen.* New York: Harcourt.

Reagon, Bernice L, ed. 1992. *We'll Understand It Better By and By: Pioneering African American Gospel Composers.* Washington, D.C: Smithsonian Institution Press.

Ricks, George Robinson. 1960. "Some Aspects of the Religious Music of the United States Negro: An Ethnomusicological Study with Special Emphasis on the Gospel Tradition." Ph.D. dissertation, Northwestern University.

Roberts, John W. 1993. "African American Diversity and the Study of Folklore." *Western Folklore* 48(2):157–171.

Roberts, Robin. 1991. "Music Videos, Performance and Resistance: Feminist Rappers." *Journal of Popular Culture* 25(2):141–152.

Rose, Tricia. 1994. *Black Noise: Rap Music and Black Culture in Contemporary America.* Hanover, N.H.: University Press of New England.

Ross, Andrew, and Tricia Rose, eds. 1994. *Microphone Fiends: Youth Music and Youth Culture.* New York: Routledge.

Rowe, Mike. 1981 [1975]. *Chicago Blues: The City and the Music.* New York: Da Capo.

Russell, Tony. 1970. *Blacks, Whites and Blues.* Ed. Paul Oliver. New York: Stein and Day.

Salaam, Mtume ya. 1995. "The Aesthetics of Rap." *African American Review* 29(2):303–315.

Sargeant, Winthrop. 1975 [1938]. *Jazz, Hot and Hybrid.* 3rd ed. New York: Da Capo.

Scarborough, Dorothy. 1963 [1925]. *On the Trail of Negro Folk-Songs.* Hatboro, Pa.: Folklore Associates.

Schuller, Gunther. 1968. *Early Jazz: Its Roots and Musical Development.* New York: Oxford University Press.

Seward, Theodore F., comp. 1872. *Jubilee Songs as Sung by the Fisk Jubilee Singers of Fisk University.* New York: Biglow and Main.

Sexton, Adam, ed. 1995. *Rap on Rap: Straight-Up Talk on Hip-Hop Culture.* New York: Delta.

Shaw, Arnold. 1970. *The World of Soul.* New York: Cowles.

———. 1978. *Honkers and Shouters: The Golden Years of Rhythm and Blues.* New York: Macmillan Collier Books.

Shusterman, Richard. 1991. "The Fine Art of Rap." *New Literary History* 22(3):613–632.

Southern, Eileen. 1983a [1971]. *The Music of Black Americans: A History.* 2nd ed. New York: Norton.

———, ed. 1983b [1971]. *Readings in the Music of Black Americans.* 2nd ed. New York: Norton.

Southern, Eileen, and Josephene Wright. 1990. *African American Traditions in Song, Sermon, Tale, and Dance, 1600s–1920: An Annotated Bibliography of Literature, Collections, and Artworks.* New York: Greenwood Press.

Spellman, A. B. 1970 [1966]. *Black Music.* New York: Schocken.

Steams, Marshall. 1956. *The Story of Jazz.* New York: Oxford University Press.

Stowe, David W. 1994. *Swing Changes: Big Band Jazz in New Deal America.* Cambridge: Harvard University Press.

Stuckey, Sterling. 1987. *Slave Culture: Nationalist Theory and the Foundations of Black America.* New York: Oxford University Press.

Tallmadge, William H. 1981. "The Black in Jackson's White Spirituals." *Black Perspective in Music* 9(2):139–160.

Tate, Greg. 1992. *Flyboy in the Buttermilk: Essays On Contemporary America.* New York: Simon and Schuster.

Taylor, Arthur. 1993 [1977]. *Notes and Tones: Musician-to-Musician Interviews.* Expanded ed. New York: Da Capo.

Thomas, Lorenzo. 1995. "Ascension: Music and the Black Arts Movement." In *Jazz among the Discourses,* ed. Krin Gabbard, 256–274. Durham, N.C.: Duke University Press.

Titon, Jeff Todd. 1993. "Reconstructing the Blues: Reflections on the 1960s Blues Revival." In *Transforming Tradition,* ed. Neil V. Rosenberg, 220–240. Urbana: University of Illinois Press.

———. 1994 [1977]. *Early Downhome Blues: A Musical and Cultural Analysis.* 2nd ed. Chapel Hill: The University of North Carolina Press.

Trotter, James M. 1881 [1878]. *Music and Some Highly Musical People.* New York: Charles T. Dillingham.

Ulanov, Barry. 1952. *A History of Jazz in America.* New York: Viking.

van Elteren, Mel. 1994. *Imagining America: Dutch Youth and Its Sense of Place.* Tilburg, Netherlands: Tilburg University.

Vincent, Rickey. 1996. *Funk: The Music, the People, and the Rhythm of the One.* New York: St. Martin's Griffin.

Walker, Wyatt Tee. 1979. *"Somebody's Calling My Name": Black Sacred Music and Social Change.* Valley Forge, Pa.: Judson Press.

Wallaschek, Richard. 1970 [1893]. *Primitive Music: An Inquiry into the Origin and Development of Music, Songs, Instruments, Dances, and Pantomimes of Savage Races.* New York: Da Capo.

Walser, Robert. 1995. "Rhythm, Rhyme, and Rhetoric in the Music of Public Enemy." *Ethnomusicology* 39(2):343–365.

———, ed. 1999. *Keeping Time: Readings in Jazz History.* New York: Oxford University Press.

Ward, Brian. 1998. *Just My Soul Responding: Rhythm and Blues, Black Consciousness, and Race Relations.* Berkeley: University of California Press.

Waterman, Richard A. 1943. "African Patterns in Trinidad Negro Music." Ph.D. dissertation, Northwestern University.

———. 1963. "On Flogging a Dead Horse: Lessons Learned from the Africanisms Controversy." *Ethnomusicology* 7(2):83–87.

———. 1967 [1952]. "African Influence on the Music of the Americas." In *Acculturation in the Americas: Proceedings and Selected Papers of the Twenty-Ninth International Congress of Americanists,* ed. Sol Tax, 207–217. New York: Cooper Square Publishers.

Werner, Craig. 1999. *A Change Is Gonna Come: Music, Race and the Soul of America.* New York: Plume.

Westcott, William. 1977. "Ideas of Afro-American Musical Acculturation in the U.S.A.: 1900 to the Present." *Journal of the Steward Anthropological Society* 8(2):107–136.

White, Newman Ivy. 1965 [1928]. *American Negro Folk Songs.* Hatboro, Pa.: Folklore Associates.

Williams, Linda Faye. 1995. "The Impact of African American Music on Jazz in Zimbabwe: An Exploration in Radical Empiricism." Ph.D. dissertation, Indiana University.

Williams, Martin. 1970. *The Jazz Tradition.* New York: Oxford University Press.

———. 1981 [1959]. *The Art of Jazz: Ragtime to Bebop.* New York: Da Capo.

Williams-Jones, Pearl. 1975. "Afro-American Gospel Music: A Crystallization of the Black Aesthetic." *Ethnomusicology* 19(3):373–385.

———. 1977. "The Musical Quality of Black Religious Folk Ritual." *Spirit* 1(1):21–30.

Wilmer, Valerie. 1980 [1977]. *As Serious as Your Life: The Story of the New Jazz.* Rev. ed. Westport, Conn.: Lawrence Hill.

Wilson, Olly. 1974. "The Significance of the Relationship between Afro-American Music and West Africa." *The Black Perspective in Music* 2(1):3–22.

———. 1977. "The Association of Movement and Music as a Manifestation of a Black Conceptual Approach to Music." In *Report of the Twelfth Congress,* ed. Daniel Heartz and Bonnie C. Wade, 98–105. Berkeley: American Musicological Society.

———. 1992. "The Heterogeneous Sound Ideal in African American Music." In *New Perspectives on Music: Essays in Honor of Eileen Southern,* ed. Josephene Wright with Samuel A. Floyd Jr., 327–338. Warren, Mich.: Harmonie Park Press.

Work, III, John W. 1969 [1915]. *Folk Songs of the American Negro.* New York: Negro Universities Press.

———. 1940. *American Negro Songs and Spirituals: A Comprehensive Collection of 230 Folk Songs, Religious and Secular.* New York: Bonanza Books.

This article was completed while Portia K. Maultsby was a Fellow at the Center for Advanced Study in the Behavioral Sciences, (1999–2000) Stanford, California.

Folk Traditions
Dena J. Epstein

A cloud of myth has surrounded African American secular folk music: blacks arrived in the New World culturally naked; African instruments could not have been transported to the New World, because the slaves could not bring anything with them; the slaves had no secular music; the banjo was invented by Joel Walker Sweeney in the 1830s.

For many years these myths were widely accepted and retold in the most respected reference books, heedless of the flourishing secular music among African Americans. The myth that the slaves had no secular music derived in part from the eighteenth-century evangelical belief that all secular music and dancing were sinful. Even the instruments associated with dancing, such as the banjo and fiddle, came to be considered disreputable. Then when abolitionists began their protest against slavery, they stressed the sufferings of the slaves, in striking contrast to the picture of the happy, carefree slave presented by the minstrel theater. Frederick Douglass wrote in his autobiography: "I have been utterly astonished, since I came to the north, to find persons who could speak of the singing among slaves, as evidence of their contentment and happiness. It is impossible to conceive of a greater mistake. Slaves sing most when they are most unhappy. The songs of the slave represent the sorrows of his heart" (Epstein 1977:179) (figure 1).

Slaves certainly were unhappy, but they had their moments of fleeting pleasure. Contemporary documents establish beyond question the continuous presence of secular music and dancing among African Americans from their introduction to mainland North America to the present, secular music that embodied distinguishing characteristics of African music. They also identified features that establish African American music as a part of an African cultural continuum.

AFRICAN MUSICAL LEGACY

Among the peoples of Africa, music was integrated into daily life, as a group activity rather than as a performance before a passive audience. Music accompanied all kinds of group work, regulating the pace of work and lessening the monotony. Even individuals working alone often sang about their work. Festivities were accompanied by music and dancing. Derisive singing, even in reference to the king, was accepted as a means of expressing sentiments that were unacceptable as speech. All these aspects of African culture were easily adapted to life in the New World.

FIGURE I   "Old Plantation," artist unknown, late eighteenth century. Found in Columbia, South Carolina. Reproduced by permission of the Abby Aldrich Rockefeller Folk Art Collection, Colonial Williamsburg.

Characteristic elements of African music have been described by J. H. Kwabena Nketia (1974) as multipart rhythmic structures, repetitive choruses with a lead singer, the call–response style of alternating phrases juxtaposed or overlapping, and scales of four to seven steps, elements that reappeared in modified form in African American music. The short, repeated phrases that accompanied vigorous dancing upset Europeans accustomed to sedate dances and regular rhythmic patterns. African polyrhythms seemed to them to be noise. Many Europeans could not acknowledge a music that did not conform to their rules and scales.

Before the invention of sound recording, the only means of preserving music was a notational system devised for European music, and those who tried to notate African or African American music had to omit or modify its distinctive characteristics: blue notes, rhythmic complexities, overlapping of leader and chorus, melodic embellishments, and timbre. At best these notated versions approximate the music as performed; at worst they distort it. Nevertheless, contemporary descriptions of African American music are meaningful. They document its existence, describe its salient features as viewed firsthand, and provide the basis for a continuing history.

Not all Europeans were repelled by African music. Richard Jobson, a British trader who visited Africa in 1620–1621, soon after the first Africans were brought to Virginia, wrote: "There is without doubt, no people on the earth more naturally affected to the sound of musicke than these people . . . singing . . . extempore upon any occasion" (Epstein 1977:4). He also described drums and an instrument made from a gourd with a neck fastened to it and up to six strings. Surely this was a prototype of the banjo. Later travelers reported similar instruments that were to be transported to the New World, sometimes by slaving captains who tried to preserve the health of their cargos by compelling the captives to dance aboard ship. In the New World, the Africans constructed familiar instruments from local materials. The British Museum has had since 1753 an African-style drum made in Virginia from native wood with a deerskin head, materials not available in Africa, although the drum is described as "typical of the Ashanti of Ghana" (Epstein 1977:49).

Besides drums, other instruments frequently described as African included various kinds of rhythm instruments, a xylophone called the *balafo or balaphon,* quills (a form of pan pipes), horns, and the banjo. The banjo is found throughout the Caribbean and the North American mainland under various names—*banza, banjah, bandore, banjar,* and others (Epstein 1975:35).

AFRICANS IN NORTH AMERICA

Although Africans arrived in Virginia in 1619, there are not many descriptions of African musical activity in North America before 1800. This lack can be explained by the slow growth of the African population. For example, in 1624 there were only twenty-two Africans in Virginia. In 1649, when there were fifteen thousand Europeans in Virginia, there were still only three hundred Africans. They worked alongside Europeans, and their status had not yet crystallized into chattel slavery. As a rule they attracted little attention.

It is important to recognize that the colonies in North America were not nearly as profitable in the seventeenth and eighteenth centuries as those in the West Indies, where the population increased rapidly and Africans were brought in vast numbers. As islands became overpopulated, planters and their work forces moved, sometimes to the mainland. Blacks who had been "seasoned" in the islands were preferred to those coming directly from Africa, as they had already become accustomed to plantation labor and knew some English or French. The relations of the West Indian colonies to mainland North America during the colonial period were close. In the West Indies, the music brought from Africa was able to survive and flourish for at least a century and a half, but on the mainland, where the black population was relatively smaller, the music became acculturated more rapidly. This was particularly true of the English colonies.

Dancing and drumming in the seventeenth and eighteenth centuries

On the mainland in the seventeenth and eighteenth centuries the dances of the Africans were usually confined to Sunday, their only day of rest, but the English clergy was bitterly opposed to this desecration of the Lord's Day and did its best to stop the dancing (figure 2). Dancing was allowed on those holidays that the planters permitted. Traditionally the Christmas holiday lasted until New Year's, and some planters allowed a holiday at Easter. The religious nature of these holidays did not rule out secular music and dancing, which became a central feature of the holiday celebrations [see RELIGIOUS MUSIC, p. 624].

In 1739 the Reverend George Whitefield complained that the Africans were permitted to "openly prophane the Lord's Day with Dancing, Piping, and such like" (Epstein 1977:39). In the same year, an insurrection at Stono, South Carolina, was accompanied by singing, dancing, and beating drums, intended to attract more Africans to join the rebellion. As a consequence, the beating of drums was forbidden by

FIGURE 2   Negro dance sketched in Lynchburg, Virginia, 18 August 1853, by Lewis Miller of York, Pennsylvania. Courtesy Virginia State Library, Richmond.

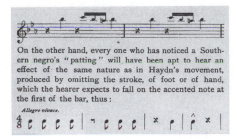

On the other hand, every one who has noticed a Southern negro's "patting" will have been apt to hear an
effect of the same nature as in Haydn's movement,
produced by omitting the stroke, of foot or of hand,
which the hearer expects to fall on the accented note at
the first of the bar, thus :

FIGURE 3   "Patting Juba," notated by Sidney
Lanier in *The Science of English Verse* (New York:
Charles Scribner's Sons, 1880), p. 189. Courtesy
Joseph Regenstein Library, University of Chicago.

law in South Carolina, as it had been earlier in the West Indies. Yet despite this ban, which was rigorously enforced, drumming continued unseen by the authorities. Former slaves in Georgia who were interviewed in the 1930s by the Georgia Writers' Project described how to make drums from hollow trees and recalled dancing to drums, dancing that must have been done in secret.

With drums so central to African music and dancing, substitutes had to be found. One was a less threatening but still rhythmic instrument described by Thomas Jefferson as "[t]he instrument proper to them ... the Banjar, which they brought hither from Africa" (Epstein 1977:34). Other rhythmic support to dancing was provided by hand-clapping, foot-stomping, and a practice apparently unique to the United States, "patting juba" (figure 3). Patting juba was an extension of simple hand-clapping, raising it to the level of a self-contained accompaniment to dancing. It was described as striking the hands on the knees, then striking the hands together, then striking the right shoulder with one hand, the left with the other—all the while keeping time with the feet and singing. The earliest reference to the practice dates from the 1820s, but by the 1830s serious attention was being paid to its rhythmic complexities, not by musicians but by poets, like Edgar Allan Poe, Beverly Tucker, and Thomas Holley Chivers. In 1880 Sidney Lanier described patting juba as a "quite complex succession of rhythm, not hesitating to syncopate, to change the rhythmic accent for the moment, or to indulge in other highly specialized variations of the current rhythmus" (Epstein 1977:142–143). A variation of patting involved the use of two sticks to beat time on the floor, either alone or with other instruments. A Christmas celebration at Eutaw Plantation in South Carolina during the Civil War had dancing accompanied by "two fiddlers, one man with bones, and another had sticks with which he kept time on the floor" (Epstein 1977:144).

The rate at which this dancing became acculturated is not known. Initially it must have been largely African, but gradually the European influence began to modify the steps. The rate of acculturation varied from colony to colony. In the northern colonies, some holidays originally observed by whites gradually became associated with the Africans. "'Lection Day," in Connecticut, Rhode Island, and Massachusetts, involving the election of a king, processions, feasting, and dancing, became known as Negro Election Day by the mid-eighteenth century. In these colonies, slaves lived singly or in small groups and had little community life. Gradually they created midyear festivals where they could enjoy their distinctive culture: drumming, dancing, and singing. Banjos, fiddles, and Guinea drums, made from logs covered with sheepskin, provided the music for the Guinea dance. As slaves were caught up in the performance, their behavior was reported as more African. In New York and New Jersey, a holiday originating with the Dutch, Pinkster, was a comparable holiday to Negro Election Day. Both holidays were celebrated in open fields with much ceremony, from the middle third of the eighteenth century (White 1994).

Although reports of African music and dancing in the southern colonies before 1800 were not common, still rarer were reports of the impact of African culture on European music and dancing. In an era when many people were preoccupied with preserving elements of their European heritage in an alien, often hostile, environment, it is hardly surprising that they recorded very little of an influence that they could not publicly acknowledge.

Yet evidence has been found that these ladies and gentlemen did indeed dance "Negro dances," not just occasionally but with some regularity ("usual" was the term found in contemporary accounts). One description of Virginia published in Dublin in 1776 stated: "Towards the close of an evening, when the company are pretty well tired with country dances, it is usual to dance jigs, ... borrowed ... from the 'Negroes'" (Epstein 1977:121). Thomas Jefferson's brother, Randolph, was described by a former Monticello slave as a "mighty simple man; used to come out among black people, play the fiddle and dance half the night" (Epstein 1977:122).

Despite the good priest's disapproval, all the Africans danced the *calinda:* the old, the young, and even the children. It seemed as if they had danced it in the wombs of their mothers.

In Richmond before 1820, the courtly black fiddler Simeon Gilliat performed at balls that began with a reel followed by contra dances, a congo (demonstrably an African term), a hornpipe, and a jig that would wind up the evening. This intermingling of cultures was embodied by Gilliat himself, who, after a career of performing at society balls, was painted playing the banjo for a group of children.

As late as 1876, Henry W. Ravenel of South Carolina reminisced about his youth (he was born in 1814): "The jig was an African dance and a famous one in old times. . . . For the jig the music would be changed. . . . The fiddle would assume a low monotonous tone, the whole tune running on three or four notes only . . . the stick-knocker changed his time, and beat a softer and slower measure" (Epstein 1977:123).

La calinda

In Louisiana and contiguous territory, areas that had been settled by the Spanish and the French, developments were quite different. Cultural and governmental ties were not to the other mainland colonies but to Spanish America and to the French West Indies. Louisiana had been settled almost one hundred years after Virginia, with its African population coming directly from Africa between 1719 and 1731. With a relatively homogeneous population, the distinctive character of New Orleans was established early. A Frenchman who had worked as a planter wrote in 1758 of the crowds of Africans who danced the *calinda,* widely reported in the French West Indies with its associated instrument, the *banza.*

La calinda had been described in Martinique by a French missionary, Jean Baptist Labat, as early as 1694. It was accompanied by two drums of unequal length, each with one open end and one covered with skin. The drummers held them between their legs and played with four fingers of both hands. The larger drum provided the basic beat, and the smaller was played more quickly. Despite the good priest's disapproval, all the Africans danced the *calinda:* the old, the young, and even the children. It seemed as if they had danced it in the wombs of their mothers.

In the mid-eighteenth century Diderot's *Encyclopédie* included special entries for *calinda* and *tamboula,* the name of one of the drums (Encyclopédie 1751–1765:2:474; 15:874). The dance was always accompanied by a guitar with four strings called *banza.* Another Frenchman, Moreau de Saint-Méry, writing in 1797, was as convinced of the African origin of the dance and instruments as Labat had been (Moreau de Saint-Méry 1797:1:44).

Other popular dances

Although in the seaboard southern states evangelical religion condemned secular music and dancing, in New Orleans African-style dancing was permitted to flourish. Popular dances included the *chica,* the *bamboula,* the *coonjine* or *counjaille,* and the congo dance. Both the French and Spanish governments had permitted such dancing, and after the Louisiana Purchase in 1803, new "Ordinances of Police" specified that the mayor should appoint places for slaves to dance on Sundays. Travelers frequently described these

dances at what is now called Congo Square, sometimes giving details of the steps and accompanying instruments.

In 1819, Benjamin Latrobe, the engineer who had supervised the rebuilding of the Capitol after the War of 1812, described what he saw on a Sunday afternoon:

> They were formed in circular groups. . . . The music consisted of two drums and stringed instrument. . . . On the top of the finger board was the rude figure of a man in a sitting posture—two pegs behind him to which the strings were fastened. The body was a calabash. . . .
>
> A man sang an uncouth song . . . which I suppose was in some African language, for it was not French. . . . The allowed amusements of Sunday have, it seems, perpetuated here those of Africa. (Epstein 1977:97)

Latrobe accompanied his account with sketches of the instruments, among the very few contemporary drawings of African instruments that have survived from the mainland (figure 4).

ACCULTURATION OF AFRICANS IN THE NEW WORLD

The gradual transformation of African culture to something that came to be called African American began almost as soon as the Africans landed in the New World. Speaking many different languages, they had to learn to communicate with each other and with their new masters. They had to adjust to new surroundings, new customs, new sounds, smells, and tastes. They observed the music and dances of these strange Europeans and gradually learned to combine them with the music and dance they had brought from Africa. The process by which this acculturation took place was described often in the West Indies but only once on the mainland. John Pierpont, a tutor from Litchfield, Connecticut, wrote from Georgetown District, South Carolina, of a Christmas celebration in 1805 when acculturated slaves danced on the portico of the plantation house while native Africans "did not join in the dance with the others, but by themselves" clapped their hands and "distorted their frames" (Epstein 1977:84). This complex of two cultures, side by side, influencing each other in intangible ways, led gradually to the formation of an African American culture.

Acculturation proceeded at different rates in different colonies. African dancing took place in New Orleans in 1819 and later, while as early as 1694 a black fiddler was playing for the dancing of whites in Virginia. This incident was recorded in a legal action brought by a minister against his daughter's friends, who had profaned his house by introducing a fiddler in the owner's absence. The dancing had continued until Sunday morning after church services had begun (Epstein 1977:80). This same fiddler might also have played for the dancing of his fellow slaves.

There also was considerable variety in the circumstances of slavery in the different colonies. Settled in 1690, Carolina had a black majority by 1708, while the northern states had only a small, scattered black population. Plantations in the southern colonies developed their distinctive society, very different from the more urban society in the North. While slavery flourished in the South with the introduction of the cotton gin after the Revolution, slavery in the northern states declined and gradually disappeared. As more and more blacks were born in the New World, African festivals in the North diminished, being replaced by processions and parades that demonstrated the dignity of the black community. With the passage of time, dancing and singing by African Americans in the northern states tended to be enjoyed in private rather than in public festivals in open fields.

Fiddlers

Although the prejudice against dancing and fiddling was widespread throughout the South, many planters not only permitted the activities but encouraged them. James H. Hammond of South Carolina penciled in his plantation manual: "Church members are privileged to dance on all holyday occasions, and the class leader or deacon who may report them shall be reprimanded or punished at the discretion of the master" (Epstein 1977:212). A more common attitude was expressed in the thirteenth annual report of the Association for the Religious Instruction of the Negroes in Liberty County, Georgia, in 1848: "[T]hey become passionately fond of dancing. . . . With the negroes dancing is a dissipating, demoralizing amusement . . . [It is incompatible with] religion or good morals" (Epstein 1977:212–213). "A Mississippi Planter" wrote to *DeBow's Review* in 1851, "I have a good fiddler, and keep him well supplied with cat-gut, and I make it his duty to play for the negroes every Saturday night until 12 o'clock" (Epstein 1977:154). Some planters went so far as to provide music teachers for talented servants.

It was customary for a planter to advertise in local newspapers if he had a slave fiddler of a good reputation whom others might wish to hire. Solomon Northup, a free Negro from upstate New York who was kidnapped and sold into slavery in Louisiana, benefited from his ability as a fiddler. His fiddle "introduced me to great houses—relieved me of many days' labor in the field—made me friends . . . gave me an honored seat at the yearly feasts" (Epstein 1977:150). These obscure musicians at times achieved what would have been a professional status if their earnings had remained in their own pockets. Many of them earned a reputation for excellence that extended for miles around.

A legal action filed in the Chancery Court of Louisville in 1844 attached the steamboat *Pike* "to recover damages for the unauthorized transportation . . . of three slaves, Reuben, Henry and George . . . from Louisville to Cincinnati, whence they escaped to Canada" (Epstein 1977:152). The slaves were described as well-trained musicians who for several years had been playing at balls and parties. Their owner had given them written permission to play in any part of the South, but of course he objected to their fleeing to Canada. The court found that the unusual privileges permitted them rendered them restless under restraint and desirous of freedom. Damages were denied.

The dances for which they played often included play-party games and songs that were almost indistinguishable from the songs of white pioneers, but modified with

African American rhythm and traditions. These games were also played by children, but few contemporary reports have been found of the play of children before 1900. The traditional children's games that were collected after 1900 surely originated much earlier, games such as "Green, Green Rocky Road," "Little Sally Walker," "Loobie Loo," and "Mary Mack." Before the invention of sound recording, these games were widely played but little noticed. Adults and children both enjoyed them, as many ex-slaves reported in their Works Progress Administration (WPA) interviews.

WORK SONGS

In Africa, singing frequently accompanied group work wherever it took place, in the fields or on the water. This practice was easily transferred to the New World wherever people worked in groups [see AFRICAN AMERICAN CRIES, CALLS, AND HOLLERS, p. 81]. Singing coordinated their movements, lifted their spirits, enabled the slower workers to keep up, and warded off fatigue. Singing could accompany hoeing, planting, harvesting, picking cotton, grinding corn, cutting brush, laying railroad tracks, cutting wood, hauling fishing nets, or rowing. Understandably, planters prized leaders with good, strong voices, commanding personalities, and a strong sense of rhythm.

Along the coast, boat songs were frequently described by travelers and in memoirs by planters' wives and daughters. Crews of four to eight rowed boats in tidal rivers from one plantation to another or to the nearest city. The leader would sing a line, and the rowers would chime in with a refrain. The words were often improvised and were sometimes compliments to the passengers, sometimes merely unconnected words and phrases. Or they could be more somber—there were songs about separation from loved ones, abuse by one's Captain, or longing for freedom. A good leader could speed the boat along, no matter how tired the crew might be.

Work and boat songs continued a tradition that had been common in Africa—integrating music into daily life. Often the chorus began to sing before the leader had finished his call. Work songs could have religious words. When William Cullen Bryant visited a tobacco factory in Richmond in 1843, the workers sang, but his guide informed him that they sang only sacred music (probably spirituals). "They will sing nothing else" (Epstein 1977:164).

Still another widely reported occasion for song throughout the southern states was corn shucking. As ears of corn were not as perishable as some other crops, the corn was allowed to stay in the field until the other crops were gathered. The ears of corn were then harvested and heaped into two enormous piles, awaiting shucking. The planter would invite workers from neighboring plantations to come on a chosen day. Gangs of workers would march, singing, to the appointed place, choose sides, and name their leaders. Each team would strive to outdo the other, spurred on by the magnificent voices of their leaders, to which the crew would respond in chorus. This ceremony had some resemblance to the English harvest home and corn huskings in the North, but the musical competition and the improvised singing were peculiar to the South. When all the corn had been shucked and the winning team acclaimed, the feasting and dancing began. The planter's family and guests watched the fun from a distance, perhaps getting a foretaste of the minstrel theater then in its infancy, initiated by white men in the North and a caricature of African-American music and dancing (see POPULAR MUSIC OF THE PARLOR AND STAGE, p. 179; BLUES, p. 637].

Other crops inspired similar harvest celebrations. In the West Indies, the cane song was reported. In middle Georgia, the Fourth of July signaled the end of the planting and cultivating season. All the tools were brought in from the fields and piled together. There followed a big celebration with much food, singing, and dancing.

Cotton picking lent itself to group singing, "some wild, simple melodies" sung in a chorus, "so loud as to be heard from one plantation to another . . . for miles with musical echoes" (Epstein 1977:163). Flailing rice, grinding hominy, and braiding

Harriet Tubman is said to have communicated her intentions to leave the plantation by singing a song of farewell as she walked about the quarters.

baskets all provided opportunities for singing, with the tempo adjusted to the task at hand.

Other opportunities for group singing were observed aboard sailing vessels. Hoisting sails, winding the capstan, and loading cargo needed song to coordinate the movements of the men. Mobile, Alabama, for example, became known as a shanty mart where sailors from different countries learned shanties from each other. Sailors from the West Indies were especially known for their prowess at singing shanties. Later when steamboats replaced sailing vessels, especially on inland rivers, firemen worked in a virtual inferno below decks. Fredrika Bremer in 1850 witnessed firemen on the Mississippi. A man standing on a pile of firewood improvised a song, which was punctuated by the sound of wood being tossed to men below. They responded in chorus while hurling firewood into the boat's furnace (Bremer 1853:2:174).

Work songs, however, did not need large groups. Plentiful reports exist of individuals singing lullabies. Weaving, spinning, shoe shining, and cooking were all accompanied by singing. A self-contained form of song was improvised by street vendors in southern cities. These street cries described what the vendor was selling in terms calculated to attract buyers. Charleston, South Carolina, and New Orleans were especially noted for the skill of their street merchants in improvising attractive cries.

CREOLE SONGS

Quite distinct from the folk songs of the eastern seaboard were the French Creole songs of Louisiana. Many blacks spoke French and enjoyed a Francophile culture. Of greater significance was the ease of manumission under the French and Spanish governments, which created a comparatively large free Afro-Creole population that was relatively prosperous but mingled freely with the slave population. Nowhere else in the United States did circumstances encourage such mingling.

French-speaking Afro-Creole families enjoyed street parades, dancing, even French opera. Although free blacks were not accepted socially by the white population before the Civil War, their presence in business and trade was familiar and customary. Within their own community, the Creoles of color could move with assurance and pride. Afro-Creole musicians were taught by teachers from the French Opera orchestra, and their folk music was heavily influenced by French music with the addition of African elements, such as rhythm and call–response forms. Traditional Creole songs were known in the French Caribbean as well as on the mainland. Unfortunately this music has been sorely neglected, and even less of it was collected in the nineteenth century than other forms of black folk music, although seven were included in *Slave Songs of the United States* (Allen 1867:109–113).

PROTEST SONGS

The African tradition of improvised derisive singing was easily adapted to the American scene. In September 1772 the *South Carolina Gazette* reported a "cabal of Negroes" near Charleston on a Saturday night, numbering about sixty people. "The entertainment was opened by the men copying (or *taking off*) the manners of their masters, and the women those of their mistresses, and relating some highly curious anecdotes, to the inexpressible diversion of that company" (Epstein 1977:82). When Europeans were present, the entertainment usually involved a more subtle satire, which permitted the expression of ideas that otherwise might have been severely punished.

Improvising satire, sometimes too subtle to be recognized, and making fun of the master and his family in ways that did not provoke offense—these were specialties of the African American improvisor. Satiric verses could easily be inserted in work songs, whether boat songs or corn songs. In 1841 a song was described that criticized a preacher for ordering his men to work on Sunday to harvest a crop before a threat of rain, thus violating traditional work arrangements. The leader sang, "Twas on a blessed Sabbath day, Here's a pretty preacher for you," to which the chorus responded, "It rain, boys, it rain" (Epstein 1977:173–174).

Fewer satirical songs than spirituals have been preserved. William Francis Allen, editor of the 1867 collection *Slave Songs of the United States,* commented, "We have succeeded in obtaining only a very few songs of this character" (Allen 1867:x) in the Sea Islands. The singers may have been reluctant to sing satiric songs, for both religious reasons and self-protection. Even after the end of slavery, it was not wise to sing critical songs in the South.

More explicit comments on the conditions of slavery were sung, sometimes interpolated into religious songs. Harriet Tubman is said to have communicated her intentions to leave the plantation by singing a song of farewell as she walked about the quarters. "Go Down, Moses" was not a safe song to sing in the South, with its refrain of "Let my people go," but a song about the promised land might seem innocuous to the casual listener. The song "Follow the Drinking Gourd" gave instructions on how to use the stars to guide a runaway to the North and freedom. Even corn-shucking songs might include verses of protest like "Grind de meal, gimme de husk; Bake de bread, gimme de crust."

THE END OF THE NINETEENTH CENTURY

Despite the influence of the music of the whites by which it was surrounded, African American secular music retained characteristics associated with African music. No matter that most of the Africans had been born in the New World, that they now spoke English in some form, that Africa was known to them only in stories and reminiscences, their music and dancing was immediately recognized by outsiders as non-European. Their skill at improvisation, at making up songs to fit the occasion, to regulate the work at hand, to compliment, or to denigrate—these were remarkable to observers.

Before the rise of recordings, the only way of preserving folk music was transcription in a notational system designed for European music (figure 5). These transcriptions might be corroborated by descriptions written mostly by Europeans of unknown musical competence. In spite of the efforts of some clergymen to disparage secular folk music and dancing, African American secular folk music persisted as a familiar part of everyday work and play, musically very similar to African American sacred music. When the immensely popular minstrel theater caricatured African Americans, their secular music was brought into discredit, leaving the spiritual (also, at times, discredited) as the preeminent form of African American music. Nevertheless, secular music continued to flourish, growing in popularity as the nineteenth century drew to a close. Although many conservative Americans considered folk music uncultured, it remained widely popular among African Americans. With the development of ragtime, a distinctly American contribution to world music became popular worldwide. As the twentieth century progressed, the blues and jazz were even more influential in demonstrating the power of African American secular music throughout the world.

FIGURE 5   "Sold Off to Georgy," from James Hungerford, *The Old Plantation and What I Gathered There in an Autumn Month* (New York: Harper, 1859), an autobiographical novel set in 1832. Courtesy The New York Public Library.

REFERENCES

Abrahams, Roger D. 1992. *Singing the Master: The Emergence of African American Folk Culture in the Plantation South.* New York: Pantheon Books.

Allen, William Francis, ed. 1867. *Slave Songs of the United States.* New York: A. Simpson.

Bremer, Fredrika. 1853. *The Homes of the New World: Impressions of America.* Trans. Mary Howitt. New York: Harper & Brothers.

Courlander, Harold. 1963. *Negro Folk Music, U.S.A.* New York: Columbia University Press.

Emery, Lynne Fauley. 1972. *Black Dance in the United States from 1619 to 1970.* Palo Alto, Calif.: National Press Books.

Encyclopédie, or Dictionnaire Raisonné des Sciences, des Arts et des Métiers. Paris: Briasson, 1751–1765.

Epstein, Dena J. 1975. "The Folk Banjo: A Documentary History." *Ethnomusicology* 19(3): 347–371.

————. 1977. *Sinful Tunes and Spirituals: Black Folk Music to the Civil War.* Urbana: University of Illinois Press.

Hare, Maude Cuney. 1936. *Negro Musicians and Their Music.* Washington, D.C.: Associated Publishers.

Levine, Lawrence W. 1977. *Black Culture and Black Consciousness: Afro-American Folk Thought from Slavery to Freedom.* New York: Oxford University Press.

Moreau de Saint-Méry, Médéric. 1797. *Déscription Topographique, Physique, Civile, Politique et Historique de . . . l'Isle Saint-Dominique . . .* Philadelphia: Chez l'Auteur.

Nketia, J. H. Kwabene. 1974. *The Music of Africa.* New York: Norton.

Parks, H. B. 1928. "Follow the Drinking Gourd." In *Texas Folk-Lore Society Publications 7,* ed. J. Frank Dobie, Austin: Texas Folk-Lore Society.

White, Shane. 1994. "It Was a Proud Day: African-American Festivals and Parades in the North, 1741–1834." *Journal of American History* 81(1):13–50.

Writers' Program. 1940. *Drums and Shadows: Survival Studies among the Georgia Coastal Negroes.* Athens: University of Georgia Press.

Concert Music
Josephine R. B. Wright

Before Emancipation (1800–1862)
Post Emancipation (1863–1900)
The Twentieth Century

A small number of classically trained composers worked professionally in North America during the early 1800s in the New England, Middle Atlantic, and midwestern states, and in a few slave-holding enclaves. Most received their initial formal training from immigrant European musicians who had settled in large metropolitan centers or from local practitioners. They composed primarily short compositions based on European models (ballads, marches, hymns, anthems, glees, overtures, dances, or descriptive pieces for piano) and produced pianoforte arrangements of patriotic songs, minstrel tunes, and popular operas that featured straightforward tuneful melodies with simple diatonic harmonies.

Emancipation brought increased opportunities for professional training and exposure for the black composer. A few studied at selected American colleges, universities, and music schools, where they received first-rate instruction, and they began to explore writing large-scale musical forms such as operas, operettas, oratorios, cantatas, chamber music, and fully orchestrated symphonic essays. Those who felt the lure of musical nationalism (a movement that had spread from Eastern Europe to North America by the dawn of the twentieth century) began incorporating materials from the African and African American folk experience in the Western art forms they wrote in affirmation of their cultural heritage.

By the early twentieth century, several prominent composers taught at traditional black colleges and universities, and a few earned critical acclaim at home and abroad for their music, which ran the gamut of contemporary forms and styles. Their legacy was passed on to composers active during the 1960s and beyond, whose impact has been felt throughout the academy and musical industry.

BEFORE EMANCIPATION (1800–1862)

Although Newport Gardner (1746–1826) reportedly composed the "Promised Anthem" (c. 1764) and is considered black America's earliest known singing-school master, the first African American school of classically trained composers thrived in Philadelphia, Pennsylvania, the nation's first capital, in the early 1800s with Frank Johnson (1792–1844), James Hemmenway (1800–1849), Isaac Hazzard (1804–c. 1864), William Appo (c. 1808–c. 1877), and Aaron J. R. Connor (d. 1850).

Ohioans boasted of Justin Miner Holland (1819–1887), a classical guitarist and composer-arranger, the earliest professional black musician to be educated at Oberlin College, one of the few American institutions of higher learning to accept black students before the Civil War.

FIGURE 1   Frank Johnson (1846). Photo courtesy the Harvard Theater Collection (Houghton Library).

Frank Johnson (figure 1), the acknowledged leader of the Philadelphia School, apparently was born in the city, according to evidence reported in the *International Dictionary of Black Composers* (Floyd 1999). A virtuoso-keyed bugler, music teacher, and band director, he seemingly first came to public notice as a composer with the publication of *Six Setts of Cotillions* (1818). Between 1820 and 1844 he organized a dance orchestra, along with a smaller military band, and toured widely with these ensembles along the East Coast, and even as far west as Missouri (then a slave state), performing much of the music that he wrote or arranged. In 1837–1838 he traveled to London, England, with Aaron J. R. Connor, Edward de Roland, William Appo, and Francis V. Seymour, becoming the first American to tour Europe with a band and give a series of concerts there. Johnson published over two hundred compositions, mostly songs, marches, dances, and pianoforte arrangements of popular music of the period, and he left many works in manuscript. Among his historic works is "General Lafayette's Grand March," commissioned by city fathers to honor the Revolutionary War hero's visit to Philadelphia in 1824.

Although the connection between Frank Johnson and James Hemmenway remains unclear, Hemmenway apparently directed the orchestra at Washington Hall in Philadelphia. His *New Year and Courtesy Cotillion* reportedly remained in print as late as 1870. Isaac Hazzard led another local orchestra in the 1830s and published several compositions for band.

William Appo, a Johnson bandsman, worked in New York City as early as the 1830s and is remembered for two compositions, the anthem "Sing Unto God" and "John Tyler's Lamentation," a work commissioned by the Utica (New York) Glee Club for the U.S. presidential campaign of 1844. William Brady (d. 1854) was also active in New York as a composer-performer, and A. J. R. Connor, another Johnson bandsman, organized an instrumental ensemble during the late 1840s and performed in Philadelphia and Saratoga Springs, New York. His ballad "My Cherished Hope, My Fondest Dream" appeared in the *Anglo-African Magazine* in 1859. The composer-arranger Peter O'Fake (1820–1883) maintained a music studio and led a society orchestra in New York City and Newark, New Jersey, during the 1840s and 1850s.

Henry F. Williams (1813–1903) operated a music studio during the early 1840s in Boston, where he composed songs, dances, overtures, anthems, and marches and arranged band music for Patrick S. Gilmore, a local white conductor. Following Frank Johnson's death, Williams went to Philadelphia as arranger for the reconstituted Johnson band and remained there until c. 1870. His career continued well past the 1870s. Among his best works are songs such as "Laurett[e]" (1840), "Come, Love and List Awhile" (1842), "It Was by Chance We Met" (1866), and "I Would I'd Never Met Thee" (1876), which are modeled after the nineteenth-century Anglo-American ballad.

Ohioans boasted of Justin Miner Holland (1819–1887) (figure 2), a classical guitarist and composer-arranger, the earliest professional black musician to be educated at Oberlin College (1841–1843, 1845), one of the few American institutions of higher

FIGURE 2   Justin Miner Holland. Photo from *Brainard's Musical World* 24 (June 1887): 204.

learning to accept black students before the Civil War. From 1845 to 1886, he resided in Cleveland, where he was highly esteemed as a performer, teacher, and composer-arranger, collaborating professionally across racial lines at a time when segregation was the norm throughout the United States. He published two important tutorials, *Holland's Comprehensive Method for the Guitar* (1874) and *Holland's Modern Method for the Guitar* (1876), as well as numerous duets and solo pieces for the guitar. Among his extant works are the collections *Gems for the Guitar* (c. 1886) and *Bouquet of Melodies* (n.d.).

Joseph William Postlewaite (c. 1827–1889), a free black from Missouri, led and managed several bands in St. Louis between about 1857 and 1860. Several of his compositions, including the popular "St. Louis Greys Quick Step," are listed in the *Complete Catalog of Sheet Music and Musical Works, 1870*, issued by the Board of Music Trade of the United States of America (1871). In antebellum Georgia, audiences marveled at the slave Thomas Green Wiggins Bethune ("Blind Tom," 1849–1908), reportedly an idiot savant, who was exhibited on the concert stage as a pianist and composer. He concertized from about 1857 through 1905 and composed dances, marches, character pieces, and programmatic music for the piano, such as his descriptive *The Battle of Manassas* (1866).

A small number of composers are recorded among the free blacks of New Orleans before the Civil War, notably Victor-Eugène McCarty (1821–1881), Edmond Dédé (1827–1901), the siblings Charles (c. 1828–1896) and Sidney Lambert (c. 1838–c. 1900/1909), Samuel Snaër (c. 1832–1896), and Basil Barés (1845–1902). McCarty, Snaër, and Barés worked primarily in the city. McCarty, an accomplished singer and pianist, performed for fashionable soirées and published *Fleurs de salon: 2 Favorite Polkas* (1854). Snaër served for many years as the organist at St. Mary's Catholic Church on Charles Street and conducted the orchestra at the Orléans Theatre. He composed liturgical music as well as orchestral music and solo compositions for voice and piano.

The Lambert brothers, who were both classically trained pianists as well as composers, pursued careers outside the United States. Charles studied in Paris in 1854. During the 1860s he emigrated to Brazil, where he opened a piano and music store. Sidney, likewise Parisian educated, eventually settled there as a performer, teacher, and composer. The catalog of the Bibliothèque Nationale in Paris lists over eighty piano pieces composed by the Lamberts, primarily dances, variations, and descriptive keyboard pieces.

Edmond Dédé similarly worked abroad. A gifted violinist, in 1857 he gained admission at the Paris Conservatory, becoming possibly the first black from North America to matriculate at that institution. There he studied violin with Jean-Delphin Alard and composition with Jacques-François Halévy. From approximately 1860 to 1889 he directed various orchestras in Bordeaux, France, and he worked in the early 1890s in Paris. Although much of Dédé's music has been lost, James Monroe Trotter published his dramatic aria "Le serment de l'Arabe" in the appendix of *Music and Some Highly Musical People* (1968 [1878]).

POST EMANCIPATION (1863–1900)

The Emancipation Proclamation of 1863, followed approximately two years later by the cessation of fighting between the Union and Confederate armies, spurred the U.S. Congress to pass the nation's first Civil Rights Acts—the Thirteenth, Fourteenth, and Fifteenth Amendments to the Constitution—between 1865 and 1867. These laws extended federal protection to black Americans, respectively abolishing slavery, granting citizenship to African Americans, and giving African American men the vote. Such legislation brought hope to many of eventual assimilation into the greater society. Their optimism was reflected in the creative and performing arts by an unprecedented flowering of musical erudition throughout black America in the late nineteenth century, opening a floodgate of pent-up hopes and desires for cultural parity with white America in the classical arts.

Concert music

Musicians born in the post-Emancipation era exerted considerable influence on the concert music of black America during the first half of the twentieth century. Representative composers of that generation included Harry T. Burleigh (1866–1949), Will Marion Cook (1869–1944), Harry L. Freeman (1870–1954), J[ohn] Rosamond Johnson (1873–1954), Clarence Cameron White (1880–1960, figure 3), R. Nathaniel Dett (1882–1943), Hall Johnson (1888–1970), Florence Price (1888–1953), Eva Jessye (1895–1992), William Grant Still (1895–1978), Shirley Graham (1896–1977), and Edward Boatner (1898–1981). Despite coming of age in a segregated society that denied them equal opportunities for advancement, a few attended selected American conservatories, universities, and schools of music and obtained excellent instruction. Burleigh studied, for example, at the now-defunct National Conservatory in New York City (1892–1896); Oberlin Conservatory claimed among its alumni Cook (1884–1888), White (1896–1901), Dett (B. Mus. 1908), Still (1917, 1919), and Shirley Graham (B. Mus. 1934; M. Mus. 1935); the New England Conservatory nurtured

FIGURE 3   Clarence Cameron White, c. 1930. Photo courtesy Schomburg Center for Research in Black Studies.

J. Rosamond Johnson (1892–1895) and Florence Price (Diploma, 1906); and Hall Johnson graduated from the University of Pennsylvania (B.A. 1910). A few even pursued additional study in Europe and/or obtained graduate degrees in music in the United States.

This generation adopted a conservative, neoromantic musical style rather than the dissonant, experimental language of early-twentieth-century European and American composers. They explored writing in small forms as well as in the more extended forms of art music. Several were inspired to rediscover their cultural roots, encouraged by the examples of musical nationalism of the famous Czech composer Antonín Dvořák and the celebrated Afro-British composer Samuel Coleridge-Taylor (1875–1912).

Harry T. Burleigh, R. Nathaniel Dett, and Clarence Cameron White were widely regarded as the leading black composers of this generation during the opening decades of the twentieth century. Burleigh was the first to gain broad acceptance as a composer. Initially a singer by profession, he composed more than three hundred art songs, several being introduced by such famous recitalists of the day as John McCormack, Ernestine Schumann-Heink, and Lucrezia Bori. Burleigh's greatest contribution lay, however, in his transformation of the Negro spiritual from the choral tradition of the Fisk Jubilee Singers to the concert tradition of the solo art song. Commencing with his arrangement of "Deep River" (1917), he published numerous concert renditions of Negro spirituals for solo voice and piano over the next twenty-one years. These arrangements have earned a permanent place in the American art song literature.

Concert arrangements of spirituals

Burleigh in turn would influence younger contemporaries of the Harlem Renaissance and beyond to write solo concert arrangements of Negro spirituals and other African American folk songs. J. Rosamond Johnson pursued this course, for example, in the *Book of American Negro Spirituals* (1925) and *Second Book of Negro Spirituals* (1926), which he published collaboratively with James Weldon Johnson (1871–1938), and he later brought out *Rolling Along in Song* (1937), a chronological survey of black folk song, and the *Album of Negro Spirituals* (1940). Edward Boatner earned a solid reputation for his arrangements of "Let Us Break Bread Together," "On Ma Journey," "Trampin'," and "Oh, What a Beautiful City." William Dawson, Eva Jessye, Hall Johnson, Florence Price, and William Grant Still also contributed to this genre.

Canadian-born Dett, who matured as a composer during the Harlem Renaissance, employed black folk idioms in his vocal and instrumental compositions, seeking to preserve traditional African American music in its original form and in art forms, in much the same way that nationalist composers in Eastern Europe had treated their folk music in the late nineteenth century. He wove the spiritual, for example, into such choral works as the oratorio *Chariot Jubilee* (1919), the motet *Don't Be Weary Traveler* (winner of Harvard University's Francis Boott Prize, 1921), the anthem *Listen to the Lambs* (1923), and the cantata *The Ordering of Moses* (1932). He further demonstrated the inherent musical value of black folk songs in two choral anthologies, *Religious Folksongs of the Negro as Sung at Hampton Institute* (1927) and *The Dett Collection of Negro Spirituals* (1936), and he experimented with secular African American folk music in such early descriptive keyboard suites as *Magnolia* (1912) and *In the Bottoms* (1913).

The choral tradition of the concert-arranged spiritual was carried into the media, theater, and film industry by Hall Johnson and Eva Jessye, who organized and led professional choirs in the mid-1920s. Hall Johnson and his choir performed, for example, in the Broadway and film productions of *Green Pastures* (1930 and 1936, respectively), for which he contributed twenty-two choral arrangements of Negro spirituals and two original compositions, "Hail de King of Babylon" and "Hallelujah, King Jesus." He published these works as the *Green Pastures Spirituals* (1932) and wrote the folk opera *Run, Little Children*, which he produced on Broadway in 1933.

A versatile composer, Still wrote four additional symphonies, several symphonic essays, extended pieces for orchestra, chorus, or soloists (for example, *And They Lynched Him on a Tree*, *Plain-Chant for America*, and *Lenox Avenue*), art songs, solo instrumental music, chamber music, and seven operas.

Eva Jessye broke new ground as one of the first professional female choral conductors, black or white, in the United States. She and her choir performed on NBC and CBS radio in the early 1930s, and they sang in the first performances of Virgil Thomson's *Four Saints in Three Acts* (1934) and George Gershwin's *Porgy and Bess* (1935). Jessye composed three oratorios, *Life of Christ in Negro Spirituals* (1931), *Paradise Lost and Regained* (1934), and *Chronicle of Job* (1936), which combine Negro spirituals with narrative dialogue.

Clarence Cameron White, perhaps the most influential composer and propagandist of the Harlem Renaissance, drew inspiration to employ black folk idioms in his music directly from personal contact with Samuel Coleridge-Taylor, during the composer's visit to the States in 1904 and through private study with him in London in 1906 and 1908–1910. White's best-known compositions include works for violin (for example, *Bandanna Sketches*, *Cabin Memories*, and *Concert Paraphrases of Traditional Negro Melodies*); his string quartet (1931); the opera *Ouanga* (1932), which explored a Haitian subject and folk culture; and *Kutamba Rhapsody* for orchestra (1942). He was also instrumental in founding the National Association of Negro Musicians, serving as its president from 1922 to 1924.

Musical theater

Noteworthy contributions to musical theater were made at the end of the nineteenth century and the turn of the new century by such composers as Harry L. Freeman, Will Marion Cook, J. Rosamond Johnson, and Shirley Graham. Freeman attracted attention in 1892–1893 with his first opera, *Epthelia*, and he wrote nineteen additional operas. The principal author of the librettos he set, he preferred black subjects, and he combined use of African American sacred and vernacular music with nineteenth-century European opera forms. Will Marion Cook, a classically trained violinist, turned to the entertainment industry in the waning years of the nineteenth century and composed *Clorindy: Or, the Origin of the Cakewalk* (1898), a ragtime operetta based on a libretto by Paul Laurence Dunbar, the inaugural black musical that introduced syncopated "hot" music on Broadway. Cook collaborated on fifteen other musicals based on black subjects, including *In Dahomey* (1903), *Bandana Land* (1908), *Darkydom* (1915), *Negro Nuances* (1924), and *Swing Along* (1929).

Although J. Rosamond Johnson and his writer brother James Weldon Johnson are generally remembered today as the authors of "Lift Every Voice and Sing" (1900), the Negro national anthem (or official song of the National Association for the Advancement of Colored People [NAACP]), they joined forces with Robert "Bob" Cole (1868–1911) to form one of the most successful popular song-writing teams in the early 1900s. J. Rosamond was coauthor with Cole of four black musicals, *The Belle of Newport* (1900), *Humpty Dumpty* and *In Newport* (1904), and *The Shoo-Fly Regiment* (1907), and he wrote the operetta *The Red Moon* (c. 1908) with Joe Jordan.

Shirley Graham (Mrs. W. E. B. Du Bois) distinguished herself as the first African American female to garner national attention as an opera composer and librettist with her first full-length musical drama, *Tom-Tom* (1932), which she wrote during her Oberlin years. This epic work traced two centuries of black music—from the music and rituals of Africa to African American slave music to the syncopated music of Harlem in the early twentieth century. Its premiere in Cleveland, Ohio, in July 1932, with Jules Bledsoe and Charlotte Murray in leading roles, along with a cast of five hundred individuals, was possibly, as Kathy Perkins (1985) has observed, the earliest black opera produced on a grandiose scale with a professional cast. Between 1936 and 1938, Graham supervised the Negro Unit of the Chicago WPA Federal Theater, where she designed and composed such musical scores as the children's opera *Little Black Sambo* (1938) and *The Swing Mikado* (1939), a syncopated parody on the Gilbert and Sullivan operetta.

Florence Price, another musician born in the post-Emancipation era, enjoys the unique position in American music as the first black woman to gain international recognition as a composer, winning two Holstein awards in composition (1925, 1927) and first prizes in the 1932 Rodman Wanamaker Foundation Awards for her piano sonata and Symphony in E Minor. The symphony received its inaugural performance one year later with Frederick Stock and the Chicago Symphony. Price's art songs were widely performed by such singers as Marian Anderson, Roland Hayes, and Leontyne Price.

William Grant Still

William Grant Still (figure 4), the "dean of African-American composers," opened new vistas for black musicians between the 1930s and 1960s. Drawing upon prior experiences in theater orchestras, with the recording studio of the Black Swan label, and in jazz, he brought an intimate knowledge of vernacular traditions of African American music to the craft of composition and was, as Eileen Southern (1982) observed, the first African American composer to apply blues and jazz to symphonic music. His watershed work, the *Afro-American Symphony* (1930), was premiered in 1931 by Howard Hanson and the Rochester Philharmonic. A versatile composer, Still wrote four additional symphonies, several symphonic essays, extended pieces for orchestra, chorus, or soloists (for example, *And They Lynched Him on a Tree, Plain-Chant for America*, and *Lenox Avenue*), art songs, solo instrumental music, chamber music, and seven operas. His *Troubled Island*, which had its debut performance in 1949 with the New York City Opera, was the first full-length opera by a black composer mounted by a major American company. Still also pioneered as a black composer in the media, creating sound tracks for the films *Lost Horizon* (1935), *Pennies from Heaven* (1936), and *Stormy Weather* (1943) and incidental music for the original *Perry Mason* television show (1954). His awards included fellowships from the Harmon (1928), Guggenheim (1934, 1935, 1938), and Rosenwald Foundations (1939–1940), as well as commissions from CBS, the New York World's Fair, the League of Composers, and leading orchestras.

FIGURE 4   William Grant Still. Photo courtesy William Grant Still Music, Flagstaff, Arizona.

THE TWENTIETH CENTURY

Dramatic social and political changes took place in the United States during the twentieth century—the two great wars; the Depression; the landmark decision in *Brown v. Board of Education of Topeka* (1954), which struck down judicial segregation of public schools; and the civil rights movement of the 1960s, which prompted passage of new legislation to protect African American citizens. Composers born in the new century reaped benefits from many of these transitions, particularly greater accessibility to higher education and expanded vistas within which to work. By the 1950s, membership of African Americans in such music-licensing organizations as ASCAP and BMI rose, which ensured them greater protection of their intellectual property. Selected black composers experienced increased offers of commissions and expanded venues for the performance, publication, and recording of their music. With a few notable exceptions, most of the well-established composers would obtain professorships at major American universities or schools of music by the 1970s, 1980s, and 1990s. Ulysses Kay (1917–1995) was a professor at Lehman College of the City University of New York; George Walker (b. 1922) at Rutgers University; Hale Smith (b. 1925) at the University of Connecticut at Storrs; T. J. Anderson (b. 1928) at Tufts University; Frederick Tillis (b. 1930) at the University of Massachusetts at Amherst; David Baker (b. 1931) at the University of Indiana; Olly Wilson (b. 1937) at the University of California at Berkeley; Wendell Logan (b. 1940) at Oberlin College Conservatory; and Tania León (b. 1943) at Brooklyn College of the City University of New York. A few such as Howard Swanson (1907–1978), Julia Perry (1924–1979), Arthur Cunningham (1928–1997), Leslie Adams (b. 1933), and Alvin Singleton (b. 1940) would maintain themselves largely through commissions, grants, or freelance work. Several obtained national exposure and coveted patronage from government agencies and private foundations— for example, the Prix de Rome: Ulysses Kay (1949, 1951); the Guggenheim Fellowship: Howard Swanson (1952, 1978), Julia Perry (1954, 1956), Ulysses Kay (1964), George Walker (1969, 1988), Olly Wilson (1971, 1977), and Wendell Logan (1991); the National Academy of Arts and Letters: Howard Swanson (1952), Olly Wilson (1974); the National Endowment for the Arts: George Walker (1971, 1975, 1978, 1984), Talib Rasul Hakim, né Stephen Chambers (1973, 1978), Wendell Logan (1973, 1978, 1985, 1995), Arthur Cunningham (1974), Tania León (1975), Valerie Capers (1976, 1994), Olly Wilson (1976, 1985), Howard Swanson (1977), Leslie Adams, Ulysses Kay, and Frederick Tillis (1979), Alvin Singleton (1980, 1990), David Baker (1981), William Cedric Banfield (1994), and Regina A. Baiocchi (1995); the American Academy and Institute of Arts and Letters: Olly Wilson (1974), George Walker (1982), Hale Smith (1988), Tania León (1991); and the Pulitzer Prize: George Walker (1996).

Mid-twentieth-century concert music

By the mid-century, Ulysses Kay, Howard Swanson, Julia Perry, and George Walker began to achieve prominence. Each embraced neoclassic concepts from a slightly different perspective. Kay, who had studied with Bernard Rogers and Howard Hanson at the Eastman School of Music (M. Mus. 1940), and later with Paul Hindemith (1941–1942) and Otto Luening (1942–1946), composed music characterized by an elegant lyricism of melody, dissonant polyphony, rich orchestration, and pulsating rhythms, with no overt hint of African American folk or vernacular music overtones. Although his extensive works lists comprised symphonic music, chamber works, art songs, and choral music, as well as operas, he excelled as a composer of orchestral music. *Markings* (1966), a symphonic essay dedicated to the memory of Dag Hammarskjöld, Secretary-General of the United Nations, and the film score for James Agee's documentary *The Quiet One* (1948) are among his masterpieces.

Howard Swanson, a graduate of the Cleveland Institute of Music (B. Mus. 1937) and a student of Nadia Boulanger at the American Academy in Fountainebleau, France (1938), consciously integrated African American musical idioms into the neoclassical forms he created. He attracted national attention in 1949 when Marian Anderson sang "The Negro Speaks of Rivers" (text by Langston Hughes) at Carnegie Hall and gained further publicity in 1951 when Dmitri Mitropoulos and the New York Philharmonic Orchestra performed his *Short Symphony*, which later received the New York Music Critics' Circle Award (1952). Although not a prolific composer, Swanson produced three symphonies, a concerto for orchestra, miscellaneous chamber pieces, two piano sonatas, and several art songs that remain staples in the modern repertoire of American recitalists.

FIGURE 5   George Walker. Photo courtesy
George Walker. Photography by Wonderland
Studios, 1990s.

Julia Perry, an alumna of Westminster Choir College in Princeton, New Jersey
(B. Mus. 1947; M. Mus. 1948), studied at Fontainebleau with Boulanger and privately
with Luigi Dallapiccola in Florence, Italy, during the 1950s and was highly regarded
during this period as one of the foremost female composers, black or white. She
worked effectively in large forms, composing ten symphonies, a string quartet, a viola
concerto, and assorted pieces for chamber instruments. In addition to the *Stabat Mater*
for contralto and string orchestra (1951) that launched her career, her best-known
offerings include *Homage to Vivaldi* for symphony orchestra (1959, rev. 1964),
Homunculus C.F. for piano, harp, and percussion (1960), and *The Cask of Amontillado*
(1953), a one-act opera.

George Walker (figure 5), an alumnus of the Oberlin Conservatory (B. Mus.
1941) and Curtis Institute (1941–1945), and of study at Fontainebleau with Boulanger
and Robert Casadesus (1947), holds the distinction of being the first African American
to earn the D.M.A. degree at the Eastman School of Music (1957), as well as the first
of his race to receive the Pulitzer Prize in music (1996). Over the years he has developed a distinctive style that fuses modern compositional techniques with jazz as well
as African American sacred and vernacular music, and he has composed for full orchestra, chamber ensemble, chorus, solo instrument, and solo voice. His Sonata for Cello
and Piano (1957), Piano Concerto (1976), Concerto for Cello and Orchestra (1981),
and four sonatas for piano (1953–1984) are among his most frequently performed
compositions.

Music of the avant-garde

Hale Smith, Olly Wilson, and Alvin Singleton are representative composers who have
experimented with a wide range of contemporary avant-garde techniques. Smith, the
senior statesman of the group, graduated from the Cleveland Institute of Music (B. Mus.
1950; M. Mus. 1952) and was active during the late 1950s and 1960s as a jazz arranger
before joining the music faculty of the University of Connecticut at Storrs (1970–
1984). His best-known work, *Contours for Orchestra* (1961), employs twelve-tone serial
technique.

Olly Wilson, The Jerry and Evelyn Hemmings Chambers Professor of Music at
the University of California, Berkeley, holds degrees from Washington University
(B. Music 1959), the University of Illinois at Urbana-Champaign (M. Mus. 1960), and
the University of Iowa (Ph.D. 1964). He won first prize in Dartmouth College's first
international electronic music contest in 1968 for *Cetus*, a composition for electronic
tape. Since the 1970s he has experimented with traditional instruments, acoustical
instruments, and electronic sounds. The influence of jazz and traditional genres of
African American as well as West African music are pronounced in his music, especially
in such pieces as *Akwan* for piano, electronic piano, and orchestra (1972), *Sometimes*
for tenor and electronic sound (1976), and *A City Called Heaven* for chamber ensemble
(1988).

In recent years Alvin Singleton has emerged as a new star among the avant-garde.
After spending much of the 1970s in Europe, he returned to the States in the mid-
1980s and has served residencies as a composer with the Atlanta Symphony Orchestra
(1985–1988), at Spelman College (1988–1991), and with the Detroit Symphony Orchestra (1996–1997). Singleton's experimentations range from the use of tonal and post-
tonal pitch classifications and sound-space structures to minimalist techniques. He has
concentrated since the 1980s on writing orchestral music, for example, *After Fallen
Crumbs* and *Shadows* (1987) for the Atlanta Symphony, *Sinfonia Diaspora* (1991) for
the Oregon Symphony, and *Durch Alles* (1992) for the Cleveland Orchestra.

Fusions and border crossings

Classical and jazz/vernacular music found a synthesis in so-called Third Stream music (a term coined in 1957 by Gunther Schuller), which has come to dominate the work of David Baker, professor and chairman of the jazz department at Indiana University (1966–2000), and Frederick Tillis, professor emeritus of the University of Massachusetts, Amherst, both of whom bring extensive experience as jazz performers to the craft of writing art music.

Baker has composed in a variety of Western forms (cantatas, oratorios, art songs, choral music, symphonies, solo sonatas, chamber music, symphonic essays) and experimented with mixed media, often combining traditional musical instruments with jazz combos, gospel choirs, or electronic instruments. Among his important works are the cantata *Le Chat qui pêche* (1974), the Concerto for Cello and Chamber Orchestra (1975), *Singers of Songs/Weavers of Dreams* for cello and percussions (1980), and *Roots II* for piano trio (1992).

Tillis has drawn eclectically from traditional African, African American, and Southeast Asian music as well as contemporary Western forms and compositional techniques. Among his representative works are *Ring Shout Concerto* for percussion and orchestra (1974), *Niger Symphony* for chamber orchestra (1975), Concerto for Pro Vivo and chamber orchestra (1980), a series of eighteen *Spiritual Fantasies* for various instruments (1980–1998), and *Kabuki Scenes* for brass quintet and timpani (1991).

Employing black folk and vernacular idioms in Western art forms remained a fairly consistent theme among many classically trained African American composers in the twentieth century. Tania León (b. 1943) (figure 6) has added to this tradition the syncretic sounds of her native Cuba, where Afro-Cuban, Yoruban, Congolese, and creole Spanish cultures comingle. Emigrating from Havana to the United States in 1967, she has established a solid reputation as a composer, conductor, and musical director. In addition to teaching composition/conducting at Brooklyn College of the City University of New York (1985–present), and conducting the Brooklyn College Orchestra (1991–present), she has held residencies as a composer at the Ravinia Festival (1991), the Cleveland Institute of Music (1992), and the New York Philharmonic (Revson Composer Fellow, 1993–1996). Through her visibility as a composer-conductor, she has sought to promote cultural exchanges between musicians within the Americas as the artistic advisor of Sonidos de las Américas. Recent examples of Afro-Caribbean influences in her music are found in *Kabiosile* for piano and orchestra (1988), *Indígena* for chamber orchestra (1991), and the symphonic essay *Carabalí* (1991).

The late twentieth century

The late twentieth century witnessed the rise of a new generation of promising composers with James Kimo Williams (b. 1950), whose *Symphony for the Sons of Nam* (1986, rev. 1990) has been programmed by National Public Radio; Anthony Davis (b. 1951), whose *X: The Life and Times of Malcolm X* was premiered in 1986 by the New York City Opera; Lettie Beckon Alston (b. 1953), a finalist in the 1993 Detroit Symphony Orchestra's Unisys African-American Composers Forum competition; Julius P. Williams (b. 1954), who directed the Bohuslav Martinů Philharmonic in a 1993 recording of his *Meditation: From Easter Celebration*; Jeffrey Mumford (b. 1955), first-prize winner of the 1994 National Black Arts Festival/Atlanta Symphony Orchestra competition; William C. Banfield (b. 1961), winner of the 1995 Detroit Symphony Orchestra's Unisys African-American Composers Forum competition for *Essay for Orchestra*; and Gregory Walker (b. 1961), son of the composer George Walker and author of *Dream N. the Hood*, a rap-symphonic essay.

FIGURE 6   Tania León. Photo courtesy Peermusic Classical.

REFERENCES

Abdul, Raoul. 1977. *Blacks in Classical Music: A Personal History.* New York: Dodd, Mead.

Ammer, Christine. 1980. *Unsung: A History of Women in American Music.* Contributions in Women's Studies 14. Westport, Conn.: Greenwood Press.

Baker, David N., Linda M. Belt, and H. C. Hudson, eds. 1978. *The Black Composer Speaks.* Metuchen, N.J.: Scarecrow Press.

Board of Music Trade of the United States of America. 1973 [1871]. *Complete Catalog of Sheet Music and Musical Works, 1870.* New York: Da Capo Press.

Boyer, Horace C., comp. 1976. "A Portfolio of Music: The New England Afro-American School." *Black Perspective in Music* 4(2):213–237.

Brown, Rae Linda. 1990. "William Grant Still, Florence Price, and William Dawson: Echoes of the Harlem Renaissance." In *Black Music in the Harlem Renaissance: A Collection of Essays,* ed. Samuel A. Floyd Jr., 71–86. Westport, Conn.: Greenwood Press.

Carter, Madison H. 1986. *An Annotated Catalog of Composers of African Ancestry.* New York: Vantage Press.

Cuney-Hare, Maud. 1974 [1936]. *Negro Musicians and Their Music.* New York: Da Capo Press.

Davidson, Celia Elizabeth. 1980. "Operas by Afro-American Composers: A Critical Survey and Analysis of Selected Works." Ph.D. dissertation, Catholic University of America.

De Lerma, Dominique-René. 1981–1984. "Bibliography of Black Music." In *Greenwood Encyclopedia of Black Music.* 4 vols. Westport, Conn.: Greenwood Press.

———. 1990. "Bibliography of the Music: The Concert Music of the Harlem Renaissance Composers, 1919–1935." In *Black Music in the Harlem Renaissance: A Collection of Essays,* ed. Samuel A. Floyd Jr., 175–217. Westport, Conn.: Greenwood Press.

De Lerma, Dominique René, and Marsha J. Reisser, comps. 1989. *Black Music and Musicians in The New Grove Dictionary of Music and The New Harvard Dictionary of Music.* CBMR Monographs, vol. 1. Chicago: Columbia College.

Floyd, Samuel A. Jr., ed. 1999. *International Dictionary of Black Composers.* Chicago: Fitzroy Dearborn.

Floyd, Samuel A. Jr., and Marsha J. Reisser. 1983. *Black Music in the United States: An Annotated Bibliography of Selected Reference and Research Materials.* Millwood, N.Y.: Kraus International.

———. 1987. *Black Music Biography: An Annotated Bibliography.* White Plains, N.Y.: Kraus International.

Garcia, William. 1974. "Church Music by Black Composers." *Black Perspective in Music* 2(2):145–157.

Gray, John, comp. 1988. *Blacks in Classical Music: A Bibliographical Guide to Composers, Performers, and Ensembles.* Westport, Conn.: Greenwood Press.

Green, Mildred Denby. 1983. *Black Women Composers: A Genesis.* Boston: Twayne.

Handy, D. Antoinette. 1995. *Black Conductors.* Lanham, Md.: Scarecrow Press.

Jones, Charles K., and Lorenzo K. Greenwich II, comps. 1982. *A Choice Collection of the Works of Francis Johnson,* vol. 1. New York: Point Two Publications.

Locke, Alain. 1936. *The Negro and His Music.* Washington, D.C.: Associates in Negro Folk Education.

Newby, John A. 1889. "Distinguished Composers: The Musical Writers of the Colored Race." *The Freeman* (Indianapolis).

Patterson, Willis C., comp. 1977. *Anthology of Art Songs by Black American Composers.* Melville, N.Y.: Edward B. Marks Music.

Perkins, Kathy A. 1985. "The Unknown Career of Shirley Graham." *Freedomways* 25(1):6–17.

Riis, Thomas L. 1989. *Just before Jazz: Black Musical Theater in New York, 1890–1915.* Washington, D.C.: Smithsonian Institution Press.

Sears, Ann. 1988. "Keyboard Music by Nineteenth-Century Afro-American Composers." In *Feel the Spirit: Studies in Nineteenth-Century Afro-American Music,* ed. George R. Keck and Sherrill V. Martin, 135–155. Westport, Conn.: Greenwood Press.

Southern, Eileen. 1975. "America's Black Composers of Classical Music." *Music Educators Journal* 62(3):46–59.

———. 1982. *A Biographical Dictionary of African and African-American Musicians. Greenwood Encyclopedia of Black Music.* Westport, Conn.: Greenwood Press.

———. 1997. *The Music of Black Americans: A History,* 3d ed. New York: W. W. Norton.

Tischler, Alice. 1981. *Fifteen Black American Composers: A Bibliography of Their Works.* Detroit Studies in Music Bibliography 45. Detroit, Mich.: Information Coordinators.

Trotter, James Monroe. 1968 [1878]. *Music and Some Highly Musical People.* New York: Johnson Reprint Corp.

Walker-Hill, Helen. 1995. *Music by Black Women Composers: A Bibliography of Available Scores.* CBMR Monographs, vol. 5. Chicago: Columbia College.

White, Evelyn Davidson, comp. 1981. *Choral Music by Afro-American Composers: A Selected, Annotated Bibliography.* Metuchen, N.J.: Scarecrow Press.

Williams, Ora. 1981. *American Black Women in the Arts and Social Sciences.* Metuchen, N.J.: Scarecrow Press.

Wilson, Olly. 1986. "The Black-American Composer and the Orchestra in the Twentieth Century." *Black Perspective in Music* 14(1):26–34.

Wright, Josephine. 1992. "Research in Afro-American Music." In *New Perspectives on Music: Essays in Honor of Eileen Southern,* ed. Josephine Wright with Samuel A. Floyd Jr., 48–515. Warren, Mich.: Harmonie Park Press.

Wyatt, Lucius R. 1987. "Composers Corner: Six Composers of Nineteenth-Century New Orleans." *Black Music Research Newsletter* 9(1):4–9.

Musical Theater
Thomas L. Riis

African Heritage
From the Revolution to the Civil War
The Black Musical Comedy: 1897 to 1930
Evolving Images on the Stage, from the Depression to the Civil Rights Era
The End of the Twentieth Century

The essence of African theatricality survived most memorably in the New World in religious rituals. These expressions of shared beliefs, celebrated communally and constructed collectively, placed few boundaries between actors and audiences. The dances, songs, and traditional stories that were re-created on the North American continent and adjacent islands preserved the rich traditions of West Africa in many guises. Whether in search of solace or strength, out of a sense of rebellion, grief, or sheer creative energy, Africans in America have always acted out and sung their sorrows, myths, dreams, and hopes.

AFRICAN HERITAGE

Descriptions of festivals such as Pinkster Day document the existence of an African theatrical practice in North America during the eighteenth century. The celebration of this holiday in Dutch colonial New York, Rhode Island, and Connecticut involved the election of a king or governor and featured elaborate costumes, processions, feasting, music, singing, and dance. John Kuner (sometimes called John Canoe or Jonkonnu) Christmas rituals in North Carolina and Jamaica also constitute important theatrical survivals, attested by many accounts from the mid-nineteenth century, which provide details about costumes, makeup (blackface and whiteface), musical instruments, parading, and occasionally song texts. "Moorish" dancing and costumes were also recorded in the early Colonial period in the American Southwest, and even modern-day Pueblo dances of New Mexico, called *matachines*, retain masks that suggest African provenance.

Other documents, such as the play *High Life Below Stairs* (1759), presented parodies of slaves imitating their white masters' habits of holiday dress, body movement, manner, and attitude. The distinctive character of African American musical theater is evident in all of these precursors: grand gesture, elaborate costumes, spirited music, dance, and parody.

FROM THE REVOLUTION TO THE CIVIL WAR

After 1750, in the English-speaking theater on the Atlantic coast, African Americans were involved in formal, text-defined theatricals only to the degree permitted within a climate generally hostile to all secular forms of theater. The conservative Christian leaders in the cities of Boston and Philadelphia, for example, frowned on the stage, which in their view acted as a magnet for licentiousness and vice of all kinds. It would long remain the dominant American middle-class belief that actors and their business were only barely respectable in the best of venues. Class, occupation, and race prejudice fenced out all but the most sanitized stage vehicles from public view and record.

New York, Charleston, and New Orleans, by contrast, took a somewhat more tolerant view. All three cities greeted foreign immigrants who brought with them the latest music, dance, and theatrical fashions from Africa, Europe, the West Indies, and South America during the 1700s. Early-nineteenth-century accounts of social dances, pit bands, and community music making in New Orleans document the presence of black entertainers. Other cities evidently supported active coteries of black theatrical musicians from time to time. Eileen Southern (1994) reports the existence of "Negro tunes" or "Negro jigs," which may have been included in the general repertoire of musical theater songs in the early years of the republic.

Shakespearean actors habitually added extra songs and dances to their plays in the early nineteenth century, and the all-black African Grove theater company in lower Manhattan was no exception when in the early 1820s it staged *Othello, Hamlet,* and *Richard III*, along with a variety of lighter entertainments and pieces by the African American playwright William Henry Brown. The African Grove on Mercer Street, though short-lived, deserves recognition because it not only featured black actors in full productions but trained at least one individual who would later achieve professional status and renown, Ira Aldridge (1807–1867). This theater arose in 1816 as a private venture, a tea garden, that finally went public in 1821, thereby incurring the wrath of hostile authorities in New York and the jealousy of the principal competing white theater, the Park. The rich variety and evidently multiracial appeal of the African Grove, as well as its attractiveness for middle-class aspirants, was undermined by the Grove's enemies, and the theater was closed finally in 1829.

In 1838, the Marigny Theater in New Orleans opened for the "free colored population" of the city, so that African Americans of means could enjoy French light comedies and musical shows but be spared the indignity of sitting in segregated theaters. (Both slaves and whites were barred from the Marigny.) The theater remained open for only a few months but revealed potential patrons among the creole citizens of New Orleans for sophisticated theater. The Theatre de la Renaissance, whose orchestra included members of the Negro Philharmonic Society, was opened in 1840 and offered full plays, comic pieces, and variety shows in the years following. Neither of these venues led to the production of new or independently created works, but they represent the passion and persistence with which the black middle class sought cultural participation and validation.

Because popular theatricals throughout history have delineated, lampooned, and translated contemporary life, African Americans were portrayed for the American public well before they had full control of the messages given out by actors or directors in formal works for the stage. Complexity in the theatrical message by and about African Americans was reflected in the changes that were taking place in American life during the first four decades of the nineteenth century. An active participant in these doings was George Washington Dixon, an early blackface (and possibly black) entertainer as well as a political gadfly, athlete, and journalist, whose popularity preceded the advent of the minstrel show.

Dixon (1801–1861) in the 1830s sang both with and without blackface makeup and made famous such songs as "Coal-Black Rose" and "Zip Coon." He performed benefit shows for black entertainers, was an ardent advocate of the working class, and may even have held abolitionist sympathies. He was described in several sources as a mulatto, although allegedly accurate sketches of him in street dress do not suggest African features or complexion. At the peak of his performing career (1836–1838) he was hailed as "*the* American Melodist," a model of patriotism, a friend of the working man, and a liberty-loving Jacksonian.

The minstrel show

Individual entertainers such as Dixon were eclipsed when the minstrel show, a more organized kind of four-man team theater event, emerged in the 1840s. Each member in blackface makeup played an African instrument (banjo, fiddle, bones, or tambourine) and performed various songs and dance skits. Although earlier actors working in blackface makeup had conveyed a wide spectrum of ideas, not all necessarily addressing race or the conditions of African Americans, the Virginia Minstrels, the Christie Minstrels, and other white minstrel teams from the 1840s claimed that they were faithfully mirroring the habits and customs of blacks. However, these white minstrel shows—popular in major theaters until the end of the century—say more about the dominant culture's wishes for, and impressions about, the groups they parodied, which included not only African Americans but women, Mormons, rubes, Native Americans, foreigners, and politicians as well.

The importance of the minstrel phenomenon cannot be overestimated, because it was so widespread and long-lived. Many groups traveled abroad. Large cities and small towns sustained them for decades. Minstrel performers generated huge amounts of music—quick, raucous, and spirited tunes—allied with nonsensical dialect poetry, clearly challenging more elite, genteel products (parlor songs) by their general high spirits, explicit politics, and irreverent attitudes. Banjo tunes, with characteristic syncopations, which some whites learned from blacks and presented on the minstrel stage, are recoverable from printed tutorials of the 1840s. The music of minstrelsy, in such songs as "Turkey in the Straw" (formerly "Zip Coon") and Stephen Foster's "Oh! Susanna," continues to be passed on in the oral tradition.

Black minstrel and touring companies of the late nineteenth century

African Americans first entered American popular theater in large numbers via the burgeoning of traveling minstrel troupes in the 1850s. They still employed burnt cork makeup, but they also sought to contradict the claim of authenticity purveyed by their white counterparts. What could be more authentic than a real black person performing as a black minstrel, they asked, and by so doing made a space in which to demonstrate black talent and to reinforce images of independence, intelligence, and black family togetherness. Throughout their skits they campaigned in favor of Emancipation, the Union, and amicable relations between the races. After the Civil War, more sentimental motifs came to dominate the minstrel song repertoire, as did the message that a new generation of young people not raised in slavery would push aside any misplaced romanticism about "good old Southern life" on the part of their elders.

Prolific black composer and singer James Bland (1854–1911), who wrote "Carry Me Back to Old Virginny" and "Oh Dem Golden Slippers," is probably the most famous of the post–Civil War minstrel men, but many other unsung entertainers made substantial careers (Billy Kersands, Sam Lucas, Ernest Hogan, for example) and participated in the companies led by Lew Johnson, Charles Callender, Sprague and Blodgett, J. H. Haverly, Richard and Pringle, W. S. Cleveland, and the Hunn Brothers. The talents of these men—males completely dominated the minstrel stage until the 1890s—were individual and hard to appreciate out of context. Usually minstrels were not allowed to address political issues (such as peonage, lynching, or segregation) except by indirection. But many rejected the use of burnt cork and, by clever subversions of well-known jokes, created a stage message with multiple meanings. By 1900, a militant young entertainer such as Robert "Bob" Cole could write an antiminstrel song called "No Coons Allowed!" and get away with performing it in whiteface makeup for a white audience.

With the increasing oppression of the Reconstruction era leading to nearly universal legalized segregation by 1900, the avenues for black expression were narrow indeed. Nevertheless, actors on the stage were often granted a certain license and could pass off social criticism in the guise of a joke, a gesture, or even an unusually inflected word, observed only by those who had ears to hear and eyes to see.

In 1876, a pair of California sisters named Anna and Emma Hyers, led by their enterprising father, formed a touring concert company. Subsequently, with the help of supportive playwrights Joseph Bradford and Pauline Hopkins, they presented the first full-fledged musical plays in American history in which African Americans themselves comment on the plight of the slaves and the relief of Emancipation without the disguises of minstrel comedy. Both *Out of Bondage* (sometimes called *Out of the Wilderness*) (1876) and *Peculiar Sam: or, The Underground Railroad* (1879), with various additions, interpolations, and revivals, enjoyed a place in the Hyers touring repertory until the sisters' official retirement in 1893.

Although they bear some unmistakable similarities to minstrel-style plays and afterpieces, the independent creations of the Hyers sisters lack blackface makeup and farcical situations; like the minstrel shows of the 1870s and 1880s, their music represents a wide array of popular stage songs of the period, including religious music. By the late 1870s, the spirituals arranged and sung by the Fisk University students had been widely copied by nonstudent professional groups, henceforth becoming the means by which secular theatricals could be justified and legitimated in the eyes of the white authorities. These spiritual parodies became an influential theatrical product. At the same time, innumerable solo and choral arrangements of the spirituals and jubilee songs constitute the major nineteenth-century American contribution to world musical culture, along with the parlor songs and minstrel show tunes of Stephen Foster [see POPULAR MUSIC OF THE PARLOR AND STAGE, p. 179].

Opera theater

The conscious separation of comic and serious strains within musical theater was pronounced and clearly class-related in the late nineteenth century. American opera (as distinct from American imitations of European works) had come into its own. Generic musical categories that had been relatively unimportant to potential viewers in earlier times now attracted more varied audiences. African Americans made efforts to enter the higher class of entertainments through the creations of full-fledged operas, and they attracted an audience within the African American community. Although the commercial impact of these shows was negligible, the landmark works deserve recognition in order to illustrate the full range of black participation long before black performers would be allowed to sing in the New York Academy of Music or the Metropolitan Opera.

Virginia's Ball (1868) by John Thomas Douglass (1847–1886), an accomplished violinist, is generally deemed to be the first opera by an African American composer. Although the music—registered for copyright—is now lost, a first performance was noted as having taken place in New York in the year of its creation. Bostonian Louisa Melvin Delos Mars was the first African American woman to have an opera produced (in Providence, Rhode Island), *Leoni, the Gypsy Queen* (1889). She finally composed no fewer than five full-length musical dramas between 1889 and 1896. The participation of educated middle-class women in amateur and church-sponsored operettas was also common by the end of the nineteenth century. Full-fledged African American divas such as Marie Selika (c. 1849–1937) and Sissieretta Jones (1869–1933) had significant careers as touring soloists at the same time.

Entrance of African Americans into the commercial mainstream of secular non-blackface theatricals occurred in the 1890s, with a handful of plays that included

By the late 1870s, the spirituals arranged and sung by the Fisk University students had been widely copied by nonstudent professional groups, henceforth becoming the means by which secular theatricals could be justified and legitimated in the eyes of the white authorities.

characteristic musical plantation scenes. Plays such as Turner Dazey's *In Old Kentucky*; Whalen and Martell's *The South Before the War*; *Darkest America*, managed by Al G. Fields; *Suwanee River*, sponsored by Davis and Keogh; and the perennial favorite *Uncle Tom's Cabin*, George Aiken and George Howard's musical play based on Harriet Beecher Stowe's 1852 novel, benefited from expanding urban populations, well-organized road tours, and production syndicates seeking ever-larger audiences, as did the variety shows conceived and created by Sam Jack's Creole Burlesque Company, John Isham's concert companies, and Sissieretta Jones's ensemble, called the Black Patti Troubadours. The appearance of many a short-lived show is noted in the pages of the trade papers of the 1890s, *Billboard*, and the New York *Dramatic Mirror*, as well as the black weekly from Indianapolis, *The Freeman*. The tendency of these shows toward vaudeville—that is, a series of acts—illustrates a general American taste for variety and episodic entertainments over narratively rich continuous plays in popular venues. As this preference also tended to support novelty and independent initiatives, black acts were able to gain a foothold in theater while being barred for allegedly financial reasons from more complex production opportunities or more overtly antistereotypical shows.

THE BLACK MUSICAL COMEDY: 1897 TO 1930

A sizable coterie of black talent gathered in New York in the 1890s, and out of this vibrant pre-Harlem community, black musical comedy was born. "Bob" Cole and his partner Billy Johnson, veterans of earlier touring companies, put together up-tempo songs, comic dialogue within a modest narrative plot, and several talented young performers to create *A Trip to Coontown* (1897). The simultaneous emergence of ragtime piano pieces and songs—in a style universally recognized as African American—with shows like *A Trip to Coontown* was a fortunate coincidence. By 1896, ragtime had invaded the stage at all levels. Between 1897 and 1930, African Americans made over three hundred shows (by Bernard Peterson's [1993] count) composed of ragtime or novelty tunes (later jazz) and comedic dialogue often embedded in the characteristic revue format (a succession of topical songs and skits using the same actors in different roles). The singing and dancing of Bert and Lottie Williams, George Walker, Aida Overton Walker, Ernest Hogan, "Bob" Cole and the Johnson brothers (James Weldon and J. Rosamond) were the featured attractions of the first decade. J. Leubrie Hill in his productions, collectively known as the Darktown Follies, inaugurated the next generation of shows (1911–1915), where the dancing and choral singing were prized above all else.

Without access to the elaborate stage apparatus and expensive trappings of full-blown operettas, the black-cast shows of the early years of the century focused on the talents of individual star players, the powerful energy of the dance with its complexities of movement, the seemingly spontaneous vernacular humor, and the overwhelming vocal power of massed choruses. The black shows used at least two conservatory-trained musicians, Will Marion Cook and J. Rosamond Johnson, whose command of the new syncopated music, together with abundant conducting and arranging skills, glued together the inevitably disparate parts of productions. Both men were hit-tune

FIGURE 1 First page of "Swing Along!" an early-twentieth-century song popular in both the United States and England. It was used by Will Marion Cook as the first big chorus in *In Dahomey* (1903) during its London run and remained popular in revival into the 1920s.

FIGURE 2 Ernest Hogan as Rufus Rastus, the title character of his first full-length musical comedy (1906). Billed as "the unbleached American" because of his avoidance of blackface makeup, Hogan was also a successful composer and business leader in the black community.

writers in 1900 ("Darktown Is Out Tonight," "Under the Bamboo Tree") and enabled the stars to be presented in well-constructed contemporary vehicles, such as *In Dahomey* (1903) (figure 1), *Abyssinia* (1906), *The Shoo Fly Regiment* (1907), *Bandana Land* (1908), and *The Red Moon* (c. 1909).

Both blacks and whites saw and knew these shows—and sat in what were, of course, segregated houses. Most of the actors did not don blackface makeup, however, and so although the shows' plots and song lyrics can appear stereotypical (if not downright slanderous) to a modern viewer, they represented an advance in some respects in their own day. Whereas a white-authored coon song of the 1890s such as Charles Trevathen's "Bully Song" could and did fling images of rampant black violence and mayhem at will (references to slashing razors and stolen chickens pervade the genre), the lyrics of "On Emancipation Day" by Paul Laurence Dunbar for Will Marion Cook's music in *In Dahomey*, filled with dialect though they were, proclaimed a kind of black joie de vivre that whites might envy.

> On Emancipation Day
> All you white folks clear de way . . .
> Coons dressed up lak masqueraders
> Porters armed like rude invaders
> When dey hear dem ragtime tunes
> White fo'ks try to pass for coons. . . . (Tilzer 1903)

The shows were generic farces, but they nevertheless made a strong impression on all viewers alert to racial politics. Black men and women were placed, through the vehicle of the stage, in a commanding expressive position night after night, all over the country. Consequently, Bert Williams, Aida Overton Walker, and Ernest Hogan (figure 2) were among the most famous African Americans of their day. They were viewed as race leaders, not merely entertainers. The most astute critics of these performers observed their mastery of mime, remarkable comic timing, vital dancing, and a distinctively animated presentation time after time. The overall impression left in the minds of the viewers after an extravaganza like Williams and Walker's *Bandana Land* (figure 3)—with multiple sets, marvelous stage effects, and live animals—must have forcefully contradicted the recollections of tired and tawdry minstrel shows from a bygone era.

After 1912, the first black triumphs on Broadway were pushed aside as Harlem grew and downtown producers feared further competition and the visibility of up-and-coming blacks. The premature deaths of black Broadway business leaders (especially Ernest Hogan in 1909) led many leading entertainers to opt for traveling vaudeville or neighborhood-based shows in the larger cities. Black ownership of theaters and audiences around the country increased dramatically between 1910 and 1920, and so naturally the places where a black audience could see black performers grew up in many urban pockets around the country (figure 4).

In 1921, the black musical came back with a blockbuster, the tuneful and energetic hit *Shuffle Along*, featuring the remarkable talents of singer-lyricist Noble Sissle, pianist-composer Eubie Blake, and comedians Flournoy Miller and Aubrey Lyles, who wrote the book on which the musical was based. The cast included a large number of fresh faces, many of whom later went on to stardom: Josephine Baker, Caterina Yarboro, Florence Mills, and Paul Robeson on stage and Hall Johnson, William Grant Still, and Leonard Jeter in the pit [see CONCERT MUSIC, p. 603]. Having originated as a 1907 Chicago show of Miller and Lyles, it required considerable updating to make a Broadway vehicle. Fortunately, Eubie Blake's years of songwriting experience served the show well ("I'm Just Wild about Harry," "Love Will Find a Way," "Dixie Moon"). The result was an outstanding success, running for over 500

FIGURE 3   The beginnings of seven songs presented in *Bandana Land* (1908). This set of excerpts was intended as a kind of teaser on the back cover or advertising sheet to encourage the purchase of each song in full piano/vocal score. *Bandana Land* was one of Williams and Walker's most critically acclaimed shows.

FIGURE 4   Vaudeville duo S. H. Dudley and his partner, Lottie Grady (c. 1915). The photo illustrates the clownish aspects of black vaudeville, with Dudley's big shoes and blackface makeup. Grady is clearly a "yaller gal," also a convention of the time.

performances, touring for two years on the road, and spawning many imitators through the decade.

As with all great shows, the reasons for *Shuffle Along*'s success were multiple. The talent was young and dedicated, but the key players drew on considerable experience. The musical material was varied. From the lyrical and romantic to the upbeat and jazzy, it accompanied a veritable kaleidoscope of dances and stage movements. Blake provided flashy piano interludes. The personalities of the stars were alluring. Everything was executed with virtuosity and struck the audience as thoroughly modern. Faced with stringent economies, the production even managed to be credited as sensibly modest. The play was familiar and genuinely funny (although nothing in the way of dramatic substance was ever expected in Broadway comedies of its type). It was produced in a theater that was accessible to regular Broadway theatergoers (at 63rd Street) and to a substantial black neighborhood on the west side of the city, if not quite in the heart of the theater district. Not unimportantly, influential critics loved it.

The stimulus provided by *Shuffle Along* and the boom of the twenties saw even more black employment in theatricals, especially song-and-dance revues. The new shows combined old-fashioned motifs (plantation scenarios, sentimental Old South clichés, and shuffling characters out of minstrelsy) with novelty updates (urban scenes, themes of black "uplift" and "improvement," glamorous female blues singers, and jazz bands). Broadway flourished in general, but shows with primarily black creators and actors made a mixed impression. The show names alone tell much about the high-spirited effervescence of the works, as well as their rather restricted dramatic palette: *Strut Miss Lizzie* (1922), *Runnin' Wild* (1923), *The Chocolate Dandies* (1924), *Lucky Sambo* (1925). The quality of the relatively new and inspired shows of the Will Marion Cook era (before 1910) and the creativity of individual black dancers and vaudevillians in vaudeville (1910–1920) were probably not surpassed in the 1920s. But at least there was a lot more to choose from. Full-fledged dramatic vehicles with substantial music—as opposed to dance revues or variety shows—are barely detectable in the historic record. This is partly because the phrase "serious musical" would have seemed self-contradictory before Jerome Kern's *Show Boat* (1927). The moneyed investors required to mount major Broadway musicals in the period had no conception that African Americans were capable of anything so revolutionary; as a result, no such shows were produced.

During the 1920s and 1930s the black creative component varied among the shows with black casts—arrangers and composers were both black and white; the financial benefits to African Americans were negligible. Individual black geniuses, such as the eminent Broadway arranger and Gershwin mentor Will Vodery, are almost lost to history. Some chose to work behind the scenes. Others developed alternative careers playing jazz and singing the blues. But the producing dictators of the musical theater stage were not yet ready to admit African Americans into full and equal participation on Broadway.

EVOLVING IMAGES ON THE STAGE, FROM THE DEPRESSION TO THE CIVIL RIGHTS ERA

Desire for heightened realism and more stringent production economies in the 1930s were reflected in the new black shows of that decade. *Brown Buddies* (1930) showed Bill Robinson and Adelaide Hall acting the romantic parts of the loyal soldier and tenderhearted civilian entertainer, respectively. *Sugar Hill* (1931) claimed to be a "sketch of life in Harlem's aristocratic section." Ethel Waters sang four songs (including a plaint about lynching) in the innovative revue *As Thousands Cheer* (1933). The Federal Theater Project of the Works Progress Administration (1935–1939) also provided work for blacks in musicals as well as straight plays in several American cities. Among the most famous of these Depression-era entries was a jazz version of the Gilbert and Sullivan operetta *The Mikado*, called *The Swing Mikado* (1939), and an opera produced in Seattle, based on the John Henry legend and incorporating black musical idioms, *Natural Man* (1937).

Two major musical works featuring black performers but with problematical scripts and contexts, again revealing the divisions and tensions within the entertainment industry of the 1930s, are Marc Connelly's religious pageant *Green Pastures* (1930), which used spirituals sung by the Hall Johnson Choir, and George and Ira Gershwin's opera *Porgy and Bess* (1935). Because creative control was racially restricted in both instances, these works generated and continue to generate controversy.

A gradual trend toward the integration of isolated black stars into white musicals and a growing allowance of more individualized black characters is perceptible in the forties, fifties, and early sixties, although there were exceptionally few all-black shows, and the amount of black participation in the preproduction process was almost invisible. (Duke Ellington's exceptional score for *Pousse-Café* (1966) couldn't save this show for more than a few days' run.) Juanita Hall sang in *South Pacific* (1949), Todd Duncan appeared in *Lost in the Stars* (1949), *Mr. Wonderful* (1956) and *Golden Boy* (1964) featured Sammy Davis, Jr., and Lena Horne glowed in *Jamaica* (1957). Richard Rodgers's *No Strings* (1962), with Diahann Carroll as the romantic lead, featured the first interracial kiss on Broadway. Despite liberalizing trends favoring racial inclusiveness in the larger post–World War II society, racial barriers still tended to restrict the creative options for black actors while reinforcing the tendency of white producers to rely on minstrel formulas in casting. Black men, women, and children continued to sing, play, and dance on the stage, but they did so largely in the makeup of comic servants, urban vagabonds, and jungle savages.

The civil rights movement and the revolutionary ideology of the late 1960s and 1970s seemed inimical to the comic conventions of musical comedy. New independent groups, especially the National Black Theater (NBT) of Harlem, 1968–1972, created works using African and West Indian rituals and dances, but longer-lived and less ideologically bound organizations, such as the Negro Ensemble Theater, did not stress musicals in their repertoires at all. The work of Melvin Van Peebles, *Ain't Supposed to Die a Natural Death* (1971) and *Don't Play Us Cheap* (1972), was probably the most artistically serious and invigorating dramatic contribution to this new theater. Its angry confrontational dialogue anticipated by a generation the powerful speech-rhythms of rap artists.

THE END OF THE TWENTIETH CENTURY

The reintroduction of black folk and religious themes into shows, such as *Black Nativity* (1962), *Tambourines to Glory* (1963), *The Prodigal Son* (1965), *A Hand at the Gate* (1966), *Your Arms Too Short to Box with God* (1976), and *The Gospel at Colonus* (1983), and the revival of older musical styles began to strengthen the black presence once again in the final third of the century. The emergence of rock and roll as the principal style of popular music—with its undeniable African American roots—accompanied the ebbing popularity of the classic productions from earlier decades. The 1970s saw more participation of African Americans on Broadway than had occurred since the thirties, although the musical contents often tended to be retrospective and nostalgic in shows like *Me and Bessie* (1975), *Bubblin' Brown Sugar* (1976), *One Mo' Time* (1979), and *Eubie* (1979). The trend toward recycling familiar African American tunes was maintained in *Sophisticated Ladies* (1982), *Williams and Walker* (1986), and *Black and Blue* (1989). In a class apart, *Bring in da Noise/Bring in da Funk* (1996) transcended its dancing show ancestors by creating a tour de force of rhythmic counterpoint realized on suspended pots, pans, and buckets, as well as with the usual tap shoes. The original moves and sustained energy flowing from this show, glossed thinly with a historical veneer, electrified audiences in a lengthy cross-country tour after its New York success.

By the end of the twentieth century, most mainline commercial American popular music was dominated by historically black elements.

Some black-cast musicals of these same decades began to draw on the proven efforts of black playwrights, in such box office hits as *Purlie* (1970), based on Ossie Davis's *Purlie Victorious*, and *Raisin* (1973), taken from Lorraine Hansberry's *Raisin in the Sun*. Other less successful shows attempted to address the problems of modern black performers: *Doctor Jazz* (1975) and *The Tap Dance Kid* (1983).

Three major award-winning shows, *Ain't Misbehavin'* (1978, revived 1988), *Dreamgirls* (1981–1985), and *Jelly's Last Jam* (1992), emphasize the point that legendary figures from African American popular musical history were more apt than other subjects in this era to inspire dynamic products with substantial box-office appeal. As in the first decades of original African American musicals (1897–1927), the elements that most attracted audiences to the revivalist shows of the 1970s–1990s were syncopated songs, dazzling dance routines, powerful choruses, and distinctive solos. But something had changed.

By the end of the twentieth century, most mainline commercial American popular music was dominated by historically black elements. More important, rock in some form had superseded pre-rock and roll idioms on the Broadway stage itself, not only in the wider market. Tin Pan Alley ballads (typically featuring a chorus of four rhymed text phrases in thirty-two bars of music), the reliable building blocks of musicals since the 1910s, now almost always had to share the bill with songs inspired by the blues, ragtime, jazz, gospel, soul, or rock.

Perhaps the most self-conscious recognition of the dominance of black aesthetics in popular music (coupled with an intuition that Broadway was now ready to accept this fact) was the fantasy-parody *The Wiz* (1975, revived 1984), which took the 1939 film classic *The Wizard of Oz* as a springboard for reinterpreting the black experience in America. Scored by the skillful Charles Smalls, *The Wiz* ran for over 1500 performances, received numerous Tony and Drama Desk awards, and succeeded with viewers despite the doubts of hostile early critics. It did so because it was far more than a protest statement, revival, sequel, or imitative revue. Its vibrancy and unapologetic embrace of black vernacular language, matched with a flamboyant visual production and superb choreography, drew on a variety of sources. Its musical style was modern and rhythmic to the core, and its hit song ("Ease On Down the Road") spoke directly to a wide audience of all races.

Although the financial control of U.S. entertainment, including Broadway, was still firmly held by white corporate interests, the creative and aesthetic impulses that gave life to the stage were strongly African American by the end of the twentieth century. Only time will tell whether just compensation will ever be received by the originators of ragtime, jazz, and rock and roll.

REFERENCES

Cockrell, Dale. 1997. *Demons of Disorder: Early Blackface Minstrels and Their World.* Cambridge: Cambridge University Press.

Cook, Will Marion. 1947. "Clorindy, the Origin of the Cakewalk." *Theater Arts* 31(9):61–65.

Flanagan, Hallie. 1940. *Arena: The History of the Federal Theater.* New York: B. Blom.

Fletcher, Tom. 1984 [1954]. *The Tom Fletcher Story: 100 Years of the Negro in Show Business.* New York: Da Capo Press.

Graziano, John. 1990. "Black Musical Theater and the Harlem Renaissance Movement." In *Black Music in the Harlem Renaissance,* ed. Samuel A. Floyd, Jr., 87–110. Westport, Conn.: Garland Press.

Hatch, James V. 1970. *Black Image on the American Stage: A Bibliography of Plays and Musicals, 1770–1970.* New York: DBS Publications.

Hay, Samuel A. 1994. *African American Theater: A Historical and Critical Analysis.* Cambridge: Cambridge University Press.

Hughes, Langston, and Milton Meltzer. 1967. *Black Magic: A Pictorial History of the Negro in American Entertainment.* Englewood Cliffs, N.J.: Prentice-Hall.

Johnson, James Weldon. 1968 [1930]. *Black Manhattan.* New York: Arno Press.

Kimball, Robert, and William Bolcom. 1973. *Reminiscing with Sissle and Blake.* New York: Viking Press.

Peterson, Bernard L., Jr. 1993. *A Century of Musicals in Black and White.* Westport, Conn.: Garland Press.

Riis, Thomas L. 1989. *Just Before Jazz: Black Musical Theater in New York, 1890 to 1915.* Washington, D.C.: Smithsonian Institution Press.

———, ed. 1996. *The Music and Scripts of In Dahomey.* Vol. 5 of *Music of the United States of America.* Madison, Wis.: A-R Editions.

Sampson, Henry. 1980. *Blacks in Blackface: A Sourcebook on Early Black Musical Shows.* Metuchen, N.J.: Scarecrow Press.

Smith, Eric Ledell. 1992. *Bert Williams: The Pioneer Black Comedian.* Jefferson, N.C.: McFarland.

Southern, Eileen, ed. 1994. *African-American Theater: Out of Bondage (1876) and Peculiar Sam; or The Underground Railroad (1879).* Vol. 9 of *Nineteenth-Century American Musical Theater,* ed. Deane Root. New York: Garland Press.

———. 1997. *The Music of Black Americans: A History.* 3d ed. New York: Norton.

Stearns, Marshall, and Jean Stearns. 1968. *Jazz Dance.* New York: Schirmer.

Stuckey, Sterling. 1987. *Slave Culture.* New York: Oxford University Press.

Tilzer, Harry Von. 1903. *In Dahomey.* London: Keith, Prowse.

Woll, Allen. 1989. *Black Musical Theater: From Coontown to Dreamgirls.* Baton Rouge: Louisiana State University Press.

Religious Music
Mellonee V. Burnim

The dynamic role that music plays in the worship of black Americans has been well documented. From the vivid descriptions of songs shouted out in the invisible church of the black slave, to the music innovations standardized in the newly independent African Methodist Episcopal (A.M.E.) congregation founded by Richard Allen, we learn of the repertoire, performance practices, and function of the eighteenth-century genre called the folk spiritual. From twentieth-century accounts by scholars in religion such as Mays and Nicholson (1933) and Drake and Cayton (1970 [1945]) and such respected musicians as the composer John Work (1983 [1949]) of Fisk University renown, we learn of the transference of these musical concepts into the modern black religious context, resulting in the development of gospel music [see RELIGION, p. 116].

Negro spirituals and gospel music are the two indigenous musical genres that have historically dominated the worship of black Americans in the United States. Although music scholars have also documented the performance of lined hymns and psalms, traditional hymns, and songs from the Western European classical music literature in black religious services, Negro spirituals and gospel music are the religious music genres actually created *by* and *for* black people themselves and which therefore reflect African American musical genius.

Negro spirituals were the products of slaves; gospel songs emerged during the first quarter of the twentieth century among members of the urban working class—the lower economic and educational strata of the black community. Although spirituals and gospel music were created well over 100 years apart, contemporary research has shown that the two genres function similarly in religion and culture for black Americans (Burnim 1988:113; Levine 1978:174–177). The black composer John Work argues that gospel music of the 1930s and 1940s was "composed *by* [emphasis mine] the same people who formerly created the spiritual, and *for* [emphasis mine] the same people who used to worship by the spiritual" (1983 [1949]:288).

This discussion of African American religious music presents a chronological history of its development that addresses both similarities and distinctions between these two major genres. The meanings and interpretations of African American religious music will be discussed from the point of view of black people themselves. The dynamics of culture as a critical determinant of musical expression will be neither minimized nor ignored, for to understand black music it is absolutely essential to understand, as deeply as possible, the culture of its creators—the attitudes, values, and beliefs that shaped their approaches and responses to the American context.

FOLK SPIRITUALS

The earliest form of black religious music to develop in the United States was what is commonly referred to as the folk spiritual. The designation *folk* is necessary to distinguish this late-eighteenth-century creation from the arranged spiritual or concert version that emerged following the Civil War. The folk spiritual was an outgrowth of slavery; it was a uniquely African response to an institution that engaged in a systematic, though unsuccessful, attack on the cultural legacy of black people in America.

When introduced to Christianity, African slaves reinterpreted their religious instruction through an African cultural lens. From a sociocultural perspective, the development of the spiritual can actually be considered as an overt act of resistance to the subjugation imposed by Europeans. Consequently, the Negro folk spiritual symbolized black cultural identity and black religious expression as it evolved on North American soil (Chase 1987:214; Raboteau 1978:67–74; Waterman 1963).

The spiritual emerged in both the North and South as a genre distinctively different from music that characterized European American musical tradition of the period. In both contexts, the critical factor that allowed blacks to articulate and advance a unique musical identity was that of autonomy. In the South, the invisible church was the spawning ground. Whether in the ravine, gully, field, or living quarters, African American slaves fiercely guarded their privacy, not merely out of fear of reprisal but out of their collective desire to express themselves in a way that was uniquely meaningful to them. Testimony from ex-slave Lucretia Alexander shows how blacks sometimes merely tolerated white religious leadership, preferring instead to conduct worship in their own time and in their own way:

> The preacher came. . . . He'd just say, "Serve your masters. Don't steal your master's turkey. Don't steal your master's hawgs. Don't steal your master's meat. Do whatsomever your master tells you to do." Same old thing all the time. My father would have church in dwelling houses, and they had to whisper. . . . Sometimes they would have church at his house. That would be when they would want a real meetin' with some real preachin'. . . . They used to sing their songs in a whisper and pray in a whisper. That was a prayer-meeting from house to house once or twice—once or twice a week. (Raboteau 1978:214)

The character of worship among blacks during slavery was closely related to that of contemporary black worship. There was prayer, communal singing, testifying, and sometimes, but not always, preaching. The most striking aspects of the worship were evident in the manner in which these elements were expressed. Prayer was described as extemporaneous, typically moving from speech to song; congregational participation, in the form of verbal affirmations, was not only accepted but expected, and highly valued. Singing involved everyone present and was accompanied by hand clapping, body movement, and, if the spirit was particularly high, shouting and religious dance, both peak forms of expressive behavior.

The following account by Sarah Fitzpatrick, an Alabama slave, reiterates the desire of blacks to worship independently of whites, and illustrates the expressive freedom that blacks often found in doing so:

> Niggers commence to wanna go to church by de'selves, even 'ef dey had ta meet in the white church. So white fo'ks have deir service in de mornin' an' "Niggers" have deirs in de evenin; after dey clean up, wash de dishes, an' look a'ter everthing. . . . Ya see "Niggers" lack to shout a hole lot an' wid de white fo'ks al' round 'em, dey couldn't shout jes lack dey want to. (Raboteau 1978:225–226)

"The only way you can ban drumming is to destroy the drummer, because drumming does not exist in an instrument. It exists within a need . . . within a human spirit."

Ecstatic worship, in which participants expressed themselves through shouting, was commonplace in the invisible church. When spirits were particularly high, services sometimes lasted far into the night, the length being determined only by the collective energy that fueled the group (Raboteau 1978:220–222). Those principles that governed the character of the worship also governed the character of the songs sung during the worship. In these early spirituals, the African-derived call–response pattern serves in one instance as an agent for stability, with the constant repetition of the chorus that encourages everyone to participate. But at the same time, this call–response structure serves as an agent for musical change, with constant variation being provided through the solo. Throughout its history, African American music has nurtured this dynamic tension between unity and diversity, individuality and collectivity.

The sequential, staggered entrances highlight the polyrhythmic element of the folk spiritual. Bans on the use of loud musical instruments, especially drums, which could be used as signaling devices did not succeed in eliminating the percussive dimension so highly valued in African music. As Bernice Johnson Reagon, former Director of the Program in Black American Culture at the Smithsonian Institution and leader of the female a capella group Sweet Honey in the Rock, states: "The only way you can ban drumming is to destroy the drummer, because drumming does not exist in an instrument. It exists within a need . . . within a human spirit" (Grauer 1993). Ernest Brown refers to this cultural resourcefulness as "something from nothing" and "more from something" (Brown 1990).

The ring shout

The specific type of folk spiritual variously known as a shout, ring shout, or "running spirchil" (Allen, Ware, and Garrison 1965 [1867]:xv) is so called because of the element of dance incorporated into its performance. As one might imagine, the practice of dancing while singing religious songs was not introduced to the slave converts by white missionaries. In fact, the practice was abhorred by the black and white Christian establishment and labeled everything from "profane" to "heathenish." Because dance had been such an integral part of cultural expression among blacks in their West and Central African homeland, missionaries failed abysmally in their efforts to eradicate this practice in the United States. Instead, specific criteria established the ring shout as sacred; when dancing, participants did *not* cross their feet.

Performance practices

The establishment of the independent African Methodist Episcopal congregation under the leadership of Richard Allen set the stage for the autonomy that fostered the growth of the spiritual in the North. After separating from the white Methodist parent church in Philadelphia in 1787, Allen made a conscious choice to reject its domination and at the same time embrace its doctrines. Allen was quite satisfied with the "plain and simple gospel" of the Methodist church, which, in his view, well suited his own congregation because it was one that "the unlearned can understand and the learned are sure to understand" (Wesley 1969 [1935]:72). Allen's selective identification with Methodism was further evident in his decision to reject the standard Methodist hymnal, choosing instead to compile his own, which included songs he felt had greater appeal for black people.

The research of Portia Maultsby (1975), Eileen Southern (1983), William Tallmadge (1981), and J. R. Braithwaite (1987) in particular details the innovations that characterized the songs in Allen's hymnal. Texts were simplified, and refrain lines and choruses were routinely added. Southern suggests that Allen quite likely wrote some of the texts for his 1801 hymnal (the book contained no music); for tunes, he probably composed some himself and used popular songs of the day as well (Southern 1983:77). Allen's goal was to generate congregational participation and assure freedom of worship for his members (Maultsby 1975:413; Southern 1983:75).

Non-black observers of Allen's worship were frequently struck by the high level of congregational involvement in spirited singing. Not surprisingly, such early commentators did not hesitate to register their displeasure at the A.M.E. song style. The following reference is from an 1819 publication by John Watson, entitled *Methodist Error or Friendly Christian Advice to Those Methodists Who Indulge in Extravagant Religious Emotions and Bodily Exercises:*

> We have too a growing evil, in the practice of singing in our places of worship, *merry* airs, adapted from old *songs,* to hymns of our composing, often miserable as poetry and senseless as matter, and most frequently composed and sung by the illiterate *blacks* of the society. (Watson 1983 [1819]:62–63)

Southern speculates that Watson, a leading figure in the Methodist Church in Philadelphia, was actually referring to Bethel, the "dominant Black Methodists in the Philadelphia conference at the time" (Southern 1983:62). Watson poses further that Mr. Wesley, Methodist church founder, was equally displeased with those who chose to reject his hymnal for questionable substitutes. Watson notes that Wesley actually went as far as expelling three ministers "for singing '*poor, bald, flat, disjointed hymns:* and . . . singing the same verse over and over again with all their might 30 or 40 times, to the utter discredit of all sober christianity [sic]" (Watson 1983 [1819]:63). In his 1953 book *Negro Slave Songs in the United States,* Miles Mark Fisher confirms that "often Negroes were not permitted to enter Methodist church buildings at all since they disturbed quiet and dignified worship by beating out the rhythm of songs with feet patting and hands clapping in place of African instruments" (Fisher 1969 [1953]:35).

Both the song texts and the aesthetic principles that affirmed musical and textual repetition—hand clapping, foot stomps, and body movement—clearly met with great disapproval from the white Methodist establishment. It was especially disconcerting that blacks were known to use secular melodies in composing sacred songs. But Watson was even more annoyed with the blacks in the church who incorporated elements of dance in their songs:

> Here ought to be considered too a most exceptionable error, which has the tolerance at least of the rulers of our camp meetings. In the *blacks'* quarter, the coloured people get together, and sing for hours together, short scraps of disjointed affirmations, pledges, or prayers, lengthened out with long repetition *choruses.* These are all sung in the merry chorus-manner of the southern harvest field, or husking-frolic method, of the slave blacks. . . . With every word so sung, they have a sinking of one or other leg of the body alternately; producing an audible sound of the feet at every step, and as manifest as the steps of actual negro dancing in Virginia, &c. If some, in the meantime sit, they strike the sounds alternately on each thigh. What in the name of religion, can countenance or tolerate such gross perversions of true religion! (Watson 1983 [1819]:63)

The practices that governed performance by these renegade Methodists were virtually identical to those of the basic folk spiritual or ring shout, illustrating the ability of African Americans to transform genres that they themselves did not create into musical expressions with cultural relevance. Watson's attitude toward the folk spiritual was echoed by Daniel Alexander Payne, nineteenth-century minister, historian, and bishop of the A.M.E. church. People in the local churches viewed the shout as the essence of religion; rings were considered necessary for conversion. Bishop Payne likened the ring shout ritual to a "bush meeting"; the songs he called "cornfield ditties," and he referred to the participants as "ignorant but well meaning." His efforts to make the bands "disgusting" and to teach the "right, fit and proper way of serving God" were, for all practical purposes, an abysmal failure among the masses of his congregants (Payne 1983 [1888]:69). The following account of one of Payne's confrontations with this ritual is an illustration:

> After the sermon they formed a ring, and with coats off sung, clapped their hands and stamped their feet in a most ridiculous and heathenish way. I requested the pastor to go and stop their dancing. At his request they stopped their dancing and clapping of hands, but remained singing and rocking their bodies to and fro. This they did for about fifteen minutes. I then went, and taking their leader by the arm requested him to desist and to sit down and sing in a rational manner. I told him also that it was a heathenish way to worship and disgraceful to themselves, the race, and the Christian name. In that instance they broke up their ring but would not sit down, and walked sullenly away. After the sermon in the afternoon, having another opportunity of speaking alone to this young leader of the singing and clapping ring, he said: "Sinners won't get converted unless there is a ring." Said I, "You might sing till you fell down dead, and you would fail to convert a single sinner, because nothing but the Spirit of God and the word of God can convert sinners." He replied: "The Spirit of God works upon people in different ways. At camp-meeting there must be a ring here, a ring there, a ring over yonder, or sinners will not get converted." This was his idea, and it is also that of many others. (Payne 1983 [1888]:69)

Payne's view of appropriate music and behavior in worship was clearly aligned with those of Watson and other white Methodists. Those blacks most likely to agree with his perspective were, in his view, ones with some degree of education. Unquestionably, a perceptual rift between the folk and the educated elite was emerging.

THE ARRANGED SPIRITUAL

The next form of religious music expression to develop among blacks on U.S. soil was the arranged spiritual. Prior to the efforts of the Fisk Jubilee Singers in the early 1870s, the Negro spiritual was known and respected almost exclusively by blacks (Dett 1918:173; Southern 1983:225). With the formation of this group, however, the spiritual assumed a character and purpose that differed radically from its folk antecedent. The original group of eleven men and women, most ex-slaves, was established under the leadership of George White, the white university treasurer who viewed musical concerts as a viable way of raising much-needed funds for the fledgling institution. According to black composer and Fisk professor John Work III,

> Mr. White decided on a style of singing the spiritual which eliminated every element that detracted from the pure emotion of the song. . . . Finish, precision and sincerity were demanded by this leader. While the program featured Spirituals, variety was given it by the use of numbers of classical standard. Mr. White strove for an art presentation (Work 1940:15).

The folk spiritual created as an expression of African American culture and religion was now transferred to the concert stage. This change in function was accompanied by a

FIGURE I   Harry Burleigh, baritone and composer, popularized Negro spirituals among concert singers by arranging them for solo voice. Photo courtesy Photographs and Prints Division, Schomburg Center for Research in Black Culture, The New York Public Library; Astor, Lenox and Tilden Foundations.

change in performance practices. The hand clapping, foot stomping, and individual latitude in interpreting the melodic line that characterized the folk spiritual were replaced by predicability, controlled reserve, and the absence of overt demonstrative behavior. The aesthetic values that characterized George White's own musical culture were now being superimposed onto the Negro spiritual. As Louis Silveri argues, "Singing spirituals in the field was one thing, singing them to sophisticated audiences [read *white*] was something else" (1988:107).

University and college groups

Early recordings of the Fisk University quartet document the continuing presence of a cappella, syllabic singing, and the same use of call–response within the larger verse–chorus form as in the folk spiritual. The melodies of the folk spiritual serve as the point of departure for the arrangements grounded in Western European compositional technique. The dialect of the earlier spiritual form remains constant. However, the vocal quality of the singers performing these choral arrangements is generally more reflective of European ideals of timbre. Heterophony is replaced with clearly defined harmonic parts, and the element of dance is eliminated altogether. Whereas folk spirituals could be repeated for indefinite periods of time, performance of the arranged spiritual is bound by the dictates of the printed score.

The Fisk campaign was an overwhelming success, generating the formation of similar groups at other black colleges. This arranged spiritual tradition has come to symbolize the best in the black college choir tradition, with generations of black composers who established careers developing folk melodies for performance on the concert stage. Notable among many are John Work II (1873–1925) and John Work III (1901–1968), William Dawson (1899–1990), R. Nathaniel Dett (1882–1943), and Undine Smith Moore (1904–1989).

Harry T. Burleigh

In 1916, Harry T. Burleigh (1866–1949) (figure 1) became the first person to arrange the Negro spiritual for solo voice [see OVERVIEW, p. 572]. As soloist for St. George's Episcopal Church in New York City for fifty-two years, Burleigh experienced a continual need and desire to present new and fresh musical literature to the congregation. "Deep River," his first arrangement, has become a standard part of the solo spiritual repertoire. Distinguished from the choral arrangement by its use of piano accompaniment, the solo arrangement otherwise shares virtually identical aesthetic values with its choral counterpart.

Harry T. Burleigh is credited with starting the practice of closing recitals with a group of spirituals. The tradition has been sustained by other pioneering black vocalists such as Roland Hayes, one of the world's leading concert tenors from the 1920s to the 1940s, and Marian Anderson, who, in 1955, was the first African American to sing at the Metropolitan Opera. The solo arranged spiritual holds a place of pride and prominence in contemporary African American worship, particularly in congregations with significant numbers of members who are college educated.

TRANSITIONAL GOSPEL MUSIC

By the time gospel music started its slow but steady climb to acceptance and widespread popularity in the 1930s, the folk spiritual had been in existence for well over 100 years. The advent of gospel music was precipitated by the migration of blacks from rural to urban contexts during the years surrounding World Wars I and II (Ricks 1960:10–13; Williams-Jones 1970:205). The natural predisposition of the migrants to continue familiar patterns of behavior was evident in virtually every aspect of their new life in the city, ranging from patterns of dress and food preferences to musical performance and worship styles.

The tradition has been sustained by other pioneering black vocalists such as Roland Hayes, one of the world's leading concert tenors from the 1920s to the 1940s, and Marian Anderson, who, in 1955, was the first African American to sing at the Metropolitan Opera.

The one-room folk church of the rural South became the storefront church of the urban North—a key setting for the emergence of gospel music. As scholars of black religious music argue:

> Black urban religious music, particularly in the newly formed Pentecostal denomination, differed little from the folk spiritual of the rural South, except for instrumental accompaniment. Both song types were based on the call-response structure; both required a demonstrative style of delivery, complete with handclapping and dancing in the spirit; and both were sung in heterophony. (Burnim and Maultsby 1987:121)

Documenting the process of musical transformation that took place in southern urban churches during the 1940s, Fisk University professor John Work writes:

> A visitor to southern Negro folk churches will hear much interesting music. Some of the music will be from the traditional hymnody. Occasionally, traditional spirituals will be heard. . . . But he will hear also some exciting new music, which possibly will disturb him. . . . Most notable of course are the instruments which are being added to the singing today. The accompaniments are just as integral a part of the performance as is the singing and in a like manner, equally an expression of the folk. (1983 [1949]:136)

What made this new music both potentially exciting and disturbing at the same time was its radical challenge to the religious status quo, what Michael Harris (1992) refers to as the traditional or "old line" church establishment. During the period from 1900 to 1930, three forms of what I refer to as transitional gospel music emerged: (1) the gospel hymn style pioneered by Charles Albert Tindley in Philadelphia, (2) the rural gospel style that served as a sacred counterpart of the rural blues, and (3) the Holiness-Pentecostal style that first rose to prominence in the Church of God In Christ.

Tindley style

The grandfather of gospel music, Charles Albert Tindley (1851–1933), was the charismatic minister of Tindley Temple Methodist Church in Philadelphia. Tindley had been influenced by the doctrines of the holiness movement, and as a result some of the services at Tindley Temple were known to continue all night long, filled with spirited congregational singing, extemporaneous prayer, and songs that Tindley himself wrote to complement his sermons. However, as Tindley was a devout Methodist, the repertoire of his church also included European anthems that readily generated congregational response, even shouting (Reagon 1992:38).

The first of Tindley's gospel hymns was published in 1901. Among his total output of forty-six songs are his enduring compositions "We Will Understand It Better By and By," "Stand by Me," and "The Storm Is Passing Over" (Boyer 1992:58, 63). Considered representative of the gospel hymn, Tindley's compositions are distinguished from the Negro spiritual by the use of instrumental accompaniment. Tindley further contributed to the evolution of a unique gospel style, as Horace Boyer describes, "allowing space in his melodic line for the interpolation of the so-called blue thirds and sevenths, . . . and for the inevitable improvisation of text, melody harmony and rhythm, so characteristic of Black American folk and popular music" (Boyer 1992:57). Tindley's compositions maintain a link to the spiritual tradition by successfully incorporating call–response into the larger verse–chorus external structure.

Rural gospel

A second form of transitional gospel music emerged as a counterpart of the rural blues. Often sung by solo blues singers with guitar or harmonica accompaniment, this subgenre was characterized by the minimal chord changes and variable rhythmic structures that typified rural blues around the turn of the twentieth century. Performers who represented this style include Blind Willie Johnson and Blind Mamie Forehand, among others.

Holiness-Pentecostal style

It was in the context of the newly formed Pentecostal denomination that the third form of transitional gospel music evolved. In this setting, the "style and feeling" of the folk spiritual is most evident. Those congregations that evolved from the 1906–1908 Azuza Street Revival in Los Angeles, under the leadership of William J. Seymour, embraced a worship style that was uninhibited and highly demonstrative. Under the anointing of the Holy Spirit, congregants sang and danced with exuberance to the accompaniment of instruments shunned by the established denominations—trombones, trumpets, mandolins, even jugs.

Arizona Dranes was one of the most celebrated pioneers of the Holiness-Pentecostal style. Although her recording career spanned only two years (1926–1928), her highly rhythmic, percussive ragtime piano style and her powerful, shouted vocal leads represent the epitome of the high-energy delivery that characterizes Pentecostal worship even today. Dranes also recorded with evangelist F. W. McGee, another pioneer whose work is highly representative of this period and style.

TRADITIONAL GOSPEL MUSIC

During the 1930s, the genre of traditional gospel music emerged, created by the meshing of the above three strands of transitional gospel. The man who figured most prominently in this merger was Thomas A. Dorsey (1899–1993), now referred to as the Father of Gospel Music. Dorsey and two other important gospel music pioneers, Mahalia Jackson (1912–1972) and Roberta Martin (1907–1969), arrived in Chicago as a part of the great migrations. In the case of Dorsey and Jackson, these pioneering spirits brought with them a musical culture rooted in the sacred and secular traditions of the African American South; the northern context provided the impetus for the growth of something new.

Born in Villa Rica, Georgia (near Atlanta), the son of an itinerant Baptist preacher, Dorsey grew up playing organ in church. As a boy, however, he also worked selling soda pop at a vaudeville theater in Atlanta, where he was regularly exposed to such blues performers as Ma Rainey and Bessie Smith. Before devoting his career to gospel music, Dorsey became a prolific composer of both blues and jazz; he acknowledged how his gospel style was influenced by his background in secular music:

> This rhythm I had, I brought with me to gospel songs. I was a blues singer, and I carried that with me into the gospel songs. . . . I always had rhythm in my bones. I like the solid beat. I like the moaning groaning tone. I like the rock. You know how they rock and shout in the church. I like it. . . . Black music calls for movement! It calls for feeling. Don't let it get away. (Dorsey 1973:190–191)

Like Dorsey, Mahalia Jackson embraced both sacred and secular musics from childhood. A native of New Orleans, Jackson was raised Baptist, finding her place in the church choir at an early age. Her religious exposure also included the Pentecostal church, whose music she loved, located next door to her home. Although her aunt, who raised her, did not expose her to "worldly" music, Jackson seized the opportunity to listen to her older cousin's blues collection whenever her aunt was not at home. Her favorite performer was Bessie Smith, whose vocal quality she greatly admired and admittedly sought to imitate: "I remember when I used to listen to Bessie Smith sing 'I Hate to See that Evening Sun Go Down,' I'd fix my mouth and try to make tones come out just like hers" (Jackson 1966:36).

As did the folk spiritual, gospel music in its formative years faced staunch opposition and criticism. When Thomas Dorsey began to promote his compositions, he faced serious rejection, in part because the music was viewed as having unacceptable links to secular music. Dorsey recounts how initially most black preachers and congregations of established Baptist and Methodist churches viewed the music with derision: "Gospel music was new and most people didn't understand. Some of the preachers used to call gospel music 'sin' music. They related it to what they called worldly things—like jazz and blues and show business. Gospel music was different from approved hymns and spirituals. It had a beat" (Duckett 1974:5).

Joining forces with Mahalia Jackson, Dorsey initiated an "audience development" strategy that bypassed the black religious and musical establishment altogether by taking the music "to the streets" (Duckett 1974:6; Goreau 1975:56). Dorsey recalls:

> There were many days and nights when Mahalia and I would be out there on the street corners. . . . Mahalia would sing songs I'd composed, and I'd sell sheet music to folk for five and ten cents. . . . We took gospel music all around the country too. (Duckett 1974:6)

In 1932, Dorsey entered into an alliance with other gospel pioneering spirits—Sallie Martin, Theodore Frye, Magnolia Lewis Butts—in Chicago to form what was to become known as the National Convention of Gospel Choirs and Choruses. With the express purpose of promoting the performance and understanding of gospel music, this organization has grown from its initial nucleus of some two hundred to an international membership of more than three thousand (Moales 1993). The Dorsey model has spawned the growth of over a dozen comparable organizations, the largest of which is the James Cleveland Gospel Music Workshop of America, founded in 1969, that boasts annual attendance of more than 20,000 (Smith 1992).

The music that Thomas Dorsey, Mahalia Jackson, and other gospel pioneers promoted so fervently has now risen to a position of prominence in the worship of African Americans of virtually every denomination across this nation. It is sung by solo and ensemble, choir and quartet, men and women, young and old, black and white (figure 2). In contrast to the simple accompaniment of piano and organ that characterizes the early years of gospel, there are now no limits to the types of instruments used to complement the voice—from saxophone to synthesizer to symphony.

The gospel quartet has evolved to such an extent that it now garners significant scholarly attention (Allen 1991; Jackson 1988; Lornell 1988). Research indicates that the evolution of the gospel quartet closely parallels that of gospel music in general. The four-member male quartet first emerged under the sponsorship of such universities as Fisk and Hampton. Their repertoire consisted largely of Negro spirituals sung without instrumental accompaniment. Ethnomusicologist Joyce Marie Jackson indicates that the transition from spirituals to gospel began during the 1930s, when the quartet was expanded to five voices, which allowed the utilization of more than one lead singer while maintaining a full four-part harmonic background. Instrumental accompaniment became a part of the quartet performance style beginning in the 1940s with the guitar (Jackson 1988:125–127). Prominent gospel quartets who pioneered in the development and proliferation of this form include The Golden Gate Quartette

FIGURE 2   The Progressive Church of God in Christ Radio Choir, a traditional Gospel Choir, 1975. Photo help by the Chicago Public Library (Courtesy Steve and Sid Ordower).

FIGURE 3   The Golden Gate Quartette, a smaller traditional Gospel ensemble. Photo help by the Chicago Public Library (Courtesy Steve and Sid Ordower).

(figure 3), the Soul Stirrers, the Dixie Hummingbirds, the Five Blind Boys of Mississippi, the Swan Silvertones, the Fairfield Four, and the Highway QCs, among others (Lornell 1988:29).

CONTEMPORARY GOSPEL

The release of the recording "O Happy Day" by the Edwin Hawkins singers in 1969 ushered in the contemporary gospel era. Initially considered innovative because of its use of the Fender bass, bongos, and horns as accompaniment (which closely paralleled popular musics of the period), this recording represented the beginning of the development of the crossover market for gospel music. Sales of "O Happy Day" exceeded one million copies, well above the 50,000 to 70,000 units most typical for gospel recording artists, even in the 1990s (May 1994).

Both the instrumental accompaniment and the vocal arrangements of contemporary gospel music are virtually indistinguishable from secular musics of the day.

FIGURE 4   Contemporary Gospel Music artist, Ce Ce Winans, who was featured as part of Kirk Franklin's *Nu Nation Tour,* 1999. Photo courtesy Debbie May and The Lee Solters Company.

"O Happy Day" was originally pressed in 1968 by the forty-six-member Church of God In Christ Northern California State Youth Choir. Conceived as a fund-raising project, eight Edwin Hawkins arrangements were recorded with only two microphones in a single two-and-a-half-hour session in a church in Berkeley. The exposure that the original recording of "O Happy Day" received on underground radio, after the recording had fallen inadvertently into the hands of an Oakland rock promoter, placed it on a trajectory that the performers had never envisioned ("Edwin Hawkins Singers," *Sepia* 1969).

With the advent of the contemporary gospel music era, gospel moved beyond the protective confines of the black church to become a music that knew neither denominational, racial, cultural, nor musical boundaries. Although striking in its distinctiveness when it was first released, "O Happy Day" now falls into the category of traditional gospel music as the musical boundaries of gospel continue to expand. Following the lead of Edwin Hawkins, other artists began to emerge who included contemporary gospel music as a significant part of their repertoire—The Clark Sisters, The Winans (figure 4), Rance Allen, Andrae Crouch, and the New York Community Choir, among others.

Unlike traditional gospel music, which is embraced by soloist, small ensemble, and mass choir, contemporary gospel music is typically performed by small ensembles. The predictability of traditional gospel music, with its easily memorized melodic lines and parallel motion in the vocal parts, is replaced with more complex forms and harmonies. Both the instrumental accompaniment and the vocal arrangements of contemporary gospel music are virtually indistinguishable from secular musics of the day.

FIGURE 5   Contemporary Gospel Music group, Take 6, 1999. Photo by Norman Seefe.

FIGURE 6   Kirk Franklin, a contemporary Gospel Music artist whose music draws on Rap and Hip Hop. Franklin's music has topped the Gospel, R&B and Contemporary Christian charts in the 1990s, and he was the leading force behind the *Nu Nation Tour*. Photo courtesy Debbie May and The Lee Solters Company.

For example, the work of contemporary gospel music group Take 6 (figure 5) is rooted primarily in jazz, whereas recordings of Kirk Franklin exemplify the sound of rap, hip-hop, and funk. The music of multi-platinum-selling recording artist Kirk Franklin (figure 6), has crossed over to rhythm and blues charts as well as the Contemporary Christian chart, which reflects a breakthrough into the white Christian market.

CONCLUSIONS

The breadth and depth of black religious musical expression in the United States represent the cultural legacy and therefore the cultural *identity* of African-derived people in this nation. Whereas the distinctiveness of African American religious music genres reflects collective adaptation to an ever-changing sociocultural and political milieu, the continuities between the spiritual and gospel music are equally indicative of the existence of a self-defining core of cultural values among African Americans that have persisted over time.

Neither spirituals nor gospel music were created out of the African American's *inability* to satisfactorily reproduce the repertoire characteristic of Euro-Americans. On the contrary, African American religious music, from its beginning, must be viewed as both a conscious and willful expression of individual and collective agency, the desire of African Americans to articulate, embrace, and celebrate those beliefs, attitudes, and values that affirm and distinguish them as a people in the United States.

REFERENCES

Allen, Ray. 1991. *Singing In the Spirit: African American Sacred Quartets in New York City.* Philadelphia: University of Pennsylvania Press.

Allen, William Francis, Charles Pickard Ware, and Lucy McKim Garrison. 1965 [1867]. *Slave Songs of the United States.* New York: Oak Publications.

Boyer, Horace. 1992. "Charles Albert Tindley: Progenitor of African American Gospel Music." In *We'll Understand It Better By and By: Pioneering African American Gospel Composers,* ed. Bernice Johnson Reagon, 53–78. Washington, D.C.: Smithsonian Institution Press.

———. 1995. *How Sweet the Sound: The Golden Age of Gospel.* Washington, D.C.: Elliott & Clark Publishing.

Braithwhite, J. Roland. 1987. Introduction to *A Collection of Hymns and Spiritual Songs* by Richard Allen. Philadelphia: Mother Bethel African Methodist Episcopal Church, 1801.

Brown, Ernest. 1990. "Something from Nothing and More from Something: The Making and Playing of Musical Instruments in African American Cultures." *Selected Reports in Ethnomusicology* 8:275–291.

Burnim, Mellonee. 1985. "The Black Gospel Music Tradition: A Complex of Ideology, Aesthetic and Behavior." In *More Than Dancing,* ed. Irene V. Jackson, 135–169. Westport, Conn.: Greenwood.

———. 1988. "Functional Dimensions of Gospel Music Performance." *Western Journal of Black Studies* 12(2):112–121.

Burnim, Mellonee, and Portia Maultsby. 1987. "From Backwoods to City Streets: The Afro-American Musical Journey." In *Expressively Black,* ed. Geneva Gay and Walter Baber, 109–135. New York: Praeger.

Chase, Gilbert. 1987. *America's Music.* Rev. 3rd ed. Urbana: University of Illinois Press.

Dett, Robert Nathaniel. 1918. "The Emancipation of Negro Music." *Southern Workman* 47:172–176.

Dorsey, Thomas A. 1973. "Gospel Music." In *Reflections on Afro-American Music,* ed. Dominique-Rene' deLerma, 189–195. Ohio: Kent State University Press.

Drake, St. Clair, and Horace R. Cayton. 1970 [1945]. *Black Metropolis: A Study of Negro Life in a Northern City.* New York: Harcourt, Brace and New World.

Duckett, Alfred. 1974. "An Interview with Thomas Dorsey." *Black World,* July 4–18.

"Edwin Hawkins Singers: 'O Happy Day.'" 1969. *Sepia* 18(8):66–68.

Epstein, Dena. 1977. *Sinful Tunes and Spirituals: Black Folk Music to the Civil War.* Urbana: University of Illinois Press.

Fisher, Miles Mark. 1969 [1953]. *Negro Slave Songs in the United States.* 2nd ed. New York: Citadel Press.

Franklin, Aretha. 1999. *Aretha: From These Roots.* New York: Villard.

Franklin, Kirk. 1998. *Church Boy: My Music and My Life.* Nashville: Word Publishing.

Goreau, Laurraine. 1975. *Just Mahalia, Baby.* Waco, Texas: Word Books.

Grauer, Rhoda, creator and executive producer. 1993. *Dancing: New Worlds, New Forms.* Thirteen/WNET and RM Arts. Chicago: Home Vision. Videorecording.

Harris, Michael. 1992. *The Rise of Gospel Blues: The Music of Thomas A. Dorsey in the Urban Church.* New York: Oxford University Press.

Hinson, Glenn. 2000. *Fire in My Bones: Transcendence and the Holy Spirit in African American Gospel.* Philadelphia: University of Pennsylvania Press.

Jackson, Joyce Marie. 1988. "The Performing Black Sacred Quartet: An Expression of Cultural Values and Aesthetics." Ph.D. dissertation, Indiana University.

Jackson, Mahalia. 1966. *Movin' On Up.* New York: Hawthorn Books.

Jones, Bobby. 1999. *Touched by God: Black Gospel Greats Share Their Stories of Finding God.* New York: Pocket Books.

Levine, Lawrence. 1978. *Black Culture and Black Consciousness.* New York: Oxford University Press.

Lincoln, E. Eric, and Lawrence H Mamiya, eds. 1990. *The Black Church in the African American Experience.* Durham, N.C.: Duke University Press.

Lornell, Kip. 1988. *"Happy in the Service of the Lord": Afro-American Gospel Quartets in Memphis.* Urbana: University of Illinois Press.

Marsh, J.B.T. 1876. *The Story of the Jubilee Singers.* London: Hodder and Stoughton.

Maultsby, Portia. 1975. "Music of Northern Independent Black Churches during the Antebellum Period." *Ethnomusicology* 19(3):401–420.

May, Debbie. 1994. Tyscot Records. Personal interview. Indiana University, Bloomington.

Mays, Benjamin, and Joseph Nicholson. 1933. *The Negro's Church.* New York: Institute of Social and Religious Research.

Moales, Kenneth. 1993. President, National Convention of Gospel Choirs and Choruses. Personal interview. Indianapolis.

Oliver, Paul. 1984. *Songsters & Saints: Vocal Traditions on Race Records.* New York: Cambridge.

Payne, Daniel Alexander. 1983 [1888]. "Recollections of Seventy Years." In *Readings in Black American Music,* 2nd ed., ed. Eileen Southern, 65–70. New York: Norton.

Raboteau, Albert. 1978. *Slave Religion.* New York: Oxford University Press.

Reagon, Bernice Johnson. 1992. "Searching for Tindley." In *We'll Understand It Better By and By: Pioneering African American Gospel Composers.* ed. Bernice Johnson Reagon, 37–52. Washington, D.C.: Smithsonian Institution Press.

Ricks, George Robinson. 1960. "Some Aspects of the Religious Music of the United States Negro: An Ethnomusicological Study with Special Emphasis on the Gospel Tradition." Ph.D. dissertation, Northwestern University.

Silveri, Louis. 1988. "The Singing Tours of the Fisk Jubilee Singers: 1870–1874." In *Feel the Spirit: Studies in Nineteenth-Century Afro-American Music,* ed. George R. Keck and Sherrill V. Martin. Westport, Conn.: Greenwood Press.

Smith, Ed. 1992. Executive director, Gospel Music Workshop of America. Personal interview. Cincinnati.

Southern, Eileen. 1983. *The Music of Black Americans: A History.* 2nd ed. New York: Norton.

Tallmadge, William. 1981. "The Black in Jackson's White Spirituals." *The Black Perspective in Music* 9(2):139–160.

Ward-Royster, Willa. 1997. *How I Got Over: Clara Ward and the World-Famous Ward Singers.* Philadelphia: Temple University Press.

Waterman, Richard. 1963. "On Flogging a Dead Horse: Lessons Learned from the Africanism Controversy." *Ethnomusicology* 7(2):83–87.

Watson, John F. 1983 [1819]. "Methodist Error." In *Readings in Black American Music,* 2nd ed., ed. Eileen Southern, 62–64. New York: Norton.

Wesley, Charles. 1969 [1935]. *Richard Allen: Apostle of Freedom.* Washington, D.C.: Associated Publishers.

Williams-Jones, Pearl. 1970. "Afro-American Gospel Music: A Brief Historical and Analytical Survey (1930–1970)." In *Development Materials for a One-Year Course in African Music for the General Undergraduate Student,* ed. Vada E. Butcher, 201–219. Washington, D.C.: U.S. Department of Health, Education and Welfare.

Winans, CeCe. 1999. *On a Positive Note.* New York: Pocket.

Wolff, Daniel. 1995. *You Send Me: The Life and Times of Sam Cooke.* New York: Quill.

Work, John. 1940. *American Negro Songs and Spirituals.* New York: Bonanza Books.

———. 1983 [1949]. "Changing Patterns in Negro Folk Songs." In *Readings in Black American Music,* 2nd ed., ed. Eileen Southern, 281–290. New York: Norton.

Blues
David Evans

Historical Background and Context
Distinctive Characteristics of Blues
Popularization of the Blues

During the first decade of the twentieth century, the term *blues* began to be applied to a new type of song emerging from black communities in the southern United States. These songs were new and different both in their formal and musical characteristics and in the topics and attitudes they expressed in their lyrics. They are discussed in contemporary accounts of folklorists and other observers and in later reminiscences of people who were involved in music at this time. The fact that blues songs seem to turn up everywhere in the Deep South more or less simultaneously—in rural areas, small towns, and cities such as New Orleans and Memphis—suggests that the form had been developing for a few years and probably allows us to place its origins in the 1890s.

HISTORICAL BACKGROUND AND CONTEXT

Blues was not the only new musical development to emerge in the decades surrounding the turn of the century. Instead it should be viewed as part of a wave of innovation in black American music at this time that also saw the first stirrings of ragtime, jazz, gospel music, and barbershop-style vocal harmony. This occurred in conjunction with significant new developments in literature, theater, and the arts in general, as well as in black political and religious life. This creativity coincided with a hardening of white resistance to black social and economic progress in the form of Jim Crow laws and the institutionalization of racial segregation, disenfranchisement of black voters, lynching and other forms of terrorism, and the loss of jobs to the swarm of new European immigrants. It was a time of the end of the American dream that had once seemed attainable for black Americans following Emancipation. A new generation that had grown up to see the erosion of its parents' hard-won freedom had to create new responses to its realization of the American situation. Earlier black folk and popular music had consisted largely of folk and concert versions of spirituals, minstrel material, and instrumental dance music played on the fiddle and other instruments, as well as work songs and children's game songs. Many of the singers and musicians had some degree of white patronage. The new musical genres all exhibited in various ways a turning inward toward utilization of black folk-musical resources, an adaptation of Western form, harmony, and instrumentation to characteristically black style, and a greater reliance on black audiences for monetary support and approval. With emphases on the performer, the creative composer, improvisation, soloing, and self-expression, the new music became more introspective, self-absorbed, individualistic, serious, and worldly at the very time that the majority of whites were viewing all blacks as an undifferentiated social caste with stereotyped mental and behavioral traits that cast them as ignorant, humorous, and carefree. The new types of music would challenge these stereotypes and lead the way in the black struggle for freedom, justice, and equality throughout most of the twentieth century.

Of all the new types of black music created at this time, blues was the most self-contained. Throughout their history blues songs have mainly been sung solo, although duet and quartet performances and background vocalizing are not unknown. The singers, especially males, usually play an instrument; in folk blues this has generally been a guitar, piano, or harmonica. Many male folk blues singers have preferred to perform solo, as have some female singers, although most of the latter have been accompanied by a single, usually male, pianist or guitarist. Even when other instruments are added, as is the case in most types of popularized blues forms, great emphasis is placed on individual expression and improvisation. Sometimes entire performances of blues—lyrics, melodies, and instrumental work—are improvised, and although some performers are highly creative in this respect, many are also aided by a body of shared and familiar lyric and musical ideas and formulas that they recombine in constantly changing ways.

European and African elements

Like most forms of black American music created in the nineteenth and twentieth centuries, blues combines elements from the European and African musical traditions. The European elements occur especially in the areas of form, harmony, and instrumentation. The use of a recurring multiphrase strophic form and basic I-IV-V harmonies in the instrumental accompaniment are clearly attributable to Western influence. The major solo and ensemble instruments are all commercially manufactured items well known in Western music, although some secondary instruments used occasionally in blues, such as washboards, jugs, kazoos, and homemade one-stringed zithers, are re-interpretations of originally African instruments. The uses to which the Western instruments are put in the blues, however, would often not be described by European-trained musicians as proper or legitimate in terms of Western music, and most of the modifications in playing technique and resultant sound are attributable to the influence of the African musical tradition. As will be noted below, the Western elements of form and harmony are also frequently altered in ways that can best be explained by reference to African patterns. Beyond this, the African elements in the blues are found chiefly in the area of style, particularly in the music's rhythmic, tonal, and timbral flexibility. Although it makes enough reference to Western norms to sound familiar to Western ears, it has essentially broken free from the notion of strict duple or triple meters and rhythmic patterns, scales with fixed intervals in multiples of 100 cents, a semitone, and idealized vocal and instrumental tone. Western musical aesthetics have, of course, broadened in the face of this challenge.

The American blues tradition has often been likened to that of the griots, members of a professional caste of musical entertainers found widely in the West African savanna region, the region that contributed a significant portion of the United States black population. Among the similarities that have been pointed out are the degree of professionalism of both types of performer, their often itinerant existence, their perceived low social status, their preference for stringed instruments, the use of a declamatory and melismatic singing style, and their songs of frank social commentary. These similarities do, indeed, suggest an African savanna origin for some elements in the blues, but it would be wrong to view blues performers simply as biological or cultural descendants of griots. Most of these characteristics can also be found elsewhere in Africa, elements from other African geographical traditions can be detected in the blues, and many of the typically African elements in the blues are simply pan-African. There is also the space of most of the nineteenth century to be accounted for between the arrival of the last griots in the United States and the beginnings of the music known as the blues. Whatever specific elements can be compared, and there are many, no complete counterpart to the blues has yet been found in any specific African ethnic group or musical genre.

Early forms that influenced the blues

If the Old World sources of the blues are rather far in its historical background, there were other, more recognizable, musical genres in existence at the end of the nineteenth century that can be identified as significant factors in the synthesis that resulted in the creation of the blues. The basic melodic resources of the blues seem to be largely derived from the field holler, a type of solo unaccompanied work song found in the rural South, characterized by great melodic, timbral, and rhythmic freedom and forceful delivery. To this one could add as influences the more individualized and improvisatory forms of religious vocal expression, such as moaning, chanted prayer, and preaching. Most blues singers throughout the twentieth century were exposed to both farmwork and the church and had plenty of opportunity to listen to and participate in these vocal genres.

The harmonic and structural form of blues comes mainly from the folk ballad. In the later decades of the nineteenth century, black American singers had adapted this originally European narrative folk song genre, until by the 1890s they had begun to create original ballads about characters and subjects of interest within the black community, often about individuals who stood outside the bounds of the law and of organized society (for example, "Stagolee," "Frankie and Albert," "Railroad Bill") or whose actions were in some way "bad" and bold (for example, "Casey Jones"). Many of these new ballads had instrumental accompaniments at fast tempos and used a three-line form consisting of a rhymed couplet plus a one-line refrain with the harmonies of each line beginning with the I, IV, and V chords, respectively. Instrumental accompaniment and the three-line form, which were black American innovations and had not been characteristic of the Euro-American ballad tradition, were adapted to the melodic material of the field holler and solo religious expression, and the outlaw content of many of the ballads undoubtedly contributed as well to the personal stance adopted by many blues singers. In the course of this adaptation, the rapid tempo of the ballads was generally slowed to accommodate the new types of couples dances such as the "slow drag," that were becoming popular at this time and with which the blues would come to be associated. It is one of the great strengths and accomplishments of the blues that it managed to synthesize elements of songs associated with work and religion on the one hand and a carefree, worldly existence on the other.

Contexts for blues performance

The geographical hearth area of the blues is the plantation country of the Deep South, stretching from the interior of Georgia to eastern Texas. Most blues singers were born and raised in this region. The music underwent a less intense, though still significant, development in Virginia and the Carolinas, and was even less developed in the border states and southern mountain regions and along the Atlantic and Gulf coasts. Within the large hearth area, certain regions, such as the Mississippi Delta and the river bottomlands of southeastern Texas, have proved especially important as places of innovation. Over the course of the twentieth century, artists from these and other regions of the hearth area migrated to cities both within the area and outside it, especially in the Midwest and California, bringing their rural styles with them and contributing to new urban musical syntheses. Over the years, blues has exhibited musical and lyrical traces of its southern rural origins as well as evidence of the desire of many performers and audience members to escape those origins.

From the beginning blues were performed as a means of making money. Some of the rural musicians were farmers and sharecroppers, and some urban musicians held weekday jobs, performing blues only on weekends.

Although blues performance sometimes occurs as a solitary activity or in intimate settings such as courtship, it has always been most often found in situations where an audience is present. It exists as music for both listening and dancing, the two often occurring in the same context. In the rural South the most common setting was the house party or outdoor picnic. Another common institution, the juke house or juke joint, was a structure, often a residence, temporarily or permanently set up for music, dancing, drinking, eating, and other activities. In the towns blues musicians would gather and perform at cafés and saloons, on sidewalks and street corners, in parks, in railroad and bus stations, and inside and in front of places of business. In the cities blues were sung in vaudeville theaters, saloons, cabarets, and at house parties, as well as in parks and on streets. Traveling tent and medicine shows often hired blues performers, providing opportunities for local and sometimes extended travel. Most of these settings persisted in black American communities until the end of the 1950s, but since then the main locations have been clubs and auditoriums. Concerts and festivals, both within and outside the black community, have provided additional settings for blues music in recent years.

For the first two decades of the twentieth century blues was generally performed alongside other types of folk and popular music. Most blues performers born in the nineteenth century and the first few years of the twentieth had eclectic repertoires that might also include ragtime pieces, older social dance songs, ballads, versions of popular songs, and even spirituals. Those born after about 1905 increasingly came to identify themselves as blues singers and often concentrated on this genre exclusively. From the beginning blues were performed as a means of making money. Some of the rural musicians were farmers and sharecroppers, and some urban musicians held weekday jobs, performing blues only on weekends. Often they could make as much in music on a weekend as a person could working all week at another job. Some used this weekend work to enable themselves and their families to live better. Others saw it as a way to make money for good times, and yet others as a way to avoid more onerous types of work during the week. The latter often became itinerant professional performers, working circuits of house parties, juke joints, clubs, or theaters. Blind and other handicapped performers also joined their ranks, often becoming some of the outstanding virtuosos and creative figures in the blues. Because blues performers were often involved in an underworld of gamblers, bootleggers, pimps, and prostitutes, blues music and blues singers gained an unsavory reputation for much of the music's history. However, this reputation has steadily improved since the 1960s, as many of the older contexts for the music have faded out of existence.

DISTINCTIVE CHARACTERISTICS OF BLUES

Although many elements of blues can be traced to antecedent musical forms, this genre was a distinct synthesis that has had an enormous impact on American and world music. Several characteristics of the blues were shocking and challenging to the norms of Western music and American popular music. They entered the larger musical world for the first time through the blues and have come to be associated with blues ever since, although some are now commonplace throughout popular music. Four characteristics in particular have this special association with the blues.

Blues texts

Blues lyrics are extremely frank and almost exclusively concerned with the self, though in relation to others. They are not only sung primarily in the first person, but when directed toward another person or about someone else, they deal with the interaction between the other person and the singer. Rather than telling stories in a chronological fashion, blues songs express feelings and emotions or describe actions based on them. These may be the real feelings and activities of the singer or those of a persona created by the singer, an exaggerated or dramatized self. The lyrics are realistic (as opposed to idealistic), nonsentimental, and serious (as opposed to light or frivolous). They may incorporate exaggeration or boasting, but these are to be taken as amplifications of essential truths. They may (and often do) contain humor, but this is usually as an expression of irony, cleverness, double or multiple meaning, or social commentary and criticism, not as an illustration of buffoonery or stupidity. This realism and seriousness, combined with the concentration on the self and a willingness to delve into sadness, deep feelings, emotions, and confessions, are probably responsible for the appellation *blues,* which became attached to this music at an early stage. Although just as many of the songs express optimism, confidence, success, and happiness, it is this melancholy or depressed side of the range of emotions that has given the genre its familiar name.

The songs deal with a full range of human feelings and describe the ups and downs of daily life. The most prominent subject by far is love and sex. This is followed by travel; work, poverty, and unemployment; alcohol, drugs, gambling, and trouble with the law; sickness and death; magic and hoodoo (often in connection with these other themes); and current events from the singer's point of view or involvement. Many of these topics rarely had been discussed before in American popular song, except in a trivial, sentimental, idealized, or moralistic way. The highly secular content of blues, its concentration on the self in the here and now, and its expression of certain emotions and subject matter that are beyond the bounds of polite society have caused it to be viewed by many both within and outside the African American community as low-down, self-centered, or even "the devil's music." On the other hand, a more positive view expressed by some intellectuals and some blues singers themselves stresses the existentialist quality of blues lyrics, their emphasis on self-reliance and self-sufficiency, and their often outstanding poetic quality.

The role of instruments

An instrument or group of instruments plays a necessary role in the construction and performance of the song itself, rather than serving simply as a more or less optional harmonic and rhythmic background to the vocal part. The instrumental part is, in fact, a second voice (sometimes several voices), punctuating and responding to the vocal lines. It is therefore an integral part of the piece itself. The role of instruments as voices is well known in most forms of African music and their New World derivatives, but seldom has the instrument had such a close conversational dialogue with the singing voice as it has in the blues. This sort of dialogue was certainly not common in nineteenth-century American popular song, but through its use in the blues and the influence of blues on other popular genres it has become commonplace.

The blue note

As the term itself suggests, blues introduced the concept of the blue note into American music. This term is used rather loosely, but essentially it means a note, sounded or suggested, that falls between two adjacent notes in the standard Western division of the octave into twelve equal intervals. Blue notes are thus sometimes described as neutral pitches and can be notated by an upward- or downward-pointing arrow printed above a note, which functions in the same way as a sharp, flat, or natural sign. These arrows, however, are not such precise indicators of pitch, because the neutral note can fall anywhere within the space of 100 cents. Blue notes are especially common at the third and seventh degrees of the scale, but they can occur at other points as well, including even such a normally stable place as the fifth. In actual practice, blue notes can be far more than neutral pitches. In fact, a variety of pitches within a single neutral range might be used in a song, suggesting aural shadings. A blue note might be expressed as a slur, usually upward from the flat toward the natural, or as a wavering between flat and natural or two other points within the interval. It might also occur as the simultaneous sounding of the flat and natural pitches or simply their use at different times in a piece, suggesting tonal ambivalence or compromise. Finally, it might simply be expressed by the sounding of a flat where a natural would be expected.

Blue notes are easy enough to achieve with the voice, but they can also be played on many instruments by the use of special techniques to "bend" notes, for example, pushing the strings on the neck of the guitar, special tonguing and blowing methods for the harmonica, woodwinds, and horns, glissandos on the slide trombone, and the slide or "bottleneck" technique on the guitar. On fixed-pitched instruments such as the piano, blue notes can only be suggested by rapid alternation of adjacent notes, a flat grace note before a natural, or the simultaneous sounding of flat and natural in a chord or in the separate melodic lines played by the two hands. Pianists have been especially ingenious in turning this emblematic instrument of Western music into a blues vehicle.

Blue notes are found in most but not all blues, leading some to use the term "blues scale." There actually is no single scale for all blues. Many pieces are pentatonic, whereas others are hexatonic and heptatonic, if one views the shading within the interval of a semitone as variations of a single scale step. The term, however, is simply a convenient designation for a scale that differs from a typical Western major or minor one by containing blue notes. Such scales certainly existed in black American folk music before the blues, but the blue notes in them were generally dismissed by musically literate observers as "wild" or "barbaric" sounds. The creation of the term "blue notes" helped greatly to give legitimacy to these sounds and make them seem less exotic. Blue notes are quite clearly an extension of African musical practices and sometimes additionally an attempt to come to terms with Western instruments whose keyboards, fretboards, valves, and fingering holes are not designed to enable the player to achieve them easily. Blue notes thus can be seen to represent symbolically both a tension between an African musical legacy and a superimposed Western system as well as a successful resolution of this tension. With respect to the African legacy, blue notes may be simply continuations of elements from African scales that employed intervals other than multiples of semitones (for example, the modes commonly found in the music of the African savanna), or they may be derived from African approaches to harmony in which singers often make slight adjustments to the pitches of notes in order to produce a richer harmonic blend. Whatever the case, blue notes have now become so familiar in American and world popular music that they are generally taken for granted and have lost their former exotic associations.

Blues forms

The majority of blues utilize the twelve-bar AAB form or some variant or approximation of it. At its most basic, the stanza consists of a line of verse (A), the same line repeated, and a third line (B) that rhymes with the first two (figure 1). Usually the B

FIGURE I   A typical twelve-bar blues stanza in the key of C major with measure divisions and imlied harmonies.

| C | C | C | C |

I'm going away, and I won't be back till fall.

| F | F | C | C |

I'm going away, and I won't be back till fall.

| G | F | C | C |

If my mind don't change, I won't be back at all.

line explains, amplifies, comments on, or contrasts with the A line, rather than following from it chronologically. Each line occupies only slightly more than the first half of a four-measure section, the other portion consisting of an instrumental response to the vocal, although the instrumental part is also heard during the singing and interacts with it. The first line usually begins with the suggestion of a tonic chord harmony, the second with the subdominant, and the third with the dominant, each of them resolving in the tonic chord by the time of the instrumental response. The third line usually passes through the subdominant on the way to the tonic figure. This simple form can be altered in a number of ways. For example, a rhymed couplet can occupy the entire first four bars, which would normally be filled by the A line and its instrumental response. The last eight bars remain the same, occupied by two lines and their instrumental responses, but these now become a refrain repeated in every stanza. The harmonic scheme can also be varied through chord substitutions, the use of passing harmonies (all serving to make the piece more harmonically complex), or through simplification to two chords or only one (that is, a strictly modal piece without any suggestion of chord changes). The number of bars can also be shortened or lengthened from the standard twelve. There are, in addition, eight-bar (two-line) and sixteen-bar (four-line) blues with their own typical harmonic patterns as well as variations, and there are some blues that are conceived in a more or less free-form manner without apparent reference to one of these standard patterns. The repetition of the A line, textually and often melodically, is a device typically found in much African music, whereas the use of a repeated multiphrase form with harmonic changes is more typically European. Another device that often occurs in the blues and that links it to the African tradition is the use of repeated short melodic-rhythmic phrases or riffs. A riff can be used both to extend the instrumental response to vocal lines and as a background behind the vocal lines, serving as an identifying marker for an entire piece. Usually several different or variant riffs are used in a single blues where this concept occurs. The twelve-bar AAB form and the use of riffs entered the mainstream of American popular music through the blues and have now become so commonplace that they are seldom noticed.

POPULARIZATION OF THE BLUES

Even from the time of its folk music origins, blues has been a commercial music in the sense that it has usually been performed with the expectation of some kind of monetary reward. It should not be surprising, then, that blues almost immediately entered the world of popular entertainment and the mass media [see TECHNOLOGY AND MEDIA, p. 235]. During the first decade of the twentieth century, almost every black community in a city or a larger town, both in the South and elsewhere, had a least one vaudeville theater serving its entertainment needs. Traveling tent shows, minstrel shows, medicine shows, and circuses also brought entertainment to these communities as well as to many of the smaller towns that could not sustain a full-time theater. Thus, there were opportunities for support of an entire class of professional black singers, musicians, dancers, and comedians, as well as composers and managers.

The Great Depression effectively killed the institution of vaudeville and the blues style that was associated with it.

By 1910 there were reports of songs called blues being sung and played by vaudeville entertainers, and twelve-bar and other typical blues strains could be detected occasionally in published ragtime piano compositions. In 1912 four songs were copyrighted with the word *blues* in their titles, including W. C. Handy's "The Memphis Blues." Black-owned publishing houses, such as Handy's in Memphis and that of Clarence Williams in New Orleans, began turning out dozens of blues in the following years. A number of southern black vaudeville singers became closely identified with this new music and rose to the status of stars, among them Gertrude "Ma" Rainey, Butler "String Beans" May, and Bessie Smith. They sang the published blues hits, their own compositions, and adaptations of folk material. Many of the vaudeville and sheet music creations that were called blues were actually popular songs or instrumental pieces in the ragtime style but incorporating one or more blues strains (for example, twelve-bar AAB) and blue notes [see MUSICAL THEATER, p. 614]. Blues were also commercially recorded at this time by vocalists and dance and jazz bands, all of them white, indicating that blues had achieved a national popularity and identity as a distinct new type of music.

Recordings

In 1920 vaudeville singer Mamie Smith became the first black vocalist to record blues commercially, having hits with "That Thing Called Love" and "Crazy Blues," both of them compositions of fellow vaudevillian Perry Bradford (figure 2). Her success resulted in the recording of many other vaudeville blues stars during the 1920s, most of them women, accompanied by a small jazz combo. At first the songs were generally the compositions of professional songwriters in the multistrain format of ragtime music, but with blue notes and the occasional twelve-bar AAB strain. Representative singers in this style, besides Mamie Smith, were Lucille Hegamin, Alberta Hunter, Trixie Smith, Lizzie Miles, Ethel Waters, and Edith Wilson. By 1923, however, a new wave of singers entered the studios, singing songs more often made up of variants of a single AAB strain and accompanied typically by a pianist, sometimes with one or two added jazz instruments. By this time more of the songs were composed by the singers themselves. Some of the more prolific and successful artists in this style were Bessie Smith, Ma Rainey, Ida Cox, Rosa Henderson, Clara Smith, Viola McCoy, Sippie Wallace, Sara Martin, Bertha "Chippie" Hill, and Victoria Spivey [MAMA YANCEY AND THE BLUES, p. 103].

A few self-accompanied male vaudeville performers had recorded in the early and mid-1920s, such as Sylvester Weaver, Papa Charlie Jackson, and Lonnie Johnson, but in 1926 a wave of folk blues artists on record was launched by the recordings of Blind Lemon Jefferson. Through the early 1930s many recordings were made of solo-guitar- or piano-accompanied blues singers, mostly male, presenting to a national audience the sounds typically heard at southern juke joints and barrelhouses and urban rent parties. Some of the important singer-guitarists who followed Jefferson in this period were Blind Blake, Blind Willie McTell (figure 3), Barbecue Bob, Sam Collins, Tommy John-

FIGURE 2   1920 sheet music cover of Perry Bradford's composition "Crazy Blues," advertising Mamie Smith's recording, the first recorded blues vocal by an African American singer. Sheet music courtesy Richard Raichelson. Photo by David Evans.

TRACK 13

FIGURE 3   Studio portrait photograph of Blind Willie McTell, Georgia blues singer and twelve-string guitarist, one of the first folk blues artists to make commercial recordings. Atlanta, 1930s or 1940s. Photo courtesy David Evans.

son, Charley Patton, Son House, Jim Jackson, Furry Lewis, Robert Wilkins, and Ramblin' Thomas, while barrelhouse pianists included Clarence "Pine Top" Smith, Speckled Red, Charles "Cow Cow" Davenport, Charlie Spand, Henry Brown, and Esau Weary (figure 4). Guitar duos, such as those of Memphis Minnie and Kansas Joe (McCoy) or the Beale Street Sheiks (Frank Stokes and Dan Sane), and the combination of harmonica and guitar, as in the work of Bobbie Leecan and Robert Cooksey, were also popular at this time. So, too, was the combination of piano and guitar, first popularized in 1928 in the recordings of Leroy Carr and Scrapper Blackwell and those of Georgia Tom (Dorsey) and Tampa Red (Hudson Whitaker).

Blues musicians also formed larger groups made up of various combinations of string, wind, and percussion instruments known as jug bands, skiffle bands, juke bands, washboard bands, string bands, and hokum bands. Some of the better known recording groups of this sort were the Memphis Jug Band, Cannon's Jug Stompers, Whistler's Jug Band, the Mississippi Sheiks, and the Hokum Boys. All of these duos and small groups were especially prominent in urban centers of both the South and North, allowing rural migrants to find common ground in their solo performance styles, explore new musical directions, and compete with more established urban musicians.

The Great Depression effectively killed the institution of vaudeville and the blues style that was associated with it. As the recording industry began to recover in the early 1930s, Chicago became the primary center of blues recording activity, and the studios concentrated on stables of reliable stars, who could sing, play their own accompaniment, help one another on records, and compose original songs to supply the increasing number of jukeboxes (figure 5). This was a decade of consolidation and homogenization in the blues. The primary instruments of folk blues were brought into small ensembles (or made to suggest their sounds), as exemplified by the work of guitarists Big Bill Broonzy and Robert Johnson, pianist Roosevelt Sykes, and harmonica player John Lee "Sonny Boy" Williamson. Other stars of this period, who sometimes performed on one another's records, were Washboard Sam, Bumble Bee Slim, Jazz Gillum, Peetie Wheatstraw, Walter Davis, Curtis Jones, Johnnie Temple, Georgia White, Lil Johnson, Merline Johnson, Rosetta Howard, Lil Green, Bill Gaither, Blind Boy Fuller, Kokomo Arnold, and Arthur "Big Boy" Crudup. In 1936 the Harlem Hamfats, a

FIGURE 4   Esau Weary, one of the last of the Piney Woods and sawmill camp blues pianists in southeastern Mississippi and Louisiana. Angie, Louisiana. Photo by David Evans, 1970.

FIGURE 5   Advertisement for "race records" of blues, *The Chicago Defender,* 2 June 1928.

seven-piece group based in Chicago and made up of Mississippi blues and New Orleans jazz musicians, pioneered a new type of blues combo sound that was a precursor of the modern blues band. Small combos continued to be popular into the 1940s, gradually adopting a louder and more rhythmic style known as jump blues. Further jazz and pop influences were heard during this decade in the singing styles of such crooners as Cecil Gant, Charles Brown, and Ivory Joe Hunter, and shouters such as Wynonie Harris, Roy Brown, and Big Joe Turner. Female singers such as Dinah Washington, Ella Johnson, Nellie Lutcher, Julia Lee, Hadda Brooks, and Big Maybelle served as counterparts to the male crooners and shouters. These styles were especially prominent in urban centers of the Midwest and California, where many African Americans had migrated during and after World War II. Most of these artists sang other material besides blues, and their familiarity with popular and jazz styles enabled their blues to approach and enter the American popular musical mainstream.

Also coming to prominence in the late 1930s and 1940s was a piano blues style known as boogie-woogie. Essentially, it is a type of rhythmic barrelhouse piano that features repeated bass figures, or riffs, often transposed to fit the tune's harmonic structure, over which the right hand plays lines that are to some degree improvised and often in a counterrhythm to the bass. Boogie-woogie is attested from the 1910s and was recorded sporadically in the 1920s and more frequently from 1929 following the success of "Pine Top" Smith's "Pine Top's Boogie Woogie." It entered spectacularly into the world of popular music through presentations at Carnegie Hall by Meade Lux Lewis, Albert Ammons, and Pete Johnson in 1938 and 1939. These artists, along with Jimmie Yancey, Camille Howard, and many others, popularized this style through the 1940s. It was often adapted by guitarists as well as swing bands and had a great influence on jazz, country and western, gospel, and the emerging rock and roll.

The electric guitar

The electric guitar was an important factor in new blues sounds that came to prominence in the late 1940s and 1950s. The guitar's role in small combos was enhanced by the louder volume and new timbres of the electric instrument, played alongside the piano and the harmonica, itself now also played through a microphone and amplifier. Such recently arrived southern musicians as Muddy Waters (McKinley Morganfield), Howlin' Wolf, Little Walter, Jimmy Reed, and Elmore James pioneered in these small electric blues combos in Chicago and other cities during this period. At the same time, a new jazz-influenced hornlike lead style of playing, featuring extensive string bending, was being developed in the cities of the West Coast and South by guitarists Aaron "T-Bone" Walker, Lowell Fulson, Clarence "Gatemouth" Brown, Pee Wee Crayton, B. B. King, and others, working usually with larger bands containing horn sections. The electric guitar also gave new life to the tradition of solo-guitar-accompanied folk blues, as exemplified in the music of artists Sam "Lightnin'" Hopkins and John Lee Hooker.

Soul blues

During the 1950s and reaching full fruition in the 1960s, a melismatic, emotional, gospel-influenced singing style, known as soul blues, became popular, as one hears in the work of B. B. King, himself a pioneer in the modern lead guitar style. Other early soul blues singers were Bobby "Blue" Bland, Ray Charles, and James Brown. None of these artists or those who followed them have restricted their singing only to blues material. This singing style, along with the introduction of the electric bass and organ toward the end of the 1950s, is perhaps the last major stylistic innovation in blues, whose popular contemporary sound is not much different from that of the 1960s (figure 6).

FIGURE 6   Members of the Hollywood All Stars, a contemporary blues band performing in a neighborhood club in Memphis, Tennessee. *Left to right:* Herbert Bryant, Ben Wilson, Calvin Valentine. Photo by David Evans, 1989.

Blues tunes form a major part of the repertoire of early jazz, and one can hardly imagine jazz music at all without blue notes, improvisation, and many other qualities doubtless introduced mainly through the blues.

Expansion of the blues audience

It was during the 1960s, however, that large numbers of white Americans, as well as people overseas, began to take an interest in blues music. This interest included historical research, recording, sponsorship of concerts and tours, and participation in the performance of the music itself. This expansion of the blues constituency from its original black American base has resulted in increased opportunities for performers as well as a revival of many older blues styles that had lost much of their popularity with the original audience. After approximately a century of survival in a kind of cultural, social, and musical underground, blues has emerged to gain worldwide respect and recognition as a distinct and influential type of music.

The role of blues in American popular music

In addition to having its own history and stylistic development, blues has played an important role in most other major popular musical genres in the United States. Its intrusion into ragtime in the first two decades of the twentieth century has already been mentioned. The tonal flexibility and improvisational performance style of blues probably hastened the decline of ragtime itself. Blues tunes form a major part of the repertoire of early jazz, and one can hardly imagine jazz music at all without blue notes, improvisation, and many other qualities doubtless introduced mainly through the blues. The blues has continued to anchor a number of new jazz styles, most notably bebop. Country music had absorbed the blues form by the 1920s, its first major manifestation being the blue yodel as popularized by Jimmie Rodgers [see COUNTRY AND WESTERN, p. 76]. Blues continued to be a major ingredient in the western swing and honky-tonk styles of the 1930s through the early 1950s and has made a comeback in contemporary country rock styles. Many early rock and roll performers of the 1950s, such as Elvis Presley, Carl Perkins, and Jerry Lee Lewis [see ROCK, p. 347], had a background in country music, which they fused with newly acquired skills in the blues inspired by contemporary black artists. Many black performers of this time, in fact, made important contributions to rock and roll, such as Little Richard, Chuck Berry, Fats Domino, and Bo Diddley, performing music that was largely blues based. Many rock styles of the 1960s, such as surf music, British rock, and psychedelic rock, made considerable use of blues repertoire and style, and blues experienced a resurgence within rock in the 1990s. Blues also influenced gospel music through the increased use of blue notes and instrumentation, particularly the guitar [see RELIGIOUS MUSIC, p. 624]. One of the leaders in introducing blues elements was Thomas A. Dorsey in the 1930s, himself an ex-blues singer, pianist, and songwriter. Rap artists also have continued to sample blues riffs from earlier recordings [see HIP-HOP AND RAP, p. 692]. Finally, a number of important twentieth-century composers in the classical tradition, such as George Gershwin and William Grant Still, were greatly influenced by blues [see OVERVIEW OF MUSIC IN THE UNITED STATES, p. 519]. If one also considers the profound influence of blues on the popular musics of Europe, Asia, Latin America, and Africa, blues would have to be a strong candidate for being the most influential music of the twentieth century.

REFERENCES

Bastin, Bruce. 1986. *Red River Blues: The Blues Tradition in the Southeast.* Urbana: University of Illinois Press.

Cohn, Lawrence. ed. 1993. *Nothing But the Blues.* New York: Abbeville.

Cowley, John, and Paul Oliver, eds. 1996. *The New Blackwell Guide to Recorded Blues.* Oxford: Blackwell.

Dixon, Robert M. W., et al. 1997. *Blues and Gospel Records, 1890–1943.* 4th ed. Oxford: Clarendon Press.

Evans, David. 1982. *Big Road Blues: Tradition and Creativity in the Folk Blues.* Berkeley: University of California Press.

Ferris, William. 1978. *Blues from the Delta.* New York: Anchor.

Groom, Bob. 1971. *The Blues Revival.* London: Studio Vista.

Handy, W. C. 1970. *Father of the Blues.* New York: Collier.

Harris, Sheldon. 1979. *Blues Who's Who.* New Rochelle, N.Y.: Arlington House.

Harrison, Daphne Duval. 1988. *Black Pearls: Blues Queens of the 1920's.* New Brunswick, N.J.: Rutgers University Press.

Hart, Mary L., et al. 1989. *The Blues: A Bibliographical Guide.* New York: Garland.

Keil, Charles. 1966. *Urban Blues.* Chicago: University of Chicago Press.

Kubik, Gerhard. 1999. *Africa and the Blues.* Jackson: University Press of Mississippi.

Leadbitter, Mike, and Neil Slaven. 1987. *Blues Records 1943–70: A Selective Discography.* London: Record Information Services.

Leadbitter, Mike, et al. 1994. *Blues Records, 1943–1970.* Vol. 2. London: Record Information Services.

Lomax, Alan. 1993. *The Land Where the Blues Began.* New York: Pantheon.

Merwe, Peter van der. 1989. *Origins of the Popular Style: The Antecedents of Twentieth-Century Popular Music.* Oxford: Clarendon Press.

Oliver, Paul. 1960. *Blues Fell This Morning.* London: Cassell.

———. 1969. *The Story of the Blues.* London: Barrie and Rockliff.

———. 1970. *Savannah Syncopaters: African Retentions in the Blues.* New York: Stein and Day.

Oster, Harry. 1969. *Living Country Blues.* Detroit: Folklore Associates.

Palmer, Robert. 1981. *Deep Blues.* New York: Viking Press.

Pearson, Barry Lee. 1984. *Sounds So Good to Me: The Bluesman's Story.* Philadelphia: University of Pennsylvania Press.

Rijn, Guido van. 1997. *Roosevelt's Blues: African-American Blues and Gospel Songs on FDR.* Jackson: University Press of Mississippi.

Rowe, Mike. 1975. *Chicago Blues: The City and the Music.* London: Eddison Press Ltd., 1973. Reprint, New York: Da Capo Press.

Russell, Tony. 1970. *Blacks, Whites, and Blues.* New York: Stein and Day.

Santelli, Robert. 1993. *The Big Book of Blues: A Biographical Encyclopedia.* New York: Penguin.

Silvester, Peter J. 1989. *A Left Hand Like God: A History of Boogie-Woogie Piano.* New York: Da Capo Press.

Titon, Jeff Todd. 1977. *Early Downhome Blues: A Musical and Cultural Analysis.* Urbana: University of Illinois Press.

Jazz
Ingrid Monson

Jazz is widely regarded as the pinnacle of African American music in the twentieth century, distinguished by the originality of its improvisation, the virtuosity and erudition of its performers and composers, and its professionalism and artistry. Many of its practitioners regard jazz as America's classical music, or African American classical music, although this definition is sometimes contested. The respectability acquired by jazz in the late twentieth century stands in stark contrast to the denigrated status of the music and its practitioners earlier in the century. Several broader social forces have shaped the history of jazz and its changing cultural meaning in the twentieth century, including urbanization, racism, the advent of recording and broadcasting technology, modernism as an aesthetic ideology, two world wars, and the civil rights movement. The musical hallmarks of jazz are improvisation, syncopation, a rhythmic propulsiveness known as swing, a blues feeling, and harmonic complexity. Unlike in most other African American musical genres, instrumental rather than vocal performance has been most prestigious and influential.

JAZZ AND RAGTIME

Several genres contributed to the formation of jazz, including ragtime, blues, marches, African American religious music, European classical music, American popular song, and musical theater. It is important to remember that these genres overlapped considerably, as the close relationships among ragtime, musical theater, and jazz at the turn of the twentieth century illustrate. Although ragtime is today most often associated with the piano compositions of Scott Joplin (1868–1917), audiences of the 1890s associated ragtime with song, especially so-called coon songs featuring lyrics about black Americans, many of which emerged from the thriving African American musical theater scene in New York. Among the most noted black American musical composers and performers of the day were Ernest Hogan (1860–1909), Will Marion Cook (1869–1944), Bob Cole (1863–1911), the Johnson brothers (J. Rosamond [1873–1954] and James Weldon [1871–1938]), Bert Williams (1874–1922), and George Walker (c. 1873–1911).

After the success of Ernest Hogan's "All Coons Look Alike to Me" (1896), which launched a fad for coon songs lasting until World War I, many of the pioneers of mainstream American musical theater began composing ragtime songs, including George M.

Cohan (1878–1942) and Irving Berlin (1888–1989). Images of African Americans in ragtime song were largely stereotypical—derived from the representational conventions of minstrelsy and vaudeville—and contributed to a debate over ragtime's merits within both the black community and mainstream American society. White society objected to the popularity of this "lowbrow" art form (at the expense of "better" European classical music), while black elites objected to the denigrating racial images in the songs.

Although ragtime made its initial impact on the musical stage, instrumental ensembles including dance bands, brass bands, and concert bands soon incorporated it into their repertoires. Piano versions of ragtime song were also published, and, in time, a distinctive piano repertoire emerged whose chief composers were Scott Joplin, James Scott (1886–1938), and Joseph Lamb (1887–1960). Perhaps the most famous piano rag, which was widely performed by pianists and instrumental ensembles, is Joplin's "Maple Leaf Rag" (1899). In addition, both sung and instrumental versions of ragtime songs were associated with popular dances of the day, including the two-step, the cake-walk, the turkey trot, and the Texas tommy. By 1913 ragtime figured prominently in a craze for social dancing that witnessed the rise to prominence of dancers Vernon (1887–1918) and Irene Castle (1893–1969). The Castles chose James Reese Europe's Society Orchestra to accompany them at their dance club, known as Castle House. This collaboration led to the first recording contract offered to a black ensemble— Europe's recording of "Down Home Rag" made in December 1913. Europe, who lived from 1881 to 1919, recorded four more pieces in February 1914 including "Castle House Rag," which is based on the form of Joplin's "Maple Leaf Rag."

The most common trait associated with ragtime is syncopation. To "rag" a piece was to syncopate its melody. Instrumental ragtime made extensive use of 2/4 meter and march form—sixteen-bar strains or themes organized into various patterns. The most common formal arrangement consisted of two themes in the tonic key (AB or ABA) followed by a trio section consisting of one or two themes in the subdominant key. March forms are widely found in early jazz. Musical innovations leading to the development of jazz as a distinctive genre occurred within instrumental ensembles that included ragtime as part of their repertoire. New Orleans occupies a special place in this process.

NEW ORLEANS

Historians place the origins of the jazz in New Orleans during the first years of the twentieth century, concurrent with the heyday of ragtime. Cornetist Buddy Bolden's band, which established a distinctive sound between 1897 and 1907, is often considered the first jazz band. Bolden (1877–1931) was known for his improvisational elaboration of melodies, an ability to play very loudly (legend has it that he could be heard across Lake Pontchartrain), and his deep feeling for the blues. Bolden's competition in New Orleans included both bands and dance bands that featured a variety of repertoire, including marches, ragtime, and waltzes. Around 1900, brass bands, which generally had featured the careful execution of written arrangements, began admitting "ear" musicians or "routiners," who created head arrangements and brought a more improvisational and blues-inflected style to the music. Brass bands were particularly important in transforming a straight march beat into the slow drag and up-tempo strut, the two basic feels of New Orleans jazz style.

Hardening racial relations in New Orleans at the end of the nineteenth century shaped the emergence of jazz as a distinctive genre. Increased contact between French-speaking Creole musicians and English-speaking African Americans was a byproduct of the emergence of Jim Crow laws in the 1890s and the use of the "one drop" rule of racial classification that enforced them. Under this criterion persons of as little as 1/32 black ancestry (sometimes even less) were considered black regardless of appearance. The traditionally three-tiered New Orleans racial hierarchy that recognized white, Creole, and black hardened into a two-tiered structure recognizing only black and white, especially after the *Plessy v. Ferguson* decision in 1896 (the Supreme Court decision that established the doctrine of "separate but equal").

Creoles of color *(gens de couleur),* who were predominantly Catholic, of French-speaking heritage, and generally of light complexion, resided "downtown" and had long cultivated an instrumental virtuosity, musical literacy, and training in classical music. They considered themselves superior to their English-speaking and less musically literate black neighbors, who resided predominantly "uptown." Uptown musicians were noted for the blues, their improvisational abilities, and their abilities as ear musicians. The emergence of jazz as an instrumentally virtuosic, improvisational tradition that also valued musical literacy emerged from a meeting of uptown and downtown. Among the Creole musicians most important to the development of jazz are pianist and composer Jelly Roll Morton (Ferdinand LeMothe, 1890–1941), clarinetist Barney Bigard (1906–1980), trombonist Kid Ory (1890–1973), and clarinetist and saxophonist Sidney Bechet (1897–1959). The most pathbreaking early soloists were uptown musicians, among them cornetist Joe "King" Oliver (1885–1938) and trumpeter Louis Armstrong (1901–1971).

CHICAGO

Despite the longstanding notion that jazz traveled up the Mississippi to Chicago (a legend that overlooks the fact the river does not pass through Chicago), California (Los Angeles and San Francisco) was an equally important market for jazz before 1917. The bands of Freddie Keppard and Kid Ory were among the many that brought jazz to California between 1914 and 1922. Chicago, nevertheless, holds a special place in the history of 1920s jazz, for it was there that Louis Armstrong's bold and virtuosic improvisational style became the talk of the town and ultimately set the direction for jazz.

In the summer of 1922 King Oliver asked Louis Armstrong to join his band in Chicago. Oliver's band played along "The Stroll," a thriving nightlife district on South State Street featuring several African American–owned clubs—the Deluxe Café, the Pekin, and the Dreamland Café. These and other clubs became sites of racial boundary crossing as interested young whites came to enjoy the music, among them saxophonist Bud Freeman (1906–1991), cornetist Jimmy McPartland (1907–1991), clarinetist Frank Teschemacher (1906–1932), and drummer Dave Tough (1908–1948). Many of Chicago's south side clubs were "blacks-and-tans," cabarets that presented African American performers and catered to both black and white audiences.

Chicago in the early 1920s tolerated greater racial mixing in such venues than New York did. Nevertheless, racial boundary crossing in Chicago was not reciprocal, for black musicians and audience members could not patronize north side white clubs. Despite the reputation of jazz as a cultural arena where there was greater interracial contact during the Jim Crow years than in other arenas of American cultural life, it is important to remember that whites had far greater mobility in crossing the color line.

Between 1925 and 1928 Louis Armstrong made a series of recordings for OKeh (arranged by his wife and pianist Lil Hardin [1898–1971]) with groups known as the Hot Five and the Hot Seven. These are among Armstrong's most celebrated recordings, and they virtually defined the expansive improvisational style that was to become the hallmark of early jazz. Armstrong moved away from melodic paraphrase to a more elaborate improvisation guided by the underlying harmonies rather than the melody alone. Armstrong's solo on "Potato Head Blues" (figure 1) offers an excellent example of his classic style. Note the expressive use of vibrato at the ends (and sometimes beginnings) of phrases, the use of arpeggiation (measures 2, 6, 8, 22), and the chromatic fills between chord tones (measures 16–17).

Armstrong's bandmates in the Hot Five included Lil Hardin, piano; Johnny Dodds (1892–1940), clarinet; Kid Ory, trombone; and Johnny St. Cyr (1890–1966),

FIGURE I Louis
Armstrong's solo on
"Potato Head Blues"
(1988).

banjo—the last three old friends from New Orleans. The Hot Seven added Baby Dodd (1898–1959), drums, and Pete Briggs, tuba. John Thomas, trombone, and Earl Hines (1903–1983), piano, were occasional sidemen. Despite the fact that these recordings were made in Chicago and that there are many earlier recordings by other bands that include improvised solos, Armstrong's style set the standard for New Orleans jazz. The Hot Five and Hot Seven recordings also established Armstrong as a cultural hero, especially in African American communities, where his tremendous success contributed to a communal sense of pride.

COMPOSERS, ENSEMBLES, AND BIG BANDS

Although the emergence of the improvising soloist is the hallmark of jazz, it is important to note that the development of the jazz ensemble (large and small) was also key. Indeed, a particular sound produced through distinctive rhythmic, harmonic, melodic, and timbral vocabularies of the ensemble are just as crucial to defining jazz as a genre as improvisation is. Among the early jazz composers and arrangers who contributed to this emerging sound were Jelly Roll Morton, Duke Ellington (1899–1974), Fletcher Henderson (1897–1952), and Don Redman (1900–1964).

Jelly Roll Morton's 1926 recordings for Victor provide examples of the creative use of the ensemble in early jazz. Among the most highly regarded compositions from these sessions are "Black Bottom Stomp," "Grandpa's Spells," "The Chant," and "Smokehouse Blues." Unlike the Hot Five recordings, which omitted bass and drums, these recordings feature one of the best rhythm sections in early jazz—Morton, piano; John Lindsay (1894–1950), bass; Andrew Hilaire, drums; and Johnny St. Cyr, banjo. In "Black Bottom Stomp," Morton and his band deploy a full range of early jazz time-feels to provide contrast and excitement to the well-planned architectural shape of the performance. The A sections of the piece proceed with a two-beat feel in cut time (bass notes on one and three). The B sections include examples of two-measure solo breaks, stop time (repetition of short-pattern as the sole accompaniment), and extended solos.

There were several keys to producing this sound—the use of a straight mute, an ordinary bathroom plunger to produce the wah-wah sound, a literal growl in the throat of the trumpeter, and the simultaneous humming of a pitch into the horn.

One B section proceeds partly in a four-beat time-feel played by the brass, a technique foreshadowing the classic walking bass line that became standard in the jazz of the 1930s. This passage is also an example of double time, a section in which the initial tempo of the piece is doubled for dramatic effect. Morton's final chorus might also be said to foreshadow the ubiquitous "shout chorus" of swing band arrangements. Here Morton's ensemble uses a back beat feel (drum on two and four) for a rousing final chorus featuring trumpet and trombone.

In New York of the 1920s Fletcher Henderson and Don Redman developed a big band sound by incorporating jazz soloists such as Louis Armstrong and Coleman Hawkins (1904–1969) into a dance band of larger instrumentation than that of the typical New Orleans jazz ensemble. Henderson's band featured three trumpets, a trombone, three reeds, and a rhythm section. Henderson and Don Redman worked as a team, developing an arranging style that featured call and response between the brass and reed sections and the use of one instrumental choir as an accompanimental background (often featuring a riff) for the other. Redman also wrote ensemble sections in the style of improvised jazz solos. All these devices and techniques became staples of big band arranging in the 1930s.

The composer who developed the most unique style for jazz ensemble in the 1920s was undoubtedly Duke Ellington. Ellington's singular style combined the "sweet" (that is, not blues inflected) dance band style with the exuberant New Orleans and blues-inspired trumpet style of New Yorker Bubber Miley (1903–1932) and Ellington's own stride- and ragtime-based piano style. Miley pioneered the growling trumpet sound that became a trademark of Ellington's so-called jungle sound. There were several keys to producing this sound—the use of a straight mute, an ordinary bathroom plunger to produce the wah-wah sound, a literal growl in the throat of the trumpeter, and the simultaneous humming of a pitch into the horn. Ellington's recordings of "East St. Louis Toodle-Oo" and *Black and Tan Fantasy* from 1926 to 1927 provide excellent examples of Miley's "talking" brass effect. Tricky Sam Nanton (1904–1946) adapted this sound to the trombone, and thereafter mastery of the growl sound was an essential for brass players in the Ellington band.

These new brass sounds were only one aspect of Ellington's interest in timbral variety and unusual orchestration. "Mood Indigo," one of the composer's most famous ballads, features an opening trio of muted trumpet, muted trombone, and clarinet that is as easily identifiable by timbre as by thematic content. The trumpet plays in a comfortable middle register, while the trombone plays in a higher tessitura and the clarinet in the low register, creating a combination of relaxation and tension in a beautifully harmonized passage (figure 2).

Ellington makes careful use of contrary motion, augmented ninth sonorities (with the ninth in the bass), and chromatic voice leading to produce an unforgettable moment. Although Ellington's musical effects are interesting analytically, Billy Strayhorn (1915–1967), Ellington's compositional collaborator, argued that there is something more to Ellington's sound: "Each member of his band is to him a distinctive tone

FIGURE 2   "Mood Indigo" (1938).

color and set of emotions, which he mixes with others equally distinctive to produce a third thing, which I like to call the Ellington Effect. Sometimes this mixing happens on paper and frequently right on the bandstand. I have often seen him exchange parts in the middle of a piece because the man and the part weren't the same character. Ellington's concern is with the individual musicians, and what happens when they put their musical characters together" (Tucker 1993:270).

In 1927 Duke Ellington got his first major break when he was hired at the Cotton Club, a Harlem nightclub catering to a whites-only clientele and decorated in plantation motif. The Cotton Club featured shows combining music, exotic dancing (some performed in pseudo-African garb), and theatrical presentation. The Ellington orchestra, now expanded from six to eleven members, provided to the wealthy white clientele the "primitive" ambience they were looking for, often through sophisticated musical means beyond their imagination. The club's regular radio broadcasts during Ellington's tenure (1927–1932) brought the "Ellington Effect" into America's living rooms and made him a national figure.

BROADCASTING AND THE SWING ERA

Radio broadcasts from major hotels, clubs, and dance halls were crucial in establishing and maintaining the reputations of the bands headed by Benny Goodman (1909–1986), Tommy Dorsey (1905–1956), Count Basie (1906–1984), and Duke Ellington, among others. There were two types of radio broadcasts, "sustaining programs" originating late at night from hotels and clubs and featuring a variety of bands, and "sponsored programs," for which a company such as Coca Cola or Lucky Strike hired particular bands for long-term contracts. Access to these radio opportunities was racially structured, with white bands at an advantage in both types of engagements. White bands were more likely to be booked at hotels and clubs with radio broadcast capability as most such venues had segregated booking policies. Even so, many black bands were able to make appearances on sustaining programs from locations that did hire black bands such as the Cotton Club, the Savoy Ballroom, or Chicago's Grand Terrace. Sponsored programs were out of the question for black bands. Not until 1946 was there an all-black sponsored radio program—NBC's *Nat King Cole Trio Time*—and even guest appearances on white programs by prominent black musicians were rare.

Segregation in the public arena caused interracial collaborations of various kinds to occur in less visible ways. Hiring arrangers from across the color line was one way; recording (but not appearing) with a mixed ensemble was another. Fletcher Henderson's compositions and arrangements, which Goodman bought in 1934, served as the principal component of the band's repertoire as it established its national profile. Goodman later hired African Americans Henderson and Jimmy Mundy (1907–1983) as staff arrangers for the band and defied the performance color line by hiring Lionel Hampton (b. 1908) and Charlie Christian (1916–1942). Teddy Wilson (1912–1986) recorded with the Benny Goodman trio a year prior to his famous 1936 appearance with the bandleader at Chicago's Congress Hotel. Although a considerable amount of interracial mixing had taken place in black venues from the very beginning, the mixing in a predominantly white setting was what was newsworthy about this event.

The ambivalent reception of Benny Goodman's title "King of Swing," especially later in the twentieth century, stems from the racially structured aspects of his rise to prominence. Goodman's story serves to illustrate several themes in ongoing debates over the relationship between black and white jazz. In late 1934 Goodman was offered a regular slot on NBC's *Let's Dance,* a radio program sponsored by the National Biscuit Company. In choosing Goodman, NBC overlooked many prominent black bands including those of Duke Ellington, Earl Hines, and Jimmie Lunceford (1902–1947). Goodman's success on the show was fueled by Fletcher Henderson's compositions and arrangements, and thus many white audience members came to know the swing music of an African American composer through the medium of white performance. Consequently, swing did not appear to be black music to the broader white public. This perception was reinforced by Jim Crow barriers that kept African American bands from being heard through the same high-visibility broadcast channels. That Goodman as an individual took actions facilitating the employment of African Americans in mainstream white dance bands (generally in advance of other white bandleaders) cannot be denied, yet he was also a beneficiary of the racial status quo in the music industry.

Swing music

The major big bands of the swing era served as important training grounds for younger musicians. Many improved their music-reading skills, understanding of harmony, ensemble skills, and (for some) composing and arranging skills under the tutelage of more experienced musicians. One hallmark of swing music is the extensive use of riffs (short ostinato figures) as ensemble textures. Riffs were used in many ways: (1) as melodies; (2) in call and response with another riff or an improvised passage; (3) as a continuous supporting texture underneath a soloist or written passage; and (4) in layers. Two shout choruses of Count Basie's "Sent for You Yesterday" (1938) (figure 3) illustrate these usages. In chorus seven, two riffs are presented in call and response between the brass and the reeds. The drums play the classic swing ride rhythm on the hi-hat cymbals, and the bass plays a walking bass, four to the bar. In chorus eight the reeds play a continuous supporting riff while the brass riff (functioning as the melody) continues in call and response with improvised drum breaks. Here the call and response of the brass and drums is layered against the continuous accompanimental riff in the reeds. Shout choruses such as these were often used at the very end of a piece as a climax. The artful use of repetition, which served as a solid anchor for dancers, was another hallmark of swing style.

Many virtuosic soloists emerged in the 1930s, from small groups as well as big bands. Expanding on Armstrong's lead, musicians strove to extend the scope of solo improvisation. Among the most prominent soloists were Roy Eldridge (1911–1989), trumpet; Lester Young (1909–1959) and Coleman Hawkins, tenor saxophone; and Art Tatum (1909–1956), piano. Vocalist Billie Holiday (1915–1959), whose inventive paraphrases of melody and timing inspired many, including Lester Young, also became prominent in the late 1930s, recording with many members of the Count Basie orchestra.

BEBOP

With World War II came not only a new aesthetic in jazz but a new attitude in African American communities as well. The Double V campaign (which called for victory over racism at home as well as victory for democracy in Europe) perhaps symbolized the transition best, as African Americans deemed fit to risk their lives in battle chafed at the glaring racial injustices at home. As Scott DeVeaux (1997) has noted, professional jazz musicians were a relatively privileged elite who worked in an industry that accorded greater personal freedom, mobility, and prosperity than did most occupations available to black Americans. The symbolic value of that hard-won success and freedom to the broader African American community was enormous.

FIGURE 3   Two shout choruses of Count
Basie's "Sent for You Yesterday" (1938).

By the late 1940s bebop had acquired a subcultural quality that shunned mainstream "squares." Bebop style included the use of "bop talk" (drawn from African American vernacular speech), a critique of the racial status quo, and the unfortunate fashionability of heroin.

During the war years musicians who had become frustrated with the limited possibilities for extended improvisation in big bands and dismayed by the dominance of white bands in the popular music market forged an ambitious improvisational style that came to be known as bebop (musicians first called it "modern music"). No longer content to be entertainers, the younger jazz musicians demanded to be taken seriously as artists. The heroes of this movement were Charlie Parker (1920–1955), alto sax; Thelonious Monk (1917–1982), piano; Dizzy Gillespie (1917–1993), trumpet; Kenny Clarke (1914–1985), drums; Max Roach (b. 1924), drums; and Bud Powell (1924–1966), piano. The series of legendary jam sessions that are said to have created the style took place in Harlem at Minton's and Monroe's Uptown House.

The musical innovations of bebop affected several dimensions of the music—instrumental virtuosity, harmony, phrasing, rhythmic feel, timbre, and tempo. Charlie Parker and Dizzy Gillespie reharmonized and/or wrote new melodies for standard jazz tunes such as "Cherokee," "I Got Rhythm," and "What Is This Thing Called Love?" increasing the harmonic rhythm (the pace at which harmonies change) and the tempo and improvising highly subdivided phrases that set a new standard for instrumental virtuosity in the music. Drummers Kenny Clarke and Max Roach, picking up where Count Basie's drummer Jo Jones left off, transferred the standard ride rhythm (figure 4) from the hi-hat cymbals to the suspended ride cymbal, altering both the timbral color of the timekeeping pattern and increasing its volume. They also began breaking up the time by inserting off-beat accents on the bass drum and snare, creating greater rhythmic variety and dialogue in the rhythm section accompaniment.

Charlie Parker's legendary solo on "Koko" (based on the chord changes to "Cherokee") (figure 5) illustrates many of the signature features of bebop melodic style. Notice the long succession of up-tempo eighth notes (throughout), the use of chromatic approach notes (chorus one, measure seventeen) often alternating with arpeggiation (chorus one, measures one to three), and the use of sequences (bridge). Parker's

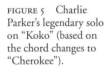

FIGURE 4   The standard ride rhythm.

FIGURE 5   Charlie Parker's legendary solo on "Koko" (based on the chord changes to "Cherokee").

particular penchant for interpolating complex figurations around skeletal melodies can be seen in his famous bridge to the second chorus of "Koko," in which the melody of "Tea for Two" serves to anchor a rapid series of arpeggiations. Parker was also widely admired for his varied accentuation of long successions of eighth notes in a manner that served to emphasize the most harmonically pleasing moments of the voice leading. Dizzy Gillespie's phrasing style was similar but made greater use of whole-tone scales and the fabled flatted fifth alteration of the dominant chord.

Among Parker's most celebrated recordings are "Koko" (1945), "Night in Tunisia" (1946), "Parker's Mood" (1948), and "Embraceable You" (1947). Among Gillespie's most admired recordings are several made with Parker, such as "Shaw 'Nuff" (1945), "Salt Peanuts" (1945), and "Hot House" (1953), as well as many under his own leadership, including "Woody'n You" (1946), "Night in Tunisia" (1946), "Manteca" (1947), "Cubana Be–Cubana Bop" (1947, a collaboration with George Russell [b. 1923] and Chano Pozo [1915–1948]), and "Con Alma" (1957).

Gillespie's trademark goatee and beret were widely emulated by fans of the new music, and by the late 1940s bebop had acquired a subcultural quality that shunned mainstream "squares." Bebop style included the use of "bop talk" (drawn from African American vernacular speech), a critique of the racial status quo, and the unfortunate fashionability of heroin. Charlie Parker's well-known addiction set the example, as many young musicians seemed to conclude that Parker achieved his genius because of, rather than in spite of, the drug. Many musicians suffered arrest, loss of their New York cabaret cards, jail time, or death in pursuit of a habit that was rumored to intensify one's hearing. Although the drug addictions of several prominent African American musicians (Charlie Parker, Miles Davis [1926–1990], Sonny Rollins [b. 1930]) are more widely known, several prominent white musicians (Stan Getz [1927–1991], Chet Baker [1929–1988], Art Pepper [1925–1982]) share similar stories.

In contrast to Parker and Gillespie, Thelonious Monk is recognized more for the originality of his compositions than for his virtuosity as a soloist. In 1947 Monk made a series of recordings for the Blue Note label that included many of his most famous compositions, "Thelonious," "Ruby My Dear," "'Round Midnight," "Well You Needn't," and "In Walked Bud" among them. Although greatly admired within the jazz world of the late 1940s (pianist Mary Lou Williams [1910–1981] was among his earliest champions), Monk did not achieve broader prominence until the late 1950s and early 1960s.

Monk's loss of his cabaret card in 1951 certainly contributed to his marginality, but perhaps a more important factor was the great difference between his aesthetic and that of mainstream bebop. If Parker and Gillespie's music emphasized dazzling virtuosity, Monk's own soloing seemed to argue that less is more. A celebrated example of Monk's ability to say more with less is his Christmas Eve 1954 recording of "Bags' Groove" with Miles Davis. Over nine choruses of the blues Monk uses spare means to build a compelling larger shape for the solo. The openings of the first three choruses illustrate one way in which Monk accomplishes this. Each chorus begins with a riff that is developed over twelve bars (figure 6). Notice that the riff for the first chorus

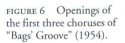

FIGURE 6   Openings of the first three choruses of "Bags' Groove" (1954).

begins with eighth notes, the second with triplets, and the third with sixteenth notes. Monk's use of rhythmic displacement (shifting a figure's position within a bar) as a means of variation are apparent in the triplet and sixteenth-note passages in choruses two and three.

COOL JAZZ AND HARD BOP

The improvisational style of Miles Davis also leaned toward an aesthetic of less is more. Davis's solo career was launched by the celebrated "Birth of the Cool" recordings made in 1949 and 1950. The "Birth of the Cool" project emerged from a think tank of composers and musicians who met in arranger Gil Evans's (1912–1988) apartment in the late 1940s to explore musical ideas and theories with potential application to jazz composition. The aesthetic that emerged from the group emphasized coloristic timbral effects achieved through unusual pairings of instruments (French horns and tuba; alto sax and baritone sax; trumpet and trombone), no vibrato, and a seamless integration of written and improvised music that often disguised the formal sectional boundaries of the music.

"Birth of the Cool" was an explicitly interracial project that distinguished itself from many others of the period by being under the leadership of an African American artist. In the early 1950s the jazz community tended to embrace a color-blind ideology in opposition to prevailing societal segregation. Miles Davis's statement that "music has no color: It's a raceless art. I don't care if a musician is green as long as he's talented" (Davis 1989:117) was typical of the way in which this ideology was publicly expressed.

Later in the 1950s the aesthetic of cool jazz, emphasizing lyrical melodic style and softer tonal colors, became coded as a "white" sound, which contrasted with hard bop, which was coded as a "black" sound. Art Blakey (1919–1990) and the Jazz Messengers (the quintessential hard bop band) often served to define the hard bop alternative. Historians emphasize Blakey's and Horace Silver's (b. 1928) active embrace of African American roots through the exuberant expressive resources of blues, gospel, and rhythm and blues. Notable examples of this style can be found on Art Blakey's "Moanin'" (1958). This simple opposition of black and white obscures the practice of some prominent white saxophonists associated with the cool sound (Stan Getz [b. 1927], Lee Konitz [b. 1927], Paul Desmond [1924–1977]) of often modeling their sound on the lyrical playing and laid-back swing of African American artists such as Lester Young and Johnny Hodges (1906–1970). Also ignored by this binary contrast is that one of the most prominent ensembles with a cool sound was the Modern Jazz Quartet, an African American group.

Dave Brubeck's (b. 1920) trios and quartets dominated the listeners's polls for a considerable portion of the 1950s. Historical ambivalence toward Brubeck's towering success, like Benny Goodman's, stems from the racially structured advantages that benefited the group. Brubeck's appearance on the cover of *Time* magazine in 1954, his popularity on white college campuses, and the comparative lack of attention to worthy African American musicians in the media all contributed to hard bop's emphasis on African American roots.

THE CIVIL RIGHTS MOVEMENT

By the mid-1950s the burgeoning civil rights movement exerted pressure on musicians to do their part in supporting efforts to end Jim Crow. The black community expected musicians to demonstrate their commitment to the larger cause of racial justice and publicly shamed those artists (such as Nat King Cole [1919–1965] and Louis Armstrong) who continued to accept engagements in performance venues that segregated audiences. The issue of audience segregation was far more important to civil rights organizations than whether or not a particular band had mixed personnel. Southern white audiences, after all, had long been comfortable with black and mixed entertainment as long as segregated seating remained. The activist climate emerging from the principal events of the civil rights movement—the Montgomery bus boycott (1956), the desegregation of Little Rock's Central High School (1957), the independence of Ghana (1957), the student lunch counter sit-ins in Greensboro (1960), the Freedom Rides (1961), the campaign to desegregate Birmingham (1963), and the assassination of Malcolm X (1965)—had important consequences for jazz of the 1950s and 1960s.

The jazz community reacted in various ways to civil rights events by performing benefit concerts, recording albums with political themes, attributing political meaning to particular jazz aesthetics, exploring African and other non-Western musical and religious ideas, and engaging in highly charged dialogues about race and racism in the jazz industry. The emergence of several of the most revered figures in jazz and the aesthetics they represent—among them Miles Davis, John Coltrane (1926–1967), Charles Mingus (1922–1979), and Ornette Coleman (b. 1930)—took place against this volatile historical backdrop.

Modal jazz

Among the most important musical innovations in this period was the development of modal jazz. Exemplified by the Miles Davis's album *Kind of Blue* (1959), modal compositions reduced the number of harmonic changes, allowing soloists to improvise for an extended period of time over one or two chords. "So What?" (1959), which has become the prototypical modal composition, is an AABA tune comprising two chord changes, one for the A section (Dm7) and one for the B section (E♭m7). Davis explored the use of the dorian mode (D–E–F–G–A–B–C) to harmonize these sonorities and construct melodies. In addition, the more open harmonic background allowed soloists greater freedom to superimpose a wide variety of modes, scales, voicings, and melodic ideas over any particular sonority.

The conceptual father of a modal approach to harmony in jazz is George Russell, whose *Lydian Concept of Tonal Organization* (1953) and *Lydian Chromatic Concept of Tonal Organization* (1959) offered the improviser and composer a complex system of associating chords with scales organized by their degree of consonance or dissonance. Russell emphasized the multiple choices available to performers and was widely known in the jazz community for his expertise in modes and scales. Both Miles Davis and pianist Bill Evans (1929–1980), who appeared on *Kind of Blue,* were familiar with Russell's ideas. The Lydian Concept, however, was intended as a more general approach to harmony that could be applied to harmonically dense as well as harmonically sparse musical settings.

Modal jazz also came to imply a more open-ended approach to form and harmonic voicings. Instead of observing a chorus structure, jazz musicians explored pieces that allowed a soloist to play indefinitely over a recurring chord pattern or rhythmic vamp. The vamp to John Coltrane's "My Favorite Things" (1960), as played by pianist McCoy Tyner (b. 1938), provides one example (figure 7). Notice the prominent use of fourths (perfect and augmented) in the structure of the chords. By the omission of certain tones (especially the tonic), these more open voicings served to articulate more than one harmony, a hallmark of modern jazz piano style. Charles Mingus's

FIGURE 7   The vamp to John Coltrane's "My Favorite Things" (1960), as played by pianist McCoy Tyner.

Critics of free jazz failed to see progress in the atonality and indefinite time feels of the music. They viewed the avant-garde as a decline, brought on by young musicians who didn't do their homework or pay their dues in the tradition.

"Pithecanthropus Erectus" (1956) and Art Blakey's extended percussion solos on "Orgy in Rhythm" (1957) and "Holiday for Skins" (1958) provide additional examples of a more open-ended conception of form. Blakey's collaborations with Afro-Cuban musicians on these albums—including Sabu Martinez (1930–1979), Patato Valdez (b. 1926), and Ubaldo Nieto—took place at the time of Ghana's independence, when there was much discussion of Africa in the African American press [see AFRO-CUBAN MUSIC, p. 783].

In the early 1960s John Coltrane shifted from a well-developed modern bebop style featuring harmonically dense compositions such as "Giant Steps" (1959) to an open-ended modal conception that actively explored not only African but Indian sources of musical and spiritual inspiration. Coltrane's legendary ensembles, featuring McCoy Tyner, piano; Elvin Jones (b. 1927), drums; and Jimmy Garrison (1934–1976), bass (among others); developed the rhythmic as well as harmonic implications of open-ended modal approaches to improvisation, something that Miles Davis's quintet of 1963–1968 did also. Freed from the necessity of delineating frequently changing harmonies, bassists expanded their use of pedal points, pianists accompanied long sections with intricate vamps and riffs, and drummers played with greater rhythmic density and cross-rhythms than had been customary in earlier styles. Among the recordings exemplifying this sound include Coltrane's *My Favorite Things* (1960), *Africa Brass* (1961), *India* (1961), *Crescent* (1964), and *A Love Supreme* (1965) and Miles Davis's *My Funny Valentine* (1964), *Miles in Berlin* (1964), and *Live at the Plugged Nickel* (1965).

Free jazz

A major aesthetic controversy erupted in the jazz world in early 1960 when alto saxophonist Ornette Coleman emerged on the New York scene. Coleman's dissonant harmonic style and abandonment of chorus structures and fixed harmonic changes as means of organizing improvisational flow were claimed by some as *The Shape of Jazz to Come* (1959) (the title of Coleman's first release after his arrival in New York), decried by others as the destruction of jazz, and by still others championed as a music of social critique. Over the next seven years an aesthetic community of jazz musicians committed to what was variously termed free jazz, the New Thing, or avant-garde jazz emerged on the New York scene. Among them were Coleman, Cecil Taylor (b. 1933), Albert Ayler (1936–1970), Archie Shepp (b. 1937), Sun Ra (1914–1993), and John Coltrane. Coltrane's turn toward free jazz gave considerable prestige to the burgeoning free jazz movement. The new approach also fostered the creation of collective musical organizations such as Chicago's Association for the Advancement of Creative Musicians (AACM) (1965) and later St. Louis's Black Artists Group (BAG) (1968).

Free jazz was claimed by its advocates as the left wing of jazz expression, its musically adventurous means taken as a sign of revolutionary social critique, spiritual awareness, and freedom. The political meanings attached to the genre must be viewed in dialogue with the riveting events of the civil rights movement that took place during its emergence. Shortly after Ornette Coleman's New York debut in late 1959, the Greensboro lunch counter sit-ins occurred (February 1960), launching the most activist phase of the civil rights movement. For many the dissonance of the music was taken as a sign of social dissidence. For modernist-oriented jazz critics, such as Gunther Schuller (b. 1925) and Martin Williams (1924–1992), the appeal of free jazz lay in its parallel with the historical development of Western classical music. These critics stressed that musical logic determined the organic evolution of music from simple to complex, from tonal music to avant-garde. Here free jazz was of interest for its modernist aesthetic, rather than its political radicalism.

Among the greatest champions of free jazz as a political music was playwright, poet, and critic Amiri Baraka (LeRoi Jones) (b. 1934), whose *Blues People* (1963a) viewed free jazz as the logical outcome of the black musician's centuries of struggle with racism in America. *Blues People* was the first major book by an African American author to advocate a sociological and culturally contextualized view of black musical history. Among musicians, Archie Shepp publicly raised the issue of racism in the jazz industry, in outspoken published pieces such as "An Artist Speaks Bluntly" (1965). Max Roach raised comparable issues and shifted toward free jazz in the 1960s as well. Later, Frank Kofsky's *Black Nationalism and the Revolution in Music* (1970) took a political view of avant-garde jazz.

For many artists, however, the politics of free jazz expression was a by-product of its spiritual implications. For Albert Ayler, John Coltrane, and Sun Ra, spiritual communion (a different sort of liberation) through avant-garde expression was a primary motivation for their expressive choices. Ayler's work drew heavily upon the African American gospel and folk traditions, turning familiar hymn melodies into abstract wails and pleas of deep emotional intensity. Both Coltrane and Sun Ra were drawn to non-Western modes of spirituality. Both men were widely read in spiritual traditions from locations as far ranging as Africa, India, China, and West Asia (the Middle East). Sun Ra's aesthetic embraced both ancient Egypt and outer space as metaphors for liberation and spiritual depth.

Critics of free jazz failed to see progress in the atonality and indefinite time feels of the music. They viewed the avant-garde as a decline, brought on by young musicians who didn't do their homework or pay their dues in the tradition. An observer for *Muhammad Speaks,* the organ of the Nation of Islam, even suggested that avant-gardists like Coltrane were pandering to white critics. Observers from the mid-1960s confirm that as the music became increasingly atonal, many black audience members defected to the immensely popular Motown and soul sound, or to soul jazz—the classic organ trio or quartet sound popularized by Jimmy Smith (b. 1925), Stanley Turrentine (1934–2000), and Shirley Scott (b. 1934)—leaving a disproportionately white audience for free jazz. During the Black Power years of 1966–1970, a tense dialogue between a militant African American radical intelligentsia and radical white audience members and musicians often took place through free jazz performances.

THE 1970s

The release of Miles Davis's *Bitches Brew* in 1969 augured a new direction for jazz in the 1970s, one that embraced rather than rejected popular musical styles. Widely heralded for its creative synthesis of jazz improvisation and rock and roll, *Bitches Brew* used electrified rock and roll time feels, as well as many of the post-production techniques of popular music, including overdubbing and looping. Davis was particularly inspired by guitarist Jimi Hendrix (1942–1970), who was able to reach a broad audience with his creative guitar pyrotechnics. Later Davis's fusion interests turned toward soul and funk in an effort to reach a younger African American audience. His albums *A Tribute to Jack Johnson* (1970) and *On the Corner* (1972) illustrate this trend. Several other bands offering various mixes among jazz, rock and roll, soul, rhythm and blues, and non-Western musics emerged in the 1970s, including, most prominently, Weather Report, John McLaughlin (b. 1942) and the Mahavishnu Orchestra, Herbie Hancock (b. 1940) and the Headhunters, and Chick Corea (b. 1941) and Return to Forever.

The 1970s also witnessed an expansion and internationalization of avant-garde jazz. Major figures and ensembles of the decade include multireedist and composer Anthony Braxton (b. 1945), the Art Ensemble of Chicago, Cecil Taylor, David Murray (b. 1955), Steve Lacy (b. 1934), and several individual members of Chicago's AACM, including Lester Bowie (1941–1999), Roscoe Mitchell (b. 1940), and Joseph Jarman (b. 1937). European audiences proved to be especially receptive to free jazz, and an indigenous European avant-garde inspired by American jazz emerged including such figures as Albert Mangelsdorff (b. 1928), Willem Breuker (b. 1944), and the Global Unity Orchestra.

LINCOLN CENTER

By the early 1980s many young jazz musicians found greater inspiration in the "golden age" of modern jazz (from 1945 to 1965) than in much of the contemporary offerings of fusion and avant-garde [see FIVE FUSIONS, p. 334]. Trumpeter Wynton Marsalis (b. 1961) made no secret of his disappointment in the jazz of the early 1980s, passionately advocating a return to basic jazz values (making the changes and swinging) through studying the classic recordings of such masters as Art Blakey, Miles Davis, John Coltrane, Thelonious Monk, and Duke Ellington. Marsalis's outspoken criticism of the jazz avant-garde and the most recent fusion efforts of Miles Davis polarized older jazz listeners, who cast Marsalis as an aesthetic conservative and latter-day "moldy fig." Marsalis nevertheless inspired and nurtured a group of young musicians who later became known as the Young Lions, among them trumpeters Roy Hargrove (b. 1969) and Terence Blanchard (b. 1962), drummer Jeff "Tain" Watts (b. 1960), bassist Christian McBride (b. 1972), and pianists Marcus Roberts (b. 1963) and Cyrus Chestnut (b. 1963). Wynton Marsalis's prominent success in both jazz and classical music (he was the first artist to win Grammy Awards in both jazz and classical performance) made him the ideal figure to actualize a long-standing dream: that someday jazz would be treated as equal in stature to classical music and accorded an institutional home. In 1988 New York City's Jazz at Lincoln Center program, dedicated to advancing jazz through performance, education, and preservation, was launched with Marsalis as its artistic director. Marsalis organized the Lincoln Center Jazz Orchestra, and in the 1990s Lincoln Center offered a highly acclaimed series of jazz concerts and educational events, often devoted to the repertoire of particular jazz figures such as Duke Ellington.

Critics of Lincoln Center have often decried the narrowness of Marsalis's programming decisions, objecting to his neglect of the avant-garde in jazz, his failure to commission more adventurous jazz compositions, and his tendency to feature his own works over those of others. This left wing of critical opinion, which aims to retain the tradition of social criticism and musical experimentation in jazz, has found a leader in clarinetist Don Byron (b. 1958). Byron's more eclectic jazz series at the Brooklyn Academy of Music has often been viewed as an alternative to Lincoln Center.

A more conservative criticism of Lincoln Center has come from white musicians who claim that white artists have been overlooked by Lincoln Center's prioritization of the African American heritage in jazz. This is the latest chapter in a long history of the charge of "reverse racism," which has generally emerged at moments of black political activism and black advancement. Historical antecedents include the 1940s, when mixed bands became possible, and the civil rights period, when many white musicians claimed that black bandleaders failed to hire them because of their color. Although jazz has historically been associated with having greater racial tolerance than the rest of American society, there has also been a significant history of white backlash in response to African American visibility and influence in the music.

The turn of the new century has amplified debates over both the legacy and the future of jazz. Lincoln Center is accused of dwelling on the past rather creating a vision of the future, even though it has attracted a new generation of musicians into its fold. Younger musicians shaped by funk and hip-hop (Steve Coleman [b. 1956], Russell Gunn [b. 1971], Don Byron, and Kenny Garrett [b. 1960]) have incorporated beats and performance conventions of contemporary urban popular music into more traditional jazz offerings, generating in the process a new wave of jazz fusion. Some musicians and critics argue that jazz is dead, having been murdered by corporate influence, mainstream marketing, lack of creativity, and the loss of responsiveness to social movements. Advocates of this perspective perceive a loss of individualism and originality among musicians associated with Wynton Marsalis. The classicization and institutionalization of jazz have, from this perspective, been a mixed blessing. Others celebrate the entry of jazz into institutional prominence and mainstream visibility. As always, debates over the legacy and future of jazz have generated a variety of aesthetic and political perspectives among musicians, audiences, and critics. As the music enters the new century the great tradition of jazz as a virtuosic improvised tradition is likely to continue to evolve in multifaceted directions.

REFERENCES

Eddie Meadows was helpful in the preparation of these references.

Armstrong, Louis. 1988. *Louis Armstrong: The Hot Fives & Hot Sevens*. Columbia CK44253.

Badger, Reid. 1995. *A Life in Ragtime: A Biography of James Reese Europe*. New York: Oxford University Press.

Basie, Count. 1938. *Big Band Jazz*. Smithsonian RD-030-02. Compact disc.

Baker, David. 1985. *How To Play Bebop*. 3 vols. Bloomington, Ind.: Frangipani Press.

Berlin, Edward A. 1980. *Ragtime: A Musical and Cultural History*. Berkeley: University of California Press.

Big Band and Quartet in Concert. 1963. Columbia C58964. LP disk.

Blesh, Rudi. 1985. *Shining Trumpets: A History of Jazz*. 2nd ed. New York: Knopf.

Bracey, John H., Jr., August Meier, and Elliott Rudwick, eds. 1970. *Black Nationalism in America*. Indianapolis: Bobbs-Merrill.

Brown, Clifford. 1953. *Clifford Brown Memorial Album*. Blue Note 857-81526. LP disk.

Brunn, N. O. 1960. *The Story of the Original Dixieland Jazz Band*. Baton Rouge: Louisiana State University Press.

Budds, Michael J. 1990. *Jazz in the Sixties: The Expansion of Musical Resources and Techniques*. Iowa City: The University of Iowa.

Buertle, Jack V., and Danny Barker. 1973. *Bourbon Street Black: The New Orleans Black Jazzman*. New York: Oxford University Press.

Byrd, Donald. 1972. "The Meaning of Black Music." *Black Scholar* 3(10):28–31.

Carno, Zita. 1959. "Art Blakey." *Jazz Review* 3(1):6–11.

Carr, Ian. 1982. *Miles Davis: A Critical Biography*. New York: Quartet Books.

Clar, Mimi. 1958–1959. "The Negro Church: Its Influence on Modern Jazz." *Jazz Review* 1(1):16–18; 2(1):6–11, 22–26; 2(2):28–30.

Cole, William. 1974. *Miles Davis*. New York: Morrow.

Collier, James Lincoln. 1983. *Louis Armstrong: An American Genius*. New York: Oxford University Press.

———. 1989. *Benny Goodman and the Swing Era*. New York: Oxford University Press.

Coltrane, John. 1960. "Coltrane on Coltrane." *Down Beat* 29:26–27.

———. 1960. *My Favorite Things*. Atlantic 1361-2. Compact disc.

Dankworth, Avril. 1968. *Jazz: An Introduction to Its Musical Basis*. London: Oxford University Press.

Davis, Miles. 1954. *Bags' Groove*. Prestige OJCCD-242-2 (P7109). Compact disc.

Davis, Miles, with Quincy Troupe. 1989. *Miles: The Autobiography*. New York: Simon and Schuster.

DeVeaux, Scott. 1997. *The Birth of Bebop: A Social and Musical History*. Berkeley: University of California Press.

Edwards, Carlos V. 1962. *The Giants of Bebop*. Urbana: University of Illinois Press.

Edwueme, Lazarus E. N. 1974. "African Music Retentions in the New World." *The Black Perspective in Music* 2(2):128–145.

Ellington, Duke. 1930. *Mood Indigo*. RCA ADL 20152(e). LP disk.

Evans, David. 1972. "Africa and the Blues." *Living Blues* 10:27–29.

Feather, Leonard. 1959. *Jazz*. Los Angeles: Trend Books.

Feather, Leonard, and Ira Gitler. 1999. *The Biographical Encyclopedia of Jazz*. New York: Oxford University Press.

Floyd, Samuel, ed. 1990. *Black Music in the Harlem Renaissance: A Collection of Essays*. New York: Greenwood Press.

Garland, Phyl. 1968. "The Many Bags of Oliver Nelson." *Ebony*, November, 108–112.

Gillespie, Dizzy, with Al Fraser. 1979 [1970]. *To Be or Not to Bop: Memoirs of Dizzy Gillespie*. New York: Da Capo.

Gitler, Ira. 1985. *Swing to Bop: An Oral History of the Transition in Jazz in the 1940s*. New York: Oxford University Press.

Goodman, Benny, and Irving Kolodin. 1939. *The Kingdom of Swing*. Harrisburg, Pa.: Stackpole Sons.

Gridley, Mark. 1991. *Jazz Styles: History and Analysis*. 4th ed. Englewood Cliffs, N.J.: Prentice-Hall.

Heckman, Don. 1965. "Inside Ornette." *Down Beat*, 9 September, 13–15; "Inside Ornette, Part a," 16 December, 20–21.

Herskovits, Melville J. 1958. *The Myth of the Negro Past*. Boston: Beacon Press.

Huggins, Nathan Irvin. 1971. *Harlem Renaissance*. New York: Oxford University Press.

Hunt, D. C. 1968. "Coleman, Coltrane and Shepp: The Need for an Educated Audience." *Jazz and Pop* 10:18–21.

"John Coltrane: Dealer in Discord." 1963. *Muhammad Speaks* 2(9):21.

Johnson, James Weldon. 1930. *Black Manhattan*. New York: Knopf.

Jones, LeRoi (Amiri Baraka). 1963a. *Blues People: Negro Music in White America*. New York: Morrow.

———. 1963b. "Jazz and the White Critic: A Provocative Essay on the Situation of Jazz Criticism. *Down Beat* 15:16–17.

Jost, Ekkehard. 1974. *Free Jazz*. Groz, Austria: Universal Edition.

Kenney, William H. 1993. *Chicago Jazz: A Cultural History, 1904–1930.* New York: Oxford University Press.

Kernfeld, Barry. 1988. *The New Grove Dictionary of Jazz.* London: Macmillan.

Kmen, Henry A. 1977. *The Roots of Jazz: The Negro and Music in New Orleans 1791–1900.* Urbana: University of Illinois Press.

Koch, Lawrence. "Ornithology: A Study of Charlie Parker's Music." *Journal of Jazz Studies* 2(1):61–88; 3(2).

Kofsky, Frank. 1966. "The Avant-Garde Revolution: Origins and Directions." *Jazz* 5(1):14–19.

———. 1970. *Black Nationalism and the Revolution in Music.* New York: Pathfinder.

Litweiler, John. 1967. "A Man with an Idea." *Down Beat* 5:23, 26, 41.

———. 1984. *The Freedom Principle: Jazz after 1958.* New York: Da Capo.

Locke, Alain. 1936. *The Negro and His Music.* Port Washington, N.Y.: Konnikat.

Lomax, John A., and Alan Lomax. 1947. *Folk Song U.S.A.* New York: Duell, Sloan and Pearce.

Longstreet, Stephen. 1965. *Sportin' House: A History of the New Orleans Sinners and the Birth of Jazz.* Los Angeles: Sherbourne Press.

Matzorkis, Gus. 1966. "Down Where We Live: Today's Avant-Garde Revolution as Seen in Light of Jazz's Long History of Internal Strife." Pt. 1. *Down Beat* 33.

McKay, Claude. 1940. *Harlem: Negro Metropolis.* New York: Dutton.

Mingus, Charles. 1971. *Beneath the Underdog.* New York: Knopf.

Meadows, Eddie S. 1981. *Jazz Reference and Research Materials: A Bibliography.* New York: Garland Publishers.

———. 1988. "The Miles Davis–Wayne Shorter Connection: Continuity and Change." *Jazzforschung* 20:55–63.

———. 1990. "African Retentions in Blues and Jazz." In *Black Studies Theory: Method and Cultural Perspectives,* ed. Talmadge Anderson, 209–216. Pullman: Washington State University Press.

Merriam, Alan P. 1952. "The African Background: An Answer to Barry Ulanov." *Record Changer* 11:7–8.

Monson, Ingrid. n.d. *Freedom Sounds: Jazz, Civil Rights, and Africa, 1950–1967.* New York: Oxford University Press. Forthcoming.

Navarro, Fats, and Tadd Dameron. 1968. *Milestone.* M-4704. LP disk.

Nisenson, Eric. 1997. *Blue: The Murder of Jazz.* New York: St. Martin's Press.

Nketia, J. H. Kwabena. 1979. "African Roots of Music in the Americas." *Jamaica Journal* 43:12–17.

Palmer, Bob. 1970. "Pharoah Sanders." *Rolling Stone,* April, 42–44.

Parker, Charlie. 1945. *The Savoy Recordings* (Master Takes). Vol 1. Savoy Records ZDS 4402. Compact disc.

Parker, Charles. 1957. *Now's The Time.* Verve 8840. LP disk.

Peretti, Burton. 1992. *The Creation of Jazz: Music, Race, and Culture in Urban America.* Urbana: University of Illinois Press.

Porter, Lewis. 1985. *Lester Young.* Boston: C. K. Hall.

Porter, Lewis, and Michael Ullman. 1993. *Jazz: From Its Origins to the Present.* Englewood Cliffs, N.J.: Prentice-Hall.

Ramsey, Frederic, Jr. 1951. "Baby Dodds: Talking and Drum Solos." Notes to *Jazz,* 1:2. Folkways Records FJ2290. LP disk.

Redkey, Edwin S. 1964. *Black Exodus: Black Nationalism and Back to Africa Movements 1890–1910.* New Haven, Conn.: Yale University Press.

Roberts, John Storm. 1972. *Black Music of Two Worlds.* New York: Praeger.

Russell, George. (1953). *Lydian Concept of Tonal Organization.* New York: Russ-Hix Music.

———. (1959). *Lydian Chromatic Concept of Tonal Organization.* New York: Concept Publishing.

Russell, George, and Martin Williams. 1960. "Ornette Coleman and Tonality." *Jazz Review* 3(5):6–11.

Russell, Ross. 1973. *Bird Lives: The High Life and Hard Times of Charlie "Yard Bird" Parker.* New York: Charterhouse.

Sargeant, Winthrop. 1975. *Jazz: Hot and Hybrid.* 3rd ed. New York: Da Capo.

Schafer, William, and Richard B. Allen. 1977. *Brass Bands and New Orleans Jazz.* Baton Rouge: Louisiana State University Press.

Schuller, Gunther. 1960. "John Lewis on the Modern Jazz Beachhead." *High Fidelity,* October, 54–56, 134–135.

———. 1968. *Early Jazz: Its Roots and Musical Development.* New York: Oxford University Press.

———. 1989. *The Swing Era: The Development of Jazz 1930–1945.* New York: Oxford University Press.

Shepp, Archie. 1965. "An Artist Speaks Bluntly." *Down Beat* 32(26):11, 42.

Simpkins, C. O. 1975. *Coltrane: A Biography.* New York: Herndon House.

Somosko, Vladimir, and Barry Tepperman. 1974. *Eric Dolphy: A Musical Biography and Discography.* Washington, D.C.: Smithsonian Institution Press.

Southern, Eileen. 1971. *The Music of Black Americans.* New York: Norton.

Spaulding, H. G. 1863. "Under The Palmetto." *Continental Monthly* 4(2):195–200.

Spellman, A. B. 1970. *Black Music: Four Lives in the Bebop Business.* New York: Pantheon.

Stearns, Marshall. 1970 [1956]. *The Story of Jazz.* New York: Oxford University Press.

Stowe, David W. 1994. *Swing Changes: Big Band Jazz in New Deal America.* Cambridge: Harvard University Press.

Sudhalter, Richard M. 1999. *Lost Chords: White Musicians and Their Contributions to Jazz, 1915–1945.* New York: Oxford University Press.

Szwed, John F. 1997. *Space Is the Place: The Life and Times of Sun Ra.* New York: Pantheon.

Tallant, Robert. 1983 [1966]. *Voodoo in New Orleans.* New York: Macmillan.

Taylor, Arthur. 1972. *Notes and Tones.* New York: Perigree.

Taylor, Billy. 1982. *Jazz Piano: History and Development.* Dubuque, Iowa: William C. Brown.

Tirro, Frank. 1977. *Jazz: A History.* New York: Norton.

Tucker, Mark. 1993. *The Duke Ellington Reader.* New York: Oxford University Press.

Williams, Martin T. 1967. *Jazz Masters of New Orleans.* New York: Macmillan.

Wilson, John S. 1996. *Jazz: The Transition Years.* New York: Meredith.

Young, Steve. 1965. Notes to *The New Wave in Jazz.* Impulse AS-90. LP disk.

R&B and Soul
Portia K. Maultsby

Rhythm and blues and soul are urban forms of black musical expression that evolved during the World War II era (1938–1945) and the two decades that followed. They are associated with southern blacks who abandoned their jobs as domestics, sharecroppers, tenant farmers, and general laborers and migrated to urban centers throughout the country. More than two million southern blacks left rural areas and small towns in the 1940s, in search of high-paying industrial jobs and to escape racial inequalities sanctioned by Jim Crow laws. In the cities, life proved challenging. Discriminatory policies in housing, restaurants, entertainment venues, and public accommodations restricted mobility and fostered the growth of segregated communities. The denial of membership in the American Federation of Musicians union (AFM) to African American musicians and the isolation of their communities created conditions ripe for the establishment of a vibrant black entertainment district in every major city. In this context, southern migrants transformed rural traditions into urban forms of expression. Rhythm and blues and soul, which captured the spirit, pace, and texture of life in the city, are products of this transformation.

DEFINITION OF TERMS

The term *rhythm and blues* was first used as a marketing label to identify all types of music recorded by African American artists. Introduced in 1949 to replace the *race music* label (a term in use since 1920), rhythm and blues encompassed all black musical traditions, including rural and urban blues, boogie-woogie, black swing, jazz combos, vocal harmony groups, and club lounge trios. It also identified a musical genre that began evolving in the mid-1940s as reinterpretations and hybridizations of vernacular traditions. Although the blues provided the foundation for rhythm and blues, other elements came from jazz, spirituals, gospel, and mainstream popular music. By the 1960s, gospel elements began to dominate and transform rhythm and blues into a distinctive genre labeled *soul*.

RHYTHM AND BLUES: THE PIONEERS

The first generation of rhythm and blues performers were blues and swing musicians who joined forces to create new musical styles in response to changes taking place in society. The war years altered the nature of social interactions and musical entertainment

Jordan's combo style, known as *jump blues,* produced a string of hits on the race/rhythm and blues and pop charts, thereby crossing established racial boundaries. Blacks and whites of various social classes related to all aspects of his performance—the musical aesthetic, novelty lyrics, and engaging showmanship.

when millions of men left America to fight abroad. Moreover, the military draft led to personnel instabilities in and the eventual demise of several swing bands, a decline in ballroom dancing, and the closing of many ballrooms. When smaller entertainment venues came into vogue in the 1940s, African American musicians adapted by forming new bands with fewer members and developing a new repertoire. The traditions they established redefined the direction of American popular music in the 1950s. Arkansas-born Louis Jordan, a singer and former alto saxophonist with Chick Webb's swing band, ushered in a new musical era in 1938 when he formed Louis Jordan and His Tympany Five. With this group, Jordan transformed big band swing into a combo sound by reducing the traditional twelve- to sixteen-member swing band to a seven-piece combo (rhythm section, alto and tenor sax, and trumpet) and creating a jazz-blues hybrid style and contemporary repertoire. While preserving the fundamental components of big band swing, his musical arrangements gave musicians more creative freedom. The sound was polished but had a spontaneous quality characterized by a 12-bar blues structure, boogie-woogie bass line, shuffle rhythms (triplet quarter note followed by a triplet eighth note), a syncopated three- and four-note horn riff pattern, a solo saxophone, and group singing on refrain lines. These features are illustrated in "What's the Use of Getting Sober (When You Gonna Get Drunk Again)" (1942), "G.I. Jive" (1943), "Caldonia" (1945), "Choo Choo Ch' Boogie" (1946), "Ain't Nobody Here but Us Chickens" (1946), and "Saturday Night Fish Fry" (1949).

Jordan's combo style, known as *jump blues,* produced a string of hits on the race/rhythm and blues and pop charts, thereby crossing established racial boundaries. Blacks and whites of various social classes related to all aspects of his performance—the musical aesthetic, novelty lyrics, and engaging showmanship. Jordan recalled: "I made as much money off of white people as I did off colored; I could play a white joint this week and a colored next (Shaw 1978:67). Working-class blacks especially identified with Jordan's humorous lyrics about urban and rural black life, which connected them to their southern roots and the performance tradition of "down home" or southern blues musicians.

Jordan's cross-cultural appeal flourished during the war years when African Americans experienced more overt discrimination in all areas of American life. Vehemently protesting these injustices, they participated in the Double V (Double Victory) campaign, a movement that supported a victory against tyranny in Europe and simultaneously demanded an end to racial inequalities in America. Society's resistance to this campaign heightened conflicts and hostilities between blacks and whites that continued decades after the war (Franklin 1994:433–473). Nevertheless, performances by Jordan's combo and swing-oriented bands led by Jimmie Lunceford, Duke Ellington, Lionel Hampton, and Lucky Millinder, among others, superficially deemphasized racial barriers in the few venues with mixed, but often segregated, audiences. After the United States declared victory over Germany in 1945, these audiences celebrated to the music of black swing bands and jazz-oriented combos. For blacks and whites, Jordan's "Let the Good Times Roll" (1946) symbolized economic prosperity and a new era in

America's social history. For African Americans, this song also signified an end to racial inequalities.

The optimism that prevailed among African Americans in the 1940s underscores the spirit of new musical styles that evolved in segregated clubs throughout the country. In this context, musicians developed a repertoire rooted in southern vernacular traditions that reflected their musical backgrounds and the musical preferences of their black working-class audiences. This segment of the African American community, according to rhythm and blues songwriter-producer Johnny Otis, "favored the blues played with a modern twist" (Otis 1984).

The clubs in Los Angeles became incubators for this music, later known as rhythm and blues (blues with rhythm). Through jam sessions, blues and jazz musicians from Arkansas, Louisiana, Oklahoma, and Texas pioneered a distinctive West Coast rhythm and blues style by adding regional vernacular elements to Jordan's combo model. The combination of guitar and piano stylings from the Texas blues tradition, horn arrangements from southwestern swing bands, rumba rhythms from Cuba via Louisiana, and the "honking" tenor saxophone style popularized by Illinois Jacquet in Lionel Hampton's remake of "Flying Home" (1942) produced an urban dance music that rocked the nation for nearly three decades. Pioneers and popularizers of the West Coast combo tradition (also known as jump blues) include Joe Liggins ("The Honeydripper" [1945]), T-Bone Walker ("Sail On Boogie" [1945]); Roy Milton ("R.M. Blues" [1946]), Eddie Vinson ("Old Maid Boogie" [1947]), Wynonie Harris ("Good Rockin' Tonight" [1948]), Mabel Scott ("Elevator Boogie" [1948]), Amos Milburn ("Chicken Shack Boogie" [1948]), Big Jay McNeely ("Deacon's Hop" [1948]), and Johnny Otis ("Head Hunter" [1950] and "Cupid's Boogie," featuring Little Esther [1950]). The West Coast combo sound spread to other parts of the country and resonated in the rhythm and blues instrumentals of Wild Bill Moore's "We're Gonna Rock, We're Gonna Roll" (1948), Hal Singer's "Cornbread" (1948), Sonny Thompson's "Long Gone (Parts I & II)" (1948), and Paul Williams's "The Huckle-Buck" (1949). Rhythm and blues combos appealed to the working class because song titles and musical features preserved the essence of southern black cultural values and musical traditions (Otis 1984; Shaw 1978:129–225).

A rhythm and blues style that differed from the combo tradition emerged from after-hours clubs in Los Angeles. Labeled *club blues* in black clubs and *cocktail music* in white clubs, this music is distinguished from combo rhythm and blues by function and instrumentation. Performers of club blues created an atmosphere for conversation rather than dancing. Chicago-born singer-pianist Nat "King" Cole is credited with originating this tradition in 1937 in Los Angeles, when he formed a trio consisting of piano, guitar, and bass.

Cole's recordings, such as "All for You" (1943), "Straighten Up and Fly Right" (1943), and "Gee, Baby, Ain't I Good to You" (1944), showcased his background in jazz, pop, and classical music. His songs appealed to both blacks and whites, especially the middle class; they related to the fluid and assimilated sound of his piano and vocal styles. The popularity of Cole's group inspired the formation of similar trios who introduced the blues aesthetic to the tradition. Blues-based trios quickly became favorites in after-hours clubs that attracted the black working class. The group Johnny Moore's Three Blazers popularized the blues-oriented trio style ("Blues at Sunrise" [1945] and "Drifting Blues" [1946]). From this group came Texas-born singer-pianists Ivory Joe Hunter ("Pretty Mama Blues" [1948]) and Charles Brown ("Trouble Blues" [1949] and "Black Night [1951]) (Pavlow 1983:15–21; Shaw 1978:89–104).

By the end of the 1940s, eight independent labels that specialized in rhythm and blues recordings had been established in Los Angeles. Despite the absence of national distribution networks, this music made its way to other parts of the country and influenced the development of other regional styles. Black Pullman porters on trains served as unofficial distributors for record labels, and the few existing black radio programs broadcast the music. Despite nationwide demand for rhythm and blues recordings, major record labels excluded the artists from their rosters. These and other exclusionary practices contributed to the proliferation of independent record labels (Shaw 1978).

THE SECOND GENERATION OF PERFORMERS

Independent labels dominated African American music production until the early 1970s. In the late 1940s and early 1950s, they began to target the rapidly growing black teenage population, signing teenage performers to attract these consumers. Imperial, Specialty, and Aladdin in Los Angeles and fledgling Atlantic in New York City were among the first labels to search for young black talent. They hired New Orleans jazz bandleader Dave Bartholomew (figure 1) and territory jazz bandleader Jesse Stone (figure 2) as talent scouts and songwriter-arranger-producers.

Bartholomew and Stone created new forms of urban dance music by modifying the rhythms and arrangements of West Coast rhythm and blues to conform to the dance styles of southern black teenagers. Drawing from the Cuban rumba that was popular in New Orleans, Bartholomew created a new rhythmic foundation. He explains:

> "Everybody was always talking about the rumba. I took the bass [pattern] from the rumba and put in my saxophone. Then I had the [string] bass do what we called the walk." Bartholomew later assigned the rumba rhythm to the [string] bass "so I could get a bigger sound doubling the horns with the bass" (Bartholomew 1985).

FIGURE 1   Dave Bartholomew, bandleader, songwriter-arranger-producer for Imperial, Specialty, and Aladdin Records. Courtesy Archives of African American Music and Culture, Indiana University.

Fats Domino added triplets and rolling fifth and octave figures from the Texas piano-blues tradition to Bartholomew's formula, producing a distinctive New Orleans rhythm and blues sound. Under Bartholomew's guidance, several artists recorded hit songs, including Fats Domino's "The Fat Man" (1949), "Goin' Home" (1952), and "Ain't That a Shame" (1955), Lloyd Price's "Lawdy Miss Clawdy" (1952), Shirley and Lee's "I'm Gone" (1952), and Smiley Lewis's "I Hear You Knocking" (1955).

Jesse Stone pioneered a slightly different regional sound by modifying the boogie-woogie bass line that he believed "was too busy and didn't fit the dances kids were doing at that particular time." Similar to Bartholomew, he adapted the boogie-woogie to the rumba and further simplified the horn arrangements "to give the kids the kind of expression they were looking for" (Stone 1982). Stone's formula, which became known as the Atlantic sound, produced hits for many of Atlantic's artists: Ruth Brown's "5–10–15 Hours" (1952), the Clovers' "Don't You Know I Love You" (1951), "One Mint Julep" (1952), and "Good Lovin'" (1953), and Joe Turner's "Shake Rattle and Roll" (1954). These and other recordings produced by Stone established Atlantic as a major recording label in the rhythm and blues market.

Paralleling the development of the Atlantic and New Orleans rhythm and blues styles was the emergence of new and youthful sounds from street corners, school gyms, and city parks. They were the voices of teenage groups who sang a cappella vocal harmony songs. Initially imitating the jazz-pop styles of the Mills Brothers, the Ink Spots, and the Ravens, they aspired to duplicate the success of these groups. Without the guidance of professional songwriter-arrangers, the teenage groups (also known as "street corner" groups) developed a musical tradition that represented their values, cultural sensibilities, and lives as city dwellers. They sang about adolescent experiences and fantasies as well as adult situations associated with the blues. They also imitated the arrangements and performance aesthetic of jubilee and gospel quartet groups rather than the jazz and pop styles of their predecessors. According to Albert "Diz" Russell, a member of the Orioles, their arrangements place the bass on the bottom of chords: "A floating tenor, which comes in and out, carries the chord up and down. The baritone

FIGURE 2   Jesse Stone, bandleader, songwriter-arranger-producer for Atlantic Records. Courtesy Archives of African American Music and Culture, Indiana University.

FIGURE 3   The Orioles, a vocal harmony group. Courtesy Archives of African American Music and Culture, Indiana University.

remains in the middle of the chord and sings the straight part" over which the lead singer freely interprets songs (Russell 1983).

The Orioles (figure 3) are credited as being the first bona fide rhythm and blues vocal harmony group. Singing sentimental ballads in a romantic style, they appealed to teenagers. This interpretation is best illustrated in "It's Too Soon to Know" (1948), "Forgive and Forget" (1949), and "Crying in the Chapel" (1953). The Orioles became the model for subsequent rhythm and blues harmony groups (Five Keys, Swallows, Penguins, and other "bird" groups), many of whom gradually developed their own unique sound.

The romantic-styled harmony groups acquired a new sound when the Spaniels introduced the doo-wop concept and the Moonglows the "blow harmony" technique. James "Pookie" Hudson, lead singer of the Spaniels, explained that the bass voice incorporated the rhythmic phrases "doo-doo-doo-wop" and "doo-doo-doo-doo-doo" to add rhythmic movement to romantic songs (Hudson 1985). These phrases imitated the string bass and became central to the background vocals of harmony groups. The Spaniels popularized this concept in "Baby, It's You" (1953) and "Goodnite Sweetheart, Goodnite" (1954), ushering in the doo-wop era. The Moonglows added yet another dimension to "doo-wop" when they instituted the technique of blowing the phrase "ooh-ooh-wee-ohh-oohwee-oohwee" into the microphone on "Sincerely" (1954) and "Most of All" (1955) to create a different kind of vocal effect.

Vocal harmony groups traditionally sang without instrumental accompaniment, but commercial production of their songs led to the use of instruments associated with rhythm and blues trios and combos. The up-tempo and bluesy style produced by combos broadened the spectrum of these groups. In addition to the previously mentioned songs recorded by the Clovers, the Dominoes' "Sixty Minute Man" (1951), "Have Mercy, Baby" (1952), and "I'd Be Satisfied" (1952) and Clyde McPhatter and the Drifters' "Money Honey" (1953) and "Whatcha Gonna Do?" (1954) are examples of this combo-based style. Moving away from the romantic lyrics of the Orioles, some combo-styled vocal groups employed double entendre, a linguistic device to mask the sexual connotations of songs.

The addition of rhythm and blues combos and the innovations of the Spaniels and Moonglows further evolved the style of vocal harmony groups. The music's aesthetic qualities and danceable character attracted the attention of white teenagers, disc jockeys, and major record labels. The music industry wanted to exploit white teenage consumer markets, and these teenagers wanted to establish their own identity through music, dance, dress, and style. African American music and culture became the foundation for this identity. To obscure the source of the new music embraced by white teenagers, record labels produced cover versions by white artists. Disc jockeys, in turn, substituted the term *rock and roll* for rhythm and blues. But when teenagers discovered the original artists through radio broadcast, they rejected the imitative versions and sought out authentic African American recordings (Garofolo 1990:57–90).

RHYTHM AND BLUES IN TRANSITION

During the era of cover records (approximately 1953–1956), rhythm and blues continued to evolve. In 1954, Little Richard introduced a new beat to the tradition that became known as *rock and roll.* Charles Conner, Little Richard's original drummer, explained:

In rhythm and blues, you had a shuffle with a back-beat, but Little Richard wanted something different. He wanted something with more energy, but he didn't know how to describe the notes. So Richard brought me down to the train station in Macon, Georgia, in 1954 and he said: "Charles, listen to the choo-choo, choo-choo, choo-choo." I said, you probably want eighth notes or sixteenth notes. We went back to his house couple of days later . . . and we came up with that beat. Now, nobody had ever played that beat before (Conner 1990).

The *choo choo* beat generated many national and crossover hits for Richard, including "Tutti Frutti" (1955), "Long Tall Sally" (1956), and "Lucille" (1957). Doo-wop groups adapted this beat to their songs, as did Frankie Lymon and the Teenagers ("I Want You To Be My Girl" [1956]), the Cadillacs ("Speedo" [1955] and "Peek-A-Boo" [1958]), and the El Dorados ("At My Front Door" [1955]).

Additional changes occurred in the rhythm and blues tradition when Bo Diddley and Chuck Berry popularized the guitar as the focal instrument. The preference for this instrument among white youth, along with Berry's novelty lyrics, made rhythm and blues even more accessible to white teenagers. Diddley's rhythmic guitar style and rumba rhythms ("Bo Diddley" [1955] and "Pretty Thing" [1955]) and Berry's more melodic approach ("Maybellene" [1955] and "Roll Over Beethoven" [1956]) appealed to the musical tastes and cultural values of all America's youth.

Labeled and promoted as rock and roll performers by the music industry, Bo Diddley, Chuck Berry, Little Richard, and black doo-wop groups generated many hits on rhythm and blues and pop charts. They also made appearances on mainstream television shows such as *The Ed Sullivan Show* and *American Bandstand,* and their music landed on jukeboxes and record players in white neighborhoods, causing consternation in mainstream society. African American performers became musical icons among white teenagers at a pivotal point in race relations in America. In the mid-1950s, the Supreme Court ruled the unconstitutionality of segregated public schools, southern blacks launched the civil rights movement, Senator Joseph P. McCarthy organized the anti-Communist campaign, and southern white citizens' councils mounted protests against school desegregation, race mixing, and the marketing of rock and roll (rhythm and blues) across racial boundaries (Garofalo 1997:169–174; Jackson 1991: 72–87).

Despite lawsuits and various forms of protests to rid the nation of this "licentious jungle" music, rhythm and blues remained popular among white youth. Record labels, eager to cater to the musical tastes of white youth, pondered new strategies to market rhythm and blues recorded by black artists across racial, class, and generational lines. They needed to garner mainstream support for this music to avoid further alienation. The solution was to record African American artists singing pop and country and western standards and pop-styled songs. Record labels also applied Tin Pan Alley or pop production concepts to dilute aesthetic qualities associated with black musical performance. In essence, record labels attempted to assimilate black artists into the mainstream of American popular music.

CROSSOVER FORMULAS

When the pop-oriented vocals and lyrics of the Platters ("Only You" [1955], "The Great Pretender" [1955], "My Prayer" [1956], and "Twilight Time" [1958]) became hits in both the rhythm and blues and pop markets, the group demonstrated its cross-cultural and cross-generational appeal. Even though Mercury had signed the Platters reluctantly, the company quickly realized the broad crossover potential of pop-flavored rhythm and blues artists. Mercury and Atlantic were the first labels to explore crossover production techniques aimed at both teenage and young adult markets. Jerry Leiber and Mike Stoller, the white songwriting and production team that replaced Jesse Stone as Atlantic's primary songwriter-producer, developed crossover formulas for both markets. Their teenage-oriented productions were mainly novelty songs that featured comic lyrics and a playful vocal style accompanied by a rhythm and blues combo. The Coasters popularized this style in "Down in Mexico" (1956), "Searching" (1957), and "Young Blood" (1957) (Gillett 1974:156–164).

To target an older audience, Leiber and Stoller employed pop production techniques. On ballads, for example, they substituted call-response or blues structures, gospel-blues harmonies, and combo arrangements with sing-along refrains, pop vocal harmonies, and elaborate orchestral arrangements (strings, marimba, tympani, and percussion). These features are heard in Clyde McPhatter's "Treasure of Love" (1956) and "Long Lonely Nights" (1957), Ivory Joe Hunter's "Since I Met You Baby" (1956), and LaVern Baker's "I Cried a Tear" (1958).

By the late 1950s, the Brazilian baion rhythms (the cha-cha beat) had infiltrated American popular music and became the foundation for many rhythm and blues songs. These rhythms landed crossover hits for the Drifters ("There Goes My Baby" [1959], "Dance with Me" [1959], "This Magic Moment" [1960], "Up on the Roof" [1962], and "On Broadway" [1963]) and Ben E. King ("Spanish Harlem" [1960]). Crossover formulas tempered the gospel vocal aesthetic and gave rhythm and blues a more urbane sound.

The "uptown" rhythm and blues concept, as scholar Charlie Gillett (1983 [1970]) called it, became standard to black music production, and it successfully launched many black female vocal groups. They were produced primarily by young white songwriter-producers, including Carole King, Gerry Goffin, Barry Mann, Cynthia Weil, Luther Dixon, and Phil Spector. The writers centered their song lyrics on the experiences and fantasies of teenagers and incorporated "hook lines" (sing-along repetitive phrases), string arrangements, and Brazilian rhythms. The Chantels' "Maybe" (1958), Shirelles' "Will You Love Me Tomorrow" (1960), Crystals' "He's a Rebel" (1962) and "Da Doo Ron Ron" (1963), Chiffons' "He's So Fine" (1963), and Ronettes' "Be My Baby" (1963) are among the many songs that crossed over into the mainstream and established the commercial viability of "girl groups" in the music industry.

While producing crossover hits, Atlantic and other record labels continued to record combo-styled rhythm and blues primarily for consumption of the black working class and southern black teenagers. Although these groups enjoyed many of the African American crossover performers, they also remained loyal to the rhythm and blues combo tradition. Among favored artists were Joe Turner ("Corrina, Corrina" [1956]), the Clovers ("Down in the Alley" [1957]), Ray Charles ("The Right Time" [1958] and "What'd I Say" [1959]), Etta James ("All I Could Do Was Cry" [1960]), and LaVern Baker ("See See Rider" [1962]).

The attempt of record companies and southern whites to prevent the penetration of black musical aesthetics and cultural traditions into the mainstream generated the reverse result. The pop elements introduced into rhythm and blues for crossover purposes actually spread black aesthetic qualities further into the arteries of society. When the diluted and toned-down uptown rhythm and blues sound recycled back into African American communities, it reentered the mainstream with a different twist. Black artists removed some pop elements and reworked others to conform to the black aesthetic ideal. Through continuous recycling, the full range of African American aesthetic qualities and popular musical expressions gradually became central to the sound reference for American popular music. In the 1960s, for example, the Motown Sound, the Memphis Sound, and soul music were mainstays on the pop, rhythm and blues, and soul music charts. Although these traditions can be distinguished from one another and mainstream popular traditions, they share aesthetic features unique to African American cultural expression.

THE MOTOWN SOUND

Motown, derived from Motor Town, the nickname for Detroit, was founded in this city by songwriter Berry Gordy in 1959. Gordy grew up in a middle-class family whose work ethic and business approach reflected the philosophy of the southern black leader and educator Booker T. Washington. His family owned a grocery store named after this leader, a commercial building, a printing company, and a plastering business. The family's work ethic, combined with Gordy's love for music, led him to pursue various business enterprises, including operating a record shop and writing songs. In his autobiography, Gordy revealed that he initially favored bebop and the music of Dinah Washington, Sarah Vaughan, Billie Holiday, the Ink Spots, and the Mills Brothers and later came to appreciate the blues and their derivative forms. This eclectic musical taste and Gordy's emphasis on good song lyrics shaped the Motown Sound (Gordy 1994: 8–46, 59–77).

Motown's first hit recordings were molded in the traditions of rhythm and blues combos (Junior Walker's "Money" [1959] and Marvin Gaye's "Can I Get a Witness" [1963]), vocal groups (the Miracles "Shop Around" [1960] and the Marvelettes "Please Mr. Postman" [1961]), and gospel-pop–styled solo singers (Mary Wells's "Two Lovers" [1962] and "You Beat Me to the Punch" [1962]). To these traditions, Gordy added his own innovations—tambourine, hand claps, a metallic ring from the guitar downstroke on beats two and four, jazz-derived bass lines, and a heavy bass drum foundation. This framework, which became the basis for the Motown Sound, appealed to teenagers across class, racial, and regional boundaries. Young America related to the music's infectious dance beat and other black aesthetic features commonplace in the popular music soundscape (Gordy 1994:110, 122–128).

Most of Motown's vocalists were teenagers who grew up in relatively impoverished neighborhoods in Detroit. Nevertheless, the innocence of their youthful voices resonated through their gospel-pop–flavored song interpretations. The company's songwriters were also young, and their songs dealt with young love, youth experiences, and feelings shared by all teenagers. Songwriter William "Mickey" Stevenson elaborates:

> We were into young people's music. We were into a different, younger approach from Stax, Atlantic, and Chess records. We had much younger writers, 18–22 years old. Writers are a reflection of the voice of people. . . . so if you have a writer, he is going to write about young love. He can't write about old love—he's never experienced it. Records by B. B. King and people like that, they are writing about experienced love. As we grew older, the music grew older, our experiences grew older—the times changed, the music changed (Stevenson 1983).

Following established songwriting principles, songwriters structured their lyrics on catchy and memorable pop- and classical-derived melodies and hook lines, to which were added vocal harmonies and call-response structures from black gospel music. By the mid-1960s, this formula catapulted Motown's artists into national and international prominence. Recordings by Martha and the Vandellas ("Dancing in the Street" [1964]), Mary Wells ("My Guy" [1964]), Marvin Gaye ("How Sweet It Is (To Be Loved by You)" [1964]), the Supremes ("Come See about Me" [1964], "Stop in the Name of Love" [1964], and "You Can't Hurry Love" [1966]), the Temptations ("My Girl" [1964] and "Ain't Too Proud to Beg" [1966]), and the Four Tops ("I Can't Help Myself" [1965]) scored big on the rhythm and blues and pop music charts.

In the late 1960s and early 1970s, the Motown Sound began to change, in part influenced by the Black Power movement and the riots in 1967 that devastated a large section of Detroit's ghetto. After World War II, Detroit's African American community suffered high unemployment when large manufacturing companies moved significant parts of their production to the suburbs. The unemployed lost their homes and, along with the constant flow of new migrants to the city, were forced to move into poorly maintained public housing and dilapidated apartments in areas that became overcrowded ghettos. Over time, frustration at ineffective government programs and an inability to rise above poverty turned into rage and riots. Changes in the Motown Sound parallel the social unrest that swept the country from the mid-1960s to early 1970s as well as internal strife within Motown. During this period, the Motown Sound slowly transformed itself into many distinct sounds that became identified as soul music (Sugrue 1996:105–177).

THE MEMPHIS SOUND

The Stax record label paralleled the development of Motown. James Stewart, a bank teller and country musician, founded the company in Memphis in 1959. An amateur recording engineer, he built a recording studio and recorded music as a hobby. Most of Stewart's clients were country musicians, but his stable of artists changed when he relocated the studio from his garage to an abandoned theater in the black community. Stax's open door policy attracted a mixture of black musicians from the neighborhood and white ones who had worked with Stewart in his first location. A core group of these musicians jammed together and became the studio's house band. Known as Booker T. and the MGs (figure 4), they created a unique southern sound, blending their individual blues, rhythm and blues, and rockabilly styles. This integrated band, which defied established social policies on race mixing and cultural exchanges, mirrored the goals of the civil rights movement (Bowman 1997:3–48).

Similar to Motown's artists, most of Stax's artists were between the ages of fifteen and twenty-two. Although they were from the South, their exposure to both southern and northern popular styles guided the company's first recordings of blues, doo-wop, rhythm and blues combo, and uptown styles. The company's initial success was built on the instrumentals of the Mar-Keys ("Last Night" [1961]) and Booker T. and the MGs ("Green Onions" [1962]), the uptown rhythm and blues tradition of Carla

FIGURE 4   Booker T. and the MGs, house band for Stax Records. Courtesy BMI Archives.

Thomas ("Gee Whiz" [1960] and "A Love of My Own" [1961]), the gospel-derived styles of William Bell ("You Don't Miss Your Water" [1961]) and Otis Redding ("These Arms of Mine" [1962] and "Pain in My Heart" [1963]), and the rhythm and blues combo sounds of Rufus Thomas ("Walking the Dog" [1963]).

The Memphis Sound was spontaneous, bold, gritty, gutsy, and warm, with an urban definition and rural undercurrents. It captured the realities and contradictions of life in the segregated South and the sensibilities of southern black culture. The warm and laid-back rhythm and blues-rockabilly stylings of Booker T. and the MGs, combined with the syncopated horn riffs of the Mar-Keys, gave a southern energy to the rhythm and blues tradition. This instrumental framework provided the foundation for vocalists, who added their individual signatures to the company sound.

Many singers, according to songwriter-vocalist Rufus Thomas (1984), wrote their own songs and collaborated with the musicians to create the musical grooves and arrangements. This process differed from Motown's creative approach. With the exception of Smokey Robinson, Marvin Gaye, and later Stevie Wonder, most of Motown singers were vehicles through which songwriter-producers, in collaboration with the studio band, presented their creations. Thus, the Motown Sound was more "produced" and less spontaneous than the Memphis Sound. Song lyrics also differed. Whereas Motown focused on teenage issues, Stax's lyrics dealt with all aspects of southern black life—daily experiences, relationships, and social issues. Some lyrics introduced new dance fads, such as Rufus Thomas's "Walking the Dog" (1963), "Do the Funky Chicken" (1970), "Do the Push and Pull" (1970), and "The Breakdown" (1971).

The Memphis Sound was largely unknown outside southern black communities until Al Bell, a black disc jockey in Washington, D.C., began promoting the music on the East Coast in 1963 and 1964. He subsequently joined the Stax label in 1965 as its first national director for promotion and, two years later, vice president and chief operating officer. Under Bell's leadership, Stax became a national and international phenomenon. As demand for the music increased, Stax expanded its roster, signing new artists and adding resident and independent black songwriter-producers and arrangers to the staff. Artists such as Sam and Dave, the Bar-Kays, Johnny Taylor, Eddie Floyd, the Staple Singers, Soul Children, the Emotions, and the Dramatics joined the roster to diversify the Memphis Sound. Songwriter-producers such as the Isaac Hayes and David Porter team, Betty Crutcher, Raymond Jackson, Carl Hamilton, Homer Banks, and later Don Davis contributed to this process beginning in the late 1960s. The songwriters who perfected and transformed the Memphis Sound into a music labeled *soul* were the team of Isaac Hayes and David Porter.

SOUL AND BLACK POWER

Soul music is a product of the Black Power movement that reflects its ethos and ideology. As the momentum of the 1950s civil rights movement continued to build, southern black college students organized under the umbrella of the Student Nonviolent Coordinating Committee (SNCC) in 1960. By the mid-1960s, these students had become increasingly impatient with the disappointingly slow pace of social change and they rejected the nonviolent and integrationist approach advocated by civil rights leaders. As an alternative, many embraced the black nationalist ideology of Malcolm X in 1966. Under the rubric Black Power, its proponents promoted national black unity, black pride, and self-determination. Thus Black Power became a political movement to which black people assigned social and cultural meanings described as soul (Marable 1991: 61–69).

SOUL MUSIC

FIGURE 5 Curtis Mayfield, songwriter-vocalist for the Impressions. Courtesy Archives of African American Music and Culture, Indiana University.

In an ethnographic study of an inner city community in Washington, D.C., Ulf Hannerz wrote: "In different ways, the soul concept has come to be employed by the black middle class and by black jazz musicians as well as by ghetto dwellers to define their identity" (Hannerz 1969: 145). These groups also applied this concept to a new style of music defined by religious overtones and sociopolitical messages. Recordings such as "Keep on Pushing" (1964), "People Get Ready" (1965), "We're a Winner" (1967), "This Is My Country" (1968), "Choice of Colors" (1969), and "We People Who Are Darker Than Blue" (1970), written by songwriter-vocalist Curtis Mayfield (figure 5) and performed by the Impressions, were embraced by African Americans from all socioeconomic classes. Music critic Tom Moon remembered that "these were the songs that really spoke to what people were feeling. They anticipated and distilled public mood in a way that no one else had ever done before" (Moon 1999). Mayfield's songs also inspired other musicians and a generation of African Americans to speak out and join the struggle for racial equality.

As Black Power evolved into a national movement, performers promoted its ideology. Themes of black pride and self-respect resonate in the Memphis Sound of Sam and Dave ("Soul Man" [1967] and "Soul Finger" [1967]) and the Staple Singers ("You've Got to Earn It" [1971] and "Respect Yourself" [1971]). On the King label, James Brown extolled racial pride in "Say It Loud—I'm Black and I'm Proud, Pt. 1" (1968) as well as self-determination in "I Don't Want Nobody to Give Me Nothing (Open up the Door I'll Get It Myself)" (1969) and "Get Up, Get into It and Get Involved" (1970).

Motown also responded to this era of activism. Berry Gordy explains: "As the new decade was beginning, the changes happening in society inspired changes in our music" (Gordy 1994:293). Songwriters Norman Whitfield, Barrett Strong, Pam Sawyer, and others introduced themes of social commentary and contemporary sounds to transform the Motown Sound. The Supremes sang about "Love Child" (1968), the Temptations recorded "Cloud Nine" (1968) and "Ball of Confusion (That's What the World Is Today)" (1970), Gladys Knight and the Pips promoted a "Friendship Train" (1969), Edwin Starr condemned "War" (1970), and Stevie Wonder recorded "Living for the City" (1973) and "Higher Ground" (1973). The musical backdrop for some songs featured wah wah and fuzz guitars and other sound effects. Introduced by Norman Whitfield, these sounds captured the turmoil and confusion in society, and they "came out of a sound of the people and the environment in which [the individual] deals" (Stevenson 1983).

The concept of soul also advocated unity and respect in personal relationships. Otis Redding elaborated on these themes in "I've Been Loving You Too Long" (1965), "Respect" (1965) and "Try a Little Tenderness" (1966), as did Sam and Dave in "When Something Is Wrong with My Baby" (1966) and Al Green in "Let's Stay Together" (1971). The "Queen of Soul," Aretha Franklin, provided a female perspective on these themes in "I Never Loved a Man (The Way I Love You)" (1967), "Do Right Woman—Do Right Man" (1967), and "I Can't See Myself Leaving You" (1968).

Soul remained a major form of black popular expression through the first half of the 1970s. During this period, social and political change came at a much slower rate for many inner-city residents than for the black middle class. Expressing feelings of the working class and the poor, the Isley Brothers expounded on the need for "Freedom" (1970) and the Chi-Lites and the O'Jays reminded society that the critical mass of African Americans had not yet been empowered in "(For God's Sake) Give More Power to the People" (1971) and "Give the People What They Want" (1975), respectively. The O'Jays also cautioned against "Back Stabbers" (1972), and Marvin Gaye deplored the social problems that continued to plague inner-city residents in "What's Going On" (1971) and "Inner City Blues" (1971). The gospel-flavored interpretation of these lyrics added a unique quality to the sound of soul.

In earlier rhythm and blues styles, performers also drew from the gospel tradition by substituting secular for religious lyrics, incorporating call-response structures and vocal harmonies, and imitating the vocal styles of gospel quartets. Ray Charles continued this practice in songs, such as "I've Got a Woman" (1954) and "This Little Girl of Mine" (1955) that are secular versions of "Jesus Is All the World to Me" and "This Little Light of Mine," respectively. Charles also broadened this musical foundation by replacing the rhythm and blues combo arrangements with those from gospel music. His original compositions, including "Drown in My Own Tears" (1956), "That's Enough" (1959), and "What'd I Say (Part I)" (1959), for example, employ the 12/8 meter, formal harmonic and rhythmic structures, and vocal and piano stylings from gospel music (Maultsby 1992:30–31).

James Brown, known as the "Godfather of Soul," also contributed to the transformation of rhythm and blues into soul by adding a southern rawness and rhythmic intensity to the tradition. His percussive vocal timbres and repetitive phrases interjected with grunts, screams, and hollers and his polyrhythmic instrumental structures further defined the gospel foundation of the soul aesthetic. The recordings "Please, Please, Please" (1956), "Bewildered" (1959), and "Think" (1960) were models for many singers in the 1960s.

The concept of soul encouraged black people to identify with the culture and traditions of the motherland—Africa. Responding to this call, performers dressed in African attire accentuated by African adornments and hairstyles. This symbolic connection carried over into album designs, which often featured African-derived art and other images. Soul performers became icons not only as cultural preservers but as economic empowerers as well. Many soul performers established businesses in the inner city and assisted in building various community programs. James Brown, for example, owned radio stations, restaurants, and other businesses where he employed inner-city residents. He and other performers contributed to youth programs and charities. Al Bell also exemplified the ideology of economic empowerment when he became the sole owner of Stax in 1972. Both Stax and Motown used their resources to preserve black cultural expressions and to aid community development. For example, they created spoken-word labels to record the speeches of African American political leaders, poets, and comedians, and they organized benefit concerts using their artists to help finance protest demonstrations and to rebuild inner cities. Stax also contributed to the election campaigns of several black politicians and to their organizations. Through political activism and economic and self-empowerment, many black performers and music industry executives inspired African Americans to pursue goals that once seemed unattainable (Bell 1983; Byrd 1984; Gordy 1994:248–52; Maultsby 1983).

Although *soul* had been a household word in African American communities since 1964, the mainstream press resisted using the term. On 28 June 1968, *Time* magazine first acknowledged the institutionalization of the term when it featured Aretha Franklin on the cover and in a lengthy article, "Lady Soul Singing It Like It Is." A year later, *Billboard,* the leading trade music magazine, changed the name of its "Rhythm and Blues" chart to "Soul." These two events signaled a cultural victory for the Black Power movement, because both magazines used a term that was first coined and used by African Americans to describe a new and distinctive black musical genre as well as a cultural style.

REFERENCES

Bartholomew, Dave. 1985. Personal interview. 14 May.

Bartlett, David W. 1993. "Housing the Underclass." In *The Underclass: Views from History,* ed. Michael B. Katz, 118–157. Princeton, N.J.: Princeton University Press.

Bell, Al. 1983. Personal interview. 26 May.

Bowman, Rob. 1997. *Soulsville U.S.A.: The Story of Stax Records.* New York: Schirmer Books.

Byrd, Bobby. 1984. Personal interview. 8 September.

Conner, Charles. 1990. Personal interview. 10 November.

DjeDje, Jacqueline Cogdell, and Eddie S. Meadows, eds. 1998. *California Soul: Music of African Americans in the West.* Berkeley: University of California Press.

Dr. Licks. 1989. *Standing in the Shadows of Motown: The Life and Music of Legendary Bassist James Jamerson.* Wynnewood, Pa.: Dr. Licks Publishing.

Franklin, John Hope. 1994. *From Slavery to Freedom: A History of African Americans.* 7th ed. New York: Knopf.

Garland, Phil. 1969. *The Sound of Soul.* Chicago: Henry Regnery.

Garofalo, Reebee. 1990. "Crossing Over: 1939." In *Split Image: African Americans in the Mass Media,* ed. Jannette L. Dates and William Barlow, 57–121. Washington, D.C.: Howard University Press.

———. 1997. *Rockin' Out: Popular Music in the USA.* Boston: Allyn and Bacon.

George, Nelson. 1985. *Where Did Our Love Go?* New York: St. Martin's Press.

———. 1988. *The Death of Rhythm and Blues.* New York: Penguin Books.

Gillett, Charlie. 1974. *Making Tracks: Atlantic Records and the Growth of a Multi-Billion-Dollar Industry.* New York: E. P. Dutton.

———. 1983 [1970]. *The Sound of the City.* Rev. and expanded ed. New York: Pantheon Books.

Gordy, Berry. 1994. *To Be Loved.* New York: Warner Books.

Guillory, Monique, and Richard C. Green, eds. 1998. *Soul.* New York: New York University Press.

Guralnick, Peter. 1986. *Sweet Soul Music.* New York: Harper and Row.

Hannerz, Ulf. 1969. *Soulside: Inquiries into Ghetto Culture and Community.* New York: Columbia University Press.

Haralambos, Michael. 1975. *Right On: From Blues to Soul in Black America.* New York: Da Capo.

———. 1985 [1974]. *Soul Music: The Birth of a Sound in Black America.* New York: Da Capo.

Holland, Brian, and Eddie Holland. 1983. Personal interview.

Hudson, James "Pookie." 1985. Telephone interview. 28 March.

Jackson, John A. 1991. *Big Beat: Alan Freed and the Early Years of Rock & Roll.* New York: Schirmer Books.

Katz, Michael, ed. 1993. *The Underclass: Views from History.* Princeton, N.J.: Princeton University Press.

[n.a.]. 1968. "Lady Soul Singing It Like It Is" *Time,* 28 June, 62–66

Lydon, Michael. 1998. *Ray Charles: Man and Music.* New York: Riverhead Books.

Marable, Manning. 1991. *Race, Reform, and Rebellion.* Rev. 2nd ed. Jackson: University Press of Mississippi.

Maultsby, Portia K. 1983. "Soul Music: Its Sociological and Political Significance in American Popular Culture." *Journal of Popular Culture* 17(2):51–60.

———. 1986. *Rhythm and Blues (1945–1955): A Survey of Styles.* In *Black American Popular Music,* ed. Bernice Johnson Reagon. Washington, D.C.: Program in Black American Culture, Museum of American History, Smithsonian Institution.

———. 1992. "The Influence of Gospel Music on the Secular Music Industry." In *We'll Understand It Better By and By: African American Pioneering Gospel Composers,* ed. Bernice Johnson Reagon, 19–33. Washington, D.C.: Smithsonian Institution Press.

Moon, Tom. 1999. Radio interview. On Talk of the Nation: "The Death of Musician Curtis Mayfield and the Impact of His Music on Today's Musicians." National Public Radio. 28 December.

Otis, Johnny. 1984. Personal interview. 13 September.

———. 1993. *Upside Your Head! Rhythm and Blues on Central Avenue.* Hanover, N.H.: University Press of New England.

Parker, Deanie. 1984. Personal interview. 6 September.

Pavlow, Al. 1983. *The R & B Book: A Disc-History of Rhythm and Blues.* Providence, R.I.: Music House Publishing.

Russell, Albert "Diz." 1983. Personal interview. 27 September.

Shaw, Arnold. 1978. *Honkers and Shouters: The Golden Years of Rhythm and Blues.* New York: Collier Books.

Spaulding, Norman W. 1981. "History of Black Oriented Radio in Chicago 1929–1963." Ph.D. dissertation, University of Illinois.

Stevenson, William "Mickey." 1983. Personal interview. 20 April.

Stone, Jesse. 1982. Personal interview. 30 November.

Sugrue, Thomas. 1996. *The Origins of the Urban Crisis: Race and Equality in Postwar Detroit.* Princeton, N.J.: Princeton University Press.

Ward, Brian. 1998. *Just My Soul Responding: Rhythm and Blues, Black Consciousness and Race Relations.* London: University College London Press.

This article was completed while the author was a Fellow at the Center for Advanced Study in the Behavioral Sciences, (1999–2000) Stanford, California.

Funk

Portia K. Maultsby

Funk is an urban form of dance music that emerged in the late 1960s, crystallized and peaked in the 1970s, and expanded in new directions in the 1980s. Its sound resonated the energy of black working-class communities, and its message, the rhetoric of Black Power and black America's response to the post–Civil Rights era. The 1960s Great Society legislation, affirmative action programs, and Black Power movement raised expectations among African Americans for a better life. Yet society's support for these programs began to wane in the mid-1970s at a time when changing economic conditions led to massive unemployment and poverty in inner-city communities.

The ubiquitous optimism that once prevailed in African American communities slowly changed in response to unfulfilled expectations. While some members of the new middle class expressed ambivalence about progress, the poor and unemployed verbalized their disillusionment at the system that failed them. The term *funk* captured these feelings. As a musical style, funk represented the resilience and creativity of African Americans under changing social conditions, becoming an expression of social change, cultural liberation, and musical experimentation.

PIONEERS, SOCIAL CHANGE, AND THE CRYSTALLIZATION OF FUNK

The pioneers of funk were revolutionaries who created a musical genre that broke rules and crossed musical, class, and racial boundaries. The interracial and intergender group Sly and the Family Stone from San Francisco led the way by redefining the direction of black popular music. This self-contained group (members sang and played instruments) introduced the technology from rock (wah-wah pedal, fuzz box, echo chamber, vocal distortion, and so on) to the tradition. They also fused a blues-rock flavored guitar ("Sex Machine" [1968]) with syncopated horn riffs and blues- and jazz-inflected horn solos laid over a polyrhythmic "groove" established by the "Godfather of Soul," James Brown. Fred Wesley, former band leader-arranger-trombonist for James Brown, described this "groove" in a British television special, *Lenny Henry En De Funk,* as "a syncopated bass line, a strong heavy backbeat from the drummer, a counter choppy line from the guitar or keyboard, and someone singing on top of that in a gospel style." James Brown popularized this groove in his soul hits "Cold Sweat (Part I)" (1967) and "There Was a Time" (1967). Another innovation of Sly and the Family Stone was the revolutionary style of bassist Larry Graham (figure 1). Graham exploited

FIGURE 1   Bassist Larry Graham of Sly and the Family Stone. Photo by Aaron Rapoport. Courtesy Archives of African American Music and Culture, Indiana University.

the instrument's melodic and rhythmic capabilities by pulling, plucking, thumping, and slapping the strings to produce a distinctive percussive style heard in the 1969 recordings "Stand!," "Hot Fun in the Summertime," and "Thank You (Falettinme Be Mice Elf Agin)."

Sly and the Family Stone epitomized the spirit, chaos, and contradictions of the late 1960s and early 1970s. Influenced by the civil rights movement and the ideology of Black Power, Sly Stone spoke out against social injustice, promoted universal harmony in "Everyday People" (1969) and "Stand!," and encouraged all races to "Dance to the Music" (1968) because "I Wanna Take You Higher" (1969). In "Thank You (Falettinme Be Mice Elf Agin)," "Don't Call Me Nigga, Whitey" (1969), and "Thank You for Talkin' to Me, Africa" (1971), Stone candidly addressed racial issues, revealing his political consciousness as a black man in America. His music also created "an open atmosphere of tolerance and truth that the wicked elements of racism were exposed and thrust into the pop dialogue like never before" (Vincent 1996:90).

The politically conscious lyrics, eclectic sounds, infectious energy, and hippie image of Sly and the Family Stone attracted multiracial audiences from all social and economic backgrounds. This form of racial integration engendered themes of universal love and world peace that became codified and promoted through the music of black artists and white folk groups. In the early 1970s, however, messages of Black Power and "let's party" began to overshadow themes of universal love and world peace. These themes revealed the response of African Americans to the changing economic and social conditions of the inner-city poor and working classes. Historian Joe Trotter explained that by the 1970s, "some middle- and working-class blacks [had] gained access to multiracial institutions and moved into integrated neighborhoods. At the same time, the onslaught of deindustrialization undercut the position of black men in heavy industries, leaving behind a growing body of permanently unemployed black poor" (Katz 1993:56). In inner-city communities, funk became a major form of cultural expression, and it provided some hope for the poor and working classes that saw little, if any, potential for improved conditions.

Kool and the Gang from New York, for example, continued the call for social and political justice in "Who's Gonna Take the Weight" (1970), employing a hybrid musical style that reflected their roots in jazz. The group War reminded society of the plight of the poor and the deteriorating conditions of ghettos in "Slipping into Darkness" (1971) and "The World Is a Ghetto" (1972). War's funk style incorporated Latin rhythms and a bluesy harmonica that symbolized the diverse racial and ethnic composition of the group as well as life in the ghettos of Los Angeles. Despite the local and national calls for social equality, a recession (1973–1975) pushed the poor and working class deeper into the margins of society and created mayhem. Without the prospect of jobs, Elijah Anderson (1990:77) noted that some of the unemployed gravitated toward the underground economy as distributors of illegal goods and services.

In black clubs, the poor and working-class blacks temporarily escaped from the uncertainties and pressures of daily life, partying to funk music. The "Dayton street funk" style of the Ohio Players (figure 2) became popular among these groups. According to bass player Marshall Jones (1997), their songs captured the flavor of black street culture and drew from the vocabulary of working-class and poor blacks. The song "Skin Tight" (1974), for example, described the bodily movements of women wearing skintight outfits; "Jive Turkey" (1974) sang of deceitful women; and "Fire" (1974) and "Sweet Sticky Thing" (1975) extolled sexual pleasures using coded language. The Ohio Players also acknowledged college life in "Streaking Cheek to Cheek" (1974), which recounts the adventures of streakers on college campuses. Other groups, such as Kool and the Gang, created a celebratory atmosphere by adding party sound effects to their music that inspired black folk to "hang loose" on the dance floor ("Funky Stuff" [1973], "Jungle Boogie" [1973], and "Hollywood Swinging" [1974]).

In inner-city communities, funk became a major form of cultural expression, and it provided some hope for the poor and working classes that saw little, if any, potential for improved conditions.

FIGURE 2   The Ohio Players, who created the Dayton street funk style. Courtesy Archives of African American Music and Culture, Indiana University.

Positioned between the black working and middle classes were African American college students. In a field study on the musical preferences of these students, many indicated that they favored funk because they could "chill," "party," and "be themselves" (Maultsby 1982 and 1983). On predominantly white campuses, this music also provided a source for personal rejuvenation and reconnected black students to their cultural roots. In studies, researchers found that these students experienced exclusion and an inhospitable environment and that their feeling of alienation increased after the assassination of Martin Luther King, Jr. Determined to influence change, African American students negotiated the implementation of black studies curricula, the recruitment of African American faculty and staff, and the establishment of black student unions, cultural centers, and all-black dormitories. Retreating from mainstream pressures, funk music created an atmosphere for unrestricted social interaction and an expression of "blackness" (Feagin and Sikes 1994:91–134, 225; F. Jones 1977:154; Willie 1972).

Although funk music appealed primarily to African American communities in the early 1970s, some groups had crossover appeal. Continuing the tradition of Sly and the Family Stone, Earth, Wind and Fire encouraged society to care for its children and to find peace on earth and meaning in life through understanding and love. These universal themes and the jazz-fusion funk style characterized the group's album *That's the Way of the World* (1975), which scored big on both the rhythm and blues and pop charts, as did Kool and the Gang's *Spirit of the Boogie* (1975), with similar messages. Despite the crossover success of Earth, Wind and Fire and occasional crossover singles from Kool and the Gang and other groups, funk largely disappeared from the mainstream in the second half of the 1970s. Contributing factors were the rise in disco music as a competing form, a slower tempo that made funk incompatible with the dance styles of whites, restrictive programming policies of Top 40 radio, and racially segmented marketing practices of record labels. In contrast, funk became central to social settings in African American communities as an outlet for frustration and a uniting force in an era of social change. This music dominated the programming of many black-oriented radio stations, the turntables in nightclubs, and the stage in performance venues (George 1988:147–156).

THE PINNACLE OF FUNK

By the mid-1970s, funk and other styles of black popular music had begun to evolve in new directions. This development paralleled the government's move toward fiscal conservatism, society's shift in views on the 1960s equal rights legislation, and the expression of disillusionment and ambivalence about progress among African Americans (Feagin and Sikes 1994:135–186; Gill 1980; Jones 1977). James Brown, the O'Jays, and Jerry Butler captured this changing mood in "Funky President (People It's Bad)" (1974), "Survival" (1975), and "(I'm Just Thinking About) Coolin' Out" (1978). In "Funky President," Brown criticized President Richard Nixon for his social and economic policies. He explained that while stock prices rose and taxes increased, jobs disappeared in the black community, leaving black people drinking from paper cups. Addressing the working-class and poor blacks, Brown declared: "We gotta' get over, before we go under." A year later, the O'Jays in "Survival" desperately pleaded for assistance to pay rent and buy shoes for a baby because they were broke and "one step away from the bread line." From the opposite end of the economic ladder, Jerry Butler expressed his weariness from chasing a "tired dream." In 1978, he acknowledged that it was time to give up the stress and strain to relax and "cool out."

In the mid-1970s, many young black professionals began retreating from their integrated neighborhoods to black clubs and other social settings in the black community to cool out. Similarly, many black faculty, staff, and graduate students in predominantly white institutions frequented clubs in the African American section of town. In these settings, they rejoined working-class and poor blacks and temporarily liberated themselves from the restrictions of and frustrating encounters in the mainstream. Funk music prevailed in all social settings, and party-funk reigned supreme (Maultsby 1984 and 1985).

Larry Graham, Sly Stone's former bass player, increased the intensity of party funk by adding familiar rhythms, harmonies, and stylings from black gospel music, accentuated by thumps, pops, and slaps on the bass guitar. The songs of Graham Central Station, "Release Yourself" (1974), "It's Alright" (1975), "The Jam" (1975), and "Now-Do-U-Wanta Dance" (1977), encouraged black people from all socioeconomic classes to "don't fight the feeling and let go." In the mid-1970s the scope of party funk broadened, reflecting the changing mood of African Americans, especially the middle class.

ONE NATION UNDER A GROOVE: THE EMERGENCE OF P-FUNK

George Clinton (figure 3) took party funk to another level when he formulated the P-funk concept, defined by a philosophy, attitude, culture, and musical style. Grounded in the ideology of Black Power, P-funk advocated self-liberation from the social and cultural restrictions of society. P-funk created new social spaces for African Americans to redefine themselves and celebrate their blackness. In a National Public Radio profile of George Clinton, producer Steve Rowland noted that various socioeconomic classes of African Americans embraced P-funk: "It appealed to the heads

FIGURE 3   George Clinton, originator of P-funk. Courtesy Archives of African American Music and Culture, Indiana University.

and to the hard core, to the intellectual and to the street" (Rowland 1994). P-funk had its own language, fashion, dances, and mythical heroes and villains, who Clinton presented as black science-fiction characters. The mastermind and producer of five P-funk groups (Parliament, Funkadelic, Parlets, the Brides of Funkenstein, and Bootsy's Rubber Band), Clinton combined these cultural components to create stories about black people and black life from a black perspective. In an interview, he revealed: "[These] stories place blacks in places where you don't conceive of them being" (Clinton 1995).

Parliament's albums *Chocolate City* (1975), *Mothership Connection* (1975), and *Clones of Dr. Funkenstein* (1976) placed blacks in the White House and on an imaginary planet, respectively. Clinton presented these stories in a humorous manner by using black slang for song titles and lyrics, such as "Groovallegiance," "Funkentelechy," and "Prosifunkstication." He also featured cartoon and science-fiction characters on the jackets of albums and brought them to life during stage performances. For Clinton, humor served a practical function: "We try to not preach but we try to bring them [social issues] up" (Clinton 1995).

The P-funk sound drew elements from the blues, rhythm and blues, jazz, funk, and psychedelic rock. The tempo of songs encouraged black people to be cool and laid back. Therefore, they were slower than the music of non-P-funk groups, centering on 88 beats per minute and rarely exceeding 104, as opposed to the 96 to 120 beats per minute of other funk groups. Clinton broadened the scope of funk by introducing new approaches to varying moods, textures, and timbres that symbolized concepts of heterogeneity and spontaneity in black cultural expression. These features are illustrated in Parliament's "Mothership Connection" (1975), "Rumpofsteelskin" (1979), "Sir Nose D'Voidoffunk" (1977), and "Night of the Thumpasorus Peoples" (1975) and in the Brides of Funkenstein's "War Ship Touchante" (1978).

Clinton's P-funk style complemented the party style of late 1970s and early 1980s associated with groups such as the Bar-Kays ("Shake Your Rump to the Funk" [1976]), Slave ("The Party Song" [1977]), Con Funk Shun ("Shake and Dance with Me" [1978]), Gap Band ("I Don't Believe You Want to Get up and Dance" [1979]), Lakeside ("Fantastic Voyage" [1980]), Cameo ("Freaky Dancin'" [1981]), and the Dazz Band ("Let It Whip" [1982]).

THE 1980s: THE RISE OF TECHNO-FUNK

In the 1980s, funk developed in new directions. New trends in popular music and the popularity of disco music following the 1978 release of the film *Saturday Night Fever* forced many funk musicians to include pop elements in their productions. The reliance on synthesizers in the production of disco influenced the reconfiguration of funk groups. Marshall Jones of the Ohio Players elaborated: "By the late 1970s, computers had started coming into the industry and the beat was more infectious because computers can do things rhythmically that musicians actually can't do" (M. Jones 1997). Changing technology as well as recording budget restrictions compelled many funk bands to reduce their personnel by replacing bass and horn players and other musicians with synthesizers to remain competitive.

Several of the 1970s groups, including the Isley Brothers, Brothers Johnson, and Rick James, successfully incorporated advanced technology to modernize their funk sound. Others, such as Kool and the Gang, Slave, and Dayton, changed musical directions by adding lead vocalists to the group in addition to disco and pop elements over the funk groove. Some funk groups had difficulty redefining their musical direction. The group Dayton, for example, reached its maturity in the transitional period between disco and funk. Trumpet and keyboard player Chris Jones recalled: "There wasn't a whole lot of deep funk with Dayton" (C. Jones 1997). Dayton's use of advanced technology resulted in a more sophisticated sound with less obvious funk roots. Similar to Heatwave's "Boogie Nights" (1977) and "The Groove Line" (1978), Dayton's sound was a funk-disco-jazz hybrid ("I Got My Eye on You" [1980] and "The Sound of Music" [1984]). Their biggest hit, "Hot Fun in the Summertime" (1982), however, was a funk-disco remake of a song by Sly and the Family Stone.

Unlike Dayton, Roger and Zapp (groups formed from one family) creatively used advanced technology to modernize the Dayton street funk sound. Their innovative and extensive use of synthesizers to produce heavy dance rhythms, timbral changes, and vocal distortion appealed to African Americans, especially the working class. This distortion, produced through a talkbox, added a unique flavor to street funk, as in "More Bounce to the Ounce" (1980), "I Heard It through the Grapevine" (1981), and "Dance Floor" (1982).

New crossover funk sounds came out of Minneapolis. The multitalented Prince of Prince and the Revolution created an eclectic repertoire and musical style rooted in rhythm and blues and rock [see THE MUSIC INDUSTRY, p. 705]. He expanded the tradition by introducing an erotic brand of synthesized funk in the albums *Dirty Mind* (1980), *1999* (1982), and *Purple Rain* (1984). Another Minneapolis group, The Time, created a new style of synthesized dance funk employing flavorings reminiscent of Graham Central Station and high-tech production techniques (*What Time Is It?* [1982] and *Ice Cream Castles* [1984]). Both Prince and The Time brought recognition to Minneapolis as another center for funk through their own recordings and productions of other artists.

The 1980s represented a transitional period not only for funk musicians but the broader African American community as well. The economic downside and President Ronald Reagan's gradual dismantling of affirmative action programs created chaos in inner-city communities. The second recession (1980–1982), ongoing fiscal and social conservatism, and the accumulative impact of deindustrialization thrust poor and working-class blacks into severe poverty marked by high unemployment and over-crowded, dilapidated, rat-infested dwellings. Moreover, the relocation of the black middle class to the suburbs and integrated neighborhoods left these communities without traditional leadership and financial resources (Landry 1987:196–233; Marable 1991:191–213; Sugrue 1996:259–271). Within this context, funk music became "a way of sustaining the everyday rituals of black folks. It soothes and comforts a wounded folk" (West 1994).

FUNK AND BLACK CULTURE

Funk as a cultural style defined an image that portrayed a lifestyle and communicated a philosophy. It is manifested in the persona adopted by groups, the fashions they wore, artwork on album jackets, and elaborate stage props. The Ohio Players, for example, chose their name and constructed an image from the street life of Dayton. Marshall Jones (1997) recalled that they were influenced by the cool persona and flashy fashions of Dayton's street hustlers as well as the players and pimps portrayed in the 1970s "blaxploitation" films such as *Shaft* (1971) and *Superfly* (1972).

On album jackets and in live performances, the Ohio Players dressed in tuxedos, furs, hats, diamond rings, and other fashionable street attire from the 1970s and 1980s. They also used extensive stage props to create the ambience of city street life. In contrast, Earth, Wind and Fire constructed an image of spirituality using Egyptian symbols that connected them with the ancient past. They dressed in sequined white and bright-colored costumes, and their stage props depicted ancient spiritual sources. These visuals and the people of different racial and ethnic backgrounds that appeared on many of Earth, Wind and Fire's album jackets conveyed themes of universality and world peace.

Live performances featured elaborate props accompanied by sound, lighting, and stage effects that transformed the stage into imagined places, including outer space, where a huge spaceship landed on the planet of funk.

George Clinton's groups, Parliament and Funkadelic, adopted images that mirrored both the P-funk philosophy and themes for each album. They dressed in outlandish costumes such as sheets, diapers, hot pants, bell-bottom pants, furs, sequined tops, space outfits, sunglasses, and masks. Moreover, live performances featured elaborate props accompanied by sound, lighting, and stage effects that transformed the stage into imagined places, including outer space, where a huge spaceship landed on the planet of funk. Stage performances of George Clinton, Earth, Wind and Fire, and the Ohio Players advanced funk to another level and influenced the productions of musicians of subsequent decades.

The funk sound, image, and stage performance of the music represented a rejection of mainstream values and norms. According to Danny Webster, guitarist and vocalist for Slave, "Funk is a black thing [because] there is a need to express yourself as an African American. You need to be your own person" (Webster 1997). In the 1970s and 1980s, many African Americans from all socioeconomic classes created new spaces for unrestricted black expression in the "land of funk," where they responded to the pressures of daily life in an "integrated" society by affirming and celebrating their black identity.

REFERENCES

Anderson, Elijah. 1990. *Street Wise: Race, Class, and Change in an Urban Community.* Chicago: University of Chicago Press.

Clinton, George. 1995. Personal interview. 5 March.

Feagin, Joe R., and Melvin P. Sikes. 1994. *Living with Racism: The Black Middle-Class Experience.* Boston: Beacon Press.

Franklin, John Hope, and Alfred A. Moss. 1994. *From Slavery to Freedom: A History of African Americans.* 7th ed. New York: Knopf.

George, Nelson. 1988. *The Death of Rhythm and Blues.* New York: Penguin Books.

Gill, Gerald. 1980. *Meanness Mania: The Changed Mood.* Washington, D.C.: Howard University Press.

Jones, Chris. 1997. Personal interview. 18 August.

Jones, Faustine Childress. 1977. *The Changing Mood in America: Eroding Commitment?* Washington, D.C.: Howard University Press.

Jones, Marshall. 1997. Personal interview. 19 August.

Katz, Michael, ed. 1993. *The Underclass: Views from History.* Princeton, N.J.: Princeton University Press.

Landry, Bart. 1987. *The New Black Middle Class.* Berkeley: University of California Press.

Marable, Manning. 1991. *Race, Reform, and Rebellion.* Rev. 2nd ed. Jackson: University Press of Mississippi.

Maultsby, Portia K. 1979. "Contemporary Pop: A Healthy Diversity Evolves from Creative Freedom." *Billboard,* June 9, BM10, BM22, BM28 [Black Music Section].

———. 1982 and 1983. Unpublished field study on the "Musical Preferences of African American College Students."

———. 1984 and 1985. Informal discussions with black faculty. Ford Foundation Postdoctoral Minority Fellows conference. Washington, D.C.

Rowland, Steve. 1994. Live commentary. On "Profile of George Clinton, the Master of Funk." Weekend Edition, National Public Radio. 6 February.

Sugrue, Thomas J. 1996. *The Origins of the Urban Crisis: Race and Inequality in Postwar Detroit.* Princeton, N.J.: Princeton University Press.

Triandis, Harry C., ed. 1976. Variations in Black and White Perceptions of the Social Environment. Urbana: University of Illinois Press.

Trotter, Joe William, Jr. 1993. "Blacks in the Urban North: The 'Underclass' Question in Historical Perspective." In *The Underclass: Views from History,* ed. Michael B. Katz, 55–81. Princeton, N.J.: Princeton University Press.

———. 1997. *River Jordan: African American Urban Life in the Ohio Valley.* Lexington: University Press of Kentucky.

———. Forthcoming. *The African American Experience.* Boston: Houghton Mifflin.

Trotter, Joe William Jr., and Eric Ledell Smith, eds. 1998. *African Americans in Pennsylvania: Shifting Historical Perspectives.* University Park: Pennsylvania State University Press.

Vincent, Rickey. 1996. *Funk: The Music, the People, and the Rhythm of the One.* New York: St. Martin's/Griffin.

Webster, Danny. 1997. Personal interview. 18 August.

West, Cornel. 1994. Radio interview. On "Profile of George Clinton, the Master of Funk." Weekend Edition, National Public Radio. 6 February.

Willie, Charles Vert. 1972. *Black Students at White Colleges.* New York: Praeger.

This article was completed while the author was a Fellow at the Center for Advanced Study in the Behavioral Sciences, (1999–2000) Stanford, California.

Disco and House Music
Kai Fikentscher

The Evolution of Disco
The Disco Backlash: Dance Music/Club Music/Hip-Hop
House Music

After 1970, American popular dance music can be summarily viewed as the development of disco music, and disco's evolution, during the 1980s and 1990s, into three main categories of dance music: club, house, and hip-hop. Disco, house, and hip-hop are thus related forms of twentieth-century American popular dance music [see Disco, p. 227; Hip-Hop and Rap, p. 692]. As such, they belong to a continuous history of American social dance that begins with the Charleston in the 1920s and to an even longer continuum of African American expressive culture.

In contrast to much rock and pop music, in which aspects of musicianship in performance are central and generally given priority, disco and postdisco dance music highlight the production process itself, exemplified in the roles of producers, recording engineers, and disc jockeys. In contrast to the world of pop music (and, to an extent, of hip-hop), the central performers in the environments of disco, club, and house music are the disc jockey and the dancers rather than the singers and musicians. In this performance environment, music is as physical as it is audible, involving, in the deejay booth, twin turntables, a mixer, and vinyl records, and on the dance floor, the human body as chief musical instruments.

THE EVOLUTION OF DISCO

Disco is a category of 1970s dance music, derived from the abbreviation for discotheque as the main venue of its performance and consumption. Before disco evolved into a stylistic category that eventually included dance routines as well as fashion and hair styles, the term referred to a new musical context, pioneered in New York underground dance venues by disc jockeys (deejays) catering to primarily minority (African American/Latino) and gay audiences. The roots of the disco phenomenon are located at the intersection of underground dance clubs and gay sensibilities and, more specifically, in gay black clubs of New York City in the late 1960s/early 1970s. Using two turntables and a repertoire of mainly soul, funk, and Latin records (before 1975, only 45-rpm singles and 33-rpm album cuts were available), deejays at that time began to create an uninterrupted flow of music at dance parties in nightclubs, lofts, and bars, following the example of Francis Grasso at New York's Sanctuary, in 1970 the first notoriously gay discotheque in America. Grasso's innovation, later called disco blending,

Comparable to the dance crazes associated with 1930s jazz and 1950s rock and roll, disco's popular success as well came at the price of rendering its sociocultural origins invisible.

became a standard for seamless mixing of prerecorded music for uninterrupted dancing that was copied and refined by other downtown disco deejays (such as Walter Gibbons, who went on to remix the first commercially available twelve-inch single, Double Exposure's "Ten Percent") and uptown deejays such as Kool Herc and Grandmaster Flash, two of the pioneers of hip-hop. Disco dance parties were held either as private, members-only events or for a more general clientele, largely by and for segments of urban society that identified themselves as being on the margins of the American mainstream. These segments consisted largely of gays, African Americans, Latinos, and women, who collectively had been largely closed out of the increasingly white, sexist, male-dominated rock music industry.

With the appeal of discotheques, such as Sanctuary, Salvation, Gallery, Le Jardin, The Loft, and Better Days, New York City became the world's disco capital during the early 1970s, with more than two hundred discotheques in Manhattan alone inviting thousands of weekly dancers by the end of the decade. Following the success of disco-hits (a term introduced by *Billboard* in 1973) such as Manu Dibango's "Soul Makossa" (1973), the Hues Corporation's "Rock the Boat" (1974), and George McCrae's "Rock Your Baby" (1974), radio stations such as WKTU changed to a disco format, while disco records began to sell so well as to compete with the sales of rock and pop singles and albums. Celebrities lined up to get into Studio 54, arguably the most famous Manhattan discotheque of that period.

Between the early and mid-1970s, with the help of radio and television exposure across the United States and Europe, disco became one of the most popular sounds of the decade. Originally based on up-tempo rhythm-and-blues-based funk and soul music (for example, MFSB's "Love Is the Message" [1974]) and popular Latin repertoire (for example, Barabas's "Checkmate" [1975]), disco's development as both style and commerce increasingly involved electronic instruments such as synthesizers and drum machines and European producers (for example, Donna Summer's "I Feel Love" [1977] was produced by Giorgio Moroder).

In 1975, disco music began to be issued in a new format, the twelve-inch single. This deejay-friendly medium established the deejay as remixer who, through rearranging, editing, and finally rerecording dance music versions for club play, became an important marketing tool for record companies eager to profit from the disco boom. In the process, discotheques became test labs for new dance music. Through deejay collectives known as record pools, advance copies of records were given to deejays before their commercial release to test audience responses on the dance floor. A famous example of this is the sixteen-minute version of Donna Summer's "Love to Love You Baby" (1975), crafted by Giorgio Moroder, who helped establish Summer's reputation as "Queen of Disco."

Disco's most profitable venture was the November 1977 release of the film (and its best-selling sound track) *Saturday Night Fever,* produced by Robert Stigwood and featuring John Travolta and the music of an Australian pop trio, the Bee Gees. Comparable to the dance crazes associated with 1930s jazz and 1950s rock and roll (both African American musical styles gaining mainstream acceptance only after their popularization by Caucasian stars such as Paul Whiteman and Elvis Presley), disco's popular success as well came at the price of rendering its sociocultural origins invisible: both John Travolta's character in the film and the Bee Gees were neither gay nor of African descent.

THE DISCO BACKLASH: DANCE MUSIC/CLUB MUSIC/HIP-HOP

The economic success of disco as America's most important mass sound of the 1970s helped to amplify the opprobrium of the mainstream rock/pop establishment, based in no small measure on the association of disco with male homosexuality and ethnic minorities. As some rock musicians jumped on the disco economic bandwagon (examples of recordings are the Rolling Stones' "Miss You" [1978], Rod Stewart's "Do Ya Think I'm Sexy?" [1978], and Queen's "Another One Bites the Dust" [1980]), others joined efforts in organized attempts to combat the "disco craze." On 12 July 1979, at a time when *Rolling Stone* magazine published advertisements for "Disco Sucks" teeshirts, rock radio deejay Steve Dahl organized a public burning of hundreds of disco records at Comiskey Park in Chicago.

By 1980, a glut of disco products coincided with an economic recession that decimated the ranks of recording companies, including those who had invested in disco acts. Disco, controversial because of its emphasis on bodily pleasures and the associated sexual, social, and ethnic connotations, lost its economic clout. In the early 1980s, the term *disco* rather quickly disappeared from the media discourse and public life. The recording industry, chiefly through *Billboard* magazine, replaced *disco* with the more neutral terms *dance music* and *club music*. Marketing subcategories of that period include DOR (dance-oriented rock) and hi-NRG, a term used for up-tempo disco music of the early and mid-1980s that appealed mainly to non–African American gays, especially in Britain but also elsewhere in Europe and Asia.

At this point, while disco's original urban core clientele continued to dance to disco, funk and soul records at underground venues known for their primarily gay patrons (in both racially segregated and mixed settings), the attention of America's mainstream media and their audiences was caught by punk and new wave, and, from the mid-1980s onward, by hip-hop. By this time, discotheques had become referred to as clubs, and disco music had been renamed club, underground music, or simply dance music. As an abbreviation, *club* eventually came to stand for the venue as much as the music, just as disco had done before. However, these 1980s terms had the advantage of not being nominally associated with disco, thus leaving open issues of musical style and associated audiences. The stylistic flexibility of this period is reflected in the eclectic repertoire of influential club deejays such as Afrika Bambaataa, who developed followings in community centers in the Bronx as well as at the Mudd Club in downtown Manhattan. While his 1980 single "Planet Rock," a reworking of Kraftwerk's "Trans-Europe-Express" (1977), enlarged audiences for rap and electro-funk, his downtown colleague Larry Levan (figure 1), residing at the Paradise Garage club on the Lower West Side, became the most influential deejay in New York, with a repertoire ranging from Philly-soul (for example, the songs of MFSB and First Choice), to German electronic music, to Caribbean pop, to songs by the Who ("Eminence Front" [1982]), the Clash ("Magnificent Dance" [1980]), and Marianne Faithfull ("Why D'Ya Do It" [1979]). In the process, the Paradise Garage, which had been voted "Most Favorite Disco" at a record industry convention in 1979, became an underground dance venue with a national and international reputation, with Levan acquiring the nickname "The Father" from his disciples among New York's growing deejay circles.

FIGURE I   The late Larry Levan in the DJ booth at The Choice, New York City, 1989. Photo by Tina Paul. Reproduced with permission.

HOUSE MUSIC

House music is generally viewed as the electronic offspring of disco music. As with disco and club music, the name refers to a location rather than to stylistic traits. Accordingly, *house* is the abbreviation of the Warehouse, an influential Chicago dance venue where a Bronx-born deejay, Frankie Knuckles, acquired the nickname "God-father of House." Knuckles was referred to the Warehouse, where he worked between 1977 and 1983, by his friend and mentor Larry Levan, who had declined the offer to relocate in order to remain resident deejay at the Paradise Garage. House also refers to the location of its production: in contrast to disco, which was produced inside the recording studio, house music began as homemade music. This points to changes in music technology associated with the then emerging home recording industry that blurred the line between the recording technology of the recording studio and the play-back technology of the deejay booth.

Disco deejays have been instrumental in lengthening disco tracks from three-minute pop songs to extended versions as long as sixteen minutes, following the intro-duction of the twelve-inch single as a deejay-friendly format by deejay-producer Tom Moulton in 1975. But whereas the typical disco production used studio musicians, technology, and production standards, house music pioneers such as Frankie Knuckles, Farley "Jackmaster Funk," Chip E., Jesse Saunders, Steve "Silk" Hurley, DJ Pierre, Marshall Jefferson, and Larry Heard, who were influenced by the music of European artists such as Kraftwerk, Manuel Göttsching, Depeche Mode, and Gary Numan, emphasized electronic technology and sounds that had recently become available and accessible with the establishment of MIDI (musical instrument digital interface) standards and the growth of the home recording industry. Accordingly, the sound of house music was characterized initially by the use of cheap analog and, later, more costly digital electronic equipment, including synthesizers, samplers, drum computers, and sequencers. Although early Chicago house records evidence a rough, unpolished, and minimalist sound related to the do-it-yourself approach of its producers, this technology eventually helped house deejays to become producers, remixers, and recording artists in their own right. In the 1990s, Frankie Knuckles became one of the highest paid remixers, one of the first deejays to receive a major label contract as recording artist, and, in 1998, the first deejay to receive a Grammy Award as best remixer, itself a newly established award category.

Chicago clubs, such as the Warehouse, the Powerplant, and the Music Box, were as important to the initial exposure of house as were radio shows on WGCI and WBMX by the Hot Mix 5, a disc jockey collective formed in 1981 by Kenny Jason and Farley Keith Williams (Farley "Jackmaster Funk"). Like their club-based colleagues Frankie Knuckles and Ron Hardy, they mixed and produced music on twelve-inch singles that were released on local independent recording companies, primarily Larry Sherman's Precision and Trax labels and Rocky Jones's DJ International company. In the late 1980s, as house gradually branched out to other urban dance scenes, several subcategories emerged, including acid house, deep house, hip house, and, later, garage and speed garage. The latter two terms, popular with British deejays, honor the Paradise Garage, as they refer to the inspiration of New York club music produced after its closure in 1987. Since then, the economic center for house has shifted from the United States to the U.K., where acid house, into the 1990s, turned into rave and techno music in the hands of British house producers, such as Jazzy M, Babyford, CJ Mackintosh, Paul Oakenfold, and Danny Rampling. Under the name techno, European derivations of British acid house have since become the soundscape in dance clubs all across Europe.

REFERENCES

Cummins, Tony. 1975. *The Sound of Philadelphia.* London: Methuen.

Fikentscher, Kai. 2000. *"You Better Work!" Underground Dance Music in New York City.* Hanover, N.H.: Wesleyan University Press/University Press of New England.

Goldman, Albert. 1978. *Disco.* New York: Hawthorn.

Harvey, Steven. 1983. "Behind the Groove: New York City's Disco Underground." *Collusion* 9:26–33.

Hughes, Walter. 1994. "In the Empire of the Beat: Discipline and Disco." In *Microphone Fiends:*

Youth Music and Youth Culture, ed. Andrew Ross and Tricia Rose, 147–157. New York: Routledge.

Joe, Radcliffe A. 1980. *This Business of Disco.* New York: Billboard Books.

Miezitis, Vita. 1980. *Night Dancin'.* New York: Ballantine.

Poschardt, Ulf. 1995. *DJ Culture.* Hamburg, Germany: Rogner & Bernard.

Shannon, Doug. 1985. *Off the Record: Everything Related to Playing Recorded Dance Music in the Nightclub Industry.* Cleveland, Ohio: Pacesetter Publishing House.

Thomas, Anthony. 1995. "The House the Kids Built: The Gay Imprint on American Dance Music." In *Out in Culture: Gay, Lesbian and Queer Essays on Popular Culture,* ed. Corey K. Creekmur and Alexander Doty, 437–448. Durham, N.C.: Duke University Press.

Tucker, Ken. 1986. "The Seventies and Beyond." In *Rock of Ages: The Rolling Stone History of Rock'n'Roll,* ed. Ed Ward, Geoffrey Stokes, and Ken Tucker, 467–624. New York: Summit.

Hip-Hop and Rap
Dawn M. Norfleet

Hip-hop (hiphop or hip hop), also called hip-hop culture, is a creative expression, aesthetic, and sensibility that developed in African American, Afro-Caribbean, and Latino communities of the Bronx and Harlem, New York City, by the mid-1970s. Hip-hop, now an internationally recognized cultural phenomenon largely due to the popularity of rap music, encompasses a wide range of competitive performance expressions that often go unnoticed by the mainstream public. These four elements are aerosol art (graffiti); b-boying/girling (break dancing); DJ-ing, or the art of using turntables, vinyl records, and mixing units as musical instruments; and MC-ing (rapping), the art of verbal musical expression (rap music). Those who consider their primary aesthetic to be shaped by hip-hop culture and/or claim a personal stake in its development form what is known as the hip-hop community. Community insiders are sometimes referred to as hip-hoppers. Rap music, which is the most popularized manifestation of hip-hop, is an African American popular musical expression that emphasizes stylized verbal delivery of rhymed couplets, typically to prerecorded accompaniment, or "tracks."

EARLY HISTORY

Rap music is rooted in cultural and verbal traditions from the Caribbean as well as the United States. Mainland traditions that remain visible in hip-hop include "jive-talking" radio personalities of the 1940s and 1950s and oral traditions of storytelling, toasting, and "playing the dozens," a competitive and recreational exchange of verbal insults. Jamaican traditions include toasting and mobile disk jockeys. Many of the hip-hop pioneers were Caribbean immigrants, who brought some of the musical practices from their native countries and adapted them for their new situation.

During World War II, Jamaicans heard African American dance music through soldiers stationed there. Additionally, music spread through record trade and American radio broadcasts could be heard on the island. Rhythm and blues, bebop, and swing offered an alternative to the two government-run, British-modeled Jamaican radio stations, which broadcast calypso-styled *mento* and other styles that appealed primarily to economically higher classes. Imported African American dance music grew in popularity, particularly at "blues dances" taking place mostly in economically poor urban areas in the 1950s. Mobile disc jockeys (DJs), who provided music for social events, featured rhythm and blues records. The DJs competed for the attention and patronage of social dancers using large sound systems ("sounds") in a battle of volume and song choices. These sounds consisted of turntables, powerful speakers, amplifiers, and a microphone. At the helm were Duke Reid and Sir Coxone, men who became legendary figures in the early era of the mobile discothèques. The DJ also enlisted a paid crew of assistants and accrued loyal audience participants. Often, two DJs were booked to perform in the same space. When this occurred, the DJs engaged in a battle of decibels and carefully selected and ordered songs designed to elicit the maximum response from the audience of social dancers.

The DJ spoke "rhythmically over the music, [using] his voice as another instrument" on the microphone (Fernando 1994:34). These spoken comments, known as toasting, included praises for dancers on their appearance and information on the next dance. With the development of the Jamaican recorded music industry in the 1950s, artists began to record instrumental versions of songs, known as "dub" versions on the "B" side of the vocal track versions, in response to the growing practice of toasting on the microphone by DJs at public dances. One of the most important figures in the Jamaican practice of toasting on record is U. Roy, who was the first to record his style of rhythmic speaking over dubs in 1970. Both Jamaican and U.S. early rapping traditions were started by rapping DJs, who only later hired people to rap exclusively as the art of DJ-ing grew increasingly complex. The rappers became known as MCs, or masters of ceremony, and were charged with motivating the crowd and delivering information about upcoming social events.

The mingling of Caribbean immigrant and native-born African American and Latino communities in the United States set the stage for the development of the new art form. A large Caribbean community had developed in the boroughs of New York, where the first rap musical dance events were said to have begun as early as 1972 in the Bronx. The native-born African American inhabitants of New York, many of whom were recent migrants from the South, had a strong and vibrant verbal culture as well. Toasting also took place in the United States, albeit in the form of long, rhymed stories, often memorized and passed on orally. "The Signifying Monkey" is one such popular toast. Another, "Hustlers' Convention," was commercially recorded by The Last Poets, a spoken word trio based in New York. *Rapping* in the 1960s and 1970s was a popular term in the African American community that referred to the art of earnest verbal engagement that was often meant to persuade the listener and did not necessitate rhyming. Rapping was perhaps most often associated with flirting, but the art also encompassed earnest political and social commentary rhetoric. Popular rhythm and blues artists of the 1960s and 1970s rapped a message-oriented section toward the end of a song. Diana Ross was well known for her raps about love and relationships, while Maurice White of Earth, Wind and Fire rapped on the topic of inner beauty in a 1975 song, "All about Love."

Rapping as a distinct musical form developed in New York in the early 1970s as only one of the cultural expressions encompassed by hip-hop. Socioeconomic conditions in the Bronx and Harlem in the 1960s and 1970s profoundly shaped the aesthetics and activities of hip-hop culture. The 1959 construction of the Cross-Bronx Expressway escalated the deterioration of buildings and the displacement of people in south Bronx communities in particular (Rose 1989, 1994). Youth gangs and gang violence escalated in these economically poor neighborhoods during this time. Despite the turbulence of the 1960s and 1970s, Bronx youths developed and/or popularized a wealth of diverse creative expressions that eventually came to be associated with hip-hop culture, then primarily consisting of graffiti and highly competitive dance. Hip-hop became a powerful cultural symbol of urban youth that within a few years spread beyond the immediate environs of the Bronx.

The earliest recordings of rap music often featured a rap artist rhyming over an instrumental version of a popular song played by a live band or a combination of simple synthesized percussion and live instruments. As was done in the Jamaican dub tracks, the rapper would add his or her voice to the layer of live instruments.

1970s: THE ERA OF THE HIP-HOP DJS

Although hip-hop began in the south and west Bronx, the accessibility of rap music was aided by several factors: residents who moved or traveled beyond the New York area; the local dissemination of the art form through the sale of home-produced cassette tapes of rap shows; and the non-Bronx residents who came to see the live performances and reported or imitated the events in their respective neighborhoods. At this time the primary mode of rap musical expression was through live performance, held in parks, community centers, school gymnasiums, neighborhood clubs, private basements, and the like. Similarly, the dominant means of establishing one's reputation as a rap artist was through performing at these events, as well as through privately taped performances of the shows and locally pressed records. Taped rap music was sold from the trunks of cars and briefcases for as much as $15.00 per cassette. These tapes, which were duplicated even further and passed on, contributed to the popularity of such acts as the Cold Crush Brothers, the Funky Four Plus One, and Kool Moe Dee and the Treacherous Three several years before the advent of music videos.

The Bronx DJs, Kool DJ Herc, Afrika Bambaataa, and Grandmaster Flash are most frequently credited with the development of hip-hop and rap music. The DJ is acknowledged among New York hip-hoppers as the foundation of hip-hop culture, and in rap music the DJ is a crucial defining element that distinguishes rapping from poetry recitation and other types of oral performance. The DJ was also the central focal point in the early stages of hip-hop, providing the music as the backdrop for the other forms of hip-hop expression. Although the DJ provided music from prerecorded discs, taking the place of a live band, the DJ makes the musical practice equivalent to a live event through techniques of spinning, cutting, mixing, and scratching, the production of percussive sounds by moving a record back and forth rhythmically under a phonographic needle. Thus DJs recontextualized the phonographs, turntables, and mixing units as musical instruments. The popularity of the MC overshadowed that of the DJ as hip-hop became more commercially recognized: "[T]he era of the [DJ] peaked around 1978, and gradually the spotlight shifted to those controlling the microphone—the MCs" (Fernando 1994:10).

Hip-hoppers acknowledge Kool DJ Herc as the "Father of Hip-hop." Having arrived in the west Bronx from Jamaica in 1967 as an adolescent, he brought with him the practice of the mobile DJ, the Jamaican tradition of toasting, and competitive musical display. By 1973 he began providing music at social events in homes (house parties), public spaces (block parties), and community centers. By the disco era of the 1970s, he became known not only for his selections of records, ranging from funk and rhythm and blues to Latin, but also for the manner in which he played the music. Using two turntables with identical records, he would select the most percussive or rhythmically appealing sections ("the breakdown"), which often featured Latin instruments such as congas, timbales, and cowbells. Then he would switch back and forth between the two turntables, finding the approximate spot where the section began.

This resulted in an extended "break" section, which was highly appealing to dancing patrons. The popular term for hip-hop dancing, or b-boying/girling, became popularized as break dancing.

Kool Herc was also recognized for his sound system with its signature massive, bass-heavy speakers, which had a reputation for overpowering competitors (who included at that time fellow "pioneer" Afrika Bambaataa) with high volume levels. Although many DJs delivered rhymes to dancers at parties, Kool Herc was known more for his musical choices and sound system, rather than his rhyming ability. For the most part, his musical speaking consisted of letting people know where the next dance would take place. Later he hired assistants to form his unit, the Herculords, who would take over the rapping roles as MCs. Just as in the earlier Jamaican mobile DJ party scene, battling for the attention of dancing patrons became a feature of the early New York hip-hop scene.

Afrika Bambaataa began as an informal student of Kool Herc's style and by 1976 emerged as his former mentor's competitor. He established his reputation as a DJ by mixing obscure and unusual records for his Bronx audiences, including rock, cartoon theme songs, and even excerpts from Western art music in his mix. Bambaataa, also of West Indian origin, promoted hip-hop expression into the late 1990s through an organization known as the Zulu Nation. This organization began as a notorious Bronx gang in the early 1970s known as the Black Spades. Bambaataa is credited with redirecting the activities of the gang toward creative competition rather than violence, through b-boying/girling and graffiti writing.

DJs Kool Herc and Bambaataa were known primarily for their musical choices and blending of one song into another, rather than for the complex turntable maneuverings, techniques, and tricks that marked later DJs. The Barbados-born, south Bronx resident Grandmaster Flash was one of several Bronx DJs who further developed the act of turntable manipulations into a distinct musical practice. Flash combined his background in electronics with his musical interests to become one of the most influential figures in hip-hop. His technological innovations with mixing units and the electronic percussion system came to characterize the hip-hop sound, particularly in the 1980s, of the electronic "beat-box."

1979–1985: RAP MUSIC ENTERS THE MAINSTREAM

The year 1979 marks rap music's first commercial release, "Rappers Delight," recorded by the New Jersey–based Sugar Hill Gang on an independent label owned by former R&B vocalist Sylvia Robinson. Although the song "King Tim III," recorded by the funk group Fatback Band, actually preceded Sugar Hill Gang's release as the first song featuring a hip-hop–style rapped section, it was the song recorded by the latter group that became the more popular.

The earliest recordings of rap music often featured a rap artist rhyming over an instrumental version of a popular song played by a live band or a combination of simple synthesized percussion and live instruments. As was done in the Jamaican dub tracks, the rapper would add his or her voice to the layer of live instruments. In 1982, however, recordings by Bambaataa's group, the Soul Sonic Force, defined the hip-hop sound of the 1980s by introducing synthesizers and electronic musical devices to rap music. Bambaataa and, later, Boogie Down Productions employed the technique of "sampling," or using snippets from previously recorded music as a basis for new material, as part of a polyphonic layer, or as a thematic reference. A popular Bronx DJ, Grandmixer D. St. was featured on versatile jazz pianist Herbie Hancock's "Rockit" (1983) (figures 1a and b). This recording was the first recorded jazz/hip-hop collaboration and the first hip-hop–influenced record to win a Grammy Award, thus extending the hip-hop audience beyond its local beginnings.

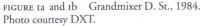
FIGURE 1a and 1b   Grandmixer D. St., 1984.
Photo courtesy DXT.

RAP MUSIC AND MAJOR LABELS

Rap music in the mid- to late 1980s experienced a stylistic and economic shift as its distribution means moved from local, predominantly black-owned labels to international conglomerates with much larger audience-reaching potential. Queens-based group Run-D.M.C., under the business partnership of Russell Simmons and Rick Rubin (Def Jam), had sold over 250,000 copies of several recordings by 1985. This attracted the attention of Columbia Records (a major label), which struck a business deal with Def Jam worth approximately one million dollars; this was the largest business contract involving rap music at the time. Columbia became the distributor for Def Jam's other rap music arts, including the white hip-hop–influenced act the Beastie Boys, who had sold over four million copies of their debut album *Licensed to Ill* (1986). Run-D.M.C. was also the first hip-hop group to commercially endorse a product, a popular sneaker. Other groups on the company roster that expanded hip-hop's popularity beyond the Bronx and Harlem were Queens-based LL Cool J and Long Island's Public Enemy.

Women have been part of hip-hop expression from its early days, primarily as part of MC crews such as the Funky Four Plus One and Sugar Hill's female group, Sequence. For most of hip-hop's recorded history, however, women MCs were mostly seen as novelty acts, with a few exceptions. In the mid-1980s, some female artists were popularized momentarily through "answer" songs, which ridiculed popular songs by male acts. These answer songs included Roxanne Shante's "Roxanne's Revenge" (responding to UTFO's 1984 song "Roxanne, Roxanne") and Peblee Poo's "Fly Guy" (responding to the Boogie Boys' 1985 song "A Fly Girl"). Some of the most enduring female hip-hop acts released premiere albums in 1986. Salt-N-Pepa (Cheryl "Salt" James, Sandi "Pepa" Denton, and DJ Dee Dee "Spinderella" Roper) was the most successful hip-hop group with its first album, *Hot, Cool and Vicious*. Queen Latifah emphasized strong social messages and female empowerment in her first album, *All Hail the Queen*. MC Lyte recorded her first album, *Lyte as a Feather*, at this time. Many female artists who appeared or recorded during the early 1990s adopted the extant masculine-oriented hip-hop images prevalent in hardcore rap music. MC Lyte, for example, recorded a hardcore album in 1993 entitled *Ain't No Other*. This album's first

697 HIP-HOP AND RAP

hit single, "Ruffneck," was MC Lyte's first "gold"-selling single. After the decline of gangsta hardcore rap music in the mid- to late 1990s, women remained on the periphery of hip-hop, with the exception of the occasional pop hit, such as the platinum-selling Atlanta-based artist DaBrat's *Funkdafied* (1994).

By the late 1990s, artists such as Lil' Kim and Foxy Brown publicly celebrated—or exploited—female sexuality through explicit lyrics and widespread publicity campaigns that presented these scantily clad artists as sex symbols. For the most part, however, female artists failed to receive respect within the hip-hop community as competent MCs and recording artists in their own right, although achieving mainstream success. Most of the writers and producers for the female groups were male, particularly through the late 1990s. The year 1998, however, was pivotal for women in hip-hop. Rapper-producer-songwriter Missy Elliot began gaining notoriety with her debut album, *Supa Dupa Fly* (1997).

Lauryn Hill (figure 2) had already established herself as a respected MC and vocalist in the mid-1990s as the frontwoman from the popular and eclectic hip-hop band The Fugees. However, Hill's first solo effort, *The Miseducation of Lauryn Hill*, was a phenomenal success; it was nominated for ten 1998 Grammy Awards and won five. For the first time, women in hip-hop achieved major success as respected artists, producers, and stars in the forefront, in the hip-hop community and in the mainstream media. Elliot's and Hill's success in diversified realms of hip-hop may indicate the beginning steps of the normalization of female voices in the male-dominated genre of rap music.

The advent of MTV (Music Television) in 1981 and use of the music video as a widespread marketing tool for music have been cited by a number of hip-hoppers as having adversely affected the live performance of rap music, although the visual format potentially permits unknown and emerging groups greater public exposure. Some rap artists have complained that attention paid by record companies to developing artists as live performers has been greatly diminished, as the companies substitute the tightly controlled performance environment of a video for the troublesome unpredictability of staged performances. Whereas the establishment of a rap artist's reputation through live performance was a mark of what came to be known in the later 1980s as old school, the new school artists heavily utilized technological innovations such as samplers and synthesizers. This phenomenon can arguably be seen as a representation of the American fascination with the computer-based technological boom in the 1980s, which had reached into the realm of hip-hop aesthetics; as a result, synthesized sounds became preferable to those produced by live instruments. Live performance, however, was further deemphasized particularly with the concurrent growth of hardcore hip-hop and the fear of violence at rap music concerts, which many owners of performance venues cited as reasons for not booking rap artists.

Once the cable station expanded beyond its initial "rock only" format, MTV came to be the prime means of popularizing emerging and existent rap artists with its video program, *Yo! MTV Raps* in 1989. Some of the early hip-hop artists, such as Kool DJ Herc, who first gained popularity through live shows and local parties did not take part in the beginning commercialization and increasing electronicization of rap music. Others, such as Bambaataa and the Soul Sonic Force, Grandmaster Flash and the Furious Five, and Kool Moe Dee, continued to record well into the decade and beyond. Many rap music videos aired on MTV and, later, on BET (Black Entertainment Television) helped spread hard-core images that stereotyped young black males as gangsters and young black women as shallow and materialistic.

The acts that emerged during the mid-1980s promoted easily commodifiable images in American culture of an idealized urban, black, macho identity, which came to be known as hardcore. Such "hardness" is one of the aspects that promoters of the new subgenre utilized as a marketing technique to separate their artists from earlier rap music's tradition of boasting and relatively simple party rhymes. Along with rap

FIGURE 2   Rapper Lauryn Hill. © Ruffhouse/Columbia Records 1998. Photo by Warren du Preez. Courtesy DXT.

Gangsta rap was considered by many West Coast hip-hoppers to represent the authentic, ignored voices of urban California youth. Many New York–area hip-hoppers considered these West Coast artists to be inauthentic "studio gangsters."

music's rising popularity as a form of mainstream entertainment grew the association between rap performance and violence. A December 1985 concert at Madison Square Garden in New York City, which included LL Cool J, Doug E. Fresh, and Kurtis Blow, greatly overexaggerated negative media attention after a concert-goer was shot. Hip-hop became a popular symbol of black life to the wider American society, embodied by the young black male, seen as exotic, dangerous, and feared, yet appealing and marketable. Negative events associated with hip-hop performances were greatly publicized, while peaceful rap music concerts, philanthropic activities of rap artists such as the Stop the Violence movement, and violence at white rock concerts were underrepresented by the media. According to one journalist, "to much of the American mainstream, rap is an outlaw music that otherwise well-informed people vilify and fear" (Pareles 1992). Despite the growing controversy surrounding rap music lyrics toward the end of the decade, acts such as Eric B. and Rakim were known for their powerful imagery, delivery, and high lyrical quality rather than violent and misogynist themes.

In the late 1980s largely African American and Latino communities of northern and southern California emerged as important new bases of hip-hop culture. In the West Coast style the hip-hop traditions of hyperbole, self-grandeur, and storytelling stemming from the African American popular toasts such as "The Signifying Monkey" and "Hustlers' Convention" blended in with themes influenced by popular black gangster movie characters such as Superfly and Dolemite. The result was a distinctive brand of hardcore known as "gangster" or "gangsta rap," exemplified in the music of Oakland's Too Short and Compton's Niggaz with Attitude (NWA). The often violent and drug-related activities of rival youth gangs such as the Bloods and the Crips, which had become highly organized by the mid-1980s, were familiar themes in West Coast street culture. Many West Coast acts claimed hip-hop authenticity because their lyrics reflected a California inner city lifestyle—albeit often idealized, exaggerated, or conjectured—depicting guns, violence, peer allegiance, sex, drugs, and the exploitation of women. The popularity and record sales of other West Coast acts such as Ice-T, Compton's Most Wanted, and, in the early 1990s after the break-up of NWA, Dr. Dre and Snoop Doggy Dogg surpassed sales of the New York artists. The hip-hop subgenre of gangsta rap was considered by many West Coast hip-hoppers to represent the authentic, ignored voices of urban California youth, some of whom considered the term *reality rap* more accurate than gangsta rap. Many New York–area hip-hoppers considered these West Coast artists to be inauthentic "studio gangsters," that is, leading a life close to mainstream society, yet creating a gangsta persona in the recording studio for the sake of commercial appeal. The East Coast/West Coast rivalry emerged at this time and was later blamed at least in part for the murders of two prominent artists, The West Coast's Tupac Shakur (1996) and the East Coast's Biggie Smalls/Notorious B.I.G. (1997).

By 1991 rap music consumers recognized distinct subgenres of hip-hop: hardcore; R&B rap (which utilized sung choruses and was exemplified by Heavy D and the Boys, and CC Music Factory); and pop or commercial rap (Vanilla Ice, MC Hammer, and

Jazzy Jeff and the Fresh Prince), which usually had the broadest popular appeal. Hardcore rap music itself could be broken down into subcategories, such as gangsta (NWA, Geto Boys); sexually explicit (2 Live Crew, Lil' Kim, Foxy Brown); political (Public Enemy, Boogie Down Productions/KRS-One, Paris); and entertainment, which combined powerful urban imagery with aggressively percussive musical accompaniment (Naughty By Nature, Eric B., and Rakim). Patrons could choose among the hard, aggressive sounds that emphasized strong electronic or sampled drum, found in the style of KRS-One; the smooth, jazz-influenced styles of A Tribe Called Quest and Digable Planets; and the funky styles that emphasized bass and/or live instruments, exemplified by the music of EPMD and Ice Cube. Producers of rap music began to use jazz samples, jazz tunes, and even live jazz musicians as source material for their new songs (Guru and Jazzmatazz, US 3) as a change from what had come to be traditional source material from James Brown and funk music of the 1960s and 1970s. The impact of rap music as an influential American expression reached into the realm of law by the early 1990s, with publicized cases involving censorship due to some rap music's sexually and violently explicit subject matter (NWA's "F—— Tha Police"; Paris's "Bush Killa"); gang violence and verbal/physical abuse of women (NWA, Ice-T, Geto Boys); and copyright infringement rulings involving common sampling practices in rap music (Biz Markie).

STYLISTIC FEATURES

The rhythmic and lyrical structure characteristic of rap music utilizes an AABB poetic scheme, or rhymed couplets (Keyes 1991). Rap artists from hip-hop's beginning to the mid-1980s kept the literal interpretation of the rhyme scheme intact, with some syncopation.

Old school

The history of rap music and hip-hop is popularly divided into old and new schools. These descriptions, which appeared by the late 1980s, were coined by professional promoters of the emerging style of rap music who sought to distinguish this new style, considered to be more street oriented, harder, and more aggressive, from that of their dance party–based predecessors. Generally, old school is (1) a temporal reference to hip-hop's early days, the 1970s to about 1985; (2) a stylistic description of the rhythmic pattern characteristic of hip-hop's early days, that is, a literal interpretation of the AABB rhyme structure; and (3) a thematic description of the lyrical content, consisting mainly of braggadocio and dance party–oriented subject matter. Old school chants that became crowd-rallying traditions throughout the history of live performances stemmed from the earliest performance contexts of hip-hop: "Throw your hands in the air / And wave them like you just don't care" and the rhythmic call and response:

> LEADER: All the fellas say, "Make money-money / Make money-money-money."
> MEN: Make money-money / Make money-money-money.
> LEADER: All the ladies say, "Take money-money / Take money-money-money."
> WOMEN: Take money-money / Take money-money-money.

The 1979 song "Spoonin' Rap: A Drive Down the Street / I Was Spanking and Freaking" was recorded by Spoonin Gee. This song utilizes the even sixteenth-note rhythms and simple syncopations typical of rap lyrics of the so-called old school, reflecting the song's roots as recreational dance music.

The early old school recordings often featured live bands and/or congas and other Latin percussion accompanying the rap artists, reflecting the Latino presence and influence in early hip-hop (examples are Sugar Hill Gang's "Rappers Delight," and Spoonie Gee and the Treacherous Three's "Love Rap" [1980]).

New school

The new school is (1) a temporal reference to the prominent rap musical styles starting at approximately 1986; (2) a stylistic description of the loose interpretation of the AABB rhyme scheme, in which rhythms are normally highly syncopated and the rhymed syllables appear at varied, irregular, or unpredictable places; and (3) a thematic reference, of which the artist and his or her overall style may be described as hardcore, smooth, gangsta, pop, and so on.

Early new school artists (1986–1990) preferred synthesized percussion, such as the electronic beat-box and other synthesized instruments, refraining from live instruments nearly altogether. Later new school artists preferred to use sampled material from popular and obscure rhythm and blues, jazz, and rock recordings from the 1970s. Sampled material used to form the basis of new songs ranged from a highly disguised snippet as short as a single chord or percussion strike to an entire section of a previously recorded popular song, literally re-presented with new lyrics or rerecorded to avoid or circumvent expensive licensing fees. For example, Dr. Dre featured Snoop Doggy Dogg's "Nothin' But a G Thang" (1992) using a rerecorded sample of the rhythm and blues popular song "I Wanna Do Something Freaky to You," and Coolio's "Fantastic Voyage" borrowed from the funk band Lakeside's song of the same name. In spite of the reemergence of live musical instruments in the later 1990s, new school recordings have nevertheless deemphasized live percussion, so that the Latin influence is not nearly as visible as in older recordings.

The application of the old or new school description to rap music or its artists is by no means precise, and there is much stylistic overlapping. A mid-1980s act such as Run-D.M.C. may have the visual and musical markings of the new school acts, but its rhyming tendencies reflect the relatively simple syncopations of the old school. Furthermore, many of the new school artists who emerged in the 1980s, such as Boogie Down Productions, Run-D.M.C., and Kool Moe Dee, were marketed as old school artists in the late 1990s to promote radio and concert programming that featured hip-hop "classics." Nevertheless, the labels are useful as a means to identify stylistic, lyrical, and thematic differences in rap music of the 1970s to the mid-1980s and the mid-1980s to the late 1990s.

Rap artists began to vary the rhyming patterns in the late 1980s, often by introducing the first rhymed word of the couplet at the beginning of the *A* line, rather than at the end. The matching rhyme would occur at the beginning of the second *A* line. By 1991 the prevailing hip-hop aesthetic preferred more intricate and complex rhyming styles and unpredictable or highly syncopated rhythmic placement. By the 1990s rap music that presented a literal interpretation of the AABB rhyme scheme with relatively predictable syncopations and regular beats was considered outdated and old school by emerging artists and their fans. The opening lines of "They Want Efx," recorded by the influential rap artists Das Efx, reflect the more intricate rhymes and rhythms that characterized the rapping style of the 1990s. Although it has become commonplace in more recent rhyming styles to vary the number of rhymed words per line and to carry over a rhyme of the second *A* into the first line of the *B* pair, the general AABB structure is maintained in the 1990s style of rapping.

Compared with live presentations of rap music in the 1990s, performances of the 1970s tended to feature "dressing up" for such shows, from the space fantasy outfits of Bambaataa typical of African American and disco groups of the 1970s to displays of exaggerated wealth by the wearing of heavy gold jewelry and other expensive accessories symbolizing "the good life" of the early 1980s. In both cases, clothes are used to heighten the distinction between onstage performers and offstage audience members. With the emergence of hardcore hip-hop and the concern of rap artists of the 1990s to "keep it real"—that is, to publicly assert one's allegiance to community and peers— "dressing down," or in a manner similar to that of the peer audience members, became the norm of live acts. With stage effects such as lighting, costumes, and jewelry kept to a minimum (compared to rock shows), the artists of the 1990s symbolically maintained their peer connection by wearing clothing similar to that of the audience members: name-brand sneakers or hiking boots, very baggy pants, and oversized sweatshirts and headgear with the names of famous European and American designers prominently displayed. Female artists who emerged during the hardcore era tended to take on dress, themes, and rhyming styles similar to those of the males. Toward the late 1990s, as the "ghetto fabulous" style (a glamourized combination of "street"-inspired designer wear and 1970s black film costuming popularized by Sean "Puffy" Combs, Mary J. Blige, and Lil' Kim) became widespread, popular female acts came to have a more distinctly feminine style that included dyed blonde hair fixtures, revealing clothes, and heavy makeup.

CULTURAL AREAS

In the 1990s stylistic distinctions became recognized in rap music, developing what can be considered cultural areas associated with regional modes of informal communication (slang), manners of speech, tempo, and thematic emphasis. Five such areas and the general characteristics with which they are associated are the East Coast, West Coast, Miami/Southwest, South, and Midwest.

East Coast

Primarily from the New York, New Jersey, and Philadelphia areas, the rhythms and timbres of the East Coast area are often described as hard or smooth. The East Coast style of the late 1980s frequently utilized sampled materials in recordings, particularly from James Brown recordings ("Funky Drummer" and "Funky President") and, later, jazz recordings (those of Lou Donaldson, Cal Tjader, and Roy Ayers). Although funk recordings such as those recorded by George Clinton are utilized in samples, hardness and smoothness are arguably more aesthetically preferable in the East than funkiness is. Philadelphia produced eclectic hip-hop acts in the 1990s, such as the fully functioning band the Roots, the hip-hop/rock band the Goats, and Bahamadia, one of the few female artists noted for being adept at verbal improvisation. With the exception of the Fugees, a popular hip-hop band formed by Haitian immigrants, New York recording acts tend to consist solely of rap artists and their accompanying DJ. The mid- to late 1990s saw a reemergence of live musical instrumental sounds in conjunction with sampled and synthesized sounds. By 2000 there was a growing trend of MCs employing live musicians, including established jazz artists with their touring bands, along with the traditional DJ.

West Coast

Primarily from the California areas of Los Angeles and Oakland, the lyrical content of rap music of this area in the late 1980s and early 1990s (as performed by NWA and Compton's Most Wanted, for example) tended to utilize gangster-oriented themes as well as musical material from black gangster movies of the 1970s. Later West Coast artists (Dr. Dre, Coolio, Ice Cube) tended to utilize live musical instruments and samples from funk recordings of George Clinton and Zapp. Relative to the East Coast style, the desired aesthetic in the accompanying musical tracks of the West Coast artists values funkiness.

Miami/Southwest

"Bass," a style of dance music prevalent in Miami and the South, uses the fastest tempos in hip-hop. As recorded by groups such as 2 Live Crew and the 69 Boys, the recorded emphasis of bass is on motivating listeners to dance; thus, there is relatively less emphasis on lyrics, which are similar to those of the New York party rhymes of the

Hip-hop is a multifaceted mode of creative expression, of which rap music is its most visible and exploited element.

1970s—only with characteristically sexually explicit themes. Stylistically, bass is closely related to the recordings done by Afrika Bambaataa in the 1980s.

The South

The description "southern fried" has been applied to rap music from Atlanta and other southern cities. Although acts from the South such as Arrested Development, Da Brat, and Kriss Kross have gained in popularity over the years, southern fried rap music in the late 1990s does not have a style markedly different from that of the West or East Coasts. The Houston, Texas, act, the Geto Boys, for example, resembles West Coast gangsta rap stylistically and thematically.

The Midwest

The huge national success of the Ohio-based group Bone Thugs-N-Harmony (originally produced by former NWA member the late Easy E), may mark a midwestern style characterized by a distinctively slower tempo in the rhythmic tracks, accompanying rapping vocals at a much faster rate. For example, to each quarter note in the rhythmic tracks, the vocalist may deliver any combination of four sixteenth notes, sixteenth-note triplets, and even thirty-second notes.

Other stylistic regions

Musical expressions associated with contemporary urban youth in a particular geographical area can be considered close relatives or equivalents of hip-hop: "go-go" from Washington, D.C., a highly percussive, funk-based street music; "dancehall" from Jamaica and New York; and "jingle music," a multilayered, polyrhythmic, electronic dance music from Britain, similar to bass and house music (a popular synthesized club music that often features heavy gospel vocals, originating from Chicago).

Hip-hop is a multifaceted mode of creative expression, of which rap music is its most visible and exploited element. Rap music, the music of hip-hop culture, has roots in both the United States and the Caribbean, particularly Jamaica. The Jamaican contributions to hip-hop culture, which was reinforced by similar traditions in the United States were (1) a development from and expression of the urban ghetto; (2) the notion of "bringing the party to the people," who had little access to more expensive means of formal entertainment, through mobile DJs; (3) an aesthetic for very high volume with greatly emphasized bass and percussion; and (4) intense competition as a means of establishing one's identity and competence in a community setting. The genre of rap music is commonly recognized as having stemmed from the contributions of DJs who are considered founders of hip-hop and rap music: three of the earliest pioneers are Kool DJ Herc, Afrika Bambaataa, and Grandmaster Flash. The terms *old* and *new schools* have been popularly utilized to refer to temporal and stylistic distinctions in rap music, although there is much overlapping that occurs between these schools. Since its start as youthful entertainment in the 1970s, hip-hop came to be considered the single most important voice and vehicle for the expression of contemporary African American urban youth in the last quarter of the twentieth century, and at the beginning of the twenty-first it has become one of the most influential cultural expressions worldwide.

REFERENCES

Anderson, Elijah. 1990. *Streetwise: Race, Class, and Change in an Urban Community.* Chicago: University of Chicago Press.

Baraka, Amiri. 1991. "The 'Blues Aesthetic' and the 'Black Aesthetic': Aesthetics as the Continuing Political History of a Culture." *Black Music Research Journal* 11(2):101–109.

Barrow, Steve. 1993. "The Story of Jamaican Music." Notes. *Tougher than Tough: The Story of Jamaican Music.* Island Records 162-539 935-2. Compact disc.

Cross, Brian. 1993. *It's Not about a Salary: Rap, Race and Resistance in Los Angeles.* New York: Verso.

Das Efx. 1992. *Dead Serious.* EastWest Records America 7 91627-4. Compact disc.

Dr. Dre. 1991. *The Chronic.* Priority Records P257129. Compact disc.

Earth, Wind and Fire. 1975. *That's the Way of the World.* Columbia PC 33280. LP disk.

Eure, Joseph D., and James G. Spady. 1991. *Nation Conscious Rap.* New York: PC International Press.

Fernando, S. H., Jr. 1994. *The New Beats: Exploring the Music, Culture, and Attitudes of Hip-Hop.* New York: Doubleday.

Fikentscher, Kai. 1995. "'You Better Work!' Music, Dance, and Marginality in Underground Dance Clubs of New York City." Ph.D. dissertation, Columbia University.

Folb, Edith. 1980. *Runnin' Down Some Lines: The Language and Culture of Black Teenagers.* Cambridge: Harvard University Press.

George, Nelson. 1988. *The Death of Rhythm & Blues.* New York: Dutton.

———. 1998. *Hip Hop America.* New York: Penguin Books.

Grand Master Flash and the Furious Five, featuring Melle Mel and Duke Bootnee. 1982. Sugar Hill Records 584. LP disk.

Hancock, Herbie. 1983. *Future Shock.* Columbia/Legacy CK 65962. Compact disc.

Hebdige, Dick. 1987. *Cut 'n' Mix: Culture, Identity and Caribbean Music.* New York: Methuen.

Hill, Lauryn. 1998. *The Miseducation of Lauryn Hill.* Ruffhouse/Columbia CK 69035. Compact disc.

Holloway, Joseph E., ed. 1990. *Africanisms in American Culture.* Bloomington: Indiana University Press.

Keyes, Cheryl. 1984. "Verbal Art Performance in Rap Music: The Conversation of the 80s." *Folklore Forum* 17:142–152.

———. 1991. "Rappin to the Beat: Rap Music as Street Culture among African Americans." Ph.D. dissertation, Indiana University.

———. 1993. "We're More than a Novelty, Boys: Strategies of Female Rappers in the Rap Music Tradition." In *Feminist Messages: Coding in Women's Folk Culture,* ed. Joan Newlon Radner, 203–220. Chicago: University of Illinois Press.

———. 1996. "At the Crossroads: Rap Music and Its African Nexus." *Ethnomusicology* 40(2): 223–248.

Kitwana, Bakari. 1994. *The Rap on Gangsta Rap.* Chicago: Third World Press.

Kochman, Thomas, ed. 1972. *Rappin' and Stylin' Out: Communication in Urban Black America.* Urbana: University of Illinois Press.

Kopytko, Tania. 1986. "Breakdance as an Identity Marker in New Zealand." *Yearbook for Traditional Music* 18:21–27.

Leland, John. 1992. "Rap and Race," *Newsweek,* 29 June, 44–52.

Norfleet, Dawn. 1993. "Hardcore as a Central Theme in Hip-Hop." Unpublished manuscript.

———. 1997. "'Hip-hop Culture' in New York City: The Role of Verbal Musical Performance in Defining a Community." Ph.D. dissertation, Columbia University.

Pareles, Jon. 1992. "On Rap, Symbolism and Fear." *The New York Times,* 2 February. 1–2, 23.

Parker, L. 1995. *The Science of Rap, by KRS-ONE* [self-published]. New York: A Street Publication.

Perkins, William Eric, ed. 1996. *Droppin' Science: Critical Essays on Rap Music and Hip Hop Culture.* Philadelphia: Temple University Press.

Potter, Russell. 1995. *Spectacular Vernaculars: Hip-Hop and the Politics of Postmodernism.* The State University of New York Series in Postmodern Culture. Albany: State University of New York Press.

Powis, Tim. 1993. "Tower of Babel: State of the Hip-Hop Nation." *Musical Express Magazine* 179 (17 January):50.

Rose, Tricia. 1989. "Orality and Technology: Rap Music and Afro-American Cultural Resistance." *Popular Music and Society* 13(4):35–44.

———. 1994. *Black Noise: Rap Music and Black Culture in Contemporary America.* Hanover, N.H.: Wesleyan University Press.

Ross, Andrew, and Tricia Rose, eds. 1994. *Microphone Fiends: Youth Music and Youth Culture.* New York: Routledge.

Smitherman, Geneva. 1985. *Talkin and Testifyin: The Language of Black America.* Detroit: Wayne State University Press.

———. 1994. *Black Talk: Words and Phrases from the Hood to the Amen Corner.* Boston: Houghton Mifflin.

Spencer, John Michael, ed. 1992. *Sacred Music of the City: From Blues to Rap.* A special issue of *Black Sacred Music: A Journal of Theomusicology* (vol. 6, no. 1). Durham, N.C.: Duke University Press.

Stephens, Robert W. 1984. "Soul: A Historical Reconstruction of Continuity and Change in Black Popular Music." *The Black Perspective in Music* 12(1):21–43.

Stephens, Ronald Jemal. 1991. "The Three Waves of Contemporary Rap Music." In *Sacred Music of the City: From Blues to Rap,* ed. Jon Michael Spencer, 25–40. Durham, N.C.: Duke University Press.

Spoonin Gee. 1979. *A Drive Down the Street/I Was Spanking and Freaking.* Sound of New York, USA. QC 708A. LP disk.

Strauss, Neil. 1995. "Rap's a 10% Slice of the Recording Industry Pie." *The New York Times,* 5 June, D8.

Sugar Hill Gang. 1992 [1979]. *"Rapper's Delight," Street Jams: Hip-Hop from the Top–Part 1.* Rhino R2 70577 [Sugar Hill #542]. Compact disc.

Thompson, Robert Farris. 1966. "An Aesthetic of the Cool: West African Dance." *African Forum* 2(2):85–102.

Toop, David. 1991. *Rap Attack 2: African Rap and Global Hiphop.* New York: Serpents' Tail.

Torp, Lisbet. 1986. "'Hip Hop Dances': Their Adoption and Function among Boys in Denmark from 1983–84." *Yearbook for Traditional Music* 18:29–36.

Vincent, Rickey. 1996. *Funk: The Music, the People, and the Rhythm of the One.* New York: St. Martin's Griffin.

Walser, Robert. 1995. "Rhythm, Rhyme, and Rhetoric in the Music of Public Enemy." *Ethnomusicology* 39(2):193–217.

Wheeler, Elizabeth. 1991. "'Most of My Heroes Don't Appear on No Stamps': The Dialogics of Rap Music." *Black Music Research Journal* 11(2):193–215.

Wilson, Olly. 1985. "The Association of Movement and Music as a Manifestation of a Black Conceptual Approach to Music-Making." In *More Than Dancing: Essays on Afro-American Music and Musicians,* ed. Irene Jackson, 10–23. Westport, Conn.: Greenwood Press.

The Music Industry
Reebee Garofalo

It is now common knowledge that African Americans have made the most significant cultural contributions to the development of American music. African Americans have created, innovated, performed, and otherwise participated in the process of music making since the United States was a colony. But if their cultural contributions have been historically undervalued or assigned to others less deserving, equally disturbing is the degree to which they have had to overcome systematic discrimination within the music industry itself.

THE NINETEENTH CENTURY

The modern music industry resulted from the gradual convergence of two quite separate nineteenth-century enterprises—the fledgling recording industry, initially devoted to spoken word applications such as stenography and books for the blind, and the music publishing business, dedicated to the sale of sheet music, initially the major source of music-related revenue. African Americans were given short shrift by both.

In the 1880s, music publishers began to centralize in an area of New York City dubbed Tin Pan Alley, with no African American firms among them [see POPULAR MUSIC OF THE PARLOR AND STAGE, p. 179]. Tin Pan Alley dominated music publishing until the end of World War II. Although these publishers had a keen ear for music and were never above borrowing from the music of African Americans when it suited their purposes, it was something of a breakthrough when white music publisher John Stillwell Stark entered into a publishing deal with composer Scott Joplin, the "King of Ragtime," at the turn of the century. Joplin's popular rags went on to sell hundreds of thousands of copies. The success of the Joplin-Stark partnership draws attention not only to the quality of Joplin's music but also to a bias inherent in the music publishing business that militated against other forms of African American music.

Ragtime was a composed music that developed alongside other forms of African American music such as jazz and the blues, which were improvisational in nature—derived more from the oral tradition of African music than from the notated (written) tradition of European music. Because U.S. copyright laws were framed in terms of melody, chord patterns, and lyrics—clearly elements of a written tradition—it was difficult for certain forms of African American music to be defined and defended as intellectual property.

In 1917, when Victor decided to take a chance on "jass," the band chosen to record was the all-white Original Dixieland Jazz Band.

Accordingly, African Americans were poorly represented in the music publishing business. When the American Society of Composers, Authors, and Publishers (ASCAP) was founded in 1914 to reap the fruits of copyright protection, membership in the society was generally skewed toward composers of pop tunes and semiserious works. Of the society's 170 charter members, six were black: Harry T. Burleigh, Will Marion Cook, J. Rosamond and James Weldon Johnson, Cecil Mack, and Will Tyers (Southern 1997:311). Although other "literate" black writers and composers (for example, W. C. Handy and Duke Ellington) would be able to gain entrance to ASCAP, the vast majority of "untutored" black artists were excluded from the society and thereby denied the full benefits of copyright protection.

The recording industry followed a similar trajectory of exclusion. Sound recording was developed primarily by Americans of European descent. Even after it became clear that the future of recording would be tied to music, the industry seldom recorded African American artists. Sheet music sales of Scott Joplin's "Maple Leaf Rag" (1899) dwarfed the sales of most early recordings, but Joplin never made a record. Even "coon" songs derived from minstrelsy, a staple of early commercial recording, were almost invariably sung by whites until World War I. Notable exceptions included George Washington Johnson, who had major hits with "The Whistling Coon" and "The Laughing Song," and Bert Williams, the extraordinary black vaudevillian.

THE EARLY TWENTIETH CENTURY

When a blues craze swept the country in the 1910s, African American composers such as the "Father of the Blues" W. C. Handy ("Memphis Blues") (figure 1) and Arthur Seals ("Baby Seals' Blues") joined the ranks of professional songwriters. Still, most of the blues compositions of the era were recorded by whites singing in "Negro dialect." With the advent of recorded jazz in the late teens, patterns of racial exclusion skewed public perceptions of African American music even more. In 1917, when Victor decided to take a chance on "jass," the band chosen to record was the all-white Original Dixieland Jazz Band. Though this group was heavily influenced by the King Oliver Band, which included Louis Armstrong, the Oliver ensemble itself didn't record until 1923.

The first ensemble of color to land a recording contract was James Reese Europe's Syncopated Society Orchestra, signed by Victor in 1914 to supervise a series of dance records for the unconventional white dance team of Vernon and Irene Castle. Europe was a talented and highly trained composer who could hold his own with any writers and arrangers of the era. He also had a talent for organization; his Clef Club and later Tempo Club organizations, which assembled bands for hire, proved quite successful. Particularly through the dances he invented for the Castles, such as the fox-trot and the turkey trot, he introduced syncopated dance music to the mainstream audience.

FIGURE 1   W. C. Handy (1873–1958), born in Florence, Alabama, was an important and prolific composer of blues whose works are still performed today. © Bettmann/CORBIS.

The race market

It wasn't until 1920, and quite by accident, that the recording industry began to take recording African Americans seriously. When an OKeh session that was to feature Sophie Tucker was canceled, the enterprising black producer-songwriter Perry Bradford talked the record company into letting him record a black contralto named Mamie Smith. Her recording of Bradford's "Crazy Blues" went on to sell 7,500 copies a week and opened up a new market for African American music. Ralph Peer, the OKeh recording director who assisted at the sessions, dubbed these records "race records," and this remained the designation for black music, by black artists, intended for a black audience, until 1949. Smith's overwhelming success ushered in a decade of classic blues recordings by African American women: Ida Cox, Chippie Hill, Sarah Martin, Clara Smith, Trixie Smith, Victoria Spivey, Sippie Wallace, and, the most famous of all, Bessie Smith, "Empress of the Blues."

The initial success of the race market encouraged the formation of a handful of black-owned independent labels, including Sunshine in Los Angeles and Meritt in Kansas City. W. C. Handy and his publishing partner, Harry Pace, started Black Swan in 1921. Mayo "Ink" Williams, head of Paramount's race series, founded Black Patti in 1927. These companies were beset with financial problems right from the start. Not a single black-owned label survived the 1920s intact. With the onset of the Depression, they were either bought up by the major companies or forced into bankruptcy, as the race market was slowly taken over by Victor, Paramount, and Columbia, which absorbed OKeh in 1926.

As the demand for classic blues grew, record companies discovered there was also a considerable demand for country blues, particularly among southern blacks. In 1924, the same year they acquired the Black Swan catalog, Paramount released Papa Charlie Jackson's "Lawdy Lawdy Blues." This record was followed with releases by Arthur "Blind" Blake and Blind Lemon Jefferson, perhaps the most popular country blues singer of the decade. The country blues artist who dominated the thirties was Big Bill Broonzy. Throughout the twenties and early thirties, a number of companies, including OKeh, Columbia, and Victor, engaged in extensive field recordings. Together with John and Alan Lomax and through the efforts of the Library of Congress, they became the unwitting folklorists of grassroots American culture. As a result, dozens of country blues artists—among them, Furry Lewis, Blind Willie McTell, "Mississippi" John Hurt, Son House, Charlie Patton, Huddie "Leadbelly" Ledbetter (figure 2), and Robert Johnson—were brought to wider public attention.

Record companies expanded into the African American market at precisely the moment when another technological development—the birth of commercial broadcasting—threatened the very survival of the recording industry. Commercial broadcasting, which offered, free, live music with better fidelity than records could provide, decimated record sales. And if record companies had finally begun to open their doors to African American artists, radio excluded them almost completely.

Aside from the financial implications of this situation, such patterns of racial segregation tended to obscure the origins of musical developments such as jazz, and Tin Pan Alley did little to correct the errors. To the average listener, then, jazz was the product of white society dance bands, George Gershwin and Irving Berlin were early pioneers, and Paul Whiteman was its king. Still, a number of African American bands managed to break through. Among the best known, Edward Kennedy "Duke" Ellington's band became famous through live broadcasts from the Cotton Club in Harlem. William Allen "Count" Basie injected jazz with a heavy dose of the blues from the Reno Club in Kansas City. The Ellington and Basie bands not only recorded for major labels, they were among the few African American ensembles that could be heard on radio.

FIGURE 2   Huddie Ledbetter (Leadbelly) (1885–1949) was an accomplished folk singer, who claimed to have over 500 songs in his memory. Also an expert 12-string guitar player, Leadbelly was widely recorded in the 1930s and 40s. © Bettmann/CORBIS.

THE 1940s: THE RISE OF RHYTHM AND BLUES

Tensions also existed between radio and the Tin Pan Alley publishers, primarily over royalty rates. The situation came to a head in 1939 when the National Association of Broadcasters (NAB), representing some six hundred radio stations, formed its own performing rights organization, Broadcast Music Incorporated (BMI), and proceeded shortly thereafter to boycott all ASCAP music. Because ASCAP represented the Broadway–Hollywood axis of popular music, BMI looked to the grass roots for its membership. This move signaled a new era in black popular music because ASCAP, with its considerable influence in shaping public taste, was challenged publicly for the first time, creating a cultural space for rhythm and blues artists like Arthur "Big Boy" Crudup, Roy Brown, Ivory Joe Hunter, Fats Domino, and Wynonie Harris.

The success of these artists in the late 1940s speaks to what critic Nelson George has referred to as "an aesthetic schism between high-brow, more assimilated black styles and working-class, grassroots sounds" (George 1988:10). Until this time, the most notable African American acts were the artists who had a more popular sound, such as Nat "King" Cole ("For Sentimental Reasons"), Ella Fitzgerald ("My Happiness"), the Mills Brothers ("Across the Valley from the Alamo"), and the Ink Spots ("The Gypsy"), all of whom recorded for major labels. These companies failed to appreciate the appeal of rhythm and blues in working-class black communities [see R&B AND SOUL, p. 667].

With more pronounced rhythm and a much smaller horn section, rhythm and blues followed from the demise of the big bands after World War II. Louis Jordan and the Tympani Five anticipated this transition and helped to define the instrumentation for the R&B combos that followed. Jordan's material was composed and arranged, but selections such as "Saturday Night Fish Fry," "Honey Chile," and "Ain't Nobody Here but Us Chickens" evoked blues images not found in most black pop of the day. "Suddenly it was as if a great deal of the Euro-American humanist facade Afro-American music had taken on had been washed away by the war" (Jones 1963:171). The raucous styles of such artists as Wynonie Harris ("Good Rockin' Tonight"), John Lee Hooker ("Boogie Chillen"), saxophonist Big Jay McNeely ("Deacon's Hop"), and pianist Amos Milburn ("Chicken Shack Boogie") deviated significantly from the sound of mainstream black pop.

As this music did not readily lend itself to the production styles of the major labels, they decided to ignore the relatively smaller rhythm and blues market. This situation made it possible for a large number of independent labels to enter the business. It is estimated that by 1949 over four hundred new labels came into existence. Most important among these were Atlantic in New York, Savoy in Newark, King in Cincinnati, Chess in Chicago, Peacock in Houston, and Modern, Imperial, and Specialty in Los Angeles. All white-owned, except for Don Robey's Peacock label, most of these labels specialized in rhythm and blues.

Throughout this period radio was embroiled in a struggle with the American Federation of Music (AFM) over the use of records ("canned music") as an alternative to live music programming. This was particularly important to the growing number of independent radio stations that depended on cheaper forms of programming for their existence. Rhythm and blues found a ready home among independent deejays, who often experimented with "specialty" musics as an antidote to the mainstream pop of network radio. Early rhythm and blues hits popular among both black and white audiences included Fats Domino's "The Fat Man," Jackie Brenston's "Rocket 88," Lloyd Price's "Lawdy Miss Clawdy," and Joe Turner's "Chains of Love," "Sweet Sixteen," and "Honey Hush." All were recorded for independent labels. Pioneer black deejays such as "Jockey" Jack Gibson in Atlanta, "Professor Bop" in Shreveport, and "Sugar Daddy" in Birmingham paved the way for white rhythm and blues deejays such as Alan Freed, the self-appointed "Father of Rock 'n' Roll."

THE 1950s AND 1960s: ROCK AND ROLL HAS SOUL

With its roots in the Deep South, the music that became rock and roll issued from just about every region in the country [see ROCK, p. 347]. Although the music was widely regarded as an amalgam of rhythm and blues and country and western, most of its formative influences as well as virtually all of its early innovators were African American: B. B. King ("The Thrill Is Gone"), Muddy Waters ("Got My Mojo Working"), Bo Diddley ("Bo Diddley"), Fats Domino ("Blueberry Hill"), Ray Charles ("I Got a Woman"), Sam Cooke ("You Send Me"), Ruth Brown ("Mama, He Treats Your Daughter Mean"), Little Richard ("Tutti Frutti"), Chuck Berry ("Johnny B. Goode") (figure 3), the Orioles ("Crying in the Chapel"), the Crows ("Gee"), the Chords ("Sh-Boom"), and the Penguins ("Earth Angel"). Even with the new name, there was no mistaking where this music came from. As late as 1956, *Billboard* referred to the music as a popularized form of rhythm and blues.

Rock and roll, produced for the most part by independent companies, made significant inroads into a musical terrain that had been dominated by major labels and ASCAP publishers. Accordingly, African American artists made significant inroads into the pop market. The majors responded with a range of strategies that included talent buying (as happened with RCA and Elvis Presley) and issuing "cover" records (pop versions of rock and roll originals). ASCAP orchestrated a series of government investigations that culminated in the payola hearings at the end of the decade. Deejays, who were considered largely responsible for the crossover of black music into the pop market, became the main target of these hearings, which imposed a tighter structure on radio.

While the payola hearings threatened to slow the advances that African American artists had made, the burgeoning civil rights movement provided a countervailing force. The 1960s thus dawned with some significant new developments in African American music. During this period, rhythm and blues producers emerged as artists in their own right, black female vocal harmony groups, known collectively as the "girl groups," emerged as a trend in mainstream popular music for the first time, and the most successful black-owned record label was founded.

Chubby Checker ushered in the decade with "The Twist," which hit number one on the pop charts twice, once in 1960 and then again in 1962. He followed up with "The Hucklebuck," "Pony Time," "The Fly," and "Limbo Rock." The Twist craze was powerful enough to force other African American artists such as Sam Cooke, Gary "US" Bonds, and the Isley Brothers to get on the bandwagon, and relative unknowns Little Eva and Dee Dee Sharp had hits with two Twist spin-offs, "The Loco-Motion" and "Mashed Potato Time," respectively.

Producers such as Luther Dixon, Phil Spector, and Berry Gordy drew on the pioneering work of Jerry Leiber and Mike Stoller with the Drifters ("There Goes My Baby," "This Magic Moment," "Save the Last Dance for Me") to create what Charlie Gillett called "uptown rhythm & blues," a precursor of soul (Gillett 1970:220). As a result, black female vocal groups such as the Shirelles ("Will You Still Love Me Tomorrow"), the Crystals ("He's a Rebel"), and Martha and the Vandellas ("Dancing in the Street") conquered the pop charts as never before.

Motown

Berry Gordy applied his business acumen to launch Motown, which soon became the largest black-owned corporation in the United States. As CEO, Gordy addressed all aspects of career development for African American artists including Martha and the Vandellas, the Marvelettes, Smokey Robinson and the Miracles, Marvin Gaye, the Temptations, the Four Tops, Stevie Wonder, and the Supremes. As a producer, he had an uncanny ability to incorporate white audience tastes without abandoning a black sound.

FIGURE 3   Chuck Berry, "Mr. Rock 'n' Roll," a consummate showman and musician, appealed to youth in a way no previous performer had done and was an inspiration to generations of younger rock 'n' roll musicians from the 1960s and later.

As the early civil rights movement gave way to the more radical demand for black power, Motown's hegemony over black pop was challenged by a resurgence of grassroots rhythm and blues from the Deep South.

FIGURE 4   James Brown "crossed over" without compromising his music. Brown became seen as a leader and role model in the African American community and his articulation of self-sufficiency and black pride in the 1960s resonated with the Civil Rights movement.

FIGURE 5   The "Lady of Soul," Aretha Franklin. Franklin drew on Gospel, Blues and R&B to emerge as a powerful and uplifting Soul performer. Her hits of the late 1960s expressed the passion of that era, and prefigured the coming feminist movement.

As the early civil rights movement gave way to the more radical demand for black power, Motown's hegemony over black pop was challenged by a resurgence of grassroots rhythm and blues from the Deep South. Chiefly responsible for the popularization of southern soul was a short-lived but highly successful collaboration between Atlantic Records and a number of southern studios, most notably Stax in Memphis and Fame in Muscle Shoals, Alabama (Guralnick 1986). From 1965 on, Otis Redding ("I've Been Loving You Too Long"), Wilson Pickett ("Land of 1,000 Dances"), Sam and Dave ("Soul Man"), Arthur Conley ("Sweet Soul Music"), Percy Sledge ("When a Man Loves a Woman"), and other artists echoed the spirit of the new militancy with raw, basic recordings easily distinguished from the cleaner, brighter Motown sound. There is, however, a certain irony in these differences.

Not only was Motown black owned, virtually all of its creative personnel—artists, writers, producers, and session musicians—were African American as well. Stax was originally a white-owned company; the "Memphis sound," created by house band Booker T. and the MGs, was the product of cross-racial teamwork [see FUNK, p. 680; DISCO AND HOUSE MUSIC, p. 687]. In the late 1960s, leadership was increasingly taken over by black vice president Al Bell, often under controversial circumstances. Paradoxically, Motown has been remembered as being "totally committed to reaching white audiences," whereas Stax recordings, by contrast, were "consistently aimed at r&b fans first, the pop market second" (George 1988:86).

James Brown and Aretha Franklin

The two artists who best expressed the spirit of the era were James Brown (figure 4) and Aretha Franklin (figure 5). In the 1950s, James Brown's music was intended for, and limited to, the black community. When he "crossed over," he did so on his own terms. His string of uncompromising Top 10 hits ("Papa's Got a Brand New Bag," "I Got You," "Cold Sweat") made few concessions to mainstream sensibilities. His 1968 hit single, "Say It Loud—I'm Black and I'm Proud," became an anthem in the struggle for black liberation. Signed to Atlantic Records in 1967, Aretha Franklin earned the title "Lady Soul" with her recording of "Respect." The vocal and emotional range of her Atlantic releases ("Baby, I Love You," "Natural Woman," "Chain of Fools," "Think," and "Young, Gifted, and Black," to name a few) uniquely expressed all the passion and forcefulness of the era.

Two black-led mixed bands in the late sixties incorporated psychedelic sounds into their music—Sly and the Family Stone ("Dance to the Music," "Everyday People," "Hot Fun in the Summertime," "Thank You Falletinme Be Mice Elf Agin," "Family Affair") and the Jimi Hendrix Experience ("Purple Haze," "All Along the Watchtower"). Chemical indulgence guided the rises and falls of both. Sly Stone married the funk and rock cultures in a way that no other artist, black or white, had done. Hendrix explored the electronic wizardry of his instrument and recording studio to a greater extent than any other African American musician. Unfortunately, Stone become more unreliable as he became more involved with drugs, and Hendrix was never able to attract a black audience to the music with which he was identified during his lifetime, which was cut tragically short by a drug overdose.

THE 1970s: SOFT SOUL AND DISCO

In the early seventies a breakthrough of sorts for African American songwriters was provided by so-called blaxploitation films. The movies *Shaft*, *Superfly*, and *Troubleman* were scored by Isaac Hayes, Curtis Mayfield, and Marvin Gaye, respectively.

If there was a dominant black sound that reflected the quieter mood of the early 1970s, it was Philadelphia soft soul, pioneered by the writer-producer team of Kenny Gamble and Leon Huff and producer-arranger Thom Bell, who joined forces with Sigma Sound Studios and collaborated in the tripartite administration of Mighty Three Music, their publishing arm. Working with Jerry Butler, the Intruders, and the Delphonics, Gamble and Huff parlayed a $700 bank loan into thirty million-selling singles in a five-year period. Gamble and Huff hit their stride in 1971, with the formation of Philadelphia International Records (PIR) and a distribution deal with CBS. Their two biggest groups were Harold Melvin and the Blue Notes ("If You Don't Know Me by Now," "The Love I Lost") and the O'Jays ("Back Stabbers," "Love Train," "I Love Music," "Use Ta Be My Girl").

Thom Bell drew on his classical training to provide lush orchestral arrangements over a polite rhythmic pulse for groups such as the Stylistics ("Betcha by Golly, Wow," "Break Up to Make Up," "You Make Me Feel Brand New"), produced for the Avco label, and the Spinners ("I'll Be Around," "Could It Be I'm Falling in Love," "The Rubberband Man," "Working My Way Back to You/Forgive Me, Girl") on Atlantic. By the mid-1970s, the massive integrated house band at Sigma Studios, MFSB (for Mother Father Sister Brother) and its backup vocal trio, the Three Degrees, had become hitmakers in their own right. Other artists such as the Chicago-based Chi-Lites ("Oh Girl") and the ever-changing Isley Brothers ("That Lady") quickly tuned into the new soft soul sound. Even Southern soul yielded the velvety smooth Al Green ("Let's Stay Together," "I'm Still in Love with You"). Together, these groups set the standard in black popular music for the first half of the decade and anticipated one strand of the disco craze that was about to erupt.

Disco

Disco began as deejay-created medleys of existing (mostly African American) dance records in black, Latino, and gay nightclubs. As it evolved into its own musical genre, its inspiration came from a number of sources: self-contained funk bands such as Kool and the Gang ("Funky Stuff," "Jungle Boogie"), the Ohio Players ("Skin Tight," "Fire"), and Earth, Wind and Fire ("Shining Star"); Philadelphia-style soft soul; and the controlled energy of what came to be known as Eurodisco. Most of the proto disco releases in the United States were by African American artists. The first disco hit to reach the charts as disco was Gloria Gaynor's "Never Can Say Good-bye" in 1974. Donna Summer's "Love to Love You Baby" moved disco closer to the surface. And by 1975, Van McCoy and The Soul City Orchestra had established the Hustle as the most important new dance craze since the Twist.

Disco was sparsely promoted by record companies and systematically ignored by radio. The music received its primary exposure in clubs, popularized only by the creative genius of club deejays. Because they were shunned by the record companies, disco deejays organized themselves into distribution networks called record pools, and, in so doing, developed an alternative to the airplay marketing structure of the industry, which represented the first time since early rock and roll that the industry was taken by surprise. Their efforts also created a new subindustry for twelve-inch singles and remixed releases that thrives to this day.

Disco was more than an underground party culture; its fanatical following turned out to be a significant record-buying public as well. By the mid-1970s, the pop charts were bursting with disco acts such as Hot Chocolate ("You Sexy Thing"), Wild Cherry ("Play That Funky Music"), K.C. and the Sunshine Band ("Shake Your Booty"), Johnny Taylor ("Disco Lady"), Maxine Nightingale ("Right Back Where We Started From"), the Emotions ("Best of My Love"), Thelma Houston ("Don't Leave Me This Way"), Rose Royce ("Car Wash"), Brick ("Dazz"), Hot ("Angel in Your Arms"), Taste of Honey ("Boogie Oogie Oogie"), Peter Brown ("Dance with Me"), Yvonne Elliman ("If I Can't Have You"), Chic ("Dance, Dance, Dance"), Heatwave ("The Groove Line"), and of course, Donna Summer. Most of these acts were black.

The importance of radio

At this point, radio could no longer ignore the phenomenon. WKTU, an obscure soft rock station in New York, pointed the way when it converted to an all-disco format in 1978 and became the most listened to station in the country. By 1979, two hundred stations broadcasting in almost every major market had converted to a disco format. Syndicated television programs such as *Disco Magic* and *Dance Fever* brought the dance craze to the heartland. Some thirty-six million adults thrilled to the musical mixes of eight thousand professional deejays who serviced a portion of the estimated twenty thousand disco clubs. The phenomenon spawned a subindustry whose annual revenues ranged from $4 billion to $8 billion. However as disco became too bloated, there was an inevitable backlash, followed by collapse. The problem was that slogans such as "Death to disco" and "Disco sucks" sounded as much like racial epithets as statements of musical preference.

THE 1980s AND THE DEVELOPMENT OF MUSIC TELEVISION

In the early 1980s, rock radio reasserted its primacy (and its avoidance of African American artists) with a vengeance. Black-oriented radio was forced to move in the direction of a new format—urban contemporary—that ultimately provided greater access for white musicians on what had been black-oriented stations. The launching of MTV in 1981 brought acts of racial exclusion to a new medium. In 1983 *People* magazine reported that "on MTV's current roster of some 800 acts, sixteen are black" (Bricker 1983). New music video outlets formed in reaction to MTV's restrictive programming policies. Black Entertainment Television (BET) and the long-standing *Soul Train* provided the primary video exposure for black talent in the early 1980s. Ironically, *Yo! MTV Raps* subsequently became one of MTV's most popular offerings.

This restriction of access to African American artists occurred during the first recession in the music business since the late 1940s. Recovery, beginning in 1983, was signaled by the multiplatinum, worldwide success of Michael Jackson's album *Thriller*, with international sales of some forty million units making it the best-selling record of all time. *Thriller* began a trend toward blockbuster LPs featuring a limited number of superstar artists as the solution to the industry's economic woes. Interestingly, many of these superstars—Michael Jackson (figure 6), Prince, Lionel Richie, Tina Turner— were African American.

The phenomenal pop successes of these artists immediately catapulted them into an upper-level industry infrastructure fully owned and operated by whites. These artists were further distinguished from their less successful African American colleagues in that they were now marketed directly to the mainstream audience, a practice that proved to be phenomenally successful with Whitney Houston and, more recently, Mariah Carey. In this rarefied atmosphere, African American artists are confronted with considerable pressure to sever their ties with the attorneys, managers, booking agents, and promoters who may have been responsible for building their careers in the

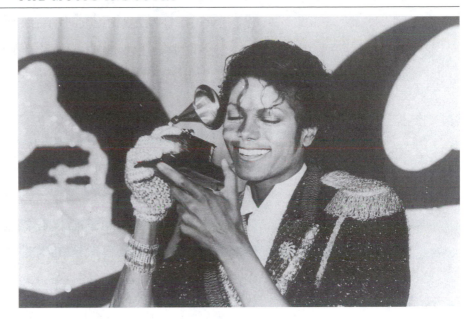

FIGURE 6   As the lead-singer of the Jackson Five in the 1970s, Michael Jackson learned his style and showmanship from the older generation of performers. This could clearly be seen in his mega-hits of the 1980s, such as *Thriller*, which rocketed him to superstar status.

first place. "Aside from Sammy Davis, Jr., Nancy Wilson, and Stephanie Mills," said Nelson George, there were "no other black household names with black management" (George 1988:177).

A number of cross-racial, pop-oriented duets brought new meaning to the term *crossover*. Releases by Stevie Wonder and Paul McCartney ("Ebony and Ivory"), Michael Jackson and Paul McCartney ("The Girl Is Mine," "Say Say Say"), Diana Ross and Julio Iglesias ("All of You"), James Ingram and Kenny Rogers ("What about Me"), Dionne Warwick and Friends ("That's What Friends Are For"), Patti LaBelle and Michael McDonald ("On My Own"), Aretha Franklin and George Michael ("I Knew You Were Waiting for Me"), and James Ingram and Linda Ronstadt ("Somewhere Out There") were designed to build market share synergistically. Michael Jackson and Lionel Richie's "We Are the World" (1985)—the ultimate crossover recording—initiated the phenomenon of "charity rock."

RAP

It remained for rap to take African American music back to the streets. Rap, one cultural element in the larger hip-hop subculture, began in the South Bronx at about the same time as disco, but given its place of origin, the movement developed in almost complete isolation for more than five years. In the late 1970s, hip-hop was "discovered" in turn, by the music business, the print media, and the film industry. Through early 1980s films such as the low budget *Wild Style* and the blockbuster *Flashdance*, followed by *Breakin'* and *Beat Street*, hip-hop was brought to the attention of a mass audience.

In the mid-1980s, early hip-hop culture heroes such as Afrika Baambaataa, Kool Herc, and Grandmaster Flash passed the baton to a second generation of artists including Whodini, the Force MDS, the Fat Boys, and Run-D.M.C., who recorded the first gold rap album, *Run-D.M.C.* (1984). This was a new wrinkle for rap, which had always been based on twelve-inch singles. In the relative absence of radio play, even on black radio, rap artists such as Run-D.M.C. *(Raising Hell, Tougher Than Leather)*, L.L. Cool J *(Bigger and Deffer)*, Whodini *(Escape)*, Heavy D. & the Boyz *(Big Tyme)*, Salt-N-Pepa *(Hot, Cool & Vicious)*, and the Fat Boys *(Crushin')* made significant inroads into the album and cassette market throughout the rest of the decade. Eight of *Billboard*'s Top 30 black albums on 28 November 1987 were rap albums.

Roundly criticized for its violence and misogyny, rap became the main target in the controversy over censorship, even as it endeavored to clean up its image.

Rap and Afrocentricity

The next development in rap was message rap, promoted most forcefully by New York's Public Enemy. Public Enemy consciously sought to advance the cause of black nationalism and Afrocentricity with tracks as compelling as they were controversial. The group hit its stride with *It Takes a Nation of Millions to Hold Us Back* (1988) and upped the ante on *Fear of a Black Planet* (1990). By this time, the Los Angeles rap scene had come into its own, and the harder rhymes of Ice-T and NWA established gangsta rap as the dominant style for the next several years and kicked off a sometimes violent East Coast/West Coast rivalry that lasted well into the 1990s. Adding to rap's penchant for controversy, Miami's 2 Live Crew released *As Nasty As They Wanna Be* (1990), the first recording to be declared legally obscene in a federal district court.

The turmoil surrounding rap presented a problem for black radio, which avoided the music like the plague, but major record companies recognized its financial potential. Beginning as a street movement, rap was initially produced by independent labels, some of which—such as Sugar Hill and Russell Simmons's Def Jam—were black owned. In putting Curtis Blow under contract, Mercury was one of the few major labels to sign a rap artist directly, but buy-ins and distribution deals with small rap labels soon became commonplace. Columbia Records concluded a custom label deal with Def Jam (L.L. Cool J, the Beastie Boys, Public Enemy) in 1985. Jive Records (Whodini, Kool Moe Dee, D.J. Jazzy Jeff and the Fresh Prince, Boogie Down Productions) worked with both RCA and Arista. In 1987, Cold Chillin' Records (Marly Marl, Roxanne Shanté, Biz Markie) signed a distribution deal with Warner, which also bought a piece of Tommy Boy (Stetsasonic, Force MDs, De La Soul, Queen Latifah, Digital Underground). Delicious Vinyl (Tone Loc, Def Jef, Young M.C.) contracted for national distribution with Island. Priority (NWA, Eazy E, Ice Cube) went with Capitol (Garofalo 1997:420).

Roundly criticized for its violence and misogyny, rap became the main target in the controversy over censorship, even as it endeavored to clean up its image. Addressing the issue of violence, a number of East Coast rap groups, including Stetsasonic, Boogie Down Productions, and Public Enemy, followed the lead of Nelson George in initiating the Stop the Violence movement aimed specifically at black-on-black crime. West Coast rappers followed with "We're All in the Same Gang." Evidence of change in the sexual politics of rap became apparent in 1988 when the overwhelming commercial success of Salt-N-Pepa's double-platinum debut LP, *Hot, Cool & Vicious,* finally convinced some rap labels to start promoting female rappers. By the end of the decade women had added a new public voice to hip-hop, with releases that included "Paper Thin" (MC Lyte), "Independent Woman" (Roxanne Shanté), and "Ladies First" (Queen Latifah).

RAP AND THE MAINSTREAM IN THE 1990s

Rap achieved a benchmark of mainstream acceptance when the National Academy of Recording Arts and Sciences (NARAS) added a rap category to the Grammy Awards in

1988. In 1990, rapper-dancer Hammer (then M.C. Hammer) scored another first for rap, as *Please Hammer Don't Hurt 'Em* logged twenty-one weeks at number one on the pop charts, becoming the best-selling rap album ever, with sales upwards of ten million copies. Rap had achieved a mainstream visibility that propelled its stars into other media as well. Following his receipt of the first rap Grammy, Will Smith (the Fresh Prince) was rewarded with a starring role in a prime-time sitcom, *The Fresh Prince of Bel Air*. Rappers also began to show up on other African American TV shows such as *A Different World, Cosby,* and *In Living Color*. Queen Latifah landed a starring role in her own television sitcom, *Living Single*. It was in film, however, that rap made some of its most powerful statements. Following Spike Lee's *Do the Right Thing* (1989), powered by the hip-hop force of Public Enemy's "Fight the Power," there appeared a rash of black-directed films in the early 1990s about life in the "hood": *Straight Outta Brooklyn, Juice, New Jack City,* and *Boyz N the Hood,* the latter two of which starred Ice-T and Ice Cube, respectively, and featured their music as well. Will Smith moved on to a significant film career, with starring roles in Hollywood blockbusters such as *Independence Day* and *Men in Black*.

The late 1980s and early 1990s was also a period that showcased the talents of African American producers, with Quincy Jones, Nile Rogers, Narada Michael Walden, Jimmy Jam, and Terry Lewis receiving top honors and paving the way for LA Reid and Babyface Edmunds. Sean "Puffy" Coombs carried the trend forward in the mid-1990s.

Rounding out the 1990s were a number of separable trends: the predictable pop of artists such as Mariah Carey, who started with five number one hits in a row; the growth of R&B vocal styles that combined the smooth ballad style of Luther Vandross with the hip-hop harmonies of groups such as Color Me Badd ("All for Love"), Boyz II Men ("End of the Road" and "One Sweet Day" with Mariah Carey), and Jodeci ("Lately"); the sexualized R&B stylings of vocalist and multi-instrumentalist R. Kelly ("Bump and Grind"); the social engagement of rap groups ranging from Arrested Development ("People Everyday") to the Fugees ("Killing Me Softly"); and the turn toward real-life violence that plagued rap artists such as Snoop Doggy Dogg (*Doggy Style*) and cost the lives of Tupac Shakur (*All Eyez on Me*) and the Notorious B.I.G. (*Ready to Die*), even as they turned in some of the best-selling albums of the era.

African American cultural traditions continue to be located at the center of what has become an increasingly broad and multicultural constituency in hip-hop. From an isolated street culture, hip-hop expanded, in less than twenty years, into a global phenomenon that surpassed all expectations. Following the collapse of alternative rock and general sluggishness in the music business in the mid-1990s, industry veterans routinely expressed the view that hip-hop and rhythm and blues–based dance music were poised to become the Next Big Thing. For many of their dedicated followers, such musics had always been there.

REFERENCES

Bricker, Rebecca. 1983. "Take One." *People,* 4 April, 31.

Garofalo, Reebee. 1990. "Crossing Over, 1939–1992." In *Split Image: African Americans in the Mass Media,* 2nd ed., ed. Jannette L. Dates and William Barlow, 57–127. Washington, D.C.: Howard University Press.

———. 1997. *Rockin' Out: Popular Music in the USA*. Boston: Allyn and Bacon.

George, Nelson. 1988. *The Death of Rhythm & Blues*. New York: Pantheon Books.

Gillett, Charlie. 1970. *The Sound of the City*. New York: Outerbridge and Dienstfrey.

Guralnick, Peter. 1986. *Sweet Soul Music*. New York: Harper and Row.

Jones, LeRoi (Amiri Baraka). 1963. *Blues People*. New York: Morrow.

Southern, Eileen. 1997. *The Music of Black Americans: A History*. 3rd ed. New York: Norton.

Section 2b
South American, Central American, Mexican, and Caribbean Musics

The Spanish were the first Europeans to establish, in the late sixteenth century, a permanent settlement in what is today the United States (in St. Augustine, Florida). From then until the present, Spanish-speaking immigrants as well as Portuguese-speaking Brazilians and mestizos (people of mixed heritage) have continued to arrive, via Mexico, the Caribbean, and Central and South America, and they now represent the second largest and fastest growing minority population in the United States. Located primarily in Texas, New Mexico, California, and New York, Hispanic musical communities have contributed their vibrant rhythms, dance forms, instruments, and musicians to the eclectic American musical landscape. Musical forms, such as the *son, conjunto, mambo, rhumba,* and *cha cha chá,* from Mexico, Cuba, Haiti, and other parts of the Caribbean, greatly influenced popular music—especially African American jazz and dance forms—in the mid- and late twentieth century, when dance crazes popularized by band leaders such as Xavier Cugat and Tito Puente were the rage. In addition to the contribution to popular and classical musics, religious systems such as "serving the spirits" (*vodou*), with its unique ritual and musical traditions, also entered the United States (mainly in New York City and New Orleans) via Haiti. Hispanic/Latin musical elements are so pervasive that they are, like African and European elements, part and parcel of what we today define as American music.

An informal group of Puerto Rican *pleneros* playing different sizes of *pandereta* 'round frame drum' performs in a procession in Manhattan for a cultural festival. Photo by Daniel Sheehy, June 1979.

Overview
Daniel Sheehy
Steven Loza

Latino Immigration
Latino Culture
Latino Music

Near the close of the twentieth century (1999), an estimated 32 million Latinos lived in the United States, representing 12 percent of the total population—nearly one of every eight Americans. Although the U.S. Bureau of the Census uses the term *Hispanic, Latino* came to prevail as the most widely accepted single label to describe a population of diverse national origins, cultures, and racial characteristics. More common terms of self-description, however, are those pointing to national or regional origin—*mexicano* 'Mexican American', *puertorriqueño* 'Puerto Rican', *cubano* 'Cuban', *guatemalteco, boliviano, tejano, nuevomexicano,* and others—or those that emerged from sociopolitical movements, such as Chicano or Nuyorican (Puerto Rican New Yorker).

According to 1996 figures, people of Mexican origin were by far the largest Latino group, comprising 65 percent of U.S. Latinos. Puerto Ricans followed, with 10 percent, those of Cuban origin 4 percent, and those from Central America and South America 14 percent. Nearly one half of Latinos in the United States were foreign born (Goldstein and Suro 2000:A24), compared to one in eleven of all U.S. residents. This statistic underscores the fact that immigration throughout the twentieth-century accounted for the vast majority of Latinos in the United States. While this is true for the Canadian Latino population as well, less than one percent of the total Canadian population of twenty-nine million identified Spanish as their "mother tongue" (Statistics Canada 1996). Consequently, this volume's treatment of Latino music in North America refers primarily to activity in the United States. At the same time, many general trends concerning Central American and South American migration and musical expression in the U.S. upper Midwest and Northeast hold true as well for Canada.

LATINO IMMIGRATION

The geographical distribution and internal variation of each of the major Latino population groups—Mexican, Puerto Rican, Cuban, Central American, Dominican, and South American—have been shaped by historical events. When the 1848 Treaty of Guadalupe Hidalgo ended the Mexican War (1846–1848), it ceded half of Mexico's territory—stretching from Texas in the east, California in the west, and southern Colorado in the north—to the United States, and the area's inhabitants became the first significant Latino population under U.S. governance. In the twentieth century, the sporadic need for foreign workers during the two world wars brought legally sanctioned Mexican railroad workers and *braceros* 'agricultural workers.' Illegal immigration spurred by the lure of greater economic prosperity in the United States occurred throughout the century, particularly during the latter decades.

Along with these "pull" forces, a major "push" force behind immigration was war in various regions of the Americas. The Mexican Revolution (1910–1917) drove many Mexican intellectuals and northern inhabitants across the border into the United States. Fidel Castro's rise to power in 1959 drove many middle- and upper-class Cubans of European descent to Miami and elsewhere in the United States. Continuing hostilities between the United States and communist Cuba brought another influx (this time of less advantaged Cubans of African heritage), most notably during the Mariel boatlift in 1980. Internal warring in El Salvador, Nicaragua, Guatemala, and other areas of Central America pushed those populations northward to the United States in the 1970s and 1980s.

Another important historical factor encouraging Latino immigration was U.S. policy toward the Commonwealth of Puerto Rico, a U.S. jurisdiction since the Spanish-American War in 1898. This post–World War I policy granted Puerto Ricans free entry and citizenship status when coming to the mainland United States. Over the twentieth century, major Puerto Rican communities formed in New York City and other large cities of the Northeast and Midwest. Musicians in particular were attracted by the opportunities for professional musical careers in New York City. A somewhat similar policy existed toward Cuba in the Castro era, as refugees reaching American soil were granted residency.

In large part due to these historical events, eight states account for four-fifths of American Latinos. According to the U.S. Bureau of the Census, in 1990 the Latino populations of California (7.7 million), Texas (4.3 million), New York (2.2 million), and Florida (1.6 million) were the largest, followed by those of Illinois, New Jersey, Arizona, and New Mexico. Latinos of Mexican descent predominate in the Southwest; from the post–World War I era to the 1990s, Puerto Ricans accounted for the majority of Latino New Yorkers; Miami became the North American locus of Cuban culture following 1959; and both Puerto Rican and Mexican communities were well established in Chicago, Detroit, and a few other midwestern cities by the mid-twentieth century. Destinations for immigration broadened at the end of the twentieth century, however, as poultry-processing, beef-packing, urban landscaping, small industry, and other nonagricultural jobs attracted Latino immigrants to virtually every American state. The Hispanic population increased over 50 percent from 1980 to 1990 and continued at this pace through the end of the century. According to a 1995 U.S. Bureau of the Census report, at this rate of growth, by the year 2050, one in four Americans may be Hispanic.

LATINO CULTURE

Historical presence in the United States, regional identity, degree of acculturation, urbanization, national origin, religion, and relative affluence are some of the major forces shaping the American Latino cultural panorama. Folklorist Américo Paredes identified "at least three kinds of folklore groups of Mexican origin" (1993:7): (1) truly regional groups, (2) groups composed of rural or semirural immigrants, and (3) urban groups. *U.S. News and World Report* (Robinson 1998:27) profiled seventeen major Latino subcultures across the United States. These consisted of the following: New Mexican and Lower Rio Grande Valley regional cultures that took root around 1600 and in the 1700s, respectively; middle-class, "*barrio*-dweller," and immigrant Mexicans in California; Central Americans in central Los Angeles; Texas Guatemalans; Houston Mexicans; Chicago's Mexican and Puerto Rican communities; Puerto Ricans, Dominicans, and Colombians in New York City; Cubans, Nicaraguans, and South Americans in Miami; and migrant workers scattered in smaller numbers throughout the country.

Overall, around 90 percent of Latinos live in urban areas, a major shift from the rural, agricultural majority prior to World War II.

The persistence of Spanish as the language of preference is a major component of acculturation, a process whereby Latinos adopt "mainstream" North American culture as their own. A 1999 survey showed that while 73 percent of first-generation Latino immigrants spoke Spanish in the home, that figure fell to 1 percent among third-generation Latinos (Goldstein and Suro 2000:A24). On the other hand, many Latinos as a point of pride maintain the ability to speak Spanish. Some other, more private, aspects of Latino cultural heritage are slower to change, such as styles of cuisine, the importance of the family social unit, and religious traditions. While the vast majority of Latinos are at least nominally Roman Catholic, for example, religious traditions and patron saint activities particular to certain nations of origin have carried over into North American life. The Virgin of Guadalupe, "a brown-appearing icon associated with the Indian-Mestizo segment of the population in Mexico, is of little interest among Cuban Americans and Puerto Ricans, and *santería* beliefs and practices (worship of African gods clothed in Catholic dogma) in those groups are far less common among Mexican Americans" (Vigil 1991:206). According to a 1997 Bureau of the Census report, a sizable portion of Latinos live below the poverty level—26.4 percent in 1996—with those of Cuban descent the most affluent of the major groups, and Puerto Ricans the least economically advantaged.

LATINO MUSIC

Latino music in the United States today reflects many of the historical and contemporary trends mentioned above. Regional traditions persist in the Lower Rio Grande Valley and in New Mexico, areas with greater connection to rural life. A high degree of musical continuity exists between certain Latin American nations of origin and their North American counterparts. This has resulted from massive immigration within recent generations, ongoing ties with nations located only hours away by air travel, and the renewal of national identities in urban areas by continued immigration. Close continuity is particularly the case with more commercially successful musical styles, and less so for musics with little footing in the popular media. Musical styles identified with a particular ethnic group, especially those popularly thought of as *"música folklórica,"* that is, representative of "old ways," often take on an added dimension of symbolic importance, as cultural minorities employ them as a vehicle to fortify their solidarity and as an emblem to represent themselves to the broader, pluralistic society.

In urban settings, proximity to North American social dance music and jazz, economic opportunities for professional musicians, and a powerful media industry that amplified the voice of commercially successful popular music offered fertile ground for musical innovation. In New York, Caribbean musicians from Puerto Rico, Cuba, and elsewhere parlayed the vogue of Cuban and pseudo-Cuban dance music in the 1930s through 1950s into a niche in the North American panorama of popular music. Some of these musicians joined Duke Ellington and other leading big bands, adding a vein of Latin Caribbean rhythm to the mix. Tito Puente and others, drawing from both popular non-Latin dance music and Caribbean rhythms, took the lead in creating Latin dance music and Latin jazz with broad appeal. In the 1930s through the 1950s, Tejano orchestras imitated or incorporated elements of nationally popular swing bands, eventually leading to the emergence of a unique regional popular music style. Los Angeles Chicano musicians, such as the group Los Lobos, drew from African American rhythm and blues in forging a new sound. Gloria Estefan headlined a nationally prominent Cuban-tinged popular musical style. Latino music has made great headway in making its presence known on the national stage. In 2000, for example, the National Academy of Recording Arts and Sciences specifically designated seven of the ninety-eight categories of the Grammy Awards for "Latin" music: Latin Pop Performance; Latin

Rock/Alternative Performance; Traditional Tropical Latin Performance; Salsa Performance; Merengue Performance; Mexican-American Performance; and Tejano Performance. In addition, that same year, Carlos Santana and Christine Aguilera garnered numerous other major Grammy awards, and a separate Latin Grammys event was inaugurated.

The four other entries on Latino music in this section—"Hispanic California," "Música Nuevomexicana," "Tejano Music," and "Latin Caribbean Music"—focus on the most prominent and most documented of these musical traditions. Regrettably, much research remains to be done on many forms of Latino music found in the United States, especially those of cultural groups who arrived in recent decades. This overview section aims to place these entries in a broader North American context and to outline musical activity not covered by them, so as not to omit entirely mention of those less-documented musical forms.

Mexican American music

Mexican American music includes all those musics of Mexican origin that are practiced in the United States as well as those created by communities historically associated with Mexico. By the former, we mean regional traditions of Mexican mestizo folk music, folk-rooted popular Mexican musics, and internationally popular urban musics. By the latter, we mean regional musical cultures from New Mexico (predating the existence of the Republic of Mexico but strongly influenced by Mexican music), the Lower Rio Grande Valley, and California, as well as hybrid creations spawned by urban life [see FIVE FUSIONS, p. 334].

The musics most long lived in the United States are those of the Nuevo-Mexicano and Tejano regional groups. It merits mention that the first documented European music education in what is now U.S. territory occurred in New Mexico, as the Spanish friars accompanying the Spanish explorer Juan de Oñate established a colony there in 1598, nearly a decade before the English settled Jamestown in the swamplands of present-day North Carolina. *Californios* also developed a regional musical culture, although it has all but faded in the face of intense acculturation and overwhelming immigration from other musical regions in Mexico. More recent Mexican American music creations include the rock and roll originals of Los Lobos and the recordings of the late Tejana vocalist Selena.

While musical distinctions reflect the broader cultural differences among Mexican American subgroups, certain unifying features are shared broadly. Baptisms, birthdays, *quinceañeras* (celebrations for fifteen-year-old girls), and weddings are universally preferred life-cycle events for music making. *Cinco de Mayo* 'Fifth of May', commemorating the Battle of Puebla in the 1860s Mexican struggle against the occupying French imperialist forces, emerged as the major annual celebration of Chicano identity, marked by performances of music and dance. Mexican Independence Day on 16 September is of similar importance, especially in communities with more recent roots in the Republic of Mexico. Mother's Day is another day for celebrations accompanied by music. The Roman Catholic feast day of the Virgin of Guadalupe on 12 December is widely celebrated with a common repertoire of hymns and other songs sung by the congregation and, when possible, live mariachi music performing a post–Vatican Council II version of certain Mass segments, known collectively as the Misa Panamericana. Social dances and concerts by touring Mexican superstar vocalists such as Vicente Fernández and Juan Gabriel attract Mexican Americans of all backgrounds. The custom of the *serenata*—a short serenade to celebrate a birthday, Mother's Day, or a man's devotion to his beloved—continues to be practiced in the North American context. The Mexican song "Las Mañanitas," sung especially on birthdays, is known widely among Mexican Americans as well as among other Latinos. The Mexican farmworker movement in the 1960s and 1970s occasioned the performance of *corridos* 'narrative

Sparked by the civil rights movement beginning in the 1960s, the Chicano movement also inspired greater interest in Mexican roots music as an important cultural symbol.

ballads' that recounted strikes, praised leader César Chávez, and aimed to reinforce general commitment to the movement (figure 1). Sparked by the civil rights movement beginning in the 1960s, the Chicano movement also inspired greater interest in Mexican roots music as an important cultural symbol. New musical compositions treating important Chicano leaders and events and calling for greater cultural pride came out of the Chicano movement as well.

Certain popular folk-rooted musical styles—two in particular—are found throughout the United States and in Canada. Mariachi ensembles are based in most American states and in at least two Canadian provinces. Typically comprising two trumpets, two or more violins, *guitarrón* 'six-stringed, convex-spined bass', *vihuela* 'five-stringed, convexed-spined guitar', and six-stringed guitar, the mariachi rose from regional roots in nineteenth-century west Mexico to become a twentieth-century pan-Mexican musical symbol (Sheehy 1997:132). It is the principal ensemble for performing *música ranchera* 'country music', popular song often treating matters of unrequited love that evokes sentiment and appeals to pan-Mexican tastes. Songs such as "El Rey" ("The King") and "Volver, Volver" ("Return, Return"), composed and recorded by the late singer/songwriter José Alfredo Jiménez, are staples of the mariachi repertoire and are known by virtually all Mexican Americans. The mariachi is also sought out to perform the Catholic Mass, particularly to celebrate the feast of the Virgin of Guadalupe. The mariachi is also widely known among non-Mexicans in the United States. Mariachi groups are frequently employed to appear at Mexican restaurants, "Mexican theme" events, and celebrations of cultural diversity. Generally speaking, mariachi

FIGURE 1 Farmworker/musicians (*left* to *right*) Jesús Figueroa, Alfredo Figueroa, and Alfredo Figueroa Jr. pose in their home in Blythe, California. Photo by Daniel Sheehy, April 1999.

groups are mobile, musically versatile, professional musical ensembles that are capable of performing a wide range of repertoire, including many non-Mexican songs.

Accordion-driven *conjuntos* 'ensembles' have migrated along with transient Mexican workers to all regions of the United States and further northward to Canada. These groups may be either of Mexican or Tejano origin. Mexican immigrant *conjuntos* of two or three musicians playing the Hohner or Gabinelli button accordion, the twelve-stringed *bajo sexto,* and, if available, the upright three-stringed *tololoche* 'bass' are more common outside Texas, reflecting the large number and wide geographic dispersal of Mexican immigrant workers. Amplified *conjuntos* with drum set often provide instrumental music such as Tejano or Mexican polkas for social dances, especially in Texas. Up-tempo, duple-meter songs such as *corridos* on current themes such as *narcotraficantes* 'drug smugglers' have gained enormous currency, however. The U.S.-based group Los Tigres del Norte (The Tigers of the North) are emblematic of this style of song. Unamplified *conjunto* duos or trios commonly perform for special events in homes, migrant camps, and bars, charging their clients hourly or by the song.

Other Mexican regional folk music styles are also present in the United States. The *banda* 'brass band', with trumpets, trombones, clarinets or saxophones, *charcheta* 'tenor horn', sousaphone, bass drum, and snare drum, originated in the states of Sinaloa and Zacatecas, routinely perform in nightclubs and rodeos in California, and tour to larger Mexican communities throughout the United States. In the 1990s, the popular media propelled a modified version of the *banda* to enormous popularity in Mexico and among many Mexican Americans. A musical style of rural Michoacán in west Mexico followed *michoacano* migrants northward to Redwood City, California, Yakima, Washington, and other places where large numbers of *michoacanos* settled (figure 2). Utilizing a large diatonic harp, one or two violins, *vihuela,* and *jarana* (deep-bodied, five-stringed rhythm guitar), these groups play fast-paced *sones, canciones rancheras, corridos,* and other pieces appealing to the Michoacán immigrants. Many Mexican marimba ensembles, traditionally identified with the southern Mexican states of Oaxaca and Chiapas but found throughout Mexico, are based in Los Angeles, Houston, and other U.S. cities. Immigrant musicians play the rapid-rhythm *son jarocho* from Veracruz on *arpa* 'thirty-four-stringed diatonic harp', regional *jarana* 'eight-stringed, narrow-bodied rhythm guitar', and *requinto jarocho* 'four-stringed melody guitar plucked with a long plastic or bone pick.' Many Chicanos, looking to Mexican roots music as a vehicle of cultural/social expression and creativity, have become

FIGURE 2   Michoacán ensemble "Los Campesinos de Michoacán," led by Salvador Baldovinos (*far right*), plays in a restaurant in Yakima, Washington. Instrumentation is two violins, *vihuela,* six-stringed guitar and *arpa grande* 'big harp.' Photo by Daniel Sheehy, October 1992.

FIGURE 3   Artemio Posadas (*left*) of San Jose, California, plays the *son huasteco* on the violin with the accompaniment of an unidentified *jarana huasteca* player (*center*) and *huapanguera* player Russell Rodríguez (*right*). Photo by Daniel Sheehy, August 1993.

accomplished performers. The Herrera family of Oxnard, California, and their group, Conjunto Hueyapan, performing the *son jarocho* of Veracruz, are a notable example. Artemio Posadas, a native of the Huastecan region in northeast Mexico and a resident of San Jose, California, and his Chicano disciples perform the *son huasteco* (figure 3). Several of the aforementioned regional Mexican mestizo musics, along with the mariachi, might also accompany the plethora of Mexican folkloric dance companies found in Mexican American communities throughout the United States.

Three significant North American trends in mariachi music overarch the regions profiled in the other entries. Large-scale mariachi festivals, numbering more than fifteen scattered throughout the Southwest in the 1990s, began in 1979 with the first San Antonio International Mariachi Conference organized by Belle and Juan Ortiz. These festivals built upon two other trends that began in the late 1960s. One was the emergence of school programs of mariachi instruction and performance in a few schools in California, Arizona, and Texas (figure 4). The other was pioneered in Los Angeles by bandleader Natividad Cano and his Mariachi Los Camperos, who "established the first

FIGURE 4   Mariachi bandleader/violinist Natividad Cano (*left of center in white shirt*) and members of his group Los Camperos lead a workshop for high school students at the Viva el Mariachi Festival in Fresno, California. Photo by Daniel Sheehy, March 1997.

FIGURE 5   Mariachi Los Camperos de Nati Cano perform in La Fonda de los Camperos restaurant in Los Angeles. Photo by Daniel Sheehy, March 1997.

night club where mariachi music was presented on stage as a dinner show, reaching a new audience of highly assimilated, middle-class, urban immigrants and their offspring" (Fogelquist 1996:20) (figure 5). The San Antonio event combined instruction of youth by master musicians with concerts by Mexico's premier group, Mariachi Vargas de Tecalitlán, and subsequently by leading U.S.-based groups as well. This combination provided a model that was imitated widely by festivals in Tucson, Arizona, Fresno and San Jose, California, Albuquerque and Las Cruces, New Mexico, Wenatchee, Washington, and elsewhere. By the late 1990s, there were hundreds of school mariachi programs in Texas, New Mexico, Arizona, Colorado, California, Washington, and Illinois, as well as numerous dinner nightclubs that featured stage-oriented mariachi shows. Following her appearance at the Tucson festival, pop music singer Linda Ronstadt, a Tucson native of Mexican American background, launched a national tour and recording, both entitled *Canciones de Mi Padre* 'Songs of my Father' in the late 1980s. The tour and recording were highly influential in spurring greater interest in mariachi music, especially among young Mexican Americans, and highlighting the music as a focal point for Mexican American cultural/social identity.

Puerto Rican music

The ceding of Puerto Rico to the United States at the conclusion of the Spanish-American war in 1898 began two processes that lasted throughout the twentieth century, especially following the end of World War I in 1918. First, the emerging influence of the North American popular music industry, radio, and cinema bombarded the island with current musical vogues. Second, the northward flow to the United States—to New York City in particular—of Puerto Rican professional musicians familiar with those vogues continued unabated. Internal economic shifts following the American takeover of the island displaced many workers, including musicians, and the hardships of the Great Depression accelerated the movement of musicians to New York, the hub of the entertainment industry (Glasser 1995:50–51). At the same time, the versatility gained by Puerto Rican musicians through exposure to both Latin and North American musics worked to their advantage (Glasser 1995:38). These events contributed to the prominent place of Puerto Rican musicians in the evolution of New York's musical life and the popular Latin musics it would spawn, especially Latin-Caribbean dance music. The multifaceted musical literacy of Puerto Rican musicians only increased as

The late Tito Puente, who made over one hundred record albums and won many Grammy Awards, was the most prominent example of Puerto Rican centrality to both Cuban-derived popular Latin dance music and Latin jazz.

Puerto Rican immigrants and their descendants became integrated into North American cultural life, borrowing from and contributing to important veins of popular music such as jazz and rock and roll. The late Tito Puente, who made over one hundred record albums and won many Grammy Awards, was the most prominent example of Puerto Rican centrality to both Cuban-derived popular Latin dance music and Latin jazz. Puerto Ricans such as singer/guitarist José Feliciano and Metropolitan Opera singer Martina Arroyo also achieved national and international prominence.

Several popular forms of Puerto Rican traditional music are actively performed in the United States. The two principal strains of popular Puerto Rican folk music—*música jíbara* and the more African-derived genres of *bomba* and *plena* (figure 6)—have long been performed in the United States and enjoyed a revival in the 1990s. *Música jíbara* centers on the music and dance form called *seis* and on the ensemble based on the ten-steel-stringed *cuatro* guitar, the six-stringed "standard" Spanish guitar, and the *güiro* 'gourd scraper.' Puerto Rican *cuatrista* ['*cuatro* player'] Estanislao Ladí was influential in the formation of the modern *conjunto jíbaro* ['*jíbaro* ensemble'], especially in the 1930s and after. He increased the music's popularity by incorporating a wide range of musical genres into the *cuatro* repertoire and including more instruments—two *cuatros*, bongo drums, and even bass and conga drum—in the ensemble. Ladí was closely linked to Puerto Rican musical life in New York City through touring and recordings. In the 1990s, several *jíbaro*-style ensembles, numerous individual musicians, and a few *jíbaro* instrument makers were active in the United States, especially in larger cities of the Midwest and Northeast such as Chicago, New York, and Hartford,

FIGURE 6   An informal group of Puerto Rican *pleneros* playing different sizes of *pandereta* 'round frame drum' performs in a procession in Manhattan for a cultural festival. Photo by Daniel Sheehy, June 1979.

Connecticut. *Cuatrista* Yomo Toro's performances of traditional *seis,* Latin dance music, and Latin jazz gained him significant renown. As in Puerto Rico, *música jíbara* and the musical genre *aguinaldo* are most favored during Christmas season. The music is often associated with an idealized rustic past and the Christmastide custom of singing from house to house, asking for small gifts of money or food, the *aguinaldo.* *Aguinaldo* texts, often improvised, refer to Christmas themes and ask the listener for the *aguinaldo.*

In the 1990s, the number of U.S.-based groups playing *bomba* and *plena* increased several fold, in great measure the result of the efforts by the group Los Pleneros de la 21 to reestablish the music's prominence in the United States. Led by musician/teacher/bandleader Juan Gutiérrez, the Pleneros elevated the prestige of *bomba* and *plena* music in the United States through innovative instrumentation, frequent performances in the Northeast and upper Midwest, educational presentations, and emphasizing the music's importance to Puerto Rican heritage. To the multilayered interlocking rhythmic core of the *plena*'s three *panderetas* 'round frame drums in graduated sizes' and the *bomba*'s two single-headed barrel drums, the Pleneros added electrified bass, melody instruments such as piano and the *cuatro,* and additional percussion. Many other groups in the region emerged, modeled in various degrees after Los Pleneros de la 21. The popularity of *bomba* also was reinforced by periodic performances by *bomba* groups from Puerto Rico such as those of the Cepeda and Ayala families.

Central American music

Immigration from Central America increased dramatically in the 1970s, as civil strife drove refugees northward. Large numbers of Salvadorans, Guatemalans, and Nicaraguans established highly visible communities in major cities such as Los Angeles, Houston, Miami, Washington, and New York, bringing with them their regional dialects of Spanish, regional foods such as the Salvadoran *pupusa* 'thick tortilla filled with cheese or meat', and musical tastes. Prior to this time, Panamanians, Costa Ricans, and Hondurans constituted a much larger proportion of Central Americans in the United States. Music in these countries had long been influenced by foreign musics from Mexico, the Caribbean, and the United States disseminated by commercial media. Central American countries by comparison had fewer means of producing and distributing local music than Mexico, the United States, and other countries. This onslaught of foreign music was at times a cause for governmental concern, occasionally prompting mandatory broadcasting of domestic music by radio stations. The making and consumption of music by Central Americans in North America reflects both the long-standing acceptance of music from other nations and identification with certain national musical icons.

Perhaps the single most distinctive and widely visible Central American musical symbol is the marimba, the Guatemalan marimba in particular (figure 7). The Guatemalan marimba, with minor exceptions, is similar in appearance to the Mexican marimba. Several octaves of tuned wooden slabs mounted on a frame and resembling a piano keyboard are played with rubber-tipped mallets by two or more musicians. Below each slab is a wooden box resonator equipped with a vibrating membrane mounted over a small hole, creating a distinctive buzzing sound as the instrument is played. The marimba might be played alone or as the centerpiece of a larger ensemble with electrified bass, percussion, or melody instruments such as saxophone, and singing. Guatemalan marimba groups are based in southern California, southern Florida, the mid-Atlantic region, and elsewhere. Most scholars point to an African origin of the marimba. Slaves imported during colonial times purportedly reconstructed the instruments of their homelands in the New World context, and the word *marimba* has close linguistic cognates in certain regions of Africa. In general, however,

FIGURE 7   Guatemalan marimba group with Jerónimo Camposeco and unidentified musicians resident in the United States rehearses offstage at the Smithsonian Folklife Festival. Photo by Daniel Sheehy, June 1985.

Guatemalans and other Central Americans identify the marimba most closely with mestizo or American Indian heritage [see SOUTHWEST, p. 428; CALIFORNIA, p. 412]. While other Central American nations are home to marimba ensembles, and while the marimba of Nicaragua's Masaya province is associated with that nation's collective identity, the Guatemalan marimba tradition is most common in the United States.

Pan-national, Caribbean-influenced dance music, often referred to as *música tropical,* maintains an important place among immigrant Central Americans. Under this general rubric, the Panamanian/Colombian-derived *cumbia,* the Dominican-origin *merengue,* and Cuban/Puerto Rican-driven *salsa* music are all staples of their musical life. While this music reaches across borders of national identity, touring bands from individual countries and North American–based groups with names identifying their country of origin attract followings from those communities.

Increasingly in the United States, non-Mexican musicians—Guatemalan and Salvadoran immigrants in particular—have joined the ranks of Mexican professional mariachi musicians. Since the 1930s, Central Americans' exposure to mariachi music through cinema, recordings, and powerful radio stations stimulated the appreciation, consumption, and performance of the music in those countries. Many Central Americans, already skilled in performing mariachi music in their homelands, found relatively lucrative employment as mariachi musicians in the United States. Some mariachi ensembles are comprised entirely of Central Americans.

Cuban music

In addition to Caribbean-derived music, other Cuban musical traditions are also practiced in the United States [see LATIN CARIBBEAN MUSIC, p. 790]. In the Cuban community around Miami that resulted from the first wave of refugees (primarily of European background) from Castro-run Cuba, a few musicians continue the rural folk tradition of the *punto guajiro,* singing often improvised poetic texts to the accompaniment of stringed instruments led by the six-stringed *tres.* The *son* is another important genre of this musical style. Practiced much more widely is music of Afro-Cuban origin, predating, but arriving principally in the wake of, the Mariel boatlift of 1980. Several Afro-Cuban religious musical traditions reflect the distinctive strains of African-derived identity in Afro-Cuban culture. Most prominent is the Yoruba-derived *lucumí* tradition popularly known as *santería.* Central to the music of *santería* are the three double-conical, two-headed drums of the *batá* ensemble. *Oru* 'songs' sung in the Yoruba-based *lucumí* language praise African deities such as Changó, Ogún, and Obatalá.

Many accomplished musicians and religious leaders in these traditions are based in large cities, particularly in New York, the mid-Atlantic region, southern Florida, and California. A few of these musicians, Francisco Aguabella for example, have been active in the United States since before the Castro era. Some, like Aguabella, who performed with popular Afro-Cuban musician Mongo Santamaría, have been very active in mainstream Latin popular music as well. Others, such as musician/instrument maker Felipe García Villamil, who arrived among the Mariel refugees, have devoted themselves mainly to religious activities. Afro-Cuban religion, ceremony, and music have attracted a growing number of devotees, including participants from outside the Cuban community.

Other than the Cuban-derived music at the core of the diverse, Caribbean-origin popular dance music collectively known as *salsa* from the 1970s forward, the rumba is most central to secular Afro-Cuban music. The rumba emerged in Cuba around the turn of the twentieth century and provided much of the rhythmic grounding for popular dance music that followed. A typical rumba ensemble might comprise three *tumbadoras* 'conga drums', one of them being the smaller lead *quinto;* the *claves* 'two short resonant sticks struck together'; and the *cajita musical* 'a mounted hollow wood block played with two sticks'. Principal types of rumba are the *guaguancó* and the *columbia.* Rumba music has attracted many other Latinos and non-Latinos as well. In recent decades, instruments and rhythms have been borrowed from the sacred repertoire and incorporated into secular Cuban music. One example is the *batá-rumba,* an amalgam of sacred and secular rhythms and instruments. Carnival music of the *comparsa* is another important secular form of Afro-Cuban music (figure 8).

South American music

South America is an immense region of many nations and hundreds of cultural groups. In North America, South American immigrants and their descendants often maintain social/cultural identities linked to their nations of origin. Large concentrations of specific South American national or cultural groups are few, however, limiting the continuity of South American musical strains in North America. There are notable exceptions to this in musical styles that have achieved sufficient notoriety and commercial success

FIGURE 8   Afro-Cuban ensemble Otonowa, based in Washington, D.C., performs *comparsa* music in a parade as part of the National Folk Festival in Johnstown, Pennsylvania, organized by the National Council for the Traditional Arts. Photo by Daniel Sheehy, July 1990.

Tens of thousands of non-Spanish flamenco music disciples have taken up this southern Spanish Gypsy tradition.

to have a broad following. Pan-Andean ensembles featuring the *quena* 'end-blown flute', *zampoña* 'panpipes', *charango* 'small, ten-stringed guitar fashioned from the shell of the *quirquincho,* a small armadillo, six-stringed guitar, *bombo* 'two-headed drum struck with two sticks, one of them padded', and other instruments emerged in many North American cities, especially following their connection with popular resistance to dictatorial regimes such as that of Augusto Pinochet in Chile following the 1973 coup d'état. The popularity of urban folk song in the 1960s and later, nightclubs called *peñas,* the *nueva canción* 'protest song movement', and the commercial success of groups such as Quilapayún and Inti-Illimani of Chile propelled this instrumental sound and style of music to international popularity throughout Europe and the entire Western Hemisphere. In the 1990s, dozens of these ensembles could be heard regularly in North American nightclubs, on street corners, in subway stations, at public concerts and folk festivals, and in other venues, particularly on the East and West Coasts.

Several other South American musics made their presence known on the North American musicscape. Argentine tango music played on the *bandoneón* 'large accordion' enjoyed a modest urban revival in the 1990s. Accordion-driven Colombian *música vallenata,* music originating in that country's northern coastal region, attained a degree of widespread popularity as a Latino popular music. In the last decades of the twentieth century, Paraguayan harp music based on the fast triple-meter Paraguayan *polca* and epitomized by the showpiece composition "Pájaro Campana" ("Bell Bird") was played regularly by Paraguayan immigrant musicians in Los Angeles, Las Vegas, New York, Washington, and beyond (figure 9).

Brazilians, often counted among the ranks of Latinos in the United States, brought the music of their *capoeira* 'martial arts/dance', played on the *berimbao* 'musi-

FIGURE 9   Paraguayan harpist Julio Flores and guitarists Alberto Ríos and Roberto Maldonado perform at the celebration of the Bicentennial of the Constitution in Philadelphia, Pennsylvania. Photo by Daniel Sheehy, July 1987.

cal bow.' In the 1980s and 1990s, *capoeira mestres* 'masters' attracted many disciples in urban areas such as New York City and the San Francisco Bay area. In New York, choreographers Loremil Machado and Jelon Vieira established *capoeira* performance ensembles. *Samba* groups emerged in New York, Washington, D.C., and other cities.

Dominican music

Following the political and social upheaval after the death of Dominican Republic dictator Rafael Trujillo in 1961, Dominican immigration to North America, particularly to New York City and other northeastern U.S. urban industrial areas, increased dramatically. Dominicans established their own community identity, such as the Washington Heights neighborhood in New York City popularly called "Quisqueya Heights"—*Quisqueya* being the indigenous name for the island shared by the Dominican Republic and Haiti. Dominicans brought their regional musical traditions and, above all, their popular music and dance form the *merengue* to North America. The *merengue cibaeño* 'regional *merengue* from Cibao' had played the lead role in the emergence of the internationally popular dance *merengue*. Set in a fast-paced duple meter, the popular *merengue* is associated with a regional musical ensemble including a button accordion playing a nonstop, dense melodic flow, a metallic rasp called *güira*, a *tambora* 'two-headed drum', and perhaps a saxophone or marimba 'bass instrument of plucked metal tongues mounted on a wooden resonator box.' The accordion-driven *merengue,* known as *perico ripiao* (Austerlitz 1997:63), became associated with Dominican national identity and was an important signifier of Dominican presence in the multicultural North American environment, as well as a primary link to the Dominican homeland (Austerlitz 1997:126).

A dramatic rise in the popularity of the *merengue* accompanied the major influx of immigration beginning in the 1960s. Accordionist Primitivo Santos was the first *merengue* bandleader to settle in the United States. He and others such as Joseíto Mateo, the "king of *merengue,*" who regularly worked in the United States, made live *merengue* performance available on a regular basis. By the 1970s, Latino dance band *merengue* was highly popular among Latinos in New York City and elsewhere. New York–based bands such as the group Millie, Jocelyn, y los Vecinos established both local and international followings (Austerlitz 1997: 125–126). In the 1990s, another Dominican roots dance music, the guitar-driven *bachata,* was also widely popular.

Other Latino musics

Spanish immigrants and North Americans of Spanish descent have both been included under the Latino rubric (as in the "Hispanic" category of the U.S. Census Bureau), given their commonalities of language, religion, and values, and excluded because of their origins in Europe, rather than in Latin America [see IBERIAN MUSIC, p. 847]. Spanish music—flamenco guitar music in particular—and dance music are regularly included in public presentations of Latino culture such as those during National Hispanic Heritage Month. Several accomplished flamenco guitarists and *cantaores* 'singers', such as fifth-generation *cante jondo* 'deep song' singer Pepe Culata (José Matallanes) of Chicago, make major North American cities their homes. Tens of thousands of other non-Spanish flamenco music disciples have taken up this southern Spanish Gypsy tradition. Basques, a linguistically distinct cultural minority from the region embracing a portion of the Spanish-French border, may or may not identify with the Spanish homeland. In the United States, Basque communities in the West might feature Basque accordion music during cultural events or occasionally teach music of the *txistu* 'cane vertical flute' and small accompanying drum to Basque Americans to instill elements of their unique heritage. Music plays a role in the cultural life of another group marginal to Latino identity, Portuguese Americans. *Fado*—an expressive form of Portuguese popular song—is performed live in the Portuguese immigrant community of Fall River, Massachusetts, and the Portuguese who made their home in the area around the town of Gustine in central California include Portuguese music in public events.

Popular music

Although the greater volume of Latino music in the United States has largely developed within Latino communities, a significant part of it has become commercially successful and musically highly influential. In fact, this was the basic theme of John Storm Roberts's important book originally published in 1979, *The Latin Tinge: The Impact of Latin American Music on the United States.* As early as 1930, Cuban bandleader Don Aspiazu had a major recording hit with the rumba/habanera "El manicero" (composed by Moises Simon), which was quickly translated into "The Peanut Vendor" and subsequently recorded by many major popular North American artists. During the same period Duke Ellington had a major impact on U.S. musical culture with his recording of "Caravan" (also based on the Afro-Cuban musical style), which he cocomposed with Juan Tizol, his Puerto Rican trombonist, who influenced the bandleader's musical compositions. Machito (Frank Grillo) and Mario Bauza assembled an orchestra, Machito and His Afro-Cubans, in 1940 and proceeded to experiment in the fusion of Cuban dance music and jazz [see FIVE FUSIONS, p. 334]. By the late 1940s Dizzy Gillespie invited Cuban *conguero* Chano Pozo to become a member of his ensembles, and the fusion of Afro-Cuban music with bebop jazz became known as Cubop. By the 1950s dance halls such as the Palladium in New York City represented an intersection of both musical styles and society, as the popular rumba, mambo, and *cha-cha-cha* became personified through the orchestras of Machito, Tito Puente, and Tito Rodríguez. By the 1970s, the use of the word *salsa* would propel the careers of veteran artists including Machito, Puente, Celia Cruz, Eddie Palmieri, Charlie Palmieri, Johnny Pacheco, Ray Barretto, Willie Colón, and Rubén Blades. The latter two, Blades and Colón, would collaborate on a highly successful and historically significant album, *Siembra,* representing salsa's association with sociopolitical themes.

On the West Coast and in the Southwest, different yet related types of Latino music entered the mainstream of popular music in the United States. By the 1930–1940s various Hollywood films were featuring bandleader Xavier Cugat and his Cuban styled orchestra, and singers such as Miguelito Valdés from Cuba and Pepe Guízar from Mexico were appearing in cameo roles. Also emerging as a major singer in the mainstream recording industry was Mexican American Andy Russell (Andrés Rábago) from Los Angeles. In the 1950s, Cuban singer, bandleader, and actor Desi Arnaz, with his actress/comedian wife Lucille Ball, produced what some consider to be the most successful television sitcom to date, *I Love Lucy.* In 1955 Cuban bandleader Pérez Prado, whose orchestra was based in Mexico City, recorded a *cha-cha-cha,* "Cherry Pink and Apple Blossom White," for a film in Hollywood; that year it became the highest-selling recording in the world. In 1959 Mexican American Ritchie Valens (Richard Valenzuela) had a major hit with "La Bamba," a rock and roll version of a popular, traditional Mexican *huapango.* Valens died the same year in an air crash along with rock stars Buddy Holly and the Big Bopper. Another Los Angeles–based singer to emerge about this time was Vikki Carr (Victoria Cardona), whose first international hits were in English but who also became established as a major popular recording artist in Latin America at the turn of the twenty-first century.

By the late 1960s, Linda Ronstadt, originally from Tucson, Arizona, began her rise in the popular rock industry and by the 1980s was also recording in the Spanish language, receiving three Grammy Awards for her mariachi albums and a tropical music album. In the late 1960s Carlos Santana, a young Mexican guitarist raised in Tijuana, Mexico, and San Francisco, California, was recorded by Columbia Records and subsequently become the major innovator in what would become known as Latin rock. Santana achieved international popularity with hits such as "Evil Ways," composed by New York Latin jazz percussionist Willie Bobo, and "Oye Como Va," composed by New York–based Tito Puente, who was like Bobo, of Puerto Rican heritage. Other artists largely inspired by Santana to attain various regional and international recognition included groups such as Malo and Azteca from San Francisco and Tierra and El Chicano from Los Angeles. On another front, rhythm and blues style in Texas, Sonny Osuna received much national attention in the 1960s with his single "Talk to Me."

Thirty years after his first recordings, Santana was still being recognized in 1999, becoming the recipient of an unprecedented eleven Grammy Awards for the year, eclipsing the previous record set by Michael Jackson for his *Thriller* album. Also awarded a 1999 Grammy (for Best New Artist) was pop singer Christina Aguilera, from Pittsburgh and of Ecuadorian/Irish American heritage. Another eclectic group to create a historical mark in the recording industry from the 1980s to the present was Los Lobos, who received Grammy Awards for two Mexican American category recordings and a nomination for Song of the Year for their triple platinum rerecording of "La Bamba," from the major film hit by the same title written and directed by Luis Valdez and based on the life of Ritchie Valens. Los Lobos was also nominated for a Grammy for a children's album recorded with Lalo Guerrero, another major Mexican American artist, who composed many of the songs adapted by Luis Valdez for his stage play and film *Zoot Suit*. Guerrero, Tito Puente, and Tejana musical artist Lydia Mendoza all received the Presidential Medal for the Arts during the late 1990s.

Another major impact in both the mainstream and Latino markets was Cuban-born vocalist Gloria Estefan, who with her husband, musician/producer Emilio Estefan, began their musical artistry in a Miami-based group called Miami Sound Machine, which achieved international recognition with its 1980s recording of "Conga." Estefan had numerous other international hits, in both English and Spanish, and for some time became the most popular artist in Latin America. Estefan's album *Mi Tierra,* released in 1993, was awarded a Grammy and established unprecedented record sales. Also achieving major crossover success during the 1990s was Texas-based Mexican American vocalist Selena. She was tragically murdered, and a major Hollywood film was made on her life in 1998 starring Jennifer López, of New York/Puerto Rican background, who would emerge as a major Hollywood actress and highly successful popular music recording artist. By the late 1990s, singers of Puerto Rican heritage based in the United States also included Marc Anthony and Ricky Martin. Martin created a sensational response in the market with his recording of "Livin' La Vida Loca" during the year 1999 and was featured on the cover of *Time* magazine. By the year 2000, popular Latino music in the United States, from Latin rock to bilingual hip-hop, was reaching heights never before imagined by a quickly changing music industry and American society.

REFERENCES

Austerlitz, Paul. 1997. *Merengue: Dominican Music and Dominican Identity.* Philadelphia: Temple University Press.

Fogelquist, Mark. 1996. "Mariachi Conferences and Festivals in the United States." In *The Changing Faces of Tradition: A Report on the Folk and Traditional Arts in the United States,* ed. Elizabeth Peterson, 18–23. Research Division Report no. 38. Washington, D.C.: National Endowment for the Arts.

Glasser, Ruth. 1995. *My Music Is My Flag: Puerto Rican Musicians and Their New York Communities, 1917–1940.* Berkeley: University of California Press.

Goldstein, Amy, and Roberto Suro. 2000. "La Nueva Vida/Latinos in America: A Journey in Stages." *The Washington Post,* 16 January, A1, A24.

Paredes, Américo. 1993. "The Folklore Groups of Mexican Origin in the United States." In *Folklore and Culture on the Texas-Mexican Border,* ed. Richard Bauman, 3–18. Austin: University of Texas, Center for Mexican American Studies.

Roberts, John Storm. 1999 [1979]. *The Latin Tinge: The Impact of Latin American Music on the United States.* 2nd ed. New York: Oxford University Press.

Robinson, Linda. 1998. "Hispanics Don't Exist." *U.S. News & World Report.* 11 May, 26–32.

Sheehy, Daniel. 1997. "Mexican Mariachi Music: Made in the USA." In *Musics of Multicultural America,* ed. Kip Lornell and Anne K. Rasmussen, 131–154. New York: Schirmer Books.

Statistics Canada. 1996. <www.statcan.ca>

Vigil, James Diego. 1991. "Latinos." In *Encyclopedia of World Cultures,* Vol. 1: *North America,* ed. Timothy J. O'Leary and David Levinson, 202–206. Boston: G. K. Hall and Company.

Hispanic California
Steven Loza

Nineteenth-Century Colonial Spanish and Mexican Musical Communities
Music of Immigration and Migration, 1830–1930
Urban Musics of the 1940s and 1950s
Mexican/Latino Styles in Los Angeles Since the 1960s
Music of the Chicano Movement

It is the consensus among scholars that with the exception of the religious music of the California missions, Latino musical culture in California has been much less studied than in Texas or New Mexico. Reasons for this have been attributed to the romanticizing of California by earlier historians who neglected to critically examine the constantly adaptive and growing Latino, and especially Mexican, population in the state. Although much recent scholarship has begun to emerge, there still exists a substantial lacunae of documentation and research.

In assessing Hispanic/Latino folk and popular music in California, Michael Heisley (1988:55) has listed five general areas: (1) the music of Colonial Spanish and Mexican communities of the nineteenth century; (2) music related to the immigration and migration of Mexicans to California from the time of the Mexican Revolution through the Depression; (3) music from urban areas such as Los Angeles that became important centers for the production of Mexican American popular music beginning in the 1940s; (4) Chicano rock and roll since the 1950s; and (5) songs of the Chicano movement of the 1960s and subsequent music related to the political movements and the cultural renaissance among many young Chicanos.

NINETEENTH-CENTURY COLONIAL SPANISH AND MEXICAN MUSICAL COMMUNITIES

The Franciscan Narciso Durán (1776–1846), who developed a basic pedagogy for teaching church music, was one of the first to be active in teaching Western music to the Indian neophytes of the California missions. In commenting on selected passages taken from Padre Durán's *Prólogo,* Howard Swann writes:

> He had determined to show his Indians how to read music. He had begun by teaching the instruments so that by seeing the distances between notes on the instruments, due to the various finger positions, the boys might gain some idea of the same intervals in singing, modulating their voices accordingly. . . . Each voice read his part from a staff dotted with notes colored red, black, yellow and white, and Father Durán deemed it advisable that instruments should always accompany the singing . . . not permitting [the boys] to go flat or sharp, as regularly happens without this precaution. (1952:87)

Alfred Robinson, visiting the same mission in 1828, wrote that "the solemn music of the mass was well selected, and the Indian voices accorded harmoniously with the flutes and violins that accompanied them" (1891:45).

The mission choirs developed an extensive repertoire. They performed plainchant for several masses in addition to the chant of the proper of the mass for Sundays and feast days. They also sang several two- and four-part homophonic masses such as the *Misa de Cataluña* and the *Misa Vizcaina,* both very likely composed by Father Durán. Also practiced as part of the mission choirs' repertoires were vespers and complines, as well as liturgical hymns (Stevenson 1988b:54–57).

MUSIC OF IMMIGRATION AND MIGRATION, 1830–1930

In 1833, relatively soon after independence from Spain, the Mexican government secularized the mission lands. Much controversy persists about the merits or demerits of this action and its consequences. Many believe that the rapid disintegration of the mission communities led to more inequities for the Indians, while others claim that the mission system itself placed the acculturated California Indians in a dependent position, destined for the chaotic social experience of the *hacienda* (*rancho*) system.

In spite of the constant political uncertainty and change that culminated in the Mexican War (1846–1848), musical life flourished in California. William Heath Davis recorded his impression that the people seemed to have a talent and a taste for music. "Many of the women played the guitar skillfully, and the young men the violin. In almost every family there were one or more musicians, and everywhere music was a familiar sound" (1929:61). Throughout California, feast days, rodeos, weddings, funerals, and other special occasions were accented by music and events were preceded or followed by a *fandango* or a *baile.* Davis also witnessed fiestas that continued for several days. One was a wedding party where he estimated that "one hundred guests danced all night, slept for three hours after daylight, enjoyed a *merienda,* or picnic in the forenoon, and then again began their dancing. This was the order for three days" (Swann 1952:91). Dance genres included traditional Spanish forms in addition to the more recent styles of the *vals* 'waltz' and *quadrillo* 'quadrille'. Especially popular was the *fandango,* which featured a *tecolero* 'master of ceremonies' who called out each woman for her turn. The Catholic Church decried the popularization of the waltz, however, which it considered indecent.

With defeat in 1848 Mexico ceded the major portion of the Southwest to the United States. The Treaty of Guadalupe Hidalgo provided for the exchange of land in return for fifteen million dollars and certain provisions to protect the rights of the Mexicans and their future offspring. Both the pact and its interpretations have been historically controversial and, from the Mexican viewpoint, have constituted a bitter issue for more than a century. When the United States incorporated California, Mexicans were still firmly established in Los Angeles. Their political and economic status changed with the 1848 gold rush, which stimulated the migration of 100,000 Anglo-Americans.

By the 1850s visiting musical attractions in Los Angeles included army bands and minstrel groups from various parts of the United States. Mexican musical traditions also continued. For example, Ignacio Coronel opened a school north of Arcadia Street in 1844. He was assisted by his daughter, Soledad, a harpist. As late as the mid-1850s the harp remained the favorite instrument of the local aristocracy. Musical performances of this period were described in newly established local newspapers, *La Estrellita de Los Angeles,* a weekly bilingual paper, and two Spanish-language newspapers, *El Clamor Público* (1855–1859) and *La Crónica* (from 1872), which gave fuller coverage to musical events (Stevenson 1986:107).

A rich Spanish/Mexican tradition that continued into the second half of the nineteenth century throughout the Southwest was that of the *pastores* and *pastorelas.*

Recounting the birth of Christ, these musical dramas depicted the journey of the shepherds to the nativity manger. *Pastorelas* were often enacted at churches or private homes in conjunction with the *posada,* a social, religious gathering at which songs celebrating the Christmas season were sung.

According to Don Arturo Bandini (1958:16–17) the last major nineteenth-century performance of the *pastores* in Los Angeles took place on Christmas Eve 1861. Bandini adds that the more dramatic and more elaborately produced *pastorela* was also enacted during the 1860s. According to his account, the priests of the order of St. Vincent de Paul, who had arrived in Los Angeles to found St. Vincent's College, contracted the highly influential Don Antonio Coronel to assist them in patronizing three performances of the *pastorela.* The plays were staged in the upstairs hall of the county courthouse.

Los Angeles, 1900–1940s

With the turn of the century, Mexicans in California entered an era of widespread change with regard to issues such as revolution, immigration, discrimination, acculturation, and, ultimately, modes of expression. In his evaluation of the musical cycle of the Mexican in California, Manuel Peña recognizes this integral stage of musical activity.

> Due to the low density of its far-flung population, California-Mexican culture . . . succumbed rather easily to the onslaught of an American invasion that began with the gold rush and culminated in the 1870s with completion of the first railroads to Southern California. It was therefore left to the later immigrants from Mexico, those who arrived beginning in the early twentieth century, to revive Mexican culture and, with it, music in the Golden State. Thus the music of California Mexicans today traces its main outlines to the early twentieth century, when the first wave of Mexican immigrants transplanted a culture that served as the foundation for later musical developments in the Golden State (1989:66).

Between 1904 and 1912 writer-photographer Charles F. Lummis produced a collection of sound recordings of Mexican folk songs. Originally recorded on 340 wax cylinders, they have been rerecorded on magnetic tape and are catalogued and housed at the Southwest Museum in Los Angeles. These may be the first sound recordings of Mexican American folk songs in California. Lummis published fourteen of the songs in 1923 (transcribed by Arthur Farwell) in *Spanish Songs of Old California.*

Among the performers on these recordings was Rosendo Uruchurtu, a talented guitarist who sang in the Mexican *canción* tradition and accompanied others on the Lummis recordings. The Southwest Museum's Braun Research Library also has lyrics and musical transcriptions of some of the songs, the latter prepared by composer Arthur Farwell, Lummis's collaborator on this project. There are also three handwritten notebooks of early California-Mexican song lyrics in the Lummis manuscript collection at the Southwest Museum. The oldest of these manuscripts dates from the late nineteenth century and is by José de la Rosa, a printer who came to California in 1833 and was an accomplished guitarist and composer. The second notebook is from Manuela Garcia and contains lyrics to most of the 150 songs that she recorded for Lummis in 1904. The notebooks in which Lummis jotted down his field notes and the lyrics to some of the Spanish language songs that he recorded are also found in this collection (Heisley 1988:57).

A great many, if not most, of these recordings reflect the Mexican *canción* that had developed by the early twentieth century. The technique of blind guitarist Rosendo Uruchurtu was quite proficient and attests to the high level of professional skill attributed to him. In many of the recorded *canciones* sung by Manuela Garcia, Uruchurtu accompanies her on guitar. Among Garcia's songs recorded by Lummis and inscribed by Garcia in her notebook are "Memorias dolorosas," "La sinaloense," "Mientras tú duermes," "La pepa," "No me niegues," "La noche está serena," and "El desvalido."

Another important collection that includes nineteenth-century Spanish-language folk songs and music from California was organized by the California Folk Music Project (1938–1942), created by the Work Projects Administration (WPA). This is presently archived at the Department of Music, University of California, Berkeley. Other collections that document nineteenth-century songs of Spanish and Mexican origin were published by Arthur Farwell (1905), William J. McCoy (1926), and Antoni Van der Voort (1928).

During the early 1900s, Mexicans in Los Angeles made their homes in the flat lowland along the Los Angeles River amidst the old housing developments that had belonged to Europeans of an earlier generation. Financially discouraged from settling in the other sections of Los Angeles, they found the inexpensive housing on the East Side more compatible with their depressed standard of living. During the era of the interurban railroad and the beginning of the age of the automobile, "the barrios became a haven for a Mexican population which faced discrimination in housing, employment, and social activities in Anglo parts of the city" (Romo 1983:8). East side Mexican residents began to organize socially and politically; they founded Spanish-language newspapers, established radio programs, and supported businesses and cultural programs that recognized and met their needs.

Growth of the Mexican community was accompanied by growth in the music of Mexicans in Los Angeles. Such growth, however, was affected not only by the transplantation of Mexican musical forms but also by factors such as migration, immigration, and the radio and recording industries. Recorded musical activity among Mexicans in California began in the 1920s and 1930s. Spanish-language broadcasts began in the late 1920s. During the mid-1920s recording companies such as Victor, Brunswick, Decca, and Columbia "began to exploit for commercial gain the musical traditions of Mexicans in California and in the Southwest" (Peña 1989:67).

Heisley (1988) notes two important trends that developed during this period. First, the traditional Mexican *corrido* became a dynamic expression of many immigrants from Mexico. The *corrido,* a narrative song form, was used extensively throughout California as it had been in Mexico, as an expression of both fortune and tragedy. Second, a dynamic Spanish-language radio and recording industry emerged, especially in the urban areas. Programs featured local artists, and by the 1930s Hispanics in California were a major market for the music industry.

The corrido *and* canción

Genres such as the *canción mexicana,* the *corrido,* the Mexican *son,* boleros, and *huapangos* were all recorded and marketed. Instrumentation was frequently based on ensembles such as the trio and the mariachi. The latter had evolved from its rural identity into a larger and more commercialized instrumental format in Mexico, incorporating, by the 1930s, violin, *vihuela* 'five-string guitar', guitar, *guitarrón* 'bass guitar', and, later, the trumpet.

Sociocultural expression marked the music of Mexicans in Los Angeles in a number of compositions and recordings during the 1920s and 1930s. Themes based on intercultural conflict, human conditions, and political actions characterize songs of the period such as "El lavaplatos," "Se acabó el WPA," "Consejos al maje," and the *corridos* dedicated to Juan Reyna.

The *corrido* "El lavaplatos" ("The Dishwasher") was composed by Jesús Osorio, who recorded the song with Manuel "El Perro" Camacho on 19 May 1930 on the Victor label. It was also recorded by Los Hermanos Banuelos on 1 July 1930 (on the Brunswick/Vocalion label) and by Chávez y Lugo on Columbia. Incorporating satire into the expression of an immigrant's illusion and disillusion with the dreams and

"Consejos al maje" satirically (yet tactfully) addresses the issue of consumerism in the United States, alluding to the commercial pretenses of clothing, two-story houses, radios, Ford automobiles, insurance, dyed hair, entertainment spots, womanizing, general foolishness, and the wasting of money.

myths of Hollywood, the song is a tragicomic sociocultural commentary. This *corrido* studies and expresses contemporary life. Peña cites this particular *corrido* as a thematically significant one because of its reference to "political and economic issues that were at the heart of the Mexican's subordination in the capitalist Anglo order that reigned over the Southwest by this time" (1989:67).

Representative of the *canción mexicana* style was "Consejos al maje" ("Advice to the Naive"), and "Se acabó el WPA" ("The WPA Has Ended"). Composed by E. Nevárez and recorded by Los Madrugadores (Chicho y Chencho) with Los Hermanos Eliceiri in 1934, "Consejos al maje" satirically (yet tactfully) addresses the issue of consumerism in the United States, alluding to the commercial pretenses of clothing, two-story houses, radios, Ford automobiles, insurance, dyed hair, entertainment spots, womanizing, general foolishness, and the wasting of money. Referring to the termination of the Work Projects Administration of President Franklin D. Roosevelt's New Deal program, "Se acabó el WPA" satirizes the project that provided food and financial support to communities throughout the United States. The song was composed by Alfredo Marín and recorded by Los Madrugadores (Chico y Chencho) in 1937.

During the early 1930s, at least six *corridos* were written about Juan Reyna, who was accused of murdering a Los Angeles policeman on 11 May 1930. Highly publicized, largely due to questions related to ethnic tensions and the nature of Reyna's arrest, the case was settled in November 1930. Reyna was convicted of manslaughter and assault with a deadly weapon and began a one- to ten-year sentence at the California State Penitentiary at San Quentin. The jury had recommended clemency, and a vigorous campaign organized by the Mexican populace in Los Angeles assisted Reyna in paying his legal fees. In May 1931, five months prior to his parole release date, Reyna committed suicide.

Important performing groups

Among Mexican artists in Los Angeles during the early 1930s, the group Los Madrugadores had perhaps the greatest commercial impact. Originally a trio consisting of the brothers Victor and Jesús Sánchez and early Spanish-language broadcaster Pedro J. González (whom the Sánchez brothers met at the music store La Casa de Música de Mauricio Calderón), the group debuted on radio station KMPC in December 1929 (Sonnichsen 1977:15). The name Los Madrugadores, which was conceived by González, means "early risers" and refers to the very early morning hours during which the group's live program was broadcast. (Air time at that hour cost much less than did prime radio time later in the day and evening.)

Another important development in California during the 1930s and 1940s was the rise of the vocal duet Las Hermanas Padilla. The sisters, Margarita and Maria, began their musical career singing at fund-raising benefits for local churches during the 1930s. Their first formal recognition came when they won first prize in a talent contest held at a park in Pico Rivera, a suburb just east of Los Angeles. Soon afterward they appeared on the Los Angeles-based radio show of Ramón B. Arnaiz, where they started singing with Chicho y Chencho. Their first recording, "La barca de oro," was an instant success (Sonnichsen 1984).

In addition to Las Hermanas Padilla, other artists featured on Arnaiz's program included the host's orchestra, singer Adelina García, Los Madrugadores, the Trío Los Porteños de Miguel Aceves Mejía, and Leopoldo González. In 1941 Arnaiz went to Mexico and the radio station replaced live entertainment with records. Other significant radio personalities who hosted programs of Mexican music in Los Angeles around this time or who would later emerge included Tony Saenz, Rodolfo Hoyos (who was also an operatic singer), Elena Salinas, Salvador Luis Hernández, Martín Becerra, and Teddy Fregozo (also a songwriter).

An individual of immense importance in the 1930s and 1940s was Manuel Acuña. After emigrating from Mexico in the early 1930s, he worked with the orchestra of Rafael Gama and eventually became one of the leading musical directors in the Mexican radio and record industries in Los Angeles. Recognized as an excellent arranger and composer, Acuña also worked extensively with Felipe Valdez Leal, with whom he cocomposed many songs recorded on the Columbia label. He later worked in A & R (artists and repertoire) for Vocalion/Decca and Imperial Records. Acuña was largely responsible for the early career promotion of Las Hermanas Padilla and composed and arranged a number of songs for Adelina García and many other major vocalists of the period.

Born in Phoenix, Arizona, Adelina García lived in Juárez, in the state of Chihuahua, Mexico, from the age of three to thirteen. On her arrival in Los Angeles in 1939 as a fifteen-year-old, García began to perform on live radio and to record on the Columbia label. A stylist of the bolero form, which was popular throughout Latin America at the time, she made several highly successful recordings during the 1940s, among them "Desesperadamente," "Vereda tropical," "Mi tormento," "Perfidia," and "Frenesí." At different points in her career, Garcia performed at Los Angeles venues such as the Mason, Mayan, and Million Dollar theaters.

One of the most influential musical artists since the late 1930s in California has been Lalo Guerrero (b. 1916, Tucson, Arizona). Guerrero represented in a dynamic fashion the bicultural experience of Mexican Americans and other Latinos in the United States. Early in his career he composed many songs that became standards in Mexican popular music, such as "Canción mexicana, " recorded by Lucha Reyes in 1940, and "Nunca jamás," recorded by both Trío Los Panchos and Javier Solís. During the 1940s, Guerrero composed and performed with his band much music that reflected both U.S. and Mexican culture. He incorporated styles based on swing, mambo, rumba, bolero, and tango as well as various Mexican genres such as the *corrido, canción ranchera,* and *son.* Guerrero would eventually gain major recognition in the Chicano communities throughout the Southwest for the many recordings of his own music on the Imperial Records label. He became especially popular as a composer of musical satire, frequently mixing Spanish, English and Caló (the Spanish slang used in the *pachuco* culture of the Southwest). Some of Guerrero's songs from this period were eventually adapted to the score of Luís Valdez's play and motion picture *Zoot Suit* in 1981 and released on MCA Records. Guerrero also wrote many songs satirizing the Chicano experience in the United States. His combination of humor and tragedy has been a main feature of such musical parodies. In 1991 Guerrero was honored by the National Endowment for the Arts as a recipient of the National Heritage Fellowship Award and in 1997 President Clinton awarded him the National Medal of Arts (Loza 1985, 1993).

URBAN MUSICS OF THE 1940s AND 1950s

During World War II the *Los Angeles Times* shifted its coverage of Mexican Americans from the "fiesta" and "old California culture" stories that glorified a mythical past to negative accounts of the subculture dramatized by the image of the zoot suit. The communities east of the Los Angeles River were the target of racist reports that made Los Angeles the symbol of the *pachuco,* the Mexican American gang member (Acuña 1984:14). Newspaper coverage exaggerated the degree of gang activity; fewer than 3 percent of the thirty thousand school-age Mexican Americans in Los Angeles actually belonged to gangs. Drug abuse was not a significant problem in 1943, for only twelve Mexican Americans were arrested on such charges (Acuña 1984:14). Stereotyping had become common practice among local journalists interested in stories of gang members and law breakers.

As World War II came to an end, musical life in the Mexican community of Los Angeles continued to be active. Performances by local musicians and other entertainers, films, and theatrical presentations from various Latin American countries were an integral part of the musical scene, with interest in the contemporary music of the period often focusing on Latin American composers such as Heitor Villa-Lobos.

Latino composers, performers, and performance venues

Mexican composer Carlos Chávez (1899–1978) conducted a concert devoted exclusively to his own music and performed by the Los Angeles Philharmonic Orchestra on 11 January 1945. The concert was well received by the public and was favorably reviewed in the 14 January issue of *La Opinión* by Samuel Martí, the Mexican violinist and musicologist. Martí was also founder of "Conciertos Martí," chamber recitals that increased recognition of Mexican artistic values in the United States and transmitted American artistic endeavors to Mexico.

Juan Aguilar (Juan Aguilar y Adame) (1893–1953) who taught at Mt. Saint Mary's College in 1949 also served as organist at St. Vibiana Cathedral in downtown Los Angeles. Born at Pueblo de Cosío near Aguascalientes, Mexico, Aguilar studied piano in Mexico City with Miramontes and composition with Godínez (composer of "Marcha Zacatecas") and eventually settled in Guadalajara. To escape the ravages of the revolution, he took his young family to Chihuahua in 1916, then to El Paso, Texas, in 1917. The next year he emigrated to Los Angeles, where he found immediate employment as pianist in the nine-member Pryor Moore instrumental ensemble that played nightly at Boos Brothers Cafeteria until the outbreak of World War II. Aguilar composed prolifically throughout his entire career and was recognized as a virtuoso organist as early as 30 June 1920, when he played for the dedication of the new organ in San Gabriel Church, Los Angeles.

Radio station XEGM, which aired Mexican music, advertised (in the 25 June edition of *La Opinión*) a program featuring Mexican singer Amalia Mendoza with José Ayala. Miguelito Valdez, the sensational Cuban singer, performed at the Avedon Ballroom on 7 July. Enjoying his recent hit "Babalú," Valdez presented a show of *valses,* sambas, rumbas, and American songs. The film *El miedo llegó a Jalisco,* starring Argentine tango singer Emilio Tuero, was also showing at that time. Songs that he interpreted in the film included "Dilo tú," "Serenata," "Sueño," "Torrente," and "No puede ser."

The Million Dollar Theater was founded in 1918 by Sid Grauman. Originally used for movies and stage shows in English, during the 1950s the ornate entertainment house, with its high ceilings, chandeliers, and winding staircases, began catering to the Latino community and became legendary throughout Latin America. Personalities booked at the Million Dollar Theater during this era included such Mexican stars as Pedro Infante, Dolores del Río, Pedro Armendáriz, José Jiménez, Augustín Lara, and María Felix. In the 1950s the Million Dollar Theater sponsored major events and showcases.

Plans for a festival at the Philharmonic Auditorium to raise funds for the Plaza Monumental de la Basílica de Guadalupe were under way in October 1953. The Orquesta Típica Mexicana gave the final concert of its 1954 season at Lincoln Park on 10 October. The highly respected and popular group was directed by Professor José

Córdova Cantú and performed a variety of Mexican and Spanish music. Featured singers with the orchestra were tenor Alfredo Margo and soprano Alicia Márquez.

Latino performers also began appearing on the new medium of television. *Fandango* debuted 29 January 1954 on the local CBS station KNXT. Produced by brothers Eddie (who wrote the show) and Pete Rodríguez, the program was sponsored by Rheingold Beer and hosted by Mauricio Jara. Marimbist Federico Salvatti and his band appeared on the premiere. The program continued into 1955 and featured musical artists Rudy Macias and his orchestra, Adelina García, Andy Russell, Los Flamingos, Manny López and his ensemble, Eddie Cano, Lalo Guerrero, Sarita Montiel, Natalie Wood, the Bobby Amos Orchestra, and the Sammy Mendoza Orchestra, among many others. Another television program of the same period was Lupita Beltrán's *Latin Time,* which aired on Sundays on KCOP, and featured entertainers such as Rita Holguín, composer Lalo Guerrero and his orchestra, and Aura San Juan (Ríos-Bustamante and Castillo 1986:173). Another prominent musician who performed during the 1950s was Miguel Sánchez, a highly rated flutist like his brother Alfonso Sánchez Chavaleis. Also part of the same musical network was Cuban flutist Issi Morales, who performed regularly at Tony's Inn.

Eventually musical activity became more intense among Mexicans and Chicanos on the east side of Los Angeles. Numerous clubs and record shops opened in the area as the population began to reflect the postwar exodus of non-Mexicans ("white flight") and the constant influx of Mexicans. Meanwhile local producers began to hold dances featuring Latin music at the Hollywood Palladium. Although the Palladium usually promoted swing bands, it instituted "Latin Holidays" featuring East Coast artists such as Celia Cruz and Tito Puente. Later, groups from Mexico such as Sonora Santanera and that of Luis Alcarz performed there. Most of the local ballroom show promoters, such as Chico Sesma and Richard Ceja, were Chicanos.

During the 1950s numerous other artists from Mexico City performed at the Palladium, such as Lobo y Melón and Sonora Santanera, both of whom specialized in tropical Caribbean music. Luis Alcaraz's big band, which played both Latin and swing music, was also frequently featured. Pérez Prado's band, consisting primarily of Mexican musicians, was becoming internationally known throughout Mexico, Cuba, the rest of Latin America, and Europe.

The recording industry that contracted with Mexican artists in Los Angeles immediately after World War II was a lucrative business, especially for the owners. Although the artists did not fare as well financially, the local industry was perhaps their only vehicle for gaining radio and market attention. U.S. laws prevented Mexican companies from recording in the United States. During the 1940s, therefore, local companies such as Imperial, Vocalion, Azteca, Tricolor, and Aguila recorded Mexican artists. Los Madrugadores (originally Los Hermanos Sánchez), the *ranchera* group Chicho y Chencho, Fernando Rosas, Lalo Guerrero, El Trío Imperial (with whom Guerrero was a soloist), and El Conjunto Los Costeños, in addition to many other well-organized duets and groups, recorded on the Imperial label. After earning considerable profits on their initial investment in recording Mexican artists, the two owners of Imperial shifted their emphasis to black artists who performed rhythm and blues [see R&B AND SOUL, p. 667]. Fats Domino and T-Bone Walker became top-sellers on the Imperial label, and Imperial became so successful in the black music market that it deleted the Mexican recording catalog.

By the mid-1950s Mexican record companies had acquired rights to export merchandise to the United States. Local recording companies began to decline because of the large quantity and marketability of the Mexican imports. U.S.-based companies such as Columbia, its affiliate Caytronics, RCA Victor, and Capitol began to record and contract Mexican artists such as María Victoria, Fernando Fernández, Pedro Vargas, and Luis Alcaraz.

"Blacks and Chicanos, isolated together, began to interact and, in large numbers, they listened to the same radio stations. There was Hunter Hancock ('Oh H.H.') on KFVD. He had a show on Sundays called 'Harlem Matinee' that featured records by Louis Jordan, Lionel Hampton, and locals Roy Milton, Joe and Jimmy Liggins, and Johnny Otis."

Swing, salsa, and Latin dance music

Although a mainstream style, swing music had considerable impact on the Mexican population in Los Angeles during the late 1930s and throughout the 1940s and 1950s. One exception to the marginal exposure received locally and nationally by most Mexican American swing musicians was Andy Russell. Named Andrés Rábago at birth, Russell adopted an anglicized stage name and became an international star, selling eight million records during the 1940s and early 1950s.

Not only were dances places for socializing, they also typified the way young Mexican Americans adapted to and assimilated different styles. Along with the tropical music of the Caribbean and traditional Mexican popular music, the bands of Cab Calloway, Jimmy Dorsey, Glenn Miller, and Duke Ellington became symbolic vehicles of change and adaptation [see JAZZ, p. 650].

The zoot suit era of the 1940s was characterized not only by the popularization of swing but also by an assortment of Latin styles including mambo, rumba, and *danzón,* all Cuban imports, often via Mexico. Mexican music was also popular among zoot-suiters. Swing and tropical rhythms were more popular among the zoot suit "cult," which adopted particular styles of dress, language (the caló dialect of Spanish), music, and dance. Zoot-suiters patronized particular entertainment spots and formed social groups that eventually became known as gangs.

During this time, a growing number of blacks were settling in Los Angeles in search of better-paying war industry jobs. The availability of low rent housing in the Mexican neighborhoods of east and south central Los Angeles prompted many blacks to settle there. Conversely, as Anglos became economically mobile they moved away from those neighborhoods. "Blacks and Chicanos, isolated together, began to interact and, in large numbers, they listened to the same radio stations. For instance, there was Hunter Hancock ('Oh H.H.') on KFVD. He had a show on Sundays called 'Harlem Matinee' that featured records by Louis Jordan, Lionel Hampton, and locals Roy Milton, Joe and Jimmy Liggins, and Johnny Otis" (Guevara 1985:116).

With the 1950s came the Korean War, the *bracero* program, and more Mexican deportations. The period also witnessed the emergence and development of rock and roll in the United States and the Mexican quarters of Los Angeles—especially the east side—were no exception [see FIVE FUSIONS, p. 334]. Guevara notes the role of radio disc jockeys, who often played particular local and regional records that eventually became national hits. In 1952, for example, Hunter Hancock aired an instrumental single titled "Pachuco Hop" by black saxophonist Chuck Higgins. Hancock later became a disc jockey at KGFJ radio, the first station to broadcast exclusively the music of black artists seven days per week. "A massive audience in East L.A. tuned in on each and every one of those days. At about the same time D.J.s like Art Laboe and Dick 'Huggy Boy' Hugg started playing jump and doo wop on the radio" (Guevara 1985:117).

Music based on Caribbean rhythms, especially Afro-Cuban, has been very popular among Hispanics in California since the rumba craze of the 1930s. Recent immigrants constituted a large portion of the Mexican population, and the community continued to transfer familiar forms popular in Mexico. These musical forms included *música tropical,* the Afro-Cuban form that in New York City would become known as salsa after the 1950s. The urban Hispanic audiences in California expanded their musical horizons as they adapted to U.S. media and record dissemination and became aficionados of the early salsa bandleaders emanating from Cuba, New York City, and Puerto Rico. During the 1940s and 1950s these included Machito (a Cuban based in New York), Tito Rodríguez (a Puerto Rican), Tito Puente (a New Yorker), and Pérez Prado (a Cuban based in Mexico).

One individual synonymous with Latin dance music throughout the 1950s and 1960s was Lionel "Chico" Sesma. A Mexican American and a product of Roosevelt High School in the Boyle Heights section of Los Angeles's east side, he began his musical profession as a trombonist in the local orchestras of Tily Lopez and Sal Cervantes, both popular Mexican American band leaders. He then toured extensively with the big bands of Johnny Richards, Pete Rugalo, Kenny Baker, and Russ Morgan.

It was on radio, however, that Sesma made his initial and long-standing impact, especially on the Mexican American population of Los Angeles. In 1949 he was hired by radio station KOWL to produce and host a bilingual program. Originally, he aired about two Latin music recordings per show which were usually chosen from discs of Tito Puente, Benny Moré, Machito, Tito Rodríguez, Pérez Prado, or other such internationally popular artists of the period. The rest of the broadcast material consisted of other popular music and jazz, including that of Billy Eckstine, Herb Jeffreys, Jimmy Lunceford, Billie Holiday, Dinah Washington, and Sarah Vaughan. After three months on the air, Sesma converted the radio show to an all-Latin music format.

In 1956, KOWL was changed to KDAY, and Sesma was featured as one of four disc jockeys headlining the station. The others were Joe Adams, Jim Ameche, and Frank Evans. In 1958 Sesma began a radio program at KALI, an all Spanish-language station, where he stayed until 1967. There he continued his bilingual format of airing contemporary Latin dance music.

The other major impact that Chico Sesma made on musical activity in Los Angeles was with his long-standing production of the Latin Holidays. Designed as Latin ballroom dances, the first took place in 1953 at the Zenda Ballroom. In 1954 Sesma changed the location of these monthly, semiannual, or annual dance concerts to the Hollywood Palladium, where they were a popular tradition, especially among Mexican Americans, until 1973. Among the many artists featured at the Latin Holidays were Celia Cruz and Sonora Matancera (for whom this was their first appearance in Los Angeles), Tito Puente, Machito, Benny Moré, Miguelito Valdez, Orquesta Aragón, Sonia López, George Shearing, Vicentico Valdez, and Pérez Prado among others. At the dances Sesma would also feature the music of local orchestras and solo artists.

Since the 1960s, tropical music and salsa musicians have continued to perform throughout California. Clubs and widely promoted dance concerts at various venues have continually featured artists such as Eddie Palmieri, Tito Puente, Celia Cruz, Sonora Mantancera, Johnny Pacheco, El Gran Combo, Sonora Ponceña, Oscar De León, Rubén Blades, Willie Colón, Justo Betancourt, Ray Barretto, Tito Nieves, Wilfrido Vargas, and Lalo Rodríguez, Marc Anthony and La India, among many others. Supporting this ambience have been specific radio stations catering to aficionados of salsa and Latin music.

MEXICAN/LATINO STYLES IN LOS ANGELES SINCE THE 1960s

The mariachi tradition

The mariachi has been popular in California since the 1930s, when it became the vogue of Mexico radio. As immigration has continuously increased, so has the growth of mariachis. Perhaps the most well-known symbol of Mexican music, scores of mariachis perform at restaurants, clubs, weddings, civil functions, holiday celebrations, and a variety of other occasions. Because so many Mexican *ranchera* singers are popular in Los Angeles, mariachis have been a mainstay of musical accompaniment for that genre in addition to performing their traditional genre, the *son jalisciense* (Pearlman 1984, 1988). Among the many well-known mariachis established in California, the three most recognized have been Mariachi Los Camperos de Nati Cano, Mariachi Los Galleros de Pedro Rey, and Mariachi Sol de México de José Hernandez.

Mariachi Los Camperos de Nati Cano, founded in Los Angeles in 1961, has continuously employed some of the most proficient mariachi musicians from Mexico and has recorded various LPs in addition to making its regular appearances at La Fonda (six nights a week) and other locales throughout the Southwest United States and Canada. The group has performed in different locations for U.S. presidents (Jimmy Carter, Gerald Ford, Ronald Reagan, George Bush, and Bill Clinton), as well as for numerous other national and international dignitaries, and in 1988 and 1989 made several television appearances with Linda Ronstadt including spots on NBC's "Tonight Show," the 1988 Grammy Awards show, and the HBO (Home Box Office) cable network's "¡Caliente y Picante!" special, in addition to touring California. Los Camperos has been featured at the major mariachi festivals in the Southwest, including those of Tucson and the Radio Bilingue Viva el Mariachi festival in Fresno, Universal Studios in Los Angeles, and San Diego, and Nati Cano has become a principal consultant for the annual Tucson International Mariachi Conference. In 1990 he was awarded the National Endowment for the Arts National Heritage Fellowship. In 1991 Cano and his Mariachi Los Camperos again recorded with Linda Ronstadt on her second LP recording of Mexican music, *Más Canciones,* and toured the United States with her. The recording also featured Mexico's Mariachi Vargas de Tecalitlán. Mariachi Los Camperos de Nati Cano toured extensively with Ronstadt throughout the United States in 1991. In 1992 Cano produced a solo album by Mariachi Los Camperos, with Ronstadt as associate producer.

Mariachi Los Galleros de Pedro Rey for many years was another very popular and long-standing mariachi also affiliated with a popular restaurant in Los Angeles County—El Rey, in Montebello, which was principally owned by family members of the mariachi (the Hernández brothers), the restaurant was opened by director Pedro Hernández (a.k.a. Pedro Rey) and other investors in 1976. Before organizing Los Galleros in 1970, Pedro Rey (Pedro Hernández) had performed with both Mariachi Vargas de Tecalitlán in Mexico and Mariachi Los Camperos de Nati Cano in Los Angeles. José Hernández, another Hernández brother, left the group to form and direct Mariachi Sol de México. In 1986, in the tradition of the show mariachi, he opened a restaurant, Cielito Lindo, in South El Monte, another eastside suburb of Los Angeles.

Mariachi festivals have become popular in several locales throughout the Southwest. The San Antonio, Texas, festival began in 1979 and the Tucson and Fresno festivals in 1983. The Universal Studios Hollywood mariachi festival originated in 1985 and continues on an annual basis. At UCLA the Mexican Arts Series staged a "minifestival" in April 1990, billed as Feria de Mariachi, which was later televised as the anchor location for a Cinco de Mayo special on KCBS. The Mariachi Los Camperos de Nati Cano and Mariachi Uclatlán de Mark Fogelquist participated, the new UCLA student mariachi group debuted, and the UCLA Grupo Folklórico interpreted a variety of traditional dance. The Mexican Arts Series introduced instructional elements into its 1991 festival. In June 1990 a major production was staged at the Hollywood Bowl. Promoted as Mariachi U.S.A., the afternoon festival featured Vikki Carr, Linda Ronstadt, Mariachi Vargas de Tecalitlán (from Mexico City), Mariachi Los Camperos de Nati Cano, Mariachi Sol de México de José Hernández, and Mariachi Las Campanas de América (from San Antonio, Texas). The festival was again staged in 1991 featuring the mariachis Vargas de Tecalitlán, Sol de México, Los Galleros, and Las Campanas de América. Featured singers included Lucha Villa and Tejano band leader Little Joe. Rodri Rodríguez, producer of Mariachi U.S.A., continued the festival on an annual basis through 2000.

In recent years one of the major contributions to the success of the mariachi tradition in Los Angeles has been singer Linda Ronstadt's recording and performance of Mexican music. Her 1988 album *Canciones de mi padre* has become both an anomaly and a milestone in the music industry. Recorded in Los Angeles, the LP employed the musical accompaniment of members of three mariachis based in Los Angeles: Los Camperos de Nati Cano, Los Galleros de Pedro Rey, and Mariachi Sol de México de José Hernández. A fourth mariachi involved in the recording, Mexico-based Mariachi Vargas de Tecalitlán, has generally been recognized as the most long-standing and successful group in the history of mariachi music. Mariachi Vargas accompanied Ronstadt on her national tour featuring the music of the album, and the group's director, Rubén Fuentes, arranged and conducted the music. José Hernández, director of Mariachi Sol de México, provided assistance and coordination in the musical production of the recording, and vocalist, composer, and actor Daniel Valdez was also featured on the album and in the concerts afterward. The album received a 1988 Grammy Award in the Mexican American category. Ronstadt's second album of Mexican music, *Más Canciones,* was released in November 1991.

Although originally from Tucson, Arizona, Ronstadt has produced most of her recordings and conducted her enterprises from the Los Angeles area since 1969, when she was still a member of the Stone Ponies. An eclectic artist who has explored various genres of popular music, she began to experiment with the mariachi style in the PBS televised performance of Luis Valdez's *Corridos* (filmed in San Francisco in 1985) and by guest appearances with mariachis at the annual Tucson International Mariachi Conference. Nati Cano has expressed on numerous occasions throughout Los Angeles and on national television that Linda Ronstadt has done more than revive the mariachi tradition for both old and new audiences; she has brought to the mariachi style an even larger, international level of commercial recognition and diffusion.

Since the 1990s, the formation of various female mariachis in California has been a growing phenomenon. One of the most successful has been Mariachi Las Reynas de Los Angeles, produced by José Hernández and originally directed by Laura Sobrino. Nydia Rojas emerged from Mariachi Las Reynas de Los Angeles to become a major solo artist, receiving wide recognition both in the United States and Mexico. Another highly successful female mariachi among others in the Southwest is Mariachi Las Adelitas, also formed in Los Angeles.

Local performing groups

Another segment of the musical network and local music industry in California that deserves mention consists of performing groups that cater exclusively to the urban Latino community, especially to Mexicans. These largely immigrant bands, generally consisting of four or more members, perform popular music sung in Spanish and usually recorded by Latin American or Spanish artists. They also record original material on local labels and have established a considerable following. The actual musical genres performed include ballads, *cumbias* (a style originally from Colombia and popular throughout Latin America), and many dance rhythms related to the Mexican *ranchera* and *norteño* styles (often with a basic polka or waltz rhythm). Among the repertoire of some of these ensembles is even a style called a *chicana.* Instrumentation consists of

One of the tragic stories was that of musician Ritchie Valens, whose real name was Richard Valenzuela. After achieving national recognition at the age of seventeen with hits like "Donna" and a rock and roll version of the traditional Mexican *huapango* "La Bamba," the young Chicano was killed in a 1959 plane crash on a snow-covered field in Iowa.

keyboards (quite frequently electric organ or synthesizer), electric guitar, electric bass, drum set, and some Latin percussion. Performance style is often modeled on that of the many popular groups in Mexico such as Los Bukis, Los Humildes, Los Yonics, and Los Freddys. In the early 1990s a phenomenal movement emerged based on the *banda* style of Mexico, derived largely from the *banda sinaloense* style from the state of Sinaloa in Mexico. Radio station KLAX, which aired *banda* music, achieved an unprecedented number one rating of radio stations in Los Angeles during the early 1990s, representing a massive change in the U.S. music industry.

There has traditionally existed in California an interplay among Latin American immigrant musicians performing in a diversity of contexts. Both immigrant Mexicans and U.S.-born Mexican Americans have performed various styles of music with Cubans, Puerto Ricans, Central Americans, Colombians, and musicians from other Latin American countries. This has been especially true in San Francisco, where many have noted a strong pan–Latin American musical culture. Popular singers such as Julio Iglesias, Rocío Durcal (who interprets Mexican mariachi music), and Rafael from Spain, Mexican artists Vicente Fernández, José José, Luis Miguel, Juan Gabriel, Lucero, and Emmanuel, and José Luis Rodriguez from Venezuela conduct concert schedules and recording promotions throughout Latin America, the United States, and Europe and are in constant demand at major commercial concert halls and arenas throughout California.

It is also important to recognize the impact of the various Mexican traditional musical styles (in addition to the mariachi tradition) in numerous locations in California. These styles, which cater to Mexican immigrants as well as Mexican Americans born in the United States and other Latinos, include the *trío* (in the style of Trío Los Panchos), the *norteño* (the northern Mexican style accented by the use of accordion), the *jarocho* (a style originally from the Mexican state of Veracruz and especially popular among Mexican *folklórico* dance groups in Los Angeles), and the marimba orchestra (originally from Guatemala and the Mexican states of Chiapas, Oaxaca, and Guerrero).

The east side sound

During the 1960s bands and individual artists that symbolized the absorption and adaptation of particular musical styles into the musical expression of the eastside community dominated the musical life of Chicanos in Los Angeles. Popular bands such as Thee Midniters, The Village Callers, Cannibal and the Headhunters, The Ambertones, El Chicano, and Tierra were just a few of the hundreds of groups that performed during the 1960s and 1970s, most of which never attained national recognition.

One of the tragic stories was that of musician Ritchie Valens, whose real name was Richard Valenzuela. After achieving national recognition at the age of seventeen with hits like "Donna" and a rock and roll version of the traditional Mexican *huapango* "La Bamba," the young Chicano was killed in a 1959 plane crash on a snow-covered field in Iowa. Valenzuela had been on tour with rock and roll stars Buddy Holly and J. P. "Big Bopper" Richardson, who also died in the crash.

Thee Midniters

From 1964 to 1970 Thee Midniters were considered by many to be the most significant rock and roll band to emanate from the Mexican community in Los Angeles. Soon after an important rock and roll concert at Salesian High School in 1964, Eddie Torres, who had become the group's manager, negotiated a record contract with Chatahoochee Records, a small Hollywood label. The song "Land of a Thousand Dances," which Thee Midniters had performed at the Salesian show, became the group's first single, attaining number sixty-seven on the Billboard charts. Regionally the record was a major hit, reaching number ten on radio station KFWB in Los Angeles during January and February 1965.

Tailored suits (similar to those of the then-popular Beatles) and group choreography were essential elements in the band's stage show. In 1965 the group recorded its first studio single, an up-tempo rock-style instrumental titled "Whittier Boulevard." "The song quickly became an anthem for young latinos in Southern California, partly because the title named one of East Los Angeles's most popular cruising spots" (Reyes and Waldman 1982:176). As a result, the band's first album, *Thee Midniters*, did very well. The album included "Whittier Boulevard" and eleven other songs, among them "Empty Heart," "Slow Down," "Stubborn Kind of Fellow," and "I Need Someone."

Thee Midniters released the single "Chicano Power" in 1969. Interestingly, in light of the intensity of the Chicano political movement at the time, the tune was an instrumental; it was also the group's last recording. Throughout most of the year the band performed regularly at the Mardi Gras club adjacent to MacArthur Park near downtown Los Angeles. Failure to obtain a major recording contract, however, coupled with some internal tension, led to the demise of Thee Midniters in 1970.

Cannibal and the Headhunters

Cannibal and the Headhunters, a group that would eventually achieve national popularity, emerged from the same network of young east side musicians. The group was not an instrumental band but rather a vocal quartet patterned after such Motown acts as the Miracles and the Temptations. Reflecting their origin in the Ramona Gardens Housing Project, the members used their street names of Scar, Yo-yo, Rabbit, and Cannibal. Their major success was "Land of 1000 Dances" in 1965. (The same song was recorded by Thee Midniters in 1964.) During the same year Cannibal and the Headhunters became the opening act for the Beatles' historic second U.S. tour. The Columbia Records subsidiary Date Records secured a contract with the group, but another hit record never materialized.

El Chicano

In 1970, the year of the East Los Angeles Moratorium and the high school blowouts, political unrest and cultural awakening manifested themselves through artistic expression, especially among young Chicanos. In that year one of the most popular and symbolic groups—El Chicano—emerged. Originally assembled as The V.I.P.s, the group recorded a rendition of a tune by jazz composer Gerald Wilson, "Viva Tirado." Wilson had written the instrumental piece in homage to the art of bullfighting and Mexican matador José Ramón Tirado.

"Viva Tirado" became a local hit within twelve weeks after being aired on radio stations such as KGFJ and KHJ. It remained the number one record for thirteen consecutive weeks. It also attained top radio ratings in Baltimore, New York, and many cities in the South and the Midwest. Rodríguez (1980b) notes that the record also became historically significant in the recording industry because it was the first single to attain positions in all popular music categories except country and western. Believing "Viva Tirado" to be the national hit that would finally propel the east side sound into nationwide exposure, producer Eddie Davis invested his finances and energy into the project. He reorganized his Rampart label and established Gordo Enterprises, advertising the theme "Chicanos Are Happening! The Sound of the New Generation."

Tierra

Of all the bands to emerge from East Los Angeles, Tierra is one of the most successful. Fronted by Rudy and Steve Salas, formerly known as the Salas Brothers (whom Eddie Davis also produced), the group was formed in 1973 after Rudy had performed as a guitarist and vocalist for short periods with El Chicano and with a group called Maya. In the band's first year it recorded its first LP, *Tierra,* on the 20th Century record label. Another member of the group at that time was David Torres Jr., who played piano and trumpet and was one of the band's principal composer-arrangers. Although a local product, having attended Garfield High School, Torres also studied music at the Berklee School of Music in Boston. Rudy Villa (reeds), Kenny Roman (drums and Latin percussion), Conrad Lozano (bass), Aaron Ballasteros (drums and vocals), Alfred Rubalcava (bass), and Leon Bisquera (keyboards) also played with Tierra in the early to mid-1970s. In 1975 the group recorded the album *Stranded* on the Salsoul Records label.

One of the outstanding aspects of Tierra during its early years was its stylistic innovation, both musical and thematic. The group's first album, for example, included a mix of rhythm and blues, rock, salsa, and ballads. Especially notable were two songs. The first, "Gema," a bolero highly popular throughout Latin America and sung by Mexican singer Javier Solís, was reinterpreted in a varied, rock-influenced format using interesting references to traditional Mexican styles. Tierra's "Gema" was like El Chicano's rendition in 1971 of "Sabor a mi," one of the first such adaptations of Mexican music recorded among the various bands of East Los Angeles. The other highly innovative cut on the album was "Barrio Suite," a multithemed composition by Steve Salas, Rudy Salas, and David Torres. The lyrics and musical contours of the piece specifically referred to the Chicano experience of the early 1970s. Social statement, idealism, and musical experimentation wove an interesting combination of sound, thought, and sentiment.

In 1979 Tierra recorded the single "Gonna Find Her," which became a radio hit in Los Angeles and throughout the Southwest. This was a self-financed project, as was their subsequent recording of a ballad called "Together," originally recorded by The Intruders. This single, featuring Steve Salas on lead vocals, reached a position in the top one hundred on a national scale, and the group was offered a contract with Boardwalk Records. The LP *City Nights* was released in 1980. With an album to Tierra's credit, their song "Together" reached number eighteen on the national top forty charts. Among the guest artists performing on the album was Willie Bobo (*timbales*), who had also been involved in the production of two of the band's recordings ("Gonna Find Her" and "Time to Dance"). Internationally, "Together" achieved the number thirty position in the Radio Free Europe top forty charts and received extensive airplay in Japan. The group also recorded a Spanish version of the song that was quite successful in Mexico.

The year 1981 was important for Tierra in terms of national and international recognition and industry success. The group appeared on numerous television programs, including *American Bandstand, Soul Train, Solid Gold, The Toni Tenille Show,* and the *American Music Awards.* An East Coast tour of the United States included concerts at the Ritz and Carnegie Hall in New York City. Press coverage was extensive throughout the country but especially in East Los Angeles and the Southwest. Tierra was featured in almost every major Latino publication in articles, interviews, and advertisements, and "Together" earned the prestigious platinum record award, in recognition of over one million records sold.

Luis Valdez

Contributing to the musical awareness of Los Angeles Chicanos was the success of Luis Valdez's play *Zoot Suit,* which was staged at the Mark Taper Forum at the Music Center in downtown Los Angeles and at the Aquarius Theater in Hollywood, as well as on Broadway, during the late 1970s. Much of the music in the play was composed by Lalo Guerrero and Daniel Valdez. The score recalled the musical ambience of the war period in Los Angeles and the *pachuco* subculture. The play was filmed in 1982 by Universal Studios under Valdez's direction and starred Edward James Olmos and Daniel Valdez. Shorty Roger's musical arrangement used the big band format in both swing and Latin styles. Musical selections adhered to those of the original theater production.

Luis Valdez also wrote and directed the musical play *Corridos.* The original version was staged by Teatro Campesino in 1972 and then in Los Angeles in 1973. An adaptation was first produced in San Juan Bautista in 1982 and arrived in Los Angeles after highly successful award-winning runs in San Francisco and San Diego. Musical director of the production was Francisco González; Miguel Delgado was choreographer as well as a member of the cast. Other performers featured in the play included Luis Valdez, Jorge Galván, Leticia Ibarra, Sal López, Alma Martínez, Irma Rangel, Diane Rodríguez, and Robert Vega. In 1985 *Corridos* was filmed in San Francisco as a PBS television special.

MUSIC OF THE CHICANO MOVEMENT

Music of the farmworkers

Musical expression has represented one of the strongest forces behind the farmworker movement in California. Much of the music expressed the organizational and social issues of farmworkers, union strikes and protests. Two records were produced by El Teatro Campesino, with another LP released in 1976 of the same recordings (issued as *¡Huelga en general!*). A collection of farmworker songs has been recorded by the University of California, Los Angeles, Center for the Study of Comparative Folklore and Mythology (*Las voces de los campesinos*) and on the LP *Corridos y canciones de Aztlán.*

Numerous artists in California have produced music relevant to both the farmworker movement and other social issues of cultural identity. Daniel Valdez, a veteran musician-actor of El Teatro Campesino, released an important album (*Mestizo*) during the 1970s on the A & M label (later reissued on cassette by El Teatro Campesino). Another musician-composer from Northern California is Agustín Lira of Fresno, who also wrote songs of the farmworker movement. Also from Fresno is singer-guitarist Al Reyes, whose album *California Corazón* featured his compositions about farmworkers, Vietnam veterans, and Chicano culture in the San Joaquin Valley. From San Diego, Los Alacranes Mojados established themselves as important troubadours of the Chicano movement, incorporating both border conflict and farmworker themes in their music. The album *¡Si se puede!* (1976) features a collection of various Chicano musicians from Los Angeles and is dedicated to the farmworker struggle.

Chicano rock and fusion musics

As interest in East Los Angeles musical activity has intensified, older out-of-press recordings have been recompiled and continue to sell, especially those of 1960s east side rock productions and artists (just as 1960s rock and roll in general is once again popular in the mainstream U.S. music industry). Such interest has also directed attention toward young east side bands involved with more contemporary styles of rock and other musical forms. Tierra is an example of one of the older groups that became associated with the modern wave because of its high point of national recognition in 1982. El Chicano has also continued to record and tour, although sporadically.

Whether or not the 1980s truly signified a rebirth of East Los Angeles bands, the period was certainly a rebirth for the group Los Lobos. Their first album, *Just Another Band from East L.A.*, was released in 1977 through New Vista Records, a local label.

Groups such as the Brat, Los Illegals, the Undertakers, and Los Cruzados (formerly called the Plugz) are some more recent representatives of musical expression emanating from Los Angeles Chicanos. Their style has relied on the punk rock and new wave movements, although certain musical nuances and literary styles still relate to aspects of the historically unique Chicano/Mexican musical tradition. Hybrid quality is quite evident, therefore, in the modern musical styles of these groups, many of which have received substantial attention in the media.

Other Los Angeles groups that began to emerge in the late 1980s included bands such as the Alienz and Los Rock Angels, both of which incorporated Mexican and other Latino musical concepts into a basic rock and rhythm and blues format. Chicano musicians in Los Angeles generally faced a completely new and constantly evolving market. Also confronted with this constant flux were musicians of the punk, new wave, and post-punk eras who had already become involved with the new music industry through various recording contracts. The Chicano rap artist Kid Frost released *Hispanic Causing Panic* in 1990 on Virgin Records. Included in it was the market hit "La Raza," which attained substantial airplay and was based on the tune "Viva Tirado" popularized by El Chicano in 1970. Kid Frost was also involved in the release of the rap project *Latin Alliance* in 1991 and his own *East Side Story* in 1992. Another group to emerge in the market in 1991 was A Lighter Shade of Brown, which released *Brown and Proud* on the Pump Records label. As with Kid Frost's music, their rap style was bilingual, in English and Spanish. Rap group Cypress Hill and rock/rap group Rage Against the Machine were other groups including Latinos to emerge in the 1990s, in addition to largely eclectic groups such as Ozomatli and Quetzal that mixed diverse popular styles.

Whether or not the 1980s truly signified a rebirth of East Los Angeles bands, the period was certainly a rebirth for the group Los Lobos. Their first album, *Just Another Band from East L.A.*, was released in 1977 through New Vista Records, a local label. After adopting a rock and roll/Mexican/*norteño* format, Los Lobos received a 1983 Grammy Award in the newly designated category of Mexican American recordings. The *norteño*-style traditional song titled "Anselma" was one cut of the group's first Slash label LP, distributed and marketed through Warner Brothers. Another album, "How Will the Wolf Survive?" followed within a year, in addition to two commercial music videos. In 1987 a third Slash LP, *By the Light of the Moon*, was rated the number two pop/rock album of the year by *Los Angeles Times* critic Robert Hilburn. The album's title track was also nominated for a Grammy Award in the Best Rock Performance category. The same year also marked the group's collaboration on the commercial sound track of the highly successful film *La Bamba*, based on the life of Ritchie Valens and written and directed by Luis Valdez. The title track, originally a Valens hit in 1959, was recorded by Los Lobos and achieved the number one spot on the national charts in twenty-seven countries. In the United States it held that spot for three weeks and earned a double platinum record for selling over two million copies. It was also nominated for a Grammy Award in the Song of the Year category.

In San Francisco, a number of rock bands emerged during the 1970s that also achieved major international success. Santana, led by guitarist Carlos Santana, became a principal innovator in the emergence of the Latin-rock style. The rise of Carlos Santana signaled a major change in the rock industry. Born in Jalisco, Mexico, and raised in Tijuana and San Francisco, the young, blues-based guitarist recorded his first album on the Columbia label in 1969. His blending of Latin and rock stylings spearheaded a movement that was followed by numerous bands of the period. He subsequently recorded a version of "¿Oye Como Va?," composed by salsa bandleader Tito Puente, which became a major hit, helping define the impact of Latin music in the United States. Santana continued recording and successfully touring through the 1990s. During the Grammy Awards of 2000, he was awarded a record nine Grammys, for his 1999 release *Supernatural.*

The National Academy of Recordings Arts and Sciences, headquartered in Los Angeles, expanded its Latin category for the Grammy Awards into three different style categories in 1983. These included Latin pop, tropical, and Mexican American. Eventually more categories were added, and in 2000 the Latin Academy of Recording Arts and Sciences initiated the Latin Grammys. The category Mexican American allowed for Mexican-based styles from both south and north of the Mexico–U.S. border, contingent on their distribution in the United States—that is, the ethnicity of the artists is not a factor for eligibility, only the location of the recording's sales. Following Los Lobos's initial award in the Mexican American category, artists receiving the recognition in subsequent years included Sheena Easton and Luis Miguel (1984) for their duet "Me gustas tal come eres" (the Grammy Award for this duet resulted in controversy among local Mexican American musicians, and a protest ensued); Vikki Carr (1985) for her LP *Simplemente mujer;* Flaco Jiménez (1986) for *Ay te dejo en San Antonio;* Los Tigres del Norte (1987) for *¡Gracias! América sin fronteras;* Linda Ronstadt (1988) for *Canciones de mi padre;* and Los Lobos (1989) for *La pistola y el corazón.*

Another group of awards instituted to recognize Latinos in music were those established by Nosotros, the Hollywood-based association developed to enhance the artistic careers of Latino entertainers. Eventually called the Golden Eagle Awards, these began in 1970 and were given to a variety of artists in the entertainment industry. Recipients of the award in the area of music have included Valentín Robles (1977); Andy Russell (1979); Charo, Chris Montez, and Tierra (1981); Freddy Fender and Lisa López (1982); Pedro Vargas, Julio Iglesias, Anacani, and Herb Alpert (1983); Irene Cara and Rita Moreno (1984); Tony Orlando and Lalo Schiffin (1985); Trío Calaveras and Mark Allen Trujillo (1987); José Feliciano, Las Hermanas Padilla, and Los Lobos (1988); Lalo Guerrero and Vikki Carr (1989); Gloria Estefan, Emmanuel, and Martica (1990); Tito Puente and Celia Cruz (1991); and Carlos Santana (1992).

Additional musical development has taken place in the educational community throughout California. Mariachi study groups are but one example of the many folkloric classes at the primary, secondary, and university levels. Mexican ballet *folklóricos* and other folk ensembles of Mexican dance and music have proliferated. Enrollment in university classes related to Mexican and Chicano folklore has also grown substantially as a consequence of the late-1960s Chicano movement and the maintenance of the ideals of that movement.

REFERENCES

Acuña, Rodolfo. 1984. *A Community under Seige: A Chronicle of Chicanos East of the Los Angeles River, 1945–1975.* Los Angeles: Chicano Studies Research Center Publications, UCLA.

"The Ballad of an Unsung Hero." 1983. PBS video broadcast. San Diego: Cinewest.

La Bamba: Original Motion Picture Soundtrack. 1987. Slash/Warner Brothers 9-25605-1. LP disk.

Bandini, Don Arturo. 1958. *Navidad: A Christmas Day with the Early Californians.* San Francisco: California Historical Society.

The Brat. n.d. *Attitudes.* Fatima Records. LP disk.

Burciaga, José Antonio. 1987. "Linda Ronstadt: My Mexican Soul." *Vista* (*Los Angeles Herald Examiner*) 2(10): 6–8.

Camarillo, Albert. 1979. *Chicanos in a Changing Society.* Cambridge: Harvard University Press.

Camacho, Ray. n.d. *Para Los Chicanos.* California Artists Corporation CAC-1003. LP disk.

Los Camperos de Nati Cano. 1972. *El super Mariachi los Camperos.* Discos Latin International DLIS 2003. LP disk.

Cano, Eddie. 1962. *His Piano and His Rhythm.* RCA Victor LPM/LSP-2636. LP disk.

Carr, Vikki. 1972. *En Espanol: Los Exitos de Hoy Y de Siempre.* CBS Records. LP disk.

El Chicano. 1971 *Revolución.* MCA (Kap) KS-3640. LP disk.

———. 1974. *El Chicano V.* MCA LP disk.

———. 1988. *¡Viva! El Chicano: Their Very Best.* MCA.

The Chicano Experience. 1975. Texas-Mexican Border Music, vol. 14. Folklyric 9021. LP disk.

Corrido de Patty Hearst. n.d. Falcon Records FLP 4077. LP disk.

Corridos, Part 1: 1930–1934. 1975. Texas-Mexican Border Music, vol. 2. Folklyric 9004. LP disk.

Corridos, Part 2: 1929–1936. 1975. Texas-Mexican Border Music, vol. 3. Folklyric 9005. LP disk.

Cruzados. n.d *After Dark.* Arista AL-8339. LP disk.

Cowell, Sidney Robertson. 1942. "The Recording of Folk Music in California." *California Folklore Quarterly* 1:7–23.

Da Silva, Owen F. 1941. *Mission Music in California.* Los Angeles: Warren F. Lewis.

Davis, William Heath. 1929. *Seventy-Five Years in California.* San Francisco: John Howell.

East Side Story, Vols. 1–12. n.d. Trojan LP-2012. LP disk.

East Side Revue: 40 Hits by East Los Angeles' Most Popular Groups. 1969 [1966]. Rampart; distributed by American Pie as LP 3303. LP disk.

Farwell, Arthur. 1905. *Folk-Songs of the West and South: Negro, Cowboy, and Spanish-American.* Newton Center, Mass.: The Wa-Wan Press.

Feliciano, José. n.d. *And The Feeling's Good.* RCA CPL1-0407. LP disk.

Fernández, Madeleine. 1966. "Romances from the Mexican Tradition of Southern Calfornia." *Folklore Americas,* 3:35–45.

García, Francisco, and Pablo and Juanita Saludado. 1977. *Las voces de los campesinos.* UCLA Center for the Study of Comparative Folklore and Mythology FMSC-01. LP disk.

Golden Treasures, Vol. 1: West Coast East Side Revue. 1966. Rampart 3303. LP disk.

Golden Treasures, Vol. 2: West Coast East Side Revue. 1969. Rampart 3305. LP disk.

Gómez-Quiñones, Juan. 1982. *Development of the Mexican Working Class North of Río Bravo.* Los Angeles: Aztlán Publications.

Guerrero, Lalo. n.d. *Las Ardillitas de Lalo Guerrero.* Discos Odeon; distributed by Alhambra as OMS-73186. LP disk.

Guevara, Rubén. 1988. "El Chicano." Notes to *Viva El Chicano.* Universal City, Calif.: MCA Records.

Hague, Eleanor. 1917. *Spanish-American Folk-Songs.* Lancaster, Pa.: American Folklore Society.

———. 1922. *Early Spanish-Californian Folk-Songs.* New York: Pantheon.

Hansen, Terrance L. 1959. "Corridos in Southern California." *Western Folklore* 18: 203–232, 295–315.

Hawes, Bess Lomax. 1974. "'El corrido de la inundación de la presa de San Francisquito': The Story of a Local Ballad." *Western Folklore* 33:219–230.

Heisley, Michael. 1988. "Sources for the Study of Mexican Music in California." In *California's Musical Wealth: Sources for the Study of Music in California,* ed. Stephen M. Fry, 55–78. Southern California Chapter, Music Library Association.

Hernández, Guillermo. 1975. "The Chicano Experience." Notes to *The Chicano Experience.* Folklyric 9021. LP disk.

———. 1978. *Cancionero de la Raza: Songs of the Chicano Experience.* Berkeley, Calif.: El Fuego de Aztlán.

———. 1983. "From Traditional to Popular Culture: Early Commercial Phonographic Recordings and the Transmission of Text." *El Mirlo: A National Chicano Studies Newsletter* 10(Summer):3.

The History of Latino Rock, Vol. 1: 1956–1965: The Eastside Sound. 1983. Zyanya; distributed by Rhino. LP disk.

Los Illegals. 1983. *Internal Exile.* A&M 7502-14925-1. LP disk.

John Biggs Consort. 1974. *California Mission Music.* KSK Recording KSK-75218, University of California, Berkeley. LP disk.

Kid Frost. 1992. *East Side Story.* Virgin Records 4-92097. Compact disc.

Latin Alliance. n.d. *Latin Alliance.* Virgin Records 91625-4. LP disk.

A Lighter Shade of Brown. n.d. Latin Active/Pump Records 4JM-15168-4. LP disk.

Lipsitz, George. 1986. "Cruising Around the Historical Block: Postmodernism and Popular Music in East Los Angeles." *Culture Critique* 5:157–177.

Little Joe. n.d. *Los Carnarnas de Hernandez de Little Joe.* Buena Suerte Records 1029. LP disk.

Little Joe and the Latinaires. n.d. *Little Joe and the Latinaires.* El Zarape Records. EZLP 1003. LP disk.

Los Lobos. 1983. *And a Time to Dance.* Slash; distributed by Warner Brothers as 7599-23963-1. LP disk.

———. 1985. *How Will the Wolf Survive?* Slash; distributed by Warner Brothers as 7599-25177-1. LP disk.

——— 1987. *By the Light of the Moon.* Slash/Warner Brothers WB25523-4. Compact disc.

——— 1992. *Kiko.* Slash/Warner Brothers 9-26786-2. Compact disc.

Loza, Steven J. 1985. "The Musical Life of the Mexican/Chicano People in Los Angeles 1945–1985: A Study in Maintenance, Change, and Adaptation." Ph.D. dissertation, University of California, Los Angeles.

———. 1993. *Barrio Rhythm: Mexican American Music in Los Angeles.* Urbana: University of Illinois Press.

Lummis, Charles F. 1923. *Spanish Songs of Old California.* New York: Schirmer.

Los Madrugadores. *Los Madrugadores.* 1985. Texas-Mexican Border Music, vol. 18. Folklyric 9036.

Malo. *Malo.* n.d. Warner Brothers, WBR 2584.

Malo. *Evolución.* n.d. Warner Brothers WBR 2702. LP disk.

Martinez, Johnny "Chano." 1974. *¡Salsa Revolution!* Sonotropic, Producción Musimex ST-7001. LP disk.

McCoy. 1926. *Folk Songs of the Spanish Californians.* San Francisco: Sherman and Clay.

Mendheim, Beverly. 1987. *Ritchie Valens: The First Latino Rocker.* Tempe, Ariz.: Bilingual Press.

Orozco, José-Luis. 1978. *160 Años del Corrido Mexicano y Chicano.* Bilingual Media Productions JL-10. LP disk.

———. 1983. *Yo Soy Chicano.* Bilingual Media Productions AMB 103. LP disk.

Pagán, Ralfi. n.d. *With Love.* Fania; distributed by Mark West as SLP 397. LP disk.

Pearlman, Steven Ray. 1984. "Standardization and Innovation in Mariachi Music Performance in Los Angeles." *Pacific Review of Ethnomusicology* 1:1–12.

———. 1988. "Mariachi Music in Los Angeles." Ph.D. diss., University of California, Los Angeles.

Peña, Manuel. 1980. "Ritual Structure in a Chicano Dance." *Latin American Music Review* 1(1):47–73.

———. 1989. "Notes Toward an Interpretive History of California-Mexican Music." In *From the Inside Out: Perspectives on Mexican and Mexican American Folk Art,* ed. Karana Hattersly-Drayton, Joyce M. Bishop, and Tomás Ybarra-Frausto, 64–75. San Francisco: The Mexican Museum.

Los Primeros Duetos Femininas/The First Women Duets 1930–1955. 1985. Texas-Mexican Border Music, vol. 17. Folklyric 9035. LP disk.

Puente, Tito. n.d. *El Rey.* Picante CJP-250. LP disk.

Reyes, Al. n.d. *California Corazón: Songs from the San Joaquin Valley.* Cuervo Records S-1001. LP disk.

Reyes, David, and Tom Waldman. 1982. "Thee Midniters." *Goldmine,* 28 February.

Reyes, Lucha. n.d. *15 Exitos de Lucha Reyes.* RCA Victor Mexico MKS 2417. LP disk.

Ríos-Bustamante, Antonio, and Pedro Castillo. 1986. *An Illustrated History of Mexican Los Angeles, 1781–1985.* Los Angeles: Chicano Studies Research Center Publications.

Roberts, John Storm. 1979. *The Latin Tinge: The Influence of Latin American Music in the United States.* New York: Oxford University Press.

Robinson, Alfred. 1891. *Life in California during a Residence of Several Years in That Territory.* San Francisco: W. Doxey.

Rodríguez, Luis. 1980a. "The History of the 'Eastside Sound.'" *L.A. Weekly,* 1–7 August.

———. 1980b. "Eastside Story, Part II." *L.A. Weekly,* 15–21 August.

Romo, Ricardo. 1983. *East Los Angeles: History of a Barrio.* Austin: University of Texas Press.

Ronstadt, Linda. 1987. *Canciones de mi padre.* Elektra/Asylum. LP disk.

Russell, Andy. 1982. *Ayer, Hoy, y Siempre.* Kim K-725. LP disk.

Sabiá. 1984. *Formando un Puente.* Redwood Records RR 2900. LP disk.

Sánchez, Poncho. 1987 *Papa Gato.* Concord (Picante) CJP-310. LP disk.

———. 1990. *Chile Con Soul.* Concord (Picante) CJP-406-C.

Santana. n.d. *Santana's Greatest Hits.* Columbia PC 33050. LP disk.

———. 1969. *Santana.* Columbia Records CS 9781. LP disk.

Shay, Anthony. 1982. "*Fandangos* and *Bailes*: Dancing Events in Early California." *Southern California Quarterly,* Summer, 99–113.

Singer, Roberta L. 1983. "Tradition and Innovation in Contemporary Latin Popular Music in New York City." *Latin American Music Review* 4-183-202.

Sonnichsen, Philip. 1975a. Notes to *Corridos, Part 1: 1930–1934.* Folklyric 9004. LP disk.

———. 1975b. Notes to *Corridos, Part 2: 1929–1936.* Folklyric 9005. LP disk.

———. 1975c. " Los Madirugadores: Early Spanish Radio in California." *La Luz,* June, 15–18.

———. 1976. "Chicano Music." In *The Folk Music Sourcebook,* ed. Larry Sandberg and Dick Weissman, 44–51. New York: Knopf.

———. 1977. "Lalo Guerrero: Pioneer in Mexican American Music." *La Luz,* May, 11–14.

———. 1984. Notes to *Los Primeros Duetos Femininas/The First Women Duets 1930–1955.* Folklyric 9035. LP disk.

Stevenson, Robert M. 1986. "Los Angeles." In *The New Grove Dictionary of American Music,* ed. H. Wiley Hitchcock and Stanley Sadie, 107–15. London: Macmillan.

———. 1988a. "Local Music History Research in Los Angeles Area Libraries: Part I." *Inter-American Music Review* 10(1):19–38.

———. 1988b. "Music in Southern California: A Tale of Two Cities (Los Angeles: The First Biennium and Beyond)." *Inter-American Music Review* 10(1):39–111.

Strachwitz, Howard. 1973. Notes to *An Introduction, 1930–1960.* Texas-Mexican Border Music, vol. 1. Folklyric. LP disk.

Summers, William John. 1980. "California Mission Music." In *The New Grove Dictionary of American Music,* ed. H. Wiley Hitchcock and Stanley Sadie, 622–623. London: Macmillan.

———. 1991. "New and Little Known Sources of Hispanic Music from California." *Inter-American Music Review* 11(2):13–24.

Swan, Howard. 1952. *Music in the Southwest, 1825–1950.* San Marino, Calif.: Huntington Library.

El Teatro Campesino. 1976. *¡Huelga en general!: Songs of the United Farm Workers.* Menyah Records TC 1352. LP disk.

The Texas Mexican Conjunto. 1975. Texas-Mexican Border Music, vol. 24. Folklyric 9049. LP disk.

Thee Midniters. n.d. *Giants.* Distributed by Marketing West as 1001-C. LP disk.

———. n.d. *Thee Midniters.* Distributed by Marketing West as 1002-C. LP disk.

———. 1983. *Best of Thee Midniters.* Zyanya; distributed by Rhino as RNLP 063. LP disk.

Tierra. n.d. *Bad City Boys.* Boardwalk 7912-33255-1. LP disk.

———. 1973. *Tierra.* 20th Century T-412. LP disk.

———. 1975. *Stranded.* Salsoul (Mericana) SSP-5500. LP disk.

Valens, Ritchie. n.d. *The History of Ritchie Valens.* Rhino RNBC 2798. LP disk.

———. 1958, 1959. *The Best of Ritchie Valens.* Del-Fi; distributed by Rhino as RNDF 200. LP disk.

Van der Voort, Antoni. 1928. *Old Spanish Songs . . .* [n.p.]

Vietnam Mascarones. n.d. Producción Mascarones.

Viva! La causa! Songs and Sounds from the Delano Strike. n.d (P.O. Box 1278, San Juan Bautista, CA 95045). LP disk.

Weber, David J. 1982. *The Mexican Frontier, 1821–1846: The American Southwest under Mexico.* Albuquerque: University of New Mexico Press.

West Coast Eastside Review, Volume 1. n.d. Rampart Records 3303. LP disk.

West Coast Eastside Review, Volume 2. n.d. Rampart Records 3305. LP disk.

Zootsuit: Music from the Original Motion Picture. n.d. MCA 5267. LP disk.

Música Nuevomexicana
James K. Leger

The History of Music in New Mexico
New Mexican Hispano Music
Musical Genres
Important Performers
Collection and Study

New Mexicans of Spanish/Mexican heritage (variously referred to as "Spanish Americans," "Mexicanos," "Hispanos," "Manitos," "Nuevomexicanos," or "Neomexicanos") possess the longest historical presence of any nonnative peoples in the United States. Originating in seventeenth- and eighteenth-century Spanish/Mexican colonization, this group's historical presence and cultural development in New Mexico have been continuous from 1598 to the present. New Mexican Hispanos are one of the least well known of American regional groups; despite their extensive history, they are much less well known than their closely related neighbors, the Mexican Americans of Texas and of California.

The music of New Mexican Hispanos descends from sixteenth-century European American culture transplanted to what is now the southwestern United States. From this original base, it has grown and adapted to local needs, influenced by a wide variety of other musical cultures. It is now a living, vital musical tradition, with a clearly defined background and heritage, grounded in the traditional culture out of which it grew and of which it is an expression. At the same time it continues to adapt and change to meet the expressive needs of the people from whom it derives as their culture and society change in response to changing social, political, and historical forces. Although New Mexican Hispano music and musicians may not be familiar to Americans in general or to the world at large, many musicians are well known to Spanish-speaking audiences throughout the Southwest, and they have occasionally achieved national and international recognition in Mexico and in Latin America.

THE HISTORY OF MUSIC IN NEW MEXICO

Music in colonial times

Spanish music came to New Mexico with the Spanish settlers, culminating in the colonizing expedition of Juan de Oñate in 1598. This constituted the founding of the New Mexican colony and the beginnings of the New Mexican Hispano people. The Spanish settlers brought with them their musical culture, formed in Renaissance Spain and developed in post-Conquest Mexico. This included both sacred and secular Spanish/Mexican musical forms, genres, and styles. To these were added influences of the musical cultures of the Native Americans with whom the colonists came into contact in New Mexico, specifically the Pueblos and Athabascans (Navajos and Apaches) [see CALIFORNIA, p. 412; SOUTHWEST, p. 428].

Little documentation exists regarding the musical life of the seventeenth- and eighteenth-century colonists of New Mexico, especially regarding secular music. Documents do exist, however, that shed some light on musical activities in the colonial missions of New Mexico during this period. Plainchant was used in the mission churches, and liturgical books, especially missals, are known to have existed since at least 1626. Polyphonic choral music had already been employed as a missionizing, indoctrinating tool with great success in the spiritual conquest of New Spain, as colonial Mexico was called. Consequently, the Franciscan missionaries sent to New Mexico doubtless would have employed this well-proven tool in their efforts to convert the local Indian population.

Although printed music or musical manuscripts actually used in colonial New Mexico are no longer known to exist (any examples that did exist would have been destroyed during the Pueblo Revolt of 1680, when the New Mexican missions were destroyed), supporting evidence makes it clear that such music was used in the New Mexican mission churches (Spiess 1965:8). Composers capable of creating polyphonic music were known to have been in the colony during the seventeenth century. Choirs of Native Americans had been formed and trained to sing in this style, and instruments for the purpose of accompanying polyphonic music existed in the colony at that time. In addition, before 1630, music schools were in operation in the colony (Spell 1927:35).

The nineteenth century

As New Mexican society developed its unique character, further influences continued to enter via Mexico, which declared its independence from Spain in 1810, influencing the repertoire and style of the musical tradition. Salon dances (*bailes de salón*) from Europe, including the waltz, polka, and mazurka, entered Mexican elite society. From there, they entered Mexican middle-class and proletarian society and were carried up the Rio Grande, along the Camino Real, into New Mexico. The lyric song (*canción*) and its later successor, the Mexican "country song" (*canción ranchera*), entered New Mexico in the same way. The *corrido,* a form of narrative ballad popular along the Texas-Mexican border in the late nineteenth and early twentieth centuries, also became a significant part of New Mexican musical culture [see TEJANO MUSICA, p. 770]. New forms relating specifically to the expressive needs of this frontier colonial society were created, including the *indita* (a narrative song) and the regional *alabado* (hymn), as well as some social dance forms such as the *cuna* and *vaquero*. Musical styles and elements from the neighboring (and subjugated) Native Americans—the Navajos, Apaches, and various Puebloan peoples—were also borrowed and incorporated into the New Mexican Hispano musical system. Elements from all these sources were combined, adapted, and redefined to meet local expressive needs.

Mexican independence eliminated the Spanish trade embargo barring outside cultural influences, and new trade opportunities and their accompanying cultural influences entered from the United States. Anglo-Americans entered after the opening of the Santa Fe Trail in 1821 and came in even greater numbers following the political takeover and occupation of New Mexico by the United States in 1846. This resulted in the development of new forms such as the *cuadrillas* and *cotilión,* as well as the modification of existing styles and genres. The coming of the railroads to New Mexico in the late nineteenth century hastened this cultural mix, and New Mexican statehood (1912) later would establish the local musical system as a regional form in the United States.

The twentieth century

The Mexican Revolution of 1910 caused massive waves of emigration to the United States, especially to areas of already large Mexican American population in the Southwest, such as Colorado and New Mexico. The new immigrants brought with them influences from contemporary Mexican culture that helped to revitalize the Mexican base of New Mexican Hispano culture. These influences continued throughout the century with the constant influx of Mexican immigrants. In addition, American popular culture had a strong, determinative effect on New Mexican Hispano music, especially among younger age groups.

The twentieth century saw the development of a new means of musical expression among New Mexican Hispanos, along with a retention of traditional expressive means. The newer musical expressions were rooted in New Mexican Hispano musical tradition but were heavily influenced by many other forms of musical expression, including (1) American popular music, such as jazz and rock, (2) Mexican popular and regional musics, (3) Mexican American popular musics, especially the *conjunto* and *orquesta* styles coming from Texas and others from California, and (4) various Latin American folk and popular music styles. Denigrated by one observer as "a rustic version of American popular music and jazz" (Robb 1952–1953:2), this style, sometimes called *música nuevomexicana,* was an amalgam of various urban popular music expressions, combined with a definite New Mexican Hispano regional style. By the end of the twentieth century, it had become the most widespread and popular form of musical expression of contemporary New Mexican Hispanos, who by then were overwhelmingly urban. It reflected their current sociocultural status, as well as their group identity, awareness, and heritage. Its most characteristic performer/composer and acknowledged leader was Al Hurricane (Alberto Sánchez) of Albuquerque, whose style has been copied and imitated by countless musicians in New Mexico and elsewhere in the Southwest.

Alongside this contemporary expression, the more deeply traditional forms of *música nuevomexicana* continued to be performed in their traditional ways as well as in newer, pop-influenced styles. New Mexican Hispano music—both new and old—continues to live on as a tradition-based system but one nevertheless responsive to the needs of the people who create and maintain it.

NEW MEXICAN HISPANO MUSIC

Although New Mexican Hispanos constitute a relatively homogeneous cultural group, stylistic variations exist between various areas of the region. These variations are reflected in linguistic patterns, folklore, and musical style and repertoire. The most traditional area of the region, that which exhibits the most clearly Spanish-derived music and culture, is northern New Mexico and adjacent southern Colorado, from the area around Santa Fe north to the San Luis Valley of Colorado. Las Vegas, New Mexico, is a center of this culture and is considered to be a center for musical tradition (Evans 1985:10; Loeffler 1983:44). Taos, Española, and Santa Fe are also important centers of musical tradition. The southern part of New Mexico that borders the Republic of Mexico, with its major city of Las Cruces, exhibits the strongest Mexican influences. The eastern plains area, around Clovis, shows strong influences from neighboring west Texas. The urban areas of Albuquerque and Santa Fe are centers for the more urban styles influenced by American pop, rock, and jazz.

MUSICAL GENRES

Many genres of New Mexican Hispano music are common to folk and popular music systems in general; others are unique to New Mexican Hispanos. The former include the *corrido, canción ranchera,* polka, and many religious songs. The latter include forms that are local variations of forms found elsewhere. One example is the expressive vocal praise song (*alabado*) of the New Mexican Hispano religious brotherhood (*La Frater-*

FIGURE I   Violinist and guitarist accompany a *matachines* dance-drama performance at the Museum of International Folk Art in Santa Fe, New Mexico. Photo by Daniel Sheehy, June 1997.

nidad Piadosa de Nuestro Padre Jesus Nazareno, popularly known as *Los Hermanos,* or *Los Penitentes*). Another is the dance-drama known as *Los matachines* (figure 1). While similar to certain dance-dramas found in various regions of the Southwest and Latin America, the New Mexican forms of *Los matachines,* found only in areas of Pueblo–Hispano interaction, incorporate elements of both Hispano and Native American music and dance into regional forms unique to New Mexico.

Song

Narrative songs

The oldest musical form still found among New Mexican Hispanos is the *romance,* the narrative ballad of sixteenth-century Spanish origin. An epic poem consisting of a series of octosyllabic quatrains (*coplas*), the *romance* entered New Mexico with the earliest Spanish *conquistadores,* explorers, and colonists and remained a favorite expressive medium for centuries. *Romances* with clear links to colonial Spain were collected in the early part of the twentieth century by Espinosa (1915) and by Campa (1946). The *romance* as a genre is nearly moribund, although it continues to exist in an attenuated form. Versions and variants of traditional *romances* have been collected in recent times by Enrique Lamadrid and Jack Loeffler (1999).

The *corrido* is also a narrative song type of more recent development than the *romance.* It dates from the nineteenth century in Mexico and the American Southwest, especially in the Texas–Mexican border area, where it developed under conditions of group contestation and conflict (Parédes 1958). The *corrido* differs from the *romance* primarily in that the themes with which it deals are more current and local than those of the *romance.* Two other distinguishing features of the *corrido* are an opening *copla* that might state the date of the event commemorated or introduce the topic, and the *despedida,* a leave-taking *copla* that marks the end of the ballad.

The *corrido* tradition is very much alive, and these songs are still used to commemorate events of significance to the local populace. Roberto Martinez is the most active composer of *corridos* in New Mexico today. He has written and recorded *corridos* concerning local Hispano politics, the Vietnam war, the Tierra Amarilla courthouse raid, the New Mexico Penitentiary riots, the Space Shuttle Challenger disaster, the Persian Gulf War, and many other current topics.

The *indita* is another narrative song form, very similar to the *corrido* but native to (or indigenous to) New Mexico. It is distinguished by influences from Southwestern Native American music, especially in its rhythms and texts. Characteristic examples include *"La Finada Pablita,"* composed around 1861, which chronicles the execution by hanging in Las Vegas, New Mexico, of Paula Angel, the first and only woman ever legally executed in New Mexico. Another well-known *indita* is *"Los Ciboleros,"* also known as *"La Indita de Manuel Maes,"* that recounts the story of a buffalo hunter killed while on a hunt on the *Llano Estacado* 'Staked Plains' of Eastern New Mexico and West Texas (Vigil 1985a, 1985b).

The *relación* is another narrative song type, similar to the *romance* but usually humorous. It is characterized by extensive lists of items. The *cuando* is yet another narrative song, marked by the inclusion of the term *cuando* 'when' in the text, usually at the beginning. The most learned poetic form of New Mexican Hispano music is the *décima,* which flourished in fifteenth-century Spain and was subsequently spread throughout the New World. *Décima* texts feature a rather intricate formal scheme: four ten-line stanzas, introduced by a four-line quatrain. All *décimas* were sung to the same basic melody.

The *trovo* is a song duel, in which two or more performers sing alternate verses. Campa (1946:18–20) notes that composer/song makers (*trovadores*) were an important part of traditional New Mexican Hispano society. Every village had its own local *poeta* or *cantador,* who performed whenever and wherever people congregated and for

When two trains met, they would camp together, and the *mayordomos* (boss or captain) of each train would often challenge each other's *trovadores* to a songfest. These songfests, which could last all night long, consisted of attempts to outdo each other's repertoires, as well as extemporaneous song contests, or *trovos*.

many types of occasion, such as birthdays, baptisms, fiestas, and weddings. These same performers frequently accompanied the pack trains that carried commerce on the Chihuahua and Santa Fe Trails. Each caravan included at least one exceptional singer, who entertained the traders and composed songs dealing with occurrences along the trade route. When two trains met, they would camp together, and the *mayordomos* (boss or captain) of each train would often challenge each other's *trovadores* to a songfest. These songfests, which could last all night long, consisted of attempts to outdo each other's repertoires, as well as extemporaneous song contests, or *trovos*. *Trovadores* from each train would compete, improvising *coplas* to a formulaic melody, posing questions to each other. The topics were usually philosophical, emphasizing theology and history, and featured wordplay such as puns. Most *trovos* are associated with famous *trovadores*, such as *El Zurdo, El Pelón, Chicoria, El Negrito, Cienfuegos, Taveras,* and the best known ones, *García* and *El Viejo Vilmas.*

Religious songs

The *entriega* (from the Spanish *entregar* 'to send forth') consists of a musical sending forth of an individual or group into the community or into a ritual function. *Entriegas* were an essential part of many ritual social occasions such as baptisms and funerals, but they occurred most often in wedding contexts, where they were referred to as the *entriega de novios* (figure 2). In times when Roman Catholic priests were very rare in New Mexican society, the *entriega de novios* actually substituted for the church wed-

FIGURE 2   A wedding procession leaving the church, Cordova, New Mexico, 1939. Photo by B. Brixner. Courtesy Museum of New Mexico.

ding ceremony. In more recent times, it has served a symbolic function. A couple might be married in the eyes of the church at the moment the priest pronounced them man and wife, but in the eyes of the community they did not form a new social unit, an integral part of the community, until the *entriega* proclaimed them to be such (Lamadrid 1990). Musically, the *entriega* takes the form of a waltz (*valse*). Its text consists of both stock (formulaic) and improvised *coplas* directed toward the bride and groom, parents, those present at the ceremony, and other community members.

The songs of the New Mexican Hispano lay religious brotherhood, *La Fraternidad Piadosa de Nuestro Padre Jesus Nazareno,* are known as *alabados.* These songs are rhythmically unmeasured and tonally based on the Church modes. Singing is in unison and unaccompanied. Two instruments are used in the ritual performances of which the *alabado* is a part: the *pito* and *matraca.* These do not accompany the singing, but rather precede or follow it. Other hymn types are frequently referred to as *alabanzas,* as distinguished from the very distinctive *alabados.* The most common and frequent contemporary arena for the performance of these hymns is the Catholic Church. Most Catholic parishes maintain amateur choirs whose repertoire includes large numbers of Spanish-language hymns for both liturgical and paraliturgical uses, along with a mix of contemporary and traditional English-language hymns. Although many are traditional in origin, many are being newly composed. New Mexico boasts a thriving school of hymn composers, including Mary Helen Reza of Albuquerque, Father George Salazar and Juan Ortega of Las Vegas, and Arcenio Córdova of Taos. Many of their compositions are contained in *Flor y Canto,* a hymnbook used by Spanish-speaking Catholic parishes throughout the United States. Many have subsequently entered the oral tradition.

Folk plays

Folk plays were common throughout New Mexican colonial society and are still performed today. The best-known are the Christmas plays, or *Pastorelas,* including *Coloquios de los Pastores* ('Colloquies of the Shepherds'), *Los Tres Reyes Magos* ('The Three Wise Kings'), and *El Niño Perdido* ('The Lost Child'). There are many others, including *Los Comanches* ('The Comanches'), *Adán y Eva* ('Adam and Eve'). These are dramatic enactments that feature a large number of songs. The songs of these plays are performed in a style very similar to that of the *alabados,* that is, rhythmically nonmetric and text-based.

Instrumental music

New Mexican Hispano instrumental music accompanies many regional dance forms, such as the *matachines*—dances performed by Pueblo Indians, with the accompanying music provided by *músicos* from the neighboring Hispano villages. They consist of double-file dances, with supplementary characters (*Monarca, Malinche, Toro,* and *Abuelos*). The music consists of a violin and guitar and is stylistically similar to the music of the secular Hispano *bailes* 'village community dance occasions.' Occasionally they are performed in a strictly "Indian" version, with drum and rattle accompaniment. The Pueblos place this dance form in their ceremonial calendars but regard it as foreign, introduced by the Spanish and not a part of their native religion. Some Hispano villages perform their own versions, with no Native American participation.

The popular interpretation of the meaning and origin of these dances is highly romantic. A medieval origin is often postulated, and many observers believe they see in them a representation of the struggle between good and evil or between paganism and Christianity. Other ritual forms include the *Comanche* or *Comanchitos* dances, which feature Plains Indian–inspired musical style elements, especially in their rhythms [see PLAINS, p. 440]. These dances are accompanied by drums and rattles rather than by guitars and violins.

The social dance tradition

The musical corpus most closely identified with New Mexican Hispano culture is the social dance music tradition, inextricably linked to the guitar-and-violin duo that traditionally provided the music for the *bailes*. Some of the dances are accompanied by the music derived from Mexican regional dance traditions, but most come from the European "salon" dances brought to Mexico during the nineteenth century. These include the two most ubiquitous of all New Mexican Hispano dance forms, *la polca* (the polka) and *el valse* (the waltz). One of the best known and most popular of all New Mexican traditional dances is the mazurka "*La varsoviana,*" familiar in Anglo-American folk dance tradition as "Put Your Little Foot."

Other dances, while stemming from Anglo-American sources, have developed unique characteristics in the Hispano cultural context. These include the *chotís*, a New Mexican version of the Anglo-American schottische, and *las cuadrillas* 'quadrille.' The New Mexican *cuadrillas* is similar to the American square dance in that it is danced in groups of two or more couples, but the *cuadrillas* does not use a caller. It is the most intricate and elaborate of the Spanish-Colonial folk dances, consisting of six or seven distinct parts, including the final *cutilio* or *cotilión* 'cotillion' [see CONTRA DANCE, p. 230; ENGLISH AND SCOTTISH MUSIC, p. 831].

Other older dance forms native to New Mexican Hispano culture are the *redondo,* a fast waltz, and the *cuna* 'cradle', whose name refers to a figure in the form of a baby's cradle that the dancers create by interweaving their arms during the course of the dance. There are also dancing games, such as *el baile de la escoba* 'broom dance' and *el baile de los paños* 'handkerchief dance', both in the form of a waltz. In *el baile de la escoba,* one person begins dancing with a broom. After a short period, he or she drops it, at which time everyone must change partners. The person left without a partner must then dance with the broom. The *baile de los paños* is danced by groups of three dancers, one male and two female. The male dancer holds one end of a handkerchief or bandana in each hand; the two women each hold the other ends of the two handkerchiefs. The dancers then execute intricate steps while attempting to avoid dropping or entangling the handkerchiefs. The native New Mexican Hispano dance type *el vaquero* 'the cowboy' reflects Anglo-American cowboy influence, and *la indita* 'the little Indian girl' reflects Native American influence. Other older dances are *la camila* (Camille) and *el taleán* (Italian dance). More newly created, although in a traditional style and serving the same social functions, are the polka "*El mosquito*" (the mosquito) by Eddie Dimas and the "*Valse de la Grama*" (the grandma's waltz) by Henry Ortiz. These demonstrate that the social dance tradition is still very much alive today.

The social significance of dancing

Dancing had a very important social significance in New Mexican Hispano society, as is frequently noted in the reports of explorers, soldiers, merchants, and others who visited the area (Lucero-White 1953:227; Thomas 1978:107–110). In New Mexico the dance was (and often still is) an accompaniment to other ceremonial events—primarily weddings, but also other community/religious social events such as baptisms, civic and church events such as *fiestas,* and public secular events such as political rallies.

The social dance tradition underwent a revitalization process in the 1960s and 1970s, under the impetus of the Chicano movement. Many school systems in New Mexico, Colorado, Texas, California, and some other Western states incorporated New Mexican folk dancing into their curricula and extracurricular activities, often by means of Lorenzo Martínez's first album, *El Redondo Largo* (Martínez n.d.). This was neither the first nor the most traditional recording of New Mexican instrumental music, but it was by far the most technically proficient and the one that was most easily available and widely distributed. Many people received their best (and in many cases only) exposure to this music and dance tradition by means of this recording.

Instruments

The guitar is by far the most important instrument in New Mexican Hispano musical culture, played alone, as an accompaniment to the voice, or in combination with other instruments. As it is generally played as an accompanying instrument, truly virtuosic lead-style guitar playing is infrequent. Some skilled performers do, however, play lead-style guitar in the manner of the Mexican *requinteros*—performers on a small six-stringed guitar (*requinto*) pitched a perfect fourth higher than the standard guitar, used particularly in small ensembles such as the Mexican *trio* or *trio romántico* to play melody. This may occur as solo playing, but it is found more often in ensemble settings. The guitar is paired with the violin so often and in all areas of the region, especially in social and ritual dance occasions, that this combination constitutes a distinguishing feature of New Mexican Hispano musical culture.

The accordion and harmonica, played in a variety of styles, are found less frequently than the guitar and violin. More Texas- and Mexican-influenced areas, such as the southern, eastern, and central regions, tend to feature the accordion more, and in more Texas Mexican–influenced playing styles. In northern New Mexico and southern Colorado, it has taken on a more regional, local character. New Mexican Hispanos consider the accordion to be a significant part of their musical culture.

The mandolin, employed to a limited extent to perform traditional New Mexican Hispano music, seems to be further diminishing in popularity in recent times. It is most often found as an accompanying instrument to the voice and secondarily as an ensemble instrument. It is rarely, if ever, heard in a solo context.

The acoustic string bass, electric bass, and, rarely, the *guitarrón* 'Mexican six-stringed bass' are sometimes found in ensembles. Even the banjo has, on occasion, found its way into New Mexican Hispano traditional music. Other less frequently found instruments include trumpet, saxophone, and various keyboard instruments (piano and organ).

Drums of various kinds are occasionally used. The *Comanche* dancers of Taos and *Comanchitos* performers of the Albuquerque area use drums in their Native American–inspired performances, and rattles are also used in Native American–influenced dance contexts, such as the *Matachines* and *Comanches*. Also, Edwin Berry of Tomé used a large drum 'tombé' to accompany his otherwise unaccompanied vocal performances (figure 3). *Alabado* performances frequently include the *pito* 'small vertical flute' and

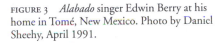

FIGURE 3   *Alabado* singer Edwin Berry at his home in Tomé, New Mexico. Photo by Daniel Sheehy, April 1991.

Popular dance bands draw from the entire pantheon of American popular instrumental usages, reflecting their heritage and influences.

matraca 'wooden ratchet.' These are used in preludes to the *alabado* performances or in other ways in the Holy Week rituals, not to accompany the singing.

Historically, Lummis (1952 [1893, 1928]:219) mentions the guitar, harmonica, concertina, and a musical bow called the *bijuela* as being the favored instruments of New Mexican Hispanos, especially the sheep herders. Espinosa (1985:38) likewise mentions the guitar, harmonica, and musical bow, which he spells *vigüela*. Campa (1946:19) mentions the *vihuela*. This instrument seems to be a mouth-bow, as Espinosa likens it to the Brazilian *berimbau*. Despite the spelling, it seems to have no connection whatsoever with either the Renaissance Spanish lute-type *vihuela*, or the contemporary Mexican mariachi guitar-type instrument of the same name.

Popular dance bands draw from the entire pantheon of American popular instrumental usages, reflecting their heritage and influences. Electric guitars and basses predominate, as do drum sets. Electric or electronic keyboard instruments (electric pianos, organs, electronic keyboards and synthesizers) are common, as are brass and woodwind instruments (trumpets, trombones, saxophones, flutes, and so on). Accordions are occasionally encountered in these contexts, but not nearly so frequently as in the neighboring Texas or California ensembles.

IMPORTANT PERFORMERS

Throughout the history of New Mexican Hispano music, certain individual performers have achieved special recognition. The early collectors, such as Lummis and Espinosa, generally neglected to obtain personal information regarding specific performers. But accomplished performers were well known to their audiences, and their names have been preserved in oral tradition. Espinosa (1985:131) mentions Don Norberto M. Abeyta of Sabinal, New Mexico, as "among the most prolific of the popular poets of New Mexico" and mentions some of his ballads on local topics. Campa (1946:22–24) mentions some near-legendary New Mexican village "troubadours" (*puetas*), including *El Pelón* (Jesús Gonzales, of Pojoaque), *Chicoria, El Viejo Vilmas, Taveras, Cienfuegos,* and *García*. Campa also was careful to record the names of, and provide biographical details concerning some of the informants with whom he worked, especially Apolinario Almanzares, "the best known troubadour in the vicinity of Las Vegas" (Campa 1946:18–20). He also mentions Próspero S. Baca of Bernalillo, who, along with Francisco S. Leyva of Leyba, served as one of Robb's principal informants (Robb:1980).

The late Cleofes Vigil of San Cristóbal, near Taos, was one of the most well known artists of the 1960s and 1970s. A former member of the so-called *penitente* brotherhood (*Fraternidad Piadosa de Nuestro Padre Jesús Nazareno*), he recorded two albums of *alabados.* He was in great demand for conferences and lectures, and many of his performances consisted of his own original material based in traditional forms and styles such as the *indita.* Known as both a storyteller and a singer, he often accompanied himself on the mandolin. In 1984, the National Endowment for the Arts awarded him a National Heritage Fellowship; he is the only New Mexican Hispano musician to be so honored.

Cleofes Ortiz of Bernal, near Las Vegas, New Mexico was one of the best known of the traditional *violinistas*. Known locally in and around the Las Vegas area, along with his longtime guitar accompanist, Augustín Chávez, he began a new career after Chávez's death, when he was discovered and promoted by Ken Keppeler and Jeannie McLearie of Bayou Seco, a band performing a mixture of traditional musics of Appalachia, Louisiana, and New Mexico. Keppeler and McLearie accompanied Ortiz, arranged performances for him, promoted his career, and introduced him to wider (especially Anglo) audiences. In the process, they made him one of the best known of all New Mexican Hispano traditional musicians. A stroke late in life curtailed, but did not end, his career. Shortly before his death he was honored with the New Mexico Governor's Award for the Arts.

Current traditional performers

The Chicano movement of the 1960s and 1970s, as well as Jack Loeffler's collecting and promotional activities of the 1980s and 1990s, brought to public awareness many still-active traditional New Mexican Hispano musicians. Many are featured in Loeffler's film *La Música de los Viejos* (1983), and excellent photographs of many of them are available in Parsons (1990).

The best known folk musician of the central Rio Grande Valley was Edwin Berry of Tomé, who was a repository of hundreds of songs, both old and recent. His vocal style and interpretation were unique. He frequently performed to his own accompaniment on a drum (*tombé*). He was a major source of material and information for the two principal collectors of New Mexican Hispano folk music: Robb, who began collecting from him in the 1940s, and Loeffler, who was still collecting from him well into the 1980s and 1990s.

A singer, guitarist, and accordionist from Rociada, near Las Vegas, Antonia Apodaca has performed throughout her life, primarily as part of a duo with her husband Macario (Max) Apodaca. After his death in December 1987, she began performing as a soloist and enjoyed a renewed career. She is currently one of the most active and best known of all New Mexican Hispano musicians, performing nationwide.

The best known performers of the southern New Mexico region, on the border of the Republic of Mexico, include Carmen Araiza, Johnny Flórez, and Johnny and Luther Whelan. Araiza was a singer, guitarist, and mandolinist from La Mesa, near Las Cruces, whose repertoire included much Mexican material. Flórez, of Las Cruces, also performs Mexican material primarily, frequently joining in a guitar/vocal duo with his longtime partner, Raúl García. The Whelans, a father and son team from Las Cruces, perform primarily rurally oriented material and specialize in the music of the cowboys and their Mexican counterparts, the *vaqueros*.

Vicente Montoya and Margarito Olivas, both of Las Vegas, New Mexico, were considered by many to be the most typical of all recent New Mexican Hispano traditional instrumentalists and "two of the finest *músicos* in New Mexico" (Loeffler 1983:44). Adept at performing the social dance music of the *bailes*, they were also accomplished vocalists, using the guitar and violin as accompaniment to their songs. Olivas continued to perform widely after Montoya's death. In 1979 these two musicians were invited to perform at the National Folk Festival at Wolf Trap Farm, Virginia. They were the first New Mexican performers ever to perform at that festival.

Groups of musicians dedicated to presenting and preserving traditional Hispano music, especially the older folk forms, exist in Taos, Las Vegas, Santa Fe, Española, and other larger population centers. La Orquesta Típica de Las Vegas is one such group. The largest such group in New Mexico, its repertoire consists primarily of traditional New Mexican Hispano music, but it also performs much Mexican material, such as *rancheras* from the mariachi repertoire. Another group is Los Alegres de Taos, a quartet consisting of Julia Jaramillo, José Archuleta, Pablo Trujillo, and Ernesto Montoya.

FIGURE 4   Cipriano Vigil. Photo by Charles Vandiver, Las Vegas, New Mexico.

Folk music interpreters

Certain performers have self-consciously worked to perpetuate "archaic" or "traditional" styles, genres, and items of New Mexican Hispano music. In an effort to remain current and acceptable to contemporary audiences, however, they also have found it necessary to incorporate various modern styles and items into their performances.

By far the most active and visible of all contemporary performers of traditional New Mexican Hispano music is singer/instrumentalist Cipriano Vigil of El Rito (figure 4), who grew up in the northern New Mexico rural community of Chamisal. A self-taught musician from an early age, he was influenced and inspired by northern New Mexican Hispano village musicians, by traveling professional musicians, and, to a great extent, by radio, including English-language broadcasts, often country music stations, from distant locations. He performs widely and lectures frequently on traditional New Mexican Hispano music in conjunction with the New Mexico Humanities Endowment's lecture series. He frequently performs New Mexican traditional music in historic reenactment events, complete with period costumes. Currently he performs primarily with his son and daughter, Cipriano Jr. and Felicita (figure 5). His group, Los Folkloristas Nuevomejicanos, uses Latin American forms, rhythms, instruments, and even complete songs, which they blend with traditional New Mexican Hispano forms.

A former lieutenant governor of New Mexico, Roberto Mondragón put his singing and guitar playing to good use in his election campaigns and thus became one of the best known traditional performers of the 1970s and 1980s. A native of La Loma, near Las Vegas, he currently resides in Santa Fe, where he is well known as a lecturer, politician, restaurateur, newspaper columnist, and radio personality.

Alex Chávez of Albuquerque taught music in the Albuquerque public schools, at the University of New Mexico, and at Adams State University in Alamosa, Colorado. In the 1960s and 1970s, he recorded two very popular and well received record albums of traditional songs, including a wide range of forms and types. He also published a comprehensive article (Chávez 1973) listing commercial and archival sources of New Mexican Hispano traditional music.

Jenny Wells Vincent, although neither Hispanic nor a native of New Mexico, has lived in San Cristóbal most of her life. She has been very influential in increasing awareness of this musical tradition through her extensive performing and recording

FIGURE 5   Cipriano Vigil (center) with his daughter, Felicita, and son, Cipriano Jr. Photo by Charles Vandiver, Las Vegas, New Mexico.

FIGURE 6   Violinist Lorenzo Martínez (*left*), his father, Roberto Martínez (*right*), and accompanying *guitarrón* player Francisco "Capiro" Castro in performance with the Raíces Musicales national tour sponsored by the National Council for the Traditional Arts. Photo by Daniel Sheehy, April 1984.

activities. Until very recently, she performed frequently with her group, El Trío de Taos. She has produced numerous significant recordings of Hispano and Native American traditional music from the Taos area, which she has distributed on her Cantemos and Taos Recordings and Publications labels.

Roberto Martínez is significant as leader/founder of the group Los Reyes de Albuquerque and for his activities in encouraging and furthering the careers of other New Mexican performers. Los Reyes is one of the best known and most influential groups in the perpetuation and dissemination of Mexican and New Mexican folk and popular music. Los Reyes is basically a mariachi-style group incorporating vocal harmonies accompanied by guitar, *vihuela, guitarrón,* violin, and trumpet. Its repertoire emphasizes equally the Mexican *ranchera* tradition and the New Mexican social dance tradition. Martínez is also the most active contemporary New Mexican composer of *corridos.* He has written and recorded many *corridos* on topics of local significance.

With the release of his first recording, *El Redondo Largo* (n.d.), Lorenzo Martínez established himself as the most significant and influential performer, preserver, and disseminator of the New Mexican social dance music tradition (figure 6). The son of Los Reyes founder Roberto Martínez, he was born into the New Mexican Hispano musical tradition. He learned the melodies of many of the social dance tunes from his grandmother. He began western classical violin training at an early age and combined this technique and discipline with traditional style and repertoire. His performances are technically impeccable and more acceptable to wider audiences than those of many older performers, who often are plagued with insecure rhythm, intonation, and tone quality. His recordings have served as models for learning by many younger musicians, inspiring them to become involved in the performance and perpetuation of this music.

Al Hurricane and family

Al Hurricane (Alberto Sánchez) and his brothers Tiny Morrie (Amador Sánchez) and Baby Gaby (Gabriel Sánchez) have been phenomenally popular throughout the Southwest since the mid-twentieth century. Known primarily for their vocal abilities, they are also very accomplished instrumentalists, composers, and arrangers. Al Hurricane (figure 7) is the most influential New Mexican Hispano musician of the second half of the twentieth century. Born in 1936, he began playing and singing Spanish songs for tips at Albuquerque's Old Town Plaza at the age of twelve. In 1954, during his senior

Morrie's son, Lorenzo Antonio, was the first member of the second generation of the Sanchez family to achieve superstar status in Mexico and Latin America. His success has since been matched, if not exceeded, by that of his sisters.

FIGURE 7   Al Hurricane. Photo by Roy Sandoval, Albuquerque, New Mexico; courtesy Albert Sánchez (Al Hurricane) and Isidro "Sider" Esquibel Jr.

year in high school, he formed a 1940s-style swing band. Later, along with his brothers, he began playing 1950s-style rock and roll (Harbert 1988:26). In the mid-1960s, he recorded the Mexican popular *ranchera "La Mula Bronca,"* which became a hit in Mexico as well as throughout the southwestern United States. He has concentrated on Spanish-language music since that time (figure 8).

Based solidly in the New Mexican Hispano musical tradition, Al Hurricane has developed a distinctive and much-imitated musical style that draws on a wide range of popular music influences, including 1940s American crooning and swing, 1950s rock and roll, Mexican *ranchera,* and Texas-Mexican *conjunto* and *orquesta.* His style is similar to Texas-Mexican *orquesta,* but it features electric guitars, brass, and saxophones. In the early 1970s the Sánchez brothers (along with the Martínez family) were widely recognized as leaders of the *Onda Chicana* 'Chicano Wave' movement. Besides their performing and touring activities, the family operated a recording studio and Spanish-language record store, as well as the Far West Club, the principal venue for New Mexican Hispano popular music. Morrie and Gaby both enjoyed tremendous success; Morrie's *"No Hay Amor"* was the first Spanish song recorded by a U.S. artist to top the charts in Mexico (Harbert 1988:31). By the mid-1980s, however, both Morrie and Gaby had retired from active public performance. Al continued headlining his own band, Bandido, and performing with his son, Al Hurricane Jr. (figure 9).

Younger members of the family have also established very successful careers. Al Hurricane Jr. is well known throughout New Mexico. Morrie's daughters, who perform throughout the United States, Mexico, and Latin America as the group named Sparx, have been especially successful. Morrie's son, Lorenzo Antonio, was the first member of the second generation of the Sanchez family to achieve superstar status in Mexico and Latin America. His success has since been matched, if not exceeded, by that of his sisters (Bowman 1996).

FIGURE 8   The Hurricane Band. Photo by Roy Sandoval, Albuquerque, New Mexico; courtesy Albert Sánchez (Al Hurricane) and Isidro "Sider" Esquibel Jr.

FIGURE 9   Al Hurricane Jr. Photo by Roy Sandoval, Albuquerque, New Mexico; courtesy Albert Sánchez (Al Hurricane) and Isidro "Sider" Esquibel Jr.

COLLECTION AND STUDY

In the first half of the twentieth century four scholars dominated the collection and study of music and folklore of Hispanos in the United States: Charles F. Lummis, Aurelio M. Espinosa, Arthur L. Campa, and Rubén Cobos. In the 1930s and early 1940s, the WPA Federal Music Project made a major contribution to the study and public awareness of traditional New Mexican Hispano music. The first technically trained musician to take an active interest in New Mexican Hispano traditional music was John Donald Robb, whose collecting career lasted over thirty-five years. His recordings form the basis of the John Donald Robb Archive of Southwestern Folk Music at the University of New Mexico, the principal repository of Southwestern traditional music, as well as of his lengthy anthology, *Hispanic Folk Music of New Mexico and the Southwest: A Self-Portrait of a People* (1980). The most active collector in the history of New Mexican folk music study, however, has been Jack Loeffler, who recorded much Hispano traditional music from all areas of the state and who has done more than anyone else in recent times to bring the traditional music of New Mexico to the attention of the general public, the academic community, and private and public funding agencies.

The standard reference on Hispano music in New Mexico and the Southwest is Robb (1980). A recent volume that covers the same range of materials but in a more limited scope is Loeffler (1999). Older but still very valuable studies of this musical tradition include Campa (1933, 1946). The best musicological study is Mendoza and Mendoza (1986). Parsons (1990) provides excellent photographs of many of the most significant performers of recent times. The most comprehensive aural survey of New Mexican Hispano traditional music is the Smithsonian Folkways collection *Music of New Mexico: Hispanic Traditions* (1992). An older compilation, still useful although somewhat dated, is *Spanish and Mexican Folk Music of New Mexico,* recorded and with notes by John D. Robb (1961 [1952]). An excellent supplement, although of more limited scope than the Smithsonian Folkways CD, is Vol. 1 of the Albuquerque Museum's Music of New Mexico Series, *Hispano Folk Music of the Past* (1998). A very useful volume is the 3-CD set *Tesoros del Espiritu: A Portrait in Sound of Hispanic New Mexico,* and its accompanying book of the same title (Lamadrid 1996). Some of the classic LP recordings of New Mexican traditional music have recently been reissued on compact disc. These include *Dark and Light in Spanish New Mexico* (1995 [1978]) and *El Testamento* by Alex J. Chavez (1995 [1965]).

The best survey of the contemporary New Mexican Hispano music scene is the series "New Mexico Spanish Super Stars" (six volumes on CD, plus a Christmas volume available on cassette only) issued by Alta Vista Records of Albuquerque. The best surveys of the career and recordings of *Los Reyes de Albuquerque* are their two retrospective CDs, *Lo Mejor de Los Reyes de Albuquerque* (1993) and *Los Reyes de Albuquerque: 30 Años de Grabaciones* (1995). Lorenzo Martinez has two retrospective CDs of his own, *Lo Mejor de Lorenzo Martinez y sus Violines* (1993) and *Lorenzo Martinez: Tocando y Cantando* (1995).

New Mexican Hispano music has been well documented in film and video. *La Música de los Viejos,* by Jack Loeffler and Jack Parsons (1983), features many of the participants in the various *"Música de los Viejitos"* projects (including a recording project and festivals). *La Música de la Gente,* also by Parsons (1993), documents the New Mexican Hispano popular music tradition and features Al Hurricane and Roberto Martínez and their families. This film presents the musicians in actual performance situations, primarily from the 1970s *Onda Chicana* period.

An extensive series of videos documenting the music of the various regions of the area has been produced by the PBS affiliate in Albuquerque, KNME-TV, as part of their weekly *Colores!* series. *Colores* 109, *"Del Norte* 'The North', documents the music of northern New Mexico and southern Colorado; *Colores* 100, *"Del Valle"* 'The Valley', presents the music of the middle Rio Grande Valley; *Colores* 130, *"Del Llano"* 'The Plains', documents the music of eastern New Mexico and its Texas border; and *Colores* 318, *"Del Sur"* 'The South', presents the music of Mexican-influenced southern New Mexico. Some segments focus on individual performers, including *Colores* 122, *"Cleofes Ortiz—Violinista Nuevo Mexicano,"* and *Colores* 206, *"El Ranchito de las Flores,"* featuring Tonie Apodaca, while others focus on specific types or genres of New Mexican Hispano music. *Colores* 123, *"Una Lucha para Mi Tierra-Tierra Amarilla,"* covers the *corridos* of the land grant struggles of the 1960s and 1970s. *Colores* 401, *"El Alma de la Divinidad*: The Soul of the Divine,"* features the Santa Fe Desert Chorale performing Spanish and Mexican polyphonic choral music of the seventeenth and eighteenth centuries that might have been performed in New Mexican colonial mission churches.

REFERENCES

Bowman, Jon. 1996. "Sparx Fly: Sisters Ignite Music World." *New Mexico* (June):34–39.

Campa, Arthur L. 1933. *The Spanish Folksong in the Southwest.* Language Series Bulletin 4:1. Albuquerque: University of New Mexico Press.

———. 1946. *Spanish Folk-Poetry in New Mexico.* Albuquerque: University of New Mexico Press.

Chávez, Alex J. 1973. "Recommended Sources for Commercially Available Discs and Field Tape Collections of Chicano Music." *Music Library Association Newsletter* 14(September–October):1–2.

———. 1995 [1965] *El Testamento.* Albuquerque Museum's Music of New Mexico Series, *Hispano Folk Music of the Past,* Cantante C95-1. Compact disc.

Dark and Light in Spanish New Mexico. 1995 [1978]. New World Records 80292–2. Compact disc.

Espinosa, Aurelio M. 1915. "Romancero nuevomejicano." *Revue Hispanique* 33:446–560.

———. 1985. *The Folklore of Spain in the American Southwest: Traditional Spanish Folk Literature in Northern New Mexico and Southern Colorado.* Ed. J. Manuel Espinosa. Norman: University of Oklahoma Press.

Espinosa, J. Manuel. 1985. "Aurelio M. Espinosa: New Mexico's Pioneer Folklorist." In *The Folklore of Spain in the American Southwest: Traditional Spanish Folk Literature in Northern New Mexico and Southern Colorado.* Ed. J. Manuel Espinosa, 1–64. Norman: University of Oklahoma Press.

Evans, Karen, with photos by Jack Parsons. 1985. "The Village Troubadours." *Impact* (*Albuquerque Journal Magazine*), 29 January, 4–10.

Harbert, Nancy. 1988. "Al Hurricane Takes the Spanish Music Scene by Storm." *New Mexico Magazine,* January, 26–31.

Heisley, Michael. 1985. "Lummis and Mexican-American Folklore." In *Charles F. Lummis: the Centennial Exhibition Commemorating His Tramp Across the Continent,* ed. Daniela P. Moneta, 60–67. Los Angeles: Southwest Museum.

Hispano Folk Music of the Past. 1998. Music of New Mexico Series, vol. 1. Albuquerque, N.M.: The Albuquerque Museum.

KANW FM Presents The Best of New Mexico Music, Vol. 1. 1993. KANW FM CD 1001.

KANW FM Presents The Best of New Mexico Music, Vol. 2. n.d. KANW FM CD 1002.

Lamadrid, Enrique. 1990. "*Las Entriegas*: Ceremonial Music and Cultural Resistance on the Upper Rio Grande. Research Notes and Catalog of the Cipriano Vigil Collection, 1985–1987." *New Mexico Historical Review* 65(1):1–19.

Lamadrid, Enrique R. 1996. *Tesoros del Espiritu. A Portrait in Sound of Hispanic New Mexico.* Jack Loeffler, producer, Miguel Gandart, photographer. Albuquerque, N.M.: Academia/El Norte Publications. Book and compact disc.

Loeffler, Jack. 1983. "*La Música de los Viejitos.*" *New Mexico* (June):45–46.

Loeffler, Jack, and Jack Parsons. 1983. *La Música de los Viejos.* Blue Sky Productions. Derry, N.H.: Chip Taylor Communications. Film.

Loeffler, Jack, with Katherine Loeffler and Enrique Lamadrid. 1999. *La Música de los Viejitos: Hispanic Folk Music of the Rio Grande del Norte.* Albuquerque: University of New Mexico Press.

Los Reyes de Albuquerque. *30 Años de Grabaciones.* 1995. MAS (Most Authentic Sound Recordings) CD MA-0827.

Lo Mejor de Lorenzo Martinez y Sus Violines. 1993. MORE (Minority Owned Record Enterprises) CD MO 0823.

Lo Mejor de los Reyes de Albuquerque. 1993. MORE (Minority Owned Record Enterprises) CD MO 0822.

Lucero-White, Lea. 1953. *Literary Folklore of the Southwest.* San Antonio: The Naylor Company.

Lummis, Charles F. 1952 [1893, 1928]. *The Land of Poco Tiempo.* New York: Charles Scribner's Sons. Albuquerque: University of New Mexico Press.

Martinez, Lorenzo. *Tocando y Cantando.* 1995. MAS (Most Authentic Sound Recordings) CD MA-0828.

Martínez, Lorenzo, with Los Reyes de Albuquerque. n.d. *El Redondo Largo.* MORE 8027. (Minority Owned Record Enterprises, 1205 Lester Dr., N. E. Albuquerque, NM 87112). LP disk.

Mendoza, Vicente T., and Virginia R. R. de Mendoza. 1986. *Estudio y Clasificación de la Música Tradicional Hispánica de Nuevo México.* Instituto de Investigaciones Estéticas, Estudios de Folklore 5. Mexico: Universidad Nacional Autónoma de Mexico.

Millenium "2000" Collectors Edition: KANW FM Presents the Best of New Mexico Music, Vol. 4. n.d. CD FM 2000.

Music of New Mexico. Hispanic Traditions. 1992. Smithsonian Folkways Recordings SF CD 40409. Compact disc.

A New Mexico Christmas: KANW FM Presents The Best of New Mexico Music, Vol. 3. n.d.

New Mexico Music 2000 (89.1 FM KANW's Gold Series). 2000. Atlantis Records CD ATL 2000.

New Mexico Spanish Superstars, Vols. 1–4. n.d. Alta Vista Enterprises.

New Mexico Spanish Superstars, Vol. 5. n.d. Alta Vista CD AV 6012.

New Mexico Spanish Superstars, Vol. 6. 1999. Alta Vista Music CD AV 9001.

Parédes, Americo. 1958. "The Mexican *Corrido*: Its Rise and Fall." In *Madstones and Twisters,* ed. Mody Boatright, Wilson M. Hudson, and Allen Maxwell, 91–105. Texas Folklore Society Publications 29. Dallas: Southern Methodist University Press.

Parsons, Jack. 1990. *Straight from the Heart: Portraits of Traditional Hispanic Musicians.* Albuquerque: University of New Mexico Press.

———, producer. 1993. *La Música de la Gente* (The Music of the People). Derry, N.H.: Chip Taylor Communications. Videocassette.

Robb, John D. 1952–1953. "The J. D. Robb Collection of Folk Music Recordings." *New Mexico Folklore Record* 7:6–20.

———. 1961 [1952]. *Spanish and Mexican Folk Music of New Mexico.* Ethnic Folkways Library FE 4426. LP disk.

———. 1980. *Hispanic Folk Music of New Mexico and the Southwest: A Self-Portrait of a People.* Norman: University of Oklahoma Press.

Spanish and Mexican Folk Music of New Mexico. 1952 (1961). Folkways Records and Service Corporation LP Ethnic Folkways Library FE 4426.

Spell, Lota M. 1927. "Music Teaching in New Mexico in the Seventeenth Century." *New Mexico Historical Review* 2(1):27–36.

Spiess, Lincoln Bunce. 1965. "Church Music in Seventeenth-Century New Mexico." *New Mexico Historical Review* 40(1):5–21.

Thomas, Anita Gonzales. 1978. "Traditional Folk Dances of New Mexico." In *The Music of the "Bailes" in New Mexico.* Comp. and ed. Richard B. Stark, 109–118. Santa Fe: Museum of New Mexico Press.

Vigil, Julián Josué. 1985a. "The Ballad of Manuel Maes." In *La Vegas Grandes on the Gallinas, 1835–1985.* Anselmo F. Arellano and Julián Josué Vigil, eds., 108–110. Las Vegas, NM: Editorial Telaraña.

———. 1985b. "Paula the Killer" 124–130. In *La Vegas Grandes on the Gallinas, 1835–1985.* Anselmo F. Arellano, and Julián Josué Vigil, eds., 108–110. Las Vegas, NM: Editorial Telaraña.

Tejano Music
José R. Reyna

The history of Spanish-speaking people in Texas begins in 1519, the year Alonso de Pineda, who had been sent by the Spanish governor of Jamaica to explore the coast from Florida to Mexico, claimed the territory in the name of Spain. A decade later, Alvar Núñez Cabeza de Vaca and several companions, shipwrecked on the site of present-day Galveston and enslaved by natives, traversed much of the territory that the Indians called *Tejas* during their nine years of captivity (1528–1536). But Spanish settlers did not come to the region until 1718, when a Spanish mission was established in San Antonio. The José de Escandón expedition, a more sizable group of settlers from the interior of Mexico, arrived in the Rio Grande region (north and south of the river) in 1749.

For three centuries, Texas was part of the Vice Royalty of New Spain (an area that included what today is Mexico). When Mexico gained its independence from Spain in 1821, Texas became part of the Republic of Mexico. That same year, wishing to populate and thus secure its sparsely settled northern frontier, Mexico encouraged immigration from other countries by offering newcomers generous land grants. During the 1820s thousands of immigrants from the United States and Europe came to Texas.

In the 1830s, Anglo immigrants, who by then were the majority of the population in Texas, began to foment revolution against the government of Mexico, declaring their independence from Mexico in 1835. Although the Anglo Texans suffered major defeats at Goliad and the Alamo, they defeated the Mexican army at San Jacinto in 1836, thus gaining their independence and becoming a separate nation—the Republic of Texas.

Continuing border hostilities between Anglo Texans and Mexicans led to the annexation of Texas by the United States in 1845 and to war between the United States and Mexico (1846–1848). By virtue of the treaty signed between Mexico and the United States at the conclusion of the war, Texas as well as most of the present-day American Southwest became part of the United States.

In short, in the nearly five hundred years since the arrival of the first Europeans, Texas has been under the flags of six different nations—Spain, France (a French settlement, Fort Saint Louis, was established on the Texas coast in 1685), Mexico, the Republic of Texas, the Confederate States of America, and the United States. From this came the popular phrase "six flags over Texas."

TEJANO CULTURE

Since the arrival of the first Spanish-speaking settlers, people have come to Texas from many other states as well as from many other parts of the world. Those people have brought with them ethnic cultures that, in turn, have taken on regional characteristics different from those of their homelands. They have also contributed to the emergence of a regional Tejano culture. Some of their ancestors came with the original settlers, while others arrived with later groups of colonists; all came "north from Mexico," as one historian noted. Throughout their history, various labels have been used in referring to these Americans of Mexican descent in Texas: Mexicans, Texas Mexicans, Latin Americans, Spanish Americans, Mexican Americans, Hispanics, and Latinos. The people themselves have preferred the Spanish terms *mexicano, tejano,* and *chicano,* each of which reflects their specific historical and cultural circumstances.

Because Texas became part of New Spain along with the rest of Mexico when the Spanish conquistador Hernán Cortés conquered the Aztecs in 1521, the label *mexicano* has been used in Texas for centuries. At the same time, Mexicans in Texas felt alienated from Mexico, in large part because the central government of Mexico had neglected its distant northern province. After Texas gained its independence from Mexico in 1845, the mexicanos in Texas began to see themselves more and more as Tejanos. Since the annexation of Texas by the United States in 1848, the differences between Mexicans in Mexico and Mexicans in the United States have become even more pronounced. Nonetheless, to this day Tejanos assert their claim to the label *mexicano,* although at some point they also began to make a distinction between *mexicanos* from Texas and *mexicanos* from Mexico by identifying themselves as *mexicanos de este lado* (Mexicans from this side of the Rio Grande) as opposed to *mexicanos del otro lado* (Mexicans from the other side of the Rio Grande).

The cultural identity of the Tejano has also been shaped by the historical conflict that has characterized relations between *mexicanos* and Texas Anglos, whom Tejanos still consider to be foreigners and interlopers. The use of nineteenth-century pejorative labels such as *americano, gringo,* and *gabacho,* all of which connote "foreigner" when referring to Anglo-Americans in general, is still common.

Perhaps the best example of a distinctly Tejano tradition born out of that clash of cultures is the *corrido* of border conflict. Although most of those folk lyric-epic ballads composed in Mexico dealt with the Mexican Revolution (1910–1930), in Texas the recurring theme was the longstanding conflict between Texas law enforcement officers—the Texas Rangers—and Tejanos. In their texts *corridos* also depicted the Tejano as a hero who, "with his pistol in his hand," always stood up to the "cowardly *Rinches de Tejas*" (Texas Rangers).

Other noteworthy examples of Tejano culture would be the Texas dialect of Mexican Spanish, which has contributed hundreds of Anglicisms to the Spanish language, and Texas-Mexican cuisine, without which Texas culture would be incomplete. But the best known expression of contemporary Tejano culture is Tejano music.

EARLY TEJANO MUSIC

Although there is little or no documentation of nineteenth-century folk music in Mexico, it is accurate to say that music tradition among Texas Mexicans was but one of many regional music traditions in Mexico until 1848. Since that time it has become a regional music of the United States, and it has been shaped and influenced by its contact with a wide range of music traditions and styles, not only from Mexico and the United States but also from other countries.

The emergence and evolution of Tejano music is best understood and appreciated in terms of its instrumentation and orchestration, that is, the instruments that constitute the various types of groups and the manner in which those instruments are played. Other aspects of the music, such as arranging, composition, songwriting, individual performers, particular groups, and dance tradition are important, to be sure, but these pertain more directly to features such as talent, style, differences between groups, economic considerations, and even more esoteric factors than to strictly musical features.

As recently as the 1920s there were various types of musical groups or combinations of instruments that came together, usually for *mexicano* dances and other public celebrations in South Texas. But based on observations from elderly informants who grew up around the turn of the twentieth century and on photographs of bands from the period, it may be said that those ensembles were essentially miscellaneous assortments of instruments, rather than set instrumental combinations. That is, their makeup seems to have been dependent largely upon availability of musicians and the instruments they happened to play, as is often the case in folk music.

The size and makeup of the early *banda típica,* as they were called, were also determined by other factors, such as the absence of electricity, microphones, electric instruments, amplifiers, and so on. Although these bands exist in various forms in Mexico today, they had disappeared completely from the music picture in South Texas by the 1930s. There were also other, smaller, combos that featured the violin (with guitar), clarinet, or piano, but these combo types also were evidently displaced by the *conjunto.*

Since the 1920s three different ensemble types have come to form the phenomenon known as Tejano music. Each has its own history and evolution yet shares many features with the others.

CONJUNTO

The first of the three genres to appear as an independent and identifiable type among Tejanos came to be called *conjunto.* In standard Spanish, the word *conjunto* means group. In most Spanish-speaking areas of the world it refers to any type of musical group or combo. But in Texas and northern Mexico the term has come to refer to a group in which the accordion plays the lead and the *bajo sexto* 'twelve-string guitar', acoustic bass, and drums play background and rhythm. This combination of instruments is one that evolved over a period of about a century. Furthermore, the Texas *conjunto* and the northern Mexican *conjunto* (called *conjunto norteño*) have had slightly different histories and characteristics.

The exact origins of *conjunto* music are impossible to determine because it is a folk music and, as such, was not notated; rather, it was and continues to be learned by ear. Perhaps more important is the fact that for many years both the *conjunto norteño* and Texas *conjunto* were considered to be unworthy of formal study or propagation as important cultural forms in their respective countries. In Mexico, for example, the *conjunto norteño* was eclipsed long ago by the mariachi and other regional forms considered to be more representative of Mexican national identity.

In Texas, *conjunto* music similarly had been a source of embarrassment to many Chicanos in the mid-twentieth century, especially to those in the emerging middle class eager to disassociate themselves from their Mexican roots and become Americanized. In recent decades, however, interest in all aspects of *conjunto* music has proliferated, and it has enjoyed a great resurgence in popularity among Chicanos as well as among non-Chicanos.

In general, this growing interest was due to the larger social, political, and cultural Chicano movement of the 1960s and 1970s, the period to which some scholars refer as the Chicano Renaissance. Thus, entrepreneurs in the Tejano music industry, for example, began to be more conscious of the role of cultural pride in promoting and marketing Tejano music in general and *conjunto* music in particular. For their part, the generation of Tejano scholars that emerged during the same period also initiated more formal, scholarly study of Tejano music. Joined by other ethnomusicologists, they have contributed a great deal toward our understanding about its origins and evolution from the nineteenth century to the present.

Origins of *conjunto* music

The beginnings of *conjunto* music can be traced to the arrival in South Texas and Northern Mexico of the accordion. Invented in 1829 by Cyrillys Damian in Vienna, the accordion probably arrived in Texas and Northern Mexico in the mid-nineteenth century. Evidently it was introduced by German immigrants who came to South Texas and Northern Mexico. They also brought the schottische, waltz, *redowa,* polka, and mazurka—all musical and dance forms historically identified with *conjunto* music. Whether *conjunto* music originated in Mexico and expanded into Texas or was created by Texas Mexicans and spread south into Mexico, however, remains a topic of interest. The most plausible *conjunto*-origin theory is that Germans and their music arrived in the Rio Grande Valley (on both sides of the river) in the mid-nineteenth century, after which different traditions emerged on either side of the border.

Texas *conjuntos*

In the late nineteenth and early twentieth century, Tejanos used a number of instrumental combinations, large and small. Perhaps the most popular type was the *banda típica,* which consisted of perhaps eight members, usually local musicians who came together to play for Saturday dances or special occasions such as weddings and *quinceañera* 'debutante' dances. Also, because electricity was not readily available for nighttime illumination, dances were usually afternoon affairs (called *tardeadas*). They were also usually held outdoors, often in wooded areas, where large dance floors (*plataformas*) were erected. Without inventions such as the microphone, electric instruments, and amplifiers, these relatively large "brass bands" were the most appropriate.

There also were smaller gatherings and venues that afforded opportunities for smaller combos. Although a violin and *bajo sexto* combo was popular until the early twentieth century, the accordion evidently replaced the violin and paired up with the *bajo sexto* to form the nucleus of the modern *conjunto.* Acoustics evidently played a part in the emergence of this combo as well. Of the various venues, it was no doubt the *cantina* 'honky-tonk', ubiquitous in both rural and urban areas, that afforded the accordion and *bajo sexto,* two relatively quiet instruments, the perfect opportunity to coalesce and thrive as a duo.

Completing the instrumentation of the modern *conjunto* were the trap set and the electric bass. The trap set, with its snare drum, bass drum, and cymbal, probably borrowed from the Tejano swing bands of the 1940s, was also added to *conjuntos* during that decade. The electric bass, invented in the 1950s, became the last of the instruments to be added permanently to the ensemble. Prior to the 1940s, accordion and *bajo sexto* duos on occasion would add the upright bass and a *tambora* (a locally made bass drum) to the ensemble.

The accordion in Texas

Although accordions with piano keyboards were invented soon after the button accordion, folk musicians in Texas (and Mexico) always have preferred the button model, particularly the Vienna- or German-style button-accordion. The earliest of these had a single row of ten treble buttons on the right side, on which only one scale could be played in three octaves, and two bass spoon keys on the left. In Texas *conjunto* music, accordionists do not use the bass keys. Instead, the bass line, played by the *bajo sexto* until the 1940s, is now played by the electric bass.

In the late 1920s, a larger, twenty-one-button double-row model, also manufactured in Germany, was incorporated into Texas Mexican and Northern Mexican *conjunto* music. That model was used until the introduction of the triple-row thirty-one-button model in the 1940s. Since the mid-1940s, the typical Texas *conjunto* accordion has been the Hohner Corona II model (figure 1), a triple-row, thirty-one-treble-button instrument, although the Italian-made Gabbanelli is also popular. Each button on

FIGURE 1   Hohner Corona II button-accordion. Standard instrument featured with Texas *conjuntos* since the 1930s. Thirty-one treble buttons on right side; twelve bass buttons on left. Tejano accordionists now play treble board only. Photo by Mary Cavazos-Reyna, February 2000.

In order to play in a wider variety of keys, professional accordionists must use more than one instrument, with additional keys included.

FIGURE 2   The Gabbanelli thirty-one-button accordion became popular with Texas and Mexican *conjunto* accordionists in the 1960s. Gabbanelli accordions have tonal switches that provide a greater range in tone quality. They are also very colorful and ornamental. Photo by Mary Cavazos-Reyna, February 2000.

FIGURE 3   The *Bajo Sexto* is a twelve-string Mexican guitar used for rhythm and chord accompaniment in Texas *conjunto* music. The bridge (often in the shape of longhorn steer horns) is much larger than on classical guitars. The instrument in this photo (with the thin A or fourth string removed) was handcrafted in Texas. Photo by Mary Cavazos-Reyna, February 2000.

these accordions plays two notes: one when the instrument is stretched, and another when it is compressed. Each row of buttons plays only one scale (in three octaves). A three-row instrument, for example, is built to play in three keys. Although accidentals in one key may be found on one of the other two rows, the fingering may be too awkward to reach them. In order to play in a wider variety of keys, professional accordionists must use more than one instrument, with additional keys included. Tonal variety may be achieved by using accordions such as the Gabbanelli (figure 2), which come equipped with tonal switches. Additional qualities may be added by changing the reeds in any given accordion, by using pickups, or by hooking the instrument up to electronic equipment.

As a lead instrument, the accordion is used not only for the melody line in instrumental pieces such as polkas, but also for introductions, background obbligato, and interludes or solos, especially as accompaniment to singing. Early recordings dating to the 1930s indicate that the typical accordionist of that era relied principally on a simple melody line, which resulted in a very lively sound in faster tempos. By the 1940s, even the average accordionist had mastered two- and three-line harmonies, which contributed to a fuller, more mature sound.

Although in recent decades large chromatic button-accordions have been used by a few accordionists (mentioned below), most Tejano accordionists have continued employing the double-row diatonic instrument. Innovation has consisted primarily of refinement of traditional introductions and passages and reflects greater mastery of the instrument. There are a number of riffs that are firmly established in the traditional accordion repertoire, that is, they are often "quoted" by modern accordionists and recognized by the public.

The bajo sexto

Since at least the early part of the twentieth century, the standard guitar used in *conjuntos* has been the *bajo sexto* (figure 3), a twelve-string Mexican guitar almost completely unknown to American musicians. The *bajo,* as it is commonly called, has steel strings and a deeper, more resonant sound than the classical guitar. It also differs from the American twelve-string guitar in the type and size of strings it requires, as well as in the way in which they are arranged and tuned. Unlike the American twelve-string guitar, which consists of six unison duplets (pairs) tuned like a six-string guitar (e′e′–BB–GG—DD—A_1A_1–E_1E_1), the *bajo* is tuned f′f′–CC–GG–Dd′–A_1a′–E_1e′; each of the three lower-register pairs on the *bajo* consists of a bass string with a treble string placed above it and tuned an octave higher. The string pairs are placed in the following manner: a third string over a sixth string; a second string over a fifth string; and a first string over a fourth string. The pairing of treble-over-bass produces a more resonant sound than the large strings can produce alone. Pickups used for amplification have enhanced the sound quality as well as technique.

For many years the function of the *bajo* was to provide both a bass line (with the three lower-register string sets) and strummed rhythmic chordal pulses (with the

FIGURE 4   The *Bajo Quinto,* a ten-string Mexican guitar also used in *conjunto* music, is a lighter instrument that has more higher-register strings than the *bajo sexto,* allowing for faster action. Photo by Mary Cavazos-Reyna, February 2000.

upper-register string sets). On waltzes, for instance, the bass would be played on beat one, and the chord accompaniment on beats two and three. On duple-metered pieces such as polkas it would be bass on one, chord on two. Since the introduction of the electric bass, however, *bajo* lower-register string sets (especially the fifth and sixth) have been rendered practically obsolete. Because the accordion is the lead instrument in *conjuntos,* the *bajo* is rarely foregrounded, although many consider the *bajo* to be the heart of the *conjunto.* Many *bajistas* 'bajo players' use a *bajo quinto* (figure 4), a ten-string *bajo* with five string pairs. It is tuned the same as the *bajo sexto,* without the sixth (lowest pitched) course of strings.

The bass

The function of the electric bass, as stated above, is strictly to provide the beat (on one in 2/4 or 3/4 time; on one and four in 6/8 time; and on one, three, and four in four-beat Latin rhythms such as that underlying the slow *bolero*). An interesting note is that there is no "walking bass" in Tejano music. In fact, the acoustic string bass, with which this style was once associated, is rarely included in contemporary Tejano groups.

The trap set

The drums, which consist of the same type of trap set used in Anglo-American dance bands, became an integral part of Texas *conjuntos* in the 1940s. The style of the drumming itself has evolved from those earlier days, when the bass drum would be pounded loudly on the downbeat, the snare drum struck on the offbeat, and the cymbal hit occasionally, to one in which the bass drum is used sparingly and muffled, and the snare drum and cymbal are tapped much more lightly.

Modernization of *conjunto*

In addition to the incorporation of modern accordions and the addition of the trap set and bass, there have been other important developments in Texas *conjunto* music since the 1950s that deserve attention. In the 1950s, for example, amplification of the *bajo,* bass, and accordion became standard. Another very important development during the 1940s and 1950s was the virtual disappearance of the schottische, *redowa,* waltz, and mazurka from the *conjunto* repertoire, although they had been identified with *conjunto* music in Texas for a century. Although *conjunto* accordionists continue to learn these forms as part of their apprenticeship, they are nearly extinct. In fact, even the polka, which continued as a staple in *conjunto* music into the 1960s, is rarely found in recordings from more recent decades, a sign perhaps of its impending demise. It is possible that this is due to the rhythmic similarity between the polka—a strictly instrumental form—and the two-beat *ranchera,* an extremely popular contemporary Mexican song genre. In fact, because of their similarity, people tend to confuse the two forms; recent album jackets, for example, often list *rancheras* as polkas. Thus although the popularity of the two-beat dance step remains strong, more two-beat *rancheras* are being composed than are polkas.

Perhaps the most noteworthy characteristic of *conjuntos* since the 1960s is that the musicians have attained a remarkable degree of proficiency, stylization, and prestige, all of which merit much more attention. While the degree of professionalism, as well as the impact of the recording industry and of broadcasting, reflects an increasing defolklorization of the *conjunto,* the standard ensemble described here is firmly established as a major genre of Tejano music tradition.

Pioneer *conjunto* musicians

Outstanding accordionists of the early era (the 1920s and 1930s) include Pedro Ayala (figure 5), Narciso Martínez (figure 6), Santiago "Flaco" Jiménez, and Bruno Villarreal. These pioneers, using the single-row and double-row accordion, not only mastered

FIGURE 5   Accordionist Pedro Ayala, known as *El Monarca del Acordeón* 'The Monarch of the Accordion', poses with Tejano bass player/guitarist Juan Viesca at the 1978 Smithsonian Folklife Festival in Washington, D.C. Photo by Daniel Sheehy, October 1978.

FIGURE 6   Pioneer *conjunto* accordionist Narciso Martínez (*center*) with bass player Juan Viesca (*right*) and partial view of unidentified *bajo sexto* player (*left*) at the 1986 Smithsonian Folklife Festival. Photo by Daniel Sheehy, July 1986.

🎵 TRACK 15

those instruments, they also learned the repertoire from the Germanic tradition and composed many tunes that became established in the South Texas *conjunto* repertoire. They also inspired several generations of accordionists. It is important to note that these musicians recorded with mainstream American labels (CBS International and Decca, for example) as early as the 1920s.

Notable *conjunto* groups

There have been countless groups since the 1940s, the best known of which are Los Alacranes de Angel Flores, Chano Cadena, Los Cuatitos Cantú, Tony de la Rosa, Los Doneños, David Lee Garza y Su Conjunto, Los Dos Gilbertos, Los Guadalupanos, Leonardo "Flaco" Jiménez, Santiago Jiménez Jr., Esteban Jordán (Steve Jordan), René Joslin, Valerio Longoria, Rubén Naranjo y Los Gamblers, Los Pavos Reales, Gilberto Pérez y Sus Compadres, Mingo Saldívar y Sus Tremendos Cuatro Espadas, Rubén Vela, and Agapito Zúñiga. The contribution of these groups, most of which were formed in the 1940s, is that they not only learned the traditions from their predecessors, that is, the old German repertoire and the compositions of the early Tejano accordionists, but that they also introduced an entirely new instrument (the triple-row button-accordion), established the definitive Texas *conjunto* style, and carried the entire tradition to its zenith in the 1960s. These groups made original contributions to the Tejano *conjunto* tradition that, as a whole, distinguish Texas *conjunto* style from that of *conjuntos norteños* (from Mexico) and that, in turn, led to greater variety in Tejano music in general. Some of the most important of these innovations are identified with several famous accordionists.

Tony de la Rosa

Tony de la Rosa, born in Sarita (though he has always been identified more closely with Kingsville), learned to play on a two-row button-accordion that he purchased through a Sears Roebuck catalog. Although his idol was Narciso Martínez, one of the pioneer *conjunto* accordionists, de la Rosa forever changed the *conjunto* by adding the drum set in the late 1940s. He is also credited with adding the bass and amplification to *conjunto* music. His impeccable musicianship includes a very distinctive deliberate staccato style.

Leonardo "Flaco" Jiménez

Leonardo "Flaco" Jiménez, son of pioneer accordionist Santiago Jiménez, began playing the button-accordion in the 1950s. By the 1980s, he had become the most widely recognized *conjunto* accordionist and the principal exponent of the genre. After being featured in the film *Chulas Fronteras* he went on to record as a sideman with many Anglo recording stars, including Ry Cooder, Emmy Lou Harris, Dwight Yoakam, Stephen Stills, and the Rolling Stones. In the 1990s he joined the Texas Tornadoes, an eclectic Texas *conjunto*. His style consists primarily of lively, rousing renditions of traditional *conjunto* tunes, although this style is not as evident when he performs with non-Tejano groups. His flashy wardrobe, which includes everything from bright-colored sequined to buckskin outfits, is indicative of the nontraditional commercial showmanship that he has brought to Texas *conjunto* music. He has won numerous awards, including five Grammys.

El Conjunto Bernal

El Conjunto Bernal was formed in Kingsville, Texas, in the 1950s. The most distinguishing characteristic of this *conjunto* was its use of the large Hohner Maestro IV chromatic accordion. Paulino Bernal, the accordionist, was the first and one of the few to use this type of instrument in Texas *conjunto* music. The chromatic accordion made it possible to play modern chord progressions, as well as much faster runs. This group also used three-part vocal harmonies in the style of Mexican *trios,* a very popular ensemble (typically consisting of two or three guitars and three voices) that originated in the 1940s.

An equally important contribution of El Conjunto Bernal to *conjunto* music is more sociological than musical. The leader, Paulino Bernal, was always conscious of the public image of *conjunto* music. In fact, his group always wore formal attire (tuxedo or suit). He has been credited with giving *conjunto* music respectability by taking *conjuntos* out of the *cantina* and into more respectable venues.

Bernal's use of the large chromatic accordion did not supplant the widespread use of the smaller Hohner Corona, but several outstanding accordionists have used it, including Oscar Hernández and Bobby Naranjo, both of whom Bernal mentored and both of whom mastered the instrument. At the height of his popularity, Bernal became a born-again Christian fundamentalist minister and changed to *conjunto*-style Christian music.

Esteban Jordán (Steve Jordan)

Esteban Jordán, one of fifteen children, was born into a family of migrant farmworkers and received no formal schooling, yet he proved to be perhaps the only true child prodigy of *conjunto* music. He not only mastered the accordion but also learned to play—also without formal instruction—more than thirty instruments. Most notably, after mastering the traditional style of *conjunto* accordion, Jordán expanded his tastes and repertoire to include jazz, blues, rock, and standard pop music, as well as the gamut of "Latin" music. As early as the 1960s, that is, long before *conjunto* music had been discovered by ethnomusicologists, Jordán began performing with his button-accordion at non-Latino, non-Tejano events. He has performed at the Monterey Jazz Festival, the Newport Jazz Festival, and the Berlin Jazz Festival.

With this background, a unique aspect of his music was the use of modern chord progressions and jazz riffs within traditional *conjunto* tunes. Unfortunately for Jordán, folklore is quite coercive, that is, it demands relatively strict adherence to tradition. Consequently, his style was considered to be too esoteric for the Tejano musical taste, and his genius went largely unappreciated. In the 1970s, however, he became quite popular with college audiences and folklife festivals, where his virtuosity could be displayed in a concert forum and could be truly appreciated. He also made a cameo appearance in the film *Born in East L.A.* But perhaps the greatest tribute to Jordán came in 1988 when the Hohner accordion company, which has been patronized by Chicano accordionists in Texas for more than a century, asked him to design a special

Although it can be argued that the bands were elitist and dropped the accordion and *bajo* because they were identified with low socioeconomic status, the bands in fact also abandoned the more prestigious Anglo (and Mexican) big band instrumentation.

instrument, the Steve Jordán Rockordion, in recognition of his mastery of the diatonic button-accordion.

EARLY TEJANO BANDS (*BANDA/ORQUESTA*): 1930s–1950s

Several social and musicological factors led to the emergence and formation of the *banda/orquesta,* the second major type of Tejano ensemble. These bands, which had their genesis in the 1930s and 1940s, were modeled after the Anglo-American swing bands of the Big Band Era (those of Glenn Miller, Benny Goodman, Tommy Dorsey, Jimmy Dorsey, and so on). These Chicano bands emerged as part of an international phenomenon in which big band music, spread through the increasingly influential media, was widely imitated. Also, by the 1930s and 1940s Chicanos were attending school in greater numbers, joining junior high and high school bands, and being imbued in Anglo American music tradition. Although public schools did not sponsor swing bands (called "stage bands" or "jazz bands") until the 1970s, the music training they provided beginning in the 1940s gave Chicanos the preparation they needed to organize their own bands. Consequently, Texas Mexican swing band instrumentation was virtually the same as that of the Anglo bands. Their repertoires also included the latest American popular tunes, as well as Mexican popular tunes, both of which were readily available in standard arrangements.

Bands popular in the region in the 1940s and 1950s include those of Ray Barrera, Mike Ornelas, Balde González, and Ralph Galván (all from Corpus Christi). These were the bands that the emerging Chicano middle class hired for major events such as weddings, *quinceañeras,* high school social club dances, school proms, and Christmas, New Year's Eve, Valentine's Day, and Easter dances. At that time, Tejano band musicians, perhaps because of their formal music training, enjoyed higher social status than did *conjunto* musicians and their music.

Nonetheless, the Tejano bands soon took on a decidedly Tejano flavor, in terms of instrumentation, style, and repertoire. Although this new sound was not typically Mexican or Latin (a generic label for Afro-Cuban–derived music), it was not typically Anglo either. Essentially, the sound consisted of a fusion of American big band instrumentation and Texas Mexican folk and popular tunes and rhythms. In the 1940s, the ascendancy of the Texas *conjunto* was closely associated with the popularity of the ubiquitous polka and *ranchera.* So popular was *conjunto* music that the bands of this early period would often employ an accordionist and *bajista* (if the guitarist did not play *bajo*) in order to meet the demand for *conjunto* music. In these musical borrowings were planted seeds from which the sound, which was to become known as the "Tejano sound," would grow.

Beto Villa

The first Tejano dance band to blend *conjunto* and band traditions, and the first whose popularity extended beyond Texas, was La Orquesta de Beto Villa from the town of Falfurrias. Although initially it played Mexican and American standards, it soon added arrangements of Mexican folk music to its repertoire. In these arrangements, a typical Beto Villa polka arrangement sounded much like a Lawrence Welk polka. More important for historical purposes, Beto Villa often included an accordionist and *bajista* within the big band.

TRANSITIONAL STAGES

Isidro López

Conjunto music, however, was too important to be relegated to permanent secondary status in Tejano music. Thus, an important transitional stage in the evolution of the Tejano bands came in the mid-1950s with the emergence and tremendous success of the Isidro López band, which illustrates unequivocally the ties between the *conjunto* and the band. Although "El Indio" (López) continued in the big band (Tejano-style) tradition of Beto Villa, he also introduced some changes that were clearly Chicano. For example, while the Beto Villa band still had essentially Anglo big-band instrumentation, the Isidro López band was much smaller by comparison, consisting of only two trumpets, two saxophones (alto and tenor), guitar, bass, drums, and piano. But López's most significant contribution was the actual incorporation of the button-accordion and *bajo sexto* within the *banda/orquesta,* clearly demonstrating the ties that existed between *conjunto* tradition and the modern big band and creating a sound that was entirely different from anything that had existed before in either Mexican or American traditions.

The first famous Chicano "crooner," López, an urban Chicano who grew up in Corpus Christi's La Cuarenta barrio, set another important precedent in Tejano band tradition. After his immense popularity and success, all big bands began to feature vocalists, while strictly instrumental arrangements especially of polkas and waltzes practically disappeared from their repertoire. Other bands from that era were those of Juan Colorado, Eugenio Gutiérrez, Chris Sandoval, and Johnny Herrera ("El Suspiro de Las Damas").

The stage represented by the Isidro López band was only a transitional stage in the evolution of Tejano band instrumentation. Once the ties between *conjunto* and band were firmly established, Tejano band tradition was ready to assume its contemporary "standard" form. In fact, that stage emerged even as Isidro López was still at the height of his popularity.

Oscar Martínez

The final stage in the evolution from Anglo big band instrumentation to the modern Tejano band was first reached by La Orquesta de Oscar Martínez. A trumpet player with the Isidro López band, Martínez formed his own group, using two trumpets, an alto sax, a tenor sax, guitar, bass, drums, and the piano (which was soon dropped). This instrumental combination became that of the standard Tejano band ensemble. At this point, the accordion and *bajo sexto* were excluded from the ensemble. Although it can be argued that the bands were elitist and dropped the accordion and *bajo* because they were identified with low socioeconomic status, the bands in fact also abandoned the more prestigious Anglo (and Mexican) big band instrumentation. Moreover, the *conjunto* repertoire and style were warmly embraced by the Tejano big bands. Also, Tejano big band arrangements continued to include parts for the button-accordion.

THE TEJANO BIG BAND ERA: 1960s–1990s

The new brassy sound of the 1960s brought a veritable proliferation of similar bands that attained even greater success not only in Texas but also throughout the Southwest and even in Mexico. And, after Isidro López, crooners became more important than instrumentation. The list of major Tejano bands dating to the 1960s includes Joe

Bravo, Johnny Canales, Sunny Ozuna and the Sunliners, Little Joe and the Latinaires (later La Familia), Freddie Martínez, Agustín Ramérez, Alfonso Ramos, Rubén Ramos, and the Royal Jesters.

Although the instrumental pattern for bands was firmly established by the 1960s, complete maturity was attained in the first half of the 1970s (two decades after the "golden age" of the *conjunto*). Since the late 1960s, the principal innovations in band music and differences among bands have been related to arranging, which is often quite complex, and to the degree of technical skill and professionalism of the musicians, many of whom have earned degrees in music and become music teachers throughout Texas. Only a very few have been willing to leave their Tejano roots to pursue careers in New York, Chicago, or California.

The most noteworthy feature of the Tejano big bands is their versatility. Being bicultural phenomena, they can simulate a very credible Latin sound, which Anglo bands can rarely accomplish. On the other hand, they can also sound like a typical Anglo band, which few if any Mexican bands can do. Thus, their repertoires include rock, jazz, Dixieland, *cumbias,* and salsa, in addition to the staples (Mexican/Tejano *rancheras,* polkas, and *boleros*). Indeed, variety was present as early as the 1950s, as the bands of that period also played everything from Tejano and Mexican to rock and roll and Country and Western.

There have been no substantive changes in Tejano band instrumentation since the 1970s. In their heyday, though, the many of the better known big bands spawned spin-offs. For example, Latin Breed was a spin-off of Sunny and the Sunliners; Jimmy Edwards was a spin-off of Latin Breed; Tortilla Factory was a spin-off of Little Joe y La Familia (formerly Little Joe and The Latinaires); and David Lee Márez was a spin-off of the Royal Jesters. All were major bands during the 1970s and 1980s. Other popular bands of the period include David Lee Garza y Los Musicales, La Connexión Mexicana, La Diferenzia, La Mafia, La Tropa F, Los Casinos, The Mexican Revolution, Ramiro "Ram" Herrera, and Tierra Tejana. This proliferation of bands certainly attests to the lasting quality of the Tejano band sound.

Although big band music is still enjoyed by the Chicano public in Texas, it has experienced a marked decline. One factor affecting the big bands is the resurgence of *conjunto* music that began in the late 1960s. *Conjuntos* are smaller and less expensive to hire than the bands. In many ways, the fate of the Tejano big bands is reminiscent of the way in which Anglo big bands were displaced by rock and roll and relegated to high school jazz programs and nostalgia events. Another factor was the emergence of a third Tejano genre, the *grupo.*

EL GRUPO

The *grupo* emerged in the 1960s, that is, after the *conjunto* had reached its peak and when the big bands were approaching their golden age. This new type of ensemble, which features synthesizers with all manner of keyboard effects rather than the accordion (as in *conjuntos*) or brass and saxes (as in big bands), did not assume the label *grupo,* however, until later.

The first such group to emerge in South Texas was Los Fabulosos Cuatro, formed in McAllen in 1964. The group has gone through many incarnations, featuring a number of singers over the years who have gone on to establish their own careers: Carlos Guzmán, Joe López, Ramiro de la Cruz ("Snowball"), Mel Villarreal ("Sonny Bono Jr."), Laura Canales, and Cha-Cha Jiménez. It also generated several spin-offs that were hugely popular: Snowball and Co., Laura Canales, Felicidad, Mazz, and Cha-Cha Jiménez y Los Chachos.

Initially, the principal goal of the early *grupos* was to distinguish their sound from *conjunto* music. There was, to be sure, the obvious influence of the *conjunto.* For instance, the earliest keyboard instrument was an organ that sounded like the accordion. *Grupos* also borrowed generously from the *conjunto* repertoire (*rancheras, boleros,* and polkas). They refused, however, to acknowledge their ties to the accordion, which they called a *congalera* 'slut' because of its association with the *cantina* and its low-class connotations. In reality, most Tejano keyboard musicians also double on the button-accordion, and, similarly, guitarists double on *bajo sexto.* With the growing pride in traditional Chicano culture in the 1970s, *conjunto* music came to be accepted by Tejano musicians in general, so that modern *grupos* as well as big bands sometimes include the accordion (but not the *bajo*) in their arrangements. Other extremely successful and established groups are Encanto, Fandango USA, Emilio Navaira, and Romance.

There are also groups that combine features from the three principal genres. For example, Roberto Pulido y Los Clásicos, in existence since the 1970s, combines the accordion with an alto and a tenor sax, and it never is referred to as a *banda, conjunto,* or *grupo.* Pulido's son, Roberto (Bobby) Pulido Jr., formed his own group in the 1990s using the same instrumentation and likewise does not fit in any of the three genres.

Selena

The most acclaimed *grupo* was Selena, named for Selena Quintanilla, who was born in Freeport in 1971 and died at the hands of an assassin in 1993. She began singing professionally at an early age and formed her first group, Selena y Los Dinos, with her sister Suzette at the age of eleven. By the age of sixteen, she had attained some recognition, and the group became known as Selena.

Although she grew up performing traditional Tejano music, she eventually became more closely identified with international Latin music, especially salsa. During her relatively brief professional career, she won numerous awards, including several Tejano Music Awards and a Grammy. She received greater national and international recognition and financial success than had any other Tejano musician before her. Her greatest ambition, successful crossover into mainstream English-language pop music, was attained posthumously.

THE TEJANO MUSIC INDUSTRY

A very important part of the success of Tejano music was the emergence, in the 1940s, of a very viable Tejano recording industry in south Texas. Major labels include Bego, Buena Suerte, Freddie, Gaviota, Hacienda, and Ideal. Radio also played an important part in the promotion of Tejano music, which for many years was overshadowed by Mexican music. In recognition of the importance of Tejano music in Texas Chicano culture, the Texas Talent Musicians' Association established the Tejano Music Awards in 1981, with an awards ceremony held every year at the Alamodrome in San Antonio. Performers are nominated in categories similar to those of the Grammy Awards, the Country Music Awards, and the People's Choice Awards.

Tejano music, influenced by nineteenth-century Mexican and European forms and later by the American swing bands, evolved into three distinctly Tejano genres—the *conjunto,* the *orquesta* or *banda,* and the *grupo. Conjunto* tradition, which features the accordion, *bajo sexto,* bass, and drums, developed over a period of approximately a century, reached maturity in the 1950s, and produced many outstanding groups. It also played an important part in the genesis, prominence, and form of the Tejano bands and *grupos* that followed. The *orquesta,* which was modeled after the Anglo swing bands of the 1940s and 1950s, gradually evolved into a distinctly Tejano big band. And, finally, in the 1960s there emerged the *grupo,* a keyboard-based hybrid ensemble with roots in both *conjunto* and *orquesta* instrumentation. All three genres remain popular.

REFERENCES

Burr, Ramiro. 1999. *The Billboard Guide to Tejano and Regional Mexican Music.* New York: Billboard Books.

¡Conjunto! Texas-Mexican Border Music. (1988) Vol. 1. Rounder Records ROUN6023. Compact disc.

———. (1988) Vol. 2. Rounder Records ROUN6024. Compact disc.

———. (1990) Vol. 3. Rounder Records ROUN6030. Compact disc.

———. (1990) Vol. 4. Rounder Records ROUN6034. Compact disc.

———. (1994) Vol. 5. Rounder Records ROUN6051. Compact disc.

———. (1994) Vol. 6. Rounder Records ROUN6052. Compact disc.

Peña, Manuel. 1985. *The Texas-Mexican Conjunto: History of a Working Class Music.* Austin: University of Texas Press.

Reyna, José. 1982. "Notes on Tejano Music." *Aztlán: International Journal of Chicano Studies Research. Thematic Issue: Mexican Folklore and Folk Art in the United States,* 13:1 and 2 (Spring and Fall). Chicano Studies Research Center, University of California, Los Angeles.

———. 1976. Tejano Music as an Expression of Cultural Nationalism. *Revista Chicano-Riqueña.* 4(3):37–41.

Taquachito Nights: Conjunto Music from South Texas. 1999. Produced by Cynthia Vidaurri and Pete Reiniger, in collaboration with the Narciso Martínez Cultural Arts Center. Smithsonian Folkways Recordings SFW CD 40477. Compact disc.

Texas–Mexican Border Music, vol. 1: *Una historia de la música de la frontera: An Introduction 1930–1960.* 1974. Folklyric Records 9003. LP disk.

Afro-Cuban Music

Steven Cornelius

Sacred Music
Secular Music
Looking toward the Future

Afro-Cuban music encompasses a highly syncretic body of material that has been evolving since the arrival of the first African slaves in Cuba in the sixteenth century. The music is a product, to varying degrees, of the assimilation and reintegration of rhythms, melodies, harmonies, and instruments from various African ethnic groups—ranging geographically from Bantu-speaking peoples of Angola to the Mandinga of Senegambia—with those of the European continent. In terms of Cuban musical heritage today, the most influential of these African peoples have been the Yoruba and the Congolese.

Afro-Cuban music has also had a long and multifaceted relationship with North America. Some styles, such as traditional street rumba and African-derived religious musics, which arrived in North America in the mid-twentieth century, have remained almost purely Afro-Cuban. In areas of popular music, however, the influence has been bilateral. Although the general flow of musical ideas has been northward from Cuba, beginning with the popularity in North America of the nineteenth-century Cuban *habanera,* Afro-Cuban popular music has also been strongly and variously influenced by ragtime, jazz, and other North American genres.

At the heart of Afro-Cuban music, and common to all the musical styles to be discussed here, is the adherence to a rhythmically based timeline (a continuously repeating rhythmic/metric motive) broadly referred to as *clave* (figure 1).

Indeed, *clave*—or variations on that principle, such as 6/8 bell, *tresillo, cinquillo,* or *baqueteo*—constitutes a fundamental building block of Afro-Cuban music. The word *clave* translates as clef, key, or keystone. It variously refers to sticks used to play rhythmic patterns, the patterns themselves, or the concepts underlying the performance of those patterns (Amira and Cornelius 1991:23). In short, *clave*'s structure, with its highlighting of on- and off-beat pulses, provides a grid or backdrop for rhythmic drive and melodic invention.

FIGURE I   Timeline played by the *clave.*

Within Santería, ritual music making—as expressed through song, drumming, and dancing—acts as a doorway through which the religion's deities (*orishas*) are praised and invoked through the phenomenon of possession trance.

SACRED MUSIC

African-derived sacred musics constitute the purest Afro-Cuban traditions currently being performed in North America. Although there has been considerable flow of musical ideas outward from these styles into secular genres, secular innovations have had virtually no impact on sacred styles.

Santería

By far the best known sacred music is that associated with the religious system variously known as Regla de Ocha, Lucumí, or, to nonpractitioners and most commonly, Santería. Within Santería, ritual music making—as expressed through song, drumming, and dancing—acts as a doorway through which the religion's deities (*orishas*) are praised and invoked through the phenomenon of possession trance.

As generally practiced, Santería is based on beliefs from the Yoruba people of West Africa. In many but certainly not all of Santería's temples, Yoruba religious concepts have been influenced by or even merged with those of Catholicism and occasionally Kardecian spiritualism.

Ceremonial music making can be divided into two distinct genres: *bembé* and the more formal *güemilere*. In addition to drums, the music ensemble may include shakers and bells. All participants are involved in responsorial singing. Dance is an essential part of any ceremony.

History

Although the earliest documentation of Santería in North America dates from the 1940s, the religion was practiced in relative obscurity until the waves of North American immigration prompted by the 1959 Cuban Revolution. It was also in 1959 that the first African Americans—who went to Matanzas, Cuba, for the ceremony—were initiated. The first stateside initiations probably took place in New York in the early 1960s.

Cuban musicians and the Santería initiates Julio Collazo and Francisco Aquabella, who came to the United States in 1957, are generally credited as catalysts for the development of North American ceremonial music making. Yet, although their activities attracted interest from musicians outside the religious culture, the two men taught the music to relatively few North Americans. Until the early 1980s, most North American musicians relied on secondary sources for their information.

Since 1981, the emigration from Cuba of important musicians such as Orlando "Puntilla" Rios and Lazaro Galarraga, the growth of public music and dance classes, and workshops based in Cuba have provided North Americans ample opportunities to work with master musicians.

By the 1990s, Latino and non-Latino musicians and practitioners could be found in virtually every major North American city. Today, the largest religious community resides in Miami, but there are extensive populations in New York, Los Angeles, and San Francisco as well.

Bembé

The most common North American ceremonial music style is *bembé* (also known as *drum and güiro*), which is itself a merging of two distinct Cuban genres: *bembé* and *iyesá*. In Cuba, *bembé* and *iyesá* have their own instrumentation and rhythmic foundation, but in North America, both rhythm genres are performed with the same instrumentation within a single ceremony. The ensemble consists of an iron bell or *guataca* (hoe blade), which provides a timeline; one to three gourds (known variously as *güiros* or *shekeres*), which provide rhythmic support; and one to three conga drums, which function as support or lead instruments.

Güemilere

Other ceremonies, called *güemilere, tambore,* or *toque,* use an ensemble of three double-headed *batá* drums. The most elevated ceremonies require the use of *fundamento* 'baptized' *batá* drums. Although in the 1960s there were perhaps no *fundamento batá* in North America, by 1998 there were as many as twelve such sets, a number of which were owned by North American drummers, in different cities throughout the United States (Mason 1992:15–16 identifies the history of some of those drums).

In both *bembés* and *güemileres,* the ritual is directed by a song leader (*akpwon*) who leads practitioners in call–response singing. The songs, which are in the *Lucumí* language (evidently a mixture of various Yoruba dialects), are designed to honor the *orishas.*

Palo Mayombe

Also known as Palomonte, or simply Palo, Palo Mayombe is a religious system of Congolese origin practiced by isolated groups in Miami, New York, Los Angeles, and perhaps other urban areas. Practitioners believe that through sacred vessels called *nganga* or *prenda,* they can control spirits of the dead. The North American musical ensemble that accompanies Palo Mayombe ceremonies consists of an iron bell and two to three drummers. Although the drumming itself is less complex than that associated with Santería, currently there are perhaps only a handful of singers in North America knowledgeable enough to lead a ceremony.

Arará and Abakuá

Arará, which shares many concepts with Santería and Haitian Vodou, is rooted in the beliefs of the Fon and Ewe peoples of the Dahomian area of West Africa. It is most strongly focused in the Matanzas and Havana provinces of Cuba.

The Abakuá (Abakwa) secret society is based on the culture and religious beliefs of peoples probably originally from the Calabar region of Nigeria. Nonpractitioners sometimes refer to Abakuá society members as *ñañigos.* It is not uncommon for members of the society, who are always male, to also belong to Santería and other religious groups.

Neither of these religions is practiced in North America, but the music is regularly heard in folkloric performances and has appeared on numerous recordings in the *salsa* genre. Abakuá in particular has had an impact on the development of rumba.

SECULAR MUSIC

Rumba

Rumba, which came to North America by the 1950s, is a noncommercial secular street dance and music style that emerged from the *cabildos* (mutual aid and religious societies) in lower-class black communities of late-nineteenth-century Cuba. Primarily a folkloric music today, rumba acts as a powerful social marker supporting traditional Afro-Cuban values and solidarity. Although some Cuban rumba ensembles—such as

FIGURE 2   The folkloric group Patakim, New York City, 1988. Standing, *left to right:* Greg Askew, Louis Bauzō, Frank Malabe, Reynaldo Rivera; Sitting, *left to right:* Lazaro Galarraga, Nydia Ocasio, Ray Romero, Reynaldo Alcantara.

Los Muñequitos de Matanzas and Los Papines—remain popular, North American rumba, except for folkloric performances, is mostly heard in informal settings within the Latino neighborhoods and parks of large metropolitan areas (figure 2).

While older rumba forms such as the *yuka* or *makuta* may be performed by folkloric ensembles, the most common styles are *yambú, columbia,* and, especially, *guaguanco.* Rumba is generally played on conga drums or, occasionally, wooden boxes called *cajones. Claves* give a timeline that is embellished by a denser rhythm called *cascara.* This rhythm is played with sticks *(palitos)* on a woodblock or bamboo tube *(gua-gua)* (figure 3).

Jazz

Although Cuban influence in New Orleans can be clearly traced back to the 1880s, when the *habanera* first became popular, Cuba's more subtle impact—as heard in *tresillo, cinquillo,* and *clave* patterns, which were embedded in rhythmic and melodic ideas—is much older. This should be expected, for New Orleans was Spanish con-

FIGURE 3   A characteristic rumba rhythm played by the *claves* and *palitos* 'sticks'.

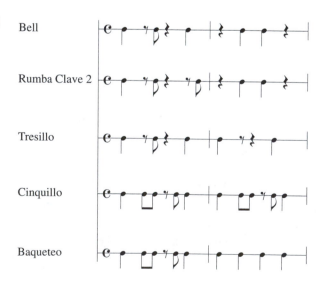

trolled for two generations before the Louisiana Purchase of 1803, and movement between the city and Cuba was commonplace. Ferdinand "Jelly Roll" Morton noted that a "Spanish tinge" was necessary for good jazz. W. C. Handy traveled with his band to Cuba in 1900, where he heard numerous street bands.

Specifically traceable Cuban elements in jazz, however, go back to Afro-Cuban flutist Alberto Socarras (who came to New York in 1927) and Machito and his Afro-Cubans. Machito's orchestra, which was formed in 1940, combined traditional Cuban elements with jazz. Its rhythm section in the early years was made up of piano, bass, bongo, and *timbale*, played by the young Tito Puente. In 1943, the same year that Mario Bauza wrote "Tanga," conga player Carlos Vidal joined the group.

Afro-Cuban jazz gained a much larger audience in 1946 when Dizzy Gillespie, who had worked alongside Bauza when both were members of the Cab Calloway Orchestra, began a brief collaboration with Cuban drummer, *rumbero,* and Arará initiate Chano Pozo.

Although Gillespie and Pozo worked together for just over two years before Pozo's untimely death, Pozo's introduction of the conga drum and the complex Afro-Cuban rhythms associated with it brought a new rhythmic energy to jazz and opened the door for the conga drum to be used in this and other non-Latin styles.

Also influenced by the Gillespie-Pozo collaboration and the Machito sound was Stan Kenton, the West Coast pianist-arranger and big band leader, who used some of Machito's percussionists in his 1948 recording of "The Peanut Vendor" and later went on to record Johnny Richards's 1956 work *Cuban Fire Suite* as well as other Latin-influenced arrangements.

Other contributors to Afro-Cuban jazz included Detroit native Les Baxter, who produced a number of LPs for Capitol in the 1940s and 1950s, and the London-born pianist George Shearing, who was strongly influenced by the 1948 Machito orchestra and went on to work with Cuban percussionists Willie Bobo, Armando Peraza, and Mongo Santamaría. Also influenced by Machito was vibist Cal Tjader, who worked with Shearing and eventually recorded some eighty LPs for various labels.

Mambo

The Cuban government's pressure during the 1930s and 1940s to keep African drums out of popular music often diluted the African presence in that country. In North America, it was commercialization and the desire to reach a mass audience that led to softened styles. This was particularly true in the late 1940s and 1950s when, based on Afro-Cuban roots, the mambo arrived. It was the first truly North American Latin development.

Probably invented in Cuba by blind percussionist and *tres* player Arsenio Rodriquez or bassist Israel "Cachao" Lopez, the early New York mambo was developed by New York bands led by Marcelino Guerra and José Curbelo (which included Tito Rodriguez, Tito Puente, and Carlos Vidal). In 1947, Tito Rodriguez and Puente left Curbelo to form their own ensembles. Along with Machito and his Afro-Cubans, they led the New York mambo style, which was centered in the Palladium Ballroom (1947–1966) but also popular at the Savoy Ballroom and Apollo Theater.

The individual most responsible for bringing mambo to a non-Latin audience was Perez Prado. Born in Matanzas, Cuba, in 1916, Prado worked mostly in Mexico and North America. His music, laced with North American pop sounds, was relatively accessible to non-Latin audiences; with a rhythm section powered at times by Mongo Santamaría and others, he enjoyed immense popularity from the late 1940s through the 1950s.

Other important bandleaders were Merced Gallego in San Francisco and, in New York, Alfredo Mendez (born Alfred Mendelsohn).

In its early development, salsa was strongly associated with the *barrio* district, working-class issues, the Afro-Cuban religions, and an emerging Latino militancy.

Charanga

The roots of the *charanga* go back to the nineteenth-century Cuban form *danzón* and the emergence from that ensemble of the *charanga francesa,* an ensemble made up of wooden flute, strings, double bass, *timbales,* and *güiro.* Although the strings are often replaced by brass, this general combination—with the addition of vocalist, piano, conga, and cowbell—remains a common instrumentation today.

Perhaps the first North American *charanga* was the short-lived Orquesta Gilberto Valdés, founded in New York in 1952. This ensemble was followed in 1956 by the Chicago-based Orquesta Nuevo Ritmo, founded by Cuban drummer Armando Sanchez and later directed by Mongo Santamaría. The year 1958 brought together the forces of pianist Charlie Palmieri and flutist Johnny Pacheco in the ensemble La Dubonney. Although drummer Ray Barretto's *charanga* enjoyed considerable crossover success with hits like "El Watusi," the 1960s and 1970s belonged to Orquesta Broadway.

Salsa

Salsa (literally, sauce) is a broad term that generally refers to contemporary popular Latin dance music. Salsa's sound not only encompasses a variety of Cuban styles such as *son,* mambo, and chachachá, but also incorporates ideas from Puerto Rico, the Dominican Republic, and to a lesser extent the rest of the Caribbean, Brazil, and black North American popular music.

Instrumentation reflects this mix. The typical salsa rhythm section consists of piano, bass, congas, bongos, *timbales, güiro,* maracas, and *claves.* The drum set, however, is often used as well. Added to the rhythm section may be any variety of horn arrangements made up of combinations of trumpets, trombones, and saxophones. Finally, the ensemble may also employ flute, violins, electric guitar, and synthesizers.

Perhaps the first use of the term salsa in a musical sense goes back to Cuban composer Ignacio Piñeiro's 1933 song "Echale Salsita" (Salazar 1991b:9). Joe Cuba's recording of Jimmy Sabater's "Salsa y Bembé" (1962), Charlie Palmieri's recording of Victor Velasquez's "Salsa Na Ma" (1963), and Cal Tjader's "Soul Sauce" were other early examples. The term *salsa* did not come into common usage until the early 1970s, when it appeared in *Latin New York* magazine and was adopted as a category for the 1975 Latin New York Music Awards.

From the mid-1970s into the early 1990s, the North American center for salsa was New York City. There, commercially empowered by the marketing of Jerry Masucci and Johnny Pacheco, who founded Fania Records in 1964, salsa became the center of popular Latin music making.

In its early development, salsa was strongly associated with the *barrio* district, working-class issues, the Afro-Cuban religions, and an emerging Latino militancy. The music and lyrics were tough, provocative, and closely aligned to Afro-Cuban culture.

Since the late 1980s, commercial considerations, in addition to the increasing Dominican presence in New York City, added a new sensibility to the music. In the 1990s, the most commercially popular Latin music—led by Eddie Santiago, Louis

Enrique, Willy Chirino, Jerry Rivera, and others—had a softer feel and was often termed *salsa romantica.*

Many musicians—including vocalist Celia Cruz, Tito Puente, Eddie Palmieri, Ray Barretto, and Israel "Cachao" Lopez, who made their mark in earlier periods—continued to be important leaders in the salsa genre. Leading musicians who came of age in the salsa era include Louis Ramírez, Rubén Blades, Willie Colon, Hector Lavoe, Gloria Estefan, and Sheila Escovedo. Since the Mariel exodus from Cuba in 1981, the genre has received creative infusions from percussionist Daniel Ponce, drummer Ignacio Berroa, saxophonist Paquito D'Rivera, and trumpet player Arturo Sandoval.

LOOKING TOWARD THE FUTURE

As the history related here suggests, Afro-Cuban music in North America continues to become more diffuse in terms of both the styles represented and the ethnic backgrounds of the musicians and audiences. While non-Cuban Latinos have long had influence on Afro-Cuban music, there is an ever-increasing involvement from non-Latinos as well.

Although sorting out that which is clearly Afro-Cuban from that which is simply African is somewhat problematic, it is important to recognize that the 1950s and 1960s *clave*-based rhythms and melodies of Delta and New Orleans–based musicians such as Bo Diddley, Antoine "Fats" Domino, and Roy "Professor Longhair" Byrd continue to influence rock and blues musicians. So, too, Carlos Santana's Afro-Cuban-derived Latin rock music remains important.

Meanwhile, a younger generation of musician-scholars, such as the New York–based percussionist Bobby Sanabria, or, on the West Coast, percussionists John Santos and Michael Spiro or pianist Rebecca Mauleón, is developing new levels of fusion among diverse Cuban styles while simultaneously informing their more traditional work with a high level of historical accuracy.

REFERENCES

Acosta, Leonardo. 1991. "The Rumba, the Guaguancó, and Tío Tom." In *Essays on Cuban Music: North American and Cuban Perspectives,* ed. Peter Manuel, 51–73. Lanham, Md.: University Press of America.

Amira, John, and Steven Cornelius. 1991. *The Music of Santería: Traditional Rhythms for the Batá Drums.* Tempe, Ariz.: White Cliffs Media, Inc.

Blum, Joseph. 1978. "Problems of Salsa Research." *Ethnomusicology* 22(1):137–149.

Boggs, Vernon, ed. 1992. *Salsiology: Afro-Cuban Music and the Evolution of Salsa in New York City.* New York: Greenwood Press.

Cornelius, Steven. 1991. "Drumming for the Orishas: Reconstruction of Tradition in New York City." In *Essays on Cuban Music: North American and Cuban Perspectives,* ed. Peter Manuel, 139–155. Lanham, Md.: University Press of America.

Manuel, Peter, ed. 1991. *Essays on Cuban Music: North American and Cuban Perspectives.* Lanham, Md.: University Press of America.

Mason, John. 1992. *Orin Orisa: Songs for Selected Heads.* New York: Yoruba Theological Archministry.

Mauleón, Rebeca. 1993. *Salsa: Guidebook for Piano and Ensemble.* Petaluma, Calif.: Sher Music Co.

Murphy, John. 1991. "The Charanga in New York and the Persistence of the Típico Style." In *Essays on Cuban Music: North American and Cuban Perspectives,* ed. Peter Manuel, 117–135. Lanham, Md.: University Press of America.

Roberts, John Storm. 1979. *The Latin Tinge: The Impact of Latin American Music on the United States.* New York: Oxford University Press.

Salazar, Max. 1991a. "Machito, Mario and Graciela: Destined for Greatness." *Latin Beat* 1(6): 25–29.

———. 1991b. "Salsa Origins." *Latin Beat* 1(10): 9–11.

———. 1992. "Who Invented the Mambo?" *Latin Beat* 2(9):9–12.

Latin Caribbean Music
Steven Loza

The Influence of Afro-Cuban Music
The Influence of Puerto Rican Music
The Dominican *Merengue*

Popular and traditional musics from the Spanish-speaking Caribbean have had a strong influence on American culture since the latter part of the nineteenth century. Musicians were very important to new immigrant communities, especially those of Cubans, Puerto Ricans, and Dominicans who traveled to the United States during the twentieth century and settled in various urban centers such as New York City, Miami, San Francisco, Chicago, and Los Angeles. Cuban music, especially, has made a profound impact in the United States.

In his landmark book *The Latin Tinge: The Impact of Latin American Music on the United States,* John Storm Roberts cites Cuba, along with Brazil, Argentina, and Mexico, as the principal exporters of musical influence to the United States (1979:3). New York City, where Cubans, Puerto Ricans, and Dominicans jointly began to create new musical traditions and popular markets for Cuban dance music, has become since the 1920s the most dynamic center of such activity in the country. Salsa, a label applied in New York to music of Afro-Cuban origin, has become the dominant form of Caribbean-influenced music in the United States. Puerto Rican and Dominican genres of music have also been highly influential.

Although a substantial amount of literature, especially from Cuba, addresses Caribbean musical development in the United States, the study of its more general influence there is more recent. While Roberts's book has emerged as a basic source, more detailed and theoretical studies in the United States have been undertaken by Roberta Singer (1982, 1983), Marina Roseman (1983), Steven Loza (1979), Danilo Lozano (1990), Robert Friedman (1978), Peter Manuel (1990, 1995), Steven Cornelius (1989), and Robbins (1990).

THE INFLUENCE OF AFRO-CUBAN MUSIC

Contemporary Afro-Cuban music has not only retained a profound and significant portion of its African tradition but has also strongly influenced music internationally, especially within the Americas. The *habanera, contradanza, danzón, son,* rumba, *charanga,* mambo, and *cha-cha-chá* all emanated from Cuba, spreading throughout other countries of Latin America and the Latin quarters of the United States. Cuban rhythms infused other Latin American rhythms in a fluid process of assimilation; in the United States, however, the mixture has created extensively hybrid forms.

Most Latin American musical forms cannot be identified or categorized according to one particular musical characteristic, as they usually incorporate a rhythm, a dance, a style or styles of playing, typical tempi, or even subject matter (Roberts 1979:5). Moreover, the precise origins and development of these forms cannot always be determined accurately, as they are hybrid manifestations that have changed frequently through time.

The *habanera*

The *habanera* was the first Cuban style to strongly influence music in the United States and was probably the most influential style throughout the Americas. Besides directly affecting jazz, it was the root of the Argentinian tango and fed Mexican styles that were to travel north. Calling the *habanera* "perhaps the most universal of our musical genres," Cuban musicologist Emilio Grenet cites the work "La Paloma" as an example of its influence (Roberts 1979:5). Written in the 1940s by a Spaniard stationed in Havana, Sebastián Yradier, it possibly came to the United States via Mexico, with which it is identified strongly. Grenet also remarks upon the resemblance of Bizet's *habanera* in the opera *Carmen* to a Spanish tango (Roberts 1979:5).

In the early nineteenth century, the *contradanza* preceded the popularity of the *habanera*. According to many sources, the *contradanza* was brought to the United States by French refugees fleeing the Haitian revolution. The dance was also influenced by certain African forms. In Cuba it developed two closely related time signatures, 6/8 and 2/4, both of which influenced the later dance form. "It was presumably black musicians who began to syncopate the *contradanza*'s rhythm. A so-called *ritmo de tango,* extremely similar to the Argentinian tango, became a feature of Cuban contradanzas, and spread into many other local forms" (Roberts 1979:5). In addition to the *merengue* of Haiti and the Dominican Republic, the *cinquillo,* a five-beat throb cast in duple meter, also became a feature of Cuban *contradanzas,* most likely via the French *contradanse.* Both the *ritmo de tango* and the *cinquillo* became fundamental to the *contradanza habanera* by the early nineteenth century. Black musicians further syncopated the *ritmo de tango,* Africanizing this widespread European dance. Though not purely a Havana style as implied by its name, and never referred to as such by its creators, the *habanera* was easily absorbed into American music largely because its rhythmic pattern was contained in a single measure of common 4/4 meter, and it was frequently incorporated into the bass line of piano compositions. The earliest known piano version of the *habanera* was "La Pimienta," written in 1836.

The *son*

The Cuban style that most influenced music in the United States was the *son,* which was the basis of the rumba's popularity during the 1930s. The *son* used Afro-Cuban rhythms such as the "anticipated bass," in which the bass line precedes the downbeat of a measure by one-half beat, and the *ritmo de tango.* In Cuba, *son* does not refer to a specific, formal musical structure. Rather, it describes a particular sound and instrumentation, characterized by a certain feeling. It originally emerged from the black population in the rural districts of Cuba as a vehicle for entertainment at informal gatherings. In the early 1900s it migrated to urban centers, eventually molding the entire phenomenon of Cuban popular music.

Although the *son* form was firmly based on African concepts, *son* guitar playing displayed a strong Spanish tradition. Most original *sones* incorporated the African tradition of call–response vocals accompanied by complex rhythmic patterns played on the drums. During both its rural and urban development in Cuba, the *son* acquired distinctive musical and dance characteristics. Odilio Urfé (1973) remarks that the Cuban *son* also contributed to the integration of various instrumental groups such as the *orquestas típicas* that had existed from 1800 to 1930 and the *charanga* groups of

Leopoldo Cervantes and Antonio María Romeu (1876–1955). Collective interpretation by instrumental ensembles, then, began to mold a most distinctive Cuban sound. Urfé comments on the social force of the *son* in dogmatic fashion:

> Because of its extraction, development, sonorous and choreographic character, and social use, the Cuban *son* evolved historically as the most ideal and representative means of expression for the humble classes of the social-economic-political structure of post–World War I Cuba, and which in the production of the Sexteto Habanero, Miguel Matamoros (1893–1971), Bienvenido J. Gutiérrez (1904–1966), and Ignacio Piñeiro achieved great works; and having as its most vibrant, lyrical voice, the undisputed, unforgettable, and immortal Benny Moré (1920–1963). (1973:199, author's translation)

An important element that typified the transition of *son* from the rural to urban contexts was the emergence of the *guajira* as a popular form. The word *guajira* 'country girl' refers to the music of the Cuban countryside. *Guajira*'s structure, text, and melodic–harmonic elements derive primarily from Spanish musical tradition; rhythmically, however, there is a definite African influence. Through the *guajira*, *trovadores* 'wandering musicians' sang nostalgically of their country life, accompanying themselves on the *tres* 'a six-stringed, three-course guitar type.' In the cities, melody and texts of the *guajira* were adapted to the *son* instrumentation, adding the *guajeo* which played "interlocking melodic and rhythmic ostinato patterns based on the clave patterns" (Friedman 1978:2). The role of the *clave* in the performance of *son* parallels the West African practice of providing a steady rhythmic pattern in instrumental ensembles. The bongos, a drum pair from which different pitches and percussive qualities may be produced, however, provide the principal means for varying the pitch and timbre of the rhythmic pulses within this pattern.

The development of *son* is characterized by three recognizable stages, each typified by a separate musical group, or *conjunto* 'ensemble': the Sexteto Habanero, the Septeto Nacional, and the *conjuntos* of Arsenio Rodríguez (1911–1972). Although the *son conjuntos* had existed and were performing in Cuban cities prior to 1918, it was the Sexteto Habanero that created and became identified with the typical *son* sound. Here, the *son* was standardized by three voices, bass, guitar, and trumpet added to the traditional *conjunto* instrumentation. The use of bongos, *claves* 'sticks', maracas, and *tres* remained while the original *laud* 'round-backed plucked lute' was deleted. Puerto Rican musicians played an essential role in spreading the form and in the broader influence of the *son* when they adopted the *septeto* 'seven instrument' style as performed by the Septeto Nacional and other *son* groups in Cuba. Both the Cubans and Puerto Ricans who migrated to the United States sustained and intensified the popularity of the *son*, especially in New York. The *tres* reached its height of importance during the late 1930s—the era of Arsenio Rodríguez.

Arsenio Rodríguez

Arsenio Rodríguez expanded the *son* sound by returning to the African-derived elements found in the rural performances of *son* that had been simplified or omitted in the music of both the Sexteto Habanero and the Septeto Nacional. Simultaneously, however, Rodríguez continued the trends of Europeanization that the two groups had initiated. Achieving a synthesis of African and European influences, Rodríguez maintained the integrity and artistic quality of both traditions. Instrumentally, he added a *campana* 'bell', a conga drum, a second trumpet, and a piano to the *son conjunto*. The contemporary *conjunto* instrumentation, similar to that of salsa, thus took its initial form. Rodríguez also emphasized the *guajeo* and incorporated the *tumbao*, an ostinato pattern resulting from interlocking rhythms played by the bass and conga. Additionally, he structured the horn

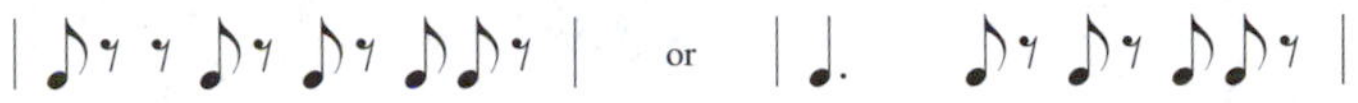

FIGURE I   Traditional *clave* pattern found in *son conjunto*.

arrangements and musical breaks around the *clave* pattern and integrated the rhythm section of bongos, congas, bass, *campana, tres,* and piano in such a way as to create a melodic–rhythmic unity also revolving around the *clave* (figure 1). Rodríguez expanded the accompanying function of the *tres* to that of a solo instrument and re-emphasized the role of the *estribillo* 'refrain.' More important, he introduced a solo section referred to as *montuno*, in which the *tres*, piano, and trumpet players demonstrated their improvisatory skills. Dynamically, the range and energy of Rodríguez's *conjuntos* grew extensively, remolding, yet preserving, the traditional *son* form.

One of Rodríguez's major innovative contributions was his incorporation of the mambo, which had been introduced by Israel "Cachao" López (b. 1918) and his brother Orestes López into the dance halls of Cuba by the late 1930s. Using *son conjunto* instrumentation and the mambo, the compositions of Arsenio Rodríguez greatly influenced the Latin popular music of New York, which eventually produced many great salsa musicians, such as Machito, Tito Puente, and Tito Rodríguez (1923–1973), all of whom incorporated mambo into their big bands. As late as the 1960s many of Rodríguez's compositions were reinterpreted by salsa musicians.

The *son* has retained its strong tradition and vigor since its emergence in Cuba in the early part of the twentieth century. It has been an important vehicle for a constantly evolving landscape of Cuban musical forms including the bolero, the conga, the rumba, and ultimately the mambo, as exemplified in the music of Arsenio Rodríguez. Since the emergence of the *son* in Cuba, unique use of anticipation in its rhythmic structure has both distinguished it as a separate musical genre and anchored it in a deeply rooted Afro-Cuban rhythmic tradition. It has come to be a symbolic expression of Cuban musical, poetic, and social innovation.

Stylists and innovators of Afro-Cuban dance music

Since the late 1930s specific musicians and bandleaders have played a central role in the development of Afro-Cuban dance music in the United States through various cycles of style and innovation. These musicians largely developed their music and catered to audiences in the highly popular Palladium Dance Hall in New York City during its height of popularity in the 1950s. Many of these artists also achieved international acclaim, made highly successful recordings, and received numerous prestigious awards ranging from Grammys to governmental honors.

Machito

Machito (1908–1984), whose real name was Frank Grillo, was perhaps the principal pioneer of the New York Latin music movement. He emigrated from his native Cuba to New York in 1937, and by 1940 had organized his own orchestra, Machito and his AfroCubans. Machito fronted the orchestra and performed as the lead vocalist. The musical arrangements of Mario Bauzá, a saxophonist-trumpeter originally from Cuba, were crucial to the development of this big band–styled ensemble.

One of the principal innovations of the Machito orchestra was its blending of Afro-Cuban dance forms such as rumba, *guaracha,* and mambo with the musical qualities of the big band jazz and bebop movements so active in New York City at this time. Heavily exposed to the music of Duke Ellington, Count Basie, Chick Webb, Charlie Parker, and Dizzy Gillespie in the Harlem district of Manhattan where they lived, Machito and Bauzá spearheaded the convergence of American and Latin musical styles, specifically those that eventually evolved into both contemporary salsa and Latin jazz.

The 1950s became the heyday of Latin dance music at the Palladium, and Rodríguez, Machito, Tito Puente, and Miguelito Valdez became institutions of the new musical movement.

Important vocalists

Vocalists were among the major stylists of Afro-Cuban dance music in the United States, especially in the growing Latin community of New York. Three of the most influential (besides Machito) have been Miguelito Valdez, Tito Rodríguez, and Celia Cruz.

Miguelito Valdez, a *sonero* 'singer of *son*' who performed in the style of the much emulated vocalist Benny Moré, a contemporary from Cuba, became a major influence among audiences in the United States by the early 1940s. Based in New York, Valdez sang with Machito's orchestra and by 1947 had formed his own band. He also enjoyed substantial success in Hollywood movies, which during the period of his popularity included many films incorporating popular Latin styles such as rumba and mambo.

Tito Rodríguez, one of the first of many Puerto Ricans to achieve major status in Latin music in New York, represents one of the most important periods of the famous Palladium Dance Hall era and the international popularization of Latin dance music. After singing with the orchestra of Xavier Cugat, Rodríguez developed his own big band and by 1949 had achieved major success. The 1950s became the heyday of Latin dance music at the Palladium, and Rodríguez, Machito, Tito Puente, and Miguelito Valdez became institutions of the new musical movement.

In 1959, Celia Cruz emigrated from her native Cuba to Mexico, where she remained until 1961 with the Cuban *conjunto* Sonora Matancera, an ensemble that had highly popularized Cuban dance music throughout the Americas. Ultimately Celia Cruz would establish herself as the most popular vocalist in the era of the development of salsa in the 1960s through the early 1990s, a tenure of unparalleled success among singers of the style. Cruz continued to record not only with Sonora Matancera but with bandleaders Tito Puente, Johnny Pacheco, Ray Barretto, and Willie Colón, among many others. She was awarded a National Medal of Arts by President Clinton in 1994.

Tito Puente

In the estimation of many experts the artist who became the major stylist and innovator following the early career of Machito was bandleader Tito Puente (1923–2000). Of Puerto Rican heritage and a virtuoso musician on *timbales* 'single-headed drum' and vibraphone, Puente began his dynamic career in his native New York performing by the early 1940s with various artists including his principal mentor, Machito. After serving in the navy during World War II, Puente returned to New York, and played with the Picadilly Boys, a group that never recorded. It was during this period that Puente first brought the percussion section of his orchestra to the front of the bandstand, an innovation that became a permanent standard for Latin dance bands into the 1990s. In 1948 Puente formed his own band, the Mambo Boys, and in 1949 recorded one of his early hits, "Abanico." During the 1950s Puente's band became internationally associated with the mambo and cha-cha eras with arrangements of tunes such as "Ran-Kan-Kan" and "Pa' los Rumberos."

With the advent of the 1960s and the beginning of the salsa era, Puente continued as one of the principal stylists of Latin music, becoming popularized as El Rey del Tim-bal 'The King of the *Timbales*'. Original tunes such as "¿Qué será mi china?" and "¿Oye cómo va?," the latter recorded by Carlos Santana in 1970, became standard arrangements in the Latin music repertoire. By 1991, Puente had received four Grammy Awards from the National Association of Recording Arts and Sciences. In 1997 he was awarded the National Medal of Arts by President Clinton.

Eddie Palmieri

Another bandleader of Puerto Rican background who merits attention among the many contemporary artists of Latin music based in New York is Eddie Palmieri (b. 1936). Although he was highly active prior to the 1970s, it was during that decade that Palmieri made a great impact on the salsa scene, emerging as an innovative pianist-arranger-composer who dynamically experimented with the blending of progressive Latin Caribbean forms and contemporary jazz shadings. Palmieri's piano style, for example, often reflected that of the then highly influential McCoy Tyner, associated primarily with the progressive jazz styles of the period.

Roberts (1979) observes that the dominant impact of twentieth-century Cuban music, which has been extensive in the United States, has come primarily from popular composers such as Moisés Simons, composer of "El Manicero" ("The Peanut Vendor") and from composers who incorporated both classical and popular elements. Of the latter, one of the most important was Ernesto Lecuona (1895–1963), who organized the Havana Orchestra and composed cantatas, operettas, and musical comedies. He was also appointed as Cuba's honorary attaché to the United States in 1943. In the 1930s, he had directed a rumba band, the Lecuona Cuban Boys, which recorded for Columbia. His profound influence is illustrated in numerous compositions of international acclaim, including "Siboney," "Maria La O," "Para Vigo me Voy," and the more complex, semiclassical immortals "Malagueña" and "Andalucía."

Other important dance forms

The *guaracha* and the bolero are also important Cuban forms that have gained immense popularity in the United States. The *guaracha* symbolizes a Cuban style of syncretism that has gained wide recognition. A mimetic dance form, it incorporates the Spanish and African vocal practice of solo verses and regular chorus refrains. The bolero, a slower rhythmic dance form that is an outgrowth of the *habanera,* became a standard genre throughout Latin America, especially in Mexico.

The popular *danzón* of the early 1870s, a descendant of the *contradanza* and thus indirectly related to the *habanera,* was until around 1916 played outdoors by *orquestas típicas,* bands characterized by a cornet sound supported by clarinet, trombone, and percussion, especially tympani. In the dance salons, the same *danzones* were performed by ensembles called *charangas francesas* 'French orchestras', eventually referred to simply as *charangas.* These ensembles used a fast-flowing flute lead accompanied by violins; the smaller *timbales* replaced the tympani.

By the 1930s, *charangas* far outnumbered *orquestas típicas* in Cuba. Initially the *charangas* did not represent the African tradition as did the *sones* of the aforementioned *septetos* but nevertheless played an essential role in providing a basis for the *danzón* mambo mix created by the influence of the *son conjuntos* of the late 1930s.

The *son conjuntos* differed from the *charanga* in instrumentation, a stronger African voice technique, and heavier use of percussion. As previously noted, the major innovator of the *son conjunto* style was the Cuban bandleader Arsenio Rodríguez. Rodríguez, who lived the latter part of his life in the United States (1950–1970), was an integral influence on the New York bandleaders of the *típico* revival of the 1960s, his compositions becoming a part of salsa groups' repertoire.

Eventually, the *charangas* adapted to the Africanization of Cuban music, influenced by the *son conjunto* sound. The *charanga* group Arcaño y sus Maravillas became one of the first groups to make this conversion, mostly due to the arrangements of bassist Israel "Cachao" López. He introduced several mambo elements into the *danzones* he composed for Arcaño (his brother Isidro López, the flutist-leader of the group), and is credited by some as being the actual originator of the dance hall *mambo*. The *charanga* as popularized by Arcaño y sus Maravillas would become the origin of the *cha-cha-chá* in the 1950s, furthering the evolution of the original *danzón*. The *charanga francesa* style of flute and violins can be heard in the recordings of Orquesta Aragón as it popularized the *cha-cha-chá*. During the late 1950s, Charlie Palmieri (1926–1988), an influential Puerto Rican musician born in New York, led a group that played many compositions by Orquesta Aragón, adapted to feature a trumpet as lead instrument. In late 1959 Palmieri hired Johnny Pacheco (b. 1935) to play flute and percussion in his Charanga Duboney. Pacheco, a Dominican, eventually led his own *charanga* group in the 1960s and subsequently became one of the most popular New York salsa musicians and bandleaders. Even Ray Barretto, a more recent forerunner in salsa and acclaimed as one of the more progressive artists indebted to the Afro-Cuban tradition, led a *charanga* during the 1960s. Today, Orquesta Aragón of Cuba is recognized as the most authentic and agile *charanga* group.

The exact origins of the mambo are the subject of much conjecture. The music and dance of the mambo originated in Cuba but then in New York evolved into a distinctive style. The height of the mambo's popularity spanned the first half of the 1950s. Pérez Prado (1916–1989) was perhaps the most widely acclaimed mambo bandleader, although his style did not hold as much appeal among the Latin population in New York as did the music of Machito, José Curbelo, Tito Puente, and Tito Rodríguez. To the general American public Prado personified the emergence of the mambo, while to the Latins he represented its commercial dilution. John Storm Roberts traces two strains of Cuban instrumental music: "[It was] Afro-Cuban on the one hand, and more white-oriented on the other (though both of course fed each other). In modern terms, one might say, the first was represented by the mambo, and the second by the cha cha chá" (1972:98). The Afro-Cuban strain grew from percussion-dominated rumba groups and Holy Week procession *comparsa* bands. The more European strain had been represented by the *charanga francesca*. The overall development of Cuba's music, however, did not divide into black versus white styles as may be heard in the *charangas* of Johnny Pacheco.

> The popular New York-based musician Johnny Pacheco's first group in the United States was called a *charanga* and featured lead flute and fiddle riffs that clearly went back to the old *charangas francesas* but were also related to the Afro-Cuban groups' trumpet and sax work. The inter-island contacts today, and the island's links with the United States, are typified by Pacheco, whose birthplace was the Dominican Republic, whose musical influences were Cuban, and who has made his name playing for Spanish-speaking audiences in the United States (Roberts 1972:98).

The original *cha-cha-chá* popularized by the Orquesta Aragón became highly popular throughout Cuba in 1953. A product of the Cuban *charangas*, the *cha-cha-chá* was an adaptation of the second thematic section of the original *danzón*, and the crisp texture of flute, violin, and *timbales* contributed to its mass appeal in Cuba. In the United States, the *cha-cha-chá* with its simple rhythm became widely accepted, while the more Afro-Cuban demanding mambo dance style made it relatively less accessible in general. Ultimately, however, the decline of the *cha-cha-chá* in the United States stemmed from the unsuitability of the *charanga* sounds that were transcribed for the heavy instrumentation of the mambo-oriented orchestras, such as those of Tito Puente, Machito, and José Curbelo. Roberts adds that "unfortunately, the cha cha chá's characteristic melody lines and simple rhythms lent themselves to a dilution that was all the more tempting because of its colossal success" (1979:132).

Machito, Fats Navarro (1923–1950), and other respected musicians in the progressive Latin and jazz waves of the late 1940s had experimented with fusions of the Afro-Cuban and Afro–North American styles, but it was Cuban *conguero* and vocalist Chano Pozo's (1915–1948) association with Dizzy Gillespie that played a prominent role in the emergence of the Cubop movement. "In Cubop, Latins and Americans were trying to work together without losing any crucial elements of either style" (Roberts 1972:119). This was in certain aspects challenging, because although there were Afro-based similarities between the rumba and the jazz "bop" styles, the Afro-Latin and Afro–North American musical traditions were at the same time quite different. Nevertheless, Pozo's impact on music in North America endured, symbolized through the fusion music known as Latin jazz. Prominent percussionist-bandleader Mongo Santamaría stresses that Pozo's essential contribution was the exposure he gave the conga drum that spearheaded its rise in popularity.

Previously, bongos and *timbales* had emigrated from Cuba to the United States in larger quantities than the conga. Among the more important Pozo–Gillespie musical collaborations were the compositions "Algo-Bueno," "Afro-Cuban Suite," and the profound "Manteca," a basic conga riff inspired by Pozo that received wide acclaim as the successful blend of the two Afro-American styles. Among the many artists who continued the school of Latin jazz were Cal Tjader (1925–1982), Mongo Santamaría (b. 1922), and Poncho Sánchez (b. 1951).

Other artists influenced by Afro-Cuban rhythms included Stan Kenton (1911–1979), who recorded the often criticized *Cuban Fire,* each of its movements based on a different Cuban rhythm. Other related Kenton works included "Viva Prado" and "28°N–82°W." Of immense importance is Chick Corea (b. 1941), whose affinity for Afro-Cuban rhythms stems from internships with both Mongo Santamaría and Willie Bobo (1934–1983). The Argentinian Gato Barbieri (b. 1934) incorporated a wide range of Afro-Cuban elements into his style, and the vibrant Latin rock texture of Carlos Santana provides a vast array of Cuban-derived rhythms.

Another important aspect of Afro-Cuban musical influence has been its continuous cross-fertilization with Mexican music. "La Paloma" inspired many Mexican composers, who considered the *habanera* to be at once ballad, typical *danza,* and sentimental *canción mexicana.* Cuba also continued to influence Mexican urban popular music throughout the twentieth century. Aaron Copland's 1937 tribute to Mexico, *El Salón México,* referred to a leading Mexico City dance hall featuring *conjuntos* that played mostly *danzones* and employed many Cuban musicians. Contemporary Mexican *música tropical* continues to reflect Afro-Cuban influence. Historically, Mexico has shared with Cuba, although to a lesser extent, an African heritage in music, particularly notable in the region of Veracruz, a seaport of slave importation during Mexico's colonial period and a constant point of contact with the Caribbean.

Salsa

Today, the word *salsa* denotes more than a category of music; it is also a major musical movement. It encompasses a multitude of genres and musical structures, but its effect transcends all labels. Born in New York City, the urban phenomenon of salsa represents a musical and social development stemming from an Afro-Cuban foundation. The works of recent artists and groups such as Tito Puente, Eddie Palmieri, Ray Barretto (b. 1929), Willie Colón (b. 1950), Johnny Pacheco, Celia Cruz (b. c. 1929), Sonora Matancera, Mongo Santamaría, Luis "Perico" Ortiz, Bobby Rodríguez, Charanga '76, Típica Ideal, Orquesta Broadway, Charanga América, Típica 73, Larry Harlow, Ruben Blades (b. 1948), and the Fania All-Stars represent a major contemporary musical trend influenced by diverse elements not bound within the confines of one musical style. Jazz, rhythm and blues, classical, and other musical styles are integrated within a traditional Afro-Cuban framework of rhythm and dance, the essential components of rumba

With the growing bicultural awareness within the United States, Latin salsa has for many provided a mode of cultural expression that bridges an inter-cultural barrier.

and *son.* No one is more dedicated to this blending than the salsa musicians themselves, who are well aware of their common training ground and school of thought inherited from Cuban immigrant musicians. Pablo "Yoruba" Guzmán writes:

> The form of Latin music known as salsa is a product of New York City streets via Afro Cuba, with stops in Puerto Rico and Santo Domingo along the way. There are those, such as Manny Oquendo, noted percussionist with such bands as Tito Rodríguez and Eddie Palmieri (now with Conjunto Libre), who insist that there is no such thing as salsa, that it is the same music (with changes) that has been played in New York for the last fifty years. The only difference, they claim, are the modem arrangements and more rock, jazz, and rhythm 'n' blues spices in the stew.
>
> The difference is not merely quantitative as this "school" would have it, but qualitative, similar to the difference between a Leadbelly and an Otis Redding (or Leadbelly and Earth, Wind and Fire). Salsa is a legitimate form within the world of Latin music (Guzmán, n.d:17).

The many Puerto Rican musicians in New York who have so closely identified with both Cuban music and U.S. jazz have played an important role in the crystallization of the hybrid salsa movement internationally, but especially in the Latin quarters of the United States. Lyrics sung in Spanish verse with a strong dance base have been fostered by a significantly growing U.S. Latino population whose Caribbean, Chicano/Mexican, Central American, and South American composition continually enhances the Latino nature of the music. With the growing bicultural awareness within the United States, Latin salsa has for many provided a mode of cultural expression that bridges an inter-cultural barrier.

In California, major exponents of Afro-Cuban musical styles and Latin jazz have also emerged. In San Francisco, an ambience referred to as "Pan-Latin Americanism" has greatly fostered the success of various Latino artists such as Francisco Aguabella (b. 1925), Pete Escovedo (b. 1935), Coke Escovedo (d. 1986), Sheila Escovedo (b. 1954), John Santos (b. 1955), Batachanga, Luis Gasca (b. 1940), Connie Caudillo, Benny Velarde, Carlos Federico, Angie Dones, Henry Caudillo, Combo Mestizo, and Carlos Gallardo (Pacheco 1986). A major musical development also occurred in San Francisco during the late 1960s with the emergence of Mexican guitarist Carlos Santana (b. 1947), who fused traditional Afro-Cuban rhythms and salsa stylings with hard rock and blues. One of Santana's major international hits was a Latin-rock rendition of Tito Puente's classic cha-cha "¿Oye cómo va?" Santana's successful explorations greatly exposed the salsa culture of the United States to the world community.

Los Angeles represents another city that has been closely integrated with the growth of Afro-Cuban musical styles. *Guaracha, rumba, mambo,* and *danzón* were all highly popular dance styles during the *"pachuco* zoot suit" period of the 1940s. During the 1950s, radio disk jockey Chico Sesma produced a series of major dance concerts at the Zenda Ballroom and the Hollywood Palladium, featuring artists such as Benny Moré (b. 1919), Machito, Pérez Prado, Tito Puente, Celia Cruz, Orquesta Aragón,

Miguelito Valdez, René Touzet (b. 1916), Eddie Cano (b. 1927), Johnny Martínez, and Manny López, among many others. Other artists active in Los Angeles have included Johnny Nelson, Ralfi Pagán, Miguel Cruz, Masacote, Melón, Rudy Regalado, Típica Antillana, José "Perico" Hernández, Henry Mora, and Rudy Macias. A major representative of the Afro-Cuban musical tradition to emerge from Los Angeles during the 1980s was Poncho Sánchez, a Chicano *conguero* who had spent seven years performing with Latin jazz exponent Cal Tjader before the latter's death in 1984.

A popular trend that emerged in the 1960s from the salsa movement in New York was *bugalú*, especially as interpreted by Joe Cuba. A blend of Latin rhythms and African American rhythm and blues, the style represented the close musical association of Latin and black music in the United States. Similar mixtures would occur in the 1970s and 1980s with groups such as Los Angeles Chicano rhythm and blues bands Tierra and El Chicano, Miami Sound Machine in Miami (featuring Cuban American lead singer Gloria Estefan), and Tito Nieves, of New York/Puerto Rican heritage. Gloria Estefan became a major success in both Spanish and English with her mixture of Latin and rhythm and blues styles.

Another important artist who emerged from the salsa movement during the 1970s was Ruben Bladés. Originally from Panama and trained in law, Bladés ventured to New York where he worked for Fania Records and eventually established himself as a lead vocalist and prolific composer. His album *Siembra* with arranger/trombonist Willie Colón, released in 1980, sold a record volume of units, and one of its tracks, "Pedro Navaja," became known in Latin America. Bladés's song texts that addressed social and political issues of Latin America gained him special recognition. With the death of the Cuban/New York bandleader Machito in 1984, many salsa critics proclaimed the end of an era in salsa, parallel to the commentary on jazz following Duke Ellington's passing. Some of the carriers of his tradition, however, still continued strongly into the turn of the twenty-first century, including Tito Puente, Celia Cruz, and Eddie Palmieri.

Also developing since the mid-1970s was a more experimental jazz fusion with the salsa world, seen in the creative work of artists Manny Oquendo, Andy Gonzales, and Jerry Gonzales and the activity of New York's New Rican Village Cultural Center. The 1980s also witnessed the success of a new breed of salsa adapted to a more international pop sound, called *salsa romántica*. Exponents included Luis Enríquez (Nicaragua/United States), José Alberto (Dominican Republic), and Eddie Santiago (Puerto Rico). Some singers of the older school, Lalo Rodríguez for example, who recorded with Eddie Palmieri in the early 1970s at the age of seventeen, successfully adapted to the new trend. Another more recent phenomenon was the international success of Orquesta de La Luz, a salsa group from Japan influenced by the New York salsa style and whose recordings were originally produced in New York by Sergio George.

THE INFLUENCE OF PUERTO RICAN MUSIC

In addition to playing a major role in the development of salsa in the United States, musicians of Puerto Rican heritage have also been important to the popularization of Puerto Rican musical genres. In New York, in particular, Puerto Ricans perform *plena, bomba, seis, aguinaldo,* and *danza*. *Plena* and *bomba* music and dance originally developed along the coastal towns of Puerto Rico. Active interpreters of *plena* and *bomba* have included Victor Montañez, Manuel "Canario" Jiménez, and the highly successful Rafael Cortijo and Ismael Rivera (the last three artists were based in Puerto Rico, but New York was a constant reference point).

The *jíbaro* styles have also played an essential role in the transplantation of Puerto Rican traditional music culture into the United States. These Hispanic-derived folk forms especially make use of the Puerto Rican *cuatro,* with ten strings grouped in five courses. Virtuosos on this instrument include Yomo Toro (New York) and Edwin Colón Zayas (Puerto Rico).

THE DOMINICAN *MERENGUE*

The Dominican *merengue* has had a major influence on the development of Latin music in the United States. A music/dance form originally developed in the Dominican Republic, it has competed with the *cumbia* as the most popular dance throughout Latin America. In recent years, the *merengue* gained a major following in the United States, led by Dominican artists such as Wilfrido Vargas, Johnny Ventura, Elvis Crespo, and Juan Luis Guerra. Guerra received a Grammy Award in 1991 in the Latin/Tropical category, demonstrating the highly prominent position of the competitive *merengue* and its related genre, *bachata,* within salsa culture in urban centers such as New York City, Miami, Chicago, and Los Angeles. In 1996 Paul Austerlitz wrote an informative book on the *merengue* titled *Merengue: Dominican Music and Dominican Identity.* Also of great significance is the 1995 book *Bachata: A Social History of a Dominican Popular Music,* written by Deborah Pacini Hernández.

REFERENCES

Alex and Orquesta Liberación. 1985. Karen Records KLP 89. LP disk.

Austerlitz, Paul. 1996. *Dominican Music and Dominican Identity.* Philadelphia: Temple University Press.

Baron, Robert. 1977. "Syncretism and Ideology: Latin New York Salsa Musicians." *Western Folklore* 36(3):209–225.

Barretto, Ray y Su Orquesta. 1983. Fania JM 623. LP disk.

Barretto, Ray. 198 1. *La Cuna.* CTI Records CTI 9002. LP disk.

Batacumbele. 1987. *Afro Caribbean Jazz.* Montieno Records MLP 525. LP disk.

Behague, Gerard. 1973. "Latin American Folk Music." In *Folk and Traditional Music of the Western Continents,* ed. Bruno Nettl, 176–206. Englewood Cliffs, N.J.: Prentice-Hall.

Bennett, John, ed. 1975. *The New Ethnicity: Perspectives from Ethnology.* Proceedings of the American Ethnological Society, 1973. St. Paul, Minn.: West.

Betancourt, Justo. *Justo Betancourt.* 1974. Fania SLP 00452. LP disk.

———. 1979. *Justo Betancourt.* Fania. JM 00553. LP disk.

Bládes, Ruben. 1983. *El que la hace la paga.* Fania JM 624. LP disk.

Blum, Joséph. 1978. "Problems of Salsa Research." *Ethnomusicology* 12(1): 137–149.

Boggs, Vernon. 1992. *Salsiology: Afro-Cuban Music and the Evolution of Salsa in New York City.* New York: Greenwood Press.

Caliente=Hot: Puerto Rican and Cuban Musical Expression in New York. 1977. New World Records NW 244. LP disk.

Canario y Su Grupo. n.d. *Plenas.* Ansonia Records LP 1232. LP disk.

Carpentier, Alejo. 1946. *La Música en Cuba.* Mexico: Fondo de Cultura Economica.

Celia, Johnny and Papo 1976. *Recordando El Ayer.* Vaya JMUS 52. LP disk.

Celia y Willie. 1981. Vaya. JMUS 93. LP disk.

Chocolate. 1981. *Prefiero el Son.* SAR Ml 5169. LP disk.

Colón, Edwin. 1988. *El Cuatro . . . Más Alla de lo Imaginable.* EC 001. LP disk.

Colón, Willie. 1977. *El Baquiné de Angelitos Negros.* Fania SLP 00506. LP disk.

Cornelius, Steven. 1989. "The Convergence of Power: An Investigation into the Music Liturgy of Santeria in New York City." Ph.D. dissertation, University of California, Los Angeles.

Crook, Larry. 1982. "A Musical Analysis of the Cuban Rumba." *Latin American Music Review* 3(1):92–123.

Cruz, Celia. 1978. *The "Brillante" Best.* Vaya SD 15. LP disk.

———. 1983. *Con la Sonora.* Matancera Peerless. LP disk.

Cruz, Celia, and Barretto, Ray. 1988. *Ritmo en El Corazón.* Fania, JM 651.

De León, Carlos. 1979. "The Most Delicate Form of Salsa." *Nuestro,* October, 49.

D'Rivera, Paquito. 1988. *Celebration.* Columbia Records AL 44077. LP disk.

El Gran Combo. 1977. *Homenaje a México.* Combo C 1011. LP disk.

Enrique, Luis. 1988. *Amor y Alegría.* CBS D-1110546. LP disk.

Fajardo, José. 1982. *Señor . . . Charanga!* Fania 24. LP disk.

Fania All Stars. 1981. *Perfect Blend.* CBS Records 10453. LP disk.

———. 1988. *Bamboleo.* Fania JM 650. LP disk.

Feliciano, Cheo. 1977. *Mi Tierra y Yo.* Vaya. JMUS 69. LP disk.

Feliciano, Cheo, and Ismael Quintana. 1983. *Los Soneros de Ponce.* Coco CLP 165. LP disk.

Fiol, Henry. 1983. *La Ley de la Jungla.* SAR SLP 1033. LP disk.

Friedman, Robert. 1978. "'If You Don't Play Good They Take the Drum Away': Performance, Communication and Acts in *Guaguancó.*" In *Discourse in Ethnomusicology: Essays in Honor of George List,* ed. C. Card, J. Hasse, R. Singer, R. Stone, 209–224. Bloomington: Indiana University Ethnomusicology Publications Group.

Friedman, Robert, and Roberta L. Singer. 1977. "Puerto Rican and Cuban Musical Expression in New York." Notes to *Caliente=Hot: Puerto Rican and Cuban Musical Expression in New York.* New World Records NW 244. LP disk.

Grenet, Emilio. 1939. *Popular Cuban Music: Eighty Revised and Corrected Compositions, Together With an Essay on the Evolution of Music in Cuba.* Havana. Carasa.

González, Jerry. 1989. *Rumba Para Monk.* Sunnyside Communications SSC 1036D. LP disk.

Guzmán, Pablo Yoruba. (n.d.) "From Afro-Cuba to New York City. Streets: An Introduction to Salsa." *City Star,* 17.

Hernández, José "Perico. " 1986. *Me Doy a Querer.* GB Records GBR 0001. LP disk.

Jiménez, Andrés. 1987. *500 Años Después.* Nuevo Arte NA 80. LP disk.

———. 1988. *Jíbaro romántico, y algo más.* Nuevo Arte NA 100. LP disk.

La India de Oriente. 1985. *La Reina de la Guajira.* Caiman CLP 9012. LP disk.

León, Argeliers. 1974. "Notas para un panorama de La Música popular cubana." *Música* 24:4–14.

Loza, Steven. 1979. "Music and the Afro-Cuban Experience: A Survey of the Yoruba Tradition in Cuba in Relation to the Origins, Form, and Development of Contemporary Afro-Cuban Rhythms." Master's thesis, University of California, Los Angeles.

Lazano, Danilo. 1990. "La Charanga Tradition in Cuba: History, Style and Ideology." Master's thesis, University of California, Los Angeles.

Machito Orchestra. 1977. *Fireworks.* Coco Records CLP 131 X. LP disk.

Machito and His Salsa Big Band. 1982. Timeless Records SJF 161. LP disk.

Machito y sus Afro-Cubanos. 1976. *Tremendo Cumbán.* Tropical Records. TRLP 5063.

Machito y sus Afro-Cuban Salseros. 1978. *Mucho Macho.* Pablo Records 2625-712. LP disk.

Manuel, Peter. 1990. *Popular Musics of the Non-Western World.* New York: Oxford University Press.

Manuel, Peter, with Kenneth Bilby and Michael Largey. 1995. *Caribbean Currents: Caribbean Music from Rumba to Reggae.* Philadelphia: Temple University Press.

Mauleon, Rebeca. 1993. *Salsa Guidebook for Piano and Ensemble.* Petaluma, Calif.: Sher Music Company.

Melón. n.d. *Melón y el Gran Pasto.* ARO Records LPS 142. LP disk.

Moré, Benny. 1984. *+15 Exitos de Benny Moré.* RCA-Victor MKS 2364. LP disk.

Orquesta Harlow. 1972. *Tribute to Arsenio Rodríguez.* Fania Records SLP 00404. LP disk.

Orquesta Broadway. 1979. *No Tiene Comparación.* Coco Records CLP 158X. LP disk.

¡Oye Listen! 1987. *Lo más caliente in Latin Music.* Globestyle Records ORB 014. LP disk.

Pacheco, Javier. 1986. "Salsa in San Francisco, 1974–1985: The Latin Music Experience." Master's thesis, University of California, Los Angeles.

Pacheco, Johnny, y Melón. 1982. *Llegó Melón.* Fania 18. LP disk.

Pacini Hernández, Deborah. 1995. *Bachata: A Social History of a Dominican Popular Music.* Philadelphia: Temple University Press.

Palmieri, Eddie. 1975. *Unfinished Masterpiece.* Coco Records CLP 120. LP disk.

Palmieri, Eddie, and Friends. 1973. *Live at the University of Puerto Rico.* Coco Records DOLP 107. LP disk.

Puente, Tito. 1979. *Homenage a Beny, Vol. 2.* Tico Records JMTS 1436. LP disk.

———. 1984. *Los Grandes Exitos de Tito Puente, Vol 2.* RCA Records IL 57294. LP disk.

———. 1987. *On Broadway.* Concord Picante Records CJP 207. LP disk.

Puente, Tito, and His Latin Ensemble. 1984. *El Rey.* Concord Picante Records CJP 250. LP disk.

Rivera, Ismael. 1978. *Esto sí es lo mío.* Fania Records JMTS 1428. LP disk.

Robbins, James Lawrence. 1990. "Making Popular Music in Cuba: A Study of the Cuban Institutes of Musical Production and Musical Life of Santiago de Cuba." Ph.D. dissertation, University of Illinois, Champaign-Urbana.

Roberts, John Storm. 1972. *Black Music of the Americas.* New York: Praeger.

———. 1979. *The Latin Tinge: The Impact of Latin American Music on the United States.* New York: Oxford University Press.

———. 1999. *Latin Jazz: The First of the Fusions, 1880s to Today.* New York: Schirmer Books.

Rodríguez, Tito. 1988. *Palladium Memories.* TR Records TR 200. LP disk.

Rodríguez, Tito, y Louie Ramirez. (n.d.). *Algo Nuevo.* TR Records TR 300. LP disk.

Rosario, Willie. 1986. *Nueva Cosecha.* Bronco Records B 142. LP disk.

Roseman, Marina. 1983. "The New Rican Village: Artists in Control of the Image-Making Machinery." *Latin American Music Review* 4(1):132–167.

Salazar, Max. 1974. "A Short History of Salsa." *Latin New York Magazine* 14 April: 12–14.

Sánchez, Armando y Su Conjunto. 1980. *Así Empezó la Cosa.* Montuno Records LP 514. LP disk.

Santamaría, Mongo. 1972. *Afro Roots.* Prestige Records 24018. LP disk.

———. 1987. *Soy Yo.* Concord Picante Records CJP 327. LP disk.

Santana. 1976. *Amigos.* Columbia Records PC 9781. LP disk.

———. 1977. *Moonflower.* Columbia Records 34914. LP disk.

Singer, Roberta L. 1982. "'My Music Is Who I Am and What I Do: Latin Popular Music and Identity in New York City." Ph.D. dissertation, Indiana University.

———. 1983. "Tradition and Innovation in Contemporary Latin Popular Music in New York City." *Latin American Music Review* 4(2):183–202.

Smith, Arnold. 1977. "Mongo Santamaría: Cuban King of Congas." *Down Beat,* 21 April.

Sonora Matancera con Justo Betancourt. 1981. Barbaro Records B 207. LP disk.

Sonora Ponceña. 1981. *Night Raider.* Inca Record JMIS 1079. LP disk.

Thompson, Robert Farris. 1975. "Nueva York's Salsa Music." *Saturday Review,* 8 June.

Urfé, Odilio. 1973. "Bosquejo histórico sobre el origen y desarollo del complejo musical y coreográfico del son cubano," *Revista de la Biblioteca Nacional José Martí,* enero/abril, 197–202.

Haitian and Franco-Caribbean Music
Gage Averill

Early Migration
Migration after World War II
***Mini-djaz* in the Diaspora**
The Haitian Recording Industry
Serving the Spirits in a Strange Land
Folkloric Troupes, Political and Apolitical
A Haven for Haitian Music

Haitian music came to North America in two waves of migration separated by two centuries. The first began around 1750 and peaked in the thirteen years preceding Haitian independence (1804). There was already a considerable flow of goods, people, armies, and expressive culture between France's territory of Louisianne (including Nouvelle Orléans) and its Caribbean holdings such as Saint-Domingue (later called Haiti).

EARLY MIGRATION

In response to a series of violent slave rebellions beginning around 1749, panic enveloped Saint-Domingue's colonists. Following the burning of Cap Haïtien, many from the northern plantocracy fled to Nouvelle Orléans; others left for Cuba or Trinidad or returned to France. The white planters and *affranchis* 'freed slaves, often of mixed race' who left Saint-Domingue brought with them thousands of African slaves, including many *bosals* 'wild ones', referring to slaves of African birth.

This migration had profound and long-lasting cultural consequences. Neo-African social dances, including the *chica, kalenda*, and *juba*, were danced and played well into the mid-nineteenth century on Sundays in Congo Square in New Orleans. *Juba* featured a drum that was laid on its side and straddled by a player who struck it with his hands while controlling the pitch of the drum with the heel of his foot. Another player beat the *kata* 'timeline' on the wood of the drum with two sticks. *Juba* drumming became the model for an African American tradition called "pattin' *juba,*" transferring the drumbeats to parts of the body in the absence of drums. Although congregational worship in the style of Afro-Haitian Vodou was rare, a number of healing, divining, and protective magic practices, mostly of Kongo origin (black cat bones, *mojos*, bottle trees, and even voodoo doll), passed into African American folklore under the general rubric voodoo.

Migrants from Saint-Domingue strengthened French creole traditions, such as funeral parade music, string bands, and military regimental brass bands, all of which were the training grounds for early New Orleans jazz instrumentalists. Slaves and *affranchis* danced creolized figure dances from Saint-Domingue, including contredanses, quadrilles, and *carrés* 'squares'. The musical accompaniment was typically characterized by a syncopated measure followed by four even beats. These dances took hold in the eastern province of Cuba (and became the Cuban *contradanza, danza*, and eventually *danzón*) as well as in Louisianne.

The syncopated rhythms that enlivened so many of the early New Orleans creole musics were linked by pianist Ferdinand "Jelly Roll" Morton to Cuban influence and later called "Latin Tinge" in African American jazz. In fact, these Cuban rhythms were a legacy of Haitian creole musics brought to New Orleans from both Cuba and Saint-Domingue.

MIGRATION AFTER WORLD WAR II

The more recent immigration of Haitians to North America occurred after World War II and is typically divided into three phases. The first took place in the 1950s and early 1960s as members of the elite fled political unrest and terrorism in Haiti. The second phase followed the liberal U.S. immigration reform of 1965 and included much of Haiti's young professional and managerial talent, disillusioned with their economic opportunities under the Duvalier dictatorship. A third phase brought many middle-level peasants and urban workers seeking an economic lifeline for their families as a result of Haiti's worsening environmental, economic, and political conditions. Some migrants came illegally—booking passage on small, rickety boats—and were dubbed "boat people" by the press. After the early 1980s, Miami was a principal terminus for Haitian migrants.

By 1957, two former presidents of Haiti and their supporters had arrived in New York City. Escalating violence during and after the election of Dr. François Duvalier to the presidency in 1957 convinced most of his opponents and their families and supporters to join the others in exile. Within a few years much of the political class had migrated to North America to form an opposition-in-exile to Duvalier. The few specifically Haitian musical events enjoyed by this community were the rare tours of the Haitian orchestras and artists of the day: Jazz des Jeunes, Orchestre Casino Nationale, singer Guy Durosier, the Ensemble Compas Direct de Nemours Jean-Baptiste, or the Ensemble Cadence Rempas de Wébert Sicot.

By the end of the 1960s, a significant Haitian presence had assembled in the New York boroughs of Manhattan (upper West Side) and Brooklyn (later in Queens). This community was relatively well educated and had disposable income for leisure pursuits. Haitian immigrants frequented dances held at rented social clubs, Friday church socials, and Haitian restaurants, and they followed the new fad in Haiti for small rock-band-like ensembles called *mini-djaz*, which played a mix of *compas direct* (*konpa* is the abbreviated creole spelling), Latin, and North American genres. *Konpa*, popularized by Nemours Jean-Baptiste and his ensembles in the 1950s, might be described as a modified *merengue* at a more leisurely tempo. The dance consists of a movement from foot to foot on an even two-beat pulse with a slight roll of the hips. It is discussed in terms denoting the closeness between partners: *tèt kole* 'cheek-to-cheek', *kole kole* 'glued together', *kole maboya* 'glued and rolling the hips', and *ploge* 'plugged together', a version frowned upon in reputable establishments. Popular in Haiti when many of these younger Haitians were leaving, *mini-djaz konpa* exercised a powerful pull on the nostalgic feelings of the Haitian *koloni* 'colony', as it was called by Haitians at the time.

MINI-DJAZ IN THE DIASPORA

Beginning about 1970, many Haitian bands on tour in the United States suffered desertions, as musicians stayed behind to start new groups in the diaspora, seeding a number of North American cities with *mini-djaz*. Most of these groups made their connection with premigration bands obvious in the choice of the name, establishing instant credibility and patronage networks in the immigrant community. Within four years, Tabou Combo, Original Shleu Shleu, Skah Shah, Gypsies de Queens, and Volo Volo de Boston were performing on the Haitian nightclub and restaurant circuit, and within another few years, *mini-djaz* found homes in Miami (Magnum Band) and other North American cities [see FRANCO-ONTARIAN MUSIC, p. 1192]. Most of these bands were modeled directly on their Haitian *mini-djaz* counterparts—a total of about nine performers played drum set, congas, a combination of bell and tamtam drum, two electric guitars,

The dance is discussed in terms denoting the closeness between partners: *tèt kole* 'cheek-to-cheek', *kole kole* 'glued together', *kole maboya* 'glued and rolling the hips', and *ploge* 'plugged together', a version frowned upon in reputable establishments.

electric bass, and saxophone, and there were one or two lead singers. In addition to weekend dances, the bands played for functions sponsored by immigrant sporting clubs and Haitian political parties; they also played at gala concerts called *spèktak* 'spectacles'.

THE HAITIAN RECORDING INDUSTRY

New York was the center of the Haitian recording industry and home to the most prolific Haitian labels: Ibo Records, Marc Records, and Mini Records. These were still rather small storefront businesses that traded records with other producers. Musicians recorded albums for a flat fee at a rate of approximately one or two per year. Albums were released to coincide with the Christmas-Carnival season or with *Vacances* 'August vacation', peak periods of music consumption in Haiti. At a time when the dictatorship monitored and regulated the circulation of people and ideas between insular and diasporic Haiti, the transnational nature of the Haitian music industry helped to maintain a sense of shared Haitian identity and a collective musical aesthetic.

SERVING THE SPIRITS IN A STRANGE LAND

The early Haitian *koloni* was solidly middle class and generally hostile to the practice of Vodou, although many Haitian Americans appreciated folkloric performances of Vodou rhythms and dances. Predominantly Catholic, but including a growing number of Protestants, most Haitian immigrants desperately wanted to live down the popular American associations of Haiti with Vodou, especially with the sensational and stereotyped images from Hollywood zombie movies. However, the widening class base of the Haitian immigrants in the mid-to-late 1970s brought many servants of the spirits to North America. (In Haiti, "serving the spirits" is a more common designation for the religion than Vodou. Spirits are known in creole as *lwa*, *zany*, or *mistè*.)

North America initially proved to be inhospitable to Vodou ceremonies. Drummers were in short supply, and if a priest was able to hire drummers, the neighbors usually called the police about noise levels. Haitian sacred drums were scarce as well, and U.S. immigration confiscated all skins for drumheads arriving from Haiti for fear of anthrax contamination. In the absence of drums, some congregations used hand claps to accompany Vodou songs. Haitian apartments were small and could not accommodate large congregations, and few apartment basements were available for such things (figure 1). Immigrants complained of having to travel long distances on the subways in the cold weather to get to Vodou ceremonies. Furthermore, the practice of animal sacrifice, an important part of the relations of mutual dependence and exchange between humans and their deities, was patently illegal in most North American municipalities. Thus, the legal system, as well as the pace of life in the cities of North America, with long hours at work and many bills to pay, seemed to discourage a rich ceremonial life. In the face of all these difficulties, however, a number of *ougan* and *manbo* 'male and female priests' succeeded in sustaining Vodou *sosyete* 'societies, congregations', some of which used live music for ceremonies. In recent years, Vodou has attracted adherents from a wide range of classes and ethnicities (figure 2).

FIGURE 1   A *manbo* (priestess), accompanied by a battery of three drums, calls the spirits at a Brooklyn Vodou ceremony. Basements have become popular sites for ceremonies in the absence of formal *peristils* (temples). Photo by Chantal Regnault.

FIGURE 2 Master drummer Frisner Augustin (right) plays for an initiate (*ounsi*) under the influence of a deity called a Gede, and she makes use of the traditional accouterments of a Gede: a black hat and cane. In 1999, Augustin was named a National Heritage Fellow by the National Endowment for the Arts for his contributions to Haitian music in the United States. Photo by Chantal Regnault.

FOLKLORIC TROUPES, POLITICAL AND APOLITICAL

Despite lingering middle-class and elite prejudice against Vodou, the *indigène* 'indigenous' movement in Haiti had established an important role for folkloric performance in the construction of national and patriotic identity. The folkloric arts flourished in Haiti during the post–World War II era, especially in the Vodou-jazz music of Jazz des Jeunes and in the stylized Vodou dances of La Troupe Folklorique Nationale d'Haïti (TFNH). By the early 1970s, following a decline in tourism in Haiti, Jazz des Jeunes and some of the founders of TFNH had relocated in New York, where they formed folkloric dance troupes such as Troupe Shango, Troupe Louinès Louinis, the Afro-Haitian Dance Company, Ibo Dancers, and Mackandal.

Haitian folkloric dance featured choreographed routines based on Vodou, *rara* (a Lenten processional ritual), Carnival, and *affranchi* figure dances. Troupes hired drummers such as Louis Celestin and Frisner Augustin, although some troupes later began to use white North American drummers. Drum rhythms were essentially those used in ceremonial contexts but typically did not include all of the complex variations found in ceremonial drumming. The *kase* 'break', a rhythmic change that helps to bring on possession in ceremonies, was preserved and synchronized with the choreography.

The diaspora was also home to a revolutionary folkloric troupe movement. After the failure of a major student strike in Haiti in the early 1960s, many anti-Duvalierist student activists took up cultural organizing among the peasants, using creole theater, song, dance, and poetry to raise political consciousness. When Duvalier suppressed leftist organizing in 1968, the majority of these activists fled to North America. There, they organized groups like Solèy Leve (Rising Sun), Atis Endepandan (Independent Artists), and Tanbou Libète (Drum of Freedom) in New York City, and Haïti Culturelle in Boston. Their music blended traditional expressive culture of Haiti's peasants (for example, music of *rara*, Vodou, work brigades, and troubadours) with urban or globally circulating forms such as international folk protest music or light bossa nova arrangements. This movement was dubbed *kilti libète* 'freedom culture', and it used the diaspora as liberated territory in the struggle against tyranny in Haiti.

The *kilti libète* movement was the incubator for a number of the artists whose *mizik angaje* 'music of social consciousness' was prominently featured in the diaspora of the 1980s, where it contributed to the movement to overthrow Duvalierism. Another crackdown on dissent in Haiti in 1981 forced *angaje* artists such as Manno Charlemagne, Ti-Manno (Antoine R. Jean-Baptiste), and Les Frères Parent into exile in the diaspora, where, along with political artists already performing in the diaspora such as Farah Juste and Fédia Laguerre, they produced songs and albums counseling the movement and protesting the situation in Haiti. The late Ti-Manno had a profound effect on the political consciousness of the diaspora. Ti-Manno's message bridged the gap between Haitian immigrants, who had worked for social change in Haiti and who hoped to return, and those resigned to staying in the United States, who were chiefly concerned with improving their economic and political situation. After Ti-Manno's death in 1985, Haitian American politicians organized a short-lived Haitian unity movement named after one of Ti-Manno's songs.

A HAVEN FOR HAITIAN MUSIC

The Haitian diaspora profoundly affected political change in Haiti, but it was also an essential component of Haitian musical growth and change. The diaspora offered new contexts for Haitian music and provided crossover exposure to wider audiences. Haitian diasporic bands joined in Labor Day Carnival in Brooklyn; played North American festivals; and performed at world beat dance clubs such as Kilimanjaro in Washington, D.C., and Sounds of Brazil in New York City (figure 3).

The diaspora nurtured new movements in Haitian music such as the *mizik rasin* 'roots music' movement, the *nouvèl jenerasyon* 'new generation', and Haitian hip-hop. Roots bands Ayizan and Sakad in New York were counterparts to the Haiti-based *mizik rasin* groups such as Boukman Eksperyans, Ram, or Foula. Fusing *rara* and Vodou rhythms and song structures with rock and reggae for a music of spiritual and political impact, *mizik rasin* swept to prominence in the early 1990s with the success of Boukman Eksperyans. Roots bands formed in New York (Rara Machine), Boston (Batwèl Rada), Miami (Kazak), and elsewhere in North America, and Miami hosted an annual *mizik rasin* festival.

The *nouvèl jenerasyon,* taking its name from an album by a Miami-based Haitian trio, pioneered a sophisticated pop sound—lighter in texture and more technically driven than *konpa. Nouvèl jenerasyon* performers, such as Phantoms or Zin or Emeline Michel, were based for much of the 1990s in North America, where they had access to studios and performance venues.

Although rap and related styles like Jamaican *ragga* were popular in Port-au-Prince after 1987, it was the North American group Fugees, featuring first-generation Haitian

FIGURE 3   Members of the *konpa* group Big Band Combo perform in Miami at a festival called "Miami Discovers Konpa." Bossa Combo was originally based in Haiti before a series of split-offs of the ensemble took up residency in the United States and Canada, including this group, which was based in Miami. Photo by Gage Averill.

American Wyclef Jean, that made rap and hip-hop arguably the most talked-about music in Haiti in the late 1990s.

The many changes since the overthrow of the Duvaliers have made the distinction between a diaspora and an insular Haiti less solid. Increased travel, electronic contact, and the circulation of recordings, videotapes, money, and goods make it ultimately more difficult to define clearly a concept as seemingly straightforward as "Haitian music in North America."

REFERENCES

Averill, Gage. 1995a. "'Mezanmi, Kouman Nou Ye? My Friends, How Are You?' Musical Constructions of the Haitian Transnation." *Diaspora, A Journal of Transnational Studies* 3(3):253–272.

———. 1995b. "Haitian Music in the Global System." In *The Reordering of Culture: Latin America, the Caribbean and Canada in the Hood*, ed. Alvina Ruprecht and Cecilia Taiana, 339–362. Ottawa: Carleton University Press.

———. 1997. *A Day for the Hunter, a Day for the Prey: Popular Music and Power in Haiti.* Chicago: University of Chicago Press.

———. 1998. "'Moving the Big Apple': Tabou Combo's Diasporic Dreams." In *Island Sounds in the Global City: Caribbean Popular Music and Identity in New York*, ed. Ray Allen and Lois Wilcken,

138–161. Special Issue of *New York Folklore* published in conjunction with the Institute for Studies in American Music.

Brown, Karen McCarthy. 1991. *Mama Lola: A Vodou Priestess in Brooklyn*. Berkeley and Los Angeles: University of California Press.

Fleurant, Gerdès. 1995. "The Song of Freedom: Vodun, Conscientization and Popular Culture of Haiti." *Compost* 5:69–73.

Juste-Constant, Vogeli. 1989. "Haitian Popular Music in Montréal: The Effect of Acculturation." *Popular Music* 9(1):79–86.

McAlister, Elizabeth A. 1995. "'Men Moun Yo'; 'Here Are the People': *Rara* Festivals and Transnational Popular Culture in Haiti and New York City." Ph.D. dissertation, Yale University.

Schiller, Nina Glick, and Georges Fouron. 1990. "'Everywhere We Go, We Are in Danger': Ti Manno and the Emergence of a Haitian Trans-national Identity." *American Ethnologist* 17(2):329–347.

Wilcken, Lois. 1991. "Music Folklore Among Haitians in New York: Staged Representations and the Negotiation of Identity." Ph.D. dissertation, Columbia University.

Wilcken, Lois, with Frisner Augustin. 1992. *The Drums of Vodou*. Crown Point, Ind.: White Cliffs Media.

British Caribbean Music
Robert Witmer

Ethnocultural and Musical Diversity
Popular Music Cultures
Folk/Traditional Music Cultures
Other Genres and Contexts
Documentation, Research, Profile

Residents of the United States who trace their roots to the British Caribbean (more commonly known to such residents as the British West Indies or simply the West Indies) hail from places in the Caribbean region formerly under British colonial rule and where English has long been the official language. The majority of British West Indian immigrants to North America have come from the countries of Jamaica, Trinidad and Tobago, and Guyana (on the northeast coast of South America but nevertheless considered a part of the British Caribbean in terms of historical and cultural ties). Others trace their roots to one or another of the numerous smaller countries and territories in the Caribbean region with a British colonial past.

The U.S. Bureau of the Census began tracking West Indian immigration as early as 1820, but it was not until the 1960s that British West Indian immigrants began arriving in the United States in substantial numbers. Thus, the British West Indian–derived population in North America is largely of quite recent origin.

Although their numbers remain small as a proportion of the total North American population, persons of British West Indies origins are a sizable presence in certain pockets of the United States. The majority have taken up residence in urban-industrial areas along the eastern seaboard of the United States (primarily in the states of New York, New Jersey, and Florida). The most populous communities are in New York City, particularly in the boroughs of Brooklyn and Queens. In these large and cosmopolitan urban centers, British Caribbean immigrants and their descendants comprise an estimated 3 to 5 percent of the total population, and in certain districts and neighborhoods they have become the majority or nearly so.

ETHNOCULTURAL AND MUSICAL DIVERSITY

The North American immigrant population mirrors the ethnocultural diversity of the British Caribbean homelands, where the population consists mainly of the descendants of African slaves but also includes the descendants of the many indentured laborers who arrived from India and China between the mid-1800s and the early 1900s, as well as smaller numbers of British and other European colonists and émigré entrepreneurs from the Middle East. Afro-Caribbeans comprise the majority of the British West Indian immigrant population in North America. Each of these population groups has its own historic musical traditions that remain somewhat exclusive to it; within the

Afro-Caribbean and Indo-Caribbean populations, which together comprise the overwhelming majority, there are musical practices that are unique to particular locales and/or subgroups. There have also been various admixtures over time, particularly between African and European strains. The transplantation of British Caribbean music cultures to North America through human migration thus encompasses a number of distinct traditions and practices carried from a multiethnic, multicultural homelands milieu.

In the populous southeastern Caribbean countries of Guyana and Trinidad and Tobago, Indo-Caribbeans are roughly as numerous as Afro-Caribbeans, and this fact is reflected in North American immigration statistics. Persons of Indo-Caribbean heritage are the second most populous group of immigrants, after Afro-Caribbeans, to North America from the British Caribbean.

POPULAR MUSIC CULTURES

In British Caribbean musical communities in North America, immigrants and their descendants have maintained virtually intact the popular music cultures of their homelands, including the quick adaptation to shifting trends. The immigrant and homelands popular music cultures operate in close tandem: the immigrant communities replicate to the extent possible the entire homelands popular music scene in the new environment and are also ongoing receptors of popular music imports from the homelands (recordings, touring musicians, print materials, and so on).

The reggae scene

Jamaican reggae music has been an established presence in British Caribbean communities in North America ever since its emergence in Jamaica in the late 1960s. This presence is not just reggae recordings and touring acts imported from Jamaica but the full reggae music infrastructure of Jamaica re-created in North America. Among the elements of this re-created infrastructure are resident professional musicians (including the all-important deejays) for stage shows, dances, and record production; specialty record shops and radio and television programming; maneuverings for coverage in print and other media; and celebration/legitimation by the music industry and cultural community (such as the annual Miami Reggae Festival). This scene is followed avidly by numerous British Caribbean expatriates, particularly those of Jamaican heritage. Reggae has also been a favorite of a segment of the general non-Caribbean popular music audience, as it has moved from an obscure regional style to an established category of international popular music, notably through the recorded output of Jamaican music superstar Bob Marley. Indicative of reggae's significance in the larger popular music marketplace is its inclusion as a separate category in the annual U.S. recording industry Grammy Awards.

Calypso, *soca*, steelband

Also well established in British West Indian immigrant communities are southeastern Caribbean (primarily Trinidadian) calypso, *soca* (soul + calypso), and steelband music. These musics have not been taken up by the non-Caribbean audience to anywhere near the extent that Jamaican reggae has, but neither are they unknown in the broader North American musical culture. Calypso and, more recently, *soca* recordings have occasionally penetrated mainstream popular music hit parade charts; in the mid-1950s there was something of an "Island music" craze in European American popular music (for example, the then superstar status of Jamaican American "West Indies folk singer" Harry Belafonte), in which calypso and calypso-tinged music were prominent. Steelband music has never been generally popular, yet there is some awareness among the broad musical public that it is Caribbean, or even specifically Trinidadian.

Indeed, Brooklyn's Labor Day carnival attracts larger crowds than Carnival in Trinidad, the event it is modeled after.

Calypso has been intertwined with the U.S. music industry almost since the music's inception. From the World War I period until the 1950s, most calypso (and other West Indian folk music) records were produced in New York City, typically using visiting Trinidad-based singer-songwriters and American-based, but generally Caribbean-derived, backup musicians. The recordings were marketed in North America, the British West Indies, and more broadly internationally. The gradual transformation of calypso from a vital but localized British Caribbean urban folk music to its present established position on the pan-Caribbean and world stage is to a considerable extent the result of activities in the United States in the first half of the twentieth century.

The current infrastructures of the calypso, *soca,* and steelband scenes in the British Caribbean immigrant community in the United States parallel those of the reggae scene outlined earlier and also include the strong emphasis on organized adjudicated competitions prevalent in southeastern Caribbean musical life. Steelband is not only being maintained in the diasporic communities in the traditional manner of the homelands—that is, as a short-term seasonal activity of mainly amateur musicians geared to a brief flurry of performances and competitions connected with Carnival festivals—but is also being taught in selected North American high school and college/university music programs, certain of which may include few, if any, students with southeastern Caribbean roots.

British Caribbean–style carnivals in the United States
North American analogues of Trinidad's annual pre-Lenten Carnival, the British Caribbean's most spectacular and well-known multi-arts festive event, are highly visible fixtures of the cultural, entertainment, and tourism calendars of several American cities. Indeed, Brooklyn's Labor Day carnival attracts larger crowds than Carnival in Trinidad, the event it is modeled after. Brooklyn's Labor Day carnival—so named because it is held on Labor Day weekend, the first weekend in September—usually attracts a range of events and huge crowds for the masquerade parade but compressed into a compact schedule.

Transformations of popular music in the United States
Although the hold of separate and distinct Caribbean homelands popular music cultures remains strong throughout the British Caribbean diaspora in the United States, certain departures from this hold are increasingly evident in the North American setting. In large and cosmopolitan centers such as New York City, musicians from the British Caribbean have more opportunities, and perhaps also more imperatives, for intercultural musical collaborations and cross-fertilizations than they may have found in their homelands. One result is the emergence of popular music groups in the British Caribbean diaspora in the United States that are, by homelands standards, unusually eclectic stylistically and exceptionally multiethnic/multinational in the makeup of

their personnel. Such groups range from pan–West Indian aggregations performing in a variety of Caribbean popular music styles to those in which Caribbean popular music styles, and musicians with Caribbean roots, are but one set of resources in a mélange of world popular music explorations. As yet, such groups perform more a mix of musics than a blend of musics: in the main they are stylistically versatile more than stylistically innovative [see FIVE FUSIONS, p. 334].

Something approaching true blending has occurred in the state of Hawai'i, with the emergence of "Jawaiian" music, a synthesis of Jamaican reggae and elements of traditional Hawaiian music [see POLYNESIAN MUSIC, p. 1047]. To the contrary, the flirtations with Jamaican reggae by a number of mainstream European American popular music acts during the 1970s and 1980s yielded a scattering of recordings featuring creative rock/pop/reggae blends but no enduring tradition. Beginning in the mid-1980s, there have been cross-fertilizations between African American hip-hop/rap musical culture and Jamaican (Jamaican–North American) deejay/dancehall reggae musical culture, evident particularly in New York City recordings and night life [see HIP-HOP AND RAP, p. 692].

It is in the North American Caribbean-style Carnival celebrations that the most radical departures from homelands practices are to be seen. In the homelands, Carnival is a somewhat insular event, reaffirming and celebrating a particular national culture, be it Trinidadian, Barbadian, or whatever. In Caribbean-style carnivals in North America, however, the flavor is pan–West Indian or pan-Caribbean and sometimes extends even beyond that. For example, during the Trinidad/British West Indies celebrations in Brooklyn's Labor Day carnival one finds not only the Trinidadian Carnival core of calypso and soca music and the focus on elaborately costumed revelers but also the active participation of, among others, the local French Caribbean (for example, the Haitian) community.

FOLK/TRADITIONAL MUSIC CULTURES

In addition to the predominant popular musical styles outlined above, the British Caribbean region has fostered a rich vein of folk and traditional music—local community-based music passed on informally from generation to generation and with little or no connection to the world of musical commerce—as an integral part of weddings, funerals, wakes, worship, work, and other recurrent community activities. The distinctions between such practices and the ones described in the previous section are more a matter of degree than kind. The state of these musical practices in the North American British Caribbean immigrant community has not as yet been systematically documented. Some commentators suggest that they are not as lively a presence in the diaspora as in the homelands, while other commentators have worried that emigration can deplete the homelands of musicians crucial to the maintenance of local traditions.

There is, however, broad evidence that some of the more prominent Afro-Christian religious sects and sociopolitical-cum-religious movements originating in the British Caribbean are flourishing on North American soil—for example, Jamaican Rastafarianism and the Trinidadian Spiritual Baptist ("Shouter Baptist") faith—and so too, necessarily, the associated musical practices.

In both the homelands and the diaspora a number of folk and traditional music genres seemingly survive today mainly in neotraditional adaptations by professional and semiprofessional folkloric ensembles. Music seemingly moribund or obscure in its original cultural context thus receives a new lease on life as nostalgia and/or cultural patrimony on the concert stage.

OTHER GENRES AND CONTEXTS

British Caribbean music cultures in the United States can by no means be defined solely by the practices outlined above. Many North American residents of British Caribbean origins actively follow (and a number perform) various non-Caribbean contemporary popular musics. For example, among adolescents and young adults prevailing African American urban music forms such as rap and rhythm and blues hold considerable sway [see R&B AND SOUL, p. 667; RAP AND HIP-HOP, p. 692]. There are also practitioners and devotees of jazz, Western (and Eastern) classical music, and various historic styles of North American and Latin American vernacular music. Among the British Caribbean–East Indian populace in North America, song hits from Indian films, Hindustani and Islamic devotional genres, *bhangra* music, and chutney music are variously important [see Indo-Caribbean Music, p. 808]. And Christian devotional music, in a broad range of styles, is vitally important across a broad spectrum of the British Caribbean–derived population in the United States. This plurality of musical tastes and allegiances has not arisen solely, or even primarily, out of the immigrant experience; it is also prevalent in the homelands.

DOCUMENTATION, RESEARCH, PROFILE

There are very few published studies dealing analytically with British Caribbean music cultures in the United States, although quite a number exist for the music cultures of the British Caribbean region itself. The references section below lists some of the more recent and informative studies in both these categories. (Recall that the immigrant musical communities operate in close tandem with the homelands—thus, publications dealing with the homelands musical cultures are usually at least somewhat germane to an understanding of the immigrant communities as well.)

The available published literature on British Caribbean music cultures in the United States consists almost entirely of topical/ephemeral "music scene news" appearing in North American Caribbean ethnic newspapers, of which there are a number, published mainly in Miami, Florida, and New York City, as well as in arts and entertainment features in alternative, and occasionally in mainstream, newspapers and news magazines. Many such publications are of limited distribution and difficult to obtain outside their local distribution areas. No systematic survey or synthesis of this material has yet been attempted. Keeping abreast of musical activities and developments in the United States on British Caribbean communities is thus quite difficult unless one is a member by birth or association, or a regular visitor. For American Caribbean popular music scenes at least, there is some coverage in widely available music magazines such as *The Beat (Reggae, African, Caribbean, World Music)*, and, increasingly, there are websites such as Jammin Reggae Archives.

REFERENCES

Allen, Ray, and Les Slater. 1997. "Trinidadian Steel Pan Music." In *Island Sounds in the Global City: Caribbean Popular Music and Identity in New York City,* ed. Ray Allen and Lois Wilkin, 114–137. New York: Institute for Studies in American Music.

Averill, Gage. 1997. " 'Pan Is We Ting': West Indian Steelbands in Brooklyn." In *Musics of Multicultural America,* ed. Kip Lornell and Anne K. Rasmussen, 101–129. New York: Schirmer Books.

Barrow, Steve, and Peter Dalton. 1997. "Reggae in the USA." In *Reggae: The Rough Guide,* 357–365. London: Rough Guides Ltd.

Bilby, Kenneth M. 1985. "The Caribbean as a Musical Region." In *Caribbean Contours,* ed. Sidney W. Mintz and Sally Price, 181–218. Baltimore: Johns Hopkins University Press.

Cowley, John. 1985. "Cultural 'Fusions': Aspects of British West Indian Music in the USA and Britain 1918–51." *Popular Music* 5:81–96.

Hill, Donald. 1997. "Calypso in the 1930s and 1940s." In *Island Sounds in the Global City: Caribbean Popular Music and Identity in New York City,* ed. Ray Allen and Lois Wilkin, 74–92. New York: Institute for Studies in American Music.

Kasinitz, Philip. 1997. "West Indian Carnival in Brooklyn." In *Island Sounds in the Global City: Caribbean Popular Music and Identity in New York City,* ed. Ray Allen and Lois Wilkin, 93–113. New York: Institute for Studies in American Music.

Manuel, Peter, Kenneth Bilby, and Michael Largey. 1995. *Caribbean Currents: Caribbean Music from Rumba to Reggae.* Philadelphia: Temple University Press.

Myers, Helen. 1993. "The West Indies." In *Ethnomusicology: Historical and Regional Studies,* ed. Helen Myers, 461–471. New York: W. W. Norton.

Nunley, John. 1988. "Festival Diffusion into the Metropole." In *Caribbean Festival Arts,* ed. John Nunley and Judith Bettelheim, 165–181. Seattle: University of Washington Press.

Okada, Yuki, director. 1995. *The Caribbean.* The JVC/Smithsonian Folkways Video Anthology of Music and Dance of the Americas, vol. 4. Barre, Vt.: Multicultural Media VTMV-288. Video.

Sealey, John, and Krister Malm. 1982. *Music in the Caribbean.* Toronto: Hodder and Stoughton.

Weintraub, Andrew. 1993. "Jawaiian Music." *Perfect Beat* 1(2):78–89.

Indo-Caribbean Music
Peter Manuel

Traditional Musics
Neotraditional Musics
Chutney and Modern Music Culture

The East Indian population of the Caribbean Basin constitutes one of the region's most culturally distinctive and yet lesser known ethnic groups. Although Trinidad's carnival, calypso, and steel band are internationally famous, few people outside that island know that the Afro-Trinidadian creoles most associated with these colorful traditions are in fact outnumbered in their homeland by people of East Indian descent, who also constitute the largest ethnic groups in nearby Guyana and Suriname.

East Indians originally migrated to the Caribbean as indentured laborers in a program sponsored by British West Indian planters, who sought to obtain cheap manual labor in the aftermath of slavery. Between 1838 and 1917, indentureship programs brought some 425,000 Indians to Trinidad and British Guiana, 35,000 to the Dutch colony of Suriname, and several thousand more to Jamaica, Martinique, and elsewhere. Some of the indenturees returned to India, but most stayed, and their descendants now number over a million people. Most of the immigrants were poor, lower caste peasants from the Bhojpuri-speaking region of northern India (Bihar and eastern Uttar Pradesh). Bhojpuri Hindi thus became a lingua franca for the first generations of indentured immigrants and is still commonly spoken, alongside Dutch and a local creole, by Indians in Suriname. In English-speaking Trinidad and Guyana, Bhojpuri is no longer widely spoken or understood [see INDIAN AND PAKISTANI MUSIC, p. 980].

The first generations of East Indians tended to remain in relatively insular communities formed around rural plantations. Since the mid-twentieth century, however, many Indo-Caribbeans have migrated to urban centers and have come to play increasingly prominent roles in the economic, political, and cultural lives of their countries. As they do so, they form new conceptions of national identity in countries traditionally dominated by creoles (blacks, Europeans, and those of mixed ancestry). At the same time, the rich and unique Indo-Caribbean music culture is beginning to earn broader recognition.

TRADITIONAL MUSICS

Indo-Caribbean music culture comprises a wide variety of distinctive idioms, which can be grouped in various categories. Much Indo-Caribbean music can be regarded as traditional in the sense of representing transplanted styles and genres that do not

Although women's folk song traditions remain strong in Suriname, they are in rapid decline in Trinidad and Guyana due to the eclipse of Bhojpuri as a living language there.

appear to have changed dramatically in the New World. Particularly prominent in this category would be traditions of women's folk songs, which correspond to counterparts in Bhojpuri India.

Women's folk songs

Many such songs are associated with particular life-cycle events, such as *sohar* (childbirth) songs, *nirgun* songs (performed at wakes), and various kinds of wedding songs. The latter include whimsical *gali* songs, in which women of the bride's family hurl abuse at the groom and his family, and ribald *matkor* (*matticore*) songs that can accompany lewd dancing, serving, perhaps, to defuse some of the sexual tension associated with marriage. Other women's folk songs are seasonal, such as those associated with the vernal *holi* or *phagwa* festival. Like most northern Indian folk song styles, these are sung in unison, often in a call-and-response style led by a knowledgeable or particularly enthusiastic lead singer. The typical instrumental accompaniment is the *dholak*, a two-headed barrel drum, and the *dantal*, a metal rod struck with a U-shaped clapper. Although women's folk song traditions remain strong in Suriname, they are in rapid decline in Trinidad and Guyana due to the eclipse of Bhojpuri as a living language there.

Devotional Hindu songs

Another substantial category of traditional musics is represented by the devotional Hindu songs (*bhajan*), performed collectively at temple functions. Typically, *bhajans* are sung by devotees, who may read the Hindi texts from songbooks, singing responsorially with a lead vocalist, who may be the *pandit* 'Hindu priest'. Muslim religious functions also often feature group or solo singing of devotional songs called *qasida* and *maulud*, with texts in Urdu. A more obscure tradition of *Mariamman* theater and music was cultivated by the descendants of lower caste migrants from southern India in Guyana, although this tradition has all but died out.

NEOTRADITIONAL MUSICS

Some Indo-Caribbean song styles seem to represent or contain traditions that have declined or perished in India itself, and thus can be seen as marginal survivals. Indo-Caribbeans had little direct interaction with India after the immigration program ceased in 1917, and, despite the advent of films and occasional holy men from India, there has been practically no contact at all with the ancestral Bhojpuri region. Thus, for example, the narrative, strophic song form called *birha*, which survives in Suriname, seems to be based on an archaic form of the genre derived from early-twentieth-century India, quite different from its modern version as performed in India today. However, most forms of Indo-Caribbean folk music appear to have evolved or changed, whether overtly or subtly, since being originally transplanted. In many cases, this evolution does not appear to involve the influence of Afro-Caribbean or creole culture but has been along purely Indian aesthetic lines, such that these styles may be called neotraditional.

Chowtal

One example of such a music tradition is *chowtal*, a vigorous *phagwa*-season genre that is sung responsorially by two groups of men, to the accompaniment of *dholak* and *dantal*. Most *chowtal* verses and melodies derive from northern India, where they are still sung. (Such songs are also performed in faraway Fiji, which is home to a large community of East Indians of Bhojpuri-region ancestry [see POLYNESIAN MUSIC, p. 1047].) But Indo-Caribbean *chowtal* has taken on a life of its own, especially in Trinidad, where each spring dozens of amateur groups compose new songs—perhaps seeking help from a Hindi-speaking elder—and vie for prizes in institutionalized competitions.

Tan-singing

Another form of neotraditional music is what is variously called "*tan*-singing," "tent-singing," "local classical music," or, in Suriname, *baithak gana* 'sitting music' (figure 1). *Tan*-singing is a sophisticated genre performed at weddings, wakes, temple and domestic ritual functions, and formal competitions by semiprofessional, predominantly male specialists. *Tan*-singing can be regarded as containing a mixture of elements, including aspects of traditional Bhojpuri folk music and garbled fragments of northern Indian classical and light-classical music. However, generations of Indo-Caribbean performers have applied their own creativity to the art, composing new melodies and rhythms and, whether intentionally or not, introducing changes and innovations into the art form. As a result, *tan*-singing, in its somewhat distinctive Trinidadian, Guyanese, and Surinamese substyles, has evolved into a coherent and unique genre that is quite distinct from anything in India. *Tan*-singing is generally performed by a solo male vocalist who also plays harmonium and is accompanied by *dholak* and *dantal*. Much of the aesthetic emphasis is on the lyrics, which are typically taken from old Hindi songbooks acquired from India. *Tan*-singers are celebrated for their extensive song repertoires, their skill at improvising melodies, and their ability to perform a variety of subgenres, such as *thumri*, *dhrupad*, and *ghazal*, which bear certain relationships to namesakes in India. *Tan*-singing has declined somewhat in recent years, especially in Guyana, although it is far from dead.

Tassa

Another kind of music performed by specialists is *tassa* drumming. The *tassa* drum ensemble is derived from northern India, where, as in Trinidad, it is heard on various occasions, especially at weddings and on the Muslim holiday of Moharrum, which

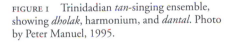

FIGURE 1   Trinidadian *tan*-singing ensemble, showing *dholak*, harmonium, and *dantal*. Photo by Peter Manuel, 1995.

FIGURE 2 *Tassa* drum ensemble, with *tazia* in background, at Trinidad's Hossay commemoration. Photo by Peter Manuel, 1995.

commemorates the martyrdom of the *Shi'a* saints Hassan and Hussein. In Trinidad this event came to be called Hossay (Hosay); its core activities are street processions in which elaborately constructed replicas of shrines called *tazia* are wheeled along by devotees to the accompaniment of the thunderous *tassa* drums (figure 2). In weddings and *matticore* festivities, women dance animatedly to *tassa* drumming. Many of the rhythms used in *tassa* drumming appear to derive from India, although others, such as *dingolay*, reflect Afro-Trinidadian influence.

CHUTNEY AND MODERN MUSIC CULTURE

Creole Caribbean influence is more overt in the secular entertainment dance music called chutney, which has flourished since the 1980s. The term chutney traditionally connoted lively, up-tempo, generally secular folk songs, often with obliquely ribald Bhojpuri texts, which accompanied sensual folk dancing at weddings and other occasions, usually in sexually segregated contexts. By the 1970s, as taboos on gender relations loosened, Trinidadian weddings started to feature informal chutney dancing by men and women—not necessarily in couples, but in the same collective space, typically after the conclusion of the *tan*-singing late at night. Chutney emerged in public culture in the 1980s, when entrepreneurs started holding weekly chutney fetes in large, public venues. Conservative moralists denounced the women's perceivedly libertine public dancing, but chutney soon became a massively popular phenomenon. Chutney dances have since become a fixture of Trinidadian culture, with hundreds of enthusiasts thronging each weekend to dance, drink, socialize, and enjoy the lively music. Chutney dancing, performed solo, or with partners of either sex, is a dynamic art form in itself, combining sensual, creole-influenced hip rotation ("wining") with graceful hand and arm gestures derived from Bhojpuri folk dance. Chutney music can be provided by a classical ensemble such as accompanies *tan*-singing, or, increasingly, acoustic instruments are supplemented by dance-band instruments, and the folk-style rhythm is supplemented by drum machines and percussion instruments playing rhythms in the style of *soca* 'modern, dance-oriented calypso'. In both formats, the thumping, pumping *dholak* provides a lively syncopated rhythmic base.

Chutney-*soca*, as the modernized hybrid is called, is now marketed on cassettes, heard on Indian-oriented radio stations, and performed in national competitions that rival the calypso contests in terms of attendance and prizes. In general, the rise of chutney in Trinidad parallels the dramatic emergence of Indo-Trinidadians into political, economic, demographic, and cultural prominence. Chutney is also popular among the substantial Trinidadian and Guyanese diaspora communities in New York and Toronto and among Indo-Surinamese in the Netherlands. Chutney's critics have had to acknowledge that its popularity has strengthened youth interest in Indian culture, albeit in a hybridized form. Even some creoles are starting to take an interest in chutney, both as performers and listeners, just as a significant handful of Indo-Trinidadians have distinguished themselves as performers of calypso and steel drum.

Film Music

Many Indo-Caribbeans have quite eclectic musical tastes. Young people tend to enjoy *soca*, dance-hall reggae, and American pop as well as chutney. Perhaps the most popular music among Indo-Caribbeans is film music imported from India, which has for several decades dominated Indian radio shows and the "Mastana Bahar" amateur performance competition in Trinidad. In recent years, such factors have contributed to a sense of cultural revival and awakening among many Indian Trinidadians and Guyanese, which, ironically, is occurring just as Hindi and Bhojpuri are dying as spoken languages in those countries. Still, many young Indo-Caribbeans acquire some familiarity with Hindi through their fondness for film songs, bhajans, and chutney; others have been able to take Hindi classes at temples. Further, with enhanced travel, communication, and media networks, many Indo-Caribbeans have become more exposed to contemporary culture in India. Such exposure enables them to cultivate enhanced ties with the ancestral motherland, but it may also intensify their realization of how different they have become from most South Asians. Indo-Caribbean culture and music are thus in a period of transition, whose present direction seems to incorporate aspects of both syncretic acculturation to creole culture and self-conscious assertion of Indianness.

REFERENCES

Arya, Usharbudh. 1968. *Ritual Songs and Folksongs of the Hindus of Surinam.* Leiden, Netherlands: E. J. Brill.

Manuel, Peter. 1995. "The Other Caribbean." In *Caribbean Currents: Caribbean Music from Rumba to Reggae*, with Michael Largey and Ken Bilby. Philadelphia: Temple University Press.

———. 1997–1998. "Music, Identity, and Images of India in the Indo-Caribbean Diaspora." *Asian Music* 29(1):17–36.

———. 1998. "Chutney and Indo-Trinidadian Cultural Identity. *Popular Music* 17(2).

Myers, Helen. 1998. *Music of Hindu Trinidad: Songs from the Indian Diaspora.* Chicago: University of Chicago Press.

Section 2c
European American Musics

European immigration to the United States began in the late sixteenth century and has continued until the present, with people of European descent then and now forming the majority population of this country. The British, who set up permanent settlements in the seventeenth century and who claimed the fledgling colonies for the Commonwealth, donated their language, much of their political and governmental organization, and their musical culture to the "new world," and their influence continues to the present day. Certainly one of the major contributions, especially of western and northern Europe, to the United States was a classical music system that was born and grew within European court and urban cultures over many centuries. So pervasive was this influence that it was not until the early twentieth century that classical music composers in the United States could establish their own "American" musical forms, based in part on materials borrowed from American Indian and African American traditions. In addition, European culture contributed much in the way of dance and instrumental musics to the American mix, and the entrance of southern and eastern Europeans, including large numbers of Ashkenazic Jews, in the late nineteenth and early twentieth centuries opened the United States to different religious and ceremonial practices as well.

Morris Dancing, Quoddy Head State Park, Lubec, Maine. © Michael S. Yamashita/ CORBIS.

Overview
Carl Rahkonen

North America is a land of immigrants. Everyone now living on this continent with the exception of Native Americans, came from, or has ancestors who came from, somewhere else. Between 1820 and 1960, an estimated fifty million immigrants came to America, the majority from Europe, in what has been described as "the greatest folk-migration in human history" (Jones 1960:94). Many immigrants formed their own ethnic communities that set them apart from other ethnicities. At the same time, they became part of a larger American society that created a culture of unity out of diverse ethnic groups. America has been called a melting pot, the theory being that immigrants from all over the world become Americanized to form a homogeneous whole. But a more accurate analogy might be that of a mosaic, with people of diverse ethnic backgrounds mixing together and coexisting. In a mosaic, each piece retains its individual integrity but also becomes an essential part of the complete picture. As we have slowly abandoned the melting pot ideal, we have come to value diversity and even to emphasize it.

FROM IMMIGRANT TO ETHNIC IDENTITY

The dominant culture of North America came from England, Spain, and France. These first immigrants established a culture and society into which subsequent immigrants would have to fit. They provided the framework within which the ethnic mosaic was created. From the very beginning, immigrants to North America differed from Europeans. Immigrant communities were internally more heterogeneous than in the Old World. Individuals who came from various regions, from urban or rural areas, tended to set aside regional differences and coalesce into a unified community. Thus, regional identities in the Old World gave way to ethnic identity in the New World. Because these groups were small in relation to the surrounding population, they tended to have more tolerance for internal diversity. Non-English-speaking first-generation immigrants were often isolated by language and thus tended to interact primarily with their own group. The music they listened to was that which they brought with them from the Old Country. Having language, religion, and music in common helped to overcome Old World regional differences.

As succeeding generations learned a common language, typically English, they communicated with others outside their group, developing a tolerance and eventually an acceptance of the surrounding American culture. The second generation, or children of immigrants, could adopt a dual identity. They would perhaps speak the language and practice Old World customs and traditions in dealing with their own ethnic community, especially with the older generation, but they could also adopt a general identity, which could be national, regional, religious, or occupational, or any combination of these four. In my research with the Jerry Intihar Ensemble (figure 1), a polka band from the Cambria City area of Johnstown, Pennsylvania (Rahkonen 1993), for example, I found that the region's various European American ethnic groups shared all four of these identities. They were all United States citizens from western Pennsylvania. Many had served together in the armed services, producing ties that transcended their ethnic backgrounds. Virtually all of them were employed in the steel mills and shared the dangers and rewards of working in this industry. A large proportion of them were Catholic, although they attended their own parishes—Slovenian, Polish, Irish, and so on. We may be tempted to believe that as second and subsequent generations of European Americans become assimilated into American culture, they somehow lose the identity of the European culture, but the process may be better described as developing an ability to shift back and forth between a specific and a general identity, depending on context.

Third and subsequent generations in America face an even more formidable force of assimilation: having multiple ethnic identities due to intermarriage. We would expect becoming a homogeneous member of American society to be the end product of the melting pot, but this has hardly ever been the case. Typically, later generations *choose* an individual ethnic identity or multiple identities. By choosing their identities, the grandchildren and great-grandchildren of immigrants are better able to appreciate the overall ethnic diversity of their society. To illustrate, answer the following question: how Irish do you have to be to be Irish on St. Patrick's Day? As a class project, I had students interview patrons of Irish pubs on St. Patrick's Day, and we found that the overwhelming majority of patrons considered themselves Irish. We found on further questioning that most were actually less than half Irish, some just "having an Irish relative in the past." Being Irish on St. Patrick's Day had less to do with lineage and more to do with the enjoyment of Irish American music and customs.

With subsequent generations, there is a shift from an immigrant identity to an ethnic identity (Dyen and Bohlman 1985; Lockwood 1986). The term *ethnic* has most frequently been applied to non-English-speaking European American immigrants (Miller 1986:356). This usage has incorrectly tended to exclude Native Americans,

FIGURE I   The Jerry Intihar Ensemble performing at the 1992 National Folk Festival in Johnstown, Pennsylvania. Photo by Carl Rahkonen.

Being Irish on St. Patrick's Day had less to do with lineage and more to do with the enjoyment of Irish American music and customs.

African Americans, and to some extent Asian Americans from being ethnic. At the same time, Irish Americans have been considered ethnic in spite of being overwhelmingly English speaking. Institutes of immigration research, which in the past have tended to concentrate solely on European Americans, have in recent years expanded their scope to include all immigrants.

INSTITUTIONS SUPPORTING ETHNIC IDENTITY

Religious institutions

As new immigrants arrived in America, they would seek out institutions that supported their ethnic identity. One of these primary institutions was the church or temple to which they belonged. It was not as simple as being Catholic, Lutheran, Orthodox, or Jewish. Frequently, local congregations were organized specifically for their own ethnic group. For example, the Cambria City section of Johnstown, Pennsylvania, has five Catholic churches within a square half mile, each defined by its ethnic composition. German and Scandinavian communities in North America were largely defined by the presence of their local Lutheran church parish. People who belonged to these congregations felt at home because they held services in the original languages of the immigrants and they featured music from the Old Country. These churches also functioned as a focal point for social activities, providing an important outlet for the community's musicians. The local church was also central to the life-cycle and year-cycle events of the immigrants. Weddings, funerals, and initiation rites; Christmas, Easter, Passover, and similar calendar celebrations became for the community a time to gather and reaffirm their identity as a community. Ethnic music and food were an essential part of these occasions.

Ethnic societies

In addition to their churches, many immigrant communities created their own lodges and clubs. They were organized for a variety of reasons: some were fraternal organizations based on language and ethnicity; some were based on politics within the ethnic community. For example, Finnish immigrants from the political left wing organized their own social clubs and halls to promote their ethnicity as well as their political views. Some clubs were based on the primary occupation of the immigrant community, such as Workers' Halls frequented by ethnic groups in one occupation. Some were commercial establishments, such as restaurants or pubs, which catered to the food, drink, and music preferences of a particular ethnic group, such as the Greek American coffeehouse [see SOUTHEASTERN EUROPEAN (BALKAN) MUSIC, p. 919] or the Italian American *caffe concerto* [see ITALIAN MUSIC, p. 860]. These lodges and clubs provided a significant venue for ethnic music, particularly dance music.

Some ethnic groups, especially those with members scattered over a wide area, formed regional, national, and even international societies based on their ethnicity. Some of these societies began as fraternal organizations or mutual benefit societies, such as the Italian Catholic Federation and the Order of the Sons of Italy [see ITALIAN MUSIC, p. 860], or grew from networks of local lodges, such as the Sons of Norway or the Finnish American Knights and Ladies of Kaleva [see SCANDINAVIAN AND BALTIC MUSIC, p. 866]. These societies provided benefits to their members and produced publications that kept more isolated immigrants abreast of the activities of their countrymen. The Finnish Suomi Seura 'Finland Society' publishes the journal *Suomen Silta* 'A Bridge to Finland', which includes articles written in Finnish, English, and Swedish and caters to the needs of Finnish immigrants not only in North America but also in Sweden, Australia, New Zealand, and elsewhere. The society supports summer workshops and clinics as well as charter flights to Finland. It provides the primary means for isolated Finnish immigrants to keep in touch with their ethnicity.

Festivals

Another institution that supports and promotes ethnic identity is the ethnic or folk festival. There are literally hundreds of such festivals on local, regional, and national levels. Local festivals may originally involve a single ethnic group and grow to become a multiethnic festival of a region or community. Such is the case with the Finnish American *Laskiainen* festival of Palo, Minnesota, which was documented by the Smithsonian Institution in a film (Vennum et al. 1983). Whereas diversity of languages and religions tends to separate people, this is not the case with music and food; people tend to try the music and food of another culture before anything else. *Laskiainen* became a combination of all the ethnic traditions of the region and was appreciated by the entire community.

The National Folk Festival, sponsored by the National Council for the Traditional Arts, is the oldest of the national American festivals, beginning in 1934. Its founder, Sarah Gertrude Knott, recognized that folk festivals go through three stages: the first features "native material traditionally learned and traditionally transmitted"; the second stage includes "basic cultural offerings from [ethnic] communities"; and the third stage adds "urban and popular" materials (Knott 1953; Lawless 1960:442). Today the National Folk Festival is held in a selected American city for three years, after which that city continues on its own. These festivals typically feature the foods, crafts, and musics of the local ethnic community, as well as some nationally known performers. The Smithsonian's annual Festival of American Folklife in Washington, D.C., has served the dual purpose of educating the nation about its various ethnic heritages and providing the premier performance opportunity for ethnic groups (figure 2). Performing at the Smithsonian Festival is for ethnic musicians analogous to playing at Carnegie Hall for the classical musician, or at the Grand Ole Opry for the Country and Western star. FinnFest USA, first held in 1985, has been a primary vehicle for the rejuvenation of Finnish American identity, particularly among the second, and subsequent generations of Finnish Americans. Each summer FinnFest attracts thousands to hear lectures on Finnish American culture, sample ethnic foods, and attend concerts of Finnish and Finnish American music. What was at one time local music is now appreciated on a national stage.

FIGURE 2   A Volga German ensemble from Nebraska playing at the 1975 Festival of American Folklife in Washington, D.C. Photo courtesy the Ralph Rinzler Folklife Archives and Collections, Center for Folklife and Cultural Heritage, Smithsonian Institution.

EUROPEAN ETHNIC MUSIC IN AMERICA

Members of European American ethnic groups were bound together by common language, customs, religion, and music. These common cultural traits took on added importance in the New World, becoming *symbols* of ethnic identity. As symbols they had, in many instances, greater stability here than in the Old World. Ethnic groups have tended to perpetuate customs, traditions, and music even after they had vanished in the lands of their origin. One example of this was the discovery of English and Scottish folk songs in the southern Appalachians by Cecil Sharp in 1916–1918 (Sharp 1932). An even more extreme case is that of the hymns of the German American

Amish, which are believed to be a marginal survivor of monophonic German hymnody (Nettl 1957a).

Hybridization

At the same time that some musical styles were being preserved in America, new musical styles were being created by a process of hybridization, or fusion. Ethnic groups came into close contact with other groups and with American popular culture. When different ethnic groups in close proximity had similar kinds of music, a performing ensemble could cross over and play at the other group's social functions. Many examples of this have been documented by Victor Greene in his history of old time ethnic music in America (1992). A large proportion of the engagements of the Intihar Ensemble, the polka band from Johnstown, for example, were at weddings or other events that mixed ethnicities: a bride, for example, might be Polish, and the bridegroom Italian. The band's repertoire included Polish, German, Italian, Greek, Irish, and Mexican pieces, which reflected the multiethnic makeup of their audiences. They performed a variety of pieces that could be appreciated by all, regardless of ethnic background. This had the overall effect of uniting their audiences despite the divergent backgrounds of individuals. Individual ethnicity became something that could be appreciated by everyone in a panethnic context. In such a context, ethnic diversity can be a unifying force, in which each person respects and values differences in others.

An additional force for hybridization has been American popular culture as spread by the mass media. This has influenced ethnic ensembles to adopt certain popular stylistic features, especially when performing in a multiethnic context. One of the best examples of this process is that of the Slovenian-style polka bands of the 1940s and 1950s. The style, popularized by Frankie Yankovic, combined old Slovenian melodies played by two accordions, with popular rhythm provided by bass, drums, and four-string banjo. During that era, its popularity stretched far beyond the Slovenian community and even that of ethnic music in general.

All the various types of music discussed here have in common that at some point they moved from being performed just for their specific ethnic community, to being performed in a broader multiethnic or panethnic context. The style and repertory of the music became adapted for broader contexts commonly found in American society. This movement could be so great that the music might no longer be associated with a single ethnic group. Some musics may enter the mainstream of American popular music and no longer be considered ethnic. Sometimes older forms of ethnic music may be revived, and the new champions of this music often come from some different ethnic background.

GENRES AND CONTEXTS

European immigrants brought with them a wide variety of music, some of which was preserved in the New World and some of which was adapted to suit different conditions or functions. The essays in this section describe a wide variety of specific styles and genres, but despite the variety, they share some general characteristics.

Vocal music

Although it may not have been easy to bring a musical instrument on the arduous journey to America, all immigrant groups brought vocal music with them; the voice took no space in the luggage. Vocal music has a text, which makes it possible to tell a story or to express an opinion. Much of the scholarship on vocal music has been concerned primarily with the text. Anglo-American ballad research began among literary scholars, who collected and studied the texts of ballads long before others studied the tunes. More than a century of research has shown a high degree of ballad preservation in America. Of the 305 English and Scottish ballad texts transcribed in the monumental collection of Sir Francis James Child, more than one hundred texts were found in the United States, as well as eighty tunes (Seeger 1980:440). Bertrand Bronson's musical counterpart to Child's work (1959a) and his additional studies (1950; 1959b) confirm the strong connection between English and North American ballad singing. Cecil Sharp (1932) showed that the same is true of Anglo-American folk songs in general.

The music that had the most relevance to the immigrant community was that which was passed down by oral tradition. Of primary importance to non-English-speaking immigrants were those songs in their original languages. Subsequent generations would learn these songs; sometimes they were the only things known to them in the original language. These songs functioned as a fundamental tie to these people's ethnic language and culture heritage.

Immigrants also created new songs featuring texts about the immigrant experience, commonly called immigrant ballads. These songs had the double function of strengthening immigrants in their newfound situations and of relating their experiences back to their home countries. Similar to these were songs with nostalgic texts about longing for the Old Country.

It was possible to express in song certain points of view that could not be expressed openly in any other way. An examination of the texts reveals that songs frequently commented on historical or current events, politics, living conditions, labor problems, or dissatisfaction with or desire for a better life. Even such genres as lullabies and humorous songs might include commentary. Songs composed about local events or local points of view could enter a stream of tradition carrying them throughout the ethnic community in North America and perhaps to other communities.

Ethnic groups also knew a great deal of vocal music outside oral tradition, such as church carols or hymns, for which the texts, at least, appeared in hymnals or other books. Many ethnic groups in North America formed choirs and singing societies, which performed choral compositions in European classical style or classical arrangements of folk songs. These choirs and singing societies generally sang their works in the original language of the immigrants, thus creating an image of national or ethnic unity (for specific examples, see Albrecht 1975; Babow 1969; and Eidbo 1956). Ethnic choirs, using the original languages, and singing societies provided an alternative means of sustaining a unified ethnic identity, a trend documented among Polish Americans by Paula Savaglio (1996).

Instrumental music

Just as in the Old World, instruments accompanied song, but purely instrumental music was most frequently associated with dance. For example, even a cursory examination of transcribed ethnic fiddle music shows that the vast majority of pieces are reels, jigs, hornpipes, waltzes, schottisches, strathspeys, and polkas, all of which are dance forms. The only exceptions are instrumental song transcriptions. Originally these pieces actually accompanied dance, but today they may be heard just as frequently at fiddle contests or on the stage at folk festivals. There has been a gradual shift from being purely functional dance music, to being music that may be listened to in a variety of contexts and appreciated for its style, rather than its function.

Of all the dance forms played by European Americans, perhaps the most pervasive is the polka, and it may be the most representative form of ethnic music in America. Charles Keil and colleagues (1992:14) cite six (or more) distinctive polka styles: southwestern Chicano and Papago Pima polkas; midwestern to western German American and Czech Bohemian American polkas; eastern to midwestern Polish American and Slovenian American polkas. Richard March (1998) includes Slovenian, Norwegian, Polish, Croatian, Bohemian (Czech), Finnish, and Dutchman (German) styles of polka *just from the state of Wisconsin* on a recent compact disc. Each of its various styles is immediately recognizable as ethnic and can be associated with a specific group. At the

Of all the dance forms played by European Americans, perhaps the most pervasive is the polka, and it may be the most representative form of ethnic music in America.

same time, all these styles embody mixtures of ethnic traditions as well as elements of popular music.

One class of instrumental music not associated with dance was that of the wind band movement. Beginning in the nineteenth century, wind bands became popular all across Europe and America, and many ethnic communities formed their own bands. Typically, these bands played the same kinds of music as other wind bands of the era: waltzes, polkas (and other dance forms primarily for listening and not for dancing), marches, opera selections, and patriotic and nationalistic music. For more information on ethnic wind bands, see Rocco (1990) and Greene (1992); on the wind band movement, see Kreitner (1990).

Certain instruments have become symbolic of ethnic groups. For example, the *tamburitza* has become a primary symbol of Croatian and Serbian immigrant groups, the button-box accordion for Slovenians, the bouzouki for Greeks, the *harding fele* for Norwegians, and bagpipes for Scottish Americans. Frequently these instruments were played only by a minority in the European areas from which they came: the *tamburitza* from northern Croatia and northeastern Bosnia, the *harding fele* from the Telemark provinces of western Norway, and so on. In America they have become general symbols for the entire nationality.

Some ethnic groups may have the same or very similar instruments as symbols of their ethnicity. For example, the Czechs use the *cymbaly* and the Ukrainians the *tsymbaly* [see CENTRAL EUROPEAN MUSIC, p. 884; EASTERN EUROPEAN MUSIC, p. 908], essentially the same instrument. The psalteries played by Baltic peoples have become symbols for each of the countries where they appear: the Finnish *kantele*, Estonian *kannel*, Latvian *kokle*, and Lithuanian *kankle*.

Joyce Hakala, a veterinarian from Minneapolis, formed Koivun Kaiku 'Echo of the Birch' (figure 3) in 1984, the first Finnish *kantele* ensemble in North America. The group was an immediate hit with the Finnish American community. Although few Finnish Americans had ever even seen a *kantele*, they had all heard of the instrument and knew it was the national instrument of Finland. As such, the *kantele* had an enormous symbolic value beyond its use for the production of music. Hakala's ensemble is made up entirely of third- and subsequent generation Finnish Americans and non-Finnish individuals interested in *kantele* music. No one speaks Finnish, but they sing many songs in this language. They were invited to perform for the 1994 Kaustinen Folk Music Festival in Finland, and toured the United States in 1997 on a Finlandia Foundation grant (Hakala 1997).

Contexts

Although many of the same forms and genres from Europe have been preserved in America, the contexts and functions of these genres may have changed. For example, music associated with calendrical rituals of agrarian societies may now provide entertainment and sustain ethnic identity. Svatava Pirkova-Jakobson (1956) said that what were rituals in Europe have become reenacted as drama in America. Still, certain year-

FIGURE 3   The Finnish American *kantele* ensemble *Koivun Kaiku* (Echoes of the Birch) dressed in Finnish national costumes, with their instruments. Photo by Charles Marabella, c. 1990. Used by permission.

cycle events associated with various saints days, Christmas, Easter, Passover, and New Year continue to be a significant venue for ethnic music.

Perhaps the most significant contexts for ethnic music continues to be life-cycle events such as weddings, initiation ceremonies, and funerals. Ritual songs and customs may still be performed in the New World, but they may lose their ritual significance and be performed outside ritual contexts.

Ethnic music was also performed simply for entertainment at dances, house parties, and similar events, as well as at concerts of singing society choirs and local wind bands. The contexts ranged from private homes, where music was just for family and friends, to church, community or local events, and ultimately regional or national festivals.

THE RECORDING INDUSTRY

One of the greatest forces for the dissemination and preservation of European American music in North America has been the recording industry. Many record companies, beginning with cylinder recordings and reaching a peak with 78s, began issuing specialized ethnic series advertised in ethnic catalogs.

Ethnic music was most often performed by amateur musicians for family and friends or for events held by their local ethnic communities. They performed a specialized repertoire for a specialized audience. Ethnic musicians almost always had to have some other kind of profession and performed their music as a hobby. When the best of these musicians issued recordings, their status in the community changed. In some cases they turned professional, touring beyond their local boundaries to other communities of their nationality. They might also perform for other nationalities who enjoyed a similar style of music.

Some sound recordings became best-sellers within their particular ethnic communities. When a recorded version of a genre of music became widely known in a community, it would homogenize, standardize, and popularize that musical style. This happened for two reasons. First, the community expected a particular piece, or type of music, in live performance to sound like the familiar recorded versions. Second, and more important, new musicians in the tradition would frequently learn their repertoire and style from recorded versions of the music.

With the advent of the audiocassette, recordings of ethnic music became even more pervasive, but the effect on the overall musical community moved largely back to local control. Almost any musical ensemble could produce its own cassette, which could be marketed at local performances. The impact of the cassette tape has been documented in studies by Roger Wallis and Krister Malm (1984) and Peter Manuel (1993). Sound recordings also leave us with a primary historical record of the music of various ethnic communities.

EUROPEAN AMERICAN MUSIC RESEARCH

Many of the sources summarizing research into European American musics point out the dearth of publications in this area. One of the best places to find information has been in general studies on folk music. Bruno Nettl's *An Introduction to Folk Music in the United States* (1949; subsequent editions 1960, 1972) examines the "ethnic backgrounds of American folk music," devoting chapters to American Indian, British, and European traditions. His *Folk and Traditional Music of Western Continents* (1973) provides a more extensive survey of the methods of folk music research and explores folk styles around the world, including European traditions in North America. Nettl's early article on urban folk music in Detroit (1957b) is still valuable. Philip V. Bohlman (1988) takes Nettl's work a step further by studying the folk music of the "modernized and urbanized world" (p. xvii), including valuable information on modern European American folk musics, especially that of German Americans. *Folk Music and Modern Sound* (Ferris and Hart 1982) contains several important essays on ethnic music in America.

Among the more specialized studies is an article by Charles Seeger (1961), which provides an excellent history of European dominance over music in the New World. Theodore C. Grame's *America's Ethnic Music* (1976) is a fine general survey, especially valuable for the vocal music of non-English-speaking European immigrants. Stephen Erdely's overview (1979) provides a substantial introduction on the vocal and instrumental traditions of a wide variety of ethnic groups, with a particular emphasis on urban traditions. Nicholas Tawa's *A Sound of Strangers* (1982) examines issues of style, acculturation, and identity in urban ethnic communities, particularly those from the Mediterranean countries and the Middle East. A special issue of *Selected Reports in Ethnomusicology*, edited by James Porter (1978a), had as its theme the "traditional musics in the Americas" (p. v). His introductory essay (1978b) is an especially strong overview of European American folklore and immigrant research in general. Articles by the folklorists Stephen Stern (1977) and James P. Leary (1984) give excellent theoretical backgrounds for studying ethnic folk traditions.

Studies on the ethnic recording industry in America provide significant sources of research. *Ethnic Recordings in America* (1982) is a collection of essays that document a wide variety of European American as well as other ethnic musics in America through sound recordings from the first half of the century. The most important discographical tools are the seven-volume *Ethnic Music on Record* by Richard Spottswood (1990) and *Ethnic and Vernacular Music* by Paul Vernon (1995). Victor Greene's *A Passion for Polka* (1992) serves as a historical counterpart to these discographies by chronicling the music of European American ethnic groups through their sound recordings.

Articles in *The New Grove Dictionary of Music and Musicians* (Seeger 1980) and in *The New Grove Dictionary of American Music* (Bohlman et al. 1986; Nettl 1986) give especially good general surveys. Important bibliographical works include a book-length annotated bibliography by Terry Miller (1986) and bibliographic essays by Helen Myers (1993a,b).

Even though the era of mass immigration from Europe has long passed, European American music is as vibrant as ever. As earlier generations pass away, there is no need to fear that their music will also pass into oblivion. There will always be someone inter-

FIGURE 4   A diverse audience enjoys the performance of Karl and the country Dutchmen in the Wisconsin Program of the 1998 Smithsonian Folklife Festival. Photo by Richard Strauss and courtesy of the Ralph Rinzler Folklife Archives and Collections, Center for Folklife and Cultural Heritage, Smithsonian Institution.

ested in Irish fiddling, Polish polka, Croatian *tamburitza*, Finnish *kantele*, or German hymn singing, if not for its ethnic symbolism, at least for the quality of its style and the aesthetic enjoyment it provides (figure 4).

REFERENCES

Albrecht, Theodore. 1975. "German Singing Societies in Texas." Ph.D. dissertation, North Texas State University.

Babow, Irving. 1969. "The Singing Societies of European Immigrant Groups in San Francisco: 1851–1953." *Journal of the History of Behavioral Sciences* 5.

Bohlman, Philip V. 1988. *The Study of Folk Music in the Modern World.* Bloomington: Indiana University Press.

Bohlman, Philip V., et al. 1986. "European-American Music." In *The New Grove Dictionary of American Music*, ed. H. Wiley Hitchcock and Stanley Sadie, New York: Grove's Dictionaries.

Bronson, Bertrand. 1950. "Some Observations about Melodic Variation in British-American Folk Tunes." *Journal of the American Musicological Society* 3:120–134.

———. 1959a. "Towards the Comparative Analysis of British-American Folk Tunes." *Journal of American Folklore* 72:165–191.

———. 1959b. *The Traditional Tunes of the Child Ballads*. Princeton, N.J.: Princeton University Press.

Dyen, Doris, and Philip V. Bohlman. 1985. "Becoming Ethnic in Western Pennsylvania: Processes of Ethnic Identification in Pittsburgh and Its Environs." Paper presented at the American Folklore Society Annual Meeting, Cincinnati, Ohio.

Eidbo, Olav H. 1956. "Songs of the Norwegian Folk in Culture and Education in the United States." Ph.D. dissertation, University of North Dakota.

Erdely, Stephen. 1979. "Ethnic Music in the United States: An Overview." *Yearbook of the International Folk Music Council* 11:114–135.

Ethnic Recordings in America: A Neglected Heritage. 1982. Washington, D.C.: Library of Congress American Folklife Center.

Ferris, William, and Mary L. Hart, eds. 1982. *Folk Music and Modern Sound*. Jackson: University Press of Mississippi.

Grame, Theodore C. 1976. *America's Ethnic Music*. Tarpon Springs, Fla.: Cultural Maintenance Associates.

Greene, Victor. 1992. *A Passion for Polka: Old Time Ethnic Music in America*. Berkeley: University of California Press.

Hakala, Joyce. 1997. *Momento of Finland: A Musical Legacy*. St. Paul, Minn.: Pikebone Music.

Jones, Maldwyn A. 1960. *American Immigration*. Chicago: University of Chicago Press.

Keil, Charles, Angeliki Keil, and Dick Blau. 1992. *Polka Happiness*. Philadelphia: Temple University Press.

Knott, Sarah Gertrude. 1953. "The Folk Festival Movement in America." *Southern Folklore Quarterly* 17 (June):143–155.

Kreitner, Kenneth. 1990. *Discoursing Sweet Music: Town Bands and Community Life in Turn of the Century Pennsylvania*. Urbana: University of Illinois Press.

Lawless, Ray M. 1960. *Folksingers and Folksongs in America*. New York: Duell, Sloan and Pearce.

Leary, James P. 1984. "Old Time Music in Northern Wisconsin." *American Music* (Spring):71–87.

Lockwood, Yvonne H. 1986. "Immigrant to Ethnic: Symbols of Identity among Finnish-Americans." In *Folklife Annual 1986*, 92–107. Washington, D.C.: Library of Congress American Folklife Center.

Manuel, Peter. 1993. *Cassette Culture: Popular Music and Technology in North India*. Chicago: University of Chicago Press.

March, Richard. 1998. *Deep Polka: Dance Music from the Midwest*. Washington, D.C.: Smithsonian Folkways SF CD 40088. Compact disc and 28-page booklet.

Miller, Terry. 1986. *Folk Music in America: A Reference Guide*. New York: Garland.

Myers, Helen. 1993a. "British-Americans." In *Ethnomusicology: Historical and Regional Studies*, ed. Helen Myers, 36–45. New York: Norton.

———. 1993b. "North America." In *Ethnomusicology: Historical and Regional Studies*, ed. Helen Myers, 401–460. New York: Norton.

Nettl, Bruno. 1949; 2nd ed. 1960. *An Introduction to Folk Music in the United States*. 3d ed., rev. and expanded by Helen Myers (1972), under the title *Folk Music in the United States: An Introduction*. Detroit: Wayne State University Press.

———. 1957a. "The Hymns of the Amish: An Example of Marginal Survival." *Journal of American Folklore* 70:323–328.

———. 1957b. "Preliminary Remarks on Urban Folk Music in Detroit." *Western Folklore* 16(1):37–42.

———. 1973. *Folk and Traditional Music of Western Continents*. 2nd ed. Englewood Cliffs, N.J.: Prentice-Hall.

————. 1986. "Folk Music." In *The New Grove Dictionary of American Music*, ed. H. Wiley Hitchcock and Stanley Sadie. New York: Grove's Dictionaries.

Pirkova-Jakobson, Svatava. 1956. "Harvest Festivals Among Czechs and Slovaks in America. In *Slavic Folklore: A Symposium*, 68–82. Philadelphia: American Folklore Society.

Porter, James, ed. 1978a. *Selected Reports in Ethnomusicology* 3(1). Special Issue. Los Angeles: UCLA Program in Ethnomusicology.

————. 1978b. "Introduction: The Traditional Music of Europeans in America." In *Selected Reports in Ethnomusicology*, 3(1):1–23. Los Angeles: UCLA Program in Ethnomusicology.

Rahkonen, Carl J. 1993. "Pan-Ethnic Polkas in Pennsylvania." Paper presented at the 32nd World Conference of the International Council for Traditional Music, Berlin, June 18.

Rocco, Emma S. 1990. *Italian Wind Bands: A Surviving Tradition in the Milltowns of Pennsylvania*. New York: Garland.

Savaglio, Paula. 1996. "Polka Bands and Choral Groups: The Musical Representation of Polish-Americans in Detroit." *Ethnomusicology* 40 (Winter):35–47.

Seeger, Charles. 1961. "The Cultivation of Various European Traditions of Music in the New World." In *Report of the Eighth Congress of the International Musicological Society, New York, 1961*, 364–375. Kassel: Barenreiter. Reprinted in *Studies in Musicology 1935–1975*, 195–210. Berkeley: University of California Press.

————. 1980. "United States of America, II. 3: British-American Folk Music." In *The New Grove Dictionary of Music and Musicians*, ed. Stanley Sadie. New York: Grove's Dictionaries.

Sharp, Cecil. 1932. *English Folk Songs from the Southern Appalachians*. London: Oxford University Press.

Spottswood, Richard K. 1990. *Ethnic Music on Record: A Discography of Ethnic Recordings Produced in the United States, 1893 to 1942*. Urbana: University of Illinois Press.

Stern, Stephen. (1977). "Ethnic Folklore and the Folklore of Ethnicity." *Western Folklore* 36(1):7–32.

Tawa, Nicholas. 1982. *A Sound of Strangers: Musical Culture, Acculturation, and the Post–Civil War Ethnic America*. Metuchen, N.J.: Scarecrow Press.

Vennum, Thomas, Elli Kongas-Maranda, and Marsha Penti.1983. *At Laskiainen in Palo, Everyone Is a Finn*. Washington, D.C.: Smithsonian Institution Film.

Vernon, Paul. 1995. *Ethnic and Vernacular Music, 1898–1960: A Resource and Guide to Recordings*. New York: Greenwood.

Wallis, Roger, and Krister Malm. 1984. *Big Sounds from Small Peoples*. New York: Pendragon.

Wilgus, D. K. 1959. *Anglo-American Folksong Scholarship since 1898*. New Brunswick, N.J.: Rutgers University Press.

English and Scottish Music

Christopher Goertzen

Music for Worship
Child Ballads and Other Folk Songs
Dance Music
Popular Music

Seventeenth-century British settlements in North America formed the nucleus of and template for the institutions and culture of the young United States and for much of Canada. Although Native American teachings in hunting and agriculture allowed the young colonies to survive, Native American music had too little in common with that of the colonists to mix with or even influence what was arriving. Colonial music at first consisted of British psalmody, ballads and other folk songs, dance music, and, by the end of the eighteenth century, popular music created in or funneled through Britain. The initial transfer of cultural materials was little different from their movement from London to some remote post in the English countryside. As time passed and the population of North America increased, American cities could imitate London more closely, although the desire to do so gradually waned. In the 1840s, when American blackface minstrelsy became the rage throughout the English-speaking world, the overall flow of culture began to reverse direction. Today, most British musicians who become popular in the Americas perform American-derived music.

MUSIC FOR WORSHIP

Wherever they settled, European immigrants brought with them two streams of music, military (briefly discussed in the section on popular music) and religious [see BANDS, p. 563; RELIGION, p. 116]. The first settlements in British North America—in Jamestown in 1607, at Plymouth Rock in 1620, and the Massachusetts Bay Colony in 1627—were founded largely for religious reasons, and musical life immediately focused on Protestant psalmody. The Pilgrims, a small conservative group that had broken away from the Puritans, brought with them the singing of psalms, for which they borrowed preexistent melodies. In theory, a tune could be employed on a given day to set any text that was in a compatible meter, here meaning having a certain number of lines and syllables per line. For example, common-meter psalms had four lines of text, the first and third with eight syllables, the second and fourth with six syllables, matching many tunes already in use for religious song as well as many secular tunes. Tunes had specific names, some of which indicated a regular association with given psalms (for example, Psalm 100 was and is still sung to the tune "Old Hundred," in long meter, that is, four lines each with eight syllables).

The lack of melodies in most of the books worshipers held in their hands was not just a matter of ease of printing: few in most congregations read music. This situation spawned a fascinating manner of performance, "lining out."

Inevitable change in the English language meant that any translation of the psalms would in time seem clumsy and would be updated by dissatisfied clergymen to achieve or restore whatever mix of grace and straightforwardness was desired. The first book printed in Britain's North American colonies was just such a revision: the 1640 publication of the *Whole Book of Psalmes Faithfully Translated into English Metre,* which became informally known as *The Bay Psalm Book.* A small book that grew in its many subsequent editions, it quickly supplanted parallel publications throughout the colonies. Seventy editions were published in British North America (through 1773), eighteen in England (through 1754), and twenty-two in Scotland (through 1759). The first edition did not contain music; its authors recommended borrowing tunes from an earlier British publication. Thirteen two-part settings of psalm tunes appeared in a supplement to the book in its ninth edition (1698), these tunes drawn from John Playford's *Brief Introduction to the Skill of Musick,* printed in London (most later editions lacked music).

Although in a literal sense the first North American publication, *The Bay Psalm Book* should be considered a British book—perhaps from a corner of the empire far from its center, but clearly British nonetheless—successful not because of its place of origin but because it presented an important body of literature in a fresh and accessible form. The early centuries of British-American life have left no documentation of any attempt to create region-specific tunes. Any regional, American quality that *The Bay Psalm Book* could be said to have possessed would have to concern its populist approach, perhaps especially important in the colonies due to the arduousness of daily life there, which left little time for wrestling with abstruse language or tricky music—indeed, for learning to read music.

How did this early psalm singing actually sound? Widespread changes in church economics and responsibilities in Britain before the colonies were founded, plus the proscription of organs and choirs in many churches, made the tidy picture of musical performance offered by musical notation deceptive (Temperley 1979). The lack of melodies in most of the books worshipers held in their hands was not just a matter of ease of printing: few in most congregations read music. This situation spawned a fascinating manner of performance, "lining out." A leader would sing a phrase to remind the congregation of the melody being used, then the group would repeat that line. Next, the leader offered the second line, the group sang it, and so on. Contemporary American accounts of the results—positive reports in the mid-seventeenth century but complaints by 1700—suggest a sound very like that of twentieth-century survivals of this practice in southern Appalachia. The congregational answers took much longer than the leader's lining out and were neither faithful copies of melodic contours nor sung in unison. Instead, singers more sincere than confident filled leaps in the melody with intervening steps and with slides between pitches, each performer managing these things in his or her own manner and pace. Contemporary reports asserted that the results were simply a mess, though this practice in its rare modern manifestations produces a rich and often lovely heterophony (a musical texture in which different variants of the same musical line are performed together).

Lining out answered by slow, varied responses, termed variously the usual, common, or "old" way of singing, began to be shunted aside by a return to singing by note—regular singing—beginning in the 1720s. In this reform movement, which remained vigorous for about a century, singing masters (the first substantial body of native-born music professionals) taught music literacy in connection with sacred music in singing schools lasting from a few weeks to no more than three months. The reform proceeded initially, just as it had a bit earlier in Britain, then took on an American cast only with the flowering of shape-note singing and repertoires of music composed in the United States, especially in New England (McKay and Crawford 1975). In participating in each of these and many later developments in singing for worship, North American communities remained part of the complex of British culture. Some correspondence continues to this day, as religious organizations pay heed to national boundaries more as a matter of practicality than of conviction. But the continued differentiation in Protestant worship on both sides of the Atlantic has naturally entailed a gradual parting of the ways in associated musical practices.

CHILD BALLADS AND OTHER FOLK SONGS

Late in the nineteenth century, Harvard English professor Francis Child traveled to England and Scotland to seek out an old, substantial body of English-language poetry, ballads that still flourished in oral tradition [see NEW ENGLAND BALLADS, p. 153]. Both lyrics and music proved appealing aesthetically, as centuries of revision by generations of singers had polished both stories and melodies. The ballads also appealed to prevailing ideologies: scholars with a romantic and nationalist bent savored tunes and poetry endorsed by history and supposedly unsullied by industrialism and other unsalubrious modern trends. This was purely Anglo-Saxon art. Child published 305 texts, many in multiple variants, in *The English and Scottish Popular Ballads* (1882–1898). Scholars following the lead of Briton Cecil Sharp found that Child had not been looking for surviving ballads in the best places. The tradition was actually more vigorous in North America than back in Britain. This body of song, still known as the Child ballads, became the focus of folk music research in both the United States and Britain: many hundreds of collections and analyses made this the most studied body of folk music in the world.

Child ballads are strophic (have the same music for each verse of text) and are set to melodies that usually arch upward at the beginning of the verse, then downward at the end. Rather than melodramatically painting the often lurid stories, melodies and singers simply present these laconically. Rhythms are straightforward, although some singers dwell on given pitches. A majority are in major mode, although much scholarship deals with other modes that contrast with major. In some of these contrasting modes, the two half-steps lie relative to the tonic (the so-called church modes); others use fewer than seven pitches per octave (Bronson 1959–1972, 1969). Indeed, pentatonic scales, more used in Scotland than in England, also are employed relatively frequently in the American South. Coffeehouse singers of the 1950s to the early 1970s often underlined the age of the Child ballads by performing ones with exotic topics and set in exotic modes, for example, "The Great Silkie of Sul Skerry" (following Child's classification, No. 113), some forms of which are in mixolydian mode (like major, but with a lowered seventh scale degree).

The texts tell stories, ones seldom tied precisely to time or place, partly through narration and partly through the voices of the characters. Verses—generally four lines long, sometimes with one or two repeated—range in number from a few to as many as several dozen. Descriptive language often follows conventions: horses are usually dapple grays or milk-white steeds, and a (fair) maid's skin is lily white. The topics of these ballads are venerable and enduring, although neither those explicitly tied to British history nor humorous ones haved fared well in America, with a few exceptions (we still laugh at "The Farmer's Curst Wife," Child 278). Many ballads relate bloody, perhaps supernatural tales that offer both titillation and moral instruction. In "Barbara Allen" (Child 84, the only of these ballads that frequently reached print in nineteenth-century America), a young man flirts clumsily, alienating the very young woman he wished to impress. She spurns him, causing him to despair and die. Filled with remorse, she herself pines away. The lesson for those listening: be careful and considerate in expressing love. In "The Golden Vanity" (Child 286), a British ship is threatened by pirates. The captain convinces a cabin boy (or carpenter boy, depending on the version) to sabotage the approaching enemy despite great personal risk. If the plan succeeds, the boy will be rewarded with great riches plus social elevation through marriage to the captain's daughter. The valiant deed is done, but the boy is abandoned to drown. The lesson: do not trust the upper classes. In "Lady Isabel and the Elf Knight" (Child 4) (figure 1), a knight with a habit of seducing, robbing, then murdering young women is finally killed by one of them. In many versions, she then returns home and admonishes her parrot not to reveal the story, whereas in other versions, she is killed. The lessons are straightforward: one should not seduce (or be seduced!), rob, or murder.

FIGURE 1   "Lady Isabel and the Elf Knight," tune and text as sung by Mrs. Moore of Rabun Gap, Georgia, on 1 May 1910. Source: Bronson 1959–1972, I:45 (originally recorded by Olive Dame Campbell, and transcribed by Cecil Sharp).

Just as a ballad's text exists in many forms, so does each tune. Samuel Bayard, the central theorist of the concept of the "tune family," described it as "a group of melodies showing basic interrelation by means of constant melodic correspondence, and presumably owing their mutual likeness to descent from a single air that has assumed multiple forms through processes of variation, imitation, and assimilation" (1950). He noted that contour and diagnostic tones (notes in rhythmically prominent positions) tend to be relatively stable and thus good signposts for identifying related tunes, whereas rhythms and modes are much more apt to fluctuate without reference to genetic connection (Bayard 1939, 1954; see contrasting views in Bronson 1959–1972, 1965; Goertzen 1985; Seeger 1977; Shapiro 1975). Complementary principles govern the flux of this folk tradition: although a tune's identity may persist across a number of highly variable forms, a gradual and multiple divergence in these forms can also occur. An air may thus be traced through many manifestations practically up to the point of its disappearance—its complete transformation into another and different tune (Bayard 1951). There is also a loose linkage between text and tune. Usually the various forms of a text are set to members of the same tune family, although some examples may be sung to other tunes, and a given tune or tune family may be associated with more than one text (figure 2).

When Cecil Sharp sought out Child ballads in the southern Appalachian mountains, he found them embedded in large personal repertoires rich in British and American broadside ballads and lyric songs [see POPULAR MUSIC OF THE PARLOR AND STAGE, p. 179]. In comparison with Child ballads, broadside ballads are usually somewhat

FIGURE 2 "Lady Isabel and the Elf Knight," tune as sung by Agnes Conners of Antigonish, Nova Scotia, on 8 March 1912. Source: Bronson 1959–1972, I:57 (originally collected and transcribed by Phillips Barry).

younger and refer explicitly to specific events in comparatively precise (though less poetic) language. Some began life as literal broadsides, that is, stories cast in verse sold as "extras," printed on one side of a sheet of newsprint, with the purchaser instructed to sing the tale "to the tune of" a song the author of the text felt was widely known. Of the tunes suggested in American nineteenth-century broadsides, two American tunes were common, "Kingdom Coming" by Henry Clay Work and "Dixie," formerly attributed to blackface minstrel Dan Emmett but more likely from a black middle-class family, the Snowdens (Sacks and Sacks 1993). However, perhaps the most common tune for this purpose was a British broadside tune, "Vilikens and His Dinah," best known today with the text "Sweet Betsy from Pike." Although such extras were most common in Europe from the sixteenth through mid-nineteenth centuries, songs that match these in character continued to be made, for example, the turn-of-the-twentieth-century North Carolina murder ballad "Omie Wise."

A wide variety of nonnarrative songs also traveled to the United States from Britain. They were sung frequently and also served as models for native composition. For example, a Scottish song, "The Cuckoo" (Lomax 1960), flourishes in the American South and has verses that we can hear again in other well-known songs such as "Stewball," "Jack of Diamonds," and so on. It is especially hard to distinguish between distinctively British and American texts (or musical elements) in this fluid repertoire.

DANCE MUSIC

A variety of instruments and music, apart from functional marches, arrived early in the British colonies, and the instruments were employed in both cultivated and casual settings. In particular, many flutes, fifes, and especially violins arrived during the seventeenth century. This last instrument has flourished since as both concert violin and folk fiddle. Fiddling is marked not just by heavy reliance on oral tradition but also by customary functions, venues, repertoires, and, especially in certain parts of the southern United States, by playing techniques and some use of scordaturas (tunings other than the usual low-to-high G–D–A–E, for example, A–E–A–E).

Although the romantic image of the illiterate backwoods fiddler bears a germ of truth, many fiddlers were educated community leaders: a steady stream of dance-tune publications attests to continued music literacy on the part of some of these men. And although modern contest fiddlers (now both men and women) include both rough-hewn and subtle musicians who play only by ear, others puzzle out tunes from print, and still others are converted classical violinists.

Violin and fiddle still look alike, but the fiddle is less narrowly defined in terms of quality and style of woodworking and varnish application and in range of desirable timbres. Indeed, in many eras and locations, the relatively nasal and cutting timbres associated with rough-and-ready construction and cheap metal strings helped a solo fiddler be heard by vigorous dancers. The fiddle was the main instrument for the performance of British American (and French American) folk music from the late eighteenth century well into the twentieth century [see FRENCH MUSIC, p. 854]. Fiddlers in the colonies that would become the United States drew primarily on British traditions (initially Scottish and English, later also Irish) for tunes, ways to compose tunes and shape repertoires, and playing styles. The young country then spawned regional styles, with the northern United States cleaving to English models and retaining a

Indeed, in many eras and locations, the relatively nasal and cutting timbres associated with rough-and-ready construction and cheap metal strings helped a solo fiddler be heard by vigorous dancers.

greater degree of music literacy. A burgeoning array of southern substyles were more strongly linked to Scottish repertoires, transmitted both through print and aurally, and they absorbed considerable African American influence in performance styles. Both imported and homegrown tunes on imported models were usually linked with dance genres. Through the early nineteenth century, a fiddler's repertoire generally supplemented these dances with vocal airs, marches, and other popular tunes. As decades passed and the solo fiddler, fifer, or flutist was replaced in cultivated circles by ensembles or keyboard instruments, fiddle music emerged as a discrete repertoire containing older dances, plus a few descriptive airs and hymn tunes. British hornpipes and reels became American hoedowns, just as other duple-time social-dance tunes eventually fit into the polka category and various triple-time dances were reworked as waltzes.

As American fiddling became less British or French and more American, other instruments more frequently joined it in performance. The fife, closely associated with the fiddle since the Revolutionary War era, was also played in fife-and-drum corps (military and dance tunes were shared between fiddle and fife). Fiddle and banjo duos became widespread in the wake of the popularity of blackface minstrelsy and of medicine shows and significantly more common when late-nineteenth-century mail-order catalogs helped disseminate a wide range of newly-cheap products, including families of instruments. Although minstrel-style banjo playing, which survives as clawhammer and frailing styles to the present day in the upper South, included African-derived playing techniques, the central repertoire for the southeastern string band (fiddle, banjo, and a few supplementary stringed instruments, including guitar, upright bass, and perhaps mandolin) has always focused on British American dance tunes.

The common-time reel and breakdown usually consists of two (or rarely more) eight-measure strains, which contrast in tessitura (emphasized pitch range). A typical performance in older, dance-oriented style consists of one strain twice, the other twice, the first twice, and so on until a few minutes have passed and the dancers are tired. Although a few northern contra dances preserve a formerly more common linkage of specific tunes with specific sets of dance figures, many tunes are used interchangeably [see CONTRA DANCE, p. 230]. That certain tunes are often irregularly phrased or otherwise inapt for dance accompaniment reflects the truth that fiddlers have always played just for their own and their peers' pleasure. Today's regional styles are characterized by the degree of melodic ornamentation and variation employed (primarily linear styles such as those of Texas are most common), the degree of affinity with older published models (New England style is most common), and the amount of African- and Scottish-derived syncopation, both bold and subtle, that is emphasized in the various styles of the southeastern United States, which are in turn differentiated by whether the high or low strain is played first and other factors.

Although most other dance genres have been assimilated into the breakdown, the British hornpipe remains vital, especially in New England, and a few marches, jigs, and descriptive pieces have survived here and there. The most widespread alternative to the breakdown remains the waltz (in 3/4), which arrived in large numbers in British and British-based publications in the 1810s–1820s, received new impetus around the turn of the twentieth century from the new pop song styles of Tin Pan Alley, and has returned as a standard ingredient in modern fiddle contests in most of North America. These contests represent a nativistic folk revival, in which a blend of rural and urban brands of nostalgia, the modern luxury of plenty of practice time for players of all socioeconomic backgrounds, and the listening-oriented venue have produced legions of polished instrumentalists, again blurring the line between folk and art performance and between violin and fiddle.

Fiddling in the southeastern United States draws heavily on blackface minstrelsy, an essentially American entertainment that spread from the United States to Britain and the rest of the English-speaking world. The first full evening of blackface entertainment was presented in 1843, and such evenings were taking place in Britain within a year. Minstrelsy took over the British stage so quickly because it stemmed from British theatrical models (blacks were often imitated on stage there as early as the late eighteenth century) and contained enough British musical elements that the music was easily accessible. Many blackface songs were recastings of British, especially Scottish, fiddle tunes and songs, sometimes with new texts, other times just with new orchestrations (and perhaps enlivened rhythms). Many such tunes were already widespread in oral tradition and, although repeatedly transformed, remain central in today's American folk music, particularly in the upper South. "Backside Albany," in 1815 among the earliest American blackface airs, borrows the melody of "Boyne Water," a British folk song whose text mocked the ineptness of the British fleet (Mahar 1988) and whose melody was frequently heard in the United States long before receiving its blackface text. "Old Zip Coon," one the best known minstrel songs, borrowed its contour from the eighteenth-century Scottish fiddle tune "Rose Tree" (which had first reached print in William Shield's ballad opera *Poor Soldier* in 1782), perhaps passing through an intermediate state as a rare antebellum fiddle tune, "Natchez on the Hill" (Goertzen and Jabbour 1987) (figure 3).

FIGURE 3   Ancestors of the American fiddle tune "Turkey in the Straw": *a,* "Rose Tree" is an eighteenth-century Scottish fiddle tune that was also a song in a ballad opera (*New and Complete Preceptor for the German Flute* 1824–1826:11); *b,* "Natchez on the Hill" is a fiddle tune adapted from "Rose Tree," one rare both in the nineteenth century and today (Knauff 1839, 4:3); *c,* "Old Zip Coon," adapted from one of the previous tunes, became one of the most popular blackface minstrel songs (and instrumental melodies) (Howe 1851:43); *d,* it survived under that title into the twentieth century (Dunham 1926:6), but more often is encountered as "Turkey in the Straw."

FIGURE 4   An old-timey fiddle band jamming in the campground at a fiddle contest in Sparta, North Carolina, in July 1996. Although such ensembles are modeled after blackface minstrel groups, much of the repertoire performed is British in origin. Photo by Christopher Goertzen.

In addition to borrowing directly more than a few Scottish melodies (and somewhat fewer Irish and English tunes), blackface minstrelsy drew on British, especially Scottish, models for harmonic and melodic formulas (Goertzen 1991). It is possible that part of the motivation for adding the fifth string to the paradigmatic minstrel instrument, the five-string banjo, has to do with Scotland. This string was played during minstrel performances unfretted, as a drone, just as in modern old-timey playing in the southeastern United States (figure 4). Although this drone is played off the beat, producing syncopation, a feature that is generally and justly taken to reflect African influence, that a drone is present at all points less to any Sub-Saharan African musical tradition than to the Scottish bagpipes and various northern European types of dulcimer. Why was there so much Scottish influence on this first important American entertainment? In the progressing industrial revolution, one refuge from soot, crowding, and alienation from the land was in a willfully rosy complex of memories of earlier rural life. For the British and other Europeans, Scotland embodied this pastoral ideal. Its inhabitants were considered on the one hand savage, crude, and generally inferior but, on the other, possessed of an unthinking contentment and a handy folk wisdom expressed in pithy sayings, all qualities to be transferred to the willful images of American blacks acted out on the minstrel stage.

POPULAR MUSIC

Popular music, as understood in contradistinction to folk music and art music, is music premiered on the secular stage, performed by professionals for a largely nonelite audience (according to Hamm 1979: xvii "persons of limited musical training and ability"), and subsequently sold to this broad audience in large numbers of inexpensive artifacts (sheet music at first, now tapes, compact discs, and so on). This category came into being as part of the industrial revolution, which created a nonelite market in the first substantial middle class as well as the streamlined technical means to produce affordable sheet music.

The transportation of British popular music to the New World began with the arrival of musically literate Britons who were not exclusively interested in church music. However, publication of sheet music in substantial amounts in North America was delayed until after two events occurred in 1789: a post-Revolution ban on theater music was finally lifted, and a U.S. copyright law came into being [see THE MUSIC INDUSTRY, p. 256; GOVERNMENT AND POLITICS, p. 288]. At first, sheet music was relatively expensive, few copies of given items came out, and few copies of British publications were imported. Because printed music was not particularly easy to come by, many enthusiasts also maintained manuscript music commonplace books, that is, initially blank books into which fiddlers, flutists, fifers, and sometimes pianists (all generally young and male) copied tunes from publications they were able to borrow. A few such manuscripts were compiled as early as during the Revolutionary War, thus predating the burgeoning of music publishing in the 1790s (Keller 1981). This practice remained common through the 1830s, when sheet music became easier to acquire because advances in publishing techniques resulted in lower prices, thus expanding markets to develop.

The contents of one typical commonplace book, assembled in and just before 1807 in rural New York by a young fiddler named Philander Seward, exemplify the broad sweep of British secular music of the day (Goertzen 1982). Among the seventy-seven items Seward wrote down were dances such as "Fisher's Hornpipe," "Flowers of Edinburgh," and "Boyne Water"; marches such as "Duke of York's March"; convivial songs such as "Drink to Me Only with Thine Eyes"; didactic pieces such as "Lesson by Morelli"; and concert excerpts such as "Duett" in William Shield's ballad opera *Rosina* and "March in the Battle of Prague," a ubiquitous selection from Franz Kotzwara's descriptive piece, itself a parlor standby in Britain.

That Seward also wrote down a few marches with American titles ("[General] Green's March," and so on) reflected a linked pair of common British practices: creating new marches or other patriotic melodies by retitling older tunes and writing tunes absolutely in line with an established style but bearing new, topical titles. The United States's central patriotic airs, for example, employ British melodies: "The Star Spangled Banner" borrows the tune of a British convivial song, "To Anacreon in Heaven," and "My Country 'Tis of Thee" puts a new text to "God Save the King [Queen]." "General Green's March" and many other tunes of this time whose names do refer to American people and places are in tried-and-true British pop music styles. In short, the era of American musical life most studied, that from its beginnings to about 1800, is the least American; it is essentially British. Most professional musicians were not native born but rather British immigrants, concert life followed that of Britain as closely as was practical, and the largest compilation of American music from this time, the enormously valuable *National Tune Index* (Keller and Rabson 1980) might better be titled *British Secular Music of the Late Eighteenth Century.*

As the nineteenth century continued, British influence on North American musical life often took the form of forwarding English borrowings from other cultures. Thomas Moore's *Irish Melodies* (1843), new texts put to Irish tunes in oral tradition, were immediate hits in North America. The birth of ballad opera with the *Beggar's Opera* (1728, but performed for over a century, including many times in the United States) was in reaction to the dominance of British concert life by Italians and Italian opera. In the service of one goal, to reject the pompous nobles and gods of Italian opera plots in favor of British commoners, the music of this and other early ballad operas was permeated with Scottish (!) tunes and style. Italian opera would return to Britain and thus to America in the nineteenth century, climaxing in the 1830s–1840s, but arias were "Englished" in Britain, that is, translated, with the arias' forms sometimes squared off when marketed as sheet music. This was precisely the treatment that many German songs received while traveling through Britain before crossing the Atlantic (Hamm 1979) [see CENTRAL EUROPEAN MUSIC, p. 884]. British singer and composer Henry Russell, the most popular performer in Canada, then the United States in the mid-1830s through the mid-1840s, set texts reeking of Irish nostalgia or Italian melodrama to simplified Italian-styled music. One way to understand the rapidness of the burgeoning of American blackface minstrelsy is to interpret this as an American extension of the British proclivity for borrowing and aggressively recasting music and musical elements from the cultures of others.

Much of the story of changing taste in music in nineteenth-century America is one of accumulation: the modern model of each new style's displacing an instantly

The same complex mix of rebellion and nostalgia that keeps the Stones economically viable, inspires synthesis after synthesis as much by North Americans as the British, who continue to produce such intellectually and musically interesting performers as Sting and ones as vacuous as the Spice Girls.

disdained older one coalesces only toward the end of the century. Compilations such as those by Bostonian Elias Howe (1844, 1851, 1864), among many others, did gather up the latest hits and youngest styles of popular music, but they abandoned nothing from earlier popular music publications. Nearly all of the British tunes laboriously written down by Philander Seward and many others at the beginning of the century were echoed dozens of times by Howe and his successors in publications distributed throughout North America. British influence finally waned later in the century but never completely disappeared (consider the durable popularity of Gilbert and Sullivan operettas).

The most interesting late manifestation of British influence in American music comes with the so-called British Invasion of the mid-1960s and its repercussions to the present day [see ROCK, p. 347]. Much of the appeal of the Beatles reflected their wonderfully eclectic synthesis of musical styles. They were less wedded to immediate trends in American popular music than were their American contemporaries, and their influences ranged from the early rock and roll of Buddy Holly and Chuck Berry forward to Bob Dylan and back to 1950s soft gospel and country (Price 1997). The British Invasion featured bands such as the Dave Clark Five, whose appeal has waned, but also the Rolling Stones, who still tour. The same complex mix of rebellion and nostalgia that keeps the Stones economically viable, inspires synthesis after synthesis as much by North Americans as the British, who continue to produce such intellectually and musically interesting performers as Sting and ones as vacuous as the Spice Girls. Today, audience members generally identify little that is British in British bands' sound: we have a single mammoth trans-Atlantic musical community based on American musical styles remixed at home and abroad.

REFERENCES

Abrahams, Roger D., and George Foss. 1968. *Anglo-American Folksong Style.* Englewood Cliffs, N.J.: Prentice-Hall.

Appel, Richard G. 1975. *The Music of the Bay Psalm Book, 9th Edition (1698).* Brooklyn, N.Y.: Institute for Studies in American Music.

Austin, William. 1975. *"Susanna," "Jeanie," and "The Old Folks at Home": The Songs of Stephen Foster from His Time to Ours.* New York: Macmillan.

Barry, Phillips, Fannie H. Eckstrom, and Mary W. Smyth. 1929. *British Ballads from Maine.* New Haven: n.p.

Bayard, Samuel P. 1939. "Aspects of Melodic Kinship and Variation in British-American Folk Tunes." In *Papers Read at the International Congress of Musicology,* 122–129. New York: Music Educators' National Conference.

———. 1944. *Hill Country Tunes: Instrumental Folk Music of Southwestern Pennsylvania.* Philadelphia: American Folklore Society.

———. 1950. "Prolegomena to a Study of the Principal Melodic Families of British-American Folk Song." *Journal of American Folklore* (63):1–44.

———. 1951. "Principal Versions of an International Folk Tune." *Journal of the International Folk Music Council* (3):44–50.

———. 1954. "Two Representative Tune Families of British Tradition." *Midwest Folklore* (4):13–34.

———. 1982. *Dance to the Fiddle, March to the Fife.* University Park: Pennsylvania State University Press.

Blake, George E. 1808–1813. *Blake's Evening Companion for the Flute, Clarinet, or Violin.* 2 vols. Philadelphia: Author.

Bronson, Bertrand. 1959–1972. *The Traditional Tunes of the Child Ballads.* 4 vols. Princeton, N.J.: Princeton University Press.

———. 1969. *The Ballad as Song.* Berkeley: University of California Press.

———. 1976. *The Singing Tradition of Child's Popular Ballads.* Princeton, N.J.: Princeton University Press.

Camus, Raoul F. 1976. *Military Music of the American Revolution.* Chapel Hill: University of North Carolina Press.

Chase, Gilbert. 1987 [1955]. *America's Music: From the Pilgrims to the Present.* Rev. 3rd ed. Urbana: University of Illinois Press.

Child, Francis James. [1882–1898]. *The English and Scottish Popular Ballads.* New York: Dover.

Coffin, Tristram P. 1963. *The British Traditional Ballad in North America.* Philadelphia: American Folklore Society.

Cormier, Bill. 1947. *44 Original Canadian Jigs and Reels for Square Dances.* Toronto: Harry E. Jarman and Co.

Dunham, Mellie. 1926. *Fiddlin' Dance Tunes.* New York: Fischer.

Ford, Ira W. 1940. *Traditional Music in America.* New York: Dutton.

Ganam, King. 1957. *Canadian Fiddle Tunes.* Don Mills, Ontario: BMI Canada.

Goertzen, Chris. 1982. "Philander Seward's 'Musical Deposit' and the History of American Instrumental Folk Music." *Ethnomusicology* 26(1):1–10.

———. 1985. "American Fiddle Tunes and the Historic-Geographic Method." *Ethnomusicology* 29(3):448–473.

———. 1991. "Mrs. Joe Person's Popular Airs: Early Blackface Minstrel Tunes in Oral Tradition." *Ethnomusicology* 35(1):31–53.

———. 1996. "Balancing Local and National Fiddle Styles at American Fiddle Contests," *American Music* 14(3):352–381.

———. 1997. "Gideon Lincecum, 'Killie Krankie', and Fiddling in Early Texas. In *Between the Cracks of History: Essays on Teaching and Illustrating Folklore,* ed. Francis Abernethy, 111–133. Publications of the Texas Folklore Society, vol. 55. Denton: University of North Texas Press.

Goertzen, Chris, and Alan Jabbour. 1987. "George P. Knauff's Virginia Reels and Fiddling in the Antebellum South." *American Music* 5(2):121–144.

Hamm, Charles. 1979. *Yesterdays: Popular Song in America.* New York: Norton.

———. 1983. *Music in the New World.* New York: Norton.

Horn, David. 1977. *The Literature of American Music in Books and Folk Music Collections.* Metuchen, N.J.: Scarecrow Press.

Howe, Elias. 1844. *The Musician's Companion.* 3 vols. Boston: Author.

———. 1851. *Howe's School for the Violin.* Boston: Author.

———. 1864. *Musician's Omnibus, Containing 1500 Pieces of Music.* Boston: Author.

Jabbour, Alan, ed. 1971. Album notes to *American Fiddle Tunes from the Library of Congress,* AFS L62. Washington, D.C.: Library of Congress.

Keller, Kate van Winkle. 1981. *Popular Secular Music in America Through 1800: A Preliminary Checklist of Manuscripts in North American Collections.* Philadelphia: Music Library Association.

Keller, Kate van Winkle, and Carolyn Rabson, eds. 1980. *National Tune Index: 18th-Century Secular Music.* New York: University Music Editions.

Knauff, George P. 1839. *Virginia Reels.* 4 vols. Baltimore: George Willig Jr.

Library of Congress, Music Division. 1942. *Checklist of Recorded Songs in the English Language in the Archive of American Folk Song to July, 1940.* Washington, D.C.: Library of Congress.

Lomax, Alan. 1960. *The Folk Songs of North America in the English Language.* New York: Doubleday.

Mahar, William J. 1988. "'Backside Albany' and Early Blackface Minstrelsy: A Contextual Study of America's First Blackface Song." *American Music* 6(1):1–27.

Marrocco, W. Thomas, and Harold Gleason. 1964. *Music in America: An Anthology from the Landing of the Pilgrims to the Close of the Civil War, 1620–1865.* New York: Norton.

McKay, David P., and Richard Crawford. 1975. *William Billings of Boston: Eighteenth-Century Composer.* Princeton, N.J.: Princeton University Press.

Mellers, Wilfrid. 1964. *Music in a New Found Land.* New York: Knopf.

Moore, Thomas. 1843. *Irish Melodies, with Original Prefatory Letter on Music: and a Supplement Containing a Selection from His Poetical Works.* 3rd complete American ed., from the 13th London ed. New York: R. P. Bixby & Co.

New and Complete Preceptor for the German Flute. 1824–1826. Albany, N.Y.: Steele.

Pichierri, Louis. 1960. *Music in New Hampshire, 1623–1800.* New York: Columbia University Press.

Playford, John. 1976 [1651]. *The English Dancing Master.* London: Author. Reprinted edition: Playford, John. 1694. *An Introduction to the Skill of Musick.* 12th edition. Reprint, with a new introduction, glossary, and index by Franklin B. Zimmerman. New York: Da Capo, 1972. Margaret Dean-Smith, ed. *Playford's English Dancing Master, 1651.* London: Schotlet Company, 1957.

Price, Charles Gower. 1997. "Sources of American Styles in the Music of the Beatles." *American Music* 15(2):208–232.

Sacks, Howard L., and Judith Rose Sacks. 1993. *Way Up North in Dixie: A Black Family's Claim to the Confederate Anthem.* Washington, D.C.: Smithsonian Institution Press.

Seeger, Charles. 1966. "Versions and Variants of the Tunes of 'Barbara Allen.'" *University of California, Los Angeles Selected Reports* 1(1):120–167.

———. 1977. *Studies in Musicology 1935–1975.* Berkeley: University of California Press.

Seward, Philander. 1807. *Philander Seward's "Musical Deposit."* Music commonplace book on deposit in the University of Illinois Music Library. Urbana, Illinois.

Shapiro, Anne Dhu. 1975. "The Tune Family Concept in British-American Folk-Song Scholarship." Ph.D. dissertation, Harvard University.

Sharp, Cecil. 1932. *English Folksongs from the Southern Appalachians.* London: Oxford University Press.

Sonneck, Oscar G. 1916. "Benjamin Franklin's Musical Side." In *Suum Cique: Essays in Music,* 59–84. New York: Schirmer.

———. 1921. "The History of Music in America." In *Miscellaneous Studies in the History of Music,* 324–344. New York: Macmillan.

Sonneck, Oscar G., and William Treat Upton. 1964 [1945]. *A Bibliography of Early American Music.* New York: Da Capo.

Stoutamire, Albert. 1972. *Music of the Old South: Colony to Confederacy.* Rutherford, N.J.: Fairleigh Dickinson University Press.

Temperley, Nicholas. 1979. *The Music of the English Parish Church.* 2 vols. Cambridge: Cambridge University Press.

Wilgus, Donald K. 1959. *Anglo-American Folksong Scholarship Since 1898.* New Brunswick, N.J.: Rutgers University Press.

Wolfe, Charles K. 1982. *Kentucky Country.* Lexington: University of Kentucky Press.

Wolfe, Richard J. *Secular Music in America: 1801–1825.* 3 vols. New York: New York Public Library.

Irish Music
Rebecca S. Miller

Irish Traditional Dance Music
Irish Song
Irish American Popular Music
The Irish Traditional Music Revival and Beyond

FIGURE I   Former resident of County Monaghan, Ireland, Matty Connolly lived for many years in Queens, New York, and is now a resident of Norwalk, Conn. He is a master of the uilleann pipes. Photo by Kathleen Collins, Grug Harbor, 1987.

One of the largest groups in America today, Irish Americans live throughout the United States, with particularly large communities found in New York City, San Francisco, Chicago, Boston, and Philadelphia. Irish immigration to the United States began in the eighteenth century and continues to this day, with new immigrants continually adding to a rich legacy of folk and popular music and song genres. This transnational exchange is also accomplished through the strength of international media and the commercial recording industry, as well as the back-and-forth migration of young Irish between Ireland and the United States.

Significant Irish American musical expressions from the twentieth century include a variety of folk and popular musical genres such as Irish traditional instrumental dance music and *sean-nós* 'old-style' song, contemporary Irish folk song, "high art" Irish American song (popularized in the 1920s and 1930s by such singers as John McCormack), hybridized Irish American popular song, Irish big band and showband musics, and Celtic rock.

IRISH TRADITIONAL DANCE MUSIC

Irish instrumental music originated centuries ago primarily as accompaniment for dancing. Today, in both Ireland and the United States, the music is played in informal community and familial contexts such as *seisúns* (sessions) and at *céilís* (group folk dancing), as well as in concert and at Irish music festivals. Playing styles and repertoire are generally learned through listening and imitation, tunes are composed more or less anonymously, and the music is, on the whole, crafted through a communal process.

Among the most commonly found instruments in traditional Irish music today are the fiddle, button accordion, wooden flute, tin whistle, and *uilleann* pipes (small, elbow-driven bagpipes) (figure 1), as well as the concertina, mandolin, harp, and tenor banjo. Traditional Irish music is primarily melodic with a subtle but propelling rhythmic pulse. Because of this reliance on an often intricate melody line, harmonic accompaniment is a relatively new development of the twentieth century and is commonly provided by piano, guitar, *bodhrán* (handheld frame drum), and, since the late 1970s, multi-stringed instruments modeled after the Greek *bouzouki* and the medieval European *cittern*.

FIGURE 2 County Kerry native Daithi Sproule (vocalist/guitarist) now a resident of Minneapolis; fiddler, Liz Carroll of Chicago; and button accordionist, Billy McComiskey of Baltimore. Photo courtesy Helen Bommarito.

Countermelodies and harmonies are uncommon in what practitioners consider strictly traditional music, although many younger Irish ensembles incorporate such arrangements in performance. Dance tunes span a range of rhythmic meters and tempi: those in duple time include lively reels (4/4) and polkas (2/4) as well as stately marches and syncopated hornpipes; tunes in triple time include jigs (6/8) and slip jigs (9/8). Also popular are waltzes in 3/4 time and slow airs and laments, which are largely free meter. Regionalism also plays a role in repertoire: musicians from the northern counties include tunes known as highlands (also called flings), mazurkas, schottisches, and barn dances in their repertoires, while players from the southwestern counties of Kerry and Cork are known for their upbeat slides (figure 2).

Traditionally, playing styles were transmitted from player to player; the recording industry (and, more recently, tape recorders) have dramatically altered this process of dissemination. Between 1900 and the early 1930s, the demand for traditional Irish music in the United States was fueled by the arrival of hundreds of thousands of Irish immigrants. Major record labels such as Decca and Columbia reacted to the market potential of this so-called Golden Age of Irish Music and made hundreds of 78-rpm recordings of outstanding Irish musicians residing in major U.S. cities (McCullough 1974; Moloney 1982). These recordings popularized specific playing styles and repertoire for generations to come and perpetuated the music of a handful of outstanding musicians. The Sligo style, for example, remains one of the most popular among Irish American players today, thanks to the early recordings of such fiddlers as Michael Coleman, Paddy Killoran, and James Morrison (see *Wheels of the World*, 1997).

IRISH SONG

Like Irish instrumental dance music, Irish traditional singing *(sean-nós)* has been passed down orally from older to younger generations. Sung in Irish Gaelic, *sean-nós* songs are performed as unaccompanied solos and feature intricate ornamentation. Once a means of recording local events and history, *sean-nós* songs today serve strictly as entertainment. Increasingly, contemporary *sean-nós* singers performing for American audiences select songs from both the Irish- and English-language repertoires and eliminate verses to fit modern attention spans.

Eliminating most of the ornamentation found in *sean-nós* singing, the Clancy Brothers and Tommy Makem performed their songs faster and with a driving beat.

Sean-nós singing was largely inaccessible to many Irish Americans and the general public because of the language barrier, so it was bypassed in the revival of Irish music in the United States in the 1960s and 1970s. Instead, songs in English, backed by guitars and banjo, took its place—a style of folk singing best exemplified by the Clancy Brothers and Tommy Makem. By capturing the attention of a vast international audience, these performers spawned a new tradition from an old. Eliminating most of the ornamentation found in *sean-nós* singing, the Clancy Brothers and Tommy Makem performed their songs faster and with a driving beat. They sang primarily in unison, which not only gave them their particular trademark as a group but also allowed for audience participation, thus increasing their appeal. Their repertoire of Irish protest and political songs was well in keeping with the prevailing antiwar sentiment of the 1960s, and their early appearances on television (then a relatively new medium) sparked an interest in Irish song among young Irish Americans as well as non-Irish.

A new folk-based Irish singing style emerged in the late 1970s, based in large part on the music of the Clancy Brothers and Tommy Makem. This style typically features a solo lead singer (sometimes with harmony vocals) and backup instrumentation, ranging from a single guitar to complicated ensemble arrangements. The singers often incorporate some of the simpler *sean-nós* vocal ornamentation into the delivery, and their repertoires, consisting of ballads, political songs, and original numbers, are typically sung in English.

IRISH AMERICAN POPULAR MUSIC

Irish American popular music is less clearly definable than its traditional counterpart, given the wide array of styles from different eras. In general, popular Irish American musics combine mainstream and Irish traditional instruments and incorporate harmonic and rhythmic accompaniment reflective of the mainstream popular genres of the time. Today, the difference between some Irish traditional bands and popular Irish ensembles is often difficult to discern as the lines between the two often blur. Some hybridized Irish American musical styles have worked their way into American culture, for example, those popularized by such composers or singers as George M. Cohan and Bing Crosby.

Beginning in the 1930s, big band Irish American ensembles were extremely popular among Irish immigrants in major U.S. cities. These bands featured piano, drums, horn and reed sections, amplified guitar and bass, and other instruments commonly found in American big bands. Most of the Irish big bands arranged parts in a style similar to the mainstream big bands, and all covered the current hits of the day to suit their immigrant audience's taste for the contemporary American, in addition to Irish and Irish American songs.

The years just after World War II saw another major surge in Irish immigration to the United States, a trend that again increased when Congress passed the Immigration and Nationality Act of 1952 (the McCarran-Walter Act), which favored Irish immigration. With these new arrivals came an increased demand for popular Irish and Irish

American musics rather than for traditional music. By the 1950s, the traditional Irish music scenes in both Ireland and the United States had waned to the point that there was little opportunity for public performance. The exceptions in the United States were the Gaelic League's monthly *céilís* in various East Coast cities and the annual New York City *Feis* (Irish music festival/competition) sponsored by the United Irish Counties Association. In general, the new Irish immigrants were eager to assimilate into American society and leave behind the vestiges of folk culture. Many Irish traditional musicians who came to the United States during this era were thus forced to set aside their instruments altogether or learn the popular styles of Irish American music on mainstream instruments (Miller 1996).

Showbands

Irish immigrants and Irish Americans flocked to dance halls where they danced to Irish big band music and then, by the late 1950s, to a new type of Irish popular music called "showband music," a craze that swept Ireland and Irish America, displaced big band music, and consistently sold out large dance halls in every major American city. Showbands performed covers of hits by early rock and roll artists (Elvis Presley in particular), skiffle, popular Irish songs, and country and western. With strong rhythm sections and an emphasis on guitars and brass, showbands offered provocative showmanship, matching stage costumes, versatile repertoires, and occasional comedy acts (Power 1990). Like the Irish big bands, showbands incorporated a traditional Irish element into their performances: a set of *céilí* dances played by an accordionist might be interspersed between covers of popular Irish songs and rock numbers. And like big band music, showbands provided the Irish American community with a musical expression that was quintessentially theirs, while reflecting the music of the mainstream. In 1965, Congress passed the Immigration and Nationality Act Amendment, which, in effect, cut off the steady stream of Irish immigrants to America. With no new audiences of young, unattached immigrants in search of a night life, Irish dance halls throughout the United States closed and the showband heyday ended.

Showband music remains a popular form of entertainment in Irish America today, particularly among the older generations. Showbands perform for wedding receptions, at dances and fundraisers, and for other community celebrations and are the preferred music at Irish American resorts in the Catskill Mountains, the Poconos, and other areas. Modern showbands feature an electronic keyboard equipped with MIDI technology, drums or drum machine, guitar, bass, and vocals. Often the keyboardist doubles on the button accordion, if only to play the occasional *céilí* dance, waltz, or polka. Showbands offer some of everything—nostalgic and political Irish songs, modern American songs with a pop beat, traditional Irish tunes, and Country-and-Western music.

Celtic rock bands

Beginning in the late 1970s, the Irish communities in New York, Boston, and Chicago saw the emergence of Celtic rock bands—ensembles that combine Irish traditional instruments, such as the *uilleann* pipes and the fiddle, with electric guitar and bass, keyboards, full drum kit, and other instruments. Drawing on a rock-and-roll aesthetic, Celtic rock bands combine rock instrumentation, technology, and rhythms with traditional tunes and original Irish songs. (The term "Celtic rock" distinguishes these types of ensembles from such groups as U2, which are strictly Irish rock bands.) A contemporary cousin to the Irish showband, Celtic rock groups perform in many of the same venues, such as Irish resorts, pubs, and at Irish music festivals; the main difference between the two ensembles is the degree of orientation to rock and roll, with showbands specializing in a diversity of pop and non-rock musics, while Celtic rock bands favor a hard rock (and sometimes rap) style. Celtic rock groups also perform political songs that challenge those in power in Ireland and comment on the life of illegal Irish immigrants in the United States (Ocasek and Kirwan 1993).

THE IRISH TRADITIONAL MUSIC REVIVAL AND BEYOND

A resurgence of interest in Irish traditional music had its beginnings in the mid-1960s thanks to the international attention brought to Irish music by the Clancy Brothers and Tommy Makem. Many young players who were initially inspired by these artists next turned their attention to the older instrumental music styles. Simultaneously, a revival of interest in traditional music in Ireland was sparked under the aegis of Comhaltas Ceolteoiri Eireann 'Irish Musicians' Association' and soon extended to America. Music *seisúns* began anew in pubs and Irish social halls in major U.S. cities, and concerts of traditional Irish bands—Planxty, the Bothy Band, the Boys of the Lough, and the Chieftains—were presented at general and Irish American venues. Many of the older traditional players who had immigrated in the 1940s and 1950s were invited to perform in similar venues. The sense of importance of ethnicity thus rekindled, the 1970s and 1980s saw an unprecedented number of Irish American youngsters flocking to schools for Irish traditional music and step dance in major American cities. With the support of state and federal folk arts funding, several annual Irish traditional music festivals were developed beginning in the late 1970s, including the Irish Arts Center's Irish Traditional Music Festival at Snug Harbor, Staten Island, New York; the Philadelphia Ceili Group's Irish Music Festival; the Milwaukee Irish Music Festival; and the Washington Irish Folk Festival at Wolf Trap, Virginia.

The Irish traditional music community in the United States in the early twenty-first century is thriving. Musicians of all ages and backgrounds—Irish immigrants, Irish Americans, and non-Irish—attend weeklong Irish music and song camps, play in music sessions in large and small cities, and attend Irish music festivals. Major record labels and folk music labels promote and produce Irish music; public and commercial radio programs give airtime to Irish traditional music as well as to Celtic rock and other popular styles; and concert venues, large and small, including Carnegie Hall and Washington, D.C.'s Kennedy Center, regularly present Irish music, song, and dance. With the recent phenomenon of the Irish dance extravaganzas *Riverdance* and *Lord of the Dance,* the popularity of Irish cultural expression is clearly growing.

Over the years, Irish American popular musics have entertained their audiences until replaced by a modern style, one that is more in keeping with an evolving Irish American aesthetic and identity. Irish music, both popular and traditional, continues to serve as an extremely visible vehicle for changing group identity. It is precisely this enduring sense of ethnicity, as well as the increasing numbers of non-Irish who are attracted to Irish music, that augurs well for its survival and creative adaptation into the future.

REFERENCES

Black 47: Fire of Freedom. 1993. New York: EMI Records. Compact disc.

The Clancy Brothers with Tommy Makem: Luck of the Irish. 1992. New York: Columbia/Legacy CK47900. Reissue of classic recording on compact disc.

McCullough, Lawrence E. 1974. "An Historical Sketch of Traditional Irish Music in the U.S." *Folklore Forum* 7(3):177–191.

Miller, Rebecca S. 1996. "Irish Traditional and Popular Music in New York City: Identity and Social Change, 1930–1975." In *The New York Irish,* ed. Ronald H. Bayor and Timothy J. Meagher, 481–

507. Baltimore: The Johns Hopkins University Press.

Moloney, Michael. 1982. "Irish Ethnic Recordings and the Irish-American Imagination." In *Ethnic Recordings in America: A Neglected Heritage, 84–101.* Washington, D.C.: American Folklife Center.

Mullins, Patrick, and Rebecca Miller. *From Shore to Shore: Irish Traditional Music in New York.* 1993. New York: Cherry Lane Productions. Video. Distributed by the Cinema Guild, Inc., 1697 Broadway, Suite 506, New York, New York 10019-5904, (800) 723-5522.

O'Neill, Francis J. 1973a [1910, 1913]. *Irish Folk Music: A Fascinating Hobby.* Darby, Pa.: Norwood Editions.

———. 1973b [1910, 1913]. *Irish Minstrels and Musicians.* Darby, Pa.: Norwood Editions.

Power, Vincent. 1990. *Send 'Em Home Sweatin': The Showbands' Story.* Dublin: Kildanore Press.

Tom Doherty: Take the Bull by the Horns. 1993. Danbury, Conn.: Green Linnet Records, GLCD 1131. Compact disc.

Wheels of the World, Vols. 1 and 2. 1997. Newton, N.J.: Shanachie Records. Yazoo 7008 and 7009. Compact disc.

Iberian Music
Janet L. Sturman

Iberian music arrived in the United States in the sixteenth century with explorers and Catholic missionaries from the Iberian Peninsula, who formed some of the first European-style settlements in America. The founding of St. Augustine in Florida in 1565 predated that of Jamestown and Plymouth Rock by more than forty years. Florida belonged to Spain until 1819. In New Mexico, Spanish settlement took place as early as 1598, nine years earlier than Jamestown was settled. In Texas and California, Spanish and Spanish-Mexican settlement happened later, beginning in the 1690s and 1790s, respectively [see Hispanic California, p. 734; Tejano Music, p. 770]. Long after migration from the east overwhelmed the Spanish-speaking majority (beginning in 1848), these areas remained strongholds of Spanish culture in the United States.

MIGRATION AND ETHNIC DIVERSITY

Migration beginning in the eighteenth century included Jewish settlers of Iberian ancestry, many of whom migrated to cities in the United States and Canada after first having lived in the Netherlands, Cuba, or elsewhere outside the Peninsula [see Jewish Music, p. 933]. The Sephardim, as these Iberian Jews were known (from *Sefarad,* Hebrew for *Spain*), brought with them music and poetry distinguished by long-standing connections with Arabic forms and featuring the Ladino language (a mixture of Hebrew and Castilian). Israel Katz (1962), Judith R. Cohen (1993), and others have collected numerous examples of the *cantiga, romance, muwashshah,* and other types of Sephardic song, and performing ensembles such as the Seattle-based Al Andalus have built careers by presenting this repertoire in concert programs that highlight the multiethnic diversity of Sephardic music, including its link to Arabic culture.

In the nineteenth century, due in part to U.S. land grant incentives, new waves of immigrants from the Basque provinces of northern Spain arrived in the United States, particularly in western states such as Idaho, Nevada, and California. In contrast to the urban Sephardim, many Basques were originally shepherds and farmers and continued to maintain a rural lifestyle on arrival. The musical practices they cultivated reflected traditions associated with village and small town life in the Basque provinces.

Portuguese presence in the United States has never matched that of the Spanish, and migration from Brazil has never equaled that from Mexico or Cuba. Nonetheless, concentrations of Portuguese can be found in Rhode Island, Massachusetts, New

Although radio and television have reduced the transmission of older Spanish music, local folk musicians continue to sing *romances* such as "La Delgadina" ("The Thin Maiden"), which can be traced back to tenth-century Europe.

Jersey, Hawai'i, and California, and these communities frequently sponsor festivals that celebrate Portuguese culture by including music. Brazilian music, much of it representing Iberian root forms transformed, has had a substantial impact on American musical practice in general, and Brazilian traditions must also be recognized as a conduit for Iberian musical presence in the United States [see LATIN CARIBBEAN MUSIC, p. 790].

Over the years, Iberian American communities have continued to be enriched by arrivals from all corners of the Luso-Hispanic world, including Mexico, the Caribbean, Latin America, and the Philippines, and from the Portuguese territories of Madeira and Azores, Brazil, Cape Verde, Angola, and Mozambique. The musical traditions maintained by people of such contrasting backgrounds are equally varied. In particular, contributions from nonpeninsular communities often embodied Iberian practices transformed by processes of accretion, acculturation, and syncretism. Furthermore, a cycle of influence has developed over time as Iberian musical practices, transformed in the colonies and New World, have returned to the peninsula, where they have developed into new, vibrant practices only to be subsequently readopted in the United States.

DEFINING IBERIAN MUSIC

Given the long history and complex nature of Spanish and Portuguese influence, it is difficult to define the music of Iberia in an American context. The Spanish and Portuguese imported a repertoire of songs types such as the *romance, villancico, copla,* and *décima,* which were cultivated in both popular and learned circles. They brought genres that mixed music with spoken drama such as the *autos sacramentales,* the *comedia,* and the *zarzuela,* as well as an array of dance traditions including elegant figure dances, such as the *contradanza,* and more rustic dances, such as the foot-stomping *zapateado.* In addition to the folk hymns or *alabados* introduced by the religious brotherhoods (today kept alive in Catholic services throughout the Southwest and cultivated especially by the Penitentes of New Mexico), festive processions, pageants, and Masses associated with Catholic worship influenced performance formats and inspired new developments evident in contemporary performances of *posadas, pastorelas,* and *matachines.* Favored instruments in preferred combinations, such as the guitar combined with violin and harp, found their way to the United States, where variant forms and combinations developed. In all instances, habits of behavior, attitudes, and values accompanied the material culture.

TRACK 18

REVIVING MISSION AND CATHEDRAL MUSIC FOR CONCERT AND WORSHIP

Modern scholars and performers have devoted considerable energy to studying the chant, hymns, polyphonic song, and instrumental music used by the Franciscan and Jesuit missionaries. Few printed sources of the actual music are extant. However, the discovery of existing manuscripts in California and Latin American sites has permitted dedicated scholars such as Robert M. Stevenson (1960, 1968), Craig Russell (1992), William John Summers (1994), and John Koegel (1993, 1994) to uncover music for study and for performance in live concerts and on recordings. In addition to such revivals, oral tradition has kept this music alive, for although the practice of performing the larger polyphonic Masses seems to have died out after the mission period, many of the Spanish hymns are still sung by American Indian congregations today.

LIVING MUSEUMS: COMMUNITIES OF PRESERVATION

The singing of narrative poetry by the Isleños of St. Bernard Parish in Louisiana offers an example of more intimate efforts to sustain old Iberian forms. Here the tradition is maintained largely by an elderly population that strives to pass on the legacy of the *décima* via private performances and through the establishment of a museum dedicated to Isleño culture. The Louisiana *décima* has come to resemble more the *corridos* of Mexico and the American Southwest than the classic *romance* from which both derive. The Isleños also sing *romances, corridos, villancicos, coplas,* and modern popular songs from Cuba and Mexico.

The Mejicanos of New Mexico and their preservation of Spanish and Mexican *canciones, coplas,* and *corridos* are better known than the Isleños. Although radio and television have reduced the transmission of older Spanish music, local folk musicians continue to sing *romances* such as "La Delgadina" ("The Thin Maiden"), which can be traced back to tenth-century Europe. Brenda Romero (1997) provides a good introduction to the living Iberian legacy in New Mexico, as do Loeffler (1999) and Lamadrid, Loeffler, and Gandert (1994).

Basque organizations in Boise, Idaho (where the largest concentration of Basques in the United States live), and in Reno, Nevada, sponsor activities that keep alive peninsular customs of music and dance and reinforce instruction and retention of the ancient Basque language, Euskara. Since 1978, the North American Basque Organization has sponsored a summer camp where Basque song and dance is taught. The Jai Aldi (Feast of the City) festival in Boise began in 1996 as a celebration of Basque culture. Among the acts featured are the Oinkari Dancers, who perform sets of male and female dances including the male sword dance, the *ezpata dantza* (figure 1), characterized by the *zortiko* rhythm in 5/8 meter. Singers include the Biotzetik community chorus with a repertoire of polyphonic hymns, and dance songs accompanied by accordion or *txistu* 'ancient Basque flute' and *tamboril* 'small drum'. Ensemble leaders make regular trips to Europe to gather new songs and dances to teach performers back in the United States, with the result that the array of songs and dance in Boise is much richer

FIGURE 1   The Oinkari Basque Dancers perform a sword dance for the Jai Aldi festival in Boise, Idaho, July 1997. Note accordion player in right rear. Photo by Estibaliz Gastesi.

than the repertoire associated with any single town or region in the Iberian Basque provinces.

Also included in the festivities are small combos featuring saxophone, accordion, and guitar performing songs and dances in the waltz and polka rhythms that swept European ballrooms and traveled with immigrants to all corners of the United States. Soft rock styles provide yet another model for contemporary American Basque musicians.

The festival format is equally important in Portuguese communities across the United States. Celebrations such as the Feast of the Blessed Sacrament celebrated in New Bedford, Massachusetts, and the *festa* 'celebration' of Our Lady of Miracles in Gustine, California, were originally conceived as reenactments of sacred festivals in Portugal. Today, after more than sixty years of practice, the emphasis is on civic celebration and ethnic pride. Featured music includes the hymns and chants appropriate for the devotional novenas, as well as dance and marching band music. Dances and songs are frequently accompanied by Portuguese instruments such as *violas de arames, violãos,* and *guitarras,* but electronic instruments are increasingly popular as the mix of entertainment expands to include modern pop styles.

ANTIQUE FORMS: FUNDAMENTAL TRANSFORMATIONS

Syncretic practices that merge worldviews even as they redefine or overtly resist the fundamental perspectives that accompanied the original import are equally important. American treatments of Iberian sacred music dramas, generally known as *autos sacramentales,* exemplify such fundamental transformations. These dramas date back to twelfth-century Europe, where they served the Crusaders. These didactic musical plays were used as tools for promoting the conversion of indigenous people to Christianity. Today in the United States the *matachines* dance dramas are performed during the Easter and Christmas seasons in New Mexico and Arizona. Variant forms of this masked pantomime appear throughout the Luso-Hispanic world; the Brazilian *chegança,* for example, merges African customs with the Iberian *auto.*

Pastorelas

Among the other types of popular religious drama performed during the Christmas season are those that depict the search for lodging, *Las Posadas,* and *Los Pastores,* dramatizations of the shepherds' visit to the infant Jesus, also known as *pastorelas. Pastorelas* are performed in Hispanic communities throughout the United States as well as throughout Latin America. In addition to ritualistic versions performed by indigenous peoples or more solemn ecclesiastical presentations, a popular type of *pastorela* incorporates comic or satiric commentary on modern concerns. Such modern theatrical versions, especially popular in the American Southwest, often feature an eclectic mixture of music: traditional Spanish hymns, *villancicos, aguinaldos* may be augmented by indigenous' *mariachi* or modern dance bands.

Matachines

Many *matachines* in the United States today are performed by American Indians (the Pueblo in New Mexico and the Yaqui in Arizona), who use the dance drama to redress power imbalances and document their own histories and worldview [see SOUTHWEST, p. 428]. In addition to reinterpreting the colonizers' sense of good and evil, indigenous communities have created their own interpretations of central characters in the drama, including the role of the controversial female convert Malinche (Champe [1983]; Robertson [1992]; Spicer [1985]).

Although both indigenous and *mestizo* people adopted the basic frame for the dramas, music and dance changed. Spanish melodies played on the violin and with guitar accompaniment are retained in Hispanic versions, but Native Americans incorporated their own dances and sometimes their own music featuring chorus and drums (Robb 1961). Romero (1997) reports that the *matachina* is the only ceremony practiced by the Pueblo that uses European music and instruments. Similarly, favored Iberian instrumental combinations from the Baroque period such as the harp with guitar and violin, or flute and drum, are retained by the Yaqui (Arizona) and employed in the deer dances *(bailes de venados)* and *pascolas,* which like the *matachines* are pantomimes reflecting the crossing of Native American and Catholic ceremonies. Griffith (1997) believes that music of these sacred ceremonies has influenced social dance practices, in particular Tohono O'odham *waila.*

SEMICLASSICAL REVIVALS: CONTINUITY AND COMMON GROUND

In recent years, professional and amateur theatrical companies along with classically trained singers working in San Francisco, Los Angeles, Tucson, Santa Fe, El Paso, New Orleans, Tampa, Chicago, Miami, and New York have worked to revive Spain's special genre of secular musical drama known as *zarzuela.* Their efforts favor nineteenth- and twentieth-century classics such as Tomás Bretón's jewel of Madrilenian taste, *La verbena de la Paloma* 'The Festival of Our Lady of the Dove' or Federico Moreno Torroba's melodramatic masterpiece *Luisa Fernanda.* As a genre, the *zarzuela* merges classical and popular perspectives, and the scores typically incorporate the lively rhythms of regional dances such as the *jota, seguidillas, bolero,* and *habanera.*

CYCLICAL TRANSMISSION OF SIGNATURE TRADITIONS: FLAMENCO AND *FADO*

Since the nineteenth century, flamenco music and dance have stood as symbols of Iberian culture and have enjoyed popularity in the United States as such. Despite such iconic associations, flamenco owes its distinctive character to a blend of influences stretching beyond the peninsula. Gypsy practices (including many of the exciting rhythms and rich harmonies) as well as Arabic contributions (melodic mode, nature of vocal delivery) have also shaped flamenco. Even the poetic structure of the song verses can be linked to Arabic practice. The web of influences became even more intricate in the late twentieth century when Latin American and Caribbean music, including Argentine tango and Cuban rumba, inspired new approaches to flamenco heard in the innovative performances of Carlos Montoya and Paco de Lucia. In recent years, non-hispanic, American-born performers, most notably Elliot Fisk, increasingly perform flamenco in the United States.

Flamenco dance attracts even more support in the United States than does flamenco guitar music. The celebrated American dance company Ballet Hispanico, under the direction of Tina Ramirez since 1970, includes in its programs a dance set that illustrates the connections between the gypsy songs of Andalusia and Eastern Europe and the paths connecting them to flamenco. Contemporary dancers and companies, including José Greco II (b. 1962) and his new company, continue the legacies of early Iberian emissaries of flamenco to the United States such as the renowned dancers La Argentina (Encarnación Lopez [1895–1945]) and José Greco (b. 1918).

In contrast with dance, *Cante jondo,* the passionate song-cycle associated with flamenco, is best appreciated by Spanish speakers. It is sometimes compared to Portugal's *fado,* a dramatic and soulful style of urban popular song sung by performers supported by the Portuguese community in Newark, New Jersey, Providence, Rhode Island and the Sacramento Valley in California. Another example of cyclical exchange between Iberia and the Americas, *fado* is believed to have originated in Brazil as a descendant of the *lundu* and was later developed in Portugal.

ART MUSIC AND CLASSICAL REPRESENTATION

The rhythms and melodies of flamenco find voice in the classical compositions of the composer Carlos Surinach. Though born in Barcelona in 1915, he became a U.S.

citizen in 1959 and lived in New York until his death in 1997. Carrying on a nationalistic perspective established by Isaac Albéniz and Enrique Granados, Surinach is best known for the music he created for world-famous choreographers and dance companies including Martha Graham (*Acrobats of God, Embattled Garden, The Owl and the Pussycat*), Doris Humphrey (*Ritmo Jondo*), Paul Taylor (*Agatha's Tale*), and the Joffrey Ballet (*Feast of Ashes*).

Opera is another arena in which performers born in Spain or Portugal have made a tremendous impact. Among the most important is Plácido Domingo, who vigorously promotes the production of Spanish music, including *zarzuela,* in the United States and now directs the National Opera in Washington, D.C. Fellow tenors José Carreras (Spain), Nico Castel (Portugal), and the late Alfredo Kraus (Canary Islands) are known for their recordings and concerts featuring music from the peninsula.

REFERENCES

Alford, Violet. 1932. "Ceremonial Dances of the Spanish Basques." *The Musical Quarterly* 18(3): 471–482.

Ammons, Darlene, and Janet Ida. 1981. "Forging a Link: The North American Basque Organization, Inc." *Basque Studies Program Newsletter* 24 (September).

Arana Martija, José Antonio. 1987. *Música Vasca.* 2nd ed. Bilbao: Caja de Ahorros Vizcaina.

Armistead, Samuel. 1992. *The Spanish Tradition in Louisiana.* Vol. I: *Isleño Folkliterature,* with transcriptions by Israel Katz. Newark, Del.: Juan de la Cuesta.

Bannert, Pamela. 1979. "Los Pastores del Valle de Mesilla." *New Mexico Magazine* 57(12):58–59, 69.

Basque Music of Boise: Tradizioa Bizirik (The Tradition Lives!). 1995. Boise, Idaho: Basque Museum and Cultural Center. Audiocassette.

Borderlands: From Conjunto to Chicken Scratch—Music of the Rio Grande Valley of Texas and Southern Arizona. 1993. Smithsonian Folkways SF-40418. Compact disc.

Boston Camerata. 1994. *Nueva España: Close Encounters in the New World, 1590–1690.* Cohen, Joel, dir. WEA/Atlantic/Erato 45977. Compact disc.

Cabral, Stephen. 1989. *Tradition and Transformation: Portuguese Feasting in New Bedford.* New York: AMS Press.

Castel, Nico. 1977. *Sefarad: The Sephardic Tradition in Ladino Song.* New York: Tara Productions. Tambour TR-590. Compact disc.

Castelo Branco, Salwa El Shawan, ed. 1997. *Portugal and the World: The Encounter of Cultures in Music.* Lisbon: Publicações Dom Quixote.

Champe, Flavia Water. 1983. *The Matachines Dance of the Upper Rio Grande: History, Music, and Choreography.* Lincoln: University of Texas Press.

Chatham Baroque. *Sol y Sombra.* 1999. Dorian Records 90263. Compact disc.

Cohen, Judith R. 1993. "Sonography of Judeo-Spanish Song (Cassettes, LP's, CDs, Video, Film)." *Jewish Folklore and Ethnology Review* 15(2): 49–55.

Collection of Our Lady of Miracles Hymns. Songs from the Portuguese Festa in Gustine, California. 1999. Kathryn Maffei, P.O. Box 485, Gustine, CA 95322.

Cowell, Sidney Robertson, collector. 1938–1940. "Alberto Mendes, Manuel Lemos, and Mr. Franks Performing Portuguese Songs and Music from the Azores, 1939." In *California Gold: Northern California Folk Music from the Thirties.* WPA California Folk Music Project. Washington, D.C.: American Folklife Center, Library of Congress. Available from website http://lcweb2.loc.gov/ammem/afcchtml/0009.html.

Daniels, Roger. 1990. *Coming to America.* New York: HarperCollins.

Dark and Light in Spanish New Mexico. 1995 [1978]. New World Records 80292-2. Compact disc.

Domingo, Plácido, Alfred Kraus, Maria Bayo, et al. (1996). *¡Viva la Zarzuela!* Avudis-Valois 4765.

Donostia, Padre José Antonio de. 1951. *Música y Músicos.* San Sebastián: Biblioteca Vascongada de los Amigos del Pais.

Euzkadil: Songs and Dances of the Basque Juan Onatibia. 1954. Smithsonian-Folkways F-6830. LP disc.

Figueroa, Frank M. 1994. *Encyclopedia of Latin American Music in New York.* St. Petersburg, Fla.: Pillar Publications.

Flores, Richard R. 1995. *Los Pastores: History and Performance in the Mexican Shepherds' Play of South Texas.* Washington, D.C.: Smithsonian Institution Press.

Gastesi-Latorre, Estibaliz. 1998. "Music of the Basque Community of Boise." Paper presented at the meeting of the Southwest Chapter of the Society for Ethnomusicology, University of New Mexico, Albuquerque, 14 March.

Griffith, James S. 1997. "*Waila*: The Social Dance Music of the Tohono O'odham." In *Musics of Multicultural America,* ed. Kip Lornell and Anne Rasmussen, 155–186. New York: Schirmer Books.

Gutiérrez, Ramon. 1986. "Unraveling America's Hispanic Past: Internal Stratification and Class Boundaries." *Aztlán: A Journal of Chicano Studies* 17(1):79–102.

Harrison, Frank L. L. 1992. "The Musical Impact of Exploration and Cultural Encounter." In *Musical Repercussions of 1492,* ed. Carol Robertson, 209–218. Washington: Smithsonian Institution Press.

Herrera-Sobek, Maria. 1993. *Northward Bound: The Mexican Emigrant Experience in Ballad and Song.* Bloomington: Indiana University Press.

Hesperus. 1990. *Spain in the New World.* Golden Apple (Koch International) 7451. Compact disc.

Hilliard Ensemble. *Spain and the New World.* 1998. EMI/Angel/Virgin Imports 61394. Compact disc.

Hispano Music and Culture of the Northern Rio Grande. 1940. The Juan B. Rael Collection. Washington, D.C.: American Folklife Center, Library of Congress. Available from website http://memory.loc.gov/ammem/rghtm/rghome.html.

Katz, Israel. 1962. "Towards a Musical Study of the Judeo-Spanish Romancero." *Western Folklore* 21:83–91.

Kingman, Daniel. 1998. *American Music: A Panorama.* New York: Schirmer Books.

Koegel, John. 1993. "Spanish Mission Music from California: Past, Present and Future Research." *American Research Center Journal* 3:78–111.

———. 1994. "Spanish and Mexican Dance Music in Early California." *Ars Musica Denver* 7(1):31–55.

Kurath, Gertrude P., and Antonio García. 1970. *Music and Drama of the Tewa Pueblos.* Santa Fe: Museum of New Mexico Press.

Lamadrid, Enrique R., Jack Loeffler, and Miguel A. Gandert. 1994. *Tesoros del Espiritu: A Portrait in Sound of Hispanic New Mexico.* Embudo, N.M.: El Norte/Academia Publications.

Lemmon, Alfred. 1979. "Preliminary Investigation: Music in the Jesuit Missions of Baja California (1698–1767)." *The Journal of San Diego History* 25(4):287–297.

Leyva Portal, Waldo, et al. 1995. *La Décima Popular en Iberoamérica.* Colección Ciencia y Sociedad. Veracruz: Instituto Veracruzano de Cultura.

Liebert, Otto. 1990. *Nouveau Flamenco.* Higher Octave Music. HOMCD 77520. Compact disc.

Limon, José. 1983. "Texas-Mexican Popular Music and Dancing: Some Notes on History and Symbolic Process." *Latin American Music Review* 4(2):229–246.

Loeffler, Jack. 1999. *La Música de los Viejitos: Hispano Folk Music of the Rio Grande del Norte.* Albuquerque: University of New Mexico Press.

Luisa Fernanda. 1997. Performed by the Jarvis Conservatory. Napa, Calif.: Jarvis Conservatory JC 9702. Live recording of an American *zarzuela* production. Compact disc.

Lyon, Luke. 1979. "Los Matachines de Nuevo Mexico." *New Mexico Magazine* 57(12):72–76.

Manuel, Peter. 1988. "Portugal and Spain." In *Popular Musics of the Nonwestern World.* New York: Oxford University Press.

McGowan, Chris, and Ricardo Pessanha. 1998. *The Brazilian Sound.* Philadelphia: Temple University Press.

McLaughlin, John, et al. 1997. *Friday Night in San Francisco.* Sony/Columbia CK 37152. Compact disc.

Montoya, Carlos. 1999. *Tango Flamenco.* Fine Tune 2227. Compact disc.

Music of New Mexico: Hispanic Traditions. 1992. Smithsonian Folkways SF-40409. Compact disc.

Nettl, Bruno. 1973. *Folk and Traditional Music of the Western Continents.* 2nd ed. Englewood Cliffs, N.J.: Prentice-Hall.

Paredes, Americo. 1958. *With His Pistol in His Hand.* Austin: University of Texas Press.

———. 1976. *A Texas-Mexican Cancionero: Folksongs of the Lower Border.* Urbana: University of Illinois Press.

Pérez, Irvan. 1988. *Spanish Décimas from St. Bernard Parish.* Dana Bowker Lee, prod. Louisiana Folklife Center at Northwestern State University in Natchitoches C-088. Cassette tape.

Rael, Juan B. 1967. *The New Mexican Alabado.* New York: AMS Press.

Robb, John, collector. 1961. *Spanish Folk Songs of New Mexico.* Folkways FA 2204. LP disk. [Available on special order as cassette or compact disc 02204.]

Robb, John Donald. 1980. *Hispanic Folk Music of New Mexico and the Southwest: A Self-Portrait of a People.* Norman: University of Oklahoma Press.

Robertson, Carol E., ed. 1992. *Musical Repercussions of 1492: Encounters in Text and Performance.* Washington, D.C.: Smithsonian Institution Press.

Rodrigues, Amália. 1996. *The Best of Fado.* Double Gold DBG53026. Compact disc.

Romero, Brenda M. 1997. "Cultural Interaction in New Mexico as Illustrated in the *Matachines* Dance. In *Musics of Multicultural America,* ed. Kip Lornell and Anne Rasmussen, 155–186. New York: Schirmer Books.

Romero, Ruben, Robert Tree Cody, and Tony Redhouse. 1999. *Native Flamenco.* Canyon Records. CR7033. Compact disc.

Russell, Craig. 1992. "Newly Discovered Treasures from Colonial California: The Masses at the San Fernando Mission." *Inter-American Music Review* 13 (Fall-Winter): 5–9.

Schindler, Kurt. 1941. *Folk Music and Poetry of Spain and Portugal.* New York: Hispanic Institute in the United States.

Seroussi, Edwin. 1993. "Sephardic Music: A Bibliographic Guide with a Checklist of Notated Sources." *Jewish Folklore and Ethnology Review* 15(2):56–62.

Singer, Roberta L. 1983. "Tradition and Innovation in Contemporary Latin Popular Music in New York City." *Latin American Music Review* 4(2):183–202.

Spicer, Edward H. 1985. *The Yaquis: A Cultural History.* Tucson: University of Arizona Press.

Stark, Richard B. 1969. *Music of the Spanish Folk Plays in New Mexico.* Sante Fe: Museum of New Mexico Press.

Stevenson, Robert M. 1960. *Spanish Music in the Age of Columbus.* The Hague: Martinus Nijhoff.

———. 1968. *Music in Aztec and Inca Territory.* Berkeley: University of California Press.

Sturman, Janet. in press. *Zarzuela: Spanish Operetta, American Stage.* Urbana: University of Illinois Press.

Summers, William John. 1994. "Recently Recovered Manuscript Source of Sacred Polyphonic Music from Spanish California." *Ars Musica Denver* 7(1):13–20.

Surinach, Carlos. *Ritmo Jondo.* 1996. Bronx Arts Ensemble. New World Records 80505-2. Compact disc.

Tinker, Edward Larocque. 1961. *Corridos and Calaveras.* Austin: University of Texas Press.

Veira Nery, Rui. 1997. "The Portuguese Seventeenth-Century Villancico: A Cross Cultural Phenomenon." In *Portugal and the World: The Encounter of Cultures in Music,* ed. Salwa El Shawan Castelo Branco, 103–113. Lisbon: Publicações Dom Quixote.

Weigle, Marta. 1976. *Brothers of Light, Brothers of Blood: The Penitentes of the Southwest.* Albuquerque: University of New Mexico Press.

Woodlee, Mary. 1979. "Las Posadas: The Patterns of a People." *New Mexico Magazine* 57(12):60–61.

French Music
Carl Rahkonen

French American Music in New England
French American Music in Louisiana
Renaissance of French American Music in Louisiana

Relatively few French immigrated directly to the United States. Those who did come directly from Europe came as individuals or families seeking economic opportunities and were scattered across the country (Hillstrom 1995:538). The majority of French Americans came by way of Canada. The two largest communities of French-speaking Americans live in New England and in Louisiana [see ACADIAN MUSIC, p. 1135; FRANCO-ONTARIAN MUSIC, p. 1192].

FRENCH AMERICAN MUSIC IN NEW ENGLAND

During the second half of the nineteenth century and early in the twentieth century, French Canadians moved in large numbers to New England to work in the textile mills, the lumber industry, or manufacturing. They established their own Catholic parishes, which served as centers for French American cultural life and counterbalanced other ethnic groups of the area, mainly English Protestants, Quakers, and Irish. They tended to remain in their own enclaves, having their own French-language newspapers and shops. Today New Englanders of French Canadian descent make up approximately 20 percent of the region's population. They refer to themselves as Franco-Americans, or simply Francos, to distinguish themselves from the French-speaking communities of Louisiana or from immigrants directly from France (Levin 1999).

The evening party

French Americans brought with them musical traditions with roots in France, but which had also evolved in Québec and the Maritime Provinces. These traditions continued to evolve in the United States. One such tradition was that of the evening party, called a *soirée* or *veillée*. These parties featured storytelling as well as vocal and instrumental music of French Canadian origin. The French-speaking Cajuns and Creoles of Louisiana held similar evening parties. In Woonsocket, Rhode Island, these traditional house parties evolved into public evening concert performances called *Soirées Canadiennes* in the 1970s, which also included popular songs translated into French (Waldman 1976:36–40).

Song genres

Traditional evening parties featured a wide variety of song genres. Many were sung as unaccompanied solos. Some of the singers from the Woonsocket community classified these songs according to functional themes: *chansons d'amour* 'love songs', *cantiques* 'religious songs', *berceuses* 'lullabies', *chansons à boire* 'drinking songs' and *chansons de marier* 'wedding songs'. Other singers classified them according to their affect: *chansons tristes* 'sad songs', *chansons tragiques* 'tragic songs', *chansons comiques* 'funny songs', *chansons foux* 'silly songs', or *chansons gaies* 'lively songs' (Waldman 1976:50–51). These songs could be learned by ear at evening parties or from printed song books called *chansonniers,* published mainly in Canada around the turn of the last century. Song melodies and texts were interchangeable. Some melodies featured shifts in meter, although multimetered melodies were less common in the United States than in Canada.

The *chansons à deux* 'songs for two', another major class of songs at evening parties, were performed by a group of singers who would repeat antiphonally part or all of a song sung first by a soloist. They featured a strict symmetrical exchange of verses between the soloist and the group, or sometimes between two soloists. In the *chansons à réprondre* 'response songs' the second verse line of one stanza becomes the first line of the next stanza, and a refrain follows each verse line. Both types of song featured humor and frivolity in their narrative verses and refrains. A related genre, the *potpourri,* linked songs together by having the downbeat of one song serve as the upbeat to the next.

Instrumental music

French American instrumental music in New England closely resembled that of the French Canadian Maritime Provinces. It was primarily dance music, played on traditional instruments such as the violin, harmonica, or accordion and accompanied by rhythm on the spoons, by clapping, or by clogging. One of the best known fiddlers of the region, Omer Marcoux, was born in Québec and emigrated to Concord, New Hampshire in 1929 (Oliver 1981). A collection of his transcribed tunes (Miskoe and Paul 1980) showed that he played a wide variety of dance music: reels, hornpipes, breakdowns, polkas, jigs, and waltzes. His style included shifts in meter, drawing out notes when he felt like it and sometimes omitting the last beat of a phrase. The transcribers had to include second "straight" versions of some tunes, so they could be more easily used for dancing. Some of Marcoux's tunes were "old timey" standards, but most had a distinctive French flavor. Many contemporary fiddlers in New England include French tunes in their repertoires but perform them together with American traditional tunes learned at fiddle contests, or through recordings, and the media.

Subsequent generations of French Americans have assimilated and intermarried with their English-speaking neighbors, hence reducing the number of those who speak French exclusively. The only French known to many younger participants at traditional *soirées* may be that of the songs. Previously music, like language and ethnicity, set the French American community apart from its neighbors. Today French American music serves more as a symbol of French heritage to the inhabitants of New England at large. This music is heard increasingly at heritage festivals, folk festivals, and other events that feature traditional New England folk music of all varieties.

Contemporary French American singer/songwriters such as Josée Vachon and Donna Hébert (from the group Chanterelle), Michèle Choinière, and Lucie Therrien have added to the traditional *chanson* repertoire with their own compositions that examine the experience of being French American in the United States (figure 1). Such performers have often become active in promoting contemporary French American culture, which today is defined less by a common language and ethnicity and more by a common musical interest (Levin 1999).

His style included shifts in meter, drawing out notes when he felt like it and sometimes omitting the last beat of a phrase. The transcribers had to include second "straight" versions of some tunes, so they could be more easily used for dancing.

FIGURE I   Franco-American artist Lucie Therrien, a native of Vermont, with her father, Eugene Therrien, a French Canadian fiddler, from whom she learned traditional music. Photo courtesy Lucie Therrien, 1990.

FRENCH AMERICAN MUSIC IN LOUISIANA

Two major groups of French-speaking Americans live in and around the Gulf Coast of Louisiana: the Cajuns and the Creoles. Both groups have adopted a mixture of cultural elements, but each has a foundation in French language and culture. Today in southern Louisiana, French-speaking whites generally call themselves Cajuns, while French-speaking blacks call themselves Creoles (Ancelet 1999 [1982]:16). There are, however, many connections in language, folklife, and music between the two groups. With the blending of cultural elements over the years, it is not always a simple or clear-cut matter to distinguish whether an individual is Cajun or Creole.

Cajun music

The term *Cajun* derives from *Acadian,* the name of a group of French immigrants who settled along coastal regions of the Canadian Maritime Provinces and Maine during the seventeenth century, forming one of the earliest colonies in the New World. Control of this colonial region shifted between the competing powers of France and Great Britain. In 1755 the British began to expel the Acadians (an action called *Le Grand Dérangement*) because they refused to swear allegiance to the king of England. The Acadians went to a number of different places, including New England, other parts of Canada, the Carolinas, and the French West Indies [see HAITIAN AND FRANCO-CARIBBEAN MUSIC, p. 802]. By 1800, several thousand Acadians found their way to Southwestern Louisiana (Brandon 1972; Heimlich 1995). They became a significant part of the multiethnic culture of the area.

Song

The roots of Cajun music may be traced to the original Acadian exiles who brought their musical styles from the Canadian Maritime Provinces and France. Cajuns continued the tradition of the evening party, or *veillée,* where they sang a wide variety of songs, unaccompanied except for the rhythm of hand clapping, foot tapping, or banging on kitchen implements. They sang French ballads, humorous songs, and particularly the *complainte,* a long, melancholy story-song of their French heritage (Ancelet 1982:21). The women sang lullabies, the men, drinking songs, and the children, play-party songs. Cajuns learned these songs from aural tradition or from printed sources. Irène Whitfield's collection, *Louisiana French Folk Songs* (1981 [1939]), showed that the themes of Cajun songs included love and marriage, lovers going to Texas, animals, people and places, and the Civil War. Claudie Marcel-Dubois (1978) published an insightful analysis of Cajun vocal music.

Instrumental music

Cajun instrumental music has always been closely tied to dancing. Originally, Cajun dances were small gatherings for family and friends, called *bals de maison,* held in private homes where the furniture had been cleared from the front room or other large space. Eventually, these events evolved into larger public parties called *fais-do-do,* baby talk for 'go to sleep'. The term may come from the practice of putting young children to sleep in a special room while their parents attended the party. After World War II, Cajuns built larger family-style dance halls to hold the *fais-do-do,* usually on Saturday evenings (Broven 1987:11–12).

Early Cajun dance music included the mazurka, polka, reel, hot-step, one-step, two-step, quadrille (contra dance), and waltz. After a while only the waltz and two-step remained popular. The original Acadian exiles arrived without instruments, so they danced to *reels à bouche,* wordless music made only with their voices (Heimlich 1995:7). Eventually the fiddle became the primary dance instrument. Dances were then played in arrangements for two fiddles, in which one would carry the melody and the other provide accompaniment. When German settlers brought the accordion to Louisiana in the late nineteenth century, it became the favored instrument of Cajun dance music. Cajuns typically used diatonic one-row or two-row accordions and developed their own style of playing that combined traditional melodies with a "push and pull" rhythmic drive (figure 2). Traditional Cajun dance ensembles consisted of the

FIGURE 2   Members of a Louisiana Cajun band play at the National Folk Festival near Cleveland, Ohio. Photo by Terry E. Miller, 1985.

FIGURE 3   This type of old-fashioned button box accordion, whose bellows drive air through sets of metal free reeds to produce sounds, is, along with the fiddle, an essential sound in Louisiana's Cajun music. Photo by Terry E. Miller, 1990.

diatonic accordion in the lead, with one or two fiddles, and simple rhythm instruments, such as the triangle.

With the coming of the oil industry to the region, improved transportation, and mass media, Cajun music absorbed influences from country and western, hillbilly, blues, western swing, and jazz. Dance ensembles began using electrical amplification and added guitar, steel guitar, bass, and drums. The use of the accordion declined in the middle decades of the twentieth century but made a comeback during the era of folk music revivals, as the traditional sound of Cajun music came back into style (figure 3).

Creole music

In eighteenth-century Louisiana, upper-class Spanish and French immigrants called their descendants born in America "creoles." Later that century, when French-speaking blacks and mulattoes from the Caribbean and South America came to Louisiana as slaves for French planters or as "free men of color," they openly exchanged cultural elements with Cajuns. French-speaking blacks were called black cajuns, black French, black creoles, or creoles of color. Gradually the term *creole* began to apply primarily to those in Louisiana French culture with an African heritage. Creole culture consists of an eclectic mix of elements, primarily Afro-Caribbean, Spanish, and French, which appear in their language, music, and cuisine.

Creoles developed a rich song tradition that was documented by Irène Whitfield (1981 [1939]) and Harry Oster (1962, 1970). Like the Cajuns, they sang many lullabies, or *fais-do-do,* and songs of love and marriage. But they also performed a large repertoire of songs about food and songs of satire, mockery, and ridicule seldom found in Cajun music (Broven 1987:101).

Like other French-speaking Americans, Creoles enjoyed evening house parties and dances. Creoles called such parties *la la* or *zydeco,* terms that also refer to their specific type of music. Zydeco draws from the same instrumental dance repertoire as Cajun music, but it adds elements of Afro-Caribbean rhythms and African American blues. The Creole version of the Cajun two-step, called the *la la,* is faster and more syncopated. The same is true of waltzes. The music has a greater emphasis on rhythm, a lesser one on melody, and frequently a blues tonality. Rural zydeco ensembles used instrumentation similar to their Cajun counterparts, namely the button accordion and fiddle as well as the *frottoir,* a metallic washboard played with thimbles, spoons, forks, or bottle openers as an essential rhythm instrument. Urban zydeco groups tended to replace the fiddle with electric guitars or saxophone and the button box with piano accordion. For rhythm they retained the *frottoir* but could also add bass guitar and drums. Such urban groups could play traditional Creole tunes as well as rhythm and blues, soul, and other forms of African American popular music (Broven 1987:101–102; Spitzer 1977:149–150).

RENAISSANCE OF FRENCH AMERICAN MUSIC IN LOUISIANA

Cajun music was first recorded in the 1920s, in the ethnic series of various labels. By mid-century, national record companies sought music that would appeal to a broader audience, and the Cajun groups of the time responded with a more popular Americanized sound. In the last half of the century, the traditional sound again asserted itself and was recorded by local and specialized folk record companies. The many Cajun and Creole performers who have attained popular success through recordings have been documented by Barry Ancelet (1989, 1999 [1982]; Ancelet and Gould 1992), John Broven (1987), and Nicholas Spitzer (1977).

Traditional Cajun and Creole musics have become among the most widely popular ethnic genres in America. This has come about through exposure at local and national folk music festivals; tourism; increased public awareness through the work of scholars, performers, and cultural activists; and direct promotion through CODOFIL (Council for the Development of French in Louisiana), the NEH (National Endowment for the Humanities), and foundation funding. Cajun and Creole musics are living traditions that will continue to change and develop but also retain a unique identity.

REFERENCES

Albert, Renaud D. 1978. *Chanson de chez-nous.* Bedford, N.H.: National Materials Development Center for French.

Ancelet, Barry Jean. 1989. *Cajun Music: Its Origins and Development.* Lafayette: Center for Louisiana Studies, University of Southwestern Louisiana.

———. 1999 [1982]. *Cajun and Creole Music Makers.* Jackson: University Press of Mississippi. New ed. of *The Makers of Cajun Music.*

Ancelet, Barry Jean, and Philip Gould. 1992. *Cajun Music and Zydeco.* Baton Rouge: Louisiana State University.

Brandon, Elizabeth. 1972. "The Socio-cultural Traits of the French Folksong in Louisiana." *Revue de Louisiana/Louisiana Review* 1(2).

Broven, John. 1987. *South to Louisiana: The Music of the Cajun Bayous.* Gretna, La.: Pelican.

Gilmore, Jeanne, and Robert C. Gilmore. 1970. *Chantez, la Louisiane!: Louisiana French Folk Songs, Selected, Edited, and Arranged for Classroom Use.* Lafayette, La.: Acadiana Music.

Gladu, André. 1972. "La musique traditionelle des francophones de la Louisiane." *Revue de Louisiana/Louisiana Review* 1(2).

Heimlich, Evan. 1995. "Acadians." In *Gale Encyclopedia of Multicultural America,* ed. Judy Galens, Anna Sheets, and Robyn V. Young, 1–14. Detroit, Mich.: Gale Research.

Hillstrom, Laurie Collier. 1995. "French Americans." In *Gale Encyclopedia of Multicultural America,* ed. Judy Galens and Robyn V. Young, 533–545. Detroit, Mich.: Gale Research.

Levin, Theodore. 1999. Liner notes for *Mademoiselle, Voulez-Vous Danser? Franco-American Music from the New England Borderlands.* Washington, D.C.: Smithsonian Folkways Recordings. SFW CD 40116. Compact disc.

Marcel-Dubois, Claudie. 1978. "Reflexions sur L'Heritage Musical Français en Louisiane." *Selected Reports in Ethnomusicology* 3(1):25–75. Los Angeles: UCLA Program in Ethnomusicology.

Miskoe, Sylvia, and Justine Paul. 1980. *Fiddle Tunes of Omer Marcoux.* Bedford, N.H.: National Materials Development Center for French.

Oliver, Julien. 1981. *Pas de gene: Omer Marcoux, violoneux et sculpteur.* Bedford, N.H.: National Materials Development Center for French.

Oster, Harry. 1962. "Negro French Spirituals of Louisiana." *Journal of the International Folk Music Council* 14.

———. 1970. "The Louisiana Acadians." In *The American Folk Music Occasional 2,* eds. Chris Strachwitz and Pete Welding. New York: Oak Pub.

Police, Anatole. 1893. *Manuel de cantiques et chants religieux.* Boston: Maison de l'Ange Guardien.

Spitzer, Nicholas. 1977. "Cajuns and Creoles: The French Gulf Coast." In *The Long Journey Home: Folklife in the South,* ed. Allen Tullos, 140–155. Chapel Hill, N.C.: Southern Exposure.

Viau, Eusèbe, and J. Ernest Philie. 1931. *Chants Populaires des Franco-Américains.* 12 vols. Woonsocket, R.I.: L'Union Saint-Jean-Baptiste d'Amérique.

Waldman, Deborah Anne. 1976. "Transcultural Folk Song Revival: Active and Passive Bearers of French Canadian Folk Song Tradition in Woonsocket, R.I., and Adjacent Towns." Master's thesis, Brown University.

Whitfield, Irène Thérèsa. 1981 [1939]. *Louisiana French Folk Songs.* 3rd ed. Eunice, La.: Hebert.

Italian Music
Mark Levy

General Characteristics of Italian American Music
Italian Americans in New York
Italian American Theater
Italian American Wind Bands
Frank Sinatra

Prior to the 1860s, most Italian immigrants to the United States were upper-class, well-educated northerners. They were followed by southern peasants from the Neapolitan and Sicilian regions with little formal education. At the turn of the twentieth century, 80 percent of the Italian immigrants in the United States were from southern Italy. Approximately four million arrived between 1880 and 1914. Very few immigrants had a significant sense of Italian national identity; most defined themselves according to their village and/or province of origin. The majority of these immigrants settled in large cities such as New York, Boston, Philadelphia, Pittsburgh, Chicago, San Francisco, and Los Angeles. Rural enclaves were also formed in agricultural or mining areas. Unskilled laborers worked in mines, on railroads, and in factories, whereas skilled artisans worked as stonecutters, masons, bricklayers, tailors, and carpenters. Fraternal organizations and mutual benefit societies were organized along regional lines and later evolved into federated membership organizations such as the Italian Catholic Federation and the Order of the Sons of Italy in America, with a network of local lodges.

GENERAL CHARACTERISTICS OF ITALIAN AMERICAN MUSIC

A commercial Italian American music market developed in the United States in the early 1900s. Firms were established that sold sheet music, gramophones, records, and piano rolls of Italian music, as well as musical instruments. By 1940, more music and language recordings had been made by Italian Americans than by any other non-English-speaking group.

These records included singing accompanied by wind bands, string orchestras, mandolin ensembles, guitar, *organetto* 'diatonic button accordion', and *fisarmonica* 'chromatic piano accordion'. Recorded vocal repertoire included opera and other classical genres, popular songs, regional folk songs, and hybrid Italian American creations. Song texts focused on love, longing for the homeland, and the difficulties of adjusting to life in America. Recorded instrumental music included the waltz, polka, quadrille, mazurka, tarantella, schottische, and march. Recordings were also made of regional instruments such as *zampogna* 'bagpipe', *ciaramella* 'oboe', and *triccaballacche* 'wooden clapper'.

Italians were extremely influential in the historical development of the American piano accordion. Italian songs and dance music became an important part of the instrument's repertoire for everyone, regardless of ethnic heritage. By the late 1930s, an accordion craze had swept the country. Many accordion schools established in the 1920s and 1930s continued to operate into the 1950s.

Opera has played a significant role in defining Italian American identity among all classes. Many working-class Italian immigrants were passionate devotees who considered Enrico Caruso a heroic figure and a symbol of hope and success. Opera was regularly heard in cafés in Italian American neighborhoods and on Italian-language radio programs.

ITALIAN AMERICANS IN NEW YORK

FIGURE I   Angelo's Novelty store on the corner of Grand and Lafayette Streets in the heart of New York's Little Italy. The windows of this store, founded in 1902, testify to the important role of music in immigrant life. Photo by Gillian Rodger, 2000.

Schlesinger (1988) describes Italian American music in the "Little Italy" of Manhattan's Lower East Side from the early twentieth century. Immigrants continued rich traditions of puppet theater, music halls, dance halls, saint's day festivals, and Christmas street music performed on *zampogna* and *ciaramella.* On some days, half a dozen wind bands could be heard simultaneously leading processions [see BANDS, p. 563]. Music continued to be an integral part of family celebrations such as holiday gatherings, birthdays, weddings, anniversaries, saints' days, baptisms, confirmations, graduations, and arrivals of relatives from Italy (figure 1).

After decades of decline following World War II, the 1980s saw a revival of interest in traditional Italian music in New York State. Folk festivals in western New York State and New York City began featuring genres such as work party music, cart driver songs, carnival music, drinking songs, regional vocal and instrumental music from southern Italy and Sardinia, Calabrian choral singing, and Neapolitan singing and percussion playing.

In New York City in the 1980s, there were still some performers of traditional rural music such as tarantellas, waltzes, polkas, and mazurkas played on button accordion. These performers also included singers of ballads, lullabies, serenades, love songs, devotional songs, and *stornello,* a genre of sung Sicilian poetry. In general, however, these rural music genres are ignored by the majority of Italian Americans in New York.

ITALIAN AMERICAN THEATER

Establishments in New York City and other urban areas known as *café concerto* or *café chantant* were gathering places for working-class Italian American immigrants that featured food, wine, music, and vaudeville. Each café commonly had a regional focus. Italian ethnic vaudeville included singing, dancing, accordion and mandolin playing, and comic vignettes on immigrant life. After the theatrical performance, musicians played for participatory singing and dancing. Italian American vaudeville continued to be popular through the late 1920s, especially in New York City.

Theater was the dominant social institution of the Italian American community in San Francisco from the turn of the century through the 1930s (Estavan 1991 [1938]). Opera, operetta, and regional folk and popular songs were performed nightly. Musical theater took the form of comedy, farce, tragedy, melodrama, or burlesque. Singing was accompanied by piano or small orchestra.

Italian theater in San Francisco entered a rapid decline in the late 1920s, due largely to changing immigration laws and the rise of motion pictures. During the 1930s the theater moved away from a close association with amateur performers and middle- and lower-class audiences to more professional "serious" works of the modern Italian theater and elite upper-class audiences.

ITALIAN AMERICAN WIND BANDS

Italian Americans played an extremely prominent role in the development of wind bands in the United States during the nineteenth and early twentieth centuries. Ensembles included professional military bands, community bands, circus and carnival bands,

Each café commonly had a regional focus. Italian ethnic vaudeville included singing, dancing, accordion and mandolin playing, and comic vignettes on immigrant life.

and bands associated with particular ethnic groups. Italians made up a large percentage of band musicians and conductors in all of these categories. During the period between 1890 and 1920, bands were indispensable in every American community for all types of outdoor events.

During the nineteenth century, Italian American band directors were often professionally trained in Italy in classical conservatories. They would compose original works for their groups in the United States, a tradition that has continued to the present day. Sometimes music teachers from Italy would be hired by a community to establish a music school, where children would be instructed and trained as future band members. This professionalism has continued to the present day, when many band members are music educators in local public schools.

By 1916, most Italian American communities had well-established uniformed bands. "Business bands" were those whose members made their livelihood by touring and performing widely to diverse audiences, often with theatrical entertainers. The heyday of these Italian traveling bands was the first two decades of the twentieth century.

The repertoire of Italian American wind bands includes military and symphonic marches, arrangements of opera overtures and arias (especially those of Rossini, Verdi, and Bellini), medleys of folk songs and dances, religious hymns, original compositions, an occasional polka, Italian and American popular and patriotic tunes, medleys of show tunes, and other repertoire from the standard American concert band literature. Contemporary bands play Italian music on special occasions such as *festa* days and a more varied Americanized repertoire, including blues, swing, jazz, and rock, at other events.

Band membership often crosses occupational and social categories and may include non-Italian ethnic backgrounds. Women are in the minority. Some bands maintain a strong religious affiliation with the community church, while others have a more secular sponsorship by a local business establishment or social club. Many have been supported by railroad companies, coal mines, steel mills, or benevolent societies. Italian American wind bands have had an especially important role in local *festas*, or feast days in honor of a holy day or saint's day. These celebrations have enabled Italian American communities to perpetuate their respective identities with particular villages, towns, or regions of the homeland. In addition to their roles within the community, these bands participate in Italian American summer festivals for the general public, or in multi-ethnic heritage festivals or nationality days honoring various ethnic groups.

FRANK SINATRA

Francis Albert Sinatra (1915–1998) grew up in an Italian American community in Hoboken, New Jersey. His father was born in Catania, Sicily, and his mother in Genoa. Although there have been a number of famous Italian American singers of popular music (Perry Como, Frankie Lane, Tony Bennett, Vic Damone), Sinatra is generally acknowledged as the first Italian American superstar (figure 2). He is regarded as an icon of success in Italian American communities and worshiped as a hero because of

FIGURE 2   Frank Sinatra, pictured here with fellow musicians Ella Fitzgerald and Count Basie, was one of the twentieth century's best-loved entertainers. In addition to his performing, Sinatra also worked to help fight discrimination within the Italian American community in the United States. © Bettmann/CORBIS.

the proud manner in which he maintained his ethnic identity throughout his career. Many Italian American establishments throughout the United States, especially in New York, New Jersey, and Pennsylvania, are filled with Sinatra photographs and other memorabilia.

In his youth, Sinatra was exposed to recordings and radio broadcasts of Enrico Caruso and other Italian bel canto singers. Inspired by Bing Crosby, he began singing in the early 1930s at local clubs, dance halls, and social lodges, at first depending on Tin Pan Alley arrangements. In succeeding years, Sinatra was influenced by performers such as Mabel Mercer, Billie Holiday, Sarah Vaughan, Fats Waller, and Count Basie. In the late 1930s and early 1940s he performed with the big swing bands of Harry James, Tommy Dorsey, and Benny Goodman. During the war years Sinatra created his own solo career and became the first mass-craze teen idol. His fifty-year career includes 58 films, 100 record albums, over 2,000 individual recordings, and innumerable awards and honors. He was named Outstanding Male Vocalist in 1941 and 1954 by *Downbeat* magazine. In 1967 Sinatra won Grammys for single Record of the Year, Album of the Year, and Top Male Vocalist. In 1973 he was voted Entertainer of the Century by the Songwriters of America. In Rio de Janeiro in 1980, he established a record for the largest live audience ever assembled for a solo performer: 175,000. He also holds the record for the longest time span between Top 40 singles: 1941 to 1981.

Frank Sinatra is considered by many to be the greatest singer of American popular songs of the twentieth century. He maintained an active performing schedule into his late seventies, finally retiring in 1995.

REFERENCES

Ackelson, Richard W. 1992. *Frank Sinatra: A Complete Recording History of Techniques, Songs, Composers, Lyricists, Arrangers, Sessions, and First-Issue Albums, 1939–1984.* Jefferson, N.C.: McFarland & Co.

Estavan, Lawrence. 1991 [1938]. *The Italian Theater in San Francisco.* San Bernadino, Calif.: Borgo Press.

Greene, Victor R. 1992. *A Passion for Polka.* Berkeley: University of California Press.

Petkov, Steven, and Leonard Mustazza, eds. 1995. *The Frank Sinatra Reader.* New York: Oxford University Press.

Rocco, Emma Scogna. 1990. *Italian Wind Bands: A Surviving Tradition in the Milltowns of Pennsylvania.* New York: Garland.

Schiavo, Giovanni Ermenegildo. 1975 [1943]. *Italian-American History.* New York: Arno Press.

Schlesinger, Michael. 1988. "Italian Music in New York." *New York Folklore* 14(3 and 4):129–138.

Snapshot:
Italian Music in Livingston County, New York
James Kimball

Italian music arrived in Livingston County long before any significant Italian immigration. From at least the 1820s professional musicians had been adapting Italian opera tunes as quadrilles and waltzes for fashionable ballroom use. In the 1850s a whole generation of young upstate performers was further influenced by operatic arias as popularized by Jenny Lind, the celebrated singer who toured the state in 1852. In the 1870s a Dansville dance band styled itself the "Italian Orchestra," not because it included Italian musicians (the leader was Charles Sedgwick) but because it featured so many Italian tunes.

A few Italian professional performers toured the area in the nineteenth century, and one, Carlo Bassini, headed an annual summer music school in Geneseo, New York, in the 1860s. Summer also brought numerous itinerant Italian street musicians to the villages of Livingston County. Street organ players, violinists and harpists, musicians with performing bears, and at least one Italian bagpipe player are recorded as touring western New York in the mid- to late-nineteenth century. The Italian street organ players in particular remained popular with local children through the first decades of the twentieth century.

The first real influx of Italian immigration into the county came in the late nineteenth century and brought with it many new musical influences. Mostly from southern Italy, from Sicily, Calabria and Naples, the new immigrants came to work on the railroads, in the fields, in the new canning factories, and in the Retsof salt mine. Some returned home with their hard-won earnings; many more remained and in spite of recurring discrimination became active and productive citizens. Several among these were musicians.

House parties, weddings, occasional festivals, and dances in clubs and barns kept some of the old culture alive as the immigrant generation sang and danced the night away. Nick Passamonte remembers one especially old tradition, his father's playing the jaw harp to accompany old-style Sicilian folk songs. True to Old World custom, the singers would cup a hand behind one ear—an age-old way of making one's own voice seem clearer. Other instruments popular with the first generation were violin, clarinet, mandolin, accordion (the small button variety), and guitar, an instrument not yet very common among non-Italians in the area.

By the 1920s a generation of American-born Italians, a generation with American-sounding first names, was learning Tin Pan Alley songs, American fox-trots, and jazz. The old jaw harp–accompanied ballads were disappearing and younger singers no longer cupped a hand behind one ear. Newer Italian popular songs were still sung, however, and dance musicians continued to play many of the beautiful old Italian polkas, mazurkas, waltzes, and tarantellas. They also played traditional Italian quadrilles. These were square dances brought from the Old Country, and, as their American counterpart did, they used a caller to guide everyone through the figures. Within the extended and very musical Passamonte family of Mt. Morris it was Gus who did the calling.

The 1920s and 1930s saw some significant changes in instrumentation among Italian dance musicians. The button accordions gradually gave way to the larger and musically more flexible piano accordions. These had been popularized by such well-known Italian American musicians as Pietro Diero of New York City and more locally by Roxy Caccamise, musician, teacher, and music dealer from Batavia. It was Roxy Caccamise, for example, who inspired both Joe Gambino and Sandy Consiglio to learn the piano accordion. The guitars and mandolins were now joined by and even physically combined with the more distinctly American banjo. Banjo-mandolin and banjo-guitar combinations, as well as tenor banjo, were all used by the Passamonte brothers in playing Italian dances throughout the area. Saxophones also became popular with Italian American musicians such as Joe LaBarbera, Charlie Runfola, and Santo Patanella, all of whom could play American standards as well as Italian tunes.

The Italian and Italian American love of the guitar is well represented in the playing of both Frank Passamonte of Mt. Morris and Peter "Al" Mastrolio of Leicester. Al's father, Giro, "Jerry," was born in Retsof's Little Italy before the turn of the century. As a child he moved with his parents back to their native village near Naples, Italy. Before World War I, however, Giro was back in Retsof, working at the salt mine and playing a great deal of music. He could play mouth organ, accordion, and piano, but his main instrument, the one he continued to play into his nineties, was the guitar.

Some of Al's earliest memories are of the evenings the Passamonte brothers and others would invade the Mastrolio home for lively sessions of Italian music. In time Al was learning guitar on his own, influenced by all the music around him (and some lessons from John Howard) and encouraged by local band musicians. Typical of his generation and of growing up in a rural Italian community, Al continues to play a wide variety of music: older Italian tunes, Tin Pan Alley, 1940s and 1950s American pop songs, rural New York square dances, commercial country, a few Polish tunes, and a bit of jazz.

The younger generation of Italian American musicians has largely forgotten the older Italian folk music traditions, as the language is lost and nobody asks for the old dances. Jazz, classical, or, especially, newer American pop styles beckon, and locally raised Italian Americans have excelled in all. Let us hope, however, that some of the older tunes and stories will be preserved, in part because of state and local arts council interest, in greater part, however, because they are such a beautiful part of local Italian American heritage.

REFERENCES

Gambino, Joe and Virginia Gambino. 1994. Interview.

Mastrolio, Al. 1994. Interview.

Passamonte, Nick. 1994. Interview.

Yasso, J. Marilyn Hannet. 1987. *History of Retsof, New York*. Lyons: Wilprint.

Scandinavian and Baltic Music

Mark Levy
Carl Rahkonen (Estonian Music)
Ain Haas (Estonian Music)

Norwegian Music
Swedish Music
Finnish Music
Lithuanian Music
Latvian Music
Estonian Music

Immigrants from Scandinavia and the Baltic countries of Lithuania, Latvia, and Estonia began arriving in the United States in the early nineteenth century. Unlike many other European immigrants, however, these Northern Europeans tended to settle in the rural farming areas of the American Midwest, creating communities that retained, as much as possible, Old World social and religious patterns as well as traditional contexts for the performance of music.

NORWEGIAN MUSIC

Between 1825 and 1925, approximately 800,000 Norwegians emigrated to the United States, the majority settling in Illinois, Iowa, Wisconsin, Minnesota, and the Dakotas. Organizations were established for Norwegian immigrants who shared a common rural settlement of origin (*bygde*) and thus a common language dialect and musical tradition. These organizations had an important role in maintaining Old Country traditions, especially at annual meetings called *stevne*. Some introduced prizes to promote excellence in fiddling, folk dancing, costume, poetry, singing, and traditional crafts. Organized activities were often aimed at attracting and educating young people. Regional rural folk dances (*bygdedanser*) such as *springar* and *halling* were generally performed for an audience, rather than in participatory social dancing. *Stev* singing, consisting of short one-strophe poems set to a number of formulaic melodies, was also included.

With the advent of World War I, suspicion concerning "hyphenated" Americans resulted in the decline of public celebrations of Norwegian traditions. The war accelerated the process of Americanization through its intense propaganda for national unity and agitation against foreign influence. Economic hardships of the 1930s made participation in *bygdelag* 'community' activities more difficult, and the outbreak of World War II saw a further decline.

The Sons of Norway, a network of fraternal organizations formed to provide illness and death benefits to members, has had a crucial role in the promotion of Norwegian American culture. These organizations have published song books that have been widely used in homes, containing folk songs, patriotic and popular songs, and a few Anglo-American songs. Texts are in Norwegian and English.

The *Leikarring* movement, which took root in the United States in the 1920s and 1930s, refers to "song dances" in which the dancers sing without any instrumental accompaniment. Societies such as the *Norrøna Leikarring* of Minneapolis and the Nordic *Leikarring* of Grand Forks, North Dakota, were formed. Sometimes groups were organized for particular festivals and then disbanded until another occasion.

In Minnesota, Norwegians settled near other Scandinavian groups as well as various Central and Northern European communities, resulting in some commonly shared music repertoire and style among these groups. In the United States, much of the music became Scandinavian American, rather than Norwegian or Swedish American. Anglo-American fiddle styles were also incorporated. "Old-time" music in immigrant communities was a multiethnic shared tradition, with commonalities among Irish, English, German, Swedish, Norwegian, Polish, and other Central and Northern European groups. Some musical changes that occurred in the transition from Europe to the United States included less melodic ornamentation, a greater reliance on chordal accompaniment, faster tempos, and a broader instrumentation.

Although secular music and dance flourished in many communities, these forms were prohibited in communities that followed the dictates of the Pietistic or Lay Religious movement, which swept Norway in the mid-1800s. Pietism, a sect of Lutheranism, renounced worldly pleasures such as drinking, card games, and dancing. Violin music was especially associated with evil. As a result, fiddling and dancing were sometimes done only in the privacy of the home or at picnics in isolated locations.

Emigrant ballads

As was the case with many European American groups, songs concerning Norwegian emigration to America and nostalgia for the homeland were sung on both sides of the Atlantic. Song texts were published from the 1880s to the 1920s in Norway as well as in American Norwegian-language newspapers. Some texts mourn the hardships of the transatlantic journey and the privations and loneliness of pioneer life, while others emphasize triumphs over difficulties. Some describe emigration as a tragic, regrettable mistake; others are full of hope for a new life. Many song texts express nostalgia for family members left behind or romantic memories of Norwegian childhoods, nature, people, and language. Some describe the strength of the Norwegian church and the state bureaucracy and the powerlessness of peasants (despite the fact that Norway had the most democratic society and government in Europe). Norway is sometimes depicted as a place of natural beauty and at other times a place of servitude, the United States generally as a place of wealth and opportunity. Some ballads portray unrealistic, romantic notions about the United States, sometimes extending these to humorous or ridiculous extremes.

Singing societies

Beginning in the late 1860s, unaccompanied Norwegian American male choruses, often including Swedes and Danes, were formed in urban areas, and concert choirs formed at Norwegian American Lutheran colleges. The repertoire of these groups included chorales, choral arrangements of hymns, rural folk songs, patriotic songs, and compositions by Norwegian composers in the European classical tradition. Most societies continue to be active in their home communities, presenting at least one annual local concert and making numerous appearances at civic and social functions of the community today.

From the mid-1880s, singing groups were organized into associations and would gather for periodic song fests. The Norwegian Singers Association of America has held biennial conventions since 1910, with as many as 1,500 singers participating. Other organizations include the Pacific Coast Norwegian Singers Association, formed in 1902.

Norway is sometimes depicted as a place of natural beauty and at other times a place of servitude, the United States generally as a place of wealth and opportunity.

Dance music

LeRoy Larson (1975) and Janet Kvam (1986) describe dance music of Norwegian American communities in Minnesota from the early twentieth century to the 1970s and 1980s. This music, known in these communities as "old-time" music, is a continuation of the *gammeldans* 'old dance' tradition in Norway: waltzes, schottisches, polkas, mazurkas, and two-steps played on instruments such as accordion, violin, guitar, bass, piano, mandolin, organ, harmonica, and banjo. Much of the dance music in Norwegian American communities is based on this repertoire, which came to Norway from Central Europe during the mid-nineteenth century and was popular throughout Norway and Sweden in the late nineteenth and early twentieth centuries.

In Norway this music, commonly shared by a number of Central and Northern European ethnic groups, is contrasted with regional rural music, or the *bygdedans* tradition: dances such as *halling, springar, springdans, gangar, pols,* and *rull,* specific to particular regions of Norway and played on regional instruments such as the *hardingfele* 'Hardanger fiddle'. In general, the *gammeldans* types of music survived in the United States; regional types died out in the 1920s and were not widely maintained beyond the first generation of immigrants.

In the late nineteenth and early twentieth centuries, barn dances were generally held in June or July, before the hay crop was harvested. Particular barns, stores, and creameries developed into Saturday night entertainment centers. Sometimes admission was charged and musicians hired and paid. Vaudeville and medicine shows would often precede the dance. During the 1930s and 1940s, bands became more diverse, playing fox-trots, two-steps, and current pop tunes in addition to Scandinavian music.

House parties, a popular activity through the 1920s, were held for visits, birthdays, holidays, and wedding anniversaries. Furniture and rugs were cleared away, and local musicians took turns playing. Dancing was often done outside on wooden platforms built for this purpose. Such events were often multiethnic, including Swedish, Finnish, German, Swiss, Bohemian, Polish, and other ethnic groups. At such dance events, younger musicians would play when the older musicians took breaks. The most common instrumentation for house party bands was one or two fiddles (playing in unison or harmony), accompanied by accordion, organ, autoharp, piano, guitar, or banjo. Accordion was also a common solo/lead instrument. A male fiddler was often accompanied by a female family member, providing rhythmic chords on piano, autoharp, accordion, or banjo. Young people learned by first accompanying and later doubling the melody, finally becoming melody soloists.

House parties and barn dances were gradually replaced by public dances in rural and urban dance halls. In the early years of immigration, these were held wherever facilities were available. Later, specifically Scandinavian facilities were built, which served as meeting places and social halls. Lodge dances and public dances were prevalent by 1900 in the more urban areas; they became popular in rural areas with the rise of the automobile. During the 1920s and 1930s, the phonograph and radio sustained, popularized, and standardized the Scandinavian American folk dance repertoire. A syncretic Scandinavian American music was created, incorporating elements of Anglo-American fiddling, country and western, and jazz.

Norwegian American vaudeville

In Minneapolis, a form of vaudeville comedy developed known as *bondkomik,* a folk play of several acts, including folk dance and presenting themes of immigrant life and humorous songs and monologues. This was followed by social dancing. Huge crowds of Scandinavian Americans would attend such events on Saturday nights. A unique style of Scandinavian American entertainment developed, unknown in Europe.

Well-known entertainers included Ernest and Clarence Iverson ("Slim Jim & the Vagabond Kid"), a Norwegian American duo from Minneapolis, grandchildren of Norwegian immigrants, who sang Norwegian and Swedish songs or folklike songs they composed, as well as American cowboy and Country and Western songs, to guitar and accordion accompaniment. The Olson sisters, American-born daughters of Chicago Norwegians, sang opera and Norwegian folk songs with piano accompaniment and performed comic monologues for Norwegian communities in the Midwest. Such entertainers often used regional language dialects.

Hardingfele

The Harding violin, Hardangar fiddle, or *hardingfele* (figure 1) is a regional instrument of the Hardanger and Telemark provinces of western Norway. It differs morphologically from the European concert violin, having inked decoration and mother-of-pearl inlay, a flat belly, raised f-holes, a lion's or woman's head scroll, sympathetic strings, and an elongated pegbox. It also has a flatter fingerboard and bridge and a shorter neck than the European concert violin has.

Many Norwegian immigrants during the early periods of migration to the United States came from the inner rural regions of Norway, areas with rich *hardingfele* traditions. These immigrants often traveled in groups, forming homogeneous settlements in the upper Midwest. Social isolation in such close-knit communities contributed to the retention of Old World cultural expressions. The use of the *hardingfele* at weddings persisted in some Norwegian American communities in Wisconsin, Iowa, and Minnesota into the early 1900s. In some smaller towns, violin and *hardingfele* were played in local taverns. The instrument was also played at informal gatherings at home and for private house parties.

The *hardingfele* began to appear on stage as a concert instrument in the mid-nineteenth century in Norway as well as in the upper Midwest of the United States. Performances were given by musicians who lived in the United States as well as by *hardingfele* players from Norway who toured periodically for enthusiastic Norwegian American audiences in Iowa, Wisconsin, Minnesota, and the Dakotas in the late nineteenth and early twentieth centuries.

The Hardanger Violinist Association of America (*Spelemanns Laget of Amerika,* or *Spelemanns Forbundet af Amerika*) was organized in 1914 at Ellsworth, Wisconsin, with the purpose of preserving and cultivating interest in the *hardingfele* as well as regional Norwegian folk dances. Its primary activity was the sponsorship of fiddling competitions, or *kappleikar,* which were held regularly until the outbreak of World War II. These competitions were usually held in conjunction with a *bygdelag stevne* 'annual community meeting' and often included dance competitions. The group disbanded in 1952. A few *bygdelags,* however, continued actively to promote demonstrations of *hardingfele* playing and dancing into the 1950s and 1960s.

Hardingfele players who emigrated to America brought the dance music derived from the older *bygdedans* repertoire (*springar, gangar,* and *halling*), as well as the newer *gammeldans* tunes (waltz, schottische or *reinlander,* and polka). Less common were *lyarslåtter* 'character pieces' and wedding marches. In certain cases Norwegian immigrant

FIGURE 1   Ron Roast, Hardinger fiddle maker, performing as part of the Wisconsin Program, 1998 Smithsonian Folklife Festival. Photo by Richard Strauss and courtesy the Ralph Rinzler Folklife Archives and Collections, Center for Folklife and Cultural Heritage, Smithsonian Institution.

fiddlers retained tunes that were no longer remembered in Norway, motivating Norwegian musicians to travel to America to learn from Norwegian Americans. The repertoire was also expanded to include Anglo-American tunes such as "Turkey in the Straw" and "The Irish Washerwoman" as well as European compositions in the classical tradition.

The *hardingfele* tradition in the United States declined during the first quarter of the twentieth century; second-generation Norwegian Americans showed a general lack of interest in their parents' music and dance traditions. It was common for descendants of *hardingfele* players to use the standard European American violin. The older *bygdedans* traditions, which varied considerably from one region to another, were easily replaced by the shared *gammeldans* music played by louder, more "modern" ensembles. By the mid-1970s, *hardingfele* playing was no longer economically rewarding, and the number of players in America had dwindled to about twenty.

Beginning in the 1970s, a renaissance of interest in the instrument occurred. In 1983 a new incarnation of the old *Spelemanns Laget af Amerika* was formed, called The Hardanger Fiddle Association of America. Since then, the organization has been conducting annual workshops in *hardingfele* playing and Norwegian regional dances. Most of the serious students of this instrument today are not of Norwegian American ancestry but became interested through their involvement in the international folk dance movement. This resurgence of interest has resulted in numerous players and dance teachers traveling regularly to the United States from Norway to teach workshops.

SWEDISH MUSIC

Religious fundamentalism sweeping Sweden in the 1840s and 1850s resulted in an exodus of believers who found coexistence with the state church extremely difficult. Many Swedes were motivated to emigrate to America in the 1860s–1880s as a result of crop failures and a general agricultural depression in northern Europe. Compulsory military service was another motivation for emigrating. In general, Swedes settled in places that reminded them of home, especially midwestern rural areas. In the twentieth century, however, Swedish craftsmen tended to settle in cities. There are communities in Wisconsin, Illinois, Minnesota, Michigan, Iowa, Nebraska, the Dakotas, Kansas, and the prairie provinces of Canada [see PRAIRIES, p. 1223]. The Swedish American population of the United States grew from about 700,000 in 1890 to more than 1.5 million in 1930.

Vocal music

Beginning in the late 1850s, song books containing both religious hymns and secular songs were published by the Swedish Lutheran Publication Society and the periodical *Det Rätta Hemlandet* 'The True Homeland'. Editions of *Hemlandssånger* 'The Homeland Singer', published from the 1870s to the 1890s, provided hundreds of hymns and songs, including Swedish, German, and English folk songs. Some hymns were composed by Swedish Americans.

Texts of Swedish emigrant ballads describe a longing for the homeland and the hardships of the journey. Sometimes new texts were set to old hymn tunes or folk songs. Ballad texts concerned the wonders of or disillusionment with the United States, sorrows of parting, nostalgia for the homeland, difficulties of the transatlantic journey, or hope for a new life. A common theme was dissatisfaction with the state church in Sweden. Some texts, such as one set to the tune of "Yankee Doodle," were humorous exaggerated descriptions of the beauties and riches of America. A number of these songs were still remembered through the mid-twentieth century.

By the late 1860s, male choruses were organized in almost every city with a large concentration of Swedish Americans. Such choruses generally performed patriotic

Swedish songs and arrangements of folk songs. Five clubs united in 1886 to form the Union of Scandinavian Singers, which held its first festival the following year in Philadelphia. The American Union of Swedish Singers was organized in Chicago in 1892 and sponsored a festival in 1893 during the Swedish Days at the World's Fair. Some of these groups later toured Sweden. In 1950 the union included seventy choruses with a total membership of 2,500 voices. In addition to songs in the Swedish language, publications of the union include Anglo-American songs in English such as "Swanee River," "America," and "The Star Spangled Banner." Well-known opera choruses with Swedish words are also included.

Dance music

Some Swedish American communities had strong Pietist prohibitions against dancing and secular music. As a result, folk dances were disguised as "singing games," which were done in the late nineteenth and early twentieth centuries by young people and adults at social gatherings and after communal work parties. In other communities without such prohibitions, the northern Central European *gammeldans* repertoire was continued, as in Norwegian American communities.

Popular Swedish American bands in the multiethnic accordion-based *gammeldans* repertoire appealed to a broad Scandinavian and Anglo-American audience. Tours of such groups throughout the Midwest during the 1930s and 1940s included an eclectic repertoire for heterogeneous audiences at state fairs, dance halls, and radio programs.

The Swedish American community of Lindsborg, Kansas

The 1960s represented a decade of Swedish American revivalism in Lindsborg and the promotion of the community as "Little Sweden, United States." A dance group of high school students was organized, with a repertoire learned from folk dance books. This group became the Lindsborg Swedish Dancers and began performing for neighboring communities, acting as a representative of Lindsborg ethnicity to these communities.

Larry William Danielson (1972) traces the history of Swedish American public festivals in Lindsborg from the late 1930s. Festival components have generally included parades, staged folk dance performances by costumed elementary school, high school, or college students, street entertainment, ethnic cuisine, exhibits, decorations, and a performance program. Such presentations were approved by local religious authorities, who tended to frown upon public street dances.

Staged folk dances performed at these festivals were generally learned from popular folk dance publications and were not actually part of the local dance repertoire. Many of the folk dances performed by public school groups described the actions of various professions (farmer, shoemaker, shepherd, weaver, and so on), with musical accompaniment provided by accordion or electric keyboard. Performance programs also included old-time fiddling and accordion music, band concerts, Country and Western music, tap dancing, and symphony orchestras performing works by Scandinavian composers in the Western classical tradition.

During the 1960s, the festivals began attracting more people from surrounding communities. The programs became more of an ethnic mix, including local square dance groups and dance groups from nearby communities representing other northern Central European ethnic communities. High school groups would sing songs learned from printed collections. Central European polka bands, consisting of clarinet, piano, bass, sousaphone, drum set, two violins, two violas, three accordions, and vocalist, became more popular. The group's repertoire included popular Swedish waltzes, schottisches, polkas, and *hambos.*

In addition to the above described festivals for the general public, Lindsborg residents celebrate several smaller in-group festivals based on calendrical rituals. Sankta Lucia includes the singing of Christmas carols in the home as well as caroling in the

Hjalmar Peterson dominated the Swedish American
vaudeville stage for two decades from World War I
to the Depression with his company of Swedish,
Norwegian, and Danish actors and musicians.

streets. From the early 1960s, the home ritual became a public event on Main Street,
including performances by the Lindsborg Swedish Dancers.

The Lindsborg King Knut Celebration, on the twentieth day after Christmas, was
held only for a few years in the mid-1960s. This provided another occasion for a performance by the Lindsborg Swedish Dancers as well as staged dramatic theater and
Anglo-American caroling. *Valborsmässoafton* (Walpurgis Night), occurring in late April
to celebrate the arrival of spring, was also celebrated only for a few years in the mid-
1960s. The student dance group performed, accompanied by a Swedish polka band.

Midsommerdag on June twenty-third includes informal dancing and singing and
social gatherings in the home. In the early 1970s it was made into a public event,
including a workshop in Scandinavian folk dance for the region's elementary and high
school students.

Swedish American vaudeville

Hjalmar Peterson dominated the Swedish American vaudeville stage for two decades
from World War I to the Depression with his company of Swedish, Norwegian, and
Danish actors and musicians. In the tradition of the *bondkomiker,* the rural peasant
comic, Peterson universalized the immigrant experience through his stage character,
Olle i Skratthult 'Olle from Laughterville', and helped forge a Scandinavian American
identity.

His company gave theatrical productions evoking Swedish rural life, with music
modeled after the popular songs of Sweden at that time. The troupe did annual tours
of Swedish American communities in Massachusetts, New York, Chicago, San Francisco, and Seattle, performing musical plays with comic monologues, followed by participatory dancing and singing by the audience with accordion accompaniment. The
dance repertoire consisted of old-time *gammeldans* dominated by polkas, schottisches,
and waltzes.

FINNISH MUSIC

Large numbers of Finns left the homeland in the 1870s, motivated by unemployment,
overcrowding in urban areas, the threat of Russification, and compulsory military service. Many settled in Oregon, Washington, Minnesota, Wisconsin, Michigan, Ohio,
Pennsylvania, New York, and Massachusetts in lumbering, farming, and mining communities. From 1890 to 1920 there were 250,000 Finnish immigrants to North America. The Finnish American population in 1930 was approximately 500,000.

Historically each community had a Lutheran church, a temperance society, and
sometimes a "Socialist Hall" for meetings of workers' associations. Local chapters of
the Finnish Socialist Federation were social and educational centers, often supporting
choirs and bands, as well as community dances in halls and parks.

Temperance societies often built halls for Finnish social events and sponsored
organized activities as alternatives to the saloon: meetings, lectures, dramatic clubs,
sports, music festivals, choirs, and brass bands. These societies began organizing music

festivals in Michigan and Ohio in the late 1890s, with the participation of vocal and instrumental groups. Later, workers' associations, mutual assistance organizations, and nationalistic organizations also supported choirs, brass bands, and dramatic clubs. Members were amateurs, but directors and hired professional singers for lead roles were often salaried.

The Knights and Ladies of *Kaleva* was an organization formed at the turn of the century, with a goal of preserving Finnish identity in America. *Kaleva* halls and lodges in many Finnish American communities continue to sponsor lectures, musical events, dances, and summer camps devoted to Finnish culture for young people.

In the early twentieth century, the most popular social event among Finnish Americans was the community festival (*iltama*). These gatherings included music performances, poetry readings, humor, plays, and social dancing to the accompaniment of brass band, accordion, or dance band. Income at such events was used to finance the activities of the local temperance society and maintenance of the community hall. Other important social events were plays, operettas, choir concerts, and summer festivals including band and choir performances.

Vocal music

Marjorie Edgar (1949) collected ballads among Finnish male immigrants in northern Minnesota during the 1930s. These were dairy cattle homesteaders, trappers, and lumberjacks who continued the tradition of Finnish woodsmen's, boatmen's, and raftmen's songs. The most common were ballads from northwestern Finland about the "knife-men," woodsmen and hunters who carried a large steel *puukko* with a birch handle and curved sheath hanging from the belt, used in woodworking and as a fighting weapon. Some texts described actual events that occurred in northwestern Finland in the 1860s—tales of the misdeeds and misfortunes of village and farmhand bullies and outlaws or Jesse James–like romantic/heroic bad men who died violent deaths or went to prison. The theme of death by knife pervades many of these texts. Some Minnesota versions interpolate American place names for Finnish ones. These songs are sung by both men and women. Some have been recorded with accordion accompaniment, sometimes in a frivolous or even comic style.

Edgar found survivals of other Finnish vocal genres among Finnish Americans in Minnesota in the 1930s. The Finnish epic *Kalevala* was still read, and sometimes sung, by Minnesota Finns at that time. Chants for bringing the cows back to the farm were sung, as were woodsmen's drinking songs. "Wake up" songs were sung at dawn by people going off to work in the fields. As in Europe, ballads, love songs, and laments were sometimes sung to the accompaniment of the plucked zither (*kantele*).

Aili Kolehmainen Johnson (1947) discusses Finnish labor songs in northern Michigan in the area of Ridge during the 1940s. Texts were created in lumber camps or mines by Finnish immigrants, sometimes set to Anglo-American tunes such as "Casey Jones." Traditional Finnish song texts were sometimes altered to American conditions and references, with the original melodies retained. Verses in Finnish sometimes alternated with refrains in English.

Some labor songs praised defenders of the working class, such as Industrial Workers of the World (I.W.W.) leader Joe Hill. Others described the poor working conditions in lumber camps and mistreatment by bosses. These song texts put forth calls to organize and liberate mistreated workers. Many texts described cruel bosses receiving their just punishments, with worker and boss roles reversed. Other songs described conditions during the Depression, when city factory workers drifted to far northern farmlands.

Lullabies sung by Finnish American women in northern Michigan in the 1940s retained European texts that reflected the poverty, semiserfdom, military tyranny, and church domination that pervaded nineteenth-century Finnish life.

Instrumental music

In the late 1800s, *soittokunta* 'brass bands' became popular in Finland as a result of the dispersion of brass instruments from military bands. The breakup of Finnish army battalions in Russia resulted in the immigration of unemployed military instrumentalists to America. These musicians formed Finnish bands in Oregon and the Upper Peninsula of Michigan from the 1870s to the early 1900s, sponsored by temperance societies and socialist organizations [see BANDS, p. 563]

Band members were often dockworkers, miners, or farmers, although some were trained professional musicians and music teachers. Membership was an expression of nationalism, ethnic pride, patriotism, and good breeding for men. Members of socialist bands tended to have more previous music training, and the bands included more female members. Some conductors had no formal music training, often relying on previous military band experience in Finland. Other bandleaders had formal conservatory training in Europe or America. Bands often began as brass ensembles, with the later addition of reeds and then strings. The repertoires of these bands included arranged Finnish folk songs, church hymns, socialist songs, temperance society songs, U.S. band marches (especially Sousa), and opera overtures. Pan-Northern Central European dances such as schottisches, waltzes, and polkas were also played.

Alaine Pakkala (1983) discusses instrumental music of Finnish American communities in the Great Lakes region in the late nineteenth and early twentieth centuries. During that period, community members classified themselves as church people or hall people. Church people centered their social life on the Lutheran Church and its related organizations [see RELIGION, p. 116]. Hall people had minimal involvement with the church, often had socialist leanings, and centered their social life on a secular meeting place or hall.

Because the Apostolic Church disapproved of music in conjunction with social entertainment, instrumental music was forbidden in church services, and social dancing was also discouraged. Some American-born second-generation Finnish Americans would secretly practice and play at local dances without the knowledge of their parents. The Evangelical Lutheran National Church and Suomi Synod Lutherans were more lenient in this regard; piano or organ accompanied congregational singing. Some churches around the turn of the century sponsored mandolin or guitar choirs, usually for young people. These groups accompanied "gospel songs" of a lighter vein than the somber hymns, as well as national songs, operatic overtures, and arias.

Secular social dancing to accordion ("the devil's lungs") was generally discouraged by the church. Other instruments used in Finnish American ensembles included violin, piano, organ, harmonica, clarinet, and to a lesser extent saxophone, mandolin, guitar, banjo, *kantele,* cornet, trombone, flute, baritone horn, and drum set.

Professional entertainers

In the early twentieth century individual troubadours toured America, promoting national Finnish identity. The golden age of Finnish American entertainment extended from just prior to World War I to the early 1930s. Well-known performers included Arthur Kylander, a mandolin player and singer who composed his own comic songs and was accompanied by his wife on piano. He published sheet music, and his ballads were humorous treatments of rural life in Europe and immigrant life in America.

Viola Turpeinen, born in Michigan's Upper Peninsula in 1909, was an extremely well-known accordionist who was active in New York City in the 1930s and 1940s. Her instrumental dance repertoire consisted primarily of polkas, waltzes, and schottisches. She was also popular among non-Finns. She was taught by Italian accordion teachers at first, which caused her to play piano rather than button accordion. During the 1920s, she played in both Finnish and Italian halls, and her repertoire included Italian opera. She recorded more than one hundred tunes for Victor and Columbia from the late 1920s to the 1950s and toured throughout the United States, Finland, and Scandinavia. A performance by Turpeinen in a community hall was often the social event of the year.

Recordings

The first Finnish recordings were made in the United States by Columbia and Victor in the 1910s and featured well-known Finnish semiclassical or romantic melodies or arranged folk songs. Singers were generally trained in the Western classical tradition and were accompanied by professional studio orchestras.

Commercial Finnish American recordings of that era did not provide a representative sample of Finnish American music, however. Choirs and brass bands, which were the most common performance groups in the communities, were hardly recorded. Recording artists were usually professional entertainers; they performed at public dances, gave concerts, and appeared in leading roles in operettas. It was felt that there was no need to record the music that anyone could sing at home. A more folksy sound became prevalent from the mid-1920s, with untrained singers and nonprofessional Finnish musicians and a repertoire focusing on political and socialist songs. Polkas, schottisches, and waltzes were the most commonly recorded dance genres.

Song texts were of Finnish origin or were translations of American songs, and others were composed in the United States. Many dealt with contemporary American themes: the Depression, Prohibition, the Scopes "Monkey Trial," difficulties of immigrant life, or portrayals of miners' or lumberjacks' lives. The accordion was the main accompanying instrument on these recordings. Other instruments included finger-picked guitar, violin, trumpet, saxophone, and occasionally xylophone.

LITHUANIAN MUSIC

Lithuanians comprise the largest group of Baltic Americans, with over 800,000 in the United States in 1980 and about 130 Lithuanian Catholic parishes (figure 2). The bulk of this immigration occurred from the late nineteenth century to World War I. After World War II, the cultural base was broadened by middle-class urban nationalists who arrived as political exiles.

In Pennsylvania mining towns in the 1880s, Lithuanian fiddle and accordion music was commonly heard in meeting halls and taverns. At that time parish choirs and brass bands were formed, and a decade later the first secular choral groups appeared. The first Lithuanian American song festival was held in 1916, preceding the first song festival in Lithuania, which was held in 1924.

Songs

Songs collected in the late 1940s and early 1950s by Jonas Balys (1951, 1958) among first-generation Lithuanian Americans include texts concerning farewells to the homeland, descriptions of the ocean crossing, and hope for a new life. Other texts unfavorably compare the lives of coal miners and steel mill workers with the sunshine and fresh air of farm work. Others deal with unemployment and nostalgia for the homeland. Most are sentimental or humorous, and many deal with hopes and expectations not met.

Through the 1950s, first-generation Lithuanian Americans had frequent social gatherings where spontaneous traditional singing was practiced, along with Anglo-American songs. The second and third generations, on the other hand, participate today in choruses led by professional conductors trained in the European classical tradition.

An archaic song genre called *sutartinė,* documented from the fourteenth century, was still performed at Lithuanian gatherings around 1950. This singing has the contrapuntal character of a choral round or canon and is generally performed by two to four singers. One singer begins and then another enters with the same melody but at the

FIGURE 2   Our Lady of Vilnius Lithuanian Catholic church on Broome Street in Manhattan is one of two Lithuanian Catholic parishes in New York City. Photo by Gillian Rodger, 2000.

It was felt that there was no need to record the music that anyone could sing at home.

interval of a second higher or lower, while the first singer continues. These songs have very small ranges and frequent harmonic major and minor seconds. Sounds are included that mimic birdcalls, flutes, sleighs, looms, and so on. The first singer, called "leader" or "collector," sings the main text. The second, the "adviser," sings nonlexical vocables or improvised commentary on the events described by the lead singer. In Europe in earlier times, people sang these songs while working or dancing. In the mid-twentieth century they were found only rarely in rural areas of northeast Lithuania, sung only by women. Balys found a number of young Lithuanian women in Chicago, all born in the United States, who learned this type of singing not orally but from a song book.

The largest category of songs sung at Lithuanian social events around 1950 were unison songs in so-called old meter (frequent changes between duple and triple meter), with three-line verses and no rhyming. The aeolian, mixolydian, dorian, and phrygian modes were most commonly used. There are numerous wedding, calendrical, and work songs, as well as narrative ballads. "Modern songs" have four-line rhymed verses, sung in parallel thirds.

Several Lithuanian American performing song-and-dance ensembles exist in large urban communities such as Cleveland and Chicago. Some groups perform unaccompanied songs learned from older members of the community, including the vocal genre *sutartine.* Such groups, as well as *kankles* 'plucked zither' ensembles and folk dance groups, are composed mainly of young people, as opposed to choral groups, whose members tend to be of the older generations. Throughout the year local community centers have folk music performances to commemorate political and cultural anniversaries. Regional and national festivals for choruses and dance troupes are held periodically in various North American locations.

Instruments

The *kanklės* is used as accompaniment in Lithuanian singing societies in many cities. There are *kanklės* ensembles in Cleveland and Chicago and a school of instruction in Cleveland. Women have an important role in the revival of this instrumental tradition. Unlike the Latvian American *kokles,* based on village models, Lithuanian American zither players tend to use modernized instruments imported from the former Soviet Union or built by United States craftsmen following that design.

By the turn of the century, there were a number of Lithuanian brass bands in eastern Pennsylvania, Chicago, Philadelphia, Cleveland, Massachusetts, and Connecticut. Members were generally factory and mine workers, many having served in Russian army bands in Europe. These bands generally had regular meetings, dues, and military-style uniforms.

In the same tradition as Italian and Scandinavian American ethnic theater, Antanas Vanagaitis came to the United States from Lithuania with a dramatic group in 1924 [see ITALIAN MUSIC, p. 860]. The comically dressed country bumpkin in various immigrant situations was a well-known figure in Lithuanian American communities.

Vanagaitis composed many songs, including several about the Lithuanian American boxer Jack Sharkey.

LATVIAN MUSIC

There was very little Latvian immigration to the United States prior to World War II. The majority who arrived as a result of the Soviet invasion were of the urban middle class. They soon established newspapers, churches, schools, and other social and political organizations. These postwar immigrants brought with them the traditions of European urban cultural organizations such as polyphonic choirs and song festivals. Regional and national festivals for choruses and dance troupes continue to attract people of Latvian heritage from all over North America.

The *kokle*

The Latvian *kokle* 'small wing-shaped plucked zither' has become a symbol of Latvian ethnic identity in America (Niles 1978). Prior to the nineteenth century in Latvia, the *kokle* was an integral part of traditional village life, accompanying singing and dancing as a solo instrument or played with duct flute and drum. During the nineteenth century, the popularity of string bands, composed of violins and bass for village dance music, caused a decline in the use of the *kokle*. A revival took place in Latvia beginning in the 1930s. Later, the instrument was adapted to concert hall performance, with up to forty strings, as opposed to the traditional five to nine strings, arranged in double courses, with added movable bridges and chromatic tuning.

Beginning in the 1960s in America, instructions for constructing *kokle*s were printed in Latvian American newspapers, resulting in a standardization of the instrument. Interest in building *kokle*s spread among wood hobbyists in many Latvian American communities. The repertoire for the instrument was standardized, and instruction methods were published. Since the 1960s, the instrument has become popular among first- and second-generation Latvian Americans who wish to support their cultural identity.

Although the old favorites of Latvian-born immigrants tend to be the German-influenced songs of the eighteenth and nineteenth centuries, the contemporary Latvian folk revival focuses more on archaic songs considered to be authentically Latvian. These have been culled from the major song collections made in the late nineteenth and early twentieth centuries and arranged for solo voice and *kokle*. In Europe, the music was learned through the oral tradition, while in the United States at the end of the twentieth century, players rely a great deal on printed music that circulates in Latvian American communities. This music is based on folk tunes but is highly classicized and standardized. Some recent creations, aiming for a wider audience through commercial recordings, have emulated the traditional texture of solo voice and accompanying folk instruments, with the incorporation of elements of medieval, baroque, and romantic forms in the European classical tradition.

Latvian Americans are generally averse to changing or modernizing the *kokle*, partly because of anti-Soviet feelings. Instrument makers tend to be first-generation Latvian Americans, while performers tend to be younger people. The instrument is used in community ensembles at social gatherings, concerts, and talent shows, at Latvian Independence Day ceremonies, and in annual nationwide *kokle* festivals. *Kokle* groups have weekly meetings, and the instrument is part of the curriculum at Latvian Saturday schools. An annual youth study camp for Latvian Americans is held in various locations each year, with participants from the United States, Canada, and South America.

ESTONIAN MUSIC

Small numbers of Estonians have immigrated to the United States since the seventeenth century. More came just after 1905, following an abortive revolution against the Russian tsar. Fewer came from 1920 to 1940, when Estonia was an independent nation and the United States imposed strict immigration quotas. The early immigrants established communities in New York, San Francisco, Astoria, Oregon, Fort Pierre, South Dakota, and elsewhere. In July 1940 Estonia was forcibly annexed by the Soviet Union and in 1941–1944 was occupied by Nazi Germany. When Soviet forces recaptured Estonia, about 10 percent of its prewar population fled, leading to the largest wave of Estonian immigration in United States history, with some 10,500 Estonians arriving between 1949 and 1952 (Pennar et al. 1975:27, 129).

The postwar immigrants established communities in Lakewood and Seabrook, New Jersey, and "Estonian Houses" (community centers) in Baltimore, Chicago, Los Angeles, Miami, Minneapolis, New York, and San Francisco. Determined to pass the cultural heritage on to descendants and numerous enough to support various organizations and activities, these immigrants preserved their musical traditions in the new land.

The earliest Estonian cultural organizations included an *Eestlaste Laulu Selts* 'Estonian Singing Society' established in San Francisco in 1904. In New York an Estonian American Music Club was established in the 1920s and an Estonian Workers' Club Choir in 1932. The New York Estonian Male Chorus was founded in 1949. Within eleven years, the ninety-voice ensemble had performed at the White House and abroad and had recorded an album (1960). In May 1953 Estonian male choruses in North America converged in Toronto for the first *Meeslaulupäevad* 'Male Chorus Days'. Subsequent events have alternated between Toronto and New York (or Lakewood, New Jersey). Similar periodic events for female choruses began in 1954.

Vocal music

Men's, women's, and mixed choruses were a continuation of the tradition of school choirs and song festivals well established in Estonia by the mid-nineteenth century, with the Baltic Germans providing a source of inspiration in repertoire and performance style. The larger Estonian American communities had choir singing on a permanent basis, but smaller centers did so more intermittently. Choir membership was generally open. The director and accompanist usually had extensive musical experience, but the singers were mainly amateurs. The repertoire drew heavily on songs found in programs of prewar song festivals in Estonia—mostly works with patriotic and nostalgic themes by Estonian composers of the late nineteenth and early twentieth centuries. A few songs composed during the Estonian "Singing Revolution" of the late 1980s, which led to renewed independence in 1991, have been incorporated into the current repertoire.

Older peasant traditions (work songs, children's songs, epic songs) continued to be sung at informal gatherings, like sing-alongs around the midsummer bonfire. Initially the accordion accompanied singing, but recently the guitar has become more popular. Such informal singing drew heavily on Estonian popular music of the 1920s and 1930s, including some German songs translated into Estonian. Such songs, as well as patriotic choir tunes, were taught to children in Estonian language schools, scout troops, and summer camps, using song books published in Sweden and Canada with prewar Estonian publications serving as guides. Estonian Americans are not very familiar with or interested in songs that became popular in Soviet Estonia, nor have they incorporated many American tunes, except old standards that became popular in Estonia long ago. The repertoire tends to preserve songs the immigrants knew before leaving their homeland.

Instrumental music

Estonian Americans play a number of traditional instruments. As in Estonia, the accordion (typically the diatonic button variety) is preferred for accompanying folk dancers, as it is loud enough to be heard over the dancing, stays in tune, and provides a rich, full sound. It supplanted two instruments that were once very important at peasant weddings and other festivities: the bagpipe and violin. After Ants Taul revived the art of bagpipe making in Estonia in the mid-1970s, his instruments began to appear in the United States, where the most active proponent of Estonian bagpipe playing is Ain Haas (b. 1950) of Indianapolis. A prominent violinist is Mart Jalakas (b. 1947) of Chicago.

The *kannel*, Estonia's version of the Baltic psaltery, is considered the national instrument in the Old Country, but it is even more revered among Estonian Americans as a symbol of their ethnic heritage. Although often mentioned in poetry, its sounds were rarely heard in the United States, as most immigrants were not able to take their instruments with them. The family of Walter Raudkivi-Stein (1902–1980), which settled in Baltimore in 1949, did bring the *kannel* he had made in Estonia, and in the late 1960s Raudkivi built three additional thirty-seven-string *kannel*s, and performed with his daughter, Lilian Esop (b. 1930).

Through her example and teaching, Lilian Esop has played a central role in advancing *kannel* playing in the United States. She organized the first Estonian *Kandlepäevad* 'Kannel Days' in 1981, which has been held every year since at the Estonian Scout Camp in Lakewood, New Jersey, or at the Estonian House in Baltimore (figure 3). In recent years it has also been organized by Tiina Ets of Laurel, Maryland. It regularly draws up to thirty *kannel* players and builders, mostly from the East Coast and Midwest, as well as Latvian, Lithuanian, and Finnish American participants. Kannel Day begins with a "friendship circle," in which each participant takes a turn performing something for everyone else. In the afternoon there is group and individual practice for a concert, which usually has a theme and features both solos and various ensemble arrangements created by the participants. *Kannel* performances may also be heard regularly in Boston, Connecticut, Chicago, Indianapolis, Seattle, and Los Angeles (Haas 1995; Rahkonen 1994).

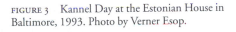 =19

FIGURE 3   Kannel Day at the Estonian House in Baltimore, 1993. Photo by Verner Esop.

Through her example and teaching, Lilian Esop has played a central role in advancing *kannel* playing in the United States.

Some players use instruments mass produced by the Tallinn Piano Factory in Estonia, but the majority use *kannel*s handmade in the United States, which have the shape and glued panel-and-frame construction of the German unfretted zither or American autoharp. The most prolific builder has been Gottlieb Peets (b. 1916), a retired cabinetmaker living in Baltimore, who has built about three dozen instruments since 1981, most modeled after Raudkivi's original. Other active builders include Karl Raidma (1918–1996) of Baltimore and Martin Kink (b. 1918) of Bellingham, Washington.

There has also been a renaissance of interest in the oldest forms of the *kannel*, smaller six- to-twelve-string instruments carved from a single block of wood. Andres Peekna (b. 1937), a research engineer living in the Chicago area, began to make this kind of *kannel* in the early 1970s, using information about Estonian museum pieces and practical construction techniques from Latvian Americans (Peekna 1997). Ain Haas of Indianapolis has made two dozen carved *kannel*s, each of them unique. Ancient runic chants and bagpipe tunes fit well within the limited range of the old-style *kannel*s.

Folk instrument performances are often featured at midsummer bonfires, Estonian Independence Day (24 February) celebrations, and Estonian language school and summer camp gatherings. The musicians often play in international festivals in their local communities, at regional Estonian meetings, and at the quadrennial Estonian World Festivals (ESTOs) (figure 4). Ensembles have rather fluid membership and often include non-Estonians such as Ed Hopf and Gita Veskimets, among the most active *kannel* players in Baltimore. As with Estonian American vocal music, the repertoire is

FIGURE 4   Members of the Chicago Estonian instrumental folk music ensemble Tuuletargad (Wind Wizards). Photo by Gina Jalakas, c. 1999.

rather conservative, drawing heavily on remembered prewar tunes and books of traditional folk dance and folk song tunes.

Estonian American Recordings

Estonian folk tunes and choral pieces may be found on recordings of popular, classical, operatic, and ESTO-festival music by Estonian Americans. A few recordings feature a special emphasis on the traditional repertoire, such as *Omad Poisid* 'Our Own Guys' (1979), *Kaja* 'Echo' (1978) and *Tuuletargad* 'Wind Wizards': *Estonian Instrumental Folk Music* (2000).

REFERENCES

Balys, Jonas, ed. 1951. "Lithuanian Folk Songs in the United States." *Journal of the International Folk Music Council* (3):67–70.

———. 1958. *Lithuanian Folksongs in America*. A Treasury of Lithuanian Folklore, no. 5. Boston: Lithuanian Encyclopedia Publishers.

Blegen, Theodore C., and Martin B. Ruud, eds. 1936. *Norwegian Emigrant Songs and Ballads*. London: Oxford University Press.

Danielson, Larry William. 1972. "The Ethnic Festival and Cultural Revivalism in a Small Midwestern Town." Ph.D. dissertation, Indiana University, Bloomington.

Edgar, Marjorie. 1936. "Finnish Charms and Folk Songs in Minnesota." *Minnesota History* 17(4):406–410.

———. 1949. "Ballads of the Knife-Men." *Western Folklore* 8(1):53–57.

Eidbo, Olav. 1956. "Songs of the Norwegian Folk in Culture and Education in the United States." Ph.D. dissertation, University of North Dakota.

Grame, Theodore C. 1976. *America's Ethnic Music*. Tarpon Springs, Fla.: Cultural Maintenance Associates.

Granquist, Mark A. 1995. "Estonian Americans." In *Gale Encyclopedia of Multicultural America*, ed. Judy Galens, and Robyn V. Young. Detroit, Mich.: Gale Research.

Greene, Victor R. 1992. *A Passion for Polka*. Berkeley: University of California Press.

Gronow, Pekka. 1971. "Finnish-American Records." *JEMF Quarterly* 7(4):176–185.

———. 1977. *Studies in Scandinavian-American Discography*. Helsinki: Finnish Institute of Recorded Sound.

Haas, Ain. 1995. "Estonian *Kannel* Players of North America: Preservation and Creation of Traditions." Paper presented at Finno-Ugric Studies Association of Canada, Montréal, 3 June.

Haugen, Einar. 1938. "Norwegian Emigrant Songs and Ballads." *Journal of American Folklore* 51:69–75.

Hoeschen, Kevin Francis. 1989. "The Norwegian Hardanger Violin in the Upper Midwest: Documentation and Interpretation of an Immigrant Music Tradition." Master's thesis, University of Minnesota.

Houser, George J. 1976. *The Swedish Community at Eriksdale, Manitoba*. Canadian Centre for Folk Culture Studies Paper, no. 14. Ottawa: National Museum of Man Mercury Series.

Jaremko, Christina. 1986. "European-American Music III, 3: Baltic." In *The New Grove Dictionary of American Music*, ed. H. Wiley Hitchcock and Stanley Sadie, 2:77–78. London: Macmillan.

Johnson, Aili Kolehmainen. 1947. "Finnish Labor Songs from Northern Michigan." *Michigan History* 31(3):331–343.

Kaja (Echo). 1978. Portland, Ore.: Kaja 42878.

Kvam, Janet. 1986. "Norwegian American Dance Music in Minnesota and Its Roots in Norway: A Comparative Study." D.M.A. dissertation, University of Missouri, Kansas City.

Larson, LeRoy. 1975. "Scandinavian American Folk Dance Music of the Norwegians in Minnesota." Ph.D. dissertation, University of Minnesota.

Lovoll, Odd Sverre. 1975. *A Folk Epic: The Bygdelag in America*. Boston: Twayne Publishers for the Norwegian American Historical Association.

Nelson, Carl Leonard. 1950. "The Sacred and Secular Music of the Swedish Settlers of the Midwest 1841–1917." Ph.D. dissertation, New York University.

New York Estonian Male Chorus. c. 1960. New York: Globe.

Niles, Christina. 1978. "The Revival of the Latvian *Kokle* in America." *Selected Reports in Ethnomusicology* 3(1):211–239.

Omad Poisi (Our Own Guys). 1979. Baltimore: Rukki Records/Sheffeld Recordings.

Pakkala, Alaine. 1983. "The Instrumental Music of the Finnish-American Community in the Great Lakes Region, 1880–1930." Master's thesis, University of Michigan.

Peekna, Andres. 1997. "Carved *Kannel* and *Kuokle* Making in America." Paper presented at the Third International Baltic Psaltery Conference, Kaustinen, Finland, 14 November.

Pennar, Jaan et al., eds. 1975. *The Estonians in America 1627–1975: A Chronology and Fact Book*. Dobbs Ferry, N.Y.: Oceana Publications.

Rahkonen, Carl. 1994. "The Estonian *Kannel* in Baltimore." Paper presented at the Second International Symposium of *Kankles* Researchers, Vilnius, Lithuania, 16 November.

Riedel, Johannes, ed. 1971. "Music of Two Finnish-Apostolic Lutheran Groups in Minnesota: The Heidemanians and the Pollarites." *Student Musicologists at Minnesota* 4:1–36.

Roucek, Joseph. 1952. "Estonian Americans." In *One America*, ed. Francis J. Brown and Joseph S. Roucek, 198–202. New York: Prentice-Hall.

Torre, L. 1978. "Of Swedish Roots: A Fiddler Returns to His Home Roof." *Swedish Pioneer Historical Quarterly* 29(4):277–287.

Tuuletargad (Wind Wizards). 2000. *Estonian Instrumental Folk Music*. Chicago: Innovative Mechanics.

Walko, M. Ann. 1989. *Rejecting the Second Generation Hypothesis: Maintaining Estonian Ethnicity in Lakewood, New Jersey*. New York: AMS Press.

Wright, Robert L. 1965. *Swedish Emigrant Ballads*. Lincoln: University of Nebraska Press.

Snapshot:
Danish Musical Traditions
in Yates County, New York
James Kimball

The Danes who settled in Yates County, in New York's Finger Lakes region, have over the years been little influenced by organized folklore or nationalist movements emanating from either Denmark itself or from major Danish concentrations in the upper Midwest. Most arrived in the late nineteenth and early twentieth centuries, coming from the north of Denmark and establishing themselves in a community of successful dairy farmers in the open land north and west of Keuka Lake. Danish music and dance have long been part of the social life within this community, although in modern times they survive in only two annual events: the Danish Christmas Tree and Dance and the Danish Day Picnic.

The Christmas Tree and Dance goes back to the early 1900s and was for a long time the biggest social event of the year. It was quite formal, professionally catered, and had music played by an established Scandinavian orchestra that generally included piano accordion, one or two violins, drum set, and piano or guitar. A 1934 advertisement for the dance reads: "Christmas Tree and Dance, auspices of the Danish Brotherhood At Grange hall, Friday, Dec. 28th. Music by the Vikings' 4-piece orchestra. Everybody invited" (*Penn Yan Chronicle Express* 20 December, 1934, p. 4).

Old-timers remember crowds of two hundred or more, with everyone dressed up. For several years there was enough interest to support two of these dances in the area, one sponsored by the Danish Brotherhood in Penn Yan and a second in the Ballona Community Hall just a few miles away. The music was mostly Scandinavian, and the dances included Danish-style waltzes, polkas, schottisches, and *hopsas* as well as several distinctive figure dances and musical games that had been passed on from older generations. Children were encouraged to attend, not only to enjoy the decorated tree, small gifts, and Christmas songs at the beginning of the evening but also to learn the old dances from parents and grandparents during the earlier part of the dance that followed. There was a slow decline in attendance and formality, however, starting in the 1950s, attributed by some to the rise of television and a general increase of holiday attractions. Others would point to a dispersion of the Danish community as younger family members lost the language and moved away or married non-Danes.

A second tradition has been the old-time folk music as played primarily by older Danes on small diatonic accordion, guitar, mouth organ, and fiddle. For the most part this music was played at home, though some musicians did (and still do) get together informally as participants at a lakeside picnic in early June to celebrate the Danish national day. Traditionally the food was potluck, and old-time dances and musical games were played in a very relaxed environment. The Danish Day picnics were started shortly after World War II and are generally the only occasions at which one is likely to see a profusion of national colors and flags, even a few traditional costumes. The local Danish Americans are not generally given to much nationalist display, and some influence here seems to be coming from other Scandinavian groups in the Finger Lakes region.

In 1985 several of these local musicians were brought together in more organized fashion by an arts council and historical society recognition of local Danish heritage, including a museum exhibit and a sale of a locally produced cassette tape. The musicians, calling themselves the Danish Day Players, were Eva Pedersen Butterfield, Chris Christensen, and Lynn Christensen on diatonic accordions, Alfred Christensen on fiddle, Ron Christensen on guitar and mouth organ, and Lester Buckholz on guitar. The music was a sampling of tunes that they had learned growing up and at the community dances.

In December of that same year, the one active Scandinavian professional band in the area was unable to play at the Christmas dance, and a quickly assembled group of the old-timers, mostly those who had been playing at the Danish Day picnic, got together to furnish the music. The group has done so ever since. The Christmas dance, while still being held, has become significantly smaller and is now generally very informal: dress is more casual, the food may be potluck rather than catered, the tree has become much smaller or is absent altogether, and some of the older tunes and dances are being forgotten as key old-timers pass away or can no longer participate. A couple of recent attempts at making the dance a more formal affair with a sit-down dinner were in certain ways very successful, although few children were present. On the other hand, participation by a few younger musicians gives hope that the tradition might persevere.

There have been occasional attempts over the years to introduce new Danish folk dances, but these do not appear to have had any lasting influence. In 1985, for example, a young immigrant couple from Copenhagen taught a local group some dances from the repertoire of an organized folk dance group in Denmark. To this couple, many of the old-time dances of the Yates County community seemed more like children's games. The new dances were performed once, at the 1985 Christmas dance, to recorded music while the musicians took an extended break. The musicians never learned the requisite tunes, however, and these "taught" dances never caught on. The tunes and dances the old-timers grew up with are still the first choice for the annual Christmas and Danish Day celebrations.

Central European Music
Mark Levy

German Music
Polish Music
Czech and Slovak Music
Slovenian Music

Central Europeans began arriving in the United States in the late seventeenth century and have continued in a steady stream from that time to the present. Establishing religious and social institutions in the New Country, they have continued to be active musically, contributing to the mainstream Western classical tradition as it developed in the United States as well as to the enrichment of their own communities. Many Central European musical traditions have thrived here, including a strong and healthy polka culture that continues to this day.

GERMAN MUSIC

The immigration of various German-speaking groups to the United States began in the 1680s and continued into the twentieth century. Large numbers arrived in the 1850s, 1870s, and 1880s. Pre-1847 immigration consisted primarily of religious exiles ("Old Lutherans"), farmers, and landless peasants from southern and eastern Germany. Political exiles emigrated to America following the 1848 revolutions.

During the eighteenth century, Pennsylvania was settled by German and Swiss immigrants speaking a variety of Middle and South German dialects that gradually became homogenized into what is popularly known as Pennsylvania Dutch. This designation includes sectarian groups such as the Mennonites, Amish, Dunkards, and Moravians, but most German Americans in Pennsylvania are Lutheran or Reformed. Early settlers used the local dialect for everyday discourse and High German in church and school.

During the nineteenth century, many settled in the Midwest in areas with high concentrations of German speakers and so were able to conduct a considerable portion of their daily affairs in that language. In general, German culture today has persisted most noticeably in rural areas.

Overview of German music

In some respects it is difficult separating German American music from the music of mainstream America. German folk music acquired traits that we associate with concepts of Western or European American music long before the musics of many other ethnic groups did. For example, much German folk music uses heptatonic 'seven-tone' major/minor melodies with a predominance of triadic melodic movement with implied harmonic function (Bohlman 1979). German folk music also has a relatively long history of interaction with urban culture and the widespread use of notated music.

German Americans have had significant influences on American literature, philosophy, visual arts, music, the educational system, agriculture, and religious movements. Music is central to German American concepts of culture; musical literacy has always been highly valued and from early years was an integral part of the curriculum in German American schools. Various genres of sacred and secular music were extremely significant in the lives of nineteenth-century German Americans and were closely tied with ethnic pride and the conservation of German identity.

During the past century, functional and contextual distinctions between religious and secular music among German Americans became hazy (Bohlman 1985:37), and today for example, hymnody is sung at home as well as in church, and secular music is also performed in church. In many communities the secular singing society is also the church choir. Similarly, the church instrumental ensemble also functions as the community social orchestra.

German Americans had a dominant role in the development of European American symphonic music in the nineteenth century [see OVERVIEW OF MUSIC IN THE UNITED STATES, p. 519]. In 1890, for example, eighty-nine of the ninety-four musicians in the New York Philharmonic were German Americans. Many orchestras, such as the Chicago Symphony, were founded by German conductors. In Texas during the 1880s, German community orchestras performed works by Wagner and Mendelssohn regularly at state festivals (Albrecht 1975:293). The influence of Germany on European American classical music decreased after World War I, when France became the preferred location for music study abroad.

Singing societies

The German American choral society, called Liedertafel, Liederkranz, Männerchor, Gesangverein, or Musikverein, is a male chorus located in an urban area, led by a classically trained director. These singing societies were established to perform elaborate four-voiced arrangements of German folk songs as well as polyphonic music by German composers in the Western classical tradition, with the intention of creating an image of national and spiritual unity of the German people. Such groups encouraged their German American members to adopt a national German identity as opposed to their regional ones. Songs previously associated with a particular region often became part of a standard repertoire (Albrecht 1975:252). During the nineteenth century, this classicized folk song repertoire was published in religious and secular song collections and periodicals used in German American homes in rural areas. Some collections contained texts only; others included music notation for piano and voice or four-part chorus.

Membership in any particular choral society tended to cut across economic, social, and occupational boundaries—a singing society could include mechanics, clerks, storekeepers, and professionals. All-male choruses have been dominant, but by 1900 mixed choruses were also common. These groups have generally opened their membership to interested individuals from other ethnic backgrounds, sometimes changing the group's name from German to English to appeal to a broader population.

Sängerbunde 'singing leagues' were formed beginning in the 1850s to coordinate competitions and festivals (*Sängerfeste*) of singing groups on local, state, national, or international levels. Such festivals included elaborate banquets, picnics, parades, concerts, and the participation of bands and orchestras. The evening banquet at these festivals was an exclusively male activity. Songs sung between elaborate toasts were mainly student songs, many in Latin.

In general, choral societies would have multiple responsibilities and functions, including performing at a variety of civic events such as building dedications, holidays,

In Texas during the 1880s, German community orchestras performed works by Wagner and Mendelssohn regularly at state festivals.

and ethnic festivals. In addition, these groups sang in church services and provided choruses for local opera, operetta, and oratorio productions. Director/conductor positions were generally salaried. A singing society in a larger city would sometimes become associated with a German American instrumental ensemble and/or drama group, with which it would collaborate on concert programs. Because their song texts tended to focus on praises of the Fatherland in the German language, the loyalties of these singing groups were questioned during World War I; this period marked the beginning of a general decline in the prestige and importance of these groups. Anti-German sentiment was created and sustained as part of the war effort. Everything German fell from esteem, and German language instruction was dropped in the schools. The speaking of the German language in public was forbidden. German music was looked down upon, and singing societies became the objects of anti-German feelings (Albrecht 1975:453).

Religious music

Lutheran music

The Lutheran Church historically has been the most important social institution for many German Americans, especially those in rural areas [see RELIGION, p. 116]. It has been the center for religious, educational, social, and musical activities and has had an important role in the perpetuation of the German language. From the early nineteenth century, classes for teaching hymn singing to young people were established in churches and parochial schools.

The Missouri Synod of the Lutheran Church, which claims the majority of German Americans, still used German in half its parishes in 1925. It favored the return to an older, more conservative hymnody, revitalizing the rhythmic style of the Reformation. This style of singing united various German American groups by providing a single style of music in a single dialect, High German.

Beginning in the 1840s, the Wisconsin and Missouri Synods published sacred and secular music for home use, including some hymns in English translation as well as some patriotic American songs. These publications formed a cultural link among German Americans throughout the Midwest.

Mennonite music

At the time of the Protestant Reformation, a small group of reformers known as Anabaptists was led by Menno Simons (1492–1559). This group believed that all worldliness was wicked and that one should lead an extremely plain, austere, and pious life, refusing to bear arms in the military. Followers of Menno were called Mennonites.

"Old Colony" Mennonites use *Gesangbuchs* 'song books' for the singing of unison hymns; these books contain texts only, without music notation. Hymns are sung informally in the home and on Sundays in the village meeting house. At the meeting house, each line of text is initiated by a *Vorsanger* 'lead singer', who is joined by the congregation. At the end of each line, the Vorsanger adds some solo notes after the congregation has stopped singing (Burkhart 1952).

Old Colony Mennonite hymns are sung in unison and in free rhythm, with no harmony or metric pattern. They are basically melismatic 'many notes to one syllable' melodically ornamented versions of old Protestant chorale tunes. Over time the tune may deviate significantly from the original through the variations of oral tradition.

Amish music

A young bishop in the Mennonite church, Jacob Amman, believed that the practice of *meidung* 'shunning of an erring member' had grown lax and should be more strictly enforced. This led to a schism in the church, and Amman and his followers broke away. They became known as Amish, after his name, and are the most orthodox of the Mennonite groups. The Amish first arrived in Pennsylvania around 1720. They maintained their attitude of separateness from the world, settling in distinct communities apart from other German-speaking dissenting religious groups, such as the Dunkards and Moravians.

Amish church music is entirely monophonic and without instrumental accompaniment. Hymns fall into two major categories according to music style: older slow hymns in free rhythm and newer fast metric hymns. Monophonic slow hymns are often highly melismatic versions of fifteenth-, sixteenth-, and seventeenth-century secular songs, Gregorian chants, or chorale melodies (Burkhart 1952). Fast tunes are generally based on German secular folk songs, well-known Lutheran hymns, American Protestant hymns, or Anglo-American folk tunes with German texts. Specific composers and dates are known for a number of these fast tunes. These melodies are not used in the church service but are sung at Sunday evening sings and weekday meetings.

In Amish communities, a worship service is held Sunday mornings at a home, in a room from which all domestic furniture has been removed. Men and women sit on opposite sides of the room on hard, backless wooden benches. A single congregation may have a half-dozen song leaders, usually older men who take turns in leading the congregation. The *Vorsanger* announces each hymn by page number in the hymnal and sings the first syllable of the line alone. The entire group joins in on the second syllable in unison. Any member of the congregation if so moved may announce the number of a hymn and proceed to lead it. Hymns are always monophonic and unaccompanied; instruments in the home or at church in conjunction with devotional singing are strictly forbidden (Frey 1949:142; Hohmann 1959:43).

Secular folk songs are sung in Amish communities in the home and on special occasions, such as the afternoon and evening of the wedding day, or during Sunday evening "singings" for young people. Music in such contexts includes faster metric hymns and songs. Popular ballads may be sung at the Sunday evening sings, often to the accompaniment of (officially forbidden) harmonicas.

In some Amish communities, weekly Saturday night barn dances are held for young people (Shaner 1963). A typical barn dance band includes some combination of guitar, fiddle, mandolin, and harmonica. Dancing is done in sets of six to eight couples in a circle formation. There is no central caller; one person in each set calls out the various steps, which others in the set must follow. Usually young women locate themselves on one side of the barn, young men on the other. At these events English rather than Pennsylvania Dutch is generally spoken, although in general no outsiders are present.

Secular German American music in Pennsylvania

Secular vocal music of this region consists of songs brought by eighteenth- and nineteenth-century immigrants, translations of Anglo-American songs, and indigenous Pennsylvania German creations. Song melodies show a great deal of influence from Anglo-American folk song.

A number of Pennsylvania German secular folk songs are identical or very similar to the following Anglo-American tunes: "Twinkle, Twinkle Little Star," "Polly, Wolly, Doodle," Stephen Foster's "Oh! Susanna," "Oats, Peas, Beans, and Barley Grow," "Yankee Doodle," "Ta-ra-ra-boom-dee-ay," "Sweet Betsy from Pike," and so on (Buffington 1974) [see ENGLISH AND SCOTTISH MUSIC, p. 831]. In some songs, a section or phrase is taken from a well-known Anglo-American tune, while the rest of the melody is a German tune. Some tunes are based on Anglo-American or Irish instrumental dance tunes, such as "Turkey in the Straw." A number of song texts are risqué. Texts are in Pennsylvania German dialect or in "Dutchified English," that is, English colored by the influence of the local dialect.

Many of the songs known by older inhabitants in the 1960s were brought from Germany, Switzerland, and Alsace in the eighteenth century. Subjects of song texts include birth, courtship, marriage, married life, family life, and farming. Humor is prevalent throughout these songs. Cumulative texts are common, where bits of each preceding verse are repeated in successive verses in a humorous manner. Other songs were created in America, with texts either in Pennsylvania Dutch dialect or High German. These texts were sometimes set to Anglo-American tunes.

Instruments are used in both sacred and secular contexts. In many homes on Sunday afternoons or winter evenings, hymns are sung with organ, zither, and/or violin accompaniment. In the early twentieth century, Sundays were also a time for male dancing and singing to fiddle accompaniment in taverns (Raichelson 1975). Annual family reunions during the summer, or at Thanksgiving or Christmas, have been important contexts for singing and instrumental music.

Eighteenth- and nineteenth-century historical records describe the prevalence of Pennsylvania Dutch dancing at wedding feasts and in taverns, even though this activity was repressed and condemned by religious leaders. Taverns and inns were social centers and would hire fiddlers to provide music for dancing, especially during the winter months. From the 1790s through the nineteenth century, such inns were located every mile along turnpikes for wagoners and other travelers. Public dances sponsored by such establishments provided an opportunity for young people to socialize. During the nineteenth century, Anglo-American square dances, reels, and contra dances, with fiddle accompaniment, prevailed among German Americans in taverns and at parties; the waltz was incorporated from the 1870s [see CONTRA DANCE, p. 230]. Fiddling was also heard in such contexts as wood-chopping matches, quiltings, and husking bees, with musicians receiving farm produce or tips as compensation (Yoder 1950). These musicians were generally members of the gathering rather than outside hired professionals, although sometimes African American musicians were engaged.

During the eighteenth and nineteenth centuries, regional fairs held during lulls in seasonal work activities were important contexts for instrumental music and dancing. These events resembled carnivals, with rides, clowns, entertainment, horse races, and parades. Bands played for dancing in taverns and inns. Historical documents also describe fiddle and zither music for dancing at Christmas celebrations and weddings.

Singing occurred at public and private social gatherings such as church picnics and family reunions. At neighborhood work bees for harvesting, flax production, husking, apple butter boiling, hog killing, quilting, wood chopping, or barn raising, singing accompanied the work activities. Later in the evening there was more singing, dancing, and eating at a "frolic," with music provided by fiddles, guitars, and zithers.

German American music in the upper Midwest

Bohlman (1979) discusses music making in the private domestic realm of the German American home in north-central Wisconsin. Both secular and religious songs are sung at social gatherings in conjunction with seasonal holidays of the Christian religious calendar. As in Pennsylvania, some German Christmas songs are versions of English-language songs. In the opposite direction, some German songs, such as "O Tannenbaum" or "Du, Du, Liebst Mir in Herzen," have achieved wide popularity outside German American communities.

If instrumentalists are found among family members, accompaniment may be provided on accordion, violin, or piano. Songs are learned at home, at church, or at school, through the oral tradition as well as from song books. There is considerable room for variation in melody, text, and rhythm, even with songs in printed collections. In general, there are hazy divisions between the oral and written traditions, between religious and secular music, and among repertoires associated with home, church, community, and school.

Variants of songs such as "Fuchs Du Hast Die Gans Gestohlen" are found in variants in German settlements throughout the world. The song genre known as *Schnadahupfl* (or *Schnaderhüpfl*), associated with Bavaria and Austria, consists of improvised texts alternating with a refrain. Hand and foot gestures may act out the text, for example, the grinding movement of a millstone. Parts of the text may be nonsensical in order to create rhyme. "Schnitzelbank," one of the most popular songs in German Wisconsin, is a good example of this genre.

Other vocal genres include funeral songs, lullabies, *Heimatlieder* 'songs about the European homeland', *Soldatenlieder* 'songs about soldiers and war', love songs, narrative ballads, and satirical/humorous songs. Pedagogical songs for children focus on issues such as language learning, counting, religious/moral lessons, or the instruments of the orchestra. Secular and religious songs are generally in the major mode, in metric patterns of 2/4, 6/8, or 3/4, and often harmonized in parallel thirds.

In rural areas of the upper Midwest, the church tends to be a focus for cultural activities and serves as the main or even sole context for social gatherings. The church has had a major role in the retention of the German language, and church-sponsored German parochial schools have provided instruction in German language and cultural traditions. Beginning in the 1860s in north-central Wisconsin, local churches formed brass bands for young people, with the purpose of training them for public music making events (figure 1). Community musicians are involved in church activities as organists and choir directors. Religious music has generally occupied a more prominent role than secular music in German American small towns.

FIGURE I   The Alte Kameraden Band of Wisconsin, playing at the 1975 Festival of American Folklife. Photo courtesy the Ralph Rinzler Folklife Archives and Collections, Center for Folklife and Cultural Heritage, Smithsonian Institution.

Secular and religious songs are generally in the major mode, in metric patterns of 2/4, 6/8, or 3/4, and often harmonized in parallel thirds.

Russian (Volga) German music

Ethnic Germans settled in the Volga and Black Sea regions of Russia during the reign of Catherine the Great. Communities of these Volga (Russian) Germans are found in Colorado, Wyoming, Nebraska, and Kansas. Members of these communities are referred to as "Dutchmen" and their public dances as "Dutch Hops" (Warren 1990).

Weddings have been important contexts for music and dance in Russian German communities in the United States, especially during the 1920s and 1930s. These ceremonies included many Eastern European Slavic customs adopted and retained by the ethnic Germans in their former homeland. Weddings in the United States were generally held during three time periods: in the spring after planting, in the fall after harvest, and in the winter after Christmas. The celebrations tended to last from two to six days; each day the band played from late morning to midnight.

During the 1920s and 1930s, band instrumentation changed according to context: string-dominated bands for indoor dancing; wind-dominated bands for outdoor processions. Often musicians needed to double on two instruments. Violin was the most common lead instrument in string bands, with clarinet the most common lead in wind bands. A typical wedding band would include two violins, *hackbrett* 'hammered dulcimer', string bass, button accordion, and possibly clarinet or harmonica. Violins were gradually replaced with accordions at weddings during the 1930s.

Prior to World War II, Russian German dances were held weekly at the halls of various fraternal organizations. After World War II, brass instruments such as trumpet and trombone were added and occasionally guitar or banjo. Bands sometimes used notated music. Band membership was flexible and could include non-Germans. Women, usually relatives of male band members, were at times included on such instruments as piano and hammered dulcimer. During the 1950s there were numerous bars with dancing and live music, and amplification became widely used. The dance music repertoire of Volga Germans includes polkas, waltzes, schottisches, and the *hochzeit,* a wedding dance in a fast duple meter. Currently the polka is the most important dance genre in this community (figure 2).

Polka bands

German Americans have had a prominent role in the American polka movement, along with Czech, Polish, and Slovenian Americans. New Ulm, Minnesota, is a major German/Czech settlement noted for its wealth of bands and well-known polka musicians. In this and other regions, Sunday evening picnic concerts have been a major context for polka band music. Groups from New Ulm are known as "Dutchman" bands and tend to have an eclectic style incorporating repertoire from their Slavic American and Scandinavian American neighbors [see SCANDINAVIAN AND BALTIC MUSIC, p. 866; EASTERN EUROPEAN MUSIC, p. 908].

The "American Dutchman" style is based on instrumental dance music of southwestern Bohemia, a Czech region that has had a great deal of German cultural influence. This style is characterized by a marchlike or military quality, with instrumentation

FIGURE 2   A Volga German ensemble from Nebraska performing at the 1975 Festival of American Folklife (Instruments: hackbrett, bass guitar, trombone, and accordion). Photo courtesy the Ralph Rinzler Folklife Archives and Collections, Center for Folklife and Cultural Heritage, Smithsonian Institution.

emphasizing button accordion, brass instruments, and drum set. Bands often consist of family members, and repertoire focuses on polkas and waltzes. Song texts are often in English and relate to the American experience of European immigrants and their descendants.

In the late 1940s, many German American bands tended to emulate mainstream swing and "sweet" bands, synthesizing old-time and modern American ballroom musical styles [see POPULAR MUSIC FOR THE PARLOR AND STAGE, p. 179]. The instrumentation of these groups included multiple saxophones, trumpets and other brass, drum set, accordions, and piano. Repertoire included two-steps, polkas, schottisches, and romantic Tin Pan Alley ballads (Greene 1992).

Lawrence Welk (1903–1992), who became a household word through television appearances from the early 1950s, integrated German American polkas and waltzes into the standard mainstream American dance band repertoire. His parents were Russian Germans from Ukraine who settled in North Dakota in 1892. His father played organ and accordion, and Welk soon began playing at local barn dances and weddings. His earliest recordings in the late 1920s and early 1930s were not "ethnic" at all, but standard contemporary popular tunes. His first polka recording was made in 1939. Welk, essentially an American bandleader of "sweet" music, had an important role in mainstreaming the acceptance of polka music, even though polkas and waltzes were always a minor part of his repertoire. His style can be characterized as smooth, bouncy, and conservative, aiming to please as wide an audience as possible. His popularity lasted into the 1960s and 1970s.

POLISH MUSIC

The Polish American population in the United States is extremely diverse, consisting of fourth-generation descendants of nineteenth-century immigrants as well as post-Solidarity émigrés of the 1990s. Polish American communities have numerous clubs, associations, churches with social halls and parochial schools, veterans' posts, Polish homes, and community centers with theaters, libraries, meeting rooms, and athletic clubs.

Choral groups

Paula Savaglio (1996) discusses choral groups in the Detroit Polish community. Such groups have thrived in the United States since the late nineteenth century, when the

Polish Singers' Alliance of America was formed. Choral groups in the Detroit area that are members of the Alliance represent the Polish community at ethnic festivals, celebrations marking significant dates in Polish history, benefit concerts for relief projects in Poland, and visits by foreign dignitaries.

These groups sing primarily in Polish, with some songs in English and a few religious songs in Latin. Some groups provide commentary during performances in both Polish and English. Their repertoire includes polyphonic arrangements of Polish patriotic songs, Christmas carols, and songs about the Solidarity movement in Poland. Choir members often dress in Polish regional costumes.

In general these choral groups tend to identify strongly with European urban Poland. Polish American polka dance bands, on the other hand, which originated as musical and social institutions in pre–World War II America, are based more on American than European models and do not incorporate such a European identity. While dance band leaders tend to be descendants of earlier pre–World War II immigrants, directors of choral groups are generally post–World War II émigrés.

Weddings

Susan Davis (1978a) discusses wedding customs among first- and second-generation Polish Americans in Utica, New York, from 1900 to World War II. Prior to the wedding day, a series of engagement parties is held, with music provided by a band of three or four musicians, including violin(s), bass, and accordion. On the wedding day, the band plays for relatives and friends at the bride's house and at a reception held in a rented community hall or restaurant after the church ceremony. At the reception, the band plays marches as each guest arrives and walks around the room with the maid of honor or bridesmaid. These marches are interspersed with polkas, waltzes, and *oberek*s, with an occasional mazurka or German *Rheinlander* (schottische). The *oberek* is in a faster triple meter, with two against three cross-rhythms and energetic leaping and stomping.

During the unveiling of the bride, bridesmaids and other guests sing songs describing the bride's loss of her youthful freedom, her love for her parents, her sadness at leaving their home, and her mixed emotions associated with the transition to married life. Guests may be provided with song sheets containing Polish texts, sometimes with modernized English translations. During the dancing that follows, guests may start singing a particular song, which is then picked up by the band. Humorous teasing songs are sung, often initiated by the older women present, giving advice to the bride and groom, with bawdy references to the wedding night. The celebration generally continues for one or several more days, with more partying at the bride's parents' home.

The wedding functions as a reaffirmation of community and family values, with an idealization of marriage and monogamy and the virginity and naïveté of the bride. Song texts, however, express the ambivalent feelings of the bride in making this difficult transition. After World War II, intermarriage, flight to the suburbs, and the increased costs of bands and halls resulted in a decline of many wedding customs. In the earlier decades of the twentieth century, bands were generally informal groupings of family members or neighbors. Later, a trend developed toward more formal groupings and greater professionalism.

Polka

Two polka traditions have existed in Central Europe since the 1830s: a rural folk tradition and an urban salon tradition. These two traditions coexisted in Poland in the latter half of the nineteenth century and were brought to the United States by immigrants. A similar dual tradition has continued to exist in the United States: the urban "Eastern" style and a revitalized and reconstructed rural "Chicago" style (Kleeman 1982:33).

Small instrumental groups with combinations such as piano, bass, and sax; concertina, trumpet, and drums; or accordion, clarinet, violin, and bass were common in Polish American communities in eastern and midwestern cities since the 1870s, but organized polka bands of six or more members did not really exist until the late 1920s (Keil 1992:31). At that time, a fusion of the rural string sound and the urban sound occurred. String-dominated bands gradually incorporated clarinet, trumpet, accordion, and drums, and the violin relinquished its lead role to these louder instruments.

In America during the 1930s and 1940s, Polish and Polish American songs in duple meter were adapted as polkas by performing them in alternation with instrumental sections called "drives." Later, songs were composed with this format in mind. By the 1940s, Polish American groups in urban areas such as Detroit were performing more and more for non-Polish audiences. This trend required them to incorporate mainstream American popular dance genres, such as the rumba, cha-cha-cha, and foxtrot (Savaglio 1996:40). The Polish American polka resulted from a syncretism of Polish folk song *krakowiak* (the Polish regional dance), pan-European polka elements, and mainstream American popular dance music.

Polish Americans have had a central role in the development of the polka tradition in the United States, a phenomenon involving the participation of many European American ethnic communities: Czechs, Germans, Slovenians, Italians, Norwegians, Swedes, Ukrainians, Russians, Lithuanians, Finns, Mexican Americans, French Americans, and Anglo-Americans. In Polish communities, however, "polka music" is synonymous with "Polish music." Post–World War II immigrants, generally from more urban, well-educated backgrounds in comparison with earlier immigrants, tend to look down on polka music as being associated with negative beer-drinking stereotypes of Poles or of the American working class. They prefer to identify themselves with European popular music, Polish composers in the Western classical tradition, or classically influenced polyphonic Polish American choral groups (Savaglio 1996:42).

Eastern-style polka

The more urban "Eastern style" was formulated by musicians such as Ed Krolikowski (Bridgeport, Connecticut) and Bernie Witkowski (New York City), both of whom were educated in Western classical music in Poland. Krolikowski absorbed musical influences from Dixieland, vaudeville, swing, jazz, and Broadway musicals, as well as a wide variety of European American ethnic traditions. As a result, he and his peers created a Polish music in an Americanized or "jazzed-up" version. Krolikowski's influence was increased by his fluency in six languages and his ownership of a music store that responded to the needs of various nationalities for printed music and recordings.

Bernie Witkowski, who had a background in classical and jazz clarinet, became a channel for the flow of ideas from big bands to polka bands in the 1930s. He expanded the role of improvisation in polka music, although most of it soon became carefully rehearsed variation. He also emphasized precise playing by the two melodic lead instruments.

Early urban-style groups that recorded in the 1920s and 1930s used a variety of instruments, usually including six or more of the following: clarinet, saxophone, trumpet, flute or piccolo, piano, concertina or accordion, banjo, xylophone, vibraphone, string bass, and drum set. Some of these recordings used non-Polish studio musicians. During the 1940s, many ethnic bands made the transition from neighborhood and home to hotel and ballroom, thus exposing themselves even more to mainstream American popular dance music.

During the 1930s and 1940s, polka music became faster, with a brass-dominated, more brilliant timbre. Professional bands played repertoire from "the Polish book"— polkas, waltzes, and *obereks*—as well as repertoire from "the English book": fox-trots, lindy-hops, swing, ballads, tangos, rumbas, and hillbilly (Keil 1992:35).

Krolikowski's influence was increased by his fluency in six languages and his ownership of a music store that responded to the needs of various nationalities for printed music and recordings.

The urban-style or ballroom polka dominated Polish American communities from the mid-1930s to 1960. During this period, rhythmic, melodic, and harmonic aspects of jazz, Latin, bluegrass, Cajun, Country and Western, and other popular musics were incorporated (Kleeman 1982:85). The classic Eastern-style band was a large ensemble with a variety of instruments, playing technically precise, well-rehearsed variations with a continuous shuffling of lead instrumental combinations during performance. By the late 1950s, most Eastern style bands had reduced their size and increased their amplification. Some groups aimed to appeal to a general working-class audience of mixed ethnic backgrounds and included rock medleys, country and western songs, Frank Sinatra and Tony Bennett classics, and Latin numbers in their repertoires. Others focused on Polish American dance music.

Chicago-style polka

During the 1920s, village-style folk orchestras from Chicago rivaled the more urbanized Eastern bands in popularity. Franciszek Dukla, a fiddler from rural Galicia living in Chicago, was a foremost exponent of the *wiejska* 'village-style Polish band' at that time. A lead clarinet and violin played in heterophonic unison, accompanied by additional violins playing upbeat chords and a bowed bass. This style echoed the string bands of the Podhale or Gorale tradition of rural Poland.

During the 1950s, a revived rural style in Chicago began to challenge the popularity of the Eastern urban style. Chicago bands played at slower tempos, with fewer sections and fewer key changes and with a greater influence from Polish folk song and *krakowiak* rhythms. The Chicago style became associated with a more improvisatory, informal quality of the melody, with irregular phrasing and syncopations (Kleeman 1982:96). The instrumentation was simpler and less arranged than that of the Eastern urban bands. The general feeling was of greater enthusiasm and emotionality, with an abandonment of complex arrangements and less reliance on notated music (Keil 1992:46). By the late 1950s, Chicago-style polka was changing the sound of polka in the East.

Eddie Blazonczyk exemplifies the multiple roles assumed by some of the more well-known, full-time professional bandleaders: singer, instrumentalist, host, emcee, promoter, producer, record company executive, disc jockey, composer, arranger, road manager, and studio engineer (Keil 1992:68). His group, the Versatones, includes rock medleys along with polkas, waltzes, and *obereks,* as well as adaptations of Country and Western songs as polkas. These adaptations feature bluegrass fiddling in addition to the usual trumpet or clarinet duets during instrumental portions of the polka [see BLUE-GRASS, p. 158]. His song texts often have a pattern of one verse in English followed by a translation into Polish. Nearly all of Blazonczyk's polkas, waltzes, and *obereks* are new compositions by himself or other composers.

A standard Chicago band has a trumpet lead, clarinet playing harmony, concertina and/or accordion providing fill-in chords, piano, string bass, and drum set. The bass, concertina, and accordion are all amplified.

Polka form and instrumentation

The nineteenth-century European urban salon polka had three or more purely instrumental sections, assigned to various keys and often with contrasting instrumentation and texture. This style rarely had song texts. The rural style, whether based on a song, *krakowiak,* or polka melody, usually had only two sections, both instrumental or alternating instrumental and vocal. These two sections were either two different melodies or a single vocal melody rendered instrumentally with considerable melodic elaboration.

The contemporary Polish American polka is based on this two-section rural model. It begins with an instrumental section called the "drive," "ride," or "push," followed by several sung verses alternating with the instrumental section (Kleeman 1982:32). In general, a particular vocal melody is associated with a particular drive melody; a catchy drive theme may be rematched with other vocal melodies.

The instrumentation in all styles of polka is generally as follows: the melody line is played by two or more lead instruments in unison or parallel thirds, supported by harmony instruments that provide a continuous chordal background, plus a bass line and drums. Lead instruments are generally clarinet, trumpet/cornet, or violin. The bass line is provided by a plucked or bowed stringed bass, electric bass guitar, or the left hand on the piano.

Recent polka trends

In the early 1950s a gradual merger of Eastern and Chicago styles took place; the quick Eastern tempo was blended with the smaller Chicago ensemble and Old Country quality. Reduction in band size corresponded with a rise in the use of amplification. This dynamic sound, developed in the late 1950s by Marion Lush and called "dyno style" or "push style," refers to the bright, brassy sound of two lead trumpets, amplified accordion, amplified bass, a large drum set, and a lively tempo. This type of band may include electric guitar and/or electric keyboard and rock-influenced drumming, thus appealing to young people. During the 1960s, the Chicago style became preeminent over the Eastern style. In many areas, large Eastern-style orchestras were replaced by smaller neighborhood Chicago-style bands.

Contemporary songs composed by Polish Americans seldom refer to the immigrant experience. Some recapture the atmosphere of the Old World rural past, but most focus on love, courtship, drinking, dancing, camaraderie, or pride in Polish heritage. Some songs, however, may address the harsh realities of life, such as war. Walt Solek introduced English-language polkas in the mid-1940s; these show influences from Country and Western lyrics and rock and roll (Kleeman 1982:159). Later, bilingual polkas became popular. Today, the use of English coexists with the continued popularity of Polish language songs.

Historically, polka bands have included only male musicians and singers. During the 1970s and 1980s, however, a few bands included female singers and instrumentalists (usually relatives of male band members), and a few all-women bands have gained popularity. Events attended primarily by recent immigrants, who tend to consider the polka movement as lowbrow culture and a source of embarrassment, prefer continental orchestras performing European tangos and Polish-language slow rock tunes, with only an occasional polka.

In the 1960s many Polish Americans left the cities for the suburbs, resulting in a decline in local polka bars. This trend, along with the end of the big ballroom era, the rise of electronic mass media entertainment, and the increasing popularity of rock and roll and country and western, resulted in less social and economic support for the polka movement. Bands could no longer play every weekend at neighborhood weddings, retirement parties, anniversaries, bars, and social events sponsored by fraternal organizations or the church. Because the polka scene was shrinking on the neighborhood

FIGURE 3 Norm Dombrowski and the Happy Notes, a Polish Polka Band in the Wisconsin Program of the 1998 Smithsonian Folklife Festival. Photo by Terry McCrea and courtesy the Ralph Rinzler Folklife Archives and Collections, Center for Folklife and Cultural Heritage, Smithsonian Institution.

level, enthusiasts and musicians began to pool their resources in order to develop polka fan clubs and associations spanning wider geographical areas and social networks (Keil 1992:75). Polka music began to be associated with special events such as Polish days and polka festivals (figure 3).

Polka festivals

The International Polka Association, incorporated in 1968, is basically a Polish American organization primarily interested in promoting Polish American music while also providing leadership to a polka world involving Slovenian, German, Czech/Bohemian and other Central European American ethnic communities (Keil 1992:73, 88). It established a Polka Music Hall of Fame and Museum in Chicago and began sponsoring annual summer polka festivals in the 1960s.

These festivals have stimulated local polka revivals through a growth in fan clubs, regional festivals, and polka dance lessons. These events have been promoted to attract young people to the movement. By being adaptable and able to compete with mainstream popular culture, the polka movement has succeeded in maintaining the active involvement of young people in Polish American communities.

CZECH AND SLOVAK MUSIC

The concept of a unified Czechoslovakia was unknown to most immigrants from Slovakia and from the Czech-language regions of Bohemia and Moravia, who left the homeland when it was under foreign domination. The western areas of Bohemia and Moravia were historically dominated by German culture and the eastern region of Slovakia dominated by Hungarian culture.

The earliest immigrants, German-speaking groups from Moravia, came to America beginning in 1741 as a result of religious persecution and settled primarily in Pennsylvania and the Carolinas. They maintained strong choral and instrumental traditions in the European classical tradition and had an important role in the development of the first American concert music. They were especially known for the brass choirs that had an important role in the church service and were also among the first instrument makers.

The greatest numbers of immigrants from Bohemia, Moravia, and Slovakia settled in the United States from the mid-nineteenth century to World War I. That period corresponds to the emergence and popularization of the polka throughout Central and

Western Europe, the flowering of brass band music, the invention and mass production of the accordion, and the rise of interest in rural folk song by urban intellectuals for nationalistic reasons (Leary 1987:80). These immigrants came primarily from agricultural areas and established farms in the Midwest and Texas.

Czech immigrants organized fraternal benevolent associations to provide illness and death benefits through low-premium insurance. These lodges built halls and pavilions for dances and organized various interest groups devoted to singing and dancing. Many Czech and Slovak social organizations unified during World War I, focusing on their similarities rather than differences, and, as a result, formerly distinct Czech and Slovak folk song repertoires began to overlap considerably.

Czech bands

Germans and Bohemians had a crucial musical role during the "Golden Age" of wind bands in the United States between the Civil War and World War I [see BANDS, p. 563]. These and other bands often performed the "polka marches" of the Bohemian "March King," František Kmoch, whose compositions were widely distributed in America in the late nineteenth and early twentieth centuries. Czech bands played at open-air beer gardens, which served as important social centers for various Central European immigrants; such ensembles played primarily for listening and singing rather than dancing. The popularity of such bands declined after World War I, due to the rise of the recording industry and jazz.

By 1920, Czech American entrepreneurs based in Chicago and Cleveland had become leaders in an "ethnic music industry." The music store and publishing business of Louis Vitak in Chicago, for example, published sheet music of polkas, marches, and waltzes. During the 1920s he and his nephew, Joseph Elsnic, expanded their inventory to include German, Polish, Lithuanian, and other Central European musics.

Czechs were extremely prominent in the dance music scene of the 1920s and served as models for German and Polish groups. Instrumental ensembles were often family bands, dressed in military uniforms and caps. In addition to the dance repertoire of polka, waltz, schottische, and *laendler* (Austrian/Swiss dance in triple meter) for participatory social dancing and singing, there was a tradition of "concert music" for Sunday afternoon picnics, emphasizing overtures and marches. During the 1930s and 1940s, ethnic crossover bands with multiethnic Central and Northern European repertoires became dominant in eastern Texas, the upper Midwest, and the urban East (Greene 1992).

Czech musicians have had a significant impact on the ethnic polka movement in North America. Czech polka bands through the 1940s generally consisted of various combinations of accordion, clarinet, saxophone, trumpet/cornet, alto horn, baritone horn, trombone, tuba, drums, and possibly piano. The Texas-Czech polka sound is distinguished by the use in some bands of the hammered dulcimer (*cymbáli*), an instrument also found in German-Russian, Ukrainian, and Hungarian communities in America [see EASTERN EUROPEAN MUSIC, p. 908].

Czechs in Texas

Czech bands have been an important music force in Texas since the 1840s and have had a history of musical interchange and cross-influences with Germans, Mexican Americans, African Americans, and Anglo-Americans. Mexican American *norteño conjunto* bands incorporated Czech-American polkas in their repertoire [see TEJANO MUSIC, p. 770]. Narciso Martinez (the "father of *conjunto*"), for example, performed for Czechs in Corpus Christi in the late 1920s. Influences have proceeded in various multiple directions: there is a noticeable Czech/German influence in western swing and country music, sometimes via Tex-Mex music (Leary 1988:92).

Wilfahrt had three million-sellers, ranking third behind Bing Crosby and the Andrews Sisters in total record sales for Decca.

Popular Czech Texas family bands include the Bača Family band, which resembled a large American swing orchestra in the late 1920s. Joseph Patek established a family band with his six sons in Texas in 1920, performing for Czechs and Germans into the 1980s. In the mid-1930s, the group Adolph & the Boys often appeared in Tyrolean costume, aiming toward a multiethnic audience. In recent decades, acoustic guitars have replaced brass instruments in many Texas-Czech bands, and electric bass has replaced the tuba (Leary 1988:91). Some bands change their instrumentation when they alternate between Country and Western and polka sets.

Dances are still regularly held at many of the 150 lodge halls of the Slavonic Benevolent Order of the State of Texas and the 100 lodge halls of the Texas Catholic Union. Many local communities sponsor annual festivals with music and dancing. Czechs in Texas also have a number of community choral groups and folk dance troupes, organized by fraternal, religious, or educational institutions.

Czechs in the Midwest

Paul Gosz formed the Empire Band in 1921 with his three sons. From the mid-1930s he incorporated elements of mainstream American jazz, show tunes, and other popular music genres. His group was broadly popular in the region by 1940 among Czechs, Dutch, German, Polish, and Belgian audiences. He performed jazzy versions of polkas, waltzes, *laendlers,* and fox-trots, and deemphasized marches and gallops. Gosz has influenced many German American polka bands.

Czech and German bands dominate the polka scene in southern Minnesota, western Wisconsin, and northern Iowa. The "Dutchman" or "Minnesota" style of Czech and German American polka music is associated with the city of New Ulm and characterized by the "oompah" sound of heavy brass, marchlike melodies, and rhythmic prominence of concertina and drum. Ensembles typically consist of a concertina, tuba, and drum set core, with larger bands including harmonizing brass and reeds (Leary 1988:88–89).

"Whoopee John" Wilfahrt, a Bohemian concertina player, performed regularly on ethnic radio programs and for local Czech and German societies and house parties from the 1920s. By the 1930s his band consisted of two saxophones, two trumpets, slide trombone, piano, drum set, and concertina. Like many other ethnic bands, his continued to do well during the Depression, touring ballrooms and hotels from Wisconsin to Nebraska and occupying a prominent position in radio and the recording industry. The rise of jukeboxes during the 1930s increased his popularity with a diverse audience. By the 1940s he was nationally recognized and had made a large number of recordings. Wilfahrt had three million-sellers, ranking third behind Bing Crosby and the Andrews Sisters in total record sales for Decca.

From the late 1930s he appeared in German *lederhosen,* Jaeger alpine hat, and other Bavarian attire and would interject frequent vocal "whoops" in performance. This constructed "Dutchman" image was motivated by the commercial incentive of gaining the widest possible audience. He performed for a variety of communities: Scandinavian,

German/Austrian, Irish, and Italian. His eclectic repertoire included British, Scandinavian, and Slavic tunes, as well as fox-trots and jazz (Greene 1992). World War II created problems for his German image, and resulted in a decline in his popularity. He experienced a resurgence in the 1950s, with numerous radio and television appearances. In the mid-1950s his was considered the most popular polka group in the United States. After his death in 1961, his son continued performing into the 1970s.

Leary makes the following general observations about Czech American polka music, which are applicable to the contemporary traditions of many (but not all) European American groups:

> Late twentieth-century music forms and styles are hybrids resulting from an interweaving of various musics, a continual mutual interchange and borrowing between various regions and ethnic groups in America, as well as between European and American repertoires. Some communities have already experienced a revival of interest in older instruments and ensembles, as young people become more knowledgeable about past traditions. In other communities, this phenomenon is yet to come. (Leary 1988:94)

Slovak music

In the late nineteenth and early twentieth centuries, singing was an important component of Slovak social gatherings in saloons, churches, and Sokol halls. The Slovak American Sokol movement involves a network of fraternal benefit societies or lodges throughout the United States and Canada. These organizations were established to assist members in times of distress or illness, conduct athletic programs and sports tournaments for young people, provide college scholarships, and raise funds for charitable causes. Song texts were created about life in America, set to Slovak folk song melodies from the Old Country (Grame 1976:21). These newly composed texts would describe prosperity in America or would reminisce nostalgically about the homeland and distant loved ones. Slovak communities in Wisconsin have had brass bands and bandoneon ensembles since the early twentieth century. There were also drum and bugle corps and singing groups that specialized in performing operettas.

In 1930 the Slovak American Home was established in Milwaukee to provide space for the social activities of various Slovak groups. The Wisconsin Slovak Historical Society and other fraternal organizations have continued to sponsor Christmas parties and picnics. The dance repertoire at these social events consists predominantly of polka, waltz, and czardas. The Federated Slovak Societies sponsor the annual Slovak Days in Milwaukee, where organized dance groups of young people perform rehearsed choreographies.

At least sixteen Slovak bands were active in Milwaukee in the late 1920s and early 1930s. These generally performed only at Slovak dance halls and social events, not for outsiders, but played a multiethnic repertoire including Bohemian waltzes, Hungarian *czardas,* and American popular dances (Greene 1992).

Fall harvest celebrations were held in many Czech and Slovak communities through the 1950s. In urban communities such as New York City these were simply community dance events. In rural areas, community members would dress as landless peasants, farmers, or landowners and reenact a Slovak village festival with accordion music, singing, dancing, and traditional foods. Participatory rituals in Europe became reenacted dramas in a performer-spectator context (Pirkova-Jakobson 1956).

On Manhattan's East Side during the 1950s, Slovak American organizations presented dramas, comedies, musicals, and operas. Old plays were adapted, with the insertion of newly composed songs, often sung by a large chorus. Topics usually concerned Old Country village life, aimed at the first-generation members of the audience.

In the 1950s, over two thousand immigrants from the Slovak mountain village of Vrbovce were living in Pennsylvania and New York. A community orchestra of two violins, clarinet, bass, and hammered dulcimer played at weddings, carnivals, picnics, national celebrations, and dances (Pirkova-Jakobson 1956:76). There was an organized community dance group with thirty-six couples that performed at international festivals in New York and on television, with profits from such appearances sent back to Europe.

Alvena Seckar (1947) describes Slovak American wedding customs in West Virginia. Festivities, including jokes, stories, and songs, began at the homes of the bride and the groom the evening before the wedding ceremony. Song texts often compared carefree bachelorhood or maidenhood with the troubles of marriage. The next day, an entourage of cars assembled at the two houses and proceeded to the church. At the dinner following the ceremony, dancing and singing were accompanied by accordion, with humorous songs concerning courtship and human frailty. After the bride's veil was removed, she danced with all of the men present, each of whom made a donation to the couple's future. As the night went on, guests exchanged songs peculiar to their own regions of origin in the Old Country (Seckar 1947:194–196).

Brownlee Waschek (1969) describes music in the Czech/Slovak community of Masaryktown in central Florida during the 1960s. Unlike those in many ethnic communities, the churches in Masaryktown have little involvement in civic or social activities, although they occasionally sponsor dinner dances. The elderly often visit each other in separate gender groups and include folk singing in their activities. Singing is also incorporated into work, travel, and celebrations; prayers are sung throughout the day. The town has a considerable population of older residents, as it attracts retired Czechs and Slovaks from the northern states.

The second generation has a number of social and sports clubs. These organizations sponsor social dances annually in the Community Hall, with themes such as Gay 90s, South Sea Islands, or Roaring 20s. The local Sokol branch sponsors weekly sessions involving music, dance, calisthenics, and choral singing for children. Sokol groups of young people perform at many community celebrations.

Music for social dancing on occasions such as Czech/Slovak Independence Day, Christmas, New Year's Day, Easter, Masaryk's Birthday, and Mother's Day is provided by a small dance band composed of men and boys of the community. Instruments were formerly violins and accordions. In the 1960s, saxophones, electric guitar, trumpet, piano, and drum set were added. The repertoire consists primarily of polkas and waltzes as well as American dance music (some learned by the younger players in their public school bands). At these events, older folks socialize while the second and third generation dance to American music.

Most wedding ceremonies are held in local churches. Some families have a traditional Slovak wedding at the community hall after the ceremony. Male guests take turns dancing with the bride, each obtaining this privilege by placing money in a bowl. Feasting, singing, and dancing continue into the night.

James P. Leary (1981) describes music in a Slovak American community in northern Wisconsin. Old-timers recollect all-night house parties and three-day weddings that prevailed through the 1930s. At these events local musicians would play in a living room or barn loft or at an outdoor dance platform. Instrumental ensembles commonly consisted of one or two fiddles, bowed bass, and perhaps clarinet. By the mid-1920s, the button accordion had superseded the fiddle as the major instrument at house and wedding dances.

The original settlers sang while they worked in the fields. At house parties in the 1920s and 1930s, certain individuals recognized for their singing ability would lead the others in song. The musicians would know the favorite songs of many of the individuals present. Especially important at the wedding were ritual songs for specific moments, for example, when the bride left her parents' home and when the bridal veil was removed and the bride given an apron. Polkas and waltzes prevailed at these house parties and weddings, as well as the Slovak *czardas*.

The Moquah Slovak Dance Group, formed in 1934, performed at camps, fairs, picnics, school assemblies, and other public events until World War II. It was revived around 1950, with a membership consisting primarily of the children of the original performers. During recent decades, there has been a decline in house parties and ethnic aspects of weddings, and there is no longer a performing dance troupe. In 1981 at the annual Pioneer Days, a garage was converted into a dance hall, with music provided by button accordion and singing.

SLOVENIAN MUSIC

The major Slovenian American center in the United States is Cleveland, where immigrants began arriving in the 1880s. They created a number of social centers and formed numerous singing societies and wind bands. Slovenians arrived as miners in St. Louis County, Minnesota, in the 1880s. Button accordions, played solo or in pairs, would provide music at picnics and weddings and in boardinghouses. Sometimes a pair of accordions would play with a guitar and/or tenor banjo.

Minnesota's iron ranges had strong connections with the large Slovenian American community in Cleveland. There were regular musical exchanges from the 1920s onward through recordings and traveling accordion makers. The community of five hundred Catholic Slovenes in western Indianapolis in the 1940s had a National Slovenian Home, which was a center for theatrical productions, wedding parties, and dances.

Polka bands

Slovenian Americans represent one of the four major "polka cultures" in the United States, along with Czech, German, and Polish Americans. Compared to other polka traditions, the Slovenian American style is noted for its precision, harmonic variety, flowing melodies, fast tempos, syncopation, articulated runs, lack of slurs and glissandos, and less melodic ornamentation.

Slovenian American style–polka music evolved primarily in Cleveland and Milwaukee. In the early decades of the twentieth century in Cleveland, the shops of well-known button accordion makers such as Anton Mervar and Matt Hoyer became music and social centers.

Charles Keil (1982) describes music in the relatively small Slovenian community in Milwaukee, which is centered on a park and community hall. Prior to the immense popularity of Slovenian American bandleader Frankie Yankovic beginning in the 1940s, the polka scene in Milwaukee was divided into a German-dominated north side and a Polish-dominated south side. Due to Yankovic's influence, however, polka bands after that time became dominated by the Slovenian style, even though Slovenians were greatly outnumbered by Germans and Poles. Slovenian bands do, however, include German and Polish tunes in their repertoires. They also play Country and Western songs and other Anglo-American favorites as requested. Slovenian bands in Milwaukee often have a multiethnic membership including Poles, Czechs, Germans, and Hungarians.

Prior to the Yankovic era, Slovenian dance music was performed mainly on the accordion. By the late 1940s, bands had expanded to include accordion, string bass, banjo, and drum set. Since the mid-1970s, there has been a revival of the older button box accordion. Button box clubs have been formed in Slovenian American communities, often with organizational support from the Slovene National Benevolent Association, whose lodges have assisted in the importation of four-row Melodija accordions from Ljubljana, Slovenia.

Frankie Yankovic

The Slovenian American accordion player and bandleader Frankie Yankovic (1915–1998) had a critical role in shaping the American polka scene during its formative

Due to Yankovic's influence, polka bands after that time became dominated by the Slovenian style, even though Slovenians were greatly outnumbered by Germans and Poles.

years. Born in Cleveland of Slovenian immigrant parents, he played three-row German-style button accordion at Slovenian community weddings and other events beginning in the late 1920s. In the early 1930s he switched to piano accordion. His eclectic approach incorporated the music styles of several European ethnic groups.

Yankovic's first band consisted of three accordions, banjo, and drum set, which was typical for Cleveland Slovenian bands of the time. In the late 1930s he added piano and string bass and, later, solovox or chordovox (electric keyboard) to facilitate the performance of the relatively complex chord progressions and key changes demanded by the hybrid Cleveland style. Amplification, which became available beginning in the 1930s, enabled touring bands to be small and mobile and facilitated the incorporation of singing.

From the late 1940s, Yankovic worked to update and Americanize Slovenian folk music and Slovenian American popular tunes, drawing from a number of European traditions, including Italian and German. He had an immense influence on the American polka scene from the 1940s, making Cleveland-style Slovenian American polka music extremely visible and popular among a diverse multiethnic working-class audience. One of his personal goals was to create a modernized, Americanized polka sound that was no longer closely associated with a particular ethnic group. In general, he retained some Old Country melodies and texts, remade others in English, and "polkacized" some Anglo-American genres.

Yankovic's major commercial hits were "Just Because" (1947–1948) and "Blue Skirt Waltz" (1948–1949). "Just Because" was originally a country tune composed and recorded in 1936 and reworked into a polka tune. In early 1948, it sold over a million copies. "Blue Skirt Waltz" was the second most popular Columbia record in 1949, after Gene Autry's "Rudolph the Red-Nosed Reindeer."

During the late 1940s, the American "polka belt" could be defined as a long southern arc around the Great Lakes, from Connecticut to Nebraska, and from Minnesota and the Dakotas to Texas. This period represents the peak of the accordion-dominated polka craze that swept the United States, equaling the popularity of big swing bands, especially in record sales. On his tours Yankovic performed a mixed repertoire of ethnic and contemporary dance tunes, with songs in English, German, Czech, Polish, and Slovenian.

Through tours and recordings, Yankovic introduced a formerly working-class ethnic music to mainstream Anglo-American middle- and upper-class society. In the 1950s his exposure was expanded through television appearances. As opposed to the German American bandleader Lawrence Welk, however, who performed old-timey Anglo-American favorites with a smattering of polka, Yankovic played a basically ethnic polka repertoire. In 1986, the National Academy of Arts and Sciences (presenter of the Grammy Awards) established a new category of polka music, and the first award recipient was Slovenian American Frankie Yankovic.

REFERENCES

Albrecht, Theodore. 1975. "German Singing Societies in Texas." Ph.D. dissertation, North Texas State University.

Bohlman, Philip V. 1979. "Music in the Culture of German Americans in North-Central Wisconsin." Master's thesis, University of Illinois.

————. 1985. "Prolegomena to the Classification of German American Music." *Yearbook of German American Studies* 20:33–48.

————. 1986. "European-American Music III, 5: Czechoslovak." In *The New Grove Dictionary of American Music,* ed. H. Wiley Hitchcock and Stanley Sadie, 2:79. London: Macmillan.

Boyer, Walter E., Albert F. Buffington, and Don Yoder, eds. 1951. *Songs along the Mahantango: Pennsylvania Dutch Folksongs.* Hatboro, Pa.: Folklore Associates.

Buffington, Albert F. 1974. *Pennsylvania German Secular Folksongs.* Publications of the Pennsylvania German Society, vol. 8. Breinigsville: Pennsylvania German Society.

Burkhart, Charles. 1952. "Music of the Old Order Amish and the Old Colony Mennonites: A Contemporary Monodic Practice." Master's thesis, Colorado College.

Davis, Susan. 1978a. "Old-Fashioned Polish Weddings in Utica, New York." *New York Folklore* 4(1–4):89–102.

————. 1978b. "Utica's Polka Music Tradition." *New York Folklore* 4(1–4):103–124.

Frey, J. William. 1949. "Amish Hymns as Folk Music." In *Pennsylvania Songs and Legends,* ed. George Korson, 129–162. Philadelphia: University of Pennsylvania Press.

Grame, Theodore C. 1976. *America's Ethnic Music.* Tarpon Springs, Fla.: Cultural Maintenance Associates.

Greene, Victor R. 1992. *A Passion for Polka.* Berkeley: University of California Press.

Hohmann, Rupert K. 1959. "The Church Music of the Old Order Amish of the United States." Ph.D. dissertation, Northwestern University.

Kardas, Jan Kleeman. 1976. "Acculturation in the Folk Music of a Polish American Community in Lackawanna, New York." Master's thesis, Brown University.

Keil, Charles. 1982. "Slovenian Style in Milwaukee." In *Folk Music and Modern Sound,* ed. William Ferris and Mary L. Hart, 32–59. Jackson: University Press of Mississippi.

————. 1992. *Polka Happiness.* Philadelphia: Temple University Press.

Kleeman, Janice Ellen. 1982. "The Origins and Stylistic Development of Polish American Polka Music." Ph.D. dissertation, University of California, Berkeley.

Leary, James P. 1981. "Ethnic Music of the North Country: The Musical Traditions of Moquah's Slovaks." *North Country Folk* 1(4):4–7.

————. 1988. "Czech Polka Styles in the United States: From America's Dairyland to the Lone Star State." In *Czech Music in Texas: A Sesquicentennial Symposium,* ed. Clinton Machann, 79–95. Komensky Press.

————. 1990. "Minnesota Polka: Polka Music, American Music." Booklet with recording, *Minnesota Polka: Dance Music from Four Traditions.* Minneapolis: Minnesota Historical Society Press.

Machann, Clinton. 1983. "Country-Western Music and the 'Now' Sound in Texas-Czech Polka Music." *JEMF Quarterly* 19(69):3–7.

Paton, Christopher Ann. 1981. "The Evolution of the Polka from 1830 to 1980 as a Symbol of Ethnic Unity and Diversity." Master's thesis, Wayne State University.

Pirkova-Jakobson, Svatova. 1956. "Harvest Festivals among Czechs and Slovaks in America." In *Slavic Folklore: A Symposium,* ed. Albert B. Lord, 68–82. American Folklore Society.

Raichelson, Richard. 1975. "The Social Context of Musical Instruments within the Pennsylvania German Culture." *Pennsylvania Folklife* 25(1):35–44.

Savaglio, Paula. 1996. "Polka Bands and Choral Groups: The Musical Self-Representation of Polish Americans in Detroit." *Ethnomusicology* 40(1):35–47.

Seckar, Alvena. 1947. "Slovak Wedding Customs." *New York Folklore Quarterly* 3(3):189–205.

Shaner, Richard H. 1963. "The Amish Barn Dance." *Pennsylvania Folklife* 13(2):24–26.

Warren, Mark. 1990. *Dutch Hops: Colorado Music of the Germans from Russia, 1865–1965.* Evergreen, Colo.: Shadow Canyon Graphics.

Waschek, Brownlee. 1969. "Czech and Slovak Folk Music in Masaryktown and Slovenska Zahrada, Florida." Ph.D. dissertation, Florida State University.

Wrazen, Louise. 1991. "Traditional Music Performance among Górale in Canada." *Ethnomusicology* 35(2):173–193.

Yoder, Don. 1950. "Pennsylvania Dutch Folk Dancing." *The Pennsylvania Dutchman* 2(5):1.

Snapshot:
German Seventh-Day Baptists
Denise A. Seachrist

The Rise of Ephrata
Religious Beliefs
Musical Style
The Decline of Ephrata

In the eighteenth century, the religious communal society of Ephrata, a precursor to the German Seventh-Day Baptists, created a unique style of choral singing and composition, some of which is still performed today. Founded by the German-born Georg Conrad Beissel (1691–1768), Ephrata flourished near Philadelphia, Pennsylvania, from 1732 to c. 1800.

THE RISE OF EPHRATA

Georg Conrad Beissel was born approximately five and one-half months after his father's death and was orphaned by the death of his mother when he was only nine years old. His older siblings apprenticed him in their father's trade of baking, and Beissel studied under a master baker who also instructed him with violin lessons. At the age of twenty-four, Beissel converted to Pietism and was arrested and jailed. Following his release, he was brought before the ecclesiastical court and banished from Mannheim and Heidelberg. Journeying to Schwarzenau and Crefeld, he came in contact with the German Baptist Brethren and the Inspirationists. This was during the period of great German emigration to Pennsylvania, and Beissel, fleeing the religious persecution in the Palatinate, eventually found his way to Lancaster County, Pennsylvania, having first arrived in Boston in 1720.

In Germantown, near Philadelphia, Beissel found little demand for his trade as a baker, which led to his serving an apprenticeship to learn the weavers' trade with Peter Becker, a Dunker (the Church of the Brethren) elder, who baptized Beissel into the church. Eventually, Beissel served as elder of a congregation of believers known as the Conestoga Congregation; however, after serving for seven years, he began preaching the precepts of celibacy and Sabbatarianism, which led to a schism with the parent church. Although the Dunkers repudiated Beissel's teaching, a few followers left with him to establish Ephrata, a communal settlement of German immigrants, in 1732.

RELIGIOUS BELIEFS

Located sixty-five miles from Philadelphia, Ephrata was founded on two main religious concepts: Beissel's aversion to marriage and sexual intercourse and his insistence on the observance of Saturday as the true Sabbath. The remaining religious observances at Ephrata were similar to those of the Dunkers: baptism by trine immersion; the laying on of hands; *pedelavia* 'feet washing', a symbolic act of humility during communion; and the observance of *agape* 'the love feast', the sharing of a common meal that was symbolic of Christian fellowship and charity.

The celibate society at Ephrata consisted of a single brotherhood and a single sisterhood; however, a third order comprising married couples known as "householders" met weekly to worship with the cloistered orders. At its height, the membership at Ephrata numbered almost three hundred. Beissel, known to his followers as *Vater Friedsam Gottrecht* 'Peaceful and Godright Father', stood as *Vorsteher* 'superintendent' of all three groups. The brotherhood and sisterhood were governed by a prior and prioress, respectively. Each leader, assisted by lesser officials, wielded strong authority within his or her own group.

The monastic brothers and sisters occupied separate buildings, lived in tiny rooms, and underwent rigorous discipline. In keeping with the ideas of humility and a commitment to the mystical way of life, the buildings at Ephrata contained narrow halls (symbolic of the straight and narrow path) and low doorways, making it necessary for the celibates to bow in humility. The members slept in cells measuring five by ten feet, each with a small window, a narrow fifteen-inch-wide bench for sleeping, and a wooden block for a pillow. The members believed that the more they denied themselves physically, the greater their rewards spiritually. Eventually the congregation at Ephrata became known as German Seventh-Day Baptists, whose early history is chronicled in a work known as the *Chronicon Ephratense,* an account written by two members of the celibate brotherhood.

MUSICAL STYLE

Beissel introduced singing and writing schools to the monastics as methods for self-improvement and discipline, and the cloister at Ephrata was recognized throughout the colonies for its unique music. The Ephrata Cloister was also known for its impressive printing establishment, which was the fourth such enterprise in the colonies. Hymnbooks were both printed and copied by hand on paper manufactured there. As part of the writing school, the members adorned pages in their books with a decorative, illuminated calligraphy known as *Fraktur.*

During a fifteen-year period (1739–1754), five main collections of Ephrata music manuscripts were created. One of the most important of these works was printed in 1747 and issued under the title *Das Gesäng der einsamen und verlassenen Turtel-Taube* 'The Song of the Solitary and Lonely Turtle Dove', which appeared in both a long and short version. The *Turtel-Taube,* which contains Beissel's works and those of his followers, is recognized as the first book of original hymns published in the colonies. The work contains what is called *Vorrede von der Singarbeit* 'Preface about the Art of Singing', a treatise on harmony written by Conrad Beissel that contains the fundamental rules of the Ephrata choral music. It also reveals that Beissel required his singers to consume a limited, rigid diet to assure purity of a flexible, clear voice.

Beissel developed his own system of harmony and composition, and he trained his followers to compose hundreds of hymns and anthems according to his compositional system, where text dominated music. The chorale-like, syllabic hymns, in which

The Ephrata Cloister was also known for its impressive printing establishment, which was the fourth such enterprise in the colonies. Hymnbooks were both printed and copied by hand on paper manufactured there.

rhythmic stress follows the natural accent of the words, is written for four to seven voices. Marked with an *alla breve* (¢) time signature, the music is freely barred, and the placement of bar lines follows no discernible pattern except when used to divide major phrases and sections. Because there is no establishment of an unchanged relationship between the long and short notes, the irregular metric formations give the compositions a flexible character. For the most part, the poetic rhythm of the words dictates the musical setting: accented syllables are set to longer notes, unaccented syllables to shorter notes. The more accented a syllable, the longer it is held, a practice reminiscent of the Renaissance humanists who typically employed longer time values for accented syllables.

Deviating from traditional functional harmony, chord progressions are governed by the melodic contour of the soprano part rather than the bass line. Thus, Beissel's system produces many unexpected chord inversions, unconventional doublings, and odd progressions. Notwithstanding skips of a third, fourth, or fifth, the works consist of prevailingly stepwise melodic movement in the upper three parts. Tunes, therefore, are largely fluctuations within a tonic chord embellished with passing notes. Octave leaps occur in the upper voice, but the basses are required regularly to execute skips of sevenths and ninths. Chords in root position are interchanged indiscriminately with those in second inversion. Most curious is the final cadential pattern: $V–I^{6/4}–I$ (dominant–second inversion of the tonic–tonic), as opposed to the more accepted perfect authentic cadence based on $I^{6/4}–V–I$ (second inversion of the tonic–dominant–tonic). Parallel octaves often occur between the alto and bass or the tenor and bass; there are often hidden fifths and octaves between the soprano and bass lines; and parallel third movement commonly occurs, all practices normally considered "mistakes" in conventional harmonic writing.

The rules of counterpoint that have been accepted as the standard for European classical choral music composition are not evident in the musical settings. Unconventional by traditional European standards in terms of voice leading, harmonic progressions, and doublings that create parallelisms viewed as unacceptable, the music might be dismissed as having little merit by those imposing such value systems in evaluating this corpus of work. However, it should be remembered that those at Ephrata did not view the physical self as disparate and unconnected from the spiritual self. They regarded their hymns as spiritual expressions of their religious beliefs, and these hymns were not created for secular entertainment.

THE DECLINE OF EPHRATA

The Ephrata communal culture declined following Beissel's death in 1768. By 1800 the celibates were almost extinct; however, the society existed until the last celibate sister died in 1813. The following year, the remaining householders and their descendants petitioned the Commonwealth of Pennsylvania for a charter, and the group was incorporated as the Seventh-Day Baptists of Ephrata. During the 1920s the property was neglected and suffered from vandalism. In 1941, the site was acquired by the Commonwealth of Pennsylvania, and the Pennsylvania Historical and Museum Commission assumed the administration of the Ephrata Cloister. Today, Ephrata is one of the most visited historic places in Pennsylvania.

Two congregations of German Seventh-Day Baptists established in the first half of the nineteenth century continue to maintain the Ephrata doctrine and musical traditions. The Snow Hill congregation (1829) in Franklin County, Pennsylvania, was established on the farm of Andreas Schneeberger (Andrew Snowberger) and housed a celibate brotherhood and sisterhood in a large community house. Married members of the congregation were permitted to worship with the celibates, as had been the custom at Ephrata. Members of the Snow Hill community continued composing and singing hymns in the Ephrata tradition until 1872, when the society dwindled to eight sisters and eight brothers. The society itself came to an end in 1889.

The physical property has been maintained by an elected board of trustees; however, despite extreme controversy, the contents of the buildings were sold at auction on August 11, 1997. Publicity for the auction induced keen interest in one of America's little-known utopian societies, and in fewer than nine hours a segment of America's history was dispersed before a crowd of fifteen hundred. The sale generated a sum of $837,860. A small congregation of five members continues to meet weekly for worship at the site.

The Salemville congregation (1847) was established in Bedford County, Pennsylvania, but monasticism was never practiced there. Seventy members continue to worship at Salemville. This congregation holds dual membership in the German Seventh-Day Baptist Church and in the Seventh-Day Baptist General Conference, a denomination of English Baptist origin. The musical traditions of Conrad Beissel's Ephrata were never practiced at Salemville.

Today the Ephrata hymns may be heard in concert and on recordings made by the Ephrata Cloister Chorus, an amateur choral group founded by the late Russell P. Getz. Rehearsing weekly to preserve this tradition, the Ephrata Cloister Chorus performs regularly throughout the year at special events taking place on this historic site.

REFERENCES

Alderfer, E. G. 1985. *The Ephrata Commune: An Early American Counterculture.* Pittsburgh: University of Pittsburgh Press.

Bach, Jeffery A. 1997. "Voices of the Turtledoves: The Mystical Language of the Ephrata Cloister." Ph.D. dissertation, Duke University.

Hark, J. M. 1972 [1889]. *Chronicon Ephratense: A History of the Community of the Seventh Day Baptists at Ephrata.* New York: Burt Franklin.

Martin, Betty Jean. 1974. "The Ephrata Cloister and Its Music, 1732–1785." Ph.D. dissertation, University of Maryland.

Sachse, Johann F. 1903. *The Music of the Ephrata Cloister; also Conrad Beissel's Preface to the "Turtel Taube" of 1747.* Lancaster: Pennsylvania German Society 12.

———. 1971 [1899–1900]. *The German Sectarians of Pennsylvania, 1708–1800: A Critical and Legendary History of the Ephrata Cloister and The Dunkers.* 2 vols. New York: AMS Press.

Seachrist, Denise A. 1993. "Snow Hill and the German Seventh-Day Baptists: Heirs to the Musical Traditions of Conrad Beissel's Ephrata Cloister." Ph.D. dissertation, Kent State University.

———. 1999. "Conrad Beissel and the Music of the Ephrata Cloister." In *Die Musik in Geschichte und Gegenwart,* 2nd ed.

———. 1999. "Ephrata Cloister." In *The New Grove Dictionary of Music and Musicians.*

Viehmeyer, L. Allen. 1995. *An Index to Hymns and Hymn Tunes of the Ephrata Cloister 1730–1766.* Ephrata, Pa.: Ephrata Cloister Associates.

Eastern European Music
Mark Levy

Hungarian Music
Romanian Music
Ukrainian Music
Russian Music

Immigrants from Eastern Europe, including Russia and Ukraine, began arriving in the United States in the mid- to late nineteenth century, settling primarily in large urban areas where they quickly established community centers and religious, political, and other social institutions. Although many traditional instruments, songs, and dances were brought to the United States from Eastern Europe, the contexts for their performance changed from rural and village rituals surrounding the seasonal calendar in the Old Country to organized musical events such as festivals and other community-wide celebrations of ethnic and religious identity in the New Country.

HUNGARIAN MUSIC

Beginning in the nineteenth century, Hungarian immigrants to the United States have tended to settle in urban industrial areas such as Cleveland, Pittsburgh, and Chicago; New Brunswick, New Jersey; Gary, Indiana; Lake County, Indiana; Norwalk, New Haven, and Bridgeport, Connecticut. Like other immigrant groups, Hungarians encountered drastic changes in music performance contexts after emigrating to America. In Hungarian villages, dances, social gatherings, weddings, calendrical celebrations, and domestic and farm work all provided contexts for music and dance. In the United States, the organized activities, programs, and productions of social clubs and music organizations replaced the functional activities of the village community. As with many Central and southeastern European groups with a great deal of gender separation in social activities, male singing at bars in Hungarian social clubs has been common. Old tunes were sometimes given new texts relating to life in America.

Performance contexts

Contemporary occasions for Hungarian American music include national folk music festivals, state and county fairs, spring festivals, town celebrations, museum presentations, banquets honoring community leaders, and church fairs. Picnics are commonly held on July 4 and St. Stephen's Day (August 20). Through the early twentieth century, nativity plays were reenacted with *regös,* songs wishing good luck to the home at which they are sung. These are based on pre-Christian winter solstice rituals.

Hungarian Americans in large cities such as Cleveland continued the European urban tradition of staging popular plays, with songs inspired by folk melodies created by late-nineteenth-century urban composers. These songs were disseminated on broadsides and were brought to the United States with rural folk songs. American-born descendants of immigrants often learn songs from recordings and published collections. Children learn traditional marching songs, game songs, holiday songs, and village folk songs in Boy Scout and Girl Scout groups and children's folk dance groups.

Vocal music

Songs dealing with emigration to the United States were created on both sides of the Atlantic. Songs created in America were generally variants of well-known Hungarian folk songs in Hungarian but included English words and American place names. Many of these song texts were published in Hungarian-language newspapers and periodicals.

Emigration song texts included complaints about poor economic conditions in Hungary, farewell to the homeland, the transatlantic journey, arrival in America, dealings with immigration authorities, humorous exaggerations of American riches, life as a miner, factory worker, or steel mill worker, accidents in mines, strikes of mine workers, longing for loved ones, disillusionment with America, homesickness, regret about emigrating, desire to return to the homeland, and returning to the homeland. Another theme was the unfaithful wife in Hungary who squandered money sent back. Sometimes English words were distorted through Hungarian grammar and pronunciation.

Immigrants from various parts of Hungary learned songs from each other in American factories and mines, resulting in a "trans-Danubian" song repertoire in the United States. Because many emigrants were only working temporarily in America, this repertoire was propagated back in Hungarian villages when the emigrants returned there. In this way folk songs traveled from one part of Hungary to another through the intermediary of America.

Stephen Erdely (1978) collected songs from three first-generation Hungarian Americans in Cleveland who had emigrated during the World War I era. Some stylistic changes were noted in comparing these songs with their European counterparts: the insertion of English words, the transformation of metric dance songs into free-rhythm songs, the ability to remember melodies more readily than texts, and the retention of old melodies with new texts describing immigrant life in America. Erdely found a varied song repertoire among these Hungarian Americans, largely depending on the rural or urban nature of their earlier lives in Hungary. A percentage of the repertoire consisted of nineteenth-century popular urban songs disseminated throughout Hungary by professional urban Gypsy musicians and theatrical groups, many of which entered the oral tradition.

Compared to that of later immigrants, the song repertoire of these early immigrants is much more conservative and less affected by settlement in the New World. Factors contributing to this conservatism include the language barrier, the high value placed on life in Hungary, and gravitation toward relatively homogeneous immigrant communities. These urban communities have functioned today as communal substitutes for village life and as cohesive agents in the perpetuation of Old World traditions.

Singing societies

Singing societies are centers of musical activity in many Hungarian American communities. Some are autonomous, whereas others are affiliated with dramatic groups, fraternal organizations, or the church. In general, these ethnic choirs perform standard choral works in the European classical tradition, in addition to arrangements of folk, popular urban, and patriotic songs in the Hungarian language. Singing societies may also stage operettas or musical comedies. Hungarian American singing societies have been strongly influenced by the German *Liedertafel* movement that spread throughout Central and Western Europe in the late nineteenth century.

Another theme was the unfaithful wife in Hungary who squandered money sent back. Sometimes English words were distorted through Hungarian grammar and pronunciation.

ROMANIAN MUSIC

In the late nineteenth and early twentieth centuries, immigrants came to America from the Romanian linguistic and cultural regions of the Austro-Hungarian empire: Banat (the northwest corner of present-day Romania, including part of northern Serbia), Bukovina (northeastern Romania, bordering Russia), and Transylvania (the central region of present-day Romania, with a large Hungarian minority). These are the three regions forming the part of present-day Romania north and west of the Carpathian Mountains. There was very little immigration from the "Old Kingdom" of Romania east and south of the Carpathians, including Moldavia and Wallachia.

In America the sense of Romanian identity thus included Transylvanians, Banatians, Bukovinians, and Romanians from the Old Kingdom. It is a common pattern that regional distinctions become less important in an immigrant community when the ethnic population is relatively small, as is the case with Romanian Americans. This did not occur, for example, with Italian Americans, where a strong sense of *campanilismo,* or regional identity, has been maintained through relatively large numbers [see ITALIAN MUSIC, p. 860]. Romanian American communities that initially had a strong identity with particular regions in Europe were eventually diluted through internal migration within the United States.

Early communities were centered on pan-Romanian religious and cultural organizations. Ethnic neighborhood contexts for music and dance performance in the early twentieth century, at which participants shared a common regional background and preserved regional music and dance styles, rapidly vanished. After 1930, and especially after World War II, regional distinctions declined in favor of tunes and styles shared by groups in urban areas such as Detroit, Cleveland, Gary, East Chicago, and Philadelphia.

Many immigrants became aware of the ethnic diversity of Romanians only after emigrating to America, where they became exposed to the cultural expressions of regions other than their own. There is a general acculturating trend toward the dominant regional music and dance style within particular Romanian American communities, depending on the origin of the majority of the population. Folk dancing in Cleveland, for example, is identified as "Transylvanian" and in Chicago as "Banatian." Tunes in these respective regional styles are sometimes identified with the corresponding American place names, such as "Invirtita din Detroit," "Invirtita din Chicago," or "Invirtita din Gary." (*Învîrtita* is a Romanian couple dance.)

Many males came to the United States only temporarily to work; they would commonly return to Europe and come back to America again, so that there was a continual reinforcement of the parent culture through contacts with the homeland. When they returned to Romania, the men were reminded of village traditions, including singing and dancing at weddings and other social events. Recordings of Romanian folk music were often brought back to America, where they were used as a part of family and community life.

In the early twentieth century, many male immigrants stayed at boardinghouses owned by other Romanian Americans. Some included saloons, providing a place for

FIGURE I   St. Dumitru Church, Eastern Orthodox Church in the Romanian Episcopate, on the Upper West Side of Manhattan. Nestled among brownstones on a residential street, this church has served Manhattan's Romanian community since 1939. Photo by Gillian Rodger, 2000.

immigrants to sing the *doina* 'a genre of Romanian lyric song'. New song texts about the American experience were composed to old tunes. Themes of these songs deal with loneliness, difficulties of factory work, and the solace of liquor in a strange land. Some of these became popular in Romania, brought back by returning emigrés. Although older Romanian songs of departure can still be found in the oral tradition, those composed in the United States, dealing with the uncertain time of temporary settlement, are rarely if ever sung today.

Performance contexts

In Eastern Orthodox communities, the local church is named after a particular saint (figure 1). Once a year, on that saint's feast day, a special service is followed by a banquet and dancing in the evening. Kin-based social events are held in the home: anniversary parties, name day celebrations, birthdays, Sunday dinners, and family get-togethers. Traditional dancing at weddings and other celebrations has been declining in many Romanian American communities since the 1940s and 1950s.

Vocal music

Songs about emigration to America were composed c. 1890 to 1910. These generally followed formulaic characteristics of the *doina,* particularly the *doina de duca* 'song of departure' or *cîntice di strain* 'songs of estrangement', sung by and about young men leaving their homes to serve in the army or find work abroad or about young women moving to another village after marriage. Texts of emigration songs were often sarcastic comments on the false promises of life in the United States. Some focused on a particular marriageable young girl left behind and fantasized about what life would have been like if the emigré had remained at home. Such songs of departure were once an important vocal genre of Romanian Americans. Most are Old World survivors that were learned in Romania before emigration, whereas others were created in America. These were popular among first-generation immigrants with rural backgrounds, because they reminded them of their own immigration experiences. They were not generally transmitted to succeeding generations because they were not as meaningful to them and were not expressions of firsthand experience.

The singing of *colinde* 'winter solstice/Christmas carols' has been a more enduring tradition. About six weeks before Christmas, these are sung at Romanian Orthodox or Byzantine Rite Catholic Sunday services after the liturgy. Churches have groups of carolers (*colindatori*), who travel in cars to visit the homes of parishioners. In Romanian villages they tend to be young men and boys, but in the United States groups are not limited by age or gender. At each home, they are invited inside to sing and are offered refreshments. The host makes a donation to the church, an American innovation. Most commonly sung *colinde* are those that had multiregional distribution in Romania. Because there are regional variants, however, carolers usually practice in advance to standardize song texts and melodies. Texts become fixed through the use of song sheets or homemade song booklets. Third-generation participants usually learn the words phonetically without understanding their meaning.

Instrumental music

In addition to differences in musical preferences resulting from varied regional backgrounds, there are important differences between pre– and post–World War II immigrants. Newcomers prefer a more contemporary urbanized music style and have a different dance repertoire. Various segments of the population do interact socially at picnics, conventions, and other social events, but there are sometimes disputes over which band a church group will hire to play for a dance or picnic: newcomers want to hire their own musicians to play their preferred style of music, whereas old-timers who run the churches and clubs prefer to hire bands that they know.

Dances frequently performed in Romanian American communities include various forms of *hora*, a circle dance, and the *sîrba*, performed in a long winding line with arms on shoulders. In some communities traditional rhythmic shouts or *strigături* still accompany the dancing of the *sîrba*, usually led by more recent immigrants.

Some performing dance ensembles strive to maintain Old World prewar regional authenticity in their dances, although they sometimes introduce a degree of choreographic manipulation. Such performed folk dances are consciously frozen retentions, learned from older community members as well as touring dance teachers from Romania. Dance ensembles often represent the community at multiethnic fairs or even yearly national events, such as the Festival of American Folklife in Washington, D.C. Members of such groups tend to assume dominant roles in leading dances at weddings, picnics, and other social gatherings.

Some post–World War II immigrants have encouraged ethnic folklore revivals focused on pre–World War II rural music and dance. Ethnic revivals have not been promoted by early immigrants but rather by American-born and recent immigrants, especially intellectuals. A frozen authenticity of dances and songs, rather than spontaneous variation, is a dominant concern of the Romanian American folk dance revival movement.

UKRAINIAN MUSIC

Ukrainian musical plays and operettas have been performed in America since the early twentieth century. The Ukrainian Music Institute was established in New York in 1952. It grew into a network of fourteen branches from Buffalo, New York, to Washington, D.C. In 1959 the Association of Ukrainian Choirs of America was formed in New York, illustrating the widespread practice of secular and religious choral singing in Ukrainian American communities.

Certain music establishments have had a huge impact, such as Myron Surmach's bookstore in New York (figure 2), established in 1916, which carried Ukrainian sheet music, recordings, piano rolls, and instruction materials and sponsored concerts and radio performances. Surmach's activities extended into the 1980s (Spottswood 1982).

Performance contexts

Centers of activity in Ukrainian American communities are local churches and community halls (figure 3). On the annual feast day of the church's patron saint, the church service is followed by a festive meal, with guests from neighboring communities. Cele-

FIGURE 2   Myron Surmach's bookstore in the East Village, New York City. This store, which was established in 1916, sells Ukranian sheet music, recordings, and books. Photo by Gillian Rodger, 2000.

brating may continue for several days in community halls as well as private homes, with eating, drinking, singing, instrumental music, and dancing (Cherwick 1992:11).

Community dances are also held on secular holidays such as Valentine's Day, Easter, and New Year's Day, as well as pre-Lenten periods prior to Easter. These may be fund-raising events for schools or community organizations. Seasonal dances or weekly dances are sponsored by seniors or singles clubs. House parties occur on Sunday afternoons after church, on holidays, or to celebrate a new house or barn. They may last all night and include local musicians playing violin and *tsymbaly* 'hammered dulcimer'.

At weddings, local musicians are paid cash or in kind with livestock, grain, or store credit. Until the 1950s, weddings were celebrated in homes or in barns with dancing on special platforms. Since then, community halls generally have been used. Weddings are the most common context for music and dance today, although many traditional European elements have been replaced by contemporary North American customs.

An important moment for traditional music in the wedding occurs when the guests arrive at the reception. The band plays up-tempo pieces, including wedding marches formerly played for the processional to and from church (Cherwick 1992: 107). Wedding songs include the *vivat* in honor of the bride and groom, sung when friends and relatives line up to greet the couple and present gifts after the feast. These tend to have contemporary texts, with Ukrainian and English words combined in humorous ways. Instrumental versions of these and other songs are also performed at this time. Music for dancing at weddings now includes Top 40 popular tunes, during which band members may switch to saxophone, guitar, and drums. The *tsymbaly* is sometimes retained and adapted to these styles.

FIGURE 3   Congregation leaving St. George's Ukranian Catholic Church on Manhattan's lower east side after a Sunday service. This thriving church, opposite the Surma bookstore, continues to be a focal point for Lithuanians in Manhattan. Photo by Gillian Rodger, 2000.

Tsymbaly

The North American *tsymbaly* repertoire includes ritual music, instrumental versions of nonritual songs, and dance music [see UKRAINIAN MUSIC, p. 1241]. Rituals that include the *tsymbaly* are primarily those associated with wedding preparations or the wedding celebration itself. Instrumental versions of nonritual songs include those in free rhythm (often played while guests are eating and socializing around a table) as well as dance songs in strict meters. The instrument provides chordal accompaniment in an ensemble, as well as assuming a solo melodic lead. In recent years there has been a trend toward emphasizing the solo melodic function.

Providing music for dancing is the most common context for *tsymbaly* music. The contemporary repertoire includes pan-Euro-American polkas, waltzes, schottisches, and fox-trots of various origins, as well as the three typically Ukrainian dances: *kolomyika, verkhovyno,* and *hopak.* Recently some younger players have begun studying old 78-rpm records in an effort to revive repertoire no longer played.

Although some contexts have declined, there is still considerable demand for the instrument through the creation of the new contexts of radio, festivals, competitions, and staged performances. *Tsymbaly* contests are modeled after old-time Anglo-American fiddle contests (Cherwick 1992:110). Competitors are grouped according to age, with each entrant performing two selections. This is followed by a public dance. Cash prizes are awarded, and winners develop a network of students and gain prestige in promoting recordings. The instrument has also been added to large orchestras that accompany staged Ukrainian dancing and integrated into non-Ukrainian music styles, thus enlarging its audience. The *tsymbaly* has adapted to change and has remained dynamically active (figure 4).

FIGURE 4   A Ukrainian-American ensemble (*tsymbaly,* violin and accordion) performing at the 1975 Festival of American Folklife. Photo courtesy the Ralph Rinzler Folklife Archives and Collections, Center for Folklife and Cultural Heritage, Smithsonian Institution.

Recordings

Pawlo Humeniuk, a rural folk fiddler from Galicia, made recordings during the 1920s that also appealed to non-Ukrainian Central and Eastern Europeans, especially Poles

Tsymbaly contests are modeled after old-time Anglo-American fiddle contests. Competitors are grouped according to age, with each entrant performing two selections. This is followed by a public dance.

and Jews. Recordings made by Ukrainian Canadians during the 1960s aimed their appeal to rural Ukrainian farmers as well as urban dwellers (Klymasz 1972). These recordings are a mixture of traditional Ukrainian songs, including popular urban songs composed in Europe in the early twentieth century, wedding ritual songs, and lyrical/humorous ditties in *kolomyika* form. Some examples are Ukrainian-language songs altered through the interpolation of English words to create a bilingual text. More than a fourth of these recordings are Anglo-American songs such as "You Are My Sunshine" and "This Land Is Your Land," translated into Ukrainian. Sometimes a traditional Ukrainian text is set to an Anglo-American melody such as "Clementine." Rarely is a Ukrainian text translated into English. Strictly instrumental items on these recordings are almost all dance pieces, including *kolomyika,* polka, waltz, and fox-trot. Instruments include violin, guitar, banjo, accordion, saxophone, drum set, and *tsymbaly.* Extremely popular in Ukrainian communities are humorous recordings based on ethnic stereotypes, including dialect jokes, songs, anecdotes, and parodies in Ukrainian-English dialect.

The transition from Europe to North America
Robert B. Klymasz's work (1973:132) in western Canada also provides a useful model for the study of Ukrainian culture in the United States. He sees Ukrainian cultural expressions in three interrelated yet fairly distinct layers, representing a chronological series of stages through which many forms of European American immigrant folklore pass:

1. "Traditional," strongly linked to Old Country antecedents. A resistance to change is associated with efforts to retain Old Country genres and behaviors, which maintain a framework for group continuity and identity in a hostile environment.
2. "Transitional," with a significant absorption of North American features. Old Country traditions are evaluated, and those that have become meaningless or dysfunctional are discontinued.
3. "Innovational," the reconstruction of the tradition, with selected retentions merging with contemporary elements to produce a streamlined, modern-day version of cultural expressions. This stage represents an adjustment to change, resolving ongoing tensions between old and new, and reformulating the folklore legacy in keeping with the demands of contemporary life.

An immigrant folklore complex is in a constant state of dynamic flux, with the coexistence of old and new. The multiple functions of folklore genres in the past, however, are often replaced with a single basic function: the expression and transmission of ethnic distinctiveness. Common patterns of innovation often include changes from agrarian calendric to urban contexts; from isolated in-group performance to unrestricted public performance; from audience participation to a greater performer-audience separation; from variation and diversity in repertoire to a more standardized, objectified, and compartmentalized repertoire; from varied and multiple functions to limited functions; from informal oral transmission to transmission through printed and recorded media; and from communal creation and performance to solo vocal performance with instrumental support. Recordings, radio, and television promote conformity, standardization, and predictability and reinforce stereotyped patterns of ethnic behavior (Klymasz 1984:49).

Loss of the mother tongue has also affected significantly the traditional folk song repertoire. The content and meaning of song texts, once common property, are currently known only by a small select group of semiprofessional and commercial vocalists. Female singers generally act as the carriers of an older traditional layer of folk song, while male vocalists and instrumentalists function in more productive and innovative ways.

RUSSIAN MUSIC

During the 1800s, Russian colonists migrated south from Alaskan territory along the west coast of Canada and the United States. Russian migration and church expansion continued eastward through the industrial Midwest. Many immigrants were minorities in ideological or religious opposition to the Russian government or the Russian Orthodox Church. At the time of the Russian Revolution, upper-class Russian immigrants settled in cosmopolitan centers of New England.

Church choirs

The Orthodox Church has been an important symbol of Russian ethnicity in the New World. Russian sacred choral music had a role in the increased interest in a cappella singing generally in the United States during the first half of the twentieth centuries. Russian immigrants gradually perceived their church music as a way of relating to American society (Reid 1983:223). Russian American churches began to develop choirs to provide music for both worship and public performance. For example, there was a phenomenal success of Russian choral groups in Minneapolis, Chicago, and New York around the turn of the century, but as the century progressed, the performance of Russian sacred music by American choirs became less frequent.

Secular music

Social contexts for secular work songs and calendrical agricultural ritual songs were lost with immigration, especially for rural groups that settled in urban areas of the eastern United States in the late nineteenth and early twentieth centuries. Genres that did survive include choral singing, instrumental performance, and the *chastushka*.

The vocal/instrumental genre known as *chastushka* consists of short, single-stanza rhymed couplets, usually of four lines. Alex Alexander (1976) examined the *chastushka* repertoire of Russian American women, all of whom were born in the Soviet Union, in New York City during the 1970s. In Russia, these are generally sung by young people to a quick, lively melody, accompanied by accordion or balalaika. Some may be danced to, whereas others are purely narrative. Texts are usually witty commentaries on love, city life, and contemporary social and political themes in Russia as they existed before the immigrants departed. The *chastushka* is not a productive form in the United States: texts have not been created pertaining to American themes, issues, or events.

A revival of interest in instrumental music began in the 1970s, based on Soviet ensemble traditions. Balalaika groups have attracted performers not only from Russian American communities but also from among non-Russians. Traditional singing has survived best in more isolated rural enclaves or among sectarian Christian communities, such as Molokans, Doukhobors, or Old Believers [see MUSIC OF THE DOUKHOBORS, p. 1267]. In the Molokan communities songs are sung at the *sobranie,* a religious and social gathering, and are learned by young people at *spevki* 'singing classes'.

Old Believers

The term Old Believers *(Staroveri)* refers to a group of Russian Christians who refused to adopt certain liturgical reforms in the Orthodox Church during the seventeenth century [see RELIGION, p. 116]. As a result of persecution, they dispersed in various directions. One group left Ukraine in the 1760s during the reign of Catherine the Great, eventually settling in Turkey, and two other groups migrated to the Harbin and Sinkiang provinces of China in the first few decades of the twentieth century. Eventually all three groups settled in Woodburn, Oregon, in the early 1960s. These groups, known in the Woodburn community as Turchani, Harbintsi, and Sinkiantsi, respectively, have established separate physical communities, although there is a great deal of intermarriage among the groups. Because these groups migrated from different regions of Russia at different times and settled in different parts of Turkey, China, and South America before emigrating to North America, the song repertoires of the three groups vary considerably in terms of language dialect, melody, rhythm, and style of performance. In Woodburn today, however, these repertoires are blending, and the style of the largest group, the Harbintsi, is becoming the dominant one.

Old Believer liturgical music

Most services take place at night, often in private homes rather than in church structures, without an officially recognized priesthood. Each church does have a chief elder (*nastayatl*), however, who is democratically elected by the group for a certain period of time. The *nastayatl* directs the order of the service, with the singing led by a designated elder. No instruments are used in church services. A choir of males stands near the icon screen. The congregation sits in family groups. Both men and women in the congregation sing, although the male voices predominate. Liturgical singing is often continued at home on Sundays after the church service.

Old Believer secular music

In the Russian Old Believer community of Woodburn, Oregon, secular singing is an important component of social gatherings such as work parties, nuptial parties, and weddings. Particular songs are historically associated with important stages of the wedding ritual: social visits of the bride's friends and relatives, negotiations between male members of the bride's and groom's families, the departure of the bride from her parents' home, the auctioning of the bride's braid of hair, and so forth. Although males occupy the most visible and dominant roles in liturgical church music, women are the primary carriers and performers of secular folk songs. These songs, however, are regarded in a negative light by many members of the community, especially the church leaders. They are considered to be frivolous indulgences or distractions from one's personal dedication to the sacred liturgy. The public performance of such songs is considered to be particularly unseemly for women. As a result, women have tended to learn such songs in their youth surreptitiously from older female friends and relatives, and the desire of these women to continue singing this repertoire has created considerable conflict in the community regarding women's roles and the balance between sacred and secular aspects of contemporary life in the United States [see GENDER AND SEXUALITY, p. 87].

In the early years of Oregon settlement, radio and television were not allowed in this community, and group singing was commonly done at work parties, social gatherings in parks and homes, and birthday and christening parties. In those days, certain older women were regarded as song leaders, but today more women are willing to assume this role. In recent years there has been a continual flow of recorded music from Russia, sent by relatives of the Harbin and Sinkiang groups. As a result, the secular song repertoire is becoming more and more eclectic and pan-Russian.

Song texts of the Harbin and Sinkiang groups tend to be about war, abandonment, loss, disaster, escape, and death. Texts of the "Turkish" group tend to be about love, nature, and courtship and include humorous and riddle songs, performed monophonically in the past but which have become polyphonic as a result of influences from the larger Harbin group. Polyphonic songs tend to be in three voices, with the middle or harmony voice often extemporized.

Old Believer weddings

A series of nuptial parties or *divizhnik*s takes place during the week preceding the wedding. The bride is visited by her unmarried female friends and relatives, and folk songs are sung while the women embroider. Correlations between specific repertoire and specific events of the wedding preparations have become rare, although the general division of the song repertoire into *divizhnik* and *svadba* 'wedding day' songs is still acknowledged. The groom and his unmarried male friends and relatives also attend the *divizhnik*s. The boys participate in nuptial "games" with the girls and "buy" songs or kisses. The final *divizhnik* is held Saturday afternoon or evening, when the bride's lament may be sung by the bride's sister or other female relative. The groom comes to bargain for the bride, and her braid is auctioned.

Weddings are the most important social events in the community. In recent times, large weddings with several hundred guests have become common, held in barns or temporary plastic-covered structures built by the groom's relatives. After the elder male church leaders leave, the women may feel free to sing secular songs if their husbands have no objection. Secular singing during the public portion of weddings in Woodburn is generally done by small groups of women in three-part polyphony without instrumental accompaniment. Instrumental music is not commonly performed in Woodburn, although, rarely, harmonica, balalaika, or accordion may be played in the home or at weddings. Dancing is officially forbidden but is done nevertheless under the guise of games. The wedding celebration continues all day Sunday and often Monday late into the night. A bride will never sing or dance at her own wedding.

REFERENCES

Alexander, Alex. 1976. "The Russian Chastushka Abroad." *Journal of American Folklore* 89:335–341.

Bandera, Mark Jaroslav. 1991. *The Tsymbaly Maker and His Craft: The Ukrainian Hammered Dulcimer in Alberta.* Canadian Series in Ukrainian Ethnology, no. 1. Edmonton: Canadian Institute of Ukrainian Studies Press, University of Alberta.

Bohlman, Philip V. 1986. "European-American Music III, 10: Russian." In *The New Grove Dictionary of American Music,* ed. H. Wiley Hitchcock and Stanley Sadie, 2:83. London: Macmillan.

Cherwick, Brian Anthony. 1992. "The Ukrainian *Tsymbaly*: Hammered Dulcimer Playing among Ukrainians in Alberta." Master's thesis, University of Alberta.

Erdely, Stephen. 1964. "Folksinging of the American Hungarians in Cleveland." *Ethnomusicology* 8(1):14–27.

———. 1978. "Traditional and Individual Traits in the Songs of Three Hungarian Americans." *Ethnomusicology* 3(1):99–151.

———. 1986. "European-American Music III, 7: Hungarian." In *The New Grove Dictionary of American Music,* ed. H. Wiley Hitchcock and Stanley Sadie, 2:80–81. London: Macmillan.

Greene, Victor R. 1992. *A Passion for Polka.* Berkeley: University of California Press.

Gunda, Béla. 1970. "America in Hungarian Folk Tradition." *Journal of American Folklore* 83:406–416.

Klymasz, Robert B. 1968. "Social and Cultural Motifs in Canadian Ukrainian Lullabies." *The Slavic and East European Journal* 12(2):176–183.

———. 1970a. "Ukrainian Folklore in Canada: An Immigrant Complex in Transition." Ph.D. dissertation, Indiana University, Bloomington.

———. 1970b. *An Introduction to the Ukrainian-Canadian Immigrant Folksong Cycle.* Bulletin no. 234, Folklore Series no. 8. Ottawa: National Museums of Canada.

———. 1970c. *The Ukrainian Winter Folksong Cycle in Canada.* Bulletin no. 236, Folklore Series no. 9. Ottawa: National Museums of Canada.

———. 1972. "'Sounds You Never Before Heard': Ukrainian Country Music in Western Canada." *Ethnomusicology* 16(3):372–380.

———. 1973. "From Immigrant to Ethnic Folklore: A Canadian View of Process and Transition." *Journal of the Folklore Institute* 10(3):131–140.

———. 1984. "Folk Music." In *Visible Symbols: Cultural Expression among Canada's Ukrainians,* ed. Manoly R. Lupul, 49–56. Edmonton: Canadian Institute of Ukrainian Studies, University of Alberta.

———. 1989. *The Ukrainian Folk Ballad in Canada.* Immigrant Communities and Ethnic Minorities in the United States and Canada, no. 65. New York: AMS Press.

Klymasz, Robert B., and James Porter. 1974. "Traditional Ukrainian Balladry in Canada." *Western Folklore* 33(2):89–132.

Patterson, G. James. 1977. *The Romanians of Saskatchewan: Four Generations of Adaptation.* Canadian Centre for Folk Culture Studies Paper, no. 23. Ottawa: National Museum of Man Mercury Series.

Peacock, Kenneth. 1970. *Songs of the Doukhobors: An Introductory Outline.* Bulletin no. 231, Folklore Series no. 7. Ottawa: The National Museums of Canada.

Reid, Robert Addison. 1983. "Russian Sacred Choral Music and Its Assimilation into and Impact on the American A Capella Choir Movement." D.M.A. dissertation, University of Texas.

Satory, Stephen. 1986. "Tánchaz: Improvisatory Folk-Dancing and String Playing in Toronto's Hungarian Community." *Hungarian Studies Review* 13(2):53–62.

Spottswood, Richard. 1982. "Commercial Ethnic Recordings in the United States." In *Ethnic Records in America: A Neglected Heritage.* Studies in American Folklife, no. 1. Washington, D.C.: Library of Congress, American Folklife Center.

Thigpen, Kenneth A. 1973. "Folklore and the Ethnicity Factor in the Lives of Romanian-Americans." Ph.D. dissertation, Indiana University, Bloomington.

———. 1986. "European-American Music III, 9: Romanian." In *The New Grove Dictionary of American Music,* ed. H. Wiley Hitchcock and Stanley Sadie, 2:82–83. London: Macmillan.

Southeastern European (Balkan) Music
Mark Levy

Croatian and Serbian Music
Macedonian and Bulgarian Music
Albanian Music
Greek Music

Immigrants from Southeastern Europe began arriving in the United States in the late nineteenth century, somewhat later than those from Central and Western Europe. Some, such as the Serbs and Croats, created communities in urban industrial areas with extremely active musical traditions. Others, such as the Bulgarians, were unable to do so due to small numbers, wide geographical dispersion, and internal factionalism. The musical activities of Balkan American communities embody the multiple identities of community members related to regional and national origin, as well as a desire to appropriate aspects of mainstream American culture. Regional rural traditions, such as those of Greek and Tosk Albanian groups, have been maintained along with more contemporary mixtures of ethnic and mainstream Euro-American styles, such as the amplified bands heard at the weddings of many of these groups.

CROATIAN AND SERBIAN MUSIC

Croats and Serbs arrived in North America in large numbers during the period 1890–1924. These were primarily peasants and unskilled workers, many of whom settled in the industrial centers and mining towns of western Pennsylvania and the Great Lakes region. The vast majority were men, whose primary social institutions were saloons and boardinghouses; these establishments became important contexts for *tamburitza* music, which is discussed elsewhere in this article. From the late nineteenth century, fraternal unions and mutual aid societies were formed that assisted in the establishment of enduring communities.

The choral tradition

Croatian choirs were formed in the United States from the turn of the century, often sponsored by mutual aid societies and modeled after singing societies in Europe. Member choirs would travel to each other's communities to perform for each other and share repertoire. These groups performed liturgical music in churches as well as secular music in concert situations. For their secular repertoire, choirs generally depended on published song arrangements from Europe. Choir repertoire also included works by Croatian composers in the European classical tradition. Choirs often became affiliated with drama groups and *tamburitza* orchestras.

The *berde* is a fretted guitar-shaped string bass with a flat bridge, plucked with a plectrum like the other instruments. It provides bass notes on strong beats or downbeats, alternating with *bugarija* chords, or may interpolate scalar passages within the harmonic framework.

The *tamburitza* tradition

The *tambura* is a fretted long-necked lute plucked with a flat plectrum, found in South Slavic areas of the Balkans. It is also called by its diminutive form *tamburica* (European spelling) or *tamburitza* (American spelling). The practice of combining a number of *tambura*s in small groups developed in rural areas in northern Croatia, northeastern Bosnia, and northern Serbia in the mid-nineteenth century, during the same period as the development of balalaika and *domra* (plucked fretted lutes with triangular- and bowl-shaped resonators, respectively) ensembles in Russia and mandolin bands in Italy.

The growth of *tamburitza* ensembles in Europe coincided with the mass migration of South Slavs to North and South America, Australia, and New Zealand. *Tamburitza* ensembles were established in these immigrant communities and, along with singing societies, became important foci of immigrant cultural activity. These musical groups became organized social institutions emphasizing music literacy, discipline, and self-improvement as a path for advancement in American society.

Instruments of the tamburitza *orchestra*

The guitar-shaped *bisernica* and pear-shaped *prim* are small lead melody instruments. The *kontrašica* or *basprim* play harmony and countermelody. The *brač* plays the melody or harmony an octave lower. The *bugarija,* in the shape of a larger guitar, provides rhythmic chords on weak beats or upbeats. The *čelo,* another large guitar-shaped instrument, provides an improvisatory elaboration of the harmonic structure, often a combination of scalar and arpeggiated figures. The *berde* is a fretted guitar-shaped string bass with a flat bridge, plucked with a plectrum like the other instruments. It provides bass notes on strong beats or downbeats, alternating with *bugarija* chords, or may interpolate scalar passages within the harmonic framework.

The *samica (kozarica, danguba)*, from an older tradition, is played only as a solo instrument, generally for family and friends rather than in public. The melody is played on the higher course of strings, while a tonic-dominant chordal accompaniment is played on the lower course. Although it resembles the pear-shaped *prim* in appearance, it is never incorporated into a *tamburitza* ensemble.

Many bands today consist exclusively of *tamburitza* instruments, although most have a string bass rather than a *berde,* and violin is commonly accepted. Other groups include accordion, guitar, or mandolin. Accordion is more common in those midwestern and eastern communities where polka music has become a panethnic genre. Some *tamburitza* groups diversify their repertoire by adding accordion for polka music, piano and winds for swing and jazz, or electric instruments and drum set for Yugoslav hits and American rock music. More affluent communities hire two bands for dance events, one for *kolo*s (line dances) and the other for contemporary American popular dancing.

History of the tamburitza movement in the United States

The *tamburitza* tradition in the United States is based primarily on musical repertoire and style from Slavonia (northeastern Croatia) and Vojvodina (northern Serbia), the regions in which the European *tamburitza* tradition developed, even though only a small minority of immigrants are from those areas. As a result, many Yugoslav immigrants had their first exposure to the *tamburitza* tradition in America. City songs from Bosnia-Hercegovina are also quite popular, despite low immigration from that region. Because of the strength of its organizational frameworks, *tamburitza* music has absorbed or supplanted other native musical forms brought by Croatian and Serbian immigrants to North America.

Prior to World War I, American *tamburitza* music differed little from that of Europe. By the 1920s, however, it had begun diverging from its European roots by developing its own distinct aesthetic. This trend was facilitated by the immigration restrictions of the 1920s, which nearly halted the flow of Croatian and Serbian immigrants to America, thus cutting off cultural contacts with the homeland. American *tamburitza* music was driven by an impulse toward greater diversity in musical expression and a desire to become more appealing to a more diverse audience. Some musicians found work in vaudeville or on the Chautauqua circuits [see POPULAR MUSIC OF THE PARLOR AND STAGE, p. 179]. Others played in pit orchestras for silent films or played elegant continental dinner music with an "exotic flavor" at swank hotels, in stylized national costumes. Some of these early groups included arrangements of classical overtures and operatic arias in their repertoires, as well as operettas composed by Croatian and Serbian Americans, performed in conjunction with singing societies.

By the early twentieth century, two main types of *tamburitza* ensembles existed: small informal tavern groups performing in the oral tradition and larger, more formally organized orchestras with classically trained directors and notated music. The latter performed light-classical pieces composed for *tamburitza* orchestra: folk song suites, polkas, waltzes, marches, and overtures.

The Duquesne University Tamburitzans, formed in 1937 in Pittsburgh, Pennsylvania, with its own music school established in 1954, has been extraordinarily influential through many years of performing for South Slavic communities throughout the United States. A visit by the group, with a concert followed by a social dance and reception, is an important community event. This organization has had a crucial role in the formation of many "junior *tamburitza*" societies for young people in Croatian and, to a lesser extent, Serbian communities throughout the Midwest. Most of these groups are affiliated with a local church or fraternal union lodge and perform choreographed folk dance suites as well as arrangements of *tamburitza* music and choral singing.

Repertoire of tamburitza groups

The repertoires of junior *tamburitza* groups include *starogradske pjesme* 'late-nineteenth-century city songs', suites of folk melodies, marches, waltzes, polkas, *kolo*s 'music for line or circle dances', *narodnjak* songs 'newly composed, accordion-dominated contemporary urban folk/popular music', and a few older American popular tunes. Events involving junior *tamburitza* groups include community concerts and social dances, fairs, ethnic day celebrations, picnics, and annual *tamburitza* conventions.

Songs sung by *tamburitza* groups are almost exclusively in the Serbo-Croatian language, despite the limited language abilities of many players. There is no significant movement toward widespread adoption of English-language texts, as has happened with polka bands. Any particular *tamburitza* group can usually perform Serbian, Croatian, Dalmatian, Bosnian, and Macedonian repertoires, regardless of the ethnicity of band members. Croatian dance music consists predominantly of polkas and waltzes in a Central European musical language, as well as *kolo*s in duple meter in the major mode. Dalmatian music shows a great deal of Italian influence. Serbian, Bosnian, and

Macedonian repertoires include many melodies with augmented seconds and other Ottoman influences. Macedonian music is also known for its additive metric patterns of short and long beats in a ratio of 2:3.

Most songs are harmonized in parallel thirds or sixths. Medleys are often constructed by combining a free-rhythm slow tune with a lively *kolo* or combining two tunes that are tonally and rhythmically similar. In songs, vocal and instrumental verses alternate. Male vocal production is characterized by a high tessitura and slow, wide vibrato.

Performers differentiate "old" songs brought to the United States during the time of mass migration (1890–1924) from "new" songs popularized by post–World War II recording artists. By the 1950s, there was considerable influence from American popular music genres, such as rock and roll, blues, and country and western. Some Country-Western songs have entered the general *tamburitza* repertoire, sometimes translated into Serbo-Croatian. Most *tamburitza* groups include some Near Eastern, Russian, Hungarian, Greek, and Jewish tunes, as well as songs from American films and musicals.

Increased music contact with Yugoslavia began in the 1960s, when the Yugoslav government encouraged men to seek work in Western Europe and America. That era saw a rapid growth in a folk-based accordion-dominated style of popular music known in Yugoslavia as *narodnjak*. Ethnic stores selling recordings of this music proliferated in the United States; as a result, *tamburitza* musicians became familiar with the latest popular hits.

In contrast to the great amount of regional diversity in Europe, the Yugoslavian American music style has undergone a significant amount of homogenization; a Serbian American group in New Jersey would tend to sound quite similar to a Croatian American group in Colorado, for example (Forry 1982:168). During the 1970s, American *tamburitza* musicians were greatly influenced by recordings of Janika Balaž with singer Zvonko Bogdan. Balaž, a professional Rom (Gypsy) musician from Vojvodina, is know for his highly improvisatory, highly ornamented style and virtuosic playing technique.

The recording industry has had a significant impact on American *tamburitza* repertoire. By the early 1940s, the large record companies such as Columbia and Victor began phasing out of the ethnic market, so small Yugoslavian American companies sprang up. Soon certain popular recordings became standards that every *tamburitza* group had to know, and the melody, harmony, and song texts on the recorded version became the model. Such recordings broke down regional distinctions between *tamburitza* groups in different cities or states.

Performance contexts for tamburitza *music*

Many European village contexts for *tamburitza* music, such as calendrical rituals and work parties, have not been retained in America. Contexts that have been retained include family and community *slava*s (celebrations in honor of the family's or the church's patron saint) and weddings. For the family *slava,* a priest is invited to the home for a small service. Relatives and friends are invited, special foods are served, and *tamburitza* musicians may be hired.

In conjunction with wedding festivities involving older immigrant family members, a *tamburitza* band is essential at prewedding gatherings and at the reception/party following the church ceremony. Weddings have incorporated mainstream North American traditions associated with the bridal shower, bachelor party, ceremony, reception, and honeymoon, while maintaining certain Slavic customs as a display of ethnicity.

Other occasions for music provided by *tamburitza* bands include holidays such as Christmas, Easter, New Year's Day, and saints' days. Newly created American contexts include picnics sponsored by local fraternal organizations, gatherings on American holidays such as Labor Day and Memorial Day, and annual gatherings of a local Kolo Club or women's auxiliary group. *Tamburitza* bands also perform at sports events such as golf, bowling, and tennis tournaments.

Music in male-dominated nightclubs tends to be directed to the taste of more recent immigrants, focusing on recently composed popular songs sung in a folk style. Songs and dances alternate through the evening, depending on the audience. At family-centered church celebrations, on the other hand, music tends to reflect the more traditional tastes of the older generation. A typical church-sponsored event in a Serbian or Croatian American community includes a program featuring young people performing arranged *tamburitza* music and choreographed folk dances, followed by social dancing, with music provided by an adult *tamburitza* group. Dances include Croatian and Serbian *kolo*s and the Macedonian *lesno oro* (line dance in a metric pattern of 3 + 2 + 2), as well as polkas, waltzes, fox-trots, and rock. At a Serbian event, the *kolo* repertoire generally includes dances such as *šest, malo kolo, kokunješte,* and *žikino.* Later in the evening, groups of men retire to the adjoining bar, where the band continues to play.

The term *becar* literally refers to a carousing, ne'er-do-well, happy-go-lucky bachelor. The *becar* event is characterized by informal singing accompanied by *tamburitza* music at a predominantly male gathering at an Orthodox Church hall, neighborhood nightclub or lodge hall bar, restaurant, picnic ground, or private party. Music at a *becar* event is similar in repertoire and style to Yugoslav immigrant music at other events; the genre is therefore defined more by context than musical style. Although *becar* activity is found in Croatian communities, Serbs are the major practitioners. Women are frequently present, although often segregated, with men having the more visible active roles.

Starogradske pjesme 'late-nineteenth-century city songs' form the major portion of the *becar* repertoire. These are primarily adapted folk melodies arranged by nineteenth-century composers, paralleling the diffusion of the *tamburitza* tradition in Europe. *Becar* songs have also adopted characteristics of Turkish-influenced Bosnian city songs known as *sevdalinka,* with their melismatic melodies and augmented seconds. Italian-influenced Dalmatian city songs have also been incorporated. Another major genre in the *becar* repertoire consists of *novokomponovana narodne pjesme* 'newly composed "folk" songs'.

Texts of *becar* songs often portray images of traditional Yugoslav rural or urban life. Some portray carefree male activities in a humorous manner, whereas others refer to the historic Ottoman past. The greatest number are love songs with the theme of unfulfilled or thwarted love, although some are humorous flirtation songs. Some texts extol the virtues of Rom musicians. In general, song texts and event behaviors express values of male heroism, honor, and virility.

In American Croatian and Serbian communities, the members of a semiprofessional *tamburitza* group often have extremely important musical roles in the community, such as teaching and directing junior *tamburitza* orchestras or choirs. Playing in a *tamburitza* band at weddings, picnics, restaurants, or taverns may provide a good supplemental income. Lavish tips are often given for requested numbers, with bills placed conspicuously on instruments or musicians' foreheads.

Since 1969 a Tamburitza Extravaganza has been held annually, sponsored by the Tamburitza Association of America. Each festival includes as many as five thousand participants and twenty to thirty *tamburitza* groups in jam sessions, formal concerts, and dance parties and an awards banquet where new inductees are admitted to the Tamburitza Hall of Fame.

Tamburitza *band membership*

Tamburitza bands generally consist of three to eight adult male musicians performing in a predominantly male domain. They are often related—brothers, cousins, fathers,

The musical repertoire of Bulgarian Americans in the United States is not as prominent in social contexts as that of other southeastern European immigrants, such as Greeks, Serbs, or Macedonian Slavs.

sons—with a common older family member as teacher. Band members are generally second- or third-generation Croatian or Serbian Americans; many groups consist entirely of young musicians. Several groups have one or two female members, and a few all-women groups have emerged since the late 1950s. Many young girls learn to play in junior groups, but few continue to perform after marriage. A regularly performing combo has an official name and business cards, and members usually belong to the local musicians' union. Prior to the 1990s, many bands had both Serbian and Croatian members; a large number of individuals were of mixed heritage. During the 1990s, wars in the former Yugoslavia created considerable tension between the two ethnic groups, and many bands of mixed heritage disbanded or reorganized.

MACEDONIAN AND BULGARIAN MUSIC

Macedonian Slavs and Bulgarians are closely related in language, customs, and music and dance traditions and as a result have formed mixed communities in North America. A number of churches and cultural organizations in the United States, especially those formed before World War II, begin their names with "Macedonian-Bulgarian" or "Bulgarian-Macedonian." The majority of immigrants in these communities are Slavic-speaking Macedonians from the former Yugoslavia and northern Greece.

After the fall of socialism in 1989, a number of professional musicians from Bulgaria emigrated temporarily or permanently to the United States. Some were trained in the state-sponsored folk music schools established in Bulgaria during the postwar socialist period, where they learned a modernized, westernized version of Bulgarian folk music that they brought to the United States. Others were specialists in the contemporary wedding music popularized by amplified bands of western instruments in Bulgaria in the 1970s and 1980s.

The musical repertoire of Bulgarian Americans in the United States is not as prominent in social contexts as that of other southeastern European immigrants, such as Greeks, Serbs, or Macedonian Slavs, for several reasons. First, the small numbers of Bulgarian Americans, their internal political factionalism, wide geographical dispersion, and frequent relocation in the United States have discouraged the establishment of concentrated communities. Second, because Bulgarian Americans come from different regions, they have very little shared vocal, instrumental, or dance repertoire. Third, when most Bulgarians emigrated during the early decades of the twentieth century, there was no established tradition of Bulgarian instrumental or vocal ensemble music that could be adapted to communal music making in the United States. Fourth, unlike the situation among Yugoslav and Greek immigrants, there has been relatively little contact with the homeland (until the 1990s) and little exchange of musicians or recordings.

Conditions among Macedonian Americans, on the other hand, have been conducive to a more prolific musical life. Their numbers are greater, and immigrants from particular regions have tended to settle together in communities. Most trace their backgrounds to a few regions along the former Yugoslav-Greek border (Aegean Macedonia) that share a common music and dance style and repertoire. There is considerable contact between the United States and Macedonia, and American musicians are constantly exposed to trends in popular urban folk music from their homeland. As a result, public music making in Bulgarian and Macedonian American communities is largely dominated by Macedonians.

Contexts and repertoire

Philip Tilney (1970) describes a Macedonian wedding in 1969 in Fort Wayne, Indiana, a community of several hundred families who emigrated from Aegean Macedonia in the World War I era. Wedding rituals and activities are adaptations of those found in Europe. The hired band, consisting of accordion, clarinet, trumpet, and drum, led processions to various relatives' houses, and provided music for activities such as the ritual shaving of the groom. The church ceremony included both mainstream Anglo-American wedding music and organ arrangements of polyphonic Eastern Orthodox choral music. The organist was also the accordionist in the band. After the ceremony, a reception was held at the Macedonian Hall in Fort Wayne, with various relatives of the bride and groom taking turns leading the dance line, in order of their closeness or importance.

Today in Macedonian-Bulgarian communities, contexts for music and dance include evening social gatherings (*vecherinki* or *igranke*), weddings, picnics, meetings of cultural and political organizations, and holidays such as Christmas, New Year's Day, Valentine's Day, and Easter. Other events in the Eastern Orthodox liturgical calendar, such as saints' days, are observed, along with American holidays such as Thanksgiving and Independence Day. Music and dance are not performed during Lent. Formal concerts may be held, with the participation of community music and dance groups. Costumed dance groups tend to perform choreographed versions of folk dances for a seated audience and are generally composed of elementary and high school children. Informal singing may occur in homes, especially on name days and during the period immediately before a wedding.

Older ritual, calendrical, or occupational songs are preserved as nostalgic reminders of the homeland by older members of the first generation with rural origins. They may be recalled at social gatherings such as christenings, engagement parties, weddings, picnics, name days, and organized church-sponsored cultural gatherings, where they serve an entertainment function and reinforce group identity.

The only songs that are commonly shared by Bulgarian immigrants from diverse regional backgrounds are the *gradski pesni* 'city songs' that were popular in Bulgaria in the early twentieth century. This genre binds and stabilizes an ethnic group that is generally highly fragmented socially and politically. Most were composed urban songs with texts by European-educated nineteenth-century Bulgarian or foreign poets, usually based on Western, Turkish, or Greek melodic and rhythmic models. Texts were published in small song books known as *pesnopoiki* and popularized through gramophone recordings in the early twentieth century. These songs were enormously popular during the period when many Bulgarians emigrated to America. They are enjoyed in North America primarily for their patriotic and nationalistic significance rather than for their regional character. These city songs tend to be in Central or Western European metric patterns and modes, with harmony in parallel thirds, as opposed to the monophonic or drone-based texture, asymmetric additive metric patterns, and melodic modes with augmented seconds and lowered seventh degrees prevalent in Macedonian and Bulgarian rural music.

Post–World War II urban songs from the former Yugoslav Macedonia are well known by Macedonians and Bulgarians in the United States, including the younger generation. Because they are not highly ornamented and have very straightforward tonic-dominant harmonic structure, such songs are conducive to communal singing.

Polyphonic arrangements of folk songs are performed by church-affiliated choirs that are usually directed by classically trained musicians.

The most common music-making context is the dance event at a church, community hall, picnic, or wedding banquet. The American-Canadian Macedonian Orthodox Diocese sponsors an annual music and dance festival, attended by thousands of Macedonian Americans from the United States and Canada and held at various locations in Ontario and the northeastern United States. Music at community events is generally provided by a four- or five-piece band of Western instruments such as clarinet, accordion, trumpet, trombone, saxophone, electric guitar, electric bass, electric keyboard, and drum set. Indigenous Macedonian-Bulgarian instruments such as the *gajda* 'bagpipe', *kaval* 'end-blown flute', and *gadulka* or *kemene* 'vertically held fiddles' are rarely played, although the *tapan* 'double-headed cylindrical drum' or *tarabuka* 'goblet-shaped hand drum' may be used if a drum set is unavailable. Bands are almost always dominated by Macedonian musicians.

The style of music performed by musicians who settled in the United States before World War II is known in the community as the "old style." This repertoire consists of traditional Macedonian, Bulgarian, Greek, and Serbian dances and includes little vocal music. Bands in this prewar style play Greek dances such as *kalamatianos* (3 + 2 + 2), *syrtos* (4 + 2 + 2 or 3 + 3 + 2), and *tsamikos* (3/4 or 6/4); Macedonian dances such as *kasapsko* (2/4), *šareni čorapi* or *niška banya* (2 + 2 + 2 + 3), *gaida* (2/4), and *nešo or beranče* (3 + 2 + 2 + 3 + 2); Bulgarian-Macedonian dances such as *pravo* (2/4 or 3 + 3), *paidushko* (2 + 3), *daichovo* (2 + 2 + 2 + 3), *eleno mome* (2 + 2 + 1 + 2), and *račenitsa* or *kičitsa* (2 + 2 + 3); and Serbian *kolo*s such a *u šest (moravac)*, *seljančica*, *žikino*, and *kukunješ*. Bands performing in the post–World War II "new style" focus on the more urban, often composed dance-songs for the Macedonian *lesno* (3 + 2 + 2), featuring an amplified solo singer. Bands composed of American-born younger musicians tend to have a pan-Balkan repertoire, learned from recordings and published collections.

In general, the style of a band is determined by the leader, often the clarinetist. Repertoires are expanded through intermarriage and contacts with other Balkan and Eastern European communities; some bands include musicians from these ethnic groups.

ALBANIAN MUSIC

Albanian Americans generally identify themselves with one of two subgroups: speakers of the Tosk dialect of central and southern Albania and the Lake Prespa region of the former Yugoslav Republic of Macedonia, or speakers of the Geg dialect of northern Albania and Kosovo. Within each group there is also a diversity of religious affiliation: Muslim, Eastern Orthodox, or Catholic. There are large Albanian American communities in the Boston, Chicago, and Toronto areas. Some immigrants maintain homes in European villages as well as in North America, making regular summer return visits to Europe.

General musical characteristics

Unlike in other Balkan American groups, traditional forms of village vocal music are still widely maintained in Albanian communities in the United States, especially among Muslim Tosks. In Tosk polyphonic singing, a lead singer and a supporting singer perform two interweaving melodic lines, while others sing a drone on a single pitch on the syllable "eh." Most of these songs are in free rhythm. Geg vocal music, on the other hand, is monophonic. In both groups, men and women generally sing separately, with distinct repertoires and vocal styles.

Eastern Orthodox Albanians in Boston in the 1930s

An article from the Federal Writers' Project of the Works Progress Administration of Massachusetts (1939) describes the holidays and festivals celebrated by Eastern Orthodox Albanians in Boston during the 1930s. As with other Orthodox groups, saints' days are extremely important events that include music and dance in the home. Each family celebrates the feast days of saints after whom family members are named. Holidays such as Easter, St. George's Day in late April, St. Demeter's Day in late August, New Year's Day, and St. John's Day in early January are observed in a more public manner. The Eastern Orthodox calendar includes periods of fasting or abstinence—prior to Easter, prior to Assumption Day in August, and prior to Christmas—during which music and dance are not performed. Life-cycle rituals involving music and dance include weddings, births, and funerals.

As with other ethnic groups, social clubs and associations were formed upon immigration to the United States. Each group's membership generally consisted of males from the same town or village, paradoxically intensifying separateness while facilitating assimilation. Albanian Americans in Boston during the 1930s also had a drama society, a string orchestra, a mandolin club, and a choral society that performed Eastern Orthodox liturgical music.

Muslim Tosk Albanians from Lake Prespa in Toronto and Chicago in the 1980s

Instrumental groups

In the Lake Prespa region of the former Yugoslav Republic of Macedonia, instrumental music in Tosk Albanian communities is almost always provided by Roma. The general absence of Gypsy musicians from that region in North America has resulted in young Albanian American males learning clarinet, accordion, guitar, bass, and drums in order to fill this gap. Several such bands have been formed in Chicago and Toronto, performing at Prespa weddings all over North America. The instrumental repertoire includes accompaniment for songs, free rhythm improvisations, and metric dance music. Popular Tosk and Geg radio music may also be included.

Weddings

Jane Sugarman (1997) discusses Tosk Albanian weddings in Toronto and Chicago during the 1980s [see OTHER EUROPEAN MUSIC, p. 1195]. The week prior to the wedding day is full of numerous social visits between the families involved. These visits include polyphonic singing. Particular women's ritual songs are associated with specific activities, such as the placement of henna on the bride's hair, the packing or unpacking of the bride's clothing, the dressing of the bride, or the presentation of clothing to the groom.

Many wedding traditions are continued in North America in somewhat altered contexts. The bride and groom may live in different cities as distant as Toronto and Chicago, and therefore walking processions between homes are transformed into automobile processions between motels. The two families may meet in the lounge area of a hotel or motel, where gift exchanges and toasts are made, and relatives and guests dance in the lounge or the parking lot. Women gather in the bridal suite, singing dance-songs and dancing in short lines, with song texts focused on the duties of the young bride. While this is occurring, the men might be dancing outside in the parking lot, joined later by the women.

The evening banquet is a blend of Albanian and American customs. Men and women sit at integrated tables. The "bride's dance" is led by a succession of relatives, first from the groom's side, then from the bride's. Line dancing during the evening is done to both Tosk and Geg songs. Although most of the music and dancing is Albanian, dances in ballroom position to slow American popular songs may also be done. Rock music is also provided for the youngsters.

At social gatherings in the home, the order in which guests enter the room and greet the family, as well as their seating locations, is directly related to gender and age, with older males given the most preferential treatment. Every adult male takes his turn leading a song, in descending age order. After that, the bride's mother leads a song,

Singing behavior embodies gender roles. Women act demurely while singing, with downcast eyes and very still bodies, publicly demonstrating female restraint and modesty.

followed by the other women in order by age. Each song ends with praises, wishes for good health, handshakes, and toasts. Late at night, as the guests become more intoxicated and exuberant, age order and seating position become less important.

Gender issues

There are distinct men's and women's repertoires, vocal styles, and behaviors. Men usually gather in the living room to talk and sing, while women may sing in another room in the house, or men and women may sit in a segregated fashion in the same room. Women bring food and drinks to the men and then retire to a nearby room, chatting and listening to the men's singing. They may sing as they prepare food or wash dishes.

At a women's gathering, the hostess serves a function similar to an elder male at a men's gathering. Singing behavior embodies gender roles. Women act demurely while singing, with downcast eyes and very still bodies, publicly demonstrating female restraint and modesty. Men sing and act in a much more outgoing, bombastic manner, with elaborate melismas, dramatic descending pitch slides, surges to the octave above the drone, interjections of intense exclamations, and dramatic body language. Men's singing embodies concepts of male strength and potency. Alcoholic beverages serve an important role in increasing camaraderie and revelry at men's gatherings. There is no alcohol at women's gatherings.

Song texts and transmission

Texts of women's wedding songs tend to deal with concerns and behaviors of the bride and groom. Men's songs, on the other hand, tend to focus on historical battles and other events, although some are concerned with love themes. Some texts have been created in North America that refer to the realities of leaving the homeland to work abroad and losing touch with one's native culture. Some songs are learned from the radio or from videos. Parents may write out song words for their children and consciously "teach" them the melodic parts, with the intention of imbuing a sense of Albanian identity. Monophonic Geg songs are sometimes taught because they are considered easier.

Europe and the United States compared

Elders are often dependent on a young couple for financial support in the United States; as a result, elders do not command the same respect or authority as in Europe. This alteration of social roles is embodied in singing behavior: elders may defer to younger family members to lead the singing at social gatherings. Middle-aged men are currently the most enthusiastic singers in America. They still identify with concepts of male honor and heroism and generally maintain a dominant role in the household.

There has also been a realignment of gender roles and a shifting sense of gender identity in the United States communities, especially in performances of younger singers. Women may perform lively rhythmic as well as subdued songs, and men perform lyric love songs as well as bombastic, heroic ones. Further, a husband and wife may sing together here, suggesting an image of equal partnership. Even though women make significant economic contributions by working outside the home, they continue to maintain a generally restrained and deferential singing behavior, reminding them of their domestic responsibilities and subordinate status. As a result, many women have lost interest in singing and participate without enthusiasm.

In the United States, there has been a greater preoccupation with economic advancement, resulting in considerably less informal socializing between families and therefore fewer opportunities for singing. There is more learning of songs from recorded media rather than through group practice; such songs tend to have fewer melodic ornaments, shorter texts, and less spontaneity in performance.

Further, there has been a general reduction in home-based events and a greater emphasis on public ones in America. At these public events, individuals from different villages mix, resulting in fewer ritual songs and more all-purpose songs that can be sung at any time. For many young people, singing represents a value system and way of life from which they hope to distance themselves. The great majority of teenagers and those in their twenties do not know how to sing Tosk songs. Although few children and young adults are learning to sing, almost all learn to dance. In the dance line, young women do not have to be as demure and self-effacing as they must be while singing.

Three-voiced Tosk singing style is still maintained in North America, and it continues to affirm ideals of cooperative interaction. Communal participation in singing conforms to egalitarian ideals, and the continuation of gender segregation in much of the singing affirms traditional patterns of village patriarchy. Prespa Albanians continue to sing in America because the singing activity emphasizes values that they continue to espouse. Singing fosters constructive relations between households, expresses deep emotional bonds among family members, and embodies gender roles and moral codes.

Instrumental dance music offers greater opportunities for males to incorporate aspects of American identity. Amplified Albanian American bands in wedding banquet halls share some of the musical aesthetics of rock music, which these young musicians perform as well. Instrumental music is also more accessible because it does not require language knowledge. Band members continue to be exclusively male, however, as it is still not acceptable for women to sing or play.

GREEK MUSIC

The largest Greek American communities today are in Boston, New York City, Detroit, Chicago, San Francisco, and Los Angeles. Churches are the focal points for social organization and ethnic identity. Most immigrants consider their regional identity of greater importance than their Greek identity, so they have tended to group themselves according to regional background. Fraternal organizations and mutual benefit societies were formed on the basis of common origin, with the goal of supporting the heritage of particular villages, towns, or districts. Since the turn of the twentieth century, Greek Americans have generally worked and socialized within their respective provincial communities.

Historical developments

Wherever Greek communities were formed, small music ensembles were organized to perform at social functions such as picnics, engagements, weddings, baptism receptions, name day celebrations, and religious and national holidays. In the early twentieth century, these ensembles were regionally oriented in personnel and repertoire, with each group performing music only from its own region and intended for immigrants from that region.

During the 1920s this sense of regionalism began to break down, and social activities were generally attended by people of various regional backgrounds. As a result, Greek American bands developed a pan-Hellenic repertoire and instrumentation, reflecting a national Hellenic identity. Until the end of World War II, this music continued to be based primarily on mainland (rather than island) Greek style, as most immigrants were from Roumeli and the Peloponnisos. Instrumental groups generally included clarinet, violin, and *santouri* 'struck zither' in heterophonic unison, with *laouto* 'fretted lute' providing rhythmic and harmonic accompaniment. Throughout the 1920s and 1930s, such pan-Hellenic ensembles focused on dance-songs as well as on the improvisatory vocal pieces in free rhythm known as *amanedhes* (sing. *amane*), which originated in Greek enclaves in Asia Minor such as Smyrna.

During the 1930s a genre known as *elafra* 'light' music developed in Greece, based on popular urban romantic songs of Europe and South America, with Western orchestral polyphonic arrangements, Latin rhythms, and Greek song texts. This genre became a fad in Greek American communities, and well-known performers from Greece toured extensively in the United States.

Rebetika (or *rembetika*), an Asia Minor–derived urban music genre that developed in the 1920s in Greek port cities, experienced a revival, modernization, and widespread acceptance in Greece during the 1950s. In New York City, two music styles developed: the Turkish-influenced urban Anatolian-rebetic school and the more rural demotic school.

The Anatolian-rebetic school developed primarily in the Greek club district of Manhattan and appealed to more recent immigrants. These ensembles performed rebetic and other Turkish-influenced music genres, often including Greek, Turkish, and Armenian musicians playing *doumbeleki* 'hourglass-shaped hand drum', guitar, *outi* 'short-necked lute without frets', *bouzouki* 'long-necked fretted lute', *kanun* 'plucked zither', and violin. The repertoire of such groups focused on dance songs of Turkish origin such as *zembekiko,* a solo dance in 9/4 (4 + 5); *tsifte teli,* a solo or couple dance in 4/4; *karsilama,* a couple dance in 9/8 (2 + 2 + 2 + 3); and, slow and fast forms of *hasapiko,* a line dance in duple meter.

At the same time in other parts of New York City, Greek American bands of the 1940s were returning to a more rural (demotic) style of performance, while retaining a good deal of Western instrumentation: *bouzouki,* clarinet, guitar, bass, and drum set. This style appealed more to older immigrants and to second- and third-generation Greek Americans. Repertoire focused on pan-Hellenic line dances such as the *kalamatiano* in 7/8 (3 + 2 + 2), *tsamiko* in 6/4, *hasipikos* or *syrtaki* in 4/4, *syrtos* (4 + 2 + 2 or 3 + 3 + 2), and *haniotikos syrtos* (4/4)—more commonly known today in the United States as "Never on Sunday" or "Miserlou."

With World War II and the rising tide of U.S. nationalism, instrumental ensembles in Boston, New York, and Chicago expanded their repertoires to include mainstream American pop music. Instrumentation resembled that of American big bands: saxophones, clarinets, trumpets, accordion, guitar, double bass, and drum set. In addition to pan-Hellenic Greek dances, these bands performed continental standards such as "La Paloma" and "Besame Mucho," as well as recent American pop hits. Organized social dances replaced weddings and picnics as the most common social contexts for music.

During the postwar period in many communities, village music was no longer considered suitable, and *rebetika* was considered to have inappropriate associations with the underworld, crime, drugs, and prisons. Modern *bouzouki* music became popular in Greece and America, with ensembles consisting of one or two amplified *bouzouki*s, amplified guitar, drum set, and other Western instruments. *Bouzouki* ensembles were booked from Greece, as were clarinetists, accompanied by amplified guitar, drum set, and electric keyboard in the newer style rather than by violin, *santouri,* and *laouto.*

In the early 1960s, many Greek American groups began performing the repertoire and style of the popular group Trio Bel Canto: vocalists singing in three-part harmony, accompanied by two *bouzouki* players in parallel thirds with rhythm guitar. Performance practices of American popular music were adopted, including the instrumentation and style of rock music, amplification with echo, electric guitar, electric keyboard, electric bass, contemporary chord progressions, and Westernized rhythmic patterns.

Performance contexts

The Greek American coffeehouse

The Greek coffeehouse (*kafenia* or *café-aman*) tradition emerged in the late nineteenth century in seaports of Asia Minor and the Aegean and was transplanted to America with the first immigrants. In both Europe and America, these establishments were favorite social gathering places where males could discuss current events and politics in Greece and problems of adjusting to American life. They provided a context for card playing and gambling as well as for urban and rural music and dance genres. Music was often performed informally by patrons, with well-known professionals hired on weekends and holidays.

During the 1920s in New York City, well-known female singers performed an eclectic pan-Balkan/western Anatolian repertoire at these *café-aman* establishments in multiple European and Near Eastern languages, appealing to their diverse audience of Greeks, Albanians, Bulgarians, Macedonians, Serbs, Romanians, Sephardic Jews, Syrians, Turks, Armenians, and Arabs. The standard *café-aman* orchestra at that time consisted of clarinet, violin, *oud, santouri,* and *doumbeleki.*

In the late twentieth century, restaurants, bakeries, billiard halls, and social clubs assumed the function of the coffeehouse, with music provided by live bands as well as recordings. Greek nightclubs have amplified bands, with presentations often including Arab- or Turkish-style belly dancing.

Community gatherings and weddings

Social functions including music and dance are sponsored by the church or various social, political, regional, and fraternal organizations: the *glendi* 'social gathering or party', *paniyiri* 'festival', dinner dances, and picnics. Family occasions with music include weddings, baptisms, name days, and reunions. Important holidays include Christmas, St. Basil's Day (New Year's), the Annunciation of the Virgin Mary (25 March, which is also Greek Independence Day), and Easter.

Nearly every Greek church sponsors one or more organized dance groups of teenagers and young people in their twenties. These church groups perform choreographies to recorded music, including suites of regional dances as well as pan-Hellenic dances. They compete at regularly held gatherings in various parts of the United States and Canada.

Anna Caraveli (1985) describes a *glendi* in a Baltimore community whose ancestry is traced to the village of Olymbos on the island of Karpathos. In this community, the *glendi* provides an opportunity for airing important social and moral concerns through songs called *mandinades*. These are composed of improvised couplets, with texts about nostalgia for the homeland, trials and benefits of emigration, or recent events. Personal grievances, enmities, and losses may be aired. A good *glendi* is judged by the range and intensity of emotions, especially weeping, and the extent of *kefi*, a festive and carefree mood with an emotionally charged and intense atmosphere. *Mandinades* are judged for their aesthetic merit and social/moral appropriateness. Successful ones may be tape-recorded and mailed from one Olymbos community to another in different parts of the world, and texts may be published in newsletters that carry praises, congratulations, and condolences from one community to another.

Men are the primary singers and instrumentalists at these *glendi*s. Women prepare and serve food, listen critically to the songs, comment on the quality of performance, and have an important role in remembering and transmitting good songs. They may

An American-style banquet is held at a Holiday Inn with a Greek American band playing a mixture of Greek and American popular tunes. Following these festivities, guests gather at the Olymbos clubhouse, where identity becomes more regionally based and less pan-Hellenic.

also sing along with men at times and participate in the dancing. Women compose and sing the same types of songs performed publicly at a *glendi* among themselves in more private situations.

Caraveli also describes a wedding in this Baltimore community, which incorporates elements of American Protestantism and a mixture of pan-Hellenic and regional identities. An American-style banquet is held at a Holiday Inn with a Greek American band playing a mixture of Greek and American popular tunes. Following these festivities, guests gather at the Olymbos clubhouse, where identity becomes more regionally based and less pan-Hellenic. Seating is arranged according to social hierarchy, and the primary mode of communication switches to stylized sung couplets. The texts of these couplets include praise for the couple and the parents, messages from those absent, remembrances of deceased members of the family, references to past family misfortunes or illnesses, nostalgic references to the homeland, comments on how the event is proceeding and on upcoming marriages, and general comments on modern life.

REFERENCES

Altankov, Nikolay G. 1979. *The Bulgarian Americans.* Palo Alto, Calif.: Ragusan Press.

Caraveli, Anna. 1985. *Scattered in Foreign Lands: A Greek Village in Baltimore.* Baltimore: Baltimore Museum of Art.

Chianis, Sotirios. 1983. "A Glimpse of Greek Folk Music in America." *Greek Music Tour Sponsored by the National Endowment for the Arts and the Ethnic Folk Arts Center.* New York: Ethnic Folk Arts Center.

———. 1988. "Survival of Greek Folk Music in New York." *New York Folklore* 14(3–4):37–48.

Erdeley, Stephen. 1986. "European-American Music III, 1: Albanian." In *The New Grove Dictionary of American Music,* ed. H. Wiley Hitchcock and Stanley Sadie, 2:77–78. London: Macmillan.

Federal Writers' Project of the Works Progress Administration of Massachusetts. 1939. *The Albanian Struggle in the Old World and New.* Boston: Albanian Historical Society of Massachusetts.

Forry, Mark. 1978. "*Becar* Music in the Serbian Community of Los Angeles: Evolution and Transformation." *Selected Reports in Ethnomusicology* 3(1):175–209.

———. 1982 "The *Becar* Music of Yugoslav-Americans." M.A. thesis, University of California, Los Angeles.

Frangos, Steve. 1991. "Greek Music in America." *The Greek American,* v. 13–15.

———. 1994. "*Marika Papagika* and the Transformations of Modern Greek Music." *Journal of the Hellenic Diaspora* 20:43–63.

Kaloyanides, Michael G. 1977. "New York and Bouzoukia: The Rise of Greek-American Music." In *Essays in Arts and Sciences* 6(1):95–102.

———. 1986. "European-American Music III, 6: Greek." In *The New Grove Dictionary of American Music,* ed. H. Wiley Hitchcock and Stanley Sadie, 2:79–80. London: Macmillan.

Kiriazis, James W. 1967. "A Study of Change in Two Rhodian Immigrant Communities." Ph.D. dissertation, University of Pittsburgh.

Kolar, Walter W. 1975. *The Tambura in America.* Vol. 2 of *A History of the Tambura.* Pittsburgh: Duquesne University Tamburitzans Institute of Folk Arts.

Levy, Mark. 1986. "European-American Music III, 4: Bulgarian and Macedonian." In *The New Grove Dictionary of American Music,* ed. H. Wiley Hitchcock and Stanley Sadie, 2:78–79. London: Macmillan.

March, Richard. 1983. "The *Tamburitza* Tradition." Ph.D. dissertation, Indiana University, Bloomington.

Markoff, Irene. 1982. "Persistence of Old World Cultural Expression in the Traditional Music of Bulgarian-Canadians." In *Culture and History of the Bulgarian People: Their Bulgarian and American Parallels,* ed. Walter Kolar, 217–239. Pittsburgh: Tamburitza Press.

Patterson, G. James. 1976. *The Greeks of Vancouver: A Study in the Preservation of Ethnicity.* Canadian Centre for Folk Culture Studies Paper, no. 18. Ottawa: National Museum of Man Mercury Series.

Smith, Ole L. 1991. "Rebetika in the United States Before World War II." In *New Directions in Greek American Studies,* ed. Dan Georgakas and Charles C. Moskos, 143–151. New York: Pella Publishing Co. Inc.

———. 1995. "Cultural Identity and Cultural Interaction: Greek Music in the United States, 1917–1941." *Journal of Modern Greek Studies* 13:125–138.

Sugarman, Jane Cicely. 1997. *Engendering Song: Singing and Subjectivity at Prespa Albanian Weddings.* Chicago: University of Chicago Press.

Tilney, Philip. 1970. "The Immigrant Macedonian Wedding in Ft. Wayne." *Indiana Folklore* 3(1):3–34.

Jewish Music
Mark Slobin

Music in Jewish Culture
Early North American Jewish Life
Jewish American Music through the 1930s
Post–World War II Jewish American Music

The approximately five million Jews who live in North America today are descendants of immigrants who, over the course of 350 years, arrived in waves from widely scattered homelands, speaking different languages and bringing extremely varied customs to the United States and Canada. This diversity has been at the core of all Jewish communities since the beginning of Diaspora in the first century C.E. Over two millennia, there has been only one unifying principle: the centrality of Hebrew/Aramaic sacred text and its implications for a daily and annual liturgical and ritual cycle. Musically, after the destruction of the Second Temple in 70 C.E., there has been no single practice. Each local community of Jews has found its own voice in the context of the surrounding sounds of its non-Jewish neighbors. Thus, it is impossible to generalize about "Jewish music," particularly given the almost total lack of written sources until the European Renaissance period. Because substantial documentation is not available even for Europe until the nineteenth century, when Jews were emigrating to North America in large numbers, our knowledge of Jewish music coincides with the period of immigration.

MUSIC IN JEWISH CULTURE

It would be convenient to divide Jewish musical heritage into sacred and secular; yet the spillover from one domain to the other has been continuous as a result of the intensive immersion in daily prayer, the weekly Sabbath/weekday round, and the intimate mixture of family life and religious holiday celebration. In pre-1939 Eastern Europe, a woman doing housework might sing either a liturgical song setting, a Yiddish adaptation of a sixteenth-century German ballad, or a current Russian or Polish popular song. In New York in the 1920s, the plays of the Yiddish theater featured liturgical songs, while, conversely, sacred singers—cantors—left their pulpits to make concert tours and recordings of material that included light-classical music and Jewish folk songs as well as liturgical music. Thus, any sacred/secular distinctions are somewhat arbitrary.

In terms of social organization, traditional Jewish societies have tended to be musically democratic, everyday singing being widespread and the number of vocal or instrumental specialists small. Among the vocal specialists, the *hazzan*, or cantor, stands out, a musically gifted prayer-leader with different functions and status among Jews of various regions and in different periods. The best known professional instru-

The organ moved into the American synagogue, albeit as part of a major controversy within each congregation, instrumental music having been officially absent in the sanctuary as a mark of respect for the passing of the Second Temple's elaborate music making.

---

mentalists are the *klezmorim* (singular: *klezmer*) of Central and Eastern Europe, who played for the celebrations of Jews and non-Jews alike with a repertoire as broad as their circuit of towns.

EARLY NORTH AMERICAN JEWISH LIFE

North American Jewish life is sharply divided into pre- and post-1881 periods. The population was rather small in the earliest period (2,500 Jews at the time of the American Revolution) and was distributed among both Sephardic (Mediterranean) and Ashkenazic (Northern and Eastern European) Jews, growing by the first large wave of immigration—German Jews of the 1840s and 1850s—to some 250,000 by 1881. This substantial figure was in turn dwarfed by the two million Eastern European Jews who flooded in until the cutoff of mass immigration in 1924. Far more research has been done on the Ashkenazim, who now constitute at least 95 percent of American Jews, so they will receive the lion's share of attention below.

The tiny early Jewish communities, beginning with those in New York in 1654, are little documented through the mid-eighteenth century. They organized themselves into one synagogue per town, each with its own rules. The leader, called the *hazzan*, was usually the most learned man, the first known *hazzan* being Saul Brown in 1686. Aside from leading prayers, early *hazzanim* might also function as teachers, ritual circumcisers, and ritual slaughterers; but real communal power resided in the hands of the synagogue's lay leadership. Major musical influence probably came from the London and Amsterdam Sephardic model of the worship service.

The influx of German Jews brought radical change. Post-Napoleonic reforms having brought the Jews into the mainstream of Western European history, Jewish music moved toward modern European models, with cantor-composers such as the giants Salomon Sulzer in Vienna, Louis Lewandowski in Berlin, and Samuel Naumbourg in Paris creating a vast corpus of liturgical music that remains an important resource even today. With the new immigrants also came an emerging Reform Jewish denomination, in which the *hazzan* was replaced by a rabbi whose functions paralleled those of the Protestant minister of the day. The organ moved into the American synagogue, albeit as part of a major controversy within each congregation, instrumental music having been officially absent in the sanctuary as a mark of respect for the passing of the Second Temple's elaborate music making. Music was consigned to an organist and choir leader, with the congregation chiming in for well-regulated, foursquare hymns.

It cannot be overemphasized that sacred music needs to be understood on a congregation-by-congregation basis throughout North America. Partly as a result of Protestant influence, each synagogue remains a world of its own. Even today, with the creation of denominational prayer books and a large body of standardized song, there is no way of predicting what melodies you will hear or be asked to sing if you walk into a local Jewish house of worship.

JEWISH AMERICAN MUSIC THROUGH THE 1930s

Persecution and desperate need drove large numbers of Jews from Poland, the Russian Empire, the Balkans, and Turkey to North America in the great wave of immigration of 1881–1924. For Eastern Europeans of the late nineteenth century, it was a musically complex period. An increasingly urbanized and proletarianized mass of Jews was inventing a Yiddish language–based popular culture (newspapers, pulp and art literature, theater, and popular song). At the same time, the cantor's role as eloquent spokesman, even intercessor with God for the community, was raised to star status. Gifted singers made a career of traveling from town to town with their own backup chorus or settling into a lucrative city pulpit and, by 1903, signing recording contracts. The operatic aria and chorus served as inspiration as much as the melodies of the older synagogue style. So it was not carriers of a settled, ancient music culture who poured into New York, but modernizing members of a mobile and volatile generation of cultural experimenters and innovators. Thus, early sound recording of Jewish sacred music was done as much in New York as in Europe, and the Yiddish-language popular song tended to be penned in that city's Lower East Side and exported to Europe.

The cantor in America

In the world of the synagogue, the cantor's moment of stardom meant that for a handful of celebrities, a move, or at least a concert tour, to America could be highly profitable. Already by 1885 a report of a thousand-dollar New York contract spread like wildfire through Eastern Europe, causing hopefuls to dream of "streets of gold." American congregations began importing cantors, supporting the synagogue's whole operating budget by selling tickets to holiday services led by superstars, some of whom, like Gershon Sirota, traveled back and forth across the Atlantic. Unfortunately, Sirota's last return to Europe coincided with the Nazi invasion of Poland, and he died in the Holocaust.

Today, this period of cantorial splendor is sometimes called the Golden Age of the Cantorate. However, it should be remembered that the gold went to very few singers. The vast majority of cantors had no job security and no pension benefits, and the ratio of applicants to synagogue positions was enormous. Some cantors eventually went into business themselves, running catering halls at which weddings and bar mitzvahs provided ample business for both entertaining and feeding guests. Still others began to advertise for products that targeted a Jewish holiday market, with endorsements such as "what famous New York Cantors Say about Maxwell House Coffee . . . the favorite coffee in the Jewish home." Once again, the sacred/secular line proves permeable in looking at Jewish musical practice.

Yiddish theater

While cantors were jockeying for jobs, the masses of early immigrants sought relief from stringent working conditions and sordid housing in the entertainment district of New York or the theaters and halls of a hundred North American cities. The Jewish population being heavily urbanized, it was possible to tour across what Yiddish theater troupes called "the provinces" by going to Philadelphia, Chicago, and Detroit. The lively, even brawling world of Yiddish theater fans and actors formed part of a sprawling scene that ranged from beer-garden vaudeville to upscale theater. We have only a single surviving Jewish American vaudeville playlet by which to judge the more plebeian fare: Minikes's *Among the Indians*, which features two dry-goods peddlers in Indian country and includes the stereotyped portrayals of both Native Americans and African Americans that typified general American shows of the day. The closing message urged the Protestant work ethic on immigrants, the whole playlet ending up as a commercial for a New York clothing manufacturer (see Slobin 1980 for the entire text in translation).

Sheet music

The energy displayed on stage spilled over into living rooms via the older medium of the parlor piano and that newer novelty, the gramophone. On New York's Lower East Side, one could easily find music dealers who sold pianos and sheet music and arranged for music lessons on the premises. The songs heard on the stage moved quickly to the streets and into shop windows and formed a separate field of study (detailed in Slobin 1982) that can only be sketched out here. The Jewish sheet music industry was not the only such ethnic enterprise in America; there were German publications in the Midwest, for example. Yet because New York's Jews lived in the heart of America's music industry in very concentrated numbers (perhaps 1,250,000 by 1914), they could produce an impressive in-group business. Of course, those with a strong drive toward upward mobility could simply walk a few blocks uptown and offer songs in English to mainstream publishers in Tin Pan Alley, as Irving Berlin did around 1910.

The Yiddish-language sheet music of the immigrant age provides a fascinating glimpse into an age of transition, when Eastern European Jews were becoming Americans. As much as mirroring that process, the popular culture of the period—theater, music, newspapers, fiction, poetry—shaped it, creating an Americanizing Yiddish language, music, and perspective that would influence the following generations. The sheet music folio is a helpful tool in excavating the culture of the immigrant age, as its cover art provides iconographic evidence, its song texts narrate the trends and tribulations of the community, and its musical style serves as a bridge from European to American taste. Shared concerns range from topics such as love to events such as the sinking of the *Titanic* in 1912. In-group interests include concerns such as the newly emerging social movement called Zionism, the need to observe Jewish holidays, and the emergence of star celebrities (singers, songwriters, actors) within the ethnic boundary. Like all newly arrived groups, Jews sang about the immigration process itself and of the world across the Atlantic. It is important not to think of Europe as "the Old World," because, until the destruction of European Jewry during World War II (1939–1945), Jews traveled back and forth, visiting relatives, finding spouses, and carrying songs across the sea. Nevertheless, the percentage of Jews who thought of America as a temporary home was far lower than among comparable immigrant groups, and the impact of Jewish American music in Europe was much stronger than the reverse, due to the power of the New York entertainment establishment.

The music of this homegrown industry began in the 1880s with the creations of Abraham Goldfaden and his colleague Sigmund Mogulesco, both of whom emigrated to America, and a small circle of contemporary songwriters such as David Meyrowitz, Joseph Brody, Louis Friedsell, and Solomon Smulewitz (who changed his last name to Small). Their style was highly eclectic, drawing on everything from Italian opera and Romanian operetta to cantorial recitative. The standard structure for many songs of the period relied on a duple meter verse moving to a waltz-time chorus, the stock American pop song verse and chorus structure being a telling sign of modernization. Yet many songs remained in the minor key, hardly an Americanism, and a significant number dealt with issues of poverty and powerlessness far removed from Tin Pan Alley's concerns with love and comedy. "Mentshen-fresser" by Solomon Small/Smulewitz (1916) is constructed around the central metaphor of the title, a rather common songwriting ploy of this repertoire. In the first verse, the man-eaters are the germs of tuberculosis, an endemic killer in the Jewish ghetto environment:

> Deeply buried in the lungs
> Lives the pale plague
> The bacilli and microbes
> Build their nest.
> They eat our bodies and lives

And multiply greatly
And we must fade away from the world before our time
And we feel how we expire
Quietly and slowly
And the pains and the suffering
Are terribly great
And the dark thoughts
Increase the pain.
For years the Angel of Death
Lives deep in our hearts.
CHORUS: Microbes, bacilli, what do you want?
Speak, whose errands are you fulfilling?
You eat the victims mercilessly
And aim only at blossoming life.
You bathe in the tears of the weepers
You extract the marrow from the bones
Microbes and bacilli, what do you want?

This relentless imagery (rhymed in Yiddish semidoggerel) extends, in subsequent verses, to other implications of the central metaphor:

Crowned heads and diplomats
To gain victory
Force us to be soldiers
Drive us to war.
Young people by the millions
Pay their price
And their flesh
Becomes cannon fodder
And the crippled and the dead
Fall here and there
New lives are prepared
To take their places
And many corpses
Are packed into big, deep graves
And the rulers, the kings
Play chess!

Unlike the music of other American ethnic groups, that of the Jews in this period of immigration has a small quotient of fantasy and a large dose of reality, even naturalistically portrayed as in "Mentshen-fresser." The "diplomats" verse ties the Jewish American experience of tenement tuberculosis to the suffering inflicted on European Jewry by the ravages of World War I, of greater interest to American Jewish immigrant groups in 1916 than to a general American public in the year before the United States entered the war.

Theater and film music

The music of the Yiddish theater grew more sophisticated in the sense of professionalism and more American in melodic line and choice of topic due to the impact of key individuals such as Joseph Rumshinsky, a prolific songwriter who set the tone in the 1910s and 1920s. Rumshinsky bridged the gap between the earlier style of the Goldfaden-Mogulesco era and the smooth, Broadway sound of later composers of the 1930s and 1940s such as Abraham Ellstein, Alexander Olshanetsky, and Sholom

FIGURE I   Molly Picon, in *A Little Girl With Big Ideas,* c. 1915. Billy Rose Theatre Collection; The New York Public Library for the Performing Arts; Astor, Lenox and Tilden Foundations.

Secunda. By the late 1930s, a song like Secunda's "Bay mir bist du sheyn" could cross over to mainstream taste and become a standard of the pop repertoire. The growth of a Yiddish-language film industry, from silent movies of the 1910s to sound movie production in the 1930s, created a brief but lively flourishing of sound track songs, some of which can still be heard at Jewish weddings today. Beginning in the 1920s, the light and lively stage personality developed by performers such as the star singer-comedienne Molly Picon on stage and screen helped keep the Yiddish-language popular song alive in a post-immigrant age (figure 1). Picon's work in the 1938 film *Yidl mitn fidl* is a fine example of the transatlantic nature of Jewish American entertainment of this period. Shot on location with local Polish Jews as extras, the musical was a joint Polish–American production. An accurate yet Hollywood-like score by Ellstein plays off scenes such as a set of authentic wedding dances, our only footage of what such a family festivity might have looked like in pre-Holocaust Poland. At the movie's end, the cross-dressed character of Yidl has become a female star along the lines of Picon's real-life persona and is sailing to America.

As this modest in-group entertainment industry struggled to keep up with a changing cultural scene, some immigrant-era performers who left the community for mainstream fame, such as the "red-hot mama" singer Sophie Tucker, kept their ties to a "home" ethnic audience. Perhaps the most compelling Jewish entertainer of this era was Al Jolson. Born Asa Yoelson in 1881, the son of a cantor, Jolson's meteoric rise to highest paid star, almost in a league of his own as an entertainer, became a myth in itself. Samson Raphaelson's 1925 Broadway hit play *The Jazz Singer* became the first successful sound film in 1927 on the strength of a movie audience's ability to see—and hear—the superstar perform on a film screen. Part of Jolson's incandescent performance must lie in the semiautobiographical quality of the plot, which shows a cantor's son being forced to choose between Broadway success and "the call of the race" as a successor to his father. Jolson's own success was partly attributed to "the tear in the voice," a supposedly Jewish trait also linked to Irving Berlin by non-Jewish show business commentators and tied to the cantorial tradition. Neil Diamond's remake of *The Jazz Singer* in 1981 only shows how durable the myth of the Jewish American entertainer has remained. The fact that Jolson, Cantor, and Sophie Tucker all used blackface in their careers, like the immigrant Irish singers of the nineteenth century before them, is eloquent testimony to the durability of black–white interaction, in all its problematic aspects, as a core concept in American popular culture to which "newcomers" must adjust.

Recordings

Parallel to both the popularity of Yiddish theater music and the emergence of ethnically marked mainstream stars, a group of talented, eclectic musicians such as Dave Tarras, Naftule Brandwine, and Abe Schwartz recorded dozens of 78-rpm recordings based on the repertoire of the *klezmorim,* the wandering professional musicians of Eastern Europe. Just as tunes made their way from Jewish neighborhoods to the Polish gentry's drawing room by way of *klezmer* ingenuity, in New York melodies traveled from downtown weddings to the studios of the major record companies, Columbia and Victor, and a host of smaller labels. At the dawn of the twentieth century, the Hebrew Disc and Cylinder Company issued what were familiar tunes of European origin for a New York public. These were generic dances, often based on southeast European styles common to a number of ethnic groups (Romanian, Greek, south Slavic, even Ukrainian, Turkish, or Armenian). Abe Schwartz used his versatility to good advantage: he and his backup musicians became a house band for Columbia Records in the 1920s, recording the music of several ethnic groups under a variety of band names. Schwartz was not the only crossover musician; David Medoff had a prolific, if short-lived, career in the

1920s singing Yiddish, Ukrainian, and Russian items, even including Christian Orthodox liturgical songs (see Slobin and Spottswood 1984 for a study of his career).

Recordings of klezmer music declined during the Great Depression of the 1930s
even before the music itself faded from the forefront of Jewish American consciousness.
Yet by the 1940s, the music that wedding guests danced to in catering halls across
America slowly yielded to more popular American-based styles, including swing and
Latin music. The term *klezmer* itself became a sign of a musician's backwardness until
the "revival" movement of the 1970s detailed below. Serious study of early Jewish
American wedding music, and of the social position of the *klezmorim* that played it,
began only late in the 1990s (e.g. Netsky 2000).

Music of social reform

A third stream of important secular music making during this period was the widespread work of activist social movements, which expressed their ideologies in song.
Among the earliest songs of the immigrant era were the broadly popular creations of
the "sweatshop poets" such as Dovid Edelshtat and Morris Rosenfeld. Items such as
Rosenfeld's "Mayn rueplats" and Edelshtat's "Es klapn di mashinen" made their way
back to the proletariat of Warsaw. Socialist-oriented movements such as the national
fraternal organization Workmen's Circle (*Arbeterring*) fielded choruses across the
United States and Canada. Choral music was enthusiastically propagated, first by Pla-
ton Brounoff in New York, then by groups started by Jacob Schaefer in Chicago, A. W.
Binder and Lazar Weiner in New York, and Henry Lefkowitch in New Jersey, all
between 1914 and 1925. Musically, this repertoire is quite eclectic, ranging from workers' standbys such as the *Internationale* and the *Marseillaise*, with Yiddish texts, to occasional pieces for particular demonstrations, often in marchlike, frequently Russian
style. One such piece was composed for New York's first community-wide procession,
in December 1905, when over 100,000 marchers snaked through the streets to protest
brutal Czarist repression. Other choral numbers reflected the emerging Zionist ideology of the day, written in Hebrew to stress the renewal of that ancient Jewish language
in the twentieth century. Beginning in the 1920s and culminating with the establishment of the State of Israel in 1948, the *halutz* (pioneer) songs of Jewish pioneers in
Palestine, based on Eastern European melodies with a Mediterranean flavor, were
widely sung in youth groups across North America. The accompanying dance forms
served as a basis for what later became the "Israeli folk dance" genre, still a viable form
across North America for Jews and non-Jews on campuses and in community centers.

Sacred music

An entirely different but highly influential stream of music making flowed into America in the 1930s with the arrival of Jewish composers from Europe's threatened lands.
Men such as Herbert Fromm, Hugo Adler, and Heinrich Schalit had been well trained
in up-to-date European compositional styles and chose to dedicate their efforts to
synagogue, rather than secular, music. Even Kurt Weill, the quintessential cabaret
composer, wrote a liturgical piece in America. Ernest Bloch's comprehensive *Avodat
Hakodesh* 'Sacred Service' of 1933 is a landmark work in this tradition. Buoyed by
American-born composers or those from an earlier immigrant generation such as Max
Helfman and younger contributors such as Ben Steinberg, this group of composers has
made a profound and durable impact on Jewish American sacred music, particularly
in the Reform movement. By the 1920s, American Jewry had divided itself into three
basic denominations: Orthodox, bent on maintaining the old patterns of rabbinic
Judaism; Reform, descended from the liberalizing trend of nineteenth-century German Jewry; and Conservative, an American-born middle path based on moderate
modernization of tradition.

This stream of liturgical music can be represented by two versions of the *Barchu*, the opening invocation of the Friday night service, an essential musical framing statement that has been set by many composers over the centuries. This key musical moment contains a call to prayer, usually sung by the cantor, and a choral/congregational response, allowing for a wide variety of musical styles within a very short compass of text in a restricted genre. Examples that hint at the great range of expression available to Jewish American composers of sacred music can be heard in the works of Heinrich Schalit (1951), a Viennese-born, highly trained composer whose setting is basically Western European in orientation and organ-oriented but contains a hint of the melismatic style of the old cantor. A second example is Michael Isaacson (1974), a younger American composer whose work is strongly influenced by popular music of our times, as can be heard in the rocklike guitar accompaniment and alternation of Hebrew and English versions of the text. Art music was also composed with different texts, notably the Yiddish-language *lieder* by such composers as Lazar Weiner, set to poems by writers working in America.

POST–WORLD WAR II JEWISH AMERICAN MUSIC

Two deeply significant historic events changed the course of Jewish American music making: what is now called the Holocaust (the destruction of European Jewry) and the aforementioned creation of the State of Israel. The Holocaust deprived North American Jews of their lifeline to a homeland, and this was as true for Jews from Greece as for those from Germany. Musically, there were several implications: (1) the decline of Yiddish as a language of song composition, begun in the postimmigrant era of 1925–1940, was drastically accelerated; (2) the training of cantors, hitherto done by the steady arrival of fresh European talent or by an apprenticeship system for the American-born, was entirely recast through the creation of cantorial training programs at the seminaries of the three major denominations within ten years after the end of World War II; (3) Eastern Europe as a topic for songs or theatrical productions was first totally taboo, then, with the appearance of *Fiddler on the Roof* (1963), was reinterpreted almost completely in terms of nostalgia, rather than as corollary to and commentary on Jewish American life.

The emergence of Israel also had multiple implications: (1) the constant presence of a stronger or weaker stream of Israeli-based or -oriented music among North American Jews, ranging from popular to liturgical song; (2) the interchange of musicians between the two countries, particularly among the ultraorthodox segments of the population; (3) the ascendance of the Sephardic pronunciation of Hebrew among American Jews and an attendant rise in interest in Mediterranean-origin Jewish musical traditions and repertoires among the dominant Ashkenazic population, from summer camp sing-alongs to highly formal synagogue music services.

Sacred music trends

Meanwhile, trends within mainstream America facilitated the growth of somewhat unexpected new musical movements among Jews. Within the sacred music sphere, the emergence of seminary training programs for cantors led to a counterpart drive for professionalization. Led by the Cantors Assembly (Conservative), sacred singers achieved such goals as the right to be recognized by Canadian and American law as clergy, with attendant tax-shelter and draft-exemption benefits. By the 1970s, the entry of women into leadership positions in Protestant churches slowly led to a similar reorientation in synagogue life. The first ordained female cantor began to work in a Reform temple in 1976, while the Conservative movement waited until 1987 to certify women as cantors and until 1990 to admit them to its professional organization, the Cantors Assembly. Only Orthodox Judaism still holds to the earlier philosophy of a sharp division of male and female ritual roles that precludes women from public leadership roles. Women's musical creativity continues to expand into new zones of expression, such as the invention by one woman in 1996 of a ritual to take place after a hysterectomy and the formation in the same year of a Jewish women's tambourine circle in New York, presumably drawing on biblical references to the prophetesses' leading of celebratory occasions, but also paralleling the 1990s American penchant for drumming circles of various sorts.

The emergence of neo-*klezmer* music

A second trend that fostered the emergence of musical innovation was the New Ethnicity movement of the mid-1960s to the 1980s, basically a response to the forceful activism and new ethos of African Americans ("black pride"). Many younger Jewish American musicians who had been busy performing Euro-American folk-based forms of diverse origins (Balkan, Anglo-Irish, bluegrass) began to reclaim the heritage of their own ethnic group, discovering, for example, the hundreds of 78-rpm recordings of the immigrant era and reevaluating that legacy. The initial thrust of this movement was the creation, in the late 1970s, of what have been called neo-*klezmer* bands on the East and West Coasts. The momentum of the early albums and concert tours by such groups as the Klezmorim (Berkeley), the Klezmer Conservatory Band (Boston), and Kapelye or Statman and Feldman (New York) spread this emerging ethnic energy across the continent through the 1980s. Older performers, particularly the *klezmer* patriarch Dave Tarras, were "discovered," tapped for material, and invited on concert tours, paralleling the older American folk revival activities that brought masters from Appalachia to folk festivals. The early neo-*klezmer* albums stressed reinterpretation of the 78-rpm classics, but gradually the scope expanded to include a wide variety of earlier Jewish American styles such as songs of the Yiddish theater, of working-class activism, and eventually of the "Borscht Belt," the entertainment circuit based in the Catskill resorts that spawned much late-twentieth-century Jewish comedy as well. The most recent albums have introduced added topical verses to older songs or whole new songs in Yiddish written by band members. Another trend has been the fusion of older Jewish tunes with various American jazz and popular music styles (figure 2). The drive of the neo-*klezmer* movement has expanded abroad, with local bands springing up across Europe, particularly

FIGURE 2 Klezamir, a local "territory" band of western Massachusetts. Photo by Lori McGlinchey, 2000. Courtesy Klezamir.

From left to right: Joe Blumenthal, Jim Armenti, Rhoda Bernard, Keith Levreault, Amy Rose

KLEZAMIR

413-253-3831
arose@crocker.com
http://www.klezamir.com

in Germany, and worldwide—for example, in Australia and Mexico. By 1996, the renowned classical violinist Itzhak Perlman had joined the *klezmer* circuit with a backup supergroup of bands, rocketing *klezmer* music to much greater visibility (his first album is reported to have sold over 200,000 copies).

In the 1990s, the *klezmer* scene extended into other musical and cultural territories as well, bringing experiments from the avant-garde composers of New York (John Zorn and his circle) and the invention of a "queer" *klezmer* sensibility including gay/lesbian concerns and an emphasis on the progressive values seen in Yiddish culture by younger musicians and audiences in New York City and elsewhere. (See Slobin 1998 and Slobin 2000 for detailed studies of the *klezmer* world.)

Hasidic music

Another somewhat unanticipated musical trend has been the penetration of Hasidic music into mainstream Jewish American practice. The Hasidim, a loose term covering a large set of ultraorthodox sects based on the teachings and dynasties of charismatic Eastern European leaders, have a special relationship to music. Hasidism (which began in the late eighteenth century) emphasized experience over learning and individual effort over normative rabbinic Judaism as a path to God, particularly supporting the liberal use of song and dance as means of transcendence. The Yiddish term *nign* (from Hebrew *nigun*, 'song' or 'melody') became a Hasidic word for tunes having particular spiritual power, sometimes composed by a charismatic rabbi himself, or perhaps by a "court" musician of his circle. The old Hasidic masters freely adapted tunes from non-Jewish sources (a march of the Napoleonic troops crossing Poland, for example), which they "liberated" for higher sacred purposes. The energy and attractiveness of many of these tunes have become apparent to non-Hasidic Jewish Americans in a particular way, beginning in the 1970s, as the Hasidim themselves became reevaluated by mainstream Jews and the media as authentic rather than as archaic or even outlandish and possibly embarrassing Jews. (See Koskoff 2000 for work on Lubavitcher Hasidim and Summit 2000 for melodic choice in sacred services.)

Music of Sephardic Jews

The music of the Sephardic (Mediterranean) Jews is another available influence that has found its way into both sacred and secular music repertoires. Viewed from the Jewish American mainstream, the Sephardim, like the Hasidim, offer exotic color to the basic musical palette. However, from the vantage point of Sephardic immigrants and their descendants, theirs is a rich tradition, neglected at best, misunderstood at worst. Research on the extremely variegated musical heritage of Jews from the Mediterranean lands (from Morocco to Syria) has been extensively carried out in Israel but has only recently begun in North America. Such work that had been done until the 1980s concentrated on just one genre, the *romance*, the ballad form in old Castilian Spanish, which scholars seized upon as representing an ancient, "authentic" form still in circulation among Sephardic Jews, who were exiled from Spain in 1492. This literature tended to bypass the majority of Sephardic musical styles, which, like those of other Jews, are tightly connected to the tastes and practices of the non-Jews (Christians or Muslims) among whom they lived. For example, at the heart of the Ottoman Empire (through c. 1914) and through the 1920s, in cities such as Istanbul and Smyrna (today's Izmir), Jews, Greeks, Armenians, Arabs, and Turks worked out musical styles that resonated among and within individual traditions. In fact, much of the style of *klezmer* music of the Ashkenazic Eastern European tradition had its roots in this exuberant, expansive musical region. The advent of commercial recording around 1900 saw the rise of a number of Sephardic Jewish stars singing in a variety of languages and styles (see "The Rebetiko of Rosa Eskenazi" [1995] for examples). Much of this music came to America, where it was not collected or studied until quite recently, when researchers such as M. Shallon and H. Weiss in Seattle began to visit older singers in retirement. This Mediterranean connection has been reframed by the younger generation of the community, who look to the popular and liturgical Sephardic music of Israel for inspiration.

To understand Sephardic music making, one has to have a grasp of the micromusical environment of each Mediterranean Jewish community. The work of Kay K. Shelemay and her student Mark Kligman on Syrian Jewish Americans in Brooklyn, New York, is instructive in demonstrating the complexity of the task (see Shelemay 1988 for details of the research project and 1998 for its findings). Shelemay found that ties to styles popular in the Arab lands of the Middle East remain very strong among Syrian Jews despite the impact of mainstream Jewish American, or even general American, musics. A core genre is the *pizmon*, a song in Hebrew set to a melody most commonly taken from the Arabic popular song repertoire. There is also considerable influence from the Sephardic music of Israel. Life-cycle events—weddings, bar mitzvahs—can stimulate *pizmon* composition, but no matter how personal the references and occasion, a good song will go out into the community to become part of the general store of songs. *Pizmon* tunes can come from a wide variety of sources, not just Arab music. One borrows the melody of "Sunrise, Sunset" from *Fiddler on the Roof*, another takes a melody from Verdi's opera *Aida*, while a third draws on the school song of New York Public School 62, itself a parody of the well-known Christmas carol *O Tannenbaum*. The odyssey from German carol to public school cheerleading to a Sephardic community's song heritage seems an incongruous journey, but it is actually quite normal in the eclectic world of Jewish American music, indeed of Jewish music as a whole.

Popular music

Meanwhile, just as earlier generations of Jewish American entertainers took their heritage out to mainstream venues, so in the 1960s musicians and producers moved into the marketplace. The most interesting Broadway vehicle of the era from the ethnic point of view is the aforementioned *Fiddler on the Roof*, the only show to attempt a representation of Jewish life in Eastern Europe. Anticipating the trend of the coming decades, the team of Jerry Bock, Sheldon Harnick, and Jerome Robbins mined the Hasidic tradition for "authentic" European scenes (tunes, dance sequences) and universalized the in-group experience being depicted by adding the concept of the generation gap and "tradition," the title of the key opening sequence, which was added almost as an afterthought when the musical was already in tryouts. *Fiddler* uses the Tevye stories of the great Yiddish writer Sholom Aleichem rather loosely, omitting some of Tevye's daughters while stressing others, and tacking on an ending suggesting that the fate of European Jews was to move to America. We have already seen in the film *Yidl mitn fidl* that the Jewish American community was used to such endings of stories set in Europe. This well-worn plot move was continued in Barbra Streisand's 1983 film *Yentl*, with its final scene in which the tortured heroine, having struggled with a fossilized traditional culture, triumphantly sails to the United States where, as she says, "I can fly."

In the 1970s, the influence of American popular music styles became ever greater, with European and Israeli influences waning. Particularly prominent was the rise of religious rock-based genres, spanning the denominational divide from the most liberal Reform summer-camp music of the National Federation of Temple Youth through the ultraorthodox bands of the Hasidic sects (*Shlock Rock*). Right-wing rock has been particularly influential, with the Piamenta Brothers influencing the *klezmer* movement. The late 1970s saw the writing of a number of religious rock operas, such as Sol Zim's *David Superstar*, a direct borrowing from the very popular *Jesus Christ Superstar*. The Orthodox movement began to stress youth choirs as a vehicle of a popular form of religious expression. Forms as old as the *purimshpil*, the folk drama performed for the carnival holiday of Purim in Eastern Europe, were continued and amplified by Hasidic groups, who took over spaces as large as New York's Madison Square Garden for large staged performances.

Ethnomusicology

A final trend to be noted is the rise of musicological and ethnomusicological investigation of Jewish American music, which began in the mid-1970s in earnest and began to burgeon by the 1990s. This movement parallels a strong revival of scholarship by younger American academics who, by the 1970s, began to feel freer to explore the history and expressive culture of their own ethnic group, an activity shunned for both practical and ideological reasons by earlier generations of researchers. An exception to the tendency just described was the work of Ruth Rubin, whose pioneering efforts to collect and perform the song tradition of the Eastern European Jews who arrived after World War II served as a benchmark for further gathering and study projects (see Rubin 2000). The most extensive of these was directed by Barbara Kirshenblatt-Gimblett in the 1970s, resulting in an archive of nearly two thousand songs and a set of intensive interviews taped from older informants.

In sum, the past of Jewish American music is an integral part of the uneven, even turbulent pattern of emigration and regrouping that characterized the history of this immigrant group. The state of Jewish American music today is, as usual, fragmented yet lively, multifaceted, and timely. Using past resources as a pool from which to draw viable older styles and combining them with the ongoing sounds of mainstream America, Jewish musicians continue to improvise a volatile and valuable ethnic tradition. The outlook for the future is contingent on factors affecting Jewry worldwide (social and cultural change in Eastern Europe, the situation of Israel), possible shifts in American immigration law, and the relationship of the Jews to North American societies, all of which directly affect musical trends, resources, and perceptions. Many internal reevaluations, such as the growth of Hasidism as an influence or the strong efflorescence of *klezmer* music, were unanticipated and hard to link to specific social causes, so we can probably look forward to more surprises.

REFERENCES

Alpert, Michael. 1993. *Like in a Different World: Leon Schwartz, a Traditional Jewish Klezmer Violinist from Ukraine.* Global Village C117. Cassette.

Feldman, Walter Zev. 1994. "*Bulgareasca/Bulgarish/Bulgar:* The Transformation of a Klezmer Dance Genre." *Ethnomusicology* 38(1):1–36.

Heskes, Irene. 1977. *The Resource Book of Jewish Music: A Bibliographical and Topical Guide to the Book and Journal Literature and Program Materials.* Westport Conn.: Greenwood Press.

———. 1992. *Yiddish American Popular Songs, 1895–1950: A Catalog Based on the Lawrence Marwick Roster of Copyright Entries.* Washington, D.C.: Library of Congress.

Jagoda, Flory. n.d. *Kantikas Di Mi Nona.* Global Village C139, and subsequent albums on this label. Cassette.

Katz, I. J., and S. G. Armistead. 1986. *Judeo-Spanish Ballads from Oral Tradition.* Berkeley: University of California Press.

Kligman, Mark. 1996. "On the Creators and Consumers of Orthodox Popular Music in Brooklyn,

New York." *YIVO Annual* 23:259. Evanston, Ill.: Northwestern University Press.

———. 1997. "Modes of Prayer: Arabic Maqamat in the Sabbath Morning Liturgical Music of the Syrian Jews in Brooklyn." Ph.D. dissertation, New York University.

Koskoff, Ellen. 2000. *Music in Lubavitcher Life.* Urbana: University of Illinois Press.

Lishner, Leon, and Lazar Weiner. 1992 [1976]. *The Yiddish Art Song.* Omega Classics OCD 3010. Compact disc reissue.

Netsky, Hankus. 2001. Forthcoming dissertation on the history of Klezmer in Philadelphia, Wesleyan University.

"The Rebetiko of Rosa Eskenazi." (1995). In series *Greatest Greek Singers.* Lyra ML 00880

Rubin, Ruth. 2000. *Voices of a People: The Story of Yiddish Folksong.* Urbana: University of Illinois Press.

Sapoznik, Henry. 1999 [1981]. *Klezmer Music: 1910–42.* Folkways Records FSS34021. Compact disc rerelease.

Schwartz, Martin. 1980, 1983. *Klezmer Music: Early Yiddish Instrumental Music.* Arhoolie Records/Folklyric 9034. LP disk.

———. 1984. *Greek-Oriental Smyrnaic-Rebetic Songs and Dances: The Golden Years, 1927–1937.* Folklyric 9033. LP disk.

Shelemay, Kay K. 1985. *Pizmon: Syrian-Jewish Religious and Social Song.* Meadowlark/Shanachie Records ML 105. Cassette.

———. 1986. "Music in the American Synagogue: A Case Study from Houston." In *The American Synagogue: A Sanctuary Transformed,* ed. Jack Wertheimer, 395–415. Cambridge: Cambridge University Press.

———. 1988. "Together in the Field: Team Research among Syrian Jews in Brooklyn. *Ethnomusicology* 32:369–384.

———. 1998. *Let Jasmine Rain Down: Song and Remembrance among Syrian Jews.* Chicago: University of Chicago Press.

Slobin, Mark. 1980. "From Vilna to Vaudeville: Minikes and *Among the Indians.*" *The Drama Review* 24:17–26.

————. 1982. *Tenement Songs: The Popular Music of the Jewish Immigrants*. Urbana: University of Illinois Press.

————. 1990a. *Chosen Voices: The Story of the American Cantorate*. Urbana: University of Illinois Press.

————. 1990b. "Engendering the Cantorate." *YIVO Annual* 19:147–168.

————. 1998. "Klezmer: History of Culture, Papers from a Conference." *Judaism* 47:1, 3–79.

————. 2000. *Fiddler on the Move: Exploring the World of Klezmer*. New York: Oxford University Press.

Slobin, Mark, and Barbara Kirshenblatt-Gimblett. 1986. *Folksongs in the East European Jewish Tradition from the Repertoire of Mariam Nirenberg*. Global Village GVM117 and subsequent Global Village solo-singer albums, for example, *Lifshe Schaechter Widman*, C111. Cassette.

Slobin, Mark, and Richard Spottswood. 1984. "David Medoff: A Case Study of Interethnic Popular Culture." *American Music* 3:261–276.

Statman, Andrew, and Walter Zev Feldman. 1978. *Dave Tarras: Master of the Jewish Clarinet: Music for the Traditional Jewish Wedding*. New York: Balkan Arts Center (now Ethnic Folk Arts Center) US 1002. Cassette.

Summit, Jeffrey. 2000. *How Shall We Sing? Music and Identity in Contemporary Jewish Worship*. New York: Oxford University Press.

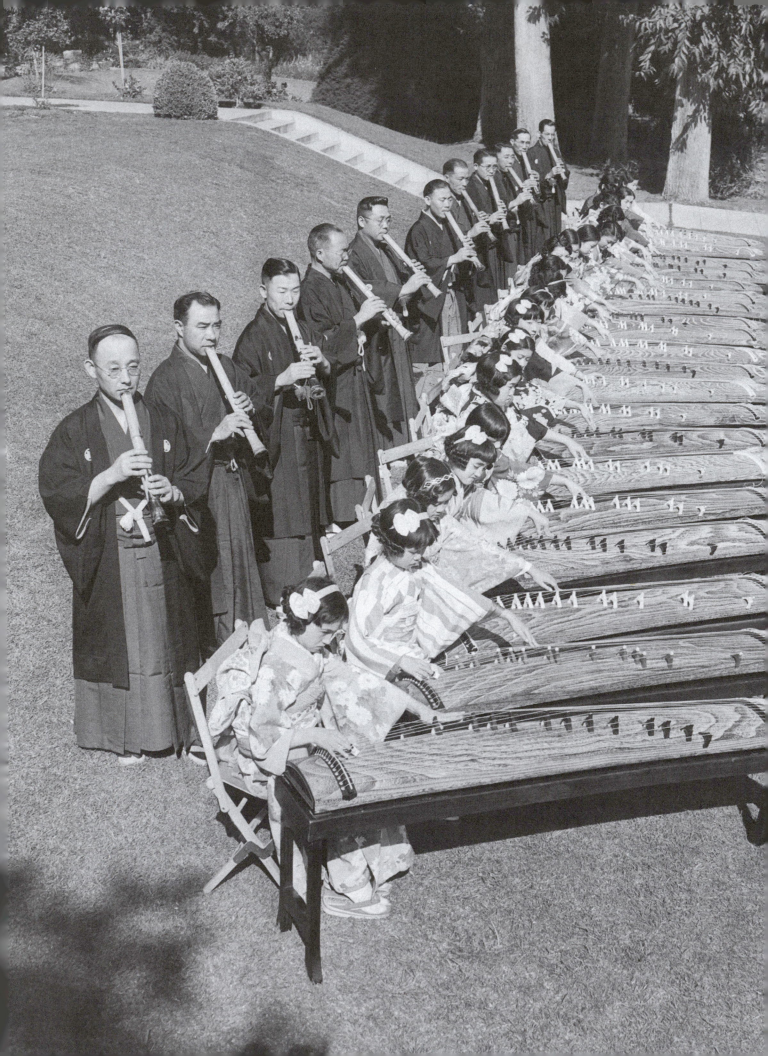

Section 2d
Asian American Musics

Asians, including people from the Middle East, south and southeast Asia, and east Asia, are the newest immigrants to arrive in the United States, beginning with the Chinese, and soon after, the Japanese, who were brought to work in the mines during the great Gold Rushes of the mid- to late nineteenth century and to help complete the transcontinental railway. Settling primarily on the west coast, in California, Oregon, and Washington, many brought with them classical music traditions hundreds of years old—ancient belief systems, religious practices, and popular musics that they, in some cases, sought to replicate in the New World. The Chinese in California, for example, still regularly perform classical Chinese opera for new immigrants as well as third- and fourth-generation Chinese Americans, and instruments such as the Japanese *koto* and *shamisen* are regularly taught in Japanese American communities in California, Hawaii, and elsewhere. Immigrants from India and Pakistan, as well as late-twentieth-century arrivals, such as the Vietnamese, Cambodians, Lao, and Indonesians, have begun to establish communities large enough to support traditional musical activities in the United States as well as to join other Asian Americans who have ventured into Western popular and classical music activities.

Traditional flutists and koto players perform during a Japanese American festival, Los Angeles, California, 1937. © Bettmann/CORBIS.

Overview
Terry E. Miller

The presence of Asian musics in the United States is a multifaceted subject requiring more than one perspective. Numerous Asian immigrant communities have coalesced throughout this country, in major cities such as San Francisco, New York, Detroit, and Chicago, as well as in many smaller ones such as Rockford, Illinois (Lao), Arlington, Virginia (Cambodian), Des Moines, Iowa (Thai Dam from Laos), and Fresno, California (Hmong from Laos). Some Asian communities, especially those composed of immigrants from China and the Philippines, have deep roots in the United States. However, most Asian immigrants came after World War II as a result of changes to immigration laws and Southeast Asian wars. As the cultures they represent tend to be quite foreign to that of the mainstream European and British Isles-derived population, they are not easily assimilated, and the musics associated with them have usually remained obscure to the mainstream population.

A second facet reflects how the non-Asian-derived population has assimilated Asian musics, often without direct contact. These contacts occur through popular recorded culture, occasional live concerts, the presence of ethnomusicology as an academic discipline, and the "world music" ensembles that have sprung up on college and university campuses. Although many such ensembles are directed by Asian musicians visiting as teachers or students, others are directed by non-Asian Americans who learned the music here or abroad. In a sense, then, Asian musics may be divided into two categories: those that are self-expressions of specific communities and those that have been appropriated by non-Asians.

ASIAN COMMUNITIES IN THE UNITED STATES

People from virtually all parts of Asia—East, Southeast, Central, South, and West—have come to the United States for a variety of reasons. Earlier groups, such as the Chinese, were originally brought in as laborers. Many Filipinos migrated to the United States during the period of American colonial rule (1898–1946). A significant number of Asians have come as students and remained, usually in professional positions, after graduation. By far the largest numbers have come seeking asylum from economic and political upheavals in their own countries. The greatest number of refugees has come from mainland Southeast Asia, especially Vietnam, Laos, and Cambodia.

As was true of earlier immigrant groups, people from Asia tended to cluster into communities, especially during the initial stages of settlement here. Some of these ethnic communities have capitalized on their "exotic" appeal by attaining status as tourist attractions. "Chinatowns," most prominent in New York, San Francisco, and Los Angeles, offer more food and souvenirs than music, however. Los Angeles's "Little Tokyo" offers excellent restaurants and shopping. Orange County, California, site of the nation's largest Vietnamese community, offers shopping malls, supermarkets, and a free-standing popular music industry.

Americans have come to associate certain Asian groups with particular economic niches: Chinese and Thai with restaurants; Indians with the medical profession, as well as independent motels; Koreans with greengrocers; and Lao with Chinese and Thai restaurants. Indeed, the most usual form of contact between Asians and non-Asians living in the United States is through ethnic restaurants. Whereas Chinese, Japanese, Middle Eastern, Indian, and Thai restaurants have sprung up throughout North America, more obscure cuisines (for example, Nepalese, Korean, Afghan) are more likely found in university towns (such as Madison, Wisconsin) or in cities having a diverse immigrant population (for example, New York).

The nature of each Asian community offers insight into whether or not its music gains significance. Working-class Asians tend to have less interest in traditional music than do professional-class Asians, but this tendency may not apply if another factor, such as a strong religious center, brings people together to maintain old-country customs.

ECONOMIC COMMUNITIES

Does a coherent business community foster the maintenance of traditional music? The most cohesive Asian communities, those called "X-town" or "little X," include Chinese, Arabs, and Vietnamese and, to lesser extents, Japanese, Koreans, Lao, Hmong, and Filipinos. North America's Chinatowns were founded primarily by Cantonese-speaking immigrants from Guangdong province (including Hong Kong) during the nineteenth and early twentieth centuries. Sharing a common language, the residents engaged in business, including both the familiar restaurants and souvenir shops as well as export-import companies, making these communities beehives of activity. Because of the language barrier, few outsiders could appreciate locally produced or itinerant musical performances, such as opera troupes performing Cantonese opera, or performances by most silk and bamboo instrumental groups, which were provided by private organizations of amateurs. Later, Chinese immigrants from both Taiwan (the Republic of China) and the People's Republic of China tended not to become part of the Chinatown community, because they spoke different languages and often came for professional reasons. *Jing xi* 'Beijing opera' in New York and Washington, D.C., for example, is not a Chinatown phenomenon. Therefore, Chinese communities have provided a context for traditional performances, but these have attracted little notice from outsiders.

In the case of Orange County's Little Saigon, however, a thriving music industry has developed. Because so many of the Republic of Vietnam's prominent popular singers and musicians escaped to the United States (and became concentrated in California), it is no surprise that they have been able to reestablish their careers within the large and increasingly prosperous Vietnamese communities of the United States. The Vietnamese music industry produces great numbers of audiotapes, music videos, and compact discs of popular songs, and artists are able to perform live in concerts that attract large audiences. Traditional music, however, attracts little interest, although locally made videos of the popularized South Vietnamese theatrical genre called *cai luong* are widely available. Live performances are few.

Because of the language barrier, few outsiders could appreciate locally produced or itinerant musical performances, such as opera troupes performing Cantonese opera, or performances by most silk and bamboo instrumental groups, which were provided by private organizations of amateurs.

RELIGIOUS COMMUNITIES

Where religion unifies a community, its religious center may provide a context for traditional music. The religions of Asia represented through organized centers in North America include Hinduism, Islam, and Buddhism. Of these, Hindu temples have provided the most hospitable context for traditional music, almost exclusively that of southern India (the Karnatic tradition). Such music includes both *bhajan* 'lay devotional songs' and classical vocal genres. Temples also provide a venue for teaching. Festivals celebrating the sacred, vocal compositions of St. Thyagaraja (1767–1847), southern India's greatest composer, often become successful by featuring both local and visiting performing artists (figure 1). Because the people of northern India are of various religious systems, the impetus for Hindustani music has tended to come from Indian professionals or community organizations (such as the cultural Indian Sunday schools) rather than religious centers.

Although Chinese, Japanese, and Vietnamese Buddhist temples, all part of the Mahayana tradition, may maintain some forms of chant, they have not been significant contexts for other kinds of traditional music. The same is largely true of the Theravada Buddhist temples established by the Lao and Cambodian communities, but the Thai Buddhist temples in Chicago, Los Angeles, and New York have brought in Thai music teachers and developed traditional ensembles. Islamic mosques have not figured prominently in encouraging the traditional musics of immigrant groups from West and Central Asia.

A number of Asian immigrant groups have also founded Christian churches. Most prominent are Koreans, Japanese, Chinese, and Filipinos. As the practices of most

FIGURE 1   Held at Cleveland State University every spring for more than twenty years, the St. Thyagaraja Festival celebrates the works of Karnatic India's most famous composer, St. Thyagaraja (1767–1847), using both local and imported talent, all supported by the local Indian community, 1984. Photo by Terry E. Miller.

Asian Christian churches are heavily, if not entirely, Westernized, and many traditional musics are associated with non-Christian cultural beliefs and activities, churches are rarely associated with such musics.

OTHER INSTITUTIONS

Some first-generation Asian immigrants were skilled musicians, but few were able to continue their professional lives in the United States. The question remains, will these musics take root and be passed to younger generations, or will they simply cease upon the passing of the carrier? Arts councils in a number of states have established apprenticeships in the traditional arts which encourage traditional masters, through modest financial incentives and public recognition, to find apprentices within the community. Reviews of this process suggest mixed levels of success. Few wish to devote the time, energy, and money needed to learn traditional music if there is neither financial reward nor ready context for its performance.

Classical Indian music and dance are likely the most systematically organized Asian traditions in the United States and Canada. A small number of masters work nearly full time teaching classical Bharata Natyam dance, *sitar* and *sarod* 'lutes', *vina* 'zither', and both *tabla* and *mridangam* 'drums'. These activities take place in private studios, under the auspices of Hindu temples, and in at least one fully established educational institution, the Ali Akbar College of Music in San Rafael, California. In addition, this training is available to non-Indian students as well as to those of Indian descent.

MEDIA

Many major cities have public access television and radio stations that allow various ethnic groups to broadcast music and programs during specified hours. Most often, popular music videos or popular songs are featured, rather than traditional music. Music videos and movies, audiotapes, compact discs, and epic-length Chinese films are often available for rental or purchase at Asian grocery stores. A number of small companies, started by immigrant Asians, manufacture and market tapes, videos, and compact discs of both material brought from Asia and newly recorded releases. Little of this material is known to the non-Asian community.

THE ROLE OF MUSIC IN MAINTAINING UNITY AND PRESERVING IDENTITY

Although popular genres (songs, film music, rock bands) outweigh traditional Asian musics in North America, both play roles in maintaining unity and identity within immigrant communities. For example, to non-Indians, all people from India may be assumed to be of the same culture, but for Indians, the distinction between Karnatic (southern) and Hindustani (northern) usually remains clear. This is especially true with regard to music performances. St. Thyagaraja Festivals only occur where there are large populations of Karnatic Indians, and a *sarod* concert will attract a large audience only where there are many Hindustani Indians. Similarly, Cantonese opera attracts Cantonese speakers, who tend to maintain an identity separate from Mandarin-speaking Chinese, who would more likely support Beijing opera. Concerts and other events offering music from the homeland not only reinforce the audience's identification with its native countries, but they often serve to subdivide audiences according to geographical, linguistic, or religious origin.

When refugees from Vietnam and Laos began arriving in North America in 1975, all were subsumed in one group, either Vietnamese or Lao. Before their arrival, however, all had clear notions of where they belonged in their homeland. Chinese-derived Vietnamese did not consider themselves to be Vietnamese in the same way that ethnic Vietnamese did, and few realized that many of the people from central Vietnam were in fact Cham, not Vietnamese. The Cham, who in Vietnam had to mute their ethnic identity, have reasserted it in the New World. Besides costume and language, a main ingredient used to invoke Cham identity is dance and music. People who had never paid much attention to these modes of expression in Vietnam now find them important in asserting a Cham identity as distinct from both Vietnamese and American identities. Other so-called Vietnamese were in fact upland Mon-Khmer speakers unrelated to the lowland ethnic Vietnamese.

For North Americans, Lao constituted a single, if obscure, ethnic identity, but within Laos distinctions are made between lowland, mid-upland, and high-upland groups, with most of the latter speaking non-Lao languages. The lowland Lao-speaking immigrants demonstrate their musical identity through (rarely heard) performances of *lam* singing (traditional Lao singing in repartee form) accompanied by *khene* 'free-reed mouth organ' and the more commonly heard rock band, which alternates traditionally derived dances and melodies with American line dances and whatever else is currently popular. Upland Lao, especially the Hmong, declare their distinctiveness in unaccompanied chanting of poetry and its realization on instruments, especially the *qeej* (gaeng), 'free-reed mouth organ'.

NON-ASIAN RESPONSES TO ASIAN MUSICS

Various Asian musics have had a strong appeal in the non-Asian community. Although by no means exhaustive, two groups dominate this area: ethnomusicology or world music programs in academia, and a counterculture of freelance composers, world music performers, and improvisers. Preceding the latter were a number of internationally known composers, some of whose works show influences from Asian musics.

ACADEMIA

Until the 1960s, ethnomusicology in the United States was primarily part of anthropology and folklore and focused on native traditions. Two institutions at opposite ends of the nation changed that. Connecticut's Wesleyan University's world music program brought in significant numbers of professional performer-teachers who trained American students to perform Asian traditions, particularly those of Indonesia and India. Mantle Hood of the University of California, Los Angeles (UCLA) espoused the concept of bimusicality as a means to learning non-Western musics. A number of his students, many of whom went on to found ethnomusicology programs throughout the United States, Canada, and elsewhere, were originally composers seeking alternative ideas for their works. Hood founded a large Javanese gamelan 'Indonesian orchestra, especially of percussion instruments', the Venerable Dark Cloud, and other ethnomusicology faculty and students offered performance training in Thai, Chinese, Arabic, and other musics. Under Hood's influence, both Javanese and Balinese gamelan were founded at institutions throughout the country, becoming so ubiquitous that having a program in ethnomusicology virtually assumed you also had a gamelan.

With the proliferation of ethnomusicology programs and the offering of courses on Asian musics to a broad range of students, an increasing number of Americans have become aware of and attracted to various Asian musics. During the 1960s and 1970s, Asian musics were sometimes associated with the youth counterculture. Partly because of the Beatles' use of Indian instruments and musicians, and George Harrison's study of the *sitar* 'Indian lute' with Ravi Shankar, Indian music remained popular until African and African-inspired drumming rose to prominence in the 1980s. Javanese and Balinese gamelan attracted many students both to play and to attend concerts. Musics from Asia took on importance for many in North America, but their meanings were often changed to fit the interests and agendas of Westerners.

Today, numerous academic institutions offer Asian performance studies. These include Chinese music (Kent State University, Florida State University, Laney College), Thai music (Kent State University), Javanese or Balinese gamelan (figure 2) (Uni-

FIGURE 2   Members of the University of Michigan's Javanese gamelan, directed by Dr. Judith Becker, rehearse for an upcoming performance, 1980. Photo by Terry E. Miller.

versity of Wisconsin, University of Michigan, Northern Illinois University, Bowling Green State University, University of Pittsburgh, Wesleyan University, Colorado College, University of Wyoming, University of Texas, Eastman School of Music, Oberlin College, UCLA, University of California–Berkeley, Mills College, Cornell University, Grinnell College, Florida State University, University of Washington, University of Hawaii), Sundanese gamelan (Evergreen State College), Arabic music (UCLA, College of William and Mary), and Indian music (UCLA, Wesleyan University). Few of these ensembles, however, have permanent status and depend on the continuous presence of individual faculty members or the availability of graduate assistants from specific countries. To use Thai-specialist David Morton's expression, these ensembles are mostly "hot-house plants" (Morton 1970:1). In 1976, several experienced players in New York founded the (Javanese) gamelan Son of Lion ensemble, using instruments built locally of steel and aluminum, and have commissioned new works.

A number of organizations have been founded to promote various Asian musics, some organized by Asian Americans, some by non-Asian Americans. These include New York's Music from China, which performs both traditional and new compositions. In Chicago, the Chinese Music Society of North America publishes a semischolarly magazine, *Chinese Music*, and provides performances by a modern-style Chinese orchestra staffed by a mixture of Chinese and non-Chinese musicians. The International Association for Research in Vietnamese Music, founded by Phong Nguyen and Terry E. Miller, encourages the performance of traditional Vietnamese music and, until 1999, published a scholarly journal, *Nhac Viet*. The Cambodian Network Council in Washington, D.C., has organized conferences on both music and art, as well as performances. The American Gamelan Institute, based in Hanover, New Hampshire, publishes *Balungan*, an occasional journal devoted primarily to Indonesian music. Other organizations offer concerts and lectures devoted to Asian musics.

COMPOSITION

Western classical composers have dabbled in Asian musics at least since the late nineteenth century, when Asian exoticism became attractive. But Europeans such as Gustav Mahler (*Das Lied von der Erde*), Giacomo Puccini (*Madama Butterfly* and *Turandot*), and Nikolai Rimsky-Korsakov ("Song of India") paid little attention to matters of authenticity. During the twentieth century, both European and American composers continued their interests in Asian musics but with increasing knowledge and firsthand experience. Lou Harrison (b. 1917) and John Cage (1912–1992) imitated the sounds of the Indonesian gamelan as early as 1941 in their *Double Music*. Colin McPhee (1901–1964) lived in Bali, Indonesia, during the 1930s and wrote not only a scholarly book on Balinese music but also compositions that suggest Balinese influence. Most prominent is *Tabuh-Tabuhan* (1936) for orchestra. Henry Cowell (1897–1965) also traveled extensively in both Eastern and Western Asia from the 1930s through the 1950s and produced numerous early recordings of Asian music for Folkways Records. Having spent 1956–1957 in Iran, Cowell wrote, among other works, *Homage to Iran* in 1957 for violin, piano, and *dombak* 'drum'. Between 1962 and 1965, he also wrote two concertos for Japanese *koto* 'zither'. Halim El-Dabh, born in Egypt in 1921, has written two works for Arabic *darabukka* 'drum', timpani, and strings, a concerto for *darabukka*, and *Fantasia-Tahmeel* for Middle Eastern percussion.

Composers active in the minimalist movement, which dates to the 1960s but continues to be a major stream in today's composition, were stimulated in part by their early participation in non-Western ensembles, particularly those of Africa and Indonesia. Philip Glass, like Beatle George Harrison, studied Indian music directly from *sitar* artist and film composer Ravi Shankar and internationally acclaimed *tabla* 'pair of hand drums' player Alla Rahka from 1964. The music of Glass, Steve Reich, Terry Riley, La Monte Young, and others often invokes a generalized atmosphere of suspension,

As early as the 1940s, John Cage's prepared pianos imitated non-Western (including Asian) instruments, and both Cage and Harrison imitated the gamelan by using brake drums, cans, pots, animal bells, etc.

cyclical structure, and contemplations created through repeated, but slowly changing, patterns. Whereas gamelan music is in fact progressive in structure, the minimalist works that suggest it only conserve its apparent monotony and the perception of suspension in time. This is clearly heard in Steve Reich's *Music for Mallet Instruments, Voices and Organ*, and *Six Pianos*.

Other composers have departed entirely from Western instruments and built their own instrumentaria. As early as the 1940s, John Cage's prepared pianos imitated non-Western (including Asian) instruments, and both Cage and Harrison imitated the gamelan by using brake drums, cans, pots, animal bells, etc. American composer and sometime hobo Harry Partch (1901–1976) composed all of his music for instruments of his own creation, many derived from Asia. In addition, Partch explored alternative tunings derived from Arabic and Chinese sources.

Composition for Asian ensembles, with or without added Western instruments, has become prominent both in the West and in Asia. Lou Harrison, who spent the years 1961–1963 traveling in East Asia, with instrument builder William Colvig, built Asian-derived instruments, including two Javanese gamelan, for use in his compositions. Harrison's works for actual Asian instruments, with added chorus, cello, violin, or horn, began in 1963 and continue to this day. Other composers who have followed this stream include David Loeb, Bruce Gaston (an American composer living and working in Thailand), and Ingram Marshall.

Also inhabiting this musical twilight zone between East and West are numerous composers and improvisers who also occupy the space between classical and popular cultures. Because this music invokes other times, other cultures, and other universes, much of it has been labeled New Age [see NEW AGE, p. 345]. Although the Windham Hill record label has been long associated with New Age music, most composer-performers publish on obscure or self-owned labels. Jaron Lanier, for example, composes and improvises music involving diverse Asian instruments, including Chinese *zheng* 'zither', Lao *khaen*, and Balinese *angklung* 'shaken bamboo rattles'. Robert Bassara's work involves great numbers of Asian percussion instruments, especially the Burmese *kyi-zi* 'metal chime'.

Few of these composer-performers using Asian instruments, alone or as part of world music ensembles, give heed to the original, authentic styles, but instead create their own styles for their own purposes. For example, No World Improvisations, consisting of Korean *kayageum* 'zither' player Jin Hi Kim and American oboist Joseph Celli, improvises new music that is neither Western nor Eastern but blends elements borrowed from each. Although using world instruments, especially those associated with the apparently mystical cultures of Asia (for example, Zen Buddhism and Sufism), has come to symbolize openness, freedom, creativity, and spirituality, it has also required a process in which Westerners assign new meanings to adopted foreign instruments and forms.

FIGURE 3   Members of a Lion Dance troupe celebrate the opening of a new restaurant in New York City's Chinatown playing gong, cymbals, and drum, 1987. Photo by Terry E. Miller.

FIGURE 3   Members of a Lion Dance troupe celebrate the opening of a new restaurant in New York City's Chinatown playing gong, cymbals, and drum, 1987. Photo by Terry E. Miller.

POPULAR CULTURE

The worlds of serious and formalized composition and of improvisation and popular forms, such as world beat, have no clear boundary [see WORLD BEAT, p. 337]. The combining of East and West within the latter's popular music began in England with the Beatles' use of Indian instruments and musicians in the albums *Revolver* (1966) and *Sgt. Pepper's Lonely Hearts Club Band* (1967) and continued with English-born John McLaughlin, who immigrated to the United States in 1968 and founded the Mahavishnu Orchestra in 1971, blending jazz, rock, and Indian music. Although Indian music waned as African influences waxed, it was India that had inspired the generation of popular musicians active in the 1960s and 1970s. Slightly later, Ancient Future, a band organized in California around 1980, invoked a variety of Asian sounds, including Balinese frogs. In addition to using Balinese instruments, Ancient Future used a number of northern Indian instruments. Jade Warrior's creations included invoking the sounds of Balinese *ketjak* (from *kecak*, 'monkey chant'). Wendy Carlos (formerly Walter Carlos) synthesized numerous Asian musics, including those of Tibet and Bali, in her 1986 album *Beauty and the Beast*. Womad Productions/Realworld has produced concert tours blending Asian and American musicians and has issued recordings of both traditional and newly blended musics. Indeed, a visit to any large record store would reveal proliferating supplies of world music recordings offering virtually everything, including traditional musics, popular musics, and various fusions [BORDER CROSSINGS AND FUSIONS, p. 321].

Asian martial arts have attracted the attention of numerous North Americans, including both Euro- and African Americans. Both the Chinese Lion Dance organizations that have proliferated in the larger cities and the martial arts groups usually associated with them often include a percussion ensemble to accompany performances. Although Lion Dance is performed by Chinese within the Chinese community in places such as New York City, and Cleveland, Ohio, all Lion Dance organizations are Asian American (figure 3).

A MULTITUDE OF MUSICS

The existence of Asian-derived musics within the United States can thus be explained from several viewpoints. Clearly, these musics exist outside their original contexts, although immigrant communities often provide authentic but new contexts. This raises questions as to whether these musics should be heard as artifacts or as part of an evolving process that not only changes the musics but assigns them new meanings. These musics, then, can be seen along a continuum from so-called pure survivals brought from places where the original music has been changed or lost, to newly fused musics created by stripping parts from world musical traditions and reuniting them in new ways. Those engaged in these processes include first-generation Asian Americans who wish to identify themselves musically with both Asia and the West, as well as non-Asians who adopt and adapt Asian musics and musical instruments in pursuit of multifarious and often conflicting agendas.

Asian musics have come to the United States through proliferating media—records, compact discs, audiocassettes, films, videos, CD-ROM, VCDs, television and radio shows, live concerts, performance courses—but most of these are experienced in new and often personal contexts (for example, the privacy of headphones or viewing rooms). As such, they usually come in objectified form, stripped of their original meaning and awaiting the assignment of new functions and meanings. Asian musics, therefore, may be given meanings connected to novelty, liberalness, liberation, spirituality and the New Age, originality, exoticism, multiculturalism, cultural diversity, environmentalism, and a host of other thoughts, agendas, and desires. The users may know, but care little (or nothing) about the musics' original intentions, functions, or meanings, but harness them to express a contemporary American music here and now.

REFERENCES

Jairazbhoy, Nazir A., and Sue Carole DeVale, eds. 1985. *Selected Reports in Ethnomusicology: Vol. VI: Asian Music in North America*. Los Angeles: UCLA Department of Music.

Morton, David. 1970. "Thai Traditional Music: Hot-house Plant or Sturdy Stock." *Journal of the Siam Society* 58(2):1–44.

Nguyen, Phong, with Adelaida Reyes Schramm and Patricia Shehan Campbell. 1995. *Searching for a Niche: Vietnamese Music at Home in America*. Kent, Ohio: Viet Music Publications.

Reyes, Adelaida. 1999. *Songs of the Caged, Songs of the Free: Music and the Vietnamese Refugee Experience*. Philadelphia: Temple University Press.

Chinese Music
Su Zheng

History of Chinese Music in America
Performance Contexts
Musical Genres

The sound of Chinese music has been resonating in North America since the mid-nineteenth century. It has been defined by the changing factors of which Chinese came to North America, why they came, and under what circumstances they stayed, on the one hand; by racialized immigration policies and societal reactions to ethnic/racial minorities in America and Canada, on the other. Until today, the music culture of Chinese in North America has been predominantly an immigrant culture, although the American-born music genre—Asian American jazz—has already left strong marks on American and Chinese American musical lives.

From its early days, music has been a significant empowering vehicle through which Chinese sojourners, or immigrants, as well as American- or Canadian-born Chinese reinforced their diasporic connections and articulated their cultural identities against oppressive and prejudiced sociopolitical environments [see CANTONESE MUSIC IN VANCOUVER, p. 1260]. At the same time, Chinese music has been perceived by the dominant society as a mystical oriental sound through which, over time, the curious majority came to know about and interpret Chinamen, Chinese immigrants, and, eventually, Chinese Americans. Contrary to the prevailing misconception that Chinese music is confined to Chinatowns, generations of Chinese American musicians and community leaders have persistently attempted to deghettoize their music—through which to deghettoize themselves—and bring it into the American public life and national cultural terrain.

At the turn of the twenty-first century, Chinese Americans and Chinese Canadians enjoy and cultivate diverse musical styles and genres. Many cities in North America, including Boston, Chicago, Honolulu, Los Angeles, New York City, San Francisco, Seattle, Toronto, Vancouver, and Washington, D.C., host numerous Chinese music groups. The states of Florida, New Jersey, Maryland, Pennsylvania, and Delaware also host such groups. Until the 1980s, San Francisco was the major home for Chinese music activities in America. Since then, New York City, as the cultural center for a more cosmopolitan and heterogeneous Chinese American society, has become the most important place for Chinese American music performance.

Women have been influential in Chinese American and Chinese Canadian music cultural productions. Left behind in China, the wives of the early sojourners wrote

Having endured years of intense racism, many of the musicians of Cantonese opera were forced to withdraw from the larger society to avoid harassment.

songs to express their feelings (Zheng 1993b), and a large number of the directors and members of today's music groups are women.

HISTORY OF CHINESE MUSIC IN AMERICA

Numbering close to 1.7 million in 1990, the Chinese were one of the earliest Asian groups to arrive in America (first recorded in 1785). However, the substantial wave of Chinese migration began in 1849, incited by the news of the discovery of gold in California. The history of Chinese American music culture can be divided into three periods: 1849 to 1949, 1950 to 1979, and 1980 to the present.

1849–1949: music among the homogeneous sojourners

During this period, almost all Chinese immigrants in America, predominantly male, of a rural agrarian background, and speaking only local dialects, came from the southern coastal region of Guangdong Province. As a result, Cantonese opera (*Yueju/Yuht kehk*), Cantonese music (*Guangdong yinyue*), and the Taishan *muyu/muk'yu* 'wooden fish' song, all popular musical forms from that region, became the dominant Chinese music genres in America for more than a hundred years. On the night of 18 October 1852, the all-male Hong Took Tong Chinese Dramatic Company from Guangdong staged the American premiere of Cantonese opera in San Francisco. In the so-called golden era of Chinese theater in America (the late 1870s to the 1880s), there were four Cantonese theaters in San Francisco, each giving frequent performances (Riddle 1983). On 12 February 1891, the members of the Boston branch of the American Folklore Society were "greatly pleased" by a Cantonese opera performance in the cellar of a Harrison Avenue hotel (Anonymous 1891). And in New York City, the first Chinese opera theater was opened in the heart of Chinatown on 26 March 1893 (Anonymous 1893). Numerous English-language reports from the 1880s recorded the activities of the "Chinese band" in the celebration of Chinese New Year (*chunjie*) and at Sunday schools (Riddle 1983; Zheng 2001). By the first half of the twentieth century, Cantonese opera lovers had formed a number of Cantonese opera clubs in San Francisco, Portland (Oregon), Boston, and New York.

Taishan *muyu,* a little-known folk genre of storytelling, is a local variation of *muyu,* an important narrative song tradition in South China. Book advertisements in San Francisco's Chinatown about *muyu* textbooks witnessed its popularity among the early immigrants. Printed *muyu* textbooks have been imported into America since the beginning of the twentieth century. A number of *muyu* song texts describe the early Chinese laborers' experience, particularly the sentiment of their wives who were left at home, prohibited from joining their husbands in America.

Soon after the completion of the transcontinental railroad in 1869, Chinese in America became victims of an anti-Chinese campaign that intensified in the 1870s and resulted in the 1882 Chinese Exclusion Act banning immigration of Chinese laborers and their wives and prohibiting the naturalization of Chinese. Between 1873 and 1875, San Francisco passed several ordinances against the use of Chinese ceremonial gongs. On 14 July 1895, Chu Fong, the proprietor and manager of the Chinese opera theater in New York, was arrested for "Sabbath breaking" because he produced "an immoral performance" on Sunday (Anonymous 1896).

Having endured years of intense racism, many of the musicians of Cantonese opera were forced to withdraw from the larger society to avoid harassment. The majority lived in Chinatowns. Many worked in restaurants or laundry businesses. Speaking very little or no English, they isolated themselves, and still do, from the mainstream of American life. In addition, Cantonese opera clubs historically functioned as substitute families for their bachelor members. Music making therefore became a private act for the members and generally did not extend beyond the Chinatown Chinese communities.

1950–1979: expansion of music genres in a polarized community

The collapse of the Chinese nationalist regime on the mainland after World War II and the establishment of the People's Republic of China by the Chinese Communist Party in 1949 dramatically, and in many cases traumatically, altered the lives of Chinese in America. For the Cantonese sojourners, their longing to return to their homeland was unexpectedly turned into a shattered dream, and some five thousand Chinese intellectuals—cosmopolitan, prosperous, and mostly from a privileged social class—became stranded in America. As a result, a homogeneous, working-class Chinese population was transformed into a polarized community separated by their different social standings, dialects, economic levels, and educational backgrounds (Kung 1955).

Chinese intellectuals contributed to the emergence of Peking opera (Jingju) clubs and minyue (music for Chinese instruments) ensembles in the early 1950s and 1960s. The members of these newer music groups spoke English as well as Mandarin in addition to their local dialects. Because they had college or graduate degrees, many worked in universities, hospitals, and companies outside Chinatowns in various professional positions. They generally resided outside Chinatowns as well. These new groups tenaciously strove to break down the ethnic boundaries and actively pursued the acceptance of Chinese music culture by mainstream Americans. In addition to serving the Chinese community, it was typical of the newer groups to give public lectures, demonstrations, and performances in universities, museums, and other institutions for non–Chinese American audiences (Zheng 1990).

After the United States Congress enacted the 1965 Immigration Act that abolished "national origins" as a basis for allocating immigration quotas to various countries, including China, the Chinese American population increased tremendously. The post-1965 Chinese immigrants from Taiwan and Hong Kong were from various social strata, including many skilled workers, technicians, and college-educated persons. Consequently, the composition of the Chinese community began to be transformed from polarity to heterogeneity and complexity (B. Wong 1987). This development was also reflected in the continuous growth of the Chinese American music groups and genres in this period.

1980–present: toward heterogeneity and complexity

In its 150-year history in America, the Chinese American community did not see anything similar to the sudden boom of music and musicians that occurred in the 1980s and 1990s. The recent flourishing of various Chinese music groups and genres is directly related to the rapid increase of the number of Chinese immigrants, including professional performers and musicians, resulting from the policy changes in China, Taiwan, and the United States. Some of these newly arrived artists, such as Hua Wenyi (Kunqu actress), Lu Siqing (violinist), Pin Chao Luo (Cantonese opera actor), Qi Shu-fang (Peking opera actress), Tang Liangxing (pipa 'four-stringed plucked lute' player), Hao Jiang Tian (tenor), Chang-yuan Wang (zheng 'sixteen- or twenty-one-stringed zither' player), and Yin Cheng-Zong (pianist), were winners of international or national prizes. The number and quality of these masters and well-known performers have radically altered the scope and level of Chinese musical performance in America.

PERFORMANCE CONTEXTS

Today's Chinese Americans are involved in a wide range of musics, including Chinese operas (*xiqu*), *minyue,* Taishan *muyu,* choral singing, Western orchestral music, new music, Chinese popular music, Western pop and rock music, rap, and Asian American jazz. New York City alone has more than forty Chinese American music groups. Other than a few formal performances at commercial venues, the majority of the performances by Chinese Americans are related to specific events or functions, including rituals and festivals (both Chinese and American), private celebrations, community services, lecture demonstrations to Chinese Americans and the general audience, American and Chinese diaspora events, and multicultural festivals.

Beginning in the 1980s, the growing Chinese ethnic media networks, which include several channels of television and radio programs transmitted via satellite from China, Taiwan, and Hong Kong, have been providing continuous news and music entertainment for the Chinese community throughout North America (Zheng 1994). Also, in countless Chinese record stores, grocery stores, and video shops, both within and outside Chinatowns, one can find the most recent hit songs in the Chinese diaspora, as well as impressive collections of compact discs, cassettes, Chinese movies, and karaoke discs. And after several decades since the 1920s and 1930s, when Cantonese opera and music in the American cities were recorded on 78-rpm discs, American record companies in the 1980s began to produce and distribute compact discs by Chinese American jazz musicians, Chinese composers of new music, and Chinese traditional instrumental music performers in the United States.

MUSICAL GENRES

Chinese operas (*xiqu*)

Currently, four different kinds of Chinese opera are being actively cultivated in the United States, all of which perform traditional repertoire consisting of remote historical stories, legends, myths, or folktales. The custom of cross-gender practice endures in Peking opera and *Yueju* (Shaoxing opera) in America. Generally, three different modes of Chinese opera performance exist: operatic song singing, individual acts or scenes extracted from operas, and complete opera. All accompanying music ensembles contain both percussion and melodic sections.

Cantonese opera (Yueju)

Cantonese opera is performed in Cantonese dialect with singing, acting, speaking, and dancing. Cantonese operatic song singing—usually one or two singers accompanied by an instrumental ensemble singing lyrical excerpts from Cantonese operas—is the most common performance mode among Chinese Americans. Nam Chung (figure 1) is the oldest Cantonese opera club in the United States. With the arrival of many new immigrants from China and Hong Kong, Cantonese opera is currently experiencing a period of revitalization.

Since the 1920s, Cantonese opera in China has absorbed several Western instruments (saxophone, electric keyboard, violin, and electric guitar). This practice was in turn imported into American cities. An ensemble (*pai he*) usually has ten to twelve musicians, playing different combinations of Chinese and Western instruments. Some Chinese instruments include *bangu* 'drum', *ban* 'hollow wood block', *wenchang luo* 'large civil gong', *wuchang luo* 'small military gong', *bo* 'cymbals', *gaohu* 'high-pitched two-stringed fiddle', *erhu* 'lower-pitched two-stringed fiddle', *yangqin* 'hammered dul-

FIGURE I   Nam Chung Musical Association.
Cantonese opera performers and musicians
participating in a fundraising parade during the
war, in Chinatown, San Francisco, 1940. Photo
courtesy Nam Chung.

FIGURE I   Nam Chung Musical Association. Cantonese opera performers and musicians participating in a fundraising parade during the war, in Chinatown, San Francisco, 1940. Photo courtesy Nam Chung.

cimer', *yueqin* 'moon-shaped four-stringed pluckcd lute', *sanxian* 'three-stringed plucked lute', and *houguan* 'double-reed wind instrument'.

Although Guandong (Cantonese) music and opera have long dominated the Chinese cultural scene in North America, a large community—around 40,000—of Chaozhou speakers from Vietnam, Cambodia, and Laos has formed in the Los Angeles area. The sound of Chaozhou music is dominated by a piercing fiddle called the *er xian* 'two string' or *tou xian* 'head string', which is joined by other more typical plucked and bowed strings and bamboo flutes. Chaozhou outdoor percussion music is distinctive for its drums with their dry rap sounds, and for gongs, some of them flat and others with a boss that makes them look Southeast Asian. The Los Angeles Chaozhou community maintains a number of skilled "silk and bamboo" ensembles, percussion ensembles, and actively performing opera troupes. Although these musicians are highly skilled, some at a professional level, the younger generation has shown little interest in learning this music, and there is concern about the survival of this old-fashioned, "traditional" version of Chaozhou culture, now very different from modern Chaozhou music in the People's Republic of China.

Peking opera (Jingju)

Historically patronized by the imperial family and the Mandarins, Peking opera is considered the national opera in both China and Taiwan. It was first brought to America by Mei Lan-fang, the most distinguished Peking opera female-role performer, during his sensational visit in 1930. The first North America *piaofang* (Peking opera club of amateur performers), Chinese Opera Club in America, was founded in 1951 in New York by Chinese students stranded in the United States.

The most popular performance mode for Peking opera in America is a set of two to four independent acts drawn from different Peking operas, performed in sequence by different sets of performers. The presentation of a complete opera is less frequent. The musical accompaniment *(changmian)* in Peking opera is quite standard, containing fewer instruments than used in Cantonese opera. They include *bangu, daluo* 'large gong', *xiaoluo* 'small gong', *cha* 'cymbals', *jinghu* 'the leading high-pitched two-stringed fiddle', *erhu, yueqin, sanxian,* and sometimes *suona* 'double-reed shawm' and *dizi* 'flute'.

Every aspect of Chinese instrumental music in America has been influenced heavily by changes in Chinese instrumental music in modern China and Taiwan, which include professionalization, standardization, and the syncretizing of Western classical music idioms and performance practices with Chinese melodies, textures, and aesthetics.

Kunqu

Kunqu, the origin of which can be traced back to the mid-fourteenth century, is one of the oldest opera genres in China and has influenced many other opera genres. Its texts and music are the most literate and archaic. Mimetic dancing is an indispensable accompaniment to the singing, for which *dizi* is the major accompanying instrument.

Because some Peking opera performers were trained in *Kunqu* as well, there were some performances of *Kunqu* excerpts in the earlier periods of Chinese immigration. In 1988 and 1989, however, a number of important *Kunqu* artists arrived in America from China, and the first *Kunqu* group in North America, Kunqu Society, was founded in New York in 1988. In a given performance, four to five individual acts from different *Kunqu* pieces are usually presented.

Shaoxing opera (Yueju)

Yueju originated in the Shaoxing area in Zhejiang province near Shanghai in the early twentieth century. It is most popular among the Zhejiang-Shanghai dialect–speaking population. The only *Yueju* club in America, Shao-Xing Opera Association of New York, was formed in 1991 and has presented several performances.

Minyue (music for Chinese instruments)

Every aspect of Chinese instrumental music in America has been influenced heavily by changes in Chinese instrumental music in modern China and Taiwan, which include professionalization, standardization, and the syncretizing of Western classical music idioms (form, harmony, and orchestration) and performance practices with Chinese melodies, textures, and aesthetics. The conventions for both performers and audience at a Chinese instrumental music concert are in many ways quite similar to those of a concert of Western classical music. Normally each piece lasts from a few minutes to about ten minutes, and an entire concert lasts about two hours with an intermission.

As in China, the three most common forms in a given instrumental music concert in America are solo music with or without accompaniment, small ensemble, and full orchestra. Although almost any melodic instrument can perform as a solo instrument, the instruments heard most often as soloists are the *erhu, dizi, zheng, pipa, yangqin,* and *sheng* 'mouth organ'. The small ensemble performances often replicate some of the regional instrumental music ensembles in China, such as Cantonese music and *jiang nan si zhu* 'silk (string instruments) and bamboo (wind instruments) music from south of Yangtze River'. The number of musicians in these small ensembles varies from five to ten. The Chinese Music Ensemble of New York (figure 2), with more than forty members, is the largest Chinese instrument orchestra outside China and Taiwan. Its repertoire covers classical pieces of elite traditions, excerpts from Chinese operas, regional ensemble music, arrangements of folk music melodies, composed modern pannational music, and tunes from films, dances, and popular songs.

FIGURE 2   The Chinese Music Ensemble of New York, 2000. Photo by Su Ming Yeh. Photo courtesy The Chinese Music Ensemble of New York.

Taishan *muyu* song

Sung in Taishan dialect, *muyu* is enjoyed by the rural population of Taishan, the county (now a city) from where most of the early Chinese immigrants originated. Many of the *muyu* stories are romances drawing from history, legend, and local folktales. *Muyu* song texts are kept in printed or hand-copied booklets and are sung to repeated basic tunes, learned aurally, with improvisational variations. Music is often performed without instrumental accompaniment, by one singer only or by a group of performers singing in turn, in the context of private gatherings, ceremonies, rituals, and festivals.

Many Chinese American senior citizens, especially women, love to listen to *muyu* and know how to sing it. One *muyu* song, "Xiu Hua Ge" ("The Embroidery Song"), depicting the sorrow and sentiment of an early immigrant's wife, is particularly popular among the senior citizens.

Sheung Chi Ng (b. 1910) (figure 3) is a well-known *muyu* singer living in New York's Chinatown. Not only did he bring *muyu* textbooks to America when he left China, he also continues to write new *muyu* texts reflecting his immigrant experiences. Ng was awarded a National Heritage Fellowship in 1992 by the National Endowment for the Arts, the first Chinese American to receive this honor.

Western symphonic orchestras and choral singing

Since the late nineteenth century, Western musical instruments and repertoire have become a vital component of Chinese musical life. The arrival in America of urban and cosmopolitan middle-class Chinese immigrants in the 1960s brought to the West the Chinese tradition of cultivating Western classical music as well as a new hybrid Chinese-Western repertoire. Two new forms of music making emerged among the Chinese Americans: symphonic orchestras for Chinese American youths, and choruses consisting of adults and/or children.

The training for and performances of the symphonic orchestras for Chinese American youths are closely tied to the Western art music tradition; their repertoires comprise mostly Western classical music, but occasionally Chinese pieces are also performed. Quite a number of choruses are affiliated with the weekend Chinese-language schools. Chinese compositions take a prominent place in the repertoire, which also includes Western classical music, religious hymns, and sacred compositions. In addition, recitals are given by Chinese American instrumental or vocal soloists. Many of

FIGURE 3   Sheung Chi Ng, a well-known *muyu* singer. Photo courtesy Asian American Arts Centre.

these musicians frequently include some Chinese compositions in their programs of mainly Western classical music.

New music

Beginning in the mid-1980s, a group of young Chinese composers, mostly from the People's Republic and directly involved in the controversial experimental movement termed *xin chao* 'new tide' in the early 1980s, came to the United States and stirred up an intense interest in Chinese new music within the American new music circle. These composers include Chen Yi (F.), Bright Sheng, Tan Dun, and Zhou Long, among others.

Inspired by the music of twentieth-century Western composers and a deeper and more comprehensive understanding of Chinese culture, these composers have explored new textures, timbres, gestures, and techniques in their orchestral and dramatic works for conventional Western symphonic orchestras or operas, chamber music for various new music ensembles, experimental works for nonconventional instruments, music for Chinese instruments, and compositions for mixed ensembles of both Chinese and Western instruments. Synthesis at different levels exists: use of tone-rows, pitch-class sets, and serialism are blended into the rhythmic patterns of Peking opera percussion and into chant tones of ritualistic ceremonies or are merged with ancient Chinese philosophical thoughts.

Chinese popular music

Popular music from Taiwan, Hong Kong, and China, with its hybrid styles of Chinese, Japanese, and Western elements, is everywhere present in the lives of Chinese Americans. It is sold on cassettes, videotapes, records, and compact discs, played on Chinese-language radio and television stations, and staged frequently by visiting pop stars at Las Vegas and Atlantic City casinos. Since 1995, a Chinese American television station, World Television based in New York, started to sponsor an annual "All-America Singing Contest" (pop songs) for Chinese Americans (figure 4).

Beginning in the late 1980s, a great number of Chinese Americans have been attracted to karaoke, or singing along with prerecorded musical accompaniments, which can be heard in many Chinese restaurants, nightclubs, and karaoke bars or KTV (Karaoke TV). It is also a popular entertainment at Chinese American gatherings, reunions, parties, and homes. Various karaoke contests have been organized, and the number of karaoke clubs is increasing (Lum 1996). Karaoke videotapes include songs of different periods and styles in Mandarin, Cantonese, and English [see JAPANESE MUSIC, p. 967; KOREAN MUSIC, p. 975].

Asian American jazz

Asian American jazz is an American-born music genre, and Chinese American musicians have played a major role in its twenty-year history. Since the beginning of the twentieth century, Chinese Americans have been involved in American popular music, including barbershop, minstrel, vaudeville, jazz, and show music, as well as more recent folk song, rock opera, and rap. San Francisco's Chinatown nightclub Forbidden City (1938–1961) was a well-known place for American popular music and dance. But Asian American jazz is the most influential of these forms of music and has attained the highest achievement. It also is the most lasting and politicized music production in defense of the ideologies of the Asian American movement that is rooted in the civil rights movement.

Through their music, Asian American jazz musicians have been searching for a new cultural identity that would empower them to be oppositional to the dominant culture and at the same time grant them the possibility of becoming part of the American social fabric. The connection with the African American musical community has

FIGURE 4   A finalist at the 2000 "All-America Singing Contest." Photo by Cheng-Hui Hsu. Photo courtesy the *World Journal.*

FIGURE 5   Fred Ho. Photo by Jack Mitchell. Photo courtesy Fred Ho.

been strongly emphasized. Since 1981, the Asian American Jazz Festival (AAJF) has been held annually in San Francisco. In 1987, the independent AsianImprov Records (AIR) was founded in the Bay Area. The first Asian American Jazz Festival in Chicago was inaugurated in November 1996. And in September 1997, the Boston Asian American Creative Music Festival took place, the first of its kind on the East Coast.

New York–based baritone saxophonist Fred Wei-han Ho (figure 5) and San Francisco–based pianist Jon Jang, both American-born Chinese, are two highly regarded Asian American jazz musicians ◉-21. Ho calls his music "an Afro-Asian new American multicultural music" or "new Chinese American multicultural music" (Ho 1995). Compositions by Ho and Jang are committed to a broad spectrum of social and political concerns, ranging from the Asian immigrant experience in America, to oriental stereotyped Chinese images, to progressive politics and panethnic coalitions [see NEW AND EXPERIMENTAL GENRES, p. 334]. Ho and Jang have collaborated frequently with Chinese immigrant musicians in their compositions and performances, employing Chinese instruments, musical elements, and language and relating their compositions to Chinese classical literature and contemporary events. Both Ho and Jang have produced several compact discs.

REFERENCES

Alley, Rewi. 1989 [1984]. *Peking Opera.* Beijing: New World Press.

Anonymous. 1891. "They Saw a Chinese Play." *The New York Times,* 13 February, 1.

———. 1893. "A Chinese 'Sacred Concert.'" *The New York Times,* 27 March, 8.

———. 1896. "Chu Fong and His Play." *The New York Times,* 20 March, 6.

Barth, Gunther. 1964. *Bitter Strength: A History of the Chinese in the United States, 1850–1870.* Cambridge, Mass.: Harvard University Press.

Beck, Louis J. 1898. *New York's Chinatown.* New York: Bohemia.

Chang, Peter. 1991. "Tan Dun's String Quartet 'Feng-Ya-Song': Some Ideological Issues." *Asian Music* 22(2):127–158.

Chen, Hsiang-shui. 1992. *Chinatown No More: Taiwan Immigrants in Contemporary New York.* Ithaca, N.Y.: Cornell University Press.

Chen, Jack. 1980. *The Chinese of America.* New York: Harper and Row.

Chen, Yuanzhu, ed. 1969 [1929]. *Taishan Geyao Ji* (A Collection of Taishan Folk Songs). Taipei, Taiwan: Folklore Books.

Chinese Students in the United States, 1948–55. 1956. New York: Committee on Educational Interchange Policy.

Chinn, Thomas W., ed. 1969. *A History of the Chinese in California: A Syllabus.* San Francisco: Chinese Historical Society of America.

———. 1989. *Bridging the Pacific: San Francisco Chinatown and Its People.* San Francisco: Chinese Historical Society of America.

Coolidge, Mary Roberts. 1909. *Chinese Immigration.* New York: Henry Holt.

Cosdon, Mark. 1995. "'Introducing Occidentals to an Exotic Art': Mei Lanfang in New York." *Asian Theatre Journal* 12(1):175–189.

Espiritu, Yen Le. 1992. *Asian American Panethnicity: Bridges, Institutions and Identities.* Philadelphia: Temple University Press.

Fong, Timothy P. 1994. *The First Suburban Chinatown: The Remaking of Monterey Park, California.* Philadelphia: Temple University Press.

Friedlander, Paul David. 1990. "Rocking the Yangtze: Impressions of Chinese Popular Music and Technology." *Popular Music and Society* 14(1):63–74.

Gray, Judith. 1979. "Additional Comments Regarding Chinese Orchestras in the United States." *Asian Music* 11(1):41–43.

Han, Kuo-Huang. 1979. "The Modern Chinese Orchestra." *Asian Music* 11(1):1–40.

Ho, Fred Wei-han. 1995. "'Jazz,' Kreolization and Revolutionary Music for the 21st Century." In *Sounding Off! Music as Subversion/Resistance/Revolution,* ed. Ron Sakolsky and Fred Wei-han Ho, 133–143. Brooklyn, N.Y.: Autonomedia.

Hoe, Ban Seng. 1989. *Beyond the Golden Mountain: Chinese Cultural Traditions in Canada.* Canada: Canadian Museum of Civilization.

Hom, Marlon K. 1987. *Songs of Gold Mountain: Cantonese Rhymes from San Francisco Chinatown.* Berkeley: University of California Press.

Horton, John. 1992. "The Politics of Diversity in Monterey Park, California." In *Structuring Diversity: Ethnographic Perspectives on the New Immigration,* ed. Louise Lamphere, 215–245. Chicago: University of Chicago Press.

Huang, Jinpei, and Alan R. Thrasher. 1993. "Cantonese Music Societies of Vancouver: A Social and Historical Survey." *Canadian Folk Music Journal* 21:31–39.

Huang, Shaorong. 1991. "Chinese Traditional Festivals." *Journal of Popular Culture* 25(3):163–180.

Kouwenhoven, Frank. 1990. "Mainland China's New Music (1)—Out of the Desert." *CHIME* 2:58–93.

———. 1991. "Mainland China's New Music (2)—Madly Singing in the Mountains." *CHIME* 3:42–75.

———. 1992. "Mainland China's New Music (3)—The Age of Pluralism." *CHIME* 5:76–134.

Kraus, Richard Curt. 1989. *Pianos and Politics in China: Middle-Class Ambitions and the Struggle over Western Music.* New York: Oxford University Press.

Kung, S. W. (Shien-woo). 1962. *Chinese in American Life: Some Aspects of Their History, Status, Problems, and Contributions.* Seattle: University of Washington Press.

Kung, Samuel Shi-shin. 1955. "Personal and Professional Problems of Chinese Students and Former Students in the New York Metropolitan Area: A Report of a Type C Project." Ph.D. dissertation, Columbia University.

Kwok, Theodore J. 1992. "A View of Chinese Music in Hawaii." *ACMR Newsletter* 5(2):20–26.

Kwong, Peter. 1987. *The New Chinatown.* New York: Hill and Wang.

Lai, Him Mark, Genny Lim, and Judy Yung. 1991 [1980]. *Island: Poetry and History of Chinese Immigrants on Angel Island, 1910–1940.* Seattle: University of Washington Press.

Lee, Rose Hum. 1958. "The Stranded Chinese in the United States." *Phylon* 19(2):180–194.

———. 1960. *The Chinese in the United States of America.* Hong Kong: Hong Kong University Press.

Leung, Pui-Chee. 1978. *Wooden-Fish Books: Critical Essays and an Annotated Catalogue Based on the Collections in the University of Hong Kong.* Hong Kong: University of Hong Kong, Centre of Asian Studies.

Li, Guangming. 1994. "Music in the Chinese Community of Los Angeles: An Overview." In *Musical Aesthetics and Multiculturalism in Los Angeles,* ed. Steven Loza, 105–127. Selected Reports in Ethnomusicology 10. Los Angeles: University of California.

Lowe, Lisa. 1996. *Immigrant Acts: On Asian American Cultural Politics.* Durham, N.C.: Duke University Press.

Lum, Casey Man Kong. 1996. *In Search of a Voice: Karaoke and the Construction of Identity in Chinese America.* Mahwah, N.J.: Lawrence Erlbaum Associates.

Lyman, Stanford M. 1974. *Chinese Americans.* New York: Random House.

MacNair, Harley F. 1925. *The Chinese Abroad: Their Position and Protection.* Shanghai, China: The Commercial Press.

Mangiafico, Luciano. 1988. *Contemporary American Immigrants: Patterns of Filipino, Korean, and Chinese Settlement in the United States.* New York: Praeger.

Mark, Diane Mei Lin, and Ginger Chih. 1982. *A Place Called Chinese America.* Dubuque, Iowa: Kendall/Hunt.

McCunn, Ruthanne Lum. 1988. *Chinese American Portraits: Personal Histories 1828–1988.* San Francisco: Chronicle Books.

Okihiro, Gary Y. 1994. *Margins and Mainstreams: Asians in American History and Culture.* Seattle: University of Washington Press.

Ong, Aihwa. 1993. "On the Edge of Empires: Flexible Citizenship among Chinese in Diaspora." *Positions* 1(3):745–778.

———. 1995. "Women Out of China: Traveling Tales and Traveling Theories in Postcolonial Feminism." In *Women Writing Culture,* ed. Ruth Behar and Deborah A. Gordon, 350–372. Berkeley: University of California Press.

Riddle, Ronald. 1983. *Flying Dragons, Flowing Streams: Music in the Life of San Francisco's Chinese.* Westport, Conn.: Greenwood Press.

Riggs, Fred W. 1950. *Pressures on Congress.* New York: King's Crown Press.

Siu, Paul. 1952. "The Sojourner." *American Journal of Sociology* 58(1):34–44.

Smith, Barbara B. 1975. "Chinese Music in Hawaii." *Asian Music* 6(1–2):225–230.

Smith, Miyoshi. 1995 [1992]. "Music Guerrilla: An Interview with Fred Wei-han Ho." In *Sounding Off! Music as Subversion/Resistance/Revolution,* ed. Ron Sakolsky and Fred Wei-han Ho, 155–160. Brooklyn, N.Y.: Autonomedia.

Stock, Jonathan. 1996. *Musical Creativity in Twentieth-Century China: Abing, His Music, and Its Changing Meanings.* Rochester, N.Y.: University of Rochester Press.

Sung, Betty Lee. 1967. *Mountain of Gold: The Story of the Chinese in America.* New York: Macmillan.

———. 1980. "Polarity in the Makeup of Chinese Immigrants." In *Sourcebook on the New Immigration: Implications for the United States and the International Community,* ed. Roy Simón Bryce-Laporte, 37–49. New Brunswick, N.J.: Transaction Books.

Tchen, John Kuo Wei. 1992. "New York Before Chinatown: Orientalism, Identity Formation, and Political Culture in the American Metropolis, 1784–1882." Ph.D. dissertation, New York University.

Thompson, Richard H. 1980. "From Kinship to Class: A New Model of Urban Overseas Chinese Social Organization." *Urban Anthropology* 9(3):265–294.

Tsai, Shin-shan Henry. 1986. *The Chinese Experience in America.* Bloomington: Indiana University Press.

Tsao, Pen-Yeh. 1989. "Structural Elements in the Music of Chinese Story-Telling." *Asian Music* 20(2):129–151.

Wang, Anguo. 1989. "A Review of the 'New Tide' in China's Musical Compositions." *Musicology in China* 1:106–126.

Wang, L. Ling-chi. 1994 [1991]. "Roots and the Changing Identity of the Chinese in the United States." In *The Living Tree: The Changing Meaning of Being Chinese Today,* ed. Tu Wei-ming, 185–212. Stanford, Calif.: Stanford University Press.

———. 1995. "The Structure of Dual Domination: Toward a Paradigm for the Study of the Chinese Diaspora in the United States." *Amerasia Journal* 21(1–2):149–169.

Wei, William. 1993. *The Asian American Movement.* Philadelphia: Temple University Press.

Whitney, James A. 1970 [1880]. *The Chinese and the Chinese Question.* San Francisco: R and E Research Associates.

Witzleben, Lawrence. 1995. *"Silk & Bamboo" Music in Shanghai: The Jiangnan Sizhu Instrumental Ensemble Tradition.* Kent, Ohio: Kent State University Press.

Wong, Bernard P. 1982. *Chinatown: Economic Adaptation and Ethnic Identity of the Chinese.* New York: Holt, Rinehart and Winston.

———. 1987. "The Chinese: New Immigrants in New York's Chinatown." In *New Immigrants in New York,* ed. Nancy Foner, 243–271, New York: Columbia University Press.

Wong, Isabel K. F. 1985. "The Many Roles of Peking Opera in San Francisco in the 1980s." In *The Asian Musician in North America,* ed. Nazir Jairazbhoy, 173–188. Selected Reports in Ethnomusicology 6. Los Angeles: University of California.

Wong, Sau-ling C. 1995. "Denationalization Reconsidered: Asian American Cultural Criticism at a Theoretical Crossroads." *Amerasia Journal* 21(1–2):1–27.

Yuan, D. Y. 1963. "Voluntary Segregation: A Study of New York Chinatown." *Phylon* 24(3):255–265.

Yung, Bell. 1989. *Cantonese Opera: Performance as Creative Process.* Cambridge: Cambridge University Press.

Zhang, Wei Hua. 1994. "The Musical Activities of the Chinese American Communities in the San Francisco Bay Area: A Social and Cultural Study." Ph.D. dissertation, University of California at Berkeley.

Zheng, Su. 1990. "Music and Migration: Chinese Traditional Music in New York City." *The World of Music* 32(3):48–67.

———. 1993a. "Immigrant Music and Transnational Discourse: Chinese American Music Culture in New York City." Ph.D. dissertation, Wesleyan University.

———. 1993b. "From Toisan to New York: *Mukyu* Songs in Folk Tradition." *CHINOPERL Papers* 16:165–205.

———. 1994. "Music Making in Cultural Displacement: The Chinese-American Odyssey." *Diaspora* 3(3):273–288.

———. 2001. *Claiming Diaspora: Music, Transnationalism, and Cultural Politics in Asian/Chinese America.* Oxford: Oxford University Press.

Zhou, Min. 1992. *Chinatown: The Socioeconomic Potential of an Urban Enclave.* Philadelphia: Temple University Press.

Zo, Kil Young. 1971. "Chinese Emigration into the United States, 1850–1880." Ph.D. dissertation, Columbia University.

Japanese Music
Susan M. Asai

Arriving on American Shores
Issei: **Japanese Music in a Foreign Land**
Nisei: **The Changing Musical Tide**
Sansei: **The Emergence of a Transculturated Music**

American musicians of Japanese descent perform and compose mainstream styles of music, such as European classical music, jazz, and assorted popular and fusion styles. In addition, they create music that expresses their cultural heritage and social or political views. This music incorporates elements of traditional Japanese music into Western genres, reinterprets aspects of Japanese music, or employs song texts that make statements about being Japanese American in this country. Third-generation Japanese Americans have been the most active and experimental in creating such music [see POLYNESIAN MUSIC, p. 1047; ASIAN MUSIC, p. 1215].

ARRIVING ON AMERICAN SHORES

In the United States, Japanese immigration before 1890 was insignificant, with the total population of this ethnic group on the American mainland and in Hawai'i barely exceeding two thousand. These low numbers reflect the Japanese government's opposition to allowing laborers to emigrate. Also, Japan was politically, socially, and economically isolated from the rest of the world during the Tokugawa period (1603–1867), a ploy used by shogun Ieyasu Tokugawa and his family to maintain their fragile power over all of Japan. Tokugawa prohibited foreign travel by Japanese, creating an insulated perspective that was not easily overcome after Japan was forced to open its doors to the world in 1868.

A dramatic increase in the Japanese population in the United States between 1890 (2,039) and 1900 (24,326) resulted from the legalization of labor emigration after 1884, when Hawaiian sugar planters coerced the Japanese government into changing their policy. Japanese immigrants continued to arrive in great numbers until 1907–1908. During the decade between 1900 and 1910, a total of 132,706 Japanese immigrants were admitted: 54,839 came to the mainland, 77,777 arrived in Hawai'i; the remaining 90 settled in Alaska.

These numbers dwindled when the anti-Asian agitation (first against the Chinese, then the Japanese) of the Pacific Coast states forced President Theodore Roosevelt to declare the proclamation of 1907, which forbade Japanese migration from Hawai'i, Canada, and Mexico to the U.S. mainland. In addition, a gentlemen's agreement between Japan and the United States, which went into effect in 1908, directly stopped further labor immigration from Japan. A drop in the numbers from 1908 to 1910 of

San Francisco was home to the Japanese Harmonica Band, which had a diverse repertoire that ranged from European classical and semiclassical pieces to arrangements of folk and popular Japanese songs (*kayokyoku*).

2,798 Japanese immigrants admitted reflects their diminished entry as a result of the immigration restrictions. The 1910 U.S. Census shows a decrease in the number of Japanese immigrants but an increase in the number of U.S.-born Japanese Americans, called *nisei* 'second generation'.

In 1921, continuing anti-Asian phobia on the West Coast forced the Japanese to end female emigration to the United States ('picture brides' for the many single male laborers) that had been allowable until this time even under the immigration restrictions of 1907 and 1908. This further restriction added to the prejudice many Japanese faced in this country, and there was a rise in the number of immigrants who returned to Japan between 1921 and 1924. Many Japanese immigrants initially came as sojourners, but large numbers ended up remaining here. During this three-year period, however, larger numbers felt compelled to return to Japan, and the immigrant population decreased by 1,210 people. The year 1924 marks a clear cutoff point for arriving *issei* 'first generation'. The United States Congress successfully legislated the Immigration Act of 1924, an exclusion law that replaced the 1908 gentlemen's agreement and singled out the Japanese.

It wasn't until the 1950s that Japanese began to arrive on American soil again. The Walter-McCarran Immigration and Naturalization Act of 1952 repealed the Immigration Act of 1924, and an immigration quota was established for Japanese and other Asian immigrants. The act also eradicated the use of race as a criterion for naturalization. The quota numbers were rather insignificant compared to the waves of immigration at the start of the twentieth century. Instead, the second-, third-, and fourth-generation offspring of these early emigrés provide a continuing history of the Japanese on the American mainland.

ISSEI: JAPANESE MUSIC IN A FOREIGN LAND

Issei, the first generation of Japanese to arrive on American shores, beginning in the 1890s and lasting until 1924, retained their language, customs, and cultural traditions as a part of their survival in the United States. Music, art, and poetry cultivated a Japanese sensibility and expressed the beauty and power of the culture they brought with them. Retention of these art forms was particularly valuable and therapeutic in countering the prejudice and inhospitable attitude of many Americans toward this immigrant population.

Music making activities of *issei* have been best documented in the urban centers of California. San Francisco and Los Angeles served as cultural hubs for Japanese immigrants, and a range of music taught in San Francisco in 1914 included *koto* 'thirteen-string zither', *shamisen* 'three-string plucked lute', *shakuhachi* 'end-blown bamboo flute, *yōkyoku* 'music for *nō* theater', and Satsuma *biwa* 'four-string plucked lute'. Also, Japanese pop music bands, such as the Teikoku Band, were active between 1877 and 1910 in San Francisco, where many *issei* first settled.

In Los Angeles, the Japanese newspaper *Rafu Shimpo* wrote about musical activities in and around the city from 1926 on. Reports of traditional Japanese music performances mention *sankyoku* 'chamber music featuring *koto, shamisen,* and *shakuhachi*', *jōruri* 'narrative *shamisen* music for puppet theater', *shigin* 'Chinese poems set to music', *nagauta* 'narrative songs for *kabuki* theater', *hauta* 'a genre of short *shamisen*-accompanied songs', and *naniwa-bushi* 'popular-style narrative *shamisen* music'.

Little is known about *issei* music making activities in rural areas, but the labor-intensive nature of agricultural work surely limited these activities. In 1909, about two-thirds of all *issei* immigrants worked within the agricultural industry in California, Hawai'i, Washington, Colorado, Utah, Oregon, Idaho, and Montana. Music was probably practiced and performed during slack seasons of the agricultural calendar, as was customary in Japan. There is some evidence that traditional Japanese music, both classical and folk, prevailed, serving as a connection for immigrants to their homeland (Hosokawa 1969:74).

Japan's exposure to Western music occurred soon after the country was forced to open its doors to the world by Commodore Matthew Perry and his fleet in 1854 and continued into the Taisho period (1912–1921). A small number of immigrants preferred European classical music and supported community and visiting artist concerts in urban centers featuring violin and piano music, opera, and art songs. John Yamauchi (1994), a *nisei* whose *issei* father was an opera singer, points out that audiences for this music consisted of the more progressive and educated classes of Japanese immigrants.

Japanese gospel societies (*fukuinkai*), as noted by Seizo Oka (1987) of the Japanese History Archives in San Francisco, were other Western-oriented musical groups that were formed at this time. These Christian hymn-singing groups were pro-Western organizations that brought together young intellectuals and encouraged assimilation into American society.

NISEI: THE CHANGING MUSICAL TIDE

The second generation of Japanese Americans *(nisei)* were born in the United States between 1910 and 1940. The musical preferences of this generation of American-born citizens began to shift as they attempted to balance Japanese family values and codes of behavior at home with democratic ideals, individualism, and other socially progressive ideas that they learned in school and experienced in American society. *Nisei* led culturally split lives, and their music making increasingly reflected this dual identity.

True to their Japanese heritage, many *nisei* continued to pursue traditional music passed on to them by *issei*—music of the *koto*, *shamisen*, and *biwa* as well as *utai* 'nō theater songs', *shigin*, and music for *kabuki* theater. The anti-Japanese hysteria of World War II and the internment of Japanese Americans during this armed conflict hurried the demise of any interest in traditional Japanese music by many *nisei*, as one's Japanese heritage often became a source of shame rather than pride.

Nisei music making encompassed a variety of musical styles that ranged from hymn singing by choirs, European classical music, Hawaiian music (popular music brought by that portion of the Japanese population that moved to California after being born and raised in Hawai'i), and musical novelties such as musical saw and mouth harp. European classical music was increasingly performed at concerts held by music societies in urban areas and at musical soirées given in the homes of music teachers or classical music lovers. Additional performances featured Boy Scout bands or drum and bugle corps and social club choruses or glee clubs that sang American folk or popular songs. Further, San Francisco was home to the Japanese Harmonica Band, which had a diverse repertoire that ranged from European classical and semiclassical pieces to arrangements of folk and popular Japanese songs (*kayokyoku*). The increased frequency of Western performances is symptomatic of the growing American identity of *nisei*.

American popular music attracted the attention of *nisei* musicians in the 1930s and 1940s. Among Japanese Americans, a growing number of young people wanted to play the big band music of Count Basie, Tommy Dorsey, and Benny Goodman.

Semiprofessional jazz orchestras, such as the Sho-Tokyans 'Lil Tokyans' in Los Angeles and the Cathayans in San Francisco, performed with a number of *nisei* and other Asian American musicians at dances and talent shows throughout California.

The unwarranted internment of 110,000 Americans of Japanese descent during World War II created unusual opportunities for music making. Music was an important activity for internees as they attempted to normalize their lives in concentration camps located in desolate parts of the United States. Music required for variety and talent shows, Christmas concerts, and other events continued, as well as music lessons, songfests, and dance bands for social dances. In fact, each of the ten concentration camps formed its own dance bands. The band Manzanar Jive Bombers of the Manzanar Relocation Camp, located in northern California, was renowned.

Traditional Japanese music was also part of the musical landscape of the camps: folk music for summer O-Bon festivals, *koto, shamisen,* and *shakuhachi* music, Japanese pop songs, *naniwa-bushi,* and music for Japanese dramas. It was primarily *issei* who retained these traditions as a way to pass the time and seek comfort in their difficult living circumstances as internees.

SANSEI: THE EMERGENCE OF A TRANSCULTURATED MUSIC

Sansei, members of the third generation who by the 1960s were entering high school and college, are diverse in their musical tastes and activities. Overall, their music making has few boundaries; many are classically trained musicians and composers in the European tradition, whereas others play rock, pop, Latin, jazz, and even traditional Irish music. However, a small number play traditional Japanese music, mostly *koto, shamisen,* and *shakuhachi,* as a way to explore or maintain their cultural connection to Japan. Of primary interest here, however, is the creation of a Japanese American sound and the musical genres that best express this transculturated music.

Sansei are the creative force in shaping Japanese American music today. Japanese American music refers to music that is for the most part composed and performed by Japanese Americans who synthesize Japanese music with Western music by incorporating Japanese instruments and their playing styles, scales, melodies, rhythms, timbres, or aesthetic concepts borrowed from or suggestive of traditional Japanese music. *Sansei* create this new transcultural music by reconciling and giving credence to their Japanese heritage; it is part of their search for self, particularly in a society where many of this ethnicity still feel marginalized.

The *sansei's* musical quest to experiment with and create music that fulfills their ethnic well-being initially began with the Asian American movement of the 1970s. This movement, inspired by the civil rights and Black Power movements, formed as Asian Americans united in building and expressing their sociopolitical views concerning education and issues of identity and empowerment. Asian American artists involved in the movement turned toward their own history and experience, and in the late 1960s and 1970s, folk music in the social commentary style of Bob Dylan served to express the struggles and prejudices faced by Asians in the United States. Two groups that traveled to college campuses and communities to express such views were Joanne, Chris, and Charlie (New York City) and Yokohama California (San Francisco).

TRACK 22

The most pervasive Japanese American music genre to emerge in the late twentieth century was *taiko* drumming (figures 1 and 2). The foundation for this music was initially based on o-Suwa *daiko,* Chichibu *yataibayashi,* and Buddhist *uchiwa daiko,* representing various drumming traditions found in Japan. Kinnara Taiko, an ensemble affiliated with the Senshin Buddhist Church in Los Angeles, inaugurated this style of group drumming more than twenty-five years ago as a way to attract *sansei* and now *yonsei* 'fourth-generation Japanese Americans' to the Buddhist faith. *Taiko* drumming exemplifies the integration of Japanese and American musics, with the folk *taiko* tradition representing Japan and various compositional and rhythmic innovations

FIGURE I   Side view of a *taiko* ensemble at the Santa Barbara Japanese O-Bon Festival, August 1981. The body stance and stylized drumming movements are an important feature of the *taiko* tradition. Photo by Susan M. Asai.

representing America. Currently more than one hundred *taiko* groups exist throughout the United States in locations as diverse as New York, Seattle, Denver, Chicago, Ogden (Utah), White River (Washington), Boston, and Bennington (Vermont). Performance contexts for *taiko* drumming include weddings, Asian cultural festivals, Japanese festivals, anniversary celebrations of Japanese American organizations, and diversity programming in public schools and on college campuses.

Jazz-based music is a rich avenue for many *sansei* composer-musicians in expressing their ethnic identity or sociopolitical views. Jazz appeals to those who take their cue from African American culture and music. According to Paul Yamazaki, a *sansei* formerly active in the Asian American Creative Music scene in San Francisco, composers choose to write in a jazz-based idiom because African American music is an "almost perfectly balanced dialectic between the individual and the collective. There is a very unique tension there, where neither the individual is subsumed underneath the collective, nor is it a totally individual act" (Auerbach 1985:37). This dialectic reinforces the social purpose and strong communal ties that certain *sansei* musicians assert. Jazz is considered to be America's greatest cultural contribution, a musical style indigenous to

FIGURE 2   Kinnara Taiko ensemble performing at the Santa Barbara Japanese O-Bon Festival, August 1981. Note the three sizes of drums, which are standard for most *taiko* groups. Photo by Susan M. Asai.

Another important piece is New York–based jazz pianist and composer Sumi Tonooka's *Out from the Silence,* inspired by her mother's own internment experience. The National Japanese American Citizens League commissioned Tonooka to write this piece.

this country and thus an expression of being an American. Yamazaki continues, "[T]he structure and spirit of jazz allows a great deal of openness. All of the open elements of the music [jazz] make it conducive for other people taking their own indigenous experiences into this music and creating more particular forms."

There are a number of jazz-based compositions by *sansei* composers that are an important part of the Japanese American music repertoire. The compositions address the conflict many *sansei* feel about the internment of members of their families and of all Japanese Americans and the race and war hysteria that created the need for such drastic measures. This music serves as a form of reconciliation for those embittered by the injustice of the internment that caused so much suffering and humiliation.

Glenn Horiuchi, a pianist and Japanese *shamisen* player, wrote *Poston Sonata* in response to his father's and other family members' testimony about the hardships they endured in the camps. Inclusion of the *shamisen* as a solo instrument, Japanese scales in slightly modified form, and *taiko* drum rhythms give Horiuchi's modern jazz-based composition a unique quality. *Poston Sonata,* named after the internment camp in Arizona where Japanese American residents of San Diego were interned (including Horiuchi's family), is written for *shamisen,* alto sax, tenor sax, bass clarinet, bass, percussion, and piano.

Another important piece is New York–based jazz pianist and composer Sumi Tonooka's *Out from the Silence,* inspired by her mother's own internment experience. The National Japanese American Citizens League commissioned Tonooka to write this piece. *Out from the Silence* is a suite for *koto, shakuhachi,* violin, clarinet, trumpet, tenor sax, trombone, vibes, rhythm section, and voice. The progression of the three movements musically represents the sociocultural evolution of each succeeding generation of Japanese Americans—*issei, nisei,* and *sansei.*

Percussionist and composer Anthony Brown has also written a piece, *E.O. 9066* (*Truth Be Told*), commemorating the indomitable spirit of Japanese Americans imprisoned during World War II. The first movement, dedicated to the *issei,* employs an arrangement of an eleventh-century *gagaku* 'music of the Imperial Japanese court' composition, *Ichikotsu-cho,* as well as the use of *taiko, koto, shakuhachi, takebue* 'bamboo transverse flute', and an assortment of Japanese folk percussion.

San Francisco is an important center for a circle of musician-composers who collectively form the Asian American Creative Music scene. Major composers in this scene include Mark Izu (bass), Vijay Iyer (piano and violin), Jon Jang (piano), Miya Masaoka (piano and *koto*), and Francis Wong (saxophone, clarinet, flute). These composers write jazz-based, contemporary, or avant-garde music. AsianImprov Arts, an umbrella organization that supports and promotes the experimental efforts of Asian American musician-composers, includes an independent recording company (AsianImprov Records) that produces recordings of Asian American musicians throughout the United States.

The Los Angeles–based group Hiroshima, which formed in the 1970s in tandem with the Asian American Movement, is notable within the jazz/rhythm and blues/pop fusion style. One of the first bands to incorporate the *koto, taiko,* and *shakuhachi,* Hiroshima provided the impetus for many bands looking for ways to give voice to their Asian heritage in an innovative and appealing style. The support of the Japanese American community in southern California made it possible for Hiroshima to launch its music, and now its members enjoy national recognition.

Rap music is also an effective political voice for *sansei* in commenting on the internment camps of World War II. Key Kool and his deejay, Rhettmatic, are part of the underground rap scene in Los Angeles, and their song "Reconcentrated" is a pointed commentary on the unmerited and unlawful treatment of Japanese Americans who endured the concentration camps euphemistically referred to as internment camps. This song serves to vent *sansei* anger concerning the humiliation and hardship of their families and to question the legality of the American government in imprisoning its own citizens without just cause.

Within the North Atlantic states on the East Coast, the Japanese American population is thin and spread out. *Taiko* drumming groups in New York (Soh Daiko) and Boston (Odaiko New England) stand out as particularly Japanese American, although many of the members of these ensembles are increasingly non-Japanese. Sumi Tonooka's big band jazz compositions *Out from the Silence* and *Taiko Jazz Project* also distinguish themselves as distinctly Japanese American. Another band that incorporates aspects of traditional Japanese music is the Far East Side Band, which seamlessly fuses jazz, ambient, and traditional Chinese, Japanese, and Korean music. Other than this, music is heard as one component of multimedia productions such as *Testimony: Japanese American Voices of Liberation,* stories of Japanese Americans interned during World War II through music, poetry, and movement; *In Their Shoes,* which uses music, dance, words, and images to speak of Japanese American families' World War II experiences; and *Bamboo and Barbed Wire,* a piece by Killer Geishas A Go-Go, an all-Asian women's writing and performing arts group. It is clear by these pieces and many others that *sansei* have a desire to reconcile the Japanese American past.

New York City is the center for Japanese American and, in general, Asian American music on the East Coast. In addition to performances in concert halls and schools and at community events, the annual Asian Pacific American Heritage Festival (presented by the City of New York), and the annual O-Bon Dance Festival, sponsored by the New York Buddhist Church, provide continuing and stable contexts for Japanese American music groups.

REFERENCES

Aoki, Tatsu. 1994. *Kioto.* AsianImprov Records AIR 0017. Compact disc.

Asai, Susan. 1985. "*Itōraku:* A Buddhist Tradition of Performing Arts and the Development of *Taiko* Drumming in the United States." In *Asian Music in North America,* ed. Nazir A. Jairazbhoy and Sue Carole DaVale, 163–172. *Selected Reports in Ethnomusicology* 6. Los Angeles: University of California.

———. 1991. "The Jazz Connection in Asian American Music." *Coda* 238 (July–August).

———. 1995. "Transformations of Tradition: Three Generations of Japanese American Music Making." *The Musical Quarterly* 79(1).

———. 1997. "*Sansei* Voices in the Community: Japanese American Musicians in California." In *Musics of Multicultural America,* 257–285. New York: Schirmer Books.

Asian American Arts Dialogue. 1995. New York: Asian American Arts Alliance.

Auerbach, Brian. 1985. "Asian American Jazz: An Oral History with Paul Yamazaki." *Options* (March–April).

Endo, Kenny. *Taiko* Ensemble. 1994. *Eternal Energy.* AsianImprov Records AIR 0021. Compact disc.

Hiroshima. 1979. *Hiroshima.* Arista Records AB 4252. LP disk.

———.1979/1980. *Ongaku.* Arista Records ARCD 8437. Compact disc.

———. 1980. *Odori.* Arista Records AL 9541. LP.

Horiuchi, Glenn. 1989a. *Issei Spirit.* AsianImprov Records. LP disk.

———. 1989b. *Manzanar Voices.* AsianImprov Records AIR 006. LP disk.

Hosokawa, Bill. 1969. *Nisei: The Quiet Americans.* New York: William Morrow.

Ichihashi, Yamato. 1932. *Japanese in the United States: A Critical Study of the Problems and the Japanese Immigrants and Their Children.* Stanford, Calif.: Stanford University Press.

Izu, Mark. 1992. *Circle of Fire.* AsianImprov Records AIR 0009. Compact disc.

Key Kool and Rhettmatic. 1995. *Kozmonautz.* Up Above Records AC-1001. Compact disc.

Korb, Ken. 1993. *Japanese Mysteries.* Toronto: Oasis Productions.

———. 1994. *Flute Traveller.* Toronto: Oasis Productions. Compact disc.

———. 1995. *Behind the Mask.* Toronto: Oasis Productions. Compact disc.

Masaokam, Miya. 1993. *Compositions/Improvisations.* AsianImprov Records AIR 00014. Compact disc.

Miyamoto, Nobuko. 1997. *Nobuko. To All Relations.* Bindu Music BIN 9602-2. Compact disc.

Murasaki Ensemble. 1994. *Niji.* A Murasaki Production. TME 8994. Compact disc.

Oka, Seizo. 1987. Interview by author. San Francisco, California, 21 July.

Sounds Like 1996: Music by Asian American Artists. 1996. AsianImprov Records IEL 0002. Compact disc.

Takaki, Ronald. 1998. *Strangers from a Different Shore: A History of Asian Americans,* rev. Back Bay Books. Boston: Little, Brown.

Tonooka, Sumi. 1987. Interview by author. Philadelphia, Pennsylvania, 10 November.

Visions. 1991/1992. *Time to Discover.* Mina Productions MPCD 75. Compact disc.

Watada, T., ed. 1997. *Collected Voices: An Anthology of Asian North American Periodical Writing.* Toronto: HpF Press.

Korean Music
Okon Hwang

Church and Music
Education and Music
Leisure and Music

The history of Korean immigration to the United States can be traced to the end of the nineteenth century, when a very small number of Koreans, mainly ginseng merchants, diplomats, or students, arrived. In 1903, approximately 7,800, mostly young single males, were sent to the United States to work on plantations in Hawai'i. Many of these regarded themselves as sojourners aspiring to wealth and, ultimately, to a return to Korea. This first wave of Korean immigration was abruptly halted in 1905, when the Japanese colonial policy on Korea stopped Korean immigration to the United States. Nevertheless, an additional 1,000 Korean picture-brides and students from Korea entered the United States between 1910 and 1924. However, by the 1940s, the number of Koreans in the United States was still fewer than 10,000. The second wave of Korean immigration lasted from 1950 to 1965. Due to the outbreak of the Korean War (1950–1953), the U.S. Congress enacted a refugee act, and a small number of orphans, war brides, and students—no more than 20,000 at most—were allowed to immigrate to the United States.

Liberalization of the United States immigration laws in 1965 accelerated the pace of Korean immigration. Since the 1970s, annual migration from South Korea to the United States has been somewhere between 20,000 and 30,000. The 1970 U.S. census data show that approximately 70,000 Koreans were living in the United States; by 1990, the number had increased to 800,000. According to a South Korean government document for 1997, approximately two million Koreans—U.S. citizens, permanent residents, or long-term sojourners—were living in the United States. Korean American population is concentrated mostly in the Los Angeles and New York City areas; most of the people are engaged in business or service industries.

Although scholars talk about ethnic solidarity as one of the major assets specifically of Korean Americans, this community is no different from any other immigrant community with respect to its issues of identity. The most defining feature that shapes the musical experience of Korean Americans is generational difference. The first generation of Korean Americans (those who came to the United States as adults after high school or college) are fluent in Korean but not in English and therefore tend to operate within a Korean cultural boundary as if still living in their ancestral land. Children who came with their families or second- and third-generation Korean Americans (those who were born in the United States) are fluent in English but not in Korean, and they

For example, as of 1998, the Manhattan School of Music in New York City had close to 20 percent Korean students in its college division and around 30 percent in the preparatory division.

are more susceptible to the cultural practices of mainstream America. Along with generational differences, the musical experience in the lives of Korean Americans is profoundly influenced by the following three factors: the church, educational patterns, and leisure time.

CHURCH AND MUSIC

Despite the fact that Christianity was introduced to Koreans only about one hundred years ago, Christianity, especially Protestantism, has been one of the major focal points of Korean American communities from the beginning of Korean immigration history. About 70 percent of Korean Americans regularly attend church, and Korean American communities are dotted with Korean churches. Queens, one of the five boroughs of New York City, for example, is densely populated with more than two hundred Korean churches.

Because Christianity is so important to the lives of Korean Americans, church is the most important context for musical performance. Most Korean churches strive to meet the various needs of their congregations, and they usually provide Korean services for the first-generation Korean Americans and English services for those who cannot speak Korean. These regular church services require congregational participation in singing hymns, and for most Korean Americans, the singing of hymns during the church service (Korean lyrics for Korean-speaking congregations) makes up the biggest portion of their regular exposure to music. Almost all Korean churches have choirs composed of amateur singers from the church membership, which provide music for regular services as well as occasional concerts (figure 1). Several times a year, Korean churches also hold special revival services to renew spirituality and to expand their congregational base. These revival services are typically centered on the singing of evangelical hymns, a hybrid of both a hymn style and the ballad style of popular music. Many Korean Americans find comfort in singing these hymns at their churches, as well as in their homes, and cassette tapes containing these hymns are distributed by churches for home listening.

The success of Korean churches in the United States, however, lies in their position as centers for not only religious but social, as well as cultural, functions. Indeed, Korean churches are the center of almost every aspect of Korean American life. Churches help new immigrants find jobs and choose schools. Churches also hold training workshops for individuals to adjust to the new society and provide day care centers and language schools for both non-English- and non-Korean speakers. Furthermore, churches provide all kinds of cultural activities, including musical events, and Korean churches have become one of the most important financial sponsors for professional Korean musicians, who are hired as conductors and accompanists. Besides holding occasional concerts by church choirs, Korean churches also facilitate various other musical activities, such as musical talent shows by Korean American children, concerts and recitals by professional musicians from other geographical areas, and various other musical gatherings, in order to boost fellowship among members. In such occasions,

FIGURE I   St. Andrew Kim Korean Catholic Church choir, Detroit, Michigan, 1995. Photo courtesy Hwa Kwon.

music is not restricted to sacred repertoire but usually consists of various selections from the Western classical musical tradition or sometimes even Korean and Western popular music.

EDUCATION AND MUSIC

Koreans have always taken education very seriously. Historically, education has been the single most important qualification for Koreans to rise in class, and it is not an overstatement that the number one priority for Korean American parents is to provide the best possible education for their children. In fact, many Koreans have immigrated to the United States in order to improve their children's education. Therefore, despite the fact that parents themselves may work long hours in low-paying jobs, they strive to meet their children's educational needs as best as they can.

Western classical music

In the minds of Korean Americans, music, especially Western classical music, is an essential part of a good education. Koreans equate Western classical music with prestige, and almost all parents aspire for their children, especially their daughters, to be able to play at least one Western classical musical instrument either as a hobby or for a possible career. Korean American children usually take lessons from private tutors, neighborhood music schools, or preparatory divisions of music colleges. In fact, many famous music conservatories have a disproportionate number of Korean students, both in the college and in preparatory divisions, and it is often possible to hear Korean spoken in the hallways of these schools. For example, as of 1998, the Manhattan School of Music in New York City had close to 20 percent Korean students in its college division and around 30 percent in the preparatory division. A high representation of Koreans is also seen in many other prestigious music schools located near areas densely populated with Korean Americans.

Their enthusiasm for Western classical music education has produced tangible results. It is now almost routine to see Korean Americans winning regional, national, and international music competitions, and some of them—Sarah Chang (violinist), Kyung Wha Chung (violinist), Myung-Whun Chung (conductor), Hei-Kyung Hong (soprano), to name a few—have even become international attractions.

The presence of Korean traditional music

Korean traditional music has been historically rather limited in popularity among Korean Americans, compared to their appetite for Western classical music. Even in their ancestral land, most Koreans delegated Korean traditional music to specialists, and studying Korean music was not considered to be very fashionable. After their immigration, most first-generation Korean Americans (who were educated in Korea at a time when the content of music education was largely devoted to the study of Western music) did not pay particular attention to Korean traditional music. As a result, this music did not occupy a large portion of the Korean American cultural landscape for a long time. But the presence of traditional music within Korean American communities is slowly rising, and as they gain more economic strength in their new land, Korean Americans have started to look into the uniqueness of their own cultural identity. Learning Korean traditional music has become popular especially with second- and third-generation Korean Americans, who are exploring their identities within the mostly white culture of the United States. The 1988 Seoul Olympics and the tremendous popularity of the music of the *samulnori* (a neo-traditional percussion quartet incorporating various rhythmic materials from folk and shaman ritual musics) in South Korea during the 1980s also provided an impetus for Korean Americans to seek and embrace Korean traditional music with cultural pride. Korean traditional dance and music have slowly started to appear as regular staples of cultural events for Korean

Americans, and more and more parents are now willing to provide an education in traditional instruments and dance for their children at such academies as the Korean Classical Music Institute of America, established in Los Angeles in 1973, and the Korean Traditional Music Institute of New York, established in 1987 (figure 2).

LEISURE AND MUSIC

Because the majority of Korean Americans in the United States are engaged in either small businesses or service industries with long working hours, Korean Americans have been able to enjoy only a limited array of leisure activities, the most prominent of which has been singing. When it comes to entertainment, Koreans in general love to sing in groups, which has eventually led to the creation of *noraebang* 'commercial singing facilities'. *Noraebang* have recently enjoyed an explosive popularity in South Korea; just during the middle of the 1990s, about twenty thousand *noraebang* popped up nationwide, taking in more than two billion dollars in annual revenue. The popularity of *noraebang* has now spread to Korean American communities in the United States.

Depending on the size of an individual singing chamber, *noraebang* can accommodate one to more than twenty people in a group, and most *noraebang* facilities have more than ten such singing chambers. As customers enter a *noraebang*, typically located in a space either above or below the ground floor of a building, a staff member guides them to an available singing chamber equipped with a karaoke machine. Customers specify the length of their stay, and the staff operates a central karaoke control machine to feed visual images and music to the chamber. Customers are given several books of menus containing various musical categories. Each menu—usually consisting of contemporary Korean popular songs, American popular songs, or Korean "oldies"—identifies various songs by code numbers, and customers specify their selections by entering a code number on a remote control. A video monitor then displays the lyrics of the chosen song, along with a picturesque or sentimental visual image usually not related to the content of the song. Meanwhile, speakers in the chamber provide an orchestral accompaniment of the song without a main vocal melody, providing an opportunity for customers to act like star singers (figure 3).

As in South Korea, *noraebang* has become the most important leisure activity for Korean Americans in recent years. People of both sexes and of all ages frequent *noraebang*, and it is now almost a routine for colleagues or friends to head for a *noraebang* for

FIGURE 3   An individual singing chamber at a *noraebang* in New York City. Photo by Okon Hwang, 1998.

entertainment. It is almost unthinkable to picture streets of Korean American communities without the presence of *noraebang* signboards.

The popularity of *noraebang* has also led to the development of karaoke machines for home use. Almost all electronic shops in Korean communities in the United States prominently display home karaoke machines manufactured in South Korea, and they have become one of the hottest-selling items in recent years. As of 1998, about 5,300 songs were available for home karaoke use. As 80 percent of these songs are Korean popular songs produced in South Korea, it is easy to conclude that *noraebang* and home karaoke are highly enjoyed by first-generation Korean Americans fluent in Korean. The second- and the third-generation Korean Americans, however, frequent *noraebang* and home karaoke as well, as they not only provide valuable entertainment opportunities among fellow Korean Americans but also assist in their study of the Korean language.

REFERENCES

Chan, Sucheng. 1991. *Asian Americans: An Interpretive History*. Boston: Twayne.

Dilling, Margaret Walker. 1994. "Kumdori Born Again in Boston: The Life Cycle of Music by a Korean American." *Korean Culture* 15(3):14–25.

Kim, Uichol. 1986. "Canada *ui han'gukin* (Korean in Canada)." *Korea Times Daily*, 28 May, 4.

———. 1994. *Korean Americans*. Princeton, N.J.: Films for the Humanities and Sciences.

Lee, Kwang-Kyu. 1991. *Chaemi Han'gukin* (Koreans in the United States). Seoul: Ilchokak.

Lehrer, Brian. 1988. *The Korean Americans*. New York: Chelsea House.

Min, Pyong Gap. 1998. *Changes and Conflicts: Korean Immigrant Families in New York*. Needham Heights, Mass.: Allyn & Bacon.

Park, Kyeyoung. 1997. *The Korean American Dream: Immigrants and Small Businesses in New York City*. Ithaca, N.Y.: Cornell University Press.

Yu, Eui-Young. 1990. *Korean Community Profile: Life and Consumer Patterns*. Los Angeles: The Korea Times.

Indian and Pakistani Music
Alison Arnold

Performance Contexts
Musical Meaning and Function
Genres and Instruments
Musical Education and Transmission
Indian American Musical Fusions
Music and Identity

The present Asian Indian population, officially estimated at between seven and eight hundred thousand in the United States, is the fastest growing American immigrant population and among the more affluent and well-educated sectors of American society. In contrast to other Asian immigrant populations, Indians and Pakistanis received relatively little scholarly attention prior to the 1980s: writers tended to focus either on the history of Indian immigration or on acculturation and adjustment to new cultural environments. In the past two decades, scholarly interest has increased, with works ranging from broad social and cultural histories and studies of religious traditions to ethnographic research on individual communities. Although this literature penetrates various facets of the immigrant experience in the United States—from the earliest arrivals in the 1890s to the post-1965 influx into the United States after the lifting of immigration quotas—none addresses the areas of Indian and Pakistani American musical cultures.

The first publication devoted to the music of this immigrant group in North America was Regula Qureshi's ethnomusicological study of East Indian (and Arab) communities in Canada (1972). Although this work laid the foundation for further research among Indian and Pakistani communities, scholarship since that time has been minimal. In 1980 Alison Geldard (now Arnold) carried out a musical ethnography of the East Indian community in the Chicago metropolitan area, and in 1985 Gordon Thompson and Medha Yodh published their research on the music and dance of the Gujarati community in southern California. Other scholars have looked at musical performance by visiting Indian artists and its impact on Indian music in North America (Erdman 1985; Neuman 1984). An interesting comparison of Indian immigrant music cultures can be drawn between the experience in North America and that of the Indian community in Felicity, Trinidad, the latter of which incorporates both Asian Indian and West Indian (Caribbean) influences (Myers 1998). Beyond these and the recent survey of South Asian American music by Nazir Jairazbhoy in *The New Grove Dictionary of American Music* (1986), studies on Indian or Pakistani immigrant music in America are rare.

PERFORMANCE CONTEXTS

Among the Indian and Pakistani American population, musical performance reflects the cultural and social organization of these immigrant groups. Indians have settled in

FIGURE 1   The grand-scale operatic ballet *Jay, Jaya, Devi* by Lalgudi Jayaraman was commissioned for and premiered at the Twentieth Anniversary Tyagaraja Festival in Cleveland, Ohio, 1997. Photo by T. Thomas Tuttle.

many metropolitan centers of the United States, with the majority now residing in the states of California, Illinois, New Jersey, New York, and Texas; and, unlike earlier European immigrants, who formed urban ethnic enclaves, Indians and Pakistanis have also dispersed throughout middle-class suburban residential areas, where they tend to socialize within their native regional communities (for example, Bengalis, Gujaratis, or Tamils). Since the mid-1960s, when urban residential clustering began to occur to some extent, Indian and Pakistani cultural and religious associations have sprung up in Atlanta, Chicago, Cleveland, Houston, New York, and other major cities, and each group organizes its own social and religious functions that promote distinct native cultural traditions, languages, dress, food, and music. Many such events include musical performance in contexts ranging from formal stage presentations to informal gatherings in private homes. Among immigrant communities, trained professional classical musicians and dancers are few; Indian classical music and dance performance by local artists is consequently infrequent and is more often the preserve of visiting artists who perform for mixed Indian and American audiences. Notably, Indian audiences for North Indian (Hindustani) and South Indian (Karnatak) classical music concerts in the United States are distinct, following the two different musical traditions and the separate communities of North and South Indians with their dissimilar cultures and languages. Perhaps the most important venue for South Indian classical performances, for example, is the annual Tyagaraja festival (honoring the revered South Indian composer [1767–1847]) held in cities throughout the United States and often featuring major performers from India. Semiprofessional and amateur artists are far more numerous and for the most part perform light-classical, folk, and popular vocal music to local business, community, and family groups (figures 1 and 2).

Although Indians generally consider music an important component of any social gathering, two common occasions for local musical performance are evening musical parties and wedding celebrations. An informal atmosphere generally characterizes such events, with audience movement and chatter during performances and audience participation through singing and clapping. At a Pakistani American Muslim wedding anniversary, for example, musicians sit on the floor in traditional fashion surrounded by family and friends and sing Pakistani folk songs in Pashto (tribal language), examples of *ghazal* 'Urdu couplet' and *qawwali* 'mystical group song', and Pakistani popular songs, with harmonium, *tabla* 'drum', violin, and tambourine accompaniment; at Sikh Canadian wedding celebrations, guests participate in dancing the traditional Punjabi *bhangra* folk dance. Social and cultural events serving extraregional groups such as

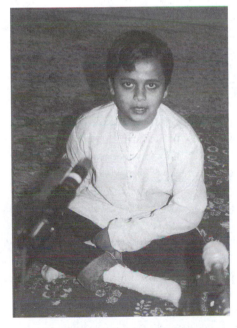

FIGURE 2   Prithvi Mohan of the Washington, D.C., area performed at the Cleveland Tyagaraja Festival from the age of ten. After winning the youth vocal competition three consecutive times, he "retired" until he is old enough for the senior division. Photo by T. Thomas Tuttle, 1996.

Among immigrant communities, trained professional classical musicians and dancers are few; Indian classical music and dance performance by local artists is consequently infrequent and is more often the preserve of visiting artists who perform for mixed Indian and American audiences.

Indian or Hindu cultural associations incorporate broader based musical entertainment, often with semiprofessional musicians performing film songs, *ghazal, qawwali, bhajan* 'devotional song', *gits* 'Hindi song', or popular regional songs, depending on the cultural and religious makeup of the audience.

Indian and Pakistani Americans also perpetuate native musical traditions and practices within religious contexts. Members of institutionalized religious traditions (Islam, Vedanta, Christianity) follow worship rituals that usually include unaccompanied solo chanting of religious texts: Qur'ān chanting in Muslim prayer sessions, prayer chanting in Vedanta temple services, and liturgical chanting within Christian congregations. Although Indian Christian worship also incorporates communal hymn singing, religious assemblies without a formal prayer-leader or priest (Hinduism, Jainism, Sathya Sai Baba movement) favor greater communal participation in musical devotion. Participatory singing of *bhajan, stavan* 'eulogy', and *shlok* 'Sanskrit couplet' forms a major part of religious worship for these assemblies.

Indian temples play an important role as cultural and musical centers, sponsoring festival celebrations and processions, religious programs and events, and music concerts on a regular basis. Over the past few decades, sizable South Asian communities have funded and supported temple building in many North American cities. In 1998, for example, a fund-raising dinner for the almost completed Murugan (Shiva) temple in Lanham, Michigan, presented Tamil devotional songs by a vocal group invited from Houston, Texas; and the Sri Guruvaayoorappan (Krishna) Temple in Marlboro, New Jersey, celebrated its grand opening with ten days of religious, cultural, and musical activities.

MUSICAL MEANING AND FUNCTION

In the new cultural environment, native music takes on new meaning and aesthetic appeal for the largely first- and second-generation Indian and Pakistani immigrant population, many of whom maintain close ties with family and friends back in their homeland. Familiar songs and musical styles create feelings of nostalgia and provide an emotional link with the past. Many amateur Indian musicians in Chicago frequently perform Indian film and popular songs of past decades because of the community's familiarity with and sentimental attachment to these old favorites.

As musical performance generally takes place within the context of the larger Indian and/or Pakistani ethnic community rather than the nuclear family, native music and language simultaneously function to preserve the community's cultural heritage and identity in the New World. On the one hand, the availability of audio- and video-cassette recordings, especially those for rent in Indian grocery stores, and the constant traffic between India and America ensure that Indian American music is not a fossilized tradition of musical memories from India and Pakistan. Especially in the realm of popular music, musicians in North America learn the latest Indian and Pakistani songs and styles to update their repertoire. On the other hand, some Indian and Pakistani American musicians are interested in creating their own immigrant musical traditions and compose music and lyrics either in popular Indian musical styles or in new musical fusions of Indian and Western traditions [see BORDER CROSSINGS AND FUSIONS, p. 321]. These hold some appeal for the younger and second-generation immigrants, whose musical tastes are greatly influenced by American pop culture.

GENRES AND INSTRUMENTS

Music performed and listened to by Indian and Pakistani Americans is for the most part native to India, Pakistan, and other countries from which these North American immigrants have originated (the Caribbean, for example). Musical fusion with Western styles and world beat experiments are not unknown among young musicians but remain outside the mainstream of this immigrant musical culture [see WORLD BEAT, p. 337]. As on the Indian subcontinent, a minority of the population performs and listens to the classical traditions of North India (Hindustani) and South India (Karnatak). Local artists generally received their training in India and practice and perform classical *raga* 'mode' as an avocation, not a profession, often also performing in lighter musical styles for the larger Indo-Pakistani community. Hindustani vocalists perform the classical *khyal* and light-classical *thumri* genres but not the older *dhrupad* form, and instrumentalists follow the traditional *raga* performance sequence of improvised *alap-jor-jhala* and *gat* but often limit their performance time to approximately one hour and include lighter pieces such as the folk-based *dhun*. With relatively little demand for classical music concerts by local artists and the necessity of *riyaz* 'practice' for the improvisatory art of classical *raga* performance, few musicians continue to practice these traditions after settling in North America.

The light-musical genres of *ghazal, qawwali, git,* and film song, widespread in India and Pakistan, are universally popular among U.S. communities. Because these forms require less musical knowledge and technique than classical forms for their comprehension and enjoyment as well as their performance, and because they are generally short in length, the incidence of semiprofessional and amateur singers and accompanists (*tabla* and harmonium) is consequently high. Folk music in the immigrant environment is less common as a result of its localized and functional nature in South Asia. In the absence of folk musicians within immigrant communities, cultural and religious organizations occasionally encourage group performance of folk songs and dances for social entertainment and for participation in larger community-wide events such as Indian Independence Day celebrations (August 16). Individual performance of traditional life-cycle or work songs in the new cultural environment is rare and limited mostly to intimate family or group gatherings.

Hindus, Muslims, Christians, and other religious groups within the Indo-Pakistani population in North America strive to maintain musical traditions as practiced in their homeland, in some cases with increased enthusiasm and orthodoxy. Among Hindus, Sathya Sai Baba followers, and Hare Krishna members, solo and group devotional singing in Hindi and other Indian languages is indispensable to communal worship. The *bhajan* repertoire is in part dependent on the musical knowledge and memory of participants, although transmission of new material occurs through contact between North American communities and with devotees abroad. Participants at the Radha Krishna Temple in Evanston, Illinois, for example, sing *bhajan* and *kirtan* devotional songs, whose texts are published by the International Society for Krishna Consciousness, but no songbooks are used in religious gatherings. Members learn songs through repetition during the leader–chorus singing, accompanied by harmonium, cymbals, and drums (fiberglass *mridangam*).

For most Muslim communities, the traditional *muezzin*'s call to prayer, broadcast from the mosque five times a day, is impractical in North American cities and is relinquished. Qur'ān chanting or recitation, in contrast, is a regular part of Muslim prayer sessions. Qur'ān chanters may not necessarily be traditionally trained in this art, nor are they all native Arabic speakers, yet Islamic groups encourage performance of this highly formalized and stylized manner of Qur'ān chanting as a fundamental component of North American Islamic worship ritual.

The experience of Indian Christians in the United States differs from that of both Hindus and Muslims, theirs being the majority religion in their new homeland. Early immigrants were able to attend American Roman Catholic or Protestant church services and participate in familiar hymn-singing traditions. Many Indian Christian groups continue to use existing American church buildings but now hold services in their own language. In Chicago, the Indian Telugu United Methodist congregation from Andhra Pradesh, for example, sings Telugu and English hymns and Western-harmonized *bhajan*s, with *tabla* (no South Indian *mridangam* 'barrel drum' was available), harmonium, cymbals, *kanjira* 'frame drum', and Hawaiian (electric) guitar accompaniment [see POLYNESIAN MUSIC, p. 1047], while the Malayalam Eastern Orthodox congregation from Kerala sings unaccompanied and in unison. The liturgical singing employs scale pitches reminiscent of the ancient melodic modes of traditional Syrian Christians in Kerala, two of which approximate the Greek phrygian and lydian modes. The use of traditional music and language among all Indian and Pakistani religious communities indicates a low degree of acculturation and assimilation in American religious life; it further provides one explanation for the popularity and cultural significance of religious gatherings among the predominantly first- and second-generation immigrant population.

Most musical instruments traditionally employed in Indian classical and light-classical music performance can be found in North American communities, and have generally been purchased in India or Pakistan and imported. The North Indian *sitar* 'long-necked, plucked lute' and *bansuri* 'bamboo flute', and the South Indian *vina* 'long-necked, plucked lute' are among the most common classical instruments. Yet the numbers of these are few in comparison with the profusion of popular and light-classical accompanying instruments: harmonium, *tabla,* and *shruti* box 'small reed organ drone instrument'. Occasional mixed groups blend Indian harmonium and *tabla* with Western drum set, electric and acoustic guitars, Afro-Cuban conga drums, and other non-Indian instruments. In virtually all musical contexts, vocalists and instrumentalists use electronic amplification. Folk instruments are far less common and are played largely among immigrants closely related by family or place of origin. In a typical gathering of Gujaratis from the Ahmedabad region, the *nal* 'barrel drum', *dholak* 'cylindrical barrel drum', *manjira* 'small hand cymbals', frame drum, and rattles accompany musical performance, while the large *dhol* 'stick-beaten barrel drum' or *dholak* is ever present for Punjabi *bhangra* stick-dance performances.

MUSICAL EDUCATION AND TRANSMISSION

Many musical performers among the Indian and Pakistani American population learned to sing and play instruments before immigrating to North America. A large percentage were introduced to music through family members at an early age and continued their musical education (often including some classical training) in school or private music lessons in India or Pakistan. Rarely did musicians experience the traditional *guru-shishya* 'master–disciple' relationship in which the student devotes his life to the practice and study of classical music. With the high demand for popular music entertainers in American communities, average performers with relatively little musical training can achieve ministardom. For self-taught singers and instrumentalists, similarly numerous among immigrant communities, the acquisition of skills and repertoire involves listening to and imitating other musicians and memorizing popular and folk songs heard in live performances and on recordings.

All musical transmission among Indian and Pakistani Americans is oral, following historical tradition in India. A strong desire among first-generation immigrants to pass

FIGURE 3   Radhika Subramaniam performs *bharatnatyam* 'Indian classical dance' and teaches students some hand gestures. Photo by T. Thomas Tuttle, 1992.

FIGURE 4   Touring artists, here flutist Dr. N. Ramani, have opportunities to lecture at local universities such as Cleveland State. Photo by T. Thomas Tuttle, 1998.

on native cultural traditions to the second and third generations has resulted in the establishment of local Indian classical music and dance schools. These organized classes for *bharatnatyam* and *kathak* dance, *sitar* performance, and so on are often held in private homes and offer regular group and solo training for South Asian immigrants as well as the general American public. Part-time classical music teachers similarly serve the larger community, charge fees, transmit musical knowledge through demonstrated performance and student imitation, and frequently include background study of Indian history, culture, and religion for non-Indian natives (figures 3 and 4). The foundation of the Ali Akbar School of Music and Ravi Shankar's Kinnara School, both in California in 1967, brought Indian classical music and dance teaching to prominence on a national level. For light-classical, popular, folk, and religious musics, in contrast, no organized methods of transmission exist. Local community musicians learn new repertoire, techniques, and styles largely from Indian and Pakistani cassette recordings available in North America, on return trips to their native land, and from visiting friends and relatives. There is little direct transmission of these musical genres to second- or third-generation immigrants through teaching, largely due to a preference among these Indian and Pakistani Americans for mainstream American culture and music.

The transmission of recorded Indian music by means of cassette and compact disc players, radio, and television forms a not insignificant part of the Indian and Pakistani American musical culture. In certain contexts prerecorded music from India and Pakistan substitutes for live performance where none is available, such as in small religious gatherings, classical dance classes, and dance performances. In private homes, musical recordings provide performances by renowned and well-loved artists who tour North America infrequently. And owners of Indian restaurants and retail stores play popular and light-classical recordings as background music to create an Indian atmosphere for their clients. Indian cassette and compact disc recordings are generally available in Indian grocery stores, and Indian classical music recordings can often be found on the shelves of larger American record stores. A relatively new source for these is the Internet, where large Indian record retail outlets such as Shrimati's in Berkeley, California, can reach a national and even international market with their mail-order service.

Unlike the government-run All India Radio, the commercial broadcasting system in the United States allows Indian program hosts to air the most popular Indian film and light music exclusively.

Indian and Pakistani American communities have also shown particular interest in radio broadcasting of their popular music and, more recently, in television broadcasting. Their reliance upon recorded music offers lower program costs than does live studio entertainment and also enables transmission of performances by popular musicians in India and Pakistan. As in India, the radio is a popular medium of communication, playing an important role in advertising local music performance for immigrant communities. Unlike the government-run All India Radio, the commercial broadcasting system in the United States allows Indian program hosts to air the most popular Indian film and light music exclusively. Television broadcasting by Indian and Pakistani Americans is much less prevalent. A common program format is the edited version of a popular commercial Indian film, but several such experiments have failed as a result of lack of financial support.

INDIAN AMERICAN MUSICAL FUSIONS

Among professional and semiprofessional Indian and Pakistani musicians in the United States, experiments blending Indian with American and Western musical traditions appeared on audiocassettes and compact discs in the 1980s and 1990s, following the pioneering efforts at Indian–Western musical combination by Ravi Shankar, Yehudi Menuhin, and Jean-Pierre Rampal in the 1970s. Several renowned classical artists now resident in the United States, including violinists L. Shankar and L. Subramaniam and *tabla* player Zakir Hussain, have produced such musical fusions with electronic synthesizers for American and international audiences. On a local level, some Indian and Pakistani American amateur music bands mix Indian and Western music, using instruments from both popular cultures, but rarely produce commercial recordings. More common among amateur musicians is the trend toward composing new melodies and song lyrics within existing Indian musical styles, thereby creating music relevant to the immigrant experience and to life in the United States. The dissemination of this distinctly immigrant music remains within urban Indian and Pakistani American communities, but its growth and popularity among the immigrant population indicates not only that Indian and Pakistani Americans no longer wish to be dependent on their homeland for their musical culture but also that they are actively creating their own music based on both Indian/Pakistani and American musical traditions.

MUSIC AND IDENTITY

As a rapidly growing but minority Asian immigrant population, Indian and Pakistani Americans maintain distinct national identities despite internal cultural and religious differences. Before 1965, a pan–South Asian unity characterized the relatively small Indo-Pakistani immigrant population in North America and was reflected in community-wide organization of social events with varied music and dance performances. With the massive post-1965 influx of South Asians to the United States following the lifting of discriminatory immigration laws, regionalism emerged and identification narrowed from Indian and Pakistani to state and religious markers such as Bengali and Sikh. Religious and cultural groups promoted separate regional identities within the larger ethnic population, and music performance often included devotional and regional traditions that served to define and segregate individual communities. However, although social organization remains diverse, umbrella groups such as the Association of Indians in America and the India and Pakistan Leagues of America seek to promote a common identity for American immigrants by fostering cooperation and consolidation. Similarly, the musical culture of Indian and Pakistani Americans includes diverse traditional classical, light-classical, religious, and folk genres, but urban popular music predominates. The widespread popularity of pop *ghazal* and film songs among this immigrant population provides Indians and Pakistanis in the United States with a sense of musical unity and common musical identity amidst the reality of musical diversity.

REFERENCES

Erdman, Joan. 1985. "Today and the Good Old Days: South Asian Music and Dance Performances in Chicago." *Selected Reports in Ethnomusicology* 6:39–58.

Geldard, Alison. 1980. "Music and Musical Performance Among the East Indians in Chicago." Master's thesis, University of Illinois at Urbana-Champaign.

Jairazbhoy, Nazir. 1986. "Asian-American Music, 1: Introduction; 5: South Asian." In *The New Grove Dictionary of American Music,* ed. H. Wiley Hitchcock and Stanley Sadie. London: Macmillan.

Myers, Helen. 1998. *Music of Hindu Trinidad: Songs from the India Diaspora.* Chicago: University of Chicago Press.

Neuman, Daniel. 1984. "The Ecology of Indian Music in North America." *Bansuri* 1:9–15.

Qureshi, Regula. 1972. "Ethnomusicological Research Among Canadian Communities of Arab and East Indian Origin." *Ethnomusicology* 16:381–396.

Thompson, Gordon, and Medha Yodh. 1985. "Garba and the Gujaratis of Southern California." *Selected Reports in Ethnomusicology* 6:59–79.

Snapshot:
The Tyagaraja Festival
in Cleveland, Ohio
Claire Martin

Cultural Awareness
Tyagaraja and the Festival at Tiruvaiyaru
Performance Practice
Music, Identity, and the Preservation of Tradition
Scholarship

FIGURE I The religious and ritual elements of the Cleveland *aradhana* are assured by the presence of Krishnamoorthy Ganapathi, head priest of the Cleveland Siva Vishnu Temple of Greater Cleveland. Photograph by T. Temple Tuttle, 1998.

The annual St. Tyagaraja music festival in Cleveland, Ohio, is a ten-day gathering held in April, celebrating the death anniversary (*aradhana*) of the great late-eighteenth- and early-nineteenth-century South Indian saint-composer who gives the festival its name. It is the largest festival of its kind outside India. Similar festivals have been organized on a smaller scale in cities such as Melbourne, Durban, Chicago, Washington, D.C., Memphis, Tokyo, and Toronto, where South Indians have settled. They gather at these festivals to pay musical homage to Tyagaraja. For many it is an occasion to remember their cultural heritage and tradition through music and *bhakti* 'religious devotion'.

The Cleveland festival began in 1978, which makes it the oldest of these festivals and the most widely attended, with over two thousand visitors from the South Indian community in Cleveland and other parts of the United States and Canada. It has been acknowledged by the U.S. House of Representatives, and the state of Ohio has formally designated the festival days as Tyagaraja Days. In addition, the government of India has taken notice of it by sanctioning the festival an official pilgrimage site (figure 1).

Currently there are more than 700,000 foreign-born Indians living in the United States, with South Indians forming the second largest group after Gujaratis (Pushkarna 1996). In the mid-1960s a large number of Asian Indians formed urban communities in cities such as Atlanta, Chicago, Cleveland, Houston, and New York (Arnold 1999:578). Since then nonresident Indians living in urban diasporas have maintained their cultural traditions in the form of festivals and other social customs and events.

CULTURAL AWARENESS

The Cleveland festival was launched in 1978 by a gathering of about seventy-five individuals in the basement of the Faith United Church of Christ in the Richmond Heights section of Cleveland. The group was motivated by a desire to preserve and promote *Carnatic* 'South Indian' music, cultural, and religious ties in an event that would reflect a culture exemplified in St. Tyagaraja's life and work. The following year Dr. T. Temple Tuttle (d. 2000), director of the Indian Cultural Studies program at Cleveland State University, arranged for the University to host the festival in the university auditorium free of charge. Today the concerts continue to be held at three venues at the university as well as at the Siva Vishnu Temple of Greater Cleveland.

Temple Tuttle regarded the role of Cleveland State University in ethnic cultural awareness as extremely important. He observed that "as an urban university serving a diverse sub-population, the CSU's main obligation is to provide educational and cultural support to all communities" ("Cleveland: North America's Tiruvaiyaru" 1996:60). The festival therefore plays a significant part in the university's mission, and non-Indians, by participating in the festival, have themselves contributed by encouraging multicultural awareness and understanding in the Cleveland area.

TYAGARAJA AND THE FESTIVAL AT TIRUVAIYARU

The logistics of the festival are organized by the Aradhana Committee, a group of South Indian volunteers living in Cleveland. Their aim is to re-create the atmosphere, music, and devotion present at the festival held in South India at Tiruvaiyaru, the composer's home town. They have achieved this aim in many respects, but the festival at Cleveland has been saved from several controversial (and some feel disappointing) political developments that have occurred in Tiruvaiyaru's *aradhana* in recent years (Jackson 1996; Pattabhi Raman 2000:23–26; Srinivasan 1999:3–5). Controversies have arisen in South India involving Tamil nationalism, for example, and disturbing social issues have crept in regarding caste inequality, commercialism, and media exploitation. It is commonly felt that these issues detract from the religious sanctity of the occasion and that they are inconsistent with Tyagaraja's ideology.

The Tyagaraja *aradhana* at Tiruvaiyaru takes place in January over a ten-day period and is attended by thousands of devotees from all over South India. It is organized so that both amateurs and professionals equally can express their devotion to Lord Rama, the seventh incarnation of Vishnu according to Hindu belief, in the form of *bhakti* and *kritis* 'songs' composed by Tyagaraja. Whereas artists at Tiruvaiyaru are restricted to renditions of Tyagaraja's work alone, Cleveland performances occasionally include compositions by other revered South Indian composers such as Syama Sastri, Muttuswami Diksitar, and Purandara Dasa.

Renowned for his pure devotion to Rama and his rejection of worldly possessions, Tyagaraja refused royal patronage on several occasions, claiming that his music was composed for no one but Lord Rama (Jackson 1996). In his lyrics he entreats Lord Rama to appear to him in a vision. He describes his helplessness as a mere human and begs of Rama to be released from earthly concerns and prejudices. Tyagaraja sang for alms and refused to accept money from his students. The appeal of his *kritis* to mankind is manifested in his themes of moral upliftment, spiritual direction, and fundamental truths in human life and existence. He believed that music is the path to salvation and the true medium for *bhakti* worship. The essence of South Indian culture is represented in Tyagaraja's works through hundreds of accounts of episodes in Rama's life.

Significantly, Tyagaraja's *kritis* are musically uncomplicated, and the lyrics are mostly composed in one of the South Indian vernaculars, Telugu, rather than in the more intellectual and ancient literary medium of Sanskrit. The most famous of his compositions is a group of five *kritis* called the *Pancharatna* 'Five Gems' *kritis*. These are usually sung in *bhajans* 'group songs', which are rendered at the commencement of the Cleveland festival by a chorus of more than sixty amateurs and professionals (figure 2). The *bhajans* in all their simplicity and accessibility can therefore be rendered by amateurs who maybe less able musically than the professionals but who wish nonetheless to participate in the devotional aspect of the festival. The composer believed that all devotees should be given the opportunity to praise Rama through music *bhakti*, regardless of musical or intellectual ability.

The festival at Tiruvaiyaru, on which the Cleveland *aradhana* is modeled, thus allows all devotees an equal chance to pay homage to Rama and Tyagaraja. Each performer, amateur or professional, is restricted to a single rendition of a *kriti* by the composer. No performer is paid for his or her concert, and entrance to the festival is free. The sole purpose of the festival is devotion and musical homage to Tyagaraja.

PERFORMANCE PRACTICE

Despite the ideals of the festival in India, the main function of the Cleveland celebrations is to provide Indians living in the United States and Canada with a wealth of professional and inspirational music by inviting over fifty world-renowned recording artists from India to perform there. Therefore, the element of (amateur) audience participation—the singing of *bhajans*—is considerably limited compared to that at Tiruvaiyaru. It is reserved for weekend slots between professional concerts.

Two or three concerts a day are scheduled for professional musicians. World-acclaimed artists such as violinist and singer, Dr. Balumarilikrishna, flutist Dr. N. Ramani, and vocalist Smt. S. Sowmya attract Indian music listeners from all over the North America to the Cleveland festival.

Professional concerts continue for up to four hours, sometimes until late into the evening—also a common performance practice in South India. Although Tyagaraja's *kritis* are vocal works, artists render them as instrumental compositions for violin, flute, *veena,* or *nadaswaram* solos, with accompaniment on instruments such as the *mrdangam* 'South Indian double-headed drum', a supporting melody instrument such as the violin or flute, and the *tambura* or *sruti*-box providing the drone or pedal point.

Soloists, whether vocal or instrumental, are expected to interpret and render the compositions according to their devotional content. Hence a knowledge of Telugu and the meaning of the *kriti* texts is essential for a true exposition of Tyagaraja's music. However, one of the festival organizers, Mr. Balusubramaniam, sees a problem. While he believes that a basic knowledge of the language is fundamental to an appreciation of Tyagaraja's work, he estimates that only about 15 percent of the audience is familiar with Telugu. Nevertheless, it is true that although they do not understand Telugu, many people are sufficiently familiar with particular songs and the translations of them to minimize language as a problem. For them the inspiration of the songs is able to come through.

MUSIC, IDENTITY, AND THE PRESERVATION OF TRADITION

Many who attend the festival view it as an opportunity chiefly to hear the main artists of *Carnatic* music and do not feel it is necessary to understand the lyrics. They may also attend for nostalgic reasons, to reconnect with their past and lost motherland in the midst of the very different host culture in America. And because the quality of Indian music concerts depends heavily on the intellectual and emotional understanding of the audience members, concerts here are often bound to relatively basic, traditional performances that cater to varied abilities in musical appreciation within the audience.

Organizers attempt to create a totally Indian ambience with the purest classical music represented; with a social gathering in which numerous South Indian languages can be heard; with traditional rituals such as *pūja* performed at Tyagaraja's altar on the stage; with the fragrance of incense burning and South Indian food cooking; and with the array of brightly colored and glittering saris and *salwars* worn by the women. Most participating families plan their vacations in the United States on the basis of this festival. It is an opportunity to meet friends made from previous years' celebrations and a time during which children especially are introduced to Indian music and society (figure 3).

For students of Indian music trained in the United States, the competition and individual singing events of the festival also serve as valuable and rare performance opportunities. The competition held during the first weekend in the presence of the great *vidwans* 'masters' of India provides a goal of high standards of performance. It helps to develop students' interest in the festival and impels them to continue seriously in their studies.

The display of local talent is especially significant in connection with the emphasis placed on the transmission and preservation of tradition and Indian heritage in the Indian diaspora (Stokes 1994). Children born of Indian parents who are growing up in America are becoming more and more distanced from their Indian roots as the pressure to merge with and adopt mainstream American culture becomes stronger. Although this is a natural development, considering that these children are generally American citizens and have rarely, if ever, traveled to India, parents who have settled in America do not easily forget or disregard their family ties and cultural values. Naturally their children are encouraged to keep the Indian classical music traditions alive and strong and to retain their ethnic identity rather than succumb to a melting pot ideology (Nair 1995) (figure 4).

FIGURE 3   The doyen of Carnatic music, vocalist K. V. Narayanaswamy, is still actively performing. Photograph by T. Temple Tuttle, 1997.

FIGURE 4   A variety of instrumentalists are represented in the individual performances, including this saxophonist from Phoenix, Arizona, accompanied by Nagarajan on the more traditional *kanjeera* 'frame drum'. Photograph by T. Temple Tuttle, 1998.

The festival contributes greatly to this aim by promoting *Carnatic* music and culture and enabling young people to feel proud of being Indian. It strives to keep non-resident Indians in touch with their great tradition. V. V. Sundaram, one of the original organizers of the festival, recalls that when the festival was first launched there was a general lack of interest among the younger generation. He acknowledges that his task in recruiting younger participants has proved easier in recent years because ethnicity has come to be more accepted in the United States.

SCHOLARSHIP

Although scholarly attention to the cultural role of the festivals in Cleveland and Tiruvaiyaru has so far been limited, a number of newspapers and magazines report on and describe the celebrations, for example, *The Lotus, Ohio Magazine, The Week, India West,* and *Sruti.* A few authors have published studies on the role of music in establishing ethnic identity and preserving and transmitting cultural traditions in diaspora (Arnold 1985, 1999; Farrell 1997; Manuel 1997–1998; Slobin 1994; Stokes 1994).

REFERENCES

Arnold, Alison. 1985. "Aspects of Asian Indian Musical Life in North America." *Selected Reports in Ethnomusicology* 6:25–38.

———. 1999. "Music and the South Asian Diaspora: United States." In *The Garland Encyclopedia of World Music:* Vol. 5. *South Asia: The Indian Subcontinent,* ed. Alison Arnold, 578–587. New York: Garland Publishing Co.

Ayyangar, R. Rangaramanuja. 1993. *History of South Indian (Carnatic) Music: From Vedic Times to the Present.* Bombay: Vipanchi Cultural Trust.

"Cleveland. North America's Tiruvaiyaru." 1996. *India West,* 7 April, 60–61.

Farrell, Gerry. 1997. *Indian Music and the West.* Oxford: Clarendon Press.

Jackson, William J. 1994. *Tyagaraja and the Renewal of Tradition.* Delhi: Motilal Banarsidass Publishers Private Ltd.

———. 1996. *Tyagaraja: Life and Lyrics.* Oxford: Oxford University Press.

Manuel, Peter. 1997–1998. "Music, Identity, and Images of India in the Indo-Caribbean Diaspora." *Asian Music* 29(1):17–36.

Nair, Savita. 1995. "Masala in the Melting Pot: History, Identity and the Indian Diaspora." *SAGAR (South Asian Graduate Research Journal)* 2:2.

Pattabhi Raman, N. 2000. "Tyagaraja Deserves Better—And So Do We." *Sruti* 188:23–26.

Pushkarna, Vijaya. 1996. "Cleveland Goes Carnatic: Exponents and Fans of Music Bring Indians Together." *The Week* 19.

Slobin, Mark. 1994. "Music in Diaspora: The View from Euro-America." *Diaspora* 3(3): 243–251.

Srinivasan, N. 1999. "Tyagaraja Mahotsavam in Tiruvaiyaru." *Sruti* 173:3–5.

Stokes, Martin, ed 1994. *Ethnicity, Identity and Music: The Musical Construction of Place.* Oxford: Berg.

Wade, Bonnie. 1997. *Music in India: The Classical Traditions.* New Delhi: Manohar Publishers.

Vietnamese Music

Phong T. Nguyễn
Terry E. Miller

The Nature of Vietnamese Music
Popular Music Culture
Performance Contexts
Religious Music
The Music of Upland Minorities
The Place of Vietnamese Music in the United States

Vietnam's involvement with the United States came about gradually. After liberation from the French in 1954, the country divided into the communist North (Democratic Republic of Vietnam) under Hồ Chí Minh, and the noncommunist South (Republic of Vietnam), under a succession of civilian and military governments increasingly supported by the United States. Its imperial past long forgotten after the 1945 abdication of Vietnam's last emperor, Bảo Đại, from the Citadel (or "Forbidden City") in Huề, Vietnam increasingly sank into a civil war that came to have universal implications for outside protagonists. Because of the more than forty thousand American soldiers killed in Vietnam, with countless more wounded both physically and psychologically, and the shock of being on the losing side when the North and the Southern Liberation Front overcame the South in 1975, for most Americans "Vietnam" remains a war, not a country or culture. For the Vietnamese, the losses were much greater, as millions were affected through deaths, injuries, and destruction.

Through secondary migration, the approximately one million Vietnamese living in the United States eventually established extensive communities in Orange County and San Jose (California), Houston, Falls Church (Virginia), Seattle, New Orleans, and other cities. Unlike other mainland Southeast Asian refugees, who had been mainly farmers and soldiers, many Vietnamese refugees had been city people, some of Chinese descent, who, based on their business experience in Vietnam, opened businesses ranging from individual restaurants and groceries to large supermarkets and shopping malls. Some were professionals, especially medical doctors, engineers, and administrators. With increasing economic success, the Vietnamese could afford to satisfy their appetite for homegrown popular culture. This led to the production of concerts, audiocassettes, compact discs, and music videos sold through a network of shops around the country. A number of vocalists, formerly stars in southern Vietnam, reestablished their careers in the United States, primarily by singing pre-1975 songs.

THE NATURE OF VIETNAMESE MUSIC

Although it resembles Chinese music superficially and because many of its instruments were derived from this culture, which dominated Vietnam for more than a thousand years, Vietnamese music is fundamentally different. Most notable are its sophisticated modal systems (hơi, điệu), which provide a comprehensive basis for composing and improvising elaborate compositions. Because several pitches in these scales fall outside the Western equal-tempered system, and particular pitches in each mode may require a specific ornament or bent tone, Vietnamese music sounds both slightly out of tune and highly ornate to Western ears. The term *traditional music* denotes numerous genres, from the imperial music of the former court in Huề, to regional folk song, theatrical, and chamber genres, to ritual and Buddhist music. Distinguishing classical from folk music in Vietnam makes no sense, however, for songs of various origins are performed by everyone from a village rice farmer to a gentleman instrumentalist in the city, and members of theatrical troupes can be urban or rural.

Virtually all Vietnamese instruments in the United States were brought or imported by immigrants, but a few amateur makers have used local materials. The *đàn tranh,* a sixteen- or seventeen-stringed board zither, is the best known instrument. Even though the guitar (both electric and acoustic) is common to both Western and Vietnamese cultures, the latter type, called *ghi-ta* or *lục huyền cầm,* is modified by scooping away wood between frets to allow for the string pulling characteristic of Vietnamese style. Also important are the *sáo* 'bamboo transverse flute', the *đàn kìm* or *đàn nguyệt* 'moon-shaped long-neck lute', and the *đàn cò* or *đàn nhị* 'two-stringed fiddle'. Attractive to both Western and Vietnamese ears is the culture's most distinctive instrument, a monochord called *đàn độc huyền* or *đàn bầu.* The instruments of the court and ritual, especially the double reeds, are virtually nonexistent outside Vietnam, however. Solo instrumental performance in the West is restricted to a few skilled individuals, while chamber ensembles are composed of amateurs within a community (figure 1).

Vocal genres are preferred over instrumental. These include popular songs (*tân nhạc*), folk songs (*dân ca*), chamber songs (*đờn ca tài tử*), and theatrical songs. Although Vietnam has theatrical genres specific to each region (North, Central, and South), only the southern theater, called *cải lương,* of early-twentieth-century origin, has survived in the West. As *cải lương* is quasi-popular and numerous practitioners live in the United States and France, it has been possible to organize ad hoc troupes for both public and video performance. Sometimes additional performers were brought from France to augment the troupe. Without a full ensemble of musicians, accompaniment is usually reduced to a synthesizer (for live performance) or multiple tracking by one performer (for video).

FIGURE I   A Vietnamese ensemble: (*left to right*) Dock Rmah (*goong* 'bamboo tube zither'), Tô Trinh (*đàn tranh* 'zither'), Miranda Arana (*sáo* 'bamboo flute'), Kim Oanh (*sinh tiền* 'coin clapper'), and Phong Nguyễn (*đàn nguyệt* 'moon-shaped lute'). Photo courtesy Loraine Tipaldy, 1998.

POPULAR MUSIC CULTURE

While the North Vietnamese listened to various kinds of revolutionary popular songs, some European- or Russian-influenced, pre-1975 South Vietnamese listened to various kinds of popular songs with French and Vietnamese roots in the style of nineteenth-century romanticism. Popular songs, first created in the late 1930s (French songs with Vietnamese lyrics), were fostered in the 1940s by students and Boy Scouts who had been musically trained in the public and Catholic schools of Saigon, Huề, and Hànội. Popular music was first called *nhạc cải cách* 'renovated music', then *tân nhạc* 'modern music' and *nhạc moi* 'new music'. These genres represented a new trend in hybridized Vietnamese music combining the distinctive Vietnamese language and a Western musical concept of composition. They came to be a powerful tool for the creation of both revolutionary and entertainment songs. Unlike the traditional songs, which are mostly anonymous, the *tân nhạc* songs are known by their composers. In the United States, whether or not these songs had political implications, most had danceable rhythms. Many such songs were written in the style of, and to accompany, various ballroom dances, such as cha-cha-cha, tango, rumba, or fox-trot. These older songs were rerecorded in the United States and by 1991 were again being played openly in Vietnam.

In the United States a small Vietnamese music industry has developed, primarily in California, where numerous audiocassettes, compact discs, and music videos are sold widely in malls, in strip shopping centers, and in Vietnamese groceries. Although influenced by American music videos, those produced by immigrant Southeast Asians have tended to be slower moving, more restrained in their emotion, and totally lacking in the challenging contents of American videos.

PERFORMANCE CONTEXTS

Concerts are often organized within communities to celebrate the *Tết* (Vietnamese New Year), *Le Phật Dan* (Buddha's Birthday Anniversary), and Christmas. Programs usually take place in schools and church halls. Musicians in California, Minnesota, Virginia, and elsewhere often assemble at friends' homes on weekends to perform *dờn ca tài tử* 'chamber-style folk songs', a genre open to all willing participants. These ensembles usually play for themselves or for a group of connoisseurs after a dinner (figure 2).

FIGURE 2 Two Vietnamese women play the seventeen-stringed zither (*đan tranh*) at a Vietnamese New Year Party in Akron, Ohio. Photo by Terry E. Miller, 1987.

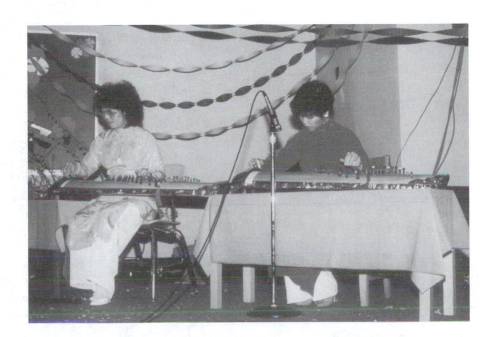

As it appears the generation of Vietnamese born in the United States has little to no interest in traditional music and only a modest interest in the older popular styles sung by artists who came from Vietnam, these styles are not likely to outlast their living proponents.

RELIGIOUS MUSIC

Vietnamese Buddhist chant constitutes an extensive genre of vocal music underlain by a rich theory. With the establishment of temples within the larger communities, there has been a partial restoration of chant traditions. Few temples outside Vietnam, however, have more than three monks in residence, making it difficult to hear the *sutras* chanted by the large groups often heard in Vietnam. In 1988, the combined temples in California formed in Westminster the largest known assembly of monks for an ordination ceremony, with over one hundred in attendance.

THE MUSIC OF UPLAND MINORITIES

Vietnam's mainstream population, the Việt or Kinh, live in the lowlands where wet rice farming is the norm. These include the vast deltas of the Mekong River (known locally as the Nine Dragons [Cuu Long]) in the South, and of the Red River in the North, as well as in coastal areas all along the 1,700-kilometer coastline, some sections being only a few kilometers wide. The vast upland plateaus are inhabited by some fifty-three minorities of both Austro-Asiatic and Malayo-Polynesian language groups. Known collectively by the French term *montagnard,* many members of these groups, such as the Bahnar, Ede, and Jarai, were employed by the U.S. military as Special Forces units. With the fall of the Republic of Vietnam in 1975, many of these men and their families fled. Some were resettled in the United States, especially in North Carolina. A few of them are musicians and maintain a part of their musical culture. Occasionally they play gongs, *goong* 'bamboo tube zithers', or *t'rung* 'bamboo xylophones', sing, and dance when observing their traditional holidays.

THE PLACE OF VIETNAMESE MUSIC IN THE UNITED STATES

Within the Vietnamese community, both American and Vietnamese popular musics predominate. Traditional styles are seldom heard and difficult to find on commercial recordings. Traditional music concerts are not easily organized but may play a minor part in a fashion show or be arranged in conjunction with professional conferences. While Buddhist chant can be heard in temples here and there, other kinds of ritual music (*chầu văn* 'possession rituals', *Cao Đài,* and *Hòa Hào* ceremonies) survive only in small, isolated communities in the United States.

To the general American public, Vietnamese music is virtually invisible. A small number of American enthusiasts attend the rare live performance of traditional music (such as offered by the World Music Institute in New York or Asian Art Museum in San Francisco) (figure 3), and many buyers of compact discs containing traditional music are Westerners. One Vietnamese traditional musician, Dr. Phong T. Nguyễn, was honored with a National Endowment for the Arts National Heritage Fellowship in 1997.

Some educators have sought to include Vietnamese music in the school curricula in areas having large Vietnamese populations. *From Rice Paddies and Temple Yards,* by Phong T. Nguyễn and Patricia Shehan Campbell (1990), is used extensively in schools.

FIGURE 3   Two lowland Cham musicians from southern Vietnam perform at an international festival called a *Katê* in San Jose, California. A single-headed frame drum accompanies the double-reed *saranai* oboe. Photo by Terry E. Miller, 1994.

As it appears the generation of Vietnamese born in the United States has little to no interest in traditional music and only a modest interest in the older popular styles sung by artists who came from Vietnam, these styles are not likely to outlast their living proponents. Young Vietnamese have instead asserted their American-ness by forming rock bands to play both American and Vietnamese styles, although they are primarily heard at Vietnamese events.

REFERENCES

Bankston, Carl L. 1995. "Vietnamese Americans." In *Gale Encyclopedia of Multicultural America,* ed. Rudolph J. Veloci, 2:1393–1407.

Eternal Voices: Traditional Vietnamese Music in the United States. 1993. New Alliance Records NAR CD 053. Compact disc.

Haines, David, ed. 1989. *Refugees and Immigrants: Cambodians, Laotians, and Vietnamese.* Totowa, N.J.: Rowan and Littlefield.

Nguyễn, Phong T. *Searching for a Niche: Vietnamese Music at Home in America.* 1995. Kent, Ohio: Viet Music Publication.

Nguyễn, Phong Thuyet, and Patricia Shehan Campbell. 1989. *From Rice Paddies and Temple Yards.* Danbury, Conn.: World Music Press.

Reyes Schramm, Adelaida. 1986. "Tradition in the Guise of Innovation: Music among a Refugee Population." In *Yearbook for Traditional Music,*

91–101. New York: International Council for Traditional Music.

Song of the Banyan: Folk Music of Vietnam by Phong Nguyễn Ensemble. 1997. Music of the World. WMI Latitudes LAT 50607. Compact disc.

Cambodian Music
Sam-Ang Sam

Several hundred thousand Cambodians began to resettle in the United States (and many more in Europe, Japan, Australia, and New Zealand) after April 1975, when the Khmer Rouge, led by Pol Pot (born Saloth Sar), invaded the capital, Phnom Penh, drove the populace into the countryside, and killed or starved at least two million of their countrymen. This four-year reign of terror ended in 1979 when the Vietnamese invaded, driving the Khmer Rouge back into the wilderness. The Khmer Rouge attempt to eradicate Cambodian (or Khmer) culture included killing or causing to die nearly 80 percent of the country's dancers, musicians, singers, and instrument makers. The education system, which included the Royal University of Fine Arts, along with other aspects of culture (for example, libraries and Buddhist temples), was destroyed. Although a small number of artists survived within Cambodia, others fled to camps in neighboring countries. Some were eventually resettled in North America.

Most of the quarter million Cambodians who live in the United States are concentrated in two locations—Long Beach, California, and Lowell, Massachusetts—but smaller groups are found in Washington, D.C., Seattle, and Philadelphia. Wherever possible, the Cambodian communities maintain traditional customs and observe many of their religious and national festivals. As with most immigrant groups, however, the younger generation now coming of age in the United States is strongly inclined to adapt to their new environment. A small minority has striven to maintain the artistic traditions of their parents' homeland.

OVERVIEW OF CAMBODIAN ARTS

The traditions brought to the United States by the new immigrants reflect the situation in Cambodia before 1975, naturally omitting later revolutionary styles. Three general types of music were then known: (1) court (or classical) arts, including ensemble instrumental music, vocal performance, dance, dance drama, and puppet theater; (2) village (or folk) arts, including instrumental and vocal music, dance, and theater; and (3) modern urban (or popular) music, primarily ballroom dance music, movie music, and popular songs.

The maintenance of these types in the United States depends on the geographical proximity of balanced groups of musicians, singers, and dancers, a coincidence of free time, and appropriate contexts for performance. All have been and continue to be problems. Obtaining good musical instruments is especially difficult. In the case of

FIGURE I Five musicians and a female singer (far right) perform a classical *mohori* ensemble for an American audience. The instruments of the ensemble are (left to right): *skor thaun* and *skor rumanea* 'drum pair', *khloy* 'fipple flute', *roneat ek* 'xylophone', *tro* 'fiddle', and *krapeu* 'floor zither'. Photo courtesy of Sam-Ang Sam.

classical ensembles (figure 1), using similar instruments from Thailand has been acceptable, although a few musicians have built their own instruments. In the case of village ensembles, substitutions have either been impossible or dissimilar (for example, using the American banjo in place of the long-necked *chapei dang veng* 'lute'). Popular music requires a distribution system for media materials (cassette tapes, compact discs, and videos), but Cambodian shops are rare outside population concentrations.

Few musicians, singers, or dancers arriving in the West could speak English. They were unable to support themselves as artists. A first priority was to learn a new language and acquire appropriate job skills. Because immigrants were resettled in widely scattered areas, it was difficult to form coherent ensembles and mount performances. The author and his wife, having lived and worked in the United States for many years, have tried to reunite ensembles and troupes, produce teaching materials and archival documents, and offer workshops and residencies, most supported by an array of private and public foundations and agencies. As a result, a number of young artists, some born in the United States, have begun learning the traditional arts of their homeland. In some cases there have been innovative projects, especially involving dance, such as those at the Portland Performing Arts Festival in Maine (July 1996) and at the Jacob's Pillow Dance Festival in Massachusetts (October 1996). The latter has included collaborations with English dancer Jonathan Lunn and American dancer Gwyneth Jones.

As Cambodia stabilized in the mid-1980s, exchanges became possible. Troupes from Cambodia have toured North America and Europe, and some artists living in the West have returned to Cambodia for research and training. The author, supported by a MacArthur Fellowship and an Asian Cultural Council Fellowship, for example, returned to Phnom Penh's restored Royal University of Fine Arts in 1996 to teach basic ethnomusicology. Even so, Cambodia's musical arts have attracted little attention beyond the community and a small group of scholars. Only Katherine McKinley, a student at Brown University, has specialized in Cambodian music, and is currently writing a dissertation on village wedding music.

COURT TRADITIONS: NEW MEANINGS

Cambodian court dance and the music accompanying it first reached its zenith during the Angkor period (ninth to fifteenth centuries C.E.) and again during the second half of the twentieth century. Until 1970 it was performed virtually by a single troupe resident at the royal palace in Phnom Penh, and from 1970 to 1975, at the Royal University

Whereas performances in Cambodia could be quite lengthy, those in the United States had to fit the new situation—modern staged presentations, short in duration, performed on weekends when performers were not working.

of Fine Arts. As the most formal expression of the Cambodian performing arts, it has come to be perceived by Cambodians as a major symbol of the culture, a reminder of most formal expression of the Cambodian performing arts. The dance itself has reflected basic socioreligious, political, and cultural facets of Cambodian life since its inception. Although the folk arts are most typically seen as reflective of a society's soul, Cambodia's case is somewhat different.

With the fall of the Cambodian monarchy in 1970 (albeit restored in 1993 when exiled Prince Silhanouk returned as King Sihanouk), the court traditions ceased to be exclusive. Court musicians and dancers living in the refugee camps had begun teaching their arts to interested commoners in the 1970s. Because the court arts were seen to embody the very soul of Cambodian culture, they quickly came to represent a common heritage that grounded and balanced all individuals no matter what their rank. Having had near sacred status before 1975, these arts came to have a similar kind of spiritual status after 1979. Their restoration represented the restoration of the Cambodian soul. Consequently, the court arts in the United States have been entirely democratic, open to anyone willing to learn. They became part of the healing process of a people deeply scarred by terrible events. The court arts were not merely elegant and sophisticated, but they became fundamental to maintaining and expressing Cambodian identity.

As Cambodian communities coalesced in the United States, and as skilled performers were identified and regrouped, certain kinds of court performances became possible, usually with help from dancers newly trained here. Traditional court dance (*robaim kbach buran*) was more possible than the extremely elaborate masked play (*lkhaon khaol*) (figure 2). The shadow play (*lkhaon sbek*), however, was impossible to

FIGURE 2   Émigré actors and actresses perform a section of a Cambodian masked dance-drama based on the Ramayana epic, called *Reamker* in Khmer. Photo by Terry E. Miller, 1982.

mount because even in Cambodia performers were rare, and, furthermore, this genre required a large set of intricate puppets cut from leather. Whereas performances in Cambodia could be quite lengthy, those in the United States had to fit the new situation—modern staged presentations, short in duration, performed on weekends when performers were not working. The principal time for these seldom-seen performances is the Cambodian New Year. North Americans not living near a significant concentration of Cambodians are unlikely to experience Cambodian music and dance unless they travel to such an area or see it on video.

FOLK ARTS

Because most traditional Cambodian folk genres required particular contexts for their performance, the lack of these in the United States discouraged their maintenance. Further, because court genres had such great meaning to communities, folk arts tended to be neglected, and few survive here. Among those that continue to be performed, though infrequently, are folk dance (*robaim prapeyney*), folk theater (*lkhaon yike*), Cambodian theater of Chinese origin (*lkhaon basakk*), and repartee singing accompanied by small ensemble (*ayai*). Epic singing (*chrieng chapei*) has not survived in the United States. Most common are wedding ensembles, as marriages occur frequently throughout the United States, but such events are generally foreshortened.

NEW TRENDS

The classical repertoire underwent numerous changes in the United States to accommodate missing instruments and the limitations of the performers. For example, the *pinn peat* ensemble, traditionally composed of *sralai* 'shawm', *roneat* 'xylophones/metallophone', *korng vung* 'circular frame of gongs', *chhing* 'small cymbals', *sampho* 'small double-headed barrel drum', *skor thomm* 'large double-headed barrel drums', and *chamrieng* 'vocals', now also includes *tror* 'two-stringed fiddles', *krapeu* 'three-stringed zither', *khimm* 'hammered dulcimer', and *khloy* 'duct flute'. Some of these modified *pinn peat* ensembles also use Western flute or recorder instead of the *khloy;* the lack of *sralai* players has led *pinn peat* ensembles to have the *roneat ek* 'high-pitched xylophone' player perform the traditional and well-known piece "Salauma," normally played on a *sralai*. Lacking *skor thomm* players, the *sampho* player now plays both parts, resulting in a decline in timbral variety; male dancers, instead of the traditional female dancers, now dance parts; and inadequate knowledge of repertoire of both music and dance has led to substitutions and abbreviations of classical pieces. For example, musicians may substitute a simpler and more familiar piece for the correct one. Sometimes when musicians cannot play all the sections of a traditional piece, they repeat what they know instead.

TRANSMISSION

Young Cambodians often feel that their parents and older relatives are too conservative, old-fashioned, and even backward. They perceive Cambodian music, song, and dance as too slow and therefore boring. Nonetheless, a few young Cambodians do seek out lessons in traditional arts and attend performance events. Cambodian associations in some communities, such as the Cambodian American Heritage in Maryland, offer classes in the traditional performing arts. Some students have little interest in learning these arts, but they come to dance and music classes for their social value, especially to meet members of the opposite sex; courtship failures usually lead to their dropping the class. There is also the problem of commitment; some come to class once and are never seen again. In addition, community arts and outreach groups, such as the Cambodian Network Council in Washington (D.C.), Portland Performing Arts Festival in Maine, Country Roads Refugee Arts Group in Boston, New England Foundation for the Arts, and the Jacob's Pillow Dance Festival in Massachusetts actively seek out and work with Cambodian artists to offer master classes, document traditional pieces on film, and sponsor concerts and festivals.

POPULAR MUSIC

Popular music has long been a part of Cambodian life, although before American influence came to dominate, it was French-style song that Europeanized Cambodians enjoyed. International styles of ballroom dance and its music, such as bolero, cha-cha, fox-trot, and rumba, were and continue to be popular both in Cambodia and in the United States. But the generation of Cambodians born here prefers American-style rock music. Cambodian youth often form rock and pop bands that are engaged for many kinds of community events. Some have managed to produce media materials (cassettes and videos), which are sold in Cambodian and other Asian groceries.

Cambodian rock bands use Western instruments such as electric guitar, electric bass, keyboard, and drum set. Most of this music is intended for dancing. The bands play popular songs composed by various groups and artists, including the Beatles, Rolling Stones, Bee Gees, Creedence Clearwater Revival, Santana, Lionel Richie, Michael Jackson, Van Halen, Rod Stewart, and Madonna. They also play popular songs in Cambodian rhythms—*roam vung, roam kbach,* and *saravane.* These dance gatherings are attended mostly by the young.

THE FUTURE OF CAMBODIAN MUSIC IN THE UNITED STATES

Although young Cambodians have had opportunities to study the musical and theatrical arts known to their parents, it is necessarily on an informal and sporadic basis, depending on the availability of teachers and spare time. More often young Cambodian Americans praise and adopt Western popular culture and discredit their own. They wish to be American rather than Cambodian, to fit in rather than stand out as possibly exotic. Their preferred instruments are guitar, keyboard, and drums. During breaks from their study of Cambodian music, which they often characterize as boring or slow, they are inclined to form small groups to rap and dance the Electric Slide or the Macarena. Few choose to express themselves in Cambodian form.

The classical tradition has been maintained but in an incomplete form. A full *pinn peat* ensemble has not been possible, making incomplete or ad hoc mixed ensembles the norm. Some older musicians possess an imperfect knowledge of the repertoire, but younger, possibly more knowledgeable, musicians are prevented from correcting their elders by customary standards of social behavior. Work schedules often conflict, even in those rare circumstances where there are enough musicians in a given area, making the scheduling of practices and performances challenging. Not surprisingly, many of the traditional ceremonies that required music in the homeland now omit it. Others have been simplified and shortened, such as the wedding ceremony—what used to take three days and three nights now lasts one day. These are the new social, economic, and logistical realities. Many wish to remain faithful to their ancestral culture, but the challenges are daunting and temptations to give in to the popular culture of the United States overwhelming.

REFERENCES

Brunet, Jacques. 1969. *Nang Sbek: Théâtre d'ombres dansé du Cambodge.* Berlin: Institut International d'Etudes Comparatives de la Musique.

Catlin, Amy, ed. 1992. *Khmer Classical Dance Songbook.* Van Nuys, Calif.: Apsara Media for Intercultural Education.

Giuriati, Giovanni. 1995. "Pambhlai: The Art of Improvisation in Khmer Traditional Music." *Cahiers d'études franco-cambodiens* 5:24–39.

Kodish, Debora, ed. 1994. *The Giant Never Wins: Lakhon Bassac (Cambodian Folk Opera) in Philadelphia.* Philadelphia: Philadelphia Folklore Project.

Sam, Chan Moly. 1987. *Khmer Court Dance.* Newington, Conn.: Khmer Studies Institute.

Sam, Sam-Ang, and Chan Moly Sam. 1987. *Khmer Folk Dance.* Newington, Conn.: Khmer Studies Institute.

Sam, Sam-Ang, and Patricia Shehan Campbell. 1991. *Silent Temples, Songful Hearts: Traditional Music of Cambodia.* Danbury, Conn.: World Music Press.

Hmong Music
Amy Catlin

Vocal Music
Instrumental Music
New Trends

The Hmong people of North America are descendants of a non-Chinese minority who began migrating from southern China to Vietnam and Laos about two hundred years ago, leaving several million still in China today. The first Hmong in the United States arrived from Laos as refugees soon after the end of the Vietnam War in 1975 and now total about 180,000, with major population centers in central California and Minnesota. These Lao Hmong had fought as guerrilla troops in the United States' unsuccessful "Secret War" against the communist Pathet Lao, in support of the Lao royalist government, and had to escape Laos. From temporary camps in Thailand many Hmong were gradually resettled in the United States in recognition of their service to the American armed forces. Some were resettled in other countries for humanitarian reasons.

Having been semimigratory agriculturalists in the mountains of southern China and northern Southeast Asia for many centuries, the Hmong (called *Miao* by the Chinese, *Meo* by the Lao) were accustomed to confining their wealth to portable items such as silver jewelry, elaborate textiles, and a rich heritage of oral literature, song, and music. Although some Hmong musicians succeeded in transmitting portions of their unique musical repertoire to their children and grandchildren born in America, most cannot compete with popular Western music and MTV for young Hmong audiences and musicians.

VOCAL MUSIC

Hmong vocal music, actually heightened speech, is always sung as an unaccompanied solo, according to intuitively learned rules for realizing the eight linguistic word tones in Hmong, a non-Chinese tonal language. Traditional Hmong vocal music includes secular poetry sung to various melody types in unmetered rhythms, and sacred texts chanted to other types of melodies for funerals, weddings, healing rituals, and various ceremonies. The secular songs may be about love, loneliness, or longing for a distant home, as the Hmong have been seminomadic for many centuries.

Hmong American songs often express the despair of refugees who remember their idyllic village life in prewar Laos, the horrors of the war, and their psychological pain due to their perceived marginality in Western society. Love songs are still sung at the annual New Year festival during courtship ball games, when boys and girls exchange

FIGURE 1 Hmong girl sings songs while tossing the courtship ball at the New Year festival in San Diego, California. Photo by Amy Catlin, December 1985.

songs while playing catch, usually under the watchful eye of parents or matchmakers (figure 1). Cassette recordings are made during these musical interactions for circulation later among potential mates belonging to the appropriate clan, as marriage is only permitted outside one's clan. There are also songs for telling legends, stories, and historical tales, as well as moral lessons. During a funeral, the surviving spouse and relatives keen (wail) their laments to the open casket in tearful outpourings of grief. Lullabies are sung by mothers to their children, but there are no songs sung by children. This seems to be because secular singing is closely associated with courtship and thus begins at puberty. Sometimes "secret languages" are sung to disguise a message whose words are obscured following rules known only to the singers, in various invented systems similar to "pig Latin." This may be done by lovers to conceal their relationship, or by parents to prevent children from understanding their plans.

INSTRUMENTAL MUSIC

Hmong melody instruments play the similar solo melodies, as players imagine poetry to guide the creation of the melody. One Hmong instrument, the *geng* (spelled *qeej* in the Hmong writing system), a free-reed mouth organ, is used to play a text-based melody in the middle range, with a two-note ostinato in the highest register. This popular instrument is played for funerals and for entertainment, and the performer often uses acrobatic dance movements. The *geng* is normally made of six bamboo tubes mounted vertically into a long horizontal wooden windchest, although plastic pipes have been substituted by some Hmong American instrument makers (figure 2). Set into the wall of each tube is a metal free reed that vibrates inside the chamber when the player inhales or exhales through the mouthpiece, thus setting the column of air in the tube in motion. Acrobatic *geng* players compete for prizes at the New Year festival, which usually occurs in December, following the Hmong calendar, although other dates have been used in North America in order to have better weather for outdoor festivities. In North America there is a shortage of *geng* players who have memorized the voluminous funeral repertoire, so players often travel long distances to participate in death rituals. A large double-headed barrel-shaped funeral drum is struck in special patterns at specified times during the rites. In order to adapt to American practices, funerals have been abbreviated from the original three-day ceremony.

Other Hmong instruments have received less attention in the American environment, perhaps because they are visually less exciting than the acrobatically played

FIGURE 2 Nhia Ka Moua demonstrating *geng (qeej)* mouth organ constructed of PVC plastic and galvanized tubes at San Diego Hmong New Year. Photo by Amy Catlin, December 1985.

FIGURE 3   Two-stringed fiddle, seesaw (*nko chaw nja; xim xo*) made of thermos bottle by Neng Yang, in playing position (Providence, R.I., June 1982). Photo by Amy Catlin.

mouth organ. These include the mouth harp (*nja, ncas,* or *guimbard*), which was used in Laos to convey words in whispery love serenades. A free-reed pipe (*chamblai* or *raj nplaim*) and a fipple flute (*chapuli* or *raj pus lim*) are still occasionally heard and can be used to suggest song texts that listeners often understand. Two-stringed fiddles called *nko chaw nja* (*nkauj nrog ncas;* Lao-derived name: *xim xo*), 'seesaw', traditionally made of bamboo or coconut shell, have been fashioned in America using such innovative materials as thermos bottles and broom handles for body and neck (figure 3). Scrimshaw designs or letters are sometimes etched into carrying cases or actual instruments as decoration or to relate memories of the passage from Laos to America.

NEW TRENDS

A few bilingual Hmong are now able to present their traditional music for non-Hmong-speaking audiences while giving their own explanations and translations in English. This contrasts with the earlier format of relying upon ethnomusicologists or folklorists for public presentations in festivals and museum programs. Mai Zong Vue of Madison, Wisconsin, is one example of a college-educated Hmong woman who self-presents Hmong music. Similarly, Chue Chang of California tells Hmong stories in English and explains and demonstrates a variety of Hmong instruments.

The first Hmong to receive a bachelor of arts degree in music was Alain Lee of Fresno (California) State University, a classical guitarist who has won several competitions. He composes in mainstream jazz and Latin styles, as well as improvising Hmong songs with instrumental accompaniments for private Hmong parties.

Although first-generation Hmong immigrants retain the most extensive musical repertoires, "generation loss" and creative adaptation to the new environment have been inevitable among second- and third-generation Hmong. Parodies of Western popular music and new compositions in the style of American pop music, using Hmong or English texts, have been most popular among the younger generation for social dancing or listening, circulated by independently produced CDs, audiocassettes, and music videos and heard on Hmong radio and TV programs. Such music sometimes accompanies stage dances by Hmong girls using movements derived from Lao folk dance, Western modern dance, and other sources. The best-known Hmong rock group, called Sounders, is based in the Fresno area. Imitations of other forms of commercial music sung in Hmong, such as Hindi film music or Thai popular song, have also been produced.

Hmong American music has also been used in dramas that reenact the history of the Hmong. Music videos feature Hmong musicians singing traditional music against a background of trees and waterfalls, intercut with similar scenery from Laos. One Hmong musician in Fresno, Vungping Yang, produces a daily radio program of Hmong music that emphasizes traditional materials. He has composed quasi-minimalist synthesizer accompaniments to his vocal renditions of Hmong poetry. Such tapes are available at Hmong grocery stores as well as New Year festival grounds, along with audiocassettes of both traditional and acculturated instrumental and vocal music by Hmong American soloists. Religious music in Protestant settings includes Western hymn tunes sung in Hmong, and Catholic pageants and masses sometimes retain authentic Hmong melodies in settings of Latin liturgical texts translated into Hmong.

The Hmong American community recognizes the increasing alienation of its Americanized youth from Hmong language and traditional culture and has devised various strategies for reconnecting younger Hmong with their cultural roots. Classes in Hmong instrumental music are offered in many Hmong communities, as well as summer camps for learning about Hmong history and culture, including music. New Year competitions function in a similar way by offering recognition and prizes for traditional costumes, song, and instrumental music, as well as for acculturated forms.

REFERENCES

Catlin, Amy. 1982. "Speech Surrogate Systems of the Hmong: From Singing Voices to Talking Reeds." In *The Hmong in the West: Observations and Reports,* ed. Bruce T. Downing and Douglas P. Olney, 170–197. Minneapolis: University of Minnesota Southeast Asia Refugee Studies Program.

———. 1985. "The Hmong and Their Music . . . A Critique of Pure Speech." In *Hmong Art: Tradition and Change,* ed. Joann Cubbs, 10–19. Sheboygan, Wisc.: The John Michael Kohler Arts Center.

———. 1988. "Virgins, Orphans, Widows, and Bards: Songs of Hmong Women." In *Textiles as Texts: Arts of Hmong Women from Laos,* ed. A. Catlin. With audiocassette. Van Nuys: Apsara Media for Intercultural Education.

———. 1992. "Homo Cantens: Why Hmong Sing During Interactive Courtship Rituals." In *Text, Context, and Performance in Cambodia, Laos, and Vietnam,* ed. A. Catlin, 43–60. Selected Reports in Ethnomusicology, Volume 9. Los Angeles: UCLA Ethnomusicology Publications.

———. 1997a. *Hmong Musicians in America: Interactions with Three Generations of Hmong American Musicians, 1978–1996.* Van Nuys, Calif.: Apsara Media for Intercultural Education. 60-minute videotape.

———. 1997b. "Puzzling the Text: Thought-Songs, Secret Languages, and Archaic Tones in Hmong Music." *The World of Music* 39(2):69–81.

Lao, Thai, and Cham Music
Terry E. Miller

Lao
Thai
Cham

Of the mainland Southeast Asian communities, those of the Viet, Lao, and Khmer are the largest because they migrated as a result of the Vietnam War, most from 1975 onwards; the Cham are a component of the Viet migration. One of the smaller groups, the Thai, are comprised mainly of professionals who came to the United States voluntarily.

LAO

Immediately after 1975, thousands of people from Laos began to resettle in the United States. Most of them were soldiers and their families, those who remained from the vanquished army of the fallen Kingdom of Laos, an American ally during the war in Vietnam. At first, little distinction was made among the many ethnic groups that made up the Lao population in the United States, but gradually the lowland Lao emerged as distinct from the upland Hmong, Khmu, and other ethnic minorities. The lowland Lao, however, maintained strong feelings of regionality, which made the formation of unified communities difficult. As a result, the Lao in the United States have remained less cohesive than other Southeast Asian populations and consequently less able to keep their cultural patterns intact. Although there are tens of thousands of Lao, there has been minimal formation of urban Lao communities similar to the "Little Saigon" and "Little Phnom Penh" phenomena. The greatest concentrations of Lao are found in California, especially in the Fresno area, but there is also a large group of Thai Dam ("Black Thai") living in the Des Moines, Iowa, area.

Two themes dominate the discussion of Lao music in North America: (1) attempts to maintain traditional music and (2) the development of a popular music. Traditional music has barely survived, whereas popular music has come to dominate the Lao music scene.

Traditional music

In Laos there were two kinds of traditional music. Classical instrumental ensembles performing music and dance were supported by the Lao court in Luang Phrabang and the School of Fine Arts in Vientiane, and a dozen or more regionally specific forms of repartee village singing, called *khap* in the north and *lam* in the south, were closely associated with rural life. Attempts were made to keep the classical ensembles together in the United States. Part of the Vientiane group moved to Nashville, Tennessee, and

Although these bands typically arrange American pop songs with newly written Lao texts, they also play a repertoire of traditional regional styles transformed into popular song style, a factor that sets them apart from the rock groups of other Southeast Asian refugees.

FIGURE 1   Famous Lao *mohlam* singer Buntong Insixiengmai of Murfreesboro, Tennessee, sings with *khene* accompaniment by Khampoun Sonsayarat, performing a regional style called *lam khon savan.* Photo by Terry E. Miller, 1981.

FIGURE 2   Lao *mawlam* singer Khamvong Insixiengmai, a recipient of a National Heritage Fellowship, accompanied by *khene* player Khamseung Syhanone, perform for a small outdoor audience in Ohio. Photo by Terry E. Miller, date unknown.

members of the Luang Phrabang group settled in Des Moines. Though the Iowa group has reformed, the classical music of Laos barely survives in the United States today.

Two major artists who specialized in *lam* were resettled in the United States: Buntong Insixiengmai (figure 1) of Murfreesboro, Tennessee, and his nephew, Khamvong Insixiengmai of Fresno. Unfortunately their female singing partners could not join them, and their performances remained incomplete. Both were able to find traditional free-reed mouth organ *(khene)* accompanists, however, and eventually Khamvong joined with female singer Thongkhio Maniwong for numerous public performances before the duo split up. Although Buntong specialized in singing one regional genre from southern Laos, *lam khon savan,* Khamvong was able to perform many southern Lao genres as well as *lam* from northeastern Thailand. Khamvong became known outside the Lao communities early on through the efforts of Cliff Sloane, then of Minneapolis, and, later, Robert Browning of the World Music Institute in New York. Eventually Khamvong recorded several commercial audiocassettes, one of which was reissued as a compact disc. In 1993 Khamvong received a National Heritage Fellowship from the National Endowment for the Arts ◉ᵀ²³.

Khamvong's accompanist, Khamseung Inthanone, is a blind master of Laos's national instrument, the *khene,* a bamboo free-reed mouth organ with sixteen pipes, which must be imported from Laos or northeastern Thailand, because neither the materials nor makers are available in the United States. There are, here and there, other *khene* players in the United States, but none approaches the talent of Khamseung (figure 2).

Popular music

The most prevalent form of music making among Lao Americans is the popular song accompanied by rock music instruments—usually electric guitars, drum set, and keyboard—primarily played by the generation born in the United States. Although these bands typically arrange American pop songs with newly written Lao texts, they also play a repertoire of traditional regional styles transformed into popular song style, a factor that sets them apart from the rock groups of other Southeast Asian refugees. Whenever there is a community event, especially celebrations of both American and Lao holidays, at least one rock band will be on hand to provide music. Although members of the older generation prefer to hear some traditional music to maintain their feelings for their former home, few communities actually have such musicians. Even when available, they are the exception rather than the rule. Indeed, when Khamvong performs in Lao events, he is normally accompanied by a *khene* plus a rock combo. Traditional Lao musicians do not view accompanying *lam* with modern Western instruments as problematic.

During the evening the band (or bands) responds to audience requests. As a result, there will be a mixture of traditional Lao circle-dance (*lamvong*) songs and modernized regional *lam* styles (especially *lam sithandone, lam khon savan, lam tangvay*, and *lam phuthai*), as well as line dances and other popular styles current in the United States. People enjoy these forms of Lao social dancing, as anyone can participate and touching, considered socially inappropriate, is not required.

A moderate number of Lao Americans have returned to their homeland to visit family and friends. While there, some purchase cassette tapes of popular songs recorded in Laos. Some of these have been reissued in the United States, even on compact disc, and are sold through a network of Lao groceries and other Asian food stores. Tapes of unmodernized traditional music are extremely rare. Large chain music stores offer the general public a limited selection of compact discs of Lao music produced in Japan, Europe, and the United States.

The future

The future of Lao musical activity in the United States will in part depend on what happens in Laos. There, the Thai media dominate, overpowering the weaker Lao stations with broadcasts of popular music and videos. These include the powerful and modernized styles emanating from northeastern Thailand, which is culturally related to Laos. It appears that poverty prevents the Lao from following a pattern of modernization such as that which has swept through northeastern Thailand during the past twenty-five years. With connections between Lao living in the United States and in Laos becoming closer, it is also possible that influences from Lao American musicians could affect matters in the home country.

THAI

Although Thai cuisine has become both popular and widespread, even in smaller cities with virtually no Thai community, Thai music has otherwise remained little known outside a small circle of followers. The vast majority of Thai in the United States came during the past thirty years to study at American universities. Many remained and became American citizens and today make their livings as doctors, engineers, computer specialists, and in business. For the most part, Thai music in the United States has consisted of imported popular music cassettes and videos available at Asian groceries in the cities. Although few Thai would normally listen to Thai classical music, most prefer to use it to represent their culture to outsiders. This is especially so on university campuses, where "Thai nights," a combination of dinner, displays of artifacts, and performances of dance, music, and simulated weddings, attract great numbers of non-Thai.

Many Thai students studied Thai classical music in their youth, but few play it now unless someone organizes a music ensemble. This has happened at a few campuses, but such ensembles rarely survive for more than a few years. Two campuses established long-running Thai ensembles—Kent State University in Ohio in 1978 and Southwestern University in Texas in 1988. Although the teachers have been Thai, most performers have been non-Thai students. At least four ensembles are known to exist within Thai communities in Seattle, Los Angeles, Chicago, and New York. Obtaining instruments requires their importation from Thailand, but one Chicago-based Thai craftsman is making Thai dulcimers (*khim*).

CHAM

When refugees began fleeing Vietnam in April 1975, everyone arriving in the United States was considered by Americans to be Vietnamese. But Vietnam is a multiethnic country, and the immigrant Vietnamese represented several ethnic groups: the dominant, lowland Viet (also called Kinh) speaking an Austro-Asiatic language; several upland minorities speaking both Austro-Asiatic and Malayo-Polynesian languages; and the lowland Cham, also Malayo-Polynesian-speakers. Although each group brought its own sense of separate identity from Vietnam, this separateness vanished for a period in the United States until communities could establish themselves and assert their uniqueness without interference from the mainstream Vietnamese.

The Cham are the descendants of the Kingdom of Champa, an Indianized Hindu-influenced state that flourished in southern Vietnam from the second century C.E. until its gradual and ultimate demise at the hands of the expanding Vietnamese in the fifteenth century. All that remains of this once-glorious kingdom are ruined and restored temples, museum-preserved carvings, and cultural pride. Most Cham in Vietnam converted to Islam, although those in Cambodia remained Hindu. The Cham consider themselves and their culture to have been suppressed by the Vietnamese, but in their new context—the United States—they have freely asserted a separate cultural identity.

Cham music is characterized by continuously derived, unphrased melody using small intervals within a narrow range. Two melodic instruments predominate, a conical oboe called *saranai* and a turtle-shell fiddle called *kanhi*. These are accompanied by single and two-headed drums playing cyclic meters. In addition to the traditional music, which may be played alone or used to accompany song or dance, there are popular songs that express the strongly emotional feelings people have for their lost homeland.

In the United States Cham music activity has centered on an annual celebration called *kate*. Although a large international *kate* to celebrate Cham identity in song, dance, and dramatic reenactments was held in San Jose, California, in 1994, subsequent *kate* are only observed locally by Hindu Cham. The organizers of these celebrations are quite serious about reestablishing the traditional dances and music known in Vietnam, and there is evidence of their success in doing so.

REFERENCES

Miller, Terry E. 1985. "The Survival of Lao Traditional Music in America." In *Selected Reports in Ethnomusicology, vol. 6: Asian Music in North America,* ed. Nazir A. Jairazbhoy and Sue Carole DeVale, 99–110. Los Angeles: University of California.

Indonesian Music

Jody Diamond
Barbara Benary

Early Exposure
Expansion of Gamelan Programs
Indonesian Teachers
American Composers
Indonesian and American Collaborators
Instrument Building
Bali, Sunda, and Sumatra
Other Regions and Arts
Other Institutions Supporting Indonesian Music
Looking Forward

In 1947, three hundred seamen on a Dutch vessel jumped ship in New York. Claiming to be Indonesian citizens, they sought asylum. At that time the United States did not recognize the Republic of Indonesia (and would not until 1949), so their status was problematic. Robert Delson, now an attorney-at-law to the American Indonesian Chamber of Commerce, represented the crew, who were eventually able to settle in America, where they formed one of the few small communities of Indonesians living on the continent—quite possibly the first such immigration from a soon-to-be born nation (Forrest 1999).

The number of Indonesian citizens living in the United States is small compared to populations from other Southeast Asian countries such as the Philippines. Many come for education or training and then return to Indonesia. In 1999 there were an estimated ten thousand Indonesian students enrolled in institutions of higher education, with adult communities of a few thousand in New York and five to ten thousand in California (Forrest 1999). Indonesians who reside in the United States tend to be diplomats, business people, students, or members of a small, specialized group of artists and scholars with permanent teaching positions in music, dance, language, and other fields. Those who are part of the diplomatic community work at the United Nations and related agencies; at the World Bank and the International Monetary Fund; at the Indonesian Embassy in Washington, D.C.; or at one of the consulates currently established in Chicago, Houston, Los Angeles, or San Francisco. The largest group of Indonesians living in the United States is concentrated in Southern California, either through business activities or by enrolling as students at universities. Indonesian students in the United States may belong to an organization known as PERMIAS, or the Association of Indonesian Students, which was founded in 1961 to unify several student groups scattered around the country at that time. In 1999 the PERMIAS website listed 140 chapters in forty-one states and Washington, D.C.

Much earlier, at the turn of the twentieth century—before a "torrent of Asian nationalism" (Toer 1992:3) and a burgeoning independence movement in the then Dutch East Indies led to the creation of Indonesia—the arts and artists of those islands had visited North America. What we call Indonesian music actually includes the musics of culturally distinct areas of a vast archipelago of 13,000 islands, now united as a nation whose identity is expressed, not surprisingly, by the motto *Bhinneka Tunggal*

Ika, 'Unity in Diversity'. In discussing the history of Indonesian arts in North America, it must be noted that the concept of *Indonesian* did not exist during the first half of the twentieth century. Most Indonesians have two identities, national and regional, and the arts that came to the United States in the twentieth century presented both of those aspects. The label *Indonesian* refers to Java, Sunda (West Java), Bali, West Sumatra, North Sumatra, Cirebon, and many other areas.

Nearly all the Indonesian music practiced in North America centers on the gamelan, which is an ensemble of melodic percussion and other instruments originating in the Indonesian islands of Java and Bali. The term *gamelan,* unlike the words "orchestra" and "ensemble," as it is often translated, means a collection of instruments that is built together, tuned together, and stored together. Musicians do not own individual instruments; rather, a full gamelan is often owned and housed by some kind of institution, be it a school, village, or palace, and the musicians go there to play it. Sometimes the gamelan will be given a name; groups of players themselves also may have a name.

A gamelan will usually include an unspecified number of metallophones and knobbed gongs, made in Indonesia of bronze, iron, and sometimes brass, and made in the United States of aluminum or iron. Depending on the musical genre and size of the ensemble, these may be augmented by drums (*kendang*), voices, flutes (*suling*), a bowed string instrument (*rebab*), and plucked zithers (*celempung, siter*), or various small percussion instruments such as sets of small cymbals (*ceng-ceng* in Bali, *kecer* in Java). Gamelans use a unique tuning system that includes *slendro,* a five-tone tuning of large intervals, and *pelog,* a seven-tone tuning of large and small intervals.

The musical styles that have become familiar in the United States and Canada are those of Bali, Central Java, and West Java (Sunda and Cirebon). Frequently taught and performed along with gamelan music are the associated arts of dance and puppet theater. In the two puppet theater styles taught most often in the United States, there is only one person who manipulates all the puppets and provides all the voices and narration for what can be an extensive performance; this multiskilled puppet master is called a *dalang.* The shadow puppet theater of Java and Bali, *wayang kulit,* is taught most frequently and uses flat leather puppets, which are perforated to make complex shadows against a white cloth screen. Also performed in the United States is *wayang golek* from the area of West Java known as Sunda; this employs carved wooden rod puppets. In both the dance and the puppet theater, characters and stories are often drawn from the *Ramayana* and the *Mahabharata,* both of Hindu origin, as well as indigenous tales from the various regions of Indonesia.

The history of Indonesian music in the United States begins with visiting Indonesian artists and arrives, nearly a century later, at a proliferation of cross-cultural, creative, collaborative communities that are connected to Indonesia and are also in the process of establishing American traditions. Groups of performers on tour or at international expositions provided America's first exposure to the traditional Indonesian arts. Later, when a significant development in ethnomusicology turned it into a hands-on field, the practice of gamelan music by Americans became more widespread. These first gamelan groups were usually taught by Indonesian experts and centered at universities. At the same time, the interest of American composers in various musics of Asia led to experiments that drew heavily on Indonesia in particular. The confluence of these influences created an environment for both the continued studies of Indonesian arts and the creation of music and instruments by Americans inspired by those arts.

EARLY EXPOSURE

Gamelan and other Indonesian arts have increased their presence in American communities to an extent far out of proportion to the representation of Indonesian citizens on the North American continent. This has occurred not so much as a result of the growth of immigrant subcommunities, as is often the case, but through programs at edu-cational institutions and the activities of independent musicians, composers, and in-strument builders. North America's first contact with Indonesian performing arts is believed to have been at the 1893 Columbian World Exposition in Chicago. Later exposure included a tour of Balinese dancers from Peliatan in Bali, organized by John Coast (1953), and the presence of Javanese and Balinese musicians and dancers at the New York World's Fair in 1964. There have been increasing numbers of groups on tour with each decade. In 1990–1991, during the yearlong Festival of Indonesia in America performance series coordinated by Rachel Cooper in the United States and by Amna S. Kusumo in Indonesia, 320 Indonesian artists toured the country, presenting court and village music from several Indonesian islands, including Java, Bali, and Sumatra, in over two hundred performances and workshops.

The sets of instruments imported for these exhibitions and tours often did not return to Indonesia but were sold or given to educational institutions and museums. With instruments procured in this manner, programs to teach both the theory and practice of Indonesian arts were founded in the 1960s at the University of Michigan, Ann Arbor, and at Wesleyan University in Middletown, Connecticut. Since the Colombian Exposition, many whole sets of instruments have been ordered, purchased, and imported, or built locally by both individuals and universities for both artistic and educational uses, a process that still continues.

EXPANSION OF GAMELAN PROGRAMS

Gamelan music in North America received a great impetus from a number of ethno-musicologists who, from the 1950s on, were dedicated to the concept of teaching world music through hands-on performance as well as academic study. Mantle Hood, an ethnomusicologist and composer, established a gamelan performance program at the University of California, Los Angeles, with Hardja Susilo as the first Javanese teacher in 1958, joined by Cokorda Mas from Bali in early 1959. Hood is credited with introducing the concept of *bimusicality,* requiring that students be able to perform the music they intended to write about. A number of graduates of that program went on to found other programs based on this idea and have maintained their dedication to educating Americans in Indonesian music over the decades. These include the late Gertrude Robinson, who was also a composer for gamelan, and Judith Becker, who later became a major scholar of Javanese music, founder of the gamelan program in Ann Arbor, and an observer of gamelan in America (1972, 1983; Becker and Feinstein 1988). Hood was also responsible for inviting several other significant Indonesian artists to UCLA to teach and study, including I Made Bandem, later to be director of first the national arts conservatory in Bali and then a major arts university in Yogya. In later generations, other Indonesian artists receiving degrees from various American institutions returned to Indonesia to a high level of artistic activity and cultural respon-sibility—for example, Endo Suanda, now head of the Indonesian Performing Arts Society; I Wayan Dibia, current director of the arts college in Bali; and Franki Raden, a prominent arts organizer and writer.

One of Hood's students to break new ground was Robert E. Brown, a Johnny Appleseed of gamelan in America. Taking Hood's bimusicality a step further, Brown emphasized performance alone as a primary form of musical knowledge. Brown founded performance-based world music programs that included Indonesian music, dance, and puppet theater at Wesleyan University (1960), California Institute of the Arts in Valencia (1970), and San Diego (California) State University (1979). Brown also directs the Center for World Music (www.centerforworldmusic.org), which was incorporated in San Francisco in 1963, has held programs in the San Francisco area and elsewhere, and moved to San Diego in 1979. In the intervening years, Brown, along with Sam and Louise Scripps, the founders of ASEA (American Society for

As of the year 2000 there were almost one hundred known active gamelan ensembles in the United States and Canada and possibly as many as a hundred additional sets of instruments privately or institutionally owned but infrequently played.

Eastern Arts), brought scores of the finest Indonesian artists to perform and to teach American students in a variety of venues. Brown and Scripps were also responsible for taking one of the earliest, and possibly the first, groups of American gamelan players to Indonesia to study and perform, in the summer of 1971. Many of the members of that group went on to to be very active in the fields of Indonesian music, literature, and culture: John Pemberton (1994), Nancy Florida (1993), Susan Walton (1987), Philip Yampolsky (1987, 1991), and Alan Feinstein (Becker and Feinstein 1988), among many others, including Jody Diamond.

Expansion in the 1970s and 1980s

The greatest expansion of university ethnomusicology programs teaching gamelan seems to have occurred in the 1970s through the early 1980s. Several ethnomusicologists specializing in Indonesia founded or developed gamelan programs as part of their departments: Martin Hatch at Cornell University in Ithaca, New York; R. Anderson Sutton at the University of Wisconsin at Madison; Roger Vetter at Grinnell College in Iowa. The growth wave leveled off in succeeding years but now seems to be picking up again as instruments become easier to import and interest in gamelan for education and composition increases. As of the year 2000 there were almost one hundred known active gamelan ensembles in the United States and Canada and possibly as many as a hundred additional sets of instruments privately or institutionally owned but infrequently played. This is nearly double the number of gamelan sets that were counted in the first North American Gamelan Directory, compiled by Barbara Benary in *Ear Magazine* in1983. Currently, new programs with new teachers and sets of instruments pop up around the country (the North American Gamelan Directory, at www.gamelan.org, lists twenty-nine states in the United States and three Canadian provinces), while others go quietly dormant as founding individuals retire or institutional powers decide to rechannel money to other educational or musical priorities. It is important to note that some of North America's music schools and conservatories have finally begun to recognize ethnomusicology and to include gamelan music in their curricula.

INDONESIAN TEACHERS

Indonesian performers, both visiting and resident teachers, have been an important and ongoing source of inspiration and knowledge in the spread of gamelan music and related arts. In nearly all cases, the universities that maintain performing programs have invited master musicians from Indonesia—representing Central Java, Bali, Sunda (West Java), and sometimes Sumatra—to teach music and accompanying dance and theater forms. Most artists stay a few years or less, but some are employed for much longer periods, often taking permanent places on the faculty of these institutions. At Wesleyan University, Javanese musician and scholar Sumarsam and master musician I. M. Harjito, as well as dancer Urip Sri Maeny and singer Denni Harjito, make an important contribution to the performance of Javanese music, dance, and *wayang* not only at that institution but in many others within commuting distance in New En-

FIGURE I   K. R. T. Wasitodiningrat giving student Lisa Gold a lesson at the University of California, Berkeley. Photo by Jody Diamond, 1986.

gland and the New York area. Hardja Susilo, first at UCLA and later for many years at the University of Hawaii, has been particularly influential to innumerable Americans through his decades of teaching and performing in the United States and Canada. K. R. T. Wasitodiningrat (familiarly known as Pak Cokro, pronounced "choke-row") was very active during his twenty years at California Institute of the Arts and the University of California at Berkeley (Diamond 1995; Wenten 1996) (figure 1). On his retirement in 1992 he was replaced by Djoko Waluyo, while his daughter Nanik and her husband, Nyoman Wenten, remained in the program.

The consulates and embassies of the Republic of Indonesia often maintain a representation of their musical culture and are the most likely place to find a large Indonesian audience for performances. Gamelan instruments are housed at several consulates in a number of cities, and a variety of groups, comprising consulate personnel and their families as well as Americans, perform in both Javanese and Balinese styles. Some diplomatic centers have Indonesian teachers in residence; others are led by highly experienced North American players. In Washington, D.C., and nearby colleges, Balinese music has been taught by I Nyoman Suadin, a permanent U.S. resident.

AMERICAN COMPOSERS

Another major force in the expansion of gamelan has been the work of American composers. Some of the earliest and most influential were Henry Cowell, Lou Harrison (Garland 1987; Miller and Leiberman 1998), and Canadian Colin McPhee (Oja 1990). Sometimes referred to in earlier decades as "Orientalists," these composers approached the assimilation of gamelan music into their own work in various ways. McPhee arranged Balinese pieces for Western instruments and used Balinese motifs in his compositions. Harrison adapted Javanese forms, built gamelan instruments with partner William Colvig (Ditrich 1983), and in his many compositions often mixed them freely with Western instruments (Harrison 1988), using just intonation as a bridge between the two tuning systems. Henry Cowell, though not approaching Indonesian music so closely or directly, was nonetheless influential through his interest in Indonesian-inspired musical ideas and his insistence that his students, among them Harrison and John Cage, be open to all forms of music. Cage, though just as sympathetic to Asian influences as Harrison, composed only one piece for gamelan (Cage 1987; Frasconi 1988).

FIGURE 2 Gamelan Son of Lion's repertoire includes a number of pieces employing pitched hubcaps as portable gongs. Photo by unknown, 1986.

Succeeding generations of musicians were more thoroughly trained in Indonesian performance techniques; this affected the nature and intention of their work and led to new directions in American composition for Indonesian and Indonesian-style instruments (Perlman 1983). Some American composers, already immersed in their own contemporary styles, brought those to bear when composing for gamelan.

Gamelan Son of Lion in New York City (figure 2), started in 1976, was one of the earliest gamelan composers' collectives. Founders Barbara Benary, Daniel Goode, and Philip Corner, along with other composer-members, produced an extensive repertoire of pieces shaped by current ideas in experimental music, including process composition, minimalism, and indeterminacy. Some of their repertoire has been documented in Benary's four volumes of scores (1993a,b,c, 1995) and Corner's Gamelan Series of over four hundred process pieces. Goode's "Eine Kleine Gamelan Music," (figure 3) which has been played all over the world in many instrumentations (including a version with computer), shows evidence of his various influences. The use of small repeating patterns with shifting emphasis is characteristic of much minimal music, the use of written instructions that lead the players to create their own parts in real time is indicative of process music, and the use of gongs to punctuate large phrases is found in most gamelan music.

Near the end of the twentieth century, there was an increased interest in compositions for gamelan and orchestra, such as *Kreasi Baru* by Robert Macht and in 2000, *Dandanggula* by I. M. Harjito. This is another indication that gamelan was gaining more acceptance as a classical orchestra ensemble accessible to American composers—one with musical as well as cultural attributes.

INDONESIAN AND AMERICAN COLLABORATORS

Another important development is the collaboration of Indonesian and American artists on works that have been performed in both Indonesia and the United States. In some cases Indonesian artists created new works for specific U.S. groups; in others the teacher–student relationship was expanded to one of collegial artistry in which new pieces were created that were "equally informed by both traditions" (Ziporyn 1992:30). Following the *Festival of Indonesia* in 1991, three Indonesian composers had residencies with American gamelan groups; each produced a piece and a recording (Diamond, 1992b). Percussionist Keith Terry has worked with Balinese choreographer

FIGURE 3   Score of "Eine Kleine Gamelan Music" by Daniel Goode.

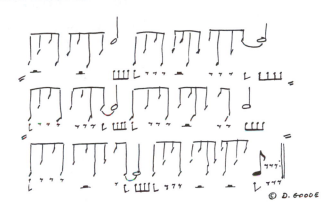

Eine Kleine Gamelan Music

by Daniel Goode

© D. GOODE

.... *for instruments of any tunings and any type* ....

Construct 3-note melodies of a step followed by a skip, *or* a skip followed by a step in any scale, mode, key, in any tuning, either upward or downward (but not both in the same melody).

Apply these melodies to the motive above, which gives the rhythm and order of the three tones. Play the same melody for *at least two* times through the motive. You can also play the motive mirror-fashion, from the highest to the lowest note and so on.

KEEP the same tone(s), the same variant for at least two repeats before changing or resting.

ENDING: When all instruments are playing the rhythmic variant (eighths in place of long notes), that becomes the last time.

VARIANTS:

—Accent either the lowest or highest tones or both.

—Omit all but the accented tones.

—Play only the long notes and fill them in with eighths including an eighth on the next beat after.* The last beat, as is.

—A sustaining instrument may play a long tone in place of the written eighths, and rest for the long notes of the motive.

—Gongs or gong-like sounds and other percussion instruments can be added to the long notes.   *see rhythmic underlay in score above*

I Wayan Dibia on the work "Body Cak," combining the interlocking rhythms of Balinese *kecak* (a theatrical unaccompanied choral style based on a kind of Balinese trance music) with body sounds. Los Angeles–based composer Elaine Barkin has co-composed pieces with Balinese artists Nyoman Wenten and Komang Astita. Jarrad Powell and Gamelan Pacifica of Seattle have worked with Javanese and Balinese composers and shadow theater masters, including Indonesian composer Tonny Prabowo and writer Goenawan Mohamad.

Many American gamelan groups play Indonesian music, learned either from Indonesian artists or from North Americans with extensive experience in Indonesia. At the same time, these ensembles, as well as others playing Indonesian or American-built instruments, have served as an experimental ground for dozens of North American composers writing in various musical styles for the instruments. Over the years, a considerable body of American new music repertoire has been developed and presented. An organization whose mission is to document both the new works and the sources that inspired them is the American Gamelan Institute (www.gamelan.org), founded in 1981 by Jody Diamond. AGI maintains an international archive of scores, recordings, and monographs representing gamelan in all forms and in 1984 began the publication of *Balungan,* a journal devoted to "gamelan, Indonesian performing arts and their international counterparts."

INSTRUMENT BUILDING

West Coast builders

On the West Coast, many composers besides Lou Harrison were building their own instruments and starting gamelan groups to play their new repertoire. Daniel Schmidt, a composer who encountered gamelan at California Institute of the Arts, built the instruments of the Berkeley Gamelan (Adler and Diamond 1985) and B.A.N.G.: Bay Area New Gamelan as well as sets for schools and groups in Texas and Oregon. Gamelan Pacifica in Seattle, led by Jarrad Powell, Paul Dresher, and Kent Devereaux, began with Schmidt's designs and added many ideas of their own. Lou Harrison and Bill Colvig (1979) and Schmidt and Dresher (1983) designed and worked in aluminum and

Murphy invented flat wooden shadow puppet characters in 1968 and then performed in a language he developed, Thoomese, which draws on Sanskrit, Tamil, Telegu, Japanese, English, and other Indo-European languages as well as including invented words.

sometimes brass, using Javanese-inspired tunings derived from just intonation. In the Southwest, Matt Finstrom of the Finestream Gamelan built several ensembles based on Indonesian models, from a variety of materials.

East Coast builders

On the East Coast of the United States, several active instrument builders emerged. Dennis Murphy (figure 4), possibly the first American to build gamelan instruments who meant to model Indonesian ensembles directly, began to experiment with gamelan building in 1959 while he was a composition student at the University of Wisconsin at Madison. As a graduate student at Wesleyan, Murphy studied with Robert E. Brown. He was later able to ask questions of Prawatasaputra (Wesleyan's first Javanese teacher in 1968), as well as Sumarsam. Murphy's 1974 dissertation at Wesleyan University, "The Autochthonous American Gamelan," documents the building of Gamelan Venerable Sir Voice of Thoom, still played by the Plainfield Village Gamelan group in Vermont. Murphy also invented flat wooden shadow puppet characters in 1968 and then performed in a language he developed, Thoomese, which draws on Sanskrit, Tamil, Telegu, Japanese, English, and other Indo-European languages as well as including invented words. While the language can be written in Roman letters, Murphy also invented a writing system of unique symbols that represent both letters and syllables.

When Barbara Benary built the instruments of Gamelan Son of Lion, she drew on Murphy's designs. Benary also built a gamelan modeled on the Balinese gamelan *angklung,* a four-tone gamelan featuring small metallophones, named for but not always including the tuned bamboo rattles called *angklung.* Benary also did extensive works for shadow puppets. At the University of Delaware, Michael Zinn pioneered his own designs, using a wide range of materials from aluminum pipes to flowerpots for his gamelan instruments. Another Wesleyan student, Gregory Acker, pioneered his Gamelan Amadindas, a xylophone-based ensemble often involved in original community-based shadow plays (1998).

In many cases the building of a homemade gamelan not only saved a great deal of import money but also provided a familiar and personal set of instruments that were less attached to an Indonesian tradition than to the musical experimentation of the composer-performers who played and wrote for them. Instruments were also built, however, by ensembles playing traditional Javanese music, as was the case with the Boston Village Gamelan, founded by Sam Quigley and Alan Robinson and later directed by Barry Drummond on a set of Javanese instruments. In the 1990s, easier access to Indonesian-made instruments slowed the impetus for building homemade gamelan, and bronze and iron-with-brass gamelan became more frequently imported.

FIGURE 4   Dennis Murphy playing an iron-keyed Javanese style gender that he built as part of the Plainfield Village Gamelan. Photo by Jody Diamond, 1999.

BALI, SUNDA, AND SUMATRA

Although the American gamelan scene has been dominated for decades by Javanese-style music, there has long been a steady presence of Balinese music, and the number of

Balinese ensembles has expanded so that by the end of the twentieth century there were nearly as many Balinese ensembles as Javanese.

The various kinds of Balinese gamelan are known by separate names, which refer both to the instruments and to the musical repertoire; each has its own place in the ceremonial and artistic practices of Bali. *Kebyar,* a twentieth-century style using a large group of gamelan instruments, grew out of older, more sedate styles. The *kebyar* style is characterized by high energy and extreme contrasts of volume and tempo. *Angklung* features portable four- or five-keyed metallophones. *Gender wayang* is an ensemble of four tube-resonated metallophones used to accompany shadow puppet theater in Bali. In American practice, a gamelan group often owns and practices the repertoire from more than one of these traditions. The choral form know as *Cak* or *Kecak* is also often taught in Balinese music programs. This involves concentric circles of seated singers, who vocalize interlocking patterns, such as those found in gamelan music, as an accompaniment for dancers in the center, who portray scenes from the *Ramayana.*

Certainly one of the most successful groups playing Balinese music is Gamelan Sekar Jaya (figure 5), founded in 1979 and currently based in El Cerrito, California (www.gsj.org). This ensemble, which has always been independent, is very active in both education and performance. A number of people have directed the ensemble, some of whom have gone on to establish other ensembles around the continent. These include cofounders Michael Tenzer and Rachel Cooper; Evan Ziporyn, who co-founded Gamelan Galak Tika at the Massachusetts Institute of Technology (M.I.T.) in Cambridge; and Sekar Jaya's current leader, Wayne Vitale. Tenzer, Ziporyn, and Vitale are also composers who have explored the wealth of possibilities of writing music for Balinese instruments. They have used composition as a way to delve further into Balinese traditions, in contrast to composers such as Schmidt or Corner, who took Javanese ideas in other directions.

Like Brown's Center for World Music in the 1970s, Sekar Jaya always works with top Indonesian artists—musicians, dancers, composers, and choreographers—all of whom spend extensive time with the group. Some of the Balinese musicians who have worked with Sekar Jaya and other groups around the continent are I Wayan Suweca (the group's first teacher), I Komang Astita, I Wayan Rai, I Wayan Tembres, I Wayan Sinti, I Nyoman Windha, and I Dewa Putu Berata. Guest dance directors have included I Wayan Dibia, Ni Made Wiratini, Ni Nyoman Sutiari, and I Made Sidia.

FIGURE 5   Gamelan Sekar Jaya in a concert of music and dance of Bali. Photo by Richard Blair, date unknown.

Sekar Jaya is also notable for having toured their Balinese and American repertoire in Bali as well as around North America.

Dozens of other Balinese groups, many community based, have also appeared in the United States. Inspired musicians have made their own instrument purchases and connected with teachers who often travel hundreds of miles to provide workshops for the musicians. I Made Lesmawan, a Balinese musician with a degree from a Javanese college of the arts, has taught as many as four different groups at once in the midwestern United States.

OTHER REGIONS AND ARTS

Other regional styles of Indonesian music are also represented in the United States, although to a lesser extent. Sundanese gamelan from West Java are found in the San Jose region of California and a few other places. Many are inspired by the programs led by Kathy Foley (herself a *dalang* in the *wayang golek* style) and Linda Burman-Hall at the University of California, Santa Cruz, as well as by local resident Lou Harrison. In the teaching of Sundanese traditions, Undang Sumarna has been a primary leader who has had many students in his long residence at UCSC. One of the most prominent *suling* players in the Sundanese area, Burhan Sukarma, settled nearby in San Jose: together Sumarna and Sukarma form the core of the group Pusaka Sunda.

The city of Cirebon in northwestern Java has a unique style, and a scattering of ensembles around the United States practice this music, including a group in Seattle directed by Richard North. Sumatra has been represented by several Indonesian artists, most from the city of Medan in North Sumatra, who have either taught or attended school in the United States. These include Rizaldi Siagian, who attended San Diego State University, and composer-performer Irwansyah Harahap, who studied at the University of Washington in Seattle, as did singer-ethnomusicologist Ritathony Huta-julu. The composer Ben M. Pasaribu (also from Medan) studied at Wesleyan University and composed a set of pieces there that are still performed in the United States and elsewhere (1999).

Wayang kulit

Associated performing arts such as dance and puppet theater, especially the Javanese and Balinese shadow puppet theater called *wayang kulit,* have developed apace with many of these music programs. Many gamelan groups are eager to try these fascinating theater forms. Since the 1990s, one of the most active *dalang* in North America has been Widiyanto S. Putro, a Javanese musician who taught for many years at Lewis and Clark College in Oregon. Sumarsam also gives an annual performance with his Wesleyan students. There are American performers of *wayang* as well, some of whom work with Indonesian theatrical and musical repertoire while speaking mostly English; they include Marc Hoffman, Kathy Foley, and Maria Bodmann. Other performers create both music and puppets themselves or use a combination of Indonesian and American resources. A notable example of a creative developer of shadow puppet theater is Larry Reed, whose company, Shadowlight Productions (www.shadowlight.com), has combined the aesthetics of film and *wayang,* using a large screen and actors as well as puppets to cast shadows. In the area of dance, there have been many active and influential teachers, both Indonesian and American. Students in the United States had the good fortune to study with some of Indonesia's most accomplished dancers, including Maridi and the late Ben Suharto. Sal Murgiyanto, a dancer as well as an important dance scholar, was a contributor to dance activities during his studies in the United States. Americans who have championed the study of Indonesian dance include Judy Mitoma at UCLA and Deena Burton, founder of Arts Indonesia, in New York City. In the Midwest, Peggy Choy and Valerie Vetter have been active as both teachers and performers. Islene Pindar, founder of the Balinese-American Dance Theater, performs Balinese dance as well as her own fusion style.

OTHER INSTITUTIONS SUPPORTING INDONESIAN MUSIC

In general, acceptance of and familiarity with gamelan instruments and music continue to grow because of continued educational and artistic presentations and availability of recordings. With increased mobility of Americans visiting Indonesia for tourism, frequent performances by American groups, and Indonesian performing groups more regularly touring the United States, Americans are becoming more aware of the wide variety of musical traditions and styles within Indonesia. What was in the 1960s and 1970s primarily a representation and study of court music of central Java now includes a fair representation of Balinese ensemble styles, a scattering of other regional styles, and growing acceptance of the idea of American compositions for traditional instruments and inclusion of such pieces in group repertoire.

While about half of the ensembles surveyed for the Gamelan Directory teach and perform a single traditional Indonesian music exclusively, increasing numbers mention additional repertoire in another musical style (contemporary or from another part of Indonesia), and a few practice repertoire of three or more styles. Approaches range from those who play music solely from Indonesian traditions to those using that music as a springboard to new experiments (Hadley 1993:60). Ongoing groups, both educational and independent, also seem to be increasingly free in crossing stylistic boundaries.

Schools and institutions are still the backbone of established gamelan and related programs, although an increasing crossover has developed within broader university communities. In fact, most university programs have come to include and rely on community performers. Likewise, independent groups have found it beneficial to affiliate themselves with universities for the housing of their instruments and support of their activities. For more than three decades, ethnomusicology programs have been producing knowledgeable scholars, not to mention the legion of people who have had short-term exposure to gamelan through introductory workshops, summer sessions, or residency in Indonesia. The number of non-college-affiliated gamelan groups has also continued to grow.

In the realm of secondary education, the gamelan-inspired Orff-Schulwerk instruments have achieved such a following as to be almost commonplace. Some educators have made the connection between Orff instruments and gamelan and are using their instruments either to teach Indonesian music or to engage in cross-cultural music education (Holtfretter and Widaryanto 1996). In addition, gamelan groups have often had regular touring schedules in schools of various levels, with residencies ranging from one day to four months. Some schools have acquired gamelan for permanent use.

LOOKING FORWARD

Other meeting grounds for Indonesian music and North American culture will undoubtedly continue to be explored. These include contemporary art music, where heterophony may be allowed; electronic music, where tunings may be controlled; and theatrical or film scoring, where the exotic is often encouraged to rub shoulders with familiar sounds. Professionals in education, music therapy, and other areas are also beginning to investigate the rich possibilities of the Indonesian arts and the art they can inspire.

What accounts for the popularity of gamelan in the United States, particularly on the part of American performers of gamelan? Direct contact with an art form of a culture other than one's own is certainly a compelling way to learn something about that culture, so gamelan provides a rich cross-cultural experience. Many American gamelan players, however, admit that the experience is as much social as musical. For some, the social aspect of playing music with a group of people is more important than musical study or connections to Indonesia. The social nature of gamelan playing may fill a special need that Americans have for community and for a group where ideally everyone's contribution is equally important regardless of individual skill.

Gamelan and other Indonesian-born performing arts have clearly found a home in North America: a recent review of recordings by gamelan groups outside of Indonesia listed seventeen American ensembles (Diamond 1998). American gamelan musicians continue to find new uses and contexts for the traditions they have both studied and created. The various ways in which North Americans interact with Indonesian arts has evolved from the first Indonesian performers on tour, to the ethnomusicologists and musicians who studied with Indonesian master artists, to the composers who invented instruments and groups to play them. In the future, Americans will no doubt continue to appreciate and study Indonesian traditions as well as to create more of their own, each generation honoring its parents while exploring new worlds.

REFERENCES

Acker, Gregory John. 1998. *To Sound Them, the Keys: Gamelan Amadindas.* Master's thesis, Wesleyan University. Distributed by the American Gamelan Institute.

Adler, Peter, and Jody Diamond. 1985. "Interview: Daniel Schmidt." *Balungan* 1(2):5–8.

American Works for Balinese Gamelan Orchestra. Gamelan Sekar Jaya, Seka Gong Abdi Budaya, and students at STSI Denpasar. 1993. Produced by Evan Ziporyn, Michael Tenzer, and Wayne Vitale. Notes by Marc Perlman. Compositions by Ziporyn, I Nyoman Windha, Tenzer, and Vitale. New World Records 80430-2. Compact disc.

Balinese Music in America. Gamelan Sekar Jaya. Directed by Wayne Vitale (*gong kebyar*) and Carla Fabrizio (*angklung*). Notes by Marc Perlman. Compositions by I Wayan Beratha, I Nyoman Windha, I Ketut Partha, Dewa Putu, Berata, and Wayne Vitale. GSJ-011. Compact disc.

B.A.N.G. (Bay Area New Gamelan). 1986. Directed by Jody Diamond and Daniel Schmidt. Instruments built by Daniel Schmidt. Compositions by Schmidt, Diamond and Ingram Marshall. Lebanon, N.H.: American Gamelan Institute. AGI01. Cassette.

Benary, Barbara. 1983. "One Perspective on Gamelan in America." *Asian Music* 15(1):82–101.

———. 1993a. *Gamelan Works Vol. 1: The Braid Pieces.* Lebanon, N.H.: American Gamelan Institute.

———. 1993b. *Gamelan Works Vol. 2: Satires.* Lebanon, N.H.: American Gamelan Institute.

———. 1993c. *Gamelan Works Vol. 3: Pieces in a Single Tuning.* Lebanon, N.H.: American Gamelan Institute.

———. 1995. *Gamelan Works Vol. 4: Seven Pieces in Mixed Tuning: Slendro and Pelog.* Lebanon, N.H.: American Gamelan Institute.

———, ed. 1983. "North American Gamelan Directory." *Ear Magazine,* 7(4).

Becker, Judith. 1972. "Western Influence in Gamelan Music." *Asian Music* 3(1):3–8.

Becker, Judith, and Alan H. Feinstein, eds. 1988. *Karawitan: Source Readings in Javanese Gamelan and Vocal Music.* 3 vols. Ann Arbor: University of Michigan, Center for South and Southeast Asian Studies.

Cage, John. 1987. *Haikai for gamelan degung.* Musical score. New York: C. F. Peters.

A Celebration of Gongs. Gamelan Lake of the Silver Bear. Directed by Michael Zinn. Instruments built by Michael Zinn. Compositions by William Naylor, Christopher Venaccio, and Zinn; also pieces from Sunda and Central Java. Independently produced cassette.

Coast, John. 1953. *Dancers of Bali.* New York: Putnam.

Diamond, Jody. 1992a. "Making Choices: American Gamelan in Composition and Education (From the Java Jive to Eine Kleine Gamelan Music)." In *Essays on Southeast Asian Performing Arts: Local Manifestations and Cross-cultural Implications,* ed. Kathy Foley. Berkeley, Calif.: Centers for South and Southeast Asian Studies.

———. 1992b. "Interaction: New Music for Gamelan." Article to accompany compact disc of same title. *Leonardo Music Journal* 2 (Fall) 1:99–110.

———. 1998. "Out of Indonesia: Global Gamelan." *Ethnomusicology* 42(1):174–183.

Diamond, Jody, ed., with I. M. Harjito, consultant. 1995. *The Vocal Notation of K.R.T. Wasitodiningrat.* 2 vols. Lebanon, N.H.: American Gamelan Institute.

Ditrich, Will. 1983. *The Mills College Gamelan: Si Darius and Si Madeleine—instrument design and construction by Lou Harrison, William Colvig, and Mills Students.* Lebanon, N.H.: American Gamelan Institute.

Dresher, Paul. 1979. "The Design and Construction of a Contemporary American Gamelan." Master's thesis, University of California, San Diego.

———. 1983. "Aluminum Bonangs." *Ear Magazine* 8(4):24–25.

East Coast–West Coast: American Music for Gamelan. Venerable Showers of Beauty/A Different Song. Directed by Vincent McDermott and Widiyanto S. Putro; Gamelan Son of Lion directed by Barbara Benary. Compositions by McDermott and Benary. Independently produced cassette.

Florida, Nancy. 1993. *Javanese Literature in Surakarta Manuscripts.* Vol. I, *Introduction and the Manuscripts of the Kraton Surakarta.* Ithaca, N.Y.: Southeast Asia Programs Publication.

———. 1995. *Writing the Past, Inscribing the Future: History as Prophecy in Colonial Java.* Durham, N.C.: Duke University Press.

Forrest, Wayne. 1999. Personal communication.

Frasconi, Miguel. 1988. "Interview: John Cage." *Balungan* 3(2):19–23.

Gamelan as a Second Language. 1995. Gamelan Son of Lion. Directed by Barbara Benary. Iron instruments built by Benary. Compositions by David Demnitz. GSOL CD-2. Compact disc.

Garland, Peter, ed. 1987. *A Lou Harrison Reader.* Santa Fe: Soundings Press.

Hadley, Peter. 1993. "New Music for Gamelan by North American Composers." Master's thesis, Wesleyan University. Distributed by the American Gamelan Institute.

Harrison, Lou. 1988. *Music for Gamelan with Western Instruments.* Scores and parts. Lebanon, N.H.: American Gamelan Institute.

Holtfretter, Lillian, and F. X. Widaryanto. 1996. *Flowing Waters: Building a Musical Bridge between Your Orff-Schulwerk Ensemble and the Javanese Gamelan.* Danbury, Conn.: World Music Press. Videocassette and study booklet.

In Celebration of Golden Rain: Kyai Udan Mas. The Scripps Javanese Gamelan of the University of California. Gamelan directed by Jody Diamond and Daniel Schmidt. Laurence Moe, organ.

Composition by Richard Felciano for organ and Javanese gamelan. Opus One 155. Compact disc.

Intergalactic Gamelan: Gamelan Galak Tika. Directed by Evan Ziporyn. 1996. Compositions for *gong kebyar* by Evan Ziporyn, I Gede Manik, and Desak Made Suarti Laksmi. Independently produced cassette.

Lolongkrang. Pusaka Sunda. 1994. Founded by Burhan Sukarma and Rae Ann Stahl. With guest artist Undang Sumarna. *Gamelan degung.* Compositions by Sukarma, Gugum Gumbira, and classical *degung* pieces. Sakti Records SAKTI 33. Compact disc.

Lou Harrison: Gamelan Music. 1992. Gamelan Si Betty. Directed by Trish Neilsen and Jody Diamond. Instruments by Lou Harrison and William Colvig. Compositions by Lou Harrison. Music Masters 01612-67091-2. Compact disc.

Miller, Leta E., and Fred Lieberman. 1998. *Lou Harrison: Composing a World.* New York: Oxford University Press.

Murphy, Dennis. 1974. "The Autochthonous American Gamelan." Ph.D. dissertation, Wesleyan University.

Music from Java and America. Venerable Showers of Beauty/A Different Song. Directed by Vincent McDermott and Widyanto S. Putro. Compositions by McDermott and Widiyanto. Independently produced casssette.

Music of Bali, Indonesia. 1995. Gamelan Tunas Mekar. Musical director, Jill Fredericksen. Artist-in-Residence, I Made Lesmawan. Notes by David Harnish. Balinese gamelan angklung. Compositions by I Wayan Beratha, I Ketut Partha, I Ketut Marya, I Nyoman Windha, and I Made Lesmawan. Prolific Records. Compact disc.

New Gamelan/New York. 1995. Gamelan Son of Lion. Directed by Barbara Benary. Compositions by Jody Kruskal, Laura Liben, David Demnitz, Mark Steven Brooks, David Simons, Daniel Goode, and Benary. GSOL CD-1. Compact disc.

Oja, Carol. 1990. *Colin McPhee: Composer in Two Worlds.* Washington, D.C.: Smithsonian Institution Press.

Palace. 1996. Evergreen Club. Directed by Blair Mackay. Artifact Music (Canada) ART-012. Compositions for Sundanese gamelan *degung* and other instruments, by Mark Duggan, Lou Harrison, John Wyre, Jon Siddal, and Alain Thibault. Compact disc.

Pasaribu, Ben M. 1999. *Between East and West: Music from 3000 Islands.* Lebanon, N.H.: American Gamelan Institute.

Pemberton, John. 1994. *On the Subject of "Java."* Ithaca, N.Y.: Cornell University Press.

Perlman, Marc. 1983. "Some Reflections on New American Gamelan Music." *Ear Magazine,* 7(4):4–5.

Suite for Javanese Gamelan and Synthesizer. Composed and recorded by Robert Macht. Javanese and Balinese instruments with synthesizer. MACH0001CD. Compact disc.

Toer, Pramoedya Ananta. 1992. *House of Glass.* Trans. Max Lane. New York: Penguin Books.

Trance Gong. 1994. Gamelan Pacifica. Directed by Jarrad Powell. Iron/brass instruments by Suhirjan (Central Java) and aluminum instruments by Schmidt, Dresher, Devereaux, Powell. Compositions by Powell, Jeff Morris, John Cage (arr. Powell), and other group members. ¿What next? Recordings WN0016.

Walton, Susan. 1987. *Mode in Javanese Music.* Athens: Ohio University Center for International Studies.

Wenten, I Nyoman. 1996. "The Creative World of Ki Wasitodipuro: The Life and Work of a Javanese Gamelan Composer." Ph.D. dissertation, University of California, Los Angeles.

Yampolsky, Philip. 1987. *Lokananta: A Discography of the National Recording Company of Indonesia, 1957–1985.* Madison, Wis.: Center for Southeast Asian Studies.

———. 1991. *Music of Indonesia.* Washington, D.C.: Smithsonian/Folkways. Compact disc series v. 1–20.

Ziporyn, Evan. 1992. "One Man's Traffic Noise: The Making of Kekembangan." In *Festival of Indonesia Conference Summaries,* ed. Marc Perlman. New York: Festival of Indonesia Foundation.

Filipino Music
Ricardo D. Trimillos

Background
Musical Activity among Filipino Americans

Three strategies characterize musical activity among Filipino Americans: continuity of homeland culture; reconstruction of a minority, alternative culture; and appropriation of majority culture(s). The history of the United States and Filipinos is critical to understanding them.

BACKGROUND

Filipino Americans occupy a unique position in America's Asian experience. They represent the only Asian population colonized by the United States. From 1898 until 1946 the Philippines was a U.S. territory and subjected to systematic assimilation by American institutions, language, and culture. Although Filipinos were known to have come to the New World as early as the sixteenth century with the Spanish galleon trade (1575–1815), the major settlement started at the beginning of the twentieth century.

Early migration was in response to two colonial objectives: an American-educated native elite and cheap agricultural labor. As early as 1905 promising young Filipinos were sent to American universities and colleges on scholarship. Known as *pensionados,* they were to be future leaders. However, some chose to remain in the United States. At the same time, Filipinos became a source of unskilled labor for the plantations of Hawai'i (also a newly acquired territory), for the agricultural industries of the West Coast, and for the fishing industries of the Northwest. Immigration was relatively unrestricted at that time.

Following the Pacific War (1946 on), Filipinos continued to emigrate to areas settled earlier by family members or town mates, so that enclaves of Filipinos emerged in agricultural areas, including Hawai'i and California's Central Valley, as well as in urban ones, including Los Angeles, Chicago, Virginia Beach, New York, Seattle, and Daly City, California. The post-1960 flow brought a significant number of educated Manila or urban-oriented professionals, primarily in medicine, engineering, and academe. The resultant Filipino American population is diverse, encompassing both American-born descendants of early laborers and families of newly arrived professionals.

MUSICAL ACTIVITY AMONG FILIPINO AMERICANS

The singular history of Filipinos with and in America manifests itself in musical activity among Filipino Americans (who often refer to themselves as "Fil-Am" or "Pinoy," a more indigenous term). As in the homeland, music in Fil-Am settings is often one component of a multifaceted activity; music events may be simultaneously dance, theater, and oral literature.

Continuity of homeland culture

Notions of homeland culture and its music are as diverse and as diachronic as the Filipino American population. Continuity is implicit in the *kundiman,* a genre of light-classical art song composed primarily for solo voice and piano with a Tagalog or Visayan language text. The musical idiom reflects appropriations from Hispanic and Italian genres of the late nineteenth century. The *kundiman,* based on an indigenous form, possesses a canon of composers and works, including Francisco Santiago (1889–1947) and his "Pakiusap" ("My Plea") (1921); Nicanor Abelardo (1893–1934), "Mutya ng Pasig" ("Pearl of the Pasig") (1926); and Constancio de Guzman (1903–1982), "Bayan Ko" ("My Country") (1928). The last song became a musical icon of resistance against the Marcos dictatorship (1972–1986) and was widely heard in the United States. *Kundiman* repertoire is part of Filipino American celebrations such as Rizal Day (30 December) and Independence Day (12 June). It is programmed in concerts by Fil-Am singers, often as encores but increasingly (in student recitals) as a group of songs in the tradition of lieder, chansons, and arias.

The folkloric dance group, with its associated instrumental and vocal music, also reflects a strategy of continuity. Such groups as Philippine Performing Arts (Florida), Fil-Am Philippine Dance Company (Alhambra, California), and Kayamanan ng Lahi (Los Angeles) generally replicate the format, choreographies, and music (often recorded) of the world-renowned Bayanihan Philippine Dance Company, whose first U.S. tour in 1959 brought an awareness of Philippine culture to American concert audiences. Continuity also includes individuals; former Bayanihan dancers now reside in the United States and lead dance groups.

The *rondalla,* a plucked string ensemble, has been active since the 1970s throughout the United States. Groups were organized principally for Fil-Am youth in such urban centers as Boston, New York, Austin, San Diego, and Honolulu in response to emergent ethnic awareness and pride. Continuity with homeland is very direct: most of the teachers are recent immigrants and the principal instruments—*bandurria* 'flat-backed, fretted mandolin with fourteen strings in six courses in soprano/alto range', *laud* 'pronounced la'ud, similar in tenor/baritone range', *oktavina* 'waisted, fretted lute identical in range and courses to the laud', and *bajo de uñas* 'fretted string bass with four strings either plucked or struck'—must be imported from the Philippines.

Continuity extends to popular culture; there is a constant flow of Philippine commercial music to the United States. The majority is mediated through the subscription television Filipino Channel and music videos and CDs carried by Filipino grocery stores. In addition, pop stars, including Sharon Cuneta and Fil-Am Martin Nievera, frequently tour the United States. These live shows provide direct access to contemporary culture.

The first three genres described enjoy widespread visibility in the United States and often serve as presentational artifact and historicized culture. That they reflect Spanish colonial influence informs a prevalent Filipino American self-image. However, it has been challenged and contested, particularly by youth.

Reconstruction of a minority, alternative culture

This strategy argues for a noncolonial culture, one that claims an Asian locus rather than a Westernized focus. Its most dramatic manifestation is the current activity in *kulintang* 'gong chime' music from the southern Philippines. The *kulintang* ensemble consists of a single row of horizontally suspended bossed gongs tuned pentatonically, which functions as the principal melodic instrument, a group of larger vertically suspended bossed gongs, which provide rhythmic and colotomic elements, and a drum (double- or single-headed depending upon the specific tradition), which articulates the rhythmic mode. The ascendance of *kulintang* in the 1980s included the founding of the World Kulintang Institute in Los Angeles and the Amauan ensemble in New York City (no longer active). *Kulintang* has clear ties with gamelan, which enjoys widespread popularity in the United States. The southern Philippines is iconic for decolonization: it successfully resisted Spanish and American domination and continues to practice Islam. This background reinforces a perception that *kulintang* is "more Asian" than *rondalla* or *kundiman*. Notably, U.S. participants are not of southern Muslim heritage. They are largely from the lowland Christian majority.

Kulintang is the single Philippine music with quasi-official U.S. recognition: the prestigious Arts Endowment Folk Heritage Fellowship has to date only one Fil-Am recipient, the Magindano *kulintang* virtuoso Danongan Kalanduyan. Based in San Francisco, he teaches and performs throughout the United States. *Kulintang,* like Japanese-American *taiko,* is a "muscular" music, which reinforces its image as minority and alternative vis-à-vis mainstream Philippine and American traditions.

The BIBAK organization represents another kind of reconstruction that resonates with homeland continuity. In the United States BIBAK is a coalition of Filipino Americans with origins among the tribes of the Cordillera, the mountains of northern Luzon. The name is an acronym for five major tribal groups: Bontoc, Ifugao, Benguet, Apayao, and Kalinga. These tribal groups have been historically marginalized by lowland majority Filipinos and theatrically exoticized by folkloric dance troupes. Through the performing arm of BIBAK they seek to transmit with accuracy and respect Cordillera heritage (including music, dance, and protocol) to their own young people, other Filipinos, and the American public. Their performances contrast with folkloric ones: the *gangsa* 'a set of four to seven flat gongs struck either with a stick or with the hands' gong rhythms use more complex interlocking hockets, the singing includes improvised texts, and dance movements are coordinated rather than choreographed. BIBAK membership emphasizes tribal lineage, contrasting with *kulintang* in the United States. However, like *kulintang,* BIBAK demarcates an identity distanced from both Philippine and American mainstreams.

Appropriation of majority culture(s)

Active involvement with American mainstream musics reinterprets the earlier colonial vision of assimilation. Evidence of appropriation/assimilation encompasses Fil-Am participation and success in American musics, including that of the concert hall, musical stage, jazz lounge, and dance club. For example, Filipino Americans (and Philippine nationals) are well represented in the various companies of *Miss Saigon* and *The King and I.*

The appropriation of American music has a history in the Philippines, from Francisco Santiago's 1924 piano concerto, through Katy de la Cruz and her jazz scatting in the 1940s, to the group Hagibis and its Village People disco covers of the 1970s. An early instance of appropriation in the United States was the proliferation of Filipino dance bands during the 1920s–1940s. Most recently Fil-Am hip-hop groups on the West Coast have achieved notoriety, and rappers express themselves in Tagalog (the national language), Taglish (an urban patois of Tagalog and English), and Black English.

Musical traditions and practices for Filipino Americans cover a broad continuum between the imaginary polarities of "pure Filipino" and "pure American" and their implicit Asian/Western dyad. Diachronic and synchronic cultural spaces inhabited by Filipino Americans provide access to and potential for rich and diverse participation in music. They also problematize issues of identity, commitment, and belonging.

REFERENCES

Gonzalves, Theo. 1995. "The Show Must Go On: Production Notes on the Filipino Cultural Night." *Critical Mass* 2:13–20.

Rafael, Vincente L. 2000. *White Love and Other Events in Filipino History.* Durham: Duke University Press.

Trimillos, Ricardo D. 1985. "Music and Ethnic Identity: Strategies for the Overseas Filipino Youth Population." *Yearbook for Traditional Music* 18:9–20.

Middle Eastern Music
Anne K. Rasmussen

Middle Eastern Immigration to North America
Early Experiences of Music Making
Modernization, Americanization, and the Nightclub
The Implications of Musical Style and Repertoire
Music Patronage and Education

Since the founding of the earliest Middle Eastern communities on the urban East Coast of North America, music has been an integral component of immigrant social life. Not only have musical instruments, repertoires, and practices prevailed in the face of hegemonic American popular culture, but Middle Eastern Americans have developed unique contexts for musical performance in which a sense of community is constructed and enacted. Middle Eastern music events in North America are not simply times to enjoy music and dance; they are also spaces where the cultural symbols and practices of the Middle East are reaffirmed for adults and passed on to children. Middle Eastern music in America is one of a number of strong cultural forces that continuously challenges the notion of European-derived American culture and begs a redefinition of American music.

There has been a Middle Eastern musical presence in North America for over one hundred years. At the end of the nineteenth century, Americans first experienced Middle Eastern culture when the "oriental" dancer "Little Egypt" and her ensemble of Egyptian musicians entertained at the Chicago World's Fair of 1893. Some twenty to thirty years later, Middle Easterners were conspicuous enough in urban America to attract accounts in the popular press of Turkish-style coffeehouses in Boston and New York where men smoked water pipes and conversed in strange tongues to the background wail of a singer accompanied by his "ood." Following World War II, immigrant musicians and dancers from Arab, Turkish, Armenian, and Greek communities captured the imagination of American audiences within the context of the Middle Eastern nightclub. At the end of the twentieth century, music of the Middle East is one of several deterritorialized musics of the world that can be heard in prestigious concert halls, at ever-popular ethnic festivals, in universities, and in the context of myriad ritual events and celebrations.

MIDDLE EASTERN IMMIGRATION TO NORTH AMERICA

Middle Eastern immigrants are likely to represent one of four broad linguistic-cultural-regional groups: Arabs, Armenians, Iranians, and Turks. They come to North America from many regions, including Turkey, Iran, the Caucasus, and countries in the Arab world. Ethnic populations, for example, Assyrians and Kurds who come from Iran, Iraq, Syria, Lebanon, and Turkey, are also represented in smaller numbers in North

America. Although often lumped together by the American mainstream, each group has a distinct history of immigration and a unique cultural life in which the role of music is paramount.

Arabs

With a population of around two million in the United States, Arab Americans are the largest subgroup of people of Middle Eastern origin in North America. Since the arrival of the first Syrian in Brooklyn, supposedly in 1854, Arab Americans have settled primarily in the large urban areas of California, New York, Michigan, and elsewhere.

Arab Americans now represent the more than twenty nations of the Arab world that are unified not by religion, race, or ethnicity but by language and culture. They came to North America in two distinct waves of immigration, the first between 1870 and 1925 and the second from 1965 to the present. Although the Arab immigrant population numbered about 110,000 by 1914, restrictive immigration quotas, inspired by antialien prejudice and enacted in 1924, limited the influx of Arab and other Middle Easterners to the United States. During the 1950s and 1960s several pieces of legislation, the most significant of which was the McCarran-Walter Act of 1952, were passed in the United States that eventually eradicated the racist national origins quota system of 1924. Although there was a noticeable increase in immigration after World War II, it was not until 1965 that legislation was passed, as a consequence of initiatives begun by President John Kennedy, that lifted the virtual ban on immigration that had endured for over forty years.

The majority of early Arab immigrants were Christians of Maronite, Melkite, and Greek and Syrian Orthodox faith from the Ottoman province of Syria, which until the 1940s included Mount Lebanon, Syria, and Palestine. A smaller number of Syrian Jews were among this first wave of emigration from the Middle East. Although the promise of economic opportunity in the New World, advertised by American missionaries and steamship captains selling voyages, has been posited by many as the predominant cause of this emigration, other accounts clearly point to the pressures of the Ottoman Turkish regime as a primary impetus for escape. Since World War II, Arabs have been drawn toward North America by promises of economic opportunity and a better life. They have also fled their homeland due to the instability resulting from the Arab-Israeli wars of 1948 and 1967, civil war in Lebanon beginning in 1975, the Iran-Iraq war (1980–1988), continuing warfare in Beirut and South Lebanon, the Palestinian uprising or *Intifadah* beginning in 1988, and the Gulf War of 1991.

First-wave immigrants who originally came with few resources are now well established both economically and socially. Groups of immigrants who came in subsequent waves of immigration include significant populations of Egyptians, Palestinians, students from the Gulf, Assyrians, Yemenis, and North Africans, as well as many Sunni Muslims and thousands of people of limited economic means who have come to work as laborers in the automotive industry in Detroit or on the farms in the central valley of California.

First-wave populations were relatively homogeneous, but today's immigrants are divided along national, regional, religious, and political lines. Because music events are supercharged with notions of ethnicity and origin as well as regional, national, and religious affiliation, reasons for migration and resettlement are central to music making in Arab American communities.

Armenians

Although Armenian history claims that a few countrymen came to Virginia with the founding fathers in the early 1600s, the first significant wave of Armenian immigrants to the United States comprised students and clergymen who sought better educational opportunities. Like many emigrés of Ottoman Syria, they came at the suggestion of

Iranian immigration to North America is unique in that it included the majority of the popular musicians of Iran.

American Protestant missionaries in Turkey, who ambitiously spread their version of Christianity and the dream of America. The horrendous massacres by Turks of the Armenian population in the mid-1890s and again in 1915 were, however, the most significant catalysts for the arrival of Armenians during the first wave of mass migration to the United States. Consequently, while post–World War II waves of Armenians emigrated from the Arab world, Iran, and what was until recently Soviet Armenia, the foundation of the Armenian American community came from Turkey.

According to immigration records that are only fairly reliable, there were about 100,000 Turkish and Russian Armenians in the United States by 1924. An estimated 2,000 people of Armenian heritage continue to come to the United States every year and now number around 500,000. Nearly half of them live in New England and the mid-Atlantic states, about 15 percent are concentrated in the Midwest, and about 25 percent have made their home in California.

Armenian Americans have maintained a musical culture in exile that dates to the turn of the twentieth century. With community members emanating from Turkish, Russian, Arab, Persian, and East European cultures, national identity, as expressed in musical style, song lyrics, and repertoire, is a dynamic source of both creativity and tension among Armenian Americans.

Turks

Immigrants from Turkey constitute the smallest national group of Middle Easterners in North America. Turkish culture (especially Turkish music), however, which spread throughout the Middle East during the nearly five hundred years of Ottoman rule, has been an important component of the cultural heritage brought by the first wave of Arab and Armenian immigrants. Few Turks, however, immigrated to America prior to the 1960s, when the relaxed immigration laws promoted Turkish immigration. Today the Turkish community numbers over 100,000.

Although the first Turks who arrived in North America brought little with them, recent immigrants tend to be well-educated and prosperous professionals. Because most Turks emigrated following the secularized social reform of Kemal Mustafa Attatürk in the 1920s, Muslim religious institutions do not play a large role in immigrant social life. Turkish associations in North America tend to revolve around either professional or social affiliation, the latter category often reflecting class and occupational status. Turkish Americans are concentrated in New York, Chicago, Detroit, Los Angeles, Philadelphia, and San Francisco.

The Turkish musical culture transplanted and perpetuated by early immigrant groups comprises the instrumentarium, the classical repertoire, and the system of melodic modes and rhythmic patterns cultivated in the elite artistic circles of the court and Sufi brotherhoods of the Ottoman world. Later, Turkish semiclassical and popular styles and repertoire were part of the eclectic polyethnic nightclub sound of the 1950s and 1960s in America. Immigrants who today bring with them a post-Attatürk cultural orientation are likely to identify not with the elite cultural traditions of the

Ottoman past but rather with the nationalized, urbanized folk music that is actively promoted by the Turkish government. On the other hand, American tours by Turkish musicians of classical Ottoman and Sufi music promote anew the cultural artifacts of the Ottoman past for both people of Turkish heritage and mainstream Americans.

Iranians

Iranian immigration became significant only during the last three or four decades of the twentieth century. A first wave of Iranians arrived before the Islamic revolution of 1978–1979, when economic and political conditions were favorable for extranational exploration and education. A second wave of emigration from Iran occurred after the revolution, when many Iranians became estranged from the strict Islamic regime in the country. Today, the United States hosts an Iranian community of about 250,000. The majority of Iranians in North America are Shi'i Muslims, but there are also groups of Armenian Christians, Jews, Baha'is, and Zoroastrians from Iran living here. Iranian Americans tend to be well educated and successful. Some of the young, primarily male, students who came prior to the revolution to pursue an education ended up staying unexpectedly, never returning to Iran. Many have brought professional skills to the United States that they have been able to put into practice almost upon arrival. The largest communities of Iranian Americans live in California, New York and New Jersey, Washington, D.C., Illinois, and Texas.

Iranian Americans' wealth has given them immediate access to most of the practices and material goods of their new host culture, and as a result many Iranians have assimilated easily into North American society. The Islamic revolution from which they fled presented not only a repressive regime but one that was especially hostile and prohibitive, if not lethal, especially for modern artists. Unlike most immigrant communities, which include only a small subpopulation of artists who are responsible for the maintenance and production of the immigrant culture's music, Iranian immigration to North America is unique in that it included the majority of the popular musicians of Iran. The lion's share of these emigré entertainers came to Los Angeles, which is now thought to be the center for Persian popular music not only for North America but for the world (Naficy 1993a:54–59). Traditional musicians, who continue to be endorsed by the postrevolutionary Iranian government, have not emigrated in such overwhelming numbers.

While there are certain connoisseurs and practitioners of Persian traditional music, much music created and consumed in Los Angeles and other North American cities reflects an enthusiastic adaptation of the styles and techniques of Western popular culture. Popular Iranian music is not simply a scaled-down reproduction of that which occurs in the more "authentic" and "traditional" homeland; it is rather a thriving musical culture-in-exile, in which creative artists set trends that are followed by musicians and audiences in other diaspora communities and even, with the exchange of audio and video recordings, in Iran itself.

EARLY EXPERIENCES OF MUSIC MAKING

During the first part of the century, music among Middle Eastern immigrant families was limited to informal gatherings, life-cycle events such as births, weddings, or funerals, and listening to recordings. It was not long, however, before a contingent of professional traveling musicians emerged who became musical and cultural curators for their communities.

Contexts for performance

Among Arab Americans, both the *haflah,* a formal music party, and the *mahrajan,* an outdoor picnic sometimes lasting an entire three-day weekend, became social and cultural axes of the community. Sponsored by church and community organizations, these events became the fulcrum of community life among Syrian and Lebanese Americans as well as the primary vehicle of fund-raising for the philanthropic causes and concerns of the community. In like fashion, Anatolian Armenians who emigrated from Turkey made music first in simple home-grown affairs and later in conjunction with functions sponsored by churches and social clubs. Their primary institution for music, dancing, and socializing was the *hantes,* described by one Armenian American as a seven-hour indoor picnic held in the church hall, where at least one if not two or three bands would play. Much later, during the 1960s and 1970s, Armenian American all-weekend music parties called *kef-time* evolved and were held regularly across the United States. Since the early decades of the century, Armenian immigrants have also participated in organized choirs that sing SATB arrangements of Armenian music, a practice popular among Armenians since the late 1800s.

In addition to large community affairs, the tradition of the coffeehouse, called *surjaran* (in Armenian) or *café aman* (in Turkish), was imported to the United States and used as a context for musical performance. In this context, which eventually gave rise to the Middle Eastern nightclub, conversation, coffee, and smoke—the fabric of male social life—were catalysts for musical creativity and exchange.

In the Arab-American community, Syrian immigrants from Aleppo, Damascus, and Beirut enjoyed an urban musical tradition, derived in part from Ottoman classical practices, involving small ensembles comprising a vocalist and three or four instruments, including an *'ud* 'pear-shaped lute', *qanun* 'trapezoid-shaped zither', violin (formerly the *kamanjah*), *riqq* 'fancy tambourine with brass jingles', and *darabukkah* 'vase-shaped ceramic or metal drum'. Immigrants from the rural area of Mount Lebanon enjoyed folk songs and especially genres of sung, improvised folk poetry.

The musical repertoire of Armenian Americans was necessarily eclectic. Musical traditions from the Caucasus and more rural areas of Mount Ararat were complemented by Turkish folk and classical music of those who immigrated from Turkish Armenia. Armenian Americans enjoyed and performed songs in the Turkish language, and with the addition of the clarinet, their instrumentarium of *'ud* (figure 1), *oud, kanoun, qanun,* violin, and *dumbeg* 'vase-shaped metal drum' resembled that of their Syrian American neighbors. Unlike Arab musicians, who played primarily folk and classical music of Egypt and the Levant as well as perhaps some Turkish instrumental music, Armenians have always been recognized for their ability to play the music of various ethnic and national groups. An interesting report documenting a Library of Congress/Works Projects Administration recording project of the late 1990s describes recordings of Turkish-influenced music played by Armenian musicians on *oud,* clarinet, *kanoun,* violin, and *dumbeg.* The musicians, who had been playing together prior to immigration, "announced they could play five kinds of music: Armenian, Turkish, Greek, Syrian, and American jazz" (figure 2) (N.a. 1942:19).

The importance of recordings

All the Middle Eastern artists who carved the musical paths for their communities in America and who are still alive today cite imported 78-rpm recordings as formative musical models. Tony Abdel Ahad, born in Boston of Syrian heritage and one of the most popular performers in the Arab American community during the 1940s, 1950s, and 1960s, remembers cranking an old Victrola phonograph for his father and uncles, who would get together almost every weekend and listen to old classical music from the Turkish/Syrian/Egyptian tradition of the early 1900s. Leo Sarkessian, an Armenian *qunun* player who grew up in Lawrence, Massachusetts, remembers the 78-rpm records of Oudi Harrant, a Turkish-Armenian *'ud* player, as being exemplary for most of the young musicians in this country. When Harrant came to North America in the late 1940s, musicians who knew his style and repertoire flocked to take a lesson or two with the great master (Sarkessian 1992). In the absence of institutions for music learn-

FIGURE 1   Viken Najarian, a luthier of Lebanese-Armenian heritage, learned how to build and repair instruments from his grandfather, formerly an instrument maker in Beirut, Lebanon. He builds and repairs *'ud*s and other Middle Eastern stringed instruments for musicians throughout the United States. His electric *'ud,* created out of the necessity to be heard over the volume of synthesizers and drum machines at community events, is his own invention. Although there is little demand in the United States for the electric *'ud,* Najarian has exported a number of them to the Middle East. This photograph was taken in his shop in Anaheim Hills, California, May 1995.

ing in North America or even a solid master-apprentice tradition, music recordings have long fulfilled a most important didactic function for musicians, who embrace such mediated performances as models for repertoire, style, and even mode, intonation, and improvisation. First-wave musicians were also recorded on big-name labels such as Victor, Columbia, and RCA Victor or on labels that emerged from within their own communities. Their records, along with recordings imported from the Middle East, were played time and again in homes as well as on the handful of Middle Eastern American radio programs as early as the 1930s.

MODERNIZATION, AMERICANIZATION, AND THE NIGHTCLUB

Following the difficult years of the Great Depression and World War II, immigrant communities, which included by that time second- and even third-generation American-born offspring, were relatively stabilized. Contexts for musical performance and the artists who performed therein were well established. Experimentation and innovation naturally superseded the imitation and reproduction that characterized musical performance of the 1920s and 1930s. A gradual erosion of Arabic, Turkish and Armenian languages took place, especially among the American born, and musicians of various ethnic backgrounds began playing together. To complement their mélange of Middle Eastern genres, the instruments, styles, and techniques of American popular music and big band jazz began to permeate their authentic Old World sounds.

The influence of American popular music and jazz

The Turkish Armenian ensembles that performed in the *hantes* and at *kef-time* celebrations began to feature a jazzier style, with more improvisation, faster tempos, more percussion, and the addition of American instruments such as saxophones and electric keyboards and guitars. Arab American musicians consistently reported that in contrast to the *haflah,* which was for serious music or "the heavy stuff," the outdoor *mahrajan* was the appropriate place for light music and popular songs (*taqatiq*), which were likely to be sung in colloquial, not classical, Arabic and were to please the young folks and, according to one prominent musician, the women. In fact, musicians who emphasized their love and promotion of authentic classical music also identified the landmarks in their careers in terms of their composition and recording of humorous and popular songs.

The nightclub

Popular music evolved and thrived within the community, but the performance context that best nurtured the modernization and Americanization of this music was the Middle Eastern nightclub. The *surjaran* and the phenomenon of *café aman* were certainly prototypes for the myriad clubs that sprang up on and around Eighth Avenue in New York City. One veteran of the scene explained that the nightclub

> is really a spin-off of the old coffee houses where musicians gathered and men sat and smoked their water pipes. [The nightclub] has a different ambiance and a different setting, but it really is an old musical tradition. (Farrah 1987)

The nightclubs that were eventually established in cities across the United States were patronized not only by families from various ethnic communities but also by cosmopolitan-minded Americans who fancied an exotic evening out on the town. For the American of European heritage, the nightclub was a temporary mecca of orientalism complete with the stereotypic decor, cuisine, music, and dance of the alluring Middle East. Belly dancing, practiced primarily by American women, was integral to this performative reinterpretation of the oriental world. Within the context of the nightclub, the Middle East was presented in a general way, as a caricature that captured all of the images and stereotypes that made the region, its history, and its culture so captivating

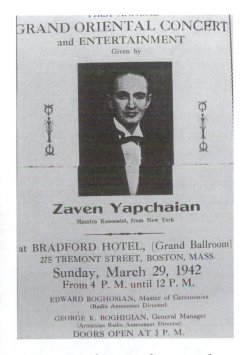

FIGURE 2   Two of ten pages of a program of Middle Eastern performers from a concert held in Boston in March 1942. Organizing Armenian-American patrons George K. Boghigian and Edward Boghosian included "Oriental," Armenian, Syrian, Greek, and Albanian performers in the program and charged $1.00 for the event. Program courtesy of Rose and Russel Bunai.

Classical musicians who have come from Iran to perform in American cities are upheld as symbols of traditional art by the intelligentsia, but they may be seen by the broader community as puppets of the regime and as representative of the repressive government that forced the musical community into exile.

to the American public. Because of the eclectic audience they entertained, musicians were careful to present only a selection of the indigenous elements of their native music as well as to exaggerate the most exotic and thus the most alluring elements of their cultural product. Eventually, nightclub musicians deemphasized the languages spoken by their parents, complicated vocal genres, and traditional musical forms and styles and replaced them with simpler strophic songs enhanced by Western instrumentation and a jazzier, faster, and louder beat. With the addition of electric keyboard, guitar, and bass, they diatonicized the scales of Middle Eastern music and harmonized a heretofore monophonic musical idiom.

With the influx of thousands of new immigrants from the Middle East following the relaxation of immigration quotas in 1965, the stylistic fusion that occurred in the nightclub has become largely a phenomenon of the past. Although there are still venues and ensembles that feature mixed groups, most Middle Eastern communities have been bolstered with new blood from the Old World. Ironically, while these new populations bring with them the cultural and linguistic tradition and authenticity of the homeland, the musical practices they have brought and continue to develop are modern and popular. Although there are still many musicians in North America who play the traditional instruments of the Middle East, it is not at all uncommon to find ensembles or bands composed solely of American Western electronic instruments. 'Uds, qanuns, and neys are difficult to find and keep in good repair, and a synthesizer can take the place of all three of these instruments. Furthermore, a certain prestige is associated with the creative adaptation of Western instruments, techniques, and technology. As they neglect tradition and adopt contemporary ideas and techniques, musicians do not seem to perceive themselves as impoverished but rather as empowered. The music of Iranians in the United States provides an excellent example.

The development of an Iranian American music culture

When mass migration to America occurred in the late 1970s and 1980s, the Iranian emigré community included most of the professional popular musicians as well as a number of conservatory-trained musicians who performed traditional and, later, popular music. Many of these musicians first came to New York, where there were Persian cabarets patronized by first-wave (prerevolution) Iranian businessmen. The majority of these musicians, however, eventually settled in Los Angeles, a city referred to by many as "little Tehran."

Immigrant musicians who perform strictly traditional Iranian music are few in the United States. Traditional instruments are brought from Iran only at great expense, and there are very few musicians who make classical instruments such as the *santur* 'trapezoidal zither struck with hammers', the *tar* and *setar* 'plucked lutes', the *ney* 'reed flute', or the *tonbak* 'wood, single-headed drum'. Nevertheless, traditional musicians are supported by cultural institutions, universities, and private patrons, the latter in the context of private musical-social events called *bazm*. While the traditional music scene is seen by some as volatile, in the Iranian American community popular music culture thrives.

Upon arrival, entertainers usually reestablished a musical scene that continued along modern prerevolutionary lines and easily incorporated the musical techniques, styles, and institutions of American culture. Hamid Naficy, in his work on Iranian American popular culture, recognizes music as "an early and favored mode of exilic communication, preservation of cultural heritage, retention of popular memory, and incorporation into the dominant host culture":

> Immediately after exiles' arrival in the United States, the classical and pop music recorded in Iran prior to the 1979 revolution was duplicated and distributed. As exile wore on, however, first the established artists who had emigrated and later a new crop of emerging talent began recording music here, turning Southern California into a "Persian Motown." (Naficy 1993a: 54)

The great majority of Iranian or Persian popular music in Los Angeles and elsewhere features topical secular love songs in a fast 6/8 meter, performed in Farsi (the national language of Iran) and accompanied almost exclusively by non-Persian instruments such as electric organ, guitar, bass, and trap drum set or drum machine. Iranian Americans have cultivated a healthy subculture that features not only performance in nightclubs, concerts, and private parties of popular musicians but also modes of music production and distribution to support artists and nourish audiences. Persian pop music is disseminated only partially through live performance; the technology of the mass media, including cassette recordings, music videos, and cable television, is also integral to its survival. And, as Naficy suggests, a sense of community is developed and maintained not only through gathering at concerts, in restaurants, nightclubs, and religious and social venues but also through the mass media itself.

THE IMPLICATIONS OF MUSICAL STYLE AND REPERTOIRE

Musicians underscore elements of ethnicity, nationality, and even regional, religious, and political affiliation with their musical style and repertoire. In the Arab American community, musicians of the 1930s and 1940s played classical music to a primarily Syrian-Lebanese Christian audience, but their task during the 1960s and 1970s in the nightclub was to perform popular Arab, Turkish, Armenian, and Greek music and even to throw in an occasional Italian or Irish tune for their eclectic, polyethnic audience. Today musicians have to keep up with the latest hits from home as well as know tunes from many Arab world countries and when to play them. In addition to the mention of countries, cities, or regions in song lyrics, musical styles and genres may be suggestive of national sentiment. For example, Levantine rural genres such as improvised sung poetry (ʿataba and mijana) and songs for dabkah dancing (a popular pan-Arab line dance), which were once considered peripheral in comparison with the mainstream classical and popular music and which might be described as "Arab country music," are enormously popular today, even among well-educated, upper-class Arab Americans.

In the culture of exile, traditional, popular, regional, and religious musical genres carry evocative messages about social class and political stance. In the Iranian American context, for example, popular music and its supporting institutions threaten some, while the traditional music network bothers others. Classical musicians who have come from Iran to perform in American cities are upheld as symbols of traditional art by the intelligentsia, but they may be seen by the broader community as puppets of the regime and as representative of the repressive government that forced the musical community into exile. In the Armenian context, the musical representation of nationalism is even more complex. Older generations of Armenian Americans were brought up singing Turkish songs and playing Turkish-style music; younger generations, however, as a result of a renewed awareness of the Turkish massacres of their ancestors, tend to boycott anything Turkish.

Sosi Setian's research among Armenian Americans on the East Coast shows the suggestive power of Turkish-style music among Armenian Americans. Even though musicians have for generations been playing Turkish-style music (also referred to as *à la Turka*) in nightclubs, and especially at *kef-time* events, they are now subject to complaints and even threats of violence from newer, second-wave community members. Ironically, although the power of Turkish songs lyrics is potentially destructive, the same audience that insists that Turkish music is unacceptable will often let a Turkish song sung in Armenian or played as a dance tune go by unnoticed.

Armenians, because they come from a handful of nations, have long been recognized for their ability to master diverse styles. Today, however, the performance of a particular style may be more a matter of survival than choice. One young musician of Lebanese Armenian heritage explained that he has had to learn to sing in Armenian, Turkish, Arabic, and Farsi in order to cater to the multinational Armenian American clientele of Southern California for whom he plays. In public venues when the audience is mixed, his choice of repertoire can be problematic, engendering impolite criticism and audible disapproval.

During these events, communities divided by ethnic politics can become united by musical styles and gestures. Sometimes conflict is voluntarily sparked by one faction or another from within a group; sometimes, however, a Middle Eastern American community and the musical aspects of their culture are involuntarily affected by the turbulent news from the Middle East. During the Gulf War of January 1991, for example, musical events in Arab American communities came to a virtual standstill. Not only were community members themselves reluctant to engage in happy music parties, but the patronage of Arab American–owned restaurants and nightclubs was sluggish due to the general American population's reluctance to associate with anything Middle Eastern.

MUSIC PATRONAGE AND EDUCATION

Among Middle Eastern Americans, individual musicians and their patrons have been, since the turn of this century, their community's managers of musical knowledge. In producing musical events, their role has not been simply to perpetuate some given age-old indigenous musical tradition imported from the homeland but rather to define a musical tradition for their community. Although musicians ultimately have the power, through their performances, to reconfirm and reinforce the traditional or modern repertoires they value as individuals, their strategies on the stage are greatly influenced by the audiences for whom they play and the patrons from whom they receive their money. Outside the commercial nightclub or restaurant, community-specific societies, clubs, associations, newspapers, religious institutions, dance groups, political committees, and charitable organizations have been, and continue to be, the backbone of musical patronage for Middle Eastern musicians in the United States.

In the final decades of the twentieth century, American institutions have become important patrons of and participants in Middle Eastern music, and Middle Eastern musical projects have received the financial support of major granting agencies. A few examples are worth noting: the University of Maryland, Baltimore County, and the New England Conservatory of Music in Boston have been sites of Turkish musical performance and scholarship. The University of California at Los Angeles, which hosts a number of performance ensembles specializing in non-Western musical traditions, has been the home of a Near East Ensemble since 1980, under the direction of Lebanese-born ethnomusicologist, performer, and composer Ali Jihad Racy, and Racy's students have gone on to direct ensembles at the universities in which they teach. Kan Zaman, the Arab-community-based ensemble for Arab traditional and folk music located in Los Angeles, is also an outgrowth of Racy's university-based group. Although university ensembles may be composed primarily of newcomers to Middle Eastern music, the ensembles, which tend to specialize in traditional acoustic music and often host guest artists, have become well known among people of Middle Eastern heritage in the surrounding communities. Community members who may find an American band playing Middle Eastern music a curious phenomenon may nevertheless hear the music as an alternative to the synthesizer-driven popular music of community events or the expensive concerts of big stars from overseas. Such groups may also serve to introduce or reintroduce Middle Eastern music to people of Middle Eastern heritage.

In New York City, the World Music Institute and the Alternative Museum have presented artists from all over the Middle East, and the Brooklyn Museum has been the site, since 1994, of the annual *Mahrajan al-Fan,* a weekend-long festival of Arab music and arts directed by Simon Shaheen. Shaheen, originally from Palestine, has also founded a week-long summer Arabic music retreat that brings together professional and amateur performers of Arab music for a week of intensive study. And since 1987, Northern California professional musicians of Turkish, Armenian, Arab, and Greek heritage gather for the Mendocino Middle Eastern Music and Dance Camp.

A unique institution of cultural patronage within the Arab American community, ACCESS (The Arab Community Center for Economic and Social Services), provides alternatives in music promotion, production, and education. Located in Dearborn, Michigan, where the largest concentration of Arabs outside of the Arab world lives, ACCESS invites Arab Americans to develop competence and pride in the culture of their heritage (figure 3). Over the years its cultural arts program has produced numerous concerts and festivals, a radio program that showcases performers in the area, and a traditional Arab music, dance, and artisans' program that features classes in music and dance (*'ud, ney, darabukkah,* and *dabkah* dancing), embroidery, and calligraphy and a summer music workshop. ACCESS draws its teachers and students from within the community and capitalizes on the energy that is already there. It also regularly invites important musical leaders such as Ali Jihad Racy and Simon Shaheen to teach workshops and give lectures and concerts, and the group sometimes even sponsors musicians from overseas. While ACCESS is a community-based, grass-roots organization, it has been enormously successful in large part because of the vision of cultural arts director Sally Howell (1987–1995). As a result of innovative programming that combines the local with the national and the global, supported by American granting agencies such as the National Endowment for the Humanities (NEH) or the Lila Wallace Reader's Digest Foundation, ACCESS has become a national model for both community-based and ethnic arts organizations.

FIGURE 3   Detroit musicians Nadim Dlaikan, playing *mizmar,* Mustapha Atat, playing *tabl baladi,* and singer Ameed perform at the Arab World Festival in Detroit, an event sponsored in part by ACCESS, Michigan, June 1988.

Since the beginning of the twentieth century, Middle Eastern music in America has been operating as a music culture in exile.

Since the beginning of the twentieth century, Middle Eastern music in America has been operating as a music culture in exile. While musicians emigrating from the Middle East may bring with them to the United States the experience of conservatory or other professional music training, those who emigrated during their childhood or the American born tend to be self-taught, a method combining listening to records and cassettes, attending music events, an occasional lesson from someone more knowledgeable, and a great deal of experience sitting in, either during informal gatherings or on stage at community events. Because of the sometimes haphazard nature of this system of musical education, complicated by the traditional low status attributed to the musical profession in general, the quality and depth of the musical culture may suffer. For example, the perpetuation of Persian traditional music in North America is problematic because the tradition of music learning, whereby students study the *radif* 'classical repertoire' with a master musician, had already been replaced by the time of the revolution in Iran by a more systematic approach to music pedagogy based on Western models and anchored in the National Conservatory. Thus, although emigré musicians may enjoy teaching students privately or in small groups, they fall into a crack between the broken master-apprentice tradition of teaching the *radif* and the institutionalized system of teaching music, which is absent in North America. Developing new contexts and institutions for music learning appropriate for people living in North America is the biggest challenge faced by Middle Eastern American music cultures today.

REFERENCES

Abraham, Nabeel. 1985. "Americans Americans." In *Gale Encyclopedia of Multicultural America,* ed. Rudolph J. Vecoli, Judy Galens, Anna Sheets, and Robyn V. Young, 84–98. Detroit: Gale Research.

Abraham, Sameer Y., and Nabeel Abraham. 1983. *Arabs in the New World., Studies on Arab-American Communities.* Detroit: Wayne State University Press.

Abu Laban, Baha. 1988a. "Arabs." In *The Canadian Encyclopedia,* vol. 1: 90. Ed. James H. Marsh. Edmonton, Alberta: Hurtig Publishers.

———. 1988b. "Iranians." In *The Canadian Encyclopedia,* vol. 2:1091. Edmonton, Alberta: Hurtig Publishers.

Ahmad, Ismael, and Nancy Adadow Gray, eds. 1988. *The Arab American Family: A Resource Manual for Human Service Providers.* Detroit: ACCESS (Arab Community Center for Economic and Social Services) and Department of Social Work, Eastern Michigan University.

Ali, Aisha. 1983. "Looking Back: The California Middle Eastern Dance Scene." *Arabesque* 9(2):6–9; 9(3):14–17.

Anderson, Benedict. 1983. *Imagined Communities: Reflections on the Origin and Spread of Nationalism.* London: Verso.

Armenians on 8th Avenue. 1996. Produced by Harold G. Hagopian. With 22-page booklet of notes, photographs, and song lyrics. Traditional Crossroads CD 4279. Compact disc.

Aswad, Barbara C., ed. 1974. *Arabic Speaking Communities in American Cities.* New York: Center for Migration Studies of New York.

Avakian, Arra S. 1977. *The Armenians in America.* Minneapolis: Lerner Publications.

Badger, R. 1979. *The Great American Fair: The World's Columbian Exposition and American Culture.* Chicago: Nelson Hall.

Bercovici, Konrad. 1924a. *Around the World in New York.* New York and London: The Century Co.

———. 1924b. "Around the World in New York, The Syrian Quarters." *The Century* 108(3): 348–356.

Borcherdt, Don. 1959. "Armenian Folk Songs and Dances in the Fresno and Los Angeles Areas." *Western Folklore* 18:1–11.

Bozorgmehr, Mehdi, Georges Sabagh, and Claudia Der-Martirosian. 1988. *Religio-Ethnic Diversity Among Iranians in Los Angeles.* Working Paper No. 6. Los Angeles: The G. E. von Grunebaum Center for Near Eastern Studies, University of California at Los Angeles.

Cameron, Charles D. 1926. "A Block from Woodward: Victor Avenue in Highland Park Where Little Arabia Meets Little Persia." *Detroit Saturday Night,* 3 July, sec. 2, 10.

Douglas-Klotz, Neil. 1997. Electronic mail to author, 13 April.

Farhat, H. 1965. "The Dastgah Concept in Persian Music." Ph.D. dissertation, University of California, Los Angeles.

Farrah, I. 1987. Personal communication, July.

Feldman, Walter. 1975. "Middle Eastern Music Among Immigrant Communities in New York City." In *Balkan-Arts Traditions,* ed. Martin Koenig, 19–25. New York: Balkan Arts Center.

Friedlander, Ira. 1992. *The Whirling Dervishes.* New York: Doubleday.

Friedlander, Jonathan, ed. 1988. *Sojourners and Settlers: The Yemeni Immigrant Experience.* Salt Lake City: University of Utah Press.

Friend, Robyn, and Neil Siegel. 1986. "Contemporary Contexts for Iranian Professional Musical Performance." In *Cultural Parameters of Iranian Musical Expression,* ed. Margaret Caton and Neil Siegel, 10–17. Redondo Beach, Calif.: The Institute of Persian Performing Arts.

Goldschmid, Arthur Jr. 1983. *A Concise History of the Middle East.* Boulder, Colo.: Westview Press; Cairo, Egypt: The American University in Cairo Press.

Gronow, Pekka. 1974. "The Record Industry Comes to the Orient." *Ethnomusicology* 25(2): 251–284.

———. 1982. "Ethnic Recordings: An Introduction." In *Ethnic Recordings in America: A Neglected Heritage,* ed. Richard K. Spottswood. Washington, D.C.: American Folklife Center, Library of Congress.

Haider, Adnan. 1989. "The Development of Lebanese *Zajal:* Genre, Meter and Verbal Duel." Unpublished paper.

Hall, Leslie. 1982. "Turkish Musical Culture in Toronto." *Canadian Folk Music Journal* 10:48–52.

Halman, Talat Sait. 1980. "Turks." In *Harvard Encyclopedia of American Ethnic Groups,* ed. Stephan Thernstron, 992–996. Cambridge, Mass.: The Belknap Press of Harvard University Press.

Hitti, Philip. 1924. *Syrians in America.* New York: George Doran.

Hoogland, Eric, ed. 1985. *Taking Root: Arab-American Community Studies.* Washington, D.C.: The Arab-American Anti-Discrimination Committee, ADC Research Institute.

Hoogland, Eric, ed. 1987. *Crossing the Waters: Arabic-Speaking Immigrants to the United States before 1940.* Washington, D.C.: Smithsonian Institution Press.

Horsman, Edward. 1917. "A Glimpse at Syrian Folk-Music." *The Syrian Review,* December:25–29.

Inayat Khan, Vilayat. 1974. *Toward the One.* New York: Harper and Row.

Ishaya, Arian and Eden Naby. 1980. "Assyrians." In *Harvard Encyclopedia of American Ethnic Groups,* ed. Stephan Thernstron, 160–163. Cambridge, Mass.: The Belknap Press of Harvard University Press.

Kaprielian, Isabel. 1988. "Armenians." *The Canadian Encyclopedia,* vol. 1:119–120. Edmonton, Alberta: Hurtig Publishers.

Kayal, Philip M., and Joseph M. Kayal. 1975. *The Syrian-Lebanese in America: A Study in Religion and Assimilation.* Boston: Twayne Publishers.

Kef Time: Exciting Sounds of the Middle East. 1994 [1986]. Produced by Harold G. Hagopian. With 6-page booklet of notes and song lyrics. Traditional Crossroads CD 4269. Compact disc.

Khalaf, Samir. 1987. "The Background and Causes of Lebanese/Syrian Immigration to the United States before World War I." In *Crossing the Waters: Arabic-Speaking Immigrants to the United States before 1940,* ed. Eric Hoogland. Washington, D.C.: Smithsonian Institution Press.

Lorentz, John H., and John T. Wertime. 1980. "Iranians." In *Encyclopedia of American Ethnic Groups,* ed. Stephan Thernstron, 521–524. Cambridge, Mass.: The Belknap Press of Harvard University Press.

Mandell, Joan. 1995. *Tales from Arab Detroit.* Detroit and Los Angeles: ACCESS and Olive Branch Productions. Film.

Marcus, Scott. 1989. "Arab Music Theory in the Modern Period." Ph.D. dissertation, University of California, Los Angeles.

Markoff, Irene. 1991. "The Ideology of Musical Practice and the Professional Turkish Folk Musician: Tempering the Creative Impulse." *Asian Music* 22(1):129–1246.

Mina, Niloofar. n.d. *"Musiqi-ye Pope Irani* and Iranian Immigrants in New York: Cultural Orientation and Identity." Ph.D. dissertation, Columbia University. Forthcoming.

———. 1992. "Female Sexuality and Power in Performances of Popular Iranians in New York." *Journal of American Folklore.*

Mirak, Robert. 1980. "Armenians." In *Harvard Encyclopedia of American Ethnic Groups,* ed. Stephan Thernstron, 136–149. Cambridge, Mass.: The Belknap Press of Harvard University.

———. 1983. *Torn between Two Lands: Armenians in America 1890 to World War I.* Cambridge, Mass.: Harvard University Press.

Moquin, Wayne, ed. 1971. *Makers of America: Emergent Minorities Vol. 10: 1955–1970.* Chicago: Encyclopaedia Educational Corp., William Benton Publishers.

The Music of Arab Americans: A Retrospective Collection. Produced by Anne K. Rasmussen. With

20-page booklet of notes, photographs, and song lyrics. Rounder CD 1122. Compact disc.

Naaf, Alexa. 1980. "Arabs." In *Harvard Encyclopedia of American Ethnic Groups*, ed. Stephan Thurston, 128–136. Cambridge, Mass.: The Belknap Press of Harvard University Press.

———. 1985. *Becoming American: The Early Arab Immigrant Experience.* Carbondale: Southern Illinois University Press.

Naficy, Hamid. 1993a. *The Making of Exile Cultures: Iranian Television in Los Angeles.* Minneapolis: University of Minnesota Press.

———. 1993b. "Popular Culture of Iranian Exiles in Los Angeles." In *Irangeles: Iranians in Los Angeles*, ed. Ron Kelly, Jonathan Friedlander, and Anita Colby. Berkeley: University of California Press.

———. 1996. "Identity Politics and Iranian Exile Music Videos." In *Middle Eastern Diaspora Communities in America*, ed. Mehdi Bozorgmehr and Alison Feldman, 105–123. New York: The Hagop Kevorkian Center for Near Eastern Studies of New York University.

Qureshi, Regula Burckhardt. 1972. "Ethnomusicological Research Among Canadian Communities of Arab and East Indian Origin." *Ethnomusicology* 16(3):381–396.

———. 1986. *Sufi Music of India and Pakistan: Sound, Context, and Meaning in Qawwali.* London: Cambridge University Press.

Racy, Ali Jihad. 1983. "Music in Nineteenth Century Egypt: An Historical Sketch." *Selected Reports in Ethnomusicology* 4(1):157–179. Peter Crossley-Holland Festschrift edition.

———. 1997. *Mystical Legacies: Ali Jihad Racy performs music of the Middle East.* With Ali Jihad Racy (*nay, buzuq, 'ud,* and bowed *tanbur*) and Souhail Kaspar (percussion). Lyrichord LYRCD 7437.

Racy, Ali Jihad, and Simon Shaheen. 1991 [1979]. *Taqasim: The Art of Improvisation in Arab Music.* Ali Jihad Racy, *buzuq,* and Simon Shaheen, *'ud.* With documentary notes by Philip Schuyler. Lyrichord LYRCD 7374.

———. 1997. "The Music of Arab Detroit: A Musical Mecca in the Midwest." In *Musics of Multicultural America: A Study of Twelve Musical Communities*, ed. Kip Lornell and Anne K. Rasmussen, 73–100. New York: Schirmer Books.

———. 1996. "Theory and Practice at the Arabic Org: Digital Practice in Contemporary Music Performance." *Popular Music* 15(3):345–365.

———. 1992. "An Evening in the Orient: The Middle Eastern Nightclub in America." *Asian Music* 23(2):63–88.

Rasmussen, Anne K. 1991. "Individuality and Social Change in the Music of Arab Americans." Ph.D. dissertation, University of California, Los Angeles.

"The Recording of Folk Music in California." 1942. *California Folklore Quarterly* 1(1):7–23.

Rouget, Gilbert. 1985. *Music and Trance.* Trans. Brunhilde Biebuyck. Chicago: University of Chicago Press.

Rydell, R. W. 1984. *All the World's a Fair: Visions of Empire at American International Expositions, 1876–1916.* Chicago: University of Illinois Press.

Sarkession, Leo. 1992. Personal interview.

Sarkissian, Margaret. 1990. "The Politics of Music: Armenian Community Choirs in Toronto." In *Ethnomusicology in Canada: Proceedings of the First Conference on Ethnomusicology in Canada,* ed. Robert Witmer, 98–105. Toronto.

Sarkissian, Margaret Lynne. 1987. "Armenian Musical Culture in Toronto: Political and Social Divisions in an Immigrant Community." Master's thesis, University of Illinois, Urbana-Champaign.

Sawaie, Mohammed. 1985. *Arabic Speaking Immigrants in the U.S. and Canada: An Annotated Bibliographic Guide.* Lexington, Ky: Mazda Publishing.

Sbait, Dirgham Hanna. 1982. "The Improvised-Sung Folk Poetry of the Palestinians." Ph.D. dissertation, University of Washington, Seattle.

Schimmel, Annemarie. 1975. *Mystical Dimensions in Islam.* Chapel Hill: University of North Carolina Press.

Setian, Sosi. 1990. *"Kef-Time: A Prohibited Style of Armenian Music."* Paper presented at the joint meeting of the *Society for Ethnomusicology,* the *American Musicological Society,* and the *Society for Music Theory,* Oakland, California.

———. 1991. *Kef-Time: A Prohibited Style of Armenian Music.* Unpublished videotape. Columbia University, New York.

Shah, Idries. 1970. *The Way of the Sufi.* New York: E. P. Dutton.

Shaheen, Simon. 1992. *Turath: Simon Shaheen Performs Masterworks of the Middle East.* With 8-page booklet of notes and photographs by Ali Jihad Racy. CMP 3006. Compact disc.

Shaker, Fouad E. 1988. "Turks." In *The Canadian Encyclopedia,* vol. 4:2202. Edmonton, Alberta: Hurtig Publishers.

Shakir, Evelyn. 1987. "Good Works, Good Times: The Syrian Ladies' Aid Society of Boston, 1917–1932." In *Crossing the Waters: Arabic-Speaking Immigrants to the United States before 1940,* ed. Eric Hoogland. Washington, D.C.: Smithsonian Institution Press.

Shryock, Andrew. 1997. "Popular Culture in Arab Detroit: Creating Arab/American Identities in a Transnational Domain." Unpublished manuscript.

Signell, Karl. 1976. "The Modernization Process in Two Oriental Cultures: Turkey and Japan." *Asian Music* 7(2):72–102.

———. 1977. *Makam: Modal Practice in Turkish Art Music.* Seattle: Asian Music Publications.

Sonneborn, Daniel Atesh. 1995. *Music and Meaning in American Sufism: The Ritual of Dhikr at Sami Mahal, a Chishtiyya-derived Sufi Center.* Ann Arbor, Mich.: University Microfilms.

Spottswood, Richard K. 1990. *Ethnic Music on Records: A Discography of Ethnic Recordings Produced in the United States, 1893–1942.* Champaign-Urbana: University of Illinois Press.

————, ed. 1982. *Ethnic Recordings in America: A Neglected Heritage.* Washington, D.C.: American Folklife Center, Library of Congress.

Sugarman, Jane. 1990. "The Electronic Village." Paper presented at the joint meeting of the Society for Ethnomusicology, the American Musicological Society, and the Society for Music Theory, Oakland, California.

Takooshian, Harold. 1995. "Armenian Americans." In *Gale Encyclopedia of Multicultural America,* ed. Rudolph J. Vecoli, Judy Galens, Anna Sheets, and Robyn V. Young, 109–119. Detroit: Gale Research.

Varzi, Morteza, with Margaret Caton, Robyn C. Friend, and Neil Siegel. 1986. "Performer-Audience Relationships in the *Bazm.*" In *Cultural Parameters of Iranian Musical Expression,* ed. Margaret Caton and Neil Siegel, 1–9. Redondo Beach, Calif.: The Institute of Persian Performing Arts.

Wasserman, Paul, and Alice E. Kennington, eds. 1983. *Ethnic Information Sources of the United States.* 2nd ed., vols. 1 and 2. Detroit: Gale Research Co.

Wilson, Howard Barrett. 1903. "Notes of Syrian Folk-Lore Collected in Boston." *The Journal of American Folk-Lore* 16(62):133–147.

Younis, Adele. 1961. "The Coming of the Arabic-Speaking People to the United States." Ph.D. dissertation, Boston University.

Zogby, John. 1990. *Arab America Today: A Demographic Profile.* Washington, D.C.: Arab American Institute.

————, ed. 1984. *Taking Root, Bearing Fruit: The Arab American Experience.* Washington, D.C.: American Arab Anti-Discrimination Committee Reports.

Snapshot: Sufi Music and Dance
D. Atesh Sonneborn

Dances of Universal Peace
Turkish Precursors
Central and South Asian Predecessors

Sufism, commonly but incompletely termed Islamic mysticism, was born and nurtured in the Middle East and Asia. Its music today is used to aid in the development of spiritual awareness and consciousness. Music is used by Sufis primarily to center and focus one's concentration on God or divine attributes. It is also seen as a means to reach a state of ecstasy, but that ecstasy is considered only a foretaste and echo of the real ecstasy, the gnosis of unity with God through the annihilation of the personal self (*fanā'*), the ultimate experiential goal of all Sufi teachings.

In North America, Sufi music is a combination of many Western and non-Western musics. Aspects of Indian, Middle Eastern, African, and Native American traditional musics may be found side by side with Western classical, American folk, and popular music, creating a true synthesis.

DANCES OF UNIVERSAL PEACE

The best known and most widespread form of North American Sufi music is that which accompanies the Dances of Universal Peace, often mistakenly called Sufi dancing. This group spiritual practice, which integrates breath, movement, and music, has spread throughout the world since its California beginnings in the mid-1960s. There are about fifty weekly meetings of recognized Dances of Universal Peace circles throughout the United States and hundreds of others that use elements of the Dances. The American Samuel L. Lewis (1896–1971), recognized during his lifetime as a Sufi master, first created the Dances in his San Francisco, California, home. Lewis, also known as Sufi Ahmed Murad Chishti, gave credit for inspiring this dance "right out of the cosmos, out of the heart of God" (Lewis 1986:320) to the modern dance pioneer Ruth St. Denis (c. 1878–1968). Of music's place in the Dances of Universal Peace, Lewis said, "One of the reasons I am teaching this music and dancing is to increase Joy, not awe towards another person, but bliss in our own self. This is finding God within, through Experience" (Lewis 1986:320). The original body of work, about fifty dances, has expanded more than tenfold by the efforts of his students and their students in turn. Today, the Dances of Universal Peace are also preserved and spread by the International Network for the Dances of Universal Peace (INDUP). INDUP is a Seattle-based organization that trains and certifies Dance teachers worldwide and maintains a publishing arm.

Compared to its nominal antecedents in Sufism, as historically manifested in Islamic cultures, the music found in the Dances of Universal Peace, especially in *dhikr* 'remembrance', shares several important characteristics with other living Sufi traditions and classical models:

1. Music is to be used in a communal assembly under the direction of a spiritual preceptor.
2. It consists of the recitation of various formulaic texts, accompanied by melodic and rhythmic instruments.
3. Music itself is said to be for the purposes of centering and as a means to enhance concentration on God.
4. The goal of the ritual is repeatedly stated as transformative, on the way to annihilation in the Divine (*fanā'*).
5. The music is self-referenced as Sufi music.
6. Participants recount experiences of ecstatic or unitive states emerging from participation in Dances of Universal Peace rituals.

The musical and textual materials that form the Dances include chants and melodies from all the world's major spiritual traditions, including Hinduism, Buddhism, Judaism, Christianity, and Islam, as well as many others, such as Zoroastrian, Native American, Aramaic, Maori, Celtic, African, and Goddess traditions. Many of the earliest melodies were simple monophonic unison chants on one or two notes. New melodies with a vocal ambitus of an octave or more were created in the 1970s. Starting late in that decade, according to Dr. Neil Douglas-Klotz (founding director of INDUP), more emphasis and attention were given to ensuring that melody and movement alike were true to their original traditions (Douglas-Klotz 1997). Since the 1980s, texts and melodies have drawn from an even broader range of cultures and traditions, using non-Western languages, modes, and polyphonic and harmonic structures. Dances are accompanied by drum, often by guitar, and, particularly since the 1980s, by additional Western and non-Western instruments. Originally conceived as folk dances with a spiritual purpose, the Dances today are also applied in therapeutic settings (for example, hospitals, drug and alcohol treatment centers, grief counseling contexts) as well as in political demonstrations for peace (for example, in Israel and Russia).

In the late 1960s, Lewis's followers invited composer W. A. Mathieu to join their circle. From that meeting developed another body of musical compositions and performances written and directed for mixed chorus and instrumental ensemble by Mathieu, who produced five Sufi Choir albums between 1970 and 1980.

TURKISH PRECURSORS

The next most familiar form of Sufi dance and music is the public *semma* 'hearing, audition', performed by the Mevlevi order founded in Konya, Turkey, by the great Sufi poet Jelāluddīn Rūmī (1207–1273). Communities in the United States have hosted a number of tours by Turkish Mevlevi dervishes. Since the 1970s at least two Mevlevi teachers, Reshad Feild and Jelaleddin Loras, have made their homes in the States and taught North American students the inner and outer forms of the turning dance and its accompanying music.

The *semma* is a highly stylized dance ritual accompanied by an orchestra of wind and string players, percussionists, and singers, traditionally all male. Our idea of

Originally conceived as folk dances with a spiritual purpose, the Dances today are also applied in therapeutic settings (for example, hospitals, drug and alcohol treatment centers, grief counseling contexts) as well as in political demonstrations for peace (for example, in Israel and Russia).

---

whirling dervishes comes from the slow turning dance of *semma*. The music of the Turkish *semma* has changed over the centuries. Most music heard in Turkey today was written between the seventeenth and nineteenth centuries, although two pieces are traditionally ascribed to Rūmī's son, Sultan Veled (d. 1312). Musically, the pieces are similar to Ottoman classical court music of 1600–1800; the texts, however, are different, being settings of Rūmī's poetry. Much of that body of work is preserved in North American Mevlevi ritual, but contemporary compositions have also been added. In the United States, brass instruments have occasionally been added to *semma*'s instrumental ensemble, and both men and women may perform either as dancers or instrumentalists.

CENTRAL AND SOUTH ASIAN PREDECESSORS

The Chishtī order of North India and Pakistan fostered another form of Sufi music, songs performed by *qawwali,* singers who track their musical lineage back to a great poet, Amīr Khusrau (1253–1325), honored as the first *qawwal*. This form of Sufism was brought to India and refined by Hazrat Khwaja Muīnuddīn Ḥasan Chishtī (c. 1142–1236), who migrated there late in the twelfth century and settled in Ajmer, Rajasthan. The Chishtī order is claimed by Idries Shah and others to have originated in Khorasan, in present-day western Afghanistan, where wandering dervishes would arrive in a town or village, "and play a rousing air with flute and drum to gather people around them before reciting a tale or legend of initiatory significance" (Shah 1970:116).

Chishtī Sufism first came to North America in the person of Hazrat Inayat Khan (1882–1927) (figure 1), a famous Indian musician who represents a direct link between Sufism in India and in the West.

His primary instrument was the *vina,* the seven-stringed (four melody strings, three drone strings) lute/stick zither of India. Inayat Khan's Sufi teacher directed him to come to the West to spread the message of Sufism in word and music. He arrived in 1910, performed his music, lectured widely in the United States and Europe, and built a Western form of Sufism. Samuel L. Lewis was among those who became followers of Inayat Khan.

Dhikr

Other Sufi music created by those who received Inayat Khan's teaching in America, and their followers, is used in the core Sufi ritual of *dhikr*. The textual content and spiritual intention of the ritual of remembrance clearly links North American Sufi circles of mystics to their Middle Eastern or Asian counterparts.

Western scholars have made considerable study of the ecstatic experiences described in classical Sufi sources, but in North American *dhikr* circles, ecstasy is considered desirable only as a transitional state (*hāl*) on the way to the goal of unity. Ecstasy is believed to be a natural occurrence that arises in a *dhikr* participant on the way to *fanā*'. As in Gilbert Rouget's description of a Mevlevi *semma*, although the participants "may

FIGURE I   Hazrat Inayat Khan, a renowned Indian *vina* master, brought Sufism to North America in the early twentieth century.

be in a trance, there are almost no outward signs of it" (Rouget 1985:270). That is the behavior we see in evidence most often in the North American rituals. The trance state is, in Rouget's term, "interiorized." Rouget concludes that music, drumming, vocal repetition, and repetitive chanting are not in themselves trance inducing. Rather, it is a combination of extramusical preparatory factors that sets up the participant's expectations for the experience. Repetition of all the elements of the musical event plays a part in the experience.

Following is a description of such a *dhikr* ritual, an amalgam of elements gleaned from many groups. In this Chishtī-derived tradition, a *dhikr* circle gathers under the leadership of a recognized Sufi teacher, a man or a woman authorized to lead such rituals by his or her own teacher. The mixed-gender participants gather, often on Thursday evenings, the onset of the Islamic Sabbath. It should be noted that the majority of American participants were raised in either the Christian or the Jewish tradition and became Sufis as adults. Prayer and an invocation are offered, "Toward the One, the Perfection of Love, Harmony and Beauty, the only Being, United with All the Illuminated Souls who Form the Embodiment of the Master, the Spirit of Guidance" (Inayat Khan, 1974a:1). The leader sings the first verse of the Qur'ān, called *Al-Fātiḥa*, 'The Opener', in an improvised solo melody built on a minor or modal tonality. If there are instrumentalists present, they are usually silent during the *Fātiḥa* or may be asked to provide a drone or pedal tone. Then the *dhikr* proper begins, which may be, at its most basic, monotonal chanting without body movements and without instrumental accompaniment of any kind. There are Chishtī circles that create new monophonic or homophonic vocal melodies to accompany their rituals and those that add instruments, often a single drum (*dumbak,* pronounced locally as dumbek, which is a vase- or goblet-shaped drum made of clay or metal; or *tār,* the single-skinned frame drum of Nubia and the Nile Valley). There are also groups accompanied by an ensemble composed of keyboard (piano or synthesizer), bass guitar, and *tār* or by amplified acoustic guitar and one or two *tār* players. Other Sufi orders active in North America tend to use percussion only to accompany their group *dhikr.*

The key text phrase of *dhikr* is in Arabic, *"Lā ilāha illa 'llāh"* 'There is no God except God', which the leader chants once and the others join in unison. Text, vocal, and instrumental elements repeat again and again in rhythmic-melodic fragments and in harmonic progressions. *Dhikr* is chanted continuously and without pause for as long as a satisfactory level of concentration can be maintained. Then it stops. Whether the group is maintaining its concentration or not is up to the leader's judgment. The chant may continue for only a few minutes or it may go on for more than an hour. The chanted texts may also be diminutions of the key phrase, such as *"Il Allāh Hū," "Allāh Hū," "Allāh,"* or *"Hū."* Other texts in Arabic are often used, for example, *"Allāhu akbar"* 'God is great'; *"Ashhadu an lā i laha illa Hū"* 'I testify that there is no God but He'; *"Ar-Rahmān, Ar-Raḥīm"* 'God, the Merciful, the Compassionate'; *"ʿishq Allāh maʿbūd li 'llāh"* (literally, "The Love of God [is] worshiped for God," often poetically rendered as "God is Love, Lover and Beloved"); or others. With the incessant repetition and focus on the sacred phrases, participants report experiencing a sense of freedom, joy, or ecstasy.

REFERENCES

The Best of the Sufi Choir: A Jubilee Selection. 1993. San Francisco: SIRS Caravan Publications CMM 010. Compact disc.

Dances of Universal Peace, Volume I. 1987 [1975]. Seattle: PeaceWorks INDUP T100. Audiocassette.

Douglas-Klotz, Neil. 1997. Electronic mail to author. April 13.

Friedlander, Ira. 1992. *The Whirling Dervishes.* New York: Doubleday.

The Hadrat. 1982. Sufi Zikr Series, no. 3. San Francisco: Sufi Islamia/Prophecy Publications SI/P 003. Audiocassette.

Inayat Khan, Hazrat. 1967. "Confessions." In *The Sufi Message of Hazrat Inayat Khan.* Vol. 12. London: Barrie and Jenkins.

———. 1973. "Music" and "The Mysticism of Sound." In *The Sufi Message of Hazrat Inayat Khan.* Vol. 2, 9–67, 69–152. London: Barrie and Jenkins.

Inayat Kahn, Vilayat. 1974. *Toward the One.* New York: Harper and Row.

Journey to the Lord of Beauty. 1982. Sufi Zikr Series, no. 2. San Francisco: Sufi Islamia/Prophecy Publications SI/P 003. Audiocassette.

Lewis, Samuel L. 1974. *Sufi Vision and Initiation.* San Francisco: Sufi Islamia/Prophecy Publications.

———. 1986. *In the Garden.* New York: Harmony Books.

———. 1990 [1975]. *Spiritual Dance and Walk: An Introduction.* Ed. Neil Douglas-Klotz. Seattle: Peace Works–INDUP.

More and More Awake: New Music from the Mevlevi Zikr. 1982. Fairfax, Calif.: Mevlevi Order of America. Audiocassette.

Qureshi, Regula Burckhardt. 1986. *Sufi Music of India and Pakistan: Sound, Context, and Meaning in Qawwali.* London: Cambridge University Press.

Remembrance. 1992. Sami Mahal Sufi Center SM 101. Audiocassette.

Rouget, Gilbert. 1985. *Music and Trance.* Trans. Brunhilde Biebuyck. Chicago: University of Chicago Press.

Schimmel, Annemarie. 1975. *Mystical Dimensions in Islam.* Chapel Hill: University of North Carolina Press.

Shah, Idries. 1970. *The Way of the Sufi.* New York: E. P. Dutton.

———. 1971. *The Sufis.* Garden City, N.Y.: Doubleday/Anchor Books.

Sonneborn, Daniel Atesh. 1995. "Music and Meaning in American Sufism: The Ritual of Dhikr at Sami Mahal, a Chishtiyya-derived Sufi Center." Ann Arbor, Mich.: University Microfilms.

Polynesian Music
Amy Ku'uleialoha Stillman

A History of Polynesian Culture in the United States
The Marketing of Hawaiian Music Outside Hawai'i
Recent Contexts for Polynesian Performance in Continental Communities

The maintenance of music and dance traditions from those island groups in the eastern Pacific known collectively as Polynesia (bounded by Hawai'i in the north, New Zealand in the south, and Rapa Nui [Easter Island] in the east) on the U.S. continent resonates as much with non-Polynesian perceptions as with cultural concerns within communities of indigenous islanders. In the 1990 census, the three largest Polynesian communities reported were as follows: native Hawaiians 211,014 (of which some 50,000 reside outside Hawai'i), Samoans 62,964, and Tongans 17,606. Continental communities are clustered mostly on the West Coast, with a sizable Mormon population in Utah as well; scattered communities are located in large urban areas in the Midwest and on the East Coast. Polynesian performance traditions are actively practiced within these communities at the turn of the twenty-first century.

A HISTORY OF POLYNESIAN CULTURE IN THE UNITED STATES

The presence of Polynesians on the U.S. continent is tied in with historical and cultural trajectories of colonization. The Hawaiian Islands were annexed as a territory in 1898 and attained statehood in 1959. Following decades of international rivalry, an administrative partitioning of the Samoan archipelago brought American Samoa under U.S. jurisdiction in 1899; Western Samoa attained independence in 1962. Because kin ties override political boundaries, American Samoa has served as an entry point to the United States for all Samoans, as well as for islanders from Tonga and other locales.

Throughout the twentieth century, Polynesian traditions also figured in American cultural consciousness. Continental conceptions of exoticness, intensified by the geographic remoteness of the islands, were initially formulated in the accounts of early explorers and subsequent travelers, including literary lions Robert Louis Stevenson, Mark Twain, and Jack London; themes of idyllic paradise were also taken up in film and television production. Several waves of national popularity of Hawaiian music have facilitated exposure for other Polynesian traditions.

THE MARKETING OF HAWAIIAN MUSIC OUTSIDE HAWAI'I

Throughout the late 1800s and early 1900s, Hawaiian music became known outside Hawai'i through two means. First, travelers who visited Hawai'i wrote descriptive

A seemingly obligatory "Hawaiian" album can be found in the discography of many lounge instrumental music recording artists of the 1950s and 1960s, including Leo Addeo, Ray Coniff, Enoch Light, country guitarist Marty Robbins, and 101 Strings.

accounts of performances that emphasized their exoticness, the aura of which has remained an important marketing tool in the tourism industry. Second, troupes began touring the United States and Europe, starting with the 1893 World Exposition in Chicago, where a troupe of hula dancers entertained daily on the Midway Plaisance for six months. Another troupe spent several months at the 1905 Exposition in Buffalo.

The Columbia and Victor record companies began commercial recording of Hawaiian music in 1905. Although performers were recorded in Honolulu by teams of traveling engineers, the recordings enjoyed national distribution and sales; remarkably, Hawaiian music was not marketed as "race" music [see AFRICAN AMERICAN MUSICS, p. 571; THE MUSIC INDUSTRY, p. 705].

The Panama-Pacific Exposition, held in 1915 in San Francisco, was the event that launched unprecedented interest in Hawaiian music on the continent. Live performances stimulated widespread interest in two domains: repertoire and instruments.

Songs

The debut of the song "On the Beach at Waikiki" at the Panama-Pacific Exposition is credited with sparking a national fad for Hawaiian songs. Its English-language lyrics play on the first line repeated in each of five verses; literally meaning "quick, let's kiss," the line is not directly translated in the song. Its representation of Hawaiian maid as siren is made explicit in the fourth verse: "'*Honi kaua, a wikiwiki,*' she was surely teasing me, So I caught that maid and kissed her on the beach at Waikiki."

Sherman Clay, a San Francisco music publisher, published Hawaiian sheet music and song folios starting in 1916 until the mid-1930s, thereby making the repertoire available to continental buyers and giving Hawaiian songwriters access to broader distribution. Compared to song folios published in Honolulu, Hawaiian language songs, especially the strophic songs known as *hula kuʻi* (literally, "interpretive hula that combines old [that is, indigenous] and new [that is, Western] components"), were frequently replaced in continental publications with songs in AABA format containing English-language lyrics, known as *hapa haole* (literally, "half foreign" [that is, English]) songs, some of which were never published in Honolulu.

Popular songwriters, based in New York's Tin Pan Alley music publishing district, were attracted to the vogue in Hawaiian songs [see POPULAR MUSIC OF THE PARLOR AND STAGE, p. 179]. Through the late 1910s and 1920s, Tin Pan Alley songwriters churned out songs with Hawaiian and other generic South Seas settings (figure 1). These songs capitalized on romanticized stereotypes of Hawaiʻi as a visitor destination. Written from a male perspective, the lyrics extolled female hula dancers with suggestive innuendo of sexual liaisons awaiting lonely travelers. Exotic distance was further increased with the use of nonsense phrases intended to mimic the Hawaiian language, evident in titles like "Oh, How She Could Yacki Hacki Wicki Wacki Woo (That's Love in Honolu [*sic*])" and "Down on Ami Ami Oni Oni Isle." This corpus of songs established the use of the thirty-two-bar popular song form (AABA) among subsequent Hawaiʻi-based songwriters of *hapa-haole* songs. Many of these songs were performed

FIGURE I   Sheet music cover, published by Shapiro, Bernstein and Co., New York, 1916.

on continental vaudeville and variety stages, and they were also recorded commercially by Hawaiian musicians.

Musical instruments

The national fad for Hawaiian music in the wake of the 1915 Panama-Pacific Exposition also sparked interest in two instruments, the 'ukulele and the so-called Hawaiian guitar. Demand for instruments and classes across the continent led to a proliferation of instrument manufacture and sales, studios offering instruction, and pedagogical publications. Hawaiian composer Ernest Ka'ai published a 'ukulele method book in Honolulu in 1916. Numerous titles followed in the 1920s and 1930s from publishers in New York (William Smith, Hawaiianized in volume titles as "Kamiki"), San Francisco (Sherman Clay), and Cleveland, Ohio (Oahu Publishing Co.). More recent publishers include pedagogical giant Mel Bay. Among continental instructional books, the quantity of non-Hawaiian songs gradually surpassed Hawaiian songs, showing evidence for a separation of the instruments from the repertoires with which they originally came to prominence. Among instrument manufacturers, Weissenborn in Los Angeles and Martin in Nazareth, Pennsylvania, became noted for quality Hawaiian guitars and 'ukuleles.

The Hawaiian guitar sound originated as a technique of melodic picking while stopping strings with a metallic bar on a guitar held across the lap; invention of the technique is most often credited to Joseph Kekuku, a Hawaiian schoolboy, in 1885. Various modifications were made to the guitar to enhance the sound, including the addition of aluminum resonators, substitution of steel for wood in the body, electrical amplification by the late 1920s, and pedals that allowed players access to multiple tunings—all factors that led to the designation *steel guitar*. The sustained sounds produced by electrically amplified instruments became iconically associated with tourist entertainment between the 1930s and 1960s. This sound also led to the adoption of the instrument and its playing techniques by honky-tonk country musicians in Nashville from the 1940s.

Amateur interest in the steel guitar across the continent, including Canada, led to the formation of associations that continue to promote the instrument and, through it, Hawaiian music. Many groups, such as the Hawaiian Steel Guitar Association, have Internet websites publicizing their activities and newsletters. Despite efforts to mentor young players, however, the steel guitar's close connection to tourist entertainment has led subsequent generations of Hawaiians to eschew the instrument, leading one scholar to conclude that its popularity at the end of the twentieth century is anachronistic (Junker 1998:390).

Film music

Fascination with the South Seas was taken up in Hollywood films beginning in the 1920s. Production numbers often involved native consultants and performers in the background, such as in *Bird of Paradise* in 1932 and especially the remake in 1951, *Waikiki Wedding* in 1937, and *Song of the Islands* in 1942. The 1963 release of *Blue Hawaii*, starring Elvis Presley (and his follow-up *Paradise Hawaiian Style* in 1966), fostered yet another wave of popularity for Hawaiian music. Films were an important means of exposure for repertoire; the song "Sweet Leilani," composed by Harry Owens, became Bing Crosby's first million-selling hit, won an Academy Award in 1937 for best song, became an iconic musical referent of Hawai'i, and subsequently became a staple of Hawaiian entertainers.

Post–World War II nostalgia

In the wake of World War II, which ended in 1945, two factors contributed to strengthening the presence of Polynesian performance traditions on the U.S. continent. First, new levels of nostalgic interest in the islands emerged among soldiers returning from stations throughout the Pacific. Film, television, and radio producers catered to this interest: the *Hawaii Calls* radio show broadcast from Honolulu had as its continental counterpart the *The Arthur Godfrey Show*, which included resident Hawaiian entertainers in the cast. Second, migration from the islands of Hawai'i and Samoa led to the establishment of communities of residents seeking wider educational and employment opportunities, particularly in the Los Angeles and San Francisco areas of California. Within these communities, studios offering dance instruction catered to homesick islanders. These community-oriented studios contrasted with studio enterprises in the 1920s and 1930s that offered limited lessons and routines for specific purposes (parties, cruises, and so on) to nonislander clientele.

Tiki culture

Throughout the 1950s, continental interest in the islands also contributed to a phenomenon known as "tiki culture." In part a reaction to the escalating Cold War and the advent of space exploration, tiki culture celebrated fabricated notions of primitivism, using Polynesian wood carvings as symbolic totems. The phenomenon spawned restaurants across the country that offered fanciful mixed cocktails, a mixture of Polynesian and Chinese cuisine, and tropical decor that included thatched walls, glowing volcanoes, vine-covered waterfalls, and torches; tiki-themed decor carried over into motels and apartment complexes as well.

The musical component of tiki culture crystallized in a 1957 album, *Exotica*, by pianist Martin Denny. Its characteristic features included lush accompaniments provided by exotic percussion, Latin rhythms, and tropical bird calls (performed by musicians in the combo). Although "exotica" music is not indigenously Hawaiian per se, musicians drew liberally on Hawaiian repertoire. Among the popular numbers that appeared repeatedly were Hawaiian-language songs adapted to instrumental versions, such as "Hawaiian War Chant" (*Kāua i ka Huahua'i*) by Leleiohoku; "Hawaiian Wedding Song" (*Ke Kali Nei Au*) and "Song of the Islands" (*Nā lei o Hawai'i*) by Charles E. King; and "Pearly Shells" (*Pūpū o 'Ewa*), adapted by Webley Edwards and Leon Pober, along with English-language songs such as "Beyond the Reef" by Jack Pitman, "Lovely Hula Hands" by R. Alex Anderson, and "Sweet Leilani" by Harry Owens. A seemingly obligatory "Hawaiian" album can be found in the discography of many lounge instrumental music recording artists of the 1950s and 1960s, including Leo Addeo, Ray Coniff, Enoch Light, country guitarist Marty Robbins, and 101 Strings. Hawaiian music profited by the national popularity of tiki culture, just as attention on Hawai'i was enhanced by its admission to statehood in 1959.

The Pan-Polynesian revue

Related to the proliferation of tropical-themed restaurants was another major hallmark in Polynesian entertainment—the pan-Polynesian revue. These productions feature live performance of music and dance from related Polynesian societies—Hawai'i, Tahiti, New Zealand Maori, Samoa, and occasionally Tonga and Fiji—in a now-standardized narrative "journey through Polynesia." The origin of these revues is as yet undocumented, but their early history is associated with tourist venues in Hawai'i, which included Waikiki hotels and especially the Polynesian Cultural Center theme park, opened on O'ahu's north shore in 1963 by the Mormon Church. The multiple-island format, adopted elsewhere in the Pacific Islands, appeared on the continent as well, in tropical-themed restaurants and nightclubs such as the Don the Beachcomber and Trader Vic's chains, the South Seas restaurant in Hollywood, Duke's in Malibu, and Disney amusement parks in California and Florida. Performers recruited from the islands on contract often served as community cultural resources and instructors; instructional studios and established troupes are populated with entertainers who have remained after their contracts expired.

The so-called pan-Polynesian approach of presenting multiple Polynesian traditions continues today, especially among troupes who work, or aspire to work, in commercial entertainment venues. However, because the majority of teachers are most knowledgeable about only one of the traditions that they teach (usually Hawaiian), the extent of repertoire in circulation from the other traditions—Samoan, Tahitian, Maori—is somewhat limited. Traveling frequently to Tahiti and New Zealand to learn new repertoire is not financially feasible for most teachers. Thus, for many troupes, the repertoire taught consists of routines that teachers themselves learned as performers from each other or from instruction sheets obtained through mail-order sources.

RECENT CONTEXTS FOR POLYNESIAN PERFORMANCE IN CONTINENTAL COMMUNITIES

Hawaiian performance activities

The resurgence of interest in Hawaiian culture since the 1970s has had ramifications for the maintenance of Polynesian performance traditions in continental communities. Many within the generation of instructors since the 1970s have sought to increase awareness about the depths of cultural knowledge that can be accessed through studying performance; this has coincided with growing numbers of students who seek out more in-depth instruction of not only the music and dance but also the culture from which they emanate. The result is the emergence of troupes that specialize in only one tradition.

Continental communities face challenges in maintaining and practicing performance traditions that are not necessarily present in the home islands. Access to resources is a major challenge. Although the Samoan language has been continuously spoken, the Hawaiian language is still in the process of revival. The availability of language classes and immersion education in Hawai'i has as yet no counterpart on the continent; as a result, Hawaiian-language facility is unevenly distributed among continental troupes. Resources for Tahitian or Maori performance are even more limited, because communities of Tahitian or Maori immigrants are virtually nonexistent.

Hula competitions

Another challenge has to do with overcoming perceptions of distance as disadvantage. Those who perpetuate Polynesian performance traditions on the continent struggle to have their efforts not regarded as second class and their creativity dismissed. This is most clearly seen in Hawaiian hula competitions, which have been major venues for hula troupes since the 1970s. No troupe from outside Hawai'i has yet won an event in Hawai'i. In California, troupes from Hawai'i routinely outscore those from outside Hawai'i in the *Iā 'Oe E Ka La* competition in northern California (begun in 1981). By restricting entry to troupes from outside Hawai'i, organizers of the *E Hula Mau* competition in southern California (begun in 1995) have ensured that a continental troupe will win.

Within Hawaiian communities, the number of hula troupes has increased dramatically since the 1970s. These troupes accommodate continental-born Hawaiians as well as more recent arrivals who relocate from the islands. Hula troupes perform at numerous community events, festivals, and hula competitions throughout the year. Troupes perform to live musical accompaniment, drawing on talent among family and friends. Fundraisers are held to assist with travel costs, especially for troupes who travel to events in Hawai'i. Individual troupes also hold annual recitals where all students perform for family and friends. Among the larger troupes (that is, more than one hundred students), recitals have become ticketed events held in a community or college campus facility and often feature popular recording artists from Hawai'i.

Concert tours

A marked increase since the 1980s in concert tours by recording artists from Hawai'i attests to the financial clout that continental communities wield as audiences and consumers. Internet websites that maintain events calendars have proliferated; these complement the efforts of the *Voice of Hawaii* newsletter, published in Los Angeles between 1971 and 1995, and the *Kapalakiko Calendar of Hawaiian Events,* published since the 1980s in San Francisco, as sources of information.

Samoan performance activities

Within Samoan communities, performance activities remain heavily based in church congregations. In addition to choirs, church sodality groups also sponsor Samoan dance teams as a youth-oriented activity. Both choirs and Samoan dance teams enter periodic interparish competitions. The major Samoan event among American Samoans is the celebration of Flag Day, which commemorates the establishment of the American protectorate on 17 April 1900. Day-long activities include performance competitions, for which groups rehearse for months.

In recent decades, Samoan community leaders have witnessed an erosion of interest in Samoan traditions among the youth, who favor adaptations of African American hip-hop culture. Rapping in English and Samoan, along with break dancing and stepping, have become regular components of school and youth talent shows; amateur groups model their efforts on professional troupes such as Nature Boys in Seattle (disbanded in the early 1990s) and Island Boiz and Kullapse in Los Angeles. The formation of the cultural troupe Penina o le Pasefika in Los Angeles in 1991, outside of the framework of a church congregation, voices a consciousness of cultural preservation not previously voiced in the Samoan community.

Tahitian performance activities

The vitality of Tahitian dance is interesting, given the lack of a community of Tahitian islanders. Two annual competitions in California, *Kiki Raina* in Merced and *Tahiti Fête* in San José, draw the participation of numerous troupes, mostly from California. Few troupes are devoted exclusively to Tahitian performance; many are *hula hālau* who enter under a Tahitian name. Initially, interest in Tahitian dance grew out of the Tahitian component of the pan-Polynesian revue. The *Tahiti Fête* in San José, established in 1990, was the first event to bring Tahitian cultural authorities as judges, thereby holding dance enthusiasts to Tahitian standards of evaluation and expectation. Troupes quickly took advantage of the Tahitian judges as sources for new repertoire, interpretation, and updates on dance trends in Tahiti.

Other contexts for Polynesian performance

At home in the islands, islander communities opt whether to associate with each other; historically, for example, Hawaiian and Samoan communities in Hawai'i do not have long experiences of interaction. On the continent, where islander communities are overwhelmed by larger mainstream populations, the formation of coalitions for political purposes gives constituent communities increased visibility. One such example is the Pacific Islander Council in Los Angeles, which has staged an annual Pacific Islander Festival each May since 1989. Through performances and crafts demonstrations, islanders celebrate island ways in an urban setting. This festival served as a prototype for subsequent festivals in San Diego and San Francisco.

Through these and other channels, communities have increased their access to traditional arts development resources from government sources at the municipal, state, and even federal levels as well as from private sources. Moreover, Polynesian traditions have come to the attention of festival presenters, who bring these traditions onstage for broader audiences at venues such as the Los Angeles Festival in 1990, the Northwest

Folklife Festival in 1993, and the 1995 San Francisco Ethnic Dance Festival. In February 1998, the program *'Ohana—We Are Family* brought three Los Angeles–based hula troupes together onstage in a noncompetitive concert event to a sellout audience at the Carpenter Performing Arts Center in Long Beach. By demonstrating the vitality of hula in southern California, the program asserted that efforts to perpetuate ancestral ways there could no longer be regarded as lacking because of geographic separation.

REFERENCES

Beloff, Jim. 1997. *The Ukulele: A Visual History.* San Francisco: Miller Freeman.

Bigelow, Brad. "The Space Age Pop Standards Page." Available from website http://home.earthlink.net/~spaceagepop/

Denny, Martin. 1957. *Exotica.* Liberty Records, LRP-3034. LP disk.

Junker, Jay. 1998. "Steel Guitars." In *Garland Encyclopedia of World Music,* Vol. 9: *Australia and the Pacific Islands,* 389–390. New York: Garland.

Reyes, Luis I. 1995. *Made in Paradise: Hollywood's Films of Hawai'i and the South Seas.* Honolulu: Mutual Publishing.

Ruymar, Lorene. 1996. *The Hawaiian Steel Guitar and Its Great Hawaiian Musicians.* Anaheim Hills, Calif.: Centerstream Publishing.

Section 3
Canada

Canada's people and music are as varied as its landscape. The second largest nation in the modern world, Canada was originally inhabited by aboriginal settlers and later by European, African, Hispanic, and Asian immigrants. Its political history as a country first colonized and dominated by the French and later by the British has helped create a musical history that has been influenced by, but is also strikingly different from, that of its neighbor to the south. We approach the diverse musics of Canada geographically here, beginning with the Atlantic provinces in the east—those that were first colonized by Europeans—moving westward to the three territories of northern Canada that have only been settled relatively recently by Europeans and, most recently, by Asians, but that have for thousands of years sustained aboriginal peoples such as the Inuit, Métis, and First Nations, who continue to maintain much of their traditional ritual and ceremonial life there.

A bagpiper wearing a traditional costume performs for visitors, Ottawa, Ontario. © Dave G. Houser/CORBIS.

Identity, Diversity, and Interaction
Beverley Diamond

National Identity, Local Identity
Global Positioning of Canadian Culture
Canadian Culture vis-à-vis the United States
Musical Interaction among Culturally Specific Communities within Canada

Already diverse prior to the arrival of Europeans, the precontact aboriginal population of the area now constituted as Canada spoke a wide range of languages, adapted to and managed remarkably contrasted environments, developed distinctive cultural practices, and established complex networks of trade and political alliance by 1500. Since the Constitution Act of 1982, the aboriginal population resident in Canada, currently estimated to be approximately two million (Royal Commission on Aboriginal People [RCAP] 1996:13), has been officially recognized as consisting of three groups: First Nations (600,000–800,000), Inuit (42,500), and Métis (153,000) (RCAP 1996:16). There are over fifty aboriginal languages (eleven different language families) spoken in Canada. Inuit arrived approximately four thousand years ago via the Bering Strait ice bridge from northern Asia. Métis, the mixed-blood descendants of aboriginal and European settlers, gradually developed a distinctive culture and societal structure since the fifteenth century.

The earliest visitors to Canada were the Norse in the tenth century, on the northern peninsula of Newfoundland (Dickason 1992:87). Europeans fished the waters along the Atlantic coast throughout the fifteenth century but are said to have first made landfall when John Cabot arrived in Newfoundland in 1497. For the next four centuries, a dominant cultural force was the fur trade; assisted by aboriginal *couriers de bois* (runners of the woods), fur traders explored interior waterways, establishing trading posts for two rival companies that largely determined alliances between indigenous and European people until the companies merged in 1824.

Considerable musical interaction seems to have taken place in early settlements, for example, at Port Royal, Québec, and Montréal, all established in the first decade of the seventeenth century. Missions (Recollets, Jesuits, and Ursuline nuns arrived after 1615) became important gathering places where many cultural practices, including both seventeenth-century aboriginal song/dance and Christian musical practices, were first documented, albeit from a Christian-centered perspective. The use of secular music in seventeenth-century settings is further described in a number of historical and diary-like accounts by settlers, explorers, and others (Diamond and Robbins 1992; Morey 1997; Robbins 1992).

The struggle for colonial control during the seventeenth and eighteenth centuries involved alliances between English and Iroquois on one hand and French and Algonquians on the other. Although at the end of the Seven Years War in 1763 the English assumed control of "British North America," the French presence was not to be denied. The American Civil War represented a juncture at which the population of what would be Canada took a unique turn. United Empire Loyalists (primarily English-born but also including some African Americans and American Indians) moved north, where their loyalty to the British Crown could be maintained. A series of legislative acts (described later in sections on Ontario and Québec) led to the confederation of a "dominion" embracing Ontario, Québec, Nova Scotia, and New Brunswick, effected by the British North America Act of 1867 (replaced when the Canadian constitution was repatriated in 1982).

Through the late nineteenth century, the French and English were positioned as the "founding nations," a designation that ignored the prior residence of aboriginal people and that rapidly became a misrepresentation of the nation's identity in light of the diversification of immigration, especially in western Canada, where large land tracts were marketed in particular to Northern and Eastern European immigrants who created relatively homogeneous bloc settlements. Others, such as the Irish potato famine victims who arrived in the late nineteenth century, fled economic adversity. Jewish immigrants arrived from the late nineteenth century onward. The Depression of the 1930s effectively slowed the early waves of European immigration. Interwar and post–World War II immigration from Northern and Eastern Europe brought a better educated, urban-oriented population, especially to the cities of Ontario and Québec. Hence the older, more rural, and often more assimilationist western communities often differed substantially from newer communities in Toronto or Montréal, in spite of their common country of birth.

Following the early importing of labor, especially for railway building, Asian and Middle Eastern immigration was severely constrained by "exclusion" acts between 1923 and 1947 and restrictive policies extending into the 1960s. Consequently families were often separated for decades, and Asian communities are often dramatically differentiated by generation and period of arrival. New waves of immigrants (Vietnamese in the 1980s or Hong Kong emigrants in the 1990s, for example) contribute further to the internal diversity of specific Asian communities.

African Canadian settlement has differed from but nevertheless been related to that of the United States. Slavery was abolished in Maritime Canada by the early eighteenth century, and by midcentury Canada was a haven for runaway slaves via the Underground Railroad. In the twentieth century, especially the 1980s and 1990s, the majority of the African Canadian population came from the Caribbean, however, resulting in a demographic profile substantially different from that of the African American population of the United States.

The diversity of every region increased exponentially in the twentieth century. By the time of the 1986 census, the ten most widely used languages were English, French, Italian, German, Ukrainian, Chinese, Portuguese, Dutch, Polish, and Greek. Between 1986 and 1996 the largest population increases were in Chinese, South Asian, and Caribbean communities. Furthermore, the diversity within communities and the intermixing of cultures are noteworthy developments in Canada (as elsewhere) at the beginning of the twenty-first century. The importance of defining local identities remains urgent, however, in the context of increasing globalization.

The issues outlined next, then, are more accurately configured as a matrix of "tensions" that have been negotiated differently by different individuals, communities, or regions at different times. What is arguably distinct about the Canadian context at the turn of the twenty-first century is what historian Ian Angus has described as "a society committed to the public relevance of diverse collective identities based on ethnocultures" (1997:137), a society in which "the core of the argument is that respect for the Other can only be established through an ethical practice that maintains a border which refuses to cannibalize the other by the self" (1997:47).

Beyond the musical sphere, the images and metaphors of national identity are diverse and as often negative as positive.

NATIONAL IDENTITY, LOCAL IDENTITY

Canadians have been variably committed to the idea of defining a national identity. As composer John Beckwith (1997:94) has noted: "[patriotism] comes and goes, and also varies from a local to a colonial to a regional to a 'national' phenomenon, sometimes creating confusion by mixing up these points of view." By the 1990s most cultural critics dispensed with any notion of a singular vision, although as Whitelaw has observed regarding art exhibitions, some cultural production can be critiqued for "replacing an outdated national essentialism with a regional one" (1997:39). Canadian scholars and artists, like their counterparts internationally, are more and more concerned with the discursive formations and performative dimensions of culture. In his work on *l'identité québécois,* cultural theorist Martin Allor, for example, finds it useful "to focus on the relations between narrations of the identity of places, and the range of practices which produce these sites as the vehicles for the performance of forms of life, and the staging of theaters marking the politics of collective identity and difference" (1997:52).

Historically, on the other hand, waves of national sentiment in which a singular identity was imagined are also identifiable. It is not coincidental that following the completion of the Canadian Pacific Railway in the 1890s, when a vision of a country built on British institutions (a structure often equated with the growth of freedom or a "rise in liberty," as Carl Berger phrases it [1986:32]) was widely shared by policy makers, we also see the rapid development of a European-derived institutional infrastructure for music, including choirs, orchestras, and training institutions. Beckwith (1997:126) regards compositions of this period as comparable to those of the Second New England School in the United States: "Interestingly, that generation of composers in Canada began thinking indigenously rather than colonially—a song-cycle refers to the Canadian northern landscape, a piano fantasia evokes impressions of an Iroquois dance-ceremony, stage works start to draw on local history and local settings rather than on legends, lands, and peoples from abroad."

Another nationalist wave coincided with the concurrent expansion of rail service and radio in the 1920s. A series of Canadian Pacific Railway–sponsored multicultural festivals and the composition of many works based on folk song are effects of this wave. Adaptable musicians such as Ernest MacMillan, composer Hector Gratton, and folklorist Marius Barbeau, who recognized the vitality of French Canadian and Native cultures, were centrally involved with this nationalist phase. At the same time, debates about national identity in music were contentious (Poirier 1994) [see OVERVIEW, p. 1146].

Yet another nationalist wave surrounded the celebration of Canada's centenary of Confederation in 1967. George Proctor (1980) has compiled a list of works commissioned for this event, among them one of the most successful contemporary Canadian operas, *Louis Riel,* a saga of the Métis hero by composer Harry Somers. Simultaneously the emergence of successful singer-songwriters such as Gordon Lightfoot, Bruce Cockburn, and others defined a Canadian perspective and even, some would argue, a Canadian sound in popular music (Rice 1995).

Beyond the musical sphere, on the other hand, the images and metaphors of national identity are diverse and as often negative as positive. One of the earliest was the depiction of Canada as a nation with a "garrison mentality," an inward-looking orientation stimulated in part by fear of the outside, the unknown, or the different. Very similar to this depiction is Gaile McGregor's identification of the "Wacousta Syndrome," a propensity to see "Wilderness" as something overwhelming and awe inspiring (1985). She acknowledges the complex shifts in representation and the social and political forces that relate to these shifts. These metaphors resonate with literary themes described in the 1970s, for example, Canadian novelist and poet Margaret Atwood's identification of "survival" as a "vantage point from which to view Canadian literature" (1972:31) or John Moss's (1974) exploration of exile and isolation as persistent themes in Canadian literature. In some ways these images seem outmoded in relation to vibrant cultural changes of the 1990s, but they have repeatedly resonated for some musicians, artists, and writers.

Another persistent image of identity, related to the preoccupation with wilderness, is the idea of "North." Composer R. Murray Schafer's sound poem *Music in the Cold* was a salient statement about this symbolic space, and in the 1990s his multiyear Wolf Project and the organization of Northern Encounters festivals marked his continued fascination with this metaphor. Andra McCartney (1997) has pointed to the extensive list of other musical works that have built upon the metaphor, ranging from Somers's *North Country* to the widely known Québécois "anthem" by Gilles Vigneault: "Mon pays, ce n'est pas un pays, c'est l'hiver."

Seven "myths," defined as "persistent images and stories," have been described by Daniel Francis in a historical reflection entitled *National Dreams* (1997). They include not only the "Myth of north," but also myths of the railway, the Royal Canadian Mounted Police, and the canoe, among others. Similar subsets of stereotypic myths were effectively parodied in the 1990s in TV series such as *Due South* or the *Royal Canadian Air Farce.*

If these images are more than stereotypic reductions, however, one must ask difficult questions about their production and usage. For whom do they resonate? Northerners themselves, for example, are less prone to rely on this imagery than are urbanites in the southern metropolises of the nation. Furthermore, South Asian literary critic Arun Mukherjee (1994), for example, has suggested that the "Great White North" is a metaphor that refers to both a geography and a racialized space, where difference is disturbing to the national ethos. In both practice and theory, then, these assertions of national identity are contested.

More compelling for many are the nationalisms within the nation. The two that are discussed most extensively are the struggle for aboriginal nationhood and the sovereignist movement in Québec. Both struggles have stimulated extensive production of popular music in particular, including the *chansonnier* tradition since the 1960s in Québec [see INTERCULTURAL AND COMMERCIAL MUSICS, p. 1154] and the more recent flourishing of aboriginal popular music on the world music scene.

GLOBAL POSITIONING OF CANADIAN CULTURE

Canada has generally occupied an ambiguous global position—historically a colony and yet economically part of the contemporary "imperializing" West; as a nation welcoming an incredibly diverse population and yet at times one with notable instances of inward-looking or even xenophobic activity. This ambiguity has marked the music historiography of the nation. Studies of ethnic minorities have until recently been ghettoized, the hyphenization of their identities maintained. Musical diversity, indeed vernacular music of any sort, has been underrepresented—particularly relative to studies in the United States (Diamond 1994). Scholarly studies of Canadian popular music and even jazz have been slow to appear and generally segregated from textbooks on

Canadian music, which have been produced discursively to focus on classical composition and modernism. In part this is a strategic means of differentiating Canadian from American music culture. The neglect of vernacular music may also be a lingering effect of colonial attitudes. A clearer sign of such attitudes is the widespread practice of confusing Self and Other through the teaching of Canadian music in courses on world music, for example, at many institutions (Diamond 1991).

Europeans other than the British and French have often had to contend with an ambiguous positioning as Other in the Canadian context. Ukrainian author Myrna Kostash has articulated this problem, particularly the "invisible minority" status occupied by Eastern and Central Europeans, a status that positions them as white and mainstream in the eyes of a Caribbean or Asian, for example, but marginal relative to the British and French onetime majority. "Where does Europe end?" she asks provocatively, as she reminds us, "An edge, a frontier, a margin becomes so because of its relationship to what comes next." She describes her communities as "Euro-ec-centrics," wrestling on the border (Kostash 1992:42–43). Evidence that Kostash's analysis also holds for Mediterranean Europeans is found in the paucity of musical information on the large Italian and Greek communities in Canada.

On the other hand, isolation (though not marginalization) has sometimes actively been sought by specific immigrant groups to maintain their language and lifeways without entirely relying on English-language institutions. Newspapers were one important way of maintaining a sense of community in a new land and sharing the process of building a new culture. Such publications were so important that in 1982 the Multicultural History Society of Ontario (MHSO) could declare that there were "more ethnic newspapers printed in Ontario, in proportion to the number of immigrants here, than there are newspapers to population in the countries of origin" (1982:1).

Although the strategies for cultural survival in different communities varied with time and place, and much remains to be learned about these processes, it would seem that Canadian communities have remained proud of their separate heritages to a large extent. Cultural policy has tended to encourage this pride in difference, especially since the 1970s, but many problems remain with policies (and labels) that perpetuate marginalization or token recognition. Folklorist Carole Carpenter (1975), for instance, has made a compelling argument for the fact that the "mosaic" image frequently applied to Canadian society (see Porter 1965 for an analysis of Canadian class structure based on this image) has also served as a tool of marginalization that reinforces the hegemony of an Anglo-French mainstream.

CANADIAN CULTURE VIS-À-VIS THE UNITED STATES

Canada and the United States have a great deal of shared history and culture. Both aboriginal nations (who regard themselves not as citizens of either Canada or the United States but rather of their own nations) and immigrants from other parts of the world have enjoyed the relatively permeable border between the two countries. Even when the border crossing enacted profound political differences—as in the case of British Loyalists who moved north in the eighteenth century to preserve their links with Europe; African Americans who entered Canada in the late eighteenth and nineteenth centuries by way of the Underground Railroad; Ukrainians and other Central and Eastern European intelligentsia who emigrated to Canada when their interwar political convictions were less welcome in the United States; or Cubans, with whom Canada has maintained cordial relations in the 1990s during the Helms–Burton era— the peopling of one country has not been isolated from the peopling of the other.

And yet there are fundamental differences, as Seymour Martin Lipset has articulated (1989). The United States began in revolution, Canada in counterrevolution. The historical watershed of the American Revolution constitutes an indelible division that "Americans do not know but Canadians cannot forget," he alleges (1989:1). The

United States was antistatist, individualistic, egalitarian, and popular; Canada was statist, collectivist, elitist, and class based. The United States was committed to bourgeois liberal democracy and laissez-faire economics; Canada remained fascinated with monarchy and hierarchy, with public responsibility for economic management. As Frank Manning (1993) observes, the two nations have tended to converge, perhaps, or even to reverse their positions on certain issues such as centralized or decentralized authority. Nevertheless, the fundamental nature of these originary premises of statehood should not be overlooked.

Among the most persistent discourses of national identity in Canada are statements contrasting the nation with the United States. Sometimes such statements posit a unified America ("melting pot") against a diversified Canada ("melting not"). The imagery of these discourses is frequently gendered. Paul Rutherford (1993:261) has pointed to Victorian distinctions between Canada, "a purer and better country (often portrayed as a young if rather stern maiden)" and the (Uncle Sam–like) United States, "an older, leaner, slightly seedy male." Others have contested the oversimplification of such images.

Elspeth Probyn, for example, has pointed to the distinctive identity of French Canada, also in gendered terms but refusing the "politics of singularity." She points to some constructions of Québec as the mature matriarch "winking at the absence of men" (1996:86) and to others that render the province sexually ambiguous in keeping with the fact that Québec identity "often rhymes with marginality" (1996:72).

Other articulations of the Canada–U.S. relationship maintain the positive–negative valence without the gender mapping. Leslie Armour states that "at one time, we defined ourselves positively by looking across the Atlantic and negatively by looking south" (1996:20). This ambivalence toward the "colonizers" of the more distant and more recent past reflects a number of factors about the hegemonic relationship between Canada and the United States. Canadians may express resentment at being overlooked or ignored, as in the case of Tom Wayman's book *A Country Not Considered* (1993), provocatively titled with a statement made by U.S. novelist Ken Kesey. They may express concern about the autonomy or sustainability of Canadian culture in the face of American ownership of Canadian industry or free trade agreements such as the North American Free Trade Agreement (NAFTA) that threaten the integrity of culture. Cultural critic Mavor Moore cites Marshal McLuhan with reference to the need for an "anti-environment" in such contexts. "The heavier the rain is, the more you need a roof. You need an anti-environment especially if the environment is particularly oppressive" (1996:230). His anti-American position aggressively iterates the need for state support and cultural control: "Canadians can't sing their own song if, as in American culture, American commerce calls the tune. That is simple enough. While some Americans believe that Canadians use culture as a smoke screen for commercial advantage, some Canadians believe that Americans use commerce as a smoke screen for cultural advantage. And the Americans know very well which is more important" (229).

Ethnomusicologist James Robbins, on the other hand, urges attention to the parallels and differences between the cultural problems faced by Canada and Latin America when he states, "We are Americans who are not Americans" (1990:48). He argues that by looking either to former colonial powers or to the United States for the "legitimizing criteria of identity (either by imitation or rejection)," we base our self-knowledge on inappropriate concepts. Further, he was one of the first music scholars to urge that we stop searching for an integrated notion of a national culture but rather "examine how Canadian plurality might differ from other American pluralities" (1990: 48–49).

A growing number of scholars adopt positions that look at the Canada–U.S. cultural relationship in more a complex and nuanced fashion (see, for example, Manning 1993; Cohnstaedt and Frenette 1997). The narrowly protectionist nationalist position

In the nineteenth century, when legal proscriptions on traditional practices generally drove music and dance underground for several decades, aboriginal performers soon learned that traditional dance was sometimes permitted in the context of European festivals or Christian holidays.

is challenged on grounds relating to both commodification and content. Some scholars (Feldthusen 1993) argue that regulation is not effective in the commercial realm or that cultural policy and industrial policy making are often at odds (Dasher 1996). Others suggest that our search for Canadian content has often ignored the many ways in which American genres and styles have been differently "inflected" (see Miller's 1993 analysis of the TV programs *Street Legal* and *LA Law;* Ames 1993), syncretized (Taft 1993), or satirized (Gilbert 1993) to reflect different cultural values.

These arguments are important with regard to Canada's music culture. Our historiography has emphasized Canadian concert music and neglected both popular and vernacular musics, a process that is arguably a "resistance strategy" vis-à-vis the United States. As Manning has said, popular culture has been trivialized in Canada "as mere imported vulgarity, a form of symbolic surrender to hegemonic domination" (1993:28). Recent music scholarship has demonstrated ways in which resistance, inflection, parody, and unique local syncretizations have operated, frequently producing distinctive cultural products.

MUSICAL INTERACTION AMONG CULTURALLY SPECIFIC COMMUNITIES WITHIN CANADA

In every part of the world a complex array of factors determines whether culturally diverse members of a nation choose to interact in the production of music and other expressive forms or else to bound their cultural practices (including their daily interactions) with a view to maintaining traditions and prescribing norms and values. These factors range from the relative proximity or isolation of the groups to the power relations among them, the competence and agency of individuals within them, and the extent to which their musics (or other art forms) have similar or compatible components (leading to what anthropologists often call syncretism). Where music is concerned, the very importance assigned to musical practices among other modes of expression/action may also determine the extent to which cross-cultural interaction takes place.

Exchanges between various First Nations cultures and nonaboriginal cultures, for instance, could serve to illustrate how these factors operate. Many traditional genres associated with ceremonial practice remained remarkably resistant to outside influence, as they were deemed appropriate only for specific occasions and often only for those who had the right to perform or hear them. Even some social music such as the drum dance songs of Inuit in the central Arctic has changed relatively little through the vast community changes that have occurred in the second half of the twentieth century (Cavanagh 1982; Vascotto 2000) [see ARCTIC CANADA AND ALASKA, p. 374; SUBARCTIC CANADA, p. 383]. On the other hand, certain social musics, the Iroquois woman's shuffle dance (*eskanye*), for instance, borrowed fragments of popular songs from surrounding European Canadians, often creating humorous quoted references within the traditional *eskanye* structure. In the nineteenth century, when legal proscriptions on traditional practices generally drove music and dance underground for several decades, aboriginal performers soon learned that traditional dance was sometimes permitted in the context of European festivals or Christian holidays. Hence many Native Canadians were willing participants in rodeos, medicine shows, or fall fairs, where they found a way to reshape their traditions for cross-cultural consumption. The reemergence of many traditional genres since the 1960s has necessarily been something of a reinvention in cases where traditional knowledge was lost, but in other cases old repertoires have reappeared with little apparent change.

Genres such as Christian hymns and fiddle musics, usually described as European derived, often present equally complex traces of interaction. According to seventeenth-century Jesuits, their aboriginal hosts were eager and able to learn European religious forms quite competently. Perhaps this relates to many documented instances in which the Christian God was equated with the Creator of precontact religions (Grant 1985) or in which Christian repertoires were used in traditional contexts (Diamond 1992). Over time, borrowed and locally composed hymn repertoires were substantially transformed in sound; the rhythms of the indigenous languages altered meter and phrase length, while vocal timbre and repetition patterns often reflected traditional practices. Particularly when the social relations were individual and at least potentially egalitarian, as in situations of intermarriage, music was part of the development of a distinctive culture of *métisage* 'mixing', 'blending'. Métis songs often move between French and the aboriginal language of the singer, for instance, while fiddle musics reflected the rhythms of aboriginal languages (see MÉTIS, p. 404).

Late-twentieth-century contemporary aboriginal musics are positioned somewhat differently. Generations of First Nations people who grew up with radio now claim the same heritage of North American popular music as do nonaboriginal people. Country music (by artists such as Ernest Monias and Jody Gaskin) and blues (by artists such as Murray Porter and Jani Lauzon, among others) have proven particularly popular in Native communities, in part because the oppression of African Canadians and rural populations resonates with the situation of First Peoples. Popular music is also widely seen as a means of encouraging creative uses of aboriginal languages by the young generation and a means of gaining a wider audience for the presentation of important social and political perspectives. Songs lyrics might constitute revisionist history, such as Manitoba Cree Buffy Sainte-Marie's "Bury My Heart at Wounded Knee," Murray Porter's "1492. Who Found Who?," or 7th Fire's "Buffalo Jump"; draw attention to challenging social issues, such as Mishi Donovan's "Forgotten Yesterday" or Susan Aglukark's "Kathy I"; or assert cultural pride, as in Edmonton rap artist Bannock's "Stand Up" (Krims 2000). Some, but not all, contemporary musicians incorporate elements of traditional music in order to mark their songs as Native. Hence vocables are integral to many songs by Kashtin and are found in Aglukark's "This Child." The Inuit duo Tudjaat incorporates traditional throat singing (vocal games), while frame drums are used by Jerry Alfred. Alfred, like many of his colleagues, simultaneously crosses beyond his own identity sphere, however, including such African instruments as *djembe* 'goblet-shaped drum' and *kora* 'harp-lute' in his band. Some recent projects assert international alliances among indigenous peoples.

In some cases, immigrant populations have adopted styles of the dominant European Canadian population around them more readily than their U.S. counterparts have. Such is the case with some early African Canadian communities in the Maritimes and in southern Ontario prior to the 1970s. Neil Rosenberg (1973) has described the musical choices of two African-descended country musicians in Newfoundland, while Richard Stewardson has studied composer Hattie Rhue Hatchett (from Buxton, Ontario), whose music resembles what has been labeled white gospel style. The relatively small and isolated population undoubtedly made the development of an independent style more difficult. More recent arrivals from the Caribbean islands have brought the transnational styles of their homelands with them.

There are many illustrations of the fine line between appropriation and respect when a noteworthy individual experiments with a mixture of styles. Often respect within the tradition is necessary before a musician dare venture outside of it. Hence, the Chinese *er hu* 'two-string bowed fiddle' player George Gao in Toronto is acclaimed for his traditional performance but also successfully collaborates with classical, New Age, or jazz musicians, while Karnatak virtuoso *mrdangam* 'double headed drum' player Trichy Sankaran is one of several musicians to compose and perform with the Toronto-based gamelan Evergreen Club. Latin jazz saxophonist Jane Bunnett enlarges her fan base by bringing a number of her Cuban collaborators to Canada. More contentious are the heavy metal arrangements of Celtic fiddler Ashley McIsaac from Cape Breton, where the authenticity of the fiddle style is frequently related to the very survival of Gaelic culture. At the beginning of the twenty-first century, the list of culturally plural ensembles is long, including such eclectic mixes as Punjabi by Nature (Toronto), who combine *bhangra* and rock with elements of Caribbean dance hall, reggae, and rap; Uzume Taiko (Vancouver), who incorporate cello, saxophone, bagpipe, or conga (Afro-Cuban drum) alongside the Japanese *taiko* 'Japanese barrel drum' drummers; or Silk Road Music (Vancouver), with Chinese, Brazilian, jazz, and Celtic elements.

REFERENCES

Allor, Marin. 1997. "Locating Cultural Activity: The 'Main' as Chronotope and Heterotopia." *Topia* 1:42–54.

Ames, Michael M. 1993. "The Canadianization of an American Fair: The Case of Expo 86." In *The Beaver Bites Back? American Popular Culture in Canada*, ed. David H. Flaherty and Frank E. Manning, 237–246. Montréal and Kingston: McGill-Queen's University Press.

Angus, Ian. 1997. *A Border Within: National Identity, Cultural Plurality, and Wilderness*. Montréal: McGill-Queen's University Press.

Armour, Leslie. 1996. "Language, Culture and Values in Canada at the Dawn of the 21st Century: A Retrospection." In *Language, Culture and Values in Canada at the Dawn of the 21st Century*, eds. André Lapierre, Patricia Smart, and Pierre Savard, 15–50. Ottawa: International Council for Canadian Studies.

Atwood, Margaret. 1972. *Survival: A Thematic Guide to Canadian Literature*. Toronto: Anansi.

Beckwith, John. 1997. *Music Papers: Articles and Talks by a Canadian Composer 1961–1994*. Ottawa: The Golden Dog Press.

Berger, Carl. 1986. *The Writing of Canadian History: Aspects of English-Canadian Historical Writing since 1900*. 2nd ed. Toronto: University of Toronto Press.

Carpenter, Carole. 1975. "The Ethnicity Factor in Anglo-Canadian Folkloristics." *Canadian Ethnic Studies* 7/2:7–18.

Cavanagh, Beverley. 1982. *Music of the Net Silik Eskimo: A Study of Stability and Change*. Ottawa: National Museums.

Cohnstaedt, Joy, and Yves Frenette, eds. 1997. *Canadian Cultures and Globalization/Cultures canadiennes et mondialisation*. Canadian Issues 19. Montréal: Association for Canadian Studies.

Diamond, Beverley. 1991. "Canadian Music Studies in University Curricula." *ACS Newsletter* 12/2:n.p.

———. 1992. "Christian Hymns in Eastern Woodlands Communities: Performance Contexts." In *Musical Repercussions of 1492: Explorations, Encounters, Identities*, ed. Carol Robertson. Washington: Smithsonian Institution.

———. "Narratives in Canadian Music History." In *Canadian Music: Issues of Hegemony and Identity*, ed. Beverley Diamond and Robert Witmer, 139–172. Toronto: Canadian Scholars Press.

Diamond and Robbins 1993. "Lessons Learned, Questions Raised: Writing a History of Ethnomusicology in Canada." *Canadian Folk Music Journal* 21:49–54.

Dickason, Olive P. 1992. *Canada's First Nations: A History of Founding Peoples from Earliest Times*. Toronto: McClelland and Stewart.

Feldthusen, Bruce. 1993. "Awakening from the National Broadcasting Dream: Rethinking Television Regulation for National Cultural Goals." In *The Beaver Bites Back? American Popular Culture in Canada*, ed. David H. Flaherty and Frank E. Manning, 42–74. Montréal and Kingston: McGill-Queen's University Press.

Francis, Daniel. 1997. *National Dreams: Myth, Memory, and Canadian History*. Vancouver: Arsenal Pulp Press.

Gasher, Mike. 1997. "From Sacred Cows to White Elephants: Cultural Policy under Siege." In *Canadian Cultures and Globalization*, eds. Joy Cohnstaedt and Yves Frenette. *Canadian Issues* 19:13–30.

Gilbert, Reid. 1993. "Mounties, Muggings, and Moose: Canadian Icons in a Landscape of American Violence. In *The Beaver Bites Back? American Popular Culture in Canada*, ed. David H. Flaherty and Frank E. Manning. Montréal and Kingston: McGill-Queen's University Press.

Grant, Jon Webster. 1984. *Moon of Wintertime: Missionaries and the Indians of Canada in Encounter since 1534*. Toronto: University of Toronto Press.

Greenhill, Pauline. 1997. *Undisciplined Women: Tradition and Culture in Canada*. Montréal: McGill-Queen's University Press.

Isajiw, Wsevelod W. 1999. "Definitions and Dimensions of Ethnicity." In *Encyclopedia of Canada's Peoples*, ed. Paul R. Magocsi, 413–422. Toronto: University of Toronto Press.

Kostash, Myrna. 1992. "Eurocentricity: Notes on Metaphors of Place." In *20 Years of Multiculturalism: Successes and Failures*, ed. Stella Hryniuk, 39–44. Winnipeg: St. John's College Press.

Krims, Adam. 2000. *Rap Music and the Poetics of Identity*. Cambridge: Cambridge University Press.

Langlois, Simon. 1999. "Canadian Identity: A Francophone Perspective." In *Encyclopedia of Canada's Peoples*, ed. Paul R. Magocsi, 323–329. Toronto: University of Toronto Press.

Lipset, Seymour Martin. 1989. *Continental Divide: The Values and Institutions of the United States and Canada*. Toronto: C. D. Howe Institute.

Magocsi, Paul R., ed. 1999. *Encyclopedia of Canada's Peoples*. Toronto: University of Toronto Press.

Manning, Frank E. 1993. 'Reversible Resistance: Canadian Popular Culture and the American Other." In *The Beaver Bites Back? American Popular Culture in Canada*, ed. David H. Flaherty and Frank E. Manning, 3–28. Montréal and Kingston: McGill-Queen's University Press.

McCartney, Andra. 1999. "Sounding Places: Situated Conversation through the Soundscape Compositions of Hldegard Westerkamp." Ph.D. dissertation, York University.

McGregor, Gaile. 1985. *The Wacousta Syndrome: Explorations in the Canadian Landscape*. Toronto: University of Toronto Press.

Miller, Mark. 1997. *Such Melodious Racket: The Lost History of Jazz in Canada, 1914–1949*. Toronto: Mercury Press.

Miller, Mary Jane. 1993. "Inflecting the Formula: The First Seasons of *Street Legal* and *L.A. Law.*" In

The Beaver Bites Back? American Popular Culture in Canada, ed. David H. Flaherty and Frank E. Manning. Montréal and Kingston: McGill-Queen's University Press.

Moore, Mavor. 1996. "A Position Paper on Canadian Cultural Policy." In *A Celebration of Canada's Art, 1930–1970,* ed. Glen Carruthers and Gordana Lazarevich, 227–232. Toronto: Canadian Scholars' Press.

Morey, Carl, comp. 1997. *Music in Canada: A Research and Information Guide.* New York and London: Garland Publishing.

Moss, John. 1974. *Patterns of Isolation.* Toronto: McClelland and Stewart.

Mukherjee, Arun. 1994. *Oppositional Aesthetics: Readings from a Hyphenated Space.* Toronto: TSAR.

Multicultural History Society of Ontario. 1982. *Polyphony.* (*The Ethnic Press in Ontario*). 4(1).

Music Directory Canada. 1997. 7th ed. St. Catharines, Ont.: Norris-Whitney Communications.

Poirier, Lucien. 1994. "A Canadian Music Style: Illusion and Reality." In *Canadian Music: Issues of Hegemony and Identity,* ed. Beverley Diamond and Robert Witmer, 239–268. Toronto: Canadian Scholars Press.

Porter, John. 1965. *The Vertical Mosaic: An Analysis of Social Class and Power in Canada.* Toronto: University of Toronto Press.

Probyn, Elspeth. 1996. *Outside Belongings.* London: Routledge.

Proctor, George A. 1980. *Canadian Music of the Twentieth Century.* Toronto: University of Toronto Press.

Rasporich, Beverly J., and Tamara Palmer Seiler. 1999. "Canadian Culture and Ethnic Diversity." In *Encyclopedia of Canada's Peoples,* ed. Paul R. Magocsi, 304–316. Toronto: University of Toronto Press.

Royal Commission on Aboriginal Peoples. 1996. *People to People, Nation to Nation: Highlights from the Report of the Royal Commission on Aboriginal Peoples.* Ottawa: The Commission.

Rice, Timothy, with Tammy Gutnik. 1995. "What's Canadian about Canadian Popular Music? The Case of Bruce Cockburn." In *Taking a Stand: Essays in Honour of John Beckwith,* ed. Timothy J. McGee, 238–258. Toronto: University of Toronto Press.

Robbins, James. 1990. "What Can We Learn When They Sing, Eh? Ethnomusicology in the American State of Canada." In *Ethnomusicology in Canada,* ed. Witmer (1990), 47–56. CanMus Documents 5. Toronto: Institute for Canadian Music.

Robbins, James. 1993. "Canada." In *Ethnomusicology: Historical and Regional Studies,* ed. Helen Myers, 63–76. New York: Norton.

Rosenberg, Neil. 1994. "Ethnicity and Class: Black Country Musicians in the Maritimes." In *Canadian Music: Issues of Hegemony and Identity,* ed. Beverley Diamond and Robert Witmer, 417–446. Toronto: Canadian Scholars Press.

Rutherford, Paul. 1993. "Made in America: The Problem of Mass Culture in Canada." In *The Beaver Bites Back? American Popular Culture in Canada,* ed. David H. Flaherty and Frank E. Manning, 260–280. Montréal and Kingston: McGill-Queen's University Press.

Stewardson, Richard. 1994. "Hattie Rhue Hatchett (1863–1958): An Interdisciplinary Study of Her Life and Music in North Buxton, Ontario." M.A. thesis, York University.

Taft, Michael. 1993. "Syncretizing Sound: The Emergence of Canadian Popular Music." In *The Beaver Bites Back? American Popular Culture in Canada,* ed. David H. Flaherty and Frank E. Manning, 197–208. Montréal and Kingston: McGill-Queen's University Press.

Vascotto, Norma. 2000. "The Transmission of Drum Songs in Pelly Bay, Nunavut, and the Contributions of Composers and Singers to Musical Norms." Ph.D. dissertation, University of Toronto.

Wayman, Tom. 1993. *A Country Not Considered. Canada, Culture, Work.* Concord, Ont.: Anansi Press.

Whitelaw, Anne. 1997. "Statistical Imperatives: Representing the Nation in Exhibitions of Contemporary Art." *Topia* 1:22–41.

Overview of Music in Canada
Beverley Diamond

Selected Cultural Policy Issues
Music Industry
Regional Histories

Canada has the second largest land mass of any nation in the modern world and is as socially diverse as its terrain and climate. Although Canadians have frequently asserted "the North" as a metaphor of nationhood, paradoxically, its over thirty million people are concentrated in communities along its southern borders. Its ten provinces and three northern territories are sometimes grouped regionally as

1. Atlantic Canada (Newfoundland, Nova Scotia, New Brunswick, and Prince Edward Island),
2. Central Canada (Québec and Ontario),
3. Western Canada, which includes the "Prairie provinces" (Manitoba, Saskatchewan, Alberta) and British Columbia, and
4. the North (the Yukon, Northwest Territory, and Nunavut).

The immense complexity and diversity within and among Canada's cultural communities precludes comprehensive coverage in either this article or indeed this volume. This article is intended as a road map to signal other articles in this volume providing detail about specific musical practices. It also attempts to frame certain interpretive issues relevant to either national or regional contexts. Within each region, selected ethnocultural groups are referenced when they are either numerically strong or of particular historical significance. Canada is one of the few nations of the world to have produced an encyclopedia of its musical practices (Kallmann, Potvin, and Winters 1992), as well as one focusing on the sociocultural development of its diverse ethnocultural communities (Magocsi 1999). These sources as well as Carl Morey's *Music in Canada: A Research and Information Guide* (1997) are good starting points for further research on music [see SOURCES, SCHOLARSHIP, AND HISTORIOGRAPHY, p. 21].

SELECTED CULTURAL POLICY ISSUES

Although Canada has yet to develop a comprehensive cultural policy, various milestone reports, speeches, or, in some cases, legislation have shaped and constrained cultural activity. Relevant in this regard are several Royal Commission reports (Massey and Levesque 1951; Applebaum and Hebert 1982) advocating on broadcasting and cultural policy, various national institutions such as the Canada Council for the Arts and the Canadian Music Center, the Canadian Broadcasting Commission, and industry infrastructure [see THE MUSIC INDUSTRY, p. 705; GOVERNMENT AND POLITICS, p. 288; RADIO, p. 1101].

Cultural critics (Gasher 1997; Zemans 1996) have described shifts in emphasis in cultural policy. Zemans, for example, identifies the strongest articulation of the defense of national identity and sovereignty in the wake of the 1929 Aird Commission (which led to the establishment of the Canadian Broadcasting Corporation). She points to vigorous support for flagship institutions in the 1950s through the 1970s, moves toward cultural democratization in the 1980s, and a shift from "a nationalist, public service, market corrective approach towards a growing emphasis on a market ideology" (1996:11) in the 1990s. The final phase that Zemans identifies is theorized further by Gasher, who observes that federal cultural policy often contradicts financial policy, industrial development, and international trade. He challenges "the state's legitimacy to govern the cultural sphere" and posits market economics as "the legitimate form of governance of more and more social activity" (1997:27). While Zemans stresses policy shifts, Gasher emphasizes the continuity of policies that have been historically rooted in arguments for nationalism, anticommercialism, and anti-Americanism and further contends that such arguments are obsolete at the end of the twentieth century.

The rhetoric of cultural "unity" and the public acknowledgment of diversity have shifted from one decade to another, particularly since 1971 when then Prime Minister Pierre Trudeau articulated a policy of federal multiculturalism within a bilingual framework. Multiculturalism was entrenched in the Charter of Rights and Freedoms in 1985 and legislated in the world's first Multiculturalism Act in 1988. Official multiculturalism in Canada, however, has been frequently contested. In the late 1970s programs focused on cultural presentation in a manner that was too often token and decorative. Some in the Maritimes, currently the only part of the country with a substantial British majority, felt multicultural programs privileged the more diverse central and western provinces. Aboriginal nations argued that the entire debate sidestepped recognition of their inherent rights. Francophones regarded multiculturalism as a threat to their equality with English-speakers as one of the two "founding nations."

The federal and Québec governments have taken contrasting approaches to the matter. Québec has vigorously sought independent nationhood for several decades, until the most recent referendum (in 1995), in which the prosovereignty side was defeated by the narrow margin of one-half percentage point. A rationale for cultural diversity in Québec usually relies on the notion of "cultural convergence," a concept that regards French as the common "vehicular" rather than "vernacular" language of the province's communities, who build together a common public culture, but one peopled with diverse imaginative worlds (Simon 1996:123–125).

MUSIC INDUSTRY

Prior to the nineteenth century, the business of music was often a mixture of service (instrument repair, piano tuning) and the importing of goods (musical instruments, especially band instruments and violins, and printed music). Kallmann (1969 [1960]) has emphasized that in the 1780s and 1790s, music reached Lower Canada soon after its European premiere. Typical of the businessmen of the time was tradesman and teacher Frederick Glackemeyer, who taught viol, bass viol, violin, and piano; imported pianos, other instruments, and sheet music; and tuned and repaired instruments in Québec. Piano building flourished from approximately 1820, reaching its height between 1890 and 1925 in southern Ontario and Québec (Kelly 1991). The work of sixty artisans, including a number who make folk or non-Western instruments, was exhibited in 1991 by the Canadian Museum of Civilization (Bégin 1992).

Music publishing began in the nineteenth century, with the 1800 edition of *Le Gradual romain* the earliest Canadian imprint. Stephen Humbert's hymn tune book

Broadcasting has been the most regulated and subsidized mode of communication in Canada. Recording, on the other hand, enjoyed little government subsidy until the 1990s.

Union Harmony (1801) was first published in St. John (though printed in New England) only one year later. Nineteenth-century music publication (Calderisi 1981), often took the form of a side activity of tradesmen who also imported foreign music and instruments, newspaper inserts, such as in Montréal's *La Minerve,* or sheet music, especially of parlor songs, dance pieces, patriotic songs, and easy keyboard pieces. The nineteenth-century pattern contrasts with the trend of the mid-twentieth century to the current period, when most Canadian music publication focuses on teaching materials (or pieces that appear on the syllabi of festivals and competitions) and on popular music. Classical scores are largely unpublished but disseminated by the Canadian Music Centre.

Broadcasting has been the most regulated and subsidized mode of communication in Canada. Recording, on the other hand, enjoyed little government subsidy until the 1990s. The regulation of Canadian content by the Canadian Radio-Television and Telecommunications Commission (CRTC) and various awards have also served to spur the industry since the 1970s.

The protection of intellectual property has been fundamentally challenged in Canada, as elsewhere, by digitization and "convergence technologies" as well as by the specific situation afforded by the North American Free Trade Agreement (NAFTA) of 1996. Even though the autonomy of the Canadian cultural industries is alleged in NAFTA, a particular concern is one clause that allows the curtailing of Canadian policy changes of which the United States does not approve.

REGIONAL HISTORIES

Atlantic Canada

The Atlantic provinces—New Brunswick, Nova Scotia, Prince Edward Island (together often called the Maritimes), and Newfoundland—were the regions of the area that is now Canada to be first visited and settled by Europeans. Norse remains at l'Anse aux Meadows in northern Newfoundland indicate contact as early as 990 C.E.; coastal fishing was established by the sixteenth century; and the earliest British and French settlements were founded in the early seventeenth century. Unlike other regions, Atlantic Canada has a sizable British majority (ranging from 35 percent in New Brunswick to 80 percent in Newfoundland). The next largest ethnocultural community is Acadian (as high as 35 percent in New Brunswick).

Factors shaping the culture of this region are (1) unique patterns of trade and travel with the New England colonies/states as well as with Britain; (2) the presence of the oldest African Canadian communities; (3) the resilience of the Acadian population; and (4) a long history of economic underdevelopment (especially vis-à-vis the industry-rich provinces of central Canada) leading, in the twentieth century, to a series of antimodernist socioeconomic strategies, including the commodification of folk song begun in the 1920s by Helen Creighton (McKay 1994).

First Nations

Aboriginal cultures have been sustained in Atlantic Canada, often with difficulty, over a longer period of intercultural contact than elsewhere in the country. The Norse reported encounters with "Skraelings," a name sometimes translated as "little people," who are thought to have been either Dorset (forerunners of contemporary Inuit) or Beothuk people (Dickason 1992:87). Inuit currently reside in several communities along the Subarctic Labrador coast, where Moravian cultural traces remain in local institutions such as the Nain brass band (Lutz 1982). Beothuk of Newfoundland had friendly relations with the Mi'kmaq and Montagnais prior to the seventeenth century but were defeated and largely exterminated (though contemporary aboriginal people claim blood ties to this nation) by the French and their Mi'kmaq allies during the eighteenth century.

The majority of aboriginal people in Atlantic Canada are members of Algonquian-speaking Mi'kmaq and Maliseet nations. The strong impact of Roman Catholicism following the conversion in 1610 of the important Mi'kmaq leader Membertou affected traditional ceremonial practices, including the use of drums (Diamond et al. 1994:185), the formats of wedding (Mechling 1958–1959) and funeral rites (Wallis and Wallis 1957:24), chief-making ceremonies, and dances (the snake dance, encountered by J. W. Fewkes), or the trading dance such as the one transcribed by Burlin (1907:16).

Nevertheless, traditional Mi'kmaq and Maliseet musical instruments (for example, a unique split ash rattle, the *jiqmaqn*) continue in use, and at the beginning of the twentieth-first century, traditional social dances are reconstructed and retaught. The drum has been brought back to communities, partly through initiatives of women such as singer Margaret Paul. Local powwow drum groups (such as Free Spirit or Sons of Membertou) became popular in the Maritimes only since the 1980s. Among the most widely known contemporary Mi'kmaq artists are Hubert Francis and his band, Eagle Feather, and the late fiddler Lee Cremo (Cronk 1990).

European

Acadian

The earliest settlers were the French ancestors of present-day Acadians, who established Port Royal (now Annapolis Royal, Nova Scotia) in 1605. Although initially they established good relations with their aboriginal neighbors, their lives were not stable for long. Forcibly deported by the British in 1755, they dispersed to the American South (particularly Louisiana), but many returned in the late eighteenth and nineteenth centuries. The contemporary culture is influenced by interaction with the Anglo and Gaelic traditions that dominate the music scene of Atlantic Canada [see ACADIAN MUSIC, p. 1135].

British

Eighteenth-century Canadian colonial practices—Christian church music, singing schools, folk song and dance, band and parlor music, as well as symphonic and chamber music—resemble those of New England, but with some significant differences, largely attributable to the influence of Loyalists who migrated from the United States in the latter half of the century. British regimental bands continued to form the backbone of community music making for 150 years after the American Revolution. Frederick Hall (1983, 1987) and Phyllis Blakeley (1949, 1951) have described the importance of bands in a garrison town such as Halifax, where bandsmen were teachers, performers, participants in musical theater, and patrons (in the case of officers). At least sixteen different comic operas were performed in Halifax during the last decade of the eighteenth century (Hall 1987:398).

Loyalist immigrants remained faithful to the Church of England (developed as the Anglican church in Canada). In Halifax, for example, St. Paul's Anglican Church (est. 1762) was a central venue for musical performance, establishing a choir in the first five years of its existence and supporting Canada's first philharmonic society. Additionally, as Nicholas Temperley has noted (McGee 1995:174), the conservative Scots who comprised the Presbyterian Church rejected psalm singing reforms that began in Scotland in the 1760s and preferred the old psalm tunes sung in the old way. This conservatism possibly contributed to the longer popularity of the fuguing tune in Maritime Canada than in New England (Blum 1987:138). Singing schools, often led by musicians who moved north from the United States (such as James Lyon, Stephen Humbert, or Amasa Braman), are documented in *The Diary of Simeon Perkins 1766–1780* (Perkins 1969).

The best known of Canadian tunebooks was Methodist Stephen Humbert's *Union Harmony* (1801). Although Newfoundland residents engaged in similar musical practices, that province's only musical history (Woodford 1988) seems replete with musical "characters" (perhaps a reflection of Newfoundland's vital storytelling traditions). Woodford records the activity of "pirate king" Peter Easton, for example, "who harried communities and shipping along the Avalon Peninsula in the early seventeenth century, . . . often taking minstrels and trumpeters with him to herald his attacks" (1988:8); Black Bart, who operated in a similar manner a century later along the island's south shore; and army lieutenant Thomas Lloyd, who played his fiddle on the Lord's Day to keep parishioners from church. By the late nineteenth century, choir directors, band masters, and classical musicians such as Charles Hutton or Georgina Stirling were more class conscious.

In the nineteenth century, the intermixing of many types of musical activity was commonplace. Sadie Harper Allen's diary of the 1890s (Peck 1992), for instance, records the juxtaposition of choir practice with step dancing, concertizing and music lessons, hymn singing and comic songs. The highbrow/lowbrow distinction articulated by Lawrence Levine (1988) with reference to the United States also developed in Canada, as Maria Tippett (1990) and others have demonstrated, but the local variants of this distinction merit careful study. In Atlantic Canada, the blurring of generic boundaries has continued into the twenty-first century, perhaps because the folk music culture assumes mainstream status in this area. The contemporary trio Peurt-a-Baroque, for example, performs medleys of Baroque dances with reels and jigs from the folk tradition, subtly effecting a shift in the "groove" from one to the other. Orchestra works featuring folk song, such as Scott Macmillan's *Celtic Mass for the Sea,* and popular music rooted in folk styles, performed by, for example, the band Great Big Sea, are well received.

Both Gaelic- and English-language folk music have thrived in Atlantic Canada since the earliest settlers arrived. Social venues ranged from domestic entertainment and social gatherings (called house parties, *ceilidhs,* or "times" in Newfoundland, as described in Quigley 1985) to isolated male-only spaces such as the lumber camps of the late nineteenth and early twentieth centuries. Folklorist Edward Ives (1964, 1978) has studied individual Maritime singer-composers such as Joe Scott and Larry Gorman. Gaelic ballads and lyric songs, *peurt a beul* (usually described as dance music sung on vocables), and milling frolics (antiphonal work songs accompanying the communal processing of cloth) have all been maintained on Cape Breton Island.

Folk music in Newfoundland has a somewhat different history, in part because of the predominance of Irish residents, but also in part because of the physical and political isolation of this rugged island. Mumming—visiting and serenading from door to door in costume—remained part of the Newfoundland tradition (Halpert and Story 1990). In isolated outport communities new preferences for such instruments as the accordion, popularized by Harry Hibbs and Minnie White, among others, and styles such as country music have produced unique stylistic syntheses, often blended with humor (for example, Buddy Wasisname). Contemporary folk groups have included

Figgy Duff, the Irish Descendants, and the Plankerdown Band. While true of folk music in Atlantic Canada more generally, it is particularly true in Newfoundland that local events—including shipwrecks, politics, logging, mining, or domestic incidents—have provided the stimulus for new song composition [see "SHE'S GONE, BOYS," p. 1138].

Fiddle music both for square and solo step dancing thrives in Atlantic Canada. The male-dominated fiddling tradition became a competitive one in the early twentieth century. On Prince Edward Island fiddle contests were banned in 1927 because they provoked fights and divided community loyalties. Subsequently, county-wide fiddler associations played a role in the maintenance of the tradition, further stimulated by the development of radio in the 1920s. Important interpreters such as Don Messer became nationally popular cultural ambassadors. Dance music also reunited emigré Maritimers or travelers temporarily "away"; Boston, for example, harbored P.E.I. nights in the 1920s (Burrill 1992).

Anglo-Celtic fiddle music in Atlantic Canada has often been influenced by Acadian fiddling, although the latter uses faster tempos and has a unique "feel." The Gaelic community identifies rhythms of their language in the fiddle style. This Anglo-Celtic style is usually slower, with more left-hand ornamentation as well as subtle changes in the pressure and speed of the bow (including the "dig" and various "cuts" as well as techniques such as what Dunlay and Greenberg (1996) call "whip-bow technique," "fat-flat strokes," "crushed bow strokes," and "up-driven bows." Dunlay and Greenberg observe differences between Cape Breton and Scottish fiddle styles: for example, dotted rhythms are more relaxed in the former.

Maritime music, especially fiddle music, has been recorded since the 1930s, when several Cape Bretoners, including Angus Chisholm and Dan J. Campbell, recorded on the Decca label. By the 1950s a local Nova Scotia–based industry was born, featuring local stars such as Dan Joe McInnis and Winston "Scotty" Fitzgerald (MacInnes 1997:141–163). By the 1980s and 1990s, a number of independent labels had extensive inventories, among them Pigeon Inlet Productions of Newfoundland, Islander and House Party Productions of Prince Edward Island, and Fiddlesticks on Cape Breton. By the mid-twentieth century, encouraged by the burgeoning tourist industry, a major Celtic revival occurred. Scottish piping thrives alongside the fiddle tradition (figure 1).

FIGURE I   Highland dancing at the College of Piping, Summerside, P.E.I., 1993. Photo by B. Diamond.

The history of music in Atlantic Canada has been
represented in a particularly uneven way in published
sources.

African

African settlers were part of the earliest communities of the Maritimes (Grant 1980:6).
There were African slaves at French Louisbourg and on Maritime ships. Free blacks are
listed in Halifax as early as 1750. The largest migration of Africans to the region was
part of the wave of Loyalists around the time of the American Revolution. The following century was a difficult period for African Maritimers as they struggled for land and
education rights. They were often forced to settle in impoverished ghettos—Africville
near Halifax or the Bog area of Charlottetown—historical sites now remembered
through song, for example, by gospel quartet Four the Moment ("Africville") or singer-
songwriter Scott Parsons ("Jupiter Wise").

A detailed historical record of music making in African Canadian communities of the
Maritimes has yet to be written. Religious music has a continuous place of importance in
community life. Spirituals and religious folk songs were collected by Helen Creighton in
the 1930s and 1940s. Neil Rosenberg (1994a) has explored the strategies of black country
musicians vis-à-vis both race and class. In the 1980s and 1990s, a number of new artistic
developments signaled a renaissance: new publications on black history in the Maritimes
(Grant 1980; Hornby 1988); the opening of a Black Community Center in Dartmouth,
Nova Scotia; and the establishment of several gospel choirs (such as the Nova Scotia
Massed Choir) and smaller, gospel-influenced ensembles or individual songwriters.

Other groups

Maritime ports have often been a first port of call for many immigrants arriving in
Canada. In Halifax, for example, Pier 21 has acquired symbolic significance as a point
of entry. In some instances, such as in the case of the Lebanese of Prince Edward Island
(Weale 1988), a community has slowly formed as a slow pattern of immigration
occurred over a century or more. Traditions are selectively maintained; the P.E.I.
Lebanese community, for example, sustains *debki* dancing, and an occasional *oud*
'long-necked, plucked chordophone' performer contributes to local festivals/concerts.

Twentieth-century classical music

Scholars of Maritime concert music have focused on the seventeenth and eighteenth
centuries (Blakeley 1951; Hall 1983; McGee 1969). As Diamond (1995) has described,
histories of Canadian music have represented the development of classical music as
congruent with the shifts in centers of economic power from Atlantic communities to
central Canada. Composers of the late twentieth century, including Robert Bauer,
Michael Parker, James Code, Michael Miller, Richard Gibson and others, have worked
hard to create the cultural infrastructure they need [see OVERVIEW, p. 1114].

Twentieth-century jazz and popular music

A thriving jazz training program is based at St. Francis Xavier University in Antigonish,
Nova Scotia. A larger proportion of the popular music production, however, is either

country and western or folk influenced. Among country and western artists are Hank Snow, Wilf Carter, and Anne Murray, as well as the nationalist songwriter Stompin' Tom Connors. Folk and country are combined in the popular radio and TV broadcasts of Don Messer and the gentle ballads of songwriter Gene McLellan. More recently, folk-influenced Maritime artists include Rita McNeil, the Rankin Family, Barra McNeils, Mary Jane Lamond, and Newfoundland's Great Big Sea. Rock artists such as Thrush, Sloan, and Jale attained national recognition in the 1990s.

Archives

Atlantic Canada houses several impressive music archives (for example, the Université de Moncton for Acadian material or MUNFLA at Memorial University of Newfoundland for material from that province). Nonetheless, the history of music in Atlantic Canada has been represented in a particularly uneven way in published sources. Those sources that reflect the central Canadian narrative privileging concert music have underrated activity in the region, while those that have celebrated the vitality of vernacular practices have acclaimed the extent of music in the same areas. The earlier phases of European settlement have received more attention than later developments, with the exception of the widely acclaimed fiddle traditions. The intermixing of practices and traditions as well as the struggle for survival faced by minority cultures have only begun to be studied.

Québec

Following Champlain's landing in 1608 at Hochelega (present-day Montréal), the French allocated land to settlers of what is now the province of Québec through the seignury system (each seignury consisted of a long strip of land with river frontage along the St. Lawrence river). During struggles between colonial powers, Innu, Cree, Algonquin, and the Iroquoian-speaking Huron usually supported the French, the Mohawk nation (and the Iroquois confederacy of which it was a part) allied with the English, and the Abenaki were buffeted between the two. The British gained control at the end of the Seven Years War (1756–1763), but the French were given language rights. The Québec Act of 1774 acknowledged further French control over what was then named Lower Canada. Lower and Upper Canada (approximately present-day Ontario) were united in 1841 but entered the new nation of Canada in 1867 as separate provinces.

Throughout the nineteenth and twentieth centuries, the influence of the Roman Catholic church on both populace and state has been a significant cultural determinant in French Canada. The image of rural, God-fearing parish communities, sometimes stereotyped as antimodernist and antiurban, was perpetuated through the church's control of education and other aspects of social life. Resistance came in the form of a series of tracts in the late 1940s and 1950s, *Le refus global* of 1948, signed by literati and artists of the period, being the most famous. The document affirmed the importance of an independent and innovative creative community.

The slow building of support for separatism in the 1960s, a period often called the Quiet Revolution, led to a major turning point with the election of the separatist Parti Québécois in 1976. The debate over Québec sovereignty, still at issue after the close referendum vote of 1995, has affected the entire country in many ways. Struggles over the definition of Québec's "distinct society" status continued in the late 1990s.

Census data since 1980 indicate that the French-speaking population of Québec has remained a relatively stable 80 percent. Countries of origin have diversified, however, with growth in the 1980s and 1990s among Asian populations and particularly significant influxes from Vietnam, the French Caribbean, Lebanon, and Morocco. Immigrants to Québec from nonfrancophone European countries, on the other hand, often arrived much earlier than elsewhere in Canada, establishing Montréal, in particular, as a cosmopolitan city already in the mid-nineteenth century. Germans contributed substantially to the establishment of the arts in Québec and Montréal from the eighteenth century. The Jewish community of Québec is an especially prominent one historically. Italians arrived in the eighteenth century, contributing to the development of the hotel trade as well as railway and steamship transportation industries. Southern European immigration to Montréal expanded following World War II, as it did in Ontario. The Portuguese (often from the continent rather than the islands of São Miguel or the Azores from which many Toronto immigrants came) and Greek communities were among the largest.

Aboriginal cultures

Eleven different aboriginal nations reside in the province of Québec. Over six thousand Inuit ally themselves with Inuit in the new northern territory of Nunavut, calling their region Nunavik. The majority of the aboriginal population speaks one of several related, and often mutually comprehensible, languages of the Algonquian language family. Among these, approximately fifteen thousand Innuat (Naskapi, Montagnais, Attikamek) live along the north shore of the St. Lawrence, in the Mauricie River valley, or further north in Matimekosh (as well as in Labrador). Anishnabek (mostly northern Cree) live along the shores of James Bay and Lac St. Jean, and Algonquins along the Ottawa river and in areas to the north of it (up to Pikogan and Lac-Simon). Québec is also home to the "Eastern door" of the Iroquois confederacy: the Mohawk (population over nine thousand) who reside near Montréal. Less numerous are members of the Wabenaki Confederacy, the Mi'kmaq in the Gaspé, the Western Abenaki between Montréal and Québec, and the Huron (Wendat) on the outskirts of Québec City.

Aboriginal families played an important role in enabling the earliest visitors and settlers to survive and in facilitating the fur trade. In the seventeenth century, annual reports of Jesuit priests to their French superiors, travelogues, or more extensive historical accounts (for example, by lawyer Marc Lescarbot) record progress in teaching Christian music to Native converts (Amtmann 1975) and describe music and dance at feasts and social gatherings, diverse healing ceremonies, divination, and other ceremonial practices. Anthropologist Eleanor Leacock (Etienne and Leacock 1980) has demonstrated that the Jesuit agenda disrupted the aboriginal emphasis on personal autonomy and gender egalitarianism.

The Innuat (plural of Innu) used songs received in dreams as hunting and divining tools; *nikumana* 'songs' were accompanied by a frame drum, the *teueigan,* with *babiche* 'snares' strung with small bird bones, quill segments, or wooden "rattlers" producing what are sometimes described as spirit voices. The same dance and song repertoires occur at the beginning of the twenty-first century, often in new contexts such as contemporary festivals or social gatherings. Until the mid-twentieth century, the shamanistic practice of the shaking tent and other healing ceremonies were used by the Innu as well as the Cree (Preston 1976). Cree maintain different practices, such as bear ceremonialism to ensure continuous relationship with the animals and other environmental forces on which human subsistence depends.

Synthetic musical practices including fiddling and hymn singing have a long history in this area (Diamond Cavanagh 1989). Fiddling thrives in Attikamek villages such as Obedjiwan. Abenaki filmmaker and songwriter Alanis Obomsawin and Innu songwriter Philip McKenzie were pioneers in the production of contemporary popular music in the 1970s. Most commercially successful is the duo Kashtin (Florent Vollant and Claude McKenzie), with three platinum albums (over 200,000 sales) exclusively in the Innu language.

Colonial institutions and entrepreneurs

Beginning with accounts by Paul LeJeune in 1632 (Thwaites 1986–1901), seventeenth-century missionaries described Christian musical practices including those of the Ursuline Mother St. Joseph, who taught religious chants accompanied by a viol;

Marie de l'Incarnation, a visionary later celebrated in an opera by Canadian composer Istvan Anhalt; Charles Amador Martin, the probable composer of plainchant for the newly established Catholic feast day *La Sainte Famille* 'Holy Family', instituted in 1684; and violinist Martin Boutet. A substantial anthology of over four hundred works, now published by Elisabeth Gallat-Morin (1988) under the title *Livre d'orgue de Montréal,* indicates that a considerable range of repertoire, including music with many theatrical elements, was popular in the early eighteenth century. In emerging urban centers such as Québec City, the sacred and secular cultural life of the eighteenth and early nineteenth centuries was sustained and stimulated by versatile amateurs and tradespeople [see OVERVIEW, p. 1146]. Those who desired the refinement of Europe, however, were sometimes dissatisfied with the colonial conditions of New France. Poet and playwright Joseph Quesnel, who composed for the musical theater, found the spirit of the land "colder than the climate" and felt unappreciated. Quesnel's work has become known to twentieth-century audiences through arrangements by Godfrey Ridout and John Beckwith, respectively, of *Colas et Colinette,* and *Lucas et Cecile.*

Mrs. John Graves Simcoe, whose diary (1973) documents social life at the end of the eighteenth century, records music at balls sponsored by garrison officers in Québec, and band music for skating, as well as concerts. As early as the 1790s Québec had a subscription series and St. Jean Baptiste Day celebrations (this holiday remains a major holiday in French Canada).

Folk music and dance

The earliest local folk music performances were by *voyageurs,* who composed or adapted songs to the rhythms of paddling (Beland 1982 is the most extensive collection). Many early references to *voyageur* singing are romanticized literary accounts that have lent mythic nuances to the genre. Some popular ballad texts were associated with *voyageur* tune variants (Barbeau 1947).

Descriptions of balls and social events involving dance music emerge by the 1640s. An often quoted description of 1770 declared: "Never have I known a nation that likes to dance more than the 'Canadiens'; they still do French contre-danses and minuets, though they intermingle English dances" (Ornstein 1982.6). The English dances were probably reels and jigs; late-nineteenth-century couple dances were not adopted widely in Québec until the twentieth century, when the waltz increased in importance and local variants of squares, reels, and more complex choreographies evolved (Voyer 1986). French Canadian fiddling often features extensive double stopping, metric changes, and asymmetrical phrase lengths, possibly due to influence from aboriginal cultures [see MÉTIS, p. 404]. The fiddle was the instrument of preference until 1800, although the occasional use of the Jew's harp and tambour as well as *turlutage* 'vocal dance music performance used when a fiddle was not available' are reported (Ornstein 1982). By the late nineteenth century, the button accordion assumed a prominent place in French Canada.

Specific tunes and the fiddle itself garnered folklore: stories record the opposition of clergy to the fiddle, the legendary talents of local players (see Fowke 1988 for accounts of Blind Louis), and evidence of the instrument's magical powers (Seguin 1986:136). The "Hangman's Reel," a classic of the Québec repertoire, is said to have originated with a condemned man who was given a violin as his last request. Although it was completely detuned (most variants of the tune require *scordatura,* or altered tuning), he managed to play harmoniously, thereby saving his life (Seguin 1986:144).

In the course of the twentieth century, the folk music traditions of Québec, like those in Atlantic Canada, were commodified. Whether in vacation packages that provide tourists with accommodations in rural households (Handler 1988), in the production of recordings (see, for example, Gabriel Labbé 1977), or in more recent staged

The early twentieth century saw a polarization between those who favored a nationalist culture and those who advocated a modernist aesthetic.

shows such as *Les Feux Follets,* folk music has been repositioned, sometimes as antimodern and often as the root of Québécois popular music. Local cafés, *les boîtes à musique* or *boîtes à chansons,* became midcentury venues for the performance of both traditional and newly composed music. As Line Grenier (1996) has described them, these sites brought together individual artists performing songs about the need for social change, about a country to be built, in front of a relatively young audience that shared their aspirations for change. For a discussion of the *chansonnier* tradition led by Leveillée, Vigneault, and others in the political context of the Quiet Revolution, as well as of other distinctive popular musics such as *yeye* 'Québec rock', see Robert Giroux (1984).

Concert music after confederation (1867–1948)

Composer Calixa Lavallée found it difficult to establish a conservatory and opera company in Canada in the 1860s and 1870s, but by the century's end a concert music infrastructure had been created by Antoine Dessane, Charles Wugk Sabatier, Wilfrid Pelletier, Alexis Contant, Guillaume Couture, and others. The early twentieth century saw a polarization between those who favored a nationalist culture and those who advocated a modernist aesthetic. The Canadian Pacific Railway festivals of the late 1920s, the first of which was in Québec, were landmarks in the construction of national pride through the celebration of ethnic diversity. Composers of the period, many of whom studied in Paris, were committed to a role in constructing a national music. Claude Champagne (in works such as *Symphonie Gaspésienne, Danse Villageoise,* and, later, *Altitude*) and Hector Gratton (for example, his folk-based *Danses canadiennes* or his symphonic poem *Légende*) responded enthusiastically. On the other hand, the early modernism of Leo Pol Morin, an energetic promoter of the music of Claude Debussy, Maurice Ravel, and their younger French contemporaries in Québec, foresaw a path that would become stronger as the century progressed.

Modernism and beyond (1948–1998)

In the decade following *le refus global,* the concert music scene came alive in new ways. Among the enabling factors were the administrative and artistic initiatives of Jean Papineau Couture, the pioneering broadcasting of composer Pierre Mercure before his untimely death in 1966, and a new music organization, la Société de musique contemporaine de Québec. Stylistic distinctions are hard to define in heterogeneous artistic scenes but many have noted the keen interest in timbral experimentation among Québec composers such as Serge Garant and Gilles Tremblay and the influence of the strong spirituality of Messiaen on some. More women composers (including Marcelle Deschenes and Micheline Coulombe Saint-Marcoux) than in any other province emerged as bold new creative voices (Lefebvre 1991). A younger generation including Claude Vivier, Jean Piche, Walter Boudreau, and others, incorporated a wide range of cosmopolitan influences.

Jazz

Montréal in particular has had a significant place in Canada's jazz history. Among the earliest recordings, the Berliner and Compo labels both recorded jazz artists, although it was Compo that advertised a specialization in what were then called race records. In the 1920s, cabaret boss Andy Tipaldi and his dance and novelty orchestra, the Melody Kings, dominated the Montréal scene. In the 1930s the St. Antoine district became the jazz center of Montréal, and Laurentian resorts were attracting a wealthy clientele with the swing bands of Myron Sutton, Irving Laing, Stan Wood, and Roland Davis. Bebop was slow to emerge in Canada. It was in this environment that Oscar Peterson formed his first trio, performing at the Alberta Lounge in the late 1940s. The same venue later featured Paul Bley and his Montréal Jazz Workshop. Other important figures nurtured in this environment were Oliver Jones, Roland Lavallee, and Nelson Symonds. The Montréal Jazz Big Band, with lead singer Ranee Lee, played an active role into the 1990s. The first ensemble to perform collectively improvised free jazz while also crossing over to play rock and classical styles was the Quatuor de Jazz Libre du Québec (1967–1974), led by saxophonist Jean Prefontaine. Other experimental genres were film scores by René Lussier and the multimedia collaboration of Walter Boudreau and poet Raoul Duguay in *L'Infonie* from 1968 to 1973.

Other musics

Country and western music artists such as Tex Lecor have often occupied the same stage as the *chansonniers* at various *boîtes à chansons* in the province, and widely popular radio programs such as CHLT Sherbrooke have served as a vehicle for country artists. Willie Lamothe, after whom an annual provincial award (the "Willie") for country music is named, hosted one such radio series.

The first Jewish settlers in Canada arrived from England and Holland. A major influx from the 1880s to late 1950s was mostly Yiddish-speaking Ashkenazim from Eastern and Northern Europe. From the late 1950s on, however, large numbers from northern Africa and the Middle East began to arrive, maintaining a wider variety of musical traditions and even, in some cases, returning to local traditions rather than Israeli ones. Sephardic music, especially that of the Moroccan community in Montréal, is maintained in part by the professional ensemble Gerinaldo.

Music of Haiti and the French Caribbean thrives in the francophone milieu, and at summer festivals such as Carifête, Festival d'été de Québec, and Francofolies. Although a wide range of contemporary Latin dance music is performed in Montréal, the tango has had a particular popularity in Québec since the 1970s. Musics of other francophone diasporic communities thrive in the cities of Québec. Among them are fusions of jazz, flamenco, and the North African music of Katjar, or the versatile ensemble Quartango. Similarly, a Vietnamese scene has emerged since the 1980s. Among African American musical practices, a variety of genres have been promoted for several decades by Trevor Payne, who led rhythm and blues bands in the 1960s. He founded the Montréal Jubilation Gospel Choir in 1982, a group that had released several CDs by the late 1990s.

Ontario

Historical background

The province of Ontario consists of a southern "horn," nestled between the Great Lakes, that contains the largest urban and industrial centers, and a much larger but less populated and less urbanized northern region. The ethnocultural profiles of the two regions differ substantially. Among the historically older populations is a large concentration of French-speaking settlers in the vicinity of Sudbury and along the Ottawa River. Upper Canada, as it was known between 1740 and 1867, received its largest influx of settlers, mostly United Empire Loyalists, after the American Revolutionary War. Mennonites had arrived from Pennsylvania in the late eighteenth century, settling primarily around the Kitchener-Waterloo area (called Berlin until World War I).

The legislature of Upper Canada was the first in the British Empire to abolish slavery, in an act of 1793. Hence, this area, especially by way of Detroit and Windsor, was a prime destination on the Underground Railroad network, bringing in over forty thousand Africans during the second half of the nineteenth century. Other nineteenth-century settlers included the first wave of Italians after the Italian civil war in the 1880s, Irish potato famine victims from about 1860 to the end of the century, and numerous Chinese, most of whom moved from western Canada.

Twentieth-century demographic changes (particularly in Southern Ontario) have been substantial. Ukrainian, Polish, Portuguese, Hungarian, Czech, and Slovakian immigrants who came to Canada between the wars were more urban-oriented than their countrymen who came earlier to farm in western Canada. A large number of between-the-wars immigrants were Jewish, mostly Ashkenazim during this period. Many Italians also arrived in the 1930s and 1940s, paradoxically choosing urban environments in contrast to the largely rural lifestyles they left in Europe. In some cases (for example, the Portuguese of Cambridge or the Finns of Welland) resettlement was localized in a specific community, while in other cases a more diffuse settlement pattern evolved.

Post–World War II refugees from war-torn nations, as well as emigrés from turbulent Greece or from countries invaded by Soviet armies in the 1950s and 1960s (Hungary, Czechoslovakia, the Baltic nations) were largely urban bound, although mining brought many eastern and northern Europeans to Northern Ontario. The post–World War II lifting of racially restrictive immigration policies brought new waves of Asians and Middle Easterners particularly to metropolitan Toronto. Canada welcomed war-scarred Vietnamese and refugees from Ethiopia and Somalia in the 1980s and 1990s, as well as many from Latin America, the Caribbean, South Asia, and Hong Kong. By the end of the twentieth century, then, Ontario had one of the most diverse populations in the world. Daily social interaction occurs in dozens of different languages; hundreds of festivals, dance and music classes, both amateur and professional performance, and culturally specific societies facilitate both traditional and innovative intra- and intercultural creative production.

Aboriginal cultures

At the time when Europeans first arrived, they encountered the powerful Iroquois confederacy in what is now Ontario and New York State, originally including the Mohawk (Eastern door), Cayuga, Onondaga (fire keepers), Oneida, and Seneca (Western door), and later the Tuscarora. Allied with the British, the Iroquois engaged in a series of commercially motivated wars in the seventeenth century, defeating the Huron, Erie, Neutral, and Petun in the northeast and the Delaware and Susquehanna to the south in the eighteenth century. Splits in their allegiance and encroachments on their land weakened the confederacy by the time of the American Revolution.

The annual cycle of thanksgiving ceremonies for the gifts of the earth and sky was already in place before colonists arrived, but associated values and beliefs had eroded during the late eighteenth century. Enabling renewal was the visionary leader Handsome Lake, who began in 1799 to teach a code of living that formed the basis of the still thriving Longhouse religion. The Longhouse tradition distinguishes among ceremonial (dances of midwinter, for example), medicine society, and social dance songs. The last, with more than thirty different genres, are performed at community socials and biannual "sings," where performing groups showcase old and new *eskanye* 'women's shuffle dance songs', the most popular traditional genre for contemporary Iroquoian composers.

More scattered over a huge area to the north, and traditionally nomadic, most Algonquian-speaking nations were allied with the French during the colonial period. The Cree maintained ceremonial practices for effective hunting, medicine, and naming ceremonies while simultaneously learning and creating new musics, including Christian hymns in their own language (the Cree were the first nation to adopt the syllabic system of writing developed by missionary James Peck).

Other Anishnabe nations, particularly those of the Three Fires Confederacy (Ojibwe, Pottawatomi, and Odawa) around Georgian Bay and Lake Superior, have played a key role in the mid-twentieth-century spiritual renewal of Ontario's aboriginal communities, including the renewal of Midewiwin ceremonies. Ontario Anishnabe communities have also played a role in the dance drum tradition (Vennum 1982) and in the development of the women's jingle dress societies, the origin of which, according to some oral histories, is in northern Ontario. Spiritual aspects are understood to underlie the intertribal tradition of powwow dancing, especially "traditional" rather than "competitive" powwows. By the 1990s the largest Ontario powwows were at Six Nations, Wikwemikong, Curve Lake, and the Skydome in Toronto.

Colonial musical practices

Several community-based studies (Hall 1973, 1974; Keillor 1988; Morey 1985, 1988) document the musical practices of colonial Ontario. Royalty was a prime topic of celebration for these loyalist settlers; in York (now Toronto), for example, Carl Morey notes music for the king's birthday as early as 1798 (1992:1292), as well as public concerts and ballad opera productions. The first organ was probably installed in St. James Anglican church in 1832. A number of transitory musical societies for choral and instrumental music were established around midcentury, and a volunteer militia band, the Queen's Own Rifles, provided music for a myriad of social occasions. In 1846, the University of Toronto conferred its first Bachelor of Music degree to James Paton Clark, known as a composer of patriotic songs and founding conductor of the Toronto Philharmonic Society (est. 1845).

A small Ontario community was the site of an unusual and interesting musical development in the mid-nineteenth century. In Hope (later Sharon), Ontario, a religious sect called the Children of Peace, led by ex-Quaker David Willson, reflected an ecumenical philosophy and creative spirit in both music and architecture [see SHARON, p. 136].

Post-confederation classical music

By the end of the nineteenth century institutions of more longevity (including the still active Toronto Mendelssohn Choir, established in 1894) and music schools (including the Canadian Academy of Music, est. 1886, and forerunner of the current Royal Conservatory of Music) were established, several led by Frederick Torrington, Edward Fisher, and Augustus Vogt. Higher professional standards became possible as many musicians from Central and Eastern European countries arrived by the 1930s and 1940s. The Hart House String Quartet (1923–1945) and individual solo performers such as Zara Nelsova and Kathleen Parlow had illustrious careers. In the 1930s through the 1950s, the multifaceted musical leadership of Ernest MacMillan as conductor, composer, examiner, administrator, writer, and teacher (Schabas 1994) was significant. The world class eminence to which classical musicians aspired in the 1930s through the 1950s was first consistently achieved in the 1960s with such groups as the Orford String Quartet (1965–1991), the Festival Singers (1954–1979, reconstituted as the Iseler Singers 1979–), and the National Arts Centre orchestra, among others. Many other Ontario orchestras, such as those of Thunder Bay, Windsor, Kitchener-Waterloo, London, Kingston, and Ottawa—where a core of professionals is complemented by amateur players—function as community ensembles.

Jazz in Ontario is, for the most part, a phenomenon of the post-1940s period.

Since the 1960s, the musical infrastructure has arguably become more specialized and diversified. Perhaps charting a course for specialization (or at least eccentric individuality) was pianist Glenn Gould, whose rejection of public performance in order to focus exclusively on recordings was radical in the 1960s [see TECHNOLOGY AND MEDIA, p. 235]. Other "niche repertoire" classical performers include the internationally acclaimed Baroque orchestra Tafelmusik (est. 1978), the Baroque opera company Opera Atelier, the Esprit Orchestra, devoted to contemporary music, the percussion ensemble Nexus, the Hannaford Street Silver Band (reviving early band and orchestral repertoire), and various new music groups including Ottawa's Espace Musicale, Toronto's New Music Concerts, and the Canadian Electronic Ensemble. Classical musical humor has been developed in Canada by the Canadian Brass and in the parodies of soprano Anna Russell in the 1940s and 1950s as well as by soprano Mary Lou Fallis in the 1980s and 1990s.

Jazz, popular music, and country music

Among the earliest pop culture artists were a vaudeville act, The Dumbells, formed in 1917 by Merton Plunkett from members of the Canadian army's third division (whose emblem was a red dumbbell). Popular in the United States and England as well as Canada, their songs (many by star crooner Al Plunkett) and skits, which incorporated blackface comedy as well as female impersonation, described army life.

The international success of the dance bands of London, Ontario–born Guy Lombardo in the 1920s and 1930s was unique in its day. Jazz in Ontario is, for the most part, a phenomenon of the post-1940s period. In the 1940s, the orchestra of Bert Nisio and Rex Battle's Maple Leaf Orchestra dominated the scene. Bebop was regarded with caution in the early days (Miller 1997). The Onyx and Café Marimba in the Church and Dundas area were the first jazz clubs in the country. Moe Kaufman, Ed Bickert, Phil Nimmons, Maynard Fergusson, and Rob McConnell were among those who transformed the local jazz aesthetic.

Country music has thrived both on the airwaves and in live performance. Wingham, Ontario's, CKNX *Barn Dance,* the longest-running show of its kind (from 1937 to 1963), featured Ontario fiddler Ward Allen and singer Tommy Hunter, who would host in the 1960s one of the most popular TV shows in Canadian history. In a statistical survey of citations in trade magazines, Tim Rogers (1990) revealed that Ontario country music featured a "full-band orientation," a more important broadcasting and club profile and less dance-band emphasis, and more attention to comedians and to bass players vis-à-vis country music in other provinces. Urban crossover artists included Willie P. Bennett and Murray McLachlan prior to the "new country" wave of the 1990s. Bluegrass has also been popular in specific localized centers in Ontario, especially Burlington. Vital centers of country music have been the rural hotels and bars of northern Ontario towns such as Timmins, where Shania Twain, among others, started her career.

Ontario has numerous old-time fiddling and step dancing contests; the largest is the Canadian Open Old Time Fiddlers' Contest (est. 1951) in Shelburne. Competitors play a reel, waltz, and jig medley or enter novelty fiddling and a variety of age-defined categories. Multiple-year winners Graham Townsend and his wife, Eleanor (also a Shelburne winner), were active in the publication of tunebooks and recordings. The Irish-dominated Ottawa River Valley is often regarded as the heartland of Ontario fiddling.

During the folk revival of the late 1960s and 1970s, particularly in the area known as Yorkville in Toronto, Gordon Lightfoot, Joni Mitchell, Bruce Cockburn, Salome Bey, and Buffy Ste. Marie became quite well known. A recent book about this folk revival movement in Yorkville (Jennings 1997) sees these songwriters as the precursers of internationally successful artists of the 1990s such as Jane Siberry, Alanis Morisette, and Shania Twain.

A number of songwriters, including Valdy, Raffi, Sharon, Lois and Bram, Fred Penner, and Dennis Lee, turned to the children's market in the 1980s. Folklorist Sheldon Posen (1993) has explored why folk music for children should have flourished in Canada, arguing that a small group of artists within a low-volume market can have an extensive impact. He posits that relative to the United States, the folk revival movement in Canada was less politically charged but more concerned with social cohesion and environmental concerns.

While Canada has always been a receptive market and participant in rock and roll, the commercial development of rock in Ontario was slow to develop until after the "British invasion" of the late 1960s. Those Canadian musicians who had successful recording careers in the 1950s (such as Paul Anka, Bobby Curtola, Percy Faith, or doo-wop groups such as the Crew-Cuts or the Diamonds) generally moved to the United States. By comparison, the annual *Live Music Directory* published by *Now* (Toronto's weekly arts and entertainment news magazine) lists over 1000 active professional bands in the 1990s. Important contributors in the 1960s include Ronnie Hawkins, who moved to Toronto around 1960 and created a market for his brand of rockabilly. Rhythm and blues was pioneered in the 1960s by singers such as Jackie Shane, the Ottawa-based Staccatos, and London's Motherlode, Mandala, and others. Bands such as Steppenwolf, probably the most successful of the Canadian imitators of the Beatles, also came on the scene in the late 1960s. The introduction of Canadian content broadcast regulations by the CRTC in 1970 was a major factor in facilitating Canadian-based success for psychedelic rockers The Paupers (formed by drummer Skip Prokop, who later played with Lighthouse), blues singer David Clayton-Thomas, or Klaatu (an unusual band that garnered a cult following on the basis of self-produced recordings alone). The hard rock trio Rush was admired by progressive rock fans for their experimentation and instrumental complexity as well as for scrupulous live performance. Ontario-based bands and performers since the 1980s include the Barenaked Ladies, Tragically Hip, the more politically oriented Parachute Club, and the intense vocal styles of Jann Arden and Alanis Morisette. By the mid-1990s, the Celtic revival had also brought longtime folk-rooted musicians such as Loreena McKennitt and Leahy to the commercial forefront.

Culturally specific musical practices

European

Although generations are variously motivated to sustain or deny their roots, many European-derived communities in Canada maintained a musical connection with their countries of origin in the contexts of private social gatherings, weddings, and more public events such as national day celebrations and multicultural events. But generalizations are impossible as specific periods of arrival, attendant religious or political issues, and degrees of similarity or difference between old and new contexts shaped communities differently. Dance has often been maintained more aggressively than music, because recordings can more easily substitute for live performance.

Just as in western Canada, the diversification of Ontario accelerated in the late nineteenth century. Several factors distinguish Ontario from the Prairie provinces, among them the urban and more nationalist orientation of many twentieth-century immigrant groups, the post-1947 increases in Asian and Middle Eastern immigration, and the recent influxes from the Caribbean and Hong Kong, South Asia, and Africa. Some of the ways these factors impacted music can be seen with reference to selected ethnocultural groups—earlier ones such as the Mennonites, Irish, and Polish; postwar immigrants such as those from Ukraine, Italy, Greece, Yugoslavia, and the Baltic countries; and more recent arrivals, such as those from Asia and the Caribbean.

The northern trek of Swiss-German Mennonites from Pennsylvania in the late eighteenth century brought Old Order, Amish, and several other religious communities, particularly to the Kitchener-Waterloo area. Over time internal diversification occurred with the arrival of Russian Mennonites, some of whom moved further west. Like most earlier groups, Mennonites have made a substantial contribution to classical music. Mennonite choirs such as the Menno Singers and singers Paul Frey, Daniel Lichti, and opera virtuoso Ben Hepner, for example, had active recording schedules in the 1980s and 1990s. Vernacular German-language music, on the other hand, seems to have had a less continuous history in Ontario than on the prairies. *Sangerfesten* and brass bands were popular in the late nineteenth century, lapsing at the onset of World War I but reviving after World War II. The Munich tradition of Oktoberfest has been transplanted to a number of Canadian cities, the largest annual event taking place in Kitchener-Waterloo.

Irish immigrants arrived after 1840 in the wake of the Irish potato famine, constituting Ontario's largest ethnic group by 1871. Settling largely in the Ottawa River valley, they maintained a lively Celtic dance music tradition with elements of American old-time fiddle style: more back bowing, slower tempos with more swing feeling, and glissandi rather than the bowing ornaments that feature so prominently in Atlantic Canadian styles. The lumber camps of the nineteenth and early twentieth century served to foster the Anglo-Celtic folk song traditions in northern Ontario as well as in Québec and the northeastern United States. Ontario folk singers, recorded since the 1960s by folklorist Edith Fowke, include O. J. Abbott and LaRena Clark.

Ukrainian immigrants who arrived in southern Ontario cities either between the world wars or after World War II created large-scale infrastructures for music production and emphasized staged concert performances in contrast to the smaller dance ensembles, *tsymbaly* 'zither' competitions, and syncretic forms (for example, Ukrainian country) that thrived in the west. Important in this regard is the Shevchenko organization, originally a male chorus (est. 1951) but shortly thereafter a choir, orchestra, and dance company. A number of choirs, such as Dibrova and Vesnika, were founded by the 1970s. Bandura 'many-stringed plucked lute-type instrument' ensembles have been particularly popular in Ontario. In addition to performance groups, sponsoring/commissioning organizations such as the Canadian Ukrainian Opera Association also emerged in the postwar period.

Their Finnish and Byelorussian neighbors, on the other hand, came to settle partly in southern cities but partly also in more northerly ones such as Sudbury or Thunder Bay, where different music infrastructures emerged. The Baltic tradition of national song festivals originating in the late nineteenth century was sustained in Canada. Latvian National Song Festivals have been held nine times in Toronto. Baltic choirs include the Lithuanian Varpas Choir, active in Toronto since the 1950s, and the Ramuneles Singers, an octet active in the 1970s and 1980s.

Croatian workers came after 1918 to work the mines of northern cities such as Timmins and Sudbury, while a later wave arrived in Toronto and other southern metropolises following World War II and again after the breakup of Yugoslavia in the 1990s. The earlier groups actively maintained folk music traditions; ethnomusicologist Tim Rice (1992:333) notes that "among traditional genres which have survived in Canada are vocal polyphony from the island of Krk and the mountains of Hercegovina, Croatian patriotic songs of the nineteenth century, and the playing of the Hercegovinian bagpipes (*mih*)." A Tamburitzan Ensemble was established in Hamilton as early as 1944. By the 1970s the Sudbury-based Croatian Folklore Federation was organizing annual festivals.

Italian immigrants, on the other hand, chose an environment radically different from the agrarian villages they left in Italy, moving to Ontario's major industrial centers—Hamilton, Guelph, Ottawa, and Toronto—where the Italian population would number over 500,000 by the mid-1980s. Historian Bruno Ramirez has pointed to the enormous importance of family and the promise of security and independence as a major factor in the establishment of Italian culture in a new land. He refers to a popular Italian song of the post–World War II era that spoke of "a little house in Canada which had a pool with fish inside, was surrounded by lots of lily flowers, and was admired by passers-by" (1989:14) as a significant statement of these values and desires. Popular music with guitar and accordion is a mainstay at weddings and social gatherings, but very little folk music was emphasized in the new context, perhaps because of the desire to leave rural practices behind.

A complex array of music is practiced by the Ontario Greek community, relating in part to the differences in region of origin (many are from Peloponnesus and Crete, and there are Macedonians from the former Yugoslavia) and economic status prior to emigration. In Toronto the largest wave of Greek immigrants arrived after 1945, settling in an area known as the Danforth in the city's east end. Saint George's Greek Orthodox Church opened its doors in 1908, both Orthodox and Eastern rites are observed in the churches of the late-twentieth-century community.

Asian

Ontario's Asian communities are generally newer than those in western Canada. In the early decades of the century, the small community suffered from ghettoization, economic hardship, and racial discrimination, as in British Columbia. The proscription on immigration similarly prevented family reunification and community development before the ban was lifted in 1947. Many first-generation Chinese moved to central Canada from the west, as did many Japanese, arriving after World War II. The largest influx of Chinese occurred in the 1980s and 1990s, with over 50,000 Hong Kong "sojourners" coming to Toronto alone, some returning to Hong Kong after 1997.

As in British Columbia, Cantonese opera clubs (among them the United Dramatic Society, Toronto, and the Wah Shing Music Group, Ottawa) were among the earliest in Ontario. The earliest production in Toronto documented to date was in 1918. Instrumental teaching of Chinese stringed instruments, such as the *yang ch'in, yueh-hu, ban-hu, yueh-ch'in, pi'pa,* and various percussion instruments was carried out in support of dramatic activities. In the 1960s through the 1980s, a number of choirs and orchestras, including Mandarin-language choirs in Guelph, Mississauga, and Hamilton, the Chinese Cantabile Chorus of Ottawa, the Chinese Canadian Choir in Toronto, and the Toronto Chinese Chamber Orchestra, were established. Perhaps because the majority of immigrants in recent decades were professionals with a high level of education and economic affluence, among them many distinguished artists such as George Gao (*er hu* 'two-string fiddle'), Fan Sheng-E (*zheng* 'zither') and others, the cultural infrastructure for Asian music and dance in Ontario has developed rapidly. The opening of the Chinese Cultural Centre in Toronto in 1998 together with the renewal of the Toronto Chinese Music Association marks the beginning of a new era. As elsewhere, a high proportion of Asian concert performers of European classical music excelled in the 1980s and 1990s.

On the other hand, relative to China, Taiwan, or Hong Kong, the celebration of calendric festivals (Hoe 1989; Chan 1996) has previously been modest in Ontario, to a large extent because of the early marginalization of the community. By the mid-1990s,

Toronto is sometimes described, by the late 1990s as the third largest Caribbean city. The Jamaican Canadian Association, the Coalition of Black Artists, Calypso Association of Canada, and the Caribana organizers, the Caribbean Cultural Committee, are among important community organizations for music and other arts.

however, the Chinese New Year, Dragon Boat Festival, and Autumn Moon Festival (more locally oriented) were widely visible events.

Japanese Canadians established Utai societies (for the production of *noh* drama and Shi-gin poetry chanting) in Ontario. The Japanese Canadian Cultural Center was established in the 1960s, and under its auspices, choirs such as the Sansei Choir of Harry Kumano, dance troupes, *koto* 'plucked zither', *shakuhachi* 'endblown flute', and *shamisen* 'plucked chordophone' instruction are available.

The earliest South Asian immigrants in Toronto were Punjabi (Sikh); the Hindu and Muslim communities have grown primarily since the 1960s. Musically they maintained both private practices such as the singing of devotional songs or *bhajans* or poetry chanting at private gatherings, weddings, and so on and an increasing number of public, concert-type performances. Bharati Kala Manram (South Indian) and Raga-Mala Societies (predominantly North Indian) were organized in major cities, bringing distinguished artists from India as well as supporting local musicians to some extent.

The artistic profile of some Asian musicians has remained more localized. Indonesians, for example, participate in gamelan performances, but the highest profile ensemble of this type is the Evergreen Club (figure 2), a Sumatran-founded ensemble that commissions new and extremely eclectic works (among them synthetic works involving Indian or West African instruments and styles) while also performing traditional Indonesian repertoire. In the 1990s, popular music activity includes karaoke in the contexts of family and friends, visiting superstar Hong Kong recording artists, and local fusion groups such as Punjabi by Nature. Toronto was an important center of *bhangra* (a popular music genre) for youth in the early 1990s.

Middle Eastern and North African

By 1986, over 100,000 people of Arabic extraction from seventeen different nations and active participants in diverse religions lived in Canada. In many Toronto communities, differences within communities (in political belief, lifeways, and so on) have helped scholars understand how new identities are negotiated in the Canadian context. As ethnomusicologist Margaret Sarkissian (1990) has shown with reference to Armenian choirs in Toronto, there is often intracultural tension concerning the pressures to conform to intercultural concert decorum or to reflect more intracultural cohesion. Her work with the Hamazkain and Ani Choirs, each affiliated with different political parties, for example, revealed correspondence between socioaesthetic principles and political leanings (1990:103).

Jane Sugarman's (1997) study of Prespa Albanian weddings, based partly on research in Toronto, revealed somewhat different intracultural tensions, between the codes of honor valued within the culture and challenges to the hierarchies and constraints that those very codes impose. These studies are significant contributions to our exploration of the complex ways in which individuals and performance groups assert agency in new contexts that partially reshape aesthetic values and social relationships.

FIGURE 2 Evergreen Club, contemporary Toronto-based gamelan rehearsing with the Aradia Baroque orchestra in 1997. Photo by Andrew Timar.

Sub-Saharan African, Afro-Caribbean, and Latin American

Although the earliest African-derived population in Ontario consisted of about 40,000 Underground Railroad travelers emanating from the United States, the contemporary demographics of southern Ontario differ substantially from those of most U.S. urban areas in that Caribbeans who arrived in the 1980s and 1990s are numerically dominant. Prior to this large influx, the African Canadian community was relatively small and survived primarily by adopting the musical practices of surrounding communities. Gospel choirs (McIntyre 1976) were maintained in Windsor churches (perhaps sustained in part by neighboring Detroit), but earlier in the century musicians in the nearby African community of Buxton composed and performed hymns in a style closer to white gospel singing (Stewardson 1994).

The 300,000-strong and rapidly growing Caribbean population in southern Ontario arrived mostly since the 1960s. Toronto is sometimes described, by the late 1990s as the third largest Caribbean city. The Jamaican Canadian Association, the Coalition of Black Artists, Calypso Association of Canada, and the Caribana organizers, the Caribbean Cultural Committee, are among important community organizations for music and other arts. The development of venues such as the Harriet Tubman Center in Toronto, which houses a gallery for local artists and sponsors music and dance programs, as well as institutions such as the Ontario Black History Society and Black History Month (February), has enhanced public awareness of African-derived cultures. Toronto's Caribana festival is one of North America's largest carnival celebrations, albeit one that is uniquely shaped by the Canadian context (Gallaugher 1995) [see CARIBANA, p. 1207].

African-derived and Latino dance musics from the Caribbean influenced the Toronto club scene in the 1980s and 1990s as elsewhere in North America. Dance bands such as Syncona (1972–1986) were among the first to bring *cadence, zouk,* reggae, and *salsa* to Toronto. Memo Acevedo (founder of Banda Brava) and Ramiro Puerta played important roles in forming and directing bands through the 1980s. In many cases, Caribbean musicians played percussion along with horn players of non-Caribbean (often jazz) background. Afro-Cuban musics have been vigorously promoted in the 1990s by jazz musicians such as Jane Bunnett and by Cuban bands such as Klave y Kongo. The diverse musics of the Caribbean countries with strong Spanish elements have often been homogenized as Hispanic or Latino in the Toronto context, creating a pan-Latin identity in spite of the different national communities. Genres such as salsa or *cumbia* became overarching symbols of Latino dance music in the club scene since the 1980s.

The Prairies

Historical background

The cultural history of the Prairie provinces of Manitoba, Saskatchewan, and Alberta has often received cursory treatment by musicologists. The reasons for this are multiple and intertwined: settlement by nonaboriginal people in this region is quite recent and thus less privileged within a historical framework. The largely rural population is sparser and thus paid less attention to within the urban-biased musicological paradigm of many Canadian studies. The historically isolated settlement patterns of different cultures often invited ethnically or regionally bounded studies. Furthermore, the Northern and Eastern European communities so central to prairie history have often been ignored for their "invisibility" vis-à-vis Caribbean or Asian cultures or their marginality relative to the British and French.

Although not forcibly removed as in the United States, many aboriginal people moved west as European Canadian settlement encroached on their land. Dickason reports (1992:194–195) that the Algonquian-speaking Blackfoot nations (the confederacy includes the Siksika, Kainah/Blood, Peigan/Peegan, and, later, the Athapascan-speaking

Sarcee) arrived first and the Gros Ventre shortly after. The Plains Cree (including the Sauteaux) came in the early eighteenth century possibly through an association with the Siouan-speaking Assiniboine, who were fellow participants in the fur trade. The newest northern Plains American Indians are the Plains Ojibwe, who arrived by the late eighteenth century. Horses were in widespread use by this time, facilitating buffalo hunting and, in turn, a period of relative prosperity in the late eighteenth and early nineteenth century until the bison herds became depleted, shortly after the fur trade waned. The widespread adoption of syllabics by the Cree (and Inuit), a writing system the development of which is usually attributed to the Methodist missionary James Evans, contributed to the rise of a messianic religious movement in the 1840s.

Settling the west after 1867 was key to the newly formed Canadian government's vision of nationhood. Manitoba and the Northwest Territories (which included Alberta and Saskatchewan at that time) joined the fledgling country in 1870. Between 1870 and 1930, treaties were signed with approximately half the Native population, but their wording does not withstand late-twentieth-century legal scrutiny. The Red River valley (Assiniboia) Métis community declared its nationhood under the leadership of Louis Riel in the face of settlers who began to move west after 1812. Skirmishes in the 1870s and 1880s (in northern Saskatchewan) led to Riel's eventual defeat and controversial hanging, an event recorded in both folk song and opera.

Inexpensive land attracted homesteaders from northern and central Europe in particular, and the population surged in the 1890s and the first two decades of the twentieth century. The French population—the earliest one and one that still constitutes a sizable minority in Manitoba, where they constituted 6.1 percent of the population in 1991—was quickly surpassed. The largest European Canadian groups in every Prairie province are the Germans, Ukrainians, and Scandinavians. The Native population is largest in Saskatchewan, constituting almost 7 percent of the population. Manitoba in particular has a large Mennonite community, especially near Steinbach in the south. Alberta has more minority religious groups than any other province, however, with active Hutterite, Mennonite, Doukhobor, Islamic, and Mormon communities. As in other provinces, the Asian and Caribbean populations have dramatically increased since the 1970s. A number of smaller communities have made significant cultural contributions; these include black emigrés from Oklahoma in Saskatchewan, the Icelandic community of Gimli, Manitoba, and the Indian/Muslim community of Edmonton, Alberta. The prairies remain substantially rural, although urban centers have grown substantially since World War II.

First nations and Métis music

Plains Indians (Algonquian-, Siouian-, and Athapaskan-language families) suffered, as did other First Nations people, from government proscriptions. An effective ban on the Sun/Thirst Dance took place in 1895, when physical endurance features of the ceremony were disallowed, and again in 1906, when all traditional dancing was banned. Music and dance practices were driven underground but were not erased. Among various responses to oppression, the Ghost Dance movement came north from the United States in the late 1890s to Round Plain, Saskatchewan, and Wood Mountain, Manitoba (Dickason 1992:287), where it was incorporated into the Medicine Feast and referred to as the Good Tidings dance.

A revival of ceremonial and social practices has taken place since the 1960s, especially through the efforts of Native-run cultural centers/museums, such as the Saskatchewan Indian Cultural Center and the Wanuskewin Heritage Park, Alberta, and increased collaboration with non-native museums. The Stoney reserve in Alberta has been at the center of a spiritual revival movement involving ecumenical conferences and annual Sun Dances.

Most Plains tribes sustained ceremonial song practices associated with medicine bundles, as well as the Sun or Thirst dance, as it is often called by Cree. Robert Witmer's research (1982) indicated that music associated with the war dance complex constituted the most vital Blood nation repertoire in the 1960s and 1970s. Patricia McArthur (1987) lists "ceremonial" dances in current use, including the Round Dance Ceremony associated with funeral rites, the Masked Dance, Bear Dance, Gift Exchange Dance, Prairie Chicken Dance, and Horse Dance, and she describes the dances of the Worthy Men's Society and "traditional" social dances including the Grass Dance, Moving Slowly or Round Dance, "Kiskipocikek," Tail Wagging Dance, and Tea Dance. Some communities also have repertoires of gambling songs, lullabies, walking or riding songs, and night serenade songs

Widely performed dances in the 1980s and 1990s are those associated with the powwow: Men's Traditional Dance and Grass Dance, Women's Traditional Dance and Jingle Dress Dance, Men's Fancy Dance, and Women's Shawl Dance. The singing is characterized by high tessitura and intense, pulsating vocal production; a large horizontal ("dry") drum played by singers, who push the tempo of the voice by drumming slightly ahead of the vocal pulse; and the practice of women surrounding the drum and joining an octave above the men's voices partway through each song. Show dances such as the hoop dance are popular, as are the triple meter couples dance (the Owl Dance) and Round Dances. Recordings by "drum groups" such as the popular Red Bull Singers (who collaborated with Buffy Sainte-Marie on her latest album), Elk's Whistle, Little Island Cree, and Mosquito Singers are currently available on the SICC label, Sunshine Records (Winnipeg), Canyon, and Indian House, among others.

The most widely known Métis music from the prairies is a distinctive style of fiddling accompanying both step dancing and square dancing. Both First Nations and Métis communities enjoy a wide range of contemporary styles and genres of music making. Country music and blues are especially popular; Mishi Donovan and Laura Vinson of Alberta, actor-musician Tom Jackson, and Manitobans Ernest Monias and Jody Thomas Gaskin are among the prominent recording artists from the prairies. The Lac La Biche Jamboree in Alberta has been an important venue for aboriginal country artists. Prairie-born Cree singer-songwriter Buffy Ste. Marie has been an important advocate for aboriginal artists, playing a role in the establishment of an annual Juno award for the Best Music of Aboriginal Canada.

The beginnings of European-derived music institutions

The development of western cities was often carefully planned and rapid, governed by the late-eighteenth-century expansion of fur-trading posts (Winnipeg and Edmonton, for example), the need for a station on the newly completed railway (Regina and Calgary), or, in the case, of Saskatoon, the rather unusual circumstance of settlement as a temperance town by a group of ex-Ontarians. Each place began with only a few hundred people but grew quickly. The establishment of cultural institutions often paralleled the energy of the population growth. Regina, for example, could boast a Musical Club, a Musical and Literary Society, a Glee Club, a Minstrel Club, several bands, and a Choral Society in the 1880s (Brundhagen 1992:1119). Saskatoon had four bands and two orchestras by 1912 (Brundhagen and Mills 1992:1180), and by 1914 the *Musical Times* would report that Edmonton is "a fine city striding the hills, but music is overdone here" (McIntosh and Berg 1992:403).

European Canadian

French

The earliest European settlers on the prairies were francophone, many descended from *couriers de bois*. Although at the end of the nineteenth century the far-flung French population was a relatively small minority, the British feared the power of the clergy. Therefore, in a move to establish an English-based culture in the West, legislation was

In the 1920s through 1940s, there was a substantial part of the community that held assimilationist views, attempting, as Subtelny puts it, "to straddle the two cultures, reading both Shevchenko and Shakespeare, celebrating Christmas on 25 December and 7 January, listening to jazz and folk songs, denouncing their elected officials and Stalin.

passed to declare English the only official language, removing the special privileges of Catholic-run "separate" schools in Manitoba in 1890 and in Alberta and Saskatchewan in 1905. Resistance was predictably strong; independent schools and colleges, newspapers, and, by the 1920s, radio stations were established. St. Boniface, Manitoba, became the cultural hub for much of the print production, although Québec-based publications, such as the various educational series (mostly compiled by Charles-Emile Gadbois) by the publishing company La bonne chanson, circulated widely after 1937.

Something of a cultural renaissance and a move to construct a cultural image independent of Québec's has occurred in francophone communities since the 1980s, evident in the bilingual success of the pop band Hart Rouge (originally a family-based folk ensemble from Willow Bunch), singer-songwriters promoted by L'association des artistes in Saskatchewan, the eclectic fiddlers of Cleaver's World, and others.

Ukrainian, German, and other Central European

The lure of inexpensive land after the Dominion Land Act of 1871, which opened the Canadian west to settlement, drew large numbers of Central and Northern Europeans to the prairies. The earliest immigrants from Poland and the Ukraine left homelands where national borders were still in dispute, hence their strongest nationalist commitment was to their adopted nation rather than to their birth nation. In some cases, such as with the Poles and Slovaks, immigrants moved east at the onset of the Depression, dissipating once strong prairie communities.

Ukrainian immigrants of the 1890s and early 1920s, for instance, from Galicia, Bukuvyna, and Transcarpathia, were farming people, while the waves following 1917 and 1945 consisted of better educated, more urban-oriented people who emigrated often for political reasons. In the west, the agrarian foundations remain fundamental. These rural communities created about 250 *Prosvita* (enlightenment) societies, reading rooms, and community centers by 1925 (Subtelny 1991:85). Communities such as Yorkton, Saskatchewan, and Vegreville, Alberta, became cultural centers. While most of this wave of immigrants was Ukrainian Catholic, some converted to the Greek Orthodox Church.

Music played an important role in settlers' lives, especially at special events such as weddings, for circle dances or *kolmekas* as well as newer waltzes and polkas (figure 3). Ritual singing was maintained and choirs established. Teodor Fedyk's *Pisni imigrantiv prostaryi I novyi krai* 'Songs of Immigrants about the Old and New Country' appeared in 1911 and sold 50,000 copies (Subtelny 1991:174). Folklorist Robert Klymasz (1970, 1971, 1992) has explored the ballad traditions of Ukrainian Canadians in western Canada, discovering archaic features including the maintenance of a ritual folk song cycle and epics. The role of the community bard or *kobza* was also maintained in Canada. Klymasz notes that traditions such as the Easter celebrations (including the well-known elaborately painted eggs, specialty breads, and so on) were experienced in Canada much as they were in the homeland.

FIGURE 3　Wedding festivities, c. 1916, in the Chipman district of Alberta. Photo courtesy Provincial Archives of Alberta.

FIGURE 4 School of Ukrainian Performing Arts at Ukrainian Labour-Farmer Temple Association, Regina. Teachers, Peter J. Lapchuk and Anna Lapchuk, 1937. Photo courtesy Saskatchewan Archives Board.

In the 1920s through 1940s, a period when divided political views emerged strongly, there was nevertheless a substantial part of the community that held assimilationist views, attempting, as Subtelny puts it, "to straddle the two cultures, reading both Shevchenko and Shakespeare, celebrating Christmas on 25 December and 7 January, listening to jazz and folk songs, denouncing their elected officials and Stalin. Some managed to draw on the best from both worlds, but most found biculturalism confusing and demanding" (1991:113). Mandolin orchestras and staged performances developed at this period (figure 4). Renowned conductor-arranger Oleksander Koshetz emigrated to Canada in 1941. From the 1950s on, a wider range of cultural institutions and festivals flourished, and new forms of popular music, such as Ukrainian country, developed. Sunshine Records has been a major producer of Ukrainian musical talent in the 1980s and 1990s, featuring comedians such as Freddie Chatybok, *tsymbaly* players such as Irene Chamzuk and the Rossburn Cymbaly Ensemble, and family bands including the Citulskys and the Hryniuks.

Scandinavian

Prairie homesteaders included many Norwegians (about 80 percent of whom settled on the prairies) and Swedes, many of whom moved north from the United States. Swedish musicians, including the Bellman Quartet and Selma Johanson, participated in the Canadian Pacific Railway–sponsored festivals of the late 1920s. Traditional calendric celebration, such as the Feast of St. Lucia in mid-December, is still practiced in some communities, and dance music has been maintained to some extent. Icelanders arrived in fewer numbers (fewer than five thousand in the area south of Lake Winnipeg, first called "New Iceland") between 1873 and 1875. Their cultural life centered in Gimli, Manitoba, where an annual Icelandic festival is still celebrated.

Middle Eastern and South and East Asian traditions

Until the 1980s, about 85 percent of Arab Canadians were Christian and were concentrated in Ontario and Québec, but the earliest Muslim communities were formed in Edmonton, Alberta, and at Lac La Biche, Alberta. The first mosque in Canada was built in Edmonton in 1938, and a group of fifteen families established another in the mink-ranching community at Lac La Biche in 1957 (Qureshi 1972:383). Regula Qureshi (1972) has described both structured performance contexts—Arab Day, sponsored by Edmonton's Canadian-Arab Friendship Society, and the celebration of the religious festival *Eid* by Calgary's Pakistan-Canadian Association—and unstructured performance at private gatherings, or *Mahfil,* where folk singing and dancing, classical music, Urdu poetry chanting, and sometimes religious chanting and singing take place. Calgary is the home of the Shastri Institute headquarters in Canada. The Asian community has also produced many internationally recognized classical music performers.

Classical music and jazz

Some distinctive features of prairie concert life emerged early in the twentieth century. First, the preeminence of choral music, especially in Manitoba, until World War II is indisputable. Second, the fervor with which western Canadians have embraced music competitions (classical music festivals, but also fiddle and other generic contests) is noteworthy. Finally, participation in concert life before World War II was ethnoculturally broader on the prairies than in central or eastern Canada, involving the British, French, German Mennonites, Ukrainian and other Slavic people, and Scandinavians.

Although the English were never demographically dominant on the Prairies, English organists and choirmasters played a major, multifaceted role in community life in the late nineteenth and early twentieth centuries. Among them were A. G. Randall in Edmonton in the 1890s; Vernon Barford (Randall's successor), who established the Edmonton Choral Society and the Operatic and Dramatic Society in 1904 and initiated a music festival in 1908; Fred Bagley, conductor of the Northwest Mounted Police Band in Calgary in 1877; and William Preston, founder of the Saskatoon Philharmonic Society in 1908.

Between the 1880s and 1910, a wide range of short-lived orchestral and choral organizations was founded: philharmonic societies (Winnipeg, 1880–1922; Edmonton, 1894–; Calgary, 1904–1908; Saskatoon 1909–), Apollo Choirs/Clubs (Winnipeg 1880–; Edmonton 1898–; Calgary 1908–1918), the Men's Musical Club (Winnipeg, 1922–), an Oratorio Society (Winnipeg, 1908–), and Women's Music Clubs (Winnipeg 1894–; Calgary 1904–1964). Among the many choirs of Winnipeg were several devoted to culturally-specific repertoire, such as the all-male Polish Sokol Choir and the Jewish Folk Choir (est. 1910). The establishment of institutions that became today's professional orchestras occurred for the most part after the Depression (Winnipeg Symphony Orchestra 1948–; Edmonton Symphony Orchestra 1952–). Although light opera and theater were established relatively early and several cities boasted of turn-of-the-century opera houses (for example Winnipeg's Theatre and Opera House, established in 1883), professional opera companies first appeared after World War II.

The earliest competitive music festival in Canada was held in Edmonton in 1908, followed by another in Regina soon after. Competitions were sufficiently popular that by 1912 the Edmonton festival boasted of twenty-eight different competitive categories. Calgary and Winnipeg joined the festival frenzy, establishing their own events in 1918. Even today the competitive spirit is arguably more alive in Western Canada than in other regions of the country.

An internationally distinguished achievement in western Canada is the Banff Center for the Arts (est. 1933), positioned in a spectacular Rocky Mountain location (Leighton 1982). Its theaters, recording studios, galleries, and visual arts studios host senior artists from around the world. Among the innovative programs are its ballet and opera division (est. 1953); the International String Quartet Competition, established in 1983; jazz workshops, which were started in 1972; and a creative program for aboriginal musicians, dancers, and multimedia artists, which was begun in the 1990s.

An early wave of classical music composition included the Hindemith-influenced work of Violet Archer in Edmonton, the tonally rooted work of Malcolm Forsyth

(Calgary and Edmonton), and the rugged neoclassicism of Murray Adaskin (Saskatoon). Since the 1990s, the Winnipeg New Music festival has attracted international superstars and has become a leading edge new music event in the country. Composers associated with this festival, including Glenn Buhr and Gary Kulesha (both now Ontario-based), Patrick Carrabré, and others, draw on eclectic compositional sources, build on their modernist training without decrying accessibility, and have arguably created a new school of Canadian music.

The significance of western Canada within the history of jazz in Canada is just coming to light in the mid-1990s. The earliest black community moved to isolated parts of Alberta (Amber Valley and Wildwood) and Saskatchewan from Oklahoma, whose statehood in 1907 disenfranchised African Americans. The first jazz performance in the country by the New Orleans Creole Band in 1914 was in Winnipeg prior to tours to other western Canadian cities (Miller 1997). Vaudeville-based acts were sometimes referred to as "jaz" bands, an example being Edmonton's Morgan Brothers' Syncopated Jaz Band around 1917. In the 1920s, a Winnipeg musicians union ban on jazz proved ineffectual when the Allen Theatre began organizing jazz weeks not only in that western city but elsewhere in Canada. In the 1930s and 1940s Ollie Wagner, a longtime resident of northern Alberta, played a major role in several cities. Mart Kenney's Western Gentlemen was reputedly the most popular swing band of the 1940s. Jazz has continued to prove particularly popular in Edmonton and Saskatoon, sites since the 1980s in the chain of Du Maurier International Jazz Festivals across the nation.

Country and popular music

Arguably the musical tradition with the broadest public impact on the prairies is country music. Based in part on Métis fiddle styles mentioned earlier, in part influenced by Maritime Canadian–born artists such as Wilf Carter and Hank Snow, whose western Canadian tours were immensely successful, in part reflecting the popularity of American cowboy songs, and in part influenced by the various European folk practices in surrounding communities, country music in the prairie provinces has been diverse and dynamic. Between the 1930s and 1950s, fancifully named bands included Bob Boyd and the Red River Playboys (Winnipeg), Sleepy and Swede and the Tumbleweeds (Saskatoon), Cactus Mack and the Saddle Tramps (Calgary), Vic Siebert and the Sons of the Saddle (Calgary), and King Ganam and the Songs of the West (Edmonton). The popular tourist attraction the Calgary Stampede sponsored barbershop and country music events. More recently Colin James and k.d. lang are among the Prairie-born musicians who have kept the Canadian west on the country music map [see GENDERING MUSIC, p. 103]. Canadian country music has been described as lower-pitched and less nasal than that of the United States; the popularity of folk-influenced ballads is noted, as well as the influence of Ukrainian and Polish folk elements in the work of some songwriters and performers (Green and Miller 1992:322). The largest of many country music festivals is the Big Valley Jamboree (est. 1983) in Craven, Saskatchewan.

Calgary was the Chatauqua capital in the 1920s. It was during the period since the 1970s, however, that Manitoba in particular produced some popular musicians of unusual innovativeness, including the BTO (Bachman-Turner-Overdrive), the Guess Who, and the Crash Test Dummies; the same city gave both Joni Mitchell and Neil Young their professional starts.

British Columbia

Historical background

Canada's third largest province is unique in its geography, history, and social demography. Approximately 70 percent of the population resides in the Georgia Straits coastal area of the southwest (including the cities of Vancouver and Victoria, on Vancouver

Often depicted are the carved heraldic emblems and crests on totem poles, house fronts, and ceremonial regalia; elaborate theatrical performance of traditional myth by dancers in colorful button blankets, elaborately carved masks, and/or headdresses; and the validation of important events or relationships through feasting and gift giving at potlatches.

Island, and communities north of Vancouver). Residents of the north/south valleys (especially the fertile Okanagan valley) interact with American neighbors along these north/south lines. The Peace River community of the northeast is more closely related to Albertan than British Columbian culture. Similarly, in the far north, a community such as Atlin relates closely to Yukon culture.

While the British (for whom James Cook claimed the land in 1778) had a dominant presence until the mid-twentieth century and still influence the character of Victoria in particular, the ethnocultural profile of British Columbia is distinctive. Both inland and more widely known coastal First Nations (eight distinct language families) are vibrant and diverse. In the south-central regions around Kootenay are Doukhobor communities. The Asian legacy in British Columbia has a long history, beginning with Chinese miners in the Fraser Valley gold rushes of 1858 and the Klondike in the 1890s and laborers for the construction of the Canadian Pacific Railway. Japanese have made a major contribution to the fisheries industries. Since the 1970s, rapid expansion of population from Southeast Asia and South Asia, as well as the Pacific islands, has occurred. Asian citizens have suffered historically from severely discriminatory attitudes and policies. The Chinese Immigration Act banned Chinese immigrants between 1923 and 1947, effectively preventing family reunification and contributing to a downturn in the Asian population. Japanese citizens were forcibly confined in camps during World War II. In the 1980s and 1990s, however, Asian investors changed both the architectural and social face of Vancouver in particular and have become major community leaders.

Factors shaping the culture of British Columbia, then, include the history of interaction between British and Asian communities, including both the earlier suppression and contemporary leadership of the latter, and the richness of the First Nations cultures in the province, as well as the long history of outsider interest in their visual arts and performing traditions.

First Nations

As elsewhere in North America, the aboriginal people of British Columbia prefer their own names for themselves, although they are, in many cases, better known by names assigned (or misheard) by outsiders. Preferred spellings for the names of coastal people are as follows (Coull 1996):

> Haida language family: Haida
>
> Ktunaxa language family: Ktunaxa (have been called Kootenay or Kutenai)
>
> Tsimshian language family: Tsimshian, Gitgsan, Nisga'a (all sometimes referred to as Tsimshian)
>
> Wakashan language family: Haisla (Kitimat), Heiltsuk (Bella Bella), Oweekeno and Kwakwaka'wakw (Kwakiutl), Nuu-chac-nulth, Ditidaht, and Pacheenaht (Nootka)

Coast Salish language family: Nuxalk (Bella Coola); Klahoose, Homalco, Sliammon, Sechelt, Halq'emeylem, Sto:lo, Hul'qumi'num, Straits (all have been called Coast Salish); Squamish

Living in the interior of the province are the following people:

Athapaskan language family : Tsilhqot'in (Chilcotin), Dakelh and Wet'suwet'en (Carrier), Nat'oot'en (Babine/Carrier), Sekani, Dunne-za (Beaver), Dene-thah (Slave[y]), Tahltan, Kaska, Tagish, Tutchone

Interior Salish language family: St'at'imc (Lilloet), Nlaka'pamux (Thompson/ Couteau), Okanagan, Secwepemc (Shuswap)

Tlingit language family: Tlingit

First Nations in British Columbia did not for the most part sign treaties with colonial authorities. In the twentieth century, they struggled to control access to resources. Heralded as a new model for intergovernmental relationships and as the first modern land claim settlement in British Columbia was a 1999 agreement between the Nisga Nation and provincial and federal governments providing a land base, resource control, self-government, and independent courts.

The rich expressive culture of the Haida, Tlingit, Tsimshian, and Wakashan nations, in particular, has been the subject of numerous studies, photographic displays, and films. Often depicted are the imposing carved heraldic emblems and crests on totem poles, house fronts, and ceremonial regalia; elaborate theatrical performance of traditional myth and clan symbolism by dancers in colorful button blankets, elaborately carved masks, and/or headdresses; and the validation of important events or relationships through feasting and gift giving at potlatches (figure 5). Widely circulated photographs of Northwest Coast cultures such as those by Edward Curtis (Graybill and Boesen 1976) have been described as "a combination of ethnographic fidelity and all-American glamour" (Maud 1982:142). The U'mista Cultural Center has played a significant role in rectifying museum representation and film production. Their film *Potlatch: A Strict Law Bids Us Dance* (1975) includes images of the 1921 potlatch given by Chief Dan Cramner, after which forty-five prosecutions took place, as well as a 1974 event hosted by the Cramner family.

More than many other forms of aboriginal creative work, Northwest Coast expressive traditions have been more readily accepted as art by mainstream scholars (Reid 1987:203). In part this may relate to the visual impact of large pieces such as totem poles and house fronts, in part to the unquestioned influence of Haida and Nootka artists on European Canadian artists such as Emily Carr, and in part to the complexity and abstraction of design. The chiefs' raven rattles are an important example of this complexity and abstraction (Holm 1983). Artistic acclaim was earned by such artists as Mungo Martin in the 1940s and Bill Reid, Robert Davidson, and Lawrence Paul (to name only a few) since the 1960s. With such extensive attention, there is widespread awareness of the problems of cross-cultural "translation" and interpretation.

Ceremonial life was organized around a bifurcation of the year, with spring/ summer marked by extensive travel to facilitate fishing and hunting activities and fall/ winter marked by residence in permanent villages where ceremonial activity could best be conducted. Song specialists were in high demand during this period. The potlatch itself was banned along with the activities of associated dancing societies by the Canadian government in 1884, and ceremonial objects (many of which entered museum collections) were confiscated. Historian Olive P. Dickason explains that "the 'give-away' aspect of potlatches was held to be incompatible with Western economic practices

FIGURE 5   Some male Kwagiulth Dancers play frame drums and a log drum during a 1999 First Peoples Festival in Wa'waditla house, Victoria, British Columbia.

and inimical to the concept of 'private property'" (1992:286). A wave of potlatch-related arrests was particularly intense in 1918–1920. The dances were not eradicated, however, but were driven underground. The anti-potlatch law was repealed in 1951, after which time a renaissance of performance traditions has occurred.

On the northwest coast, complex aboriginal traditions of intellectual property have been negotiated differently in different eras. Some collectors have released recordings of traditional music for summer and winter ceremonials, clan songs, music associated with the myth of Baxbakwalanuxsiwae, which forms part of the *hamatsa* or chief-making ceremony, and mourning songs (Halpern 1967, 1981, 1986).

Coast and Interior Salish traditional song and dance are distinct in many regards from that of the more northerly Wakashan-speaking communities. The complex of practices relating to guardian spirit beliefs, renewed since the 1950s, and the more extensive influence of the Ghost Dance movement after the 1890s are historical differences. Published information about the music cultures of interior communities is less extensive. Among several recent Okanagan cultural initiatives is a monograph by storyteller Harry Robinson together with Wendy Wickwire (1989). The Sen Klip Theatre Company, blending traditional and modern arts, is acquiring an international profile.

With more northerly Dunna-ze people, anthropologist Robin Ridington (1988, 1990) has explored relationships between prophet dancing, dreaming, and singing, as well as between storied and experienced worlds.

An unusually strong interest in brass bands emerged in many British Columbian–based Native communities in the late nineteenth century, the earliest band instituted being the Metlakatla community band formed by missionary William Duncan in 1875 (McIntosh 1989:44–49). Nass River communities also have a longtime interest in band music; the Kincolith band and Nelson's [Silver] Cornet Band (figure 6) (named after conductor Job Nelson who also conducted at Kincolith for a period of time), for example, flourished from the 1880s, and the former endured into the 1970s. In the late twentieth century, British Columbia–based musicians such as David Campbell and Fara have had national recognition. Contemporary aboriginal music plays a major role on local radio stations such as "Mahowyah: The Aboriginal Voice" (FM 102.7, Vancouver).

European musical practices

In the eighteenth century British and Spanish interests in the area were in contestation. The Spanish, however, withdrew by 1795. Consequently the cultural infrastructure of the region was developed and largely controlled by British settlers, whose musical practices such as brass bands and English-language music theater have been well documented by Robert Dale McIntosh (1981, 1989). He observes that "in the nineteenth century, communities such as Vancouver and Victoria could support several community-based ensembles as well as at least one military band at the same time and Kamloops could boast three active bands at one point in its history" (1989:17). He documents over a century of existence for a number of ensembles such as the Nanaimo Silver Comet Band (est. 1872) and traces their role in marches, parades, and concerts under such bandmasters as William Haynes, Phillip Brandon, John Morris Finn, and, more recently, Arthur W. Delamont.

Choral music, often patronized by Christian churches, enjoyed a similarly significant role, with major choirs often predating their counterparts in Ontario, among them St. John's Choral Society, established in 1868 in Victoria, the Victoria Choral Society (1878), the New Westminster Choral Union (1882), the Vancouver Musical Club (1888), and the Arion Club's Male Voice Choir (1893). The Vancouver Bach Choir, formed in 1930 with founding conductor Herbert Mason Drost, is the longest continuous choral organization. Orchestras were later to develop; the earliest recorded

FIGURE 6 Nelson's Cornet Band of Port Simpson, British Columbia, in 1900, dressed in Tsimshian regalia. Photo courtesy the Vancouver Public Library.

by McIntosh was probably the Victoria Amateur Orchestra, founded in 1878. The "new" Vancouver Symphony Orchestra, directed by Allard de Ridder, emerged in 1930.

McIntosh suggests that musical theater and light opera has played an especially important role. The Vancouver Opera House (built in 1891) was one of many Canadian Pacific Railway–sponsored cultural projects. In the mid-twentieth century a distinctive performance venue was Vancouver's Stanley Park, where from 1936 to 1963 the Theatre under the Stars (TUTS) produced successful summer shows. Outdoor venues remain popular in the relative mildness of the Vancouver and Victoria climate. Smaller communities were hardly left behind, however, as demonstrated by such groups as the Summerland Singers and Players and indigenous productions by companies in Salmon Arm and Cowichan.

Doukhobors

This distinctive religious community, led by Peter Veregin, emigrated to Canada in 1899 and settled in south-central British Columbia as well as in many prairie communities. The Doukhobors left their Russian homeland because of religious persecution and opposition to their belief in pacifism. Establishing farming communes where they could maintain their spiritual practices, they have demonstrated their commitment to ideas of justice, compassion for all life, spiritual beauty, and social service, thus questioning "the right of material and institutional power," as Mark Mealing puts it (1995:39). Their religious precepts were collected in the *Book of Life* and transmitted by means of a capella choral singing.

Asians

Chinese

As mentioned earlier, the first wave of Cantonese-speaking Chinese, who arrived from Guangdong to work in gold mines in the 1850s and subsequently to build the Canadian Pacific Railway or seek their fortunes in the Klondike, were almost exclusively men. Despite the hard labor, extreme cold, illness, and racism in the newly emerging cities, a cultural community was able to sustain a distinctive way of life in the segregated community around Vancouver's Pendle Street area. This area remains the heart of the Chinese community in that city. Photographic evidence attests to the presence of Chinese orchestra and opera performances by the 1890s. Early performances not only effected a sense of community but raised money for community projects and relief work in Asia (Hoe 1989:30) (figure 7). After 1947, when wives and families of many

FIGURE 7   Ching Wong Musical Society, Vancouver, British Columbia, 1934. Photo courtesy Vancouver Public Library.

Japanese first immigrated to Canada in 1877, establishing a thriving community by 1940 in the Powell Street area. Interned during World War II following the attack on Pearl Harbor and subsequently dispersed across the country, the community struggled to regain its earlier stature and solidarity.

residents were finally able to immigrate to Canada, an emphasis on family celebration was able to develop for the first time. Under the umbrella of the Chinese Benevolent Society, many cultural, especially musical, associations developed.

In recent decades the Chinese community has expanded exponentially and become both more diversified and more economically powerful. Products of this diversification are new opera associations and dance troupes (the Lorita Leung Dance Studio is one of the best established). The Vancouver Chinese Music Ensemble (established in the 1980s) includes both Cantonese and musicians from more northerly regions. The Vancouver Chinese Choir Association celebrated its tenth anniversary in 1995 with the production of a new self-titled recording, made live at the Orpheus Theatre. By the 1990s, the Dr. Sun Yat Sen Classical Chinese Garden hosted an annual summer series of Asian musics and served as a venue for the Vancouver Jazz Festival. New styles of popular music flourish today in Vancouver, with songwriters such as Kokuho Rose Prohibited and Terry Watada, among others, articulating Asian experiences in Canada.

Japanese, Korean, South Asian, and Southeast Asian

Japanese first immigrated to Canada in 1877, establishing a thriving community by 1940 in the Powell Street area. Interned during World War II following the attack on Pearl Harbor and subsequently dispersed across the country, the community struggled to regain its earlier stature and solidarity. Since 1977, an annual Powell Street Festival commemorates the history of the original community. Contemporary Vancouver-based performance groups include the Kokoro Dance ensemble and several *taiko* drum ensembles, including the Katari Taiko drummers and Uzume.

Until the 1960s, Sikhs constituted the largest South Asian population in British Columbia; Qureshi (1972) notes at least seven *gurdwaras* 'temples' in the province, some established as early as the 1920s. Peacock (1970) has collected music from British Columbia Sikh communities in the late 1960s.

Concerts and festivals

British Columbia's concert life, especially that of Vancouver at the beginning of the twenty-first century, is vibrant. The Vancouver Chamber Choir (founding director Jon Washburn) and the women's choir Elektra (Morna Edmundson and Diane Loomer, co-directors) have international profiles and active recording schedules. The Vancouver Symphony Orchestra has been a leader in adopting new directions, such as collaboration with Celtic-rockers Spirit of the West, in recent times. The CBC Vancouver Orchestra remained the only CBC-sponsored orchestra in the 1980s. Little research to date has been done on early British Columbian composers such as George Sandrie, Frederick S. Bushell, William M. Cross, George Jennings Burnett, the Deloume family of Mill Bay, Jesse Longfield, Eugene Aubin, Job Nelson, Ezra Read, or Harry L. Stone. The first generation of widely influential composers in British Columbia included two notable women, Jean Coulthard and Barbara Pentland. Pentland's vigorous modernism, Coulthard's somewhat impressionistic sound idioms, the subtle folk influences in the choral music of Latvian Canadian Imant Raminsh, and the more romantically oriented minimalism of Michael Conway Baker are among the styles that coexist in the contemporary concert scene.

Vancouver is the birthplace of folk revivalist Ian Tyson and an important city in the career development of Bryan Adams, who got a start as the lead singer of the local rock band Sweeney Todd in the late 1970s before his successful songwriting contributions to Prism, Loverboy, and others. The alternative band Moist as well as jazz stylist Diane Krall are among the best known Vancouver-based artists.

Outdoor venues were mentioned earlier as particularly important during the Vancouver summer. The Vancouver Folk Festival (est. 1975), one of the oldest in the country, is based at Jericho Beach Park. Many venues for the Vancouver Jazz Festival are outdoors, as is the Merritt Mountain (Country) Music Festival, Victoria's Symphony Splash, at which the Victoria Symphony performs on a barge in the inner harbor, and the Caribbean Festival at Waterfront Park in North Vancouver.

The North: Yukon, Northwest Territories, and Nunavut

The three northernmost territories of Canada (the most recent, the territory of Nunavut created 1 April 1999) differ from the provinces demographically and politically. The majority of residents are Inuit, First Nations, and/or Métis, although natural resources have attracted many others to the North since the late nineteenth century. The musical traditions of Inuit, various First Nations, Métis, and nonaboriginal people as well as the unique history of broadcasting and the recent development of cultural institutions for performance, production, and recording are discussed elsewhere in this volume [see OVERVIEW, p. 1274; ARCTIC CANADA AND ALASKA, p. 374; SUBARCTIC CANADA, p. 383].

REFERENCES

Amtmann, Willy. 1975. *Music in Canada 1600–1800.* Montréal: Habitex.

Anthology of Canadian Music. 1978–1991. Canadian Broadcasting Corporation and Canadian Music Center. 39 boxed sets. Originally LP disks but rereleased as compact discs.

Applebaum, Louis, and Jacques Hebert. 1982. *Report of the Federal Cultural Policy Review Committee.* Ottawa: Minister of Supply and Services.

Barbeau, Marius. 1947. "Trois Beau Canards." *Archives de Folklore* 2:97–138.

Beckwith, John, and F. A. Hall, eds. 1988. *Musical Canada: Words and Music Honouring Helmut Kallmann.* Toronto: University of Toronto Press.

Bégin, Carmelle. 1992. *Opus: The Making of Musical Instruments in Canada.* Hull: Canadian Museum of Civilization.

Beland, Madeleine. 1982. *Chansons de voyageurs, couriers de bois, et forestiers.* Québec: Les Presses de l'Université Laval.

Berg, Wesley. 1985. *From Russia with Love: A Study of the Mennonite Choral Singing Tradition in Canada.* Winnipeg: Hyperion.

Berg, Wesley. 1986. "Music in Edmonton, 1880–1905." *Canadian University Music Review* 7:141–170.

Blakeley, Phyllis R. 1949. "The Theatre and Music in Halifax." *The Dalhousie Review* 29(1):8–20.

———. 1951. "Music in Nova Scotia 1605–1867." *The Dalhousie Review* 31(2):94–101; 31(3):223–230.

Blum, Stephen. 1987. "The Fuging Tune in British North America." *Sing Out the Glad News: Hymn Tunes in Canada.* CanMus Documents 1. Toronto: Institute for Canadian Music.

Brandhagen, William L. 1992. "Regina." In *Encyclopedia of Music in Canada,* 2nd ed., ed. Helmut Kallmann, Gilles Potvin, and Kenneth Winters, 1119–1120. Toronto: University of Toronto Press.

Brandhagen, William L., and Isabelle M. Mills. 1992. "Saskatoon." In *Encyclopedia of Music in Canada,* 2nd ed., ed. Helmut Kallmann, Gilles Potvin, and Kenneth Winters, 1180–1181. Toronto: University of Toronto Press.

Burlin, Natalie Curtis. 1968 [1907]. *The Indians Book.* New York: Dover.

Burrill, Gary, ed. 1992. *Away: Maritimers in Massachusetts, Ontario, and Alberta: An Oral History of Leaving Home.* Montréal: McGill-Queen's University Press.

Calderisi, Maria. 1981. *Music Publishing in the Canadas, 1800–1867.* Ottawa: National Library.

Carruthers, Glen, and Gordana Lazarevich, eds. 1996. *A Celebration of Canada's Arts 1930–1970.* Toronto: Canadian Scholars' Press.

Chan, Margaret. 1996. "The Yellow River Piano Concerto as a Site for Negotiating Cultural Space for a Diasporic Chinese Community in Toronto." Master's thesis, York University.

Cohen, Judith R. 1982. "Judeo-Spanish Traditional Songs in Montréal and Toronto." *Canadian Folk Music Journal/Revue de Musique Folklorique Canadienne* 10:40–47.

Cohnstaedt, Joy, and Yves Frenette, eds. 1997. *Canadian Cultures and Globalization/Cultures canadiennes et mondialisation.* Canadian Issues 19. Montréal: Association for Canadian Studies.

Coull, Cheryl. 1996. *A Traveller's Guide to Aboriginal B.C.* Vancouver: Whitecap Books.

Creighton, Helen. 1961. *Maritime Folk Songs.* Toronto: Ryerson.

———. 1966. *Songs and Ballads from Nova Scotia.* New York: Dover.

Cronk, M. S., comp. 1990. *The Sound of the Drum.* Brantford, Ont.: Woodland Cultural Center.

Diamond, Beverley. 1995. "Narratives in Canadian Music History. " In *Taking a Stand,* ed. Timothy McGee, 273–305. Toronto: University of Toronto Press.

Diamond, Beverley, and R. Witmer, eds. 1994. *Canadian Music: Issues of Hegemony and Identity.* Toronto: Canadian Scholars' Press.

Diamond, Beverley, et al. 1994. *Visions of Sound: Musical Instruments of First Nations Communities in Northeastern America.* Chicago: University of

Chicago Press, and Waterloo: Wilfrid Laurier University Press.

Diamond Cavanagh, Beverley. 1989. "Writing about Music and Gender in the Sub-Arctic Algonkian Area." In *Women in North American Indian Music: Six Essays*, ed. Richard Keeling, 55–66. SEM Special Series, no. 6. Bloomington, Ind.: Society for Ethnomusicology.

Dickason, Olive P. 1992. *Canada's First Nations: A History of Founding Peoples from Earliest Times*. Toronto: McClelland and Stewart.

Drakich, Janice, et al., eds. 1995. *With a Song in Her Heart: A Celebration of Canadian Women Composers*. Windsor: University of Windsor Humanities Research Group.

Dunlay, Kate, and David Greenberg. 1996. *Traditional Celtic Violin Music of Cape Breton*. Toronto: DunGreen Music.

Einarsson, Magnús. 1992. *Icelandic-Canadian Memory Lore*. Ottawa: Canadian Museum of Civilization.

Etienne, Mona, and Eleanor Leacock, eds. 1980. *Women and Colonization: Anthropological Perspectives*. New York: Praeger.

Fedyk, I. Teodor. 1927 [1911]. *Pisni imigrantiv pro staryi i novyi krai*. (Immigrant Songs of the Old and New Country). Winnipeg: Nakladom Ukains'koi Kniharni.

Fewkes, Jesse. 1890. "A Contribution to Passamaquoddy Folklore." *Journal of American Folklore* 3.

Fleming, Lee, ed. 1997. *Rock, Rhythm and Reels: Canada's East Coast Musicians on Stage*. Charlottetown: Ragweed Press.

Fowke, Edith. 1988. *Canadian Folklore*. Toronto: Oxford University Press.

Gallat-Morin, Elisabeth. 1988. *Un manuscrit de musique française classique; étude critique et historique: Le Livre d'orgue de Montréal*. Montréal: Les Presses de l'Université de Montréal.

Gallaugher, Annemarie. 1995. "Constructing Caribbean Culture in Toronto: The Representation of Caribana." In *The Reordering of Culture: Latin America, the Caribbean and Canada in the Hood*, ed. Alvina Ruprecht and Cecilia Taiana, 397–408. Ottawa: Carleton University Press.

Garrison, Virginia. 1985. "Traditional and Non-Traditional Teaching and Learning Practices in Folk Music: An Ethnographic Field Study of Cape Breton." Ph.D. dissertation, University of Wisconsin.

Gasher, Mike. 1997. "From Sacred Cows to White Elephants: Cultural Policy Under Siege." In *Canadian Cultures and Globalization/Cultures canadiennes et mondialisation,* ed. Joy Cohnstaedt and Yves Frenette, 13–30. Canadian Issues 19. Montréal: Association for Canadian Studies.

Gasser, Alan. 1996. Notes to *Introduction to Canadian Music* (Orchestral music, Choral Music, Chamber Music, Electroacoustic Music). Naxos 8.550171-2. 2 compact discs.

Gesser, Samuel. 1994. Notes to *A Folksong Portrait of Canada/Un portrait folklorique*. Folkways/Polygram. 3 compact discs.

Gibbons, Roy. 1981. *Folk Fiddling in Canada: A Sampling*. Ottawa: National Museums.

Gilmore, John. 1989. *Who's Who of Jazz in Montréal: Ragtime to 1970*. Montréal: Véhicule Press.

Giroux, Robert. 1984. *Les Aires de la Chanson Québécoise*. Montréal: Editions Triptyque.

Grant, John N. 1980. *Black Nova Scotians*. Halifax: Nova Scotia Museum.

Graybill, Florence Curtis, and Victor Boesen. 1976. *Edward Sheriff Curtis*. New York: Crowell.

Grenier, Line. 1996. "Making Music Matter: The Effectivity of the *Chanson Dispositif* in Québec." Paper delivered at the Inaugural Conference on Culture and Citizenship at the Australian Key Center for Cultural and Media Policy.

Guertin, Marcelle, ed. 1984. *Musique contemporaine au Québec*. Montréal: Diffusion parallèle.

Hall, Frederick. 1973. "Musical Life in Windsor, 1875–1901." *Canada Music Book* 6:11–24.

———. 1974. "Hamilton 1846–1946: A Century of Music." *Journal of the Canadian Association of University Schools of Music* 4(1–2):98–114.

———. 1983. "Musical Life in Eighteenth-Century Halifax." *Canadian University Music Review* 4:278–307.

———. 1987. "Musical Yankees and Tories in Maritime Settlements of Eighteenth-Century Canada." *American Music* 5(4):391–402.

Halpern, Ida. 1967. Notes to *Indian Music of the Pacific Northwest Coast*. Folkways FE 4523. LP disks.

———. 1974. *Nootka Indian Music of the Pacific Northwest Coast*. Folkways FE 4524. LP disk.

———. 1981. *Kwakiutl Indian Music of the Pacific Northwest*. Folkways FE 4122. LP disk.

———. 1986. *Haida Indian Music of the Pacific Northwest*. Folkways FE 4119. LP disk.

Halpert, Herbert, and G. M. Story. 1990 [1969]. *Christmas Mumming in Newfoundland*. Toronto: University of Toronto Press.

Handler, Richard. 1988. *Nationalism and the Politics of Culture in Québec*. Madison: University of Wisconsin Press.

Hatch, Peter, and J. Beckwith, eds. 1991. *The Fifth Stream*. Toronto: Institute for Canadian Music.

Henry, Frances. 1975. "Black Music in the Maritimes." *Canadian Folk Music Journal/Revue de Musique Folklorique Canadienne* 3:3–10.

Here and Now/En nos temps et lieux: A Celebration of Canadian Music/Une Célébration de la Musique Canadienne. 1995. Music of the First Peoples and Folk Music, Classical Music, Jazz and World Music, Artists and Styles of Historical Importance. The Canada Council, produced in partnership with the Canadian Broadcasting Corporation CDSP 4510, 4511, 4512, 4513. 4 compact discs.

Hoe, Ban Seng. 1989. *Beyond the Golden Mountain: Chinese Cultural Traditions in Canada*. Ottawa: Canadian Museum of Civilization.

Holm, Bill. 1983. *The Box of Daylight: Northwest Coast Indian Art*. Vancouver: Douglas and McIntyre.

Hornby, James. 1988. *Black Islanders*. Charlottetown: Institute for Island Studies.

Humbert, Stephen. 1801. *Union Harmony*. Saint John: Stephen Humbert.

Ives, Edward D. 1964. *Larry Gorman: The Man Who Made the Songs*. Fredericton: Goose Lanes Press.

———. 1978. *Joe Scott: The Woodsman-Songmaker*. Urbana: University of Illinois Press.

Jennings, N. 1997. *Before the Gold Rush: Flashbacks to the Dawn of the Canadian Sound*. New York: Viking.

Jin Pei, Huang, and Alan R. Thrasher. 1993. "Cantonese Music Societies of Vancouver: A Social and Historical Survey." *Canadian Folk Music Journal/Revue de Musique Folklorique Canadienne* 21:31–39.

Joyal, Jean-Pierre. 1980. "Le Processus de composition dans la musique instrumental du Québec." *Canadian Folk Music Journal/Revue de Musique Folklorique Canadienne,* 8:49–53.

Kallmann, Helmut. 1969 [1960]. *A History of Music in Canada 1534–1914*. Toronto: University of Toronto Press.

Kallmann, Helmut, Gilles Potvin, and Kenneth Winters, eds. 1992. *Encyclopedia of Music in Canada*. 2nd ed. Toronto: University of Toronto Press.

Keillor, Elaine. 1988. "Musical Activity in Canada's New Capital City in the 1870s." In *Musical Canada: Words and Music Honouring Helmut Kallmann,* ed. John Beckwith and F. A. Hall, 115–133. Toronto: University of Toronto Press.

Kelly, Wayne. 1991. *Downright Upright: A History of the Canadian Piano Industry*. Toronto: National Heritage/National History Inc.

Klymasz, Robert B. 1970. *An Introduction to the Ukrainian Canadian Immigrant Folksong Cycle*. Ottawa: National Museums.

———. 1971. *The Ukrainian Winter Folksong Cycle*. Ottawa: National Museums.

———. 1989. *The Ukrainian Folk Ballad in Canada*. Transcriptions by Ken Peacock, New York: AMS Press.

———. 1992. *Svieto: Celebrating Ukrainian Canadian Ritual in East Central Alberta through the Generations*. Edmonton: Alberta Culture and Multiculturalism, Historical Resources Division.

Labbé, Gabriel. 1977. *Les Pionniers du disque folklorique québécois, 1920–1950*. Montréal: L'Aurore.

Lederman, Anne. 1991. "Old Indian and Métis Fiddling in Manitoba: Origins, Structure, and Question of Syncretism. *Canadian Folk Music Journal/Revue de Musique Folklorique Canadienne* 18:40–60.

Lefebvre, Marie-Thérèse. 1991. *La Création musicale des femmes au Québec*. Montréal: Les éditions du remue-ménage.

Leighton, David. 1982. *Artists, Builders and Dreamers: 50 Years at the Banff School*. Toronto: McClelland and Stewart.

Lescarbot, Marc. 1907–1914 [1618]. *The History of New France*. Trans. W. L. Grant. 3 vols. Toronto: Champlain Society.

Levine, Lawrence. 1988. *Highbrow/Lowbrow: The Emergence of Cultural Hierarchy in America.* Cambridge: Harvard University Press.

Lutz, Maja. 1982. *Musical Traditions of the Labrador Coast Inuit.* Ottawa: National Museums.

MacInnes, Sheldon. 1997. *A Journey in Celtic Music: Cape Breton Style.* Sydney: University College of Cape Breton Press.

MacMillan, Keith and John Beckwith, eds. 1975. *Contemporary Canadian Composers.* Toronto: Oxford University Press.

Magocsi, Paul R., ed. 1999. *Encyclopedia of Canada's Peoples.* Toronto: University of Toronto Press.

Massey, Vincent, and R. Levesque. 1951. *Report of the Royal Commission on Development in the Arts, Letters and Sciences, 1949–51.* Ottawa: King's Printer.

Maud, Ralph. 1982. *A Guide to B.C. Indian Myth and Legend.* Vancouver: Talonbooks.

McArthur, Patricia. 1987. *Dances of the Northern Plains.* Saskatoon: Saskatchewan Indian Cultural Center.

McGee, Timothy J. 1969. "Music in Halifax 1749–1799." *The Dalhousie Review* 49(3): 377–387.

———. 1985. *The Music of Canada.* New York: Norton.

———, ed. 1995. *Taking a Stand: Essays in Honour of John Beckwith.* Toronto: University of Toronto Press.

McIntosh, Robert Dale. 1981. *A Documentary History of Music in Victoria, British Columbia. Vol. 1: 1850–1899.* Victoria: University of Victoria.

———. 1989. *History of Music in British Columbia 1850–1950.* Victoria: Sono Nis Press.

———. 1994. *A Documentary History of Music in Victoria, British Columbia. Vol. II: 1900–1950.* Victoria: Beach Holme Publishers.

McIntosh, Robert Dale, and Wesley Berg. 1992. "Edmonton." In *Encyclopedia of Music in Canada,* 2nd ed., ed. Helmut Kallmann, Gilles Potvin, and Kenneth Winters, 403–404. Toronto: University of Toronto Press.

McIntyre, Paul. 1976. *Black Pentecostal Music in Windsor.* Ottawa: National Museums.

McKay, Ian. 1994. *The Quest of the Folk: Antimodernism and Cultural Selection in Twentieth-Century Nova Scotia.* Montréal and Kingston: McGill-Queen's University Press.

Mealing, Mark F. 1995. "Doukhobor Psalms: Adornment to the Soul." In *Spirit Wrestlers: Centennial Papers in Honour of Canada's Doukhobor Heritage,* ed. Koozma J. Tarasoff and Robert B. Klymasz, 39–50. Ottawa: Canadian Museum of Civilization.

Mechling, William H. 1958–1959. "The Malecite Indians, with Notes on the Micmacs, 1916." *Anthropologica* 7:1–160; 8:161–274.

Miller, Mark. 1997. *Such Melodious Racket: The Lost History of Jazz in Canada, 1914–1949.* Toronto: Mercury Press.

Morey, Carl. 1984. "The Beginnings of Modernism in Toronto." In *Célébration,* ed. Godfrey Ridout and Talivaldis Kenins, 80–86. Toronto: Canadian Music Center.

———. 1985. "Music and Modernism: Toronto 1920–1950." In *Regionalism and National Identity,* ed. Reginald Berry and James Acheson, 117–125. Christchurch, New Zealand: Association for Canadian Studies in Australia and New Zealand.

———. 1988. "Orchestras and Orchestral Repertoire in Toronto before 1914." In *Musical Canada: Words and Music Honouring Helmut Kallmann,* ed. J. Beckwith and F. Hall, 100–114. Toronto: University of Toronto Press.

Morey, Carl, and Helmut Kallman. 1992. "Toronto." In *Encyclopedia of Music in Canada,* 2nd ed., ed. Helmut Kallmann, Gilles Potvin, and Kenneth Winters, 1292–1296. Toronto: University of Toronto Press.

Morey, Carl, comp. 1997. *Music in Canada: A Research and Information Guide.* New York and London: Garland Publishing, Inc.

Oh! What a Feeling: A Vital Collection of Canadian Music, 25 years of Juno Award Winners. 1996. Canadian Academy of Recording Arts and Sciences JUNO 251-4. 4 compact discs.

Ornstein, Lisa. 1982. "Instrumental Folk Music of Québec: An Introduction." *Canadian Folk Music Journal/Revue de Musique Folklorique Canadienne* 10: 3–11.

Peacock, Kenneth. 1965a. *Songs of the Newfoundland Outports.* 3 vols. Ottawa: National Museums.

———. 1965b. *A Survey of Ethnic Folk Music across Western Canada.* Ottawa: National Museums.

———. 1970. *Songs of the Doukhobors.* Ottawa: National Museums.

Peck, Mary Biggar. 1992. *A Full House and Fine Singing: Diaries and Letters of Sadie Harper Allen.* Fredericton: Goose Lane Editions.

Perkins, Simeon. 1969. *The Diary of Simeon Perkins.* New York: Greenwood Press.

Pevere, Geoff, and Greig Dymond. 1996. *Mondo Canuck: A Canadian Pop Culture Odyssey.* Scarborough, Ont.: Prentice-Hall.

Posen, I. Sheldon. 1993. "The Beginnings of the Children's (Folk) Music Industry in Canada: An Overview." *Canadian Folk Music Journal/Revue de Musique Folklorique Canadienne* 21:19–30.

Preston, Richard. 1976. *Cree Narrative: Expressing the Personal Meaning of Events.* Ottawa: National Museums.

Proctor, George A. 1980. *Canadian Music of the Twentieth Century.* Toronto: University of Toronto Press.

Quigley, Colin. 1985. *Close to the Floor: Folk Dance in Newfoundland.* St. John's: Memorial University of Newfoundland, Folklore Department.

Qureshi, Regula. 1972. "Ethnomusicological Research among Canadian Communities of Arab and East Indian Origin." *Ethnomusicology* 16(3):381–396.

Ramirez, Bruno. 1989. *The Italians in Canada.* Canada's Ethnic Groups, Booklet 14. Ottawa: Canadian Historical Association.

Reid, Martine. 1987. "Silent Speakers: Arts of the Northwest Coast." In *The Spirit Sings,* 201–236. Calgary: Glenbow Museum.

Rice, Timothy. 1992. "Croatia." In *Encyclopedia of Music in Canada,* 2nd ed., ed. Helmut Kallmann, Gilles Potvin, and Kenneth Winters, 333. Toronto: University of Toronto Press.

Ridington, Robin. 1988. *Trail to Heaven: Knowledge and Narrative in a Northern Native Community.* Vancouver: Douglas and McIntyre.

———. 1990. *Little Bit Know Something: Stories in a Language of Anthropology.* Vancouver: Douglas and McIntyre.

Ridout, Godfrey, and Talivaldis Kenins, eds. 1984. *Célébration.* Toronto: Canadian Music Center.

Robinson, Harry, and Wendy Wickwire. 1989. *Write It on Your Heart: The Epic World of an Okanagan Storyteller.* Vancouver: Talon Books/Thetus.

Rogers, Tim B. 1990. "Country Music Bands in Canada during the 1950s: A Comparative Survey." In *Ethnomusicology in Canada,* ed. Robert Witmer, 226–234. CanMus Documents 5. Toronto: Institute for Canadian Music.

Rosenberg, Neil V. 1994a. "Ethnicity and Class: Black Country Music in the Maritimes." In *Canadian Music: Issues of Hegemony and Identity,* ed. Beverley Diamond and Robert Witmer, 417–446. Toronto: Canadian Scholars' Press.

———. 1994b. "Don Messer's Modern Canadian Fiddle Canon." *Canadian Folk Music Journal/Revue de Musique Folklorique Canadienne* 22:23–35.

Sarkissian, Margaret. 1990. "The Politics of Music: Armenian Community Choirs in Toronto." In *Ethnomusicology in Canada,* ed. Robert Witmer, 98–105. CanMus Documents 5. Toronto: Institute for Canadian Music.

Schabas, Ezra. 1994. *Sir Ernest MacMillan: The Importance of Being Canadian.* Toronto: University of Toronto Press.

Seguin, Robert-Lionel. 1986. *La danse traditionnelle à Québec.* Québec: Les Presses de l'Université du Québec.

Simcoe, Mrs. John Graves. 1973 [1911]. *The Diary of Mrs. John Graves Simcoe, 1792–1796.* Toronto: Coles.

Simon, Sherry. 1996. "National Membership and Forms of Contemporary Belonging in Québec." In *Language, Culture and Values in Canada at the Dawn of the 21st Century,* 121–132. Ottawa: International Council for Canadian Studies.

Stewardson, Richard G. 1994. "Hattie Rhue Hatchett (1863–1958): An Interdisciplinary Study of Her Life and Music in North Buxton, Ontario." Master's thesis, York University.

Subtelny, Orest. 1991. *Ukrainians in North America: An Illustrated History.* Toronto: University of Toronto Press.

Sugarman, Jane. 1997. *Embodied Subjectivities: Singing and Subjectivity at Prespa Albanian Weddings.* Chicago: University of Chicago Press.

Taft, Michael. 1993. "Syncretizing Sound: The Emergence of Canadian Popular Music." In *The*

Beaver Bites Back? American Popular Culture in Canada, ed. David H. Flaherty and Frank E. Manning, 197–208. Montréal and Kingston: McGill-Queen's University Press.

Tarasoff, Koozma J., and Robert B. Klymasz. 1995. *Spirit Wrestlers: Centennial Papers in Honour of Canada's Doukhobor Heritage.* Ottawa: Canadian Museum of Civilization.

Temperley, Nicholas. 1995. "Worship Music in English-Speaking North America, 1608–1820." In *Taking a Stand: Essays in Honour of John Beckwith,* ed. Timothy J. McGee, 166–184. Toronto: University of Toronto Press.

Thwaites, Reuben G. 1896–1901. *The Jesuit Relations and Allied Documents.* Cleveland: Burrows.

Tippett, Maria. 1990. *Making Culture: English-Canadian Institutions and the Arts before the Massey Commission.* Toronto: University of Toronto Press.

Trowsdale, G. Campbell. 1984. "The Furthest West: The Beginnings of Modernism in Vancouver." In *Célébration,* ed. Godfrey Ridout and Talivaldis Kenins, 87–98. Toronto: Canadian Music Center.

Vennum, Thomas. 1982. *The Ojibwe Dance Drum.* Washington, D.C.: Library of Congress.

Voyer, Simonne. 1986. *La Danse traditionelle dans l'est du Canada: Quadrilles et cotillons.* Québec: Les Presses de l'Université Laval.

Wallis, Wilson D., and Ruth S. Wallis. 1955. *The Micmac Indians of Eastern Canada.* Minneapolis: University of Minneapolis Press.

———. 1957. *The Malecite Indians of New Brunswick.* Ottawa: National Museums.

Weale, David. 1988. *A Stream out of Lebanon.* Charlottetown: Institute of Island Studies.

Wheeler, Dennis. 1975. *Potlatch: A Strict Law Bids Us Dance.* Vancouver: U'Mista Cultural Center.

White, Paul, prod. 1990. *Made in Canada: Our Rock and Roll History.* BMG Canada KCD1-7156, 7157, 7158, 7159. 4 Compact discs.

Witmer, Robert. 1982. *The Musical Life of the Blood Indians.* Ottawa: National Museums.

Witmer, Robert, ed. 1990. *Ethnomusicology in Canada.* CanMus Documents 5. Toronto: Institute for Canadian Music.

Woodford, Paul, 1988. *'We Love the Place, O Lord.'* St. John's, Newfoundland: Creative Publishers.

Zemans, Joyce. 1997. *Where Is Here? Canadian Cultural Policy in a Globalized World.* Toronto: Robarts Center for Canadian Studies, York University.

Snapshot:
Four Views of Music in Canada

Jody Berland
Mark Miller
Beverley Diamond
Neil V. Rosenberg

Radio—Jody Berland
Jazz 1914–1949—Mark Miller
The Canadian Musical Heritage Society—Beverley Diamond
Whose Music Is Canadian Country Music?—Neil V. Rosenberg

Following are four different views of music and musical activity that are uniquely Canadian. They do not, of course, represent the total picture of musical life in Canada but were chosen because each discusses a specific social and musical context that helps define Canada as a country. The reader is encouraged to consult cross-referenced articles within this one for further information about many related musical activities.

RADIO

Radio has played a pivotal role in the history and dissemination of music in Canada. The establishment of a strong professional apparatus for the creation of concert music came about only after the formation of the public radio network; the recording industry became accessible to Canadian musicians only with the financial intervention of Canada's commercial broadcasters. These idiosyncrasies explain much of Canada's musical culture. Since 1932 broadcasters have been required by legislation to promote and support Canadian culture and artists. This requirement, inspired by the early dominance of American radio and recorded music and now administered by the Canadian Radio-Television and Telecommunications Commission (CRTC), has been unevenly observed but largely successful. Radio continues to be an important part of musical culture in Canada. Today 95 percent of Canadians spend an average of twenty-two hours weekly listening to radio; radio listening far exceeds the time Canadians spend reading books, newspapers, and periodicals. Over 70 percent of broadcast time is dedicated to music (Filion 1996).

Canadian Broadcasting Corporation (CBC)

Between the 1936 founding of the CBC and the late 1950s, the CBC was the primary patron and commissioner of diverse musical works in Canada. Because recording was negligible, private patronage minimal, touring prohibitively expensive, and the public a small one, radio was central to the forming of a professional musical culture. Many ensembles and works were developed specifically for radio performance, and radio

Canada's radio was transformed by a sharpened demarcation between "light" and "serious" music, the growing dominance of commercial radio, and, after television, the change from block to format programming in commercial radio in response to the invention of the hit parade in the United States and the proliferation of competing radio services in Canada.

became the dominant site of interaction among composers, musicians, and audiences. Most Canadians heard their first orchestral or live band performances on the CBC. Access to radio time became more valuable—in both monetary and prestige terms—than performance alone, and Canadian composers lobbied for increased radio time. At the same time, opera, choir, orchestral, and instrumental concerts grew more distinct in organization and repertoire; this specialization led to a broadening of repertoire to include lesser-known works by familiar composers and greater marginalization of works and styles outside the classical canon. Works written and performed by Canadians tended to retain stylistic traits out of fashion in their country of origin.

The CBC introduced many contemporary works when local performers were still reluctant to confront them. They introduced a number of composers successfully established in Europe, including Schoenberg and most notably Stravinsky, who guest conducted a number of his own works with the CBC Symphony Orchestra (1952–1964). Ten recordings of works conducted by the composer were released on record by the CBC, including "4 Etudes for Orchestra," "Scenes de ballet," "Symphony of Psalms, and Symphony in C." This encounter encouraged commissions of Canadian compositions and performances. Indeed, "No other single organization," the *Encyclopedia of Music in Canada* maintains, "has played so large a role in making Canadians and the outside world aware of Canadian cultural pursuits and in helping these to flourish . . . no other organization is acknowledged as often as the CBC, whether as a performance medium, an employer, a sponsor, or a discoverer of talent" (Kallmann, Potvin, and Winters, 1992:166).

Performances by Canadian performers were common through the 1940s and 1950s, and there was a higher proportion of original Canadian composition during that period than there is today. The CBC Symphony Orchestra gave a weekly broadcast of classical and contemporary works from 1952 to 1964. The greatest proportion of music broadcast on the CBC, however, was that classified as "light music"; neither the CBC nor its listeners yet perceived the CBC as an alternative to commercial broadcasting. The CBC's weekly schedule included jazz, folk and traditional, choral and religious, and other light musics as well as classical music. After the advent of television and the delineation of a narrower role for public radio in relation to commercial radio, "serious" drama and music continued on CBC radio—now unique in North America—but no longer buttressed by the popular appeal of the lighter mass programming. Emphasis shifted from studio broadcasts to recorded music. By the 1970s the audience for CBC's serious music programming had shrunk to a small percentage of Canadian listeners (Berland 1986).

Both CBC Radio One (primarily talk, with some concerts, interviews, and evening music programs) and Radio Two ("classics and beyond," with an after-midnight pop-experimental-alternative music program modeled on community radio) remain free from the constraints of advertising and can offer programs that do not have to compete with commercial radio for audience shares. However, marginal ratings have rendered the CBC vulnerable to budget cuts in an era of government downsizing. The

CBC now has coproduction relationships with many Canadian arts organizations that save money and enable the CBC to make its tax-supported productions available as both broadcasts and public events. Since 1945 the CBC has produced excellent recordings of Canadian music performances for broadcasters worldwide, first under RCI (Radio Canada International) and, after 1966, under the labels CBC-SM and CBC-LM. These record and distribute concerts by leading Canadian performers and ensembles and by top names in light music, jazz, and pop music in Canada.

Commercial radio

Canada's radio was transformed by a sharpened demarcation between "light" and "serious" music, the growing dominance of commercial radio, and, after television, the change from block to format programming in commercial radio in response to the invention of the hit parade in the United States and the proliferation of competing radio services in Canada. By the mid-1950s, Canadian stations were switching format to follow the example of U.S. broadcasters. Adaptation of the American model was achieved through the regulation of radio formats and the enforcement of regulations through licensing.

Format is a determining component of the license, which specifies, besides the style of music, the minimum percentage of Canadian music, the proportion and the type of advertisement, the maximum number of repetitions of a composition per week, and the programming styles of stations. CRTC regulation divides music into two categories, music/general, and music/traditional and special interests. The first category includes five subdivisions: popular music and soft rock, popular music and hard rock, country, folk-oriented, and jazz-oriented musics. These make up the programming of most commercial radio.

In 1984 the CRTC simplified FM radio formats, gathering them into four main groups: (1) softer music: from instrumental to middle-of-the-road (MOR) and soft rock, including easy listening; (2) rock: hard rock and "accentuated" popular music; (3) country music; (4) other kinds: includes folk oriented and jazz oriented.

The second category includes classical music, opera (*operette* and *théâtre lyrique*), folk, jazz, and nonclassical religious music.

Broadcasters seeking an FM license or license renewal must prove the viability and need for their chosen format in the particular city and promise to devote 70 percent of music programming to the music of that format. When applying for an FM license or a license renewal, broadcasters sign a "promise of performance" that lists their programming obligations: the type and range of music to be programmed, the intended percentage of Canadian content ("Cancon" regulations), maximum repeat quotas for hits, proportions of hits to other musical selections (Canadian selections are exempt from the 50 percent limit), amount of "foreground" programming, and so on. Such regulation aims to maintain musical diversity, given an increasingly competitive market and the tendency for broadcasters to duplicate successful formats as long as they can draw sufficient advertising revenue. It aims to improve the balance between viable market conditions and nonmarket cultural objectives like musical diversity and Canadian content.

As a condition of license (and to ensure enough Canadian recordings to fulfill the Cancon quotas), radio stations are required to demonstrate support for local music talent. In 1982 CHUM Limited (owner of a multi-city group of pop radio stations, and later of MuchMusic, Canada's national music video channel), Moffat Communications, Rogers Broadcasting Limited, CIRPA (The Canadian Independent Record Producers Association), and CMPA (the Canadian Music Publishers Association) together created FACTOR, the Fund to Assist Canadian Talent on Record. FACTOR's francophone equivalent is Musicaction. Through FACTOR's juried support for music recording, touring, and promotion, commercial broadcasters subsidize the Canadian music industry. FACTOR has proven highly effective, particularly in supporting French-language music in Québec. Canadians thus hear more music by Canadian artists and buy more Canadian recorded music and by the mid-1990s were celebrating the national success of popular performers like Tragically Hip and Barenaked Ladies. Some critics argue that protectionism limits the ability of indigenous companies and artists to compete outside Canada. Cancon regulations and the subsidization of the recording industry cannot produce a competitive Canadian recording industry, they argue, because these mechanisms have evolved into means of improving Canadian musicians' chances in a global industry dominated by the multinationals (Wright 1991).

Community radio

Soon after its establishment in 1968 the CRTC developed a policy for community programming on cable and welcomed the arrival of community radio. The first campus–community station, CKWR-FM, was incorporated in Kitchener-Waterloo, Ontario, and licensed in 1973. Today community radio takes three forms: (1) Native radio, mainly serving communities in the North; (2) student radio, broadcast university campuses with programming that often includes material produced and intended for reception by communities in the area; and (3) community radio, which took as its model the American Pacifica network of community stations modeled, in turn, on the CBC.

Native radio

The Native Communications Program and the Northern Native Broadcast Access Program, both publicly funded, support a network of stations across northern Canada operating in aboriginal languages. There are only two nonaboriginal English-speaking community stations outside Québec—in Kingston and Vancouver. Other English-speaking community stations are actually campus stations with community outreach. Fewer than 10 percent of Canada's more than one thousand three hundred radio stations are community radio stations. The National Campus Radio Organization produces a newsletter, a website, policy briefs for the CRTC, and conferences for member stations.

Campus–community radio

Campus–community radio is "committed to providing alternative radio to an audience that is recognized as being diverse in ethnicity, culture, gender, sexual orientation, age and physical and mental ability" (NCCRA 1987:1). Unique among urban broadcasters in their willingness to commit program time and promotion to local, independent musicians and multicultural communities, they consequently receive many cassette tapes and local recordings, including high-quality music on disc and recorded at concerts, without the mediation of the large record companies. Volunteer music programmers are specialists who seek to contextualize the music within a group's culture. Weekly programs offer several hours of continuous programming, wherein long sequences of music are interspersed with information concerning histories and issues affecting that music. Programmers encourage listener participation in music selection and promote local live performance.

Program slots may include music in many different categories—local, experimental (electronic and improvisational) jazz, black (current and "roots"), women's, gay and lesbian, ethnic ("pan-ethnic fourth world"), funk, reggae, classical and contemporary classical, folk and traditional, hardcore or "aggressive rock," blues, contemporary Christian, and gospel—as well as spoken/poetic word. These stations are primarily government funded but also draw on limited advertising revenues and listeners' support. They help to build communities or "scenes" whose loyal networks of musicians and fans are also important resources for national and international recording companies (Straw 1996).

Radio art

Canada's Glenn Gould and Murray Schafer are renowned not only for, respectively, award-winning piano recordings and world class composition and important writings on music, technology, and soundscape ecology, but also for contributing to the emergence of a new genre of radio art. Gould's 1967 seminal *Idea of North,* produced by the CBC, employs the contrapuntal structure of a fugue to arrange voices and sounds of people traveling by train to northern Canada. Other radio art explores urban and rural soundscapes, the expression of interior landscapes, montage, live performance, travel, and the political aesthetics of technology. The Banff Center for Fine Art, McGill University Radio, Vancouver's Co-op Radio, Toronto's Music Gallery, the Media Arts Section of the Canada Council, the Canadian Society for Independent Radio Production (http://www.web.net/csirp/index.html), and many artist-run galleries and campus–community stations have advanced practices that use radio as a medium for artworks.

New directions

New technologies like satellite, cable, and digital audio continue to transform radio and its acoustic communities. Canada's Department of Industry proposes to transform the radio spectrum into the digital audio format over the next decade, in part to support Canada's leading research and investment in digital audio technologies. An increasing number of cable systems in Canada offer radio signals. In the nearly five hundred areas where radio services are delivered via cable, the ratio of distant Canadian signals to local is 2 to 1. With the addition of U.S. radio signals offered by cable television systems, the ratio of distant radio signals to local radio signals increases to 2.5 to 1. New cable specialty services, now basic service in most Canadian homes, provide programming in areas where radio has traditionally been strong: news, weather, music and sports. This will further fragment the radio environment.

Over one hundred stations now relay rock or country music programs by satellite from the Canadian Radio Networks (CRN). Programs are live, DJ-hosted, cheap and continuous; they replicate local stations stylistically but function to replace them along with local DJs and staffs. As technology continues to transform radio, the soundscapes of community radio will increase in importance as a place for musical expression and innovation among Canada's diverse musical communities.

—JODY BERLAND

JAZZ 1914–1949

Typically, the early history of jazz in Canada is a history of jazz in the major cities, each an insular "scene" with only tenuous links to the others (figure 1). The connections that were so important to early American jazz history—between New Orleans and Chicago, Chicago and New York, and later Kansas City and New York—had few if any parallels in Canada, where musicians generally limited themselves to their own regions. Those of a mind to advance their careers looked to the United States as often as they looked elsewhere in Canada.

Musicians in Montréal and Toronto, for example, were more likely to know about jazz in New York, Chicago, or Los Angeles than in each others' cities—let alone in Vancouver, more than four thousand kilometers away. Indeed, the flow of recordings from the United States and the strength of U.S. radio in Canada, not to mention the availability of publications like *Down Beat* and *Metronome,* kept Canadian musicians and fans alike fully abreast of the American scene. Jazz in Canada, meanwhile, had no comparable means of promulgating itself either nationally or internationally, which made the American influence that much more indomitable.

FIGURE I Time Line of Jazz Activities in Canada 1914–1949.

FIGURE I Time Line of Jazz Activities in Canada 1914–1949.

1914	The Creole Band's first Canadian tour
1916	The Creole Band returns
1917	Morgan Brothers' Syncopated Jazz Band at Cabaret Garden in Calgary; the Tennessee Ten's first Canadian tour; George Paris forms band for Patricia Cabaret in Vancouver
1918	Westmount Jazz Band at Victoria Hall in Montréal
1919	Jelly Roll Morton arrives in Vancouver; Original Winnipeg Jazz Babies tour western Canada
1920	Yerkes's Blue Bird Orchestra records in Montréal; Millard Thomas and Famous Chicago Jazz Band in first season at Princess Theater in Québec City
1921	Jelly Roll Morton leaves Vancouver
1922	Shirley Oliver and Gumps Jazz Hounds on CJCA in Edmonton; Melody Kings record in Montréal
1924	Charles (Bass) Foster at Star Theater in St. John's; Guy Lombardo and Royal Canadians record in Richmond, Indiana; Millard Thomas and Famous Chicago Novelty Orchestra record in Montréal; New Princes' Toronto Band records in London
1925	Carroll Dickerson's *Charleston Revue* tours western Canada; Smiling Billy Steward's Alabama Jazz Band at the Zenith Café in Saskatoon; Gilbert Watson records in Montréal
1926	Dave Caplan's "Toronto-Band from Canada" records in Berlin
1927	Orange Blossoms at Casa Loma in Toronto; Chocolate Dandies at Silver Slipper in Toronto
1929	Alphonso Trent's 12 Black Aces in southern Ontario
1931	Noel Allen forms Harlem Aces in Toronto; Myron Sutton and Canadian Ambassadors at Gatineau Country Club in Aylmer, Québec
1933	Bert Niosi starts seventeen-year association with Palais Royale in Toronto
1935	Ollie Wagner's Knights of Harlem tour western Canada; Rex Battle's Maple Leaf Orchestra at Bob-Lo Island, Detroit River
1936	Bert Niosi proclaimed Canada's King of Swing; Irving Laing at Auditorium, Montréal
1937	Sandy De Santis at Palomar Ballroom in Vancouver, challenges Niosi's title
1938	Trump Davidson Orchestra tours Britain with Ray Noble; Onyx Club opens in Toronto
1939	Ollie Wagner reorganizes Knights of Harlem in Winnipeg
1941	Ray Norris's *Serenade in Rhythm* on air from CBC Vancouver
1943	Chris Gage leads first band at Silver Dell in Regina
1944	Cy McLean Orchestra opens at Club Top Hat in Toronto
1945	Oscar Peterson begins recording career in Montréal; Maynard Ferguson leads first orchestra at Verdum Pavilion; Bert Niosi Orchestra tours western Canada
1946	Oscar Peterson tours western Canada; Queen City Jazz Band active in Toronto
1947	Louis Metcalf's International Band starts two-and-a-half year engagement at Café St. Michel in Montréal; Bert Niosi Septet records in Montréal; Oscar Peterson Trio begins two-year engagement at Alberta Lounge in Montréal
1948	Moe Koffman records for Main Stem in Buffalo
1949	Oscar Peterson makes U.S. debut at Carnegie Hall, New York

Only a few jazz recordings were made in Canada during the 1920s, virtually none in the 1930s, and a few more beginning in the mid-1940s, among them Oscar Peterson's (b. 1925) first efforts. Private (or commercial) radio initially offered jazz some exposure (including a broadcast by a black quartet, Gumps Jazz Hounds, on Edmonton station CJCA at the remarkably early date of October 1922), but private radio was also generally local radio. Network radio, on the other hand, first organized in Canada by the Canadian National Railway in 1923, offered the country's jazz musicians very limited exposure—when it offered them any exposure at all.

The CNR was followed as a national broadcaster by the Canadian Radio Broadcasting Commission in 1932 and the CRBC by the Canadian Broadcasting Corporation in 1936. To these organizations, the last two publicly owned, fell the task of giving Canadians a voice on airways that were dominated by the powerful U.S. networks—CBS, NBC, Mutual, and, in time, ABC. American programming, which included jazz and dance music, could be heard in Canada either directly from nearby U.S. cities or selectively, by relay on private Canadian stations and, in some instances, on the Canadian network of the day. In other words, even Canadian broadcast content could be of U.S. origin.

Jazz was most often presented nationally on the CBC in the context of variety shows. The young Robert Farnon, later an inestimably influential arranger and conductor in London studios, contributed the occasional jazzy cornet solo to *The Happy Gang* from Toronto, while Oscar Peterson was featured on *Light Up and Listen* from Montréal. Programs devoted exclusively to jazz were rare, however, and not often broadcast outside their originating region. The Ray Norris Quintet's *Serenade in Rhythm* and Bob Smith's long-running record show *Hot Air*, for example, were heard from Vancouver during the 1940s only in western Canada. Bert Niosi, Canada's King of Swing, nevertheless had both national and regional series throughout the decade, and Oscar Peterson was eventually heard on his own cross-country broadcasts—fifteen-minute spots weekly during the summers of 1946 and 1947. So it was that Niosi and Peterson, who also toured and recorded during the late 1940s, became the first musicians to transcend the regionalism of the Canadian jazz scene. Niosi, at that time nearing forty, appeared content with his achievement. Not so Peterson, a generation younger; his move to the international stage was as inevitable as it would be dramatic.

In the years since his Carnegie Hall debut in 1949, Oscar Peterson (figure 2) has enjoyed undiminished celebrity as a recording and touring artist. His discography exceeded 130 albums under his own name alone by the mid-1990s and his concert itinerary has taken him from his home in Montréal—later Toronto, and still later nearby Mississauga—to halls throughout the world. Few jazz musicians, whatever their country of origin, could claim greater popularity.

Jazz in Canada, meanwhile, flourished rather more modestly for many years, the country's musicians generally following at a cautious distance the lead of their American contemporaries through bebop and its variant styles in the 1950s, the avant-garde of the 1960s, and fusion jazz of the 1970s. Significantly, two Canadians who have been in the forefront of the music's continuing evolution, the Montréal-born (1932) pianist Paul Bley and the Toronto-born (1930) trumpeter Kenny Wheeler, left Canada in the early 1950s, Bley for the United States and Wheeler for England.

In the 1980s and 1990s, finally, Canada caught up with the world. The country's jazz festivals, led by events in Montréal and Vancouver, have become justly renowned for their vision and integrity, while several Canadians have made impressive strides on the world stage, among them the veterans Ed Bickert, Oliver Jones, Peter Leitch, and Rob McConnell—the last with his big band the Boss Brass—and the younger Seamus Blake, Jane Bunnett, D. D. Jackson, Diana Krall, and Renee Rosnes. Many others are waiting in the wings.

—Mark Miller

FIGURE 2   Oscar Peterson 1980. © Hulton-Deutsch Collection/CORBIS.

The keyboard volumes are among those where the popular, the gentrified, and the very serious are juxtaposed: quadrilles, galops, marches, and polkas sit beside fugues and toccatas.

THE CANADIAN MUSICAL HERITAGE SOCIETY

Although there are few parallels in Canada to the huge publication industry that supports music in the United States, there have been several important projects, including the *Anthology of Canadian Music* (1978–1991), published jointly by the CBC and the Canadian Music Center during the 1970s and 1980s, and, more recently, the work of the Canadian Musical Heritage Society, a group founded in 1982 to produce early (mostly pre-1939) printed music by Canadian composers. Furthermore, the society's innovative approaches to technology and distribution have made such material available in versatile formats that resist the reification of a canon of early Canadian music.

The project emerged in the wake of the production of the *Encyclopedia of Music in Canada* (1981), which contained numerous references to compositions that were not available to readers. EMC editor Helmut Kallmann, together with composers John Beckwith and Clifford Ford, musicologists Elaine Keillor, Lucien Poirier (later Marie-Thérèse Lefebvre), and Fred Hall, devised a plan for publishing twenty-five volumes of music, an objective met by 1999.

The series is roughly organized by genre: piano music (four volumes), songs (two volumes each in French and English), choral music (seven volumes, including hymns, sacred and secular works, oratorio, cantata, and movements from masses), opera and operetta (one volume), music for organ (two volumes), orchestra music (three volumes), music for band (two volumes), and chamber music (three volumes). While the medium of print and the generic divisions clearly give priority to art music, the series demonstrates that the divisions between "high-brow" and "low-brow" or oral/print transmission were often blurred in practice. Hymns, marches, popular song, and parlor music all have variants in the oral tradition and in various vernacular practices. Some volumes include material in languages other than English and French. The final sacred music volume, for instance, includes Ukrainian Catholic, Jewish, Roman Catholic, and Protestant works. The hymn volume includes sources from several aboriginal hymnbooks.

With regard to the roster of professional composers included, there is work by romanticists ranging from the light-hearted operettas, keyboard works, and songs of Calixa Lavallée to the almost somber late romantic work of Guillaume Couture in his oratorio *Jean Le Precurseur* or of Alexis Contant in his *Piano Trio*. There are folk song–influenced works by nationalists such as Ernest MacMillan and Hector Gratton, as well as the early hints of modernism in works such as Papineau Couture's *Eglogues* or Rudolph Mathieu's *Piano Sonata*. But the anthology also includes such things as early singing-school psalm settings, hymns, and anthems, popular songs by Geoffery O'Hara, and Christmas carols by Jesuit priests. The keyboard volumes are among those where the popular, the gentrified, and the very serious are juxtaposed: quadrilles, galops, marches, and polkas sit beside fugues and toccatas. The extensive introductions historicize the production and, in some cases, the use of each piece.

Several spin-off projects enhance the pedagogical usefulness of the series. A series of audio CDs, named in honor of the composer of Canada's national anthem, Calixa Lavallée, has been produced in collaboration with Marquis Classics. By 2000, *Canadian Songs for Parlor and Stage, Theater Music, Popular Songs to English Texts, Art Songs on English Texts,* and *Noel: Early Canadian Christmas Music* were available, all performed by distinguished Canadians.

The CMHS also maintains an inventory of notated Canadian music to 1950, available on their website (www.cmhs.carleton.ca), and can produce sheet music copies of specific works, a clever way to meet demand without risking overruns. The inventory can also be tapped to substitute works in the widely used original *Historical Anthology of Canadian Music* (1996), described next. Furthermore, in addition to published music the inventory does include some archival sources for manuscripts relating to vernacular traditions (for example, the Allen Ash collection of fiddle tunes he copied for private use).

The *Historical Anthology of Canadian Music* (HACM) is a one-volume anthology of 122 compositions and historical notes designed for use in high school and university courses. An innovative aspect of this project is the fact that the "anthology" may be customized to suit individual instructors or performers by substituting works from the CMHS inventory. Altogether, the CMHS has enriched the corpus of Canadian music available for study and performance, effectively using digital technologies in creative ways to reach their market.

—BEVERLEY DIAMOND

WHOSE MUSIC IS CANADIAN COUNTRY MUSIC?

The question posed above requires answers on two levels. First, what aspects of national culture, character, or soul can be found in this commercial people's music? If, as Martin Laba argues, "Canadian culture must be realized in the recognition of the nature of Canadianism as limited, unblended, regional, and popular" (1988:419), where then does country music fit? But there is a second level to my question that I want to consider first. It has to do with the way in which folklorists and ethnomusicologists can become advocates for those whom they study. Often they do so without examining their own premises. What is the social role of the student of country music? I agree with Barbara Kirshenblatt-Gimblett that "advocacy can distort inquiry" (1988:142) and that our approach to country music as scholars should be grounded in a critically informed theory of culture. Before we can describe country music historically or ethnographically we must know what we think and why.

The interlocking dualism of business and culture
Bill C. Malone's standard history, *Country Music, U.S.A.* (1985), neglects the business side of the music in favor of a fan's-eye point of view that focuses on artists. The complexities of the Canadian country music business reflect the ways in which it is intertwined with and dependent on the American business.

Imperialism and creolization
The role of southern culture in the United States is characterized in terms of what I call the soul/power exchange, an apparently simple situation in which there is a trade-off of soul (the South) for power (the rest of the country). In this setting a monolithic and all-embracing American conception of country music has emerged—a kind of national cultural imperialism. There are problems with applying this concept in Canada, for there are many soul/power exchanges in Canada. The question is thus raised: is Canada's "down East" truly equivalent to the American South as the heartland for

country music? Further problems are presented by Canada's more firmly entrenched multicultural and bilingual setting. Finally, country music in Canada frequently seems to provoke among those Canadians who are not part of its system a fear of creolization. This is linked to fears of loss of cultural autonomy.

Regional syncretism

Simon Bronner (1987) critiques the American idea of country music as a Southern music, arguing that the concept of regionalization of culture is a recent romantic construct. In Canada, where regional issues dominate national politics, students of country music face a very different cultural landscape. They must take into account the complexities of soul/power exchanges both within and between regions.

Ethnic syncretism

The major points of Robert Klymasz's pioneering work on Ukrainian country music (1972) underscore the notion that multiculturalism has a strong political dimension. Country music as a form that subsumes or borrows from ethnic music can be seen, for example, in the music of Newfoundland (where, for official political reasons, region has become ethnicity), French Canada, Native peoples, and African Canadians. In some parts of the nation, country music becomes a competing alternative to ethnic music.

Class

Is country music's working-class image truly meaningful given the middle-class business control of important aspects of its system? Five specific questions are put regarding class: (1) What about the upward mobility of the star? (2) What about country music in Canadian one-industry and company towns? (3) What about country music in the Armed Forces? (4) What about the influence of folk revivals, an urban and middle-class phenomenon, on Canadian country music? (5) What about the influences of rock and roll?

A universal process

Letters from home? Cross-cultural comparisons, particularly recent work by sociologists of music and ethnomusicologists on the popular musics of many parts of the world, indicate that country music–type systems exist wherever emigration–immigration patterns exist, in which members of ethnic or regional groups move to urban areas for industrial work. In Canada, steel band, reggae, Irish, and polka music typify such parallel systems.

The mute Canadian symbol

One of the most popular and influential Canadian country musicians, Don Messer, never spoke in public. He just played the fiddle. Fiddling, like dancing (another important component of the Messer show), is linguistically neutral. Perhaps it is only on such neutral ground that a completely national musical popularity is possible.

I posed these questions at the first conference on ethnomusicology in Canada in 1988 (Rosenberg 1991). For further information about Canadian country music, see Green and Miller (1992), and Miller (1992). Although the emergence of such phenomena as "new country," the international success of Canadian country artists such as k.d. lang and Shania Twain, and the surge of attention to Celtic music may cast the soul/power tension differently than in 1988, the issues outlined here have continuing relevance. I hope that, when the definitive work on country music in Canada is written, it will take all of them into account. I expect that it will find others to consider as well.

—Neil V. Rosenberg

REFERENCES

Anthology of Canadian Music. 1978–1991. Toronto: Canadian Broadcasting Corporation and Canadian Music Center.

Augaitis, D., and D. Lander, eds. 1994. *Radio Rethink: Art, Sound and Transmission.* Banff: Walter Phillips Gallery, The Banff Centre for the Arts.

Berland, Jody. 1986. "Cultural Re/Percussions: The Social Production of Music Broadcasting in Canada." Ph.D. dissertation, York University.

———. 1994a. "Radio Space and Industrial Time: The Case of Music Formats." In *Canadian Music: Issues of Hegemony and Identity,* ed. Beverley Diamond and Robert Witmer, 173–188. Toronto: Canadian Scholars' Press.

———. 1994b. "Toward a Creative Anachronism: Radio, the State and Sound Government." In *Radio Rethink: Art, Sound and Transmission,* ed. D. Augaitis and D. Lander, 33–44. Banff: Walter Phillips Gallery, The Banff Centre for the Arts.

Bronner, Simon. 1987. *Old-Time Music Makers of New York State.* Syracuse: Syracuse University Press.

CBC. 1981. *Culture, Broadcasting, and the Canadian Identity.* S.L.: Canadian Broadcasting Corporation. Pamphlet

———. 1983. *The English Radio Development Project.*

Ellis, David. 1979. *Evolution of the Canadian Broadcasting System: Objectives and Realities, 1928–1968.* Ottawa: Minister of Supply and Services Canada.

Filion, Michel. 1996. "Radio." In *The Cultural Industries in Canada: Problems, Policies and Prospects,* ed. Michael Dorland, 118–141. Toronto: James Lorimer and Company.

Green, Richard, and Mark Miller. 1992. "Country Music." In *Encyclopedia of Music in Canada,* ed. Helmut Kallmann, Gilles Potvin, and Kenneth Winters, 320–323. Toronto: University of Toronto Press.

Grenier, Line. 1990. "Radio Broadcasting in Canada: The Case of 'Transformat' Music." *Popular Music* 9(2):221–233.

Hahn, R. Richard. 1981. *The Role of Radio in the Canadian Music Industry.* Toronto: Canadian Association of Broadcasters. (Prepared for submission to the CRTC.)

Historical Anthology of Canadian Music. 1996. Ottawa: Canadian Music Heritage Society.

Kallmann, Helmut, Gilles Potvin, and Kenneth Winters. 1992. "CBC." In *Encyclopedia of Music in Canada,* 2nd ed., ed. Helmut Kallman and Gilles Potvin, 228–229. Toronto: University of Toronto Press.

Kirshenblatt-Gimblett, Barbara. 1988. "Mistaken Dichotomies." *Journal of American Folklore* 101: 140–155.

Klymasz, Robert. 1972. "'Sounds You Never Heard Before': Ukrainian Country Music in Western Canada." *Ethnomusicology* 16:372–380.

Laba, Martin. 1988. "Popular Culture as Local Culture: Regions, Limits and Canadianism." In *Communication Canada: Issues in Broadcasting and New Technologies,* ed. R. M. Lorimer and D. C. Wilson, 82–101. Toronto: Kazan and Woo.

Lewis, Peter, and Jerry Booth. 1990. *The Invisible Medium: Public, Commercial and Community Radio.* Washington, D.C.: Howard University Press.

MacMillan, Keith. 1992. "Broadcasting." In *Encyclopedia of Music in Canada,* 2nd ed., ed. Helmut Kallmann and Gilles Potvin, 162–167. Toronto: University of Toronto Press.

Malone, Bill. 1985. *Country Music, U.S.A.* Rev. ed. Austin: University of Texas Press.

Miller, Mark. 1992. "Country Music News." In *Encyclopedia of Music in Canada,* 2nd ed., ed. Helmut Kallmann and Gilles Potvin, 323. Toronto: University of Toronto Press.

———. 1997. *Such Melodious Racket: The Lost History of Jazz in Canada 1914–1949.* Toronto: Mercury Press.

NCCRA (National Community and Campus Radio Association). 1987. *NCRA Statement of Principles.* Available at http://www.ams.ubc.ca/media/citr/ncra/ncrastat.htm.

A New Deal for Radio: The Canadian Association of Broadcasters' Response to the CRTC. 1990. Canadian Association of Broadcasters, May.

Rosenberg, Neil V. 1991. "Whose Music Is Canadian Country Music?—A Precis." In *Ethnomusicology in Canada,* ed. Robert Witmer, 236–238. Toronto: Institute for Canadian Music.

Schafer, R. Murray. 1977. *The Tuning of the World.* Toronto: McLelland and Stewart.

Stiles, J. Mark, and Jacques Lachance. 1988. *History and Present Status of Community Radio in Québec.* Ottawa: Stiles Associates Inc. (Ministry of Culture and Communications, Government of Ontario).

Straw, Will. 1996. "Sound Recording." In *The Cultural Industries in Canada: Problems, Policies and Prospects,* ed. Michael Dorland, 95–117. Toronto: James Lorimer and Company.

Wilkinson, Kealy, and Associates. 1988. *Community Radio in Ontario.* Toronto: Ministry of Culture and Communications.

Wright, Robert. 1991. "'Gimme Shelter': Observations on Cultural Protectionism and the Recording Industry in Canada." *Cultural Studies* 5(3): 306–316.

Parts of the article "Whose Music Is Canadian Country Music?" were excerpted from the contribution of bluegrass and country music scholar Neil Rosenberg to the first conference on ethnomusicology in Canada in 1988 and published in R. Witmer, ed. Ethnomusicology in Canada. *(Toronto: Institute for Canadian Studies, 1990). Although the emergence of such phenomena as "new country," the international success of Canadian country artists such as k. d. lang and Shania Twain, and the surge of attention to Celtic music may cast the "soul/power" tension differently than in 1988, the issues outlined here have continuing relevance. For further information about Canadian country music, see Green and Miller (1992) and Miller (1992).*

Section 3a
Atlantic Canada

Atlantic Canada comprises the eastern provinces of New Brunswick, Nova Scotia, Prince Edward Island, and Newfoundland, where the current population is overwhelmingly of British origin. The French were the first Europeans to settle in the area, however, establishing communities in Acadia (present-day Nova Scotia) in the seventeenth century with close ties with First Nations peoples (predominantly the Algonquian-speaking Mi'qmaq). The British were soon to follow, establishing trade with the New England colonies to the south. Atlantic Canada is also the first Canadian area to have a sizable portion of African Canadians—predominantly slaves who came to Canada as property of British Loyalists during the American Revolutionary War. From its very beginnings, then, Atlantic Canada has hosted many different social and musical communities experiencing a variety of musics, from French Catholic church music to American Indian ceremonial practices; from British, Scottish, and Irish secular dance traditions to African Canadian minstrel songs. And since much of the economy of Atlantic Canada depended and continues to depend on fishing, a longstanding Anglo-inspired ballad tradition of sea songs and chanties still thrives.

Tom Jennings of the Torbay Fiddles entertains in his living room, Newfoundland, 1950. © Hulton-Deutsch Collection/CORBIS.

Overview
Nancy F. Vogan

The region currently known as Atlantic Canada consists of the east coast provinces of Nova Scotia, New Brunswick, and Prince Edward Island and the province of Newfoundland and Labrador. Nova Scotia, New Brunswick, and Prince Edward Island are referred to as the Maritime Provinces or the Maritimes. Nova Scotia and New Brunswick became part of Canada in 1867 as part of the four founding provinces; Prince Edward Island joined the confederation in 1873. Newfoundland did not join Canada until 1949; until then it was a separate colony belonging to Great Britain.

EARLY SETTLEMENT IN THE MARITIMES

A variety of settlers, including French, British, German, and people from the American colonies, came to the region beginning in the seventeenth century, but the two primary groups were the French and the British. In fact, rivalry between France and Britain for control of this area of North America played the dominant role in the history of the region.

Settlement patterns differed, even for the English-speaking settlers who came from various regions of England, Scotland, and Ireland as well as from these same countries by way of the American colonies. This meant that there were differences in their social and political experiences, including folk traditions that they brought with them, as well as variations in religious denominations and the role that music played in their services of worship. The early French settlers were a more homogenous group, coming from the same general area of northern France and sharing a common heritage and, for the most part, a common religion—Roman Catholicism.

Music of the early settlers

One of the earliest references to music in the region is in the history of the colony established by the French in Port Royal, Nova Scotia, in 1604. The entertainment *Le Théatre de Neptune,* presented in the colony in 1606, is known to have contained music. Music was part of the celebrations of the l'Ordre du Bon Temps, often referred to as one of the earliest social clubs in North America. These early settlers interacted with aboriginal residents (for example, *Le Théatre de Neptune* had both aboriginal and European participants) and attempted to write down some of the native songs they heard. There are also references to members of the clergy teaching natives to sing the simpler chants of the Roman Catholic service.

Although several French settlements developed in this area of New France (referred to as Acadia), the one at Port Royal did not develop as originally intended and most of the key personnel returned to France. Similarly, although music played an important role in daily life in the French colony established at the fortress of Louisbourg on Cape Breton Island, this transplanted European musical tradition did not continue to develop after the fall of the fortress to the British in 1758.

DEVELOPMENTS IN THE EIGHTEENTH CENTURY

European wars between France and Britain had a direct effect on the region. With the Treaty of Utrecht in 1713 Britain obtained all of Acadia or Nova Scotia (the land now known as Nova Scotia and New Brunswick) with the exception of Isle Royale (Cape Breton Island) and Isle St. Jean (Prince Edward Island). The British established more settlements in the region; in 1749 Halifax was founded as a major military port and garrison town.

Expulsion of the Acadians

In 1755 nearly six thousand French settlers (Acadians) who had remained in Nova Scotia were forcibly removed to communities further down the Atlantic coast. Three years later the British captured the French fortress of Louisbourg. The Treaty of Paris (1763), which settled the Seven Years' War in Europe, gave Britain complete control of Canada, which included the land known as Acadia. Although a few French remained in the area, settlers from Britain (English, Scottish, and Irish) and others from the British colonies in New England were recruited, thus making British culture the dominant one in the region.

Arrival of British settlers and the Loyalists

The growing population of the region and the arrival of the American colonists who remained loyal to Britain following the Revolutionary War in 1783 led to a geographical division of the area, creating the political divisions of Nova Scotia and the new colony of New Brunswick, each with a separate government.

The port cities of Halifax, Nova Scotia, and Saint John, New Brunswick, became the chief musical centers. Several British and European, as well as American, musicians came to these cities as performers and instructors. The musicians in the British regimental bands stationed in Halifax performed at numerous nonmilitary functions, and several also provided instrumental music instruction, especially after their retirement from the military.

EXPANSION OF MUSICAL ACTIVITIES IN THE EIGHTEENTH AND NINETEENTH CENTURIES

Influence of churches and singing schools

As in many parts of the continent, churches were important centers of musical life for members of both the Roman Catholic faith and various Protestant denominations. Singing schools similar to those in New England played an important role in music training for the Protestant traditions; references to singing schools can be found as early as the 1770s. The tradition continued throughout the nineteenth century and was retained in several rural areas well into the twentieth century. Early singing school instructors in Maritime Canada included Amasa Braman and Reuben McFarlane in Nova Scotia and Stephen Humbert in New Brunswick.

Individuals responsible for music in the churches often became musical leaders in their communities, conducting local choral and instrumental ensembles and providing

The Maritime School for the Blind, founded in
Halifax in 1871, had music as a vital component
for its students, offering various aspects of music
instruction including pianoforte tuning.

musical instruction, particularly for the young. In addition to the important community role played by church organists and choir directors, members of the clergy influenced the musical life of a community. A notable example is the Oxford-educated first
Anglican Bishop of Fredericton, John Medley. Pipe organs were placed in churches in
the region as early as 1765 in Halifax, 1801 in Saint John, 1848 in Fredericton, New
Brunswick, and around 1840 in Charlottetown, Prince Edward Island.

Convents, private schools, and institutions

Music instruction was provided by several Roman Catholic orders, including the Sisters of Charity, the Sisters of the Sacred Heart, les Soeurs de la Congrégation de Notre-
Dame, Les Pères de la St.-Croix, and les Pères Eudistes. Several of these orders operated
schools that became noted for music.

Private music schools, such as the Halifax Conservatory under Charles Porter and
the church-affiliated Acadia and Mount Allison conservatories were established in the
second half of the nineteenth century. The Maritime School for the Blind, founded in
Halifax in 1871, had music as a vital component for its students, offering various
aspects of music instruction including pianoforte tuning. The auditorium at this
school was used for many performances in the city. Beginning in the 1880s, instruction
in Curwen's tonic solfa method, developed in Britain, became popular in many communities throughout the region.

Choral and philharmonic societies

During the nineteenth century several choral and philharmonic societies were formed;
military and town bands were also popular, and some centers had small orchestras with
varied instrumentation. Concerts of large groups of school children were reported in
both Halifax (one thousand five hundred in 1868) and Saint John (one thousand in
1870). As port cities, both Halifax and Saint John enjoyed performances of leading
concert and operatic ensembles traveling between Europe and the United States.

Music publishing and instrument manufacturing

The first music book in the region (*Union Harmony*) was published in Saint John
in 1801, with further editions in 1816, 1831, and 1840. The printing of this New
England-style tunebook by Stephen Humbert was done in New Hampshire. In 1838,
James Dawson of Pictou, Nova Scotia, imported music type and published a tunebook (*The Harmonicon*), which was printed at his own newspaper office. Music was
published a few decades later in Charlottetown. From the 1870s onward music was
published in both Halifax and Saint John.

Some instrument making began in the region during the nineteenth century, particularly piano manufacturing. More recently there has also been interest in the building of folk instruments and early instruments in several areas, although on a limited
scale. However, the internationally known cymbal manufacturer Sabian Ltd. is located
on the Saint John River near Fredericton.

MUSICAL ACTIVITIES IN THE EARLY TWENTIETH CENTURY

By the beginning of the twentieth century, music clubs, particularly ladies' morning musical clubs, played both a social and an educational role in several communities and promoted performances by local and visiting artists. Despite the hardships brought on by the Great Depression there were improvements in the cultural life of the Maritime Provinces between the two world wars; music was a major part of this development. During the 1930s the Carnegie Corporation of New York made many significant contributions to the area that included musical scores and recordings for conservatory libraries. Churches continued as important musical centers, with church musicians still being involved in community activities, but there were also cultural ventures that were completely independent.

Concerts

Concerts by visiting artists increased throughout the region. Community Concert Associations, affiliated with Columbia Artists Management, Inc., in New York City, were established. Many concerts were held in church halls and gymnasiums as well as in several new high school auditoriums. Other tours of artists continued to be arranged locally by ladies' musical clubs, Imperial Order of the Daughters of the Empire (IODE) chapters, Rotary Clubs, and other associations. One of the most frequently heard ensembles during this time was the Hart House String Quartet from Toronto. This group made yearly tours from 1931 until its dissolution at the end of World War II, performing not only in major centers but also in more remote communities.

The expansion of local performing groups also added to the concert life of the area. The number of philharmonic societies, madrigal and choral societies, small orchestras, and town bands increased. Several groups devoted themselves to the production of works by Gilbert and Sullivan, which became popular in the region. The introduction of local radio stations created the need for studio orchestras, which provided further opportunities for local musicians.

Festivals and music instruction

Choral organizations, such as the Choral Society in Truro, Nova Scotia, sponsored special festivals for school music groups in some centers; the event begun in Truro developed into an ongoing annual music festival, one of the oldest in the Maritime region. Some of the rural areas held special folk song and folk dance festivals. Events such as the Apple Blossom Festival in Nova Scotia's Annapolis Valley featured performances by school children on a regular basis, and the Provincial Exhibition in that province featured a School Music Contest. British-style competitive music festivals were organized in both Halifax and Saint John in 1836, laying the foundation for the development of similar events following World War II.

Increased influence came from the United States, particularly concerning the offering of music in the schools. Programs expanded, and, with the introduction of the phonograph, classes in listening to music were included. Most instructional programs did not extend to the high school level until the 1950s, but the number of high school performing ensembles continued to grow in the time between the wars.

Music in Newfoundland and Labrador before 1949

Newfoundland is Canada's newest province, but it is one of the oldest areas in the country. Until the early 1800s most of the population stayed for only the summer months, as the area was an important migratory fishing resource for Britain and permanent settlement was discouraged. (The population of St. John's in 1766, for example, was one thousand in the winter but ten thousand in the summer.) Over the years there has been a strong English and Irish influence in the colony, with small pockets of French culture. Until well into the twentieth century, many settlements were accessible only by water. The isolation from the rest of North America helped to retain a strong tradition of folk music that has become well recognized.

There is documentation of music being used in religious services in some of the earliest settlements—Renews, Ferryland, and the French settlement of Placentia. References to music in Labrador are sparse, but it is known that the Moravian missionaries who served in Nain on the Labrador coast taught many of the Inuit to play both string and brass instruments.

St. John's became the main center for cultural activities. References to early concerts can be found, and a ballad opera was produced as early as 1820. Church choirs, and later choral societies, were important factors in the musical culture of St. John's and many of the other smaller communities. Unlike in the Maritime Provinces, the influence of the singing school movement was not present. A number of bands operated under the auspices of various organizations, and a St. John's Orchestral Society was formed in 1890. Concerts by visiting artists traveling from Europe to the United States were given, as they had been in the ports of Halifax and Saint John.

Much of the private teaching in St. John's was associated with convent schools or private denominational colleges operated by Roman Catholics, Anglicans, and Methodists. There was little opportunity for instruction in the more remote communities apart from convents that offered music lessons to both Roman Catholic and Protestant children.

The existence of a denominationally based school system has helped to maintain a religious influence in music education. Many schools, particularly those run by Roman Catholic orders, became well known for both choral and instrumental music, including orchestras. The Salvation Army, one of the four major denominations operating schools, introduced instrumental music (brass bands) into its schools. Service bands stationed at the U.S. bases in Newfoundland during World War II led to a strong American influence in instrumental music.

MUSIC IN ATLANTIC CANADA SINCE 1950

Music in Acadian communities

Music has been valued as a vehicle for cultural expression among French-speaking Acadians throughout the Maritimes. Several outstanding choral ensembles organized by Roman Catholic orders, such as Chorale de l'Université Saint-Joseph in Memramcook, N.B., and Chorale Notre Dame d'Acadie in Moncton, have won international awards. Numerous school and community groups were organized to participate in the Acadian nationalism celebration of 1955. Many of these ensembles continued to develop following these celebrations, helping to preserve and promote the rich heritage of folk material and the strong choral tradition in Acadian communities. Les Jeunesses Musicales has been active in sponsoring concerts in francophone communities. The formation of a music department at New Brunswick's Université de Moncton (formerly Université St. Joseph in Memramcook) during the 1960s has played an important role for Acadians.

Festivals

Competitive music festivals

During the 1950s the competitive festival movement expanded throughout the Atlantic region. Participants included not only individual performers but also school, church, and community chamber groups and ensembles. Service organizations, such as local Kiwanis and Rotary Clubs, often act as sponsors. Competitive music festivals continue throughout the region, with one of the largest in St. John's.

Summer music festivals

Summer music activities have increased in the region with a variety of professional and semiprofessional events, and this has led to increased tourism in Atlantic Canada. The Charlottetown Festival was established in 1965 to present original Canadian musical theater as well as occasional concerts by well-known artists. Held on an annual basis in the Confederation Centre for the Arts, it has presented many new Canadian productions; the musical *Anne of Green Gables,* which was featured at the opening, has been produced every year. A chamber music festival and a jazz festival have been organized at the University of New Brunswick in Fredericton since the mid-1960s. The International Baroque Music Festival, held on Lameque Island on the northeast coast of New Brunswick since 1975, features artists of international stature each summer. The summer Festival-by-the-Sea, held annually in Saint John, features a variety of performers. Scotia Festival of Music has been held in Halifax each spring since 1980. This chamber music festival features a composer-in-residence, a professional development program for young musicians, and a series of concerts, recitals, and master classes. Musique Royale, a festival of early music held in historic settings across Nova Scotia, was organized in 1985.

In St. John's, the Sound Symposium, an International Festival of New Music and the Arts first held in July 1983, has become a biennial event that attracts participants from many different countries. More recently, Festival 500 Sharing the Voices, An International Festival of Choral Music and Celebration of Song, has been developed, which also meets in St. John's on a biennial basis.

Various jazz and blues festivals as well as numerous folk festivals, such as the Lunenburg Folk Harbour Festival, are popular events throughout the region. The Nova Scotia Tattoo held in Halifax each year features many performers, including the local armed forces Stadacona Band.

Organizations and institutions

Expansion of music instruction

Music programs in public schools expanded in the Atlantic region during the 1960s to 1980s; many of the elementary programs adopted the Orff, Kodály, or Martenot approaches, which used folk songs of the region, thus keeping many of these songs alive. Programs in secondary schools also expanded, with accredited courses in music being introduced in all four provinces. Choral and instrumental groups, including jazz ensembles, reached high levels of performance. In addition to concerts, school productions of musical theater pieces have become annual events in many areas.

A large number of private teachers as well as private music schools continue to offer music instruction. Associations for both private and school music teachers, as well as chapters of the Royal Canadian College of Organists (RCCO), have been active in sponsoring recitals, workshops, and festivals.

Several universities in the region offer postsecondary instruction in music. Acadia, Dalhousie, and St. Francis Xavier in Nova Scotia; Mount Allison and Université de Moncton in New Brunswick; the University of Prince Edward Island in Charlottetown; and Memorial University of Newfoundland in St. John's. In addition to providing both professional music instruction and the study of music within a liberal arts curriculum, these music departments serve as cultural centers for their areas, providing recitals, ensemble concerts, lectures, and venues for the performance of new music. Other postsecondary institutions offer concert series and some music courses, and a few, such as the University of New Brunswick, host musicians-in-residence.

Summer music camps have been held throughout the region, sponsored by universities, local school boards and cultural organizations such as provincial choral

Pride in the musical heritage of the area is not a new phenomenon—much of this music had been kept alive in the smaller rural communities—but the increase in performances of traditional music from the region in the larger urban centers is a newer trend.

federations. Centers for the study of traditional music such as the Gaelic College in Cape Breton and the Scottish School of Piping in Summerside, Prince Edward Island, have flourished.

Theaters and cultural centers

Until the 1950s many concerts took place in school auditoriums, gymnasiums, and church halls. By the 1960s, however, the need for more performance venues was felt in many areas, and new buildings, many associated with the Canadian Centennial celebrations, began to appear. Some examples are the Confederation Centre for the Arts in Charlottetown, the Beaverbrook Playhouse in Fredericton, the Rebecca Cohn Auditorium in Halifax, and several new arts and culture centers in Newfoundland, including those in St. John's and Corner Brook. Restoration of early-twentieth-century theaters was undertaken, ranging from the small Savoy Theatre in Glace Bay, Nova Scotia, to the major renovations projects at the Capitol and Imperial Theatres in Moncton and Saint John.

Performing ensembles

Local and regional symphonies, both amateur and semiprofessional, have been active throughout the region. Provincial symphonies operate in Saint John and in Charlottetown; a semiprofessional orchestra has been active in St. John's since 1961. The only fully professional group is Symphony Nova Scotia (a successor to the Atlantic Symphony), based in Halifax. This ensemble offers a full season of concerts featuring many notable guest artists and also tours the province. Provincial youth orchestras were founded in New Brunswick (1965), Nova Scotia (1977), and Newfoundland (1981).

The Nova Scotia Opera Association operated in the 1950s and produced shows in Halifax that then toured to other Maritime centers. Organizations including the Canadian Opera Company have toured the region, and small-scale productions of operas are given by some of the universities. Opera New Brunswick has recently given annual performances at the newly renovated Imperial Theatre.

Choral singing continues to be popular throughout the Atlantic region. Although there are no professional choirs, there are many fine amateur groups, for both youth and adult singers. Several chamber music ensembles, including string quartets, are associated with either regional orchestras or universities. The number of jazz groups and new music concerts has increased.

Arts boards and cultural organizations

Artists, ensembles, and composers have been eligible to apply for awards from the Canada Council since its inception in 1957. In addition, provincial arts boards and other private foundations, such as the Nova Scotia Talent Trust, provide support. Debut Atlantic has played an important role in sponsoring and arranging tours of rising young Canadian artists. The East Coast Music Association currently sponsors the annual East Coast Music Awards, which recognize accomplishments in all aspects of the music industry, including concert music.

Composition in the Atlantic region

Composers in the Atlantic region formed their own organization, Atlantic Association of Composers, in 1979, which works to promote regional composition through live concerts and radio broadcasts. Several composers are faculty members at university music departments or composers-in-residence at various institutions. The Halifax-based Canadian Broadcasting Corporation (CBC) and the Moncton-based French-speaking Radio-Canada both offer programs featuring regional performances of new music concerts, as does the regional CBC in Newfoundland. The Atlantic Regional Centre of the Canadian Music Centre is located at Mount Allison University in Sackville, New Brunswick.

Revival of interest in traditional music

A revival of interest in traditional music has influenced both the popular and concert music scene. This revival has been felt strongly in Cape Breton, in Newfoundland, and in French-speaking Acadian areas, but its influence has been felt throughout the Atlantic region and beyond. It has led to a fusion of popular and concert musics in many different ways, including symphony concerts. Pride in the musical heritage of the area is not a new phenomenon—much of this music had been kept alive in the smaller rural communities—but the increase in performances of traditional music from the region in the larger urban centers (many times in place of more commercial pop/rock groups) is a newer trend.

REFERENCES

Amtmann, Willy. 1975. *Music in Canada, 1600–1800.* Montréal: Habitex.

Beaton, Virginia, and Stephen Pederson. 1992. *Maritime Music Greats: Fifty Years of Hits and Heartbreak.* Halifax: Nimbus Publishing.

Beckwith, John, ed. 1986. *Hymn Tunes.* The Canadian Musical Heritage, vol. 5. Ottawa: Canadian Musical Heritage Society.

Beckwith, John, and Frederick A. Hall, eds. 1988. *Music Canada: Words and Music Honouring Helmut Kallmann.* Toronto: University of Toronto Press.

Blakeley, Phyllis. 1949. "The Theater and Music in Halifax." *Dalhousie Review* 29:8–20.

———. 1951. "Music in Nova Scotia, 1605–1867." *Dalhousie Review* 31/2:94–101 and 31/3:223–230.

Brown, Howard, ed. 1960. *Report of Conference on Music in the Schools of the Atlantic Provinces.* Sackville, N.B.: Mount Allison University.

Croft, Clary. 1999. *Helen Creighton: Canada's First Lady of Folklore.* Halifax: Nimbus Publishing.

Daigle, Jean, ed. 1982. *The Acadians of the Maritimes: Thematic Studies.* Moncton: Centre d'études acadiennes.

Diamond, Beverley, and Robert Witmer, eds. 1994. *Canadian Music: Issues of Hegemony and Identity.* Toronto: Canadian Scholars' Press Inc.

Fancy, Margaret, ed. 1987. *The Proceedings of the Art and Music in New Brunswick Symposium.* Fredericton: Goose Lane Editions.

Farquharson, Dorothy H. 1983. *O for a Thousand Tongues to Sing: A History of Singing Schools in Early Canada.* Waterdown, Ont.:

Ford, Clifford. 1982. *Canada's Music: An Historical Survey.* Agincourt, Ont.: GLC Publishers.

Green, J. Paul, and Nancy F. Vogan. 1991. *Music Education in Canada: A Historical Account.* Toronto: University of Toronto Press.

Hall, Frederick A. 1983. "Musical Life in Eighteenth-Century Halifax." *Canadian University Music Review* 4:278–307.

———. 1994. "Musical Yankees and Tories in Maritime Settlements of 18th-Century Canada." In *Canadian Music: Issues of Hegemony and Identity,* ed. Beverley Diamond and Robert Witmer, 447–458. Toronto: Canadian Scholar's Press, Inc.

Harper, J. Russell. 1954. "The Theatre in Saint John 1789–1817." *Dalhousie Review* 34:260–269.

Kallmann, Helmut. 1960. *A History of Music in Canada, 1534–1914.* Toronto: University of Toronto Press.

Kallmann, Helmut, and Gilles Potvin, eds. 1992. *Encyclopedia of Music in Canada.* 2nd ed. Toronto: University of Toronto Press.

Kallmann, Helmut, Gilles Potvin, and Kenneth Winters, eds. 1981. *Encyclopedia of Music in Canada.* Toronto: University of Toronto Press.

Kemp, Walter H. 1988. "Three Masses by Maritime Composers." In *Musical Canada: Words and Music Honouring Helmut Kallmann,* ed. John Beckwith and Frederick A. Hall, 274–285. Toronto: University of Toronto Press.

MacDonald, Bertrum H., and Nancy F. Vogan. 2000. "James Dawson of Pictou and the Harmonicon: Sacred Music for Victorian Maritimers." *Papers of the Bibliographical Society of Canada* 38, no. 1.

MacMillan, Sir Ernest, ed. 1955. *Music in Canada.* Toronto: University of Toronto Press.

Martel, Paul. 1998. *Music in Nova Scotia—The Written Tradition: 1752–1893.* Halifax: Nova Scotia Museum Curatorial Report Number 85.

McCullagh, Harold. 1977. *The Man Who Made New Brunswick Sing.* St. Stephen, N.B.: Print'N Press.

McGee, Timothy J. 1969. "Music in Halifax, 1741–1799." *Dalhousie Review* 49:377–387.

———. 1985. *The Music of Canada.* New York: Norton.

McGuire, Matthew D. 1998. *Music in Nova Scotia: The Oral Tradition.* Halifax: Nova Scotia Museum Curatorial Report Number 84.

O'Neill, Paul. 1975. *The Oldest City: The Story of St. John's, Newfoundland.* Erin, Ont.: Press Porcepic.

Proctor, George. 1980. *Canadian Music of the Twentieth Century.* Toronto: University of Toronto Press.

Rowe, Frederick W. 1976. *Education and Culture in Newfoundland.* Toronto: McGraw-Hill.

Ryerson, Talbot Hugo, ed. 1904. *Musical Halifax, 1903–4.* Halifax: McAlpine Publishing Co.

Temperley, Nicholas. 1987. "Stephen Humbert's Union Harmony, 1816: 'Sing Out Glad News.'" CanMus Documents 1. Toronto: University of Toronto.

Tweedie, R. A., Fred Cogswell and W. Stewart MacNutt, eds. 1967. *Arts in New Brunswick.* Fredericton: Brunswick Press.

Vogan, Nancy F. 1987. "The Maritime-Leipzig Connection." In *The Red Jeep and Other Landscapes of Interest to Douglas Lochhead,* ed. Peter Thomas, 69–75. Fredericton: Fiddlehead/Goose Lane Editions.

———. 1988. "Music Instruction in Nova Scotia before 1914." In *Musical Canada: Words and Music Honouring Helmut Kallmann,* ed. John Beckwith and Frederick A. Hall 71–78. Toronto: University of Toronto Press.

———. 1991. "The Musical Traditions of the Planters and 'Mary Miller Her Book.'" In *Making Adjustments: Change and Continuity in Planter Nova Scotia 1759–1800,* ed. Margaret Conrad, 247–252. Fredericton: Acadiensis Press.

———. 1993. "Music Education in the Maritimes between the Wars: A Period of Transition." In *Myth and Milieu: Atlantic Literature and Culture, 1918–1939,* ed. G Davies, 77–86. Fredericton: Acadiensis Press.

———. 2000. "The Robert Moor Tunebook and Musical Culture in Eighteenth-Century Nova Scotia." In *Planter Links: Community and Culture in Colonial Nova Scotia,* ed. Margaret Conrad. Fredericton: Acadiensis Press. In press.

Walter, Arnold, ed. 1969. *Aspects of Music in Canada.* Toronto: University of Toronto Press.

Woodford, Paul. 1983. *Charles Hutton.* St. John's: Creative Printers and Publishers.

———. 1984. *Nish Rumboldt.* St. John's: Creative Printers and Publishers.

———. 1988. *We Love the Place, O Lord: A History of the Written Musical Tradition of Newfoundland and Labrador to 1949.* St. John's: Creative Printers and Publishers.

Anglo Music
Anne Lederman

Story Songs: Ballads and Occupational Songs
Comic Songs
Instrumental Music
Collecting and Current Practices

Atlantic Canada comprises Newfoundland and Labrador, Nova Scotia, Prince Edward Island, and New Brunswick. People of British and Irish origin are the majority in all these provinces, but there are significant Scottish Gaelic traditions in Cape Breton and eastern Prince Edward Island (P.E.I.) that are outside the scope of this article. Atlantic Canada was historically dependent on the sea. Musically these provinces share an Old World song repertoire of traditional English and Scottish ballads and newer "broadside" ballads, as well as a fondness for comic and mocking songs, generally locally composed.

Nova Scotia, New Brunswick, and Prince Edward Island further share a strong lumbering tradition that is also common to the northeastern United States and parts of Québec, Ontario, and the Prairies. Newfoundland was settled earlier and has always been culturally distinct. It is both the oldest British colony and the oldest European settlement in North America and has the largest repertoire of indigenous English-language folk songs of any area in Canada.

STORY SONGS: BALLADS AND OCCUPATIONAL SONGS

Atlantic Canada was fertile ground for collectors throughout most of the twentieth century. Whether centuries old or recently composed, story songs about historical, mythical, or local events have always been favored. Until the mid-twentieth century, these songs were generally sung a capella in homes, at sea, or in lumber camps and were "characterized by a straightforward, undramatic solo performance with little dynamic variation from stanza to stanza" (Rosenberg 1992:473). High notes tended to be held and last lines spoken, revealing the strong Irish influence in the music. Some singers embellished the melody while others sang quite plainly. Songs were often associated with particular singers, so that others would not perform them.

The oldest songs are the ballads collected by Sir Frances James Child, known in North America as the Child Ballads, with forty-four collected from Newfoundland, forty-seven from Nova Scotia, and thirty-eight from New Brunswick (Child 1965 [1882–1898]; Doucette and Quigley 1981:3–19). However, Child ballads are generally a very small part of the repertoire of the male singers from whom most of the collecting has been done. Edward Ives notes that women tended to know far more Child Ballads than men but often sang them only in private, so that we may never know to what extent they were known overall (1978:17 23). According to the collections we have, the most popular in Newfoundland was "Sweet William's Ghost" (Child 77), while in all other areas "Bonny Barbara Allen" (Child 84) was favored. Almost all of Child's comic and riddling ballads turn up, the latter featuring a devil figure who asks a child riddles that he must solve to save himself.

Broadside ballads are more popular than Child ballads overall. Especially well known were stories of separated lovers in which the man returns in disguise and tests his sweetheart's faithfulness in various ways. These turn up under many names: "The Pretty Fair Maid," "The Dark-Eyed Sailor," "The Mantle So Green," "The Plains of Waterloo." "It would seem that romance, adventure and tragedy are the chief reasons for the appeal of a majority of ballad stories" (Doucette and Quigley 1981:9).

More favored by male singers were songs specifically related to work away from home: at sea, in the lumber camps (Nova Scotia, New Brunswick, and P.E.I.), and at the seal and cod fisheries (Newfoundland). Older sea songs include shanties as well as stories of pirates and disasters, many featuring ghosts and other supernatural elements. Woods songs were frequently adapted from sea songs; certain elements, such as coming ashore after a long voyage, might change into coming back to town after a winter in the woods. Like disasters at sea, songs were written to commemorate accidents on the drive or in the camps, but with far less supernatural content. Camps were known for their music. Ives reports, "I know of one man who went to work in the woods because he liked the singing, and several have told me how when they had come home from the woods, they would be asked if they had learned any 'new' songs" (1989:10). Sealing songs (*swilin*) in Newfoundland are similar in style to woods songs, relating details of work, telling stories of particular trips and hardships, and commemorating death.

COMIC SONGS

In all provinces there is a stock of comic songs or "ditties," most locally composed. Some woods songmakers became legendary for such songs, for example, Larry Gorman of Prince Edward Island, whose parodies and mocking songs were sung throughout the northeast. In Newfoundland, such songs typically make fun of individuals or of people from certain places (figure 1).

INSTRUMENTAL MUSIC

Newfoundland is the only area of Canada in which the fiddle is not the favored dance instrument. There, that honor goes to the button accordion. Known for fast tempos

FIGURE 1 "Mussels in the Corner," traditional Newfoundland song. Transcribed by Anne Lederman from the singing of Harry Hibbs.

'Deed I am in love with you   Out all night in the fog-gy dew

'Deed I am in love with you,   mus-sels in the cor-   ner.

CHORUS: 'Deed I am in love with you
Out all night in the foggy dew
'Deed I am in love with you
Mussels in the corner

Ask a Bayman for a smoke
He will say his pipe is broke
Ask a Bayman for a chew
He will bite it off for you

All the people on Belle Isle
Don't get up 'til half past nine
Wash their face in kerosene oil
Paddy, you're a corker

I took Nellie to the ball
But she wouldn't dance at all
Nailed her up against the wall
Left her there 'til Sunday

and simple chords (the standard one-row accordion had only two chords on it), accordions pump out "singles" (2/4 tunes with generally two notes to a beat, also called polkas), "doubles" (6/8 or 9/8 tunes, also called jigs), and "triples" (2/4 tunes with four notes to a beat, also called reels or breakdowns) for both group and step dances. Fiddles, tin whistles, and harmonicas are also played, and dance tunes were frequently sung, a practice known as "gob," "mouth," or "chin" music, the last named after the practice of resting one's chin on one's hands while singing. Like the songs, the instrumental tune repertoire is heavily Irish influenced, although much of it is unique to the island. There is a fair amount of asymmetric phrasing, resulting in "crooked tunes." Harry Hibbs and Dick Nolan greatly popularized the accordion tradition with their recordings in the 1960s, which alternate instrumentals with sentimental Irish, country and western, and native Newfoundland songs. Two older fiddlers, Emile Benoit and Rufus Guinchard, both French Newfoundlanders, have also achieved national recognition, largely because of the support given them by younger revival players.

In the other Atlantic provinces, fiddle reigns supreme. Gaelic and French Acadian areas have their own styles and repertoires, but English areas have favored what has become known west of the Maritimes as the "down east" sound. Originally popularized by Don Messer and the Islanders of P.E.I. through national radio and television programs, this style is a smooth, relatively unornamented distillation of older Anglo-Irish and Scottish repertoires. It favors waltzes, jigs, and reels, with some clogs, also called "schottisches," for step dancing and some polkas and specialty dance tunes. The slow airs and strathspeys of Gaelic tradition are mainly gone in "down east" style (although some survive as clogs), while many Irish and American hornpipes have been sped up to the tempo of reels. Promoted through contests and recordings, this style has come to dominate many parts of Canada. Well-known proponents of this style, not all from Atlantic Canada, include Ned Landry, King Ganarn, Ward Allen, Graham and Eleanor Townsend (all deceased), Peter Dawson of Ontario, and Ivan Hicks of New Brunswick.

COLLECTING AND CURRENT PRACTICES

The first published scholarly collection in the Maritimes was Roy Mackenzie's *Ballads and Sea Songs from Nova Scotia* (1928). That and his *Quest of the Ballad* inspired many others, such as Kenneth Peacock in Newfoundland, Helen Creighton in Nova Scotia and New Brunswick, and Louise Manny in New Brunswick. Both Creighton and Manny had radio shows featuring traditional singers for a time, and Manny started the legendary Miramichi Festival devoted to traditional singing in 1958. Pigeon Inlet has released many recordings of Newfoundland material, but most other traditional recordings in the Maritimes were made by American companies, especially Folkways. Memorial University in Newfoundland has the only program of Folklore Studies in Canada and holds a large archive of traditional folklore and song. Newfoundland also has many small local music festivals, some of which still feature traditional singing.

However, in spite of the greater collecting activity in the Atlantic provinces than in any other part of Canada, certain areas, especially P.E.I., and kinds of repertoire, such as women's songs, have been missed. Also, little comparative work has been done on the melodies in order to determine how widespread certain tune types are.

Overall, the a capella tradition throughout the Maritimes has gradually given way to guitar and band accompaniment and, consequently, a more regular rhythm and less ornamented singing style. In Newfoundland, many revival groups and individuals have become popular, such as Figgy Duff, The Wonderful Grand Band, Simani, Kelly Russell, Jim Payne, and Ron Hines, all of whom write original material. In Cape Breton a local songwriting tradition has also flourished, partly related to the annual *Cape Breton Follies,* a musical revue.

REFERENCES

Benoit, Emile. 1979. *Emile's Dream* (and others). Pigeon Inlet Productions PIP 732. LP disk.

Child, Francis James. 1965 [1882–1898]. *The English and Scottish Popular Ballads*. Vols. 1–6. New York: Dover.

Creighton, Helen. 1966. *Songs and Ballads from Nova Scotia*. New York: Dover.

———. 1971. *Folksongs from Southern New Brunswick*. Ottawa: National Museum of Civilization.

———. 1979. *Maritime Folk Songs*. Toronto: The Ryerson Press.

———. 1992. "Folk Music: Nova Scotia and New Brunswick." In *Encyclopedia of Music in Canada*, 2nd ed., ed. Helmut Kallmann, Gilles Potvin, and Kenneth Winters, 474–475. Toronto: University of Toronto Press.

Creighton, Helen, and Doreen Senior. 1950. *Traditional Songs from Nova Scotia*. Toronto: The Ryerson Press.

Croft, Clary. c. 1980s. *False Knight upon the Road*. Solar SAR-3015. LP disk.

Dibblee, Randall, and Dorothy Dibblee. 1973. *Folksongs from Prince Edward Island*. Summerside: Williams and Crue.

Doucette, Laurel, and Colin Quigley. 1981. "The Child Ballad in Canada: A Survey." *Canadian Folk Music Journal* 9:3–19.

Figgy Duff. 1991. *Weather Out the Storm* (and others). Hypnotic 71356-1000. Compact disc.

Folksongs of the Miramichi. 1962. Folkways FM 4053. LP disk.

Fowke, Edith. 1992. "Ballads." In *Encyclopedia of Music in Canada*, 2nd ed., ed. Helmut Kallmann,

Gilles Potvin, and Kenneth Winters, 70. Toronto: University of Toronto Press.

Gledhill, Christopher. 1973. *Folksongs of Prince Edward Island*. Summerside: Williams and Crue.

Guinchard, Rufus. 1981. *Steptunes and Dances* (and others). Pigeon Inlet Productions PIP 737. LP disk.

Hibbs, Harry. c. 1970s. *At the Caribou Club* (and others). ARC 794. LP disk.

Hicks, Ivan. 1987. *Shingle the Roof* (and others). N.p. LP disk.

Hynes, Ron. 1996. *Face to the Gale* (and others). Artisan Music E2/E436187. Compact disc.

Island Folk Festival. 1985. Institute of Island Studies FH001. LP disk.

Ives, Edward D. 1964. *Larry Gorman: The Man Who Made the Songs*. Bloomington: Indiana University Press.

———. 1971. *Lawrence Doyle: The Farmer Poet of Prince Edward Island*. Orono: University of Maine Press.

———. 1978. "Lumbercamp Singing: Up from the Valley of Dry Bones." *Canadian Folk Music Journal* 5:17–23.

———. 1989. *Folksongs of New Brunswick*. Fredericton: Goose Lane Editions.

———. 1992. "Folk Music: Prince Edward Island." In *Encyclopedia of Music in Canada*, 2nd ed., ed. Helmut Kallmann, Gilles Potvin, and Kenneth Winters, 475. Toronto: University of Toronto Press.

Landry, Ned. c. 1960s. *Saturday Night Breakdown* (and others). RCA Camden CAL 780. LP disk.

Lehr, Genevieve. 1985. *Come and I Will Sing You: A Newfoundland Songbook*. Toronto: University of Toronto Press.

Manny, Louise, and J. R. Wilson. 1968. *Songs of the Miramichi*. Fredericton: University Press of New Brunswick.

Maritime Folk Songs. 1962. Folkways FE-4307. LP disk.

Messer, Don, and His Islanders. 1979. *The Good Old Days* (and others). MCA Records TVLP 99052. LP disk.

O'Donnell, John C. 1975. *The Men of the Deeps*. Waterloo: Waterloo Music Co.

Payne, Jim. 1992. *Empty Nets* (and others). SingSong SS 9192. Compact disc.

Peacock, Kenneth. 1965. *Songs of the Newfoundland Outports*. Vols. 1–3. Ottawa: National Museum of Civilization.

Prince Edward Island Fiddlers. Vols. 1 and 2. Islander Records SVC-002, SVC-001387.

Rosenberg, Neil V. 1992. "Folk Music: Newfoundland." In *Encyclopedia of Music in Canada*, 2nd ed., ed. Helmut Kallmann, Gilles Potvin, and Kenneth Winters, 473. Toronto: University of Toronto Press.

Ryan, Shannon, and Larry Small. 1978. *Haulin' Rope and Gaff: Songs and Poetry in the History of the Newfoundland Seal Fishery*. Toronto: Breakwater Books.

Simani. 1986. *Outport People*. SWC Productions SD-758A. LP disk.

Songs of the Newfoundland Outports. 1984. Pigeon Inlet Productions PP-7319. LP disk.

Snapshot:
The Celtic Revival in Cape Breton
Kate Dunlay

Traditional Culture and Its Decline
The Vanishing Cape Breton Fiddler Makes a Comeback
Traditional Music as an Economic Resource

During the 1990s the popularity of Celtic music rose dramatically throughout various parts of the world. Canadians played a large part in this revival, especially musicians from Cape Breton Island in Nova Scotia and also from nearby Prince Edward Island (P.E.I.). Cape Breton in particular is now widely recognized as an important homeland for Celtic music. Formerly much of the public associated the "Celtic" genre mainly with the music of Ireland.

To the casual outside observer it may seem as if talented musicians suddenly started emerging from Cape Breton in limitless supply. The East Coast Music Awards, founded in 1989, helped raise the profile of Maritime Celtic artists. In 1994 the groundbreaking Rankin Family from Cape Breton won four (national) Juno Awards, having created their own brand of Celtic-folk-country-pop. Soon afterward, fiddlers Ashley MacIsaac and Natalie MacMaster—practically neighbors in Cape Breton—and Richard Wood of PEI achieved international recognition. MacIsaac single-handedly gained a new following for traditional music with a best-selling CD that fused fiddling with alternative music (winning him five awards at the East Coast Music Awards including pop rock and hip-hop artist of the year), which he then followed up with a strictly traditional CD (MacIsaac 1995, 1996). Perhaps even more remarkable is the commercial success of Mary Jane Lamond, who sings primarily in Gaelic; although her music crosses into contemporary genres as well, it is thoroughly rooted in the Cape Breton Scottish tradition.

In retrospect, it can be seen that many factors contributed to setting the stage for the Celtic revival in Cape Breton and PEI. There were earlier organized efforts to perpetuate elements of existing culture, to resuscitate extinct or declining elements, and to introduce new elements of related culture. Popularization, commercialization, and formalization also have their roots in earlier movements.

TRADITIONAL CULTURE AND ITS DECLINE

The Maritimes (the Atlantic Provinces) were settled so thickly by Highland Scots in the late eighteenth and early nineteenth centuries that even in 1900 much of Inverness County in Cape Breton and parts of Kings County in Prince Edward Island were still culturally Gaelic (Gibson 1998:236). A large number of Irish also settled in both PEI and Cape Breton.

For many years, relative isolation and a strong value placed on musical culture kept traditional music alive. Rock music, television, and a high rate of emigration due to unemployment are reasons often given for the eventual decline of the fiddle tradition during the 1960s. By this time, a rapid decrease in the number of Gaelic speakers threatened the Gaelic song tradition in Cape Breton. Traditional Cape Breton–style bagpiping was on the verge of being lost as well, having been replaced by a modern Scottish style.

THE VANISHING CAPE BRETON FIDDLER MAKES A COMEBACK

The fiddling revival in Cape Breton is usually dated to the first Glendale Festival in 1973. Two years earlier a Canadian Broadcast Corporation (CBC) documentary, *The Vanishing Cape Breton Fiddler,* had predicted the demise of Cape Breton fiddling unless the younger generation started taking more of an interest in the tradition (MacInnis 1971). Community response to the challenge was immediate. The Cape Breton Fiddlers' Association was formed, and 130 fiddlers came together for the Glendale Festival (MacGillivray 1981:4). The popularity of similar outdoor concerts has continued to grow, and at least one festival takes place in Cape Breton almost every weekend of the summer. The annual Rollo Bay Fiddlers Festival in PEI was founded in 1977 under similar circumstances.

Early commercialization of fiddle music

Local radio programs in Cape Breton and the nearby mainland featured fiddle music from the beginning. Some of these programs could be heard in PEI, where they reinforced the Scottish element of PEI fiddling (Perlman 1993:5–6). From the 1930s to the 1960s the Celtic label (a Nova Scotia company) released at least eighty-seven fiddle records (McKinnon 1989). Rodeo Records also released a considerable number. Only a few commercial records of Gaelic singing or bagpiping were issued.

These fiddle records were sold primarily to people who already had some connection to Cape Breton culture. However, in the 1970s Rounder Records, an American folk revival label, started its "7000 series" consisting almost entirely of Cape Breton fiddlers and piano players. These disks reached a new audience that ultimately was to grow significantly. As more people in the United States, Scotland, and other countries discovered the Cape Breton tradition, more musicians from Cape Breton were invited to play concerts and festivals in these areas, as well as to teach at music camps and workshops. Fans also started traveling to Cape Breton in increasing numbers.

The heart of the fiddle tradition

Despite the commercialization of Cape Breton fiddle music, home and community activities have remained its lifeblood. At the heart of the fiddle tradition is the dance. Scottish-style step dance, a percussive form of dance related to tap dance, has been preserved in both Cape Breton and PEI (and recently reintroduced into Scotland by Cape Breton teachers). Square dancing (figure 1) is also a strong part of the culture, as is the house party, or *cèilidh,* which remains a common venue for fiddle music. Some people believe that the cadence of the Gaelic language is essential to Cape Breton fiddle music. They fear that elements of the old style are being lost as the link with the language weakens.

Piping

During the last two decades of the twentieth century, a movement was begun to revive a nearly extinct style of piping. Formerly one of the primary roles of pipers in Cape

FIGURE I   Roadside sign in Cape Breton. Photo by Kate Dunlay, 1989.

Breton had been, like that of fiddlers, to provide music for social dancing and solo step dancing. However, with the advent of amplification, pipes lost their advantage over fiddles (Shears 1995:i). The old style of aurally transmitted piping had begun to be considered technically inferior as well and began to be supplanted by a more formal modern style of Scottish piping around the time of World War I (Gibson 1998:14, 206–207; Shears 1995:ii).

There are, however, old-style pipers in some of the contemporary mixed instrument ensembles spawned by the Celtic revival. For this type of music, the drive and individual expression of old-style dance piping are assets once again valued over technical virtuosity. Small-pipes have also been introduced, which blend well with the fiddle in traditional settings.

Meanwhile, Nova Scotia has remained a center for conventional pipe band and competition-oriented bagpiping. PEI has also become a center with the establishment in 1990 of the College of Piping and Celtic Performing Arts of Canada (affiliated with the College of Piping in Glasgow, Scotland).

Gaelic song

Although the number of people who use Gaelic in their everyday lives has dwindled, lately there has been a resurgence of interest in the language within Cape Breton. It is also not uncommon for revivalist singers who have little or no Gaelic background to come to Cape Breton to begin their study of the language. *Cèilidhs,* Gaelic choirs, and milling frolics also continue to bring together traditional singers in Cape Breton. Milling songs were once sung while pounding newly woven wool cloth on a table to preshrink it. Although this type of labor is no longer done, the rhythmic music and the social occasion have been preserved.

TRACK 26

An influential songster

The larger folk music revival of the 1960s and 1970s stirred up some interest in Scottish and Irish song in the Maritimes. However, Cape Breton folk singer John Allan Cameron was ahead of his time in performing and recording Gaelic songs for a general audience. He was also a pioneer in playing pipe and fiddle tunes on the guitar and combining fiddle pieces with songs. Because he has been featured on national television shows and toured internationally, he has had a large impact. At the beginning of the new century, his musical career is still going strong.

TRADITIONAL MUSIC AS AN ECONOMIC RESOURCE

In 1999 the Center for Community and Enterprise Networking at the University College of Cape Breton reported: "Music, and particularly Celtic music with the associated Gaelic culture and tourism, has now become the primary resource of Cape Breton Island and its largest employment sector" (Gurstein 1999). The center created an e-mail discussion list for Cape Breton music in 1995 and then a website to support the music industry.

From an economic point of view the Celtic music revival has been successful beyond expectations. Nevertheless, some individuals suggest that more needs to be done to sustain the Gaelic-based culture that produced the music. For example, in her critique of the first Celtic Colours International Festival held in Cape Breton, Gaelic magazine editor Frances MacEachen accused the festival of "capitalizing on Celtic" without making any concrete plans to fulfill their mandate to "preserve . . . the Gaelic language, music, arts and crafts" (MacEachen 1997a:6). In a related article she pointed out that there was no traditional, a capella Gaelic singing represented on the first festival CD, whereas non-Celtic Acadian and Québécois music was included (MacEachen 1997b).

FIGURE 2 Big Pond Concert, Cape Breton. Photo by Kate Dunlay, 1985.

Public discussion of the management of culture in Cape Breton has resulted in changes in the past. In the 1970s the Gaelic College of Celtic Arts and Crafts faced a crisis. Members of the teaching staff objected to the College's being run "not as an institution for the promotion and preservation of the Gaelic culture . . . but as a tartan circus with the attraction of tourists as the first priority" (Foster 1988:100). Founded in 1939 by a Scot, the school first brought instructors from Scotland to teach Gaelic, piping, and highland dancing. Older locally preserved styles of piping, dancing, and fiddling were given little attention (MacInnes 1997:177–178). Cape Breton–style fiddle and step dance classes were finally introduced in the late 1970s (Foster 1988: 98–102). By the 1990s the fiddle program especially had expanded greatly, and course offerings were balanced between local and imported Celtic traditions (figure 2).

There has been a growing recognition that Cape Breton's strength is in what is unique about its heritage. As long as Cape Breton and PEI can be portrayed accurately as regions that support authentic Celtic culture, that culture can be used as a resource. Traditional musicians will continue to emerge, and innovators and revivalists will have a wellspring from which to draw.

—KATE DUNLAY

REFERENCES

The Cape Breton Music Center On-line. Available: http://cbmusic.com (21 July 1999).

Cranford, Paul Stewart. 1997. *Winston Fitzgerald: A Collection of Fiddle Tunes.* Englishtown, N.S.: Cranford Publications.

Creighton, Helen, and Calum MacLeod. 1979. *Gaelic Songs in Nova Scotia.* Ottawa: National Museums of Canada.

Doherty, Elizabeth A. 1996. "The Paradox of the Periphery: Evolution of the Cape Breton Fiddle Tradition 1928–1995." Ph.D. dissertation, University of Limerick.

Dunlay, Kate, and David Greenberg. 1996. *Traditional Celtic Violin Music of Cape Breton, the Dun-Green Collection.* Mississauga, Ont.: DunGreen Music.

Fergusson, Donald A. 1977. *Beyond the Hebrides.* Halifax: Donald A. Fergusson.

Fleming, Lee. 1997. *Rock Rhythm and Reels: Canada's East Coast Musicians on Stage.* Charlottetown: Ragweed Press.

Foster, Gilbert. 1988. *Language and Poverty, the Persistence of Scottish Gaelic in Eastern Canada.* St. John's: Institute of Social and Economic Research, Memorial University of Newfoundland.

Garrison, Virginia Hope. 1985. "Traditional and Non-Traditional Teaching and Learning Practices in Folk Music: An Ethnographic Field Study of Cape Breton Fiddling." Ph.D. dissertation, University of Wisconsin.

Gibson, John G. 1998. *Traditional Gaelic Bagpiping, 1745–1945.* Montréal: McGill-Queen's University Press.

Gurstein, Michael. 1999. "Fiddlers on the Wire: Music, Electronic Commerce and Local Economic Development on a Virtual Cape Breton Island." In *Doing Business on the Internet: Opportunities and Pitfalls,* ed. Celia T. Romm and Fay Sudweeks. Berlin: Springer Verlag.

Hornby, Jim. 1982. "The Fiddle on the Island: Fiddling Tradition on Prince Edward Island." Master's thesis, Memorial University of Newfoundland.

MacDonell, Margaret. 1982. *The Emigrant Experience: Songs of Highland Emigrants in North America.* Toronto: University of Toronto Press.

MacEachen, Frances. 1997a. "Capitalizing on Celtic." *Am Bràighe* 5(2):6.

———. 1997b. "Getting Lost on the Road Home." *Am Bràighe* 5(2):8.

MacGillivray, Allister. 1981. *The Cape Breton Fiddler.* Sydney, N.S.: College of Cape Breton Press.

———. 1988. *A Cape Breton Ceilidh.* Sydney, N.S.: Sea Cape Music Ltd.

MacInnes, Sheldon. 1997. *A Journey in Celtic Music–Cape Breton Style.* Sydney, N.S.: UCCB Press.

MacInnis, Ron, prod. 1971. *The Vanishing Cape Breton Fiddler.* Halifax: CBC. Film.

MacIsaac, Ashley. 1995. *Hi™ How Are You Today?* Ancient Music/A&M Records 31454 0522 2. Compact disc.

———. 1996. *Fine® Thank You Very Much.* Ancient Music/A&M Records 79602 2002-2. Compact disc.

McKinnon, Ian Francis. 1989. "Fiddling to Fortune: The Role of Commercial Recordings Made by Cape Breton Fiddlers in the Fiddle Music Tradition of Cape Breton Island." Master's thesis, Memorial University of Newfoundland.

Moore, Maggie. 1995. *Scottish Step Dancing.* Scottish Arts Council. Available: http://metalab. unc.edu/gaelic/john/scottishstepdancing.html or http://www.tullochgorn.com/scottish.html (21 July 1999).

Murphy, Peter, prod. 1996. *The Pipes, the Pipes Are Calling.* Antigonish, N.S.: Seabright Video Productions. Videocassette.

Perlman, Ken. 1993. *The Old Time Fiddlers of Prince Edward Island.* Booklet accompanying Marimac Recordings C-6501. Audiocassette.

———. 1996. *The Fiddle Music of Prince Edward Island: Celtic and Acadian Tunes in Living Tradition.* Pacific, Mo.: Mel Bay Publications.

Shears, Barry. 1991. *The Gathering of the Clans Collection.* Halifax: Taigh a' Chiuil/The House of Music.

———. 1995. *The Cape Breton Collection of Bagpipe Music.* Halifax: Taigh a' Chiuil/The House of Music.

African Canadian Music
Anne Lederman

Religious Music
Secular Music

The first free blacks to arrive in any numbers in Atlantic Canada were those emancipated by the British government during the American Revolution (in order to attract them to the British side as soldiers) [see OVERVIEW OF MUSIC IN CANADA, p. 1066]. Only about a third of them, however, were given the land grants in Nova Scotia that they had been promised. After the War of 1812, another offer of freedom in exchange for British loyalty prompted more than two thousand to come. About one-quarter moved on to New Brunswick, where most eventually went to the larger centers of Fredericton and Saint John, although small black communities continued at Elm Hill, Willow Grove, Kingsclear, and Loch Lomond. In Nova Scotia a fairly large community called Campbell River, later Africville, was established on the outskirts of Halifax, but every county has some small black settlements. Some blacks returned to the United States after the American Civil War (1861–1865), and a few Barbadians came to Sydney around the turn of the century to work in the coal mines, but overall the Maritime black population remained relatively stable from the mid-1800s until the 1940s, when more Caribbean immigrants began to arrive.

RELIGIOUS MUSIC

In the 1700s black Maritimers tended to be part of Anglican and Presbyterian congregations, but in the late eighteenth century the Newlight Movement attracted many black converts. "They held camp meetings in which crying, shouting, fainting and 'fits,' seeing visions and hearing voices were important elements of the service" (Henry 1973:123). However, under white leadership, there was a trend away from fundamentalism in the mid-1800s, which also affected the early all-black churches, whose leaders were often trained in England. Henry does note the use of the words *sing-song, hymn sing, shouts,* and *jubilees* for musical gatherings, but at least in the areas where she worked, "the hymns are those which can be heard in any Baptist or other Protestant church, and with few exceptions 'Shouting' Spirituals are heard only occasionally in an average Service" (Henry 1973:126). The Africville Church was such an exception. Known for its intense emotionalism, its choir often performed at other churches. However, Africville was torn down in 1966 and all residents transplanted to different parts of Halifax.

Helen Creighton recorded songs all over Nova Scotia in the 1940s, including eighty-one from black residents. Her collection is now housed in the Canadian Museum of Civilization in Ottawa/Hull. These are mainly spirituals from published collections such as those of the Fisk Jubilee Singers. Both EMO and Newsflash Sounds, recording companies of New Brunswick and Newfoundland respectively, have recorded local gospel groups. A 1975 National Film Board Production, *Seven Shades of Pale,* depicts the Nova Scotia community of Tracadie, with shots of older singers singing "Way Down in Alabama," "Where Shall I Be When the First Trumpet Sounds?," and other country and gospel songs. Gospel is still the most popular music in the black Maritime community, and such groups as the Nova Scotia Mass Choir and The Gospel Heirs are now bringing it to a wider audience. A recent anthology, *Lord, You Brought Me a Mighty Long Way: An African Nova Scotian Musical Journey* (1998) gives an overview of sacred music during the past fifty years.

SECULAR MUSIC

According to newspaper accounts, there were several itinerant black performers in the late 1800s. The most celebrated were brothers James and George Bohee, banjoists with Haverly's Genuine Colored Minstrels, who spent the latter part of their lives performing to great success in England. Minstrel shows put on by local blacks were apparently common in the early twentieth century, and influenced many white Maritime country musicians.

In 1923 American anthropology student Arthur Huff Fauset collected folklore and eleven song texts, but no melodies, from black residents of Nova Scotia, including British ballads, sea shanties, and six minstrel songs (1931). There are other reports of blacks singing shanties and British ballads, but "country music has been the preferred form since the 1940's" (Rosenberg 1988:147). Brent Williams and Harry Cromwell, from the Weymouth, Nova Scotia area, made up two-thirds of the Birch Mountain Boys, one of the first bluegrass bands in Canada to record in the 1950s. However, after an initial acceptance, they were refused an appearance on Don Messer's prestigious CBC television show, *Don Messer's Jubilee,* when they forwarded their picture. George Hector of Grand Bay, New Brunswick, met with more success as "the singing chauffeur" and leader of The Maritime Farmers; he performed on radio for twenty years and on television for six.

Henry (1975:11–21) traces the reasons for what she considers a lack of musical tradition in the Maritimes compared with other North American black communities, citing church influences and economic dependency on the dominant white community as factors. But Neil Rosenberg takes issue with Henry's assertion that music was lacking in these communities, pointing out that the continued influence of British folk traditions and American popular music, both white and black in origin, is not surprising given the history and size of the community (Rosenberg 1988:145). In any case, later oral reports would seem to dispute Henry's notion. From Africville, for example, comes the following:

> Had plenty of musicians here just as good as what you hear on records. Boysie Dixon could make a piano sing like a bird in the sky. Archie Dixon played the saxophone and clarinet. We had guitar players, fiddle players, and drummers, too. Some folks even made their own instruments. Flutes carved from a tree branch, spoons, washboards—anything and everything . . . you could get a whole concert going at the drop of a hat. Why, we even had some of our people study at the Halifax Conservatory of Music. (Carver 1989:5–6)

Maritime black communities have produced several professional classical and jazz musicians, such as contralto Portia White from Truro, Nova Scotia, who had a brief international career in the early 1940s culminating in a celebrated recital at New York's

The best known contemporary secular performers with black Maritime roots are songwriter Faith Nolan, whose 1984 recording, *Africville,* pays tribute to many black Canadian women, and vocal quartet Four the Moment, many of whose songs address Maritime black experience.

Town Hall. The best known contemporary secular performers with black Maritime roots are songwriter Faith Nolan, whose 1984 recording, *Africville,* pays tribute to many black Canadian women, and vocal quartet Four the Moment, many of whose songs address Maritime black experience. They have released three recordings: *We're Still Standing* (1984), *Four the Moment: Live* (1993), and *In My Soul* (1996). Africville also inspired Montréal pianist Joe Sealy's 1997 composition *Africville Suite,* a tribute to his father's community.

REFERENCES

Black Cultural Centre of Nova Scotia. 1998. *Lord You Have Brought Me a Mighty Long Way: An African Nova Scotian Musical Journey.* CBC/BCCNS.

Black Mother, Black Daughter. 1990. Ottawa: National Film Board of Canada. Videocassette.

Carver, Irvine, et al. 1989. *Africville.* Halifax: Mount St. Vincent University.

Clairmont, D. H., and Magill, Dennis W. 1974. *Africville: The Life and Death of a Canadian Black Community.* Toronto: McLelland and Stewart.

Creighton, Helen. 1950. *Traditional Songs from Nova Scotia.* Toronto: Ryerson Press.

Fauset, Arthur Huff. 1931. *Folklore of Nova Scotia.* New York: American Folklore Society.

Four the Moment. 1987. *We're Still Standing.* JAM FTM 1987. Compact disc.

———. 1993. *Four the Moment: Live.* JAM FTM 101. Compact disc.

———. 1996. *In My Soul.* Atlantic. Compact disc.

Henry, Frances. 1973. *Forgotten Canadians: The Blacks of Nova Scotia.* Don Mills, Ont.: Longman Canada Ltd.

———. 1975. "Black Music in the Maritimes." *Canadian Folk Music Journal* 3:11–21.

National Film Board of Canada. 1975. *Seven Shades of Pale.* Documentary film.

Nolan, Faith. 1984. *Africville.* M.W.I.C. Records 11161A. Compact disc.

Nova Scotia Mass Choir. 1998. *Heaven.* Halifax CBC Maritimes. Compact disc.

Overlords. 1999. *Overlords Caravan 2000.* Trobiz Records. Compact disc.

Rosenberg, Neil. 1988. "Ethnicity and Class: Black Country Musicians in the Maritimes." *Journal of Canadian Studies* 23:138–156.

Sealy, Joe. 1996. *Africville Suite.* SEA JAM Records. Compact disc.

Seven Shades of Pale. 1975. Ottawa: National Film Board of Canada. Videocassette.

Sparks, Jamie. 1998. *The Time.* Smash Trash Distribution. Compact disc.

Sparks, Jeremiah. 1998. *Let Go and Get God.* N.p.

Winks, Robin, 1971. *The Blacks in Canada: A History.* Montréal: McGill–Queen's University Press.

Acadian Music
Beverley Diamond

History
Songs
Dance Music
Contemporary Performers

The first European settlers to arrive and remain in Atlantic Canada—and to substantially interact and influence the local culture—were the French ancestors of present-day Acadians, who established Port Royal (now Annapolis Royal, Nova Scotia) in 1605. While it is hard to make a clear distinction between the Acadians in Atlantic Canada and the Québec French populations on the basis of where they come from, in general Acadians emigrated from the region south of the Loire, especially around Poitou, while Québécois are predominantly from Normandy and Breton. There are many exceptions to this pattern, however, and many historians attribute the distinctiveness of the two cultures to their history in the Americas rather than to their European roots.

HISTORY

Heavily reliant on their indigenous neighbors for subsistence, the earliest settlers seem to have had extensive interaction with the Mi'kmaq and Maliseet neighbors. A masquelike theatrical production by lawyer and historian Marc Lescarbot, the *Theater of Neptune* (1606), performed "on the waves" (in canoes) to celebrate the return of a local dignitary, was a case in point: the extant libretto contains musical cues and indicates participation of both French and Native performers.

During the seventeenth and eighteenth centuries, the Acadians were buffeted between the French and English, but because they maintained control of strategic shipping routes (especially from Ile St. Jean [now Prince Edward Island], Il Royale [now Cape Breton], and Havre St. Pierre on the north shore of the St. Lawrence), they were needed by both sides and managed to live in relative stability. With the Treaty of Utrecht in 1713, however, their security became more tenuous. In 1755 a proclamation was issued to deport all Acadians from British North America, an event that was physically and emotionally devastating, as recorded in song and story. The defiant Acadian woman Evangeline, for example, who lost her life in an effort to resist forcible removal, has been celebrated in the poetry of Longfellow, in numerous songs, and in at least one Canadian opera (by Graham George, 1948, predating one by U.S. composer Otto Luening on the same theme in the same year).

The expulsion of approximately six thousand people to the thirteen New England colonies was, however, temporary. Some moved further south to Louisiana, where they

Acadian singing style is generally less accented than Québécois folk song, and the timbre of some singers has a distinctive quality.

constituted Cajun communities. Others returned to the Maritime Provinces after the Seven Years' War ended in 1763. The Treaty of Paris, which ended this war, guaranteed religious rights for French inhabitants, but this provision did not extend to the Acadians. The latter were permitted to return, however, provided they took an oath of allegiance to the British Crown. The return took place gradually between the mid-1760s and the late 1820s (Ross and Deveau 1992:76).

More recently, a significant musical reminder of this traumatic historic episode is the 1970s band 1755, whose members effected a virtual explosion of interest in Acadian music, spawning the rock-influenced zydeco style of Zacharie Richard and the more folk-based music of Les Mechants Maquereaux, Suroît, Maniak, and Les Habitants.

In the nineteenth century, Acadians attempted to reclaim land and learn to exist in the midst of a British milieu. They were numerically the strongest in New Brunswick; cultural infrastructures developed most extensively there and continue to be reflected in the important role played, for example, by French-language radio based in Moncton and the Centre d'études acadiennes at the Université de Moncton. (See Cormier [1975] for a survey of the archival holdings at the university relating to Acadian music.) Fishing increased in importance, but both farming and fishing communities remained poor and isolated in comparison to their British neighbors. The introduction of the Cooperative movement in the 1930s improved economic prospects to some extent.

SONGS

While nationalist movements date from the mid-nineteenth century and folk songs were printed in a local newspaper, *La Voix d'Evangeline,* in the 1930s, scholarly attention to Acadian folk song was scant until the work in Cape Breton by Père Anselme Chiasson, whose five-volume *Chansons d'Acadie* (1942–1979) presented some of the musical richness of this tradition. Subsequent collections of note include Cormier's *Ecoutez tous petits et grands* (1978), Deschene's *C'était la plus jolie des filles: Répertoire des chansons d'Angélina Paradis-Fraser* (1982), Creighton's *La Fleur du Rosier* (1988), Arsenault's *Complaintes acadiennes de L'Ile-du-Prince-Édouard* (1980), and his anthology *Par un dimanche au soir* (1993).

Arsenault (1980) has categorized local compositions into five groups: *les complaintes* (narrative songs analogous to English ballads), satirical songs, political and electoral songs, songs about special events, and miscellaneous songs. The repertoire of individual singers provides interesting points of comparison for this list. For example, Prince Edward Islander Leah Maddix, one of Arsenault's consultants, about whom he has written (1993), performed numerous narrative *complaintes,* religious songs for major holidays of the year (especially *la fête de noël* and *la fête de l'an*), and songs to accompany various work-related "frolics" (milling cloth, for example, or rug hooking). The influence of the English milieu is sometimes apparent in Leah Maddix's frequent exhortations of "le fun" of Acadian music and in her choice of tunes such as "Silver Threads among the Gold" or "My Bonny Lies over the Ocean." Acadian singing style is generally less accented than Québécois folk song, and the timbre of some singers has a distinctive quality.

DANCE MUSIC

Acadian dance music is, thus far, less well documented than folk song, although Acadian fiddlers from Prince County, Prince Edward Island, have released several recordings. One of the most respected of the older generation is Eddy Arsenault, whose recordings of the 1990s (1993, 1995) feature a number of his own tunes, such as "Herring Reel," "Rocky Point Reel," and "The Draggers."

Acadian fiddlers perform regularly at the Acadian Jamboree held annually in Abrams Village, Prince Edward Island. Both the repertoire and style of Acadian and Gaelic fiddlers in the Maritimes are closely related, but Prince Edward Islanders observe that Acadian fiddling is faster and more frequently involves harmonic cross-relations from one octave to another. Acadian folk dance ensembles play a significant role in acquainting a younger generation with traditional music. The extent to which the exchange between Acadian and Anglo-Celtic fiddle traditions have joined to constitute a distinctive style and repertoire is significant.

In Newfoundland, the francophone population is concentrated along the south and west coasts in the most isolated communities of the island. Their roots are closely connected to the Acadian population of the Maritime Provinces. The best known Acadian fiddlers from Newfoundland are Rufus Guinchard (1899–1990) and Emile Benoit (1913–1992) (Quigley 1987:11).

CONTEMPORARY PERFORMERS

Contemporary Acadian song writers have enjoyed strong support both locally and in the larger francophone (and to some extent anglophone) community. Edith Butler and compatriots who moved to Québec—Angele Arsenault and Suroit—played a major role during the folk revival era in the 1970s and continue to participate in the construction of a francophone cultural identity. A younger generation includes Prince Edward Islanders La Sagouine, Nova Scotians Les Tymeux de la Baie, and New Brunswickers Les Mechants Maquereaux.

REFERENCES

Arsenault, Eddy. 1993. *Piling on the Bois Sec.* Wellington, PEI: House Party Productions, HPP1. Compact disc.

———. N.d.: Les Productions de L'Ile, ILE 1001. Compact disc.

Arsenault, Georges. 1980. *Complaintes acadiennes de L'Ile-du-Prince-Édouard.* Montréal: Lemeac.

———. 1993. *Par un dimanche au soir: Leah Maddix, chanteuse et conteuse acadienne.* Moncton: Editions d'Acadie.

Chiasson, Père Anselme. 1942–1979. *Chansons d'Acadie.* Vols. 1–3, Pointe-aux-Trembles, P.Q.: La Réparation. Vols. 4–5, Moncton: Les Editions des Aboiteaux.

Cormier, Charlotte. 1975. "Situation de la recherche en folklore acadien." *Canadian Folk Music Journal* 3:30–34.

———. 1978. *Ecoutez tous petits et grands.* Moncton: Les Editions d'Acadie.

Creighton, Helen. 1988. *La Fleur du Rosier: Chansons folkloriques d'Acadie,* ed. Ronald Labelle. Ottawa and Sydney: Canadian Museum of Civilization and University College of Cape Breton.

Deschenes, Donald. 1982. *C'était la plus jolie des filles: Répertoire des chansons d'Angélina Paradis-Fraser.* Montréal: Editions Quinze.

Party Acadien. 1995. House Party Productions. Compact disc.

Quicley, Colin. 1987. "Creative Processes in Musical Composition: French–Newfoundland Fiddler Emile Benoit." Ph.D. dissertation, University of California.

Ross, Sally, and Alphonse Deveau. 1992. *The Acadians of Nova Scotia: Past and Present.* Halifax: Nimbus.

Snapshot: "She's Gone, Boys": Songs in Response to the Moratorium on Fishing in Newfoundland

Peter Narváez

Musical Styles
Lyrics
The Arrest of the Spanish Trawler *Estai* **and the "Turbot War"**

Traditions of song making and versifying that respond to local events continue to thrive in Atlantic Canada, especially in Newfoundland. As with the sealing protests and counterprotests of the 1970s, area residents view the moratorium on fishing northern cod, first announced on 2 July 1992, as a tragedy severe enough to prompt vernacular poetics and music—expressive elements of culture the people of a particular region identify as their own.

Unlike the demise of the limited seal fishery, the moratorium on fishing northern cod has directly undercut the basis of the North Atlantic fisheries. Described by Canadian historian Jack Granatstein as the "biggest layoff in Canadian history" (1992:2), this fishing ban is an economic tragedy of unprecedented proportions. Originally imposed for two years, it has been extended by the Canadian government, and moratoria on the fishing of other species (capelin, salmon, turbot) have followed. These actions have put approximately fifty thousand fishers and fish-plant workers out of work in the region, thirty thousand of these in Newfoundland.

Although the federal government has instituted two major compensation and retraining programs (NCARP, the Northern Cod Adjustment and Recovery Program, 1 August 1992 to 15 May 1994, and TAGS, The Atlantic Groundfish Strategy, 16 May 1994 to 15 May 1999), these have not offset what is widely perceived as the loss of a traditional way of life.

This snapshot examines musical and other expressive responses to the fisheries crisis and owes much to the cooperation and generosity of journalists in electronic and print media. I have occasionally discussed my interest in such songs on Canadian Broadcast Corporation (CBC) radio and in the *St. John's Evening Telegram* and subsequently learned of items of which I had been unaware. At some point what I had termed "songs responding to the fisheries crisis" came to be called "Moratorium songs," a descriptive phrase I use here.

The songs considered in this snapshot were created between July 1992 and spring 1996 and were collected from and performed by individuals or groups from Newfoundland and from Newfoundlanders on the mainland of Canada and from Prince Edward Island. Many of the singers are women, of whom seven wrote their own songs. To my knowledge, only a few performers are full-time entertainers. For most, entertaining publicly in their localities is an enjoyable avocation, whereas a few perform only in their own homes.

Most of the songs are commercially available on audiocassette or CD. Usually produced privately in small home-recording studios, they have had very limited distribution. Because the largest sales have been in singers' home communities, I liken the songs to the broadsides of yesteryear, especially as they consist of formulaic commercial verse on topics of local interest [see POPULAR MUSIC OF THE PARLOR AND STAGE, p. 179]. Other pieces have not been for sale but have been transcribed to paper and/or prerecorded and sent to radio programs or have been directly recorded on answering machines for radio shows, especially the *Fisheries Broadcast* (formerly *Fisherman's Broadcast* [Narváez 1991]), one of the CBC's oldest continuous programs. Several have been performed at special public entertainments and then aired on radio and television.

MUSICAL STYLES

The songs are composed in many musical styles. Some feature popular folk-revival and singer-songwriter styles, frequently characterized by heavily accented chordal accompaniments and minor melodies, whereas others combine tragic-ballad and rousing male chorus conventions of the Irish folk revival. But almost half are performed in country music styles and the related Newfoundland style, a musical syncretism in which traditional melodies, rhythms, and button accordion are joined with musical content and traditional forms from Britain and Ireland and with country music of the United States, the Maritimes, and mainland Canada (Narváez 1978).

Composed by Wayne Bartlett of Quirpon, "She's Gone, Boys, She's Gone" beautifully illustrates this Newfoundland style (figure 1).

FIGURE 1 "She's Gone, Boys, She's Gone." Copyright Wayne Bartlett, 1992.

[Bartlett] saw what was happening to a way of life that I loved when I way a boy lose its interest in the lives of my son and his friends. . . . The fishery and the whole system failed my son in that his last chance at a decent job was taken away from him by the closure, the Moratorium. One time, if a young man could not find a job, he could always depend on the fishery to earn a living for himself and his family. In the song, "She's Gone Boys, She's Gone," there's an old man and a young boy. The old man tells of what he saw when he was younger, tells the young boy that none of the younger generations will ever see those things because now she's gone. (Bartlett 1996)

The old man looked down in his dory
As he stood on the wharf one more time.
With the wind in his hair, he stood there and stared
"Look at her now, what a crime!"
Said, "I can recall when I built her,
When I lived in the place I called home.
'Twas a good life back then, but never again,
Cause now, she's gone, boys, she's gone.

He said, "My father once told me
That surely there would come a day
When the fish that you'd get would be too small to split
And too big to just throw away."
I never thought that I'd ever live to see such going on.
To think that the end could ever have been,
But now, she's gone, boys, she's gone.

REFRAIN: She's gone, boys, she's gone, she's gone,
She's gone boys, she's gone.
What we didn't destroy, we allowed to die.
And now, she's gone, boys, she's gone,
She's gone, boys, she's gone, boys, she's gone.

He stopped for a moment, just stood there
With a handkerchief, he wiped his eyes.
He looked out to sea, then he looked at me
He said, "I pities you, boy.
You'll never see the great big old codfish
Float up in the trap and go on
Out over the heads like one time thy did,
Cause now, she's gone, boys, she's gone."

He said, "You see that old dory;
One day I thought she'd be yours:
She's still just as good, you know, as she was,
Except for the gunwhales and oars.
She might need a new plank there somewhere.
And the bottom might be a bit drawn."
Then a lump in his throat as the old man spoke:
"She's gone, boys, she's gone, boys. She's gone."

Since outport Newfoundland has borne the brunt of the Moratorium—four hundred communities thrown onto the brink of dissolution—it is hardly surprising that the vast majority of songs performed in Newfoundland style and country styles have been composed, played, and sung by outport residents, virtually all having a stake in the fisheries.

LYRICS

The lyrics of Moratorium songs respond explicitly to the fisheries crisis. Not nearly as well known as other Newfoundland folk songs and very limited in their distribution, Moratorium songs are topical and express specific opinions on occupation and employment. They can be considered insider occupational songs in the broad sense of depicting the milieu of a trade, of expressing concerns about it, and of creating performance contexts where "singer and audience are part of that same milieu" (Porter 1992:14).

Lyrical responses to loss

While the often used image of an old fisherman may index the passing of an entire way of life, many problems of loss cited in the songs are quite precise: from the loss of a favorite Newfoundland dish, "fish and brewis":

> Last year we were out fishing; this year we're on the land:
> Me and brother George, me son, we started up a band.
> There's no use to ignore it, there's nothing else to do:
> Tonight we're cooking up some beans instead of fish 'n' brewis. (Buffett 1993)

to the loss of song tradition itself, as indicated by the traditional song titles illustrated in the lyrics of Owen Morsden's song, "I'se the B'y," also known as "Lukey's Boat," "The Tiny Red Light," "The Little Boats of Newfoundland," and "Hard, Hard Times":

> I wonder what folklore changes will come,
> Now that the word is Moratorium?
>
> REFRAIN: You see, I'se the b'y can't sell his boat;
> Lukey's crew won't need the grub;
> No need to place the tiny red light.
> The little boats don't go to sea;
> There's no fish off Cape St. Mary's:
> Those are hard, hard times. (Hewison 1993)

Diachronically, Moratorium song texts have changed from the positive and sometimes humorous responses to the initial federal financial "package," thought by some to be a "windfall":

> REFRAIN: Oh the Moratorium, the Moratorium,
> We'll buy ourselves a brand new car
> On the Moratorium.
>
> I got myself a Big Bear, and George, he got a Skidoo,
> We're running round the rabbit roads, so you can join us too.
> With the money that we're making . . . pretty good, my son,
> I'll buy myself a brand new car on the Moratorium. (Buffett 1993)

to later expressions of frustration and anxiety as the Moratorium has continued and the extent of the ecological disaster has become apparent, as in the Irish Descendants' recording of John Phippard's 1994 song "Will They Lie There Evermore?":

> I was born under the star, never meant to journey far,
> From all the faces and the places that I called home.

And my father lived the same, and his father before him,
But now I see in my son's eyes, something has changed.
And the smoke it has stopped rising from the chimney up the road,
And the light no longer shines over the door.
Last year I lent a hand to haul the boats onto the land:
They've been lying there for nineteen months or more,
And I wonder, will they lie there evermore. (John Phippard 1994)

THE ARREST OF THE SPANISH TRAWLER *ESTAI* AND THE "TURBOT WAR"

Perhaps the most dramatic episode of the fisheries crisis was the Canadian government's arrest of the Spanish trawler *Estai* on the Grand Banks in January 1995 and the subsequent "turbot war" with the European Union. These events inspired expressions that vented pent-up anger at the Moratorium by providing an unambiguous culprit: Spain. Significantly, these expressions voiced positive support for the government of Canada, specifically praise for Newfoundlander Brian Tobin—at the time federal fisheries minister, now premier of Newfoundland and Labrador—who was the subject of many Moratorium songs and poems, such as the one by Gideon Sheppard whose first few lines are quoted here:

I am an inshore fisherman from Lark Harbor, Newfoundland,
Who due to the Moratorium is now upon the land.
There has been much overfishing by the foreign fleet;
It's been talked about by everyone who I've chanced to meet.
It's been told at meetings and at forums too,
We all knew what was happening, but what could we do? (Sheppard 1995)

In explaining to me why he penned his poem, Sheppard (1996) articulated how creating verse centering on events provides an important traditional outlet for expressively communicating concerns about critical social issues:

I was a fisherman who had noticed the decline in fish stocks in the last few years. It had been very hard to make a living at the inshore fishery. I realized that there was a lot of overfishing, not only by the foreign fleet, but by our own as well. Our other ministers on Fisheries and our scientists failed to do anything about it. When Mr. Brian Tobin decided to do something about it I was thrilled and decided to write about it. I only started to write poems in 1992. I find that it is the best way I can express myself (Sheppard 1996).

Tobin's elevation to the status of a national hero rose so high that he was eventually lampooned on CBC Radio by Ontario resident Kirk Elliot in his song "The Ballad of Brian Tobin or 'Let My Turbot Go,'" sung triumphantly to the melody of the country music classic "Ghost Riders in the Sky":

Once there was a turbot way down in the sea,
Swimming by his lonesome, saying, "What will become of me?
The Spanish fleet's a-coming, and can you tell me why
They're fishing off the nose and tail 'til the Grand Banks run dry?"

He'd seen the Spanish fishing nets, his mortal enemy;
He'd seen them sweep the cod that once swam proud and free.
So he stuck his little head above the waves that were so high
And he called for Brian Tobin to hear his mortal cry.

REFRAIN: Yippee aye ay
Yippee aye oh
Let my turbot go. (Elliot 1995)

The songs and poems cited here and in the References that follow, as well as many others publicly issued over the past decade, thus clearly show that traditional song making and versifying continue to be alive and well in Atlantic Canada as its residents adjust, through lament or satire, to economic, political, and social realities.

—PETER NARVÁEZ

REFERENCES

Baker, Kristin, and Leo Baker. 1994. "Moratorium." SWC Productions. Audiocassette.

Bartlett, Wayne. 1992. "She's Gone Boys, She's Gone." SWC Productions. Audiocassette.

Best, Anita. 1995. "Which Side Are You On?" CBC Radio, *Morningside,* 2 March.

Buffett, Jim, and Chris Buffett. 1993. "The Moratorium Song." Audiocassette.

Butler, Hedley. 1994. "We Took Enough." CBC Radio, St. John's, *Fisheries Broadcast.*

Cat Fud. 1995. "They Boys from Spain." CBC Radio, St. John's, *The Morning Show.*

Coffey, Eddie, and Marty Delaney. 1996. "Tribute to Brian Tobin." RMS 0196. Audiocassette.

Denisoff, R. Serge. 1972. *Sing a Song of Social Significance.* Bowling Green, Ohio: Bowling Green University Popular Press.

Elliot, Kirk. 1995. "The Ballad of Brian Tobin or 'Let My Turbot Go.'" CBC Radio, St. John's, *The Morning Show.*

Evans, Bobby. 1994. "Jig One on the Sly." Audiocassette.

Fitzgerald, Dennis. 1994. "The Patrick and Elizabeth." CBC-TV, St. John's, *Land and Sea.*

Fowlow, Susan. 1995. "Dad Was a Fisherman." Private recording from Francesa Swan.

Gallant, Lennie. 1994. "Peter's Dream." *The Open Window.* Columbia CD CK80196. Compact disc.

Granatstein, Jack. 1992. "Northern Cod Shutdown: Biggest Layoff in Canada." *St. John's Evening Telegram,* 3 July.

Great Big Sea. 1993. "Fisherman's Lament." *Great Big Sea.* NRA Productions Ltd. CD NRA3-1002. Compact disc.

Hewison, George, and The Rank 'n' File Band. 1993. "I'se the B'y and Other Stuff." RFCD9301. Audiocassette.

Hillier, Calvin. 1993a. "I'm Going Back to School." Audiocassette.

———. 1993b. "When the Last Ship Comes Sailing In." Audiocassette.

Irish Descendants. 1994. "Will They Lie There Evermore?" *Gypsies Lovers.* Warner Music Canada Ltd. CD W88. Compact disc.

Joyce, Jim. 1991. "Hard, Hard Times." On *Another Time: The Songs of Newfoundland,* Kelly Russell and Don Walsh, producers. Pigeon Inlet Production CD PIPCD 7326. Compact disc.

Lamson, Cynthia. 1979. "Bloody Decks and a Bumper Crop: The Rhetoric of Sealing Counterprotest." *Social and Economic Studies* 24. St. John's: Institute for Social and Economic Research.

Lee, Fred. 1994a. "Back in School." Audiocassette.

———. 1994b. "We All Knew 'Twas Comin'." Audiocassette.

Mercer, Paul. 1979. *Newfoundland Songs and Ballads in Print, 1842–1974: A Title and First Line Index.* St. John's: Memorial University of Newfoundland.

Moonshiners, The. 1993. "The Good Days Are Gone." SWC Productions 99321. Audiocassette.

Narváez, Peter. 1978. "Country Music in Diffusion: Juxtaposition and Syncretism in the Popular Music of Newfoundland." *Journal of Country Music* 7(2):93–101.

———. 1991. "Folk Talk and Hard Facts: The Role of Ted Russell's 'Uncle Mose' on CBC's 'Fishermen's Broadcast.'" In *Studies in Newfoundland Folklore: Community and Process,* ed. Gerald Thomas and J. D. A. Widdowson, 191–212. St. John's: Breakwater.

———. 1995. "Newfoundland Vernacular Song." In *Popular Music: Style and Identity,* ed. Will Straw et al., 215–219. Montréal: Center for Research on Canadian Cultural Industries and Institutions.

Norman, Wayne. 1992. "Way of Life." Private recording. Audiocassette.

Overton, Jim. 1993. "Newfoundland in the 1930s: Voices of the Unemployed." *Socialist Studies Bulletin* 33:8–19; 34:3–29.

Payne, Jim. 1994. "Empty Nets." Mary Brown's, TWP-093. Audiocassette.

Phippard, John. 1996. Personal correspondence, 6 October.

Porter, Gerald. 1992. *The English Occupational Song.* Umea, Sweden: University of Umea.

Porter, Harris. 1994. "Searching for a Rainbow." SWC Productions. Audiocassette.

Power (O'Rourke), Ernestine. 1994. "Boy by My Side." CBC Radio, St. John's, *Radio Noon.*

Prince, John, and A Piece of the Rock. 1994. "Let's All Pull Together" and "Where Do Old Boats Go? *Take Me Back.* Rattle Falls Publishing CD JP-001. Compact disc.

Rosenberg, Neil V. 1991. "The Gerald S. Doyle Songsters and the Politics of Newfoundland Folksong." *Canadian Folklore canadien* 13(1):45–57.

Sheppard, Gideon. 1995. Untitled recitation. CBC Radio, St. John's, *Fisheries Broadcast.*

———. 1996. Personal correspondence, 25 October.

Simani. 1994. "It Could Be Worse." SWC Productions. Audiocassette.

Smith, Jennifer. 1996. "Song of the Dory Man." *The Evening Telegram,* 17 July.

Soirees, The. 1993. "Crisis in the Fishery." TS-93. Audiocassette.

Split Peas, The. 1995. "Where Are the Fishing Boats?" Audiocassette.

Stuffed Squid. 1994a. "The Moratorium Blues." SWC Productions. Audiocassette.

———. 1994b. "Package Song." SWC Productions. Audiocassette.

———. 1995. "The Last Water Haul." CBC-TV, *Land and Sea.*

Wallace, Len, 1994. "Leaving the Fishing Behind." CBC Radio, St. John's, *Fisheries Broadcast.*

Walsh, Junior. 1993. "I Used to Be a Fisherman." Audiocassette.

Wareham, Wilfred. 1984. "The Monologue in Newfoundland Folk Culture." In *The Encyclopedia of Newfoundland,* Vol. 2, ed. J. R. Smallwood et al., 252–262. St. John's: Newfoundland Book Publishers.

Whyatt, Sabrina. 1994. "What Has Gone Wrong?" Lloyd Bartlett Productions. LBP5 12301. Audiocassette.

Section 3b
Québec

The province of Québec, first explored by Samuel Champlain in the early seventeenth century, continues to be dominated by French culture, institutions, and language. Although the British gained control of Québec in 1763, the French have retained much control and autonomy within this province. Early French settlers interacted with the local American Indian population, predominantly Algonquian-language speakers, the Mohawk of the Iroquois Confederation, and the Inuit, who today identify culturally and politically with the Inuit of the newest Canadian territory, Inuvut. Along with secular traditions such as fiddling and dance musics, the Catholic church, with its centuries-old religious musics and institutions, helped promote both French and Catholic culture in Canada. Today a vibrant popular music, derived from the *chanson* tradition, as well as classical music, jazz, and a lively Sephardic Jewish musical tradition, among many others, thrive in Québec.

A street violinist leans against a pillar in Montréal, Québec. © Kit Kittle/CORBIS.

Overview
Marie-Thérèse Lefebvre

The story of Québec's musical creativity, a mirror image of its cultural diversity, is as rich and complex as the society it reflects.

HISTORICAL CONTEXT

This vast territory where the Inuit and other Native Americans lived was initially colonized by France, which introduced the music of the Versailles School, especially that of the Louis XIV and Louis XV periods. Having incurred heavy debts following battles for the Spanish throne (1701–1713) and the Seven Years War in Europe (1756–1763), France ceded the young colony to England in 1763.

Sixty thousand inhabitants, the majority of whom were Catholic and French speaking, were now governed by a Protestant English parliamentary regime that by the Québec Act of 1774 gave them the right to religious freedom, use of the French language, and the French civil law system. Accelerating westward expansion and development caused the government to divide the colony into two administrative territories in 1791, Upper Canada (Ontario) and Lower Canada (Québec).

The arrival in the early nineteenth century of English, Scots, and then Irish immigrants profoundly changed the relatively homogeneous nature of this population. Political tensions between French- and English-speakers increased. These tensions resulted in Deputy Louis-Joseph Papineau's calls for change, which led to the Patriots' revolt in 1837–1838. To resolve the conflict, Lord Durham proposed to the British Parliament in 1840 that the two territories be fused so as to weaken or neutralize the larger number of French-speakers. The proposal was doomed to failure, and it gradually engendered nationalist sentiment and led to the confederation of four provinces to form the nation of Canada in 1867. Thus a nation was born. Much of the music of this period stems from an oral tradition and bears witness to the nation's search for identity: old French folk songs, nostalgic Scots and Irish ones, and the political and nationalist songs that animated popular gatherings.

The period 1867–1914 was marked by great economic growth: a network of railways from east to west, commercial and cultural exchange with the United States, particularly with New England, and the reopening of diplomatic relations with France were all elements that prepared Québec to enter the modern era and had an impact on the development of its musical institutions.

A number of French-speaking students, freethinkers, and artists such as writers Guy Delahaye, Paul Morin, and Marcel Dugas and musician Léo-Pol Morin traveled to Paris and discovered new artistic trends there. On their return in 1914 they attempted to implant this modern vision of society in Québec, an effort immediately thwarted by the bourgeoisie and the clergy. Acerbic debate between the proponents of a land-based, agrarian nationalism—who believed in a Canadian style of art rooted in Canadian folklore—and modernists—who advocated a more ecumenical vision of art—marked the political and intellectual life of this period (1914–1939) as well as all realms of artistic creation such as literature, painting, and music. In the minority and without serious support, the modernists remained isolated despite siding with modern American and European trends during this first half of the twentieth century. "Full of hope and promises, the twenties ended in disillusionment brought about by economic crisis," wrote Ramsay Cook (Brown 1987:510). Not until the postwar generation would the pendulum swing back.

From 1939 to 1979, Québec leaped into the technological era. Modernity infiltrated every corner, helped in its diffusion this time by a variety of organizations. Calls for change in opposition to the governing political party of the province, the Union Nationale, came from every side: from unions and leftists against the clergy's hegemony; from feminists; and also, perhaps even more radically, from artists, especially after the publication in 1948 of Paul-Emile Borduas's *Le Refus global,* a manifesto signed by fifteen artists challenging the agrarian values of Québec society and advocating a refusal of any ideology that curbed creative spontaneity. This lively flowering of new ideas occurred during a period of unprecedented economic expansion that placed 1960s Québec into networks of international exchange, under first the Liberals and then the Parti Québécois.

After 1979 new circumstances changed Québec's direction. On the one hand, the rise of conservative and far right political movements, together with the spiraling government deficit, wars and famines (elsewhere in the world) that caused great upheavals in the population, and mergers of industrial megacomplexes, changed people's ways of acting and living. On the other hand, growing awareness of the fragility of the environment, growing ethnic diversity, questioning of modernity's theoretical discourse, and the exponential development of information and communication technologies also combined to explain the phenomenon of postmodernity as a new historical paradigm.

Artistic expression today is individualistic, personal, and subjective, and thus much more varied. Artistic trends have multiplied, and many creators bring environmental concerns or intercultural diversity into their work or draw inspiration from past styles and genres to renew their own musical language. While at the turn of the twenty-first century many deplore the abandonment of rationalist discourse consisting of clearly defined structures and points of references that allow clear value judgments, young postmodernists turn their backs on this recent past and project in their works a vision of the future that is theirs to build. It is in this historical context that I now address Québec's musical history.

MUSIC IN NEW FRANCE (1608–1763)

When France ceded its immense territory to England in 1763, many of the roughly sixty thousand people who lived there had already imported instruments, performance styles, and sheet music (both handwritten and printed by musicians of the Versailles School) and had in their memories a repertoire of religious, instrumental, vocal, folk, and dance music. During the French regime, music was a subject learned in school and part of political meetings. A vehicle for conveying social values, it accompanied the rhythms of the seasons and of family life and helped differentiate social classes. It was also a weapon the savvy clergy used to conquer souls and "facilitate" encounters between Jesuits and indigenous peoples, as discussed in recent studies by Elisabeth Gallat-Morin, Jean-Pierre Pinson, and Paul-André Dubois (1995).

MUSIC IN THE ENGLISH COLONY (1763–1867)

A French-based musical culture was already well established when the English-speaking community began to take root in the young colony at the end of the eighteenth century. The Protestant aesthetic advocated that religious music not be reserved for an elite body like the Catholic choirs trained in the *schola cantorum* (musical schools specialized in the learning of Georgian chant) but more democratically sung by all, within the family as well as at church. The new availability of printing technology allowed the clergy to publish anthologies of *cantiques* 'hymns' and choral songs as early as 1802. A major economic base began to grow, the effects of which remain unstudied.

In the same spirit of new accessibility the musical amateur was born. With more and more musical instruments being imported (thanks in part to Frederick Glacke-meyer [1795–1836], a musician who had immigrated to Québec in 1777), chamber music could be heard in intimate gatherings and at governors' speeches or during visits by the royal family. String and wind instruments constituted the earliest orchestras that gathered under the direction of Charles Sauvageau at the earliest banquets held by the Saint John the Baptist Society in 1842. In the meantime, theatrical companies multiplied—there were a dozen before 1867—and foreign troupes came to perform operas. Verdi's *Il Trovatore* was performed in Montréal in 1858, five years after it was written. As Mireille Barrière has pointed out, over 1,705 stage shows were performed in Montréal between 1840 and 1913 (1989:331). Music teachers such as Jean Chrysostome Brauneiss II (1814–1871) in Montréal and Antoine Dessane (1826–1873) in Québec were among the earliest classically trained musicians to teach the European repertoire before confederation. Finally, new Irish, Scots, and English immigrants brought with them a body of folk music that joined the patriotic and nationalist songs heard at gatherings. In fact, who would remember Octave Crémazie's poem "Le Drapeau de Carillon" ("The Carillon Flag") if Charles W. Sabatier's music had not engraved it in our memories?

The return of the French sailing vessel *La Capricieuse* to the port of Québec in 1855 reestablished diplomatic ties to France. This political event presaged important consequences for the history of Québec's music: French-Canadian musicians could now go to France to study, establish contacts and sometimes even friendships with European composers, and become professional composers themselves.

MUSIC OF CONFEDERATION (1867–1914)

During the period following the confederation of Canada at the turn of the twentieth century, various structures for spreading music were in place—theaters, impresarios, professional musicians sufficiently trained to join the various musical groups that already existed, and a public now ready to pay for tickets to concerts. In the ensuing years, musical Québec enjoyed economic prosperity thanks to flourishing industries in musical instruments (especially pianos and organs), printing, and publishing. Even more important was the importation of sheet music from Boston and Paris featuring compositions by nineteenth-century composers such as Cécile Chaminade, Paul Delmet, Théodore Dubois, Charles Gounod, Benjamin Godard, Édouard Lalo, Jules Massenet, and Camille Saint-Saëns, who, together with Romain Bussine, founded the Société Nationale de Musique (SNM) in Paris 1871. These composers specialized in light music—pieces they wrote in order to pay the bills and eat—written in a conservative, accessible salon style. It was not an unusual occurrence in this era to attend performances of this very lucrative musical genre.

Yet there is no comparison between the effervescence of musical life at the turn of the twentieth century (1867–1914) and what we know of it today. For example, during his stay in Paris from 1873 to 1875, Calixa Lavallée (1842–1891) attended classes taught by François-Antoine Marmontel, François Bazin, and Adrien-Louis Boieldieu. We know very little about his stay except that one of his *études* for piano, "Le Papillon" ("The Butterfly"), was added to the list of works recommended by the Paris Conservatory; that *A Suite for Orchestra* was conducted by orchestra director Adolphe Maton; and that Marmontel dedicated one of his fifty salon *études* to Lavallée and gave him a letter of recommendation when he returned to Canada in July 1875.

Lavallée sought the creation of a conservatory and organized concerts with an eye to amassing the subsidies necessary for it, but facing the inertia of a conservative government, he preferred to exile himself to the United States, where he became president of the American Music Teachers Association and organized the first concert consisting entirely of works by American composers at the Congress of Cleveland on 3 July 1884.

We should also acknowledge the imposing career of Guillaume Couture (1851–1915), a friend of Camille Saint-Saëns, Romain Bussine (a renowned singing teacher who willed part of his musical library to Couture), and Théodore Dubois, the professor of harmony with whom Debussy so disagreed. We are indebted to him for having forged close ties with American musicians and orchestra leaders in Boston and New York, for establishing a great choral, orchestral, and operatic repertoire in Montréal—most notably by creating the Montréal Philharmonic Society—and for conducting the Montréal Symphony Orchestra between 1894 and 1896. This orchestra, founded in 1891 by Ernest Lavigne, later became part of the cultural offerings of Sohmer Park, one of the first public spaces in Montréal to hold simultaneous cultural events.

Couture's pilgrimage to Bayreuth in 1897 constitutes the high point of a life's work of nearly twenty years dedicated to introducing, among other things, the Wagnerian repertoire. Soon after the death of the famous composer, Couture completed this endeavor by publishing a series of ten articles in the newspaper *La Patrie* ("The Country") in 1884.

Although his music, particularly the oratorio *Jean le Précurseur,* reflects the academic view upheld by the Parisian composers of the SNM (especially Dubois), Couture left his students with a profound knowledge of music and a demanding conception of composition. Traces of conservatory training can be found in the scores of Achille Fortier (1864–1939), who studied at the Paris Conservatory during 1886–1890 with Ernest Guiraud, Debussy's composition teacher. On his return to Montréal, Couture directed a concert entirely devoted to works by this young composer, who left us melodies of great expressive quality before leaving Québec for California, returning later in his life.

More cautious by nature, Alexis Contant (1858–1918) received his training most exclusively from Lavallée in Boston and completed it on his own using the great repertoire of Johann Sebastian Bach, César Franck, Charles Gounod, Camille Saint-Saëns, and Richard Wagner. An organist for over thirty years at the Church of St. John the Baptist in Montréal, he wrote little, preferring to devote himself to teaching. His Trio for Violin, Cello, and Piano of 1907 remains his best known work.

History also recalls the names of performers who had an international career in Europe and the United States, including singers Emma Albani (1847–1930) and Eva Gauthier (1885–1958) as well as several other musicians who shaped Québec's turn-of-the-century musical culture, among them Paul and Arthur Letondal, Arthur Laurendeau, and Joseph-Jean Goulet, who directed the Montréal Symphony Orchestra after Couture's departure.

THE EARLY MODERN PERIOD (1914–1939)

It is hard to explain in a few words what motivated the young intellectuals and artists who gathered almost secretly at the dawn of the twentieth century and then left for Paris to board modernity's train. Forced to return—surely too soon—by the start of World War I to a still very conservative environment that believed a nationalism rooted in rural parish life was necessary in order to survive, they could be found at the Arche, their clandestine meeting place on Montréal's Notre Dame Street, discussing plans for the publication of a multidisciplinary magazine *Le Nigog,* which began publishing in 1918.

Pianist and music critic Léo-Pol Morin (1892–1941), who had attended the premier of Stravinsky's *Rite of Spring,* joined in these discussions. His first article opened debate on the thorny question of nationalism in music. Should pieces incorporate a land-based ideology in order to become specifically Canadian? No, he answered, and his strong support for the trend of modernity prompted several retorts from traditionalists Gustave Comte, Arthur Letondal, and Frédéric Pelletier, supported on their side by the "right-minded" public and by the clergy, particularly the ineffable Monsignor Olivier Maurault, a sultician who had an influence on the cultural life at the time.

In the same vein, Morin's references to contemporary French composers were met with acerbic criticism by pianist Alfred Laliberté, a passionate supporter of Alexander Scriabin, Nicholas Medtner, and German music. Morin, unrelenting, increased the recitals he held and had the works of Debussy performed (by the Ladies Morning Musical Club in 1905) as well as those of Enrique Granados, Manuel De Falla, Maurice Ravel, and Albert Roussel. He also introduced the young Québec composer Rodolphe Mathieu (1890–1962) to the public. This freethinking, self-taught artist, through his reading and reflection, explored the process of musical creation, in contrast to his predecessors and contemporaries, for whom composing was above all the application of nearly immutable music-writing rules whose results had to conform to the expectations of the bourgeois and clergy.

Mathieu was the first Canadian musician to consider composition a form of personal and original expression of artistic thought and the first to mine all the potential of music-writing tools without regard for established rules. For Mathieu, composition was no longer a function of or a frill added to the job of the instrumental teacher, but an authentic art designed to produce an original work corresponding to its author's deep personality. Mathieu was thus far ahead of his time in making a distinction between composing and creating.

After the *Nigog* adventure and the war's end, a number of Québécois moved to France between 1919 and 1928, among them Morin and Mathieu. They established close ties with musicians there, including Albert Roussel, Arthur Honegger, and Maurice Ravel, whom Morin accompanied on his North American tour with its last stop of Montréal in 1928, as well as Robert Schmidt, founder of New York's Pro Musica. During this time, the Delphic Study Club, created in New York and run by English-speaking women, organized an annual music week, 1923–1939, during which several French-speaking musicians performed. As morose as the decade of the thirties was—the consequence of the economic crisis, which brought with it right-wing politics—this remains an important musical period. Deserving particular mention is the work of composer Claude Champagne on his return to Québec from Paris in 1928. His work included the development of music education in the province's public schools; the founding of French-speaking music organizations such as the Variétés Lyriques, the Disciples of Massenet, and the Montréal Symphony Orchestra; and, above all, the 1936 creation of a state-sponsored radio station, the Sociéte Radio Canada, where Jean Beaudet (1908–1996), the first musical director and head of the Radio Canada orchestra, played an essential role in the ensuing decades in popularizing Canadian works.

MID-TWENTIETH-CENTURY MUSIC (1940–1979)

Major changes shaped composers' behavior and the musical environment starting in 1939. On the one hand, the career of composer increasingly demanded specialized training, resulting in the creation of the Conservatoire de Musique du Québec in 1942, led by Wilfrid Pelletier (1896–1982), Claude Champagne (1891–1965), and Jean Vallerand (1915–1996). This new institution joined private schools founded by nuns, especially the Vincent D'Indy Music School created in 1933, and the music departments created at Québec universities—McGill (1920), Laval (1922), and Montréal (1950).

On the other hand, with the creation of the Canadian Composers' League in 1951 and the Canadian Music Center (CMC) in 1959, composers approved by the league could house their manuscripts at one of the CMC's regional centers, facilitating access to and research on music written after 1939. Finally, the creation of the Canada Arts Council in 1957 and later the Conseil des Arts et des Lettres du Québec contributed to the development of a new phenomenon—subsidized commissions for musical works. This process gave composers the assurance of a public hearing of some of their works.

The publication of the four hundred copies of the *Refus Global* in 1948 marks a milestone in Québec's cultural history. Even though no musician signed this manifesto, the formalist and abstract musical trend that emerged from it lasted until the end of the 1970s. This trend converged with artistic thinking inspired by Stravinsky (endorsed by Jean Papineau-Couture [1916–2000]) and Olivier Messiaen, the famous French pedagogue and composer, who taught an analysis class frequently used as a point of reference by several Québec composers.

The Société de Concert de Musique Canadienne (1954–1968), headed by Papineau-Couture (1959–1967; also president of the Société de Musique Contemporaine de Québec, 1966–1972), continued the work begun by Jean Beaudet, and the contemporary music concerts organized in 1954, 1955, and 1958 by Serge Garant (1929–1986), Otto Joachim (b. 1910), François Morel (b. 1926), Gilles Tremblay (b. 1932), Gabriel Charpentier (b. 1925), Jeanne Landry (b. 1922), and Jocelyne Binet (1923–1968) allowed audiences to position Canadian works within the broader context of international production. These concerts paralleled the movement in contemporary visual arts shown in the era's galleries.

Yet other composers held themselves apart from these trends, Clermont Pépin (b. 1926), André Prévosit (b. 1934), and Jacques Hétu (b. 1938) among them. They pursued their creative work without adhering to the line of modernist thought defended so forcefully in polemical articles by Pierre Boulez (b. 1925) in Europe and Serge Garant in Montréal. With historical distance, this debate appears to mark an important point. Composers could now claim strongly and clearly a freedom of artistic expression in new terms without making reference to classical forms or traditional rules of harmony. Instead, they could develop a personal musical language and find an authentic path to express what was most profound within them as individuals. This "contemporary" music (the name of this movement) is what made promoter, organizer, commentator, cultural advocate, and emeritus professor Maryvonne Kendergi (b. 1915) so enormously popular; it is also the music that Serge Garant conducted for twenty years with the Ensemble of the Société de Musique Contemporaine du Québec (SMCQ), and it is this music that Bruce Mather (b. 1939), François Morel (b. 1926), and Gilles Tremblay (b. 1932) also supported, with perhaps greater modesty. The 1961 meeting in Montréal of Québec and American experimental musicians during the International New Music Week organized by Pierre Mercure (1927–1966) put an end to European hegemony in Québec's music production and gave rise to new artistic thinking.

MUSIC AND POSTMODERNITY (1980 TO THE PRESENT)

The adventure of the Evénéments du Neuf (1979–1989), founded by Lorraine Vaillancourt (b. 1947), José Evangelista (b. 1943), John Rea (b. 1944), and Claude Vivier (1948–1983), and the shock caused by the autobiographical content and use of new musical forms found in Claude Vivier's 1980 work *Lonely Child* mark the beginnings of the postmodern period. While this new paradigm is generally analyzed in the other disciplines of the social sciences in its historical and contextual dimension, with regard to intellectual history it is seen in music—particularly in Québec—as a generational conflict between proponents of modernity who have become a "school" in the eyes of many and those who claim the right to a more individualist, more subjective way of thinking.

The formal concerns of and membership in the organizational system of the post-serialists have given way to simpler structures that are sometimes just as imaginative but with fewer, less complex musical elements, which are more easily perceived. Sources of inspiration are many: biography, history, the environment, ethnicity. Artists seek to abolish cultural borders that were used in modernist times to cordon off the great musical schools from each other. Each work seeks to be unique, in the image of human diversity. Women composers, such as Micheline Coulombe Saint-Marcoux (1938–1985), Marcelle Dechênes (b. 1939), Isabelle Panneton (b. 1955), Linda Bouchard (b. 1959), and many others, have made a path in this musical community and are very much a part of it.

The postmodern attitude fragments the European way of thinking that until this point was relatively homogenous. Artistic orientations are multiplying, resulting in more groups, diversified audiences, and more varied concert sites. Further, each circle has its own magazine or radio show. For example, the electroacoustic and multimedia music of the Association pour la Création et la Recherche Electroacoustiques du Québec (ACREQ) supports a music publishing house called Empreintes Digitales, directed by Jean-François Denis, and new music, which combines improvisation, jazz, and experimental music elements, also has its own publishing house, Ambiances Magnétiques. The very diverse music written for the past twenty years by contemporary composers—with or without postserialist allegiances—is offered by Walter Boudreau, director of the SMCQ Ensemble, Lorraine Vaillancourt, director of the Nouvel Ensemble Moderne, and Denys Bouliane, head of the Atelier de Musique Contemporaine of McGill University. The Chants Libres company offers the contemporary opera and musical theater music of Pauline Vaillancourt, its founder, and new compositions by men and women under the age of forty are performed by the Code d'Accès group and the Ensemble Contemporain de Montréal, led by Véronique Lacroix. These trends are now fully established internationally and encounter each other each year during a Festival of this or Week of that and at national and international roundtables, engendering much discussion—a testament to the milieu's dynamism (figures 1 and 2).

The musical history of Québec resembles in numerous ways the history of the countries of the New World. The musical life of French Canadians also added its own specific qualities to this history. After benefiting from the cultural contributions of its two colonizers (from countries with very different aesthetics), French-speaking Cana-

FIGURES I AND 2   Two CD covers representing the beginning and ending of a four-hundred-year period of music in Québec. The cover on the left was designed for *Un concert en Nouvelle-France,* recorded in 1995 by L'Ensemble Arion; on the right is the cover for *Ne blâmez jamais les bédouins,* recorded in 1992 by Chants Libres, dir. Pauline Vaillancourt.

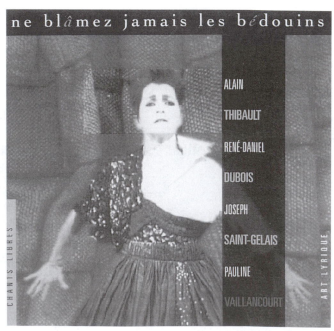

dian composers evolved differently from their English-speaking colleagues as early as the Confederation by their independence of spirit, will to venture from beaten paths, and greater disinclination to remain under the thumb of the motherland.

Their way of seeing also caused them to look with interest at American culture, whose pragmatism, experimental character and structures for popularizing and teaching music to the public they greatly appreciated. Many were self-taught and sought a more personal way to express new emotions in music. Was this initially a result of their minority status in relation to an immense America?

We can see in the response of Canadian composers a specificity that marked the period between 1867 and 1939, a period in which musical discourse was intimately tied to politics. Even within one city (Montréal), debates between the English-speaking and French-speaking cultures regarding language and its influence on repertoire choice are sharply divided, especially in the activities of the annual music week between 1923 and 1939. After 1939, a political base developed on aesthetic values influenced by the American experimental composers rather than the older European musical structures. The International New Music Week of 1961 and New Music America in Montréal (1990) were held in the middle of these discussions. This diversity of artistic expression led French-speakers to gradually take more initiative in musical organizations, and their music became increasingly distinctive and hence visible in the vast sea of Americanness. Starting in the 1980s, Québec's diverse musical culture has begun to spread to performance stages throughout the world.

REFERENCES

Anthologie de la musique canadienne (Anthology of Canadian Music). 1978–1991. Radio-Canada International. Boxed set of 32 LP disks and 6 compact discs.

Anthologie d'œuvres musicales canadiennes (Anthology of Canadian Music). 1983–. Collection of 25 volumes of printed Canadian music written before 1950. Ottawa: Canadian Musical Heritage Society.

Arcuri, Serge. n.d. *Les méandres du rêve.* Empreintes Digitales IMED-9310. Compact disc.

Barrière, Mireille. 1989. "La société canadienne-français et le théâtre lyrique à Montréal entre 1840 et 1913." Thèse de doctorat, Université Laval.

Boivin, Jean. 1992. *La Classe de Messiaen.* Paris: Bourgois.

Brown, Craig, et al., eds. 1987. *The Illustrated History of Canada.* Toronto: Lester and Orpen Dennys.

Les Cahiers de la Société Québécoise de Recherche en Musique (SQRM). 1983–. (Previously named l'Association pour l'Avancement de la Recherche en Musique du Québec.) Montréal.

Le Canada Romantique. n.d. Réjean Coallier, piano; Liette Turner et Eric Oland, chanteurs. SNE 557.

Un concert en Nouvelle-France. 1995. L'Ensemble Arion, CBC Records SRC-MVCD 1081. Compact disc.

L'époque de Julie Papineau. 1997. Musiques du Québec, vol. 1. Ensemble Nouvelle-France. Lanoraie ORCD41081, Interdisq Distr. Compact disc.

Fin de siécle, Nouvelle musique montréalaise. 1994. L'Ensemble Contemporain de Montréal, dir. Véronique Lacroix. SNE 590. Compact disc.

Gallat-Morin, Elisabeth, Jean-Pierre Pinson, and Paul-André Dubois. 1995. Booklet to accompany *Le Chant de la Jerusalem des Terres Froides* (Song of a Cold Holy Land). Studio de Musique en Cienne de Montréal, dir. Christopher Jackson. Compact disc.

Garant, Serge. n.d. *Edition Souvenir.* Société de Musique Contemporaine du Québec (SMCQ), dir. Walter Doudreau. Analekta AN 29804. Compact disc.

Kallmann, Helmut, Gilles Potvin, and Kenneth Winters, eds. 1992. *Encyclopedia of Music in Canada.* 2nd ed. Toronto: University of Toronto Press.

Mathieu, Rodolphe. 1998. *Musique de chambre.* Réjean Coallier, piano; Marie-Josée Arpin, violon; Annie Parent, alto; Chantal Marcil, violoncelle. Fonovox 79112. Compact disc.

Montréal Postmoderne. 1994. Centrediscs. Compact disc.

Morel, Francois. n.d. *Musique à l'Université Laval.* Vol. 2. SNE 521.

Morey, Carl. 1997. *Music in Canada: A Research and Information Guide.* New York: Garland Publications.

Musiques de Montréal. n.d. Nouvel Ensemble Moderne, dir. Lorraine Vaillancourt. UMMUS 105. Compact disc.

Ne blâmez jamais les bédouins. 1992. Chants Libres, dir. Pauline Vaillancourt. Diffusion i MéDIA IMSO 9202. Compact disc.

Oeuvres symphoniques, Patrimoine musical du Canada français. 1990. L'Orchestre Métropolitain, dir. Gilles Auger et Louis Lavigueur. SRC SMCD 5090. Compact disc.

Panneton, Isabelle. n.d. *Cantate de la fin du jour.* Fonovox VOX 7824-2. Compact disc.

Prévost, André. n.d. *Sonates et Improvisations.* UMMUS 103. Compact disc.

Le Souvenir (série Lavallée). n.d. Carolyn Maule, piano; Sally Dibblee et Russell Braun, chanteurs. Centrediscs CMC.

Tremblay, Gilles. n.d. *Vêpres de la Vierge.* Analekta FL 2 3102.

Intercultural and Commercial Musics
Val Morrison

Early Recording History
***Chanson* and the *Chansonnier* Movement**
The Recording Industry in Québec, 1970–1990
At the Beginning of the Twenty-first Century

Contemporary French-language popular music in Québec traces its roots to early-twentieth-century singers and songwriters. Some of the earliest musical publications and recordings were those of French Canadians Ovila Légaré, Charles Marchant, Conrad Gauthier, Hector Charland, and Madame Bolduc, known simply and affectionately as La Bolduc. In the 1920s, these artists were known primarily through public performances such as *Les Veillées du bon vieux temps* in larger urban centers such as Québec and Montréal or through radio performances and songwriting/singing contests and festivals organized by industries such as the Canadian Pacific Railway (CPR).

EARLY RECORDING HISTORY

The first sound recording of popular music in the province dates to 1903 and reflects the heterogeneous array of music popular at that time. The collection, associated with Emile Berliner's new technology, contained folklore and vernacular songs as well as a number of interpretations of French songs. Throughout the 1920s, recordings of popular music from the burlesque-inspired *music-hall québécois,* French romantic songs, and folk and religious music continued to gain popularity. It was not until the end of the decade, though, that Québec would have its first popular music star: La Bolduc.

La Bolduc and the beginnings of the *chansonnier* movement

La Bolduc (née Mary Travers) first recorded her own songs on the Starr label in 1927. Her first records sold more than twelve thousand copies, an unprecedented number in Québec during that time, given both the newness of the technology and the relative poverty of French Canadians. La Bolduc became known for her bold use of vernacular lyrics, head-on tackling of economic struggle, and celebration of local ritual and daily life. In a career that lasted less than fifteen years and spanned most of the Great Depression, La Bolduc recorded more than forty 78-rpm records and performed regularly in Québec, Canada, and the United States (Thérien and D'Amours 1992). Although her style and use of the French language offended the clerical sensibilities of the era and caused many to label her as a populist, her songs continue to be associated with the origins of the *chansonnier* movement.

In part as a reaction to the popularity of La Bolduc and other performers and music judged to be vulgar, the Catholic Church reacted by editing and promoting a series of folk, romantic, and patriotic songs under the direction of Abbey Charles-Émile Gadbois in the late 1930s. The series was published under the title *La Bonne Chanson* (Right or Good Music) and was quickly recommended for distribution in schools. In addition to publishing sheet music, Gadbois was also able to produce three 78-rpm records featuring singers Albert Viau and François Brunet. The collection was meant to reflect the Church's vision of good music—and good French Canadians—as well as to perpetuate its ongoing role in defining intellectual and cultural life and pursuits in the *patrie* (fatherland).

Other singers and styles

Through World War II and into the 1950s, popular music in Québec continued to thrive and develop indigenous styles and genres. Singers and radio personalities such as Fernand Robidoux and Robert L'Herbier took on the cause of French Canadian artists as their own, and radio became instrumental in its roles as promoter and as organizer of a series of contests (*La feuille d'érable, Concours de la chanson canadienne,* and so on). These contests and various radio shows played a key role in encouraging singer-songwriters to develop a distinctly French Canadian style. One particular artist of this era is notable for his career and style that was almost wholly dependent on the war. Roland Lebrun, known as Le Soldat 'the soldier' Lebrun is remarkable both for accompanying himself on the guitar, an instrument that was more the exception than the rule at that time, and for incorporating elements of American country and western music in his songs.

Country music would continue to grow as a genre in Québec, sometimes in the mainstream but mostly in the margins. Those artists who had wide-ranging success writing in a country style include Willie Lamothe, who composed original songs and translated such American country hits as Hank Williams's "Jambalaya"; Marcel Martel, who began by interpreting songs written by Le Soldat Lebrun in the 1940s and would go on to be a country music star in the 1950s in Québec; and Pier Beland and Renée Martel (Marcel's daughter), who are among the best known mainstream country music singers in Québec currently. It is worth noting that the country and western music played by Lamothe, Lebrun, and Martel also influenced *chanson*. *Chansonniers* of the 1960s and 1970s would import the tradition of the lone singer-songwriter accompanying himself on the guitar, and the idioms of country music can be heard in many of the songs of artists from the *chansonnier* era. In 1950s Québec all of these types of music as well as many popular variety shows and cabaret cultures would pave the way for what would become the most important musical style to guide Québec through the Quiet Revolution.

CHANSON AND THE *CHANSONNIER* MOVEMENT

The decade of the 1960s was as turbulent in Québec as it was elsewhere in North America, although for somewhat different reasons.

The Quiet Revolution

Profound changes known as the Quiet Revolution would be the harbinger of Québec's social, economic, and cultural modernization. Among the most striking of these changes was the secularization of Québécois society. The Catholic Church had been as important a branch of government in the province as any elected body, and it was only in the second half of the twentieth century that it relinquished its stranglehold, particularly over education. Other changes included the expansion of universities and the extension of free education to include college, the nationalization of industries such as Hydro-Québec, and the increasing urbanization of society.

This economic and social modernization led to a cultural awakening among French Canadians in the province. While rural and under the control of the Catholic

Chanson 'song' and the *chansonnier* 'song-maker' were seen as the poetic voice of the people whose aspirations were embodied in the lyrical texts and the simplistic music.

Church, French-speakers had little contact with the English-speaking economic elite in Québec. During the decades leading up to the Quiet Revolution, increased contact, combined with the aspiration of younger generations to succeed in the modern capitalist economy, led to an awareness of the relative deprivation of French-speakers. The contradiction of being an overwhelming numerical majority (in the 1960s, citizens of French origin represented well over 80 percent of the provincial population while those of British origin made up less than 10 percent) yet decidedly under the power of English-speaking decision-makers, led an increasing number of people to rebel against the common belief that in order to succeed, a French person in Québec must learn to speak English.

In 1961 the liberal government of Jean Lesage created *L'Office de la Langue Française* 'the Office of the French Language', and with this official act began a social and cultural movement that embraced French as the language of the people *and* as that of business, government, and popular culture. It was in the wake of the Quiet Revolution that the term *French Canadian* began to be replaced by *Québécois*. The tone set by the Quiet Revolution would reverberate in very specific ways for popular music in the second half of the century.

The musical tradition known as the *chansonnier* movement began in earnest in the 1950s and peaked during the 1960s. *Chanson* 'song' and the *chansonnier* 'song-maker' were seen as the poetic voice of the people whose aspirations were embodied in the lyrical texts (both sung and in the form of monologues) and the simplistic music. Thus the vast majority of the artists associated with this tradition were young men who performed in the popular *boîtes à chansons* 'song clubs', the night clubs that were the live venue of choice for performers during this period. These sprang up, in many cases literally overnight, all over the province. More often than not the performers, including Félix Leclerc, Georges D'Or, Raymond Levesque, Jean-Pierre Ferland, Sylvain Lelièvre, Pierre Létourneau, Claude Gauthier, Jacques Blanchet, Claude Léveillée, Robert Charlebois, and Gilles Vigneault, were also the composers and lyricists of the songs they performed. Although undeniably as dominated by men as the rock tradition was in the United States (there is indeed no equivalent word in French to designate a female *chansonnier*), the decade also saw a number of female artists perform as part of the movement, notably Clémence Dérochers, Monique Miville-Deschênes, Monique Leyrac, and Pauline Julien.

The *chansonniers* spoke and sang the reality of Québec; its land (Leclerc's "Hymne au printemps" ["Hymn to spring"], Léveillée's "Pour quelques arpents de neige" ["For a few acres of snow"]); its climate (Vigneault's "Mon pays" ["My country"], Charlebois's "Demain l'hiver" ["Tomorrow, winter"]); its geography (Ferland's "St.-Adèle P.Q.," D'Or's "La manic"); its people (Vigneault's "Les gens de mon pays" ["The people of my country"], La Bolduc's "Nos braves habitants" ["Our brave people"]); and its cultural and political aspirations (Levesque's "Bozo-les-culottes" ["Bozo-the-pants"] and Gauthier's "Le grand six pieds" ["The big six footer"]). Audiences in Québec were able to see themselves, their histories, their daily struggles, and their hopes for the future through the music performed by the *chansonniers*. For this and other reasons (the perceived originality of *chanson* as a genre, the status of *chansonniers* as artist-poets, and the consequent support they received from literary and other institutions), *chanson* was, and in many cases remains, lauded as the most important cultural emblem of Québec.

Félix Leclerc

Although La Bolduc is often credited as the first truly Québécois popular songstress, Félix Leclerc is viewed as the indisputable father of *chanson* in Québec. The annual music awards in Québec bear his name (the Felix Awards); the origin of Québec's motto, *Je me souviens* 'I remember', is usually attributed to a radio show that he animated in the 1940s; and there is scarcely a public performance in celebration of Québécois culture that does not feature a performance of one of his songs by a contemporary artist, regardless of the genre for which he or she is known. When Québécois hockey hero Maurice Richard died in the summer of 2000, a vast array of media personalities commented on the fact that he was one of Québec's three biggest heroes (the other two being René Levesque, founder of le Parti Québécois, and Félix Leclerc). The common claim is that without Félix Leclerc, to whom all subsequent Québécois musicians and performers owe an artistic debt, Québécois popular music would not have developed as it did.

Leclerc's career began in the 1930s in radio and during the 1950s he became known as a performing musician, composer, and singer. Interestingly, it was following a series of successful performances in Paris that Leclerc became a star in Québec. It is arguable that this "if you can make it there, you can make it here" relationship between success in France and at home continued to be a mainstay of stardom in Québec until the 1980s.

The heyday of the *chansonnier* movement peaked at the end of the 1960s, when it ushered in changes that defined the more group- and rock-oriented 1970s in the province. This is not to say that the figures popular in the 1960s were eclipsed. Indeed, throughout the next three decades many of them would continue actively to compose and perform and, in many cases, be the centerpieces for live performances at such festivities as the annual free concert in celebration of Québec's national holiday. It was from among their ranks, however, that a more diverse *chansonnier* tradition emerged.

The modern era of *chanson: L'Osstidcho*

As unfathomable as it may seem, a single live show in Québec and the recordings that accompanied it are viewed as bringing about nothing short of a revolution in song in the province. *L'Osstidcho*, a concert that combined music and theater (monologues, improvisation, and comedy), was presented in Montréal in the summer of 1968. This show and the song "Lindberg" are commonly credited with ushering in the modern era of *chanson* in Québec.

There are many reasons why a single performance could accomplish this. The years 1967–1968 can be isolated as a particular moment when Québécois culture began to demand attention. French president DeGaulle made his now infamous "Vive le Québec libre" ("Long live free Québec") statement in Montréal in the summer of 1967. The world exposition (Expo '67) was also held there, an event viewed as the first instance of presenting Montréal and, by extension, Québec to the world. Michel Tremblay's play *Les belles soeurs* 'The sisters-in-law' unashamedly presented working-class Montréal, its familial disputes, its less-than-perfect use of the French language, and its everyday mundaneness.

The performance event *L'Osstidcho*, viewed in the context of an awakening of national pride in Québec, represents a completely secular (one might say sacrilegious) manifestation of popular culture in a society that was only beginning to separate Church and State. The name of the concert is a homonymous play on words that combines Québécois vernacular with what is likely considered the worst swear word in the French language: *Ostie,* literally 'the host' in a Catholic Mass, and *cho,* which is vernacular word play on the English word *show.* The show, often referred to as an anti-concert, featured Robert Charlebois, Louise Forestier, Yvon Deschamps, Mouffe, and musicians from Le Jazz Libre du Québec in a partially improvised mixture of music, monologue, and theater. This type of performance was unheard of in the *chansonnier* tradition, and the combination of the use of local vernacular, the presence of several performers, and electrified instruments makes the event a point of crystallization for popular music.

Chansonniers who followed closely in Charlebois's electrified group format included Claude Dubois, Jean-Pierre Ferland, Jacques Michel, and others. An indigenous rock tradition would also follow from these innovations with groups such as Offenbach, Beau Dommage, and Harmonium, not shying away from *joual* 'slang', but rather embracing it as something typically Québécois and thus integral part of local culture.

Later developments of *chanson*

The duality typical of that between *La Bonne Chanson* and the populism of pre-1950 music in Québec continued well into the second half of the twentieth century, at that time pitting pop against *chanson.* Québec followed many other Western industrialized nations by integrating the innovations and sounds of the rock and roll explosion into the local scene. As early as 1956, French translations and lyrical improvizations on popular rock and roll tunes began being recorded in the province. This tradition took off following the arrival of the Beatles in North America. Québec's answer to the British Invasion took the form of what came to be called *yé-yé* (borrowed and translated from the use of repeated "yeah-yeah"'s in pop music of the period, such as in the Beatles "She Loves You . . . Yeah Yeah Yeah.") In many cases the pop charts were dominated by translations of popular English and American songs, but a vast number of original compositions were popular as well. The pop singers included such individuals as Michel Louvain, Michèle Richard, Joël Denis, Pierre Lalonde, Donald Lautrec, and Jenny Rock, as well as a number of groups: Les Classels, Les Gants Blancs, Les Sultans, Les Baronets, Les Sinners, and César et ses Romains. Along with this English-language inspired vein of the pop music of the 1960s was an equally popular group of artists who sang more in the French pop tradition, Ginette Reno, Jean Lapointe, and Renée Claude, among others. While popular memory along with tangibles such as radio playlists and charts as well as the long-running success of television shows such as *Jeunesse d'aujourd'hui* attest to the enormous popularity of pop styles in the 1960s, *chanson* was usually seen as the only truly Québécois form of popular music. Indeed, until well into the 1980s books and articles that purported to tell the history of Québécois music in fact told the story of *chanson.*

The virtual monopoly of *chanson* as the only acceptable expression of Québécois identity in popular music was carried on in the 1970s and early 1980s by many of the artists originally associated with the scene, as well as by a number of newcomers. An indigenous rock tradition married *chanson* with political and art-oriented veins from the United States and Britain in the music of Séguin and Fiori, Aut'Chose, Harmonium, Octobre, and Offenbach, among others.

As is true of popular music elsewhere in Western Europe and North America, the decade of the 1970s showed seemingly endless growth in the industry. Profits in the music business grew each year during the decade, and, along with them, a proliferation of styles, genres, and stars filled the airwaves in Québec as elsewhere. The first crack in the armor of *chanson*'s guardianship of Québécois identity and culture would come in the wake of the crisis that hit the music industry in the late 1970s.

THE RECORDING INDUSTRY IN QUÉBEC, 1970–1990

As a market for mainly French-language recordings, Québec developed a comparatively strong independent recording industry during the 1970s. However, although a number of independent record companies were formed and a large proportion of distribution was controlled by local companies, many of these were small and short-lived. As with most small nations at that time, Québec's industry was largely in the hands of a few multinational major record companies who operated affiliates in Canada that handled English Canadian and Québécois recordings. The dramatic decrease in sales in the industry by 1978–1979 led to many of the majors pulling out of small markets or, at the very least, drastically reducing their production of untested artists. For example, in 1978 the proportion of total production for Canadian affiliates of multinational record companies of French-language recordings stood at 61 percent, while in 1987 it represented a mere 5.5 percent. In 1979 these companies released some 180 Québécois albums, but in 1987 they released only 38 (Grenier 1993). Many of the small independent labels that had sprung up in Québec during the prosperous 1970s were forced out of business, and indigenous production in the province suffered further. Overall, between 1978 and 1983 the production of French-language recordings dropped more than 54 percent (Blain and Cloutier 1986). The market in Québec was thus affected drastically by the crisis in the international music business. The lack of economic input was further exacerbated by a cultural and political "depression" among Québécois artists, particularly those of the *chansonnier* tradition.

The 1980 referendum

The cultural fervor that began during the Quiet Revolution culminated in the 1976 election of Réné Lévesque's Parti Québécois, which was elected on the promise to hold a referendum that would see Québec become a nation separate and distinct from Canada. The results of the 1980 referendum on Québec sovereignty, during which 60 percent of Québec's polled citizens voted for the *no* side, left something of a cultural void for several years to follow. The vast majority of *chansonniers* were associated with a strong commitment to Québec and its culture, and many were active in the campaign for Québec sovereignty.

The defeat of the referendum left many of these activists-in-song disenchanted with Québécois politics. This too was reflected in patterns of cultural consumption: record and book sales dropped, as did theater attendance figures. Although albums by Québécois artists usually represented around 20 percent of total sales in the province, in the early years of the 1980s this figure dropped to 10 percent (Grenier 1993:211). Both artists and consumers suffered a disillusion, and the transformations of the political and cultural scene that would change the narrow association of *chanson* and nationalism would reverberate in the final two decades of the twentieth century.

Aftereffects of the crisis on the recording industry

The local music industry managed to pick up the pieces after the fallout from the crisis in the business and showed signs of recovery as early as the mid-1980s. During the years of the crisis, both provincial and federal levels of government created programs to encourage cultural development, and many of these provided much needed financial support for the music industry. Moreover, Québec and Canada's radio music quota programs (65 percent French-language music on French radio in Québec and 30 percent Canadian content in the country as a whole) made for many an enviable small market. Indeed, other small countries have considered or attempted to apply quota models based on those in Québec and Canada (notably France and New Zealand). Perhaps more important, though, Québec's industry rapidly and quite effectively took up the vacancies left by the exodus of multinational record companies. In all, there were more than sixty independent labels operating in Québec in the 1990s, and of the

What is now considered to be "authentic" Québécois music includes a much broader array of styles and artists than was earlier the case.

twenty most active, seventeen were founded during the 1980s. These companies are now responsible for over 85 percent of the production of Québécois popular music and control approximately 25 percent of the local market.

Distribution

While Québécois control of the local market had earlier been sporadic in terms of production, control over distribution had in fact been stronger than was common in small markets and became a stronghold of the industry in the wake of the crisis. Multinational labels often controlled their own distribution as well as that of many independent labels. This was the case in English Canada, for example, where many local labels produced records that were then distributed by the majors. During the 1980s, Québec's independent distributors took on an even greater importance. By the end of the decade, independent Québécois companies distributed 80 percent of all locally produced records, whereas in English Canada, multinationals were responsible for 88 percent of the distribution of records produced there (Lapointe 1994:16).

The restructuring of the local industry also included the founding of a great number of independent record labels as well as more local control of concert venues. The most important example of the vertical integration that took place in the industry is that of record label Audiogram, music retailer Archambault Musique, music distributor Distribution Select, and concert, studio, festival, and audiovisual producer L'Équipe Spectra. These four are among the oldest and strongest in their categories. Archambault Musique is the oldest music retailer and among the original music publishers in the province, and Distribution Select, which is owned by Archambault Musique, distributes exclusively for some fifty local labels accounting for an estimated 60 percent of Québécois product as well as for a sizable number of French labels. Audiogram is also fiscally connected to Archambault, Select, and Spectra and is undeniably the most influential and successful independent label in Québec, with popular artists such as Laurence Jalbert, Paul Piché, Richard Séguin, and Michel Rivard all recording on Audiogram. Finally, L'Équipe Spectra rounds out this group by providing concert venues (Montréal's Spectrum and Théâtre Olympia) and a recording studio (Morin-Height's Le Studio) as well as being the producers (and reproducers for television) of popular annual festivals such as Le festival international de Jazz de Montréal— one of the most successful and profitable jazz festivals in the world—as well as Les Francofolies de Montréal, an annual showcase for the music of Francophone artists around the world. These four companies are joined by other labels and distributors such as record companies Kébec-disques, Les Disques Star, Production Guy Cloutier, Isba, and Disques Doubles and distributors Musicor, Fusion, and Cargo. This consolidation and integration in the industry was in part responsible for the regeneration of public interest in Québécois music in the late 1980s and 1990s and can partially explain how the defining categories used to delineate authentically Québécois music changed considerably from those used during the height of popularity of the *chansonnier* movement.

Pop versus chanson

Another equally important restructuring within the music business can be found in the alignment of industry interests that began to reconsider the early pop versus *chanson* duality. The industry trade organization, Association du disque et de l'industrie du spectacle et de la vidéo du Québec (ADISQ), was formed in 1978 with the original mandate of organizing in 1979 the first of what would then be the annual music awards in Québec. From the outset, ADISQ was the site of controversy and confrontation. The two camps, representing the *chanson* tradition on the one hand and the pop/variety side on the other, were involved in a battle to determine the boundaries of definition for Québécois music. The pop side—publicly represented by producer Guy Cloutier—argued that the *chanson* side—publicly represented by producer Guy Latraverse—was attempting to foist a patronizing, overly intellectualized, and nationalist-oriented definition of Québécois culture and music on the people, whose favorite artists included both pop singers and interpreters as well as *chansonniers.* As ADISQ developed, increasingly acting as a lobby group in the interests of the music industry in Québec, it began to build bridges between the two camps and to recognize the important contribution of pop. The industry and its lobby have become more closely aligned in the past fifteen years or so in such a way that what is now considered to be "authentic" Québécois music includes a much broader array of styles and artists than was earlier the case.

AT THE BEGINNING OF THE TWENTY-FIRST CENTURY

The field of popular music in Québec continued to thrive in the 1990s. The position of the indigenous industry remains strong at the start of the twenty-first century, although the recovery of the international industry has led to a renewed interest of multinational labels in local product. The majors have signed a number of local artists. Sony, for example, recently signed popular group Lili Fatale and continues to make millions with Céline Dion's English and French products. BMG, in addition to signing local artists such as Térez Montcalm, has openly offered to purchase Québec's most successful label, Audiogram. Naturally the prospect of losing control of an industry that has come into its own worries many in the business, who fear that the next slow period for international record sales will once again mean that popular music in Québec will suffer.

These worries are exacerbated by the increasingly globalized music industry. It remains to be seen how the local industry and its products will fare in the coming decades. What can be said, though, is that the consolidation and restructuring of the industry in the 1980s has led to a wider array of music being counted as genuinely Québécois. Moreover, the last several years have witnessed a reclaiming of the pop *yé-yé* tradition of the 1960s as one that honestly reflects the taste of a generation of Québécois. For example, a number of artists who would earlier have been excluded from the local scene constantly show up at various public performances and on albums that might earlier have been limited to *chansonniers* and those closely associated with the nationalist movements of the 1960s and 1970s. Publicly, in places such as the mid-1990s museum exhibit on the history of popular music in Québec, *Je vous entends chanter* 'I hear you singing', increasingly accorded an importance to the history of pop in the province. Moreover, artists associated with the *chansonnier* tradition began to integrate commercial concerns into their performances and recordings. Richard Séguin, for example, released radio and extended versions of his late-1980s hit "Double Vie" ("Double Life").

This is not to say that *chanson* and singers associated with the movement have disappeared; indeed, many argue that *chanson* is still the sole truly Québécois genre, and popular music and musicians continue to align themselves and be aligned with cultural pride and often with nationalism. For example, during the final rally leading up to the October 1995 referendum on Québec sovereignty, the Parti Québécois, the political party in power, which represented the *yes* vote, invited singer-songwriter Gilles Vigneault to perform. The rally was held in then Premier Jacques Parizeau's home. Radio and televised broadcasts showed Parizeau and the crowd singing along to the lyrics of Vigneault's "Tu peux ravaler ta romance" ("You can take back your romance"), a song that tells the history of Québec–Canada relations in a mocking and provocative fashion, using the metaphor of an unhappy marriage in which the man (Canada) has done all in his power to alienate and take for a fool the woman (Québec), who has finally wised up, telling him that she believes they are no longer "from the same country." During the same heated political campaign, Paul Piché, another singer-songwriter aligned with the sovereignist movement in Québec, joined Lucien Bouchard, then leader of the political opposition in Canada and subsequently premier of Québec, on a series of public appearances in Montréal.

There is little doubt that where there are nationalist politics in Québec there will be nationalist artists, but now in the twenty-first century, these artists are increasingly sharing the stage with singers who reflect changing cultural, linguistic, and social realities as well as a less narrowly defined nationalism in Québec. Many artists, some aligned with the *chansonnier* tradition, are increasingly singing and recording in English, something that a few short years ago would have been viewed as selling out Québec culture. Kevin Parent, for example, includes English titles to French songs ("Father on the Go") and has recorded a number of original English-language songs. Other groups, such as pop/hip-hop group No Déjà, mix languages both in the group name and within their songs ("Quelque chose about you").

Others still are equally comfortable singing in both strict pop or *chanson* genres as well as crossing boundaries in what they choose to sing and listen to. For example, in 1989 the aboriginal group Kashtin, whose songs are recorded in the Innu language (a language spoken by some ten thousand people in northern Québec), was nominated for nine Félix awards and won several of them, including that for best first album. Contemporary *chansonnier* Daniel Bélanger has performed and recorded a popular *yé-yé* song from the 1960s, and newcomer Daniel Boucher sings rock cover versions of Félix Leclerc songs.

Popular music in Québec at the beginning of the twenty-first century has undergone many changes in terms of both its music and its industrial base. The past twenty years have seen an indigenous industry built and subsequently restructured in such a way that the dualism that was characteristic of popular music in Québec for decades is progressively being dismantled.

REFERENCES

Blain, Francois, and B. Cloutier. 1986. "En bonne compagnie avec Audiogramme." *Chanson d'aujourd'hui* 9(5):11–13.

Drapeau, Renée-Berthe. 1984. "Le yéyé dans la marge du nationalisme québécois (1960–1974)." In *Les aires de la chanson québécoise*, ed. Robert Giroux, 174–205. Montréal: Tryptique.

Grenier, Line. 1993. "The Aftermath of a Crisis: Québec Music Industries in the 1980s." *Popular Music* 12(3):209–228.

Lapointe, Jean-francois. 1994. *Portrait de la distribution indépendante de phonogrammes au Québec: Principaux rôles et enjeux.* Montréal: Mémoire de maîtrise, Université de Montréal.

Roy, Bruno. 1991. *Pouvoir chanter.* Montréal: V1B.

Thérien, Robert, and Isabelle D'Amours. 1992. *Dictionnaire de la musique populaire au Québec 1955–1992.* Montréal: Institut québécois de recherche sur la culture.

Tremblay, Danielle. 1993. *Le développement historique et le fonctionnement de l'industrie de la chanson québécoise.* Research report presented to the Québec City Museum of Civilization, 26 March 1996, 1–83.

Folk Musics
Gordon E. Smith

Early Folk Song Scholarship
Research Directions and the Popularization of Québécois Folklore from the 1940s
Contemporary Contexts and Performers

The singing of folk songs and playing of traditional instruments by French settlers in Québec (sometimes referred to historically as New France) was an important part of the social fabric in the first centuries of European colonization. Folk songs were brought to Canada from France by settlers, many of whom originated in rural regions of Normandy as well as the Loire valley. Serving as a means of entertainment and also a sustaining force in a harsh physical climate, music played a central role in peoples' lives. Collecting folk songs, forces of creativity and change, processes of oral transmission, and ideas surrounding origins and variants traditionally have been the focus of scholarly attention, while recent creative and performative trends reflect the blending of different musical contexts (popular, traditional, First Nations, world music, and even concert music). Thus, broadly considered, folk music in Québec continues to be a powerful symbol of regional (some would argue national) identity.

TRACK 28

EARLY FOLK SONG SCHOLARSHIP

The first to comment on the rich musical folklore of French Canada were seventeenth- and eighteenth-century visitors (explorers, travelers, missionaries) who made references in their travel reports and diaries to various aspects of music making (Robbins 1993:63–65).

Voyageur songs

Of particular notice were the paddling songs of the *voyageurs,* boatmen who traveled in canoes between trading centers in what was then known as Lower Canada (*le pays en bas* or Québec) and Upper Canada (*le pays en haut* or Ontario). First known as *coureurs de bois,* these men, many of whom were French or Métis, were crucial to the development of the fur trade in Canada. They formed alliances with Indian peoples, learning their languages and often taking Indian wives. Of mixed French and Indian ancestry, these people came to be known by the French as the Métis, an important racial group in the Canadian ethnic context [see MÉTIS, p. 404].

The romantic image of the *voyageurs* had a particular appeal to European visitors, who were impressed by the extent to which song was an integral part of the *voyageur's* work. On a visit to Canada in 1804 the Irish poet Thomas Moore was so inspired by the sight of *voyageurs* on the St. Lawrence River that he composed the "Canadian Boat

FIGURE 1   Marius Barbeau transcribing from an Edison cylinder. c. 1940. Photo by permission of the Canadian Museum of Civilization, Hull, Québec, Canada.

Song" (London 1805), the spirit and opening of which resemble the *voyageur* song "Dans mon chemin j'ai rencontré." Early collections of *voyageur* songs include Lieutenant George Back's *Canadian Airs* (London 1823), a volume of melodies compiled by Back during his work with Captain John Franklin's Arctic expedition in the early 1820s. Intended for commercial use and reflecting the popular taste of the period for salon entertainment, this song book contained new words supplied by the editors as well as typically elaborate piano accompaniments. Another important early collection is that of Edward Ermatinger, a fur trader of Swiss and Italian descent. Gathered during the ten-year period (1818–1828) when Ermatinger worked for the Hudson's Bay Company, his collection contains eleven songs (texts and melodies). Edited and published by the Québec folklorist Marius Barbeau (1883–1969) (figure 1) in 1954, the Ermatinger collection demonstrates the pervasiveness of the *voyageur* repertoire (Québec, Ontario, and Manitoba) and is musical evidence of the substantial distances traveled by the *voyageurs*. A recent large compilation of *voyageur* songs is that of Madeleine Béland (1982).

Dance music

The other historic folk genre was dance music, which is also referred to in descriptions of balls and social events from the mid-seventeenth century. Discussion of dance genres (French contredanses and minuets that were often mixed in with English-style reels and jigs) and local variants, as well as a substantial repertoire of dance music, is in Simone Voyer's study (1986). Québécois fiddle music is often described with reference to specific regional stylistic inflections, including frequent double stopping, asymmetrical phrase lengths, and fast tempo. Because fiddle playing was often the object of opposition by the powerful Roman Catholic clergy, a certain folklore emerged surrounding magical powers of the fiddle (Seguin 1986). Stories developed around certain tunes as well, one of the most notable of which is "The Hangman's Reel." In addition to the fiddle, from the late nineteenth century the button accordion has become an important folk instrument in social contexts.

Collecting paradigms

In the nineteenth century the documentation of French folk song in Canada followed European paradigms. Aside from isolated instances such as the works of Back and Ermatinger, the first collections typically contained texts only, following the philological preference of early German, French, and British collectors. The Québécois folklorist Conrad Laforte (1993 [1976]) has compiled a list of manuscript and printed collections beginning with Cécile Lagueux's (1817) through the numerous college and seminary song books of the 1840s, 1850s, and 1860s in Québec. As in France, the collecting of folk song texts in Québec was begun by literary figures and historians (from approximately 1840) with nationalist intentions. Inspired by romantic ideals of the folk, folk song became a pervasive vehicle for expressing national identity and local color in the nineteenth century. Québec writers such as Philippe Aubert de Gaspé, Joseph-Olivier Chauveau, and Joseph Charles Taché followed the example of their French counterparts, notably François René Chateaubriand, Champfleury, Gérard de Nerval, and George Sand. Believing in the intrinsic value of oral tradition, these writers employed the technique of incorporating folk song texts into their literary works in order to provide local color and to illustrate more vividly the qualities of peasant life.

A point of comparison between the French and French Canadian folk song movements was that whereas France emphasized above all the collecting (preservation) of the folk song repertoire (for example, the French government–sponsored folk song inquiry of the late 1850s), in Québec folk song was regarded as a means of heightening historical and literary self-consciousness as well as national identity. Historical and patriotic orientation was a hallmark of the mid-nineteenth-century literary movement that produced the first collections of folk song texts in Québec (for example, Philippe Aubert de Gaspé's *Les Anciens Canadiens* [1863] and Joseph-Charles Taché's *Forestiers et voyageurs* [1863]). Such writings were typically romantic and realist insofar as everyday life was intertwined with idealized, ultra-Montanist characterizations of a chosen people.

The nationalist literary movement in Québec in the 1860s produced two seminal folk song collections in the 1860s. The first is Hubert LaRue's *Les Chansons populaires et historiques du Canada* (1863, 1865), which is as much an essay as a song collection (texts only). In this work, LaRue provides historical discussion of selected folk songs—comparisons of variants, origins, and so on. He also included the texts of well-known songs of the day, some of which he compiled from printed sources such as the local press. The lack of music in LaRue's essay was the impetus for Ernest Gagnon's *Chansons populaires du Canada* (1880 [1865–1867]), which was reprinted more than a dozen times through the 1950s. Gagnon's *Chansons populaires* is important because it contains integral textual and musical renditions of more than one hundred songs, some of which Gagnon collected in the field; the rest he included as pervasive representatives of the current song tradition. Gagnon also provides commentaries for each of the songs and a concluding essay in which he examines musical aspects of the repertoire among other topics.

One of the dominant analytical and ideological themes in Gagnon's work is the hypothesis that there is a link between the modality in the song melodies and that of Gregorian chant. The hypothesis is explained by Gagnon in technical terms, taking into account French theoretical stances (those of François-Joseph Fétis, Louis Niedermeyer, and Joseph d'Ortigue) and articulating a metaphorical framework of the French Canadian people. Gagnon concludes that because the rural population is "honest and religious" (1880 [1865–1867]:315–346), they would avoid chromaticism and leading tones in their singing. Although Gagnon's argument did not have lasting support, within a paradigm deriving from particular notions of the French Canadian "race," his interpretation is important within both the context of the contemporaneous nationalist movement in Québec and the wider, emergent context of nineteenth-century ideas of ethnic identity [see RACE, ETHNICITY, AND NATIONHOOD, p. 63].

The idea of Gagnon's *Chansons populaires* as definitive and exhaustive was dispelled by the work of Édouard-Zotique Massicotte (1847–1947), who had begun collecting in the Montréal region in the 1880s, and by Marius Barbeau, whose long career as a collector and scholar of French folk song began soon after he was hired as an anthropologist by the Museum Branch of the Geological Survey of Canada in 1911. Educated in anthropology, archaeology, and ethnology at Oxford in England and the Sorbonne in Paris (1906–1910), Barbeau was inspired initially by his linguist colleague German-born anthropologist Edward Sapir (1884–1939) (who worked with the Canadian government from 1910 to 1926) and George Herzog (1901–1983), whom he met through the American Folklore Society. In conjunction with Massicotte, Barbeau published transcriptions of Massicotte's field recordings in 1919 and, with Sapir, the landmark *Folk Songs of French Canada* (1925).

Untrained as a musician, Barbeau used a combination of his own considerable self-taught skill and the help of others to provide accurate musical transcriptions of the melodies he collected. The *Romancero du Canada* (with Marguerite d'Harcourt [1937]) and the *Jongleur Songs of Old Québec* (with Jean Beck [1962]) are two examples. In the latter collection, Barbeau and Beck treat the subject of the modes and folk song with a view to establishing links between French medieval secular song and the folk repertoire, an idea that is also discussed in the collection of Marguente and Raoul d'Harcourt, *Chansons folkloriques françaises du Canada* (1956).

Many of Barbeau's more than ten thousand field recordings appear in his numerous collections, the largest of which is the multivolume *Répertoire de la Chanson folklorique*

Barbeau's prodigious collecting efforts were part of a nationalist desire to carve out a French Canadian identity through the discovery and documentation of folk traditions.

française au Canada, including *Le Rossignol y chante* (1979 [1962]) and *En Roulant ma boule* (1982) and *Le Roi boit* (1987), both published posthumously.

Barbeau's prodigious collecting efforts were part of a nationalist desire to carve out a French Canadian identity through the discovery and documentation of folk traditions. To this end Barbeau encouraged the performance of folk music through the establishment of festivals and concerts. The two folk and handicraft festivals held at the Château Frontenac Hotel in Québec City (1927, 1928) sponsored by the Canadian Pacific Railway (CPR) and organized by Barbeau and the CPR's publicity agent, John Murray Gibbon, featured performances by both traditional and concert musicians (figure 2). In historical terms, the commercial motives of the CPR were overshadowed by Barbeau's goal of bringing together musicians of different backgrounds and encouraging composers to create a distinctly national music based on folk traditions.

While the art music repertoire that resulted from Barbeau's efforts was limited, arrangements of traditional songs from his collections were made by Ernest MacMillan, François Brassard, Oscar O'Brien, Alfred Whitehead, and Healey Willan, among others. Another context was the *Veillées du bon vieux temps* at the Monument National in Montréal (1921–1941), regular concerts that brought together traditional performers. Combining folk music with popular idioms, often with creativity and humor, Conrad Gauthier, Lionel Daunais, Ovila Légaré, Gustave Lanctot, Adélard Lambert, Charles Marchand, the Alouette Vocal Quartet, the Bytown Troubadours, and Evelyn Bolduc

FIGURE 2   Folk Arts Festival at the Château Frontenac Hotel, Québec City, 1927. Photo by permission of the Canadian Museum of Civilization, Hull, Québec, Canada.

had successful careers as performing artists in the period up to and including World War II. Another important means of public dissemination, as well as an educational offshoot, was the popular *La Bonne Chanson* series (eleven books dating from 1937), as well as over fifty recordings (78s) of the same title produced for RCA Victor. These recordings featured popular musicians of the era, including those mentioned in the preceding list.

RESEARCH DIRECTIONS AND THE POPULARIZATION OF QUÉBÉCOIS FOLKLORE FROM THE 1940s

The influence of Barbeau's work also contributed to the establishment of the Archives de Folklore at Laval University in 1944 by Barbeau, Félix-Antoine Savard, and Luc Lacourcière (1910–1989), a pupil of Barbeau's and director of the archives from its inception until 1975. Lacourcière and his colleague Conrad Laforte played central roles in developing research directions in French traditional music. Studies by instructors and students in the folklore programme at Laval have included song collections—Sr. Marie-Ursule's *Civilisation traditionnelle des Lavalois* (1951) and Russell Scott Young's *Vieilles Chansons de la Nouvelle-France* (1956)—as well as the sound recording *Acadie et Québec* by Roger Matton and his subsequent collection with Dominique Gauthier, *Les Chansons de Shippagan* (1975). The musical analyses in both the Young and Matton/Gauthier volumes focus on rhythmic considerations in the song repertoires.

Expanding on the approach of French scholars who studied textual variants and established a song's critical text, Lacourcière (1946) and Barbeau (1947), in two later studies ("Les Écoliers de Pontoise" and "Trois beaux canards: ninety-two Canadian versions," respectively), included textual variants and musical versions of a single song with the idea of re-creating a complete restoration of each original song version. Inspired by this work, Laforte developed the *Catalogue de la chanson folklorique française,* a large ongoing research project begun in 1958. His goal of a global methodological classification of French folk songs (including North America and French-speaking Europe) is discussed in *Poétiques de la chanson traditionnelle française* (1993 [1976]). The six categories discussed in this study are the basis of the complete edition of the *Catalogue* (1977–1987): *chansons en laisse* 'chansons in the medieval *lai* form'; strophic songs; songs in the form of dialogue; enumerative songs; short songs; and *chansons sur les timbres* 'songs on preexisting tunes'. Based on poetic characteristics in the song texts, each type is discussed in a separate volume with substantial bibliographies for both North America and Europe; some details about the music are also included. Besides Laforte's scholarly work, many folk-based categorizations of repertoire exist. Terminology that has been used to categorize French folk songs includes *complainte* 'an unaccompanied freely cast modal song' and *turlutages,* which are dance pieces performed vocally.

The *chansonniers*

In the period following World War II, a new generation of popular performing artists, the *chansonniers,* emerged in Québec. Coinciding with the advent of television in the 1950s and major changes on the popular music scene in that and the following decades, the *chansonniers* extended the trend of combining folk and popular music idioms. This was especially true in songs that reflected the cultural, spiritual and political themes of emancipation and identity of the so-called Quiet Revolution in Québec, a movement dating from the 1950s and 1960s arising from the repudiation of the historic domination of the Roman Catholic Church, among other forces, in Québec.

The Quiet Revolution is often referred to as a spiritual beginning of the separatist movement. Inspired by folk music, indigenous poetry, and songwriters from France such as Georges Brassens and Jacques Brel, successful Québécois *chansonniers* include Hélène Baillergeon, Clémence Desrochers, Félix Leclerc, Claude Léveillée, Monique

Leyrac, Ginette Reno, and Gilles Vigneault, among numerous other individuals and performing groups. Some of these performers (for example, Robert Charlebois, Roch Voisine, and Céline Dion) have had international as well as national careers.

CONTEMPORARY CONTEXTS AND PERFORMERS

Other important venues for the performance of traditional and newly composed music were *les boites à chansons* 'song clubs', local cafés that attracted young audiences and artists performing songs concerning the need for social and political change as well as nationalist aspirations. In addition to individuals, groups such as Harmonium, Beau Dommage, and Suroit have blended folk forms in distinctive ways. Fiddlers, one of the most notable of whom was Jean Carignan, have had successful careers as well.

Beginning in the 1980s the popularization of Québécois folklore is the result of the interface of traditional forms with popular and world music trends, combined with a pervasive sense in Québec of folk music (now broadly considered) as a symbol of history and identity. In this context, music in contemporary Québec society continues to play a vital role, perpetuating constructions of the local, regional, national, and international identities that characterize modern Québec.

REFERENCES

Barbeau, Marius. 1947. "Trois beaux canards." Les Archives de Folklore 2:97–138. Québec: Les Presses de l'Université Laval.

———. 1954. "The Ermatinger Collection of Voyageur Songs." *Journal of American Folklore* 67:147–161.

———. 1979 [1962]. *Le Rossignol y chante.* Ottawa: National Museum of Canada.

———. 1982. *En Roulant ma boule.* Ottawa: National Museum of Canada.

———. 1987. *Le Roi boit.* Ottawa: National Museum of Canada.

Barbeau, Marius, and Jean Beck. 1962. *Jongleur Songs of Old Québec.* New Brunswick, N.J.: Rutgers University Press.

Barbeau, Marius, and Marguerite d'Harcourt. 1937. *The Romancero du Canada.* Toronto: Macmillan.

Barbeau, Marius, and Edward Sapir. 1925. *Folk Songs of French Canada.* New Haven, Conn.: Yale University Press.

Bégin, Carmelle. 1992. *La Musique Traditionnelle pour Violon: Jean Carignon.* Ottawa: National Museum of Canada.

Béland, Madeleine. 1982. *Chansons de voyageurs, coureurs de bois et forestiers.* Québec: Les Presses de l'Université Laval.

d'Harcourt, Marguerite, and Raoul d'Harcourt. 1956. *Chansons folkloriques du Canada.* Québec: Les Presses de L'Université Laval.

Gagnon, F. Ernest A. 1880 [1865–1867]. *Chansons populaires du Canada.* Montréal: Beauchemin.

Giroux, Robert. 1984. *Les aires de la chanson québécoise.* Montréal: Éditions Triptyque.

Katz, lsrael. 1970. "Marius Barbeau 1883–1969." *Ethnomusicology* 14(1):129.

Laforte, Conrad. 1993 [1976]. *Poétiques de la chanson traditionnelle française.* Québec: Les Presses de l'Université Laval.

Lacourciere, Luc. 1946. "Les Écoliers de Pontoise: Étude critique d'une chanson populaire." Les Archives de Folklore 1. Montréal: Fides.

"Le Catalogue de la Chanson Française." 1977–1987. Les Archives de Folklore, Vols. 18–23. Québec: Les Presses de l'Université Laval.

Massicotte, Emest-Zotique. 1919. "Chants populaires du Canada." *Journal of American Folklore* 32:1–89.

Matton, Roger. n.d. *Acadie et Québec: Field Recordings.* Québec: Les Archives de Folklore. RCA Records CGP-139. LP disk.

Matton, Roger, and Dominique Gaulthier. 1975. "Chansons de Shippagan Québec." Les Archives de Folklore 16. Québec: Les Presses de L'Université Laval.

Nowry, Lawrence. 1995. *Man of Mana: Marius Barbeau.* Toronto: NC Press Ltd.

Robbins, James. 1993. "Canada" In *Ethnomusicology: Historical and Regional Studies,* ed. Helen Myers, 63–76. New York: Norton.

Seguin, Robert-Lionel. 1986. *La Danse traditionnelle à Québec.* Québec: Les Presses de l'Université Laval.

Voyer, Simone. 1986. *La Danse traditionnelle dans l'est du Canada: Quadrilles et cotillon.* Québec: Les Presses de l'Université Laval.

Young, Russell Scott. 1956. "Vieilles Chansons de Nouvelle France." *Les Archives de Folklore* 7. Québec: Les Presses de L'Université Laval.

African Canadian Music
Anne Lederman

The St.-Henri Community
Caribbean and Continental African Musics

The first documented black musician in Canada is a runaway slave from Québec named Lowcanes who, it says on the notice for his recapture, *"jouant trés bien du violin"* (plays the violin very well) (Miller 1992:129). Slavery was rejected in principle in 1793, although not officially outlawed for another forty years. Throughout this time, Montréal, along with southern Ontario and the Maritimes, became home for many African Americans. A community was established in the St. Henri area of Montréal, which exists to this day. Throughout the twentieth century a small number of English Caribbean immigrants mostly from Barbados, came to Canada, and in the 1960s francophones from the Caribbean (primarily Haiti) and from Africa began to arrive.

THE ST.-HENRI COMMUNITY

There has been movement back and forth across the border with the United States throughout the life of this community, tying it culturally and musically to American popular trends—first ragtime, then jazz and swing. Pianist Millard Thomas from this community led the Famous Chicago Novelty Orchestra until 1928. Clubs featuring black musicians were popular from the 1920s to the 1950s. Many St. Henri musicians have achieved international fame as jazz artists, such as pianists Oscar Peterson, Oliver Jones and Joe Sealy (all of whom studied with Peterson's sister, Daisy). What we know of day-to-day musical life comes largely from their biographies. Peterson's entire family were musicians, for example, performing as a band at community events. Jones first played in church at age five.

In St.-Henri, as in other black Canadian communities, churches were important centers of musical activity, fostering gospel choirs and the singing of hymns and spirituals. The best known of these is the Montréal Jubilation Gospel Choir, started under Barbadian Trevor W. Payne in 1982 for the seventy-fifth anniversary of Union United Church, the oldest black church in Montréal. They and their predecessors, the Montréal Black Community Youth Choir, have both made several recordings. They have appeared at the Festival International de Jazz de Montréal and with pop singers like Céline Dion. Payne also had a rhythm and blues band, The Soul Brothers, in the 1960s. However, other oral music traditions in the St.-Henri community await further study.

CARIBBEAN AND CONTINENTAL AFRICAN MUSICS

The first Haitians to arrive in the 1960s were mostly students and professionals who came to escape political repression, joined by others throughout the 1970s. Drummer-choreographer Georges Rodriquez founded Mapou Guinin and, later, Rada, two ensembles devoted to ritual music and dance. In the late 1970s, *les grands bals* were held, like those in Haiti, and clubs featured Haitian music. The English Caribbean community, largely from Jamaica, Trinidad, and Barbados, held its first Afro-Festival in 1972, accompanied by CariFête, a Carnaval-style parade, and has maintained calypso and *soca* events since that time.

Continental African musicians from Mali, Senegal, Zaire, Cameroon, Guine-Bissau, and, more recently, Ghana have encouraged both traditional music and hybridization. Yaya Diallo of Mali, who arrived in 1967, is known especially for his book *The Healing Drum* (1989) and his teaching in the United States and Canada, but he has also formed the fusion groups Kléba and Kanza. Senegalese *kora* master Boubakar Diabaté has performed with many Canadian and international groups. Other fusionist performers and groups include South African singer Lorraine Klaasen, The Lofimbo Stars, Diori Sinn led by the Senegalise Ndiouga Sarr, Njacko Backo (figure 1) of Cameroon who has since moved to Toronto, and Takadja.

Fusion trends involve both inter-African blendings as well as the combination of African, Caribbean, Latin, and North American styles. In the 1970s musicians of many backgrounds began to work together on the streets of the old city and in parks, dance schools, and clubs. Sunday drum jams began on Mont-Royal, an open event that sometimes attracts upwards of five hundred participants. In the early 1980s, the group Aganman was formed to promote black Montréal culture, organizing festivals to encourage such cross-cultural explorations. A kind of Québec "Afro-rock" was spurred by Michel Seguin's group, Toubabou. Robert Villefranche and Yves Bernard (1989:23) feel that Montréal may be one of the most important centers in the world for such new Afrocentric musical creations.

Haitian, African, Afro-Cuban, and many of the fusion groups began to record in the 1980s. Festivals have played a large part in popularizing African and Caribbean music in Québec: the Superfrancofête of 1974 that brought together francophone artists from around the world; film festival *Vues d'Afrique* 'Views of Africa' started in 1983; *Nuits d'Afrique* 'African Nights', founded in 1987 at Club Balattou; the annual *Rhythme du Monde* 'Rhythm of the World' promoting local and international black culture; and the Festival internationale de jazz de Montréal, which has featured African music as a regular part of its programming since the 1980s.

FIGURE I   Njacko Backo. Photo by Anand Maharaj. Photo courtesy Njacko Backo.

REFERENCES

Desroches, Monique, and Marie Therese Lefebvre. 1992. "Black Africa." In *Encyclopedia of Music in Canada,* 2nd ed., ed. Helmut Kallmann, Gilles Potvin, and Kenneth Winters, 126–128. Toronto: University of Toronto Press.

Diallo, Yaya, and Mitchell Hall. 1989. *The Healing Drum: African Wisdom Teachings.* Rochester, N.Y.: Destiny Books.

Miller, Mark. 1997. *Such a Melodious Racket: The Lost History of Jazz in Canada.* Toronto: Mercury Press.

Miller, Mark. 1992a. "Black Music and Musicians." In *Encyclopedia of Music in Canada,* 2nd ed., ed. Helmut Kallmann, Gilles Potvin, and Kenneth Winters, 129–130. Toronto: University of Toronto Press.

———. 1992b. "The Montréal Jubilation Gospel Choir." In *Encyclopedia of Music in Canada,* 2nd ed., ed. Helmut Kallmann, Gilles Potvin, and Kenneth Winters, 876–877. Toronto: University of Toronto Press.

———. 1992c. "Oscar Peterson." In *Encyclopedia of Music in Canada,* 2nd ed., ed. Helmut Kallmann, Gilles Potvin, and Kenneth Winters, 1047–1048. Toronto: University of Toronto Press.

———. 1992d. "Oliver Jones." In *Encyclopedia of Music in Canada,* 2nd ed., ed. Helmut Kallmann, Gilles Potvin, and Kenneth Winters, 665–666. Toronto: University of Toronto Press.

Villefranche, Robert, and Yves Bernard. 1989. "Petites Histoire des Musiques Afro-Montréalaises." *Canadian Folk Music Journal* 17:19–23.

Snapshot:
Musical Life in Montréal's Judeo-Spanish Community

Judith R. Cohen

Immigration

Sephardic Songs and Performance Contexts

The Promotion of Sephardic Musical Culture in Montréal

"En la ciudad de Toledo . . . B-69! Brigitte Bardot! Bingo!" ("In the city of Toledo . . . B-69! Brigitte Bardot! Bingo!") I recorded this unlikely rendition of an old *romance,* the narrative ballad "Diego León", in a new context in Montréal's Moroccan Sephardic community: instead of accompanying embroidery, rocking the cradle, or swinging in the enclosed courtyard, it was sung by an elderly Moroccan woman playing bingo at her weekly club meeting with the attendant conversation in a mixture of French and Spanish.

IMMIGRATION

While Canada is home to about thirty thousand Sephardic Jews (in the broadest sense of "Sephardic"), only a few thousand speak Judeo-Spanish ("Ladino"). In the early twentieth century, many eastern Mediterranean Judeo-Spanish Sephardim emigrated to the United States, and it is from among them and their descendants that the major Judeo-Spanish song collections in the United States have been recorded. In Canada, however, only a few Sephardim arrived in the late eighteenth century, and there was negligible Sephardic immigration until the late 1950s. There never have been many from the former Ottoman lands of the eastern Mediterranean. Most of Canada's Sephardim came from North Africa and the Middle East; they settled in Montréal and Toronto, with several small groups settling elsewhere. Montréal's French-speaking milieu was a natural choice for those who had grown up under Morocco's French Protectorate and/or had attended the schools of the Alliance Israélite le Universelle. The main umbrella organization in Montréal, the Communauté Sépharade du Québec (CSQ), was established in 1976; also in Montréal are Sephardic schools and synagogues, as well as the Grand Rabbinat Sépharade du Québec.

SEPHARDIC SONGS AND PERFORMANCE CONTEXTS

Liturgical singing in Hebrew, traditionally the domain of men, is strong in Montréal's Sephardic synagogues. Outside the synagogue, there are several religious and ceremonial events associated with music, with both men and women participating. One event

Against the sonic backdrop of rather boisterous bingo games, I have recorded ballads, wedding songs, stories, *pasodobles,* popular Israeli songs, multilingual versions of "Happy Birthday," and a memorable, if somewhat incongruous, rendition of "Deck the Halls," intoned in a rather absentminded and grumpy fashion by one woman focusing on her bingo card.

peculiar to Moroccan Sephardim is the *hiloulá,* the pilgrimage to the tomb of a revered rabbi or other particularly revered person. As the actual tombs are in Israel or Morocco, the event in Canada has been modified to be either a local event without the actual tomb or, for those with the time and budget, a *"hiloulá* package," including charter flights, visits to tombs, and multistar hotel accommodations.

Judeo-Spanish songs are typically sung during life-cycle and calendar-cycle events, as well as in domestic contexts and for recreational purposes. The simplification of elaborate life-cycle ceremonies and activities, especially the traditional wedding, has eroded the accompanying song repertoires. Aspects of religious and ceremonial singing do take place, however. A marked change in lifestyle that began well before emigration and, of course, was further altered upon arrival in Canada severely reduced the traditional contexts for many narrative ballads (*romances*) and recreational songs. Among the many changes is the disappearance of the traditional wedding, with songs accompanying each of its many phases, and, as well, the absence of the *matesha,* the large outdoor swing where people often sat in the evenings, singing *cantares de matesha* 'songs of the swing', which are ballads or light songs. *Romances* are often referred to as being *de matesha* or not *de matesha.* In fact, the association between swinging and singing was so close that the following citation included no explanatory note: "[Mon mari] me faisait un balançoire, mais m'interdisait de chanter" ("[my husband] made me a swing, but forbade me to sing") (Berdugo-Cohen and Levy 1987:102).

Senior citizens' clubs, as already noted, have become important contexts for collecting, and to some extent transmitting, Judeo-Spanish songs and lore. Against the sonic backdrop of rather boisterous bingo games, I have recorded ballads, wedding songs, stories, *pasodobles,* popular Israeli songs, multilingual versions of "Happy Birthday," and a memorable, if somewhat incongruous, rendition of "Deck the Halls," intoned in a rather absentminded and grumpy fashion by one woman focusing on her bingo card. The presence of the group helps elicit songs in a relatively spontaneous way; at the same time it alters performance practice. *Romances* that a woman would usually sing alone in a slow, unmeasured style may be sung by the group with a regular rhythm at accelerating tempo, as the excitement of the bingo game mounts, even with accompanying drumming on tabletops. Transmission may be fostered as well. For example, women learn versions from each other or pass around scraps of paper with new or long-forgotten words jotted down by a faraway friend or relative.

Over the years, I have recorded some five hundred songs in Canadian Judeo-Spanish communities, mostly from Moroccan Sephardim, with a few notable exceptions such as Buena Sarfatty Garfinkle, who contributed an extensive repertoire of songs, stories, oral history, and proverbs from Salonica, and Nina Vučkovič, certainly the only Bosnian Sephardi living on a Mohawk reservation. Singers from the Eastern Mediterranean were usually younger than those from Morocco and had left their homes at a younger age, often living in Israel before coming to Canada, while Moroccans had spent much of their adult lives in Morocco. *"Mi generación no canta ya"* ("My generation doesn't sing any more") was a poignant remark made by one Izmirli grandmother, echoed by several people from Greece and Turkey. In general, Moroccan Judeo-Spanish speakers sang much more of the older repertoire, ballads and life-cycle songs than did those from the Eastern Mediterranean communities.

Romances and life-cycle songs

Romances and life-cycle songs, especially wedding songs, constitute the main repertoire of Moroccan Sephardic women. Jumol Edéry from Larache described the painting of wedding announcements on houses, the singing, the procession, the ritual bath, the food (in mouthwatering detail), and the dressing of the cow in sumptuous garments before it is slaughtered. In a mixture of French and *khaketía* (Moroccan Judeo-Spanish), she described the procession to the groom's house: *"Yo estaba ya cansada . . . con mi voile . . . tout le monde allume avec des bougies, et todo el mundo paytineando todos, piyyutim, piyyutim, hasta la casa del novio"* ("I was already tired . . . with my veil . . . everyone lit up by candlelight, and everyone singing *piyyutim* 'Hebrew hymns', everyone, *piyyutim, piyyutim,* right up to the groom's house") (Cohen 1982a).

Calendar-cycle songs are sung by both women and men. Their use of contrafactum (using a known melody for a selected song text), which goes back a long time, may occasionally appear inappropriate. However, as in the Hasidic tradition, a melody adapted for sacred use loses its profane associations (Koskoff 1978). Melodic sources from texts in Hebrew varied from *romances* to lyric songs or songs from outside the tradition altogether. The *piyyut* "Az vashir Moshe" ("So sang Moses") was sung by two different men to the tune for a bawdy ballad about a priest's adventures in the convent ("Fray Pedro"). One woman interviewed felt this was inappropriate; the other, equally observant, shrugged and said tunes came from all over. The *piyyut* "Eshet ne'urim" ("A Woman of Valour") was sung to the tune of the Moroccan version of a pan-European adultery ballad, "La Blancaniña" (related to "Four Nights Drunk/Our Goodman"). The Sabbath hymn "Lekha dodi" ("Welcome Sabbath Bride") was recorded sung to several melodies: a short bawdy ditty in *khaketía* ("Jacób y Mazaltóv"), "Scarborough Fair," and a tune identified by the singer only as *moruna árabe* 'Moorish-Arabic'. In a musical skit for a Sephardic audience, Gerineldo (figure 1), a Sephardi ensemble, sang the same text to a Spanish *pasodoble,* and, to the delight of both native and new Québécois, Solly Lévy of the group set it to the famous tune by Vigneault and Rochon, "Gens du pays" (Cohen 1982b).

Lyric songs

Lyric songs are part of an Eastern rather than a Moroccan repertoire, but Moroccans contributed several recreational and satirical songs. "Me vaya kappará" (a Moroccan Sephardic expression, roughly, "may I be sacrificed [for you]") pokes fun at "current" (1930s–1940s) fashions in dress and behavior (figure 2), and Gerineldo's Solly Lévy added a verse about the icy climate of Canada (Cohen 1985). The theme of being cold in Canada is echoed in several songs composed in Toronto by Tangier-born Jack Benlolo, including "Avramico y Davico" ("Abe and Davie"), which is set to the delightfully incongruous tune "Dominique," made popular by Soeur Sourire, the "Singing Nun" of the 1960s. Consciously or not, these references to cold weather may also reflect the differences felt by the immigrants between the emotional climates of the Mediterranean and Canada. Other Moroccan satirical and topical songs I have recorded include parodies—the tune of the popular wedding song/*romance* "Rahél lastimosa" ("Tearful Rachel"), for example, is adjusted to fit the story of a famous Spanish bullfighter, and the devotional "Coplas de las flores" ("Verses of the Flowers") lends its graceful melody to a parody about Roosevelt and Churchill.

Salonican and Turkish Sephardim borrowed melodies from French, Latin American, Italian, Serbian, and other popular songs. Various languages might appear in the same song, as in the following rather chaotic mixture sung to the tune of "La

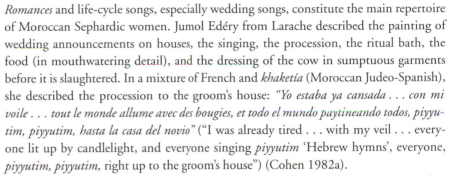

FIGURE I   Gerineldo 1985. Clockwise from upper left: Solly Lévy, Judith Cohen, Kelly Sultan Amar, Oro Anahory-Librowicz. Photo by R. S. Adams, Montréal, 1985.

TRACK 29

FIGURE 2   "Me vaya
kappará," a song about
youth and fashion in
early twentieth century
Jewish Tangier, composed
by Solomon Lévy, re-
corded by Judith Cohen,
Gerineldo rehearsal,
Montréal, June 11, 1988.

FIGURE 2   "Me vaya kappará," a song about youth and fashion in early twentieth century Jewish Tangier, composed by Solomon Lévy, recorded by Judith Cohen, Gerineldo rehearsal, Montréal, June 11, 1988.

Madelón": *"Se fué con su musiu . . . à la plage . . . una vez cada el Shabbat . . . si . . . vos azen amotzi, dezilde en francés 'au revoir et merci'"* ("She went with her *monsieur* . . . to the beach . . . every Sabbath . . . if . . . they say the blessing over bread . . . say in French 'good-bye and thanks'").

Abandonment of a young girl by her boyfriend, who sometimes left her pregnant, was a common theme, and topical songs include the story of the Great Fire of Salonica ("El Dió que mate a la grega"), an account of life at the Alliance Israélite Universelle (AIU) schools ("A la Eskola de la Aliança"), and sly innuendos about "El vendedor de frutas" ("The Fruit Vendor"). Affectionate references abound to "el char-less-tón" (the Charleston). Parodies are numerous: "La muzher que cale tomar" ("The woman one should choose"), to the tune of "Valentine," made popular by Maurice Chevalier, features a young man who sighs for a woman *de famiya* ("of good family"), who can play violin and piano, hold her own at a "salon," and *"que tenga sex appeal . . . como flamma a la cama"* ("who should have sex appeal . . . like a flame in bed")! His friend accuses him of wanting a *"kukla de vitrina"* ("a window mannequin").

Few performing artists from the Sephardic community focus specifically on Judeo-Spanish song. Synagogue choirs and *hazzanim* 'cantors' often include a few selections, but many performers from within the community work in non-Judeo-Spanish repertoires. The Reverend Salomon Amzallag has been well known for decades to audiences in Morocco, France, Israel, and Canada as *Samy el-Maghribi*, 'Samy of the Maghreb', performing Hebrew and Judeo-Spanish songs, Arab-Andalusian music, and his own compositions. Many younger Sephardim are involved in contemporary classic and popular musical forms. Dance orchestras advertise such unlikely sounding repertoires as *"chants hébreux, Rock 'n' roll, nigunim hassidiques, musique orientale et espagnole"* ("Hebrew songs, rock and roll, Hassidic niguns, Oriental, and Spanish music"), while the band Geoulah is advertised as *"un groupe de musique reggae, aux accents jazz, rock et funk"* ("a reggae music group with jazz, rock, and funk influences").

THE PROMOTION OF SEPHARDIC MUSICAL CULTURE IN MONTRÉAL

The Centre Communautaire Juif (CCJ) of the Communuaté Sépharade du Québec (CSQ) is actively involved in promoting aspects of Sephardic culture. Two musical groups have been affiliated with the CCJ, the Chorale Kinor (ongoing) and Gerineldo (1981–1994). Kinor has an eclectic repertoire that includes, but is not restricted to, Sephardic songs. Gerineldo specialized in research and authentic performance of

Moroccan Judeo-Spanish songs, language, and customs through concerts, original plays by group member Solly Lévy, and audio and video recordings.

A *Soirée Orientale* is sometimes put on as a gala benefit for a synagogue or community center. Live Moroccan, Andalusian, or popular Middle Eastern music is featured, with the "oriental" atmosphere enhanced by the women's embroidered kaftans. Most songs are in French and Arabic, but performers often include some in Judeo-Spanish, usually from commercial recordings. The biennial *Quinzaine Sépharade* 'Sephardic Fortnight' may include theater, music, dance, lectures, discussion groups, art exhibits, films, and so on, with an international roster of artists and speakers. Specifically Judeo-Spanish content is usually limited. The 2000 Quinzaine's musical events included the Israel Andalusian Orchestra, the Moroccan-Israeli cantor Emile Zrihan, who began to appear in World Music festivals in the late 1990s, Russian Jewish immigrant musicians, and a local flamenco guitarist, as well as a musical version of *Oliver Twist* adapted to a Moroccan Sephardic context and concerts of Western concert music by several of the community's *"jeunes virtuoses."*

It is increasingly rare to find the older Judeo-Spanish repertoire in Montréal's Sephardic community today, although as in other communities worldwide, the actual Sephardic presence is a flourishing and vital one.

—JUDITH R. COHEN

REFERENCES

Armistead, Samuel G. 1973. "El cancionero judeo-español de Marruecos en el siglo XVIII (incipits de los Ben-Çur)." *Nueva Revista de Filología Hispánica* 22:280–290.

Armistead, Samuel, and Joseph A. Silverman. 1981. "El antiguo romancero sefardí: citas de romances en himnarios hebreos (siglos XVI–XIX)." *Nueva Revista de Filología Hispánica* 30:450–512.

Avenary, Hanoch. 1971. "Cantos españoles antiguos mencionados en la literatura hebrea." *Anuario Musical* 25:67–79.

Berdugo-Cohen, Yolande, and Joseph Levy. 1987. *Juifs Marocains à Montréal.* Montréal: VLB Editeur.

Cohen, Judith. 1982a. Personal interview, Jumol (Julia) Edéry. Montréal.

———. 1982b. Personal interview, Solly Lévy. Montréal.

———. 1985. Personal collection. Songs recorded 28 January.

———. 1987. "Ya salió de la mar: Judeo-Spanish Wedding Songs among Moroccan Jews in Canada." In *Women and Music in Cross-Cultural Perspective,* ed. Ellen Koskoff, 55–68. Westport, Conn.: Greenwood Press.

———. 1990. "Musical Bridges: The Contrafact Tradition in Judeo-Spanish Song." In *Cultural Marginality in the Western Mediterranean,* ed. F. Gerson and A. Percival, 121–128. Toronto: New Aurora.

———. 1995. "A Bosnian Sephardic Woman in Kahnewake, Québec." *Canadian Women's Studies/Les Cahiers de la Femme* 16(4):112–113.

———. 1996/2000. "Sonography of Judeo-Spanish Song." *Jewish Folklore and Ethnology Review* 18(1–2):95–100.

Katz, Israel J. 1988. "Contrafact and the Judeo-Spanish Romancero: A Musicological View." In *Hispanic Studies in Honor of Joseph A. Silverman,* ed. Joseph R. Recapito, 169–187. Newark, N.J.: Juan de la Cuesta Hispanic Monographs.

Koskoff, Ellen. 1978. "Nigun Composition in an American Hasidic Community." In *Selected Reports in Ethnomusicology,* vol. 3, ed. James Porter. Los Angeles: University of California.

Section 3c
Ontario

Ontario is Canada's most populous province as well as one of the world's most culturally varied areas, and social and musical interactions among and between diverse populations are the norm, especially in Toronto. The American Indian population, consisting primarily of members of the Iroquois confederacy, Algonquian-speakers such as the Cree, and the Anishnabe nations such as the Ojibwe, were crucial in the seventeenth and eighteenth centuries to the survival of early French and British settlers who joined with them in various wars to protect their hunting interests. Today these groups have been instrumental in reviving the intertribal tradition of the powwow, where Indian tribes from all over the United States and Canada come together to perform and exchange rituals and music. Ontario is also home to a large African Canadian and more recently a Caribbean Canadian population, whose yearly festival, Caribbana, is known worldwide. Post World War II immigration resulted in the establishment of sizable southern European, Middle Eastern, and South Asian musical communities as well, and concerts of Indian and Arabic, as well as of Western European classical music traditions, are common.

The Toronto Symphony performs with a chorus at the Roy Thompson Hall in Toronto. © Kelly-Mooney Photography/CORBIS.

Overview
Elaine Keillor
Robin Elliott

The 1800s to Confederation
The Years of Rapid Expansion, 1867 to 1918
From World War I to 1960
Developments after 1960

Ontario is the second largest in area and the largest in population of the ten provinces of Canada. Its capital, Toronto, is the most populous city in Canada. Ottawa, the federal capital, is also located in Ontario, on the border with Québec; other major cities in Ontario include Hamilton, London, Windsor, Kitchener, and Sudbury. The southern part of the province was called Upper Canada from 1791 to 1841 and Canada West from 1841 to 1867. The name Ontario—an Iroquoian word sometimes translated as "beautiful water"—was first applied to the easternmost of the Great Lakes in 1641. It was adopted as the name of the province at the time of Confederation in 1867. The northern part of the province, formerly part of Rupert's Land, was purchased from the Hudson's Bay Company in 1870.

In precontact times Ontario was inhabited by both sedentary and nomadic indigenous cultures that hunted in its dense forests, fished in its numerous lakes and rivers, and cultivated the land to grow corn, squash, and beans. As a result of wars and devastating diseases brought by the Europeans, however, over half of the indigenous population had perished by 1650. Father Francesco Giuseppe Bressani (1612–1672) described one indigenous group, the Neutrals, in the early 1600s as having "exceedingly acute vision, excellent hearing, [and] an ear for music" (Jury 1977:7). Music played an important role in the efforts of European missionaries to convert the indigenous groups to Christianity. One famous example is the first North American Christmas carol, "Jesous Ahatonhia" ("Huron Carol"), which was created at a mission established near Georgian Bay in the 1640s.

The fur trade dominated the economic life of what is now Ontario for many years. Life in the fur-trading forts was occasionally brightened by music: in records for the Moose Factory dating from 1749, there is mention of three fiddlers who helped with dancing and singing. Many of the Hudson's Bay Company employees were of Scottish heritage, so secular musical repertoire associated with the fur trade consisted mostly of Scottish reels, jigs, and hornpipes [see ENGLISH AND SCOTTISH MUSIC, p. 831]. Except for the occasional fort and the surviving indigenous peoples, Ontario remained largely uninhabited until the last decade of the eighteenth century. As more settlers of European heritage arrived, they brought the cultivated and vernacular music of their native countries to Ontario. This provided the basis of the varied and vibrant music scene that has developed in the province.

THE 1800s TO CONFEDERATION

In 1796 Elizabeth Simcoe wrote in her diary about the kind of music to be heard in York, which had been founded by her husband, John Graves Simcoe, three years earlier (York was renamed Toronto in 1834): "[A] band of music [is] stationed near. . . . Jacob, the Mohawk, . . . danced Scotch reels with more ease and grace than any person I ever saw. . . . A large party from the garrison to dinner. A boat with music accompanied them; we heard it in the evening until they had passed the town. It sounds delightfully" (Simcoe 1965:174).

This observation reveals two important elements in the development of music in Ontario: the enormous influence of British garrison bands and the mingling or *rubbaboo* 'Canadian soup' created when one culture adapts the musical idiom of another [see BORDER CROSSINGS AND FUSIONS, p. 321]. By 1840 the population of Upper Canada was about 400,000; the settlers were scattered in small communities from the Ottawa River to the head of the Great Lakes. Aside from the garrison bands, music making was predominantly a matter of individual enterprise, but it was also becoming an important feature in the churches, especially those of the Protestant denominations [see RELIGION, p. 116]. Many of the settlers were Loyalists who had come from the United States and were thus familiar with singing schools, the aim of which was to improve singing in the church services and to teach participants the basics of musical notation. The singing of moralistic texts to psalm tunes was also a prominent feature of sacred music in Ontario. Judith Humphrey's notebook, dated 1813, is a collection of twelve psalm tunes, each with a secular verse; it was used in the area of Simcoe (Beckwith 1987:10).

The community of Hope, renamed Sharon in the 1830s, has more extant musical artifacts than any other nineteenth-century Canadian community. It was home to the religious sect of the charismatic leader David Willson [see SHARON, p. 136]. A singing school was active there by 1819, and among other musical records there are copies of the first tune books published in Ontario: Mark Burnham's *Colonial Harmonist* (Port Hope, 1832) and Alexander Davidson's *Sacred Harmony* (Toronto, 1838). The Canadian tune books were intended for use in church services, as school manuals, and for secular enjoyment.

As the singing standards improved, church or community choirs would perform more ambitious works for which an accompaniment might be provided by the local band, supplemented by whatever string players were available. Thus, in Toronto the Musical Society was organized by 1835, and the Harmonic Society was giving concerts in 1840. Various organizations known as the Toronto Philharmonic Society were active in the years 1845–1850 and 1853–1855, giving six or so concerts each year. An advertisement for one concert on 23 April 1847 stated: "The Members will be assisted in the vocal and Instrumental departments by several Amateurs, and by the Band of the 81st. Regiment under the direction of Mr. Crozier. The Choruses will be accompanied on a new Organ of great power and richness of tone, which has been lent for the occasion, and erected in the hall, by the builder, Mr. Thomas, of this city. J. P. Clarke, conductor, will preside at the organ" (Sale 1968:72).

This particular concert included one symphony by Mozart and two by Beethoven (not identified either in the program or the press coverage) plus choruses from Handel's *Messiah* and Haydn's *The Creation,* two oratorios that were frequently performed in the 1800s (Sale 1968:72). Original Canadian compositions were heard increasingly in Ontario parlors and concerts by the 1850s. Some Canadian content appeared in the various tune books and also in periodicals that often included one or two pieces of music in each issue. In the *Anglo-American Magazine* (Toronto, 1852–1855), for example, works by J. P. Clarke can be found.

Abraham Nordheimer (1816–1862) settled about 1842 in Kingston, where he taught piano, voice, and violin privately and operated a music store. By 1844 he had

When the Germania Musical Society, an orchestra of twenty-two to twenty-five musicians originally from Berlin, gave concerts in Kingston and Toronto in 1850 and 1852, it had to repeat its program to meet the demand for tickets.

FIGURE I   Front cover of a Nordheimer publication. By permission of the Music Division, National Library of Canada.

moved to Toronto and was operating a music store and the first publishing firm in Canada that was dedicated solely to music (figure 1). The Nordheimer catalog included reprints of U.S. or European material, but also an ever-increasing number of piano and vocal works composed by Canadians, among them R. S. Ambrose (1824–1908), J. P. Clarke (c. 1807–1877) (the first Canadian to receive a bachelor of music degree, Kings College, Toronto, 1846), William Horatio Clarke (1840–1913) (father of the famed cornetist Herbert L. Clarke), W. O. Forsyth (1859–1937), Mrs. H. E. Gilbert (fl. 1870s), Edwin Gledhill (1830–1919), Henry Herbert Godfrey (1858–1908), Moritz Relle (fl. 1860s), E[lizabeth] H[arriet?] Ridout, Henry F. Sefton (1882), Henry Schallehn (1813?–1891?), Hattie Stephens (not known), G. W. Strathy (1818–1890) (the first Canadian known to have received the degree doctor of music, Trinity College, Toronto, 1858), and Thomas Turvey (fl. 1860s–1870s) (Calderisi 1981). Some of these works have been republished in the Canadian Musical Heritage volumes.

Although singing schools continued to flourish in Ontario to the 1870s, music education increasingly became the preserve of private teachers and was also offered as a subject in primary and secondary schools [see LEARNING, p. 274]. Henry Frost, who taught in a small school in York County, prepared a set of manuals between 1835 and 1850 to cover the rudiments of music notation through three- and four-part songs. Egerton Ryerson, appointed superintendent of education for Canada West in 1844, prescribed vocal music as a subject in the Common School Act of 1846. Because Ryerson decided that it should be taught by nonspecialized teachers, arrangements were made to provide training in the normal schools based on the Wilhem-Hullah method using the fixed *do* system (Green and Vogan 1991:51).

Famous musicians, such as the singers Jenny Lind and Adelina Patti, the pianists Anton Rubinstein and Sigismund Thalberg, and the violinists Ole Bull and Henri Vieuxtemps, began to tour Ontario from the 1840s onward. The building of railway lines in the 1850s made for better traveling conditions for touring artists. When Lind performed at St. Lawrence Hall, Toronto, in 1851, more than a thousand people paid a minimum of three dollars to attend each of her two concerts. And when the Germania Musical Society, an orchestra of twenty-two to twenty-five musicians originally from Berlin, gave concerts in Kingston and Toronto in 1850 and 1852, it had to repeat its program to meet the demand for tickets (Keillor 1997:56). Louis Moreau Gottschalk wrote vividly about his experiences performing in Kingston, Toronto, St. Catherines, and Ottawa in 1862 and 1864 (1964:84, 201, 224–225).

Until the 1860s the building of instruments, mainly organs, pianos, and string instruments, was done by individuals such as the Mr. Thomas mentioned above or Richard Coates, who made three organs for the community at Sharon. Even Theodor August Heintzman (1817–1899), the founder of Canada's most important piano manufacturing firm, built (in his kitchen) his first instruments in his spare time after moving to Toronto about 1858. In 1864 Robert and William Bell began turning out one melodeon a week in Guelph. Within three years they could not keep up with the local demand for their instruments. The Bell Piano and Organ Co. rapidly expanded its production of harmoniums or large cabinet organs, melodeons, and pianos that were shipped around the world. Customers included Queen Victoria and the Sultan of Turkey, and the company reported that 75,000 of its instruments were in use by 1895 (Kelly 1991:44).

THE YEARS OF RAPID EXPANSION, 1867 TO 1918

On 1 July 1867 Canada West (Ontario) joined Canada East (Québec), New Brunswick, and Nova Scotia to form the Dominion of Canada, the capital of which was to be Ottawa, a small lumber industry town formerly known as Bytown. Writing in 1871, Charles Roger described the rapid changes that were taking place in this Ontario community as a result: "Fine shops, vying with those of Montréal or New York in the character of their goods have sprung up; societies for the improvement of knowledge in literature and science have been instituted; agreeable promenades have been constructed . . . and all the banks are doing business in elegant and substantial stone structures. . . . Ottawa is, we repeat, making rapid progress, covering a space of three miles in length and about as many in breadth but having no good place of amusement, no theatre, nor any proper Music Hall, and a wretchedly ugly looking City Hall" (1871: 52–53, 88). Within a decade several bands were formed, one of which, the Governor-General's Foot Guards, has remained active to the present. Band concerts included marches, dances, hymn and folk song tunes, operatic selections, and the occasional locally composed work (figure 2).

When Gowan's Opera House opened in Ottawa in 1875, the Canadian-based Holman English Opera Company presented seven different works, including Bellini's *La Sonnambula,* Rossini's *La Cenerentola,* and Donizetti's *L'Elisir d'Amore.* Other new venues were used for chamber music concerts, such as those by the Canadian artists Frantz Jehin-Prume, Rosita del Vecchio, and Calixa Lavallée. Such events probably encouraged the formation of local organizations such as the Quintette Club, Musical Union, and various choral groups.

The provision of better halls, the proliferation of musical organizations, and the drive for higher standards in musical education occurred in similar fashion in Ontario communities into the twentieth century. Choral groups predominated, employing an instrumental group as needed (figure 3). The Toronto Mendelssohn Choir, formed in 1894 by A. S. Vogt, is still active today and played a major role in establishing Toronto as the choral capital of North America in the early twentieth century. The Ottawa

FIGURE 2   Citizen's Band, Perth, Ontario, c. 1889. This community has had at least one civilian and/or militia band in existence for over 150 years. Each gave regular concerts during the warm weather in the park or in the winter at the town hall, as well as leading parades and appearing at strawberry festivals, lawn socials, firemen's nights, skating rinks, and county fairs. From the collection of Daphne Overhill. Used by permission.

FIGURE 3 Elgin County Male Choir, c. 1928, conducted by Lenore Stevens Keillor, seated at the organ. This is just one of the numerous choirs active in Ontario prior to 1930, many of which participated in competitive music festivals for which trophies and certificates were awarded. By permission of the Music Division, National Library of Canada.

Orpheus Glee Club, formed in 1906, became the Orpheus Operatic Society and still produces operettas and musicals today. In many communities, concert giving was initiated by a local women's musical club; the first such group in Canada was the Duet Club of Hamilton, founded in 1889 and still active today.

Several teaching studios had been using the grand title of conservatory, but the first Canadian institution to offer instruction in a wide range of instruments and voice with basic training in theoretical subjects was the Toronto Conservatory of Music (TCM), formed in 1886. Offering both class and private instruction, the TCM established syllabi of required repertoire and initiated a graded examination system. In 1899 the Associated Musicians of Ontario was formed to oppose the introduction of music examinations into Canada from the Royal Schools of Music in Britain (Jones 1989:129). After that skirmish the TCM developed examination centers throughout Ontario and beyond. The TCM became the Royal Conservatory of Music (RCM) in 1947, and today it is the largest national integrated music conservatory in the world. Other notable music conservatories in Ontario have included the Hambourg Conservatory of Music in Toronto (1911–1951) and the Western Ontario Conservatory of Music, established in London, Ontario, in 1891. The latter institution merged with the Western (Canada) Board in 1997 to become Conservatory Canada, which also has an extensive national examination system.

Even though more systematic musical education became available during this period, Ontario musicians who wished to pursue composition or international performing careers tended to go abroad for further education: W. O. Forsyth (1859–1937) went to Leipzig, Clarence Lucas (1866–1947) to Paris, and Gena Branscombe (1881–1977) to Chicago and later Berlin. These composers wrote in the larger genres and managed to have their orchestral and/or large-scale operatic/choral works performed abroad. On occasion homegrown operettas were seen on the stages of the opera house found in any Ontario town. One of these was *Leo, The Royal Cadet* with music by Oscar Telgmann (1855–1946) and a libretto by G. F. Cameron (1854–1885), set in part at Kingston's Royal Military College. It premiered on 11 July 1889 in Kingston and by 1925 had been performed over 150 times (figure 4). Meanwhile, Torontonians from 1887 on could see the staple operas by Rossini, Verdi, Gounod, Massenet, and Wagner performed by touring companies.

Technology began to influence music making in Ontario in the nineteenth century. In November 1879 the telephone was used to transmit the sounds of a concert taking place at St. James Hall, Ottawa, to persons sitting in the offices of the Dominion Telegraph Company (Keillor 1997:63). By the 1900s telephone companies were often providing concerts of recorded music through the telephone to their subscribers

FIGURE 4   Cast of *Leo, The Royal Cadet,* Grand
Opera House, Kingston, Ontario, 15 June 1915.
Used by permission of Queen's University
Archives.

FIGURE 4   Cast of *Leo, The Royal Cadet,* Grand Opera House, Kingston, Ontario, 15 June 1915. Used by permission of Queen's University Archives.

on Sunday afternoons (Keillor 1997:64). Some Ontario piano-manufacturing companies by 1901 were making mechanical player pianos, and between 1906 and 1925 every major piano manufacturer did so. Meanwhile, the production of grand and upright pianos was at its height in Ontario; the major companies in Toronto were Heintzman, Nordheimer, and Mason and Risch. The company W. Doherty of Clinton began manufacturing organs in 1875; by 1900 it was making seventy-four types and had also moved into upright and grand piano production. The Sherlock-Manning Piano Company opened in Clinton in 1890 and was the last of all of the Canadian piano-manufacturing companies to close its doors in 1988. R. S. Williams, who made mandolins, banjos, guitars, violins, brass instruments, and pianos as well as reed and pipe organs, moved his factory in 1888 from Toronto to Oshawa, where it continued until 1932.

FROM WORLD WAR I TO 1960

World War I decisively accelerated Canada's emerging sense of nationhood, but at great loss of human life. Many organizations that seemed to be well established early in the century faded away during the war due to a loss of personnel or leadership. Frank Welsman formed the Toronto (Conservatory) Symphony Orchestra in 1906; it weathered the war years only to cease activity in 1918. Donald Heins formed an orchestra in Ottawa in 1905 that won the Earl Grey Orchestra Competition (created in 1907 and usually entered by four or five orchestras annually) three times; it was once described by a New York critic as the finest community orchestra he had ever heard. The orchestra folded in 1927 when Heins moved to Toronto. Most instrumental musicians depended on playing for vaudeville shows and silent movies for a living. Even before the talkies arrived in 1927, some musicians wanted a respite from playing commercial theater music and tried to organize orchestras. This was the case when the present Toronto Symphony Orchestra (TSO) was formed and gave its first concert at 5:00 P.M. on 23 April 1923. The young Toronto pianist Colin McPhee performed his Second Piano Concerto with the TSO that year, and a near-riot broke out over its avant-garde sounds, even though the conductor had not allowed the use of Chinese wind chimes as the composer had intended. By 1928, twenty-five TSO concerts were being broadcast annually on a trans-Canada network under the auspices of the Canadian National

The young Toronto pianist Colin McPhee performed his Second Piano Concerto with the TSO that year, and a near-riot broke out over its avant-garde sounds, even though the conductor had not allowed the use of Chinese wind chimes as the composer had intended.

Railways. Many Ontario orchestras began as community ensembles and later developed into semiprofessional or professional organizations, among them the London Civic Symphony Orchestra (founded in 1937), Kitchener-Waterloo Symphony Orchestra (1944), Windsor Symphony Orchestra (1947), Hamilton Philharmonic Orchestra (1949), Kingston Symphony (1953), International Symphony Orchestra of Sarnia and Port Huron (1957), and Thunder Bay (originally Lakehead) Symphony Orchestra (1960).

In 1936 the Canadian Broadcasting Corporation (CBC) was formed, creating employment for many musicians, especially in Toronto, the CBC's main English-language center. The CBC Symphony Orchestra (1952–1964) was noted for its performances of contemporary works, many of which were commissioned from Ontario composers, including Harry Somers (1925–1999), Norman Symonds (1920–1998), and John Weinzweig (b. 1913). The orchestra participated in a famed series of performances and recordings of the works of Stravinsky and Schoenberg, frequently with the Festival Singers of Canada, founded by the conductor Elmer Iseler in 1954. The Festival Singers became Canada's first professional choir in 1968.

Other smaller ensembles continued to be formed for chamber music. The most notable was the Hart House String Quartet (figure 5), formed in Toronto in 1924 as Canada's first fully subsidized chamber group. The Quartet included some works by Canadian composers in its repertoire and appeared throughout North America and Europe to high acclaim until its dissolution in 1946. In 1941 the noted Canadian violinist Kathleen Parlow formed a quartet based in Toronto that was active until 1956.

While various choral organizations continued and new ones were created, operatic productions by touring companies were becoming fewer due to traveling expenses. As a result, more groups formed to concentrate on operetta and opera production: at least half a dozen such groups were active in Toronto during the interwar years. But it was only with the establishment of the Conservatory Opera School in 1946 and the formation of the CBC Opera Company in 1948 that local professional opera production became firmly established.

The CBC actively promoted Canadian performers and commissioned composers, as did the National Film Board (NFB), formed in Ottawa in 1939. During the war John Weinzweig, Barbara Pentland, and Godfrey Ridout, among others, were hired to write incidental music for radio plays and films. The first opera commissioned by the CBC was *Deirdre,* composed by Healey Willan (1880–1968), who settled in Toronto in 1913 and was widely recognized for his organ music and sacred choral compositions. The opera was broadcast in 1946 and again in 1951; a staged version of *Deirdre* was presented by the Royal Conservatory Opera School in 1965 and by the Canadian Opera Company in 1966. The latter organization, the leading opera company in Canada, began using its present name in 1958, after emerging from various groups producing opera in Toronto after World War II.

FIGURE 5   Hart House String Quartet, c. 1926. *Left to right:* Harry Adaskin, Milton Blackstone, Geza de Krez, and Boris Hambourg. By permission of the Public Archives Canada.

Prior to 1960 the foundation was laid for Ontario's subsequent rich production of electro-acoustic music. Morse Robb of Belleville patented the world's first electric organ in 1927. His experiments became known to a young physicist interested in music, Hugh Le Caine (1914–1977), who worked at the National Research Council in Ottawa. By the mid-1940s Le Caine had developed the Sackbut, the first music synthesizer. In 1955 he composed *Dripsody,* using the sound of the fall of a single drop of water, manipulated by another of his inventions, the multitrack tape recorder. Le Caine's inventions were used to create the first electronic music studio in Canada (and the second one in North America) at the University of Toronto in 1959. Arnold Walter (1902–1973) was a guiding light in this development.

Walter had become the director of the University of Toronto's faculty of music in 1952 and was putting into place a strong academic program including graduate work in musicology, music education, and composition. He also introduced to North America the educational theories of Carl Orff by providing English translations of his manuals in collaboration with Doreen Hall. Students were thus better prepared to teach in the secondary school system, where increasingly vocal and band programs were becoming part of the daily agenda rather than an extracurricular activity dependent on an interested individual teacher. Also at the University of Toronto, students were learning about twentieth-century compositional techniques from teachers such as John Weinzweig, who had composed his first serial-based work in 1938. Weinzweig, along with some of his friends and former students, initiated the Canadian League of Composers in Toronto in 1951, mainly in response to the difficulty of getting their works published and performed.

The increased musical activity in Ontario during the 1940s and 1950s was due in no small measure to the large number of recently arrived immigrants from Europe who were accustomed to having the opportunity to attend chamber, symphonic, and operatic performances. There was as yet no consistent governmental support for such activities, apart from the publicly funded CBC and NFB. With the establishment of the Canada Council as a Crown Corporation in 1957, funding for jury-approved projects of arts organizations became available. One of the first funded projects in music was the establishment in 1959 of the Canadian Music Centre in Toronto, which provides a library of scores and an information center for the dissemination and promotion of the music composed by its associates.

Summer festivals began in the 1950s and proliferated thereafter. The Stratford Festival was founded in 1953 and became an important promoter of both musical and dramatic events prior to 1970. Louis Applebaum (b. 1918) organized the musical program from 1955 to 1960, featuring performances of jazz, opera, chamber, and symphonic music. Applebaum also wrote incidental music for the festival's productions of Shakespeare plays. In 1960 the International Conference of Composers and the International String Congress were held in Stratford.

DEVELOPMENTS AFTER 1960

A frequent performer at Stratford was Glenn Gould, a Toronto-born and -trained musician who established an international career as a pianist. He is perhaps the best known of the many Ontario musicians who have achieved worldwide recognition in recent years. Every aspect of musical activity has flourished greatly since 1960, and governmental support for music has also increased during this period. Funding has been supplied by the Ontario Arts Council (created in 1963) and various municipal arts councils, in addition to the Canada Council. Further, greater opportunities to study music at an advanced level have become available as more universities (Western Ontario, York, Wilfrid Laurier, Ottawa, and Carleton) have expanded their graduate offerings in music disciplines

An important classical-sized orchestra, the National Arts Centre Orchestra, was formed in 1969 and is resident in a state-supported theater and auditorium complex in Ottawa. Chamber music ensembles based in Ontario have included the Lyric Arts Trio (1964–1983), Orford String Quartet (1965–1991), Canadian Brass (formed 1970), York Winds (1972–1988), and Camerata Canada (1974–1985). Ensembles active at the turn of the twenty-first century include Thirteen Strings, the St. Lawrence and Penderecki String Quartets, Amici, and the Rembrandt and Gryphon Trios.

There has been considerable interest in Ontario in early music. A consort of viols was given to Hart House at the University of Toronto in the 1920s and was used for performances by Leo Smith, Wolfgang Grunsky, and Peggy Sampson. In 1972 the Toronto Consort was formed to perform repertoire of the medieval period and the Renaissance, frequently using editions prepared by its members from manuscript sources. It has commissioned modern compositions for period instruments from Walter Buczynski, Lothar Klein, Ben McPeek, John Beckwith, Hope Lee, and David Eagle. A larger professional ensemble is the period instrument orchestra Tafelmusik, formed in 1978. Through its Toronto concert series, worldwide tours, and recordings, it has revived many works, including Baroque operas performed with Opera Atelier, founded in 1983. Many organizations have concentrated on performing contemporary repertoire. Ten Centuries Concerts (active 1962–1967) organized programs highlighting and contrasting unfamiliar (pre-1700) repertoire with twentieth-century works and Canadian commissions. In 1972 New Music Concerts and Arraymusic were both founded in Toronto to perform contemporary repertoire. Professional organizations founded more recently include Espace Musique (Ottawa, 1979), the Esprit Orchestra (Toronto, 1983), Trillium Plus Music and More (London, 1987), and Opera Anonymous (Toronto, 1994). The Glass Orchestra, founded in 1977, is the only ensemble in the world creating and performing contemporary compositions entirely with instruments of glass. The Evergreen Club Gamelan Ensemble and the Toronto performance group Cinnamon Sphere indicate the ever-increasing influences of Asian music in Ontario; this influence is also evident in the music of the composers Alexina Louie and Chan Ka Nin, among others [see AN OVERVIEW OF ASIAN AMERICAN MUSICS, p. 947; CANTONESE MUSIC IN VANCOUVER, p. 1260].

Music festivals have also proliferated. The Guelph Spring Festival began in 1968, although in 1929 a festival was held in Guelph in which Edward Johnson, a Guelph native, leading tenor of his day, and manager of the Metropolitan Opera (1935–1950), had performed. Other festivals held in the province include the Algoma Fall Festival (Sault Saint Marie, 1973–), Festival Franco-Ontarien (Ottawa, 1976–), Music at Sharon (1981–1990), Peterborough Festival of the Arts (1984–), Quinte Summer Festival (Picton, 1984–), Boris Brott Summer Festival (Hamilton, 1988–), and Festival Alexandria (1991–). Among the most highly regarded and varied are the Elora Festival and the Festival of the Sound (Parry Sound), both founded in 1979. The Ottawa Chamber Music Festival, within five years of its founding in 1994, had become the largest festival of its kind in the world. Festivals devoted to popular or jazz music idioms include the Mariposa Folk Festival, Caribana, the Ottawa International Jazz Festival, and Ottawa's Bluesfest [see CARIBANA, p 1207]. The variety of music making in these festivals is a reflection of the eclecticism, diversity, and excellence of Ontario's musical life.

REFERENCES

Beckwith, John. 1987. "On Compiling an Anthology of Canadian Hymn Tunes." In *Sing Out the Glad News: Hymn Tunes in Canada. CanMus Documents* 1:3–32.

Calderisi, Maria. 1981. *Music Publishing in Canada, 1800–1867.* Ottawa: National Library of Canada.

The Canadian Musical Heritage /Le patrimoine musical canadien. 1983–1999. Twenty-five vol-

umes of pre-1950 Canadian notated music, each edition preceded by an essay on the genre concerned. Website: http://www.cmhs.carleton.ca

Gottschalk, Louis Moreau. 1964. *Notes of a Pianist.* Ed. Jeanne Behrend. New York: Knopf.

Green, J. Paul, and Nancy F. Vogan. 1991. *Music Education in Canada: A Historical Account.* Toronto: University of Toronto Press.

Jones, Gaynor. 1989. "The Fisher Years: The Toronto Conservatory of Music, 1886–1913." In *Three Studies: College Songbooks, Toronto Conservatory, Arraymusic. CanMus Documents* 4:59–146.

Jury, Elsie McLeod. 1977. *The Neutral Indians of Southwestern Ontario.* Bulletin 13, Museum of Indian Archaeology. London: The University of Western Ontario.

Kallmann, Helmut. 1985. "Music in Upper Canada." In *The Shaping of Ontario from Explo-ration to Confederation,* comp. Nick and Helma Mika, 220–227. Belleville, Ont.: Mika Publishing Company:

Keillor, Elaine. 1988. "Musical Activity in Canada's New Capital City in the 1870s." In *Musical Canada: Words and Music Honoring Helmut Kallmann,* ed. John Beckwith and Frederick A. Hall, 115–133. Toronto: University of Toronto Press.

———. 1997. "*Auf Kanadischer Welle:* The Es-tablishment of the Germanic Musical Canon in Canada." In *Kanada-Studien: Music in Canada,* ed. Guido Bimberg, 49–76. Bochum, Germany: Brockmeyer.

Kelly, Wayne. 1991. *Downright Upright: A History of the Canadian Piano Industry.* Toronto: Natural Heritage/Natural History.

Roger, Charles. 1871. *Ottawa Past and Present.* Ottawa: Time Print and Publishing Co.

Sale, David. 1968. *Toronto's Pre-confederation Music Societies.* Master's thesis, University of Toronto.

Simcoe, Elizabeth. 1965. *Mrs. Simcoe's Diary.* Ed. M. Q. Innis. Toronto: Macmillan.

Anglo-Ontarian Music
Anne Lederman

Song Traditions
Instrumental Music

Ontario's first European residents were those at fur-trading posts, largely French, Scottish and Métis, and British military personnel attached to forts [see MÉTIS, p. 404]. There are reports of Scottish fiddling at Hudson's Bay posts in the 1700s and descriptions of garrison bands that played both country dances and minuets for fortnightly balls in addition to their military duties.

In the 1790s a large influx of British Empire Loyalists from the United States prompted the creation of Upper Canada, later Canada West, then Ontario. These immigrants included a significant number of German origin, who were fairly well assimilated. These early settlers were augmented throughout the nineteenth century by more Scots, Irish, English, and Germans, as well as African Americans and, eventually, immigrants of other European backgrounds. However, those of British Isles origin, including Ireland, have remained the largest group in Ontario to the present day.

SONG TRADITIONS

Reflecting the origins of the people in nineteenth-century Ontario, English-language song repertoire was influenced by both the United States and the British Isles. One might sing "The Man on the Flying Trapeze" or "Barbara Allen" or a locally composed ballad set to an old Irish melody. However, no serious collecting of folk song was done until the mid-twentieth century, so we do not know the proportions of different types of repertoire at earlier dates. Edith Fowke is the main collector of Ontario song, working originally around the Peterborough area, then into the Ottawa Valley and Haliburton and Glengarry counties from the 1950s on. She focused mainly on the ballad tradition: Child ballads, of which she found twenty-two; broadside ballads; Irish songs; and locally composed songs set to English, Irish, and Scottish melodies [see ENGLISH AND SCOTTISH MUSIC, p. 831; IRISH MUSIC, p. 842]. However, other studies of the repertoires of individual singers have revealed that these songs usually took their place beside new popular repertoire—sentimental parlor songs, minstrel and music hall songs, bawdy songs, satiric songs, parodies, and, in the twentieth century, vaudeville, swing, and country and western. Hymns, temperance songs, and other morality tales were also frequently sung in nonreligious settings.

Certain occupations, primarily lumbering and Great Lakes shipping, fostered local song traditions. In both occupations, men were gone for long periods of time from their families and worked in an all-male environment. Although songs did not accompany the work itself, entertainment was highly valued, and someone with a good repertoire or who could pen a verse or play an instrument was prized. In both lumbering and shipping traditions, songs give detailed pictures of the nature of the work, of living conditions (especially food), and of social life. Some are records of a particular voyage or camp, with different verses, often comic, devoted to each of the men involved.

Lumbering songs are generally set to older tunes, primarily Irish, even though there were sometimes few or no Irishmen in camp. This reflects the tendency for lumbering work to move westward from the Maritimes through Québec and into Ontario over the nineteenth and early twentieth centuries, taking the musical repertoire with it. Songs were generally sung a cappella, with a somewhat free rhythm and often a spoken last line—another legacy of Irish tradition (figure 1).

Bridging the gap between the oral tradition and formal music training in early Ontario was a singing school practice in which itinerant teachers would hold classes in the winter months to teach the rudiments of music, using tune books consisting largely of hymns arranged in four-part harmony. Some of these were published in Canada but largely copied from American sources.

Country and popular music largely supplanted the older folk material in the mid-twentieth century. There has been a small revival of older material since 1970 or so, through groups such as Muddy York, Tamarack, and Tanglefoot and traditional singers such as Ian Robb and Shelly Posen, many of whom also write original material in traditional styles. In revival hands, the songs are frequently arranged with instrumental accompaniment and adapted to a regular rhythm [see REVIVALS, p. 55].

INSTRUMENTAL MUSIC

The violin or fiddle has been the main folk dance instrument of rural Ontario from the first European settlement to the present day. In lumber camps and on board ships, fiddles were probably played solo more often than not, as were other easily transported melody instruments such as bagpipes, harmonica, button-accordion, concertina, and flute. Simple percussion instruments such as mouth harp, bones, and spoons were also

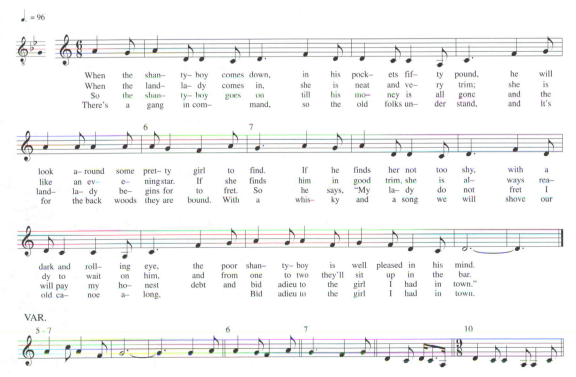

FIGURE 1 "When the Shantyboy Comes Down," from *Lumbering Songs from the Northern Woods* (Fowke 1985:159). Tune transcribed by Norman Cazden, words by Edith Fowke, from the singing of Jim Doherty, Peterborough, Ontario, June 1957. A woods version of an older sailors' ballad called "Jack Tar in Town," it is also known as "The Lumberman in Town."

All melodies were fodder for the fiddler's bow as long as they could be played in danceable rhythms.

popular. At community dances, and at the contests that have tended to replace them in popularity, piano has been the main accompaniment. In the past, many people had pump organs in their homes, and there are references to hammered dulcimers, mandolins, banjos, guitars, zithers, and hybrid stringed instruments such as the mandolin-guitarophone and the banjolin, as well as cornet, fife, and other instruments borrowed from the local marching band.

In the nineteenth century, repertoire was a mixture of Scottish (favored in Glengarry County), Irish, and French (in the Ottawa Valley especially), and a general Anglo blend held somewhat in common with the Maritimes and northeastern United States. What we know of particular tunes comes largely from concert playbills and musicians' handwritten manuscripts. The most detailed is that of Allen Ash, fiddler and inventor from Newcastle, Ontario, whose book contains slip jigs, double jigs, waltzes, quicksteps (6/8 marches), hornpipes (including one triple—an old British Isles form that has not survived), marches (the largest group), reels, and song tunes. Most are of British origin, but some are American, some are drawn from classical music and operettas, and some may have been locally composed. All melodies were fodder for the fiddler's bow as long as they could be played in danceable rhythms. Published tune books from the United States, England, and Scotland were also used, especially *Ryan's Mammoth Collection* (c. 1880, later published as *1001 Fiddle Tunes,* c. 1940) and *Harding's All-Round Collection of Jigs, Reels, and Country Dances* (1905). Older round dances gave way to newer three-part quadrilles from the United States, later simply called "square dances," mixed with popular couple dances—waltzes, polkas, and those requiring particular tunes, such as "The French Minuet," "The Jersey," "The Rye Waltz," and "The Waltz Quadrille."

The advent of radio, recordings, and published Canadian collections in the early twentieth century altered the musical landscape. The earliest fiddle records were by Québec fiddlers, and now common tunes such as "St. Anne's Reel" (Joseph Allard's "Reel de Ste. Anne," recorded in the 1930s) probably entered the repertoire from these. George Wade and the Cornhuskers, based in Toronto, was one of the first groups heard on national radio, from the late 1920s to the late 1930s. The group also recorded medleys of tunes with square dance calls in the early 1930s and published books of traditional and original tunes (Jarman 1937, 1938).

The "down-east" style popularized by Don Messer and the Islanders on national radio from 1934 and television from 1959 somewhat replaced older repertoires in the province. Radio station CKNX in Wingham, Ontario, began to broadcast its *Barn Dance* in the early 1930s, featuring "old-time" Canadian and American music as well as following the new trends in country music and western swing. At one point, more than forty musicians were on full-time staff at CKNX, putting on shows in the surrounding area several nights a week. Fiddlers who went on to later TV and recording fame, such as Ward Allen, Al Czerny, and Graham Townsend, all worked for CKNX at one time.

Fiddle and step-dancing contests began in the early 1950s [see CONTRA DANCE, p. 230]. Several dozen are held throughout the province in the summer months, the largest being the Canadian Open Old-Time Fiddle Contest in Shelbourne, Ontario. Competitors play a waltz, a jig, and a reel in down-east style, although other Canadian and Celtic styles are often featured as special show presentations. There is also an active revival of Irish traditional music with regular sessions held in many urban centers. Concert presentations of fiddling, often with step dancing, have recently become popular again, featuring such groups as the Leahys, Cindy Thompson (who pioneered the art of fiddling and step dancing simultaneously in Ontario), and Pierre Shreyer.

REFERENCES

Allen, Ward. *Ward Allen Presents Maple Leaf Hoedown.* Spartan Records SP–203, SP–210, SP–213. LP.

Bell, Ian. 1990. *A Grand Musical Entertainment.* Sound Reconstructions. Cassette.

Carpenter, Carole Henderson. 1979. *Many Voices: A Study of Folklore Activities in Canada and Their Role in Canadian Culture.* Ottawa: National Museums of Canada.

Czerny, Al. *Fiddle Country.* TeeVee Records TA–1019. LP. Many others available.

Clark, LaRena. 1965. *Canadian Garland.* Topic 12T–140. LP.

Daly, Margaret, and Mark Miller. "George Wade and His Cornhuskers." In *Encyclopedia of Music in Canada,* 2nd ed., ed. Helmut Kallman, Gilles Potvin, and Kenneth Winters, 1380–1381. Toronto: University of Toronto Press.

Doucette, Laurel. 1975. "An Introduction to the Puckett Collection of Ontario Folklore." *Canadian Folk Music Journal* 3:22–29.

Folk Songs of Ontario. Folkways FM 4005. LP.

Fowke, Edith. 1965. *Traditional Singers and Songs from Ontario.* Hatboro: Folklore Associates.

———. 1985. *Lumbering Songs from the Northern Woods.* Toronto: NC Press.

———. 1992a. "Ballads." In *Encyclopedia of Music in Canada,* 2nd ed., ed. Helmut Kallman, Gilles Potvin, and Kenneth Winters, 70. Toronto: University of Toronto Press.

———. 1992b. " Folk Music: Anglo-Canadian: Ontario and the Prairies." In *Encyclopedia of Music in Canada,* 2nd ed., ed. Helmut Kallman, Gilles Potvin, and Kenneth Winters, 475–476. Toronto: University of Toronto Press.

Fowke, Edith, and Jay Rahn. 1994. *A Family Heritage: LaRena Clark's Story and Songs.* Calgary: University of Calgary Press.

Harding, Ed. 1905. *Harding's All-Round Collection of Jigs, Reels, and Country Dances.* England: Lewis Music Publishing Co.

Jarman, Harry E., comp. 1937. *The Cornhuskers Book of Square Dance Tunes.* Toronto: Harry E. Jarman and Co.

Jarman, Harry E., comp. 1938. *The Cornhuskers Book of Old Time Fiddlin' Tunes.* Toronto: Harry E. Jarman and Co.

Old Time Couple Dances. Folkways FW 8827. LP.

1001 Fiddle Tunes. c. 1940 [c. 1880]. Reprint of *Ryan's Mammoth Collection.* Chicago: M. M. Cole.

Ontario Ballads and Folksongs. 1962. Prestige/International INT 25014. LP.

Posen, I. Sheldon. 1988. *For Singing and Dancing and All Sorts of Fun.* Toronto: Deneau Publishers.

Shreyer, Pierre. 1997. *New Canadian Waltz.* New Canadian Records NCCD–9610. CD, Cassette.

Songs of the Great Lakes. Folk FM 4018. LP.

Tamarack. 1984. *200 Musical Years.* SGB Productions SBB5–1984. Cassette.

Tanglefoot. 1999. *Full Throated Abandon.* The Borealis Recording Company BCD115. CD.

Thompson, Cindy. 1997. *Through Gates.* RBM Associates RBM 001. CD.

Townsend, Graham. *The Great Canadian Fiddle.* Rounder Records 7002. LP. Many others available.

York, Muddy. 1984. *Scatter the Ashes: Music of Old Ontario.* Boot BOS 7244. LP, Cassette.

Franco-Ontarian Music
Anne Lederman

Songs
Instrumental Music

Forts and trading posts established the first French settlements in Ontario, mostly along the major fur-trade route from Montréal—up the Ottawa River to Mattawa, the Mattawa River through Lake Nipissing, the French River into Georgian Bay, across to Sault Sainte Marie, across Lake Superior to Fort William, and through a network of lakes and rivers to Lake of the Woods and into Manitoba. Many of these older communities have strong Métis ancestry (a mixed heritage of French, Ojibwa, and Cree), frequently unacknowledged for various political and historical reasons [see Métis, p. 404].

After 1840, francophones from Québec began to move into the Ottawa Valley and eastern Ontario and later into the Sudbury and Haileybury areas, as well as to larger centers in the south. Immigrants also came from France, Switzerland, Belgium, and North Africa. By the late 1880s there were almost 500,000 francophones in Ontario, about 40 percent in the eastern sector, 33 percent in the north, and the rest in southern Ontario. Because they have come together at different times from quite different cultural backgrounds, frequently two or more distinct francophone cultures are active even in sparsely populated areas. Today, there are francophones active in all musical genres. However, this article will concentrate on the older French-language song traditions and instrumental music.

SONGS

What we know of Franco-Ontarian songs comes almost completely from the work of Germain Lemieux, a Jesuit priest who began to collect French songs and stories in the Sudbury area in 1948, eventually reaching out to Timmins, North Bay, and other northern areas. Still active, Lemieux has recorded over three thousand songs, housed in Le Centre Franco-Ontarien de Folklore at the University of Sudbury. Some are in his two books, *Chansonnier franco-ontarien I* and *II* (1974, 1975), including some of Canadian origin. These latter are about voyages by canoe, life in the shanties, and the hardships of traveling on the Grand Trunk Railway. There are two about the death of voyagers in the woods, one with an Ojibwa refrain. Typically, the refrains of French Canadian songs and melodies are locally composed and most subject to change, whereas the verses often go back to medieval France. Lemieux identifies the influence of the Ojibwa language as one of the main elements distinguishing Franco-Ontarian songs and stories from those of other French areas of Canada, affecting vocabulary, pronunciation, and refrains. There are also songs with English refrains.

The largest group of songs in Lemieux's published books are *amants* 'love songs', which are divided into "adventures" and "separations." A typical scenario, common to other European and North American traditions as well, is the story of a lover who must leave the morning of his wedding, usually to go to war, only to return seven years later and find that his intended is about to marry someone else [see OVERVIEW, p. 820]. Some ballad stories in French Canada seem to have been translated directly from English versions through contact in the lumber camps. Songs of separation seem to have been especially popular in early Canada, when voyageurs and lumbermen were away from their families for months at a time.

The best known song, however, for both men and women alike, is "Le Petit Mari," the story of the little husband who gets lost in the bedclothes on his wedding night, burned by the fire of the candle his new bride uses to search for him, and, in some cases, eaten by the cat. "Rare are the French-Canadian informants who do not know one or two versions" (Lemieux 1974:22).

> Mon père m'a donné un p'tit mari
> My gosh, my soul, my poor little man
> Mon père m'a donné un p'tit mari
> My gosh, qu'il était p'tit
>
> Il me l'a donné si petit, My gosh, my soul, etc.
> Que dans mon lit je le perdis . . .
> Je pris la lampe et le cherchis . . .
> J'ai mis le feu dedans mon lit . . .
> J'ai trouvé mon mari rôti . . .
> Sur la corniche, je l'ai mis . . .
> Le chat, l'a pris pour un' souris . . .
> Gros chat, gros chat, lâch' mon mari. . . .
>
> Translation
> My father gave me a little husband
> He gave me one that was so small
> That I lost him in the bed
> I took my lamp and looked for him
> I set the bed on fire
> I found my husband roasted
> I put him on the ledge
> The cat took him for a mouse
> Big cat, big cat, let my husband go! (Lemieux 1974:112–113)

Strong French elements in the repertoire include messages carried by swallows or nightingales to bereaved lovers and many metaphors for sexual relations, especially fountains, streams, and bouquets of flowers or herbs. Phrasing is frequently irregular, as it is in France. One trait that occurs frequently in songs of Canadian origin is a final signature verse, in which the author either names himself or gives some characteristic, for example, "Who has composed this song? It's a little blacksmith, sitting in his shop, smoking his pipe" (Lemieux 1974:23). Almost all Franco-Ontarian songs are in *chanson à répondre* 'response style', in which everyone participates by singing refrain lines and/or by repeating the verse lines (sometimes called *chanson doublée*). As soon as the group knows the responses, the leader will generally stop singing them, and the song will proceed by alternating phrases between the leader and the other participants.

The best known song for both men and women alike is "Le Petit Mari," the story of the little husband who gets lost in the bedclothes on his wedding night, burned by the fire of the candle his new bride uses to search for him, and, in some cases, eaten by the cat.

Contemporary Franco-Ontarian performers include songwriters Jean-Guy (Chuck) Labelle and Robert Paquette, who write frequently about northern Ontario, and the groups Brouhaha, who write in both French and English, and Deux Saisons, who perform traditional material. Rock group CANO (Co-opérative des Artistes du Nouvel-Ontario) created a modern sound that incorporated traditional and original material. Two long-running festivals in Ontario have been instrumental in promoting francophone traditions: La Nuit sur l'Étang and Festival Boréal, both in Sudbury.

INSTRUMENTAL MUSIC

There are many fiddlers with French roots in Ontario. However, the music has not been studied or collected in any formal way. Also, instrumental repertoire, in general, changes much more rapidly than song does and is much more subject to local influences. Some fiddlers still play repertoire passed down in their families from Québécois roots or from the fur trade tradition, but usually alongside other fiddle repertoire. Some Franco-Ontarian fiddlers practice the two-foot clogging patterns common to other French and Métis areas of Canada, but this is not universal. Melodies are also played on mandolin, harmonica, and, occasionally, hammered dulcimer. Both guitar and piano are used for accompaniment.

Franco-Ontarian musicians include the Shreyer family (Raymond, Julie, Pierre, Louis, and Daniel), Bobby Lalonde, and René Coté, all from the Sault Sainte Marie area, and Paul Menard from Sudbury.

REFERENCES

Beaunoyer, Jean. 1985. "Paquette joue le grand jeu impeccable." *La Presse* [Montréal], 20 January.

Beland, Madeleine. 1982. *Chansons de voyageurs, coureurs de bois et forestiers.* Québec: L'Université Laval.

Brouhaha. c. 1980s. *Vision.* Brouhaha Music BENT CD 001. Compact disc.

CANO. c. 1970s. *Tous dans l'même bateau.* A&M SP 9024.

Deux Saisons. 1998. *Au bal des bois.* AGCD 98020. Compact disc.

Huronia Old Time Country Band. c. 1980s. *Old Time Fiddle Music with Marcel, Martin, Eric and Gerrard.* n.p. MRD 001. Cassette.

Laforte, Conrad. 1992. "Folk Music, Franco-canadian." In *Encyclopedia of Music in Canada,* 2nd ed., ed. Helmut Kallman, Gilles Potvin, and Kenneth Winters, 477–481. Toronto: University of Toronto Press.

Lemieux, Germain. 1974. *Chansonnier franco-ontarien I.* Sudbury: Centre Franco-Ontarien de Folklore, University of Sudbury.

———. 1975. *Chansonnier franco-ontarien II.* Sudbury: Centre Franco-Ontarien de Folklore, University of Sudbury.

Lemieux, Germain, comp. 1998. *Ce qu'ils m'ont chanté: 1948–1958.* Sudbury: Centre Franco-Ontarien de Folklore, University of Sudbury.

Menard, Denise. 1992. "Lemieux, Germain." In *Encyclopedia of Music in Canada,* 2nd ed., ed. Helmut Kallman, Gilles Potvin, and Kenneth Winters, 743. Toronto: University of Toronto Press.

Menard, Paul. 1998. *Fiddle Goldmine.* Holbourne 4424. Compact disc.

Paquette, Robert. c. 1980s. *Gare à vous.* Saisons SNS4–90.004. Cassette, compact disc.

Shreyer, Pierre. 1996. *New Canadian Waltz.* New Canadian Records NCCD–9610. Cassette, compact disc.

Other European Music
Irene Markoff

Germany, Austria, and the Netherlands

Sweden and Finland

Estonia, Latvia, and Lithuania

Italy, Spain, and Portugal

Hungary and Poland

Czechoslovakia and Slovakia

Slovenia, Croatia, Serbia, Macedonia, and Bulgaria

Turkey and Greece

Russia and Ukraine

According to the 1996 government census, individuals from Europe (1,353,290) continue to account for the largest proportion of immigrants in the province of Ontario, despite a large influx of newcomers from Asia and the Middle East beginning in the early 1990s. This continues a trend that began at the turn of the twentieth century with the first great wave of foreign immigration. Ontarians with origins in Northern (other than the United Kingdom) and Western Europe total 235,135; those from Eastern Europe, 264,320; and those from Southern Europe, 482,325. European immigrants (other than those from Britain or France) make up 26 percent of the total population of the province, with two-thirds living in the metropolitan area of Toronto.

GERMANY, AUSTRIA, AND THE NETHERLANDS

A singing society revival in German Canadian communities in the 1950s generated the creation of choirs such as Concordia (Kitchener), Germania (Hamilton), and Harmonie (Toronto) (Kallmann 1992). The Kitchener-Waterloo region, with a highly concentrated German settlement, organizes the Oktoberfest Munich tradition every year, at which professional bands such as The Harmony Brass, The Golden Keys, and the Matt Lebar Ensemble play an important role in accompanying dance. These groups (accordion, drum set, trumpet and saxophone or clarinet) perform polkas, waltzes, and tangos and accompany sing-alongs at German and Austrian clubs (Lebar 2000). Austrians have their own choirs, such as two sponsored by the Austrian club Edelweiss in Toronto (Soundship 2000).

Credit unions and social clubs in the Dutch community support choirs such as the Liberation Choir (Toronto), the New Ottawa Carleton Male Choir (Ottawa), and the Vrij en Blij Choir (Hamilton) that sing arrangements of traditional music by Dutch composers. Dance bands such as The Touch of Class (Kitchener) and Orkestar Politour (accordion, solo and rhythm guitar, contrabass) provide entertainment at Dutch clubs, social functions, and festivals (Tulip Festival, Ottawa; International Villages Festival, Brantford), as does the brass Tomato Soup Band that contributes to Carnaval celebrations just before Lent. The dance bands perform waltzes, fox-trots, polkas, and a general North American dance repertoire. All communities organize St. Nicholas parties for children with special songs (*sinterklaas*) for the occasion (Kooy 2000).

SWEDEN AND FINLAND

Traditional Swedish music can be heard at annual celebrations such as the Santa Lucia Festival Pageant, Swedish Flag Day, and the Midsummer Solstice. Choirs are often associated with churches and perform traditional and composed music. The Toronto Swedish Folk Dancers and Singers perform traditional and arranged songs and dances such as quadrilles, court dances (minuet and gavotte), waltzes, schottisches, *polskas* and *hambos* (both couple dances in triple meter), and polkas (Thompson 2000). At the heart of Swedish folk music are the accordion and the violin, instruments that combine with percussion, double bass, and keyboards in bands that play modern, big band, and traditional music for formal occasions.

Finnish cultural associations continue to support local choirs throughout Ontario such as Vox Finlandia and the Toronto Finnish Male Singers (conducted by Pieter Sigmundt) that sing unaccompanied arrangements of folk songs and art songs. Choral works are often inspired by the Finnish national epic *Kalevala,* which is still sung with *kantele* 'zither' accompaniment at special events (Sigmundt 2000). Dance bands such as the Räimo Ärvenpää band of Toronto (accordion, saxophone, and drums) play tangos (of the Argentinian variety), polkas, and waltzes, while the accordion accompanies dance ensembles such as The Sisu Finnish Folk Dancers of Toronto (Temisevä 2000).

ESTONIA, LATVIA, AND LITHUANIA

Folk dance and choral singing are strong traditions among Estonian Canadians, who participate in local and international festivals of Estonian song with arrangements of Estonian folk songs and composed music such as that of Roman Toi, a Toronto-based composer and conductor (Toi 2000). The *kannel* 'zither' is taught in Estonian-language schools and sometimes accompanies choral concerts and folk dance ensembles such as Kungla in Toronto. Kungla's suites of regional dances are also accompanied by accordions and the Estonian bagpipe (*torupill*) (Olup 2000). Ad hoc dance bands that feature instruments such as violin, guitar, accordion, saxophone, clarinet, string bass, and keyboards perform all forms of dances including waltzes, polkas, schottisches, and *tuljak* 'a standard set of polkas at weddings and the finale at dance festivals' at community functions (Holmes 2000).

Latvian communities also favor choral singing and folk dance activities, their traditional zither (*kokle*) taught at community schools. The dance ensembles Daugavina, Dizdancis, and Menestins (Toronto) are accompanied by accordion and drums, while deejays are employed for weddings and other events (Maksins 2000).

Secular and religious music join forces in performances by Lithuanian choral groups such as the Volunge mixed chorus, and the Aras male choir (Toronto), who often integrate *kankle* 'zither' and the *birbyne* 'wooden reed instrument' into liturgical music performances. Folk dance festivals are very popular and involve ensembles such as the Gintaras folk dance group of Toronto, which is accompanied by double bass, accordion, *birbyne,* fiddles, and percussion (Viskontas 2000).

ITALY, SPAIN, AND PORTUGAL

Most Italians in Ontario demonstrate a proclivity toward contemporary popular Italian music, although there is also a fondness for Neapolitan ballads. Bands perform a few token tarantellas and waltzes at weddings, and old regional repertoire is sung in established choirs in Toronto such as The Santa Cecilia Chorus, Coro Verdi, and the Coro San Marco. Folk dance ensembles are active in smaller communities such as St. Catherines (Club Roma Dancers) and London (the Marconi Dancers). Instrumental ensembles are diverse and include Giuliano Saracini's symphonic band that performs marches, waltzes, and arrangements of old Italian songs for saints' days (Saracini 2000). The Continental Six and New Image are Toronto bands that emulate the modern Euro-pop sound with their ballads and up-tempo dance tunes. Emerging young innovative Italian Canadian artists such as Dominic Mancuso can be heard on student-produced radio programs on CHRY, York University, Toronto. Mancuso incorporates Italian ballads into his Middle Eastern–influenced contemporary rock sound (Porco 2000).

Spanish folk music and dance have been sustained by several amateur ensembles. In addition, a number of professional flamenco dancers in Toronto have formed dance companies with professional guitarists and singers of Spanish origin. Of these, Esmeralda Enrique is unique in having collaborated with Kathak dancers and the Toronto Tabla Ensemble. Another visionary in the community is artist Mel Mirabet (Ottawa), who creates a jazz–folk fusion with his blending of traditional Andalusian and flamenco music with Middle Eastern elements.

Local Portuguese Catholic churches and associations organize and support regional folk dance ensembles and brass bands and organize special *fado* 'urban songs accompanied by classical guitar (*viola*) and Portuguese twelve-string *guitarra*' evenings (Hall 1992). Dance bands use drum sets, synthesizers, and guitars and play a variety of popular Portuguese music. Alvorada, a professional ensemble devoted to traditional music, was formed by Nuno Christo in the 1980s but disbanded in the 1990s. Instruments included *gaita de fole* 'bagpipe', *adute* 'square drum', *cazaquinho* 'ukelele', accordion, bass guitar, classical guitar, and voice. Christo has since formed the Banza Duo, which performs instrumental *fados* and original compositions (Christo 2000).

HUNGARY AND POLAND

The folk dance revival (*tanchaz* movement) of the mid-1970s in Hungary spread to Canada and led to the formation of groups such as the exemplary Kodaly Ensemble of Toronto with its dancers, singers, and instrumental ensemble consisting of two violins, a three-stringed viola, flutes, and accordion. Similar ensembles in Ontario perform regional dance suites from Hungary proper and from Transylvania, Slovakia, Voivodina, and Moldavia.

In 1997 three members of the Kodaly ensemble created the Vastaghuros Ensemble, which plays Hungarian, Romanian, Polish, and Gypsy folk music in traditional styles (Horvath, Etynkowski 2000). An older Toronto band, Fekete Föld, utilizes hurdy-gurdy, *cimbalom* 'hammered dulcimer', the *ütő gardon* 'struck cello', and flutes as well as fiddles and viola (*kontra*). For their *báls* 'dinner dances', Hungarians hire folk pop bands (drum machine, violins, accordion, saxophone, clarinet, bass, and guitar) that perform a wide variety of music including *csardas,* polkas, and waltzes.

Poles in Ontario also maintain their cultural heritage with folk music and dance ensembles. Three Toronto-based ensembles, Lechowia, Bialy Orzel, and the Harnasie Highlanders incorporate singing into their performances and are accompanied by violins, clarinet, trumpet, double bass, and *cymbaly* 'hammered dulcimer', depending on the region. The Highlanders group uses two violins and a three-stringed cello. Preferred dances include *krakowiak, kujlawiak, mazurka, oberek, polonaise,* and *goralski* (Etynkowski 2000). Dynamix, a newly formed polka band from Barrie, appeals to tastes of Canadian Poles by performing tangos, waltzes, polkas, *obereks,* and contemporary North American tunes.

CZECHOSLOVAKIA AND SLOVAKIA

Czech and Slovak cultural traditions have been kept alive through church groups, auxiliary schools, and community associations. In 1998 many folk dance ensembles throughout Ontario (such as the seventy-five-year-old Krivan folklore group, Sudbury, and the Toronto Slovak Dancers) were brought together at St. Mary's Church Hall for the seventy-fifth anniversary of Slovak folklore. Moravanka, a Czech folk dance ensemble, continues to be active in Toronto. Violins, piano, accordion, drums, trumpet, and string bass constitute Slovak ensembles that play waltzes, polkas, and other repertoire for

Almost every Serbian community in Ontario takes pride in church choirs that sing liturgical music as well as folk music arranged by Serbian composers.

their fellow countrymen. Young Czech musicians gravitate toward urban musical forms such as jazz, blues, and Czech country and western (Rollerova 2000). A recent arrival (1997) is the professional Roma vocal-guitar duo Romani Yag.

SLOVENIA, CROATIA, SERBIA, MACEDONIA, AND BULGARIA

Choral singing is important in Slovenian communities, as are bands (accordion, clarinet, trumpet, drums, and vocals) that play Alpine region polkas and waltzes at weddings and community gatherings. Two top polka bands that entertain Slovenian and other ethnic communities are those of Matt Lebar, and Walter Ostanek (Canada's polka king and Grammy winner). Lebar has incorporated swing, salsa, and pop tunes into his repertoire (Lebar 2000). Younger bands such as Toronto's Alpine Septet have revived older traditional styles by abandoning drums and adding guitars and the euphonium.

Makedonka and the Selyani Macedonian Folklore group are two major dance and folk song ensembles that are still active in Toronto's Macedonian community. Selyani, the older of the two, has committed to avoiding highly stylized choreographies and has integrated traditional songs and instruments (*gajda* 'bagpipe', *kaval* 'end-blown vertical flute', *tambura* 'long-necked plucked lute with frets', and *tapan* 'double-headed, cylindrical drum played with a beater and a stick') into their performances. A number of professional Toronto wedding bands (clarinet, accordion, drums, saxophone, keyboards, and electric guitar) perform traditional dance music as well as newly composed urban folk tunes. Some of these are Bisser, Makedonija, Izgrev, Ohrid, Ilinden 1903, The Boys from Bouf, Gerdan, and Makedonski Melos (using folk instruments such as *gaida, kaval,* and *zurla*) (Nikoloff 2000).

Croatians in Ontario continue the tradition of folk dance ensembles with *tamburica* orchestras, which consist of plucked lutes in varying sizes, and singing. The ensemble Sljeme in Mississauga performs regional dance suites from various villages, towns, and regions (Split, Lika, Medimurje, Pokuplje) with accompaniment provided by the *tamburica* orchestra Stare Tambure (*brać* 'pear-shaped lute that doubles melody', *prim* 'small, pear-shaped lute, lead instrument', *bugarija* 'guitar-sized lute that plays harmonic rhythm on weak beats') and the vocal ensemble Croatia. Dance bands (accordion, electric guitar, drums) supply traditional music for various events, while modern Croatian repertoire can be heard by groups such as the Toronto band Nova Generacija, consisting of an electric guitar, bass, synthesizer, and drums.

Almost every Serbian community in Ontario takes pride in church choirs that sing liturgical music as well as folk music arranged by Serbian composers. Some choirs participate in annual choral festivals organized by the Serbian Singing Federation. Church-supported folk dance ensembles such as Stražilovo and Hajduk Veljko of Toronto, the Mississauga Oplenac Dancers, and Kolo in Hamilton regularly present suites of regional dances. Community members continue the tradition of circle dances (*kolo*) such as *u šest, žikino, čačak,* and so on and sing old traditional songs such as *bećarac* and *svatovac.* At least seven folk orchestras are now active, most using accordion, guitars, drums, and sometimes saxophone, flute, and clarinet. The band Lika adds *tamburicas* to their accordion, bass, and drum set ensemble. Worth noting is a group of epic singers (*guslari*) in Toronto and Kitchener who sing epic songs ("Kraljević Marko," "Kosovo" cycle, and newly composed repertoire) to the accompaniment of the one-string *gusle* 'bowed lute' (Dragasevic 2000).

Bulgarian folk musical traditions in Ontario have been in decline since the 1950s, when choirs, orchestras, and folk dance ensembles were thriving. Four church choirs performed liturgical music, and a women's choir, Balgarka, sang light urban folk songs until the mid-1990s. The ensemble Balkan Connection was formed in 1995 (in Toronto) as an outgrowth of the vocal trio Zornitza, which specialized in regional folk songs as well as three-part arranged and composed repertoire representative of the state ensembles that were a product of the Soviet era. Balkan Connection instrumentalists include a Bulgarian accordionist and four professional Canadian (some non-Balkan) musicians who play *tambura*, *ud* 'plucked lute', *darabuka* 'goblet-shaped drum', and clarinet. The group performs Bulgarian, Macedonian, and Gypsy repertoire for mainly Canadian audiences. An ad hoc folk dance group, affiliated with the Saints Cyril and Methodius Macedono–Bulgarian Orthodox Cathedral in Toronto, assembles for annual cultural celebrations where circle dances (*horo*) and urban songs (*gradski pesni*) are still relished. Among recent immigrants is Anton Apostolov, a professional guitarist who is part of the internationally recognized Bulgarian folk/jazz fusion trio Acoustic (acoustic guitar, *tambura*, percussion).

TURKEY AND GREECE

Turkish communities (Turkey, Azerbaijan, Iraq) support authentic folk music and dance through performances of the Toronto-based Anatolian Folk Dancers in collaboration with the Ezgi folk music ensemble, including *bağlamas* 'plucked lutes', *darabuka*, *davul* 'double-headed log drum', accordion, and vocalists. The Turkish Classical Music Chorus (chorus and instrumental ensemble) stages annual concerts of *makam* 'Turkish modal music' (Ozkan 2000). Turkish Sufi groups have also appeared in concert with their *ilahis* 'hymns', accompanied by *ud* and *bendir* 'frame drum', and *semas* 'ritual dance of the Alevi heterodox sect', accompanied by *bağlamas* and voice (Gokcen 1992).

Many Greek regional associations lend their support to folk music (*demotiki*) and dance ensembles (Dionysus [Toronto]; Odyssey [Ottawa]) that use regional folk lutes such as the bowed Pontic and Cretan *liras* and the plucked *laouto*. Commercial *bouzouki* 'long-necked plucked lute' music is still performed at clubs and elsewhere by bands that use clarinet, flute, electric *bouzouki*, keyboards, and drums. Nevertheless, contemporary pop Greek music has increased in popularity with bands such as New Generation and Piriaiki (Klein 2000). Also popular are deejays such as the Mbabatsikos brothers (also known as Club Pandemonium), who are hired for Greek Nights at clubs and weddings where they play Greek/Arabic crossover tunes to accompany upbeat *tsiftetelli*, *syrtos*, *zeibekiko*, and *tsamikos* dances (Mbabatsikos 2000).

RUSSIA AND UKRAINE

Musical activity in the Russian community is limited at the moment. The choir of Christ the Savior Cathedral in Toronto performs folk and liturgical music, and a mixed community choir in Ottawa sings unaccompanied folk songs. Folk dance is perpetuated through the Berioska women's folk dance ensemble (Toronto) that is accompanied by *balalaika* and accordion. When Russian Canadians gather for annual balls they engage Canadian bands that play music for waltzes, tangos, polkas, and mazurkas (Kurms 2000).

Ukrainian Canadians revere choral music and sing liturgical music as well as choral settings of folk music. Some choirs of importance are the Ukrainian Women's choir of Thunder Bay, the Dibrova Men and Women's Choir of Toronto, and the Toronto Vesnivka Women's Choir (Syrotynski 2000). Folk dance ensembles (Svitanok Ukrainian Dance Ensemble [Ottawa]; the Dunai Dancers [St. Catherines]) and choirs are often accompanied by traditional instruments such as the *cymbaly* 'hammered dulcimer', *bandura* 'zither-like instrument', *kobza* 'plucked lute', *lira* 'hurdy-gurdy', mandolins, and accordion. A folk ensemble par excellence is the 120-member Schevchenko ensemble of Toronto (chorus, orchestra, and dance group), which has performed throughout Canada and in Ukraine (Klymasz 1992).

REFERENCES

Anderson, Grace M., and David Higgs. 1976. *A Future to Inherit: The Portuguese Communities in Canada.* Toronto: McClelland and Stewart.

Bassa, Philip. "Ukrainian Musical Culture in Canada." 1951. Master's thesis, University of Montréal.

Calderisi, Maria. 1992. "Portugal." In *Encyclopedia of Music in Canada,* 2nd ed., ed. Helmut Kallmann, Gilles Potvin, and Kenneth Winters, 639–640. Toronto: University of Toronto Press.

Chimbos, Peter D. 1980. *The Canadian Odyssey: The Greek Experience in Canada.* Toronto: McClelland and Stewart.

Christo, Nuno. 2000. Personal interview, 27 January.

Čulig, David. 2000. Personal interview, 3 February.

Dragaševich, Draga. 2000. Personal interviews, February, March.

Erickson, Kim. 1987. "Stella Trylinski and the Ukrainian Women's Choir of Thunder Bay." *Musicworks* 38.

Etynkowski, Mateusz. 2000. Personal interview, 18 January.

Gellner, John, and John Smerek. 1968. *The Czechs and Slovaks in Canada.* Toronto: University of Toronto Press.

Gokcen, Ilhami. 1992. "Turkey." In *Encyclopedia of Music in Canada,* 2nd ed., ed. Helmut Kallmann, Gilles Potvin, and Kenneth Winters, 1321. Toronto: University of Toronto Press.

Hall, Leslie. 1982. "Turkish Musical Culture in Toronto." *Canadian Folk Music Journal* 10:48–52.

———. 1992. "Portugal." In *Encyclopedia of Music in Canada,* 2nd ed., ed. Helmut Kallmann, Gilles Potvin, and Kenneth Winters, 1071–1072. Toronto: University of Toronto Press.

Holmes, Ramona. 2000. Personal interviews, 16, 21 February.

Horvath, Peter. 2000. Personal interview, 19 January.

Kallmann, Helmut. 1992. "Germany." In *Encyclopedia of Music in Canada,* 2nd ed., ed. Helmut

Kallmann, Gilles Potvin, and Kenneth Winters, 523–525. Toronto: University of Toronto Press.

Kallmann, Helmut, Gilles Potvin, and Kenneth Winters, eds. 1992. *Encyclopedia of Music in Canada.* 2nd ed. Toronto: University of Toronto Press.

Klein, Leigh. 2000. Personal interview, 10 January.

Klymasz, Robert B. 1971a. "Ukrainian folklore in Canada: An Immigrant Complex in Transition." Ph.D. dissertation, Indiana University.

———. 1992. "Ukraine." In *Encyclopedia of Music in Canada,* 2nd ed., ed. Helmut Kallmann, Gilles Potvin, and Kenneth Winters, 1326–1327. Toronto: University of Toronto Press.

Kooy, Leendert. 2000. Personal interview, 20 January.

Kurms, Herman. 2000. Personal interview, 3 March.

Lebar, Matt. 2000. Personal interview, 15 January.

Markoff, Irene. 1984. "Persistence of Old-World Cultural Expression in the Traditional Music of Bulgarian-Canadians." *Polyphony* 6(1):73–74.

Mbabatsikos, George. 2000. Personal interview, 4 February.

Nikoloff, James and Dena. 2000. Personal interview, 25 January.

Olup, Aime. 2000. Personal interview, 22 February.

Ozkan, Oguz. 2000. Personal interview, 29 February.

Peacock, Kenneth. 1971. *A Garland of Rue: Lithuanian Folksongs of Love and Betrothal.* Ottawa: National Museums of Canada.

Pelinski, Ramon. 1975. "The Music of Canada's Ethnic Minorities." *Canadian Music Book* 10:59–83

Perkowski, Jan L. 1973–74. Gusle *and* Ganga *among the Herzegovians of Toronto.* Ann Arbor, Mich.: University Microfilms International.

Porco, Carla. 2000. Personal interview, 26 January.

Rice, Timothy. 1992a. "Croatia." In *Encyclopedia of Music in Canada,* 2nd ed., ed. Helmut Kall-

mann, Gilles Potvin, and Kenneth Winters, 333. Toronto: University of Toronto Press.

———. 1992b. "Macedonia." In *Encyclopedia of Music in Canada,* 2nd ed., ed. Helmut Kallmann, Gilles Potvin, and Kenneth Winters, 785. Toronto: University of Toronto Press.

———. 1992c. "Serbia." In *Encyclopedia of Music in Canada,* 2nd ed., ed. Helmut Kallmann, Gilles Potvin, and Kenneth Winters, 1207. Toronto: University of Toronto Press.

Saracini, Giuliano. 2000. Personal interview, 11 January.

Satory, Stephen. 1987. *"Tanchaz* in Toronto: A Transplanted Tradition." *Canadian University Music Review* 8.

Sigmundt, Pieter. 2000. Personal interview, 17 February.

Signell, Karl. 1992. "Greece." In *Encyclopedia of Music in Canada,* 2nd ed., ed. Helmut Kallmann, Gilles Potvin, and Kenneth Winters, 553. Toronto: University of Toronto Press.

Soundship, Franz. 2000. Personal interview, 10 January.

Syrotynsky, Olenka. 2000. Personal interview, 28 February.

Temisevä, Matti. 2000. Personal interview, 15 February.

Thompson, Lloyd. 2000. Personal interview, 23 February.

Toi, Roman. 2000. Personal interview, 15 February.

Viskontas, Dalia. 2000. Personal interview, 8 February.

Wrazen, Louise. 1983. "Continuity and Change in the Music of the Polish Highlanders of Toronto." *Canadian Folk Music Journal* 11:18–27.

———. 1988. "The Goralski of the Polish Highlanders: Old World Musical Tradition from a New World Perspective." Ph.D. dissertation, University of Toronto.

———. "Traditional Music Performance among *Gorale* in Canada." 1991. *Ethnomusicology* 35:173–193.

Latin American and Caribbean Music

Robert Witmer

Latin American and Caribbean immigrants and their descendants have settled all across Canada. A majority resides in the urban areas in the southwestern portion of the province of Ontario, particularly in the Greater Toronto area (population about five million at the turn of the millennium), where Latin American and Caribbean immigrants and their descendants comprise roughly 8 percent of the total population; elsewhere in Ontario their concentration is much smaller. The Latin American and Caribbean communities are of quite recent origin, with the first major wave of settlers arriving in the late 1960s and early 1970s.

The Caribbean-derived populace hails almost entirely from the former British West Indies and in particular the countries of Jamaica, Trinidad and Tobago, Barbados, and Guyana (on the northeast coast of South America but nevertheless considered a part of the British Caribbean in terms of historical and cultural ties). The Latin American–derived population hails mainly from the Spanish-speaking countries of Ecuador, Colombia, El Salvador, Chile, and Argentina. The Latin American and Caribbean immigrant populations in Ontario mirror the ethnocultural diversity of their homelands and have brought a broad range of musical practices to the province's multicultural musicscape.

POPULAR CARIBBEAN MUSIC SCENES

Within the British Caribbean musical communities in Ontario, immigrants and their descendants have maintained virtually intact the popular music cultures of their homelands, including the quick adaptation to shifting trends. The immigrant and homelands popular music cultures operate in close tandem: the immigrant communities replicate (to the extent possible) the homelands popular music scene in the new environment and are also ongoing receptors of popular music imports from the homelands through recordings, touring musicians, print materials, and so on.

The reggae scene

Jamaican reggae music has been an established presence in British Caribbean communities in Ontario ever since its emergence in Jamaica in the late 1960s. This presence is not just reggae recordings and touring acts imported from Jamaica but the full reggae music infrastructure of Jamaica as re-created in Ontario. Among the elements of this re-created infrastructure are resident professional musicians (including the all-important deejays) for stage shows, dances, and record production; specialty record shops and radio and television programming; maneuverings for coverage in print and other media; and celebration/legitimation by the music industry and cultural community (for example, the annual Canadian Reggae Music Awards). This scene is followed avidly by numerous British Caribbean expatriates, particularly those of Jamaican heritage. Reggae has also been a favorite of a segment of the general non-Caribbean popular music audience as it has moved from an obscure regional style to an established category of international popular music, notably through the recorded output of Jamaican music superstar Bob Marley. Indicative of reggae's significance in the larger popular music marketplace is its inclusion as a separate category in the annual Canadian recording industry Juno Awards.

Calypso, *soca*, and steelband

Also well established in British West Indian immigrant communities are southeastern Caribbean (primarily Trinidadian) calypso, *soca* (soul + calypso) and steelband musics. These musics have not been taken up by the non-Caribbean audience to anywhere near the extent that Jamaican reggae has, but neither are they unknown in the broader musical culture. Calypso and, more recently, *soca* recordings have occasionally penetrated mainstream popular music hit parade charts, and in the mid-1950s there was something of an "Island music" craze in European American popular music (for example, the then superstar status of Jamaican-American "West Indies folk singer" Harry Belafonte), in which calypso and calypso-tinged music were prominent. Steelband music has never been general popular music fare, yet there is some awareness among the broad musical public that it is Caribbean, or even specifically Trinidadian.

The current infrastructures of the calypso, *soca,* and steelband scenes in the British Caribbean immigrant community parallel those of the reggae scene outlined earlier and also include the strong emphasis on organized adjudicated competitions prevalent in southeastern Caribbean musical life. Groups such as the Organization of Calypso Performing Artists and the Pan Trinbago Steelband Association of Ontario promote and monitor such activities. Steelband is not only being maintained in Ontario in the traditional manner of the homelands—as a short-term seasonal activity of mainly amateur musicians geared to a brief flurry of performances and competitions connected with Carnival festivals—but is also being taught in selected Ontario schools, certain of which may include few, if any, students with southeastern Caribbean roots.

Caribbean-style carnivals

North American analogues of Trinidad's annual pre-Lenten Carnival are highly visible fixtures of the cultural, entertainment, and tourism calendars of several North American cities, prominent among them Toronto. Toronto's Caribana, sometimes billed as North America's largest West Indian celebration, is a two-week summer extravaganza of cultural display and reaffirmation, including formal organized competitions in various categories of West Indian performance and visual arts; it climaxes with the Caribana Parade, an all-day street party that attracts in the range of 700,000 to 1,000,000 spectators and 10,000 parading/dancing masqueraders on the first Saturday of August [see Two Views of Music in Toronto, p. 1207]. More modest annual events with a Caribbean carnival flavor include the Grape and Wine Festival, held in the city of St. Catharines.

TRANSFORMATIONS

While the hold of separate and distinct Caribbean homelands popular music cultures remains strong throughout the British Caribbean diaspora, certain departures from this hold are increasingly evident in the North American setting. In large and cosmopolitan North American centers such as Toronto, musicians from the British Caribbean have more opportunities, and perhaps also more imperatives, for intercultural musical collaborations and cross-fertilizations than they may have found in their homelands. One result is the emergence of popular music groups in the British Caribbean diaspora that are, by homelands standards, unusually eclectic stylistically and exceptionally multiethnic/multinational in the makeup of their personnel. Such groups range from pan–West Indian aggregations performing in a variety of Caribbean popular music styles to those in which Caribbean popular music styles and musicians with Caribbean roots are but one set of resources in a mélange of world popular music explorations. As yet, such groups perform more a mix of musics than a blend of musics: in the main they are stylistically versatile more than stylistically innovative.

Beginning in the mid-1980s, there have been cross-fertilizations between African American hip-hop/rap musical culture and Jamaican North American deejay/dancehall reggae musical culture, evident particularly in New York City recordings and night life, but also in Toronto [see HIP-HOP AND RAP, p. 692].

It is in the North American Caribbean-style Carnival celebrations that the most radical departures from homelands practices are to be seen. In the homelands, Carnival is a somewhat insular event, reaffirming and celebrating a particular national culture, be it Trinidadian, Barbadian, or whatever. In Caribbean-style carnivals in North America, however, the flavor is pan–West Indian or pan-Caribbean and sometimes extends even beyond that. For example, within the time frame of Toronto's Caribana festival one finds not only the Trinidadian Carnival core of calypso and *soca* music and the focus on elaborately costumed revelers but also events such as Reggaebana (a three-night showcase of Canadian reggae acts), AfriCaribeat (a four-night showcase of world beat acts), and Centre Island Music Fest (hip-hop and rhythm and blues acts). In the Caribana Parade itself there have been the occasional hip-hop and Latin American music floats.

POPULAR LATIN AMERICAN MUSIC SCENES

The Latin American communities, like the Caribbean communities, have attempted to replicate the popular music cultures of their respective homeland countries in the new environment. In this they have had more challenges than the Caribbean communities, as the population figures for each Latin American nation in Ontario are relatively small and a national immigrant community may in effect be only a "partial culture" (Bhabha 1998:30) in relation to the cultural scope available in the national homeland (for example, the Brazilian community in the Greater Toronto area probably consists of no more than 10 thousand persons, whereas the population of Brazil is around 160 million and musically very heterogeneous). This state of affairs has produced a number of principal music scenes, sometimes illustrative of the workings of intercultural alliances and accommodations, outlined briefly next.

The Latin music scene

The regular presence of Latin American musicians in Ontario predates the emergence of Latin American communities by several decades. Early migration of Latin American musicians had to do with Ontario entrepreneurs who attempted to take advantage of the international popularity of so-called Latin music—social dance music genres such as rumba, samba, mambo, and cha-cha-cha developed among and initially popularized by professional Latin American musical entertainers during the middle third of the twentieth century.

In Ontario today, Latin American musicians and communities at large continue to participate in the transnational Latin music market. Through the consumption of Latin music videos, recordings, films, television programs, and print media, Latin Americans in Ontario connect with, and maintain musical currency with, the main

Music seemingly moribund or obscure in its original cultural context receives a new lease on life as nostalgia and/or cultural patrimony on the concert stage.

centers in Latin America and the United States. The infrastructure of the Latin music scene in Ontario parallels that of the reggae scene outlined earlier. The Latin music in Ontario is first and foremost a club/dance scene, with the predominant bands on the circuit having some facility in many or at least several of the current main genres of transnational Latin music at large, such as salsa, merengue, *cumbia, vallenato, bachata,* traditional Cuban music, and Latin jazz. The horn players in Latin music ensembles in Ontario are typically freelancers from outside the Latin American community, while rhythm players and vocalists are typically of Latin American or Caribbean origins. The audience for Latin music in Ontario is, like the Ontario-based performers of Latin music, multiethnic and multicultural.

Regionally specific popular music scenes

Certain Latin American popular music scenes remain isolated from, or only partially absorbed into, the pan–Latin American Latin music scene outlined earlier. For example, Brazilian popular music activity in Ontario is fairly insular, owing mainly to linguistic factors (song lyrics are in Portuguese, and the Brazilian community is to a considerable degree "nested" within Toronto's large Portuguese community, lessening the opportunities and needs for interaction with Spanish-speaking Latin American communities). The Argentinian tango maintains a certain independence from the overall commercial Latin music scene by virtue of the complex choreography of the dance: the tango scene in Ontario is decidedly centered on dance studios, lessons, and competitions. The styles and repertoires of Mexican mariachi and bolero are generally not incorporated into the multicultural mix of commercial Latin music ensembles, but there are mariachi ensembles and groups that perform boleros for hire in the Greater Toronto area. Even some of the regionally specific styles and genres that the Latin music bands commonly feature in their repertoires are also represented by specialized ensembles.

The *nueva canción* and Andean folkloric music scene

The newly arrived Latin American musical elements that were the most noticeable to the general populace in Ontario in the early years of the Latin American settlement (1970s) were the Andean folkloric music ensembles and the performers of *nueva canción,* the pan–Latin American singer-songwriter movement that addressed the political oppression occurring in countries such as El Salvador and Chile with hard-hitting songs of social protest. In a related development, musical ensembles emulating traditional Andean highlands stylings and instrumentation were formed by urban middle-class youths, often university students, and became emblematic of a pan-Latin–leftist alliance. In the Greater Toronto area, as elsewhere, *nueva canción* and Andean folkloric music typically has been presented in folk music clubs and coffeehouses and at rallies, fundraisers, and various other solidarity events in a multicultural and multiethnic milieu. Andean folkloric ensembles also became a fixture of the busking circuit and remain so to this day, not always exclusively using Latin American musicians.

FOLK AND TRADITIONAL MUSIC CULTURES

In addition to the predominant popular musical styles outlined earlier, the Latin American and Caribbean nations have fostered a rich vein of folk and traditional music (local community-based music passed on informally from generation to generation and with little or no connection to the world of musical commerce) as an integral part of weddings, funerals, wakes, worship, work, and other recurrent community activities. The distinctions between such practices and the ones described in the previous section are more a matter of degree than kind. The state of these musical practices in Ontario's Latin American and Caribbean immigrant communities has not as yet been systematically documented. Some commentators suggest that they are not as lively a presence in the diaspora as in the homelands, while other commentators have worried that emigration can deplete the homelands of musicians crucial to the maintenance of local traditions.

There is, however, broad evidence that some of the more prominent African Christian religious sects and sociopolitical-cum-religious movements originating in the British Caribbean are flourishing on Ontario soil—for example, Jamaican Rastafarianism and the Trinidadian Spiritual Baptist ("Shouter Baptist") faith—and so too, necessarily, the associated musical practices. There are also adherents in Ontario of the Afro-Cuban santería religion, which employs Yoruba-based voice-and-percussion music in its rites [see AFRO-CUBAN MUSIC, p. 783].

In both the homelands and the diaspora, a number of folk and traditional music genres seemingly survive today mainly in neotraditional adaptations by professional and semiprofessional folkloric ensembles. Dozens of such groups, generally combining music, dance, and rustic costuming, are active in Ontario. Music seemingly moribund or obscure in its original cultural context thus receives a new lease on life as nostalgia and/or cultural patrimony on the concert stage.

OTHER GENRES AND CONTEXTS

Latin American and Caribbean music cultures in Ontario can by no means be defined solely by the practices outlined here. Many Ontario residents of Latin America and Caribbean origins actively follow (and a number perform) various contemporary popular musics. For example, among adolescents and young adults, prevailing African American urban music forms such as rap and rhythm and blues hold considerable sway. There are also practitioners and devotees of jazz, Western (and Eastern) classical music, and various historic styles of North American vernacular music. Among the British Caribbean–East Indian populace in Ontario, song hits from Indian films, Hindustani and Islamic devotional genres, *bhangra* music, and chutney music are variously important [see INDO-CARIBBEAN MUSIC, p. 813]. Also, Christian devotional music, in a broad range of styles, is vitally important across a broad spectrum of the Latin American and Caribbean-derived populations in Ontario. This plurality of musical tastes and allegiances has not arisen solely, or even primarily, out of the immigrant experience: it is also prevalent in the homelands.

DOCUMENTATION AND RESEARCH

The available published literature on Latin American and Caribbean music cultures in Ontario consists almost entirely of topical/ephemeral "music scene news" appearing in ethnic newspapers (of which there are a number, published mainly in Toronto) and in arts and entertainment features in alternative (and occasionally in mainstream) Canadian newspapers and news magazines. Many such publications are of limited distribution and difficult to obtain outside their local distribution areas. No systematic survey or synthesis of this material has yet been attempted. Several unpublished master's theses have dealt with aspects of Latin American and Caribbean music in Ontario.

REFERENCES

Bhabha, Homi. 1998. "Culture's Inbetween." In *Multicultural States: Rethinking Difference and Identity,* ed. David Bennett, 29–36. London: Routledge.

Caudeiron, Daniel. 1992a. "Reggae." In *Encyclopedia of Music in Canada,* 2nd ed., ed. Helmut Kallmann, Gilles Potvin, and Kenneth Winters, 187–188. Toronto: University of Toronto Press.

———. 1992b. "Calypso." In *Encyclopedia of Music in Canada,* 2nd ed., ed. Helmut Kallmann, Gilles Potvin, and Kenneth Winters, 1118–1119. Toronto: University of Toronto Press.

Gallaugher, Annemarie. 1991. "From Trinidad to Toronto: Calypso as a Way of Life." Master's thesis, York University.

———. 1992. "Caribana." In *Encyclopedia of Music in Canada,* 2nd ed., ed. Helmut Kallmann, Gilles Potvin, and Kenneth Winters, 220. Toronto: University of Toronto Press.

———. 1994. "Trinbago North: Calypso Culture in Toronto." In *Canadian Music: Issues of Hegemony and Identity,* ed. Beverley Diamond and Robert Witmer, 359–382. Toronto: Canadian Scholars' Press.

———. 1995. "Constructing Caribbean Culture in Toronto: The Representation of Caribana." In *The Reordering of Culture: Latin America, The Caribbean and Canada in the Hood,* ed. Alvina Ruprecht and Cecilia Taiana, 397–407. Ottawa: Carleton University Press.

———. 1999. "Articulations of Locality: Portraits and Narratives from the Toronto-Cuban Musicscape." *Canadian University Music Review* 19(2):102–114.

Galván, Brígido. 1996. "Partially-Automated Live Performance by Latin American Musicians in Two Canadian Cities: Musical Identity and Authenticity in a Globalized Cultural Economy." Master's thesis, University of Ottawa.

Haslebacher, Pauline. 1988. "Pan on the Move: A Historical and Ethnomusicological Overview of the Toronto Steelband Community." Master's thesis, York University.

Hunt, Krystyna. 1979. "Toronto's Trojan Horse: A Coffee House for Greeks, Latin Americans and WASPS." *Toronto Star,* 27 December, F6.

Jennings, Nicholas. 1996. "Some Like It Hot: Canadians Warm to the Sizzling Sounds of Home-grown Latin Music." *Words & Music* 3(3):12–13.

Kastner, Jamie. 1996. "The Sattalites." *Canadian Musician* 28(3):44–49.

Nunley, John. 1988. "Festival Diffusion into the Metropole." In *Caribbean Festival Arts,* ed. John Nunley and Judith Bettelheim, 165–181. Seattle: University of Washington Press.

Robbins, James. 1992. "Cuba." In *Encyclopedia of Music in Canada,* 2nd ed., ed. Helmut Kallmann, Gilles Potvin, and Kenneth Winters, 335–336. Toronto: University of Toronto Press.

Rojas, Leuten P. 1982. *From the Strings of My Guitar.* Ottawa: Cordillera Films.

Waxer, Lise. 1991. "Latin Popular Musicians in Toronto: Issues of Ethnicity and Cross-Cultural Integration." Master's thesis, York University.

Snapshot:
Two Views of Music in Toronto
Annemarie Gallaugher
Robin Elliott

Caribana—*Annemarie Gallaugher*
The Toronto Women's Musical Club—*Robin Elliott*

CARIBANA

Based primarily on Trinidad's world-renowned pre-Lenten Carnival, Caribana—a two-week-long festival of the arts showcasing the multiple and diverse expressive traditions of the Caribbean—has become a well-established centerpiece of Toronto's annual summer cultural fare. Begun in Canada's centennial year, 1967, as a somewhat modest affair celebrating the multicultural presence of the small and newly arrived Caribbean community in Toronto, the event now, at the beginning of the twenty-first century, attracts between some 750,000 and one million people and pours considerable revenue into the local tourist economy. It thus takes its rightful place among a series of large and lucrative (for local businesses and entrepreneurs if not for organizers and participants themselves) carnival-type celebrations in major centers throughout the Caribbean diaspora, including London, England, New York, and Miami.

Caribana has tended to stand out among its sister festivals in its attention to the masquerade element. Although frequently beset in recent years by funding problems and other types of local-level political controversy, occasionally to the extent that some masquerade bands and other participants have threatened boycotts, the show has always managed to go on as some forty masquerade bands (some with upwards of seven hundred to one thousand members) delight the crowds with lavish and spectacular costumes representing all manner of Caribbean flora and fauna, personages and themes from world history and current events, local and global environmental issues, and flights of unparalleled fantasy and imagination. Masquerade designers and players, who often spend an entire year carefully laboring over their costume presentations, have a number of opportunities to display their talents during the festival, including the Junior Carnival, the King and Queen of the Bands Competition, and the Caribana Parade, the festival's main highlight, in which masqueraders compete for the title of Band of the Year (figure 1).

The parade, held initially on Yonge Street and then, by 1970, on University Avenue, has since 1991 been moved to the CNE (Canadian National Exhibition) Grandstand and nearby Lakeshore Boulevard. Although this setting is preferred by some as the view of Lake Ontario and nearby Toronto Islands provide nostalgic reminiscences of home, others have seen the move as yet another attempt by authorities to

control and contain public expression of African Caribbeanness. The increasing use of police barricades all along the parade route has also been critically regarded as a further act of containment, although some masqueraders themselves appear to be in favor of the barricades given the protection they afford to their massive yet delicate costumes. Some members of the Caribbean Cultural Committee (the official Caribana organization) also seem to have been in favor of the move because it would allow the opportunity to charge for admission tickets. Nevertheless, the change in venue of the parade from a core downtown street to the city's waterfront edge does seem to have marginalized some of its original political energy, something of an irony given that the parade is scheduled on the first Saturday in August in commemoration of the emancipation of African Trinidadians from slavery in 1834.

Propelling the parade, which lasts for upward of eight hours rain or shine, are the music bands and sound systems, which pump out calypso, *soca,* reggae, salsa, samba, and other familiar Caribbean and Latin-tinged rhythms at ear-splitting volume. Mounted on huge tractor-trailer trucks, musicians, deejays, and their towering entourages of equipment provide a riotous soundscape to accompany the frenzied revelry of dancing masqueraders and parade watchers. At one time, the Caribbean Cultural Committee instituted a live-music requirement for the parade, but this has given way in recent years to the pressures and popularity of technology. Live steel bands are nevertheless still an important component; their music can be heard not only in the parade but also at the official Pan Trinbago Panorama competition, a part of the festival proceedings since 1995 and a further means to ensure the Trinidad Carnival tradition remains well entrenched. Percussion groups (for example, East Indian–Trinidadian tassa drumming and Brazilian batucada) add further variety to the multiplex soundscape.

Apart from the parade, other festival events include calypso "tents" (shows), "jump-ups" (dances), "fetes" (parties), "mas" (masquerade) competitions, mas camp tours, fashion shows, craft sales, a junior carnival, "pan blockos" or "blockoramas" (steel band street parties), "talk tents" (shows featuring storytellers, comedians, and others expert in the oral traditions), a series of moonlight cruises on Lake Ontario, and a Caribana picnic on Toronto Island. Although Caribana is the official name for events sponsored by the Caribbean Cultural Committee, other organizations and individuals mount carnival-type events during the Caribana season. For example, the Organization of Calypso Performing Artists holds an annual Calypso Monarch of Canada Competition featuring the talents of local calypsonians (calypso performers) who comment in witty and satirical fashion (often with the use of stage props and costumes) on local and international issues relevant to the Caribbean population.

—ANNEMARIE GALLAUGHER

THE TORONTO WOMEN'S MUSICAL CLUB

The Women's Musical Club of Toronto (hereafter WMCT) claims our attention not solely on account of its own merits but also because it is a flourishing and venerable representative of what was arguably one of the largest and most important musical movements in the history of North America.

The women's musical club movement was an outgrowth of the larger women's study club movement, which began in the United States in the aftermath of the Civil War. Improvements in domestic technology, together with a gradually declining birth rate and the introduction of compulsory education in 1871, provided a greater amount of leisure time for middle-class women in the late nineteenth century. The need for companionship and the impulse to help others and accomplish something worthwhile led to the rise and growth of women's study clubs. These clubs have been regarded as service organizations, educational institutions, and latent feminist groups. There is likely some truth in each of these views, for no single framework can embrace the range and variety of a movement that claimed millions of members at its peak in the early years of the twentieth century.

The first women's musical club seems to have been the Rossini Club of Portland, Maine. It was officially founded in 1869 but had already existed informally several years prior to that time (Whitesitt 1991:664). The National Federation of Music Clubs, an all-women organization, was founded in Springfield, Illinois in 1898; by 1930 it had 400,000 members. There was no national organization for the women's musical club movement in Canada. Some Canadian clubs joined the U.S. federation, but most existed independently, and as a result the extent of the movement in Canada is difficult to estimate. The oldest women's musical club in Canada is the Duet Club of Hamilton, which was founded in 1889 and still active in 1999. By the early years of the twentieth century, women's musical clubs were operating in towns large and small across the country. In many municipalities it was the local women's musical club that first organized a concert series for the community.

In Toronto no fewer than eight women's musical clubs were in operation by 1900. The WMCT was founded on 23 January 1899, when a group of women musicians and music lovers met in a studio in the Yonge Street Arcade and decided to begin holding biweekly recitals by club members. The first president was Mary Henderson Flett Dickson. Up to 1914 there were two categories of membership: active (performers) and associate (nonperformers). Most recitals were given by active club members and were private events; only one or two concerts each year were open to the general public. In the course of its first twenty-five seasons, though, the WMCT was gradually transformed from a private club that sponsored a few public events into an organization presenting solo and chamber music recitals by professional musicians rather than club members.

During World War I the WMCT proved its relevance during straitened circumstances with a vigorous campaign of charitable works, in keeping with the Presbyterian ethos of social service that in part motivated the club's founders. This urge to do good works surfaced again during World War II, when the WMCT raised thousands of dollars for the Red Cross. But the strain of the war effort took its toll, and in fact the WMCT was inactive from 1942 to 1946. Since the resumption of activities after the war, the charitable urge has centered on granting scholarships to young musicians, which is an ongoing and vital part of the club's agenda.

The sponsoring of recitals has always been the central activity of the WMCT; by 1999 the club had given almost nine hundred concerts. Artists who have appeared in recital for the WMCT have included the Kneisel Quartet and Olga Samaroff in the 1900s, the Flonzaley Quartet and Guiomar Novaes in the 1910s, Myra Hess and Wanda Landowska in the 1920s, Andrés Segovia and Marian Anderson in the 1930s, Dorothy Maynor and Rosalyn Tureck in the 1940s, Dietrich Fischer-Dieskau, Christa Ludwig, and Leontyne Price in the 1950s, Jean-Pierre Rampal, the Juilliard Quartet, and the Beaux Arts Trio in the 1960s, Elly Ameling and Murray Perahia in the 1970s, Mitsuko Uchida and Michala Petri in the 1980s, and Michael Schade and the St. Lawrence String Quartet in the 1990s. Most of these artists were being featured in their Toronto or Canadian debut recital.

The WMCT has had occasion to celebrate its accomplishments over the years. For the seventy-fifth anniversary season Helen Goudge, a past president, wrote a short account of the history of the club (Goudge 1972), and for the centennial season a longer and more thoroughly researched book was commissioned (Elliott 1997). These two sources tell how the fortunes of the WMCT have fluctuated over the years; in 1929, for instance, there were fewer than three hundred members and the club was in danger of folding, while in the early 1960s there were 1,000 members and sold-out concerts were the norm. Men were first admitted to become associate members of the WMCT in 1958, though without the right to vote. Full membership for men arrived in 1989, and today men are well represented in the rank and file and also on the executive committee of the WMCT.

The women's musical club movement is but a pale shadow of what it once was. Seventy-five years ago, women's musical clubs existed in towns large and small across Canada, but today only a handful is still active. There are many reasons for the decline of the movement, from the rise of radio and television to demographic considerations such as the increasing number of women in the work force. The ability to adapt to the changing circumstances of the past century has allowed the WMCT to continue to thrive as a vital remnant of a movement that changed the musical landscape of North America.

—ROBIN ELLIOTT

REFERENCES

Elliott, Robin. 1997. *Counterpoint to a City: The First One Hundred Years of the Women's Musical Club of Toronto.* Toronto: ECW Press.

Gallaugher, Annemarie. 1995. "Constructing Caribbean Culture in Toronto: The Representation of Caribana." In *The Re-Ordering of Culture: Latin America, the Caribbean and Canada in the Hood,* ed. Alvina Ruprecht and Cecilia Taiana, 397–407. Ottawa: Carleton University Press.

Goudge, Helen. 1972. *Look Back in Pride: A History of the Women's Musical Club of Toronto 1897–98 to 1972–73.* Toronto: Women's Musical Club of Toronto.

Haslebacher, Pauline. 1998. "Pan on the Move: A Historical and Ethnomusicological Overview of the Toronto Steelband Community." Master's thesis, York University.

Jackson, Peter. 1992. "The Politics of the Streets: A Geography of Caribana." *Political Geography* 11(2):130–151.

Malcolm, C. James. 1990. "Caribana: The Art of Carnival in Toronto." *Performing Arts in Canada* 26 (summer).

Manning, Frank. 1983. "Carnival and the West Indian diaspora." *The Round Table* 286:186–196.

Nunley, John, and Bettleheim, Judith. 1988. *Caribbean Festival Arts: Each and Every Bit of Difference.* Seattle: The Saint Louis Art Museum and the University of Washington Press.

Reed-Olsen, Joan, prod. and dir. 1991. *Mas Camp to Parade.* Hands Over Time series. [28 mins.] TV Ontario and Ontario Educational Communications Authority. Video.

Shepherd, Patrick. 1984. "Caribana." *Polyphony: Bulletin of the Multicultural History Society of Ontario.* 6(1):135–139.

Whitesitt, Linda. 1991. "'The Most Potent Force' in American Music: The Role of Women's Music Clubs in American Concert Life." In *The Musical Woman: An International Perspective,* vol. 3, ed. Judith Lang Zaimont, 663–681. Westport, Conn.: Greenwood Press.

African Canadian Music

Anne Lederman

African Canadian Music
Caribbean Music
Continental African Music

There are essentially three cultural communities of African descent in Ontario: black communities established from the late 1700s to the mid-1800s (African Canadian), a Caribbean community centered in Toronto established in the mid- to late twentieth century, and a continental African community of recent arrival, also largely centered in Toronto.

AFRICAN CANADIAN MUSIC

There were black slaves in Ontario, but we have no information on their musical activities. In 1793, anti-slavery legislation was passed forbidding the importation of slaves into Canada, prompting many fugitives from the United States to seek freedom in southern Ontario. They settled in the Sandwich-Windsor area, Essex county, Fort Erie, Hamilton, Toronto, London, the Niagara Peninsula, Owen Sound, and Conestoga (between Guelph and Waterloo). Virtually all-black communities were established at Dawn, Elgin, Wilberforce, and North Buxton. Although many blacks returned to the United States after emancipation, many stayed.

There has been very little study of music in these communities. What is known comes largely from history books, newspapers, and personal accounts. Emancipation Day parades featuring brass bands were held at Niagara soon after 1814 and, by 1840, in almost all of Ontario's black communities, usually on the first weekend of August. These celebrations continued into the mid-twentieth century. The black chapter of the Masons had a band in Windsor before 1850. Chatham had a black band and glee club in the 1850s, and Owen Sound had a black orchestra at one time (Winks 1971:325). There are scattered reports of fiddlers. Two 1850s papers, *The Voice of the Fugitive* and *The Provincial Freeman,* published poems, some meant to be sung to well-known tunes. The following was printed in *The Voice of the Fugitive,* in Sandwich, Ontario, 29 January 1851, with eight verses, to be sung to the tune of "Oh! Susannah":

I'm on my way to Canada, that cold and dreary land
The dire effects of slavery I can no longer stand.
My soul is mixed within me so, to think that I'm a slave
I'm now resolved to strike the blow for freedom or the grave.
O Righteous Father, wilt Thou not pity me
And aid me on to Canada, where colored men are free?

I heard old Queen Victoria say if we would all forsake
Our native land of slavery and come across the lake
That she was standing on the shore with arms extended wide
To give us all a peaceful home beyond the rolling tide.
Farewell, old master, this is enough for me
I'm going straight to Canada, where colored men are free.

I've served my master all my days without a dime's reward
And now I'm forced to run away to flee the lot abhorred.
The hounds are baying on my track, the master's just behind
Resolved that he will bring me back before I cross the line.
And so, old master, don't come after me
I'm going up to Canada, where colored men are free. (Fowke 1984:80)

Many black churches in Ontario were known for their music, especially the British Methodist Episcopal Churches of Oakville and Toronto and Toronto's First Baptist Church in the 1930s, which gave rise to the vocal group The Radio Kings of Harmony. Kenneth Peacock and Paul McIntyre recorded Pentecostal services in the 1960s and 1970s in the Windsor area, which are now housed in the Canadian Center for Folk Culture Studies (Ottawa), including a study of the music (McIntyre 1976). Church choirs also fostered many singers who went on to professional careers in pop and swing, such as Jay Jackson of the 1960s group The Pharoahs.

The most comprehensive picture of African Ontarian musical life is organist and choir leader Vivian Robbins's *Musical Buxton* (1969), a small book that spans almost one hundred years, discussing individual musicians, groups, and types of performances, professional and amateur. There were several church choirs in Buxton, as well as a school choir, a male quartet, a glee club, the North Buxton Maple Leaf Band, and several female vocal groups. Songwriter Shelton Brooks, composer of "Darktown Strutters Ball," "Some of These Days," and other tunes, came from Buxton.

Southern Ontario was also the birthplace of composer Nathaniel Dett (Niagara Falls), singer Phyllis Marshall (Barrie), drummer Archie Alleyne, guitarist Sonny Greenwich (Toronto), and singer, guitarist, and piano player Jackie Washington (Hamilton). Musicians of local African ancestry are active in blues, disco, rhythm and blues, jazz, folk, and classical music, although these forms are all dominated by non-blacks in Ontario.

Given the close links older Ontario black communities have had with the United States, it is not surprising that their cultural expressions have followed similar lines [see AFRICAN AMERICAN MUSICS, p. 571]. Many black musicians born in the United States have also chosen to live and perform in Ontario, including Salome Bey, Leon Bibb and Billy Newton-Davis.

CARIBBEAN MUSIC

Although students and other individuals came to Ontario from the Caribbean throughout the 1900s, immigration greatly increased from the 1950s on, to a population in Toronto of over 300,000 by 1990. Ontario Caribbean music loosely divides into two areas: on the one hand, calypso, steel band, and *soca* (a newer dance-oriented blend of soul and calypso) music stemming from Carnival traditions in Trinidad and the British Caribbean, and on the other reggae, ska, dub poetry, rap, and hip-hop, rooted in Jamaica.

Carnival traditions

The first Caribana Festival was held in Toronto on 1 August 1967 (the date of the old Emancipation Day Parades) [see CARIBANA, p. 1207]. Caribana features calypso competitions (first held in 1980), "jump ups" (dances), parties, *mas* 'costume' competitions, steel band street parties, "talk tents" featuring storytellers, cruises, and picnics, as well as the all-day parade with dozens of elaborately costumed groups, each led by a king and queen. Calypso monarch competitions are held in tents around the city just prior to Caribana and feature local singers performing original songs with full band arrangements, which are then judged on the basis of lyrics, melody, presentation and originality.

Several Caribbean clubs were established in Toronto in the late 1960s and 1970s, including the Bermuda Tavern, the Latin Quarter, and the Little Trinidad Club. One of the first local groups was the Tradewinds, led by Guyanese musician Dave Martin. Steel bands and community brass bands also formed in the 1980s, including many school programs to teach the technique of playing the steel drum.

Reggae, ska, dub, and hip-hop

The earliest local reggae bands began in the 1960s—the Rivals, the Sheiks, the Cougars, and the Cavaliers. The 1970s and 1980s saw the rise of bands Truth and Rights, featuring Lillian Allen as lyricist, and Messenjah and the Satellites, among others. Allen went on to become Canada's leading dub poet (in the dub form, words are spoken over music, usually heavily reggae influenced). The closely related forms of rap and hip-hop, along with a comeback of ska, have been popular in the 1990s [see AFRICAN AMERICAN MUSICS, p. 571; HIP-HOP AND RAP, p. 692].

The Canadian Reggae Awards, the Juno Award for Best Reggae/Calypso Recording, and the Black Music Association of Canada Awards honor these Caribbean forms annually.

CONTINENTAL AFRICAN MUSIC

There were approximately 100,000 black Africans and Somalis (many of whom do not identify themselves as black) living in Toronto in 1993, most of whom came since 1980 (Lederman 1993). Over half are Somali, but West Africans, mainly from southern Ghana and Nigeria, Lingala speakers from Central Africa, Ethiopians, Eritreans, and South Africans are also well represented. Whereas in 1993 most musical/cultural activities were confined to African audiences, there have been remarkable changes in this regard since that time. The annual Afrofest Festival, sponsored by Music Africa, along with regular activities at Harbourfront Center and in various clubs throughout the city, now draws many non-Africans as well.

Toronto became a recording center for Ghanaian "high-life" music in the 1980s. The Highlife World record label, under the direction of Thaddeus Ulzen and Sam Mensah, recorded singers Jewel Ackah, AB Crentsil, and Pat Thomas. The Hi-Life Stars, an ongoing Toronto group, are still regularly employed to back up visiting Ghanaian singers.

Both the University of Toronto and York University, as well as various community organizations such as Worlds of Music Toronto, regularly teach African traditions. Several organizations, such as the Ewe Cultural Association, the Fontonfrom Drum Ensemble, and the Oromo Association, maintain traditional drum and dance ensembles. Other professional performers have included Soukous groups, Somali singers and pop bands, South African *mbaquanga* (a popular style that mixed African and American sounds) groups, West and Central African traditional drum/dance ensembles, and contemporary African bands. The annual African Music Awards honor current performers.

REFERENCES

AfroCan Routes. 1992. CBC Variety Recordings World Music Series 2, VRCD 1015. Compact disc.

Bell, Ian. 1990. *A Grand Musical Entertainment.* Sound Reconstructions. Audiocassette.

Caudeiron, Daniel. 1992a. "Rap." In *Encyclopedia of Music in Canada,* 2nd ed., ed. Helmut Kallman, Gilles Potvin, and Kenneth Winters, 1106–1107. Toronto: University of Toronto Press.

———. 1992b. "Reggae." In *Encyclopedia of Music in Canada,* 2nd ed., ed. Helmut Kallman, Gilles Potvin, and Kenneth Winters, 1118–1119. Toronto: University of Toronto Press.

Faith Chorale. 1996. *Caught Up.* n.p.

Gallaugher, Annemarie. 1990. "'Some of We Is One': Calypso by Association." In *Ethnomusicology in Canada,* ed. Robert Witmer, 286–290. Toronto: Institute for Canadian Music.

———. 1991. "From Trinidad to Toronto: Calypso as a Way of Life." Master's thesis, York University.

———. 1992. "Calypso." In *Encyclopedia of Music in Canada,* 2nd ed., ed. Helmut Kallmann, Gilles Potvin, and Kenneth Winters, 187–188. Toronto: University of Toronto Press.

Fowke, Edith. 1984. *Singing Our History.* Toronto: Doubleday Canada.

Harris Family Gospel Singers. 1967. *Trust in God.* L.R.C. Records 120153. LP disk.

Haslebacher, Pauline. 1988. "Pan on the Move: A Historical and Ethnomusicological Overview of the Toronto Steelband Community." Master's thesis, York University.

Hill, Daniel. 1981. *The Freedom Seekers: Blacks in Early Canada.* Agincourt, Ontario: The Book Society of Canada.

Lederman, Anne. 1993. "Music in African Communities in Toronto." Research Report for the Canadian Center for Folk Culture Studies, Canadian Museum of Civilization, Ottawa.

McIntyre, Paul. 1976. *Black Pentecostal Music in Windsor.* Mercury Series, No. 15. Ottawa: National Museums of Man.

Miller, Mark. 1992a. "Allen, Lillian." In *Encyclopedia of Music in Canada,* 2nd ed., ed. Helmut Kallman, Gilles Potvin, and Kenneth Winters, 19. Toronto: University of Toronto Press.

———. 1992b. "Black Music and Musicians." In *Encyclopedia of Music in Canada,* 2nd ed., ed. Helmut Kallman, Gilles Potvin, and Kenneth Winters, 129–130. Toronto: University of Toronto Press.

———. 1992c. "Jazz." In *Encyclopedia of Music in Canada,* 2nd ed. ed. Helmut Kallman, Gilles

Potvin, and Kenneth Winters, 645–649. Toronto: University of Toronto Press.

———. 1992d. "Washington, Jackie." In *Encyclopedia of Music in Canada,* 2nd ed., ed. Helmut Kallman, Gilles Potvin, and Kenneth Winters, 1387–1388. Toronto: University of Toronto Press.

———. 1997. *Such Melodious Racket: The Lost History of Jazz in Canada.* Toronto: Mercury Press.

Moogk, Edward B. 1980. *Roll Back the Years.* Québec: Ministry of Supply and Services Canada.

Richmond, Norman Otis. 1979. "The Uphill Struggle of Our Black Musicians." *Toronto Star,* 14 April, H1.

Robbins, Vivian. 1969. *Musical Buxton.* Buxton: n.p.

Thomas, Pat. 1980. *Pat Thomas '80 and Mbrepa.* Highlife World. Audiocassette.

Winks, Robin. 1971. *The Blacks in Canada: A History.* Montréal: McGill–Queen's University Press.

Witmer, Robert. 1992. "Caribbean." In *Encyclopedia of Music in Canada,* 2nd ed., ed. Helmut Kallman, Gilles Potvin, and Kenneth Winters, 220–221. Toronto: University of Toronto Press.

Asian Music
James R. Kippen

Ontario, Canada's most populous and prosperous province, has long been a primary destination for immigrants. With one-third of the country's population living within a one-hundred-mile radius of Ontario's thriving capital, Toronto, the province has enjoyed a strong economic reputation that has attracted people from every part of the world. Past patterns favoring immigrants from all regions of Europe have given way in recent decades to newcomers from other areas, most of all Asia. Toronto itself is currently considered to be the world's most multiethnic and multicultural city; one person in three is identified as a visible minority. Half the South Asian population of Canada lives in Toronto, along with about two-fifths of the country's Chinese, Koreans, and Filipinos. In addition there are large numbers of Japanese, and there is a growing trend in immigration from Arab and West Asian countries, particularly Iran.

There are small Asian communities in large urban centers such as the federal capital Ottawa, Hamilton, London, Windsor, and Kitchener-Waterloo, but Toronto accounts for the bulk of Ontario's Asian ethnic and cultural diversity: Toronto received eighty thousand immigrants in 1997 from 169 countries; over eighty languages can be heard regularly in the streets, prominent among which are Chinese (many varieties), Punjabi, Hindi, Urdu, and Tamil; and by 2001, foreign-born residents will comprise more than 50 percent of its population. Yet it is important to remember that for most Asian musics the practitioners are not just Asians performing their own traditions but also Canadians from all ethnic and cultural backgrounds, some having learned their skills in Canada, others having studied in Asia itself.

CONTEXTS FOR PERFORMANCE

As with any large, vibrant, multicultural urban environment, the Toronto music scene has become a microcosmic representation of the world's musics and dances. Artists of international repute have made it a routine stop on world tours; some, like Indian sitar maestro Ravi Shankar or the Japanese Kodo drummers, have drawn a broad spectrum of listeners from every community, while Iranian vocalist Mohammad Reza Shajarian and Pakistani *qawwali* singers the Sabri brothers have in the recent past filled vast suburban auditoriums with almost exclusively expatriate audiences (and with remarkably little advertising).

Harbourfront, both a location and an organization whose mandate is to showcase the best in contemporary Canadian culture side by side with the best from around the world, has become the focal point of festivals that attract around three million people annually. It also acts as a liaison for over 450 community groups that together form a rich local artistic resource. Harbourfront's massive World of Music Arts and Dance (WOMAD) Festival of former years has now been replaced with a multitude of smaller thematic festivals: Rhythms of the World and Panorama India are recent examples.

In addition there is the annual celebration of Toronto's ethnic communities called Caravan, occurring in late June. Neighborhoods host pavilions from all parts of the world providing visitors with an extraordinary array of sights, tastes, and sounds. Aside from the communities themselves, much funding for individuals and organizations performing and promoting world music comes from the Toronto Arts Council, the Ontario Arts Council, the Canada Council, and the Laidlaw Foundation.

ARABIC AND PERSIAN MUSIC COMMUNITIES

Arabic and Persian music thrive in Toronto, but these are essentially amateur traditions carried on by individuals who have studied with great masters. They occur in private homes, are rarely heard by the general public, and are thus very difficult to document. The Egyptian *qānūn* 'trapezoid plucked zither of the Middle East' player George Sawa, for example, teaches and performs the Syrian repertoire and is internationally respected for his scholarship.

INDIAN MUSIC COMMUNITIES

Toronto is a major center for musics of the Indian subcontinent. Organizations like the Raag-Mala Music Society (Hindustani music) and Bharathi Kala Mandram (Karnatak music) have for decades sponsored concerts featuring all the great artists of Northern and Southern India. The *mridangam* 'South Indian barrel drum' master Trichy Sankaran joined York University in the early 1970s, and his influence has been felt by a generation of percussionists. More recently, sitar player Irshad Khan (son of Imrat Khan) and *sārangī* 'North Indian bowed lute' player Aruna Narayan Kalle (figure 1) (daughter of Ram Narayan) have made Toronto their home and are active performers and teachers.

Dance performances abound, and several classical traditions are well represented. For example, successful schools for *bharata natyam* have been established by Menaka Thakkar and Lata Pada, and for *kathak* by Rina Singha and Joanna Das. ●᪲᪲31 Many excellent tabla drummers are active in Toronto, and there is even a Toronto Tabla Ensemble, created by Ritesh Das, performing experimental percussion and popular fusion music. A great deal of instruction in all kinds of music and dance is carried on within the traditional master-disciple relationship, but recently the Kalai Kovil Academy has been catering to the burgeoning South Indian and Sri Lankan Tamil community, many of them recent refugees, by creating a systematic syllabus for practical and theory training with an examination system along the lines of an Indian music conservatory. Outside Toronto, Ottawa is host to a number of Indian music concerts annually, organized by the Hindustani Sangeet Mandal and the South Indian Cultural Association.

FIGURE I   Aruna Narayan Kalle, the Toronto-based *sārangī* player. Photo by Eric Parker, 1996.

INDONESIAN AND JAPANESE MUSIC COMMUNITIES

Indonesian gamelan orchestras have a long history in North America, and the University of Toronto and York University have Balinese and Javanese ensembles respectively. The Evergreen Gamelan Club of Toronto has for many years specialized in the Sundanese gamelan tradition, and the Central Javanese tradition is practiced by Gamelan Toronto, which operates out of the city's Indonesian consulate. The Indonesian embassy in Ottawa also houses a Javanese gamelan that is played by a local group.

Japanese music is represented in Toronto by several individuals and groups. Prominent among these are the Kiyoshi Nagata Taiko Drumming Ensemble and an all-women's *shakuhachi* flute group under the direction of *shakuhachi* expert Debbie Danbrook.

CHINESE MUSIC COMMUNITIES

Chinese music came to Ontario with the first immigrant workers on the railroads in the nineteenth century. To entertain themselves and to maintain cultural links with the homeland, these early communities established their own opera clubs, Cantonese opera being by far the most prominent style. Opera burgeoned in the 1960s and 1970s, when most of the clan associations in North America began organizing Cantonese operas for festive occasions such as Chinese New Year and the Midautumn Festival.

Toronto, with North America's largest Chinese population, is now home to about thirty such clubs; singing Cantonese opera has become one of the most important social and cultural activities in Chinese communities. Singers pay to sing with a resident group of about five to seven traditional musicians; these musicians are in great demand, and with so many clubs there is a great deal of work to be found. Many famous actor-singers of Cantonese opera have settled in Toronto, and many of them continue to perform and teach.

Although there is no fully professional Chinese orchestra in Toronto, there is an active Toronto Chinese Music Association comprising both professionals and amateurs who rehearse and perform regularly. Founded in 1992, the ensemble now operates under the name Toronto Chinese Orchestra. There is also an active children's choir, attached to the Yip's Children's Choral and Performing Arts Centre, that fosters an enthusiasm in the young for their Chinese musical heritage as well as the Western choral tradition. Many dance groups operate in the city (Panda Dance Theatre, Chi Ping Dance Group, Canadian Chinese Folk Dance Institute, and so on), as do several outstanding instrumentalists who make a living from teaching traditional music (for example, the *erh-hu* 'Chinese two-string spike fiddle' player George Gao).

It is at the festivals that all join together to celebrate the vitality of the community and its arts: Toronto is home to an annual Lion Dance Festival, a Chinese New Year Festival (also held in Vancouver) until recently sponsored by Canadian Airlines, and the huge midsummer Toronto International Dragon Boat Race Festival organized by the Toronto Chinese Business Association. The Dragon Boat Race Festival is a multicultural event that includes, among other things, a good deal of Filipino music and dance in addition to the Chinese performing arts. Smaller Dragon Boat Festivals are held in several other Ontario cities.

Middle Eastern Music
George Dimitri Sawa

Performance Contexts
The Traditional Arabic Music Ensemble
Festivals and Concerts
Studying Middle Eastern Music in Ontario

People from the Middle East, mainly Syrians and Lebanese, first began to arrive in Ontario in 1882. Successive waves of immigration from 1946 onward brought Palestinians and Egyptians. These four nationalities were the most prominent, but by the 1970s, however, all nationalities from the Arab-speaking world were present in Ontario. The early immigrants were small merchants and blue-collar workers, but later migrations brought a large proportion of white-collar professionals.

Among the immigrants and their descendants today are amateur musicians and a few professionals. The latter earn their living outside the music field and at the same time join the amateurs to provide performances of popular music for their community. They perform on both traditional and nontraditional instruments—the former include the *'üd* 'lute'; *qänün* 'psaltery'; *näy* 'end-blown flute', *riqq, duff, mazhar* 'three varieties of tambourine'; *darabukka* 'conical cylindrical drum'; and *kamanja* 'adapted Western violin'. Traditional instruments include the accordion and keyboard with Arabic tuning as well as electric guitar and Western percussion instruments. The introduction of Western instruments is not a result of acculturation in Canada but, rather, a result of close to two hundred years of Western influence in the homeland.

PERFORMANCE CONTEXTS

Performance contexts include the *ḥafla,* which is an Arabic musical party held to celebrate a wedding, a wedding anniversary, a high school or university graduation, a baptism for Christian Arabs, or social, political, and religious events; and performances in restaurants and night clubs, where instruments are used to accompany Middle Eastern dances. The latter are often performed by non–Middle Eastern women who have developed great admiration for this art form and who are trained in many of Ontario's Middle Eastern dance schools. At the *ḥafla,* the audience always joins in clapping, singing, and dancing. To cater to the younger generation as well as to those who are Westernized, popular dance music is provided by a Western band or a disc jockey. As for authentic folk music, it is sometimes performed by members of the audience during the *ḥafla* but more so in private gatherings.

FIGURE I   The Traditional Arabic Music Ensemble in 1984. *Left to right:* Ebrahim Eleish (*ʿūd*), Dahlia Obadia (dancer), George Sawa (*qānūn*), Sonia Belkacem (singer), Suzanne Meyers Sawa (*darabukka*).

THE TRADITIONAL ARABIC MUSIC ENSEMBLE

Side by side with Middle Eastern musicians performing popular music for their own communities, a group was formed in 1973 for the purpose of performing a repertoire of not only popular music but also folk music and the much-neglected Arabic classical repertoire for both the Middle Eastern community and Canadian society at large. This was the Classical Arabic Music Quintet, founded in 1973 by the late Ebrahim Eleish (d. 1994) and George Sawa and renamed The Traditional Arabic Music Ensemble in 1978 (figure 1). The group has performed extensively in North America; in Ontario it has performed at music and dance festivals (Mariposa, World of Music and Dance [WOMAD], Metro Caravan, Arab Canadian Heritage Day in Toronto, Earthsong in Hamilton) and in museums and art galleries (Royal Ontario Museum, Art Gallery of Ontario, in Toronto, Canada Museum of Civilization in Ottawa/Hull). It has given concerts and lecture demonstrations at various Ontario universities (Universities of Toronto, York, McMaster) and at various scholarly societies' meetings (Society for Ethnomusicology and Middle East Studies Association of North America). The Traditional Arabic Music Ensemble has also presented lecture-demonstrations to junior and high school students, has cooperated in composition and performance with Canadian composer R. Murray Schafer's RA (a recreation of an ancient Egyptian ritual), and has recorded audio and video performances for the CBC and the Canada Museum of Civilization.

FESTIVALS AND CONCERTS

Although Middle Eastern music can be heard regularly in a variety of nightclubs and restaurants, it is also featured in a number of special concerts and in the many productions of the Arabesque Dance Company at the Harbourfront in Toronto. It is also performed at the Hummingbird Center, the Fringe Festival of Independent Dance Artists in Toronto, and at the Dancenet, a monthly event featuring world dances where Middle Eastern dances are often accompanied by live performances from music students. The Metro Caravan in Toronto, Carassauga in Mississauga, and the Arab Canadian Heritage Day at the Harbourfront are yearly events for the Middle Eastern community.

At midnight the star sings at least three suites, each
lasting an hour-and-a-half, and the concert ends at
six o'clock in the morning.

In addition to events provided by the amateur and professional musicians are others
featuring famous musicians from the homeland. The music performed can be broadly
classified into two styles, the first being a commercialized music with a supranational
approach speaking to diverse nationalities, such as concerts by the Lebanese popular
songstress Feiruz, Iraqi popular singer Kazim al-Sahir, or Egyptian star Amr Diyab;
these different musical styles and instrumentation exhibit Western influence, such as
the presence of keyboard instruments and electric guitars side by side with traditional
Arabic instruments. The other style is the music of a particular area, which appeals primarily to people originally from that region. Among the memorable concerts of this
type of music are those sponsored by particular communities. The Syrian community
has sponsored renowned classical singer Sabah Fakhri and popular singer Georges Was-
suf; the Lebanese community has sponsored the traditional singer Wadi al-Safi; the
Egyptian community, together with its embassy, has sponsored the Reda Dance Troupe,
the Umm Kulthum orchestra and choir, and the Samer theater group that included
twenty-seven folk musicians and dancers. Some of these concerts follow the Western
style of presenting two parts, approximately one hour each, with an intermission. Others, such as the concerts of Sabah Fakhri, follow the traditional Arabic format. They
start around nine o'clock with an hour of instrumental music, then each of two vocalists from the chorus sings for an hour. At midnight the star sings at least three suites,
each lasting an hour and a half, and the concert ends at six o'clock in the morning. The
suites are built on contrasting sections: instrumental versus vocal, solo versus chorus,
measured versus unmeasured, improvised versus precomposed. Often the audience
participates by clapping, dancing, and singing along, as well as by sending special
requests to the star.

STUDYING MIDDLE EASTERN MUSIC IN ONTARIO

The Centre for Studies in Middle Eastern Music, located in Toronto and directed
by George Sawa, was created in 1992 to respond to a strong demand to study vocal
and instrumental Middle Eastern music outside colleges and universities. The students
are Canadian professional musicians who learn theory and analysis, compositions,
vocal techniques, and instrumental music, as well as dancers who perform traditional
Middle Eastern dances but also want to learn more about Middle Eastern culture
and rituals, music appreciation, and percussion instruments (*darabukka,* tambourines,
and finger cymbals). George Sawa teaches *qänün, näy,* basic percussion techniques, and
voice; Ramon Sarweh, Maroun Tannous, and Nabil Shehadeh teach *'üd;* and Ramon
Sarweh and Amer Mitri teach advanced percussion at the Centre. Instruction is also
given by those mentioned at the Arabesque Dance Company in Toronto. Among the
students of the center are members of the now popular Toronto-based trio Doula and
Maza Meze, a group of eleven musicians who perform Arabic and Greek music and
experiment successfully with fusion styles.

REFERENCES

Meyers Sawa, Suzanne. 1994. "The Odyssey of Dahlia Obadia: Morocco, Israel, Canada." In *Canadian Music: Issues of Hegemony and Identity,* ed. Beverley Diamond and Robert Witmer, 529–540. Toronto: Canadian Scholars' Press.

Qureshi, Regula. 1972. "Ethnomusicological Research among Canadian Communities of Arab and East Indian Origin." *Ethnomusicology* 16:381–396.

Qureshi, Regula, and George D. Sawa. 1992. "Arabic Music." In *Encyclopedia of Music in Canada,* 2nd ed., ed. Helmut Kallman, Gilles Potvin, and Kenneth Winters, 34. Toronto: University of Toronto Press.

Sawa, George D. 1975. "Musical Acculturation of the Arab-Canadian in Toronto." Unpublished report. Ottawa: National Museum of Man.

———. 1992a. "Egypt." In *Encyclopedia of Music in Canada,* 2nd ed., ed. Helmut Kallman, Gilles Potvin, and Kenneth Winters, eds, 409. Toronto: University of Toronto Press.

———. 1992b. "Lebanon." In *Encyclopedia of Music in Canada,* 2nd ed., ed. Helmut Kallman, Gilles Potvin, and Kenneth Winters, 734. Toronto: University of Toronto Press.

———. 1992c. "Syria." In *Encyclopedia of Music in Canada,* 2nd ed., ed. Helmut Kallman, Gilles Potvin, and Kenneth Winters, 1271. Toronto: University of Toronto Press.

Section 3d
Prairies

The Prairie provinces (Manitoba, Saskatchewan, and Alberta) were settled, by both First Nations Peoples and by Europeans, somewhat later than the eastern provinces, but by the end of the eighteenth century various groups of Algonkian- and Athapascan-speaking Indians and Plains Cree had established communities there. The French soon followed, interacting with the aboriginal population there, creating within the next 100 years or so a new cultural group, the Métis, who developed their own language and musical forms, and who in the late nineteenth century, under the leadership of Louis Riel, declared their own nationhood—an act that was quickly deterred. A place where the British were never a majority, the Prairies became in the nineteenth and early twentieth centuries home to German, Ukrainian, and Scandinavian immigrants, who, attracted by government land grants, quickly established farming communities and a northern-European-based musical life. The latest immigrants to arrive on the Prairies in the 1980s were a small group of North Indian Muslims who settled in Edmonton, Alberta, and who brought with them their poetry, folk songs, dances, and classical and ritual musics. The Banff Center for the Arts, established in 1933 in Alberta, has quickly become a world-renowned center for the performance of Western classical music, and jazz and country and western music also thrive there.

Performances such as this one held at the Pysanka Festival in Saskatchewan help to celebrate Ukrainian culture on the Canadian Prairies and to create musical ties between generations within the Ukrainian community. © Natalie Forbes/CORBIS.

Overview
Wesley Berg

Nineteenth Century
1900–1920
1920–1950
1950 to the Present

The Canadian Prairies are the northern portion of the Great Plains of North America, bounded on the east by the Precambrian Shield and on the west by the Rocky Mountains and stretching from the forty-ninth parallel to the Arctic coast. The most heavily populated regions are the provinces of Manitoba, Saskatchewan, and Alberta. The region was inhabited by the prairie bison and nomadic Indian tribes until the beginning of the twentieth century, when a flood of immigration made possible by the building of a transcontinental railroad transformed its grasslands by replacing fur traders and bison hunters with farmers and ranchers, and fur trading posts with towns and cities.

NINETEENTH CENTURY

Until the last two decades of the nineteenth century the music heard on the Canadian prairies was that of the Indians—the original inhabitants of this vast territory—and toward the end of the century that of the Europeans coming to the area in search of furs and buffalo. The music of the traders consisted mostly of the folk and popular songs of their homelands, Great Britain and France, while the Métis, the offspring of French-speaking traders and their Indian wives, and the mixed bloods, the offspring of similar unions of British traders and Indian women, developed a musical tradition that combined elements of musical style from both cultures [see MÉTIS, p. 404]. Their fiddling tradition is particularly well developed, and Métis fiddlers often participated in social dances at which all three cultures—Indian, Métis, and European—were present.

The first substantial European settlement on the prairies was established at the confluence of the Red and Assiniboine Rivers, where Winnipeg, the capital of Manitoba, now stands. It was a fur-trading post as early as 1738, but in 1870, the year Manitoba became a province, it still had only two hundred inhabitants. By 1882 its population had grown to seven thousand, making possible the growth of musical institutions associated with urban centers. A band was established in 1871 using instruments left behind by the First Ontario Rifles, the regiment that had been sent to deal with the Red River Rebellion of 1869. A pipe organ had been placed in a church in St. Boniface in 1875, and in 1880 the first Philharmonic Society on the prairies came into being.

Similar developments across the prairies occurred somewhat later. Edmonton had been the center of the fur trade since 1795 in what was to become northern Alberta, but it was still a hamlet of 275 traders and their helpers and wives in 1880. Musical instruments were brought to the region by freighter canoes on the North Saskatchewan River or by oxcart via the Carlton Trail from Winnipeg. In spite of these difficulties, residents of such prairie outposts were quick to organize organ funds and choirs for their churches, as well as glee clubs and amateur orchestras when capable musicians happened to move to the community.

The other major urban centers in the region began as creations of the Canadian Pacific Railway, pushed across the southern prairies in order to provide a link between Ontario and the new province of British Columbia (1871) on the west coast. Between 1881 and 1883, Brandon, Regina, Saskatoon, and Calgary became important regional centers because of the arrival of the railway. Edmonton had to wait until 1891 to have a spur from Calgary arrive and until 1905 to be connected by a transcontinental line. In addition to the rapid increase in population made possible by the coming of the railroad, the railroad also opened up the region to touring operatic companies, national and international solo artists, and the North American network of vaudeville and light opera companies, dramatically expanding the entertainment horizons of prairie audiences [see POPULAR MUSIC OF THE PARLOR AND STAGE, p. 179].

The Canadian prairies were opened up to immigration after 1890, with the extirpation of the prairie bison, the resettlement of the aboriginal population on reserves, and the completion of the transcontinental railroad in 1885. Small settlements had been established before 1890, including a group of Mennonites in southern Manitoba in 1874 and groups of Icelandic settlers around Lake Winnipeg in Manitoba in 1875 and 1876. The largest number of immigrants came from Ontario and Great Britain; more than one-half million Americans arrived between 1898 and 1914; the balance consisted of immigrants from central and eastern Europe, including 170,000 Ukrainians, with much smaller numbers of immigrants from Asia.

Immigration officials encouraged bloc settlements as a means of luring, retaining, controlling, and assisting groups of agricultural immigrants. This made it possible for some ethnic groups at least to postpone immediate assimilation to the prevailing British values and institutions established by the earliest settlers from Ontario. It was also easier for these groups to maintain their particular forms of religious expression in their new homeland.

The extent to which different ethnocultural communities developed an institutional infrastructure for their cultural activities varied, partly in relation to their own priorities with regard to external circumstances. Aboriginal practices were often conducted secretly after the legal banning of their rites and dances beginning in the 1880s. Some groups, Icelandic residents of Manitoba, for instance, emphasized language maintenance and hence literary production, while others, including the large Ukrainian communities in all three provinces, fostered artistic production of many forms and developed institutions to promote and maintain them.

1900–1920

The populations of the five largest prairie cities increased very rapidly between 1901 and 1916: Winnipeg (from 42,340 to 163,000), Regina (from 2,249 to 26,127), Saskatoon (from 113 to 21,048), Calgary (from 4,392 to 56,514), and Edmonton (from 4,176 to 53,846). As a result, by the end of the second decade western Canadian cities were able to support a range and level of musical activities that corresponded in quantity if not always in quality to that of eastern Canadian cities like Toronto, Montréal, and Québec City that had flourished since the early nineteenth century. Calgary, Edmonton, and Saskatoon supported operatic societies that gave regular performances of light operas and Gilbert and Sullivan operettas until 1920 (figure 1). Winnipeg was known for the excellence and abundance of its choral ensembles, most notably the Winnipeg Male Voice Choir (1916), although it was not alone in supporting oratorio choirs that regularly presented Handel's *Messiah* and other large choral works (figure 2).

FIGURE 1 Edmonton Operatic Society presenting Gilbert and Sullivan's *Trial by Jury* in Robertson Hall, 1905. Photo courtesy Provincial Archives of Alberta, E. Brown Collection.

FIGURE 2 Winnipeg Male Voice Choir departing on a U.S. tour, 1922. Photo courtesy Provincial Archives of Manitoba, Foote Collection. 1951.

Festivals

Perhaps because of the population diversity, festivals seem to have thrived on the prairies, arguably earlier and more tenaciously than in other regions. The Gimli Icelandic Festival, for instance, was founded in 1890. The idea of competitive music festivals had originated in Great Britain, but the first such festival to be held in Canada occurred in 1908 in Edmonton in a clear demonstration of the independence and self-reliance that living so near the frontier required. Governor General Earl Grey had encouraged musical and dramatic groups from across Canada to come to Ottawa for a festival of the arts. As worthy as this idea might have been, it was difficult for the musicians in Edmonton to see their way clear to participating in such a remote event, so they decided to establish their own festival. The festival was open to competitors from across Alberta and ended with a concert by a mass choir and orchestra. The idea spread quickly to Saskatchewan, where the first festival was held in Regina in 1909, after which it moved around to other large centers in the province. The first Winnipeg festival was held in 1919 under the auspices of the Men's Musical Club.

Until the 1960s the adjudicators for the larger festivals were drawn mainly from Great Britain, a demonstration of the strong British influence in Canada's musical life in the first half of the century. The festival associations coordinated their events so that the adjudicators could be shared. More recently the British adjudicators have been replaced by Canadian musicians. The festival associations produce a syllabus each year that influences the annual choice of repertoire of many music students and school music classes in each province. The Federation of Canadian Music Festivals (FCMF) was established in 1926, sponsoring conferences and providing adjudicators for affiliated associations until 1983. Since 1972 local festivals affiliated with the FCMF can send their winners to a provincial competition, from which the winners move on to a national competition sponsored by the Canadian Imperial Bank of Commerce. Competitors at all levels compete for trophies, scholarships, and cash prizes.

Women's musical clubs

Another important institution in the early part of the century was the women's musical club, first established in the East but followed soon by women's musical clubs in Winnipeg (1894), Calgary (1904), Regina (1907), Edmonton (1908), and Saskatoon (1912) [see Two Views of Music in Toronto, p. 1207]. These clubs began as meetings in the homes of wives of well-to-do citizens to discuss music and the arts, to hear talks given by local musicians, and to encourage performances by local musicians. Before long they began to organize recitals by touring artists, in many cases providing the main concert series in their city for the next few decades. Another valuable contribution took the form of raising funds in order to provide promising young artists with scholarships. Although most of the clubs had disbanded by 1980, they played an important role in the musical life of the prairies in the first half of the century.

Important musical leaders

The almost exclusive use of British musicians as adjudicators in Canadian music festivals is indicative of a thoroughgoing British influence in all aspects of Canadian music in the first half of the century. Trained as singers, organists, instrumentalists, and composers in English conservatories and cathedral choir schools, musical immigrants from Great Britain fanned out across the country to become leaders wherever they settled. Healy Willan (1880–1968), who came to Toronto in 1913, is the best known of these men, but the prairie provinces had their share. W. H. Anderson (1882–1955) came to Winnipeg from London in 1910, where he had a career as a composer, singing teacher, and choral conductor for more than four decades. Vernon Barford (1876–1963) arrived in Edmonton in 1900 and served All Saints Anglican Cathedral and the wider community for more than fifty years as pianist, conductor, composer, teacher and organizer of festivals and operatic and choral societies. W. J. Hendra (1878–1966) was a Welsh singer and violist who came to Edmonton in 1906 and worked as a singing teacher, conductor of the Edmonton Male Choir (1917–1941), and member of the Edmonton Symphony Orchestra for the next sixty years. Similar work was done by Clifford Higgins (1876–1951) in Calgary, who arrived in 1920, and by Frank Laubach (1857–1923) in Regina. Laubach was a bandmaster, cellist, conductor, and composer from Scotland who arrived in Regina in 1904 and proceeded to organize the Philharmonic and Orchestral Society. Their activities as teachers of a generation of Canadian musicians who would take their places by the middle of the century were as important as their contributions as practicing musicians.

Having just acquired concentrations of population sufficient to support orchestral subscription series and regular operatic performances, the region was hit very hard by the Great Depression (1929–1939).

1920–1950

The years from the end of World War I to the end of World War II were difficult years for musical organizations on the prairies. Having just acquired concentrations of population sufficient to support orchestral subscription series and regular operatic performances, the region was hit very hard by the Great Depression (1929–1939). The effects of the Depression were magnified in the West by low prices for agricultural products, the foundation of the prairie economy, and by drought, dust storms, and grasshopper infestations that devastated crops and produced widespread unemployment, poverty, and radical political reform movements.

The history of orchestras in Edmonton was typical of this period. The Edmonton Symphony Orchestra was established in 1920 and gave annual subscription concerts until 1933, when it ceased to exist until resurrected in 1952. The Regina Symphony Orchestra was one of the few to have an uninterrupted history from its beginnings in 1926. Community orchestras continued to provide access to orchestral music, especially of the lighter kind, but these groups tended to be somewhat ephemeral.

Opera companies were even more difficult to sustain. While amateur productions of Gilbert and Sullivan operettas and other light operas still took place, the development of opera associations presenting a series of operas every season did not occur until after 1950. The most successful undertaking between the wars was the Edmonton Civic Opera Society (1935–1971), founded and conducted by Mrs. J. B. Carmichael, a violinist, singer, and conductor trained in Chicago who emigrated to Edmonton in 1920.

Broadcasting

In spite of the difficulties faced by those trying to sustain musical life on the prairies during this period, a number of significant developments took place. One of the most important was the arrival of radio broadcasts in the West. The founding of the Canadian Broadcasting Corporation (CBC) in 1936 made it possible for prairie residents to hear both Canadian and international broadcasts of orchestral, operatic, vocal, and chamber music. Opera productions from New York's Metropolitan Opera continue to be broadcast to this day. The CBC also established regional broadcast orchestras. The CBC Winnipeg Orchestra became a permanent ensemble in 1947 after seven years as a string ensemble. Orchestras and chamber groups in other centers were broadcast as well, although less frequently. The CBC thus gave employment to musicians, sustained orchestras in several centers, and permitted audiences that otherwise would not have been able to attend concerts to hear a wide variety of music.

Struggles to establish broadcasting in languages other than English began almost with the advent of radio. For far-flung French communities on the prairies, for instance, the establishment of French-language radio was a hard-fought victory in the 1940s (Gareau 1990).

School broadcasts

School music broadcasts began in Manitoba as early as 1927, when orchestral rehearsal sessions were broadcast across the province from CKY, a private station in Winnipeg.

They continued until 1949. Regular broadcasts on the CBC began in 1941 when the four western provinces agreed to share school broadcast programming. Each province also produced its own programs. The national CBC network produced music appreciation programming that included orchestral and operatic concerts. While schools in larger centers may have had music programs and specialized music teachers, these were rare in rural schools, and the broadcasts provided instruction in music rudiments and singing and allowed children to hear music they would otherwise not have been able to experience (figure 3).

Piano teachers

School music programs try to instill a love and understanding of music in students and provide opportunities for group music making in orchestral and choral programs, but the foundation of musical performance in the North American context rests with students receiving instruction on their instruments from teachers working in conservatories or in private studios. By far the largest number of such students study the piano, and in each region there were piano teachers who established reputations for excellence. Eva Clare (1884–1961) was born in Neepawa, Manitoba, studied in Berlin and New York, and began teaching in Winnipeg in 1918. She was a prime mover in the organizing of the Manitoba Registered Music Teachers Association and was director of music at the University of Manitoba from 1937 until her retirement in 1949. Lyell Gustin (1895–1988) was born in Sherbrooke, Québec, studied in Chicago and New York, and began teaching in Saskatoon in 1920. In over sixty years of teaching his studio produced a number of well-known Canadian pianists. Gladys Egbert (1896–1968) was born near Brandon, Manitoba, studied in London, and in 1914 established a studio in Calgary, where she remained Calgary's most important piano teacher for fifty years. The only one of this group not born in Canada, Jenny Lerouge LeSaunier (1886–1971), was born in Brussels. She studied in Paris and Berlin and established a studio in Edmonton in 1922, where she became a prominent teacher for the next half-century. Early musical leaders among other ethnocultural communities included Ukrainians Vasile Avramenko and Oleksander Koshetz (1875–1994), the latter an important Winnipeg teacher who started his career in the 1920s.

FIGURE 3   Sister Francesca and her recorder class, Saskatchewan school broadcast, 1959. Courtesy Saskatchewan Archives Board.

Examining boards

The efforts of most young music students in Canada for much of the century have revolved around preparations for conservatory examinations leading at the highest level to an Associate or Licentiate diploma. Each level consists of a practical examination accompanied by examinations in music theory and history. Examining boards publish syllabuses and have also sponsored the publication of collections of graded examination pieces. The idea was borrowed from Great Britain, where the Associated Board of the Royal Schools of Music was the primary examining body. Although the Associated Board did operate in Canada as well, Canadian conservatories were quick to establish their own examining boards.

The largest and most influential of these was the Toronto Conservatory of Music (Royal Toronto Conservatory of Music [RTCM] after 1947). Examiners would be sent out to local centers across the country, where they might give master classes and recitals as well. The RTCM was and remains the largest examining board in the prairies, but in 1936 music educators in three prairie provinces, concerned about a multitude of examining bodies, inconsistent standards, and the flow of fees to Toronto, Montréal, and London, decided to establish an examining board that would be tailored to western Canadian needs, especially those of music teachers and students in rural and northern areas. Affiliated for much of the time with the departments of music of the seven prairie universities, the Western Board of Music was a force in music instruction in the four western provinces for more than thirty years.

1950 TO THE PRESENT

The second half of the twentieth century witnessed the development of a full range of musical activities across the prairies. Contributing factors were the relative affluence of the past fifty years, an influx of well-educated European immigrants for whom attending operas and going to concerts are a necessary part of a civilized life, and the growth of private and government bodies that have provided funding for musical activities. The large urban centers have professional or semiprofessional symphony orchestras that sponsor annual series of subscription concerts, perform school and CBC broadcasts, and provide instrumentalists for operatic, chamber, and choral concerts in their communities as well (figure 4). Opera associations have been established in Winnipeg (Rainbow Stage, 1954; Manitoba Opera Association, 1969), Edmonton (1963), Cal-

FIGURE 4   Calgary Philharmonic Orchestra in the Jack Singer Concert Hall, 1995. Photo courtesy the Calgary Philharmonic Orchestra

gary (1972), and Saskatoon (1978), offering three or four operas a year. Culturally specific institutions such as the large Ukrainian festivals—which still attract huge numbers—also began in this period. Universities in the larger cities have fully developed music programs, including graduate degrees, and community colleges in smaller centers have music programs of varying sizes. Universities have also been the loci for composition on the prairies, providing employment as teachers of theory and composition for composers.

Arts councils

In response to the recommendation of the Massey Commission, a royal commission investigating the development of the arts, literature, and science in Canada, the Canada Council was formed in 1957. Funded by annual grants from Parliament, the Council has established over one hundred programs that support individual artists and composers and arts organizations and a touring office that helps to make the arts accessible in all parts of the country. Individual provinces have established arts councils that perform a similar function within provinces. The Saskatchewan Arts Board (1948) preceded the Canada Council by a decade and has worked to encourage greater participation in the arts throughout the province and to support and encourage professional activities. The Manitoba Arts Council (1965) assists nonprofit arts organizations, commissions works by Manitoba composers, and funds artists-in-the-schools and community programs. The Alberta Cultural Development Branch (1946), now Alberta Culture and Multiculturalism, has a similar agenda. It also publishes a list of artists willing to tour the province and provides assistance in coordinating tours.

At the beginning of the twenty-first century

As the name change of the Alberta arts board suggests, consciousness of the diversity of musical practices on the prairies is slowly being transformed at the beginning of the twenty-first century. Asian students arriving from Hong Kong and elsewhere have taken to the examination system and the competitive festivals with verve and relish. Mennonite choirs have taken the singing traditions they brought with them to the grasslands of Manitoba from Russia to Winnipeg, where they are now front and center in the performance of large choral works in the city. The children and grandchildren of Ukrainian immigrants who settled on the open prairie in sod huts at the beginning of the twentieth century have entered the concert halls of Canada and the world. At the same time, many of these groups have retained aspects of their traditional musical identity. There is now a multitude of sounds, sounds that are beginning to penetrate even the staid and tradition-bound symphonic and operatic halls. The days of community socials where only the songs of the British Isles would be sung are now just a distant memory.

REFERENCES

Berg, Wesley. 1986. "Music in Edmonton, 1880–1905." *Canadian University Music Review* 7:141–170.

Berg, Wesley, and Gerry Paulsen. 1997. "Mrs. J. B. Carmichael and the Edmonton Civic Opera Society, 1935–1971." *Canadian University Music Review* 17:30–48.

Eagle, John A. 1989. *The Canadian Pacific Railway and the Development of Western Canada, 1896–1914.* Kingston: McGill–Queen's University Press.

Frances, R. Douglas, and Howard Palmer, eds. 1992. *The Prairie West: Historical Readings.* Edmonton: Pica Pica Press.

Friesen, Gerald. 1984. *The Canadian Prairies: A History.* Toronto: University of Toronto Press.

Gareau, Laurier. 1990. *Le défi de la radio francaise en Saskatchewan.* Regina: La Société historique de la Saskatchewan.

Kallmann, Helmut. 1960. *A History of Music in Canada 1534–1914.* Toronto: University of Toronto Press.

Kallmann, Helmut, Gilles Potvin, and Kenneth Winters, eds. 1992. *Encyclopedia of Music in Canada.* 2nd ed. Toronto: University of Toronto Press.

Snapshot: Winnipeg Festivals
Pauline Greenhill

The Winnipeg Folk Festival
Folklorama

Festivals include a variety of very different kinds of events—some sacred, some profane; some private, some public; some innovative, some traditional. Alessandro Falassi defines festival as "a periodically recurrent, social occasion in which, through a multiplicity of forms and a series of coordinated events, [members] participate directly or indirectly and to various degrees [and where] members of a whole community, united by ethnic, linguistic, religious, historical bonds, and sharing a worldview" participate together. (Falassi 1987:2) [see Blurring the Boundaries of Social and Musical Identities, p. 322].

Music is fundamental to most festivals, where it serves to mark transitions, focus ritual attention, allow competitive displays of skill, and indicate a time set apart from the ordinary. It can enhance festival aims and purposes or provide a focus for these events. In Winnipeg, Manitoba, Canada, festivals thrive throughout the year, because they attract locals and outsiders alike and because they appeal to a range of tastes and sociocultural groupings. (A full list of festivals across Canada is published annually by the Canadian Society for Traditional Music in its *Bulletin*.)

Summer events like the Fringe Theater festival and A Taste of Manitoba are pivotal to the city's—and the province's—strategy to attract tourists. The nearest large city, Minneapolis, is an eight-hour drive away; the nearest Canadian city, Calgary, is even farther. So Winnipeg draws audiences from a quite extensive area—albeit sparsely populated—in both Canada and the United States. And while many music-related festivals take place during the summer's good weather, Winnipeg's challenging winters are also a time for festival and musical activities. The success of winter festivals like the New Music festival and the Festival Du Voyageur (French Manitoban) reflects residents' need to defy the freezing climate and enjoy the warmth of sociability.

Although many events focus on musical styles and traditions—the new music and jazz festivals, for example—almost every Winnipeg festival incorporates music in some way. As might be expected, given the city's multicultural population, music-focused festivals in Winnipeg highlight a wide range of genres: classical European, traditional, jazz, and so on.

THE WINNIPEG FOLK FESTIVAL

The Winnipeg Folk Festival (WFF) (figure 1) makes music its focus but includes other elements such as craft sales. To avoid the tedious "What is folk music?" question, the WFF characterizes its "folk" as "people and music." When the July weather is fine and the Northern Prairie skies a clear blue—and even sometimes when they are not—the location of the festival, Birds Hill Provincial Park, some forty kilometers distance from the city, becomes the temporary home of thousands of Winnipeggers and others. Many camp out there for the entire duration from Thursday to Sunday. The WFF is the quintessential must-do event for the midsummer and also the main festival venue for traditional, revival, folk, roots, or world music in the city.

The WFF began in 1974 under the direction of Mitch Podolak. It has been an artistic and popular success ever since and has survived artistic and financial crises that destroyed many of its Canadian and American predecessors. Some 25,000 to 30,000 people from Winnipeg and beyond—almost one-third of the audience is American—attend annually. Over one thousand volunteers work, many year-round, to ensure the event's success.

The festival's musical ideology is resolutely pluralist, but there is no apparent attempt to represent any particular geographic region or series of groups. One year, the brochure's musical categories were Brittany, Blues, Women in Celtic Music, World Music, Singer-Songwriters, In the Tradition, and On the Edge. Current artistic Director Pierre Guerin commented that while he tries to address the WFF's various constituencies, often with no preconceived concept of the kinds of music he wants to include, usually "something else emerges that happened without my even realizing that it was there. It does take on a life of its own" (Guerin 1995).

Performers are invited primarily on musical and aesthetic grounds. Yet Guerin avoids a star system that would favor the Anglo North American mainstream. Although other festivals book big names, Guerin says, "Two years ago we removed the performers' names entirely from the poster . . . to basically send out as a message. . . . 'Don't worry. We pick good music. We have for twenty-three years. Don't worry about that part. What you have to think about is that this is a fairly unique context that you can experience'" (1995).

FIGURE I   From the main stage, Winnipeg Folk Festival, 1998. Photo by David Landy.

The WFF counterposes, rather than separates, cultural differences. There are four main stage evenings (Thursday through Sunday) and three days of workshops (Friday through Sunday) (figure 2). Thus musics and performances not suitable for large concert presentations find another venue; indeed, the majority of WFF performers do not get a main stage gig. Solo and group performances are often presented simultaneously. Most groups and individual performers get half-hour morning or afternoon concerts at one of the workshop stages, but there are also workshops that position very different musics under a single rubric.

Workshops can link musicians by instrument ("Mother Earth's Heartbeat [Percussion Jam]") or place ("Yes, But It's a Dry Cold!!! [Manitoba Songwriters]"). They can be serious ("Singing Our Way into the New Millennium") or more lighthearted ("My Dog Ate My Database . . . or Was It the Other Way Around [Life in the Late '90s]"). Indeed, the connections can be quite arbitrary, as in the recurring alphabet series ("S Is for Shetland's Young Heritage; Sisa Pacari"). Workshops can turn into mini concerts, without interaction or conversation—musical or otherwise—between performers, but they can also be sources for novel personal and musical combinations and discourses. Just as each audience member quite literally composes his or her own festival by selecting workshops, those who present workshops can compose different sorts of experiences for themselves within that structure.

The evening main stages can be seen as a series of sequential individual/group presentations or as whole choreographed events. They offer in turn very different musical sources and aesthetics—The Nields to Steve Riley and the Mamou Playboys to Punjabi by Nature. Audiences can, of course, walk away from, talk during, sleep through, or otherwise ignore any of the music. But the possibility for a synthesis is available at the listeners' pleasure. Artistic Director Guerin commented, "You can feel the audience out there working as opposed to just sitting there saying 'OK, come on, entertain me, and make it snappy.' . . . It takes on a life of its own and becomes so much more than anything you could have imagined" (1995).

The Sunday evening main stage finale brings a variety of performers together with the audience in song. Although what they sing ("Wild Mountain Thyme," "The Mary Ellen Carter," "Hard Times," and "Amazing Grace") may represent white European North American sensibilities, the festival's final invocation is to collectivity and to a rapprochement between diverse performers and their implicitly diverse audiences.

FOLKLORAMA

The WFF presents professional or professional-caliber music in styles and contexts that are palatable to mainstream bourgeois tastes. In contrast, the annual multicultural Folklorama, usually held (since 1970) for two weeks in August, tends to present more varied amateur fare. The quality of music may be extremely disparate from one location to another, but each pavilion is organized and sponsored by local community members, usually through ethnic group societies. This means that the music and musicians are chosen by a given group to represent itself, not, as in the WFF, by someone outside the group for more purely aesthetic or musical reasons.

Yet Folklorama is not primarily about self-presentation; instead, it combines local boosterism with big corporate sponsorship to create a tourist event. What was originally conceived as a one-time celebration of Manitoba's centennial as a province has become a self-termed extravaganza with as many as forty-five pavilions and more than twenty thousand volunteers. In pavilions located at different venues throughout the city—mainly in ethnic society halls, community centers, and public education buildings—various ethnic, linguistic, national, and/or geographical groupings are showcased.

Some groups have more than one venue, such as the Pearl of the Orient Philippine Pavilion and Philippine Pavilion–Nayong Pilipino, or the Ireland/Irish Pavilion and Isle of the Shamrock–Ireland Pavilion. One might expect that cultural distinctiveness within ethnic groups provided the impetus for multiple pavilions, but some pavilion organizers feel that profit is the primary motive. Such splitting of community resources is not problematic for the larger ethnic communities in Winnipeg; it can, however, severely strain the volunteer pool in smaller ones. Throughout, the distinctiveness of cultural presentations is mitigated by the rigid Folklorama structure. Contrasts within and between groups are masked by common presentation of three elements: music/dance, food/drink, and the display and sale of crafts.

To give Folklorama its due, it is remarkably successful at representing geographic and national "there" as actually "here," and ethnic and cultural "other" as truly part of the "self." Folklorama's venues are actually in Winnipeg (unlike the WFF's rural location). From pavilion to pavilion, musical performers seem equally drawn from home countries ("Back by popular demand from Paraguay is the acclaimed, internationally renowned harpist Ramon Romero"), from other areas of North America ("Chicago's Polonia choir and dance group will perform on stage"; "Celebrate with Toronto's Greek Folk Dancing Group"), and from the local context ("Experience the sound of Winnipeg's famous Hinode Taiko drumming group"). Although Folklorama's governing body has reportedly resisted attempts to extend its inclusion of sociocultural groupings (for example, having a Deaf Culture or Queer Culture pavilion), the event does aim to represent and express Winnipeg's sociocultural and linguistic diversity.

Further, the WFF is primarily a series of performances by professional musicians; there are few opportunities for those attending it to be part of the music making (although dancing is encouraged). But many Folklorama pavilions explicitly include audience participation in musical activities: the German pavilion invites attendees to "sing along and dance beneath the big top outdoor tent"; in the Serbian pavilion one can "join in the famous Kolo dance" and at the Greek Islands pavilion "participate in a 'Zorba the Greek' dance lesson"; both Philippine pavilions advertise karaoke; and so on. However, visitors are hustled in and out of the pavilions for shows presented at standard times, thus containing their experience in time and space.

Folklorama and the WFF are by no means representative of the totality of Winnipeg festivals, but they give some idea of the range of events associated with the city. Clearly, while reflecting the makeup of city's population, Winnipeg festivals also express, rehearse, and sometimes even exacerbate some of the conflicts that inevitably arise between individuals and groups. Nevertheless, in their variety, each provides an unusual series of musical alternatives.

—PAULINE GREENHILL

REFERENCES

Falassi, Alessandro. 1987. "Festival Definition and Morphology." *In Time Out of Time: Essays on the Festival,* ed. Alessandro Falassi, 1–10. Albuquerque: University of New Mexico Press.

Guerin, Pierre. Personal interview. 1995.

Music of Christian Minorities
Wesley Berg

Mennonites
Hutterites

Both the policy of bloc immigration and the relative isolation of communities on the prairies facilitated the maintenance of particular forms of religious expression by various groups in their new Canadian homeland. Architectural signs of this phenomenon are the domes of Ukrainian Orthodox churches in rural Alberta and Manitoba, the temple in Cardston, Alberta, where Mormons began to settle in southern Alberta in 1887, the bell towers of Lutheran churches in Icelandic and German communities, and the simple meetinghouses of Old Colony Mennonites in southern Manitoba and northern Alberta.

MENNONITES

Mennonites are the descendants of the Anabaptists of the early Reformation, emphasizing adult baptism, pacifism, and separation of church and state. One portion of the Mennonites of North America came from Switzerland and South Germany to Pennsylvania in the seventeenth century, with two thousand of them moving to Ontario after the American Revolution. The other portion originated in Holland and northern Germany, fled persecution by finding refuge in Poland, migrated to southern Russia in the late eighteenth century, and then came to North America in three waves of immigration: to Kansas, Minnesota, and Manitoba after 1874; to Canada in the 1920s after the Bolshevik Revolution; and finally, after World War II, having come from Russia to Germany with the retreating German army after 1943, they scattered across Canada, which by this time was much more uniformly settled than when the first two waves arrived.

The history of music among the Mennonites on the prairies is characterized by two sharply diverging trajectories. The larger portion has moved toward accommodation and assimilation, while a smaller group has emphasized reaction and isolation. Mennonites in Russia sang chorales in an oral tradition until the middle of the nineteenth century, when reforms leading to musical literacy using numbers, the equivalent of sol-fa syllables, as a substitute for conventional notation, the adoption of the evangelical hymnody of the late nineteenth century, and the formation of choirs in churches were instituted. These reforms were just becoming widespread when the first Mennonites came to Manitoba in 1874. They separated very early into a group that wished to use the new methods in their congregations and another group, now known as the Old Colony Mennonites, which saw the move to Manitoba as an opportunity to

FIGURE I　Title page, hymnal of the Old Colony Mennonites.

return to and maintain the old way of singing as part of a concerted effort to avoid worldly influences in all aspects of life.

Old Colony Mennonites

Like Hutterites, the Old Order Amish of Pennsylvania, and the Old Order Mennonites of Waterloo County in southern Ontario, Old Colony Mennonites are characterized by their simple, austere clothing and rural way of life and by their avoidance of technological developments that might compromise their attempts to remain separated from the world. Unlike their more liberal colleagues, who, although they retained many distinctive aspects of their ethnic and religious heritage, were willing to accommodate and assimilate such new ideas as English-language instruction in schools and Sunday schools in church, the conservative Mennonites resisted such changes, making further treks to Saskatchewan, northern Alberta, Mexico, Belize, and, most recently, Texas, in search of areas where they could live in isolation. Their music is a reflection of this very traditional outlook on life. Social songs are mostly in Low German, the language of every day (Klassen 1989). The music of the church consists of Lutheran chorales contained in a hymnal reprinted in the style of the first German hymnal prepared for the Mennonites of Polish Prussia in 1767, sung to melodies transmitted in an oral tradition going back to the late eighteenth century (figure 1). The melodies are melismatic (many notes to one syllable) and rhythmically amorphous as a result of several centuries of oral transmission and are led by a group of song leaders singing in a slow, stentorian vocal style (Berg 1996).

Into the mainstream

Although willing to adopt many of the advantages that their new country had to offer them, Mennonites in the more liberal group still lived mostly traditional rural lives until 1950, concentrated around Steinbach in eastern Manitoba, in south central Manitoba, and in areas north of Saskatoon and south of Swift Current in Saskatchewan and north and southeast of Calgary in Alberta. Music took place in the home as hymns and German and Low German folk songs were sung, and in church, where hearty congregational singing in four-part harmony and the nurturing of choirs filled with the young people of the congregations were the primary avenues of musical expression. Congregational and choral singing have been associated with Mennonites and can be seen as one means of creative expression in a life governed by the principles of hard work, frugality, and humility and as an expression of the importance of family unity, both biological and congregational. Itinerant choral conductors spent summers in the 1930s and 1940s traveling from area to area holding choral festivals and workshops for local choir conductors, most of whom would have had little or no formal musical training (figures 2, 3).

FIGURE 2　Choral festival in Southern Manitoba, 14 June 1936. Photo courtesy Mrs. Susie Penner.

FIGURE 3   K. H. Neufeld conducting a mass choir in Southern Manitoba, 1935. Photo courtesy of Mrs. Susie Penner.

Since 1950 urbanization has been a major influence in the lives of prairie Mennonites. They have availed themselves of the opportunities for musical education in private studios, high schools, and universities, moving to an ever-increasing professionalism that would have been viewed with suspicion by their grandfathers (figure 4). However, private high schools (Rosthern Junior College, Mennonite Collegiate Institute, Westgate Collegiate Institute, Mennonite Brethren Collegiate Institute) and Bible colleges (Canadian Mennonite Bible College and Mennonite Brethren Bible College, now Concord College) have added a distinctive Mennonite flavor to the training of many Mennonite musicians, with an emphasis on choral singing that has made the Mennonite Oratorio Choir associated with the two Winnipeg Bible colleges a prominent organization in that city's musical life.

Music among the Mennonites of the prairies at the end of the twentieth century displayed a wide range of expression, from revivals of traditional singing of Low German songs, to the acceptance of the latest trends in church music as promulgated by television evangelists, to professional choirs and singers like Ben Hepner, Tracy Dahl, and Henriette Schellenberg, who have performed at the highest international levels.

FIGURE 4   North Star Mennonite Church Band, Drake, Saskatchewan, n.d. Notice the white patches on performers' foreheads where workday caps had sheltered them from the sun. Courtesy of Saskatchewan Archives Board.

They live by the precepts of their founder, Peter Rideman, who instructed them to sing to the glory of God and not for "carnal pleasure."

HUTTERITES

Hutterites trace their origins back to the earliest days of the Reformation. Theologically similar to the Mennonites, they are distinguished by their commitment to communal living that has survived essentially unchanged to this day. After moving about Europe for centuries in an attempt to find a place where they could live free from persecution, they left Russia in 1874, settling in South Dakota, and moved to the Canadian prairies following World War I after receiving harsh treatment because of their refusal to participate in military service. There are now more than two hundred colonies in the three prairie provinces, each containing an average of fourteen families. They combine a life in closed communities that bans access to mass media and other forms of entertainment with highly mechanized farming methods that have allowed them to prosper. They live by the precepts of their founder, Peter Rideman, who instructed them to sing to the glory of God and not for "carnal pleasure."

Their hymnody, along with that of the Old Order Amish, dates back to the mid-sixteenth century. The main collection consists of hymns written by early Anabaptists and Hutterites, many of whom became martyrs. The hymns may contain dozens of stanzas, all of which are sung during performance. The tunes are mostly sixteenth-century secular German folk songs, but also Meistersinger songs and Reformation hymns preserved in an unbroken oral tradition. These hymns are sung primarily in worship services. Singing is important in everyday life as one of the primary forms of recreation and learning, especially for women as they go about their household duties, for children as they are taught the ways of the colony, and for families in their evening devotions. Here they use other collections of more recent hymns, including the hymnal used by the Old Colony Mennonites.

REFERENCES

Berg, Wesley. 1985. *From Russia with Music: A Study of the Mennonite Choral Singing Tradition in Canada.* Winnipeg: Hyperion Press.

———. 1988. "From Piety to Sophistication: Developments in Canadian–Mennonite Music after World War II." *Journal of Mennonite Studies* 6:89–99.

———. 1996. "Hymns of the Old Colony Mennonites and the Old Way of Singing." *The Musical Quarterly* 80:71–117.

Brednich, Rolf Wilhelm. 1977. *Mennonite Folklife and Folklore: A Preliminary Report.* Canadian Center for Folk Culture Studies, Paper no. 22. Ottawa: National Museums of Canada.

———. 1981. "Beharrung und Wandel im Liedgut der hutterischen Brüder: Ein Beitrag zur empirischen Hymnologie." *Jahrbuch für Volksliedforschung* 26:44–60.

Burkhart, Charles. 1953. "The Church Music of the Old Order Amish and Old Colony Mennonites." *The Mennonite Quarterly Review* 27:34–54.

Driedger Leo, ed. 1978. *The Canadian Ethnic Mosaic: A Quest for Identity.* Toronto: McClelland and Stewart.

———. 1987. *Ethnic Canada: Identities and Inequalities.* Toronto: Copp Clark Pitman.

Epp, Frank H. 1974. *Mennonites in Canada, 1786–1920: The History of a Separate People.* Toronto: Macmillan of Canada.

———. 1982. *Mennonites in Canada, 1920–1940: A People's Struggle for Survival.* Toronto: Macmillan of Canada.

Kauffman, J. Howard, and Leo Driedger. 1991. *The Mennonite Mosaic: Identity and Modernization.* Scottdale, Pa.: Herald Press.

Klassen, Doreen Helen. 1989. *Singing Mennonite: Low German Songs among the Mennonites.* Winnipeg: The University of Manitoba Press.

Martens, Helen. 1968. "Hutterite Songs: The Origins and Aural Transmission of Their Melodies from the Sixteenth Century." Ph.D. dissertation, Columbia University.

———. 1974. "Hutterite Melodies from the Strassburg Psalter." *Mennonite Quarterly Review* 48:201–214.

Redekop, Calvin. 1969. *The Old Colony Mennonites: Dilemmas of Ethnic Minority Life.* Baltimore: The John Hopkins University Press.

Regehr, T. D. 1996. *Mennonites in Canada, 1939–1970: A People Transformed.* Toronto: University of Toronto Press.

Ukrainian Music
Brian Cherwick

Ukrainian Musical Genres
Instrumental Ensembles
Contexts
Electronic Media and Commercial Recordings

Ukrainian immigration to Canada occurred in three predominant waves: the first and largest beginning in the 1890s and lasting until World War I; the second during the interwar years; and the third following World War II. The first two waves of immigration, comprising predominantly peasant agriculturists, settled primarily in rural bloc settlements in the Canadian prairie provinces.

UKRAINIAN MUSICAL GENRES

Music in many forms has played an important role in the social life of Ukrainians in Canada. It is an integral part of most calendar and life-cycle rituals. Often these musical forms continue to be maintained long after their ritual functions have lost their significance. While the role of instrumental ensembles or orchestras is of central importance for the completion of many social rituals and for entertainment, many of other genres are also significant parts of the Ukrainian musical picture.

Choral singing is perhaps the most widespread of all Ukrainian musical genres. Multipart singing is often recognized as one of the most distinguishing features of Ukrainian culture (Iashchenko 1962). It is connected to religious life as an integral part of the eastern Christian liturgy and services (Matsenko 1973), and to social and political life. Choral singing as part of Christmas celebrations was noted among the most popular activities of the early Ukrainian settlers to Canada (Boulton 1942). Notable choirs in western Canada are the O. Koshetz Choir of Winnipeg and the Dnipro Choir of Edmonton.

One of the first systematically organized forms of music making to appear among the Ukrainian community in Canada was the mandolin orchestra. The first such orchestra was founded in Winnipeg in 1921, with similar groups established soon after at Ukrainian Labor and Farmer Temple Association halls across the prairies (Kravchuk 1996). Similar string and mandolin orchestras were organized at schools and other halls, often providing the first musical instruction for many (Klymasz 1992; Lupul 1984). Later, wind bands also became popular in some areas.

Drama productions offered another vehicle for musical expression. Many community groups staged performances of simple plays complete with music, singing, and dancing, as well as more ambitious musicals (Klymasz 1982). The development of staged folk dance provided yet another genre of performance with music as a central component.

Festivals provide an array of performance possibilities, ranging from concert-style grandstand performances, to music for late night dances, to performances on parade floats.

INSTRUMENTAL ENSEMBLES

The small instrumental ensembles of violin, *tsymbaly* 'hammered dulcimer', and drum popular in the villages of western Ukraine served as the prototype for most similar ensembles among the early Ukrainians settlers in western Canada. This kind of instrumentation continued to serve as the core for western Canadian Ukrainian bands well into the 1970s.

As Ukrainians came into greater contact with North American musical styles some changes were made in the composition of their bands. Ukrainian musicians in Canada have more recently been influenced by trends in popular music and have incorporated new instruments and new repertoires. The music performed by these bands still consists largely of traditional Ukrainian pieces; however, there has been an increasing emphasis on providing music for dancing rather than ritual music.

Because of its rural roots, Ukrainian traditional music was closely connected to other rural-based genres like American country music [see TWO VIEWS OF MUSIC, RACE, ETHNICITY, AND NATIONHOOD, p. 76]. Both share similar origins in acoustic string band music, with the violin or fiddle taking a prominent role. The popularity of country music in rural regions of western Canada led to the further development of this connection, with its ultimate manifestation occurring in the 1960s in the hybrid music performed by groups such as Mickey and Bunny and the Interlake Polka Kings (Klymasz 1972). While country music remains an important influence for Ukrainian bands, rural and Old Country connections are often mistaken for country connections by those outside the western Canadian community ("Metro Radomsky" 1981).

Another genre closely related to country music and equally significant was old-time music. Again, the prominence of the fiddle and the popularity of nationally known stars such as Don Messer and Andy DeJarlis had a profound influence on many Ukrainian Canadian violinists. The high profile visibility of Ukrainian Canadian fiddler Al Cherny on weekly broadcasts of CBC television's *The Tommy Hunter Show* helped solidify the link between Ukrainian and old-time fiddling. The music of sweet and swing dance bands was also of considerable influence. Local groups adopted not only the instrumentation and repertoire of such groups but also their modes of dress and stage presentation, such as sitting behind large wooden music stands.

As popular music changed, so did the repertoire of Ukrainian bands. As rock and other genres gained popularity, they also became part of the repertoire for bands in western Canada. For most Ukrainian bands, versatility has long been of central importance in securing work. In this way they are not unlike club date musicians working in other locations.

CONTEXTS

Weddings

Perhaps the most celebrated social event among Ukrainians is the wedding. In Ukraine, the traditional village wedding usually extended over several days, filled with ritual, feasting, music and dancing. Each action included ritual singing, accompanied by musicians. These musicians usually remained after the ceremonies to play music for dancing, which could last until the following morning.

Ukrainian wedding celebrations in Canada preserved patterns set in Ukraine. Weddings lasting several days continued to be held at the family homes of the couples being married. Special preparations were made for dancing outdoors with platforms or dance floors constructed in the farmhouses or in the barn. These traditions lasted into the 1950s, when the community hall became the preferred location for such large events (Klymasz 1992; Makuch 1988). Other prominent contexts for the performance of instrumental music were house parties, community dances, and annual church celebrations known as the *kram* or *praznyk*.

Festivals

Since the mid-1960s, ethnic folk festivals have assumed an increasingly important role as a forum for Ukrainian music. Currently in western Canada major Ukrainian festivals are presented at Dauphin, Manitoba (Canada's National Ukrainian Festival), and Vegreville, Alberta (Vegreville Ukrainian Pysanka Festival). Smaller festivals are held in Gardenton, Teulon, and Valley River in Manitoba; at Saskatoon, Foam Lake, and Prince Albert in Saskatchewan; and at Sherwood Park and the Ukrainian Cultural Heritage Village in Alberta. Ukrainian pavilions are also a part of multicultural festivals in Winnipeg (Folklorama), Regina (Mosaic), Saskatoon (Folkfest), and Edmonton (Heritage Days).

Festivals provide an array of performance possibilities, ranging from concert-style grandstand performances, to music for late night dances, to performances on parade floats. Musicians also demonstrate instruments. The festival is also the most likely forum for the exchange of ideas between musicians from various strata of the community.

ELECTRONIC MEDIA AND COMMERCIAL RECORDINGS

Commercial recordings have not only provided a further forum for musicians, they have helped unite and define the community. For the early immigrants a gramophone was among the first "luxury" items purchased (Klymasz 1991). The early commercial recordings produced by the large American firms (Columbia, OKeh, Stinson) often attempted to package not only the music but the dialogues and rituals of old country life (Spottswood 1982).

The recording industry

The development of an indigenous Canadian Ukrainian recording industry began at the end of the 1940s, when Alex Groshak of Winnipeg produced an album of Ukrainian songs performed by the Ukrainian Male Chorus (of Winnipeg) on the Quality Record label. The success of these recordings led him to start his own label, Regis Records, which recorded a number of Ukrainian dance bands from Manitoba.

The 1960s saw a boom in Ukrainian recording in Canada. Groshak established the highly successful V-Records label, producing recordings of artists from across the prairies and shipping those products around the world. His success spawned a number of similar competing labels, Galaxy, UK, and Eagle Records, among others. All focused principally on prairie dance bands and singers of traditional and ritual (primarily wedding) songs. In the 1970s, Heritage Records of Edmonton and Sunshine Records (and its later subsidiary Baba's Records) of Winnipeg also joined this market. Eventually numerous independent and self-produced products entered the market, and with the development of recording technology, an explosion of this "homegrown" type of product occured in the 1980s and especially the 1990s.

Radio

Radio is another medium that provides both a forum for musicians and a unifying force for the community. Broadcasts of Ukrainian programs began in Alberta on CKUA in the 1940s. CBC Radio occasionally aired programs of Ukrainian music and current events, with artists like fiddler Tommy Buick presenting regular live broadcasts. Eventually commercial radio stations, like CFCW of Camrose, Alberta, and CKDM of Dauphin, Manitoba, also began to broadcast Ukrainian programs. For many years *The Ukrainian Hour* with Dan Chomlak on CFCW was one of the top-rated shows of any kind in the Edmonton market and was rebroadcast in other markets, like Winnipeg and Regina. These broadcasts provided communities separated by immense distances with some common point of reference and helped to acquaint residents in one part of the country with the music of groups from another.

In the 1970s, full-time multilingual broadcasters entered the radio market. In Winnipeg, CKJS featured a daily Ukrainian program that was soon followed by a similar program on CKER in Edmonton. These programs continue to broadcast Ukrainian music while also informing the Ukrainian listening audience of current affairs and public events.

Ukrainian instrumental and vocal music is an integral part of Ukrainian life in western Canada. Once a popular form of leisure activity for many members of the community, it has increasingly become the realm of a shrinking body of specialists. Through live performance events like parties, dances, weddings, festivals, and club dates, Ukrainian musicians have had intimate interaction with the listening community. Through the media of commercial recordings and broadcasting, musicians reach a wider audience while drawing the community closer together.

REFERENCES

Avramenko, Vasile. 1947. *Ukrains'ki natsional'ni tanky, muzyka i strii: Ukrainian National Dances, Music and Costumes.* Published by the Author.

Balan, Jars. 1991. "Backdrop to an Era: The Ukrainian Canadian Stage in the Interwar Years." *Journal of Ukrainian Studies* 16(1–2):89–114.

Boulton, Laura. 1942. *Ukrainian Winter Holidays.* National Film Board of Canada. Film.

Iashchenko, Leonid. 1962. *Ukrains'ke narodne bahatoholossia.* Kyiv: Vydavnytstvo Akademii Nauk.

Klymasz, Robert B. 1972. "'Sounds You Never Before Heard': Ukrainian Country Music in Canada." *Ethnomusicology* 16(3):372–380.

———. 1976. "The Ethnic Folk Festival in North America Today." In *Ukrainsti v Amerykan'skomu ta Kanads'komu suspil'stakh* (Ukrainians in American and Canadian society), ed. Wsevolod Isajiw, 199–211. Jersey City: M. P. Kots Publishing.

———. 1982. "The Fine Arts." In *A Heritage in Transition: Essays in the History of Ukrainians in*

Canada, ed. Manoly R. Lupul, 281–295. Toronto: McClelland and Stewart.

———. 1991. *Art and Ethnicity: The Ukrainian Tradition in Canada.* Hull, P.Q.: Canadian Museum of Civilization.

———. 1992. *Svieto: Celebrating Ukrainian Canadian Ritual in East Central Alberta.* Edmonton: Alberta Culture and Multiculturalism Historic Resources Division.

Knysh, Zynovii. ed. 1992. *Na shliakhu do natsional'noi iednosty: Piatdesiat rokiv pratsi Ukrains'koho national'noho obiednannia, 1932–1982* (Toward national unity: Fifty years of service by the Ukrainian National Federation, 1932–1982). Toronto: Ukrains'ke National'ne Ob'iednannia Kanady Kraiova Ekzekutyva.

Kravchuk, Petro. 1996. *Our History: The Ukrainian Labor-Farmer Movement.* Toronto: Lugus.

Lupul, Manoly R., ed. 1984. *Visible Symbols: Cultural Expression among Canada's Ukrainians.* Edmonton: Canadian Institute of Ukrainian Studies.

Makuch, Andrij. 1978. "A Ukrainian Wolfman Jack." *Student,* 9 August.

———. 1988. "Narodni Domy in East Central Alberta." In *Continuity and Change: The Cultural Life of Alberta's First Ukrainians,* ed. Manoly R. Lupul, 202–210. Edmonton: Canadian Institute of Ukrainian Studies.

Matsenko, P. 1973. *Konspekt istorii ukrains'koi tserkovnoi muzyky* (A summary of the history of Ukrainian church music). Winnipeg: Vydavnytstvo Kolegii sv. Andreia.

"Metro Radomsky: Orchestra Leader of Ukrainian Country Music." 1981. *Forum* 47:8–10.

Spottswood, Richard. K. 1982. "Commercial Ethnic Recordings in the United States." In *Ethnic Recordings in America: A Neglected Heritage.* Studies in American Folklife, vol. 1. Washington, D.C.: American Folklife Center, Library of Congress.

Middle Eastern and Asian Music
Regula Burckhardt Qureshi
Brian Cherwick

Immigration
Multiculturalism

Across the Prairies, Middle Eastern and Asian music making is urban, concentrated in Edmonton, Calgary, and Winnipeg. Even within the region's brief history of settlement (little over one hundred years), this music making is recent and continuously evolving. Its growth and practice are intimately tied to governmental immigration and multiculturalism policies as well as wartime internment and professional recruitment for the following major Asian and Middle Eastern ethnocultural groups: Arab, Chinese, South Asian, Vietnamese, and Japanese.

IMMIGRATION

An Asian presence on the prairies began in the late nineteenth and early twentieth centuries with sporadic male immigration. First came the Chinese, who were brought to help build the railroad, and then the Arabs, who were willing to settle in northern Canadian areas to escape the Turkish draft. Both groups established small business-oriented communities in the major cities. Immigration from India followed much later, mainly in response to recruitment of teachers by the government during the 1950s and 1960s. Until the late 1960s the immigration quota for Asian countries was limited to one hundred per year, which kept numbers low and families nuclear. At that time a new and open immigration policy was established with a special focus on family reunification, which enabled Middle Eastern and Asian communities to grow in both numbers and cohesion. Also, beginning in the early 1970s, a liberalized refugee policy gave a further boost to Asian immigration. South Asians from Uganda, mainland Chinese fleeing the Cultural Revolution, Vietnamese, and, most recently, Chinese from Hong Kong added to and diversified the already thriving Asian cultural and musical presence on the Prairies. Japanese immigrants who were removed from the Canadian West Coast and resettled on the Prairies during World War II were a small but significant early presence.

MULTICULTURALISM

Cultural and musical activities thrived and were made public through the policy of multiculturalism practiced by both the federal and provincial governments since the early 1970s. Grants for ethnocultural groups were given to support cultural centers, associations, and performances, and institutions such as "heritage days" created a public

Beginning in the 1960s with small groups of disparate amateurs who wanted to keep their music alive, Indian musical activity was enhanced occasionally by a few Beatles-influenced local enthusiasts.

presence and mainstream audience for Middle Eastern and Asian music and dance. They also facilitated the building of intercommunity institutions for teaching and practicing social and religious heritage. What follows are musical sketches of several communities, based on the growing ethnomusicological research done at the University of Alberta. They can be considered cases of the general situation on the prairies.

South Asian music

The most prominent Asian musical presence on the Canadian prairies comes from India. Beginning in the 1960s with small groups of disparate amateurs who wanted to keep their music alive, Indian musical activity was enhanced occasionally by a few Beatles-influenced local enthusiasts. Forty years later Indian music is thriving, thanks to a composite web of support and commitment within the community but also in the wider society, including the University of Alberta, where an Indian music ensemble runs every year, offering Hindustani music through voice, *sitar* 'plucked lute', *tabla* 'paired drum', *sarangi* 'bowed lute', and flute. Within the community are several quasi-professional private teachers and a well-established school of music and dance. Most remarkable is the degree of second-generation competence, thanks to devoted parents who want their children to retain their culture, even sending them to India for a summer or to one of the Indian music schools on the Canadian West Coast. Voice and dance are preferred; both devotional songs (*bhajans*) and South Indian classical dance (*bharata natyam*) contribute to Hindu religious practice and representation. Some Sikh boys also learn the *tabla* in order to provide accompaniment to the scriptural hymns presented in the *gurdwara* 'place of worship'. Muslims generally stay away from formal music learning, but some of their children do chant religious hymns or even the Arabic verses of the Qur'an, a strictly religious activity, in contrast to the explicitly "musical" hymns of Hindus and Sikhs that motivate believers to learn music formally.

Core support and practice for Indian music, however, is located within the community, especially among North Indians, and its basis is both religious and social. Music is foundational to Hindu thought and to all South Asian devotional practice. In Hindu temples and Sikh *gurdwaras,* Sunday service resounds with religious hymns and chants (*kirtan, shabad*), accompanied by *tabla* and harmonium. Unaccompanied hymns are also central to Muslim devotional practice, especially among Shi'as and Ismailis.

Where Indian music really lives, however, is in homes, at the congenial social gatherings of first-generation South Asian Canadians, especially those from the Hindu–Urdu language areas. Favorites are poems set to music in the form of the ubiquitous *ghazal* 'art song' or of older film songs; both bring on nostalgia and above all a sense of shared delight and heightened occasion. Song performance is also an essential part of formal parties and especially weddings, including, of course, the traditional weddings songs sung by women to the beat of a barrel drum (*dholak*).

A musical practice deemed nonmusical and hence favored by Muslims is chanted Urdu and Hindi poetry, performed at formal but highly interactive recitals (*mushaira*).

The Canadian prairies harbor a number of competent amateur poets who present their verses in chanted tunes. In addition, renowned poets are invited to *mushairas* from North America as well as South Asia. As this poetry is savored aurally rather than by silent reading, good reciters present verses by other poets at "fake" *mushairas* and at other social gatherings, especially among Muslims who consider these chanted verses poetry, not music.

Finally, music is a centerpiece of Indian national culture. When the prominent Canadian Women's Association of Alberta wanted to make a donation to the Provincial Museum symbolizing the contribution of Indian settlers to Alberta, they chose a musical instrument, the *veena* 'South Indian long-necked lute chordophone'. Concerts and workshops by established Indian performers have long been part of the musical scene on the prairies, thanks to volunteer based music societies that exist in every major city, best known among them the Ragamala Societies in both Edmonton and Calgary.

What is unique in this rich and multifarious Indian musical life on the prairies? Surely one factor is the commitment to make it happen despite the relative remoteness from major performance circuits; others are the strongly multiethnic urban population, especially in Alberta, and the relative openness of the Western musical establishment, both of which have enabled the Indian Canadian community to make a major place for its music.

Chinese music

A large percentage of the Chinese population of Edmonton and other prairie cities is made up of Cantonese speakers from the Fukien and Kwangtung regions of China and from Hong Kong [see CANTONESE MUSIC IN VANCOUVER, p. 1260]. Often based on surname, locality, dialect group or occupation (Hoe 1979:125–126), their community organizations include nonprofessional ensembles affiliated with traditional social clubs that also promote sports and culture. Performing ability is not necessarily required, and many members are fans of the style, attending the club for social purposes. Outside performances are rare except during the time of Chinese New Year. Opera ensembles such as that of the Edmonton Jin Wah Sing Society are often twenty or more years old; they include restaurant workers who make time to rehearse arias at night after closing or on Sundays.

Edmonton is also home to another kind of ensemble founded more recently in the larger prairie cities. The Chinese Art Society is composed largely of Mandarin-speaking immigrants who have recently arrived in Canada from mainland China. Many had been professional musicians in China, while others are highly skilled amateur musicians. The ensemble consists of three sections: (1) an instrumental section that features an orchestra of traditional Chinese instruments, sometimes referred to by its members as the Chinese Band, as well as soloists who perform on Western instruments; (2) adult and children's dance groups; and (3) vocalists who perform as soloists and in various ensemble groupings.

Unlike the Cantonese opera clubs, which meet primarily for recreational purposes, the Chinese Art Society has a somewhat more ambitious agenda. While the group functions as a social outlet for its members, many of whom are otherwise occupied with nonmusical pursuits, it also has assumed the responsibility of providing both the Chinese and the non-Chinese communities of Edmonton with the best possible examples of traditional Chinese music. By performing and also offering musical instruction, the group works toward legitimizing Chinese music and establishing an identity for Chinese musicians in Edmonton's music scene.

One of the interesting phenomena surrounding the musical activity of recent immigrants from mainland China is the status given to forms of folk music, which is treated as a type of art music. Because China has such an old recorded history, it is easy for Chinese musicians and scholars to draw on ancient material from both the classical and folk realms (Zhang 1985:267). The repertoire performed by ensembles of traditional instruments consists of contemporary compositions, rearranged pieces from folk sources, and revived traditional repertoire. These pieces include concerti or concert solos for traditional instruments such as the *pi'pa* 'plucked lute', *erhu* 'bowed fiddle', or *yangqin* 'hammered board zither'.

Another trend present among recent immigrants from mainland China is the use of instruments that have been redesigned in the interest of increasing technical performance possibilities. This is a result of the ideology of the Communist regime in China, which encouraged an expansion of solo instrumental styles and promoted the development of "professional" folk musicians. Many of the recent immigrant musicians are products of this system, trained in Chinese music conservatories.

Japanese music

The most prominent Japanese musical presence on the prairies is the very popular *taiko* drumming, a relatively recent urban innovation that in Edmonton has been practiced by the popular Kito na Taiko ensemble for at least fifteen years and performed in a variety of settings, including parks and shopping centers. Very few members of the ensemble are Japanese, for neither language, melodic system, nor technique are a hurdle to accessing this compelling, spiritually connected musical practice. Within the small but highly educated Japanese community the presence of one skilled performer can generate a thriving musical practice. In Edmonton, a dancing teacher has generated a women's group that performs to recorded music, mainly for Japanese-Canadian events.

REFERENCES

Han Kuo-Huang. 1979. "The Modern Chinese Orchestra." *Asian Music* 11(1):1–41.

Hoe, Ban Seng. 1979. *Structural Changes of Two Chinese Communities in Alberta, Canada.* Canadian Center for Folk Culture Studies Paper 19. Ottawa: National Museums of Canada.

Qureshi, Regula Burckhardt. 1972. "Ethnomusicological Research among Canadian Communities of Arab and East Indian Origin." *Ethnomusicology* 16(3):381–396.

Qureshi, Regula. Forthcoming. "Indian Music—World Music: The Work of Culture in a Globalized World." In *Critical Research Directions India-Canada*, ed. Jayant Lele. Toronto: Scholars' Press.

———, researcher. 1988. "Cantonese Opera in Edmonton." Segment of *View: A Heritage in Music.* CTV (CFRN) Television Production. Edmonton: Center for Ethnomusicology Collection, University of Alberta.

Tan, Jin, and Patricia E. Roy. 1985. *The Chinese in Canada.* Ottawa: Canadian Historical Association.

Northern and Central European Music

Beverley Diamond

Central Europeans
Scandinavians

The opening of the prairies to homesteaders of diverse national origins is usually said to have begun with the Dominion Lands Act of 1872. Northern and Central Europeans were specifically targeted by various campaigns to attract hard-working immigrants. By the 1880s the relative scarcity of good farm land in the western United States together with the boost to settlement given by the completion of a transcontinental railway in 1885 were further enabling factors. The window of opportunity to acquire free farmland was relatively short. By the beginning of the Great Depression in 1930, the immigration opportunity was severely curtailed. Later waves of immigrants from Germany, Poland, Ukraine and the Baltic States, Czechoslovakia, and the Scandinavian countries would be more urban oriented and equally if not more prone to settle in Ontario cities than in the west. Ukrainian communities are treated in a separate article because of their size and musical diversity. Other nationalities from northern and central Europe are introduced here.

CENTRAL EUROPEANS

Residents of German, Hungarian, and Polish descent have been active in Canada's public cultural life since the eighteenth century, contributing substantially to the development of classical music institutions. German-speaking settlers came from all over Germany, Austria, and Switzerland as well as from Eastern European countries and Latin America. Gerhard Bassler (1999:600) suggests there was less class consciousness in Canada than in the United States as well as weak nationalist sentiment prior to World War I. As with many other groups, their cultural expression was sustained by means of local social and fraternal clubs, the German Society of Winnipeg founded in 1871 being one of the earliest. The Lutheran church also played an important role in the cultural life of the communities, many of which were located in rather rugged bush country in Saskatchewan or the Alberta drylands.

Most study of German musical traditions has centered on the music of religious minorities, especially the Mennonites and Hutterites [see MUSIC OF CHRISTIAN MINORITIES, p. 1237]. Mennonites came directly to the prairies from Russia or Ukraine in three waves: in 1870, during the 1920s, and again following World War II. The Mennonite Children's Choir of Winnipeg (est. 1957) is one of the longest standing organizations, and Winnipeg also has a Mennonite Symphony Orchestra.

Perhaps church disapproval accounts for the sparsity of instrumental music found in the Canadian Norwegian community when the National Museum of Canada commissioned a study of Norwegian Canadian culture in the 1970s.

Annual *Sangerfesten* were first sponsored in Canada in 1862. Over two hundred Low German folk songs have been collected in southern Manitoba by Doreen Klassen (1990) since 1976. The repertoire ranges from "ballads of social comment to love songs to songs commemorating historical events" (Klassen 1990:93). Some of these were locally composed after 1970 during a "Low German renaissance" (96). The tunes, however, are mostly borrowed from the High German repertoire or from Anglo-American folk song and country music repertoires.

The Polish settlers on the prairies gravitated to Winnipeg, where more than one thousand already resided before 1895. A later post–World War I wave moved to the Peace River district; this group came from what was now an independent Poland and had a much clearer sense of the national identity of their homeland. The Depression effectively eroded Polish community life in the west; many Poles moved east to seek a more prosperous life.

The Sokol Choir of Winnipeg is internationally renowned. The *Encyclopedia of Music in Canada* (Kallmann, Potvin, and Winters 1992:1068) reports over forty dance, choral, and instrumental ensembles (not regionally desegregated) and a preference for the following dance types: *krakowiak, polonaise, kujiawiak, mazurka, oberek, troyak,* and *goralski* (a reference to mountain dwellers).

Many Hungarians came in 1886 to the Qu-Appelle valley region of Saskatchewan by way of the United States. Others came somewhat later to mining jobs at Medicine Hat and Lethbridge. Their culture was maintained, like that of most other prairie communities, via mutual aid societies, clubs, and churches, including the Hungarian Canadian Cultural Council in Winnipeg and the Szechenyi Society in Calgary. Prior to the 1930s, when the majority of Hungarians migrated east (primarily to Ontario), folk song and poetry thrived, as evidenced in a selectively published collection by Kenneth Peacock (1966) for the National Museums. Among the best known ensembles is the Hungarian Kapisztran Folk Ensemble of Winnipeg, a mixed choir, orchestra, and folk dance group founded in 1960 by conductor Gertrud Edenhoffer.

Over forty thousand Slovaks and Czechs came to the prairies by the 1920s to work in coal mining in Alberta and British Columbia or to homestead in Saskatchewan. A large number moved east to Fort William, Ontario (at the head of Lake Superior) after World War I, leaving only about five thousand on the prairies by the late twentieth century. Early fraternal societies sustained calendric celebrations at Christmas and Easter in particular.

SCANDINAVIANS

Scandinavians have sometimes collaborated with one another in the establishment of institutions on the prairies, an example being the Scandinavian Center of Calgary, which is shared by the Swedish Vasa Lodge, Club Finlandia, Icelandic Club, and Sons of Norway and used to promote cultural activities including folk dance and theater of all constituents. Another instance of cooperation was the long-running *Scandinavian Program* on CKUA Radio, Edmonton, from 1952 to 1994.

The history of specific national communities from Scandinavia, however, is rather distinct. The Norwegians arrived in the largest numbers in the second half of the nineteenth century (about one-half million, making their group second in size only to the Irish during this period). Over 90 percent were engaged in agriculture, and most were affiliated with the Lutheran church. Perhaps church disapproval accounts for the sparsity of instrumental music found in the Canadian Norwegian community when the National Museum of Canada commissioned a study of Norwegian Canadian culture in the 1970s. However, noted accordionist Olaf Sveen, who has produced more than 180 original compositions, moved to Saskatchewan (and later Alberta) around 1954. He played for dances with the Southern Playboys, the Western Five Orchestra, and Olle and His Playmates, performing waltzes, polkas, and dance tunes that drew on folk and country traditions. Choral music also abounded within the Norwegian community. Camrose Lutheran College in Alberta developed a distinguished concert choir and male quartet. The Bardo Male Chorus and Una Orchestra of Viceroy, Saskatchewan, and the Choral Union of the Young People's Luther League were also well known.

Swedes, on the other hand, arrived more often via the United States. A group from Gammalsvenskby in Ukraine constituted 20 percent of Swedes in Alberta in 1920, and immigrants from Sweden comprised 28 percent of the population of Saskatchewan by 1931, often settling in both southern towns such as Stockholm and northern areas around Maidstone, later in areas south of Edmonton and in Calmar. Dances, cultural celebrations, theater, and music were promoted by a series of Vasa lodges, the earliest at Edmonton in 1929. Calendric holidays such as Midsummer's Eve and the Feast of St. Lucia in December, celebrated by the singing of traditional songs, led by a young woman bedecked with a crown of candles, were maintained in Canada.

Although Finns and Danes were also sought as homesteaders, they came in fewer numbers to this part of Canada. Nevertheless, organizations such as the Dania Club in Edmonton, the Danish Canadian Club in Winnipeg, or, from the 1920s to 1950s, the Dalum Folkefest in Alberta, were active at Midsummer's Eve, Shrovetide, and Martinmas celebrations, especially in urban areas.

The Icelandic community is different yet again. Because of a series of concurrent problems at home, a sizable group moved to Canada in the 1870s, settling on the west side of Lake Winnipeg, including Hecla Island, and naming their new location New Iceland. They maintained their own legal and judicial system until 1887. The contemporary community is centered in Gimli, Manitoba, although communities also exist in other prairie locales. The Islendinga Dagurinn (Icelandic festival of Manitoba) began in 1890 and continues to the present day, moving to Gimli in 1932. Since 1969, it has been a multiday event with concerts and dances.

The central symbol of Icelandic romantic nationalism continues to be the *fjallkona* 'a female representing Mother Iceland', although this symbol is contentious at the turn of the century (see Brydon 2000). Folklorist Magnus Einarsson (1992) has documented Icelandic Canadian musical traditions, including the practice of improvising quatrains by *husgangar*, poets who go from house to house, and repertoires of narrative songs, drinking songs, dances and reels, and children's rhymes. Among traditional instruments, the *langspil* 'bowed box zither' is occasionally found in Canada.

REFERENCES

Bassler, Gerhard. 1999. "Germans." In *Encyclopedia of Canada's Peoples*, ed. Paul R. Magocsi, 586–612. Toronto: University of Toronto Press.

Brydon, Anne. 2000. "Mother to Her Distant Children: The Icelandic *Fjallkona* in Canada," in *Undisciplined Women: Tradition and Culture in Canada*, Pauline Greenhill and Diane Tye, ed. 87–100. Montréal: McGill–Queen's University Press.

Einarsson, Magnús. 1992. *Icelandic-Canadian Memory Lore*. Ottawa: Canadian Museum of Civilization.

Kallmann, Helmut, Gilles Potvin, and Kenneth Winters, eds. 1992. *Encyclopedia of Music in Canada*. 2nd ed. Toronto: University of Toronto Press.

Klassen, Doreen. 1990. "Musical Borrowing and Sociopolitical Power: Low German Songs of the Southern Manitoba Mennonites." In *Ethnomusicology in Canada*, ed. Robert Witmer, CanMus Documents 5. Toronto: Institute for Canadian Music.

Peacock, Kenneth. 1966. *Twenty Ethnic Songs from Western Canada*. Ottawa: National Museums.

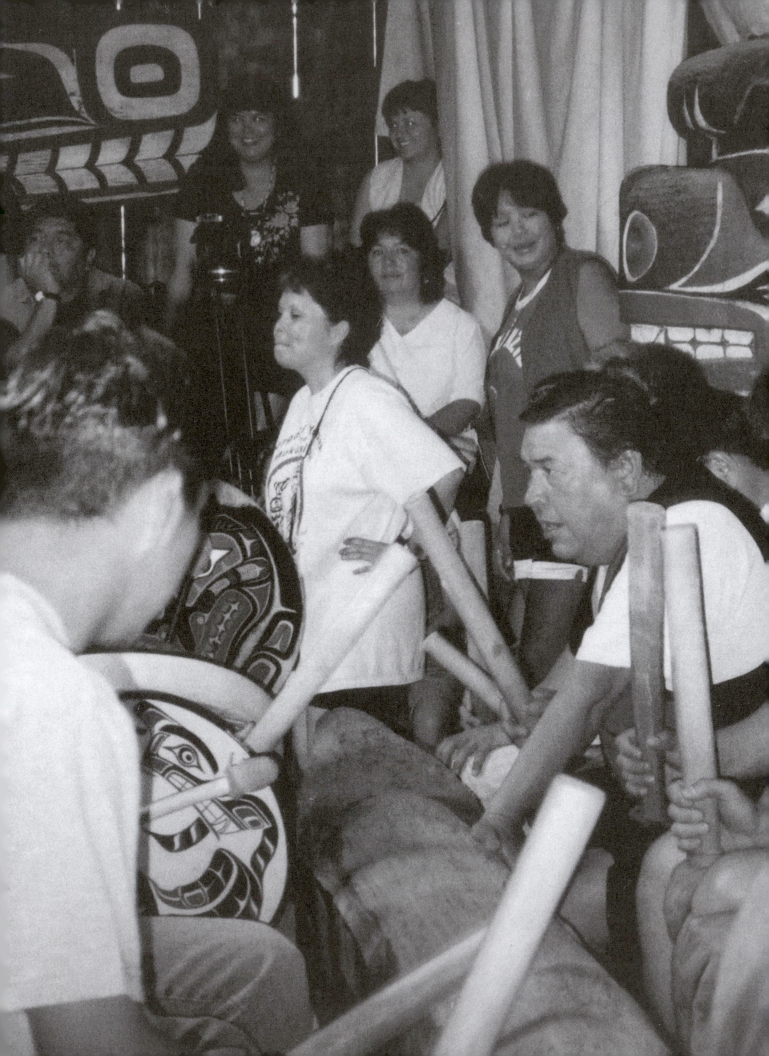

Section 3e
British Columbia

British Columbia, claimed for the British by James Cook in 1778, had already been inhabited by First Nations peoples (predominantly the Haida, Tlingit, and Nookta) who had migrated west from the great prairies or south from the Yukon and arctic polar cap centuries before. Northwest coast carvings, especially the intricately carved totem poles and ceremonies (such as the potlatch), with their own distinctive music and dance, have become perhaps the best known of all American Indian cultural expressions throughout the world. In the mid-nineteenth century large groups of Chinese, primarily from Canton, were brought to British Columbia to work in the gold mines and as laborers on the transcontinental railway. These immigrants quickly established communities, especially in Vancouver, and promoted the performance of Chinese opera through many associations and clubs that both taught the demanding repertoires and patronized performances. European immigration came in the late nineteenth century, bringing Ukrainians, Russians, and a distinctive religious and musical community, the Doukhobors, to British Columbia. Since the mid-twentieth century, immigrants from southeast and south Asia, as well as the Pacific Islands, have come to western Canada, bringing with them their traditional theatrical and dance forms as well as classical instrumental genres. Vancouver was also a major force in the revival of interest in European folk traditions, being one of the first cities in Canada to establish a yearly folk festival in 1975.

Some male Kwagiulth Dancers play frame drums and a log drum during a 1999 First Peoples Festival in Wa'waditla house, Victoria, British Columbia.

Overview
Norman Stanfield

The Early Years
The Settlers
Non-Native Music in British Columbia

British Columbia is one of the five regions of Canada, defined by its vast eastern and western mountain ranges lying north to south, separated by a sea of rolling hills. Its principal geographic zones, the rain forest coastal region on the Pacific side, the dry plateau in its southern interior, and the subarctic terrain in the north, itself composed of Cordilleran and woodland features, comprise the physical background for the province's history and evolution.

THE EARLY YEARS

The earliest occupants of the province were the First Nations peoples. Archeologists have located materials that date the occupation of the coast from between ten thousand and five thousand years ago, which is halfway along the First Nations time line in ancient America, beginning with the first migrations across Beringia from Asia. It would seem that the various waves of nomads made their way down the eastern slopes of the Cordilleran Glacier Field along an ice-free corridor and possibly even down the western "seaward" side.

Because of the province-wide ice cap, the interior of British Columbia does not have the same ancient archaeological history as the coast does. By the time of the arrival of the first European explorers, these First Nations peoples were roughly divided among the Coastal Wakashan, Haidan, Tsimshian, and Salishan peoples, the southern Interior Plateau Salishan and Kootenayan Nations, and the northern Interior Subarctic Cordilleran and Woodland Athapaskan tribes. A full account of their places in the province, as well as their musics, is provided elsewhere in this volume [see NORTH-WEST COAST, p. 394; SUBARCTIC CANADA, p. 383; OVERVIEW OF MUSIC IN CANADA, p. 1066].

Lying on the northwest coast of the New World, the Pacific Rim of the province was about the farthest reach possible for the earliest explorers and traders. They came by three-masted ships into the empty stretches of the newly discovered Pacific Ocean via the distant southern tip of South America or by canoe along the farthest reaches of the fur trade river routes extending westward from eastern Canada, or across the endless tundra of Siberia from Russia, thence by ship through the Bering Sea. The first incentives to ply these coastal waters stemmed from the desire to find the entrance to "the other side" of the Northwest Passage (West to East), but this dream was quickly replaced by the far more practical consideration of enormous wealth accrued from sea otter pelts, destined for Guangzhou (Canton) (Gibson 1992).

The first explorers on the northwest coast were the Russians in 1741, then the Spanish in 1774, who were the first to sight the coast of British Columbia, followed by the English (under Captain James Cook), who eventually negotiated sole control of the province and its waterways, as laid out in the Nootka Convention of 1790. Thus began the groundwork for the first of two British colonies (Vancouver Island and New Caledonia, both within modern-day British Columbia), officially surveyed by Captain George Vancouver in 1792–1793.

In one of those remarkable moments of historical synchronicity, Captain Vancouver was in the same vicinity at almost the same time in 1793 as Alexander Mackenzie, one of the greatest land explorers of all time. Mackenzie was also in search of a route to the sea otter trade, but his approach was via the great expanse of the interior of Canada along the fur trade rivers rather than following the arduous route up the coast. He was followed by other "Nor-westers" (North West Company men rivaling the Hudson Bay and American Fur Companies), Simon Fraser (1808) and finally David Thompson (1811). Fraser named his newfound land New Caledonia and was instrumental in establishing a series of northwest Canada trading forts in the interior, beginning with Fort St. James (Stuart Lake) in 1805. All this trading activity culminated in the building of Fort Langley on the Fraser River very near the Pacific Ocean in 1827, the first fort on the coast of British Columbia.

THE SETTLERS

The fur trade in sea otter pelts was in serious decline during the mid-1820s, and the interior beavers became scarce in the 1830s. Ironically, fashion also hastened the end of both trade commodities, as felt replaced beaver and otter as the material of choice for men's hats. The traders were progressively replaced by settlers, beginning with Fort Victoria in 1841 on Vancouver Island, then the interior in the wake of the gold rush in 1864. In order to combat the influx of acquisitive Americans, James Douglas consolidated the English presence in British Columbia by becoming governor of the crown colonies of Vancouver Island and New Caledonia in 1858. They were combined into one colony named British Columbia (as an acknowledgment of Christopher Columbus, not a reference to the Columbia River) in 1866, establishing Victoria as its capital.

In 1867 the province sank into a financial crisis following the collapse of the gold rush a year earlier. It had three options: continue to be a colony of England, join with the newly created confederated country of (eastern) Canada, or be embraced by the rapidly expanding United States of America. England was uninterested in bailing out the debt-ridden province, but the United States held out its hand because it was investing heavily in the west, beginning with its purchase of Alaska that same year. However, following promises to assist with the debt load and extend the proposed national railway to the Pacific Ocean, British Columbia chose to join the Canadian Confederation in 1871. By this time the lands and waterways were becoming valued for settlement as well as long-term economic exploitation. For example, the canning of sockeye salmon began in earnest in 1870. As if to complete the picture, the newly formed Canadian government had purchased all of the Northwest Territories, including the northernmost interior of British Columbia, from the Hudson's Bay Company in 1869. The Dominion Lands Act laid the groundwork for mass immigration to Canada in 1872. And as the train tracks were laid out during the mid-1880s, all of western Canada became flooded with immigrants intending to make a new life, or new wealth, for themselves. Although most immigrants came from Europe, there are records of East and South Asian families establishing themselves as early as 1858, in the case of the Chinese, and 1904, for South Asians, to cite two examples.

NON-NATIVE MUSIC IN BRITISH COLUMBIA

British-derived forms and contexts

The history and music of the province from the vantage of the immigrants is bound up principally with its relationship to Britain. This is made patently obvious by the astounding record of transplanted May Days found throughout the province, not to be found in any other part of Canada, including staunchly loyalist Ontario. The city of New Westminster has the longest uninterrupted history of May Day celebrations in the entire British Commonwealth, beginning in 1870, just three years after confederation. This record exceeds the same kind of event in England (because of interruptions during the two wars). The oldest recorded May Day was in Clinton in 1858 (the same year as the Fraser River gold strike and the subsequent proclamation of mainland British Columbia as a Crown Colony). These dates are remarkable in that they are within just a few decades of that period in English history when it was newly exploring its heritage in the form of Victorian May Day pageants—imagined manifestations of its Merrie England past (Judge 1991).

British Columbia has not been a bountiful source of the kind of long-standing folk song variants such as the Child ballads that attracted Cecil Sharp to the Appalachians and his assistant, Maud Karpeles, to Newfoundland, no doubt because of its more recent immigrant history, although some examples have been found by Philip Thomas (1979). Other similar, parallel folk traditions such as the Ukrainian Malanka were regularly found on the Canadian prairies so the mystery of the absence of British time-honored customs only deepens. Because folk songs are part of the lifestyle of the "working poor," often resorted to in order to survive hard times, it may be that the particular class or character of the original British settlers militated against this tradition. Certainly many of these pay-for-play traditions fell by the wayside as enlightened legislation in nineteenth-century England began to provide various forms of government-assisted welfare, coupled with active unionism that fought for better and more secure wages, thus eliminating the necessity of such activities, sometimes seen as "begging." Many British union organizers made their way to British Columbia, and even today the various British accents are not uncommon in the pro-union and leftist movements.

Old-time music

Another major factor in the folk culture and music of the province is the prevalence of old-time and country and western music played on the violin with piano and/or guitar accompaniment, enjoyed by the cowboy culture of the plateau interior. Today the term *cowboys* is also understood to refer to First Nations peoples, who were central to maintaining the vast and rambling ranches introduced in the 1860s, some twenty years before the introduction of cattle to southern Alberta. The huge cattle herds were brought up from the northern United States via the American region of the plateau. Horses were already well established, so much so that the competitions called rodeos, popular with the First Nations peoples (within the contexts of their powwows) as well as the settlers, were a staple of the summer recreations.

Old-time fiddling is active throughout the province and currently sustained by a society with over a dozen branches. They organize two summer camps in the interior, an orchestra composed entirely of young fiddle players (named The Daniel Lapp Fiddleharmonic), and a full roster of five young players sent to the National Championships in Neppean, Ontario, each year.

The old-time genre is a style of dance music that features couple dances such as waltzes and foxtrots, as opposed to the cowboy genre of square dance, which requires the specialized and increasingly rare services of a caller—a person who directs the choreography of the dance in an improvisatory manner, harmonizing the vocal directions to the melody by employing a melodic chanting technique. The genre of old-time fiddling is also referred to as the Anglo-Canadian fiddle tradition, one of six Canadian styles that also include Cape Breton/Scottish, French Canadian, Métis and Athapaskan (Yukon) First Nations, Ukrainian, and country and western (Lederman 1992:325–326). Its characteristics are its successful melding of Irish, Scottish, and even classical techniques into a smooth, less ornamented style (Gibbons 1982).

The British Columbia Old Time Fiddlers Association is the first organization of its type in Canada, founded in 1978 but tracing most of its roots back to influences from the rural towns and farms of the prairies, where most of its players originated. It also counts Don Messer and His Islanders—regularly featured in a weekly television program *Don Messer's Jubilee* (1958–1969), broadcast by CBC from Halifax—as one of the most seminal influences in all of Canada. Many Canadians are under the impression that fiddle music is most prominent in Canada's Maritime Provinces, especially Cape Breton, but that impression has been created by the media and the publicity machines of the new performers. One finds excellent fiddlers throughout Canada, but without the same drive for public exposure and lucrative careers. Also, most Maritime fiddlers have not had to grapple with the problem of huge distances between performers and venues, as they have in the West.

The principal collector of British Columbia's indigenous fiddle music is Daniel Lapp, the 1993 provincial champion, who maintains an active career as a touring and session musician. Beginning in 1990, thanks to a Canada Council grant, he has traveled throughout the province and collected over a thousand tunes. They are heavily influenced by Don Messer, Grand Ol' Opry, and the great prairie fiddlers Al Cherny, Ned Landry, Frankie Rodgers, Ward Allen, King Gaanam, Graham Townsend, and Andy DeJarlis. In private correspondence, however, Lapp is quick to add that they have a unique touch that marks them as "BC interior." We look forward to the results of his research.

Scholarship of British-derived folk song

The single most important collector of folk songs in British Columbia has been Philip J. Thomas (b. 1921) (Lyon 1998), whose important book, *Songs of the Pacific Northwest* (1979), is an excellent sample of his collection of almost two hundred taped performances (currently held in the provincial archives [Bartlett 1976]). Because the earliest immigrants were largely from Great Britain (England, Wales, Scotland, and Ireland), many via Ontario and the United States, the earliest records show those influences. Thomas's book offers a musical tour of the history of the province, providing examples of vocal repertoire that touch on most of the major genres in ballad and lyric song literature. The collection is completely eclectic, unlike some of the early collections made in England that were focused on rural ballads. The repertoire of songs reflects a great diversity of lifestyles and contexts, from rural ballads to urban settings of occupational protests. Thomas's only criteria were stated in his foreword. "In addition to traditional songs and ballads, the term 'folk song' may be given to newer and authored songs of the same general type if the writer's primary intent is social and communicative rather than commercial" (1979:6). In addition, the book has taken the high road with regard to detailed essays on historical context of each song and careful documentation of sources. The beginning of the book provides examples of broadside ballads generated in the United States, in keeping with this country's fur trading interests on the West Coast of British Columbia. Later examples are parodies of well-known British songs (such as "The Grand Hotel," to the tune of "Villikens and His Dinah," or "Sweet Betsy from Pike"), songs of labor struggles including a fascinating description of a song ("Where the Fraser River Flows" [1979:95–99]) commemorating the union organizing of the famous American Joe Hill, who was in British Columbia on behalf of the Industrial Workers of the World (nicknamed "Wobblies") and the rail workers in 1912.

What is interesting in the list of performers is the relegation and recognition of England as simply one of several ethnic communities, as opposed to the unspoken understanding that the resident English were the common denominator of all.

Equally interesting are songs using the Northwest Coast First Nations "pidgin language," Chinook, particularly in the interior.

Bluegrass

Another equally popular form, more recently introduced, is bluegrass music, in keeping with the multitude of accompanying instruments common to the area: banjo, guitar, piano, and string bass. The yearly competitions and the weekly jam sessions (which can attract some fifty people every Thursday night in Prince George, ranging in age from seven to seventy) are considered a healthy and logical extension of the tradition of making music in the home and the community, but like similar musics around the world, they are in deep competition with modern forms of electronic, passive music experiences.

Other traditional musics

Several other ethnic groups were settling in the province at the same time, such as the Chinese (beginning in 1858 as members of the gold rush), bringing with them their leisure and religious music and dance. Although their cultural activities did not constitute the mainstream of society at the beginning, their presence became steadily more pronounced. In the 1930s Vancouver's foreign consulates co-hosted a folk dance and song festival that in 1936 included music and dance from thirty different ethnic groups, including the English. What is interesting in the list of performers is the relegation and recognition of England as simply one of several ethnic communities, as opposed to the unspoken understanding that the resident English were the common denominator of all. England's contribution consisted of the latest research and revival of folk dance, including "ritual dance" (morris and linked swords) and the social "country dance," imported by Beatrice Cave Browne-Cave (1883–1987), a recent graduate of Cecil Sharp's program of folk dance certification.

Dale McIntosh provides an incredibly detailed study of the concert and jazz music of British Columbia in his *History of Music in British Columbia, 1850–1950* (1989). "More than five thousand documents were consulted and several dozen interviews conducted" (11), although the book manages to avoid any references to folk music. The book has a staggering wealth of detail organized by genre, ranging from opera to orchestras, music in education to music in print, making it very comprehensive. Of particular interest is the entry on brass bands, which again points out the debt to English music on many levels, including political. Within the brass band genre, the proliferation of First Nations brass bands is especially interesting.

Today the English are an inconspicuous presence in the company of a multitude of other ethnic communities (which now include the Welsh, Scots, and Irish). Because of Vancouver's position as Canada's port of call nearest to Asia, it has a very large and diverse Asian population, reflected in institutions such as the University of British Columbia, whose ethnomusicology department includes specialists in Asian music, and its yearly urban folk festival called Cityfest, at which for example, several schools of

South Asian dance vie for public attention. It is most likely in British Columbia (and perhaps Ontario) that the multicultural imperative within Canada will be played out to its fullest extent, so music and dance from many ethnic groups will no doubt form an important component of the nation's growing appreciation of and its adaptation to its emerging cultural diversity.

REFERENCES

Barman, Jean. 1996. *The West beyond the West: A History of British Columbia.* Rev. ed. Toronto: University of Toronto Press.

Bartlett, John. 1976. "The P. J. Thomas Collection of British Columbia Folk Songs." *Canadian Folk Music Journal* 4:29–30.

Canada's Year of Asia Pacific Multicultural Bibliography. 1997. Vancouver, B.C.: British Columbia Teacher-Librarians' Association.

Davies, Sandra, et al. 1982. *The Chinese People: Music, Instruments, Folklore.* Vancouver, B.C.: Western Education Development Group.

———. 1986. *Japanese People: Music, Instruments, Arts, Crafts.* Vancouver, B.C.: Western Education Development Group.

Gibbons, Roy W. 1982. *As It Comes: Folk Fiddling in Prince George, British Columbia.* Mercury Series 42. Ottawa: National Museum of Man.

Gibson, James R. 1992. *Otter Skins, Boston Ships, and China Goods: The Maritime Fur Trade of the Northwest Coast, 1785–1841.* Montréal: McGill–Queens University Press.

Hayes, Derek. 1999. *Historical Atlas of British Columbia and the Pacific Northwest.* Delta, B.C.: Cavendish Books.

Judge, Roy. 1991. "May Day and Merrie England." *Folklore* 102(2):131–148.

Kallmann, Helmut, Gilles Potvin, and Kenneth Winters, eds. 1992. *Encyclopedia of Music in Canada.* 2nd ed. Toronto: University of Toronto Press.

Lederman, Anne. 1992. "Fiddling." In *Encyclopedia of Music in Canada,* 2nd ed., ed. Helmut Kallmann, Gilles Potvin, and Kenneth Winters. Toronto: University of Toronto Press.

Lyon, George W. 1998. "'The Singing Was the Important Thing': An Interview with Phil Thomas." *Canadian Folk Music Journal/Revue de musique folklorique canadiennes* 32(2):3–18.

McIntosh, Dale. 1989. *History of Music in British Columbia, 1850–1950.* Victoria, B.C.: Sono Nis Press.

Thomas, Philip J. 1979. *Songs of the Pacific Northwest.* Saanichton, B.C.: Hancock House.

———. 1992. "Folk Music, Anglo-Canadian: 5. British Columbia." In *Encyclopedia of Music in Canada,* 2nd ed., ed. Helmut Kallmann, Gilles Potvin, and Kenneth Winters. Toronto: University of Toronto Press.

Woodcock, George. 1990. *British Columbia: A History of the Province.* Vancouver: Douglas and McIntyre.

Cantonese Music in Vancouver

Huang Jinpei
Alan R. Thrasher

Cantonese Opera and Instrumental Music
The Music Societies
The Social Setting
Preservation

The Guangdong (Cantonese) subculture of South China is one the largest in China. While its center is the city of Guangzhou (or Canton), there are also four counties to its west, notably Taishan, Kaiping, Enping, and Xinhui, which reflect many cultural similarities and speak closely related dialects. The earliest Cantonese-speakers to come to Vancouver were the working peoples of Taishan (Toisan), around 1858, soon followed by peoples from the neighboring counties (Lee 1967). It would be much later that Cantonese-speakers from Hong Kong, Malaysia, Vietnam, and Taiwan would arrive. As the Taishan people spoke a dialect only slightly different from Cantonese, they quite naturally developed an affection for Cantonese opera and instrumental music. This they brought to Vancouver in the late nineteenth and early twentieth centuries, and it has dominated Chinese music making in Canada to the present day.

CANTONESE OPERA AND INSTRUMENTAL MUSIC

Cantonese opera was derived primarily from the Han Chinese opera of North China. Before the 1920s texts were sung in the Zhongzhou dialect, which is similar to Mandarin. The opera stories also came from the North, most dating from before the Qing dynasty (1644-1911). During this period between two and three dozen operas were regularly performed. Musicians followed scripts, in which melodies were written in traditional character notation (*gongche pu*). Instruments were tempered in the old seven-tone equidistant system, utilizing both whole-step and 3/4-step intervals. Both notation and temperament have remained relatively unchanged in contemporary practice.

However, by the 1930s other aspects of Cantonese opera had changed. The texts were increasingly sung in Cantonese dialect; melodic structure changed as local idioms were incorporated; and to the traditional ensemble of *erxian* 'short-neck fiddle', *suona* 'shawm', and other instruments with strong projecting tonal qualities, newly introduced instruments from the West were added, such as saxophone, violin, and Hawaiian guitar. The opera sung in Vancouver at this time was already a combination of both the old and new styles.

Cantonese instrumental music developed side by side with the opera tradition. It was performed by instrumentalists who did not necessarily sing opera music. Small instruments, such as the *dizi* 'bamboo flute', *gaohu* 'fiddle', and *qinqin* 'long-neck lute', were relatively inexpensive, easy to play, and not so loud as to annoy the neighbors. Because the instrumental melodies were learned without reference to notation, an amateur instrumental ensemble was considerably easier to form than was an amateur opera troupe. We have little documentation on the activities of these early groups, but they were certainly very popular among the local population and with overseas Chinese as well. Professor Huang, coauthor of this article, recalls from his own experience as a boy in Singapore (1928 to 1931), that Cantonese instrumental music was heard everywhere. He learned the music by listening to other boys play. Once learned, it is never forgotten. Friends of the same age tell him they remember these same experiences.

During the late nineteenth and early twentieth centuries, both opera songs and instrumental music were performed in the larger teahouses (*chaguan*) of Guangzhou and Hong Kong, a milieu similar to that used in the performance of narrative song in Suzhou and "silk-bamboo" instrumental music in Shanghai. The teahouse tradition declined sharply in the South during the 1950s, and Cantonese music is rarely heard in this environment any longer. At any rate, it was within the context of the amateur society that both vocal and instrumental traditions survived best. In Guangzhou there were dozens of amateur societies. Most disappeared between the 1950s and 1980s; some are now being revived. In Hong Kong there was an equal number, and these have survived well. The nature and organization of the amateur society is well preserved in Vancouver, as seen in the following discussion.

According to the old Vancouver Chinese-language newspapers, Cantonese opera troupes visited Vancouver regularly (often annually) between 1916 and 1941, performing full-length programs in Chinatown. From the 1920s onward, 78-rpm recordings of the famous songs were also available to the public. However, no music society was established in Vancouver until the mid-1930s.

At this time there was an organization in Guangzhou called the Bahe Huiguan, a strong union responsible for organizing all Cantonese opera activity. It also exercised strict control over its actors. The first society of Vancouver, Jin Wah Sing, which served initially as a broker agent to invite opera troupes, contacted this organization and registered itself as an opera troupe. As a result, the Vancouver society was able to invite famous actors from China, such as Sun Ju, Gui Ming-young, and as many as thirty others. After the 1950s, the Bahe Huiguan was disbanded, thereby losing this control. In its place, the Hong Kong opera troupes grew in prominence, and greater numbers of musicians and actors traveled out from this colony.

During this same period, though especially in the 1930s, instrumental music became very popular in local urban culture. Between fifty and sixty composers were active, among them Chen Deju, Yan Laolie, Lu Wencheng, and He Liutang. Their compositions, unlike the older repertoire of the Confucian heritage, were mostly bright and lively, reflecting the high spirit and optimism of the time. Examples of this lively repertoire include *Hantianlei* (*Thunder in the Drought*) and *Sailong Duojin* (*Challenge of the Dragon Boat*). Indeed, many pieces were performed for dance accompaniment in ballrooms, usually with added harmony and percussion.

Ultimately the introduction into South China of electronic media during the 1920s and 1930s proved to be the decisive factor for the widespread dissemination of Cantonese opera and instrumental music. Most of the repertoire was recorded by skilled artists, released on 78-rpm disks and purchased by an enthusiastic public. Performers were paid for these recordings. The recordings were also broadcast on radio, which further broadened support. And in the newly constructed cinema halls, instrumental music was played during intermissions, most notably by the very famous instrumentalist and composer Lu Wencheng. If there was a "classical" period of Cantonese music, this was it.

THE MUSIC SOCIETIES

Of the many Cantonese music societies in Vancouver, the most prominent are Jin Wah Sing, Ching Won, and Ngai Lum. All are centrally located in Chinatown. Established in 1935, Jin Wah Sing is the oldest, largest, and most conservative. It has a membership of about one hundred, meets on Sunday afternoons, and occupies one of the old landmark buildings of Chinatown (on the northeast corner of Pender and Carroll Streets). The society has a stage on which Cantonese opera can be performed for an audience of up to two hundred persons. It possesses its own complete set of stage properties, including stage lights and sets, costumes, recording equipment, and musical instruments.

For the most part, these properties were presented to the society by Cantonese opera troupes in Hong Kong or Guangzhou. New costumes have been purchased more recently. In fact, their properties are so complete that it is common for other troupes, both visiting and local, to request loans of equipment and sometimes even of musicians and actors. A recent example involved a visiting opera troupe from Taishan county, which the Jin Wah Sing helped by lending musicians for an evening performance.

The society's teacher (*shifu*) through the early 1990s has been Wong Tou, a famous musician from Hong Kong who came to Vancouver in 1961. Now in his late seventies, he still teaches part time and continues to play. Other prominent musicians include Owen Wong, past president for eleven years, Yu Kwong-hon and Lee Bing-chuen, who has made a special effort to collect old songs.

During the late 1930s and early 1940s, some Jin Wah Sing actors returned to China to perform in support of the Sino-Japanese war. Jin Wah Sing stopped meeting during this period (Wong 1983). (For an interesting account of Jin Wah Sing during the late 1930s, see Leung 1977:10.) In 1954, the society was revived; the name was changed to Jin Wah Sing Music Association and registered with the Ministry of Culture in Vancouver. For its opening ceremony, the society presented the Cantonese opera *Xixiang Daiyue* 'Waiting for the Moon in the West Chamber'. The show was performed at the Majestic Theater to a full house, and the Cantonese audience was quite happy to see its native opera on stage again. Since the 1950s, the association has regularly presented operas for charities and entertainment and has been known as a strong force for traditional Chinese opera promotion.

Ching Won Music Society was also established in the 1930s and, like the Jin Wah Sing, disbanded for a few years during the war. It occupies a second-floor complex of rooms directly across from the Chinese Cultural Center on Pender Street and meets every Saturday night (often until 2:00 A.M.). Their resources being somewhat more limited than those of Jin Wah Sing, Ching Won has some musical instruments and costumes, but fewer stage properties. Its membership of less than one hundred is, like Jin Wah Sing's, composed of older, established Cantonese Canadians. Ching Won, though it has no *shifu*, is led by several highly skilled musicians, notably the eighty-eight-year-old Louis Chang (Chang Long-you), performer of *yangqin* 'zither' and instrument maker, and, until recently, Lee Bing, student of the famous Cantonese violinist Won Ji-jong. There is at present some turnover of personnel at Ching Won, and other musicians are now emerging.

Ngai Lum, formed in the early 1960s, is considered a younger brother to the two older societies. Having recently moved its meeting hall because of urban renovation, it presently occupies a ground-level facility across from the Sun Yat Sen Classical Garden on Carroll Street; it meets on Sunday afternoons. It has about fifty members, generally somewhat younger and better educated than those of the larger societies and including recently arrived musicians from Hong Kong and the Chinese mainland. Its *shifu* is Yan Jun-ho, who is also a part-time Chinese herbal doctor and teacher of martial arts. Also prominent as a player of percussion and saxophone is Raymond Li, who serves as the society's spokesperson as well. In terms of outreach and of welcoming of non-Chinese visitors, Ngai Lum is more open than the other societies, no doubt because of the energy and education of its younger members. For the society's yearly Spring Festival (the Chinese New Year), more than four hundred friends typically attend a banquet, which is always a lively event with ongoing staged performances during and after the meal.

There are other music societies outside of Chinatown as well, but these come and go, and membership is considerably more fluid. The most active is Fai Lok San Chinese Music Society (est. 1982), which is attached to the Mount Pleasant Community Center. Fai Lok San rents a room for its music making every Wednesday afternoon. The founders and leaders of this society, Wong Wun-wah and her husband, Mak Shu-wing, contribute all the musical instruments for performances and provide refreshments for each meeting. There are about thirty regular members, all between fifty and seventy years of age. Their performance standard is somewhat more relaxed than that of the other societies, but the members are extremely enthusiastic and they attend regularly. Other societies exist as well, and there are also home parties that meet occasionally but have no formal basis. There is also a Cantonese opera school in Vancouver, the Yuet Sing Guangdong Song-Arts Research Academy (est. 1987), that specifically provides singing lessons. Yuet Sing collects fees directly from students. The president is its principal teacher, with others teaching part time. Students include wealthy women, though very few young people.

The Vancouver Chinese Music Ensemble, not specifically a Cantonese ensemble, was organized in 1979 to play the more recent "national music" (*guoyue*), although this ensemble also includes some Cantonese music in its repertoire. Its members are mostly Cantonese, together with a few performers from North China. There is also a Peking opera society in Vancouver, but owing to sharp differences in dialect and musical style, there is little contact between its members and the Cantonese music societies.

THE SOCIAL SETTING

The members of Vancouver's Cantonese music societies are mostly middle-aged and older people. Approximately 95 percent are first-generation immigrants from Hong Kong. Most work five or six days a week at other jobs, especially those associated with the restaurant business, though including other fields as well. They have little time or cultural diversion. It is primarily for this occupational reason they consider themselves "amateurs," but not for lack of skill. Each club has a president, a rotating position elected annually. Membership is dominated by a large group of female and male singers, together with a smaller group of instrumentalists. Instrumentalists are mostly men between fifty and seventy years of age. Only a few are in their thirties or forties or late seventies or eighties. Although some instrumentalists have had formal music instruction, most are self-taught.

There are no fully professional Cantonese musicians in Vancouver, although at present there are two *shifu* who function as part-time ensemble directors and teachers and other less prominent instructors. The teaching of Cantonese opera singing is a difficult and time-consuming job. A teacher is required to provide his own notation, usually hand copied, in about ten copies for the accompanying musicians. Notations of older pieces are obtainable in Hong Kong. However, if a student wishes to learn a new piece, this must be written out by the teacher, a tedious task taking nearly a week. Since students are generally untrained in the technical aspects of music (such as in the singing of scales and knowledge of music theory), teachers generally rely upon the method of demonstration, imitation, and repetition. Within the last two decades, students have also learned to sing by listening to cassette tapes of Hong Kong singers. Over time, the student is able to sing one piece well.

Because singers stand behind microphones at the center of the ensemble and take pride in their accomplishment, most teachers are very hesitant to correct errors in public. This would be too embarrassing.

The societies meet once a week, primarily to sing Cantonese opera songs in unstaged settings and occasionally to play instrumental music as well. Meetings are essentially get-togethers, in which actual "rehearsal" (as this term is used in the West) is relatively modest. Songs and instrumental pieces are typically performed from beginning to end without stopping unless a serious musical problem arises (for example, if the singer loses his place in the music). Because singers stand behind microphones at the center of the ensemble and take pride in their accomplishment, most teachers are very hesitant to correct errors in public. This would be too embarrassing (and it might also estrange the student).

The atmosphere is usually casual, with nonperforming members talking among themselves and drinking tea or coffee. The Chinese concept is of a "happy garden" (*leyuan*), where self-entertainment is one of the principal functions. In performance, some members sing the same one or two opera excerpts each week, while others perform a wider variety of old and new songs. Often certain songs become associated with specific singers, and gradually it happens that only those singers will perform them. As with most Cantonese music making, singers rotate in performing. The accompanying instrumentalists, however, usually play without a break. Professor Huang has been at meetings at which he played for more than two hours at a sitting. Even though he was very tired, the singers kept coming up, one after another, and it would have been impolite to stop playing accompaniment.

Particularly scarce among Vancouver's instrumentalists are percussionists, who traditionally assume an important role in ensembles. As a result, it is common for a society to have only one person playing all the percussion instruments at the same time, cymbals with the left hand, gong with the right, and wood blocks when the cymbals and gong are not in use. The several players in the city who have this skill travel among the different societies and are always welcomed by all.

Unlike the instrumental music, songs are predominantly slow and set in a minor-sounding mode utilizing neutral fa and ti (known as *yifan*). Such songs are thought to express a sad and melancholy feeling. This favored style is technically simple to perform and so widely known that musicians may meet and perform together without preparation or rehearsal. Texts of the chosen songs express a variety of emotions and well-known old stories. Some songs are about faith, love, and loyalty, traditional concepts that still exist in the minds of the older Chinese. Other songs revere the past. Some express grievances, and as they are written in the first person, the singer himself/herself sings as if the misfortune were really his or hers. One old man more than sixty years of age has tears in his eyes when he sings "The Death of Liang Shanbo." He sings this song at every meeting, so it may be that he himself was disappointed in love when he was young.

Of interest to the better trained instrumental performers is a type of paid accompaniment known as the "special engagement" (*teyue*). This involves the weekly traveling to private homes to accompany the singing of women. Skilled performers can work as many as five half-days per week, rotating among different homes. For a full after-noon (or evening) of accompaniment work, a musician may receive about $40. For this, he is expected to accompany the singers one after another. While this "special engagement" is one of the more invisible aspects of music making in Vancouver, in social terms it is an important setting and is eagerly sought by accompanists.

Funding for society activities is based on membership fees and donations. Annual fees average between about $5 and $20 per member, with wealthier members some-times contributing as much as $100. At Chinese New Year and/or at special festivals, other donations may be made as well. Some funding is occasionally available from the British Columbia provincial government through its support of multicultural enter-prises. However, the best sources of income are found in the sale of tickets for opera performances and banquets. In 1985, for example, the Jin Wah Sing association held its fifty-first anniversary celebration at the Queen Elizabeth Theatre, and the Can-tonese community responded enthusiastically by buying tickets for all twenty-eight hundred seats. Similarly, annual $25-a-plate banquets, which attract Euro-Canadians as well as Cantonese, produce worthwhile profits.

Society expenses are low in general, with rent, electricity, and amplification/recording equipment being the large cost items. The *shifu* also receives a small salary from weekly student fees, but the society pays him nothing. All other work for upkeep is done on a volunteer basis, each member having a specific position, such as accoun-tant, secretary, and so on.

The Vancouver societies are quite active. Each has a regular performance schedule, playing for events throughout the year, of which the most important are commemora-tions of the Chinese New Year and annual celebrations of the societies themselves. The other societies are often invited to attend annual celebrations. In addition, city-wide events such as Vancouver's occasional Asia Pacific Festival, the 1986 Vancouver Exposi-tion, radio/television performances, and a host of banquets involve performances by the more active societies.

PRESERVATION

Major Western-influenced changes have occurred among the professional opera troupes of South China. For instance, ensemble accompaniment is now fully arranged and written out in cipher notation, the parts played in harmony rather than in tradi-tional heterophonic texture (one line of music realized in simultaneous variations) and performed in equal temperament. Ensembles now have conductors who formally rehearse their groups. In 1986, this new style of opera was introduced to Vancouver, but it met with considerable criticism from traditionalists who did not like such strict-ness and formality. Their complaint was that the opportunity for spontaneous creativ-ity and inspiration had been taken out of opera performance and actors' roles had become like those of puppets.

Of perhaps greater threat to the societies and the traditional music is the disen-chantment and lack of interest among younger, second-generation Cantonese people. The old stories, performance styles, and temperaments are not suited to the changing tastes of young people, who like brighter and more joyful songs in faster tempos. In today's world, love affairs and marriage systems are not the same as in traditional China, and young people have little understanding or sympathy for the old conven-tions. Also, the texts of these songs are written in the old literary style and are difficult for the young to follow. Professor Huang recalled that during his first term of residency at the University of British Columbia (1987), he was asked by the Hon Sing Athletic Association to teach young people to play Cantonese music. These children, whose ages ranged between eleven and fourteen, could speak only English and had adopted very Euro-Canadian cultural attitudes. After studying for little over a month, they abandoned their music classes for other activities, such as *gongfu* 'boxing'. This was a disappointment for their parents, amateur musicians themselves, who had hoped their children would share in their interest.

There are some younger men and women in the Ngai Lum society who appreciate Cantonese opera and its songs. But youths in Vancouver for the most part tend to favor either the excitement of pop music, in which they seldom participate in creation, or Western classical music, in which they are quite active as pianists and violinists.

The older style of Cantonese music is well preserved in Vancouver, but principally among the older immigrant generation. A statement attributed to Confucius puts this type of marginal survival in partial perspective: "You can find the ritual in neighboring countries when it is lost [at home]." But for how long? About abandonment of the heritage by youth, Confucius was silent.

REFERENCES

Huang Jinpei. 1982. "Lun Guangdong Yinyuede Xingti" (On the waxing and waning of Cantonese music). *Guangzhou Yinyue Xueyuan Xuebao* (*Journal of the Guangzhou Conservatory of Music*) 1:8–17.

Lee, David T. H. 1967. *A History of Chinese in Canada*. Vancouver: The Chinese Voice.

Leung Chun-kin. 1977. "Notes on Cantonese Opera in North America." *Chinoperl Papers* 7.

Wong Toa. 1983. "Brief History of the Jin Wah Sing Musical Association." Unpublished manuscript.

The initial research for this paper was undertaken by Huang Jinpei in 1987, with support of a "Foreign Scholars" grant awarded by the Social Sciences and Humanities Research Council of Canada. Huang Jinpei, professor at the Xinghai Conservatory of Music in Guangzhou and presently in residence at the University of British Columbia, is one of the leading experts on Cantonese music. The paper was updated and revised in 1993, with some additional social observations by Alan Thrasher.

Music of the Doukhobors
F. Mark Mealing

Music Forms and Genres
Scholarship

Doukhobors first emigrated from Russia to Canada in 1899. In southern Russia they had been pacifist sectarians for two hundred fifty years, during which time their numbers grew despite severe oppression. Doukhobors rejected the values of Orthodox belief and secular government, seeking a purer way of life guided by oral Christian tradition and by rural values of labor and consensus. Their path proved difficult indeed, but at such times as the Burning of Arms in 1894, when communities across southern Russia defied militarism, they bore powerful and enduring witness.

In Canada, Doukhobors settled first in the Prairies, the most devout moving shortly to the West Kootenay region of south central British Columbia. They established a communal social, religious, and economic entity, the Christian Community of Universal Brotherhood (CCUB); this collapsed during the Depression of the 1930s. They also experienced new and profound troubles, externally from the aggressive pressures of North American capitalism but also internally. From the 1930s to 1960s one group, the Freedomites (*Svobodniki*), attacked the new materialism by destroying their own homes and sometimes those of the community people, a tactic that did not succeed in restoring purity to earth or the Doukhobors to Russia. Despised in ignorance by many of their neighbors, discredited by internal strife, and pressed to adopt the forms and values of the surrounding culture, Doukhobors nevertheless upheld and still maintain their values and communities today. Although many have prospered, many question their security in Canada and some visit Russia, yet the community continues to gather under the new aegis of the Union of Spiritual Communities of Christ (USCC).

MUSIC FORMS AND GENRES

Doukhobors believe that their greatest cultural tool to support cherished beliefs and values is their music, expressed through numerous community choirs in the Prairies and British Columbia and at the Sunday prayer meetings (*Molenye*) and cyclic festivals where they gather to sing. The psalms are central to Doukhobor religion and song; their uniquely melismatic (many notes to one syllable of text) style is apparently ancient but was refined in the eighteenth century, when most of the texts were created within the community.

The harmony used in Doukhobor music is archaic, predominantly using fourths, fifths, and octaves, with melody carried by lower female and upper male voices in unison or organum (identical melodic lines a few intervals apart). Usually straightforward countermelodies are often carried in lower male and upper female voices. Skilled choirs may include one or more women and perhaps one man who sing extreme upper and lower outer voices (*Utvod*) with great freedom. The core melodies apparently derive from ancient Russian ecclesiastical chant with melismas, containing complex internal structures. Psalms contain verses, today only one to three are sung, but one verse might extend for four minutes: a single vowel sung for dozens of seconds, followed by a rush of words and then the next vowel chain. This technique traditionally served complex social purposes, such as concealing in its auditory maze doctrines that spies must not recognize or allowing an imprisoned singer to let other Doukhobors know they were not alone in misery and hope.

Doukhobors today divide their music into sacred and secular categories, with psalms (*psalmi*) and hymns (*stikhi*) in the former and traditional songs (*pesni*) in the latter. The hymn tradition especially is alive and flourishing today. Performers frequently appropriate external song and tune texts. When secular texts are adapted, conventional harmonies and rhythms prevail; however, secular or church texts adapted to sacred use are quickly adjusted to Doukhobor harmonic style.

SCHOLARSHIP

Doukhobors have long valued the distinction and power of their musical heritage, but written collections and scholarship are scarce within as well as outside the community. Yet Doukhobors were recording and distributing reproductions of their music as early as the late 1940s, especially under the extinct Dominion label of Toronto. Doukhobors view writing as inferior to memory: better to "Write it on the heart, Reveal it through the mouth" (*Napishite vo serdtsakh, Vosvestite vo ustakh*), declares a Doukhobor proverb. Recordings (78s, LPs, cassette tapes, CDs) have been widely published and may be found in the Doukhobor centers of Kamsack and Prince Albert, Saskatchewan, and Grand Forks and Castlegar in British Columbia, where two generations of a vigorous home music archiving tradition have developed involving a project (currently under way) to assemble and archive outstanding materials from the past half-century.

"From the Beginning to the Present Time" (figure 1) is commonly used at funerals. Its text is typical in that it uses open dialogue between God and His people in crisis, employing special apocalyptic imagery unique to Doukhobor tradition.

> From the beginning [of time] and to this day
> the Lord calls his children:
>> Come to me, children,
>> come to me, my darlings,
>> For you the Kingdom of heaven is prepared,
>>> by the Lord God,
>>>> our heavenly ruler.
>> Have no regret for your father [and] mother,
>>> all your kinfolk,
>>> all your perishable estate in the flesh.
>> Take pity on me, your Father,
>>> heavenly king in the spirit.
> The children call to him,
> the darlings pray to him:
>> Lord, Lord! It is so hard for us
>>> to enter your heavenly kingdom:
>> all the ways to you are blocked.
>> On the paths stand doors of iron,
>>> gates of brass,
>> at the gates stand foul watchers.

FIGURE I   Doukhobor
psalm (Bonch-Bruevich
#150), "From the Begin-
ning to the Present Time";
transcribed by Kenneth
Peacock (PEA 334-2145),
as sung by a group of
mixed elders, Saskatoon,
Saskatchewan, 8 July
1964. Courtesy Canadian
Museum of Civilization.

FIGURE I   (*continued*)

The Lord speaks back to them:
        Do not fear, my children, do not fear, my darlings;
                for I the mighty champion go in strength before you,
                I shall break down the iron doors,
                I shall tear down the gates of brass,
                and shall scatter the foul watchers,
                but you I shall lead into my heavenly kingdom
                        and be with you forever to reign in paradise;
        Behold the heaven of heavens,
                the face of the God of Jacob.

There are few scholars of Doukhobor song texts. A century ago the Russian populist Vladimir Bonch-Bruevich traveled to Canada with emigrating Doukhobors, with whom he lived for almost a year collecting and recording psalms and related texts, published secretly in Geneva in 1901 as *Zhivotnaia Kniga Dukhobortsev* 'From the Book of Life of the Doukhobor'. Bonch-Breuvich was to become V. I. Lenin's confidential secretary and a significant advocate for peasant groups. In 1966 the National Museum's musicologist Kenneth Peacock recorded a substantial body of Doukhobor music and in 1970 published a superb sampler, *Songs of the Doukhobors,* including three LP inserts; unfortunately, no further music transcriptions have been published to date. In 1972 I completed a dissertation, "Our People's Way," which included 134 psalm texts and translations and much other cultural material. Independent Doukhobor Michael Kalmikoff published a compact printed collection of hymns and songs in 1973; Peter Legebokoff and Anna Markova published a fine major collection including psalms (1978); George Woodcock and Ivan Avakumovic's *The Doukhobors* (1968) and Koozma Tarasoff's *Plakun Trava* 'Willow-herb' (a waterplant believed to grow against the current, and thus a symbol of Doukhobor resistance to secular social values) (1982) provide a broad introduction to Doukhobor history.

REFERENCES

Bonch-Bruevich, Vladimir. 1979 [1954]. *Zhivotnaig Kniga Dukhobortsev* (Book of Life of Doukhobors). Trans. V. Boyniak. Blame Lake, Sask.: privately published.

Kalmikoff, Michael. 1973. *Dukhovnie Stikhi i Narodnie Pesni* (Spiritual Hymns and Folk Songs) Richmond, B.C.: privately published.

Mealing, F. Mark. 1972. "Our People's Way: A Study in Doukhobor Hymnody and Folklife." Ph.D. dissertation, University of Pennsylvania.

Legebokoff, Peter, and Anna Markova, eds. 1978. *Sbornik: Dukhoborcheskikh Psalmov, Stikhov i Pesen* (Collection of Doukhobor Psalms, Hymns and Songs). Grand Forks, B.C.: Union of Spiritual Communities of Christ.

Peacock, Kenneth. 1966. *Twenty Ethnic Songs from Western Canada*. Bulletin 211, Anthropology Series 76. Ottawa: National Museum of Man.

———. 1970. *Songs of the Doukhobors*. Bulletin 231, Folklore Series 7. Includes 3 LP disks. (Flexidiscs TM 3). Ottawa: National Museum of Man.

Tarasoff, Koozma. 1982. *Plakun Trava* (Willowherb). Grand Forks, B.C.: Mir Publishing.

Woodcock, George, and Ivan Avakumovic. 1968. *The Doukhobors*. Toronto: Oxford University Press.

Section 3f
Northern Canada

It may seem that the rugged and harsh terrain and extreme temperatures of the three northern Canadian territories—the Yukon, the Northwest Territory, and Nunavut—would have prevented the establishment of communities large enough to sustain any musical traditions. Yet thousands of Inuit, representing the majority population of Nunavut, and American Indian groups, such as the Dene, Tutchone, and Tlingit in the Yukon, have lived here in scattered communities for over four thousand years, carrying on their ceremonial and ritual life and performing drum dance and gambling songs and games, including the women's vocal genre, referred to by nonaboriginals as "throat singing." Interactions with Europeans in the eighteenth and nineteenth centuries promoted the development of native fiddling and brass band traditions as well. The gold rushes of the mid- and late nineteenth century saw the immigration of many people from the United States, who brought with them theatrical traditions such as vaudeville shows that quickly became popular entertainments. One of the most remarkable developments in Northern Canada in the last twenty years has been the establishment of the Inuit Broadcasting Corporation and the spread of popular music recording studios there.

An Inuit mother and son pose next to an Inuit rock formation in the Nunavut region. © Galen Rowell/CORBIS.

Overview
Beverley Diamond

Inuit
First Nations and Métis
Yukon First Nations
Nonaboriginal Performers
Northern Broadcasting and Recording Industry

Music in each of the three territories of Northern Canada—the Yukon, the Northwest Territories, and the newly formed (1 April 1999) Nunavut—is shaped differently, as the demography of the Inuit, First Nations, and nonaboriginal population varies for each and the Arctic environment ranges widely both in climate and terrain. Although all three territories have majority aboriginal populations (over 70 percent in the Northwest Territory and Nunavut and about 50 percent in the Yukon), their demographic profiles are otherwise contrasted. Over 41,000 Inuit residents constitute the majority population of Nunavut and a sizable proportion of the Northwest Territory (1996 census data). The Athabaskan-speaking Dene predominate in the Northwest Territory. The Yukon is home to diverse First Nations—the northern and southern Tutchone, Tsimshian, Tlingit, and Kaska as well as the Gwich'in (primarily of Old Crow) and the Athapaskan-speaking Han along the Alaska border. Additionally, the population includes residents who have moved from other parts of Canada, the United States, and elsewhere. In all of Canada, the Yukon has the highest proportion of U.S.-born residents, a few of whom are descendants of gold seekers who trekked north in the 1890s.

The only cities are the capitals: Whitehorse, Yukon (approximately 20,000); Yellowknife, Northwest Territory (over 17,000); and Iqaluit, Nunavut (over 4,000). Other communities are generally small and far-flung. In some cases, Inuit people moved into permanent settlements such as Pelly Bay as late as the 1960s, and many still rely on caribou hunting, sealing, or fishing. The geography of Nunavut varies from the mountains of Baffin Island to the rather flat terrain west of Hudson Bay. Of the many communities located on Arctic islands, some are icebound all year. The mineral-rich Northwest Territories (a name that applied to a larger land area before the creation of Nunavut in 1999) has the McKenzie River running through it as well as two sizable lakes; the capital, Yellowknife, is located on Great Slave Lake. The Yukon varies from the moderate climate of the south around the capital city of Whitehorse located on the river of the same name, to the mountainous Kluane region, tourist-oriented towns such as Skagway and Dawson City, and isolated villages in the north. The building of the Alaska Highway in the 1940s is regarded by many residents as the change that effected the most radical transformation of life in this region.

INUIT

Inuit, who arrived in North America about four thousand years ago, perform a variety of traditional and contemporary music. Vocal games, sometimes called "throat singing" by southerners, are practiced by women only in the eastern and central Arctic (from Gjoa Haven east). Called *katajjait* on Baffin Island, in Iglulik, Cape Dorset, and Inoudjouac, similar games are given individual names in central Arctic communities of the Netsilingmiut, where the games are more often texted rather than sung on abstract sounds or vocables. The performance mode, in which two women face one another very closely and alternate sounds or produce them canonically, is described further by Nicole Beaudry in this volume [see ARCTIC CANADA AND ALASKA, p. 374; SUB-ARCTIC CANADA, p. 383]. Juggling games, which share certain structures with the vocal games and concatenate a variety of short repeated motives, are widely performed across the Canadian Arctic. Their texts are nearly incomprehensible, with obscure references to myth, obsolete words, and joking scatological references. Short songs also occur in the context of myth narration; the myth of "Kiviuq," for example, contains a song contest between animals such as the wolf and wolverine.

The most highly esteemed songs in the central and western Arctic are the drum dance songs (called *pisiq,* pl. *pisiit,* in central Arctic villages). Solo, male-only drum dancers in the central Arctic are accompanied by the chanting of a women's chorus. Songs are personal to individuals and are often long narratives recording hunting exploits and other personal experiences. Formerly drum dance songs might be mocking caricatures of fellow hunters, used as contests between rivals. The songs' careful record of travel in the north has traditionally served to establish land use and has been cited as evidence in such documents as the Inuit Land Use and Occupancy Project (1976). Further west, the tradition of drum dancing resembles that in Alaska, in which a group of seated drummer-singers accompanies a dancer (figure 1). The use of decorated dance gloves and mimetic dance enactments of story songs are other distinguishing features of the western tradition.

Inuit have adapted a number of traditions first learned from European visitors as their own. The unique bowed zither called the *tautirut* closely resembles an instrument found in northern Finland, although the link between these two is not proven, and some believe that sinew-strung instruments predate European contact. In Nain, Labrador, where Moravian missionaries have resided since the eighteenth century, a brass band tradition developed (Lutz 1982). Button accordion and fiddle players have been integral to social dances in northern communities since at least the late nineteenth century. Musical interaction of Inuit and whalers in the Cumberland Sound area has been reconstructed by Maija Lutz (1978), who notes that accordion-based music in the community of Pangnirtung is called "Eskimo music." Among well-known Inuit fiddlers of the 1990s are Charlie Tumik from Umiujaq and Eddie Kikoak of Gjoa Haven. Leah Surusila has recorded button accordion improvization on *The Inuit Artist World Showcase* (1995).

Since the 1970s, singer-songwriters using Western harmonies and drawing on hymns, folk songs, country music, and to a lesser extent rock and roll have been central spokespersons in the representation of northern issues and lifestyles to a larger audience. The work of artists such as the pioneer Charlie Panagoniak, first-generation singers such as Charlie Adams, William Tagoona, Etulu Etidloiee, and Tumasi Quissaq, and younger artists such as the duo Tudjaat, Lucie Idlout, and the northern superstar Susan Aglukark are discussed elsewhere in this volume [see POPULAR MUSIC, p. 1279].

FIGURE I   Inuit drummers and dancers from Inuvik, N.W.T., performing at the Yukon International Storytelling Festival in 1998. Photo by Beverley Diamond.

FIRST NATIONS AND MÉTIS

The territory of the Dene nation, centered in the area around and between Great Slave and Great Bear Lakes in the Northwest Territory, extends across the boundaries of the

1276 MUSICAL CULTURES AND REGIONS

Yukon and British Columbia. Through the twentieth century, the Dene struggled to prevent a McKenzie Valley pipeline from being built through their territory.

Some contemporary Eastern Dene festivities may have emerged out of treaty day celebrations, as Nancy Lurie notes with regard to the Dogrib, with whom she did research in the 1960s. Observing the feasting, hand games, and dances associated with a contemporary treaty day celebration at Rae, she notes: "Dancing during the evening of the treaty feast was all of the type known as the tea dance. The name derives from the fact that traditionally the Hudson's Bay Company provided the chief with tea and bannock to feed the assembled group when the people came into the fort with their winter's fur take. The tea dance has no accompaniment except the human voice, the dancers gathering into an ever-widening circle, moving with mincing steps clockwise, crowding tightly, shoulder to shoulder, and facing into the centre of the circle" (Helm and Lurie 1962:10). Frame drums with snares on the top of the membrane are used for social occasions as well as for private use (Keillor 1985–1986). Tea dances were replaced by drum dances as the most popular events in the late-twentieth century. Drum dances among the Slavey are either Rabbit dances or Cree dances (Asch 1988). Different dance formations here involve the whole community, including choreographies in which lines move toward one another and back. Asch (1988) relates drum dancing to kinship. In western Dene communities (as in the Yukon), potlatches commemorating a deceased relative continue to be practiced, although on a smaller scale than formerly.

The drum was also considered a private instrument, a tool used to communicate with spirit guides; such personal repertoires were usually associated with dreams. Asch describes the divination skill of certain Slavey individuals in "dreaming true" (1988:30–31). Several scholars have observed, however, that the marked individuality of Dene spirituality has often been misrepresented by outsiders (Ridington 1990:100–118). Jean-Guy Goulet, for instance, has observed that "among Athapaskans a person with religious experience is described not as a believer but as someone who 'knows'" while "generally anthropologists do not share in the kinds of experiences—dreams, visions, power of songs, ceremonies—that are at the foundation of aboriginal religious experience and knowledge" (1987:4). One spiritual practice that recognizes the power of individual dreams and visions but has been made more public is the century-old tradition of prophet singing (Beaudry 1992), a blend of indigenous and Christian belief systems.

A widely performed traditional repertoire of drumming and singing at the beginning of the twenty-first century, however, accompanies hand or gambling games. These team sports, in which small marked sticks are exchanged among the members of one team under a blanket while the other team guesses the location of the sticks, are especially popular with youth. These games are now highly competitive, and aspects of magic attributed to earlier generations are generally no longer practiced. Contemporary singer-songwriters of Dene ancestry include Leela Gilday and David Gon.

YUKON FIRST NATIONS

The central ceremonial practice of Yukon First Nations, as well as western Dene in the Northwest Territory and coastal nations, is the potlatch, a ceremony marking and validating a major social change such as the death of a relative, the anniversary of the death of a relative, the installation of a new chief, and so on. Marked by elaborate gift giving, feasting, formal oratory, the displaying of clan crests (worn, for example, on button blankets), and the performance of specialized dance and music repertoires, contemporary potlatches are more localized and less elaborate than they were in previous times. The clan and moiety systems facilitate the potlatch, as one moiety hosts the event for the individual from the other. In the Yukon these moiety groups are usually the Crow and Wolf. Traditional knowledge of songs and stories has been transmitted in the

Yukon by a group of remarkable women performers including Annie Ned, Angela Sydney, and Kittie Smith. Their oral histories have been published by anthropologist Julie Cruikshank (1990).

An instance of a large contemporary potlatch was one hosted in 1998 in Whitehorse by Judy Gingell, the first Native woman to be commissioner of the Yukon Territory. After opening prayers in different aboriginal languages of the Yukon First Nations and the singing of the Tlinkit national anthem, Gingell observed that this was the first time in approximately one hundred years that all First Peoples in the territory had potlatched together. Others noted that the first potlatch, recorded in myth, was hosted by a Crow woman and that this 1998 event marked a new cycle, as it too was hosted by a Crow woman. A stick gambling tent was busy all day. On stage, performers included groups of youth who learn traditional dance styles—the local Dakwakada Dancers, the Upper Tanana Scottie Creek dancers, the Tagish Nation Dancers from Carcross, Yukon, and the Tahltan dancers among others; fiddle and step dancers from Old Crow, a remote northern community; and visiting performers, including Inuit recording artist Willie Thrasher and a contemporary ensemble, Sun Dog, as well as a large group of singers from the Han Nation who were publicly performing repertoire that had not been heard for a long time. Gifts of songs were made during the feasting. A giveaway including tee-shirts or posters for all participants followed the feast.

The gambling song repertoire is the root of contemporary Northern Tutchone singer Jerry Alfred's music. He also writes folklike songs, many describing specific places or events, in his native language. A number of Yukon country and western, rhythm and blues, or rock bands include members who are First Nations affiliated. Fiddling has remained particularly popular in the more northerly communities. Craig Mishler (1993) has documented the tunes of Gwitchin and Métis players in both the Yukon and Alaska.

NONABORIGINAL PERFORMERS

The earliest documentation of nonaboriginal performers in the north relates to the Yukon gold rushes of the 1890s. Vaudeville shows thrived in the local saloons, and they continue to be reinvented a century later for the tourist market in summer cabarets, especially in Whitehorse and Dawson City hotels. The history of this genre reveals a distinctive negotiation of respectability and gentility. Prominent within the saloon culture were dancers such as Klondike Kate, the exotic Little Egypt, or the "40 shapely ladies" (broadside description) who performed alongside juggling and other musical acts at venues such as the Palace Grand in Dawson City. One response to such acts was the establishment of the Family Theatre in 1898, a venue that advertised itself as "the first theatre ever opened in the Northwest not in any way connected with a saloon. The entertainments will be of the highest order. The patrons can be assured there will be no slang or obscene language used on the stage at any time" (Yukon Archives). Paradoxically, gentility did not preclude parody: this theater presented a minstrel show as its first production.

In the early twentieth century, settlers favored the fiddle, mandolin, button accordion, guitar (figure 2), and, after 1930, the saxophone for domestic entertainment or local dancing. Even mining compounds formed musical ensembles. In the 1930s, for example, the Wernecke Camp Orchestra in the Yukon consisted of two banjos, two fiddles, two saxophones, and a bass drum.

Songwriters throughout the century have written about the spectacular wilderness of the north, often fetishizing stereotypic symbols of northern life. Folk-inspired songs with northern themes continue in the work of Yukon artists Manfred Jansen, Steve Slade, Kim Barlow, Len Osland, and others. More diverse is the band Inconnu, the repertoire of which blends Cajun, jazz, and pop elements. In Nunavut and the Northwest Territories, the Gumboots (led by Bill Gilday) and singers such as Moira Cameron similarly favor northern narratives. Country styles prevail in the work of many N.W.T.

FIGURE 2   Yukon homesteaders c. 1900 at Eldorado Creek. Photo courtesy of Yukon Archives.

FIGURE 3   Whitehorse Arts Centre, Yukon.
Photo by Beverley Diamond.

songwriters such as Tom Hudson. The development of northern festivals in the 1980s stimulated popular music production, showcasing local talent alongside national and international acts while capitalizing on the growing tourist market. Folk on the Rocks (Yellowknife) and the Dawson City Festival are the largest events. A small classical music and jazz scene also finds a place in the north. Both local musicians and, increasingly, visiting performers are involved, particularly since the opening of the modern Whitehorse Arts Centre (figure 3) and the Northern Arts and Cultural Center in Yellowknife.

NORTHERN BROADCASTING AND RECORDING INDUSTRY

Radio reached many areas of the north by the 1920s but was used primarily for medical emergencies and business. By the 1990s, in the Northwest Territories, the Native Communications Society linked about thirty community stations; CKNM-FM in Yellowknife is one of the largest, broadcasting in five Dene languages.

The Anik A satellite, launched in 1972, brought television to most northern communities; concurrently in the 1970s, film and video production workshops such as the Nunatsiakmiut Native Communications Society (Iqaluit) began producing northern programming. Following intense lobbying by the Inuit Tapirisat of Canada for Inuktitut-language programming, the Iqaluit-based Inuit Broadcasting Corporation was established in 1981 and, soon after, the production-oriented Taqramiut Nipingat Incorporated.

In 1992 Television Northern Canada began producing one hundred hours of programming per week in eleven native languages as well as English and French. In 1999 TVNC was replaced by a nationwide network, the Aboriginal Broadcast Network, which brings northern productions for the first time to millions of southern viewers.

Inuit and First Nations musicians were first recorded by the CBC in the 1970s. Montréal producer Les McLaughlin played an important role in promoting these artists. The initial recordings of both traditional and contemporary musical styles were intended for local distribution and broadcast. In the 1990s, however, recording studios proliferated due to the economic feasibility of high-quality digital technologies and the Internet, which facilitates the marketing of independent labels more effectively. Consequently a small boom in the northern recording industry has occurred. Inukshuk Productions (established 1994 in Inukjuak) is exemplary. Their popular first CD, the *Inuit Artist World Showcase,* was recorded live in 1994 and included artists from Canada, Alaska, and Greenland performing gospel, throat singing, country and western, "electro-pop," fiddle, accordion, folk, and blues. In the Yukon, high-quality professional recording facilities (particularly Old Crow Studio) and production companies (Caribou Records, Whispering Willows Records) are important components of the international success of Jerry Alfred, Inconnu, Kim Barlow, and Matthew Lien.

REFERENCES

Asch, Michael. 1988. "Kinship and the Drum Dance in a Northern Dene Community." Boreal Institute for Northern Studies.

Beaudry, Nicole. 1992. "The Language of Dreams. Songs of the Dene Indians." In *Music and Spiritual Power among the Indians of North America,* ed. Richard Keeling. Special Issue, *World of Music* 92(2):72–90.

Cruikshank, Julie. 1990. *Life Lived like a Story: Life Stories of Three Yukon Elders.* Lincoln: University of Nebraska Press.

Goulet, Jean-Guy. 1987. "Ways of Knowing with the Mind: An Ethnography of Aboriginal Beliefs."

Paper presented at CESCE Conference, Québec City.

Helm, June, and Nancy Lurie. 1962. *The Dogrib Hand Game.* Ottawa: National Museum of Man.

The Inuit Artist World Showcase. 1995. Inukjuak: Inukshuk Productions.

Inuit Land Use and Occupancy Project. 1976. Ottawa: Ministry of Supply and Services.

Keillor, Elaine. 1985–1986. "Les Tambours des Athapaskan du nord." *Recherches Amerindiennes au Québec* 15(4):43–52.

Lutz, Maija M. 1978. *The Effects of Acculturation on Eskimo Music of Cumberland Peninsula.* Ottawa: National Museum of Man.

———. 1982. *Musical Traditions of the Labrador Coast Inuit.* Ottawa: National Museums.

Mishler, Craig. 1993. *The Crooked Stovepipe: Athapaskan Fiddle Music and Square Dancing in Northeast Alaska and Northwest Canada.* Urbana: University of Illinois Press.

Ridington, Robin. 1990. *Little Bit Know Something: Stories in a Language of Anthropology.* Vancouver: Douglas and McIntyre.

Statistics Canada. *1996 Census.* Available at <www.statcan.ca>.

Yukon Archives. Whitehorse: Al Johnson Collection.

Popular Music
Beverley Diamond

Early Inuit Performers
Contemporary Inuit, First Nations, and Métis Performers
Nonaboriginal Performers

This articles focuses on late-twentieth-century popular music, defined as commercially oriented, commodified music produced by recording artists from northern Canada. Musics that served such social functions of popular music as entertainment or dance accompaniment, for instance, would constitute a broader category. Some genres of traditional Inuit and First Nations music would fall into the latter: Inuit women's vocal games, for instance, or arguably, the stick gambling songs of northern Dene and Yukon First Nations. Similarly, the music performed by the vaudevillians of turn-of-the-century saloons or homemade entertainment using fiddle, mandolin, or button accordion is also popular music broadly defined [see OVERVIEW, p. 1274]. The narrower topic of late-twentieth-century recorded popular music, on the other hand, is an important one, as a number of factors have coincided to enable its flourishing. One is the general popularity of world music, a factor that has particularly enabled performers of Inuit, Métis, and First Nations descent. Another is the increasing economic feasibility of owning first-rate studio equipment, both digital and analog. A third is the marketing opportunity afforded by the Internet. In northern Canada, the production has involved aboriginal and nonaboriginal musicians including a remarkable number of bands that include members from a range of ethnocultural backgrounds.

EARLY INUIT PERFORMERS

Among the pioneers of Inuit recording, Charlie Panagoniak (Eskimo Point) learned to play guitar while recovering from tuberculosis in a southern sanitorium. His songs, first recorded by the CBC in 1973, are stylistically influenced by hymns, folk songs, and country music. He has made LPs, including *Inuktitut Christmas and Gospel Songs*, and has been active through the 1990s, performing at various northern festivals as well as at WOMAD (World of Music, Arts, Dance) in Toronto. Etulu Etidloiee was one of the earliest Inuit songwriters to try to incorporate traditional style elements (from juggling games, for example) into contemporary idioms. Noteworthy is the fact that some musicians in the 1970s used the guitar analogously to the drum, keeping the rhythm but not always coordinating chord changes with those implied in the tune. Lyrics concerned relationships—more often those with family or friends rather than with romantic partners—memories of earlier times, travels, or local belief and customs. Others who made CBC recordings in the 1970s and early 1980s included Charlie Adams, William Tagoona, Willie Thrasher, Alexis and Victor Utanaq, and the comic singer Tumasi Quissa (later spelled Quitsaq).

CONTEMPORARY INUIT, FIRST NATIONS, AND MÉTIS PERFORMERS

Unique syntheses of traditional and contemporary styles emerged after the 1980s. Laina Tulluga and Martha Sivuarapik performed vocal games with guitar accompaniment at the 1986 Innu Nikamu festival in Uashat, Québec. Aqsarniit (based in Ontario but consisting of Inuit from different Arctic communities) and Komatsiutiksak blend both throat singing and drum dance with contemporary pop styles, while the duo Tudjaat (Madeleine Allakarialak and Phoebe Atagotaaluk) combines synthesized accompaniment and expressive dance with throat singing. On the other hand, Lucie Idlout asserts her right to sing hard-hitting rock and roll without identifiable "aboriginal" elements, although the subject matter of her songs deals with challenging issues in the region, including the high suicide rate in Inuit communities.

FIGURE I   Jerry Alfred and The Medicine Beat in performance. *Left to right:* Andrea McColeman (keyboards), Marie Gogo (backup vocals), Jerry Alfred (guitar), Bob Hamilton (guitar), Mark Paradis (percussion). Jerry Alfred belongs to the Crow Clan of the Northern Tutchone First Nation. Photo by Beverley Diamond.

The most commercially successful Inuit artist to date is unquestionably Susan Aglukark. She frequently acknowledges her musical beginnings in the choir of her father's church in Arviat, N.W.T., as well as the importance of Christianity in her life, reflected, for instance, in the unaccompanied rendition of "Amazing Grace" in Inuktitut at the end of her *Arctic Rose* album (1992). Her clear voice, folk-influenced compositions, and acoustically uncluttered arrangements are gentler than many of her lyrics. Among songs that address tough social issues are "Suffer in Silence" (about sexual abuse) and "Kathy I" (about suicide). More celebratory are "O Siem" and "This Child," the latter incorporating "a ya yai" refrains reminiscent of traditional drum dance songs. EMI Canada released her fourth album, *This Child* (1995), and her fifth, *Unsung Heroes* (1999), both produced by Chad Irshick.

In the Northwest Territories and Yukon, Dene artists Leela Gilday and David Gon, southern Tutchone Daniel Tlen, and the award-winning northern Tutchone singer-songwriter Jerry Alfred are leading the way. Alfred, who won a Juno award in 1995 for the best album in aboriginal Canada, has toured Germany with his band, The Medicine Beat, and has performed at major festivals in North America (figure 1). His repertoire includes traditional gambling songs, most often accompanied simply by his frame drum but occasionally arranged for keyboard, percussion, guitar, and electronics, as in "Stick Gambling Rock" on his third album, *Kehlonn* (1998). He writes contemporary songs mostly on primary chords, many of which describe places of importance in his experience. He favors heavy reverberation, relating the echo to the sense of space that is rooted in his experience growing up in a remote community in the northern Yukon. His band draws on jazz stylings (the keyboard player Andrea McColeman) and country guitar influences (Bob Hamilton) in the (often extended) instrumental solos.

NONABORIGINAL PERFORMERS

Among the nonaboriginal artists of note in the Canadian north is Bill Gilday. With his band, the Gumboots, he wrote "The Resurrection of Billy Adamache" in 1989 about wilderness survival. The north inspires the lyrics of the Celtic folk trio Northern Skies (Suzanne Montreuil, Ron Kent, and Greg O'Neil). The rawness of Yukon life is captured in the music of Kim Barlow from Whitehorse. The rather unusual sounds of plucked cello, marimba, and very dry percussion depart from the expected arrangements for popular song but connect her to singers such as Suzanne Vega or Veda Hille, whom she admires. Eclecticism is also the mark of the popular Whitehorse band Inconnu, in which Cajun elements (conveyed by francophone singer Lucy Desaulniers and evident in songs such as "Jigi Dou") combine with punk, jazz, and rock. The semi-spoken, short-phrased lyrics of the male lead (Nick de Graf) are distinctive. Hip-hop and related genres had by the late 1990s only just begun to impact the northern popular music scene. The Yellowknife rappers Unonymous (Taj Johnson and Aaron Hernandez) played the Folk on the Rocks festival in 1998.

Northern Canada, then, has produced a remarkable number of musicians relative to its small population. In part this relates to the fact that there are relatively fewer other social outlets in the region as compared with southern cities. In part the wilderness experience seems to continue to inspire poetry and music. Furthermore, the distinctions among ethnocultural groups and genres are not so easily drawn here. Musicians who play one type of music are quickly drawn into projects with different genres and instrumental mixes, depending on who is available in these relatively small communities. Inuit, Métis, and First Nations residents have adopted the popular musics of the day as theirs for several centuries (ceremonial musics are still used only in appropriate contexts). Hence issues of authenticity and identity are cast differently here. Many bands that include both aboriginal and nonaboriginal members find that their eclecticism is initially confusing to southern audiences, although this is becoming less and less the case. Furthermore, the northern scene may seem "local" compared to that of major urban centers in the south, but there are often unexpected international linkages such as those between Canadian and other indigenous groups.

REFERENCES

Aglukark, Susan. 1992. *Arctic Rose.* Independently produced by Susan Aglukark.

———. 1995. *This Child.* EMI Canada. E2 7243 8 32075 2 7. Compact disc.

———. 1999. *Unsung Heroes.* EMI Canada. 7243 8 53393 2 5. Compact disc.

Alfred, Jerry. 1994. *Etsi Shon.* Independently produced by Jerry Alfred. Compact disc.

———. 1998. *Kehlonn.* Caribou Records. CRCD004. Compact disc.

Panagoniak, Charlie, n.d. *Inuktitut Christmas and Gospel Songs.* Boot Records. NCB 501. LP disk.

Statistics Canada. *1996 Census.* Available at <www.statcan.ca>.

Glossary

à la Turka Turkish style of music played at Armenian community events (1036)

accordion Portable wind instrument with a keyboard (*see* index)

acid house Subcategory of house music repertoire that media often associate with drugs, especially Ecstasy (or "E") (691)

aerophone Musical instrument whose sound is produced by vibrating air, such as a flute (*see* index)

aguinaldo In Puerto Rico, a genre of strophic song particularly associated with Christmas season, taking its name from the small Christmas offering called *aguinaldo* (727, 799, 850)

alabado Form of free meter religious folk song developed in late-nineteenth/early-twentieth-century New Mexico, typically sung unaccompanied and in unison by a group of worshipers; occasionally a *pito* or small flute accompanies the singers (9, 437, 755–756, 759, 761–762, 848, 8530)

alabanza 'Praise', New Mexican Hispano hymn type that is distinguished from the very distinctive *alabados*; the most common and frequent contemporary arena for the performance of these hymns is the Catholic Church (437, 759)

alap-jor-jhala Sequence of musical sections at the beginning of a Hindustani instrumental performance (983)

amane (pl. *amanedes*) Improvisatory vocal pieces in free rhythm that originated in Greek enclaves in Asia Minor (930)

Aqausiq Arctic song composed by a relative at the birth of a child, consecrating a lifelong link between the two people (376, 378)

Arbeterring 'Workmen's Circle', a fraternal, socialist-leaning organization among East European Jewish immigrants (939)

arpa harp Diatonic harp with many regional variants in Mexico and Central and South America (473, 493, 723)

'ataba and *mijana* Improvised sung folk poetry, with alternation of metric and nonmetric sections (1035)

autoharp String instrument similar to a zither, used as accompaniment in folk and country and western music (78, 240, 868, 880)

autos sacramentales Short Spanish religious dramas typically performed on the occasion of religious feast days and including music and dance (848, 850)

ayai Cambodian repartee singing accompanied by a small ensemble, sometimes performed by Cambodians in the United States (1001)

backbeat Emphasis placed on beats two and four, usually by the snare drum (671)

baile de venado Deer dance performed by the Yaqui Indians during the Easter season (851)

bajista bajo sexto or *bajo quinto* player (775, 778–779)

bajo de uñas Fretted, flat-backed lute with four strings that are either plucked or struck with a mallet; similar to the orchestral string bass in shape and function (1025)

bajo quinto Bajo sexto without the sixth (E/e) string pair (775)

bajo sexto Guitar with six double courses of steel strings, used in Texas–Mexican *conjunto* music (723, 772–776, 779, 781)

balafo (*balaphon*) African xylophone (593)

balalaika Russian/Balkan plucked fretted lute with a triangle-shaped resonator (57–58, 59, 529, 915, 917, 920, 1199)

ballad opera Originating in eighteenth-century England, a comic play with songs in which new texts are set to familiar tunes (46, 137, 179–182, 189, 542, 837, 839, 1079, 1118)

ban Chinese hollow wood block instrument (*see* index)

banda/orquesta synonymous terms for Tejano dance bands similar in instrumentation to Anglo-American swing bands

banda (1) Brass band, wind band; (2) in Mexico, particular regional styles and repertoires of music; (3) in the 1990s, a highly popular commercial music based on regional bandas (723, 746, 770, 772–773, 778–779, 781, 1085)

banda sinaloense Performing style from the state of Sinaloa in Mexico (746)

banda típica Early-twentieth century Texas–Mexican string band (772–773)

bandoneón Large button accordion, particularly popular in the revival of Argentine tango music in the late twentieth century (730)

bandurria (*bandurría*) Fretted, flat-backed plucked lute with fourteen strings in six courses used for soprano and alto voices in the *rondalla*, found in Spain and Latin America (1025)

bangu Type of Chinese drum (960–961)

banjo Fretted chordophone of African origin with four or five strings on a neck attached to a drumlike body; depending on the number of strings, played with a plectrum or finger picks (*see* index)

bazm Iranian private musical social event (1034, 1041)

Bear Dance Ute ceremony usually (but not always) conducted in the spring; characterized by women's choice couple dancing and the use of a large rasp that accompanies the singing (415, 422–427, 525, 1087)

beat box Also drum machine, (1) electronic percussion characteristic of hip-hop music from the 1980s; (2) an orally produced percussion sound emulating electronic beatbox or drum machine; (3) to produce hip-hop oral percussion, usually to accompany an MC

bel canto Italian opera style of the eighteenth and early nineteenth centuries that emphasizes beautiful vocal tone and lyrical phrasing (181, 528, 551, 863, 930)

Bembe Afro-Cuban religious music celebration

berimbao Used to accompany the Brazilian *capoeira* dance, a musical bow with gourd resonator held against the chest and struck on its metal string with a small stick (730)

bhajan Hindu devotional song genre (814, 817, 950, 982–984, 989–990, 1084, 1246)

bijuela Musical bow found in New Mexican Hispano communities (762)

bitsitsi Reed instrument played by the Zuni Indians (478)

biwa Japanese pear-shaped plucked lute with a bent neck, usually having four or five strings and played with a large plectrum (968–969)

blackface Practice commonly used in American minstrelsy, in which African Americans are portrayed by performers whose faces have been blackened by burnt cork (*see* index)

blow harmony Technique used by singers to blow vocables into a microphone for sound effects (671)

blue note In blues and blues-influenced music (for example, jazz, rock and roll), a note that falls between two adjacent notes in the modern Western division of the octave (twelve equal intervals), expressed variously as a neutral pitch, an upward slur within a semitone range, a wavering of pitch, or a simultaneous sounding of flat and natural pitches (457, 523, 539, 593, 641–642, 644, 648, 659, 665, 711)

bluegrass Hybrid of Appalachian "old-time" (hillbilly) music developed by Bill Munroe in 1938 in Kentucky; usually performed by four to seven people singing and accompanying themselves on acoustic chordophones including guitar, mandolin, fiddle, five-string banjo, and bass (*see* index)

blues scale a scale incorporating one or more blue notes (642)

bo Chinese cymbals mainly used in theatres and on ceremonial occasions (960)

bodhrán Traditional Irish hand-held frame drum (326, 842)

bolero (1) Spanish dance in triple meter, originating in the late eighteenth century and frequently performed by a pair of dancers with castanets; (2) Cuban duple meter dance and song form characterized by distinctive, interlocking rhythmic patterns; (3) romantic song of Mexican origin with a slow rumba beat (737, 739, 775, 781, 793, 795)

bomba Genre of Afro-Puerto Rican music and dance centered on the *bomba* drums (337, 516, 726–727, 799)

bongo drums (*bongoes*) Pair of small hand-played conical single-headed Afro-Cuban drums from which different pitches and percussive qualities may be produced (726)

boogie-woogie bass line Rhythmic pattern that outlines chord structures on the first, third, fifth, sixth, and eighth degrees of the scale in a series of eighth notes; played by the left hand on the piano or a bass guitar in a combo against a syncopated pattern in the right hand (668, 670)

bouzouki Greek multistringed instrument that since the late 1970s has been incorporated into Irish traditional music (504, 529–530, 826, 842, 930, 1199)

box drum Box-shaped wooden drum, open at both ends, sometimes played at North Alaskan feasts (375, 400)

box fiddle In the Eastern Arctic, a three-stringed box-shaped fiddle, presumably inspired by the fiddles observed in the hands of the early whalers (375)

brass band Musical ensemble popular during the nineteenth century, normally consisting of brass and percussion instruments (11, 1094)

break Section of a popular R&B, disco, or funk song of the 1970s and early 1980s in which harmonic instruments drop out and percussion (that is, congas, bongos, cowbells, and timbales) is featured; considered by DJs and dancers to be the most rhythmically exciting section

bridge (1) Mechanical device made of wood, metal, bone, or some combination of these, located at or near the center of the body of a chordophone and over which the strings pass, causing the body of the instrument to resonate the vibrations produced by the strings; (2) term used to describe melodic structure in popular music, the bridge being the second or B part of a two-part A, B melody or a contrasting instrumental section in songs

broadside ballad Songs published cheaply on large pieces of newspaper (broadsides) that present stories in a straightforward manner, accompanied by blocky, often undistinguished tunes that may be reused (180, 834, 1123–1124, 1188, 1257)

bugalú Blend of Latin rhythms and African American rhythm and blues (799)

bugle Military trumpet developed around 1880 that contains side holes operated by keys (83, 899, 969)

bullroarer Friction aerophone, or wind instrument, typically constructed as a trapezoid-shaped wooden slab tied to a string or leather thong and whirled in the air to produce a buzzing sound, found in the Arctic and elsewhere in the world

bygdelag Community life and traditional activities of Norwegian settlers; in the United States these practices fell into decline in the early twentieth century (866, 869, 881)

café aman Coffeehouse tradition of music, conversation, and refreshment found in American Middle Eastern communities (1032–1033)

cajita musical 'Small musical box', mounted on a stand and played with two sticks as part of the Afro-Cuban rumba ensemble (729)

cajones Boxes played like drums in Afro-Cuban music (786)

calinda African dance performed in French West Indies and Louisiana (596)

call–response style Antiphonal singing between leader and chorus; major musical characteristic of African American music, especially work songs and blues (814)

caller Person who calls out the choreography to the dancers during a performance of social square dance music (231, 233–234, 746, 760, 865, 887, 1256)

canción (pl. *canciones*) (1) Popular Mexican song genre; (2) topical song (730, 736–739, 755–756, 797, 1204)

canción ranchera Mexican country song, embracing a variety of formal structures, meters, and tempos; evocative of rural life or themes (739, 755–756)

CanCon regulations Regulations introduced by the Canadian Radio and Telecommunications Commission in 1970 requiring Canadian radio stations to play a certain quota of Canadian music (18, 314, 1103–1104)

canned music (1) Prerecorded music, as opposed to live performance; (2) expression used by musicians to refer derogatorily to recorded music (708)

cante jondo 'Deep song', the throaty, impassioned improvised flamenco song (731, 851)

cantiga Monophonic song in the Luso-Galician troubadour tradition dating back to the thirteenth century (847)

cantor Singer of sacred music hired by a Jewish congregation to act as messenger of their prayers; more recently, a member of the staff clergy (12, 98, 544, 933, 935, 938, 940, 1175)

capoeira Brazilian tradition of dance of a martial arts character, with accompanying music played on the berimbao musical bow (210, 730–731)

Cha Cymbals used in Afro-Cuban music (717, 796, 961)

cha-cha-cha Cuban dance style originating in the 1950s

chamblai (*raj nplaim*) Hmong free-reed side-blown pipe with a high falling tone, short low tone, and glottalized ending pattern (1005)

chamrieng 'Vocals', Cambodian singing featured in the *pinnpeat* ensemble (1001)

Changmian Peking opera music ensemble (961)

chanson à repondre (*chanson doubleé*) 'Response style', in which everyone participates by singing refrain lines and/or by repeating the verse line

chapei dang veng lute Long-necked Cambodian lute used in the Khmer wedding and epic singing ensembles (999)

chapuli (*raj pus lim*) Hmong fipple flute with low- to mid-level tone, short low tone and glottalized ending pattern (1005)

charanga Afro-Cuban dance band style originating in the 1950s (788–791, 795–797, 800)

charango Small guitar of Andean origin, constructed from the shell of the *quirquincho* (a regional variety of armadillo), usually with five double courses of nylon strings (730)

charcheta Three-valve tenor horn used to play off-beats in the Sinaloan *banda* ensemble (723)

chegança (1) Brazilian dance drama and procession depicting the Christians battling the Moors; (2) a sensuous Afro-Brazilian dance (850)

chhing 'Small cymbals', Cambodian percussion instrument played as part of the *pinnpeat* ensemble, serves as the time keeper in the ensemble (1001)

chica Neo-African social dance practiced by Afro-Haitians in nineteenth-century New Orleans (596, 802)

Child ballads (1) Oldest substantial body of oral tradition sung English-language poetry, often concerning love; (2) a repertoire first systematically collected by Sir Francis James Child (1825–1896) in Great Britain and North America (29, 511, 519–520, 833–834, 1123–1124, 1188–1189)

Choctaw social dance songs Set of songs originally associated with the Ballgame cycle performed among American Indians of the Eastern Woodlands and Great Lakes but now performed in secular contexts such as festivals (468–469, 471)

chorale Hymn tune of the German Protestant Church (10, 138, 768, 867, 887, 1118, 1174, 1214, 1237–1238)

chotis *Waila* dance form whose name is derived from the German *schottisch*, originally brought to Madrid from Scotland; later became popular in Latin America (490)

chowtal In Indo-Caribbean culture, a vigorous, responsorial male song genre performed during the springtime *phagwa* festival (815)

chrieng chapei Cambodian epic singing in which a vocalist accompanies himself on a long-necked lute; has not survived within the U.S. Cambodian community (1001)

chordophone musical instrument such as a violin or guitar, whose sound is produced by a vibrating string (*see* index)

chromatic In Western music, pertaining to a scale or passage that contains only half steps (126–127, 165–166, 652, 654, 658, 661, 666, 774, 777, 860, 877)

ciaramella Italian oboe (860–861)

cinquillo Five-beat "throb" cast in duple meter; also a feature of Cuban *contradanzas*, most likely via the French *contradanse* (783, 786, 791)

circle of fifths Schematic representation depicting the major keys most closely related to one another within the Western tonal system, located a fifth apart (783, 786, 791)

cittern Long-necked, multistringed instrument used to play Irish traditional music (842)

clave One of a pair of sticks used to play a rhythm that serves as the rhythmic base of Afro-Cuban music (280, 729, 783, 786, 788, 792–793)

comedia Full-length Spanish drama, lasting up to three hours, in several (usually three) acts and typically incorporating song, dance, and instrumental music (848)

comparsa (1) Form of percussive Afro-Cuban processional music used in *carnaval* and other festive settings; (2) ensemble of musicians playing *comparsa* music (729, 796)

compas direct (*konpa*) Modified *merengue* danced at a leisurely tempo, which became popular among Haitians and Haitian Americans in the 1950s and 1960s (803)

concertina Small reed instrument in the accordion family (231, 762, 842, 893–894, 898, 1189)

conga drum Narrow barrel-shaped Afro-Cuban drum (729, 785–786, 984)

conguero Player of the conga drum (732, 797, 799)

conjunto 'combo', used to describe many regional Latin musical ensembles; in Texas, synonymous with *conjunto tejano*, the accordion-driven Texas–Mexican ensemble (*see* index)

conjunto norteño Mexican label for *conjunto* (772)

container rattle Rattle that contains seed or other small objects that when shaken produce sound (429, 463, 474–475)

contradanza Iberian and Hispanic American dance derived from the English country dance; in Cuba, a variant of French Creole *contradanse* (790–791, 795, 802, 848)

contredanse Type of French Creole figure dance practiced in Louisiana by French and Haitian immigrants (213, 802, 1164)

coplas Spanish term for couplets typically performed in sets as four-line stanzas with lines two and four ending in rhyme and operating either as independent songs or as part of longer forms such as the romance or *villancico* (757–759, 849, 1173)

corn songs Songs improvised at or associated with seasonal harvest celebrations called corn shuckings (601)

cornet Soprano brass instrument similar to the trumpet, but with a conical rather than cylindrical bore producing a more mellow timbre; popular in military bands in the nineteenth and early twentieth centuries and in jazz (60, 232, 564–565, 568, 795, 874, 895, 897, 1094, 1107, 1190)

corrido Mexican folk ballad and strophic song stemming from the romance tradition, featuring sets of *coplas* with eight-syllable lines (*see* index)

cover record (1) Remake of an old recording; (2) imitative recordings of black music by white artists (671, 709)

cowboy genre Also known as country and western, a later hybrid of hillbilly music developed in western North America in the 1930s and 1940s by film stars such as Gene Autry and Roy Rogers (1256)

coyote Belt rattle used among the O'odham Indians

Creole musics Musics practiced by French and Caribbean settlers in the U.S. gulf states, characterized by syncopated rhythms (803, 858–859)

crooning songs (1) Songs or intoned formulas that include loving crooning sounds of a mother for her child; (2) popular singing style of the 1930s (386)

crossover Originally the process by which a recording released in a secondary market achieves hit status in the mainstream or pop market (*see* index)

cuadrilla 'Quadrille'; New Mexican *cuadrilla* is similar to the American square dance in that it is danced in groups of two or more couples, but cuadrilla does not employ a caller (755, 760)

cuando Hispanic narrative song, marked by the inclusion of the term *cuando* 'when' in the text, usually at the beginning (757)

cuatro In Puerto Rico, a guitar with five double courses of steel strings, central to *música jíbara* (726–727, 776, 780, 799–800)

cumbia Popular lively dance music in duple meter, with origins in Panama and Colombia, now popular in many communities of Latin America and the United States (728, 800, 1085, 1204)

cuna 'Cradle,' referring to a figure in the form of a baby's cradle that Hispano dancers create by interweaving their arms during the course of a dance (755, 760, 800)

cymbály Czech hammered dulcimer (826, 897, 1197, 1200)

dabkah In Arabic music, a folk line dance and accompanying song or music (1035, 1037)

daiko Japanese drum; same word as *taiko*, but *t* changes to *d* when it used in a compound word (970, 973)

daluo Large Chinese gong (961)

dance hall (1) Style of music from Jamaica, West Indies, and New York City; (2) hip-hop and reggae-influenced genre, delivered in Jamaican patois, directly linked to earlier "toasting" Jamaican DJs who rhymed over prerecorded music at public dances (dance halls) in the 1950s and 1960s (702, 811, 1203)

Dances of Universal Peace Body of spiritual practices that integrate breath, movement, and music, originating in California in the mid-1960s and now found worldwide (1042–1043, 1045)

dantal In Indo-Caribbean culture and Bhojpuri-region North India, a metal rod struck rhythmically with a U-shaped clapper (814–815)

danza (*danzón*) Cuban variant of French Creole *contradanse* (797, 799, 802)

darabukka Arabic single-headed ceramic cylindrical drum (953, 1218–1220)

décima Most learned poetic form of New Mexican Hispano music that flourished in fifteenth-century Spain and was subsequently spread throughout the New World; *decima* texts feature a rather intricate formal scheme: four ten-line stanzas, introduced by a four-line quatrain (757, 848–849, 852)

deep house Subcategory of house music, known as soulful house in the U.K., and characterized by either a gospel-influenced vocal track, a minimalist instrumental arrangement, or both (691)

Delaware Big House song Song performed as part of the annual harvest rituals of the Delaware Indians (463–464)

dhikr [Arabic] recollection, remembrance, reiteration, or mentioning, from the verb *dhakara* 'to remember'; often spelled *zikr* or *zekar* (1040, 1043–1046)

dholak Double-headed barrel drum common in Indian and Indo-Caribbean music (814–816, 984, 1246)

didgeridu Australian Aborigine drone instrument whose distinctive sound has become a staple of world beat recordings (337, 340)

digital sampler Computer program that allows any recorded sound to be translated into digital code and thereby combined with other sounds in order to create novel compositions (265)

disco Category of 1970s dance music, derived from the abbreviation of discothèque, the main venue of consumption (*see* index)

disco blending Construction of an uninterrupted flow of music inside a discothèque, by a disc jockey using two or more turntables and an audio mixer; also referred to as mixing (687)

dizi Chinese bamboo flute (961–962, 1260)

dobro Six-stringed guitar with a metal resonator beneath the bridge and a raised nut, noted (or fretted) with a steel bar and plucked with finger picks (79, 160, 164, 166, 240)

domra Russian/Balkan plucked fretted lute with a bowl-shaped resonator (57–59, 61, 920)

doo-wop groups Vocal harmony groups that emphasize the rhythmic delivery of a phrase consisting of vocables such as "doo-wop-doo-wop" or "doo-doo-doo" in the song arrangement (672, 1081)

DOR Abbreviation for dance-oriented rock (689)

doumbeleki Greek hourglass-shaped hand drum (930–931)

dream songs In Subarctic regions, songs that emanate from a person's dreams or visions and that signal the confirmation of a relationship with one's spirit helpers (457)

drone Tone or interval that continues throughout a piece to help sustain a melodic line, especially in Indian music (837)

duff Arabic tambourine (1071, 1125–1126, 1218)

dulcimer Name for two types of folk zither: the Appalachian lap dulcimer, a slender strummed instrument with three or four strings, and the much rarer hammered dulcimer, a trapezoidal

instrument with several dozen pairs of strings, descended from the Persian/Indian *santour* or Hungarian *cimbalom* (*see* index)

el grupo Tejano ensemble consisting of keyboards, guitar, bass, and drums (770, 780)

entriega (from the Spanish *entregar*, 'to send forth') Consists of a musical sending forth of a group or social entity into the community or into a ritual function, used primarily in Hispanic wedding contexts (758–759, 768)

entriega de novios In times when Roman Catholic priests were very rare in New Mexican society, the *entriega de novios* actually substituted for the church wedding ceremony (758)

er xian Two-stringed fiddle of southeastern China (961)

erhu Low-pitched two-stringed fiddle from China (960–962, 1248)

ezpata dantza Basque sword dance (849)

fado Melancholy Portuguese solo song type generally accompanied by the *guitarra* (ten- or twelve-stringed Portuguese guitar) or the *violao* (Spanish guitar); features aspects of the Portuguese ballad tradition (*modhinha*), including rhyming quatrains (*coplas*) and dance rhythms; popular in grassroots Portuguese communities (731, 847, 851, 853, 1197)

Farfisa Single-manual electronic organ produced by the Italian Farfisa company, with electronic oscillators instead of reeds; the portability and distinctive timbre of the Farfisa organ made it a natural choice for popular musicians of the 1960s as well as such conservatory-trained composer-performers as David Borden, Philip Glass, and Steve Reich (254)

festa Italian feast day, typically including a procession with music (850, 852, 862)

fiddle Alternate name for violin; typically describes a violin used to perform vernacular (as opposed to concert) music (*see* index)

field music Military musicians performing on drums, fifes, bagpipes, trumpets, or bugles, who beat or sound the camp duty calls that regulate military life, (298, 564)

fife Traditionally, a one-piece cylindrical transverse wooden flute with mouth and six finger holes, commonly pitched in B♭ but transposing to D, primarily used with drum accompaniment in military and military-styled civilian marching bands (7, 240, 563, 835–836, 840, 1190)

fisarmonica Italian chromatic piano accordion (860)

flamenco (1) Song, dance, and guitar style developed in Andalucia in the south of Spain blending elements of local practice with that from Morocco, Egypt, India, Pakistan, Greece, and other parts of the Near and Far East; (2) a style of Gypsy music with guitar, song, and hand clapping, of southern Spanish origin but diffused throughout the Americas and beyond (*see* index)

Forty-niners (49ers) Social song genre that incorporates English lyrics with American Indian vocables found in Puerto Rico and elsewhere (213, 425)

frame drum Most typical in Arctic and Subarctic regions, a drum consisting of a single (rarely double) membrane stretched over a variably sized bent wood or bone round frame and tied with lacing around the frame or in the back; in the Arctic, the handheld frame drum features a handle (*see* index)

fret (1) a thin metal bar inlaid across the fingerboard on the neck of a chordophone, beneath the strings, which protrudes above the surface, enabling the player to press a string or strings behind it and thus shorten the vibrating portion of the string to change the pitch; (2) to change the pitch of a string or strings on a chordophone (165–166, 930, 994, 1198)

fukuinkai Japanese-American Christian gospel society (969)

funk Syncopated, eclectic form of R&B, beginning in the late 1960s (*see* index)

funk groove Polyrhythmic foundation built on a syncopated bass line that locks with the bass drum pattern and is accentuated by a heavy backbeat (684)

Gaelic song Vocal music in the Scottish Gaelic or Irish Gaelic language (292, 303, 1128–1130)

gamelan Multi-timbred melodic percussion ensemble from Indonesia similar to other "gong-chime" ensembles of Southeast Asia; most gamelan have a low gongs to punctuate melodic phrases, metallophones or other keyed instruments to play a trunk melody, a variety of instruments that elaborate on the melodic structure, and drums that lead changes in tempo (*see* index)

gangsa Generic term in the Cordillera (upland Luzon, Philippines) for flat gongs played in ensembles and struck either with mallets or with the hands using hocket techniques (1026)

gaohu High-pitched two-stringed fiddle used in Cantonese opera or music (960, 1260)

garage British term for American club music of the late 1980s and early 1990s, referring to the most influential underground dance venue of the time, New York City's Paradise Garage (49, 172, 283–284, 355, 675, 689–691, 901)

ge'e tambio O'odham Indian term for big drum (473)

geng (*qeej*) Hmong (Vietnamese) six-tubed free-reed mouth organ (1004)

Gesangbuch Mennonite song book (886)

Ghost Dance Native revivalist movement of the late nineteenth century that sprang up among the Paiute people in the 1880s, spreading rapidly, particularly across the Great Plains, in which believers received songs while in trancelike states induced by a rapidly accelerating dance; it was believed that participation in Ghost Dance activities would bring back the world as it had been prior to the white invasion, and that whites would disappear (*see* index)

gigue Lively dance in triple time, popular in France in the early eighteenth century, featuring complex, rhythmical footwork; still danced in Québec (223, 344, 360, 408, 411)

glee Unaccompanied choral work in three or more parts for male voices, (66, 183, 304, 310, 604, 969, 1087, 1182, 1211–1212, 1225)

glendi Greek social gathering or party featuring the singing and playing of *mandinades* (931–932)

go-go Style of music popular in Washington, D.C., and parts of the South that prominently features live percussion (congas, *timbales*, cowbells) (702, 973)

gongche pu Traditional notational system used in common-practice Chinese music (1260)

gospel Style of vernacular religious music originally associated with evangelistic revival meetings (*see* index)

gradski pesni Bulgarian city songs (925, 1199)

guaguancó Popular form of Afro-Cuban rumba music that also has been incorporated into popular salsa music (729, 789, 800)

guajira (Spanish, 'country girl'); refers to the music of the Cuban countryside (792, 800)

Guangdong yinyue 'Cantonese music', instrumental ensemble music popular in the Pearl River Delta in the southern part of Guangdong province of China (958)

guaracha Cuban mimetic dance form that incorporates the Spanish and African vocal practice of solo verses and regular chorus refrains (793, 795, 798)

Guataca Hoe blade that is used to keep the rhythmic timeline in Afro-Cuban music (785)

guimbard Jew's harp (1005)

guitarra 'Guitar', often used to refer to the electric guitar (850, 1197)

guitarrón Mexican six-stringed bass (722, 737, 761, 765)

habanera Nineteenth-century Cuban song and dance form featuring a slow to moderate duple meter and a characteristic dotted eighth sixteenth rhythm followed by two even eighth notes; its name reflects its origins in Havana, from where it spread to Spain, Europe, and throughout Latin America (13, 732, 783, 786, 790–791, 795, 797, 851)

hackbrett Hammered dulcimer often used in Russian (Volga) German wedding bands (890–891)

haflah Arab American party with music, food, drink, and dance (1031, 1033)

halling Rural Norwegian folk dance performed for an audience (866, 868–869)

hambo Modernized nonimprovised version of the Swedish *polska* (233, 871, 1196)

hantes All-day church picnic with music; sometimes held indoors within the Armenian American community (1032–1033)

Hardingfele Type of violin originating in western Norway, with a flatter fingerboard and bridge and a shorter neck than the European concert violin; played by Norwegian immigrants at both weddings and informal gatherings (826, 868–870)

harmoniemusik Musical wind ensemble, usually five to eight instruments, consisting of pairs of oboes and/or clarinets, horns, and one or two bassoons, without drums; popular during the eighteenth century (563)

harmonium Hand-pumped keyboard instrument commonly used to accompany Indian and Indo-Caribbean music has recently become popular in the United States and Canada, due in part to its popularization by the late Nusrat Fatah Ali Khan, one of the greatest stars of world music/world beat (815, 981, 983–984, 1246)

hautboys (*hautbois*) (1) Literally, the oboe, a double-reed musical instrument; (2) musical wind ensemble usually consisting of three oboes and a bass oboe or bassoon, with snare drums, popular in military units from the end of the seventeenth to the middle of the eighteenth century (563)

hazzan Hebrew for cantor (933–934)

Heimatlieder For German Americans, songs about the European homeland (889)

heterophony Musical texture deriving from the simultaneous performance of many variations of a musical line

highland dancing Formal, balletlike, athletic, and frequently competitive type of dancing that developed in Scotland and is usually performed to bagpipe music (1071, 1130)

highlife West African popular music style that combines international pop with traditional rhythms and textures, well known to fans of world music/world beat (338, 1213–1214)

hi-NRG Also high energy, a category of 1980s dance music geared toward a mainly white, gay audience; used to describe non-R&B derived dance music, often by European, especially British, artists and producers; *see also* **disco** (689)

hip house House music featuring rap rhymes (691)

hip-hop Beginning in the early 1970s, a primarily black and Latino street culture that comprised rap music, break dancing, and graffiti art (*see* index)

hocket Ensemble performance technique that produces a single composite melody from a number of interlocking rhythmic ostinatos; akin to Euro-American bell ringing (1026)

hook lines Short repetitive phrases of text, set to sing-along-type melodies (673–674)

hornpipe (1) Wooden or bone pipe having a single reed and holes for fingering; (2) lively English and Irish dance in 4/4 time, originally accompanied by a hornpipe (231, 596, 825, 836, 839, 855)

houguan Double-reed wind instrument (961)

house Style of dance music originating at gay black clubs in Chicago in the early 1980s, whose musical elements reflect the heritage of disco while incorporating production techniques characteristic of the emerging home studio industry that helped DJs to become producers and artists (*see* index)

huapango (1) Genre of folk music and dance rooted in the rural mestizo cultures of several east Mexican states; (2) a popular Mexican musical form with a distinctive rhythm and the frequent use of falsetto vocal embellishments (732, 737, 746)

Hutterites Group in the Anabaptist tradition that practices communal living (1237–1238, 1240, 1249)

hymnody (1) Hymn singing; (2) hymn writing; (3) the hymns of a time, place, or church; (4) the study of hymn singing practices (121, 123, 128, 480, 484, 531–534, 576, 630, 824, 885–886, 1237, 1240, 1271)

hyperinstrument Specially modified acoustic instrument whose performance involves the use of computer technology; the additional computer hardware and software allows the performer to play music that exceeds the normal limitations of the instrument or to send triggers to other digital music instruments; hyperinstruments were pioneered by the American composer Tod Machover (b. 1953) (254)

idiophone Musical instrument whose whole body vibrates to produce the sound, such as a rattle or chime (445, 463–464, 473–475, 477)

iltama Finnish American community festival featuring musical performance, poetry, plays, and social dancing (873)

indita Narrative song form very similar to the *corrido*, but found in a particular locality within New Mexico; further distinguished by influences from Southwestern Native American music, especially in its rhythms (755, 757, 760, 762)

Iroquois Social Dance song Music performed in association with the longhouse tradition (371, 463–465)

iscathamiya Secular male a cappella performance tradition from South Africa that became popular worldwide through rock star Paul Simon's famous collaboration with Ladysmith Black Mambazo (338)

jarana (1) Mexican folk guitar with several regional types, played primarily as a harmonic or metrical accompaniment to singing or melody instruments; (2) dance similar to the Spanish *jota* found in the Mexican state of Yucatan (723–724)

jarocho Dance style originally from the Mexican state of Veracruz and especially popular among Mexican *folklorico* dance groups in Los Angeles (723–724, 746)

Jiang nan si zhu Literally, silk; music performed on string and bamboo instruments from south of the Yangtse River (962)

jinghu Leading high-pitched two-stringed fiddle used in Peking opera (961)

jōruri Traditional Japanese narrative ballad originally accompanied by the *biwa* and later by the *shamisen*; combined with puppet theater to develop a musical drama of high artistic quality called *bunraku*

jota Spanish folk dance and song in triple meter, developed from ancient poetic forms (851)

juba Neo-African social dance featuring a two-player drum, practiced by Afro-Haitians in nineteenth-century New Orleans (595, 802)

juju Yoruba (Nigerian) popular music that has become a successful world beat genre (338)

jungle music Also, "drum'n bass," mostly instrumental dance style of music emanating from black communities in Britain (354, 672)

kabuki Highly stylized traditional Japanese play with singing, instrumental music, and dancing (218, 612, 969)

kalenda Neo-African social dance practiced by Afro-Haitians in nineteenth-century New Orleans (802)

kamanja Adapted Arabic violin (1218)

kankles Lithuanian plucked zither often used to accompany singing, played by ensembles composed mainly of young people (876, 881)

kantele Finnish plucked zither (826–827, 829, 873–874, 1196)

kanun Greek plucked zither (930)

kappleikar Finnish American fiddle competition held until the outbreak of World War II (869)

kase Rhythmic change believed to bring on possession in Haitian Vodou ceremonies (805)

kata Time pattern beat on the wooden part of the drum that is played during Afro-Haitian *juba* dancing (802)

katajjaq Women's game played in the Eastern Arctic, using extremely varied vocal sound patterns (376–378, 381)

keen To wail, lament (154, 279, 284, 705, 907, 1004, 1076)

kef-time Weekend-long music retreat featuring multiple bands within the Armenian American community (1032–1033, 1036, 1040)

keyed-bugle (Royal Kent Bugle) Soprano brass instrument similar to the trumpet, but with a conical rather than cylindrical bore, to which five to seven woodwind-like keys have been attached to make the instrument chromatic (564)

khimm 'Hammered dulcimer', Cambodian string instrument played in contemporary versions of the *pinnpeat* ensemble (1001)

khloy 'Duct flute', Cambodian wind instrument played in contemporary versions of the *pinnpeat* ensemble, sometimes replaced by the Western flute or recorder (999, 1001)

khyal Important Hindustani vocal genre (983)

klezmer music (1) Ensemble music of Eastern European Jewish origin; (2) important revival

music in the United States; (3) professional instrumental musician who appeared most commonly at celebrations, particularly weddings (325, 330, 939, 942, 944)

kolo Serbo-Croatian line or circle dance music (920–923, 926, 1198, 1235)

kora Traditional West African harp, one of many non-Western instruments used frequently in world beat recording projects (339, 1063, 1170)

korng vung 'Circular frame of gongs', Cambodian percussion instrument played as part of the *pinnpeat* ensemble (1001)

koto Japanese thirteen-stringed board zither (336, 346, 527, 947, 953, 968–970, 972–973, 1084)

krakowiak Polish regional dance (893–895, 1197, 1250)

krapeu 'three-stringed zither', Cambodian string instrument played in contemporary versions of the *pinnpeat* ensemble (999, 1001)

kulintang (1) Gong chime melodic instrument; (2) gong ensemble that features this melodic instrument from the southern Philippines (1025–1026)

kundiman Filipino genre of composed and published love songs; stylistically related to romantic European light classical forms (1025–1026)

laendler Austrian/Swiss dance in triple meter (897–898)

laouto Greek fretted lute (930, 1199)

laud Spanish fretted, flat-backed plucked lute with fourteen strings in six courses, used for tenor and baritone voices in the *rondalla* and sounding an octave lower than the *bandurria* (792, 1025)

Leikarring movement Revival of "song dancing"—dancers singing without accompaniment—in the Norwegian American community in the 1920s and 1930s (867)

lesno oro Macedonian line dance in a metric pattern of 3 + 2 + 2 (923)

letter notation Musical notation that uses the letters of the alphabet to designate pitches, (135)

libretto 'little book', the text of a work, particularly an opera, for the musical theater (196, 608, 1135, 1182)

lieder (German, 'song') (940, 1025)

line dance Popular social dance form in which dancers in long lines execute identical steps (229, 430, 434, 438, 469, 529, 920, 923, 930, 952, 1009, 1035)

lining out Style of singing religious songs in which a leader sings a phrase to remind the congregation of its contour; the congregation then repeats the phrase much more slowly (119, 125, 832–833)

lkhaon basakk Cambodian theater of Chinese origin sometimes performed in the United States (1001)

lkhaon khaol Elaborate masked play practiced in Cambodia by men only; rarely staged by Cambodian immigrants in the United States, (1000)

lkhaon sbek Rarely performed Cambodian shadow play featuring a set of large leather puppets (1000)

lkhaon yike Cambodian folk theater of Muslim origin, sometimes performed in the United States (1001)

log drum Musical instrument constructed from a wooden log that is beaten with a stick; although called a drum, it is really an idiophone (429, 476, 1093, 1199, 1253)

lundu (*lundum*) Afro-Brazilian song and dance of Angolan origin brought to Brazil by Bantu slaves; the song and couple dance featured sensuous exchange partners that later gave rise to many contemporary song forms including the Portuguese *fado* (851)

lute/stick zither Chordophone whose strings are stretched over a broad neck that extends from a resonant body (1044)

Lwa Also *mistè*, *zany*, deities of the Afro-Haitian religion Vodou (804)

mahrajan Outdoor weekend-long festival or picnic with music within the Arab American community (1031, 1033, 1037)

mambo Cuban ballroom dance popular in the 1940s (see index)

mandinade Greek song composed of improvised couplets with texts about recent events or issues (931)

mandolin Lute-shaped fretted chordophone of Italian origin with eight strings in double courses, tuned like a violin and played with a plectrum (see index)

mariachi (1) Mexican-style musical ensemble typically consisting of *guitarrón* (bass guitar), *vihuela* (five-stringed guitarlike instrument), violins, and trumpets; (2) individual mariachi musician (see index)

marimba In Mexican and Central American traditions, a xylophone played by several musicians (723, 727–28, 731, 746)

Matachines Ceremonial dance drama featuring Native American and Ibero-European elements (614, 757, 759, 761, 848, 850–853)

mazhar Arabic tambourine (1218)

mazurka Polish-origin dance or tune in 2/4 time resembling the polka (see index)

mbaqanga South African popular music that has found much success in the international world music/world beat market (338–339)

Meistersinger songs Songs written by a guild of fifteenth- and sixteenth-century German musicians (1240)

melismatic Pertaining to a way of vocalizing the text of a song in which one syllable of text is sung to many notes of music (164, 414, 638, 647, 887, 923, 940, 1238, 1267)

membranophone Musical instrument such as a drum, whose sound is produced by a vibrating membrane or skin (445, 473, 475, 477)

merengue Fast-paced, duple-meter form of Dominican music and dance, played by small, regional, accordion-driven ensembles as well as by contemporary salsa dance orchestras (337, 728, 731, 790–791, 800, 1204)

merengue cibaeño Regional form of *merengue* from the Dominican region of Cibao, though popular far beyond that region

mexicanos de este lado Mexican Americans (771)

mexicanos del otro lado Mexican nationals (771)

MIDI Abbreviation for Musical Instrument Digital Interface, a system developed in the early 1980s by several electronic instrument manufacturers to allow their products to communicate with each other; allows for compatibility of analog and digital instruments, such as sequencers, computers, synthesizers, and drum machines; became a recording studio standard by the mid-1980s (95, 240, 245, 691, 845)

minidjaz Small rock band–like ensembles that originated in Haiti in the 1960s and later formed in North American cities with Haitian communities (803–804)

minimalism Musical style that emerged in America in the mid-1960s, in which repeating patterns of diatonic or modal music in a regular (usually fast) pulse are developed over time (175–176, 254, 541, 1016, 1097)

MiniMoog Compact and portable version of the professional studio electronic music synthesizer developed by Robert Moog in the late 1960s; oscillators generate audio signals that are modified by means of voltage-controlled devices that allow the user to shape attacks, decays, sculpt timbre, and so on (254)

minstrel show Full-length theatrical entertainment featuring performers in blackface who perform songs, dances, and comic skits based on parodies and stereotypes of African American life and manners (184–187, 544, 615–617, 837–838)

Minyue Music for Chinese instruments (959–960, 962)

mizik angaje 'Engaged music', Haitian protest music developed within the *kilti libete* movement (805)

mizik rasin 'Roots music,' a Haitian musical movement that arose in the 1980s devoted to fusing popular commercial dance music with traditional music of Vodou and *rara* and gained prominence in the United States in the early 1990s (806)

mode (1) Set of pitches that are used hierarchically in a musical structure; (2) set of pitches and a grammar for their use, often written graphically as a scale; (3) way of generating a piece of music, given a set of pitches; (4) in Western music, scales codified by the early Roman Catholic church (*see* index)

mojos Magical spells or charms of African origin, later associated with the practice of African American Vodou (802)

morache Rasp instrument used by the Utes in the Bear Dance ceremony (423, 425–426)

morris dance Folk dance once common throughout England, featuring men (very rarely, women) who perform vigorous, intricate choreographies in three or four couples, accompanied by folk instruments such as the pipe and tabor, melodeon, or fiddle, in streets or garden spaces in the manner of street theater (322, 323–324)

Motown Slang for Motor Town (Detroit), where Motown Records, the most successful black-owned record company ever, was founded (673–679, 709–710)

música jíbara Multifaceted tradition of music associated with rural communities of Puerto Rico, in which stringed instruments dominate and improvised texts are common (726–727)

música ranchera Mexican country music associated particularly with the mariachi ensemble (722)

música vallenata Accordion-driven dance music of coastal Colombia (730)

musical area concept Term borrowed from anthropology's culture area concept; posits that societies sharing common musical traits can be said to constitute a single musical area (512)

musical theater Popular form of theatrical entertainment incorporating drama, music, and dance in various combinations and proportions (*see* index)

musique concrete Form of electronic music that first appeared in 1948 in Paris; involves recording naturally occurring sounds (such as the human voice or breaking glass) and then using electronic devices (such as a tape recorder or filters that attenuate certain frequencies) to modify the sounds, sometimes beyond recognition (252–253, 540)

muwashshah Form of Arabic (or Andalucian) strophic poetry set to song, especially cultivated in southern Spain and Morocco (847)

muyu/mukíyu 'Wooden fish song' an important narrative song tradition in South China (958, 960, 963)

nagauta Japanese long epic song or ballad chanted to the accompaniment of *shamisen*, often with drums and flutes added, for dances performed in the kabuki theater (969)

naniwa-bushi Popular narrative style of Japanese singing that combines storytelling with *shamisen*-accompanied singing (969–970)

nay Also *ney* or *nai*, a reed flute, rarely heard at first in the United States, but heard more and more as professional immigrants from the Arab world came to this country to perform (1040)

Negro jig African dance adapted by Europeans in eighteenth-century Virginia and Carolina

Negro spiritual a nineteenth-century sacred folk song of African-American origin (75, 575–578, 585, 589, 607, 624, 628–630, 632)

ñe'icuda Term used for song makers among the O'odham Indians (472)

neo-klezmer music Music of North American bands that reinterprets and revitalizes the klezmer tradition beginning in the mid-1970s (941)

Ng Sheung Chi Muyu 'fish song' singer from South China (963, 994, 1025)

Nign From Hebrew *nigun*, 'melody', used among Hasidic Jews to refer to spiritually powerful tunes (942)

nja (*ncas*) Hmong guimbard or Jew's harp, made of a flat piece of metal into which the vibrating tongue is excised (1005)

nō Traditional Japanese drama, developed in the fourteenth century from religious sources and folk myths, characterized by highly stylized acting, unique vocalizations, wooden masks, elaborate costumes, and symbolism presented in a minimalist setting and performance style (1084)

noraebang Commercial place where customers can sing songs in a small room equipped with a video monitor, speakers, and microphones, popular in Korea (978–979)

norteno Northern Mexican style distinguished by the use of accordion (355)

Nouvèl jenerasyon 'New generation', a Haitian cosmopolitan pop music of the late 1980s and 1990s that aimed for international markets (806)

nueva canción Stream of urban song and its accompanying music, often drawing from South American folk elements and representing some form of social protest (730, 733, 801, 852, 1175, 1204)

oberek Polish dance in fast triple meter, with two against three cross-rhythms and energetic leaping and stomping (892–894, 1197, 1250)

oktavina Fretted flat-backed plucked waisted lute with fourteen strings in six courses in the tenor range typically used for countermelodies (1025)

old-time genre Folk music originating in the Appalachian Mountains of the United States over a hundred years ago, also known as hillbilly music, mainly involving fiddle, guitar, and banjo (1256)

organetto Italian diatonic button accordion (860)

oru Afro-Cuban song in praise of one of more deities of the Yoruba-derived lucumí religious tradition (729)

outi Greek short-necked flute without frets (930)

Pai he Cantonese opera music ensemble (960)

paired phrasing Simple repetition of a musical phrase, including words and melody, as a stylistic identifier (421, 423)

pandereta In Puerto Rico, a round frame drum grouped in several sizes, playing in multilayered, interlocking rhythms and used to accompany the *plena* (717, 726–727)

pascolas Sacred dance of the Yaqui Indians featuring dancers wearing masks and ankle rattles, accompanied by a fiddle and harp (218, 437–438, 851)

pastorelas (*pastores*) based on the birth of Christ, these musical dramas performed in Hispanic communities depict the journey of the shepherds to the nativity manger (735–736, 759, 848, 850)

pattin' juba (patting *juba*) African American style of drumming in which drumbeats are played on parts of the body; derived from drumming accompanying the Afro-Haitian *juba* dance (802)

payola (pay for play) Industry term given for money, or other forms of compensation, given in order to have a composition played in public (260, 355, 709)

pegbox Part of a stringed instrument that holds the tuning keys or pegs (869)

peña Folk music nightclub of South American origin (62, 517–518, 553, 730, 736–738, 752, 782)

perico ripiao Regional folk *merengue* music and couples dance form, promoted by former dictator Rafael Trujillo as a symbol of Dominican national identity (731)

peyote song Song associated with the Native American Church (426, 445, 458, 486–488)

Piaofang Peking opera club of amateur performers (961)

Pilates System of physical rehabilitation developed by Joseph Pilates; studied by many dancers to help develop strength and flexibility (225)

pinkster Midyear celebration, originated by the Dutch, later associated with African Americans (595, 614)

pipa Four-stringed plucked lute (959, 962)

piping Playing the bagpipes (594, 1071, 1120, 1128–1130)

pisirk In the Eastern Arctic, song that expresses personal emotions and feelings or specific anecdotes (376, 378)

pito Small vertical Mexican flute (759, 761)

pizmon Hymn sung by Sephardic Jews (513, 943–944)

plena Strophic song genre with percussion accompaniment rooted in African-derived communities of coastal Puerto Rico (337, 516, 726–727, 799–800)

polca Spanish for polka, similar to the European-derived dance form except in the Paraguayan tradition, in which it is a triple-metered genre particularly favored by harpists (522, 730, 760)

polka Lively dance or tune of Bohemian or Polish origin in 2/4/ meter (*see* index)

Posadas Plays about Mary and Joseph seeking lodging on the night of Christ's birth (724, 848, 850, 853)

powwow American Indian intertribal context for music and dance performance (*see* index)

praznyk Annual celebration held on the feast day of the saint to which a Church is dedicated (1243)

psalmody The singing of Psalms; became the basis in the early eighteenth century for learning to read music (*see* index)

punto guajiro Spanish-derived musical form associated with rural Cuban populations, marked by improvised song texts and accompanied by an ensemble consisting mainly of stringed instruments (728)

Purimshpil Traditional folk drama staged among European Jews for the springtime holiday of Purim (944)

puukko Knife with a birch handle and curved sheath used by Finnish woodsman as a tool and weapon; Finnish "knifemen" figured prominently in Finnish American ballads of the nineteenth and early twentieth centuries (873)

qanun Also *kanun, kanoon,* plucked zither with approximately seventy-two strings in triple courses that are fine tuned during performance with a series of small levers that are moved up and down (1032, 1034, 1216)

qawwali Plural of *qawwal,* a body of Pakistani ecstatic devotional song and the hereditary group of singers and instrumentalists who perform them; originated in thirteenth-century India (338, 340, 981–983, 1040, 1044, 1046, 1215)

qinqin Chinese two-stringed plucked lute with frets (1260)

quadrille (1) Square dance for four couples in a set of five or six figures mainly in 2/4 and 6/8 time; (2) type of French Creole figure dance practiced in Louisiana by French and Haitian immigrants (*see* index)

quenacane Open-ended notch-flute associated with the music of the South American Andean region (730)

quinto Small drum of the *tumbadora* type that often plays a lead role in rumba music (729, 775)

R&B Short for rhythm and blues, a form of black popular music that combined elements of jazz and the blues beginning in the late 1940s (*see* index)

rabbit dance Male-female partner dances performed in the context of a Native American powwow (368, 408, 447, 483, 489, 1276)

ragga Jamaican music similar to reggae but played entirely (or mostly) with digital instrumentation (806)

ragtime Style of music popular at the turn of the twentieth century characterized by a syncopated melody placed against a steady bass line (*see* index)

rai Energetic Algerian popular music that has found a limited audience among Canadian and American world beat enthusiasts (338, 1019)

ranchera Popular Mexican song resembling American country and western (722, 744, 763, 765, 766, 775, 778, 781)

rap Form of primarily African American spoken-word music, originally one element of hip-hop culture (*see* index)

Rara Widespread and popular processional ritual in Haiti that takes place over the Lenten season and culminates on Easter weekend; *Rara* ensembles have been organized in recent years in Haitian communities of North America, and *rara* music was a major influence in the *mizik rasin* movement (805–807)

rasp Percussive instrument consisting of a notched stick or gourd scraped with another object (*see* index)

rattle drum Drum made from the sapling of a tree with metal objects inserted (476)

rave Legal or illegal dance party, originally held outdoors to accommodate thousands of dancers; features European and especially British forms of house and techno music, supplied by several DJs playing on separate stages or taking turns on one set (691)

rebetika (*rembetika*) Asia Minor–derived urban music genre that developed in the 1920s in Greek port cities (930, 932)

redondo Fast Mexican/Spanish waltz (760, 765, 768, 1039, 1041)

redowa Dance or tune in 3/4 or 2/4 meter of Bohemian origin resembling the mazurka (522, 773, 775)

reel Couples dance from Scotland, accompanied by brisk duple-time binary melodies, disseminated in North America and now flourishing in folk fiddling as the breakdown (*see* index)

reggae Popular Jamaican style of music that combines native styles with elements of rock and soul music; characterized by an accent on the offbeat (*see* index)

requinto jarocho Thin-bodied four-stringed guitar used to play melody in the *son jarocho,* folk music of southern coastal Veracruz in Mexico (723, 761)

rumba (*rhumba*) (1) Short repetitive and syncopated rhythmic pattern of Afro-Cuban origin defined by a quarter note followed by an eighth rest, an eighth note tied to a quarter note, and a quarter note; (2) dance featuring this rhythmic pattern (717)

riff In blues and related African American musics, a repeated short melodic rhythmic phrase

riqq Also *daff,* Arabic tambourine with heavy brass jingles (1032, 1218)

robaim kbach buran Traditional Cambodian court dance performed by females only (1000)

robaim prapeyney Cambodian folk dance sometimes performed by Cambodian Americans (1001)

romance (1) narrative song in the ballad tradition with a poetic text typically set as a series of sixteen-syllable strophes and concerning topics associated with historic or legendary persons; (2) Sephardic songs based on medieval Spanish balladry (84, 757, 848, 849, 942, 1171, 1172, 1173)

romantica 'Romantic', a popular style of 1980s salsa (789)

rondalla Plucked string band ubiquitous throughout the Lowland Philippines appropriated from Iberian *cumparsa* and *estudiantina* ensembles (1025–1026)

roneat 'Xylophone/metallophone', Cambodian percussion instrument played as part of the *pinn-peat* ensemble (999, 1001)

roneat ek 'High-pitched xylophone', Cambodian percussion instrument played as part of the *pinnpeat* ensemble (999, 1001)

salsa 'Sauce', popular Latin dance style (*see* index)

samba Form of popular Brazilian music and dance with prominent percussion accompaniment and group song, especially important during Carnival (522, 731, 740, 1203, 1208)

sampho 'small double-headed barreled drum', Cambodian percussion instrument played as part of the *pinnpeat* ensemble (1001)

Sängerbunde German singing league (885)

Sängerfeste German singing festival (885)

sankyoku Traditional Japanese chamber music, featuring *koto, shamisen,* and *shakuhachi* or *kokyū,* a bowed lute (968)

sansei Third-generation Japanese American, the second generation to be born on American soil (967, 970–973, 1084)

santouri Greek struck zither (930–931)

santur Iranian trapezoidal zither struck with hammers (1034)

sanxian Chinese three-stringed plucked lute (961)

saravane Type of Cambodian rhythm, often used by Cambodian rock bands playing popular songs with Western instruments (1002)

Schnadahupfl (*Schnaderhüpfl*) Song genre associated with Bavaria and Austria; consists of improvised tests alternating with a refrain (889)

schottische Dance or tune in 2/4 time similar to the polka, but somewhat slower (*see* index)

scratch To produce percussive sounds from a vinyl recording by manually moving a selected part of a song rhythmically back and forth under a phonograph needle; common technique of hip-hop DJs (turntablists) (436, 439, 473, 488–489, 852)

***sean-nós* song** 'old style' song; unaccompanied solo song performed in Irish or English (843)

seguidillas (1) Song form with strophes of four or seven lines, each between five and seven syllables, frequently set to music in 6/8 meter; (2) one of the most popular Spanish dance types (851)

seisúns Irish traditional instrumental music sessions (842, 846)

semma (Arabic *sama*) Audition, listening, or concert among the Sufis (1043–1044)

serenata 'Serenade', among professional mariachi musicians, a short performance of several songs (721, 740)

serpent Lip-vibrated wind instrument in serpentine form with six finger holes used as a bass instrument in military and church bands in the seventeenth and eighteenth centuries (563, 589, 704)

setar Iranian plucked lute (1034)

shakuhachi Traditional Japanese bamboo flute whose sound has become familiar to Western audiences via New Age, world beat, and other popular genres (340, 346, 527, 968, 970, 972–973, 1084, 1217)

shamisen Japanese 3-stringed plucked lute with a square-shaped body, played with a large plectrum (527, 947, 968–970, 972, 1084)

shape-note notation Type of notation in which the shape of the note head indicates the solmization syllable of the note (119, 135)

shekeres Beaded gourd rattle used in Afro-Cuban music (785)

sheng Chinese mouth organ (962, 964)

shifu Teacher, within the context of Cantonese music societies (1262–1263, 1265)

shigin Melodies set to Chinese poems (969)

shuffle In country and bluegrass fiddle music, a term used to describe bowing techniques that produce rhythmic two-note chord patterns (6, 166, 194, 619–620, 668, 671, 1062, 1078)

shuffle rhythm Triplet pattern characterized by a quarter-note triplet followed by an eighth note triplet (166, 668)

sitar Long-necked lute from North India (340, 504, 951–953, 984–985, 1215–1216, 1246)

skiffle Music played on folk instruments and on "found" instrumentation such as jugs, washboards, and so on; popular among African-Americans in the 1920s and experienced a revival of interest in England and Ireland in the 1950s and 1960s (645, 845)

skor thomm 'Large double-headed barreled drum', Cambodian percussion instrument played as part of the *pinnpeat* ensemble (1001)

slava Serbo-Croatian celebration in honor of a family's or a church's patron saint, for which musicians may be hired (922)

slip jig Irish traditional dance tune and dance step in 9/8 rhythm (843, 1190)

slow air Type of Irish traditional instrumental tune; also known as a lament (843, 1125)

soittokunta Finnish brass bands that developed in the United States in the late nineteenth and early twentieth centuries, sponsored by temperance societies and socialist organizations (874)

Soldatenlieder German songs about soldiers and war (889)

someak Inuit/Eskimo single-headed frame drum with a short handle of wood, ivory, or bone on the lower side of the instrument (476)

son jarocho Variety of *son* associated with the *jarocho* regional culture of southern coastal Veracruz in Mexico (723–724)

son (pl. *sones*) (1) In Mexico, a mestizo musical genre marked by regional traditions, usually with vigorous rhythm, simple harmony, and strophic form; (2) Cuban strophic song with interludes of instrumental improvisation and fixed *clave* (13, 728, 788, 790, 791–93, 798)

song plugging Music industry designation for the promotional work done by a publisher on behalf of its compositions (258)

sorry songs Western Subarctic regions songs expressive of sad feelings when recalling the memory of a deceased friend or relative; also called mourning songs (388)

soukous Highly danceable, Latin-influenced popular music style from Zaire that has met with some success in the world music/world beat market (338, 1213)

sound instrument Object that makes a sound, not necessarily used within a musical context (429, 431, 472–475, 478–479)

spèktak 'Spectacle', an elaborate concert of Haitian music featuring a variety of entertainment, often including dance bands, folkloric troupes, comedians, and singers (804)

square dance Social dance in which sets of four couples form squares and execute a series of patterns shouted out by a caller (160, 223, 559, 760, 841, 865, 871, 888, 1190–1191, 1256)

sralai 'Shawm', Cambodian quadruple-reed wind instrument played as part of the *pinnpeat* ensemble, in the court, and at funerals (1001)

starogradske pjesme Late-nineteenth-century city songs from Croatia and Serbia (921, 923)

step dance Solo dance in hard-soled shoes, executed with quick, rhythmical footwork close to the ground; still performed in the Maritimes and Québec, where step dance competitions are popular (223, 284, 344, 846, 1125, 1128, 1130)

stev Practiced by Norwegian immigrants in the nineteenth century, singing consisting of short one-strophe poems set to formulaic melodies (866)

Stomp Dance Songs performed among the Creek Indians in the summer (368–370, 464, 467–471)

stornello Genre of sung Sicilian poetry (861)

suona Chinese shawm-type double-reed wind instrument (961, 1260)

surjaran Coffeehouse tradition of music, conversation, and refreshment within the Armenian American community (1032–1033)

suspension rattle Rattle made by suspending objects from a stick or other device so that when shaken the objects strike one another and produce sound; also called jingle rattles (429, 434, 474)

sutartinès Archaic Lithuanian song genre that features contrapuntal singing and is usually performed by two to four people (875–876)

syllabic Style of vocalizing the text of a song in which there is one syllable of text to one note of music (378, 389, 401, 416–417, 426, 629, 905, 1079, 1086)

syncopation In Western music, the displacement or shifting of an accent so that it falls on a weak metric beat (*see* index)

tabla North Indian small drums played as a pair (339–340, 504, 951, 953, 981, 983–984, 986, 1197, 1216, 1246)

taiko Japanese drum (336, 527, 970–973, 1026, 1064, 1096, 1217, 1235, 1248)

takebue Japanese transverse bamboo flute (972)

tambora Small drum used especially to accompany the *merengue* with prominent percussion accompaniment and group song, especially important during Dominican carnival (731, 773)

tamboril Small Basque drum typically played by the right hand to accompany oneself while playing the *txistu* (flute) with the left hand (849)

tamboula African drum associated with La Calinda (596)

tamburitza Fretted long-necked lute plucked with a flat plectrum, found in South Slavic areas of the Balkans (529, 826, 829, 919–923, 932)

tango Ballroom dance of Argentine origin in 4/4 time featuring stylized bodily postures (*see* index)

tan-singing Form of Indo-Caribbean neotraditional music sung by semiprofessional specialists (815–816)

tar (1) Single membrane frame drum, widespread in the Near East; often called *dāff* (2) Iranian plucked lute (1034, 1045, 1189)

tarantella Italian and Corsican dance in vivacious 6/8 time that derives its name from a dance-therapy ritual supposedly prescribed to cure a person bitten by a tarantula (860–861, 865, 1196)

tardeada Hispanic afternoon dance (773)

tassa Drum and drum ensemble, played at weddings, Muslim Moharrum commemorations (in Trinidad Hosay), and other events (815–816, 1208)

techno Category of 1980s fast electronic dance music (230, 341, 355, 359, 691)

Tejano music Popular music from the border regions of Texas and Mexico (720, 721, 770,-781)

tessitura Most comfortable or general range of a voice or instrument (125, 654, 836, 922, 1087)

timbales Metal-shelled, single-headed drums popular in Cuban dance styles (694, 748, 788, 794–797)

timbre Quality of a musical sound, interval or ensemble that distinguishes it from another (*see* index)

Tin Pan Alley Nickname given to an area of New York City where many music publishers were located in the early twentieth century; name is credited to a newspaperman who thought the sound of so many pianos in one locale sounded like tin pans being banged together (12, 194–195, 260, 548–549, 705)

tololoche Mexican-style string bass, often with three strings rather than the four strings typical of the symphonic string bass (723)

tonbak Iranian wooden singleheaded drum (1034)

tone cluster Group of pitches contiguous either diatonically or chromatically, played together; pioneered by the American composer Henry Cowell (1897–1965) (174)

tremolo Right hand plectrum technique used on the mandolin especially but also on other chordophones played with the plectrum in which the plectrum is moved rapidly back and forth over one or more strings to produce a sustained sound consisting of thirty-second or sixty-fourth notes (166, 368, 397, 400–402, 423, 445)

tres Cuban guitarlike instrument (728, 759, 787, 792–793)

tresillo Three-note rhythmic ostinato found in Cuban popular music (783, 786)

triccaballacche Italian wooden clapper (860)

tror 'Two-stringed fiddle', Cambodian string instrument played in contemporary versions of the *pinnpeat* ensemble (1001)

trovadore Composer-songmakers who were an important part of traditional New Mexican Hispano society (757–758, 792)

trovo Song duel within Hispano culture, in which two or more performers sing alternate verses (757–758)

tsymbaly Ukrainian hammered dulcimer (345, 826, 913–914, 917, 1082, 1089, 1242)

tumbadora Single-headed, elongated, barrel-shaped drum, commonly called conga, used particularly in Afro-Cuban rumba music (729)

tumbao Ostinato pattern resulting from interlocking rhythms played by the bass and conga, found in *son* (792)

tune family Group of related melodies descending from a common ancestor that share melodic contours and important structural pitches; most often applied to groups of Child ballads (511, 834, 841)

turntable Phonograph; an essential component of a hip-hop DJ's equipment (166–167, 169–170, 229–230, 683, 687, 692–695)

tuvan throat singing Striking vocal tradition from the steppes of Mongolia that has been promoted successfully to an international world music audience (339, 340)

txistu Basque flute, usually played in conjunction with a small drum (731, 849)

'ud Also *oud, ood*, Fretless pear-shaped lute with a round belly, bent neck, and eleven strings, ten of which are in double courses (1025, 1032, 1034, 1037, 1040, 1199)

uilleann pipes Traditional Irish bellows-blown bagpipe (326, 842, 845)

utai Vocalization of *nō* drama chanting sometimes performed outside the theater by amateur performers (969, 1084)

vaudeville Theatrical form consisting of a variety of unrelated performing acts, including actors, singers, dancers, acrobats, comedians, magicians, trained animals, and other specialty acts (*see* index)

vihuela Five-stringed Mexican guitar with spined, convex back, used in the mariachi ensemble and in the *conjunto de arpa grande* ensemble (722–723, 737, 762, 765)

villancico Luso-Hispanic song genre whose form and character changed over its long history; today the term refers to a Christmas carol or a popular song featuring verses and a refrain (848–850, 853) *vina* Seven-stringed (four melody strings, three drone strings) lute/stick zither of Indian classical music (951, 984, 1044)

violão Portuguese (Brazilian) guitar (850)

violas de arames Portuguese and Brazilian guitar-like instruments whose number of strings (five, seven, eight, ten, twelve, fourteen) vary according to the region of origin (850)

vocable A syllable that is consistent with the phonemes of a language but which carries no referential meaning; used to vocalize music, as in "fa-la-la"; often carries emotional meaning

Vorsanger Lead singer of hymns in Mennonite services (886–887)

waila Social dance music, sometimes called "chicken scratch," of the Tohono O'odham people featuring accordion, bass, guitar, drums, and saxophone (fiddles in the old style) (213, 436–437, 439, 473, 479, 489–490, 851–852)

waltz Pan-European dance in triple time that became popular in North America early in the nineteenth century and became the dominant basis for popular song at the turn of the twentieth century; survives today both in the ballroom and in folk fiddling (*see* index)

water drum American Indian drum that is partially filled with water (431–432, 454–455, 463, 468, 472, 476–477, 487)

wayang golek Puppet theater using rod puppets with wooden heads, torso, and arms particularly popular in West Java (Sunda) but also found in Central Java (1012, 1020)

wayang kulit Shadow puppet theater using perforated leather puppets against an illuminated cloth screen, often accompanied by gamelan music; in Java the performance sometimes lasts up to nine hours and audiences view both sides of the screen; in Bali a performance may last three to four hours with the audience mostly on the shadow side; the stories most often dramatized are from the Hindu epics the *Mahabharata* and the *Ramayana,* with local characters and topics added (1012, 1020)

wenchang luo Civil gong, large size, used in Chinese music (960)

wiejska Village-style Polish band (894)

Wolf Dance In the Western Arctic, a dance named according to the animal honored in the song text (375, 399, 482)

world beat Term used to describe hybrid music that combines traditional and/or non-Western musical elements with contemporary pop styles and production values; often the result of cross-cultural collaboration between producers and musicians (74, 334, 337–342, 359–360, 489, 806, 955, 983, 1203)

world music Label used to market folk, classical, and popular musics from outside the Anglo-American mainstream to Western audiences (*see* index)

wuchang luo Small military gong used in Chinese music (960)

xiaoluo Small gong (961)

xiqu (Chinese operas) General term for about 350 distinct types of music-drama in contemporary China (960)

yangqin Chinese hammered dulcimer (960, 962, 1248, 1262)

yataibayashi Musical ensemble seated on a float used in processions for traditional Japanese festivals (970)

yifan Cantonese mode in which the intervals *fa* and *ti* are prominent (264)

yonsei Fourth-generation Japanese American; third generation to be born on American soil (970)

Yueju/Yuht kehk (Cantonese opera) Major southern Chinese operatic genre from the Pearl River Delta, as well as Hong Kong (958, 960, 962)

yueqin Moon-shaped four-stringed Chinese plucked lute (961)

yuka Older style of rumba (786)

zampogna Italian bagpipe (860–861)

zampoña Cane panpipes, often played in complementary pairs, associated with the Andean region of South America (730)

zapateado Dance patterns involving the stamping of the feet characteristic of an array of Spanish and Hispanic American dances (848)

zarzuela Distinctively Spanish musical theatrical genre with origins dating back to sixteenth-century court entertainment and today sharing features with opera and operetta (848, 851–853)

zheng Sixteen- or twenty-one-stringed Chinese zither (518, 954, 957–960, 962, 966, 1083)

zither Stringed instrument with a shallow horizontal soundboard, played with pick and fingers (*see* index)

zortiko Dance song in a rapid 5/8 meter, generally divided into units of three and two beats (849)

A Guide to Publications

Entries in this Guide were chosen from the references sections following each article in this volume and represent a mere fraction of all references cited. The reader is urged to go back to specific articles to find other important sources.

GENERAL

Abrahams, Roger D. 1992. *Singing the Master: The Emergence of African American Folk Culture in the Plantation South.* New York: Pantheon Books.

Adjaye, Joseph K. and Adrianne R. Andrews, eds. 1997. *Language, Rhythm and Sound: Black Popular Cultures into the Twenty-First Century.* Pittsburgh: University of Pittsburgh Press.

Adorno, Theodor. 1988. *Introduction to the Sociology of Music.* Trans. E. B. Ashton. New York: Continuum.

Ahlquist, Karen. 1997. *Democracy at the Opera: Music, Theater, and Culture in New York City, 1815–60.* Chicago: University of Illinois Press.

Alba, Richard D. 1990. *Ethnic Identity: The Transformation of White America.* New Haven, Conn.: Yale University Press.

Allen, James Paul. 1988. *We the People: An Atlas of America's Ethnic Diversity.* New York: Macmillan.

Allen, Ray, and Lois Wilcken, eds. 1998. *Island Sounds in the Global City: Caribbean Popular Music and Identity in New York.* New York: Brooklyn College and New York Folklore Society and the Institute for Studies in American Music.

Ammer, Christine. 1980. *Unsung: A History of Women in American Music.* Contributions in Women's Studies 14. Westport, Conn.: Greenwood Press.

Amoss, Pamela. 1978. *Coast Salish Spirit Dancing: The Survival of an Ancestral Religion.* Seattle: University of Washington Press.

Aparicio, Frances R. 1998. *Listening to Salsa: Gender, Latin Popular Music, and Puerto Rican Cultures.* Middletown, Conn.: Wesleyan University Press.

Arts in America 1990: The Bridge between Creativity and Community. 1990. Washington, D.C.: National Endowment for the Arts.

Attali, Jacques. 1985. *Noise: The Political Economy of Music.* Trans. Brian Massumi. Minneapolis: University of Minnesota Press.

Auerbach, Susan. 1994. *Encyclopedia of Multiculturalism.* New York: Marshall Cavendish.

Austin, William W. 1987. *"Susanna," "Jeanie," and "The Old Folks at Home": The Songs of Stephen C. Foster from His Time to Ours.* 2nd ed. Urbana: University of Illinois Press.

Barbeau, Marius. 1946. *Alouette.* Montréal: Thériens.

Barlow, William. 1999. *Voice Over: The Making of Black Radio.* Philadelphia: Temple University Press.

Beckwith, John. 1997. *Music Papers: Articles and Talks by a Canadian Composer 1961–1994.* Ottawa: The Golden Dog Press.

Berland, Jody. 1988. "Locating Listening: Technological Space, Popular Music, Canadian Mediations." *Cultural Studies* 2(3):343–358.

———. 1990. "Radio Space and Industrial Time: Music Formats, Local Narratives and Technological Mediation." *Popular Music* 9(2):179–192.

———. 1994a. "Radio Space and Industrial Time: The Case of Music Formats." In *Canadian Music: Issues of Hegemony and Identity,* ed. Beverley Diamond and Robert Witmer, 173–188. Toronto: Canadian Scholars' Press.

———. 1994b. "Toward a Creative Anachronism: Radio, the State and Sound Government." In *Radio Rethink: Art, Sound and Transmission,* ed. D. Augaitis and D. Lander, 33–44. Banff: Walter Phillips Gallery, The Banff Centre for the Arts.

———. 1998. "Locating Listening: Technological Space, Popular Music, and Canadian Mediations." In *The Place of Music,* ed. Andrew Leyshon, David Matless, and George Revill, 129–150. New York: The Guilford Press

Bindas, Kenneth J. 1995. *All of This Music Belongs to the Nation: The WPA's Federal Music Project and American Society, 1935–1939.* Knoxville: University of Tennessee Press.

Birosek, Patti Jean. 1989. *The New Age Music Guide.* New York: Collier Books.

Boas, Franz. 1966. *Kwakiutl Ethnography,* ed. Helen Codere. Chicago: University of Chicago Press.

Boggs, Vernon, ed. 1992. *Salsiology: Afro-Cuban Music and the Evolution of Salsa in New York City.* New York: Greenwood Press.

Breton, Raymond. 1980. *Cultural Boundaries and the Cohesion of Canada.* Montréal: Institute for Research on Public Policy.

Broughton, Simon, et al., eds. 1994. *World Music: The Rough Guide.* London: Rough Guides.

Brown, Charles T. 1983. *The Rock and Roll Story: From the Sounds of Rebellion to an American Art Form.* Englewood Cliffs, N.J.: Prentice-Hall.

Brown, Royal S. 1994. *Overtones and Undertones: Reading Film Music.* Berkeley: University of California Press.

Broyles, Michael. 1992. *"Music of the Highest Class": Elitism and Populism in Antebellum Boston.* New Haven, Conn.: Yale University Press.

Burnett, Robert. 1996. *The Global Jukebox.* London: Routledge.

Cage, John. 1961. *Silence: Lectures and Writings.* Middletown, Conn.: Wesleyan University Press.

Camus, Raoul François. 1980. "Military Music of Colonial Boston." In *Music in Colonial Massachusetts, 1630–1820,* vol 1: *Music in Public Places,* 75–103. Boston: The Colonial Society of Massachusetts and the University Press of Virginia.

Carder, Polly, ed. 1990. *The Eclectic Curriculum in American Music Education.* Rev. 2nd ed. Reston, Va.: Music Educators National Conference.

Casey, Betty. 1985. *Dance Across Texas.* Austin: University of Texas Press.

Cateforis, Theo, and Elena Humphreys. 1997. "Constructing Communities and Identities: Riot Grrl New York City." In *Musics of Multicultural America,* ed. Kip Lornell and Anne K. Rasmussen, 317–342. New York: Prentice Hall.

Cavanagh, Beverley (Diamond). 1989. "Writing about Music and Gender in the Sub-Arctic Algonquian Area." In *Women in North American Music: Six Essays,* ed. Richard Keeling, 55–66. Special Series, no. 6. Bloomington, Ind.: The Society for Ethnomusicology.

Chadabe, Joel. 1997. *Electric Sound: The Past and Promise of Electronic Music.* Englewood Cliffs, N.J.: Prentice Hall.

Chase, Gilbert. 1987 [1955]. *America's Music: From the Pilgrims to the Present.* New York: McGraw-Hill.

Child, Francis James. 1882–1898. *The English and Scottish Popular Ballads.* Boston: Houghton, Mifflin.

Chiswick, Barry R., ed. 1992. *Immigration, Language and Ethnicity: Canada and the United States.* Washington, D.C.: AEI Press.

Choksy, Lois, Robert Abramson, David Woods, and Avon Gillespie. 1986. *Teaching Music in the Twentieth Century.* Englewood Cliffs, N.J.: Prentice-Hall.

Clément, Catherine. 1988. *Opera, or the Undoing of Women.* Trans. Betsy Wong. Minneapolis: University of Minnesota Press.

Cockrell, Dale. 1997. *Demons of Disorder: Early Blackface Minstrels and Their World.* Cambridge: Cambridge University Press.

Cohen, Norm. 1981. *Long Steel Rail: The Railroad in American Folksong.* Urbana: University of Illinois Press.

Cohen, Selma Jeanne, ed. 1998. *International Encyclopedia of Dance.* New York: Oxford University Press.

Collier, Cliff, and Pierre Guilmette. 1982. *Dance Resources in Canadian Libraries.* Ottawa: National Library of Canada.

Cook, Susan C., and Judy S. Tsou, eds. 1994. *Cecilia Reclaimed: Feminist Perspectives on Gender and Music.* Urbana: University of Illinois Press.

Covach, John, and Graeme M. Boone, eds. 1997. *Understanding Rock: Essays in Musical Analysis.* New York: Oxford University Press.

Crawford, Richard. 1993. *The American Musical Landscape.* Berkeley: University of California Press.

Daniel, Linda J. 1999. "Singing Out! Canadian Women in Country Music." D.Ed dissertation, Ontario Institute for the Study of Education, University of Toronto.

Daniel, Ralph. 1966. *The Anthem in New England before 1800.* Evanston, Ill.: Northwestern University Press.

Dannen, Frederic. 1990. *Record Men: Power Brokers and Fast Money inside the Music Business.* New York: Times Books.

Davis, Mary B., ed. 1994. *Native America in the Twentieth Century: An Encyclopedia.* New York: Garland.

Denisoff, R. Serge. 1971. *Great Day Coming: Folk Music and the American Left.* Chicago: University of Illinois Press.

Densmore, Frances. 1918. *Teton Sioux Music.* Bureau of American Ethnology Bulletin 61. Washington, D.C.: Smithsonian Institution.

———. 1923. *Mandan and Hidatsa Music.* Bureau of American Ethnology Bulletin 80. Washington, D.C.: Smithsonian Institution.

———. 1939. *Nootka and Quileute Music.* Bureau of American Ethnology Bulletin 124. Washington, D.C.: Smithsonian Institution.

———. 1943. *Music of the Indians of British Columbia.* Bureau of American Ethnology Bulletin 136. Washington, D.C.: Smithsonian Institution.

Desmond, Jane C. 1997. "Embodying Difference: Issues in Dance and Cultural Studies." In *Everynight Life: Culture and Dance in Latino America,* ed. Celeste Frasier Delgado and José Esteban Muñoz, 33–64. Durham, N.C.: Duke University Press.

Diamond, Beverley. 2000. *Gender and Music: Negotiating Shifting Worlds.* Urbana: University of Illinois Press.

Diamond, Beverley, and Robert Witmer, eds. 1994. *Canadian Music: Issues of Hegemony and Identity.* Toronto: Canadian Scholars' Press.

DiMaggio, Paul. 1972. "Country Music: Ballad of the Silent Majority." In *The Sounds of Social Change,* ed. R. Denisoff and R. Peterson, 31–56. Chicago: Rand McNally.

Dorland, Michael. 1996. *The Cultural Industries in Canada: Problems, Policies and Prospects.* Toronto: James Lorimer and Co.

Driedger, Leo, ed. 1978. *The Canadian Ethnic Mosaic.* Canadian Ethnic Studies Association Series 6. Toronto: McClelland and Stewart, Ltd.

Drucker, Philip. 1940. "Kwakiutl Dancing Societies." *Anthropological Records* 2(6):201–230. Berkeley: University of California Press.

———. 1951. *The Northern and Central Nootkan Tribes.* Bureau of American Ethnology Bulletin 144. Washington, D.C.: Smithsonian Institution.

———. 1963. *Indians of the Northwest Coast.* Garden City, N.Y.: The Natural History Press.

———. 1965. *Cultures of the North Pacific Coast.* San Francisco: Chandler Publishing Company.

Dwight, John Sullivan, ed. 1852–1881. *Dwight's Journal of Music.* Boston: Houghton, Osgood.

Eisenberg, Evan. 1987. *The Recording Angel: Music, Records and Culture from Aristotle to Zappa.* New York: McGraw-Hill.

Eisler, Hanns, and Theodor Adorno. 1947. *Composing for the Films.* New York: Oxford University Press.

Epstein, Dena J. 1977. *Sinful Tunes and Spirituals: Black Folk Music to the Civil War.* Urbana: University of Illinois Press.

Escott, Colin, and Martin Hawkins. 1991. *Good Rockin' Tonight: Sun Records and the Birth of Rock 'n' Roll.* New York: St. Martin's Press.

Ewen, David. 1962. *Popular American Composers, from Revolutionary Times to the Present.* New York: H. W. Wilson, Co.

———. 1977. *All the Years of American Popular Music.* Englewood Cliffs, N.J.: Prentice-Hall.

Ewen, David, ed. 1966. *American Popular Songs from the Revolutionary War to the Present.* New York: Random House.

Faris, James C. 1990. *The Nightway: A History and a History of Documentation of a Navajo Ceremonial.* Albuquerque: University of New Mexico Press.

Fiske, Roger. 1973. *English Theater Music in the Eighteenth Century.* London: Oxford University Press.

Fletcher, Alice C., and Francis La Flesche. 1970 [1911]. "The Omaha Tribe." In *27th Annual Report of the U.S. Bureau of American Ethnology to the Secretary of the Smithsonian Institution, 1905–06,* 19–672. Reprint, New York: Johnson Reprint.

Flinn, Caryl. 1992. *Strains of Utopia: Gender, Nostalgia, and Hollywood Film Music.* Princeton, N.J.: Princeton University Press.

Ford, Clifford. 1982. *Canada's Music: An Historical Survey.* Agincourt, Ont.: GLC Publishers.

Friedlander, Paul. 1996. *Rock and Roll: A Social History.* Boulder, Colo.: Westview Press.

Frisbie, Charlotte J. 1987. *Navajo Medicine Bundles or Jish: Acquisition, Transmission, and Disposition in the Past and Present.* Albuquerque: University of New Mexico Press.

Frith, Simon. 1978. *The Sociology of Rock.* London: Constable.

Frith, Simon, and Andrew Goodwin, eds. 1990. *On Record: Rock, Pop, and the Written Word.* New York: Pantheon.

Gaar, Gillian G. 1992. *She's a Rebel: The History of Women in Rock & Roll.* Seattle: Seal Press.

Gagnon, Ernest. 1865. *Chansons populaires du Canada.* Québec: Bureau du "Foyer canadien."

———. 1935 [1865, 1880]. *Chansons populaires du Canada.* Montréal: Beauchemin.

Garofalo, Reebee. 1997. *Rockin' Out: Popular Music in the U.S.A.* Boston: Allyn and Bacon.

Garofalo, Reebee, and Steve Chapple. 1977. *Rock & Roll Is Here to Pay: The History and Politics of the Music Industry.* Chicago: Nelson Hall.

Giglio, Virginia. 1994. *Southern Cheyenne Women's Songs.* Norman: University of Oklahoma Press.

Gillett, Charlie. 1970. *The Sound of The City: The Rise of Rock and Roll.* London: Souvenir Press.

Goldstein, Paul. 1994. *Copyright's Highway: From Gutenberg to the Celestial Jukebox.* New York: Hill and Wang.

Green, J. Paul, and Nancy F. Vogan. 1991. *Music Education in Canada: A Historical Account.* Toronto: University of Toronto Press.

Green, Mildred Denby. 1983. *Black Women Composers: A Genesis.* Boston: Twayne.

Grenier, Line. 1993. "Policing French-Language Music on Canadian Radio: The Twilight of the Popular Record Era?" In *Rock and Popular Music: Politics, Policies, Institutions,* ed. Tony Bennett, Simon Frith, Lawrence Grossberg, John Shepherd, and Graeme Turner, 119–141. London: Routledge.

Guralnick, Peter. 1994. *Last Train to Memphis: The Rise of Elvis Presley.* New York: Little, Brown.

Halpern, Ida. 1968. "Music of the B.C. Northwest Coast Indians." In *Centennial Workshop on Ethnomusicology,* 23–42. Vancouver: University of British Columbia.

Hamm, Charles. 1979. *Yesterdays: Popular Song in America.* New York: Norton.

———. 1983. *Music in the New World.* New York: Norton.

Hampton, Wayne. 1986. *Guerrilla Minstrels.* Knoxville: University of Tennessee Press.

Handy, D. Antoinette. 1981. *Black Women in American Bands and Orchestras.* Metuchen, N.J.: Scarecrow.

Hayward, Victoria. 1922. *Romantic Canada.* Toronto: The Macmillan Company of Canada.

Hitchcock, H. Wiley. 1988. *Music in the United States: A Historical Introduction.* 3rd ed. Englewood Cliffs, N.J.: Prentice-Hall.

Hitchcock, H. Wiley, and Stanley Sadie, eds. 1986. *The New Grove Dictionary of American Music.* London: Macmillan.

Hood, George. 1846. *History of Music in New England; with Biographical Sketches of Reformers and Psalmists.* Boston: Wilkins, Carter.

Howard, John Tasker. 1931. *Our American Music: Three Hundred Years of It.* New York: Crowell. Rev. eds., 1939, 1946, 1965.

Jackson, George Pullen. 1943. *White and Negro Spirituals.* Locust Valley N.Y.: J. J. Augustin.

Johnston, Thomas F. 1975. "Eskimo Music of the Northern Interior Alaska." *Polar Notes* 14:54–57.

Kallmann, Helmut. 1960. *A History of Music in Canada 1534–1914.* Toronto: University of Toronto Press.

Kallmann, Helmut, Gilles Potvin, and Kenneth Winters, eds. 1992. *Encyclopedia of Music in Canada.* 2nd ed. Toronto: Toronto University Press.

Kassabian, Anahid. 2000. *Hearing Film: Tracking Identifications in Contemporary Hollywood Film Music.* New York: Routledge.

Keeling, Richard, ed. 1989. *Women in North American Indian Music: Six Essays.* Special Series, no. 6. Bloomington, Ind.: The Society for Ethnomusicology.

Keil, Charles, and Steven Feld, eds. 1994. *Music Grooves.* Chicago: University of Chicago Press.

Kingman, Daniel. 1998. *American Music: A Panorama.* New York: Schirmer Books.

Kivi, K. Linda. 1992. *Canadian Women Making Music.* Toronto: Green Dragon Press.

Klassen, Doreen Helen. 1989. *Singing Mennonite: Low German Songs among the Mennonites.* Winnipeg: The University of Manitoba Press.

Kodish, Debora. 1986. *Good Friends and Bad Enemies: Robert Winslow Gordon and the Study of American Folksong.* Urbana: University of Illinois Press.

Korson, George. 1927. *Songs and Ballads of the Anthracite Miner.* New York: F. H. Hitchcock.

Koskoff, Ellen, ed. 1989. *Women and Music in Cross-Cultural Perspective.* Urbana: University of Illinois Press.

Kostelanetz, Richard, ed. 1996. *Classic Essays on Twentieth-Century Music: A Continuing Symposium.* New York: Schirmer Books.

Laing, Dave. 1985. *One Chord Wonders: Power and Meaning in Punk Rock.* Philadelphia: Open University Press.

Lambert, Barbara, ed. 1985. *Music in Colonial Massachusetts, 1630–1820.* 2 vols. Boston: The Colonial Society of Massachusetts.

Lang, Andrew. 1895. *Border Ballads.* London: Lawrence and Bullen.

Larson, Gary O. 1983. *The Reluctant Patron: The United States Government and the Arts, 1943–1965.* Philadelphia: University of Pennsylvania Press.

Lewis, Lisa A. 1990. *Gender Politics and MTV.* Philadelphia: Temple University Press.

Linn, Karen. 1991. *That Half-Barbaric Twang: The Banjo in American Popular Culture.* Urbana: University of Illinois Press.

Lomax, John. 1910. *Cowboy Songs and Other Frontier Ballads.* New York: Sturgis and Walton.

Lomax, John A., and Alan Lomax. 1934. *American Ballads and Folk Songs.* New York: Macmillan.

———. 1947. *Folk Song U.S.A.* New York: Duell, Sloan and Pearce.

Lott, Eric. 1993. *Love and Theft: Blackface Minstrelsy and the American Working Class.* New York: Oxford University Press.

Lull, James, ed. 1987. *Popular Music and Communication.* Newbury Park, Calif.: Sage.

Lum, Casey Man Kong. 1996. *In Search of a Voice: Karaoke and the Construction of Identity in Chinese America.* Mahwah, N.J.: Lawrence Erlbaum Associates.

Magocsi, Paul, ed. 1988. *Encyclopedia of Canada's Peoples.* Toronto: University of Toronto Press.

Malm, Krister, and Roger Wallace. 1992. *Media Policy and Music Activity.* London: Routledge.

Malone, Bill C. 1985. *Country Music U.S.A.* Rev ed. Austin: University of Texas Press.

Manning, Peter. 1993. *Electronic and Computer Music.* Oxford: Clarendon Press.

Marco, Guy A., ed. 1993. *Encyclopedia of Recorded Sound in the United States.* New York: Garland.

Marcus, Greil. 1975. *Mystery Train: Images of America in Rock 'n' Roll Music.* New York: E. P. Dutton.

Mark, Michael L., and Charles L. Gary. 1992. *A History of American Music Education.* New York: Schirmer Books.

Mason, Lowell. 1839. "Historical Sketches of Sacred and Church Music, from the Earliest Times to the Present." *The Boston Musical Gazette* 1:51, 57, 65–66, 83, 97–98, 105, 113, 122, 130, 139.

Mates, Julian. 1985. *America's Musical Stage: Two Hundred Years of Musical Theater.* Westport, Conn.: Greenwood Press.

Mayer, Margaret M. 1994. *The American Dream: American Popular Music.* Bethesda, Md.: Front Desk Publishing.

McClary, Susan. 1991. *Feminine Endings: Music, Gender, Sexuality.* Minneapolis: University of Minnesota Press.

McGee, Timothy J., ed. 1995. *Taking a Stand., Essays in Honour of John Beckwith.* Toronto: University of Toronto Press.

McKay, Ian. 1994. *The Quest of the Folk: Antimodernism and Cultural Selection in Twentieth-Century Nova Scotia.* Montréal and Kingston: McGill-Queen's University Press.

Mellers, Wilfrid. 1964. *Music in a New Found Land: Themes and Developments in the History of American Music.* London: Barrie and Rockcliffe.

Millard, André. 1995. *America on Record: A History of Recorded Sound.* Cambridge: Cambridge University Press.

Mishler, Craig. 1993. *The Crooked Stovepipe: Athapaskan Fiddle Music and Square Dancing in Northeast Alaska and Northwest Canada.* Urbana: University of Illinois Press.

Moffitt, W. O. 1878. *The National Temperance Songster.* Debuque, Iowa: Gay and Schermerhorn.

Moogk, Edward B. 1975. *Roll Back the Years: A History of Canadian Recorded Sound and Its Legacy, Genesis to 1930.* Ottawa: National Library of Canada.

Morris, Robert. 1997. "Milton Babbitt's Electronic Music: The Medium and the Message." *Perspectives of New Music* 35(2):85–99.

Naimpally, Anuradha. 1988. "The Teaching of Bharata Natyam in Canada: Modifications within the Canadian Context." Master's thesis, York University.

Negus, Keith. 1992. *Producing Pop: Culture and Conflict in the Popular Music Industry.* London: Edward Arnold.

Peacock, Kenneth. 1966. *Twenty Ethnic Songs from Western Canada.* Ottawa: National Museum of Canada.

Pegley, Karen. 1998. "Femme Fatale and Lesbian Representation in Alban Berg's Lulu." In *Encrypted Messages in Alban Berg's Music,* ed. Siglind Bruhn, 249–277. New York: Garland Press.

———. 1999. "An Analysis of the Construction of National, Racial and Gendered Identities on MuchMusic (Canada) and MTV (US)." Ph.D. dissertation, York University.

Pendle, Karin, ed. 1997. "American Women Composers." *Contemporary Music Review* 16(1/2).

Peretti, Burton W. 1992. *The Creation of Jazz: Music, Race and Culture in Urban America.* Urbana: University of Illinois Press.

Peterson, Elizabeth. 1996. *The Changing Faces of Tradition: A Report on the Folk and Traditional Arts in the United States.* Washington, D.C.: National Endowment for the Arts.

Porter, Susan L. 1991. *With an Air Debonair: Musical Theater in America, 1785–1815.* Washington, D.C.: Smithsonian Institution Press.

Preston, Katherine K. 1993. *Opera on the Road: Traveling Opera Companies in the United States, 1825–60.* Urbana: University of Illinois Press.

Proctor, George A. 1980. *Canadian Music of the Twentieth Century.* Toronto: University of Toronto Press.

Qureshi, Regula Burckhardt. 1972. "Ethnomusicological Research among Canadian Communities of Arab and East Indian Origin." *Ethnomusicology* 16(3):381–396.

Radano, Ronald and Philip V. Bohlman, eds. 2000. *Music and the Racial Imagination.* Chicago Studies in Ethnomusicology. Chicago: University of Chicago Press.

Rapée, Erno. 1978 [1970]. *Encyclopedia of Music for Pictures.* New York: Ayer Co.

Riis, Thomas L. 1989. *Just before Jazz: Black Musical Theater in New York, 1890–1915.* Washington, D.C.: Smithsonian Institution Press.

Roberts, Helen H. 1936. *Musical Areas in Aboriginal North America.* Publications in Anthropology 12. New Haven, Conn.: Yale University Press.

Rockwell, John. 1983. *All American Music.* New York: Knopf.

Root, Deane L. 1981. *American Popular Stage Music: 1860–1880.* Ann Arbor, Mich.: UMI Research Press.

Rose, Tricia. 1994. *Black Noise: Rap Music and Black Culture in Contemporary America.* Hanover, N.H.: University Press of New England.

Rosenberg, Neil V., ed. 1993. *Transforming Tradition: Folk Music Revivals Examined.* Chicago: University of Illinois Press.

Ryan, John. 1985. *The Production of Culture in the Music Music Industry: The ASCAP–BMI Controversy.* Lanham, Md.: University Press of America.

Sakolsky, Ron, and Fred Ho. 1995. *Sounding Off: Music as Subversion/Resistance/Revolution.* New York: Autonomedia.

Sanjek, Russell. 1988. *American Popular Music and Its Business: The First Four Hundred Years.* New York: Oxford University Press.

Sanjek, Russell, and David Sanjek. 1991. *American Popular Music Business in the 20th Century.* New York: Oxford University Press.

Schramm, A. Reyes. 1975. "The Role of Music in the Interaction of Black Americans and Hispanos in New York City's East Harlem." Ph.D. dissertation, Columbia University.

Scott, Derek. 1989. *The Singing Bourgeois: Songs of the Victorian Drawing Room and Parlour.* Milton Keynes, Eng.: Open University Press.

Seeger, Charles. 1945. "Music in the Americas: Oral and Written Traditions in the Americas." *Bulletin of the Pan American Union* 79:290–293, 341–344.

Shepherd, John, Phil Virden, Graham Vulliamy, and Trevor Wishart, eds. 1977. *Whose Music? A Sociology of Musical Languages.* New Brunswick, N.J.: Transaction Books.

Slobin, Mark. 1993. *Subcultural Sounds: Micromusics of the West.* Hanover & London: Wesleyan University Press.

Small, Christopher. 1996. *Music, Society, Education.* Hanover, N.H.: University Press of New England.

Smith, Jeff. 1998. *The Sounds of Commerce: Marketing Popular Film Music.* New York: Columbia University Press.

Sonneck, O. G. 1916 [1913]. *A Survey of Music in America.* Reprinted in O. G. Sonneck, *Suum Cuique: Essays on Music,* 121–124. New York: G. Schirmer.

Sonneck, Oscar George Theodore. 1983. *Oscar Sonneck and American Music.* Urbana: University of Illinois Press.

Spaeth, Sigmund. 1948. *A History of Popular Music in America.* New York: Random House.

Spencer, Peter. 1992. *World Beat: A Listener's Guide to Contemporary World Music on CD.* Pennington, N.J.: A Capella Books.

Stevenson, Robert. 1970. *Philosophies of American Music History.* Washington, D.C.: Library of Congress.

Straw, Will. 1996. "Sound Recording." In *The Cultural Industries in Canada: Problems, Policies and Prospects,* ed. Michael Dorland, 95–117. Toronto: James Lorimer and Company.

Supiciİ, Ivan. 1987. *Music in Society: A Guide to the Sociology of Music (Elementi sociologije muzike).* Stuyvesant, N.Y.: Pendragon Press.

Swain, Joseph P. 1990. *The Broadway Musical: A Critical and Musical Survey.* New York: Oxford University Press.

Swiss, Thomas, John Sloop, and Andrew Herman, eds. 1997. *Mapping the Beat: Popular Music and Contemporary Theory.* London: Blackwell.

Szatmary, David P. 1996. *A Time to Rock: A Social History of Rock-and-Roll.* New York: Schirmer Books.

Tawa, Nicholas E. 1980. *Sweet Songs for Gentle Americans: The Parlor Song in America, 1790–1860.* Bowling Green, Ohio: Bowling Green University Popular Press.

———. 1982. *A Sound of Strangers: Musical Culture, Acculturation, and the Post–Civil War Ethnic American.* Metuchen, N.J.: Scarecrow Press.

———. 1990. *The Way to Tin Pan Alley: American Popular Song.* New York: Schirmer Books.

Taylor, Timothy D. 1997. *Global Pop: World Music, World Markets.* New York: Routledge.

Théberge, Paul. 1997. *Any Sound You Can Imagine: Making Music/Consuming Technology.* Hanover, N.H.: University Press of New England.

Tick, Judith. 1983. *American Women Composers before 1870.* Rochester, N.Y.: University of Rochester.

Tosches, Nick. 1984. *Unsung Heroes of Rock 'n' Roll.* New York: Charles Scribner's Sons.

Van Zile, Judy. 1982. *The Japanese Bon Dance in Hawaii.* Kailua, Hawai'i: Press Pacifica.

Vander, Judith. 1988. *Songprints: The Musical Experience of Five Shoshone Women.* Urbana and Chicago: University of Illinois Press.

Ventura, Michael. 1985. "White Boys Dancing." In *Shadow Dancing in the USA,* 42–51. Los Angeles: J. P. Tarchor.

Voyer, Simone. 1986. *La Danse traditionnelle dans l'est du Canada: Quadrilles et cotillon.* Québec: Les Presses de l'Université Laval.

Waksman, Steve. 1999. *Instruments of Desire: The Electric Guitar and the Shaping of Musical Experience.* Cambridge: Harvard University Press.

Walser, Robert. 1993. *Running with the Devil: Power Gender and Madness in Heavy Metal Music.* Hanover, N.H.: University Press of New England.

Walter, Arnold, ed. 1969. *Aspects of Music in Canada.* Toronto: University of Toronto Press.

Ward, Brian. 1998. *Just My Soul Responding: Rhythm and Blues, Black Consciousness and Race Relations.* London: University College London Press.

Wilgus, Donald K. 1959. *Anglo-American Folksong Scholarship Since 1898.* New Brunswick, N.J.: Rutgers University Press.

Wilson, Pamela. 1998. "Mountains of Contradictions: Gender, Class, and Region in the Star Image of Dolly Parton." In *Reading Country Music,* ed. Cecelia Tichi, 98–120. Durham, N.C.: Duke University Press.

Witmer, Robert, ed. 1990. *Ethnomusicology in Canada: Proceedings of the First Conference on Ethnomusicology in Canada.* Toronto: Institute for Canadian Music.

AMERICAN INDIANS/FIRST NATIONS

Adams, Robert H. 1991 [1977]. *Songs of Our Grandfathers: Music of the Unami Delaware Indians.* Dewey, Okla.: Touching Leaves Indian Crafts.

American Folklife Center. 1984–1990. *The Federal Cylinder Project: A Guide to Field Cylinder Collections in Federal Agencies.* Washington, D.C.: American Folklife Center, Library of Congress.

Amoss, Pamela. 1978. *Coast Salish Spirit Dancing: The Survival of an Ancestral Religion.* Seattle: University of Washington Press.

———. 1978. *Coast Salish Spirit Dancing: The Survival of an Ancestral Religion.* Seattle: University of Washington Press.

Asch, Michael. 1988. *Kinship and the Drum Dance in a Northern Community.* Edmonton: The Boreal Institute for Northern Studies.

Bahr, Donald M., and Richard J. Haefer. 1974. *Piman Shamanism and Staying Sickness (Ka:cim Mumkidag).* Tucson: University of Arizona Press.

Bahti, Tom. 1970. *Southwestern Indian Ceremonials.* Flagstaff, Ariz.: KC Publications.

Beaudry, Nicole. 1986. "La danse à tambour des Esquimaux yupik du sud-ouest de l'Alaska: performance et contexte." Ph.D. dissertation, Université de Montréal.

Black Bear, Ben Sr., and R. D. Theisz. 1976. *Songs and Dances of the Lakota.* Rosebud, S. Dak.: Sinte Gleska College.

Boas, Franz. 1966. *Kwakiutl Ethnography,* ed. Helen Codere. Chicago: University of Chicago Press.

———. 1888. *The Central Eskimo.* Sixth Annual Report of the Bureau of American Ethnology. Washington: Smithsonian Institution.

Brown, Donald N. 1962. *Masks, Mantas, and Moccasins: Dance Costumes of the Pueblo Indians.* Colorado Springs: Taylor Museum.

Browner, Tara Colleen. 1995. *Transposing Cultures: The Appropriation of Native North American Musics, 1890–1990.* Ph.D. dissertation, University of Michigan.

Callahan, Alice A. 1990. *The Osage Ceremonial Dance I'n-Lon-Schka.* Norman: University of Oklahoma Press.

Cavanagh, Beverley. 1982. *Music of the Netsilik Eskimo: A Study of Stability and Change.* 2 vols. Mercury Series 82. Ottawa: National Museum of Man. Record included. LP disk.

Cole, Douglas, and Ira Chaikin. 1990. *An Iron Hand upon the People: The Law against the Potlatch on the Northwest Coast.* Seattle: University of Washington Press.

Curtis, Natalie. 1905. *Songs of Ancient America: Three Pueblo Indian Corn-Grinding Songs from Laguna, New Mexico.* New York: Schirmer.

Densmore, Frances. 1910–1913. *Chippewa Music.* 2 vols. Bureau of American Ethnology Bulletin 45, 53. Washington, D.C.: Smithsonian Institution.

———. 1918. *Teton Sioux Music and Culture.* Washington, D.C.: U.S. Government Printing Office. Bureau of American Ethnology, Bulletin 61.

Reprint, Lincoln: University of Nebraska Press, 1992.

———. 1921. *Indian Action Songs.* Boston: C. C. Birchard.

———. 1922. *Northern Ute Music.* Bureau of American Ethnology Bulletin 75. Washington, D.C.: Smithsonian Institution.

———. 1923. *Mandan and Hidatsa Music.* Bureau of American Ethnology Bulletin 80. Washington, D.C.: Smithsonian Institution.

———. 1926. *The American Indians and Their Music.* New York: The Woman's Press.

———. 1929. *Chippewa Customs.* Bureau of American Ethnology Bulletin 86. Washington, D.C.: Smithsonian Institution.

———. 1929. *Papago Music.* Bureau of American Ethnology Bulletin 90. Washington, D.C.: Smithsonian Institution.

———. 1932. *Menominee Music.* Bureau of American Ethnology Bulletin 102. Washington, D.C.: Smithsonian Institution.

———. 1936. *Cheyenne and Arapaho Music.* Southwest Museum Papers, no. 10. Los Angeles: Southwest Museum.

———. 1939. *Nootka and Quileute Music.* Bureau of American Ethnology Bulletin 124. Washington, D.C.: Smithsonian Institution.

———. 1942. "The Study of Indian Music." From the Annual Report of the Smithsonian Institution for 1941. Publication 3671. Washington, D.C.: U.S. Government Printing Office.

———. 1953. "The Use of Music in the Treatment of the Sick by American Indians." From the Annual Report of the Smithsonian Institution for 1952. Publication 4128. Washington, D.C.: U.S. Government Printing Office.

———. 1957. *Music of Acoma, Isleta, Cochiti, and Zuñi Pueblos.* Bureau of American Ethnology Bulletin 165. Washington, D.C.: Smithsonian Institution.

———. 1958. *Music of the Maidu Indians of California.* Los Angeles: Southwest Museum.

———. 1958. *Seminole Music.* Bureau of American Ethnology Bulletin No. 141. Washington, D.C.: Smithsonian Institution.

———. 1972 [1943]. *Choctaw Music.* New York: Da Capo.

———. 1979. *Chippewa Customs.* Minneapolis, Minn: Minnesota Historical Society Press.

Diamond, Beverley, et al. 1994. *Visions of Sound: Musical Instruments of First Nations Communities in Northeastern America.* Chicago: University of Chicago Press, and Waterloo: Wilfrid Laurier University Press.

Dyal, Susan. 1985. *Preserving Traditional Arts: A Toolkit for Native American Communities.* Los Angeles: University of California American Indian Studies Center.

Enrico, John, and Wendy Bross Stuart. 1996. *Northern Haida Songs.* Lincoln: University of Nebraska Press.

Evers, Larry, and Felipe S. Molina. 1987. *Yaqui Deer Songs: Maso Bwikan: a Native American Poetry.* Tucson: Sun Tracks, University of Arizona Press.

Fenton, William N. 1940. *Masked Medicine Societies of the Iroquois.* Annual Report of the Smithsonian Institution for 1940. Washington, D.C.: Government Printing Office, 397–429.

———. 1978. *Iroquois Social Dance Songs.* 3 vols. Iroqrafts, Ont.: Ohsweken.

Fletcher, Alice C. 1893. "A Study of Omaha Indian Music." *Archaeological and Ethnological Papers of the Peabody Museum* 1:237-287.

Frisbie, Charlotte J. 1977. *Music and Dance Research of Southwestern United States Indians: Past Trends, Present Activities and Suggestions for Future Research.* Detroit Studies in Music Bibliography 36. Detroit: Information Coordinators.

———. 1987. *Navajo Medicine Bundles or Jish: Acquisition, Transmission, and Disposition in the Past and Present.* Albuquerque: University of New Mexico Press.

———. 1993 [1967]. *Kinaldá. A Study of the Navajo Girls' Puberty Ceremony.* Middletown, Conn.: Wesleyan University Press.

Frisbie, Charlotte J., and David P. McAllester. 1978. *Navajo Blessingway Singer: The Autobiography of Frank Mitchell, 1881–1967.* Tucson: University of Arizona Press.

Frisbie, Charlotte J., ed. 1989 [1980]. *Southwest Indian Ritual Drama.* Prospect Heights, Ill.: Waveland Press, Inc.

Gibbons, Roy. 1980b. "Ethnomusicology of the Métis in Alberta and Saskatchewan: A Distinct Cultural Display of Anglo-Celtic, French and Native Elements." Audiotape, Video Collection, and Field Report. Canadian Centre for Folk Culture Studies, National Museum of Civilization.

Gifford, Edward. 1955. *Central Miwok Ceremonies.* University of California Anthropological Records, vol. 14, no. 4. Berkeley, 261–318.

Giglio, Virginia. 1994. *Southern Cheyenne Women's Songs.* Norman: University of Oklahoma Press.

Goldschmidt, Walter, and Harold Driver. 1940. *The Hupa White Deerskin Dance.* University of California Publications in American Archeology and Ethnology, vol. 35. Berkeley, 103–142.

Gombert, Greg. 1994. *A Guide to Native American Music Recordings.* Fort Collins, Colo.: Multi Cultural Publishing.

Goodman, Linda J. 1977. *Music and Dance in Northwest Coast Indian Life.* Occasional Papers, vol. III, Music and Dance Series no. 3. Tsaile, Ariz.: Navajo Community College Press.

Gray, John, comp. 1988. *Blacks in Classical Music: A Bibliographical Guide to Composers, Performers, and Ensembles.* Westport, Conn.: Greenwood Press.

Haefer, J. Richard. 1977. *Papago Music and Dance.* Tsalie, Ariz.: Navajo Community College Press.

Halpern, Abraham M. 1988. *Southeastern Pomo Ceremonials: The Kuksu Cult and Its Successors.* University of California Anthropological Records, vol. 29. Berkeley.

Hawkes, Ernest W. 1914. *The Dance Festivals of the Alaskan Eskimos.* University of Pennsylvania Anthropological Publications 6(2): 1-41.

Herzog, George. 1936. *Research in Primitive and Folk Music in the United States: A Survey.* Washington, D.C.: American Council of Learned Societies.

Hodge, Frederick W., ed. 1913. *The North American Indian,* vol. 9. Norwood, Mass.: Plimpton Press.

Hoffman, Walter J. 1885–1886. *The Midéwiwin or "Grand Medicine" Society of the Ojibwe.* Bureau of American Ethnology Annual Report 7:143–300.

Howard, James H., and Victoria Lindsay Levine. 1990. *Choctaw Music and Dance.* Norman: University of Oklahoma Press.

Howard, James Henri. 1981. *Shawnee!: The Ceremonialism of a Native Indian Tribe and Its Cultural Background.* Athens: Ohio University Press.

———. 1984. *The Canadian Sioux.* Lincoln: University of Nebraska Press.

Institute of Alaska Native Arts. 1987. *Interior Tunes: Athapaskan Old-Time Music.* Fairbanks: Institute of Alaska Native Arts.

Jenness, Diamond. 1935. *The Ojibwa Indians of Parry Sound, Their Social and Religious Life.* Bulletin 78. Ottawa: Department of Mines, National Museum of Canada.

———. 1943. *The Carrier Indians of the Bulkley River: Their Social and Religious Life.* Bureau of Ethnology Paper 25, Bulletin 133. Washington, D.C.: Smithsonian Institution.

———. 1943. *The Sekani Indians of British Columbia.* Bulletin 84, Anthropological Series 20. Ottawa: Department of Mines and Resources.

Jilek, Wolfgang. 1982. *Indian Healing: Shamanic Ceremonialism in the Pacific Northwest Today.* Surrey, B.C.: Hancock House.

Johnston, Basil. 1990. *Ojibwey Ceremonies.* Lincoln: University of Nebraska Press.

Johnston, Thomas A. 1976. *Eskimo Music, a Comparative Circumpolar Study.* Mercury Series 32. Ottawa: National Museum of Man.

Johnston, Thomas F., et al. 1978. *Koyukan Athapaskan Dance Songs.* Anchorage, Alaska: National Bilingual Materials Development Center.

Keeling, Richard. 1997. *North American Indian Music: A Guide to Published Sources and Selected Recordings (1535–1995).* Garland Library of Music Ethnology 5. New York: Garland Publishing Company.

Keeling, Richard H. 1992. *Cry for Luck: Sacred Song and Speech among the Yurok, Hupa, and Karok Indians of Northwestern California.* Berkeley: University of California Press.

Koranda, Lorraine. 1972. *Alaskan Eskimo Songs and Stories.* Seattle: University of Washington Press.

Kurath, Gertrude. 1968. *Dance and Song Rituals of Six Nations Reserve.* Bulletin No. 220. Ottawa: National Museum.

Kurath, Gertrude P. with Antonio Garcia. 1970. *Music and Dance of the Tewa Pueblos.* Museum of New Mexico Records 8. Santa Fe: Museum of New Mexico Press.

Kurath, Gertrude Prokosch. 1964. *Iroquois Music and Dance: Ceremonial Arts of Two Seneca Longhouses.* Bureau of American Ethnology Bulletin 187. Washington, D.C.: Smithsonian Institution.

———. 1966. *Michigan Indian Festivals.* Ann Arbor, Mich.: Ann Arbor Publishers.

———. 1968. *Dance and Song Rituals of Six Nations Reserve, Ontario.* Bulletin of the National Museum of Canada, no. 220; Folklore series, no. 4. Ottawa: Queen's Printer.

———. 1968. *Dance and Song Rituals of Six Nations Reserve, Ontario.* Bulletin of the National Museum of Canada, no. 220; Folklore series, no. 4. Ottawa: Queen's Printer.

———. 1977. *Iroquois Music and Dance: Ceremonial Arts of Two Seneca Longhouses.* St. Clair Shores, Mich.: Scholarly Press.

———. 1981. *Tutelo Rituals on Six Nations Reserve, Ontario.* Ann Arbor, Mich.: Society for Ethnomusicology.

Lederman, Anne. 1984. "Fiddling in Western Manitoba." Audiotape Collection and Field Report. Canadian Centre for Folk Culture Studies, Canadian Museum of Civilization.

Lee, Dorothy Sara. 1979. *Native North American Music and Oral Data: A Catalogue of Sound Recordings 1893–1976 (at the Archives of Traditional Music, Indiana University).* Bloomington: Indiana University Press.

Lowie, Robert. 1915. *Dances and Societies of the Plains Shoshone.* Anthropological Papers of the American Museum of Natural History, vol. 11, no. 1, 803–835.

Lutz, Maija. 1982. *Musical Traditions of the Labrador Coast Inuit.* Mercury Series 79. Ottawa: National Museum of Man.

Mason, Alden F. 1946. *Notes on the Indians of the Great Slave Lake Area.* Publications in Anthropology 34. New Haven, Conn.: Yale University.

McAllester, David P. 1964. *Peyote music.* New York: Johnson Reprint Corporation.

———. 1973. *Enemy Way Music: A Study of Social and Esthetic Values as Seen in Navaho Music.* Milwood, N.Y.: Kraus Reprint Co.

———. 1980. *Hogans: Navajo Houses and House Songs,* translated and arranged by David P. McAllester. Middletown, Conn.: Wesleyan University Press.

McIlwraith, Thomas F. 1948. *The Bella Coola Indians,* 2 vols. Toronto: University of Toronto Press.

Merriam, Alan P. 1967. *Ethnomusicology of the Flathead Indians.* Chicago: Aldine.

Messenger, Phyllis Mauch, ed. 1989. *The Ethics of Collecting Cultural Property: Whose Culture? Whose Property?* Albuquerque: University of New Mexico Press.

Mishler, Craig. 1993. *The Crooked Stovepipe: Athapaskan Fiddle Music and Square Dancing in Northeast Alaska and Northwest Canada.* Urbana: University of Illinois Press.

Mooney, James. 1973 [1896]. *The Ghost Dance Religion and Wounded Knee.* Reprint of the Fourteenth Annual Report (Part 2) of the Bureau of Ethnology to the Smithsonian Institution, 1892–93; *The Ghost-Dance Religion and the Sioux Outbreak of 1890.* Mineola, N.Y.: Dover Publications.

Morgan, Lewis Henry. 1962 [1851]. *League of the Ho-dé-no-sau-nee or Iroquois.* Secaucus, N.J.: Citadel Press.

Murdock, George P. 1936. "Rank and Potlatch among the Haida." *Anthropology* 13. New Haven, Conn.: Yale University Publications.

Nettl, Bruno. 1954. *North American Indian Musical Styles.* Memoirs of the American Folklore Society, vol. 45. Philadelphia: American Folklore Society.

———. 1954. *North American Indian Musical Styles.* Memoirs of the American Folklore Society, vol. 45. Philadelphia: American Folklore Society.

———. 1979. *An Historical Album of Blackfoot Indian Music.* New York: Folkways Records.

Painter, Muriel Thayer. 1986. *With Good Heart: Yaqui Beliefs and Ceremonies in Pascua Village.* Tucson: University of Arizona Press.

Pelinski, Ramon, et al. 1979. *Inuit Songs from Eskimo Point.* Mercury Series 60. Ottawa: National Museum of Man. Record included. LP disk.

Peterson, Jacquelin, and J. Brown, eds. 1987. *The New Peoples: Being and Becoming Métis in North America.* Winnipeg: University of Manitoba Press.

Powers, William K. 1977. *Oglala Religion.* Lincoln: University of Nebraska Press.

———. 1982. *Yuwipi, Vision and Experience in Oglala.* Lincoln: University of Nebraska Press.

———. 1987. *Beyond the Vision: Essays on American Indian.* The Civilization of the American Indian Series, vol. 184. Norman: University of Oklahoma Press.

———. 1990a. *Voices from the Spirit World: Lakota Ghost Dance Songs.* Kendall Park, N.J.: Lakota Books.

———. 1990b. *War Dance: Plains Indian Musical Performance.* Tucson: University of Arizona Press.

———. 1998. *Lakota Cosmos: Religion and the Reinvention of Culture.* Kendall Park, N.J.: Lakota Books.

Ridington, Robin. 1978. *Swan People: A Study of the Dunne-Za Prophet Dance.* Mercury Series 38. Ottawa: National Museum of Man.

Roberts, Helen, and Diamond Jenness. 1925. "Songs of the Copper Eskimos." In *Report of the Canadian Arctic Expedition, 1913–1918,* vol. 14. Ottawa: F. A. Ackland.

Roberts, Helen H. 1933. *Form in Primitive Music: An Analytical and Comparative Study of the Melodic Form of Some Ancient Southern California Indian Songs.* American Library of Musicology. New York: Norton.

Roberts, Helen H., and Morris Swadesh. 1955. *Songs of the Nootka Indians of Western Vancouver Island.* Philadelphia: American Philosophical Society.

Ross, W. Gillies. 1984. "The Earliest Sound Recordings among the North American Inuit." *Arctic* 37(3):291–292.

Seeger, Anthony, and Louise S. Spear, eds. 1987. *Early Field Recordings: A Catalogue of the Cylinder Collections at the Indiana University Archives of Traditional Music.* Bloomington: Indiana University Press.

Shimkin, Demitri B. 1953. *The Wind River Shoshone Sun Dance.* Bureau of American Ethnology Bulletin 151. Washington, D.C.: Smithsonian Institution, 399–491.

Smyth, Willie and Esme Ryan, ed. 1999. *Spirit of the First People: Native American Music Traditions of Washington State.* Seattle: University of Washington Press.

Speck, Frank G., and George Herzog. 1942. *The Tutelo Adoption Ceremony: Reclothing the Living in the Name of the Dead.* Harrisburg: Pennsylvania Historical Commission.

Speck, Frank G., and Leonard Broom. 1983. *Cherokee Dance and Drama,* 2nd ed. Norman: University of Oklahoma Press.

Speck, Frank Gouldsmith. 1911. *Ceremonial Songs of the Creek and Yuchi Indians.* University of Pennsylvania. The University Museum Anthropological Publications 50(2):157–245.

Sturtevant, William C., and David Damas, eds. 1984. *Handbook of North American Indians,* vol. 5: *Arctic.* Washington, D.C.: Smithsonian Institution.

Swanton, John R. 1912. *Haida Songs.* Publications of the American Ethnological Society 3:1–63.

Sweet, Jill D. 1985. *Dances of the Tewa Pueblo Indians*. Santa Fe: School of American Research.

Underhill, Ruth Murray. 1973 [1938]. *Singing for Power: The Song Magic of the Papago Indians of Southern Arizona*. New York: Ballantine Books.

Vander, Judith. 1986. *Ghost Dance Songs and Religion of a Wind River Shoshone Woman*. Urbana: University of Illinois Press.

———. 1988. *Songprints: The Musical Experience of Five Shoshone Women*. Urbana and Chicago: University of Illinois Press.

———. 1997. *Shoshone Ghost Dance Religion: Poetry Songs and Great Basin Context*. Urbana: University of Illinois Press.

Vennum, Thomas Jr. 1982. *The Ojibwa Dance Drum: Its History and Construction*. Smithsonian Folklife Studies 2. Washington, D.C.: Smithsonian Institution Press.

Whiddon, Lynn. 1993. *Métis Songs: Visiting was the Métis Way*. New York: Gabriel Dumont Institute.

———. 1986. "An Ethnomusicological Study of the Traditional Songs of the Chisasibi Cree." Ph.D. dissertation, Université de Montréal.

Wyman, Leland Clifton. 1970. *Blessingway*. Tucson: University of Arizona Press.

———. 1975. *The Mountainway of the Navajo*. Tucson: University of Arizona Press.

UNITED STATES

Abrahams, Roger D., and George Foss. 1968. *Anglo-American Folksong Style*. Englewood Cliffs, N.J.: Prentice-Hall.

Alderfer, E. G. 1985. *The Ephrata Commune: An Early American Counterculture*. Pittsburgh: University of Pittsburgh Press.

Allen, Ray. 1991. *Singing in the Spirit: African American Sacred Quartets in New York City*. Philadelphia: University of Pennsylvania Press.

Allen, Ray, and Lois Wilcken, eds. 1998. *Island Sounds in the Global City: Caribbean Popular Music and Identity in New York*. New York: Brooklyn College and New York Folklore Society and the Institute for Studies in American Music.

Allen, William Francis, Charles Pickard Ware, and Lucy McKim Garrison, comp. 1951 [1867]. *Slave Songs of the United States*. New York: Peter Smith.

Allen, William Francis, Charles Pickard Ware, and Lucy McKim Garrison, eds. 1965 [1867]. *Slave Songs of the United States*. New York: Oak Publications.

Ancelet, Barry Jean. 1989. *Cajun Music: Its Origins and Development*. Lafayette: Center for Louisiana Studies, University of Southwestern Louisiana.

Ancelet, Barry Jean, and Philip Gould. 1992. *Cajun Music and Zydeco*. Baton Rouge: Louisiana State University.

Andrews, Edward Deming. 1962 [1940]. *The Gift to Be Simple: Songs, Dances and Rituals of the American Shakers*. New York: Dover Publications.

Arapaho Music and Spoken Word Collection. The Alice Cunningham Fletcher Collection. Archive of Folk Culture, Library of Congress AFS 20308 and 20324.

Armistead, Samuel. 1992. *The Spanish Tradition in Louisiana*. Vol. I: *Isleño Folkliterature*, with transcriptions by Israel Katz. Newark, Del.: Juan de la Cuesta.

Arnold, Alison. 1985. "Aspects of Asian Indian Musical Life in North America." *Selected Reports in Ethnomusicology* 6:25–38.

Artis, Bob. 1975. *Bluegrass*. New York: Hawthorne.

Arya, Usharbudh. 1968. *Ritual Songs and Folksongs of the Hindus of Surinam*. Leiden, Netherlands: E. J. Brill.

Attali, Jacques. 1985. *Noise: The Political Economy of Music*. Trans. Brian Massumi. Minneapolis: University of Minnesota Press.

Austerlitz, Paul. 1996. *Dominican Music and Dominican Identity*. Philadelphia: Temple University Press.

———. 1997. *Merengue: Dominican Music and Dominican Identity*. Philadelphia: Temple University Press.

Averill, Gage. 1997. *A Day for the Hunter, a Day for the Prey: Popular Music and Power in Haiti*. Chicago: University of Chicago Press.

Baker, David. 1985. *How To Play Bebop*. 3 vols. Bloomington, Ind.: Frangipani Press.

Balys, Jonas, ed. 1958. *Lithuanian Folksongs in America*. A Treasury of Lithuanian Folklore, no. 5. Boston: Lithuanian Encyclopedia Publishers.

Bandera, Mark Jaroslav. 1991. *The Tsymbaly Maker and His Craft: The Ukrainian Hammered Dulcimer in Alberta*. Canadian Series in Ukrainian Ethnology, no. 1. Edmonton: Canadian Institute of Ukrainian Studies Press, University of Alberta.

Barlow, William. 1989. *"Looking Up at Down": The Emergence of Blues Culture*. Philadelphia: Temple University Press.

Barrand, Anthony G. 1991. *Six Fools and a Dancer: The Timeless Way of the Morris*. Plainfield, Vt.: Northern Harmony.

Bastin, Bruce. 1986. *Red River Blues: The Blues Tradition in the Southeast*. Urbana: University of Illinois Press.

Bauman, Richard, ed. 1993. *Folklore and Culture on the Texas-Mexican Border*. Austin: Center for Mexican American Studies, University of Texas.

Bayard, Samuel P. 1944. *Hill Country Tunes: Instrumental Folk Music of Southwestern Pennsylvania*. Philadelphia: American Folklore Society.

Beckwith, John. 1997. *Music Papers: Articles and Talks by a Canadian Composer 1961–1994*. Ottawa: The Golden Dog Press.

Behague, Gerard H., ed.. 1994. *Music and Black Ethnicity: The Caribbean and South America*. Miami: University of Miami North-South Center.

Benary, Barbara. 1983. "One Perspective on Gamelan in America." *Asian Music* 15(1):82–101.

———. 1993a. *Gamelan Works Vol. 1: The Braid Pieces*. Lebanon, N.H.: American Gamelan Institute.

Berendt, Joachim. 1975. *The Jazz Book: From New Orleans to Rock and Free Jazz*. Trans. Dan Morgenstern and Helmut and Barbara Bredigkeit. Westport, Conn.: Lawrence Hill and Co.

Berlin, Edward A. 1980. *Ragtime: A Musical and Cultural History*. Berkeley: University of California Press.

Berliner, Paul F. 1994. *Thinking in Jazz: The Infinite Art of Improvisation*. Chicago: University of Chicago Press.

Bierley, Paul. 1984. *The Works of John Philip Sousa*. Columbus, Ohio: Integrity Press.

Blegen, Theodore C., and Martin B. Ruud, eds. 1936. *Norwegian Emigrant Songs and Ballads*. London: Oxford University Press.

Blesh, Rudi. 1946. *Shining Trumpets. A History of Jazz*. New York: Knopf.

———. 1985. *Shining Trumpets: A History of Jazz*. 2nd ed. New York: Knopf.

Blesh, Rudi, and Harriet Janis. 1971 [1966]. *They All Played Ragtime*. 4th ed. New York: Oak Publications.

Boggs, Vernon, ed. 1992. *Salsiology: Afro-Cuban Music and the Evolution of Salsa in New York City*. New York: Greenwood Press.

Bohlman, Philip V. 1988. *The Study of Folk Music in the Modern World*. Bloomington: Indiana University Press.

Bowman, Rob. 1997. *Soulsville U.S.A.: The Story of Stax Records*. New York: Schirmer Books.

Boyer, Horace. 1995. *How Sweet the Sound: The Golden Age of Gospel*. Washington, D.C.: Elliott & Clark Publishing.

Boyer, Walter E., Albert F. Buffington, and Don Yoder, eds. 1951. *Songs along the Mahantango: Pennsylvania Dutch Folksongs*. Hatboro, Pa.: Folklore Associates.

Bronson, Bertrand. 1959–1972. *The Traditional Tunes of the Child Ballads*. 4 vols. Princeton, N.J.: Princeton University Press.

———. 1976. *The Singing Tradition of Child's Popular Ballads*. Princeton, N.J.: Princeton University Press.

Bronson, Bertrand H. 1976. *The Singing Tradition of Child's Popular Ballads*. Abridgment of *The Traditional Tunes of the Child Ballads*. 4 vols., 1959–1972. Princeton, N.J.: Princeton University Press.

Brown, Rae Linda. 1990. "William Grant Still, Florence Price, and William Dawson: Echoes of the Harlem Renaissance." In *Black Music in the Harlem Renaissance: A Collection of Essays*, ed. Samuel A. Floyd Jr., 71–86. Westport, Conn.: Greenwood Press.

Broyles, Michael. 1992. *"Music of the Highest Class": Elitism and Populism in Antebellum Boston*. New Haven, Conn.: Yale University Press.

Bryant, Carolyn. 1975. *And the Band Played On, 1776–1976*. Washington, D.C.: Smithsonian Institution Press.

Budds, Michael J. 1990. *Jazz in the Sixties: The Expansion of Musical Resources and Techniques*. Iowa City: The University of Iowa.

Buertle, Jack V., and Danny Barker. 1973. *Bourbon Street Black: The New Orleans Black Jazzman*. New York: Oxford University Press.

Buffington, Albert F. 1974. *Pennsylvania German Secular Folksongs*. Publications of the Pennsylvania German Society, vol. 8. Breinigsville: Pennsylvania German Society.

Bufwack, Mary A., and Robert K. Oermann. 1993. *Finding Her Voice: The Saga of Women in Country Music*. New York: Crown.

Burr, Ramiro. 1999. *The Billboard Guide to Tejano and Regional Mexican Music*. New York: Billboard Books.

Cage, John. 1961. *Silence: Lectures and Writings*. Middletown, Conn.: Wesleyan University Press.

California's Musical Wealth: Sources for the Study of Music in California, ed. Stephen M. Fry, 55–78. Southern California Chapter, Music Library Association.

Camus, Raoul F. 1976. *Military Music of the American Revolution*. Chapel Hill: University of North Carolina Press.

———. 1992. *American Wind and Percussion Music.* Three Centuries of American Music, Vol. 12. Boston: G. K. Hall.

Cantwell, Bob. 1984. *Bluegrass Breakdown.* Urbana: University of Illinois Press.

Cantwell, Robert. 1996. *When We Were Good: The Folk Revival.* Cambridge: Harvard University Press.

Carter, Madison H. 1986. *An Annotated Catalog of Composers of African Ancestry.* New York: Vantage Press.

Catlin, Amy, ed. 1992. *Khmer Classical Dance Songbook.* Van Nuys, Calif.: Apsara Media for Intercultural Education.

Cavanagh, Beverley. 1982. *Music of the Net Silik Eskimo: A Study of Stability and Change.* Ottawa: National Museums.

Champe, Flavia Water. 1983. *The Matachines Dance of the Upper Rio Grande: History, Music, and Choreography.* Lincoln: University of Texas Press.

Chapple, Steve, and Reebee Garofalo. 1977. *Rock 'n' Roll Is Here to Pay: The History of Politics in the Music Industry.* Chicago: Nelson-Hall.

Charters, Samuel B. 1959. *The Country Blues.* New York: Rinehart.

Chen, Jack. 1980. *The Chinese of America.* New York: Harper and Row.

Chinn, Thomas W., ed. 1989. *Bridging the Pacific: San Francisco Chinatown and Its People.* San Francisco: Chinese Historical Society of America.

Cipolla, Frank, J., and Donald Hunsberger, eds. 1994. *The Wind Ensemble and Its Repertoire.* Rochester, N.Y.: University of Rochester Press.

Coffin, Tristram P. 1963. *The British Traditional Ballad in North America.* Philadelphia: American Folklore Society.

Colcord, Joanna C. 1938. *Songs of American Sailormen.* New York: Norton.

Cole, Bill. 1993 [1976]. *John Coltrane.* New York: Da Capo.

Collier, James Lincoln. 1978. *The Making of Jazz: A Comprehensive History.* Boston: Houghton Mifflin.

Cornelius, Steven. 1989. "The Convergence of Power: An Investigation into the Music Liturgy of Santeria in New York City." Ph.D. dissertation, University of California, Los Angeles.

Courlander, Harold. 1963. *Negro Folk Music, U.S.A.* New York: Columbia University Press.

Cowell, Henry, ed. 1961 [1933]. *American Composers on American Music: A Symposium.* New York: Frederick Ungar Publishing Co.

Cowell, Sidney Robertson, collector. 1938–1940. "Alberto Mendes, Manuel Lemos, and Mr. Franks Performing Portuguese Songs and Music from the Azores, 1939." In *California Gold: Northern California Folk Music from the Thirties.* WPA California Folk Music Project. Washington, D.C.: American Folklife Center, Library of Congress. Available from website http://lcweb2.loc.gov/ammem/afcchtml/0009.html.

Cowley, John, and Paul Oliver, eds. 1996. *The New Blackwell Guide to Recorded Blues.* Oxford: Blackwell.

Crawford, Richard, ed. 1984. *The Core Repertory of Early American Psalmody.* Recent Researches in American Music, vols. 11 and 12. Madison, Wisc.: A-R Editions.

Cross, Brian. 1993. *It's not about a Salary: Rap, Race and Resistance in Los Angeles.* New York: Verso.

Cuney-Hare, Maud. 1974 [1936]. *Negro Musicians and Their Music.* New York: Da Capo.

Da Silva, Owen F. 1941. *Mission Music in California.* Los Angeles: Warren F. Lewis.

Davis, Angela Y. 1998. *Blues Legacies and Black Feminism: Gertrude "Ma" Rainey, Bessie Smith, and Billie Holiday.* New York: Pantheon.

Davis, Stephen. 1985. *Hammer of the Gods: The Led Zeppelin Saga.* New York: Ballantine Books.

DeVeaux, Scott. 1997. *The Birth of Bebop: A Social and Musical History.* Berkeley: University of California Press.

Diamond, Beverley. 1991. "Canadian Music Studies in University Curricula," *ACS Newsletter* 12/2:n.p.

Diamond, Beverley and Robert Witmer, eds. 1994. *Canadian Music: Issues of Hegemony and Identity.* Toronto: Canadian Scholars' Press.

Diamond, Beverley, M. Sam Cronk, and Franziska von Rosen. 1994. *Visions of Sound: Musical Instruments of First Nations Communities in Northeastern America.* Chicago Studies in Ethnomusicology. Chicago: University of Chicago Press.

Diamond, Jody. 1992a. "Making Choices: American Gamelan in Composition and Education (From the Java Jive to Eine Kleine Gamelan Music)." In *Essays on Southeast Asian Performing Arts: Local Manifestations and Cross-cultural Implications,* ed. Kathy Foley. Berkeley, Calif.: Centers for South and Southeast Asian Studies.

Dilling, Margaret Walker. 1994. "Kumdori Born Again in Boston: The Life Cycle of Music by a Korean American." *Korean Culture* 15(3):14–25.

Dixon, Robert M. W., and John Godrich. 1963. *Blues and Gospel Records (1902–1942).* Middlesex, Eng.: Storyville.

DjeDje, Jacqueline Cogdell, and Eddie S. Meadows, eds. 1998. *California Soul: Music of African Americans in the West.* Berkeley: University of California Press.

Dyson, Michael E. 1996. *Between God and Gangsta Rap: Bearing Witness to Black Culture.* New York: Oxford University Press.

Emery, Lynne Fauley. 1972. *Black Dance in the United States from 1619 to 1970.* Palo Alto, Calif.: National Press Books.

Epstein, Dena J. 1977. *Sinful Tunes and Spirituals: Black Folk Music to the Civil War.* Urbana: University of Illinois Press.

Eskew, Harry, David W. Music, and Paul A. Richardson. 1994. *Singing Baptists: Studies in Baptist Hymnody in America.* Nashville, Tenn.: Church Street Press.

Estavan, Lawrence. 1991 [1938]. *The Italian Theater in San Francisco.* San Bernadino, Calif.: Borgo Press.

Ethnic Recordings in America: A Neglected Heritage. 1982. Washington, D.C.: Library of Congress American Folklife Center.

Evans, David. 1982. *Big Road Blues: Tradition and Creativity in the Folk Blues.* Berkeley: University of California Press.

Farrell, Gerry. 1997. *Indian Music and the West.* Oxford: Clarendon Press.

Feather, Leonard, and Ira Gitler. 1999. *The Biographical Encyclopedia of Jazz.* New York: Oxford University Press.

Feintuch, Burt. 1993. "Musical Revival as Musical Transformation." In *Transforming Tradition: Folk Music Revivals Examined,* ed. Neil V. Rosenberg. Urbana: University of Illinois Press.

Feldman, Walter. 1975. "Middle Eastern Music Among Immigrant Communities in New York City." In *Balkan-Arts Traditions,* ed. Martin Koenig, 19–25. New York: Balkan Arts Center.

Fernando, S. H. Jr. 1994. *The New Beats: Exploring the Music, Culture and Attitudes of Hip-Hop.* New York: Anchor Books/Doubleday.

Ferris, William, and Mary L. Hart, eds. 1982. *Folk Music and Modern Sound.* Jackson: University Press of Mississippi.

Ferris, William, Jr. 1970. *Blues from the Delta.* London: Studio Vista.

Figueroa, Frank M. 1994. *Encyclopedia of Latin American Music in New York.* St. Petersburg, Fla.: Pillar Publications.

Fikentscher, Kai. 2000. *"You Better Work!" Underground Dance Music in New York City.* Hanover, N.H.: Wesleyan University Press/University Press of New England.

Flaherty, David H. and Frank E. Manning, eds. 1993. *The Beaver Bites Back? American Popular Culture in Canada.* Montréal and Kingston: McGill-Queen's University Press.

Fletcher, Alice C., Francis La Flesche, and John C. Fillmore. 1893. *A Study of Omaha Indian Music.* Peabody Museum Archaeological and Ethnological Papers, vol. 1, no. 5. Cambridge, Mass.: Peabody Museum of American Archaeology and Ethnology, Harvard University.

Flores, Richard R. 1995. *Los Pastores: History and Performance in the Mexican Shepherds' Play of South Texas.* Washington, D.C.: Smithsonian Institution Press.

Floyd, Samuel A. Jr., and Marsha J. Reisser. 1983. *Black Music in the United States: An Annotated Bibliography of Selected Reference and Research Materials.* Millwood, N.Y.: Kraus International.

———. 1987. *Black Music Biography: An Annotated Bibliography.* White Plains, N.Y.: Kraus International.

Floyd, Samuel, ed. 1990. *Black Music in the Harlem Renaissance: A Collection of Essays.* New York: Greenwood Press.

Folb, Edith. 1980. *Runnin' Down Some Lines: The Language and Culture of Black Teenagers.* Cambridge: Harvard University Press.

Fong-Torres, Ben. 1998. *The Hits Just Keep on Coming: The History of Top 40 Radio.* San Francisco: Miller Freeman Books.

Frey, J. William. 1949. "Amish Hymns as Folk Music." In *Pennsylvania Songs and Legends,* ed. George Korson, 129–162. Philadelphia: University of Pennsylvania Press.

Friedlander, Paul David. 1990. "Rocking the Yangtze: Impressions of Chinese Popular Music and Technology." *Popular Music and Society* 14(1):63–74.

Friend, Robyn, and Neil Siegel. 1986. "Contemporary Contexts for Iranian Professional Musical Performance." In *Cultural Parameters of Iranian Musical Expression,* ed. Margaret Caton and Neil Siegel, 10–17. Redondo Beach, Calif.: The Institute of Persian Performing Arts.

Frigyesi, Judit. 1996. "The Aesthetic of the Hungarian Revival Movement." In *Retuning Culture: Musical Changes in Central and Eastern Europe,* ed. Mark Slobin, 54–75. Durham, N.C.: Duke University Press.

Frith, Simon, and Andrew Goodwin, eds. 1990. *On Record: Rock, Pop, and the Written Word.* New York: Pantheon.

Ganam, King. 1957. *Canadian Fiddle Tunes.* Don Mills, Ontario: BMI Canada.

Garofalo, Reebee. 1997. *Rockin' Out: Popular Music in the U.S.A.* Boston: Allyn and Bacon.

Geldard, Alison. 1980. "Music and Musical Performance Among the East Indians in Chicago." Master's thesis, University of Illinois at Urbana-Champaign.

George, Nelson. 1998. *Hip Hop America.* New York: Penguin Books.

Gillett, Charlie. 1983 [1970]. *The Sound of the City.* Rev. and expanded ed. New York: Pantheon Books.

Gitler, Ira. 1985. *Swing to Bop: An Oral History of the Transition in Jazz in the 1940s.* New York: Oxford University Press.

Goldman, Albert. 1978. *Disco.* New York: Hawthorn.

Gould, Nathaniel D. 1972 [1853]. *Church Music in America, Comprising Its History and Its Peculiarities of Different Periods with Cursory Remarks.* New York: AMS Press.

Grame, Theodore C. 1976. *America's Ethnic Music.* Tarpon Springs, Fla.: Cultural Maintenance Associates.

Green, Mildred Denby. 1983. *Black Women Composers: A Genesis.* Boston: Twayne.

Greene, Victor. 1992. *A Passion for Polka: Old Time Ethnic Music in America.* Berkeley: University of California Press.

Greenhill, Pauline. 1997. *Undisciplined Women: Tradition and Culture in Canada.* Montréal: McGill-Queen's University Press.

Grenet, Emilio. 1939. *Popular Cuban Music: Eighty Revised and Corrected Compositions, Together With an Essay on the Evolution of Music in Cuba.* Havana. Carasa.

Gridley, Mark. 1991. *Jazz Styles: History and Analysis.* 4th ed. Englewood Cliffs, N.J.: Prentice-Hall.

Griffiths, John. 1788. *A Collection of the Newest and Most Fashionable Country Dances and Cotillions, The Greater Part by Mr. John Griffiths, Dancing Master, in Providence.* Providence, R.I.

Gronow, Pekka. 1977. *Studies in Scandinavian-American Discography.* Helsinki: Finnish Institute of Recorded Sound.

Groom, Bob. 1971. *The Blues Revival.* London: November Books Ltd.

Guralnick, Peter. 1986. *Sweet Soul Music: Rhythm and Blues and the Southern Dream of Freedom.* New York: Harper and Row.

Hadley, Peter. 1993. "New Music for Gamelan by North American Composers." Master's thesis, Wesleyan University. Distributed by the American Gamelan Institute.

Haefer, J. Richard. 1989 [1980]. "O'odham Celkona: The Papago Skipping Dance." In *Southwest Indian Ritual Drama,* ed. Charlotte J. Frisbie. Prospect Heights, Ill.: Waveland Press.

Hague, Eleanor. 1917. *Spanish-American Folk-Songs.* Lancaster, Pa.: American Folklore Society.

———. 1922. *Early Spanish-Californian Folk-Songs.* New York: Pantheon.

Hakala, Joyce. 1997. *Momento of Finland: A Musical Legacy.* St. Paul, Minn.: Pikebone Music.

Hall, Leslie. 1982. "Turkish Musical Culture in Toronto." *Canadian Folk Music Journal* 10:48–52.

Hambly, Scott. 1977. "Mandolins in the United States: An Industrial and Sociological History since 1880." Ph.D. dissertation, University of Pennsylvania.

Hamm, Charles. 1979. *Yesterdays: Popular Song in America.* New York: Norton.

———. 1983. *Music in the New World.* New York: Norton.

Handy, D. Antoinette. 1995. *Black Conductors.* Lanham, Md.: Scarecrow Press.

Haralambos, Michael. 1985 [1974]. *Soul Music: The Birth of a Sound in Black America.* New York: Da Capo.

Hark, J. M. 1972 [1889]. *Chronicon Ephratense: A History of the Community of the Seventh Day Baptists at Ephrata.* New York: Burt Franklin.

Harris, Michael W. 1992. *The Rise of Gospel Blues: The Music of Thomas Andrew Dorsey in the Urban Church.* New York: Oxford University Press.

Hart, Mary L., et al. 1989. *The Blues: A Bibliographical Guide.* New York: Garland.

Haskell, Harry. 1988. *The Early Music Revival: A History.* London: Thames and Hudson.

Hast, Dorothea. 1994. "Music, Dance, and Community: Contra Dance in New England." Ph.D. dissertation, Wesleyan University.

Hatch, James V. 1970. *Black Image on the American Stage: A Bibliography of Plays and Musicals, 1770–1970.* New York: DBS Publications.

Haugen, Einar, and Camilla Cai. 1993. *Ole Bull: Norway's Romantic Musician and Cosmopolitan Patriot.* Madison: University of Wisconsin Press.

Hay, Samuel A. 1994. *African American Theater: A Historical and Critical Analysis.* Cambridge: Cambridge University Press.

Hazen, Margaret Hindle, and Robert M. Hazen. 1987. *The Music Men. An Illustrated History of Brass Bands in America, 1800–1920.* Washington, D.C.: Smithsonian Institution Press.

Heilbut, Anthony. 1971. *The Gospel Sound: Good News and Bad Times.* New York: Simon and Schuster.

Hentoff, Nat. 1961. *The Jazz Life.* New York: Dial Press.

Hernández, Guillermo. 1978. *Cancionero de la Raza: Songs of the Chicano Experience.* Berkeley, Calif.: El Fuego de Aztlán.

Herrera-Sobek, Maria. 1993. *Northward Bound: The Mexican Emigrant Experience in Ballad and Song.* Bloomington: Indiana University Press.

Herskovits, Melville J. 1958 [1941]. *The Myth of the Negro Past.* Boston: Beacon Press.

Heskes, Irene. 1977. *The Resource Book of Jewish Music: A Bibliographical and Topical Guide to the Book and Journal Literature and Program Materials.* Westport Conn.: Greenwood Press.

Heth, Charlotte, ed. 1992. *Native American Dance: Ceremonies and Social Traditions.* Washington, D.C.: Smithsonian Institution.

Hines, Michele. 1997. *Radio Voices: American Broadcasting, 1922–1952.* Minneapolis: University of Minnesota Press.

Hispano Folk Music of the Past. 1998. Music of New Mexico Series, vol. 1. Albuquerque, N.M.: The Albuquerque Museum.

Hispano Music and Culture of the Northern Rio Grande. 1940. The Juan B. Rael Collection. Washington, D.C.: American Folklife Center, Library of Congress. Available from website http://memory.loc.gov/ammem/rghtm/rghome.html.

Hitchcock, H. Wiley, and Stanley Sadie, eds. 1986. *The New Grove Dictionary of American Music.* London: Macmillan.

Hoe, Ban Seng. 1989. *Beyond the Golden Mountain: Chinese Cultural Traditions in Canada.* Canada: Canadian Museum of Civilization.

Hohmann, Rupert K. 1959. "The Church Music of the Old Order Amish of the United States." Ph.D. dissertation, Northwestern University.

Hom, Marlon K. 1987. *Songs of Gold Mountain: Cantonese Rhymes from San Francisco Chinatown.* Berkeley: University of California Press.

Hood, George. 1970 [1846]. *A History of Music in New England: With Biographical Sketches of Reformers and Psalmists.* New York: Johnson Reprint Corp.

Hoogland, Eric, ed. 1987. *Crossing the Waters: Arabic-Speaking Immigrants to the United States before 1940.* Washington, D.C.: Smithsonian Institution Press.

Horn, David. 1977. *The Literature of American Music in Books and Folk Music Collections.* Metuchen, N.J.: Scarecrow Press.

Houser, George J. 1976. *The Swedish Community at Eriksdale, Manitoba.* Canadian Centre for Folk Culture Studies Paper, no. 14. Ottawa: National Museum of Man Mercury Series.

Hubbard, W. L., ed. 1910. *The American History and Encyclopedia of Music.* Irving Squire.

Intergalactic Gamelan: Gamelan Galak Tika. Directed by Evan Ziporyn. 1996. Compositions for *gong kebyar* by Evan Ziporyn, I Gede Manik, and Desak Made Suarti Laksmi. Independently produced cassette.

Ishaya, Arian and Eden Naby. 1980. "Assyrians." In *Harvard Encyclopedia of American Ethnic Groups,* ed. Stephan Thernstron, 160–163. Cambridge, Mass.: The Belknap Press of Harvard University Press.

Jackson, George P. 1933. *White Spirituals in the Southern Uplands.* Chapel Hill: University of North Carolina Press.

———. 1975 [1943]. *White and Negro Spirituals: Their Life-Span and Kinship.* New York: Da Capo.

Jackson, George Pullen. 1965 [1933]. *White Spirituals in the Southern Uplands.* New York: Dover.

Jackson, Irene V., ed. 1985. *More Than Dancing.* Westport, Conn.: Greenwood Press.

Jairazbhoy, Nazir A., and Sue Carole DeVale, eds. 1985. *Selected Reports in Ethnomusicology: Vol. VI: Asian Music in North America.* Los Angeles: UCLA Department of Music.

Jairazbhoy, Nazir, and Sue Carole de Vale, eds. 1985. *Asian Music in North America.* Vol. 6 of *Selected Reports in Ethnomusicology.* Los Angeles: University of California Press.

John Biggs Consort. 1974. *California Mission Music.* KSK Recording KSK-75218, University of California, Berkeley. LP disk.

Jones, LeRoi (Amiri Baraka). 1963a. *Blues People: Negro Music in White America.* New York: Morrow.

Keck, George R. and Sherrill V. Martin, ed. 1988. *Feel the Spirit: Studies in Nineteenth-Century Afro-American Music.* Westport, Conn.: Greenwood Press.

Keil, Charles, Angeliki Keil, and Dick Blau. 1992. *Polka Happiness.* Philadelphia: Temple University Press.

———. 1966. *Urban Blues.* Chicago: University of Chicago Press.

———. 1992. *Polka Happiness.* Philadelphia: Temple University Press.

Kelly, Ron, Jonathan Friedlander and Anita Colby, eds. 1993b. *Irangeles: Iranians in Los Angeles.* Berkeley: University of California Press.

Kenney, William H. 1993. *Chicago Jazz: A Cultural History 1904–1930.* New York: Oxford University Press.

Kernfeld, Barry. 1988. *The New Grove Dictionary of Jazz.* London: Macmillan.

Key Kool and Rhettmatic. 1995. *Behind the Mask.* Toronto: Lasis Productions.

Kingsbury, Paul, ed. 1998. *The Encyclopedia of Country Music.* New York: Oxford University Press.

Kivy, Peter. 1995. *Authenticities: Philosophical Reflections on Music Performance.* Ithaca, N.Y.: Cornell University Press.

Klymasz, Robert B. 1970b. *An Introduction to the Ukrainian-Canadian Immigrant Folksong Cycle.* Bulletin no. 234, Folklore Series no. 8. Ottawa: National Museums of Canada.

———. 1970c. *The Ukrainian Winter Folksong Cycle in Canada.* Bulletin no. 236, Folklore Series no. 9. Ottawa: National Museums of Canada.

———. 1989. *The Ukrainian Folk Ballad in Canada.* Immigrant Communities and Ethnic Minorities in the United States and Canada, no. 65. New York: AMS Press.

Kmen, Henry A. 1977. *The Roots of Jazz: The Negro and Music in New Orleans 1791–1900.* Urbana: University of Illinois Press.

Kodish, Debora, ed. 1994. *The Giant Never Wins: Lakhon Bassac (Cambodian Folk Opera) in Philadelphia.* Philadelphia: Philadelphia Folklore Project.

Kofsky, Frank. 1970. *Black Nationalism and the Revolution in Music.* New York: Pathfinder.

Kolar, Walter W. 1975. *The Tambura in America.* Vol. 2 of *A History of the Tambura.* Pittsburgh: Duquesne University Tamburitzans Institute of Folk Arts.

Koskoff, Ellen. 2000. *Music in Lubavitcher Life.* Urbana: University of Illinois Press.

Krasnow, Carolyn. 1993. "Fear and Loathing in the Seventies: Race, Sexuality, and Disco." *Stanford Humanities Review* 3(2):37–45.

Kraus, Richard Curt. 1989. *Pianos and Politics in China: Middle-Class Ambitions and the Struggle over Western Music.* New York: Oxford University Press.

Krehbiel, Henry. 1962 [1914]. *Afro-American Folk Songs.* New York: Frederick Ungar.

Kreitner, Kenneth. 1990. *Discoursing Sweet Music: Brass Bands and Community Life in Turn-of-the-Century Pennsylvania.* Urbana: University of Illinois Press.

Krims, Adam. 2000. *Rap Music and the Poetics of Identity.* Cambridge: Cambridge University Press.

Lamadrid, Enrique R., Jack Loeffler, and Miguel A. Gandert. 1994. *Tesoros del Espiritu: A Portrait in Sound of Hispanic New Mexico.* Embudo, N.M.: El Norte/Academia Publications.

Larkin, Rochelle. 1970. *Soul Music.* New York: Lancer Books.

Lawless, Ray M. 1960. *Folksingers and Folksongs in America.* New York: Duell, Sloan and Pearce.

Laws, George Malcolm. 1950. *Native American Balladry: A Descriptive Study and a Bibliographical Syllabus.* Philadelphia: American Folklore Society.

———. 1957. *American Balladry from British Broadsides: A Guide for Students and Collectors of Traditional Song.* Philadelphia: American Folklore Society.

Leary, James P. 1990. "Minnesota Polka: Polka Music, American Music." Booklet with recording, *Minnesota Polka: Dance Music from Four Traditions.* Minneapolis: Minnesota Historical Society Press.

Lebrecht, Norman. 1997. *Who Killed Classical Music? Maestros, Managers, and Corporate Politics.* Secaucus, N.J.: Birch Lane Press.

Levine, Lawrence W. 1977. *Black Culture and Black Consciousness: Afro-American Folk Thought from Slavery to Freedom.* New York: Oxford University Press.

Lewis, Samuel L. 1990 [1975]. *Spiritual Dance and Walk: An Introduction.* Ed. Neil Douglas-Klotz. Seattle: Peace Works–INDUP.

Li, Guangming. 1994. "Music in the Chinese Community of Los Angeles: An Overview." In *Musical Aesthetics and Multiculturalism in Los Angeles,* ed. Steven Loza, 105–127. Selected Reports in Ethnomusicology 10. Los Angeles: University of California.

Library of Congress, Music Division. 1942. *Checklist of Recorded Songs in the English Language in the Archive of American Folk Song to July, 1940.* Washington, D.C.: Library of Congress.

Lieb, Sandra R. 1981. *Mother of the Blues: A Study of Ma Rainey.* Amherst: University of Massachusetts Press.

Lipsitz, George. 1994. *Dangerous Crossroads: Popular Music, Postmodernism and the Poetics of Place.* London: Verso.

Loeffler, Jack, with Katherine Loeffler and Enrique Lamadrid. 1999. *La Música de los Viejitos: Hispanic Folk Music of the Rio Grande del Norte.* Albuquerque: University of New Mexico Press.

Loesser, Arthur. 1954. *Men, Women, and Pianos: A Social History.* New York: Simon and Schuster.

Lomax, Alan. 1960. *The Folk Songs of North America in the English Language.* New York: Doubleday.

———. 1975. *The Folk Songs of North America.* New York: Doubleday/Dolphin.

Longstreet, Stephen. 1965. *Sportin' House: A History of the New Orleans Sinners and the Birth of Jazz.* Los Angeles: Sherbourne Press.

Lornell, Kip, and Anne K. Rasmussen, ed. 1997. *Musics of Multicultural America.* New York: Schirmer Books.

Lornell, Kip, and Anne K. Rasmussen, eds. 1997. *Musics of Multicultural America: A Study of Twelve Musical Communities.* New York: Schirmer Books.

Lovell, John Jr. 1972. *Black Song: The Forge and the Flame.* New York: Macmillan.

Lovoll, Odd Sverre. 1975. *A Folk Epic: The Bygdelag in America.* Boston: Twayne Publishers for the Norwegian American Historical Association.

Lowe, Lisa. 1996. *Immigrant Acts: On Asian American Cultural Politics.* Durham, N.C.: Duke University Press.

Loza, Steven J. 1993. *Barrio Rhythm: Mexican American Music in Los Angeles.* Urbana: University of Illinois Press.

Magocsi, Paul R., ed. 1999. *Encyclopedia of Canada's Peoples.* Toronto: University of Toronto Press.

Malone, Bill C. 1985. *Country Music U.S.A.* Rev ed. Austin: University of Texas Press.

Malone, Bill, and Judith McCulloh. 1975. *Stars of Country Music.* Urbana: University of Illinois Press.

Manuel, Peter, ed. 1991. *Essays on Cuban Music: North American and Cuban Perspectives.* Lanham, Md.: University Press of America.

Manuel, Peter L. 1988. *Popular Musics of the Non-Western World: An Introductory Survey.* New York: Oxford University Press.

Manuel, Peter, with Kenneth Bilby and Michael Largey. 1995. *Caribbean Currents: Caribbean Music from Rumba to Reggae.* Philadelphia: Temple University Press.

Manuel, Peter. 1990. *Popular Musics of the Non-Western World.* New York: Oxford University Press.

Mates, Julian. 1985. *America's Musical Stage: Two Hundred Years of Musical Theater.* Westport, Conn.: Greenwood Press.

Mattfeld, Julius. 1952. *Variety Musical Cavalcade, 1620–1950. A Chronology of Vocal and Instrumental Music Popular in the United States.* New York: Prentice-Hall.

McAllester, David P. 1954. *Enemy Way Music.* Cambridge, Mass.: Peabody Museum of American Archaeology and Ethnology, Harvard University.

McCoy. 1926. *Folk Songs of the Spanish Californians.* San Francisco: Sherman and Clay.

McGowan, Chris, and Ricardo Pessanha. 1998. *The Brazilian Sound.* Philadelphia: Temple University Press.

McKay, Ian. 1994. *The Quest of the Folk: Antimodernism and Cultural Selection in Twentieth-Century Nova Scotia.* Montréal and Kingston: McGill-Queen's University Press.

Meadows, Eddie S. 1981. *Jazz Reference and Research Materials: A Bibliography.* New York: Garland Publishers.

Mertens, Wim. 1983. *American Minimal Music: La Monte Young, Terry Riley, Steve Reich, Philip Glass.* Trans. J. Hautekiet. New York: Alexander Broude.

Miller, Jim, ed. 1980. *The Rolling Stone Illustrated History of Rock and Roll.* New York: Random House/Rolling Stone Press.

Miller, Mark. 1997. *Such Melodious Racket: The Lost History of Jazz in Canada 1914–1949.* Toronto: Mercury Press.

Miller, Terry. 1986. *Folk Music in America: A Reference Guide.* New York: Garland.

Monson, Ingrid. 1996. *Saying Something: Jazz Improvisation and Interaction.* Chicago: University of Chicago Press.

Monson, Ingrid. n.d. *Freedom Sounds: Jazz, Civil Rights, and Africa, 1950–1967.* New York: Oxford University Press. Forthcoming.

Montell, William Lynwood. 1991. *Singing the Glory Down: Amateur Gospel Music in South Central Kentucky, 1900–1990.* Lexington: University Press of Kentucky.

Morrison, Craig. 1996. *Go Cat Go!: Rockabilly and Its Makers.* Urbana: University of Illinois Press.

Myers, Helen. 1993b. "North America." In *Ethnomusicology: Historical and Regional Studies,* ed. Helen Myers, 401–460. New York: Norton.

———. 1998. *Music of Hindu Trinidad: Songs from the Indian Diaspora.* Chicago: University of Chicago Press.

Naficy, Hamid. 1993a. *The Making of Exile Cultures: Iranian Television in Los Angeles.* Minneapolis: University of Minnesota Press.

Narváez, Peter, and Martin Laba, eds. 1986. *Media Sense: The Folklore–Popular Culture Continuum.* Bowling Green, Ohio: Bowling Green State University Popular Press.

Negus, Keith. 1992. *Producing Pop: Culture and Conflict in the Popular Music Industry.* London: Edward Arnold.

Nettl, Bruno. 1949; 2nd ed. 1960. *An Introduction to Folk Music in the United States.* 3d ed., rev. and expanded by Helen Myers (1972), under the title *Folk Music in the United States: An Introduction.* Detroit: Wayne State University Press.

Neuman, Daniel. 1984. "The Ecology of Indian Music in North America." *Bansuri* 1:9–15.

Nguy-n, Phong T. *Searching for a Niche: Vietnamese Music at Home in America.* 1995. Kent, Ohio: Viet Music Publication.

Nguyen, Phong, with Adelaida Reyes Schramm and Patricia Shehan Campbell. 1995. *Searching for a Niche: Vietnamese Music at Home in America.* Kent, Ohio: Viet Music Publications.

Nicholls, David, ed. 1999. *The Cambridge History of American Music.* Cambridge: Cambridge University Press.

O'Leary, Timothy J., and David Levinsohn, eds. *Encyclopedia of World Cultures,* Vol. 1: *North America.* Boston: G. K. Hall and Company.

Oja, Carol. 1990. *Colin McPhee: Composer in Two Worlds.* Washington, D.C.: Smithsonian Institution Press.

Oliver, Paul. 1984. *Songsters & Saints: Vocal Traditions on Race Records.* New York: Cambridge.

———. 1998. *The Story of the Blues.* New Ed. Boston: Northeastern University Press.

Olson, Kenneth E. 1981. *Music and Musket: Bands and Bandsmen of the American Civil War.* Westport, Conn.: Greenwood Press.

Otis, Johnny. 1993. *Upside Your Head! Rhythm and Blues on Central Avenue.* Hanover, N.H.: University Press of New England.

Pacini Hernández, Deborah. 1995. *Bachata: A Social History of a Dominican Popular Music.* Philadelphia: Temple University Press.

Palmer, Robert. 1981. *Deep Blues.* New York: Viking Press.

Panassié, Hugues. 1970 [1936]. *Hot Jazz: The Guide to Swing Music.* Westport, Conn.: Negro Universities Press.

Paredes, Americo. 1958. *With His Pistol in His Hand.* Austin: University of Texas Press.

———. 1976. *A Texas-Mexican Cancionero: Folksongs of the Lower Border.* Urbana: University of Illinois Press.

Patterson, Beverly Bush. 1995. *The Sound of the Dove: Singing in Appalachian Primitive Baptist Churches.* Urbana: University of Illinois Press.

Patterson, Daniel W. 1979. *The Shaker Spiritual.* Princeton, N.J.: Princeton University Press.

Peacock, Kenneth. 1970. *Songs of the Doukhobors: An Introductory Outline.* Bulletin no. 231, Folklore Series no. 7. Ottawa: The National Museums of Canada.

Pearson, Barry Lee. 1984. *Sounds So Good to Me: The Bluesman's Story.* Philadelphia: University of Pennsylvania Press.

Peña, Manuel H. 1985. *The Texas-Mexican Conjunto: History of a Working Class Music.* Austin: University of Texas Press.

Peretti, Burton W. 1992. *The Creation of Jazz: Music, Race and Culture in Urban America.* Urbana: University of Illinois Press.

Perkins, William Eric, ed. 1996. *Droppin' Science: Critical Essays on Rap Music and Hip Hop Culture.* Philadelphia: Temple University Press.

Perlman, Marc. 1983. "Some Reflections on New American Gamelan Music." *Ear Magazine,* 7(4):4–5.

Peterson, Bernard L., Jr. 1993. *A Century of Musicals in Black and White.* Westport, Conn.: Garland Press.

Peterson, Elizabeth. 1996. *The Changing Faces of Tradition: A Report on the Folk and Traditional Arts in the United States.* Washington, D.C.: National Endowment for the Arts.

Peterson, Richard, 1997. *Creating Country Music: Fabricating Authenticity.* Chicago: University of Chicago Press.

Petkov, Steven, and Leonard Mustazza, eds. 1995. *The Frank Sinatra Reader.* New York: Oxford University Press.

Porter, Lewis, and Michael Ullman. 1993. *Jazz: From Its Origins to the Present.* Englewood Cliffs, N.J.: Prentice-Hall.

Porter, Susan L. 1991. *With an Air Debonair: Musical Theater in America, 1785–1815.* Washington, D.C.: Smithsonian Institution Press.

Poschardt, Ulf. 1995. *DJ Culture.* Hamburg, Germany: Rogner & Bernard.

Potter, Keith. 2000. *Four Musical Minimalists: La Monte Young, Terry Riley, Steve Reich, Philip Glass.* New York and Cambridge: Cambridge University Press.

Potter, Russell. 1995. *Spectacular Vernaculars: Hip-Hop and the Politics of Postmodernism.* The State University of New York Series in Postmodern Culture. Albany: State University of New York Press.

Preston, Katherine K. 1992. *Music for Hire: A Study of Professional Musicians in Washington (1877–1900).* Stuyvesant, N.Y.: Pendragon Press.

Pritchett, James. 1993. *The Music of John Cage.* New York and Cambridge: Cambridge University Press.

Pruter, Robert. 1996. *Doowop: The Chicago Scene.* Urbana: University of Illinois Press.

Qureshi, Regula. 1972. "Ethnomusicological Research Among Canadian Communities of Arab and East Indian Origin." *Ethnomusicology* 16:381–396.

Racy, Ali Jihad, and Simon Shaheen. 1992. "An Evening in the Orient: The Middle Eastern Nightclub in America." *Asian Music* 23(2):63–88.

Rasmussen, Anne K. 1991. "Individuality and Social Change in the Music of Arab Americans." Ph.D. dissertation, University of California, Los Angeles.

Reagon, Bernice L, ed. 1992. *We'll Understand It Better By and By: Pioneering African American Gospel Composers.* Washington, D.C: Smithsonian Institution Press.

Redhead, Steve. 1990. *The End-of-the-Century Party: Youth and Pop Towards 2000.* Manchester, Eng.: Manchester University Press.

Rehrig, William H. 1991. *The Heritage Encyclopedia of Band Music: Composers and Their Music.* Ed. Paul Bierley. 2 vols. Westerville, Ohio: Integrity Press.

Reich, Steve. 1974. *Writings about Music.* Halifax: Press of Nova Scotia College of Art and Design.

Reyes, Adelaida. 1999. *Songs of the Caged, Songs of the Free: Music and the Vietnamese Refugee Experience.* Philadelphia: Temple University Press.

Reyes, Luis I. 1995. *Made in Paradise: Hollywood's Films of Hawai'i and the South Seas.* Honolulu: Mutual Publishing.

Reynolds, Simon, and Joy Press. 1995. *The Sex Revolts: Gender, Rebellion and Rock 'n' Roll.* Cambridge: Harvard University Press.

Riddle, Ronald. 1983. *Flying Dragons, Flowing Streams: Music in the Life of San Francisco's Chinese.* Westport, Conn.: Greenwood Press.

Riis, Thomas L. 1989. *Just before Jazz: Black Musical Theater in New York, 1890–1915.* Washington, D.C.: Smithsonian Institution Press.

Robb, John Donald. 1980. *Hispanic Folk Music of New Mexico and the Southwest: A Self-Portrait of a People.* Norman: University of Oklahoma Press.

Roberts, Helen Heffron. 1970 [1936]. *Musical Areas in Aboriginal North America.* Yale University Publications in Anthropology, no. 12. New Haven, Conn.: Yale University Press.

Roberts, John Storm. 1972. *Black Music of the Americas.* New York: Praeger.

———. 1979. *The Latin Tinge: The Impact of Latin American Music on the United States.* New York: Oxford University Press.

———. 1999 [1979]. *The Latin Tinge: The Impact of Latin American Music on the United States.* 2nd ed. New York: Oxford University Press.

Robertson, Carol E., ed. 1992. *Musical Repercussions of 1492: Encounters in Text and Performance.* Washington, D.C.: Smithsonian Institution Press.

Rochberg, George. 1984. *The Aesthetics of Survival: A Composer's View of Twentieth-Century Music.* Ann Arbor: University of Michigan Press.

Rose, Tricia. 1994. *Black Noise: Rap Music and Black Culture in Contemporary America.* Hanover, N.H.: University Press of New England.

Rosenberg, Neil V. 1985. *Bluegrass: A History.* Urbana: University of Illinois Press.

Rosenberg, Neil V., ed. 1993. *Transforming Tradition: Folk Music Revivals Examined.* Chicago: University of Illinois Press.

Ross, Andrew, and Tricia Rose, eds. 1994. *Microphone Fiends: Youth Music and Youth Culture.* New York: Routledge.

Rowe, Mike. 1981 [1975]. *Chicago Blues: The City and the Music.* New York: Da Capo.

Russell, Tony. 1970. *Blacks, Whites and Blues.* Ed. Paul Oliver. New York: Stein and Day.

Ruymar, Lorene. 1996. *The Hawaiian Steel Guitar and Its Great Hawaiian Musicians.* Anaheim Hills, Calif.: Centerstream Publishing.

Sablosky, Irving L. 1969. *American Music.* Chicago: University of Chicago Press.

Sachse, Johann F. 1903. *The Music of the Ephrata Cloister; also Conrad Beissel's Preface to the "Turtel Taube" of 1747.* Lancaster: Pennsylvania German Society 12.

Sakolsky, Ron, and Fred Ho. 1995. *Sounding Off: Music as Subversion/Resistance/Revolution.* New York: Autonomedia.

Sam, Sam-Ang, and Patricia Shehan Campbell. 1991. *Silent Temples, Songful Hearts: Traditional Music of Cambodia.* Danbury, Conn.: World Music Press.

Sargeant, Winthrop. 1975 [1938]. *Jazz, Hot and Hybrid.* 3rd ed. New York: Da Capo.

Sarkissian, Margaret Lynne. 1987. "Armenian Musical Culture in Toronto: Political and Social Divisions in an Immigrant Community." Master's thesis, University of Illinois, Urbana-Champaign.

Sawaie, Mohammed. 1985. *Arabic Speaking Immigrants in the U.S. and Canada: An Annotated Bibliographic Guide.* Lexington, Ky: Mazda Publishing.

Schafer, William J., with Richard B. Allen. 1977. *Brass Bands and New Orleans Jazz.* Baton Rouge: Louisiana State University Press.

Schuller, Gunther. 1968. *Early Jazz: Its Roots and Musical Development.* New York: Oxford University Press.

———. 1989. *The Swing Era: The Development of Jazz 1930–1945.* New York: Oxford University Press.

Sealey, John, and Krister Malm. 1982. *Music in the Caribbean.* Toronto: Hodder and Stoughton.

Seeger, Anthony. 1992. "Ethnomusicology and Music Law." *Ethnomusicology* 36(3):345–359.

Sexton, Adam, ed. 1995. *Rap on Rap: Straight-Up Talk on Hip-Hop Culture.* New York: Delta.

Shanet, Howard. 1975. *Philharmonic. A History of New York's Orchestra.* New York: Doubleday.

Shank, Barry. 1994. *Dissonant Identities: The Rock 'n' Roll Scene in Austin, Texas.* Hanover. N.H.: Wesleyan University Press.

Shannon, Doug. 1982. *Off the Record: The Disco Concept.* Cleveland: Pacesetter.

Sharp, Cecil. 1932. *English Folk Songs from the Southern Appalachians.* London: Oxford University Press.

Singer, Roberta L. 1982. "'My Music is Who I Am and What I Do: Latin Popular Music and Identity in New York City." Ph.D. dissertation, Indiana University.

Slobin, Mark. 1982. *Tenement Songs: The Popular Music of the Jewish Immigrants.* Urbana: University of Illinois Press.

———. 1990a. *Chosen Voices: The Story of the American Cantorate.* Urbana: University of Illinois Press.

———. 1993. *Subcultural Sounds: Micromusics of the West.* Hanover & London: Wesleyan University Press.

———. 2000. *Fiddler on the Move: Exploring the World of Klezmer.* New York: Oxford University Press.

Smith, Barbara B. 1975. "Chinese Music in Hawaii." *Asian Music* 6(1–2):225–230.

Smyth, Williw, ed. 1989. *Songs of Indian Territory: Native American Music Traditions of Oklahoma.* Oklahoma City: Center of the American Indian.

Sonneborn, Daniel Atesh. 1995. *Music and Meaning in American Sufism: The Ritual of Dhikr at Sami Mahal, a Chishtiyya-derived Sufi Center.* Ann Arbor, Mich.: University Microfilms.

Southern, Eileen. 1983a [1971]. *The Music of Black Americans: A History.* 2nd ed. New York: Norton.

———. 1997 [1983, 1971]. *The Music of Black Americans: A History.* 3rd ed. New York: Norton.

Southern, Eileen, and Josephine Wright, comps. 1990. *African American Traditions in Song, Sermon, Tale, and Dance, 1600s–1920: An Annotated Bibliography of Literature, Collections, and Artworks.* Westport, Conn.: Greenwood Press.

Southern, Eileen, ed. 1983 [1867]. *Readings in Black American Music,* 2nd ed. New York: Norton.

———. 1983b [1971]. *Readings in the Music of Black Americans.* 2nd ed. New York: Norton.

———. 1994. *African-American Theater: Out of Bondage (1876) and Peculiar Sam; or The Underground Railroad (1879).* Vol. 9 of *Nineteenth-Century American Musical Theater,* ed. Deane Root. New York: Garland Press.

Spicer, Edward H. 1985. *The Yaquis: A Cultural History.* Tucson: University of Arizona Press.

Spottswood, Richard K., ed. 1982. *Ethnic Recordings in America: A Neglected Heritage.* Washington, D.C.: American Folklife Center, Library of Congress.

Stark, Richard B. 1969. *Music of the Spanish Folk Plays in New Mexico.* Sante Fe: Museum of New Mexico Press.

Stearns, Marshall. 1970 [1956]. *The Story of Jazz.* New York: Oxford University Press.

Stevenson, Robert M. 1960. *Spanish Music in the Age of Columbus.* The Hague: Martinus Nijhoff.

———. 1988a. "Local Music History Research in Los Angeles Area Libraries: Part I." *Inter-American Music Review* 10(1):19–38.

———. 1988b. "Music in Southern California: A Tale of Two Cities (Los Angeles: The First Biennium and Beyond)." *Inter-American Music Review* 10(1):39–111.

Stowe, David W. 1994. *Swing Changes: Big Band Jazz in New Deal America.* Cambridge: Harvard University Press.

Stuessy, Joe. 1990. *Rock and Roll: Its History and Stylistic Development.* Englewood Cliffs, N.J.: Prentice-Hall.

Sturman, Janet. in press. *Zarzuela: Spanish Operetta, American Stage.* Urbana: University of Illinois Press.

Sudhalter, Richard M. 1999. *Lost Chords: White Musicians and Their Contributions to Jazz, 1915–1945.* New York: Oxford University Press.

Sugarman, Jane Cicely. 1997. *Engendering Song: Singing and Subjectivity at Prespa Albanian Weddings.* Chicago: University of Chicago Press.

Summit, Jeffrey A. 1993. "'I'm a Yankee Doodle Dandy'?: Identity and Melody at an American *Simhat Torah* Celebration." *Ethnomusicology* 37(1):41–62.

Sung, Betty Lee. 1967. *Mountain of Gold: The Story of the Chinese in America.* New York: Macmillan.

Swan, Howard. 1952. *Music in the Southwest, 1825–1950.* San Marino, Calif.: Huntington Library.

Tallant, Robert. 1983 [1966]. *Voodoo in New Orleans.* New York: Macmillan.

Talley, Thomas V. 1922. *Negro Folk Rhymes: Wise and Otherwise.* New York: Macmillan Co.

Tawa, Nicholas. 1995. *American Composers and Their Public: A Critical Look.* Metuchen, N.J.: Scarecrow.

Tawa, Nicholas E. 1982. *A Sound of Strangers: Musical Culture, Acculturation, and the Post–Civil War Ethnic American.* Metuchen, N.J.: Scarecrow Press.

The Emergence of Black and the Emergency of Rap, special issue of *Black Sacred Music* 5(1).

Thomas, J. C. 1975. *Chasin' the Trane: The Music and Mystique of John Coltrane.* Garden City, N.Y.: Doubleday.

Thompson, Gordon, and Medha Yodh. 1985. "Garba and the Gujaratis of Southern California." *Selected Reports in Ethnomusicology* 6:59–79.

Thomson, Virgil. 1971. *American Music since 1910.* New York: Holt, Rinehart and Winston.

Tick, Judith. 1997. *Ruth Crawford Seeger: A Composer's Search for American Music.* New York: Oxford University Press.

Tinker, Edward Larocque. 1961. *Corridos and Calaveras.* Austin: University of Texas Press.

Tirro, Frank. 1977. *Jazz: A History.* New York: Norton.

Tischler, Barbara L. 1986. *An American Music: The Search for an American Musical Identity.* New York: Oxford University Press.

Titon, Jeff Todd. 1994 [1977]. *Early Downhome Blues: A Musical and Cultural Analysis.* 2nd ed. Chapel Hill: The University of North Carolina Press.

Turner, Frederick. 1994. *Remembering Song: Encounters with the New Orleans Jazz Tradition.* New York: Da Capo.

Tuuletargad (Wind Wizards). 2000. *Estonian Instrumental Folk Music.* Chicago: Innovative Mechanics.

Varzi, Morteza, with Margaret Caton, Robyn C. Friend, and Neil Siegel. 1986. "Performer-Audience Relationships in the *Bazm.*" In *Cultural Parameters of Iranian Musical Expression,* ed. Margaret Caton and Neil Siegel, 1–9. Redondo Beach, Calif.: The Institute of Persian Performing Arts.

Vecoli, Rudolph J., Judy Galens, Anna Sheets and Robyn V. Young, eds. 1985. *Gale Encyclopedia of Multicultural America.* Detroit: Gale Research.

Vincent, Rickey. 1996. *Funk: The Music, the People, and the Rhythm of the One.* New York: St. Martin's/Griffin.

Walser, Robert, ed. 1999. *Keeping Time: Readings in Jazz History.* New York: Oxford University Press.

Ward, Brian. 1998. *Just My Soul Responding: Rhythm and Blues, Black Consciousness and Race Relations.* London: University College London Press.

Warren, Mark. 1990. *Dutch Hops: Colorado Music of the Germans from Russia, 1865–1965.* Evergreen, Colo.: Shadow Canyon Graphics.

Watkins, Glenn. 1988. *Soundings: Music in the Twentieth Century.* New York: Schirmer Books.

Weinstein, Deena. 1991. *Heavy Metal: A Cultural Sociology.* New York: Lexington Books.

Whisnant, David. 1983. *All That Is Native and Fine: The Politics of Culture in an American Region.* Chapel Hill: University of North Carolina Press.

White, William C. 1944. *A History of Military Music in America.* New York: Exposition Press.

Whiteley, Sheila, ed. 1997. *Sexing the Groove: Popular Music and Gender.* New York: Routledge.

Whitfield, Irène Thérèsa. 1981 [1939]. *Louisiana French Folk Songs.* 3rd ed. Eunice, La.: Hebert.

Wilcken, Lois E. 1991. *Music Folklore among Haitians in New York: Staged Representations and the Negotiation of Identity.* Ph.D. dissertation, Columbia University.

Wilcken, Lois, with Frisner Augustin. 1992. *The Drums of Vodou.* Crown Point, Ind.: White Cliffs Media.

Wilgus, Donald K. 1959. *Anglo-American Folksong Scholarship Since 1898.* New Brunswick, N.J.: Rutgers University Press.

Williams, Martin. 1970. *The Jazz Tradition.* New York: Oxford University Press.

Witmer, Robert, ed. 1990. *Ethnomusicology in Canada: Proceedings of the First Conference on Ethnomusicology in Canada.* Toronto: Institute for Canadian Music.

Wolfe, Charles K. 1976. *Tennessee Strings: The Story of Country Music in Tennessee.* Knoxville: The University of Tennessee Press.

———. 1982. *Kentucky Country.* Lexington: University of Kentucky Press.

———. 1999. *A Good Natured Riot: The Birth of the Grand Ole Opry.* Nashville: Vanderbilt University Press and the Country Music Hall of Fame.

Wolfe, Richard J. *Secular Music in America: 1801–1825.* 3 vols. New York: New York Public Library.

Woll, Allen. 1989. *Black Musical Theater: From Coontown to Dreamgirls.* Baton Rouge: Louisiana State University Press.

Wong, Isabel K. F. 1985. "The Many Roles of Peking Opera in San Francisco in the 1980s." In *The Asian Musician in North America,* ed. Nazir Jairazbhoy, 173–188. Selected Reports in Ethnomusicology 6. Los Angeles: University of California.

Work, III, John W. 1940. *American Negro Songs and Spirituals: A Comprehensive Collection of 230 Folk Songs, Religious and Secular.* New York: Bonanza Books.

Wright, Robert L. 1965. *Swedish Emigrant Ballads.* Lincoln: University of Nebraska Press.

Zhang, Wei Hua. 1994. "The Musical Activities of the Chinese American Communities in the San Francisco Bay Area: A Social and Cultural Study." Ph.D. dissertation, University of California at Berkeley.

Zheng, Su de San. 1993. *Immigrant Music and Transnational Discourse: Chinese American Music Culture in New York City.* Ph.D. dissertation, Wesleyan University.

Zheng, Su. 2001. *Claiming Diaspora: Music, Transnationalism, and Cultural Politics in Asian/Chinese America.* Oxford: Oxford University Press.

[n.a.]. 1968. "Lady Soul Singing It Like It Is" *Time,* 62–66. 28 June.

CANADA

Amtmann, Willy. 1975. *Music in Canada 1600–1800*. Montréal: Habitex.

Anthologie d'œuvres musicales canadiennes (Anthology of Canadian Music). 1983–. Collection of 25 volumes of printed Canadian music written before 1950. Ottawa: Canadian Musical Heritage Society.

Barbeau, Marius. 1979 [1962]. *Le Rossignol y chante*. Ottawa: National Museum of Canada.

Barbeau, Marius, and Edward Sapir. 1925. *Folk Songs of French Canada*. New Haven, Conn.: Yale University Press.

Barbeau, Marius, and Jean Beck. 1962. *Jongleur Songs of Old Quebec*. New Brunswick, N.J.: Rutgers University Press.

Barbeau, Marius, and Marguerite d'Harcourt. 1937. *The Romancero du Canada*. Toronto: Macmillan.

Beaton, Virginia, and Stephen Pederson. 1992. *Maritime Music Greats: Fifty Years of Hits and Heartbreak*. Halifax: Nimbus Publishing.

Beckwith, John. 1987. "On Compiling an Anthology of Canadian Hymn Tunes." In *Sing Out the Glad News: Hymn Tunes in Canada. CanMus Documents* 1:3–32.

Beckwith, John, and Frederick A. Hall, eds. 1988. *Musical Canada: Words and Music Honouring Helmut Kallmann*. Toronto: University of Toronto Press.

Beckwith, John, ed. 1986. *Hymn Tunes*. The Canadian Musical Heritage, vol. 5. Ottawa: Canadian Musical Heritage Society.

Bégin, Carmelle. 1992. *La Musique Traditionnelle pour Violon: Jean Carignon*. Ottawa: National Museum of Canada.

———. 1992. *Opus: The Making of Musical Instruments in Canada*. Hull: Canadian Museum of Civilization.

Béland, Madeleine. 1982. *Chansons de voyageurs, coureurs de bois et forestiers*. Québec: Les Presses de l'Université Laval.

Berdugo-Cohen, Yolande, and Joseph Levy. 1987. *Juifs Marocains à Montréal*. Montréal: VLB Editeur.

Berg, Wesley. 1985. *From Russia with Love: A Study of the Mennonite Choral Singing Tradition in Canada*. Winnipeg: Hyperion.

Berland, Jody. 1986. "Cultural Re/Percussions: The Social Production of Music Broadcasting in Canada." Ph.D. dissertation, York University.

Bohlman, Philip V. 1988. *The Study of Folk Music in the Modern World*. Bloomington: Indiana University Press.

Bonner, Simon. 1987. *Old Time Music Makers of New York State*. Syracuse, N.Y.: Syracuse University Press.

Brednich, Rolf Wilhelm. 1981. "Beharrung und Wandel im Liedgut der hutterischen Brüder: Ein Beitrag zur empirischen Hymnologie." *Jahrbuch für Volksliedforschung* 26:44–60.

Brydon, Anne. 2000. "Mother to Her Distant Children: The Icelandic *Fjallkona* in Canada," in *Undisciplined Women: Tradition and Culture in Canada*, Pauline Greenhill and Diane Tye, ed. 87–100. Montreal: McGill–Queen's University Press.

Burlin, Natalie Curtis. 1968 [1907]. *The Indians Book*. New York: Dover.

Calderisi, Maria. 1981. *Music Publishing in the Canadas, 1800–1867*. Ottawa: National Library.

Canada's Year of Asia Pacific Multicultural Bibliography. 1997. Vancouver, B.C.: British Columbia Teacher-Librarians' Association.

The Canadian Musical Heritage /Le patrimoine musical canadien. 1983–1999. Twenty-five volumes of pre-1950 Canadian notated music, each edition preceded by an essay on the genre concerned. Website: http://www.cmhs.carleton.ca

Carpenter, Carole Henderson. 1979. *Many Voices: A Study of Folklore Activities in Canada and Their Role in Canadian Culture*. Ottawa: National Museums of Canada.

Carruthers, Glen, and Gordana Lazarevich, eds. 1996. *A Celebration of Canada's Arts 1930–1970*. Toronto: Canadian Scholars' Press.

Cass-Beggs, Barbara. 1967. *Seven Métis Songs*. Don Mills: BMI Canada.

CBC. 1981. *Culture, Broadcasting, and the Canadian Identity*. S.L.: Canadian Broadcasting Corporation. Pamphlet

Chiasson, Père Anselme. 1942–1979. *Chansons d'Acadie*. Vols. 1–3, Pointe-aux-Trembles, P.Q.: La Réparation. Vols. 4–5, Moncton: Les Editions des Aboiteaux.

Clairmont, D. H., and Magill, Dennis W. 1974. *Africville: The Life and Death of a Canadian Black Community*. Toronto: McLelland and Stewart.

Creighton, Helen. 1961. *Maritime Folk Songs*. Toronto: The Ryerson Press.

———. 1966. *Songs and Ballads from Nova Scotia*. New York: Dover.

———. 1971. *Folksongs from Southern New Brunswick*. Ottawa: National Museum of Civilization.

———. 1988. *La Fleur du Rosier: Chansons folkloriques d'Acadie*, ed. Ronald Labelle. Ottawa and Sydney: Canadian Museum of Civilization and University College of Cape Breton.

Creighton, Helen, and Calum MacLeod. 1979. *Gaelic Songs in Nova Scotia*. Ottawa: National Museums of Canada.

Creighton, Helen, and Doreen Senior. 1950. *Traditional Songs from Nova Scotia*. Toronto: The Ryerson Press.

Croft, Clary. 1999. *Helen Creighton: Canada's First Lady of Folklore*. Halifax: Nimbus Publishing.

d'Harcourt, Marguerite, and Raoul d'Harcourt. 1956. *Chansons folkloriques du Canada*. Québec: Les Presses de L'Université Laval.

Daigle, Jean, ed. 1982. *The Acadians of the Maritimes: Thematic Studies*. Moncton: Centre d'études acadiennes.

Davies, Sandra, et al. 1982. *The Chinese People: Music, Instruments, Folklore*. Vancouver, B.C.: Western Education Development Group.

———. 1986. *Japanese People: Music, Instruments, Arts, Crafts*. Vancouver, B.C.: Western Education Development Group.

Denisoff, R. Serge. 1972. *Sing a Song of Social Significance*. Bowling Green, Ohio: Bowling Green University Popular Press.

Deschenes, Donald. 1982. *C'était la plus jolie des filles: Répertoire des chansons d'Angélina Paradis-Fraser*. Montréal: Editions Quinze.

Diamond, Beverley, and James Robbins. 1992. "Ethnomusicology." In *Encyclopedia of Music in Canada*, ed. Helmut Kallmann et al., 422–431. Toronto: University of Toronto.

Diamond, Beverley and Robert Witmer, eds. 1994. *Canadian Music: Issues of Hegemony and Identity*. Toronto: Canadian Scholars' Press.

Diamond, Beverley, et al. 1994. *Visions of Sound: Musical Instruments of First Nations Communities in Northeastern America*. Chicago: University of Chicago Press, and Waterloo: Wilfrid Laurier University Press.

Dibblee, Randall, and Dorothy Dibblee. 1973. *Folksongs from Prince Edward Island*. Summerside: Williams and Crue.

Doherty, Elizabeth A. 1996. "The Paradox of the Periphery: Evolution of the Cape Breton Fiddle Tradition 1928–1995." Ph.D. dissertation, University of Limerick.

Drakich, Janice, Edward Kovarik, and Ramona Lumpkin, eds. 1995. *With a Song in Her Heart: A Celebration of Canadian Women Composers*. Windsor, Ont.: University of Windsor Humanities Research Group.

Driedger, Leo, ed. 1978. *The Canadian Ethnic Mosaic: A Quest for Identity*. Toronto: McClelland and Stewart.

Dunlay, Kate, and David Greenberg. 1996. *Traditional Celtic Violin Music of Cape Breton, the DunGreen Collection*. Mississauga, Ont.: DunGreen Music.

Eagle, John A. 1989. *The Canadian Pacific Railway and the Development of Western Canada, 1896–1914*. Kingston: McGill–Queen's University Press.

Einarsson, Magnús. 1992. *Icelandic-Canadian Memory Lore*. Ottawa: Canadian Museum of Civilization.

Elliott, Robin. 1997. *Counterpoint to a City: The First One Hundred Years of the Women's Musical Club of Toronto*. Toronto: ECW Press.

Epp, Frank H. 1982. *Mennonites in Canada, 1920–1940: A People's Struggle for Survival*. Toronto: Macmillan of Canada.

Farquharson, Dorothy H. 1983. *O for a Thousand Tongues to Sing: A History of Singing Schools in Early Canada*. Waterdown, Ont.:

Fleming, Lee. 1997. *Rock, Rhythm and Reels: Canada's East Coast Musicians on Stage*. Charlottetown: Ragweed Press.

Fowke, Edith. 1965. *Traditional Singers and Songs from Ontario*. Hatboro: Folklore Associates.

———. 1985. *Lumbering Songs from the Northern Woods*. Toronto: NC Press.

———. 1988. *Canadian Folklore*. Toronto: Oxford University Press.

Fowke, Edith, and Jay Rahn. 1994. *A Family Heritage: LaRena Clark's Story and Songs*. Calgary: University of Calgary Press.

Friesen, Gerald. 1984. *The Canadian Prairies: A History*. Toronto: University of Toronto Press.

Gagnon, F. Ernest A. 1880 [1865–1867]. *Chansons populaires du Canada*. Montréal: Beauchemin.

Gareau, Laurier. 1990. *Le défi de la radio francaise en Saskatchewan*. Regina: La Société historique de la Saskatchewan.

Gibbons, Roy W. 1982. *As It Comes: Folk Fiddling in Prince George, British Columbia*. Mercury Series 42. Ottawa: National Museum of Man.

Gibson, John G. 1998. *Traditional Gaelic Bagpiping, 1745–1945*. Montréal: McGill–Queen's University Press.

Giroux, Robert, ed. 1984. *Les aires de la chanson québécoise*. Montréal: Tryptique.

Gledhill, Christopher. 1973. *Folksongs of Prince Edward Island*. Summerside: Williams and Crue.

Green, J. Paul, and Nancy F. Vogan. 1991. *Music Education in Canada: A Historical Account*. Toronto: University of Toronto Press.

Hahn, R. Richard. 1981. *The Role of Radio in the Canadian Music Industry*. Toronto: Canadian Association of Broadcasters. (Prepared for submission to the CRTC.)

Helm, June, and Nancy Lurie. 1962. *The Dogrib Hand Game*. Ottawa: National Museum of Man.

Henry, Frances. 1975. "Black Music in the Maritimes." *Canadian Folk Music Journal/Revue de Musique Folklorique Canadienne* 3:3–10.

Historical Anthology of Canadian Music. 1996. Ottawa: Canadian Music Heritage Society.

Hoe, Ban Seng. 1979. *Structural Changes of Two Chinese Communities in Alberta, Canada*. Canadian Center for Folk Culture Studies Paper 19. Ottawa: National Museums of Canada.

Ives, Edward D. 1989. *Folksongs of New Brunswick*. Fredericton: Goose Lane Editions.

Jackson, Peter. 1992. "The Politics of the Streets: A Geography of Caribana." *Political Geography* 11(2):130–151.

Kallmann, Helmut. 1960. *A History of Music in Canada 1534–1914*. Toronto: University of Toronto Press.

Kallmann, Helmut, and Gilles Potvin, eds. 1992. *Encyclopedia of Music in Canada*. 2nd ed. Toronto: University of Toronto Press.

Keeling, Richard, ed. 1992. *Music and Spiritual Power among the Indians of North America*. Special Issue, *World of Music* 92(2).

Keillor, Elaine. 1997. "*Auf Kanadischer Welle*: The Establishment of the Germanic Musical Canon in Canada." In *Kanada-Studien: Music in Canada*, ed. Guido Bimberg, 49–76. Bochum, Germany: Brockmeyer.

Kelly, Wayne. 1991. *Downright Upright: A History of the Canadian Piano Industry*. Toronto: National Heritage/National History Inc.

Klassen, Doreen Helen. 1989. *Singing Mennonite: Low German Songs among the Mennonites*. Winnipeg: The University of Manitoba Press.

Klymasz, Robert B. 1972. "'Sounds You Never Before Heard': Ukrainian Country Music in Western Canada." *Ethnomusicology* 16(3):372–380.

———. 1989. *The Ukrainian Folk Ballad in Canada*. Transcriptions by Ken Peacock, New York: AMS Press.

———. 1991. *Art and Ethnicity: The Ukrainian Tradition in Canada*. Hull, P.Q.: Canadian Museum of Civilization.

———. 1992. *Sviéto: Celebrating Ukrainian Canadian Ritual in East Central Alberta through the Generations*. Edmonton: Alberta Culture and Multiculturalism, Historical Resources Division.

Lapointe, Jean-françois. 1994. *Portrait de la distribution indépendante de phonogrammes au Québec: Principaux rôles et enjeux*. Montréal: Mémoire de maîtrise, Université de Montréal.

Lehr, Genevieve. 1985. *Come and I Will Sing You: A Newfoundland Songbook*. Toronto: University of Toronto Press.

Lemieux, Germain. 1974. *Chansonnier franco-ontarien I*. Sudbury: Centre Franco-Ontarien de Folklore, University of Sudbury.

———. 1975. *Chansonnier franco-ontarien II*. Sudbury: Centre Franco-Ontarien de Folklore, University of Sudbury.

Les Cahiers de la Société Québécoise de Recherche en Musique (SQRM). 1983–. (Previously named l'Association pour l'Avancement de la Recherche en Musique du Québec.) Montréal.

Levine, Lawrence W. 1988. *Highbrow/Lowbrow: The Emergence of Cultural Hierarchy in America*. Cambridge, Mass.: Harvard University Press.

Lutz, Maija. 1978. *The Effects of Acculturation on Eskimo Music of Cumberland Sound Peninsula*. Mercury Series 41. Ottawa: National Museum of Man. Record included.

Lutz, Maja. 1982. *Musical Traditions of the Labrador Coast Inuit*. Ottawa: National Museums.

MacDonell, Margaret. 1982. *The Emigrant Experience: Songs of Highland Emigrants in North America*. Toronto: University of Toronto Press.

MacGillivray, Allister. 1981. *The Cape Breton Fiddler*. Sydney, N.S.: College of Cape Breton Press.

MacMillan, Keith and John Beckwith, eds. 1975. *Contemporary Canadian Composers*. Toronto: Oxford University Press.

Magocsi, Paul R., ed. 1999. *Encyclopedia of Canada's Peoples*. Toronto: University of Toronto Press.

McGee, Timothy J. 1985. *The Music of Canada*. New York: Norton.

McGuire, Matthew D. 1998. *Music in Nova Scotia: The Oral Tradition*. Halifax: Nova Scotia Museum Curatorial Report Number 84.

McIntosh, Dale. 1989. *History of Music in British Columbia, 1850–1950*. Victoria, B.C.: Sono Nis Press.

McIntyre, Paul. 1976. *Black Pentecostal Music in Windsor*. Mercury Series, No. 15. Ottawa: National Museums of Canada.

Mercer, Paul. 1979. *Newfoundland Songs and Ballads in Print, 1842–1974: A Title and First Line Index*. St. John's: Memorial University of Newfoundland.

Morey, Carl. 1997. *Music in Canada: A Research and Information Guide*. New York and London: Garland Publishing.

Peacock, Kenneth. 1965a. *Songs of the Newfoundland Outports*. 3 vols. Ottawa: National Museums.

———. 1965b. *A Survey of Ethnic Folk Music across Western Canada*. Ottawa: National Museums.

———. 1966. *Twenty Ethnic Songs from Western Canada*. Ottawa: National Museum of Canada.

———. 1970. *Songs of the Doukhobors*. Bulletin 231, Folklore Series 7. Includes 3 LP disks. (Flexidiscs TM 3). Ottawa: National Museum of Man.

———. 1970. *Songs of the Doukhobors*. Ottawa: National Museums.

———. 1971. *A Garland of Rue: Lithuanian Folksongs of Love and Betrothal*. Ottawa: National Museums of Canada.

Pelinski, Ramon. 1975. "The Music of Canada's Ethnic Minorities." *Canadian Music Book* 10:59–83

Perkowski, Jan L. 1973–74. *Gusle and Ganga among the Herzegovians of Toronto*. Ann Arbor, Mich.: University Microfilms International.

Proctor, George A. 1980. *Canadian Music of the Twentieth Century*. Toronto: University of Toronto Press.

Quigley, Colin. 1985. *Close to the Floor: Folk Dance in Newfoundland*. St. John's: Memorial University of Newfoundland, Folklore Department.

Qureshi, Regula Burckhardt. 1972. "Ethnomusicological Research among Canadian Communities of Arab and East Indian Origin." *Ethnomusicology* 16(3):381–396.

Rogers, Tim B. 1990. "Country Music Bands in Canada during the 1950s: A Comparative Survey." In *Ethnomusicology in Canada*, ed. Robert Witmer, 226–234. CanMus Documents 5. Toronto: Institute for Canadian Music.

Ruprecht, Alvina and Cecilia Taiana, eds. 1995. *The Reordering of Culture: Latin America, the Caribbean and Canada in the Hood*. Ottawa: Carleton University Press.

Sale, David. 1968. *Toronto's Pre-confederation Music Societies*. Master's thesis, University of Toronto.

Schafer, R. Murray. 1977. *The Tuning of the World*. Toronto: McLelland and Stewart.

Seguin, Robert-Lionel. 1986. *La Danse traditionnelle à Québec*. Québec: Les Presses de l'Université Laval.

Stiles, J. Mark, and Jacques Lachance. 1988. *History and Present Status of Community Radio in Québec*. Ottawa: Stiles Associates Inc. (Ministry of Culture and Communications, Government of Ontario).

Straw, Will et al, ed. 1995. *Popular Music: Style and Identity*. Montréal: Center for Research on Canadian Cultural Industries and Institutions.

Sugarman, Jane. 1997. *Embodied Subjectivities: Singing and Subjectivity at Prespa Albanian Weddings*. Chicago: University of Chicago Press.

Thérien, Robert, and Isabelle D'Amours. 1992. *Dictionnaire de la musique populaire au Québec 1955–1992*. Montréal: Institut québécois de recherche sur la culture.

Thomas, Philip J. 1979. *Songs of the Pacific Northwest*. Saanichton, B.C.: Hancock House.

Tippett, Maria. 1990. *Making Culture: English-Canadian Institutions and the Arts before the Massey Commission*. Toronto: University of Toronto Press.

Trance Gong. 1994. Gamelan Pacifica. Directed by Jarrad Powell. Iron/brass instruments by Suhirjan (Central Java) and aluminum instruments by Schmidt, Dresher, Devereaux, Powell. Compositions by Powell, Jeff Morris, John Cage (arr. Powell), and other group members. ¿What next? Recordings WN0016.

Tremblay, Danielle. 1993. *Le développement historique et le fonctionnement de l'industrie de la chanson québécoise*. Research report presented to the Québec City Museum of Civilization, 26 March 1996, 1–83.

Vennum, Thomas Jr. 1982. *The Ojibwa Dance Drum: Its History and Construction*. Smithsonian Folklife Studies 2. Washington, D.C.: Smithsonian Institution Press.

Walter, Arnold, ed. 1969. *Aspects of Music in Canada*. Toronto: University of Toronto Press.

Wilkinson, Kealy, and Associates. 1988. *Community Radio in Ontario*. Toronto: Ministry of Culture and Communications.

Witmer, Robert. 1982. *The Musical Life of the Blood Indians*. Ottawa: National Museums.

Witmer, Robert, ed. 1990. *Ethnomusicology in Canada*. CanMus Documents 5. Toronto: Institute for Canadian Music.

Woodford, Paul. 1988. *We Love the Place, O Lord: A History of the Written Musical Tradition of Newfoundland and Labrador to 1949*. St. John's: Creative Printers and Publishers.

Wrazen, Louise. 1991. "Traditional Music Performance among *Gorale* in Canada." *Ethnomusicology* 35:173–193.

Young, Russell Scott. 1956. "Vieilles Chansons de Nouvelle France." *Les Archives de Folklore* 7. Québec: Les Presses de L'Université Laval.

A Guide to Recordings

Entries in this Guide were chosen from the references sections following each article in this volume and represent a mere fraction of all references cited. The reader is urged to go back to specific articles to find other important sources.

GENERAL

After the Ball: A Treasury of Turn-of-the-Century Popular Songs. Elektra-Nonesuch 79148-2. Compact disc.

American Dreamer: Songs of Stephen Foster. 1992. Angel CDC 07777–54621-28. Compact disc.

American Popular Song: Six Decades of Songwriters and Singers. 1984. Smithsonian R031 P7 17983. Compact disc.

Boley, Raymond. 1976. *Gourd Dance Songs of the Kiowa.* Canyon Records C-6148.

Brand, Oscar. 1960. *Election Songs of the United States.* New York: Folkways Records. FH5280. LP disk.

Cohen, Norm. 1991. Notes to "Folk Song America: A 20th Century Revival." Notes for *Smithsonian Collection of Recordings* R 046/P6 21489. Compact disc.

Densmore, Frances. 1952. *Songs of the Nootka and Quileute.* Library of Congress AAFS L32. LP disk.

Fenton, William N. 1942. *Songs from the Iroquois Longhouse.* Library of Congress AFS L6. LP.

The Great American Composers: Cole Porter. 1989. CBS C21/2 7926. Compact disc.

The Great American Composers: George and Ira Gershwin. 1989. CBS C21/2 7925. Compact disc.

The Great American Composers: Irving Berlin. 1989. CBS C21/2 7929. Compact disc.

The Great American Composers: Jerome Kern. 1990. CBS C21/2 7973. Compact disc.

The Great American Composers: Rodgers and Hart. 1990. CBS C21/2 7971. Compact disc.

Indian Music of the Pacific Northwest Coast. 1967. Collected and recorded by Ida Halpern. Folkways Records FE 4523. LP disk.

Kwakiutl, Indian Music of the Pacific Northwest. n.d. Ethnic Folkways Record Library FF. 4122. LP disk.

Moore's Irish Melodies. 1984. Nonesuch 79059. LP disk.

Rhodes, Willard. 1950. *Northwest (Puget Sound).* Library of Congress AFS L34. LP disk.

Simon, Paul. 1986. *Graceland.* Warner Bros. 9 26098–2. Compact disc.

Sing along with Millard Fillmore: The Life Album of Presidential Campaign Songs. Columbia Mono-CL 2260. LP disk.

The Smithsonian Collection of American Musical Theater: Shows, Songs, and Stars. 1989. Smithsonian RD 036 A4 20483. Compact disc.

AMERICAN INDIANS/FIRST NATIONS

Anon. 1970. *Songs of the Muskogee Creek, pts. 1-2.* Indian House IH 3001, IH 3002. LP.

———. 1971, 1974. *American Indian Music of the Mississippi Choctaws, vols. 1–2.* United Sound Recorders USR 3519, USR 7133. LP.

———. 1976. *Songs of the Caddo.* Canyon Records C 6146. LP.

Beaudry, Nicole. 1984. *Inuit Traditional Songs and Games.* Canadian Broadcasting Corporation, Northern Québec Service. SQN 108. LP disk.

Boley, Raymond. 1976. *Gourd Dance Songs of the Kiowa.* Canyon Records C-6148.

Boulton, Laura. 1954. *The Eskimos of Hudson Bay and Alaska.* Folkways Records FE 4444. LP disk.

———. 1992 [1933, 1940/1992]. *Navajo Songs.* Notes by Charlotte J. Frisbie and David P. McAllester. Smithsonian Folkways CD SF 40403. Compact disc.

Bouvette, Reg. c.1970. *Red River Jig.* Sunshine Records SSB 402. LP disk and cassette.

d'Azevedo, Warren L. 1972. *Washo-Peyote Songs: Songs of the American Indian Native Church-Peyotist.* Twelve-page reprint of a 1957 study by Alan P. Merriam and Warren L. d'Azevedo. Ethnic Folkways Library Album No. FE 4384. LP disk.

Haida Indian Music of the Pacific Northwest. 1986. Recorded and annotated by Ida Halpern. Folkways Records. LP disk.

Healing Songs of the American Indians. 1965. Notes by Charles Hofmann. Ethnic Folkways Library FE 4251. LP disk.

Honor the Earth Powwow: Songs of the Great Lakes Indians. 1991. Thomas Vennum Jr., notes; Mickey Hart, Jens McVoy, and Thomas Vennum Jr., research and recording. Rykodisc RACS 0199.

Indian Music of the Pacific Northwest Coast. 1967. Collected and recorded by Ida Halpern. Folkways Records FE 4523. LP disk.

Jones, Owen R. Jr. 1972. *Music of the Algonkians: Woodland Indians (Cree, Montagnais, Naskapi).* Folkways FE 4253. LP disk.

Kwakiutl: Indian Music of the Pacific Northwest. 1981. Collected, recorded, and annotated by Ida Halpern. Folkways Records. LP disk.

Lederman, Anne. 1987a. *Old Native and Métis Fiddling in Manitoba,* vols. I and II. Falcon Productions FP 187, FP 287. Compact discs.

Le Mouël, J. F., and M. Le Mouël. n.d. *Music of the Inuit. The Copper Eskimo Tradition.* Unesco Collection, Musical Atlas. EMI-Odon 64-2402781. LP disk.

Meilleur, Marcel. 1984. *Turtle Mountain Music.* Folkways FES 4140. Compact disc.

Mishler, Craig. 1974. *Music of the Alaskan Kutchin Indians.* Folkways FE 4070. LP disk.

Nattiez, Jean-Jacques. 1989. *Jeux vocaux des Inuit (Inuit du Caribou, Netsilik et Igloolik).* Ocora. CD HM83.

Ned, Buster. 1976–1977. *Choctaw-Chickasaw Dance Songs,* vols. 1–2. Mannsville, Okla.: Choctaw-Chickasaw Heritage Committee. LP disk.

Nootka Indian Music of the Pacific Northwest Coast. 1974. Collected, recorded, and annotated by Ida Halpern. Folkways Records FE 4524. LP disk.

Plains Chippewa/Métis Music from Turtle Mountain: Drums, Fiddles, Chansons and Rock and Roll. 1992. Smithsonian/Folkways SF 40411. Compact disc.

Relocation. Originally Canyon Records C-7121, released in 1977. Since 1990, available on CD and cassette as S.O.A.R. 131 [Sound of America Record].

Rhodes, Willard, ed. 1984. *Music of the American Indian, Great Basin: Paiute, Washo, Ute, Bannock, Shoshone.* Library of Congress Archive of Folk Culture, Recording Laboratory AFS L38. Cassette.

Rhodes, Willard. n.d. *Delaware, Cherokee, Choctaw, Creek.* Library of Congress AFS L37. LP.

Seneca Social Dance Music. 1980. Smithsonian Folkways Recordings FE 4072. Compact disc.

Songs and Dances of the Great Lakes Indians. 1956. Recording and liner notes by Gertrude Prokosch Kurath. Monograph Series of the Ethnic Folkways Library. Smithsonian-Folkways Recordings P 1003. LP disk.

Songs of the Chippewa, Volume I: Game and Social Dance Songs. 1977. Recording and liner notes by Paul Parthun. Smithsonian-Folkways FE 4392.

Songs of Earth, Water, Fire, and Sky: Music of the American Indians. 1976. New World Records NW 246. LP.

Southern Ute Singers. 1974. Canyon Records CR-6113-C.

Sryker, Miriam. 1966. *Eskimo Songs from Alaska.* Record FE 4069 and booklet. New York: Folkways.

Suluk, Donald, and Alice Suluk. n.d. *Inuit Songs and Dances.* Canadian Broadcasting Corporation, Northern Québec Services. Cassette.

Vennum, Thomas Jr. 1973. *Chippewa Grass Dance Songs: The Kingbird Singers of Ponemah, Minnesota.* Canyon Records C-6106.

Wood That Sings: Indian Fiddle Music of the Americas. 1997. Smithsonian Folkways SF CD 40472. Compact disc.

UNITED STATES

Alpert, Michael. 1993. *Like in a Different World: Leon Schwartz, a Traditional Jewish Klezmer Violinist from Ukraine.* Global Village C117. Cassette.

American Fiddle Tunes from the Library of Congress, AFS L62. Washington, D.C.: Library of Congress.

American Works for Balinese Gamelan Orchestra. Gamelan Sekar Jaya, Seka Gong Abdi Budaya, and students at STSI Denpasar. 1993. Produced by Evan Ziporyn, Michael Tenzer, and Wayne Vitale. Notes by Marc Perlman. Compositions by Ziporyn, I Nyoman Windha, Tenzer, and Vitale. New World Records 80430-2. Compact disc.

B.A.N.G. (Bay Area New Gamelan). 1986. Directed by Jody Diamond and Daniel Schmidt. Instruments built by Daniel Schmidt. Compositions by Schmidt, Diamond and Ingram Marshall. Lebanon, N.H.: American Gamelan Institute. AGI01. Cassette.

Basque Music of Boise: Tradizioa Bizirik (The Tradition Lives!). 1995. Boise, Idaho: Basque Museum and Cultural Center. Audiocassette.

Batacumbele. 1987. *Afro Caribbean Jazz.* Montieno Records MLP 525. LP disk.

Big Band and Quartet in Concert. 1963. Columbia C58964. LP disk.

Black 47: Fire of Freedom. 1993. New York: EMI Records. Compact disc.

Bládes, Ruben. 1983. *El que la hace la paga.* Fania JM 624. LP disk.

Borderlands: From Conjunto to Chicken Scratch— Music of the Rio Grande Valley of Texas and Southern Arizona. 1993. Smithsonian Folkways SF-40418. Compact disc.

Boston Camerata. 1994. *Nueva España: Close Encounters in the New World, 1590–1690.* Cohen, Joel, dir. WEA/Atlantic/Erato 45977. Compact disc.

Botkin, Benjamin Albert. 1959 [1942]. Notes to *Negro Work Songs and Calls.* Library of Congress, Division of Music, Recording Laboratory AAFS L8. LP disk.

Caliente=Hot: Puerto Rican and Cuban Musical Expression in New York. 1977. New World Records NW 244. LP disk.

Castel, Nico. 1977. *Sefarad: The Sephardic Tradition in Ladino Song.* New York: Tara Productions. Tambour TR-590. Compact disc.

Chávez, Alex J. 1995 [1965] *El Testamento.* Albuquerque Museum's Music of New Mexico Series, *Hispano Folk Music of the Past,* Cantante C95-1. Compact disc.

Coltrane, John. 1968. *Om.* Impulse A-9140. LP disk.

¡Conjunto! Texas-Mexican Border Music. (1988) Vol. 1. Rounder Records ROUN6023. Compact disc.

———. (1988) Vol. 2. Rounder Records ROUN6024. Compact disc.

———. (1990) Vol. 3. Rounder Records ROUN6030. Compact disc.

———. (1990) Vol. 4. Rounder Records ROUN6034. Compact disc.

———. (1994) Vol. 5. Rounder Records ROUN6051. Compact disc.

———. (1994) Vol. 6. Rounder Records ROUN6052. Compact disc.

Corridos, Part 1: 1930–1934. 1975. Texas-Mexican Border Music, vol. 2. Folklyric 9004. LP disk.

Corridos, Part 2: 1929–1936. 1975. Texas-Mexican Border Music, vol. 3. Folklyric 9005. LP disk.

Dances of Universal Peace, Volume I. 1987 [1975]. Seattle: PeaceWorks INDUP T100. Audiocassette.

Dark and Light in Spanish New Mexico. 1995 [1978]. New World Records 80292–2. Compact disc.

Das Efx. 1992. *Dead Serious.* EastWest Records America 7 91627-4. Compact disc.

Denny, Martin. 1957. *Exotica.* Liberty Records, LRP-3034. LP disk.

Dr. Dre. 1991. *The Chronic.* Priority Records P257129. Compact disc.

East Coast–West Coast: American Music for Gamelan. Venerable Showers of Beauty/A Different Song. Directed by Vincent McDermott and Widiyanto S. Putro; Gamelan Son of Lion directed by Barbara Benary. Compositions by McDermott and Benary. Independently produced cassette.

East Side Revue: 40 Hits by East Los Angeles' Most Popular Groups. 1969 [1966]. Rampart; distributed by American Pie as LP 3303. LP disk.

East Side Story, Vols. 1–12. n.d. Trojan LP-1012. LP disk.

El Chicano. 1988. *¡Viva! El Chicano: Their Very Best.* MCA.

El Gran Combo. 1977. *Homenaje a México.* Combo C 1011. LP disk.

Endo, Kenny. *Taiko* Ensemble. 1994. *Eternal Energy.* AsianImprov Records AIR 0021. Compact disc.

Eternal Voices: Traditional Vietnamese Music in the United States. 1993. New Alliance Records NAR CD 053. Compact disc.

Euzkadil: Songs and Dances of the Basque Juan Onatibia. 1954. Smithsonian-Folkways F-6830. LP disk.

Evans, David. 1978. Notes to *Let's Get Loose: Folk and Popular Blues Styles from the Beginnings to the Early 1940s.* New World Records NW 290. LP disk.

Fania All Stars. 1981. *Perfect Blend.* CBS Records 10453. LP disk.

Flatt, Lester, and Earl Scruggs. 1991. *Flatt & Scruggs, 1948–1959.* Notes by Neil V. Rosenberg. Bear Family BCD 15472. Compact disc.

Golden Treasures, Vol. 1: West Coast East Side Revue. 1966. Rampart 3303. LP disk.

Golden Treasures, Vol. 2: West Coast East Side Revue. 1969. Rampart 3305. LP disk.

Hancock, Herbie. 1983. *Future Shock.* Columbia/Legacy CK 65962. Compact disc.

Heth, Charlotte, ed. 1976. *New World Records.* Vol. 1. New York, N246. LP New World Records.

Hiroshima. 1979. *Hiroshima.* Arista Records AB 4252. LP disk.

———. 1979/1980. *Ongaku.* Arista Records ARCD 8437. Compact disc.

———. 1980. *Odori.* Arista Records AL 9541. LP.

Horiuchi, Glenn. 1989a. *Issei Spirit.* AsianImprov Records. LP disk.

Hot Rize. 1990. *Take It Home.* Sugar Hill SH-CD-3784. Compact disc.

James, Willis Laurence. 1970. *Afro-American Music: A Demonstration Recording by Dr. Willis James.* ASCH Records AA702. LP disk.

Journey to the Lord of Beauty. 1982. Sufi Zikr Series, no. 2. San Francisco: Sufi Islamia/Prophecy Publications SI/P 003. Audiocassette.

Kef Time: Exciting Sounds of the Middle East. 1994 [1986]. Produced by Harold G. Hagopian. With 6-page booklet of notes and song lyrics. Traditional Crossroads CD 4269. Compact disc.

Krauss, Alison. 1990. *I've Got That Old Feeling.* Rounder CD 0275. Compact disc.

Kurath, Gertrude Prokosch. 1956. "Voices of the Waterways." Liner notes for *Songs and Dances of the Great Lakes Indians.* Monograph Series of the Ethnic Folkways Library. Smithsonian-Folkways Recordings P 1003. LP disk.

Latin Alliance. n.d. *Latin Alliance.* Virgin Records 91625-4. LP disk.

Lawson, Doyle, and Quicksilver. 1990 [1979]. *Rock My Soul.* Sugar Hill SH-CD-3717. Compact disc.

Leadbitter, Mike, and Neil Slaven. 1987. *Blues Records 1943–70: A Selective Discography.* London: Record Information Services.

Leadbitter, Mike, et al. 1994. *Blues Records, 1943–1970.* Vol. 2. London: Record Information Services.

Levin, Theodore. 1996. Liner notes for *Mademoiselle, Voulez-Vous Danser? Franco- American Music from the New England Borderlands.* Washington, D.C.: Smithsonian Folkways Recordings. SFW CD 40116. Compact disc.

Liebert, Otto. 1990. *Nouveau Flamenco.* Higher Octave Music. HOMCD 77520. Compact disc.

Lomax, Alan. 1956 [1942]. *Afro-American Spirituals, Work Songs and Ballads,* record notes. Library of Congress, Division of Music, Recording Laboratory AAFS L3. LP disk.

Lornell, Christopher "Kip" 1978. *Non-Blues Secular Black Music,* record notes. BRI Records BRI 001.

Los Camperos de Nati Cano. 1972. *El super Mariachi los Camperos.* Discos Latin International DLIS 2003. LP disk.

Los Madrugadores. *Los Madrugadores.* 1985. Texas-Mexican Border Music, vol. 18. Folklyric 9036.

Lou Harrison: Gamelan Music. 1992. Gamelan Si Betty. Directed by Trish Neilsen and Jody Diamond. Instruments by Lou Harrison and William Colvig. Compositions by Lou Harrison. Music Masters 01612-67091-2. Compact disc.

Machito and His Salsa Big Band. 1982. Timeless Records SJF 161. LP disk.

March, Richard. 1998. *Deep Polka: Dance Music from the Midwest.* Washington, D.C.: Smithsonian Folkways SF CD 40088. Compact disc and 28-page booklet.

Monroe, Bill. 1989. *Blue Grass 1950–1958*. Notes by Neil V. Rosenberg and Charles K. Wolfe. Bear Family BCD 15423. Compact disc.

Montoya, Carlos. 1999. *Tango Flamenco*. Fine Tune 2227. Compact disc.

More and More Awake: New Music from the Mevlevi Zikr. 1982. Fairfax, Calif.: Mevlevi Order of America. Audiocassette.

Mountain Music Bluegrass Style. 1991 [1959]. Recorded, edited, and with notes by Mike Seeger. Smithsonian/Folkways CD SF 40038. Compact disc.

Murasaki Ensemble. 1994. *Niji*. A Murasaki Production. TME 8994. Compact disc.

Music of New Mexico. Hispanic Traditions. 1992. Smithsonian Folkways Recordings SF CD 40409. Compact disc.

Navarro, Fats, and Tadd Dameron. 1968. *Milestone*. M-4704. LP disk.

New Gamelan/New York. 1995. Gamelan Son of Lion. Directed by Barbara Benary. Compositions by Jody Kruskal, Laura Liben, David Demnitz, Mark Steven Brooks, David Simons, Daniel Goode, and Benary. GSOL CD-1. Compact disc.

Omad Poisi (Our Own Guys). 1979. Baltimore: Rukki Records/Sheffeld Recordings.

Orquesta Broadway. 1979. *No Tiene Comparación*. Coco Records CLP 158X. LP disk.

Palace. 1996. Evergreen Club. Directed by Blair Mackay. Artifact Music (Canada) ART-012. Compositions for Sundanese gamelan *degung* and other instruments, by Mark Duggan, Lou Harrison, John Wyre, Jon Siddal, and Alain Thibault. Compact disc.

Palmieri, Eddie, and Friends. 1973. *Live at the University of Puerto Rico*. Coco Records DOLP 107. LP disk.

Puente, Tito. 1984. *Los Grandes Exitos de Tito Puente, Vol 2*. RCA Records IL 57294. LP disk.

———. 1987. *On Broadway*. Concord Picante Records CJP 207. LP disk.

Puente, Tito, and His Latin Ensemble. 1984. *El Rey*. Concord Picante Records CJP 250. LP disk.

Racy, Ali Jihad. 1997. *Mystical Legacies: Ali Jihad Racy performs music of the Middle East*. With Ali Jihad Racy (*nay, buzuq, 'ud*, and bowed *tanbur*) and Souhail Kaspar (percussion). Lyrichord LYRCD 7437.

Racy, Ali Jihad, and Simon Shaheen. 1991 [1979]. *Taqasim: The Art of Improvisation in Arab Music*. Ali Jihad Racy, *buzuq*, and Simon Shaheen, *'ud*. With documentary notes by Philip Schuyler. Lyrichord LYRCD 7374.

Ramsey, Frederic. 1960. Notes to *Been Here and Gone*. Folkways Records FA 2659. LP disk.

Reyes, Al. n.d. *California Corazón: Songs from the San Joaquin Valley*. Cuervo Records S-1001. LP disk.

Rhodes, Willard. 1950. *Northwest (Puget Sound)*. Library of Congress AFS L34. LP disk.

———. 1954. *Music of the American Indian from the Archive of Folk Culture: Northwest (Puget Sound)*. Library of Congress AFS L34. Accompanying booklet revised in 1984.

Rinzler, Ralph. 1957. Notes to *American Banjo Scruggs Style*. Folkways FA 2314. LP disk.

Robb, John D. 1961 [1952]. *Spanish and Mexican Folk Music of New Mexico*. Ethnic Folkways Library FE 4426. LP disk.

Robb, John, collector. 1961. *Spanish Folk Songs of New Mexico*. Folkways FA 2204. LP disk. [Available on special order as cassette or compact disc 02204.]

Rodrigues, Amália. 1996. *The Best of Fado*. Double Gold DBG53026. Compact disc.

Rodríguez, Tito, y Louie Ramirez. (n.d.). *Algo Nuevo*. TR Records TR 300. LP disk.

Santamaría, Mongo. 1972. *Afro Roots*. Prestige Records 24018. LP disk.

Santana. n.d. *Santana's Greatest Hits*. Columbia PC 33050. LP disk.

Sapoznik, Henry. 1999 [1981]. *Klezmer Music: 1910–42*. Folkways Records FSS34021. Compact disc rerelease.

Seeger, Mike. 1959. Notes to *Mountain Music Bluegrass Style*. Folkways FA 2318. LP disk.

Shaheen, Simon. 1992. *Turath: Simon Shaheen Performs Masterworks of the Middle East*. With 8-page booklet of notes and photographs by Ali Jihad Racy. CMP 3006. Compact disc.

Shelemay, Kay K. 1985. *Pizmon: Syrian-Jewish Religious and Social Song*. Meadowlark/Shanachie Records ML 105. Cassette.

Slobin, Mark, and Barbara Kirshenblatt-Gimblett. 1986. *Folksongs in the East European Jewish Tradition from the Repertoire of Mariam Nirenberg*. Global Village GVM117 and subsequent Global Village solo-singer albums, for example, *Lifshe Schaechter Widman*, C111. Cassette.

Song of the Banyan: Folk Music of Vietnam by Phong Nguy-n Ensemble. 1997. Music of the World. WMI Latitudes LAT 50607. Compact disc.

Sonora Matancera con Justo Betancourt. 1981. Barbaro Records B 207. LP disk.

Sounds Like 1996: Music by Asian American Artists. 1996. AsianImprov Records IEL 0002. Compact disc.

Spanish and Mexican Folk Music of New Mexico. 1952 (1961). Folkways Records and Service Corporation LP Ethnic Folkways Library FE 4426.

Sugar Hill Gang. 1992 [1979]. *"Rapper's Delight," Street Jams: Hip-Hop from the Top—Part 1*. Rhino R2 70577 [Sugar Hill #542]. Compact disc.

Surinach, Carlos. *Ritmo Jondo*. 1996. Bronx Arts Ensemble. New World Records 80505-2. Compact disc.

Taquachito Nights: Conjunto Music from South Texas. 1999. Produced by Cynthia Vidaurri and Pete Reiniger, in collaboration with the Narciso Martínez Cultural Arts Center. Smithsonian Folkways Recordings SFW CD 40477. Compact disc.

Texas–Mexican Border Music, vol. 1: *Una historia de la música de la frontera: An Introduction 1930–1960*. 1974. Folklyric Records 9003. LP disk.

The Best of the Sufi Choir: A Jubilee Selection. 1993. San Francisco: SIRS Caravan Publications CMM 010. Compact disc.

The Clancy Brothers with Tommy Makem: Luck of the Irish. 1992. New York: Columbia/Legacy CK47900. Reissue of classic recording on compact disc.

The Hadrat. 1982. Sufi Zikr Series, no. 3. San Francisco: Sufi Islamia/Prophecy Publications SI/P 003. Audiocassette.

The History of Latino Rock, Vol. 1: 1956–1965: The Eastside Sound. 1983. Zyanya; distributed by Rhino. LP disk.

The Music of Arab Americans: A Retrospective Collection. Produced by Anne K. Rasmussen. With 20-page booklet of notes, photographs, and song lyrics. Rounder CD 1122. Compact disc.

The Stanley Brothers. 1990 [c. 1964]. *Long Journey Home*. Notes by Bill Vernon. Rebel CD 1110. Compact disc.

The Texas Mexican Conjunto. 1975. Texas-Mexican Border Music, vol. 24. Folklyric 9049. LP disk.

Trance Gong. 1994. Gamelan Pacifica. Directed by Jarrad Powell. Iron/brass instruments by Suhirjan (Central Java) and aluminum instruments by Schmidt, Dresher, Devereaux, Powell. Compositions by Powell, Jeff Morris, John Cage (arr. Powell), and other group members. ¿What next? Recordings WN0016.

Valens, Ritchie. 1958, 1959. *The Best of Ritchie Valens*. Del-Fi; distributed by Rhino as RNDF 200. LP disk.

Wheels of the World, Vols. 1 and 2. 1997. Newton, N.J.: Shanachie Records. Yazoo 7008 and 7009. Compact disc.

CANADA

AfroCan Routes. 1992. CBC Variety Recordings World Music Series 2, VRCD 1015. Compact disc.

Aglukark, Susan. 1999. *Unsung Heroes*. EMI Canada. 7243 8 53393 2 5. Compact disc.

Alfred, Jerry. 1998. *Kehlonn*. Caribou Records. CRCD004. Compact disc.

Anthologie de la musique canadienne (Anthology of Canadian Music). 1978–1991. Radio-Canada International. Boxed set of 32 LP disks and 6 compact discs.

Anthology of Canadian Music. 1978–1991. Canadian Broadcasting Corporation and Canadian Music Center. 39 boxed sets. Originally LP disks but rereleased as compact discs.

Arsenault, Eddy. 1993. *Piling on the Bois Sec*. Wellington, PEI: House Party Productions, HPP1. Compact disc.

Bartlett, Wayne. 1992. "She's Gone Boys, She's Gone." SWC Productions. Audiocassette.

Brouhaha. c. 1980s. *Vision*. Brouhaha Music BENT CD 001. Compact disc.

Czerny, Al. *Fiddle Country*. TeeVee Records TA–1019. LP. Many others available.

Figgy Duff. 1991. *Weather Out the Storm* (and others). Hypnotic 71356-1000. Compact disc.

Fin de siècle, Nouvelle musique montréalaise. 1994. L'Ensemble Contemporain de Montréal, dir. Véronique Lacroix. SNE 590. Compact disc.

Folksongs of the Miramichi. 1962. Folkways FM 4053. LP disk.

Four the Moment. 1993. *Four the Moment: Live*. JAM FTM 101. Compact disc.

———. 1996. *In My Soul*. Atlantic. Compact disc.

Freed, Don, and Prince Albert students. 1996. *Singing About the Métis*. Bush League Records BL8. Cassette.

Gasser, Alan. 1996. Notes to *Introduction to Canadian Music* (Orchestral music, Choral Music, Chamber Music, Electroacoustic Music). Naxos 8.550171-2. 2 compact discs.

Haida Indian Music of the Pacific Northwest. 1986. Folkways FE 4119. LP disk.

Here and Now/En nos temps et lieux: A Celebration of Canadian Music/Une Célébration de la Musique Canadienne. 1995. Music of the First Peoples and Folk Music, Classical Music, Jazz and World Music, Artists and Styles of Historical Importance. The Canada Council, produced in partnership with the Canadian Broadcasting Corporation. CDSP 4510, 4511, 4512, 4513. 4 compact disks.

Hibbs, Harry. c. 1970s. *At the Caribou Club* (and others). ARC 794. LP disk.

Huronia Old Time Country Band. c. 1980s. *Old Time Fiddle Music with Marcel, Martin, Eric and Gerrard.* n.p. MRD 001. Cassette.

Indian Music of the Pacific Northwest Coast. 1967. Collected and recorded by Ida Halpern. Folkways Records FE 4523. LP disk.

Irish Descendants. 1994. "Will They Lie There Evermore?" *Gypsies Lovers.* Warner Music Canada Ltd. CD W88. Compact disc.

Joyce, Jim. 1991. "Hard, Hard Times." On *Another Time: The Songs of Newfoundland,* Kelly Russell and Don Walsh, producers. Pigeon Inlet Production CD PIPCD 7326. Compact disc.

Kwakiutl Indian Music of the Pacific Northwest. 1981. Folkways FE 4122. LP disk.

Landry, Ned. c. 1960s. *Saturday Night Breakdown (and others).* RCA Camden CAL 780. LP disk.

L'époque de Julie Papineau. 1997. Musiques du Québec, vol. 1. Ensemble Nouvelle-France. Lanoraie ORCD41081, Interdisq Distr. Compact disc.

MacIsaac, Ashley. 1995. *Hi™ How Are You Today?* Ancient Music/A and M Records, 31454 0522 2. Compact disc.

———. 1996. *Fine® Thank You Very Much.* Ancient Music/A and M Records. 79602 2002-2. Compact disc.

Made in Canada: Our Rock and Roll History. 1990. BMG Canada KCD1-7156, 7157, 7158, 7159. 4 Compact discs.

Maritime Folk Songs. 1962. Folkways FE-4307. LP disk.

Matton, Roger. n.d. *Acadie et Québec: Field Recordings.* Québec: Les Archives de Folklore. RCA Records CGP-139. LP disk.

Montréal Postmoderne. 1994. Centrediscs. Compact disc.

Ne blâmez jamais les bédouins. 1992. Chants Libres, dir. Pauline Vaillancourt. Diffusion i MéDIA IMSO 9202. Compact disc.

Nolan, Faith. 1984. *Africville.* M.W.I.C. Records 11161A. Compact disc.

Nootka Indian Music of the Pacific Northwest Coast. 1974. Collected, recorded, and annotated by Ida Halpern. Folkways Records FE 4524. LP disk.

Oeuvres symphoniques, Patrimoine musical du Canada français. 1990. L'Orchestre Métropolitain, dir. Gilles Auger et Louis Lavigueur. SRC SMCD 5090. Compact disc.

Oh! What a Feeling: A Vital Collection of Canadian Music, 25 years of Juno Award Winners. 1996. Canadian Academy of Recording Arts and Sciences JUNO 251-4. 4 compact discs.

Old Time Couple Dances. Folkways FW 8827. LP.

Ontario Ballads and Folksongs. 1962. Prestige/International INT 25014. LP.

Overlords. 1999. *Overlords Caravan 2000.* Trobiz Records. Compact disc.

Panneton, Isabelle. n.d. *Cantate de la fin du jour.* Fonovox VOX 7824-2. Compact disc.

Party Acadien. 1995. House Party Productions. Compact disc.

Perlman, Ken. 1993. *The Old Time Fiddlers of Prince Edward Island.* Booklet accompanying Marimac Recordings C-6501. Audiocassette.

Prince Edward Island Fiddlers. Vols. 1 and 2. Islander Records SVC-002, SVC-001387.

Puamuna-Montagnais Hunting Songs. 1982. Canadian Broadcasting Corporation, Northern Quebec Service SQN 100. LP disk.

Sealy, Joe. 1996. *Africville Suite.* SEA JAM Records. Compact disc.

Shreyer, Pierre. 1996. *New Canadian Waltz.* New Canadian Records NCCD–9610. Compact disc, cassette.

Songs of the Great Lakes. Folk FM 4018. LP.

Songs of the Newfoundland Outports. 1984. Pigeon Inlet Productions PP-7319. LP disk.

Townsend, Graham. *The Great Canadian Fiddle.* Rounder Records 7002. LP. Many others available.

Un concert en Nouvelle-France. 1995. L'Ensemble Arion, CBC Records SRC-MVCD 1081. Compact disc.

York, Muddy. 1984. *Scatter the Ashes: Music of Old Ontario.* Boot BOS 7244. LP, Cassette.

A Guide to Films and Videos

Entries in this Guide were chosen from the references sections following each article in this volume and represent a mere fraction of all references cited. The reader is urged to go back to specific articles to find other important sources.

AMERICAN INDIANS/FIRST NATIONS

Loukinen, Michael. 1992. *Medicine Fiddle*. Marquette, Mich.: Up Front Films.

UNITED STATES

Catlin, Amy. 1997a. *Hmong Musicians in America: Interactions with Three Generations of Hmong American Musicians, 1978–1996*. Van Nuys, Calif.: Apsara Media for Intercultural Education. 60-minute videotape.

Mandell, Joan. 1995. *Tales from Arab Detroit*. Detroit and Los Angeles: ACCESS and Olive Branch Productions. Film.

Mullins, Patrick, and Rebecca Miller. *From Shore to Shore: Irish Traditional Music in New York*. 1993. New York: Cherry Lane Productions. Video. Distributed by the Cinema Guild, Inc., 1697 Broadway, Suite 506, New York, New York 10019-5904, (800) 723-5522.

Okada, Yuki, director. 1995. *The Caribbean*. The JVC/Smithsonian Folkways Video Anthology of

Music and Dance of the Americas, vol. 4. Barre, Vt.: Multicultural Media VTMV-288. Video.

Parsons, Jack, producer. 1993. *La Música de la Gente* (The Music of the People). Derry, N.H.: Chip Taylor Communications. Videocassette.

CANADA

Boulton, Laura. 1942. *Ukrainian Winter Holidays*. National Film Board of Canada. Film.

MacInnis, Ron, prod. 1971. *The Vanishing Cape Breton Fiddler*. Halifax: CBC. Film.

National Film Board of Canada. 1975. *Seven Shades of Pale*. Documentary film.

Reed-Olsen, Joan, prod. and dir. 1991. *Mas Camp to Parade*. Hands Over Time series. [28 mins.] TV

Ontario and Ontario Educational Communications Authority. Video.

Rojas, Leuten P. 1982. *From the Strings of My Guitar*. Ottawa: Cordillera Films.

Notes on the Audio Examples

The musical examples provided here are a small fraction of the total amount of recorded music now available from the United States and Canada. The reader is urged to seek out other recordings, especially of western classical, jazz, and contemporary popular musics.

1. "My Little Annie, So Sweet" (2:08)

    Field holler sung by Horace Sprott while chopping cotton in Alabama.

    From *Been Here and Gone: Music from the South,* vol. 10. Recorded and compiled by Frederic Ramsey during the 1960s. Folkways Records FA 02659 (1960). Courtesy of Smithsonian Folkways.

2. "Coiled Chalk Circle" (2:07)

    In the old stories, a wise judge calls for each of the parents who claim a child to take an arm and pull. When one lets go, the judge declares that this is the real parent, who would rather lose than see the child torn apart. The new stories are not so clear and wise. Counselors' questions, court assessments, and custody hearings bring us back into the circle again and again. Parents who let go live with pain, loss, and often community condemnation. This piece expresses the struggle to find ways to love children at arms' length. It is dedicated with hope to Sian and Daniel. Thanks to Barry Truax for the use of the realtime granular synthesis system at Simon Fraser University, and to Trish Armstrong for assistance.

    By Andra McCartney. From *The Mix: An Audio Document of Selections from Live Recording of the Sound Art Festival.*

3. "Exhortation" (first line: "Now, in the heat of youthful blood") (1:35)

    Recorded by Terry E. Miller on June 12, 1971, at Hopewell Primitive Baptist Church near Oneonta, Alabama, on the second day of a three-day singing (with "dinner on the ground"). This song is a fuging tune, and as is customary the singers use the "fasola" (four shape) solfege the first time through, then sing the words.

    From the *Original Sacred Harp (Denson Revision)*, p. 272.

4. "True Life Blues" (2:40)

    Bill Monroe, musical innovator and performer, developed a new style of music during the 1950s and 1960s known as bluegrass, a synthesis of southern string band, blues, and country music.

    Bill Monroe and the Blue Grass Boys. From *Live Recordings 1956–1969, Off the Record*, vol. 1, 1993. Smithsonian Folkways SF CD 40063. Courtesy of Smithsonian Folkways.

5. "Beautiful Dreamer" (2:33)

    This song, along with countless others composed by Stephen C. Foster (1826–1864), was hugely popular in the late nineteenth and early twentieth centuries.

    By Stephen Collins Foster; sung by Richard Dyer-Bennet. From *Richard Dyer-Bennet Sings Songs from Stephen Foster*. Richard Dyer-Bennet Recordings, D-11 (1962). Courtesy of Smithsonian Folkways.

6. "Clay and Frelinghuysen" (1:17)

    Sung to the tune "Old Dan Tucker" for the election of 1884, this song represents an important historical genre of American political song, popular from about 1840 to 1920.

    From *Election Songs of the United States*, sung by Oscar Brand with Billy Faier on guitar and banjo. Folkways Records FH5280 (1960). Courtesy of Smithsonian Folkways.

7. "Personal Song" (0:45)

    Among the Dene, a Personal Song gives voice to individual thoughts and feelings. A recognizable melodic and rhythmic style leaves room for individual variations that identify the song maker. Typically, personal songs use very few words. Here, the elderly singer reminisces about a long ago boyfriend who has gone hunting. She indirectly wishes him a safe return by flattering the lead dog of his team, telling him how good he is.

    Field recording by Nicole Beaudry, February, 1988. Singer: Eliza Blondin, Fort Franklin, Northwest Territories, Canada.

8. "Haste to the Wedding" (1:00)

    Old Native and Métis Fiddling in Manitoba, Canada. A well-known tune, often called simply "The Wedding Tune," it is usually played for the first dance at a wedding party.

    Performed by Willie Mousseau (1903–1985), Ebb and Flow Reserve, Manitoba. Recorded by Willie Henry in spring 1984 at Mr. Mousseau's home. Falcon Productions, FP 01.

9. "Brush Dance Heavy Song" (1:01)

    Sung by Ewing Davis and recorded by Frank Quin in 1956.

10. "Song of Happiness" (1:06)

    Performed by a children's chorus, drum, and harmonica. This song was sung by the women to sustain the morale and hope of the men during the confinement of the Navajo at Fort Sumner following their capitulation to Kit Carson in 1864. It is recorded here as sung by a group of students at the Fort Wingate Indian School.

    From *Music of the Sioux and the Navajo* (1949). Folkways Records F4401 (1953). Courtesy of Smithsonian Folkways.

11. "Fireman's Polka" (2:58)

Taken from a manuscript dated c.1862, this is a modern favorite with brass bands; it describes a peaceful day in the firehouse interrupted by the fire bell, which calls the volunteers to rush to answer in polka rhythm.

By W. S. Ripley. Performed by Saxton's Cornet Band at the Great American Brass Band Festival, June 1999. Saxton's Cornet Band is a reconstructed Civil War band that performs in blue or gray uniforms.

12. "Were You There?" (2:03)

The Fisk Jubilee Singers, directed by John W. Work, 1955. The Fisk Jubilee Singers made their debut in 1871 in Cincinnati, Ohio, and were largely responsible for the popularization of the Negro Spiritual throughout the United States and Europe.

Folkways Records FA 02372 (1955). Courtesy of Smithsonian Folkways.

13. "In the Pines" ("Black Girl," "Where Did You Sleep Last Night?") (2:06)

An important composer and performer of blues and ballads, Huddie Ledbetter (Lead Belly 1888–1949) influenced a whole generation of revival musicians.

Recorded in 1947. From *Lead Belly, Where Did You Sleep Last Night? Lead Belly Legacy,* vol. 1. Smithsonian Folkways SF 40044 (1996). Courtesy of Smithsonian Folkways.

14. "La Finada Pablita" (2:29)

One of the best known *inditas* ('narrative song form'), "La finada Pablita" tells the story of Paula Angel, the first and only woman to be legally executed in New Mexico.

Sung by Julia Jaramillo of Taos, New Mexico. Recorded in Taos, August 27, 1986. *Music of New Mexico: Hispanic Traditions* (1992). Smithsonian Folkways CD SF 40409. Courtesy of Smithsonian Folkways.

15. "Asi se baila en Tejas" ("This is the Way They Dance in Texas") (1:32)

One of the founders of the Texas-style *conjunto*, Tony de la Rosa has come to epitomize the second generation of *conjuncto* accordionists. During the 1940s and 1950s he brought innovative changes to the older *conjunto* style, introducing the drum set, the electric bass, and the amplified *bajo sexto* ('12-string guitar').

Rounder CD 6046 (1991).

16. "Heavenly Father, Lead Us" (4:00)

From the Anglican hymnal, *Hymns Ancient and Modern*; sung by members of St. John's Spiritual Baptist Church in the Flatbush section of Brooklyn, New York. Although Trinidad's Spiritual Baptists make use of the standard Anglican hymnal, they recall the tunes from memory and improvise the harmony. After singing two verses, some lines of which are "lined" by Leader Violet, the singing turns into "doption," during which the words change to instrumental-inspired syllables. This indicates a beginning level of an altered state which, if it deepens, results in the singing changing to rhythmic breathing.

Recorded on June 8, 1986, by Terry E. Miller.

17. "The Glouster Witch" ("Old Meg") (1:23)

This song recounts the changes in attitude toward witches in the centuries following the Salem, Massachusetts, witch trials in 1692. No longer seen as the agents of Satan, old women and eccentrics such as Margaret Wesson of Glouster tended to be scorned, pitied, and, as in this song, ridiculed.

From *Witches and War-Whoops: Early New England Ballads,* collected and sung by John Allison. Folkways Records F 05211 (1962). Courtesy of Smithsonian Folkways.

18. "Habanera of the Savoyard" (2:56)

From the *zarzuela, Luisa Fernanda,* by Fredrico Moreno Torroba; libretto by Fredrico Romero and Guillermo Fernández Shaw. Composed in 1932, the story takes place in 1868 during the reign of Queen Isabella II of Spain and tells the story of Luisa Fernanda, who is being courted by Vidal, a wealthy landowner, but who loves Javier, a colonel in the Royal Hussars. The *habanera* presented here is sung by a blind wandering musician who sings prophetically of the betrayal of love during war.

Jarvis Conservatory, JC 9702 Stereo Compact Disk (1997).

19. "Vigala reinlender" ("Vigala Schottische") (1:56)

From *Tuuletargat (Wind Wizards): Estonian Instrumental Folk Music Ensemble of Chicago.* Sponsor/Copyright: Innovative Mechanics, Inc., 2000, in a version written down by the *kannel* player Alfred Kuus of Toronto. Harmony part arranged by Andres Peekna. Performers: Andres Peekna (12 string *kannel*), Garrett Derner (guitar), Mart Jalakas (violin), Paul Höglund (*nyckelharpa*), and Christina von Wunder (*nyckelharpa*).

20. "Dortn, Dortn Ibern Vasserl" ("There, Across the Water") (2:02)

A love song from a young man "across the water" to his girlfriend back home in Eastern Europe, "Dortn, Dortn" is sung here by Ruth Rubin, one of the foremost scholars and interpreters of Yiddish songs, who has recorded, taught, and published on Jewish music over the last fifty years.

From *Yiddish Folksongs,* sung by Ruth Rubin; collected from Dora Wasserman, Montreal, Canada, 1955. Folkways Records F 08720 (1978). Courtesy of Smithsonian Folkways.

21. "Heartsong Aria" (3:29)

From *Night Vision, A First to Third World Vampyre Opera.* The opera is about a female Vampyre, Ajlinna, born 2000 years ago (and resurrected in each century), who sings with two hearts (third and first world), and who is propelled to stardom in this century by a Thrall (the Spin Doctor). Her voice is said to transfix anyone who hears it. "Heartsong Aria," her signature hit single in this century, is performed here by Daphne Gaines, Dr. Sa'di Al-Hadithi, Funda Duyal, and chorus.

Concept and music by Fred Ho; libretto and lyrics by Ruth Margraff. Autonomedia & Big Red, Inc., 2000.

22. "Something About Me Today" (2:30)

This is a song of protest about the role of the media—seen here as a tool of the white ruling class—in forming "American" images and values.

From *A Grain of Sand: Music for the Struggle by Asians in America.* Chris Kando Iijima, Joanne Nobuko Miyamoto, and "Charlie" Chin. Folkways P 1020 (1973). Courtesy of Smithsonian Folkways.

23. "Lam khon savane" (3:14)

Traditional repartee singing (*lam*) from southern Laos sung by Lao Americans Khamvong Insixiengmai (male) and Thongkhio Manivong (female), accompanied on the sixteen-pipe free-reed mouth organ (*khene*) by Khamseung Syhanone. Khamvong, who later won a National Heritage Fellowship from the National Endowment for the Arts, alternates with singing partner Thongkhio in singing a southern Lao genre that originated in the Savannakhet area along the Maekong River. Such singing consists of memorized and extemporized poetry that may continue for hours, often taking the form of an imaginary love affair.

Recorded by Terry E. Miller on April 24, 1987, in New York City before a concert.

24. "Gending Erhu," excerpt (3:18)

The main melody in this piece is played by the erhu, a Chinese spike fiddle with the bow hairs threaded between its two strings. The erhu evokes a similar instrument in Indonesia, the rebab, which plays an especially important melodic role in the Javanese gamelan. The gamelan instruments played in "Gending Erhu" are made of aluminum and were designed and built by Daniel Schimdt, Paul Dresher, and Kent Devereaux. By Jarrad Powell (1983).

From *Trance Gong*. Performed by Warren Chang on the erhu and the Gamelan Pacifica of Seattle (Randy Doak, Jay Hamilton, Jana Hawley, Margaret Johnstone, Brenda Kramer, Jim Madara, Joanne McDonald, Chris McFee, Rebecca Morgan, Jarrad Powell, and Allan Vaupell).

25. "Sabá Medley" (3:03)

Improvisation (*taqasim*) and medley of Arab folk songs in the musical mode of *Sabá,* played on the Arab reed flute (*nay*) by the performer, composer, and professor of ethnomusicology Ali Jihad Racy. Percussion accompaniment on the ceramic, vase-shaped drum (*tablah* or *darabukkha*) by Souhail Kaspar.

From a live concert recording of 1993 at the J. Paul Getty Museum in Los Angeles, California. *Mystical Legacies: Ali Jihad Racy Performs Music of the Middle East*, accompanied by Soulhail Kaspar. Lyrichord Discs: LYRCH 7437 (1994).

26. "He Mo Leannan" ("Hey, My Darling") (1:32)

A girl sings of her sweetheart who is not as faithful as he should be. Songs such as "He Mo Leannan" were often sung during milling parties where young men and women would meet and court.

Sung by Dan J. Morrison, *Songs from Cape Breton Island*, recorded by Sidney Robertson Cowell and John P. Hughes at Briton Cove, Nova Scotia. Folkways FE 04450 (1955). Courtesy of Smithsonian Folkways.

27. "Acadian Dance" (:55)

Collected by the folklorist Helen Creighton, this tune with its graceful fiddle style and unusual meter is characteristic of Acadian dance tunes.

Hilaire Pothier (fiddle) and Laure Irène McNeil (piano). Performed and recorded in Hilaire Pothier's home. From *Folk Music from Nova Scotia*. Folkways 04006 (1964). Courtesy of Smithsonian Folkways.

28. "A la Claire Fontaine" (1:32)

One of the best known folk songs of French Canada, "A la Claire Fontaine" tells the story of a young man whose sweetheart is angry with him for not giving her a bouquet of roses. One day, while bathing in a brook, he hears a nightingale singing and pours out his troubles to the bird.

Sung by Alan Mills. From *French Canadian Folk Songs*. Folkways Records FW 6929 (1960).

29. "El Pájaro Verde" ("The Green Bird") (2:16)

A Moroccan Judeo-Spanish romance tells of a beautiful girl from Madrid who plans to elope with her beloved to avoid an unpalatable arranged marriage. When her family kills her beloved, the girl dies of a broken heart (in some versions she stabs herself to death). The family opens the door to confess to her and finds only a green bird ("pájaro verde") singing. The two lovers are buried together and flowers grow from the graves. This *romance* ('narrative ballad') exists only in the Moroccan tradition.

Performed by Rafael and Algeri'a Benamron and recorded by Judith Cohen, Montreal, November 1990. The Benamrons are from the small northern Moroccan town of Alcazarquivir (KsaralKabir), which was once home to a thriving Jewish community where the ballad repertoire was particularly rich.

30. "Mosaic" (3:38)

A historical and musical portrait of Toronto, this piece uses fragments of the "Marseillaise" (France), "The British Grenadiers" (England), "The Purple Bamboo" (China), and "Ma Bella Bimba" (Italy), as well as tunes of Polish and calypso origin. The title refers to the *rubbaboo* ('spicy soup') of musics to be heard in Ontario.

By Mary Gardiner (1984). From *Piano Music by Torontonians*, Kinck Sound Productions, Scarborogh, WRC1-3315.

31. "Aläp in Räg Bhairav" (2:36)

From a musical score created for *Medicine Wheel,* scripted and performed by *kathak* dancer Joanna Das.

Recorded in Toronto in July 1991 by Donald Quan, Q-Music. Aruna Narayan Kalle on *särangii*; Eric Parker on *tänpuuraa*; voiceover by FirstNations actor Jack Burning.

32. "Saskatchewan" (2:32)

A song commemorating the "dirty thirties" (the Depression years, 1929–1939) on the Canadian prairies, set to the well-known hymn tune "Beulah Land."

By William W. Smith; performed by Alan Mills. From *A History of Canada in Song*. Folkways Records FW 3000 (1960). Courtesy of Smithsonian Folkways.

33. Cherwick "Hutsulka" (1:45)

From *Easy Aces Five Play Old Country Dances*, Easy Aces Five. Bill Boychuk (violin), Bob Mason (accordion), Con Malayko (drum), John D. Lugose (*tsymbaly*), and Steve Osypchuck (guitar). DSF Records, DSLP-3, n.d.

Index